SCOTT

2018
STANDARD POSTAGE
STAMP CATALOGUE

ONE HUNDRED AND SEVENTY-FOURTH EDITION IN SIX VOLUMES

VOLUME 1A

U.S., U.N. A-Australia

EDITOR	Donna Houseman
MANAGING EDITOR	Charles Snee
EDITOR EMERITUS	James E. Kloetzel
SENIOR EDITOR /NEW ISSUES & VALUING	Martin J. Frankevicz
SENIOR VALUING ANALYST	Steven R. Myers
ADMINISTRATIVE ASSISTANT/CATALOGUE LAYOUT	Eric Wiessinger
PRINTING AND IMAGE COORDINATOR	Stacey Mahan
SENIOR GRAPHIC DESIGNER	Cinda McAlexander
ADVERTISING/SALES – EAST	Stephanie Campana
	David Pistello
ADVERTISING/SALES – WEST & FL	Eric Roth

Released April 2017
Includes New Stamp Listings through the February 2017 *Linn's Stamp News Monthly* Catalogue Update

Copyright© 2017 by

AMOS MEDIA

911 Vandemark Road, Sidney, OH 45365-0828
Publishers of *Linn's Stamp News*, *Linn's Stamp News Monthly*, *Coin World* and *Coin World Monthly*.

Table of Contents

See Volumes 1B through 6B for Countries of the World, Austria-Z

Volume 1B: Austria-B
Volume 2A: C-Cur; Volume 2B: Cyp-F
Volume 3A: G; Volume 3B: H, I
Volume 4A: J-L; Volume 4B: M
Volume 5A: N, O, Phil; Volume 5B: Pit-Sam
Volume 6A: San-Tete; Volume 6B: Thai, U-Z

Scott Catalogue Mission Statement

The Scott Catalogue Team exists to serve the recreational,
educational and commercial hobby needs of stamp collectors and dealers.

We strive to set the industry standard for philatelic information and products by developing and
providing goods that help collectors identify, value, organize and present their collections.

Quality customer service is, and will continue to be, our highest priority.
We aspire toward achieving total customer satisfaction.

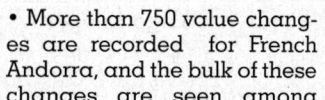

What's new for 2018 Scott Standard Volume 1A?

The 2018 edition of the Scott *Standard Postage Stamp Catalogue* celebrates the 150th anniversary of the Scott catalogs. The title page of this volume and other volumes in the 2018 Standard catalog states that this is the 174th edition of the catalogs (and it is). In September 1868, John Walter Scott published his first stamp catalog. The catalog, titled *A Descriptive Catalogue of America and Foreign Postage Stamps, Issued from 1840 to Date*, is considered to be the first Scott stamp catalog.

The Scott catalog has come a long way since its humble beginnings as a 24-page bound pamphlet. The Scott Standard catalog lists more than 700,000 stamps from more than 600 stamp-issuing entities. Because the catalog volumes had grown so large that they were literally bursting at the seams, each 2018 Scott Standard catalog has been split into two volumes, A and B.

Slightly more value changes (1,022) were made in United States for Vol. 1A of the 2018 Scott Standard catalog than were made last year (783), with greater numbers of changes made in all categories from Postage through Stamped Envelopes (cut squares). Once again, there are few changes in the Postage areas through No. 771. Dealers have not raised prices, and at auction, true very fine stamps are realizing prices close to Scott values, with higher grades realizing more. A few items show slight value declines, and a very few show increases.

• Among the U.S. 20th-century coils, used singles of Nos. 349 and 352 show increases, and the scarce 2¢ coil (388) climbs slightly, to $1,400 unused, from $1,350 in the 2017 Scott *Specialized Catalogue of United States Stamps and Covers*.

• Large selections of error stamps appeared in several auctions during the past six months, and the realizations, quite frankly, were disappointing (unless you were an eager buyer). Even the scarcer errors did not fare well. The results mirror other auctions from recent years. As a result, several errors had their catalog values further trimmed for 2018. Countering the general trend were Liberty series perforation errors Nos. 1035b,1035f and 1054c, each of which shows significant value increases.

• Other errors that show large value increases include Nos. 2484c, 2853b, 2884b and 2992c. Several error stamps that previously were dashed in the value columns have been assigned values, which should be helpful to buyers and sellers.

A newly added error is the imperforate Quilled Paper Heart stamp. (Scott 5036b).

• Official stamps performed well, because some quality examples made their way to the marketplace. The scarcer Official special printings did especially well. Several of these stamps had large value increases, and two of the rarest, Nos. O70S and O71S, saw huge increases in catalog value.

• Values for mint cut squares of stamped envelopes, like errors, have been weak for a few years, and values fell for many of them. Revenue stamps stand firm, with a couple of the inverted centers from the third issue showing value increases.

• Elsewhere in Vol. 1A, take note of the substantial increases in used condition for the 26 stamps of La Aguera. The 1920 10-peseta orange, for example, advances from $100 in the 2017 catalog to $125 this year.

• More than 750 value changes are recorded for French Andorra, and the bulk of these changes are seen among

Angola's 1947 1-angola airpost stamp jumps from $11.50 unused to $16.

stamps issued during 1976-2010. Overall, values are down 10 percent to 25 percent. The three high denominations of the 1949-51 regular issue (Scott 121-123) go against this trend by increasing in value in both mint never-hinged and used condition. The 30-franc ultramarine Provost stamp (Scott 123) jumps to $40 mint and $22.50 used, from $35 and $13.50, respectively, last year.

• Angola received a thorough review this year, resulting in almost 2,700 value changes, which reflect mostly downward movement. Scattered increases can be found among the scarce issues and varieties. The 1-angolar airmail stamp (Scott C10) soars from $11.50 unused to $16 but decreases from $7 used to $5.25.

• The modern issues of Armenia come in with more than 800 value changes. A small number of increases are scatterd among mostly decreases. The 1992 7-ruble Eagle and Mt. Ararat souvenir sheet (Scott 431) jumps from $50 mint and used in 2017 to $55 both ways in the 2018 catalog.

Editorial enhancements for Vol. 1A

In addition to the many updated notes of clarification throughout the listings, new listings for U.S. error stamps have been added. Perhaps the most interesting is No. 5036b, the imperforate error of the 2016 Quilled Paper Heart stamp. This stamp was issued in imperforate press sheets, but all of those were printed from Plate S11111. A later printing was printed from plate B11111, and it is from this printing that the imperforate errors come. But in order to differentiate the error stamps from the more commonnly issued imperforates, examples of the error must be collected with the B11111 selvage attached.

• Much new work has been done on the Computer Vended Postage section, mostly in clarifying listings and footnotes.

• In the Hunting Permit Stamps section, a footnote has been added after No. RW13 explaining that the previously listed No. RW13a shade variety was deleted because it has been determined that it is a chemically induced changeling.

• Another new listing of a postmaster's provisional appears in the Confederate States of America section. This is the unique 5¢ Danville, Va., No. 21XU3B.

As always, we encourage you to pay special attention to the Number Additions, Deletions & Changes found on page 830 in this volume.

While you settle in with your stamp album and Scott catalog, relax and enjoy the world's greatest hobby.

Donna Houseman

Donna Houseman/Catalogue Editor

Acknowledgments

Our appreciation and gratitude go to the following individuals who have assisted us in preparing information included in this year's Scott Catalogues. Some helpers prefer anonymity. These individuals have generously shared their stamp knowledge with others through the medium of the Scott Catalogue.

Those who follow provided information that is in addition to the hundreds of dealer price lists and advertisements and scores of auction catalogues and realizations that were used in producing the catalogue values. It is from those noted here that we have been able to obtain information on items not normally seen in published lists and advertisements. Support from these people goes beyond data leading to catalogue values, for they also are key to editorial changes.

A special acknowledgment to Liane and Sergio Sismondo of The Classic Collector for their assistance and knowledge sharing that have aided in the preparation of this year's Standard and Classic Specialized Catalogues.

Roland Austin
Robert Ausubel (Great Britain Collectors Club)
John Birkinbine II
Roger S. Brody
Peter Bylen
Tina & John Carlson (JET Stamps)
Richard A Champagne (Richard A. Champagne, Ltd.)
Henry Chlanda
David & Julia Crawford
Steven D. Crippe (Gradedstamps.com)
Tony L. Crumbley (Carolina Coin & Stamp, Inc.)
Christopher Dahle
Ubaldo Del Toro
Leon Djerahian
Bob & Rita Dumaine (Sam Houston Duck Co.)
Sister Theresa Durand
Mark Eastzer (Markest Stamp Co.)
Paul G. Eckman
George Epstein (Allkor Stamp Co.)
Henry Fisher
Jeffrey M. Forster
Robert S. Freeman
Michael Fuchs
Bob Genisol (Sultan Stamp Center)
Stan Goldfarb
Daniel E. Grau
Jan E. Gronwall
Bruce Hecht (Bruce L. Hecht Co.)
Peter Hoffman
Armen Hovsepian (Armenstamp)
Philip J. Hughes
Doug Iams
John Jamieson (Saskatoon Stamp and Coin)
N. M. Janoowalla
Peter Jeannopoulos
Stephen Joe (International Stamp Service)
William A. Jones
Allan Katz (Ventura Stamp Co.)
Stanford M. Katz
Lewis Kaufman (The Philatelic Foundation)
Jon Kawaguchi (Ryukyu Philatelic Specialist Society)
Roland Kretschmer

William V. Kriebel (Brazil Philatelic Association)
George Krieger
Victor Krievans
Frederick P. Lawrence
Ken Lawrence
John R. Lewis (The William Henry Stamp Co.)
Ulf Lindahl
Ignacio Llach (Filatelia Llach S.L.)
Marilyn R. Mattke
Gary Morris (Pacific Midwest Co.)
Peter Mosiondz, Jr.
Bruce M. Moyer (Moyer Stamps & Collectibles)
Richard H. Muller
Leonard Nadybal
Dr. Tiong Tak Ngo
Nik & Lisa Oquist
Dr. Everett Parker
Donald J. Peterson (International Philippine Philatelic Society)
Stanley M. Piller (Stanley M. Piller & Associates)
Virgil Pirvulescu
Todor Drumev Popov
Peter W. W. Powell
Siddique Mahmudur Rahman
Ghassan D. Riachi
Mehrdad Sadri (Persiphila)
Theodosios Sampson PhD
Alexander Schauss (Schauss Philatelics)
Jacques C. Schiff, Jr. (Jacques C. Schiff, Jr., Inc.)
Chuck & Joyce Schmidt
Michael Schreiber
Jeff Siddiqui
Sergio & Liane Sismondo (The Classic Collector)
Jay Smith
Frank J. Stanley, III
Alfred E. Staubus
Peter Thy
Scott R. Trepel (Siegel Auction Galleries)
Dan Undersander (United Postal Stationery Society)
Herbert R. Volin
Philip T. Wall
Giana Wayman
Gary B. Weiss

Ralph Yorio
Val Zabijaka (Zabijaka Auctions)
Michal Zika
Steven Zirinsky (Zirinsky Stamps)
Alfonso G. Zulueta, Jr.

Addresses, Telephone Numbers, Web Sites, E-Mail Addresses of General & Specialized Philatelic Societies

Collectors can contact the following groups for information about the philately of the areas within the scope of these societies, or inquire about membership in these groups. Aside from the general societies, we limit this list to groups that specialize in particular fields of philately, particular areas covered by the Scott Standard Postage Stamp Catalogue, and topical groups. Many more specialized philatelic society exist than those listed below. These addresses are updated yearly, and they are, to the best of our knowledge, correct and current. Groups should inform the editors of address changes whenever they occur. The editors also want to hear from other such specialized groups not listed. Unless otherwise noted all website addresses begin with http://

American Philatelic Society
100 Match Factory Place
Bellefonte PA 16823-1367
Ph: (814) 933-3803
www.stamps.org
E-mail: apsinfo@stamps.org

American Stamp Dealers Association, Inc.
P.O. Box 692
Leesport PA 19553
Ph: (800) 369-8207
www.americanstampdealer.com
E-mail: asda@americanstampdealer.com

National Stamp Dealers Association
Richard Kostka, President
3643 Private Road 18
Pinckneyville IL 62274-3426
Ph: (800) 875-6633
www.nsdainc.org
E-mail: nsda@nsdainc.org

International Society of Worldwide Stamp Collectors
Joanne Berkowitz, MD
P.O. Box 19006
Sacramento CA 95819
www.iswsc.org
E-mail: executivedirector@iswsc.org

Royal Philatelic Society
41 Devonshire Place
London, W1G 6JY
UNITED KINGDOM
www.rpsl.org.uk
E-mail: secretary@rpsl.org.uk

Royal Philatelic Society of Canada
P.O. Box 929, Station Q
Toronto, ON, M4T 2P1
CANADA
Ph: (888) 285-4143
www.rpsc.org
E-mail: info@rpsc.org

Young Stamp Collectors of America
Janet Houser
100 Match Factory Place
Bellefonte PA 16823-1367
Ph: (814) 933-3820
www.stamps.org/ysca/intro.htm
E-mail: ysca@stamps.org

Philatelic Research Resources
(The Scott editors encourage any additional research organizations to submit data for inclusion in this listing category)

American Philatelic Research Library
Tara Murray
100 Match Factory Place
Bellefonte PA 16823
Ph: (814) 933-3803
www.stamplibrary.org
E-mail: library@stamps.org

Institute for Analytical Philately, Inc.
P.O. Box 8035
Holland MI 49422-8035
Ph: (616) 399-9299
www.analyticalphilately.org
E-mail: info@analyticalphilately.org

The Western Philatelic Library
P.O. Box 2219
1500 Partridge Ave.
Sunnyvale CA 94087
Ph: (408) 733-0336
www.fwpf.org

Groups focusing on fields or aspects found in worldwide philately (some might cover U.S. area only)

American Air Mail Society
Stephen Reinhard
P.O. Box 110
Mineola NY 11501
www.americanairmailsociety.org
E-mail: sreinhard1@optonline.net

American First Day Cover Society
Douglas Kelsey
P.O. Box 16277
Tucson AZ 85732-6277
Ph: (520) 321-0880
www.afdcs.org
E-mail: afdcs@afdcs.org

American Revenue Association
Eric Jackson
P.O. Box 728
Leesport PA 19533-0728
Ph: (610) 926-6200
www.revenuer.org
E-mail: eric@revenuer.com

American Topical Association
Vera Felts
P.O. Box 8
Carterville IL 62918-0008
Ph: (618) 985-5100
www.americantopicalassn.org
E-mail: americantopical@msn.com

Christmas Seal & Charity Stamp Society
John Denune
234 E. Broadway
Granville OH 43023
Ph: (740) 587-0276
www.seal-society.org
E-mail: john@christmasseals.net

Errors, Freaks and Oddities Collectors Club
Scott Shaulis
P.O. Box 549
Murrysville PA 15668-0549
Ph: (724) 733-4134
www.efocc.org

First Issues Collectors Club
Kurt Streepy, Secretary
3128 E. Mattatha Drive
Bloomington IN 47401
www.firstissues.org
E-mail: secretary@firstissues.org

International Society of Reply Coupon Collectors
Peter Robin
P.O. Box 353
Bala Cynwyd PA 19004
E-mail: peterrobin@verizon.net

The Joint Stamp Issues Society
Richard Zimmermann
29A Rue Des Eviats
Lalaye F-67220
FRANCE
www.philarz.net
E-mail: richard.zimmermann@club-internet.fr

National Duck Stamp Collectors Society
Anthony J. Monico
P.O. Box 43
Harleysville PA 19438-0043
www.ndscs.org
E-mail: ndscs@ndscs.org

No Value Identified Club
Albert Sauvanet
Le Clos Royal B, Boulevard des Pas Enchantes
St. Sebastien-sur Loire, 44230
FRANCE
E-mail: alain.vailly@irin.univ nantes.fr

The Perfins Club
Ken Masters
111 NW 94th Street Apt. 102
Kansas City MO 64155-2993
Ph: (816) 835-5907
www.perfins.org
E-mail: kmasters@aol.com

Postage Due Mail Study Group
John Rawlins
13, Longacre
Chelmsford, CM1 3BJ
UNITED KINGDOM
E-mail: john.rawlins2@ukonline.co.uk.

Post Mark Collectors Club
Bob Milligan
7014 Woodland Oaks
Magnolia TX 77354
Ph: (281) 259-2735
www.postmarks.org
E-mail: bob.milligan@gmail.net

Postal History Society
George McGowan
P.O. Box 482
East Schodack NY 12063-0482
www.postalhistorysociety.org
E-mail: geolotus2003@nycap.rr.com

Precancel Stamp Society
Charles Adrion
P.O. Box 10295
Rochester NY 14610
Ph: (585) 319-0600
www.precancels.com
E-mail: pss.promotion@rochester.rr.com

United Postal Stationery Society
Stuart Leven
1659 Branham Lane Suite F-307
San Jose CA 95118-2291
www.upss.org
E-mail: poststat@gmail.com

United States Possessions Philatelic Society
Daniel F. Ring
P.O. Box 113
Woodstock IL 60098
www.uspps.net
E-mail: danielfring@hotmail.com

Groups focusing on U.S. area philately as covered in the Standard Catalogue

Canal Zone Study Group
Tom Brougham
737 Neilson St.
Berkeley CA 94707
www.CanalZoneStudyGroup.com
E-mail: czsgsecretary@gmail.com

Carriers and Locals Society
Martin Richardson
P.O. Box 74
Grosse Ile MI 48138
www.pennypost.org
E-mail: martinr362@aol.com

Confederate Stamp Alliance
Patricia A. Kaufmann
10194 N. Old State Road
Lincoln DE 19960
Ph: (302) 422-2656
www.csalliance.org
E-mail: trishkauf@comcast.net

Hawaiian Philatelic Society
Kay H. Hoke
P.O. Box 10115
Honolulu HI 96816-0115
Ph: (808) 521-5721

Plate Number Coil Collectors Club
Gene Trinks
16415 W. Desert Wren Court
Surprise AZ 85374
Ph: (623) 322-4619
www.pnc3.org
E-mail: gctrinks@cox.net

Ryukyu Philatelic Specialist Society
Laura Edmonds, Secy.
P.O. Box 240177
Charlotte NC 28224-0177
Ph: (336) 509-3739
www.ryukyustamps.org
E-mail: secretary@ryukyustamps.org

United Nations Philatelists
Blanton Clement, Jr.
P.O. Box 146
Morrisville PA 19067-0146
www.unpi.com
E-mail: bclemjr@yahoo.com

United States Stamp Society
Executive Secretary
P.O. Box 6634
Katy TX 77491-6634
www.usstamps.org

U.S. Cancellation Club
Joe Crosby
E-mail: joecrosby@cox.nat

U.S. Philatelic Classics Society
Rob Lund
2913 Fulton St.
Everett WA 98201-3733
www.uspcs.org
E-mail: membershipchairman@uspcs.org

Groups focusing on philately of foreign countries or regions

Aden & Somaliland Study Group
Gary Brown
P.O. Box 106
Briar Hill, Victoria, 3088
AUSTRALIA
E-mail: garyjohn951@optushome.com.au

American Society of Polar Philatelists
(Antarctic areas)
Alan Warren
P.O. Box 39
Exton PA 19341-0039
www.polarphilatelists.org

Andorran Philatelic Study Circle
D. Hope
17 Hawthorn Drive
Stalybridge, Cheshire, SK15 1UE
UNITED KINGDOM
E-mail: andorranpsc@btinternet.com

Australian States Study Circle of The
Royal Sydney Philatelic Club
Ben Palmer
GPO 1751
Sydney, N.S.W., 2001
AUSTRALIA
www.philas.org.au/states

Austria Philatelic Society
Ralph Schneider
P.O. Box 23049
Belleville IL 62223
Ph: (618) 277-6152
www.austriaphilatelicsociety.com
E-mail: rschneiderstamps@att.net

American Belgian Philatelic Society
Edward de Bary
11 Wakefield Drive Apt. 2105
Asheville NC 28803
E-mail: emdeb@charter.net

Bechuanalands and Botswana Society
Neville Midwood
69 Porlock Lane
Furzton, Milton Keynes, MK4 1JY
UNITED KINGDOM
www.nevsoft.com
E-mail: bbsoc@nevsoft.com

Bermuda Collectors Society
John Pare
405 Perimeter Road
Mount Horeb WI 53572
www.bermudacollectorssociety.com
E-mail: pare16@mhtc.net

Brazil Philatelic Association
William V. Kriebel
1923 Manning St.
Philadelphia PA 19103-5728
www.brazilphilatelic.org
E-mail: info@brazilphilatelic.org

British Caribbean Philatelic Study Group
Duane Larson
2 Forest Blvd.
Park Forest IL 60466
www.bcpsg.com
E-mail: dlarson283@aol.com

The King George VI Collectors Society
(British Commonwealth)
Brian Livingstone
21 York Mansions, Prince of Wales Drive
London, SW11 4DL
UNITED KINGDOM
www.kg6.info
E-mail: livingstone484@btinternet.com

British North America Philatelic Society
(Canada & Provinces)
Andy Ellwood
10 Doris Avenue
Gloucester, ON, KIT 3W8
CANADA
www.bnaps.org
E-mail: secretary@bnaps.org

British West Indies Study Circle
John Seidl
4324 Granby Way
Marietta GA 30062
Ph: (770) 642-6424
www.bwisc.org
E-mail: john.seidl@gmail.com

Burma Philatelic Study Circle
Michael Whittaker
1, Ecton Leys, Hillside
Rugby, Warwickshire, CV22 5SL
UNITED KINGDOM
www.burmastamps.homecall.co.uk
E-mail: manningham8@mypostoffice.co.uk

Cape and Natal Study Circle
Dr. Guy Dillaway
P.O. Box 181
Weston MA 02493
www.nzsc.demon.co.uk

Ceylon Study Circle
R. W. P. Frost
42 Lonsdale Road, Cannington
Bridgewater, Somerset, TA5 2JS
UNITED KINGDOM
www.ceylonsc.org
E-mail: rodney.frost@tiscali.co.uk

Channel Islands Specialists Society
Richard Flemming
64, Falconers Green, Burbage
Hinckley, Leicestershire, LE10 2SX
UNITED KINGDOM
www.ciss1950.org.uk
E-mail: secretary@ciss1950.org.uk

China Stamp Society
H. James Maxwell
1050 West Blue Ridge Boulevard
Kansas City MO 64145-1216
www.chinastampsociety.org
E-mail: president@chinastampsociety.org

Colombia/Panama Philatelic Study Group
(COPAPHIL)
Thomas P. Myers
P.O. Box 522
Gordonsville VA 22942
www.copaphil.org
E-mail: tpmphil@hotmail.com

Association Filatelic de Costa Rica
Giana Wayman
c/o Interlink 102, P.O. Box 52-6770
Miami FL 33152
E-mail: scotland@racsa.co.cr

Society for Costa Rica Collectors
Dr. Hector R. Mena
P.O. Box 14831
Baton Rouge LA 70808
www.socorico.org
E-mail: hrmena@aol.com

International Cuban Philatelic Society
Ernesto Cuesta
P.O. Box 34434
Bethesda MD 20827
www.cubafil.org
E-mail: ecuesta@philat.com

Cuban Philatelic Society of America ®
P.O. Box 141656
Coral Gables FL 33114-1656
www.cubapsa.com
E-mail: cpsa.usa@gmail.com

Cyprus Study Circle
Colin Dear
10 Marne Close, Wem
Shropshire, SY4 5YE
UNITED KINGDOM
www.cyprusstudycircle.org/index.htm
E-mail: colindear@talktalk.net

Society for Czechoslovak Philately
Tom Cossaboom
P.O. Box 4124
Prescott AZ 86302
Ph: (928) 771-9097
www.csphilately.org
E-mail: klfck1@aol.com

Danish West Indies Study Unit of the
Scandinavian Collectors Club
Arnold Sorensen
7666 Edgedale Drive
Newburgh IN 47630
Ph: (812) 480-6532
www.scc-online.org
E-mail: valbydwi@hotmail.com

East Africa Study Circle
Michael Vesey-Fitzgerald
Gambles Cottage, 18 Clarence Road
Lyndhurst, SO43 7AL
UNITED KINGDOM
www.easc.org.uk
E-mail: secretary@easc.org.uk

Egypt Study Circle
Mike Murphy
109 Chadwick Road
London, SE15 4PY
UNITED KINGDOM
Trent Ruebush: North American Agent
E-mail: tkruebrush@gmail.com
www.egyptstudycircle.org.uk
E-mail: egyptstudycircle@hotmail.com

Estonian Philatelic Society
Juri Kirsimagi
29 Clifford Ave.
Pelham NY 10803
Ph: (914) 738-3713

Ethiopian Philatelic Society
Ulf Lindahl
21 Westview Place
Riverside CT 06878
Ph: (203) 722-0769
http://ethiopianphilatelicsociety.weebly.com
E-mail: ulindahl@optonline.net

Falkland Islands Philatelic Study Group
Carl J. Faulkner
615 Taconic Trail
Williamstown MA 01267-2745
Ph: (413) 458-4421
www.fipsg.org.uk
E-mail: cfaulkner@taconicwilliamstown.
com

Faroe Islands Study Circle
Norman Hudson
40 Queen's Road, Vicar's Cross
Chester, CH3 5HB
UNITED KINGDOM
www.faroeislandssc.org
E-mail: jntropics@hotmail.com

Former French Colonies Specialist Society
COLFRA
BP 628
75367 Paris, Cedex 08
FRANCE
www.colfra.org
E-mail: secretaire@colfra.org

France & Colonies Philatelic Society
Edward Grabowski
111 Prospect St., 4C
Westfield NJ 07090
www.franceandcolps.org
E-mail: edjjg@alum.mit.edu

Germany Philatelic Society
P.O. Box 6547
Chesterfield MO 63006
www.germanyphilatelicusa.org

Plebiscite-Memel-Saar Study Group of the
German Philatelic Society
Clayton Wallace
100 Lark Court
Alamo CA 94507
E-mail: claytonwallace@comcast.net

Gibraltar Study Circle
Eric D. Holmes
29 Highgate Road
Woodley, Berkshire RG5 3ND
UNITED KINGDOM
www.gibraltarstudycircle.wordpress.com
E-mail: ericholmes@talktalk.net

Great Britain Collectors Club
Steve McGill
10309 Brookhollow Circle
Highlands Ranch CO 80129
www.gbstamps.com/gbcc
E-mail: steve.mcgill@comcast.net

International Society of Guatemala
Collectors
Jaime Marckwordt
449 St. Francis Blvd.
Daly City CA 94015-2136
www.guatemalastamps.com
E-mail:
membership@guatamalastamps.com

Haiti Philatelic Society
Ubaldo Del Toro
5709 Marble Archway
Alexandria VA 22315
www.haitiphilately.org
E-mail: u007ubi@aol.com

Federacion Filatelica de la Republica
de Honduras (Honduran Philatelic
Federation, FFRH)
Mauricio Mejia
Apartado postal 1465
Tegucigalpa
HONDURAS

Hong Kong Stamp Society
Ming W. Tsang
P.O. Box 206
Glenside PA 19038
www.hkss.org
E-mail: hkstamps@yahoo.com

Society for Hungarian Philately
Robert Morgan
2201 Roscomare Road
Los Angeles CA 90077-2222
Ph: (978) 682-0242
www.hungarianphilately.org
E-mail: alan@hungarianstamps.com

India Study Circle
John Warren
P.O. Box 7326
Washington DC 20044
Ph: (202) 564-6876
www.indiastudycircle.org
E-mail: warren.john@epa.gov

Indian Ocean Study Circle
E. S. Hutton
29 Patermoster Close
Waltham Abby, Essex, EN9 3JU
UNITED KINGDOM
www.indianoceanstudycircle.com
E-mail: secretary@indianoceanstudy-
circle.com

Society of Indo-China Philatelists
Ron Bentley
2600 N. 24th St.
Arlington VA 22207
www.sicp-online.org
E-mail: ron.bentley@verizon.net

Iran Philatelic Study Circle
Mehdi Esmaili
P.O. Box 750096
Forest Hills NY 11375
www.iranphilatelic.org
E-mail: m.esmaili@earthlink.net

Eire Philatelic Association (Ireland)
David J. Brennan
P.O. Box 704
Bernardsville NJ 07924
www.eirephilatelicassoc.org
E-mail: brennan704@aol.com

Society of Israel Philatelists
Becky Dean
100 Match Factory Place
Bellefonte PA 16823-1367
Ph: (814) 933-3802 ext. 212
www.israelstamps.com
E-mail: israelstamps@gmail.com

Italy and Colonies Study Circle
Richard Harlow
7 Duncombe House, 8 Manor Road
Teddington, TW11 8BE
UNITED KINGDOM
www.icsc.pwp.blueyonder.co.uk
E-mail: harlowr@gmail.com

International Society for Japanese
Philately
William Eisenhauer
P.O. Box 230462
Tigard OR 97281
www.isjp.org
E-mail: secretary@isjp.org

Korea Stamp Society
John E. Talmage
P.O. Box 6889
Oak Ridge TN 37831
www.pennfamily.org/KSS-USA
E-mail: jtalmage@usit.net

Latin American Philatelic Society
Jules K. Beck
30½ St. #209
St. Louis Park MN 55426-3551

Liberian Philatelic Society
William Thomas Lockard
P.O. Box 106
Wellston OH 45692
Ph: (740) 384-2020
E-mail: tlockard@zoomnet.net

Liechtenstudy USA (Liechtenstein)
Paul Tremaine
410 SW Ninth St.
Dundee OR 97115
Ph: (503) 538-4500
www.liechtenstudy.org
E-mail: editor@liechtenstudy.org

Lithuania Philatelic Society
John Variakojis
8472 Carlisle Court
Burr Ridge IL 60527
Ph: (630) 974-6525
www.lithuanianphilately.com/lps
E-mail: variakojis@sbcglobal.net

Luxembourg Collectors Club
Gary B. Little
7319 Beau Road
Sechelt, BC, V0N 3A8
CANADA
lcc.luxcentral.com
E-mail: gary@luxcentral.com

Malaya Study Group
David Tett
16 Broadway, Gustard Wood
Wheathampstead, Herts, AL4 8LN
UNITED KINGDOM
www.m-s-g.org.uk
E-mail: davidtett@aol.com

Malta Study Circle
Rodger Evans
Ravensbourne, Hook Heath Road
Woking, Surrey, GU22 0LB
UNITED KINGDOM
www.maltastudycircle.org.uk
E-mail: carge@hotmail.co.uk

Mexico-Elmhurst Philatelic Society
International
Thurston Bland
50 Regato
Rancho Santa Margarita CA 92688-3003
www.mepsi.org

Asociacion Mexicana de Filatelia
AMEXFIL
Jose Maria Rico, 129, Col. Del Valle
Mexico City DF, 03100
MEXICO
www.amexfil.mx
E-mail: amexfil@gmail.com

Society for Moroccan and Tunisian Philately
S.P.L.M.
206, bld. Pereire
Paris 75017
FRANCE
splm-philatelie.org
E-mail: splm206@aol.com

Nepal & Tibet Philatelic Study Group
Roger D. Skinner
1020 Covington Road
Los Altos CA 94024-5003
Ph: (650) 968-4163
www.fuchs-online.com/ntpsc/
E-mail: colinhepper@hotmail.co.uk

American Society for Netherlands Philately
Hans Kremer
50 Rockport Court
Danville CA 94526
Ph: (925) 820-5841
www.asnp1975.com
E-mail: hkremer@usa.net

New Zealand Society of Great Britain
Michael Wilkinson
121 London Road
Sevenoaks, Kent, TN13 1BH
UNITED KINGDOM
www.nzsgb.org.uk
E-mail: mwilkin799@aol.com

Nicaragua Study Group
Erick Rodriguez
11817 SW 11th St.
Miami FL 33184-2501
clubs.yahoo.com/clubs/
nicaraguastudygroup
E-mail: nsgsec@yahoo.com

Society of Australasian Specialists/Oceania
David McNamee
P.O. Box 37
Alamo CA 94507
www.sasoceania.org
E-mail: treasurer@sasoceania.org

Orange Free State Study Circle
J. R. Stroud
24 Hooper Close
Burnham-on-sea, Somerset, TA8 1JQ
UNITED KINGDOM
orangefreestatephilately.org.uk
E-mail: richardstroudph@gofast.co.uk

Pacific Islands Study Circle
John Ray
24 Woodvale Ave.
London, SE25 4AE
UNITED KINGDOM
www.pisc.org.uk
E-mail: info@pisc.org.uk

Pakistan Philatelic Study Circle
Jeff Siddiqui
P.O. Box 7002
Lynnwood WA 98046
E-mail: jeffsiddiqui@msn.com

Centro de Filatelistas Independientes de
Panama
Vladimir Berrio-Lemm
Apartado 0823-02748
Plaza Concordia Panama
PANAMA
E-mail: panahistoria@gmail.com

Papuan Philatelic Society
Steven Zirinsky
P.O. Box 49, Ansonia Station
New York NY 10023
Ph: (718) 706-0616
www.communigate.co.uk/york/pps
E-mail: szirinsky@cs.com

International Philippine Philatelic Society
Donald J. Peterson
P.O. Box 122
Brunswick MD 21716
Ph: (301) 834-6419
www.theipps.info
E-mail: dpeterson4526@gmail.com

Pitcairn Islands Study Group
Dr. Everett L. Parker
117 Cedar Breeze South
Glenburn ME 04401-1734
Ph: (386) 688-1358
www.pisg.net
E-mail: eparker@hughes.net

Polonus Philatelic Society (Poland)
Daniel Lubelski
P.O. Box 60438
Rossford OH 43460
Ph: (419) 410-9115
www.polonus.org
E-mail: info@polonus.org

International Society for Portuguese
Philately
Clyde Homen
1491 Bonnie View Road
Hollister CA 95023-5117
www.portugalstamps.com
E-mail: ispp1962@sbcglobal.net

Rhodesian Study Circle
William R. Wallace
P.O. Box 16381
San Francisco CA 94116
www.rhodesianstudycircle.org.uk
E-mail: bwall8rscr@earthlink.net

Rossica Society of Russian Philately
Alexander Kolchinsky
1506 Country Lake Drive
Champaign IL 6821-6428
www.rossica.org
E-mail: alexander.kolchinsky@rossica.org

St. Helena, Ascension & Tristan Da Cunha
Philatelic Society
Dr. Everett L. Parker
117 Cedar Breeze South
Glenburn ME 04401-1734
Ph: (386) 688-1358
www.shatps.org
E-mail: eparker@hughes.net

St. Pierre & Miquelon Philatelic Society
James R. (Jim) Taylor
2335 Paliswood Road SW
Calgary, AB, T2V 3P6
CANADA
www.stamps.org/spm

Associated Collectors of El Salvador
Joseph D. Hahn
1015 Old Boalsburg Road Apt G-5
State College PA 16801-6149
www.elsalvadorphilately.org
E-mail: jdhahn2@gmail.com

Fellowship of Samoa Specialists
Donald Mee
23 Leo St.
Christchurch, 8051
NEW ZEALAND
www.samoaexpress.org
E-mail: donanm@xtra.co.nz

Sarawak Specialists' Society
Stephen Schumann
2417 Cabrillo Drive-
Hayward CA 94545
Ph: (510) 785-4794
www.britborneostamps.org.uk
E-mail: sdsch@earthlink.net

Scandinavian Collectors Club
Steve Lund
P.O. Box 16213
St. Paul MN 55116
www.scc-online.org
E-mail: steve88h@aol.com

Slovakia Stamp Society
Jack Benchik
P.O. Box 555
Notre Dame IN 46556

Philatelic Society for Greater Southern
Africa
Alan Hanks
34 Seaton Drive
Aurora, ON, L4G 2K1
CANADA
www.psgsa.thestampweb.com

South Sudan Philatelic Society
William Barclay
1370 Spring Hill Road
South Londonderry VT 05155
E-mail: barclayphilatelics@gmail.com

Spanish Philatelic Society
Robert H. Penn
1108 Walnut Drive
Danielsville PA 18038
Ph: (610) 844-8963
E-mail: roberthpenn43@gmail.com

Sudan Study Group
Paul Grigg
19 Howmead
Berkeley, GLOS, GL13 9AR
England
UNITED KINGDOM
www.sudanstamps.org

American Helvetia Philatelic Society
(Switzerland, Liechtenstein)
Richard T. Hall
P.O. Box 15053
Asheville NC 28813-0053
www.swiss-stamps.org
E-mail: secretary2@swiss-stamps.org

Tannu Tuva Collectors Society
Ken R. Simon
P.O. Box 385
Lake Worth FL 33460-0385
Ph: (561) 588-5954
www.tuva.tk
E-mail: yurttuva@yahoo.com

Society for Thai Philately
H. R. Blakeney
P.O. Box 25644
Oklahoma City OK 73125
E-mail: HRBlakeney@aol.com

Transvaal Study Circle
Chris Board
36 Wakefield Gardens
London, SE19 2NR
UNITED KINGDOM
www.transvaalstamps.org.uk
E-mail: c.board@macace.net

Ottoman and Near East Philatelic Society
(Turkey and related areas)
Bob Stuchell
193 Valley Stream Lane
Wayne PA 19087
www.oneps.org
E-mail: rstuchell@msn.com

Ukrainian Philatelic & Numismatic Society
Martin B. Tatuch
5117 8th Road N.
Arlington VA 22205-1201
www.upns.org
E-mail: treasurer@upns.org

Vatican Philatelic Society
Sal Quinonez
1 Aldersgate, Apt. 1002
Riverhead NY 11901-1830
Ph: (516) 727-6426
www.vaticanphilately.org

British Virgin Islands Philatelic Society
Giorgio Migliavacca
P.O. Box 7007
St. Thomas VI 00801-0007
www.islandsun.com/category/collectables/
E-mail: issun@candwbvi.net

West Africa Study Circle
Martin Bratzel
1233 Virginia Ave.
Windsor, ON, N8S 2Z1
CANADA
www.wasc.org.uk
E-mail: marty_bratzel@yahoo.ca

Western Australia Study Group
Brian Pope
P.O. Box 423
Claremont, Western Australia, 6910
AUSTRALIA
www.wastudygroup.com
E-mail: black5swan@yahoo.com.au

Yugoslavia Study Group of the Croatian Philatelic Society
Michael Lenard
1514 N. Third Ave.
Wausau WI 54401
Ph: (715) 675-2833
E-mail: mjlenard@aol.com

Topical Groups

Americana Unit
Dennis Dengel
17 Peckham Road
Poughkeepsie NY 12603-2018
www.americanaunit.org
E-mail: ddengel@americanaunit.org

Astronomy Study Unit
John Budd
728 Sugar Camp Way
Brooksville FL 34604
Ph: (352) 345-4799
E-mail: jwgbudd@gmail.com

Bicycle Stamp Club
Steve Andreasen
2000 Alaskan Way, Unit 157
Seattle WA 98121
E-mail: steven.w.andreasen@gmail.com

Biology Unit
Alan Hanks
34 Seaton Drive
Aurora, ON, L4G 2K1
CANADA
Ph: (905) 727-6993

Bird Stamp Society
S. A. H. (Tony) Statham
Ashlyns Lodge, Chesham Road,
Berkhamsted, Hertfordshire HP4 2ST
UNITED KINGDOM
www.bird-stamps.org/bss
E-mail: tony.statham@sky.com

Captain Cook Society
Jerry Yucht
8427 Leale Ave.
Stockton CA 95212
www.captaincooksociety.com
E-mail: US@captaincooksociety.com

The CartoPhilatelic Society
Marybeth Sulkowski
2885 Sanford Ave, SW, #32361
Grandville MI 49418-1342
www.mapsonstamps.org
E-mail: secretary@mapsonstamps.org

Casey Jones Railroad Unit
Roy W. Menninger MD
P.O. Box 5511
Topeka KS 66605
Ph: (785) 231-8366
www.uqp.de/cjr/index.htm
E-mail: roymenn85@gmail.com

Cats on Stamps Study Unit
Robert D. Jarvis
2731 Teton Lane
Fairfield CA 94533
www.catstamps.info
E-mail: bobmarci@aol.com

Chemistry & Physics on Stamps Study Unit
Dr. Roland Hirsch
20458 Water Point Lane
Germantown MD 20874
www.cpossu.org
E-mail: rfhirsch@cpossu.org

Chess on Stamps Study Unit
Ray C. Alexis
608 Emery St.
Longmont CO 80501
E-mail: chessstuff911459@aol.com

Christmas Philatelic Club
Jim Balog
P.O. Box 774
Geneva OH 44041
www.christmasphilatelicclub.org
E-mail: jpb4stamps@windstream.net

Cricket Philatelic Society
A.Melville-Brown, President
11 Weppons, Ravens Road
Shoreham-by-Sea
West Sussex, BN43 5AW
UNITED KINGDOM
www.cricketstamp.net
E-mail: mel.cricket.100@googlemail.com

Dogs on Stamps Study Unit
Morris Raskin
202A Newport Road
Monroe Township NJ 08831
Ph: (609) 655-7411
www.dossu.org
E-mail: mraskin@cellurian.com

Earth's Physical Features Study Group
Fred Klein
515 Magdalena Ave.
Los Altos CA 94024
epfsu.jeffhayward.com

Ebony Society of Philatelic Events and Reflections, Inc. (African-American topicals)
Manuel Gilyard
800 Riverside Drive, Suite 4H
New York NY 10032-7412
www.esperstamps.org
E-mail: gilyardmani@aol.com

Europa Study Unit
Tonny E. Van Loij
3002 S. Xanthia St.
Denver CO 80231-4237
Ph: (303) 752-0189
www.europastudyunit.org
E-mail: tvanloij@gmail.com

Fine & Performing Arts
Deborah L. Washington
6922 S. Jeffery Blvd., #7 - North
Chicago IL 60649
E-mail: brasslady@comcast.net

Fire Service in Philately
John Zaranek
81 Hillpine Road
Cheektowaga NY 14227-2259
Ph: (716) 668-3352
E-mail: jczaranek@roadrunner.com

Gay & Lesbian History on Stamps Club
Joe Petronie
P.O. Box 190842
Dallas TX 75219-0842
www.facebook.com/glhsc
E-mail: glhsc@aol.com

Gems, Minerals & Jewelry Study Unit
Mrs. Gilberte Proteau
138 Lafontaine
Beloeil QC J3G 2G7
CANADA
Ph: (978) 851-8283
E-mail: gilberte.ferland@sympatico.ca

Graphics Philately Association
Mark H. Winnegrad
P.O. Box 380
Bronx NY 10462-0380
www.graphics-stamps.org
E-mail: indybruce1@yahoo.com

Journalists, Authors & Poets on Stamps
Ms. Lee Straayer
P.O. Box 6808
Champaign IL 61826
E-mail: lstraayer@dcbnet.com

Lighthouse Stamp Society
Dalene Thomas
1805 S Balsam St., #106
Lakewood CO 80232
Ph: (303) 986-6620
www.lighthousestampsociety.org
E-mail: dalene@lighthousestampsociety.org

Lions International Stamp Club
John Bargus
108-2769 Barry Road RR 2
Mill Bay, BC, V0R 2P2
CANADA
Ph: (250) 743-5782

Mahatma Gandhi On Stamps Study Circle
Pramod Shivagunde
Pratik Clinic, Akluj
Solapur, Maharashtra, 413101
INDIA
E-mail: drnanda@bom6.vsnl.net.in

Masonic Study Unit
Stanley R. Longenecker
930 Wood St.
Mount Joy PA 17552-1926
Ph: (717) 669-9094
E-mail: natsco@usa.net

Mathematical Study Unit
Monty Strauss
4209 88th St.
Lubbock TX 79423-2941
www.mathstamps.org

Medical Subjects Unit
Dr. Frederick C. Skvara
P.O. Box 6228
Bridgewater NJ 08807
E-mail: fcskvara@optonline.net

Military Postal History Society
Ed Dubin
1 S. Wacker Drive, Suite 3500
Chicago IL 60606
www.militaryPHS.org
E-mail: dubine@comcast.net

Mourning Stamps and Covers Club
James Camak, Jr.
3801 Acapulco Ct.
Irving TX 75062
www.mscc.ms
E-mail: jamescamak7@gmail.com

Napoleonic Age Philatelists
Ken Berry
4117 NW 146th St.
Oklahoma City OK 73134-1746
Ph: (405) 748-8646
www.nap-stamps.org
E-mail: krb4117@att.net

Old World Archeological Study Unit
Caroline Scannell
11 Dawn Drive
Smithtown NY 11787-1761
www.owasu.org
E-mail: editor@owasu.org

Petroleum Philatelic Society International
Feitze Papa
922 Meander Dr.
Walnut Creek CA 94598-4239
E-mail: oildad@astound.net

Rotary on Stamps Unit
Gerald L. Fitzsimmons
105 Calla Ricardo
Victoria TX 77904
rotaryonstamps.org
E-mail: glfitz@suddenlink.net

Scouts on Stamps Society International
Lawrence Clay
P.O. Box 6228
Kennewick WA 99336
Ph: (509) 735-3731
www.sossi.org
E-mail: rfrank@sossi.org

Ships on Stamps Unit
Les Smith
302 Conklin Ave.
Penticton, BC, V2A 2T4
CANADA
Ph: (250) 493-7486
www.shipsonstamps.org
E-mail: lessmith440@shaw.ca

Space Unit
David Blog
P.O. Box 174
Bergenfield NJ 07621
www.space-unit.com
E-mail: davidblognj@gmail.com

Sports Philatelists International
Mark Maestrone
2824 Curie Place
San Diego CA 92122-4110
www.sportstamps.org
Email: president@sportstamps.org

Stamps on Stamps Collectors Club
Alf Jordan
156 W. Elm St.
Yarmouth ME 04096
www.stampsonstamps.org
E-mail: ajordan1@maine.rr.com

Windmill Study Unit
Orville Tysseling
9740 Washington Church Rd.
Miamisburg OH 45342-4510
www.wsu.world

Wine On Stamps Study Unit
David Wolfersberger
768 Chain Ridge Road
St. Louis MO 63122-3259
Ph: (314) 961-5032
www.wine-on-stamps.org
E-mail: dewolf2@swbell.net

Women on Stamps Study Unit
Hugh Gottfried
2232 26th St.
Santa Monica CA 90405-1902
E-mail: hgottfried@adelphia.net

Expertizing Services

The following organizations will, for a fee, provide expert opinions about stamps submitted to them. Collectors should contact these organizations to find out about their fees and requirements before submiting philatelic material to them. The listing of these groups here is not intended as an endorsement by Amos Media Co.

General Expertizing Services

American Philatelic Expertizing Service (a service of the American Philatelic Society)
100 Match Factory Place
Bellefonte PA 16823-1367
Ph: (814) 237-3803
Fax: (814) 237-6128
www.stamps.org
E-mail: ambristo@stamps.org
Areas of Expertise: Worldwide

B. P. A. Expertising, Ltd.
P.O. Box 1141
Guildford, Surrey, GU5 0WR
UNITED KINGDOM
E-mail: sec@bpaexpertising.org
Areas of Expertise: British Commonwealth, Great Britain, Classics of Europe, South America and the Far East

Philatelic Foundation
341 W. 38th St., 5th Floor
New York NY 10018
Ph: (212) 221-6555
Fax: (212) 221-6208
www.philatelicfoundation.org
E-mail: philatelicfoundation@verizon.net
Areas of Expertise: U.S. & Worldwide

Philatelic Stamp Authentication and Grading, Inc.
P.O. Box 41-0880
Melbourne FL 32941-0880
Customer Service: (305) 345-9864
www.psaginc.com
E-mail: info@psaginc.com
Areas of Expertise: U.S., Canal Zone, Hawaii, Philippines, Canada & Provinces

Professional Stamp Experts
P.O. Box 6170
Newport Beach CA 92658
Ph: (877) STAMP-88
Fax: (949) 833-7955
www.collectors.com/pse
E-mail: pseinfo@collectors.com
Areas of Expertise: Stamps and covers of U.S., U.S. Possessions, British Commonwealth

Royal Philatelic Society Expert Committee
41 Devonshire Place
London, W1N 1PE
UNITED KINGDOM
www.rpsl.org.uk/experts.html
E-mail: experts@rpsl.org.uk
Areas of Expertise: Worldwide

Expertizing Services Covering Specific Fields Or Countries

China Stamp Society Expertizing Service
1050 W. Blue Ridge Blvd.
Kansas City MO 64145
Ph: (816) 942-6300
E-mail: hjmesq@aol.com
Areas of Expertise: China

Confederate Stamp Alliance Authentication Service
Gen. Frank Crown, Jr.
P.O. Box 278
Capshaw AL 35742-0396
Ph: (302) 422-2656
Fax: (302) 424-1990
www.csalliance.org
E-mail: csaas@knology.net
Areas of Expertise: Confederate stamps and postal history

Errors, Freaks and Oddities Collectors Club Expertizing Service
138 East Lakemont Drive
Kingsland GA 31548
Ph: (912) 729-1573
Areas of Expertise: U.S. errors, freaks and oddities

Estonian Philatelic Society Expertizing Service
39 Clafford Lane
Melville NY 11747
Ph: (516) 421-2078
E-mail: esto4@aol.com
Areas of Expertise: Estonia

Hawaiian Philatelic Society Expertizing Service
P.O. Box 10115
Honolulu HI 96816-0115
Areas of Expertise: Hawaii

Hong Kong Stamp Society Expertizing Service
P.O. Box 206
Glenside PA 19038
Fax: (215) 576-6850
Areas of Expertise: Hong Kong

International Association of Philatelic Experts
United States Associate members:

Paul Buchsbayew
119 W. 57th St.
New York NY 10019
Ph: (212) 977-7734
Fax: (212) 977-8653
Areas of Expertise: Russia, Soviet Union

William T. Crowe
P.O. Box 2090
Danbury CT 06813-2090
E-mail: wtcrowe@aol.com
Areas of Expertise: United States

John Lievsay
(see American Philatelic Expertizing Service and Philatelic Foundation)
Areas of Expertise: France

Robert W. Lyman
P.O. Box 348
Irvington on Hudson NY 10533
Ph and Fax: (914) 591-6937
Areas of Expertise: British North America, New Zealand

Robert Odenweller
P.O. Box 401
Bernardsville NJ 07924-0401
Ph and Fax: (908) 766-5460
Areas of Expertise: New Zealand, Samoa to 1900

Sergio Sismondo
The Regency Tower, Suite 1109
770 James Street
Syracuse NY 13203
Ph: (315) 422-2331
Fax: (315) 422-2956
Areas of Expertise: British East Africa, Camerouns, Cape of Good Hope, Canada, British North America

International Society for Japanese Philately Expertizing Committee
132 North Pine Terrace
Staten Island NY 10312-4052
Ph: (718) 227-5229
Areas of Expertise: Japan and related areas, except WWII Japanese Occupation issues

International Society for Portuguese Philately Expertizing Service
P.O. Box 43146
Philadelphia PA 19129-3146
Ph and Fax: (215) 843-2106
E-mail: s.s.washburne@worldnet.att.net
Areas of Expertise: Portugal and Colonies

Mexico-Elmhurst Philatelic Society International Expert Committee
P.O. Box 1133
West Covina CA 91793
Areas of Expertise: Mexico

Ukrainian Philatelic & Numismatic Society Expertizing Service
30552 Dell Lane
Warren MI 48092-1862
Areas of Expertise: Ukraine, Western Ukraine

V. G. Greene Philatelic Research Foundation
P.O. Box 204, Station Q
Toronto, ON, M4T 2M1
CANADA
Ph: (416) 921-2073
Fax: (416) 921-1282
www.greenefoundation.ca
E-mail: vggfoundation@on.aibn.com
Areas of Expertise: British North America

Information on Catalogue Values, Grade and Condition

Catalogue Value

The Scott Catalogue value is a retail value; that is, an amount you could expect to pay for a stamp in the grade of Very Fine with no faults. Any exceptions to the grade valued will be noted in the text. The general introduction on the following pages and the individual section introductions further explain the type of material that is valued. The value listed for any given stamp is a reference that reflects recent actual dealer selling prices for that item.

Dealer retail price lists, public auction results, published prices in advertising and individual solicitation of retail prices from dealers, collectors and specialty organizations have been used in establishing the values found in this catalogue. Amos Media Co. values stamps, but Amos Media is not a company engaged in the business of buying and selling stamps as a dealer.

Use this catalogue as a guide for buying and selling. The actual price you pay for a stamp may be higher or lower than the catalogue value because of many different factors, including the amount of personal service a dealer offers, or increased or decreased interest in the country or topic represented by a stamp or set. An item may occasionally be offered at a lower price as a "loss leader," or as part of a special sale. You also may obtain an item inexpensively at public auction because of little interest at that time or as part of a large lot.

Stamps that are of a lesser grade than Very Fine, or those with condition problems, generally trade at lower prices than those given in this catalogue. Stamps of exceptional quality in both grade and condition often command higher prices than those listed.

Values for pre-1900 unused issues are for stamps with approximately half or more of their original gum. Stamps with most or all of their original gum may be expected to sell for more, and stamps with less than half of their original gum may be expected to sell for somewhat less than the values listed. On rarer stamps, it may be expected that the original gum will be somewhat more disturbed than it will be on more common issues. Post-1900 unused issues are assumed to have full original gum. From breakpoints in most countries' listings, stamps are valued as never hinged, due to the wide availability of stamps in that condition. These notations are prominently placed in the listings and in the country information preceding the listings. Some countries also feature listings with dual values for hinged and never-hinged stamps.

Grade

A stamp's grade and condition are crucial to its value. The accompanying illustrations show examples of Very Fine stamps from different time periods, along with examples of stamps in Fine to Very Fine and Extremely Fine grades as points of reference. When a stamp seller offers a stamp in any grade from fine to superb without further qualifying statements, that stamp should not only have the centering grade as defined, but it also should be free of faults or other condition problems.

FINE stamps (illustrations not shown) have designs that are quite off center, with the perforations on one or two sides very close to the design but not quite touching it. There is white space between the perforations and the design that is minimal but evident to the unaided eye. Imperforate stamps may have small margins, and earlier issues may show the design just touching one edge of the stamp design. Very early perforated issues normally will have the perforations slightly cutting into the design. Used stamps may have heavier than usual cancellations.

FINE-VERY FINE stamps will be somewhat off center on one side, or slightly off center on two sides. Imperforate stamps will have two margins of at least normal size, and the design will not touch any edge. For perforated stamps, the perfs are well clear of the design, but are still noticeably off center. *However, early issues of a country may be printed in such a way that the design naturally is very close to the edges. In these cases, the perforations may cut into the design very slightly.* Used stamps will not have a cancellation that detracts from the design.

VERY FINE stamps will be just slightly off center on one or two sides, but the design will be well clear of the edge. The stamp will present a nice, balanced appearance. Imperforate stamps will be well centered within normal-sized margins. *However, early issues of many countries may be printed in such a way that the perforations may touch the design on one or more sides. Where this is the case, a boxed note will be found defining the centering and margins of the stamps being valued.* Used stamps will have light or otherwise neat cancellations. This is the grade used to establish Scott Catalogue values.

EXTREMELY FINE stamps are close to being perfectly centered. Imperforate stamps will have even margins that are slightly larger than normal. Even the earliest perforated issues will have perforations clear of the design on all sides.

Amos Media Co. recognizes that there is no formally enforced grading scheme for postage stamps, and that the final price you pay or obtain for a stamp will be determined by individual agreement at the time of transaction.

Condition

Grade addresses only centering and (for used stamps) cancellation. *Condition* refers to factors other than grade that affect a stamp's desirability.

Factors that can increase the value of a stamp include exceptionally wide margins, particularly fresh color, the presence of selvage, and plate or die varieties. Unusual cancels on used stamps (particularly those of the 19th century) can greatly enhance their value as well.

Factors other than faults that decrease the value of a stamp include loss of original gum, regumming, a hinge remnant or foreign object adhering to the gum, natural inclusions, straight edges, and markings or notations applied by collectors or dealers.

Faults include missing pieces, tears, pin or other holes, surface scuffs, thin spots, creases, toning, short or pulled perforations, clipped perforations, oxidation or other forms of color changelings, soiling, stains, and such man-made changes as reperforations or the chemical removal or lightening of a cancellation.

Grading Illustrations

On the following two pages are illustrations of various stamps from countries appearing in this volume. These stamps are arranged by country, and they represent early or important issues that are often found in widely different grades in the marketplace. The editors believe the illustrations will prove useful in showing the margin size and centering that will be seen on the various issues.

In addition to the matters of margin size and centering, collectors are reminded that the very fine stamps valued in the Scott catalogues also will possess fresh color and intact perforations, and they will be free from defects.

Examples shown are computer-manipulated images made from single digitized master illustrations.

Stamp Illustrations Used in the Catalogue

It is important to note that the stamp images used for identification purposes in this catlaogue may not be indicative of the grade of stamp being valued. Refer to the written discussion of grades on this page and to the grading illustrations on the following two pages for grading information.

Fine-Very Fine

SCOTT CATALOGUES VALUE STAMPS IN THIS GRADE

Very Fine

Extremely Fine

Fine-Very Fine

SCOTT CATALOGUES VALUE STAMPS IN THIS GRADE

Very Fine

Extremely Fine

For purposes of helping to determine the gum condition and value of an unused stamp, Scott presents the following chart which details different gum conditions and indicates how the conditions correlate with the Scott values for unused stamps. Used together, the Illustrated Grading Chart on the previous pages and this Illustrated Gum Chart should allow catalogue users to better understand the grade and gum condition of stamps valued in the Scott catalogues.

Gum Categories:	MINT N.H.	ORIGINAL GUM (O.G.)				NO GUM
	Mint Never Hinged *Free from any disturbance*	**Lightly Hinged** *Faint impression of a removed hinge over a small area*	**Hinge Mark or Remnant** *Prominent hinged spot with part or all of the hinge remaining*	**Large part o.g.** *Approximately half or more of the gum intact*	**Small part o.g.** *Approximately less than half of the gum intact*	**No gum** *Only if issued with gum*
Commonly Used Symbol:	★★	★	★	★	★	(★)
Pre-1900 Issues (Pre-1881 for U.S.)	*Very fine pre-1900 stamps in these categories trade at a premium over Scott value*			Scott Value for "Unused"		Scott "No Gum" listings for selected unused classic stamps
From 1900 to breakpoints for listings of never-hinged stamps	Scott "Never Hinged" listings for selected unused stamps	Scott Value for "Unused" (Actual value will be affected by the degree of hinging of the full o.g.)				
From breakpoints noted for many countries	Scott Value for "Unused"					

Never Hinged (NH; ★★): A never-hinged stamp will have full original gum that will have no hinge mark or disturbance. The presence of an expertizer's mark does not disqualify a stamp from this designation.

Original Gum (OG; ★): Pre-1900 stamps should have approximately half or more of their original gum. On rarer stamps, it may be expected that the original gum will be somewhat more disturbed than it will be on more common issues. Post-1900 stamps should have full original gum. Original gum will show some disturbance caused by a previous hinge(s) which may be present or entirely removed. The actual value of a post-1900 stamp will be affected by the degree of hinging of the full original gum.

Disturbed Original Gum: Gum showing noticeable effects of humidity, climate or hinging over more than half of the gum. The significance of gum disturbance in valuing a stamp in any of the Original Gum categories depends on the degree of disturbance, the rarity and normal gum condition of the issue and other variables affecting quality.

Regummed (RG; (★)): A regummed stamp is a stamp without gum that has had some type of gum privately applied at a time after it was issued. This normally is done to deceive collectors and/or dealers into thinking that the stamp has original gum and therefore has a higher value. A regummed stamp is considered the same as a stamp with none of its original gum for purposes of grading.

Understanding the Listings

On the opposite page is an enlarged "typical" listing from this catalogue. Below are detailed explanations of each of the highlighted parts of the listing.

❶ Scott number — Scott catalogue numbers are used to identify specific items when buying, selling or trading stamps. Each listed postage stamp from every country has a unique Scott catalogue number. Therefore, Germany Scott 99, for example, can only refer to a single stamp. Although the Scott catalogue usually lists stamps in chronological order by date of issue, there are exceptions. When a country has issued a set of stamps over a period of time, those stamps within the set are kept together without regard to date of issue. This follows the normal collecting approach of keeping stamps in their natural sets.

When a country issues a set of stamps over a period of time, a group of consecutive catalogue numbers is reserved for the stamps in that set, as issued. If that group of numbers proves to be too few, capital-letter suffixes, such as "A" or "B," may be added to existing numbers to create enough catalogue numbers to cover all items in the set. A capital-letter suffix indicates a major Scott catalogue number listing. Scott generally uses a suffix letter only once. Therefore, a catalogue number listing with a capital-letter suffix will seldom be found with the same letter (lower case) used as a minor-letter listing. If there is a Scott 16A in a set, for example, there will seldom be a Scott 16a. However, a minor-letter "a" listing may be added to a major number containing an "A" suffix (Scott 16Aa, for example).

Suffix letters are cumulative. A minor "b" variety of Scott 16A would be Scott 16Ab, not Scott 16b.

There are times when a reserved block of Scott catalogue numbers is too large for a set, leaving some numbers unused. Such gaps in the numbering sequence also occur when the catalogue editors move an item's listing elsewhere or have removed it entirely from the catalogue. Scott does not attempt to account for every possible number, but rather attempts to assure that each stamp is assigned its own number.

Scott numbers designating regular postage normally are only numerals. Scott numbers for other types of stamps, such as air post, semi-postal, postal tax, postage due, occupation and others have a prefix consisting of one or more capital letters or a combination of numerals and capital letters.

❷ Illustration number — Illustration or design-type numbers are used to identify each catalogue illustration. For most sets, the lowest face-value stamp is shown. It then serves as an example of the basic design approach for other stamps not illustrated. Where more than one stamp use the same illustration number, but have differences in design, the design paragraph or the description line clearly indicates the design on each stamp not illustrated. Where there are both vertical and horizontal designs in a set, a single illustration may be used, with the exceptions noted in the design paragraph or description line.

When an illustration is followed by a lower-case letter in parentheses, such as "A2(b)," the trailing letter indicates which overprint or surcharge illustration applies.

Illustrations normally are 70 percent of the original size of the stamp. Oversized stamps, blocks and souvenir sheets are reduced even more. Overprints and surcharges are shown at 100 percent of their original size if shown alone, but are 70 percent of original size if shown on stamps. In some cases, the illustration will be placed above the set, between listings or omitted completely. Overprint and surcharge illustrations are not placed in this catalogue for purposes of expertizing stamps.

❸ Paper color — The color of a stamp's paper is noted in italic type when the paper used is not white.

❹ Listing styles — There are two principal types of catalogue listings: major and minor.

Major listings are in a larger type style than minor listings. The catalogue number is a numeral that can be found with or without a capital-letter suffix, and with or without a prefix.

Minor listings are in a smaller type style and have a small-letter suffix or (if the listing immediately follows that of the major number) may show only the letter. These listings identify a variety of the major item. Examples include perforation and shade differences, multiples (some souvenir sheets, booklet panes and se-tenant combinations), and singles of multiples.

Examples of major number listings include 16, 28A, B97, C13A, 10N5, and 10N6A. Examples of minor numbers are 16a and C13Ab.

❺ Basic information about a stamp or set — Introducing each stamp issue is a small section (usually a line listing) of basic information about a stamp or set. This section normally includes the date of issue, method of printing, perforation, watermark and, sometimes, some additional information of note. *Printing method, perforation and watermark apply to the following sets until a change is noted.* Stamps created by overprinting or surcharging previous issues are assumed to have the same perforation, watermark, printing method and other production characteristics as the original. Dates of issue are as precise as Scott is able to confirm and often reflect the dates on first-day covers, rather than the actual date of release.

❻ Denomination — This normally refers to the face value of the stamp; that is, the cost of the unused stamp at the post office at the time of issue. When a denomination is shown in parentheses, it does not appear on the stamp. This includes the non-denominated stamps of the United States, Brazil and Great Britain, for example.

❼ Color or other description — This area provides information to solidify identification of a stamp. In many recent cases, a description of the stamp design appears in this space, rather than a listing of colors.

❽ Year of issue — In stamp sets that have been released in a period that spans more than a year, the number shown in parentheses is the year that stamp first appeared. Stamps without a date appeared during the first year of the issue. Dates are not always given for minor varieties.

❾ Value unused and Value used — The Scott catalogue values are based on stamps that are in a grade of Very Fine unless stated otherwise. Unused values refer to items that have not seen postal, revenue or any other duty for which they were intended. Pre-1900 unused stamps that were issued with gum must have at least most of their original gum. Later issues are assumed to have full original gum. From breakpoints specified in most countries' listings, stamps are valued as never hinged. Stamps issued without gum are noted. Modern issues with PVA or other synthetic adhesives may appear ungummed. Unused self-adhesive stamps are valued as appearing undisturbed on their original backing paper. Values for used self-adhesive stamps are for examples either on piece or off piece. For a more detailed explanation of these values, please see the "Catalogue Value," "Condition" and "Understanding Valuing Notations" sections elsewhere in this introduction.

In some cases, where used stamps are more valuable than unused stamps, the value is for an example with a contemporaneous cancel, rather than a modern cancel or a smudge or other unclear marking. For those stamps that were released for postal and fiscal purposes, the used value represents a postally used stamp. Stamps with revenue cancels generally sell for less.

Stamps separated from a complete se-tenant multiple usually will be worth less than a pro-rated portion of the se-tenant multiple, and stamps lacking the attached labels that are noted in the listings will be worth less than the values shown.

❿ Changes in basic set information — Bold type is used to show any changes in the basic data given for a set of stamps. These basic data categories include perforation gauge measurement, paper type, printing method and watermark.

⓫ Total value of a set — The total value of sets of three or more stamps issued after 1900 are shown. The set line also notes the range of Scott numbers and total number of stamps included in the grouping. The actual value of a set consisting predominantly of stamps having the minimum value of 25 cents may be less than the total value shown. Similarly, the actual value or catalogue value of se-tenant pairs or of blocks consisting of stamps having the minimum value of 25 cents may be less than the catalogue values of the component parts.

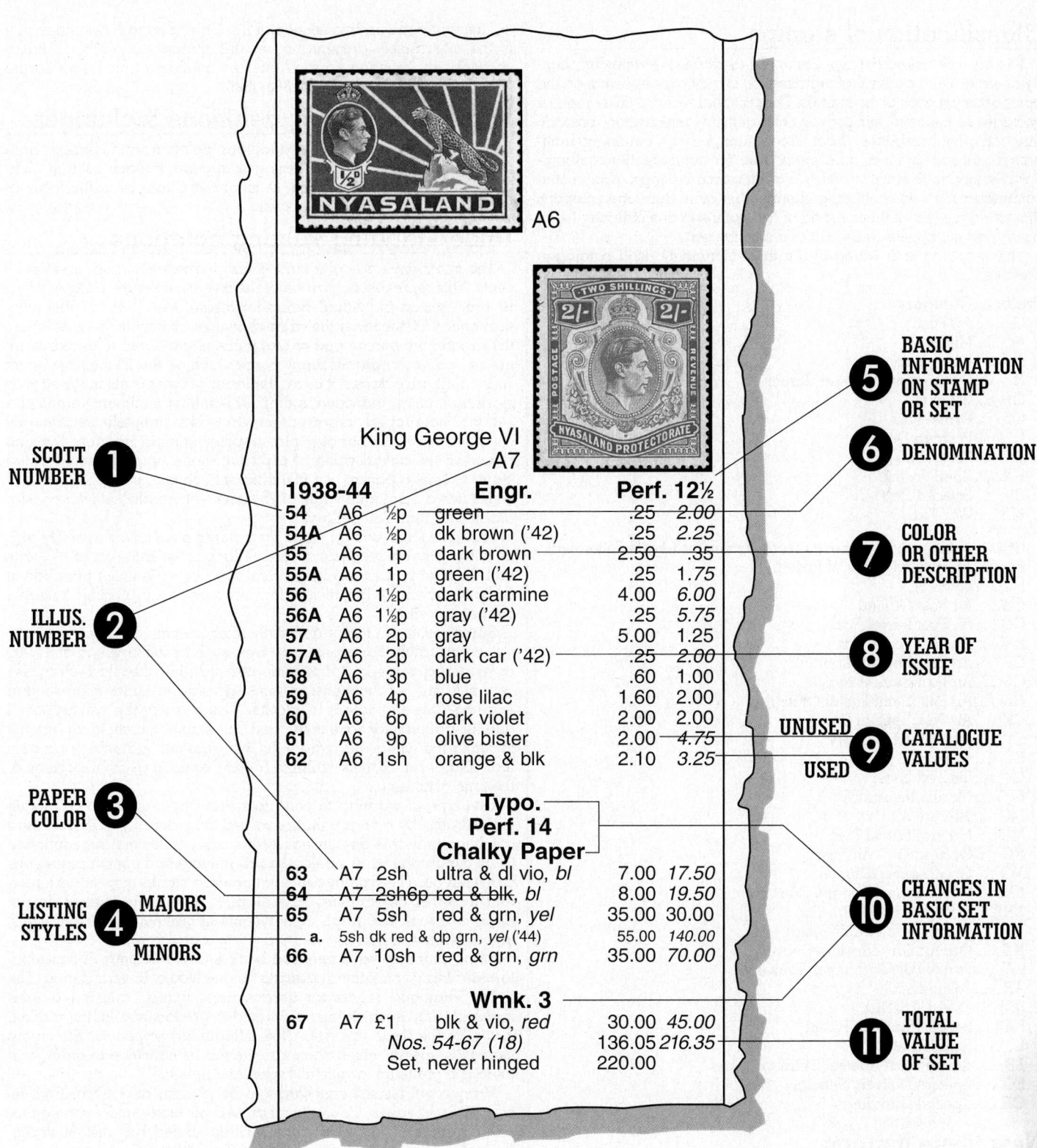

A6

King George VI
A7

BASIC INFORMATION ON STAMP OR SET — ⑤

DENOMINATION — ⑥

SCOTT NUMBER — ①

ILLUS. NUMBER — ②

PAPER COLOR — ③

LISTING STYLES — ④ — MAJORS / MINORS

COLOR OR OTHER DESCRIPTION — ⑦

YEAR OF ISSUE — ⑧

CATALOGUE VALUES — ⑨ (UNUSED / USED)

CHANGES IN BASIC SET INFORMATION — ⑩

TOTAL VALUE OF SET — ⑪

Scott No.	Illus.	Denom.	Description	Unused	Used
1938-44			**Engr.**	**Perf. 12½**	
54	A6	½p	green	.25	*2.00*
54A	A6	½p	dk brown ('42)	.25	*2.25*
55	A6	1p	dark brown	2.50	.35
55A	A6	1p	green ('42)	.25	1.75
56	A6	1½p	dark carmine	4.00	*6.00*
56A	A6	1½p	gray ('42)	.25	5.75
57	A6	2p	gray	5.00	1.25
57A	A6	2p	dark car ('42)	.25	*2.00*
58	A6	3p	blue	.60	1.00
59	A6	4p	rose lilac	1.60	2.00
60	A6	6p	dark violet	2.00	2.00
61	A6	9p	olive bister	2.00	*4.75*
62	A6	1sh	orange & blk	2.10	*3.25*

Typo.
Perf. 14
Chalky Paper

Scott No.	Illus.	Denom.	Description	Unused	Used
63	A7	2sh	ultra & dl vio, *bl*	7.00	*17.50*
64	A7	2sh6p	red & blk, *bl*	8.00	*19.50*
65	A7	5sh	red & grn, *yel*	35.00	30.00
a.		5sh	dk red & dp grn, *yel* ('44)	55.00	*140.00*
66	A7	10sh	red & grn, *grn*	35.00	*70.00*

Wmk. 3

Scott No.	Illus.	Denom.	Description	Unused	Used
67	A7	£1	blk & vio, *red*	30.00	*45.00*
			Nos. 54-67 (18)	136.05	*216.35*
			Set, never hinged	220.00	

Special Notices

Classification of stamps

The *Scott Standard Postage Stamp Catalogue* lists stamps by country of issue. The next level of organization is a listing by section on the basis of the function of the stamps. The principal sections cover regular postage, semi-postal, air post, special delivery, registration, postage due and other categories. Except for regular postage, catalogue numbers for all sections include a prefix letter (or number-letter combination) denoting the class to which a given stamp belongs. When some countries issue sets containing stamps from more than one category, the catalogue will at times list all of the stamps in one category (such as air post stamps listed as part of a postage set).

The following is a listing of the most commonly used catalogue prefixes.

Prefix ....Category

C	Air Post
M	Military
P	Newspaper
N	Occupation - Regular Issues
O	Official
Q	Parcel Post
J	Postage Due
RA	Postal Tax
B	Semi-Postal
E	Special Delivery
MR	War Tax

Other prefixes used by more than one country include the following:

H	Acknowledgment of Receipt
I	Late Fee
CO	Air Post Official
CQ	Air Post Parcel Post
RAC	Air Post Postal Tax
CF	Air Post Registration
CB	Air Post Semi-Postal
CBO	Air Post Semi-Postal Official
CE	Air Post Special Delivery
EY	Authorized Delivery
S	Franchise
G	Insured Letter
GY	Marine Insurance
MC	Military Air Post
MQ	Military Parcel Post
NC	Occupation - Air Post
NO	Occupation - Official
NJ	Occupation - Postage Due
NRA	Occupation - Postal Tax
NB	Occupation - Semi-Postal
NE	Occupation - Special Delivery
QY	Parcel Post Authorized Delivery
AR	Postal-fiscal
RAJ	Postal Tax Due
RAB	Postal Tax Semi-Postal
F	Registration
EB	Semi-Postal Special Delivery
EO	Special Delivery Official
QE	Special Handling

New issue listings

Updates to this catalogue appear each month in the *Linn's Stamp News* monthly magazine. Included in this update are additions to the listings of countries found in the *Scott Standard Postage Stamp Catalogue* and the *Specialized Catalogue of United States Stamps and Covers*, as well as corrections and updates to current editions of this catalogue.

From time to time there will be changes in the final listings of stamps from the *Linn's Stamp News* magazine to the next edition of the catalogue. This occurs as more information about certain stamps or sets becomes available.

The catalogue update section of the *Linn's Stamp News* magazine is the most timely presentation of this material available. Annual subscriptions to *Linn's Stamp News* are available from Linn's Stamp News, Box 926, Sidney, OH 45365-0926.

Number additions, deletions & changes

A listing of catalogue number additions, deletions and changes from the previous edition of the catalogue appears in each volume. See Catalogue Number Additions, Deletions & Changes in the table of contents for the location of this list.

Understanding valuing notations

The *minimum catalogue value* of an individual stamp or set is 25 cents. This represents a portion of the cost incurred by a dealer when he prepares an individual stamp for resale. As a point of philatelic-economic fact, the lower the value shown for an item in this catalogue, the greater the percentage of that value is attributed to dealer mark up and profit margin. In many cases, such as the 25-cent minimum value, that price does not cover the labor or other costs involved with stocking it as an individual stamp. The sum of minimum values in a set does not properly represent the value of a complete set primarily composed of a number of minimum-value stamps, nor does the sum represent the actual value of a packet made up of minimum-value stamps. Thus a packet of 1,000 different common stamps — each of which has a catalogue value of 25 cents — normally sells for considerably less than 250 dollars!

The *absence of a retail value* for a stamp does not necessarily suggest that a stamp is scarce or rare. A dash in the value column means that the stamp is known in a stated form or variety, but information is either lacking or insufficient for purposes of establishing a usable catalogue value.

Stamp values in *italics* generally refer to items that are difficult to value accurately. For expensive items, such as those priced at $1,000 or higher, a value in italics indicates that the affected item trades very seldom. For inexpensive items, a value in italics represents a warning. One example is a "blocked" issue where the issuing postal administration may have controlled one stamp in a set in an attempt to make the whole set more valuable. Another example is an item that sold at an extreme multiple of face value in the marketplace at the time of its issue.

One type of warning to collectors that appears in the catalogue is illustrated by a stamp that is valued considerably higher in used condition than it is as unused. In this case, collectors are cautioned to be certain the used version has a genuine and contemporaneous cancellation. The type of cancellation on a stamp can be an important factor in determining its sale price. Catalogue values do not apply to fiscal, telegraph or non-contemporaneous postal cancels, unless otherwise noted.

Some countries have released back issues of stamps in canceled-to-order form, sometimes covering as much as a 10-year period. The Scott Catalogue values for used stamps reflect canceled-to-order material when such stamps are found to predominate in the marketplace for the issue involved. Notes frequently appear in the stamp listings to specify which items are valued as canceled-to-order, or if there is a premium for postally used examples.

Many countries sell canceled-to-order stamps at a marked reduction of face value. Countries that sell or have sold canceled-to-order stamps at *full* face value include United Nations, Australia, Netherlands, France and Switzerland. It may be almost impossible to identify such stamps if the gum has been removed, because official government canceling devices are used. Postally used examples of these items on cover, however, are usually worth more than the canceled-to-order stamps with original gum.

Abbreviations

Scott uses a consistent set of abbreviations throughout this catalogue to conserve space, while still providing necessary information.

COLOR ABBREVIATIONS

amb. amber	crim. crimson	ol ..... olive
anil.. aniline	cr ..... cream	olvn . olivine
ap.... apple	dk... dark	org... orange
aqua aquamarine	dl..... dull	pck .. peacock
az .... azure	dp..... deep	pnksh pinkish
bis ... bister	db.... drab	Prus. Prussian
bl..... blue	emer emerald	pur... purple
bld... blood	gldn. golden	redsh reddish
blk... black	gryshgrayish	res ... reseda
bril... brilliant	grn... green	ros ... rosine
brn... brown	grnsh greenish	ryl.... royal
brnsh brownish	hel ... heliotrope	sal ... salmon
brnz. bronze	hn.... henna	saph sapphire
brt.... bright	ind... indigo	scar. scarlet
brnt . burnt	int .... intense	sep .. sepia
car... carmine	lav ... lavender	sien . sienna
cer ... cerise	lem .. lemon	sil..... silver
chlky chalky	lil ..... lilac	sl...... slate
chamchamois	lt ...... light	stl .... steel
chnt . chestnut	mag. magenta	turq.. turquoise
choc chocolate	man. manila	ultra ultramarine
chr... chrome	mar.. maroon	Ven.. Venetian
cit .... citron	mv ... mauve	ver ... vermilion
cl...... claret	multi multicolored	vio ... violet
cob .. cobalt	mlky milky	yel ... yellow
cop .. copper	myr.. myrtle	yelsh yellowish

When no color is given for an overprint or surcharge, black is the color used. Abbreviations for colors used for overprints and surcharges include: "(B)" or "(Blk)," black; "(Bl)," blue; "(R)," red; and "(G)," green.

Additional abbreviations in this catalogue are shown below:

Adm.	Administration
AFL................	American Federation of Labor
Anniv.............	Anniversary
APS	American Philatelic Society
Assoc.	Association
ASSR.	Autonomous Soviet Socialist Republic
b.	Born
BEP................	Bureau of Engraving and Printing
Bicent............	Bicentennial
Bklt.	Booklet
Brit................	British
btwn.	Between
Bur.	Bureau
c. or ca..........	Circa
Cat.	Catalogue
Cent.	Centennial, century, centenary
CIO	Congress of Industrial Organizations
Conf.	Conference
Cong.............	Congress
Cpl.	Corporal
CTO	Canceled to order
d.	Died
Dbl.	Double
EDU...............	Earliest documented use
Engr.	Engraved
Exhib.............	Exhibition
Expo..............	Exposition
Fed.	Federation
GB	Great Britain
Gen.	General
GPO	General post office
Horiz.	Horizontal
Imperf.	Imperforate
Impt...............	Imprint

Intl.	International
Invtd.............	Inverted
L	Left
Lieut., lt........	Lieutenant
Litho.............	Lithographed
LL	Lower left
LR	Lower right
mm	Millimeter
Ms.	Manuscript
Natl.	National
No.................	Number
NY	New York
NYC	New York City
Ovpt.	Overprint
Ovptd...........	Overprinted
P	Plate number
Perf...............	Perforated, perforation
Phil...............	Philatelic
Photo............	Photogravure
PO	Post office
Pr.	Pair
P.R.................	Puerto Rico
Prec.............	Precancel, precanceled
Pres..............	President
PTT	Post, Telephone and Telegraph
R	Right
Rio................	Rio de Janeiro
Sgt................	Sergeant
Soc.	Society
Souv.	Souvenir
SSR...............	Soviet Socialist Republic, see ASSR
St..................	Saint, street
Surch.	Surcharge
Typo.	Typographed
UL.................	Upper left
Unwmkd.	Unwatermarked
UPU..............	Universal Postal Union
UR	Upper Right
US	United States
USPOD	United States Post Office Department
USSR	Union of Soviet Socialist Republics
Vert..............	Vertical
VP	Vice president
Wmk.............	Watermark
Wmkd.	Watermarked
WWI	World War I
WWII............	World War II

Examination

Amos Media Co. will not comment upon the genuineness, grade or condition of stamps, because of the time and responsibility involved. Rather, there are several expertizing groups that undertake this work for both collectors and dealers. Neither will Amos Media Co. appraise or identify philatelic material. The company cannot take responsibility for unsolicited stamps or covers sent by individuals.

All letters, E-mails, etc. are read attentively, but they are not always answered due to time considerations.

How to order from your dealer

When ordering stamps from a dealer, it is not necessary to write the full description of a stamp as listed in this catalogue. All you need is the name of the country, the Scott catalogue number and whether the desired item is unused or used. For example, 'Japan Scott 422 unused" is sufficient to identify the unused stamp of Japan listed as "422 A206 5y brown."

Catalogue Listing Policy

It is the intent of Amos Media Co. to list all postage stamps of the world in the *Scott Standard Postage Stamp Catalogue*. The only strict criteria for listing is that stamps be decreed legal for postage by the issuing country and that the issuing country actually have an operating postal system. Whether the primary intent of issuing a given stamp or set was for sale to postal patrons or to stamp collectors is not part of our listing criteria. Scott's role is to provide basic comprehensive postage stamp information. It is up to each stamp collector to choose which items to include in a collection.

It is Scott's objective to seek reasons why a stamp should be listed, rather than why it should not. Nevertheless, there are certain types of items that will not be listed. These include the following:

1. Unissued items that are not officially distributed or released by the issuing postal authority. If such items are officially issued at a later date by the country, they will be listed. Unissued items consist of those that have been printed and then held from sale for reasons such as change in government, errors found on stamps or something deemed objectionable about a stamp subject or design.

2. Stamps "issued" by non-existent postal entities or fantasy countries, such as Nagaland, Occusi-Ambeno, Staffa, Sedang, Torres Straits and others. Also, stamps "issued" in the names of legitimate, stamp-issuing countries that are not authorized by those countries.

3. Semi-official or unofficial items not required for postage. Examples include items issued by private agencies for their own express services. When such items are required for delivery, or are valid as prepayment of postage, they are listed.

4. Local stamps issued for local use only. Postage stamps issued by governments specifically for "domestic" use, such as Haiti Scott 219-228, or the United States non-denominated stamps, are not considered to be locals, since they are valid for postage throughout the country of origin.

5. Items not valid for postal use. For example, a few countries have issued souvenir sheets that are not valid for postage. This area also includes a number of worldwide charity labels (some denominated) that do not pay postage.

6. Egregiously exploitative issues such as stamps sold for far more than face value, stamps purposefully issued in artificially small quantities or only against advance orders, stamps awarded only to a selected audience such as a philatelic bureau's standing order customers, or stamps sold only in conjunction with other products. All of these kinds of items are usually controlled issues and/or are intended for speculation. These items normally will be included in a footnote.

7. Items distributed by the issuing government only to a limited group, club, philatelic exhibition or a single stamp dealer or other private company. These items normally will be included in a footnote.

8. Stamps not available to collectors. These generally are rare items, all of which are held by public institutions such as museums. The existence of such items often will be cited in footnotes.

The fact that a stamp has been used successfully as postage, even on international mail, is not in itself sufficient proof that it was legitimately issued. Numerous examples of so-called stamps from non-existent countries are known to have been used to post letters that have successfully passed through the international mail system.

There are certain items that are subject to interpretation. When a stamp falls outside our specifications, it may be listed along with a cautionary footnote.

A number of factors are considered in our approach to analyzing how a stamp is listed. The following list of factors is presented to share with you, the catalogue user, the complexity of the listing process.

Additional printings — "Additional printings" of a previously issued stamp may range from an item that is totally different to cases where it is impossible to differentiate from the original. At least a minor number (a small-letter suffix) is assigned if there is a distinct change in stamp shade, noticeably redrawn design, or a significantly different perforation measurement. A major number (numeral or numeral and capital-letter combination) is assigned if the editors feel the "additional printing" is sufficiently different from the original that it constitutes a different issue.

Commemoratives — Where practical, commemoratives with the same theme are placed in a set. For example, the U.S. Civil War Centennial set of 1961-65 and the Constitution Bicentennial series of 1989-90 appear as sets. Countries such as Japan and Korea issue such material on a regular basis, with an announced, or at least predictable, number of stamps known in advance. Occasionally, however, stamp sets that were released over a period of years have been separated. Appropriately placed footnotes will guide you to each set's continuation.

Definitive sets — Blocks of numbers generally have been reserved for definitive sets, based on previous experience with any given country. If a few more stamps were issued in a set than originally expected, they often have been inserted into the original set with a capital-letter suffix, such as U.S. Scott 1059A. If it appears that many more stamps

than the originally allotted block will be released before the set is completed, a new block of numbers will be reserved, with the original one being closed off. In some cases, such as the U.S. Transportation and Great Americans series, several blocks of numbers exist. Appropriately placed footnotes will guide you to each set's continuation.

New country — Membership in the Universal Postal Union is not a consideration for listing status or order of placement within the catalogue. The index will tell you in what volume or page number the listings begin.

"No release date" items — The amount of information available for any given stamp issue varies greatly from country to country and even from time to time. Extremely comprehensive information about new stamps is available from some countries well before the stamps are released. By contrast some countries do not provide information about stamps or release dates. Most countries, however, fall between these extremes. A country may provide denominations or subjects of stamps from upcoming issues that are not issued as planned. Sometimes, philatelic agencies, those private firms hired to represent countries, add these later-issued items to sets well after the formal release date. This time period can range from weeks to years. If these items were officially released by the country, they will be added to the appropriate spot in the set. In many cases, the specific release date of a stamp or set of stamps may never be known.

Overprints — The color of an overprint is always noted if it is other than black. Where more than one color of ink has been used on overprints of a single set, the color used is noted. Early overprint and surcharge illustrations were altered to prevent their use by forgers.

Personalized Stamps — Since 1999, the special service of personalizing stamp vignettes, or labels attached to stamps, has been offered to customers by postal administrations of many countries. Sheets of these stamps are sold, singly or in quantity, only through special orders made by mail, in person, or through a sale on a computer website with the postal administrations or their agents for which an extra fee is charged, though some countries offer to collectors at face value personalized stamps having generic images in the vignettes or on the attached labels. It is impossible for any catalogue to know what images have been chosen by customers. Images can be 1) owned or created by the customer, 2) a generic image, or 3) an image pulled from a library of stock images on the stamp creation website. It is also impossible to know the quantity printed for any stamp having a particular image. So from a valuing standpoint, any image is equivalent to any other image for any personalized stamp having the same catalogue number. Illustrations of personalized stamps in the catalogue are not always those of stamps having generic images.

Personalized items are listed with some exceptions. These include:

1. Stamps or sheets that have attached labels that the customer cannot personalize, but which are nonetheless marketed as "personalized," and are sold for far more than the franking value.

2. Stamps or sheets that can be personalized by the customer, but where a portion of the print run must be ceded to the issuing country for sale to other customers.

3. Stamps or sheets that are created exclusively for a particular commercial client, or clients, including stamps that differ from any similar stamp that has been made available to the public.

4. Stamps or sheets that are deliberately conceived by the issuing authority that have been, or are likely to be, created with an excessive number of different face values, sizes, or other features that are changeable.

5. Stamps or sheets that are created by postal administrations using the same system of stamp personalization that has been put in place for use by the public that are printed in limited quantities and sold above face value.

6. Stamps or sheets that are created by licensees not directly affiliated or controlled by a postal administration.

Excluded items may or may not be footnoted.

Se-tenants — Connected stamps of differing features (se-tenants) will be listed in the format most commonly collected. This includes pairs, blocks or larger multiples. Se-tenant units are not always symmetrical. An example is Australia Scott 508, which is a block of seven stamps. If the stamps are primarily collected as a unit, the major number may be assigned to the multiple, with minors going to each component stamp. In cases where continuous-design or other unit se-tenants will receive significant postal use, each stamp is given a major Scott number listing. This includes issues from the United States, Canada, Germany and Great Britain, for example.

Basic Stamp Information

A stamp collector's knowledge of the combined elements that make a given stamp issue unique determines his or her ability to identify stamps. These elements include paper, watermark, method of separation, printing, design and gum. On the following pages each of these important areas is briefly described.

Paper

Paper is an organic material composed of a compacted weave of cellulose fibers and generally formed into sheets. Paper used to print stamps may be manufactured in sheets, or it may have been part of a large roll (called a web) before being cut to size. The fibers most often used to create paper on which stamps are printed include bark, wood, straw and certain grasses. In many cases, linen or cotton rags have been added for greater strength and durability. Grinding, bleaching, cooking and rinsing these raw fibers reduces them to a slushy pulp, referred to by paper makers as "stuff." Sizing and, sometimes, coloring matter is added to the pulp to make different types of finished paper.

After the stuff is prepared, it is poured onto sieve-like frames that allow the water to run off, while retaining the matted pulp. As fibers fall onto the screen and are held by gravity, they form a natural weave that will later hold the paper together. If the screen has metal bits that are formed into letters or images attached, it leaves slightly thinned areas on the paper. These are called watermarks.

When the stuff is almost dry, it is passed under pressure through smooth or engraved rollers - dandy rolls - or placed between cloth in a press to be flattened and dried.

Wove   Laid   Granite

Quadrille   Oblong Quadrille   Laid Batonne

Stamp paper falls broadly into two types: wove and laid. The nature of the surface of the frame onto which the pulp is first deposited causes the differences in appearance between the two. If the surface is smooth and even, the paper will be of fairly uniform texture throughout. This is known as *wove paper*. Early papermaking machines poured the pulp onto a continuously circulating web of felt, but modern machines feed the pulp onto a cloth-like screen made of closely interwoven fine wires. This paper, when held to a light, will show little dots or points very close together. The proper name for this is "wire wove," but the type is still considered wove. Any U.S. or British stamp printed after 1880 will serve as an example of wire wove paper.

Closely spaced parallel wires, with cross wires at wider intervals, make up the frames used for what is known as *laid paper*. A greater thickness of the pulp will settle between the wires. The paper, when held to a light, will show alternate light and dark lines. The spacing and the thickness of the lines may vary, but on any one sheet of paper they are all alike. See Russia Scott 31-38 for examples of laid paper.

Batonne, from the French word meaning "a staff," is a term used if the lines in the paper are spaced quite far apart, like the printed ruling on a writing tablet. Batonne paper may be either wove or laid. If laid, fine laid lines can be seen between the batons.

Quadrille is the term used when the lines in the paper form little squares. *Oblong quadrille* is the term used when rectangles, rather than squares, are formed. Grid patterns vary from distinct to extremely faint. See Mexico-Guadalajara Scott 35-37 for examples of oblong quadrille paper.

Paper also is classified as thick or thin, hard or soft, and by color. Such colors may include yellowish, greenish, bluish and reddish.

Brief explanations of other types of paper used for printing stamps, as well as examples, follow.

Colored — Colored paper is created by the addition of dye in the paper-making process. Such colors may include shades of yellow, green, blue and red. *Surface-colored papers*, most commonly used for British colonial issues in 1913-14, are created when coloring is added only to the surface during the finishing process. Stamps printed on surface-colored paper have white or uncolored backs, while true colored papers are colored through. See Jamaica Scott 71-73.

Pelure — Pelure paper is a very thin, hard and often brittle paper that is sometimes bluish or grayish in appearance. See Serbia Scott 169-170.

Native — This is a term applied to handmade papers used to produce some of the early stamps of the Indian states. Stamps printed on native paper may be expected to display various natural inclusions that are normal and do not negatively affect value. Japanese paper, originally made of mulberry fibers and rice flour, is part of this group. See Japan Scott 1-18.

Manila — This type of paper is often used to make stamped envelopes and wrappers. It is a coarse-textured stock, usually smooth on one side and rough on the other. A variety of colors of manila paper exist, but the most common range is yellowish-brown.

Silk — Introduced by the British in 1847 as a safeguard against counterfeiting, silk paper contains bits of colored silk thread scattered throughout. The density of these fibers varies greatly and can include as few as one fiber per stamp or hundreds. U.S. revenue Scott R152 is a good example of an easy-to-identify silk paper stamp.

Silk-thread paper has uninterrupted threads of colored silk arranged so that one or more threads run through the stamp or postal stationery. See Great Britain Scott 5-6 and Switzerland Scott 14-19.

Granite — Filled with minute cloth or colored paper fibers of various colors and lengths, granite paper should not be confused with either type of silk paper. Austria Scott 172-175 and a number of Swiss stamps are examples of granite paper.

Chalky — A chalk-like substance coats the surface of chalky paper to discourage the cleaning and reuse of canceled stamps, as well as to provide a smoother, more acceptable printing surface. Because the designs of stamps printed on chalky paper are imprinted on what is often a water-soluble coating, any attempt to remove a cancellation will destroy the stamp. *Do not soak these stamps in any fluid.* To remove a stamp printed on chalky paper from an envelope, wet the paper from underneath the stamp until the gum dissolves enough to release the stamp from the paper. See St. Kitts-Nevis Scott 89-90 for examples of stamps printed on this type of chalky paper.

India — Another name for this paper, originally introduced from China about 1750, is "China Paper." It is a thin, opaque paper often used for plate and die proofs by many countries.

Double — In philately, the term double paper has two distinct meanings. The first is a two-ply paper, usually a combination of a thick and a thin sheet, joined during manufacture. This type was used experimentally as a means to discourage the reuse of stamps.

The design is printed on the thin paper. Any attempt to remove a cancellation would destroy the design. U.S. Scott 158 and other Banknote-era stamps exist on this form of double paper.

The second type of double paper occurs on a rotary press, when the end of one paper roll, or web, is affixed to the next roll to save time feeding the paper through the press. Stamp designs are printed over the joined paper and, if overlooked by inspectors, may get into post office stocks.

Goldbeater's Skin — This type of paper was used for the 1866 issue of Prussia, and was a tough, translucent paper. The design was printed in reverse on the back of the stamp, and the gum applied over the printing. It is impossible to remove stamps printed on this type of paper from the paper to which they are affixed without destroying the design.

Ribbed — Ribbed paper has an uneven, corrugated surface made by passing the paper through ridged rollers. This type exists on some copies of U.S. Scott 156-165.

Various other substances, or substrates, have been used for stamp manufacture, including wood, aluminum, copper, silver and gold foil, plastic, and silk and cotton fabrics.

Watermarks

Watermarks are an integral part of some papers. They are formed in the process of paper manufacture. Watermarks consist of small designs, formed of wire or cut from metal and soldered to the surface of the mold or, sometimes, on the dandy roll. The designs may be in the form of crowns, stars, anchors, letters or other characters or symbols. These pieces of metal - known in the paper-making industry as "bits" - impress a design into the paper. The design sometimes may be seen by holding the stamp to the light. Some are more easily seen with a watermark detector. This important tool is a small black tray into which a stamp is placed face down and dampened with a fast-evaporating watermark detection fluid that brings up the watermark image in the form of dark lines against a lighter background. These dark lines are the thinner areas of the paper known as the watermark. Some watermarks are extremely difficult to locate, due to either a faint impression, watermark location or the color of the stamp. There also are electric watermark detectors that come with plastic filter disks of various colors. The disks neutralize the color of the stamp, permitting the watermark to be seen more easily.

Multiple watermarks of Crown Agents and Burma

Watermarks of Uruguay, Vatican City and Jamaica

WARNING: Some inks used in the photogravure process dissolve in watermark fluids (Please see the section on Soluble Printing Inks). Also, see "chalky paper."

Watermarks may be found normal, reversed, inverted, reversed and inverted, sideways or diagonal, as seen from the back of the stamp. The relationship of watermark to stamp design depends on the position of the printing plates or how paper is fed through the press. On machine-made paper, watermarks normally are read from right to left. The design is repeated closely throughout the sheet in a "multiple-watermark design." In a "sheet watermark," the design appears only once on the sheet, but extends over many stamps. Individual stamps

may carry only a small fraction or none of the watermark.

"Marginal watermarks" occur in the margins of sheets or panes of stamps. They occur on the outside border of paper (ostensibly outside the area where stamps are to be printed). A large row of letters may spell the name of the country or the manufacturer of the paper, or a border of lines may appear. Careless press feeding may cause parts of these letters and/or lines to show on stamps of the outer row of a pane.

Soluble Printing Inks

WARNING: Most stamp colors are permanent; that is, they are not seriously affected by short-term exposure to light or water. Many colors, especially of modern inks, fade from excessive exposure to light. There are stamps printed with inks that dissolve easily in water or in fluids used to detect watermarks. Use of these inks was intentional to prevent the removal of cancellations. Water affects all aniline inks, those on so-called safety paper and some photogravure printings - all such inks are known as fugitive colors. *Removal from paper of such stamps requires care and alternatives to traditional soaking.*

Separation

"Separation" is the general term used to describe methods used to separate stamps. The three standard forms currently in use are perforating, rouletting and die-cutting. These methods are done during the stamp production process, after printing. Sometimes these methods are done on-press or sometimes as a separate step. The earliest issues, such as the 1840 Penny Black of Great Britain (Scott 1), did not have any means provided for separation. It was expected the stamps would be cut apart with scissors or folded and torn. These are examples of imperforate stamps. Many stamps were first issued in imperforate formats and were later issued with perforations. Therefore, care must be observed in buying single imperforate stamps to be certain they were issued imperforate and are not perforated copies that have been altered by having the perforations trimmed away. Stamps issued imperforate usually are valued as singles. However, imperforate varieties of normally perforated stamps should be collected in pairs or larger pieces as indisputable evidence of their imperforate character.

PERFORATION

The chief style of separation of stamps, and the one that is in almost universal use today, is perforating. By this process, paper between the stamps is cut away in a line of holes, usually round, leaving little bridges of paper between the stamps to hold them together. Some types of perforation, such as hyphen-hole perfs, can be confused with roulettes, but a close visual inspection reveals that paper has been removed. The little perforation bridges, which project from the stamp when it is torn from the pane, are called the teeth of the perforation.

As the size of the perforation is sometimes the only way to differentiate between two otherwise identical stamps, it is necessary to be able to accurately measure and describe them. This is done with a perforation gauge, usually a ruler-like device that has dots or graduated lines to show how many perforations may be counted in the space of two centimeters. Two centimeters is the space universally adopted in which to measure perforations.

Perforation gauge

perce en arc   perce en lignes

perce en points   oblique roulette

perce en scie   perce serpentin

To measure a stamp, run it along the gauge until the dots on it fit exactly into the perforations of the stamp. If you are using a graduated-line perforation gauge, simply slide the stamp along the surface until the lines on the gauge perfectly project from the center of the bridges or holes. The number to the side of the line of dots or lines that fit the stamp's perforation is the measurement. For example, an "11" means that 11 perforations fit between two centimeters. The description of the stamp therefore is "perf. 11." If the gauge of the perforations on the top and bottom of a stamp differs from that on the sides, the result is what is known as *compound perforations*. In measuring compound perforations, the gauge at top and bottom is always given first, then the sides. Thus, a stamp that measures 11 at top and bottom and 10½ at the sides is "perf. 11 x 10½." See U.S. Scott 632-642 for examples of compound perforations.

Stamps also are known with perforations different on three or all four sides. Descriptions of such items are clockwise, beginning with the top of the stamp.

A perforation with small holes and teeth close together is a "fine perforation." One with large holes and teeth far apart is a "coarse perforation." Holes that are jagged, rather than clean-cut, are "rough perforations." *Blind perforations* are the slight impressions left by the perforating pins if they fail to puncture the paper. Multiples of stamps showing blind perforations may command a slight premium over normally perforated stamps.

The term *syncopated perfs* describes intentional irregularities in the perforations. The earliest form was used by the Netherlands from 1925-33, where holes were omitted to create distinctive patterns. Beginning in 1992, Great Britain has used an oval perforation to help prevent counterfeiting. Several other countries have started using the oval perfs or other syncopated perf patterns.

A new type of perforation, still primarily used for postal stationery, is known as microperfs. Microperfs are tiny perforations (in some cases hundreds of holes per two centimeters) that allows items to be intentionally separated very easily, while not accidentally breaking apart as easily as standard perforations. These are not currently measured or differentiated by size, as are standard perforations.

ROULETTING

In rouletting, the stamp paper is cut partly or wholly through, with no paper removed. In perforating, some paper is removed. Rouletting derives its name from the French roulette, a spur-like wheel. As the wheel is rolled over the paper, each point makes a small cut. The number of cuts made in a two-centimeter space determines the gauge of the roulette, just as the number of perforations in two centimeters determines the gauge of the perforation.

The shape and arrangement of the teeth on the wheels varies. Various roulette types generally carry French names:

Perce en lignes - rouletted in lines. The paper receives short, straight cuts in lines. This is the most common type of rouletting. See Mexico Scott 500.

Perce en points - pin-rouletted or pin-perfed. This differs from a small perforation because no paper is removed, although round, equidistant holes are pricked through the paper. See Mexico Scott 242-256.

Perce en arc and *perce en scie* - pierced in an arc or saw-toothed designs, forming half circles or small triangles. See Hanover (German States) Scott 25-29.

Perce en serpentin - serpentine roulettes. The cuts form a serpentine or wavy line. See Brunswick (German States) Scott 13-18.

Once again, no paper is removed by these processes, leaving the stamps easily separated, but closely attached.

DIE-CUTTING

The third major form of stamp separation is die-cutting. This is a method where a die in the pattern of separation is created that later cuts the stamp paper in a stroke motion. Although some standard stamps bear die-cut perforations, this process is primarily used for self-adhesive postage stamps. Die-cutting can appear in straight lines, such as U.S. Scott 2522, shapes, such as U.S. Scott 1551, or imitating the appearance of perforations, such as New Zealand Scott 935A and 935B.

Printing Processes

ENGRAVING (Intaglio, Line-engraving, Etching)

Master die — The initial operation in the process of line engraving is making the master die. The die is a small, flat block of softened steel upon which the stamp design is recess engraved in reverse.

Master die

Photographic reduction of the original art is made to the appropriate size. It then serves as a tracing guide for the initial outline of the design. The engraver lightly traces the design on the steel with his graver, then slowly works the design until it is completed. At various points during the engraving process, the engraver hand-inks the die and makes an impression to check his progress. These are known as progressive die proofs. After completion of the engraving, the die is hardened to withstand the stress and pressures of later transfer operations.

Transfer roll

Transfer roll — Next is production of the transfer roll that, as the name implies, is the medium used to transfer the subject from the master die to the printing plate. A blank roll of soft steel, mounted on a mandrel, is placed under the bearers of the transfer press to allow it to roll freely on its axis. The hardened die is placed on the bed of the press and the face of the transfer roll is applied to the die, under pressure. The bed or the roll is then rocked back and forth under increasing pressure, until the soft steel of the roll is forced into every engraved line of the die. The resulting impression on the roll is known as a "relief" or a "relief transfer." The engraved image is now positive in appearance and stands out from the steel. After the required number of reliefs are "rocked in," the soft steel transfer roll is hardened.

Different flaws may occur during the relief process. A defective relief may occur during the rocking in process because of a minute piece of foreign material lodging on the die, or some other cause. Imperfections in the steel of the transfer roll may result in a breaking away of parts of the design. This is known as a relief break, which will show up on finished stamps as small, unprinted areas. If a damaged relief remains in use, it will transfer a repeating defect to the plate. Deliberate alterations of reliefs sometimes occur. "Altered reliefs" designate these changed conditions.

Plate — The final step in pre-printing production is the making of the printing plate. A flat piece of soft steel replaces the die on the bed of the transfer press. One of the reliefs on the transfer roll is positioned over this soft steel. Position, or layout, dots determine the correct position on the plate. The dots have been lightly marked on the plate in advance. After the correct position of the relief is determined,

the design is rocked in by following the same method used in making the transfer roll. The difference is that this time the image is being transferred from the transfer roll, rather than to it. Once the design is entered on the plate, it appears in reverse and is recessed. There are as many transfers entered on the plate as there are subjects printed on the sheet of stamps. It is during this process that double and shifted transfers occur, as well as re-entries. These are the result of improperly entered images that have not been properly burnished out prior to rocking in a new image.

Modern siderography processes, such as those used by the U.S. Bureau of Engraving and Printing, involve an automated form of rocking designs in on preformed cylindrical printing sleeves. The same process also allows for easier removal and re-entry of worn images right on the sleeve.

Transferring the design to the plate

Following the entering of the required transfers on the plate, the position dots, layout dots and lines, scratches and other markings generally are burnished out. Added at this time by the siderographer are any required *guide lines*, *plate numbers* or other *marginal markings*. The plate is then hand-inked and a proof impression is taken. This is known as a *plate proof*. If the impression is approved, the plate is machined for fitting onto the press, is hardened and sent to the plate vault ready for use.

On press, the plate is inked and the surface is automatically wiped clean, leaving ink only in the recessed lines. Paper is then forced under pressure into the engraved recessed lines, thereby receiving the ink. Thus, the ink lines on engraved stamps are slightly raised, and slight depressions (debossing) occur on the back of the stamp. Prior to the advent of modern high-speed presses and more advanced ink formulations, paper had to be dampened before receiving the ink. This sometimes led to uneven shrinkage by the time the stamps were perforated, resulting in improperly perforated stamps, or misperfs. Newer presses use drier paper, thus both *wet* and *dry printings* exist on some stamps.

Rotary Press — Until 1914, only flat plates were used to print engraved stamps. Rotary press printing was introduced in 1914, and slowly spread. Some countries still use flat-plate printing.

After approval of the plate proof, older *rotary press plates* require additional machining. They are curved to fit the press cylinder. "Gripper slots" are cut into the back of each plate to receive the "grippers," which hold the plate securely on the press. The plate is then hardened. Stamps printed from these bent rotary press plates are longer or wider than the same stamps printed from flat-plate presses. The stretching of the plate during the curving process is what causes this distortion.

Re-entry — To execute a re-entry on a flat plate, the transfer roll is re-applied to the plate, often at some time after its first use on the press. Worn-out designs can be resharpened by carefully burnishing out the original image and re-entering it from the transfer roll. If the original impression has not been sufficiently removed and the transfer roll is not precisely in line with the remaining impression, the resulting double transfer will make the re-entry obvious. If the registration is true, a re-entry may be difficult or impossible to distinguish. Sometimes a stamp printed from a successful re-entry is identified by having a much sharper and clearer impression than its neighbors. With the advent of rotary presses, post-press re-entries were not possible. After a plate was curved for the rotary press, it was impossible to make a re-entry. This is because the plate had already been bent once (with the design distorted).

However, with the introduction of the previously mentioned modern-style siderography machines, entries are made to the preformed cylindrical printing sleeve. Such sleeves are dechromed and softened. This allows individual images to be burnished out and re-entered on the curved sleeve. The sleeve is then rechromed, resulting in longer press life.

Double Transfer — This is a description of the condition of a transfer on a plate that shows evidence of a duplication of all, or a portion of the design. It usually is the result of the changing of the registration between the transfer roll and the plate during the rocking in of the original entry. Double transfers also occur when only a portion of the design has been rocked in and improper positioning is noted. If the worker elected not to burnish out the partial or completed design, a strong double transfer will occur for part or all of the design.

It sometimes is necessary to remove the original transfer from a plate and repeat the process a second time. If the finished re-worked image shows traces of the original impression, attributable to incomplete burnishing, the result is a partial double transfer.

With the modern automatic machines mentioned previously, double transfers are all but impossible to create. Those partially doubled images on stamps printed from such sleeves are more than likely re-entries, rather than true double transfers.

Re-engraved — Alterations to a stamp design are sometimes necessary after some stamps have been printed. In some cases, either the original die or the actual printing plate may have its "temper" drawn (softened), and the design will be re-cut. The resulting impressions from such a re-engraved die or plate may differ slightly from the original issue, and are known as "re-engraved." If the alteration was made to the master die, all future printings will be consistently different from the original. If alterations were made to the printing plate, each altered stamp on the plate will be slightly different from each other, allowing specialists to reconstruct a complete printing plate.

Dropped Transfers — If an impression from the transfer roll has not been properly placed, a dropped transfer may occur. The final stamp image will appear obviously out of line with its neighbors.

Short Transfer — Sometimes a transfer roll is not rocked its entire length when entering a transfer onto a plate. As a result, the finished transfer on the plate fails to show the complete design, and the finished stamp will have an incomplete design printed. This is known as a "short transfer." U.S. Scott No. 8 is a good example of a short transfer.

TYPOGRAPHY (Letterpress, Surface Printing, Flexography, Dry Offset, High Etch)

Although the word "Typography" is obsolete as a term describing a printing method, it was the accepted term throughout the first century of postage stamps. Therefore, appropriate Scott listings in this catalogue refer to typographed stamps. The current term for this form of printing, however, is "letterpress."

As it relates to the production of postage stamps, letterpress printing is the reverse of engraving. Rather than having recessed areas trap the ink and deposit it on paper, only the raised areas of the design are inked. This is comparable to the type of printing seen by inking and using an ordinary rubber stamp. Letterpress includes all printing where the design is above the surface area, whether it is wood, metal or, in some instances, hardened rubber or polymer plastic.

For most letterpress-printed stamps, the engraved master is made in much the same manner as for engraved stamps. In this instance, however, an additional step is needed. The design is transferred to another surface before being transferred to the transfer roll. In this way, the transfer roll has a recessed stamp design, rather than one done in relief. This makes the printing areas on the final plate raised, or relief areas.

For less-detailed stamps of the 19th century, the area on the die not used as a printing surface was cut away, leaving the surface area raised. The original die was then reproduced by stereotyping or electrotyping. The resulting electrotypes were assembled in the required number and format of the desired sheet of stamps. The plate used in printing the stamps was an electroplate of these assembled electrotypes.

Once the final letterpress plates are created, ink is applied to the raised surface and the pressure of the press transfers the ink impression to the paper. In contrast to engraving, the fine lines of letterpress are impressed on the surface of the stamp, leaving a debossed surface. When viewed from the back (as on a typewritten page), the corresponding line work on the stamp will be raised slightly (embossed) above the surface.

PHOTOGRAVURE (Gravure, Rotogravure, Heliogravure)

In this process, the basic principles of photography are applied to a chemically sensitized metal plate, rather than photographic paper. The design is transferred photographically to the plate through a halftone, or dot-matrix screen, breaking the reproduction into tiny dots. The plate is treated chemically and the dots form depressions, called cells, of varying depths and diameters, depending on the degrees of shade in the design. Then, like engraving, ink is applied to the plate and the surface is wiped clean. This leaves ink in the tiny cells that is lifted out and deposited on the paper when it is pressed against the plate.

Gravure is most often used for multicolored stamps, generally using the three primary colors (red, yellow and blue) and black. By varying the dot matrix pattern and density of these colors, virtually any color can be reproduced. A typical full-color gravure stamp will be created from four printing cylinders (one for each color). The original multicolored image will have been photographically separated into its component colors.

Modern gravure printing may use computer-generated dot-matrix screens, and modern plates may be of various types including metal-coated plastic. The catalogue designation of Photogravure (or "Photo") covers any of these older and more modern gravure methods of printing.

For examples of the first photogravure stamps printed (1914), see Bavaria Scott 94-114.

LITHOGRAPHY (Offset Lithography, Stone Lithography, Dilitho, Planography, Collotype)

The principle that oil and water do not mix is the basis for lithography. The stamp design is drawn by hand or transferred from engraving to the surface of a lithographic stone or metal plate in a greasy (oily) substance. This oily substance holds the ink, which will later be transferred to the paper. The stone (or plate) is wet with an acid fluid, causing it to repel the printing ink in all areas not covered by the greasy substance.

Transfer paper is used to transfer the design from the original stone or plate. A series of duplicate transfers are grouped and, in turn, transferred to the final printing plate.

Photolithography — The application of photographic processes to lithography. This process allows greater flexibility of design, related to use of halftone screens combined with line work. Unlike photogravure or engraving, this process can allow large, solid areas to be printed.

Offset — A refinement of the lithographic process. A rubber-covered blanket cylinder takes the impression from the inked lithographic plate. From the "blanket" the impression is *offset* or transferred to the paper. Greater flexibility and speed are the principal reasons offset printing has largely displaced lithography. The term "lithography" covers both processes, and results are almost identical.

EMBOSSED (Relief) Printing

Embossing, not considered one of the four main printing types, is a method in which the design first is sunk into the metal of the die. Printing is done against a yielding platen, such as leather or linoleum. The platen is forced into the depression of the die, thus forming the design on the paper in relief. This process is often used for metallic inks.

Embossing may be done without color (see Sardinia Scott 4-6); with color printed around the embossed area (see Great Britain Scott 5 and most U.S. envelopes); and with color in exact registration with the embossed subject (see Canada Scott 656-657).

HOLOGRAMS

For objects to appear as holograms on stamps, a model exactly the same size as it is to appear on the hologram must be created. Rather than using photographic film to capture the image, holography records an image on a photoresist material. In processing, chemicals eat away at certain exposed areas, leaving a pattern of constructive and destructive interference. When the photoresist is developed, the result is a pattern of uneven ridges that acts as a mold. This mold is then coated with metal, and the resulting form is used to press copies in much the same way phonograph records are produced.

A typical reflective hologram used for stamps consists of a reproduction of the uneven patterns on a plastic film that is applied to a reflective background, usually a silver or gold foil. Light is reflected off the background through the film, making the pattern present on the film visible. Because of the uneven pattern of the film, the viewer will perceive the objects in their proper three-dimensional relationships with appropriate brightness.

The first hologram on a stamp was produced by Austria in 1988 (Scott 1441).

FOIL APPLICATION

A modern technique of applying color to stamps involves the application of metallic foil to the stamp paper. A pattern of foil is applied to the stamp paper by use of a stamping die. The foil usually is flat, but it may be textured. Canada Scott 1735 has three different foil applications in pearl, bronze and gold. The gold foil was textured using a chemical-etch copper embossing die. The printing of this stamp also involved two-color offset lithography plus embossing.

THERMOGRAPHY

In the 1990s stamps began to be enhanced with thermographic printing. In this process, a powdered polymer is applied over a sheet that has just been printed. The powder adheres to ink that lacks drying or hardening agents and does not adhere to areas where the ink has these agents. The excess powder is removed and the sheet is briefly heated to melt the powder. The melted powder solidifies after cooling, producing a raised, shiny effect on the stamps. See Scott New Caledonia C239-C240.

COMBINATION PRINTINGS

Sometimes two or even three printing methods are combined in producing stamps. In these cases, such as Austria Scott 933 or Canada 1735 (described in the preceding paragraph), the multiple-printing technique can be determined by studying the individual characteristics of each printing type. A few stamps, such as Singapore Scott 684-684A, combine as many as three of the four major printing types (lithography, engraving and typography). When this is done it often indicates the incorporation of security devices against counterfeiting.

INK COLORS

Inks or colored papers used in stamp printing often are of mineral origin, although there are numerous examples of organic-based pigments. As a general rule, organic-based pigments are far more subject to varieties and change than those of mineral-based origin.

The appearance of any given color on a stamp may be affected by many aspects, including printing variations, light, color of paper, aging and chemical alterations.

Numerous printing variations may be observed. Heavier pressure or inking will cause a more intense color, while slight interruptions in the ink feed or lighter impressions will cause a lighter appearance. Stamps printed in the same color by water-based and solvent-based inks can differ significantly in appearance. This affects several stamps in the U.S. Prominent Americans series. Hand-mixed ink formulas (primarily from the 19th century) produced under different conditions (humidity and temperature) account for notable color variations in early printings of the same stamp (see U.S. Scott 248-250, 279B, for example). Different sources of pigment can also result in significant differences in color.

Light exposure and aging are closely related in the way they affect stamp color. Both eventually break down the ink and fade colors, so that a carefully kept stamp may differ significantly in color from an identical copy that has been exposed to light. If stamps are exposed to light either intentionally or accidentally, their colors can be faded or completely changed in some cases.

Papers of different quality and consistency used for the same stamp printing may affect color appearance. Most pelure papers, for example, show a richer color when compared with wove or laid papers. See Russia Scott 181α, for an example of this effect.

The very nature of the printing processes can cause a variety of differences in shades or hues of the same stamp. Some of these shades are scarcer than others, and are of particular interest to the advanced collector.

Luminescence

All forms of tagged stamps fall under the general category of luminescence. Within this broad category is fluorescence, dealing with forms of tagging visible under longwave ultraviolet light, and phosphorescence, which deals with tagging visible only under shortwave light. Phosphorescence leaves an afterglow and fluorescence does not. These treated stamps show up in a range of different colors when exposed to UV light. The differing wavelengths of the light activates the tagging material, making it glow in various colors that usually serve different mail processing purposes.

Intentional tagging is a post-World War II phenomenon, brought about by the increased literacy rate and rapidly growing mail volume. It was one of several answers to the problem of the need for more automated mail processes. Early tagged stamps served the purpose of triggering machines to separate different types of mail. A natural outgrowth was to also use the signal to trigger machines that faced all envelopes the same way and canceled them.

Tagged stamps come in many different forms. Some tagged stamps have luminescent shapes or images imprinted on them as a form of security device. Others have blocks (United States), stripes, frames (South Africa and Canada), overall coatings (United States), bars (Great Britain and Canada) and many other types. Some types of tagging are even mixed in with the pigmented printing ink (Australia Scott 366, Netherlands Scott 478 and U.S. Scott 1359 and 2443).

The means of applying taggant to stamps differs as much as the intended purposes for the stamps. The most common form of tagging is a coating applied to the surface of the printed stamp. Since the taggant ink is frequently invisible except under UV light, it does not interfere with the appearance of the stamp. Another common application is the use of phosphored papers. In this case the paper itself either has a coating of taggant applied before the stamp is printed, has taggant applied during the papermaking process (incorporating it into the fibers), or has the taggant mixed into the coating of the paper. The latter method, among others, is currently in use in the United States.

Many countries now use tagging in various forms to either expedite mail handling or to serve as a printing security device against counterfeiting. Following the introduction of tagged stamps for public use in 1959 by Great Britain, other countries have steadily joined the parade. Among those are Germany (1961); Canada and Denmark (1962); United States, Australia, France and Switzerland (1963); Belgium and Japan (1966); Sweden and Norway (1967); Italy (1968); and Russia (1969). Since then, many other countries have begun using forms of tagging, including Brazil, China, Czechoslovakia, Hong Kong, Guatemala, Indonesia, Israel, Lithuania, Luxembourg, Netherlands, Penrhyn Islands, Portugal, St. Vincent, Singapore, South Africa, Spain and Sweden to name a few.

In some cases, including United States, Canada, Great Britain and Switzerland, stamps were released both with and without tagging. Many of these were released during each country's experimental period. Tagged and untagged versions are listed for the aforementioned countries and are noted in some other countries' listings. For at least a few stamps, the experimentally tagged version is worth far more than its untagged counterpart, such as the 1963 experimental tagged version of France Scott 1024.

In some cases, luminescent varieties of stamps were inadvertently created. Several Russian stamps, for example, sport highly fluorescent ink that was not intended as a form of tagging. Older stamps, such as early U.S. postage dues, can be positively identified by the use of UV light, since the organic ink used has become slightly fluorescent over time. Other stamps, such as Austria Scott 70a-82a (varnish bars) and Obock Scott 46-64 (printed quadrille lines), have become fluorescent over time.

Various fluorescent substances have been added to paper to make it appear brighter. These optical brightners, as they are known, greatly affect the appearance of the stamp under UV light. The brightest of these is known as Hi-Brite paper. These paper varieties are beyond the scope of the Scott Catalogue.

Shortwave UV light also is used extensively in expertizing, since each form of paper has its own fluorescent characteristics that are impossible to perfectly match. It is therefore a simple matter to detect filled thins, added perforation teeth and other alterations that involve the addition of paper. UV light also is used to examine stamps that have had cancels chemically removed and for other purposes as well.

Gum

The Illustrated Gum Chart in the first part of this introduction shows and defines various types of gum condition. Because gum condition has an important impact on the value of unused stamps, we recommend studying this chart and the accompanying text carefully.

The gum on the back of a stamp may be shiny, dull, smooth, rough, dark, white, colored or tinted. Most stamp gumming adhesives use gum arabic or dextrine as a base. Certain polymers such as polyvinyl alcohol (PVA) have been used extensively since World War II.

The *Scott Standard Postage Stamp Catalogue* does not list items by types of gum. The *Scott Specialized Catalogue of United States Stamps and Covers* does differentiate among some types of gum for certain issues.

Reprints of stamps may have gum differing from the original issues. In addition, some countries have used different gum formulas for different seasons. These adhesives have different properties that may become more apparent over time.

Many stamps have been issued without gum, and the catalogue

will note this fact. See, for example, United States Scott 40-47. Sometimes, gum may have been removed to preserve the stamp. Germany Scott B68, for example, has a highly acidic gum that eventually destroys the stamps. This item is valued in the catalogue with gum removed.

Reprints and Reissues

These are impressions of stamps (usually obsolete) made from the original plates or stones. If they are valid for postage and reproduce obsolete issues (such as U.S. Scott 102-111), the stamps are *reissues*. If they are from current issues, they are designated as *second, third,* etc., *printing*. If designated for a particular purpose, they are called *special printings*.

When special printings are not valid for postage, but are made from original dies and plates by authorized persons, they are *official reprints. Private reprints* are made from the original plates and dies by private hands. An example of a private reprint is that of the 1871-1932 reprints made from the original die of the 1845 New Haven, Conn., postmaster's provisional. *Official reproductions* or imitations are made from new dies and plates by government authorization. Scott will list those reissues that are valid for postage if they differ significantly from the original printing.

The U.S. government made special printings of its first postage stamps in 1875. Produced were official imitations of the first two stamps (listed as Scott 3-4), reprints of the demonetized pre-1861 issues (Scott 40-47) and reissues of the 1861 stamps, the 1869 stamps and the then-current 1875 denominations. Even though the official imitations and the reprints were not valid for postage, Scott lists all of these U.S. special printings.

Most reprints or reissues differ slightly from the original stamp in some characteristic, such as gum, paper, perforation, color or watermark. Sometimes the details are followed so meticulously that only a student of that specific stamp is able to distinguish the reprint or reissue from the original.

Remainders and Canceled to Order

Some countries sell their stock of old stamps when a new issue replaces them. To avoid postal use, the *remainders* usually are canceled with a punch hole, a heavy line or bar, or a more-or-less regular-looking cancellation. The most famous merchant of remainders was Nicholas F. Seebeck. In the 1880s and 1890s, he arranged printing contracts between the Hamilton Bank Note Co., of which he was a director, and several Central and South American countries. The contracts provided that the plates and all remainders of the yearly issues became the property of Hamilton. Seebeck saw to it that ample stock remained. The "Seebecks," both remainders and reprints, were standard packet fillers for decades.

Some countries also issue stamps *canceled-to-order (CTO)*, either in sheets with original gum or stuck onto pieces of paper or envelopes and canceled. Such CTO items generally are worth less than postally used stamps. In cases where the CTO material is far more prevalent in the marketplace than postally used examples, the catalogue value relates to the CTO examples, with postally used examples noted as premium items. Most CTOs can be detected by the presence of gum. However, as the CTO practice goes back at least to 1885, the gum inevitably has been soaked off some stamps so they could pass as postally used. The normally applied postmarks usually differ slightly from standard postmarks, and specialists are able to tell the difference. When applied individually to envelopes by philatelically minded persons, CTO material is known as *favor canceled* and generally sells at large discounts.

Cinderellas and Facsimiles

Cinderella is a catch-all term used by stamp collectors to describe phantoms, fantasies, bogus items, municipal issues, exhibition seals, local revenues, transportation stamps, labels, poster stamps and many other types of items. Some cinderella collectors include in their collections local postage issues, telegraph stamps, essays and proofs, forgeries and counterfeits.

A *fantasy* is an adhesive created for a nonexistent stamp-issuing authority. Fantasy items range from imaginary countries (Occusi-Ambeno, Kingdom of Sedang, Principality of Trinidad or Torres Straits), to non-existent locals (Winans City Post), or nonexistent transportation lines (McRobish & Co.'s Acapulco-San Francisco Line).

On the other hand, if the entity exists and could have issued stamps (but did not) or was known to have issued other stamps, the items are considered *bogus* stamps. These would include the Mormon postage stamps of Utah, S. Allan Taylor's Guatemala and Paraguay inventions, the propaganda issues for the South Moluccas and the adhesives of the Page & Keyes local post of Boston.

Phantoms is another term for both fantasy and bogus issues.

Facsimiles are copies or imitations made to represent original stamps, but which do not pretend to be originals. A catalogue illustration is such a facsimile. Illustrations from the Moens catalogue of the last century were occasionally colored and passed off as stamps. Since the beginning of stamp collecting, facsimiles have been made for collectors as space fillers or for reference. They often carry the word "facsimile," "falsch" (German), "sanko" or "mozo" (Japanese), or "faux" (French) overprinted on the face or stamped on the back. Unfortunately, over the years a number of these items have had fake cancels applied over the facsimile notation and have been passed off as genuine.

Forgeries and Counterfeits

Forgeries and counterfeits have been with philately virtually from the beginning of stamp production. Over time, the terminology for the two has been used interchangeably. Although both forgeries and counterfeits are reproductions of stamps, the purposes behind their creation differ considerably.

Among specialists there is an increasing movement to more specifically define such items. Although there is no universally accepted terminology, we feel the following definitions most closely mirror the items and their purposes as they are currently defined.

Forgeries (also often referred to as *Counterfeits*) are reproductions of genuine stamps that have been created to defraud collectors. Such spurious items first appeared on the market around 1860, and most old-time collections contain one or more. Many are crude and easily spotted, but some can deceive experts.

An important supplier of these early philatelic forgeries was the Hamburg printer Gebruder Spiro. Many others with reputations in this craft included S. Allan Taylor, George Hussey, James Chute, George Forune, Benjamin & Sarpy, Julius Goldner, E. Oneglia and L.H. Mercier. Among the noted 20th-century forgers were Francois Fournier, Jean Sperati and the prolific Raoul DeThuin.

Forgeries may be complete replications, or they may be genuine stamps altered to resemble a scarcer (and more valuable) type. Most forgeries, particularly those of rare stamps, are worth only a small fraction of the value of a genuine example, but a few types, created by some of the most notable forgers, such as Sperati, can be worth as much or more than the genuine. Fraudulently produced copies are known of most classic rarities and many medium-priced stamps.

In addition to rare stamps, large numbers of common 19th- and early 20th-century stamps were forged to supply stamps to the early packet trade. Many can still be easily found. Few new philatelic forgeries have appeared in recent decades. Successful imitation of well-engraved work is virtually impossible. It has proven far easier to produce a fake by altering a genuine stamp than to duplicate a stamp completely.

Counterfeit (also often referred to as *Postal Counterfeit* or *Postal Forgery*) is the term generally applied to reproductions of stamps that have been created to defraud the government of revenue. Such items usually are created at the time a stamp is current and, in some cases, are hard to detect. Because most counterfeits are seized when the perpetrator is captured, postal counterfeits, particularly used on cover, are usually worth much more than a genuine example to specialists. The first postal counterfeit was of Spain's 4-cuarto carmine of 1854 (the real one is Scott 25). Apparently, the counterfeiters were not satisfied with their first version, which is now very scarce, and they soon created an engraved counterfeit, which is common. Postal counterfeits quickly followed in Austria, Naples, Sardinia and the Roman States. They have since been created in many other countries as well, including the United States.

An infamous counterfeit to defraud the government is the 1-shilling Great Britain "Stock Exchange" forgery of 1872, used on telegraph forms at the exchange that year. The stamp escaped detection until a stamp dealer noticed it in 1898.

Fakes

Fakes are genuine stamps altered in some way to make them more desirable. One student of this part of stamp collecting has estimated that by the 1950s more than 30,000 varieties of fakes were known. That number has grown greatly since then. The widespread existence of fakes makes it important for stamp collectors to study their philatelic holdings and use relevant literature. Likewise, collectors should buy from reputable dealers who guarantee their stamps and make full and prompt refunds should a purchased item be declared faked or altered by some mutually agreed-upon authority. Because fakes always have some genuine characteristics, it is not always possible to obtain unanimous agreement among experts regarding specific items. These students may change their opinions as philatelic knowledge increases. More than 80 percent of all fakes on the philatelic market today are regummed, reperforated (or perforated for the first time), or bear forged overprints, surcharges or cancellations.

Stamps can be chemically treated to alter or eliminate colors. For example, a pale rose stamp can be re-colored to resemble a blue shade of high market value. In other cases, treated stamps can be made to resemble missing color varieties. Designs may be changed by painting, or a stroke or a dot added or bleached out to turn an ordinary variety into a seemingly scarcer stamp. Part of a stamp can be bleached and reprinted in a different version, achieving an inverted center or frame. Margins can be added or repairs done so deceptively that the stamps move from the "repaired" into the "fake" category.

Fakers have not left the backs of the stamps untouched either. They may create false watermarks, add fake grills or press out genuine grills. A thin India paper proof may be glued onto a thicker backing to create the appearance an issued stamp, or a proof printed on cardboard may be shaved down and perforated to resemble a stamp. Silk threads are impressed into paper and stamps have been split so that a rare paper variety is added to an otherwise inexpensive stamp. The most common treatment to the back of a stamp, however, is regumming.

Some in the business of faking stamps have openly advertised fool-proof application of "original gum" to stamps that lack it, although most publications now ban such ads from their pages. It is believed that very few early stamps have survived without being hinged. The large number of never-hinged examples of such earlier material offered for sale thus suggests the widespread extent of regumming activity. Regumming also may be used to hide repairs or thin spots. Dipping the stamp into watermark fluid, or examining it under longwave ultraviolet light often will reveal these flaws.

Fakers also tamper with separations. Ingenious ways to add margins are known. Perforated wide-margin stamps may be falsely represented as imperforate when trimmed. Reperforating is commonly done to create scarce coil or perforation varieties, and to eliminate the naturally occurring straight-edge stamps found in sheet margin positions of many earlier issues. Custom has made straight-edged stamps less desirable. Fakers have obliged by perforating straight-edged stamps so that many are now uncommon, if not rare.

Another fertile field for the faker is that of overprints, surcharges and cancellations. The forging of rare surcharges or overprints began in the 1880s or 1890s. These forgeries are sometimes difficult to detect, but experts have identified almost all. Occasionally, overprints or cancellations are removed to create non-overprinted stamps or seemingly unused items. This is most commonly done by removing a manuscript cancel to make a stamp resemble an unused example. "SPECIMEN" overprints may be removed by scraping and repainting to create non-overprinted varieties. Fakers use inexpensive revenues or pen-canceled stamps to generate unused stamps for further faking by adding other markings. The quartz lamp or UV lamp and a high-powered magnifying glass help to easily detect removed cancellations.

The bigger problem, however, is the addition of overprints, surcharges or cancellations - many with such precision that they are very difficult to ascertain. Plating of the stamps or the overprint can be an important method of detection.

Fake postmarks may range from many spurious fancy cancellations to a host of markings applied to transatlantic covers, to adding normally appearing postmarks to definitives of some countries with stamps that are valued far higher used than unused. With the increased popularity of cover collecting, and the widespread interest in postal history, a fertile new field for fakers has come about. Some have tried to create entire covers. Others specialize in adding stamps, tied by fake cancellations, to genuine stampless covers, or replacing less expensive or damaged stamps with more valuable ones. Detailed study of postal rates in effect at the time a cover in question was mailed, including the analysis of each handstamp used during the period, ink analysis and similar techniques, usually will unmask the fraud.

Restoration and Repairs

Scott bases its catalogue values on stamps that are free of defects and otherwise meet the standards set forth earlier in this introduction. Most stamp collectors desire to have the finest copy of an item possible. Even within given grading categories there are variances. This leads to a controversial practice that is not defined in any universal manner: stamp *restoration*.

There are broad differences of opinion about what is permissible when it comes to restoration. Carefully applying a soft eraser to a stamp or cover to remove light soiling is one form of restoration, as is washing a stamp in mild soap and water to clean it. These are fairly accepted forms of restoration. More severe forms of restoration include pressing out creases or removing stains caused by tape. To what degree each of these is acceptable is dependent upon the individual situation. Further along the spectrum is the freshening of a stamp's color by removing oxide build-up or the effects of wax paper left next to stamps shipped to the tropics.

At some point in this spectrum the concept of *repair* replaces that of restoration. Repairs include filling thin spots, mending tears by reweaving or adding a missing perforation tooth. Regumming stamps may have been acceptable as a restoration or repair technique many decades ago, but today it is considered a form of fakery.

Restored stamps may or may not sell at a discount, and it is possible that the value of individual restored items may be enhanced over that of their pre-restoration state. Specific situations dictate the resultant value of such an item. Repaired stamps sell at substantial discounts from the value of sound stamps.

Terminology

Booklets — Many countries have issued stamps in small booklets for the convenience of users. This idea continues to become increasingly popular in many countries. Booklets have been issued in many sizes and forms, often with advertising on the covers, the panes of stamps or on the interleaving.

The panes used in booklets may be printed from special plates or made from regular sheets. All panes from booklets issued by the United States and many from those of other countries contain stamps that are straight edged on the sides, but perforated between. Others are distinguished by orientation of watermark or other identifying features. Any stamp-like unit in the pane, either printed or blank, that is not a postage stamp, is considered to be a *label* in the catalogue listings.

Scott lists and values booklet panes. Modern complete booklets also are listed and valued. Individual booklet panes are listed only when they are not fashioned from existing sheet stamps and, therefore, are identifiable from their sheet stamp counterparts.

Panes usually do not have a used value assigned to them because there is little market activity for used booklet panes, even though many exist used and there is some demand for them.

Cancellations — The marks or obliterations put on stamps by postal authorities to show that they have performed service and to prevent their reuse are known as cancellations. If the marking is made with a pen, it is considered a "pen cancel." When the location of the post office appears in the marking, it is a "town cancellation." A "postmark" is technically any postal marking, but in practice the term generally is applied to a town cancellation with a date. When calling attention to a cause or celebration, the marking is known as a "slogan cancellation." Many other types and styles of cancellations exist, such as duplex, numerals, targets, fancy and others. See also "precancels," below.

Coil Stamps — These are stamps that are issued in rolls for use in dispensers, affixing and vending machines. Those coils of the United States, Canada, Sweden and some other countries are perforated horizontally or vertically only, with the outer edges imperforate. Coil stamps of some countries, such as Great Britain and Germany, are perforated on all four sides and may in some cases be distinguished from their sheet stamp counterparts by watermarks, counting numbers on the reverse or other means.

Covers — Entire envelopes, with or without adhesive postage stamps, that have passed through the mail and bear postal or other markings of philatelic interest are known as covers. Before the introduction of envelopes in about 1840, people folded letters and wrote the address on the outside. Some people covered their letters with an extra sheet of paper on the outside for the address, producing the term "cover." Used airletter sheets, stamped envelopes and other items of postal stationery also are considered covers.

Errors — Stamps that have some major, consistent, unintentional deviation from the normal are considered errors. Errors include, but are not limited to, missing or wrong colors, wrong paper, wrong watermarks, inverted centers or frames on multicolor printing, inverted or missing surcharges or overprints, double impressions, missing perforations, unintentionally omitted tagging and others. Factually wrong or misspelled information, if it appears on all examples of a stamp, are not considered errors in the true sense of the word. They are errors of design. Inconsistent or randomly appearing items, such as misperfs or color shifts, are classified as freaks.

Color-Omitted Errors — This term refers to stamps where a missing color is caused by the complete failure of the printing plate to deliver ink to the stamp paper or any other paper. Generally, this is caused by the printing plate not being engaged on the press or the ink station running dry of ink during printing.

Color-Missing Errors — This term refers to stamps where a color or colors were printed somewhere but do not appear on the finished stamp. There are four different classes of color-missing errors, and the catalog indicates with a two-letter code appended to each such listing what caused the color to be missing. These codes are used only for the United States' color-missing error listings.

FO = A *foldover* of the stamp sheet during printing may block ink from appearing on a stamp. Instead, the color will appear on the back of the foldover (where it might fall on the back of the selvage or perhaps on the back of the stamp or another stamp). FO also will be used in the case of foldunders, where the paper may fold underneath the other stamp paper and the color will print on the platen.

EP = A piece of *extraneous paper* falling across the plate or stamp paper will receive the printed ink. When the extraneous paper is removed, an unprinted portion of stamp paper remains and shows partially or totally missing colors.

CM = A misregistration of the printing plates during printing will result in a *color misregistration*, and such a misregistraion may result in a color not appearing on the finished stamp.

PS = A *perforation shift* after printing may remove a color from the finished stamp. Normally, this will occur on a row of stamps at the edge of the stamp pane.

Measurements – When measurements are given in the Scott catalogues for stamp size, grill size or any other reason, the first measurement given is always for the top and bottom dimension, while the second measurement will be for the sides (just as perforation gauges are measured). Thus, a stamp size of 15mm x 21mm will indicate a vertically oriented stamp 15mm wide at top and bottom, and 21mm tall at the sides. The same principle holds for measuring or counting items such as U.S. grills. A grill count of 22x18 points (B grill) indicates that there are 22 grill points across by 18 grill points down.

Overprints and Surcharges — Overprinting involves applying wording or design elements over an already existing stamp. Overprints can be used to alter the place of use (such as "Canal Zone" on U.S. stamps), to adapt them for a special purpose ("Porto" on Denmark's 1913-20 regular issues for use as postage due stamps, Scott J1-J7) or to commemorate a special occasion (United States Scott 647-648).

A *surcharge* is a form of overprint that changes or restates the face value of a stamp or piece of postal stationery.

Surcharges and overprints may be handstamped, typeset or, occasionally, lithographed or engraved. A few hand-written overprints and surcharges are known.

Personalized Stamps — In 1999, Australia issued stamps with se-tenant labels that could be personalized with pictures of the customer's choice. Other countries quickly followed suit, with some offering to print the selected picture on the stamp itself within a frame that was used exclusively for personalized issues. As the picture used on these stamps or labels vary, listings for such stamps are for any picture within the common frame (or any picture on a se-tenant label), be it a "generic" image or one produced especially for a customer, almost invariably at a premium price.

Precancels — Stamps that are canceled before they are placed in the mail are known as precancels. Precanceling usually is done to expedite the handling of large mailings and generally allow the affected mail pieces to skip certain phases of mail handling.

In the United States, precancellations generally identified the point of origin; that is, the city and state. This information appeared across the face of the stamp, usually centered between parallel lines. More recently, bureau precancels retained the parallel lines, but the city and state designations were dropped. Recent coils have a service inscription that is present on the original printing plate. These show the mail service paid for by the stamp. Since these stamps are not intended to receive further cancellations when used as intended, they are considered precancels. Such items often do not have parallel lines as part of the precancellation.

In France, the abbreviation *Affranchts* in a semicircle together with the word *Postes* is the general form of precancel in use. Belgian precancellations usually appear in a box in which the name of the city appears. Netherlands precancels have the name of the city enclosed between concentric circles, sometimes called a "lifesaver." Precancellations of other countries usually follow these patterns, but may be any arrangement of bars, boxes and city names.

Precancels are listed in the Scott catalogues only if the precancel changes the denomination (Belgium Scott 477-478); if the precanceled stamp is different from the non-precanceled version (such as untagged U.S. precancels); or if the stamp exists only precanceled (France Scott 1096-1099, U.S. Scott 2265).

Proofs and Essays — Proofs are impressions taken from an approved die, plate or stone in which the design and color are the same as the stamp issued to the public. Trial color proofs are impressions taken from approved dies, plates or stones in colors that vary from the final version. An essay is the impression of a design that differs in some way from the issued stamp. "Progressive die proofs" generally are considered to be essays.

Provisionals — These are stamps that are issued on short notice and intended for temporary use pending the arrival of regular issues. They usually are issued to meet such contingencies as changes in government or currency, shortage of necessary postage values or military occupation.

During the 1840s, postmasters in certain American cities issued stamps that were valid only at specific post offices. In 1861, postmasters of the Confederate States also issued stamps with limited validity. Both of these examples are known as "postmaster's provisionals."

Se-tenant — This term refers to an unsevered pair, strip or block of stamps that differ in design, denomination or overprint.

Unless the se-tenant item has a continuous design (see U.S. Scott 1451a, 1694a) the stamps do not have to be in the same order as shown in the catalogue (see U.S. Scott 2158a).

Specimens — The Universal Postal Union required member nations to send samples of all stamps they released into service to the International Bureau in Switzerland. Member nations of the UPU received these specimens as samples of what stamps were valid for postage. Many are overprinted, handstamped or initial-perforated "Specimen," "Canceled" or "Muestra." Some are marked with bars across the denominations (China-Taiwan), punched holes (Czechoslovakia) or back inscriptions (Mongolia).

Stamps distributed to government officials or for publicity purposes, and stamps submitted by private security printers for official approval, also may receive such defacements.

The previously described defacement markings prevent postal use, and all such items generally are known as "specimens."

Tete Beche — This term describes a pair of stamps in which one is upside down in relation to the other. Some of these are the result of intentional sheet arrangements, such as Morocco Scott B10-B11. Others occurred when one or more electrotypes accidentally were placed upside down on the plate, such as Colombia Scott 57a. Separation of the tete-beche stamps, of course, destroys the tete beche variety.

Pronunciation Symbols

ə .... banana, collide, abut

ˈə, ˌə .... humdrum, abut

ə .... immediately preceding \l\, \n\, \m\, \ŋ\, as in battle, mitten, eaten, and sometimes open \ˈō-pᵊm\, lock and key \-ᵊŋ-\; immediately following \l\, \m\, \r\, as often in French table, prisme, titre

ər .... further, merger, bird

ˈər-
ˈə-r } .... as in two different pronunciations of hurry \ˈhər-ē, ˈhə-rē\

a .... mat, map, mad, gag, snap, patch

ā .... day, fade, date, aorta, drape, cape

ä .... bother, cot, and, with most American speakers, father, cart

à .... father as pronounced by speakers who do not rhyme it with bother; French patte

aù .... now, loud, out

b .... baby, rib

ch .... chin, nature \ˈnā-chər\

d .... did, adder

e .... bet, bed, peck

ˈē, ˌē .... beat, nosebleed, evenly, easy

ē .... easy, mealy

f .... fifty, cuff

g .... go, big, gift

h .... hat, ahead

hw .... whale as pronounced by those who do not have the same pronunciation for both whale and wail

i .... tip, banish, active

ī .... site, side, buy, tripe

j .... job, gem, edge, join, judge

k .... kin, cook, ache

k̲ .... German ich, Buch; one pronunciation of loch

l .... lily, pool

m .... murmur, dim, nymph

n .... no, own

ⁿ .... indicates that a preceding vowel or diphthong is pronounced with the nasal passages open, as in French un bon vin blanc \œⁿ -bōⁿ -vaⁿ -blän\

ŋ .... sing \ˈsiŋ\, singer \ˈsiŋ-ər\, finger \ˈfiŋ-gər\, ink \ˈiŋk\

ō .... bone, know, beau

ȯ .... saw, all, gnaw, caught

œ .... French boeuf, German Hölle

œ̄ .... French feu, German Höhle

ȯi .... coin, destroy

p .... pepper, lip

r .... red, car, rarity

s .... source, less

sh .... as in shy, mission, machine, special (actually, this is a single sound, not two); with a hyphen between, two sounds as in grasshopper \ˈgras-ˌhä-pər\

t .... tie, attack, late, later, latter

th .... as in thin, ether (actually, this is a single sound, not two); with a hyphen between, two sounds as in knighthood \ˈnīt-ˌhu̇d\

t̲h̲ .... then, either, this (actually, this is a single sound, not two)

ü .... rule, youth, union \ˈyün-yən\, few \ˈfyü\

u̇ .... pull, wood, book, curable \ˈkyu̇r-ə-bəl\, fury \ˈfyu̇r-ē\

ue .... German füllen, hübsch

ūe .... French rue, German fühlen

v .... vivid, give

w .... we, away

y .... yard, young, cue \ˈkyü\, mute \ˈmyüt\, union \ˈyün-yən\

ʸ .... indicates that during the articulation of the sound represented by the preceding character the front of the tongue has substantially the position it has for the articulation of the first sound of yard, as in French digne \dēnʸ\

z .... zone, raise

zh .... as in vision, azure \ˈa-zhər\ (actually, this is a single sound, not two); with a hyphen between, two sounds as in hogshead \ˈhȯgz-ˌhed, ˈhägz-\

\ .... slant line used in pairs to mark the beginning and end of a transcription: \ˈpen\

ˈ .... mark preceding a syllable with primary (strongest) stress: \ˈpen-mən-ˌship\

ˌ .... mark preceding a syllable with secondary (medium) stress: \ˈpen-mən-ˌship\

- .... mark of syllable division

( ) .... indicate that what is symbolized between is present in some utterances but not in others: factory \ˈfak-t(ə-)rē\

÷ .... indicates that many regard as unacceptable the pronunciation variant immediately following: cupola \ˈkyü-pə-lə, ÷-ˌlō\

The system of pronunciation is used by permission from Merriam-Webster's Collegiate® Dictionary, Tenth Edition ©1993 by Merriam-Webster Inc., publisher of the Merriam-Webster® dictionaries.

COMMON DESIGN TYPES

Pictured in this section are issues where one illustration has been used for a number of countries in the Catalogue. Not included in this section are overprinted stamps or those issues which are illustrated in each country. Because the location of Never Hinged breakpoints varies from country to country, some of the values in the listings below will be for unused stamps that were previously hinged.

EUROPA

Europa, 1956

The design symbolizing the cooperation among the six countries comprising the Coal and Steel Community is illustrated in each country.

Belgium	496-497
France	805-806
Germany	748-749
Italy	715-716
Luxembourg	318-320
Netherlands	368-369

Nos. 496-497 (2)	9.00	.70
Nos. 805-806 (2)	5.25	1.00
Nos. 748-749 (2)	7.30	1.20
Nos. 715-716 (2)	11.50	1.25
Nos. 318-320 (3)	73.00	50.00
Nos. 368-369 (2)	72.50	1.75
Set total (13) Stamps	178.55	55.90

Europa, 1958

"E" and Dove — CD1

European Postal Union at the service of European integration.

1958, Sept. 13

Belgium	527-528
France	889-890
Germany	790-791
Italy	750-751
Luxembourg	341-343
Netherlands	375-376
Saar	317-318

Nos. 527-528 (2)	4.25	.60
Nos. 889-890 (2)	1.65	.55
Nos. 790-791 (2)	3.65	.65
Nos. 750-751 (2)	1.85	.60
Nos. 341-343 (3)	2.35	1.15
Nos. 375-376 (2)	2.50	.75
Nos. 317-318 (2)	1.05	2.30
Set total (15) Stamps	17.30	6.60

Europa, 1959

6-Link Enless Chain — CD2

1959, Sept. 19

Belgium	536-537
France	929-930
Germany	805-806
Italy	791-792
Luxembourg	354-355
Netherlands	379-380

Nos. 536-537 (2)	1.55	.60
Nos. 929-930 (2)	1.40	.80
Nos. 805-806 (2)	1.55	.65
Nos. 791-792 (2)	.80	.50
Nos. 354-355 (2)	3.50	1.40
Nos. 379-380 (2)	9.90	1.25
Set total (12) Stamps	18.70	5.20

Europa, 1960

19-Spoke Wheel CD3

First anniverary of the establishment of C.E.P.T. (Conference Europeenne des Administrations des Postes et des Telecommunications.) The spokes symbolize the 19 founding members of the Conference.

1960, Sept.

Belgium	553-554
Denmark	379
Finland	376-377
France	970-971
Germany	818-820
Great Britain	377-378
Greece	688
Iceland	327-328
Ireland	175-176
Italy	809-810
Luxembourg	374-375
Netherlands	385-386
Norway	387
Portugal	866-867
Spain	941-942
Sweden	562-563
Switzerland	400-401
Turkey	1493-1494

Nos. 553-554 (2)	1.25	.55
No. 379 (1)	.55	.50
Nos. 376-377 (2)	1.70	1.80
Nos. 970-971 (2)	.50	.50
Nos. 818-820 (3)	2.25	1.50
Nos. 377-378 (2)	9.00	5.00
No. 688 (1)	5.00	2.00
Nos. 327-328 (2)	1.30	1.30
Nos. 175-176 (2)	75.00	14.00
Nos. 809-810 (2)	.70	.50
Nos. 374-375 (2)	1.00	.80
Nos. 385-386 (2)	3.65	1.50
No. 387 (1)	1.25	1.25
Nos. 866-867 (2)	2.25	1.25
Nos. 941-942 (2)	1.50	.75
Nos. 562-563 (2)	1.05	.55
Nos. 400-401 (2)	1.25	.65
Nos. 1493-1494 (2)	2.10	1.35
Set total (34) Stamps	111.30	35.75

Europa, 1961

19 Doves Flying as One — CD4

The 19 doves represent the 19 members of the Conference of European Postal and Telecommunications Administrations C.E.P.T.

1961-62

Belgium	572-573
Cyprus	201-203
France	1005-1006
Germany	844-845
Great Britain	382-384
Greece	718-719
Iceland	340-341
Italy	845-846
Luxembourg	382-383
Netherlands	387-388
Spain	1010-1011
Switzerland	410-411
Turkey	1518-1520

Nos. 572-573 (2)	.75	.50
Nos. 201-203 (3)	2.10	1.20
Nos. 1005-1006 (2)	.50	.50
Nos. 844-845 (2)	.60	.75
Nos. 382-384 (3)	.75	.90
Nos. 718-719 (2)	.80	.50
Nos. 340-341 (2)	.90	.90
Nos. 845-846 (2)	.55	.50
Nos. 382-383 (2)	.70	.70
Nos. 387-388 (2)	.55	.50
Nos. 1010-1011 (2)	.70	.55
Nos. 410-411 (2)	1.25	.60
Nos. 1518-1520 (3)	2.45	1.30
Set total (29) Stamps	12.60	9.40

Europa, 1962

Young Tree with 19 Leaves CD5

The 19 leaves represent the 19 original members of C.E.P.T.

1962-63

Belgium	582-583
Cyprus	219-221
France	1045-1046
Germany	852-853
Greece	739-740
Iceland	348-349
Ireland	184-185
Italy	860-861
Luxembourg	386-387
Netherlands	394-395
Norway	414-415
Switzerland	416-417
Turkey	1553-1555

Nos. 582-583 (2)	.65	.65
Nos. 219-221 (3)	76.25	4.40
Nos. 1045-1046 (2)	.60	.50
Nos. 852-853 (2)	.70	.80
Nos. 739-740 (2)	2.25	1.15
Nos. 348-349 (2)	.85	.85
Nos. 184-185 (2)	2.00	1.50
Nos. 860-861 (2)	1.35	.55
Nos. 386-387 (2)	.85	.70
Nos. 394-395 (2)	1.40	.75
Nos. 414-415 (2)	2.25	2.25
Nos. 416-417 (2)	1.65	1.00
Nos. 1553-1555 (3)	3.00	1.55
Set total (28) Stamps	93.80	16.65

Europa, 1963

Stylized Links, Symbolizing Unity — CD6

1963, Sept.

Belgium	598-599
Cyprus	229-231
Finland	419
France	1074-1075
Germany	867-868
Greece	768-769
Iceland	357-358
Ireland	188-189
Italy	880-881
Luxembourg	403-404
Netherlands	416-417
Norway	441-442
Switzerland	429
Turkey	1602-1603

Nos. 598-599 (2)	1.60	.55
Nos. 229-231 (3)	54.75	5.15
No. 419 (1)	1.25	.55
Nos. 1074-1075 (2)	.60	.50
Nos. 867-868 (2)	.50	.55
Nos. 768-769 (2)	5.25	1.90
Nos. 357-358 (2)	1.50	1.50
Nos. 188-189 (2)	4.75	3.25
Nos. 880-881 (2)	.65	.50
Nos. 403-404 (2)	1.00	.80
Nos. 416-417 (2)	2.25	1.00
Nos. 441-442 (2)	4.75	3.00
No. 429 (1)	.90	.60
Nos. 1602-1603 (2)	1.40	.60
Set total (27) Stamps	81.15	20.45

Europa, 1964

Symbolic Daisy — CD7

5th anniversary of the establishment of C.E.P.T. The 22 petals of the flower symbolize the 22 members of the Conference.

1964, Sept.

Austria	738
Belgium	614-615
Cyprus	244-246
France	1109-1110
Germany	897-898
Greece	801-802
Iceland	367-368
Ireland	196-197
Italy	894-895
Luxembourg	411-412
Monaco	590-591
Netherlands	428-429
Norway	458
Portugal	931-933
Spain	1262-1263
Switzerland	438-439
Turkey	1628-1629

No. 738 (1)	1.20	.80
Nos. 614-615 (2)	1.40	.60
Nos. 244-246 (3)	35.75	3.45
Nos. 1109-1110 (2)	.50	.50
Nos. 897-898 (2)	.50	.50
Nos. 801-802 (2)	5.00	1.90
Nos. 367-368 (2)	2.00	1.65
Nos. 196-197 (2)	20.00	4.25
Nos. 894-895 (2)	.55	.50
Nos. 411-412 (2)	.90	.55
Nos. 590-591 (2)	2.50	.70
Nos. 428-429 (2)	1.80	.60
No. 458 (1)	4.50	4.50
Nos. 931-933 (3)	10.00	2.00
Nos. 1262-1263 (2)	1.30	.80
Nos. 438-439 (2)	1.60	.50
Nos. 1628-1629 (2)	2.65	1.35
Set total (34) Stamps	92.15	25.15

Europa, 1965

Leaves and "Fruit" CD8

1965

Belgium	636-637
Cyprus	262-264
Finland	437
France	1131-1132
Germany	934-935
Greece	833-834
Iceland	375-376
Ireland	204-205
Italy	915-916
Luxembourg	432-433
Monaco	616-617
Netherlands	438-439
Norway	475-476
Portugal	958-960
Switzerland	469
Turkey	1665-1666

Nos. 636-637 (2)	.50	.50
Nos. 262-264 (3)	25.35	3.80
No. 437 (1)	1.25	.55
Nos. 1131-1132 (2)	.70	.55
Nos. 934-935 (2)	.50	.50
Nos. 833-834 (2)	2.25	1.15
Nos. 375-376 (2)	2.50	1.75
Nos. 204-205 (2)	20.00	3.35
Nos. 915-916 (2)	.50	.50
Nos. 432-433 (2)	.80	.60
Nos. 616-617 (2)	3.25	1.65
Nos. 438-439 (2)	.75	.55
Nos. 475-476 (2)	4.00	3.10
Nos. 958-960 (3)	10.00	2.75
No. 469 (1)	1.15	.25
Nos. 1665-1666 (2)	3.50	2.10
Set total (32) Stamps	77.00	23.65

Europa, 1966

Symbolic Sailboat — CD9

1966, Sept.

Andorra, French	172
Belgium	675-676
Cyprus	275-277
France	1163-1164
Germany	963-964

Greece	862-863
Iceland	384-385
Ireland	216-217
Italy	942-943
Liechtenstein	415
Luxembourg	440-441
Monaco	639-640
Netherlands	441-442
Norway	496-497
Portugal	980-982
Switzerland	477-478
Turkey	1718-1719

No. 172 (1)	3.00	3.00
Nos. 675-676 (2)	.80	.50
Nos. 275-277 (3)	4.75	1.90
Nos. 1163-1164 (2)	.55	.50
Nos. 963-964 (2)	.50	.55
Nos. 862-863 (2)	2.25	1.05
Nos. 384-385 (2)	5.00	3.80
Nos. 216-217 (2)	7.00	2.00
Nos. 942-943 (2)	.50	.50
No. 415 (1)	.40	.35
Nos. 440-441 (2)	.80	.60
Nos. 639-640 (2)	2.00	.65
Nos. 441-442 (2)	1.50	.65
Nos. 496-497 (2)	5.00	3.00
Nos. 980-982 (3)	9.75	2.25
Nos. 477-478 (2)	1.60	.60
Nos. 1718-1719 (2)	3.35	1.75
Set total (34) Stamps	48.75	23.65

Europa, 1967

Cogwheels
CD10

1967

Andorra, French	174-175
Belgium	688-689
Cyprus	297-299
France	1178-1179
Germany	969-970
Greece	891-892
Iceland	389-390
Ireland	232-233
Italy	951-952
Liechtenstein	420
Luxembourg	449-450
Monaco	669-670
Netherlands	444-447
Norway	504-505
Portugal	994-996
Spain	1465-1466
Switzerland	482
Turkey	B120-B121

Nos. 174-175 (2)	10.75	6.25
Nos. 688-689 (2)	1.05	.55
Nos. 297-299 (3)	4.25	1.75
Nos. 1178-1179 (2)	.55	.50
Nos. 969-970 (2)	.55	.55
Nos. 891-892 (2)	3.75	1.00
Nos. 389-390 (2)	3.00	2.00
Nos. 232-233 (2)	6.15	2.30
Nos. 951-952 (2)	.60	.50
No. 420 (1)	.45	.40
Nos. 449-450 (2)	1.00	.70
Nos. 669-670 (2)	2.75	.70
Nos. 444-447 (4)	5.00	1.85
Nos. 504-505 (2)	3.25	2.75
Nos. 994-996 (3)	9.50	1.85
Nos. 1465-1466 (2)	.50	.50
No. 482 (1)	.70	.25
Nos. B120-B121 (2)	3.50	2.75
Set total (38) Stamps	57.30	27.15

Europa, 1968

Golden Key with C.E.P.T. Emblem
CD11

1968

Andorra, French	182-183
Belgium	705-706
Cyprus	314-316
France	1209-1210
Germany	983-984
Greece	916-917
Iceland	395-396
Ireland	242-243
Italy	979-980

Liechtenstein	442
Luxembourg	466-467
Monaco	689-691
Netherlands	452-453
Portugal	1019-1021
San Marino	687
Spain	1526
Switzerland	488
Turkey	1775-1776

Nos. 182-183 (2)	16.50	10.00
Nos. 705-706 (2)	1.25	.50
Nos. 314-316 (3)	2.90	1.75
Nos. 1209-1210 (2)	.85	.55
Nos. 983-984 (2)	.50	.55
Nos. 916-917 (2)	3.75	1.65
Nos. 395-396 (2)	3.00	2.50
Nos. 242-243 (2)	3.75	3.00
Nos. 979-980 (2)	.50	.50
No. 442 (1)	.45	.40
Nos. 466-467 (2)	.80	.70
Nos. 689-691 (3)	5.40	.95
Nos. 452-453 (2)	2.10	.70
Nos. 1019-1021 (3)	9.75	2.10
No. 687 (1)	.55	.35
No. 1526 (1)	.25	.25
No. 488 (1)	.45	.25
Nos. 1775-1776 (2)	5.00	2.00
Set total (35) Stamps	57.75	28.70

Europa, 1969

"EUROPA" and "CEPT"
CD12

Tenth anniversary of C.E.P.T.

1969

Andorra, French	188-189
Austria	837
Belgium	718-719
Cyprus	326-328
Denmark	458
Finland	483
France	1245-1246
Germany	996-997
Great Britain	585
Greece	947-948
Iceland	406-407
Ireland	270-271
Italy	1000-1001
Liechtenstein	453
Luxembourg	475-476
Monaco	722-724
Netherlands	475-476
Norway	533-534
Portugal	1038-1040
San Marino	701-702
Spain	1567
Sweden	814-816
Switzerland	500-501
Turkey	1799-1800
Vatican	470-472
Yugoslavia	1003-1004

Nos. 188-189 (2)	18.50	12.00
No. 837 (1)	.65	.30
Nos. 718-719 (2)	.75	.50
Nos. 326-328 (3)	3.00	1.35
No. 458 (1)	.75	.75
No. 483 (1)	3.50	.75
Nos. 1245-1246 (2)	.55	.50
Nos. 996-997 (2)	.80	.50
No. 585 (1)	.25	.25
Nos. 947-948 (2)	5.00	1.50
Nos. 406-407 (2)	4.20	2.40
Nos. 270-271 (2)	4.00	2.00
Nos. 1000-1001 (2)	.70	.50
No. 453 (1)	.45	.45
Nos. 475-476 (2)	1.00	.70
Nos. 722-724 (3)	10.50	2.00
Nos. 475-476 (2)	2.60	1.15
Nos. 533-534 (2)	3.75	2.35
Nos. 1038-1040 (3)	17.85	2.40
Nos. 701-702 (2)	.90	.90
No. 1567 (1)	.25	.25
Nos. 814-816 (3)	4.00	2.85
Nos. 500-501 (2)	1.85	.60
Nos. 1799-1800 (2)	3.85	2.25
Nos. 470-472 (3)	.75	.75
Nos. 1003-1004 (2)	4.00	4.00
Set total (51) Stamps	94.40	43.95

Europa, 1970

Interwoven Threads
CD13

1970

Andorra, French	196-197
Belgium	741-742
Cyprus	340-342
France	1271-1272
Germany	1018-1019
Greece	985, 987
Iceland	420-421
Ireland	279-281
Italy	1013-1014
Liechtenstein	470
Luxembourg	489-490
Monaco	768-770
Netherlands	483-484
Portugal	1060-1062
San Marino	729-730
Spain	1607
Switzerland	515-516
Turkey	1848-1849
Yugoslavia	1024-1025

Nos. 196-197 (2)	20.00	8.50
Nos. 741-742 (2)	1.10	.55
Nos. 340-342 (3)	2.70	1.90
Nos. 1271-1272 (2)	.65	.50
Nos. 1018-1019 (2)	.60	.50
Nos. 985,987 (2)	7.75	2.00
Nos. 420-421 (2)	6.00	4.00
Nos. 279-281 (3)	9.50	3.30
Nos. 1013-1014 (2)	.65	.50
No. 470 (1)	.45	.45
Nos. 489-490 (2)	.80	.80
Nos. 768-770 (3)	6.35	2.10
Nos. 483-484 (2)	2.50	1.15
Nos. 1060-1062 (3)	9.85	2.35
Nos. 729-730 (2)	.90	.55
No. 1607 (1)	.25	.25
Nos. 515-516 (2)	1.85	.60
Nos. 1848-1849 (2)	5.00	2.25
Nos. 1024-1025 (2)	.80	.80
Set total (40) Stamps	77.70	33.05

Europa, 1971

"Fraternity, Cooperation, Common Effort"
CD14

1971

Andorra, French	205-206
Belgium	803-804
Cyprus	365-367
Finland	504
France	1304
Germany	1064-1065
Greece	1029-1030
Iceland	429-430
Ireland	305-306
Italy	1038-1039
Liechtenstein	485
Luxembourg	500-501
Malta	425-427
Monaco	797-799
Netherlands	488-489
Portugal	1094-1096
San Marino	749-750
Spain	1675-1676
Switzerland	531-532
Turkey	1876-1877
Yugoslavia	1052-1053

Nos. 205-206 (2)	20.00	7.75
Nos. 803-804 (2)	1.30	.55
Nos. 365-367 (3)	2.60	1.75
No. 504 (1)	5.00	.75
No. 1304 (1)	.45	.40
Nos. 1064-1065 (2)	.60	.50
Nos. 1029-1030 (2)	4.00	1.80
Nos. 429-430 (2)	5.00	3.75
Nos. 305-306 (2)	5.00	1.50
Nos. 1038-1039 (2)	.65	.50
No. 485 (1)	.45	.45
Nos. 500-501 (2)	1.00	.80
Nos. 425-427 (3)	.80	.80
Nos. 797-799 (3)	15.00	2.80
Nos. 488-489 (2)	2.50	1.15
Nos. 1094-1096 (3)	9.75	1.75
Nos. 749-750 (2)	.65	.55
Nos. 1675-1676 (2)	.75	.55
Nos. 531-532 (2)	1.85	.65
Nos. 1876-1877 (2)	5.60	2.50
Nos. 1052-1053 (2)	.50	.50
Set total (43) Stamps	83.45	31.75

Europa, 1972

Sparkles, Symbolic of Communications
CD15

1972

Andorra, French	210-211
Andorra, Spanish	62
Belgium	825-826
Cyprus	380-382
Finland	512-513
France	1341
Germany	1089-1090
Greece	1049-1050
Iceland	439-440
Ireland	316-317
Italy	1065-1066
Liechtenstein	504
Luxembourg	512-513
Malta	450-453
Monaco	831-832
Netherlands	494-495
Portugal	1141-1143
San Marino	771-772
Spain	1718
Switzerland	544-545
Turkey	1907-1908
Yugoslavia	1100-1101

Nos. 210-211 (2)	21.00	7.00
No. 62 (1)	45.00	45.00
Nos. 825-826 (2)	.95	.55
Nos. 380-382 (3)	5.95	2.45
Nos. 512-513 (2)	7.00	1.40
No. 1341 (1)	.50	.35
Nos. 1089-1090 (2)	1.30	.55
Nos. 1049-1050 (2)	2.00	1.55
Nos. 439-440 (2)	2.90	2.65
Nos. 316-317 (2)	13.00	4.50
Nos. 1065-1066 (2)	.65	.50
No. 504 (1)	.45	.45
Nos. 512-513 (2)	1.00	.80
Nos. 450-453 (4)	1.05	1.40
Nos. 831-832 (2)	5.00	1.40
Nos. 494-495 (2)	3.25	1.15
Nos. 1141-1143 (3)	9.85	1.50
Nos. 771-772 (2)	.70	.50
No. 1718 (1)	.50	.40
Nos. 544-545 (2)	1.65	.60
Nos. 1907-1908 (2)	7.50	3.00
Nos. 1100-1101 (2)	1.20	1.20
Set total (44) Stamps	132.40	78.85

Europa, 1973

Post Horn and Arrows
CD16

1973

Andorra, French	219-220
Andorra, Spanish	76
Belgium	839-840
Cyprus	396-398
Finland	526
France	1367
Germany	1114-1115
Greece	1090-1092
Iceland	447-448
Ireland	329-330
Italy	1108-1109
Liechtenstein	528-529
Luxembourg	523-524
Malta	469-471
Monaco	866-867
Netherlands	504-505
Norway	604-605
Portugal	1170-1172
San Marino	802-803
Spain	1753
Switzerland	580-581
Turkey	1935-1936
Yugoslavia	1138-1139

Nos. 219-220 (2)	20.00	11.00
No. 76 (1)	.65	.55
Nos. 839-840 (2)	1.00	.65
Nos. 396-398 (3)	4.25	2.10
No. 526 (1)	1.25	.55
No. 1367 (1)	1.25	.75
Nos. 1114-1115 (2)	.90	.50
Nos. 1090-1092 (3)	2.10	1.40
Nos. 447-448 (2)	7.00	4.05

Nos. 329-330 (2)	5.25	2.00
Nos. 1108-1109 (2)	.65	.50
Nos. 528-529 (2)	.60	.60
Nos. 523-524 (2)	.90	1.00
Nos. 469-471 (3)	.90	1.20
Nos. 866-867 (2)	15.00	2.40
Nos. 504-505 (2)	2.85	1.10
Nos. 604-605 (2)	6.25	2.40
Nos. 1170-1172 (3)	13.00	2.15
Nos. 802-803 (2)	1.00	.60
No. 1753 (1)	.35	.25
Nos. 580-581 (2)	1.55	.60
Nos. 1935-1936 (2)	10.00	4.50
Nos. 1138-1139 (2)	1.15	1.10
Set total (46) Stamps	97.85	41.95

Europa, 2000

CD17

2000

Albania	2621-2622
Andorra, French	522
Andorra, Spanish	262
Armenia	610-611
Austria	1814
Azerbaijan	698-699
Belarus	350
Belgium	1818
Bosnia & Herzegovina (Moslem)	358
Bosnia & Herzegovina (Serb)	111-112
Croatia	428-429
Cyprus	959
Czech Republic	3120
Denmark	1189
Estonia	394
Faroe Islands	376
Finland	1129
Aland Islands	166
France	2771
Georgia	228-229
Germany	2086-2087
Gibraltar	837-840
Great Britain (Jersey)	935-936
Great Britain (Isle of Man)	883
Greece	1959
Greenland	363
Hungary	3699-3700
Iceland	910
Ireland	1230-1231
Italy	2349
Latvia	504
Liechtenstein	1178
Lithuania	668
Luxembourg	1035
Macedonia	187
Malta	1011-1012
Moldova	355
Monaco	2161-2162
Poland	3519
Portugal	2358
Portugal (Azores)	455
Portugal (Madeira)	208
Romania	4370
Russia	6589
San Marino	1480
Slovakia	355
Slovenia	424
Spain	3036
Sweden	2394
Switzerland	1074
Turkey	2762
Turkish Rep. of Northern Cyprus	500
Ukraine	379
Vatican City	1152

Nos. 2621-2622 (2)	11.00	11.00
No. 522 (1)	2.00	1.00
No. 262 (1)	1.60	.70
Nos. 610-611 (2)	4.75	4.75
No. 1814 (1)	1.40	1.40
Nos. 698-699 (2)	6.00	6.00
No. 350 (1)	1.75	1.75
No. 1818 (1)	1.40	.60
No. 358 (1)	4.75	4.75
Nos. 111-112 (2)	110.00	110.00
Nos. 428-429 (2)	6.25	6.25
No. 959 (1)	2.10	1.40
No. 3120 (1)	1.00	.40
No. 1189 (1)	3.50	2.25
No. 394 (1)	1.25	1.25
No. 376 (1)	2.40	2.40
No. 1129 (1)	2.00	.60
No. 166 (1)	2.00	1.10
No. 2771 (1)	1.25	.40
Nos. 228-229 (1)	9.00	9.00
Nos. 2086-2087 (2)	4.15	1.90
No. 837-840 (4)	5.50	5.30

Nos. 935-936 (2)	2.40	2.40
No. 883 (1)	1.50	1.50
No. 1959 (1)	3.00	3.00
No. 363 (1)	1.90	1.90
Nos. 3699-3700 (2)	6.50	2.50
No. 910 (1)	2.00	2.00
Nos. 1230-1231 (2)	4.75	4.75
No. 2349 (1)	1.50	.40
No. 504 (1)	5.00	2.40
No. 1178 (1)	2.25	1.75
No. 668 (1)	1.50	1.50
No. 1035 (1)	1.40	1.00
No. 187 (1)	3.25	3.25
Nos. 1011-1012 (2)	4.35	4.35
No. 355 (1)	3.50	3.50
Nos. 2161-2162 (2)	2.80	1.40
No. 3519 (1)	1.10	.50
No. 2358 (1)	1.25	.65
No. 455 (1)	1.25	.50
No. 208 (1)	1.25	.50
No. 4370 (1)	2.50	1.25
No. 6589 (1)	2.00	.85
No. 1480 (1)	1.00	1.00
No. 355 (1)	1.25	.55
No. 424 (1)	3.25	1.60
No. 3036 (1)	.75	.40
No. 2394 (1)	3.00	2.25
No. 1074 (1)	2.10	.75
No. 2762 (1)	2.00	2.00
No. 500 (1)	2.50	2.50
No. 379 (1)	4.50	3.00
No. 1152 (1)	1.25	1.25
Set total (68) Stamps	263.60	231.35

The Gibraltar stamps are similar to the stamp illustrated, but none have the design shown above. All other sets listed above include at least one stamp with the design shown, but some include stamps with entirely different designs. Bulgaria Nos. 4131-4132, Guernsey Nos. 802-803 and Yugoslavia Nos. 2485-2486 are Europa stamps with completely different designs.

PORTUGAL & COLONIES
Vasco da Gama

Fleet Departing CD20

Fleet Arriving at Calicut — CD21

Embarking at Rastello CD22

Muse of History CD23

San Gabriel, da Gama and Camoens CD24

Archangel Gabriel, the Patron Saint CD25

Flagship San Gabriel — CD26

Vasco da Gama — CD27

Fourth centenary of Vasco da Gama's discovery of the route to India.

1898

Azores	93-100
Macao	67-74
Madeira	37-44
Portugal	147-154
Port. Africa	1-8
Port. Congo	75-98
Port. India	189-196
St. Thomas & Prince Islands	170-193
Timor	45-52

Nos. 93-100 (8)	122.00	76.25
Nos. 67-74 (8)	136.00	96.75
Nos. 37-44 (8)	44.55	34.00
Nos. 147-154 (8)	169.30	43.45
Nos. 1-8 (8)	23.95	21.70
Nos. 75-98 (24)	41.15	34.45
Nos. 189-196 (8)	20.25	12.95
Nos. 170-193 (24)	38.75	34.30
Nos. 45-52 (8)	21.50	10.45
Set total (104) Stamps	617.45	364.30

Pombal
POSTAL TAX
POSTAL TAX DUES

Marquis de Pombal — CD28

Planning Reconstruction of Lisbon, 1755 — CD29

Pombal Monument, Lisbon — CD30

Sebastiao Jose de Carvalho e Mello, Marquis de Pombal (1699-1782), statesman, rebuilt Lisbon after earthquake of 1755. Tax was for the erection of Pombal monument. Obligatory on all mail on certain days throughout the year. Postal Tax Dues are inscribed "Multa."

1925

Angola	RA1-RA3, RAJ1-RAJ3
Azores	RA9-RA11, RAJ2-RAJ4
Cape Verde	RA1-RA3, RAJ1-RAJ3
Macao	RA1-RA3, RAJ1-RAJ3
Madeira	RA1-RA3, RAJ1-RAJ3
Mozambique	RA1-RA3, RAJ1-RAJ3
Nyassa	RA1-RA3, RAJ1-RAJ3
Portugal	RA11-RA13, RAJ2-RAJ4
Port. Guinea	RA1-RA3, RAJ1-RAJ3
Port. India	RA1-RA3, RAJ1-RAJ3
St. Thomas & Prince Islands	RA1-RA3, RAJ1-RAJ3
Timor	RA1-RA3, RAJ1-RAJ3

Nos. RA1-RA3,RAJ1-RAJ3 (6)	6.60	6.60
Nos. RA9-RA11,RAJ2-RAJ4 (6)	6.60	9.30
Nos. RA1-RA3,RAJ1-RAJ3 (6)	6.00	5.40
Nos. RA1-RA3,RAJ1-RAJ3 (6)	19.50	4.20
Nos. RA1-RA3,RAJ1-RAJ3 (6)	4.35	12.45
Nos. RA1-RA3,RAJ1-RAJ3 (6)	2.55	2.70
Nos. RA1-RA3,RAJ1-RAJ3 (6)	52.50	38.25
Nos. RA11-RA13,RAJ2-RAJ4 (6)	5.80	5.20
Nos. RA1-RA3,RAJ1-RAJ3 (6)	3.30	2.70
Nos. RA1-RA3,RAJ1-RAJ3 (6)	3.45	3.45
Nos. RA1-RA3,RAJ1-RAJ3 (6)	3.60	3.60
Nos. RA1-RA3,RAJ1-RAJ3 (6)	2.10	3.90
Set total (72) Stamps	116.35	97.75

Vasco da Gama CD34

Mousinho de Albuquerque CD35

Dam CD36

Prince Henry the Navigator CD37

Affonso de Albuquerque CD38

Plane over Globe CD39

1938-39

Angola	274-291, C1-C9
Cape Verde	234-251, C1-C9
Macao	289-305, C7-C15
Mozambique	270-287, C1-C9
Port. Guinea	233-250, C1-C9
Port. India	439-453, C1-C8
St. Thomas & Prince Islands	302-319, 323-340, C1-C18
Timor	223-239, C1-C9

Nos. 274-291,C1-C9 (27)	132.90	22.85
Nos. 234-251,C1-C9 (27)	100.00	31.20
Nos. 289-305,C7-C15 (26)	701.70	135.60
Nos. 270-287,C1-C9 (27)	63.45	11.20
Nos. 233-250,C1-C9 (27)	88.05	30.70
Nos. 439-453,C1-C8 (23)	74.75	25.50
Nos. 302-319,323-340,C1-C18 (54)	319.25	190.35
Nos. 223-239,C1-C9 (26)	149.25	73.15
Set total (237) Stamps	1,629.	520.55

Lady of Fatima

Our Lady of the Rosary, Fatima, Portugal — CD40

1948-49

Angola	315-318
Cape Verde	266
Macao	336
Mozambique	325-328
Port. Guinea	271
Port. India	480
St. Thomas & Prince Islands	351
Timor	254

Nos. 315-318 (4)	68.00	17.25
No. 266 (1)	8.50	4.50
No. 336 (1)	40.00	12.00
Nos. 325-328 (4)	20.00	4.50
No. 271 (1)	3.25	3.00
No. 480 (1)	2.50	2.25
No. 351 (1)	7.25	6.50
No. 254 (1)	3.00	3.00
Set total (14) Stamps	152.50	53.00

A souvenir sheet of 9 stamps was issued in 1951 to mark the extension of the 1950 Holy Year. The sheet contains: Angola No. 316, Cape Verde No. 266, Macao No. 336, Mozambique No. 325, Portuguese Guinea No. 271, Portuguese India Nos. 480, 485, St. Thomas & Prince Islands No. 351, Timor No. 254. The sheet also contains a portrait of Pope Pius XII and is inscribed "Encerramento do

Ano Santo, Fatima 1951." It was sold for 11 escudos.

Holy Year

Church Bells and Dove CD41

Angel Holding Candelabra CD42

Holy Year, 1950.

1950-51

Angola	331-332
Cape Verde	268-269
Macao	339-340
Mozambique	330-331
Port. Guinea	273-274
Port. India	490-491, 496-503
St. Thomas & Prince Islands	353-354
Timor	258-259

Nos. 331-332 (2)	7.60	1.35
Nos. 268-269 (2)	4.75	2.20
Nos. 339-340 (2)	55.00	12.50
Nos. 330-331 (2)	1.75	.85
Nos. 273-274 (2)	3.50	2.60
Nos. 490-491,496-503 (10)	12.80	5.40
Nos. 353-354 (2)	7.50	4.40
Nos. 258-259 (2)	3.75	3.25
Set total (24) Stamps	96.65	32.55

A souvenir sheet of 8 stamps was issued in 1951 to mark the extension of the Holy Year. The sheet contains: Angola No. 331, Cape Verde No. 269, Macao No. 340, Mozambique No. 331, Portuguese Guinea No. 275, Portuguese India No. 490, St. Thomas & Prince Islands No. 354, Timor No. 258, some with colors changed. The sheet contains doves and is inscribed 'Encerramento do Ano Santo, Fatima 1951.' It was sold for 17 escudos.

Holy Year Conclusion

Our Lady of Fatima — CD43

Conclusion of Holy Year. Sheets contain alternate vertical rows of stamps and labels bearing quotation from Pope Pius XII, different for each colony.

1951

Angola	357
Cape Verde	270
Macao	352
Mozambique	356
Port. Guinea	275
Port. India	506
St. Thomas & Prince Islands	355
Timor	270

No. 357 (1)	5.25	1.50
No. 270 (1)	1.50	1.25
No. 352 (1)	37.50	10.00
No. 356 (1)	2.25	1.00
No. 275 (1)	1.00	.65
No. 506 (1)	1.60	1.00
No. 355 (1)	2.50	2.00
No. 270 (1)	2.00	1.75
Set total (8) Stamps	53.60	19.15

Medical Congress

CD44

First National Congress of Tropical Medicine, Lisbon, 1952. Each stamp has a different design.

1952

Angola	358
Cape Verde	287
Macao	364

Mozambique	359
Port. Guinea	276
Port. India	516
St. Thomas & Prince Islands	356
Timor	271

No. 358 (1)	1.50	.50
No. 287 (1)	.70	.50
No. 364 (1)	9.75	4.25
No. 359 (1)	1.10	.55
No. 276 (1)	.45	.35
No. 516 (1)	4.75	2.00
No. 356 (1)	.30	.30
No. 271 (1)	1.00	1.00
Set total (8) Stamps	19.55	9.45

Postage Due Stamps

CD45

1952

Angola	J37-J42
Cape Verde	J31-J36
Macao	J53-J58
Mozambique	J51-J56
Port. Guinea	J40-J45
Port. India	J47-J52
St. Thomas & Prince Islands	J52-J57
Timor	J31-J36

Nos. J37-J42 (6)	4.05	3.15
Nos. J31-J36 (6)	2.80	2.30
Nos. J53-J58 (6)	17.45	6.85
Nos. J51-J56 (6)	1.80	1.55
Nos. J40-J45 (6)	2.55	2.55
Nos. J47-J52 (6)	6.10	6.10
Nos. J52-J57 (6)	4.15	4.15
Nos. J31-J36 (6)	3.50	3.50
Set total (48) Stamps	42.40	30.15

Sao Paulo

Father Manuel da Nobrega and View of Sao Paulo — CD46

Founding of Sao Paulo, Brazil, 400th anniv.

1954

Angola	385
Cape Verde	297
Macao	382
Mozambique	395
Port. Guinea	291
Port. India	530
St. Thomas & Prince Islands	369
Timor	279

No. 385 (1)	.80	.50
No. 297 (1)	.70	.60
No. 382 (1)	14.00	3.00
No. 395 (1)	.40	.30
No. 291 (1)	.35	.25
No. 530 (1)	.80	.40
No. 369 (1)	.80	.60
No. 279 (1)	.85	.70
Set total (8) Stamps	18.70	6.35

Tropical Medicine Congress

CD47

Sixth International Congress for Tropical Medicine and Malaria, Lisbon, Sept. 1958. Each stamp shows a different plant.

1958

Angola	409
Cape Verde	303
Macao	392
Mozambique	404
Port. Guinea	295
Port. India	569
St. Thomas & Prince Islands	371

Timor	289

No. 409 (1)	3.50	1.10
No. 303 (1)	5.50	2.10
No. 392 (1)	8.00	3.00
No. 404 (1)	4.00	.85
No. 295 (1)	2.75	1.10
No. 569 (1)	1.75	.75
No. 371 (1)	2.75	2.25
No. 289 (1)	3.00	2.75
Set total (8) Stamps	31.25	13.90

Sports

CD48

Each stamp shows a different sport.

1962

Angola	433-438
Cape Verde	320-325
Macao	394-399
Mozambique	424-429
Port. Guinea	299-304
St. Thomas & Prince Islands	374-379
Timor	313-318

Nos. 433-438 (6)	5.50	3.20
Nos. 320-325 (6)	15.25	5.20
Nos. 394-399 (6)	74.00	14.60
Nos. 424-429 (6)	5.70	2.45
Nos. 299-304 (6)	4.95	2.15
Nos. 374-379 (6)	6.75	3.20
Nos. 313-318 (6)	6.40	3.70
Set total (42) Stamps	118.55	34.50

Anti-Malaria

Anopheles Funestus and Malaria Eradication Symbol — CD49

World Health Organization drive to eradicate malaria.

1962

Angola	439
Cape Verde	326
Macao	400
Mozambique	430
Port. Guinea	305
St. Thomas & Prince Islands	380
Timor	319

No. 439 (1)	1.75	.90
No. 326 (1)	1.40	.90
No. 400 (1)	6.50	2.00
No. 430 (1)	1.40	.40
No. 305 (1)	1.25	.45
No. 380 (1)	2.00	1.50
No. 319 (1)	.75	.60
Set total (7) Stamps	15.05	6.75

Airline Anniversary

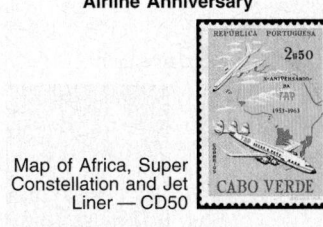

Map of Africa, Super Constellation and Jet Liner — CD50

Tenth anniversary of Transportes Aereos Portugueses (TAP).

1963

Angola	490
Cape Verde	327
Mozambique	434
Port. Guinea	318
St. Thomas & Prince Islands	381

No. 490 (1)	1.00	.35
No. 327 (1)	1.10	.70
No. 434 (1)	.40	.25

No. 318 (1)	.65	.35
No. 381 (1)	.70	.60
Set total (5) Stamps	3.85	2.25

National Overseas Bank

Antonio Teixeira de Sousa — CD51

Centenary of the National Overseas Bank of Portugal.

1964, May 16

Angola	509
Cape Verde	328
Port. Guinea	319
St. Thomas & Prince Islands	382
Timor	320

No. 509 (1)	.90	.30
No. 328 (1)	1.10	.75
No. 319 (1)	.65	.40
No. 382 (1)	.70	.50
No. 320 (1)	.75	.60
Set total (5) Stamps	4.10	2.55

ITU

ITU Emblem and the Archangel Gabriel — CD52

International Communications Union, Cent.

1965, May 17

Angola	511
Cape Verde	329
Macao	402
Mozambique	464
Port. Guinea	320
St. Thomas & Prince Islands	383
Timor	321

No. 511 (1)	1.25	.65
No. 329 (1)	2.10	1.40
No. 402 (1)	5.00	2.00
No. 464 (1)	.40	.25
No. 320 (1)	1.90	.75
No. 383 (1)	1.50	1.00
No. 321 (1)	1.50	.90
Set total (7) Stamps	13.65	6.95

National Revolution

CD53

40th anniv. of the National Revolution. Different buildings on each stamp.

1966, May 28

Angola	525
Cape Verde	338
Macao	403
Mozambique	465
Port. Guinea	329
St. Thomas & Prince Islands	392
Timor	322

No. 525 (1)	.50	.25
No. 338 (1)	.60	.45
No. 403 (1)	5.00	2.00
No. 465 (1)	.50	.30
No. 329 (1)	.55	.35
No. 392 (1)	.75	.50
No. 322 (1)	1.50	.90
Set total (7) Stamps	9.40	4.75

Navy Club

CD54

Centenary of Portugal's Navy Club. Each stamp has a different design.

1967, Jan. 31

Angola	527-528
Cape Verde	339-340
Macao	412-413
Mozambique	478-479
Port. Guinea	330-331
St. Thomas & Prince Islands	393-394
Timor	323-324

Nos. 527-528 (2)	1.75	.75
Nos. 339-340 (2)	2.00	1.40
Nos. 412-413 (2)	9.50	3.75
Nos. 478-479 (2)	1.20	.65
Nos. 330-331 (2)	1.20	.90
Nos. 393-394 (2)	3.20	1.25
Nos. 323-324 (2)	4.00	2.00
Set total (14) Stamps	22.85	10.70

Admiral Coutinho

CD55

Centenary of the birth of Admiral Carlos Viegas Gago Coutinho (1869-1959), explorer and aviation pioneer. Each stamp has a different design.

1969, Feb. 17

Angola	547
Cape Verde	355
Macao	417
Mozambique	484
Port. Guinea	335
St. Thomas & Prince Islands	397
Timor	335

No. 547 (1)	.85	.35
No. 355 (1)	.35	.25
No. 417 (1)	3.75	1.50
No. 484 (1)	.25	.25
No. 335 (1)	.35	.25
No. 397 (1)	.50	.35
No. 335 (1)	1.10	.85
Set total (7) Stamps	7.15	3.80

Administration Reform

Luiz Augusto Rebello da Silva — CD56

Centenary of the administration reforms of the overseas territories.

1969, Sept. 25

Angola	549
Cape Verde	357
Macao	419
Mozambique	491
Port. Guinea	337
St. Thomas & Prince Islands	399
Timor	338

No. 549 (1)	.35	.25
No. 357 (1)	.35	.25
No. 419 (1)	5.00	1.00
No. 491 (1)	.25	.25
No. 337 (1)	.25	.25
No. 399 (1)	.45	.45
No. 338 (1)	.40	.25
Set total (7) Stamps	7.05	2.70

Marshal Carmona

CD57

Birth centenary of Marshal Antonio Oscar Carmona de Fragoso (1869-1951), President of Portugal. Each stamp has a different design.

1970, Nov. 15

Angola	563
Cape Verde	359
Macao	422
Mozambique	493
Port. Guinea	340
St. Thomas & Prince Islands	403
Timor	341

No. 563 (1)	.45	.25
No. 359 (1)	.55	.25
No. 422 (1)	2.25	1.25
No. 493 (1)	.40	.25
No. 340 (1)	.35	.25
No. 403 (1)	.75	.45
No. 341 (1)	.25	.25
Set total (7) Stamps	5.00	3.05

Olympic Games

CD59

20th Olympic Games, Munich, Aug. 26-Sept. 11. Each stamp shows a different sport.

1972, June 20

Angola	569
Cape Verde	361
Macao	426
Mozambique	504
Port. Guinea	342
St. Thomas & Prince Islands	408
Timor	343

No. 569 (1)	.65	.25
No. 361 (1)	.65	.30
No. 426 (1)	3.25	1.00
No. 504 (1)	.30	.25
No. 342 (1)	.45	.25
No. 408 (1)	.35	.25
No. 343 (1)	.50	.50
Set total (7) Stamps	6.15	2.80

Lisbon-Rio de Janeiro Flight

CD60

50th anniversary of the Lisbon to Rio de Janeiro flight by Arturo de Sacadura and Coutinho, March 30-June 5, 1922. Each stamp shows a different stage of the flight.

1972, Sept. 20

Angola	570
Cape Verde	362
Macao	427
Mozambique	505
Port. Guinea	343
St. Thomas & Prince Islands	409
Timor	344

No. 570 (1)	.35	.25
No. 362 (1)	1.50	.30
No. 427 (1)	22.50	7.50
No. 505 (1)	.25	.25
No. 343 (1)	.25	.25
No. 409 (1)	.35	.25
No. 344 (1)	.25	.40
Set total (7) Stamps	25.45	9.20

WMO Centenary

WMO Emblem — CD61

Centenary of international meterological cooperation.

1973, Dec. 15

Angola	571
Cape Verde	363
Macao	429
Mozambique	509
Port. Guinea	344
St. Thomas & Prince Islands	410

Timor		345
No. 571 (1)	.45	.25
No. 363 (1)	.65	.30
No. 429 (1)	6.25	1.75
No. 509 (1)	.30	.25
No. 344 (1)	.45	.35
No. 410 (1)	.60	.50
No. 345 (1)	1.75	2.00
Set total (7) Stamps	10.45	5.40

FRENCH COMMUNITY

Upper Volta can be found under Burkina Faso in Vol. 1
Madagascar can be found under Malagasy in Vol. 3

Colonial Exposition

People of French Empire CD70

Women's Heads CD71

France Showing Way to Civilization CD72

"Colonial Commerce" CD73

International Colonial Exposition, Paris.

1931

Cameroun	213-216
Chad	60-63
Dahomey	97-100
Fr. Guiana	152-155
Fr. Guinea	116-119
Fr. India	100-103
Fr. Polynesia	76-79
Fr. Sudan	102-105
Gabon	120-123
Guadeloupe	138-141
Indo-China	140-142
Ivory Coast	92-95
Madagascar	169-172
Martinique	129-132
Mauritania	65-68
Middle Congo	61-64
New Caledonia	176-179
Niger	73-76
Reunion	122-125
St. Pierre & Miquelon	132-135
Senegal	138-141
Somali Coast	135-138
Togo	254-257
Ubangi-Shari	82-85
Upper Volta	66-69
Wallis & Futuna Isls.	85-88

Nos. 213-216 (4)	23.00	18.25
Nos. 60-63 (4)	22.00	22.00
Nos. 97-100 (4)	26.00	26.00
Nos. 152-155 (4)	22.00	22.00
Nos. 116-119 (4)	19.75	19.75
Nos. 100-103 (4)	18.00	18.00
Nos. 76-79 (4)	30.00	30.00
Nos. 102-105 (4)	19.00	19.00
Nos. 120-123 (4)	17.50	17.50
Nos. 138-141 (4)	19.00	19.00
Nos. 140-142 (3)	11.50	11.50
Nos. 92-95 (4)	22.50	22.50
Nos. 169-172 (4)	7.90	5.00
Nos. 129-132 (4)	21.00	21.00
Nos. 65-68 (4)	22.00	22.00
Nos. 61-64 (4)	20.50	20.50
Nos. 176-179 (4)	24.00	24.00
Nos. 73-76 (4)	21.50	21.50
Nos. 122-125 (4)	22.00	22.00
Nos. 132-135 (4)	24.00	24.00
Nos. 138-141 (4)	20.00	20.00
Nos. 135-138 (4)	22.00	22.00
Nos. 254-257 (4)	22.00	22.00

Nos. 82-85 (4)	21.00	21.00
Nos. 66-69 (4)	19.00	19.00
Nos. 85-88 (4)	35.00	35.00
Set total (103) Stamps	552.15	544.50

Paris International Exposition
Colonial Arts Exposition

"Colonial Resources"
CD74   CD77

Overseas Commerce CD75

Exposition Building and Women CD76

"France and the Empire" CD78

Cultural Treasures of the Colonies CD79

Souvenir sheets contain one imperf. stamp.

1937

Cameroun	217-222A
Dahomey	101-107
Fr. Equatorial Africa	27-32, 73
Fr. Guiana	162-168
Fr. Guinea	120-126
Fr. India	104-110
Fr. Polynesia	117-123
Fr. Sudan	106-112
Guadeloupe	148-154
Indo-China	193-199
Inini	41
Ivory Coast	152-158
Kwangchowan	132
Madagascar	191-197
Martinique	179-185
Mauritania	69-75
New Caledonia	208-214
Niger	73-83
Reunion	167-173
St. Pierre & Miquelon	165-171
Senegal	172-178
Somali Coast	139-145
Togo	258-264
Wallis & Futuna Isls.	89

Nos. 217-222A (7)	18.80	20.30
Nos. 101-107 (7)	23.60	27.60
Nos. 27-32, 73 (7)	28.10	32.10
Nos. 162-168 (7)	22.50	24.50
Nos. 120-126 (7)	24.00	28.00
Nos. 104-110 (7)	21.15	36.50
Nos. 117-123 (7)	58.50	75.00
Nos. 106-112 (7)	23.60	27.60
Nos. 148-154 (7)	19.55	21.05
Nos. 193-199 (7)	17.70	19.70
No. 41 (1)	19.00	22.50
Nos. 152-158 (7)	22.20	26.20
No. 132 (1)	9.25	11.00
Nos. 191-197 (7)	19.25	21.75
Nos. 179-185 (7)	19.95	21.70
Nos. 69-75 (7)	20.50	24.50
Nos. 208-214 (7)	39.00	50.50
Nos. 73-83 (11)	42.70	46.70
Nos. 167-173 (7)	21.70	23.20
Nos. 165-171 (7)	49.60	64.00
Nos. 172-178 (7)	21.00	23.80
Nos. 139-145 (7)	25.60	32.60
Nos. 258-264 (7)	20.40	20.40
No. 89 (1)	28.50	37.50
Set total (154) Stamps	616.15	738.70

Curie

Pierre and Marie Curie CD80

40th anniversary of the discovery of radium. The surtax was for the benefit of the Intl. Union for the Control of Cancer.

1938

Cameroun	B1
Cuba	B1-B2
Dahomey	B2
France	B76
Fr. Equatorial Africa	B1
Fr. Guiana	B3
Fr. Guinea	B2
Fr. India	B6
Fr. Polynesia	B5
Fr. Sudan	B1
Guadeloupe	B3
Indo-China	B14
Ivory Coast	B2
Madagascar	B2
Martinique	B2
Mauritania	B3
New Caledonia	B4
Niger	B1
Reunion	B4
St. Pierre & Miquelon	B3
Senegal	B3
Somali Coast	B2
Togo	B1

No. B1 (1)	10.00	10.00
Nos. B1-B2 (2)	8.50	2.40
No. B2 (1)	9.50	9.50
No. B76 (1)	21.00	12.50
No. B1 (1)	24.00	24.00
No. B3 (1)	13.50	13.50
No. B2 (1)	8.75	8.75
No. B6 (1)	10.00	10.00
No. B5 (1)	20.00	20.00
No. B1 (1)	12.50	12.50
No. B3 (1)	11.00	10.50
No. B14 (1)	12.00	12.00
No. B2 (1)	11.00	7.50
No. B2 (1)	11.00	11.00
No. B3 (1)	13.00	13.00
No. B3 (1)	7.75	7.75
No. B4 (1)	16.50	17.50
No. B1 (1)	15.00	15.00
No. B4 (1)	14.00	14.00
No. B3 (1)	21.00	22.50
No. B3 (1)	10.50	10.50
No. B2 (1)	7.75	7.75
No. B1 (1)	20.00	20.00
Set total (24) Stamps	308.25	292.15

Caillie

Rene Caillie and Map of Northwestern Africa — CD81

Death centenary of Rene Caillie (1799-1838), French explorer. All three denominations exist with colony name omitted.

1939

Dahomey	108-110
Fr. Guinea	161-163
Fr. Sudan	113-115
Ivory Coast	160-162
Mauritania	109-111
Niger	84-86
Senegal	188-190
Togo	265-267

Nos. 108-110 (3)	1.20	3.60
Nos. 161-163 (3)	1.20	3.20
Nos. 113-115 (3)	1.20	3.20
Nos. 160-162 (3)	1.05	2.55
Nos. 109-111 (3)	1.05	3.80
Nos. 84-86 (3)	1.05	2.35
Nos. 188-190 (3)	1.05	2.90
Nos. 265-267 (3)	1.05	3.30
Set total (24) Stamps	8.85	24.90

New York World's Fair

Natives and New York Skyline CD82

1939

Cameroun	223-224
Dahomey	111-112
Fr. Equatorial Africa	78-79
Fr. Guiana	169-170
Fr. Guinea	164-165
Fr. India	111-112
Fr. Polynesia	124-125
Fr. Sudan	116-117
Guadeloupe	155-156
Indo-China	203-204
Inini	42-43
Ivory Coast	163-164
Kwangchowan	133-134
Madagascar	209-210
Martinique	186-187
Mauritania	112-113
New Caledonia	215-216
Niger	87-88
Reunion	174-175
St. Pierre & Miquelon	205-206
Senegal	191-192
Somali Coast	179-180
Togo	268-269
Wallis & Futuna Isls.	90-91

Nos. 223-224 (2)	2.80	2.40
Nos. 111-112 (2)	1.60	3.20
Nos. 78-79 (2)	1.60	3.20
Nos. 169-170 (2)	2.60	2.60
Nos. 164-165 (2)	1.60	3.20
Nos. 111-112 (2)	3.00	8.00
Nos. 124-125 (2)	4.80	4.80
Nos. 116-117 (2)	1.60	3.20
Nos. 155-156 (2)	2.50	2.50
Nos. 203-204 (2)	2.05	2.05
Nos. 42-43 (2)	7.50	9.00
Nos. 163-164 (2)	1.50	3.00
Nos. 133-134 (2)	2.50	2.50
Nos. 209-210 (2)	1.50	2.50
Nos. 186-187 (2)	2.35	2.35
Nos. 112-113 (2)	1.40	2.80
Nos. 215-216 (2)	3.35	3.35
Nos. 87-88 (2)	1.40	2.80
Nos. 174-175 (2)	2.80	2.80
Nos. 205-206 (2)	4.80	6.00
Nos. 191-192 (2)	1.40	2.80
Nos. 179-180 (2)	1.40	2.80
Nos. 268-269 (2)	1.40	2.80
Nos. 90-91 (2)	6.00	6.00
Set total (48) Stamps	63.45	86.65

French Revolution

Storming of the Bastille CD83

French Revolution, 150th anniv. The surtax was for the defense of the colonies.

1939

Cameroun	B2-B6
Dahomey	B3-B7
Fr. Equatorial Africa	B4-B8, CB1
Fr. Guiana	B4-B8, CB1
Fr. Guinea	B3-B7
Fr. India	B7-B11
Fr. Polynesia	B6-B10, CB1
Fr. Sudan	B2-B6
Guadeloupe	B4-B8
Indo-China	B15-B19, CB1
Inini	B1-B5
Ivory Coast	B3-B7
Kwangchowan	B1-B5
Madagascar	B3-B7, CB1
Martinique	B3-B7
Mauritania	B4-B8
New Caledonia	B5-B9, CB1
Niger	B2-B6
Reunion	B5-B9, CB1
St. Pierre & Miquelon	B4-B8
Senegal	B4-B8, CB1
Somali Coast	B3-B7
Togo	B2-B6
Wallis & Futuna Isls.	B1-B5

Nos. B2-B6 (5)	60.00	60.00
Nos. B3-B7 (5)	47.50	47.50
Nos. B4-B8,CB1 (6)	120.00	120.00
Nos. B4-B8,CB1 (6)	79.50	79.50
Nos. B3-B7 (5)	47.50	47.50
Nos. B7-B11 (5)	28.75	32.50
Nos. B6-B10,CB1 (6)	122.50	122.50
Nos. B2-B6 (5)	50.00	50.00
Nos. B4-B8 (5)	50.00	50.00
Nos. B15-B19,CB1 (6)	85.00	85.00
Nos. B1-B5 (5)	75.00	87.50
Nos. B3-B7 (5)	43.75	43.75
Nos. B1-B5 (5)	46.25	46.25
Nos. B3-B7,CB1 (6)	65.50	65.50
Nos. B3-B7 (5)	52.50	52.50
Nos. B4-B8 (5)	42.50	42.50
Nos. B5-B9,CB1 (6)	101.50	101.50
Nos. B2-B6 (5)	60.00	60.00
Nos. B5-B9,CB1 (6)	87.50	87.50
Nos. B4-B8 (5)	67.50	72.50
Nos. B4-B8,CB1 (6)	56.50	56.50
Nos. B3-B7 (5)	45.00	45.00
Nos. B2-B6 (5)	42.50	42.50
Nos. B1-B5 (5)	95.00	95.00
Set total (128) Stamps	1,572.	1,593.

Plane over Coastal Area CD85

All five denominations exist with colony name omitted.

1940

Dahomey	C1-C5
Fr. Guinea	C1-C5
Fr. Sudan	C1-C5
Ivory Coast	C1-C5
Mauritania	C1-C5
Niger	C1-C5
Senegal	C12-C16
Togo	C1-C5

Nos. C1-C5 (5)	4.00	4.00
Nos. C1-C5 (5)	4.00	4.00
Nos. C1-C5 (5)	4.00	4.00
Nos. C1-C5 (5)	3.80	3.80
Nos. C1-C5 (5)	3.50	3.50
Nos. C1-C5 (5)	3.50	3.50
Nos. C12-C16 (5)	3.50	3.50
Nos. C1-C5 (5)	3.15	3.15
Set total (40) Stamps	29.45	29.45

Defense of the Empire

Colonial Infantryman — CD86

1941

Cameroun	B13B
Dahomey	B13
Fr. Equatorial Africa	B8B
Fr. Guiana	B10
Fr. Guinea	B13
Fr. India	B13
Fr. Polynesia	B12
Fr. Sudan	B12
Guadeloupe	B10
Indo-China	B19B
Inini	B7
Ivory Coast	B13
Kwangchowan	B7
Madagascar	B9
Martinique	B9
Mauritania	B14
New Caledonia	B11
Niger	B12
Reunion	B11
St. Pierre & Miquelon	B8B
Senegal	B14
Somali Coast	B9
Togo	B10B
Wallis & Futuna Isls.	B7

No. B13B (1)	1.60
No. B13 (1)	1.20
No. B8B (1)	3.50
No. B10 (1)	1.40
No. B13 (1)	1.40
No. B13 (1)	1.25
No. B12 (1)	3.50
No. B12 (1)	1.40
No. B10 (1)	1.00
No. B19B (1)	1.60
No. B7 (1)	1.75
No. B13 (1)	1.25
No. B7 (1)	.85
No. B9 (1)	1.50
No. B9 (1)	1.40
No. B14 (1)	.95
No. B11 (1)	1.60
No. B12 (1)	1.40
No. B11 (1)	1.60
No. B8B (1)	3.75
No. B14 (1)	1.25
No. B9 (1)	1.60
No. B10B (1)	1.10
No. B7 (1)	2.40
Set total (24) Stamps	40.25

Each of the CD86 stamps listed above is part of a set of three stamps. The designs of the other two stamps in the set vary from country to country. Only the values of the Common Design stamps are listed here.

Colonial Education Fund

CD86a

1942

Cameroun	CB3
Dahomey	CB4
Fr. Equatorial Africa	CB5
Fr. Guiana	CB4
Fr. Guinea	CB4
Fr. India	CB3
Fr. Polynesia	CB4
Fr. Sudan	CB4
Guadeloupe	CB3
Indo-China	CB5
Inini	CB3
Ivory Coast	CB4
Kwangchowan	CB4
Malagasy	CB5
Martinique	CB3
Mauritania	CB4
New Caledonia	CB4
Niger	CB4
Reunion	CB4
St. Pierre & Miquelon	CB3
Senegal	CB5
Somali Coast	CB3
Togo	CB3
Wallis & Futuna	CB3

No. CB3 (1)	1.10	
No. CB4 (1)	.80	5.50
No. CB5 (1)	.80	
No. CB4 (1)	1.10	
No. CB4 (1)	.40	5.50
No. CB3 (1)	.90	
No. CB4 (1)	2.00	
No. CB4 (1)	.40	5.50
No. CB3 (1)	1.10	
No. CB5 (1)	1.10	
No. CB3 (1)	1.25	
No. CB4 (1)	1.00	5.50
No. CB4 (1)	1.00	
No. CB5 (1)	.65	
No. CB3 (1)	1.00	
No. CB4 (1)	.80	
No. CB4 (1)	1.60	
No. CB4 (1)	.35	
No. CB4 (1)	.90	
No. CB3 (1)	5.25	
No. CB5 (1)	.80	6.50
No. CB3 (1)	.70	
No. CB3 (1)	.35	
No. CB3 (1)	2.25	
Set total (24) Stamps	27.60	28.50

Cross of Lorraine & Four-motor Plane CD87

1941-5

Cameroun	C1-C7
Fr. Equatorial Africa	C17-C23
Fr. Guiana	C9-C10
Fr. India	C1-C6
Fr. Polynesia	C3-C9
Fr. West Africa	C1-C3
Guadeloupe	C1-C2
Madagascar	C37-C43

Martinique	C1-C2
New Caledonia	C7-C13
Reunion	C18-C24
St. Pierre & Miquelon	C1-C7
Somali Coast	C1-C7

Nos. C1-C7 (7)	6.30	6.30
Nos. C17-C23 (7)	10.40	6.35
Nos. C9-C10 (2)	3.80	3.10
Nos. C1-C6 (6)	9.30	15.00
Nos. C3-C9 (7)	13.75	10.00
Nos. C1-C3 (3)	9.50	3.90
Nos. C1-C2 (2)	3.75	2.50
Nos. C37-C43 (7)	5.60	3.80
Nos. C1-C2 (2)	3.00	1.60
Nos. C7-C13 (7)	8.35	8.35
Nos. C18-C24 (7)	7.05	5.00
Nos. C1-C7 (7)	11.60	9.40
Nos. C1-C7 (7)	13.95	11.10
Set total (71) Stamps	106.35	86.40

Transport Plane CD88

Caravan and Plane CD89

1942

Dahomey	C6-C13
Fr. Guinea	C6-C13
Fr. Sudan	C6-C13
Ivory Coast	C6-C13
Mauritania	C6-C13
Niger	C6-C13
Senegal	C17-C25
Togo	C6-C13

Nos. C6-C13 (8)	7.15
Nos. C6-C13 (8)	5.75
Nos. C6-C13 (8)	8.00
Nos. C6-C13 (8)	11.15
Nos. C6-C13 (8)	9.75
Nos. C6-C13 (8)	6.90
Nos. C17-C25 (9)	9.45
Nos. C6-C13 (8)	6.75
Set total (65) Stamps	64.90

Red Cross

Marianne CD90

The surtax was for the French Red Cross and national relief.

1944

Cameroun	B28
Fr. Equatorial Africa	B38
Fr. Guiana	B12
Fr. India	B14
Fr. Polynesia	B13
Fr. West Africa	B1
Guadeloupe	B12
Madagascar	B15
Martinique	B11
New Caledonia	B13
Reunion	B15
St. Pierre & Miquelon	B13
Somali Coast	B13
Wallis & Futuna Isls.	B9

No. B28 (1)	2.00	1.60
No. B38 (1)	1.60	1.20
No. B12 (1)	1.75	1.25
No. B14 (1)	1.50	1.25
No. B13 (1)	2.00	1.60
No. B1 (1)	6.50	4.75
No. B12 (1)	1.40	1.00
No. B15 (1)	.90	.90
No. B11 (1)	1.20	1.20
No. B13 (1)	1.50	1.50
No. B15 (1)	1.60	1.10
No. B13 (1)	2.75	2.40
No. B13 (1)	1.75	2.00
No. B9 (1)	4.50	3.25
Set total (14) Stamps	30.95	25.00

Eboue

CD91

Felix Eboue, first French colonial administrator to proclaim resistance to Germany after French surrender in World War II.

1945

Cameroun	296-297
Fr. Equatorial Africa	156-157
Fr. Guiana	171-172
Fr. India	210-211
Fr. Polynesia	150-151
Fr. West Africa	15-16
Guadeloupe	187-188
Madagascar	259-260
Martinique	196-197
New Caledonia	274-275
Reunion	238-239
St. Pierre & Miquelon	322-323
Somali Coast	238-239

Nos. 296-297 (2)	2.40	1.95
Nos. 156-157 (2)	2.55	2.00
Nos. 171-172 (2)	2.45	2.00
Nos. 210-211 (2)	2.20	1.95
Nos. 150-151 (2)	3.60	2.85
Nos. 15-16 (2)	2.40	2.40
Nos. 187-188 (2)	2.05	1.60
Nos. 259-260 (2)	2.00	1.45
Nos. 196-197 (2)	2.05	1.55
Nos. 274-275 (2)	3.40	3.00
Nos. 238-239 (2)	2.40	2.00
Nos. 322-323 (2)	4.40	3.45
Nos. 238-239 (2)	2.45	2.10
Set total (26) Stamps	34.35	28.30

Victory

Victory — CD92

European victory of the Allied Nations in World War II.

1946, May 8

Cameroun	C8
Fr. Equatorial Africa	C24
Fr. Guiana	C11
Fr. India	C7
Fr. Polynesia	C10
Fr. West Africa	C4
Guadeloupe	C3
Indo-China	C19
Madagascar	C44
Martinique	C3
New Caledonia	C14
Reunion	C25
St. Pierre & Miquelon	C8
Somali Coast	C8
Wallis & Futuna Isls.	C1

No. C8 (1)	1.60	1.20
No. C24 (1)	1.60	1.25
No. C11 (1)	1.75	1.25
No. C7 (1)	1.00	4.00
No. C10 (1)	2.75	2.00
No. C4 (1)	1.60	1.20
No. C3 (1)	1.25	1.00
No. C19 (1)	1.00	.55
No. C44 (1)	1.00	.35
No. C3 (1)	1.30	1.00
No. C14 (1)	2.25	1.25
No. C25 (1)	1.10	.90
No. C8 (1)	2.10	1.75
No. C8 (1)	1.75	1.40
No. C1 (1)	2.50	1.90
Set total (15) Stamps	24.55	21.00

Chad to Rhine

Leclerc's Departure from Chad — CD93

Battle at Cufra Oasis — CD94

Tanks in Action, Mareth — CD95

Normandy Invasion — CD96

Entering Paris — CD97

Liberation of Strasbourg — CD98

"Chad to the Rhine" march, 1942-44, by Gen. Jacques Leclerc's column, later French 2nd Armored Division.

1946, June 6

Cameroun	C9-C14
Fr. Equatorial Africa	C25-C30
Fr. Guiana	C12-C17
Fr. India	C8-C13
Fr. Polynesia	C11-C16
Fr. West Africa	C5-C10
Guadeloupe	C4-C9
Indo-China	C20-C25
Madagascar	C45-C50
Martinique	C4-C9
New Caledonia	C15-C20
Reunion	C26-C31
St. Pierre & Miquelon	C9-C14
Somali Coast	C9-C14
Wallis & Futuna Isls.	C2-C7

Nos. C9-C14 (6)	12.05	9.70
Nos. C25-C30 (6)	14.70	10.80
Nos. C12-C17 (6)	12.65	10.35
Nos. C8-C13 (6)	12.80	15.00
Nos. C11-C16 (6)	17.55	13.40
Nos. C5-C10 (6)	16.05	11.95
Nos. C4-C9 (6)	12.00	9.60
Nos. C20-C25 (6)	6.40	6.40
Nos. C45-C50 (6)	10.30	8.40
Nos. C4-C9 (6)	8.85	7.30
Nos. C15-C20 (6)	13.40	11.90
Nos. C26-C31 (6)	10.25	6.55
Nos. C9-C14 (6)	17.30	14.35

Nos. C9-C14 (6)	18.10	12.65
Nos. C2-C7 (6)	13.75	10.45
Set total (90) Stamps	196.15	158.80

UPU

French Colonials, Globe and Plane — CD99

Universal Postal Union, 75th anniv.

1949, July 4

Cameroun	C29
Fr. Equatorial Africa	C34
Fr. India	C17
Fr. Polynesia	C20
Fr. West Africa	C15
Indo-China	C26
Madagascar	C55
New Caledonia	C24
St. Pierre & Miquelon	C18
Somali Coast	C18
Togo	C18
Wallis & Futuna Isls.	C10

No. C29 (1)	8.00	4.75
No. C34 (1)	16.00	12.00
No. C17 (1)	11.50	8.75
No. C20 (1)	20.00	15.00
No. C15 (1)	12.00	8.75
No. C26 (1)	4.75	4.00
No. C55 (1)	4.00	2.75
No. C24 (1)	8.25	5.25
No. C18 (1)	20.00	14.00
No. C18 (1)	14.00	10.50
No. C18 (1)	8.50	7.00
No. C10 (1)	12.50	8.25
Set total (12) Stamps	139.50	99.00

Tropical Medicine

Doctor Treating Infant CD100

The surtax was for charitable work.

1950

Cameroun	B29
Fr. Equatorial Africa	B39
Fr. India	B15
Fr. Polynesia	B14
Fr. West Africa	B3
Madagascar	B17
New Caledonia	B14
St. Pierre & Miquelon	B14
Somali Coast	B14
Togo	B11

No. B29 (1)	7.25	5.50
No. B39 (1)	7.25	5.50
No. B15 (1)	6.00	4.00
No. B14 (1)	10.50	8.00
No. B3 (1)	9.50	7.25
No. B17 (1)	5.50	5.50
No. B14 (1)	6.75	5.25
No. B14 (1)	17.00	13.00
No. B14 (1)	7.75	6.25
No. B11 (1)	5.00	3.50
Set total (10) Stamps	82.50	63.75

Military Medal

Medal, Early Marine and Colonial Soldier — CD101

Centenary of the creation of the French Military Medal.

1952

Cameroun	322
Comoro Isls.	39
Fr. Equatorial Africa	186

Fr. India		233
Fr. Polynesia		179
Fr. West Africa		57
Madagascar		286
New Caledonia		295
St. Pierre & Miquelon		345
Somali Coast		267
Togo		327
Wallis & Futuna Isls.		149

No. 322 (1)	7.25	3.25
No. 39 (1)	50.00	40.00
No. 186 (1)	8.00	5.50
No. 233 (1)	5.50	3.25
No. 179 (1)	13.50	10.00
No. 57 (1)	8.75	6.50
No. 286 (1)	3.75	2.50
No. 295 (1)	7.50	6.00
No. 345 (1)	17.00	13.00
No. 267 (1)	9.00	8.00
No. 327 (1)	5.50	4.75
No. 149 (1)	9.50	7.00
Set total (12) Stamps	145.25	113.50

Liberation

Allied Landing, Victory Sign and Cross of Lorraine — CD102

Liberation of France, 10th anniv.

1954, June 6

Cameroun		C32
Comoro Isls.		C4
Fr. Equatorial Africa		C38
Fr. India		C18
Fr. Polynesia		C22
Fr. West Africa		C17
Madagascar		C57
New Caledonia		C25
St. Pierre & Miquelon		C19
Somali Coast		C19
Togo		C19
Wallis & Futuna Isls.		C11

No. C32 (1)	7.25	4.75
No. C4 (1)	35.00	20.00
No. C38 (1)	12.00	8.00
No. C18 (1)	11.00	8.00
No. C22 (1)	10.00	8.00
No. C17 (1)	12.00	5.50
No. C57 (1)	3.25	2.00
No. C25 (1)	8.25	5.00
No. C19 (1)	18.00	12.00
No. C19 (1)	10.50	8.50
No. C19 (1)	7.00	5.50
No. C11 (1)	12.50	8.25
Set total (12) Stamps	146.75	95.50

FIDES

Plowmen CD103

Efforts of FIDES, the Economic and Social Development Fund for Overseas Possessions (Fonds d' Investissement pour le Developpement Economique et Social). Each stamp has a different design.

1956

Cameroun		326-329
Comoro Isls.		43
Fr. Equatorial Africa		189-192
Fr. Polynesia		181
Fr. West Africa		65-72
Madagascar		292-295
New Caledonia		303
St. Pierre & Miquelon		350
Somali Coast		268-269
Togo		331

Nos. 326-329 (4)	6.90	3.20
No. 43 (1)	2.25	1.60
Nos. 189-192 (4)	3.20	1.65
No. 181 (1)	4.00	2.00
Nos. 65-72 (8)	16.00	6.35
Nos. 292-295 (4)	2.25	1.20
No. 303 (1)	1.90	1.10
No. 350 (1)	6.50	3.50

Nos. 268-269 (2)	5.35	3.15
No. 331 (1)	4.25	2.10
Set total (27) Stamps	52.60	25.85

Flower

CD104

Each stamp shows a different flower.

1958-9

Cameroun		333
Comoro Isls.		45
Fr. Equatorial Africa		200-201
Fr. Polynesia		192
Fr. So. & Antarctic Terr.		11
Fr. West Africa		79-83
Madagascar		301-302
New Caledonia		304-305
St. Pierre & Miquelon		357
Somali Coast		270
Togo		348-349
Wallis & Futuna Isls.		152

No. 333 (1)	1.60	.80
No. 45 (1)	5.50	4.50
Nos. 200-201 (2)	3.60	1.60
No. 192 (1)	6.50	4.00
No. 11 (1)	10.00	8.00
Nos. 79-83 (5)	10.45	5.60
Nos. 301-302 (2)	1.60	.60
Nos. 304-305 (2)	9.25	3.00
No. 357 (1)	4.50	2.40
No. 270 (1)	4.25	1.40
Nos. 348-349 (2)	1.10	.50
No. 152 (1)	4.50	2.50
Set total (20) Stamps	62.85	34.90

Human Rights

Sun, Dove and U.N. Emblem CD105

10th anniversary of the signing of the Universal Declaration of Human Rights.

1958

Comoro Isls.		44
Fr. Equatorial Africa		202
Fr. Polynesia		191
Fr. West Africa		85
Madagascar		300
New Caledonia		306
St. Pierre & Miquelon		356
Somali Coast		274
Wallis & Futuna Isls.		153

No. 44 (1)	11.00	11.00
No. 202 (1)	2.40	1.25
No. 191 (1)	13.00	8.75
No. 85 (1)	2.40	2.00
No. 300 (1)	.80	.40
No. 306 (1)	3.00	1.50
No. 356 (1)	3.50	2.50
No. 274 (1)	3.50	2.10
No. 153 (1)	5.75	4.00
Set total (9) Stamps	45.35	33.50

C.C.T.A.

CD106

Commission for Technical Cooperation in Africa south of the Sahara, 10th anniv.

1960

Cameroun		339
Cent. Africa		3
Chad		66
Congo, P.R.		90
Dahomey		138
Gabon		150
Ivory Coast		180
Madagascar		317

Mali		9
Mauritania		117
Niger		104
Upper Volta		89

No. 339 (1)	1.60	.75
No. 3 (1)	1.90	.65
No. 66 (1)	1.90	.50
No. 90 (1)	1.00	1.00
No. 138 (1)	.50	.25
No. 150 (1)	1.40	1.10
No. 180 (1)	1.10	.50
No. 317 (1)	.60	.30
No. 9 (1)	1.40	.50
No. 117 (1)	.75	.40
No. 104 (1)	.85	.45
No. 89 (1)	.45	.40
Set total (12) Stamps	13.45	6.80

Air Afrique, 1961

Modern and Ancient Africa, Map and Planes — CD107

Founding of Air Afrique (African Airlines).

1961-62

Cameroun		C37
Cent. Africa		C5
Chad		C7
Congo, P.R.		C5
Dahomey		C17
Gabon		C5
Ivory Coast		C18
Mauritania		C17
Niger		C22
Senegal		C31
Upper Volta		C4

No. C37 (1)	1.00	.50
No. C5 (1)	1.00	.55
No. C7 (1)	1.00	.25
No. C5 (1)	1.75	.90
No. C17 (1)	.80	.40
No. C5 (1)	11.00	6.00
No. C18 (1)	2.00	1.25
No. C17 (1)	2.50	1.25
No. C22 (1)	1.75	.90
No. C31 (1)	.80	.30
No. C4 (1)	.65	.45
Set total (11) Stamps	24.25	12.75

Anti-Malaria

CD108

World Health Organization drive to eradicate malaria.

1962, Apr. 7

Cameroun		B36
Cent. Africa		B1
Chad		B1
Comoro Isls.		B1
Congo, P.R.		B3
Dahomey		B15
Gabon		B4
Ivory Coast		B15
Madagascar		B19
Mali		B1
Mauritania		B16
Niger		B14
Senegal		B16
Somali Coast		B15
Upper Volta		B1

No. B36 (1)	1.00	.45
No. B1 (1)	1.40	1.40
No. B1 (1)	1.25	.50
No. B1 (1)	4.00	4.00
No. B3 (1)	1.40	1.00
No. B15 (1)	.75	.75
No. B4 (1)	1.00	1.00
No. B15 (1)	1.25	1.25
No. B19 (1)	.75	.50
No. B1 (1)	1.25	.60
No. B16 (1)	.80	.80
No. B14 (1)	.60	.60

No. B16 (1)	1.10	.65
No. B15 (1)	7.00	7.00
No. B1 (1)	.95	.95
Set total (15) Stamps	24.50	21.45

Abidjan Games

CD109

Abidjan Games, Ivory Coast, Dec. 24-31, 1961. Each stamp shows a different sport.

1962

Cent. Africa		19-20, C6
Chad		83-84, C8
Congo, P.R.		103-104, C7
Gabon		163-164, C6
Niger		109-111
Upper Volta		103-105

Nos. 19-20, C6 (3)	3.90	2.60
Nos. 83-84, C8 (3)	6.30	1.55
Nos. 103-104, C7 (3)	3.85	1.80
Nos. 163-164, C6 (3)	5.00	3.00
Nos. 109-111 (3)	2.60	1.10
Nos. 103-105 (3)	3.15	1.80
Set total (18) Stamps	24.80	11.85

African and Malagasy Union

Flag of Union CD110

First anniversary of the Union.

1962, Sept. 8

Cameroun		373
Cent. Africa		21
Chad		85
Congo, P.R.		105
Dahomey		155
Gabon		165
Ivory Coast		198
Madagascar		332
Mauritania		170
Niger		112
Senegal		211
Upper Volta		106

No. 373 (1)	2.00	.75
No. 21 (1)	1.25	.60
No. 85 (1)	1.25	.25
No. 105 (1)	1.50	.50
No. 155 (1)	1.25	.90
No. 165 (1)	1.60	1.25
No. 198 (1)	2.10	.75
No. 332 (1)	.80	.80
No. 170 (1)	.75	.40
No. 112 (1)	.80	.50
No. 211 (1)	.80	.50
No. 106 (1)	1.50	.90
Set total (12) Stamps	15.60	8.10

Telstar

Telstar and Globe Showing Andover and Pleumeur-Bodou — CD111

First television connection of the United States and Europe through the Telstar satellite, July 11-12, 1962.

1962-63

Andorra, French		154
Comoro Isls.		C7
Fr. Polynesia		C29
Fr. So. & Antarctic Terr.		C5
New Caledonia		C33
St. Pierre & Miquelon		C26
Somali Coast		C31
Wallis & Futuna Isls.		C17

No. 154 (1)	2.00	1.60
No. C7 (1)	5.00	3.00
No. C29 (1)	11.50	8.00

No. C5 (1)	29.00	21.00
No. C33 (1)	30.00	18.50
No. C26 (1)	7.25	5.50
No. C31 (1)	1.00	1.00
No. C17 (1)	3.50	3.50
Set total (8) Stamps	89.25	62.10

Freedom From Hunger

World Map and Wheat Emblem CD112

U.N. Food and Agriculture Organization's "Freedom from Hunger" campaign.

1963, Mar. 21

Cameroun	B37-B38
Cent. Africa	B2
Chad	B2
Congo, P.R.	B4
Dahomey	B16
Gabon	B5
Ivory Coast	B16
Madagascar	B21
Mauritania	B17
Niger	B15
Senegal	B17
Upper Volta	B2

Nos. B37-B38 (2)	2.25	.75
No. B2 (1)	1.25	1.25
No. B2 (1)	2.00	.50
No. B4 (1)	1.40	1.00
No. B16 (1)	.80	.80
No. B5 (1)	1.00	1.00
No. B16 (1)	1.50	1.50
No. B21 (1)	.60	.45
No. B17 (1)	.80	.80
No. B15 (1)	.60	.60
No. B17 (1)	.80	.50
No. B2 (1)	.95	.95
Set total (13) Stamps	13.95	10.10

Red Cross Centenary

CD113

Centenary of the International Red Cross.

1963, Sept. 2

Comoro Isls.	55
Fr. Polynesia	205
New Caledonia	328
St. Pierre & Miquelon	367
Somali Coast	297
Wallis & Futuna Isls.	165

No. 55 (1)	9.50	7.00
No. 205 (1)	15.00	12.00
No. 328 (1)	9.00	6.75
No. 367 (1)	12.00	6.75
No. 297 (1)	6.25	6.25
No. 165 (1)	4.00	3.50
Set total (6) Stamps	55.75	42.25

African Postal Union, 1963

UAMPT Emblem, Radio Masts, Plane and Mail CD114

Establishment of the African and Malagasy Posts and Telecommunications Union.

1963, Sept. 8

Cameroun	C47
Cent. Africa	C10
Chad	C9
Congo, P.R.	C13

Dahomey	C19
Gabon	C13
Ivory Coast	C25
Madagascar	C75
Mauritania	C22
Niger	C27
Rwanda	36
Senegal	C32
Upper Volta	C9

No. C47 (1)	2.25	1.00
No. C10 (1)	1.90	.85
No. C9 (1)	2.40	.60
No. C13 (1)	1.40	.75
No. C19 (1)	.75	.25
No. C13 (1)	1.90	.80
No. C25 (1)	2.50	1.50
No. C75 (1)	1.25	.80
No. C22 (1)	1.50	.60
No. C27 (1)	1.25	.60
No. 36 (1)	.90	.55
No. C32 (1)	1.75	.50
No. C9 (1)	1.50	.75
Set total (13) Stamps	21.25	9.55

Air Afrique, 1963

Symbols of Flight — CD115

First anniversary of Air Afrique and inauguration of DC-8 service.

1963, Nov. 19

Cameroun	C48
Chad	C10
Congo, P.R.	C14
Gabon	C18
Ivory Coast	C26
Mauritania	C26
Niger	C35
Senegal	C33

No. C48 (1)	1.25	.40
No. C10 (1)	2.40	.60
No. C14 (1)	1.60	.60
No. C18 (1)	1.40	.65
No. C26 (1)	1.00	.50
No. C26 (1)	.70	.25
No. C35 (1)	.90	.50
No. C33 (1)	2.00	.65
Set total (8) Stamps	11.25	4.15

Europafrica

Europe and Africa Linked — CD116

Signing of an economic agreement between the European Economic Community and the African and Malagasy Union, Yaounde, Cameroun, July 20, 1963.

1963-64

Cameroun	402
Cent. Africa	C12
Chad	C11
Congo, P.R.	C16
Gabon	C19
Ivory Coast	217
Niger	C43
Upper Volta	C11

No. 402 (1)	2.25	.60
No. C12 (1)	2.50	1.75
No. C11 (1)	2.00	.50
No. C16 (1)	1.60	1.00
No. C19 (1)	1.40	.75
No. 217 (1)	1.10	.35
No. C43 (1)	.85	.50
No. C11 (1)	1.50	.80
Set total (8) Stamps	13.20	6.25

Human Rights

Scales of Justice and Globe CD117

15th anniversary of the Universal Declaration of Human Rights.

1963, Dec. 10

Comoro Isls.	56
Fr. Polynesia	206
New Caledonia	329
St. Pierre & Miquelon	368
Somali Coast	300
Wallis & Futuna Isls.	166

No. 56 (1)	9.50	7.50
No. 205 (1)	15.00	12.00
No. 329 (1)	8.00	6.00
No. 368 (1)	6.50	3.50
No. 300 (1)	8.50	8.50
No. 166 (1)	8.00	7.50
Set total (6) Stamps	55.50	45.00

PHILATEC

Stamp Album, Champs Elysees Palace and Horses of Marly CD118

Intl. Philatelic and Postal Techniques Exhibition, Paris, June 5-21, 1964.

1963-64

Comoro Isls.	60
France	1078
Fr. Polynesia	207
New Caledonia	341
St. Pierre & Miquelon	369
Somali Coast	301
Wallis & Futuna Isls.	167

No. 60 (1)	4.50	4.00
No. 1078 (1)	.25	.25
No. 206 (1)	15.00	10.00
No. 341 (1)	8.50	6.75
No. 369 (1)	11.00	8.00
No. 301 (1)	7.75	7.75
No. 167 (1)	3.50	3.50
Set total (7) Stamps	50.50	40.25

Cooperation

CD119

Cooperation between France and the French-speaking countries of Africa and Madagascar.

1964

Cameroun	409-410
Cent. Africa	39
Chad	103
Congo, P.R.	121
Dahomey	193
France	1111
Gabon	175
Ivory Coast	221
Madagascar	360
Mauritania	181
Niger	143
Senegal	236
Togo	495

Nos. 409-410 (2)	2.50	.50
No. 39 (1)	1.00	.55
No. 103 (1)	1.00	.25
No. 121 (1)	.80	.35
No. 193 (1)	.80	.35
No. 1111 (1)	.25	.25
No. 175 (1)	.90	.60
No. 221 (1)	1.10	.35

No. 360 (1)	.60	.25
No. 181 (1)	.60	.35
No. 143 (1)	.80	.40
No. 236 (1)	1.60	.85
No. 495 (1)	.70	.25
Set total (14) Stamps	12.65	5.30

ITU

Telegraph, Syncom Satellite and ITU Emblem CD120

Intl. Telecommunication Union, Cent.

1965, May 17

Comoro Isls.	C14
Fr. Polynesia	C33
Fr. So. & Antarctic Terr.	C8
New Caledonia	C40
New Hebrides	124-125
St. Pierre & Miquelon	C29
Somali Coast	C36
Wallis & Futuna Isls.	C20

No. C14 (1)	20.00	10.00
No. C33 (1)	80.00	52.50
No. C8 (1)	200.00	160.00
No. C40 (1)	12.00	9.00
Nos. 124-125 (2)	40.50	34.00
No. C29 (1)	24.00	11.00
No. C36 (1)	15.00	9.00
No. C20 (1)	21.00	15.00
Set total (9) Stamps	412.50	300.50

French Satellite A-1

Diamant Rocket and Launching Installation — CD121

Launching of France's first satellite, Nov. 26, 1965.

1965-66

Comoro Isls.	C16a
France	1138a
Reunion	359a
Fr. Polynesia	C41a
Fr. So. & Antarctic Terr.	C10a
New Caledonia	C45a
St. Pierre & Miquelon	C31a
Somali Coast	C40a
Wallis & Futuna Isls.	C23a

No. C16a (1)	11.00	11.00
No. 1138a (1)	.65	.65
No. 359a (1)	3.50	3.00
No. C41a (1)	14.00	14.00
No. C10a (1)	29.00	24.00
No. C45a (1)	8.25	7.00
No. C31a (1)	15.00	15.00
No. C40a (1)	7.00	7.00
No. C23a (1)	9.25	9.25
Set total (9) Stamps	97.65	90.90

French Satellite D-1

D-1 Satellite in Orbit — CD122

Launching of the D-1 satellite at Hammaguir, Algeria, Feb. 17, 1966.

1966

Comoro Isls.	C17
France	1148

Fr. Polynesia.............................C42
Fr. So. & Antarctic Terr. C11
New Caledonia..........................C46
St. Pierre & Miquelon....................C32
Somali Coast............................C49
Wallis & Futuna Isls. C24

No. C17 (1)	4.00	4.00
No. 1148 (1)	.25	.25
No. C42 (1)	7.00	4.75
No. C11 (1)	57.50	40.00
No. C46 (1)	3.00	2.00
No. C32 (1)	10.50	6.50
No. C49 (1)	4.25	2.75
No. C24 (1)	3.50	3.50
Set total (8) Stamps	90.00	63.75

Air Afrique, 1966

Planes and Air Afrique
Emblem — CD123

Introduction of DC-8F planes by Air Afrique.

1966

Cameroun C79
Cent. Africa C35
Chad.......................................C26
Congo, P.R................................C42
Dahomey C42
Gabon C47
Ivory Coast C32
Mauritania C57
Niger.......................................C63
Senegal C47
Togo C54
Upper Volta...............................C31

No. C79 (1)	.80	.25
No. C35 (1)	1.00	.40
No. C26 (1)	1.00	.25
No. C42 (1)	1.00	.25
No. C42 (1)	.75	.25
No. C47 (1)	.90	.35
No. C32 (1)	1.00	.60
No. C57 (1)	.80	.30
No. C63 (1)	.65	.35
No. C47 (1)	.80	.30
No. C54 (1)	.80	.25
No. C31 (1)	.75	.50
Set total (12) Stamps	10.25	4.05

African Postal Union, 1967

Telecommunications Symbols and Map
of Africa — CD124

Fifth anniversary of the establishment of the African and Malagasy Union of Posts and Telecommunications, UAMPT.

1967

Cameroun C90
Cent. Africa C46
Chad.......................................C37
Congo, P.R................................C57
Dahomey C61
Gabon C58
Ivory Coast C34
Madagascar C85
Mauritania C65
Niger.......................................C75
Rwanda C1-C3
Senegal C60
Togo C81
Upper Volta...............................C50

No. C90 (1)	2.40	.65
No. C46 (1)	2.25	.85
No. C37 (1)	2.00	.60
No. C57 (1)	1.60	.60
No. C61 (1)	1.75	.95
No. C58 (1)	2.25	.95
No. C34 (1)	3.50	1.50
No. C85 (1)	1.25	.60
No. C65 (1)	1.25	.60
No. C75 (1)	1.40	.60

Nos. C1-C3 (3)	2.30	1.25
No. C60 (1)	1.75	.50
No. C81 (1)	1.90	.30
No. C50 (1)	1.80	.70
Set total (16) Stamps	27.40	10.65

Monetary Union

Gold Token of the
Ashantis, 17-18th
Centuries — CD125

West African Monetary Union, 5th anniv.

1967, Nov. 4

Dahomey 244
Ivory Coast 259
Mauritania 238
Niger.......................................204
Senegal 294
Togo 623
Upper Volta...............................181

No. 244 (1)	.65	.65
No. 259 (1)	.85	.40
No. 238 (1)	.45	.25
No. 204 (1)	.45	.25
No. 294 (1)	.60	.25
No. 623 (1)	.60	.25
No. 181 (1)	.70	.35
Set total (7) Stamps	4.30	2.40

WHO Anniversary

Sun,
Flowers
and WHO
Emblem
CD126

World Health Organization, 20th anniv.

1968, May 4

Afars & Issas 317
Comoro Isls. 73
Fr. Polynesia.............................241-242
Fr. So. & Antarctic Terr. 31
New Caledonia..........................367
St. Pierre & Miquelon....................377
Wallis & Futuna Isls. 169

No. 317 (1)	3.00	3.00
No. 73 (1)	2.75	2.00
Nos. 241-242 (2)	22.00	12.75
No. 31 (1)	65.00	45.00
No. 367 (1)	4.50	2.25
No. 377 (1)	12.00	8.00
No. 169 (1)	6.50	4.50
Set total (8) Stamps	115.75	77.50

Human Rights Year

Human Rights
Flame — CD127

1968, Aug. 10

Afars & Issas 322-323
Comoro Isls. 76
Fr. Polynesia.............................243-244
Fr. So. & Antarctic Terr. 32
New Caledonia..........................369
St. Pierre & Miquelon....................382
Wallis & Futuna Isls. 170

Nos. 322-323 (2)	6.50	3.70
No. 76 (1)	3.50	3.50
Nos. 243-244 (2)	24.00	14.00
No. 32 (1)	60.00	45.00
No. 369 (1)	3.00	1.50
No. 382 (1)	10.00	5.50
No. 170 (1)	3.75	3.75
Set total (9) Stamps	110.75	76.95

2nd PHILEXAFRIQUE

CD128

Opening of PHILEXAFRIQUE, Abidjan, Feb. 14. Each stamp shows a local scene and stamp.

1969, Feb. 14

Cameroun C118
Cent. Africa C65
Chad.......................................C48
Congo, P.R................................C77
Dahomey C94
Gabon C82
Ivory Coast C38-C40
Madagascar C92
Mali C65
Mauritania C80
Niger.......................................C104
Senegal C68
Togo C104
Upper Volta...............................C62

No. C118 (1)	3.25	1.25
No. C65 (1)	1.90	1.90
No. C48 (1)	2.40	1.00
No. C77 (1)	2.00	1.75
No. C94 (1)	2.25	2.25
No. C82 (1)	2.25	2.25
Nos. C38-C40 (3)	14.50	14.50
No. C92 (1)	1.75	.85
No. C65 (1)	2.00	1.00
No. C80 (1)	1.90	.75
No. C104 (1)	2.75	1.90
No. C68 (1)	2.00	1.40
No. C104 (1)	2.25	.45
No. C62 (1)	4.00	3.75
Set total (16) Stamps	45.20	35.00

Concorde

Concorde in
Flight
CD129

First flight of the prototype Concorde supersonic plane at Toulouse, Mar. 1, 1969.

1969

Afars & Issas C56
Comoro Isls. C29
France.....................................C42
Fr. Polynesia.............................C50
Fr. So. & Antarctic Terr. C18
New Caledonia..........................C63
St. Pierre & Miquelon....................C40
Wallis & Futuna Isls. C30

No. C56 (1)	25.00	16.00
No. C29 (1)	24.00	16.00
No. C42 (1)	.75	.35
No. C50 (1)	55.00	35.00
No. C18 (1)	55.00	37.50
No. C63 (1)	35.00	20.00
No. C40 (1)	32.50	12.00
No. C30 (1)	15.00	10.00
Set total (8) Stamps	242.25	146.85

Development Bank

Bank
Emblem — CD130

African Development Bank, fifth anniv.

1969

Cameroun 499
Chad.......................................217
Congo, P.R.............................181-182

Ivory Coast 281
Mali 127-128
Mauritania 267
Niger.......................................220
Senegal 317-318
Upper Volta...............................201

No. 499 (1)	.80	.25
No. 217 (1)	.70	.25
Nos. 181-182 (2)	.80	.50
No. 281 (1)	.70	.40
Nos. 127-128 (2)	1.25	.50
No. 267 (1)	.60	.25
No. 220 (1)	.60	.30
Nos. 317-318 (2)	1.55	.50
No. 201 (1)	.70	.30
Set total (12) Stamps	7.70	3.25

ILO

ILO Headquarters, Geneva, and
Emblem — CD131

Intl. Labor Organization, 50th anniv.

1969-70

Afars & Issas 337
Comoro Isls. 83
Fr. Polynesia.............................251-252
Fr. So. & Antarctic Terr. 35
New Caledonia..........................379
St. Pierre & Miquelon....................396
Wallis & Futuna Isls. 172

No. 337 (1)	2.75	2.00
No. 83 (1)	1.25	.75
Nos. 251-252 (2)	24.00	12.50
No. 35 (1)	18.50	11.00
No. 379 (1)	2.25	1.10
No. 396 (1)	10.00	5.50
No. 172 (1)	3.00	2.90
Set total (8) Stamps	61.75	35.75

ASECNA

Map of
Africa,
Plane and
Airport
CD132

10th anniversary of the Agency for the Security of Aerial Navigation in Africa and Madagascar (ASECNA, Agence pour la Securite de la Navigation Aerienne en Afrique et a Madagascar).

1969-70

Cameroun 500
Cent. Africa 119
Chad.......................................222
Congo, P.R................................197
Dahomey 269
Gabon 260
Ivory Coast 287
Mali 130
Niger.......................................221
Senegal 321
Upper Volta...............................204

No. 500 (1)	2.00	.60
No. 119 (1)	2.25	.80
No. 222 (1)	1.00	.25
No. 197 (1)	2.00	.40
No. 269 (1)	.90	.55
No. 260 (1)	1.75	.75
No. 287 (1)	.90	.40
No. 130 (1)	1.00	.40
No. 221 (1)	1.25	.70
No. 321 (1)	1.60	.50
No. 204 (1)	1.75	1.00
Set total (11) Stamps	16.40	6.35

U.P.U. Headquarters

CD133

New Universal Postal Union headquarters, Bern, Switzerland.

1970

Afars & Issas	342
Algeria	443
Cameroun	503-504
Cent. Africa	125
Chad	225
Comoro Isls.	84
Congo, P.R.	216
Fr. Polynesia	261-262
Fr. So. & Antarctic Terr.	36
Gabon	258
Ivory Coast	295
Madagascar	444
Mali	134-135
Mauritania	283
New Caledonia	382
Niger	231-232
St. Pierre & Miquelon	397-398
Senegal	328-329
Tunisia	535
Wallis & Futuna Isls.	173

No. 342 (1)	2.50	1.40
No. 443 (1)	1.10	.40
Nos. 503-504 (2)	2.60	.55
No. 125 (1)	1.90	.70
No. 225 (1)	1.00	.25
No. 84 (1)	5.50	2.00
No. 216 (1)	.80	.25
Nos. 261-262 (2)	20.00	10.00
No. 36 (1)	45.00	29.00
No. 258 (1)	.90	.55
No. 295 (1)	1.10	.50
No. 444 (1)	.55	.25
Nos. 134-135 (2)	1.25	.50
No. 283 (1)	.60	.30
No. 382 (1)	3.00	1.50
Nos. 231-232 (2)	1.20	.60
Nos. 397-398 (2)	34.00	17.50
Nos. 328-329 (2)	1.55	.55
No. 535 (1)	.60	.25
No. 173 (1)	4.00	4.00
Set total (26) Stamps	129.15	71.05

De Gaulle

CD134

First anniversay of the death of Charles de Gaulle, (1890-1970), President of France.

1971-72

Afars & Issas	356-357
Comoro Isls.	104-105
France	1325a
Fr. Polynesia	270-271
Fr. So. & Antarctic Terr.	52-53
New Caledonia	393-394
Reunion	380a
St. Pierre & Miquelon	417-418
Wallis & Futuna Isls.	177-178

Nos. 356-357 (2)	14.50	9.50
Nos. 104-105 (2)	9.00	5.75
No. 1325a (1)	3.00	2.50
Nos. 270-271 (2)	51.50	29.50
Nos. 52-53 (2)	47.00	33.50
Nos. 393-394 (2)	25.00	11.75
No. 380a (1)	9.25	8.00
Nos. 417-418 (2)	57.50	30.00
Nos. 177-178 (2)	24.00	16.25
Set total (16) Stamps	240.75	146.75

African Postal Union, 1971

UAMPT Building, Brazzaville, Congo — CD135

10th anniversary of the establishment of the African and Malagasy Posts and Telecommunications Union, UAMPT. Each stamp has a different native design.

1971, Nov. 13

Cameroun	C177
Cent. Africa	C89
Chad	C94
Congo, P.R.	C136
Dahomey	C146
Gabon	C120
Ivory Coast	C47
Mauritania	C113
Niger	C164
Rwanda	C8
Senegal	C105
Togo	C166
Upper Volta	C97

No. C177 (1)	2.00	.50
No. C89 (1)	2.25	.85
No. C94 (1)	1.50	.50
No. C136 (1)	1.60	.75
No. C146 (1)	1.75	.80
No. C120 (1)	1.75	.70
No. C47 (1)	2.00	1.00
No. C113 (1)	1.20	.65
No. C164 (1)	1.25	.60
No. C8 (1)	2.75	2.25
No. C105 (1)	1.60	.50
No. C166 (1)	1.25	.40
No. C97 (1)	1.50	.70
Set total (13) Stamps	22.40	10.20

West African Monetary Union

African Couple, City, Village and Commemorative Coin — CD136

West African Monetary Union, 10th anniv.

1972, Nov. 2

Dahomey	300
Ivory Coast	331
Mauritania	299
Niger	258
Senegal	374
Togo	825
Upper Volta	280

No. 300 (1)	.65	.25
No. 331 (1)	1.00	.50
No. 299 (1)	.75	.25
No. 258 (1)	.55	.30
No. 374 (1)	.50	.30
No. 825 (1)	.60	.25
No. 280 (1)	.60	.25
Set total (7) Stamps	4.65	2.10

African Postal Union, 1973

Telecommunications Symbols and Map of Africa — CD137

11th anniversary of the African and Malagasy Posts and Telecommunications Union (UAMPT).

1973, Sept. 12

Cameroun	574
Cent. Africa	194
Chad	294
Congo, P.R.	289
Dahomey	311
Gabon	320
Ivory Coast	361
Madagascar	500
Mauritania	304
Niger	287
Rwanda	540
Senegal	393
Togo	849
Upper Volta	297

No. 574 (1)	1.75	.40
No. 194 (1)	1.25	.75
No. 294 (1)	1.75	.40
No. 289 (1)	1.60	.50
No. 311 (1)	1.25	.55
No. 320 (1)	1.40	.75
No. 361 (1)	2.50	1.00
No. 500 (1)	1.10	.35
No. 304 (1)	1.10	.40
No. 287 (1)	.90	.60
No. 540 (1)	3.75	2.00
No. 393 (1)	1.60	.50
No. 849 (1)	1.00	.35
No. 297 (1)	1.25	.70
Set total (14) Stamps	22.20	9.25

Philexafrique II — Essen

CD138

CD139

Designs: Indigenous fauna, local and German stamps. Types CD138-CD139 printed horizontally and vertically se-tenant in sheets of 10 (2x5). Label between horizontal pairs alternately commemorates Philexafrique II, Libreville, Gabon, June 1978, and 2nd International Stamp Fair, Essen, Germany, Nov. 1-5.

1978-1979

Benin	C286a
Central Africa	C201a
Chad	C239a
Congo Republic	C246a
Djibouti	C122a
Gabon	C216a
Ivory Coast	C65a
Mali	C357a
Mauritania	C186a
Niger	C292a
Rwanda	C13a
Senegal	C147a
Togo	C364a

No. C286a (1)	9.00	8.50
No. C201a (1)	7.50	7.50
No. C239a (1)	8.00	4.00
No. C246a (1)	7.00	7.00
No. C122a (1)	8.50	8.50
No. C216a (1)	6.50	4.00
No. C65a (1)	9.00	9.00
No. C357a (1)	7.50	3.00
No. C186a (1)	4.50	4.00
No. C292a (1)	6.00	5.00
No. C13a (1)	4.00	4.00
No. C147a (1)	10.00	4.00
No. C364a (1)	3.00	1.50
Set total (13) Stamps	90.50	70.00

BRITISH COMMONWEALTH OF NATIONS

The listings follow established trade practices when these issues are offered as units by dealers. The Peace issue, for example, includes only one stamp from the Indian state of Hyderabad. The U.P.U. issue includes the Egypt set. Pairs are included for those varieties issued with bilingual designs se-tenant.

Silver Jubilee

Windsor Castle and King George V CD301

Reign of King George V, 25th anniv.

1935

Antigua	77-80
Ascension	33-36
Bahamas	92-95
Barbados	186-189
Basutoland	11-14
Bechuanaland Protectorate	117-120
Bermuda	100-103
British Guiana	223-226
British Honduras	108-111
Cayman Islands	81-84
Ceylon	260-263
Cyprus	136-139
Dominica	90-93
Falkland Islands	77-80
Fiji	110-113
Gambia	125-128
Gibraltar	100-103
Gilbert & Ellice Islands	33-36
Gold Coast	108-111
Grenada	124-127
Hong Kong	147-150
Jamaica	109-112
Kenya, Uganda, Tanzania	42-45
Leeward Islands	96-99
Malta	184-187
Mauritius	204-207
Montserrat	85-88
Newfoundland	226-229
Nigeria	34-37
Northern Rhodesia	18-21
Nyasaland Protectorate	47-50
St. Helena	111-114
St. Kitts-Nevis	72-75
St. Lucia	91-94
St. Vincent	134-137
Seychelles	118-121
Sierra Leone	166-169
Solomon Islands	60-63
Somaliland Protectorate	77-80
Straits Settlements	213-216
Swaziland	20-23
Trinidad & Tobago	43-46
Turks & Caicos Islands	71-74
Virgin Islands	69-72

The following have different designs but are included in the omnibus set:

Great Britain	226-229
Offices in Morocco (Sp. Curr.)	67-70
Offices in Morocco (Br. Curr.)	226-229
Offices in Morocco (Fr. Curr.)	422-425
Offices in Morocco (Tangier)	508-510
Australia	152-154
Canada	211-216
Cook Islands	98-100
India	142-148
Nauru	31-34
New Guinea	46-47
New Zealand	199-201
Niue	67-69
Papua	114-117
Samoa	163-165
South Africa	68-71
Southern Rhodesia	33-36
South-West Africa	121-124

Nos. 77-80 (4)	20.25	20.50
Nos. 33-36 (4)	58.50	120.00
Nos. 92-95 (4)	25.00	43.00
Nos. 186-189 (4)	30.15	49.30
Nos. 11-14 (4)	12.10	23.00
Nos. 117-120 (4)	17.00	31.25
Nos. 100-103 (4)	18.00	58.25
Nos. 223-226 (4)	18.35	35.50
Nos. 108-111 (4)	15.25	15.35
Nos. 81-84 (4)	19.95	19.50
Nos. 260-263 (4)	10.15	19.10
Nos. 136-139 (4)	39.75	34.40
Nos. 90-93 (4)	18.85	19.85
Nos. 77-80 (4)	51.00	13.75
Nos. 110-113 (4)	15.25	29.00
Nos. 125-128 (4)	12.65	29.25
Nos. 100-103 (4)	32.00	47.50
Nos. 33-36 (4)	34.50	53.50
Nos. 108-111 (4)	26.25	62.85
Nos. 124-127 (4)	18.60	45.00
Nos. 147-150 (4)	76.50	21.00
Nos. 109-112 (4)	19.70	39.00
Nos. 42-45 (4)	8.75	11.00
Nos. 96-99 (4)	35.75	49.60
Nos. 184-187 (4)	22.00	33.70
Nos. 204-207 (4)	47.60	58.25
Nos. 85-88 (4)	10.25	20.25
Nos. 226-229 (4)	17.50	12.05
Nos. 34-37 (4)	13.25	59.75
Nos. 18-21 (4)	16.75	16.25
Nos. 47-50 (4)	39.75	80.25
Nos. 111-114 (4)	31.15	33.25
Nos. 72-75 (4)	11.55	18.50
Nos. 91-94 (4)	16.00	20.80
Nos. 134-137 (4)	9.45	21.25
Nos. 118-121 (4)	17.50	32.50
Nos. 166-169 (4)	24.25	56.00
Nos. 60-63 (4)	27.25	38.00
Nos. 77-80 (4)	18.75	50.75
Nos. 213-216 (4)	15.00	25.10
Nos. 20-23 (4)	6.80	18.25
Nos. 43-46 (4)	14.05	27.75
Nos. 71-74 (4)	9.25	16.25
Nos. 69-72 (4)	24.20	55.25
Nos. 226-229 (4)	7.25	7.45

Nos. 67-70 (4)	14.35	26.10
Nos. 226-229 (4)	8.20	28.90
Nos. 422-425 (4)	3.90	2.00
Nos. 508-510 (3)	18.80	23.85
Nos. 152-154 (3)	45.75	60.35
Nos. 211-216 (6)	26.30	13.35
Nos. 98-100 (3)	9.65	12.00
Nos. 142-148 (7)	23.25	11.80
Nos. 31-34 (4)	12.60	13.85
Nos. 46-47 (2)	4.35	1.70
Nos. 199-201 (3)	21.75	31.75
Nos. 67-69 (3)	10.55	26.50
Nos. 114-117 (4)	9.20	17.00
Nos. 163-165 (3)	4.40	5.50
Nos. 68-71 (4)	57.00	155.00
Nos. 33-36 (4)	27.75	45.25
Nos. 121-124 (4)	14.50	36.10
Set total (245) Stamps	1,346.	2,113.

Coronation

Queen
Elizabeth
and King
George VI
CD302

1937

Aden	13-15
Antigua	81-83
Ascension	37-39
Bahamas	97-99
Barbados	190-192
Basutoland	15-17
Bechuanaland Protectorate	121-123
Bermuda	115-117
British Guiana	227-229
British Honduras	112-114
Cayman Islands	97-99
Ceylon	275-277
Cyprus	140-142
Dominica	94-96
Falkland Islands	81-83
Fiji	114-116
Gambia	129-131
Gibraltar	104-106
Gilbert & Ellice Islands	37-39
Gold Coast	112-114
Grenada	128-130
Hong Kong	151-153
Jamaica	113-115
Kenya, Uganda, Tanzania	60-62
Leeward Islands	100-102
Malta	188-190
Mauritius	208-210
Montserrat	89-91
Newfoundland	230-232
Nigeria	50-52
Northern Rhodesia	22-24
Nyasaland Protectorate	51-53
St. Helena	115-117
St. Kitts-Nevis	76-78
St. Lucia	107-109
St. Vincent	138-140
Seychelles	122-124
Sierra Leone	170-172
Solomon Islands	64-66
Somaliland Protectorate	81-83
Straits Settlements	235-237
Swaziland	24-26
Trinidad & Tobago	47-49
Turks & Caicos Islands	75-77
Virgin Islands	73-75

The following have different designs but are included in the omnibus set:

Great Britain	234
Offices in Morocco (Sp. Curr.)	82
Offices in Morocco (Fr. Curr.)	439
Offices in Morocco (Tangier)	514
Canada	237
Cook Islands	109-111
Nauru	35-38
Newfoundland	233-243
New Guinea	48-51
New Zealand	223-225
Niue	70-72
Papua	118-121
South Africa	74-78
Southern Rhodesia	38-41
South-West Africa	125-132

Nos. 13-15 (3)	3.00	5.75
Nos. 81-83 (3)	1.85	3.75
Nos. 37-39 (3)	2.75	2.75
Nos. 97-99 (3)	1.15	3.05
Nos. 190-192 (3)	1.10	1.95
Nos. 15-17 (3)	1.15	3.00
Nos. 121-123 (3)	.95	3.35
Nos. 115-117 (3)	1.25	5.00
Nos. 227-229 (3)	1.45	3.05
Nos. 112-114 (3)	1.20	2.35
Nos. 97-99 (3)	1.10	2.30
Nos. 275-277 (3)	8.25	10.35

Nos. 140-142 (3)	3.75	6.50
Nos. 94-96 (3)	.85	2.40
Nos. 81-83 (3)	2.90	2.30
Nos. 114-116 (3)	1.35	5.75
Nos. 129-131 (3)	1.00	4.70
Nos. 104-106 (3)	2.60	6.45
Nos. 37-39 (3)	.85	2.00
Nos. 112-114 (3)	3.10	10.00
Nos. 128-130 (3)	1.00	.85
Nos. 151-153 (3)	27.00	12.50
Nos. 113-115 (3)	1.35	1.25
Nos. 60-62 (3)	1.00	2.35
Nos. 100-102 (3)	1.55	4.00
Nos. 188-190 (3)	1.25	1.60
Nos. 208-210 (3)	2.05	3.75
Nos. 89-91 (3)	1.00	3.35
Nos. 230-232 (3)	7.00	2.80
Nos. 50-52 (3)	3.25	8.50
Nos. 22-24 (3)	.95	2.25
Nos. 51-53 (3)	1.05	1.30
Nos. 115-117 (3)	1.45	2.05
Nos. 76-78 (3)	.95	2.05
Nos. 107-109 (3)	1.05	2.05
Nos. 138-140 (3)	.80	4.75
Nos. 122-124 (3)	1.20	1.90
Nos. 170-172 (3)	1.95	5.65
Nos. 64-66 (3)	.90	2.00
Nos. 81-83 (3)	1.10	3.40
Nos. 235-237 (3)	3.25	1.60
Nos. 24-26 (3)	1.05	1.75
Nos. 47-49 (3)	1.00	1.00
Nos. 75-77 (3)	1.30	1.55
Nos. 73-75 (3)	2.20	6.90
Nos. 234 (1)	.25	.25
No. 82 (1)	.80	.80
No. 439 (1)	.35	.25
No. 514 (1)	.55	.55
No. 237 (1)	.35	.25
Nos. 109-111 (3)	.85	.80
Nos. 35-38 (4)	1.15	5.50
Nos. 233-243 (11)	42.20	30.40
Nos. 48-51 (4)	1.40	7.90
Nos. 223-225 (3)	1.40	2.75
Nos. 70-72 (3)	.80	2.05
Nos. 118-121 (4)	1.60	5.25
Nos. 74-78 (5)	9.25	10.80
Nos. 38-41 (4)	3.55	15.50
Nos. 125-132 (8)	5.50	8.45
Set total (189) Stamps	178.25	259.40

Peace

King
George VI
and
Parliament
Buildings,
London
CD303

Return to peace at the close of World War II.

1945-46

Aden	28-29
Antigua	96-97
Ascension	50-51
Bahamas	130-131
Barbados	207-208
Bermuda	131-132
British Guiana	242-243
British Honduras	127-128
Cayman Islands	112-113
Ceylon	293-294
Cyprus	156-157
Dominica	112-113
Falkland Islands	97-98
Falkland Islands Dep	1L9-1L10
Fiji	137-138
Gambia	144-145
Gibraltar	119-120
Gilbert & Ellice Islands	52-53
Gold Coast	128-129
Grenada	143-144
Jamaica	136-137
Kenya, Uganda, Tanzania	90-91
Leeward Islands	116-117
Malta	206-207
Mauritius	223-224
Montserrat	104-105
Nigeria	71-72
Northern Rhodesia	46-47
Nyasaland Protectorate	82-83
Pitcairn Islands	9-10
St. Helena	128-129
St. Kitts-Nevis	91-92
St. Lucia	127-128
St. Vincent	152-153
Seychelles	149-150
Sierra Leone	186-187
Solomon Islands	80-81
Somaliland Protectorate	108-109
Trinidad & Tobago	62-63
Turks & Caicos Islands	90-91
Virgin Islands	88-89

The following have different designs but are included in the omnibus set:

Great Britain	264-265

Offices in Morocco (Tangier)	523-524
Aden	
Kathiri State of Seiyun	12-13
Qu'aiti State of Shihr and Mukalla	
	12-13
Australia	200-202
Basutoland	29-31
Bechuanaland Protectorate	137-139
Burma	66-69
Cook Islands	127-130
Hong Kong	174-175
India	195-198
Hyderabad	51-53
New Zealand	247-257
Niue	90-93
Pakistan-Bahawalpur	O16
Samoa	191-194
South Africa	100-102
Southern Rhodesia	67-70
South-West Africa	153-155
Swaziland	38-40
Zanzibar	222-223

Nos. 28-29 (2)	.95	2.50
Nos. 96-97 (2)	.50	.80
Nos. 50-51 (2)	.90	1.80
Nos. 130-131 (2)	.50	1.40
Nos. 207-208 (2)	.50	1.10
Nos. 131-132 (2)	.55	.55
Nos. 242-243 (2)	1.05	1.40
Nos. 127-128 (2)	.50	.50
Nos. 112-113 (2)	.60	.80
Nos. 293-294 (2)	.60	2.10
Nos. 156-157 (2)	1.00	.70
Nos. 112-113 (2)	.50	.50
Nos. 97-98 (2)	.90	1.35
Nos. 1L9-1L10 (2)	1.40	1.00
Nos. 137-138 (2)	.50	1.75
Nos. 144-145 (2)	.50	.95
Nos. 119-120 (2)	.75	1.00
Nos. 52-53 (2)	.50	.50
Nos. 128-129 (2)	1.85	3.75
Nos. 143-144 (2)	.50	.95
Nos. 136-137 (2)	.90	12.50
Nos. 90-91 (2)	.65	.65
Nos. 116-117 (2)	.50	1.50
Nos. 206-207 (2)	.65	2.00
Nos. 223-224 (2)	.50	1.05
Nos. 104-105 (2)	.50	.50
Nos. 71-72 (2)	.70	2.75
Nos. 46-47 (2)	1.25	2.00
Nos. 82-83 (2)	.50	.50
Nos. 9-10 (2)	1.40	1.40
Nos. 128-129 (2)	.65	.70
Nos. 91-92 (2)	.50	.50
Nos. 127-128 (2)	.50	.60
Nos. 152-153 (2)	.50	.50
Nos. 149-150 (2)	.55	.50
Nos. 186-187 (2)	.50	.50
Nos. 80-81 (2)	.50	1.30
Nos. 108-109 (2)	.70	.50
Nos. 62-63 (2)	.50	.50
Nos. 90-91 (2)	.50	.50
Nos. 88-89 (2)	.50	.50
Nos. 264-265 (2)	.50	.70
Nos. 523-524 (2)	1.50	3.00
Nos. 12-13 (2)	.50	.90
Nos. 12-13 (2)	.50	1.25
Nos. 200-202 (3)	1.60	3.00
Nos. 29-31 (3)	2.10	2.60
Nos. 137-139 (3)	2.05	4.75
Nos. 66-69 (4)	1.60	1.30
Nos. 127-130 (4)	2.00	1.85
Nos. 174-175 (2)	7.25	3.15
Nos. 195-198 (4)	4.75	3.60
Nos. 51-53 (3)	1.50	1.70
Nos. 247-257 (11)	3.95	3.90
Nos. 90-93 (4)	1.70	2.20
No. O16 (1)	5.50	7.00
Nos. 191-194 (4)	2.05	1.00
Nos. 100-102 (3)	1.20	4.00
Nos. 67-70 (4)	1.40	1.75
Nos. 153-155 (3)	2.55	3.50
Nos. 38-40 (3)	2.40	5.50
Nos. 222-223 (2)	.65	1.00
Set total (151) Stamps	75.75	114.50

Silver Wedding

King George VI and Queen
Elizabeth

CD304   CD305

1948-49

Aden	30-31
Kathiri State of Seiyun	14-15
Qu'aiti State of Shihr and Mukalla	
	14-15

Antigua	98-99
Ascension	52-53
Bahamas	148-149
Barbados	210-211
Basutoland	39-40
Bechuanaland Protectorate	147-148
Bermuda	133-134
British Guiana	244-245
British Honduras	129-130
Cayman Islands	116-117
Cyprus	158-159
Dominica	114-115
Falkland Islands	99-100
Falkland Islands Dep.	1L11-1L12
Fiji	139-140
Gambia	146-147
Gibraltar	121-122
Gilbert & Ellice Islands	54-55
Gold Coast	142-143
Grenada	145-146
Hong Kong	178-179
Jamaica	138-139
Kenya, Uganda, Tanzania	92-93
Leeward Islands	118-119
Malaya	
Johore	128-129
Kedah	55-56
Kelantan	44-45
Malacca	1-2
Negri Sembilan	36-37
Pahang	44-45
Penang	1-2
Perak	99-100
Perlis	1-2
Selangor	74-75
Trengganu	47-48
Malta	223-224
Mauritius	229-230
Montserrat	106-107
Nigeria	73-74
North Borneo	238-239
Northern Rhodesia	48-49
Nyasaland Protectorate	85-86
Pitcairn Islands	11-12
St. Helena	130-131
St. Kitts-Nevis	93-94
St. Lucia	129-130
St. Vincent	154-155
Sarawak	174-175
Seychelles	151-152
Sierra Leone	188-189
Singapore	21-22
Solomon Islands	82-83
Somaliland Protectorate	110-111
Swaziland	48-49
Trinidad & Tobago	64-65
Turks & Caicos Islands	92-93
Virgin Islands	90-91
Zanzibar	224-225

The following have different designs but are included in the omnibus set:

Great Britain	267-268
Offices in Morocco (Sp. Curr.)	93-94
Offices in Morocco (Tangier)	525-526
Bahrain	62-63
Kuwait	82-83
Oman	25-26
South Africa	106
South-West Africa	159

Nos. 30-31 (2)	37.90	45.00
Nos. 14-15 (2)	18.85	40.30
Nos. 14-15 (2)	18.55	14.75
Nos. 98-99 (2)	12.55	12.75
Nos. 52-53 (2)	60.55	57.95
Nos. 148-149 (2)	45.25	40.30
Nos. 210-211 (2)	18.35	13.05
Nos. 39-40 (2)	52.80	55.25
Nos. 147-148 (2)	45.35	50.25
Nos. 133-134 (2)	47.75	55.25
Nos. 244-245 (2)	24.25	28.45
Nos. 129-130 (2)	22.75	53.20
Nos. 116-117 (2)	22.75	28.50
Nos. 158-159 (2)	58.50	78.05
Nos. 114-115 (2)	25.25	32.75
Nos. 99-100 (2)	112.10	83.60
Nos. 1L11-1L12 (2)	4.25	6.00
Nos. 139-140 (2)	18.20	10.75
Nos. 146-147 (2)	22.75	25.25
Nos. 121-122 (2)	66.00	83.00
Nos. 54-55 (2)	16.25	24.25
Nos. 142-143 (2)	35.25	37.75
Nos. 145-146 (2)	25.25	25.25
Nos. 178-179 (2)	363.90	136.60
Nos. 138-139 (2)	30.35	72.75
Nos. 92-93 (2)	52.75	72.75
Nos. 118-119 (2)	7.00	8.25
Nos. 128-129 (2)	29.25	53.25
Nos. 55-56 (2)	35.25	50.25
Nos. 44-45 (2)	35.75	62.75
Nos. 1-2 (2)	35.40	49.75
Nos. 36-37 (2)	28.10	38.20
Nos. 44-45 (2)	28.00	38.05
Nos. 1-2 (2)	40.50	37.80

Nos. 99-100 (2)	27.80	37.75
Nos. 1-2 (2)	33.50	58.00
Nos. 74-75 (2)	30.25	25.30
Nos. 47-48 (2)	35.25	62.75
Nos. 223-224 (2)	40.55	45.25
Nos. 229-230 (2)	17.75	45.25
Nos. 106-107 (2)	9.25	18.25
Nos. 73-74 (2)	17.85	22.80
Nos. 48-49 (2)	92.80	90.25
Nos. 85-86 (2)	19.25	32.75
Nos. 11-12 (2)	49.25	51.00
Nos. 130-131 (2)	32.80	42.80
Nos. 93-94 (2)	11.25	7.25
Nos. 129-130 (2)	22.25	45.25
Nos. 154-155 (2)	27.75	30.25
Nos. 174-175 (2)	55.40	60.40
Nos. 151-152 (2)	16.25	45.75
Nos. 188-189 (2)	24.75	26.25
Nos. 21-22 (2)	116.25	45.40
Nos. 82-83 (2)	13.40	13.40
Nos. 110-111 (2)	8.40	8.75
Nos. 48-49 (2)	40.30	47.75
Nos. 64-65 (2)	32.75	38.25
Nos. 92-93 (2)	15.25	20.30
Nos. 90-91 (2)	15.35	21.35
Nos. 224-225 (2)	29.60	38.00
Nos. 267-268 (2)	40.40	40.25
Nos. 93-94 (2)	20.10	25.35
Nos. 525-526 (2)	23.10	29.25
Nos. 62-63 (2)	38.45	72.50
Nos. 82-83 (2)	45.50	45.50
Nos. 25-26 (2)	46.00	47.50
No. 106 (1)	.90	1.25
No. 159 (1)	1.25	.35
Set total (134) Stamps	2,549.	2,742.

U.P.U.

Mercury and Symbols of
Communications — CD306

Plane, Ship and
Hemispheres — CD307

Mercury
Scattering
Letters over
Globe
CD308

U.P.U.
Monument,
Bern
CD309

Universal Postal Union, 75th anniversary.

1949

Aden	32-35
Kathiri State of Seiyun	16-19
Qu'aiti State of Shihr and Mukalla	
	16-19
Antigua	100-103
Ascension	57-60
Bahamas	150-153
Barbados	212-215
Basutoland	41-44
Bechuanaland Protectorate	149-152
Bermuda	138-141
British Guiana	246-249
British Honduras	137-140
Brunei	79-82
Cayman Islands	118-121
Cyprus	160-163
Dominica	116-119
Falkland Islands	103-106
Falkland Islands Dep	1L14-1L17
Fiji	141-144
Gambia	148-151
Gibraltar	123-126
Gilbert & Ellice Islands	56-59

Gold Coast	144-147
Grenada	147-150
Hong Kong	180-183
Jamaica	142-145
Kenya, Uganda, Tanzania	94-97
Leeward Islands	126-129
Malaya	
Johore	151-154
Kedah	57-60
Kelantan	46-49
Malacca	18-21
Negri Sembilan	59-62
Pahang	46-49
Penang	23-26
Perak	101-104
Perlis	3-6
Selangor	76-79
Trengganu	49-52
Malta	225-228
Mauritius	231-234
Montserrat	108-111
New Hebrides, British	62-65
New Hebrides, French	79-82
Nigeria	75-78
North Borneo	240-243
Northern Rhodesia	50-53
Nyasaland Protectorate	87-90
Pitcairn Islands	13-16
St. Helena	132-135
St. Kitts-Nevis	95-98
St. Lucia	131-134
St. Vincent	170-173
Sarawak	176-179
Seychelles	153-156
Sierra Leone	190-193
Singapore	23-26
Solomon Islands	84-87
Somaliland Protectorate	112-115
Southern Rhodesia	71-72
Swaziland	50-53
Tonga	87-90
Trinidad & Tobago	66-69
Turks & Caicos Islands	101-104
Virgin Islands	92-95
Zanzibar	226-229

The following have different designs but are included in the omnibus set:

Great Britain	276-279
Offices in Morocco (Tangier)	546-549
Australia	223
Bahrain	68-71
Burma	116-121
Ceylon	304-306
Egypt	281-283
India	223-226
Kuwait	89-92
Oman	31-34
Pakistan-Bahawalpur	26-29, O25-O28
South Africa	109-111
South-West Africa	160-162

Nos. 32-35 (4)	5.50	7.80
Nos. 16-19 (4)	3.10	3.60
Nos. 16-19 (4)	2.95	3.95
Nos. 100-103 (4)	4.15	6.85
Nos. 57-60 (4)	12.40	10.00
Nos. 150-153 (4)	5.60	9.55
Nos. 212-215 (4)	4.40	14.15
Nos. 41-44 (4)	4.75	10.00
Nos. 149-152 (4)	3.35	7.25
Nos. 138-141 (4)	4.75	5.55
Nos. 246-249 (4)	2.75	4.20
Nos. 137-140 (4)	3.35	4.75
Nos. 79-82 (4)	7.75	6.75
Nos. 118-121 (4)	4.00	6.40
Nos. 160-163 (4)	4.60	8.30
Nos. 116-119 (4)	2.30	5.65
Nos. 103-106 (4)	14.90	17.10
Nos. 1L14-1L17 (4)	15.50	14.00
Nos. 141-144 (4)	3.35	14.00
Nos. 148-151 (4)	3.50	7.85
Nos. 123-126 (4)	6.25	9.50
Nos. 56-59 (4)	4.85	8.75
Nos. 144-147 (4)	3.05	6.95
Nos. 147-150 (4)	2.30	3.55
Nos. 180-183 (4)	74.25	23.60
Nos. 142-145 (4)	2.70	6.00
Nos. 94-97 (4)	2.90	3.40
Nos. 126-129 (4)	3.05	9.60
Nos. 151-154 (4)	4.70	8.90
Nos. 57-60 (4)	4.80	12.00
Nos. 46-49 (4)	4.25	12.65
Nos. 18-21 (4)	4.25	17.30
Nos. 59-62 (4)	3.50	10.75
Nos. 46-49 (4)	3.00	7.25
Nos. 23-26 (4)	5.10	11.75
Nos. 101-104 (4)	3.65	10.75
Nos. 3-6 (4)	3.95	14.25
Nos. 76-79 (4)	4.90	12.30
Nos. 49-52 (4)	4.95	9.75
Nos. 225-228 (4)	4.50	4.85
Nos. 231-234 (4)	4.35	6.70
Nos. 108-111 (4)	3.40	3.85
Nos. 62-65 (4)	1.60	4.10
Nos. 79-82 (4)	24.25	24.25
Nos. 75-78 (4)	2.80	9.25
Nos. 50-53 (4)	5.00	6.50

Nos. 87-90 (4)	4.05	4.05
Nos. 13-16 (4)	18.50	16.50
Nos. 132-135 (4)	4.85	7.10
Nos. 95-98 (4)	3.35	4.70
Nos. 131-134 (4)	2.55	3.85
Nos. 170-173 (4)	2.20	5.05
Nos. 176-179 (4)	9.00	11.10
Nos. 153-156 (4)	3.25	4.10
Nos. 190-193 (4)	3.00	5.10
Nos. 23-26 (4)	20.75	14.20
Nos. 84-87 (4)	4.35	4.90
Nos. 112-115 (4)	3.95	8.70
Nos. 71-72 (2)	1.95	2.25
Nos. 50-53 (4)	2.80	4.65
Nos. 87-90 (4)	3.25	5.25
Nos. 66-69 (4)	3.15	3.15
Nos. 101-104 (4)	3.65	4.00
Nos. 92-95 (4)	2.60	5.90
Nos. 226-229 (4)	5.45	13.50
Nos. 276-279 (4)	1.35	2.10
Nos. 546-549 (4)	3.20	10.15
No. 223 (1)	.60	.55
Nos. 68-71 (4)	5.00	16.75
Nos. 116-121 (6)	7.15	5.30
Nos. 304-306 (3)	3.35	4.25
Nos. 281-283 (3)	5.75	2.70
Nos. 223-226 (3)	35.50	10.50
Nos. 89-92 (4)	6.10	10.25
Nos. 31-34 (4)	5.55	15.75
Nos. 26-29, O25-O28 (8)	2.00	42.00
Nos. 109-111 (3)	2.20	3.00
Nos. 160-162 (3)	3.95	6.00
Set total (309) Stamps	489.60	683.55

University

Arms of
University
College
CD310

Alice, Princess
of Athlone
CD311

1948 opening of University College of the West Indies at Jamaica.

1951

Antigua	104-105
Barbados	228-229
British Guiana	250-251
British Honduras	141-142
Dominica	120-121
Grenada	164-165
Jamaica	146-147
Leeward Islands	130-131
Montserrat	112-113
St. Kitts-Nevis	105-106
St. Lucia	149-150
St. Vincent	174-175
Trinidad & Tobago	70-71
Virgin Islands	96-97

Nos. 104-105 (2)	1.35	3.25
Nos. 228-229 (2)	1.85	1.55
Nos. 250-251 (2)	1.10	1.25
Nos. 141-142 (2)	1.40	2.15
Nos. 120-121 (2)	1.40	1.75
Nos. 164-165 (2)	1.20	1.60
Nos. 146-147 (2)	.95	.85
Nos. 130-131 (2)	1.35	4.00
Nos. 112-113 (2)	.85	1.50
Nos. 105-106 (2)	.90	1.50
Nos. 149-150 (2)	1.40	1.50
Nos. 174-175 (2)	1.00	2.15
Nos. 70-71 (2)	.75	.75
Nos. 96-97 (2)	1.50	3.40
Set total (28) Stamps	17.00	27.20

Coronation

Queen Elizabeth
II — CD312

1953

Aden	47
Kathiri State of Seiyun	28
Qu'aiti State of Shihr and Mukalla	
	28
Antigua	106
Ascension	61

Bahamas	157
Barbados	234
Basutoland	45
Bechuanaland Protectorate	153
Bermuda	142
British Guiana	252
British Honduras	143
Cayman Islands	150
Cyprus	167
Dominica	141
Falkland Islands	121
Falkland Islands Dependencies	1L18
Fiji	145
Gambia	152
Gibraltar	131
Gilbert & Ellice Islands	60
Gold Coast	160
Grenada	170
Hong Kong	184
Jamaica	153
Kenya, Uganda, Tanzania	101
Leeward Islands	132
Malaya	
Johore	155
Kedah	82
Kelantan	71
Malacca	27
Negri Sembilan	63
Pahang	71
Penang	27
Perak	126
Perlis	28
Selangor	101
Trengganu	74
Malta	241
Mauritius	250
Montserrat	127
New Hebrides, British	77
Nigeria	79
North Borneo	260
Northern Rhodesia	60
Nyasaland Protectorate	96
Pitcairn Islands	19
St. Helena	139
St. Kitts-Nevis	119
St. Lucia	156
St. Vincent	185
Sarawak	196
Seychelles	172
Sierra Leone	194
Singapore	27
Solomon Islands	88
Somaliland Protectorate	127
Swaziland	54
Trinidad & Tobago	84
Tristan da Cunha	13
Turks & Caicos Islands	118
Virgin Islands	114

The following have different designs but are included in the omnibus set:

Great Britain	313-316
Offices in Morocco (Tangier)	579-582
Australia	259-261
Bahrain	92-95
Canada	330
Ceylon	317
Cook Islands	145-146
Kuwait	113-116
New Zealand	280-284
Niue	104-105
Oman	52-55
Samoa	214-215
South Africa	192
Southern Rhodesia	80
South-West Africa	244-248
Tokelau Islands	4

No. 47 (1)	1.25	1.25
No. 28 (1)	.40	1.50
No. 28 (1)	1.10	.60
No. 106 (1)	.50	.75
No. 61 (1)	1.25	2.50
No. 157 (1)	1.25	.75
No. 234 (1)	1.00	.25
No. 45 (1)	.50	.60
No. 153 (1)	.75	.35
No. 142 (1)	.85	.40
No. 252 (1)	.45	.25
No. 143 (1)	.55	.40
No. 150 (1)	.40	1.00
No. 167 (1)	1.50	1.00
No. 141 (1)	.40	.40
No. 121 (1)	.90	1.50
No. 1L18 (1)	1.50	1.50
No. 145 (1)	1.75	.60
No. 152 (1)	.50	.50
No. 131 (1)	.50	.50
No. 60 (1)	.65	2.25
No. 160 (1)	.95	.25
No. 170 (1)	.30	.25
No. 184 (1)	7.00	.35
No. 153 (1)	.95	.25
No. 101 (1)	.40	.25
No. 132 (1)	1.00	2.25

No. 155 (1)	1.40	.30
No. 82 (1)	2.25	.60
No. 71 (1)	1.60	1.60
No. 27 (1)	1.10	1.50
No. 63 (1)	1.40	.65
No. 71 (1)	2.25	.25
No. 27 (1)	1.75	.30
No. 126 (1)	1.60	.25
No. 28 (1)	1.75	4.00
No. 101 (1)	1.75	.25
No. 74 (1)	1.50	1.00
No. 241 (1)	.50	.25
No. 250 (1)	1.00	.25
No. 127 (1)	.65	.50
No. 77 (1)	.75	.60
No. 79 (1)	.45	.25
No. 60 (1)	.70	.25
No. 96 (1)	.75	.75
No. 19 (1)	2.25	2.25
No. 139 (1)	1.25	1.25
No. 119 (1)	.35	.25
No. 156 (1)	.70	.35
No. 185 (1)	.50	.30
No. 196 (1)	2.25	2.25
No. 172 (1)	.80	.80
No. 194 (1)	.40	.40
No. 27 (1)	2.50	.40
No. 88 (1)	1.10	1.10
No. 127 (1)	.40	.25
No. 54 (1)	.30	.25
No. 84 (1)	.25	.25
No. 13 (1)	1.00	1.75
No. 118 (1)	.40	1.10
No. 114 (1)	.40	1.00
Nos. 313-316 (4)	16.35	8.75
Nos. 579-582 (4)	7.40	5.20
Nos. 259-261 (3)	4.60	3.25
Nos. 92-95 (4)	15.25	12.75
No. 330 (1)	.25	.25
No. 317 (1)	1.50	.25
Nos. 145-146 (2)	2.65	2.65
Nos. 113-116 (4)	16.00	8.50
Nos. 280-284 (5)	5.65	6.85
Nos. 104-105 (2)	1.75	1.75
Nos. 52-55 (4)	15.25	6.50
Nos. 214-215 (2)	2.10	1.00
No. 192 (1)	.30	.25
No. 80 (1)	7.25	7.25
Nos. 244-248 (5)	4.90	3.50
No. 4 (1)	2.75	2.75
Set total (105) Stamps	170.50	121.40

Separate designs for each country for the visit of Queen Elizabeth II and the Duke of Edinburgh.

Royal Visit 1953

1953

Aden	62
Australia	267-269
Bermuda	163
Ceylon	318
Fiji	146
Gibraltar	146
Jamaica	154
Kenya, Uganda, Tanzania	102
Malta	242
New Zealand	286-287

No. 62 (1)	.65	2.00
Nos. 267-269 (3)	2.35	1.90
No. 163 (1)	.50	.25
No. 318 (1)	1.25	.25
No. 146 (1)	.65	.35
No. 146 (1)	.50	.30
No. 154 (1)	.50	.25
No. 102 (1)	.50	.25
No. 205 (1)	.50	.25
No. 242 (1)	.35	.25
Nos. 286-287 (2)	.50	.50
Set total (13) Stamps	7.75	6.30

West Indies Federation

Map of the Caribbean
CD313

Federation of the West Indies, April 22, 1958.

1958

Antigua	122-124
Barbados	248-250
Dominica	161-163
Grenada	184-186
Jamaica	175-177
Montserrat	143-145
St. Kitts-Nevis	136-138
St. Lucia	170-172
St. Vincent	198-200
Trinidad & Tobago	86-88

Nos. 122-124 (3)	5.80	3.80
Nos. 248-250 (3)	1.60	2.90
Nos. 161-163 (3)	1.95	1.85

Nos. 184-186 (3)	1.50	1.20
Nos. 175-177 (3)	3.10	4.20
Nos. 143-145 (3)	2.35	1.35
Nos. 136-138 (3)	3.00	1.85
Nos. 170-172 (3)	2.05	2.80
Nos. 198-200 (3)	1.50	1.75
Nos. 86-88 (3)	.75	.90
Set total (30) Stamps	23.60	22.60

Freedom from Hunger

Protein Food
CD314

U.N. Food and Agricultural Organization's "Freedom from Hunger" campaign.

1963

Aden	65
Antigua	133
Ascension	89
Bahamas	180
Basutoland	83
Bechuanaland Protectorate	194
Bermuda	192
British Guiana	271
British Honduras	179
Brunei	100
Cayman Islands	168
Dominica	181
Falkland Islands	146
Fiji	198
Gambia	172
Gibraltar	161
Gilbert & Ellice Islands	76
Grenada	190
Hong Kong	218
Malta	291
Mauritius	270
Montserrat	150
New Hebrides, British	93
North Borneo	296
Pitcairn Islands	35
St. Helena	173
St. Lucia	179
St. Vincent	201
Sarawak	212
Seychelles	213
Solomon Islands	109
Swaziland	108
Tonga	127
Tristan da Cunha	68
Turks & Caicos Islands	138
Virgin Islands	140
Zanzibar	280

No. 65 (1)	1.75	1.75
No. 133 (1)	.35	.35
No. 89 (1)	1.00	1.00
No. 180 (1)	.65	.65
No. 83 (1)	.50	.25
No. 194 (1)	.50	.50
No. 192 (1)	1.00	.50
No. 271 (1)	.45	.25
No. 179 (1)	.65	.25
No. 100 (1)	3.25	2.25
No. 168 (1)	.50	.30
No. 181 (1)	.30	.30
No. 146 (1)	11.50	3.50
No. 198 (1)	5.25	2.75
No. 172 (1)	.50	.25
No. 161 (1)	4.00	2.25
No. 76 (1)	1.40	.40
No. 190 (1)	.30	.25
No. 218 (1)	57.50	8.75
No. 291 (1)	2.00	2.00
No. 270 (1)	.50	.50
No. 150 (1)	.55	.45
No. 93 (1)	.60	.25
No. 35 (1)	10.00	4.50
No. 173 (1)	2.25	1.10
No. 179 (1)	.40	.40
No. 201 (1)	.90	.50
No. 212 (1)	1.60	1.75
No. 213 (1)	.85	.35
No. 109 (1)	2.00	.85
No. 108 (1)	.50	.50
No. 127 (1)	.70	.35
No. 68 (1)	.90	.40
No. 138 (1)	.50	.50
No. 140 (1)	.50	.50
No. 280 (1)	1.50	.80
Set total (36) Stamps	117.60	42.20

Red Cross Centenary

Red Cross and Elizabeth II
CD315

1963

Antigua	134-135
Ascension	90-91
Bahamas	183-184
Basutoland	84-85
Bechuanaland Protectorate	195-196
Bermuda	193-194
British Guiana	272-273
British Honduras	180-181
Cayman Islands	169-170
Dominica	182-183
Falkland Islands	147-148
Fiji	203-204
Gambia	173-174
Gibraltar	162-163
Gilbert & Ellice Islands	77-78
Grenada	191-192
Hong Kong	219-220
Jamaica	203-204
Malta	292-293
Mauritius	271-272
Montserrat	151-152
New Hebrides, British	94-95
Pitcairn Islands	36-37
St. Helena	174-175
St. Kitts-Nevis	143-144
St. Lucia	180-181
St. Vincent	202-203
Seychelles	214-215
Solomon Islands	110-111
South Arabia	1-2
Swaziland	109-110
Tonga	134-135
Tristan da Cunha	69-70
Turks & Caicos Islands	139-140
Virgin Islands	141-142

Nos. 134-135 (2)	1.10	1.50
Nos. 90-91 (2)	8.25	2.70
Nos. 183-184 (2)	2.30	2.55
Nos. 84-85 (2)	1.20	.90
Nos. 195-196 (2)	.95	.85
Nos. 193-194 (2)	2.75	2.55
Nos. 272-273 (2)	1.05	.80
Nos. 180-181 (2)	1.00	2.25
Nos. 169-170 (2)	.95	2.00
Nos. 182-183 (2)	.70	1.05
Nos. 147-148 (2)	19.75	6.00
Nos. 203-204 (2)	4.00	3.55
Nos. 173-174 (2)	.85	.85
Nos. 162-163 (2)	6.25	5.40
Nos. 77-78 (2)	2.25	3.25
Nos. 191-192 (2)	.80	.50
Nos. 219-220 (2)	39.50	8.85
Nos. 203-204 (2)	.75	1.65
Nos. 292-293 (2)	2.50	4.75
Nos. 271-272 (2)	.90	.90
Nos. 151-152 (2)	1.00	.80
Nos. 94-95 (2)	1.00	.50
Nos. 36-37 (2)	6.50	5.50
Nos. 174-175 (2)	1.70	2.30
Nos. 143-144 (2)	.90	.90
Nos. 180-181 (2)	1.25	1.25
Nos. 202-203 (2)	.90	.90
Nos. 214-215 (2)	1.10	.90
Nos. 110-111 (2)	1.25	1.15
Nos. 1-2 (2)	1.25	1.25
Nos. 109-110 (2)	1.10	1.10
Nos. 134-135 (2)	1.00	1.25
Nos. 69-70 (2)	1.50	1.00
Nos. 139-140 (2)	.95	1.10
Nos. 141-142 (2)	.80	.80
Set total (70) Stamps	120.00	73.55

Shakespeare

Shakespeare Memorial Theatre, Stratford-on-Avon — CD316

400th anniversary of the birth of William Shakespeare.

1964

Antigua	151
Bahamas	201
Bechuanaland Protectorate	197
Cayman Islands	171
Dominica	184
Falkland Islands	149
Gambia	192
Gibraltar	164
Montserrat	153
St. Lucia	196
Turks & Caicos Islands	141
Virgin Islands	143

No. 151 (1)	.40	.25
No. 201 (1)	.60	.35
No. 197 (1)	.35	.35

No. 171 (1)	.35	.30
No. 184 (1)	.35	.35
No. 149 (1)	1.75	.50
No. 192 (1)	.35	.25
No. 164 (1)	.65	.55
No. 153 (1)	.35	.25
No. 196 (1)	.45	.25
No. 141 (1)	.40	.40
No. 143 (1)	.45	.45
Set total (12) Stamps	6.45	4.25

ITU

ITU Emblem
CD317

Intl. Telecommunication Union, cent.

1965

Antigua	153-154
Ascension	92-93
Bahamas	219-220
Barbados	265-266
Basutoland	101-102
Bechuanaland Protectorate	202-203
Bermuda	196-197
British Guiana	293-294
British Honduras	187-188
Brunei	116-117
Cayman Islands	172-173
Dominica	185-186
Falkland Islands	154-155
Fiji	211-212
Gibraltar	167-168
Gilbert & Ellice Islands	87-88
Grenada	205-206
Hong Kong	221-222
Mauritius	291-292
Montserrat	157-158
New Hebrides, British	108-109
Pitcairn Islands	52-53
St. Helena	180-181
St. Kitts-Nevis	163-164
St. Lucia	197-198
St. Vincent	224-225
Seychelles	218-219
Solomon Islands	126-127
Swaziland	115-116
Tristan da Cunha	85-86
Turks & Caicos Islands	142-143
Virgin Islands	159-160

Nos. 153-154 (2)	1.65	1.35
Nos. 92-93 (2)	1.90	1.50
Nos. 219-220 (2)	1.35	1.35
Nos. 265-266 (2)	1.50	1.25
Nos. 101-102 (2)	.85	.65
Nos. 202-203 (2)	1.10	.75
Nos. 196-197 (2)	2.15	2.25
Nos. 293-294 (2)	.60	.55
Nos. 187-188 (2)	.85	.85
Nos. 116-117 (2)	1.75	1.75
Nos. 172-173 (2)	1.00	1.00
Nos. 185-186 (2)	.55	.55
Nos. 154-155 (2)	7.75	3.65
Nos. 211-212 (2)	2.70	2.70
Nos. 167-168 (2)	9.00	5.95
Nos. 87-88 (2)	.95	.75
Nos. 205-206 (2)	.50	.50
Nos. 221-222 (2)	32.00	4.55
Nos. 291-292 (2)	1.20	.65
Nos. 157-158 (2)	1.25	1.15
Nos. 108-109 (2)	.65	.50
Nos. 52-53 (2)	6.25	4.30
Nos. 180-181 (2)	.80	.60
Nos. 163-164 (2)	.60	.60
Nos. 197-198 (2)	1.25	1.25
Nos. 224-225 (2)	.80	.90
Nos. 218-219 (2)	.90	.60
Nos. 126-127 (2)	.70	.55
Nos. 115-116 (2)	.75	.75
Nos. 85-86 (2)	1.15	.65
Nos. 142-143 (2)	.90	.90
Nos. 159-160 (2)	.95	.95
Set total (64) Stamps	86.30	46.25

Intl. Cooperation Year

ICY Emblem
CD318

1965

Antigua	155-156
Ascension	94-95
Bahamas	222-223
Basutoland	103-104

Bechuanaland Protectorate......204-205
Bermuda...........................199-200
British Guiana.....................295-296
British Honduras..................189-190
Brunei..............................118-119
Cayman Islands...................174-175
Dominica...........................187-188
Falkland Islands..................156-157
Fiji.................................213-214
Gibraltar...........................169-170
Gilbert & Ellice Islands...........104-105
Grenada............................207-208
Hong Kong 223-224
Mauritius..........................293-294
Montserrat 176-177
New Hebrides, British 110-111
New Hebrides, French...........126-127
Pitcairn Islands.....................54-55
St. Helena.........................182-183
St. Kitts-Nevis.....................165-166
St. Lucia...........................199-200
Seychelles.........................220-221
Solomon Islands..................143-144
South Arabia 17-18
Swaziland..........................117-118
Tristan da Cunha....................87-88
Turks & Caicos Islands 144-145
Virgin Islands......................161-162

Nos. 155-156 (2)	.60	.50
Nos. 94-95 (2)	1.30	1.50
Nos. 222-223 (2)	.65	1.40
Nos. 103-104 (2)	.75	.85
Nos. 204-205 (2)	.85	1.00
Nos. 199-200 (2)	2.25	1.25
Nos. 295-296 (2)	.65	.60
Nos. 189-190 (2)	.60	.55
Nos. 118-119 (2)	.85	.85
Nos. 174-175 (2)	1.00	.95
Nos. 187-188 (2)	.55	.55
Nos. 156-157 (2)	7.00	1.90
Nos. 213-214 (2)	2.60	2.35
Nos. 169-170 (2)	1.25	2.75
Nos. 104-105 (2)	.95	.60
Nos. 207-208 (2)	.50	.50
Nos. 223-224 (2)	26.00	4.10
Nos. 293-294 (2)	.70	.70
Nos. 176-177 (2)	.80	.65
Nos. 110-111 (2)	.50	.50
Nos. 126-127 (2)	12.00	12.00
Nos. 54-55 (2)	6.35	4.50
Nos. 182-183 (2)	.95	.50
Nos. 165-166 (2)	.70	.60
Nos. 199-200 (2)	.55	.55
Nos. 220-221 (2)	.90	.65
Nos. 143-144 (2)	.70	.60
Nos. 17-18 (2)	1.20	.50
Nos. 117-118 (2)	.75	.75
Nos. 87-88 (2)	1.35	.75
Nos. 144-145 (2)	.85	.85
Nos. 161-162 (2)	.80	.80
Set total (64) Stamps	77.45	47.10

Churchill Memorial

Winston Churchill and St. Paul's, London, During Air Attack — CD319

1966

Antigua 157-160
Ascension 96-99
Bahamas 224-227
Barbados 281-284
Basutoland 105-108
Bechuanaland Protectorate......206-209
Bermuda...........................201-204
British Antarctic Territory.............16-19
British Honduras 191-194
Brunei 120-123
Cayman Islands...................176-179
Dominica...........................189-192
Falkland Islands..................158-161
Fiji.................................215-219
Gibraltar...........................171-174
Gilbert & Ellice Islands...........106-109
Grenada............................209-212
Hong Kong 225-228
Mauritius..........................295-298
Montserrat 178-181
New Hebrides, British 112-115
New Hebrides, French...........128-131
Pitcairn Islands.....................56-59
St. Helena.........................184-187
St. Kitts-Nevis.....................167-170
St. Lucia...........................201-204
St. Vincent.........................241-244
Seychelles.........................222-225
Solomon Islands..................145-148
South Arabia 19-22
Swaziland..........................119-122

Tristan da Cunha...................89-92
Turks & Caicos Islands 146-149
Virgin Islands......................163-166

Nos. 157-160 (4)	3.05	2.55
Nos. 96-99 (4)	10.00	7.15
Nos. 224-227 (4)	2.30	3.20
Nos. 281-284 (4)	3.00	4.45
Nos. 105-108 (4)	2.80	3.25
Nos. 206-209 (4)	2.50	2.50
Nos. 201-204 (4)	4.00	4.00
Nos. 16-19 (4)	41.35	20.00
Nos. 191-194 (4)	2.55	1.80
Nos. 120-123 (4)	8.00	7.25
Nos. 176-179 (4)	3.40	3.55
Nos. 189-192 (4)	1.15	1.15
Nos. 158-161 (4)	12.75	7.80
Nos. 215-218 (4)	5.15	3.45
Nos. 171-174 (4)	3.05	5.30
Nos. 106-109 (4)	1.75	1.30
Nos. 209-212 (4)	1.10	1.10
Nos. 225-228 (4)	68.00	12.15
Nos. 295-298 (4)	4.05	4.05
Nos. 178-181 (4)	1.60	1.55
Nos. 112-115 (4)	2.30	1.00
Nos. 128-131 (4)	10.25	10.25
Nos. 56-59 (4)	11.00	6.75
Nos. 184-187 (4)	1.85	1.95
Nos. 167-170 (4)	1.70	1.70
Nos. 201-204 (4)	1.50	1.50
Nos. 241-244 (4)	1.50	1.75
Nos. 222-225 (4)	3.20	3.60
Nos. 145-148 (4)	1.75	1.75
Nos. 19-22 (4)	2.95	2.20
Nos. 119-122 (4)	1.70	2.55
Nos. 89-92 (4)	5.95	2.70
Nos. 146-149 (4)	1.60	1.75
Nos. 163-166 (4)	1.90	1.90
Set total (136) Stamps	230.70	138.90

Royal Visit, 1966

Queen Elizabeth II and Prince Philip CD320

Caribbean visit, Feb. 4 - Mar. 6, 1966.

1966

Antigua 161-162
Bahamas 228-229
Barbados 285-286
British Guiana.....................299-300
Cayman Islands...................180-181
Dominica...........................193-194
Grenada............................213-214
Montserrat 182-183
St. Kitts-Nevis.....................171-172
St. Lucia...........................205-206
St. Vincent.........................245-246
Turks & Caicos Islands 150-151
Virgin Islands......................167-168

Nos. 161-162 (2)	3.80	2.60
Nos. 228-229 (2)	3.05	3.05
Nos. 285-286 (2)	3.00	2.00
Nos. 299-300 (2)	3.35	1.60
Nos. 180-181 (2)	3.45	1.80
Nos. 193-194 (2)	3.00	.60
Nos. 213-214 (2)	.90	.50
Nos. 182-183 (2)	1.70	1.00
Nos. 171-172 (2)	.80	.75
Nos. 205-206 (2)	1.50	1.35
Nos. 245-246 (2)	2.75	1.35
Nos. 150-151 (2)	1.20	.70
Nos. 167-168 (2)	2.25	2.25
Set total (26) Stamps	30.75	19.55

World Cup Soccer

Soccer Player and Jules Rimet Cup CD321

World Cup Soccer Championship, Wembley, England, July 11-30.

1966

Antigua 163-164
Ascension 100-101
Bahamas 245-246
Bermuda...........................205-206
Brunei 124-125
Cayman Islands...................182-183
Dominica...........................195-196
Fiji.................................219-220
Gibraltar...........................175-176
Gilbert & Ellice Islands...........125-126
Grenada............................230-231

New Hebrides, British 116-117
New Hebrides, French 132-133
Pitcairn Islands.....................60-61
St. Helena.........................188-189
St. Kitts-Nevis.....................173-174
St. Lucia...........................207-208
Seychelles.........................226-227
Solomon Islands..................167-168
South Arabia 23-24
Tristan da Cunha...................93-94

Nos. 163-164 (2)	.85	.50
Nos. 100-101 (2)	2.50	1.80
Nos. 245-246 (2)	.65	.65
Nos. 205-206 (2)	1.75	1.75
Nos. 124-125 (2)	1.40	1.00
Nos. 182-183 (2)	.75	.75
Nos. 195-196 (2)	1.20	.75
Nos. 219-220 (2)	2.00	1.20
Nos. 175-176 (2)	1.85	1.75
Nos. 125-126 (2)	.80	.60
Nos. 230-231 (2)	.65	.95
Nos. 116-117 (2)	1.00	1.00
Nos. 132-133 (2)	7.00	7.00
Nos. 60-61 (2)	5.50	5.00
Nos. 188-189 (2)	1.25	.60
Nos. 173-174 (2)	.85	.80
Nos. 207-208 (2)	1.15	.90
Nos. 226-227 (2)	.85	.85
Nos. 167-168 (2)	.70	.70
Nos. 23-24 (2)	1.90	.55
Nos. 93-94 (2)	1.25	.80
Set total (42) Stamps	35.85	29.90

WHO Headquarters

World Health Organization Headquarters, Geneva — CD322

1966

Antigua 165-166
Ascension 102-103
Bahamas 247-248
Brunei 126-127
Cayman Islands...................184-185
Dominica...........................197-198
Fiji.................................224-225
Gibraltar...........................180-181
Gilbert & Ellice Islands...........127-128
Grenada............................232-233
Hong Kong 229-230
Montserrat 184-185
New Hebrides, British 118-119
New Hebrides, French 134-135
Pitcairn Islands.....................62-63
St. Helena.........................190-191
St. Kitts-Nevis.....................177-178
St. Lucia...........................209-210
St. Vincent.........................247-248
Seychelles.........................228-229
Solomon Islands..................169-170
South Arabia 25-26
Tristan da Cunha...................99-100

Nos. 165-166 (2)	1.05	.55
Nos. 102-103 (2)	6.60	3.50
Nos. 247-248 (2)	.80	.80
Nos. 126-127 (2)	1.35	1.00
Nos. 184-185 (2)	2.25	1.40
Nos. 197-198 (2)	.75	.75
Nos. 224-225 (2)	5.10	3.90
Nos. 180-181 (2)	6.50	4.50
Nos. 127-128 (2)	.80	.70
Nos. 232-233 (2)	.80	.50
Nos. 229-230 (2)	14.25	2.30
Nos. 184-185 (2)	1.00	1.00
Nos. 118-119 (2)	.75	.50
Nos. 134-135 (2)	8.75	8.75
Nos. 62-63 (2)	7.25	6.50
Nos. 190-191 (2)	3.50	1.50
Nos. 177-178 (2)	.65	.65
Nos. 209-210 (2)	.80	.80
Nos. 247-248 (2)	1.15	1.05
Nos. 228-229 (2)	1.25	.75
Nos. 169-170 (2)	.80	.80
Nos. 25-26 (2)	2.10	.70
Nos. 99-100 (2)	1.90	1.25
Set total (46) Stamps	70.15	44.15

UNESCO Anniversary

"Education" — CD323

"Science" (Wheat ears & flask enclosing globe). "Culture" (lyre & columns). 20th anniversary of the UNESCO.

1966-67

Antigua 183-185
Ascension 108-110
Bahamas 249-251
Barbados 287-289
Bermuda...........................207-209
Brunei 128-130
Cayman Islands...................186-188
Dominica...........................199-201
Gibraltar...........................183-185
Gilbert & Ellice Islands...........129-131
Grenada............................234-236
Hong Kong 231-233
Mauritius..........................299-301
Montserrat 186-188
New Hebrides, British 120-122
New Hebrides, French 136-138
Pitcairn Islands.....................64-66
St. Helena.........................192-194
St. Kitts-Nevis.....................179-181
St. Lucia...........................211-213
St. Vincent.........................249-251
Seychelles.........................230-232
Solomon Islands..................171-173
South Arabia 27-29
Swaziland..........................123-125
Tristan da Cunha..................101-103
Turks & Caicos Islands 155-157
Virgin Islands......................176-178

Nos. 183-185 (3)	1.90	2.50
Nos. 108-110 (3)	11.00	6.15
Nos. 249-251 (3)	2.35	2.35
Nos. 287-289 (3)	2.50	2.15
Nos. 207-209 (3)	4.30	3.90
Nos. 128-130 (3)	5.00	7.40
Nos. 186-188 (3)	2.50	1.70
Nos. 199-201 (3)	1.60	.75
Nos. 183-185 (3)	6.50	3.25
Nos. 129-131 (3)	2.50	1.65
Nos. 234-236 (3)	1.10	1.20
Nos. 231-233 (3)	89.00	20.00
Nos. 299-301 (3)	2.10	1.50
Nos. 186-188 (3)	2.40	2.40
Nos. 120-122 (3)	1.90	1.90
Nos. 136-138 (3)	7.75	7.75
Nos. 64-66 (3)	7.10	4.75
Nos. 192-194 (3)	5.25	3.65
Nos. 179-181 (3)	.90	.90
Nos. 211-213 (3)	1.15	1.15
Nos. 249-251 (3)	2.30	1.35
Nos. 230-232 (3)	2.40	2.40
Nos. 171-173 (3)	2.00	1.50
Nos. 27-29 (3)	5.50	5.50
Nos. 123-125 (3)	1.45	1.45
Nos. 101-103 (3)	2.00	1.40
Nos. 155-157 (3)	1.05	1.05
Nos. 176-178 (3)	1.30	1.30
Set total (84) Stamps	176.80	92.95

Silver Wedding, 1972

Queen Elizabeth II and Prince Philip — CD324

Designs: borders differ for each country.

1972

Anguilla 161-162
Antigua 295-296
Ascension 164-165
Bahamas 344-345
Bermuda...........................296-297
British Antarctic Territory.............43-44
British Honduras 306-307
British Indian Ocean Territory.......48-49
Brunei 186-187
Cayman Islands...................304-305
Dominica...........................352-353
Falkland Islands 223-224
Fiji.................................328-329
Gibraltar...........................292-293
Gilbert & Ellice Islands...........206-207
Grenada............................466-467
Hong Kong 271-272
Montserrat 286-287
New Hebrides, British 169-170
Pitcairn Islands...................127-128
St. Helena.........................271-272
St. Kitts-Nevis.....................257-258
St. Lucia...........................328-329
St. Vincent.........................344-345

Seychelles		309-310
Solomon Islands		248-249
South Georgia		35-36
Tristan da Cunha		178-179
Turks & Caicos Islands		257-258
Virgin Islands		241-242

Nos. 161-162 (2)	1.30	1.50
Nos. 295-296 (2)	.50	.50
Nos. 164-165 (2)	.80	.80
Nos. 344-345 (2)	.60	.60
Nos. 296-297 (2)	.50	.50
Nos. 43-44 (2)	7.75	6.10
Nos. 306-307 (2)	.90	.90
Nos. 48-49 (2)	2.30	1.00
Nos. 186-187 (2)	.65	.85
Nos. 304-305 (2)	.75	.75
Nos. 352-353 (2)	.65	.65
Nos. 223-224 (2)	1.10	1.10
Nos. 328-329 (2)	1.00	1.00
Nos. 292-293 (2)	.50	.50
Nos. 206-207 (2)	.50	.50
Nos. 466-467 (2)	.70	.70
Nos. 271-272 (2)	2.10	1.75
Nos. 286-287 (2)	.55	.55
Nos. 169-170 (2)	.50	.50
Nos. 127-128 (2)	.90	.85
Nos. 271-272 (2)	.70	1.20
Nos. 257-258 (2)	.65	.50
Nos. 328-329 (2)	.75	.75
Nos. 344-345 (2)	.55	.55
Nos. 309-310 (2)	.95	.95
Nos. 248-249 (2)	.60	.60
Nos. 35-36 (2)	1.40	1.40
Nos. 178-179 (2)	.70	.70
Nos. 257-258 (2)	.50	.50
Nos. 241-242 (2)	.50	.50
Set total (60) Stamps	31.85	29.25

Princess Anne's Wedding

Princess Anne and Mark Phillips — CD325

Wedding of Princess Anne and Mark Phillips, Nov. 14, 1973.

1973

Anguilla		179-180
Ascension		177-178
Belize		325-326
Bermuda		302-303
British Antarctic Territory		60-61
Cayman Islands		320-321
Falkland Islands		225-226
Gibraltar		305-306
Gilbert & Ellice Islands		216-217
Hong Kong		289-290
Montserrat		300-301
Pitcairn Islands		135-136
St. Helena		277-278
St. Kitts-Nevis		274-275
St. Lucia		349-350
St. Vincent		358-359
St. Vincent Grenadines		1-2
Seychelles		311-312
Solomon Islands		259-260
South Georgia		37-38
Tristan da Cunha		189-190
Turks & Caicos Islands		286-287
Virgin Islands		260-261

Nos. 179-180 (2)	.55	.55
Nos. 177-178 (2)	.65	.65
Nos. 325-326 (2)	.50	.50
Nos. 302-303 (2)	.50	.50
Nos. 60-61 (2)	1.10	1.10
Nos. 320-321 (2)	.55	.55
Nos. 225-226 (2)	.75	.75
Nos. 305-306 (2)	.55	.55
Nos. 216-217 (2)	.50	.50
Nos. 289-290 (2)	3.25	2.25
Nos. 300-301 (2)	.65	.65
Nos. 135-136 (2)	.70	.60
Nos. 277-278 (2)	.50	.50
Nos. 274-275 (2)	.50	.50
Nos. 349-350 (2)	.50	.50
Nos. 358-359 (2)	.50	.50
Nos. 1-2 (2)	.50	.50
Nos. 311-312 (2)	.70	.70
Nos. 259-260 (2)	.70	.70
Nos. 37-38 (2)	.75	.75
Nos. 189-190 (2)	.50	.50
Nos. 286-287 (2)	.50	.50
Nos. 260-261 (2)	.50	.50
Set total (46) Stamps	16.40	15.30

Elizabeth II Coronation Anniv.

CD326   CD327

CD328

Designs: Royal and local beasts in heraldic form and simulated stonework. Portrait of Elizabeth II by Peter Grugeon. 25th anniversary of coronation of Queen Elizabeth II.

1978

Ascension		229
Barbados		474
Belize		397
British Antarctic Territory		71
Cayman Islands		404
Christmas Island		87
Falkland Islands		275
Fiji		384
Gambia		380
Gilbert Islands		312
Mauritius		464
New Hebrides, British		258
St. Helena		317
St. Kitts-Nevis		354
Samoa		472
Solomon Islands		368
South Georgia		51
Swaziland		302
Tristan da Cunha		238
Virgin Islands		337

No. 229 (1)	2.25	2.25
No. 474 (1)	1.35	1.35
No. 397 (1)	1.75	1.75
No. 71 (1)	6.00	6.00
No. 404 (1)	2.00	2.50
No. 87 (1)	3.50	4.00
No. 275 (1)	4.00	4.00
No. 384 (1)	2.75	2.75
No. 380 (1)	1.50	1.50
No. 312 (1)	1.25	1.25
No. 464 (1)	2.75	2.75
No. 258 (1)	1.75	1.75
No. 317 (1)	1.75	1.75
No. 354 (1)	1.00	1.00
No. 472 (1)	2.00	2.00
No. 368 (1)	3.00	3.00
No. 51 (1)	3.00	3.00
No. 302 (1)	1.75	1.75
No. 238 (1)	1.50	1.50
No. 337 (1)	2.25	2.25
Set total (20) Stamps	47.10	48.10

Queen Mother Elizabeth's 80th Birthday

CD330

Designs: Photographs of Queen Mother Elizabeth. Falkland Islands issued in sheets of 50; others in sheets of 9.

1980

Ascension		261
Bermuda		401
Cayman Islands		443
Falkland Islands		305
Gambia		412
Gibraltar		393
Hong Kong		364
Pitcairn Islands		193
St. Helena		341
Samoa		532
Solomon Islands		426

Tristan da Cunha		277

No. 261 (1)	.50	.50
No. 401 (1)	.45	.45
No. 443 (1)	.45	.45
No. 305 (1)	.40	.40
No. 412 (1)	.40	.50
No. 393 (1)	.35	.35
No. 364 (1)	1.10	1.00
No. 193 (1)	.60	.60
No. 341 (1)	.50	.50
No. 532 (1)	.55	.55
No. 426 (1)	.50	.50
No. 277 (1)	.45	.45
Set total (12) Stamps	6.25	6.25

Royal Wedding, 1981

Prince Charles and Lady Diana — CD331   CD331a

Wedding of Charles, Prince of Wales, and Lady Diana Spencer, St. Paul's Cathedral, London, July 29, 1981.

1981

Antigua		623-627
Ascension		294-296
Barbados		547-549
Barbuda		497-501
Bermuda		412-414
Brunei		268-270
Cayman Islands		471-473
Dominica		701-705
Falkland Islands		324-326
Falkland Islands Dep		1L59-1L61
Fiji		442-444
Gambia		426-428
Ghana		759-764
Grenada		1051-1055
Grenada Grenadines		440-443
Hong Kong		373-375
Jamaica		500-503
Lesotho		335-337
Maldive Islands		906-909
Mauritius		520-522
Norfolk Island		280-282
Pitcairn Islands		206-208
St. Helena		353-355
St. Lucia		543-549
Samoa		558-560
Sierra Leone		509-518
Solomon Islands		450-452
Swaziland		382-384
Tristan da Cunha		294-296
Turks & Caicos Islands		486-489
Caicos Island		8-11
Uganda		314-317
Vanuatu		308-310
Virgin Islands		406-408

Nos. 623-627 (5)	7.55	2.55
Nos. 294-296 (3)	1.10	1.10
Nos. 547-549 (3)	10.95	10.95
Nos. 497-501 (5)	10.95	10.95
Nos. 412-414 (3)	2.00	2.00
Nos. 268-270 (3)	2.15	4.50
Nos. 471-473 (3)	1.35	1.35
Nos. 701-705 (5)	8.35	2.35
Nos. 324-326 (3)	1.65	1.70
Nos. 1L59-1L61 (3)	1.45	1.45
Nos. 442-444 (3)	1.70	1.70
Nos. 426-428 (3)	.80	.80
Nos. 759-764 (9)	5.00	5.00
Nos. 1051-1055 (5)	9.85	1.85
Nos. 440-443 (4)	2.35	2.35
Nos. 373-375 (3)	3.30	3.10
Nos. 500-503 (4)	1.50	1.25
Nos. 335-337 (3)	1.10	1.10
Nos. 906-909 (4)	1.70	1.80
Nos. 520-522 (3)	2.75	2.75
Nos. 280-282 (3)	1.35	1.35
Nos. 206-208 (3)	1.10	1.10
Nos. 353-355 (3)	.85	.85
Nos. 543-549 (3)	8.50	8.50
Nos. 558-560 (3)	.85	.85
Nos. 509-518 (10)	15.50	15.50
Nos. 450-452 (3)	1.05	1.05
Nos. 382-384 (3)	1.30	1.25
Nos. 294-296 (3)	.90	.90
Nos. 486-489 (4)	2.20	2.20
Nos. 8-11 (4)	6.25	6.25
Nos. 314-317 (4)	3.30	3.00
Nos. 308-310 (3)	1.15	1.15
Nos. 406-408 (3)	1.30	1.30
Set total (131) Stamps	113.10	95.80

Princess Diana

CD332

CD333

Designs: Photographs and portrait of Princess Diana, wedding or honeymoon photographs, royal residences, arms of issuing country. Portrait photograph by Clive Friend. Souvenir sheet margins show family tree, various people related to the princess. 21st birthday of Princess Diana of Wales, July 1.

1982

Antigua		663-666
Ascension		313-316
Bahamas		510-513
Barbados		585-588
Barbuda		544-547
British Antarctic Territory		92-95
Cayman Islands		486-489
Dominica		773-776
Falkland Islands		348-351
Falkland Islands Dep		1L72-1L75
Fiji		470-473
Gambia		447-450
Grenada		1101A-1105
Grenada Grenadines		485-491
Lesotho		372-375
Maldive Islands		952-955
Mauritius		548-551
Pitcairn Islands		213-216
St. Helena		372-375
St. Lucia		591-594
Sierra Leone		531-534
Solomon Islands		471-474
Swaziland		406-409
Tristan da Cunha		310-313
Turks and Caicos Islands		531-534
Virgin Islands		430-433

Nos. 663-666 (4)	9.70	9.70
Nos. 313-316 (4)	3.95	3.95
Nos. 510-513 (4)	6.00	3.85
Nos. 585-588 (4)	3.40	3.25
Nos. 544-547 (4)	9.75	7.70
Nos. 92-95 (4)	5.30	3.45
Nos. 486-489 (4)	5.40	2.70
Nos. 773-776 (4)	7.05	7.05
Nos. 348-351 (4)	3.10	3.10
Nos. 1L72-1L75 (4)	2.50	2.60
Nos. 470-473 (4)	4.50	4.50
Nos. 447-450 (4)	2.85	2.85
Nos. 1101A-1105 (7)	16.05	15.55
Nos. 485-491 (7)	17.65	17.65
Nos. 372-375 (4)	4.00	4.00
Nos. 952-955 (4)	7.25	7.25
Nos. 548-551 (4)	5.50	5.50
Nos. 213-216 (4)	2.15	2.15
Nos. 372-375 (4)	2.95	2.95
Nos. 591-594 (4)	9.90	9.90
Nos. 531-534 (4)	7.20	7.20
Nos. 471-474 (4)	2.90	2.90
Nos. 406-409 (4)	3.85	2.25
Nos. 310-313 (4)	3.65	1.45
Nos. 486-489 (4)	2.20	2.20
Nos. 430-433 (4)	3.55	3.55
Set total (110) Stamps	152.30	139.20

250th anniv. of first edition of Lloyd's List (shipping news publication) & of Lloyd's marine insurance.

CD335

Designs: First page of early edition of the list; historical ships, modern transportation or harbor scenes.

1984

Ascension	351-354
Bahamas	555-558
Barbados	627-630
Cayes of Belize	10-13
Cayman Islands	522-526
Falkland Islands	404-407
Fiji	509-512
Gambia	519-522
Mauritius	587-590
Nauru	280-283
St. Helena	412-415
Samoa	624-627
Seychelles	538-541
Solomon Islands	521-524
Vanuatu	368-371
Virgin Islands	466-469

Nos. 351-354 (4)	3.30	2.55
Nos. 555-558 (4)	4.55	2.95
Nos. 627-630 (4)	6.10	5.15
Nos. 10-13 (4)	3.05	3.05
Nos. 522-526 (5)	9.30	8.45
Nos. 404-407 (4)	3.65	4.00
Nos. 509-512 (4)	6.15	6.15
Nos. 519-522 (4)	4.20	4.30
Nos. 587-590 (4)	8.95	8.95
Nos. 280-283 (4)	2.40	2.35
Nos. 412-415 (4)	2.40	2.40
Nos. 624-627 (4)	2.75	2.55
Nos. 538-541 (4)	5.25	5.25
Nos. 521-524 (4)	4.65	3.95
Nos. 368-371 (4)	2.40	2.40
Nos. 466-469 (4)	5.00	5.00
Set total (65) Stamps	74.10	69.45

Queen Mother 85th Birthday

CD336

Designs: Photographs tracing the life of the Queen Mother, Elizabeth. The high value in each set pictures the same photograph taken of the Queen Mother holding the infant Prince Henry.

1985

Ascension	372-376
Bahamas	580-584
Barbados	660-664
Bermuda	469-473
Falkland Islands	420-424
Falkland Islands Dep.	1L92-1L96
Fiji	531-535
Hong Kong	447-450
Jamaica	599-603
Mauritius	604-608
Norfolk Island	364-368
Pitcairn Islands	253-257
St. Helena	428-432
Samoa	649-653
Seychelles	567-571
Zil Elwannyen Sesel	101-105
Solomon Islands	543-547
Swaziland	476-480
Tristan da Cunha	372-376
Vanuatu	392-396

Nos. 372-376 (5)	5.35	5.35
Nos. 580-584 (5)	7.95	6.45
Nos. 660-664 (5)	8.00	6.70
Nos. 469-473 (5)	9.90	9.90
Nos. 420-424 (5)	8.25	7.60
Nos. 1L92-1L96 (5)	8.25	8.25
Nos. 531-535 (5)	7.05	7.05
Nos. 447-450 (4)	10.25	8.50
Nos. 599-603 (5)	7.30	8.00
Nos. 604-608 (5)	11.80	11.80
Nos. 364-368 (5)	5.05	5.05
Nos. 253-257 (5)	5.25	5.95
Nos. 428-432 (5)	5.25	5.25
Nos. 649-653 (5)	8.65	7.80
Nos. 567-571 (5)	8.70	8.70
Nos. 101-105 (5)	7.15	7.15
Nos. 543-547 (5)	4.20	4.20
Nos. 476-480 (5)	8.00	7.50
Nos. 372-376 (5)	5.40	5.40
Nos. 392-396 (5)	5.25	5.25
Set total (99) Stamps	147.00	141.85

Queen Elizabeth II, 60th Birthday

CD337

1986, April 21

Ascension	389-393
Bahamas	592-596
Barbados	675-679
Bermuda	499-503
Cayman Islands	555-559
Falkland Islands	441-445
Fiji	544-548
Hong Kong	465-469
Jamaica	620-624
Kiribati	470-474
Mauritius	629-633
Papua New Guinea	640-644
Pitcairn Islands	270-274
St. Helena	451-455
Samoa	670-674
Seychelles	592-596
Zil Elwannyen Sesel	114-118
Solomon Islands	562-566
South Georgia	101-105
Swaziland	490-494
Tristan da Cunha	388-392
Vanuatu	414-418
Zambia	343-347

Nos. 389-393 (5)	2.80	2.80
Nos. 592-596 (5)	2.75	3.70
Nos. 675-679 (5)	3.35	3.20
Nos. 499-503 (5)	4.90	4.90
Nos. 555-559 (5)	4.55	4.45
Nos. 441-445 (5)	3.95	4.95
Nos. 544-548 (5)	4.05	4.05
Nos. 465-469 (5)	9.60	6.85
Nos. 620-624 (5)	2.95	3.05
Nos. 470-474 (5)	2.10	2.10
Nos. 629-633 (5)	3.70	3.70
Nos. 640-644 (5)	4.50	4.50
Nos. 270-274 (5)	2.70	2.70
Nos. 451-455 (5)	3.05	3.05
Nos. 670-674 (5)	2.90	2.90
Nos. 592-596 (5)	2.70	2.70
Nos. 114-118 (5)	2.25	2.25
Nos. 562-566 (5)	2.50	2.50
Nos. 101-105 (5)	3.55	3.55
Nos. 490-494 (5)	2.30	2.30
Nos. 388-392 (5)	3.00	3.00
Nos. 414-418 (5)	3.10	3.10
Nos. 343-347 (5)	1.75	1.75
Set total (115) Stamps	79.00	78.05

Royal Wedding

Marriage of Prince Andrew and Sarah Ferguson
CD338

1986, July 23

Ascension	399-400
Bahamas	602-603
Barbados	687-688
Cayman Islands	560-561
Jamaica	629-630
Pitcairn Islands	275-276
St. Helena	460-461
St. Kitts	181-182
Seychelles	602-603
Zil Elwannyen Sesel	119-120
Solomon Islands	567-568
Tristan da Cunha	397-398
Zambia	348-349

Nos. 399-400 (2)	1.60	1.60
Nos. 602-603 (2)	2.75	2.75
Nos. 687-688 (2)	2.25	1.25
Nos. 560-561 (2)	1.50	2.15
Nos. 629-630 (2)	1.75	1.75
Nos. 275-276 (2)	2.40	2.40
Nos. 460-461 (2)	1.05	1.05
Nos. 181-182 (2)	1.50	1.50
Nos. 602-603 (2)	2.50	2.50
Nos. 119-120 (2)	2.30	2.30
Nos. 567-568 (2)	1.00	1.00
Nos. 397-398 (2)	1.40	1.40
Nos. 348-349 (2)	1.10	1.30
Set total (26) Stamps	23.10	22.95

Queen Elizabeth II, 60th Birthday

Queen Elizabeth II & Prince Philip, 1947 Wedding Portrait — CD339

Designs: Photographs tracing the life of Queen Elizabeth II.

1986

Anguilla	674-677
Antigua	925-928
Barbuda	783-786
Dominica	950-953
Gambia	611-614
Grenada	1371-1374
Grenada Grenadines	749-752
Lesotho	531-534
Maldive Islands	1172-1175
Sierra Leone	760-763
Uganda	495-498

Nos. 674-677 (4)	8.00	8.00
Nos. 925-928 (4)	6.75	6.75
Nos. 783-786 (4)	23.15	23.15
Nos. 950-953 (4)	7.25	7.25
Nos. 611-614 (4)	8.25	7.90
Nos. 1371-1374 (4)	6.80	6.80
Nos. 749-752 (4)	6.75	6.75
Nos. 531-534 (4)	5.50	5.50
Nos. 1172-1175 (4)	7.00	7.00
Nos. 760-763 (4)	6.30	6.30
Nos. 495-498 (4)	8.50	8.50
Set total (44) Stamps	94.25	93.90

Royal Wedding, 1986

CD340

Designs: Photographs of Prince Andrew and Sarah Ferguson during courtship, engagement and marriage.

1986

Antigua	939-942
Barbuda	809-812
Dominica	970-973
Gambia	635-638
Grenada	1385-1388
Grenada Grenadines	758-761
Lesotho	545-548
Maldive Islands	1181-1184
Sierra Leone	769-772
Uganda	510-513

Nos. 939-942 (4)	8.25	8.25
Nos. 809-812 (4)	14.55	14.55
Nos. 970-973 (4)	7.25	7.25
Nos. 635-638 (4)	8.55	8.55
Nos. 1385-1388 (4)	8.30	8.30
Nos. 758-761 (4)	9.00	9.00
Nos. 545-548 (4)	7.95	7.95
Nos. 1181-1184 (4)	10.20	10.20
Nos. 769-772 (4)	5.35	5.35
Nos. 510-513 (4)	9.25	10.00
Set total (40) Stamps	88.65	89.40

Lloyds of London, 300th Anniv.

CD341

Designs: 17th century aspects of Lloyds, representations of each country's individual connections with Lloyds and publicized disasters insured by the organization.

1986

Ascension	454-457
Bahamas	655-658
Barbados	731-734
Bermuda	541-544
Falkland Islands	481-484
Liberia	1101-1104
Malawi	534-537
Nevis	571-574
St. Helena	501-504
St. Lucia	923-926
Seychelles	649-652
Zil Elwannyen Sesel	146-149
Solomon Islands	627-630
South Georgia	131-134
Trinidad & Tobago	484-487
Tristan da Cunha	439-442
Vanuatu	485-488

Nos. 454-457 (4)	5.00	5.00
Nos. 655-658 (4)	8.90	4.95
Nos. 731-734 (4)	12.50	8.35
Nos. 541-544 (4)	8.25	5.60
Nos. 481-484 (4)	6.30	4.55
Nos. 1101-1104 (4)	4.25	4.25
Nos. 534-537 (4)	11.00	7.85
Nos. 571-574 (4)	8.35	8.35
Nos. 501-504 (4)	8.70	7.15
Nos. 923-926 (4)	9.40	9.40
Nos. 649-652 (4)	13.10	13.10
Nos. 146-149 (4)	11.25	11.25
Nos. 627-630 (4)	7.90	4.45
Nos. 131-134 (4)	6.30	3.70
Nos. 484-487 (4)	10.25	6.35
Nos. 439-442 (4)	7.60	7.60
Nos. 485-488 (4)	5.90	5.90
Set total (68) Stamps	144.95	117.80

Moon Landing, 20th Anniv.

CD342

Designs: Equipment, crew photographs, spacecraft, official emblems and report profiles created for the Apollo Missions. Two stamps in each set are square in format rather than like the stamp shown; see individual country listings for more information.

1989

Ascension	468-472
Bahamas	674-678
Belize	916-920
Kiribati	517-521
Liberia	1125-1129
Nevis	586-590
St. Kitts	248-252
Samoa	760-764
Seychelles	676-680
Zil Elwannyen Sesel	154-158
Solomon Islands	643-647
Vanuatu	507-511

Nos. 468-472 (5)	9.40	8.60
Nos. 674-678 (5)	23.00	19.70
Nos. 916-920 (5)	27.40	23.50
Nos. 517-521 (5)	12.50	12.50
Nos. 1125-1129 (5)	8.50	8.50
Nos. 586-590 (5)	7.50	7.50
Nos. 248-252 (5)	8.00	8.00
Nos. 760-764 (5)	9.60	9.05
Nos. 676-680 (5)	16.05	16.05
Nos. 154-158 (5)	26.85	26.85
Nos. 643-647 (5)	12.75	11.60
Nos. 507-511 (5)	9.90	9.90
Set total (60) Stamps	171.45	161.75

Queen Mother, 90th Birthday

CD343   CD344

Designs: Portraits of Queen Elizabeth, the Queen Mother. See individual country listings for more information.

1990

Ascension	491-492
Bahamas	698-699
Barbados	782-783
British Antarctic Territory	170-171
British Indian Ocean Territory	106-107
Cayman Islands	622-623
Falkland Islands	524-525
Kenya	527-528
Kiribati	555-556
Liberia	1145-1146
Pitcairn Islands	336-337
St. Helena	532-533
St. Lucia	969-970
Seychelles	710-711
Zil Elwannyen Sesel	171-172
Solomon Islands	671-672
South Georgia	143-144
Swaziland	565-566
Tristan da Cunha	480-481

Nos. 491-492 (2)	4.75	5.65
Nos. 698-699 (2)	5.65	5.65
Nos. 782-783 (2)	4.00	3.70
Nos. 170-171 (2)	6.75	6.75
Nos. 106-107 (2)	20.75	21.25
Nos. 622-623 (2)	5.10	6.75
Nos. 524-525 (2)	5.25	5.25
Nos. 527-528 (2)	7.00	7.00
Nos. 555-556 (2)	5.60	5.60
Nos. 1145-1146 (2)	3.25	3.25
Nos. 336-337 (2)	4.25	4.25
Nos. 532-533 (2)	5.25	5.25
Nos. 969-970 (2)	5.25	5.25
Nos. 710-711 (2)	6.60	6.60
Nos. 171-172 (2)	8.25	8.25
Nos. 671-672 (2)	6.50	6.40
Nos. 143-144 (2)	5.75	5.75
Nos. 565-566 (2)	4.35	4.35
Nos. 480-481 (2)	5.60	5.60
Set total (38) Stamps	119.90	122.55

Queen Elizabeth II, 65th Birthday, and Prince Philip, 70th Birthday

CD345

CD346

Designs: Portraits of Queen Elizabeth II and Prince Philip differ for each country. Printed in sheets of 10 + 5 labels (3 different) between. Stamps alternate, producing 5 different triptychs.

1991

Ascension	506a
Bahamas	731a
Belize	970a
Bermuda	618a
Kiribati	572a
Mauritius	734a
Pitcairn Islands	349a
St. Helena	555a
St. Kitts	319a
Samoa	791a
Seychelles	724a
Zil Elwannyen Sesel	178a
Solomon Islands	689a
South Georgia	150a
Swaziland	587a
Vanuatu	541a

No. 506a (1)	3.50	3.75
No. 731a (1)	4.00	4.00
No. 970a (1)	3.75	3.75
No. 618a (1)	4.00	4.00
No. 572a (1)	4.00	4.00
No. 734a (1)	3.75	3.75
No. 349a (1)	3.25	3.25
No. 555a (1)	2.75	2.75
No. 319a (1)	3.00	3.00
No. 791a (1)	4.25	4.25
No. 724a (1)	5.00	5.00
No. 178a (1)	6.50	6.50
No. 689a (1)	4.50	4.50
No. 150a (1)	7.00	7.00
No. 587a (1)	4.25	4.25
No. 541a (1)	2.50	2.50
Set total (16) Stamps	66.00	66.25

Royal Family Birthday, Anniversary

CD347

Queen Elizabeth II, 65th birthday, Charles and Diana, 10th wedding anniversary: Various photographs of Queen Elizabeth II, Prince Philip, Prince Charles, Princess Diana and their sons William and Henry.

1991

Antigua	1446-1455
Barbuda	1229-1238
Dominica	1328-1337
Gambia	1080-1089
Grenada	2006-2015
Grenada Grenadines	1331-1340
Guyana	2440-2451
Lesotho	871-875
Maldive Islands	1533-1542
Nevis	666-675
St. Vincent	1485-1494
St. Vincent Grenadines	769-778
Sierra Leone	1387-1396
Turks & Caicos Islands	913-922
Uganda	918-927

Nos. 1446-1455 (10)	21.95	20.30
Nos. 1229-1238 (10)	125.00	119.50
Nos. 1328-1337 (10)	30.20	30.20
Nos. 1080-1089 (10)	24.65	24.40
Nos. 2006-2015 (10)	25.45	22.10
Nos. 1331-1340 (10)	23.85	23.35
Nos. 2440-2451 (12)	21.40	21.15
Nos. 871-875 (5)	13.55	13.55
Nos. 1533-1542 (10)	29.60	29.60
Nos. 666-675 (10)	25.65	25.65
Nos. 1485-1494 (10)	26.75	25.90
Nos. 769-778 (10)	25.40	25.40
Nos. 1387-1396 (10)	26.55	26.55
Nos. 913-922 (10)	31.65	30.00
Nos. 918-927 (10)	26.60	26.60
Set total (147) Stamps	478.25	464.25

Queen Elizabeth II's Accession to the Throne, 40th Anniv.

CD348

Various photographs of Queen Elizabeth II with local Scenes.

1992

Antigua	1513-1518
Barbuda	1306-1311
Dominica	1414-1419
Gambia	1172-1177
Grenada	2047-2052
Grenada Grenadines	1368-1373
Lesotho	881-885
Maldive Islands	1637-1642
Nevis	702-707
St. Vincent	1582-1587
St. Vincent Grenadines	829-834
Sierra Leone	1482-1487
Turks and Caicos Islands	978-987
Uganda	990-995
Virgin Islands	742-746

Nos. 1513-1518 (6)	16.00	14.10
Nos. 1306-1311 (6)	125.25	83.65
Nos. 1414-1419 (6)	12.50	12.50
Nos. 1172-1177 (6)	16.60	16.35
Nos. 2047-2052 (6)	15.95	15.95
Nos. 1368-1373 (6)	17.00	15.35
Nos. 881-885 (5)	11.90	11.90
Nos. 1637-1642 (6)	17.55	17.55
Nos. 702-707 (6)	13.80	13.80
Nos. 1582-1587 (6)	14.40	14.40
Nos. 829-834 (6)	19.65	19.65
Nos. 1482-1487 (6)	22.50	22.50
Nos. 913-922 (10)	31.65	30.00
Nos. 990-995 (6)	19.50	19.50
Nos. 742-746 (5)	15.50	15.50
Set total (92) Stamps	369.75	322.70

CD349

1992

Ascension	531-535
Bahamas	744-748
Bermuda	623-627
British Indian Ocean Territory	119-123
Cayman Islands	648-652
Falkland Islands	549-553
Gibraltar	605-609
Hong Kong	619-623
Kenya	563-567
Kiribati	582-586
Pitcairn Islands	362-366
St. Helena	570-574
St. Kitts	332-336
Samoa	805-809
Seychelles	734-738
Zil Elwannyen Sesel	183-187
Solomon Islands	708-712
South Georgia	157-161
Tristan da Cunha	508-512
Vanuatu	555-559
Zambia	561-565

Nos. 531-535 (5)	6.35	6.35
Nos. 744-748 (5)	6.90	4.70
Nos. 623-627 (5)	8.20	7.30
Nos. 119-123 (5)	24.75	21.00
Nos. 648-652 (5)	7.60	7.10
Nos. 549-553 (5)	6.80	8.20
Nos. 605-609 (5)	5.15	5.50
Nos. 619-623 (5)	5.65	2.65
Nos. 563-567 (5)	9.10	9.10
Nos. 582-586 (5)	3.85	3.85
Nos. 362-366 (5)	5.35	5.35
Nos. 570-574 (5)	5.70	5.70
Nos. 332-336 (5)	6.60	5.50
Nos. 805-809 (5)	8.10	6.15
Nos. 734-738 (5)	10.80	10.80
Nos. 183-187 (5)	9.40	9.40
Nos. 708-712 (5)	7.95	7.30
Nos. 157-161 (5)	5.85	5.75
Nos. 508-512 (5)	8.75	8.30
Nos. 555-559 (5)	3.65	3.65
Nos. 561-565 (5)	5.60	5.60
Set total (105) Stamps	162.10	149.25

Royal Air Force, 75th Anniversary

CD350

1993

Ascension	557-561
Bahamas	771-775
Barbados	842-846
Belize	1003-1008
Bermuda	648-651
British Indian Ocean Territory	136-140
Falkland Is.	573-577
Fiji	687-691
Montserrat	830-834
St. Kitts	351-355

Nos. 557-561 (5)	16.70	14.85
Nos. 771-775 (5)	26.00	22.20
Nos. 842-846 (5)	13.65	12.35
Nos. 1003-1008 (6)	19.40	18.70
Nos. 648-651 (4)	10.50	9.95
Nos. 136-140 (5)	17.50	17.50
Nos. 573-577 (5)	11.25	11.25
Nos. 687-691 (5)	18.95	18.95
Nos. 830-834 (5)	14.35	14.35
Nos. 351-355 (5)	24.45	23.95
Set total (50) Stamps	172.75	164.05

Royal Air Force, 80th Anniv.

Design CD350 Re-inscribed

1998

Ascension	697-701
Bahamas	907-911
British Indian Ocean Terr	198-202
Cayman Islands	754-758
Fiji	814-818
Gibraltar	755-759
Samoa	957-961
Turks & Caicos Islands	1258-1265
Tuvalu	763-767
Virgin Islands	879-883

Nos. 697-701 (5)	17.35	17.35
Nos. 907-911 (5)	14.25	13.55
Nos. 136-140 (5)	17.50	17.50
Nos. 754-758 (5)	15.75	15.75
Nos. 814-818 (5)	15.50	15.50
Nos. 755-759 (5)	9.70	9.70
Nos. 957-961 (5)	16.70	15.90
Nos. 1258-1265 (2)	32.00	32.00
Nos. 763-767 (5)	9.75	9.75
Nos. 879-883 (5)	17.00	17.00
Set total (47) Stamps	165.50	164.00

End of World War II, 50th Anniv.

CD351

CD352

1995

Ascension	613-617
Bahamas	824-828
Barbados	891-895
Belize	1047-1050
British Indian Ocean Territory	163-167
Cayman Islands	704-708
Falkland Islands	634-638
Fiji	720-724
Kiribati	662-668
Liberia	1175-1179
Mauritius	803-805
St. Helena	646-654
St. Kitts	389-393
St. Lucia	1018-1022
Samoa	890-894
Solomon Islands	799-803
South Georgia	198-200
Tristan da Cunha	562-566

Nos. 613-617 (5)	21.50	21.50
Nos. 824-828 (5)	22.00	18.70
Nos. 891-895 (5)	14.20	11.90
Nos. 1047-1050 (4)	7.45	6.75
Nos. 163-167 (5)	16.25	16.25
Nos. 704-708 (5)	18.15	14.45
Nos. 634-638 (5)	17.90	17.40
Nos. 720-724 (5)	21.35	21.35
Nos. 662-668 (7)	16.30	16.30
Nos. 1175-1179 (5)	15.25	11.15
Nos. 803-805 (3)	7.50	7.50
Nos. 646-654 (9)	26.10	26.10
Nos. 389-393 (5)	13.60	13.60
Nos. 1018-1022 (5)	14.25	11.15
Nos. 890-894 (5)	14.25	13.50
Nos. 799-803 (5)	17.50	17.50
Nos. 198-200 (3)	14.00	14.00
Nos. 562-566 (5)	20.10	20.10
Set total (91) Stamps	297.65	279.20

UN, 50th Anniv.

CD353

1995

Bahamas		839-842
Barbados		901-904
Belize		1055-1058
Jamaica		847-851
Liberia		1187-1190
Mauritius		813-816
Pitcairn Islands		436-439
St. Kitts		398-401
St. Lucia		1023-1026
Samoa		900-903
Tristan da Cunha		568-571
Virgin Islands		807-810

Nos. 839-842 (4)	8.00	7.05
Nos. 901-904 (4)	7.00	5.75
Nos. 1055-1058 (4)	5.70	5.60
Nos. 847-851 (5)	6.50	5.95
Nos. 1187-1190 (4)	9.65	9.65
Nos. 813-816 (4)	3.90	3.90
Nos. 436-439 (4)	8.15	8.15
Nos. 398-401 (4)	6.15	6.15
Nos. 1023-1026 (4)	7.50	7.25
Nos. 900-903 (4)	9.35	8.20
Nos. 568-571 (4)	13.50	13.50
Nos. 807-810 (4)	9.45	9.45
Set total (49) Stamps	94.85	90.60

Queen Elizabeth, 70th Birthday

CD354

1996

Ascension		632-635
British Antarctic Territory		240-243
British Indian Ocean Territory		176-180
Falkland Islands		653-657
Pitcairn Islands		446-449
St. Helena		672-676
Samoa		912-916
Tokelau		223-227
Tristan da Cunha		576-579
Virgin Islands		824-828

Nos. 632-635 (4)	5.90	5.90
Nos. 240-243 (4)	10.50	8.90
Nos. 176-180 (5)	11.50	11.50
Nos. 653-657 (5)	14.35	11.90
Nos. 446-449 (4)	8.60	8.60
Nos. 672-676 (5)	12.70	12.70
Nos. 912-916 (5)	11.50	11.50
Nos. 223-227 (5)	11.35	11.35
Nos. 576-579 (4)	8.35	8.35
Nos. 824-828 (5)	12.30	12.30
Set total (46) Stamps	107.05	103.00

Diana, Princess of Wales (1961-97)

CD355

1998

Ascension		696
Bahamas		901A-902
Barbados		950
Belize		1091
Bermuda		753
Botswana		659-663
British Antarctic Territory		258
British Indian Ocean Terr.		197
Cayman Islands		752A-753

Falkland Islands		694
Fiji		819-820
Gibraltar		754
Kiribati		719A-720
Namibia		909
Niue		706
Norfolk Island		644-645
Papua New Guinea		937
Pitcairn Islands		487
St. Helena		711
St. Kitts		437A-438
Samoa		955A-956
Seychelles		802
Solomon Islands		866-867
South Georgia		220
Tokelau		252B-253
Tonga		980
Niuafo'ou		201
Tristan da Cunha		618
Tuvalu		762
Vanuatu		718A-719
Virgin Islands		878

No. 696 (1)	5.50	5.50
Nos. 901A-902 (2)	5.30	5.30
No. 950 (1)	5.00	5.00
No. 1091 (1)	5.50	5.50
No. 753 (1)	5.50	5.50
Nos. 659-663 (5)	10.25	10.10
No. 258 (1)	6.25	6.25
No. 197 (1)	6.50	6.50
Nos. 752A-753 (3)	7.75	7.75
No. 694 (1)	4.75	4.75
Nos. 819-820 (2)	6.00	6.00
No. 754 (1)	4.75	4.75
Nos. 719A-720 (2)	4.85	4.85
No. 909 (1)	1.90	1.90
No. 706 (1)	5.50	5.50
Nos. 644-645 (2)	5.25	5.25
No. 937 (1)	6.50	6.50
No. 487 (1)	4.75	4.75
No. 711 (1)	4.25	4.25
Nos. 437A-438 (2)	5.15	5.15
Nos. 955A-956 (2)	7.00	7.00
No. 802 (1)	6.25	6.25
Nos. 866-867 (2)	6.90	6.90
No. 220 (1)	5.25	5.25
Nos. 252B-253 (2)	6.75	6.75
No. 980 (1)	5.75	5.75
No. 201 (1)	7.75	7.75
No. 618 (1)	5.00	5.00
No. 762 (1)	4.00	4.00
Nos. 718A-719 (2)	8.00	8.00
No. 878 (1)	5.50	5.50
Set total (46) Stamps	179.35	179.20

Wedding of Prince Edward and Sophie Rhys-Jones

CD356

1999

Ascension		729-730
Cayman Islands		775-776
Falkland Islands		729-730
Pitcairn Islands		505-506
St. Helena		733-734
Samoa		971-972
Tristan da Cunha		636-637
Virgin Islands		908-909

Nos. 729-730 (2)	5.90	5.90
Nos. 775-776 (2)	5.50	5.50
Nos. 729-730 (2)	15.00	15.00
Nos. 505-506 (2)	7.00	7.00
Nos. 733-734 (2)	5.00	5.00
Nos. 971-972 (2)	5.00	5.00
Nos. 636-637 (2)	7.50	7.50
Nos. 908-909 (2)	8.30	8.30
Set total (16) Stamps	59.20	59.20

1st Manned Moon Landing, 30th Anniv.

CD357

1999

Ascension		731-735
Bahamas		942-946
Barbados		967-971
Bermuda		778
Cayman Islands		777-781
Fiji		853-857
Jamaica		889-893
Kiribati		746-750
Nauru		465-469
St. Kitts		460-464
Samoa		973-977
Solomon Islands		875-879
Tuvalu		800-804
Virgin Islands		910-914

Nos. 731-735 (5)	13.90	13.90
Nos. 942-946 (5)	14.10	14.10
Nos. 967-971 (5)	8.65	7.75
No. 778 (1)	8.00	8.00
Nos. 777-781 (5)	10.30	10.30
Nos. 853-857 (5)	10.40	10.40
Nos. 889-893 (5)	10.20	10.00
Nos. 746-750 (5)	8.85	8.85
Nos. 465-469 (5)	8.90	10.15
Nos. 460-464 (5)	12.00	12.00
Nos. 973-977 (5)	13.45	13.30
Nos. 875-879 (5)	10.00	9.85
Nos. 800-804 (5)	7.45	7.45
Nos. 910-914 (5)	15.00	15.00
Set total (66) Stamps	151.20	151.05

Queen Mother's Century

CD358

1999

Ascension		736-740
Bahamas		951-955
Cayman Islands		782-786
Falkland Islands		734-738
Fiji		858-862
Norfolk Island		688-692
St. Helena		740-744
Samoa		978-982
Solomon Islands		880-884
South Georgia		231-235
Tristan da Cunha		638-642
Tuvalu		805-809

Nos. 736-740 (5)	17.00	17.00
Nos. 951-955 (5)	14.00	12.90
Nos. 782-786 (5)	9.15	9.15
Nos. 734-738 (5)	30.75	27.75
Nos. 858-862 (5)	15.00	15.00
Nos. 688-692 (5)	10.30	10.30
Nos. 740-744 (5)	16.15	16.15
Nos. 978-982 (5)	12.50	12.10
Nos. 880-884 (5)	10.00	9.45
Nos. 231-235 (5)	30.25	29.75
Nos. 638-642 (5)	18.00	18.00
Nos. 805-809 (5)	8.65	8.65
Set total (60) Stamps	191.75	186.20

Prince William, 18th Birthday

CD359

2000

Ascension		755-759
Cayman Islands		797-801
Falkland Islands		762-766
Fiji		889-893
South Georgia		257-261
Tristan da Cunha		664-668
Virgin Islands		925-929

Nos. 755-759 (5)	17.75	17.75
Nos. 797-801 (5)	13.05	12.75
Nos. 762-766 (5)	27.15	23.75
Nos. 889-893 (5)	14.00	14.00
Nos. 257-261 (5)	29.00	29.00
Nos. 664-668 (5)	21.50	21.50
Nos. 925-929 (5)	14.75	14.75
Set total (35) Stamps	137.20	133.50

Reign of Queen Elizabeth II, 50th Anniv.

CD360

2002

Ascension		790-794
Bahamas		1033-1037
Barbados		1019-1023
Belize		1152-1156
Bermuda		822-826
British Antarctic Territory		307-311
British Indian Ocean Territory		239-243
Cayman Islands		844-848
Falkland Islands		804-808
Gibraltar		896-900
Jamaica		952-956
Nauru		491-495
Norfolk Island		758-762
Papua New Guinea		1019-1023
Pitcairn Islands		552
St. Helena		788-792
St. Lucia		1146-1150
Solomon Islands		931-935
South Georgia		274-278
Swaziland		706-710
Tokelau		302-306
Tonga		1059
Niuafo'ou		239
Tristan da Cunha		706-710
Virgin Islands		967-971

Nos. 790-794 (5)	16.25	16.25
Nos. 1033-1037 (5)	15.75	15.75
Nos. 1019-1023 (5)	13.15	13.15
Nos. 1152-1156 (5)	15.50	15.15
Nos. 822-826 (5)	18.50	18.50
Nos. 307-311 (5)	25.00	25.00
Nos. 239-243 (5)	22.00	22.00
Nos. 844-848 (5)	14.25	14.25
Nos. 804-808 (5)	23.50	22.50
Nos. 896-900 (5)	6.65	6.65
Nos. 952-956 (5)	18.25	18.25
Nos. 491-495 (5)	18.75	18.75
Nos. 758-762 (5)	19.50	19.50
Nos. 1019-1023 (5)	14.50	14.50
No. 552 (1)	9.25	9.25
Nos. 788-792 (5)	19.75	19.75
Nos. 1146-1150 (5)	12.25	12.25
Nos. 931-935 (5)	16.00	16.00
Nos. 274-278 (5)	28.50	28.50
Nos. 706-710 (5)	12.75	12.75
Nos. 302-306 (5)	17.00	17.00
No. 1059 (1)	8.00	8.00
No. 239 (1)	7.00	7.00
Nos. 706-710 (5)	18.50	18.50
Nos. 967-971 (5)	19.00	19.00
Set total (113) Stamps	409.55	408.20

Queen Mother Elizabeth (1900-2002)

CD361

2002

Ascension		799-801
Bahamas		1044-1046
Bermuda		834-836
British Antarctic Territory		312-314

British Indian Ocean Territory 245-247
Cayman Islands......................857-861
Falkland Islands 812-816
Nauru.....................................499-501
Pitcairn Islands.......................561-565
St. Helena 808-812
St. Lucia 1155-1159
Seychelles 830
Solomon Islands......................945-947
South Georgia 281-285
Tokelau 312-314
Tristan da Cunha.....................715-717
Virgin Islands..........................979-983

Nos. 799-801 (3)	9.75	9.75
Nos. 1044-1046 (3)	9.35	9.35
Nos. 834-836 (3)	12.50	12.50
Nos. 312-314 (3)	19.25	19.25
Nos. 245-247 (3)	19.50	19.50
Nos. 857-861 (5)	15.00	15.00
Nos. 812-816 (5)	31.50	31.50
Nos. 499-501 (3)	16.00	16.00
Nos. 561-565 (5)	15.25	15.25
Nos. 808-812 (5)	12.00	12.00
Nos. 1155-1159 (5)	13.00	13.00
No. 830 (1)	6.50	6.50
Nos. 945-947 (3)	11.00	11.00
Nos. 281-285 (5)	20.00	20.00
Nos. 312-314 (3)	14.25	13.75
Nos. 715-717 (3)	16.25	16.25
Nos. 979-983 (5)	26.50	26.50
Set total (63) Stamps	267.60	267.10

Head of Queen Elizabeth II

CD362

2003

Ascension.......................................822
Bermuda...865
British Antarctic Territory.................322
British Indian Ocean Territory 261
Cayman Islands...............................878
Falkland Islands 828
St. Helena 820
South Georgia 294
Tristan da Cunha............................731
Virgin Islands................................1003

No. 822 (1)	13.50	13.50
No. 865 (1)	55.00	55.00
No. 322 (1)	10.00	10.00
No. 261 (1)	12.50	12.50
No. 878 (1)	17.00	17.00
No. 828 (1)	10.00	10.00
No. 820 (1)	9.00	9.00
No. 294 (1)	9.00	9.00
No. 731 (1)	10.00	10.00
No. 1003 (1)	10.00	10.00
Set total (10) Stamps	156.00	156.00

Coronation of Queen Elizabeth II, 50th Anniv.

CD363

2003

Ascension................................823-825
Bahamas 1073-1075
Bermuda...............................866-868
British Antarctic Territory.........323-325
British Indian Ocean Territory 262-264
Cayman Islands.......................879-881
Jamaica 970-972
Kiribati 825-827
Pitcairn Islands.......................577-581
St. Helena 821-823
St. Lucia 1171-1173
Tokelau 320-322
Tristan da Cunha....................732-734
Virgin Islands.......................1004-1006

Nos. 823-825 (3)	13.50	13.50
Nos. 1073-1075 (3)	13.00	13.00
Nos. 866-868 (3)	14.25	14.25
Nos. 323-325 (3)	26.00	26.00
Nos. 262-264 (3)	31.00	31.00
Nos. 879-881 (3)	20.25	20.25

Nos. 970-972 (3)	11.75	11.75
Nos. 825-827 (3)	13.50	13.50
Nos. 577-581 (5)	14.40	14.40
Nos. 821-823 (3)	7.25	7.25
Nos. 1171-1173 (3)	8.75	8.75
Nos. 320-322 (3)	20.00	20.00
Nos. 732-734 (3)	16.75	16.75
Nos. 1004-1006 (3)	25.00	25.00
Set total (44) Stamps	235.40	235.40

Prince William, 21st Birthday

CD364

2003

Ascension.......................................826
British Indian Ocean Territory 265
Cayman Islands.......................882-884
Falkland Islands 829
South Georgia 295
Tokelau 323
Tristan da Cunha............................735
Virgin Islands.......................1007-1009

No. 826 (1)	7.50	7.50
No. 265 (1)	9.00	9.00
Nos. 882-884 (3)	7.65	7.65
No. 829 (1)	14.50	14.50
No. 295 (1)	9.00	9.00
No. 323 (1)	7.25	7.25
No. 735 (1)	6.00	6.00
Nos. 1007-1009 (3)	10.00	10.00
Set total (12) Stamps	70.90	70.90

50A

2016 Minkus Supplements

Whether you're updating your album or decided to start collecting a new country, Minkus supplements are the way to go. Heavy acid-free paper and the use of Scott numbers for easy identification makes collecting easy.

Country	Item No.	Retail	AA	Release Date
All-American				
All-American Part 1: US Reg Issues & Commems	MAA116	22.99	19.99	February
All-American Part 3: United Nations	MAA316	25.99	21.99	March
All-American Part 4: US Booklet Panes	MAA416	16.99	13.99	April
All-American Part 5: US Sheetlets	MAA516	22.99	19.99	April
All-American Part 6: US Plate Number Coils	MAA616	11.99	9.99	January
U.S. & U.N 3-Ring				
U.S. Booklet Panes	MUBK16	19.99	16.99	April
U.S. Commemoratives	MUSC16	16.99	13.99	February
U.S. Plate Blocks	MSPB16	22.99	19.99	April
U.S. Plate Number Coils	MPNC16	11.99	9.99	January
U.S. Regular Issues	MUSR16	16.99	13.99	February
U.S. Sheetlets	MSH16	22.99	19.99	April
U.N. Imprint Blocks	MUIB16	22.99	19.99	March
U.N. Postal Stationery	MNPS16	11.99	9.99	March
U.N. Singles	MUN16	25.99	21.99	March
Worldwide				
Andorra - French & Spanish	MAND16	11.99	9.99	July
Australia	MBO116	22.99	19.99	September
Austria	MAU16	19.99	16.99	May
Belgium	MBL16	22.99	19.99	August
Dependencies of Australia	MBO216	22.99	19.99	September
Brazil	MBR16	19.99	16.99	September
Canada	MCA16	34.99	29.99	May
Cyprus	MBE516	16.99	13.99	May
Czech Republic & Slovakia	MCZ16	22.99	19.99	August
Denmark/Faroe Islands/ Greenland/Iceland	MSC116	28.99	24.99	June
Finland	MSC216	22.99	19.99	June
France	MFR16	34.99	29.99	May
Germany	MGM16	16.99	13.99	May
Gibraltar	MBE416	16.99	13.99	May

Country	Item No.	Retail	AA	Release Date
Worldwide				
Great Britian, Ireland	MBE116	28.99	24.99	May
Greece	MGR16	22.99	19.99	June
Guernsey, Jersey, Isle of Man	MBE216	37.99	32.99	May
Hong Kong	MBA216	22.99	19.99	May
Hungary	MHU16	22.99	19.99	August
India	MIN116	22.99	19.99	July
Ireland	MIR16	16.99	13.99	May
Israel Singles	MIS16	16.99	13.99	August
Israel Tab Singles	MIST16	19.99	16.99	August
Italy	MIT16	22.99	19.99	July
Japan	MJA16	45.99	39.99	July
Latvia, Lithuania, Estonia	MSC516	19.99	16.99	August
Liechtenstein	MLT16	16.99	13.99	June
Luxembourg	MLX16	11.99	9.99	August
Malta	MBE316	16.99	13.99	May
Mexico	MMX16	19.99	16.99	September
Monaco	MMO16	16.99	13.99	May
Netherlands	MNE16	37.99	32.99	August
New Zealand	MBO316	22.99	19.99	September
Norway	MSC316	11.99	9.99	June
People's Republic of China	MPRC16	22.99	19.99	July
Poland	MPO16	19.99	16.99	August
Portugal	MPT16	22.99	19.99	July
Republic of China-Taiwan	MCT16	22.99	19.99	July
Russia	MRU16	34.99	29.99	September
San Marino	MSM16	11.99	9.99	July
Spain	MSP16	22.99	19.99	July
Sweden	MSC416	16.99	13.99	September
Switzerland	MSWZ16	16.99	13.99	June
Vatican City	MVA16	11.99	9.99	July
Global				
Global Part 1 (Countries U.S. & A-K)	MGL117	160.99	140.00	December
Global Part 2 (Countries L-Z)	MGL217	160.99	140.00	December

Visit AmosAdvantage.com

or Call 1-800-572-6885

Outside U.S. & Canada 937-498-0800
Mail to: P.O. Box 4129, Sidney OH 45365

British Commonwealth of Nations

Dominions, Colonies, Territories, Offices and Independent Members

Comprising stamps of the British Commonwealth and associated nations.

A strict observance of technicalities would bar some or all of the stamps listed under Burma, Ireland, Kuwait, Nepal, New Republic, Orange Free State, Samoa, South Africa, South-West Africa, Stellaland, Sudan, Swaziland, the two Transvaal Republics and others but these are included for the convenience of collectors.

1. Great Britain

Great Britain: Including England, Scotland, Wales and Northern Ireland.

2. The Dominions, Present and Past

AUSTRALIA

The Commonwealth of Australia was proclaimed on January 1, 1901. It consists of six former colonies as follows:

New South Wales	Victoria
Queensland	Tasmania
South Australia	Western Australia

The following islands and territories are, or have been, administered by Australia: Australian Antarctic Territory, Christmas Island, Cocos (Keeling) Islands, Nauru, New Guinea, Norfolk Island, Papua.

CANADA

The Dominion of Canada was created by the British North America Act in 1867. The following provinces were former sepa- rate colonies and issued postage stamps:

British Columbia and Vancouver Island	Newfoundland
New Brunswick	Nova Scotia
	Prince Edward Island

FIJI

The colony of Fiji became an independent nation with dominion status on Oct. 10, 1970.

GHANA

This state came into existence Mar. 6, 1957, with dominion status. It consists of the former colony of the Gold Coast and the Trusteeship Territory of Togoland. Ghana became a republic July 1, 1960.

INDIA

The Republic of India was inaugurated on January 26, 1950. It succeeded the Dominion of India which was proclaimed August 15, 1947, when the former Empire of India was divided into Pakistan and the Union of India. The Republic is composed of about 40 predominantly Hindu states of three classes: governor's provinces, chief commissioner's provinces and princely states. India also has various territories, such as the Andaman and Nicobar Islands.

The old Empire of India was a federation of British India and the native states. The more important princely states were autonomous. Of the more than 700 Indian states, these 43 are familiar names to philatelists because of their postage stamps.

CONVENTION STATES

Chamba	Jhind
Faridkot	Nabha
Gwalior	Patiala

FEUDATORY STATES

Alwar	Jammu and Kashmir
Bahawalpur	Jasdan
Bamra	Jhalawar
Barwani	Jhind (1875-76)
Bhopal	Kashmir
Bhor	Kishangarh
Bijawar	Kotah
Bundi	Las Bela
Bussahir	Morvi
Charkhari	Nandgaon
Cochin	Nowanuggur
Dhar	Orchha
Dungarpur	Poonch
Duttia	Rajasthan
Faridkot (1879-85)	Rajpeepla
Hyderabad	Sirmur
Idar	Soruth
Indore	Tonk
Jaipur	Travancore
Jammu	Wadhwan

NEW ZEALAND

Became a dominion on September 26, 1907. The following islands and territories are, or have been, administered by New Zealand:

Aitutaki	Ross Dependency
Cook Islands (Rarotonga)	Samoa (Western Samoa)
Niue	Tokelau Islands
Penrhyn	

PAKISTAN

The Republic of Pakistan was proclaimed March 23, 1956. It succeeded the Dominion which was proclaimed August 15, 1947. It is made up of all or part of several Moslem provinces and various districts of the former Empire of India, including Bahawalpur and Las Bela. Pakistan withdrew from the Commonwealth in 1972.

SOUTH AFRICA

Under the terms of the South African Act (1909) the self-governing colonies of Cape of Good Hope, Natal, Orange River Colony and Transvaal united on May 31, 1910, to form the Union of South Africa. It became an independent republic May 3, 1961.

Under the terms of the Treaty of Versailles, South-West Africa, formerly German South-West Africa, was mandated to the Union of South Africa.

SRI LANKA (CEYLON)

The Dominion of Ceylon was proclaimed February 4, 1948. The island had been a Crown Colony from 1802 until then. On May 22, 1972, Ceylon became the Republic of Sri Lanka.

3. Colonies, Past and Present; Controlled Territory and Independent Members of the Commonwealth

Aden	Bechuanaland
Aitutaki	Bechuanaland Prot.
Anguilla	Belize
Antigua	Bermuda
Ascension	Botswana
Bahamas	British Antarctic Territory
Bahrain	British Central Africa
Bangladesh	British Columbia and
Barbados	Vancouver Island
Barbuda	British East Africa
Basutoland	British Guiana
Batum	

British Honduras
British Indian Ocean Territory
British New Guinea
British Solomon Islands
British Somaliland
Brunei
Burma
Bushire
Cameroons
Cape of Good Hope
Cayman Islands
Christmas Island
Cocos (Keeling) Islands
Cook Islands
Crete,
  British Administration
Cyprus
Dominica
East Africa & Uganda
  Protectorates
Egypt
Falkland Islands
Fiji
Gambia
German East Africa
Gibraltar
Gilbert Islands
Gilbert & Ellice Islands
Gold Coast
Grenada
Griqualand West
Guernsey
Guyana
Heligoland
Hong Kong
Indian Native States
  (see India)
Ionian Islands
Jamaica
Jersey

Kenya
Kenya, Uganda & Tanzania
Kuwait
Labuan
Lagos
Leeward Islands
Lesotho
Madagascar
Malawi
Malaya
  Federated Malay States
  Johore
  Kedah
  Kelantan
  Malacca
  Negri Sembilan
  Pahang
  Penang
  Perak
  Perlis
  Selangor
  Singapore
  Sungei Ujong
  Trengganu
Malaysia
Maldive Islands
Malta
Man, Isle of
Mauritius
Mesopotamia
Montserrat
Muscat
Namibia
Natal
Nauru
Nevis
New Britain
New Brunswick
Newfoundland
New Guinea

New Hebrides
New Republic
New South Wales
Niger Coast Protectorate
Nigeria
Niue
Norfolk Island
North Borneo
Northern Nigeria
Northern Rhodesia
North West Pacific Islands
Nova Scotia
Nyasaland Protectorate
Oman
Orange River Colony
Palestine
Papua New Guinea
Penrhyn Island
Pitcairn Islands
Prince Edward Island
Queensland
Rhodesia
Rhodesia & Nyasaland
Ross Dependency
Sabah
St. Christopher
St. Helena
St. Kitts
St. Kitts-Nevis-Anguilla
St. Lucia
St. Vincent
Samoa
Sarawak
Seychelles
Sierra Leone
Solomon Islands
Somaliland Protectorate
South Arabia
South Australia
South Georgia

Southern Nigeria
Southern Rhodesia
South-West Africa
Stellaland
Straits Settlements
Sudan
Swaziland
Tanganyika
Tanzania
Tasmania
Tobago
Togo
Tokelau Islands
Tonga
Transvaal
Trinidad
Trinidad and Tobago
Tristan da Cunha
Trucial States
Turks and Caicos
Turks Islands
Tuvalu
Uganda
United Arab Emirates
Victoria
Virgin Islands
Western Australia
Zambia
Zanzibar
Zululand

**POST OFFICES IN
FOREIGN COUNTRIES**
  Africa
    East Africa Forces
    Middle East Forces
  Bangkok
  China
  Morocco
  Turkish Empire

Colonies, Former Colonies, Offices, Territories Controlled by Parent States

Belgium
Belgian Congo
Ruanda-Urundi

Denmark
Danish West Indies
Faroe Islands
Greenland
Iceland

Finland
Aland Islands

France
COLONIES PAST AND PRESENT, CONTROLLED TERRITORIES
Afars & Issas, Territory of
Alaouites
Alexandretta
Algeria
Alsace & Lorraine
Anjouan
Annam & Tonkin
Benin
Cambodia (Khmer)
Cameroun
Castellorizo
Chad
Cilicia
Cochin China
Comoro Islands
Dahomey
Diego Suarez
Djibouti (Somali Coast)
Fezzan
French Congo
French Equatorial Africa
French Guiana
French Guinea
French India
French Morocco
French Polynesia (Oceania)
French Southern & Antarctic Territories
French Sudan
French West Africa
Gabon
Germany
Ghadames
Grand Comoro
Guadeloupe
Indo-China
Inini
Ivory Coast
Laos
Latakia
Lebanon
Madagascar
Martinique
Mauritania
Mayotte
Memel
Middle Congo
Moheli
New Caledonia
New Hebrides
Niger Territory
Nossi-Be
Obock
Reunion
Rouad, Ile
Ste.-Marie de Madagascar
St. Pierre & Miquelon
Senegal
Senegambia & Niger
Somali Coast
Syria
Tahiti
Togo
Tunisia
Ubangi-Shari
Upper Senegal & Niger
Upper Volta
Viet Nam
Wallis & Futuna Islands

POST OFFICES IN FOREIGN COUNTRIES
China
Crete
Egypt
Turkish Empire
Zanzibar

Germany
EARLY STATES
Baden
Bavaria
Bergedorf
Bremen
Brunswick
Hamburg
Hanover
Lubeck
Mecklenburg-Schwerin
Mecklenburg-Strelitz
Oldenburg
Prussia
Saxony
Schleswig-Holstein
Wurttemberg

FORMER COLONIES
Cameroun (Kamerun)
Caroline Islands
German East Africa
German New Guinea
German South-West Africa
Kiauchau
Mariana Islands
Marshall Islands
Samoa
Togo

Italy
EARLY STATES
Modena
Parma
Romagna
Roman States
Sardinia
Tuscany
Two Sicilies
  Naples
  Neapolitan Provinces
  Sicily

FORMER COLONIES, CONTROLLED TERRITORIES, OCCUPATION AREAS
Aegean Islands
  Calimno (Calino)
  Caso
  Cos (Coo)
  Karki (Carchi)
  Leros (Lero)
  Lipso
  Nisiros (Nisiro)
  Patmos (Patmo)
  Piscopi
  Rodi (Rhodes)
  Scarpanto
  Simi
  Stampalia
Castellorizo
Corfu
Cyrenaica
Eritrea
Ethiopia (Abyssinia)
Fiume
Ionian Islands
  Cephalonia
  Ithaca
  Paxos
Italian East Africa
Libya
Oltre Giuba
Saseno
Somalia (Italian Somaliland)
Tripolitania

POST OFFICES IN FOREIGN COUNTRIES
"ESTERO"*
Austria
China
  Peking
  Tientsin
Crete
Tripoli
Turkish Empire
  Constantinople
  Durazzo
  Janina
Jerusalem
Salonika
Scutari
Smyrna
Valona
*Stamps overprinted "ESTERO" were used in various parts of the world.

Netherlands
Aruba
Caribbean Netherlands
Curacao
Netherlands Antilles (Curacao)
Netherlands Indies
Netherlands New Guinea
St. Martin
Surinam (Dutch Guiana)

Portugal
COLONIES PAST AND PRESENT, CONTROLLED TERRITORIES
Angola
Angra
Azores
Cape Verde
Funchal
Horta
Inhambane
Kionga
Lourenco Marques
Macao
Madeira
Mozambique
Mozambique Co.
Nyassa
Ponta Delgada
Portuguese Africa
Portuguese Congo
Portuguese Guinea
Portuguese India
Quelimane
St. Thomas & Prince Islands
Tete
Timor
Zambezia

Russia
ALLIED TERRITORIES AND REPUBLICS, OCCUPATION AREAS
Armenia
Aunus (Olonets)
Azerbaijan
Batum
Estonia
Far Eastern Republic
Georgia
Karelia
Latvia
Lithuania
North Ingermanland
Ostland
Russian Turkestan
Siberia
South Russia
Tannu Tuva
Transcaucasian Fed. Republics
Ukraine
Wenden (Livonia)
Western Ukraine

Spain
COLONIES PAST AND PRESENT, CONTROLLED TERRITORIES
Aguera, La
Cape Juby
Cuba
Elobey, Annobon & Corisco
Fernando Po
Ifni
Mariana Islands
Philippines
Puerto Rico
Rio de Oro
Rio Muni
Spanish Guinea
Spanish Morocco
Spanish Sahara
Spanish West Africa

POST OFFICES IN FOREIGN COUNTRIES
Morocco
Tangier
Tetuan

Dies of British Colonial Stamps

DIE A:

1. The lines in the groundwork vary in thickness and are not uniformly straight.

2. The seventh and eighth lines from the top, in the groundwork, converge where they meet the head.

3. There is a small dash in the upper part of the second jewel in the band of the crown.

4. The vertical color line in front of the throat stops at the sixth line of shading on the neck.

DIE B:

1. The lines in the groundwork are all thin and straight.

2. All the lines of the background are parallel.

3. There is no dash in the upper part of the second jewel in the band of the crown.

4. The vertical color line in front of the throat stops at the eighth line of shading on the neck.

DIE I:

1. The base of the crown is well below the level of the inner white line around the vignette.

2. The labels inscribed "POSTAGE" and "REVENUE" are cut square at the top.

3. There is a white "bud" on the outer side of the main stem of the curved ornaments in each lower corner.

4. The second (thick) line below the country name has the ends next to the crown cut diagonally.

DIE Ia.	DIE Ib.
1 as die II.	1 and 3 as die II.
2 and 3 as die I.	2 as die I.

DIE II:

1. The base of the crown is aligned with the underside of the white line around the vignette.

2. The labels curve inward at the top inner corners.

3. The "bud" has been removed from the outer curve of the ornaments in each corner.

4. The second line below the country name has the ends next to the crown cut vertically.

Wmk. 1
Crown and C C

Wmk. 2
Crown and C A

Wmk. 3
Multiple Crown
and C A

Wmk. 4
Multiple Crown
and Script C A

Wmk. 4a

Wmk. 314
St. Edward's Crown
and C A Multiple

Wmk. 373

Wmk. 384

Wmk. 406

British Colonial and Crown Agents Watermarks

Watermarks 1 to 4, 314, 373, 384 and 406, common to many British territories, are illustrated here to avoid duplication.

The letters "CC" of Wmk. 1 identify the paper as having been made for the use of the Crown Colonies, while the letters "CA" of the others stand for "Crown Agents." Both Wmks. 1 and 2 were used on stamps printed by De La Rue & Co.

Wmk. 3 was adopted in 1904; Wmk. 4 in 1921; Wmk. 314 in 1957; Wmk. 373 in 1974; Wmk. 384 in 1985; Wmk 406 in 2008.

In Wmk. 4a, a non-matching crown of the general St. Edwards type (bulging on both sides at top) was substituted for one of the Wmk. 4 crowns which fell off the dandy roll. The non-matching crown occurs in 1950-52 printings in a horizontal row of crowns on certain regular stamps of Johore and Seychelles, and on various postage due stamps of Barbados, Basutoland, British Guiana, Gold Coast, Grenada, Northern Rhodesia, St. Lucia, Swaziland and Trinidad and Tobago. A variation of Wmk. 4a, with the non-matching crown in a horizontal row of crown-CA-crown, occurs on regular stamps of Bahamas, St. Kitts-Nevis and Singapore.

Wmk. 314 was intentionally used sideways, starting in 1966. When a stamp was issued with Wmk. 314 both upright and sideways, the sideways varieties usually are listed also – with minor numbers. In many of the later issues, Wmk. 314 is slightly visible.

Wmk. 373 is usually only faintly visible.

ScottMounts

PRE-CUT SINGLE MOUNTS

ITEM	W x H (MM)	DESCRIPTION	MOUNTS	RETAIL	AA*
901	40 x 25	U.S. Standard Comm. Horizontal Water Activated	40	$3.50	$2.39
902	25 x 40	U.S. Standard Comm. Vertical Water Activated	40	$3.50	$2.39
903	25 x 22	U.S. Regular Issue – Horizontal Water Activated	40	$3.50	$2.39
904	22 x 25	U.S. Regular Issue – Vertical Water Activated	40	$3.50	$2.39
905	41 x 31	U.S. Semi-Jumbo - Horizontal	40	$3.50	$2.39
906	31 x 41	U.S. Semi-Jumbo – Vertical	40	$3.50	$2.39
907	50 x 31	U.S. Jumbo - Horizontal	40	$3.50	$2.39
908	31 x 50	U.S. Jumbo – Vertical	40	$3.50	$2.39
909	25 x 27	U.S. Regular Issues Self-Adhesive	40	$3.50	$2.39
910	33 x 27	United Nations	40	$3.50	$2.39
911	40 x 27	U.S. Commemoratives; United Nations Self-Adhesive	40	$3.50	$2.39
976	67 x 25	U.S. Plate Number Coil Strips of 3	40	$6.25	$3.99
984	67 x 34	Triangle shaped (Pacific '97)	10	$3.50	$2.39
985	111 x 25	U.S. Plate Number Coil Strips of 5	25	$6.25	$3.99
986	51 x 36	U.S. Hunting Permit (Duck Stamps); Express Mail	40	$6.25	$3.99
1045	40 x 26	U.S. Commemorative - Horizontal Self-Adhesive	40	$3.50	$2.39
1046	25 x 41	U.S. Commemorative - Vertical Self-Adhesive	40	$3.50	$2.39
1047	22 x 26	U.S. Definitives - Vertical Self-Adhesive	40	$3.50	$2.39
966	Value Pack	(Assortment Pre-Cut Sizes 40 ea)	320	$23.25	$15.25
975 B	Best Pack	((Assortment Pre-Cut Sizes 20 ea - Black Only))	160	$14.75	$9.99

PRE-CUT PLATE BLOCK, FDC, POSTAL CARD MOUNTS

ITEM	W x H (MM)	DESCRIPTION	MOUNTS	RETAIL	AA*
912	57 x 55	U.S. Regular Issue Plate Block	25	$6.25	$3.99
913	73 x 63	U.S. Champions of Liberty Plate Block	25	$6.25	$3.99
914	106 x 55	U.S. Rotary Press Standard Comm. Plate Block	20	$6.25	$3.99
915	105 x 57	U.S. Giori Press Standard Comm. Plate Block	20	$6.25	$3.99
916	127 x 70	U.S. Giori Press Jumbo Comm. Plate Block	10	$6.25	$3.99
917	165 x 94	U.S. First Day Cover	10	$6.25	$3.99
918	140 x 90	U.S. Postal Card, Submarine Booklet Pane, Cycling S/S	10	$6.25	$3.99
1048	152 x 107	Modern/Large U.S. Postal Cards	8	$10.25	$6.99

STRIPS 215MM LONG

ITEM	W x H (MM)	DESCRIPTION	MOUNTS	RETAIL	AA*
919	20	U.S. 19th Century, Horizontal Coil	22	$7.99	$5.25
920	22	U.S. Early Air Mail, 20th Century Horizontal Coils, Windmills strip	22	$7.99	$5.25
921	24	U.S. Vertical Coils, Xmas, Jamestown, Canada, Great Britain	22	$7.99	$5.25
922	25	U.S. Commemoratives and Regulars	22	$7.99	$5.25
1049	26	U.S. Commemoratives and Regulars Self-Adhesive	22	$7.99	$5.25
923	27	U.S. Self-Adhesive	22	$7.99	$5.25
924	28	U.S. Famous American, Champions of Liberty, 19th Century	22	$7.99	$5.25
925	30	U.S. 19th Century, Foreign	22	$7.99	$5.25
926	31	U.S. Horizontal Jumbo and Semi-Jumbo (Elvis, Cats, etc)	22	$7.99	$5.25
927	33	U.S. Speedboats strip; United Nations	22	$7.99	$5.25
928	36	U.S. Hunting Permit, Express Mail, Canada	15	$7.99	$5.25
929	39	U.S. Early 20th Century; 8c Magsaysay	15	$7.99	$5.25
930	41	U.S. Vertical Semi-Jumbo (1977 Lafayette, Pottery, etc)	15	$7.99	$5.25
931		Multiple Assortment: 1 Strip of each size 22-41 (2 x 25mm strips)	12	$7.99	$5.25
932	44	U.S. Vertical Coil Pair, Garden Flowers booklet panes	15	$7.99	$5.25
933	48	U.S. Farleys, Gutter Pair	15	$7.99	$5.25
934	50	U.S. Jumbo (Lyndon Johnson, 1974 UPU, etc)	15	$7.99	$5.25
935	52	U.S. Standard Commemorative. Horizontal Block	15	$7.99	$5.25
936	55	U.S. Standard Plate Block - Normal Margins	15	$7.99	$5.25
937	57	U.S. Standard Plate Block - Wider Margins	15	$7.99	$5.25
938	61	U.S. Christmas Madonna Booklet Pane	15	$7.99	$5.25

STRIPS 240MM LONG

ITEM	W x H (MM)	DESCRIPTION	MOUNTS	RETAIL	AA*
939	63	U.S. Jumbo Comm. Horizontal Block; Air Mail Plate Blocks	10	$9.25	$5.99
940	66	U.S. Self-Adhesive Booklet Panes, Space Achievement block of 8	10	$9.25	$5.99
941	68	U.S. CIPEX S/S; U.S. ATM Booklet Panes, Ducks Panes	10	$9.25	$5.99
942	74	U.S. Souvenir Sheets (FIPEX, TIPEX, CAPEX, etc.)	10	$9.25	$5.99
943	80	U.S. Comm. Vertical Blocks, Rio Grande Blankets	10	$9.25	$5.99
944	82	U.S. Large Blocks, U.N. Chagall Souvenir Sheet	10	$9.25	$5.99
945	84	Washington 2006, Mars Pathfinder, Diplomats, Israel Tab Block	10	$9.25	$5.99
946	89	2013 Jenny Invert, Supreme Court Justices, Postal Cards	10	$9.25	$5.99
947	100	U.S. 1974 UPU Block, U.N. Margin Block	7	$9.25	$5.99
948	120	Souvenir Sheets (Franklin/Washington, etc) & Blocks	7	$9.25	$5.99

STRIPS 265MM LONG

ITEM	W x H (MM)	DESCRIPTION	MOUNTS	RETAIL	AA*
1035	25	U.S. Long Coil Strips of 10 or 11, U.S. Horizontal Comm.	12	$9.25	$5.99
949	40	U.S. Commemorative Strip (Postal People, Historic Flags)	10	$9.25	$5.99
981	44	U.S. Long Self-Adhesive Booklet Panes of 15	10	$9.25	$5.99
1030	45	U.S. $9.35 Express Mail, Canada #1725-34, etc.	10	$9.25	$5.99
1036	46	U.S. Long Self-Adhesive Booklet Panes of 15 & 20	10	$9.25	$5.99
950	55	U.S. Regular Plate Block or Strip of 20	10	$9.25	$5.99
951	59	U.S. Double Issue Strip	10	$9.25	$5.99
952	70	Children's Book Animals, U.S. Jumbo Comm. Plate Block	10	$12.50	$8.50
1031	72	Various, Canada, etc.	10	$12.50	$8.50
1032	75	Plate Blocks: Louis Armstrong, Prehistoric Animals, Canada, etc.	10	$12.50	$8.50
953	91	U.S. Self-Adhesive Booklet Pane (Love Swans, '98 Wreaths, etc)	10	$12.50	$8.50
1033	95	U.S. Old Glory Booklet Pane, Mini-Sheet Plate Blocks, Canada	10	$12.50	$8.50
954	105	U.S. Comm. Plate Block Strip of 20; Harry Potter, Postal Cards	10	$12.50	$8.50
955	107	Same as Above - Wider Margins	10	$12.50	$8.50
956	111	Large Postal Cards; U.S. Gravure - Intaglio Plate Number Strip	10	$14.75	$9.99
957	127	U.S. Purple Heart sheet, Jumbo Comm. Plate Strip	10	$17.50	$11.99
958	137	2002 Snowmen sheet, Great Britain Coronation	10	$17.50	$11.99
959	158	Tail Fins & Chrome, Civil Rights Pioneers, American Glass	10	$17.99	$12.50

STRIPS 265MM LONG - Continued

ITEM	W x H (MM)	DESCRIPTION	MOUNTS	RETAIL	AA*
960	175	Sheets: Wilt Chamberlain, Speedboats, All Aboard!, Caulder	5	$12.50	$8.50
961	231	U.S. Full Sheets: State Flags, Birds & Flowers, Wildflowers, etc.	5	$17.99	$12.50

SOUVENIR SHEETS/SMALL PANES

ITEM	W x H (MM)	DESCRIPTION	MOUNTS	RETAIL	AA*
962	204 x 153	U.S. Bicentennial, White Plains, New Year Baby	4	$9.25	$5.99
963	187 x 144	U.S. Earthscapes, Cloudscapes, Cinco de Mayo, U.N. Flag	9	$15.50	$10.25
964	160 x 200	U.N., Israel Sheets	10	$15.50	$10.25
965	120 x 207	U.S. AMERIPEX	4	$6.25	$3.99
968	229 x 131	World War II S/S Plate Block Only	5	$9.25	$5.99
970	111 x 91	Columbus Souvenir Sheets	6	$6.25	$4.75
972	148 x 196	Apollo Moon Landing/Carnivorous Plants	4	$7.99	$5.25
989	129 x 122	U.S. Definitive Sheet- Harte, Hopkins, etc.	8	$10.25	$6.99
990	189 x 151	Chinese New Year Sheets (regular gum)	5	$10.25	$6.99
991	150 x 185	Frank Sinatra, Ronald Reagan, Arthur Ashe, Breast Cancer, etc.	5	$10.25	$6.99
992	198 x 151	1993 Cherokee Strip Sheet	5	$10.25	$6.99
993	185 x 151	Chinese New Year, 2009 Lincoln, 99-06 U.S. Airmail sheets, etc.	5	$10.25	$6.99
994	198 x 187	Postal Museum, Popular Singers (mounted sideways)	4	$10.25	$6.99
995	156 x 187	Innovative Choreographers, Sign Language	5	$10.25	$6.99
996	188 x 197	Alzheimer's, Illustrators, Gospel, Reptiles, Comic Superheroes	4	$10.25	$6.99
997	151 x 192	World Stamp Show-NY 2016, Lighthouses, Olympics	5	$10.25	$6.99
998	174 x 185	Buffalo Soldiers	5	$10.25	$6.99
999	130 x 198	Silent Screen Stars Block of 20	5	$10.25	$6.99
1000	190 x 199	Stars Stripes, Soldiers, Baseball Legends, Civil War, Comics	4	$10.25	$6.99
1001	178 x 181	Janis Joplin, Elvis, Jimi Hendrix, Ray Charles, Johnny Cash, etc.	4	$10.25	$6.99
1002	183 x 212	Let's Dance, Wonders of the Sea	3	$10.25	$6.99
1003	156 x 264	$14 Eagle Sheet	4	$10.25	$6.99
1004	159 x 270	$9.95 Moon Landing Sheet	4	$10.25	$6.99
1005	159 x 259	$2.90 Priority, $9.95 Express Mail	4	$10.25	$6.99
1006	223 x 187	Batman, Hollywood Legends, Early TV Memories, Hubble Space	3	$10.25	$6.99
1007	185 x 181	Motorcycles, X-Planes, Deep Sea Creatures, Challenger Shuttle	4	$10.25	$6.99
1008	152 x 228	Indian Dances, Antique Autos Sheets	3	$10.25	$6.99
1009	165 x 150	Happy Birthday, Riverboats, Hanukkah, Shelter Pets (trimmed)	6	$10.25	$6.99
1010	275 x 200	World of Dinosaurs Sheets, Large Gutter Blocks	2	$10.25	$6.99
1011	161 x 160	Poets (trimmed)	6	$10.25	$6.99
1012	174 x 130	Road Runner, Daffy Duck, Bugs Bunny, Sylvester/Tweety	6	$10.25	$6.99
1013	196 x 158	Football Coaches, American Glass Sheets, Civil Rights Pioneers	4	$10.25	$6.99
1014	184 x 184	Greta Garbo, Child Health, Football Heroes, American Dolls	4	$10.25	$6.99
1015	186 x 230	Classic Movie Monsters Sheet	3	$10.25	$6.99
1016	187 x 160	Muscle Cars, Civil Rights, Peanuts, Trans-Mississippi	4	$10.25	$6.99
1017	192 x 230	Celebrate the Century	3	$10.25	$6.99
1018	156 x 204	Black Cinema, 1998 Space Discovery Sheet	5	$10.25	$6.99
1019	182 x 209	American Ballet, Disney, Teddy Bears	5	$10.25	$6.99
1020	139 x 151	Christmas Wreaths Sheet (use sideways for Xmas Deer)	5	$10.25	$6.99
1021	129 x 126	10¢ Clock, 60¢ Coverlet Eagle, Claude Pepper, J. Stillwell	8	$10.25	$6.99
1022	184 x 165	Baseball All-Stars, Cherry Blossoms, Baseball Fields	4	$10.25	$6.99
1023	185 x 172	Shuttle Landing Sheet	4	$10.25	$6.99
1024	172 x 233	Civil War, Kelp Forest, Dunes, Wetlands, Reef, Tundra, Prairie	3	$10.25	$6.99
1025	150 x 166	Prostate Cancer Sheet	5	$10.25	$6.99
1026	201 x 176	All Aboard!, Trains Sheet	4	$10.25	$6.99
1027	176 x 124	Canada - Historic Vehicles	5	$10.25	$6.99
1028	245 x 114	Canada - Provincial Leaders	5	$10.25	$6.99
1029	177 x 133	Canada - Year of the Family	5	$10.25	$6.99
1034	181 x 213	Arctic Animals Sheet	3	$10.25	$6.99
1037	179 x 242	Louise Nevelson Sheet	3	$10.25	$6.99
1038	179 x 217	Jamestown (mounted sideways), Library of Congress Sheets	3	$10.25	$6.99
1039	182 x 232	Youth Team Sports Sheet	3	$10.25	$6.99
1040	183 x 216	Bob Hope Sheet (mounted sideways)	3	$10.25	$6.99
1041	182 x 244	Star Wars (not Yoda), American Photography Sheets	3	$10.25	$6.99
1042	185 x 255	Andy Warhol Sheet	3	$10.25	$6.99
1043	165 x 190	Filmmaking Sheet	4	$10.25	$6.99
1044	28 x 290	American Eagle PNC Strips of 11	12	$9.25	$6.99

Available in clear or black backgrounds. Please specify color choice when ordering.

2016 NATIONAL, MINUTEMAN OR ALL-AMERICAN SUPPLEMENT MOUNT PACKS

ITEM	DESCRIPTION	RETAIL	AA*
2016 B	2016 National, Minuteman or All-American Supplement Mount Pack - BLACK	$49.99	$39.99
2016 C	2016 National, Minuteman or All-American Supplement Mount Pack - CLEAR	$49.99	$39.99

Visit AmosAdvantage.com
Call 1-800-572-6885
Outside U.S. & Canada 937-498-0800
Mail to: P.O. Box 4129, Sidney OH 45365

AMOS ADVANTAGE

UNITED STATES

yu-ˌnī-təd 'stāts

GOVT. — Republic
AREA — 3,615,211 sq. mi.
POP. — 308,745,538 (2010)
CAPITAL — Washington, DC

In addition to the 50 States and the District of Columbia, the Republic includes Guam, the Commonwealth of Puerto Rico, the Virgin Islands, American Samoa, Wake, Midway, and a number of small islands in the Pacific Ocean, all of which use stamps of the United States.

100 Cents = 1 Dollar

Catalogue values for unused stamps in this country are for Never Hinged items, beginning with Scott 772 in the regular postage section, Scott C19 in the air post section, Scott E17 in the special delivery section, Scott FA1 in the certified mail section, Scott O127 in officials section, Scott J88 in the postage due section, Scott RW1 in the hunting permit stamps section.

Watermarks

Wmk. 190 — "USPS" in Single-lined Capitals

Wmk. 191 — Double-lined "USPS" in Capitals

Watermark 191 has 9 letters for each horizontal row of 10 stamps. Watermark 190 has 8 to 9 letters for each horizontal row. Each watermark has 9 letters for each vertical row of 10 stamps This results in a number of stamps in each pane showing only a small portion of 1 or more watermark letters. This is especialy true of watermark 190.

Wmk. 190PI — PIPS, used in the Philippines
Wmk. 191PI — PIPS, used in the Philippines
Wmk. 191C — US-C, used for Cuba
Wmk. 191R — USIR

PROVISIONAL ISSUES BY POSTMASTERS

Values for Envelopes are for entires.

ALEXANDRIA, VA.

A1

All known examples are cut to shape.
Type I — 40 asterisks in circle.
Type II — 39 asterisks in circle.

1846	Typeset	Imperf.
1X1	A1 5c black, buff, type I	325,000.
a.	5c black, buff, type II	625,000.
1X2	A1 5c black, blue, type I, on cover	—

ANNAPOLIS, MD.

E1

1846
2XU1 E1 5c carmine red, white 600,000.

Handstamped impressions of the circular design with "2" in blue or red exist on envelopes and letter sheets. Values: blue $17,500, red $30,000.

A letter sheet exists with circular design and "5" handstamped in red. Values: blue $10,000, red $12,500.

A similar circular design in blue was used as a postmark.

BALTIMORE, MD.

Signature of Postmaster — A1

Printed from a plate of 12 (2x6) containing nine 5c stamps and three 10c.

1845	Engr.	Imperf.
3X1	A1 5c black	6,000.
3X2	A1 10c black, on cover	80,000.
3X3	A1 5c black, bluish	65,000. 6,000.
3X4	A1 10c black, bluish	50,000.

Nos. 3X1-3X4 were printed from a plate of 12 (2x6) containing nine 5c and three 10c.

Envelopes

E1

The color given is that of the "PAID 5" and oval. "James M. Buchanan" is handstamped in black, blue or red. The paper is manila, buff, white, salmon or grayish.

1845		Handstamped
	Various Papers	
3XU1	E1 5c blue	6,500.
3XU2	E1 5c red	10,000.
3XU3	E1 10c blue	20,000.
3XU4	E1 10c red	20,000.

On the formerly listed "5+5" envelopes, the second "5" in oval is believed not to be part of the basic prepaid marking.

BOSCAWEN, N. H.

A1

1846 (?)	Typeset	Imperf.
4X1	A1 5c dull blue, yellowish, on cover	300,000.

BRATTLEBORO, VT.

Initials of Postmaster (FNP) — A1

Plate of 10 (5x2).

1846		Imperf.
Thick Softwove Paper Colored Through		
5X1	A1 5c black, buff	7,500.

LOCKPORT, N. Y.

A1

"Lockport, N.Y." oval and "PAID" separately handstamped in red, "5" in black ms.

1846		Imperf.
6X1	A1 5c red, buff, on cover	300,000.

MILLBURY, Mass.

George Washington — A1

Printed from a woodcut, singly, on a hand press.

1846		Imperf.
7X1	A1 5c black, bluish	— 50,000.

NEW HAVEN, CONN.

ENVELOPES

E1

Impressed from a handstamp at upper right of envelope.

Signed in blue, black or magenta ms., as indicated in parentheses.

1845		
8XU1	E1 5c red (M)	100,000.
8XU2	E1 5c red, light bluish (Bk)	125,000.
8XU3	E1 5c dull blue, buff (Bl)	75,000.
8XU4	E1 5c dull blue (Bl)	60,000.

Values of Nos. 8XU1-8XU4 are a guide to value. They are based on auction realizations and other sales, and take condition into consideration. All New Haven envelopes are of equal rarity (each is unique), with the exception of No. 8XU2, of which two exist. An entire of No. 8XU2 is the finest example known, and this is reflected in the value. The other envelopes are valued according to condition, and cut squares are valued according to condition as much as rarity.

Reprints were made at various times between 1871 and 1932. They can be distinguished from the originals, primarily due to differences in paper. See the Scott Specialized Catalogue of United States Stamps and Covers for more detail and values.

NEW YORK, N. Y.

George Washington — A1

Plate of 40 (5x8). Nos. 9X1-9X3 and varieties unused are valued without gum. Examples with original gum are extremely scarce and will command higher prices.

9X1	A1 5c black, signed ACM, connected, 1846	1,500.	500.
a.	Signed ACM, AC connected	1,750.	575.
b.	Signed A.C.M.	4,500.	700.
c.	Signed MMJr		10,000.
d.	Signed RHM	13,000.	3,500.
e.	Without signature	3,750.	950.

These stamps were usually initialed "ACM" in magenta ink, as a control, before being sold or passed through the mails.

A plate of 9 (3x3) was made from which proofs were printed in black on white and deep blue papers; also in blue, green, brown and red on white bond paper. Stamps from this plate were not issued, and it is possible that it is an essay, as the design differs slightly from the issued stamps from the sheet of 40. No examples from the plate of nine are known used.

1847	Engr.	Imperf.
Blue Wove Paper		
9X2	A1 5c black, signed ACM connected	6,500. 3,500.
a.	Signed RHM	
b.	Signed ACM, AC connected	8,000.
d.	Without signature	11,000. 7,500.

On the only example known of No. 9X2a the "R" is illegible and does not match those of the other "RHM" signatures.
No. 9X2b is unique.

1847	Engr.	Imperf.
Gray Wove Paper		
9X3	A1 5c black, signed ACM connected	5,250. 2,250.
a.	Signed RHM	7,000.
b.	Without signature	13,000.

PROVIDENCE, R. I.

A1 & A2

10X1	A1 5c gray black	350.	1,900.
10X2	A2 10c gray black	1,150.	16,500.
a.	Se-tenant with 5c	2,000.	

Plate of 12 (3x4) contains 11-5c and 1-10c.
Reprints were made in 1898. Each stamp bears one of the following letters on the back: B. O. G. E. R. T. D. U. R. B. I. N. Value of 5c, $65; 10c, $160; sheet, $1,000.
Reprint singles or sheets without back print sell for more.

ST. LOUIS, MO.

A1 A2

A3

Missouri Coat of Arms

Nos. 11X1-11X8 unused are valued without gum.

Wove Paper Colored Through

1845, Nov.-1846   *Imperf.*

11X1	A1	5c black, greenish	50,000. 8,000.
11X2	A2	10c black, greenish	50,000. 8,000.
11X3	A3	20c black, greenish	160,000.

Printed from Plate 1 (3 varieties each of the 5c and 10c) and Plate 2 (1 variety of the 5c, 3 of the 10c, 2 of the 20c).

1846

11X4	A1	5c black, (III), gray lilac	— 55,000.
11X5	A2	10c black, gray lilac	50,000. 12,500.
11X6	A3	20c black, gray lilac	100,000. 60,000.

One variety of 5c, 3 of 10c, 2 of 20c.
No. 11X6 unused is unique. It is in the grade of fine and valued thus.

1847   **Pelure Paper**

11X7	A1	5c black, bluish	— 11,000.
11X8	A2	10c black, bluish	17,500. 15,000.
a.		Impression of 5c on back	77,500.

Three varieties of 5c, 3 of 10c.
Values of Nos. 11X7-11X8 reflect the usual poor condition of these stamps, which were printed on fragile pelure paper. Attractive examples with minor defects sell for considerably more.
Used values are for pen-canceled stamps.
No. 11X8a is unique.

Please Note:

Stamps are valued in the grade of very fine unless otherwise indicated. Values for early and valuable stamps are for examples with certificates of authenticity from acknowledged expert committees, or examples sold with the buyer having the right of certification. This applies to examples with original gum as well as examples without gum. Beware of stamps offered "as is," as the gum on some unused stamps offered with "original gum" may be fraudulent, and stamps offered as unused without gum may in some cases be altered or faintly canceled used stamps.

Manuscript Cancels on Used Stamps

Manuscript (pen) cancels reduce the value of used stamps by about 50%. See the Scott U.S. Specialized Catalogue for individual valuations.

GENERAL ISSUES
All Issues from 1847 through 1894 are unwatermarked.

Benjamin Franklin — A1

1847, July 1   **Engr.**   *Imperf.*
Thin Bluish Wove Paper

1	A1	5c red brown	6,500.	375.
		No gum	2,300.	
		Pen Cancel		200.
a.		5c dark brown	8,750.	800.
		No gum	3,250.	
b.		5c orange brown	10,000.	750.
		No gum	3,500.	
c.		5c red orange	25,000.	9,500.
		No gum	9,500.	
d.		5c brown orange		1,000.
		No gum	4,500.	

George Washington — A2

2	A2	10c black	35,000.	800.
		No gum	15,000.	
		Pen Cancel		500.

REPRODUCTIONS of 1847 ISSUE

    A3   A4

Actually, official imitations made from new plates of 50 subjects made by the Bureau of Engraving and Printing by order of the Post Office Department. These were not valid for postal use.

5c. On the originals the left side of the white shirt frill touches the oval on a level with the top of the "F" of "Five." On the reproductions it touches the oval about on a level with the top of the figure "5." On the originals, the bottom of the right leg of the "N" in "CENTS" is blunt. On the reproductions, the "N" comes to a point at the bottom.

10c. On the reproductions, line of coat at left points to right tip of "X" and line of coat at right points to center of "S" of CENTS. On the originals, line of coat points to "T" of TEN and between "T" and "S" of CENTS. The bottom of the right leg of the "N" of "CENTS" shows the same difference as on the 5c originals and reproductions. On the reproductions, the gap between the bottom legs of the left "X" is noticeably wider than the gap on the right "X." On the originals, the gaps are of equal width. On the reproductions, the eyes have a sleepy look, the line of the mouth is straighter, and in the curl of hair near the left cheek is a strong black dot, while the originals have only a faint one.

(See Nos. 948a and 948b for 1947 reproductions—5c blue and 10c brown orange in larger size.)

1875   *Imperf.*
Bluish paper, without gum

3	A3	5c red brown	850.
4	A4	10c black	1,050.

Numbers in parentheses are quantities sold.

Except as noted here and in footnotes for selected issues, values for 1851-57 issues are for examples that clearly show all of the illustrated type characteristics. Stamps that have weakly defined or missing type characteristics sell for less.

In Nos. 5-17, the 1¢, 3¢ and 12¢ have very small margins between the stamps. The 5¢ and 10¢ have moderate size margins. The values of these stamps take the margin size into consideration.

Values for Nos. 5A, 6b and 19b are for the less distinct positions. Best examples sell for more.

Values for No. 16 are for outer line recut at top. Other recuts sell for more.

Franklin — A5

Type I

Type Ib

ONE CENT. Issued July 1, 1851.
Type I. Has complete curved lines outside the labels with "U. S. Postage" and "One Cent." The scrolls below the lower label are turned under, forming little balls. The ornaments at top are substantially complete.
Type Ib. As type I, but balls below bottom label are not as clear. Plume-like scrolls at bottom are incomplete.

1851-57   *Imperf.*

5	A5	1c blue, type I (7R1E)	225,000.	67,500.
5A	A5	1c blue, type 1b	32,500.	8,000.
		No gum	12,000.	

A6

Type Ic

Type Ia. Same as type I at bottom, but top ornaments and outer line at top are partly cut away.
Type Ic. Same as type Ia, but bottom right plume and ball ornament incomplete. Bottom left plume is complete or nearly complete.

6	A6	1c blue, type 1a ('57)	45,000.	10,500.
		No gum	20,000.	
6b	A6	1c blue, type 1c	7,000.	3,250.
		No gum	3,000.	

A7

Type II — Same as Type I at top, but the little balls of the bottom scrolls and the bottoms of the lower plume ornaments are missing. The side ornaments are substantially complete.

7	A7	1c blue, type II	1,000.	130.
		No gum	375.	

A8

Great collections have ONE NAME *in common*

Newbury 1961

Lilly 1967

Kapiloff 1992

Honolulu Advertiser 1995

Zoellner 1998

Golden 1999

Islander 2008

Whitman 2009

Twigg-Smith 2009

Frelinghuysen 2012

Gross 2013

Walske 2013

Robert A. Siegel

AUCTION GALLERIES, INC.

siegelauctions.com

Siegel offers unparalleled expertise, a worldwide client base, financial reliability,
intelligent marketing, and the best internet resources and search tools.
To discuss the sale of your U.S. stamps or postal history, call Scott Trepel at 212-753-6421.
If you have a worldwide collection, call Charles Shreve at 214-754-5991.

Type IIIa

Type III. The top and bottom curved lines outside the labels are broken in the middle. The side ornaments are substantially complete.

Type IIIa. Similar to type III with the outer line broken at top or bottom but not both.

8	A8	1c blue, type III	25,000.	1,900.
	No gum		7,500.	

Values for type III are for at least a 2mm break in each outer line. Examples of type III with wider breaks in outer lines command higher prices; those with smaller breaks sell for much less.

8A	A8	1c blue, type IIIa	6,000.	825.
	No gum		2,250.	

Stamps of type IIIa with bottom line broken command higher prices than those with top line broken. See note after No. 8 on width of break of outer lines.

A9

Type IV. Similar to type II, but with the curved lines outside the labels recut at top or bottom or both.

9	A9	1c blue, type IV ('52)	725.00	90.00
	No gum		240.00	
a.	Printed on both sides, reverse inverted			50,000.

No. 9a is unique.

The No. 9b cover, a printed-matter circular mailed in 1853, is unique. The circular likely should have been sent at the 1c rate for printed matter in effect at the time. However, both the sending (New Haven, Conn.) and receiving (Hartford, Conn.) post offices treated it as fully prepaid with ½c postage applied. Value is based on 2013 auction realization.

Washington — A10

All of the 3c stamps of the 1851 and 1857 issues were recut at least to the extent of the outer frame lines, sometimes the inner lines at the sides (type II stamps), and often other lines in triangles, diamond blocks, label blocks and/or top/bottom frame lines. Some of the most prominent varieties are listed below each major listing (others are described in "The 3c Stamp of U.S. 1851-57 Issue," by Carroll Chase).

OUTER FRAME LINE

Type I

THREE CENTS.

Type I — There is an outer frame line on all four sides. The outer frame lines at the sides are always recut.

10	A10	3c org brown, type I	4,000.	190.00
	No gum		1,500.	

OUTER FRAME LINE

INNER LINE

Type II

Type II — As type I, but with the inner lines at the sides added by recutting on the plate.

10A	A10	3c org brown, type II	3,250.	150.00
	No gum		1,250.	
b.	Printed on both sides			55,000.

Only one example of No. 10Ab is recorded.

11	A10	3c dull red, type I ('55)	275.00	15.00
	No gum		100.00	

11A	A10	3c dull red, type II ('53-'55)	250.00	15.00
	No gum		85.00	
e.	Double impression			30,000.

Thomas Jefferson — A11

FIVE CENTS.

Type I — Projections on all four sides.

12	A11	5c red brown, type I ('56)	30,000.	700.
	No gum		11,000.	

Washington — A12

TEN CENTS

Type I — The "shells" at the lower corners are practically complete. The outer line below the label is very nearly complete. The outer lines are broken above the middle of the top label and the "X" in each upper corner.

13	A12	10c green, type I ('55)	19,000.	850.
	No gum		8,500.	

A13

Type II — The design is complete at the top. The outer line at the bottom is broken in the middle. The shells are partly cut away, as shown.

14	A13	10c green, type II ('55)	5,000.	150.
	No gum		1,800.	

A14

Type III — The outer lines are broken above the top label and the "X" numerals. The outer line at the bottom and the shells are partly cut away, as shown, similar to type II.

15	A14	10c green, type III ('55)	5,000.	150.
	No gum		1,800.	

A15

Type IV. The outer lines have been recut at top or bottom or both.

Types I, II, III and IV have complete ornaments at the sides of the stamps and three pearls at each outer edge of the bottom panel.

16	A15	10c green, type IV ('55)	37,500.	1,700.
	No gum		15,000.	

Washington — A16

17	A16	12c gray black	6,250.	250.
	No gum		2,100.	
c.	Printed on both sides		40,000.	

Values for 1857-61 issues are for examples that clearly show all the illustrated type characteristics. Stamps that have weakly defined or missing type characteristics sell for less.

Nos. 18-39 have small or very small margins. The values take into account the margin size. See footnotes for more specific information on selected issues.

SAME DESIGNS AS 1851-57 ISSUES

1857-61   **Perf. 15½**

18	A5	1c blue, type I ('61)	2,100.	550.
	No gum		800.	
	Short ornaments at either top or bottom			—
19	A6	1c blue, type Ia	42,500.	9,000.
	No gum		20,000.	
b.	blue, type Ic	4,250.	2,750.
	No gum		1,750.	
20	A7	1c blue, type II	900.	250.
	No gum		400.	
21	A8	1c blue, type III	17,500.	1,750.
	No gum		6,000.	
a.	Horiz. pair, imperf between			20,000.
22	A8	1c blue, type IIIa	2,400.	500.
	No gum		850.	

Beware of pairs of No. 22 with faint blind perforations between that sometimes are offered as pairs imperf. between.

23	A9	1c blue, type IV	10,000.	1,000.
	No gum		4,250.	

Franklin — A20

Type V — Similar to type III of 1851-57 but with side ornaments partly cut away. About one-half of all positions have side scratches. Wide breaks in top and bottom framelines.

Type Va — Stamps from Plate 5 with almost complete ornaments at right side and no side scratches. Many, but not all, stamps from

Plate 5 are Type Va, the remainder being Type V.

24	A20	1c blue, type V	140.00	40.00
		No gum	60.00	
b.		Laid paper		7,500.
25	A10	3c rose, type I	2,750.	175.00
		No gum	950.	
b.		Vert. pair, imperf. hori-zontally		10,000.
25A	A10	3c rose, type II	9,000.	900.00
		No gum	4,000.	

CONTIN-UOUS FRAME LINE   CONTIN-UOUS FRAME LINE

Washington Type III — A21

Type III — There are no outer frame lines at top and bottom. The side frame lines were recut so as to be continuous from the top to the bottom of the plate. Stamps from the top or bottom rows show the ends of the side frame lines and may be mistaken for Type IV.

26	A21	3c dull red, type III	65.00	10.00
		No gum	27.50	
b.		Horiz. pair, imperf. verti-cally	14,000.	
c.		Vert. pair, imperf. hori-zontally	16,000.	
d.		Horizontal pair, imperf. between	—	
e.		Double impression	15,000.	

BROKEN FRAME LINE   BROKEN FRAME LINE

Washington Type IV — A21a

Type IV — As type III, but the side frame lines extend only to the top and bottom of the stamp design. All Type IV stamps are from plates 10 and 11 (each of which exists in three states), and these plates produced only Type IV. The side frame lines were recut individually for each stamp, thus being broken between the stamps vertically.

Beware of type III stamps with frame lines that stop at the top of the design (from top row of plate) or bottom of the design (from bottom row of plate). These are often mistakenly offered as No. 26A.

26A	A21a	3c dull red, type IV	600.00	150.00
		No gum	260.00	

No. 26Af is unique.

27	A11	5c brick red, type I ('58)	80,000.	1,600.
		No gum	20,000.	
		N.Y. Ocean Mail		+1,000.
28	A11	5c red brown, type I	60,000.	1,100.
		No gum	15,000.	
b.		Bright red brown	70,000.	2,300.
		No gum	20,000.	
28A	A11	5c Indian red, type I ('58)	175,000.	3,500.
		No gum	40,000.	

No. 28A unused is valued in the grade of fine. Only four examples are recorded with any amount of gum.

29	A11	5c brown, type I ('59)	5,500.	375.
		No gum	1,750.	

Jefferson — A22

FIVE CENTS.

Type II — The projections at top and bottom are partly cut away.

30	A22	5c orange brown, type II ('61)	1,200.	1,400.
		No gum	500.	
30A	A22	5c brown, type II ('60)	2,200.	290.
		No gum	825.	
b.		Printed on both sides		35,000.
31	A12	10c green, type I	35,000.	1,200.
		No gum	11,500.	
32	A13	10c green, type II	6,000.	200.
		No gum	2,150.	
33	A14	10c green, type III	6,000.	200.
		No gum	2,150.	
34	A15	10c green, type IV	50,000.	2,100.
		No gum	20,000.	

Example I   Example II

Washington (Two typical examples) — A23

TEN CENTS

Type V — The side ornaments are slightly cut away. Usually only one pearl remains at each end of the lower label, but some copies show two or three pearls at the right side. At the bottom the outer line is complete and the shells nearly so. The outer lines at top are complete except over the right "X."

35	A23	10c green, type V ('59)	225.00	65.00
		No gum	100.00	

No. 36 outer frame lines recut on plate

TWELVE CENTS. Printed from two plates. Plate 1 (No. 36) — Outer frame lines were recut on the plate and are complete. Very narrow spacing of stamps on the plate.

36	A16	12c black (Plate 1)	1,850.	325.
		No gum	575.	
c.		Horizontal pair, imperf. between		12,500.

Typical No. 36B, outer frame lines not recut

Plate III (No. 36B) — Weak outer frame lines from the die were not recut and are noticeably uneven or broken, sometimes partly missing. Somewhat wider spacing of stamps on the plate.

36B	A16	12c black, plate III ('59)	700.	275.
		No gum	325.	

Washington A17   Franklin A18

37	A17	24c gray lilac ('60)	1,450.	400.
a.		24c gray	1,450.	400.
		No gum	525.	
38	A18	30c orange ('60)	2,000.	425.
		No gum	750.	

Washington — A19

39	A19	90c blue ('60)	3,000.	10,000.
		No gum	1,200.	

See Die and Plate proofs in the Scott United States Specialized Catalogue for imperfs. of the 12c, 24c, 30c, 90c.

Genuine cancellations on the 90c are rare. Used examples must be accompanied by certificates of authenticity issued by recognized expertizing committees.

REPRINTS OF 1857-60 ISSUE
White paper, without gum.

1875   **Perf. 12**

40	A5	1c bright blue	600.	
41	A10	3c scarlet	3,000.	
42	A22	5c orange brown	1,250.	
43	A12	10c blue green	2,750.	13,000.
44	A16	12c greenish black	3,000.	
45	A17	24c blackish violet	3,250.	10,000.
46	A18	30c yellow orange	3,250.	
47	A19	90c deep blue	3,850.	

Nos. 41-46 are valued in the grade of fine.

Nos. 40-47 exist imperforate. Very infrequent sales preclude establishing a value at this time. One set of imperforate pairs is recorded and it sold for $110,000 in a 2009 auction.

Essays-Trial Color Proofs

The paper of former Nos. 55-62 (Nos. 63E11e, 65-E15h, 67-E9e, 69-E6e, 72-E7h, Essay section, Nos. 70eTC, 71bTC, Trial Color Proof section, Scott U.S. Specialized) is thin and semitransparent. That of the postage issues is thicker and more opaque, except Nos. 62B, 70c and 70d.

Franklin — A24

A24

Washington — A25

A25

Jefferson — A26

A26

Washington — A27

A27

A27a

Washington — A28

A28

Washington A29   Franklin A30

Washington — A31

A31

1c — There is a dash under the tip of the ornament at right of the numeral in upper left corner.

3c — Ornaments at corners end in a small ball.

5c — There is a leaflet in the foliated ornaments at each corner.

10c (A27) — A heavy curved line has been cut below the stars and an outer line added to the ornaments above them.

12c — There are corner ornaments consisting of ovals and scrolls.

90c — Parallel lines form an angle above the ribbon with "U. S. Postage"; between these lines there is a row of dashes and a point of color at the apex of the lower line.

1861   *Perf. 12*

62B	A27a 10c dark green	8,250.	1,600.
	No gum	3,500.	

1861-62   *Perf. 12*

63	A24 1c blue	300.00	50.00
	No gum	110.00	
a.	1c ultramarine	2,500.	950.00
	No gum	1,000.	
b.	1c dark blue	800.00	850.00
	No gum	300.00	
c.	Laid paper, horiz. or vert.	8,500.	4,500.
d.	Vertical pair, imperf. horiz.		—
e.	Printed on both sides, reverse inverted	—	35,000.

The editors would like to see authenticated evidence of the existence of No. 63d.

64	A25 3c pink	14,000.	650.00
	No gum	5,000.	
a.	3c pigeon blood pink	50,000.	4,500.
	No gum	15,000.	
b.	3c rose pink, Aug. 17, 1861	600.00	150.00
	No gum	225.00	
65	A25 3c rose	125.00	3.00
	No gum	50.00	
b.	Laid paper, horiz. or vert.	—	1,100.
d.	Vertical pair, imperf. horiz.	15,000.	1,500.
	No gum	6,500.	
e.	Printed on both sides, reverse inverted	40,000.	8,000.
f.	Double impression		12,500.

The 3c lake can be found under No. 66 in the Trial Color Proofs section of the Scott U.S. Specialized Catalogue. The imperf 3c lake under No. 66P in the same section. The imperf 3c rose can be found in the Die and Plate Proofs section of the Specialized.

67	A26 5c buff	27,500.	800.
	No gum	10,500.	
a.	5c brown yellow	30,000.	1,100.
	No gum	11,500.	
b.	5c olive yellow		4,750.

Values of Nos. 67, 67a, 67b reflect the normal small margins.

68	A27 10c green	1,000.	55.00
	No gum	400.	
a.	10c dark green	1,400.	85.00
	No gum	500.	
b.	Vertical pair, imperf. horiz.		30,000.
69	A28 12c black	1,800.	100.00
	No gum	725.	
70	A29 24c red lilac ('62)	3,000.	300.00
	No gum	1,150.	
a.	24c brown lilac	3,250.	325.00
	No gum	1,250.	
b.	24c steel blue ('61)	16,500.	850.00
	No gum	6,250.	
c.	24c violet, thin paper, Aug. 20, 1861	35,000.	2,250.
	No gum	13,500.	
d.	24c pale gray violet, thin paper	25,000.	3,000.
	No gum	6,000.	

There are numerous shades of the 24c stamp in this and the following issue. Color changelings, especially of No. 78, are frequently offered as No. 70b. Obtaining a certificate from an acknowledged expert committee is strongly advised.

Nos. 70c and 70d are on a thinner, harder and more transparent paper than Nos. 70, 70a, 70b or the latter Nos. 78, 78a, 78b and 78c.

71	A30 30c orange	2,750.	200.
	No gum	1,000.	
a.	Printed on both sides		—

Values for No. 71 are for examples with small margins, especially at sides. Large-margined examples sell for much more.

72	A31 90c blue	3,250.	600.
	No gum	1,300.	
a.	90c pale blue	3,250.	650.
	No gum	1,300.	
b.	90c dark blue	4,000.	1,000.
	No gum	1,600.	

DESIGNS AS 1861 ISSUE

Andrew Jackson A32   Abraham Lincoln A33

1861-66   *Perf. 12*

73	A32 2c black ('63)	350.00	60.00
	No gum	150.00	
f.	Printed on both sides, reverse not inverted		27,500.
g.	Laid paper	—	11,500.

No. 73f unused is unique. It has perfs cut off on two sides and is valued thus.

The 3c scarlet can be found under No. 74 in the Scott U.S. Specialized Catalogue Trial Color Proofs section.

75	A26 5c red brown ('62)	5,750.	425.
	No gum	2,100.	

Values for No. 75 reflect the normal small margins.

76	A26 5c brown ('63)	1,350.	120.
	No gum	525.	
a.	5c black brown	2,250.	400.
	No gum	850.	
b.	Laid paper		—

Values of Nos. 76, 76a reflect the normal small margins.

77	A33 15c black ('66)	4,750.	180.
	No gum	1,750.	
78	A29 24c lilac ('62)	2,750.	375.
	No gum	950.	
a.	24c grayish lilac	2,900.	425.
	No gum	1,000.	
b.	24c gray	2,900.	450.
	No gum	1,000.	
c.	24c blackish violet	100,000.	20,000.
	No gum	30,000.	

Only three examples are recorded of No. 78c unused with original gum. No. 78c unused with and without gum are valued in the grade of fine-very fine.

d.	Printed on both sides, reverse inverted		22,500.

SAME DESIGNS AS 1861-66 ISSUES

Grill

Embossed with grills of various sizes. Some authorities believe that more than one size of grill probably existed on one of the grill rolls.

A peculiarity of the United States issues from 1867 to 1870 is the grill or embossing. The object was to break the fiber of the paper so that the ink of the canceling stamp would soak in and make washing for a second using impossible. The exact date at which grilled stamps came into use is unsettled. Luff's "Postage Stamps of the United States" places the date as probably August 8, 1867.

Horizontal measurements are given first.

GRILL WITH POINTS UP

Grills A and C were made by a roller covered with ridges shaped like an inverted V. Pressing the ridges into the stamp paper forced the paper into the pyramidal pits between the ridges, causing irregular breaks in the paper. Grill B was made by a roller with raised bosses.

A. GRILL COVERING THE ENTIRE STAMP

1867   *Perf. 12*

79	A25 3c rose	8,500.	1,500.
	No gum	2,750.	
b.	Printed on both sides		—

Nos. 79, 79b, are valued for fine-very fine centering but with minor perforation faults.

An essay which is often mistaken for No. 79 (#79-E15) shows the points of the grill as small squares faintly impressed in the paper, but not cutting through it.

On No. 79 the grill breaks through the paper. Examples free from defects are rare.

80	A26 5c brown	260,000.	
a.	5c dark brown	260,000.	
81	A30 30c orange	240,000.	

Four examples of Nos. 80 and 80a (two of each shade), and eight examples of No. 81 (one in the New York Public Library Miller collection and not available to collectors) are known. All are more or less faulty and/or off center. Values are for off-center examples with small perforation faults.

B. GRILL ABOUT 18x15mm (22x18 POINTS)

82	A25 3c rose	900,000.	

The four known examples of No. 82 are valued in the grade of fine.

Earliest documented use: Feb. 1?, 1869 (dated cancel on off-cover stamp).

C. GRILL ABOUT 13x16mm (16 TO 17 BY 18 TO 21 POINTS)

The grilled area on each of four C grills in the sheet may total about 18x15mm when a normal C grill adjoins a fainter grill extending to the right or left edge of the stamp.

This is caused by a partial erasure on the grill roller when it was changed to produce C grills instead of the all-over A grill.

The imperf. can be found in the *Scott U.S. Specialized Catalogue* Die and Plate Proofs section.

83	A25 3c rose	6,000.	1,100.
	No gum	2,150.	

GRILL WITH POINTS DOWN

The grills were produced by rollers with the surface covered, or partly covered, by pyramidal bosses. On the D, E and F grills the tips of the pyramids are vertical ridges. On the Z grill the ridges are horizontal.

D. GRILL ABOUT 12x14mm (15 BY 17 TO 18 POINTS)

84	A32 2c black	16,000.	4,500.
	No gum	6,500.	

No. 84 is valued in the grade of fine.

85	A25 3c rose	8,500.	1,050.

Z. GRILL ABOUT 11x14mm (13 TO 14 BY 18 POINTS)

85A	A24 1c blue		3,000,000.

Two examples of No. 85A are known. One is contained in the New York Public Library collection, which is on long-term loan to the Smithsonian National Postal Museum.

85B	A32 2c black	17,500.	1,200.
	No gum	6,750.	
85C	A25 3c rose	25,000.	3,500.
	No gum	9,000.	
85D	A27 10c green		600,000.

Six examples of No. 85D are known. One is contained in the New York Public Library collection. Value is for a well-centered example with small faults.

85E	A28 12c intense black	17,500.	2,500.
	No gum	6,500.	
85F	A33 15c black		2,000,000.

Two examples of No. 85F are documented, one in the grade of very good, the other extremely fine. Value is for the extremely fine example.

E. GRILL ABOUT 11x13mm (14 BY 15 TO 17 POINTS)

86	A24 1c blue	3,250.	425.
	No gum	1,200.	
a.	1c dull blue	3,250.	400.
	No gum	1,200.	
87	A32 2c black	1,700.	200.
	No gum	650.	

88	A25 3c rose	1,000.	30.00
	No gum	375.	
a.	3c lake red	1,250.	70.00
	No gum	475.	
89	A27 10c green	5,250.	350.
	No gum	2,100.	
90	A28 12c black	5,000.	400.
	No gum	2,000.	
91	A33 15c black	12,500.	625.
	No gum	4,500.	

F. GRILL ABOUT 9x13mm (11 TO 12 BY 15 TO 17 POINTS)

92	A24 1c blue	3,000.	450.
	No gum	1,000.	
a.	1c pale blue	2,500.	400.
	No gum	750.	
93	A32 2c black	450.	60.00
	No gum	160.	
94	A25 3c red	350.	10.00
a.	3c rose	350.	10.00
	No gum	150.	
c.	Vertical pair, imperf. horiz.	15,000.	
d.	Printed on both sides	9,000.	42,500.

The imperf. 3c can be found in the Scott U.S. Specialized Catalogue Die and Plate Proofs section.

95	A26 5c brown	3,500.	900.
	No gum	1,300.	
a.	5c black brown	4,750.	2,400.
	No gum	1,850.	

Values of Nos. 95, 95a reflect the normal small margins.

96	A27 10c yel grn	2,750.	225.
	No gum	900.	
97	A28 12c black	3,000.	250.
	No gum	1,100.	
98	A33 15c black	4,250.	275.
	No gum	1,600.	
99	A29 24c gray lilac	9,000.	1,600.
	No gum	3,500.	
100	A30 30c orange	9,500.	1,000.
	No gum	3,500.	

Values for No. 100 are for examples with small margins, especially at sides. Large-margined examples sell for much more.

101	A31 90c blue	14,500.	2,250.
	No gum	5,500.	

RE-ISSUE OF 1861-66 ISSUES
Without Grill, Hard White Paper
White Crackly Gum

1875   *Perf. 12*

102	A24 1c blue	800.	1,600.
	No gum	350.	

103	A32	2c black	3,500.	12,500.
		No gum	1,650.	
104	A25	3c brown red	4,000.	16,000.
		No gum	1,850.	
105	A26	5c brown	2,600.	7,000.
		No gum	1,225.	
106	A27	10c green	3,100.	125,000.
		No gum	1,500.	
107	A28	12c black	3,750.	15,000.
		No gum	1,750.	
108	A33	15c black	4,500.	35,000.
		No gum	2,100.	
109	A29	24c deep violet	5,750.	20,000.
		No gum	2,750.	
110	A30	30c brownish org	6,000.	20,000.
		No gum	2,800.	
111	A31	90c blue	6,750.	225,000.
		No gum	3,250.	

These stamps can be distinguished from the 1861-66 issues by the shades and the paper which is hard and very white instead of yellowish. The gum is white and crackly.

Franklin — A34   Post Horse and Rider — A35

G. Grill measuring 9½x9mm
(12 by 11 to 11½ points)

1869   Hard Wove Paper   Perf. 12

112	A34	1c buff	600.	140.
		No gum	225.	
b.		Without grill	32,500.	
113	A35	2c brown	525.	80.
		No gum	200.	
b.		Without grill	14,000.	
d.		Printed on both sides		62,500.

Locomotive A36   Washington A37

114	A36	3c ultramarine	250.	17.50
		No gum	100.	
a.		Without grill	13,000.	18,000.
		Without grill, gray paper		3,750.
d.		Double impression	15,000.	
e.		Printed on both sides, reverse inverted		55,000.

Two examples recorded of No. 114a on normal paper: one with pen cancel but with original gum, 1994 Philatelic Foundation certificate; and one lifted from a cover, original gum adhering, examined, and placed back, 2011 Philatelic Foundation certificate. Also, four examples of No. 114a on gray paper: a single lifted from cover, examined, and hinged back in place, 1991 Philatelic Foundation certificate; and a strip of three on piece, mostly detached from piece, with full gum, 1978 and 2006 Philatelic Foundation certificates.
Nos. 114d and 114e each are unique. No. 114d has a pre-printing paper fold.

115	A37	6c ultramarine	2,750.	225.
		No gum	1,000.	500.

Shield and Eagle — A38   S. S. Adriatic — A39

116	A38	10c yellow	2,000.	120.
		No gum	800.	
117	A39	12c green	1,900.	130.
		No gum	750.	

Landing of Columbus — A40

A40a

Type I. Picture unframed. No. 118 has horizontal shading lines at the left and right sides of the vignette.

118	A40	15c brn & bl, type I	9,500.	850.
		No gum	3,250.	
a.		Without grill		11,500.

A40a

Type II. Picture framed. No. 119 has diagonal shading lines at the left and right sides of the vignette.

119	A40a	15c brn & bl, type II	3,250.	220.
		No gum	1,150.	
b.		Center inverted	1,000,000.	22,500.
		No gum	700,000.	
c.		Center double, one inverted		80,000.

Declaration of Independence — A41

120	A41	24c green & violet	8,000.	650.
		No gum	2,800.	
a.		Without grill	14,000.	
b.		Center inverted	750,000.	37,500.

Shield, Eagle and Flags — A42   Lincoln — A43

121	A42	30c ultra & carmine	4,500.	425.
		No gum	1,600.	
a.		Without grill	10,000.	
b.		Flags inverted	750,000.	100,000.
		No gum	300,000.	

Seven examples of No. 121b unused are recorded. Only one has part of its original gum.

122	A43	90c carmine & black	12,000.	1,800.
		No gum	4,000.	
a.		Without grill	22,500.	

Values of varieties of Nos. 112-122 without grill are for examples with original gum.
Most examples of Nos. 119b, 120b are faulty. Values are for stamps with fine centering and only minimal faults. No. 120b unused is valued without gum, as all of the three examples available to collectors are without gum.

RE-ISSUE OF 1869 ISSUE
Without grill, hard white paper, with white crackly gum.

The gum is almost always somewhat yellowed with age, and unused stamps with original gum are valued with such gum.
A new plate of 150 subjects was made for the 1c. The plate for the frame of the 15c was made using the same die as that used to make the type I frame for No. 118. For No. 118, the lines on each side of the vignette area were entered onto the plate itself, one position at a time. Upon close examination, each stamp position will be found to exhibit minute differences in these horizontal fringe lines.

1875   **Perf. 12**

123	A34	1c buff	550.	450.
			230.	

124	A35	2c brown	650.	800.
		No gum	275.	
125	A36	3c blue	5,000.	27,500.
		No gum	2,500.	

Used value for No. 125 is for an attractive fine to very fine example with minimal faults.

126	A37	6c blue	1,750.	3,250.
		No gum	775.	
127	A38	10c yellow	1,650.	2,000.
		No gum	725.	
128	A39	12c green	2,250.	3,250.
		No gum	1,025.	
129	A40	15c brn & bl, Type III	1,350.	1,250.
		No gum	600.	
a.		Imperf. horizontally, single	14,000.	30,000.
		No gum	5,000.	

Two used examples of No. 129a are recorded. Both have faults and are valued thus.

130	A41	24c grn & violet	2,100.	1,700.
		No gum	900.	
131	A42	30c ultra & car	2,500.	2,900.
		No gum	1,100.	
132	A43	90c car & blk	3,750.	6,000.
		No gum	1,500.	

Soft Porous Paper
1880-82

133	A34	1c buff, issued with gum	325.	550.
		No gum	140.	
a.		1c brown orange, issued without gum ('81 and '82)	300.	

PRODUCED BY THE NATIONAL BANK NOTE COMPANY

Franklin — A44

A44

Jackson — A45

A45

Washington — A46

A46

Lincoln — A47

Edwin M. Stanton — A48

A48

Jefferson — A49

A49

Henry Clay — A50

A50

Daniel Webster — A51

A51

Gen. Winfield Scott A52   Alexander Hamilton A53

Commodore O.H. Perry — A54

H. GRILL ABOUT 10x12mm
(11 TO 13 BY 14 TO 16 POINTS)

The "H" grills can be separated into early state and late state, based on the shape of the tip of the grill. Early-state grills show a point or very small vertical line at the tip of the pyramid, while late-state grills show the pyramid tips truncated and flat.

Early-state "H" grills tend to be on vertical-mesh wove paper, while later printings and all late-state grills were printed on horizontal-mesh wove paper, resulting in stamp designs being approximately ¼mm shorter than the designs printed on vertical-mesh wove paper. The late-stage "H" grills virtually all seem to have been used only after Jan. 1873.

Poor printing quality often resulted in grills that show only a few grill points or a very few rows of points. This is especially true of the "H" grills. When there are not enough grill points to clearly identify whether the grill is an "H" or an "I", it must be assumed it is the lower-valued "H" grill variety. Authentication is advised for these stamps with high catalogue values.

White Wove Paper, Thin to Medium Thick.

1870-71			Perf. 12
134	A44	1c ultramarine	2,000.	225.00
	No gum		700.
b.	Pair, one without grill		—
135	A45	2c red brown	1,000.	75.00
	No gum		360.
136	A46	3c green	575.	32.50
	No gum		190.
b.	Printed on both sides		—

The imperf. 3c can be found in the Scott U.S. Specialized Catalogue Die and Plate Proofs section.

137	A47	6c carmine	5,000.	450.00
	No gum		1,750.
b.	Pair, one without grill		—
138	A48	7c vermilion	4,250.	500.
	No gum		1,550.
b.	Pair, one without grill		—
139	A49	10c brown	7,000.	850.
	No gum		2,550.
140	A50	12c dull violet	30,000.	3,600.
	No gum		14,000.
141	A51	15c orange	7,500.	1,500.
	No gum		2,500.
142	A52	24c purple		6,750.
143	A53	30c black	20,000.	4,000.
	No gum		7,500.
144	A54	90c carmine	25,000.	2,500.
	No gum		10,000.

I. GRILL ABOUT 8½x10mm
(10 TO 11 BY 10 TO 13 POINTS)

The "I" grills can be separated into early state and late state, based on the shape of the tip of the grill. Early state grills show small tips of the pyramid, while late state grills show the pyramid tips truncated and flat.

Early state "I" grills tend to be on vertical-mesh wove paper, while later printings and all late-state grills were printed on horizontal-mesh wove paper, resulting in stamp designs being approximately ¼mm shorter than the designs printed on vertical-mesh wove paper. The late-stage "I" grills all seem to have been used only after Jan. 1873.

Values are for stamps with grills that are clearly identifiable. Poor printing quality often resulted in grills that show only a few grill points or a very few rows of points. When there are not enough grill points to clearly identify whether the grill is an "H" or an "I", it must be assumed it is the lower-valued "H" grill variety. Authentication is advised for these stamps with high catalogue values.

134A	A44	1c ultramarine	2,750.	350.00
	No gum		800.00
135A	A45	2c red brown	2,000.	300.00
136A	A46	3c green	800.00	100.00
a.	Pair, one without grill		—
137A	A47	6c carmine	7,000.	900.00
138A	A48	7c vermilion ('71)	6,500.	850.00
	No gum		2,200.
139A	A49	10c brown	17,500.	8,500.

There are two unused examples of No. 139A recorded. One is fine and the other is very fine plus. The catalogue value is for the latter. Only one cover is recorded.

140A A50 12c dull violet 30,000.

Two examples are recorded of No. 140A unused and it is valued in the grade of fine.

141A A51 15c orange 16,500. 7,500.

Three examples are recorded of No. 141A unused, and value is for a fine example.

Earliest documented use: June 15, 1870.

143A A53 30c black 75,000.

Only one recorded example of No. 143A, which is valued in the grade of fine-very fine.

144A A54 90c carmine — 15,000.

The unused No. 144A has a vertically split grill and is unique.

White Wove Paper Without Grill.

1870-71			Perf. 12
145	A44	1c ultra	675.	25.00
	No gum		250.
146	A45	2c red brown	325.	20.00
	No gum		125.
d.	Double impression		9,000.

147	A46	3c green	225.	2.00
	No gum		90.
a.	Printed on both sides, reverse inverted		17,500.
b.	Double impression		30,000.

Nos. 147a and 147b are valued in the grade of fine.

The imperf. 3c can be found in the Scott U.S. Specialized Catalogue Die and Plate Proofs section.

148	A47	6c carmine	1,000.	25.00
	No gum		320.
c.	Double paper		100.00

No. 148b is unique.

149	A48	7c ver ('71)	1,000.	100.00
	No gum		320.
150	A49	10c brown	2,150.	35.00
	No gum		850.
151	A50	12c dull violet	3,000.	220.00
	No gum		1,100.
152	A51	15c brt org	3,500.	220.00
	No gum		1,300.
a.	Double impression		9,000.

No. 152a is unique. It has fine centering and faults and is valued thus.

153	A52	24c purple	1,800.	230.00
	No gum		625.
a.	Double paper		—
154	A53	30c black	7,500.	300.00
	No gum		2,750.
155	A54	90c carmine	5,000.	325.00
	No gum		1,900.

PRINTED BY THE CONTINENTAL BANK NOTE COMPANY

Designs of the 1870-71 Issue with secret marks on the values from 1c to 15c, as described and illustrated:

The object of secret marks was to provide a simple and positive proof that these stamps were produced by the Continental Bank Note Company and not by their predecessors.

Almost all of the stamps of the Continental Bank Note Co. printing including the Department stamps and some of the Newspaper stamps may be found upon a paper that shows more or less the characteristics of a ribbed paper. The ribbing may be oriented either vertically or horizontally, with horizontal ribbing being far more common than vertical ribbing. Values are for the most common varieties.

Franklin — A44a

1c. In the pearl at the left of the numeral "1" there is a small crescent.

Jackson — A45a

2c. Under the scroll at the left of "U. S." there is a small diagonal line. This mark seldom shows clearly. The stamp, No. 157, can be distinguished by its color.

Washington — A46a

3c. The under part of the upper tail of the left ribbon is heavily shaded.

Lincoln — A47a

6c. The first four vertical lines of the shading in the lower part of the left ribbon have been strengthened.

Stanton — A48a

7c. Two small semi-circles are drawn around the ends of the lines that outline the ball in the lower right hand corner.

Jefferson — A49a

10c. There is a small semi-circle in the scroll at the right end of the upper label.

Clay — A50a

12c. The balls of the figure "2" are crescent shaped.

Webster — A51a

15c. In the lower part of the triangle in the upper left corner two lines have been made heavier forming a "V." This mark can be found on some of the Continental and American (1879) printings, but not all stamps show it.

Secret marks were added to the dies of the 24c, 30c and 90c but new plates were not made from them. The various printings of the 30c and 90c can be distinguished only by the shades and paper.

Experimental J. Grill about 7x9½mm exists on all values except 24c and 90c. Grill was composed of truncated pyramids and was so strongly impressed that some points often broke through the paper.

White Wove Paper, Thin to Thick Without Grill

1873, July (?)			Perf. 12
156	A44a	1c ultra	225.	6.00
	No gum		95.
e.	With grill		2,000.
f.	Imperf., pair	—	1,500.
157	A45a	2c brown	350.	25.00
	No gum		135.
c.	With grill		1,850.	750.00
d.	Double impression		16,500.

No. 157d is unique.

158	A46a	3c green	110.	1.00
	No gum		40.
a.	Double paper		600.	100.00
e.	With grill		550.
h.	Horizontal pair, imperf. vert.		—
i.	Horizontal pair, imperf. between		1,300.
j.	Double impression		7,000.
k.	Printed on both sides		20,000.

Nos. 158j and 158k are valued in the grade of fine.

The imperf 3c, with and without grill, can be found in the Scott U.S. Specialized Catalogue Die and Plate Proofs section.

159	A47a	6c dull pink	400.	20.00
	No gum		130.
b.	With grill		1,800.
160	A48a	7c org ver	1,150.	90.00
	No gum		350.
a.	With grill		3,500.
161	A49a	10c brown	900.	27.50
	No gum		275.
a.	Double paper		3,500.	900.00
c.	With grill		3,750.
d.	Horizontal pair, imperf. between		17,500.
162	A50a	12c blkish vio	2,400.	145.00
	No gum		800.
a.	With grill		5,500.

163	A51a	15c yel org	2,250.	160.00
	No gum		750.
a.	With grill		5,750.
164	A52	24c purple		357,500.

The Philatelic Foundation has certified as genuine a 24c on vertically ribbed paper, and that is the unique stamp listed as No. 164. Specialists believe that only Continental used ribbed paper. It is not known for sure whether or not Continental also printed the 24c value on regular paper; if it did, specialists currently are not able to distinguish these from No. 153. The catalogue value represents a 2004 auction sale price realized.

165	A53	30c gray black	4,000.	140.
	No gum		1,300.
a.	Double paper		—
c.	With grill		22,500.
166	A54	90c rose car	2,250.	300.00
	No gum		750.

Special Printing of the 1873 Issue
Hard, White Wove Paper
Without Gum

1875			Perf. 12
167	A44a	1c ultramarine	15,000.
168	A45a	2c dark brown	6,750.
169	A46a	3c blue green	23,500.
170	A47a	6c dull rose	20,000.
171	A48a	7c reddish ver	4,500.
172	A49a	10c pale brown	19,000.
173	A50a	12c dark violet	6,250.
174	A51a	15c bright org	17,000.
175	A52	24c dull purple	3,750.	22,500.
176	A53	30c greenish blk	13,500.
177	A54	90c vio carmine	20,000.

Although perforated, these stamps were usually cut apart with scissors. As a result, the perforations are often much mutilated and the design is frequently damaged.

These can be distinguished from the 1873 issue by the shades; also by the paper, which is very white instead of yellowish.

These and the subsequent issues listed under the heading of "Special Printings" are special printings of stamps then in current use which, together with the reprints and re-issues, were made for sale to collectors. They were available for postage except for the Officials, Newspaper and Periodical, and demonetized issues.

Only three examples of No. 175 used have been certified. They all have small faults and are valued thus.

Yellowish Wove Paper

1875			Perf. 12
178	A45a	2c vermilion	350.	15.00
	No gum		110.
c.	With grill		900.	2,750.

The imperf 2c can be found in the Scott U.S. Specialized Catalogue Die and Plate Proofs section.

Zachary Taylor — A55

179	A55	5c blue	675.	25.00
	No gum		225.
c.	With grill		4,500.

SPECIAL PRINTING OF 1875 ISSUE
Hard, White Wove Paper
Without Gum

1875			
180	A45a	2c carmine ver	70,000.
181	A55	5c bright blue	450,000.

Unlike Nos. 167-177, Nos. 180-181 were not cut apart with scissors.

Please Note:

Stamps are valued in the grade of very fine unless otherwise indicated.

Values for early and valuable stamps are for examples with certificates of authenticity from acknowledged expert committees, or examples sold with the buyer having the right of certification.

This applies to examples with original gum as well as examples without gum.

Beware of stamps offered "as is," as the gum on some unused stamps offered with "original gum" may be fraudulent, and stamps offered as unused without gum may in some cases be altered or faintly canceled used stamps.

IMPORTANT INFORMATION REGARDING VALUES FOR NEVER-HINGED STAMPS

Collectors should be aware that the values given for never-hinged stamps from No. 182 on are for stamps in the grade of very fine, just as the values for all stamps in the catalogue are for very fine stamps unless otherwise indicated. The never-hinged premium as a percentage of value will be larger for stamps in extremely fine or superb grades, and the premium will be smaller for fine-very fine, fine or poor examples. This is particularly true of the issues of the late-19th and early-20th centuries.

VALUES FOR NEVER-HINGED STAMPS PRIOR TO SCOTT 182

This catalogue does not value pre-1879 stamps in never-hinged condition. Premiums for never-hinged condition in the classic era invariably are even larger than those premiums listed for the 1879 and later issues. Generally speaking, the earlier the stamp is listed in the catalogue, the larger will be the never-hinged premium.

For values of the most popular U.S. stamps in various conditions, including never hinged from No. 182 on, and in the grades of very good, fine, fine to very fine, very fine, very fine to extremely fine, extremely fine, extremely fine to superb, and superb, see the *Scott Stamp Values U.S. Specialized by Grade*, updated and issued each year as part of the U.S. specialized catalogue.

PRINTED BY THE AMERICAN BANK NOTE COMPANY
SAME AS 1870-75 ISSUES
Soft Porous Paper
Varying from Thin to Thick

1879   *Perf. 12*

182	A44a	1c dark ultra	225.	6.00
		Never hinged	775.	
		No gum	90.	
183	A45a	2c vermilion	100.	5.00
		Never hinged	370.	
		No gum	40.	
a.		Double impression	—	5,500.

No. 183a is valued in the grade of fine.

184	A46a	3c green	90.	1.00
		Never hinged	330.	
		No gum	35.	
b.		Double impression		5,000.

No. 184b is valued in the grade of fine.

The imperf 3c can be found in the Scott U.S. Specialized Catalogue Die and Plate Proofs section.

185	A55	5c blue	450.	17.50
		Never hinged	1,500.	
		No gum	140.	
186	A47a	6c pink	900.	25.00
		Never hinged	3,100.	
		No gum	275.	
187	A49	10c brn, without secret mark	3,250.	42.50
		Never hinged	11,000.	
		No gum	1,100.	
a.		Double paper	10,000.	—
188	A49a	10c brn, with secret mark	1,800.	32.50
		Never hinged	6,500.	
		No gum	625.	
189	A51a	15c red orange	200.	30.00
		Never hinged	675.	
		No gum	80.	
190	A53	30c full black	900.	95.00
		Never hinged	3,000.	
		No gum	325.	
191	A54	90c carmine	2,000.	360.00
		Never hinged	7,000.	
		No gum	650.	

The Continental Bank Note Co. was consolidated with the American Bank Note Co. on February 4, 1879. The American Bank Note Company used many plates of the Continental Bank Note Company to print the ordinary postage, Departmental and Newspaper stamps. Therefore, stamps bearing the Continental Company's imprint were not always its product.

The A. B. N. Co. also used the 30c and 90c plates of the N. B. N. Co. Some of No. 190 and all of No. 217 were from A. B. N. Co. plate 405.

Early printings of No. 188 were from Continental plates 302 and 303 which contained the normal secret mark of 1873. After those plates were re-entered by the A. B. N. Co. in 1880, pairs or multiple pieces contained combinations of normal, hairline or missing marks. The pairs or other multiples usually found contain at least one hairline mark which tended to disappear as the plate wore.

A. B. N. Co. plates 377 and 378 were made in 1881 from the National transfer roll of 1870. No. 187 from these plates has no secret mark.

The imperf. 90c can be found in the Scott U.S. Specialized Catalogue Die and Plate Proofs section.

Special Printing of the 1879 Issue
Soft Porous Paper
Without Gum

1880   *Perf. 12*

192	A44a	1c dark ultra	62,500.
193	A45a	2c black brown	19,000.
194	A46a	3c blue green	120,000.
195	A47a	6c dull rose	72,250.
196	A48a	7c scarlet ver	7,500.
197	A49a	10c deep brown	38,000.
198	A50a	12c blkish pur	10,500.
199	A51a	15c orange	32,500.
200	A52	24c dark violet	10,000.
201	A53	30c grnish blk	22,500.
202	A54	90c dull carmine	32,500.
203	A45a	2c scarlet ver	110,000.
204	A55	5c deep blue	260,000.

Nos. 192 and 194 are valued in the grade of fine.

No. 197 was printed from Continental plate 302 (or 303) after plate was re-entered. Therefore, the stamp may show normal, hairline or missing secret mark.

The Post Office Department did not keep separate records of the 1875 and 1880 Special Printings of the 1873 and 1879 issues, but the total quantity sold of both is recorded.

Unlike the 1875 hard-paper Special Printings (Nos. 167-177), the 1880 soft-paper Special Printings were never cut apart with scissors.

While use of Nos. 192-204 for postage was legal, no used examples are recorded. Expertization by competent authorities would be required to establish use.

James A. Garfield — A56

1882

205	A56	5c yellow brown	240.	12.00
		Never hinged	775.	
		No gum	90.	

Special Printing
1882   *Perf. 12*
Soft porous paper, without gum

205C	A56	5c gray brown	60,000.

DESIGNS OF 1873 RE-ENGRAVED

Franklin — A44b

1c — The vertical lines in the upper part of the stamp have been so deepened that the background often appears to be solid. Lines of shading have been added to the upper arabesques.

1881-82

206	A44b	1c gray blue	70.00	1.00
		Never hinged	225.00	
		No gum	25.00	
a.		Double impression		—

No. 206a is a partial double impression, with "ONE 1 CENT," etc. at bottom doubled.
Earliest documented use: Oct. 11, 1881.

Washington — A46b

3c. The shading at the sides of the central oval appears only about one-half the previous width. A short horizontal dash has been cut about 1mm below the "TS" of "CENTS."

207	A46b	3c blue green	70.00	.80
		Never hinged	225.00	
		No gum	25.00	
c.		Double impression		5,000.

Lincoln — A47b

6c. On the original stamps four vertical lines can be counted from the edge of the panel to the outside of the stamp. On the re-engraved stamps there are but three lines in the same place.

208	A47b	6c rose	750.	110.00
		Never hinged	2,350.	
		No gum	225.	
a.		6c deep brown red	550.	180.00
		Never hinged	1,750.	
		No gum	150.	

Jefferson — A49b

10c. On the original stamps there are five vertical lines between the left side of the oval and the edge of the shield. There are only four lines on the re-engraved stamps. In the lower part of the latter, also, the horizontal lines of the background have been strengthened.

209	A49b	10c brown	160.	6.00
		Never hinged	475.	
		No gum	65.	
b.		10c black brown	3,000.	350.00
		Never hinged	6,000.	
		No gum	950.	
c.		Double impression		—

Specimen stamps (usually overprinted "Sample") without overprint exist in a brown shade that differs from No. 209. The unoverprinted brown specimen is cheaper than No. 209. Expertization is recommended.

Washington   Jackson
A57   A58

Nos. 210-211 were issued to meet the reduced first class rate of 2 cents for each half ounce, and the double rate, which Congress approved Mar. 3, 1883, effective Oct. 1, 1883.

1883, Oct. 1   *Perf. 12*

210	A57	2c red brown	42.50	.75
		Never hinged	130.00	
		No gum	16.00	
211	A58	4c blue green	250.	27.50
		Never hinged	900.	
		No gum	90.	

Imperfs can be found in the Scott U.S. Specialized Catalogue Die and Plate Proofs section.

Special Printing
1883-85   Soft porous paper   *Perf. 12*

211B	A57	2c pale red brn, with gum ('85)	375.	—
		Never hinged	1,000.	
		No gum	130.	
c.		Horizontal pair, imperf. between	2,000.	
		Never hinged	3,000.	
211D	A58	4c deep blue grn	50,000.	

No. 211D is without gum.

Franklin — A59

1887   *Perf. 12*

212	A59	1c ultramarine	90.00	2.50
		Never hinged	290.00	
		No gum	35.00	
213	A57	2c green	40.00	.60
		Never hinged	120.00	
		No gum	15.00	
b.		Printed on both sides		

Imperf 1c, 2c can be found in the Scott U.S. Specialized Catalogue Die and Plate Proofs section.

214	A46b	3c vermilion	60.00	55.00
		Never hinged	180.00	
		No gum	25.00	
		Nos. 212-214 (3)	190.00	58.10

1888   *Perf. 12*

215	A58	4c carmine	190.	27.50
		Never hinged	550.	
		No gum	65.	
216	A56	5c indigo	225.	17.50
		Never hinged	700.	
		No gum	85.	
217	A53	30c orange brn	250.	100.00
		Never hinged	900.	
		No gum	80.	
218	A54	90c purple	850.	250.00
		Never hinged	2,600.	
		No gum	275.	
		Nos. 215-218 (4)	1,515.	395.00

Imperfs can be found in the Scott U.S. Specialized Catalogue Die and Plate Proofs section.

Franklin   Washington
A60   A61

Jackson   Lincoln
A62   A63

Ulysses S. Grant   Garfield
A64   A65

William T. Sherman   Daniel Webster
A66   A67

Henry Clay
A68

Jefferson
A69

Perry — A70

1890-93   *Perf. 12*

219	A60	1c dull blue	20.	.75
		Never hinged	65.	
219D	A61	2c lake	175.	5.50
		Never hinged	550.	
220	A61	2c carmine	20.00	.70
		Never hinged	60.00	
a.		Cap on left "2"	150.00	12.50
		Never hinged	425.00	
c.		Cap on both "2's"	650.00	35.00
		Never hinged	1,800.	
221	A62	3c purple	60.00	9.00
		Never hinged	190.00	
222	A63	4c dark brown	90.00	4.75
		Never hinged	275.00	
223	A64	5c chocolate	65.00	4.75
		Never hinged	200.00	
224	A65	6c brown red	60.00	25.00
		Never hinged	190.00	
225	A66	8c lilac ('93)	50.00	17.00
		Never hinged	150.00	
226	A67	10c green	175.00	5.00
		Never hinged	525.00	
227	A68	15c indigo	200.00	27.50
		Never hinged	600.00	
228	A69	30c black	300.00	35.00
		Never hinged	900.00	
229	A70	90c orange	475.00	150.00
		Never hinged	1,450.	
		Nos. 219-229 (12)	1,690.	284.95

The No. 220 with "cap on right 2" variety is due to imperfect inking, not a plate defect.

Imperfs. can be found in the *Scott U.S. Specialized Catalogue* Die and Plate Proofs section.

COLUMBIAN EXPOSITION ISSUE

Columbus in Sight of Land — A71

Landing of Columbus
A72

Flagship of Columbus
A73

Fleet of Columbus
A74

Columbus Soliciting Aid from Isabella
A75

Columbus Welcomed at Barcelona
A76

Columbus Restored to Favor — A77

Columbus Presenting Natives
A78

Columbus Announcing his Discovery
A79

Columbus at La Rábida
A80

Recall of Columbus
A81

Isabella Pledging her Jewels
A82

Columbus in Chains
A83

Columbus Describing his Third Voyage
A84

Isabella & Columbus
A85

Columbus
A86

1893   *Perf. 12*

230	A71	1c deep blue	15.00	.40
		Never hinged	35.00	
231	A72	2c brn vio	14.00	.30
		Never hinged	35.00	
232	A73	3c green	37.50	17.50
		Never hinged	105.00	
233	A74	4c ultra	55.00	9.00
		Never hinged	160.00	
a.		4c blue (error)	17,500.	16,500.
		Never hinged	32,500.	

No. 233a exists in two shades. No. 233a used is valued with small faults, as almost all examples come thus.

234	A75	5c chocolate	55.00	9.50
		Never hinged	160.00	
235	A76	6c purple	55.00	25.00
		Never hinged	160.00	
a.		6c red violet	55.00	25.00
		Never hinged	160.00	
236	A77	8c magenta	52.50	12.00
		Never hinged	160.00	
237	A78	10c blk brn	100.00	9.00
		Never hinged	285.00	
238	A79	15c dark green	225.00	82.50
		Never hinged	675.00	
239	A80	30c org brn	240.00	100.00
		Never hinged	725.00	
240	A81	50c slate blue	500.00	200.00
		Never hinged	1,450.	
		No gum	225.	
241	A82	$1 salmon	1,100.	550.
		Never hinged	3,750.	
		No gum	550.	
242	A83	$2 brown red	1,150.	550.
		Never hinged	3,800.	
		No gum	550.	
243	A84	$3 yel grn	1,500.	800.
		Never hinged	4,750.	
		No gum	750.	
a.		$3 olive green	1,500.	800.
		Never hinged	4,750.	
		No gum	750.	
244	A85	$4 crim lake	2,000.	1,000.
		Never hinged	7,000.	
		No gum	1,000.	
a.		$4 rose carmine	2,000.	1,050.
		Never hinged	7,000.	
		No gum	1,000.	
245	A86	$5 black	2,400.	1,200.
		Never hinged	10,000.	
		No gum	1,200.	

World's Columbia Expo., Chicago, May 1-Oct. 30, 1893.

Nos. 230-245 are known imperf., but were not regularly issues.

See Scott U.S. Specialized Catalogue Die and Plate Proofs section for the 2c.

Never-Hinged Stamps
See note before No. 182 regarding premiums for never-hinged stamps.

Bureau Issues
Starting in 1894, the Bureau of Engraving and Printing at Washington produced most U.S. postage stamps.

Until 1965 Bureau-printed stamps were engraved except Nos. 525-536 which were offset.

The combination of lithography and engraving (see #1253) was first used in 1964, and photogravure (see #1426) in 1971.

Franklin
A87

Washington
A88

Jackson
A89

Lincoln
A90

Grant
A91

Garfield
A92

Sherman
A93

Webster
A94

Clay
A95

Jefferson
A96

Perry
A97

James Madison
A98

John Marshall — A99

1894   Unwmk.   *Perf. 12*

246	A87	1c ultramarine	30.00	7.00
		Never hinged	90.00	
247	A87	1c blue	65.00	4.00
		Never hinged	190.00	

TWO CENTS:

Triangle A (Type I)

Type I (Triangle A). The horizontal lines of the ground work run across the triangle and are of the same thickness within it as without.

Triangle B (Type II)

Type II (Triangle B). The horizontal lines cross the triangle but are thinner within it than without. Other minor design differences exist, but the change to Triangle B is a sufficient determinant.

Triangle C (Types III and IV)

Type III (Triangle C). The horizontal lines do not cross the double lines of the triangle. The lines within the triangle are thin, as in Type II. The rest of the design is the same as Type II, except that most of the designs had the dot in the "S" of "CENTS" removed. Stamps with this dot present are listed; some specialists refer to them as "Type IIIa" varieties.

Type IV

Type IV (Triangle C). See No. 279B and its varieties. Type IV is from a new die with many major and minor design variations including, (1) re-cutting and lengthening of hairline, (2) shaded toga button, (3) strengthening of lines on sleeve, (4) additional dots on ear, (5) "T" of "TWO" straight at right, (6) background lines extend into white oval opposite "U" of "UNITED." Many other differences exist.

For further information concerning type IV, see also George Brett's article in the Sept. 1993 issue of the "The United States Specialist" and the 23-part article by Kenneth Diehl in the Dec. 1994 through Aug. 1997 issues of the "The United States Specialist."

248	A88	2c pink, type I	30.00	9.00
		Never hinged	90.00	
a.		Vert. pair, imperf. horiz.	5,500.	
249	A88	2c car lake, type I	150.00	7.00
		Never hinged	450.00	
a.		Double impression		—
250	A88	2c car, type I	30.00	3.00
		Never hinged	90.00	
a.		2c rose, type I	37.50	6.00
		Never hinged	110.00	
b.		2c scarlet, type I	27.50	3.00
		Never hinged	82.50	
d.		Horizontal pair, imperf. between	2,000.	
251	A88	2c car, type II	375.00	15.00
		Never hinged	1,100.	
a.		2c scarlet, type II	350.00	14.00
		Never hinged	1,050.	
252	A88	2c car, type III	125.00	14.00
		Never hinged	375.00	
		On cover		22.50
a.		2c scarlet, type III	110.00	16.00
		Never hinged	325.00	
b.		Horiz. pair, imperf. vert.	5,000.	
c.		Horiz. pair, imperf. between	5,500.	
253	A89	3c purple	110.00	13.00
		Never hinged	325.00	
254	A90	4c dark brown	190.00	12.50
		Never hinged	550.00	
255	A91	5c chocolate	110.00	10.00
		Never hinged	325.00	
c.		Vert. pair, imperf. horiz.	3,500.	
256	A92	6c dull brown	160.00	30.00
		Never hinged	475.00	
a.		Vert. pair, imperf. horiz.	3,000.	
257	A93	8c vio brn	160.00	22.50
		Never hinged	475.00	
258	A94	10c dark green	275.00	22.50
		Never hinged	850.00	
259	A95	15c dark blue	275.00	70.00
		Never hinged	850.00	
260	A96	50c orange	500.00	150.
		Never hinged	1,500.	

Type I

Type II

ONE DOLLAR

Type I. The circles enclosing "$1" are broken where they meet the curved line below "One Dollar."

Type II. The circles are complete.

261	A97	$1 blk, type I	1,000.	375.
		Never hinged	3,150.	
		No gum	400.	
261A	A97	$1 blk, type II	2,100.	825.
		Never hinged	6,500.	
		No gum	850.	
262	A98	$2 bright blue	2,750.	1,250.
		Never hinged	8,750.	
		No gum	1,100.	
263	A99	$5 dark green	4,250.	2,750.
		Never hinged	15,000.	
		No gum	2,200.	

For imperfs. and the 2c pink, vert. pair, imperf. hoirz., see Scott U.S. Specialized Catalogue Die and plate Proofs.

Same as 1894 Issue

Wmk. 191 Horizontally or Vertically

1895   **Perf. 12**

264	A87	1c blue	6.00	.60
		Never hinged	17.50	
265	A88	2c car, type I	35.00	3.50
		Never hinged	105.00	
266	A88	2c car, type II	40.00	5.50
		Never hinged	120.00	
267	A88	2c car, type III	5.50	.50
		Never hinged	16.00	
a.		2c pink, type III	20.00	5.00
		Never hinged	60.00	
b.		2c vermilion, type III	50.00	15.00
c.		2c rose carmine, type III	—	

The three left vertical rows from plate 170 are type II, the balance being type III.

268	A89	3c purple	37.50	2.25
		Never hinged	115.00	
269	A90	4c dark brown	42.50	3.50
		Never hinged	125.00	
270	A91	5c chocolate	35.00	3.50
		Never hinged	105.00	

271	A92	6c dull brown	120.00	8.50
		Never hinged	360.00	
a.		Wmkd. USIR	15,000.	8,500.
272	A93	8c violet brown	70.00	2.75
		Never hinged	210.00	
a.		Wmkd. USIR	6,000.	950.00
273	A94	10c dark green	95.00	2.25
		Never hinged	280.00	
274	A95	15c dark blue	210.00	17.50
		Never hinged	625.00	
275	A96	50c orange	260.	40.00
		Never hinged	775.	
a.		50c red orange	350.	47.50
		Never hinged	1,050.	
276	A97	$1 black, type I	600.	100.
		Never hinged	1,800.	
		No gum	250.	
276A	A97	$1 black, type II	1,250.	210.
		Never hinged	3,750.	
		No gum	500.	
277	A98	$2 bright blue	900.	425.
		Never hinged	2,900.	
		No gum	375.	
a.		$2 dark blue	900.	425.
		Never hinged	2,900.	
		No gum	375.	
278	A99	$5 dark green	2,000.	625.
		Never hinged	6,250.	
		No gum	800.	

For imperfs. and the 1c horiz. pair, imperf. vert., see Scott U.S. Specialized Catalogue Die and Plate Proofs.
For "I.R." overprints see Nos. R155, R156-R158.
No. 271a unused is valued in the grade of fine.

Wmk. 191 Horizontally or Vertically
1897-1903   **Perf. 12**

279	A87	1c dp grn, horiz. wmk ('98)	9.00	.50
		Never hinged	25.00	
a.		Vert. wmk (error)	50.00	7.50
		Never hinged	150.00	
279B	A88	2c red, type IV ('99)	9.00	.40
		Never hinged	25.00	
c.		2c rose carmine, type IV ('99)	275.00	220.00
		Never hinged	850.00	
d.		2c orange red, type IV, horiz. wmk. ('00)	11.50	2.00
		Never hinged	32.50	
e.		2c orange red, type IV, vert. wmk.	45.00	12.50
		Never hinged	140.00	
f.		2c carmine, type IV	10.00	2.00
		Never hinged	27.50	
g.		2c pink, type IV	55.00	7.50
		Never hinged	165.00	
h.		2c vermilion, type IV ('99)	11.00	3.00
		Never hinged	30.00	
i.		2c brown org, type IV ('99)	350.00	100.00
		Never hinged	900.00	
j.		Booklet pane of 6, red, type IV, horiz. wmk. ('00)	500.00	3,000.
		Never hinged	1,000.	
k.		Booklet pane of 6, red, type IV, vertical watermark ('02)	500.00	—
		Never hinged	1,000.	
l.		As No. 279B, all color missing (FO)	500.00	

No. 279Bl must be collected se-tenant with a partially printed stamp.

280	A90	4c rose brn ('98)	30.00	3.25
		Never hinged	80.00	
a.		4c lilac brown	30.00	3.25
		Never hinged	80.00	
b.		4c orange brown	30.00	3.00
		Never hinged	80.00	
281	A91	5c dk blue ('98)	32.50	2.25
		Never hinged	100.00	
282	A92	6c lake ('98)	45.00	6.50
		Never hinged	140.00	
a.		6c purple lake	75.00	20.00
		Never hinged	225.00	

Type I. The tips of the foliate ornaments do not impinge on the white curved line below "ten cents."

282C	A94	10c brn, type I ('98)	175.00	6.50
		Never hinged	525.00	

Type II. The tips of the ornaments break the curved line below the "e" of "ten" and the "t" of "cents."

283	A94	10c org brn, type II, horiz. wmk.	150.00	6.00
		Never hinged	450.00	
a.		Vert. wmk. ('00)	225.00	15.00
		Never hinged	700.00	
284	A95	15c ol grn ('98)	150.00	13.00
		Never hinged	475.00	
		Nos. 279-284 (8)	600.50	38.40

For "I.R." overprints, see Nos. R153-R155A.

VALUES FOR VERY FINE STAMPS
Please note: Stamps are valued in the grade of Very Fine unless otherwise indicated.

TRANS-MISSISSIPPI EXPOSITION ISSUE

Marquette on the Mississippi A100

Farming in the West — A101

Indian Hunting Buffalo A102

Frémont on the Rocky Mountains A103

Troops Guarding Wagon Train — A104

Hardships of Emigration A105

Western Mining Prospector A106

Western Cattle in Storm A107

Mississippi River Bridge A108

1898, June 17   Wmk. 191   Perf. 12

285	A100	1c dk yel grn	27.50	7.00
		Never hinged	75.00	
286	A101	2c copper red	25.00	2.75
		Never hinged	67.50	
287	A102	4c orange	110.00	27.50
		Never hinged	300.00	

288	A103	5c dull blue	100.00	25.00
		Never hinged	275.00	
289	A104	8c violet brown	150.00	50.00
		Never hinged	425.00	
a.		Vert. pair, imperf. horiz.	27,500.	
290	A105	10c gray vio	150.00	35.00
		Never hinged	425.00	
291	A106	50c sage grn	600.00	200.00
		Never hinged	1,800.	
292	A107	$1 black	1,400.	725.
		Never hinged	3,500.	
		No gum	800.	
293	A108	$2 org brn	1,900.	1,100.
		Never hinged	6,000.	
		No gum	875.	
		Nos. 285-293 (9)	4,463.	2,172.

Trans-Mississippi Exposition, Omaha, Neb., June 1 to Nov. 1, 1898.
For "I.R" overprints see #R158A-R158B.

Never-Hinged Stamps
See note before No. 182 regarding premiums for never-hinged stamps.

PAN-AMERICAN EXPOSITION ISSUE

Fast Lake Navigation A109

"Empire State" Express A110

Electric Automobile A111

Bridge at Niagara Falls — A112

Canal Locks at Sault Ste. Marie — A113

Fast Ocean Navigation — A114

1901, May 1   Wmk. 191   Perf. 12

294	A109	1c grn & blk	16.50	3.00
		Never hinged	42.50	
a.		Center inverted	12,500.	25,000.
		Never hinged	22,500.	
295	A110	2c car & blk	15.50	1.00
		Never hinged	40.00	
a.		Center inverted	55,000.	55,000.
296	A111	4c dp red brn & blk	70.00	19.00
		Never hinged	170.00	
a.		Center inverted	85,000.	—
297	A112	5c ultra & black	75.00	18.00
		Never hinged	180.00	
298	A113	8c brn vio & blk	90.00	55.00
		Never hinged	230.00	
299	A114	10c yel brn & blk	115.00	32.50
		Never hinged	300.00	
		Nos. 294-299 (6)	382.00	128.50
		Nos. 294-299, never hinged	962.50	

No. 296a was a special printing. Almost all unused examples of Nos. 295a and 296a have partial or disturbed gum. Values are for examples with full original gum that is slightly disturbed.

Franklin A115

Washington A116

Jackson A117

Grant A118

Lincoln
A119

Garfield
A120

Martha
Washington
A121

Webster
A122

Benjamin
Harrison
A123

Clay
A124

Jefferson
A125

David G.
Farragut
A126

Madison
A127

Marshall
A128

1902-03		**Wmk. 191**		*Perf. 12*
300	A115	1c blue grn		
		('03)	11.00	.25
		Never hinged	27.50	
b.		Booklet pane of 6	600.00	11,500.
		Never hinged	1,150.	
		Wmk. horiz.	2,000.	
301	A116	2c car ('03)	15.00	.50
		Never hinged	37.50	
c.		Booklet pane of 6	500.00	6,000.
		Never hinged	950.00	
302	A117	3c brt vio		
		('03)	50.00	4.00
		Never hinged	130.00	
303	A118	4c brn ('03)	55.00	2.50
		Never hinged	140.00	
304	A119	5c blue ('03)	60.00	2.25
		Never hinged	150.00	
305	A120	6c claret		
		('03)	60.00	5.75
		Never hinged	150.00	
306	A121	8c vio black	45.00	3.50
		Never hinged	110.00	
307	A122	10c pale red		
		brn ('03)	60.00	3.25
		Never hinged	150.00	
308	A123	13c purple blk	40.00	11.00
		Never hinged	100.00	
309	A124	15c ol grn		
		('03)	180.00	14.00
		Never hinged	475.00	
310	A125	50c org ('03)	375.	37.50
		Never hinged	1,150.	
311	A126	$1 black ('03)	600.00	95.00
		Never hinged	1,900.	
		No gum	240.00	
312	A127	$2 dk bl ('03)	825.00	200.00
		Never hinged	2,550.	
		No gum	350.00	
313	A128	$5 dk grn		
		('03)	2,100.	700.00
		Never hinged	6,250.	
		No gum	800.00	
		Nos. 300-313 (14)	4,476.	1,080.

For listings of designs A127 and A128 with Perf. 10 see Nos. 479 and 480.

1906-08				*Imperf.*
314	A115	1c blue green	15.00	20.00
		Never hinged	32.50	
314A	A118	4c brn ('08)	100,000.	52,500.
		Never hinged	230,000.	
315	A119	5c blue ('08)	325.00	1,250.
		Never hinged	600.00	

No. 314A was issued imperforate but all examples were privately perforated with large oblong perforations at the sides (Schermack type III).

Beware of examples of No. 303 with trimmed perforations and fake private perfs added.

Used examples of Nos. 314 and 315 must have contemporaneous cancels.

COIL STAMPS

Warning! Imperforate stamps are known fraudulently perforated to resemble coil stamps and part-perforate varieties. Fully perforated stamps and booklet stamps also are known with perforations fraudulently trimmed off to resemble coil stamps.

1908			*Perf. 12 Horizontally*	
316	A115	1c blue green	125,000.	
317	A119	5c blue	5,750.	—
		Never hinged	12,000.	

		Perf. 12 Vertically		
318	A115	1c blue green	4,250.	
		Never hinged	9,500.	

Coil stamps for use in vending and affixing machines are perforated on two sides only, either horizontally or vertically.

They were first issued in 1908, using perf. 12. This was changed to 8 ½ in 1910, and to 10 in 1914.

Imperforate sheets of certain denominations were sold to the vending machine companies which applied a variety of private perforations and separations.

Several values of the 1902 and later issues are found on an apparently coarse ribbed paper caused by worn blankets on the printing press and are not true paper varieties.

All examples of Nos. 316-318 must be accompanied by certificates of authenticity issued by recognized expertizing committees.

No. 318 mint never hinged is valued in the grade of fine.

Washington — A129

Type I

Type II

The two large arrows in the illustrations highlight the two major differences of the type II stamps: closing of the thin left border line next to the laurel leaf, and strengthening of the inner frame line at the lower left corner. The small arrows point out three minor differences that are not always easily discernible: strengthening of shading lines under the ribbon just above the "T" of "TWO," a shorter shading line to the left of the "P" in "POST-AGE," and shortening of a shading line in the left side ribbon.

Type I

1903, Nov. 12		**Wmk. 191**		*Perf. 12*
319	A129	2c car, type I	6.00	.25
		Never hinged	15.00	
a.		2c lake	—	
b.		2c carmine rose	15.00	.40
		Never hinged	45.00	
c.		2c scarlet	10.00	.30
		Never hinged	25.00	
d.		Vert. pair, imperf. horiz.,		
		No. 319	7,500.	
		Never hinged	17,500.	
e.		Vert. pair, imperf. between		
r.		Vert. pair, rouletted between	4,000.	

During the use of No. 319, the postmaster of San Francisco discovered in his stock panes that had the perforations missing between the top two rows of stamps. To facilitate their separation, the imperf rows were rouletted, and the stamps were sold over the counter. These vertical pairs with regular perfs all around and rouletted between are No. 319r. No 319e is from a different source. One example has been authenticated, and collectors are warned that other pairs exist with faint blind perfs or indentations from the perforating machine.

g.		Booklet pane of 6, carmine	125.00	450.00
		Never hinged	240.00	
n.		Booklet pane of 6, carmine rose	275.00	700.00
		Never hinged	500.00	
p.		Booklet pane of 6, scarlet	185.00	625.00
		Never hinged	350.00	

Type II

1908		**Wmk. 191**		*Perf. 12*
319F	A129	2c lake	10.00	.30
		Never hinged	25.00	
i.		2c carmine	65.00	50.00
		Never hinged	150.00	
j.		2c carmine rose	100.00	1.75
		Never hinged	225.00	
k.		2c scarlet	70.00	2.00
		Never hinged	160.00	
l.		Booklet pane of 6, scarlet	—	
q.		Booklet pane of 6, lake	300.00	800.00
		Never hinged	575.00	

Type I

1906, Oct. 2		**Wmk. 191**		*Imperf.*
320	A129	2c carmine	15.00	19.00
		Never hinged	32.50	
c.		2c carmine rose	75.00	42.50
		Never hinged	150.00	

Type II

1908		**Wmk. 191**		*Imperf.*
320A	A129	2c lake	45.00	50.00
		Never hinged	100.00	
d.		2c carmine	125.00	25.00
		Never hinged	190.00	

No. 320Ad was issued imperforate, but all examples were privately perforated with large oblong perforations at the sides (Schermack type III).

COIL STAMPS

1908			*Perf. 12 Horizontally*	
321	A129	2c car, type I,		
		pair	450,000.	250,000.

Four authenticated unused pairs of No. 321 are known and available to collectors. A fifth, unauthenticated pair is in the New York Public Library Miller collection, which is on long-term loan to the Smithsonian National Postal Museum. The value for an unused pair is for a fine-very fine example. Two fine pairs are recorded and one very fine pair.

There are no authenticated unused single stamps recorded. The used value is for a single on cover, of which two authenticated examples are known, both used from Indianapolis in 1908.

Numerous counterfeits exist.

322	A129	2c carmine,		
		type II	7,000.	—
		Never hinged	15,000.	

This Government Coil Stamp should not be confused with those of the International Vending Machine Co., which are perforated 12 ½.

All examples of Nos. 321-322 must be accompanied by certificates of authenticity issued by recognized expertizing committees.

VALUES FOR VERY FINE STAMPS
Please note: Stamps are valued in the grade of Very Fine unless otherwise indicated.

1904, Apr. 30		**Wmk. 191**		*Perf. 12*
323	A130	1c green	25.00	5.00
		Never hinged	65.00	
324	A131	2c carmine	25.00	2.00
		Never hinged	65.00	
a.		Vertical pair, imperf. horiz.	25,000.	

325	A132	3c violet	70.00	30.00
		Never hinged	185.00	
326	A133	5c dark blue	75.00	25.00
		Never hinged	200.00	
327	A134	10c red brown	130.00	30.00
		Never hinged	310.00	
		Nos. 323-327 (5)	325.00	92.00
		Nos. 323-327, never hinged	845.00	

JAMESTOWN EXPOSITION ISSUE

Captain John Smith — A135

Founding of Jamestown A136

Pocahontas A137

1907		Wmk. 191		Perf. 12
328	A135	1c green	25.00	5.00
		Never hinged	65.00	
329	A136	2c carmine	27.50	4.50
		Never hinged	75.00	
a.		2c carmine lake	—	
330	A137	5c blue	120.00	35.00
		Never hinged	290.00	
		Nos. 328-330 (3)	172.50	44.50
		Nos. 328-330, never hinged	430.00	

Franklin A138   Washington A139

There are several types of some of the 2c and 3c stamps of this and succeeding issues. These types are described under the dates at which they first appeared.

Illustrations of Types I-VII of the 2c (A140) and Types I-IV of the 3c (A140) are reproduced by permission of H. L. Lindquist.

1908-09		Wmk. 191		Perf. 12
331	A138	1c green	6.75	.40
		Never hinged	17.00	
a.		Booklet pane of 6	150.00	700.00
		Never hinged	300.00	

No. 331 exists in horizontal pair, imperforate between, a variety resulting from booklet experiments. Not regularly issued. Value in the grade of fine, $3,750.

No. 331a used is valued with a contemporaneous cancel. A certificate of authenticity is advised.

332	A139	2c carmine	6.25	.35
		Never hinged	15.00	
a.		Booklet pane of 6	135.00	500.00
		Never hinged	240.00	
b.		2c lake	4,250.	

No. 332a used is valued with a contemporaneous cancel. A certificate of authenticity is advised.

No. 332b is valued in the grade of fine.

Washington — A140

TYPE I

THREE CENTS.

Type I. The top line of the toga rope is weak and the rope shading lines are thin. The 5th line from the left is missing. The line between the lips is thin. (For descriptions of 3c types II, III and IV, see notes and illustrations preceding Nos. 484, 529-530.)

Used on both flat plate and rotary press printings.

333	A140	3c dp vio, type I	30.00	3.00
		Never hinged	75.00	
334	A140	4c org brn	37.50	1.50
		Never hinged	92.50	
335	A140	5c blue	50.00	2.50
		Never hinged	120.00	
336	A140	6c red orange	65.00	6.50
		Never hinged	150.00	
337	A140	8c olive green	45.00	3.00
		Never hinged	105.00	
338	A140	10c yellow ('09)	67.50	2.00
		Never hinged	160.00	
339	A140	13c bl grn ('09)	37.50	19.00
		Never hinged	90.00	
340	A140	15c pale ultra ('09)	65.00	6.50
		Never hinged	150.00	
341	A140	50c violet ('09)	300.00	22.50
		Never hinged	700.00	
342	A140	$1 vio brn ('09)	475.00	100.00
		Never hinged	1,100.	
		Nos. 331-342 (12)	1,186.	167.25

For listings of other perforated sheet stamps of A138, A139 and A140 see:
Nos. 357-366 Bluish paper
Nos. 374-382, 405-407 Single line wmk. Perf. 12
Nos. 423A-423C Single line wmk. Perf 12x10
Nos. 423D-423E Single line wmk. Perf 10x12
Nos. 424-430 Single line wmk. Perf. 10
Nos. 461 Single line wmk. Perf. 11
Nos. 462-469 unwmk. Perf. 10
Nos. 498-507 unwmk. Perf. 11
Nos. 519 Double line wmk. Perf. 11
Nos. 525-530 and 536 Offset printing
Nos. 538-546 Rotary press printing

Imperf

343	A138	1c green	5.00	5.50
		Never hinged	10.00	
344	A139	2c carmine	5.00	3.25
		Never hinged	10.00	
345	A140	3c dp violet, type I	10.00	22.50
		Never hinged	20.00	
346	A140	4c org brn ('09)	14.50	25.00
		Never hinged	29.00	
347	A140	5c blue ('09)	30.00	37.50
		Never hinged	60.00	
		Nos. 343-347 (5)	64.50	93.75
		Nos. 343-347, never hinged	129.00	

For listings of other imperforate stamps of designs A138, A139 and A140 see Nos. 383, 384, 408, 409 and 459 Single line wmk.
Nos. 481-485 unwmk.
Nos. 531-535 Offset printing

The values for used coil stamps are for examples with contemporaneous cancels that can be authenticated by expertizing committees. Used coils with cancels most commonly from the 1950s exist, and these and stamps with other non-contemporaneous cancels sell for less than the values shown.

COIL STAMPS

1908-10		Perf. 12 Horizontally		
348	A138	1c green	40.00	55.00
		Never hinged	80.00	
349	A139	2c carmine ('09)	100.00	150.00
		Never hinged	225.00	
350	A140	4c org brn ('10)	140.00	240.00
		Never hinged	325.00	
351	A140	5c blue ('09)	140.00	300.00
		Never hinged	325.00	
		Nos. 348-351 (4)	420.00	745.00

1909		Perf. 12 Vertically		
352	A138	1c green	100.00	225.00
		Never hinged	230.00	
353	A139	2c carmine	90.00	220.00
		Never hinged	200.00	
354	A140	4c org brn	200.00	275.00
		Never hinged	425.00	
355	A140	5c blue	210.00	300.00
		Never hinged	450.00	
356	A140	10c yellow	3,250.	4,500.
		Never hinged	8,000.	

For listings of other coil stamps of designs A138, A139 and A140, see #385-396, 410-413, 441-458 (single line wmk.), #486-496 (unwatermarked).

Beware of stamps offered as No. 356 which may be examples of No. 338 with perfs. trimmed at top and/or bottom. Beware also of plentiful fakes in the marketplace of Nos. 348-355, made by fraudulently perforating imperforate stamps or by fraudulently trimming perforations off fully perforated stamps. Authentication of all these coils is advised.

BLUISH PAPER

This was made with 35 percent rag stock instead of all wood pulp. The "bluish" color (actually grayish blue) goes through the paper showing clearly on the back as well as on the face.

1909				Perf. 12
357	A138	1c green	85.00	150.00
		Never hinged	180.00	
358	A139	2c carmine	80.00	150.00
		Never hinged	170.00	
359	A140	3c dp vio, type I	1,800.	9,000.
		Never hinged	4,000.	
360	A140	4c org brn	27,500.	
361	A140	5c blue	5,750.	17,500.
		Never hinged	14,500.	

Only two examples of No. 361 used off cover (three additional on cover) are recorded. Value used is for the better of the two examples, which is well-centered but has two reattached perforations.

362	A140	6c red org	1,250.	12,500.
		Never hinged	3,000.	
363	A140	8c olive green	30,000.	
		Never hinged	85,000.	
364	A140	10c yellow	1,600.	10,000.
		Never hinged	4,000.	
365	A140	13c blue green	2,600.	4,000.
		Never hinged	6,000.	
366	A140	15c pale ultra	1,250.	12,500.
		Never hinged	3,000.	

Nos. 360 and 363 were not regularly issued.

Used examples of Nos. 357-366 must bear contemporaneous cancels, and Nos. 359-366 used must be accompanied by certificates of authenticity issued by recognized expertizing committees.

LINCOLN CENTENARY OF BIRTH ISSUE

Lincoln — A141

1909, Feb. 12		Wmk. 191		Perf. 12
367	A141	2c carmine	5.00	2.00
		Never hinged	10.50	

Imperf

368	A141	2c carmine	14.00	22.50
		Never hinged	25.00	

BLUISH PAPER Perf. 12

369	A141	2c carmine	150.00	250.00
		Never hinged	320.00	

Used examples of No. 369 must bear contemporaneous cancels. Expertizing is recommended.

ALASKA-YUKON-PACIFIC EXPOSITION ISSUE

William H. Seward — A142

1909, June 1		Wmk. 191		Perf. 12
370	A142	2c carmine	7.50	2.25
		Never hinged	16.00	
a.		Imperf. (error), P#5209 block of 6	—	

No. 370a comes from error panes found in perforated stock. Plate 5209 was used only to print the perforated Alaska-Yukon-Pacific Exposition issue. No. 370a can only be collected as a plate-number stamp or multiple. Without an attached plate number 5209, the stamps from this pane cannot be differentiated from No. 371.

Imperf

371	A142	2c carmine	16.00	24.00
		Never hinged	32.50	

Seattle, Wash., June 1 to Oct. 16.

HUDSON-FULTON CELEBRATION ISSUE

"Half Moon" and Steamship A143

1909, Sept. 25		Wmk. 191		Perf. 12
372	A143	2c carmine	10.00	4.75
		Never hinged	21.00	

Imperf

373	A143	2c carmine	20.00	27.50

Tercentenary of the discovery of the Hudson River and Centenary of Robert Fulton's steamship.

DESIGNS OF 1908-09 ISSUES

1910-11		Wmk. 190		Perf. 12
374	A138	1c green	6.50	.25
		Never hinged	15.00	
a.		Booklet pane of 6	225.00	400.00
		Never hinged	375.00	
b.		Double impression	300.00	
375	A139	2c carmine	6.50	.25
		Never hinged	15.00	
a.		Booklet pane of 6	125.00	300.00
		Never hinged	200.00	
b.		2c lake	800.00	—
		Never hinged	1,750.	
c.		As "b," booklet pane of 6	10,000.	
d.		Double impression	750.00	—
		Never hinged	1,500.	
376	A140	3c dp vio, type I ('11)	20.00	2.00
		Never hinged	45.00	
377	A140	4c brown ('11)	30.00	1.00
		Never hinged	70.00	
378	A140	5c blue ('11)	30.00	.75
		Never hinged	70.00	
379	A140	6c red org ('11)	40.00	1.25
		Never hinged	90.00	
380	A140	8c ol grn ('11)	100.00	15.00
		Never hinged	225.00	
381	A140	10c yellow ('11)	95.00	6.00
		Never hinged	220.00	
382	A140	15c pale ultra ('11)	240.00	22.50
		Never hinged	525.00	
		Nos. 374-382 (9)	568.00	49.00

1910, Dec.				Imperf.
383	A138	1c green	2.50	2.75
		Never hinged	5.00	
384	A139	2c carmine	4.00	2.75
		Never hinged	8.00	

The values for used coil stamps are for examples with contemporaneous cancels that can be authenticated by expertizing committees. Used coils with cancels most commonly from the 1950s exist, and these and stamps with other non-contemporaneous cancels sell for less than the values shown.

COIL STAMPS

1910, Nov. 1		Perf. 12 Horizontally		
385	A138	1c green	45.00	50.00
		Never hinged	100.00	
386	A139	2c carmine	130.00	100.00
		Never hinged	280.00	

1910-11		Perf. 12 Vertically		
387	A138	1c green	190.00	140.00
		Never hinged	400.00	
388	A139	2c carmine	1,400.	2,250.
		Never hinged	3,250.	

Stamps offered as No. 388 frequently are privately perforated examples of No. 384, or examples of No. 375 with top and/or bottom perfs trimmed.

389	A140	3c dp vio, type I ('11)	110,000.	10,000.
		Never hinged	240,000.	

No. 389 is valued in the grade of fine.

Stamps offered as No. 389 sometimes are examples of No. 376 with top and/or bottom perfs trimmed.

Beware of plentiful fakes in the marketplace of Nos. 385-387.

Expertization by competent authorities is recommended.

1910		Perf. 8½ Horizontally		
390	A138	1c green	4.50	14.00
		Never hinged	10.00	
391	A139	2c carmine	42.50	50.00
		Never hinged	90.00	

1910-13		Perf. 8½ Vertically		
392	A138	1c green	27.50	55.00
		Never hinged	65.00	
393	A139	2c carmine	45.00	45.00
		Never hinged	105.00	

394	A140	3c dp vio, type I	
		('11)	60.00 70.00
		Never hinged	135.00
395	A140	4c brown ('12)	60.00 70.00
		Never hinged	135.00
396	A140	5c blue ('13)	60.00 70.00
		Never hinged	135.00
		Nos. 392-396 (5)	252.50 310.00

Beware also of plentiful fakes in the market-place of Nos. 390-393.

PANAMA-PACIFIC EXPOSITION ISSUE

Vasco Nunez de Balboa — A144

Pedro Miguel Locks, Panama Canal — A145

Golden Gate — A146

Discovery of San Francisco Bay — A147

1913		**Wmk. 190**	**Perf. 12**
397	A144	1c green	16.50 2.00
		Never hinged	40.00
398	A145	2c carmine	18.00 1.00
		Never hinged	40.00
a.		2c carmine lake	1,500.
		Never hinged	2,500.
b.		2c lake	5,250. 3,000.
		Never hinged	8,500.
399	A146	5c blue	70.00 10.00
		Never hinged	160.00
400	A147	10c orange yel	120.00 22.50
		Never hinged	270.00
400A	A147	10c orange	180.00 20.00
		Never hinged	400.00
		Nos. 397-400A (5)	404.50 55.50
		Nos. 397-400A, never hinged	910.00

1914-15			**Perf. 10**
401	A144	1c green	25.00 7.00
		Never hinged	60.00
402	A145	2c car ('15)	70.00 2.75
		Never hinged	170.00
403	A146	5c blue ('15)	160.00 20.00
		Never hinged	390.00
404	A147	10c org ('15)	700.00 75.00
		Never hinged	1,700.
		Nos. 401-404 (4)	955.00 104.75
		Nos. 401-404, never hinged	2,320.

1912-14		**Wmk. 190**	**Perf. 12**
405	A140	1c green	6.50 .25
		Never hinged	15.00
a.		Vert. pair, imperf. horiz.	2,000.
b.		Booklet pane of 6	65.00 75.00
		Never hinged	110.00
c.		Double impression	5,500.

TYPE I

TWO CENTS

Type I. There is one shading line in the first curve of the ribbon above the left "2" and one in the second curve of the ribbon above the right "2."

The button of the toga has only a faint outline.

The top line of the toga rope, from the button to the front of the throat, is also very faint.

The shading lines of the face terminate in front of the ear with little or no joining, to form a lock of hair.

Used on both flat plate and rotary press printings.

406	A140	2c car, type I	6.50 .25
		Never hinged	15.00
a.		Booklet pane of 6	65.00 90.00
		Never hinged	110.00
b.		Double impression	1,250.
c.		2c lake, type I	2,000. 6,000.
		Never hinged	3,750.
407	A140	7c black ('14)	70.00 14.00
		Never hinged	150.00
		Nos. 405-407 (3)	83.00 14.50

1912			**Imperf.**
408	A140	1c green	1.00 1.00
		Never hinged	2.00
409	A140	2c car, type I	1.20 1.20
		Never hinged	2.40

COIL STAMPS

1912		**Perf. 8½ Horizontally**	
410	A140	1c green	6.00 12.50
		Never hinged	13.00
411	A140	2c carmine, type I	10.00 17.50
		Never hinged	22.50

		Perf. 8½ Vertically	
412	A140	1c green	25.00 40.00
		Never hinged	55.00
413	A140	2c carmine, type I	60.00 50.00
		Never hinged	130.00
		Nos. 410-413 (4)	101.00 120.00

Beware also of plentiful fakes in the market-place of Nos. 410-413.

Franklin — A148

1912-14		**Wmk. 190**	**Perf. 12**
414	A148	8c pale ol grn	42.50 2.00
		Never hinged	100.00
415	A148	9c sal red ('14)	52.50 14.00
		Never hinged	120.00
416	A148	10c orange yel-low	42.50 .80
		Never hinged	100.00
a.		10c brown yellow	1,250.
		Never hinged	2,750.
417	A148	12c cl brn ('14)	42.50 5.00
		Never hinged	100.00
418	A148	15c gray	85.00 4.50
		Never hinged	190.00
419	A148	20c ultra ('14)	190.00 19.00
		Never hinged	400.00
420	A148	30c org red ('14)	115.00 19.00
		Never hinged	250.00
421	A148	50c violet ('14)	350.00 30.00
		Never hinged	775.00
		Nos. 414-421 (8)	920.00 94.30

No. 421 almost always has an offset of the frame lines on the back under the gum. No. 422 does not have this offset.

VALUES FOR VERY FINE STAMPS
Please note: Stamps are valued in the grade of Very Fine unless otherwise indicated.

1912, Feb. 12		**Wmk. 191**	**Perf. 12**
422	A148	50c violet	225.00 25.00
		Never hinged	500.00
423	A148	$1 violet brown	475.00 80.00
		Never hinged	1,000.

Perforated sheet stamps of type A148: #431-440 (single line wmk., perf. 10), #460 (double line wmk. perf. 10), #470-478 (unwmkd., perf. 10), #508-518 (unwmkd., perf. 11).

1914		**Wmk. 190**	**Perf. 12x10**
423A	A140	1c green	15,000. 5,500.
		Never hinged	—
423B	A140	2c rose red, type I	175,000. 14,000.
423C	A140	5c blue	16,000.

Nos. 423A-423C formerly were Nos. 424a, 425d and 428a, respectively.

No. 423A unused is valued in the grade of fine. Values for 423A used and 423B-423C are for fine-very fine examples.

1914		**Wmk. 190**	**Perf. 10x12**
423D	A140	1c green	10,000.
423E	A140	2c rose red, type I	

Nos. 423D and 423E formerly were Nos. 424b and 425c, respectively. Only one example is recorded of No. 423E.

No. 423D is valued in the grade of fine-very fine.

1913-15		**Wmk. 190**	**Perf. 10**
424	A140	1c grn ('14)	2.50 .25
		Never hinged	5.25
c.		Vert. pair, imperf. horiz.	3,000. 2,500.
		Never hinged	4,500.
d.		Booklet pane of 6 ('13)	5.25 7.50
		Never hinged	8.75
e.		As "d," imperf.	1,350.
f.		Vert. pair, imperf. between and with straight edge at top	13,000.

All known examples of No. 424e are without gum.

425	A140	2c rose red, type I ('14)	2.30 .25
		Never hinged	4.75
e.		Booklet pane of 6 ('13)	17.50 25.00
		Never hinged	30.00

For former Nos. 425c and 425d, see Nos. 423A and 423D.

426	A140	3c dp vio, type I ('14)	14.00 1.50
		Never hinged	32.50
427	A140	4c brn ('14)	32.50 1.00
		Never hinged	75.00
428	A140	5c blue ('14)	32.50 1.00
		Never hinged	75.00

For former No. 428a, see No. 423C.

429	A140	6c red org ('14)	45.00 2.00
		Never hinged	105.00
430	A140	7c black ('14)	90.00 5.00
		Never hinged	200.00
431	A148	8c pale olive grn ('14)	35.00 3.00
		Never hinged	82.50
a.		Double impression	—
432	A148	9c salmon red ('14)	45.00 9.00
		Never hinged	105.00
433	A148	10c org yel ('14)	45.00 1.00
		Never hinged	105.00
434	A148	11c dk grn ('15)	22.50 8.50
		Never hinged	55.00
435	A148	12c clar brn ('14)	25.00 6.00
		Never hinged	60.00
a.		12c copper red	30.00 7.00
		Never hinged	72.50
437	A148	15c gray ('14)	125.00 7.25
		Never hinged	280.00
438	A148	20c ultra ('14)	190.00 6.00
		Never hinged	430.00
439	A148	30c org red ('14)	220.00 20.00
		Never hinged	500.00
440	A148	50c violet ('15)	450.00 20.00
		Never hinged	1,050.
		Nos. 424-440 (16)	1,376. 91.75

The values for used coil stamps are for examples with contemporaneous cancels that can be authenticated by expertizing committees. Used coils with cancels most commonly from the 1950s exist, and these and stamps with other non-contemporaneous cancels sell for less than the values shown.

COIL STAMPS

1914		**Perf. 10 Horizontally**	
441	A140	1c green	1.00 1.50
		Never hinged	2.00
442	A140	2c carmine, type I	10.00 45.00
		Never hinged	22.50

1914		**Perf. 10 Vertically**	
443	A140	1c green	30.00 45.00
		Never hinged	65.00
444	A140	2c car, type I	50.00 40.00
		Never hinged	120.00
a.		2c lake	2,000.
445	A140	3c violet, type I	210.00 250.00
		Never hinged	500.00
446	A140	4c brown	130.00 150.00
		Never hinged	280.00
447	A140	5c blue	45.00 125.00
		Never hinged	100.00
		Nos. 443-447 (5)	465.00 610.00

Beware also of plentiful fakes in the market-place of Nos. 441-447.

ROTARY PRESS STAMPS

The Rotary Press Stamps are printed from plates that are curved to fit around a cylinder. This curvature produces stamps that are slightly larger, either horizontally or vertically, than those printed from flat plates. Designs of stamps from flat plates measure about 18½-19mm wide by 22mm high.

When the impressions are placed sidewise on the curved plates the designs are 19½-20mm wide; when they are placed vertically the designs are 22½ to 23mm high. A line of color (not a guide line) shows where the curved plates meet or join on the press.

ROTARY PRESS COIL STAMPS
Stamp designs: 18½-19x22½mm

1915-16		**Perf. 10 Horizontally**	
448	A140	1c green	7.50 17.50
		Never hinged	16.00

Type II

TWO CENTS.
Type II. Shading lines in ribbons as on type I.
The toga button, rope and rope shading lines are heavy.
The shading lines of the face at the lock of hair end in a strong vertical curved line.
Used on rotary press printings only.

Type III

Type III. Two lines of shading in the curves of the ribbons.
Other characteristics similar to type II.
Used on rotary press printings only.

Fraudulently altered examples of type III (Nos. 455, 488, 492 and 540) have had one line of shading scraped off to make them resemble type II (Nos. 454, 487, 491 and 539).

449	A140	2c red, type I	2,500. 600.00
	Never hinged		5,500.
450	A140	2c car, type III ('16)	12.50 *25.00*
	Never hinged		27.50

1914-16   Perf. 10 Vertically
Stamp designs: 19½-20x22mm

452	A140	1c green	10.00 *17.50*
	Never hinged		21.00
453	A140	2c carmine rose, type I	140.00 40.00
	Never hinged		300.00
454	A140	2c red, type II	70.00 22.50
	Never hinged		160.00
455	A140	2c carmine, type III	8.00 3.50
	Never hinged		18.00
456	A140	3c vio, type I ('16)	225.00 170.00
	Never hinged		500.00
457	A140	4c brown ('16)	25.00 30.00
	Never hinged		55.00
458	A140	5c blue ('16)	27.50 30.00
	Never hinged		60.00
Nos. 452-458 (7)			505.50 313.50

Horizontal Coil

1914, June 30   Imperf.

459	A140	2c car, type I	200. *1,300.*
	Never hinged		300.

When the value for a used stamp is higher than the unused value, the stamp must have a contemporaneous cancel. Valuable stamps of this type should be accompanied by certificates of authenticity issued by recognized expertizing committees. The used value for No. 459 is for an example with such a certificate.
Beware of examples of No. 453 with perforations fraudulently trimmed to resemble single examples of No. 459.

FLAT PLATE PRINTINGS

1915, Feb. 8   Wmk. 191   Perf. 10

460	A148	$1 violet black	650. 140.
	Never hinged		1,450.

1915, June 17   Wmk. 190   Perf. 11

461	A140	2c pale carmine red, type I	150. *375.*
	Never hinged		325.

Beware of fraudulently perforated examples of No. 409 being offered as No. 461.
See note on used stamps following No. 459.

Unwatermarked
From 1916 onward all postage stamps except Nos. 519 and 832b are on unwatermarked paper.

1916-17   Unwmk.   Perf. 10

462	A140	1c green	7.00 .35
	Never hinged		16.00
a.		Booklet pane of 6	9.50 *12.50*
	Never hinged		16.00
463	A140	2c carmine, type I	4.50 .40
	Never hinged		10.00 .45
a.		Booklet pane of 6	110.00 *110.00*
	Never hinged		180.00

See No. 467 for P# block of 6 from plate 7942.

464	A140	3c violet, type I	70.00 19.00
	Never hinged		175.00

Beware of fraudulently perforated examples of No. 483 being offered as No. 464.

465	A140	4c org brn	40.00 2.50
	Never hinged		90.00
466	A140	5c blue	70.00 2.50
	Never hinged		160.00
467	A140	5c car (error in plate of 2c, '17)	475.00 *1,500.*
	Never hinged		850.00

No. 467 is an error caused by using a 5c transfer roll in re-entering three subjects: 7942 UL 74, 7942 UL 84, 7942 LR 18; the balance of the subjects on the plate being normal 2c entries. No. 467 imperf. is listed as No. 485. The error perf 11 on unwatermarked paper is No. 505.

468	A140	6c red orange	85.00 9.00
	Never hinged		190.00
469	A140	7c black	120.00 15.00
	Never hinged		270.00
470	A148	8c olive green	55.00 8.00
	Never hinged		125.00
471	A148	9c salmon red	60.00 20.00
	Never hinged		135.00
472	A148	10c orange yel	100.00 2.50
	Never hinged		230.00
473	A148	11c dark green	45.00 20.00
	Never hinged		95.00
474	A148	12c claret brn	50.00 7.50
	Never hinged		115.00
475	A148	15c gray	180.00 16.00
	Never hinged		400.00
476	A148	20c lt ultra	225.00 20.00
	Never hinged		525.00
476A	A148	30c orange red	2,000.
	Never hinged		4,250.

No. 476A is valued in the grade of fine.

477	A148	50c lt violet ('17)	900. 85.00
	Never hinged		2,000.
478	A148	$1 violet black	625.00 30.00
	Never hinged		1,450.
Nos. 462-466,468-476,477-478 (16)			2,637. 257.75

TYPES OF 1902-03 ISSUE

1917, Mar. 22   Unwmk.   Perf. 10

479	A127	$2 dark blue	210.00 40.00
	Never hinged		475.00
480	A128	$5 light green	170.00 35.00
	Never hinged		375.00

1916-17   Imperf.

481	A140	1c green	1.25 .95
	Never hinged		1.90

Type Ia

TWO CENTS
Type Ia. The design characteristics are similar to type I except that all of the lines of the design are stronger.
The toga button, toga rope and rope shading lines are heavy.
The latter characteristics are those of type II, which, however, occur only on impressions from rotary plates.
Used only on flat plates 10208 and 10209.

482	A140	2c carmine, type I	1.50 1.30
	Never hinged		2.60
482A	A140	2c deep rose, type Ia	— *65,000.*

No. 482A was issued imperforate but all examples were privately perforated with large oblong perforations at the sides (Schermack type III).

Type II

THREE CENTS
Type II. The top line of the toga rope is strong and the rope shading lines are heavy and complete.
The line between the lips is heavy.
Used on both flat plate and rotary press printings.

483	A140	3c violet, type I ('17)	12.00 10.00
	Never hinged		24.00
484	A140	3c violet, type II	10.00 8.00
	Never hinged		20.00
485	A140	5c car (error in plate of 2c) ('17)	9,000.
	Never hinged		14,000.

Although No. 485 is valued as a single stamp, such examples are seldom seen in the marketplace.
No. 485 usually is seen as the center stamp in a block of 9 with 8 No. 482 (value with #485 never hinged, $22,500) or as two center stamps in a block of 12 (value with both No. 485 never hinged, $42,500).

ROTARY PRESS COIL STAMPS
(See note over No. 448)

1916-18   Perf. 10 Horizontally
Stamp designs: 18½-19x22½mm

486	A140	1c green ('18)	.85 .85
	Never hinged		1.75
487	A140	2c carmine, type II	12.50 14.00
	Never hinged		27.50
488	A140	2c carmine, type III	3.00 *5.00*
	Never hinged		6.50
489	A140	3c vio, type I ('17)	4.50 2.25
	Never hinged		10.00
Nos. 486-489 (4)			20.85 22.10

1916-22   Perf. 10 Vertically
Stamp designs: 19½-20x22mm

490	A140	1c green	.50 .60
	Never hinged		1.05
491	A140	2c carmine, type II	2,500. 800.00
	Never hinged		5,250.
492	A140	2c carmine, type III	9.00 1.00
	Never hinged		19.00
493	A140	3c vio, type I ('17)	14.00 4.50
	Never hinged		30.00
494	A140	3c vio, type II ('18)	10.00 2.50
	Never hinged		21.50
495	A140	4c org brn ('17)	10.00 7.00
	Never hinged		21.50
496	A140	5c blue ('19)	3.25 2.50
	Never hinged		7.00
497	A148	10c org yel ('22)	17.50 17.50
	Never hinged		35.00

Blind Perfs
Listings of imperforate-between varieties are for examples which show no trace of "blind perfs," traces of impressions from the perforating pins which do not cut into the paper.
Some unused stamps have had the gum removed to eliminate the impressions from the perforating pins. These stamps do not qualify as the listed varieties.

TYPES OF 1913-15 ISSUE
FLAT PLATE PRINTINGS

1917-19   Unwmk.   Perf. 11

498	A140	1c green	.35 .25
	Never hinged		.75
a.		Vertical pair, imperf. horiz.	800.00
	Never hinged		1,600.
b.		Horizontal pair, imperf. between	600.00
	Never hinged		1,350.
c.		Vertical pair, imperf. between	700.00
d.		Double impression	250.00 *3,750.*
e.		Booklet pane of 6	2.50 *2.00*
	Never hinged		4.25
f.		Booklet pane of 30	1,050. *12,500.*
	Never hinged		1,700.
g.		Perf. 10 at top or bottom	15,000. *20,000.*
	Never hinged		27,500.

No. 498g used is valued in the grade of fine.

499	A140	2c rose, type I	.35 .25
	Never hinged		.75
a.		Vertical pair, imperf. horiz., type I	1,000.
	Never hinged		2,000.
b.		Horiz. pair, imperf. vert., type I	550.00 *600.00*
	Never hinged		1,100.
c.		Vert. pair, imperf. btwn., type I	900.00 *300.00*
e.		Booklet pane of 6, type I	4.00 *2.50*
	Never hinged		6.75

---

f.		Booklet pane of 30, type I	22,500. —
	Never hinged		32,500.
g.		Double impression, type I	200.00 *2,000.*
	Never hinged		400.00
h.		2c lake, type I	500.00 800.00
	Never hinged		1,000.
i.		As "e," single stamp, lake	—

No. 499b is valued in the grade of fine. No. 499g used is valued in the grade of fine.

500	A140	2c deep rose, type Ia	250.00 240.00
	Never hinged		550.00
501	A140	3c lt vio, type I	10.00 .40
	Never hinged		22.50
b.		Booklet pane of 6, type I	75.00 *80.00*
	Never hinged		125.00
c.		Vert. pair, imper. horiz., type I	2,100.
	Never hinged		3,250.
d.		Double impression	3,500. *3,500.*

No. 501d is valued in the grade of fine.

502	A140	3c dark violet, type II	13.00 .75
	Never hinged		30.00
b.		Bklt. pane of 6, type II	60.00 *75.00*
	Never hinged		100.00
c.		Vert. pair, imperf. horiz., type II	1,400. *850.00*
	Never hinged		2,750.
d.		Double impression	800.00 *1,000.*
	Never hinged		1,600.
e.		Perf. 10 at top or bottom	15,000. *30,000.*
	Never hinged		21,500.
503	A140	4c brown	9.00 .40
	Never hinged		20.00
b.		Double impression	
504	A140	5c blue	8.00 .35
	Never hinged		18.00
a.		Horizontal pair, imperf. between	20,000.
b.		Double impression	1,750. *1,600.*
505	A140	5c rose (error in plate of 2c)	350.00 *600.00*
	Never hinged		625.00
506	A140	6c red orange	12.00 .40
	Never hinged		27.50
a.		Perf. 10 at top or bottom	30,000. 8,000.
b.		Double impression, never hinged	2,000.

No. 506a also exists as a transitional stamp gauging partly perf 10 and partly perf 11 at top. Value thus the same as normal 506a.
No. 506b is a partial double impression. Two authenticated examples are documented.

507	A140	7c black	26.00 1.25
	Never hinged		60.00
508	A148	8c olive bister	10.00 .65
	Never hinged		27.50
b.		Vertical pair, imperf. between	— 9,000.
c.		Perf. 10 at top or bottom	
509	A148	9c salmon red	12.00 1.75
	Never hinged		27.50
a.		Perf. 10 at top or bottom	37,500. 7,500.

No. 509a also exists as a transitional stamp gauging partly perf 10 and partly perf 11 at top or bottom. Value thus the same as normal 509a.

510	A148	10c orange yellow	16.00 .25
	Never hinged		36.00
a.		10c brown yellow	1,400.
	Never hinged		3,250.
511	A148	11c lt green	8.00 2.50
	Never hinged		18.00
a.		Perf. 10 at top or bottom	4,000. 3,750.
	Never hinged		7,500.

No. 511a also exists as a transitional stamp gauging partly perf 10 and partly perf 11 at top or bottom. Value thus the same as normal 511a.

512	A148	12c claret brown	8.00 .40
	Never hinged		18.00
a.		12c brown carmine	9.00 .50
	Never hinged		20.00
b.		Perf. 10 at top or bottom	27,500. 15,000.
513	A148	13c apple grn ('19)	10.00 6.00
	Never hinged		22.00
514	A148	15c gray	35.00 1.50
	Never hinged		80.00
a.		Perf. 10 at bottom	10,000.
515	A148	20c lt ultra	42.50 .45
	Never hinged		90.00
b.		Vertical pair, imperf. between	1,750. *3,250.*
c.		Double impression	1,250.
	Never hinged		2,500.
d.		Perf. 10 at top or bottom	— 12,500.

No. 515b is valued in the grade of fine.
Beware of pairs with blind perforations inside the design of the top stamp that are offered as No. 515b.
No. 515c is a partial double impression.

516	A148	30c orange red	30.00 1.50
	Never hinged		70.00
a.		Perf. 10 at top or bottom	20,000. 15,000.
	Never hinged		37,500.
b.		Double impression	

No. 516a used is valued in the grade of fine.

517	A148	50c red violet	47.50 .75
	Never hinged		115.00
b.		Vertical pair, imperf. between & with natural straight edge at bottom	6,000.
c.		Perf. 10 at top or bottom	17,500.

No. 517b is valued in average condition and may be a unique used pair (precanceled). The editors would like to see authenticated evidence of an unused pair.

518	A148	$1 violet brown	37.50	1.50
		Never hinged	95.00	
b.		$1 deep brown	1,900.	1,250.
		Never hinged	4,000.	

Nos. 498-504,506-518 (20) 587.20 261.30

No. 518b is valued in the grade of fine to very fine.

TYPE OF 1908-09 ISSUE
1917, Oct. 10   Wmk. 191   *Perf. 11*

519	A139	2c carmine	400.00	1,750.
		Never hinged	850.00	

Beware of examples of No. 344 fraudulently perforated and offered as No. 519. Obtaining a certificate from a recognized expertizing committee is strongly recommended.
Warning: See note following No. 459 regarding used stamps.

Franklin — A149

1918, Aug.   Unwmk.   *Perf. 11*

523	A149	$2 org red & blk	525.	250.
		Never hinged	1,150.	
524	A149	$5 dp grn & blk	170.	35.00
		Never hinged	360.	

See No. 547 for $2 carmine & black.

TYPES OF 1917-19 ISSUE
OFFSET PRINTING
1918-20   Unwmk.   *Perf. 11*

525	A140	1c gray green	2.50	.90
		Never hinged	6.00	
a.		1c dark green	10.00	1.75
		Never hinged	25.00	
c.		Horizontal pair, imperf.		
		between	750.00	650.00
d.		Double impression	40.00	750.00
		Never hinged	90.00	

No. 525c is valued in the grade of fine and with natural straight edge at right, as virtually all recorded examples come thus. No. 525d used is valued in the grade of very good.

Type IV

TWO CENTS
Type IV — Top line of the toga rope is broken.
The shading lines in the toga button are so arranged that the curving of the first and last form "D (reversed) ID."
The line of color in the left "2" is very thin and usually broken.
Used on offset printings only.

Type V

Type V — Top line of the toga is complete. There are five vertical shading lines in the toga button.
The line of color in the left "2" is very thin and usually broken.
The shading dots on the nose are as shown on the diagram.
Used on offset printings only.

Type Va

Type Va — Characteristics are the same as type V except in the shading dots of the nose. The third row of dots from the bottom has four dots instead of six. The overall height is ⅓mm shorter than the other types.
Used on offset printings only.

Type VI

Type VI — General characteristics the same as type V except that the line of color in the left "2" is very heavy.
Used on offset printings only.

TYPE VII

Type VII — The line of color in the left "2" is invariably continuous, clearly defined and heavier than in type V or Va but not as heavy as type VI.
An additional vertical row of dots has been added to the upper lip.
Numerous additional dots have been added to the hair on top of the head.
Used on offset printings only.

526	A140	2c car, type IV		
		('20)	25.00	4.00
		Never hinged	57.50	
527	A140	2c car, type V		
		('20)	18.00	1.25
		Never hinged	40.00	
a.		Double impression	100.00	—
		Never hinged	225.00	
b.		Vert. pair, imperf. horiz.	850.00	—
c.		Horiz. pair, imperf. vert.	1,000.	—
528	A140	2c car, type Va		
		('20)	8.00	.40
		Never hinged	20.00	
c.		Double impression	60.00	
		Never hinged	150.00	
g.		Vert. pair, imperf. be-		
		tween	3,500.	
528A	A140	2c car, type VI		
		('20)	47.50	2.00
		Never hinged	115.00	
d.		Double impression	200.00	900.00
		Never hinged	450.00	
f.		Vert. pair, imperf. horiz.	—	
h.		Vert. pair, imperf. be-		
		tween	5,000.	
528B	A140	2c car, type VII		
		('20)	20.00	.75
		Never hinged	50.00	
e.		Double impression	77.50	400.00

No. 528Be used is valued in the grade of very good to fine.

TYPE III

THREE CENTS
Type III — The top line of the toga rope is strong but the 5th shading line is missing as in type I.
Center shading line of the toga button consists of two dashes with a central dot.
The "P" and "O" of "POSTAGE" are separated by a line of color.
The frame line at the bottom of the vignette is complete.
Used on offset printings only.

TYPE IV

Type IV — The shading lines of the toga rope are complete.
The second and fourth shading lines in the toga button are broken in the middle and the third line is continuous with a dot in the center.
The "P" and "O" of "POSTAGE" are joined.
The frame line at the bottom of the vignette is broken.
Used on offset printings only.

529	A140	3c vio, type III	3.50	.50
		Never hinged	7.75	
a.		Double impression	50.00	800.00
		Never hinged	115.00	
b.		Printed on both sides	2,500.	

No. 529a used is valued in the grade of very good.

530	A140	3c pur, type IV	2.00	.30
		Never hinged	4.50	
a.		Double impression	40.00	750.00
		Never hinged	90.00	
b.		Printed on both sides	750.00	
		Never hinged	1,100.	
c.		Triple impression	1,750.	—

Nos. 525-530 (8) 126.50 10.10

No. 530a used is valued in the grade of fine.

1918-20   *Imperf.*

531	A140	1c green ('19)	12.00	12.00
		Never hinged	21.00	
532	A140	2c car rose,		
		type IV		
		('20)	37.50	42.50
		Never hinged	70.00	
533	A140	2c car, type V		
		('20)	110.00	125.00
		Never hinged	175.00	
534	A140	2c car, type Va		
		('20)	15.00	15.00
		Never hinged	26.00	
534A	A140	2c car, type VI		
		('20)	40.00	40.00
		Never hinged	75.00	
534B	A140	2c car, type VII		
		('20)	2,000.	1,400.
		Never hinged	3,750.	
535	A140	3c vio, type IV	10.00	6.00
		Never hinged	18.00	
a.		Double impression	100.00	—
		Never hinged	200.00	

Nos. 531-534A,535 (6) 224.50 240.50

1919, Aug. 15   *Perf. 12½*

536	A140	1c gray green	20.00	35.00
		Never hinged	45.00	
a.		Horiz. pair, imperf. vert.	1,000.	

"Victory" and Flags of the Allies — A150

FLAT PLATE PRINTING
1919, Mar. 3   Engr.   *Perf. 11*

537	A150	3c violet	10.00	3.25
		Never hinged	20.00	
a.		3c deep red violet	1,250.	1,750.
		Never hinged	2,300.	
b.		3c light reddish violet	150.00	50.00
		Never hinged	300.00	
c.		3c red violet	200.00	60.00
		Never hinged	400.00	

Victory of the Allies in World War I.
No. 537a is valued in the grade of fine.

ROTARY PRESS PRINTINGS
1919   *Perf. 11x10*
Stamp designs: 19½-20x22-22¼mm

538	A140	1c green	10.00	9.00
		Never hinged	23.00	
a.		Vert. pair, imperf. horiz.	60.00	125.00
		Never hinged	125.00	
539	A140	2c carmine		
		rose, type		
		II	2,700.	17,500.
		Never hinged	4,250.	
540	A140	2c car rose,		
		type III	12.00	9.50
		Never hinged	27.50	
a.		Vert. pair, imperf. horiz.	60.00	140.00
		Never hinged	125.00	
b.		Horiz. pair, imperf. vert.	2,000.	
541	A140	3c vio, type II	40.00	32.50
		Never hinged	100.00	

The part perforate varieties of Nos. 538a and 540a were issued in sheets and may be had in blocks; similar part perforate varieties, Nos. 490 and 492, are from coils and are found only in strips.
See note over No. 448 regarding No. 539.
No. 539 is valued in the grade of fine.
No. 540b is valued in the grade of fine.

1920, May 26 — Perf. 10x11
Stamp design: 19x22½-22¾mm

542	A140	1c green	12.50	1.50
		Never hinged	30.00

1921 — Perf. 10
Stamp design: 19x22½mm

543	A140	1c green	.70	.40
		Never hinged	1.75
a.		Horizontal pair, imperf. between	5,000.

1922 — Perf. 11
Stamp design: 19x22½mm

544	A140	1c green	22,500.	3,500.
		Never hinged	35,000.

No. 544 is valued in the grade of fine.

1921
Stamp designs: 19½-20x22mm

545	A140	1c green	170.00	200.00
		Never hinged	450.00
546	A140	2c carmine rose, type III	105.00	190.00
		Never hinged	230.00
a.		Perf. 10 on left side	7,500.	17,500.

No. 546a used is valued in the grade of very good. It is unique used.

FLAT PLATE PRINTING
1920, Nov. 1 — Perf. 11

547	A149	$2 carmine & black	125.	40.
		Never hinged	270.
a.		$2 lake & black	200.	40.
		Never hinged	425.

PILGRIM TERCENTENARY ISSUE

"Mayflower" A151

Landing of the Pilgrims — A152

Signing of the Compact — A153

1920, Dec. 21 — Perf. 11

548	A151	1c green	4.00	2.25
		Never hinged	10.00
549	A152	2c carmine rose	5.25	1.60
		Never hinged	12.50
550	A153	5c deep blue	35.00	14.00
		Never hinged	75.00
		Nos. 548-550 (3)	44.25	17.85
		Nos. 548-550, never hinged	97.50

Tercentenary of the landing of the Pilgrims at Plymouth, Mass.

Nathan Hale A154

Franklin A155

Harding A156

Washington A157

Lincoln A158

Martha Washington A159

Theodore Roosevelt A160

Garfield A161

McKinley A162

Grant A163

Jefferson A164

Monroe A165

Rutherford B. Hayes A166

Grover Cleveland A167

American Indian A168

Statue of Liberty A169

Golden Gate — A170

Niagara Falls — A171

American Buffalo A172

Arlington Amphitheater A173

Lincoln Memorial A174

U.S. Capitol A175

Head of Freedom Statue, Capitol Dome — A176

FLAT PLATE PRINTINGS

1922-25 — Unwmk. — Perf. 11

551	A154	½c ol brn ('25)	.25	.25
		Never hinged	.50
552	A155	1c dp grn ('23)	1.40	.25
		Never hinged	3.00
a.		Booklet pane of 6	7.50	4.00
		Never hinged	12.50
553	A156	1½c yel brn ('25)	2.25	.25
		Never hinged	4.60
554	A157	2c carmine ('23)	1.30	.25
		Never hinged	3.00
a.		Horiz. pair, imperf. vert.	250.00
b.		Vert. pair, imperf. horiz.	6,000.
			10,000.
c.		Booklet pane of 6	7.00	3.00
		Never hinged	12.00
d.		Perf. 10 at top or bottom	17,500.	9,500.
555	A158	3c violet ('23)	14.00	1.20
		Never hinged	30.00
556	A159	4c yel brn ('23)	17.50	.50
		Never hinged	37.50
a.		Vert. pair, imperf. horiz.	12,500.
b.		Perf. 10 at top or bottom	3,500.	22,500.

No. 556a is unique. It resulted from a sheet that was damaged and patched during production.

No. 556b used also exists as a transitional stamp gauging 10 at left top and 11 at right top. Value the same.

557	A160	5c dark blue	17.50	.30
		Never hinged	37.50
a.		Imperf., pair	2,000.
		Never hinged	4,000.
b.		Horiz. pair, imperf. vert.
c.		Perf. 10 at top or bottom	—	9,500.
558	A161	6c red orange	32.50	1.00
		Never hinged	70.00
559	A162	7c black ('23)	7.75	.75
		Never hinged	16.50
560	A163	8c ol grn ('23)	40.00	1.00
		Never hinged	90.00
561	A164	9c rose ('23)	12.50	1.25
		Never hinged	27.00
562	A165	10c orange ('23)	15.00	.35
		Never hinged	32.50
a.		Vert. pair, imperf. horiz.	2,000.
		Never hinged	3,250.
b.		Imperf., pair	1,900.
c.		Perf. 10 at top or bottom	70,000.	15,000.

No. 562a is valued in the grade of fine, with gum and without blue defacing lines. No. 562b is valued without gum and without blue pencil defacing lines. No. 562c is valued in the grade of fine.

563	A166	11c greenish blue	1.40	.60
		Never hinged	3.00
a.		11c light bluish green	1.40	.60
		Never hinged	3.00
d.		Imperf., pair	20,000.

Many other intermediate shades exist for Nos. 563 and 563a, all falling within the blue or green color families.

564	A167	12c brn vio ('23)	.35
		Never hinged	11.50
a.		Horiz. pair, imperf. vert.	3,750.
565	A168	14c blue ('23)	4.75	.90
		Never hinged	10.50
566	A169	15c gray	17.50	.30
		Never hinged	37.50
567	A170	20c car rose ('23)	17.50	.30
		Never hinged	37.50
a.		Horiz. pair, imperf. vert.	2,500.
		Never hinged	5,000.

No. 567a is valued in the grade of fine.

568	A171	25c yel grn	15.00	.75
		Never hinged	32.50
b.		Vert. pair, imperf. horiz.	3,250.
c.		Perf. 10 at one side	5,000.	11,000.
		Never hinged	7,500.

No. 568b is valued in the grade of fine. No. 568c used is valued in the grade of fine.

569	A172	30c ol brn ('23)	25.00	.60
		Never hinged	55.00
570	A173	50c lilac	35.00	.40
		Never hinged	75.00
571	A174	$1 vio brn ('23)	37.50	.80
		Never hinged	80.00
572	A175	$2 dp blue ('23)	60.00	9.00
		Never hinged	125.00
573	A176	$5 car & bl ('23)	100.00	15.00
		Never hinged	180.00
a.		$5 car lake & dk bl	175.00	30.00
		Never hinged	350.00
		Nos. 551-573 (23)	480.85	36.35
		Nos. 551-573, never hinged	1,075.

No. 556a is unique. No. 554b is valued in the grade of fine. No. 562b is valued without gum and without blue pencil defacing lines. No. 568b is valued in the grade of fine.

For other listings of perforated stamps of designs A154 to A173 see:

Nos. 578 & 579, Perf. 11x10
Nos. 581-591, Perf. 10
Nos. 594-596, Perf. 11
Nos. 632-642, 653, 692-696, Perf. 11x10½
Nos. 697-701, Perf. 10½x11
This series also includes #622-623 (perf. 11), 684-687 & 720-723.

1923-25 — Imperf.
Stamp design 19¼x22¼mm

575	A155	1c green	5.00	5.00
		Never hinged	11.00
576	A156	1½c yel brn ('25)	1.25	1.50
		Never hinged	2.70

The 1½c A156 Rotary press imperforate is listed as No. 631.

577	A157	2c carmine	1.30	1.25
		Never hinged	2.90
a.		2c carmine lake	2.70
		Nos. 575-577 (3)	7.55	7.75
		Nos. 575-577, never hinged	16.60

ROTARY PRESS PRINTINGS
(See note over No. 448)

1923 — Perf. 11x10

578	A155	1c green	75.00	160.00
		Never hinged	160.00
579	A157	2c carmine	70.00	140.00
		Never hinged	150.00

Nos. 578-579 were made from coil waste of Nos. 597, 599 and measure approximately 19¾x22¼mm.

1923-26 — Perf. 10

581	A155	1c green	10.00	.75
		Never hinged	22.50
582	A156	1½c brown ('25)	6.00	.65
		Never hinged	13.50
583	A157	2c car ('24)	3.00	.30
		Never hinged	6.50
a.		Booklet pane of 6	110.00	150.00
		Never hinged	200.00
584	A158	3c violet ('25)	27.50	3.00
		Never hinged	62.50
585	A159	4c yel brn ('25)	17.50	.65
		Never hinged	37.50
586	A160	5c blue ('25)	17.50	.40
		Never hinged	37.50
a.		Horizontal pair, imperf. vertically	7,500.

No. 586a is unique, precanceled, with average centering and small faults, and it is valued as such.

587	A161	6c red org ('25)	9.25	.60
		Never hinged	21.00
588	A162	7c black ('26)	12.50	6.25
		Never hinged	27.50
589	A163	8c ol grn ('26)	27.50	4.50
		Never hinged	60.00
590	A164	9c rose ('26)	6.00	2.50
		Never hinged	13.50
591	A165	10c org ('25)	45.00	.50
		Never hinged	90.00
		Nos. 581-591 (11)	181.75	20.10
		Nos. 581-591, never hinged	402.00

1923 — Perf. 11

594	A155	1c green	35,000.	11,000.
		With gum	65,000.

The main listing for No. 594 unused is for an example without gum; both unused and used are valued with perforations just touching frameline on one side.

595	A157	2c carmine	240.00	375.00
		Never hinged	475.00

Nos. 594-595 were made from coil waste of Nos. 597 and 599, and measure approximately 19¾x22¼mm.

596	A155	1c green	150,000.
		Precanceled	100,000.

No. 596 was made from rotary press sheet waste and measures approximately 19¼x22½mm. A majority of the examples carry the Bureau precancel "Kansas City, Mo." No. 596 is valued in the grade of fine.

COIL STAMPS
ROTARY PRESS

1923-29 — Perf. 10 Vertically
Stamp designs approximately 19¾x22¼mm

597	A155	1c green	.30	.25
		Never hinged	.60
598	A156	1½c brown ('25)	.90	.25
		Never hinged	1.80

Type I

Type II

Type I   Type II

TYPE I. No line outlining forehead. No heavy hair lines at top center of head. Outline of left acanthus scroll generally faint at top and toward base at left side.

TYPE II. Thin line outlining forehead. Three heavy hair lines at top center of head; two being outstanding in the white area. Outline of left acanthus scroll very strong and clearly defined at top (under left edge of lettered panel) and at lower curve (above and to left of numeral oval). This type appears only on Nos. 599A and 634A.

599	A157	2c car, type I	.35	.25
		Never hinged	.70	
b.		2c carmine lake, type I,		
		never hinged	300.00	—
599A	A157	2c car, type II		
		('29)	105.00	17.50
		Never hinged	200.00	
600	A158	3c violet ('24)	6.25	.25
		Never hinged	12.50	
601	A159	4c yel brn	3.75	.35
		Never hinged	7.50	
602	A160	5c dk blue ('24)	1.75	.25
		Never hinged	3.50	
603	A165	10c orange ('24)	3.50	.25
		Never hinged	7.00	

The 6c design A161 coil stamp is listed as No. 723.

1923-25   *Perf. 10 Horizontally*
Stamp designs: 19¼x22½mm

604	A155	1c green ('24)	.40	.25
		Never hinged	.80	
605	A156	1½c yel brn ('25)	.40	.25
		Never hinged	.80	
606	A157	2c carmine	.40	.25
		Never hinged	.80	
a.		2c carmine lake	75.00	—
		Never hinged	150.00	

Nos. 597-599,600-606 (10)   18.00   2.60
Nos. 597-599, 600-606,
never hinged   36.00

HARDING MEMORIAL ISSUE

Warren G. Harding — A177

FLAT PLATE PRINTING
Stamp designs: 19¼x22¼mm

1923   *Perf. 11*

610	A177	2c black	.55	.25
		Never hinged	1.10	
a.		Horiz. pair, imperf. vert.	2,000.	
b.		Imperf. (error), P#14870		
		block of 6	25,000.	

No. 610a is valued in the grade of fine.
No. 610b comes from left side error panes found in a normal pad of No. 610 stamps before No. 611 was issued. Two left side plate blocks and one top position plate block are recorded. Plate #14870 was not used to print No. 611. Loose stamps separated from the top and left plate blocks are indistinguishable from No. 611.

Imperf

611	A177	2c black	4.75	4.00
		Never hinged	9.50	

ROTARY PRESS PRINTING
Stamp designs: 19¼x22½mm

612	A177	2c black	15.00	1.75
		Never hinged	32.50	

Perf. 11

613	A177	2c black		40,000.

Tribute to President Warren G. Harding, who died August 2, 1923.
No. 613 was produced from rotary press sheet waste. It is valued in the grade of fine.

HUGUENOT-WALLOON TERCENTENARY ISSUE

"New Netherland" A178

Landing at Fort Orange A179

Monument to Jan Ribault at Duvall County, Fla. — A180

FLAT PLATE PRINTINGS

1924, May 1   *Perf. 11*

614	A178	1c dark green	2.40	3.25
		Never hinged	4.50	
615	A179	2c carmine rose	4.00	2.25
		Never hinged	7.50	
616	A180	5c dark blue	16.00	13.00
		Never hinged	30.00	
		Nos. 614-616 (3)	22.40	18.50
		Nos. 614-616, never hinged	42.00	

Tercentenary of the settling of the Walloons and in honor of the Huguenots.

LEXINGTON-CONCORD ISSUE

Washington at Cambridge A181

"Birth of Liberty," by Henry Sandham A182

The Minute Man, by Daniel Chester French A183

1925, Apr. 4   *Perf. 11*

617	A181	1c deep green	2.10	2.50
		Never hinged	4.00	
618	A182	2c carmine rose	3.75	4.00
		Never hinged	7.00	
619	A183	5c dark blue	15.00	13.00
		Never hinged	28.00	
		Nos. 617-619 (3)	20.85	19.50
		Nos. 617-619, never hinged	39.00	

150th anniv. of the Battle of Lexington-Concord.

NORSE-AMERICAN ISSUE

A184   A185

1925, May 18   *Perf. 11*

620	A184	2c carmine & black	3.25	3.00
		Never hinged	6.50	
621	A185	5c dark blue & black	10.00	10.00
		Never hinged	20.00	

100th anniv. of the arrival in NY on Oct. 9, 1825, of the sloop "Restaurationen" with the first group of immigrants from Norway to the U.S.

Benjamin Harrison A186   Woodrow Wilson A187

1925-26   *Perf. 11*

622	A186	13c green ('26)	10.00	.75
		Never hinged	20.00	
623	A187	17c black	10.00	.30
		Never hinged	20.00	

SESQUICENTENNIAL EXPOSITION ISSUE

Liberty Bell — A188

1926, May 10   *Perf. 11*

627	A188	2c carmine rose	2.25	.50
		Never hinged	4.25	

150th anniv. of the Declaration of Independence, Philadelphia, June 1-Dec. 1.

ERICSSON MEMORIAL ISSUE

Statue of John Ericsson — A189

1926, May 29   *Perf. 11*

628	A189	5c gray lilac	5.25	3.25
		Never hinged	9.00	

John Ericsson, builder of the "Monitor."

BATTLE OF WHITE PLAINS ISSUE

Alexander Hamilton's Battery — A190

1926, Oct. 18   *Perf. 11*

629	A190	2c carmine rose	1.75	1.70
		Never hinged	3.00	

Battle of White Plains, NY, 150th anniv.

INTERNATIONAL PHILATELIC EXHIBITION ISSUE
Souvenir Sheet

A190a

Condition valued:
Centering: Overall centering will average very fine, but individual stamps may be better or worse.
Perforations: No folds along rows of perforations.
Gum: There may be some light gum bends but no gum creases.
Hinging: There may be hinge marks in the selvage and on up to two or three stamps, but no heavy hinging or hinge remnants (except in the ungummed portion of the wide selvage.
Margins: Top panes should have about ½ inch bottom margin and 1 inch top margin.
Bottom panes should have about ½ inch top margin and just under ¾ inch bottom margin. Both will have one wide side (usually 1 inch plus) and one narrow (½ inch) side margin. The wide margin corner will have a small diagonal notch on top panes.

1926, Oct. 18   *Perf. 11*

630	A190a	2c carmine rose,		
		pane of 25	350.00	475.00
		Never hinged	600.00	

Issued in panes measuring 158-160¼x136-146½mm containing 25 stamps with inscription "International Philatelic Exhibition, Oct. 16th to 23rd, 1926" in top margin.

VALUES FOR VERY FINE STAMPS
Please note: Stamps are valued in the grade of Very Fine unless otherwise indicated.

TYPES OF 1922-26 ISSUE
REGULAR ISSUE
ROTARY PRESS PRINTINGS
(See note above No. 448.)

1926, Aug. 27   *Imperf.*

631	A156	1½c yellow brown	2.00	1.70
		Never hinged	3.00	

1926-34   *Perf. 11x10½*

632	A155	1c green ('27)	.25	.25
		Never hinged	.35	
a.		Booklet pane of 6	5.00	4.00
		Never hinged	8.00	
b.		Vertical pair, imperf. between	3,000.	3,250.

	Never hinged	5,500.	
c.	Horiz. pair, imperf. between	5,000.	

No. 632b is valued in the grade of fine. No. 632c is valued in the grade of fine and never hinged. It is possibly unique.

633	A156	1½c yel brn ('27)	1.70	.25
		Never hinged	2.60	
634	A157	2c car, type I	.25	.25
		Never hinged	.30	
b.		2c carmine lake	180.00	500.00
		Never hinged	425.00	
c.		Horiz. pair, imperf. btwn.	6,000.	
d.		Booklet pane of 6, carmine	1.50	1.50
		Never hinged	2.50	
e.		As "d," carmine lake	400.00	1,000.
		Never hinged	750.00	

Shades of the carmine exist.
No. 634c is valued in the grade of fine.

634A	A157	2c car, type II ('28)	325.00	13.50
		Never hinged	650.00	
635	A158	3c violet ('27)	.75	.25
		Never hinged	1.20	
a.		3c bright violet ('34)	.35	.25
		Never hinged	.45	
636	A159	4c yel brn ('27)	1.90	.25
		Never hinged	3.00	
637	A160	5c dk blue ('27)	1.90	.25
		Never hinged	3.00	
638	A161	6c red org ('27)	2.00	.25
		Never hinged	3.20	
639	A162	7c black ('27)	2.00	.25
		Never hinged	3.20	
a.		Vertical pair, imperf. between	550.00	400.00
		Never hinged	1,000.	
640	A163	8c ol grn ('27)	2.00	.25
		Never hinged	3.20	
641	A164	9c rose ('27)	1.90	.25
		Never hinged	3.00	
642	A165	10c org ('27)	3.25	.25
		Never hinged	5.50	
	Nos. 632-634,635-642 (11)		17.90	2.75
	Nos. 632-634, 635-642 never hinged		28.00	

The 1½c, 2c, 4c, 5c, 6c, 8c imperf. (dry print) are printer's waste.
For ½c, 11c-50c see Nos. 653, 692-701.

VERMONT SESQUICENTENNIAL ISSUE

Battle of Bennington, 150th anniv. and State independence.

Green Mountain Boy — A191

FLAT PLATE PRINTING

1927, Aug. 3			**Perf. 11**	
643	A191	2c carmine rose	1.20	.80
		Never hinged	2.00	

BURGOYNE CAMPAIGN ISSUE

Battles of Bennington, Oriskany, Fort Stanwix and Saratoga.

"The Surrender of General Burgoyne at Saratoga," by John Trumbull A192

1927, Aug. 3			**Perf. 11**	
644	A192	2c carmine rose	3.10	2.10
		Never hinged	5.50	

VALLEY FORGE ISSUE

150th anniversary of Washington's encampment at Valley Forge, Pa.

Washington at Prayer — A193

1928, May 26			**Perf. 11**	
645	A193	2c carmine rose	1.20	.50
		Never hinged	1.90	
a.		2c lake	—	
		Never hinged	—	

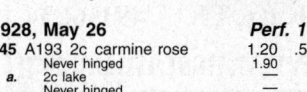

BATTLE OF MONMOUTH ISSUE

150th anniv. of the Battle of Monmouth, N.J., and "Molly Pitcher" (Mary Ludwig Hayes), the heroine of the battle.

No. 634 Overprinted

ROTARY PRESS PRINTING

1928, Oct. 20			**Perf. 11x10½**	
646	A157	2c carmine	1.00	1.00
		Never hinged	1.60	
a.		"Pitcher" only	675.00	
b.		2c carmine lake		2,500.

No. 646a is valued in the grade of fine.
Normally the overprints were placed 18mm apart vertically, but pairs exist with a space of 28mm between the overprints.

HAWAII SESQUICENTENNIAL ISSUE

Sesquicentennial Celebration of the discovery of the Hawaiian Islands.

Nos. 634 and 637 Overprinted

ROTARY PRESS PRINTING

1928, Aug. 13			**Perf. 11x10½**	
647	A157	2c carmine	4.00	4.00
		Never hinged	7.25	
648	A160	5c dark blue	11.00	12.50
		Never hinged	21.50	

Nos. 647-648 were sold at post offices in Hawaii and at the Postal Agency in Washington, D.C. They were valid throughout the nation.
Normally the overprints were placed 18mm apart vertically, but pairs exist with a space of 28mm between the overprints.

AERONAUTICS CONFERENCE ISSUE

Intl. Civil Aeronautics Conf., Washington, D.C., Dec. 12 - 14, 1928, and 25th anniv. of the 1st airplane flight by the Wright Brothers, Dec. 17, 1903.

Wright Airplane A194

Globe and Airplane A195

FLAT PLATE PRINTING

1928, Dec. 12			**Perf. 11**	
649	A194	2c carmine rose	1.10	.80
		Never hinged	1.75	
650	A195	5c blue	4.50	3.25
		Never hinged	7.25	

GEORGE ROGERS CLARK ISSUE

150th anniv. of the surrender of Fort Sackville, the present site of Vincennes, Ind., to Clark.

Surrender of Fort Sackville A196

1929, Feb. 25			**Perf. 11**	
651	A196	2c carmine & black	.70	.50
		Never hinged	1.15	

TYPE OF 1922-26 ISSUE
ROTARY PRESS PRINTING

1929, May 25			**Perf. 11x10½**	
653	A154	½c olive brown	.25	.25
			.35	

ELECTRIC LIGHT'S GOLDEN JUBILEE ISSUE

Invention of the 1st incandescent electric lamp by Thomas Alva Edison, Oct. 21, 1879, 50th anniv.

Edison's First Lamp — A197

FLAT PLATE PRINTING

1929			**Perf. 11**	
654	A197	2c carmine rose	.65	.65
		Never hinged	1.10	
		2c lake	—	

ROTARY PRESS PRINTING
Perf. 11x10½

655	A197	2c carmine rose	.65	.25
		Never hinged	1.10	

ROTARY PRESS COIL STAMP
Perf. 10 Vertically

656	A197	2c carmine rose	11.00	1.75
		Never hinged	21.00	

SULLIVAN EXPEDITION ISSUE

150th anniversary of the Sullivan Expedition in New York State during the Revolutionary War.

Maj. Gen. John Sullivan — A198

FLAT PLATE PRINTING

1929, June 17			**Perf. 11**	
657	A198	2c carmine rose	.55	.55
		Never hinged	1.00	
a.		2c lake	350.00	250.00
		Never hinged	625.00	
b.		Vert. pair, imperf. btwn.	4,000.	

The unique No. 657b resulted from a paper foldover before perfing, and it has angled errant perfs from another row of horiz. perfs through the left side of the stamps.

Nos. 632-634, 635-642 Overprinted

This special issue was authorized as a measure of preventing losses from post office burglaries. Approximately a year's supply was printed and issued to postmasters. The P.O. Dept. found it desirable to discontinue the State overprinted stamps after the initial supply was used.

ROTARY PRESS PRINTING

1929, May 1			**Perf. 11x10½**	
658	A155	1c green	2.50	2.00
		Never hinged	5.00	
a.		Vertical pair, one without ovpt.	300.00	
		Never hinged	500.00	
659	A156	1½c brown	3.25	2.90
		Never hinged	6.50	
a.		Vertical pair, one without ovpt.	475.00	
660	A157	2c carmine	4.00	1.00
		Never hinged	7.50	
661	A158	3c violet	17.50	15.00
		Never hinged	35.00	
a.		Vertical pair, one without ovpt.	600.00	
		Never hinged	800.00	
662	A159	4c yellow brown	17.50	9.00
		Never hinged	35.00	
a.		Vertical pair, one without ovpt.	600.00	
		Never hinged	800.00	
663	A160	5c deep blue	12.50	9.75
		Never hinged	25.00	
664	A161	6c red orange	25.00	18.00
		Never hinged	50.00	
665	A162	7c black	25.00	27.50
		Never hinged	50.00	
666	A163	8c olive green	72.50	65.00
		Never hinged	145.00	
667	A164	9c light rose	14.00	11.50
		Never hinged	27.50	

668	A165	10c org yel	22.50	12.50
		Never hinged	45.00	
	Nos. 658-668 (11)		216.25	174.15
	Nos. 658-668, never hinged		431.50	

See notes following No. 679.

Overprinted

1929, May 1				
669	A155	1c green	3.25	2.25
		Never hinged	6.50	
b.		No period after "Nebr." (19338, 19339 UR 26, 36)	50.00	
670	A156	1½c brown	3.00	2.50
		Never hinged	6.00	
671	A157	2c carmine	3.00	1.30
		Never hinged	6.00	
672	A158	3c violet	11.00	12.00
		Never hinged	22.00	
a.		Vertical pair, one without ovpt.	500.00	
673	A159	4c yellow brown	17.50	15.00
		Never hinged	35.00	
674	A160	5c deep blue	15.00	15.00
		Never hinged	30.00	
675	A161	6c red orange	35.00	24.00
		Never hinged	70.00	
676	A162	7c black	22.50	18.00
		Never hinged	45.00	
677	A163	8c olive green	30.00	25.00
		Never hinged	60.00	
678	A164	9c light rose	35.00	27.50
		Never hinged	70.00	
a.		Vertical pair, one without ovpt.	750.00	
679	A165	10c org yel	90.00	22.50
		Never hinged	180.00	
	Nos. 669-679 (11)		265.25	165.05
	Nos. 669-679, never hinged		530.50	

Nos. 658-661, 669-673, 677-678 are known with the overprints on vertical pairs spaced 32mm apart instead of the normal 22mm.
Important: Nos. 658-679 with original gum have either one horizontal gum breaker ridge per stamp or portions of two at the extreme top and bottom of the stamps, 21mm apart. Multiple complete gum breaker ridges indicate a fake overprint. Absence of the gum breaker ridge indicates either regumming or regumming and a fake overprint.

BATTLE OF FALLEN TIMBERS ISSUE

Memorial to Gen. Anthony Wayne and for 135th anniv. of the Battle of Fallen Timbers, Ohio.

Gen. Anthony Wayne Memorial — A199

FLAT PLATE PRINTING

1929, Sept. 14			**Perf. 11**	
680	A199	2c carmine rose	.65	.65
		Never hinged	1.10	

OHIO RIVER CANALIZATION ISSUE

Completion of the Ohio River Canalization Project, between Cairo, Ill. and Pittsburgh, Pa.

Lock No. 5, Monongahela River — A200

1929, Oct. 19			**Perf. 11**	
681	A200	2c carmine rose	.55	.55
		Never hinged	.90	
a.		2c lake	425.00	
		Never hinged	650.00	
b.		2c carmine lake, never hinged	—	

MASSACHUSETTS BAY COLONY ISSUE

300th anniversary of the founding of the Massachusetts Bay Colony.

Mass. Bay Colony
Seal — A201

1930, Apr. 8 *Perf. 11*
682 A201 2c carmine rose .65 .50
Never hinged .95

CAROLINA-CHARLESTON ISSUE

260th anniv. of the founding of the Province of Carolina and the 250th anniv. of the city of Charleston, S.C.

Gov. Joseph West &
Chief Shadoo, a
Kiowa — A202

1930, Apr. 10 *Perf. 11*
683 A202 2c carmine rose 1.00 1.00
Never hinged 1.50

TYPES OF 1922-26 ISSUE

Warren G.
Harding
A203

William H. Taft
A204

ROTARY PRESS PRINTING

1930 *Perf. 11x10½*
684 A203 1½c brown .50 .25
Never hinged .70
685 A204 4c brown .80 .25
Never hinged 1.25

ROTARY PRESS COIL STAMPS
Perf. 10 Vertically
686 A203 1½c brown 1.75 .25
Never hinged 2.60
687 A204 4c brown 3.00 .45
Never hinged 4.50

BRADDOCK'S FIELD ISSUE

175th anniversary of the Battle of Braddock's Field, otherwise the Battle of Monongahela.

Statue of Col. George
Washington — A205

FLAT PLATE PRINTING

1930, July 9 *Perf. 11*
688 A205 2c carmine rose .85 .85
Never hinged 1.30

VON STEUBEN ISSUE

Baron Friedrich Wilhelm von Steuben (1730-1794), participant in the American Revolution.

General von
Steuben — A206

FLAT PLATE PRINTING

1930, Sept. 17 *Perf. 11*
689 A206 2c carmine rose .50 .50
Never hinged .75
a. Imperf., pair 2,000.
Never hinged 3,000.
b. 2c carmine lake 950.00

PULASKI ISSUE

150th anniversary (in 1929) of the death of Gen. Casimir Pulaski, Polish patriot and hero of the American Revolutionary War.

General Casimir
Pulaski — A207

1931, Jan. 16 *Perf. 11*
690 A207 2c carmine rose .30 .25
Never hinged .40

TYPE OF 1922-26 ISSUES
ROTARY PRESS PRINTING

1931 *Perf. 11x10½*
692 A166 11c light blue 2.50 .25
Never hinged 3.75
693 A167 12c brown violet 5.00 .25
Never hinged 8.00
694 A186 13c yellow green 2.25 .25
Never hinged 3.50
695 A168 14c dark blue 4.00 .60
Never hinged 6.25
696 A169 15c gray 7.75 .25
Never hinged 12.00

Perf. 10½x11
697 A187 17c black 4.75 .25
Never hinged 7.25
698 A170 20c carmine rose 7.75 .25
Never hinged 12.50
699 A171 25c blue green 8.00 .25
Never hinged 13.00
700 A172 30c brown 13.00 .25
Never hinged 22.50
701 A173 50c lilac 30.00 .25
Never hinged 52.50
Nos. 692-701 (10) 85.00 2.85
Nos. 692-701, never hinged 141.25

RED CROSS ISSUE

50th anniversary of the founding of the American Red Cross Society.

"The Greatest
Mother" — A208

FLAT PLATE PRINTING

1931, May 21 *Perf. 11*
702 A208 2c black & red .25 .25
Never hinged .35
a. Red cross missing (FO) 40,000.

One example of No. 702a is documented; believed to be unique. Value reflects most recent sale price at auction in 1994.

YORKTOWN ISSUE

Surrender of Cornwallis at Yorktown, 1781.

Count de Rochambeau, Washington,
Count de Grasse — A209

1931, Oct. 19 *Perf. 11*
703 A209 2c carmine rose &
black .35 .25
Never hinged .50
a. 2c lake & black 4.50 .75
Never hinged 6.25
b. 2c dark lake & black 400.00
Never hinged 750.00
c. Horiz. pair, imperf. vertically 7,000.
Never hinged 8,500.

No. 703c is valued in the grade of fine.

WASHINGTON BICENTENNIAL ISSUE

200th anniversary of the birth of George Washington. Various Portraits of George Washington.

A210   A211

A212

A213

A214

A215

A216

A217

A218   A219

A220

A221

ROTARY PRESS PRINTINGS

1932, Jan. 1 *Perf. 11x10½*
704 A210 ½c olive brown .25 .25
Never hinged .35
705 A211 1c green .25 .25
Never hinged .35
706 A212 1½c brown .45 .25
Never hinged .60
707 A213 2c carmine rose .30 .25
Never hinged .45
708 A214 3c purple .55 .25
Never hinged .80
709 A215 4c light brown .60 .25
Never hinged .85
710 A216 5c blue 1.50 .25
Never hinged 2.25
711 A217 6c red orange 3.00 .25
Never hinged 4.50
712 A218 7c black .60 .25
Never hinged .85
713 A219 8c olive bister 2.75 .50
Never hinged 4.00
714 A220 9c pale red 2.25 .25
Never hinged 3.25
715 A221 10c orange yellow 10.00 .25
Never hinged 15.00
Nos. 704-715 (12) 22.50 3.25
Nos. 704-715, never hinged 33.25

OLYMPIC WINTER GAMES ISSUE

3rd Olympic Winter Games, held at Lake Placid, N.Y., Feb. 4-13, 1932.

Skier — A222

FLAT PLATE PRINTING

1932, Jan. 25 *Perf. 11*
716 A222 2c carmine rose .35 .25
Never hinged .55
a. 2c lake 500.00
Never hinged 1,000.

ARBOR DAY ISSUE

Boy and Girl Planting
Tree — A223

ROTARY PRESS PRINTING

1932, Apr. 22 *Perf. 11x10½*
717 A223 2c carmine rose .25 .25
Never hinged .35

60th anniv. of the 1st observance of Arbor Day in Nebr., April, 1872.
Birth centenary of Julius Sterling Morton, who conceived the plan and the name "Arbor Day," while a member of the Nebr. State Board of Agriculture.

OLYMPIC GAMES ISSUE

Issued in honor of the 10th Olympic Games, held at Los Angeles, Calif., July 30 to Aug. 14, 1932.

Runner at
Starting Mark
A224

Myron's
Discobolus
A225

ROTARY PRESS PRINTING

1932, June 15 *Perf. 11x10½*
718 A224 3c purple 1.50 .25
Never hinged 2.00
719 A225 5c blue 2.25 .25
Never hinged 2.90

Washington — A226

ROTARY PRESS PRINTING

1932, June 16		Perf. 11x10½	
720	A226 3c purple	.35	.25
	Never hinged	.45	
b.	Booklet pane of 6	35.00	12.50
	Never hinged	60.00	
c.	Vertical pair, imperf. between	700.00	1,750.
	Never hinged	1,400.	

ROTARY PRESS COIL STAMPS

1932		Perf. 10 Vertically	
721	A226 3c purple	2.75	.25
	Never hinged	3.50	

	Perf. 10 Horizontally		
722	A226 3c purple	1.50	.35
	Never hinged	2.00	

Issued: #721, 6/24; #722, 10/12.

TYPE OF 1922-26 ISSUES

1932, Aug. 18		Perf. 10 Vertically	
723	A161 6c deep orange	11.00	.30
	Never hinged	15.00	

WILLIAM PENN ISSUE

250th anniv. of the arrival in America of Penn (1644-1718), English Quaker and founder of Pennsylvania.

William Penn — A227

FLAT PLATE PRINTING

1932, Oct. 24		Perf. 11	
724	A227 3c purple	.45	.25
	Never hinged	.60	
a.	Vert. pair, imperf. horiz.	—	

DANIEL WEBSTER ISSUE

Daniel Webster — A228

FLAT PLATE PRINTING

1932, Oct. 24		Perf. 11	
725	A228 3c purple	.45	.25
	Never hinged	.60	

Daniel Webster (1782-1852), statesman.

GEORGIA BICENTENNIAL ISSUE

200th anniv. of the founding of the Colony of Georgia, and honoring Oglethorpe, who landed from England, Feb. 12, 1733, and personally supervised the establishing of the colony.

Gen. James Edward Oglethorpe — A229

FLAT PLATE PRINTING

1933, Feb. 12		Perf. 11	
726	A229 3c purple	.50	.25
	Never hinged	.65	

PEACE OF 1783 ISSUE

150th anniv. of the issuance by George Washington of the official order containing the Proclamation of Peace marking officially the ending of hostilities in the War for Independence.

Washington's Headquarters, Newburgh, NY — A230

ROTARY PRESS PRINTING

1933, Apr. 19		Perf. 10½x11	
727	A230 3c violet	.25	.25
	Never hinged	.30	

See No. 752.

CENTURY OF PROGRESS ISSUES

"Century of Progress" Intl. Exhibition, Chicago, which opened June 1, 1933, and centenary of the incorporation of Chicago as a city.

Restoration of Fort Dearborn A231

Federal Building at Chicago, 1933 A232

ROTARY PRESS PRINTING

1933, May 25		Perf. 10½x11	
728	A231 1c yellow green	.25	.25
	Never hinged	.30	
729	A232 3c purple	.25	.25
	Never hinged	.35	

AMERICAN PHILATELIC SOCIETY ISSUE
SOUVENIR SHEETS

Restoration of Fort Dearborn — A231a

Federal Building at Chicago, 1933 — A232a

FLAT PLATE PRINTING

1933, Aug. 25		Imperf.	
		Without Gum	
730	A231a 1c deep yellow green, pane of 25	22.50	25.00
a.	Single stamp	.75	.50
731	A232a 3c purple, pane of 25	20.00	22.50
a.	Single stamp	.65	.50

Issued in panes measuring 134x120mm.
See Nos. 766-767.

NATIONAL RECOVERY ACT ISSUE

Issued to direct attention to and arouse the support of the nation for the National Recovery Act.

Group of Workers — A233

ROTARY PRESS PRINTING

1933, Aug. 15		Perf. 10½x11	
732	A233 3c purple	.25	.25
	Never hinged	.30	

BYRD ANTARCTIC ISSUE

Issued in connection with the Byrd Antarctic Expedition of 1933 and for use on letters mailed through the Little America Post Office established at the Base Camp of the Expedition in the territory of the South Pole.

World Map on van der Grinten's Projection — A234

FLAT PLATE PRINTING

1933, Oct. 9		Perf. 11	
733	A234 3c dark blue	.50	.50
	Never hinged	.60	

See Nos. 735, 753.

KOSCIUSZKO ISSUE

Kosciuszko (1746-1817), Polish soldier and statesman served in the American Revolution, on the 150th anniv. of the granting to him of American citizenship.

Statue of Gen. Tadeusz Kosciuszko — A235

FLAT PLATE PRINTING

1933, Oct. 13		Perf. 11	
734	A235 5c blue	.55	.25
	Never hinged	.65	
a.	Horiz. pair, imperf. vert.	1,750.	
	Never hinged	2,750.	

NATIONAL STAMP EXHIBITION ISSUE
SOUVENIR SHEET

A235a

1934, Feb. 10		Imperf.	
		Without Gum	
735	A235a 3c dark blue, pane of 6	10.00	9.00
a.	Single stamp	1.60	1.25

Issued in panes measuring 87x93mm.
See No. 768.

MARYLAND TERCENTENARY ISSUE

300th anniversary of the founding of Maryland.

"The Ark" and "The Dove" — A236

FLAT PLATE PRINTING

1934, Mar. 23		Perf. 11	
736	A236 3c carmine rose	.30	.25
	Never hinged	.40	
a.	Horizontal pair, imperf between	4,000.	
b.	3c lake	—	
c.	3c carmine lake, never hinged	—	

The unique No. 736a resulted from a paper foldover before perfing, and it has angled errant perfs from another column of vert. perfs through the upper-left corner of the left stamp.

MOTHERS OF AMERICA ISSUE

Issued to commemorate Mother's Day.

Adaptation of Whistler's Portrait of his Mother A237

ROTARY PRESS PRINTING

1934, May 2		Perf. 11x10½	
737	A237 3c purple	.25	.25
	Never hinged	.30	

FLAT PLATE PRINTING
Perf. 11

738	A237 3c purple	.25	.25
	Never hinged	.30	

See No. 754.

WISCONSIN TERCENTENARY ISSUE

Arrival of Jean Nicolet, French explorer, on the shores of Green Bay, 300th anniv. According to historical records, Nicolet was the 1st white man to reach the territory now comprising the State of Wisconsin.

Nicolet's Landing A238

FLAT PLATE PRINTING

1934, July 7		Perf. 11	
739	A238 3c purple	.25	.25
	Never hinged	.40	
a.	Vert. pair, imperf. horiz.	575.00	
	Never hinged	1,050.	
b.	Horiz. pair, imperf. vert.	1,000.	
	Never hinged	1,750.	

See No. 755.

NATIONAL PARKS YEAR ISSUE

El Capitan, Yosemite (California) A239

Old Faithful, Yellowstone (Wyoming) A243

Grand Canyon (Arizona) A240

Mt. Rainier and Mirror Lake
(Washington) — A241

Mesa Verde
(Colorado)
A242

Crater Lake
(Oregon)
A244

Great
Head,
Acadia Park
(Maine)
A245

Great White
Throne, Zion
Park (Utah)
A246

Great Smoky
Mts. (North
Carolina)
A248

Mt. Rockwell (Mt. Sinopah) and Two
Medicine Lake, Glacier Natl. Park
(Montana)
A247

FLAT PLATE PRINTING

1934		**Unwmk.**	**Perf. 11**	
740	A239	1c green	.30	.25
		Never hinged	.40	
a.		Vert. pair, imperf. horiz.,		
		with gum	1,750.	
		Never hinged	3,000.	
741	A240	2c red	.30	.25
		Never hinged	.40	
a.		Vert. pair, imperf. horiz.,		
		with gum	800.00	
		Never hinged	1,450.	
b.		Horiz. pair, imperf. vert.,		
		with gum	900.00	
		Never hinged	1,600.	
c.		Imperf. P# 21261 block of		
		20	7,500.	

No. 741c is a unique bottom margin plate #21261 block of 20. This plate was not used to print the imperforate Farley special printing, No. 757. Loose stamps separated from this block or from other possible imperforate No. 741 Plate #21261 blocks are indistinguishable from gummed examples of No. 757.

742	A241	3c purple	.40	.25
		Never hinged	.50	
a.		Vert. pair, imperf. horiz.,		
		with gum	1,000.	
		Never hinged	1,850.	
743	A242	4c brown	.50	.40
		Never hinged	.70	
a.		Vert. pair, imperf. horiz.,		
		with gum	3,500.	
		Never hinged	8,000.	
744	A243	5c blue	.80	.65
		Never hinged	1.10	
a.		Horiz. pair, imperf. vert.,		
		with gum	1,500.	
		Never hinged	4,000.	
745	A244	6c dark blue	1.20	.85
		Never hinged	1.65	
746	A245	7c black	.80	.75
		Never hinged	1.10	
a.		Horiz. pair, imperf. vert.,		
		with gum	1,250.	
		Never hinged	2,000.	

747	A246	8c sage green	1.75	1.50
		Never hinged	2.70	
748	A247	9c red orange	1.60	.65
		Never hinged	2.40	
749	A248	10c gray black	3.25	1.25
		Never hinged	5.00	
		Nos. 740-749 (10)	10.90	6.80
		Nos. 740-749, never hinged	15.95	

Beware of fakes of the part-perforate errors of Nos. 740-749, including those with gum (see "without gum" note before No. 752). See Nos. 750-751, 756-765, 769-770, 797.

AMERICAN PHILATELIC SOCIETY ISSUE
SOUVENIR SHEET

A248a

1934, Aug. 28			**Imperf.**	
750	A248a	3c purple, pane of		
		6	22.50	27.50
		Never hinged	32.50	
a.		Single stamp	3.75	3.25
		Never hinged	4.75	

Issued in panes measuring approximately 98x93mm.
See No. 770.

TRANS-MISSISSIPPI PHILATELIC EXPOSITION ISSUE
SOUVENIR SHEET

A248b

1934, Oct. 10			**Imperf.**	
751	A248b	1c green, pane of 6	10.00	12.50
		Never hinged	15.00	
a.		Single stamp	1.65	1.60
		Never hinged	2.25	

Issued in panes measuring approximately 92x99mm.
See No. 769.

SPECIAL PRINTING
(Nos. 752-771 inclusive)

"Issued for a limited time in full sheets as printed, and in blocks thereof, to meet the requirements of collectors and others who may be interested." — From Postal Bulletin No. 16614.

Issuance of the following 20 stamps in complete sheets resulted from the protest of collectors and others at the practice of presenting, to certain government officials, complete sheets of unsevered panes, imperforate (except Nos. 752 and 753) and generally ungummed.

Designs of Commemorative Issues
Without Gum

NOTE: In 1940 the P.O. Department offered to and did gum full sheets of Nos. 756-765 and 769-770 sent in by owners. No other Special Printings were accepted for gumming.

TYPE OF PEACE ISSUE
Issued in sheets of 400
ROTARY PRESS PRINTING
Perf. 10½x11

1935, Mar. 15			**Unwmk.**	
752	A230	3c purple	.25	.25

TYPE OF BYRD ISSUE
Issued in sheets of 200
FLAT PLATE PRINTING
Perf. 11

753	A234	3c dark blue	.50	.45

No. 753 is similar to No. 733. Positive identification is by blocks or pairs showing guide line between stamps. These lines between stamps are found only on No. 753.

TYPE OF MOTHERS OF AMERICA ISSUE
Issued in sheets of 200
FLAT PLATE PRINTING
Imperf

754	A237	3c deep purple	.60	.60

TYPE OF WISCONSIN ISSUE
Issued in sheets of 200
FLAT PLATE PRINTING
Imperf

755	A238	3c deep purple	.60	.60

TYPES OF NATIONAL PARKS ISSUE
Issued in sheets of 200
FLAT PLATE PRINTING
Imperf

756	A239	1c green	.25	.25
757	A240	2c red	.25	.25
758	A241	3c deep purple	.50	.45
759	A242	4c brown	1.00	.95
760	A243	5c blue	1.60	1.40
761	A244	6c dark blue	2.40	2.25
762	A245	7c black	1.60	1.40
763	A246	8c sage green	1.90	1.50
764	A247	9c red orange	2.00	1.75
765	A248	10c gray black	4.00	3.50
		Nos. 756-765 (10)	15.50	13.70
		Nos. 756-765, with original		
		gum, never hinged	114.35	
		Nos. 756-765, P# blocks of		
		6	274.25	

SOUVENIR SHEETS

Note: Single items from these sheets are identical with other varieties, 766 and 730, 766a and 730a, 767 and 731, 767a and 731a, 768 and 735, 768a and 735a, 769a and 756, 770a and 758.

Positive identification is by blocks or pairs showing wide gutters between stamps. These wide gutters occur only on Nos. 766-770 and measure, horizontally, 13mm on Nos. 766-767; 16mm on No. 768, and 23mm on Nos. 769-770.

TYPE OF CENTURY OF PROGRESS ISSUE
Issued in sheets of 9 panes of 25 stamps each
FLAT PLATE PRINTING
Imperf

766	A231a	1c yellow green,		
		pane of 25	30.00	30.00
a.		Single stamp	.80	.50
767	A232a	3c deep purple,		
		pane of 25	25.00	25.00
a.		Single stamp	.70	.50

NATIONAL EXHIBITION ISSUE TYPE OF BYRD ISSUE
Issued in sheets of 25 panes of 6 stamps each
FLAT PLATE PRINTING
Imperf

768	A235a	3c dark blue, pane		
		of six	20.00	15.00
a.		Single stamp	2.80	2.40

TYPES OF NATIONAL PARKS ISSUE
Issued in sheets of 20 panes of 6 stamps each
FLAT PLATE PRINTING
Imperf

769	A248b	1c green, pane of		
		six	12.50	11.00
a.		Single stamp	1.85	1.80
770	A248a	3c deep purple,		
		pane of six	30.00	24.00
a.		Single stamp	3.25	3.10

Hinged examples of Nos. 769-770 with original gum sell for approximately half the values shown for never-hinged stamps.

TYPE OF AIR POST SPECIAL DELIVERY
Issued in sheets of 200
FLAT PLATE PRINTING
Imperf

771	APSD1	16c dark blue	2.75	2.60

> Catalogue values for unused stamps in this section, from this point to the end, are for Never Hinged items.

VALUES FOR HINGED STAMPS AFTER NO. 771
This catalogue does not value unused stamps after No. 771 in hinged condition. Hinged unused stamps from No. 772 to the present are worth considerably less than the values given for unused stamps, which are for never-hinged examples.

CONNECTICUT TERCENTENARY ISSUE
300th anniv. of the settlement of Connecticut.

Charter
Oak
A249

ROTARY PRESS PRINTING
Perf. 11x10½

1935, Apr. 26			**Unwmk.**	
772	A249	3c rose purple	.35	.25

CALIFORNIA PACIFIC EXPOSITION ISSUE
California Pacific Exposition at San Diego.

View of
San Diego
Exposition
A250

1935, May 29			**Unwmk.**	
773	A250	3c purple	.35	.25

BOULDER DAM ISSUE
Dedication of Boulder Dam.

Boulder Dam — A251

FLAT PLATE PRINTING

1935, Sept. 30		**Unwmk.**	**Perf. 11**	
774	A251	3c purple	.35	.25

MICHIGAN CENTENARY ISSUE
Advance celebration of Michigan Statehood centenary.

Michigan
State Seal
A252

ROTARY PRESS PRINTING

1935, Nov. 1		**Unwmk.**	**Perf. 11x10½**	
775	A252	3c purple	.35	.25

TEXAS CENTENNIAL ISSUE

Centennial of Texas independence.

Sam Houston, Stephen F. Austin and the Alamo A253

1936, Mar. 2   **Unwmk.**
776 A253 3c purple   .35 .25

RHODE ISLAND TERCENTENARY ISSUE

300th anniv. of the settlement of Rhode Island.

Statue of Roger Williams — A254

1936, May 4 Unwmk. Perf. 10½x11
777 A254 3c purple   .35 .25

THIRD INTERNATIONAL PHILATELIC EXHIBITION ISSUE
SOUVENIR SHEET

A254a

FLAT PLATE PRINTING

1936, May 9 Unwmk. Imperf.
778 A254a 3c purple, pane of 4   1.75 1.25
    a.   3c Type A249   .40 .30
    b.   3c Type A250   .40 .30
    c.   3c Type A252   .40 .30
    d.   3c Type A253   .40 .30

Issued in panes measuring 98x66mm containing four stamps, inscribed in the margins: "Printed by the Treasury Department, Bureau of Engraving and Printing, under authority of James A. Farley, Postmaster General, in compliment to the third International Philatelic Exhibition of 1936. New York, N. Y., May 9-17, 1936. Plate No. 21557 (or 21558)."

ARKANSAS CENTENNIAL ISSUE

100th anniv. of the State of Arkansas.

Arkansas Post, Old and New State Houses A255

ROTARY PRESS PRINTING
Perf. 11x10½

1936, June 15   **Unwmk.**
782 A255 3c purple   .35 .25

OREGON TERRITORY ISSUE

Opening of the Oregon Territory, 1836, 100th anniv.

Map of Oregon Territory A256

1936, July 14   **Unwmk.**
783 A256 3c purple   .35 .25

SUSAN B. ANTHONY ISSUE

Susan Brownell Anthony (1820-1906), woman-suffrage advocate, and 16th anniv. of the ratification of the 19th Amendment which grants American women the right to vote.

Susan B. Anthony — A257

1936, Aug. 26   **Unwmk.**
784 A257 3c purple   .25 .25

ARMY ISSUE

Issued in honor of the United States Army.

George Washington, Nathanael Greene and Mount Vernon — A258

Andrew Jackson, Winfield Scott and the Hermitage A259

Generals Sherman, Grant and Sheridan A260

Generals Robert E. Lee, "Stonewall" Jackson and Stratford Hall A261

U.S. Military Academy, West Point A262

1936-37   **Unwmk.**
785 A258 1c green   .30 .25
786 A259 2c carmine ('37) .30 .25
787 A260 3c purple ('37)   .40 .25
788 A261 4c gray ('37)   .60 .25
789 A262 5c ultra ('37)   .75 .25
    Nos. 785-789 (5)   2.35 1.25

NAVY ISSUE

Issued in honor of the United States Navy.

John Paul Jones and John Barry A263

Stephen Decatur and Thomas MacDonough — A264

Admirals David G. Farragut and David D. Porter A265

Admirals William T. Sampson, George Dewey and Winfield S. Schley A266

Seal of U.S. Naval Academy and Naval Midshipmen — A267

1936-37   **Unwmk.**
790 A263 1c green   .30 .25
791 A264 2c carmine ('37) .30 .25
792 A265 3c purple ('37)   .40 .25
793 A266 4c gray ('37)   .60 .25
794 A267 5c ultra ('37)   .75 .25
    Nos. 790-794 (5)   2.35 1.25

ORDINANCE OF 1787 SESQUICENTENNIAL ISSUE

150th anniv. of the adoption of the Ordinance of 1787 and the creation of the Northwest Territory.

Manasseh Cutler, Rufus Putnam and Map of Northwest Territory A268

1937, July 13   **Unwmk.**
795 A268 3c rose purple   .30 .25

VIRGINIA DARE ISSUE

350th anniv. of the birth of Virginia Dare, 1st child born in America of English parents (Aug. 18, 1587), and the settlement at Roanoke Island.

Virginia Dare and Parents — A269

FLAT PLATE PRINTING

1937, Aug. 18 Unwmk. Perf. 11
796 A269 5c gray blue   .35 .25

SOCIETY OF PHILATELIC AMERICANS ISSUE
SOUVENIR SHEET

A269a

TYPE OF NATIONAL PARKS ISSUE

1937, Aug. 26 Unwmk. Imperf.
797 A269a 10c blue green   .60 .40

Issued in panes measuring 67x78mm.

CONSTITUTION SESQUICENTENNIAL ISSUE

150th anniversary of the signing of the Constitution on September 17, 1787.

Signing of the Constitution A270

Perf. 11x10½

1937, Sept. 17   **Unwmk.**
798 A270 3c bright reddish purple   .40 .25

TERRITORIAL ISSUES
Hawaii

Statue of Kamehameha I, Honolulu — A271

Alaska

Landscape with Mt. McKinley A272

Puerto Rico

La Fortaleza, San Juan A273

Virgin Islands

Charlotte Amalie A274

1937 Unwmk. Perf. 10½x11
799 A271 3c violet   .35 .25

Perf. 11x10½

800	A272	3c violet	.40	.25
801	A273	3c bright purple	.40	.25
802	A274	3c rose violet	.40	.25
		Nos. 799-802 (4)	1.55	1.00

PRESIDENTIAL ISSUE

Benjamin Franklin
A275

George Washington
A276

Martha Washington
A277

John Adams
A278

Thomas Jefferson
A279

James Madison
A280

White House
A281

James Monroe
A282

John Q. Adams
A283

Andrew Jackson
A284

Martin Van Buren
A285

William H. Harrison
A286

John Tyler — A287

James K. Polk — A288

Zachary Taylor
A289

Millard Fillmore
A290

Franklin Pierce
A291

James Buchanan
A292

Abraham Lincoln
A293

Andrew Johnson
A294

Ulysses S. Grant
A295

Rutherford B. Hayes
A296

James A. Garfield
A297

Chester A. Arthur
A298

Grover Cleveland
A299

Benjamin Harrison
A300

William McKinley
A301

Theodore Roosevelt
A302

William Howard Taft
A303

Woodrow Wilson
A304

Warren G. Harding
A305

Calvin Coolidge
A306

1938   **Unwmk.**

803	A275	½c deep orange	.25	.25
804	A276	1c green	.25	.25
b.		Booklet pane of 6	2.00	.50
c.		Horiz. pair, imperf between (from booklet pane)	—	
805	A277	1½c bister brown	.25	.25
b.		Horiz. pair, imperf. between	100.00	20.00

No. 805b unused is not precanceled. Precanceled examples are considered used and are valued in the used column. They are valued with gum; pairs without gum are worth less.

806	A278	2c rose carmine	.25	.25
b.		Booklet pane of 6	5.50	1.00
807	A279	3c light violet	.25	.25
a.		Booklet pane of 6	8.50	2.00
b.		Horiz. pair, imperf. between	2,000.	—
c.		Imperf., pair	3,500.	—
d.		As "a," imperf between vert.	—	
808	A280	4c bright rose purple	.75	.25
809	A281	4½c dark gray	.40	.25
810	A282	5c bright blue	.35	.25
811	A283	6c red orange	.40	.25
812	A284	7c sepia	.40	.25
813	A285	8c olive green	.40	.25
814	A286	9c rose pink	.45	.25
815	A287	10c brown red	.45	.25
816	A288	11c ultramarine	.75	.25
817	A289	12c bright mauve	1.00	.25
818	A290	13c blue green	1.30	.25
819	A291	14c blue	1.00	.25
820	A292	15c blue gray	.90	.25
821	A293	16c black	1.50	.25
822	A294	17c rose red	1.00	.25
823	A295	18c brown carmine	2.25	.25
824	A296	19c bright mauve	1.30	.35
825	A297	20c bright blue green	1.20	.25
826	A298	21c dull blue	1.30	.25
827	A299	22c vermilion	1.20	.40
828	A300	24c gray black	3.25	.25
829	A301	25c deep red lilac	1.20	.25
830	A302	30c dp ultra	3.50	.25
a.		30c blue	15.00	—
b.		30c deep blue	240.00	—
831	A303	50c mauve	5.50	.25

FLAT PLATE PRINTING

1938   **Perf. 11**

832	A304	$1 purple & black	7.00	.25
a.		Vert. pair, imperf. horiz.	1,100.	
b.		Watermarked USIR ('51)	200.00	65.00
c.		$1 red violet & black ('54)	6.00	.25
d.		As "c," vert. pair, imperf. horiz.	900.00	
e.		Vert. pair, imperf. btwn.	7,500.	
f.		As "c," vert. pair, imperf. btwn.	10,000.	
g.		As "c," bright magenta & black	75.00	50.00
h.		As No. 832, red violet & black		

No. 832c is dry printed from 400-subject flat plates on thick white paper with smooth, colorless gum.

No. 832g is the far end of the color spectrum for the No. 832c stamp, trending toward a more pinkish shade, but the shade is not pink. No. 832g is known in bright magenta and deep bright magenta; both shades qualify as No. 832g.

No. 832h is a shade variety of the wet printing (No. 832), but the shade essentially matches the red violet normally seen on the dry printing (No. 832c).

833	A305	$2 yel grn & blk	17.50	3.75
834	A306	$5 car & blk	85.00	3.00
a.		$5 red brown & black	3,000.	7,000.
		Nos. 803-834 (32)	142.50	14.50

No. 834 can be chemically altered to resemble Scott 834a. No. 834a should be purchased only with competent expert certification.

Watermarks

All stamps from No. 835 on are unwatermarked.

CONSTITUTION RATIFICATION ISSUE

150th anniversary of the ratification of the United States Constitution.

Old Court House, Williamsburg, Va. — A307

ROTARY PRESS PRINTING

1938, June 21   **Perf. 11x10½**

835	A307	3c deep violet	.45	.25

SWEDISH-FINNISH TERCENTENARY ISSUE

Tercentenary of the founding of the Swedish and Finnish Settlement at Wilmington, Delaware.

Landing of the Swedes and Finns — A308

FLAT PLATE PRINTING

1938, June 27   **Perf. 11**

836	A308	3c bright reddish purple	.35	.25

NORTHWEST TERRITORY SESQUICENTENNIAL

Statue Symbolizing Colonization of the West — A309

ROTARY PRESS PRINTING

1938, July 15   **Perf. 11x10½**

837	A309	3c bright rose purple	.30	.25

IOWA TERRITORY CENTENNIAL ISSUE

Old Capitol, Iowa City
A310

1938, Aug. 24

838	A310	3c violet	.40	.25

TYPES OF 1938
ROTARY PRESS COIL STAMPS

1939, Jan. 20   **Perf. 10 Vertically**

839	A276	1c green	.30	.25
840	A277	1½c bister brown	.30	.25

The reported and authenticated "small holes" examples of No. 840 are precanceled Salt Lake City/Utah.

841	A278	2c rose carmine	.40	.25
842	A279	3c light violet	.50	.25
843	A280	4c red violet	7.50	.40
844	A281	4½c dark gray	.70	.40
845	A282	5c bright blue	5.00	2.50
846	A283	6c red orange	1.10	.55
847	A287	10c brown red	11.00	1.00

1939, Jan. 27   **Perf. 10 Horizontally**

848	A276	1c green	.85	.25
849	A277	1½c bister brown	1.25	.30
850	A278	2c rose carmine	2.50	.40
851	A279	3c light violet	2.50	.40
		Nos. 839-851 (13)	33.90	7.20

GOLDEN GATE INTL. EXPOSITION, SAN FRANCISCO

"Tower of the Sun" — A311

ROTARY PRESS PRINTING

1939, Feb. 18   **Perf. 10½x11**

852	A311	3c bright purple	.30	.25

NEW YORK WORLD'S FAIR ISSUE

Trylon and Perisphere — A312

1939, Apr. 1

853	A312	3c violet	.30	.25

WASHINGTON INAUGURATION ISSUE

Sesquicentennial of the inauguration of George Washington as First President.

George Washington Taking Oath of Office — A313

FLAT PLATE PRINTING

1939, Apr. 30   **Perf. 11**
854 A313 3c bright purple   .60   .25

BASEBALL CENTENNIAL ISSUE

Sand-lot Baseball Game A314

ROTARY PRESS PRINTING

1939, June 12   **Perf. 11x10½**
855 A314 3c violet   1.75   .25

PANAMA CANAL ISSUE

25th anniv. of the opening of the Panama Canal.

Theodore Roosevelt, Gen. George W. Goethals and Gaillard Cut — A315

FLAT PLATE PRINTING

1939, Aug. 15   **Perf. 11**
856 A315 3c reddish purple   .40   .25

PRINTING TERCENTENARY ISSUE

Issued in commemoration of the 300th anniversary of printing in Colonial America. The Stephen Daye press is in the Harvard University Museum.

Stephen Daye Press — A316

ROTARY PRESS PRINTING

1939, Sept. 25   **Perf. 10½x11**
857 A316 3c violet   .25   .25

50th ANNIVERSARY OF STATEHOOD ISSUE

Map of North and South Dakota, Montana and Washington A317

1939, Nov. 2   **Perf. 11x10½**
858 A317 3c rose purple   .35   .25

FAMOUS AMERICANS ISSUES
AMERICAN AUTHORS

Washington Irving — A318   James Fenimore Cooper — A319

Ralph Waldo Emerson A320   Louisa May Alcott A321

Samuel L. Clemens (Mark Twain) — A322

1940   **Perf. 10½x11**
859 A318 1c bright blue green   .25   .25
860 A319 2c rose carmine   .25   .25
861 A320 3c bright purple   .25   .25
862 A321 5c ultramarine   .35   .25
863 A322 10c dark brown   1.75 1.20
     Nos. 859-863 (5)   2.85 2.20

AMERICAN POETS

Henry W. Longfellow A323   John Greenleaf Whittier A324

James Russell Lowell A325   Walt Whitman A326

James Whitcomb Riley — A327

864 A323 1c bright blue green   .25   .25
865 A324 2c rose carmine   .25   .25
866 A325 3c bright purple   .25   .25
867 A326 5c ultramarine   .50   .25
868 A327 10c dark brown   1.75 1.25
     Nos. 864-868 (5)   3.00 2.25

AMERICAN EDUCATORS

Horace Mann — A328   Mark Hopkins — A329

Charles W. Eliot — A330   Frances E. Willard — A331

Booker T. Washington — A332

869 A328 1c bright blue green   .25   .25
870 A329 2c rose carmine   .25   .25
871 A330 3c bright purple   .25   .25
872 A331 5c ultramarine   .50   .25
873 A332 10c dark brown   2.25 1.10
     Nos. 869-873 (5)   3.50 2.10

AMERICAN SCIENTISTS

John James Audubon A333   Dr. Crawford W. Long A334

Luther Burbank — A335   Dr. Walter Reed — A336

Jane Addams — A337

874 A333 1c bright blue green   .25   .25
875 A334 2c rose carmine   .25   .25
876 A335 3c bright purple   .25   .25
877 A336 5c ultramarine   .50   .25
878 A337 10c dark brown   1.50   .85
     Nos. 874-878 (5)   2.75 1.85

AMERICAN COMPOSERS

Stephen Collins Foster — A338   John Philip Sousa — A339

Victor Herbert A340   Edward MacDowell A341

Ethelbert Nevin — A342

879 A338 1c bright blue green   .25   .25
880 A339 2c rose carmine   .25   .25
881 A340 3c bright purple   .25   .25
882 A341 5c ultramarine   .50   .25
883 A342 10c dark brown   3.75 1.35
     Nos. 879-883 (5)   5.00 2.35

AMERICAN ARTISTS

Gilbert Charles Stuart — A343   James A. McNeill Whistler — A344

Augustus Saint-Gaudens A345   Daniel Chester French A346

Frederic Remington — A347

884 A343 1c bright blue green   .25   .25
885 A344 2c rose carmine   .25   .25
886 A345 3c bright purple   .30   .25
887 A346 5c ultramarine   .50   .25
888 A347 10c dark brown   1.75 1.25
     Nos. 884-888 (5)   3.05 2.25

AMERICAN INVENTORS

Eli Whitney — A348   Samuel F. B. Morse — A349

Cyrus Hall McCormick A350   Elias Howe A351

Alexander Graham Bell — A352

889 A348 1c brt blue grn   .25   .25
890 A349 2c rose carmine   .30   .25
891 A350 3c bright purple   .30   .25
892 A351 5c ultramarine   1.10   .30
893 A352 10c dark brown   11.00 2.00
     Nos. 889-893 (5)   12.95 3.05
     Nos. 859-893 (35)   33.10 16.05

PONY EXPRESS, 80th ANNIV. ISSUE

Pony Express Rider A353

1940, Apr. 3   *Perf. 11x10½*
894 A353 3c henna brown   .50   .25

PAN AMERICAN UNION ISSUE

Founding of the Pan American Union, 50th anniv.

The Three Graces from Botticelli's "Spring" — A354

1940, Apr. 14   *Perf. 10½x11*
895 A354 3c bright rose purple   .30   .25

IDAHO STATEHOOD, 50th ANNIV.

Idaho Capitol, Boise A355

1940, July 3   *Perf. 11x10½*
896 A355 3c bright mauve   .35   .25

WYOMING STATEHOOD, 50th ANNIV.

Wyoming State Seal — A356

1940, July 10   *Perf. 10½x11*
897 A356 3c brown violet   .35   .25

CORONADO EXPEDITION, 400th ANNIV.

"Coronado and His Captains," painted by Gerald Cassidy A357

1940, Sept. 7   *Perf. 11x10½*
898 A357 3c bright violet   .35   .25

NATIONAL DEFENSE ISSUE

Statue of Liberty — A358

90-millimeter Anti-aircraft Gun — A359

Torch of Enlightenment — A360

1940, Oct. 16
899 A358 1c bright blue green   .25   .25
   a. Vertical pair, imperf. between   600.00   —
   b. Horizontal pair, imperf. between   32.50   —
900 A359 2c rose carmine   .25   .25
   a. Horizontal pair, imperf. between   37.50   —
901 A360 3c bright mauve   .25   .25
   a. Horizontal pair, imperf. between   22.50   —
    Nos. 899-901 (3)   .75   .75

THIRTEENTH AMENDMENT ISSUE

75th anniv. of the 13th Amendment to the Constitution abolishing slavery.

"Emancipation," Statue of Lincoln and Slave, by Thomas Ball — A361

1940, Oct. 20   *Perf. 10½x11*
902 A361 3c violet   .50   .25

VERMONT STATEHOOD, 150th ANNIV.

Vermont Capitol, Montpelier A362

1941, Mar. 4   *Perf. 11x10½*
903 A362 3c light violet   .45   .25

KENTUCKY STATEHOOD, 150th ANNIV.

Daniel Boone and Three Frontiersmen, from mural by Gilbert White — A363

1942, June 1
904 A363 3c purple   .30   .25

WIN THE WAR ISSUE

American Eagle — A364

1942, July 4
905 A364 3c bright lilac   .25   .25
   b. 3c reddish purple   750.00   500.00

All examples of No. 905b are precanceled either Los Angeles, Calif., or Fremont, Ohio. Value is for Los Angeles, which is the more common. Value of Fremont, unused $1,750.

CHINESE RESISTANCE ISSUE

Issued to commemorate the Chinese people's five years of resistance to Japanese aggression.

Lincoln, Sun Yat-sen & Map A365

1942, July 7
906 A365 5c bright blue   3.00   .50

ALLIED NATIONS ISSUE

Allegory of Victory — A366

1943, Jan. 14
907 A366 2c rose carmine   .25   .25
   Bureau Precancels: Denver, Baltimore.

FOUR FREEDOMS ISSUE

A367

1943, Feb. 12
908 A367 1c bright blue green   .25 .25

OVERRUN COUNTRIES ISSUE

Printed by the American Bank Note Co.

FRAMES ENGRAVED, CENTERS OFFSET LETTERPRESS ROTARY PRESS PRINTING

Flag of Poland A368

1943-44   *Perf. 12*
909 A368 5c Poland   .25   .25
   a. Double impression of "Poland"   200.00
   b. Double impression of black flag color and red "Poland"   —
910 A368a 5c Czechoslovakia   .25   .25
   a. Double impression of "Czechoslovakia"   650.00
911 A368b 5c Norway   .25   .25
   a. Double impression of "Norway"   225.00
912 A368c 5c Luxembourg   .25   .25
   a. Double impression of "Luxembourg"   —
913 A368d 5c Netherlands   .25   .25
914 A368e 5c Belgium   .25   .25
   a. Double impression of "Belgium"   225.00
915 A368f 5c France   .25   .25
916 A368g 5c Greece   .50   .25
917 A368h 5c Yugoslavia   .40   .25
   b. Double impression of black   200.00   200.00
918 A368i 5c Albania   .25   .25
   a. Double impression of "Albania"   —   600.00
919 A368j 5c Austria   .30   .25
   a. Double impression of "Austria"   200.00
   c. Double impression of black   —

---

920 A368k 5c Denmark (blue violet, red and black)   .30   .25
   b. 5c blue violet, red & gray   .30   .25
921 A368m 5c Korea   .25   .25
   a. Double impression of light blue (including "Korea")   —
   c. Double impression of red   —
    Nos. 909-921 (13)   3.75   3.25

TRANSCONTINENTAL RAILROAD ISSUE

Completion of the 1st transcontinental railroad, 75th anniv.

"Golden Spike Ceremony" Painting by John McQuarrie A369

ENGRAVED ROTARY PRESS PRINTING

1944, May 10   *Perf. 11x10½*
922 A369 3c violet   .25   .25

STEAMSHIP ISSUE

1st steamship to cross the Atlantic, 125th anniv.

"Savannah" A370

1944, May 22
923 A370 3c violet   .25   .25

TELEGRAPH ISSUE

1st message transmitted by telegraph, cent.

Telegraph Wires & the First Transmitted Words "What Hath God Wrought" A371

1944, May 24
924 A371 3c bright purple   .25   .25

PHILIPPINE ISSUE

Final resistance of the US and Philippine defenders on Corregidor to the Japanese invaders in 1942.

View of Corregidor A372

1944, Sept. 27
925 A372 3c deep violet   .25   .25

MOTION PICTURE, 50th ANNIV.

Motion Picture Showing for the Armed Forces in South Pacific A373

1944, Oct. 31
926 A373 3c deep violet   .25   .25

FLORIDA STATEHOOD, CENTENARY

Old Florida Seal, St. Augustine Gates and State Capitol A374

1945, Mar. 3
927　A374　3c bright red violet　.25　.25

UNITED NATIONS CONFERENCE ISSUE

United Nations Conference, San Francisco, Calif.

A375

1945, Apr. 25
928　A375　5c ultramarine　.25　.25

IWO JIMA (MARINES) ISSUE

Battle of Iwo Jima and honoring the achievements of the US Marines.

Marines Raising the Flag on Mt. Suribachi, Iwo Jima, from a Photograph by Joel Rosenthal — A376

1945, July 11　　Perf. 10½x11
929　A376　3c yellow green　.30　.25

FRANKLIN D. ROOSEVELT ISSUE

Franklin Delano Roosevelt (1882-1945).

Roosevelt and Hyde Park Home A377

Roosevelt and "Little White House," Warm Springs, Georgia A378

Roosevelt and White House A379

Roosevelt, Globe and Four Freedoms A380

1945-46　　Perf. 11x10½
930　A377　1c blue green　.25　.25
931　A378　2c carmine rose　.25　.25
932　A379　3c purple　.25　.25
933　A380　5c bright blue　.25　.25
　　Nos. 930-933 (4)　1.00　1.00

ARMY ISSUE

Achievements of the US Army in World War II.

U.S. Troops Passing Arch of Triumph, Paris A381

1945, Sept. 28
934　A381　3c olive　.25　.25

NAVY ISSUE

Achievements of the U.S. Navy in World War II.

U.S. Sailors A382

1945, Oct. 27
935　A382　3c blue　.25　.25

COAST GUARD ISSUE

Achievements of the US Coast Guard in World War II.

Coast Guard Landing Craft and Supply Ship A383

1945, Nov. 10
936　A383　3c bright blue green　.25　.25

ALFRED E. SMITH ISSUE

Alfred E. Smith — A384

1945, Nov. 26
937　A384　3c purple　.25　.25

TEXAS STATEHOOD, 100th ANNIV.

U.S. and Texas State Flags A385

1945, Dec. 29
938　A385　3c dark blue　.25　.25

MERCHANT MARINE ISSUE

Achievements of the US Merchant Marine in World War II.

Liberty Ship Unloading Cargo A386

1946, Feb. 26
939　A386　3c blue green　.25　.25

VETERANS OF WORLD WAR II ISSUE

Issued to honor all veterans of World War II.

Honorable Discharge Emblem — A387

1946, May 9
940　A387　3c dark violet　.25　.25

TENNESSEE STATEHOOD, 150th ANNIV.

Andrew Jackson, John Sevier & Tennessee Capitol A388

1946, June 1
941　A388　3c dark violet　.25　.25

IOWA STATEHOOD, 100th ANNIV.

Iowa State Flag & Map A389

1946, Aug. 3
942　A389　3c deep blue　.25　.25

SMITHSONIAN INSTITUTION ISSUE

100th anniversary of the establishment of the Smithsonian Institution, Washington, D.C.

Smithsonian Institution A390

1946, Aug. 10
943　A390　3c violet brown　.25　.25

KEARNY EXPEDITION ISSUE

100th anniversary of the entry of General Stephen Watts Kearny into Santa Fe.

"Capture of Santa Fe" by Kenneth M. Chapman A391

1946, Oct. 16
944　A391　3c brown violet　.25　.25

THOMAS A. EDISON ISSUE

Thomas A. Edison, Birth Centenary — A392

1947, Feb. 11　　Perf. 10½x11
945　A392　3c bright red violet　.25　.25

JOSEPH PULITZER ISSUE

Joseph Pulitzer & Statue of Liberty A393

1947, Apr. 10　　Perf. 11x10½
946　A393　3c purple　.25　.25

POSTAGE STAMP CENTENARY ISSUE

Centenary of the first postage stamps issued by the United States Government

Washington & Franklin; Early and Modern Mail-carrying Vehicles — A394

1947, May 17
947　A394　3c deep blue　.25　.25

CENTENARY INTERNATIONAL PHILATELIC EXHIBITION ISSUE
SOUVENIR SHEET

A395

FLAT PLATE PRINTING

1947, May 19　　Imperf.
948　A395　Pane of 2　.55　.45
　a.　5c blue, type A1　.25　.25
　b.　10c brown orange, type A2　.25　.25
　　Pane size varies: 96-98x66-68mm.

DOCTORS ISSUE

Issued to honor the physicians of America.

"The Doctor," by Sir Luke Fildes A396

ROTARY PRESS PRINTING

1947, June 9　　Perf. 11x10½
949　A396　3c brown violet　.25　.25

UTAH ISSUE

Centenary of the settlement of Utah.

Pioneers Entering the Valley of Great Salt Lake A397

1947, July 24
950　A397　3c dark violet　.25　.25

U.S. FRIGATE CONSTITUTION ISSUE

150th anniversary of the launching of the U.S. frigate Constitution ("Old Ironsides").

Naval Architect's Drawing of Frigate Constitution A398

1947, Oct. 21
951　A398　3c blue green　.25　.25

EVERGLADES NATIONAL PARK ISSUE

Dedication of the Everglades National Park, Florida, Dec. 6, 1947.

Great White Heron and Map of Florida — A399

1947, Dec. 5   *Perf. 10½x11*
952 A399 3c bright green   .25   .25

GEORGE WASHINGTON CARVER ISSUE

5th anniversary of the death of Dr. George Washington Carver, (1864-1943), botanist.

Dr. George Washington Carver — A400

1948, Jan. 5
953 A400 3c bright red violet   .25   .25

CALIFORNIA GOLD CENTENNIAL ISSUE

Sutter's Mill, Coloma, California A401

1948, Jan. 24   *Perf. 11x10½*
954 A401 3c dark violet   .25   .25

MISSISSIPPI TERRITORY ISSUE

Mississippi Territory establishment, 150th anniv.

Map, Seal and Gov. Winthrop Sargent A402

1948, Apr. 7
955 A402 3c brown violet   .25   .25

FOUR CHAPLAINS ISSUE

George L. Fox, Clark V. Poling, John P. Washington and Alexander D. Goode, the 4 chaplains who sacrificed their lives in the sinking of the S.S. Dorchester, Feb. 3, 1943.

Four Chaplains and Sinking S.S. Dorchester A403

1948, May 28
956 A403 3c gray black   .25   .25

WISCONSIN STATEHOOD, 100th ANNIV.

Map on Scroll & State Capitol A404

1948, May 29
957 A404 3c dark violet   .25   .25

SWEDISH PIONEER ISSUE

Centenary of the coming of the Swedish pioneers to the Middle West.

Swedish Pioneer with Covered Wagon Moving Westward — A405

1948, June 4
958 A405 5c deep blue   .25   .25

PROGRESS OF WOMEN ISSUE

Century of progress of American Women.

Elizabeth Stanton, Carrie C. Catt & Lucretia Mott A406

1948, July 19
959 A406 3c dark violet   .25   .25

WILLIAM ALLEN WHITE ISSUE

William Allen White, Editor and Author — A407

1948, July 31   *Perf. 10½x11*
960 A407 3c bright red violet   .25   .25

UNITED STATES-CANADA FRIENDSHIP ISSUE

Century of friendship between the US and Canada.

Niagara Railway Suspension Bridge A408

1948, Aug. 2   *Perf. 11x10½*
961 A408 3c blue   .25   .25

FRANCIS SCOTT KEY ISSUE

Francis Scott Key (1779-1843), Maryland lawyer and author of "The Star-Spangled Banner" (1813).

Key and American Flags of 1814 and 1948 A409

1948, Aug. 9
962 A409 3c rose pink   .25   .25

SALUTE TO YOUTH ISSUE

Issued to honor the Youth of America and to publicize "Youth Month," September, 1948.

Girl and Boy Carrying Books A410

1948, Aug. 11
963 A410 3c deep blue   .25   .25

OREGON TERRITORY ISSUE

Centenary of the establishment of Oregon Territory.

John McLoughlin, Jason Lee & Wagon on Oregon Trail A411

1948, Aug. 14
964 A411 3c brown red   .25   .25

HARLAN F. STONE ISSUE

Chief Justice Harlan Fiske Stone — A412

1948, Aug. 25   *Perf. 10½x11*
965 A412 3c bright red violet   .25   .25

PALOMAR MOUNTAIN OBSERVATORY ISSUE

Dedication, August 30, 1948.

Observatory, Palomar Mt., Cal. — A413

1948, Aug. 30
966 A413 3c blue   .25   .25
   a.   Vert. pair, imperf. between   300.00

CLARA BARTON ISSUE

Founder of the American Red Cross (1882) A414

Designed by Charles R. Chickering.

1948, Sept. 7   *Perf. 11x10½*
967 A414 3c rose pink   .25   .25

POULTRY INDUSTRY CENTENNIAL ISSUE

Light Brahma Rooster A415

1948, Sept. 9
968 A415 3c sepia   .25   .25

GOLD STAR MOTHERS ISSUE

Issued to honor the mothers of deceased members of the United States armed forces.

Star and Palm Frond — A416

1948, Sept. 21   *Perf. 10½x11*
969 A416 3c orange yellow   .25   .25

FORT KEARNY ISSUE

Establishment of Fort Kearny, Neb., centenary.

Fort Kearny and Pioneer Group A417

1948, Sept. 22   *Perf. 11x10½*
970 A417 3c violet   .25   .25

VOLUNTEER FIREMEN ISSUE

300th anniv. of the organization of the 1st volunteer firemen in America by Peter Stuyvesant.

Peter Stuyvesant; Early and Modern Fire Engines A418

1948, Oct. 4
971 A418 3c bright rose carmine   .25   .25

INDIAN CENTENNIAL ISSUE

Centenary of the arrival in Indian Territory, later Oklahoma, of the Five Civilized Indian Tribes: Cherokee, Chickasaw, Choctaw, Muscogee and Seminole.

Map of Indian Territory & Seals of Five Tribes A419

1948, Oct. 15
972 A419 3c dark brown   .25   .25

ROUGH RIDERS ISSUE

50th anniversary of the organization of the Rough Riders of the Spanish-American War.

Statue of Capt. William O. (Bucky) O'Neill A420

1948, Oct. 27
973 A420 3c violet brown   .25   .25

JULIETTE LOW ISSUE

Low (1860-1927), founder of the Girl Scouts of America. Mrs. Low organized the 1st Girl Guides troop in 1912 at Savannah. The name was changed to Girl Scouts in 1913 and headquarters moved to New York.

Low and Girl Scout Emblem A421

1948, Oct. 29
974 A421 3c blue green   .25   .25

WILL ROGERS ISSUE

Will Rogers — A422

1948, Nov. 4   *Perf. 10½x11*
975 A422 3c bright red violet   .25   .25

Will Rogers, 1879-1935, humorist and political commentator.

FORT BLISS CENTENNIAL ISSUE

Fort Bliss and Rocket — A423

1948, Nov. 5
976 A423 3c henna brown .25 .25

MOINA MICHAEL ISSUE

Moina Michael (1870-1944), educator who originated (1918) the Flanders Field Poppy Day idea as a memorial to the war dead.

Moina Michael and Poppy Plant A424

1948, Nov. 9 *Perf. 11x10½*
977 A424 3c rose pink .25 .25

GETTYSBURG ADDRESS ISSUE

85th anniversary of Abraham Lincoln's address at Gettysburg, Pennsylvania.

Lincoln and Quotation from Gettysburg Address A425

1948, Nov. 19
978 A425 3c bright blue .25 .25

AMERICAN TURNERS ISSUE

Formation of the American Turners Soc., cent.

Torch and American Turners' Emblem — A426

1948, Nov. 20 *Perf. 10½x11*
979 A426 3c carmine .25 .25

JOEL CHANDLER HARRIS ISSUE

Joel Chandler Harris — A427

1948, Dec. 9
980 A427 3c bright red violet .25 .25
Harris (1848-1908), editor and author.

MINNESOTA TERRITORY ISSUE

Establishment of Minnesota Territory, cent.

Pioneer and Red River Oxcart A428

1949, Mar. 3 *Perf. 11x10½*
981 A428 3c blue green .25 .25

WASHINGTON AND LEE UNIVERSITY ISSUE

Bicentenary of Washington and Lee University.

George Washington, Robert E. Lee and University Building — A429

1949, Apr. 12
982 A429 3c ultramarine .25 .25

PUERTO RICO ELECTION ISSUE

First gubernatorial election in the Territory of Puerto Rico, Nov. 2, 1948.

Puerto Rican Farmer Holding Cogwheel and Ballot Box A430

1949, Apr. 27
983 A430 3c green .25 .25

ANNAPOLIS TERCENTENARY ISSUE

Founding of Annapolis, Maryland, 300th anniv.

Stoddert's 1718 Map of Regions about Annapolis, Redrawn A431

1949, May 23
984 A431 3c aquamarine .25 .25

G.A.R. ISSUE

Final encampment of the Grand Army of the Republic, Indianapolis, Aug. 28 - Sept. 1, 1949.

Union Soldier and GAR Veteran of 1949 A432

1949, Aug. 29
985 A432 3c bright rose carmine .25 .25

EDGAR ALLAN POE ISSUE

Edgar Allan Poe (1809-1849), Poet, Story Writer and Editor — A433

1949, Oct. 7 *Perf. 10½x11*
986 A433 3c bright red violet .25 .25

AMERICAN BANKERS ASSOCIATION ISSUE

75th anniv. of the formation of the Association.

Coin, Symbolizing Fields of Banking Service — A434

1950, Jan. 3 *Perf. 11x10½*
987 A434 3c yellow green .25 .25

SAMUEL GOMPERS ISSUE

Samuel Gompers (1850-1924), Labor Leader — A435

1950, Jan. 27 *Perf. 10½x11*
988 A435 3c bright red violet .25 .25

NATIONAL CAPITAL SESQUICENTENNIAL ISSUE

150th anniversary of the establishment of the National Capital, Washington, D.C.

Statue of Freedom on Capitol Dome — A436

Executive Mansion A437

Supreme Court Building A438

United States Capitol A439

1950 *Perf. 10½x11, 11x10½*
989 A436 3c bright blue .25 .25
990 A437 3c deep green .25 .25
991 A438 3c light violet .25 .25
992 A439 3c bright red violet .25 .25
Nos. 989-992 (4) 1.00 1.00

RAILROAD ENGINEERS ISSUE

Issued to honor the Railroad Engineers of America. Stamp portrays John Luther (Casey) Jones (1864-1900), locomotive engineer killed in train wreck near Vaughn, Miss.

"Casey" Jones and Locomotives of 1900 and 1950 — A440

1950, Apr. 29 *Perf. 11x10½*
993 A440 3c violet brown .25 .25

KANSAS CITY, MISSOURI, CENTENARY ISSUE

Kansas City, Missouri, incorporation.

Kansas City Skyline, 1950 and Westport Landing, 1850 A441

1950, June 3
994 A441 3c violet .25 .25

BOY SCOUTS ISSUE

Honoring the Boy Scouts of America on the occasion of the 2nd National Jamboree, Valley Forge, Pa.

Three Boys, Statue of Liberty and Scout Badge A442

1950, June 30
995 A442 3c sepia .25 .25

INDIANA TERRITORY ISSUE

Establishment of Indiana Territory, 150th anniv.

Gov. William Henry Harrison & First Indiana Capitol, Vincennes A443

1950, July 4
996 A443 3c bright blue .25 .25

CALIFORNIA STATEHOOD ISSUE

Gold Miner, Pioneers and S.S. Oregon A444

1950, Sept. 9
997 A444 3c yellow orange .25 .25

UNITED CONFEDERATE VETERANS FINAL REUNION ISSUE

Final reunion of the United Confederate Veterans, Norfolk, Virginia, May 30, 1951.

Confederate Soldier & United Confederate Veteran A445

1951, May 30
998 A445 3c gray .25 .25

NEVADA CENTENNIAL ISSUE

Centenary of the settlement of Nevada.

Carson Valley, c. 1851 A446

Designed by Charles R. Chickering.

1951, July 14
999 A446 3c light olive green .25 .25

LANDING OF CADILLAC ISSUE

250th anniversary of the landing of Antoine de la Mothe Cadillac at Detroit.

Detroit Skyline and Cadillac Landing A447

1951, July 24
1000 A447 3c blue .25 .25

COLORADO STATEHOOD, 75th ANNIV.

Colorado Capitol and Mount of the Holy Cross A448

1951, Aug. 1
1001 A448 3c blue violet .25 .25

AMERICAN CHEMICAL SOCIETY ISSUE

75th anniv. of the formation of the Society.

A.C.S. Emblem and Symbols of Chemistry A449

1951, Sept. 4
1002 A449 3c violet brown .25 .25

BATTLE OF BROOKLYN, 175th ANNIV.

Gen. George Washington Evacuating Army A450

1951, Dec. 10
1003 A450 3c violet .25 .25

BETSY ROSS ISSUE

200th anniv. of the birth of Betsy Ross, maker of the first American flag.

Betsy Ross Showing Flag to Gen. George Washington, Robert Morris & George Ross — A451

1952, Jan. 2
1004 A451 3c carmine rose .25 .25

4-H CLUB ISSUE

Farm, Club Emblem, Boy and Girl — A452

1952, Jan. 15
1005 A452 3c blue green .25 .25

B. & O. RAILROAD ISSUE

125th anniv. of the granting of a charter to the Baltimore and Ohio Railroad Company by the Maryland Legislature.

Charter and Three Stages of Rail Transportation — A453

1952, Feb. 28
1006 A453 3c bright blue .25 .25

A. A. A. ISSUE

50th anniversary of the formation of the American Automobile Association.

School Girls and Safety Patrolman, Automobiles of 1902 and 1952 — A454

1952, Mar. 4
1007 A454 3c deep blue .25 .25

NATO ISSUE

Signing of the North Atlantic Treaty, 3rd anniv.

Torch of Liberty and Globe — A455

1952, Apr. 4
1008 A455 3c deep violet .25 .25

GRAND COULEE DAM ISSUE

50 years of Federal cooperation in developing the resources of rivers and streams in the West.

Spillway, Grand Coulee Dam A456

1952, May 15
1009 A456 3c blue green .25 .25

LAFAYETTE ISSUE

175th anniversary of the arrival of Marquis de Lafayette in America.

Marquis de Lafayette, Flags, Cannon and Landing Party A457

1952, June 13
1010 A457 3c bright blue .25 .25

MT. RUSHMORE MEMORIAL ISSUE

Dedication of the Mt. Rushmore National Memorial in the Black Hills of South Dakota, 25th anniv.

Sculptured Heads on Mt. Rushmore — A458

1952, Aug. 11 Perf. 10½x11
1011 A458 3c blue green .25 .25

ENGINEERING CENTENNIAL ISSUE

American Society of Civil Engineers founding.

George Washington Bridge & Covered Bridge of 1850s A459

1952, Sept. 6 Perf. 11x10½
1012 A459 3c violet blue .25 .25

SERVICE WOMEN ISSUE

Women in the United States Armed Services.

Women of the Marine Corps, Army, Navy and Air Force A460

1952, Sept. 11
1013 A460 3c deep blue .25 .25

GUTENBERG BIBLE ISSUE

Printing of the 1st book, the Holy Bible, from movable type, by Johann Gutenberg, 500th anniv.

Gutenberg Showing Proof to the Elector of Mainz A461

1952, Sept. 30
1014 A461 3c violet .25 .25

NEWSPAPER BOYS ISSUE

Newspaper Boy, Torch and Group of Homes A462

1952, Oct. 4
1015 A462 3c violet .25 .25

RED CROSS ISSUE

Globe, Sun and Cross A463

1952, Nov. 21
1016 A463 3c deep blue & carmine .25 .25

NATIONAL GUARD ISSUE

National Guardsman and Amphibious Landing A464

1953, Feb. 23
1017 A464 3c bright blue .25 .25

OHIO STATEHOOD, 150th ANNIV.

Map and Ohio State Seal — A465

1953, Mar. 2
1018 A465 3c chocolate .25 .25

WASHINGTON TERRITORY ISSUE

Organization of Washington Territory, cent.

Medallion, Pioneers and Washington Scene A466

1953, Mar. 2
1019 A466 3c green .25 .25

LOUISIANA PURCHASE, 150th ANNIV.

Monroe, Livingston and Barbé-Marbois — A467

1953, Apr. 30
1020 A467 3c violet brown .25 .25

OPENING OF JAPAN CENTENNIAL ISSUE

Centenary of Commodore Matthew Calbraith Perry's negotiations with Japan, which opened her doors to foreign trade.

Commodore Perry and 1st Anchorage off Tokyo Bay — A468

1953, July 14
1021 A468 5c green .25 .25

AMERICAN BAR ASSOCIATION, 75th ANNIV.

Section of Frieze, Supreme Court Room A469

1953, Aug. 24
1022 A469 3c rose violet .25 .25

SAGAMORE HILL ISSUE

Opening of Sagamore Hill, Theodore Roosevelt's home, as a national shrine.

Home of Theodore Roosevelt A470

1953, Sept. 14
1023 A470 3c yellow green   .25   .25

FUTURE FARMERS ISSUE

25th anniversary of the organization of Future Farmers of America.

Agricultural Scene and Future Farmer A471

1953, Oct. 13
1024 A471 3c deep blue   .25   .25

TRUCKING INDUSTRY ISSUE

50th anniv. of the Trucking Industry in the US.

Truck, Farm and Distant City A472

1953, Oct. 27
1025 A472 3c violet   .25   .25

GENERAL PATTON ISSUE

Honoring Gen. George S. Patton, Jr. (1885-1945), and the armored forces of the US Army.

Gen. George S. Patton, Jr., and Tank in Action A473

1953, Nov. 11
1026 A473 3c blue violet   .25   .25

NEW YORK CITY, 300th ANNIV.

Dutch Ship in New Amsterdam Harbor A474

1953, Nov. 20
1027 A474 3c bright red violet   .25   .25

GADSDEN PURCHASE ISSUE

Centenary of James Gadsden's purchase of territory from Mexico to adjust the US-Mexico boundary.

Map and Pioneer Group A475

1953, Dec. 30
1028 A475 3c copper brown   .25   .25

COLUMBIA UNIVERSITY, 200th ANNIV.

Low Memorial Library A476

1954, Jan. 4
1029 A476 3c blue   .25   .25

Wet and Dry Printings

In 1953 the Bureau of Engraving and Printing began experiments in printing on "dry" paper (moisture content 5-10 per cent). In previous "wet" printings the paper had a moisture content of 13-35 per cent.

The new process required a thicker, stiffer paper, special types of inks and greater pressure to force the paper into the recessed plates. The "dry" printings show whiter paper, a higher sheen on the surface, feel thicker and stiffer, and the designs stand out more clearly than on the "wet" printings.

Nos. 832c and 1041 (flat plate) were the first "dry" printings to be issued of flat-plate, regular-issue stamps. No. 1063 was the first rotary-press stamp to be produced entirely by "dry" printing. Nos. QE1a, QE2a and QE3a, RF26A and RW21 (all flat plate) were the first "dry" printings of back-of-the-book issue stamps.

All postage stamps have been printed by the "dry" process since the late 1950's.

See the Scott *Specialized Catalogue of United States Stamps* for listings of the wet and dry printings and for No. 1033 on Silkote paper.

LIBERTY ISSUE

Franklin A477

Washington A478

Palace of the Governors, Santa Fe — A478a — 1031A

Mount Vernon — A479

Thomas Jefferson A480

Bunker Hill Monument, Mass. Flag, 1776 A481

Statue of Liberty A482

Abraham Lincoln A483

The Hermitage A484

James Monroe A485

Theodore Roosevelt A486

Woodrow Wilson A487

Statue of Liberty A489

A488

The Alamo A490

Independence Hall — A491

Statue of Liberty — A491a

Benjamin Harrison A492

John Jay A493

Monticello A494

Paul Revere A495

Robert E. Lee A496

John Marshall A497

Susan B. Anthony A498

Patrick Henry A499

Alexander Hamilton — A500

ROTARY PRESS PRINTING

1954-68				*Perf. 11x10½, 10½x11*	
1030	A477	½c red orange ('55)		.25	.25
1031	A478	1c dark green		.25	.25
1031A	A478a	1¼c turquoise ('60)		.25	.25
1032	A479	1½c brn car ('56)		.25	.25
1033	A480	2c car rose		.25	.25
1034	A481	2½c gray blue ('59)		.25	.25
1035	A482	3c deep violet		.25	.25
a.		Booklet pane of 6, June 30, 1954		4.00	1.25
b.		Horiz. pairs, imperf. btwn in #1035a with foldover (two pairs recorded in two full panes) or miscut (three pairs from pane)		5,000.	
e.		Tagged ('66)		.35	.25
f.		Imperf., pair		3,000.	
g.		Horiz. pair, imperf. between		1,000.	

No. 1057b measures about 19½x22mm; No. 1035f, about 18¾x22½mm.

1036	A483	4c red violet		.25	.25
b.		Booklet pane of 6 ('58)		2.75	1.25
c.		As "b," imperf. horiz.		10,000.	
d.		Horiz. pair, imperf between		4,000.	
e.		Tagged ('63)		.65	.40
1037	A484	4½c blue green ('59)		.25	.25
1038	A485	5c deep blue		.25	.25
1039	A486	6c carmine ('55)		.40	.25
		Pair with full vert. gutter btwn.		2,750.	
b.		Imperf., block of 4 (unique)		23,000.	
1040	A487	7c rose car ('56)		.25	.25
a.		dk rose car		.25	.25

FLAT PLATE PRINTING
Size: 22.7mm high
Perf. 11

1041	A488	8c dk vio blue & car		.25	.25
a.		Double impression of carmine		575.00	—

ROTARY PRESS PRINTING
Size: 22.9mm high

1041B	A488	8c dk vio blue & car		.40	.25

GIORI PRESS PRINTING
Redrawn design

1042	A489	8c dk vio bl & car rose ('58)		.25	.25

The 8c John J. Pershing stamp, formerly No. 1042A, is now included with the regular issue of 1961-66. See No. 1214.

ROTARY PRESS PRINTING
Perf. 10½x11

1043	A490	9c rose lilac ('56)		.30	.25
a.		9c dark rose lilac		.30	.25
1044	A491	10c rose lake ('56)		.30	.25
b.		10c dark rose lake		.25	.25
d.		Tagged		2.00	1.00

GIORI PRESS PRINTING
Perf. 11

1044A	A491a	11c car & dk vio bl ('61)	.30	.25
c.		Tagged	2.50	1.60

Perf. 11x10½, 10½x11

1045	A492	12c red ('59)	.35	.25
a.		Tagged ('68)	.35	.25
1046	A493	15c rose lake	.60	.25
a.		Tagged	1.10	.80
1047	A494	20c ultra ('56)	.50	.25
a.		deep bright ultra	.50	.25
1048	A495	25c green ('58)	1.00	.75
1049	A496	30c black ('55)	1.20	.75
b.		30c intense black	.80	.25

No. 1049b is from later printings and is on a harder, whiter paper than No. 1049.

1050	A497	40c brown red ('55)	1.75	.25
1051	A498	50c brt pur ('55)	1.75	.25
1052	A499	$1 purple ('55)	5.00	1.00

FLAT PLATE PRINTING
Perf. 11

1053	A500	$5 black	50.00	6.75
		Nos. 1030-1053 (27)	67.10	15.00

Luminescence
During 1963 quantities of certain issues (Nos. C64a, 1213b, 1213c and 1229a) were overprinted with phosphorescent coating, "tagged," for use in testing automated facing and canceling machines. Listings for tagged varieties of stamps previously issued without tagging start with Nos. 1035b and C59a.

The entire printings of Nos. 1238, 1278, 1280-1281, 1283B, 1286-1288, 1298-1305, 1323-1340, 1342-1362, 1364, and C69-C75 and all following listings, unless otherwise noted, were tagged.

Stamps tagged with zinc orthosilicate glow yellow green. Airmail stamps with calcium silicate overprint glow orange red. Both tagging overprints are activated only by shortwave ultraviolet light.

ROTARY PRESS COIL STAMPS
Perf. 10 Vert., Horiz. (1¼c, 4½c)
1954-80

1054	A478	1c dark green	.60	.25
c.		Imperf., pair	5,000.	1,000.
1054A	A478a	1¼c turquoise ('60)	.25	.25
d.		Imperf., pair	—	—

All examples of No. 1054Ad are precanceled "SEATTLE/WASH." No. 1054A with large holes exists non-precanceled as well as precanceled. The values shown are for the non-precanceled variety; precanceled stamps with large holes are quite common.

1055	A480	2c car rose	.60	.25
b.		Tagged ('68)	.25	.25
c.		Imperf. pair, (Bureau precanceled)	325.00	
d.		As "b," Imperf. pair	450.00	
1056	A481	2½c gray blue ('59)	.30	.25
1057	A482	3c deep violet	.35	.25
b.		Imperf., pair	1,250.	800.00
d.		Tagged ('66)	1.00	.50

No. 1057b measures about 19½x22mm; No. 1035f, about 18¾x22½mm.

1058	A483	4c red violet ('58)	.75	.25
a.		Imperf., pair	75.00	70.00
1059	A484	4½c blue green ('59)	1.50	1.00
1059A	A495	25c green ('65)	.50	.30
b.		Tagged	.80	.25
d.		Imperf., pair, tagged	30.00	

Value for No. 1059Ad is for fine centering.

NEBRASKA TERRITORY ISSUE
Establishment of the Nebraska Territory, centenary.

Mitchell Pass, Scotts Bluff & "The Sower," by Lee Lawrie A507

ROTARY PRESS PRINTING
1954, May 7   **Perf. 11x10½**

1060	A507	3c violet	.25	.25

KANSAS TERRITORY ISSUE
Establishment of the Kansas Territory, centenary

Wheat Field and Pioneer Wagon Train A508

1954, May 31

1061	A508	3c brown orange	.25	.25

GEORGE EASTMAN ISSUE

George Eastman (1854-1932), Inventor & Philanthropist A509

1954, July 12   **Perf. 10½x11**

1062	A509	3c violet brown	.25	.25

LEWIS AND CLARK EXPEDITION
150th anniv. of the Lewis and Clark expedition.

Landing of Lewis and Clark A510

1954, July 28   **Perf. 11x10½**

1063	A510	3c violet brown	.25	.25

PENNSYLVANIA ACADEMY OF THE FINE ARTS ISSUE
150th anniversary of the founding of the Pennsylvania Academy of the Fine Arts, Philadelphia.

Charles Willson Peale in his Museum, Self-portrait — A511

1955, Jan. 15   **Perf. 10½x11**

1064	A511	3c rose brown	.25	.25

LAND GRANT COLLEGES ISSUE
Centenary of the founding of Michigan State College and Pennsylvania State University, first of the land grant institutions.

Open Book and Symbols of Subjects Taught A512

1955, Feb. 12   **Perf. 11x10½**

1065	A512	3c green	.25	.25

ROTARY INTERNATIONAL, 50th ANNIV.

Torch, Globe and Rotary Emblem A513

1955, Feb. 23

1066	A513	8c deep blue	.25	.25

ARMED FORCES RESERVE ISSUE

Marine, Coast Guard, Army, Navy, & Air Force Personnel A514

1955, May 21

1067	A514	3c purple	.25	.25

NEW HAMPSHIRE ISSUE
Sesquicentennial of the discovery of the "Old Man of the Mountains."

Great Stone Face — A515

1955, June 21   **Perf. 10½x11**

1068	A515	3c green	.25	.25

SOO LOCKS ISSUE
Centenary of the opening of the Soo Locks.

Map of Great Lakes and Two Steamers A516

1955, June 28   **Perf. 11x10½**

1069	A516	3c blue	.25	.25

ATOMS FOR PEACE ISSUE
Issued to promote an Atoms for Peace policy.

Atomic Energy Encircling the Hemispheres — A517

1955, July 28

1070	A517	3c deep blue	.25	.25

FORT TICONDEROGA ISSUE
Bicentenary of Fort Ticonderoga, New York.

Map of the Fort, Ethan Allen and Artillery A518

1955, Sept. 18

1071	A518	3c light brown	.25	.25

ANDREW W. MELLON ISSUE

Andrew W. Mellon — A519

1955, Dec. 20   **Perf. 10½x11**

1072	A519	3c rose carmine	.25	.25

Mellon, U.S. Sec. of the Treasury (1921-32), financier and art collector.

BENJAMIN FRANKLIN ISSUE
250th anniv. of the birth of Benjamin Franklin.

"Franklin Taking Electricity from the Sky," by Benjamin West — A520

1956, Jan. 17

1073	A520	3c bright carmine	.25	.25

BOOKER T. WASHINGTON ISSUE
Washington (1856-1915), black educator, founder and head of Tuskegee Institute in Alabama.

Log Cabin A521

1956, Apr. 5   **Perf. 11x10½**

1074	A521	3c deep blue	.25	.25

FIFTH INTERNATIONAL PHILATELIC EXHIBITION ISSUES
FIPEX, New York City, Apr. 28 - May 6, 1956.

SOUVENIR SHEET

A522

FLAT PLATE PRINTING

1956, Apr. 28   **Imperf.**

1075	A522	Pane of 2	1.20	1.50
a.		A482 3c deep violet	.75	.60
b.		A488 8c dark violet blue & carmine	.85	.75

No. 1075 measures 108x73mm. Nos. 1075a and 1075b measure 24x28mm.

Inscriptions printed in dark violet blue; scrolls and stars in carmine.

New York Coliseum & Columbus Monument A523

ROTARY PRESS PRINTING

1956, Apr. 30   *Perf. 11x10½*
1076 A523 3c deep violet   .25   .25

WILDLIFE CONSERVATION ISSUE

Issued to emphasize the importance of Wildlife Conservation in America.

Wild Turkey A524

Pronghorn Antelope A525

King Salmon A526

1956
1077 A524 3c rose lake   .25   .25
1078 A525 3c brown   .25   .25
1079 A526 3c blue green   .25   .25
    Nos. 1077-1079 (3)   .75   .75

PURE FOOD AND DRUG LAWS, 50th ANNIV.

Harvey W. Wiley — A527

1956, June 27   *Perf. 10½x11*
1080 A527 3c dark blue green   .25   .25

WHEATLAND ISSUE

President Buchanan's Home, "Wheatland," Lancaster, PA — A528

1956, Aug. 5
1081 A528 3c black brown   .25   .25

LABOR DAY ISSUE

Mosaic, AFL-CIO Headquarters A529

1956, Sept. 3   *Perf. 10½x11*
1082 A529 3c deep blue   .25   .25

NASSAU HALL ISSUE

200th anniv. of Nassau Hall, Princeton University.

Nassau Hall, Princeton, NJ — A530

1956, Sept. 22
1083 A530 3c black, *orange*   .25   .25

DEVILS TOWER ISSUE

Issued to commemorate the 50th anniversary of the Federal law providing for protection of American natural antiquities. Devils Tower National Monument, Wyoming, is an outstanding example.

Devils Tower — A531

1956, Sept. 24   *Perf. 10½x11*
1084 A531 3c violet   .25   .25

CHILDREN'S ISSUE

Issued to promote friendship among the children of the world.

Children of the World A532

1956, Dec. 15   *Perf. 11x10½*
1085 A532 3c dark blue   .25   .25

ALEXANDER HAMILTON (1755-1804)

Alexander Hamilton (1757-1804) and Federal Hall A533

1957, Jan. 11
1086 A533 3c rose red   .25   .25

POLIO ISSUE

Honoring "those who helped fight polio," and on for 20th anniv. of the Natl. Foundation for Infantile Paralysis and the March of Dimes.

Allegory — A534

1957, Jan. 15   *Perf. 10½x11*
1087 A534 3c red lilac   .25   .25

COAST AND GEODETIC SURVEY ISSUE

150th anniversary of the establishment of the Coast and Geodetic Survey.

Flag of Coast and Geodetic Survey and Ships at Sea A535

1957, Feb. 11   *Perf. 11x10½*
1088 A535 3c dark blue   .25   .25

ARCHITECTS ISSUE

American Institute of Architects, centenary.

Corinthian Capital and Mushroom Type Head & Shaft A536

1957, Feb. 23
1089 A536 3c red lilac   .25   .25

STEEL INDUSTRY ISSUE

Centenary of the steel industry in America.

American Eagle and Pouring Ladle — A537

1957, May 22   *Perf. 10½x11*
1090 A537 3c bright ultramarine   .25   .25

INTERNATIONAL NAVAL REVIEW ISSUE

Issued to commemorate the International Naval Review and the Jamestown Festival.

Aircraft Carrier and Jamestown Festival Emblem A538

1957, June 10   *Perf. 11x10½*
1091 A538 3c blue green   .25   .25

OKLAHOMA STATEHOOD, 50th ANNIV.

Map of Oklahoma, Arrow and Atom Diagram A539

1957, June 14
1092 A539 3c dark blue   .25   .25

SCHOOL TEACHERS ISSUE

Teacher and Pupils A540

1957, July 1
1093 A540 3c rose lake   .25   .25

FLAG ISSUE

"Old Glory" (48 Stars) A541

GIORI PRESS PRINTING

1957, July 4   *Perf. 11*
1094 A541 4c dark blue & deep carmine   .25   .25

SHIP BUILDING ISSUE

350th anniversary of shipbuilding in America.

"Virginia of Sagadahock" and Seal of Maine — A542

ROTARY PRESS PRINTING

1957, Aug. 15   *Perf. 10½x11*
1095 A542 3c deep violet   .25   .25

CHAMPION OF LIBERTY ISSUE

Magsaysay (1907-57), Pres. of the Philippines.

Ramon Magsaysay, (1907-1957), Philippines President A543

GIORI PRESS PRINTING

1957, Aug. 31   *Perf. 11*
1096 A543 8c car, ultra & ocher   .25   .25

For other Champion of Liberty issues, see Nos. 1110-1111, 1117-1118, 1125-1126, 1136-1137, 1147-1148, 1159-1160, 1165-1166, 1168-1169, 1174-1175.

LAFAYETTE BICENTENARY ISSUE

Marquis de Lafayette — A544

1957. Sept. 6   *Perf. 10½x11*
1097 A544 3c rose lake   .25   .25

WILDLIFE CONSERVATION ISSUE

Issued to emphasize the importance of Wildlife Conservation in America.

Whooping Cranes — A545

GIORI PRESS PRINTING

1957, Nov. 22   *Perf. 11*
1098 A545 3c blue, ocher & green   .25   .25

RELIGIOUS FREEDOM ISSUE

300th anniv. of the Flushing Remonstrance.

Bible, Hat and Quill Pen — A546

ROTARY PRESS PRINTING
1957, Dec. 27   *Perf. 10½x11*
1099 A546 3c black   .25 .25

GARDENING HORTICULTURE ISSUE

Issued to honor the garden clubs of America and in connection with the centenary of the birth of Liberty Hyde Bailey, horticulturist.

"Bountiful Earth" — A547

1958, Mar. 15
1100 A547 3c green   .25 .25

BRUSSELS EXHIBITION ISSUE

Issued in honor of the opening of the Universal and International Exhibition at Brussels, April 17.

U.S. Pavilion at Brussels A551

1958, Apr. 17   *Perf. 11x10½*
1104 A551 3c deep claret   .25 .25

JAMES MONROE ISSUE

James Monroe, by Gilbert Stuart — A552

1958, Apr. 28
1105 A552 3c purple   .25 .25

MINNESOTA STATEHOOD, 100th ANNIV.

Minnesota Lakes and Pines A553

1958, May 11
1106 A553 3c green   .25 .25

GEOPHYSICAL YEAR ISSUE

International Geophysical Year, 1957-58.

Solar Disc and Hands from Michelangelo's "Creation of Adam" — A554

GIORI PRESS PRINTING
1958, May 31   *Perf. 11*
1107 A554 3c black & red orange   .25 .25

GUNSTON HALL ISSUE

Issued for the bicentenary of Gunston Hall and to honor George Mason, author of the Constitution of Virginia and the Virginia Bill of Rights.

Gunston Hall, Virginia A555

ROTARY PRESS PRINTING
1958, June 12   *Perf. 11x10½*
1108 A555 3c light green   .25 .25

MACKINAC BRIDGE ISSUE

Dedication of Mackinac Bridge, Michigan.

Mackinac Bridge — A556

1958, June 25   *Perf. 10½x11*
1109 A556 3c brt greenish blue   .25 .25

CHAMPION OF LIBERTY ISSUE

Simon Bolívar, South American freedom fighter.

Simon Bolivar — A557

1958, July 24
1110 A557 4c olive bister   .25 .25

GIORI PRESS PRINTING
Perf. 11
1111 A557 8c car, ultra & ocher   .25 .25

ATLANTIC CABLE CENTENNIAL ISSUE

Centenary of the Atlantic Cable, linking the Eastern and Western hemispheres.

Neptune, Globe and Mermaid A558

ROTARY PRESS PRINTING
1958, Aug. 15   *Perf. 11x10½*
1112 A558 4c reddish purple   .25 .25

LINCOLN SESQUICENTENNIAL ISSUE

Sesquicentennial of the birth of Abraham Lincoln. No. 1114 also for the centenary of the founding of Cooper Union, New York City. No. 1115 marks the centenary of the Lincoln-Douglas Debates.

Lincoln, by George Healy — A559   Lincoln, by Gutzon Borglum — A560

Abraham Lincoln and Stephen A. Douglas Debating A561

Lincoln, by Daniel Chester French A562

1958-59   *Perf. 10½x11*
1113 A559 1c green ('59)   .25 .25
1114 A560 3c dark rose ('59)   .25 .25
Perf. 11x10½
1115 A561 4c sepia   .25 .25
1116 A562 4c dark blue ('59)   .25 .25
Nos. 1113-1116 (4)   1.00 1.00

CHAMPION OF LIBERTY ISSUE

Lajos Kossuth, Hungarian freedom fighter.

Lajos Kossuth, (1802-1892) — A563

1958, Sept. 19   *Perf. 10½x11*
1117 A563 4c green   .25 .25

GIORI PRESS PRINTING
Perf. 11
1118 A563 8c car, ultra & ocher   .25 .25

FREEDOM OF PRESS ISSUE

Honoring Journalism and freedom of the press in connection with the 50th anniv. of the 1st School of Journalism at the University of Missouri.

Early Press and Hand Holding Quill — A564

ROTARY PRESS PRINTING
1958, Sept. 22   *Perf. 10½x11*
1119 A564 4c black   .25 .25

OVERLAND MAIL ISSUE

Centenary of Overland Mail Service.

Mail Coach and Map of Southwest U.S. A565

1958, Oct. 10   *Perf. 11x10½*
1120 A565 4c crimson rose   .25 .25

NOAH WEBSTER ISSUE

Webster (1758-1843), lexicographer and author.

Noah Webster — A566

1958, Oct. 16   *Perf. 10½x11*
1121 A566 4c dark carmine rose   .25 .25

FOREST CONSERVATION ISSUE

Issued to publicize forest conservation and the protection of natural resources and to honor Theodore Roosevelt, a leading forest conservationist, on the centenary of his birth.

Forest Scene — A567

GIORI PRESS PRINTING
1958, Oct. 27   *Perf. 11*
1122 A567 4c green, yellow & brown   .25 .25

FORT DUQUESNE ISSUE

Bicentennial of Fort Duquesne (Fort Pitt) at future site of Pittsburgh.

Occupation of Fort Duquesne A568

ROTARY PRESS PRINTING
1958, Nov. 25   *Perf. 11x10½*
1123 A568 4c blue   .25 .25

OREGON STATEHOOD, 100th ANNIV.

Covered Wagon and Mt. Hood A569

1959, Feb. 14
1124 A569 4c blue green   .25 .25

CHAMPION OF LIBERTY ISSUE

San Martin, So. American soldier and statesman.

José de San Martin — A570

1959, Feb. 25   *Perf. 10½x11*
1125 A570 4c blue   .25 .25
  a.   Horiz. pair, imperf. between 900.00

GIORI PRESS PRINTING
Perf. 11
1126 A570 8c car, ultra & ocher   .25 .25

NATO ISSUE

North Atlantic Treaty Organization, 10th anniv.

NATO Emblem — A571

ROTARY PRESS PRINTING

1959, Apr. 1   *Perf. 10½x11*
1127 A571 4c blue   .25   .25

ARCTIC EXPLORATIONS ISSUE

Conquest of the Arctic by land by Rear Admiral Robert Edwin Peary in 1909 and by sea by the submarine "Nautilus" in 1958.

North Pole, Dog Sled and "Nautilus" A572

1959, Apr. 6   *Perf. 11x10½*
1128 A572 4c bright greenish
     blue   .25   .25

WORLD PEACE THROUGH WORLD TRADE ISSUE

Issued in conjunction with the 17th Congress of the International Chamber of Commerce, Washington, D.C., April 19-25.

Globe and Laurel A573

1959, Apr. 20
1129 A573 8c rose lake   .25   .25

SILVER CENTENNIAL ISSUE

Discovery of silver at the Comstock Lode, Nevada.

Henry Comstock at Mount Davidson Site A574

1959, June 8
1130 A574 4c black   .25   .25

ST. LAWRENCE SEAWAY ISSUE

Opening of the St. Lawrence Seaway.

Great Lakes, Maple Leaf and Eagle Emblems A575

GIORI PRESS PRINTING

1959, June 26   *Perf. 11*
1131 A575 4c red & dark blue   .25   .25
    See Canada No. 387.

49-STAR FLAG ISSUE

U.S. Flag, 1959 A576

1959, July 4
1132 A576 4c ocher, dark blue &
     deep carmine   .25   .25

SOIL CONSERVATION ISSUE

Issued as a tribute to farmers and ranchers who use soil and water conservation measures.

Modern Farm A577

1959, Aug. 26
1133 A577 4c blue, green &
     ocher   .25   .25

PETROLEUM INDUSTRY ISSUE

Centenary of the completion of the nation's first oil well at Titusville, Pa.

Oil Derrick — A578

ROTARY PRESS PRINTING

1959, Aug. 27   *Perf. 10½x11*
1134 A578 4c brown   .25   .25

DENTAL HEALTH ISSUE

Issued to publicize Dental Health and for the centenary of the American Dental Association.

Children A579

1959, Sept. 14   *Perf. 11x10½*
1135 A579 4c green   .25   .25

CHAMPION OF LIBERTY ISSUE

Ernst Reuter, Mayor of Berlin, 1948-53.

Ernst Reuter — A580

1959, Sept. 29   *Perf. 10½x11*
1136 A580 4c gray   .25   .25

GIORI PRESS PRINTING
Perf. 11

1137 A580 8c car, ultra &
     ocher   .25   .25
   a.   Ocher missing (EP)   3,250.
   b.   Ultramarine missing (EP)   4,000.
   c.   Ocher & ultramarine miss-
      ing (EP)   4,250.
   d.   All colors missing (EP)   2,250.

DR. EPHRAIM McDOWELL ISSUE

Honoring McDowell (1771-1830) on the 150th anniv. of the 1st successful ovarian operation in the US, performed at Danville, Ky., 1809.

Dr. Ephraim McDowell — A581

ROTARY PRESS PRINTING

1959, Dec. 3   *Perf. 10½x11*
1138 A581 4c rose lake   .25   .25
   a.   Vert. pair, imperf. btwn.   375.00
   b.   Vert. pair, imperf. horiz.   200.00

AMERICAN CREDO ISSUE

Issued to re-emphasize the ideals upon which America was founded and to honor those great Americans who wrote or uttered the credos.

Quotation from Washington's Farewell Address, 1796 — A582

Benjamin Franklin Quotation A583

Thomas Jefferson Quotation A584

Francis Scott Key Quotation A585

Abraham Lincoln Quotation A586

Patrick Henry Quotation A587

Designed by Frank Conley.

GIORI PRESS PRINTING
Plates of 200 subjects in four panes of 50.

1960-61   **Perf. 11**
1139 A582 4c dk vio bl & car   .25   .25
1140 A583 4c ol bister & grn   .25   .25
1141 A584 4c gray & vermilion   .25   .25
1142 A585 4c car & dark blue   .25   .25
1143 A586 4c magenta & green   .25   .25
1144 A587 4c green & brown   .25   .25
    Nos. 1139-1144 (6)   1.50   1.50

Issued: 1/20; 3/31; 5/8; 9/14; 11/19; 1/11/61.

BOY SCOUT JUBILEE ISSUE

50th anniv. of the Boy Scouts of America.

Boy Scout Giving Scout Sign A588

1960, Feb. 8
1145 A588 4c red, dark blue &
     dark bister   .25   .25

OLYMPIC WINTER GAMES ISSUE

Opening of the 8th Olympic Winter Games, Squaw Valley, Feb. 18-29, 1960.

Olympic Rings and Snowflake — A589

ROTARY PRESS PRINTING

1960, Feb. 18   *Perf. 10½x11*
1146 A589 4c dull blue   .25   .25

CHAMPION OF LIBERTY ISSUE

Issued to honor Thomas G. Masaryk, founder and president of Czechoslovakia (1918-35), on the 110th anniversary of his birth.

Thomas G. Masaryk — A590

1960, Mar. 7
1147 A590 4c blue   .25   .25
   a.   Vert. pair, imperf. between   2,000.

GIORI PRESS PRINTING
Perf. 11

1148 A590 8c car, ultra & ocher   .25   .25
   a.   Horiz. pair, imperf. between   —

WORLD REFUGEE YEAR ISSUE

World Refugee Year, July 1, 1959-June 30, 1960.

Refugee Family Walking Toward New Life A591

ROTARY PRESS PRINTING

1960, Apr. 7   *Perf. 11x10½*
1149 A591 4c gray black   .25   .25

WATER CONSERVATION ISSUE

Issued to stress the importance of water conservation and to commemorate the 7th Watershed Congress, Washington, D.C.

Water, from Watershed to Consumer A592

GIORI PRESS PRINTING

1960, Apr. 18   *Perf. 11*
1150 A592 4c dk bl, brn org
     & grn   .25   .25
   a.   Brown orange missing
      (EP)   2,750.

SEATO ISSUE

South-East Asia Treaty Organization and for the SEATO Conf., Washington, D.C., May 31-June 3.

SEATO Emblem — A593

ROTARY PRESS PRINTING

1960, May 31   *Perf. 10½x11*
1151 A593 4c blue   .25   .25
   a.   Vertical pair, imperf. be-
      tween   125.00

AMERICAN WOMAN ISSUE

Issued to pay tribute to American women and their accomplishments in civic affairs, education, arts and industry.

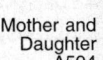

Mother and
Daughter
A594

1960, June 2   *Perf. 11x10½*
1152 A594 4c deep violet   .25 .25

50-STAR FLAG ISSUE

U.S. Flag,
1960 — A595

GIORI PRESS PRINTING

1960, July 4   *Perf. 11*
1153 A595 4c dark blue & red   .25 .25

PONY EXPRESS CENTENNIAL ISSUE

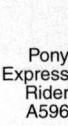

Pony
Express
Rider
A596

ROTARY PRESS PRINTING

1960, July 19   *Perf. 11x10½*
1154 A596 4c sepia   .25 .25

EMPLOY THE HANDICAPPED ISSUE

Promoting the employment of the physically handicapped and publicizing the 8th World Congress of the Intl. Soc. for the Welfare of Cripples, New York City.

Man in Wheelchair
Operating Drill
Press — A597

1960, Aug. 28   *Perf. 10½x11*
1155 A597 4c dark blue   .25 .25

WORLD FORESTRY CONGRESS ISSUE

5th World Forestry Cong., Seattle, Wash., Aug. 29-Sept. 10.

5th World Forestry
Congress
Seal — A598

1960, Aug. 29
1156 A598 4c green   .25 .25

MEXICAN INDEPENDENCE, 150th ANNIV.

A599

GIORI PRESS PRINTING

1960, Sept. 16   *Perf. 11*
1157 A599 4c green & rose red   .25 .25
        See Mexico No. 910.

US-JAPAN TREATY ISSUE

Centenary of the United States-Japan Treaty of Amity and Commerce.

A600

1960, Sept. 28
1158 A600 4c blue & pink   .25 .25

CHAMPION OF LIBERTY ISSUE

Jan Paderewski, Polish statesman and musician.

Ignacy Jan
Paderewski — A601

ROTARY PRESS PRINTING

1960, Oct. 8   *Perf. 10½x11*
1159 A601 4c blue   .25 .25

GIORI PRESS PRINTING
Perf. 11
1160 A601 8c car, ultra & ocher .25 .25

SENATOR TAFT MEMORIAL ISSUE

Senator Robert A. Taft (1889-1953) of Ohio.

Robert A.
Taft — A602

ROTARY PRESS PRINTING

1960, Oct. 10   *Perf. 10½x11*
1161 A602 4c dull violet   .25 .25

WHEELS OF FREEDOM ISSUE

Issued to honor the automotive industry and in connection with the National Automobile Show, Detroit, Oct. 15-23.

Globe and
Steering
Wheel with
Tractor, Car
and Truck
A603

1960, Oct. 15   *Perf. 11x10½*
1162 A603 4c dark blue   .25 .25

BOYS' CLUBS OF AMERICA ISSUE

Boys' Clubs of America movement, centenary.

Profile of a
Boy — A604

GIORI PRESS PRINTING

1960, Oct. 18   *Perf. 11*
1163 A604 4c indigo, slate &
            rose red   .25 .25

FIRST AUTOMATED POST OFFICE IN THE US ISSUE

Publicizing the opening of the 1st automated post office in the US at Providence, R.I.

Architect's
Sketch of
New Post
Office,
Providence,
RI — A605

1960, Oct. 20
1164 A605 4c dark blue & car-
            mine   .25 .25
  a.   Red missing (PS)   250.00

CHAMPION OF LIBERTY ISSUE

Baron Karl Gustaf Emil Mannerheim (1867-1951), Marshal and President of Finland.

Baron Gustaf Emil
Mannerheim — A606

ROTARY PRESS PRINTING

1960, Oct. 26   *Perf. 10½x11*
1165 A606 4c blue   .25 .25

GIORI PRESS PRINTING

Plates of 288 subjects in four panes of 72 each.
Perf. 11
1166 A606 8c car, ultra & ocher .25 .25

CAMP FIRE GIRLS ISSUE

50th anniv. of the Camp Fire Girls' movement and in connection with the Golden Jubilee Convention celebration of the Camp Fire Girls.

Camp Fire Girls
Emblem — A607

GIORI PRESS PRINTING

1960, Nov. 1   *Perf. 11*
1167 A607 4c dark blue & bright
            red   .25 .25

CHAMPION OF LIBERTY ISSUE

Giuseppe Garibaldi (1807-1882), Italian patriot and freedom fighter.

Giuseppe Garibaldi
(1807-1882) — A608

ROTARY PRESS PRINTING

1960, Nov. 2   *Perf. 10½x11*
1168 A608 4c green   .25 .25

GIORI PRESS PRINTING
Perf. 11
1169 A608 8c car, ultra & ocher .25 .25

SENATOR GEORGE MEMORIAL ISSUE

Walter F. George (1878-1957) of Georgia.

Walter F. George
(1878-1957) — A609

ROTARY PRESS PRINTING

1960, Nov. 5   *Perf. 10½x11*
1170 A609 4c dull violet   .25 .25

ANDREW CARNEGIE ISSUE

Carnegie (1835-1919), industrialist & philanthropist.

Andrew
Carnegie — A610

1960, Nov. 25
1171 A610 4c deep claret   .25 .25

JOHN FOSTER DULLES MEMORIAL ISSUE

Dulles (1888-1959), Secretary of State (1953-59).

John Foster
Dulles — A611

1960, Dec. 6
1172 A611 4c dull violet   .25 .25

ECHO I — COMMUNICATIONS FOR PEACE ISSUE

World's 1st communications satellite, Echo I, placed in orbit by the Natl. Aeronautics and Space Admin., Aug. 12, 1960.

Radio
Waves
Connecting
Echo I and
Earth
A612

1960, Dec. 15   *Perf. 11x10½*
1173 A612 4c deep violet   .25 .25

CHAMPION OF LIBERTY ISSUE

Mohandas K. Gandhi, leader in India's struggle for independence.

Mahatma Gandhi — A613

1961, Jan. 26 **Perf. 10½x11**
1174 A613 4c red orange .25 .25

GIORI PRESS PRINTING
Perf. 11
1175 A613 8c car, ultra & ocher .25 .25

RANGE CONSERVATION ISSUE

Issued to stress the importance of range conservation and to commemorate the meeting of the American Society of Range Management. "The Trail Boss" from a drawing by Charles M. Russell is the Society's emblem.

The Trail Boss and Modern Range A614

1961, Feb. 2 **Perf. 11**
1176 A614 4c blue, slate & brown orange .25 .25

HORACE GREELEY ISSUE

Horace Greeley (1811-1872), Publisher and Editor — A615

ROTARY PRESS PRINTING
1961, Feb. 3 **Perf. 10½x11**
1177 A615 4c dull violet .25 .25

CIVIL WAR CENTENNIAL ISSUE

Centenaries of the firing on Fort Sumter (No. 1178), the Battle of Shiloh (No. 1179), the Battle of Gettysburg (No. 1180), the Battle of the Wilderness (No. 1181) and the surrender at Appomattox (No. 1182).

Sea Coast Gun of 1861 A616

Rifleman at Shiloh, 1862 A617

Blue and Gray at Gettysburg, 1863 A618

Battle of the Wilderness, 1864 A619

Appomattox, 1865 — A620

1961-65 **Perf. 11x10½**
1178 A616 4c light green .25 .25
1179 A617 4c black, *peach blossom* .25 .25

GIORI PRESS PRINTING
Plates of 200 subjects in four panes of 50.
Perf. 11
1180 A618 5c gray & blue .25 .25
1181 A619 5c dk red & black .25 .25
1182 A620 5c Prus. blue & blk .30 .25
  a. Horiz. pair, imperf. vert. 3,500.
  Nos. 1178-1182 (5) 1.30 1.25
  Issued: #1178-1182, 4/12; 4/7/62; 7/1/63; 5/5/64; 4/9/65.

KANSAS STATEHOOD, 100th ANNIV.

Sunflower, Pioneer Couple and Stockade A621

1961, May 10 **Perf. 11**
1183 A621 4c brown, dark red & green, *yellow* .25 .25

SENATOR NORRIS ISSUE

Norris and Norris Dam, Tenn. A622

ROTARY PRESS PRINTING
1961, July 11 **Perf. 11x10½**
1184 A622 4c blue green .25 .25

NAVAL AVIATION, 50th ANNIV.

Navy's First Plane (Curtiss A-1 of 1911) and Naval Air Wings A623

1961, Aug. 20
1185 A623 4c blue .25 .25

WORKMEN'S COMPENSATION ISSUE

50th anniv. of the 1st successful Workmen's Compensation Law, enacted by the Wisconsin legislature.

Scales of Justice, Factory, Worker and Family — A624

1961, Sept. 4 **Perf. 10½x11**
1186 A624 4c ultramarine, *grayish* .25 .25

FREDERIC REMINGTON ISSUE

Remington (1861-1909), artist of the West. The design is from an oil painting, Amon Carter Museum of Western Art, Fort Worth, Texas.

Remington's "Smoke Signal" — A625

GIORI PRESS PRINTING
1961, Oct. 4 **Perf. 11**
1187 A625 4c multicolored .25 .25

REPUBLIC OF CHINA ISSUE

50th anniversary of the Republic of China.

Sun Yat-sen — A626

ROTARY PRESS PRINTING
1961, Oct. 10 **Perf. 10½x11**
1188 A626 4c blue .35 .25

NAISMITH — BASKETBALL ISSUE

Honoring basketball and James Naismith (1861-1939), Canada-born director of physical education, who invented the game in 1891 at Y.M.C.A. College, Springfield, Mass.

Basketball — A627

1961, Nov. 6
1189 A627 4c brown .25 .25

NURSING ISSUE

Issued to honor the nursing profession.

Student Nurse Lighting Candle — A628

GIORI PRESS PRINTING
1961, Dec. 28 **Perf. 11**
1190 A628 4c bl, grn, org & blk .25 .25

NEW MEXICO STATEHOOD, 50th ANNIV.

Shiprock A629

1962, Jan. 6
1191 A629 4c lt. blue, maroon & bister .25 .25

ARIZONA STATEHOOD, 50th ANNIV.

Giant Saguaro Cactus — A630

1962, Feb. 14
1192 A630 4c carmine, violet blue & green .25 .25

PROJECT MERCURY ISSUE

1st orbital flight of a US astronaut, Lt. Col. John H. Glenn, Jr., Feb. 20, 1962.

"Friendship 7" Capsule and Globe A631

1962, Feb. 20
1193 A631 4c dark blue & yellow .25 .25
  Imperfs. are printers waste.

MALARIA ERADICATION ISSUE

World Health Organization's drive to eradicate malaria.

Great Seal of U.S. and WHO Symbol A632

1962, Mar. 30
1194 A632 4c blue & bister .25 .25

CHARLES EVANS HUGHES ISSUE

Hughes (1862-1948), Governor of New York, Chief Justice of the US.

Charles Evans Hughes — A633

ROTARY PRESS PRINTING
1962, Apr. 11 **Perf. 10½x11**
1195 A633 4c black, *buff* .25 .25

SEATTLE WORLD'S FAIR ISSUE

"Century 21" International Exposition, Seattle, Wash., Apr. 21-Oct. 21.

Space Needle and Monorail — A634

GIORI PRESS PRINTING
1962, Apr. 25 **Perf. 11**
1196 A634 4c red & dark blue .25 .25

LOUISIANA STATEHOOD, 150th ANNIV.

Riverboat on the Mississippi A635

1962, Apr. 30
1197 A635 4c blue, dark slate green & red .25 .25

HOMESTEAD ACT, CENTENARY

Sod Hut and Settlers A636

ROTARY PRESS PRINTING
1962, May 20   *Perf. 11x10½*
1198 A636 4c slate .25 .25

GIRL SCOUTS ISSUE

50th anniversary of the Girl Scouts of America.

Senior Girl Scout & Flag A637

1962, July 24
1199 A637 4c rose red .25 .25

SENATOR BRIEN McMAHON ISSUE

McMahon (1903-52) of Connecticut had a role in opening the way to peaceful uses of atomic energy through the Atomic Energy Act establishing the Atomic Energy Commission.

Brien McMahon & Atomic Diagram A638

1962, July 28
1200 A638 4c purple .25 .25

APPRENTICESHIP ISSUE

National Apprenticeship Program and 25th anniv. of the National Apprenticeship Act.

Machinist Handing Micrometer to Apprentice A639

1962, Aug. 31
1201 A639 4c blk, *yellow bister* .25 .25

SAM RAYBURN ISSUE

Sam Rayburn and Capitol — A640

GIORI PRESS PRINTING
1962, Sept. 16   *Perf. 11*
1202 A640 4c dark blue & red brown .25 .25

DAG HAMMARSKJOLD ISSUE

UN Headquarters & Dag Hammarskjold, U.N. Sec. Gen., 1953-61 — A641

1962, Oct. 23
1203 A641 4c black, brown & yellow .25 .25

No. 1203a can only be collected on a cover postmarked before Nov. 16, 1962 (the date the Hammarskjold Special Printing, No. 1204, was issued), or tied on dated piece (unique used pair). Covers are known machine postmarked Cuyahoga Falls, Ohio, Nov. 14, 1962, and notarized in the lower left corner by George W. Schwartz, Notary Public. Other covers are reported postmarked Oct. 26, 1962, Brooklyn, NY, Vanderveer Station. Unaddressed, uncacheted first day covers also exist. Other covers may exist. All covers must be accompanied by certificates from recognized expertizing committees. Value of first-day cover, $3,000.

An unused pane of 50 was signed in the selvage by ten well-known philatelists attesting to its genuineness. This pane was donated to the American Philatelic Society in 1987.

An unknown number of "first day covers" exist bearing Artmaster cachets. These were contrived using examples of No. 1204.

Hammarskjold Special Printing
1962, Nov. 16
1204 A641 4c black, brown & yel (yellow inverted) .25 .25

No. 1204 was issued following discovery of No. 1203 with yellow background inverted.

CHRISTMAS ISSUE

Wreath and Candles — A642

1962, Nov. 1
1205 A642 4c green & red .25 .25

HIGHER EDUCATION ISSUE

Higher education's role in American cultural and industrial development and the centenary celebrations of the signing of the law creating land-grant colleges and universities.

Map of U.S. and Lamp A643

1962, Nov. 14
1206 A643 4c blue green & black .25 .25

WINSLOW HOMER ISSUE

Homer (1836-1910), painter, showing his oil, "Breezing Up," which hangs in the National Gallery, Washington, D.C.

"Breezing Up" — A644

1962, Dec. 15
1207 A644 4c multicolored .25 .25
　　a. Horiz. pair, imperf. btwn. and at right 7,000.

FLAG ISSUE

Flag over White House — A645

1963-66
1208 A645 5c blue & red .25 .25
　　a. Tagged ('68) .25 .25
　　b. Horiz. pair, imperf. between, tagged 2,250.

Beware of pairs with faint blind perfs between offered as No. 1208b.

REGULAR ISSUE

Andrew Jackson A646　　George Washington A650

John J. Pershing A651

ROTARY PRESS PRINTING
1961-66   *Perf. 11x10½*
1209 A646 1c green ('63) .25 .25
　　a. Tagged ('66) .25 .25
1213 A650 5c dk gray blue .25 .25
　　a. Booklet pane of 5 + label 2.75 2.00
　　b. Tagged ('63) .50 .25
　　c. As "a," tagged, ('63) 2.50 1.50
　　d. Horiz. pair, imperf. between, in #1213a with foldover or miscut 1,750.
1214 A651 8c brown ('61) .25 .25

See Luminescence note after No. 1053.

Three different messages are found on the label in No. 1213a, and two messages on that of No. 1213c.

No. 1213d resulted from a paper foldover after perforating and before cutting into panes.

Unused catalogue numbers were left vacant for additional denominations.

COIL STAMPS
(Rotary Press)
1962-66   *Perf. 10 Vertically*
1225 A646 1c green ('63) .40 .25
　　a. Tagged ('66) .40 .25
1229 A650 5c dk blue gray 1.50 .25
　　a. Tagged ('63) 2.50 .25
　　b. Imperf., pair 300.00

CAROLINA CHARTER ISSUE

Tercentenary of the Carolina Charter granting to 8 Englishmen lands extending coast-to-coast roughly along the present border of Virginia to the north and Florida to the south. Original charter on display at Raleigh.

First Page of Carolina Charter A662

GIORI PRESS PRINTING
1963, Apr. 6   *Perf. 11*
1230 A662 5c dark carmine & brown .25 .25

FOOD FOR PEACE-FREEDOM FROM HUNGER ISSUE

American "Food for Peace" program and the "Freedom from Hunger" campaign of the FAO.

Wheat — A663

1963, June 4
1231 A663 5c green, buff & red .25 .25

WEST VIRGINIA STATEHOOD, 100th ANNIV.

Map of West Virginia & State Capitol A664

1963, June 20
1232 A664 5c green, red & black .25 .25

EMANCIPATION PROCLAMATION ISSUE

Centenary of Lincoln's Emancipation Proclamation freeing about 3,000,000 slaves in 10 southern states.

Severed Chain A665

1963, Aug. 16
1233 A665 5c dark blue, black & red .25 .25

ALLIANCE FOR PROGRESS ISSUE

2nd anniv. of the Alliance for Progress, which aims to stimulate economic growth and raise living standards in Latin America.

Alliance Emblem A666

1963, Aug. 17
1234 A666 5c ultramarine & green .25 .25

CORDELL HULL ISSUE

Hull (1871-1955), Secretary of State (1933-44).

Cordell Hull (1871-1955), Sec. of State (1933-44) — A667

ROTARY PRESS PRINTING
1963, Oct. 5   *Perf. 10½x11*
1235 A667 5c blue green .25 .25

ELEANOR ROOSEVELT ISSUE

Mrs. Franklin D. Roosevelt (1884-1962).

Mrs. Franklin D. Roosevelt (1884-1962) A668

1963, Oct. 11   **Perf. 11x10½**
1236 A668 5c bright purple   .25 .25

SCIENCE ISSUE

Honoring the sciences and in connection with the centenary of the Natl. Academy of Science.

"The Universe" A669

GIORI PRESS PRINTING
1963, Oct. 14   **Perf. 11**
1237 A669 5c Prussian blue & black   .25 .25

CITY MAIL DELIVERY ISSUE

Centenary of free city mail delivery.

Letter Carrier, 1863 — A670

1963, Oct. 26   **Tagged**
1238 A670 5c gray, dark blue & red   .25 .25

RED CROSS CENTENARY ISSUE

A671

1963, Oct. 29
1239 A671 5c bluish black & red   .25 .25

CHRISTMAS ISSUE

Natl. Christmas Tree & White House — A672

1963, Nov. 1
1240 A672 5c dk bl, bluish blk & red   .25 .25
a.   Tagged   .65 .50
b.   Horiz. pair, imperf between   7,500.
c.   Red missing (PS)

JOHN JAMES AUDUBON ISSUE

Audubon (1785-1851), ornithologist and artist. The birds pictured are actually Collie's magpie jays. See No. C71.

Columbia Jays — A673

1963, Dec. 7
1241 A673 5c dk blue & multi   .25 .25

SAM HOUSTON ISSUE

Houston (1793-1863), soldier, president of Texas, US senator.

Sam Houston — A674

ROTARY PRESS PRINTING
1964, Jan. 10   **Perf. 10½x11**
1242 A674 5c black   .25 .25

CHARLES M. RUSSELL ISSUE

Russell (1864-1926), painter. The design is from a painting, Thomas Gilcrease Institute of American History and Art, Tulsa, Okla.

"Jerked Down" A675

GIORI PRESS PRINTING
1964, Mar. 19   **Perf. 11**
1243 A675 5c multicolored   .25 .25

NEW YORK WORLD'S FAIR ISSUE

New York World's Fair, 1964-65.

Mall with Unisphere & "Rocket Thrower," by Donald De Lue — A676

ROTARY PRESS PRINTING
1964, Apr. 22   **Perf. 11x10½**
1244 A676 5c blue green   .25 .25
a.   All color omitted   —

On No. 1244a, a clear albino impression of the design is present.

JOHN MUIR ISSUE

Muir (1838-1914), naturalist and conservationist.

John Muir (1838-1914), naturalist and conservationist and Redwood Forest — A677

GIORI PRESS PRINTING
1964, Apr. 29   **Perf. 11**
1245 A677 5c brown, green, yellow green & olive   .25 .25

KENNEDY MEMORIAL ISSUE

President John Fitzgerald Kennedy, (1917-1963).

Pres. John F. Kennedy (1917-63) and Eternal Flame A678

ROTARY PRESS PRINTING
1964, May 29   **Perf. 11x10½**
1246 A678 5c blue gray   .25 .25

NEW JERSEY TERCENTENARY ISSUE

300th anniv. of English colonization of New Jersey. The design is from a mural by Howard Pyle in the Essex County Courthouse, Newark, N.J.

Philip Carteret Landing at Elizabethtown & Map of New Jersey — A679

1964, June 15   **Perf. 10½x11**
1247 A679 5c brt. ultramarine   .25 .25

NEVADA STATEHOOD, 100th ANNIV.

Virginia City and Map of Nevada A680

GIORI PRESS PRINTING
1964, July 22   **Perf. 11**
1248 A680 5c red, yellow & blue   .25 .25

REGISTER AND VOTE ISSUE

Campaign to draw more voters to the polls.

Flag — A681

1964, Aug. 1
1249 A681 5c dark blue & red   .25 .25

SHAKESPEARE ISSUE

William Shakespeare (1564-1616).

William Shakespeare A682

ROTARY PRESS PRINTING
1964, Aug. 14   **Perf. 10½x11**
1250 A682 5c black brown, *tan*   .25 .25

DOCTORS MAYO ISSUE

Dr. William James Mayo (1861-1939) and his brother, Dr. Charles Horace Mayo (1865-1939), surgeons who founded the Mayo Foundation for Medical Education and Research in affiliation with the Univ. of Minnesota at Rochester. Heads on stamp are from a sculpture by James Earle Fraser.

Drs. William and Charles Mayo — A683

1964, Sept. 11
1251 A683 5c green   .25 .25

AMERICAN MUSIC ISSUE

50th anniv. of the founding of the American Society of Composers, Authors and Publishers (ASCAP).

Lute, Horn, Laurel, Oak and Music Score A684

GIORI PRESS PRINTING
1964, Oct. 15   **Perf. 11**
Gray Paper with Blue Threads
1252 A684 5c red, black & blue   .25 .25
a.   Blue omitted   650.00
b.   Blue missing (PS)

Beware of examples offered as No. 1252a which have traces of blue.

HOMEMAKERS ISSUE

Honoring American women as homemakers and for the 50th anniv. of the passage of the Smith-Lever Act. By providing economic experts under an extension service of the U.S. Dept. of Agriculture, this legislation helped to improve homelife.

Farm Scene Sampler A685

Engraved (Giori Press); Background Lithographed
1964, Oct. 26
1253 A685 5c multicolored   .25 .25

CHRISTMAS ISSUE

Holly A686   Mistletoe A687

Poinsettia A688   Sprig of Conifer A689

GIORI PRESS PRINTING
1964, Nov. 9
1254 A686 5c green, car & black   .25 .25
a.   Tagged   .75 .50
b.   Printed on gummed side   1,850.
c.   All color missing (FO)   2,000.
1255 A687 5c car, green & black   .25 .25
a.   Tagged   .75 .50
1256 A688 5c car, green & black   .25 .25
a.   Tagged   .75 .50

1257 A689 5c black, green &
car .25 .25
a. Tagged .75 .50
b. Block of 4, #1254-1257 1.00 1.00
c. Block of 4, tagged 3.00 2.25

Tagged stamps issued Nov. 10.
No. 1254b resulted from a paper foldover
before printing and perforating.
No. 1254c is unique and is in a block of four
with the other three stamps missing parts of
the designs.

VERRAZANO-NARROWS BRIDGE ISSUE

Opening of the Verrazano-Narrows
Bridge connecting Staten Island and
Brooklyn.

Verrazano-Narrows
Bridge and Map of
NY Bay — A690

ROTARY PRESS PRINTING
1964, Nov. 21 *Perf. 10½x11*
1258 A690 5c blue green .25 .25

FINE ARTS ISSUE

Abstract
Design by
Stuart
Davis
A691

GIORI PRESS PRINTING
1964, Dec. 2 *Perf. 11*
1259 A691 5c ultra., black & dull
red .25 .25

AMATEUR RADIO ISSUE

Issued to honor the radio amateurs
on the 50th anniversary of the American Radio Relay League.

Radio Waves and
Dial — A692

ROTARY PRESS PRINTING
1964, Dec. 15 *Perf. 10½x11*
1260 A692 5c red lilac .25 .25

BATTLE OF NEW ORLEANS ISSUE

Battle of New Orleans, Chalmette
Plantation, Jan. 8-18, 1815, established
150 years of peace and friendship
between the US and Great Britain.

General Andrew Jackson and
Sesquicentennial Medal — A693

GIORI PRESS PRINTING
1965, Jan. 8 *Perf. 11*
1261 A693 5c deep carmine, violet blue & gray .25 .25

PHYSICAL FITNESS-SOKOL ISSUE

Publicizing the importance of physical
fitness and for the centenary of the
founding of the Sokol (athletic) organization in America.

Discus
Thrower — A694

1965, Feb. 15
1262 A694 5c maroon & black .25 .25

CRUSADE AGAINST CANCER ISSUE

Issued to publicize the "Crusade
Against Cancer" and to stress the
importance of early diagnosis.

Microscope and
Stethoscope — A695

1965, Apr. 1
1263 A695 5c black, purple & red
orange .25 .25

CHURCHILL MEMORIAL ISSUE

Sir Winston Spencer Churchill (1874-
1965), British statesman and World War
II leader.

Winston
Churchill — A696

ROTARY PRESS PRINTING
1965, May 13 *Perf. 10½x11*
1264 A696 5c black .25 .25

MAGNA CARTA ISSUE

750th anniversary of the Magna
Carta, the basis of English and American common law.

Procession
of Barons
and King
John's
Crown
A697

GIORI PRESS PRINTING
1965, June 15 *Perf. 11*
1265 A697 5c black, yellow ocher
& red lilac .25 .25

INTERNATIONAL COOPERATION YEAR

ICY, 1965, and 20th anniv. of the UN.

ICY
Emblem
A698

1965, June 26
1266 A698 5c dull blue & black .25 .25

SALVATION ARMY ISSUE

Centenary of the founding of the Salvation Army by William Booth in
London.

A699

1965, July 2
1267 A699 5c red, black & dark
blue .25 .25

DANTE ISSUE

Dante Alighieri (1265-1321), Italian
poet.

A700

ROTARY PRESS PRINTING
1965, July 17 *Perf. 10½x11*
1268 A700 5c maroon, *tan* .25 .25

HERBERT HOOVER ISSUE

President Herbert Clark Hoover,
(1874-1964).

A701

1965, Aug. 10
1269 A701 5c rose red .25 .25

ROBERT FULTON ISSUE

Fulton (1765-1815), inventor of the
1st commercial steamship.

Robert
Fulton &
Clermont
A702

GIORI PRESS PRINTING
1965, Aug. 19 *Perf. 11*
1270 A702 5c black & blue .25 .25

FLORIDA SETTLEMENT ISSUE

400th anniv. of the settlement of Florida, and the 1st permanent European
settlement in the continental US, St.
Augustine, Fla.

Spanish Explorer,
Royal Flag of Spain
and Ships — A703

1965, Aug. 28
1271 A703 5c red, yel & blk .25 .25
a. Yellow omitted 200.00

See Spain No. 1312.

TRAFFIC SAFETY ISSUE

Issued to publicize traffic safety and
the prevention of traffic accidents.

Traffic
Signal
A704

1965, Sept. 3
1272 A704 5c emer, red & blk .25 .25

JOHN SINGLETON COPLEY ISSUE

Copley (1738-1815), painter. The
portrait of the artist's daughter is from
the oil painting "The Copley Family,"
which hangs in the National Gallery of
Art, Washington, D.C.

Elizabeth Clarke
Copley — A705

1965, Sept. 17
1273 A705 5c blk, brn & olive .25 .25

INTERNATIONAL TELECOMMUNICATION UNION, 100th ANNIV.

Gall
Projection
World Map
& Radio
Sine Wave
A706

1965, Oct. 6
1274 A706 11c blk, car & bister .35 .25

ADLAI STEVENSON ISSUE

Adlai Ewing Stevenson (1900-65),
governor of Illinois, US ambassador to
the UN.

Adlai E.
Stevenson — A707

LITHOGRAPHED, ENGRAVED (Giori)
1965, Oct. 23
1275 A707 5c pale bl, blk, car &
vio bl .25 .25

CHRISTMAS ISSUE

Angel with
Trumpet — A708

GIORI PRESS PRINTING
1965, Nov. 2
1276 A708 5c carmine, dark olive
green & bister .25 .25
a. Tagged .75 .25

PROMINENT AMERICANS ISSUE

Thomas Jefferson A710

Albert Gallatin A711

Frank Lloyd Wright & Guggenheim Museum A712

Francis Parkman A713

Lincoln A714

Washington A715

Washington (Redrawn) A715a

Franklin D. Roosevelt A716

Albert Einstein A717

Andrew Jackson — A718

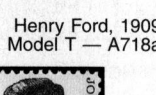
Henry Ford, 1909 Model T — A718a

John F. Kennedy A719

Oliver Wendell Holmes A720

Type 3 — A720a

George Catlett Marshall A721

Frederick Douglass A722

John Dewey — A723

Thomas Paine — A724

Lucy Stone A725

Eugene O'Neill A726

John Bassett Moore — A727

Types of 15c:

I. Necktie barely touches coat at bottom; crosshatching of tie strong and complete. Flag of "5" is true horizontal. Crosshatching of "15" is colorless when visible.

II. Necktie does not touch coat at bottom; LL to UR crosshatching lines strong, UL to LR lines very faint. Flag of "5" slants down slightly at right. Crosshatching of "15" is colored and visible when magnified.

III. Used only for No. 1288B; smaller in overall size and "15¢" is ¾mm closer to head.

ROTARY PRESS PRINTING

1965-78   Perf. 11x10½, 10½x11

1278	A710	1c green, tagged	.25	.25
a.		Booklet pane of 8	1.00	.75
b.		Bklt. pane of 4+2 labels	.75	.60
c.		Untagged (Bureau precanceled)	6.25	1.25
1279	A711	1¼c light green	.25	.25
1280	A712	2c dk blue gray, tagged	.25	.25
a.		Bklt. pane of 5 + label	1.25	.80
b.		Untagged (Bureau precanceled)	1.35	.40
c.		Bklt. pane of 6	1.00	.75
1281	A713	3c violet, tagged	.25	.25
a.		Untagged (Bureau precanceled)	3.00	.75
1282	A714	4c black	.25	.25
a.		Tagged	.25	.25
1283	A715	5c blue	.25	.25
a.		Tagged	.25	.25
1283B	A715a	5c blue, tagged	.25	.25
d.		Untagged (Bureau precanceled)	12.50	1.00

No. 1283B is redrawn; highlights, shadows softened.

1284	A716	6c gray brown	.25	.25
a.		Tagged	.25	.25
b.		Booklet pane of 8	1.50	1.00
c.		Bklt. pane of 5+ label	1.40	1.00
d.		Horiz. pair, imperf. between	2,250.	
1285	A717	8c violet	.25	.25
a.		Tagged	.25	.25
1286	A718	10c lilac, tagged	.25	.25
b.		Untagged (Bureau precanceled)	55.00	1.75
1286A	718a	12c black, tagged	.25	.25
c.		Untagged (Bureau precanceled)	4.75	1.00
1287	A719	13c brown, tagged	.30	.25
a.		Untagged (Bureau precanceled)	6.00	1.00
1288	A720	15c mag, type I, tagged	.30	.25
a.		Untagged (Bureau precanceled)	.75	.75
d.		Type II	.55	.25

Imperforates exist from printer's waste.

Values for No. 1288a are for the bars-only precancel. Also exists with city precancels, and worth more thus.

Perf. 10 on 2 or 3 Sides

1288B	A720a	15c magenta, type III	.35	.25
c.		Booklet pane of 8	2.80	1.75
e.		As "c," vert. imperf. between	1,500.	

No. 1288B issued in booklets only. All stamps have one or two straight edges. Plates made from redrawn die.

Perf. 11x10½, 10½x11

1289	A721	20c deep olive	.40	.25
a.		Tagged	.40	.25
b.		black olive	.50	.25
c.		As "a," double impression	500.00	
1290	A722	25c rose lake	.55	.25
a.		Tagged	.45	.25
b.		25c magenta	25.00	

Shades of No. 1290 rose lake exist that tend toward magenta, but are not. Competent identification is important for No. 1290b.

1291	A723	30c red lilac	.65	.25
a.		Tagged	.50	.25
1292	A724	40c blue black	.80	.25
a.		Tagged	.75	.25
1293	A725	50c rose magenta	1.00	.25
a.		Tagged	.80	.25
1294	A726	$1 dull purple	2.25	.25
a.		Tagged	1.75	.25
b.		$1 black violet	100.00	350.00
1295	A727	$5 gray black	10.00	2.25
a.		Tagged	8.50	2.00
		Nos. 1278-1295 (21)	19.35	7.25

Issued (without tagging) — 1965: 4c, 11/19.
1966: 5c, 2/22; 6c, 1/29; 8c, 3/14; $5, 12/3.
1967: 1¼c, 1/30; 20c, 10/24; 25c, 2/14; $1, 10/16.
1968: 30c, 10/21; 40c, 1/29; 50c, 8/13.
Dates for tagged: 1965: 4c, 12/1.
1966: 2c, 6/8; 5c, 2/23; 6c, 12/29; 8c, 7/6.
1967: 3c, 9/16; #1283B, 11/17; #1284b, 12/28; 10c, 3/15; 13c, 5/29.
1968: 1c, #1284c, 1/12; #1280a, 1/8; 12c, 7/30; 15c, 3/8.
1973: 20c, 25c, 30c, 40c, 50c, $1, $5, 4/3.
1978: No. 1288B, 6/14.

COIL STAMPS
Perf. 10 Horizontally

1966-81   Tagged

1297	A713	3c violet	.25	.25
a.		Imperf., pair	22.50	
b.		Untagged (Bureau precanceled)	.40	.25
c.		As "b," imperf. pair	8.00	—
1298	A716	6c gray brown	.25	.25
a.		Imperf., pair	1,500.	

Franklin D. Roosevelt — A727a

Perf. 10 Vertically

1299	A710	1c green	.25	.25
a.		Untagged (Bureau precanceled)	8.00	1.75
b.		Imperf., pair	22.50	
1303	A714	4c black	.25	.25
a.		Untagged (Bureau precanceled)	8.75	.75
b.		Imperf., pair	600.00	
1304	A715	5c blue	.25	.25
a.		Untagged (Bureau precanceled)	6.50	.65
b.		Imperf., pair	110.00	
e.		As "a," imperf., pair	250.00	
f.		Tagging omitted (not Bureau precanceled)		

No. 1304b is valued in the grade of fine.
No. 1304e is precanceled Mount Pleasant, Iowa. Also exists from Chicago, Illinois; value $1,500 for pair.

1304C	A715a	5c blue	.25	.25
d.		Imperf., pair	375.00	
1305	A727a	6c gray brown	.25	.25
a.		Imperf., pair	55.00	
b.		Untagged (Bureau precanceled)	20.00	1.00
m.		Pair, imperf. between	250.00	
1305E	A720	15c magenta, type I	.25	.25
f.		Untagged (Bureau precanceled)	32.50	
g.		Imperf., pair, type I	20.00	
h.		Pair, imperf. between	125.00	
i.		Type II	1.50	
j.		Imperf., pair, type II	55.00	
1305C	A726	$1 dull purple	3.25	.40
d.		Imperf., pair	1,250.	
		Nos. 1297-1305C (9)	5.25	2.40

Issued: 1c, 1/12/68; 3c, 11/4/75; 4c, 5/28/66; #1304, 9/8/66; 6c, #1298, 12/28/67; #1305, 2/28/68;
$1, 1/12/73; 15c, 6/14/78.

MIGRATORY BIRD TREATY ISSUE

Migratory Birds over Canada-U.S. Border — A728

GIORI PRESS PRINTING

1966, Mar. 16   Perf. 11
1306	A728	5c black, crimson & dark blue	.25	.25

HUMANE TREATMENT OF ANIMALS ISSUE

Issued to promote humane treatment of all animals and for the centenary of the American Society for the Prevention of Cruelty to Animals.

Mongrel A729

LITHOGRAPHED, ENGRAVED (Giori)

1966, Apr. 9
1307	A729	5c orange brown & black	.25	.25

INDIANA STATEHOOD, 150th ANNIV.

Sesquicentennial Seal — A730

GIORI PRESS PRINTING

1966, Apr. 16
1308	A730	5c ocher, brown & violet blue	.25	.25

AMERICAN CIRCUS ISSUE

Issued to honor the American Circus on the centenary of the birth of John Ringling.

Clown — A731

1966, May 2
1309	A731	5c multicolored	.25	.25

SIXTH INTERNATIONAL PHILATELIC EXHIBITION ISSUES

Sixth International Philatelic Exhibition (SIPEX), Washington, D.C., May 21-30.

Stamped Cover A732

LITHOGRAPHED, ENGRAVED (Giori)

1966
1310	A732	5c multicolored	.25	.25

A733

SOUVENIR SHEET
Imperf

1311 A733 5c multicolored .25 .25

No. 1311 measures 108x74mm.

BILL OF RIGHTS, 175th ANNIV.

"Freedom" Checking
"Tyranny" — A734

GIORI PRESS PRINTING

1966, July 1 **Perf. 11**
1312 A734 5c carmine, dark &
light blue .25 .25

POLISH MILLENNIUM ISSUE

Adoption of Christianity in Poland, 1000th anniv.

Polish Eagle and
Cross — A735

ROTARY PRESS PRINTING

1966, July 30 **Perf. 10½x11**
1313 A735 5c red .25 .25

Tagging Extended

During 1966, experimental use of tagged stamps was extended to the Cincinnati Postal Region covering offices in Indiana, Kentucky and Ohio. To supply these offices about 12 percent of the following nine issues (Nos. 1314-1322) were tagged.

NATIONAL PARK SERVICE ISSUE

50th anniv. of the Natl. Park Service of the Interior Dept. The design "Parkscape U.S.A." identifies Natl. Park Service facilities.

National
Park
Service
Emblem
A736

LITHOGRAPHED, ENGRAVED (Giori)

1966, Aug. 25 **Perf. 11**
1314 A736 5c yellow, black &
green .25 .25
a. Tagged .35 .35

MARINE CORPS RESERVE ISSUE

US Marine Corps Reserve founding, 50th anniv.

A737

1966, Aug. 29
1315 A737 5c black, bister,
red & ultra .25 .25
a. Tagged .40 .25
b. Black & bister (en-
graved) missing (EP) 16,000.

GENERAL FEDERATION OF WOMEN'S CLUBS ISSUE

75 years of service by the General Federation of Women's Clubs.

Women of
1890 and
1966
A738

GIORI PRESS PRINTING

1966, Sept. 12
1316 A738 5c black, pink & blue .25 .25
a. Tagged .40 .25

AMERICAN FOLKLORE ISSUE
Johnny Appleseed

Issued to honor Johnny Appleseed (John Chapman 1774-1845), who wandered over 100,000 square miles planting apple trees, and who gave away and sold seedlings to Midwest pioneers.

Johnny
Appleseed — A739

1966, Sept. 24
1317 A739 5c green, red & black .25 .25
a. Tagged .40 .25

BEAUTIFICATION OF AMERICA ISSUE

Issued to publicize President Johnson's "Plant for a more beautiful America" campaign.

Jefferson
Memorial
A740

1966, Oct. 5
1318 A740 5c emerald, pink &
black .25 .25
a. Tagged .40 .25

Compare with No. 4716c.

GREAT RIVER ROAD ISSUE

Issued to publicize the 5,600-mile Great River Road connecting New Orleans with Kenora, Ontario, and following the Mississippi most of the way.

Central U.S. Map
With Great River
Road — A741

LITHOGRAPHED, ENGRAVED (Giori)

1966, Oct. 21
1319 A741 5c vermilion, yellow,
blue & green .25 .25
a. Tagged .45 .25

SAVINGS BOND-SERVICEMEN ISSUE

25th anniv. of US Savings Bonds, and honoring American servicemen.

Statue of Liberty &
"Old Glory" — A742

1966, Oct. 26
1320 A742 5c red, dk bl, lt bl &
blk .25 .25
a. Tagged .40 .25
b. Red, dark blue & black missing (EP) 3,750.
c. Dark blue (engr.) missing
(EP) 5,000.

CHRISTMAS ISSUE

Madonna and
Child — A743

Modeled after "Madonna and Child with Angels," by the Flemish artist Hans Memling (c.1430-1494), Mellon Collection, National Gallery of Art, Washington, D.C.

1966, Nov. 1
1321 A743 5c multicolored .25 .25
a. Tagged .40 .25

MARY CASSATT ISSUE

Cassatt (1844-1926), painter. The painting "The Boating Party" is in the Natl. Gallery of Art, Washington, D.C.

"The
Boating
Party"
A744

GIORI PRESS PRINTING

1966, Nov. 17
1322 A744 5c multicolored .25 .25
a. Tagged .40 .25

Cassatt (1844-1926), painter. The original painting is in the Natl. Gallery of Art, Washington, DC.

NATIONAL GRANGE ISSUE

Centenary of the founding of the National Grange, American farmers' organization.

Grange Poster,
1870 — A745

1967, Apr. 17
1323 A745 5c org, yel, brn, grn &
blk .25 .25

Phosphor Tagging

From No. 1323 onward, all postage issues are tagged, unless otherwise noted.

Tagging Omitted

Inadvertent omissions of tagging occurred on Nos. 1238, 1278, 1281, 1298 and 1305. In addition many tagged issues from 1967 on exist with tagging unintentionally omitted. These errors are listed in the *Scott Specialized Catalogue of United States Stamps and Covers.*

CANADA CENTENARY ISSUE

Centenary of Canada's emergence as a nation.

Canadian
Landscape
A746

1967, May 25
1324 A746 5c lt bl, dp grn, ultra,
olive & blk .25 .25

ERIE CANAL ISSUE

150th anniversary of the Erie Canal ground-breaking ceremony at Rome, N.Y. The canal links Lake Erie and New York City.

Stern of
Early Canal
Boat
A747

LITHOGRAPHED, ENGRAVED (Giori)

1967, July 4
1325 A747 5c ultra., greenish
blue, black &
crimson .25 .25

"SEARCH FOR PEACE" — LIONS ISSUE

Issued to publicize the search for peace. "Search for Peace" was the theme of an essay contest for young men and women sponsored by Lions International on its 50th anniversary.

Peace
Dove
A748

GIORI PRESS PRINTING

1967, July 5
Gray Paper with Blue Threads
1326 A748 5c blue, red & black .25 .25

HENRY DAVID THOREAU ISSUE

Henry David
Thoreau (1817-
1862),
Writer — A749

1967, July 12
1327 A749 5c carmine, black &
blue green .25 .25
b. Carmine missing (PS) —

NEBRASKA STATEHOOD, 100th ANNIV.

Hereford Steer and Corn A750

LITHOGRAPHED, ENGRAVED (Giori)

1967, July 29
1328 A750 5c dark red brown, lemon & yellow .25 .25

VOICE OF AMERICA ISSUE

25th anniv. of the radio branch of the United States Information Agency (USIA).

Radio Transmission Tower and Waves — A751

1967, Aug. 1
1329 A751 5c red, blue, black & carmine .25 .25

AMERICAN FOLKLORE ISSUE

Davy Crockett (1786-1836), frontiersman, hunter, and congressman from Tennessee who died at the Alamo.

Davy Crockett & Scrub Pines A752

1967, Aug. 17
1330 A752 5c green, black, & yellow .25 .25
a. Vertical pair, imperf. between —
b. Green (engr.) missing (FO) 7,500.
c. Black & green (engr.) missing (FO) —

A foldover on a pane of No. 1330 resulted in one example each of Nos. 1330b-1330c. Part of the colors appear on the back of the selvage and one freak stamp. An engraved black-and-green-only impression appears on the gummed side of one almost-complete "stamp."

ACCOMPLISHMENTS IN SPACE ISSUE

US accomplishments in space. Printed with continuous design in horizontal rows of 5. In the left panes the astronaut stamp is 1st, 3rd and 5th, the spaceship 2nd and 4th. This arrangement is reversed in the right panes.

Space-Walking Astronaut — A753

Gemini 4 Capsule and Earth A754

1967, Sept. 29
1331 A753 5c multicolored .55 .25
1332 A754 5c multicolored .55 .25
b. Pair, #1331-1332 1.25 1.25

URBAN PLANNING ISSUE

Publicizing the importance of Urban Planning in connection with the Intl. Conf. of the American Institute of Planners, Washington, D.C., Oct. 1-6.

View of Model City — A755

1967, Oct. 2
1333 A755 5c dark blue, light blue & black .25 .25

FINNISH INDEPENDENCE, 50th ANNIV.

Finnish Coat of Arms — A756

ENGRAVED (Giori)

1967, Oct. 6
1334 A756 5c blue .25 .25

THOMAS EAKINS ISSUE

Eakins (1844-1916), painter and sculptor. The painting is in the Natl. Gallery of Art, Washington, D.C.

"The Biglin Brothers Racing" (Sculling on Schuylkill River, Philadelphia) — A757

Printed by Photogravure & Color Co., Moonachie, N.J.

PHOTOGRAVURE

1967, Nov. 2 **Perf. 12**
1335 A757 5c gold & multicolored .25 .25

CHRISTMAS ISSUE

Madonna and Child, by Hans Memling — A758

LITHOGRAPHED, ENGRAVED (Giori)

1967, Nov. 6 **Perf. 11**
1336 A758 5c multicolored .25 .25
See note on painting above No. 1321.

MISSISSIPPI STATEHOOD, 150th ANNIV.

Magnolia A759

GIORI PRESS PRINTING

1967, Dec. 11
1337 A759 5c brt grnsh bl, grn & red brn .25 .25

FLAG ISSUE

Flag and White House — A760

1968, Jan. 24 **Size: 19x22mm**
1338 A760 6c dk bl, red & grn .25 .25
k. Vert. pair, imperf. btwn. 250.00 150.00
s. Red missing (FO) —
u. Vert. pair, imperf horiz. 325.00
v. All color omitted —

No. 1338s is unique.
Beware of regumming on No. 1338u. Most examples have had the gum washed off to make it difficult or impossible to detect blind perfs. Check carefully for blind perfs. Value is for pair with original gum.
On No. 1338v, an albino impression of the engraved plate is present.

COIL STAMP
MULTICOLOR HUCK PRESS

1969, May 30 **Perf. 10 Vertically**
Size: 18¼x21mm
1338A A760 6c dk bl, red & grn .25 .25
b. Imperf., pair 350.00

MULTICOLOR HUCK PRESS

1970-71 **Perf. 11x10½**
Size: 18¼x21mm
1338D A760 6c dk bl, red & grn .25 .25
e. Horiz. pair, imperf. between 115.00
1338F A760 8c dk bl, red & slate gren ('71) .25 .25
i. Imperf., vert. pair 35.00
j. Horiz. pair, imperf. between 45.00
p. Slate green omitted 300.00
t. Horiz. pair, imperf. vertically —

Issued: #1338D, 8/7/70

COIL STAMP
MULTICOLOR HUCK PRESS

1971, May 10 **Perf. 10 Vertically**
Size: 18¼x21mm
1338G A760 8c dk bl, red & slate grn .30 .25
h. Imperf., pair 45.00

ILLINOIS STATEHOOD, 150th ANNIV.

Farm House & Fields of Ripening Grain — A761

LITHOGRAPHED, ENGRAVED (Giori)

1968, Feb. 12 **Perf. 11**
1339 A761 6c dk blue, blue, red & ocher .25 .25

HEMISFAIR '68 ISSUE

HemisFair '68 exhibition, San Antonio, Texas, Apr. 6-Oct. 6, for the 250th anniv. of San Antonio.

Map of North & South America — A762

1968, Mar. 30
1340 A762 6c blue, rose red & white .25 .25
a. White omitted 650.00

AIRLIFT ISSUE

Eagle Holding Pennant A763

1968, Apr. 4 **Untagged**
1341 A763 $1 sepia, dk. blue, ocher & brown red 2.00 1.25

Issued to pay for airlift of parcels from and to U.S. ports to servicemen overseas and in Alaska, Hawaii and P.R. Valid for all regular postage.
On Apr. 26, 1969, the POD ruled that henceforth No. 1341 "may be used toward paying the postage or fees for special services on airmail articles."

"SUPPORT OUR YOUTH" — ELKS ISSUE

Support Our Youth program, and honoring the Benevolent and Protective Order of Elks, which extended its youth service program in observance of its centennial year.

Girls & Boys A764

1968, May 1 **Tagged**
1342 A764 6c ultramarine & orange red .25 .25

LAW AND ORDER ISSUE

Publicizing the policeman as protector and friend and to encourage respect for law and order.

Policeman and Small Boy — A765

GIORI PRESS PRINTING

1968, May 17
1343 A765 6c chalky blue, black & red .25 .25

REGISTER AND VOTE ISSUE

Campaign to draw more voters to the polls. The weather vane is from an old house in the Russian Hill section of San Francisco, Cal.

Eagle Weather Vane — A766

LITHOGRAPHED, ENGRAVED (Giori)

1968, June 27
1344 A766 6c black, yellow & orange .25 .25

HISTORIC FLAG SERIES

Flags carried by American colonists and by citizens of the new United States. Printed se-tenant in vertical columns of 10. The flag sequence on the 2 upper panes is as listed. On the 2 lower panes the sequence is reversed with the Navy Jack in the 1st row and the Fort Moultrie flag in the 10th.

Ft. Moultrie, 1776 A767

Ft. McHenry, 1795-1818 A768

Washington's Cruisers, 1775 — A769

Bennington, 1777 A770

Rhode Island, 1775 A771

First Stars and Stripes, 1777 A772

Bunker Hill, 1775 A773

Grand Union, 1776 A774

Philadelphia Light Horse, 1775 — A775

First Navy Jack, 1775 A776

ENGR. (Giori) (#1345-1348, 1350); ENGR. & LITHO. (#1349, 1351-1354).

1968, July 4

1345	A767	6c dark blue	.40	.25
1346	A768	6c dark blue & red	.40	.25
1347	A769	6c dark blue & olive green	.30	.25
1348	A770	6c dark blue & red	.30	.25
1349	A771	6c dark blue, yellow & red	.30	.25
1350	A772	6c dark blue & red	.30	.25
1351	A773	6c dark blue, olive green & red	.30	.25
1352	A774	6c dark blue & red	.30	.25
1353	A775	6c dark blue, yellow & red	.30	.25

1354	A776	6c dark blue, red & yellow	.30	.25
a.	Strip of ten, #1345-1354		3.25	3.25
b.	#1345b-1354b, any single, tagging omitted		65.00	
c.	As "a," imperf		4,500.	

WALT DISNEY ISSUE

Walt Disney (1901-1966), cartoonist, film producer and creator of Mickey Mouse.

Disney and Children of the World — A777

Printed by Achrovure Division of Union-Camp Corp., Englewood, N.J.

PHOTOGRAVURE

1968, Sept. 11   **Perf. 12**

1355	A777	6c multicolored	.40	.25
a.	Ocher omitted ("Walt Disney," "6c," etc.)		375.00	—
b.	Vert. pair, imperf. horiz.		575.00	
c.	Imperf., pair		425.00	
d.	Black omitted		1,750.	
e.	Horiz. pair, imperf. between		5,000.	
f.	Blue omitted		1,500.	

FATHER MARQUETTE ISSUE

Father Jacques Marquette (1637-1675), French Jesuit missionary, who together with Louis Jolliet explored the Mississippi River and its tributaries.

Father Marquette and Louis Jolliet Exploring the Mississippi A778

LITHOGRAPHED, ENGRAVED (Giori)

1968, Sept. 20   **Perf. 11**

1356	A778	6c black, apple green & orange brown	.25	.25

AMERICAN FOLKLORE ISSUE

Daniel Boone (1734-1820), frontiersman and trapper.

Pennsylvania Rifle, Powder Horn, Tomahawk Pipe & Knife — A779

LITHOGRAPHED, ENGRAVED (Giori)

1968, Sept. 26

1357	A779	6c yel, dp yel, mar & blk	.25	.25

ARKANSAS RIVER NAVIGATION ISSUE

Opening of the Arkansas River to commercial navigation.

Ship's Wheel, Power Transmission Tower & Barge — A780

1968, Oct. 1

1358	A780	6c bright blue, dark blue & black	.25	.25

LEIF ERIKSON ISSUE

Leif Erikson, 11th century Norse explorer, called the 1st European to set foot on the American continent, at a place he called Vinland. The statue by the American sculptor A. Stirling Calder is in Reykjavik, Iceland.

Leif Erikson, by Stirling Calder — A781

1968, Oct. 9

1359	A781	6c light gray brown & black brown	.25	.25

The luminescent element is in the light gray brown ink of the background. The engraved parts were printed on a rotary currency press.

CHEROKEE STRIP ISSUE

75th anniversary of the opening of the Cherokee Strip to settlers, Sept. 16, 1893.

Homesteaders Racing to Cherokee Strip — A782

ROTARY PRESS PRINTING

1968, Oct. 15   **Perf. 11x10½**

1360	A782	6c brown	.25	.25

JOHN TRUMBULL ISSUE

Trumbull (1756-1843), painter. The stamp shows Lt. Thomas Grosvenor and his attendant Peter Salem. The painting hangs at Yale University.

Detail from "The Battle of Bunker's Hill" — A783

LITHOGRAPHED, ENGRAVED (Giori)

1968, Oct. 18   **Perf. 11**

1361	A783	6c multicolored	.25	.25
b.	Black (engr.) missing (FO)		11,000.	

WATERFOWL CONSERVATION ISSUE

Wood Ducks A784

1968, Oct. 24

1362	A784	6c blk & multi	.25	.25
a.	Vertical pair, imperf. between		250.00	—
b.	Red & dark blue omitted		400.00	—
c.	Red omitted		1,750.	

Dangerous fakes exist of Nos. 1362b and 1362c. Authentication by experts is required.

CHRISTMAS ISSUE

"The Annunciation" by the 15th century Flemish painter Jan van Eyck is in the National Gallery of Art, Washington, D.C.

Gabriel, from van Eyck's Annunciation — A785

ENGRAVED (Multicolor Huck press)

1968, Nov. 1

1363	A785	6c multicolored	.25	.25
a.	Untagged		.25	.25
b.	Imperf., pair, tagged		140.00	
c.	Light yellow omitted		50.00	—
d.	Imperf., pair, untagged		225.00	

AMERICAN INDIAN ISSUE

Honoring the American Indian and to celebrate the opening of the Natl. Portrait Gallery, Washington, D.C. Chief Joseph (Indian name, Thunder Traveling over the Mountains), a leader of the Nez Percé, was born in eastern Oregon about 1840 and died at the Colesville Reservation in Washington State in 1904.

Chief Joseph, by Cyrenius Hall — A786

LITHOGRAPHED, ENGRAVED (Giori)

1968, Nov. 4

1364	A786	6c black & multi	.25	.25

BEAUTIFICATION OF AMERICA ISSUE

Publicizing the Natural Beauty Campaign for more beautiful cities, parks, highways and streets. In the left panes Nos. 1365 and 1367 appear in 1st, 3rd and 5th place, Nos. 1366 and 1368 in 2nd and 4th place. This arrangement is reversed in the right panes.

Capitol, Azaleas and Tulips A787

Washington Monument, Potomac River and Daffodils A788

Poppies and Lupines along Highway A789

Blooming Crab Apples along Street A790

1969, Jan. 16   **Tagged**

1365	A787	6c multicolored	.25	.25
1366	A788	6c multicolored	.25	.25
1367	A789	6c multicolored	.25	.25
1368	A790	6c multicolored	.25	.25
a.	Block of 4, #1365-1368		1.00	1.25

Compare with Nos. 4716a, 4716b, 4716d, 4716e.

AMERICAN LEGION, 50th ANNIV.

Eagle from Great Seal of U.S. — A791

1969, Mar. 15
1369 A791 6c red, blue & black   .25   .25

AMERICAN FOLKLORE ISSUE

Grandma Moses (Anna Mary Robertson Moses, 1860-1961), primitive painter of American life.

July Fourth, by Grandma Moses — A792

1969, May 1
1370 A792 6c multicolored   .25   .25
  a.   Horizontal pair, imperf. be-
      tween   140.00   —
  b.   Engraved black ("6c U.S.
      Postage") & Prus. blue
      ("Grandma Moses") omit-
      ted   500.00

Beware of pairs with blind perfs. being offered as No. 1370a.
No. 1370b often comes with mottled or disturbed gum. Such stamps sell for about two-thirds as much as examples with perfect gum.

APOLLO 8 ISSUE

Apollo 8 mission, which 1st put men into orbit around the moon, Dec. 21-27, 1968. The astronauts were: Col. Frank Borman, Capt. James Lovell and Maj. William Anders.

Moon Surface and Earth — A793

LITHOGRAPHED, ENGRAVED (Giori)
1969, May 5
1371 A793 6c black, blue & ocher   .25   .25
Imperfs. exist from printer's waste.

W.C. HANDY ISSUE

Handy (1873-1958), jazz musician and composer.

W. C. Handy (1873-1958), Jazz Musician and Composer — A794

LITHOGRAPHED, ENGRAVED (Giori)
1969, May 17
1372 A794 6c violet, deep lilac
    & blue   .25   .25

CALIFORNIA SETTLEMENT, 200th ANNIV.

Carmel Mission Belfry — A795

1969, July 16
1373 A795 6c orange, red,
    black & light
    blue   .25   .25
  b.   Red (engr.) missing (CM)   400.00

JOHN WESLEY POWELL ISSUE

Powell (1834-1902), geologist who explored the Green and Colorado Rivers 1869-75, and ethnologist.

Powell Exploring Colorado River A796

1969, Aug. 1
1374 A796 6c black, ocher & light
    blue   .25   .25

ALABAMA STATEHOOD, 150th ANNIV.

Camellia & Yellow-shafted Flicker — A797

1969, Aug. 2
1375 A797 6c mag, rose red, yel,
    dk, grn & brn   .25   .25

BOTANICAL CONGRESS ISSUE

11th Intl. Botanical Cong., Seattle, Wash., Aug. 24-Sept. 2. In left panes Nos. 1376 and 1378 appear in 1st, 3rd and 5th place; Nos. 1377 and 1379 in 2nd and 4th place. This arrangement is reversed in right panes.

Douglas Fir (Northwest) A798

Lady's-slipper (Northeast) — A799

Ocotillo (Southwest) A800

Franklinia (Southeast) A801

1969, Aug. 23

1376 A798 6c multicolored   .35   .25
1377 A799 6c multicolored   .35   .25
1378 A800 6c multicolored   .35   .25
1379 A801 6c multicolored   .35   .25
  a.   Block of 4, #1376-1379   1.40   1.75

DARTMOUTH COLLEGE CASE ISSUE

150th anniv. of the Dartmouth College Case, which Daniel Webster argued before the Supreme Court, reasserting the sanctity of contracts.

Daniel Webster & Dartmouth Hall — A802

ROTARY PRESS PRINTING
1969, Sept. 22   **Perf. 10½x11**
1380 A802 6c green   .25   .25

PROFESSIONAL BASEBALL, 100th ANNIV.

Batter A803

LITHOGRAPHED, ENGRAVED (Giori)
1969, Sept. 24   **Perf. 11**
1381 A803 6c yellow, red,
    black & green   .45   .25
  a.   Black omitted ("1869-1969,
     United States, 6c, Profes-
     sional Baseball")   500.00
  c.   Double impression of black
     (engr.)   5,750.

INTERCOLLEGIATE FOOTBALL, 100th ANNIV.

Football Player & Coach A804

1969, Sept. 26
1382 A804 6c red & green   .25   .25
  b.   Vert. pair, imperf horiz.   5,750.
  c.   Double impression   2,500.

The engraved parts were printed on a rotary currency press.
No. 1382b is unique.
Two examples of No. 1382c are recorded, with the double impression on the left part of the left stamps within a lower left plate block of 4. Value given is for the plate block.

DWIGHT D. EISENHOWER ISSUE

Dwight D. Eisenhower A805

Designed by Robert J. Jones; photograph by Bernie Noble.

GIORI PRESS PRINTING
1969, Oct. 14
1383 A805 6c blue, black &
    red   .25   .25
  b.   Blue ("U.S. 6c Postage")
     missing (PS)   600.00

CHRISTMAS ISSUE

The painting, painted about 1870 by an unknown primitive artist, is the property of the N.Y. State Historical Association, Cooperstown, N.Y.

Winter Sunday in Norway, Maine A806

ENGRAVED (Multicolor Huck)
1969, Nov. 3   **Perf. 11x10½**
1384 A806 6c dark green &
    multicolored   .25   .25
    Precancel   .60   .25
  b.   Imperf., pair   700.00
  c.   Light green omitted   25.00
  d.   Light green, red & yellow
     omitted   600.00
  e.   Yellow omitted   1,500.
  g.   Red & yellow omitted   2,250.
  h.   Light green and yellow
     omitted   500.00
  i.   Light green and red omit-
     ted   —
  j.   Vert. pair, top stamp Balti-
     more precancel, bottom
     stamp precancel missing
     (FO)   —
  k.   Baltimore precancel
     printed on gum side   150.00
  l.   Baltimore precancel, vert.
     pair, one stamp missing
     precancel, other stamp
     with precancel printed
     inverted on reverse (FO)   500.00
  m.   Inverted Baltimore precan-
     cel   200.00
  n.   Baltimore precancel
     printed inverted on re-
     verse (FO)   150.00
  p.   Double impression of New
     Haven precancel   —
  q.   Inverted Memphis precan-
     cel   100.00

The precancel value applies to the least expensive of experimental precancels printed locally in four cities, on tagged stamps, with the names between lines 4 ½mm apart: in black or green, "ATLANTA, GA" and in green only "BALTIMORE, MD," "MEMPHIS, TN" and "NEW HAVEN, CT." They were sold freely to the public and could be used on any class of mail at all post offices during the experimental program and thereafter.
Most examples of No. 1384c show orange where the offset green was. Value is for this variety. Examples without orange sell for more.
On No. 1384i, almost all of the yellow is also omitted. Do not confuse with No. 1384d.

Cured Child — A807

HOPE FOR CRIPPLED ISSUE

Issued to encourage the rehabilitation of crippled children and adults and to honor the National Society for Crippled Children and Adults (Easter Seal Society) on its 50th anniversary.

LITHOGRAPHED, ENGRAVED (Giori)
1969, Nov. 20   **Perf. 11**
1385 A807 6c multicolored   .25   .25

WILLIAM M. HARNETT ISSUE

"Old Models" — A808

Harnett (1848-1892), painter. The painting hangs in the Museum of Fine Arts, Boston.

1969, Dec. 3
1386 A808 6c multicolored .25 .25
  a. Red (engr.) missing (CM) —

NATURAL HISTORY ISSUE

Centenary of the American Museum of Natural History, New York City. Nos. 1387-1388 alternate in 1st row, Nos. 1389-1390 in 2nd row. This arrangement is repeated throughout the pane.

American Bald Eagle — A809

African Elephant Herd — A810

Tlingit Chief in Haida Ceremonial Canoe — A811

Brontosaurus, Stegosaurus & Allosaurus — A812

1970, May 6
1387	A809	6c multicolored	.25	.25
1388	A810	6c multicolored	.25	.25
1389	A811	6c multicolored	.25	.25
1390	A812	6c multicolored	.25	.25
	a.	Block of 4, #1387-1390	1.00	1.00

MAINE STATEHOOD, 150th ANNIV.

The painting hangs in the Metropolitan Museum of Art, New York City.

Lighthouse at Two Lights, Maine A813

1970, July 9   Tagged   Perf. 11
1391 A813 6c black & multi .25 .25

WILDLIFE CONSERVATION ISSUE

American Buffalo A814

ROTARY PRESS PRINTING

1970, July 20   Perf. 11x10½
1392 A814 6c black, *light brown* .25 .25

REGULAR ISSUE
Dwight David Eisenhower

Dot between "R" and "U" A815

No dot between "R" and "U" — A815a

Benjamin Franklin A816

USPS Emblem A817

Fiorello H. LaGuardia A817a

Ernest Taylor Pyle — A818

Dr. Elizabeth Blackwell A818a

Amadeo P. Giannini A818b

ROTARY PRESS PRINTING

1970-74
1393	A815	6c dk blue gray	.25	.25
	a.	Booklet pane of 8	2.00	2.00
	b.	Booklet pane of 5 + label	1.40	1.40
	c.	Untagged (Bureau precanceled)	12.75	3.00

Perf. 10½x11
1393D	A816	7c bright blue ('73)	.25	.25
	e.	Untagged (Bureau precanceled)	4.25	1.00

GIORI PRESS PRINTING
Perf. 11
1394	A815a	8c blk, red & bl gray ('71)	.25	.25
	b.	Red missing (PS)	150.00	
	c.	Red missing (FO)	1,250.	
	d.	Red and blue gray missing (PS)	—	
	e.	Red and blue gray missing (FO or preprinting paper crease)	1,000.	
	f.	All colors and tagging missing (FO)	1,000.	
	g.	Printed on gum side, tagged	1,000.	

No. 1394f must be collected se-tenant with No. 1394c, 1394e, or with a partially printed No. 1394.

ROTARY PRESS PRINTING
Perf. 11x10½ on 2 or 3 Sides
1395	A815	8c deep claret ('71)	.25	.25
	a.	Booklet pane of 8	2.00	2.00
	b.	Booklet pane of 6	1.50	1.50
	c.	Booklet pane of 4 +2 ('72)	1.65	1.10
	d.	Booklet pane of 7 + label ('72)	1.90	1.90
	e.	Vert. pair, imperf. between, in #1395a or 1395d with foldover	600.00	

No. 1395 was issued only in booklets. At least 4 pairs of No. 1395e are recorded from 3 panes (one No. 1395a and two 1395d) with different foldover patterns. A pane of No. 1395d also is known with a foldover resulting in a vertical pair of stamp and label, imperf between.

PHOTOGRAVURE (Andreotti)

Plates of 400 subjects in four panes of 100.
Perf. 11x10½
1396 A817 8c multi ('71) .25 .25

ROTARY PRESS PRINTING
1397	A817a	14c gray brown ('72)	.25	.25
	a.	Untagged (Bureau precanceled)	125.00	17.50
1398	A818	16c brown ('72)	.35	.25
	a.	Untagged (Bureau precanceled)	22.50	5.00
1399	A818a	18c violet ('74)	.35	.25
1400	A818b	21c green ('73)	.40	.25
		Nos. 1393-1400 (9)	2.60	2.25

Issued: 6c, 8/6/70; 7c, 10/20/72; #1394-1395, 5/10/71; #1396, 7/1/71; 14c, 4/24/72; 16c, 5/7/71; 18c, 1/23/74; 21c, 6/27/73.

COIL STAMPS
ROTARY PRESS PRINTING

1970-71   Perf. 10 Vert.
1401	A815	6c dk blue gray	.25	.25
	a.	Untagged (Bureau precanceled)	19.50	3.00
	b.	Imperf., pair	2,500.	
1402	A815	8c dp claret ('71)	.25	.25
	a.	Imperf., pair	37.50	
	b.	Untagged (Bureau precanceled)		
	c.	Pair, imperf. between	6.75	.75
			6,250.	

No. 1401b often found with small faults and/or without gum. Such examples sell for considerably less.
Issue dates: 6c, Aug. 6; 8c, May 10, 1971.

EDGAR LEE MASTERS ISSUE

A819

LITHOGRAPHED, ENGRAVED (Giori)
1970, Aug. 22   Perf. 11
1405 A819 6c black & olive bister .25 .25

WOMAN SUFFRAGE ISSUE

50th anniversary of the 19th Amendment, which gave the vote to women.

Suffragettes, 1920 & Woman Voter, 1970 — A820

GIORI PRESS PRINTING
1970, Aug. 26
1406 A820 6c blue .25 .25

SOUTH CAROLINA ISSUE

300th anniv. of the founding of Charles Town (Charleston), the 1st permanent settlement of South Carolina. Against a background of pine wood the line drawings of the design represent the economic and historic development of South Carolina: the spire of St. Phillip's Church, Capitol, state flag, a ship, 17th century man and woman, a Fort Sumter cannon, barrels, cotton, tobacco and yellow jasmine.

Symbols of South Carolina A821

LITHOGRAPHED, ENGRAVED (Giori)
1970, Sept. 12
1407 A821 6c bister, black & red .25 .25

STONE MOUNTAIN MEMORIAL ISSUE

Dedication of the Stone Mountain Confederate Memorial, Georgia, May 9, 1970.

A822

GIORI PRESS PRINTING
1970, Sept. 19
1408 A822 6c gray .25 .25

FORT SNELLING ISSUE

150th anniv. of Fort Snelling, Minnesota, an important outpost for the opening of the Northwest.

Fort Snelling, Keelboat & Tepees A823

LITHOGRAPHED, ENGRAVED (Giori)
1970, Oct. 17
1409 A823 6c yellow & multi .25 .25

ANTI-POLLUTION ISSUE

Issued to focus attention on the problems of pollution.
In left panes Nos. 1410 and 1412 appear in 1st, 3rd and 5th place; Nos. 1411 and 1413 in 2nd and 4th place. This arrangement is reversed in right panes.

Globe and Wheat A824

Globe and City A825

Globe and Bluegill A826

Globe and Seagull A827

PHOTOGRAVURE
1970, Oct. 28   Perf. 11x10½
1410	A824	6c multicolored	.25	.25
1411	A825	6c multicolored	.25	.25
1412	A826	6c multicolored	.25	.25
1413	A827	6c multicolored	.25	.25
	a.	Block of 4, #1410-1413	1.00	1.25

CHRISTMAS ISSUE

In left panes Nos. 1415 and 1417 appear in 1st, 3rd and 5th place; Nos. 1416 and 1418 in 2nd and 4th place. This arrangement is reversed in right panes.

Christmas 6¢US. Nativity — A828

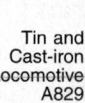

Tin and
Cast-iron
Locomotive
A829

Toy Horse
on Wheels
A830

Mechanical
Tricycle
A831

Doll
Carriage
A832

1970, Nov. 5   **Perf. 10½x11**
1414 A828 6c multicolored .25 .25
  a.   Precanceled .25 .25
  b.   Black omitted 400.00
  c.   As "a," blue omitted 1,100.
  d.   Type II .25 .25
  e.   Type II, precanceled .25 .25

No. 1414 has a slightly blurry impression, snowflaking in the sky and no gum breaker ridges. No. 1414d had shiny surfaced paper, sharper impression, no snowflaking and vertical and horizontal gum breaker ridges.

No. 1414a has a slightly blurry impression, snowflaking in the sky, no gum breaker ridges and the precancel is grayish black. No. 1414e has sharper impression, no snowflaking, gum breaker ridges and the precancel is intense black.

     Perf. 11x10½
1415 A829 6c multicolored .30 .25
  a.   Precanceled .65 .25
  b.   Black omitted 2,000.
1416 A830 6c multicolored .30 .25
  a.   Precanceled .65 .25
  b.   Black omitted 2,000.
  c.   Imperf., pair (#1416, 1418) 2,500.
1417 A831 6c multicolored .30 .25
  a.   Precanceled .65 .25
  b.   Black omitted 2,000.
1418 A832 6c multicolored .30 .25
  a.   Precanceled .65 .25
  b.   Block of 4, #1415-1418 1.25 1.40
  c.   As "b," precanceled 3.75 3.50
  d.   Black omitted 2,000.
  e.   As "b," black omitted 9,000.
  f.   As "b," black omitted on #1417 & 1418 4,500.
  g.   P# block of 8, black omitted on #1415 & 1416 4,500.
  Nos. 1415-1418 (4) 1.20 1.00

Nos. 1415-1418 and 1415a-1418a are known both without gum breaker ridges (common) and with gum breaker ridges (scarce).

The precanceled stamps, Nos. 1414a-1418a, were furnished to 168 cities. The plates include two straight (No. 1414a) or two wavy (Nos. 1415a-1418a) black lines that make up the precancelation. Unused values are for stamps with gum and used values are for stamps with an additional cancellation or without gum.

UNITED NATIONS, 25th ANNIV.

"UN" & UN
Emblem
A833

LITHOGRAPHED, ENGRAVED (Giori)
1970, Nov. 20   **Perf. 11**
1419 A833 6c blk, verm & ultra .25 .25

LANDING OF THE PILGRIMS ISSUE

350th anniv. of the landing of the Mayflower.

Mayflower &
Pilgrims — A834

1970, Nov. 21
1420 A834 6c blk, org, yel, magenta, bl & brn .25 .25
  a.   Orange & yellow omitted 575.00

DISABLED AMERICAN VETERANS AND SERVICEMEN ISSUE

No. 1421 for the 50th anniv. of the Disabled Veterans of America Organization; No. 1422 honors the contribution of servicemen, particularly those who were prisoners of war, missing or killed in action. Nos. 1421-1422 are printed se-tenant in horizontal rows of 10.

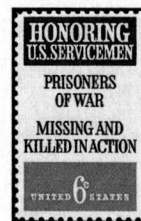

A835   A836

1970, Nov. 24
1421 A835 6c dark blue, red & multicolored .25 .25
ENGRAVED
1422 A836 6c dark blue, black & red .25 .25
  a.   Pair, #1421-1422 .50 .50

AMERICAN WOOL INDUSTRY ISSUE

450th anniv. of the introduction of sheep to the North American continent and the beginning of the American wool industry.

Ewe and
Lamb — A837

Plates of 200 subjects in four panes of 50.

1971, Jan. 19
1423 A837 6c multicolored .25 .25
  b.   Teal blue ("United States") missing (CM) 400.00

GEN. DOUGLAS MacARTHUR ISSUE

MacArthur (1880-1964), Chief of Staff, Supreme Commander for the Allied Powers in the Pacific Area during World War II and Supreme Commander in Japan after the war.

Douglas
MacArthur — A838

GIORI PRESS PRINTING
1971, Jan. 26
1424 A838 6c black, red & dark blue .25 .25
  a.   Red missing (PS) —
  c.   Blue missing (PS) —

BLOOD DONOR ISSUE

Salute to blood donors and spur to increased participation in the blood donor program.

Giving
Blood
Saves
Lives
A839

LITHOGRAPHED, ENGRAVED (Giori)
1971, Mar. 12
1425 A839 6c bl, scarlet & ind .25 .25

MISSOURI STATEHOOD, 150th ANNIV.

The stamp design shows a Pawnee facing a hunter-trapper and a group of settlers. It is from a mural by Thomas Hart Benton in the Harry S Truman Library, Independence, Mo.

"Independence and the Opening of the West" — A840

PHOTOGRAVURE (Andreotti)
1971, May 8   **Perf. 11x10½**
1426 A840 8c multicolored .25 .25

See note on Andreotti printings and their color control markings in Information for Collectors under Printing, Photogravure.

WILDLIFE CONSERVATION ISSUE

Nos. 1427-1428 alternate in first row, Nos. 1429-1430 in second row. This arrangement repeated throughout pane.

Trout
A841

Alligator — A842

Polar
Bear,
Cubs
A843

California Condor — A844

LITHOGRAPHED, ENGRAVED (Giori)
1971, June 12   **Perf. 11**
1427 A841 8c multicolored .25 .25
  a.   Red omitted 1,250.
  b.   Green (engr.) omitted
1428 A842 8c multicolored .25 .25
1429 A843 8c multicolored .25 .25
1430 A844 8c multicolored .25 .25
  a.   Block of 4, #1427-1430 1.00 1.00
  b.   As "a," light green & dark green omitted from #1427-1428 3,250.
  c.   As "a," red omitted from #1427, 1429-1430 3,000.

ANTARCTIC TREATY ISSUE

Map of
Antarctica
A845

Adapted from emblem on official documents of Consultative Meetings.

GIORI PRESS PRINTING
1971, June 23
1431 A845 8c red & dark blue .25 .25
  b.   Both colors missing (EP) 500.00

No. 1431b should be collected se-tenant with a normal stamp and/or a partially printed stamp.

AMERICAN REVOLUTION BICENTENNIAL

Bicentennial
Commission
Emblem — A846

LITHOGRAPHED, ENGRAVED (Giori)
1971, July 4
1432 A846 8c gray, red, blue & black .25 .25
  a.   Gray & black missing (EP) 350.00
  b.   Gray ("U.S. Postage 8c") missing (EP) 650.00

JOHN SLOAN ISSUE

John Sloan (1871-1951), painter. The painting hangs in the Phillips Gallery, Washington, D.C.

The Wake
of the
Ferry
A847

1971, Aug. 2
1433 A847 8c multicolored .25 .25
  b.   Red engr. ("John Sloan" and "8") missing (CM) 950.00

SPACE ACHIEVEMENT DECADE ISSUE

Decade of space achievements and the Apollo 15 moon exploration mission, July 26-Aug. 7. In the left panes the earth and sun stamp is 1st, 3rd and 5th, the rover 2nd and 4th. This arrangement is reversed in the right panes.

Earth, Sun, Landing Craft on Moon
A848

Lunar Rover
A849

1971, Aug. 2
1434 A848 8c blk, bl, gray,
                yel & red   .25   .25
1435 A849 8c blk, bl, gray,
                yel & red   .25   .25
   b.   Pair, #1434-1435   .50   .50
   d.   As "b," blue & red (litho.)
        omitted   950.00

EMILY DICKINSON ISSUE

Emily Elizabeth Dickinson — A850

1971, Aug. 28
1436 A850 8c **multi**, green-
                ish   .25   .25
   a.   Black & olive (engr.) omit-
        ted   500.00
   b.   Pale rose missing (EP)   5,000.00
   c.   Red omitted   —

SAN JUAN ISSUE

450th anniversary of San Juan, Puerto Rico.

Sentry Box, Morro Castle, San Juan — A851

1971, Sept. 12
1437 A851 8c pale brn, blk, yel,
                red brn & dk brn   .25   .25
   b.   Dark brown (engr.) omitted   1,750.   —

VALUES FOR HINGED STAMPS AFTER NO. 771

This catalogue does not value unused stamps after No. 771 in hinged condition. Hinged unused stamps from No. 772 to the present are worth considerably less than the values given for unused stamps, which are for never-hinged examples.

PREVENT DRUG ABUSE ISSUE

Drug Abuse Prevention Week, Oct. 3-9.

Young Woman Drug Addict — A852

PHOTOGRAVURE (Andreotti)
1971, Oct. 4   *Perf. 10½x11*
1438 A852 8c blue, deep blue &
                black   .25   .25

CARE ISSUE

25th anniversary of CARE, a US-Canadian Cooperative for American Relief Everywhere.

Hands Reaching for CARE — A853

1971, Oct. 27
1439 A853 8c blue, blk, vio &
                red lilac   .25   .25
   a.   Black omitted   1,250.

HISTORIC PRESERVATION ISSUE

Nos. 1440-1441 alternate in 1st row, Nos. 1442-1443 in 2nd row. This arrangement is repeated throughout the pane.

Decatur House, Washington, DC — A854

Whaling Ship Charles W. Morgan, Mystic, Conn. — A855

Cable Car, San Francisco — A856

San Xavier del Bac Mission, Tucson, Ariz. — A857

LITHOGRAPHED, ENGRAVED (Giori)
1971, Oct. 29   Tagged   Perf. 11
1440 A854 8c blk brn &
                ocher, *buff*   .25   .25
1441 A855 8c blk brn &
                ocher, *buff*   .25   .25
1442 A856 8c blk brn &
                ocher, *buff*   .25   .25
1443 A857 8c blk brn &
                ocher, *buff*   .25   .25
   a.   Block of 4, #1440-1443   1.00 1.00
   b.   As "a," black brown omit-
        ted   800.00
   c.   As "a," ocher omitted   2,500.

CHRISTMAS ISSUE

Adoration of the Shepherds, by Giorgione
A858

Partridge in a Pear Tree, by Jamie Wyeth
A859

No. 1444 after a painting by Giorgione in the National Gallery of Art, Washington D.C.

PHOTOGRAVURE (Andreotti)
1971, Nov. 10   *Perf. 10½x11*
1444 A858 8c gold & multi   .25   .25
   a.   Gold omitted   350.00
1445 A859 8c dark green, red
                & multicolored   .25   .25

SIDNEY LANIER ISSUE

Lanier (1842-81), poet, musician, lawyer, educator.

Sidney Lanier (1842-1881) — A860

GIORI PRESS PRINTING

1972, Feb. 3   *Perf. 11*
1446 A860 8c black, brown &
                light blue   .25   .25

PEACE CORPS ISSUE

Peace Corps Poster, by David Battle — A861

PHOTOGRAVURE (Andreotti)
1972, Feb. 11   *Perf. 10½x11*
1447 A861 8c dark blue, light
                blue & red   .25   .25

NATIONAL PARKS CENTENNIAL ISSUE

Centenary of Yellowstone National Park, the 1st National Park, and of the entire National Park System. See No. C84.

Hulk of Ship
A862

Cape Hatteras Lighthouse
A863

Laughing Gulls on Driftwood
A864

Laughing Gulls and Dune
A865

Wolf Trap Farm, Vienna, Va. — A866

Old Faithful, Yellowstone
A867

Mt. McKinley, Alaska
A868

LITHOGRAPHED, ENGRAVED (Giori)
1972   *Perf. 11*
Plates of 400 subjects in 4 panes of 100 each
1448 A862 2c black & multi   .25   .25
1449 A863 2c black & multi   .25   .25
1450 A864 2c black & multi   .25   .25
1451 A865 2c black & multi   .25   .25
   a.   Block of 4, #1448-1451   .50   .50
   b.   As "a," black (litho.) omit-
        ted   1,000.
1452 A866 6c black & multi   .25   .25
1453 A867 8c blk, bl, brn &
                multi   .25   .25
1454 A868 15c black & multi   .30   .25
   b.   Yellow omitted   3,500.

FAMILY PLANNING ISSUE

Family — A869

1972, Mar. 18
1455 A869 8c blk & multi   .25   .25
   a.   Yellow omitted   325.00
   c.   Dark brown missing (FO)   9,500.

AMERICAN BICENTENNIAL ISSUE
Colonial American Craftsmen

In left panes Nos. 1456 and 1458 appear in 1st, 3rd and 5th place; Nos. 1457 and 1459 in 2nd and 4th place. This arrangement is reversed in right panes.

Glassmaker
A870

Silversmith
A871

Wigmaker
A872

Hatter
A873

ENGRAVED

1972, July 4   *Perf. 11x10½*

1456	A870	8c deep brown	.25	.25
1457	A871	8c deep brown	.25	.25
1458	A872	8c deep brown	.25	.25
1459	A873	8c deep brown	.25	.25
a.		Block of 4, #1456-1459	1.00	1.00

OLYMPIC GAMES ISSUE

11th Winter Olympic Games, Sapporo, Japan, Feb. 3-13 and 20th Summer Olympic Games, Munich, Germany, Aug. 26-Sept. 11. See No. C85.

Bicycling and Olympic Rings
A874

Bobsledding
A875

Running
A876

PHOTOGRAVURE (Andreotti)

1972, Aug. 17   *Perf. 11x10½*

1460	A874	6c blk, bl, red, emer & yel	.25	.25
1461	A875	8c blk, bl, red, emer & yel	.25	.25
1462	A876	15c blk, bl, red, emer & yel	.30	.25
		Nos. 1460-1462 (3)	.80	.75

PARENT TEACHER ASSN., 75th ANNIV.

Blackboard
A877

1972, Sept. 15

1463	A877	8c yellow & black	.25	.25

WILDLIFE CONSERVATION ISSUE

Nos. 1464-1465 alternate in 1st row, Nos. 1468-1469 in 2nd row. This arrangement repeated throughout pane.

Fur Seals
A878

Cardinal — A879

Brown Pelican — A880

Bighorn Sheep — A881

LITHOGRAPHED, ENGRAVED (Giori)

1972, Sept. 20   *Perf. 11*

1464	A878	8c multicolored	.25	.25
1465	A879	8c multicolored	.25	.25
1466	A880	8c multicolored	.25	.25
1467	A881	8c multicolored	.25	.25
a.		Block of 4, #1464-1467	1.00	1.00
b.		As "a," brown omitted	2,750.	
c.		As "a," green & blue omitted	2,750.	
d.		As "a," red & brown omitted	3,250.	

MAIL ORDER BUSINESS ISSUE

Centenary of mail order business, originated by Aaron Montgomery Ward, Chicago. Design based on Headsville, W.Va., post office in Smithsonian Institution, Washington, D.C.

Rural Post Office Store
A882

PHOTOGRAVURE (Andreotti)

1972, Sept. 27   *Perf. 11x10½*

1468	A882	8c multicolored	.25	.25

OSTEOPATHIC MEDICINE ISSUE

75th anniv. of the American Osteopathic Assoc., founded by Dr. Andrew T. Still (1828-1917), who developed the principles of osteopathy in 1874.

Man's Quest for Health — A883

1972, Oct. 9   *Perf. 10½x11*

1469	A883	8c multicolored	.25	.25

AMERICAN FOLKLORE ISSUE

Tom Sawyer, by Norman Rockwell — A884

Designed by Bradbury Thompson.

LITHOGRAPHED, ENGRAVED (Giori)

1972, Oct. 13   *Perf. 11*

1470	A884	8c blk, red, yel, tan, bl & rose red	.25	.25
a.		Horiz. pair, imperf. between	6,750.	
b.		Red & black (engr.) omitted	800.00	

c.		Yellow & tan (litho.) omitted	1,100.	
e.		Red (engr. 8c) missing (CM)	750.	

CHRISTMAS ISSUE

Angel from "Mary, Queen of Heaven" — A885

Santa Claus — A886

No. 1471, detail from a painting by the Master of the St. Lucy Legend in the National Gallery of Art, Washington, D.C.

PHOTOGRAVURE (Andreotti)

1972, Nov. 9   *Perf. 10½x11*

1471	A885	8c multicolored	.25	.25
a.		Pink omitted	100.00	
b.		Black omitted	2,500.	
1472	A886	8c multicolored	.25	.25

PHARMACY ISSUE

Honoring American druggists in connection with the 120th anniversary of the American Pharmaceutical Association.

Mortar & Pestle, Bowl of Hygeia, 19th Century Medicine Bottles
A887

LITHOGRAPHED, ENGRAVED (Giori)

1972, Nov. 10   *Perf. 11*

1473	A887	8c black & multicolored	.25	.25
a.		Blue & orange omitted	600.00	
b.		Blue omitted	1,250.	
c.		Orange omitted	1,250.	
e.		Vertical pair, imperf horiz.	2,000.	

STAMP COLLECTING ISSUE

Issued to publicize stamp collecting.

U.S. No. 1 Under Magnifying Glass
A888

1972, Nov. 17

1474	A888	8c multicolored	.25	.25
a.		Black (litho.) omitted	375.00	

LOVE ISSUE

"Love," by Robert Indiana
A889

PHOTOGRAVURE (Andreotti)

1973, Jan. 26   *Perf. 11x10½*

1475	A889	8c red, emerald & violet blue	.25	.25

AMERICAN BICENTENNIAL ISSUE
Communications in Colonial Times

Printer and Patriots Examining Pamphlet
A890

Posting a Broadside
A891

Postrider
A892

Drummer
A893

GIORI PRESS PRINTING

1973   *Perf. 11*

1476	A890	8c ultra, greenish blk & red	.25	.25
b.		Red missing (PS)	—	
1477	A891	8c blk, vermilion & ultra	.25	.25

LITHOGRAPHED, ENGRAVED (Giori)

1478	A892	8c bl, blk, red & grn	.25	.25
a.		Red missing (CM)	—	
1479	A893	8c bl, blk, yel & red	.25	.25
a.		Blue missing (CM)	—	
		Nos. 1476-1479 (4)	1.00	1.00

AMERICAN BICENTENNIAL ISSUE
Boston Tea Party

In left panes Nos. 1480 and 1482 appear in 1st, 3rd and 5th place, Nos. 1481 and 1483 appear in 2nd and 4th place. This arrangement is reversed in right panes.

British Merchantman — A894

British Three-master — A895

Boats and Ship's Hull
A896

Boat and Dock
A897

1973, July 4

1480	A894	8c black & multi	.25	.25
1481	A895	8c black & multi	.25	.25
1482	A896	8c black & multi	.25	.25
1483	A897	8c black & multi	.25	.25
a.		Block of 4, #1480-1483	1.00	1.00
b.		As "a," black (engraved) omitted	950.00	
c.		As "a," black (litho.) omitted	900.00	
e.		As "a," dk blue omitted	1,500.	750.00

AMERICAN ARTS ISSUE

George Gershwin (1898-1937), composer (No. 1484); Robinson Jeffers (1887-1962), poet (No. 1485); Henry Ossawa Tanner (1859-1937), black painter (No. 1486); Willa Cather (1873-1947), novelist (No. 1487).

Gershwin, Sportin' Life, Porgy & Bess A898

Robinson Jeffers, Man & Children of Carmel with Burro A899

Henry Ossawa Tanner, Palette & Rainbow A900

Willa Cather, Pioneer Family & Covered Wagon A901

PHOTOGRAVURE (Andreotti)

1973

1484	A898	8c dp grn & multi	.25	.25
a.		Vertical pair, imperf. horiz.	160.00	
1485	A899	8c Prus bl & multi	.25	.25
a.		Vertical pair, imperf. horiz.	160.00	
1486	A900	8c yel brn & multi	.25	.25
1487	A901	8c dp brn & multi	.25	.25
a.		Vertical pair, imperf. horiz.	175.00	
		Nos. 1484-1487 (4)	1.00	1.00

Honoring: No. 1484, George Gershwin (1898-1937), composer. No. 1485, Robinson Jeffers (1887-1962), poet. No. 1486, Henry Ossawa Tanner (1859-1937), black painter (portrait by Thomas Eakins). No. 1487, Willa Sibert Cather (1873-1947), novelist.

Issued: No. 1484, Feb. 28; No. 1485, Aug. 13; No. 1486, Sept. 10; No. 1487, Sept. 20.

COPERNICUS ISSUE

Nicolaus Copernicus (1473-1543), Polish Astronomer — A902

LITHOGRAPHED, ENGRAVED (Giori)

1973, Apr. 23

1488	A902	8c black & orange	.25	.25
a.		Orange omitted	500.00	
b.		Black (engraved) omitted	600.00	

The orange can be chemically removed. Expertization of No. 1488a is required.

POSTAL SERVICE EMPLOYEES ISSUE

A tribute to US Postal Service employees. Nos. 1489-1498 are printed se-tenant in horizontal rows of 10. Emerald inscription on back, printed beneath gum in water-soluble ink, includes Postal Service emblem, "People Serving You" and a statement, differing for each of the 10 stamps, about some aspect of postal service.

Each stamp in top or bottom row has a tab with blue inscription enumerating various jobs in postal service.

Stamp Counter A903

Mail Collection A904

Letter Facing on Conveyor Belt — A905

Parcel Post Sorting — A906

Mail Canceling A907

Manual Letter Routing A908

Electronic Letter Routing — A909

Loading Mail on Truck — A910

Mailman A911

Rural Mail Delivery A912

PHOTOGRAVURE (Andreotti)

1973, Apr. 30   **Perf. 10½x11**

1489	A903	8c multicolored	.25	.25
1490	A904	8c multicolored	.25	.25
1491	A905	8c multicolored	.25	.25
1492	A906	8c multicolored	.25	.25
1493	A907	8c multicolored	.25	.25
1494	A908	8c multicolored	.25	.25
1495	A909	8c multicolored	.25	.25
1496	A910	8c multicolored	.25	.25
1497	A911	8c multicolored	.25	.25
1498	A912	8c multicolored	.25	.25
a.		Strip of 10, #1489-1498	2.50	2.50

HARRY S. TRUMAN ISSUE

Harry S Truman, 33rd President (1884-1972) A913

GIORI PRESS PRINTING

1973, May 8   **Perf. 11**

1499	A913	8c carmine rose, black & blue	.25	.25

ELECTRONICS PROGRESS ISSUE

See No. C86.

Marconi's Spark Coil and Gap A914

Transistors and Printed Circuit Board A915

Microphone, Speaker, Vacuum Tube, TV Camera Tube A916

LITHOGRAPHED, ENGRAVED (Giori)

1973, July 10

1500	A914	6c lilac & multi	.25	.25
1501	A915	8c tan & multi	.25	.25
a.		Black (inscriptions & "U.S. 8c") omitted	300.00	
b.		Tan (background) & lilac omitted	700.00	

Many examples of No. 1501b are hinged. Value about one-half never hinged value.

1502	A916	15c gray green & multicolored	.30	.25
a.		Black (inscriptions & "U.S. 15c") omitted	900.00	
		Nos. 1500-1502 (3)	.80	.75

See No. C86.

LYNDON B. JOHNSON ISSUE

Lyndon B. Johnson (1908-1973), 36th President A917

PHOTOGRAVURE (Andreotti)

1973, Aug. 27

1503	A917	8c black & multi	.25	.25
a.		Horiz. pair, imperf. vert.	200.00	

RURAL AMERICA ISSUE

Centenary of the introduction of Aberdeen Angus cattle into the US (#1504); of the Chautauqua Institution (#1505); and of the introduction of hard winter wheat into Kansas by Mennonite immigrants (#1506).

Angus and Longhorn Cattle A918

Chautauqua Tent and Buggies — A919

Wheat Fields and Train A920

No. 1504 after painting by F.C. "Frank" Murphy.

LITHOGRAPHED, ENGRAVED (Giori)

1973-74

1504	A918	8c multi	.25	.25
a.		Green & red brown omitted	675.00	
b.		Vert. pair, imperf. between		5,000.
d.		Blue (engr.) missing (PS)	—	
1505	A919	10c multi	.25	.25
a.		Black (litho.) omitted	1,750.	
1506	A920	10c multi	.25	.25
a.		Black and blue (engr.) omitted	450.00	
		Nos. 1504-1506 (3)	.75	.75

CHRISTMAS ISSUE

Small Cowper Madonna, by Raphael A921

Christmas Tree in Needlepoint A922

No. 1507 after painting in the National Gallery of Art, Washington, D.C.

PHOTOGRAVURE (Andreotti)

1973, Nov. 7   **Perf. 10½x11**

1507	A921	8c multicolored	.25	.25
1508	A922	8c multicolored	.25	.25
a.		Vertical pair, imperf. between	225.00	

50-Star & 13-Star Flags A923

Jefferson Memorial & Signature A924

Mail Transport A925

Liberty Bell A926

MULTICOLOR HUCK PRESS

1973-74   **Perf. 11x10½**

1509	A923	10c red & blue	.25	.25
a.		Horizontal pair, imperf. between	40.00	—
b.		Blue omitted	150.00	
c.		Imperf., vert. pair	450.00	

d.	Horiz. pair, imperf. vert.	*900.00*
f.	Vert. pair, imperf between	—

No. 1509 exists imperf and with red omitted from printer's waste.

ROTARY PRESS PRINTING

1510	A924 10c blue	.25	.25
a.	Untagged (Bureau precanceled)	*4.00*	*1.00*
b.	Booklet pane of 5 + label	*1.65*	*1.25*
c.	Booklet pane of 8	*2.00*	*2.00*
d.	Booklet pane of 6 ('74)	*5.00*	*1.75*
e.	Vert. pair, imperf. horiz.	*300.00*	
f.	Vert. pair, imperf. btwn., in #1510c with miscut or with foldover	*475.00*	
i.	As "b," double booklet pane of 10 plus stamps with 2 horiz. pairs imperf. btwn. plus stamp and label imperf. btwn. (FO)	*1,750.*	

No. 1510f resulted from a paper foldover after perforating and before cutting into booklet panes.

PHOTOGRAVURE (Andreotti)

1511	A925 10c multi	.25	.25
a.	Yellow omitted	*40.00*	

Beware of stamps with yellow chemically removed offered as No. 1511a.

COIL STAMPS
ROTARY PRESS PRINTING

1973-74		**Perf. 10 Vert.**	
1518	A926 6.3c brick red	.25	.25
a.	Untagged (Bureau precanceled)	*.35*	*.25*
b.	Imperf., pair	*130.00*	
c.	As "a," imperf., pair	*75.00*	

No. 1518c is precanceled Washington, DC. Columbus, Ohio and Garden City, N.Y. Values for Columbus pair $400, for Garden City pair $850.

MULTICOLOR HUCK PRESS

1519	A923 10c red & blue	.25	.25
a.	Imperf., pair	*35.00*	

Huck press printings often show parts of a joint line, but this feature is not consistent.

ROTARY PRESS PRINTING

1520	A924 10c blue	.25	.25
a.	Untagged (Bureau precanceled)	*5.50*	*1.25*
b.	Imperf., pair	*30.00*	

VETERANS OF FOREIGN WARS ISSUE

75th anniversary of Veterans of Spanish-American and Other Foreign Wars.

V.F.W. Emblem A928

GIORI PRESS PRINTING

1974, Mar. 11		**Perf. 11**	
1525	A928 10c red & dark blue	.25	.25
b.	Blue missing (PS)	—	

ROBERT FROST ISSUE

Robert Frost (1874-1963), Poet — A929

1974, Mar. 26		**Perf. 10½x11**	
1526	A929 10c black	.25	.25

EXPO '74 WORLD'S FAIR ISSUE

EXPO '74 World's Fair "Preserve the Environment," Spokane, Wash., May 4-Nov. 4.

"Cosmic Jumper" A930

PHOTOGRAVURE (Andreotti)

1974, Apr. 18		**Perf. 11**	
1527	A930 10c multicolored	.25	.25

HORSE RACING ISSUE

Kentucky Derby, Churchill Downs, centenary.

Horses Rounding Turn A931

1974, May 4		**Perf. 11x10½**	
1528	A931 10c yellow & multicolored	.25	.25
a.	Blue ("Horse Racing") omitted	*700.00*	
b.	Red ("U.S. postage 10 cents") omitted	*1,750.*	

Beware of stamps offered as No. 1528b that have traces of red.

SKYLAB ISSUE

First anniversary of the launching of Skylab I, honoring all who participated in the Skylab project.

Skylab A932

LITHOGRAPHED, ENGRAVED (Giori)

1974, May 14		**Perf. 11**	
1529	A932 10c multicolored	.25	.25
a.	Vert. pair, imperf. between	—	
c.	Vert. pair, imperf. horiz.	—	

UNIVERSAL POSTAL UNION ISSUE

UPU cent. In the 1st row Nos. 1530-1537 are in sequence as listed. In the 2nd row Nos. 1534-1537 are followed by Nos. 1530-1533. Every row of 8 and every horizontal block of 8 contains all 8 designs. The letter writing designs are from famous works of art; some are details. The quotation on every second stamp, "Letters mingle souls," is from a letter by poet John Donne.

Michelangelo, from School of Athens — A933

Five Feminine Virtues — A934

Old Time Letter Rack — A935

Mlle. La Vergne — A936

Lady Writing Letter — A937

Inkwell and Quill — A938

Mrs. John Douglas — A939

Don Antonio Noreiga — A940

PHOTOGRAVURE (Andreotti)

1974, June 6			
1530	A933 10c multicolored	.25	.25
1531	A934 10c multicolored	.25	.25
1532	A935 10c multicolored	.25	.25
1533	A936 10c multicolored	.25	.25
1534	A937 10c multicolored	.25	.25
1535	A938 10c multicolored	.25	.25
1536	A939 10c multicolored	.25	.25

1537	A940 10c multicolored	.25	.25
a.	Block or strip of 8 (#1530-1537)	*2.00*	*2.00*
b.	As "a," (block), imperf. vert.	*2,500.*	

MINERAL HERITAGE ISSUE

The sequence of stamps in 1st horizontal row is Nos. 1538-1541, 1538-1539. In 2nd row Nos. 1540-1541 are followed by Nos. 1538-1541.

Petrified Wood A941

Tourmaline — A942

Amethyst — A943

Rhodochrosite — A944

1974, June 13			
1538	A941 10c blue & multi	.25	.25
a.	Light blue & yellow (litho.) omitted	—	
1539	A942 10c blue & multi	.25	.25
a.	Light blue (litho.) omitted	—	
b.	Black & purple (engr.) omitted	—	
1540	A943 10c blue & multi	.25	.25
a.	Light blue & yellow (litho.) omitted	—	
1541	A944 10c blue & multi	.25	.25
a.	Block or strip of 4, #1538-1541	*1.00*	*1.00*
b.	As "a," light blue & yellow (litho.) omitted	*1,000.*	—
c.	Light blue (litho.) omitted	—	
d.	Black & red (engr.) omitted	—	
e.	Block of 4, two right stamps being Nos. 1539b and 1541d	*7,000.*	

No. 1541e is usually collected as a transition block of six or larger.

KENTUCKY SETTLEMENT, 200th ANNIV.
Fort Harrod, first settlement in Kentucky.

Fort Harrod — A945

1974, June 15

1542 A945 10c green & multi	.25	.25
a. Dull black (litho.) omitted	475.00	
b. Green (engr. & litho.), black (engr. & litho.) & blue missing (EP)	2,250.	
c. Green (engr.) missing (EP)	3,000.	
d. Green (engr.) & black (litho.) missing (EP)		
f. Blue (litho.) omitted	—	

No. 1542f was caused by an occurrence that seems to be unique for U.S. total color omitted/missing errors. According to the BEP, oil on the printing blanket made a small area unreceptive to the blue ink. No blue at all was printed on one unique error stamp.

AMERICAN REVOLUTION BICENTENNIAL ISSUE
First Continental Congress

Nos. 1543-1544 alternate in 1st row, Nos. 1545-1546 in 2nd row. This arrangement is repeated throughout the pane.

Carpenters' Hall A946

A947

A948

Independence Hall — A949

1974, July 4

1543 A946 10c dark blue & red	.25	.25
1544 A947 10c gray, dark blue & red	.25	.25
1545 A948 10c gray, dark blue & red	.25	.25
1546 A949 10c red & dark blue	.25	.25
a. Block of 4, #1543-1546	1.00	1.00

ENERGY CONSERVATION ISSUE

Publicizing the importance of conserving all forms of energy.

A950

LITHOGRAPHED, ENGRAVED (Giori)
1974, Sept. 23

1547 A950 10c multicolored	.25	.25
a. Blue & orange omitted	600.00	
b. Orange & green omitted	300.00	
c. Green omitted	575.00	

AMERICAN FOLKLORE ISSUE
Legend of Sleepy Hollow

The Headless Horseman in pursuit of Ichabod Crane from "Legend of Sleepy Hollow," by Washington Irving.

Legend of Sleepy Hollow A951

1974, Oct. 10

1548 A951 10c dk bl, blk, org & yel	.25	.25

RETARDED CHILDREN ISSUE

Retarded Children Can Be Helped, theme of annual convention of the National Association of Retarded Citizens.

Retarded Child — A952

GIORI PRESS PRINTING
1974, Oct. 12

1549 A952 10c brown red & dark brown	.25	.25

CHRISTMAS ISSUE

Angel, from Perussis Altarpiece, 1480 — A953

"The Road-Winter," by Currier & Ives — A954

No. 1550, detail from the Perusus altarpiece painted by anonymous French artist, 1480, in Metropolitan Museum of Art, New York City. Currier and Ives print from drawing by Otto Knirsch

PHOTOGRAVURE (Andreotti)
1974, Oct. 23 *Perf. 10½x11*

1550 A953 10c multicolored	.25	.25

Perf. 11x10½

1551 A954 10c multicolored	.25	.25
a. Buff omitted	12.50	

No. 1551a is difficult to identify. Competent expertization is necessary.

Dove Weather Vane — A955

Die Cut, Paper Backing Rouletted
1974, Nov. 15 **Untagged**
Self-adhesive; Inscribed "Precanceled"

1552 A955 10c multicolored	.25	.25
Nos. 1550-1552 (3)	.75	.75

Unused value of No. 1552 is for stamp on rouletted paper backing as issued. Used value is for stamp on piece, with or without postmark. **Most examples are becoming discolored from the adhesive. The Catalogue value is for discolored examples.**

Die cutting includes crossed slashes through dove, applied to prevent removal and re-use of the stamp. The stamp will separate into layers if soaked.

AMERICAN ARTS ISSUE

Benjamin West (1738-1820), painter (No. 1553); Paul Laurence Dunbar (1872-1906), poet (No. 1554); David (Lewelyn) Wark Griffith (1875-1948), motion picture producer (No. 1555).

Benjamin West — A956

Paul Laurence Dunbar — A957

D. W. Griffith & Projector A958

PHOTOGRAVURE (Andreotti)
1975 *Perf. 10½x11*

1553 A956 10c multicolored	.25	.25

Perf. 11

1554 A957 10c multicolored	.25	.25
a. Imperf., pair	800.00	

LITHOGRAPHED, ENGRAVED (Giori)
Perf. 11

1555 A958 10c brown & multicolored	.25	.25
a. Brown (engr.) omitted	425.00	
Nos. 1553-1555 (3)	.75	.75

SPACE ISSUES

US space accomplishments with unmanned craft. Pioneer 10 passed within 81,000 miles of Jupiter, Dec. 10, 1973. Mariner 10 explored Venus and Mercury in 1974 and Mercury again in 1975.

Pioneer 10 Passing Jupiter A959

Mariner 10, Venus & Mercury A960

LITHOGRAPHED, ENGRAVED (Giori)
1975 *Perf. 11*

1556 A959 10c lt yel, dk yel, red, bl & 2 dk blues	.25	.25
a. Red & dark yellow omitted	800.00	
b. Dark blues (engr.) omitted	500.00	
d. Dark yellow omitted		

Imperfs. exist from printer's waste.

1557 A960 10c blk, red, ultra & bister	.25	.25
a. Red omitted	275.00	
b. Ultramarine & bister omitted	1,000.	
d. Red missing (PS)	525.00	—

COLLECTIVE BARGAINING ISSUE

Collective Bargaining law, enacted 1935, in Wagner Act.

"Labor and Management" — A961

PHOTOGRAVURE (Andreotti)
1975, Mar. 13

1558 A961 10c multicolored	.25	.25

Imperforates exist from printer's waste.

AMERICAN BICENTENNIAL ISSUE
Contributors to the Cause

Sybil Ludington, age 16, rallied militia, Apr. 26, 1777; Salem Poor, black freeman, fought in Battle of Bunker Hill; Haym Salomon, Jewish immigrant, raised money to finance Revolutionary War; Peter Francisco, Portuguese-French immigrant, joined Continental Army at 15. Emerald inscription on back, printed beneath gum in water-soluble ink, gives thumbnail sketch of portrayed contributor.

Sybil Ludington A962

Salem Poor A963

Haym Salomon A964

Peter Francisco A965

1975, Mar. 25 *Perf. 11x10½*

1559 A962 8c multicolored	.25	.25
a. Back inscriptions omitted	125.00	
1560 A963 10c multicolored	.25	.25
a. Back inscription omitted	125.00	
b. Black missing (PS)		
1561 A964 10c multicolored	.25	.25
a. Back inscription omitted	125.00	
1562 A965 18c multicolored	.35	.25
Nos. 1559-1562 (4)	1.10	1.00

On No. 1560, two black plates were used. No. 1560b is missing the impression from one of those plates ("Salem Poor - U.S. Bicentennial symbol - Gallant Soldier") due to an upward shift of the horizontal perforations.

Dangerous fakes exist of No. 1561 with red apparently omitted. Professional authentication is mandatory in order to establish such a stamp as a genuine error.

Lexington-Concord Battle, 200th Anniv.

"Birth of Liberty," by Henry Sandham A966

1975, Apr. 19 *Perf. 11*

1563 A966 10c multicolored	.25	.25
a. Vert. pair, imperf. horiz.	300.00	

Bunker Hill Battle, 200th Anniv.

Battle of Bunker
Hill, by John
Trumbull — A967

1975, June 17

1564   A967   10c multicolored   .25   .25

Military Uniforms

Bicentenary of US Military Services.
Nos. 1565-1566 alternate in one row,
Nos. 1567-1568 in next row.

Soldier with
Flintlock Musket,
Uniform
Button — A968

Sailor with
Grappling Hook,
First Navy Jack,
1775 — A969

Marine with
Musket, Full-
rigged
Ship — A970

Militiaman with
Musket, Powder
Horn — A971

1975, July 4

1565   A968   10c multicolored   .25   .25
1566   A969   10c multicolored   .25   .25
1567   A970   10c multicolored   .25   .25
1568   A971   10c multicolored   .25   .25
   a.   Block of 4, #1565-1568   1.00   1.00

APOLLO SOYUZ SPACE ISSUE

Apollo Soyuz space test project,
Russo-American cooperation, launched
July 15; link-up, July 17. Nos. In the 1st
row, No. 1569 is in 1st and 3rd space,
No. 1570 is 2nd space; in the 2nd row
No. 1570 is in 1st and 3rd space, No.
1569 in 2nd space, etc.

Participating US and USSR crews:
Thomas P. Stafford, Donald K. Slayton,
Vance D. Brand, Aleksei A. Leonov,
Valery N. Kubasov.

Apollo & Soyuz After Docking,
Earth — A972

Spacecraft Before Docking, Earth &
Project Emblem — A973

1975, July 15

1569   A972   10c multicolored   .25   .25
1570   A973   10c multicolored   .25   .25
   a.   Pair, #1569-1570   .50   .50
   c.   As "a," vert. pair, imperf.
        horiz.   800.00
   d.   As "a," yellow omitted   900.00

Nos. 1569-1570 totally imperforate are
printer's waste.
See Russia Nos. 4339-4340.

INTERNATIONAL WOMEN'S YEAR ISSUE

International Women's Year 1975.

Worldwide
Equality for
Women
A974

1975, Aug. 26   Perf. 11x10½

1571   A974   10c blue, orange &
           dark blue   .25   .25

US POSTAL SERVICE BICENTENNIAL ISSUE

Nos. 1572-1573 alternate in 1st row,
Nos. 1574-1575 in 2nd row. This
arrangement is repeated throughout the
pane.

Stagecoach
and Trailer
Truck
A975

Old and New Locomotives — A976

Early Mail
Plane and
Jet — A977

Satellite for Transmission of
Mailgrams — A978

1975, Sept. 3

1572   A975   10c multicolored   .25   .25
1573   A976   10c multicolored   .25   .25
1574   A977   10c multicolored   .25   .25
1575   A978   10c multicolored   .25   .25
   a.   Block of 4, #1572-1575   1.00   1.00
   b.   As "a," red "10c" omitted   —

WORLD PEACE THROUGH LAW ISSUE

A prelude to 7th World Law Conference of the World Peace Through Law
Center at Washington, D.C., Oct. 12-17.

Law Book,
Olive
Branch and
Globe
A979

GIORI PRESS PRINTING

1975, Sept. 29   Perf. 11

1576   A979   10c green, Prus-
            sian blue &
            rose brown   .25   .25
   b.   Horiz. pair, imperf vert.   7,500.
   c.   All colors omitted   —

No. 1576c is collected in a horiz. strip as
two errors se-tenant with a partially printed
stamp.

BANKING AND COMMERCE ISSUE

Banking and commerce in the U.S.,
and for the Centennial Convention of
the American Bankers Association.

Engine
Turning,
Indian
Head
Penny &
Morgan
Silver
Dollar
A980

Seated
Liberty
Quarter,
$20 Gold
(Double
Eagle),
Engine
Turning
A981

LITHOGRAPHED, ENGRAVED (Giori)

1975, Oct. 6

1577   A980   10c multicolored   .25   .25
1578   A981   10c multicolored   .25   .25
   a.   Pair, #1577-1578   .50   .50
   b.   As "a," brown & blue (litho)
        omitted   1,400.
   c.   As "a," brown, blue & yellow
        (litho) omitted   1,750.

CHRISTMAS ISSUE

Madonna, by
Domenico
Ghirlandaio
A982

Christmas Card,
by Louis Prang,
1878
A983

PHOTOGRAVURE (Andreotti)

1975, Oct. 14

1579   A982   (10c) multicolored   .25   .25
   a.   Imperf., pair   75.00

          Perf. 11.2

1580   A983   (10c) multicolored   .25   .25
   a.   Imperf., pair   85.00
   c.   Perf. 10.9   .25   .25

         Perf. 10.5x11.3

1580B   A983   (10c) multicolored   .65   .25

AMERICANA ISSUE

Inkwell and
Quill
A984

Speaker's
Stand
A985

Early Ballot
Box
A987

Books,
Bookmark,
Eyeglasses
A988

Dome of
Capitol
A994

Contemplation
of Justice
A995

Early
American
Printing
Press — A996

Torch — A997

Liberty Bell
A998

Eagle and
Shield
A999

Fort McHenry
Flag
A1001

Head, Statue
of Liberty
A1002

Old North
Church,
Boston
A1003

Fort Nisqually
A1004

Sandy Hook
Lighthouse,
NJ — A1005

Morris
Township
School No. 2,
Devils Lake,
ND — A1006

Iron "Betty"
Lamp, 17th-
18th Cent.
A1007

Rush Lamp
and Candle
Holder
A1008

Kerosene
Table Lamp
A1009

Railroad
Conductor's
Lantern,
c. 1850
A1010

ROTARY PRESS PRINTING

1975-81   Perf. 11¼x10½
     Size: 18½x22½mm

1581   A984   1c dk bl,
            grnish   .25   .25
   a.   Untagged (Bureau pre-
        canceled)   4.50   1.50
   c.   White paper, dull gum   —
1582   A985   2c red brn,
            grnish   .25   .25
   a.   Untagged (Bureau pre-
        canceled)   4.50   1.50
   b.   Cream paper ('81)   .25   .25

1584 A987 3c olive, *grnsh* .25 .25
　a. Untagged (Bureau pre-
　　canceled) .75 .50

Values for No. 1584a are for the lines-only precancel. Also known with city precancels, and valued at $100 thus.

1585 A988 4c rose mag,
　　cream .25 .25
　a. Untagged (Bureau pre-
　　canceled) 1.00 .75

The pair with horiz. gutter between also is misperfed through the stamps horizontally.
Values for No. 1585a are for the lines-only precancel. Also known with city precancels, and worth more thus.

Size: 17½x20½mm
Perf. 11x10½ on 3 Sides

1590 A994 9c slate green .45 20.00

From bklt. pane #1623a.

Perf. 10x9¾ on 3 Sides

1590A A994 9c slate green 12.50 50.00

From bklt. pane #1623Bc.

Nos. 1590 and 1590A used are valued with contemporaneous cancels only.

Size: 18½x22½mm
Perf. 11¼x10½

1591 A994 9c sl grn, *gray* .25 .25
　a. Untagged (Bureau pre-
　　canceled) 1.75 1.00

Values for No. 1591a are for the lines-only precancel. Also known with city precancels, and valued at $32.50 thus.

1592 A995 10c violet, *gray* .25 .25
　a. Untagged (Bureau pre-
　　canceled, Chicago) 9.50 5.00
1593 A996 11c orange,
　　gray .25 .25
1594 A997 12c red brown,
　　beige .25 .25

Perf. 11¼x10½ on 2 or 3 Sides

1595 A998 13c brown .30 .25
　a. Booklet pane of 6 2.25 1.50
　b. Booklet pane of 7 + la-
　　bel 2.25 1.50
　c. Booklet pane of 8 2.25 1.50
　d. Booklet pane of 5 + la-
　　bel, Apr. 2, 1976 1.75 1.25
　e. Vert. pair, imperf. btwn.,
　　in #1595c with
　　foldover 1,250.
　g. Horiz. pair, imperf.
　　btwn., in #1595d with
　　foldover —

Nos. 1595e and 1595g resulted from paper foldovers after perforating and before cutting into panes. Beware of printer's waste consisting of complete panes with perfs around all outside edges.

PHOTOGRAVURE (Andreotti)
Perf. 11¼x10½

1596 A999 13c multicolored .25 .25
　a. Imperf., pair 40.00 —
　b. Yellow omitted 75.00

ENGRAVED (Combination Press)

1597 A1001 15c gray, dk bl &
　　red .30 .25
　b. Gray omitted 325.00
　c. Vert. pair, imperf btwn and
　　with natural straight edge
　　at bottom 350.00
　e. Imperf., vert. pair 15.00

ENGRAVED
Perf. 11x10½ on 2 or 3 Sides

1598 A1001 15c gray, dk bl
　　& red .40 .25
　a. Booklet pane of 8 3.75 1.50

Perf. 11¼x10½

1599 A1002 16c blue .35 .25
1603 A1004 24c red, *blue* .50 .25
1604 A1004 28c brown, *blue* .55 .25
1605 A1005 29c blue, *blue* .60 .25
1606 A1006 30c green, *blue* .55 .25

LITHOGRAPHED AND ENGRAVED
Perf. 11

1608 A1007 50c tan, blk &
　　org .85 .25
　a. Black omitted 325.00
　b. Vert. pair, imperf. horiz. 1,200.

Beware of examples offered as No. 1608b that have blind perfs.

1610 A1008 $1 tan, brn, org
　　& yel 2.00 .25
　a. Brown (engraved) omitted 200.00
　b. Tan, orange & yellow
　　omitted 200.00
　c. Brown (engraved) invert-
　　ed 17,500.
1611 A1009 $2 tan, dk grn,
　　org & yel 3.75 .75
1612 A1010 $5 tan, red brn,
　　yel & org 8.50 1.75
　Nos. 1581-1612 (23) 33.85 77.25

Nos. 1590, 1590A, 1595, 1598, 1623 and 1623b were issued only in booklets. All stamps have one or two straight edges.
Years of issue: #1591; 1595-1596, 11c, 24c, 1975. #1590, 1c-4c, 10c, 1977. #1597-1598,

16c, 28c, 29c, $2, 1978. 30c-$1, $5, 1979. 12c, 1981.

Guitar
A1011

Saxhorns
A1012

Drum
A1013

Piano
A1014

Designers: 3.1c, George Mercer. 7.7c, Susan Robb. 7.9c, Bernard Glassman. 10c, Walter Brooks. 15c, V. Jack Ruther.

COIL STAMPS
ENGRAVED

1975-79 **Perf. 10 Vertically**

1613 A1011 3.1c brown
　　('79) .25 .25
　a. Untagged (Bureau pre-
　　canceled, lines only) .35 .35
　b. Imperf., pair 850.00
1614 A1012 7.7c brown
　　('76) .25 .25
　a. Untagged (Bureau pre-
　　canceled) .40 .30
　b. As "a," imperf., pair 1,250.

No. 1614b is precanceled Washington, DC. Also exists with Marion, OH precancel; value $1,950 for pair.

1615 A1013 7.9c carmine
　　('76) .25 .25
　a. Untagged (Bureau pre-
　　canceled) .40 .40
　b. Imperf., pair 400.00
1615C A1014 8.4c dak blue
　　('78) .25 .25
　d. Untagged (Bureau pre-
　　canceled) .50 .40
　e. As "d," pair, imperf.
　　between 45.00
　f. As "d," imperf. pair,
　　shiny gum 15.00

No. 1615Ce is precanceled with lines only. No. 1615Cf is precanceled with lines only (value shown) and also exists in pairs precanceled Newark, N.J. ($25), Brownstown, Ind. ($900), Oklahoma City, Okla. ($1,500.) and Washington, DC ($900).

1616 A994 9c slate
　　green
　　('75) .25 .25
　a. Imperf., pair 125.00
　b. Untagged (Bureau pre-
　　canceled) .75 .75
　c. As "b," imperf., pair 600.00

Value for No. 1616b is for stamp with dull gum.
No. 1616c is precanceled Pleasantville, NY.

1617 A995 10c violet
　　('77) .25 .25
　a. Untagged (Bureau pre-
　　canceled) 1.35 1.35
　b. Imperf., pair 55.00
　c. As "a," imperf pair 3,750.

Values for No. 1617a and 1617b are for stamps with dull gum. These varieties with shiny gum are worth considerably more.

1618 A998 13c brown
　　('75) .25 .25
　a. Untagged (Bureau pre-
　　canceled) .75 .75
　b. Imperf., pair 22.50
　g. Pair, imperf. between 600.00
　h. As "a," imperf., pair —

Value for No. 1618a is for stamp with dull gum.

1618C A1001 15c gray, dk
　　bl & red
　　('78) .75 .25
　d. Imperf., pair 20.00
　e. Pair, imperf. between 100.00
　f. Gray omitted 30.00
1619 A1002 16c ultra ('78) .35 .25
　a. Huck Press Printing .50 .25
　Nos. 1613-1619 (9) 2.85 2.25

No. 1619a (the B press printing) has a white background without bluish tinge, is a fraction of a millimeter smaller than No. 1619 (the Cottrell press printing) and has no joint lines.
See Nos. 1811, 1813, 1816.

13-Star Flag,
Independence
Hall — A1015

Flag over
Capitol — A1016

1975-81 **Perf. 11x10¾**

1622 A1015 13c dk bl, red
　　& brn red .25 .25
　a. Horiz. pair, imperf. be-
　　tween 40.00
　b. Vertical pair, imperf. 300.00
　e. Horiz. pair, imperf. vert. —

No. 1622 was printed on the Multicolored Huck Press. Plate markings are at top or bottom of pane.

Perf. 11¼

1622C A1015 13c dk bl, red
　　& brn red
　　('81) 1.00 .25
　d. Vertical pair, imperf 100.00

No. 1622C was printed on the Combination Press. Plate markings are at sides of pane.

BOOKLET STAMPS
Perf. 11x10½ on 2 or 3 Sides

1977, Mar. 11

1623 A1016 13c blue & red .25 .25
　a. Booklet pane, 1 #1590
　　+ 7 #1623 2.25 2.00
　d. Pair, #1590 & #1623 .70 1.00

Perf. 10x9¾ on 2 or 3 Sides

1623B A1016 13c blue & red .65 .75
　c. Booklet pane, 1 #1590A
　　+ 7 #1623B 17.50 —
　d. Pair, #1590A & #1623B 15.00 15.00

COIL STAMP

1975, Nov. 15 **Perf. 10 Vertically**

1625 A1015 13c dk blue,
　　red &
　　brown red .35 .25
　a. Imperf., pair 20.00

AMERICAN BICENTENNIAL ISSUE
The Spirit of '76

Designed after painting by Archibald M. Willard in Abbot Hall, Marblehead, Massachusetts. Nos. 1629-1631 printed in continuous design.
Left panes contain 3 No. 1631a and one No. 1629; right panes contain one No. 1631 and 3 No. 1631a.

Drummer Boy
A1019

Old Drummer
A1020

Fifer — A1021

PHOTOGRAVURE (Andreotti)

1976, Jan. 1 **Perf. 11**

1629 A1019 13c blue violet &
　　multi .25 .25
　a. Imperf., vert. pair —
1630 A1020 13c blue violet &
　　multi .25 .25
1631 A1021 13c blue violet &
　　multi .25 .25
　a. Strip of 3, #1629-1631 .75 .75
　b. As "a," imperf. 700.00
　c. Imperf., vert. pair, #1631 500.00

INTERPHIL ISSUE

Interphil 76 International Philatelic Exhibition, Philadelphia, Pa., May 29-June 6.

"Interphil
76"
A1022

LITHOGRAPHED, ENGRAVED (Giori)

1976, Jan. 17

1632 A1022 13c dark blue & red
　　(engr.), ultra. &
　　red (litho.) .25 .25
　a. Dark blue & red (engr.) miss-
　　ing (CM) —
　c. Red (engr.) missing (CM) —

State Flags
A1023

Photo.

1976, Feb. 23

1633	A1023	13c	Delaware	.30 .25
1634	A1024	13c	Pennsylvania	.30 .25
1635	A1025	13c	New Jersey	.30 .25
1636	A1026	13c	Georgia	.30 .25
1637	A1027	13c	Connecticut	.30 .25
1638	A1028	13c	Massachu-
setts	.30 .25
1639	A1029	13c	Maryland	.30 .25
1640	A1030	13c	South Caroli-
na	.30 .25
1641	A1031	13c	New Hamp-
shire	.30 .25
1642	A1032	13c	Virginia	.30 .25
1643	A1033	13c	New York	.30 .25
1644	A1034	13c	North Caroli-
na	.30 .25
1645	A1035	13c	Rhode Island	.30 .25
1646	A1036	13c	Vermont	.30 .25
1647	A1037	13c	Kentucky	.30 .25
1648	A1038	13c	Tennessee	.30 .25
1649	A1039	13c	Ohio	.30 .25
1650	A1040	13c	Louisiana	.30 .25
1651	A1041	13c	Indiana	.30 .25
1652	A1042	13c	Mississippi	.30 .25
1653	A1043	13c	Illinois	.30 .25
1654	A1044	13c	Alabama	.30 .25
1655	A1045	13c	Maine	.30 .25
1656	A1046	13c	Missouri	.30 .25
1657	A1047	13c	Arkansas	.30 .25
1658	A1048	13c	Michigan	.30 .25
1659	A1049	13c	Florida	.30 .25
1660	A1050	13c	Texas	.30 .25
1661	A1051	13c	Iowa	.30 .25
1662	A1052	13c	Wisconsin	.30 .25
1663	A1053	13c	California	.30 .25
1664	A1054	13c	Minnesota	.30 .25
1665	A1055	13c	Oregon	.30 .25
1666	A1056	13c	Kansas	.30 .25
1667	A1057	13c	West Virginia	.30 .25
1668	A1058	13c	Nevada	.30 .25
1669	A1059	13c	Nebraska	.30 .25
1670	A1060	13c	Colorado	.30 .25
1671	A1061	13c	North Dakota	.30 .25
1672	A1062	13c	South Dakota	.30 .25
1673	A1063	13c	Montana	.30 .25
1674	A1064	13c	Washington	.30 .25
1675	A1065	13c	Idaho	.30 .25
1676	A1066	13c	Wyoming	.30 .25
1677	A1067	13c	Utah	.30 .25
1678	A1068	13c	Oklahoma	.30 .25
1679	A1069	13c	New Mexico	.30 .25
1680	A1070	13c	Arizona	.30 .25
1681	A1071	13c	Alaska	.30 .25
1682	A1072	13c	Hawaii	.30 .25
		a.	Pane of 50	17.50 15.00

TELEPHONE CENTENNIAL ISSUE

Centenary of first telephone call by Alexander Graham Bell, March 10, 1876.

Bell's
Telephone
Patent
Application
A1073

ENGRAVED (Giori)

1976, Mar. 10

1683	A1073	13c black, purple & red, tan	.25	.25
a.	Black & purple missing (EP)		450.00
b.	Red missing (EP)		—
c.	All colors missing (EP)		—

On No. 1683a, the errors have only tiny traces of red present, so are best collected as a horiz. strip of 5 with 2 or 3 error stamps. No. 1683c also must be collected as a transitional strip.

COMMERCIAL AVIATION ISSUE

50th anniversary of first contract airmail flights: Dearborn, Mich. to Cleveland, Ohio, Feb. 15, 1926; and Pasco, Wash. to Elko, Nev., Apr. 6, 1926.

A1074

PHOTOGRAVURE (Andreotti)

1976, Mar. 19   Tagged   Perf. 11

1684	A1074	13c blue & multicolored	.25	.25

CHEMISTRY ISSUE

Honoring American chemists, in conjunction with the centenary of the American Chemical Society.

A1075

PHOTOGRAVURE (Andreotti)

1976, Apr. 6

1685	A1075	13c multicolored	.25	.25

AMERICAN BICENTENNIAL ISSUES
SOUVENIR SHEETS

Designs, from Left to Right, No. 1686: a, Two British officers. b, Gen. Benjamin Lincoln. c, George Washington. d, John Trumbull, Col. Cobb, von Steuben, Lafayette, Thomas Nelson. e, Alexander Hamilton, John Laurens, Walter Stewart (all vert.).

No. 1687: a, John Adams, Roger Sherman, Robert R. Livingston. b, Jefferson, Franklin. c, Thomas Nelson, Jr., Francis Lewis, John Witherspoon, Samuel Huntington. d, John Hancock, Charles Thomson, Edward Rutledge (a, d, vert., b, c, e, horiz.).

No. 1688: a, Boatsman. b, Washington. c, Flag bearer. d, Men in boat. e, Men on shore (a, d, horiz., b, c, e, vert.).

No. 1689: a, Two officers. b, Washington. c, Officer, black horse. d, Officer, white horse. e, Three soldiers (a, c, e, horiz., b, d, vert.).

LITHOGRAPHED

1976, May 29

1686	A1076	Pane of 5	2.75	2.25
a.-e.		13c multicolored	.40	.40
f.	"USA/13c" omitted on "b," "c" & "d," imperf, tagging omitted		—
g.	"USA/13c" omitted on "a" & "e"		1,750.
h.	Imperf., tagging omitted		500.00	300.00
i.	"USA/13c" omitted on "b," "c" & "d"		2,500.
j.	"USA/13c" double on "b"		500.00
k.	"USA/13c" omitted on "c" & "d"		—
l.	"USA/13c" omitted on "e"		750.00
m.	"USA/13c" omitted, imperf., tagging omitted		475.00
n.	As "g," imperf., tagging omitted		—
o.	"USA/13c" missing on "a" (PS)		—
q.	"USA/13c" omitted on "a"		450.00
r.	Imperf., tagged		750.00
			—

s.	"USA/13c" missing on "b" and "d" (PS)		—
1687	A1077	Pane of 5	3.75	3.25
a.-e.		18c multicolored	.50	.50
f.	Design & marginal inscriptions omitted		2,500.
g.	"USA/18c" omitted on "a" & "c"		550.00	—
h.	"USA/18c" omitted on "b," "d" & "e"		350.00
i.	"USA/18c" omitted on "d"		425.00	475.00
j.	Black omitted in design		1,500.
k.	"USA/18c" omitted, imperf., tagging omitted		1,500.
m.	"USA/18c" omitted on "b" & "e"		500.00
n.	"USA/18c" omitted on "b" & "d"		1,000.
p.	Imperf. (tagged)		1,000.
q.	"USA/18c" missing on "c" (CM)		—
r.	Yellow omitted		5,000.
s.	"USA/18c" missing on "a," "c" and "d" (PS)		—
t.	"USA/18c" missing on "a" and "d" (PS)		300.00
1688	A1078	Pane of 5	4.75	4.25
a.-e.		24c multicolored	.65	.65
f.	"USA/24c" omitted, imperf., tagging omitted		950.00
g.	"USA/24c" omitted on "d" & "e"		400.00	400.00
h.	Design & marginal inscriptions omitted		2,500.
i.	"USA/24c" omitted on "a," "b" & "c"		400.00	400.00
j.	Imperf., tagging omitted		1,250.
k.	"USA/24c" of "d" & "e" inverted		12,500.
l.	As "i," imperf, tagging omitted		3,250.
n.	As No. 1688, perfs inverted and reversed		7,500.
p.	"USA/24c" omitted on "d" and "e" (CM)		—
q.	"USA/24c" omitted on "b" and "c"		—
r.	"USA/24c" omitted on "a"		400.00
s.	As No. 1688, imperf.		400.00
1689	A1079	Pane of 5	5.75	5.25
a.-e.		31c multicolored	.80	.80
f.	"USA/31c" omitted, imperf.		950.00
g.	"USA/31c" omitted on "a" & "c"		375.00
h.	"USA/31c" omitted on "b," "d" & "e"		450.00	—

i.	"USA/31c" omitted on "e"		375.00
j.	Black omitted in design		1,450.
k.	Imperf., tagging omitted		2,000.
l.	"USA/31c" omitted on "b" & "d"		300.00
m.	"USA/31c" omitted on "a," "c" & "e"		750.00
n.	As "m," imperf., tagging omitted		—
p.	As "h," imperf., tagging omitted		1,250.
q.	As "g," imperf., tagging omitted		2,500.
r.	As "d" & "e"		600.00
s.	As "f," tagging omitted		2,000.
t.	"USA/31c" omitted on "d"		500.00
v.	As No. 1689, perfs and tagging inverted		10,000.
w.	"USA/31c" missing on "a," "b," "c" and "d" (PS)		500.00
x.	"USA/31c" missing on "e" (CM)		—
y.	"USA/31c" omitted on "a"		—

Nos. 1686-1689 (4)   17.00

Issued in connection with Interphil 76 International Philatelic Exhibition, Philadelphia, Pa., May 29-June 6. Size of panes: 203x152mm.

A1076

The Surrender of Lord Cornwallis at Yorktown
From a Painting by John Trumbull

A1077

The Declaration of Independence, 4 July 1776 at Philadelphia
From a Painting by John Trumbull

Washington Crossing the Delaware
From a Painting by Emanuel Leutze/Eastman Johnson

A1078

Washington Reviewing His Ragged Army at Valley Forge
From a Painting by William T. Trego

A1079

Benjamin Franklin

American Bicentennial: Benjamin Franklin (1706-1790), deputy postmaster general for the colonies (1753-1774) and statesman. Design based on marble bust by anonymous Italian sculptor after terra cotta bust by Jean Jacques Caffieri, 1777. Map published by R. Sayer and J. Bennett in London.

Franklin & Map of North America, 1776 A1080

LITHOGRAPHED, ENGRAVED (Giori)
1976, June 1

1690	A1080	13c multicolored	.25	.25
a.		Light blue omitted	150.00	

See Canada No. 691.

American Bicentennial Issue

A1081

A1082

A1083

A1084

Declaration of Independence, by John Trumbull
PHOTOGRAVURE (Andreotti)
1976, July 4

1691	A1081	13c multicolored	.30	.25
1692	A1082	13c multicolored	.30	.25
1693	A1083	13c multicolored	.30	.25
1694	A1084	13c multicolored	.30	.25
a.		Strip of 4, #1691-1694	1.20	1.10

OLYMPIC GAMES ISSUE

12th Winter Olympic Games, Innsbruck, Austria, Feb. 4-15, and 21st Summer Olympic Games, Montreal, Canada, July 17-Aug. 1. Nos. 1695-1696 alternate in one row, Nos. 1697-1698 in other row.

Diving — A1085

Skiing — A1086

Running A1087

Skating A1088

1976, July 16

1695	A1085	13c multicolored	.30	.25
1696	A1086	13c multicolored	.30	.25
1697	A1087	13c multicolored	.30	.25
1698	A1088	13c multicolored	.30	.25
a.		Block of 4, #1695-1698	1.20	1.20
b.		As "a," imperf.	375.00	

CLARA MAASS ISSUE

Clara Louise Maass (1876-1901), volunteer in fight against yellow fever, birth centenary.

Clara Maass, Newark German Hospital Pin — A1089

1976, Aug. 18

1699	A1089	13c multicolored	.25	.25
a.		Horiz. pair, imperf. vert.	350.00	
b.		Dark blue missing (PS)	—	

On No. 1699, two blue plates were used. No 1699b is missing the dark blue ("She gave her life") at bottom due to an upward shift of the horizontal perforations.

ADOLPH S. OCHS ISSUE

Adolph S. Ochs, Publisher of the NY Times, 1896-1935 A1090

GIORI PRESS PRINTING
1976, Sept. 18

1700	A1090	13c black & gray	.25	.25

CHRISTMAS ISSUE

Nativity, by John Singleton Copley A1091

Winter Pastime, by Nathaniel Currier A1092

PHOTOGRAVURE (Andreotti)
1976, Oct. 27

1701	A1091	13c multicolored	.25	.25
a.		Imperf., pair	85.00	
1702	A1092	13c multi, overall tagging	.25	.25
a.		Imperf., pair	75.00	

COMBINATION PRESS

1703	A1092	13c multicolored	.25	.25
a.		Imperf., pair	75.00	
b.		Vert. pair, imperf. between	275.00	
d.		Red omitted	500.00	
e.		Yellow omitted	—	

No. 1702 has overall tagging. Lettering at base is black and usually ½mm below design. As a rule, no "snowflaking" in sky or pond. Pane of 50 has margins on 4 sides with slogans. Plate Nos. 37465-37478.

No. 1703 has block tagging the size of printed area. Lettering at base is gray black and usually ¾mm below design. "Snowflaking" generally in sky and pond. Plate Nos. 37617-37621 or 37634-37638.

Examples of No. 1703 are known with various amounts of red or yellow missing. Nos. 1703d-1703e are stamps with the colors totally omitted. Expertization is recommended.

AMERICAN BICENTENNIAL ISSUE
Washington at Princeton

Washington's Victory over Lord Cornwallis at Princeton, N.J., bicentenary.

Washington, Nassau Hall, Hessians, 13-Star Flag — A1093

1977, Jan. 3

1704	A1093	13c multicolored	.25	.25
a.		Horiz. pair, imperf. vert.	425.00	
b.		Black (inscriptions) missing (PS)	—	

SOUND RECORDING ISSUE

Centenary of the invention of the phonograph by Thomas Alva Edison and development of sophisticated recording industry.

Tin Foil Phonograph A1094

LITHOGRAPHED, ENGRAVED (Giori)
1977, Mar. 23

1705	A1094	13c black & multi	.25	.25

AMERICAN FOLK ART SERIES
Pueblo Pottery

Pueblo art, 1880-1920, from Museums in New Mexico, Arizona and Colorado.

Zia — A1095

San Ildefonso A1096

Hopi — A1097

Acoma — A1098

PHOTOGRAVURE (Andreotti)
1977, Apr. 13

1706	A1095	13c multicolored	.25	.25
1707	A1096	13c multicolored	.25	.25
1708	A1097	13c multicolored	.25	.25
1709	A1098	13c multicolored	.25	.25
a.		Block or strip of 4, #1706-1709	1.00	1.00
b.		As "a," imperf. vert.	1,250.	

LINDBERGH FLIGHT ISSUE

Charles A. Lindbergh's solo transatlantic flight from New York to Paris, 50th anniversary.

Spirit of St. Louis A1099

1977, May 20

1710	A1099	13c multicolored	.25	.25
a.		Imperf., pair	700.00	

COLORADO STATEHOOD ISSUE

Issued to honor Colorado as the "Centennial State." It achieved statehood in 1876.

Columbine & Rocky Mountains — A1100

1977, May 21

1711	A1100	13c multicolored	.25	.25
a.		Horiz. pair, imperf. between and with natural straight edge at right	650.00	
b.		Horiz. pair, imperf. vertically	500.00	
c.		Perf. 11.2	.70	.25

BUTTERFLY ISSUE

Nos. 1712-1713 alternate in 1st row, Nos. 1714-1715 in 2nd row. This arrangement is repeated throughout the pane. Butterflies represent different geographic US areas.

Swallowtail A1101

Checkerspot — A1102

Dogface A1103

Orange Tip A1104

			Tagged	*Perf. 11*
1977, June 6				
1712	A1101	13c tan & multi	.25	.25
1713	A1102	13c tan & multi	.25	.25
1714	A1103	13c tan & multi	.25	.25
1715	A1104	13c tan & multi	.25	.25
a.		Block of 4, #1712-1715	1.00	1.00
b.		As "a," imperf. horiz.	9,500.	

AMERICAN BICENTENNIAL ISSUES
Marquis de Lafayette

200th anniversary of Lafayette's Landing on the coast of South Carolina, north of Charleston.

Marquis de Lafayette
A1105

GIORI PRESS PRINTING
1977, June 13

1716	A1105	13c blue, black & red	.25	.25
a.		Red missing (PS)	250.00	

Skilled Hands for Independence

Nos. 1717-1718 alternate in 1st row, Nos. 1719-1720 in 2nd row. This arrangement is repeated throughout the pane.

Seamstress
A1106

Blacksmith
A1107

Wheelwright — A1108

Leatherworker — A1109

1977, July 4

1717	A1106	13c multicolored	.25	.25
1718	A1107	13c multicolored	.25	.25
1719	A1108	13c multicolored	.25	.25
1720	A1109	13c multicolored	.25	.25
a.		Block of 4, #1717-1720	1.00	1.00

PEACE BRIDGE ISSUE

50th anniversary of the Peace Bridge, connecting Buffalo (Fort Porter), N.Y. and Fort Erie, Ontario.

Peace Bridge & Dove
A1110

ENGRAVED
1977, Aug. 4   *Perf. 11x10½*

1721	A1110	13c blue	.25	.25

AMERICAN BICENTENNIAL ISSUE
Battle of Oriskany

200th anniv. of the Battle of Oriskany, American Militia led by Brig. Gen. Nicholas Herkimer (1728-77).

Herkimer at Oriskany, by Yohn
A1111

PHOTOGRAVURE (Andreotti)
1977, Aug. 6   *Perf. 11*

1722	A1111	13c multicolored	.25	.25

ENERGY ISSUE

Conservation and development of nation's energy resources. Nos. 1723-1724 se-tenant vertically.

Energy Conservation — A1112

Energy Development — A1113

1977, Oct. 20

1723	A1112	13c multicolored	.25	.25
1724	A1113	13c multicolored	.25	.25
a.		Pair, #1723-1724	.50	.50

ALTA CALIFORNIA ISSUE

Founding of El Pueblo de San José de Guadalupe, first civil settlement in Alta California, 200th anniversary.

Farm Houses
A1114

LITHOGRAPHED, ENGRAVED (Giori)
1977, Sept. 9   **Tagged**   *Perf. 11*

1725	A1114	13c black & multi	.25	.25

AMERICAN BICENTENNIAL ISSUE
Articles of Confederation

200th anniversary of drafting the Articles of Confederation, York Town, Pa.

Members of Continental Congress in Conference
A1115

ENGRAVED (Giori)
1977, Sept. 30

1726	A1115	13c red & brn, cream	.25	.25
b.		Red omitted	500.00	
c.		Red & brown omitted	300.00	

No. 1726b also has most of the brown omitted. No. 1726c must be collected as a transition multiple, certainly with No. 1726b and preferably also with No. 1726.

TALKING PICTURES, 50th ANNIV.

Movie Projector and Phonograph
A1116

LITHOGRAPHED, ENGRAVED (Giori)
1977, Oct. 6

1727	A1116	13c multicolored	.25	.25

AMERICAN BICENTENNIAL ISSUE
Surrender at Saratoga

200th anniversary of Gen. John Burgoyne's surrender at Saratoga.

Surrender of Burgoyne, by John Trumbull
A1117

PHOTOGRAVURE (Andreotti)
1977, Oct. 7

1728	A1117	13c multicolored	.25	.25

CHRISTMAS ISSUE

Washington at Valley Forge
A1118

Rural Mailbox
A1119

PHOTOGRAVURE (Combination Press)
1977, Oct. 21

1729	A1118	13c multicolored	.25	.25
a.		Imperf., pair	55.00	

See Combination Press note after No. 1703.

PHOTOGRAVURE (Andreotti)
1977, Oct. 21

1730	A1119	13c multicolored	.25	.25
a.		Imperf., pair	175.00	

CARL SANDBURG ISSUE

Carl Sandburg (1878-1967), poet, biographer and collector of American folk songs, birth centenary.

Carl Sandburg, by William A. Smith, 1952 — A1120

GIORI PRESS PRINTING
1978, Jan. 6

1731	A1120	13c black & brown	.25	.25
a.		Brown omitted	1,750.	
c.		All colors omitted		

No. 1731c is tagged and has a faint black tagging ghost. Authentication is advised.

CAPTAIN COOK ISSUE

Capt. James Cook, 200th anniversary of his arrival in Hawaii, at Waimea, Kauai, Jan. 20, 1778, and of his anchorage in Cook Inlet, near Anchorage, Alaska, June 1, 1778. Nos. 1732-1733 printed in panes of 50, containing 25 each of Nos. 1732-1733 including 5 No. 1733b.

Capt. Cook, by Nathaniel Dance, 1776 — A1121

"Resolution" and "Discovery," by John Webber — A1122

1978, Jan. 20

1732	A1121	13c dark blue	.25	.25
1733	A1122	13c green	.25	.25
a.		Vert. pair, imperf. between	1,000.	
b.		Pair, #1732-1733	.50	.50
c.		As "b," imperf. between	4,000.	

Indian Head Penny, 1877
A1123

Eagle
A1124

Roses — A1126

ENGRAVED (Giori)
1978

1734	A1123	13c brown & blue green, *bister,* Jan. 11, 1978	.25	.25
a.		Horiz. pair, imperf. vert.	175.00	

PHOTOGRAVURE (Andreotti)

1735	A1124	(15c) orange, *May 22, 1978*	.30	.25
a.		Imperf., pair	70.00	
b.		Vert. pair, imperf. horiz.	500.00	
c.		Perf. 11.2	.35	.25

BOOKLET STAMPS
ENGRAVED
Perf. 11x10½ on 2 or 3 Sides

1736	A1124	(15c) orange	.30	.25
a.		Booklet pane of 8, *May 22, 1978*	2.50	1.50
c.		Vert. pair, imperf. btwn., in #1736a with foldover	1,000.	

Perf. 10 on 2 or 3 Sides

1737	A1126	15c multi	.30	.25
a.		Booklet pane of 8, *July 11, 1978*	2.50	2.00
b.		Imperf, pair	450.00	
c.		As "a," imperf	2,250.	

Robertson Windmill, Williamsburg
A1127

Old Windmill, Portsmouth
A1128

Cape Cod Windmill, Eastham
A1129

Dutch Mill, Batavia
A1130

Southwestern Windmill — A1131

BOOKLET STAMPS
ENGRAVED
Perf. 11 on 2 or 3 Sides

1980, Feb. 7

1738	A1127	15c sepia, *yellow*	.30	.25
1739	A1128	15c sepia, *yellow*	.30	.25
1740	A1129	15c sepia, *yellow*	.30	.25
1741	A1130	15c sepia, *yellow*	.30	.25
1742	A1131	15c sepia, *yellow*	.30	.25
a.		Booklet pane of 10, 2 each #1738-1742	3.50	3.00
b.		Strip of 5, #1738-1742	1.50	1.40

COIL STAMP

1978, May 22   *Perf. 10 Vert.*

1743	A1124	(15c) orange	.30	.25
a.		Imperf., pair	65.00	

No. 1743a is valued in the grade of fine.

BLACK HERITAGE SERIES

Harriet Tubman (1820-1913), born a slave, helped more than 300 slaves escape to freedom.

Harriet Tubman (1820-1913), Cart Carrying Slaves — A1133

PHOTOGRAVURE (Andreotti)

1978, Feb. 1   *Perf. 10½x11*

1744	A1133	13c multicolored	.25	.25

AMERICAN FOLK ART SERIES
Quilts
Basket Design

A1134

A1135

A1136

A1137

1978, Mar. 8   *Perf. 11*

1745	A1134	13c multicolored	.25	.25
1746	A1135	13c multicolored	.25	.25
1747	A1136	13c multicolored	.25	.25
1748	A1137	13c multicolored	.25	.25
a.		Block of 4, #1745-1748	1.00	1.00

AMERICAN DANCE ISSUE

Ballet A1138

Theater A1139

Folk Dance A1140

Modern Dance A1141

1978, Apr. 26

1749	A1138	13c multicolored	.25	.25
1750	A1139	13c multicolored	.25	.25
1751	A1140	13c multicolored	.25	.25
1752	A1141	13c multicolored	.25	.25
a.		Block of 4, #1749-1752	1.00	1.00

AMERICAN BICENTENNIAL ISSUE

French Alliance, signed in Paris, Feb. 6, 1778 and ratified by Continental Congress, May 4, 1778.

Louis XVI and Franklin, Porcelain Sculpture by C. G. Sauvage A1142

GIORI PRESS PRINTING

1978, May 4

1753	A1142	13c blue, black & red	.25	.25
a.		Red missing (PS)	—	

EARLY CANCER DETECTION ISSUE

George Papanicolaou, M.D. (1883-1962), cytologist and developer of Pap Test, early cancer detection in women.

Dr. George Papanicolaou (1883-1962) A1143

ENGRAVED

1978, May 18   *Perf. 10½x11*

1754	A1143	13c brown	.25	.25

PERFORMING ARTS SERIES

Jimmie Rodgers (1897-1933), the "Singing Brakeman, Father of Country Music" (No. 1755); George M. Cohan (1878-1942), actor and playwright (No. 1756).

Jimmie Rodgers and Locomotive A1144

George M. Cohan, "Yankee Doodle Dandy" and Stars A1145

PHOTOGRAVURE (Andreotti)

1978   *Perf. 11*

1755	A1144	13c multicolored	.25	.25
1756	A1145	15c multicolored	.30	.25

CAPEX ISSUE

CAPEX '78, Canadian International Philatelic Exhibition, Toronto, Ont., June 9-18.

Wildlife from Canadian-U.S. Border — A1146

LITHOGRAPHED, ENGRAVED (Giori)

1978, June 10

1757	A1146	Block of 8, multicolored	2.00	2.00
a.		13c Cardinal	.25	.25
b.		13c Mallard	.25	.25
c.		13c Canada goose	.25	.25
d.		13c Blue jay	.25	.25
e.		13c Moose	.25	.25
f.		13c Chipmunk	.25	.25
g.		13c Red fox	.25	.25
h.		13c Raccoon	.25	.25
i.		As No. 1757, yellow, green, red, brown, blue, black (litho) omitted	6,000.	
j.		Strip of 4 (a-d), imperf. vert.	5,000.	
k.		Strip of 4 (e-h), imperf. vert.	2,000.	
l.		As No. 1757, "d" and "h" with black (engr.) omitted	—	
m.		As No. 1757, "b" with blue missing (PS)	—	
o.		Strip of 4 (e-h), all colors except black missing on "e," "f" and "g," all colors except black and brown missing on "h" (PS)	1,250.	
p.		As No. 1757, yellow, red, brown omitted, pane of 48	—	

No. 1757k is worth more when contained in the block of 8. Value is for strip only.

PHOTOGRAPHY ISSUE

Photography's contribution to communications and understanding.

Photographic Equipment A1147

PHOTOGRAVURE (Andreotti)

1978, June 26

1758	A1147	15c multicolored	.30	.25

VIKING MISSIONS TO MARS ISSUE

Second anniv. of landing of Viking 1 on Mars.

Viking 1 Lander Scooping Up Soil on Mars A1148

LITHOGRAPHED, ENGRAVED (Giori)

1978, July 20

1759	A1148	15c multicolored	.30	.25

WILDLIFE CONSERVATION

Nos. 1760-1761 alternate in one horizontal row. Nos. 1762-1763 in the next.

Great Gray Owl — A1149

Saw-whet Owl — A1150

Barred Owl — A1151

Great Horned Owl — A1152

1978, Aug. 26

1760	A1149	15c multicolored	.30	.25
1761	A1150	15c multicolored	.30	.25
1762	A1151	15c multicolored	.30	.25
1763	A1152	15c multicolored	.30	.25
a.		Block of 4, #1760-1763	1.25	1.25
c.		As "a," yellow and magenta (litho) omitted	—	

Two panes of No. 1763c have been reported. On one pane, the black (engr.) is shifted to the left.

AMERICAN TREES ISSUE

Giant Sequoia A1153

White Pine A1154

White Oak
A1155

Gray Birch
A1156

PHOTOGRAVURE (Andreotti)

1978, Oct. 9

1764	A1153	15c multicolored	.30	.25
1765	A1154	15c multicolored	.30	.25
1766	A1155	15c multicolored	.30	.25
1767	A1156	15c multicolored	.30	.25
a.		Block of 4, #1764-1767	1.25	1.25
b.		As "a," imperf. horiz.	17,500.	

No. 1767b is unique.

CHRISTMAS ISSUE

Madonna and
Child with
Cherubim, by
Andrea della
Robbia
A1157

Child on
Hobby-horse
and
Christmas
Trees
A1158

No. 1768, after terra cotta sculpture in
National Gallery, Washington, D.C.

1978, Oct. 18   *Perf. 11*

1768	A1157	15c blue & multi	.30	.25
a.		Imperf., pair	70.00	

Value for No. 1768a is for an uncreased pair.

1769	A1158	15c red & multi	.30	.25
a.		Imperf., pair	75.00	
b.		Vert. pair, imperf. horiz.	1,000.	

ROBERT F. KENNEDY ISSUE

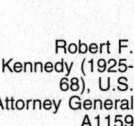

Robert F.
Kennedy (1925-
68), U.S.
Attorney General
A1159

ENGRAVED

1979, Jan. 12

1770	A1159	15c blue	.35	.25

BLACK HERITAGE SERIES

Dr. Martin Luther King, Jr. (1929-
1968), Civil Rights leader.

Dr. Martin Luther
King, Jr. (1929-68),
and Civil Rights
Marchers — A1160

PHOTOGRAVURE (Andreotti)

1979, Jan. 13

1771	A1160	15c multicolored	.40	.25
a.		Imperf., pair	900.00	

INTERNATIONAL YEAR OF THE CHILD ISSUE

Children
A1161

ENGRAVED

1979, Feb. 15

1772	A1161	15c orange red	.30	.25

LITERARY ARTS SERIES

John
Steinbeck — A1162

1979, Feb. 27   *Perf. 10½x11*

1773	A1162	15c dark blue	.30	.25

ALBERT EINSTEIN ISSUE

Albert
Einstein — A1163

1979, Mar. 4

1774	A1163	15c chocolate	.30	.25

AMERICAN FOLK ART SERIES

Pennsylvania Toleware, c. 1800.

Coffeepot
A1164

Tea
Caddy — A1165

Sugar
Bowl — A1166

Coffeepot
A1167

PHOTOGRAVURE (Andreotti)

1979, Apr. 19   *Perf. 11*

1775	A1164	15c multicolored	.30	.25
1776	A1165	15c multicolored	.30	.25
1777	A1166	15c multicolored	.30	.25
1778	A1167	15c multicolored	.30	.25
a.		Block of 4, #1775-1778	1.25	1.25
b.		As "a," imperf. horiz.	2,000.	

AMERICAN ARCHITECTURE SERIES

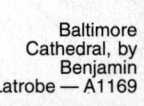

Virginia Rotunda,
by Thomas
Jefferson
A1168

Baltimore
Cathedral, by
Benjamin
Latrobe — A1169

Boston State
House, by
Charles Bulfinch
A1170

Philadelphia
Exchange, by
William
Strickland
A1171

ENGRAVED (Giori)

1979, June 4

1779	A1168	15c blk & brick red	.30	.25
1780	A1169	15c blk & brick red	.30	.25
1781	A1170	15c blk & brick red	.30	.25
1782	A1171	15c blk & brick red	.30	.25
a.		Block of 4, #1779-1782	1.25	1.25

ENDANGERED FLORA ISSUE

Persistent
Trillium
A1172

Hawaiian Wild
Broadbean
A1173

Contra Costa
Wallflower
A1174

Antioch Dunes
Evening
Primrose
A1175

PHOTOGRAVURE (Andreotti)

1979, June 7

1783	A1172	15c multicolored	.30	.25
1784	A1173	15c multicolored	.30	.25
1785	A1174	15c multicolored	.30	.25
1786	A1175	15c multicolored	.30	.25
a.		Block of 4, #1783-1786	1.25	1.25
b.		As "a," imperf.	200.00	

SEEING EYE DOGS ISSUE

1st guide dog program in the US,
50th anniv.

German Shepherd
Leading
Man — A1176

PHOTOGRAVURE (Combination Press)

1979, June 15

1787	A1176	15c multicolored	.30	.25
a.		Imperf., pair	325.00	

SPECIAL OLYMPICS ISSUE

Special Olympics for special children,
Brockport, N.Y., Aug. 8-13.

Child Holding
Winner's
Medal — A1177

PHOTOGRAVURE (Andreotti)

1979, Aug. 9

1788	A1177	15c multicolored	.30	.25

JOHN PAUL JONES ISSUE

John Paul Jones (1747-1792), Naval
Commander, American Revolution.

John Paul Jones, by
Charles Willson
Peale — A1178

PHOTOGRAVURE (Champlain)

1979, Sept. 23   *Perf. 11x12*

1789	A1178	15c multi	.30	.25
c.		Vert. pair, imperf. horiz.	125.00	

Imperforates on gummed stamp paper,
including gutter pairs and blocks, are proofs
from the ABNCo. archives. See No. 1789P in
Proofs section of the Scott United States Specialized Catalogue.

Perf. 11

1789A	A1178	15c multi	.55	.25
d.		Vertical pair, imperf. horiz.	115.00	

Perf. 12

1789B	A1178	15c multi	3,000.	3,500.

OLYMPIC GAMES ISSUE

22nd Summer Olympic Games, Moscow, July 19-Aug. 3, 1980. Nos. 1791-1792 alternate in one horizontal row, Nos. 1793-1794 in next.

Javelin — A1179

Running
A1180

Swimming
A1181

Rowing
A1182

Equestrian
A1183

PHOTOGRAVURE

1979, Sept. 5			**Perf. 11**	
1790	A1179	10c multicolored	.25	.25

1979, Sept. 28				
1791	A1180	15c multicolored	.30	.25
1792	A1181	15c multicolored	.30	.25
1793	A1182	15c multicolored	.30	.25
1794	A1183	15c multicolored	.30	.25
a.		Block of 4, #1791-1794	1.25	1.25
b.		As "a," imperf.	1,000.	

OLYMPIC GAMES ISSUE

13th Winter Olympic Games, Lake Placid, N.Y., Feb. 12-24. Nos. 1795-1796 alternate in one horizontal row, Nos. 1797-1798 in next.

Speed
Skating
A1184

Downhill
Skiing
A1185

Ski Jump
A1186

Ice Hockey
A1187

1980, Feb. 1			**Perf. 11¼x10½**	
1795	A1184	15c multicolored	.35	.25
1796	A1185	15c multicolored	.35	.25
1797	A1186	15c multicolored	.35	.25
1798	A1187	15c multicolored	.35	.25
b.		Block of 4, #1795-1798	1.50	1.40
		Perf. 11		
1795A	A1184	15c multicolored	1.10	.60
1796A	A1185	15c multicolored	1.10	.60
1797A	A1186	15c multicolored	1.10	.60
1798A	A1187	15c multicolored	1.10	.60
c.		Block of 4, #1795A-1798A	4.50	3.50

CHRISTMAS ISSUE

Virgin and
Child, by
Gerard David
A1188

Santa Claus,
Christmas
Tree
Ornament
A1189

No. 1799 is designed after a painting in National Gallery of Art, Washington, D.C.

PHOTOGRAVURE (Andreotti)

1979, Oct. 18			**Perf. 11**	
1799	A1188	15c multicolored	.30	.25
a.		Imperf., pair	70.00	
b.		Vert. pair, imperf. horiz.	450.00	
c.		Vert. pair, imperf. between	950.00	
		Perf. 11x10½		
1800	A1189	15c multicolored	.30	.25
a.		Green & yellow omitted	450.00	
b.		Green, yellow & tan omitted	400.00	
c.		Vert. se-tenant pair, #1800a & 1800b	850.00	

Nos. 1800a and 1800b always have the remaining colors misaligned.
Nos. 1800a, 1800b and 1800c are valued in the grade of fine.

VALUES FOR HINGED STAMPS AFTER NO. 771

This catalogue does not value unused stamps after No. 771 in hinged condition. Hinged unused stamps from No. 772 to the present are worth considerably less than the values given for unused stamps, which are for never-hinged examples.

PERFORMING ARTS SERIES

Will Rogers (1879-1935), Actor and Humorist — A1190

1979, Nov. 4	**Tagged**		**Perf. 11**	
1801	A1190	15c multicolored	.30	.25
a.		Imperf., pair	135.00	

VIETNAM VETERANS ISSUE

A tribute to veterans of the Vietnam War.

Ribbon for
Viet Nam
Service
Medal
A1191

1979, Nov. 11				
1802	A1191	15c multicolored	.30	.25

PERFORMING ARTS SERIES

W.C. Fields (1880-1946), actor and comedian.

W.C. Fields (1880-1946), Actor and Comedian — A1192

PHOTOGRAVURE

1980, Jan. 29				
1803	A1192	15c multicolored	.30	.25
a.		Imperf., pair	—	

BLACK HERITAGE SERIES

Benjamin Banneker (1731-1806), astronomer and mathematician.

Benjamin Banneker (1731-1806), Astronomer and Mathematician, Transverse — A1193

1980, Feb. 15				
1804	A1193	15c multicolored	.30	.25
a.		Horiz. pair, imperf. vert.	275.00	

Imperfs, including gutter pairs and blocks, exist from printer's waste. These have been fraudulently perforated to simulate No. 1804a. Genuine examples of No. 1804a do not have colors misregistered.

NATIONAL LETTER WRITING WEEK ISSUE

National Letter Writing Week, Feb. 24-Mar. 1. Nos. 1805-1810 are printed vertically se-tenant.

Letters Preserve
Memories
A1194

P.S. Write Soon
A1195

Letters Lift
Spirits
A1196

Letters Shape
Opinions
A1197

1980, Feb. 25				
1805	A1194	15c multicolored	.30	.25
1806	A1195	15c purple & multi	.30	.25
1807	A1196	15c multicolored	.30	.25
1808	A1195	15c green & multi	.30	.25
1809	A1197	15c multicolored	.30	.25
1810	A1195	15c red & multi	.30	.25
a.		Vertical strip of 6, #1805-1810	1.85	2.00
		Nos. 1805-1810 (6)	1.80	1.50

AMERICANA TYPE

Weaver
Violins — A1199

COIL STAMPS

1980-81	**Engr.**		**Perf. 10 Vertically**	
1811	A984	1c dk blue, grnish	.25	.25
a.		Imperf., pair	60.00	
1813	A1199	3.5c pur, yel	.25	.25
a.		Untagged (Bureau precanceled, lines only)	.25	.25
b.		Imperf., pair	125.00	
1816	A997	12c red brown, beige ('81)	.25	.25
a.		Untagged (Bureau precanceled), red brown, beige	1.25	1.25
b.		Imperf., pair	135.00	
c.		As "a," brownish red, reddish beige	1.25	1.25
		Nos. 1811-1816 (3)	.75	.75

A1207

PHOTOGRAVURE

1981, Mar. 15	**Tagged**		**Perf. 11x10½**	
1818	A1207	(18c) violet	.35	.25

BOOKLET STAMP
ENGRAVED
Perf. 10 on 2 or 3 Sides

1819	A1207	(18c) violet	.40	.25
a.		Booklet pane of 8	3.50	2.25

COIL STAMP
Perf. 10 Vert.

1820	A1207	(18c) violet	.40	.25
a.		Imperf., pair	75.00	

FRANCES PERKINS ISSUE

Frances Perkins (1882-1965), Secretary of Labor, 1933-1945 (first woman cabinet member).

Frances
Perkins — A1208

ENGRAVED

1980, Apr. 10			**Perf. 10½x11**	
1821	A1208	15c Prussian blue	.30	.25

DOLLEY MADISON ISSUE

Dolley Madison (1768-1849), First Lady, 1809-1817.

Dolley Madison — A1209

1980, May 20			**Perf. 11**	
1822	A1209	15c red brown & sepia	.30	.25
a.		Red brown missing (PS)	575.00	

EMILY BISSELL ISSUE

Emily Bissell (1861-1948), social worker; introduced Christmas seals in United States.

Emily Bissell — A1210

1980, May 31

1823	A1210	15c black & red	.30	.25
a.		Vert. pair, imperf. horiz.	250.00	
b.		All colors missing (EP)	—	
c.		Red missing (FO)	—	

HELEN KELLER ISSUE

Helen Keller (1880-1968), blind and deaf writer and lecturer taught by Anne Sullivan (1867-1936).

Helen Keller and Anne Sullivan — A1211

LITHOGRAPHED AND ENGRAVED

1980, June 27

1824	A1211	15c multicolored	.30	.25

VETERANS ADMINISTRATION, 50th ANNIV.

Veterans Administration Emblem — A1212

PHOTOGRAVURE

Plates of 200 subjects in four panes of 50.

1980, July 21

1825	A1212	15c car & vio blue	.30	.25
a.		Horiz. pair, imperf. vert.	375.00	

BERNARDO DE GALVEZ ISSUE

Gen. Bernardo de Galvez (1746-1786), helped defeat British in Battle of Mobile, 1780.

Gen. Bernardo de Galvez — A1213

LITHOGRAPHED & ENGRAVED

1980, July 23

1826	A1213	15c multicolored	.30	.25
a.		Red, brown & blue (engr.) omitted	550.00	
b.		Light yellow, red, blue & brown (litho.) omitted	550.00	

CORAL REEFS ISSUE

Brain Coral, Beaugregory Fish A1214

Elkhorn Coral, Porkfish A1215

Chalice Coral, Moorish Idol Fish — A1216

Finger Coral, Sabertooth Blenny Fish — A1217

PHOTOGRAVURE

1980, Aug. 26

1827	A1214	15c multi	.30	.25
1828	A1215	15c multi	.30	.25
1829	A1216	15c multi	.30	.25
1830	A1217	15c multi	.30	.25
a.		Block of 4, #1827-1830	1.25	1.10
b.		As "a," imperf.	350.00	
c.		As "a," vert. imperf. between	1,750.	
d.		As "a," imperf. vert.	2,750.	

ORGANIZED LABOR ISSUE

American Bald Eagle — A1218

1980, Sept. 1

1831	A1218	15c multi	.30	.25
a.		Imperf., pair	275.00	

LITERARY ARTS SERIES

Edith Wharton (1862-1937), novelist.

Edith Wharton — A1219

ENGRAVED

1980, Sept. 5   **Perf. 10½x11**

1832	A1219	15c purple	.30	.25

EDUCATION ISSUE

"Homage to the Square: Glow," by Josef Albers — A1220

PHOTOGRAVURE

1980, Sept. 12   **Perf. 11**

1833	A1220	15c multi	.30	.25
a.		Horiz. pair, imperf. vert.	150.00	

AMERICAN FOLK ART SERIES

Pacific Northwest Indian Masks

Heiltsuk, Bella Bella Tribe — A1221

Chilkat Tlingit Tribe — A1222

Tlingit Tribe — A1223

Bella Coola Tribe — A1224

1980, Sept. 25

1834	A1221	15c multi	.35	.25
1835	A1222	15c multi	.35	.25
1836	A1223	15c multi	.35	.25
1837	A1224	15c multi	.35	.25
a.		Block of 4, #1834-1837	1.50	1.25

AMERICAN ARCHITECTURE SERIES

Smithsonian Institution, by James Renwick A1225

Trinity Church, Boston, by Henry Hobson Richardson A1226

Pennsylvania Academy of Fine Arts, by Frank Furness — A1227

Lyndhurst, Tarrytown, NY, by Alexander Jackson Davis A1228

ENGRAVED (Giori)

1980, Oct. 9

1838	A1225	15c black & red	.30	.25
a.		Red missing (PS)	—	
1839	A1226	15c black & red	.30	.25
1840	A1227	15c black & red	.30	.25
1841	A1228	15c black & red	.30	.25
a.		Block of 4, #1838-1841	1.25	1.25
b.		As "a," red missing on Nos. 1838, 1839 (PS)	400.00	

CHRISTMAS ISSUE

Madonna and Child A1229

Wreath, Toys on Windowsill A1230

Design of No. 1842 after Epiphany Window, Washington Cathedral.

PHOTOGRAVURE

1980, Oct. 31

1842	A1229	15c multi	.30	.25
a.		Imperf., pair	40.00	

PHOTOGRAVURE (Combination Press)

1843	A1230	15c multi	.30	.25
a.		Imperf., pair	35.00	
b.		Buff omitted	22.50	
c.		Vert. pair, imperf. horiz.	—	
d.		Horiz. pair, imperf. between	3,250.	

No. 1843b is difficult to identify and should have a competent certificate.

GREAT AMERICANS ISSUE

Dorothea Dix A1231   Igor Stravinsky A1232

Henry Clay A1233   Carl Schurz A1234

Pearl Buck A1235   Walter Lippmann A1236

Abraham Baldwin A1237   Henry Knox A1238

A1239

A1240

A1241

A1242

A1243

A1244

A1245

A1246

A1247

A1248

A1249

A1250

A1251

A1252

A1253

A1254

A1255

A1256

ENGRAVED
Perf. 11x10½, 11 (1c, 6c-11c, 14c,
No. 1862, 22c, 30c, 39c, 40c, 50c)
1980-85

1844	A1231	1c black ('83)	.25	.25
a.		Imperf., pair	250.00	
b.		Vert. pair, imperf. btwn. and with natural straight edge at bottom	1,000.	
e.		Vert. pair, imperf. horiz.	1,000.	
1845	A1232	2c brn blk ('82)	.25	.25
1846	A1233	3c ol grn ('83)	.25	.25
1847	A1234	4c violet ('83)	.25	.25
1848	A1235	5c henna brn ('83)	.30	.25

1849	A1236	6c org verm ('85)	.25	.25
a.		Vert. pair, imperf. between and with natural straight edge at bottom	1,000.	
1850	A1237	7c brt car ('85)	.25	.25
1851	A1238	8c ol blk ('85)	.25	.25
1852	A1239	9c dk grn ('86)	.25	.25
1853	A1240	10c Prussian bl ('84)	.25	.25
b.		Vert. pair, imperf. between	550.00	
c.		Horiz. pair, imperf. between	1,250.	
d.		Vert. pair, imperf horiz.		

Almost all examples of No. 1853b also have a natural straight edge at bottom. At least one pair has perfs at bottom and partial perfs at top.

Completely imperforate tagged or untagged stamps are from printer's waste. Known unused and used.

1854	A1241	11c dk blue ('85)	.40	.25
1855	A1242	13c lt maroon ('82)	.40	.25
1856	A1243	14c slate grn ('85)	.30	.25
b.		Vert. pair, imperf. horiz.	90.00	
c.		Horiz. pair, imperf. between	8.00	
d.		Vert. pair, imperf. between	1,250.	
e.		All color omitted		

No. 1856e comes from a partially printed pane and should be collected as a vertical strip of 10, one stamp normal, one stamp transitional and 8 stamps with color omitted.

1857	A1244	17c green ('81)	.35	.25
1858	A1245	18c dk blue ('81)	.35	.25
1859	A1246	19c brown	.45	.25
1860	A1247	20c claret ('82)	.40	.25
1861	A1248	20c green ('83)	.50	.25
1862	A1249	20c black ('84)	.40	.25
1863	A1250	22c dk chalky bl ('85)	.75	.25
d.		Vert. pair, imperf. horiz.	1,300.	
f.		Horiz. pair, imperf. between	1,300.	
1864	A1251	30c ol gray ('84)	.60	.25
b.		Perf. 11.2, overall tagging	3.75	.25
1865	A1252	35c gray ('81)	.75	.25
1866	A1253	37c blue ('82)	.80	.25
1867	A1254	39c rose lilac ('85)	1.00	.25
a.		Vert. pair, imperf. horiz.	350.00	
b.		Vert. pair, imperf. between	1,500.	
1868	A1255	40c dk green ('84)	1.00	.25
1869	A1256	50c brown ('85)	.95	.25
		Nos. 1844-1869 (26)	11.95	6.50

EVERETT DIRKSEN (1896-1969)
Senate minority leader, 1960-1969.

A1261

ENGRAVED
1981, Jan. 4   **Perf. 11**

1874	A1261	15c gray	.30	.25
a.		All color omitted	500.00	

No. 1874a comes from a partially printed pane and may be collected as a vertical strip of 3 or 5 (1 or 3 stamps normal, one stamp transitional and one stamp with color omitted) or as a pair with one partially printed stamp.

BLACK HERITAGE SERIES
Whitney Moore Young, Jr. (1921-1971), civil rights leader.

A1262

PHOTOGRAVURE
1981, Jan. 30

1875	A1262	15c multi	.35	.25

FLOWER ISSUE

A1263

A1264

A1265

A1266

1981, Apr. 23

1876	A1263	18c multicolored	.35	.25
1877	A1264	18c multicolored	.35	.25
1878	A1265	18c multicolored	.35	.25
1879	A1266	18c multicolored	.35	.25
a.		Block of 4, #1876-1879	1.40	1.25

AMERICAN WILDLIFE

A1267

A1268

A1269

A1270

A1271

A1272

A1273

A1274

A1275

A1276

No. 1880, Bighorn. No. 1881, Puma. No. 1882, Harbor seal. No. 1883, American Buffalo. No. 1884, Brown bear. No. 1885, Polar bear. No. 1886, Elk (wapiti). No. 1887, Moose. No. 1888, White-tailed deer. No. 1889, Pronghorn.

ENGRAVED
1981, May 14

1880	A1267	18c multicolored	.50	.25
1881	A1268	18c multicolored	.50	.25
1882	A1269	18c multicolored	.50	.25
1883	A1270	18c multicolored	.50	.25
1884	A1271	18c multicolored	.50	.25
1885	A1272	18c multicolored	.50	.25
1886	A1273	18c multicolored	.50	.25
1887	A1274	18c multicolored	.50	.25
1888	A1275	18c multicolored	.50	.25
1889	A1276	18c multicolored	.50	.25
b.		Booklet pane of 10, #1880-1889	5.00	5.00
		Nos. 1880-1889 (10)	5.00	2.50

Nos. 1880-1889 issued in booklet only. All stamps have one or two straight edges. Imperfs are from printer's waste.

FLAG AND ANTHEM ISSUE

A1277

A1278

A1279

A1280

ENGRAVED
1981, Apr. 24   **Perf. 11**

1890	A1277	18c multicolored	.35	.25
a.		Imperf., pair	75.00	
b.		Vert. pair, imperf. horiz.	550.00	
c.		Vert. pair, imperf. between	550.00	

Coil Stamp
Perf. 10 Vert.

1891	A1278	18c multicolored	.35	.25
a.		Imperf., pair	17.50	
b.		Pair, imperf. between	1,750.	

Beware of pairs offered as No. 1891b that have faint blind perfs.
Vertical pairs and blocks exist from printer's waste.

Booklet Stamps
Perf. 11x10½ on 3 Sides

1892	A1279	6c dark blue & red	.50	.25

Perf. 11x10½ on 2 or 3 Sides

1893	A1280	18c multicolored	.30	.25
a.		Booklet pane of 8 (2 #1892, 6 #1893)	3.00	2.50
b.		As "a," vert. imperf. between	60.00	
c.		Se-tenant pair, #1892 & #1893	.90	1.00

Bureau Precanceled Coils
Starting with No. 1895b, Bureau precanceled coil stamps are valued unused as well as used. The coils issued with dull gum may be difficult to distinguish.

When used normally these stamps do not receive any postal markings so that used stamps with an additional postal cancellation of any kind are worth considerably less than the values shown here.

FLAG OVER SUPREME COURT ISSUE

A1281

1981, Dec. 17   **Perf. 11**

1894	A1281	20c blk, dk bl & red	.40	.25
a.		Vert. pair, imperf.	30.00	
b.		Vert. pair, imperf. horiz.	350.00	
c.		Dark blue omitted	60.00	
d.		Black omitted	225.00	

Coil Stamp
Perf. 10 Vert.

1895	A1281	20c blk, dk bl & red	.40	.25
b.		Untagged (Bureau precanceled, lines only)	.50	.50
d.		Imperf., pair	8.00	
e.		Pair, imperf. between	600.00	
f.		Black omitted	45.00	
g.		Dark blue omitted	1,000.	
h.		Black field of stars instead of blue		

BOOKLET STAMP
Perf. 11x10½ on 2 or 3 Sides

1896	A1281 20c blk, dk bl & red	.40	.25
a.	Booklet pane of 6	3.00	2.25
b.	Booklet pane of 10, *June 1, 1982*	5.25	3.25

TRANSPORTATION ISSUE

A1283   A1284

COIL STAMPS
ENGRAVED

1981-84			**Perf. 10 Vert.**
1897	A1283 1c violet ('83)	.25	.25
b.	Imperf., pair	325.00	

See No. 2225.

| **1897A** | A1284 2c black ('82) | .25 | .25 |
| c. | Imperf., pair | 45.00 | |

See No. 2226.

A1284a   A1285

1898	A1284a 3c dk grn ('83)	.25	.25
1898A	A1285 4c reddish brn ('82)	.25	.25
b.	Untagged (Bureau precanceled, Nonprofit Org.)	.25	.25
c.	As "b," imperf., pair	375.00	
d.	As No. 1898A, imperf. pair	400.00	—

See No. 2228.

A1286   A1287

1899	A1286 5c gray grn ('83)	.25	.25
a.	Imperf., pair	1,750.	
1900	A1287 5.2c car ('83)	.25	.25
a.	Untagged (Bureau precanceled, lines only)	.25	.25

A1288   A1289

1901	A1288 5.9c blue ('82)	.25	.25
a.	Untagged (Bureau precanceled, lines only)	.25	.25
b.	As "a," imperf., pair	140.00	
1902	A1289 7.4c brown ('84)	.25	.25
a.	Untagged (Bureau precanceled, Blk. Rt. CAR-RT SORT)	.25	.25

A1290   A1291

1903	A1290 9.3c car rose	.30	.25
a.	Untagged (Bureau precanceled, lines only)	.25	.25
b.	As "a," imperf., pair	90.00	
1904	A1291 10.9c pur ('82)	.30	.25
a.	Untagged (Bureau precanceled, lines only)	.30	.25
b.	As "a," imperf., pair	125.00	

A1292   A1293

1905	A1292 11c red ('84)	.30	.25
a.	Untagged *Sept. 1991*	.25	.25

Untagged stamps from plate 1 come only Bureau precanceled with lines. Untagged stamps from plate 2 come only without precancel lines.

1906	A1293 17c ultra	.35	.25
a.	Untagged (Bureau precanceled, Presorted First Class)	.35	.35
b.	Imperf., pair	130.00	
c.	As "a," imperf., pair	400.00	

A1294   A1295

1907	A1294 18c dk brn	.35	.25
a.	Imperf., pair	95.00	
1908	A1295 20c vermilion	.35	.25
a.	Imperf., pair	75.00	
	Nos. 1897-1908 (14)	3.95	3.50

A1296

Booklet Stamp
PHOTOGRAVURE

Perf. 10 Vert. on 1 or 2 Sides

1983, Aug. 12		**Untagged**	
1909	A1296 $9.35 multicolored	19.00	15.00
a.	Booklet pane of 3	57.50	—

AMERICAN RED CROSS CENTENNIAL

A1297

Plates of 200 subjects in four panes of 50.

1981, May 1		**Perf. 10½x11**	
1910	A1297 18c multicolored	.35	.25

SAVINGS & LOAN SESQUICENTENNIAL

A1298

1981, May 8		**Perf. 11**	
1911	A1298 18c multicolored	.35	.25

SPACE ACHIEVEMENT ISSUE

A1299   A1302

A1300

A1301

A1303   A1306

A1304

A1305

Designs: A1299, Moon walk. A1300-A1301, A1304-A1305, Columbia space shuttle. A1302, Skylab. A1303, Pioneer 11. A1306, Telescope.

1981, May 21			
1912	A1299 18c multicolored	.35	.25
1913	A1300 18c multicolored	.35	.25
1914	A1301 18c multicolored	.35	.25
1915	A1302 18c multicolored	.35	.25
1916	A1303 18c multicolored	.35	.25
1917	A1304 18c multicolored	.35	.25
1918	A1305 18c multicolored	.35	.25
1919	A1306 18c multicolored	.35	.25
a.	Block of 8, #1912-1919	2.80	3.00
b.	As "a," imperf.	5,500.	
c.	As "a," imperf. vert.	2,000.	
e.	As "a," top 4 stamps part perf, bottom 4 stamps imperf	—	

No. 1919c is unique and has blind horiz. perfs.

PROFESSIONAL MANAGEMENT EDUCATION CENTENARY

Joseph Wharton
A1307

1981, June 18			
1920	A1307 18c blue & black	.35	.25

PRESERVATION OF WILDLIFE HABITATS

A1308   A1309

A1310   A1311

1981, June 26			
1921	A1308 18c multicolored	.35	.25
1922	A1309 18c multicolored	.35	.25
1923	A1310 18c multicolored	.35	.25
1924	A1311 18c multicolored	.35	.25
a.	Block of 4, #1921-1924	1.50	1.25

INTERNATIONAL YEAR OF THE DISABLED

Man Looking through Microscope
A1312

1981, June 29			
1925	A1312 18c multicolored	.35	.25
a.	Vert. pair, imperf. horiz.	1,500.	

EDNA ST. VINCENT MILLAY ISSUE

A1313

LITHOGRAPHED AND ENGRAVED

1981, July 10			
1926	A1313 18c multicolored	.35	.25
a.	Black (engr., inscriptions) omitted	200.00	—

ALCOHOLISM

A1314

ENGRAVED

1981, Aug. 19			
1927	A1314 18c blue & black	.45	.25
a.	Imperf., pair	325.00	
b.	Vert. pair, imperf. horiz.	2,000.	

AMERICAN ARCHITECTURE SERIES

New York University Library by Sanford White
A1315

Biltmore House by Richard Morris Hunt
A1316

Palace of the Arts by Bernard Maybeck
A1317

National Farmer's Bank by Louis Sullivan
A1318

1981, Aug. 28

1928	A1315	18c black & red	.40	.25
1929	A1316	18c black & red	.40	.25
a.		Red missing (PS)	—	
1930	A1317	18c black & red	.40	.25
b.		Red missing (PS)	—	
1931	A1318	18c black & red	.40	.25
a.		Block of 4, #1928-1931	1.65	1.65

SPORTS PERSONALITIES

Mildred Didrikson Zaharias A1319   Robert Tyre Jones A1320

1981, Sept. 22   *Perf. 10½x11*

1932	A1319	18c purple	.40	.25
1933	A1320	18c green	.60	.25

FREDERIC REMINGTON

Coming Through the Rye A1321

LITHOGRAPHED AND ENGRAVED
1981, Oct. 9   *Perf. 11*

1934	A1321	18c gray, olive green & brown	.35	.25
a.		Vert. pair, imperf. between	160.00	
b.		Brown omitted	200.00	

JAMES HOBAN

Irish-American Architect of White House — A1322

PHOTOGRAVURE
1981, Oct. 13

1935	A1322	18c multicolored	.35	.25
1936	A1322	20c multicolored	.35	.25

See Ireland No. 504.

AMERICAN BICENTENNIAL

Battle of Yorktown A1323

Battle of Virginia Capes A1324

LITHOGRAPHED AND ENGRAVED
1981, Oct. 16

1937	A1323	18c multicolored	.35	.25
1938	A1324	18c multicolored	.35	.25
a.		Pair, #1937-1938	.90	.75
b.		As "a," black (engr., inscriptions) omitted	300.00	
d.		As "a," black (litho.) omitted	—	

CHRISTMAS

Madonna and Child, Botticelli — A1325

Felt Bear on Sled A1326

PHOTOGRAVURE
1981, Oct. 28

1939	A1325	(20c) multicolored	.40	.25
a.		Imperf., pair	90.00	
b.		Vert. pair, imperf. horiz.	750.00	
1940	A1326	(20c) multicolored	.40	.25
a.		Imperf., pair	175.00	
b.		Vert. pair, imperf. horiz.	2,000.	

JOHN HANSON

First President of Continental Congress — A1327

1981, Nov. 5

1941	A1327	20c multicolored	.40	.25

DESERT PLANTS

Barrel Cactus — A1328

Agave — A1329

Beavertail Cactus — A1330

Saguaro — A1331

LITHOGRAPHED AND ENGRAVED
1981 Dec. 11

1942	A1328	20c multicolored	.35	.25
1943	A1329	20c multicolored	.35	.25
1944	A1330	20c multicolored	.35	.25
1945	A1331	20c multicolored	.35	.25
a.		Block of 4, #1942-1945	1.50	1.25
b.		As "a," deep brown (litho.) omitted	3,000.	
c.		No. 1945 imperf., vert. pair	3,000.	
d.		As "a," dark green & dark blue (engr.) missing (EP)	—	
e.		As "a," dark green (engr.) missing (EP) on left stamp (EP)	—	

A1332   A1333

PHOTOGRAVURE
1981, Oct. 11   *Perf. 11x10½*

1946	A1332	(20c) brown	.40	.25
b.		All color omitted	425.00	

No. 1946b comes from a partially printed pane with most stamps normal. It must be collected as a vertical pair or strip with normal or partially printed stamps attached.

ENGRAVED
COIL STAMP
Perf. 10 Vert.

1947	A1332	(20c) brown	.60	.25
a.		Imperf. pair	700.00	

BOOKLET STAMPS
Perf. 11 on 2 or 3 Sides

1948	A1333	(20c) brown	.40	.25
a.		Booklet pane of 10	4.50	3.25

A1334

BOOKLET STAMP
ENGRAVED
Perf. 11 on 2 or 3 Sides
1982, Jan. 8

1949	A1334	20c dark blue	.50	.25
a.		Booklet pane of 10	5.00	2.50
b.		As "a," imperf. vert.	90.00	
c.		Type II	1.40	.25
d.		Type II, booklet pane of 10	14.00	—

No. 1949 is 18¾mm wide and has overall tagging. No. 1949c is 18½mm wide and has block tagging.
See No. 1880.

A1335

1982, Jan. 30   *Perf. 11*

1950	A1335	20c blue	.40	.25

LOVE ISSUE

A1336

PHOTOGRAVURE
1982, Feb. 1   *Perf. 11¼*

1951	A1336	20c multicolored	.40	.25
b.		Imperf., pair	200.00	
c.		Blue omitted	200.00	
d.		Yellow omitted	600.00	
e.		Purple omitted	—	

No. 1951c is valued in the grade of fine.

Perf. 11¼x10½

1951A	A1336	20c multicolored	.75	.25

GEORGE WASHINGTON

A1337

1982, Feb. 22   *Perf. 11*

1952	A1337	20c multicolored	.40	.25

STATE BIRDS AND FLOWERS ISSUE

A1338

1982, Apr. 14   *Perf. 10½x11¼*

1953	A1338	20c Alabama	.55	.30
1954	A1339	20c Alaska	.55	.30
1955	A1340	20c Arizona	.55	.30
1956	A1341	20c Arkansas	.55	.30
1957	A1342	20c California	.55	.30
1958	A1343	20c Colorado	.55	.30
1959	A1344	20c Connecticut	.55	.30
1960	A1345	20c Delaware	.55	.30
1961	A1346	20c Florida	.55	.30
1962	A1347	20c Georgia	.55	.30
1963	A1348	20c Hawaii	.55	.30
1964	A1349	20c Idaho	.55	.30
1965	A1350	20c Illinois	.55	.30
1966	A1351	20c Indiana	.55	.30
1967	A1352	20c Iowa	.55	.30
1968	A1353	20c Kansas	.55	.30
1969	A1354	20c Kentucky	.55	.30
1970	A1355	20c Louisiana	.55	.30
1971	A1356	20c Maine	.55	.30
1972	A1357	20c Maryland	.55	.30
1973	A1358	20c Massachusetts	.55	.30
1974	A1359	20c Michigan	.55	.30
1975	A1360	20c Minnesota	.55	.30
1976	A1361	20c Mississippi	.55	.30
1977	A1362	20c Missouri	.55	.30
1978	A1363	20c Montana	.55	.30
1979	A1364	20c Nebraska	.55	.30
1980	A1365	20c Nevada	.55	.30
1981	A1366	20c New Hampshire	.55	.30
b.		Black missing (EP)	4,000.	
1982	A1367	20c New Jersey	.55	.30
1983	A1368	20c New Mexico	.55	.30
1984	A1369	20c New York	.55	.30
1985	A1370	20c North Carolina	.55	.30

1986	A1371	20c North Dako-ta	.55	.30
1987	A1372	20c Ohio	.55	.30
1988	A1373	20c Oklahoma	.55	.30
1989	A1374	20c Oregon	.55	.30
1990	A1375	20c Pennsylvania	.55	.30
1991	A1376	20c Rhode Is-land	.55	.30
b.		Black missing (EP)	4,000.	
1992	A1377	20c South Caro-lina	.55	.30
1993	A1378	20c South Dako-ta	.55	.30
1994	A1379	20c Tennessee	.55	.30
1995	A1380	20c Texas	.55	.30
1996	A1381	20c Utah	.55	.30
1997	A1382	20c Vermont	.55	.30
1998	A1383	20c Virginia	.55	.30
1999	A1384	20c Washington	.55	.30
2000	A1385	20c West Virgin-ia	.55	.30
2001	A1386	20c Wisconsin	.55	.30
b.		Black missing (EP)	4,000.	
2002	A1387	20c Wyoming	.55	.30
b.		A1338-A1387 Pane of 50, Nos. 1953-2002	27.50	20.00
d.		Pane of 50, imperf.	21,000.	

Perf. 11¼x11

1953A	A1338	20c Alabama	.65	.30
1954A	A1339	20c Alaska	.65	.30
1955A	A1340	20c Arizona	.65	.30
1956A	A1341	20c Arkansas	.65	.30
1957A	A1342	20c California	.65	.30
1958A	A1343	20c Colorado	.65	.30
1959A	A1344	20c Connecticut	.65	.30
1960A	A1345	20c Delaware	.65	.30
1961A	A1346	20c Florida	.65	.30
1962A	A1347	20c Georgia	.65	.30
1963A	A1348	20c Hawaii	.65	.30
1964A	A1349	20c Idaho	.65	.30
1965A	A1350	20c Illinois	.65	.30
1966A	A1351	20c Indiana	.65	.30
1967A	A1352	20c Iowa	.65	.30
1968A	A1353	20c Kansas	.65	.30
1969A	A1354	20c Kentucky	.65	.30
1970A	A1355	20c Louisiana	.65	.30
1971A	A1356	20c Maine	.65	.30
1972A	A1357	20c Maryland	.65	.30
1973A	A1358	20c Massachu-setts	.65	.30
1974A	A1359	20c Michigan	.65	.30
1975A	A1360	20c Minnesota	.65	.30
1976A	A1361	20c Mississippi	.65	.30
1977A	A1362	20c Missouri	.65	.30
1978A	A1363	20c Montana	.65	.30
1979A	A1364	20c Nebraska	.65	.30
1980A	A1365	20c Nevada	.65	.30
1981A	A1366	20c New Hamp-shire	.65	.30
1982A	A1367	20c New Jersey	.65	.30
1983A	A1368	20c New Mexico	.65	.30
1984A	A1369	20c New York	.65	.30
1985A	A1370	20c North Caroli-na	.65	.30
1986A	A1371	20c North Dako-ta	.65	.30
1987A	A1372	20c Ohio	.65	.30
1988A	A1373	20c Oklahoma	.65	.30
1989A	A1374	20c Oregon	.65	.30
1990A	A1375	20c Penn-sylvania	.65	.30
1991A	A1376	20c Rhode Is-land	.65	.30
1992A	A1377	20c South Caro-lina	.65	.30
1993A	A1378	20c South Dako-ta	.65	.30
1994A	A1379	20c Tennessee	.65	.30
1995A	A1380	20c Texas	.65	.30
1996A	A1381	20c Utah	.65	.30
1997A	A1382	20c Vermont	.65	.30
1998A	A1383	20c Virginia	.65	.30
1999A	A1384	20c Washington	.65	.30
2000A	A1385	20c West Virgin-ia	.65	.30
2001A	A1386	20c Wisconsin	.65	.30
2002A	A1387	20c Wyoming	.65	.30
c.		A1338-A1387 Pane of 50, Nos. 1953A-2002A	32.50	22.50

Nos. 1953-2002 are line perforated. The perforations do not meet perfectly at the corners of each stamp and extend into the narrow selvage margins of an intact pane. Nos. 1953A-2002A are comb perforated. The perforations meet perfectly at the corners of each stamp and do not extend into the narrow selvage margins of an intact pane.

US-NETHERLANDS

200th Anniv. of Diplomatic Recognition by the Netherlands A1388

1982, Apr. 20   *Perf. 11*
2003 A1388 20c multicolored   .40 .25
a.   Imperf., pair   250.00

See Netherlands Nos. 640-641.

LIBRARY OF CONGRESS

A1389

ENGRAVED

1982, Apr. 21
2004 A1389 20c red & black   .40 .25
a.   All color missing   4,000.

No. 2004a must be collected as a right margin horiz. strip of 3, 4 or 5 with one No. 2004a, one transitional stamp and one or more normal stamps.

CONSUMER EDUCATION

A1390

Coil Stamp

1982, Apr. 27   *Perf. 10 Vert.*
2005 A1390 20c sky blue   .55 .25
a.   Imperf., pair   70.00

KNOXVILLE WORLD'S FAIR

A1391

A1392

A1393

A1394

PHOTOGRAVURE

1982, Apr. 29   *Perf. 11*
2006 A1391 20c multicolored   .45 .25
2007 A1392 20c multicolored   .45 .25
2008 A1393 20c multicolored   .45 .25
2009 A1394 20c multicolored   .45 .25
a.   Block of 4, #2006-2009   1.80 1.50

HORATIO ALGER

Frontispiece from "Ragged Dick" — A1395

ENGRAVED

1982, Apr. 30
2010 A1395 20c red & black, tan   .40 .25
a.   Red and black omitted   —

The Philatelic Foundation has issued a certificate for a pane of 50 with red and black colors omitted. Recognition of this error is by the paper and by a tiny residue of red ink from the tagging roller. The engraved plates did not strike the paper.

AGING TOGETHER

A1396

ENGRAVED

1982, May 21
2011 A1396 20c brown   .40 .25

PERFORMING ARTS SERIES

A1397

PHOTOGRAVURE

1982, June 8
2012 A1397 20c multicolored   .40 .25
a.   Black missing (EP)   —

John (1882-1942), Ethel (1879-1959), and Lionel (1878-1954) Barrymore, actors.

DR. MARY WALKER

A1398

1982, June 10
2013 A1398 20c multicolored   .40 .25

Dr. Mary Walker (1832-1919), 1865 recipient of Medal of Honor.

INTERNATIONAL PEACE GARDEN

A1399

LITHOGRAPHED AND ENGRAVED

1982, June 30
2014 A1399 20c multicolored   .45 .25
a.   Black (engr.) omitted   200.00

AMERICA'S LIBRARIES

A1400

ENGRAVED

1982, July 13
2015 A1400 20c red & black   .40 .25
a.   Vert. pair, imperf. horiz.   200.00
c.   All colors missing (EP)   175.00

On No. 2015c, an albino impression of the design is present.

BLACK HERITAGE SERIES

Jackie Robinson (1919-72), baseball player.

A1401

PHOTOGRAVURE

1982, Aug. 2   *Perf. 10½x11*
2016 A1401 20c multicolored   1.10 .25

TOURO SYNAGOGUE

A1402

PHOTOGRAVURE AND ENGRAVED

1982, Aug. 22   *Perf. 11*
2017 A1402 20c multicolored   .40 .25
a.   Imperf., pair   1,400.

WOLF TRAP FARM PARK

A1403

PHOTOGRAVURE

1982, Sept. 1
2018 A1403 20c multicolored   .40 .25

AMERICAN ARCHITECTURE SERIES

Fallingwater, Mill Run, Pa., by Frank Lloyd Wright — A1404

Illinois Institute of Technology by Ludwig Mies van der Rohe A1405

Gropius House, Lincoln, Mass., by Walter Gropius A1406

Dulles Airport, by Eero Saarinen A1407

ENGRAVED

1982, Sept. 30
2019 A1404 20c black & brown   .45 .25
b.   Red missing (PS)   —
2020 A1405 20c black & brown   .45 .25
a.   Red missing (PS)   —
2021 A1406 20c black & brown   .45 .25
2022 A1407 20c black & brown   .45 .25
a.   Block of 4, #2019-2022   2.00 1.75

FRANCIS OF ASSISI

A1408

PHOTOGRAVURE

1982, Oct. 7
2023 A1408 20c multicolored .40 .25

PONCE DE LEON

A1409

PHOTOGRAVURE (Combination press)

1982, Oct. 12
2024 A1409 20c multicolored .40 .25
a. Imperf., pair 250.00
b. Vert. pair, imperf. between and at top 500.00

CHRISTMAS ISSUES

A1410

A1411

A1412

A1413

A1414

A1415

PHOTOGRAVURE

1982, Nov. 3
2025 A1410 13c multicolored .25 .25
a. Imperf., pair 300.00

PHOTOGRAVURE (Combination Press)

1982, Oct. 28
2026 A1411 20c multicolored .40 .25
a. Imperf. pair 90.00
b. Horiz. pair, imperf. vert. 900.00
c. Vert. pair, imperf. horiz. —

PHOTOGRAVURE

2027 A1412 20c multicolored .60 .25
2028 A1413 20c multicolored .60 .25

2029 A1414 20c multicolored .60 .25
2030 A1415 20c multicolored .60 .25
a. Block of 4, #2027-2030 2.40 1.50
b. As "a," imperf. 1,250.
c. As "a," imperf. horiz. 700.00
Nos. 2025-2030 (6) 3.05 1.50

SCIENCE & INDUSTRY

A1416

LITHOGRAPHED AND ENGRAVED

1983, Jan. 19
2031 A1416 20c multicolored .40 .25
a. Black (engr.) omitted 800.00

BALLOONS

A1417

A1420

A1418

A1419

PHOTOGRAVURE

1983, Mar. 31 Tagged *Perf. 11*
2032 A1417 20c multicolored .50 .25
2033 A1418 20c multicolored .50 .25
2034 A1419 20c multicolored .50 .25
2035 A1420 20c multicolored .50 .25
a. Block of 4, #2032-2035 2.00 1.50
b. As "a," imperf. 2,750.
c. As "a," right stamp perf., otherwise imperf. 2,750.

US-SWEDEN

A1421

ENGRAVED

1983, Mar. 24
2036 A1421 20c blue, blk & red brn .40 .25
See Sweden No. 1453.

CCC, 50th ANNIV.

A1422

PHOTOGRAVURE

1983, Apr. 5
2037 A1422 20c multicolored .40 .25
a. Imperf., pair 2,250. —
b. Vert. pair, imperf. horiz.

JOSEPH PRIESTLEY

A1423

1983, Apr. 13
2038 A1423 20c multicolored .40 .25

VOLUNTEERISM

A1424

ENGRAVED (Combination Press)

1983, Apr. 20
2039 A1424 20c red & black .40 .25
a. Imperf., pair 225.00

US-GERMANY

Concord, 1683
A1425

ENGRAVED

1983, Apr. 29
2040 A1425 20c brown .40 .25
See Germany No. 1397.

BROOKLYN BRIDGE

A1426

1983, May 17
2041 A1426 20c blue .40 .25
b. All color missing (EP) 90.00
On No. 2041b, an albino impression of part of the design is evident.

TVA

A1427

PHOTOGRAVURE AND ENGRAVED (Combination Press)

1983, May 18
2042 A1427 20c multicolored .40 .25

A1428

PHOTOGRAVURE (Combination Press)

1983, May 14
2043 A1428 20c multicolored .40 .25

BLACK HERITAGE SERIES

A1429

PHOTOGRAVURE

1983, June 9
2044 A1429 20c multicolored .50 .25
a. Imperf., pair 300.00

MEDAL OF HONOR

A1430

LITHOGRAPHED AND ENGRAVED

1983, June 7
2045 A1430 20c multicolored .55 .25
a. Red omitted 150.00

GEORGE HERMAN RUTH (1895-1948)

A1431

ENGRAVED

1983, July 6 *Perf. 10½x11*
2046 A1431 20c blue 1.30 .25

LITERARY ARTS SERIES

Nathaniel Hawthorne (1804-1864), novelist.

A1432

PHOTOGRAVURE

1983, July 8 *Perf. 11*
2047 A1432 20c multicolored .40 .25

1984 SUMMER OLYMPICS

Discus
A1433

High Jump
A1434

Archery
A1435

Boxing
A1436

1983, July 28

2048	A1433	13c multicolored	.35	.25
2049	A1434	13c multicolored	.35	.25
2050	A1435	13c multicolored	.35	.25
2051	A1436	13c multicolored	.35	.25
a.		Block of 4, #2048-2051	1.50	1.25

SIGNING OF TREATY OF PARIS

John Adams, Franklin, John Jay, David Hartley
A1437

1983, Sept. 2
2052 A1437 20c multicolored   .40   .25

CIVIL SERVICE

A1438

PHOTOGRAVURE AND ENGRAVED
1983, Sept. 9
2053 A1438 20c buff, blue & red   .40   .25

METROPOLITAN OPERA

A1439

LITHOGRAPHED AND ENGRAVED
1983, Sept. 14
2054 A1439 20c yellow & maroon   .40   .25

AMERICAN INVENTORS

A1440

A1441

A1442

A1443

LITHOGRAPHED AND ENGRAVED

1983, Sept. 21

2055	A1440	20c multicolored	.50	.25
2056	A1441	20c multicolored	.50	.25
2057	A1442	20c multicolored	.50	.25
2058	A1443	20c multicolored	.50	.25
a.		Block of 4, #2055-2058	2.00	1.50
b.		As "a," black omitted	275.00	

STREETCARS

A1444

A1445

A1446

A1447

PHOTOGRAVURE AND ENGRAVED

1983, Oct. 8

2059	A1444	20c multicolored	.50	.25
2060	A1445	20c multicolored	.50	.25
a.		Horiz. pair, black (engr.) missing on Nos. 2059, 2060 (EP)	—	
2061	A1446	20c multicolored	.50	.25
a.		Vert. pair, black (engr.) missing on Nos. 2059, 2061 (EP)	—	
2062	A1447	20c multicolored	.50	.25
a.		Block of 4, #2059-2062	2.00	1.50
b.		As "a," black (engr.) omitted	250.00	
c.		As "a," black (engr.) omitted on #2059, 2061	—	

CHRISTMAS

A1448

A1449

PHOTOGRAVURE

1983, Oct. 28

2063	A1448	20c multicolored	.40	.25
2064	A1449	20c multicolored	.40	.25
a.		Imperf., pair	100.00	

MARTIN LUTHER (1483-1546)

Martin Luther (1483-1546), German Religious Leader — A1450

1983, Nov. 11
2065 A1450 20c multicolored   .40   .25

ALASKA STATEHOOD, 25th ANNIV.

Caribou and Alaska Pipeline — A1451

1984, Jan. 3
2066 A1451 20c multicolored   .40   .25
a.   Vert. pair, imperf. horiz.   —

14th WINTER OLYMPIC GAMES

Ice Dancing
A1452

Downhill Skiing
A1453

Cross-country Skiing
A1454

Hockey
A1455

1984, Jan. 6   *Perf. 10½x11*

2067	A1452	20c multicolored	.55	.25
2068	A1453	20c multicolored	.55	.25
2069	A1454	20c multicolored	.55	.25
2070	A1455	20c multicolored	.55	.25
a.		Block of 4, #2067-2070	2.20	1.75

FEDERAL DEPOSIT INSURANCE CORPORATION, 50TH ANNIV.

A1456

1984, Jan. 12   *Perf. 11*
2071 A1456 20c multicolored   .40   .25

LOVE

A1457

PHOTOGRAVURE AND ENGRAVED
(Combination Press)
1984, Jan. 31   *Perf. 11x10½*
2072 A1457 20c multicolored   .40   .25
a.   Horiz. pair, imperf. vert.   125.00

BLACK HERITAGE SERIES

Carter G. Woodson (1875-1950), Historian.

A1458

PHOTOGRAVURE
1984, Feb. 1   *Perf. 11*
2073 A1458 20c multicolored   .40   .25
a.   Horiz. pair, imperf. vert.   800.00

SOIL & WATER CONSERVATION

A1459

1984, Feb. 6
2074 A1459 20c multicolored   .40   .25

50TH ANNIV. OF CREDIT UNION ACT

Dollar Sign, Coin — A1460

1984, Feb. 10
2075 A1460 20c multicolored   .40   .25

ORCHIDS

A1461

A1462

A1463

A1464

1984, Mar. 5
2076	A1461	20c multicolored	.50	.25
2077	A1462	20c multicolored	.50	.25
2078	A1463	20c multicolored	.50	.25
2079	A1464	20c multicolored	.50	.25
a.		Block of 4, #2076-2079	2.00	1.50

HAWAII STATEHOOD, 25th ANNIV.

Eastern Polynesian Canoe, Golden Plover, Mauna Loa Volcano A1465

1984, Mar. 12
2080	A1465	20c multicolored	.40	.25

50TH ANNIV., NATIONAL ARCHIVES

Abraham Lincoln, George Washington A1466

1984, Apr. 16
2081	A1466	20c multicolored	.40	.25

LOS ANGELES SUMMER OLYMPICS

Diving — A1467

Long Jump — A1468

Wrestling A1469

Kayak A1470

1984, May 4
2082	A1467	20c multicolored	.55	.25
2083	A1468	20c multicolored	.55	.25
2084	A1469	20c multicolored	.55	.25
2085	A1470	20c multicolored	.55	.25
a.		Block of 4, #2082-2085	2.40	1.90
b.		As "a," imperf between vertically		9,500.

LOUISIANA WORLD EXPOSITION

River Wildlife A1471

1984, May 11
2086	A1471	20c multicolored	.50	.25

HEALTH RESEARCH

Lab Equipment A1472

1984, May 17
2087	A1472	20c multicolored	.40	.25

PERFORMING ARTS

A1473

PHOTOGRAVURE AND ENGRAVED (Combination Press)

1984, May 23
2088	A1473	20c multicolored	.40	.25
b.		Horiz. pair, imperf between	—	

JIM THORPE

A1474

ENGRAVED

1984, May 24
2089	A1474	20c dark brown	.60	.25
a.		All color omitted	—	

On No. 2089a, an albino impression of the design is evident.

PERFORMING ARTS

Tenor John McCormack (1884-1945) A1475

PHOTOGRAVURE

1984, June 6
2090	A1475	20c multicolored	.40	.25

See Ireland No. 594.

ST. LAWRENCE SEAWAY, 25th ANNIV.

Aerial View of Seaway, Freighters A1476

1984, June 26
2091	A1476	20c multicolored	.40	.25

WATERFOWL PRESERVATION ACT, 50th ANNIV.

"Mallards Dropping In," by Jay N. Darling A1477

ENGRAVED

1984, July 2   *Perf. 11*
2092	A1477	20c blue	.50	.25
a.		Horiz. pair, imperf. vert.	275.00	

ROANOKE VOYAGES

The Elizabeth — A1478

PHOTOGRAVURE

1984, July 13
2093	A1478	20c multicolored	.40	.25

LITERARY ARTS SERIES

Herman Melville (1819-1891), Author — A1479

ENGRAVED

1984, Aug. 1
2094	A1479	20c sage green	.40	.25

HORACE MOSES (1862-1947), FOUNDER OF JUNIOR ACHIEVEMENT

Junior Achievement Founder — A1480

ENGRAVED (Combination Press)

1984, Aug. 6
2095	A1480	20c org & dark brn	.40	.25

SMOKEY BEAR

Smokey Bear — A1481

LITHOGRAPHED AND ENGRAVED

1984, Aug. 13
2096	A1481	20c multicolored	.40	.25
a.		Horiz. pair, imperf. btwn.	175.00	
b.		Vert. pair, imperf. btwn.	150.00	
c.		Block of 4, imperf. btwn. vert. and horiz.	2,500.	
d.		Horiz. pair, imperf. vert.	500.00	

ROBERTO CLEMENTE (1934-1972)

Clemente, Puerto Rican Flag — A1482

PHOTOGRAVURE

1984, Aug. 17
2097	A1482	20c multicolored	1.30	.25
a.		Horiz. pair, imperf. vert.	1,250.	

DOGS

Beagle, Boston Terrier A1483

Chesapeake Bay Retriever, Cocker Spaniel — A1484

Alaskan Malamute, Collie A1485

Black & Tan Coonhound, American Foxhound A1486

1984, Sept. 7
2098	A1483	20c multicolored	.50	.25
2099	A1484	20c multicolored	.50	.25
2100	A1485	20c multicolored	.50	.25
2101	A1486	20c multicolored	.50	.25
a.		Block of 4, #2098-2101	2.00	1.90
b.		As "a," imperf horiz.	5,500.	

CRIME PREVENTION

McGruff, The Crime Dog — A1487

1984, Sept. 26
2102	A1487	20c multicolored	.40	.25

HISPANIC AMERICANS

A1488

1984, Oct. 31
2103   A1488   20c multicolored   .40   .25
    a.   Vert. pair, imperf. horiz.   1,250.

FAMILY UNITY

A1489

PHOTOGRAVURE AND ENGRAVED
(Combination Press)
1984, Oct. 1
2104   A1489   20c multicolored   .40   .25
    a.   Horiz. pair, imperf. vert.   325.00
    c.   Vert. pair, imperf. btwn. and
        at bottom   —
    d.   Horiz. pair, imperf. between   —

ELEANOR ROOSEVELT (1884-1962)

A1490

ENGRAVED
1984, Oct. 11
2105   A1490   20c deep blue   .40   .25

NATION OF READERS

Lincoln, Son
Tad — A1491

1984, Oct. 16
2106   A1491   20c brown & maroon   .40   .25

CHRISTMAS

Madonna and   Santa
Child by Fra   Claus — A1493
Filippo
Lippi — A1492

PHOTOGRAVURE
1984, Oct. 30
2107   A1492   20c multicolored   .40   .25
    a.   Imperf., pair   1,750.
2108   A1493   20c multicolored   .40   .25
    a.   Horiz. pair, imperf. vert.   750.00

No. 2108a is valued in the grade of fine.

VIETNAM VETERANS MEMORIAL

Memorial Wall — A1494

ENGRAVED
1984, Nov. 10
2109   A1494   20c multicolored   .50   .25

PERFORMING ARTS

Composer Jerome
Kern (1885-1945)
A1495

PHOTOGRAVURE
1985, Jan. 23
2110   A1495   22c multicolored   .45   .25

A1496   A1497

PHOTOGRAVURE
1985, Feb. 1   **Perf. 11**
2111   A1496   (22c) green   .60   .25
    a.   Vert. pair, imperf.   35.00
    b.   Vert. pair, imperf. horiz.   750.00

COIL STAMP
Perf. 10 Vert.
2112   A1496   (22c) green   .60   .25
    a.   Imperf., pair   45.00

BOOKLET STAMP
ENGRAVED
Perf. 11 on 2 or 3 Sides
2113   A1497   (22c) green   .70   .25
    a.   Booklet pane of 10   7.00   3.00
    b.   As "a," Horiz. imperf. btwn.   —

A1498

Flag over
Capitol
Dome
A1499

ENGRAVED
1985, Mar. 29   **Perf. 11**
2114   A1498   22c blue, red &
                  black   .45   .25
    a.   All color missing (EP)   —

No. 2114a should be collected se-tenant
with a normal or a partially printed stamp.

COIL STAMP
Perf. 10 Vert.
2115   A1498   22c blue, red &
                  black   .45   .25
    c.   Inscribed "T" at bottom ('87)   .55   .40
    d.   Black field of stars instead of
        blue   —
    f.   Imperf., pair, wide block tag-
        ging   10.00
    g.   Imperf., pair, narrow block
        tagging   10.00

BOOKLET STAMP
Perf. 10 Horiz.
2116   A1499   22c blue, red &
                  black   .50   .25
    a.   Booklet pane of 5   2.50   1.25

BOOKLET STAMPS

Frilled   Reticulated
Dogwinkle   Helmet
A1500   A1501

New England   Calico Scallop
Neptune   A1503
A1502

Lightning
Whelk — A1504

ENGRAVED
Perf. 10 on 2 or 3 Sides
1985, Apr. 4
2117   A1500   22c black & brown   .45   .25
2118   A1501   22c black & multi   .45   .25
2119   A1502   22c black & brown   .45   .25
2120   A1503   22c black & violet   .45   .25
2121   A1504   22c black & multi   .45   .25
    a.   Booklet pane of 10, 2 ea
        #2117-2121   4.50   3.00
    b.   As "a," violet omitted on
        both Nos. 2120   400.00
    c.   As "a," vert. imperf. be-
        tween   350.00
    d.   As "a," imperf.   —
    e.   Strip of 5, Nos. 2117-2121   2.00   —

Eagle and Half Moon — A1505

TYPE I: washed out, dull appearance most
evident in the black of the body of the eagle,
and the red in the background between the
eagle's shoulder and the moon. "$10.75"
appears splotchy or grainy (P# 11111).
TYPE II: brighter, more intense colors most
evident in the black on the eagle's body, and
red in the background. "$10.75" appears
smoother, brighter, and less grainy (P#
22222).

PHOTOGRAVURE
Perf. 10 Vert. on 1 or 2 Sides
1985, Apr. 29   **Untagged**
2122   A1505 $10.75 multi, type I   18.50   7.50
    a.   Booklet pane of 3   55.00   —
    b.   Type II, June 19, 1989   20.00   10.00
    c.   As "b," booklet pane of 3   60.00

TRANSPORTATION ISSUE

A1506   A1507

A1508   A1509

A1510   A1511

A1512   A1513

A1514   A1515

A1516   A1517

A1518   A1519

COIL STAMPS
ENGRAVED
1985-89   **Tagged**   **Perf. 10 Vert.**
2123   A1506   3.4c dk bluish
                green   .25   .25
    a.   Untagged (Bureau pre-
        cancel, Nonprofit Org.
        CAR-RT SORT)   .25   .25
2124   A1507   4.9c brn blk   .25   .25
    a.   Untagged (Bureau pre-
        cancel, Nonprofit Org.)   .25   .25
2125   A1508   5.5c dp mag
                ('86)   .25   .25
    a.   Untagged (Bureau pre-
        cancel, Nonprofit Org.
        CAR-RT SORT)   .25   .25
2126   A1509   6c red brn   .35   .25
    a.   Untagged (Bureau pre-
        cancel, Nonprofit Org.)   .25   .25
    b.   As "a," imperf., pair   175.00
2127   A1510   7.1c lake ('87)   .25   .25
    a.   Untagged (Bureau pre-
        cancel)   .25   .25
    c.   As "a," black (precancel)
        omitted   —

On No. 2127c, an albino impression of the
precancel is present.

2128   A1511   8.3c green   .25   .25
    a.   Untagged (Bureau pre-
        cancel, Blk. Rt. CAR-
        RT SORT)   .25   .25

On No. 2231 "Ambulance 1860s" is 18mm
long; on No. 2128, 18½mm long.

2129   A1512   8.5c dk Prus
                grn ('87)   .25   .25
    a.   Untagged (Bureau pre-
        cancel, Nonprofit Org.)   .25   .25
2130   A1513   10.1c slate blue   .55   .25
    a.   Untagged (Bureau pre-
        cancel "Bulk Rate
        Carrier Route Sort" in
        red) ('88)   .25   .25
    b.   As "a," red precancel,
        imperf. pair   15.00
        As "a," black precancel,
        imperf. pair   70.00
2131   A1514   11c dk green   .25   .25
2132   A1515   12c dk bl, I   .35   .25
    a.   Untagged, type I (Bu-
        reau precancel,
        PRESORTED FIRST-
        CLASS)   .25   .25
    b.   Untagged, type II (Bu-
        reau precancel,
        PRESORTED FIRST-
        CLASS) ('87)   .40   .30

Type II has "Stanley Steamer 1909" ½mm
shorter (17⅔mm) than No. 2132 (18mm).

2133   A1516   12.5c ol grn   .35   .25
    a.   Untagged (Bureau pre-
        cancel, Bulk Rate)   .25   .25
    b.   As "a," imperf., pair   40.00

2134	A1517	14c sky bl, I	.30	.25
a.		Imperf., pair	80.00	
b.		Type II ('86)	.30	.25
c.		Tagging omitted, type I	35.00	—

Type II design is ¼mm narrower (17¼mm) than the original stamp (17½mm) and has block tagging. No. 2134 has overall tagging.

2135	A1518	17c brt bl ('86)	.55	.25
a.		Imperf., pair	300.00	
2136	A1519	25c org brn ('86)	.50	.25
a.		Imperf., pair	10.00	
b.		Pair, imperf. between	525.00	
		Nos. 2123-2136 (14)	4.70	3.50

See Nos. 1897-1908, 2225-2231, 2252-2266, 2451-2468.

BLACK HERITAGE SERIES

Mary McLeod Bethune (1875-1955), Educator — A1520

PHOTOGRAVURE

1985, Mar. 5   **Perf. 11**

2137	A1520	22c multicolored	.60	.25

AMERICAN FOLK ART SERIES
Duck Decoys

Broadbill A1521

Mallard A1522

Canvasback — A1523

Redhead A1524

1985, Mar. 22

2138	A1521	22c multicolored	.90	.25
2139	A1522	22c multicolored	.90	.25
2140	A1523	22c multicolored	.90	.25
2141	A1524	22c multicolored	.90	.25
a.		Block of 4, #2138-2141	3.60	2.75

WINTER SPECIAL OLYMPICS

Ice Skater, Emblem, Skier A1525

1985, Mar. 25

2142	A1525	22c multicolored	.50	.25
a.		Vert. pair, imperf. horiz.	300.00	

LOVE

A1526

1985, Apr. 17

2143	A1526	22c multicolored	.45	.25
a.		Imperf., pair	800.00	

RURAL ELECTRIFICATION ADMINISTRATION

Electrified Farm A1527

PHOTOGRAVURE & ENGRAVED
(Combination Press)

1985, May 11

2144	A1527	22c multicolored	.50	.25
a.		Vert. pair, imperf between	—	

AMERIPEX '86

U.S. No. 134 — A1528

LITHOGRAPHED & ENGRAVED

1985, May 25

2145	A1528	22c multicolored	.45	.25
a.		Red, black & blue (engr.) omitted	125.00	
b.		Red & black omitted	1,250.	
c.		Red omitted	1,750.	
d.		Black missing (PS)	—	

ABIGAIL ADAMS (1744-1818)

Abigail Adams (1744-1818) A1529

PHOTOGRAVURE

1985, June 14

2146	A1529	22c multicolored	.45	.25
a.		Imperf., pair	200.00	

FREDERIC AUGUSTE BARTHOLDI (1834-1904)

Frederic Auguste Bartholdi (1834-1904), Statue of Liberty — A1530

LITHOGRAPHED & ENGRAVED

1985, July 18

2147	A1530	22c multicolored	.45	.25

Examples of No. 2147 exist with most, but not all, of the engraved black omitted.

George Washington, Washington Monument A1532

Envelopes A1533

COIL STAMPS
PHOTOGRAVURE

1985   **Perf. 10 Vertically**

2149	A1532	18c multicolored	.40	.25
a.		Untagged (Bureau precancel)	.35	.35
b.		Imperf., pair	750.00	
c.		As "a," imperf., pair	575.00	
2150	A1533	21.1c multicolored	.40	.25
a.		Untagged (Bureau Precancel)	.40	.40

Precancellations on Nos. 2149a ("PRESORTED FIRST-CLASS") and 2150a ("ZIP+4") do not have lines.

KOREAN WAR VETERANS

American Troops in Korea A1535

ENGRAVED

1985, July 26   **Perf. 11**

2152	A1535	22c gray green & rose red	.45	.25

SOCIAL SECURITY ACT, 50th ANNIV.

Men, Women, Children, Corinthian Columns A1536

PHOTOGRAVURE

1985, Aug. 14

2153	A1536	22c deep & light blue	.45	.25

WORLD WAR I VETERANS

The Battle of Marne, France, by Harvey Dunn A1537

ENGRAVED

1985, Aug. 26

2154	A1537	22c gray green & rose red	.45	.25
a.		Red missing (PS)	225.00	

HORSES

Quarter Horse A1538

Morgan A1539

Saddlebred A1540

Appaloosa A1541

PHOTOGRAVURE

1985, Sept. 25

2155	A1538	22c multicolored	1.10	.25
2156	A1539	22c multicolored	1.10	.25
2157	A1540	22c multicolored	1.10	.25
2158	A1541	22c multicolored	1.10	.25
a.		Block of 4, #2155-2158	4.40	4.00

PUBLIC EDUCATION IN AMERICA

Quill Pen, Apple, Spectacles, Penmanship Quiz — A1542

1985, Oct. 1

2159	A1542	22c multicolored	.45	.25

INTERNATIONAL YOUTH YEAR

YMCA Youth Camping, Cent. A1543

Boy Scouts, 75th Anniv. A1544

Big Brothers/Big Sisters Fed., 40th Anniv. — A1545

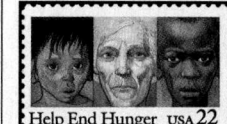

Camp Fire, Inc., 75th Anniv. A1546

1985, Oct. 7

2160	A1543	22c multicolored	.70	.25
2161	A1544	22c multicolored	.70	.25
2162	A1545	22c multicolored	.70	.25
2163	A1546	22c multicolored	.70	.25
a.		Block of 4, #2160-2163	3.00	2.25

HELP END HUNGER

Youths and the Elderly Suffering from Malnutrition A1547

PHOTOGRAVURE
1985, Oct. 15
2164 A1547 22c multicolored .45 .25

CHRISTMAS

Genoa Madonna, Enameled Terra-Cotta by Luca Della Robbia (1400-1482) A1548

Poinsettia Plants A1549

1985, Oct. 30
2165 A1548 22c multicolored .45 .25
  a. Imperf., pair 55.00
2166 A1549 22c multicolored .45 .25
  a. Imperf., pair 50.00

ARKANSAS STATEHOOD, 150th ANNIV.

Old State House, Little Rock A1550

1986, Jan. 3
2167 A1550 22c multicolored .65 .25
  a. Vert. pair, imperf. horiz. 500.00

GREAT AMERICANS ISSUE

A1551 A1552

ENGRAVED
Perf. 11, 11½x11 (#2185), 11.2x11.1 (#2179)
1986-94
2168 A1551 1c brnsh ver .25 .25
  b. 1c red brown .30 .30
2169 A1552 2c brt bl ('87) .25 .25
  a. Untagged .40 .25

A1553 A1554

2170 A1553 3c bright blue .25 .25
  a. Untagged ('94) .30 .25
2171 A1554 4c blue violet .25 .25
  a. 4c grayish violet, untagged .25 .25
  b. 4c deep grayish blue, untagged .35
  d. All color missing (EP) —

No. 2171d has an albino impression, and it also may be collected with a fully or partially printed stamp.

A1555 A1556

2172 A1555 5c dk ol grn .25 .25
  b. 5c lt ol grn .35 .25
2173 A1556 5c car ('90) .25 .25
  a. Untagged .25 .25

A1557 A1558

2175 A1557 10c lake ('87) .25 .25
  e. 10c carmine .80 .25
  f. All color omitted 125.00

No. 2175f may be collected se-tenant with a partially printed stamp or longer vertical strip. Stamps not se-tenant with a partially printed stamp are identified by a light setoff on the gum side.

2176 A1558 14c crimson ('87) .30 .25

A1559 A1560

2177 A1559 15c claret ('88) 1.00 .25
  d. All color omitted 200.00

No. 2177d resulted from partially printed panes. It must be collected se-tenant with a partially printed stamp or in a longer horizontal strip showing error stamps plus partially/completely printed stamps.

2178 A1560 17c dull bl grn .35 .25

A1561 A1562

2179 A1561 20c red brn ('94) .40 .25
  a. 20c orange brown .75 .25
  b. 20c bright red brown 1.25 .25
2180 A1562 21c bl vio ('88) .45 .25

A1563 A1564

2181 A1563 23c pur ('88) .45 .25
2182 A1564 25c blue ('88) .50 .25
  a. Booklet pane of 10, May 3, 1988 5.00 3.75
  d. Horiz. pair, imperf between 750.00
  e. As "a," all color omitted on right stamps 1,250.
  f. As No. 2182 (sheet stamp), vert. pair, bottom stamp all color omitted —

No. 2182f may be collected se-tenant with a partially printed stamp or longer vertical strip. See Nos. 2197, 2197a.

A1565 A1566

2183 A1565 28c myrtle grn ('89) .65 .35
2184 A1566 29c blue ('92) .70 .25

A1567 A1568

2185 A1567 29c indigo ('93) .65 .25
2186 A1568 35c black ('91) .75 .25

A1569 A1570

2187 A1569 40c dk bl ('90) .85 .25
2188 A1570 45c brt bl ('88) 1.00 .25
  a. 45c blue ('90) 2.75 .25

Almost all examples of No. 2188a are in the grade of fine or fine-very fine. Values are for stamps in the grade of fine-very fine.

A1571 A1572

2189 A1571 52c pur ('91) 1.10 .25
2190 A1572 56c scarlet 1.20 .25

A1573 A1574

2191 A1573 65c dk bl ('88) 1.30 .25
2192 A1574 75c dp mag ('92) 1.75 .25

A1575 A1576

2193 A1575 $1 dk Prus grn 3.00 .50
  a. All color omitted —

No. 2193a must be collected se-tenant vertically with partially printed stamps.

2194 A1576 $1 intense dp bl ('89) 2.25 .50
  b. $1 dp bl ('90) 2.50 .50
  d. $1 dk bl ('92) 2.50 .50
  e. $1 blue ('93) 2.75 .60

The intense deep blue of No. 2194 is much deeper than the deep blue and dark blue of the other $1 varieties.

A1577 A1578

2195 A1577 $2 brt violet 4.50 .50
2196 A1578 $5 copper red ('87) 9.00 1.00
  Nos. 2168-2196 (28) 33.90 8.60

Booklet Stamp
Perf. 10 on 2 or 3 Sides
2197 A1564 25c blue ('88) .55 .25
  a. Booklet pane of 6 3.30 2.50

Issued: No. 2182, 1/11; No. 2172, 2/27; $2, 3/19; 17c, 6/18; 1c, 6/30; 4c, 7/14; 56c, 9/3; 3c, 9/15; No. 2193, 9/23; 14c, 2/12/87; 2c, 2/28/87; 10c, 8/15/87; $5, 8/25/87; Nos. 2182a, 2197, 5/3/88; 15c, 6/6/88; 45c, 6/17/88; 21c, 10/21/88; 23c, 11/4/88; 65c, 11/5/88; No. 2194, 6/7/89; 28c, 9/14/89; No. 2173, 2/18/90; 40c, 9/6/90; Nos. 2188a, 2194b, 1990; 35c, 4/3/91; 52c, 6/3/91; No. 2173a, 1991; 75c, 2/16/92; No. 2184, 3/9/92; No. 2194d, 1992; No. 2185, 4/13/93; Nos. 2171b, 2194e, 1993; 20c, 10/24/94; Nos. 2170a, 2175e, 1994.

UNITED STATES - SWEDEN STAMP COLLECTING

Handstamped Cover, No. 213, Philatelic Memorabilia — A1581

Boy Examining Stamp Collection A1582

No. 836 Under Magnifying Glass, Sweden Nos. 268, 271 — A1583

1986 Presidents Miniature Sheet on First Day Cover A1584

BOOKLET STAMPS
LITHOGRAPHED & ENGRAVED
Perf. 10 Vert. on 1 or 2 Sides
1986, Jan. 23
2198 A1581 22c multicolored .45 .25
2199 A1582 22c multicolored .45 .25
2200 A1583 22c multicolored .45 .25
2201 A1584 22c multicolored .45 .25
  a. Bklt. pane of 4, #2198-2201 2.00 1.75
  b. As "a," black omitted on Nos. 2198, 2201 45.00
  c. As "a," blue (litho.) omitted on Nos. 2198-2200 1,500.
  d. As "a," buff (litho.) omitted —

See Sweden Nos. 1585-1588.

LOVE ISSUE

A1585

PHOTOGRAVURE
1986, Jan. 30 *Perf. 11*
2202 A1585 22c multicolored .55 .25

BLACK HERITAGE SERIES

Sojourner Truth (c. 1797-1883), Abolitionist — A1586

PHOTOGRAVURE

1986, Feb. 4
2203 A1586 22c multicolored .55 .25

REPUBLIC OF TEXAS, 150th ANNIV.

Texas State Flag and Silver Spur — A1587

1986, Mar. 2
2204 A1587 22c dk bl, dk red
& grayish
blk .50 .25
a. Horiz. pair, imperf. vert. 600.00
b. Dark red omitted 1,750.
c. Dark blue omitted 5,000.

FISH

Muskellunge — A1588

Atlantic Cod A1589

Largemouth Bass — A1590

Bluefin Tuna A1591

Catfish A1592

BOOKLET STAMPS
PHOTOGRAVURE
Perf. 10 Horiz. on 1 or 2 Sides
1986, Mar. 21
2205 A1588 22c multicolored 1.00 .25
2206 A1589 22c multicolored 1.00 .25
2207 A1590 22c multicolored 1.00 .25
2208 A1591 22c multicolored 1.00 .25
2209 A1592 22c multicolored 1.00 .25
a. Bklt. pane of 5, #2205-2209 5.00 2.75

The magenta used to print this issue is extremely fugitive. Dangerous fakes purported to be magenta omitted exist. No genuine examples are known. Panes apparently lacking red must be certified, and examples presently with certificates should be recertified.

PUBLIC HOSPITALS

A1593

1986, Apr. 11   *Perf. 11*
2210 A1593 22c multicolored .45 .25
a. Vert. pair, imperf. horiz. 250.00
b. Horiz. pair, imperf. vert. 800.00

PERFORMING ARTS

Edward Kennedy "Duke" Ellington (1899-1974), Jazz Composer — A1594

1986, Apr. 29
2211 A1594 22c multicolored .45 .25
a. Vert. pair, imperf. horiz. 500.00

AMERIPEX '86 ISSUE
Miniature Sheets

35 Presidents — A1599a

No. 2216: a, George Washington. b, John Adams. c, Thomas Jefferson. d, James Madison. e, James Monroe. f, John Quincy Adams. g, Andrew Jackson. h, Martin Van Buren. i, William H. Harrison.
No. 2217: a, John Tyler. b, James Knox Polk. c, Zachary Taylor. d, Millard Fillmore. e, Franklin Pierce. f, James Buchanan. g, Abraham Lincoln. h, Andrew Johnson. i, Ulysses S. Grant.
No. 2218: a, Rutherford B. Hayes. b, James A. Garfield. c, Chester A. Arthur. d, Grover Cleveland. e, Benjamin Harrison. f, William McKinley. g, Theodore Roosevelt. h, William H. Taft. i, Woodrow Wilson.
No. 2219: a, Warren G. Harding. b, Calvin Coolidge. c, Herbert Hoover. d, Franklin Delano Roosevelt. e, White House. f, Harry S. Truman. g, Dwight D. Eisenhower. h, John F. Kennedy. i, Lyndon B. Johnson.

LITHOGRAPHED & ENGRAVED

1986, May 22
2216 A1599a Pane of 9 6.50 4.00
a.-i. 22c, any single .65 .40
j. Blue (engr.) omitted 2,000.
k. Black inscription omitted 1,000.
l. Imperf. 10,500.
m. As "k," double impression of red —
n. Blue omitted on b-c, e-f, i —
2217 A1599b Pane of 9 6.50 4.00
a.-i. 22c, any single .65 .40
j. Black inscription omitted 1,500.
2218 A1599c Pane of 9 6.50 4.00
a.-i. 22c, any single .65 .40
j. Brown (engr.) omitted —
k. Black inscription omitted 1,500.

2219 A1599d Pane of 9 6.50 4.00
a.-i. 22c, any single .65 .40
j. Blackish blue (engr.) inscription omitted on a-b, d-e, g-h 2,250.
l. Blackish blue (engr.) omitted on all stamps —
Nos. 2216-2219 (4) 26.00 16.00

Issued in conjunction with AMERIPEX '86 Intl. Philatelic Exhibition, Chicago, IL May 22-June 1.

ARCTIC EXPLORERS

Elisha Kent Kane A1600

Adolphus W. Greely A1601

Vilhjalmur Stefansson A1602

Robert E. Peary and Matthew Alexander Henson A1603

PHOTOGRAVURE

1986, May 28
2220 A1600 22c multicolored .65 .25
2221 A1601 22c multicolored .65 .25
2222 A1602 22c multicolored .65 .25
2223 A1603 22c multicolored .65 .25
a. Block of 4, #2220-2223 2.75 2.25
b. As "a," black omitted 4,500.
c. As "a," Nos. 2220, 2221 black omitted 1,000.
d. As "a," Nos. 2222, 2223 black omitted 1,000.

STATUE OF LIBERTY, 100th
ANNIVERSARY

Statue of Liberty, Cent. — A1604

ENGRAVED

1986, July 4
2224 A1604 22c scar & dk bl .45 .25
a. Scarlet omitted —

On No. 2224a, virtually all of the dark blue also is omitted, so the error stamp should be collected as part of a transition strip.
See France No. 2014.

TRANSPORTATION ISSUE
Types of 1982-85 and

A1604a

A1604b

COIL STAMPS
ENGRAVED

1986-90   *Perf. 10 Vert.*
2225 A1604a 1c violet .25 .25
b. Untagged .25 .25
c. Imperf., pair 1,750.

2226 A1604b 2c black .25 .25
a. Untagged .25 .25

REDUCED SIZE

2228 A1285 4c reddish brown .25 .25
b. Imperf., pair 175.00

Untagged

2231 A1511 8.3c green (Bureau precancel) .65 .25
Nos. 2225-2231 (4) 1.40 1.00

Issued: 1c, 11/26; 2c, 3/6/87. Earliest known usage of 4c, 8/15/86; 8.3c, 8/29.
On No. 2228 "Stagecoach 1890s" is 17¾mm long, on No. 1898A, 19½mm long. On No. 2231 "Ambulance 1860s" is 18mm long, on No. 2128, 18½mm long.
No. 2226 inscribed "2 USA"; No. 1897A inscribed "USA 2c".

AMERICAN FOLK ART SERIES
Navajo Art

A1605

A1606

A1607

A1608

LITHOGRAPHED & ENGRAVED

1986, Sept. 4   *Perf. 11*
2235 A1605 22c multicolored .80 .25
a. Black (engr.) omitted 65.00
2236 A1606 22c multicolored .80 .25
a. Black (engr.) omitted 65.00
2237 A1607 22c multicolored .80 .25
a. Black (engr.) omitted 65.00
2238 A1608 22c multicolored .80 .25
a. Black (engr.) omitted 65.00
b. Block of 4, #2235-2238 3.25 2.25
c. As "b," black (engr.) omitted 300.00

LITERARY ARTS SERIES

T. S. Eliot (1888-1965), Poet — A1609

ENGRAVED

1986, Sept. 26
2239 A1609 22c copper red .45 .25

AMERICAN FOLK ART SERIES
Woodcarved Figurines

Highlander Figure A1610

Ship Figurehead A1611

Nautical Figure — A1612

Cigar Store Figure — A1613

PHOTOGRAVURE
1986, Oct. 1

2240	A1610	22c multicolored	.50	.25
2241	A1611	22c multicolored	.50	.25
2242	A1612	22c multicolored	.50	.25
2243	A1613	22c multicolored	.50	.25
a.		Block of 4, #2240-2243	2.00	1.50
b.		As "a," imperf. vert.	750.00	

CHRISTMAS

Madonna, by Perugino (c. 1450-1523) A1614

Village Scene A1615

1986, Oct. 24

2244	A1614	22c multicolored	.45	.25
a.		Imperf., pair	425.00	
2245	A1615	22c multicolored	.45	.25

MICHIGAN STATEHOOD, 150th ANNIV.

White Pine — A1616

1987, Jan. 26

2246	A1616	22c multicolored	.50	.25

PAN AMERICAN GAMES

Runner in Full Stride A1617

1987, Jan. 29

2247	A1617	22c multicolored	.45	.25
a.		Silver omitted	575.00	

No. 2247a is valued in the grade of fine.

LOVE ISSUE

A1618

PHOTOGRAVURE
1987, Jan. 30   **Perf. 11½x11**

2248	A1618	22c multicolored	.45	.25

BLACK HERITAGE SERIES

Jean Baptiste Pointe du Sable (c. 1750-1818), Pioneer Trader, Founder of Chicago — A1619

1987, Feb. 20   **Perf. 11**

2249	A1619	22c multicolored	.40	.25

PERFORMING ARTS SERIES

Enrico Caruso (1873-1921), Opera Tenor — A1620

PHOTOGRAVURE
1987, Feb. 27

2250	A1620	22c multicolored	.45	.25
a.		Black omitted	3,750.	

GIRL SCOUTS, 75TH ANNIVERSARY

Fourteen Achievement Badges — A1621

LITHOGRAPHED & ENGRAVED
1987, Mar. 12

2251	A1621	22c multicolored	.45	.25
a.		All litho. colors omitted	1,750.	
b.		Red & black (engr.) omitted	1,500.	

All known examples of No. 2251a have been expertized and certificate must accompany purchase. The unique pane of No. 2251b has been expertized and a certificate exists for the pane of 50.

TRANSPORTATION ISSUE

A1622

A1623

A1624

A1625

A1626

A1627

A1628

A1629

A1630

A1631

A1632

A1633

A1634

A1635

A1636

COIL STAMPS
ENGRAVED
1987-88   **Perf. 10 Vert.**

2252	A1622	3c claret ('88)	.25	.25
a.		Untagged	.25	.25
b.		As "a," imperf. pair	1,350.	
2253	A1623	5c black	.25	.25
2254	A1624	5.3c black (Bureau precancel in red), untagged ('88)	.25	.25
2255	A1625	7.6c brown (Bureau precancel in red), untagged ('88)	.25	.25
2256	A1626	8.4c dp clar (Bureau precancel in red), untagged ('88)	.25	.25
a.		Imperf., pair	350.00	
2257	A1627	10c blue	.40	.25
e.		Imperf., pair	1,000.	
2258	A1628	13c black (Bureau precancel in red), untagged ('88)	.65	.25
2259	A1629	13.2c slate grn (Bureau precancel in red), untagged ('88)	.25	.25
a.		Imperf., pair	75.00	
2260	A1630	15c violet ('88)	.30	.25
c.		Imperf., pair	500.00	
2261	A1631	16.7c rose (Bureau precancel in black), untagged ('88)	.30	.30
a.		Imperf., pair	125.00	

All known examples of No. 2261a are miscut top to bottom.

2262	A1632	17.5c dk vio	.75	.25
a.		Untagged (Bureau precancel in red)	.65	.30
b.		Imperf., pair	1,250.	
2263	A1633	20c blue vio ('88)	.35	.25
a.		Imperf., pair	50.00	
2264	A1634	20.5c rose (Bureau precancel in black), untagged ('88)	.75	.40
2265	A1635	21c olive grn (Bureau precancel in red), untagged ('88)	.50	.40
a.		Imperf., pair	35.00	

2266	A1636	24.1c deep ultra (Bureau precancel in red), untagged ('88)	.80	.45
		Nos. 2252-2266 (15)	6.30	4.30

5.3c, 7.6c, 8.4c, 13.2c, 16.7c, 20.5c, 21c and 24.1c only available precanceled.
See Nos. 1897-1908, 2123-2136, 2225-2231, 2451-2468.

SPECIAL OCCASIONS

A1637

A1638

A1639

A1640

A1641

A1642

A1643

A1644

BOOKLET STAMPS
PHOTOGRAVURE
Perf. 10 on 1, 2 or 3 Sides
1987, Apr. 20

2267	A1637	22c multicolored	.75	.25
2268	A1638	22c multicolored	.90	.25
2269	A1639	22c multicolored	.90	.25
2270	A1640	22c multicolored	.90	.25
2271	A1641	22c multicolored	.90	.25
2272	A1642	22c multicolored	.75	.25
2273	A1643	22c multicolored	1.50	.25
2274	A1644	22c multicolored	.90	.25
a.		Bklt. pane of 10 (#2268-2271, 2273-2274, 2 each #2267, 2272)	9.00	5.00
		Nos. 2267-2274 (8)	7.50	2.00

UNITED WAY, 100th ANNIV.

Six Profiles A1645

LITHOGRAPHED & ENGRAVED
1987, Apr. 28   **Perf. 11**

2275	A1645	22c multicolored	.45	.25

A1646

A1647

A1648

A1649

Pheasant
A1649a

Grosbeak
A1649b

Owl —
A1649c

Honeybee
A1649d

Photo., Engr. (No. 2280). Litho. &
Engr. (No. 2281)

1987-88			*Perf. 11*	
2276	A1646	22c multi	.45	.25
a.		Booklet pane of 20, Nov. 30	9.00	—
b.		As "a," vert. pair, imperf. btwn.	1,450.	
c.		As "a," miscut and inserted upside down into booklet cover, imperf between stamps and right selvage		
d.		Yellow omitted		—

All documented examples of No. 2276d show significant misregistration of the red ink.

2277	A1647	(25c) multi ('88)	.50	.25
2278	A1648	25c multi ('88)	.50	.25
	Nos. 2276-2278 (3)		1.45	.75

COIL STAMPS
Perf. 10 Vert.

2279	A1647	(25c) multi ('88)	.50	.25
a.		Imperf., pair	60.00	
2280	A1649	25c multi ('88)	.50	.25
c.		Imperf. pair	10.00	
e.		Black trees	90.00	—
f.		Pair, imperf. between	375.00	
2281	A1649d	25c multi ('88)	.50	.25
a.		As No. 2281, imperf. pair	45.00	
b.		Black (engr. - details on bee) omitted	45.00	—
c.		Black (litho. - "25 USA") omitted	400.00	
d.		Pair, imperf. between	600.00	
e.		Yellow (litho.) omitted	700.00	
	Nos. 2279-2281 (3)		1.50	.75

Beware of stamps with traces of the litho. black that are offered as No. 2281c.

Vertical pairs or blocks of No. 2281 and imperfs. with the engr. black missing are from printer's waste.

BOOKLET STAMPS
PHOTOGRAVURE
Perf. 10 on 2 or 3 Sides

2282	A1647	(25c) multi ('88)	.50	.25
a.		Booklet pane of 10	6.50	3.50

Perf. 11 on 2 or 3 Sides

2283	A1649a	25c multi ('88)	.50	.25
a.		Booklet pane of 10	6.00	3.50
b.		25c multicolored, red removed from sky	4.50	.25
c.		As "b," bklt. pane of 10	45.00	—
d.		Vert. pair, imperf. btwn.	275.00	

Imperf. panes exist from printers waste, and a large number exist. No. 2283d resulted from a foldover. Non-foldover pairs and multiples are printer's waste.

Perf. 10 on 2 or 3 Sides

2284	A1649b	25c multi ('88)	.50	.25
2285	A1649c	25c multi ('88)	.50	.25
b.		Bklt. pane of 10, 5 each #2284-2285	5.00	3.50
d.		Pair, Nos. 2284-2285	1.10	.50
2285A	A1648	25c multi ('88)	.50	.25
c.		Booklet pane of 6	3.00	2.00
	Nos. 2282-2285A (5)		2.50	1.25

Issued: #2276, 5/9; #2277, 2279, 2282, 3/22; #2278, 5/6; #2280, 5/20; #2281, 9/2; #2283, 4/29; #2284-2285, 5/28; #2285A, 7/5.

NORTH AMERICAN WILDLIFE

North American
Wildlife — A1650

PHOTOGRAVURE

1987, June 13   *Perf. 11*

2286	A1650	22c Barn swallow	1.00	.50
2287	A1651	22c Monarch butterfly	1.00	.50
2288	A1652	22c Bighorn sheep	1.00	.50
2289	A1653	22c Broad-tailed hummingbird	1.00	.50
2290	A1654	22c Cottontail	1.00	.50
2291	A1655	22c Osprey	1.00	.50
2292	A1656	22c Mountain lion	1.00	.50
2293	A1657	22c Luna moth	1.00	.50
2294	A1658	22c Mule deer	1.00	.50
2295	A1659	22c Gray squirrel	1.00	.50
2296	A1660	22c Armadillo	1.00	.50
2297	A1661	22c Eastern chipmunk	1.00	.50
2298	A1662	22c Moose	1.00	.50
2299	A1663	22c Black bear	1.00	.50
2300	A1664	22c Tiger swallowtail	1.00	.50
2301	A1665	22c Bobwhite	1.00	.50
2302	A1666	22c Ringtail	1.00	.50
2303	A1667	22c Red-winged blackbird	1.00	.50
2304	A1668	22c American lobster	1.00	.50
2305	A1669	22c Black-tailed jack rabbit	1.00	.50
2306	A1670	22c Scarlet tanager	1.00	.50
2307	A1671	22c Woodchuck	1.00	.50
2308	A1672	22c Roseate spoonbill	1.00	.50
2309	A1673	22c Bald eagle	1.00	.50
2310	A1674	22c Alaskan brown bear	1.00	.50
2311	A1675	22c Iiwi	1.00	.50
2312	A1676	22c Badger	1.00	.50
2313	A1677	22c Pronghorn	1.00	.50
2314	A1678	22c River otter	1.00	.50
2315	A1679	22c Ladybug	1.00	.50
2316	A1680	22c Beaver	1.00	.50
2317	A1681	22c White-tailed deer	1.00	.50
2318	A1682	22c Blue jay	1.00	.50
2319	A1683	22c Pika	1.00	.50
2320	A1684	22c Bison	1.00	.50
2321	A1685	22c Snowy egret	1.00	.50
2322	A1686	22c Gray wolf	1.00	.50
2323	A1687	22c Mountain goat	1.00	.50
2324	A1688	22c Deer mouse	1.00	.50
2325	A1689	22c Black-tailed prairie dog	1.00	.50
2326	A1690	22c Box turtle	1.00	.50
2327	A1691	22c Wolverine	1.00	.50
2328	A1692	22c American elk	1.00	.50
2329	A1693	22c California sea lion	1.00	.50
2330	A1694	22c Mockingbird	1.00	.50
2331	A1695	22c Raccoon	1.00	.50
2332	A1696	22c Bobcat	1.00	.50
2333	A1697	22c Black-footed ferret	1.00	.50
2334	A1698	22c Canada goose	1.00	.50
2335	A1699	22c Red fox	1.00	.50
a.		Pane of 50, #2286-2335	50.00	35.00
2286b-2335b		Any single, red omitted	2,000.	

RATIFICATION OF THE CONSTITUTION BICENTENNIAL

Dec 7, 1787 USA 22 Delaware
A1700

Dec 12, 1787 Pennsylvania
A1701

Dec 18, 1787 USA New Jersey 22
A1702

January 2, 1788 Georgia
A1703

January 9, 1788 USA Connecticut
A1704

Feb 6, 1788 Massachusetts
A1705

April 28, 1788 USA Maryland 22
A1706

May 23, 1788 South Carolina
A1707

June 21, 1788 New Hampshire
A1708

June 25, 1788 USA Virginia 25
A1709

July 26, 1788 USA New York 25
A1710

November 21, 1789 North Carolina
A1711

May 29, 1790 Rhode Island
A1712

LITHOGRAPHED & ENGRAVED, PHOTOGRAVURE (#2337-2339, 2343-2344, 2347), ENGRAVED (#2341).

1987-90				
2336	A1700	22c multi	.55	.25
2337	A1701	22c multi	.55	.25
2338	A1702	22c multi	.55	.25
a.		Black (engr.) omitted	2,750.	
2339	A1703	22c multi	.55	.25
2340	A1704	22c multi	.55	.25
2341	A1705	22c dk bl & dk red	.55	.25
2342	A1706	22c multi	.55	.25
2343	A1707	22c multi	.55	.25
a.		Strip of 3, vert. imperf btwn.	12,500.	
b.		Red missing (PS)		—
2344	A1708	25c multi	.55	.25
2345	A1709	25c multi	.55	.25
2346	A1710	25c multi	.55	.25
2347	A1711	25c multi	.55	.25
2348	A1712	25c multi	.55	.25
	Nos. 2336-2348 (13)		7.15	3.25

No. 2343b resulted either from a shifting of all colors or from a shift of both the perforations and the cutting of the pane.

Issued: No. 2336, 7/4; No. 2337, 8/26; No. 2338, 9/11; No. 2339, 1/6/88; No. 2340, 1/9/88; No. 2341, 2/6/88; No. 2342, 2/15/88; No. 2343, 5/23/88; No. 2344, 6/21/88; No. 2345, 6/25/88; No. 2346, 7/26/88; No. 2347, 8/22/89; No. 2348, 5/29/90.

US-MOROCCO DIPLOMATIC RELATIONS, 200th ANNIV.

Arabesque, Dar
Batha Palace,
Fez — A1713

Friendship with Morocco 1787-1987 USA 22

LITHOGRAPHED & ENGRAVED

1987, July 17				
2349	A1713	22c scar & blk	.50	.25
a.		Black (engr.) omitted	200.00	

See Morocco No. 642.

LITERARY ARTS SERIES

William Faulkner USA 22

William Cuthbert
Faulkner (1897-
1962),
Novelist — A1714

ENGRAVED

1987, Aug. 3				
2350	A1714	22c bright green	.50	.25

Used untagged imperfs exist from printer's waste.

AMERICAN FOLK ART SERIES
Lacemaking

Lacemaking USA 22
A1715

Lacemaking USA 22
A1716

Lacemaking USA 22
A1717

Lacemaking USA 22
A1718

LITHOGRAPHED & ENGRAVED
1987, Aug. 14

2351	A1715	22c ultra & white	.45	.25
2352	A1716	22c ultra & white	.45	.25
2353	A1717	22c ultra & white	.45	.25
2354	A1718	22c ultra & white	.45	.25
a.		Block of 4, #2351-2354	1.90	1.90
b.		As "a," white omitted	350.00	
c.		Any single stamp, white omitted	90.00	

DRAFTING OF THE CONSTITUTION BICENTENNIAL
Excerpts from the Preamble

A1719

The Bicentennial of the Constitution of the United States of America 1787-1987 USA 22

We the people of the United States, in order to form a more perfect Union... Preamble, U.S. Constitution USA 22
A1720

Establish justice, insure domestic tranquility, provide for the common defense, promote the general welfare... Preamble, U.S.Constitution USA 22
A1721

And secure the blessings of liberty to ourselves and our posterity... Preamble, U.S.Constitution USA 22
A1722

Do ordain and establish this Constitution for the United States of America. Preamble, U.S.Constitution USA 22
A1723

BOOKLET STAMPS
PHOTOGRAVURE
Perf. 10 Horiz. on 1 or 2 Sides
1987, Aug. 28

2355	A1719	22c multicolored	.75	.25
a.		Grayish green (background) omitted	400.00	
2356	A1720	22c multicolored	.75	.25
a.		Grayish green (background) omitted	400.00	
2357	A1721	22c multicolored	.75	.25
a.		Grayish green (background) omitted	400.00	
2358	A1722	22c multicolored	.75	.25
a.		Grayish green (background) omitted	400.00	
2359	A1723	22c multicolored	.75	.25
a.		Bklt. pane of 5, #2355-2359	3.75	2.25
b.		Grayish green (background) omitted	400.00	

SIGNING OF THE CONSTITUTION

A1724

LITHOGRAPHED & ENGRAVED
1987, Sept. 17   *Perf. 11*

2360	A1724	22c multicolored	.55	.25

CERTIFIED PUBLIC ACCOUNTING

CPA
A1725

1987, Sept. 21

2361	A1725	22c multicolored	.70	.25
a.		Black (engr.) omitted	450.00	

LOCOMOTIVES

Stourbridge Lion, 1829 — A1726

Best Friend of Charleston, 1830 — A1727

John Bull, 1831 A1728

Brother Jonathan, 1832 — A1729

Gowan & Marx, 1839 A1730

BOOKLET STAMPS
Perf. 10 Horiz. on 1 or 2 Sides
1987, Oct. 1

2362	A1726	22c multi	.50	.25
2363	A1727	22c multi	.50	.25
2364	A1728	22c multi	.50	.25
2365	A1729	22c multi	.50	.25
a.		Red omitted	1,000.	250.00
2366	A1730	22c multi	.50	.25
a.		Bklt. pane of 5, #2362-2366	2.50	2.00
b.		As No. 2366, black (engr.) omitted (single)	—	
c.		As No. 2366, blue omitted (single)	—	

CHRISTMAS

Moroni Madonna A1731

Christmas Ornaments A1732

PHOTOGRAVURE
1987, Oct. 23   *Perf. 11*

2367	A1731	22c multicolored	.45	.25
2368	A1732	22c multicolored	.45	.25

1988 WINTER OLYMPICS, CALGARY

Skiing — A1733

1988, Jan. 10

2369	A1733	22c multicolored	.50	.25

AUSTRALIA BICENTENNIAL

Caricature of Australian Koala & American Bald Eagle — A1734

1988, Jan. 26

2370	A1734	22c multicolored	.45	.25

See Australia No. 1052.

BLACK HERITAGE SERIES

James Weldon Johnson, Author, Lyricist — A1735

1988, Feb. 2

2371	A1735	22c multicolored	.50	.25

CATS

Siamese, Exotic Shorthair A1736

Abyssinian, Himalayan A1737

Maine Coon, Burmese A1738

CATS (continued)

American Shorthair, Persian A1739

1988, Feb. 5

2372	A1736	22c multicolored	.70	.25
2373	A1737	22c multicolored	.70	.25
2374	A1738	22c multicolored	.70	.25
2375	A1739	22c multicolored	.70	.25
a.		Block of 4, #2372-2375	2.80	1.90

AMERICAN SPORTS

Knute Rockne (1888-1931), Notre Dame football coach.

A1740

LITHOGRAPHED & ENGRAVED
1988, Mar. 9

2376	A1740	22c multicolored	.50	.25

AMERICAN SPORTS

Francis Ouimet (1893-1967), 1st amateur golfer to win the US Open championship.

A1741

PHOTOGRAVURE
1988, June 13

2377	A1741	25c multicolored	.60	.25

LOVE ISSUE (Roses)

Rose A1742

Roses A1743

1988

2378	A1742	25c multi	.50	.25
a.		Imperf. pair	1,500.	
2379	A1743	45c multi	.85	.25

1988 SUMMER OLYMPICS, SEOUL

Gymnastic Rings A1744

1988, Aug. 19

2380	A1744	25c multicolored	.50	.25

CLASSIC AUTOMOBILES

1928 Locomobile — A1745

1929 Pierce-Arrow A1746

1931 Cord A1747

1932 Packard A1748

1935 Duesenberg — A1749

LITHOGRAPHED & ENGRAVED BOOKLET STAMPS
Perf. 10 Horiz. on 1 or 2 Sides
1988, Aug. 25

2381	A1745	25c multicolored	.65	.25
2382	A1746	25c multicolored	.65	.25
2383	A1747	25c multicolored	.65	.25
2384	A1748	25c multicolored	.65	.25
2385	A1749	25c multicolored	.65	.25
a.		Bklt. pane of 5, #2381-2385	3.25	2.50

ANTARCTIC EXPLORERS

Nathaniel Palmer (1799-1877) A1750

Lt. Charles Wilkes (1798-1877) A1751

Richard E. Byrd (1888-1957) A1752

Lincoln Ellsworth (1880-1951) A1753

PHOTOGRAVURE
1988, Sept. 14 — **Perf. 11**

2386	A1750	25c multicolored	.65	.25
2387	A1751	25c multicolored	.65	.25
2388	A1752	25c multicolored	.65	.25
2389	A1753	25c multicolored	.65	.25
a.		Block of 4, #2386-2389	2.75	2.00
b.		As "a," black omitted	750.00	
c.		As "a," imperf. horiz.	1,500.	

AMERICAN FOLK ART SERIES
Carousel Animals

Deer — A1754

Horse — A1755

Camel — A1756

Goat — A1757

LITHOGRAPHED & ENGRAVED
1988, Oct. 1

2390	A1754	25c multicolored	.75	.25
2391	A1755	25c multicolored	.75	.25
2392	A1756	25c multicolored	.75	.25
2393	A1757	25c multicolored	.75	.25
a.		Block of 4, #2390-2393	3.00	2.00
b.		As "a," red omitted	800.00	

EXPRESS MAIL RATE

Eagle in Flight — A1758

1988, Oct. 4
2394 A1758 $8.75 multicolored 13.50 8.00

SPECIAL OCCASIONS

Happy Birthday — A1759

Best Wishes — A1760

Thinking of You — A1761

Love You — A1762

BOOKLET STAMPS
PHOTOGRAVURE
Perf. 11 on 2 or 3 Sides
1988, Oct. 22

2395	A1759	25c multicolored	.50	.25
2396	A1760	25c multicolored	.50	.25
a.		Bklt. pane of 6, 3 #2395 + 3 #2396 with gutter between	3.50	3.25
2397	A1761	25c multicolored	.50	.25
2398	A1762	25c multicolored	.50	.25
a.		Bklt. pane of 6, 3 #2397 + 3 #2398 with gutter between	3.50	3.25
b.		As "a," imperf. horiz.	2,250.	
c.		As "a," imperf.		
		Nos. 2395-2398 (4)	2.00	1.00

CHRISTMAS

Madonna and Child, by Botticelli A1763

One-horse Open Sleigh & Village Scene A1764

LITHOGRAPHED & ENGRAVED (No. 2399), PHOTOGRAVURE (No. 2400)
1988, Oct. 20 — **Perf. 11½**

2399	A1763	25c multicolored	.50	.25
a.		Gold omitted	25.00	
2400	A1764	25c multicolored	.50	.25

MONTANA STATEHOOD, 100th ANNIV.

C.M. Russell and Friends, by Charles M. Russell (1865-1926) A1765

LITHOGRAPHED & ENGRAVED
1989, Jan. 15 — **Perf. 11**

2401 A1765 25c multicolored .55 .25

Imperfs without gum exist from printer's waste.

BLACK HERITAGE SERIES

Asa Philip Randolph (1889-1979), Labor & Civil Rights Leader — A1766

PHOTOGRAVURE
1989, Feb. 3

2402 A1766 25c multicolored .50 .25

NORTH DAKOTA STATEHOOD, 100th ANNIV.

Grain Elevator A1767

1989, Feb. 21

2403 A1767 25c multicolored .50 .25

WASHINGTON STATEHOOD, 100th ANNIV.

Mt. Rainier — A1768

1989, Feb. 22

2404 A1768 25c multicolored .50 .25

STEAMBOATS

Experiment, 1788-1790 — A1769

Phoenix, 1809 — A1770

New Orleans, 1812 — A1771

Washington, 1816 — A1772

Walk in the Water, 1818 — A1773

LITHOGRAPHED & ENGRAVED BOOKLET STAMPS
Perf. 10 Horiz. on 1 or 2 Sides
1989, Mar. 3

2405	A1769	25c multicolored	.60	.25
2406	A1770	25c multicolored	.60	.25
2407	A1771	25c multicolored	.60	.25
2408	A1772	25c multicolored	.60	.25
2409	A1773	25c multicolored	.60	.25
a.		Booklet pane of 5, #2405-2409	3.00	1.75

WORLD STAMP EXPO '89
Nov. 17-Dec. 3. Washington, D.C.

No. 122 — A1774

1989, Mar. 16 — **Perf. 11**

2410 A1774 25c grayish brn, blk & car rose .50 .25

PERFORMING ARTS

Arturo Toscanini
(1867-1957),
Conductor — A1775

PHOTOGRAVURE

1989, Mar. 25
2411 A1775 25c multicolored   .50   .25

CONSTITUTION BICENTENNIAL SERIES

House of
Representatives
A1776

Senate
A1777

Executive
Branch
A1778

Supreme Court
A1779

LITHOGRAPHED & ENGRAVED

1989-90
2412 A1776 25c multi   .50   .25
2413 A1777 25c multi   .50   .25
2414 A1778 25c multi   .50   .25
2415 A1779 25c multi   .50   .25
Nos. 2412-2415 (4)   2.00   1.00

Issued: No. 2412, 4/4; No. 2413, 4/6; No. 2414, 4/16; No. 2415, 2/2/90.

SOUTH DAKOTA STATEHOOD, 100th ANNIV.

Pasque Flowers, Pioneer Woman and
Sod House on Grasslands
A1780

PHOTOGRAVURE

1989, May 3
2416 A1780 25c multicolored   .60   .25
Imperfs exist from printer's waste.

AMERICAN SPORTS

Lou Gehrig (1903-
1941), New York
Yankee Baseball
Player — A1781

1989, June 10
2417 A1781 25c multicolored   .60   .25

LITERARY ARTS SERIES

Ernest Hemingway
(1899-1961), Nobel
Prize-winner for
Literature,
1954 — A1782

1989, July 17
2418 A1782 25c multicolored   .50   .25
a.   Vert. pair, imperf horiz.   800.00

Imperforates on gummed stamp paper, including gutter pairs and blocks, are proofs from the ABNCo. archives. See No. 2418P in Proofs section of the Scott U.S. Specialized Catalogue.

MOON LANDING, 20th ANNIVERSARY

Raising the
Flag on Lunar
Surface, July
20, 1969
A1783

LITHOGRAPHED & ENGRAVED

1989, July 20   *Perf. 11x11½*
2419 A1783 $2.40 multi   4.75   2.00
a.   Black (engr.) omitted   1,500.
b.   Imperf., pair   400.00
c.   Black (litho.) omitted   1,500.

LETTER CARRIERS

Letter
Carriers
A1784

PHOTOGRAVURE

2420 A1784 25c multicolored   .50   .25

CONSTITUTION BICENTENNIAL

Bill of
Rights — A1785

LITHOGRAPHED & ENGRAVED

1989, Sept. 25
2421 A1785 25c multicolored   .50   .25
a.   Black (engr.) omitted   225.00

PREHISTORIC ANIMALS

Tyrannosaurus Rex — A1786

Pteranodon
A1787

Stegosaurus — A1788

Brontosaurus — A1789

1989, Oct. 1
2422 A1786 25c multicolored   .70   .25
a.   Black (engr.) omitted   80.00
2423 A1787 25c multicolored   .70   .25
a.   Black (engr.) omitted   80.00
2424 A1788 25c multicolored   .70   .25
a.   Black (engr.) omitted   80.00
2425 A1789 25c multicolored   .70   .25
a.   Black (engr.) omitted   80.00
b.   Block of 4, #2422-2425   2.80   2.00
c.   As "b," black (engr.) omitted   325.00

The correct scientific name for Brontosaurus is Apatosaurus.
No. 2425c is valued in the grade of fine. Very fine blocks exist and sell for approximately $600.

PRE-COLUMBIAN AMERICA ISSUE

Southwest Carved
Figure, A. D. 1150-
1350 — A1790

PHOTOGRAVURE

1989, Oct. 12
2426 A1790 25c multicolored   .60   .25
See No. C121.

CHRISTMAS

Madonna and
Child, by
Caracci
A1791

Sleigh Full of
Presents
A1792

LITHOGRAPHED & ENGRAVED,
PHOTOGRAVURE (#2428-2429)

1989, Oct. 19   *Perf. 11½*
2427 A1791 25c multicolored   .50   .25
a.   Booklet pane of 10   5.00   3.50
b.   Red (litho.) omitted   400.00
c.   As "a," imperf.   —

Perf. 11
2428 A1792 25c multicolored   .50   .25
a.   Vert. pair, imperf. horiz.   500.00

BOOKLET STAMP
Perf. 11½ on 2 or 3 Sides
2429 A1792 25c multicolored   .50   .25
a.   Booklet pane of 10   5.00   3.50
b.   Vert. pair, imperf. btwn.
(from miscut bklt pane)   500.00

c.   As "a," horiz. imperf. between   2,250.
d.   As "a," red omitted   3,250.
e.   Imperf., pair   750.00

Marked differences exist between Nos. 2428 and 2429: No. 2429 was printed in four colors, No. 2428 in five colors. The runners on the sleigh in No. 2429 are twice as thick as those on No. 2428. On No. 2429 the package at the upper left in the sleigh has a red bow, whereas the same package in No. 2428 has a red and black bow; and the ribbon on the upper right package in No. 2429 is green, whereas the same ribbon in No. 2428 is black.

Eagle and
Shield — A1793

PHOTOGRAVURE
BOOKLET STAMP

1989, Nov. 10   *Die Cut*
Self-Adhesive
2431 A1793 25c multicolored   .50   .25
a.   Booklet pane of 18   10.00
b.   Vert. pair, die cutting omitted between   325.00
c.   Die cutting omitted, pair   200.00

Panes sold for $5.
Also available in strips of 18 with stamps spaced for use in affixing machines to service first day covers. Sold for $5.
No. 2431c will include part of the margins around the stamps.
Sold only in 15 test cities (Atlanta, Chicago, Cleveland, Columbus, OH, Dallas, Denver, Houston, Indianapolis, Kansas City, MO, Los Angeles, Miami, Milwaukee, Minneapolis, Phoenix, St. Louis) and through the philatelic agency.

WORLD STAMP EXPO '89

World Stamp Expo, Washington, DC,
Nov. 17-Dec. 3 — A1794

LITHOGRAPHED & ENGRAVED

1989, Nov. 17   *Imperf.*
2433 A1794   Pane of 4   13.00   14.00
a.   90c like No. 122   3.25   3.00
b.   90c like 132TC4j   3.25   3.00
c.   90c like 132TC4i   3.25   3.00
d.   90c like 132TC4d   3.25   3.00

20th UPU CONGRESS
Traditional Mail Delivery

Stagecoach, c.
1850 — A1795

Paddlewheel
Steamer
A1796

Biplane — A1797

Depot-hack Type Automobile
A1798

1989, Nov. 19   **Perf. 11**

2434	A1795	25c multicolored	.50	.25
2435	A1796	25c multicolored	.50	.25
2436	A1797	25c multicolored	.50	.25
2437	A1798	25c multicolored	.50	.25
a.		Block of 4, #2434-2437	2.00	1.75
b.		As "a," dark blue (engr.)		
		omitted	325.00	

No. 2437b is valued in the grade of fine. Very fine blocks exist and sell for approximately $450.

Souvenir Sheet
Souvenir Sheet

1989, Nov. 28   **Imperf.**

2438		Sheet of 4	5.00	3.75
a.		A1795 25c multicolored	1.25	.80
b.		A1796 25c multicolored	1.25	.80
c.		A1797 25c multicolored	1.25	.80
d.		A1798 25c multicolored	1.25	.80
e.		Dark blue & gray (engr.) omitted	4,000.	

20th Universal Postal Union Congress.

VALUES FOR HINGED STAMPS AFTER NO. 771
This catalogue does not value unused stamps after No. 771 in hinged condition. Hinged unused stamps from No. 772 to the present are worth considerably less than the values given for unused stamps, which are for never-hinged examples.

IDAHO STATEHOOD, 100th ANNIV.

Mountain Bluebird, Sawtooth Mountains — A1799

PHOTOGRAVURE

1990, Jan. 6   **Perf. 11**
2439	A1799	25c multicolored	.55	.25

LOVE

A1800

PHOTOGRAVURE

1990, Jan. 18   **Perf. 12½x13**
2440	A1800	25c multi	.50	.25
a.		Imperf., pair	550.00	

BOOKLET STAMP
Perf. 11½ on 2 or 3 Sides
2441	A1800	25c multi	.50	.25
a.		Booklet pane of 10	5.00	3.50
b.		Bright pink omitted	85.00	
c.		As "a," bright pink omitted	950.00	

No. 2441b may be obtained from booklet panes containing both normal and color-omitted stamps.

BLACK HERITAGE SERIES

Ida B. Wells (1862-1931), Journalist — A1801

1990, Feb. 1   **Perf. 11**
2442	A1801	25c multicolored	.75	.25

Beach Umbrella — A1802

BOOKLET STAMP
Perf. 11 on 2 or 3 Sides
1990, Feb. 3
2443	A1802	15c multicolored	.30	.25
a.		Booklet pane of 10	3.00	2.50
b.		Blue omitted	100.00	
c.		As "a," blue omitted	1,000.	

WYOMING STATEHOOD, 100th ANNIV.

High Mountain Meadows, by Conrad Schwiering
A1803

LITHOGRAPHED & ENGRAVED

1990, Feb. 23   **Perf. 11**
2444	A1803	25c multicolored	.80	.25
a.		Black (engr.) omitted	900.00	—

CLASSIC FILMS

Judy Garland and Toto (The Wizard of Oz) — A1804

Clark Gable & Vivien Leigh (Gone With the Wind) — A1805

Gary Cooper (Beau Geste) — A1806

John Wayne (Stagecoach) A1807

PHOTOGRAVURE

1990, Mar. 23
2445	A1804	25c multicolored	1.25	.25
2446	A1805	25c multicolored	1.25	.25
2447	A1806	25c multicolored	1.25	.25
2448	A1807	25c multicolored	1.25	.25
a.		Block of 4, #2445-2448	5.00	3.50

LITERARY ARTS SERIES

Marianne Craig Moore (1887-1972), Poet — A1808

1990, Apr. 18
2449	A1808	25c multicolored	.55	.25
a.		All colors missing (EP)	—	

No. 2449a must be collected se-tenant with a partially printed stamp or in longer horizontal strips with a partially printed stamp and normal stamps.

TRANSPORTATION ISSUE

A1810   A1811

A1811a   A1812

A1816   A1822

A1823   A1825

A1827

COIL STAMPS
ENGRAVED, PHOTOGRAVURE
(#2452B, 2452D, 2454, 2458)

1990-95   **Perf. 9.8 Vert.**
Untagged (Nos. 2452B, 2452D, 2453, 2454, 2457-2458)
Bureau Precancel in Gray (#2453-2458)
2451	A1810	4c claret	.25	.25
a.		Imperf., pair	450.00	
b.		Untagged	.25	
2452	A1811	5c carmine	.25	.25
a.		Untagged, dull gum	.25	
c.		Imperf., pair	350.00	
2452B	A1811	5c carmine	.25	.25
2452D	A1811a	5c carmine	.25	.25
e.		Imperf., pair	115.00	
2453	A1812	5c brown	.40	.25
a.		Imperf., pair	225.00	
b.		Gray omitted	—	

2454	A1812	5c red	.45	.25
2457	A1816	10c green	.45	.25
a.		Imperf., pair	110.00	
b.		All color omitted	—	

No. 2457b must be accompanied by a 2012 certificate of authentication confirming that stamps are from the discovery coil roll that also contained normal and partially printed stamps.

2458	A1816	10c green	.55	.25
2463	A1822	20c green	.40	.25
a.		Imperf., pair	75.00	
2464	A1823	23c dark blue	.45	.25
a.		Imperf., pair	100.00	
2466	A1825	32c blue	.80	.25
a.		Imperf., pair, shiny gum	375.00	
b.		bright blue	3.00	2.25

Some specialists refer to No. 2466b as "Bronx blue," and it is considered to be an error of color.

2468	A1827	$1 bl & scar	2.25	.50
a.		Imperf., pair	1,750.	1,150.
		Nos. 2451-2468 (12)	6.75	3.25

Some mint pairs of No. 2468 appear to be imperf. but have faint blind perforations on the gum. Beware of examples with the gum removed.

Issued: $1, 4/20; No. 2452, 8/31; 4c, 1/25/91; 23c, 4/12/91; Nos. 2453, 2457, 5/25/91; No. 2454, 10/22/91; No. 2452B, 12/8/92; No. 2458, 5/25/94; Nos. 2452D, 3/20/95; 32c, 6/2/95; 20c, 6/9/95.

LIGHTHOUSES

Admiralty Head, WA — A1829

Cape Hatteras, NC — A1830

West Quoddy Head, ME — A1831

American Shoals, FL — A1832

Sandy Hook, NJ — A1833

BOOKLET STAMPS
LITHOGRAPHED & ENGRAVED
Perf. 10 Vert. on 1 or 2 Sides
1990, Apr. 26
2470	A1829	25c multicolored	1.00	.25
2471	A1830	25c multicolored	1.00	.25
2472	A1831	25c multicolored	1.00	.25
2473	A1832	25c multicolored	1.00	.25
2474	A1833	25c multicolored	1.00	.25
a.		Bklt. pane of 5, #2470-2474	5.00	2.00
b.		As "a," white ("USA 25") omitted	65.00	—

Perforations on Lighthouse booklet panes separate very easily. Careful handling is required.

FLAG

A1834

PHOTOGRAVURE

1990, May 18   **Untagged**   *Die Cut*
Self-adhesive
Printed on Plastic

2475 A1834 25c dk red & dk bl		.55	.25
a.	Pane of 12	6.60	

Sold only in panes of 12; peelable plastic backing inscribed in light ultramarine. Available for a test period of six months at 22 First National Bank automatic teller machines in Seattle.

FLORA AND FAUNA

A1840

American Kestrel
A1841

Eastern Bluebird
A1842

Fawn
A1843

Cardinal
A1844

Pumpkinseed Sunfish — A1845

Bobcat
A1846

LITHOGRAPHED

Perf. 11, 11.2 (#2477)

1990-95   **Untagged (1c, 3c)**

2476 A1840 1c multi		.25	.25
a.	Quadruple impression of black inscriptions and denomination	850.00	

Other colors on Nos. 2476a, 2476b and 2476c are misregistered and the stamps are poorly centered.

b.	Quintuple impression of black inscriptions and denomination	1,500.	
2477 A1841 1c multi		.25	.25
2478 A1842 3c multi		.25	.25
a.	Vert. pair, imperf. horiz.	—	
b.	Double impression of all colors except yellow	200.00	
c.	Double impression of blue, triple impression of black	—	

Imperforates on gummed stamp paper, plus imperforate and perforated gutter pairs and blocks (including imperforate and perforated gutter pairs and blocks of No. 2476 se-tenant with No. 2478), are proofs from the ABNCo. archives. See Nos. 2476P and 2478P in Proofs section of the Scott U.S. Specialized Catalogue.

See Nos. 3031, 3031A, 3044. Compare design A1842 with design A2336.

PHOTOGRAVURE

2479 A1843 19c multi		.35	.25
b.	Red omitted	425.00	
c.	Imperf, pair	900.00	

On No. 2479b other colors are shifted.

2480 A1844 30c multicolored, June 22, 1991		.60	.25

LITHOGRAPHED & ENGRAVED

2481 A1845 45c multi		.90	.25
a.	Black (engr.) omitted	325.00	—
2482 A1846 $2 multi		3.50	1.25
a.	Black (engr.) omitted	200.00	

Nos. 2476-2482 (7)   6.10   2.75

Issued: $2, 6/1; 19c, 3/11/91; No. 2476, 3c, 30c, 6/22/91; 45c, 12/2/92; No. 2477, 5/10/95.

Blue Jay — A1847

Wood Duck — A1848

African Violets
A1849

Peach
A1850

Pear
A1851

Rose
A1853

Red Squirrel
A1852

Pine Cone
A1854

PHOTOGRAVURE
BOOKLET STAMPS

Perf. 10.9x9.8 on 2 or 3 Sides

1991-95

2483 A1847 20c multi		.50	.25
a.	Booklet pane of 10	5.25	2.50
b.	As "a," imperf		

Perf. 10 on 2 or 3 sides

2484 A1848 29c blk & multi		.60	.25
a.	Booklet pane of 10	6.00	3.75
b.	Vert. pair, imperf. horiz.	175.00	
c.	As "b," bklt. pane of 10	875.00	
f.	Vert. pair, imperf between and with natural straight edge at top or bottom	175.00	
g.	As "f," bklt. pane of 10	875.00	

Perf. 11 on 2 or 3 Sides

2485 A1848 29c red & multi		.60	.25
a.	Booklet pane of 10	6.00	4.00
b.	Vert. pair, imperf. between	2,500.	
c.	Imperf, pair	4,500.	

Perf. 10x11 on 2 or 3 Sides

2486 A1849 29c multi		.60	.25
a.	Booklet pane of 10	6.00	4.00

Perf. 11x10 on 2 or 3 Sides

2487 A1850 32c multi		.65	.25
2488 A1851 32c multi		.65	.25
a.	Booklet pane, 5 each #2487-2488	6.50	4.25
b.	Pair, #2487-2488	1.30	.30

Issued: Nos. 2484-2485, 4/12; No. 2486, 10/8/93; 20c, 6/15/95; 32c, 7/8/95.

PHOTOGRAVURE, ENGRAVED
(#2491)

1993-95   *Die Cut*

Self-Adhesive
Booklet Stamps

2489 A1852 29c multi		.60	.25
a.	Booklet pane of 18	11.00	
b.	As "a," die cutting omitted	—	

2490 A1853 29c red, green & black		.60	.25
a.	Booklet of 18	11.00	
2491 A1854 29c multi		.60	.25
a.	Booklet pane of 18	11.00	
b.	Horiz. pair, die cutting omitted between	175.00	125.00
c.	Coil with plate # B1		6.00

Stamps without plate number from coil strips are indistinguishable from booklet stamps once they are removed from the backing paper.

Serpentine Die Cut 11.3x11.7 on 2, 3 or 4 Sides

2492 A1853 32c pink, green & black		.65	.25
a.	Booklet pane of 20 + label	13.00	
b.	Booklet pane of 15 + label	9.75	
c.	Horiz. pair, die cutting omitted between	—	
d.	As "a," 2 stamps and parts of 7 others printed on backing liner	—	
e.	Booklet pane of 14	20.00	
f.	Booklet pane of 16	20.00	
g.	Coil with plate # S111		5.50
h.	Vert. pair, die cutting omitted between (from No. 2492b)	400.00	
i.	As "a," 6 pairs plus stamp and label die cutting omitted vert. btwn. (due to miscutting)	800.00	
j.	As "f," with 2 vert. pairs at bottom die cutting omitted horiz., in full bklt. #BK178D	—	

Serpentine Die Cut 8.8 on 2, 3 or 4 Sides

2493 A1850 32c multi		.65	.25
2494 A1851 32c multi		.65	.25
a.	Booklet pane, 10 each #2493-2494 + label	13.00	
b.	Pair, #2493-2494	1.30	
c.	As "b," die cutting omitted	—	

COIL STAMPS
Serpentine Die Cut 8.8 Vert.

2495 A1850 32c multi		2.00	.25
2495A A1851 32c multi		2.00	.25
b.	Pair, #2495-2495A	4.00	

Issued: No. 2489, 6/25; No. 2490, 8/19; No. 2491, 11/5; No. 2492, 6/2/95; Nos. 2493-2495A, 7/8/95.
See Nos. 3048-3049, 3053-3054.

Values for used self-adhesive stamps are for examples either on piece or off piece.

OLYMPIANS

Jesse Owens, 1936
A1855

Ray Ewry, 1900-08
A1856

Hazel Wightman, 1924
A1857

Eddie Eagan, 1920, 1932
A1858

Helene Madison, 1932
A1859

PHOTOGRAVURE

1990, July 6   *Perf. 11*

2496 A1855 25c multicolored		.60	.25
2497 A1856 25c multicolored		.60	.25
2498 A1857 25c multicolored		.60	.25
2499 A1858 25c multicolored		.60	.25
2500 A1859 25c multicolored		.60	.25
a.	Strip of 5, 2496-2500	3.25	2.50
b.	As "a," blue omitted	—	

Imperforates on gummed stamp paper, including gutter pairs, strips and blocks, are proofs from the ABNCo. archives. See No. 2500aP in Proofs section of the Scott U.S. Specialized Catalogue.

INDIAN HEADDRESSES

Assiniboin
A1860

Cheyenne
A1861

Comanche
A1862

Flathead
A1863

Shoshone
A1864

LITHOGRAPHED & ENGRAVED
BOOKLET STAMPS

Perf. 11 on 2 or 3 Sides

1990, Aug. 17

2501 A1860 25c multicolored		1.00	.25
2502 A1861 25c multicolored		1.00	.25
2503 A1862 25c multicolored		1.00	.25
a.	Black (engr.) omitted	—	
2504 A1863 25c multicolored		1.00	.25
2505 A1864 25c multicolored		1.00	.25
a.	Bklt. pane of 10, 2 each #2501-2505	10.00	6.00
b.	As "a," black (engr.) omitted	2,500.	
c.	Strip of 5, #2501-2505	5.00	2.50
d.	As "a," horiz. imperf. between	2,250.	

At least one of the examples of No. 2505d that have been reported is actually split at the booklet fold and is a block of 4 and a block of 6.

MICRONESIA & MARSHALL ISLANDS

Canoe & Federated States of Micronesia Flag
A1865

Stick Chart, Canoe & Republic of the Marshall Islands Flag
A1866

1990, Sept. 28 **Perf. 11**
2506 A1865 25c multicolored .50 .25
2507 A1866 25c multicolored .50 .25
a. Pair, #2506-2507 1.00 .75
b. As "a," black (engr.) omitted 1,400.

See Micronesia Nos. 124-126, Marshall Islands No. 381.

SEA CREATURES

Killer Whales A1867

Northern Sea Lions A1868

Sea Otter A1869

Common Dolphin A1870

1990, Oct. 3
2508 A1867 25c multicolored .55 .25
2509 A1868 25c multicolored .55 .25
2510 A1869 25c multicolored .55 .25
2511 A1870 25c multicolored .55 .25
a. Block of 4, #2508-2511 2.25 1.90
b. As "a," black (engr.) omitted 250.00

See Russia Nos. 5933-5936.

PRE-COLUMBIAN AMERICA ISSUE

Grand Canyon A1871

PHOTOGRAVURE
1990, Oct. 12
2512 A1871 25c multicolored .55 .25

See No. C127.

DWIGHT D. EISENHOWER, BIRTH CENTENARY

A1872

1990, Oct. 13 **Tagged** **Perf. 11**
2513 A1872 25c multicolored .80 .25

Imperforates on gummed stamp paper are proofs from the ABNCo. archives. See No.

2513P in Proofs section of the Scott U.S. Specialized Catalogue.

CHRISTMAS

Madonna and Child by Antonello da Messina A1873

Christmas Tree A1874

LITHOGRAPHED & ENGRAVED
1990, Oct. 18 **Perf. 11½**
2514 A1873 25c multi .50 .25
b. Booklet pane of 10 5.00 3.25

PHOTOGRAVURE
Perf. 11
2515 A1874 25c multicolored .50 .25
a. Vert. pair, imperf. horiz. 500.00
b. All colors missing (EP) —

No. 2515b must be collected se-tenant with normal and/or partially printed stamp(s).

BOOKLET STAMP
Perf. 11½x11 on 2 or 3 Sides
2516 A1874 25c multicolored .60 .25
a. Booklet pane of 10 6.00 3.25

Marked differences exist between Nos. 2515 and 2516. The background red on No. 2515 is even while that on No. 2516 is splotchy. The bands across the tree and "Greetings" are blue green on No. 2515 and yellow green on No. 2516.

A1875

This U.S. stamp, along with 25¢ of additional U.S. postage, is equivalent to the 'F' stamp rate
A1876

1991, Jan. 22 **Perf. 13**
2517 A1875 (29c) yel, blk, red & yel grn .60 .25
a. Imperf., pair 1,000.
b. Horiz. pair, imperf. vert. 1,000.

See note after No. 2518.
Gutter pairs and blocks, and cross gutter blocks, all perforated, are proofs from the ABNCo. archives. See No. 2517P in Proofs section of the Scott U.S. Specialized Catalogue.
No. 2517a is usually collected as a vertical pair, though No. 2517 can be distinguished from the other "F" stamp issues.

COIL STAMP
Perf. 10 Vert.
2518 A1875 (29c) yel, blk, dull red & dk yel grn .60 .25
a. Imperf., pair 25.00

"For U.S. addresses only" is 17½mm long on No. 2517, 16½mm long on No. 2518. Design of No. 2517 measures 21½x17½mm, No. 2518, 21x18mm.

BOOKLET STAMPS
Perf. 11 on 2 or 3 Sides
2519 A1875 (29c) yel, blk, dull red & dk grn .60 .25
a. Booklet pane of 10 6.50 4.50
2520 A1875 (29c) pale yel, blk, red & brt grn 1.50 .25
a. Booklet pane of 10 15.00 4.50
b. As "a," imperf. horiz. —
c. Horiz. pair, imperf btwn., in error booklet pane of 12 stamps 450.00
d. Horiz. pair, imperf. vert. —

No. 2519 has bullseye perforations that measure approximately 11.2. No. 2520 has less pronounced black lines in the leaf, which is a much brighter green than on No. 2519.
No. 2520c is from a paper foldover before perforating.

LITHOGRAPHED
1991, Jan. 22 **Untagged** **Perf. 11**
2521 A1876 (4c) bister & carmine .25 .25
a. Vert. pair, imperf. horiz. 70.00
b. Imperf., pair 60.00

FLAG

A1877

PHOTOGRAVURE
1991, Jan. 22 **Untagged** **Die Cut**
Self-Adhesive
Printed on Plastic
2522 A1877 (29c) blk, blue & dk red .60 .25
a. Pane of 12 7.25

Sold only in panes of 12; peelable plastic backing inscribed in light ultramarine. Available during a test period at First National Bank automatic teller machines in Seattle.

Flag Over Mt. Rushmore — A1878

COIL STAMPS
ENGRAVED
1991, Mar. 29 **Tagged** **Perf. 10 Vert.**
2523 A1878 29c bl, red & claret .75 .25
b. Imperf., pair 20.00
c. blue, red & brown 3.00 —

Specialists often call No. 2523c the "Toledo brown" variety.

PHOTOGRAVURE
1991, July 4
2523A A1878 29c blue, red & brown .75 .25

On No. 2523A, USA and 29 are not outlined in white and are farther from the bottom of the design.

Flower — A1879

PHOTOGRAVURE
1991-92 **Perf. 11**
2524 A1879 29c dull yel, blk, red & yel grn .60 .25

See note after No. 2527.

Perf. 13x12¾
2524A A1879 29c dull yel, blk, red & yel grn 1.00 .25

COIL STAMPS
Rouletted 10 Vert.
2525 A1879 29c pale yel, blk, red & yel grn .60 .25

Perf. 10 Vert.
2526 A1879 29c pale yel, blk, red & yel grn .80 .25

BOOKLET STAMP
Perf. 11 on 2 or 3 Sides
2527 A1879 29c pale yel, blk, red & bright grn .60 .25
a. Booklet pane of 10 6.00 3.50
b. Horiz. pair, imperf. between —
c. Horiz. pair, imperf. vert. 150.00
d. As "a," imperf. horiz. 750.00
e. As "a," imperf. vert. 500.00

Flower on Nos. 2524-2524A has grainy appearance, inscriptions look rougher.
Issued: Nos. 2524, 2524A,2527, 4/5; No. 2525, 8/16; No. 2526, 3/3/92.

Flag, Olympic Rings — A1880

BOOKLET STAMP
Perf. 11 on 2 or 3 Sides
1991, Apr. 21
2528 A1880 29c multicolored .60 .25
a. Booklet pane of 10 6.00 3.50
b. As "a," imperf. horiz. 2,750.
c. Vert. pair, imperf. between, perfed at top and bottom 225.00
d. Vert. strip of 3, top or bottom pair imperf. between —
e. Vert. pair, imperf. horiz. 650.00
f. As "d," two pairs in #2528a with foldover —

No. 2528c comes from misperfed booklet panes. No. 2528d resulted from paper foldovers after normal perforating and before cutting into panes. Two No. 2528d are known. No. 2528e is valued in the grade of fine.

Fishing Boat A1881

Balloon A1882

COIL STAMPS
1991, Aug. 8 **Perf. 9.8 Vert.**
2529 A1881 19c multicolored, type I .40 .25
a. Type II ('93) .40 .25
b. As "a," untagged ('93) 1.00 .40

Design on Type II stamps is created by a finer dot pattern. Vertical sides of "1" are smooth on Type II and jagged on Type I stamps.
Imperforates are from printer's waste.
Nos. 2529 and 2529a have two loops of rope tying boat to piling.

1994, June 25
2529C A1881 19c multicolored .50 .25

No. 2529C has one loop of rope tying boat to piling.

BOOKLET STAMP
Perf. 10 on 2 or 3 Sides
1991, May 17
2530 A1882 19c multicolored .40 .25
a. Booklet pane of 10 4.00 2.75

Flags on Parade — A1883

1991, May 30 **Perf. 11**
2531 A1883 29c multi .60 .25

Liberty Torch — A1884

1991, June 25 **Die Cut**
Self-Adhesive
2531A A1884 29c black, gold & green .60 .25
b. Booklet pane of 18 11.00
c. Die cutting omitted, pair 1,000.

Sold only in panes of 18; peelable paper backing inscribed in light blue. Available for consumer testing at First National Bank automatic teller machines in Seattle, WA.

SWITZERLAND

Switzerland, 700th Anniv. — A1887

1991, Feb. 22 **Perf. 11**
2532 A1887 50c multicolored 1.00 .25
a. Vert. pair, imperf. horiz. 1,500.

See Switzerland No. 888.

Imperfs exist from printer's waste.

VERMONT STATEHOOD, 200th ANNIV.

A1888

1991, Mar. 1
2533 A1888 29c multicolored .80 .25

SAVINGS BONDS, 50TH ANNIVERSARY

A1889

1991, Apr. 30 **Perf. 11**
2534 A1889 29c multicolored .60 .25

LOVE

A1890 A1891

1991, May 9 **Perf. 12½x13**
2535 A1890 29c multi .60 .25
b. Imperf., pair 1,650.

Perf. 11
2535A A1890 29c multi 1.00 .25

BOOKLET STAMP (#2536)
Perf. 11.1x11.3 on 2 or 3 Sides
2536 A1890 29c multi .60 .25
a. Booklet pane of 10 6.00 3.50

"29" is closer to edge of design on No. 2536 than on No. 2535.

Perf. 11
2537 A1891 52c multi .90 .25

LITERARY ARTS SERIES

William Saroyan A1892

1991, May 22 **Perf. 11**
2538 A1892 29c multicolored .60 .25
a. All colors missing (EP) —
b. All colors except black missing (EP) 11,000.

No. 2538a must be collected se-tenant with a partially printed stamp. On No. 2538b, only part of the black is present; it is unique. See Russia No. 6002.

Eagle, Olympic Rings — A1893

A1894

A1895

A1896

Futuristic Space Shuttle A1897

Space Shuttle Challenger A1898

Space Shuttle Endeavour — A1898a

1991, Sept. 29
2539 A1893 $1 gold & multi 2.00 .50
a. Black omitted

LITHOGRAPHED & ENGRAVED
1991, July 7
2540 A1894 $2.90 multicolored 6.00 1.50
a. Vert. pair, imperf horiz. 900.00
b. Black (engr.) omitted 750.00

Imperforates on gummed stamp paper, including gutter pairs and blocks, are proofs from the ABNCo. archives. From the same source also come imperforate progressive proofs. See No. 2540P in Proofs section of the Scott U.S. Specialized Catalogue.

1991, June 16 **Untagged**
2541 A1895 $9.95 multicolored 20.00 6.00
a. Imperf., pair

No. 2541 exists imperf plus black (engr.) omitted from printer's waste.

1991, Aug. 31 **Untagged**
2542 A1896 $14 multicolored 25.00 15.00
a. Red (engr. inscriptions) omitted 750.00

No. 2542 exists imperf plus red omitted from printer's waste.

PHOTOGRAVURE
1993, June 3 **Perf. 11x10½**
2543 A1897 $2.90 multicolored 6.00 1.75

Faked examples of No. 2543, unused and used, exist with red omitted due to bleaching.

1995, June 22 **Perf. 11.2**
2544 A1898 $3 multicolored, dated "1995" 5.75 1.75
b. Dated "1996" 5.75 1.75
c. As "b," horiz. pair, imperf between 1,000.
d. As "b," imperf pair 1,000.

1995, Aug. 4 **Perf. 11**
2544A A1898a $10.75 multi 20.00 9.00

No. 2544A was printed on paper embedded with red fibers.

FISHING FLIES

Royal Wulff A1899

Jock Scott A1900

Apte Tarpon Fly A1901

Lefty's Deceiver A1902

Muddler Minnow A1903

PHOTOGRAVURE BOOKLET STAMPS
Perf. 11 Horiz. on 1 or 2 Sides
1991, May 31
2545 A1899 29c multicolored 1.10 .25
a. Black omitted —
b. Horiz. pair, imperf. btwn., in #2549a with foldover 2,400.
2546 A1900 29c multicolored 1.10 .25
a. Black omitted —
2547 A1901 29c multicolored 1.10 .25
a. Black omitted —
2548 A1902 29c multicolored 1.10 .25
2549 A1903 29c multicolored 1.10 .25
a. Bklt. pane of 5, #2545-2549 5.50 3.00

Horiz. pairs, imperf vert., exist from printer's waste.

No. 2545b is unique and resulted from a foldover after perfing but before cutting. Both stamps are creased.

PERFORMING ARTS

Cole Porter (1891-1964), Composer — A1904

1991, June 8 **Perf. 11**
2550 A1904 29c multicolored .60 .25
a. Vert. pair, imperf. horiz. 400.00

OPERATIONS DESERT SHIELD & DESERT STORM

S. W. Asia Service Medal — A1905

1991, July 2
2551 A1905 29c multicolored .60 .25
a. Vert. pair, imperf. horiz. 700.00

No. 2551 is 21mm wide.

BOOKLET STAMP
Perf. 11 Vert. on 1 or 2 Sides
2552 A1905 29c multicolored .60 .25
a. Booklet pane of 5 3.00 2.25

No. 2552 is 20½mm wide. Inscriptions are shorter than on No. 2551.
No. 2552 Vert. pairs, imperf horiz., are from printer's waste.

1992 SUMMER OLYMPICS, BARCELONA

Pole Vault A1907

Discus A1908

Women's Sprints A1909

Javelin A1910

Women's Hurdles A1911

1991, July 12 **Perf. 11**
2553 A1907 29c multicolored .60 .25
2554 A1908 29c multicolored .60 .25
2555 A1909 29c multicolored .60 .25
2556 A1910 29c multicolored .60 .25
2557 A1911 29c multicolored .60 .25
a. Strip of 5, #2553-2557 3.00 2.25

NUMISMATICS

1858 Flying Eagle Cent, 1907 Standing Liberty Double Eagle, Series 1875 $1 Note, Series 1902 $10 National Currency Note — A1912

LITHOGRAPHED & ENGRAVED

1991, Aug. 13
2558 A1912 29c multicolored .60 .25

WORLD WAR II

A1913

Designs and events of 1941: a, Military vehicles (Burma Road, 717-mile lifeline to China). b, Recruits (America's first peacetime draft). c, Shipments for allies (U.S. supports allies with Lend-Lease Act). d, Franklin D. Roosevelt, Winston Churchill (Atlantic Charter sets war aims of allies). e, Tank (America becomes the "arsenal of democracy."). f, Sinking of Destoyer Reuben James, Oct. 31. g, Gas mask, helmet (Civil defense mobilizes Americans at home). h, Liberty Ship, sea gull (First Liberty ship delivered December 30). i, Sinking ships (Japanese bomb Pearl Harbor, December 7). j, Congress in session (U.S. declares war on Japan, December 8). Central label is the size of 15 stamps and shows world map, extent of axis control.

LITHOGRAPHED & ENGRAVED

1991, Sept. 3
2559	A1913	Block of 10	7.50 5.00
a.-j.		29c any single	.75 .45
k.		Black (engr.) omitted	6,500.

No. 2559 has selvage at left and right and either top or bottom.

BASKETBALL, 100TH ANNIVERSARY

Basketball, Hoop, Players' Arms — A1914

PHOTOGRAVURE

1991, Aug. 28
2560 A1914 29c multicolored .60 .25

DISTRICT OF COLUMBIA BICENTENNIAL

Capitol Building from Pennsylvania Avenue, Circa 1903 — A1915

LITHOGRAPHED & ENGRAVED

1991, Sept. 7
2561	A1915	29c multicolored	.60 .25
a.		Black (engr.) omitted	85.00

COMEDIANS

Stan Laurel and Oliver Hardy A1916

Edgar Bergen and Charlie McCarthy A1917

Jack Benny A1918

Fanny Brice A1919

Bud Abbott and Lou Costello A1920

BOOKLET STAMPS
Perf. 11 on 2 or 3 Sides

1991, Aug. 29
2562	A1916	29c multicolored	1.00	.25
2563	A1917	29c multicolored	1.00	.25
2564	A1918	29c multicolored	1.00	.25
2565	A1919	29c multicolored	1.00	.25
2566	A1920	29c multicolored	1.00	.25
a.		Strip of 5, #2562-2566	5.00	2.25
b.		Bklt. pane of 10, 2 each #2562-2566	10.00	5.00
c.		As "b," scar & brt violet (engr.) omitted	350.00	

BLACK HERITAGE SERIES

Jan E. Matzeliger (1852-1889), Inventor — A1921

PHOTOGRAVURE

1991, Sept. 15 *Perf. 11*
2567	A1921	29c multicolored	.60	.25
a.		Horiz. pair, imperf. vert.	600.00	
b.		Vert. pair, imperf. horiz.	600.00	
c.		Imperf., pair	275.00	

SPACE EXPLORATION

Mercury, Mariner 10 A1922

Venus, Mariner 2 A1923

Earth, Landsat A1924

Moon, Lunar Orbiter A1925

Mars, Viking Orbiter A1926

Jupiter, Pioneer 11 A1927

Saturn, Voyager 2 A1928

Uranus, Voyager 2 A1929

Neptune, Voyager 2 A1930

Pluto A1931

PHOTOGRAVURE BOOKLET STAMPS
Perf. 11 on 2 or 3 Sides

1991, Oct. 1
2568	A1922	29c multicolored	.90	.25
2569	A1923	29c multicolored	.90	.25
2570	A1924	29c multicolored	.90	.25
2571	A1925	29c multicolored	.90	.25
2572	A1926	29c multicolored	.90	.25
2573	A1927	29c multicolored	.90	.25
2574	A1928	29c multicolored	.90	.25
2575	A1929	29c multicolored	.90	.25
2576	A1930	29c multicolored	.90	.25
2577	A1931	29c multicolored	.90	.25
a.		Bklt. pane of 10, #2568-2577	9.00	4.50

CHRISTMAS

Madonna and Child by Antoniazzo Romano A1933

Santa Claus in Chimney A1934

Santa Checking List — A1935

Santa with Present — A1936

Santa at Fireplace A1937

Santa and Sleigh — A1938

LITHOGRAPHED & ENGRAVED

1991, Oct. 17 *Perf. 11*
2578	A1933	(29c) multi	.60	.25
a.		Booklet pane of 10	6.00	3.25
b.		Red & black (engr.) omitted	2,250.	

PHOTOGRAVURE
2579	A1934	(29c) multi	.60	.25
a.		Horiz. pair, imperf. vert.	150.00	
b.		Vert. pair, imperf. horiz.	300.00	

BOOKLET STAMPS
Size: 25x18 ½mm
Perf. 11 on 2 or 3 Sides

2580	A1934	(29c) Type I	2.00	.25
2581	A1934	(29c) Type II	2.00	.25
a.		Pair, #2580-2581	4.00	.55
b.		Bklt. pane, 2 each, #2580, 2581	8.00	1.25
2582	A1935	(29c) multi	.50	.25
a.		Bklt. pane of 4	2.00	1.25
2583	A1936	(29c) multi	.50	.25
a.		Bklt. pane of 4	2.00	1.25
2584	A1937	(29c) multi	.50	.25
a.		Bklt. pane of 4	2.00	1.25
2585	A1938	(29c) multi	.50	.25
a.		Bklt. pane of 4	2.00	1.25
		Nos. 2578-2585 (8)	7.20	2.00

The far left brick from the top row of the chimney is missing from Type II, No. 2581.
Imperfs of Nos. 2581, 2583-2585 are printer's waste.

 A1939

A1942

A1944

ENGRAVED

1994-95 *Perf. 11.2*
2587	A1939	32c red brown	.65	.25

Perf. 11.5
2590	A1942	$1 blue	1.90	.50
2592	A1944	$5 slate green	8.00	2.50

Issued: $2, 5/5; $5, 8/19; 32c, 11/2/95.

Flag — A1946

Eagle and Shield — A1947

A1950

Statue of
Liberty — A1951

BOOKLET STAMPS
PHOTOGRAVURE
Perf. 10 on 2 or 3 Sides
1992, Sept. 8

2593	A1946	29c black & multi	.60	.25
a.		Booklet pane of 10	6.00	4.25
d.		Imperf, pair	500.00	

Perf. 11x10 on 2 or 3 Sides

2593B	A1946	29c blk & multi	2.00	.50
c.		Bklt. pane of 10, shiny gum	25.00	7.50

Perf. 11x10 on 2 or 3 Sides
1993, Apr. 8 (?)

2594	A1946	29c red & multi	.65	.25
a.		Booklet pane of 10	6.50	4.25

Denomination is red on #2594 and black on
#2593 and 2593B.

LITHOGRAPHED & ENGRAVED
(#2595), PHOTOGRAVURE
1992, Sept. 25   Die Cut
Self-Adhesive

2595	A1947	29c brown & multicolored	.60	.25
a.		Bklt. pane of 17 + label	10.50	
b.		Die cutting omitted, pair	90.00	
c.		Brown omitted	250.00	
d.		As "a," die cutting omitted	725.00	
2596	A1947	29c green & multicolored	.60	.25
a.		Bklt. pane of 17 + label	10.50	
2597	A1947	29c red & multicolored	.60	.25
a.		Bklt. pane of 17 + label	10.50	

Plate No. and inscription reads down on No.
2595a and up on Nos. 2596a-2597a. Design is
sharper and more finely detailed on Nos.
2595, 2597.
Nos. 2595a-2597a sold for $5 each.
Nos. 2595-2597 also available in strips with
stamps spaced for use in affixing machines to
service first day covers.

1994   Die Cut
Self-Adhesive

2598	A1950	29c red, cream & blue	.60	.25
a.		Booklet pane of 18	11.00	
b.		Coil with P#111	—	5.00
c.		Die cutting omitted, pair	1,000.	
2599	A1951	29c multi	.60	.25
a.		Booklet pane of 18	11.00	
b.		Coil with P#D1111	—	5.00

Except for Nos. 2598b and 2599b with plate
numbers, coil stamps of Nos. 2595-2599 are
indistinguishable from booklet stamps once
they are removed from the backing paper.
See Nos. 3122-3122E.
Issued: No. 2598, 2/4; No. 2599, 6/24.

> **Scott values for used self-adhesive stamps are for examples either on piece or off piece.**

A1956

A1957

A1959

A1960

A1961   Flag Over White
House — A1961

COIL STAMPS
1991-93   Untagged   Perf. 10 Vert.

2602	A1956	(10c) multi	.30	.25
a.		Imperf., pair	—	
2603	A1957	(10c) org yel & multi	.30	.25
a.		Imperf., pair	20.00	
2604	A1957	(10c) gold & multi	.25	.25
2605	A1959	23c multi	.45	.40
a.		Imperf, pair		

Vertical pairs uncut between on gummed
stamp paper are proofs from the ABNCo.
archives. See No. 2605P in Proofs section of
the Scott U.S. Specialized Catalogue.

2606	A1960	23c multi	.45	.40

"First-Class" is 9½mm long and "23" is 6mm
long on No. 2606.

2607	A1960	23c multi	.45	.40
c.		Imperf., pair	65.00	

"First-Class" is 9mm long and "23" is 6½mm
long on No. 2607.

2608	A1960	23c vio bl, red & blk	.80	.40

"First-Class" is 8½mm long and "23" is
6½mm long on No. 2608.
Nos. 2602-2608 are considered precancels
by the USPS.

ENGRAVED
Tagged

2609	A1961	29c blue & red	.60	.25
a.		Imperf., pair	15.00	
b.		Pair, imperf. between	75.00	
c.		Indigo blue & red	22.50	
		Nos. 2602-2609 (8)	3.60	2.60

Beware of pairs with blind perfs sometimes
offered as No. 2609b.
Issued: No. 2605, 9/27; No. 2602, 12/31;
29c, 4/23/92; No. 2606, 7/21/92; No. 2607,
10/9/92; Nos. 2603-2604, 5/29/93; No. 2608,
5/14/93.
See Nos. 2907, 3270-3271.

WINTER OLYMPICS

Hockey
A1963

Figure
Skating
A1964

Speed
Skating
A1965

Skiing
A1966

Bobsledding — A1967

PHOTOGRAVURE
1992, Jan. 11   Perf. 11

2611	A1963	29c multicolored	.60	.25
2612	A1964	29c multicolored	.60	.25
2613	A1965	29c multicolored	.60	.25
2614	A1966	29c multicolored	.60	.25
2615	A1967	29c multicolored	.60	.25
a.		Strip of 5, #2611-2615	3.00	2.50

WORLD COLUMBIAN STAMP EXPO

Portion of Vignette
of No. 129 — A1968

LITHOGRAPHED & ENGRAVED
1992, Jan. 24

2616	A1968	29c multicolored	.60	.25

BLACK HERITAGE SERIES

W.E.B. Du Bois
(1868-1963), Civil
Rights
Leader — A1969

1992, Jan. 31

2617	A1969	29c multicolored	.60	.25

LOVE

A1970

PHOTOGRAVURE
1992, Feb. 6

2618	A1970	29c multicolored	.60	.25
a.		Horiz. pair, imperf. vert.	300.00	
b.		As "a," green omitted on right stamp	1,750.	

OLYMPIC BASEBALL

A1971

1992, Apr. 3   Tagged   Perf. 11

2619	A1971	29c multicolored	.60	.25

VOYAGES OF COLUMBUS

Seeking
Queen
Isabella's
Support
A1972

Crossing
the Atlantic
A1973

Approaching Land — A1974

Coming
Ashore
A1975

LITHOGRAPHED & ENGRAVED
1992, Apr. 24

2620	A1972	29c multicolored	.65	.25
2621	A1973	29c multicolored	.65	.25
2622	A1974	29c multicolored	.65	.25
2623	A1975	29c multicolored	.65	.25
a.		Block of 4, #2620-2623	2.60	2.00

See Italy Nos. 1877-1880.

Souvenir Sheets

A1976

A1977

A1978

A1979

A1980

A1981

1992, May 22   *Perf. 10½*
Tagged (15c-$5), Untagged

2624	A1976	Pane of 3	2.25	1.50
a.	A71 1c deep blue	.25	.25
b.	A74 4c ultramarine	.25	.25
c.	A82 $1 salmon	1.75	1.00
2625	A1977	Pane of 3	7.50	5.00
a.	A72 2c brown violet	.25	.25
b.	A73 3c green	.25	.25
c.	A85 $4 crimson lake	7.00	4.00
2626	A1978	Pane of 3	1.75	1.25
a.	A75 5c chocolate	.25	.25
b.	A80 30c orange brown	.60	.30
c.	A81 50c slate blue	.90	.50
2627	A1979	Pane of 3	6.00	3.75
a.	A76 6c purple	.25	.25
b.	A77 8c magenta	.25	.25
c.	A84 $3 yellow green	5.50	3.00
2628	A1980	Pane of 3	4.25	3.00
a.	A78 10c black brown	.25	.25
b.	A79 15c dark green	.30	.25
c.	A83 $2 brown red	3.50	2.00
2629	A1981	$5 Pane of 1	8.75	6.00
a.	A86 $5 black, single stamp	8.50	5.00
	Nos. 2624-2629 (6)	30.50	20.50

See Italy Nos. 1883-1888, Portugal Nos. 1918-1923 and Spain Nos. 2677-2682.

Imperforate souvenir sheets on gummed stamp paper, singly or in pairs and blocks, are proofs from the ABNCo. archives. Additionally, one imperforate essay, with the background of No. 2622 combined with the stamps of No. 2620, is recorded. See Nos. 2624P-2629P in Proofs section of the Scott U.S. Specialized Catalogue.

NEW YORK STOCK EXCHANGE BICENTENNIAL

A1982

1992, May 17   *Perf. 11*

2630	A1982	29c green, red & black	.60	.25
a.	Black missing (EP)	4,000.	
b.	Black missing (CM)	4,000.	
c.	Center (black engr.) inverted	17,000.	
d.	Se-tenant pair, #2630b and #2630c	22,500.	

No. 2630a resulted from extraneous paper that blocked the black from appearing on the stamp paper. It is from a unique pane that contained four color-missing errors plus a fifth stamp missing half the black center.

No. 2630a must be collected se-tenant with a normal stamp or with a stamp with half of black engraving missing, or se-tenant with a normal stamp and an additional 2630a.

No. 2630b may be collected alone or se-tenant with No. 2630c.

Two panes, each containing 28 No. 2630c and 12 No. 2630b, have been documented.

SPACE ACCOMPLISHMENTS

Cosmonaut, U.S. Space Shuttle A1983

Astronaut, Russian Space Station A1984

Sputnik, Vostok, Apollo Command & Lunar Modules A1985

Soyuz, Mercury and Gemini Spacecraft A1986

PHOTOGRAVURE
1992, May 29

2631	A1983	29c multicolored	.60	.25
2632	A1984	29c multicolored	.60	.25
2633	A1985	29c multicolored	.60	.25
2634	A1986	29c multicolored	.60	.25
a.	Block of 4, #2631-2634	2.40	2.00
b.	As "a," yellow omitted	4,750.	

The yellow color in Nos. 2631-2634 is easily removed by exposure to sunlight. Expertization of No. 2634b is essential.
See Russia Nos. 6080-6083.

ALASKA HIGHWAY, 50th ANNIVERSARY

A1987

LITHOGRAPHED & ENGRAVED
1992, May 30

2635	A1987	29c multicolored	.60	.25
a.	Black (engr.) omitted	575.00	

Almost half the recorded No. 2635a errors are poorly centered. These sell for approximately $400.

KENTUCKY STATEHOOD BICENTENNIAL

A1988

PHOTOGRAVURE
1992, June 1

2636	A1988	29c multicolored	.60	.25
a.	Dark blue missing (EP)	—	
b.	Dark blue and red missing (EP)	—	
c.	All colors missing (EP)	—	

Nos. 2636a-2636c must be collected se-tenant with normal stamps.

SUMMER OLYMPICS

Soccer A1989

Gymnastics A1990

Volleyball A1991

Boxing A1992

Swimming A1993

1992, June 11

2637	A1989	29c multicolored	.60	.25
2638	A1990	29c multicolored	.60	.25
2639	A1991	29c multicolored	.60	.25
2640	A1992	29c multicolored	.60	.25
2641	A1993	29c multicolored	.60	.25
a.	Strip of 5, #2637-2641	3.00	2.50

HUMMINGBIRDS

Ruby-throated A1994

Broad-billed A1995

Costa's A1996

Rufous A1997

Calliope — A1998

BOOKLET STAMPS
Perf. 11 Vert. on 1 or 2 Sides
1992, June 15

2642	A1994	29c multicolored	.60	.25
2643	A1995	29c multicolored	.60	.25
2644	A1996	29c multicolored	.60	.25
2645	A1997	29c multicolored	.60	.25
2646	A1998	29c multicolored	.60	.25
a.	Bklt. pane of 5, #2642-2646	3.00	2.50

Imperforate singles, booklet panes and pane multiples or varieties on gummed stamp paper are proofs from the ABNCo. archives. From the same source also come imperforate progressive proofs. See No. 2646aP in Proofs section of the Scott U.S. Specialized Catalogue.

WILDFLOWERS

A1999

LITHOGRAPHED
1992, July 24   *Perf. 11*

2647	A1999	29c Indian paintbrush	.80	.60
2648	A2000	29c Fragrant water lily	.80	.60
2649	A2001	29c Meadow beauty	.80	.60
2650	A2002	29c Jack-in-the-pulpit	.80	.60
2651	A2003	29c California poppy	.80	.60
2652	A2004	29c Large-flowered trillium	.80	.60
2653	A2005	29c Tickseed	.80	.60
2654	A2006	29c Shooting star	.80	.60
2655	A2007	29c Stream violet	.80	.60
2656	A2008	29c Bluets	.80	.60
2657	A2009	29c Herb Robert	.80	.60
2658	A2010	29c Marsh marigold	.80	.60
2659	A2011	29c Sweet white violet	.80	.60
2660	A2012	29c Claret cup cactus	.80	.60
2661	A2013	29c White mountain avens	.80	.60
2662	A2014	29c Sessile bellwort	.80	.60
2663	A2015	29c Blue flag	.80	.60
2664	A2016	29c Harlequin lupine	.80	.60
2665	A2017	29c Twinflower	.80	.60
2666	A2018	29c Common sunflower	.80	.60
2667	A2019	29c Sego lily	.80	.60
2668	A2020	29c Virginia bluebells	.80	.60
2669	A2021	29c Ohi'a lehua	.80	.60
2670	A2022	29c Rosebud orchid	.80	.60
2671	A2023	29c Showy evening primrose	.80	.60
2672	A2024	29c Fringed gentian	.80	.60
2673	A2025	29c Yellow lady's slipper	.80	.60
2674	A2026	29c Passionflower	.80	.60
2675	A2027	29c Bunchberry	.80	.60
2676	A2028	29c Pasqueflower	.80	.60
2677	A2029	29c Round-lobed hepatica	.80	.60
2678	A2030	29c Wild columbine	.80	.60
2679	A2031	29c Fireweed	.80	.60
2680	A2032	29c Indian pond lily	.80	.60
2681	A2033	29c Turk's cap lily	.80	.60
2682	A2034	29c Dutchman's breeches	.80	.60
2683	A2035	29c Trumpet honeysuckle	.80	.60
2684	A2036	29c Jacob's ladder	.80	.60
2685	A2037	29c Plains prickly pear	.80	.60
2686	A2038	29c Moss campion	.80	.60
2687	A2039	29c Bearberry	.80	.60
2688	A2040	29c Mexican hat	.80	.60
2689	A2041	29c Harebell	.80	.60
2690	A2042	29c Desert five spot	.80	.60
2691	A2043	29c Smooth Solomon's seal	.80	.60
2692	A2044	29c Red maids	.80	.60
2693	A2045	29c Yellow skunk cabbage	.80	.60
2694	A2046	29c Rue anemone	.80	.60
2695	A2047	29c Standing cypress	.80	.60
2696	A2048	29c Wild flax	.80	.60
a.	A1999-A2048 Pane of 50, #2647-2696	40.00	—

WORLD WAR II

A2049

No. 2697 — Events of 1942: a, B-25's take off to raid Tokyo, Apr. 18. b, Ration coupons (Food and other commodities rationed). c, Divebomber and deck crewman (US wins Battle of the Coral Sea, May). d, Prisoners of war (Corregidor falls to Japanese, May 6). e, Dutch Harbor buildings on fire (Japan invades Aleutian Islands, June). f, Headphones, coded message (Allies decipher secret enemy codes). g, Yorktown lost, U.S. wins at Midway. h, Woman with drill (Millions of women join war effort). i, Marines land on Guadalcanal, Aug. 7. j, Tank in desert (Allies land in North Africa, Nov.).

Central label is the size of 15 stamps and shows world map, extent of axis control.

LITHOGRAPHED & ENGRAVED
1992, Aug. 17

2697	A2049	Block of 10	7.50	5.00
a.-j.		29c any single	.75	.30
k.		Red (litho.) omitted	4,000.	

No. 2697 has selvage at left and right and either top or bottom.

LITERARY ARTS SERIES

A2050

PHOTOGRAVURE
1992, Aug. 22

2698 A2050 29c multicolored   .60   .25
Dorothy Parker (1893-1967), author.

THEODORE VON KARMAN

A2051

1992, Aug. 31

2699 A2051 29c multicolored   .60   .25
Von Karman (1881-1963), rocket scientist.

MINERALS

Azurite — A2052

Copper — A2053

Variscite
A2054

Wulfenite
A2055

LITHOGRAPHED & ENGRAVED
1992, Sept. 17

2700	A2052	29c multicolored	.60	.25
2701	A2053	29c multicolored	.60	.25
2702	A2054	29c multicolored	.60	.25
2703	A2055	29c multicolored	.60	.25
a.		Block or strip of 4, #2700-2703	2.40	2.00
b.		As "a," silver (litho.) omitted	6,000.	
d.		As "a," silver omitted on two stamps	—	

JUAN RODRIGUEZ CABRILLO

Cabrillo, Ship, Map of San Diego Bay Area — A2056

1992, Sept. 28

2704	A2056	29c multicolored	.60	.25
a.		Black (engr.) omitted	1,750.	

WILD ANIMALS

Giraffe
A2057

Giant Panda
A2058

Flamingo
A2059

King Penguins
A2060

White Bengal Tiger
A2061

PHOTOGRAVURE
BOOKLET STAMPS
Perf. 11 Horiz. on 1 or 2 Sides
1992, Oct. 1

2705	A2057	29c multicolored	.65	.25
2706	A2058	29c multicolored	.65	.25
2707	A2059	29c multicolored	.65	.25
2708	A2060	29c multicolored	.65	.25
2709	A2061	29c multicolored	.65	.25
a.		Booklet pane of 5, #2705-2709	3.25	2.25
b.		As "a," imperf.	2,000.	

CHRISTMAS

Madonna and Child, by Giovanni Bellini — A2062

Horse and Rider — A2063

Fire Pumper — A2064

Train Engine — A2065

Riverboat A2066

LITHOGRAPHED & ENGRAVED
1992   **Perf. 11½x11**

2710	A2062	29c multicolored	.60	.25
a.		Booklet pane of 10	6.00	3.50

LITHOGRAPHED

2711	A2063	29c multicolored	.75	.25
2712	A2064	29c multicolored	.75	.25
2713	A2065	29c multicolored	.75	.25
2714	A2066	29c multicolored	.75	.25
a.		Block of 4, #2711-2714	3.00	1.10

Booklet Stamps
PHOTOGRAVURE
Perf. 11 on 2 or 3 Sides

2715	A2063	29c multicolored	.90	.25
2716	A2064	29c multicolored	.90	.25
2717	A2065	29c multicolored	.90	.25
2718	A2066	29c multicolored	.90	.25
a.		Booklet pane of 4, #2715-2718	3.60	1.25

Imperforates and part-perforates on gummed stamp paper are proofs from the ABNCo. archives. From the same source come imperforates with Toys only and imperforates without denominations. See No. 2718aP in Proofs section of the Scott U.S. Specialized Catalogue.

Self-Adhesive
Die Cut

2719	A2065	29c multicolored	.65	.25
a.		Booklet pane of 18	12.00	

"Greetings" is 27mm long on Nos. 2711-2714, 25mm long on Nos. 2715-2718 and 21½mm long on No. 2719. Nos. 2715-2719 differ in color from Nos. 2711-2714.
Issued: #2710-2718, 10/22; #2719, 10/28.

CHINESE NEW YEAR

Year of the Rooster A2067

LITHOGRAPHED & ENGRAVED
1992, Dec. 30   **Perf. 11**

2720 A2067 29c multicolored   .60   .25
See No. 3895j.

AMERICAN MUSIC SERIES

Elvis Presley A2068

Oklahoma! A2069

Hank Williams A2070

Elvis Presley A2071

Bill Haley A2072

Clyde McPhatter A2073

Ritchie Valens A2074

Otis Redding A2075

Buddy Holly A2076

Dinah Washington
A2077

PHOTOGRAVURE

1993			**Perf. 11**	
2721	A2068	29c multicolored	.60	.25
a.	Imperf, pair		—	
		Perf. 10		
2722	A2069	29c multicolored	.60	.25
2723	A2070	29c multicolored	.75	.25
		Perf. 11.2x11.5		
2723A	A2070	29c multicolored	17.50	10.00
1993, June 16			**Perf. 10**	
2724	A2071	29c multicolored	.70	.25
2725	A2072	29c multicolored	.70	.25
2726	A2073	29c multicolored	.70	.25
2727	A2074	29c multicolored	.70	.25
2728	A2075	29c multicolored	.70	.25
2729	A2076	29c multicolored	.70	.25
2730	A2077	29c multicolored	.70	.25
a.	Vert. strip of 7, #2724-2730		5.50	3.00

Booklet Stamps
Perf. 11 Horiz. on 1 or 2 Sides

2731	A2071	29c multicolored	.65	.25
2732	A2072	29c multicolored	.65	.25
2733	A2073	29c multicolored	.65	.25
2734	A2074	29c multicolored	.65	.25
2735	A2075	29c multicolored	.65	.25
2736	A2076	29c multicolored	.65	.25
2737	A2077	29c multicolored	.65	.25
a.	Booklet pane, 2 #2731, 1 each #2732-2737		5.25	2.25
b.	Booklet pane, #2731, 2735-2737 + tab		2.60	1.50

Nos. 2731-2737 have smaller design sizes, brighter colors and shorter inscriptions than Nos. 2724-2730, as well as framelines around the designs and other subtle design differences.

No. 2737b without tab is indistinguishable from broken No. 2737a.

Imperforates of both No. 2737a and 2737b on gummed stamp paper are proofs from the ABNCo. archives. Perforated booklet pane multiples and varieties also exist from the same source. See Nos. 2737aP-2737bP in Proofs section of the Scott U.S. Specialized Catalogue.

See Nos. 2769, 2771, 2775 and designs A2112-A2117.

SPACE FANTASY

A2086

A2087

A2088

A2089

A2090

BOOKLET STAMPS

1993, Jan. 25			**Perf. 11 Vert.**	
2741	A2086	29c multicolored	.60	.25
2742	A2087	29c multicolored	.60	.25
2743	A2088	29c multicolored	.60	.25
2744	A2089	29c multicolored	.60	.25
2745	A2090	29c multicolored	.60	.25
a.	Booklet pane of 5, #2741-2745		3.00	2.25

BLACK HERITAGE SERIES

Percy Lavon Julian (1899-1975), Chemist — A2091

LITHOGRAPHED & ENGRAVED

1993, Jan. 29			**Perf. 11**	
2746	A2091	29c multicolored	.60	.25

OREGON TRAIL

A2092

1993, Feb. 12				
2747	A2092	29c multicolored	.60	.25
b.	Blue omitted		550.00	

WORLD UNIVERSITY GAMES

A2093

PHOTOGRAVURE

1993, Feb. 25				
2748	A2093	29c multicolored	.60	.25

GRACE KELLY (1929-1982)

Actress, Princess of Monaco — A2094

ENGRAVED

1993, Mar. 24				
2749	A2094	29c blue	.60	.25

See Monaco No. 1851.

CIRCUS

Clown — A2095

Ringmaster
A2096

Trapeze Artist — A2097

Elephant
A2098

LITHOGRAPHED

1993, Apr. 6				
2750	A2095	29c multicolored	.60	.25
2751	A2096	29c multicolored	.60	.25
2752	A2097	29c multicolored	.60	.25
2753	A2098	29c multicolored	.60	.25
a.	Block of 4, #2750-2753		2.40	1.75

CHEROKEE STRIP LAND RUN, CENTENNIAL

A2099

LITHOGRAPHED & ENGRAVED

1993, Apr. 17				
2754	A2099	29c multicolored	.60	.25

Imperforates on gummed stamp paper, including gutter pairs and blocks, are proofs from the ABNCo. archives. From the same source also come perforated gutter pairs and blocks, plus imperforates missing the red text and black denomination and "USA." An approved die proof also is recorded. See No. 2754P in Proofs section of the Scott U.S. Specialized Catalogue.

DEAN ACHESON (1893-1971)

Secretary of State — A2100

ENGRAVED

1993, Apr. 21				
2755	A2100	29c greenish gray	.60	.25

SPORTING HORSES

Steeplechase — A2101

Thoroughbred Racing — A2102

Harness Racing
A2103

Polo
A2104

LITHOGRAPHED & ENGRAVED

1993, May 1			**Perf. 11x11½**	
2756	A2101	29c multicolored	.60	.25
2757	A2102	29c multicolored	.60	.25
2758	A2103	29c multicolored	.60	.25
2759	A2104	29c multicolored	.60	.25
a.	Block of 4, #2756-2759		2.40	2.00
b.	As "a," black (engr.) omitted		500.00	

GARDEN FLOWERS

Hyacinth
A2105

Daffodil
A2106

Tulip — A2107

Iris — A2108

Lilac — A2109

LITHOGRAPHED & ENGRAVED
BOOKLET STAMPS

1993, May 15			**Perf. 11 Vert.**	
2760	A2105	29c multicolored	.70	.25
2761	A2106	29c multicolored	.70	.25
2762	A2107	29c multicolored	.70	.25
2763	A2108	29c multicolored	.70	.25
2764	A2109	29c multicolored	.70	.25
a.	Booklet pane of 5, #2760-2764		3.50	2.25
b.	As "a," black (engr.) omitted		135.00	
c.	As "a," imperf.		850.00	

WORLD WAR II

A2110

Designs and events of 1943: a, Destroyers (Allied forces battle German U-boats). b, Military medics treat the wounded. c, Amphibious landing craft on beach (Sicily attacked by Allied forces, July). d, B-24s hit Ploesti refineries, August. e, V-mail delivers letters from home. f, PT boat (Italy invaded by Allies, Sept.). g, Nos. WS7, WS8, savings bonds, (Bonds and stamps help war effort). h, "Willie and Joe" keep spirits high. i, Banner in window (Gold Stars mark World War II losses). j, Marines assault Tarawa, Nov.

Central label is the size of 15 stamps and shows world map with extent of Axis control and Allied operations.

1993, May 31   *Perf. 11*
2765   A2110   Block of 10   7.50   5.00
   a.-j.   29c any single   .75   .40

No. 2765 has selvage at left and right and either top or bottom.

JOE LOUIS (1914-1981)

A2111

LITHOGRAPHED & ENGRAVED
1993, June 22
2766   A2111   29c multicolored   .60   .25

AMERICAN MUSIC SERIES
Oklahoma! Type and

Show Boat
A2112

Porgy & Bess
A2113

My Fair Lady
A2114

BOOKLET STAMPS
PHOTOGRAVURE
Perf. 11 Horiz. on 1 or 2 Sides
1993, July 14
2767   A2112   29c multicolored   .60   .25
2768   A2113   29c multicolored   .60   .25
2769   A2069   29c multicolored   .60   .25
2770   A2114   29c multicolored   .60   .25
   a.   Booklet pane of 4, #2767-2770   2.75   2.25

No. 2769 has smaller design size, brighter colors and shorter inscription than No. 2722, as well as a frameline around the design and other subtle design differences.

Imperforate booklet panes, singly or in multiples, on gummed stamp paper are proofs from the ABNCo. archives. From the same source come imperforate progressive proofs, plus imperforate proofs/essays showing slightly altered designs. See No. 2770aP in Proofs section of the Scott U.S. Specialized Catalogue.

AMERICAN MUSIC SERIES
Hank Williams Type and

Patsy Cline
A2115

The Carter Family
A2116

Bob Wills
A2117

PHOTOGRAVURE
1993, Sept. 25   *Perf. 10*
2771   A2070   29c multicolored   .75   .25
2772   A2115   29c multicolored   .75   .25
2773   A2116   29c multicolored   .75   .25
2774   A2117   29c multicolored   .75   .25
   a.   Block or horiz. strip of 4, #2771-2774   3.00   1.75

Booklet Stamps
Perf. 11 Horiz. on one or two sides
With Black Frameline
2775   A2070   29c multicolored   .60   .25
2776   A2116   29c multicolored   .60   .25
2777   A2115   29c multicolored   .60   .25
2778   A2117   29c multicolored   .60   .25
   a.   Booklet pane of 4, #2775-2778   2.50   2.00

Inscription at left measures 27½mm on No. 2723, 27mm on No. 2771 and 22mm on No. 2775. No. 2723 shows only two tuning keys on guitar, while No. 2771 shows those two and parts of two others.

Imperforate booklet panes on gummed stamp paper, singly or in multiples, are proofs from the ABNCo. archives. From the same source come panes perfed horiz. but uncut vertically, plus imperforate progressive proofs and other die proof varieties. See No. 2778aP in Proofs section in the Scott U.S. Specialized Catalogue.

NATIONAL POSTAL MUSEUM

Independence Hall, Benjamin Franklin, Printing Press, Colonial Post Rider — A2118

Pony Express Rider, Civil War Soldier, Concord Stagecoach A2119

JN-4H Biplane, Charles Lindbergh, Railway Mail Car, 1931 Model A Ford Mail Truck A2120

California Gold Rush Miner's Letter, Nos. 39, 295, C3a, C13, Barcode & Circular Date Stamp A2121

LITHOGRAPHED AND ENGRAVED
1993, July 30   *Tagged*   *Perf. 11*
2779   A2118   29c multicolored   .60   .25
2780   A2119   29c multicolored   .60   .25
2781   A2120   29c multicolored   .60   .25
2782   A2121   29c multicolored   .60   .25
   a.   Block or strip of 4, #2779-2782   2.40   2.00
   b.   As "a," engr. maroon (USA/29) and black ("My dear...") omitted   2,500.
   c.   As "a," imperf   2,500.

AMERICAN SIGN LANGUAGE

A2122

A2123

PHOTOGRAVURE
1993, Sept. 20   *Perf. 11½*
2783   A2122   29c multicolored   .60   .25
2784   A2123   29c multicolored   .60   .25
   a.   Pair, #2783-2784   1.20   .75

CLASSIC BOOKS

A2124

A2125

A2126

A2127

Designs: No. 2785, Rebecca of Sunnybrook Farm, by Kate Douglas Wiggin. No. 2786, Little House on the Prairie, by Laura Ingalls Wilder. No. 2787, The Adventures of Huckleberry Finn, by Mark Twain. No. 2788, Little Women, by Louisa May Alcott.

LITHOGRAPHED & ENGRAVED
1993, Oct. 23   *Perf. 11*
2785   A2124   29c multicolored   .60   .25
2786   A2125   29c multicolored   .60   .25
2787   A2126   29c multicolored   .60   .25
2788   A2127   29c multicolored   .60   .25
   a.   Block or horiz. strip of 4, #2785-2788   2.40   2.00

Imperforates on gummed stamp paper, including gutter pairs and blocks, are proofs from the ABNCo. archives. See No. 2788aP in Proofs section of the Scott U.S. Specialized Catalogue.

CHRISTMAS

Madonna and Child in a Landscape, by Giovanni Battista Cima — A2128

Jack-in-the-Box A2129

Red-Nosed Reindeer A2130

Snowman A2131

Toy Soldier Blowing Horn A2132

1993, Oct. 21
2789   A2128   29c multicolored   .60   .25
Booklet Stamp
Size: 18x25mm
Perf. 11½x11 on 2 or 3 Sides
2790   A2128   29c multicolored   .60   .25
   a.   Booklet pane of 4   2.40   1.75
   b.   Imperf., pair   —
   c.   As "a," imperf   —

Nos. 2789-2790 have numerous design differences.

1993   *Perf. 11½*
PHOTOGRAVURE
2791   A2129   29c multicolored   .60   .25
2792   A2130   29c multicolored   .60   .25
2793   A2131   29c multicolored   .60   .25
2794   A2132   29c multicolored   .60   .25
   a.   Block or strip of 4, #2791-2794   2.40   2.00
Booklet Stamps
Size: 18x21mm
Perf. 11x10 on 2 or 3 Sides
2795   A2132   29c multicolored   .85   .25
2796   A2131   29c multicolored   .85   .25
2797   A2130   29c multicolored   .85   .25
2798   A2129   29c multicolored   .85   .25
   a.   Booklet pane, 3 each #2795-2796, 2 each #2797-2798   8.50   4.00
   b.   Booklet pane, 3 each #2797-2798, 2 each #2795-2796   8.50   4.00
   c.   Block of 4, #2795-2798   3.40   1.75

Self-Adhesive
Size: 19½x26½mm
Die Cut

2799	A2131	29c multicolored	.75	.25
a.		Coil with plate # V1111111	—	6.00
2800	A2132	29c multicolored	.75	.25
2801	A2129	29c multicolored	.75	.25
2802	A2130	29c multicolored	.75	.25
a.		Booklet pane, 3 each #2799-2802		9.00
b.		Block of 4, #2799-2802		3.00

Except for No. 2799a with plate number, coil stamps are indistinguishable from booklet stamps once they are removed from the backing paper.

Size: 17x20mm

2803	A2131	29c multicolored	.60	.25
a.		Booklet pane of 18	11.00	

Snowman on Nos. 2793, 2799 has three buttons and seven snowflakes beneath nose (placement differs on both stamps). No. 2796 has two buttons and five snowflakes beneath nose. No. 2803 has two orange buttons and four snowflakes beneath nose.

Issued: #2791-2798, 10/21; #2799-2803, 10/28.

MARIANA ISLANDS

A2133

LITHOGRAPHED AND ENGRAVED
1993, Nov. 4   **Perf. 11**

2804	A2133	29c multicolored	.60	.25

COLUMBUS' LANDING IN PUERTO RICO, 500th ANNIVERSARY

A2134

PHOTOGRAVURE
1993, Nov. 19   **Perf. 11.2**

2805	A2134	29c multicolored	.60	.25

AIDS AWARENESS

A2135

1993, Dec. 1

2806	A2135	29c black & red	.60	.25
a.		Perf. 11 vert. on 1 or 2 sides, from bklt. pane	.70	.25
b.		As "a," booklet pane of 5	3.50	2.00

WINTER OLYMPICS

Slalom — A2136

Luge — A2137

Ice Dancing
A2138

Cross-Country Skiing
A2139

Ice Hockey — A2140

LITHOGRAPHED
1994, Jan. 6

2807	A2136	29c multicolored	.60	.25
2808	A2137	29c multicolored	.60	.25
2809	A2138	29c multicolored	.60	.25
2810	A2139	29c multicolored	.60	.25
2811	A2140	29c multicolored	.60	.25
a.		Strip of 5, #2807-2811	3.00	2.50

EDWARD R. MURROW, JOURNALIST (1908-65)

A2141

ENGRAVED
1994, Jan. 21

2812	A2141	29c brown	.60	.25

LOVE

A2142

A2143

A2144

Booklet Stamps
LITHOGRAPHED & ENGRAVED
1994   **Die Cut**
Self-adhesive

2813	A2142	29c multicolored	.60	.25
a.		Booklet pane of 18	11.00	
b.		Coil with plate # B1	—	3.75

Except for No. 2813b with plate number, coil stamps are indistinguishable from booklet stamps once they are removed from the backing paper.

PHOTOGRAVURE
Perf. 10.9x11.1 on 2 or 3 sides

2814	A2143	29c multicolored	.60	.25
a.		Booklet pane of 10	6.00	3.50
b.		Imperf, pair		
d.		As "a," imperf.		

Horiz. pairs, imperf between, are printer's waste.

No. 2814 was issued in booklets only.

LITHOGRAPHED & ENGRAVED
Perf. 11.1

2814C	A2143	29c multicolored	.70	.25

Size of No. 2814C is 20x28mm. No. 2814 is 18x24½mm.

PHOTOGRAVURE & ENGRAVED
Perf. 11.2

2815	A2144	52c multicolored	1.00	.25

Issued: No. 2813, Jan. 27; Nos. 2814-2815, Feb. 14; No. 2814C, June 11.

BLACK HERITAGE SERIES

Dr. Allison Davis (1902-83), Social Anthropologist, Educator — A2145

ENGRAVED
1994, Feb. 1   **Perf. 11.2**

2816	A2145	29c red brown & brown	.60	.25

CHINESE NEW YEAR

Year of the Dog
A2146

PHOTOGRAVURE
1994, Feb. 5

2817	A2146	29c multicolored	.80	.25

See No. 3895k.

BUFFALO SOLDIERS

A2147

LITHOGRAPHED & ENGRAVED
1994, Apr. 22   **Perf. 11.5x11.2**

2818	A2147	29c multicolored	.60	.25
a.		Double impression (second impression light) of red brown (engr. inscriptions)	—	

SILENT SCREEN STARS

Rudolph Valentino (1895-1926)
A2148

Clara Bow (1905-65)
A2149

Charlie Chaplin (1889-1977)
A2150

Lon Chaney (1883-1930)
A2151

John Gilbert (1895-1936)
A2152

Zasu Pitts (1898-1963)
A2153

Harold Lloyd (1894-1971)
A2154

Keystone Cops
A2155

Theda Bara (1885-1955)
A2156

Buster Keaton (1895-1966)
A2157

1994, Apr. 27   **Perf. 11.2**

2819	A2148	29c red, blk & brt vio	1.10	.30
2820	A2149	29c red, blk & brt vio	1.10	.30
2821	A2150	29c red, blk & brt vio	1.10	.30
2822	A2151	29c red, blk & brt vio	1.10	.30
2823	A2152	29c red, blk & brt vio	1.10	.30
2824	A2153	29c red, blk & brt vio	1.10	.30
2825	A2154	29c red, blk & brt vio	1.10	.30
2826	A2155	29c red, blk & brt vio	1.10	.30
2827	A2156	29c red, blk & brt vio	1.10	.30
2828	A2157	29c red, blk & brt vio	1.10	.30
a.		Block of 10, #2819-2828	11.00	5.00
b.		As "a," black (litho.) omitted		
c.		As "a," blk, red & brt vio (litho.) omitted	—	

GARDEN FLOWERS

Lily — A2158

Zinnia — A2159

Gladiola
A2160

Marigold
A2161

Rose — A2162

1994, Apr. 28   *Perf. 10.9 Vert.*
Booklet Stamps

2829	A2158	29c multicolored	.60	.25
2830	A2159	29c multicolored	.60	.25
2831	A2160	29c multicolored	.60	.25
2832	A2161	29c multicolored	.60	.25
2833	A2162	29c multicolored	.60	.25
a.		Booklet pane of 5, #2829-2833	3.00	2.25
b.		As "a," imperf	400.00	
c.		As "a," black (engr.) omitted	125.00	

1994 WORLD CUP SOCCER CHAMPIONSHIPS

A2163

A2163a

A2164

A2165

Design: 40c, Soccer player, diff.

PHOTOGRAVURE

1994, May 26   *Perf. 11.1*

2834	A2163	29c multicolored	.60	.25
2835	A2163a	40c multicolored	.80	.25
2836	A2164	50c multicolored	1.00	.25
	Nos. 2834-2836 (3)		2.40	.75

Souvenir Sheet of 3

2837	A2165	#a.-#c.	4.50	3.00

No. 2837c has a portion of the yellow map in the LR corner.

WORLD WAR II

A2166

Designs and events of 1944: a, Allied forces retake New Guinea. b, P-51s escort B-17s on bombing raids. c, Troops running from landing craft (Allies in Normandy, D-Day, June 6). d, Airborne units spearhead attacks. e, Officer at periscope (Submarines shorten war in Pacific). f, Parade (Allies free Rome, June 4; Paris, Aug. 25).

g, Soldier firing flamethrower (US troops clear Saipan bunkers). h, Red Ball Express speeds vital supplies. i, Battleship firing main battery (Battle for Leyte Gulf, Oct. 23-26). j, Soldiers in snow (Bastogne and Battle of the Bulge, Dec.).

Central label is size of 15 stamps and shows world map with extent of Axis control and Allied operations.

Illustration reduced.

LITHOGRAPHED & ENGRAVED

1994, June 6   *Perf. 10.9*

2838	A2166	Block of 10	17.00	10.00
a.-j.		29c any single	1.70	.50

No. 2838 has selvage at left and right and either top or bottom.

NORMAN ROCKWELL

A2167

A2168

1994, July 1   *Perf. 10.9x11.1*

2839	A2167	29c multicolored	.60	.25

Souvenir Sheet

LITHOGRAPHED

2840	A2168	Sheet of 4	4.50	2.75
a.		50c Freedom From Want	1.10	.65
b.		50c Freedom From Fear	1.10	.65
c.		50c Freedom of Speech	1.10	.65
d.		50c Freedom of Worship	1.10	.65

Moon Landing, 25th Anniv.

A2169

A2170

Miniature Sheet

1994, July 20   *Perf. 11.2x11.1*

2841	A2169	29c Sheet of 12	10.50	—
a.		Single stamp	.85	.60

LITHOGRAPHED & ENGRAVED
Perf. 10.7x11.1

2842	A2170	$9.95 multicolored	20.00	16.00

LOCOMOTIVES

Hudson's General
A2171

McQueen's Jupiter
A2172

Eddy's No. 242
A2173

Ely's No. 10
A2174

Buchanan's No. 999
A2175

PHOTOGRAVURE

1994, July 28   *Perf. 11 Horiz.*
Booklet Stamps

2843	A2171	29c multicolored	.75	.25
2844	A2172	29c multicolored	.75	.25
2845	A2173	29c multicolored	.75	.25
2846	A2174	29c multicolored	.75	.25
2847	A2175	29c multicolored	.75	.25
a.		Booklet pane of 5, #2843-2847	3.75	2.00
b.		As "a," imperf.	2,500.	

GEORGE MEANY, LABOR LEADER (1894-1980)

A2176

ENGRAVED

1994, Aug. 16   *Perf. 11.1x11*

2848	A2176	29c blue	.60	.25

AMERICAN MUSIC SERIES
Popular Singers

Al Jolson (1886-1950)
A2177

Bing Crosby (1904-77)
A2178

Ethel Waters (1896-1977)
A2179

Nat "King" Cole (1919-65)
A2180

Ethel Merman (1908-84)
A2181

Jazz Singers

Bessie Smith (1894-1937)
A2182

Muddy Waters (1915-83)
A2183

Billie Holiday (1915-59)
A2184

Robert Johnson (1911-38)
A2185

Jimmy Rushing (1902-72)
A2186

"Ma" Rainey (1886-1939)
A2187

Mildred Bailey (1907-51)
A2188

Howlin' Wolf (1910-76)
A2189

PHOTOGRAVURE

1994, Sept. 1   **Perf. 10.1x10.2**

2849	A2177	29c multicolored	.85	.25
2850	A2178	29c multicolored	.85	.25
2851	A2179	29c multicolored	.85	.25
2852	A2180	29c multicolored	.85	.25
2853	A2181	29c multicolored	.85	.25
a.		Vert. strip of 5, #2849-2853	4.25	2.00
b.		Pane of 20, imperf	10,000.	

1994, Sept. 17   **Perf. 11x10.8**

LITHOGRAPHED

2854	A2182	29c multicolored	1.50	.25
2855	A2183	29c multicolored	1.50	.25
2856	A2184	29c multicolored	1.50	.25
2857	A2185	29c multicolored	1.50	.25
2858	A2186	29c multicolored	1.50	.25
2859	A2187	29c multicolored	1.50	.25
2860	A2188	29c multicolored	1.50	.25
2861	A2189	29c multicolored	1.50	.25
a.		Block of 10, #2854-2861 +2 additional stamps	15.00	4.50

LITERARY ARTS SERIES

James Thurber (1894-1961) A2190

LITHOGRAPHED & ENGRAVED

1994, Sept. 10   **Perf. 11**

2862	A2190	29c multicolored	.60	.25

WONDERS OF THE SEA

Diver, Motorboat A2191

Diver, Ship A2192

Diver, Ship's Wheel A2193

Diver, Coral A2194

LITHOGRAPHED

1994, Oct. 3   **Perf. 11x10.9**

2863	A2191	29c multicolored	.75	.25
2864	A2192	29c multicolored	.75	.25
2865	A2193	29c multicolored	.75	.25
2866	A2194	29c multicolored	.75	.25
a.		Block of 4, #2863-2866	3.00	1.50
b.		As "a," imperf	500.00	

CRANES

Black-Necked Crane A2195

Whooping Crane A2196

LITHOGRAPHED & ENGRAVED

1994, Oct. 9   **Perf. 10.8x11**

2867	A2195	29c multicolored	.70	.25
2868	A2196	29c multicolored	.70	.25
a.		Pair, #2867-2868	1.40	.75
b.		As "a," black & magenta (engr.) omitted	1,250.	
c.		As "a," double impression of engr. black (Birds' names and "USA") & magenta ("29")	3,000.	
d.		As "a," double impression of engr. black ("USA") & magenta ("29")	3,000.	

See People's Republic of China Nos. 2528-2529.

LEGENDS OF THE WEST

A2197

g. Bill Pickett (1870-1932) (Revised)

Designs: a, Home on the Range. b, Buffalo Bill Cody (1846-1917). c, Jim Bridger (1804-81). d, Annie Oakley (1860-1926). e, Native American Culture. f, Chief Joseph (c. 1840-1904). h, Bat Masterson (1853-1921). i, John C. Fremont (1813-90). j, Wyatt Earp (1848-1929). k, Nellie Cashman (c. 1849-1925). l, Charles Goodnight (1826-1929). m, Geronimo (1823-1909). n, Kit Carson (1809-68). o, Wild Bill Hickok (1837-76). p, Western Wildlife. q, Jim Beckwourth (c. 1798-1866). r, Bill Tilghman (1854-1924). s, Sacagawea (c. 1787-1812). t, Overland Mail.

PHOTOGRAVURE

1994, Oct. 18   **Perf. 10.1x10**

2869	A2197	Pane of 20	15.00	10.00
a.-t.		29c any single	.75	.50
u.		As No. 2869, a.-e. imperf.		
		f.-j. part perf.	—	

LEGENDS OF THE WEST (Recalled)

g. Bill Pickett (Recalled)

Nos. 2870b-2870d, 2870f-2870o, 2870q-2870s have a frameline around the vignette that is half the width of the frameline on similar stamps in No. 2869. Other design differences may exist.

1994

2870	A2197	29c Pane of 20	220.00	—

150,000 panes of No. 2870 were made available through a drawing. Panes were delivered in an envelope. Value is for pane without envelope. Panes with envelopes sell for somewhat more.

CHRISTMAS

Madonna and Child, by Elisabetta Sirani A2200

Stocking A2201

Santa Claus A2202

Cardinal in Snow A2203

LITHOGRAPHED & ENGRAVED

1994, Oct. 20   **Perf. 11¼**

2871	A2200	29c multi	.60	.25

BOOKLET STAMP
Perf. 9¾x11

2871A	A2200	29c multi	.60	.25
b.		Booklet pane of 10	6.25	3.50
c.		Imperf., pair	350.00	

LITHOGRAPHED
Perf. 11¼

2872	A2201	29c multi	.60	.25
a.		Booklet pane of 20	12.50	6.00
b.		Imperf., pair	—	
c.		Vert. pair, imperf. horiz.	—	
d.		Quadruple impression of black, triple impression of blue, double impressions of red and yellow, green normal	900.00	
e.		Vert. pair, imperf. between	125.00	
f.		As "a," imperf.	—	

PHOTOGRAVURE
BOOKLET STAMPS
Self-Adhesive
Die Cut

2873	A2202	29c multi	.70	.25
a.		Booklet pane of 12	8.50	
b.		Coil with plate #V1111	—	6.00

Except for No. 2873b with plate number, coil stamps are indistinguishable from booklet stamps once they are removed from the backing paper.

2874	A2203	29c multi	.60	.25
a.		Booklet pane of 18	11.00	

BUREAU OF ENGRAVING & PRINTING
Souvenir Sheet

A2204

LITHOGRAPHED & ENGRAVED

1994, Nov. 3   **Perf. 11**

2875	A2204	$2 Pane of 4	16.00	13.50
a.		Single stamp	4.00	2.00
b.		Pane of 4 with double impression of the brown lettering panel	1,100.	

The double impression is clear, but may be seen best in the scrolls at lower right.

CHINESE NEW YEAR

Year of the Boar A2205

PHOTOGRAVURE

1994, Dec. 30   **Perf. 11.2x11.1**

2876	A2205	29c multicolored	.70	.25

See No. 3895l.

A2206

A2207

A2208

A2208a

A2209

LITHOGRAPHED
Perf. 11x10.8

1994, Dec. 13   **Untagged**

2877	A2206	(3c) tan, brt bl & red	.25	.25
a.		Imperf., pair	115.00	
b.		Double impression of red	175.00	

No. 2877 imperf and with blue omitted is known from printer's waste.

Perf. 10.8x10.9
Untagged

2878	A2206	(3c) tan, dk bl & red	.25	.25

Inscriptions on #2877 are in a thin typeface. Those on #2878 are in heavy, bold type.

PHOTOGRAVURE
Perf. 11.2x11.1

2879	A2207	(20c) black "G," yel & multi	.40	.25
a.		Imperf., pair		

Perf. 11x10.9

2880	A2207	(20c) red "G," yel & multi	.75	.25

Perf. 11.2x11.1

2881	A2208	(32c) black "G" & multi	1.25	.25
a.		Booklet pane of 10	12.50	5.00

Perf. 11x10.9

2882	A2208a	(32c) red "G" & multi	.60	.25

Distance on #2882 from bottom of red G to top of flag immediately above is 13¾mm. Illustration A2208a shows #2885 superimposed over #2882.

BOOKLET STAMPS
Perf. 10x9.9 on 2 or 3 Sides

2883	A2208	(32c) black "G" & multi	.65	.25
a.		Booklet pane of 10	6.50	3.75

Perf. 10.9 on 2 or 3 Sides

2884	A2208	(32c) blue "G" & multi	.65	.25
a.		Booklet pane of 10	6.50	3.75
b.		As "a," imperf	4,500.	

Perf. 11x10.9 on 2 or 3 Sides

2885	A2208a	(32c) red "G" & multi	.90	.25
a.		Booklet pane of 10	9.00	4.50
b.		Horiz. pair, imperf vert.	750.00	
c.		Horiz. pair, imperf. btwn., in #2885a with foldover		

Distance on #2885 from bottom of red G to top of flag immediately above is 13½mm. See note below #2882.

No. 2885c resulted from a paper foldover after perforating and before cutting into panes.

A2208b

A2208c

Die Cut
Self-Adhesive

2886	A2208b (32c) gray, bl, lt bl, red & blk	.70	.25
a.	Booklet pane of 18	12.50	
b.	Coil with plate # V11111	—	10.00

No. 2886 is printed on prephosphored paper that is opaque, thicker and brighter than that of No. 2887 and has only a small number of blue shading dots in the white stripes immediately below the flag's blue field.

Except for No. 2886b with plate number, coil stamps are indistinguishable from booklet stamps once they are removed from the backing paper.

2887	A2208c (32c) black, blue & red	.70	.25
a.	Booklet pane of 18	12.50	

No. 2887 has noticeable blue shading in the white stripes immediately below the blue field and has overall tagging. The paper is translucent, thinner and duller than No. 2886.

COIL STAMPS
Perf. 9.8 Vert.

2888	A2209	(25c) black "G"	.90	.50
2889	A2208	(32c) black "G"	1.50	.25
a.	Imperf., pair		250.00	
2890	A2208	(32c) blue "G"	.65	.25
2891	A2208	(32c) red "G"	.85	.25

Rouletted 9.8 Vert.

2892	A2208	(32c) red "G"	.75	.25

A2210

Flag Over
Porch — A2212

COIL STAMP

1995　Untagged　Perf. 9.8 Vert.

2893	A2210 (5c) green & multi	.50	.25

1995, May 19　Perf. 10.4

2897	A2212 32c multicolored	.75	.25
a.	Imperf., vert. pair	55.00	

See Nos. 2913-2916, 2920-2921, 3133.

Butte
A2217

Mountain
A2218

Auto — A2220

Auto Tail
Fin — A2223

Juke Box
A2225

Flag Over
Field
A2230

COIL STAMPS
Self-Adhesive (#2902B, 2904A-2904B, 2906-2907, 2910, 2912A, 2912B, 2915-2915D, 2919-2921)

1995-97　　Perf. 9.8 Vert.
Untagged (Nos. 2902-2912B)

2902	A2217	(5c) yel, red & bl	.25	.25
a.	Imperf., pair		350.00	

Serpentine Die Cut 11.5 Vert.
Untagged

2902B	A2217	(5c) yel, red & bl ('96)	.35	.25

Perf. 9.8 Vert.
Untagged

2903	A2218	(5c) purple & multi ('96)	.25	.25

Letters of inscription "USA NONPROFIT ORG." outlined in purple on No. 2903. No. 2903 has purple "1996" at left bottom.

Untagged

2904	A2218	(5c) blue & multi ('96)	.25	.25
c.	Imperf., pair		225.00	

Letters of inscription have no outline on No. 2904. No. 2904 has blue "1996" at bottom left.

Serpentine Die Cut 11.2 Vert.
Untagged

2904A	A2218	(5c) purple & multi ('96)	.40	.25

Serpentine Die Cut 9.8 Vert.
Untagged

2904B	A2218	(5c) purple & multi ('97)	.25	.25

Letters of inscription outlined in purple on No. 2904B, not outlined on No. 2904A. No. 2904A has large purple "1996" at bottom left. No. 2904B has small purple "1997" at bottom left.

Perf. 9.8 Vert.
Untagged

2905	A2220	(10c) blk, red brn & brn, small "1995" date	.25	.25
a.	Medium "1995" date		.35	.25
b.	Large "1995" date ('96)		.60	.25
c.	As "b," brown omitted, P#S33 single		400.00	

Date on 2905 is approximately 1.9mm long, on No. 2905a 2mm long, and on No. 2905b 2.1mm long.

Serpentine Die Cut 11.5 Vert.
Untagged

2906	A2220	(10c) blk, brn & red brn ('96)	.50	.25

Untagged

2907	A1957	(10c) gold & multi ('96)	.75	.25

Perf. 9.8 Vert.
Untagged

2908	A2223	(15c) dk org yel & multi	.30	.30

No. 2908 has "2005" in blue and has dark, bold colors, heavy shading lines and heavily shaded chrome.

Untagged

2909	A2223	(15c) buff & multi	.30	.30

No. 2909 has "2005" in black and has shinier chrome, more subdued colors and finer details than No. 2908.

Serpentine Die Cut 11.5 Vert.
Untagged

2910	A2223	(15c) buff & multi ('96)	.30	.30

Perf. 9.8 Vert.
Untagged

2911	A2225	(25c) dk red, dk yel grn & multi	.50	.50
a.	Imperf, pair		400.00	

No. 2911 has dark, saturated colors and dark blue lines in the music selection board.

Untagged

2912	A2225	(25c) brt org red, brt yel grn & multi	.75	.50

No. 2912 has bright colors, less shading and light blue lines in the music selection board.

Serpentine Die Cut 11.5 Vert.
Untagged

2912A	A2225	(25c) brt org red, brt yel grn & multi ('96)	.50	.50

Serpentine Die Cut 9.8 Vert.
Untagged

2912B	A2225	(25c) dk red, dk yel grn & multi ('97)	.75	.50

See No. 3132.

Perf. 9.8 Vert.

2913	A2212	32c bl, tan, brn, red & lt bl	.65	.25
a.	Imperf., pair		30.00	

No. 2913 has pronounced light blue shading in the flag and red "1995" at left bottom. See No. 3133.

2914	A2212	32c bl, yel brn, red & gray	.80	.25

No. 2914 has pale gray shading in the flag and blue "1995" at left bottom.

Serpentine Die Cut 8.7 Vert.

2915	A2212	32c multi	1.25	.30

No. 2915 has blue "1995" at bottom left.

Serpentine Die Cut 9.8 Vert.

2915A	A2212	32c dk bl, tan, brn, red & lt bl ('96)	.65	.25
h.	Die cutting omitted, pair		32.50	
i.	Tan omitted		—	
j.	Double die cutting		30.00	

No. 2915A has red "1996" at left bottom. Sky on No. 3133 shows color gradation at LR not on No. 2915A.
On No. 2915Ai all other colors except brown are severely shifted.
On No. 2915Aj, the second die cutting is a different gauge than the normal 9.8.

Serpentine Die Cut 11.5 Vert.

2915B	A2212	32c dk bl, tan, brn, red & lt bl ('96)	1.00	.90

Serpentine Die Cut 10.9 Vert.

2915C	A2212	32c dk bl, tan, brn, red & lt bl	3.50	.40

Serpentine Die Cut 9.8 Vert.

2915D	A2212	32c dk bl, tan, brn, red & lt bl ('97)	2.00	.90

Stamps on multiples of No. 2915A touch, and are on a peelable backing the same size as the stamps, while those of No. 2915D are separated on the peelable backing, which is larger than the stamps.
No. 2915D has red "1997" at left bottom; No. 2915A has red "1996" at left bottom.
Sky on No. 3133 shows color gradation at LR not on No. 2915D, and it has blue "1996" at left bottom.

BOOKLET STAMPS
Perf. 10.8x9.8 on 2 or 3 Adjacent Sides

2916	A2212	32c bl, tan, brn, red & lt bl	.65	.25
a.	Booklet pane of 10		6.50	3.25
b.	As "a," imperf.		—	

Die Cut

2919	A2230	32c multi	.65	.25
a.	Booklet pane of 18		12.00	
b.	Vert. pair, die cutting omitted btwn.		—	

Serpentine Die Cut 8.7 on 2, 3 or 4 Adjacent Sides

2920	A2212	32c multi, dated blue "1995"	.65	.25
a.	Booklet pane of 20+label		13.00	
b.	Small date		6.00	.35
c.	As "b," booklet pane of 20+label		120.00	
f.	As No. 2920, pane of 15+label		9.75	
g.	As "a," partial pane of 10, 3 stamps and parts of 7 stamps printed on backing liner		—	
h.	As No. 2920, booklet pane of 15		47.50	
i.	As No. 2920, die cutting omitted, pair		—	
j.	Dark blue omitted (from No. 2920a)		2,100.	
k.	Vert. pair, die cutting missing btwn., three examples in No. 2920a with shift in die cutting (PS)		—	

Date on No. 2920 is nearly twice as large as date on No. 2920b. No. 2920f comes in various configurations.
No. 2920h is a pane of 16 with one stamp removed. The missing stamp is the lower right stamp in the pane or (more rarely) the upper left stamp. No. 2920h cannot be made from No. 2920f, a pane of 15 + label. The label is located in the sixth or seventh row of the pane and is die cut. If the label is removed, an impression of the die cutting appears on the backing paper.

Serpentine Die Cut 11.3 on 3 sides

2920D	A2212	32c multi, dated blue "1996" ('96)	.80	.25
e.	Booklet pane of 10		8.00	

Serpentine Die Cut 9.8 on 2 or 3 Adjacent Sides

2921	A2212	32c dk bl, tan, brn, red & lt bl, dated red "1996" ('96)	.90	.25
a.	Booklet pane of 10, dated red "1996"		9.00	
b.	As No. 2921, dated red "1997," Jan. 24, 1997		1.20	.25
c.	As "a," dated red "1997"		12.00	
d.	Booklet pane of 5 + label, dated red "1997," Jan. 24, 1997		8.00	
e.	As "a," die cutting omitted		200.00	

Issued: #2902, 2905, 3/10/95; #2908-2909, 2911-2912, 2919, 3/17/95; #2915, 2920, 4/18/95; #2897, 2913-2914, 2916, 5/19/95; #2920d, 1/20/96; #2904B, 2912B, 2915D, 2921b-2921d, 1/24/97; #2903-2904, 3/16/96; #2915A, 5/21/97; #2907, 2921, 5/21/96; #2902B, 2904A, 2906, 2910, 2912A, 2915B, 6/15/96; #2915C, 5/21/96.
See Nos. 3132-3133.

Scott values for used self-adhesive stamps are for examples either on piece or off piece.

GREAT AMERICANS ISSUE

A2248

A2249

A2250

A2251

A2253

A2255

A2256

A2257

A2258

ENGRAVED

1995-99
Self-Adhesive (#2941-2942)
Perf. 11.2, Serpentine Die Cut
11.7x11.5 (#2941-2942)

2933	A2248	32c brown	.75	.25
2934	A2249	32c green ('96)	.75	.25
2935	A2250	32c lake ('98)	.65	.35
2936	A2251	32c blue ('98)	.65	.35
a.		32c light blue	.65	.35
2938	A2253	46c carmine	.90	.30
2940	A2255	55c green	1.15	.25
a.		Imperf, pair	—	
2941	A2256	55c black ('99)	1.10	.25
2942	A2257	77c blue ('98)	1.50	.40
2943	A2258	78c bright violet	1.60	.25
a.		78c dull violet	1.60	.25
b.		78c pale violet	3.00	.30
		Nos. 2933-2943 (9)	9.05	2.65

The pale violet ink on No. 2943b luminesces bright pink under long-wave ultraviolet light.

LOVE

A2263

Cherub from Sistine Madonna, by Raphael — A2264

LITHOGRAPHED & ENGRAVED

1995, Feb. 1　　　　　　　*Perf. 11.2*
2948	A2263	(32c) multi	.65	.25

Self-Adhesive
Die Cut
2949	A2264	(32c) multi	.65	.25
a.		Booklet pane of 20 + label	13.00	
b.		Red (engr.) omitted	100.00	
c.		As "a," red (engr.) omitted	2,000.	
d.		Red (engr.) missing (CM)		

No. 2949d must be collected se-tenant with a normal stamp.
See Nos. 2957-2960, 3030.

FLORIDA STATEHOOD

A2265

LITHOGRAPHED

1995, Mar. 3　　　　　　　*Perf. 11.1*
2950	A2265	32c multicolored	.65	.25

EARTH DAY

Earth Clean-Up
A2266

Solar Energy
A2267

Tree Planting
A2268

Beach Clean-Up
A2269

1995, Apr. 20　　　　　　*Perf. 11.1x11*
2951	A2266	32c multicolored	.65	.25
2952	A2267	32c multicolored	.65	.25
2953	A2268	32c multicolored	.65	.25
2954	A2269	32c multicolored	.65	.25
a.		Block of 4, #2951-2954	2.60	1.75

RICHARD M. NIXON
37th President (1913-94)

Richard M. Nixon, 37th President (1913-94) — A2270

LITHOGRAPHED & ENGRAVED

1995, Apr. 26　　　　　　*Perf. 11.2*
2955	A2270	32c multicolored	.65	.25
a.		Red (engr.) missing (CM)	700.00	

No. 2955 is known with red (engr. "Richard Nixon") inverted, and with red engr. omitted but only half the Nixon portrait present, both from printer's waste. No. 2955a shows a complete Nixon portrait.

BLACK HERITAGE SERIES

Bessie Coleman, Aviator — A2271

ENGRAVED

1995, Apr. 27
2956	A2271	32c red & black	.85	.25

LOVE

A2272

A2273

A2274

LITHOGRAPHED & ENGRAVED

1995, May 12
2957	A2272	32c multicolored	.65	.25

Compare with No. 3030.

2958	A2273	55c multicolored	1.10	.25

BOOKLET STAMPS
Perf. 9.8x10.8
2959	A2272	32c multicolored	.65	.25
a.		Booklet pane of 10	6.50	3.25
b.		Imperf, pair	100.00	
c.		As "a," imperf.	500.00	

Self-Adhesive
Die Cut
2960	A2274	55c multicolored	1.10	.25
a.		Booklet pane of 20 + label	22.50	

RECREATIONAL SPORTS

Volleyball
A2275

Softball
A2276

Bowling
A2277

Tennis
A2278

Golf
A2279

LITHOGRAPHED

1995, May 20
2961	A2275	32c multicolored	.65	.25
2962	A2276	32c multicolored	.65	.25
2963	A2277	32c multicolored	.65	.25
2964	A2278	32c multicolored	.65	.25
2965	A2279	32c multicolored	.65	.25
a.		Vert. strip of 5, #2961-2965	3.25	2.00
b.		As "a," imperf	1,750.	
c.		As "a," yellow omitted	1,600.	
d.		As "a," yellow, blue & magenta omitted	1,600.	

PRISONERS OF WAR & MISSING IN ACTION

A2280

1995, May 29
2966	A2280	32c multicolored	.65	.25

LEGENDS OF HOLLYWOOD

Marilyn Monroe (1926-62) — A2281

PHOTOGRAVURE

1995, June 1　　　　　　*Perf. 11.1*
2967	A2281	32c multicolored	.80	.25
a.		Imperf., pair	225.00	

Perforations in corner of each stamp are star-shaped.

TEXAS STATEHOOD

A2282

LITHOGRAPHED

1995, June 16　　　　　　*Perf. 11.2*
2968	A2282	32c multicolored	.70	.25

GREAT LAKES LIGHTHOUSES

Split Rock, Lake Superior
A2283

St. Joseph, Lake Michigan
A2284

Spectacle Reef, Lake Huron — A2285

Marblehead, Lake Erie — A2286

Thirty Mile Point, Lake Ontario — A2287

PHOTOGRAVURE
BOOKLET STAMPS

1995, June 17　　　*Perf. 11.2 Vert.*
2969	A2283	32c multicolored	1.00	.30
2970	A2284	32c multicolored	1.00	.30
2971	A2285	32c multicolored	1.00	.30
2972	A2286	32c multicolored	1.00	.30
2973	A2287	32c multicolored	1.00	.30
a.		Booklet pane of 5, #2969-2973	5.00	2.50
b.		As "a," two vert. pairs imperf. horiz. of #2972 and 2973, in pane of 7+ stamps in cplt. bklt. #BK230 (due to foldover)	—	

U.N., 50th ANNIV.

A2288

ENGRAVED

1995, June 26　　　　　　*Perf. 11.2*
2974	A2288	32c blue	.65	.25

CIVIL WAR

A2289

Designs: a, Monitor and Virginia. b, Robert E. Lee. c, Clara Barton. d, Ulysses S. Grant. e, Battle of Shiloh. f, Jefferson Davis. g, David Farragut. h, Frederick Douglass. i, Raphael Semmes. j, Abraham Lincoln. k, Harriet Tubman. l, Stand Watie. m, Joseph E. Johnston. n, Winfield Hancock. o, Mary Chesnut. p, Battle of Chancellorsville. q, William T. Sherman. r, Phoebe Pember. s, "Stonewall" Jackson. t, Battle of Gettysburg.

PHOTOGRAVURE

			1995, June 29	**Perf. 10.1**
2975	A2289	Pane of 20	32.50	17.50
a.-t.		32c any single	1.50	.60
u.		As No. 2975, a.-e. imperf, f.-j. part perf, others perf	800.00	
v.		As No. 2975, k.-t. imperf, f.-j. part perf, others perf	1,250.	
w.		As No. 2975, imperf	800.00	
x.		Block of 9 (f.-h., k.-m., p.-r.) k.-l. & p.-q. imperf, vert.	800.00	
y.		As No. 2975, a.-b. perf, c., f.-h. part perf, others imperf	800.00	
z.		As No. 2975, o. and t. imperf, j., n. & s. part perf, others perf	—	
aa.		As No. 2975, c.-e. imperf, b., g.-j. part perf, others perf	500.00	

AMERICAN FOLK ART SERIES
Carousel Horses

A2290

A2291

A2292

A2293

LITHOGRAPHED

			1995, July 21	**Perf. 11**
2976	A2290	32c multicolored	.65	.25
2977	A2291	32c multicolored	.65	.25
2978	A2292	32c multicolored	.65	.25
2979	A2293	32c multicolored	.65	.25
a.		Block of 4, #2976-2979	2.60	2.00

WOMAN SUFFRAGE

A2294

LITHOGRAPHED & ENGRAVED

			1995, Aug. 26	**Perf. 11.1x11**
2980	A2294	32c multicolored	.65	.25
a.		Black (engr.) omitted	275.00	
b.		Imperf., pair	750.00	
c.		Vert. pair, imperf between and at bottom	500.00	

No. 2980a is valued in the grade of fine. Very fine examples exist and sell for much more.

WORLD WAR II

A2295

Designs and events of 1945: a, Marines raise flag on Iwo Jima. b, Fierce fighting frees Manila by March 3, 1945. c, Soldiers advancing (Okinawa, the last big battle). d, Destroyed bridge (US and Soviets link up at Elbe River). e, Allies liberate Holocaust survivors. f, Germany surrenders at Reims. g, Refugees (By 1945, World War II has uprooted millions). h, Truman announces Japan's surrender. i, Sailor kissing nurse (News of victory hits home). j, Hometowns honor their returning veterans.

Central label is size of 15 stamps and shows world map with extent of Axis control and Allied operations.

			1995, Sept. 2	**Perf. 11.1**
2981	A2295	Block of 10	15.00	7.50
a.-j.		32c any single	1.50	.50

No. 2981 has selvage at left and right and either top or bottom.

AMERICAN MUSIC SERIES

Louis Armstrong A2296

Coleman Hawkins A2297

James P. Johnson A2298

Jelly Roll Morton A2299

Charlie Parker A2300

Eubie Blake A2301

Charles Mingus A2302

Thelonious Monk A2303

John Coltrane A2304

Erroll Garner A2305

LITHOGRAPHED
Plates of 120 in six panes of 20

			1995	**Perf. 11.1x11**
2982	A2296	32c white denomination	.90	.25
a.		Imperf, pair		
2983	A2297	32c multicolored	2.25	.30
2984	A2296	32c black denomination	2.25	.30
2985	A2298	32c multicolored	2.25	.30
2986	A2299	32c multicolored	2.25	.30
2987	A2300	32c multicolored	2.25	.30
2988	A2301	32c multicolored	2.25	.30
2989	A2302	32c multicolored	2.25	.30
2990	A2303	32c multicolored	2.25	.30
2991	A2304	32c multicolored	2.25	.30
2992	A2305	32c multicolored	2.25	.30
a.		Vert. block of 10, #2983-2992	23.00	7.50
b.		Pane of 20, dark blue (inscriptions) omitted	—	
c.		Imperf pair of Nos. 2991-2992	5,000.	

GARDEN FLOWERS

A2306

A2307

A2308

A2309

A2310

LITHOGRAPHED & ENGRAVED
BOOKLET STAMPS

			1995, Sept. 19	**Perf. 10.9 Vert.**
2993	A2306	32c multicolored	.65	.25
2994	A2307	32c multicolored	.65	.25
2995	A2308	32c multicolored	.65	.25
2996	A2309	32c multicolored	.65	.25
2997	A2310	32c multicolored	.65	.25
a.		Booklet pane of 5, #2993-2997	3.25	2.25
b.		As "a," imperf	2,250.	

EDDIE RICKENBACKER (1890-1973), AVIATOR

A2311

PHOTOGRAVURE

			1995, Sept. 25	**Perf. 11¼**
2998	A2311	60c multicolored, small "1995" year date	1.40	.50
a.		Large "1995" date, Oct., 1999	2.00	.50

Date on No. 2998 is 1mm long, on No. 2998a 1 ½mm long.

REPUBLIC OF PALAU

A2312

LITHOGRAPHED

			1995, Sept. 29	**Perf. 11.1**
2999	A2312	32c multicolored	.65	.25

See Palau Nos. 377-378.

COMIC STRIPS

A2313

Designs: a, The Yellow Kid. b, Katzenjammer Kids. c, Little Nemo in Slumberland. d, Bringing Up Father. e, Krazy Kat. f, Rube Goldberg's Inventions. g, Toonerville Folks. h, Gasoline Alley. i, Barney Google. j, Little Orphan Annie. k, Popeye. l, Blondie. m, Dick Tracy. n, Alley Oop. o, Nancy. p, Flash Gordon. q, Li'l Abner. r, Terry and the Pirates. s, Prince Valiant. t, Brenda Starr, Reporter.

PHOTOGRAVURE

1995, Oct. 1   **Perf. 10.1**

3000	A2313	Pane of 20	13.00 10.00
a.-t.		32c any single	.65 .50
u.		As No. 3000, a.-h. imperf., i.-l. part perf	3,250.
v.		As No. 3000, m.-t. imperf., i.-l. part perf	3,250.
w.		As No. 3000, a.-l. im- perf.,m.-t. imperf vert.	3,250.
x.		As No. 3000, imperf	5,250.

U.S. NAVAL ACADEMY, 150th ANNIVERSARY

A2314

LITHOGRAPHED

1995, Oct. 10   **Perf. 10.9**

3001	A2314	32c multicolored	.65 .25

LITERARY ARTS SERIES

Tennessee Williams (1911-83) A2315

1995, Oct. 13   **Perf. 11.1**

3002	A2315	32c multicolored	.65 .25

CHRISTMAS

Madonna and Child A2316

Santa Claus Entering Chimney A2317

Child Holding Jumping Jack — A2318   Child Holding Tree — A2319

Santa Claus Working on Sled A2320   Midnight Angel A2321

Children Sledding — A2322

LITHOGRAPHED & ENGRAVED

1995   **Perf. 11.2**

3003	A2316	32c mul- ticolored	.65 .25
c.		Black (engr., denomina- tion) omitted	250.00 —

BOOKLET STAMP
Perf. 9.8x10.9

3003A	A2316	32c mul- ticolored	.65 .25
b.		Booklet pane of 10	6.50 4.00

LITHOGRAPHED
Perf. 11.25

3004	A2317	32c mul- ticolored	.70 .25
3005	A2318	32c mul- ticolored	.70 .25
3006	A2319	32c mul- ticolored	.70 .25
3007	A2320	32c mul- ticolored	.70 .25
a.		Block or strip of 4, #3004-3007	2.80 1.25
b.		Booklet pane of 10, 3 each #3004-3005, 2 each #3006-3007	8.00 4.00
c.		Booklet pane of 10, 2 each #3004-3005, 3 each #3006-3007	8.00 4.00
d.		As "a," imperf	350.00
e.		As "b," miscut and in- serted upside down into booklet cover, with full bottom selvage	—

PHOTOGRAVURE
Self-Adhesive Stamps
Serpentine Die Cut 11.25 on 2, 3 or 4 sides

3008	A2320	32c mul- ticolored	.95 .25
3009	A2318	32c mul- ticolored	.95 .25
3010	A2317	32c mul- ticolored	.95 .25
3011	A2319	32c mul- ticolored	.95 .25
a.		Booklet pane of 20, 5 each #3008-3011 + label	19.00

LITHOGRAPHED
Serpentine Die Cut 11.3x11.6 on 2, 3 or 4 sides

3012	A2321	32c mul- ticolored	.65 .25
a.		Booklet pane of 20 + la- bel	13.00
b.		Vert. pair, die cutting omitted between	—
c.		Booklet pane of 15 + la- bel, 1996	12.00
d.		Booklet pane of 15	30.00

No. 3012a comes either with no die cutting in the label (1995 printing) or with the die cut- ting from the 1996 printing.
No. 3012d is a pane of 16 with one stamp removed. The missing stamp can be from either row 1, 2, 3, 7 or 8 of the pane. No. 3012d cannot be made from No. 3012c, a pane of 15 + label. The label is die cut. If the label is removed, an impression of the die cut- ting appears on the backing paper.

PHOTOGRAVURE
Die Cut

3013	A2322	32c mul- ticolored	.65 .25
a.		Booklet pane of 18	12.00

Self-Adhesive Coil Stamps
Serpentine Die Cut 11.2 Vert.

3014	A2320	32c mul- ticolored	3.00 .30
3015	A2318	32c mul- ticolored	3.00 .30
3016	A2317	32c mul- ticolored	3.00 .30
3017	A2319	32c mul- ticolored	3.00 .30
a.		Strip of 4, #3014-3017	12.00

LITHOGRAPHED
Serpentine Die Cut 11.6 Vert.

3018	A2321	32c mul- ticolored	1.10 .30

Nos. 3005-3006 have "USA" printed in green. It is red on the self-adhesive stamps.
Issued: #3003-3003A, 3012-3013, 3018, 10/19; #3004-3011, 3014-3017, 9/30.

ANTIQUE AUTOMOBILES

1893 Duryea A2323

1894 Haynes A2324

1898 Columbia A2325

1899 Winton A2326

1901 White A2327

PHOTOGRAVURE

1995, Nov. 3   **Perf. 10.1x11.1**

3019	A2323	32c multicolored	.90 .25
3020	A2324	32c multicolored	.90 .25
3021	A2325	32c multicolored	.90 .25
3022	A2326	32c multicolored	.90 .25
3023	A2327	32c multicolored	.90 .25
a.		Vert. or horiz. strip of 5, #3019-3023	4.50 2.00

Vert. and horiz. strips are all in different order.

UTAH STATEHOOD CENTENARY

Delicate Arch, Arches Natl. Park — A2328

LITHOGRAPHED

1996, Jan. 4   **Perf. 11.1**

3024	A2328	32c multicolored	.75 .25

GARDEN FLOWERS

Crocus A2329

Winter Aconite A2330

Pansy A2331   Snowdrop A2332

Anemone — A2333

LITHOGRAPHED & ENGRAVED
BOOKLET STAMPS

1996, Jan. 19   **Perf. 10.9 Vert.**

3025	A2329	32c multi	.70 .25
3026	A2330	32c multi	.70 .25
3027	A2331	32c multi	.70 .25
3028	A2332	32c multi	.70 .25
3029	A2333	32c multi	.70 .25
a.		Booklet pane of 5, #3025-3029	3.50 2.50
b.		As "a," imperf.	—

LOVE

Cherub from Sistine Madonna, by Raphael — A2334

BOOKLET STAMP
Serpentine Die Cut 11.3x11.7

1996, Jan. 20
Self-Adhesive

3030	A2334	32c multicolored	.65 .25
a.		Booklet pane of 20 + label	13.00
b.		Booklet pane of 15 + label	9.75
c.		Red (engr. "Love") omitted	75.00
d.		Red (engr. "Love") missing (CM)	—
e.		Double impression of red (engr. "Love")	450.00
f.		Die cutting omitted, pair	225.00
g.		As "a," stamps 1-5 double impression of red (engr. "LOVE")	1,000.
h.		As "a," red (engr. "LOVE") omitted	1,500.
i.		As "a," die cutting omitted	1,000.
j		As "e," two examples in booklet pane of 20 (No. 3030a)	1,000.

No. 3030d must be collected se-tenant with a stamp bearing the red engraving.

FLORA AND FAUNA SERIES
Kestrel, Blue Jay and Rose Types of 1993-95 and

Red-headed Woodpecker A2335

Eastern Bluebird A2336

Red Fox A2339

Ring-necked Pheasant A2350

Coral Pink Rose — A2351

Serpentine Die Cut 10½

1996-2002   **Untagged**
Self-Adhesive (#3031, 3031A)

3031	A1841	1c multicolored	.25 .25
c.		Die cutting omitted, pair	—

Serpentine Die Cut 11¼
Untagged

3031A	A1841	1c multicolored	.25 .25
b.		Die cutting omitted, pane of 50	325.00

No. 3031A has blue inscription and year.

Perf. 11
Untagged

3032	A2335	2c multicolored	.25 .25
3033	A2336	3c multicolored	.25 .25

Serpentine Die Cut 11½x11¼
Self-Adhesive

3036	A2339	$1 multicolored	4.50 .50
a.		Serpentine die cut 11¾x11 ('02)	4.75 .50

Beginning with Nos. 3036 and 3036a, hidden 3-D images can be seen on some stamps when they are viewed with a special "Stamp Decoder" lens sold by the USPS. See the *Scott Specialized Catalogue of U.S. Stamps and Covers* for descriptions of these images. Stamps with 3-D images are 3036-3036a, 3167, 3168-3172, 3178, 3206, 3230-3234, 3238-3242, 3261-3262, 3321-3324, 3472-3473, 3647-3648, 3651, 3771, 3787-3791, 3808-3811, 3838 and 3862.

COIL STAMPS
Untagged
Perf. 9¾ Vert.

3044   A1841 1c multicolored,
         small date   .25   .25
   a.   Large date   .25   .25

Date on No. 3044 is 1mm long, on No. 3044a 1.5mm long.

Untagged

3045   A2335 2c multicolored   .25   .25

Issued: #3032, 2/2/96; #3033, 4/3/96; #3044, 1/20/96; #3036, 8/14/98; #3045, 6/22/99; #3031, 11/19/99; #3031A, 10/00.

BOOKLET STAMPS
PHOTOGRAVURE
Serpentine Die Cut 10.4x10.8 on 3 Sides
Tagged
Self-Adhesive

3048   A1847 20c multi   .40   .25
   a.   Booklet pane of 10   4.00
   b.   Booklet pane of 4   70.00
   c.   Booklet pane of 6   100.00

Nos. 3048b-3048c are from the vending machine booklet No. BK237 that has a glue strip at the top edge of the top pane, the peel-able strip removed and the rouletting line 2mm lower than on No. 3048a on some booklets, when the panes are compared with bottoms aligned. Vending booklets with plate #S2222 always have gauge 8½ rouletting on booklet covers. Convertible booklets (No. 3048a) with plate #S2222 always have gauge 12½ rouletting on booklet covers. Vending booklets with plate #S1111 can have either 8½ or 12½ gauge rouletting on booklet cover, and it may be impossible to tell a vending booklet with 12½ gauge rouletting and plate #S1111 from a convertible booklet with peelable strip removed.

Serpentine Die Cut 11.3x11.7 on 2, 3 or 4 Sides

3049   A1853 32c yel, org, grn
          & blk   .65   .25
   a.   Booklet pane of 20 + label   13.00
   b.   Booklet pane of 4   2.60
   c.   Booklet pane of 5 + label   3.50
   d.   Booklet pane of 6   4.00

Serpentine Die Cut 11.2 on 3 Sides

3050   A2350 20c multi   .65   .25
   a.   Booklet pane of 10, all
       stamps upright   6.50
   b.   Serpentine die cut 11   3.25
   c.   As "b," booklet pane of 10,
       all stamps upright   35.00

Serpentine Die Cut 10½x11 on 3 Sides

3051   A2350 20c multi   .75   .25

Serpentine Die Cut 10.6x10.4 on 3 Sides

3051A A2350 20c multicolored   7.00   .50
   b.   Booklet pane of 5, 4
       #3051, 1 #3051A turned
       sideways at top   10.00
   c.   Booklet pane of 5, 4
       #3051, 1 #3051A turned
       sideways at bottom   10.00

No. 3051 represents the eight upright stamps on the booklet panes Nos. 3051Ab and 3051Ac. The two stamps turned sideways on those panes are No. 3051A.

Serpentine Die Cut 11½x11¼ on 2, 3 or 4 Sides

3052   A2351 33c multi   .90   .25
   a.   Booklet pane of 4   3.60
   b.   Booklet pane of 5 + label   4.50
   c.   Booklet pane of 6   5.50
   d.   Booklet pane of 20 + label   17.50
   j.   Die cutting omitted, pair   —
   k.   As "d," die cutting omitted   *1,000.*

Serpentine Die Cut 10¾x10½ on 2 or 3 sides

3052E A2351 33c multi   .75   .25
   f.   Booklet pane of 20   15.00
   g.   Black ("33 USA," etc.) omit-
       ted   350.00
   h.   As "f," all 12 stamps on
       one side with black omit-
       ted   —

---

   i.   Horiz. pair, die cutting
       missing between (PS)   —
   j.   As "f," vert. die cutting
       missing between (PS)   —

No. 3052Ef is a double-sided booklet pane with 12 stamps on one side and 8 stamps plus label on the other side.

COIL STAMPS
Serpentine Die Cut 11½ Vert.

3053   A1847 20c multi   .50   .25
   a.   Die cutting omitted, pair   —

Yellow Rose, Ring-necked Pheasant Types of 1996-98
COIL STAMPS
LITHOGRAPHED
Self-Adhesive

3054   A1853 32c yel, mag,
          blk & grn   .65   .25
   a.   Die cutting omitted,
       pair   85.00
   b.   Black, yellow & green
       omitted   —
   c.   Black, yellow & green
       omitted, die cutting
       omitted, pair   —
   d.   Black omitted   200.00
   e.   Black omitted, die cut-
       ting omitted, pair   250.00
   f.   All colors omitted, die
       cutting omitted   —
   g.   Pair, die cutting omit-
       ted, containing one
       stamp each of "c"
       and "e"   —

Nos. 3054b and 3054d also are miscut and with shifted die cuttings. No. 3054f must be collected se-tenant with a partially printed stamp(s).

3055   A2350 20c multi   .40   .25
   a.   Die cutting omitted,
       pair   125.00

No. 3055a exists miscut. It is more common in this form and is valued thus.
Issued: #3048, 3053, 8/2/96; #3049, 10/24/96; #3054, 8/1/97; #3050, 3055, 7/31/98; #3051, 7/99; #3052, 8/13/99; #3052E, 4/7/00.

BLACK HERITAGE SERIES

Ernest E. Just (1883-1941), Marine Biologist — A2358

LITHOGRAPHED
1996, Feb. 1   **Perf. 11.1**
3058   A2358 32c gray & black   .65   .25

SMITHSONIAN INSTITUTION, 150TH ANNIVERSARY

A2359

1996, Feb. 7
3059   A2359 32c multicolored   .65   .25

CHINESE NEW YEAR

Year of the Rat — A2360

PHOTOGRAVURE
1996, Feb. 8
3060   A2360 32c multicolored   .90   .25
   a.   Imperf., pair   625.00
      See No. 3895a.

PIONEERS OF COMMUNICATION

Eadweard Muybridge A2361

Ottmar Mergenthaler — A2362

Frederic E. Ives A2363

William Dickson A2364

LITHOGRAPHED
1996, Feb. 22   **Perf. 11.1x11**
3061   A2361 32c multicolored   .65   .25
3062   A2362 32c multicolored   .65   .25
3063   A2363 32c multicolored   .65   .25
3064   A2364 32c multicolored   .65   .25
   a.   Block or strip of 4, #3061-
       3064   2.60   2.00

Muybridge (1830-1904), Photographer; Mergenthaler (1854-99), Inventor of Linotype; Ives (1856-1937), Developer of Halftone Process; Dickson (1860-1935), Co-developer of Kinetoscope.

FULBRIGHT SCHOLARSHIPS, 50th ANNIVERSARY

A2365

LITHOGRAPHED & ENGRAVED
1996, Feb. 28   **Perf. 11.1**
3065   A2365 32c multicolored   .75   .25

JACQUELINE COCHRAN (1910-80), PILOT

A2366

1996, Mar. 9
3066   A2366 50c multicolored   1.00   .40
   a.   Black (engr.) omitted   45.00

MARATHON

A2367

LITHOGRAPHED
1996, Apr. 11
3067   A2367 32c multicolored   .65   .25

1996 SUMMER OLYMPIC GAMES

A2368

Designs: a, Decathlon (javelin). b, Men's canoeing. c, Women's running. d, Women's diving. e, Men's cycling. f, Freestyle wrestling. g, Women's gymnastics. h, Women's sailboarding. i, Men's shot put. j, Women's soccer. k, Beach volleyball. l, Men's rowing. m, Men's sprints. n, Women's swimming. o, Women's softball. p, Men's hurdles. q, Men's swimming. r, Men's gymnastics (pommel horse). s, Equestrian. t, Men's basketball.

PHOTOGRAVURE
1996, May 2   **Perf. 10.1**
3068   A2368   Pane of 20   14.00   10.00
   a.-t.   32c any single   .70   .50
   u.   As No. 3068, imperf   *700.00*
   v.   As No. 3068, back in-
       scriptions omitted on
       a., f., k. & p., incorrect
       back inscriptions on
       others
   w.   As No. 3068, e. imperf,
       d., i.-j. part perf, all
       others perf   *750.00*

GEORGIA O'KEEFFE (1887-1986)

A2369

PHOTOGRAVURE
1996, May 23   **Perf. 11.6x11.4**
3069   A2369 32c multicolored   .85   .25
   a.   Imperf., pair   125.00

TENNESSEE STATEHOOD BICENTENNIAL

A2370

1996, May 31   **Perf. 11.1**
3070   A2370 32c multicolored   .65   .25

Booklet Stamp
Self-Adhesive
Serpentine Die Cut 9.9x10.8

3071 A2370 32c multicolored .65 .30
  a. Booklet pane of 20, #S11111 13.00
  b. Horiz. pair, die cutting omitted btwn. 300.00 —
  c. Die cutting omitted, pair —
  d. Horiz. pair, die cutting omitted vert. — —

AMERICAN INDIAN DANCES

A2371

A2372

A2373

A2374

A2375

LITHOGRAPHED
1996, June 7   *Perf. 11.1*

3072 A2371 32c Fancy 1.20 .25
3073 A2372 32c Butterfly 1.20 .25
3074 A2373 32c Traditional 1.20 .25
3075 A2374 32c Raven 1.20 .25
3076 A2375 32c Hoop 1.20 .25
  a. Strip of 5, #3072-3076 6.00 2.50

PREHISTORIC ANIMALS

A2376

A2377

A2378

A2379

1996, June 8   *Perf. 11.1x11*
3077 A2376 32c Eohippus .65 .25
3078 A2377 32c Woolly Mammoth .65 .25
3079 A2378 32c Mastodon .65 .25
3080 A2379 32c Saber-tooth Cat .65 .25
  a. Block or strip of 4, #3077-3080 2.60 2.00

BREAST CANCER AWARENESS

A2380

1996, June 15   *Perf. 11.1*
3081 A2380 32c multicolored .65 .25

LEGENDS OF HOLLYWOOD

A2381

PHOTOGRAVURE
1996, June 24
3082 A2381 32c multicolored .65 .25
  a. Imperf., pair 100.00
  b. As "a," red (USA 32c) missing (CM) and tan (JAMES DEAN) omitted —
  c. As "a," tan (JAMES DEAN) omitted —
  d. As "a," top stamp red missing (CM) and tan (JAMES DEAN) omitted, bottom stamp tan omitted —
  e. As No. 3082 pane of 20, right two columns perf, left three columns imperf 1,750.

Perforations in corner of each stamp are star-shaped. No. 3082 was also available on the first day of issue in at least 127 Warner Bros. Studio stores.

Nos. 3082b-3082d come from the same error pane. The top row is No. 3082b; rows 2-4 are No. 3082c. No. 3082d is a vertical pair with one stamp from No. 3082b at top and one stamp from No. 3082c at bottom.

FOLK HEROES

A2382

A2383

A2384

A2385

LITHOGRAPHED
1996, July 11   *Perf. 11.1x11*
3083 A2382 32c multicolored .65 .25
3084 A2383 32c multicolored .65 .25
3085 A2384 32c multicolored .65 .25
3086 A2385 32c multicolored .65 .25
  a. Block or strip of 4, #3083-3086 2.60 2.00

CENTENNIAL OLYMPIC GAMES

Myron's Discobolus — A2386

ENGRAVED
1996, July 19   **Tagged**   *Perf. 11.1*
3087 A2386 32c brown .75 .25
  Sheet margin of the pane of 20 is lithographed.

IOWA STATEHOOD, 150TH ANNIVERSARY

Young Corn, by Grant Wood — A2387

LITHOGRAPHED
1996, Aug. 1
3088 A2387 32c multicolored .80 .25
BOOKLET STAMP
Self-Adhesive
Serpentine Die Cut 11.6x11.4
3089 A2387 32c multicolored .65 .30
  a. Booklet pane of 20 13.00

RURAL FREE DELIVERY, CENT.

A2388

LITHOGRAPHED & ENGRAVED
1996, Aug. 7   *Perf. 11.2x11*
3090 A2388 32c multicolored .80 .25

RIVERBOATS

Robt. E. Lee A2389

Sylvan Dell A2390

Far West A2391

Rebecca Everingham A2392

Bailey Gatzert A2393

PHOTOGRAVURE
Serpentine Die Cut 11x11.1
1996, Aug. 22
Self-Adhesive

3091 A2389 32c multicolored .65 .40
3092 A2390 32c multicolored .65 .40
3093 A2391 32c multicolored .65 .40
3094 A2392 32c multicolored .65 .40
3095 A2393 32c multicolored .65 .40
  a. Vert. strip of 5, #3091-3095 3.25
  b. Strip of 5, #3091-3095, with special die cutting, die cut 11¼ 45.00 45.00

The serpentine die cutting runs through the peelable backing to which Nos. 3091-3095 are affixed. No. 3095a exists with stamps in different sequences.

On the long side of each stamp in No. 3095b, the die cutting is missing 3 "perforations" between the stamps, one near each end and one in the middle. This allows a complete strip to be removed from the backing paper for use on a first day cover.

AMERICAN MUSIC SERIES
Big Band Leaders

Count Basie A2394

Tommy & Jimmy Dorsey A2395

Glenn Miller A2396

Benny Goodman A2397

Songwriters

Harold Arlen A2398

Johnny Mercer A2399

Dorothy Fields A2400

Hoagy Carmichael A2401

LITHOGRAPHED

1996, Sept. 11				*Perf. 11.1x11*	
3096	A2394	32c multicolored		.75	.25
3097	A2395	32c multicolored		.75	.25
3098	A2396	32c multicolored		.75	.25
3099	A2397	32c multicolored		.75	.25
a.		Block or strip of 4, #3096-3099		3.00	2.00
3100	A2398	32c multicolored		.75	.25
3101	A2399	32c multicolored		.75	.25
3102	A2400	32c multicolored		.75	.25
3103	A2401	32c multicolored		.75	.25
a.		Block or strip of 4, #3100-3103		3.00	2.00

LITERARY ARTS SERIES

F. Scott Fitzgerald (1896-1940) A2402

PHOTOGRAVURE

1996, Sept. 27				*Perf. 11.1*	
3104	A2402	23c multicolored		.55	.25

ENDANGERED SPECIES

A2403

Designs: a, Black-footed ferret. b, Thick-billed parrot. c, Hawaiian monk seal. d, American crocodile. e, Ocelot. f, Schaus swallowtail butterfly. g, Wyoming toad. h, Brown pelican. i, California condor. j, Gila trout. k, San Francisco garter snake. l, Woodland caribou. m, Florida panther. n, Piping plover. o, Florida manatee.

LITHOGRAPHED

1996, Oct. 2				*Perf. 11.1x11*	
3105	A2403	Pane of 15		12.00	8.00
a.-o.		32c any single		.80	.50

See Mexico No. 1995.

COMPUTER TECHNOLOGY

A2404

LITHOGRAPHED & ENGRAVED

1996, Oct. 8				*Perf. 10.9x11.1*	
3106	A2404	32c multicolored		.65	.25

CHRISTMAS

Madonna and Child from Adoration of the Shepherds, by Paolo de Matteis — A2405

Family at Fireplace A2406

Decorating Tree A2407

Dreaming of Santa Claus A2408

Holiday Shopping A2409

Skaters — A2410

LITHOGRAPHED & ENGRAVED

1996				*Perf. 11.1x11.2*	
3107	A2405	32c multicolored		.65	.25
a.		Black (engr.) omitted at bottom		600.00	
b.		Black (engr.) missing (PS)		—	

On No. 3107a, an albino impression of the lettering at bottom is present, but there is no trace of black ink.
No. 3107b is missing the black lettering at bottom due to a small upward shift of the horizontal perforations. This lettering is the only engraved black on the stamp.

LITHOGRAPHED

				Perf. 11.3	
3108	A2406	32c multicolored		.65	.25
3109	A2407	32c multicolored		.65	.25
3110	A2408	32c multicolored		.65	.25
3111	A2409	32c multicolored		.65	.25
a.		Block or strip of 4, #3108-3111		2.60	1.75
b.		Strip of 4, #3110-3111, 3108-3109, with #3109 imperf., #3108 imperf. at right		1,000.	
c.		Strip of 4, #3108-3111, with #3111 imperf, #3110 imperf at right		1,000.	

BOOKLET STAMPS
Self-Adhesive
LITHOGRAPHED & ENGRAVED
Serpentine Die Cut 10 on 2, 3 or 4 Sides

3112	A2405	32c multicolored		.75	.25
a.		Booklet pane of 20 + label		15.00	
b.		Die cutting omitted, pair		40.00	
c.		As "a," die cutting omitted		400.00	

LITHOGRAPHED
Serpentine Die Cut 11.8x11.5 on 2, 3 or 4 Sides

3113	A2406	32c multicolored		.65	.25
3114	A2407	32c multicolored		.65	.25
3115	A2408	32c multicolored		.65	.25
3116	A2409	32c multicolored		.65	.25
a.		Booklet pane of 20, 5 ea #3113-3116		13.00	
b.		Strip of 4, #3113-3116, die cutting omitted		500.00	
c.		Block of 6, die cutting omitted		700.00	
d.		As "a," die cutting omitted		1,250.	

PHOTOGRAVURE
Die Cut

3117	A2410	32c multicolored		.65	.25
a.		Booklet pane of 18		12.00	

Issued: #3108-3111, 3113-3117, 10/8; #3107, 3112, 11/1.

HANUKKAH

A2411

Serpentine Die Cut 11.1
1996, Oct. 22
Self-Adhesive

3118	A2411	32c multicolored		.65	.25

See Nos. 3352, 3547, 3672, Israel No. 1289. For booklet see No. BK258.

CYCLING
Souvenir Sheet

A2412

1996, Nov. 1				*Perf. 11x11.1*	
3119	A2412	Sheet of 2		2.75	2.00
a.		50c orange & multi		1.30	1.00
b.		50c blue green & multi		1.30	1.00

No. 3119 exists overprinted in gold and in silver for the Tour of China '96. This overprint is a private production. Value, set of 2 sheets $17.50.

CHINESE NEW YEAR

Year of the Ox A2413

1997, Jan. 5				*Perf. 11.2*	
3120	A2413	32c multicolored		.80	.25

See No. 3895b.

BLACK HERITAGE SERIES

Brig. Gen. Benjamin O. Davis, Sr. (1880-1970) A2414

LITHOGRAPHED
Serpentine Die Cut 11.4
1997, Jan. 28
Self-Adhesive

3121	A2414	32c multicolored		.70	.25

Statue of Liberty Type of 1994
PHOTOGRAVURE
Serpentine Die Cut 11 on 2, 3 or 4 Sides
1997, Feb. 1
Self-Adhesive

3122	A1951	32c red, lt bl, dk bl & yel		.70	.25
a.		Booklet pane of 20 + label		14.00	
b.		Booklet pane of 4		2.80	
c.		Booklet pane of 5 + label		3.75	
d.		Booklet pane of 6		4.25	
h.		As "a," die cutting omitted		—	

Serpentine Die Cut 11.5x11.8 on 2, 3 or 4 Sides
1997
Self-Adhesive

3122E	A1951	32c red, lt bl, dk bl & yel		1.50	.25
f.		Booklet pane of 20 + label		40.00	
g.		Booklet pane of 6		9.00	

LOVE

A2415   Swans — A2416

LITHOGRAPHED
Serpentine Die Cut 11.8x11.6 on 2, 3 or 4 Sides
1997, Feb. 4
Self-Adhesive

3123	A2415	32c multicolored		.65	.25
a.		Booklet pane of 20 + label		13.00	
b.		Die cutting omitted, pair		100.00	
c.		As "a," die cutting omitted		1,000.	
d.		As "a," black omitted		—	

Serpentine Die Cut 11.6x11.8 on 2, 3 or 4 Sides

3124	A2416	55c multicolored		1.10	.25
a.		Booklet pane of 20 + label		22.00	

HELPING CHILDREN LEARN

A2417

PHOTOGRAVURE
Serpentine Die Cut 11.6x11.7
1997, Feb. 18
Self-Adhesive

3125	A2417	32c multicolored		.65	.25

MERIAN BOTANICAL PRINTS

Citron, Moth, Larvae, Pupa, Beetle A2418   Flowering Pineapple, Cockroaches A2419

No. 3128 (r), No. 3129 (l), No. 3128a below

Serpentine Die Cut 10.9x10.2 on 2, 3 or 4 Sides
1997, Mar. 3
Self-Adhesive

3126	A2418	32c multicolored		.65	.25
3127	A2419	32c multicolored		.65	.25
a.		Booklet pane, 10 ea #3126-3127 + label		13.00	
b.		Pair, #3126-3127		1.30	
c.		Vert. pair, die cutting omitted between		350.00	

Size: 18.5x24mm
Serpentine Die Cut 11.2x10.8 on 2 or 3 Sides

3128	A2418	32c multicolored		1.00	.25
a.		See footnote		2.50	.25
b.		Booklet pane, 2 ea #3128-3129, 1 #3128a		6.50	

3129	A2419	32c multicolored	1.00	.25
a.		See footnote	4.50	.35
b.		Booklet pane, 2 ea #3128-3129, 1 #3129a	8.50	
c.		Pair, #3128-3129	2.00	

Nos. 3128a-3129a are placed sideways on the pane and are serpentine die cut 11.2 on top and bottom, 10.8 on left side. One of the two No. 3128a per pane has a straight edge at left. The right side is 11.2 broken by a sloping die cut where the stamp meets the vertical die cutting of the two stamps above it. See illustration above.

PACIFIC 97

Sailing Ship — A2420

Stagecoach — A2421

ENGRAVED				
1997, Mar. 13		**Tagged**		**Perf. 11.2**
3130	A2420	32c blue	.65	.30
3131	A2421	32c red	.65	.30
a.		Pair, #3130-3131	1.30	.75

Juke Box and Flag Over Porch Types of 1995
PHOTOGRAVURE
COIL STAMPS
1997, Mar. 14   Untagged   *Imperf.*
Self-Adhesive

3132	A2225	(25c) brt org red, brt yel grn & multi	1.50	.50

Tagged
Serpentine Die Cut 9.9 Vert.

3133	A2212	32c dk bl, tan, brn, red & lt bl	1.75	.25

Nos. 3132-3133 were issued without backing paper. No. 3132 has simulated perforations ending in black bars at the top and bottom edges of the stamp. Sky on No. 3133 shows color gradation at LR not on Nos. 2915A or 2915D, and it has blue "1996" at left bottom.

LITERARY ARTS SERIES

Thornton Wilder (1897-1975) A2422

LITHOGRAPHED				
1997, Apr. 17				**Perf. 11.1**
3134	A2422	32c multicolored	.65	.25

RAOUL WALLENBERG (1912-47)

Wallenberg and Jewish Refugees A2423

1997, Apr. 24				
3135	A2423	32c multicolored	.65	.25

DINOSAURS

A2424

Designs: a, Ceratosaurus. b, Camptosaurus. c, Camarasaurus. d, Brachiosaurus. e, Goniopholis. f, Stegosaurus. g, Allosaurus. h, Opisthias. i, Edmontonia. j, Einiosaurus. k, Daspletosaurus. l, Palaeosaniwa. m, Corythosaurus. n, Ornithomimus. o, Parasaurolophus.

1997, May 1				**Perf. 11x11.1**
3136	A2424	Sheet of 15	10.00	8.00
a.-o.		32c any single	.65	.50
p.		As No. 3136, bottom 7 stamps imperf.	2,500.	
q.		As No. 3136, top 8 stamps imperf	2,500.	
r.		As No. 3136, all colors and tagging missing (EP)	—	

No. 3136r resulted from double sheeting in the sheet-fed press. It is properly gummed and perforated.

BUGS BUNNY

A2425

PHOTOGRAVURE
1997, May 22 *Serpentine Die Cut 11*
Self-Adhesive

3137		Pane of 10 #3137a	6.75	
a.	A2425	32c single	.65	.25
b.		Pane of 9 #3137a	6.00	
c.		Pane of 1 #3137a	.65	

Die cutting on #3137 does not extend through the backing paper.

3138		Pane of 10 #3138c, 9 #3138a	175.00	
a.	A2425	32c single	3.50	
b.		Pane of 9 #3138a	32.50	
c.		Pane of 1, no die cutting	120.00	

Die cutting on No. 3138b extends through the backing paper.

An untagged promotional piece similar to No. 3137c exists on the same backing paper as the pane, with the same design image, but without Bugs' signature and the single stamp. Replacing the stamp is an enlarged "32 / USA" in the same style as used on the stamp. This promotional piece was not valid for postage.

PACIFIC 97

Franklin A2426   Washington A2427

LITHOGRAPHED & ENGRAVED				
1997				**Perf. 10.5x10.4**
3139		Pane of 12	12.00	9.00
a.	A2426	50c single	1.00	.50
3140		Pane of 12	14.50	11.00
a.	A2427	60c single	1.20	.60

Selvage on Nos. 3139-3140 is lithographed.
Issued: No. 3139, 5/29; No. 3140, 5/30.

MARSHALL PLAN, 50TH ANNIV.

Gen. George C. Marshall, Map of Europe — A2428

1997, June 4				**Perf. 11.1**
3141	A2428	32c multicolored	.65	.25

CLASSIC AMERICAN AIRCRAFT

A2429

Designs: a, Mustang. b, Model B. c, Cub. d, Vega. e, Alpha. f, B-10. g, Corsair. h, Stratojet. i, GeeBee. j, Staggerwing. k, Flying Fortress. l, Stearman. m, Constellation. n, Lightning. o, Peashooter. p, Tri-Motor. q, DC-3. r, 314 Clipper. s, Jenny. t, Wildcat.

PHOTOGRAVURE

1997, July 19				**Perf. 10.1**
3142	A2429	Pane of 20	13.00	10.00
a.-t.		32c any single	.65	.50

FOOTBALL COACHES

Bear Bryant A2430

Pop Warner A2431

Vince Lombardi A2432

George Halas A2433

LITHOGRAPHED				
1997				**Perf. 11.2**
3143	A2430	32c multicolored	.65	.25
3144	A2431	32c multicolored	.65	.25
3145	A2432	32c multicolored	.65	.25
3146	A2433	32c multicolored	.65	.25
a.		Block or strip of 4, #3143-3146	2.60	1.50

With Red Bar Above Coach's Name
Perf. 11

3147	A2432	32c multicolored	.65	.45
3148	A2430	32c multicolored	.65	.45
3149	A2431	32c multicolored	.65	.45
3150	A2433	32c multicolored	.65	.45

Issued: #3143-3146, 7/25; #3147, 8/5; #3148, 8/7; #3149, 8/8; #3150, 8/16.

AMERICAN DOLLS

A2434

Designs: a, "Alabama Baby," and doll by Martha Chase. b, "Columbian Doll." c, Johnny Gruelle's "Raggedy Ann." d, Doll by Martha Chase. e, "American Child." f, "Baby Coos." g, Plains Indian. h, Doll by Izannah Walker. i, "Babyland Rag." j, "Scootles." k, Doll by Ludwig Greiner. l, "Betsy McCall." m, Percy Crosby's "Skippy." n, "Maggie Mix-up." o, Dolls by Albert Schoenhut.

1997, July 28				**Perf. 10.9x11.1**
3151	A2434	Pane of 15	13.50	—
a.-o.		32c any single	.90	.60

LEGENDS OF HOLLYWOOD
Humphrey Bogart (1899-1957).

A2435

PHOTOGRAVURE

1997, July 31				**Perf. 11.1**
3152	A2435	32c multicolored	.85	.25

Perforations in corner of each stamp are star-shaped.

"THE STARS AND STRIPES FOREVER!"

A2436

1997, Aug. 21				
3153	A2436	32c multicolored	.65	.25

AMERICAN MUSIC SERIES
Opera Singers

Lily Pons A2437

Richard Tucker A2438

Lawrence
Tibbett
A2439

Rosa
Ponselle
A2440

Classical Composers & Conductors

Leopold
Stokowski
A2441

Arthur
Fiedler
A2442

George
Szell
A2443

Eugene
Ormandy
A2444

Samuel
Barber
A2445

Ferde
Grofé
A2446

Charles
Ives
A2447

Louis
Moreau
Gottschalk
A2448

LITHOGRAPHED

1997			**Perf. 11**	
3154	A2437	32c multicolored	.75	.25
3155	A2438	32c multicolored	.75	.25
3156	A2439	32c multicolored	.75	.25
3157	A2440	32c multicolored	.75	.25
a.		Block or strip of 4, #3154-3157	3.00	2.00
3158	A2441	32c multicolored	1.50	.25
3159	A2442	32c multicolored	1.50	.25
3160	A2443	32c multicolored	1.50	.25
3161	A2444	32c multicolored	1.50	.25
3162	A2445	32c multicolored	1.50	.25
3163	A2446	32c multicolored	1.50	.25
3164	A2447	32c multicolored	1.50	.25
3165	A2448	32c multicolored	1.50	.25
a.		Block of 8, #3158-3165	12.00	4.00

Issued: #3154-3157, 9/10; #3158-3165, 9/12.

PADRE FÉLIX VARELA (1788-1853)

A2449

1997, Sept. 15			**Perf. 11.2**	
3166	A2449	32c purple	.65	.25

DEPARTMENT OF THE AIR FORCE, 50TH ANNIV.

Thunderbirds Aerial Demonstration
Squadron — A2450

1997, Sept. 18			**Perf. 11.2x11.1**	
3167	A2450	32c multicolored	.65	.25

CLASSIC MOVIE MONSTERS

A2451

A2452

A2453

A2454

A2455

PHOTOGRAVURE

1997, Sept. 30			**Perf. 10.2**	
3168	A2451	32c multicolored	.75	.25
3169	A2452	32c multicolored	.75	.25
3170	A2453	32c multicolored	.75	.25
3171	A2454	32c multicolored	.75	.25
3172	A2455	32c multicolored	.75	.25
a.		Strip of 5, #3168-3172	3.75	2.25

FIRST SUPERSONIC FLIGHT, 50TH ANNIV.

A2456

LITHOGRAPHED

Serpentine Die Cut 11.4
1997, Oct. 14
Self-Adhesive

3173	A2456	32c multicolored	.65	.25

WOMEN IN MILITARY SERVICE

A2457

1997, Oct. 18			**Perf. 11.1**	
3174	A2457	32c multicolored	.65	.25

KWANZAA

A2458

PHOTOGRAVURE

1997, Oct. 22 Serpentine Die Cut 11
Self-Adhesive

3175	A2458	32c multicolored	.65	.25

See Nos. 3368, 3548, 3673.

CHRISTMAS

Madonna and
Child
A2459

Holly
A2460

LITHOGRAPHED

Serpentine Die Cut 9.9 on 2, 3 or 4
Sides
1997

Booklet Stamps
Self-Adhesive

3176	A2459	32c multicolored	.65	.25
a.		Booklet pane of 20 + label	13.00	

Serpentine Die Cut 11.2x11.6 on 2, 3
or 4 Sides

3177	A2460	32c multicolored	.65	.25
a.		Booklet pane of 20 + label	13.00	
b.		Booklet pane of 4	2.60	
c.		Booklet pane of 5 + label	3.25	
d.		Booklet pane of 6	3.90	

Madonna and Child, by Sano di Pietro.
Issued: No. 3176, 10/27; No. 3177, 10/30.

MARS PATHFINDER
Souvenir Sheet

Mars Rover Sojourner — A2461

PHOTOGRAVURE

1997, Dec. 10 Tagged			**Perf. 11x11.1**	
3178	A2461	$3 multicolored	6.00	4.00
a.		$3, single stamp	5.50	3.00
b.		Single souvenir sheet from sheet of 18	7.50	—

The perforations at the bottom of the stamp
contain the letters "USA." Vertical rouletting
extends from the vertical perforations of the
stamp to the bottom of the souvenir sheet.

Sheet of 18 has vertical perforations separating the three columns of souvenir sheets.
These were cut away when No. 3178 was produced. Thus, the souvenir sheet from the
sheet of 18 is wider and has vertical perforations on one or two sides.

CHINESE NEW YEAR

Year of the Tiger — A2462

1998, Jan. 5			**Perf. 11.2**	
3179	A2462	32c multicolored	.80	.25

See No. 3895c.

ALPINE SKIING

A2463

LITHOGRAPHED

1998, Jan. 22			**Perf. 11.2**	
3180	A2463	32c multicolored	.75	.25

BLACK HERITAGE SERIES

A2464

Serpentine Die Cut 11.6x11.3
1998, Jan. 28
Self-Adhesive

3181 A2464 32c sepia & black .70 .25

CELEBRATE THE CENTURY

1900s — A2465

No. 3182: a, Model T Ford. b, Theodore Roosevelt. c, Motion picture "The Great Train Robbery," 1903. d, Crayola Crayons introduced, 1903. e, St. Louis World's Fair, 1904. f, Design used on Hunt's Remedy stamp (#RS56), Pure Food & Drug Act, 1906. g, Wright Brothers first flight, Kitty Hawk, 1903. h, Boxing match shown in painting "Stag at Sharkey's," by George Bellows of the Ash Can School. i, Immigrants arrive. j, John Muir, preservationist. k, "Teddy" Bear created. l, W.E.B. Du Bois, social activist. m, Gibson Girl. n, First baseball World Series, 1903. o, Robie House, Chicago, designed by Frank Lloyd Wright.

1910s — A2466

No. 3183: a, Charlie Chaplin as the Little Tramp. b, Federal Reserve System created, 1913. c, George Washington Carver. d, Avant-garde art introduced at Armory Show, 1913. e, First transcontinental telephone line, 1914. f, Panama Canal opens, 1914. g, Jim Thorpe wins decathlon at Stockholm Olympics, 1912. h, Grand Canyon National Park, 1919. i, U.S. enters World War I. j, Boy Scouts started in 1910, Girl Scouts formed in 1912. k, Woodrow Wilson. l, First crossword puzzle published, 1913. m, Jack Dempsey wins heavyweight title, 1919. n, Construction toys. o, Child labor reform.

1920s — A2467

No. 3184: a, Babe Ruth. b, The Gatsby style. c, Prohibition enforced. d, Electric toy trains. e, 19th Amendment (woman voting). f, Emily Post's Etiquette. g, Margaret Mead, anthropologist. h, Flappers do the Charleston. i, Radio entertains America. j, Art Deco style (Chrysler Building). k, Jazz flourishes. l, Four Horsemen of Notre Dame. m, Lindbergh flies the Atlantic. n, American realism (Automat, by Edward Hopper). o, Stock Market crash, 1929.

1930s — A2468

No. 3185: a, Franklin D. Roosevelt. b, The Empire State Building. c, 1st Issue of Life Magazine, 1936. d, Eleanor Roosevelt. e, FDR's New Deal. f, Superman arrives, 1938. g, Household conveniences. h, "Snow White and the Seven Dwarfs," 1937. i, "Gone with the Wind," 1936. j, Jesse Owens. k, Streamline design. l, Golden Gate Bridge. m, America survives the Depression. n, Bobby Jones wins golf Grand Slam, 1938. o, The Monopoly Game.

1940s — A2469

No. 3186: a, World War II. b, Antibiotics save lives. c, Jackie Robinson. d, Harry S Truman. e, Women support war effort. f, TV entertains America. g, Jitterbug sweeps nation. h, Jackson Pollock, Abstract Expressionism. i, GI Bill, 1944. j, Big Band Sound. k, Intl. style of architecture (UN Headquarters). l, Postwar baby boom. m, Slinky, 1945. n, "A Streecar Named Desire," 1947. o, Orson Welles' "Citizen Kane."

1950s — A2470

No. 3187: a, Polio vaccine developed. b, Teen fashions. c, The "Shot Heard 'Round the World." d, US launches satellites. e, Korean War. f, Desegregating public schools. g, Tail fins, chrome. h, Dr. Seuss' "The Cat in the Hat." i, Drive-in movies. j, World Series rivals. k, Rocky Marciano, undefeated boxer. l, "I Love Lucy." m, Rock 'n Roll. n, Stock car racing. o, Movies go 3-D.

1960s — A2471

No. 3188: a, Martin Luther King, Jr., "I Have a Dream." b, Woodstock. c, Man walks on the moon. d, Green Bay Packers. e, Star Trek. f, The Peace Corps. g, Viet Nam War. h, Ford Mustang. i, Barbie Doll. j, Integrated circuit. k, Lasers. l, Super Bowl I. m, Peace symbol. n, Roger Maris, 61 in '61. o, The Beatles "Yellow Submarine."

1970s — A2472

No. 3189: a, Earth Day celebrated. b, "All in the Family" television series. c, "Sesame Street" television series character, Big Bird. d, Disco music. e, Pittsburgh Steelers win four Super Bowls. f, US Celebrates 200th birthday. g, Secretariat wins Triple Crown. h, VCRs transform entertainment. i, Pioneer 10. j, Women's rights movement. k, 1970s fashions. l, "Monday Night Football." m, Smiley face buttons. n, Jumbo jets. o, Medical imaging.

1980s — A2473

No. 3190: a, Space shuttle program. b, "Cats" Broadway show. c, San Francisco 49ers. d, Hostages in Iran come home. e, Figure skating. f, Vietnam Veterans Memorial. h, Compact discs. i, Cabbage Patch Kids. j, "The Cosby Show" television series. k, Fall of the Berlin Wall. l, Video games. m, "E.T. The Extra-Terrestrial" movie. n, Personal computers. o, Hip-hop culture.

1990s — A2474

No. 3191: a, New baseball records. b, Gulf War. c, "Seinfeld" television series. d, Extreme sports. e, Improving education. f, Computer art and graphics. g, Recovering species. h, Return to space. i, Special Olympics. j, Virtual reality. k, Movie "Jurassic Park." l, Movie "Titanic." m, Sport utility vehicles. n, World Wide Web. o, Cellular phones.

LITHOGRAPHED, ENGRAVED
(#3182m, 3183f, 3184m, 3185b, 3186k, 3187a, 3188c, 3189h)

1998-2000			Perf. 11½	
3182	A2465	Pane of 15	10.00	8.50
a.-o.		32c any single	.75	.65
p.		Engr. red (No. 3182m, Gibson girl) omitted, in pane of 15	3,000.	
3183	A2466	Pane of 15	10.00	8.50
a.-o.		32c any single	.75	.65
p.		Nos. 3183g, 3183 l-3183o imperf, in pane of 15	7,000.	
3184	A2467	Pane of 15	12.50	8.50
a.-o.		32c any single	.80	.65
3185	A2468	Pane of 15	12.50	8.50
a.-o.		32c any single	.80	.65
3186	A2469	Pane of 15	13.00	8.50
a.-o.		33c any single	.85	.65
3187	A2470	Pane of 15	13.00	8.50
a.-o.		33c any single	.85	.65
3188	A2471	Pane of 15	13.00	8.50
a.-o.		33c any single	.85	.65
3189	A2472	Pane of 15	13.00	8.50
a.-o.		33c any single	.85	.65
3190	A2473	Pane of 15	13.00	8.50
a.-o.		33c any single	.85	.65
3191	A2474	Pane of 15	13.00	8.50
a.-o.		33c any single	.85	.65
	Nos. 3182-3191 (10)		123.00	85.00

Issued: #3182-3183, 2/3; #3184, 5/28; #3185, 9/10; #3186, 2/18/99; #3187, 5/26/99; #3188, 9/17/99; #3189, 11/18/99; #3190, 1/12/00; #3191, 5/2/00.

"REMEMBER THE MAINE"

A2475

LITHOGRAPHED & ENGRAVED
1998, Feb. 15 **Perf. 11.2x11**
3192 A2475 32c red & black .70 .25

FLOWERING TREES

Southern Magnolia
A2476

Blue Paloverde
A2477

Yellow Poplar — A2478

Prairie Crab Apple — A2479

Pacific Dogwood A2480

LITHOGRAPHED
1998, Mar. 19   *Die Cut Perf 11.3*
Self-Adhesive

3193	A2476	32c multicolored	1.10	.40
3194	A2477	32c multicolored	1.10	.40
3195	A2478	32c multicolored	1.10	.40
3196	A2479	32c multicolored	1.10	.40
3197	A2480	32c multicolored	1.10	.40
a.		Strip of 5, #3193-3197		5.50
b.		As "a," die cutting omitted		—

ALEXANDER CALDER (1898-1976), SCULPTOR

Black Cascade, 13 Verticals, 1959 — A2481

Untitled, 1965 — A2482

Rearing Stallion, 1928 — A2483

Portrait of a Young Man, c. 1945 — A2484

Un Effet du Japonais, 1945 — A2485

PHOTOGRAVURE
1998, Mar. 25   **Perf. 10.2**

3198	A2481	32c multicolored	.65	.25
3199	A2482	32c multicolored	.65	.25
3200	A2483	32c multicolored	.65	.25
3201	A2484	32c multicolored	.65	.25
3202	A2485	32c multicolored	.65	.25
a.		Strip of 5, #3198-3202	3.25	2.25

CINCO DE MAYO

A2486

Serpentine Die Cut 11.7x10.9
1998, Apr. 16
Self-Adhesive

3203	A2486	32c multicolored	.65	.25

See Mexico No. 2066. For 33c version, see No. 3309.

SYLVESTER & TWEETY

A2487

Serpentine Die Cut 11.1
1998, Apr. 27
Self-Adhesive

3204		Pane of 10 #3204a	6.75	
a.	A2487	32c single	.65	.25
b.		Pane of 9 #3204a	6.00	
c.		Pane of 1 #3204a	.65	

Die cutting on No. 3204b does not extend through the backing paper.

3205		Pane of 10, #3205c, 9 #3205a	12.50
a.	A2487	32c single	.90
b.		Pane of 9 #3205a	8.00
c.		Pane of 1, no die cutting	4.00

Die cutting on #3205a extends through the backing paper.

WISCONSIN STATEHOOD

A2488

Serpentine Die Cut 10.8x10.9
1998, May 29
Self-Adhesive

3206	A2488	32c multicolored	.65	.30

Wetlands A2489

Diner A2490

COIL STAMPS
1998   **Untagged**   **Perf. 10 Vert.**

3207	A2489	(5c) multicolored	.25	.25

Serpentine Die Cut 9.8 Vert.
Self-adhesive
Untagged

3207A	A2489	(5c) multicolored, small date	.25	.25
b.		Large date	.30	.25

Date on No. 3207A is approximately 1.4mm long, on No. 3207Ab approx. 1.6mm long.

Perf. 10 Vert.
Untagged

3208	A2490	(25c) multicolored	.50	.50

Serpentine Die Cut 9.8 Vert.
Self-Adhesive
Untagged

3208A	A2490	(25c) multicolored	.50	.50

Issued: #3207-3208, 6/5; #3208A, 9/30; #3207A, 12/14.

1898 TRANS-MISSISSIPPI STAMPS, CENT.

A2491

LITHOGRAPHED & ENGRAVED
1998, June 18   **Perf. 12x12.4**

3209	A2491	Pane of 9	9.50	7.00
a.	A100	1c green & black	.25	.25
b.	A108	2c red brown & black	.25	.25
c.	A102	4c orange & black	.25	.25
d.	A103	5c blue & black	.25	.25
e.	A104	8c dark lilac & black	.25	.25
f.	A105	10c purple & black	.25	.25
g.	A106	50c green & black	1.25	.60
h.	A107	$1 red & black	2.50	1.25
i.	A101	$2 red brown & black	4.25	2.50

Vignettes on Nos. 3209b and 3209i are reversed in comparison to the original issue.

3210	A107	$1 Pane of 9 #3209h	22.50	—

BERLIN AIRLIFT, 50th ANNIV.

A2492

PHOTOGRAVURE
1998, June 26   **Perf. 11.2**

3211	A2492	32c multicolored	.65	.25

AMERICAN MUSIC SERIES
Folk Singers

Huddie "Leadbelly" Ledbetter A2493

Woody Guthrie A2494

Sonny Terry A2495

Josh White A2496

1998, June 26   **Perf. 10.1x10.2**

3212	A2493	32c multicolored	.90	.25
3213	A2494	32c multicolored	.90	.25
3214	A2495	32c multicolored	.90	.25
3215	A2496	32c multicolored	.90	.25
a.		Block or strip of 4, #3212-3215	3.60	2.00

AMERICAN MUSIC SERIES
Gospel Singers

Mahalia Jackson A2497

Roberta Martin A2498

Clara Ward A2499

Sister Rosetta Tharpe A2500

1998, July 15   **Perf. 10.1x10.3**

3216	A2497	32c multicolored	1.00	.25
3217	A2498	32c multicolored	1.00	.25
3218	A2499	32c multicolored	1.00	.25
3219	A2500	32c multicolored	1.00	.25
a.		Block or strip of 4, #3216-3219	4.00	2.00

SPANISH SETTLEMENT OF THE SOUTHWEST

La Mision de San Miguel de San Gabriel, Española, NM — A2501

LITHOGRAPHED
1998, July 11   ***Perf. 11.2***
3220 A2501 32c multicolored   .65 .25

LITERARY ARTS SERIES

Stephen Vincent Benét — A2502

1998, July 22   ***Perf. 11.2***
3221 A2502 32c multicolored   .65 .25

TROPICAL BIRDS

Antillean Euphonia — A2503

Green-throated Carib — A2504

Crested Honeycreeper — A2505

Cardinal Honeyeater A2506

1998, July 29
3222 A2503 32c multicolored   .65 .25
3223 A2504 32c multicolored   .65 .25
3224 A2505 32c multicolored   .65 .25
3225 A2506 32c multicolored   .65 .25
  a.   Block or strip of 4, #3222-
       3225   2.60 2.00

LEGENDS OF HOLLYWOOD

A2507

PHOTOGRAVURE
1998, Aug. 3   ***Perf. 11.1***
3226 A2507 32c multicolored   .75 .25
  Perforations in corner of each stamp are star-shaped.

ORGAN & TISSUE DONATION

A2508

Serpentine Die Cut 11.7
1998, Aug. 5
    Self-Adhesive
3227 A2508 32c multicolored   .65 .25

MODERN BICYCLE

A2509

COIL STAMP
Serpentine Die Cut 9.8 Vert.
1998, Aug. 14   **Untagged**
    Self-Adhesive (#3228)
3228 A2509 (10c) multicolored,
             small "1998"
             year date   .25 .25
  a.   Large date   .35 .25
  Date on No. 3228a is approximately 1 ½mm; on No. 3228 approximately 1mm.

        Untagged
     Perf. 9.9 Vert.
3229 A2509 (10c) multicolored   .25 .25
  Date on No. 3229 is approximately 2mm wide.

BRIGHT EYES

Dog A2510

Fish A2511

Cat A2512

Parakeet A2513

Hamster A2514

Serpentine Die Cut 9.9
1998, Aug. 20
    Self-Adhesive
3230 A2510 32c multicolored   .75 .40
3231 A2511 32c multicolored   .75 .40
3232 A2512 32c multicolored   .75 .40
3233 A2513 32c multicolored   .75 .40
3234 A2514 32c multicolored   .75 .40
  a.   Strip of 5, #3230-3234   3.75

KLONDIKE GOLD RUSH, CENTENNIAL

A2515

LITHOGRAPHED
1998, Aug. 21   ***Perf. 11.1***
3235 A2515 32c multicolored   .65 .25

AMERICAN ART

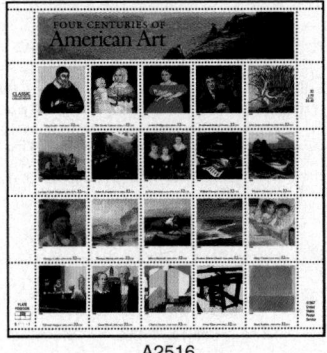

A2516

Paintings: a, "Portrait of Richard Mather," by John Foster. b, "Mrs. Elizabeth Freake and Baby Mary," by The Freake Limner. c, "Girl in Red Dress with Cat and Dog," by Ammi Phillips. d, "Rubens Peale with a Geranium," by Rembrandt Peale. e, "Long-billed Curlew, Numenius Longrostris," by John James Audubon. f, "Boatmen on the Missouri," by George Caleb Bingham. g, "Kindred Sprits," by Asher B. Durand. h, "The Westwood Children," by Joshua Johnson. i, "Music and Literature," by William Harnett. j, "The Fog Warning," by Winslow Homer. k, "The White Cloud, Head Chief of the Iowas," by George Catlin. l, "Cliffs of Green River," by Thomas Moran. m, "The Last of the Buffalo," by Alfred Bierstadt. n, "Niagara," by Frederic Edwin Church. o, "Breakfast in Bed," by Mary Cassatt. p, "Nighthawks," by Edward Hopper. q, "American Gothic," by Grant Wood. r, "Two Against the White," by Charles Sheeler. s, "Mahoning," by Franz Kline. t, "No. 12," by Mark Rothko.

PHOTOGRAVURE
1998, Aug. 27   ***Perf. 10.2***
3236 A2516 Pane of 20   18.00 10.00
  a.-t. 32c any single   .90   .60

AMERICAN BALLET

A2517

LITHOGRAPHED
1998, Sept. 16   ***Perf. 10.9x11.1***
3237 A2517 32c multicolored   .65 .25

SPACE DISCOVERY

A2518   A2519

A2520   A2521

A2522

PHOTOGRAVURE
1998, Oct. 1   ***Perf. 11.1***
3238 A2518 32c multicolored   .65 .25
3239 A2519 32c multicolored   .65 .25
3240 A2520 32c multicolored   .65 .25
3241 A2521 32c multicolored   .65 .25
3242 A2522 32c multicolored   .65 .25
  a.   Strip of 5, #3238-3242   3.25 2.25

GIVING AND SHARING

A2523

PHOTOGRAVURE
Serpentine Die Cut 11.1
1998, Oct. 7
    Self-Adhesive
3243 A2523 32c multicolored   .65 .25

CHRISTMAS

Madonna and Child — A2524

Evergreen   Victorian
A2525   A2526

Chili Pepper   Tropical
A2527   A2528

LITHOGRAPHED
Serpentine Die Cut 10.1x9.9 on 2, 3 or 4 Sides
1998, Oct. 15
    Self-Adhesive
    Booklet Stamps
3244 A2524 32c multicolored   .65 .25
  a.   Booklet pane of 20 + label 13.00 —
  b.   Die cutting omitted, pair   —

    Size: 22x25mm
Serpentine Die Cut 11.3x11.7 on 2 or 3 Sides
3245 A2525 32c multicolored   4.25 .25
3246 A2526 32c multicolored   4.25 .25
3247 A2527 32c multicolored   4.25 .25
3248 A2528 32c multicolored   4.25 .25
  a.   Booklet pane of 4, #3245-
       3248   17.00
  b.   Booklet pane of 5, #3245-
       3246, 3248, 2 #3247 +
       label   21.50
  c.   Booklet pane of 6, #3247-
       3248, 2 each #3245-
       3246   26.00
  d.   As "a," die cutting omitted —
  e.   As "b," die cutting omitted —
  f.   As "c," die cutting omitted —
  g.   Block of 4, #3245-3248 17.00

Size: 23x30mm
Serpentine Die Cut 11.4x11.5 on 2, 3, or 4 Sides

3249	A2525	32c multicolored	1.75	.25
a.		Serp. die cut 11.7x11.6 on 2, 3, or 4 sides	2.00	.25
3250	A2526	32c multicolored	1.75	.25
a.		Serp. die cut 11.7x11.6 on 3 or 4 sides	2.00	.25
3251	A2527	32c multicolored	1.75	.25
a.		Serp. die cut 11.7x11.6 on 3 or 4 sides	2.00	.25
3252	A2528	32c multicolored + label	1.75	.25
a.		Serp. die cut 11.7x11.6 on 2, 3, or 4 sides	2.00	.25
b.		Block or strip of 4, #3249-3252	7.00	
c.		Booklet pane of 20, 5 each #3249-3252 + label	35.00	
d.		Block or strip of 4, #3249a-3252a	8.00	
e.		Booklet pane of 20, 5 each #3249a-3252a + label	40.00	
f.		Block or strip of 4, #3249-3252, red ("Greetings 32 USA" and "1998") omitted on #3249, 3252	625.00	
g.		Block or strip of 4, #3249-3252, red ("Greetings 32 USA" and "1998") omitted on #3249, 3252; green (same) omitted on #3250, 3251	—	
h.		As "b," die cutting omitted	—	
i.		As "c," die cutting omitted	4,500.	

Madonna and Child, Florence, 15th Cent.

Dedicated printing plates were used to print the red and green denominations, salutations and dates. Red and green appearing in the wreaths come from other plates and, therefore, are not part of the color omissions.

Weather Vane — A2529

Uncle Sam — A2530

Uncle Sam's Hat — A2531

Space Shuttle Landing — A2532

Piggyback Space Shuttle — A2533

1998   Untagged   Perf. 11.2

3257	A2529	(1c) multi	.25	.25
a.		Black omitted	125.00	
b.		Horiz. pair, imperf. vert. and at top	—	

Untagged

3258	A2529	(1c) multi	.25	.25

No. 3257 is 18mm high, has thin letters, white USA, and black 1998. No. 3258 is 17mm high, has thick letters, pale blue USA and blue 1998.

PHOTOGRAVURE
Serpentine Die Cut 10.8
Self-Adhesive (#3259, 3261-3263, 3265-3269)

3259	A2530	22c multi	.45	.25
a.		Die cut 10.8x10.5	2.50	.25
b.		Vert. pair, No. 3259 + 3259a	3.50	

See No. 3353.

Perf. 11.2

3260	A2531	(33c) multi	.65	.25

LITHOGRAPHED
Serpentine Die Cut 11.5

3261	A2532	$3.20 multi	6.00	1.50
3262	A2533	$11.75 multi	22.50	10.00

Hidden 3-D images (ENTERPRISE/COLUMBIA /CHALLENGER/ATLANTIS/ENDEAVOR/DISCOVERY) can be seen on Nos. 3261 and 3262 when viewed with a special "Stamp Decoder" lens sold by the USPS.

COIL STAMPS
PHOTOGRAVURE
Serpentine Die Cut 9.9 Vert.

3263	A2530	22c multi	.45	.25
a.		Die cutting omitted, pair	750.00	

See No. 3353.

Perf. 9.8 Vert.

3264	A2531	(33c) multi	.65	.25
a.		Imperf, pair	325.00	

Serpentine Die Cut 9.9 Vert.

3265	A2531	(33c) multi	.80	.25
a.		Die cutting omitted, pair	65.00	
b.		Red omitted	300.00	
c.		Black omitted	1,500.	
d.		Black omitted, die cutting omitted, pair	675.00	
e.		Red omitted, die cutting omitted, pair	500.00	
f.		Blue omitted	—	

Unused examples of No. 3265 are on backing paper the same size as the stamps. Corners of the stamp are 90 degree angles.
On No. 3265b, the blue and gray colors are shifted down and to the right.
On No. 3265f, the red is misregistered to right by 10½ stamps and gray by 3mm.

Serpentine Die Cut 9.9 Vert.

3266	A2531	(33c) multi	2.25	.25

Unused examples of No. 3266 are on backing paper larger than the stamps, and the stamps are spaced approximately 2mm. apart. Corners of stamps are rounded.

BOOKLET STAMPS
Serpentine Die Cut 9.9 on 2 or 3 Sides

3267	A2531	(33c) multi	.75	.25
a.		Booklet pane of 10	7.50	

Serpentine Die Cut 11¼ on 3 Sides (#3268, 3268a) or 11 on 2, 3 or 4 sides (#3268b, 3268c)

3268	A2531	(33c) multi	.75	.25
a.		Booklet pane of 10	7.50	
b.		Serpentine die cut 11	.75	.25
c.		As "b," booklet pane of 20 + label	15.00	

Die Cut 8 on 2, 3 or 4 Sides

3269	A2531	(33c) multi	.65	.25
a.		Booklet pane of 18	12.00	

Issued: No. 3262, 11/19; others, 11/9.

Unused and used examples of an "H" nondenominated stamp inscribed "Postcard Rate" exist in the marketplace. There is no evidence that these stamps were ever officially issued. Values: unused $2,500; used $2,150.

A2534

PHOTOGRAVURE
COIL STAMPS
Perf. 9.8 Vert.

1998, Dec. 14   Untagged

3270	A2534	(10c) multicolored, small date	.25	.25
a.		Large date	.45	.25

Self-Adhesive
Untagged
Serpentine Die Cut 9.9 Vert.

3271	A2534	(10c) multicolored, small date	.25	.25
a.		Large date	1.00	.25

Dates on Nos. 3270a and 3271a are approximately 1¾mm; on Nos. 3270-3271 approximately 1¼mm.
Compare to Nos. 2602-2604, 2907.

> Scott values for used self-adhesive stamps are for examples either on piece or off piece.

CHINESE NEW YEAR

Year of the Rabbit — A2535

1999, Jan. 5   Perf. 11.2

3272	A2535	33c multicolored	.80	.25

See No. 3895d.

BLACK HERITAGE SERIES

Malcolm X — A2536

LITHOGRAPHED
Serpentine Die Cut 11.4
1999, Jan. 20
Self-Adhesive

3273	A2536	33c multicolored	.85	.25

LOVE

A2537   A2538

PHOTOGRAVURE
1999, Jan. 28   Die Cut
Booklet Stamp
Self-Adhesive

3274	A2537	33c multicolored	.65	.25
a.		Booklet pane of 20	13.00	
b.		Die cutting omitted, pair	100.00	
c.		As "a," die cutting omitted	1,000.	
3275	A2538	55c multicolored	1.10	.25

HOSPICE CARE

A2539

LITHOGRAPHED
Serpentine Die Cut 11.4
1999, Feb. 9

3276	A2539	33c multicolored	.65	.25
a.		Horiz. pair, vert. die cutting omitted	—	

Flag & City — A2540

PHOTOGRAVURE
1999, Feb. 25   Perf. 11.2
Self-Adhesive (#3278, 3278F, 3279, 3281-3282)

3277	A2540	33c multi	.70	.25

No. 3277 has red date.

Serpentine Die Cut 11 on 2, 3 or 4 Sides

3278	A2540	33c multi	.65	.25
a.		Booklet pane of 4	2.60	
b.		Booklet pane of 5 + label	3.25	
c.		Booklet pane of 6	3.90	
d.		Booklet pane of 10	13.00	
e.		Booklet pane of 20 + label	17.00	
h.		As "e," die cutting omitted	—	
i.		Serpentine die cut 11¼	1.20	.25
j.		As "i," booklet pane of 10	12.00	

No. 3278 has black date.

BOOKLET STAMPS
Serpentine Die Cut 11½x11¾ on 2, 3 or 4 Sides

3278F	A2540	33c multi	1.40	.25
g.		Booklet pane of 20 + label	28.00	

No. 3278F has black date.

Serpentine Die Cut 9.8 on 2 or 3 Sides

3279	A2540	33c multi	.85	.25
a.		Booklet pane of 10	8.50	

No. 3279 has red date.

COIL STAMPS
Perf. 9.9 Vert.

3280	A2540	33c multi, small "1999" year date	.65	.25
a.		Large date	2.00	.25
b.		As No. 3280, imperf pair	200.00	150.00

Serpentine Die Cut 9.8 Vert.

Two types of No. 3281: Type I, Long vertical feature at left and at tallest building consists of 3 separate lines; Type II, Same features consist of solid color.

3281	A2540	33c multi, type I, large "1999" year date	.65	.25
a.		As No. 3281, die cutting omitted, pair	30.00	
b.		Light blue and yellow omitted	275.00	
c.		Small date, type II	.65	.25
d.		Small date, type I	5.00	.30
e.		As "c," die cutting omitted, pair	—	

Corners are square on #3281. Unused examples are on backing paper the same size as the stamps, and the stamps are adjoining.
Date on Nos. 3280a and 3281 is approximately 1¾mm; on Nos. 3280, 3281c and 3281d approximately 1¼mm.

3282	A2540	33c multi	.65	.25

Corners are rounded on #3282. Unused examples are on backing paper larger than the stamps, and the stamps are spaced approximately 2mm. apart.

Flag & Chalkboard — A2541

PHOTOGRAVURE
Serpentine Die Cut 7.9 on 2, 3 or 4 Sides
1999, Mar. 13
Self-Adhesive
BOOKLET STAMP

3283	A2541	33c multicolored	.65	.25
a.		Booklet pane of 18	12.00	

IRISH IMMIGRATION

A2542

LITHOGRAPHED

1999, Feb. 26   *Perf. 11.2*

3286 A2542 33c multicolored   .65   .25

See Ireland No. 1168.

PERFORMING ARTS SERIES
Alfred Lunt (1892-1977), Lynn Fontanne (1887-1983), Actors

A2543

LITHOGRAPHED

1999, Mar. 2   *Perf. 11.2*

3287 A2543 33c multicolored   .65   .25

ARCTIC ANIMALS

A2544

A2545

A2546

A2547

A2548

LITHOGRAPHED

1999, Mar. 12   *Perf. 11*

3288 A2544 33c Arctic Hare   .85   .25
3289 A2545 33c Arctic Fox   .85   .25
3290 A2546 33c Snowy Owl   .85   .25

3291 A2547 33c Polar Bear   .85   .25
3292 A2548 33c Gray Wolf   .85   .25
   a.   Strip of 5, #3288-3292   4.25   —

SONORAN DESERT

A2549

Designs: a, Cactus wren, brittlebush, teddy bear cholla. b, Desert tortoise. c, White-winged dove, prickly pear. d, Gambel quail. e, Saguaro cactus. f, Desert mule deer. g, Desert cottontail, hedgehog cactus. h, Gila monster. i, Western diamondback rattlesnake, cactus mouse. j, Gila woodpecker.

LITHOGRAPHED
Serpentine Die Cut Perf 11.2
1999, Apr. 6
Self-Adhesive

3293 A2549   Pane of 10   8.00
   a.-j.   33c any single   .80   .50

BERRIES

Blueberries
A2550

Raspberries
A2551

Strawberries
A2552

Blackberries
A2553

PHOTOGRAVURE
Serpentine Die Cut 11¼x11½ on 2, 3 or 4 Sides (Nos. 3294-3297), or 2 or 3 sides (Nos. 3294a-3297a)
1999, Apr. 10
Self-Adhesive

3294 A2550 33c multicolored   .85   .25
   a.   Dated "2000"   1.25   .25
3295 A2551 33c multicolored   .85   .25
   a.   Dated "2000"   1.25   .25
3296 A2552 33c multicolored   .85   .25
   a.   Dated "2000"   1.25   .25
3297 A2553 33c multicolored   .85   .25
   a.   Dated "2000"   1.25   .25
   b.   Booklet pane of 20, 5 each #3294-3297 + label   17.50
   c.   Block of 4, #3294-3297   3.50
   d.   Booklet pane of 20, 5 #3297e + label   25.00
   e.   Block of 4, #3294a-3297a   5.00

No. 3297d is a double-sided booklet pane, with 12 stamps on one side and eight stamps plus label on the other side.

Serpentine Die Cut 9½x10 on 2 or 3 Sides

3298 A2550 33c multicolored   1.00   .25
3299 A2552 33c multicolored   1.00   .25
3300 A2551 33c multicolored   1.00   .25
3301 A2553 33c multicolored   1.00   .25
   a.   Booklet pane of 4, #3298-3301   4.00
   b.   Booklet pane of 5, #3298, 3299, 3301, 2 #3300 + label   5.00
   c.   Booklet pane of 6, #3300, 3301, 2 #3298, 3299   6.00
   d.   Block of 4, #3298-3301   4.00

COIL STAMPS
Serpentine Die Cut 8.5 Vert.

3302 A2550 33c multicolored   2.25   .25
3303 A2551 33c multicolored   2.25   .25
3304 A2553 33c multicolored   2.25   .25
3305 A2552 33c multicolored   2.25   .25
   a.   Strip of 4, #3302-3305   9.00

See Nos. 3404-3407.

DAFFY DUCK

A2554

PHOTOGRAVURE
Serpentine Die Cut 11.1
1999, Apr. 16
Self-Adhesive

3306   Pane of 10 #3306a   6.75
   a.   A2554 33c single   .65   .25
   b.   Pane of 9 #3306a   6.00
   c.   Pane of 1 #3306a   .65

Die cutting on #3306b does not extend through the backing paper.

3307   Pane of 10, #3307c, 9 #3307a   15.00
   a.   A2554 33c single   1.25
   b.   Pane of 9 #3307a   12.00
   c.   Pane of 1, no die cutting   2.75
   d.   As "a," vert. pair, die cutting omitted btwn. pos. 6 and 9 (unique)   4,250.

Die cutting on #3307b extends through the backing paper.

LITERARY ARTS SERIES
Ayn Rand (1905-82).

A2555

LITHOGRAPHED

1999, Apr. 22   *Perf. 11.2*

3308 A2555 33c multicolored   .65   .25

Cinco De Mayo Type of 1998
LITHOGRAPHED
Serpentine Die Cut 11.6x11.3
1999, Apr. 27
Self-Adhesive

3309 A2486 33c multicolored   .70   .25

TROPICAL FLOWERS

Bird of Paradise
A2556

Royal Poinciana
A2557

Gloriosa Lily
A2558

Chinese Hibiscus
A2559

PHOTOGRAVURE
BOOKLET STAMPS
Serpentine Die Cut 10.9 on 2 or 1 Sides
1999, May 1
Self-Adhesive

3310 A2556 33c multicolored   .65   .30
3311 A2557 33c multicolored   .65   .30
3312 A2558 33c multicolored   .65   .30
3313 A2559 33c multicolored   .65   .30
   a.   Block of 4, #3310-3313   2.60
   b.   Booklet pane, 5 each #3313a   13.00

No. 3313b is a double-sided booklet pane with 12 stamps on one side and 8 stamps plus label on the other side.

JOHN (1699-1777) & WILLIAM (1739-1823) BARTRAM, BOTANISTS

A2560

LITHOGRAPHED
Serpentine Die Cut 11½
1999, May 18
Self-Adhesive

3314 A2560 33c Franklinia alatamaha, by William Bartram   .65   .25

PROSTATE CANCER AWARENESS

A2561

PHOTOGRAVURE
1999, May 28   *Serpentine Die Cut 11*
Self-Adhesive

3315 A2561 33c multicolored   .65   .25

CALIFORNIA GOLD RUSH, 150TH ANNIV.

A2562

LITHOGRAPHED

1999, June 18   *Perf. 11¼*

3316 A2562 33c multicolored   .65   .25

AQUARIUM FISH
Reef Fish

A2563

A2564

A2565

A2566

Designs: No. 3317, Yellow fish, red fish, cleaner shrimp. No. 3318, Fish, thermometer. No. 3319, Red fish, blue & yellow fish. No. 3320, Fish, heater/aerator.

LITHOGRAPHED
Serpentine Die Cut 11½
1999, June 24
Self-Adhesive

3317	A2563	33c multicolored	.65	.30
3318	A2564	33c multicolored	.65	.30
3319	A2565	33c multicolored	.65	.30
3320	A2566	33c multicolored	.65	.30
b.		Strip of 4, #3317-3320	2.60	

EXTREME SPORTS

A2567

A2568

A2569

A2570

PHOTOGRAVURE
Serpentine Die Cut 11
1999, June 25
Self-Adhesive

3321	A2567	33c multicolored	.75	.30
3322	A2568	33c multicolored	.75	.30
3323	A2569	33c multicolored	.75	.30
3324	A2570	33c multicolored	.75	.30
a.		Block or strip of 4, #3321-3324	3.00	

AMERICAN GLASS

Free-Blown
Glass — A2571

Mold-Blown
Glass — A2572

Pressed
Glass — A2573

Art
Glass — A2574

LITHOGRAPHED
1999, June 29   *Perf. 11*

3325	A2571	33c multicolored	1.90	.25
3326	A2572	33c multicolored	1.90	.25
3327	A2573	33c multicolored	1.90	.25
3328	A2574	33c multicolored	1.90	.25
a.		Strip or block of 4, #3325-3328	7.75	3.00

LEGENDS OF HOLLYWOOD
James Cagney (1899-1986)

A2575

PHOTOGRAVURE
1999, July 22   *Perf. 11*
3329   A2575 33c multicolored   .80   .25

Perforations in corner of each stamp are star-shaped.

GEN. WILLIAM "BILLY" L. MITCHELL (1879-1936), AVIATION PIONEER

A2576

Serpentine Die Cut 9¾x10
1999, July 30
Self-Adhesive
3330   A2576 55c multicolored   1.10   .30

HONORING THOSE WHO SERVED

A2577

Serpentine Die Cut 11
1999, Aug. 16
Self-Adhesive
3331   A2577 33c black, blue & red   .65   .25

UNIVERSAL POSTAL UNION

A2578

LITHOGRAPHED
1999, Aug. 25   *Perf. 11*
3332   A2578 45c multicolored   1.00   .45

FAMOUS TRAINS

Daylight
A2579

Congressional — A2580

20th
Century
Limited
A2581

Hiawatha
A2582

Super Chief
A2583

1999, Aug. 26				
3333	A2579	33c multicolored	.75	.25
3334	A2580	33c multicolored	.75	.25
3335	A2581	33c multicolored	.75	.25
3336	A2582	33c multicolored	.75	.25
3337	A2583	33c multicolored	.75	.25
a.		Strip of 5, #3333-3337	3.75	—

Stamps in No. 3337a are arranged in four different orders.

FREDERICK LAW OLMSTED (1822-1903), LANDSCAPE ARCHITECT

A2584

1999, Sept. 12
3338   A2584 33c multicolored   .65   .25

AMERICAN MUSIC SERIES
Hollywood Composers

Max Steiner
(1888-1971)
A2585

Dimitri
Tiomkin
(1894-1975)
A2586

Bernard
Herrmann
(1911-75)
A2587

Franz
Waxman
(1906-67)
A2588

Alfred
Newman
(1907-70)
A2589

Erich
Wolfgang
Korngold
(1897-1957)
A2590

1999, Sept. 16			*Perf. 11*	
3339	A2585	33c multicolored	1.40	.25
3340	A2586	33c multicolored	1.40	.25
3341	A2587	33c multicolored	1.40	.25
3342	A2588	33c multicolored	1.40	.25
3343	A2589	33c multicolored	1.40	.25
3344	A2590	33c multicolored	1.40	.25
a.		Block of 6, #3339-3344	8.50	4.50

AMERICAN MUSIC SERIES
Broadway Songwriters

Ira (1896-1983) &
George
(1898-1937)
Gershwin
A2591

Alan Jay
Lerner
(1918-86) &
Frederick
Loewe
(1901-88)
A2592

Lorenz Hart
(1895-1943)
A2593

Richard Rodgers (1902-79) & Oscar
Hammerstein II (1895-1960) — A2594

Meredith
Willson
(1902-84)
A2595

Frank
Loesser
(1910-69)
A2596

1999, Sept. 21

3345	A2591	33c multicolored	1.25	.25
3346	A2592	33c multicolored	1.25	.25
3347	A2593	33c multicolored	1.25	.25
3348	A2594	33c multicolored	1.25	.25
3349	A2595	33c multicolored	1.25	.25
3350	A2596	33c multicolored	1.25	.25
a.		Block of 6, 3345-3350	7.50	4.50

INSECTS & SPIDERS

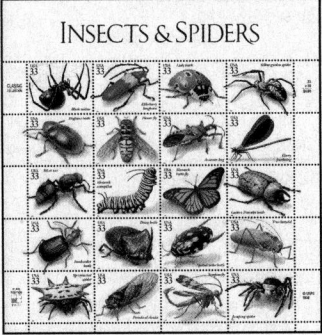

A2597

Designs: a, Black widow. b, Elderberry longhorn. c, Lady beetle. d, Yellow garden spider.
e, Dogbane beetle. f, Flower fly. g, Assassin
bug. h, Ebony jewelwing. i, Velvet ant. j, Monarch caterpillar. k, Monarch butterfly. l, Eastern Hercules beetle. m, Bombardier beetle. n,
Dung beetle. o, Spotted water beetle. p, True
katydid. q, Spinybacked spider. r, Periodical
cicada. s, Scorpionfly. t, Jumping spider.

1999, Oct. 1			**Perf. 11**	
3351	A2597	Pane of 20	14.00	10.00
a.-t.		33c any single	.70	.50

Hanukkah Type of 1996
PHOTOGRAVURE

1999, Oct. 8		*Serpentine Die Cut 11*		
Self-Adhesive				
3352	A2411	33c multicolored	.65	.25

Uncle Sam Type of 1998
COIL STAMP

1999, Oct. 8			**Perf. 9¾ Vert.**	
3353	A2530	22c multicolored	.45	.25

NATO, 50TH ANNIV.

A2598

LITHOGRAPHED

1999, Oct. 13			**Perf. 11¼**	
3354	A2598	33c multicolored	.65	.25

CHRISTMAS

Madonna and
Child, by
Bartolomeo
Vivarini
A2599

Deer
A2600

*Serpentine Die Cut 11¼ on 2 or 3
sides*

1999, Oct. 20
Booklet Stamp
Self-Adhesive

3355	A2599	33c multicolored	.90	.25
a.		Booklet pane of 20	18.00	

Serpentine Die Cut 11¼

3356	A2600	33c gold & red	2.25	.25
3357	A2600	33c gold & blue	2.25	.25
3358	A2600	33c gold & purple	2.25	.25
3359	A2600	33c gold & green	2.25	.25
a.		Block or strip of 4, #3356-3359	9.00	

Booklet Stamps
*Serpentine Die Cut 11¼ on 2, 3 or 4
sides*

3360	A2600	33c gold & red	1.25	.25
3361	A2600	33c gold & blue	1.25	.25
3362	A2600	33c gold & purple	1.25	.25
3363	A2600	33c gold & green	1.25	.25
a.		Booklet pane of 20, 5 each #3360-3363	25.00	
b.		Block of 4, 3360-3363	5.00	
c.		As "b," die cutting omitted	100.00	
d.		As "a," die cutting omitted	500.00	

Size: 21x19mm
*Serpentine Die Cut 11½x11¼ on 2
or 3 sides*

3364	A2600	33c gold & red	1.50	.25
3365	A2600	33c gold & blue	1.50	.25
3366	A2600	33c gold & purple	1.50	.25
3367	A2600	33c gold & green	1.50	.25
a.		Booklet pane of 4, #3364-3367	6.00	
b.		Booklet pane of 5, #3364, 3366, 3367, 2 #3365 + label	7.50	
c.		Booklet pane of 6, #3365, 3367, 2 each #3364 & 3366	9.00	
d.		Block of 4, 3364-3367	6.00	

The frame on Nos. 3356-3359 is narrow and
the space between it and the hoof is a hairline.
The frame on Nos. 3360-3363 is much thicker,
and the space between it and the hoof is
wider.

Kwanzaa Type of 1997
PHOTOGRAVURE

1999, Oct. 29		*Serpentine Die Cut 11*		
Self-Adhesive				
3368	A2458	33c multicolored	.65	.25

YEAR 2000

Baby New
Year — A2601

LITHOGRAPHED
Serpentine Die Cut 11¼

1999, Dec. 27				
Self-Adhesive				
3369	A2601	33c multicolored	.65	.25

CHINESE NEW YEAR

Year of the Dragon — A2602

2000, Jan. 6			**Perf. 11¼**	
3370	A2602	33c multicolored	.80	.25
		See No. 3895e.		

BLACK HERITAGE SERIES

Patricia Roberts
Harris — A2603

Serpentine Die Cut 11½x11¼
2000, Jan. 27
Self-Adhesive

3371	A2603	33c indigo	.65	.25

SUBMARINES

S Class
A2604

Los
Angeles
Class
A2605

Ohio Class
A2606

USS
Holland
A2607

Gato Class — A2608

2000, Mar. 27			**Perf. 11**	
3372	A2605	33c multicolored, with microprinted "USPS" at base of sail	.75	.25

BOOKLET STAMPS

3373	A2604	22c multicolored	.75	.75
3374	A2605	33c multicolored, no microprinting	1.00	1.00
3375	A2606	55c multicolored	1.75	1.25
3376	A2607	60c multicolored	2.50	1.50
3377	A2608	$3.20 multicolored	14.00	5.00
a.		Booklet pane of 5, #3373-3377	20.00	

No. 3377a was issued with two types of text
in the selvage.

PACIFIC COAST RAIN FOREST

A2609

Designs: a, Harlequin duck. b, Dwarf
oregongrape, snail-eating ground beetle. c,
American dipper, horiz. d, Cutthroat trout,
horiz. e, Roosevelt elk. f, Winter wren. g,

Pacific giant salamander, Rough-skinned
newt. h, Western tiger swallowtail, horiz. i,
Douglas squirrel, foliose lichen. j, Foliose
lichen, banana slug.

*Serpentine Die Cut 11¼x11½, 11½
(horiz. stamps)*
2000, Mar. 29
Self-Adhesive

3378	A2609	Pane of 10	10.00	
a.-j.		33c any single	1.00	.50

LOUISE NEVELSON (1899-1988),
SCULPTOR

Silent Music
I — A2610

Royal Tide
I — A2611

Black
Chord — A2612

Nightsphere-Light — A2613

Dawn's Wedding Chapel I — A2614

2000, Apr. 6			**Perf. 11x11¼**	
3379	A2610	33c multicolored	.65	.25
3380	A2611	33c multicolored	.65	.25
3381	A2612	33c multicolored	.65	.25
3382	A2613	33c multicolored	.65	.25
3383	A2614	33c multicolored	.65	.25
a.		Strip of 5, #3379-3383	3.25	—

HUBBLE SPACE TELESCOPE IMAGES

Eagle Nebula — A2615

Ring Nebula — A2616

Lagoon Nebula — A2617

Egg Nebula — A2618

Galaxy NGC 1316 — A2619

PHOTOGRAVURE

2000, Apr. 10   *Perf. 11*

3384	A2615	33c multicolored	.65	.25
3385	A2616	33c multicolored	.65	.25
3386	A2617	33c multicolored	.65	.25
3387	A2618	33c multicolored	.65	.25
3388	A2619	33c multicolored	.65	.25
a.		Strip of 5, #3384-3388	3.25	2.00
b.		As "a," imperf	900.00	

AMERICAN SAMOA

Samoan Double Canoe A2620

LITHOGRAPHED

2000, Apr. 17

3389	A2620	33c multicolored	.85	.25

LIBRARY OF CONGRESS

A2621

2000, Apr. 24

3390	A2621	33c multicolored	.65	.25

ROAD RUNNER & WILE E. COYOTE

A2622

Serpentine Die Cut 11
2000, Apr. 26
Self-Adhesive

3391		Pane of 10 #3391a	10.00
a.		A2622 33c single	.85 .25
b.		Pane of 9 #3391a	8.00
c.		Pane of 1 #3391a	1.50
d.		All die cutting omitted, pane of 10	2,250.

Die cutting on #3391b does not extend through the backing paper.

3392		Pane of 10, #3392c, 9 #3392a	40.00
a.		A2622 33c single	2.75
b.		Pane of 9 #3392a	30.00
c.		Pane of 1, no die cutting	5.00

Die cutting on #3392a extends through the backing paper. Used examples of No. 3392a are identical to those of No. 3391a.
Nos. 3391b-3391c and 3392b-3392c are separated by a vertical line of microperforations.

DISTINGUISHED SOLDIERS

A2623

A2624

A2625

A2626

Designs: No. 3393, Maj. Gen. John L. Hines. No. 3394, Gen. Omar N. Bradley. No. 3395, Sgt. Alvin C. York. No. 3396, Second Lt. Audie L. Murphy.

2000, May 3   *Perf. 11*

3393	A2623	33c multicolored	.70	.25
3394	A2624	33c multicolored	.70	.25
3395	A2625	33c multicolored	.70	.25
3396	A2626	33c multicolored	.70	.25
a.		Block or strip of 4, #3393-3396	2.80	1.50

SUMMER SPORTS

Runners A2627

2000, May 5

3397	A2627	33c multicolored	.65	.25

ADOPTION

Stick Figures — A2628

Serpentine Die Cut 11½
2000, May 10
Self-Adhesive

3398	A2628	33c multicolored	.65	.25
a.		Die cutting omitted, pair	2,500.	

See note after No. 1549.

YOUTH TEAM SPORTS

A2629

A2630

A2631

A2632

2000, May 27   *Perf. 11*

3399	A2629	33c Basketball	.70	.25
3400	A2630	33c Football	.70	.25
3401	A2631	33c Soccer	.70	.25
3402	A2632	33c Baseball	.70	.25
a.		Block or strip of 4, #3399-3402	2.80	1.75

THE STARS AND STRIPES

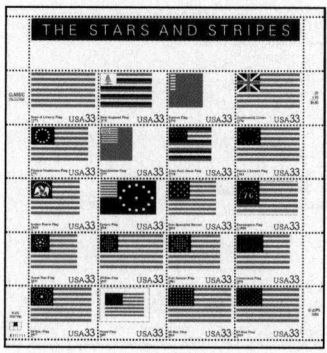
A2633

Designs: a, Sons of Liberty Flag, 1775. b, New England Flag, 1775. c, Forster Flag, 1775. d, Continental Colors, 1776. e, Francis Hopkinson Flag, 1777. f, Brandywine Flag, 1777. g, John Paul Jones Flag, 1779. h, Pierre L'Enfant Flag, 1783. i, Indian Peace Flag, 1803. j, Easton Flag, 1814. k, Star-Spangled Banner, 1814. l, Bennington Flag, c. 1820. m, Great Star Flag, 1837. n, 29-Star Flag, 1847. o, Fort Sumter Flag, 1861. p, Centennial Flag, 1876. q, 38-Star Flag, 1877. r, Peace Flag, 1891. s, 48-Star Flag, 1912. t, 50-Star Flag, 1960.

2000, June 14   *Perf. 10½x11*

3403	A2633	Pane of 20	15.00	11.00
a.-t.		33c any single	.75	.50

BERRIES

Blueberries A2634

Strawberries A2635

Blackberries A2636

Raspberries A2637

See designs A2550-A2553.

PHOTOGRAVURE
COIL STAMPS
Serpentine Die Cut 8½ Horiz.
2000, June 16   **Tagged**
Self-Adhesive

3404	A2634	33c multicolored	3.50	.25
3405	A2635	33c multicolored	3.50	.25
3406	A2636	33c multicolored	3.50	.25
3407	A2637	33c multicolored	3.50	.25
a.		Strip of 4, #3404-3407	15.00	

Nos. 3404-3407 are linerless coils issued without backing paper. The adhesive is strong and can remove the ink from stamps in the roll.

LEGENDS OF BASEBALL

A2638

Designs: a, Jackie Robinson. b, Eddie Collins. c, Christy Mathewson. d, Ty Cobb. e, George Sisler. f, Rogers Hornsby. g, Mickey Cochrane. h, Babe Ruth. i, Walter Johnson. j, Roberto Clemente. k, Lefty Grove. l, Tris Speaker. m, Cy Young. n, Jimmie Foxx. o, Pie Traynor. p, Satchel Paige. q, Honus Wagner. r, Josh Gibson. s, Dizzy Dean. t, Lou Gehrig.

LITHOGRAPHED
Serpentine Die Cut 11¼
2000, July 6
Self-Adhesive

3408	A2638	Pane of 20	15.00	
a.-t.		33c any single	.75	.50

SPACE
Souvenir Sheets

A2639

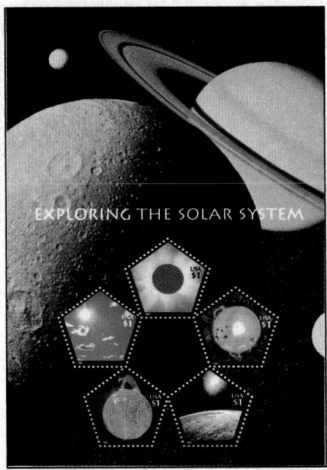

EXPLORING THE SOLAR SYSTEM

A2640

ESCAPING THE GRAVITY OF EARTH

$3.20 $3.20

A2641

SPACE ACHIEVEMENT AND EXPLORATION

WORLD STAMP EXPO 2000

USA $11.75

A2642

LANDING ON THE MOON

A2643

Designs: No. 3409: a, Hubble Space Telescope. b, Radio interferometer very large array, New Mexico. c, Optical and infrared telescopes, Keck Observatory, Hawaii. d, Optical telescopes, Cerro Tololo Observatory, Chile. e, Optical telescope, Mount Wilson Observatory, California. f, Radio telescope, Arecibo Observatory, Puerto Rico.

No. 3410: a, Sun and corona. b, Cross-section of sun. c, Sun and earth. d, Sun and solar flare. e, Sun and clouds.

No. 3411: a, Space Shuttle and Space Station. b, Astronauts working in space.

PHOTOGRAVURE

2000   **Perf. 10½x11**

3409	A2639	Sheet of 6	15.00	7.00
a.-f.		60c any single	2.25	1.00

Perf. 10¾

3410	A2640	Sheet of 5 + label	17.50	10.00
a.-e.		$1 any single	3.00	1.75
f.		As No. 3410, imperf	2,000.	
g.		As No. 3410, with hologram from No. 3411b applied	1,500.	

Untagged

Photogravure with Hologram Affixed

Perf. 10½, 10¾ (#3412)

3411	A2641	Sheet of 2	22.50	10.00
a.-b.		$3.20 any single	10.00	4.00
c.		Hologram omitted on right stamp		
3412	A2642	multicolored	40.00	17.50
a.		$11.75 single	35.00	15.00
b.		Hologram omitted		
c.		Hologram omitted on No. 3412 in uncut sheet of 5 panes		
3413	A2643	multicolored	40.00	17.50
a.		$11.75 single	35.00	15.00
b.		Double hologram	3,000.	
c.		Double hologram on No. 3413 in uncut sheet of 5 panes		
d.		Hologram omitted on No. 3413 in uncut sheet of 5 panes		
		Nos. 3409-3413 (5)	135.00	62.00

Issued: No. 3409, 7/10; No. 3410, 7/11; No. 3411, 7/9; No. 3412, 7/7; No. 3413, 7/8.
The holograms on Nos. 3411-3413 scratch easily. Values are for examples with minimal scratches. Examples without scratches are worth more.
Warning: Soaking in water may affect holographic images.

STAMPIN' THE FUTURE CHILDREN'S STAMP DESIGN CONTEST WINNERS

by Zachary Canter
A2644

by Sarah Lipsey
A2645

by Morgan Hill
A2646

by Ashley Young
A2647

LITHOGRAPHED

Serpentine Die Cut 11¼

2000, July 13

Self-Adhesive

3414	A2644	33c multicolored	.65	.30
3415	A2645	33c multicolored	.65	.30
3416	A2646	33c multicolored	.65	.30
3417	A2647	33c multicolored	.65	.30
a.		Horiz. strip of 4, #3414-3417	2.60	

DISTINGUISHED AMERICANS

Gen. Joseph W. Stilwell
A2650

Wilma Rudolph (1940-94), Athlete
A2652

Sen. Claude Pepper
A2656

Sen. Margaret Chase Smith (1897-1995)
A2657

James A. Michener (1907-97), Author — A2657a

Dr. Jonas Salk (1914-95), Polio Vaccine Pioneer
A2658

Harriet Beecher Stowe (1811-96), Author
A2660

Sen. Hattie Caraway (1878-1950) — A2661

Edward Trudeau (1848-1915), Phthisiologist — A2661a

Mary Lasker (1900-94), Philanthropist — A2661b

Edna Ferber (1887-1968), Writer
A2662

Edna Ferber (With Curving Shoulder)
A2663

Dr. Albert Sabin (1906-93), Polio Vaccine Pioneer — A2664

LITHOGRAPHED & ENGRAVED, LITHOGRAPHED (#3436)

Perf. 11 (#3420, 3426), Serpentine Die Cut 11¼x10¾ (#3422, 3430, 3432B), 11¼x11 (#3427A, 3428, 3432A, 3435), 11 (#3427, 3431), 11½x11 (#3432), 11x11¾ (#3433), 11¼ (#3434)

2000-09

Self-Adhesive (All Except #3420, 3426)

3420	A2650	10c red & blk	.25	.25
a.		Imperf, pair	200.00	
3422	A2652	23c red & blk	.45	.25
a.		Imperf, pair	—	
3426	A2656	33c red & blk	.65	.25
3427	A2657	58c red & blk	1.25	.25
b.		Black (engr.) omitted	400.00	
3427A	A2657a	59c multi	1.30	.25
3428	A2658	63c red & blk	1.25	.25
b.		Black (litho.) omitted	275.00	
3430	A2660	75c red & blk	1.50	.25
3431	A2661	76c red & blk	1.50	.25
3432	A2661	76c red & blk	4.00	2.00
3432A	A2661a	76c multi	2.00	.25
3432B	A2661b	78c multi	1.60	.25
3433	A2662	83c red & blk	1.70	.30
3434	A2663	83c red & blk	1.60	.30
3435	A2664	87c red & blk	1.75	.30

BOOKLET STAMP

Serpentine Die Cut 11¼x10¾ on 3 Sides

Self-Adhesive

3436	A2652	23c red & blk	.45	.25
a.		Booklet pane of 4	1.80	
b.		Booklet pane of 6	2.70	
c.		As "a" & "b" in cplt booklet of 10 (No. BK279A), die cutting omitted and peel strip intact, P#P44	—	
d.		Booklet pane of 10	4.50	
e.		As "d," die cutting omitted	—	

The backing on No. 3436b has a different product number (672900) than that found on the lower portion of No. 3436d (673000).
Issued: 10c, 8/24; 33c, 9/7; No. 3432, 2/21/01; No. 3433, 7/29/02; No. 3434, Aug. 2003; 23c, 7/14/04; 63c, 87c, 3/2/06; 58c, 75c, 6/13/07; 59c, 3432A, 5/12/08; No. 3432B, 5/15/09.

CALIFORNIA STATEHOOD, 150TH ANNIV.

Big Sur and Iceplant — A2668

PHOTOGRAVURE

2000, Sept. 8   Serpentine Die Cut 11

Self-Adhesive

3438	A2668	33c multicolored	.75	.25

DEEP SEA CREATURES

Fanfin Anglerfish
A2669

Sea Cucumber
A2670

Fangtooth
A2671

Amphipod
A2672

Medusa
A2673

2000, Oct. 2   Tagged   Perf. 10x10¼
3439	A2669	33c multicolored	.75	.25
3440	A2670	33c multicolored	.75	.25
3441	A2671	33c multicolored	.75	.25
3442	A2672	33c multicolored	.75	.25
3443	A2673	33c multicolored	.75	.25
a.		Vert. strip of 5, #3439-3443	3.75	2.00

LITERARY ARTS SERIES

Thomas Wolfe (1900-38),
Novelist — A2674

LITHOGRAPHED

2000, Oct. 3   Perf. 11
3444	A2674	33c multicolored	.65	.25

WHITE HOUSE, 200TH ANNIV.

A2675

Serpentine Die Cut 11¼
2000, Oct. 18
Self-Adhesive
3445	A2675	33c multicolored	1.00	.25

LEGENDS OF HOLLYWOOD

Edward G. Robinson
(1893-1973),
Actor — A2676

PHOTOGRAVURE

2000, Oct. 24   Perf. 11
3446	A2676	33c multicolored	1.60	.25

Perforations in corner of each stamp are
star-shaped.

New York Public
Library Lion — A2677

PHOTOGRAVURE
COIL STAMP

Serpentine Die Cut 11½ Vert.
2000, Nov. 9   Untagged
Self-Adhesive
3447	A2677	(10c) multicolored, "2000" year date	.25	.25
a.		"2003" year date	.25	.25

See No. 3769.

Flag Over
Farm — A2678

LITHOGRAPHED (#3448-3449),
PHOTOGRAVURE (#3450)
2000, Dec. 15   Perf. 11¼
3448	A2678	(34c) multicolored	1.00	.25

Self-Adhesive
Serpentine Die Cut 11¼
3449	A2678	(34c) multicolored	1.00	.25

Booklet Stamp
Self-Adhesive
Serpentine Die Cut 8 on 2, 3 or 4 Sides
3450	A2678	(34c) multicolored	.85	.25
a.		Booklet pane of 18	16.00	
b.		Die cutting omitted, pair		—

A2679

Statue of
Liberty — A2680

PHOTOGRAVURE
Serpentine Die Cut 11 on 2, 3 or 4 Sides
2000, Dec. 15
Self-Adhesive (#3451, 3453)
Booklet Stamp
3451	A2679	(34c) multicolored	.70	.25
a.		Booklet pane of 20	14.00	
b.		Booklet pane of 4	3.00	
c.		Booklet pane of 6	5.75	
d.		As "a," die cutting omitted		—

Coil Stamps
Perf. 9¾ Vert.
3452	A2680	(34c) multicolored	.70	.25

Serpentine Die Cut 10 Vert.
3453	A2680	(34c) multicolored, small date	.70	.25
a.		Die cutting omitted, pair	300.00	
b.		Large date	.75	.25

The date on No. 3453 is 1.4mm long, on No.
3453b 1.55mm long and darker in color.

A2681

A2682

A2683

Flowers — A2684

PHOTOGRAVURE
Serpentine Die Cut 10½x10¾ on 2 or 3 Sides
2000, Dec. 15
Booklet Stamps
Self-Adhesive
3454	A2681	(34c) purple & multi	1.25	.25
3455	A2682	(34c) tan & multi	1.25	.25
3456	A2683	(34c) green & multi	1.25	.25

3457	A2684	(34c) red & multi	1.25	.25
a.		Block of 4, #3454-3457	5.00	
b.		Booklet pane of 4, #3454-3457	5.00	
c.		Booklet pane of 6, #3456, 3457, 2 each #3454-3455	7.50	
d.		Booklet pane of 6, #3454, 3455, 2 each #3456-3457	7.50	
e.		Booklet pane of 20, 5 each #3454-3457 + label	25.00	

No. 3457e is a double-sided booklet pane,
with 12 stamps on one side and eight stamps
plus label on the other side.

Serpentine Die Cut 11½x11¾ on 2 or 3 Sides
3458	A2681	(34c) purple & multi	5.00	.25
3459	A2682	(34c) tan & multi	5.00	.25
3460	A2683	(34c) green & multi	5.00	.25
3461	A2684	(34c) red & multi	5.00	.25
a.		Block of 4, #3458-3461	20.00	
b.		Booklet pane of 20, 2 each #3461a, 3 each #3457a	60.00	
c.		Booklet pane of 20, 2 each #3457a, 3 each #3461a	100.00	

Nos. 3461b and 3461c are double-sided
booklet panes, with 12 stamps on one side
and eight stamps plus label on the other side.

Coil Stamps
Serpentine Die Cut 8½ Vert.
3462	A2683	(34c) green & multi	4.50	.25
3463	A2684	(34c) red & multi	4.50	.25
3464	A2682	(34c) tan & multi	4.50	.25
3465	A2681	(34c) purple & multi	4.50	.25
a.		Strip of 4, #3462-3465	20.00	

Lettering on No. 3462 has black outline not
found on No. 3456. Zeroes of "2000" are
rounder on Nos. 3454-3457 than on Nos.
3462-3465.

Statue of
Liberty
A2685

George
Washington
A2686

American
Buffalo
A2687

Flag Over
Farm
A2688

Statue of
Liberty — A2689

A2690

A2691

A2692

Flowers
A2693

Apple
A2694

Orange
A2695

Eagle
A2696

Capitol
Dome — A2697

Washington
Monument
A2698

Serpentine Die Cut 9¾ Vert.
2001, Jan. 7
Coil Stamp
Self-Adhesive
3466	A2685	34c multi	.70	.25

Sheets of 400 in four panes of 100
(#3467), Sheets of 200 in 10 panes of
20 (#3468), Sheets of 200 in two
panes of 100 (#3469), Sheets of 120
in six panes of 20 (#3468A, 3470-
3473), Sheets of 160 in eight panes of
20 (#3471A)

Self-Adhesive (#3468-3468A, 3470-3473)
2001   Perf. 11¼x11
3467	A2687	21c multi	.50	.25

Serpentine Die Cut 11
3468	A2687	21c multi	.50	.25

Litho.
Serpentine Die Cut 11¼x11¾
3468A	A2686	23c green	.50	.25

Photo.
Perf. 11¼
3469	A2688	34c multi	.75	.25

Serpentine Die Cut 11¼
3470	A2688	34c multi	.75	.25

Serpentine Die Cut 10¾
3471	A2696	55c multi	1.10	.25
3471A	A2696	57c multi	1.10	.25

Serpentine Die Cut 11¼x11½
Litho.
3472	A2697	$3.50 multi	7.00	2.00
a.		Die cutting omitted, pair	500.00	
3473	A2698	$12.25 multi	22.50	10.00

COIL STAMPS
Self-Adhesive (#3475-3475A, 3477-3481)
Photo.
Serpentine Die Cut 8½ Vert.
3475	A2687	21c multi	.50	.25
3475A	A2686	23c green	.75	.25

Compare No. 3475A ("2001" date at lower
left) with No. 3617 ("2002" date at lower left).

Perf. 9¾ Vert.
3476	A2685	34c multi	.90	.25

Serpentine Die Cut 9¾ Vert.
3477	A2685	34c multi	.80	.25
a.		Die cutting omitted, pair	65.00	

No. 3477 has right angle corners and backing paper as high as the stamp. No. 3466 has
rounded corners and is on backing paper
larger than the stamp.

Serpentine Die Cut 8½ Vert.
3478	A2690	34c green & multi	1.50	.25
3479	A2691	34c red & multi	1.50	.25
3480	A2692	34c tan & multi	1.50	.25
3481	A2693	34c purple & multi	1.50	.25
a.		Strip of 4, #3478-3481	6.00	

BOOKLET STAMPS
Litho.
Self-Adhesive
Serpentine Die Cut 11¼x11 on 3 Sides

3482	A2686	20c dk car	.55	.25
a.	Booklet pane of 10		5.50	
b.	Booklet pane of 4		2.20	
c.	Booklet pane of 6		3.30	

Serpentine Die Cut 10½x11 on 3 Sides

3483	A2686	20c dk car	5.50	1.25
a.	Booklet pane of 4, 2 #3482 at L, 2 #3483 at R		12.50	
b.	Booklet pane of 6, 3 #3482 at L, 3 #3483 at R		20.00	
c.	Booklet pane of 10, 5 #3482 at L, 5 #3483 at R		30.00	
d.	Booklet pane of 4, 2 #3483 at L, 2 #3482 at R		12.50	
e.	Booklet pane of 6, 3 #3483 at L, 3 #3482 at R		20.00	
f.	Booklet pane of 10, 5 #3483 at L, 5 #3482 at R		30.00	
g.	Pair, #3482 at L, #3483 at R		6.00	
h.	Pair, #3483 at L, #3482 at R		6.00	

Serpentine Die Cut 11¼ on 3 Sides

3484	A2687	21c multi	.60	.25
b.	Booklet pane of 4		2.40	
c.	Booklet pane of 6		3.60	
d.	Booklet pane of 10		6.00	

Serpentine Die Cut 10½x11¼

3484A	A2687	21c multi	5.50	1.50
e.	Booklet pane of 4, 2 #3484 at L, 2 #3484A at R		12.50	
f.	Booklet pane of 6, 3 #3484 at L, 3 #3484A at R		20.00	
g.	Booklet pane of 10, 5 #3484 at L, 5 #3484A at R		30.00	
h.	Booklet pane of 4, 2 #3484A at L, 2 #3484 at R		12.50	
i.	Booklet pane of 6, 3 #3484A at L, 3 #3484 at R		20.00	
j.	Booklet pane of 10, 5 #3484A at L, 5 #3484 at R		30.00	
k.	Pair, #3484 at L, #3484A at R		6.00	
l.	Pair, #3484A at L, #3484 at R		6.00	

Photo.
Serpentine Die Cut 11 on 2, 3 or 4 Sides

3485	A2689	34c multi	.70	.25
a.	Booklet pane of 10		7.00	
b.	Booklet pane of 20		14.00	
c.	Booklet pane of 4		3.00	
d.	Booklet pane of 6		4.50	
e.	Die cutting omitted, pair (from No. 3485b)		—	
f.	As "e," booklet pane of 20		—	

Serpentine Die Cut 10½x10¾ on 2 or 3 Sides

3487	A2693	34c purple & multi	.85	.25
3488	A2692	34c tan & multi	.85	.25
3489	A2690	34c green & multi	.85	.25
3490	A2691	34c red & multi	.85	.25
a.	Block of 4, #3487-3490		3.50	
b.	Booklet pane of 4, #3487-3490		3.50	
c.	Booklet pane of 6, #3489-3490, 2 each #3487-3488		5.00	
d.	Booklet pane of 6, #3487-3488, 2 each #3489-3490		5.00	
e.	Booklet pane of 20, 5 each #3490a + label		20.00	

No. 3490e is a double-sided booklet pane, with 12 stamps on one side and eight stamps plus label on the other side.

Litho.
Serpentine Die Cut 11¼ on 2, 3 or 4 Sides

3491	A2694	34c multi	.70	.25
3492	A2695	34c multi	.70	.25
a.	Pair, #3491-3492		1.40	
b.	Booklet pane, 10 each #3491-3492		14.00	
c.	As "a," black ("34 USA") omitted		—	
d.	As "a," die cutting omitted		1,100.	
e.	As "b," die cutting omitted		5,500.	
f.	As "b," right four stamps yellow omitted		3,500.	

Serpentine Die Cut 11½x10¾ on 2 or 3 Sides

3493	A2694	34c multi	1.15	.25
3494	A2695	34c multi	1.15	.25
a.	Pair, #3493-3494		2.30	
b.	Booklet pane, 2 each #3493-3494		4.60	

c.	Booklet pane, 3 each #3493-3494, #3493 at UL	7.00
d.	Booklet pane, 3 each #3493-3494, #3494 at UL	7.00

Serpentine Die Cut 8 on 2, 3, or 4 Sides

3495	A2688	34c multi	1.25	.25
a.	Booklet pane of 18		22.50	

Issued: Nos. 3472-3473, 1/29; Nos. 3469, 3476-3481, 3485, 3487-3490, 2/7; Nos. 3468, 3471, 3475, 3482, 3483, 2/22; Nos. 3470, 3491-3492, 3/6; Nos. 3493-3494, May; Nos. 3467, 3468A, 3471A, 3475A, 3483, 3484A, 9/20; No. 3495, 12/17.
See Nos. 3616-3619.

LOVE

Rose, Apr. 20, 1763 Love Letter by John Adams
A2699

Rose, Apr. 20, 1763 Love Letter by John Adams
A2700

Rose, Aug. 11, 1763 Love Letter by Abigail Smith (Abigail Adams in 1764) — A2701

LITHOGRAPHED
Serpentine Die Cut 11¼ on 2, 3 or 4 Sides

2001

Self-Adhesive
Booklet Stamps (Nos. 3496-3498)

3496	A2699	(34c) multi	.90	.25
a.	Booklet pane of 20		18.00	
b.	Vert. pair, die cutting omitted between		—	

Serpentine Die Cut 11¼ on 2, 3 or 4 Sides

3497	A2700	34c multi	.90	.25
a.	Booklet pane of 20		18.00	
b.	Vertical pair, die cutting omitted between		—	

Size: 18x21mm
Serpentine Die Cut 11½x10¾ on 2 or 3 Sides

3498	A2700	34c multi	1.00	.25
a.	Booklet pane of 4		4.00	
b.	Booklet pane of 6		6.00	

Serpentine Die Cut 11¼

3499	A2701	55c multi	1.10	.25

Issued: No. 3496, 1/19; others, 2/14.
See No. 3551.

CHINESE NEW YEAR

Year of the Snake
A2702

2001, Jan. 20			**Perf. 11¼**	
3500	A2702	34c multicolored	.75	.25

See No. 3895f.

BLACK HERITAGE SERIES

Roy Wilkins (1901-81), Civil Rights Leader — A2703

Serpentine Die Cut 11½x11¼
2001, Jan. 24
Self-Adhesive

3501	A2703	34c blue	.70	.25

AMERICAN ILLUSTRATORS

A2704

No. 3502: a, Marine Corps poster "First in the Fight, Always Faithful," by James Montgomery Flagg. b, "Interlude (The Lute Players)," by Maxfield Parrish. c, Advertisement for Arrow Collars and Shirts, by J. C. Leyendecker. d, Advertisement for Carrier Corp. Refrigeration, by Robert Fawcett. e, Advertisement for Luxite Hosiery, by Coles Phillips. f, Illustration for correspondence school lesson, by Al Parker. g, "Br'er Rabbit," by A. B. Frost. h, "An Attack on a Galleon," by Howard Pyle. i, Kewpie and Kewpie Doodle Dog, by Rose O'Neill. j, Illustration for cover of True Magazine, by Dean Cornwell. k, "Galahad's Departure," by Edwin Austin Abbey. l, "The First Lesson," by Jessie Willcox Smith. m, Illustration for cover of McCall's Magazine, by Neysa McMein. n, "Back Home For Keeps," by Jon Whitcomb. o, "Something for Supper," by Harvey Dunn. p, "A Dash for the Timber," by Frederic Remington. q, Illustration for "Moby Dick," by Rockwell Kent. r, "Captain Bill Bones," by N. C. Wyeth. s, Illustration for cover of The Saturday Evening Post, by Norman Rockwell. t, "The Girl He Left Behind," by John Held, Jr.

PHOTOGRAVURE
Serpentine Die Cut 11¼
2001, Feb. 1
Self-Adhesive

3502	A2704	Pane of 20	19.00	
a.-t.	34c any single		.90	.60

DIABETES AWARENESS

A2705

LITHOGRAPHED
Serpentine Die Cut 11¼x11½
2001, Mar. 16
Self-Adhesive

3503	A2705	34c multicolored	.65	.25

NOBEL PRIZE CENTENARY

Alfred Nobel and Obverse of Medals
A2706

LITHOGRAPHED & ENGRAVED
2001, Mar. 22   **Perf. 11**

3504	A2706	34c multicolored	.70	.25
a.	Imperf, pair		—	

See Sweden No. 2415.

PAN-AMERICAN EXPOSITION
INVERT STAMPS, CENT.

A2707

No. 3505: Reproductions (dated 2001) of: a, #294a. b, #295a. c, #296a. d, Commemorative "cinderella" stamp depicting a buffalo.

LITHOGRAPHED (#3505d), ENGRAVED (others)
Perf. 12 (#3505d), 12½x12 (others)
2001, Mar. 29
Tagged (#3505d), Untagged (others)

3505	A2707	Pane of 7, #3505a-3505c, 4 #3505d	10.00	7.00
a.	A109	1c green & black	.75	.25
b.	A110	2c carmine & black	.75	.25
c.	A111	4c deep red brown & black	.75	.25
d.		80c red & blue	1.90	.35

GREAT PLAINS PRAIRIE

A2708

No. 3506 — Wildlife and flowers: a, Pronghorns, Canada geese. b, Burrowing owls, American buffalos. c, American buffalo, Black-tailed prairie dogs, wild alfalfa, horiz. d, Black-tailed prairie dog, American buffalos,. e, Painted lady butterfly, American buffalo, prairie coneflowers, prairie wild roses, horiz. f, Western meadowlark, camel cricket, prairie coneflowers, prairie wild roses. g, Badger, harvester ants. h, Eastern short-horned lizard, plains pocket gopher. i, Plains spadefoot, dung beetle, prairie wild roses, horiz. j, Two-striped grasshopper, Ord's kangaroo rat.

LITHOGRAPHED
Serpentine Die Cut 10
2001, Apr. 19
Self-Adhesive

3506	A2708	Pane of 10	10.00	
a.-j.	34c Any single		1.00	.50

PEANUTS COMIC STRIP

Snoopy
A2709

Serpentine Die Cut 11¼x11½
2001, May 17
Self-Adhesive

3507	A2709	34c multicolored	.80	.25

HONORING VETERANS

A2710

2001, May 23
Self-Adhesive
3508 A2710 34c multicolored .80 .25

FRIDA KAHLO (1907-54), PAINTER

Self-portrait
A2711

2001, June 21 *Perf. 11¼*
3509 A2711 34c multicolored .70 .25

LEGENDARY PLAYING FIELDS

Ebbets
Field
A2712

Tiger
Stadium
A2713

Crosley
Field
A2714

Yankee
Stadium
A2715

Polo
Grounds
A2716

Forbes
Field
A2717

Fenway
Park
A2718

Comiskey
Park
A2719

Shibe
Park
A2720

Wrigley
Field
A2721

PHOTOGRAVURE
Serpentine Die Cut 11¼x11½
2001, June 27 **Self-Adhesive**
3510 A2712 34c multicolored .90 .60
3511 A2713 34c multicolored .90 .60
3512 A2714 34c multicolored .90 .60
3513 A2715 34c multicolored .90 .60
3514 A2716 34c multicolored .90 .60
3515 A2717 34c multicolored .90 .60
3516 A2718 34c multicolored .90 .60
3517 A2719 34c multicolored .90 .60
3518 A2720 34c multicolored .90 .60
3519 A2721 34c multicolored .90 .60
   a. Block of 10, #3510-3519 9.00

ATLAS STATUE, NEW YORK CITY

A2722

COIL STAMP
Serpentine Die Cut 8½ Vert.
2001, June 29 **Untagged**
Self-Adhesive
3520 A2722 (10c) multicolored .25 .25

No. 3520 is dated 2001. See No. 3770.
No. 3520 is known with extremely faint tagging, most likely from contamination in the paper-making process.

LEONARD BERNSTEIN (1918-90), CONDUCTOR

A2723

LITHOGRAPHED
2001, July 10 *Perf. 11¼*
3521 A2723 34c multicolored .70 .25

WOODY WAGON

A2724

PHOTOGRAVURE
COIL STAMP
Serpentine Die Cut 11½ Vert.
2001, Aug. 3 **Untagged**
Self-Adhesive
3522 A2724 (15c) multicolored .30 .25

LEGENDS OF HOLLYWOOD

Lucille Ball (1911-89) — A2725

LITHOGRAPHED
2001, Aug. 6 *Serpentine Die Cut 11*
Self-Adhesive
3523 A2725 34c multicolored 1.00 .25
   a. Die cutting omitted, pair 800.00

AMERICAN TREASURES SERIES
Amish Quilts

Diamond in the
Square, c.
1920 — A2726

Lone Star, c.
1920 — A2727

Sunshine and
Shadow, c.
1910 — A2728

Double
Ninepatch
Variation
A2729

Serpentine Die Cut 11¼x11½
2001, Aug. 9
Self-Adhesive
3524 A2726 34c multicolored .70 .30
3525 A2727 34c multicolored .70 .30
3526 A2728 34c multicolored .70 .30
3527 A2729 34c multicolored .70 .30
   a. Block or strip of 4, #3524-3527 2.80

CARNIVOROUS PLANTS

Venus Flytrap
A2730

Yellow Trumpet
A2731

Cobra
Lily — A2732

English
Sundew — A2733

PHOTOGRAVURE
Serpentine Die Cut 11½
2001, Aug. 23
Self-Adhesive
3528 A2730 34c multicolored .70 .25
3529 A2731 34c multicolored .70 .25
3530 A2732 34c multicolored .70 .25

3531 A2733 34c multicolored .70 .25
   a. Block or strip of 4, #3528-3531 2.80

EID

"Eid
Mubarak" — A2734

Serpentine Die Cut 11¼
2001, Sept. 1
Self-Adhesive
3532 A2734 34c multicolored .70 .25
See Nos. 3674, 4117, 4202, 4351, 4416.

ENRICO FERMI (1901-54), PHYSICIST

A2735

LITHOGRAPHED
2001, Sept. 29 *Perf. 11*
3533 A2735 34c multicolored .70 .25

THAT'S ALL FOLKS!

Porky Pig at
Mailbox — A2736

PHOTOGRAVURE
2001, Oct. 1 *Serpentine Die Cut 11*
Self-Adhesive
3534 Pane of 10 #3534a 7.00
   a. A2736 34c single .70 .25
   b. Pane of 9 #3534a 6.25
   c. Pane of 1 #3534a .70

Die cutting on No. 3534b does not extend through the backing paper.

3535 Pane of 10, #3535c, 9 #3535a 60.00
   a. A2736 34c single 3.00
   b. Pane of 9 #3535a 27.50
   c. Pane of 1, no die cutting 30.00

Die cutting on No. 3535a extends through backing paper.
Nos. 3534b-3534c and 3535b-3535c are separated by a vertical line of microperforations.

CHRISTMAS

Virgin and Child, by
Lorenzo
Costa — A2737

A2738   A2739

A2740   A2741

19th Century Chromolithographs of Santa Claus

Serpentine Die Cut 11½ on 2, 3 or 4 Sides

2001, Oct. 10

Self-Adhesive

Booklet Stamps (#3536, 3537a-3540a, 3537b, 3538b, 3539b, 3540e, 3541-3544)

3536	A2737	34c multicolored	.75	.25
a.		Booklet pane of 20	15.00	

Serpentine Die Cut 10¾x11

Black Inscriptions

3537	A2738	34c multicolored, large date	.70	.25
a.		Small date (from booklet pane)	.90	.25
b.		Large date (from booklet pane)	2.00	.25
3538	A2739	34c multicolored, large date	.70	.25
a.		Small date (from booklet pane)	.90	.25
b.		Large date (from booklet pane)	2.00	.25
3539	A2740	34c multicolored, large date	.70	.25
a.		Small date (from booklet pane)	.90	.25
b.		Large date (from booklet pane)	2.00	.25
3540	A2741	34c multicolored, large date	.70	.25
a.		Small date (from booklet pane)	.90	.25
b.		Block of 4, #3537-3540	2.80	
c.		Block of 4, small date, #3537a-3540a	3.60	
d.		Booklet pane of 20, 5 #3540c + label	18.00	
e.		Large date (from booklet pane)	2.00	.25
f.		Block of 4, large date, #3537b-3539b, 3540e	8.00	
g.		Booklet pane of 20, 5 #3540f + label	40.00	

Nos. 3540d and 3540g are double-sided booklet panes, with 12 stamps on one side and eight stamps plus label on the other side.

Numerals "3" and "4" are distinctly separate on Nos. 3537-3540, and touching or separated by a slight hairline on the booklet pane stamps.

Designs of booklet stamps Nos. 3537a-3539a and 3537b-3539b are slightly taller than Nos. 3537-3539. Nos. 3540a and 3540e measure the same as No. 3540.

Serpentine Die Cut 11 on 2 or 3 Sides

Size: 21x18½mm

Green and Red Inscriptions

3541	A2738	34c multicolored	1.10	.25
3542	A2739	34c multicolored	1.10	.25
3543	A2740	34c multicolored	1.10	.25
3544	A2741	34c multicolored	1.00	.25
a.		Block of 4, #3541-3544	4.00	
b.		Booklet pane of 4, #3541-3544	4.00	
c.		Booklet pane of 6, #3543-3544, 2 #3541-3542	6.00	
d.		Booklet pane of 6, #3541-3542, 2 #3543-3544	6.00	
		Nos. 3536-3544 (9)	7.85	2.25

JAMES MADISON (1751-1836)

Madison and His Home, Montpelier A2742

LITHOGRAPHED & ENGRAVED

2001, Oct. 18   *Perf. 11x11¼*

3545	A2742	34c green & black	.70	.25

THANKSGIVING

Cornucopia A2743

LITHOGRAPHED

Serpentine Die Cut 11¼

2001, Oct. 19

Self-Adhesive

3546	A2743	34c multicolored	.70	.25

Hanukkah Type of 1996

PHOTOGRAVURE

2001, Oct. 21   *Serpentine Die Cut 11*

Self-Adhesive

3547	A2411	34c multicolored	.70	.25

Kwanzaa Type of 1997

2001, Oct. 21

Self-Adhesive

3548	A2458	34c multicolored	.70	.25

UNITED WE STAND

A2744

LITHOGRAPHED

BOOKLET STAMPS

Serpentine Die Cut 11¼ on 2, 3, or 4 Sides

2001, Oct. 24

Self-Adhesive

3549	A2744	34c multicolored	.75	.25
a.		Booklet pane of 20	15.00	

PHOTOGRAVURE

Serpentine Die Cut 10½x10¾ on 2 or 3 Sides

2002, Jan.

Self-Adhesive

3549B	A2744	34c multicolored	.90	.25
c.		Booklet pane of 4	3.60	
d.		Booklet pane of 6	5.40	
e.		Booklet pane of 20	20.00	

No. 3549Be is a double-sided booklet pane, with 12 stamps on one side and eight stamps plus label on the other side.

"First day covers" of No. 3549B are dated Oct. 24, 2001.

COIL STAMPS

Serpentine Die Cut 9¾ Vert.

2001, Oct. 24

Self-Adhesive

3550	A2744	34c multicolored	1.25	.25
3550A	A2744	34c multicolored	1.75	.25

No. 3550 has right angle corners and backing paper as high as the stamp. No. 3550A has rounded corners, the backing paper larger than the stamp, and the stamps are spaced approximately 2mm apart.

Love Letters Type of 2001

LITHOGRAPHED

Serpentine Die Cut 11¼

2001, Nov. 19

Self-Adhesive

3551	A2701	57c multicolored	1.10	.25

WINTER OLYMPICS

Ski Jumping A2745

Snowboarding — A2746

Ice Hockey A2747

Figure Skating A2748

PHOTOGRAVURE

Serpentine Die Cut 11½x10¾

2002, Jan. 8

Self-Adhesive

3552	A2745	34c multicolored	.70	.35
3553	A2746	34c multicolored	.70	.35
3554	A2747	34c multicolored	.70	.35
3555	A2748	34c multicolored	.70	.35
a.		Block or strip of 4, #3552-3555	2.80	
b.		Die cutting inverted, pane of 20	—	
c.		Die cutting omitted, block of 4	825.00	

MENTORING A CHILD

Child and Adult A2749

Serpentine Die Cut 11x10¾

2002, Jan. 10

Self-Adhesive

3556	A2749	34c multicolored	.70	.25

BLACK HERITAGE SERIES

Langston Hughes (1902-67), Writer — A2750

LITHOGRAPHED

Serpentine Die Cut 10¼x10½

2002, Feb. 1

Self-Adhesive

3557	A2750	34c multicolored	.70	.25
a.		Die cutting omitted, pair	850.00	

Beware of pairs/panes with extremely faint die cutting offered as imperf errors.

HAPPY BIRTHDAY

A2751

PHOTOGRAVURE

2002, Feb. 8   *Serpentine Die Cut 11*

Self-Adhesive

3558	A2751	34c multicolored	.75	.25

See Nos. 3695, 4079.

CHINESE NEW YEAR

Year of the Horse A2752

LITHOGRAPHED

Serpentine Die Cut 10½x10¼

2002, Feb. 11

Self-Adhesive

3559	A2752	34c multicolored	.75	.25
a.		Horiz. pair, vert. die cutting omitted	—	

See No. 3895g.

U.S. MILITARY ACADEMY, BICENT.

Military Academy Coat of Arms — A2753

PHOTOGRAVURE

Serpentine Die Cut 10½x11

2002, Mar. 16

Self-Adhesive

3560	A2753	34c multicolored	.75	.25

GREETINGS FROM AMERICA

Alabama A2754

Serpentine Die Cut 10¾

2002, Apr. 4

Self-Adhesive

3561	A2754	34c Alabama	.70	.60
3562	A2755	34c Alaska	.70	.60
3563	A2756	34c Arizona	.70	.60
3564	A2757	34c Arkansas	.70	.60
3565	A2758	34c California	.70	.60
3566	A2759	34c Colorado	.70	.60
3567	A2760	34c Connecticut	.70	.60
3568	A2761	34c Delaware	.70	.60
3569	A2762	34c Florida	.70	.60
3570	A2763	34c Georgia	.70	.60
3571	A2764	34c Hawaii	.70	.60
3572	A2765	34c Idaho	.70	.60
3573	A2766	34c Illinois	.70	.60
3574	A2767	34c Indiana	.70	.60
3575	A2768	34c Iowa	.70	.60
3576	A2769	34c Kansas	.70	.60
3577	A2770	34c Kentucky	.70	.60
3578	A2771	34c Louisiana	.70	.60
3579	A2772	34c Maine	.70	.60
3580	A2773	34c Maryland	.70	.60
3581	A2774	34c Massachusetts	.70	.60
3582	A2775	34c Michigan	.70	.60
3583	A2776	34c Minnesota	.70	.60
3584	A2777	34c Mississippi	.70	.60
3585	A2778	34c Missouri	.70	.60
3586	A2779	34c Montana	.70	.60
3587	A2780	34c Nebraska	.70	.60
3588	A2781	34c Nevada	.70	.60
3589	A2782	34c New Hampshire	.70	.60
3590	A2783	34c New Jersey	.70	.60
3591	A2784	34c New Mexico	.70	.60
3592	A2785	34c New York	.70	.60
3593	A2786	34c North Carolina	.70	.60
3594	A2787	34c North Dakota	.70	.60
3595	A2788	34c Ohio	.70	.60
3596	A2789	34c Oklahoma	.70	.60
3597	A2790	34c Oregon	.70	.60
3598	A2791	34c Pennsylvania	.70	.60
3599	A2792	34c Rhode Island	.70	.60
3600	A2793	34c South Carolina	.70	.60
3601	A2794	34c South Dakota	.70	.60
3602	A2795	34c Tennessee	.70	.60
3603	A2796	34c Texas	.70	.60
3604	A2797	34c Utah	.70	.60
3605	A2798	34c Vermont	.70	.60
3606	A2799	34c Virginia	.70	.60
3607	A2800	34c Washington	.70	.60
3608	A2801	34c West Virginia	.70	.60
3609	A2802	34c Wisconsin	.70	.60
3610	A2803	34c Wyoming	.70	.60
a.		Pane of 50, #3561-3610	35.00	

See Nos. 3696-3745.

LONGLEAF PINE FOREST

LONGLEAF PINE FOREST

A2804

No. 3611 — Wildlife and flowers: a, Bachman's sparrow. b, Northern bobwhite, yellow pitcher plants. c, Fox squirrel, red-bellied woodpecker. d, Brown-headed nuthatch. e, Broadhead skink, yellow pitcher plants, pipeworts. f, Eastern towhee, yellow pitcher plants, Savannah meadow beauties, toothache grass. g, Gray fox, gopher tortoise, horiz. h, Blind click beetle, sweetbay, pine woods treefrog. i, Rosebud orchid, pipeworts, southern toad, yellow pitcher plants. j, Grass-pink orchid, yellow-sided skimmer, pipeworts, yellow pitcher plants, horiz.

Serpentine Die Cut 10½x10¾,
10¾x10½

2002, Apr. 26

Self-Adhesive

3611	A2804	Pane of 10	19.00	
a.-j.		34c Any single	1.90	.50
k.		As No. 3611, die cutting omitted	2,500.	

AMERICAN DESIGN SERIES

Toleware
Coffeepot — A2805

PHOTOGRAVURE
COIL STAMP
Perf. 9¾ Vert.

2002, May 31   **Untagged**

3612	A2805	5c multicolored	.25	.25
a.		Imperf, pair	—	

No. 3612a is valued with disturbed gum. It is also known without gum and is valued only slightly less thus.
See Nos. 3756-3756A.

Star — A2806

LITHOGRAPHED, PHOTOGRAVURE
(No. 3614, 3615)

Serpentine Die Cut 11

2002, June 7   **Untagged**

Self-Adhesive (#3613-3614)

Year at Lower Left

3613	A2806	3c red, blue & black	.25	.25
a.		Die cutting omitted, pair		

Serpentine Die Cut 10

Year at Lower Right
Untagged

3614	A2806	3c red, blue & black	.25	.25

Coil Stamp
Perf. 9¾ Vert.

Year at Lower Left
Untagged

3615	A2806	3c red, blue & black	.25	.25

Washington Type of 2001
LITHOGRAPHED, PHOTOGRAVURE
(#3617)

2002, June 7   **Perf. 11¼**

3616	A2686	23c green	.50	.25

Self-Adhesive
Coil Stamp
Serpentine Die Cut 8½ Vert.

3617	A2686	23c gray green	.45	.25
a.		Die cutting omitted, pair		

Compare No. 3617 ("2002" date at lower left) with No. 3475A ("2001" date at lower left).

Booklet Stamps
Serpentine Die Cut 11¼x11 on 3 Sides

3618	A2686	23c green	.50	.25
a.		Booklet pane of 4	2.00	
b.		Booklet pane of 6	3.00	
c.		Booklet pane of 10	5.00	

Serpentine Die Cut 10½x11 on 3 Sides

3619	A2686	23c green	4.50	1.75
a.		Booklet pane of 4, 2 #3619 at L, 2 #3618 at R	10.00	
b.		Booklet pane of 6, 3 #3619 at L, 3 #3618 at R	15.00	
c.		Booklet pane of 4, 2 #3618 at L, 2 #3619 at R	10.00	
d.		Booklet pane of 6, 3 #3618 at L, 3 #3619 at R	15.00	
e.		Booklet pane of 10, 5 #3619 at L, 5 #3618 at R	27.50	
f.		Booklet pane of 10, 5 #3618 at L, 5 #3619 at R	27.50	
g.		Pair, #3619 at L, #3618 at R	5.00	
h.		Pair, #3618 at L, #3619 at R	5.00	
i.		Nos. 3619c and 3619d, in bklt. of 10 (#BK289A), imperf. vert. btwn. on both panes		

Flag — A2807

LITHOGRAPHED, PHOTOGRAVURE
(#3622, 3624, 3625)

2002, June 7   **Perf. 11¼x11**

3620	A2807	(37c) multicolored	.85	.25

Self-Adhesive
Serpentine Die Cut 11¼x11

3621	A2807	(37c) multicolored	1.00	.25

Coil Stamp
Serpentine Die Cut 10 Vert.

3622	A2807	(37c) multicolored	.75	.25
a.		Die cutting omitted, pair		

Booklet Stamps
Serpentine Die Cut 11¼ on 2, 3 or 4 Sides

3623	A2807	(37c) multicolored	.75	.25
a.		Booklet pane of 20	15.00	

No. 3623 has "USPS" microprinted in the top red stripe of the flag.

Serpentine Die Cut 10½x10¾ on 2 or 3 Sides

3624	A2807	(37c) multicolored	1.00	.25
a.		Booklet pane of 4	4.00	
b.		Booklet pane of 6	6.00	
c.		Booklet pane of 20	20.00	

No. 3624 does not have a microprinted "USPS."

Serpentine Die Cut 8 on 2, 3 or 4 Sides

3625	A2807	(37c) multicolored	.90	.25
a.		Booklet pane of 18	16.50	

Toy Mail Wagon
A2808

Toy Locomotive
A2809

Toy Taxicab
A2810

Toy Fire Pumper
A2811

PHOTOGRAVURE
Serpentine Die Cut 11 on 2, 3 or 4 Sides

2002, June 7

Booklet Stamps
Self-Adhesive

3626	A2808	(37c) multicolored	.75	.25
3627	A2809	(37c) multicolored	.75	.25
3628	A2810	(37c) multicolored	.75	.25
3629	A2811	(37c) multicolored	.75	.25
a.		Block of 4, #3626-3629	3.00	
b.		Booklet pane of 4, #3626-3629	3.00	
c.		Booklet pane of 6, #3627, 3629, 2 each #3626, 3628	4.50	
d.		Booklet pane of 6, #3626, 3628, 2 each #3627, 3629	4.50	
e.		Booklet pane of 20, 5 each #3626-3629	15.00	

Flag — A2812

LITHOGRAPHED, PHOTOGRAVURE
(#3631-3633, 3634, 3636, 3636D)

2002-05   **Perf. 11¼**

3629F	A2812	37c multi	.90	.25
g.		Imperf, pair	100.00	

No. 3629F has microprinted "USA" in top red stripe of flag.

Serpentine Die Cut 11¼x11
Self-Adhesive (#3630, 3632-3637)

3630	A2812	37c multi	.90	.25

No. 3630 has microprinted "USA" in top red stripe of flag.

COIL STAMPS
Perf. 9¾ Vert.

3631	A2812	37c multi	.75	.25

Serpentine Die Cut 9¾ Vert.

3632	A2812	37c multi	.75	.25
b.		Die cutting omitted, pair	55.00	55.00

Serpentine Die Cut 10¼ Vert.

3632A	A2812	37c multi	.75	.25
f.		Die cutting omitted, pair	250.00	
g.		Vert. pair, horiz. die-cut slits omitted	750.00	

No. 3632A lacks points of stars at margin at left top, and was printed in "logs" of adjacent coil rolls that are connected at the top or bottom, wherein each roll could be separated from an adjacent roll as needed.
No. 3632 has "2002" date at left bottom. No. 3632A has "2003" date at left bottom.

Serpentine Die Cut 11¾ Vert.

3632C	A2812	37c multi	1.50	.25

No. 3632C is the only 37c Flag coil stamp with a "2004" date at left bottom.

Serpentine Die Cut 8½ Vert.

3633	A2812	37c multi	.75	.25
3633A	A2812	37c multi	2.25	.25

No. 3633A has right angle corners and backing paper as high as the stamp, and is dated "2003." No. 3633 is dated "2002," has rounded corners, the backing paper larger than the stamp, and the stamps are spaced approximately 2mm apart.

Serpentine Die Cut 9½ Vert.

3633B	A2812	37c multi	9.00	.25

No. 3633B has microprinted "USA" in top red stripe of flag, and has "2005" date at bottom left.

Booklet Stamps
Serpentine Die Cut 11.1 on 3 Sides (#3634)

3634	A2812	37c multi, large "2002" year date	.75	.25
a.		Booklet pane of 10	7.50	
b.		Small "2003" date, die cut 11	.75	.25
c.		Booklet pane, 4 #3634b	3.00	
d.		Booklet pane 6 #3634b	4.50	
e.		As #3634, die cut 11.3	1.00	.25
f.		As "e," booklet pane of 10	10.00	

Serpentine Die Cut 11.3 on 2, 3 or 4 Sides

3635	A2812	37c multi	.75	.25
a.		Booklet pane of 20	15.00	
b.		Black omitted	3,000.	

No. 3635 has "USPS" microprinted in the top red flag stripe and has a small "2002" year date.

Serpentine Die Cut 10½x10¾ on 2 or 3 Sides

3636	A2812	37c multi	.75	.25
a.		Booklet pane of 4	3.00	
b.		Booklet pane of 6	4.50	
c.		Booklet pane of 20	15.00	
f.		As "c," 11 stamps and part of 12th stamp on reverse printed on backing liner, the 8 stamps on front side die cutting omitted	—	

No. 3636c is a double-sided booklet pane, with 12 stamps on one side and eight stamps plus label on the other side.

Serpentine Die Cut 11¼x11 on 2 or 3 Sides

3636D	A2812	37c multi	1.25	.25
e.		Booklet pane of 20	25.00	

No. 3636D lacks points of stars at margin at UL. No. 3636D is the only 37c Flag booklet stamp with a "2004" date at left bottom. No. 3636De is a double-sided booklet pane with 12 stamps on one side and eight stamps plus label on the other side.

Serpentine Die Cut 8 on 2, 3 or 4 Sides

3637	A2812	37c multi	.75	.25
a.		Booklet pane of 18	13.50	

Issued: Nos. 3630-3632, 3633, 3634, 3635-3636, 6/7; No. 3637, 2/4/03; No. 3633A, Apr. 2003; No. 3632A, 8/7/03; No. 3634b, 10/23/03; No. 3629F, 11/24/03; No. 3636D, July 2004; No. 3632C, 2004; No. 3633B, 6/7/05.

Toy Locomotive
A2813

Toy Mail Wagon
A2814

Toy Fire Pumper
A2815

Toy Taxicab
A2816

PHOTOGRAVURE
Serpentine Die Cut 8½ Horiz.

2002-03

Self-Adhesive
Coil Stamps

3638	A2813	37c multi	1.50	.25
3639	A2814	37c multi	1.50	.25
3640	A2815	37c multi	1.50	.25
3641	A2816	37c multi	1.50	.25
a.		Strip of 4, #3638-3641	6.00	

Serpentine Die Cut 11 on 2, 3 or 4 Sides

Booklet Stamps

3642	A2814	37c multi, "2002" year date	.75	.25
a.		Serpentine die cut 11x11¼ on 2 or 3 sides, dated "2003"	.75	.25
3643	A2813	37c multi, "2002" year date	.75	.25
a.		Serpentine die cut 11x11¼ on 2 or 3 sides, dated "2003"	.75	.25
3644	A2816	37c multi, "2002" year date	.75	.25
a.		Serpentine die cut 11x11¼ on 2 or 3 sides, dated "2003"	.75	.25
3645	A2815	37c multi, "2002" year date	.75	.25
a.		Block of 4, #3642-3645	3.00	
b.		Booklet pane of 4, #3642-3645	3.00	
c.		Booklet pane of 6, #3643, 3645, 2 each #3642, 3644	4.50	
d.		Booklet pane of 6, #3642, 3644, 2 each #3643, 3645	4.50	
e.		Booklet pane of 20, 5 each #3642-3645	15.00	
f.		Serpentine die cut 11x11¼ on 2 or 3 sides, dated "2003"	.75	.25
g.		Block of 4, #3642a, 3643a, 3644a, 3645f	3.00	
h.		Booklet pane of 20, 5 #3645g	15.00	

No. 3645h is a double-sided booklet with 12 stamps on one side and 8 stamps plus label (booklet cover) on the other side. Nos. 3642a, 3643a, 3644a and 3645f have slightly narrower designs than Nos. 3642-3645.

Issued: Nos. 3638-3645, 7/26; Nos. 3642a, 3643a, 3644a, 3645f, 9/3/03.

Coverlet
Eagle — A2817

LITHOGRAPHED
Serpentine Die Cut 11x11¼
2002, July 12
Self-Adhesive

3646 A2817 60c multicolored   1.25   .25

Jefferson
Memorial
A2818

Capitol
Dome — A2819

*Serpentine Die Cut 11¼ (#3647,
3648), 11x10¾ (#3647A)*
2002-03   **Tagged**
Self-Adhesive

3647   A2818 $3.85 multi   7.50   2.00
3647A A2818 $3.85 multi   8.50   2.00
3648   A2819 $13.65 multi   27.50 10.00

No. 3647 is dated 2002, and No. 3647A is
dated 2003.

MASTERS OF AMERICAN PHOTOGRAPHY

A2820

No. 3649: a, Portrait of Daniel Webster, by
Albert Sands Southworth and Josiah Johnson
Hawes. b, Gen. Ulysses S. Grant and Officers,
by Timothy H. O'Sullivan. c, "Cape Horn,
Columbia River," by Carleton E. Watkins. d,
"Blessed Art Thou Among Women," by Ger-
trude Käsebier. e, "Looking for Lost Luggage,
Ellis Island," by Lewis W. Hine. f, "The Octo-
pus," by Alvin Langdon Coburn. g, "Lotus,
Mount Kisco, New York," by Edward Steichen.
h, "Hands and Thimble," by Alfred Stieglitz. i,
"Rayograph," by Man Ray. j, "Two Shells," by
Edward Weston. k, "My Corsage," by James
VanDerZee. l, "Ditched, Stalled, and Stranded,
San Joaquin Valley, California," by Dorothea
Lange. m, "Washroom and Dining Area of
Floyd Burroughs' Home, Hale County, Ala-
bama," by Walker Evans. n, "Frontline Soldier
with Canteen, Saipan," by W. Eugene Smith.
o, "Steeple," by Paul Strand. p, "Sand Dunes,
Sunrise," by Ansel Adams. q, "Age and Its
Symbols," by Imogen Cunningham. r, New
York cityscape, by André Kertész. s, Photo-
graph of pedestrians, by Garry Winogrand. t,
"Bristol, Vermont," by Minor White.

PHOTOGRAVURE
Serpentine Die Cut 10½x10¾
2002, June 13
Self-Adhesive

3649 A2820 Pane of 20   22.50
  a.-t.   37c Any single   1.00   .50
  u.   As No. 3649, die cutting
          omitted   —

AMERICAN TREASURES SERIES

Scarlet and
Louisiana Tanagers,
by John James
Audubon — A2821

Serpentine Die Cut 10¾
2002, June 27
Self-Adhesive

3650 A2821 37c multicolored   1.00   .25

HARRY HOUDINI (1874-1926), MAGICIAN

A2822

LITHOGRAPHED
Serpentine Die Cut 11¼
2002, July 3
Self-Adhesive

3651 A2822 37c multicolored   .75   .25

ANDY WARHOL (1928-87), ARTIST

Self-Portrait
A2823

PHOTOGRAVURE
Serpentine Die Cut 10½x10¾
2002, Aug. 9
Self-Adhesive

3652 A2823 37c multicolored   .75   .25

TEDDY BEARS, CENTENNIAL

Bruin Bear, c.
1907 — A2824

"Stick" Bear,
1920s — A2825

Gund Bear, c.
1948 — A2826

Ideal Bear, c.
1905 — A2827

Serpentine Die Cut 10½
2002, Aug. 15
Self-Adhesive

3653 A2824 37c multicolored   1.00   .30
3654 A2825 37c multicolored   1.00   .30
3655 A2826 37c multicolored   1.00   .30
3656 A2827 37c multicolored   1.00   .30
  a.   Block or vert. strip of 4,
        #3653-3656   4.00

LOVE

A2828   A2829

**LITHOGRAPHED (#3657),
PHOTOGRAVURE**
*Serpentine Die Cut 11 on 2, 3 or 4
Sides*
2002, Aug. 16
Booklet Stamp (#3657)
Self-Adhesive

3657 A2828 37c multicolored   .75   .25
  a.   Booklet pane of 20   15.00
  b.   As "a," silver ("Love 37
        USA") missing on top five
        stamps (CM)   750.00
  c.   Strip of 5, silver ("Love 37
        USA") omitted on one
        stamp   1,000.

Serpentine Die Cut 11

3658 A2829 60c multicolored   1.25   .25

Beware of examples of No. 3658 with gold
ink fraudulently removed.

LITERARY ARTS

Ogden
Nash (1902-
71), Poet
A2830

PHOTOGRAVURE
Serpentine Die Cut 11
2002, Aug. 19
Self-Adhesive

3659 A2830 37c multicolored   .75   .25

DUKE KAHANAMOKU (1890-1968), "FATHER OF SURFING" AND OLYMPIC SWIMMER

Kahanamoku
and Surfers at
Waikiki
Beach — A2831

PHOTOGRAVURE
Serpentine Die Cut 11½x11¾
2002, Aug. 24
Self-Adhesive

3660 A2831 37c multicolored   .75   .25

AMERICAN BATS

Red Bat
A2832

Leaf-nosed
Bat
A2833

Pallid Bat
A2834

Spotted Bat
A2835

Serpentine Die Cut 10¾
2002, Sept. 13
Self-Adhesive

3661 A2832 37c multicolored   .75   .30
3662 A2833 37c multicolored   .75   .30
3663 A2834 37c multicolored   .75   .30
3664 A2835 37c multicolored   .75   .30
  a.   Block or horiz. strip of 4,
        #3661-3664   3.00

WOMEN IN JOURNALISM

Nellie Bly (1864-1922) — A2836

Ida M. Tarbell (1857-1944) — A2837

Ethel L.
Payne
(1911-91)
A2838

Marguerite
Higgins
(1920-66)
A2839

Serpentine Die Cut 11x10½
2002, Sept. 14
Self-Adhesive

3665 A2836 37c multicolored   1.25   .35
3666 A2837 37c multicolored   1.25   .35
3667 A2838 37c multicolored   1.25   .35
3668 A2839 37c multicolored   1.25   .35
  a.   Block or horiz. strip of 4,
        #3665-3668   5.00

IRVING BERLIN (1888-1989), COMPOSER

Berlin and Score of "God Bless America" — A2840

Serpentine Die Cut 11
2002, Sept. 15
Self-Adhesive

3669 A2840 37c multicolored .75 .25

NEUTER AND SPAY

Kitten A2841

Puppy A2842

Serpentine Die Cut 10¾x10½
2002, Sept. 20
Self-Adhesive

3670	A2841	37c multicolored	1.00	.25
3671	A2842	37c multicolored	1.00	.25
a.		Horiz. or vert. pair, #3670-3671		2.00

Hanukkah Type of 1996
2002, Oct. 10 Serpentine Die Cut 11
Self-Adhesive

3672 A2411 37c multicolored .75 .25

Kwanzaa Type of 1997
2002, Oct. 10 Serpentine Die Cut 11
Self-Adhesive

3673 A2458 37c multicolored .75 .25

Eid Type of 2001
2002, Oct. 10 Serpentine Die Cut 11
Self-Adhesive

3674 A2734 37c multicolored .75 .25

CHRISTMAS

Madonna and Child, by Jan Gossaert — A2843

LITHOGRAPHED
Serpentine Die Cut 11x11¼ on 2, 3 or 4 Sides
2002, Oct. 10
Self-Adhesive
Booklet Stamp
Design size: 19x27mm

| 3675 | A2843 | 37c multicolored | .75 | .25 |
| a. | | Booklet pane of 20 | 15.00 | |

Compare to No. 3820, which measures 19½x28mm

CHRISTMAS

Snowman with Red and Green Plaid Scarf — A2844

Snowman with Blue Plaid Scarf — A2845

Snowman with Pipe — A2846

Snowman with Top Hat — A2847

Snowman with Blue Plaid Scarf — A2848

Snowman with Pipe — A2849

Snowman with Top Hat — A2850

Snowman with Red and Green Plaid Scarf — A2851

PHOTOGRAVURE
Serpentine Die Cut 11
2002, Oct. 28 **Tagged**
Self-Adhesive

3676	A2844	37c multicolored	.90	.25
3677	A2845	37c multicolored	.90	.25
3678	A2846	37c multicolored	.90	.25
3679	A2847	37c multicolored	.90	.25
a.		Block or vert. strip of 4, #3676-3679	3.75	

COIL STAMPS
Serpentine Die Cut 8½ Vert.

3680	A2848	37c multicolored	3.25	.25
3681	A2849	37c multicolored	3.25	.25
3682	A2850	37c multicolored	3.25	.25
3683	A2851	37c multicolored	3.25	.25
a.		Strip of 4, #3680-3683	13.00	

BOOKLET STAMPS
Serpentine Die Cut 10¾x11 on 2 or 3 Sides

3684	A2844	37c multicolored	1.25	.25
3685	A2845	37c multicolored	1.25	.25
3686	A2846	37c multicolored	1.25	.25
3687	A2847	37c multicolored	1.25	.25
a.		Block of 4, #3684-3687	5.00	
b.		Booklet pane of 20, 5 #3687a + label	25.00	

No. 3687b is a double-sided booklet pane with 12 stamps on one side and eight stamps plus label on the other side.
Colors of Nos. 3684-3687 are deeper and designs are slightly smaller than those found on Nos. 3676-3679.

Serpentine Die Cut 11 on 2 or 3 Sides

3688	A2851	37c multicolored	1.15	.25
3689	A2848	37c multicolored	1.15	.25
3690	A2849	37c multicolored	1.15	.25
3691	A2850	37c multicolored	1.15	.25
a.		Block of 4, #3688-3691	4.60	
b.		Booklet pane of 4, #3688-3691	4.60	
c.		Booklet pane of 6, #3690-3691, 2 each #3688-3689	7.00	
d.		Booklet pane of 6, #3688-3689, 2 each #3690-3691	7.00	
		Nos. 3676-3691 (16)	26.20	4.00

LEGENDS OF HOLLYWOOD

Cary Grant (1904-86), Actor — A2852

Serpentine Die Cut 10¾
2002, Oct. 15
Self-Adhesive

3692 A2852 37c multicolored 1.25 .25

Sea Coast — A2853

PHOTOGRAVURE
COIL STAMP
Serpentine Die Cut 8½ Vert.
2002, Oct. 21
Self-Adhesive

3693 A2853 (5c) multicolored .25 .25

See Nos. 3775, 3785, 3864, 3874, 3875, 4348.

HAWAIIAN MISSIONARY STAMPS

A2854

No. 3694: a, 2c stamp of 1851 (Hawaii Scott 1). b, 5c stamp of 1851 (Hawaii Scott 2) c, 13c stamp of 1851 (Hawaii Scott 3). d, 13c stamp of 1852 (Hawaii Scott 4).

LITHOGRAPHED

2002, Oct. 24		**Tagged**	**Perf. 11**	
3694	A2854	Pane of 4	5.00	2.50
a.-d.		37c Any single	1.25	.50

Happy Birthday Type of 2002
PHOTOGRAVURE
2002, Oct. 25 Serpentine Die Cut 11
Self-Adhesive

3695 A2751 37c multicolored .75 .25

Greetings From America Type of 2002
Serpentine Die Cut 10¾
2002, Oct. 25
Self-Adhesive

3696	A2754	37c Alabama	.75	.60
3697	A2755	37c Alaska	.75	.60
3698	A2756	37c Arizona	.75	.60
3699	A2757	37c Arkansas	.75	.60
3700	A2758	37c California	.75	.60
3701	A2759	37c Colorado	.75	.60
3702	A2760	37c Connecticut	.75	.60
3703	A2761	37c Delaware	.75	.60
3704	A2762	37c Florida	.75	.60
3705	A2763	37c Georgia	.75	.60
3706	A2764	37c Hawaii	.75	.60
3707	A2765	37c Idaho	.75	.60
3708	A2766	37c Illinois	.75	.60
3709	A2767	37c Indiana	.75	.60
3710	A2768	37c Iowa	.75	.60
3711	A2769	37c Kansas	.75	.60
3712	A2770	37c Kentucky	.75	.60
3713	A2771	37c Louisiana	.75	.60
3714	A2772	37c Maine	.75	.60
3715	A2773	37c Maryland	.75	.60
3716	A2774	37c Massachusetts	.75	.60
3717	A2775	37c Michigan	.75	.60
3718	A2776	37c Minnesota	.75	.60
3719	A2777	37c Mississippi	.75	.60
3720	A2778	37c Missouri	.75	.60
3721	A2779	37c Montana	.75	.60
3722	A2780	37c Nebraska	.75	.60
3723	A2781	37c Nevada	.75	.60
3724	A2782	37c New Hampshire	.75	.60
3725	A2783	37c New Jersey	.75	.60
3726	A2784	37c New Mexico	.75	.60
3727	A2785	37c New York	.75	.60
3728	A2786	37c North Carolina	.75	.60
3729	A2787	37c North Dakota	.75	.60
3730	A2788	37c Ohio	.75	.60
3731	A2789	37c Oklahoma	.75	.60
3732	A2790	37c Oregon	.75	.60
3733	A2791	37c Pennsylvania	.75	.60
3734	A2792	37c Rhode Island	.75	.60
3735	A2793	37c South Carolina	.75	.60
3736	A2794	37c South Dakota	.75	.60
3737	A2795	37c Tennessee	.75	.60
3738	A2796	37c Texas	.75	.60
3739	A2797	37c Utah	.75	.60
3740	A2798	37c Vermont	.75	.60
3741	A2799	37c Virginia	.75	.60
3742	A2800	37c Washington	.75	.60
3743	A2801	37c West Virginia	.75	.60
3744	A2802	37c Wisconsin	.75	.60
3745	A2803	37c Wyoming	.75	.60
a.		Pane of 50, #3696-3745	37.50	

BLACK HERITAGE SERIES

Thurgood Marshall (1908-93), Supreme Court Justice — A2855

LITHOGRAPHED
Serpentine Die Cut 11½
2003, Jan. 7
Self-Adhesive

3746 A2855 37c black & gray .75 .25

CHINESE NEW YEAR

Year of the Ram A2856

Serpentine Die Cut 11½
2003, Jan. 15
Self-Adhesive

3747 A2856 37c multicolored .75 .25

See No. 3895h.

LITERARY ARTS

Zora Neale Hurston (1891-1960), Writer — A2857

PHOTOGRAVURE
Serpentine Die Cut 10¾
2003, Jan. 24
Self-Adhesive

3748 A2857 37c multicolored .90 .25

AMERICAN DESIGN SERIES

Toleware Coffeepot Type of 2002 and

Navajo Necklace A2858

Chippendale Chair A2859

American Clock
A2860

Tiffany Lamp
A2866

Silver Coffeepot — A2868

LITHOGRAPHED, PHOTOGRAVURE (#3750, 3751, 3756, 3758, 3758A, 3758B, 3759, 3761, 3761A, 3762)
Self-Adhesive (#3749-3757)

2003-11 *Serpentine Die Cut 11¼x11*

3749	A2866	1c multi	.25	.25
3749A	A2866	1c multi	.25	.25

No. 3749A has "USPS" microprinted on a white field high on the lamp stand, just below the shade and is dated "2008." No. 3749 has "USPS" microprinted lower on the lamp stand and not on a white field and is dated "2007."

Serpentine Die Cut 11

3750	A2858	2c multi	.25	.25

A reprinting of No. 3750 shows the borders in a much brighter deep turquoise blue shade.

Serpentine Die Cut 11¼x11½

3751	A2858	2c multi	.30	.25

Serpentine Die Cut 11¼x11
With "USPS" Microprinting

3752	A2858	2c multi	.25	.25

Serpentine Die Cut 11¼x10¾

3753	A2858	2c multi	.25	.25

Serpentine Die Cut 11¼x11

3754	A2868	3c multi	.25	.25

Microprinted "USPS" on No. 3752 is found on top silver appendage next to and below the middle turquoise stone on the right side of the necklace. Microprinting on No. 3753 is found on the top silver appendage next to and below the lower turquoise stone on the left side of the necklace. Nos. 3751 and 3752 are dated "2006." No. 3753 is dated "2007."

Serpentine Die Cut 10¾x10¼

3755	A2859	4c multi	.25	.25

Serpentine Die Cut 11¼x11¾

3756	A2805	5c multi	.25	.25

Serpentine Die Cut 11¼x10¾

3756A	A2805	5c multi	.25	.25
b.		Die cutting omitted, pair		

No. 3756A has microprinting on the lower part of the coffeepot handle and is dated "2007." No. 3756 has no microprinting and is dated "2004." Existence of No. 3756A was reported in Aug. 2008.

No. 3756A is known printed with non-reactive cream-colored background ink and also with luminescent cream-colored ink that glows orange under both shortwave and longwave ultraviolet light.

3757	A2860	10c multi	.25	.25
a.		Die cutting omitted, pair		—

COIL STAMPS
Perf. 9¾ Vert.

3758	A2866	1c multi	.25	.25
3758A	A2866	1c multi	.25	.25
3758B	A2858	2c multi	.25	.25

No. 3758A has microprinted "USPS" on lamp stand just below the lampshade and is dated "2008." No. 3758 lacks microprinting and is dated "2003."

3759	A2868	3c multi	.25	.25
3761	A2859	4c multi, dated "2007" at LL	.25	.25
3761A	A2859	4c multi, dated "2013" at UL	.25	.25

On plate number singles, the plate number is at the lower right on No. 3761 and centered at bottom on No. 3761A.

3762	A2860	10c multi	.25	.25
3763	A2860	10c multi	.25	.25

No. 3763 is dated "2008," has a microprinted "USPS" as the middle "I" in "VIII," and has a network of beige dots on clock face. No. 3762 is dated "2006," lacks microprinting, and has network of gray dots on clock face.

Issued: No. 3757, 1/24; No. 3758, 3/1; No. 3755, 3/5/04; No. 3756, 6/25/04; No. 3750, 8/20/04; No. 3759, 9/16/05; Nos. 3751-3752, 12/8/05; No. 3762, 8/4/06; Nos. 3749, 3754,

---

3/16/07; No. 3753, 5/12/07; No. 3761, 7/19/07; No. 3749A, 3/7/08; No. 3758A, 6/7/08; No. 3758B, 2/12/11; No. 3763, 7/15/08; No. 3756A, Aug. 2008.

This is an ongoing set. Numbers may change.
See No. 3612.

AMERICAN CULTURE SERIES

Wisdom, Rockefeller Center, New York City — A2875

LITHOGRAPHED
Serpentine Die Cut 11¼x11
2003, Feb. 28
Self-Adhesive

3766	A2875	$1 multicolored	2.00	.40
a.		Dated "2008"	2.00	.40

New York Public Library Lion Type of 2000
PHOTOGRAVURE
COIL STAMP
Perf. 9¾ Vert.
2003, Feb. 4   Untagged

3769	A2677	(10c) multicolored	.25	.25

Atlas Statue Type of 2001
PHOTOGRAVURE
Serpentine Die Cut 11 Vert.
2003, Oct.   Untagged
Coil Stamp
Self-Adhesive

3770	A2722	(10c) multicolored	.25	.25

No. 3770 is dated 2003.

SPECIAL OLYMPICS

Athlete with Medal — A2879

Serpentine Die Cut 11
2003, Feb. 13
Self-Adhesive

3771	A2879	80c multicolored	1.60	.35

AMERICAN FILMMAKING: BEHIND THE SCENES

A2880

No. 3772: a, Screenwriting (segment of script from *Gone With the Wind*). b, Directing (John Cassavetes). c, Costume design (Edith Head). d, Music (Max Steiner working on score). e, Makeup (Jack Pierce working on Boris Karloff's makeup for *Frankenstein*). f, Art direction (Perry Ferguson working on sketch for *Citizen Kane*). g, Cinematography (Paul Hill, assistant cameraman for *Nagana*). h, Film editing (J. Watson Webb editing *The Razor's Edge*). i, Special effects (Mark Siegel working on model for *E.T. The Extra-Terrestrial*). j, Sound (Gary Summers works on control panel).

Serpentine Die Cut 11 Horiz.
2003, Feb. 25
Self-Adhesive

3772	A2880	Pane of 10	12.00	
a.-j.		37c Any single	1.20	.50

OHIO STATEHOOD BICENTENNIAL

Aerial View of Farm Near Marietta — A2881

LITHOGRAPHED
Serpentine Die Cut 11¾x11½
2003, Mar. 1
Self-Adhesive

3773	A2881	37c multicolored	.75	.25

PELICAN ISLAND NATIONAL WILDLIFE REFUGE, CENT.

Brown Pelican — A2882

Serpentine Die Cut 12x11½
2003, Mar. 14
Self-Adhesive

3774	A2882	37c multicolored	.75	.25

Sea Coast Type of 2002
PHOTOGRAVURE
COIL STAMP
Perf. 9¾ Vert.
2003, Mar. 19   Untagged

3775	A2853	(5c) multicolored	.25	.25

See No. 3864. No. 3775 has "2003" year date in blue, dots that run together in surf area, and a distinct small orange cloud. No. 3864 has "2004" year date in black, rows of distinctly separated dots in surf area, and the small orange cloud is indistinct.

OLD GLORY

Uncle Sam on Bicycle with Liberty Flag, 20th Cent. — A2883

1888 Presidential Campaign Badge — A2884

1893 Silk Bookmark A2885

Modern Hand Fan A2886

Carving of Woman with Flag and Sword, 19th Cent. — A2887

LITHOGRAPHED BOOKLET STAMPS
Serpentine Die Cut 10x9¾
2003, Apr. 3
Self-Adhesive

3776	A2883	37c multicolored	.75	.50
3777	A2884	37c multicolored	.75	.50
3778	A2885	37c multicolored	.75	.50
3779	A2886	37c multicolored	.75	.50
3780	A2887	37c multicolored	.75	.50
a.		Horiz. strip of 5, #3776-3780	3.75	
b.		Booklet pane, 2 #3780a	7.50	

No. 3780b was issued with two types of backing.

CESAR E. CHAVEZ (1927-93), LABOR ORGANIZER

A2888

Serpentine Die Cut 11¾x11½
2003, Apr. 23
Self-Adhesive

3781	A2888	37c multicolored	.75	.25

LOUISIANA PURCHASE, BICENTENNIAL

English Translation of Treaty, Map of U.S., Treaty Signers — A2889

PHOTOGRAVURE
Serpentine Die Cut 10¾
2003, Apr. 30
Self-Adhesive

3782	A2889	37c multicolored	.95	.40

FIRST FLIGHT OF WRIGHT BROTHERS, CENT.

Orville Wright Piloting 1903 Wright Flyer A2890

2003, May 22 *Serpentine Die Cut 11*
Self-Adhesive

3783		Pane of 10	9.00	
a.		A2890 37c single	.90	.40
b.		Pane of 9 #3783a	8.00	
c.		Pane of 1 #3783a	.90	

PURPLE HEART

A2891

LITHOGRAPHED
2003 *Serpentine Die Cut 11¼x10¾*
Self-Adhesive

3784	A2891	37c multi	.75	.25
b.		Printed on back of backing paper	—	
d.		Die cutting omitted, pair	—	

Serpentine Die Cut 10¾x10¼

3784A	A2891	37c multi	.75	.25
e.		Die cutting omitted, pair	150.00	

See Nos. 4032, 4164, 4263-4264, 4390.

Sea Coast Type of 2002
COIL STAMP
PHOTOGRAVURE
Serpentine Die Cut 9½x10
2003, June   **Untagged**
Self-Adhesive

3785	A2853	(5c) multicolored	.25	.25
a.		Serp. die cut 9¼x10	.25	.25

On No. 3785, the stamps are spaced on backing paper that is taller than the stamps. One printing of No. 3785 has more of a scarlet shade in the sky than do other examples of Nos. 3785 and 3785a. Nos. 3785 and 3785a have black "2003" year date.

LEGENDS OF HOLLYWOOD

Audrey Hepburn
(1929-93),
Actress — A2892

Serpentine Die Cut 10¾
2003, June 11
Self-Adhesive

3786	A2892	37c multicolored	1.25	1.00

SOUTHEASTERN LIGHTHOUSES

Old Cape Henry, Virginia A2893   Cape Lookout, North Carolina A2894

Morris Island, South Carolina A2895   Tybee Island, Georgia A2896

Hillsboro Inlet, Florida — A2897

Serpentine Die Cut 10¾
2003, June 13
Self-Adhesive

3787	A2893	37c multicolored	1.10	.30
3788	A2894	37c multicolored	1.10	.30
a.		Bottom of "USA" even with top of upper half-diamond of lighthouse (pos. 2)	4.00	2.50
3789	A2895	37c multicolored	1.10	.30
3790	A2896	37c multicolored	1.10	.30

3791	A2897	37c multicolored	1.10	.30
a.		Strip of 5, #3787-3791	5.50	
b.		Strip of 5, #3787, 3788a, 3789-3791	9.50	

Eagle in Gold on Colored Background A2898   Colored Eagle on Gold Background A2899

COIL STAMPS
Dated "2003"

Serpentine Die Cut 11¾ Vert.
2003, June 26   **Untagged**
Self-Adhesive

3792	A2898	(25c) gray & gold	.50	.25
3793	A2899	(25c) gold & red	.50	.25
3794	A2898	(25c) dull blue & gold	.50	.25
3795	A2899	(25c) gold & Prussian blue	.50	.25
3796	A2898	(25c) green & gold	.50	.25
3797	A2899	(25c) gold & gray	.50	.25
3798	A2898	(25c) Prussian blue & gold	.50	.25
3799	A2899	(25c) gold & dull blue	.50	.25
3800	A2898	(25c) red & gold	.50	.25
3801	A2899	(25c) gold & green	.50	.25
b.		Strip of 10, #3792-3801	5.00	

Dated "2005"

Serpentine Die Cut 11½ Vert.
2005, Aug. 5   **Untagged**

3792d	A2898	(25c) gray & gold	.50	.25
3793d	A2899	(25c) gold & red	.50	.25
3794d	A2898	(25c) dull blue & gold	.50	.25
3795d	A2899	(25c) gold & Prussian blue	.50	.25
3796d	A2898	(25c) green & gold	.50	.25
3797d	A2899	(25c) gold & gray	.50	.25
3798d	A2898	(25c) Prussian blue & gold	.50	.25
3799d	A2899	(25c) gold & dull blue	.50	.25
3800d	A2898	(25c) red & gold	.50	.25
3801d	A2899	(25c) gold & green	.50	.25
e.		Strip of 10, #3792d-3801d	5.00	

See Nos. 3844-3853.

ARCTIC TUNDRA

A2900

No. 3802 — Wildlife and vegetation: a, Gyrfalcon. b, Gray wolf, vert. c, Common raven, vert. d, Musk oxen and caribou, vert. e, Grizzly bears, caribou. f, Caribou, willow ptarmigans. g, Arctic ground squirrel, vert. h, Willow ptarmigan, bearberry. i, Arctic grayling. j, Singing vole, thin-legged wolf spider, lingonberry, Labrador tea.

LITHOGRAPHED
Serpentine Die Cut 10¾x10½, 10½x10¾
2003, July 2
Self-Adhesive

3802	A2900	Pane of 10	8.50	
a.-j.		37c Any single	.85	.50

KOREAN WAR VETERANS MEMORIAL

Memorial in Snow A2901

Serpentine Die Cut 11½x11¾
2003, July 27
Self-Adhesive

3803	A2901	37c multicolored	.75	.25

MARY CASSATT PAINTINGS

Young Mother, 1888 — A2902   Children Playing on the Beach, 1884 — A2903

On a Balcony, 1878-79 A2904   Child in a Straw Hat, c. 1886 A2905

PHOTOGRAVURE
Serpentine Die Cut 10¾ on 2 or 3 Sides
2003, Aug. 7
Self-Adhesive
Booklet Stamps

3804	A2902	37c multicolored	.75	.30
3805	A2903	37c multicolored	.75	.30
3806	A2904	37c multicolored	.75	.30
3807	A2905	37c multicolored	.75	.30
a.		Block of 4, #3804-3807	3.00	
b.		Booklet pane of 20, 5 #3807a	15.00	

No. 3807b is a double-sided booklet with 12 stamps on one side and 8 stamps plus label (booklet cover) on the other side.

EARLY FOOTBALL HEROES

Bronko Nagurski (1908-90) A2906

Ernie Nevers (1903-76) A2907

Walter Camp (1859-1925) A2908

Red Grange (1903-91) A2909

Serpentine Die Cut 11½x11¾
2003, Aug. 8
Self-Adhesive

3808	A2906	37c multicolored	.75	.35
3809	A2907	37c multicolored	.75	.35
3810	A2908	37c multicolored	.75	.35
3811	A2909	37c multicolored	.75	.35
a.		Block of 4, #3808-3811	3.00	

ROY ACUFF

Acuff (1903-92), Country Music Artist, and Fiddle — A2910

Serpentine Die Cut 11
2003, Sept. 13
Self-Adhesive

3812	A2910	37c multicolored	.75	.25

DISTRICT OF COLUMBIA

Map, National Mall, Row Houses and Cherry Blossoms — A2911

2003, Sept. 23
Self-Adhesive

3813	A2911	37c multicolored	.80	.25

REPTILES AND AMPHIBIANS

Scarlet Kingsnake A2912

Blue-Spotted Salamander — A2913

Reticulate Collared Lizard A2914

Ornate Chorus Frog A2915

Ornate Box Turtle A2916

2003, Oct. 7
Self-Adhesive

3814	A2912	37c multicolored	.80	.40
3815	A2913	37c multicolored	.80	.40
3816	A2914	37c multicolored	.80	.40
3817	A2915	37c multicolored	.80	.40
3818	A2916	37c multicolored	.80	.40
a.		Vert. strip of 5, #3814-3818	4.00	

Washington Type of 2002
PHOTOGRAVURE

2003, Oct. *Serpentine Die Cut 11*
Self-Adhesive

3819	A2686	23c gray green	1.00	.25

Christmas Type of 2002
LITHOGRAPHED
Serpentine Die Cut 11¼ on 2 or 3 Sides

2003, Oct. 23
Self-Adhesive
Booklet Stamp
Size: 19½x28mm

3820	A2843	37c multicolored	.75	.25
a.		Booklet pane of 20	15.00	
b.		Die cutting omitted, pair		

No. 3820a is a double-sided booklet with 12 stamps on one side and 8 stamps plus label (booklet cover) on the other side.
Compare to No. 3675, which measures 19x27mm.

CHRISTMAS

Reindeer with Pan Pipes A2917

Santa Claus with Drum A2918

Santa Claus with Trumpet A2919

Reindeer with Horn A2920

Reindeer with Pan Pipes A2921

Santa Claus with Drum A2922

Santa Claus with Trumpet A2923

Reindeer with Horn A2924

PHOTOGRAVURE
Serpentine Die Cut 11¾x11

2003, Oct. 23
Self-Adhesive

3821	A2917	37c multicolored	1.00	.25
3822	A2918	37c multicolored	1.00	.25
3823	A2919	37c multicolored	1.00	.25
3824	A2920	37c multicolored	1.00	.25
a.		Block of 4, #3821-3824	4.00	
b.		Booklet pane of 20, 5 each #3821-3824	20.00	

No. 3824b is a double-sided booklet with 12 stamps on one side and 8 stamps plus label (booklet cover) on the other side.

BOOKLET STAMPS
Serpentine Die Cut 10½x10¾ on 2 or 3 Sides

3825	A2921	37c multicolored	1.10	.25
3826	A2922	37c multicolored	1.10	.25
3827	A2923	37c multicolored	1.10	.25
3828	A2924	37c multicolored	1.10	.25
a.		Block of 4, #3825-3828	4.40	
b.		Booklet pane of 4, #3825-3828	4.40	
c.		Booklet pane of 6, #3827-3828, 2 each #3825-3826	6.60	
d.		Booklet pane of 6, #3825-3826, 2 each #3827-3828	6.60	

Snowy Egret — A2925

COIL STAMPS
PHOTOGRAVURE
Serpentine Die Cut 8½ Vert.

2003-04 **Tagged**
Self-Adhesive

3829	A2925	37c multi	.75	.25
b.		Black omitted		

LITHOGRAPHED
Serpentine Die Cut 9½ Vert.

3829A	A2925	37c multi	.85	.25

Serpentine Die Cut 11½x11 on 2, 3 or 4 Sides
Booklet Stamps
PHOTOGRAVURE

3830	A2925	37c multi	.75	.25
a.		Booklet pane of 20	15.00	
b.		As "a," die cutting omitted		

With "USPS" Microprinted on Bird's Breast
Litho.

3830D	A2925	37c multi	5.50	.25
e.		Booklet pane of 20	110.00	
f.		Die cutting omitted, pair	150.00	
g.		As "e," die cutting omitted	1,200.	

Issued: No. 3829, 10/24; No. 3830, 1/30/04; No. 3829A, Mar. 2004; No. 3830D, 2004.

PACIFIC CORAL REEF

A2926

No. 3831 — Marine life: a, Emperor angelfish, blue coral, mound coral, vert. b, Humphead wrasse, Moorish idol. c, Bumphead parrotfish, vert. d, Black-spotted puffer, threadfin butterflyfish, staghorn coral. e, Hawksbill turtle, palette surgeonfish. f, Pink anemonefish, magnificent sea anemone, vert. g, Snowflake moray eel, Spanish dancer. h, Lionfish, vert. i, Triton's trumpet. j, Oriental

---

sweetlips, bluestreak cleaner wrasse, mushroom coral, vert.

PHOTOGRAVURE
Serpentine Die Cut 10¾

2004, Jan. 2
Self-Adhesive

3831	A2926	Pane of 10	9.00	
a.-j.		37c Any single	.90	.40

CHINESE NEW YEAR

Year of the Monkey A2927

Serpentine Die Cut 10¾

2004, Jan. 13
Self-Adhesive

3832	A2927	37c multicolored	.75	.25

See No. 3895i.

LOVE

Candy Hearts — A2928

BOOKLET STAMP
Serpentine Die Cut 10¾ on 2, 3 or 4 Sides

2004, Jan. 14
Self-Adhesive

3833	A2928	37c multicolored	.75	.25
a.		Booklet pane of 20	15.00	

BLACK HERITAGE SERIES

Paul Robeson (1898-1976), Actor, Singer, Athlete and Activist — A2929

PHOTOGRAVURE
Serpentine Die Cut 10¾

2004, Jan. 20
Self-Adhesive

3834	A2929	37c multicolored	.85	.25

THEODOR SEUSS GEISEL (DR. SEUSS)

Dr. Seuss (1904-91), Children's Book Writer, and Book Characters A2930

PHOTOGRAVURE
Serpentine Die Cut 10¾x10½

2004, Mar. 2
Self-Adhesive

3835	A2930	37c multicolored	.85	.25
a.		Die cutting omitted, pair	1,750.	

FLOWERS

White Lilacs and Pink Roses A2931

Five Varieties of Pink Roses A2932

LITHOGRAPHED (#3836), PHOTOGRAVURE
BOOKLET STAMP (#3836)
Serpentine Die Cut 10¾ on 2, 3 or 4 Sides

2004, Mar. 4
Self-Adhesive

3836	A2931	37c multicolored	.75	.25
a.		Booklet pane of 20	15.00	

Serpentine Die Cut 11½x11

3837	A2932	60c multicolored	1.40	.25

UNITED STATES AIR FORCE ACADEMY, 50TH ANNIV.

Cadet Chapel A2933

PHOTOGRAVURE
Serpentine Die Cut 10¾

2004, Apr. 1
Self-Adhesive

3838	A2933	37c multicolored	.75	.25

HENRY MANCINI

Henry Mancini (1924-94), Composer, and Pink Panther A2934

2004, Apr. 13
Self-Adhesive

3839	A2934	37c multicolored	.75	.25

AMERICAN CHOREOGRAPHERS

Martha Graham (1893-1991) — A2935

Alvin Ailey (1931-89), and Dancers A2936

Agnes de Mille (1909-93), and Dancers A2937

George Balanchine (1904-83), and Dancers A2938

LITHOGRAPHED
2004, May 4
Self-Adhesive

3840	A2935	37c multicolored	.75	.35
3841	A2936	37c multicolored	.75	.35
3842	A2937	37c multicolored	.75	.35
3843	A2938	37c multicolored	.75	.35
a.		Horiz. strip of 4, #3840-3843	3.00	
b.		Strip of 4, die cutting omitted	250.00	
c.		Pane of 20 misprinted and miscut to show 5 #3843 and half of 5 #3842 at left, lower center plate position diagram at center, and 10 blank stamps at right.	—	

Eagle Types of 2003
PHOTOGRAVURE
COIL STAMPS
Perf. 9¾ Vert.
2004, May 12   **Untagged**

3844	A2898	(25c) gray & gold	.70	.25
3845	A2899	(25c) gold & green	.70	.25
3846	A2899	(25c) red & gold	.70	.25
3847	A2899	(25c) gold & dull blue	.70	.25
3848	A2898	(25c) Prussian blue & gold	.70	.25
3849	A2899	(25c) gold & gray	.70	.50
3850	A2898	(25c) green & gold	.70	.25
3851	A2899	(25c) gold & Prussian blue	.70	.25
3852	A2898	(25c) dull blue & gold	.70	.25
3853	A2899	(25c) gold & red	.70	.25
a.		Strip of 10, #3844-3853	7.00	—

LEWIS & CLARK EXPEDITION, BICENTENNIAL

Meriwether Lewis (1774-1809) and William Clark (1770-1838) On Hill — A2939

Lewis — A2940

Clark — A2941

LITHOGRAPHED & ENGRAVED
Serpentine Die Cut 10¾
2004, May 14
Self-Adhesive

3854	A2939	37c green & multi	1.10	.25

Booklet Stamps
Serpentine Die Cut 10½x10¾

3855	A2940	37c blue & multi	.90	.45
3856	A2941	37c red & multi	.90	.45
a.		Horiz. or vert. pair, #3855-3856	1.80	
b.		Booklet pane, 5 each #3855-3856	9.00	

Nos. 3855-3856 were issued in booklets containing two No. 3856b, each with a different backing. The booklets sold for $8.95.

ISAMU NOGUCHI (1904-88), SCULPTOR

Akari 25N — A2942

Margaret La Farge Osborn A2943

Black Sun — A2944

Mother and Child — A2945

Figure (Detail) — A2946

LITHOGRAPHED
Serpentine Die Cut 10½x10¾
2004, May 18
Self-Adhesive

3857	A2942	37c black	.90	.40
3858	A2943	37c black	.90	.40
3859	A2944	37c black	.90	.40
3860	A2945	37c black	.90	.40
3861	A2946	37c black	.90	.40
a.		Horiz. strip of 5, #3857-3861	4.50	

NATIONAL WORLD WAR II MEMORIAL

A2947

Serpentine Die Cut 10¾
2004, May 29
Self-Adhesive

3862	A2947	37c multicolored	.75	.25

Scott values for used self-adhesive stamps are for examples either on piece or off piece.

OLYMPIC GAMES, ATHENS, GREECE

Stylized Runner A2948

2004, June 9
Self-Adhesive

3863	A2948	37c multicolored	.75	.25

Sea Coast Type of 2002
PHOTOGRAVURE
COIL STAMP
Perf. 9¾ Vert.
2004, June 11   **Untagged**

3864	A2853	(5c) multicolored	.25	.25

No. 3864 has "2004" year date in black, rows of distinctly separated dots in surf area, and the small orange cloud is indistinct. No. 3775 has "2003" year date in blue, dots that run together in surf area, and a distinct small orange cloud.

THE ART OF DISNEY: FRIENDSHIP

Goofy, Mickey Mouse, Donald Duck — A2949

Bambi, Thumper A2950

Mufasa, Simba — A2951

Jiminy Cricket, Pinocchio A2952

LITHOGRAPHED
Serpentine Die Cut 10½x10¾
2004, June 23
Self-Adhesive

3865	A2949	37c multicolored	1.00	.30
3866	A2950	37c multicolored	1.00	.30
3867	A2951	37c multicolored	1.00	.30
3868	A2952	37c multicolored	1.00	.30
a.		Block or vert. strip of 4, #3865-3868	4.00	

U.S.S. CONSTELLATION

A2953

ENGRAVED
Serpentine Die Cut 10½
2004, June 30
Self-Adhesive

3869	A2953	37c brown	.75	.25

R. BUCKMINSTER FULLER (1895-1983), ENGINEER

Time Magazine Cover Depicting Fuller, by Boris Artzybasheff A2954

LITHOGRAPHED
Serpentine Die Cut 10½x10¾
2004, July 12
Self-Adhesive

3870	A2954	37c multicolored	.75	.25

LITERARY ARTS

James Baldwin (1924-87), Writer A2955

Serpentine Die Cut 10¾
2004, July 23
Self-Adhesive

3871	A2955	37c multicolored	.75	.25
a.		Die cutting omitted, pair	750.00	

AMERICAN TREASURES SERIES

Giant Magnolias on a Blue Velvet Cloth, by Martin Johnson Heade A2956

PHOTOGRAVURE
BOOKLET STAMP
Serpentine Die Cut 10¾ on 2 or 3 Sides
2004, Aug. 12
Self-Adhesive

3872	A2956	37c multicolored	.70	.25
a.		Booklet pane of 20	15.00	
b.		Die cutting omitted, pair, in #3872a with foldover	—	

No. 3872a is a double-sided booklet pane with 12 stamps on one side and eight stamps plus label on the other side.

ART OF THE AMERICAN INDIAN

A2957

No. 3878: a, Mimbres bowl. b, Kutenai parfleche. c, Tlingit sculptures. d, Ho-Chunk bag. e, Seminole doll. f, Mississippian effigy. g, Acoma pot. h, Navajo weaving. i, Seneca carving. j, Luiseño basket.

Serpentine Die Cut 10¾x11

2004, Aug. 21

Self-Adhesive

3873	A2957	Pane of 10	25.00	
a.-j.		37c Any single	2.50	.40

Sea Coast Type of 2002
PHOTOGRAVURE
COIL STAMPS

Serpentine Die Cut 10 Vert.

2004-05   **Untagged**

Self-Adhesive

3874	A2853	(5c) multicolored, large "2003" year date	.25	.25
a.		Small "2003" year date ('05)	.25	.25

Serpentine Die Cut 11½ Vert.

Untagged

3875	A2853	(5c) multicolored, "2004" year date	.25	.25

On Nos. 3874, 3874a and 3875, the stamps are spaced on backing paper that is taller than the stamps.

LEGENDS OF HOLLYWOOD

John Wayne (1907-79), Actor — A2958

Serpentine Die Cut 10¾

2004, Sept. 9

Self-Adhesive

3876	A2958	37c multicolored	.85	.25

SICKLE CELL DISEASE AWARENESS

Mother and Child — A2959

Serpentine Die Cut 11

2004, Sept. 29

Self-Adhesive

3877	A2959	37c multicolored	.75	.25

CLOUDSCAPES

A2960

No. 3878 — Clouds: a, Cirrus radiatus. b, Cirrostratus fibratus. c, Cirrocumulus undulatus. d, Cumulonimbus mammatus. e, Cumulonimbus incus. f, Altocumulus stratiformis. g, Altostratus translucidus. h, Altocumulus undulatus. i, Altocumulus castellanus. j, Altocumulus lenticularis. k, Stratocumulus undulatus. l, Stratus opacus. m, Cumulus humilis. n, Cumulus congestus. o, Cumulonimbus with tornado.

2004, Oct. 4

Self-Adhesive

3878	A2960	Pane of 15	15.00	
a.-o.		37c Any single	1.00	.50

CHRISTMAS

Madonna and Child, by Lorenzo Monaco — A2961

LITHOGRAPHED
BOOKLET STAMP

Serpentine Die Cut 10¾x11 on 2 or 3 Sides

2004, Oct. 14

Self-Adhesive

3879	A2961	37c multicolored	.75	.25
a.		Booklet pane of 20	15.00	
b.		As "a," die cutting omitted	—	

No. 3879a is a double-sided booklet pane with 12 stamps on one side and eight stamps plus label that serves as a booklet cover on the other side.

HANUKKAH

Dreidel — A2962

Serpentine Die Cut 10¾

2004, Oct. 15

Self-Adhesive

3880	A2962	37c multicolored	.75	.25
a.		Die cuts applied to wrong sides of stamp (hyphen-hole die cuts and wavy line on face, die cut 10¾ on reverse)	—	—

See Nos. 4118, 4219, 4372.

KWANZAA

People in Robes — A2963

Serpentine Die Cut 10¾

2004, Oct. 16

Self-Adhesive

3881	A2963	37c multicolored	.75	.25

See Nos. 4119, 4220, 4373.

LITERARY ARTS

Moss Hart (1904-61), Playwright — A2964

PHOTOGRAVURE

2004, Oct. 25   *Serpentine Die Cut 11*

Self-Adhesive

3882	A2964	37c multicolored	.75	.25

CHRISTMAS

Purple Santa Ornament A2965

Green Santa Ornament A2966

Blue Santa Ornament A2967

Red Santa Ornament A2968

Purple Santa Ornament A2969

Green Santa Ornament A2970

Blue Santa Ornament A2971

Red Santa Ornament A2972

Serpentine Die Cut 11½x11

2004, Nov. 16

Self-Adhesive

3883	A2965	37c purple & multi	1.00	.25
3884	A2966	37c green & multi	1.00	.25
3885	A2967	37c blue & multi	1.00	.25
3886	A2968	37c red & multi	1.00	.25
a.		Block or strip of 4, #3883-3886	4.00	
b.		Booklet pane of 20, 5 #3886a blocks	20.00	

Booklet Stamps

Serpentine Die Cut 10¼x10¾ on 2 or 3 Sides

3887	A2969	37c purple & multi	.90	.25
3888	A2970	37c green & multi	.90	.25
3889	A2971	37c blue & multi	.90	.25
3890	A2972	37c red & multi	.90	.25
a.		Block of 4, #3887-3890	3.60	
b.		Booklet pane of 4, #3887-3890	3.60	
c.		Booklet pane of 6, #3889-3890, 2 each #3887-3888	5.50	
d.		Booklet pane of 6, #3887-3888, 2 each #3889-3890	5.50	

Serpentine Die Cut 8 on 2, 3 or 4 Sides

3891	A2970	37c green & multi	1.35	.25
3892	A2969	37c purple & multi	1.35	.25
3893	A2972	37c red & multi	1.35	.25
3894	A2971	37c blue & multi	1.35	.25
a.		Block of 4, #3891-3894	8.00	
b.		Booklet pane of 18, 6 each #3891, 3893, 3 each # 3892, 3894	26.50	
		Nos. 3883-3894 (12)	13.00	3.00

No. 3886b is a double-sided booklet with 12 stamps on one side and 8 stamps plus label that serves as a booklet cover on the other side.

The design of No. 3894b shows ornaments in a wooden box. The pattern of the wooden box dividers creates three types of each design. Rows 1 and 4 are Type 1, with a top horizontal strip of frame extending from edge to edge while the bottom strip of frame stops at the design's width. Rows 2 and 5 are Type 2, with both top and bottom strips of frame stopping at the design's width. Rows 3 and 6 are Type 3, with the top strip of frame stopping at design's width while the bottom strip of frame extends from edge to edge. Each variety is equally common.

Chinese New Year Types of 1992-2004

Serpentine Die Cut 10¾

2005, Jan. 6

Self-Adhesive

3895		Double sided pane of 24, 2 each #a-l	18.00	
a.	A2360	37c Rat	.75	.40
b.	A2413	37c Ox	.75	.40
c.	A2462	37c Tiger	.75	.40
d.	A2535	37c Rabbit	.75	.40
e.	A2602	37c Dragon	.75	.40
f.	A2702	37c Snake	.75	.40
g.	A2752	37c Horse	.75	.40
h.	A2856	37c Ram	.75	.40
i.	A2927	37c Monkey	.75	.40
j.	A2067	37c Rooster	.75	.40
k.	A2146	37c Dog	.75	.40
l.	A2205	37c Boar	.75	.40

m.	As No. 3895, die cutting missing on "a," "b," and "c" reverse side (PS)	1,100.	

No. 3895h has "2005" year date and is photogravure while No. 3747 has "2003" year date and is lithographed.

Stamps are on the right side of the front and on the left side of the reverse.

BLACK HERITAGE SERIES

Marian Anderson (1897-1993), Singer — A2973

2005, Jan. 27

Self-Adhesive

3896	A2973	37c multicolored	.85	.25

RONALD REAGAN

Ronald Reagan (1911-2004), 40th President — A2974

2005, Feb. 9

Self-Adhesive

3897	A2974	37c multicolored	.75	.25

See No. 4078.

LOVE

Hand and Flower Bouquet — A2975

BOOKLET STAMP

Serpentine Die Cut 10¾x11 on 2, 3 or 4 Sides

2005, Feb. 18

Self-Adhesive

3898	A2975	37c multicolored	.75	.25
a.		Booklet pane of 20	15.00	

NORTHEAST DECIDUOUS FOREST

A2976

No. 3899 — Wildlife: a, Eastern buckmoth, vert. b, Red-shouldered hawk. c, Eastern red bat. d, White-tailed deer. e, Black bear. f, Long-tailed weasel, vert. g, Wild turkey, vert. h, Ovenbird, vert. i, Red eft. j, Eastern chipmunk.

Serpentine Die Cut 10¾

2005, Mar. 3

Self-Adhesive

3899	A2976	Pane of 10	8.50	
a.-j.		37c Any single	.85	.40

SPRING FLOWERS

Hyacinth
A2977

Daffodil
A2978

Tulip — A2979

Iris — A2980

LITHOGRAPHED BOOKLET STAMPS
Serpentine Die Cut 10¾ on 2 or 3 Sides

2005, Mar. 15
Self-Adhesive

3900	A2977	37c multicolored	.85	.30
3901	A2978	37c multicolored	.85	.30
3902	A2979	37c multicolored	.85	.30
3903	A2980	37c multicolored	.85	.30
a.		Block of 4, #3900-3903	3.40	
b.		Booklet pane of 20, 5 each #3900-3903	17.00	
c.		As "b," die cutting omitted on side with 8 stamps	—	

No. 3903b is a double-sided booklet with 12 stamps on one side and 8 stamps plus label (booklet cover) on the other side.

LITERARY ARTS

Robert Penn Warren (1905-89), Writer A2981

PHOTOGRAVURE
Serpentine Die Cut 10¾
2005, Apr. 22
Self-Adhesive

3904	A2981	37c multicolored	.75	.25

EDGAR Y. "YIP" HARBURG

Harburg (1896-1981), Lyricist — A2982

LITHOGRAPHED
2005, Apr. 28
Self-Adhesive

3905	A2982	37c multicolored	.75	.25

AMERICAN SCIENTISTS

Barbara McClintock (1902-92), Geneticist A2983

Josiah Willard Gibbs (1839-1903), Thermodynamicist — A2984

John von Neumann (1903-57), Mathematician — A2985

Richard Feynman (1918-88), Physicist A2986

2005, May 4
Self-Adhesive

3906	A2983	37c multicolored	1.00	.35
3907	A2984	37c multicolored	1.00	.35
3908	A2985	37c multicolored	1.00	.35
a.		Vert. pair, die cutting omitted, #3906 & 3908	—	
3909	A2986	37c multicolored	1.00	.35
a.		Block or horiz. strip of 4, #3906-3909	4.00	
b.		All colors omitted, tagging omitted, pane of 20	—	
c.		As "a," printing on back of stamps omitted	—	
d.		Vert. pair, die cutting omitted, #3907 & 3909	—	

On No. 3909b, the printing on the back of the pane and all die cutting is normal.

MODERN AMERICAN ARCHITECTURE

A2987

No. 3910 — Buildings: a, Guggenheim Museum, New York. b, Chrysler Building, New York. c, Vanna Venturi House, Philadelphia. d, TWA Terminal, New York. e, Walt Disney Concert Hall, Los Angeles. f, 860-880 Lake Shore Drive, Chicago. g, National Gallery of Art, Washington, DC. h, Glass House, New Canaan, CT. i, Yale Art and Architecture Building, New Haven, CT. j, High Museum of Art, Atlanta. k, Exeter Academy Library, Exeter, NH. l, Hancock Center, Chicago.

Serpentine Die Cut 10¾x11
2005, May 19
Self-Adhesive

3910	A2987	Pane of 12	11.00	
a.-l.		37c Any single	.90	.50
m.		As No. 3910, orange yellow omitted	400.00	—

LEGENDS OF HOLLYWOOD

Henry Fonda (1905-82), Actor — A2988

Sheets of 180 in nine panes of 20
Serpentine Die Cut 11x10¾
2005, May 20
Self-Adhesive

3911	A2988	37c multicolored	.90	.25

THE ART OF DISNEY: CELEBRATION

Pluto, Mickey Mouse — A2989

Mad Hatter, Alice — A2990

Flounder, Ariel — A2991

Snow White, Dopey — A2992

Serpentine Die Cut 10½x10¾
2005, June 30
Self-Adhesive

3912	A2989	37c multicolored	.85	.30
3913	A2990	37c multicolored	.85	.30
3914	A2991	37c multicolored	.85	.30
3915	A2992	37c multicolored	.85	.30
a.		Block or vert. strip of 4, #3912-3915	3.40	
b.		Die cutting omitted, pane of 20	—	1,400.
c.		Printed on backing paper, pane of 20	—	

On the unique used pane of No. 3915b, the outer selvage was removed by cutting.

ADVANCES IN AVIATION

Boeing 247 A2993

Consolidated PBY Catalina — A2994

Grumman F6F Hellcat A2995

Republic P-47 Thunderbolt A2996

Engineering and Research Corporation Ercoupe 415 A2997

Lockheed P-80 Shooting Star A2998

Consolidated B-24 Liberator — A2999

Boeing B-29 Superfortress — A3000

Beechcraft 35 Bonanza A3001

Northrop YB-49 Flying Wing A3002

Serpentine Die Cut 10¾x10½
2005, July 29
Self-Adhesive

3916	A2993	37c multicolored	.80	.40
3917	A2994	37c multicolored	.80	.40
3918	A2995	37c multicolored	.80	.40
3919	A2996	37c multicolored	.80	.40
3920	A2997	37c multicolored	.80	.40
3921	A2998	37c multicolored	.80	.40
3922	A2999	37c multicolored	.80	.40
3923	A3000	37c multicolored	.80	.40
3924	A3001	37c multicolored	.80	.40
3925	A3002	37c multicolored	.80	.40
a.		Block of 10, #3916-3925	8.00	

RIO GRANDE BLANKETS

A3003

A3004

A3005 A3006

LITHOGRAPHED BOOKLET STAMPS

Serpentine Die Cut 10¾ on 2 or 3 Sides

2005, July 30
Self-Adhesive

3926	A3003 37c multicolored	.75	.30
3927	A3004 37c multicolored	.75	.30
3928	A3005 37c multicolored	.75	.30
3929	A3006 37c multicolored	.75	.30
a.	Block of 4, #3926-3929	3.00	
b.	Booklet pane, 5 each #3926-3929	15.00	

No. 3929b is a double-sided booklet with 12 stamps on one side and 8 stamps plus label (booklet cover) on the other side.

PRESIDENTIAL LIBRARIES ACT, 50th ANNIV.

Presidential Seal — A3007

Serpentine Die Cut 10¾
2005, Aug. 4
Self-Adhesive

3930	A3007 37c multicolored	.80	.25

SPORTY CARS OF THE 1950S

1953 Studebaker Starliner A3008

1954 Kaiser Darrin A3009

1953 Chevrolet Corvette A3010

1952 Nash Healey A3011

1955 Ford Thunderbird — A3012

BOOKLET STAMPS
Serpentine Die Cut 10¾ on 2 or 3 Sides

2005, Aug. 20
Self-Adhesive   **Tagged**

3931	A3008 37c multicolored	.90	.40
3932	A3009 37c multicolored	.90	.40
3933	A3010 37c multicolored	.90	.40
3934	A3011 37c multicolored	.90	.40
3935	A3012 37c multicolored	.90	.40
a.	Vert. strip of 5, #3931-3935	4.50	
b.	Booklet pane, 4 each #3931-3935	18.00	

Stamps in No. 3935a are not adjacent, as rows of selvage are between stamps one and two, and between stamps three and four.

No. 3935b is a double-sided booklet pane with 12 stamps on one side (2 each #3931, 3933, and 3 each #3932, 3934) and eight stamps (1 each #3932, 3934, and 2 each #3931, 3933, 3935) plus label on the other side.

ARTHUR ASHE

Arthur Ashe (1943-93), Tennis Player — A3013

Serpentine Die Cut 10¾
2005, Aug. 27
Self-Adhesive

3936	A3013 37c multicolored	.75	.25

TO FORM A MORE PERFECT UNION

A3014

No. 3937 — Inscriptions and artwork: a, 1948 Executive Order 9981 (Training for War, by William H. Johnson). b, 1965 Voting Rights Act (Youths on the Selma March, 1965, photograph by Bruce Davidson). c, 1960 Lunch Counter Sit-ins (National Civil Rights Museum exhibits, by StudioEIS). d, 1957 Little Rock Nine (America Cares, by George Hunt). e, 1955 Montgomery Bus Boycott (Walking, by Charles Alston). f, 1961 Freedom Riders (Freedom Riders, by May Stevens). g, 1964 Civil Rights Act (Dixie Café, by Jacob Lawrence). h, 1963 March on Washington (March on Washington, by Alma Thomas). i, 1965 Selma March (Selma March, by Bernice Sims). j, 1954 Brown v. Board of Education (The Lamp, by Romare Bearden).

Serpentine Die Cut 10¾x10½
2005, Aug. 30
Self-Adhesive

3937	A3014 Pane of 10	11.00	
a.-j.	37c Any single	1.10	.40

CHILD HEALTH

Child and Doctor — A3015

PHOTOGRAVURE
Serpentine Die Cut 10½x11
2005, Sept. 7
Self-Adhesive

3938	A3015 37c multicolored	.75	.25

LET'S DANCE

Merengue A3016

Salsa — A3017

Cha Cha Cha — A3018

Mambo A3019

Serpentine Die Cut 10¾
2005, Sept. 17
Self-Adhesive

3939	A3016 37c multicolored	1.00	.35
3940	A3017 37c multicolored	1.00	.35
3941	A3018 37c multicolored	1.00	.35
3942	A3019 37c multicolored	1.00	.35
a.	Vert. strip of 4, #3939-3942	4.00	

Stamps in the vertical strip are not adjacent as rows of selvage are between the stamps. The backing paper of stamps from the 2nd and 4th columns have Spanish inscriptions, while the other columns have English inscriptions.

GRETA GARBO

Garbo (1905-90), Actress A3020

ENGRAVED
2005, Sept. 23
Self-Adhesive

3943	A3020 37c black	.75	.25

See Sweden No. 2517.

JIM HENSON AND THE MUPPETS

A3021

No. 3944: a, Kermit the Frog. b, Fozzie Bear. c, Sam the Eagle and flag. d, Miss Piggy. e, Statler and Waldorf. f, The Swedish Chef and fruit. g, Animal. h, Dr. Bunsen Honeydew and Beaker. i, Rowlf the Dog. j, The Great Gonzo and Camilla the Chicken. k, Jim Henson.

Nos. 3944a-3944j are 30x30mm; No. 3944k, 28x37mm.

PHOTOGRAVURE
Serpentine Die Cut 10½, 10½x10¾ (#3944k)
2005, Sept. 28
Self-Adhesive

3944	A3021 Pane of 11	9.00	
a.-k.	37c Any single	.80	.50

CONSTELLATIONS

Leo — A3022

Orion — A3023

Lyra A3024

Pegasus A3025

LITHOGRAPHED
Serpentine Die Cut 10¾
2005, Oct. 3
Self-Adhesive

3945	A3022 37c multicolored	.85	.35
3946	A3023 37c multicolored	.85	.35
3947	A3024 37c multicolored	.85	.35
3948	A3025 37c multicolored	.85	.35
a.	Block or vert. strip of 4, #3945-3948	3.40	
b.	As "a," die cutting omitted	750.00	

CHRISTMAS COOKIES

Santa Claus A3026

Snowmen A3027

Angel — A3028

Elves — A3029

Santa Claus
A3030

Snowmen
A3031

Angel
A3032

Elves
A3033

LITHOGRAPHED, PHOTOGRAVURE
(#3953-3960)

Serpentine Die Cut 10¾x11

2005, Oct. 20

Self-Adhesive

Design Size: 19x26mm

3949	A3026	37c multicolored	.85	.25
3950	A3027	37c multicolored	.85	.25
3951	A3028	37c multicolored	.85	.25
3952	A3029	37c multicolored	.85	.25
a.	Block or vert. strip of 4, #3949-3952		3.50	

Booklet Stamps

Serpentine Die Cut 10¾x11 on 2 or 3 Sides

Design Size: 19½x27mm

3953	A3026	37c multicolored	1.00	.25
3954	A3027	37c multicolored	1.00	.25
3955	A3028	37c multicolored	1.00	.25
3956	A3029	37c multicolored	1.00	.25
a.	Block of 4, #3953-3956		4.00	
b.	Booklet pane of 20, 5 #3956a		20.00	

Serpentine Die Cut 10½x10¾

3957	A3030	37c multicolored	1.10	.25
3958	A3031	37c multicolored	1.10	.25
3959	A3032	37c multicolored	1.10	.25
3960	A3033	37c multicolored	1.10	.25
a.	Block of 4, #3957-3960		4.50	
b.	Booklet pane of 4, #3957-3960		4.50	
c.	Booklet pane of 6, #3959-3960, 2 each #3957-3958		7.00	
d.	Booklet pane of 6, #3957-3958, 2 each #3959-3960		7.00	

No. 3956b is a double-sided booklet pane with 12 stamps on one side and eight stamps plus label that serves as a booklet cover on the other side. Nos. 3949-3952 have a small "2005" year date, while Nos. 3953-3956 have a large year date. Other design differences caused by different cropping of the images can be found, with Nos. 3953-3956 showing slightly more design features on one or more sides.

DISTINGUISHED MARINES

Lt. Gen. John A. Lejeune (1867-1942), 2nd Infantry Division Insignia — A3034

Lt. Gen. Lewis B. Puller (1898-1971), 1st Marine Division Insignia — A3035

Sgt. John Basilone (1916-45), 5th Marine Division Insignia A3036

Sgt. Major Daniel J. Daly (1873-1937), 73rd Machine Gun Company, 6th Marine Regiment Insignia — A3037

LITHOGRAPHED

Serpentine Die Cut 11x10½

2005, Nov. 10

Self-Adhesive

3961	A3034	37c multicolored	1.00	.35
3962	A3035	37c multicolored	1.00	.35
3963	A3036	37c multicolored	1.00	.35
3964	A3037	37c multicolored	1.00	.35
a.	Block or horiz. strip of 4, #3961-3964		4.00	

Flag and Statue of Liberty — A3038

LITHOGRAPHED (#3965, 3966, 3970, 3974), PHOTOGRAVURE

2005, Dec. 8   **Perf. 11¼**

3965	A3038	(39c) multicolored	.80	.25

Self-Adhesive (#3966, 3968-3975)

Serpentine Die Cut 11¼x10¾

3966	A3038	(39c) multicolored	.80	.25
a.	Booklet pane of 20		16.00	
b.	As "a," die cutting omitted		—	

COIL STAMPS

Perf. 9¾ Vert.

3967	A3038	(39c) multicolored	.80	.25

Serpentine Die Cut 8½ Vert.

3968	A3038	(39c) multicolored	.80	.25

Serpentine Die Cut 10¼ Vert.

3969	A3038	(39c) multicolored	1.50	.25

Serpentine Die Cut 9½ Vert.

3970	A3038	(39c) multicolored	3.50	.25

BOOKLET STAMPS

Serpentine Die Cut 11¼x10¾ on 2 or 3 Sides

3972	A3038	(39c) multicolored	.80	.25
a.	Booklet pane of 20		16.00	

Serpentine Die Cut 10½x10¾ on 2 or 3 Sides

3973	A3038	(39c) multicolored	.80	.25
a.	Booklet pane of 20		16.00	

On both Nos. 3972 and 3973, the sky immediately above the date is bright blue and extends from the left side to beyond the "6" in the date, the left arm of the star at the upper left barely touches the frame line and is without the "USPS" microprinting. They are distinguishable by the die cutting. Nos. 3872a and 3973a are double-sided booklet panes with 12 stamps on one side and eight stamps plus label that serves as a booklet cover on the other side.

No. 3973 was not available until January 2006.

Serpentine Die Cut 11¼x10¾ on 2 or 3 Sides

3974	A3038	(39c) multicolored	.80	.25
a.	Booklet pane of 4		3.20	
b.	Booklet pane of 6		4.80	

Serpentine Die Cut 8 on 2, 3 or 4 Sides

3975	A3038	(39c) multicolored	.80	.25
a.	Booklet pane of 18		14.50	
	Nos. 3965-3975 (10)		11.40	2.50

Nos. 3965-3975 are dated "2006."

On No. 3966, the sky immediately above the date is bright blue and extends from the left side to beyond the "6" in the date, the left arm of the star at upper left is clear of the top frame, and "USPS" is microprinted on the top red flag stripe.

On No. 3974, the sky immediately above the date is dark blue and extends from the left side to the second "0" in the date, the left arm of the star at upper left touches the top frame, and lacks the microprinting found on No. 3966.

Nos. 3965 and 3970 also have "USPS" microprinted on the top red flag stripe.

Nos. 3966a and 3972a are double-sided booklet panes with 12 stamps on one side and eight stamps plus label that serves as a booklet cover on the other side. On No. 3966a, the stamps on one side are upside-down with relation to the stamps on the other side. On No. 3972a the stamps are all aligned the same on both sides.

LOVE

Birds — A3039

PHOTOGRAVURE

Serpentine Die Cut 11 on 2, 3, or 4 Sides

2006, Jan. 3

BOOKLET STAMP

Self-Adhesive

3976	A3039	(39c) multicolored	1.00	.25
a.	Booklet pane of 20		20.00	

Flag and Statue of Liberty — A3040

LITHOGRAPHED (#3978, 3981), PHOTOGRAVURE (#3979-3980, 3982-3983, 3985)

2006   **Serpentine Die Cut 11¼x10¾**

Self-Adhesive (#3978, 3980-3985)

3978	A3040	39c multi	.85	.25
a.	Booklet pane of 10		8.50	
b.	Booklet pane of 20		17.00	
c.	As "b," die cutting omitted on side with 8 stamps		—	

No. 3978 has "USPS" microprinted on top red flag stripe.

No. 3978b is a double-sided booklet with 12 stamps on one side and 8 stamps plus label (booklet cover) on the other side.

COIL STAMPS

Perf. 9¾ Vert.

3979	A3040	39c multi	1.00	.25

Serpentine Die Cut 11 Vert.

3980	A3040	39c multi	.80	.25

No. 3980 has rounded corners and lacks microprinting. Unused examples are on backing paper taller than the stamp, and the stamps are spaced approximately 3mm apart.

Serpentine Die Cut 9½ Vert.

3981	A3040	39c multi	1.40	.25
a.	Die cutting omitted, pair		—	

No. 3981 has "USPS" microprinted on top red flag stripe.

Serpentine Die Cut 10¼ Vert.

3982	A3040	39c multi	1.25	.25
a.	Vert. pair, unslit between	500.00		

Serpentine Die Cut 8½ Vert.

3983	A3040	39c multi	.80	.25

BOOKLET STAMP

Serpentine Die Cut 11¼x10¾ on 2 or 3 Sides

3985	A3040	39c multi	.80	.25
a.	Booklet pane of 20		16.00	
b.	Serpentine die cut 11.1 on 2 or 3 sides		.80	.25
c.	Booklet pane of 4 #3985b		3.20	
d.	Booklet pane of 6 #3985b		4.80	

Nos. 3983 and 3985 lack the microprinting found on Nos. 3978 and 3981. No. 3982 was not made available until June, despite the official first day of issue. No. 3983 was not made available until July and No. 3985 was not made available until August, despite the official first day of issue. No. 3985a is a double-sided booklet with 12 stamps on one side and 8 stamps plus label (booklet cover) on the other side.

Issued: No. 3980, 1/9; No. 3979, 3/8; Nos. 3978, 3981, 3982, 3985, 4/8.

CHILDREN'S BOOK ANIMALS

The Very Hungry Caterpillar, from *The Very Hungry Caterpillar*, by Eric Carle A3041

Wilbur, from *Charlotte's Web*, by E. B. White A3042

Fox in Socks, from *Fox in Socks*, by Dr. Seuss A3043

Maisy, from *Maisy's ABC*, by Lucy Cousins A3044

Wild Thing, from *Where the Wild Things Are*, by Maurice Sendak A3045

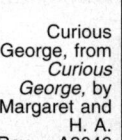
Curious George, from *Curious George*, by Margaret and H. A. Rey — A3046

Olivia, from *Olivia*, by Ian Falconer A3047

Frederick, from *Frederick*, by Leo Lionni A3048

PHOTOGRAVURE

Serpentine Die Cut 10¾

2006, Jan. 10

Self-Adhesive

3987	A3041	39c multicolored	.80	.40
3988	A3042	39c multicolored	.80	.40
3989	A3043	39c multicolored	.80	.40
3990	A3044	39c multicolored	.80	.40
3991	A3045	39c multicolored	.80	.40
3992	A3046	39c multicolored	.80	.40

3993	A3047	39c multicolored	.80	.40
3994	A3048	39c multicolored	.80	.40
a.		Block of 8, #3987-3994	6.50	

See Great Britain Nos. 2340-2341.

2006 WINTER OLYMPICS, TURIN, ITALY

Skier
A3049

LITHOGRAPHED
2006, Jan. 11
Self-Adhesive

3995	A3049	39c multicolored	.80	.25

BLACK HERITAGE SERIES

Hattie McDaniel
(1895-1952),
Actress — A3050

2006, Jan. 25
Self-Adhesive

3996	A3050	39c multicolored	.80	.25

Chinese New Year Types of 1992-2004

2006, Jan. 29
Self-Adhesive

3997		Pane of 12	12.00	
a.	A2360	39c Rat	1.00	.50
b.	A2413	39c Ox	1.00	.50
c.	A2462	39c Tiger	1.00	.50
d.	A2535	39c Rabbit	1.00	.50
e.	A2602	39c Dragon	1.00	.50
f.	A2702	39c Snake	1.00	.50
g.	A2752	39c Horse	1.00	.50
h.	A2856	39c Ram	1.00	.50
i.	A2927	39c Monkey	1.00	.50
j.	A2067	39c Rooster	1.00	.50
k.	A2146	39c Dog	1.00	.50
l.	A2205	39c Boar	1.00	.50

WEDDING DOVES

Dove Facing
Left — A3051

Dove Facing
Right — A3052

BOOKLET STAMPS
Serpentine Die Cut 10¾x11 on 2, 3 or 4 Sides
2006, Mar. 1
Self-Adhesive

3998	A3051	39c pale lilac	.80	.25
a.		Booklet pane of 20	16.00	
b.		As "a," die cutting omitted	—	

Serpentine Die Cut 10¾x11

3999	A3052	63c pale yellow green	1.40	.50
a.		Booklet pane, 20 each #3998-3999	45.00	
b.		Horiz. pair, #3998-3999 with vertical gutter between	2.25	1.50

Common Buckeye
Butterfly — A3053

LITHOGRAPHED (#4000), PHOTOGRAVURE (#4001-4002)
2006, Mar. 8   **Perf. 11¼**

4000	A3053	24c multicolored	.50	.25

Self-Adhesive
Serpentine Die Cut 11

4001	A3053	24c multicolored	.55	.25
a.		Serpentine die cut 10¾x11¼ on 3 sides (from booklet panes)	.50	.25
b.		Booklet pane of 10 #4001a	5.00	
c.		Booklet pane of 4 #4001a	2.00	
d.		Booklet pane of 6 #4001a	3.00	

No. 4001b is a convertible booklet that was sold flat. It has a self-adhesive panel that covers the rouletting on the inside of the booklet cover. Nos. 4001c and 4001d are component panes of a vending machine booklet, which was sold pre-folded and sealed, and which does not have the self-adhesive panel covering the rouletting on the inside of the booklet cover.

COIL STAMP
Serpentine Die Cut 8½ Horiz.

4002	A3053	24c multicolored	.50	.25

CROPS OF THE AMERICAS

Chili Peppers
A3054

Beans
A3055

Sunflower and
Seeds
A3056

Squashes
A3057

Corn — A3058

PHOTOGRAVURE (#4003-4012), LITHOGRAPHED (#4013-4017)
Serpentine Die Cut 10¼ Horiz.
2006, Mar. 16
Self-Adhesive
Coil Stamps

4003	A3054	39c multicolored	2.40	.35
4004	A3055	39c multicolored	2.40	.35
4005	A3056	39c multicolored	2.40	.35
4006	A3057	39c multicolored	2.40	.35
4007	A3058	39c multicolored	2.40	.35
a.		Strip of 5, #4003-4007	12.00	

Booklet Stamps
Serpentine Die Cut 10¾x10½ on 2 or 3 Sides

4008	A3058	39c multicolored	1.25	.35
4009	A3057	39c multicolored	1.25	.35
4010	A3056	39c multicolored	1.25	.35
4011	A3055	39c multicolored	1.25	.35
4012	A3054	39c multicolored	1.25	.35
a.		Horiz. strip of 5, #4008-4012	6.25	
b.		Booklet pane, 4 each #4008-4012	25.00	

Serpentine Die Cut 10¾x11¼ on 2 or 3 Sides

4013	A3054	39c multicolored	1.10	.35
4014	A3058	39c multicolored	1.10	.35
4015	A3057	39c multicolored	1.10	.35
4016	A3056	39c multicolored	1.10	.35
a.		Booklet pane of 4, #4013-4016	4.50	
4017	A3055	39c multicolored	1.10	.35
a.		Horiz. strip of 5, #4013-4017	5.50	
b.		Booklet pane of 4, #4013-4015, 4017	4.50	
c.		Booklet pane of 6, #4013-4016, 2 #4017	6.75	
d.		Booklet pane of 6, #4013-4015, 4017, 2 #4016	6.75	

Stamps in Nos. 4012a and 4017a are not adjacent, as one or two rows of selvage is between stamps (or a blank space where selvage was removed by the manufacturer).

No. 4012b is a double-sided booklet with 12 stamps on one side and 8 stamps plus label (booklet cover) on the other side.

"USA" is at right of "39" on No. 4004, at left of "39" on Nos. 4011, 4017. Top of "USA" is aligned with top of "39" on No. 4013, with bottom of "39" on Nos. 4003, 4012.

X-PLANES

A3059

A3060

LITHOGRAPHED WITH HOLOGRAM AFFIXED
Serpentine Die Cut 10¾x10½
2006, Mar. 17   **Self-Adhesive**

4018	A3059	$4.05 multi	8.00	5.00
a.		Silver foil ("X") omitted		
4019	A3060	$14.40 multi	27.50	15.00

Beware of Nos. 4018 and 4019 with "X" hologram chemically removed. Certification is strongly recommended.

SUGAR RAY ROBINSON (1921-89), BOXER

A3061

PHOTOGRAVURE
2006, Apr. 7   *Serpentine Die Cut 11*
Self-Adhesive

4020	A3061	39c red & blue	.80	.25

BENJAMIN FRANKLIN (1706-90)

Statesman
A3062

Scientist
A3063

Printer
A3064

Postmaster
A3065

2006, Apr. 7

4021	A3062	39c multicolored	1.25	.35
4022	A3063	39c multicolored	1.25	.35
4023	A3064	39c multicolored	1.25	.35
4024	A3065	39c multicolored	1.25	.35
a.		Block or horiz. strip of 4	5.00	

THE ART OF DISNEY: ROMANCE

Mickey and
Minnie
Mouse — A3066

Cinderella and
Prince Charming
A3067

Beauty and the
Beast — A3068

Lady and
Tramp — A3069

LITHOGRAPHED
Serpentine Die Cut 10½x10¾
2006, Apr. 21
Self-Adhesive

4025	A3066	39c multicolored	.80	.30
4026	A3067	39c multicolored	.80	.30
4027	A3068	39c multicolored	.80	.30
4028	A3069	39c multicolored	.80	.30
a.		Block or vert. strip of 4, #4025-4028	3.20	

LOVE

Birds — A3070

PHOTOGRAVURE
Serpentine Die Cut 11 on 2, 3 or 4 Sides
2006, May 1
Self-Adhesive
Booklet Stamp

4029	A3070	39c multicolored	.95	.25
a.		Booklet pane of 20	19.00	

LITERARY ARTS

Katherine Anne Porter (1890-1980),
Author — A3071

LITHOGRAPHED
Serpentine Die Cut 10¾
2006, May 15
Self-Adhesive

4030	A3071	39c multicolored	.80	.25

AMBER ALERT

Mother and Child
A3072

PHOTOGRAVURE
Serpentine Die Cut 10¾
2006, May 25
Self-Adhesive

| 4031 | A3072 | 39c multicolored | .80 | .25 |

Purple Heart Type of 2003
LITHOGRAPHED
Serpentine Die Cut 11¼x11
2006, May 26
Self-Adhesive

| 4032 | A2891 | 39c multicolored | .80 | .25 |

WONDERS OF AMERICA

American
Alligator — A3073

Designs: No. 4033, American alligator, largest reptile. No. 4034, Moloka'i, highest sea cliffs. No. 4035, Saguaro, tallest cactus. No. 4036, Bering Glacier, largest glacier. No. 4037, Great Sand Dunes, tallest dunes. No. 4038, Chesapeake Bay, largest estuary. No. 4039, Cliff Palace, largest cliff dwelling. No. 4040, Crater Lake, deepest lake. No. 4041, American bison, largest land mammal. No. 4042, Off the Florida Keys, longest reef. No. 4043, Pacific Crest Trail, longest hiking trail. No. 4044, Gateway Arch, tallest man-made monument. No. 4045, Appalachians, oldest mountains. No. 4046, American lotus, largest flower. No. 4047, Lake Superior, largest lake. No. 4048, Pronghorn, fastest land animal. No. 4049, Bristlecone pines, oldest trees. No. 4050, Yosemite Falls, tallest waterfall. No. 4051, Great Basin, largest desert. No. 4052, Verrazano-Narrows Bridge, longest span. No. 4053, Mount Washington, windiest place. No. 4054, Grand Canyon, largest canyon. No. 4055, American bullfrog, largest frog. No. 4056, Oroville Dam, tallest dam. No. 4057, Peregrine falcon, fastest bird. No. 4058, Mississippi River Delta, largest delta. No. 4059, Steamboat, tallest geyser. No. 4060, Rainbow Bridge, largest natural bridge. No. 4061, White sturgeon, largest freshwater fish. No. 4062, Rocky Mountains, longest mountain chain. No. 4063, Coast redwoods, tallest trees. No. 4064, American beaver, largest rodent. No. 4065, Mississippi-Missouri, longest river system. No. 4066, Mount Wai'ale'ale, rainiest spot. No. 4067, Kilauea, most active volcano. No. 4068, Mammoth Cave, longest cave. No. 4069, Blue whale, loudest animal. No. 4070, Death Valley, hottest spot. No. 4071, Cornish-Windsor Bridge, longest covered bridge. No. 4072, Quaking aspen, largest plant.

PHOTOGRAVURE
Serpentine Die Cut 10¾
2006, May 27
Self-Adhesive

4033	A3073	39c multicolored	.80	.60
4034	A3074	39c multicolored	.80	.60
4035	A3075	39c multicolored	.80	.60
4036	A3076	39c multicolored	.80	.60
4037	A3077	39c multicolored	.80	.60
4038	A3078	39c multicolored	.80	.60
4039	A3079	39c multicolored	.80	.60
4040	A3080	39c multicolored	.80	.60
4041	A3081	39c multicolored	.80	.60
4042	A3082	39c multicolored	.80	.60
4043	A3083	39c multicolored	.80	.60
4044	A3084	39c multicolored	.80	.60
4045	A3085	39c multicolored	.80	.60
4046	A3086	39c multicolored	.80	.60
4047	A3087	39c multicolored	.80	.60
4048	A3088	39c multicolored	.80	.60
4049	A3089	39c multicolored	.80	.60
4050	A3090	39c multicolored	.80	.60
4051	A3091	39c multicolored	.80	.60
4052	A3092	39c multicolored	.80	.60
4053	A3093	39c multicolored	.80	.60
4054	A3094	39c multicolored	.80	.60
4055	A3095	39c multicolored	.80	.60
4056	A3096	39c multicolored	.80	.60
4057	A3097	39c multicolored	.80	.60
4058	A3098	39c multicolored	.80	.60
4059	A3099	39c multicolored	.80	.60
4060	A3100	39c multicolored	.80	.60
4061	A3101	39c multicolored	.80	.60
4062	A3102	39c multicolored	.80	.60
4063	A3103	39c multicolored	.80	.60
4064	A3104	39c multicolored	.80	.60
4065	A3105	39c multicolored	.80	.60
4066	A3106	39c multicolored	.80	.60
4067	A3107	39c multicolored	.80	.60
4068	A3108	39c multicolored	.80	.60
4069	A3109	39c multicolored	.80	.60
4070	A3110	39c multicolored	.80	.60
4071	A3111	39c multicolored	.80	.60
4072	A3112	39c multicolored	.80	.60
a.		Pane of 40, #4033-4072	32.00	

EXPLORATION OF EAST COAST BY SAMUEL DE CHAMPLAIN, 400TH ANNIV.

Ship and Map — A3113

A3114

LITHOGRAPHED & ENGRAVED
Serpentine Die Cut 10¾
2006, May 28
Self-Adhesive (#4073)

| 4073 | A3113 | 39c multicolored | .85 | .25 |

Souvenir Sheet
Perf. 11

| 4074 | A3114 | Pane of 4, 2 each #4074a, Canada #2156a | 8.50 | 8.50 |
| a. | | A3113 39c multicolored | 2.00 | .25 |

Washington 2006 World Philatelic Exhibition (#4074). Canada No. 2156, which was sold only by Canada Post, has a bar code in the lower left margin of the pane. No. 4074, which was sold only by the United States Postal Service for $1.75, lacks this bar code.

WASHINGTON 2006 WORLD PHILATELIC EXHIBITION
Souvenir Sheet

A3115

LITHOGRAPHED (MARGIN) & ENGRAVED

2006, May 29			Perf. 10¾x10½	
4075	A3115	Pane of 3	16.00	6.00
a.		A174 $1 violet brown	2.00	.50
b.		A175 $2 deep blue	4.00	1.00
c.		A176 $5 carmine & blue	10.00	2.50

DISTINGUISHED AMERICAN DIPLOMATS
Souvenir Sheet

A3116

No. 4076: a, Robert D. Murphy (1894-1978). b, Frances E. Willis (1899-1983). c, Hiram Bingham IV (1903-88). d, Philip C. Habib (1920-92). e, Charles E. Bohlen (1904-74). f, Clifton R. Wharton, Sr. (1899-1990).

PHOTOGRAVURE
Serpentine Die Cut 10¾
2006, May 29
Self-Adhesive

| 4076 | A3116 | Pane of 6 | 6.00 | |
| a.-f. | | 39c any single | 1.00 | .40 |

LEGENDS OF HOLLYWOOD

Judy Garland (1922-69), Actress — A3117

LITHOGRAPHED
2006, June 10
Self-Adhesive

| 4077 | A3117 | 39c multicolored | 1.00 | .25 |
| a. | | Pair, die cutting omitted | — | |

Ronald Reagan Type of 2005
PHOTOGRAVURE
2006, June 14
Self-Adhesive

| 4078 | A2974 | 39c multicolored | .90 | .25 |

Happy Birthday Type of 2002
Serpentine Die Cut 11
2006, June 23
Self-Adhesive

| 4079 | A2751 | 39c multicolored | .80 | .25 |

BASEBALL SLUGGERS

Roy Campanella (1921-93)
A3118

Hank Greenberg (1911-86)
A3119

Mel Ott (1909-58)
A3120

Mickey Mantle (1931-95)
A3121

Serpentine Die Cut 10¾
2006, July 15
Self-Adhesive

4080	A3118	39c multicolored	.80	.30
4081	A3119	39c multicolored	.80	.30
4082	A3120	39c multicolored	.80	.30
4083	A3121	39c multicolored	.80	.30
a.		Block or vert. strip of 4, #4080-4083	3.20	

DC COMICS SUPERHEROES

A3122

No. 4084: a, Superman. b, Green Lantern. c, Wonder Woman. d, Green Arrow. e, Batman. f, The Flash. g, Plastic Man. h, Aquaman. i, Supergirl. j, Hawkman. k, Cover of *Superman #11*. l, Cover of *Green Lantern #4*. m, Cover of *Wonder Woman #22 (Second Series)*. n, Cover of *Green Arrow #15*. o, Cover of *Batman #1*. p, Cover of *The Flash #111*. q, Cover of *Plastic Man #4*. r, Cover of *Aquaman #5 (of 5)*. s, Cover of *The Daring New Adventures of Supergirl #1*. t, Cover of *The Brave and the Bold Presents Hawkman #36*.

Serpentine Die Cut 10½x10¾
2006, July 20
Self-Adhesive

4084	A3122	Pane of 20	16.00	
a.-t.		39c Any single	.80	.50
u.		As No. 4084, all inscriptions omitted on reverse	2,000.	

MOTORCYCLES

1940 Indian Four
A3123

1918 Cleveland
A3124

Generic "Chopper," c. 1970
A3125

1965 Harley-Davidson Electra-Glide — A3126

Serpentine Die Cut 10¾x10½
2006, Aug. 7
Self-Adhesive

4085	A3123	39c multicolored	1.00	.35
4086	A3124	39c multicolored	1.00	.35
4087	A3125	39c multicolored	1.00	.35
4088	A3126	39c multicolored	1.00	.35
a.		Block or horiz. strip of 4, #4085-4088	4.00	

AMERICAN TREASURES SERIES
Quilts of Gee's Bend, Alabama

Housetop Variation, by Mary Lee Bendolph A3127

Pig in a Pen Medallion, by Minnie Sue Coleman A3128

Nine Patch, by Ruth P. Mosely A3129

Housetop Four Block Half Log Cabin Variation, by Lottie Mooney A3130

Roman Stripes Variation, by Loretta Pettway A3131

Chinese Coins Variation, by Arlonzia Pettway A3132

Blocks and Strips, by Annie Mae Young A3133

Medallion, by Loretta Pettway A3134

Bars and String-pieced Columns, by Jessie T. Pettway A3135

Medallion With Checkerboard Center, by Patty Ann Williams A3136

BOOKLET STAMPS
Serpentine Die Cut 10¾ on 2 or 3 Sides
2006, Aug. 24
Self-Adhesive

4089	A3127	39c multicolored	1.10	.40
4090	A3128	39c multicolored	1.10	.40
4091	A3129	39c multicolored	1.10	.40
4092	A3130	39c multicolored	1.10	.40
4093	A3131	39c multicolored	1.10	.40
4094	A3132	39c multicolored	1.10	.40
4095	A3133	39c multicolored	1.10	.40

4096	A3134	39c multicolored	1.10	.40
4097	A3135	39c multicolored	1.10	.40
4098	A3136	39c multicolored	1.10	.40
a.		Block of 10, #4089-4098	11.00	
b.		Booklet pane of 20, 2 each #4089-4098	22.50	

No. 4098b is a double-sided booklet pane with 12 stamps on one side (1 each #4090-4093, 4095-4098, and 2 each #4089, 4094) and eight stamps (1 each #4090-4093, 4095-4098) plus label (booklet cover) on the other side.

SOUTHERN FLORIDA WETLAND

A3137

No. 4099 — Wildlife: a, Snail kite. b, Wood storks. c, Florida panther. d, Bald eagle, horiz. e, American crocodile, horiz. f, Roseate spoonbills, horiz. g, Everglades mink. h, Cape Sable seaside sparrow, horiz. i, American alligator, horiz. j, White ibis.

Serpentine Die Cut 10¾
2006, Oct. 4
Self-Adhesive

4099	A3137	Pane of 10	9.00	
a.-j.		39c any single	.90	.40

CHRISTMAS

Madonna and Child with Bird, by Ignacio Chacón A3138

Snowflake A3139

Snowflake A3140

Snowflake A3141

Snowflake — A3142

LITHOGRAPHED, PHOTOGRAVURE
(#4113-4116)
Serpentine Die Cut 10¾x11 on 2 or 3 Sides
2006
Self-Adhesive
Booklet Stamps (#4100, 4105-4116)

4100	A3138	39c multi	.80	.25
a.		Booklet pane of 20	16.00	

Base of Denomination Higher Than Year Date
Serpentine Die Cut 11¼x11

4101	A3139	39c multi	.90	.25
4102	A3140	39c multi	.90	.25
4103	A3141	39c multi	.90	.25
4104	A3142	39c multi	.90	.25
a.		Block or vert. strip of 4, #4101-4104	3.60	

Base of Denominations Even With Year Date
Serpentine Die Cut 11¼x11½ on 2 or 3 Sides

4105	A3139	39c multi	.90	.25
a.		Red missing (PS)	—	
4106	A3140	39c multi	.90	.25
a.		Red missing (PS)	—	

4107	A3141	39c multi	.90	.25
4108	A3142	39c multi	.90	.25
a.		Block of 4, #4105-4108	3.60	
b.		Booklet pane of 20, 5 #4108a	18.00	
c.		As "a," red ("USA") and green ("39") omitted	—	

Serpentine Die Cut 11¼x10¾ on 2 or 3 Sides

4109	A3139	39c multi	1.00	.25
4110	A3140	39c multi	1.00	.25
4111	A3141	39c multi	1.00	.25
4112	A3142	39c multi	1.00	.25
a.		Block of 4, #4109-4112	4.00	
b.		Booklet pane of 4, #4109-4112	4.00	
c.		Booklet pane of 6, #4111-4112, 2 each #4109-4110	6.00	
d.		Booklet pane of 6, #4109-4110, 2 each #4111-4112	6.00	

Serpentine Die Cut 8 on 2, 3 or 4 Sides

4113	A3139	39c multi	1.50	.35
a.		Red and green missing (PS)		
4114	A3141	39c multi	1.50	.35
4115	A3140	39c multi	1.50	.35
4116	A3142	39c multi	1.50	.35
a.		Block of 4, #4113-4116	6.00	
b.		Booklet pane of 18, 4 each #4114, 4116, 5 each #4113, 4115	27.00	
		Nos. 4100-4116 (17)	18.00	4.65

No. 4108b is a double-sided booklet pane with 12 stamps on one side and eight stamps plus label that serves as a booklet cover on the other side. Snowflakes on Nos. 4101-4104 are slightly smaller than those on Nos. 4105-4116.

Issued: No. 4100, 10/17, Nos. 4101-4116, 10/5.

Eid Type of 2001
PHOTOGRAVURE
2006, Oct. 6 *Serpentine Die Cut 11*
Self-Adhesive

4117	A2734	39c multicolored	.80	.25

Hanukkah Type of 2004
LITHOGRAPHED
Serpentine Die Cut 10¾x11
2006, Oct. 6
Self-Adhesive

4118	A2962	39c multicolored	.80	.25
a.		Die cutting omitted, pane of 20	—	

Kwanzaa Type of 2004
Serpentine Die Cut 11x10¾
2006, Oct. 6
Self-Adhesive

4119	A2963	39c multicolored	.80	.25

BLACK HERITAGE SERIES

Ella Fitzgerald (1917-96), Singer — A3143

Serpentine Die Cut 11
2007, Jan. 10
Self-Adhesive

4120	A3143	39c multicolored	.80	.25

OKLAHOMA STATEHOOD, 100TH ANNIV.

Cimarron River A3144

2007, Jan. 11
Self-Adhesive

4121	A3144	39c multicolored	.80	.25

LOVE

Hershey's Kiss — A3145

PHOTOGRAVURE
Serpentine Die Cut 10¾x11 on 2, 3 or 4 Sides
2007, Jan. 13
BOOKLET STAMP
Self-Adhesive

4122	A3145	39c multicolored	.80	.25
a.		Booklet pane of 20	16.00	

INTERNATIONAL POLAR YEAR
Souvenir Sheet

A3146

No. 4123: a, Aurora borealis. b, Aurora australis.

LITHOGRAPHED
Serpentine Die Cut 10¾
2007, Feb. 21
Self-Adhesive

4123	A3146	Pane of 2	4.00	
a.-b.		84c Either single	2.00	.50

LITERARY ARTS

Henry Wadsworth Longfellow (1807-82), Poet A3147

2007, Mar. 15
Self-Adhesive

4124	A3147	39c multicolored	.80	.25

Beginning with No. 4125, the United States Postal Service began issuing "Forever" stamps that satisfy the domestic 1-ounce first-class letter rate and the 1-ounce international letter rate regardless of future rate increases. The denomination in parentheses in the catalogue listing represents the face value at the time of issue. The face value increases to the new letter rate whenever rates change.

"FOREVER" STAMP

Liberty Bell — A3148

Large Microprinting (#4125, 4128)

Small Microprinting (#4126)

Medium Microprinting (#4127)

PHOTOGRAVURE, LITHOGRAPHED
(#4126, 4127)

Serpentine Die Cut 11¼x10¾ on 2 or 3 Sides

2007-09

Booklet Stamps
Self-Adhesive
Large Microprinting, Bell 16mm Wide

4125	A3148 (41c) multicolored, dated "2007," Apr. 12	.90	.25
a.	Booklet pane of 20	18.00	
b.	(42c) Dated "2008"	.90	.25
c.	Booklet pane of 20 #4125b	18.00	
d.	As "c," copper ("FOREVER") omitted	1,000.	
e.	As "c," copper ("FOREVER") omitted on side with 12 stamps, copper splatters on side with 8 stamps	—	
f.	(44c) Dated "2009" ('09)	.90	.25
g.	Booklet pane of 20 #4125f	18.00	
h.	As No. 4125, copper ("FOR-EVER") omitted	—	
i.	As No. 4125, die cutting missing, horiz. pair (PS)	—	
j.	As "b," copper ("FOREVER") omitted	50.00	

Small Microprinting, Bell 16mm Wide

4126	A3148 (41c) multicolored, dated "2007"	.90	.25
a.	Booklet pane of 20	18.00	
b.	(42c) Dated "2008" ('08)	.90	.25
c.	Booklet pane of 20 #4126b	18.00	
d.	(44c) Dated "2009" in copper ('09)	.90	.25
e.	Booklet pane of 20 #4126d	18.00	
f.	As "b," copper ("FOREVER") omitted	1,400.	
g.	As "c," die cutting omitted	—	

Medium Microprinting, Bell 15mm Wide

4127	A3148 (41c) multicolored, dated "2007" ('07)	.90	.25
a.	Booklet pane of 20	18.00	
b.	Booklet pane of 4	3.60	
c.	Booklet pane of 6	5.50	
d.	(42c) Dated "2008" ('08)	.90	.25
e.	As "d," booklet pane of 20	18.00	
f.	(42c) Dated "2008," date in smaller type ('08)	.90	.25
g.	As "f," booklet pane of 4	3.60	
h.	As "f," booklet pane of 6	5.50	
i.	(44c) Dated "2009" in copper ('09)	.90	.25
j.	As "i," booklet pane of 20	18.00	
k.	As "i," die cutting omitted, pair	—	
l.	As No. 4127, copper ("FOR-EVER") and "USA FIRST-CLASS" missing (PS)	—	
m.	As "e," die cutting omitted	500.00	

Large Microprinting, Bell 16mm Wide

Serpentine Die Cut 8 on 2, 3 or 4 Sides

4128	A3148 (41c) multicolored, dated "2007"	.90	.25
a.	Booklet pane of 18	16.50	
b.	(42c) Dated "2009" ('09)	.90	.25
c.	As "b," booklet pane of 18	16.50	
	Nos. 4125-4128 (4)	3.60	1.00

Nos. 4125-4128 were sold for 41c on the day of issue and will be valid for the one ounce first class postage rate after any new rates go into effect. As of May 12, 2008, any "Forever" stamp (Nos. 4125-4128 and 4127d) in stock was sold for 42c. As of May 15, 2009, all "Forever" stamps in stock were sold for 44c, etc.

Nos. 4125a, 4125c, 4126a, 4126c, 4127a, 4127e and 4127j are double-sided booklet panes, with 12 stamps on one side and eight stamps plus a label that serves as a booklet cover on the other side.

Nos. 4127b and 4127c exist with rouletting on backing paper of either gauge 9½ or 13.

See No. 4437.

Flag — A3149

LITHOGRAPHED, PHOTOGRAVURE
(#4134, 4135)

2007, Apr. 12   Perf. 11¼

4129	A3149 (41c) multicolored	.90	.40

Self-Adhesive (#4130, 4132-4135)
Serpentine Die Cut 11¼x10¾

4130	A3149 (41c) multicolored	.90	.25

COIL STAMPS
Perf. 9¾ Vert.

4131	A3149 (41c) multicolored	.90	.40

With Perpendicular Corners
Serpentine Die Cut 9½ Vert.

4132	A3149 (41c) multicolored	1.20	.25

Serpentine Die Cut 11 Vert.

4133	A3149 (41c) multicolored	1.20	.25
a.	Die cutting omitted, pair	1,250.	

Serpentine Die Cut 8½ Vert.

4134	A3149 (41c) multicolored	.90	.25

With Rounded Corners
Serpentine Die Cut 11 Vert.

4135	A3149 (41c) multicolored	1.25	.75
	Nos. 4129-4135 (7)	7.25	2.55

Nos. 4132-4134 are on backing paper as high as the stamp. No. 4135 is on backing paper that is larger than the stamp.

SETTLEMENT OF JAMESTOWN, 400TH ANNIV.

Ships Susan Constant, Godspeed and Discovery — A3150

LITHOGRAPHED
Serpentine Die Cut 10½x10½x10¾

2007, May 11

Self-Adhesive

4136	A3150 41c multicolored	1.10	.25

WILDLIFE

Bighorn Sheep   Florida
A3151   Panther
                 A3152

LITHOGRAPHED, PHOTOGRAVURE
(#4138, 4142)

2007   Perf. 11¼x11

4137	A3152 26c multi	.60	.25

Self-Adhesive
Serpentine Die Cut 11

4138	A3151 17c multi	.35	.25

Serpentine Die Cut 11¼x11

4139	A3152 26c multi	.55	.25

Coil Stamps
Serpentine Die Cut 11 Vert.

4140	A3151 17c multi	.35	.25
4141	A3152 26c multi	.75	.25
a.	Die cutting omitted, pair	500.00	

Booklet Stamp
Serpentine Die Cut 11¼x11 on 3 Sides

4142	A3152 26c multi	.55	.25
a.	Booklet pane of 10	5.50	

Nos. 4137 and 4139 have microprinted "USPS" to the left and above the lower left whisker. No. 4140 has microprinted "USPS" on right horn. No. 4141 has microprinted "USPS" along the right edge of the stamp just above the panther. Nos. 4138 and 4142 lack microprinting.
Issued: Nos. 4137, 4139, 4141, 4142, 5/12; No. 4138, 5/14; No. 4140, 5/21.

PREMIERE OF MOVIE "STAR WARS," 30TH ANNIVERSARY

A3153

No. 4143: a, Darth Vader (40x53mm). b, Millennium Falcon (47x25mm). c, Emperor Palpatine (41x26mm). d, Anakin Skywalker and Obi-Wan Kenobi (41x33mm). e, Luke Skywalker (31x41mm). f, Princess Leia and R2-D2 (41x33mm). g, C-3PO (21x65mm). h, Queen Padmé Amidala (26x48mm). i, Obi-Wan Kenobi (31x48mm). j, Boba Fett (32x40mm). k, Darth Maul (26x41mm). l, Chewbacca and Han Solo (48x31mm). m, X-wing Starfighter (41x26mm). n, Yoda (31x48mm). o, Stormtroopers (41x31mm).

LITHOGRAPHED
2007, May 25   Serpentine Die Cut 11
Self-Adhesive

4143	A3153 Pane of 15	15.00	
a.-o.	41c Any single	1.00	.50

PRESIDENTIAL AIRCRAFT

Air Force One
A3154

Marine One
A3155

LITHOGRAPHED & ENGRAVED
(#4144), LITHOGRAPHED (#4145)
Serpentine Die Cut 10¾

2007, June 13

Self-Adhesive

4144	A3154 $4.60 multi	9.25	5.00
a.	Black (engr.) omitted	225.00	
4145	A3155 $16.25 multi	30.00	16.00

PACIFIC LIGHTHOUSES

Diamond Head   Five Finger
Lighthouse,   Lighthouse,
Hawaii — A3156   Alaska — A3157

Grays Harbor   Umpqua River
Lighthouse,   Lighthouse,
Washington   Oregon
A3158   A3159

St. George Reef
Lighthouse,
California — A3160

PHOTOGRAVURE
Serpentine Die Cut 11
2007, June 21
Self-Adhesive

4146	A3156 41c multicolored	1.20	.40
4147	A3157 41c multicolored	1.20	.40
4148	A3158 41c multicolored	1.20	.40
4149	A3159 41c multicolored	1.20	.40
4150	A3160 41c multicolored	1.20	.40
a.	Horiz. strip of 5, #4146-4150	6.00	

WEDDING HEARTS

Heart With Lilac   Heart With Pink
Background   Background
A3161   A3162

LITHOGRAPHED (#4151),
PHOTOGRAVURE (#4152)
BOOKLET STAMP (#4151)
Serpentine Die Cut 10¾ on 2, 3 or 4 Sides

2007, June 27
Self-Adhesive

4151	A3161 41c multicolored	1.00	.25
a.	Booklet pane of 20	20.00	

Serpentine Die Cut 10¾x11

4152	A3162 58c multicolored	1.25	.25

POLLINATION

Purple Nightshade, Morrison's Bumblebee
A3163

Hummingbird Trumpet, Calliope Hummingbird — A3164

Saguaro, Lesser Long-nosed Bat
A3165

Prairie Ironweed, Southern Dogface Butterfly A3166

No. 4153: Type I, Tip of bird wing is directly under center of "U" in "USA," straight edge at left. Type II, Tip of bird wing is directly under the right line of the "U" in "USA," straight edge at right.

No. 4154: Type I, Tip of bird wing is even with the top of denomination, straight edge at right. Type II, Tip of bird wing is well above denomination, straight edge at left.

No. 4155: Type I, Top of "USA" is even with the lower portion of the nearest unopened green saguaro flower bud, straight edge at left. Type II, Top of "USA" is even with the point where the flower and unopened green saguaro bud meet, straight edge at right.

No. 4156: Type I, Bottom of denomination is even with top point of the white triangle found between the bottom of the purple flower and the green leaf below it, straight edge at right. Type II, Bottom of denomination is even with the lower point of the white triangle found between the bottom of the purple flower and the green leaf below it, straight edge at left.

LITHOGRAPHED
Serpentine Die Cut 11 on 2, 3 or 4 Sides

2007, June 29   **Tagged**

Self-Adhesive

Booklet Stamps

4153	A3163	41c multicolored, Type I	.85	.30
a.		Type II	.85	.30
4154	A3164	41c multicolored, Type I	.85	.30
a.		Type II	.85	.30
4155	A3165	41c multicolored, Type I	.85	.30
a.		Type II	.85	.30
4156	A3166	41c multicolored, Type I	.85	.30
a.		Type II	.85	.30
b.		Block of 4, #4153-4156	3.40	
c.		Block of 4, #4153a-4156a	3.40	
d.		Booklet pane of 20, 3 each #4153-4156, 2 each #4153a-4156a	17.00	

No. 4156d is a double-sided booklet with 12 stamps (2 each #4153-4156, 1 each #4153a-4156a) on one side and 8 stamps plus label (booklet cover) on the other side.

Patriotic Banner — A3167

PHOTOGRAVURE (#4157), LITHOGRAPHED (#4158)
Serpentine Die Cut 11 Vert.

2007, July 4   **Untagged**

Coil Stamps

Self-Adhesive

4157	A3167	(10c) red, gold & blue	.25	.25

Serpentine Die Cut 11¾ Vert.

4158	A3167	(10c) red, gold & blue	.25	.25

See No. 4385.

MARVEL COMICS SUPERHEROES

A3168

No. 4159: a, Spider-man. b, The Hulk. c, Sub-Mariner. d, The Thing. e, Captain America. f, Silver Surfer. g, Spider-Woman. h, Iron Man. i, Elektra. j, Wolverine. k, Cover of *The Amazing Spider-Man #1.* l, Cover of *The Incredible Hulk #1.* m, Cover of *Sub-Mariner #1.* n, Cover of *The Fantastic Four #3.* o, Cover of *Captain America #100.* p, Cover of *The Silver Surfer #1.* q, Cover of *Marvel Spotlight on The Spider-Woman #32.* r, Cover of *Iron Man #1.* s, Cover of *Daredevil #176 Featuring Elektra.* t, Cover of *The X-Men #1.*

PHOTOGRAVURE
Serpentine Die Cut 10½x10¾

2007, July 26

Self-Adhesive

4159	A3168	Pane of 20	17.00	
a.-t.		41c Any single	.85	.50

VINTAGE MAHOGANY SPEEDBOATS

1915 Hutchinson A3169

1954 Chris-Craft A3170

1939 Hacker-Craft A3171

1931 Gar Wood — A3172

LITHOGRAPHED
Serpentine Die Cut 10½

2007, Aug. 4

Self-Adhesive

4160	A3169	41c multicolored	.85	.35
4161	A3170	41c multicolored	.85	.35
4162	A3171	41c multicolored	.85	.35
4163	A3172	41c multicolored	.85	.35
a.		Horiz. strip of 4, #4160-4163	3.40	

Purple Heart Type of 2003
LITHOGRAPHED
Serpentine Die Cut 11¼x10¾

2007, Aug. 7

Self-Adhesive

4164	A2891	41c multicolored	.85	.25

AMERICAN TREASURES SERIES

Magnolia and Irises, Stained Glass by Louis Comfort Tiffany — A3173

BOOKLET STAMP
Serpentine Die Cut 10¾ on 2 or 3 Sides

2007, Aug. 9

Self-Adhesive

4165	A3173	41c multicolored	.85	.25
a.		Booklet pane of 20	17.00	

No. 4165a is a double-sided booklet pane with 12 stamps on one side and eight stamps plus label (booklet cover) on the other side.

FLOWERS

Iris — A3174

Dahlia — A3175

Magnolia A3176

Red Gerbera Daisy A3177

Coneflower A3178

Tulip A3179

Water Lily — A3180

Poppy — A3181

Chrysanthemum A3182

Orange Gerbera Daisy A3183

LITHOGRAPHED, PHOTOGRAVURE (#4176-4185)
Serpentine Die Cut 9½ Vert.

2007, Aug. 10

COIL STAMPS

Self-Adhesive

4166	A3174	41c multicolored	2.00	.35
4167	A3175	41c multicolored	2.00	.35
4168	A3176	41c multicolored	2.00	.35
4169	A3177	41c multicolored	2.00	.35
4170	A3178	41c multicolored	2.00	.35
4171	A3179	41c multicolored	2.00	.35
4172	A3180	41c multicolored	2.00	.35
4173	A3181	41c multicolored	2.00	.35
4174	A3182	41c multicolored	2.00	.35
4175	A3183	41c multicolored	2.00	.35
a.		Strip of 10, #4166-4175	20.00	

BOOKLET STAMPS
Serpentine Die Cut 11¼x11½ on 2 or 3 Sides

4176	A3182	41c multicolored	1.25	.35
4177	A3183	41c multicolored	1.25	.35
4178	A3174	41c multicolored	1.25	.35
4179	A3175	41c multicolored	1.25	.35
4180	A3176	41c multicolored	1.25	.35
4181	A3177	41c multicolored	1.25	.35
4182	A3180	41c multicolored	1.25	.35
4183	A3181	41c multicolored	1.25	.35
4184	A3178	41c multicolored	1.25	.35
4185	A3179	41c multicolored	1.25	.35
a.		Booklet pane of 20, 2 each #4176-4185	25.00	
b.		As "a," die cutting missing on Nos. 4178 & 4183 on side with 8 stamps (PS)	750.00	

No. 4185a is a double-sided booklet pane with 12 stamps on one side (2 each #4176-4177, 1 each #4178-4185) and eight stamps (#4178-4185) plus label (booklet cover) on the other side.

Flag — A3184

LITHOGRAPHED, PHOTOGRAVURE (#4188, 4189)
Serpentine Die Cut 9½ Vert.

2007, Aug. 15

COIL STAMPS

Self-Adhesive

With "USPS" Microprinted on Right Side of Flagpole

With Perpendicular Corners

4186	A3184	41c multicolored	1.20	.25

With "USPS" Microprinted on Left Side of Flagpole

Serpentine Die Cut 11 Vert.

4187	A3184	41c multicolored	1.20	.25

Without "USPS" Microprinting on Flagpole

Serpentine Die Cut 8½ Vert.

4188	A3184	41c multicolored	.85	.25

Serpentine Die Cut 11 Vert.

With Rounded Corners

4189	A3184	41c multicolored	.85	.25

No. 4188 is on backing paper as high as the stamp. No. 4189 is on backing paper that is larger than the stamp.

BOOKLET STAMPS
Serpentine Die Cut 11¼x10¾ on 3 Sides

With "USPS" Microprinted on Right Side of Flagpole

4190	A3184	41c multicolored	.85	.25
a.		Booklet pane of 10	8.50	

With "USPS" Microprinted on Left Side of Flagpole

Serpentine Die Cut 11¼x10¾ on 2 or 3 Sides

4191	A3184	41c multicolored	.85	.25
a.		Booklet pane of 20	17.00	

The microprinting on Nos. 4190 and 4191 is under the ball of the flagpole. The flagpole is light gray on No. 4190 and dark gray on No. 4191. No. 4191a is a double-sided booklet with 12 stamps on one side of the peelable backing and 8 stamps plus label (booklet cover) on the other side.

THE ART OF DISNEY: MAGIC

Mickey Mouse A3185

Peter Pan and Tinker Bell — A3186

Dumbo and Timothy Mouse A3187

(#4178-4185) plus label (booklet cover) on the other side.

Aladdin and Genie — A3188

PHOTOGRAVURE
Serpentine Die Cut 10½x10¾
2007, Aug. 16
Self-Adhesive

4192	A3185	41c multicolored	.85	.30
4193	A3186	41c multicolored	.85	.30
4194	A3187	41c multicolored	.85	.30
4195	A3188	41c multicolored	.85	.30
a.		Block of 4, #4192-4195	3.40	

CELEBRATE

A3189

LITHOGRAPHED
Serpentine Die Cut 10¾
2007, Aug. 17
Self-Adhesive

4196	A3189	41c multicolored	.85	.25

See Nos. 4335, 4407.

LEGENDS OF HOLLYWOOD

James Stewart (1908-97), Actor — A3190

2007, Aug. 17
Self-Adhesive

4197	A3190	41c multicolored	1.00	.25

ALPINE TUNDRA

A3191

No. 4198 — Wildlife: a, Elk. b, Golden eagle, horiz. c, Yellow-bellied marmot. d, American pika. e, Bighorn sheep. f, Magdalena alpine butterfly. g, White-tailed ptarmigan. h, Rocky Mountain parnassian butterfly. i, Melissa arctic butterfly, horiz. j, Brown-capped rosy-finch, horiz.

PHOTOGRAVURE
2007, Aug. 28
Self-Adhesive

4198	A3191	Pane of 10	8.50	
a.-j.		41c any single	.85	.40

GERALD R. FORD

Gerald R. Ford (1913-2006), 38th President — A3192

LITHOGRAPHED
Serpentine Die Cut 11
2007, Aug. 31
Self-Adhesive

4199	A3192	41c multicolored	.85	.25

JURY DUTY

Twelve Jurors — A3193

Serpentine Die Cut 10½
2007, Sept. 12
Self-Adhesive

4200	A3193	41c multicolored	.85	.25

MENDEZ v. WESTMINSTER, 60th ANNIV.

A3194

LITHOGRAPHED
Serpentine Die Cut 11
2007, Sept. 14
Self-Adhesive

4201	A3194	41c multicolored	.85	.25

Eid Type of 2001
PHOTOGRAVURE
Serpentine Die Cut 11
2007, Sept. 28
Self-Adhesive

4202	A2734	41c multicolored	.90	.25

AURORAS

Aurora Borealis A3195

Aurora Australis A3196

LITHOGRAPHED
Serpentine Die Cut 10¾
2007, Oct. 1
Self-Adhesive

4203	A3195	41c multicolored	1.25	.30
4204	A3196	41c multicolored	1.25	.30
a.		Horiz. or vert. pair, #4203-4204	2.50	

YODA

A3197

Serpentine Die Cut 10½x10¾
2007, Oct. 25
Self-Adhesive

4205	A3197	41c multicolored	.85	.25

CHRISTMAS

Madonna of the Carnation, by Bernardino Luini A3198

Knit Reindeer A3199

Knit Christmas Tree A3200

Knit Snowman A3201

Knit Bear A3202

Knit Reindeer A3203

Knit Christmas Tree A3204

Knit Snowman A3205

Knit Bear — A3206

LITHOGRAPHED, PHOTOGRAVURE (#4215-4218)
Serpentine Die Cut 10¾x11 on 2 or 3 Sides
2007, Oct. 25
Self-Adhesive
Booklet Stamps (#4206, 4210b, 4211-4218)

4206	A3198	41c multicolored	.85	.25
a.		Booklet pane of 20	17.00	

No. 4206a is a double-sided booklet pane with 12 stamps on one side and eight stamps plus label that serves as a booklet cover on the other side.

Serpentine Die Cut 10¾ on 2, 3 or 4 Sides

4207	A3199	41c multicolored	.85	.25
4208	A3200	41c multicolored	.85	.25
4209	A3201	41c multicolored	.85	.25

4210	A3202	41c multicolored, overall tagging	.85	.25
b.		Block or vert. strip of 4, #4207-4210	3.40	
d.		Booklet pane of 20	17.00	

No. 4210d is a double-sided booklet pane with 12 stamps on one side and eight stamps plus label that serves as a booklet cover on the other side.

Serpentine Die Cut 11¼x11 on 2 or 3 Sides

4211	A3203	41c multicolored	1.25	.25
4212	A3204	41c multicolored	1.25	.25
4213	A3205	41c multicolored	1.25	.25
4214	A3206	41c multicolored	1.25	.25
a.		Block of 4, #4211-4214	5.00	
b.		Booklet pane of 4, #4211-4214	5.00	
c.		Booklet pane of 6, #4213-4214, 2 each #4211-4212	7.50	
d.		Booklet pane of 6, #4211-4212, 2 each #4213-4214	7.50	

Serpentine Die Cut 8 on 2, 3 or 4 Sides

4215	A3203	41c multicolored	1.30	.25
4216	A3204	41c multicolored	1.30	.25
4217	A3205	41c multicolored	1.30	.25
4218	A3206	41c multicolored	1.30	.25
a.		Block of 4, #4215-4218	5.20	
b.		Booklet pane of 18, 4 each #4215, 4218, 5 each #4216, 4217	23.50	
		Nos. 4206-4218 (13)	14.45	3.25

Hanukkah Type of 2004
LITHOGRAPHED
Serpentine Die Cut 10¾x11
2007, Oct. 26
Self-Adhesive

4219	A2962	41c multicolored	.85	.25

Kwanzaa Type of 2004
LITHOGRAPHED
Serpentine Die Cut 11x10¾
2007, Oct. 26
Self-Adhesive

4220	A2963	41c multicolored	.85	.25

CHINESE NEW YEAR

Year of the Rat A3207

PHOTOGRAVURE
Serpentine Die Cut 10¾
2008, Jan. 9　　**Self-Adhesive**

4221	A3207	41c multicolored	.85	.25

BLACK HERITAGE SERIES

Charles W. Chesnutt (1858-1932), Writer — A3208

Serpentine Die Cut 11
2008, Jan. 31　　**Self-Adhesive**

4222	A3208	41c multicolored	.85	.25

LITERARY ARTS SERIES

Marjorie Kinnan Rawlings (1896-1953), Writer — A3209

Self-Adhesive

4223	A3209	41c multicolored	.85	.25

AMERICAN SCIENTISTS

Gerty Cori (1896-1957), Biochemist — A3210

Linus Pauling (1901-94), Structural Chemist A3211

Edwin Hubble (1889-1953), Astronomer — A3212

John Bardeen (1908-91), Theoretical Physicist A3213

2008, Mar. 6
Self-Adhesive

4224	A3210	41c multicolored	1.00	.35
4225	A3211	41c multicolored	1.00	.35
4226	A3212	41c multicolored	1.00	.35
4227	A3213	41c multicolored	1.00	.35
a.		Horiz. strip of 4, #4224-4227	4.00	

Flag at Dusk — A3214

Flag at Night — A3215

Flag at Dawn A3216

Flag at Midday A3217

PHOTOGRAVURE (#4228-4231, 4240-4247), LITHOGRAPHED (#4232-4239)

2008, Apr. 18 *Perf. 9¾ Vert.*
COIL STAMPS

4228	A3214	42c multicolored	2.50	.40
4229	A3215	42c multicolored	2.50	.40
4230	A3216	42c multicolored	2.50	.40
4231	A3217	42c multicolored	2.50	.40
a.		Horiz. strip of 4, #4228-4231	10.00	1.60

Self-Adhesive
With Perpendicular Corners
Serpentine Die Cut 9½ Vert.

4232	A3214	42c multicolored	2.25	.25
4233	A3215	42c multicolored	2.25	.25
4234	A3216	42c multicolored	2.25	.25
4235	A3217	42c multicolored	2.25	.25
a.		Horiz. strip of 4, #4232-4235	9.00	

Serpentine Die Cut 11 Vert.

4236	A3214	42c multicolored	2.50	.25
4237	A3215	42c multicolored	2.50	.25
4238	A3216	42c multicolored	2.50	.25
4239	A3217	42c multicolored	2.50	.25
a.		Horiz. strip of 4, #4236-4239	10.00	

Serpentine Die Cut 8½ Vert.

4240	A3214	42c multicolored	2.00	.25
4241	A3215	42c multicolored	2.00	.25
4242	A3216	42c multicolored	2.00	.25
4243	A3217	42c multicolored	2.00	.25
a.		Horiz. strip of 4, #4240-4243	8.00	

Serpentine Die Cut 11 Vert.
With Rounded Corners

4244	A3214	42c multicolored	1.25	.30
4245	A3215	42c multicolored	1.25	.30
4246	A3216	42c multicolored	1.25	.30
4247	A3217	42c multicolored	1.25	.30
a.		Horiz. strip of 4, #4244-4247	6.00	
		Nos. 4228-4247 (20)	42.00	5.80

Nos. 4232-4243 are on backing paper as high as the stamp. Nos. 4244-4247 are on backing paper that is larger than the stamp. Nos. 4232-4235 have "USPS" microprinted on the right side of a white flag stripe. Nos. 4236-4239 have "USPS" microprinted on red flag stripes. On Nos. 4244-4247, the paper, vignette size and "2008" year date are slightly larger than those features on Nos. 4236-4239.

AMERICAN JOURNALISTS

Martha Gellhorn (1908-98) A3218

John Hersey (1914-93) A3219

George Polk (1913-48) A3220

Ruben Salazar (1928-70) A3221

Eric Sevareid (1912-92) A3222

LITHOGRAPHED
Serpentine Die Cut 10¾x10½
2008, Apr. 22
Self-Adhesive

4248	A3218	42c multicolored	1.40	.40
4249	A3219	42c multicolored	1.40	.40
4250	A3220	42c multicolored	1.40	.40
4251	A3221	42c multicolored	1.40	.40
4252	A3222	42c multicolored	1.40	.40
a.		Vert. strip of 5, #4248-4252	7.00	

TROPICAL FRUIT

Pomegranate A3223

Star Fruit A3224

Kiwi A3225

Papaya A3226

Guava — A3227

LITHOGRAPHED (#4253-4257), PHOTOGRAVURE (#4258-4262)
Serpentine Die Cut 11¼x10¾
2008, Apr. 25
Self-Adhesive

4253	A3223	27c multicolored	.90	.25
4254	A3224	27c multicolored	.90	.25
4255	A3225	27c multicolored	.90	.25
4256	A3226	27c multicolored	.90	.25
4257	A3227	27c multicolored	.90	.25
a.		Horiz. strip of 5, #4253-4257	4.50	

COIL STAMPS
Serpentine Die Cut 8½ Vert.

4258	A3226	27c multicolored	1.80	.25
4259	A3227	27c multicolored	1.80	.25
4260	A3223	27c multicolored	1.80	.25
4261	A3224	27c multicolored	1.80	.25
4262	A3225	27c multicolored	1.80	.25
a.		Strip of 5, #4258-4262	9.00	
b.		As No. 4262, light green ("27 USA," "Kiwi" and year date) omitted	—	
		Nos. 4253-4262 (10)	13.50	2.50

Purple Heart Type of 2003
LITHOGRAPHED

2008, Apr. 30 *Perf. 11¼*
4263	A2891	42c multicolored	.90	.25

Self-Adhesive
Serpentine Die Cut 11¼x10¾
4264	A2891	42c multicolored	.85	.25

FRANK SINATRA

Frank Sinatra (1915-98), Singer and Actor — A3228

Serpentine Die Cut 10¾
2008, May 13
Self-Adhesive
4265	A3228	42c multicolored	.85	.25

MINNESOTA STATEHOOD, 150th ANNIV.

Bridge Over Mississippi River Near Winona — A3229

Serpentine Die Cut 10¾
2008, May 17
Self-Adhesive
4266	A3229	42c multicolored	.85	.25

WILDLIFE

Dragonfly — A3230

LITHOGRAPHED
Serpentine Die Cut 11¼x11
2008, May 19
Self-Adhesive
4267	A3230	62c multicolored	2.50	.25

AMERICAN LANDMARKS

Mount Rushmore A3231

Hoover Dam A3232

2008 *Serpentine Die Cut 10¾x10½*

4268	A3231	$4.80 multi	12.00	5.00
4269	A3232	$16.50 multi	35.00	17.00

Issued: $4.80, 6/6; $16.50, 6/20.

LOVE

Man Carrying Heart — A3233

PHOTOGRAVURE
Serpentine Die Cut 10¾ on 2, 3, or 4 Sides
2008, June 10
Booklet Stamp
Self-Adhesive
4270	A3233	42c multicolored	.95	.25
a.		Booklet pane of 20	19.00	

WEDDING HEARTS

Heart With Light Green Background A3234

Heart With Buff Background A3235

LITHOGRAPHED (#4271), PHOTOGRAVURE (#4272)
BOOKLET STAMP (#4271)
Serpentine Die Cut 10¾ on 2, 3 or 4 Sides
2008, June 10
Self-Adhesive
4271	A3234	42c multicolored	.90	.25
a.		Booklet pane of 20	18.00	

Serpentine Die Cut 10¾
4272	A3235	59c multicolored	1.25	.25

FLAGS OF OUR NATION

American Flag and Clouds — A3236

Alabama Flag and Shrimp
Boat — A3237

Alaska Flag and Humpback
Whale — A3238

American Samoa Flag and Island
Peaks and Trees — A3239

Arizona
Flag
and
Saguaro
Cacti
A3240

Arkansas Flag and Wood
Duck — A3241

California Flag and Coast — A3242

Colorado Flag and Mountain — A3243

Connecticut Flag, Sailboats and
Buoy — A3244

Delaware Flag and Beach — A3245

PHOTOGRAVURE
Serpentine Die Cut 11 Vert.
2008, June 14
Self-Adhesive
Coil Stamps

4273	A3236	42c multicolored	1.00	.30
4274	A3237	42c multicolored	1.00	.30
4275	A3238	42c multicolored	1.00	.30
4276	A3239	42c multicolored	1.00	.30
4277	A3240	42c multicolored	1.00	.30
a.		Strip of 5, #4273-4277	5.00	
4278	A3241	42c multicolored	1.00	.30
4279	A3242	42c multicolored	1.00	.30
4280	A3243	42c multicolored	1.00	.30
4281	A3244	42c multicolored	1.00	.30

4282	A3245	42c multicolored	1.00	.30
a.		Strip of 5, #4278-4282	5.00	
b.		P # set of 10, #4277a + 4282a	10.00	

No. 4273 always has a plate number. No. 4282b may be collected as one continuous strip, but the item will not fit in any standard album.

District of Columbia Flag and Cherry
Tree — A3246

Florida
Flag
and
Anhinga
A3247

Georgia Flag, Fence and
Lamppost — A3248

Guam Flag, Fish and
Tropicbird — A3249

Hawaii
Flag
and
Ohia
Lehua
Flowers
A3250

Idaho Flag and Rainbow
Trout — A3251

Illinois
Flag
and
Windmill
A3252

Indiana
Flag
and
Tractor
A3253

Iowa Flag, Farm Field and
Cornstalks — A3254

Kansas Flag and Farm
Buildings — A3255

2008, Sept. 2
Self-Adhesive
Coil Stamps

4283	A3246	42c multicolored	1.00	.30
4284	A3247	42c multicolored	1.00	.30
4285	A3248	42c multicolored	1.00	.30
4286	A3249	42c multicolored	1.00	.30
4287	A3250	42c multicolored	1.00	.30
a.		Strip of 5, #4283-4287	5.00	
4288	A3251	42c multicolored	1.00	.30
4289	A3252	42c multicolored	1.00	.30
4290	A3253	42c multicolored	1.00	.30
4291	A3254	42c multicolored	1.00	.30
4292	A3255	42c multicolored	1.00	.30
a.		Strip of 5, #4288-4292	5.00	
b.		P # set of 10, #4287a + 4192a	10.00	

No. 4283 always has a plate number. No. 4292b may be collected as one continuous strip, but the item will not fit in any standard album.

Kentucky Flag, Fence and
Horses — A3256

Louisiana Flag and Brown
Pelicans — A3257

Maine
Flag
and
Moose
A3258

Maryland Flag and Red-winged
Blackbird — A3259

Massachusetts Flag, Sea Birds and
Sailboats — A3260

Michigan Flag and Great Lakes
Ships — A3261

Minnesota Flag, Swans and Grain
Elevator — A3262

Mississippi Flag and Black
Bears — A3263

Missouri
Flag
and
Paddle
Wheeler
A3264

American Flag and Wheat — A3265

2009, Aug. 6
Self-Adhesive
Coil Stamps

4293	A3256	44c multicolored	1.00	.30
4294	A3257	44c multicolored	1.00	.30
4295	A3258	44c multicolored	1.00	.30
4296	A3259	44c multicolored	1.00	.30
4297	A3260	44c multicolored	1.00	.30
a.		Strip of 5, #4293-4297	5.00	
4298	A3261	44c multicolored	1.00	.30
4299	A3262	44c multicolored	1.00	.30
4300	A3263	44c multicolored	1.00	.30
4301	A3264	44c multicolored	1.00	.30
4302	A3265	44c multicolored	1.00	.30
a.		Strip of 5, #4298-4302	5.00	
b.		P # set of 10, #4297a + 4302a	10.00	

No. 4293 always has a plate number. No. 4302b may be collected as one continuous strip, but the item will not fit in any standard album.

American Flag and
Mountains — A3266

Montana Flag and Mountain
Lion — A3267

Nebraska Flag and Central-pivot
Irrigation System — A3268

Nevada Flag, Mountains and
Ocotillos — A3269

New Hampshire Flag and
Loon — A3270

New
Jersey
Flag
and
Sand
Castle
A3271

New Mexico Flag, Mountains and Hot Air Balloons — A3272

New York Flag, Fireboats and City Skyline — A3273

North Carolina Flag, Great Blue Heron and Cape Hatteras Lighthouse — A3274

North Dakota Flag and Elk A3275

2010, Apr. 16
Self-Adhesive
Coil Stamps

4303	A3266	44c multicolored	1.00	.30
4304	A3267	44c multicolored	1.00	.30
4305	A3268	44c multicolored	1.00	.30
4306	A3269	44c multicolored	1.00	.30
4307	A3270	44c multicolored	1.00	.30
a.		Strip of 5, #4303-4307	5.00	
4308	A3271	44c multicolored	1.00	.30
4309	A3272	44c multicolored	1.00	.30
4310	A3273	44c multicolored	1.00	.30
4311	A3274	44c multicolored	1.00	.30
4312	A3275	44c multicolored	1.00	.30
a.		Strip of 5, #4308-4312	5.00	
b.		P # set of 10, #4307a + 4312a	10.00	

No. 4303 always has a plate number. No. 4312b may be collected as one continuous strip, but the item will not fit in any standard album.

Northern Marianas Flag, Beach and Palm Trees — A3276

Ohio Flag, Butterfly, Milkweed Flowers and River — A3277

Oklahoma Flag and Oil Pumps — A3278

Oregon Flag, Mount Hood and Camas Lilies A3279

Pennsylvania Flag and White-tailed Deer — A3280

Puerto Rico Flag and Puerto Rican Tody Bird A3281

Rhode Island Flag and Sailboat A3282

South Carolina Flag, Marsh and Gazebo A3283

South Dakota Flag and Bison A3284

Tennessee Flag and Scarlet Tanagers — A3285

PHOTOGRAVURE
Serpentine Die Cut 11 Vert.
2011, Aug. 11
Self-Adhesive
Coil Stamps

4313	A3276	(44c) multicolored	1.25	.30
4314	A3277	(44c) multicolored	1.25	.30
4315	A3278	(44c) multicolored	1.25	.30
4316	A3279	(44c) multicolored	1.25	.30
4317	A3280	(44c) multicolored	1.25	.30
a.		Strip of 5, #4313-4317	6.25	
4318	A3281	(44c) multicolored	1.25	.30
4319	A3282	(44c) multicolored	1.25	.30
4320	A3283	(44c) multicolored	1.25	.30
4321	A3284	(44c) multicolored	1.25	.30
4322	A3285	(44c) multicolored	1.25	.30
a.		Strip of 5, #4318-4322	6.25	
b.		P# set of 10, #4317a + 4322a	12.50	

Alternating examples of the five examples of No. 4313 in the roll have a plate number. No. 4322b may be collected as one continuous strip, but the item will not fit in any standard album.

Texas Flag, Cotton Plant and Field A3286

Utah Flag, Cactus and Rock Arch A3287

Vermont Flag and Owls A3288

Virgin Islands Flag, Sailfish and Boat A3289

Virginia Flag and Replicas of Ships that Carried Settlers to Jamestown — A3290

Washington Flag and Evergreen Forest — A3291

West Virginia Flag and Wild Turkeys A3292

Wisconsin Flag and Dairy Cows — A3293

Wyoming Flag and Bighorn Sheep — A3294

American Flag and Fruited Plain — A3295

PHOTOGRAVURE
Serpentine Die Cut 11 Vert.
2012, Aug. 16
Self-Adhesive
Coil Stamps

4323	A3286	(45c) multicolored	1.25	.30
4324	A3287	(45c) multicolored	1.25	.30
4325	A3288	(45c) multicolored	1.25	.30
4326	A3289	(45c) multicolored	1.25	.30
4327	A3290	(45c) multicolored	1.25	.30
a.		Strip of 5, #4323-4327	6.25	
4328	A3291	(45c) multicolored	1.25	.30
4329	A3292	(45c) multicolored	1.25	.30
4330	A3293	(45c) multicolored	1.25	.30
4331	A3294	(45c) multicolored	1.25	.30
4332	A3295	(45c) multicolored	1.25	.30
a.		Strip of 5, #4328-4332	6.25	
b.		P# set of 10, #4327a + 4332a	12.50	

Alternating examples of the five examples of No. 4323 in the roll have a plate number. No. 4332b may be collected as one continuous strip, but the item will not fit in any standard album.

CHARLES (1907-78) AND RAY (1912-88) EAMES, DESIGNERS

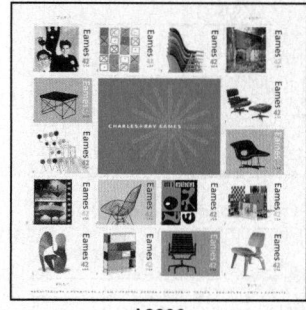

A3296

No. 4333: a, Christmas card depicting Charles and Ray Eames. b, "Crosspatch" fabric design. c, Stacking chairs. d, Case Study House #8, Pacific Palisades, CA. e, Wire-base table. f, Lounge chair and ottoman. g, Hang-it-all. h, La Chaise. i, Scene from film, "Tops." j, Wire mesh chair. k, Cover of May 1943 edition of *California Arts & Architecture* Magazine. l, House of Cards. m, Molded plywood sculpture. n, Eames Storage Unit. o, Aluminum group chair. p, Molded plywood chair.

PHOTOGRAVURE
Serpentine Die Cut 10¾x10½
2008, June 17
Self-Adhesive

4333	A3296	Pane of 16 + label	18.00	
a.-p.		42c Any single	1.10	.50

SUMMER OLYMPIC GAMES, BEIJING, CHINA

Gymnast A3297

LITHOGRAPHED
Serpentine Die Cut 10¾
2008, June 19
Self-Adhesive

4334	A3297	42c multicolored	.85	.25

Celebrate Type of 2007
Serpentine Die Cut 10¾
2008, July 10
Self-Adhesive

4335	A3189	42c multicolored	.85	.25

VINTAGE BLACK CINEMA

Poster for "Black and Tan" — A3298

Poster for "The Sport of the Gods" — A3299

Poster for "Prinsesse Tam-Tam" A3300

Poster for "Caldonia" A3301

Poster for "Hallelujah" — A3302

Serpentine Die Cut 10¾
2008, July 16　　　　　　　　**Tagged**
Self-Adhesive
4336	A3298	42c multicolored	.95	.45
4337	A3299	42c multicolored	.95	.45
4338	A3300	42c multicolored	.95	.45
4339	A3301	42c multicolored	.95	.45
4340	A3302	42c multicolored	.95	.45
a.		Horiz. strip of 5, #4336-4340	4.75	

"TAKE ME OUT TO THE BALLGAME," CENT.

Baseball Players and First Six Notes of Song — A3303

PHOTOGRAVURE
Serpentine Die Cut 11
2008, July 16
Self-Adhesive
4341	A3303	42c multicolored	.85	.25

THE ART OF DISNEY: IMAGINATION

Pongo and Pup — A3304

Steamboat Willie — A3305

Princess Aurora, Flora, Fauna and Merryweather A3306

Mowgli and Baloo — A3307

Serpentine Die Cut 10½x10¾
2008, Aug. 7
Self-Adhesive
4342	A3304	42c multicolored	.85	.30
4343	A3305	42c multicolored	.85	.30
4344	A3306	42c multicolored	.85	.30
4345	A3307	42c multicolored	.85	.30
a.		Block of 4, #4342-4345	3.40	

AMERICAN TREASURES SERIES

Valley of the Yosemite, by Albert Bierstadt A3308

LITHOGRAPHED
BOOKLET STAMP
Serpentine Die Cut 11 on 2 or 3 Sides
2008, Aug. 14
Self-Adhesive
4346	A3308	42c multicolored	.85	.25
a.		Booklet pane of 20	17.00	

No. 4346a is a double-sided booklet pane with 12 stamps on one side and eight stamps plus label (booklet cover) on the other side.

Sunflower — A3309

BOOKLET STAMP
Serpentine Die Cut 11¼x10¾ on 2 or 3 Sides
2008, Aug. 15
Self-Adhesive
4347	A3309	42c multicolored	.85	.25
a.		Booklet pane of 20	17.00	

No. 4347a is a double-sided booklet pane with 12 stamps on one side and eight stamps plus label (booklet cover) on the other side.

Sea Coast Type of 2002
LITHOGRAPHED
COIL STAMP
Perf. 9¾ Vert.
2008, Sept. 5　　　　　　　**Untagged**
4348	A2853	(5c) multicolored	.25	.25

No. 4348 has "2008" year date in black, and microprinted "USPS" at the end of the purple rock to the right of the crashing wave.

LATIN JAZZ

Musicians A3310

PHOTOGRAVURE
Serpentine Die Cut 11x10¾
2008, Sept. 8
Self-Adhesive
4349	A3310	42c multicolored	.85	.25

LEGENDS OF HOLLYWOOD

Bette Davis (1908-89), Actress — A3311

LITHOGRAPHED
Serpentine Die Cut 10¾
2008, Sept. 18
Self-Adhesive
4350	A3311	42c multicolored	1.00	.25

Eid Type of 2001
PHOTOGRAVURE
Serpentine Die Cut 11
2008, Sept. 23
Self-Adhesive
4351	A2734	42c multicolored	.85	.25

GREAT LAKES DUNES

A3312

No. 4352 — Wildlife: a, Vesper sparrow. b, Red fox, vert. c, Piping plover. d, Eastern hognose snake. e, Common mergansers. f, Spotted sandpiper, vert. g, Tiger beetle, vert. h, White-footed mouse, vert. i, Piping plover nestlings. j, Red admiral butterfly, vert.

Serpentine Die Cut 10¾
2008, Oct. 2
Self-Adhesive
4352	A3312	Pane of 10	10.00	
a.-j.		42c Any single	1.00	.40

AUTOMOBILES OF THE 1950s

1959 Cadillac Eldorado A3313

1957 Studebaker Golden Hawk A3314

1957 Pontiac Safari A3315

1957 Lincoln Premiere A3316

1957 Chrysler 300C A3317

LITHOGRAPHED
2008, Oct. 3
Self-Adhesive
4353	A3313	42c multicolored	.85	.45
4354	A3314	42c multicolored	.85	.45
4355	A3315	42c multicolored	.85	.45
4356	A3316	42c multicolored	.85	.45
4357	A3317	42c multicolored	.85	.45
a.		Vert. strip of 5, #4353-4357	4.25	

ALZHEIMER'S DISEASE AWARENESS

A3318

PHOTOGRAVURE
Serpentine Die Cut 10¾
2008, Oct. 17
Self-Adhesive
4358	A3318	42c multicolored	.85	.25

CHRISTMAS

Virgin and Child with the Young John the Baptist, by Sandro Botticelli A3319

Drummer Nutcracker A3320

Santa Claus Nutcracker A3321

King Nutcracker A3322

Soldier Nutcracker A3323

Drummer Nutcracker A3324

Santa Claus Nutcracker A3325

King Nutcracker A3326

Soldier Nutcracker — A3327

LITHOGRAPHED, PHOTOGRAVURE
(#4368-4371)

Serpentine Die Cut 10¾x11 on 2 or 3 Sides

2008, Oct. 23
Self-Adhesive
Booklet Stamps

4359	A3319 42c multicolored	.85	.25
a.	Booklet pane of 20	17.00	
b.	Die cutting omitted, pair	—	
4360	A3320 42c multicolored	1.00	.25
4361	A3321 42c multicolored	1.00	.25
4362	A3322 42c multicolored	1.00	.25
4363	A3323 42c multicolored	1.00	.25
a.	Block of 4, #4360-4363	4.00	
b.	Booklet pane of 20, 5 each #4360-4363	20.00	

No. 4359a is a double-sided booklet pane with 12 stamps on one side and eight stamps plus label that serves as a booklet cover on the other side. No. 4363b is a double-sided booklet pane with 12 stamps on one side (3 each of Nos. 4360-4363) and eight stamps (2 each of Nos. 4360-4363) plus label that serves as a booklet cover on the other side.

Serpentine Die Cut 11¼x11 on 2 or 3 Sides

4364	A3324 42c multicolored	1.25	.25
4365	A3325 42c multicolored	1.25	.25
4366	A3326 42c multicolored	1.25	.25
4367	A3327 42c multicolored	1.25	.25
a.	Block of 4, #4364-4367	5.00	
b.	Booklet pane of 4, #4364-4367	5.00	
c.	Booklet pane of 6, #4366-4367, 2 each #4364-4365	7.50	
d.	Booklet pane of 6, #4364-4365, 2 each #4366-4367	7.50	

Serpentine Die Cut 8 on 2, 3 or 4 Sides

4368	A3324 42c multicolored	1.25	.25
4369	A3325 42c multicolored	1.25	.25
4370	A3326 42c multicolored	1.25	.25
4371	A3327 42c multicolored	1.25	.25
a.	Block of 4, #4368-4371	5.00	
b.	Booklet pane of 18, 5 each #4368-4369, 4 each #4370-4371	22.50	
	Nos. 4359-4371 (13)	14.85	3.25

Hanukkah Type of 2004
LITHOGRAPHED

Serpentine Die Cut 10¾x11

2008, Oct. 24
Self-Adhesive

4372	A2962 42c multicolored	.85	.25

Kwanzaa Type of 2004
Serpentine Die Cut 11x10¾
2008, Oct. 24
Self-Adhesive

4373	A2963 42c multicolored	.85	.25

ALASKA STATEHOOD, 50TH ANNIV.

Dogsledder Near Rainy Pass A3328

Serpentine Die Cut 10¾
2009, Jan. 3
Self-Adhesive

4374	A3328 42c multicolored	.85	.25

CHINESE NEW YEAR

Year of the Ox A3329

2009, Jan. 8
Self-Adhesive

4375	A3329 42c multicolored	.85	.25

OREGON STATEHOOD, 150TH ANNIV.

Pacific Coast of Oregon A3330

2009, Jan. 14
Self-Adhesive

4376	A3330 42c multicolored	.85	.25

EDGAR ALLAN POE

Edgar Allan Poe (1809-49), Writer — A3331

PHOTOGRAVURE
2009, Jan. 16
Self-Adhesive

4377	A3331 42c multicolored	.90	.25

AMERICAN LANDMARKS

Redwood Forest A3332

Old Faithful A3333

LITHOGRAPHED
Serpentine Die Cut 10¾x10½
2009, Jan. 16
Self-Adhesive

4378	A3332 $4.95 multi	11.00	5.00
4379	A3333 $17.50 multi	40.00	20.00

ABRAHAM LINCOLN (1809-65), 16TH PRESIDENT

Lincoln as Rail-splitter A3334

Lincoln as Lawyer A3335

Lincoln as Politician A3336

Lincoln as President A3337

Serpentine Die Cut 10¾
2009, Feb. 9
Self-Adhesive

4380	A3334 42c multicolored	1.50	.35
4381	A3335 42c multicolored	1.50	.35
4382	A3336 42c multicolored	1.50	.35
4383	A3337 42c multicolored	1.50	.35
a.	Horiz. strip of 4, #4380-4383	6.00	

CIVIL RIGHTS PIONEERS

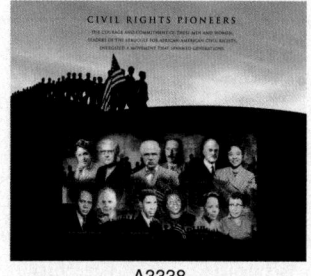

A3338

No. 4384: a, Mary Church Terrell (1863-1954), writer, Mary White Ovington (1865-1951), journalist. b, J. R. Clifford (1848-1933), attorney, Joel Elias Spingarn (1875-1939), educator. c, Oswald Garrison Villard (1872-1949), co-founder of National Association for the Advancement of Colored People (NAACP), Daisy Gatson Bates (1914-99), mentor of black Little Rock Central High School students. d, Charles Hamilton Houston (1895-1950), lawyer, Walter White (1893-1955), chief secretary of NAACP. e, Medgar Evers (1925-63), assassinated Mississippi NAACP field secretary, Fannie Lou Hamer (1917-77), voting rights activist. f, Ella Baker (1903-86), activist, Ruby Hurley (1909-80), NAACP Southeast Regional Director.

PHOTOGRAVURE
2009, Feb. 21
Self-Adhesive

4384	A3338 Pane of 6	9.00	
a.-f.	42c Any single	1.50	.40

Patriotic Banner Type of 2007
LITHOGRAPHED
COIL STAMP
Perf. 9¾ Vert.
2009, Feb. 24 **Untagged**

4385	A3167 (10c) multicolored	.25	.25

LITERARY ARTS

Richard Wright (1908-60), Author A3339

Serpentine Die Cut 10¾
2009, Apr. 9
Self-Adhesive

4386	A3339 61c multicolored	1.25	.25

WILDLIFE

Polar Bear A3340

Dolphin A3341

LITHOGRAPHED (#4387),
PHOTOGRAVURE
2009 *Serpentine Die Cut 11¼x11*
Self-Adhesive

4387	A3340 28c multi	.75	.25
a.	Die cutting omitted, pane of 20	7,250.	

Serpentine Die Cut 11

4388	A3341 64c multi	1.40	.25

COIL STAMP
Serpentine Die Cut 8½ Vert.

4389	A3340 28c multi	.60	.25

Issued: Nos. 4387, 4389, 4/16; No. 4388, 6/12.

Purple Heart Type of 2003
LITHOGRAPHED
Serpentine Die Cut 11¼x10¾
2009, Apr. 28
Self-Adhesive

4390	A2891 44c multicolored	.90	.25

Flag — A3342

LITHOGRAPHED, PHOTOGRAVURE
(#4394, 4395, 4396)

2009 *Perf. 9¾ Vert.*
COIL STAMPS

4391	A3342 44c multi	1.00	1.00

Self-Adhesive
Serpentine Die Cut 11 Vert.
With Pointed Corners

4392	A3342 44c multi	2.00	.25
a.	Die cutting omitted, pair	—	

Serpentine Die Cut 9½ Vert.

4393	A3342 44c multi	1.50	.25

Serpentine Die Cut 8½ Vert.

4394	A3342 44c multi	1.50	.25

Serpentine Die Cut 11 Vert.
With Rounded Corners

4395	A3342 44c multi	1.25	.25

BOOKLET STAMP
Serpentine Die Cut 11¼x10¾ on 3 Sides

4396	A3342 44c multi	.90	.25
a.	Booklet pane of 10	9.00	

Nos. 4392-4394 are on backing paper as high as the stamp. No. 4395 is on backing paper that is taller than the stamp. No. 4393 has microprinted "USPS" on white stripe below the blue field.
Issued: Nos. 4391, 4395, 5/1; Nos. 4392-4394, 5/8, No. 4396, 6/5.

WEDDINGS

Wedding Rings — A3343

Wedding Cake — A3344

LITHOGRAPHED, PHOTOGRAVURE
(#4398)
Serpentine Die Cut 10¾
2009, May 1
Self-Adhesive

4397	A3343 44c multicolored	.90	.25
4398	A3344 61c multicolored	1.25	.25

See Nos. 4521, 4602, 4735, 4867.

THE SIMPSONS TELEVISION SHOW, 20TH ANNIV.

Homer Simpson A3345

Marge Simpson A3346

Bart Simpson A3347

Lisa Simpson A3348

Maggie Simpson — A3349

LITHOGRAPHED BOOKLET STAMPS

Serpentine Die Cut 10¾ on 2, 3 or 4 Sides

2009, May 7

Self-Adhesive

4399	A3345	44c multicolored	1.15	.40
4400	A3346	44c multicolored	1.15	.40
4401	A3347	44c multicolored	1.15	.40
4402	A3348	44c multicolored	1.15	.40
4403	A3349	44c multicolored	1.15	.40
a.		Horiz. strip of 5, #4399-4403	5.75	
b.		Booklet pane of 20, 4 each #4399-4403	23.00	

LOVE

King of Hearts
A3350

Queen of Hearts
A3351

PHOTOGRAVURE BOOKLET STAMPS

Serpentine Die Cut 10¾ on 2, 3 or 4 Sides

2009, May 8

Self-Adhesive

4404	A3350	44c multicolored	1.15	.25
4405	A3351	44c multicolored	1.15	.25
a.		Horiz. or vert. pair, #4404-4405	2.30	
b.		Booklet pane of 20, 10 each #4404-4405	23.00	

BOB HOPE

Bob Hope (1903-2003), Actor, Comedian — A3352

LITHOGRAPHED

Serpentine Die Cut 10¾

2009, May 29

Self-Adhesive

4406	A3352	44c multicolored	1.00	.25

Celebrate Type of 2007

2009, June 10

Self-Adhesive

4407	A3189	44c multicolored	.90	.25
a.		Die cutting omitted, pair		

BLACK HERITAGE

Anna Julia Cooper (c. 1858-1964), Educator — A3353

2009, June 11

Self-Adhesive

4408	A3353	44c multicolored	.90	.25

GULF COAST LIGHTHOUSES

Matagorda Island Lighthouse, Texas
A3354

Sabine Pass Lighthouse, Louisiana
A3355

Biloxi Lighthouse, Mississippi
A3356

Sand Island Lighthouse, Alabama
A3357

Fort Jefferson Lighthouse, Florida — A3358

Serpentine Die Cut 11x10¾

2009, July 23

Self-Adhesive

4409	A3354	44c multicolored	.90	.40
4410	A3355	44c multicolored	.90	.40
4411	A3356	44c multicolored	.90	.40
4412	A3357	44c multicolored	.90	.40
4413	A3358	44c multicolored	.90	.40
a.		Horiz. strip of 5, #4409-4413	4.50	

EARLY TV MEMORIES

A3359

No. 4414: a, Milton Berle in "Texaco Star Theater." b, Lucille Ball and Vivian Vance in "I Love Lucy." c, Red Skelton in "The Red Skelton Show." d, Marionette Howdy Doody in "Howdy Doody." e, Jack Webb in "Dragnet." f, Lassie in "Lassie." g, William Boyd and horse, Topper, in "Hopalong Cassidy." h, Groucho Marx in "You Bet Your Life." i, Dinah Shore in "The Dinah Shore Show." j, Ed Sullivan in "The Ed Sullivan Show." k, Fran Allison and puppets, Kukla and Ollie in "Kukla, Fran and Ollie." l, Phil Silvers in "The Phil Silvers Show." m, Clayton Moore and horse, Silver, in "The Lone Ranger." n, Raymond Burr and William Talman in "Perry Mason." o, Alfred Hitchcock in "Alfred Hitchcock Presents." p, George Burns and Gracie Allen in "Burns and Allen." q, Ozzie and Harriet Nelson in "Ozzie and Harriet." r, Steve Allen in "The Tonight Show." s, Rod Serling in "The Twilight Zone." t, Jackie Gleason and Art Carney in "The Honeymooners."

Serpentine Die Cut 10¾x10½

2009, Aug. 11

Self-Adhesive

4414	A3359	Pane of 20	20.00	
a.-t.		44c Any single	1.00	.50

HAWAII STATEHOOD, 50TH ANNIV.

Surfer and Outrigger Canoe
A3360

PHOTOGRAVURE

Serpentine Die Cut 11

2009, Aug. 21

Self-Adhesive

4415	A3360	44c multicolored	1.25	.25

Eid Type of 2001

2009, Sept. 3

Self-Adhesive

4416	A2734	44c multicolored	.90	.25

THANKSGIVING DAY PARADE

Crowd, Street Sign, Bear Balloon
A3361

Drum Major, Musicians
A3362

Musicians, Balloon, Horse
A3363

Cowboy, Turkey Balloon, Crowd, Television Cameraman — A3364

Serpentine Die Cut 11x10¾

2009, Sept. 9

Self-Adhesive

4417	A3361	44c multicolored	.90	.35
4418	A3362	44c multicolored	.90	.35
4419	A3363	44c multicolored	.90	.35
4420	A3364	44c multicolored	.90	.35
a.		Horiz. strip of 4, #4417-4420	3.60	

LEGENDS OF HOLLYWOOD

Gary Cooper (1901-61), Actor — A3365

Serpentine Die Cut 11

2009, Sept. 10

Self-Adhesive

4421	A3365	44c multicolored	1.00	.25

SUPREME COURT JUSTICES

Souvenir Sheet

A3366

No. 4422: a, Felix Frankfurter (1882-1965). b, William J. Brennan, Jr. (1906-97). c, Louis D. Brandeis (1856-1941). d, Joseph Story (1779-1845).

LITHOGRAPHED

Serpentine Die Cut 11x10½

2009, Sept. 22

Self-Adhesive

4422	A3366	Pane of 4	4.00	
a.-d.		44c Any single	1.00	.30

KELP FOREST

A3367

Wildlife: a, Brown pelican. b, Western gull, southern sea otters, red sea urchin. c, Harbor seal. d, Lion's mane nudibranch, vert. e, Yellowtail rockfish, white-spotted rose anemone. f, Vermilion rockfish. g, Copper rockfish. h, Pacific rock crab, jeweled top snail. i, Northern kelp crab, vert. j, Treefish, Monterey turban snail, brooding sea anemones.

PHOTOGRAVURE

Serpentine Die Cut 10¾

2009, Oct. 1

Self-Adhesive

4423	A3367	Pane of 10	11.00	
a.-j.		44c Any single	1.10	.40

CHRISTMAS

Madonna and Sleeping Child, by Sassoferrato (Giovanni Battista Salvi)
A3368

Reindeer
A3369

Snowman
A3370

Gingerbread Man
A3371

Toy Soldier
A3372

Reindeer
A3373

Snowman
A3374

Gingerbread
Man
A3375

Toy Soldier — A3376

LITHOGRAPHED, PHOTOGRAVURE
(#4429-4432)
Serpentine Die Cut 10¾x11 on 2 or 3 Sides
2009
Self-Adhesive
Booklet Stamps

4424	A3368	44c multicolored	.90	.25
a.		Booklet pane of 20	18.00	
4425	A3369	44c multicolored	1.10	.25
4426	A3370	44c multicolored	1.10	.25
4427	A3371	44c multicolored	1.10	.25
4428	A3372	44c multicolored	1.10	.25
a.		Block of 4, #4425-4428	4.40	
b.		Booklet pane of 20, 5 each #4425-4428	22.00	
c.		As "b," die cutting omitted on side with 12 stamps	—	
d.		As "b," die cutting omitted on side with 8 stamps	—	
e.		As "a," die cutting omitted	375.00	

Serpentine Die Cut 8 on 2, 3 or 4 Sides

4429	A3373	44c multicolored	1.10	.25
4430	A3374	44c multicolored	1.10	.25
4431	A3375	44c multicolored	1.10	.25
4432	A3376	44c multicolored	1.10	.25
a.		Block of 4, #4429-4432	4.40	
b.		Booklet pane of 18, 5 each #4429, 4431, 4 each #4430, 4432	20.00	
		Nos. 4424-4432 (9)	9.70	2.25

No. 4424a is a double-sided booklet pane with 12 stamps on one side and eight stamps plus label that serves as a booklet cover on the other side. No. 4428b is a double-sided booklet pane with 12 stamps on one side (3 each of Nos. 4425-4428) and eight stamps (2 each of Nos. 4425-4428) plus label that serves as a booklet cover on the other side.

HANUKKAH

Menorah — A3377

LITHOGRAPHED
Serpentine Die Cut 10¾x11
2009, Oct. 9
Self-Adhesive

4433	A3377	44c multicolored	.90	.25

KWANZAA

Family — A3378

2009, Oct. 9
Self-Adhesive

4434	A3378	44c multicolored	.90	.25

CHINESE NEW YEAR

Year of the
Tiger
A3379

Designed by Ethel Kessler. Printed by Avery Dennison.

PHOTOGRAVURE
Serpentine Die Cut 11
2010, Jan. 14   **Tagged**
Self-Adhesive

4435	A3379	44c multicolored	1.10	.25

2010 WINTER OLYMPICS, VANCOUVER

Snowboarder
A3380

Designed by Howard E. Paine. Printed by Avery Dennison.

PHOTOGRAVURE
Serpentine Die Cut 11
2010, Jan. 22   **Tagged**
Self-Adhesive

4436	A3380	44c multicolored	.90	.25
		P# block of 4, 6# + V	4.00	
		Pane of 20	20.00	

"Forever" Liberty Bell Type of 2007
Printed by Ashton-Potter (USA) Ltd.

Serpentine Die Cut 11¼x10¾ on 2, 3 or 4 Sides
2010, Feb. 3   **Litho.**
Booklet Stamp
Self-Adhesive
Medium Microprinting, Bell 16mm Wide
Dated "2009" in Copper

4437	A3148	(44c) multicolored	1.00	.25
a.		Booklet pane of 18	18.00	

On No. 4437, the "2009" date is smaller than that on No. 4127i, which has a 15mm wide bell. The bell on No. 4437 is also 17mm tall while No. 4127i is 16mm tall. The microprinted "Forever" is on a dotted background on No. 4437 and on a white background on No. 4127i.
See also No. 4128c.

AMERICAN LANDMARKS

Mackinac
Bridge,
Michigan
A3381

Bixby
Creek
Bridge,
California
A3382

PHOTOGRAVURE
Serpentine Die Cut 10¾x10½
2010, Feb. 3   **Tagged**
Self-Adhesive

4438	A3381	$4.90 multi	11.00	5.00
		P# block of 4, 4# +V	45.00	
		Pane of 20	220.00	
4439	A3382	$18.30 multi	45.00	18.00
		P# block of 4, 4# +V	180.00	
		Pane of 20	900.00	

DISTINGUISHED SAILORS

Admiral William S. Sims (1858-1936), Emblem of USS W.S. Sims — A3383

Admiral Arleigh A. Burke (1901-96), Emblem of USS Arleigh Burke A3384

Lieutenant Commander John McCloy (1876-1945), Emblem of USS McCloy — A3385

Petty Officer 3rd Class Doris Miller (1919-43), Emblem of USS Miller A3386

PHOTOGRAVURE
Serpentine Die Cut 10¾x10½
2010, Feb. 4   **Tagged**
Self-Adhesive

4440	A3383	44c multicolored	.90	.40
4441	A3384	44c multicolored	.90	.40
4442	A3385	44c multicolored	.90	.40
4443	A3386	44c multicolored	.90	.40
a.		Block or horiz. strip of 4, #4440-4443	3.60	
		P# block of 4, 6# + V	4.00	
		P# block of 8, 2 sets of 6# + V + top label	7.20	
		Pane of 20	19.50	

ABSTRACT EXPRESSIONISTS

A3387

No. 4444: a, The Golden Wall, by Hans Hofmann (30x30mm). b, Asheville, by Willem de Kooning (38x38mm). c, Orange and Yellow, by Mark Rothko (35x49mm). d, Convergence, by Jackson Pollock (63x43mm). e, The Liver Is the Cock's Comb, by Arshile Gorky (39x32mm). f, 1948-C, by Clyfford Still (35x49mm). g, Elegy to the Spanish Republic No. 34, by Robert Motherwell (54x49mm). h, La Grande Vallée 0, by Joan Mitchell (35x49mm). i, Romanesque Façade, by Adolph Gottlieb (35x49mm). j, Achilles, by Barnett Newman (35x49mm).

LITHOGRAPHED
Serpentine Die Cut 10¾x11, 10¾ (#4444a, 4444b, 4444e), 11x10¾ (#4444d)
2010, Mar. 11   **Tagged**
Self-Adhesive

4444	A3387	Pane of 10	11.00	
a.-j.		44c Any single	1.10	.40

BILL MAULDIN (1921-2003), CARTOONIST

A3388

LITHOGRAPHED
Serpentine Die Cut 10¾
2010, Mar. 31   **Tagged**
Self-Adhesive

4445	A3388	44c multicolored	.90	.25
		P# block of 4, 4# + P	3.60	
		Pane of 20	18.00	

COWBOYS OF THE SILVER SCREEN

Roy Rogers
(1911-98)
A3389

Tom Mix (1880-1940)
A3390

William S. Hart
(1864-1946)
A3391

Gene Autry
(1907-98)
A3392

LITHOGRAPHED
Serpentine Die Cut 10½x10¾
2010, Apr. 17
Self-Adhesive

4446	A3389	44c multicolored	1.25	.35
4447	A3390	44c multicolored	1.25	.35
4448	A3391	44c multicolored	1.25	.35
4449	A3392	44c multicolored	1.25	.35
a.		Block of 4, #4446-4449	5.00	

LOVE

Pansies in a
Basket — A3393

PHOTOGRAVURE
Serpentine Die Cut 10¾
2010, Apr. 22
Self-Adhesive

4450	A3393	44c multicolored	.90	.25

ANIMAL RESCUE

Wire-haired Jack Russell Terrier — A3394

Maltese — A3395

Calico — A3396

Yellow Labrador Retriever A3397

Golden Retriever A3398

Gray, White and Tan Cat — A3399

Black, White and Tan Cat — A3400

Australian Shepherd A3401

Boston Terrier — A3402

Orange Tabby — A3403

LITHOGRAPHED
Serpentine Die Cut 10¾
2010, Apr. 30
Self-Adhesive

4451	A3394	44c multicolored	1.25	.40
4452	A3395	44c multicolored	1.25	.40
4453	A3396	44c multicolored	1.25	.40
4454	A3397	44c multicolored	1.25	.40
4455	A3398	44c multicolored	1.25	.40
4456	A3399	44c multicolored	1.25	.40
4457	A3400	44c multicolored	1.25	.40
4458	A3401	44c multicolored	1.25	.40
4459	A3402	44c multicolored	1.25	.40
4460	A3403	44c multicolored	1.25	.40
a.		Block of 10, #4451-4460	12.50	

LEGENDS OF HOLLYWOOD

Katharine Hepburn (1907-2003), Actress — A3404

PHOTOGRAVURE
Serpentine Die Cut 10¾
2010, May 12
Self-Adhesive

4461	A3404	44c black	1.00	.25

MONARCH BUTTERFLY

A3405

PHOTOGRAVURE
Serpentine Die Cut 10½
2010, May 17
Self-Adhesive

4462	A3405	64c multicolored	1.50	.25

KATE SMITH

Kate Smith (1907-86), Singer — A3406

PHOTOGRAVURE
2010, May 27 *Serpentine Die Cut 11*
Self-Adhesive

4463	A3406	44c multicolored	.90	.25

BLACK HERITAGE

Oscar Micheaux (1884-1951), Film Director — A3407

Serpentine Die Cut 11
2010, June 22
Self-Adhesive

4464	A3407	44c multicolored	.90	.25

NEGRO LEAGUES BASEBALL

Play at the Plate A3408

Andrew "Rube" Foster (1879-1930), Founder of Negro National League — A3409

PHOTOGRAVURE
Serpentine Die Cut 11
2010, July 15
Self-Adhesive

4465	A3408	44c multicolored	.90	.30
4466	A3409	44c multicolored	.90	.30
a.		Horiz. pair, #4465-4466	1.80	

SUNDAY FUNNIES

Beetle Bailey — A3410

Calvin and Hobbes A3411

Archie — A3412

Garfield A3413

Dennis the Menace A3414

LITHOGRAPHED
Serpentine Die Cut 10½x10¾
2010, July 16
Self-Adhesive

4467	A3410	44c multicolored	1.00	.30
4468	A3411	44c multicolored	1.00	.30
4469	A3412	44c multicolored	1.00	.30
4470	A3413	44c multicolored	1.00	.30
4471	A3414	44c multicolored	1.00	.30
a.		Horiz. strip of 5, #4467-4471	5.00	

BOY SCOUTS OF AMERICA, CENTENNIAL

Boy Scouts — A3415

PHOTOGRAVURE
Serpentine Die Cut 11
2010, July 27
Self-Adhesive

4472	A3415	44c multicolored	.90	.25

Boys in a Pasture, by Winslow Homer (1836-1910) — A3416

Serpentine Die Cut 10¾
2010, Aug. 12
Self-Adhesive

4473	A3416	44c multicolored	1.00	.25

HAWAIIAN RAIN FOREST

A3417

No. 4474: a, Hawaii 'amakihi, Hawaii 'elepaio, ohi'a lehua. b, 'Akepa, 'ope'ape'a, vert. c, 'I'iwi, haha. d, 'Oma'o, kanawao, 'ohelo kau la'au, vert. e, 'Oha, vert. f, Pulelehua butterfly, kolea lau nui, 'ilihia. g, Koele Mountain damselfly, 'akala, vert. h, 'Apapane, Hawaiian mint, vert. i, Jewel orchid, vert. j, Happyface spider, 'ala'ala wai nui, vert.

LITHOGRAPHED
Serpentine Die Cut 10¾
2010, Sept. 1
Self-Adhesive

4474	A3417	Pane of 10	10.00	
a.-j.		44c Any single	1.00	.40

MOTHER TERESA

Mother Teresa (1910-97), Humanitarian, 1979 Nobel Peace Laureate — A3418

PHOTOGRAVURE
2010, Sept. 5 *Serpentine Die Cut 11*
Self-Adhesive

4475	A3418	44c multicolored	.90	.25

LITERARY ARTS

Julia de Burgos (1914-53), Poet A3419

PHOTOGRAVURE
Serpentine Die Cut 11
2010, Sept. 14
Self-Adhesive

4476	A3419	44c multicolored	.90	.25

CHRISTMAS

Angel with Lute, Detail of Fresco by Melozzo da Forli — A3420

Ponderosa Pine — A3421

Eastern Red Cedar A3422

Balsam Fir A3423

Blue Spruce A3424

Ponderosa Pine A3425

Eastern Red Cedar A3426

Balsam Fir A3427

Blue Spruce — A3428

Designed by Terrence W. McCaffrey (#4477), Howard E. Paine
Printed by Avery Dennison (#4477), Banknote Corporation of America for Sennett Security Products (#4478-4481), Ashton-Potter (USA) Ltd. (#4482-4485).

PHOTOGRAVURE (#4477), LITHOGRAPHED
Serpentine Die Cut 10¾
2010, Oct. 21   Tagged
Self-Adhesive

4477 A3420 44c multicolored   1.00   .25

Booklet Stamps
Serpentine Die Cut 11 on 2 or 3 Sides

4478 A3421 (44c) multicolored   1.00   .25
4479 A3422 (44c) multicolored   1.00   .25
4480 A3423 (44c) multicolored   1.00   .25
4481 A3424 (44c) multicolored   1.00   .25
  a. Block of 4, #4478-4481   4.00
  b. Booklet pane of 20, 5 each
     #4478-4481   20.00
  c. As "a," die cutting omitted   —
  d. As "b," die cutting omitted
     on side with 12 stamps   500.00
  e. As "b," die cutting omitted
     on side with 8 stamps   700.00
  f. As "b," die cutting omitted
     on side with 12 stamps,
     die cutting omitted on
     bottom 4 stamps on side
     with 8 stamps   —

Serpentine Die Cut 11¼x10¾ on 2, 3 or 4 Sides

4482 A3425 (44c) multicolored   1.00   .25
4483 A3426 (44c) multicolored   1.00   .25
4484 A3427 (44c) multicolored   1.00   .25

4485 A3428 (44c) multicolored   1.00   .25
  a. Block of 4, #4482-4485   4.00
  b. Booklet pane of 18, 5 each
     #4482, 4484, 4 each
     #4483, 4485   18.00
     Nos. 4477-4485 (9)   9.00 2.25

No. 4481b is a double-sided booklet pane with 12 stamps on one side (3 each of Nos. 4478-4481) and eight stamps (2 each of Nos. 4478-4481) plus label that serves as a booklet cover on the other side.

Statue of Liberty A3429

Flag A3430

LITHOGRAPHED (#4486-4489), PHOTOGRAVURE
Serpentine Die Cut 9½ Vert.
2010, Dec. 1
COIL STAMPS
Self-Adhesive

4486 A3429 (44c) multicolored   1.50   .25
4487 A3430 (44c) multicolored   1.50   .25
  a. Pair, #4486-4487   3.00

Serpentine Die Cut 11 Vert.

4488 A3429 (44c) multicolored   1.50   .25
  a. Vert. pair, horiz. unslit btwn.
4489 A3430 (44c) multicolored   1.50   .25
  a. Pair, #4488-4489   3.00
  b. Block of 4 (one pair each from
     two different coil rolls), horiz.
     unslit btwn.   —

Serpentine Die Cut 8½ Vert.

4490 A3429 (44c) multicolored   1.50   .25
4491 A3430 (44c) multicolored   1.50   .25
  a. Pair, #4490-4491   3.00
     Nos. 4486-4491 (6)   9.00 1.50

Microprinting reads "4evR" on Nos. 4486-4487, "4evr" on Nos. 4488-4489, and "4EVR" on Nos. 4490-4491. The microprinting is found above the Statue of Liberty's hair, and at the bottom of the lowest red stripe of the flag.
See Nos. 4518-4519, 4559-4564.

CHINESE NEW YEAR

Year of the Rabbit A3431

PHOTOGRAVURE
Serpentine Die Cut 11
2011, Jan. 22
Self-Adhesive

4492 A3431 (44c) multicolored   1.00   .25

KANSAS STATEHOOD, 150TH ANNIV.

Windmill and Wind Turbines A3432

LITHOGRAPHED
Serpentine Die Cut 11
2011, Jan. 27
Self-Adhesive

4493 A3432 (44c) multicolored   1.00   .25

PRES. RONALD REAGAN (1911-2004)

Pres. Ronald Reagan — A3433

PHOTOGRAVURE
Serpentine Die Cut 10½
2011, Feb. 10
Self-Adhesive

4494 A3433 (44c) multicolored   1.00   .25

Art Deco Bird — A3434

LITHOGRAPHED
Serpentine Die Cut 10 Vert.
2011, Feb. 11   Untagged
COIL STAMP
Self-Adhesive

4495 A3434 (5c) multicolored   .25   .25

Quill and Inkwell — A3435

LITHOGRAPHED
Serpentine Die Cut 11¾ Vert.
2011, Feb. 14
COIL STAMP
Self-Adhesive

4496 A3435 44c multicolored   .95   .25

LATIN MUSIC LEGENDS

Tito Puente (1923-2000) A3436

Carmen Miranda (1909-55) A3437

Selena (1971-95) A3438

Carlos Gardel (1890-1935) A3439

Celia Cruz (1925-2003) A3440

PHOTOGRAVURE
Serpentine Die Cut 10¾
2011, Mar. 16
Self-Adhesive

4497 A3436 (44c) multicolored   1.00   .40
4498 A3437 (44c) multicolored   1.00   .40
4499 A3438 (44c) multicolored   1.00   .40
4500 A3439 (44c) multicolored   1.00   .40
4501 A3440 (44c) multicolored   1.00   .40
  a. Horiz. strip of 5, #4497-4501   5.00

CELEBRATE

A3441

PHOTOGRAVURE
Serpentine Die Cut 11x11½
2011, Mar. 25
Self-Adhesive

4502 A3441 (44c) multicolored   1.00   .25
Compare with type A3855.

JAZZ

Musicians A3442

PHOTOGRAVURE
Serpentine Die Cut 10¾
2011, Mar. 26
Self-Adhesive

4503 A3442 (44c) multicolored   1.00   .25
See note after No. 1549.

Statue of Liberty and Flag Types of 2010 and

George Washington A3443

Oregano A3444

Flax A3445

Foxglove A3446

Lavender A3447

Sage A3448

Oveta Culp Hobby (1905-95), First Health, Education and Welfare Department Secretary A3449

New River Gorge Bridge, West Virginia — A3450

LITHOGRAPHED (#4504, 4511, 4512, 4518-4519), PHOTOGRAVURE (#4505-4510, 4513-4517)

2011   *Serpentine Die Cut 11¼x10¾*
Self-Adhesive

4504	A3443	20c multicolored	.40	.25

Serpentine Die Cut 11

4505	A3444	29c multicolored	.75	.25
4506	A3445	29c multicolored	.75	.25
4507	A3446	29c multicolored	.75	.25
4508	A3447	29c multicolored	.75	.25
4509	A3448	29c multicolored	.75	.25
a.		Horiz. strip of 5, #4505-4509	3.75	
4510	A3449	84c multicolored	1.75	.35

Serpentine Die Cut 10¾x10½

4511	A3450	$4.95 multicolored	10.00	5.00
		Nos. 4504-4511 (7)	14.15	6.50

Coil Stamps
Serpentine Die Cut 9½ Vert.

4512	A3443	20c multicolored	.40	.25

No. 4512a is recorded only on a single cover bearing a strip of 9 and three strips of 10. The editors would welcome reports of unused examples.

Serpentine Die Cut 8½ Vert.

4513	A3446	29c multicolored	1.20	.25
4514	A3447	29c multicolored	1.20	.25
4515	A3448	29c multicolored	1.20	.25
4516	A3444	29c multicolored	1.20	.25
4517	A3445	29c multicolored	1.20	.25
a.		Horiz. strip of 5, #4513-4517	6.00	
		Nos. 4512-4517 (6)	6.40	1.50

Booklet Stamps
Thin Paper
Serpentine Die Cut 11¼x10¾ on 2, 3, or 4 Sides

4518	A3429	(44c) multicolored	1.00	.25
4519	A3430	(44c) multicolored	1.00	.25
a.		Pair, #4518-4519	2.00	
b.		Booklet pane of 18, 9 each #4518-4519	18.00	

Issued: Nos. 4504, 4511, 4512, 4/11; Nos. 4505-4509, 4513-4517, 4/7; No. 4510, 4/15; Nos. 4518-4519. 4/8.

Wedding Cake Type of 2009 With "USA" in Serifed Type and

Wedding Roses — A3450a

LITHOGRAPHED (#4520), PHOTOGRAVURE (#4521)

2011   *Serpentine Die Cut 11*
Self-Adhesive

4520	A3450a	(44c) multicolored	1.00	.25
a.		Die cutting omitted, pair		
4521	A3344	64c multicolored	1.35	.25

Issued: No. 4520, 4/21; No. 4521, 4/11.

CIVIL WAR SESQUICENTENNIAL

Battle of Fort Sumter — A3451

First Battle of Bull Run — A3452

LITHOGRAPHED
Serpentine Die Cut 11
2011, Apr. 12
Self-Adhesive

4522	A3451	(44c) multicolored	1.00	.30
4523	A3452	(44c) multicolored	1.00	.30
a.		Pair, #4522-4523	2.00	

GO GREEN

A3453

No. 4524 — Messages: a, Buy local produce, reuse bags. b, Fix water leaks. c, Share rides. d, Turn off lights not in use. e, Choose to walk. f, Go Green, reduce our environmental footprint step by step. g, Compost. h, Let nature do the work. i, Recycle more. j, Ride a bike. k, Plant trees. l, Insulate the home. m, Use public transportation. n, Use efficient light bulbs. o, Adjust the thermostat. p, Maintain tire pressure.

PHOTOGRAVURE
Serpentine Die Cut 10¾
2011, Apr. 14
Self-Adhesive

4524	A3453	Pane of 16	16.00	
a.-p.		(44c) Any single	1.00	.50

HELEN HAYES

Helen Hayes (1900-93), Actress — A3454

Serpentine Die Cut 11
2011, Apr. 25   **Tagged**
Self-Adhesive

4525	A3454	(44c) multicolored	1.00	.25

LEGENDS OF HOLLYWOOD

Gregory Peck (1916-2003), Actor — A3455

Serpentine Die Cut 10¾
2011, Apr. 28
Self-Adhesive

4526	A3455	(44c) black	1.25	.25

SPACE FIRSTS

Alan B. Shepard, Jr. (1923-98), First American in Space A3456

Messenger, First Spacecraft to Orbit Mercury — A3457

LITHOGRAPHED
2011, May 4   *Serpentine Die Cut 11*
Self-Adhesive

4527	A3456	(44c) multicolored	1.00	.30
4528	A3457	(44c) multicolored	1.00	.30
a.		Horiz. pair, #4527-4528	2.00	

Purple Heart and Ribbon — A3458

Serpentine Die Cut 11¼x10¾
2011, May 5
Self-Adhesive

4529	A3458	(44c) multicolored	1.00	.25

INDIANAPOLIS 500, CENT.

Ray Harroun Driving Marmon Wasp A3459

Designed by Phil Jordan. Printed by Banknote Corporation of America for Sennett Security Products.

LITHOGRAPHED
Serpentine Die Cut 10¾
2011, May 20
Self-Adhesive

4530	A3459	(44c) multicolored	1.00	.25

GARDEN OF LOVE

Pink Flower A3460   Red Flower A3461

Blue Flowers A3462   Butterfly A3463

Green Vine Leaves A3464   Blue Flower A3465

Doves A3466   Orange Red Flowers A3467

Strawberry A3468   Yellow Orange Flowers A3469

Designed by Derry Noyes. Printed by Avery Dennison.

PHOTOGRAVURE
Serpentine Die Cut 10¾
2011, May 23
Self-Adhesive

4531	A3460	(44c) multicolored	1.50	.40
4532	A3461	(44c) multicolored	1.50	.40
4533	A3462	(44c) multicolored	1.50	.40
4534	A3463	(44c) multicolored	1.50	.40
4535	A3464	(44c) multicolored	1.50	.40
4536	A3465	(44c) multicolored	1.50	.40
4537	A3466	(44c) multicolored	1.50	.40
4538	A3467	(44c) multicolored	1.50	.40
4539	A3468	(44c) multicolored	1.50	.40
4540	A3469	(44c) multicolored	1.50	.40
a.		Block of 10, #4531-4540	15.00	
		Nos. 4531-4540 (10)	15.00	4.00

The two blocks of 10 on the pane are separated by a gutter.

AMERICAN SCIENTISTS

Melvin Calvin (1911-97), Chemist A3470

Asa Gray (1810-88), Botanist A3471

Maria Goeppert Mayer (1906-72), Physicist A3472

Severo Ochoa (1905-93), Biochemist A3473

LITHOGRAPHED
Serpentine Die Cut 11
2011, June 16
Self-Adhesive

4541	A3470	(44c) multicolored	1.00	.50
4542	A3471	(44c) multicolored	1.00	.50
4543	A3472	(44c) multicolored	1.00	.50
4544	A3473	(44c) multicolored	1.00	.50
a.		Horiz. strip of 4, #4541-4544	4.00	
b.		Horiz. strip of 4, die cutting missing on backing paper (from misaligned die-cutting mat)	—	

LITERARY ARTS

Mark Twain (Samuel L. Clemens) (1835-1910), Writer — A3474

PHOTOGRAVURE
Serpentine Die Cut 11
2011, June 25
Self-Adhesive

4545	A3474	(44c) multicolored	1.00	.25

PIONEERS OF AMERICAN INDUSTRIAL DESIGN

A3475

No. 4546: a, "Normandie" pitcher, designed by Peter Müller-Munk (1904-67). b, Fiesta dinnerware, designed by Frederick Hurten Rhead (1880-1942). c, Streamlined pencil sharpener, designed by Raymond Loewy (1893-1986). d, Table lamp, designed by Donald Deskey (1894-1989). e, Kodak "Baby Brownie" camera, designed by Walter Dorwin Teague (1883-1960). f, Model 302 Bell telephone, designed by Henry Dreyfuss (1904-72). g, Emerson "Patriot" radio, designed by Norman Bel Geddes (1893-1958). h, Streamlined sewing machines, designed by Dave Chapman (1909-78). i, "Anywhere" lamp, designed by Greta von Nessen (1900-74). j, IBM "Selectric" typewriter, designed by Eliot Noyes (1910-77). k, "Highlight/Pinch" flatware, designed by Russel Wright (1904-76). l, Herman Miller electric clock, designed by Gilbert Rohde (1894-1944).

PHOTOGRAVURE
Serpentine Die Cut 10¾
2011, June 29
Self-Adhesive

4546	A3475	Pane of 12	12.00	
a.-l.		(44c) Any single	1.00	.50

OWNEY, THE POSTAL DOG

Owney, His Medals and Tags A3476

PHOTOGRAVURE
Serpentine Die Cut 11
2011, July 27
Self-Adhesive

4547	A3476	(44c) multicolored	1.50	.25

U.S. MERCHANT MARINE

Clipper Ship A3477

Auxiliary Steamship A3478

Liberty Ship A3479

Container Ship A3480

PHOTOGRAVURE
Serpentine Die Cut 11
2011, July 28
Self-Adhesive

4548	A3477	(44c) multicolored	1.00	.35
4549	A3478	(44c) multicolored	1.00	.35
4550	A3479	(44c) multicolored	1.00	.35
4551	A3480	(44c) multicolored	1.00	.35
a.		Block or horiz. strip of 4, #4548-4551	4.00	

EID

"Eid Mubarak" — A3481

PHOTOGRAVURE
Serpentine Die Cut 11¼
2011, Aug. 12
Self-Adhesive

4552	A3481	(44c) mar, gray & gold	1.00	.25

CHARACTERS FROM DISNEY-PIXAR FILMS
Send a Hello

Lightning McQueen and Mater from *Cars* — A3482

Remy the Rat and Linguini from *Ratatouille* A3483

Buzz Lightyear and Aliens from *Toy Story* — A3484

Carl Fredricksen and Dug the Dog from *Up* — A3485

WALL-E from *WALL-E* A3486

PHOTOGRAVURE
Serpentine Die Cut 10½
2011, Aug. 19
Self-Adhesive

4553	A3482	(44c) multicolored	1.10	.40
4554	A3483	(44c) multicolored	1.10	.40
4555	A3484	(44c) multicolored	1.10	.40
4556	A3485	(44c) multicolored	1.10	.40
4557	A3486	(44c) multicolored	1.10	.40
a.		Horiz. strip of 5, #4553-4557	5.50	

Adjacent horizontal or vertical stamps will have selvage between the stamps.

AMERICAN TREASURES SERIES

The Long Leg, by Edward Hopper (1882-1967) — A3487

PHOTOGRAVURE
Serpentine Die Cut 11
2011, Aug. 24
Self-Adhesive

4558	A3487	(44c) multicolored	1.00	.25

Statue of Liberty and Flag Types of 2010
LITHOGRAPHED (#4559-4562), PHOTOGRAVURE
Serpentine Die Cut 11¼x11 on 2 or 3 Sides
2011, Sept. 14
BOOKLET STAMPS
Self-Adhesive

4559	A3429	(44c) multicolored	1.25	.25
4560	A3430	(44c) multicolored	1.25	.25
a.		Pair, #4559-4560	2.50	
b.		Booklet pane of 20, 10 each #4559-4560	25.00	
4561	A3429	(44c) multicolored	1.00	.25
4562	A3430	(44c) multicolored	1.00	.25
a.		Pair, #4561-4562	2.00	
b.		Booklet pane of 20, 10 each #4561-4562	20.00	

Serpentine Die Cut 11¼x11½ on 2 or 3 Sides

4563	A3429	(44c) multicolored	1.00	.25
4564	A3430	(44c) multicolored	1.00	.25
a.		Pair, #4563-4564	2.00	
b.		Booklet pane of 20, 10 each #4563-4564	20.00	
		Nos. 4559-4564 (6)	6.50	1.50

Microprinting reads "4evR" on Nos. 4559-4560, "4evr" on Nos. 4561-4562, and "4EVR" on Nos. 4563-4564. The microprinting is found above the Statue of Liberty's hair, and at the bottom of the lowest red stripe of the flag. Nos. 4560b, 4562b and 4564b are double-sided booklet panes with 12 stamps one one side (6 each of types A3429-A3430) and 8 stamps (4 each of types A3429-A3430) on the other side. The paper used on Nos. 4561-4562 is thicker than that used on Nos. 4518-4519.

BLACK HERITAGE

Barbara Jordan (1936-96), Congresswoman A3488

LITHOGRAPHED
Serpentine Die Cut 10¾
2011, Sept. 16
Self-Adhesive

4565	A3488	(44c) multicolored	1.00	.25

ART OF ROMARE BEARDEN (1911-88)

Conjunction A3489

Odysseus: Poseidon, The Sea God - Enemy of Odysseus A3490

Prevalence of Ritual: Conjur Woman A3491

Falling Star — A3492

PHOTOGRAVURE
Serpentine Die Cut 10¾
2011, Sept. 28
Self-Adhesive

4566	A3489	(44c) multicolored	1.00	.40
4567	A3490	(44c) multicolored	1.00	.40
4568	A3491	(44c) multicolored	1.00	.40
4569	A3492	(44c) multicolored	1.00	.40
a.		Horiz. strip of 4, #4566-4569	4.00	

CHRISTMAS

Madonna of the Candelabra, by Raphael — A3493

A3494   A3495

A3496   A3497

A3498   A3499

Ornaments
A3500   A3501

LITHOGRAPHED
Serpentine Die Cut 10¾x 11 on 2 or 3 Sides
2011, Oct. 13
Booklet Stamps
Self-Adhesive

4570	A3493	(44c) multicolored	1.00	.25
a.		Booklet pane of 20	20.00	

With "USPS" Microprinted on Collar of Ornament

4571	A3494	(44c) multicolored	1.00	.25
4572	A3495	(44c) multicolored	1.00	.25
4573	A3496	(44c) multicolored	1.00	.25
4574	A3497	(44c) multicolored	1.00	.25
a.		Block of 4, #4571-4574	4.00	
b.		Booklet pane of 20, 5 each #4571-4574	20.00	

Microprinted "USPS" in Places Other Than Collar of Ornament

4575	A3494	(44c) multicolored	1.00	.25
4576	A3495	(44c) multicolored	1.00	.25
4577	A3496	(44c) multicolored	1.00	.25
4578	A3497	(44c) multicolored	1.00	.25
a.	Block of 4, #4575-4578		4.00	
b.	Booklet pane of 20, 5 each #4575-4578		20.00	

Serpentine Die Cut 11¼x11 on 2, 3 or 4 Sides

4579	A3498	(44c) multicolored	1.00	.25
4580	A3499	(44c) multicolored	1.00	.25
4581	A3500	(44c) multicolored	1.00	.25
4582	A3501	(44c) multicolored	1.00	.25
a.	Block of 4, #4579-4582		4.00	
b.	Booklet pane of 18, 5 each #4579, 4582, 4 each #4580-4581		18.00	
	Nos. 4570-4582 (13)		13.00	3.25

The microprinted "USPS" is to the left of the third stripe on Nos. 4575 and 4579, on the left side of the bottom ribbon of the ribbon cluster above the ornament collar on Nos. 4576 and 4578, below the bottom stripe near the bottom tip on No. 4577, on the vertical ribbon on No. 4580, on a curved ribbon above the collar on No. 4581, and on the left side of the ornament, below the collar, on No. 4582.

No. 4570a is a double-sided booklet with 12 stamps on one side and eight stamps plus a label that serves as a booklet cover on the other side. Nos. 4574b and 4578b are double sided booklets with 12 stamps (3 each of types A3494-A3497) on one side and eight stamps (2 each of types A3494-A3497) plus a label that serves as a booklet cover on the other side.

HANUKKAH

A3502

Serpentine Die Cut 11x10¾
2011, Oct. 14
Self-Adhesive

4583	A3502	(44c) multicolored	1.00	.25

KWANZAA

Family — A3503

Serpentine Die Cut 10¾x11
2011, Oct. 14
Self-Adhesive

4584	A3503	(44c) multicolored	1.00	.25

Eagle — A3504

PHOTOGRAVURE
Serpentine Die Cut 11 Vert.
2012, Jan. 3
Coil Stamps
Self-Adhesive
Color Behind "USA"

4585	A3504	(25c) green	.50	.25
4586	A3504	(25c) blue green	.50	.25
4587	A3504	(25c) blue	.50	.25
4588	A3504	(25c) red violet	.50	.25
4589	A3504	(25c) brown orange	.50	.25
4590	A3504	(25c) yellow orange	.50	.25
a.	Strip of 6, #4585-4590		3.00	

NEW MEXICO STATEHOOD CENTENNIAL

Sanctuary II, Painting by Doug West
A3505

PHOTOGRAVURE
2012, Jan. 6   *Serpentine Die Cut 11*
Self-Adhesive

4591	A3505	(44c) multicolored	1.00	.25

ALOHA SHIRTS

Surfers and Palm Trees A3506   Surfers A3507

Bird of Paradise Flowers A3508   Kilauea Volcano A3509

Fossil Fish, Shells and Starfish — A3510

PHOTOGRAVURE, LITHOGRAPHED
(#4597-4601)
Serpentine Die Cut 11
2012, Jan. 19
Self-Adhesive

4592	A3506	32c multicolored	2.00	.30
4593	A3507	32c multicolored	2.00	.30
4594	A3508	32c multicolored	2.00	.30
4595	A3509	32c multicolored	2.00	.30
4596	A3510	32c multicolored	2.00	.30
a.	Horiz. strip of 5, #4592-4596		10.00	

Coil Stamps
Serpentine Die Cut 11 Vert.

4597	A3510	32c multicolored	1.40	.30
4598	A3506	32c multicolored	1.40	.30
4599	A3507	32c multicolored	1.40	.30
4600	A3508	32c multicolored	1.40	.30
4601	A3509	32c multicolored	1.40	.30
a.	Strip of 5, #4597-4601		7.00	—
b.	As "a," die cutting omitted			
	Nos. 4592-4601 (10)		17.00	3.00

On Nos. 4592-4596, the top of the shirt collars are all higher than the cross line of the "A" in "USA," and on Nos. 4597-4601, they are even with or slightly below the cross line.

Wedding Cake Type of 2009
LITHOGRAPHED
Serpentine Die Cut 10¾
2012, Jan. 20
Self-Adhesive

4602	A3344	65c multicolored	1.35	.25

BALTIMORE CHECKERSPOT BUTTERFLY

A3511

PHOTOGRAVURE
Serpentine Die Cut 10¾
2012, Jan. 20
Self-Adhesive

4603	A3511	65c multicolored	1.50	.25

DOGS AT WORK

Seeing Eye Dog — A3512   Therapy Dog — A3513

Military Dog — A3514   Rescue Dog — A3515

PHOTOGRAVURE
Serpentine Die Cut 10¾
2012, Jan. 20
Self-Adhesive

4604	A3512	65c multicolored	1.30	.30
4605	A3513	65c multicolored	1.30	.30
4606	A3514	65c multicolored	1.30	.30
4607	A3515	65c multicolored	1.30	.30
a.	Block or vert. strip of 4, #4604-4607		5.20	

BIRDS OF PREY

Northern Goshawk A3516   Peregrine Falcon A3517

Golden Eagle A3518   Osprey A3519

Northern Harrier — A3520

LITHOGRAPHED
Serpentine Die Cut 11¼x10¾
2012, Jan. 20
Self-Adhesive

4608	A3516	85c multicolored	1.75	.35
4609	A3517	85c multicolored	1.75	.35
4610	A3518	85c multicolored	1.75	.35
4611	A3519	85c multicolored	1.75	.35
4612	A3520	85c multicolored	1.75	.35
a.	Horiz. strip of 5, #4608-4612		8.75	

WEATHER VANES

Rooster With Perch — A3521   Cow — A3522

Eagle — A3523   Rooster Without Perch — A3524

Centaur — A3525

LITHOGRAPHED
Serpentine Die Cut 11¾ Vert.
2012, Jan. 20
Coil Stamps
Self-Adhesive

4613	A3521	45c multicolored	1.50	.30
4614	A3522	45c multicolored	1.50	.30
4615	A3523	45c multicolored	1.50	.30
4616	A3524	45c multicolored	1.50	.30
4617	A3525	45c multicolored	1.50	.30
a.	Strip of 5, #4613-4617		7.50	

BONSAI

Sierra Juniper — A3526

Black Pine — A3527

Banyan — A3528

Trident Maple — A3529

Azalea — A3530

LITHOGRAPHED
Serpentine Die Cut 11x10¾ on 2 or 3 Sides
2012, Jan. 23
Booklet Stamps
Self-Adhesive

4618	A3526	(45c) multicolored	1.20	.40
4619	A3527	(45c) multicolored	1.20	.40
4620	A3528	(45c) multicolored	1.20	.40
4621	A3529	(45c) multicolored	1.20	.40
4622	A3530	(45c) multicolored	1.20	.40
a.	Vert. strip of 5, #4618-4622		6.00	
b.	Booklet pane of 20, 4 each #4618-4622		24.00	

Stamps in No. 4622a are not adjacent, as rows of selvage are between stamps two and three, and between stamps four and five.

No. 4622b is a double-sided booklet with 12 stamps on one side (3 each #4618, 4621, 2 each #4619, 4620, 4622) and eight stamps (#4618, 4621, 2 each #4619, 4620, 4622) plus label that serves as a booklet cover on the other side.

CHINESE NEW YEAR

Year of the Dragon A3531

PHOTOGRAVURE
Serpentine Die Cut 11x10¾
2012, Jan. 23
Self-Adhesive

4623 A3531 (45c) multicolored   1.15   .25

BLACK HERITAGE

John H. Johnson (1918-2005), Magazine Publisher — A3532

LITHOGRAPHED
Serpentine Die Cut 10¾
2012, Jan. 31
Self-Adhesive

4624 A3532 (45c) multicolored   1.00   .25

HEART HEALTH

Tree, Man, Sun and Apple — A3533

PHOTOGRAVURE
2012, Feb. 9   *Serpentine Die Cut 11*
Self-Adhesive

4625 A3533 (45c) multicolored   1.00   .25

LOVE

Ribbons A3534

LITHOGRAPHED
Serpentine Die Cut 10¾
2012, Feb. 14
Self-Adhesive

4626 A3534 (45c) red   1.00   .25
  a.   Die cutting omitted, pair   —

Postal Service officials declared on Feb. 2 that No. 4626 could be sold in post offices as of that date to make the stamp available to customers before St. Valentine's Day, but the first day ceremony for the stamp was held Feb. 14 in Colorado Springs, CO. Official first day covers have that date and city.

ARIZONA STATEHOOD CENTENNIAL

Cathedral Rock A3535

PHOTOGRAVURE
Serpentine Die Cut 11
2012, Feb. 14
Self-Adhesive

4627 A3535 (45c) multicolored   1.00   .25

DANNY THOMAS

Thomas (1912-91), Comedian, and St. Jude's Children's Research Hospital, Memphis
A3536

LITHOGRAPHED
Serpentine Die Cut 10¾x10½
2012, Feb. 16
Self-Adhesive

4628 A3536 (45c) multicolored   1.00   .25

Flag and "Equality" A3537   Flag and "Justice" A3538

Flag and "Freedom" A3539   Flag and "Liberty" A3540

PHOTOGRAVURE (#4629-4632), LITHOGRAPHED (#4633-4648)
Serpentine Die Cut 8½ Vert.
2012, Feb. 22
Coil Stamps
Self-Adhesive

4629	A3537	(45c)	multicolored	1.50	.25
4630	A3538	(45c)	multicolored	1.50	.25
4631	A3539	(45c)	multicolored	1.50	.25
4632	A3540	(45c)	multicolored	1.50	.25
a.		Strip of 4, #4629-4632		6.00	

Serpentine Die Cut 9½ Vert.

4633	A3537	(45c)	multicolored	1.00	.25
4634	A3538	(45c)	multicolored	1.00	.25
4635	A3539	(45c)	multicolored	1.00	.25
4636	A3540	(45c)	multicolored	1.00	.25
b.		Strip of 4, #4633-4636		4.00	

Serpentine Die Cut 11 Vert.

4637	A3537	(45c)	multicolored	1.50	.25
4638	A3538	(45c)	multicolored	1.50	.25
4639	A3539	(45c)	multicolored	1.50	.25
4640	A3540	(45c)	multicolored	1.50	.25
a.		Strip of 4, #4637-4640		6.00	
b.		As "a," die cutting omitted		350.00	
	Nos. 4629-4640 (12)			16.00	3.00

Booklet Stamps
Colored Dots in Stars
18½mm From Lower Left to Lower
Right Corners of Flag
Serpentine Die Cut 11¼x10¾ on 2 or 3 Sides

4641	A3539	(45c)	multicolored	1.25	.25
4642	A3540	(45c)	multicolored	1.25	.25
4643	A3537	(45c)	multicolored	1.25	.25
4644	A3538	(45c)	multicolored	1.25	.25
b.		Block of 4, #4641-4644		5.00	
c.		Booklet pane of 20, 5 each #4641-4644		25.00	

Dark Dots Only in Stars
19mm from Lower Left to Lower
Right Corners of Flag

4645	A3539	(45c)	multicolored	1.50	.25
4646	A3540	(45c)	multicolored	1.50	.25
4647	A3537	(45c)	multicolored	1.50	.25
4648	A3538	(45c)	multicolored	1.50	.25
a.		Block of 4, #4645-4648		6.00	
b.		Booklet pane of 20, 5 each #4645-4648		30.00	
	Nos. 4641-4648 (8)			11.00	2.00

On Nos. 4641-4644, the blue canton of the flag is made up of blue and red inks. The paper is tagged over each block of 4, with no tagging on the paper between the blocks. The tagging is a dull yellow green under ultraviolet light. The words are slightly longer than those on Nos. 4645-4648.

On Nos. 4645-4648, the blue canton is made up of blue and dull blue inks. The paper is prephosphored with the tagging appearing bright yellow green under ultraviolet light. The words are slightly shorter than those on Nos. 4641-4644.

No. 4644b is a double-sided booklet with 12 stamps on one side (3 each #4641-4644) and eight stamps (2 each #4641-4644) plus label that serves as a booklet cover on the other side.

No. 4648b is a double-sided booklet with 12 stamps on one side (3 each #4645-4648) and eight stamps (2 each #4645-4648) plus label that serves as a booklet cover on the other side.

See Nos. 4673-4676.

AMERICAN LANDMARKS ISSUE

Sunshine Skyway Bridge, Florida A3541

Carmel Mission, Carmel, CA A3542

LITHOGRAPHED
Serpentine Die Cut 10¾x10½
2012, Feb. 28
Self-Adhesive

4649 A3541 $5.15 multi   11.00   5.75
4650 A3542 $18.95 multi   42.50   19.00

CHERRY BLOSSOM CENTENNIAL

Cherry Blossoms and Washington Monument — A3543

Cherry Blossoms and Jefferson Memorial A3544

LITHOGRAPHED
Serpentine Die Cut 10¾
2012, Mar. 24   **Tagged**
Self-Adhesive

4651 A3543 (45c) multicolored   1.00   .25
4652 A3544 (45c) multicolored   1.00   .25
  a.   Horiz. pair, #4651-4652   2.00

See Japan No. 3413.

AMERICAN TREASURES SERIES

Flowers, by William H. Johnson (1901-70) — A3545

PHOTOGRAVURE
Sheets of 200 in 10 panes of 20
Serpentine Die Cut 10¾
2012, Apr. 11   **Tagged**
Self-Adhesive

4653 A3545 (45c) multicolored   1.15   .35

TWENTIETH CENTURY POETS

Joseph Brodsky (1940-96) A3546   Gwendolyn Brooks (1917-2000) A3547

William Carlos Williams (1883-1963) A3548   Robert Hayden (1913-80) A3549

Sylvia Plath (1932-63) A3550   Elizabeth Bishop (1911-79) A3551

Wallace Stevens (1879-1955) A3552   Denise Levertov (1923-97) A3553

E. E. Cummings (1894-1962) A3554   Theodore Roethke (1908-63) A3555

LITHOGRAPHED
Sheets of 160 in eight panes of 20
Serpentine Die Cut 10¾x11
2012, Apr. 21   **Tagged**
Self-Adhesive

4654	A3546	(45c)	multicolored	1.00	.50
4655	A3547	(45c)	multicolored	1.00	.50
4656	A3548	(45c)	multicolored	1.00	.50
4657	A3549	(45c)	multicolored	1.00	.50
4658	A3550	(45c)	multicolored	1.00	.50
4659	A3551	(45c)	multicolored	1.00	.50
4660	A3552	(45c)	multicolored	1.00	.50
4661	A3553	(45c)	multicolored	1.00	.50
4662	A3554	(45c)	multicolored	1.00	.50
4663	A3555	(45c)	multicolored	1.00	.50
a.		Block of 10, #4654-4663		10.00	
	Nos. 4654-4663 (10)			10.00	5.00

CIVIL WAR SESQUICENTENNIAL

Battle of New Orleans — A3556

Battle of Antietam — A3557

LITHOGRAPHED
Double-sided sheets of 72 in six
panes of 12 (60 on one side, 12 on
other side)
Serpentine Die Cut 11
2012, Apr. 24   Tagged
Self-Adhesive

4664	A3556	(45c) multicolored	1.00	.30
4665	A3557	(45c) multicolored	1.00	.30
a.		Pair, #4664-4665	2.00	

DISTINGUISHED AMERICANS

José Ferrer (1912-
92), Actor — A3558

LITHOGRAPHED
Sheets of 160 in eight panes of 20
Serpentine Die Cut 10¾x11
2012, Apr. 26   Tagged
Self-Adhesive

4666	A3558	(45c) multicolored	1.00	.25

LOUISIANA STATEHOOD BICENTENNIAL

Sunset Over Flat
Lake — A3559

PHOTOGRAVURE
Sheets of 160 in eight panes of 20
Serpentine Die Cut 11
2012, Apr. 30   Tagged
Self-Adhesive

4667	A3559	(45c) multicolored	1.00	.25

GREAT FILM DIRECTORS

John Ford (1894-1973), Scene From
The Searchers, Starring John
Wayne — A3560

Frank Capra (1897-1991), Scene From
It Happened One Night, Starring Clark
Gable and Claudette Colbert — A3561

Billy Wilder (1906-2002), Scene From
Some Like It Hot, Starring Marilyn
Monroe — A3562

John Huston (1906-87), Scene From
The Maltese Falcon, Starring
Humphrey Bogart
A3563

PHOTOGRAVURE
Serpentine Die Cut 10¾
2012, May 23
Self-Adhesive

4668	A3560	(45c) multicolored	1.00	.40
4669	A3561	(45c) multicolored	1.00	.40
4670	A3562	(45c) multicolored	1.00	.40
4671	A3563	(45c) multicolored	1.00	.40
a.		Block or horiz. strip of 4, #4668-4671	4.00	

WILDLIFE

Bobcat — A3564

LITHOGRAPHED
Serpentine Die Cut 10 Vert.
2012, June 1
Coil Stamp
Self-Adhesive

4672	A3564	1c multicolored	.25	.25
a.		Dated "2015"	.25	.25

Issued: No. 4672a, 2/21/15. Microprinting is
on bobcat's ear on No. 4672 and on the bobcat's leg on No. 4672a. See No. 4802.

Flags Type of 2012
PHOTOGRAVURE
*Serpentine Die Cut 11¼x10¾ on 3
Sides*
2012, June 1   Tagged
Booklet Stamps
Self-Adhesive
Colored Dots in Stars
19¼mm From Lower Left to Lower
Right Corners of Flag

4673	A3539	(45c) multicolored	1.00	.25
4674	A3540	(45c) multicolored	1.00	.25
4675	A3537	(45c) multicolored	1.00	.25
4676	A3538	(45c) multicolored	1.00	.25
a.		Block of 4, #4673-4676	4.00	
b.		Booklet pane of 10, 3 each #4673-4674, 2 each #4675-4676	10.00	

Nos. 4673 and No. 4675 have straight edge
on left side only. Nos. 4674 and 4676 have
straight edge on right side only. Nos. 4641-
4648 each have a straight edge at top or bottom. The letters in the "USPS" microprinting
on Nos. 4673-4676, found at the right side of
the bottom white flag stripe, are printed in a
distinct curve, with the tops of the middle letters, "SP," being below the tops of the outside
letters, "U" and "S," and the letters can be
difficult to distinguish against the shading on
the stripe. The letters in the microprinting on
Nos. 4641-4648, found in the same place on
the stamp, are printed in a straight line, and
are printed boldly, making them easily distinguishable from the shading. The lettering on
Nos. 4673-4767 has a fuzzier, less distinct
appearance under magnification than the lettering on Nos. 4641-4648, which is most evident in the year "2012."

CHARACTERS FROM DISNEY-PIXAR FILMS
Mail a Smile

Flik and Dot
From *A Bug's
Life* — A3565

Bob Parr and
Dashiell Parr
From *The
Incredibles*
A3566

Nemo and
Squirt From
*Finding
Nemo* — A3567

Jessie, Woody
and Bullseye
From *Toy Story
2* — A3568

Boo, Mike
Wazowski and
James P.
"Sulley" Sullivan
From *Monsters,
Inc.* — A3569

PHOTOGRAVURE
Serpentine Die Cut 10½
2012, June 1
Self-Adhesive

4677	A3565	(45c) multicolored	1.00	.40
4678	A3566	(45c) multicolored	1.00	.40
4679	A3567	(45c) multicolored	1.00	.40
4680	A3568	(45c) multicolored	1.00	.40
4681	A3569	(45c) multicolored	1.00	.40
a.		Horiz. strip of 5, #4677-4681	5.00	

Adjacent horizontal or vertical stamps will
have selvage between the stamps.

Aloha Shirts Type of 2012
LITHOGRAPHED
Tagged
*Serpentine Die Cut 11¼x10¾ on 3
Sides*
2012, June 2
Booklet Stamps
Self-Adhesive

4682	A3506	32c multicolored	2.50	.30
4683	A3508	32c multicolored	2.50	.30
4684	A3510	32c multicolored	2.50	.30
4685	A3507	32c multicolored	2.50	.30
4686	A3509	32c multicolored	2.50	.30
a.		Vert. strip of 5, #4682-4686	12.50	
b.		Booklet pane of 10, 2 each #4682-4686	25.00	

BICYCLING

Child on
Bicycle
with
Training
Wheels
A3570

Commuter
on Bicycle
with
Panniers
A3571

Road
Racer
A3572

BMX Rider
A3573

LITHOGRAPHED
Serpentine Die Cut 10¾
2012, June 7
Self-Adhesive

4687	A3570	(45c) multicolored	1.00	.35
4688	A3571	(45c) multicolored	1.00	.35
4689	A3572	(45c) multicolored	1.00	.35
4690	A3573	(45c) multicolored	1.00	.35
a.		Horiz. strip of 4, #4687-4690	4.00	

GIRL SCOUTS OF AMERICA, CENT.

Girl
Scouts — A3574

LITHOGRAPHED
Serpentine Die Cut 10¾
2012, June 9
Self-Adhesive

4691	A3574	(45c) multicolored	1.00	.25
a.		Die cutting omitted, pair	—	

MUSICIANS

Edith Piaf (1915-
63),
Singer — A3575

Miles Davis
(1926-91), Jazz
Trumpet
Player — A3576

PHOTOGRAVURE
Serpentine Die Cut 10¾x11
2012, June 12
Self-Adhesive

4692	A3575	(45c) multicolored	1.00	.30
4693	A3576	(45c) multicolored	1.00	.30
a.		Horiz. pair, #4692-4693	2.00	

See France Nos. 4256-4257.

Imperforate Uncut Press Sheets
Beginning with Nos. 4694-4697,
the United States Postal Service
made available for sale imperforate
uncut press sheets of selected commemorative and definitive issues.
These sheets, along with their corresponding multiples, are described
and valued in footnotes following
each issue in the Scott *Specialized
Catalogue of United States Stamps
and Covers.* For descriptions and
illustrations of typical press-sheet
multiples, see the note after No. 2868
in the Scott U.S. Specialized
catalogue.

MAJOR LEAGUE BASEBALL ALL-STARS

Ted Williams (1918-2002) — A3577

Larry Doby (1923-2003) — A3578

Willie Stargell (1940-2001) — A3579

Joe DiMaggio (1914-99) A3580

PHOTOGRAVURE
Serpentine Die Cut 10¾x11
2012, July 20
Self-Adhesive

4694	A3577	(45c) multicolored	1.00	.30
a.		Imperforate	2.00	—
4695	A3578	(45c) multicolored	1.00	.30
a.		Imperforate	2.00	—
4696	A3579	(45c) multicolored	1.00	.30
a.		Imperforate	2.00	—
4697	A3580	(45c) multicolored	1.00	.30
a.		Imperforate	2.00	—
b.		Horiz. strip or block of 4, #4694-4697	4.00	
c.		Imperf. horiz. strip or block of 4, #4694a-4697a	12.00	—

Panes containing 20 of the same stamp were issued on July 21 in Boston, MA (for No. 4694), Cleveland, OH (for No. 4695), Pittsburgh, PA (for No. 4696) and New York, NY (for No. 4697).

INNOVATIVE CHOREOGRAPHERS

Isadora Duncan (1877-1927) A3581

José Limón (1908-72) A3582

Katherine Dunham (1909-2006) A3583

Bob Fosse (1927-87) A3584

LITHOGRAPHED
Serpentine Die Cut 10¾x11
2012, July 28
Self-Adhesive

4698	A3581	(45c) multicolored	1.00	.35
4699	A3582	(45c) multicolored	1.00	.35
4700	A3583	(45c) multicolored	1.00	.35
4701	A3584	(45c) multicolored	1.00	.35
a.		Vert. strip of 4, #4698-4701	4.00	

EDGAR RICE BURROUGHS

Edgar Rice Burroughs (1875-1950), Writer, and Tarzan — A3585

LITHOGRAPHED
Serpentine Die Cut 10¾
2012, Aug. 17
Self-Adhesive

4702	A3585	(45c) multicolored	1.00	.25

WAR OF 1812 BICENTENNIAL

Painting of U.S.S. Constitution, by Michele Felice Corné — A3586

PHOTOGRAVURE
Serpentine Die Cut 10¾x10½
2012, Aug. 18
Self-Adhesive

4703	A3586	(45c) multicolored	1.75	.25
a.		Imperforate	2.50	—

Purple Heart and Ribbon — A3587

Designed by Jennifer Arnold. Printed by Avery Dennison or CCL Label, Inc.

PHOTOGRAVURE
Sheets of 420 in 21 panes of 20
2012, Sept. 4 *Serpentine Die Cut 11*
Self-Adhesive

4704	A3587	(45c) multicolored	1.00	.25
a.		Imperforate	1.75	—
b.		Dated "2014"	1.00	.25

Compare with Type A3458.

LITERARY ARTS

O. Henry (William S. Porter) (1862-1910), New York City Buildings and Elevated Trains — A3588

PHOTOGRAVURE
Serpentine Die Cut 11
2012, Sept. 11
Self-Adhesive

4705	A3588	(45c) multicolored	1.00	.25

Flags Type of 2012
LITHOGRAPHED
Serpentine Die Cut 11¼x10¾ on 2, 3 or 4 Sides
2012, Sept. 22
Booklet Stamps
Self-Adhesive
Colored Dots in Stars
18½mm From Lower Left to Lower Right Corners of Flag
Thin Paper

4706	A3539	(45c) multicolored	1.00	.25
4707	A3540	(45c) multicolored	1.00	.25
4708	A3537	(45c) multicolored	1.00	.25

4709	A3538	(45c) multicolored	1.00	.25
a.		Block of 4, #4706-4709	4.00	
b.		Booklet pane of 18, 5 each #4706-4707, 4 each #4708-4709	18.00	
		Nos. 4706-4709 (4)	4.00	1.00

The overall-tagged paper used for Nos. 4706-4709 is glossier than that used on Nos. 4641-4644. The blue canton of the flag on Nos. 4706-4709 is made up of blue and red inks, similar to Nos. 4641-4644.

EARTHSCAPES

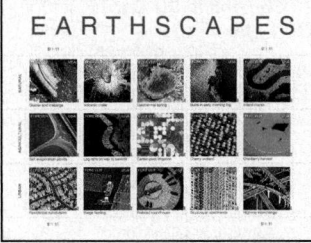

A3589

No. 4710: a, Glacier and icebergs. b, Volcanic crater. c, Geothermal spring. d, Butte in early morning fog. e, Inland marsh. f, Salt evaporation ponds. g, Log rafts on way to sawmill. h, Center-pivot irrigation. i, Cherry orchard. j, Cranberry harvest. k, Residential subdivision. l, Barge fleeting. m, Railroad roundhouse. n, Skyscraper apartments. o, Highway interchange.

LITHOGRAPHED
Serpentine Die Cut 10¾
2012, Oct. 1
Self-Adhesive

4710	A3589	Pane of 15	22.50	
a.-o.		(45c) Any single	1.50	.50
p.		Imperforate pane of 15	55.00	

CHRISTMAS

Holy Family and Donkey A3590

Reindeer in Flight, Moon A3591

Santa Claus and Sleigh — A3592

Reindeer Over Roof — A3593

Snow-covered Buildings A3594

LITHOGRAPHED
Serpentine Die Cut 11 on 2 or 3 Sides
2012
Booklet Stamps
Self-Adhesive

4711	A3590	(45c) multi	1.00	.25
a.		Booklet pane of 20	20.00	
b.		Imperforate	1.50	—
c.		Imperforate booklet pane of 20	30.00	

Serpentine Die Cut 11x10¾ on 2 or 3 sides

4712	A3591	(45c) multi	1.00	.25
4713	A3592	(45c) multi	1.00	.25
4714	A3593	(45c) multi	1.00	.25
4715	A3594	(45c) multi	1.00	.25
a.		Block of 4, #4712-4715	4.00	
b.		Booklet pane of 20, 5 each #4712-4715	20.00	
c.		Imperforate block of 4	8.00	—
d.		Imperforate booklet pane of 20	40.00	
		Nos. 4711-4715 (5)	4.50	1.25

Issued: No. 4711, Oct. 10, Nos. 4712-4715, Oct. 13.

No. 4711a is a double-sided booklet with 12 stamps on one side and eight stamps plus a label that serves as a booklet cover on the other side. No. 4715b is a double-sided booklet with 12 stamps on one side (3 each of Nos. 4712-4715) and eight stamps (2 each of Nos. 4712-4715) plus a label that serves as a booklet cover on the other side.

See No. 4813.

LADY BIRD JOHNSON

A3595

No. 4716: a, Blooming crab apples lining avenue (Plant for more Beautiful Streets). b, Washington Monument, Potomac River and daffodils (Plant for more Beautiful Parks). c, Jefferson Memorial, Tidal Basin and cherry blossoms (Plant for a more Beautiful America). d, Poppies and lupines along highway (Plant for more Beautiful Highways). e, Capitol, azaleas and tulips (Plant for more Beautiful Cities). f, Lady Bird Johnson (1912-2007), First Lady, vert.

LITHOGRAPHED
Serpentine Die Cut 10¾
2012, Nov. 30
Self-Adhesive

4716	A3595	Pane of 6	6.00	
a.-f.		(45c) Any single	1.00	.40
g.		Imperforate pane of 6	22.50	

WAVES OF COLOR

A3596

A3597

A3598

A3599

LITHOGRAPHED & ENGRAVED
Serpentine Die Cut 11, 10¾ (#4719)
2012, Dec. 1
Self-Adhesive

4717	A3596	$1 multi	2.00	.50
4718	A3597	$2 multi	3.75	1.25
4719	A3598	$5 multi	8.75	2.50
4720	A3599	$10 multi	17.50	9.00
	Nos. 4717-4720 (4)		32.00	13.25

Adjacent horizontal or vertical stamps have selvage between the stamps. Plate blocks have sheet margins on the top or bottom and both sides.

EMANCIPATION PROCLAMATION, 150th ANNIV.

A3600

PHOTOGRAVURE
2013, Jan. 1   *Serpentine Die Cut 11*
Self-Adhesive

4721	A3600	(45c) multicolored	1.00	.25
a.		Imperforate	1.50	—

KALEIDOSCOPE FLOWERS

A3601   A3602

A3603   A3604

LITHOGRAPHED
Serpentine Die Cut 11 Vert.
2013, Jan. 14
Coil Stamps
Self-Adhesive
Color of Large Outer Leaves

4722	A3601	46c yellow orange	1.25	.25
4723	A3602	46c yellow green	1.25	.25
4724	A3603	46c red violet	1.25	.25
4725	A3604	46c red	1.25	.25
a.		Strip of 4, #4722-4725	5.00	
	Nos. 4722-4725 (4)		5.00	1.00

CHINESE NEW YEAR

Year of the Snake A3605

PHOTOGRAVURE
Serpentine Die Cut 11
2013, Jan. 16
Self-Adhesive

4726	A3605	(45c) multicolored	1.00	.25
a.		Imperforate	2.00	—

APPLES

Northern Spy Apple A3606   Golden Delicious Apple A3607

Granny Smith Apple A3608   Baldwin Apple A3609

LITHOGRAPHED
Serpentine Die Cut 11¼x10¾
2013, Jan. 17
Self-Adhesive

4727	A3606	33c multicolored	1.00	.25
4728	A3607	33c multicolored	1.00	.25
4729	A3608	33c multicolored	1.00	.25
4730	A3609	33c multicolored	1.00	.25
a.		Block of 4, #4727-4730	4.00	
b.		Imperforate block of 4	6.00	—

Coil Stamps
Serpentine Die Cut 11 Vert.

4731	A3609	33c multicolored	1.25	.25
4732	A3606	33c multicolored	1.25	.25
4733	A3607	33c multicolored	1.25	.25
4734	A3608	33c multicolored	1.25	.25
a.		Strip of 4, #4731-4734	5.00	
	Nos. 4727-4734 (8)		9.00	2.00

Wedding Cake Type of 2009
LITHOGRAPHED
Serpentine Die Cut 10¾
2013, Jan. 18
Self-Adhesive

4735	A3344	66c multicolored	1.40	.25
a.		Imperforate	2.50	—

SPICEBUSH SWALLOWTAIL BUTTERFLY

A3610

PHOTOGRAVURE
Serpentine Die Cut 10¾
2013, Jan. 23
Self-Adhesive

4736	A3610	66c multicolored	1.40	.25
a.		Imperforate	2.25	—

TUFTED PUFFINS

A3611

LITHOGRAPHED
Serpentine Die Cut 11¼x10¾
2013, Jan. 23
"2013" in Orange Red
Solid Color in "Tufted Puffins" and "86"
Self-Adhesive

4737	A3611	86c multicolored	1.80	.35
b.		Imperforate	3.00	—

"2013" in Black
With Dots in "Tufted Puffins" and "86"

4737A	A3611	86c multi	2.50	.35

AMERICAN LANDMARKS ISSUE

Arlington Green Bridge, Vermont A3612

Grand Central Terminal, New York City A3613

PHOTOGRAVURE
2013   *Serpentine Die Cut 10¾x10½*
Self-Adhesive

4738	A3612	$5.60 multi	11.00	6.25
4739	A3613	$19.95 multi	40.00	21.00

Earth A3614

PHOTOGRAVURE
2013, Jan. 28   *Serpentine Die Cut*
Self-Adhesive

4740	A3614	($1.10) multi	2.25	.50
		Imperforate	3.75	—

Unused values are for stamps with surrounding selvage. Adjacent stamps are separated by rouletting.

LOVE

Envelope With Wax Seal — A3615

PHOTOGRAVURE
Serpentine Die Cut 10¾
2013, Jan. 30
Self-Adhesive

4741	A3615	(46c) multicolored	1.00	.25
a.		Imperforate	1.50	—

ROSA PARKS

Parks (1913-2005), Civil Rights Pioneer — A3616

PHOTOGRAVURE
Serpentine Die Cut 10¾
2013, Feb. 4
Self-Adhesive

4742	A3616	(46c) multicolored	1.00	.25
a.		Imperforate	1.75	—

MUSCLE CARS

1969 Dodge Charger Daytona A3617

1966 Pontiac GTO A3618

1967 Ford Mustang Shelby GT 500 A3619

1970 Chevrolet Chevelle SS A3620

1970 Plymouth Hemi Barracuda A3621

Designed by Carl T. Herrman. Printed by Avery Dennison.

PHOTOGRAVURE
Serpentine Die Cut 10¾
2013, Feb. 22   Tagged
Self-Adhesive

4743	A3617	(46c) multicolored	1.00	.30
4744	A3618	(46c) multicolored	1.00	.30
4745	A3619	(46c) multicolored	1.00	.30
4746	A3620	(46c) multicolored	1.00	.30
4747	A3621	(46c) multicolored	1.00	.30
a.		Vert. strip of 5, #4743-4747	5.00	
		Vert. P# block of 10, 5#+ V	10.00	
		Horiz. P# block of 8, 2 sets of 5#+ V	8.00	
b.		Imperforate vert. strip of 5	9.00	—
	Nos. 4743-4747 (5)		5.00	1.50

MODERN ART IN AMERICA

A3622

No. 4748: a, I Saw the Figure 5 in Gold, by Charles Demuth (37x51mm). b, Sunset, Maine Coast, by John Marin (43x43mm). c, House and Street, by Stuart Davis (51x41mm). d, Painting, Number 5, by Marsden Hartley (37x51mm). e, Black Mesa Landscape, New Mexico/Out Back of Marie's II, by Georgia O'Keeffe (51x41mm). f, Noire et Blanche, by Man Ray (43x41mm). g, The Prodigal Son, by Aaron Douglas (34x51mm). h, American Landscape, by Charles Sheeler (43x41mm). i, Brooklyn Bridge, by Joseph Stella (38x47mm). j, Razor, by Gerald Murphy (43x43mm). k, Nude Descending a Staircase, No. 2, by Marcel Duchamp (34x58mm). l, Fog Horns, by Arthur Dove (43x37mm).

PHOTOGRAVURE
Serpentine Die Cut 10½
2013, Mar. 7
Self-Adhesive

4748	A3622	Pane of 12	13.25	
a.-l.		(46c) Any single	1.10	.50
m.		Imperforate pane of 12	60.00	

Armory Show, cent.

Patriotic Star — A3623

LITHOGRAPHED
Serpentine Die Cut 10¾ Vert.
2013, Mar. 19
Coil Stamp
Self-Adhesive

4749	A3623	46c multicolored	.95	.25

LA FLORIDA

A3624 A3625

A3626 A3627

PHOTOGRAVURE
Serpentine Die Cut 10½
2013, Apr. 3
Self-Adhesive

4750	A3624	(46c)	multicolored	1.00	.25
4751	A3625	(46c)	multicolored	1.00	.25
4752	A3626	(46c)	multicolored	1.00	.25
4753	A3627	(46c)	multicolored	1.00	.25
a.	Block of 4, #4750-4753			4.00	
b.	Imperforate block of 4			9.00	—
	Nos. 4750-4753 (4)			4.00	1.00

Naming of Florida, 500th anniv.

VINTAGE SEED PACKETS

Phlox
A3628

Calendula
A3629

Digitalis
A3630

Linum
A3631

Alyssum
A3632

Zinnias
A3633

Pinks
A3634

Cosmos
A3635

Aster
A3636

Primrose
A3637

PHOTOGRAVURE
Serpentine Die Cut 10¾ on 2 or 3 Sides
2013, Apr. 5
Booklet Stamps
Self-Adhesive

4754	A3628	(46c)	multicolored	1.30	.25
4755	A3629	(46c)	multicolored	1.30	.25
4756	A3630	(46c)	multicolored	1.30	.25
4757	A3631	(46c)	multicolored	1.30	.25
4758	A3632	(46c)	multicolored	1.30	.25
4759	A3633	(46c)	multicolored	1.30	.25
4760	A3634	(46c)	multicolored	1.30	.25
4761	A3635	(46c)	multicolored	1.30	.25
4762	A3636	(46c)	multicolored	1.30	.25
4763	A3637	(46c)	multicolored	1.30	.25
a.	Block of 10, #4754-4763			13.00	
b.	Booklet pane of 20, 2 each				
	#4754-4763			26.00	
	Nos. 4754-4763 (10)			13.00	2.50

No. 4763b is a double-sided booklet pane with 12 stamps on one side (2 each #4754, 4759, 1 each #4755-4758, 4760-4763), and eight stamps (1 each #4755-4758, 4760-4763) plus label (booklet cover) on the other side.

WEDDING FLOWERS

Flowers — A3638

Flowers and "Yes I Do"
A3639

LITHOGRAPHED
Serpentine Die Cut 10¾
2013, Apr. 11
Self-Adhesive

4764	A3638	(46c)	multicolored	1.00	.25
a.	Dated "2014"			1.00	.25
b.	Imperforate			2.00	
4765	A3639	66c	multicolored	1.40	.30
a.	Imperforate			2.50	—

Flag in Autumn
A3640

Flag in Winter
A3641

Flag in Spring
A3642

Flag in Summer
A3643

PHOTOGRAVURE (#4766-4769), LITHOGRAPHED (#4770-4785)
2013 *Serpentine Die Cut 8½ Vert.*
Coil Stamps
Self-Adhesive

4766	A3640	(46c)	multicolored	1.00	.25
4767	A3641	(46c)	multicolored	1.00	.25
4768	A3642	(46c)	multicolored	1.00	.25
4769	A3643	(46c)	multicolored	1.00	.25
a.	Strip of 4, #4766-4769			4.00	

Serpentine Die Cut 9½ Vert.

4770	A3640	(46c)	multicolored	1.10	.25
4771	A3641	(46c)	multicolored	1.10	.25
4772	A3642	(46c)	multicolored	1.10	.25
4773	A3643	(46c)	multicolored	1.10	.25
a.	Strip of 4, #4770-4773			4.40	

Serpentine Die Cut 11 Vert.

4774	A3641	(46c)	multicolored	1.25	.25
4775	A3642	(46c)	multicolored	1.25	.25
4776	A3643	(46c)	multicolored	1.25	.25
4777	A3640	(46c)	multicolored	1.25	.25
a.	Strip of 4, #4774-4777			5.00	
	Nos. 4766-4777 (12)			13.40	3.00

Booklet Stamps
With Microprinted "USPS" at Lower Left Corner of Flag
Serpentine Die Cut 11¼x10¾ on 2 or 3 Sides

4778	A3642	(46c)	multicolored	1.25	.25
4779	A3643	(46c)	multicolored	1.25	.25
4780	A3640	(46c)	multicolored	1.25	.25
4781	A3641	(46c)	multicolored	1.25	.25
a.	Block of 4, #4778-4781			6.00	
b.	Booklet pane of 20, 5 each				
	#4778-4781			30.00	

With Microprinted "USPS" Near Top of Pole or at Lower Left Corner Near Rope (#4783, 4783b)
Pre-phosphored Paper

4782	A3642	(46c)	multicolored	1.00	.25
b.	As #4782, dated "2014"			1.00	.25
4783	A3643	(46c)	multicolored	1.00	.25
b.	As #4783, dated "2014"			1.00	.25
4784	A3640	(46c)	multicolored	1.00	.25
b.	As #4784, dated "2014"			1.00	.25
4785	A3641	(46c)	multicolored	1.00	.25
b.	As #4785, dated "2014"			1.00	.25
c.	Block of 4, #4782-4785			4.00	
d.	Booklet pane of 20, 5 each				
	#4782-4785			20.00	
f.	Booklet pane of 10, 3 each				
	#4782a, 4783a, 2 each				
	#4784a, 4785a			10.00	
g.	Block of 4, #4782b, 4783b,				
	4784b, 4785b			4.00	
h.	Booklet pane of 20, 5 each				
	#4782b, 4783b, 4784b,				
	4785b			20.00	
	Nos. 4778-4785 (8)			9.00	2.00

Issued: Nos. 4766-4777, 5/3; Nos. 4778-4785, 5/17. No. 4781b is a double-sided booklet with 12 stamps on one side (3 each #4778-4781) and eight stamps (2 each #4778-4781) plus label that serves as a booklet cover on the other side.

No. 4785c is a double-sided booklet with 12 stamps on one side (3 each #4782-4785) and eight stamps (2 each #4782-4785) plus label that serves as a booklet cover on the other side.

A microprinted "USPS" is found on tree trunk to the left of the "F" in "Forever" on No. 4766, on tree trunk near lower left corner of flag on No. 4767, on white flag stripe at lower right on No. 4768, and on the top of the flagpole below the ball on No. 4769. Nos. 4770-4773 are microprinted "USPS" in the same places as on Nos. 4778-4781. Nos. 4774-4777 are microprinted "USPS" in the same places as on Nos. 4782-4785.

No. 4785e comprises stamps printed on paper with overall tagging. For detailed listings, see the *Scott Specialized Catalogue of United States Stamps and Covers.*

See Nos. 4796-4799.

Issued: Nos. 4782b, 4783b, 4784b, 4785b, 3/17/14. Nos. 4782b, 4783b, 4784b and 4785b each sold for 49c on day of issue.

MUSIC ICONS

Lydia Mendoza (1916-2007), Tejano Music Recording Artist — A3644

PHOTOGRAVURE
Serpentine Die Cut 10¾
2013, May 15
Self-Adhesive

4786	A3644	(46c)	multicolored	1.00	.25
a.	Imperforate			1.50	—

Adjacent horizontal or vertical stamps have selvage between the stamps.

CIVIL WAR SESQUICENTENNIAL

Battle of Vicksburg — A3645

Battle of Gettysburg — A3646

LITHOGRAPHED
2013, May 23 *Serpentine Die Cut 11*
Self-Adhesive

4787	A3645	(46c)	multicolored	1.00	.30
4788	A3646	(46c)	multicolored	1.00	.30
a.	Pair, #4787-4788			2.00	
b.	Imperforate pair, #4787-4788			5.50	—

MUSIC ICONS

Johnny Cash (1932-2003), Country Music Recording Artist — A3647

PHOTOGRAVURE
Serpentine Die Cut 10¾
2013, June 5
Self-Adhesive

4789	A3647	(46c)	multicolored	1.00	.25
a.	Imperforate			1.50	—

WEST VIRGINIA STATEHOOD, 150th ANNIV.

Hills in Monongahela National Forest — A3648

PHOTOGRAVURE
Serpentine Die Cut 11
2013, June 20
Self-Adhesive

4790	A3648	(46c)	multicolored	1.00	.25
a.	Imperforate			1.50	—

NEW ENGLAND COASTAL LIGHTHOUSES

Portland Head Lighthouse, Maine
A3649

Portsmouth Harbor Lighthouse, New Hampshire
A3650

Boston Harbor Lighthouse, Massachusetts
A3651

Point Judith Lighthouse, Rhode Island
A3652

New London Harbor Lighthouse, Connecticut
A3653

LITHOGRAPHED
Serpentine Die Cut 11x10¾
2013, July 13
Self-Adhesive

4791	A3649	(46c) multicolored	1.00	.40
a.		"FOREVER" and "USA" 1mm higher than normal (pos. 1)	2.00	1.00
b.		Horiz. strip of 5, #4791a, 4792-4795	6.00	
4792	A3650	(46c) multicolored	1.00	.40
4793	A3651	(46c) multicolored	1.00	.40
4794	A3652	(46c) multicolored	1.00	.40
4795	A3653	(46c) multicolored	1.00	.40
a.		Horiz. strip of 5, #4791-4795	5.00	
b.		Imperforate horiz. strip of 5	10.00	—
c.		Imperforate horiz. strip of 5, pos. 1 as No. 4791a	12.00	—
		Nos. 4791-4795 (5)	5.00	2.00

Flag Types of 2013
PHOTOGRAVURE
Serpentine Die Cut 11¼x11½ on 2 or 3 Sides
2013, Aug. 8
Booklet Stamps
Self-Adhesive

4796	A3642	(46c) multicolored	1.25	.25
4797	A3643	(46c) multicolored	1.25	.25
4798	A3640	(46c) multicolored	1.25	.25
4799	A3641	(46c) multicolored	1.25	.25
a.		Block of 4, #4796-4799	5.00	
b.		Booklet pane of 20, 5 each #4796-4799	25.00	
		Nos. 4796-4799 (4)	5.00	1.00

No. 4799b is a double-sided booklet with 12 stamps on one side (3 each #4796-4799) and eight stamps (2 each #4796-4799) plus label that serves as a booklet cover on the other side. Nos. 4796-4799 are microprinted "USPS" in the same places as Nos. 4766-4769.

EID

"Eid Mubarak" — A3654

LITHOGRAPHED
2013, Aug. 8   *Serpentine Die Cut 11*
Self-Adhesive

4800	A3654	(46c) dk grn, gray & gold	1.00	.25
a.		Imperforate	1.75	—

BUILDING A NATION

Airplane Mechanic, Photograph by Lewis Hine — A3655

Derrick Man on Empire State Building, Photograph by Lewis Hine — A3656

Millinery Apprentice, Photograph by Lewis Hine — A3657

Man on Hoisting Ball on Empire State Building, Photograph by Lewis Hine — A3658

Linotype Operator, Photograph by Lewis Hine — A3659

Welder on Empire State Building, Photograph by Lewis Hine — A3660

Coal Miner, by Anonymous Photographer A3661

Riveters on Empire State Building, Photograph by Lewis Hine — A3662

Powerhouse Mechanic, Photograph by Lewis Hine — A3663

Railroad Track Walker, Photograph by Lewis Hine — A3664

Textile Worker, Photograph by Lewis Hine — A3665

Man Guiding Beam on Empire State Building, Photograph by Lewis Hine — A3666

PHOTOGRAVURE
Serpentine Die Cut 10½x10¾
2013, Aug. 8
Self-Adhesive

4801		Pane of 12	12.00	
a.	A3655	(46c) black & gray	1.00	.50
b.	A3656	(46c) black & gray	1.00	.50
c.	A3657	(46c) black & gray	1.00	.50
d.	A3658	(46c) black & gray	1.00	.50
e.	A3659	(46c) black & gray	1.00	.50
f.	A3660	(46c) black & gray	1.00	.50
g.	A3661	(46c) black & gray	1.00	.50
h.	A3662	(46c) black & gray	1.00	.50
i.	A3663	(46c) black & gray	1.00	.50
j.	A3664	(46c) black & gray	1.00	.50
k.	A3665	(46c) black & gray	1.00	.50
l.	A3666	(46c) black & gray	1.00	.50
m.		Imperforate pane of 12	70.00	

No. 4801 was printed with five different sheet margins depicting coal miner from No. 4801g, man on hoisting ball on Empire State Building, man measuring bearings in large gearwheel, man on cable at Empire State Building, and woman welder. Value is for sheet with any margin.

Bobcat Type of 2012
LITHOGRAPHED
2013, Aug. 9   *Perf. 9¾ Vert.*
Coil Stamp

4802	A3564	1c multicolored	.25	.25

BLACK HERITAGE

Althea Gibson (1927-2003), Tennis Player — A3667

PHOTOGRAVURE
Serpentine Die Cut 11
2013, Aug. 23
Self-Adhesive

4803	A3667	(46c) multicolored	1.00	.25
a.		Imperforate	1.50	—

MARCH ON WASHINGTON, 50th ANNIV.

Marchers and Washington Monument — A3668

PHOTOGRAVURE
Serpentine Die Cut 10¾
2013, Aug. 23
Self-Adhesive

4804	A3668	(46c) multicolored	1.00	.25
a.		Imperforate	1.50	—

WAR OF 1812 BICENTENNIAL

Painting of Battle of Lake Erie, by William Henry Powell A3669

LITHOGRAPHED
Serpentine Die Cut 10¾
2013, Sept. 10
Self-Adhesive

4805	A3669	(46c) multicolored	1.00	.25
a.		Imperforate	1.50	—

INVERTED JENNY
Miniature Sheet

A3670

LITHOGRAPHED & ENGRAVED
Serpentine Die Cut 10½x11¼
2013, Sept. 22
Self-Adhesive

4806	A3670	multicolored	24.00	
a.		$2 Single stamp	4.00	1.25
b.		Imperforate pane of 6	65.00	—
c.		As "b," single stamp	11.00	—
d.		Pane of 6, airplane right-side up	75,000.	
e.		As "d," single stamp	13,500.	

No. 4806, along with a piece of white cardboard backing, was placed in a sealed envelope. The envelope, along with a piece of gray cardboard backing, was inside a sealed plastic outerwrap. One hundred panes were produced that contain the airplane right-side up. These panes were included in the same envelope and outerwrap and were distributed randomly. No returns or refunds were offered for any opened packages. Values for No. 4806 are for panes removed from the envelope.

A book containing an unused and a first-day canceled example of No. 4806, along with items that are termed "proofs" and "die wipes" sold for $200.

MUSIC ICONS

Ray Charles (1930-2004), Recording Artist — A3671

LITHOGRAPHED
Serpentine Die Cut 10½
2013, Sept. 23
Self-Adhesive

4807	A3671	(46c) multicolored	1.00	.25
a.		Imperforate	1.50	—

Adjacent horizontal or vertical stamps have selvage between the stamps.

SNOWFLAKES

A3672   A3673

A3674   A3675

A3676

PHOTOGRAVURE
Serpentine Die Cut 11 Vert.
2013, Oct. 1
Coil Stamps
Self-Adhesive

4808	A3672	(10c) lt bl & multi	.25	.25
4809	A3673	(10c) pale bl & multi	.25	.25
4810	A3674	(10c) lt bl & multi	.25	.25
4811	A3675	(10c) pale bl & multi	.25	.25
4812	A3676	(10c) lil & multi	.25	.25
a.		Strip of 5, #4808-4812	1.25	
		Nos. 4808-4812 (5)	1.25	1.25

Holy Family and Donkey Type of 2012 Dated "2013" and

Wreath
A3677

Virgin and Child, by Jan Gossaert
A3678

Poinsettia
A3679

Gingerbread House With Red Door — A3680

Gingerbread House With Blue Door — A3681

Gingerbread House With Green Door — A3682

Gingerbread House With Orange Door — A3683

Poinsettia — A3684

LITHOGRAPHED, PHOTOGRAVURE (#4821)
2013 **Serpentine Die Cut 11**
Self-Adhesive

4813	A3590	(46c) multicolored	1.00	.25
a.		Imperforate	1.50	—

Serpentine Die Cut

4814	A3677	($1.10) multicolored	2.25	.50
a.		Imperforate	4.00	

Booklet Stamps
Serpentine Die Cut 11 on 2 or 3 Sides

4815	A3678	(46c) multicolored	1.00	.25
a.		Booklet pane of 20	20.00	
b.		Imperforate	1.50	
c.		Imperforate booklet pane of 20	30.00	
4816	A3679	(46c) multicolored	1.00	.25
a.		Booklet pane of 20	20.00	
b.		Dated "2014"	1.00	.25
c.		As #4816a, dated "2014"	20.00	
d.		Imperforate, dated "2013"	1.50	—
e.		Imperforate booklet pane of 20	30.00	
4817	A3680	(46c) multicolored	1.00	.25
4818	A3681	(46c) multicolored	1.00	.25
4819	A3682	(46c) multicolored	1.00	.25
4820	A3683	(46c) multicolored	1.00	.25
a.		Block of 4, #4817-4820	4.00	
b.		Booklet pane of 20, 5 each #4817-4820	20.00	
c.		Imperforate block of 4	7.00	—
d.		Imperforate booklet pane of 20	35.00	

Serpentine Die Cut 8 on 2, 3 or 4 Sides

4821	A3684	(46c) multicolored	1.00	.25
a.		Booklet pane of 18	18.00	
		Nos. 4815-4821 (7)	7.00	1.75

Issued: Nos. 4813, 4815, 10/11; No. 4814, 10/24; Nos. 4816, 4821, 10/10; Nos. 4817-4820, 11/6.

MEDALS OF HONOR

Navy Medal of Honor — A3685

Army Medal of Honor — A3686

LITHOGRAPHED
Serpentine Die Cut 11
2013, Nov. 11
Self-Adhesive

4822	A3685	(46c) multicolored	1.00	.30
a.		Dated "2014"	1.00	.30
b.		Dated "2015"	1.00	.30
4823	A3686	(46c) multicolored	1.00	.30
a.		Dated "2014"	1.00	.30
b.		Dated "2015"	1.00	.30
c.		Pair, #4822-4823	2.00	
d.		Pair, #4822a-4823a	2.00	
e.		Imperf. pair, #4822-4823	3.50	—
f.		Imperf. pair, #4822a-4823a	3.50	—

HANUKKAH

Menorah
A3687

LITHOGRAPHED
Sheets of 160 in eight panes of 20
Serpentine Die Cut 11
2013, Nov. 19
Self-Adhesive

4824	A3687	(46c) multicolored	1.00	.25
a.		Imperforate	1.50	—

Postal Service officials declared on Nov. 8 that No. 4824 could be sold in post offices on Nov. 9, but the first day ceremony was held on Nov. 19 in New York, NY. Official first day covers have that date and city.

SCENES FROM HARRY POTTER MOVIES

Harry Potter — A3688

Harry Potter and Ron Weasley
A3689

Harry Potter, Ron Weasley, Hermione Granger
A3690

Hermione Granger — A3691

Harry Potter and Fawkes the Phoenix
A3692

Hedwig the Owl — A3693

Dobby the House Elf — A3694

Harry Potter and Buckbeak the Hippogriff
A3695

Headmaster Albus Dumbledore
A3696

Professor Severus Snape
A3697

Rubeus Hagrid
A3698

Professor Minerva McGonagall
A3699

Harry Potter, Ron Weasley, Hermione Granger
A3700

Luna Lovegood
A3701

Fred and George Weasley
A3702

Ginny Weasley
A3703

Draco Malfoy — A3704

Harry Potter
A3705

Lord Voldemort
A3706

Bellatrix Lestrange — A3707

LITHOGRAPHED
Serpentine Die Cut 11
2013, Nov. 19
Booklet Stamps
Self-Adhesive

4825	A3688	(46c) multicolored	1.00	.30
4826	A3689	(46c) multicolored	1.00	.30
4827	A3690	(46c) multicolored	1.00	.30
4828	A3691	(46c) multicolored	1.00	.30
a.		Booklet pane of 4, #4825-4828, + central label	4.00	
b.		Imperf. booklet pane of 4	12.50	—
4829	A3692	(46c) multicolored	1.00	.30
4830	A3693	(46c) multicolored	1.00	.30
4831	A3694	(46c) multicolored	1.00	.30
4832	A3695	(46c) multicolored	1.00	.30
a.		Booklet pane of 4, #4829-4832, + central label	4.00	
b.		Imperf. booklet pane of 4	12.50	—
4833	A3696	(46c) multicolored	1.00	.30
4834	A3697	(46c) multicolored	1.00	.30
4835	A3698	(46c) multicolored	1.00	.30
4836	A3699	(46c) multicolored	1.00	.30
a.		Booklet pane of 4, #4833-4836, + central label	4.00	
b.		Imperf. booklet pane of 4	12.50	—
4837	A3700	(46c) multicolored	1.00	.30
4838	A3701	(46c) multicolored	1.00	.30
4839	A3702	(46c) multicolored	1.00	.30
4840	A3703	(46c) multicolored	1.00	.30
a.		Booklet pane of 4, #4837-4840, + central label	4.00	
b.		Imperf. booklet pane of 4	12.50	—
4841	A3704	(46c) multicolored	1.00	.30
4842	A3705	(46c) multicolored	1.00	.30
4843	A3706	(46c) multicolored	1.00	.30
4844	A3707	(46c) multicolored	1.00	.30
a.		Booklet pane of 4, #4841-4844, + central label	4.00	
b.		Imperf. booklet pane of 4	12.50	—
		Nos. 4825-4844 (20)	20.00	6.00

KWANZAA

People, Candles and Book — A3708

LITHOGRAPHED
Serpentine Die Cut 11
2013, Nov. 26
Self-Adhesive

| 4845 | A3708 | (46c) multicolored | 1.00 | .25 |
| *a.* | | Imperforate | 1.50 | |

CHINESE NEW YEAR

Year of the Horse
A3709

PHOTOGRAVURE
Serpentine Die Cut 11
2014, Jan. 15
Self-Adhesive

| 4846 | A3709 | (46c) multicolored | 1.00 | .25 |
| *a.* | | Imperforate | 1.50 | — |

LOVE

Heart — A3710

PHOTOGRAVURE
Serpentine Die Cut 10¾
2014, Jan. 21
Self-Adhesive

| 4847 | A3710 | (46c) multicolored | 1.00 | .25 |
| *a.* | | Imperforate | 1.50 | — |

FERNS

Fortune's Holly Fern — A3711　　Soft Shield Fern — A3712

Autumn Fern — A3713　　Goldie's Wood Fern — A3714

Painted Fern — A3715

PHOTOGRAVURE
Serpentine Die Cut 11 Vert.
2014, Jan. 27
Coil Stamps
Self-Adhesive

4848	A3711	49c multicolored	1.50	.25
4849	A3712	49c multicolored	1.50	.25
4850	A3713	49c multicolored	1.50	.25
4851	A3714	49c multicolored	1.50	.25
4852	A3715	49c multicolored	1.50	.25
a.		Strip of 5, #4848-4852	7.50	
		Nos. 4848-4852 (5)	7.50	1.25

Fort McHenry Flag and Fireworks — A3716

PHOTOGRAVURE (#4853),
LITHOGRAPHED (#4854-4855)
Serpentine Die Cut 8½ Vert.
2014, Jan. 28
Coil Stamps
Self-Adhesive

| 4853 | A3716 | (49c) multicolored | 1.00 | .25 |

Serpentine Die Cut 9½ Vert.

| 4854 | A3716 | (49c) multicolored | 1.00 | .25 |
| *a.* | | Die cutting omitted, pair | 200.00 | |

Booklet Stamp
Serpentine Die Cut 11¼x10¾ on 2 or 3 Sides

| 4855 | A3716 | (49c) multicolored | 1.00 | .25 |
| *a.* | | Booklet pane of 20 | 20.00 | |

No. 4855a is a double-sided booklet with 12 stamps on one side and eight stamps plus a label that serves as the booklet cover on the other side.

Nos. 4854 and 4855 each have a microprinted "USPS" on the right side of the flag.

See Nos. 4868-4871.

BLACK HERITAGE

Shirley Chisholm (1924-2005), Congresswoman A3717

PHOTOGRAVURE
Serpentine Die Cut 11
2014, Jan. 31
Self-Adhesive

| 4856 | A3717 | (49c) multicolored | 1.00 | .25 |
| *a.* | | Imperforate | 1.50 | — |

WILDLIFE ISSUE

Hummingbird A3718

LITHOGRAPHED
Serpentine Die Cut 11¼x10¾
2014, Feb. 7
Self-Adhesive

| 4857 | A3718 | 34c multicolored | .70 | .25 |

Coil Stamp
Serpentine Die Cut 9½ Vert.

4858	A3718	34c multicolored	.70	.25
a.		Overall tagging	.70	.25
b.		As "a," die cutting omitted, pair	—	

GREAT SPANGLED FRITILLARY BUTTERFLY

A3719

PHOTOGRAVURE
Serpentine Die Cut 10¾
2014, Feb. 10
Self-Adhesive

| 4859 | A3719 | 70c multicolored | 1.40 | .25 |
| *a.* | | Imperforate | 3.00 | — |

Statue of Abraham Lincoln in Lincoln Memorial — A3720

PHOTOGRAVURE
Serpentine Die Cut 11
2014, Feb. 12
Self-Adhesive

| 4860 | A3720 | 21c multicolored | .45 | .25 |
| *a.* | | Imperforate | 1.00 | — |

Coil Stamp
Serpentine Die Cut 8½ Vert.

| 4861 | A3720 | 21c multicolored | .45 | .25 |

WINTER FLOWERS

Amaryllis A3721　　Cyclamen A3722

Paperwhite A3723　　Christmas Cactus A3724

LITHOGRAPHED
Serpentine Die Cut 11 on 2 or 3 Sides
2014, Feb. 14
Booklet Stamps
Self-Adhesive

4862	A3721	(49c) multicolored	1.00	.30
4863	A3722	(49c) multicolored	1.00	.30
4864	A3723	(49c) multicolored	1.00	.30
4865	A3724	(49c) multicolored	1.00	.30
a.		Block of 4, #4862-4865	4.00	
b.		Booklet pane of 20, 5 each #4862-4865	20.00	
c.		Imperforate block of 4	6.00	—
d.		Imperforate booklet pane of 20	30.00	—
		Nos. 4862-4865 (4)	4.00	1.20

No. 4865b is a double-sided booklet pane with 12 stamps on one side (3 each #4862-4865), and eight stamps (2 each #4862-4865) plus label (booklet cover) on the other side.

LITERARY ARTS

Ralph Ellison (1913-94), Buildings in Harlem A3725

PHOTOGRAVURE
Serpentine Die Cut 11
2014, Feb. 18
Self-Adhesive

| 4866 | A3725 | 91c multicolored | 1.90 | .45 |
| *a.* | | Imperforate | 3.25 | — |

Wedding Cake Type of 2009
LITHOGRAPHED
Serpentine Die Cut 10¾
2014, Feb. 22
Self-Adhesive

| 4867 | A3344 | 70c multicolored | 1.40 | .25 |

Fort McHenry Flag and Fireworks Type of 2014
LITHOGRAPHED (#4868, 4870-4871),
PHOTOGRAVURE (#4869)
Coil Stamp Self-Adhesive With "USPS" Microprinted in Fireworks Above Flagpole

Serpentine Die Cut 11 Vert.
2014, Mar. 3

4868	A3716	(49c) multicolored	1.00	.25
a.		Vert. strip of 3 (one single each from three different coil rolls), horiz. unslit between	60.00	
b.		Pair, die cutting omitted		

Booklet Stamps
Without Microprinted "USPS"
Serpentine Die Cut 11¼x11½ on 2 or 3 Sides

| 4869 | A3716 | (49c) multicolored | 1.00 | .25 |
| *a.* | | Booklet pane of 20 | 20.00 | |

With "USPS" Microprinted in Fireworks Above Flagpole
Serpentine Die Cut 11¼x10¾ on 2 or 3 Sides

| 4870 | A3716 | (49c) multicolored | 1.00 | .25 |
| *a.* | | Booklet pane of 20 | 20.00 | |

The actual design images on Nos. 4855, 4869 and 4870 differ slightly in size. This is easiest seen by measuring the height of the flagpole: No. 4855 is 13mm, No. 4869 is 14mm, and No. 4870 is 12mm.

Thin Paper
Serpentine Die Cut 11¼x11 on 2, 3 or 4 Sides

| 4871 | A3716 | (49c) multicolored | 1.00 | .25 |
| *a.* | | Booklet pane of 18 | 18.00 | |

Nos. 4869a and 4870a are double-sided booklets with 12 stamps on one side and eight stamps plus a label that serves as the booklet cover on the other side.

AMERICAN LANDMARKS ISSUE

Verrazano-Narrows Bridge, New York — A3726

USS Arizona Memorial, Hawaii A3727

LITHOGRAPHED
2014　*Serpentine Die Cut 10¾x10½*
Self-Adhesive

4872	A3726	$5.60 multi	11.00	6.25
4873	A3727	$19.99 multi	40.00	21.00
a.		Imperforate	55.00	—

Issued: $5.60, 3/4; $19.99, 3/13.

FERNS

Fortune's Holly Fern — A3728　　Soft Shield Fern — A3729

Autumn Fern — A3730　　Goldie's Wood Fern — A3731

Painted Fern — A3732

PHOTOGRAVURE
Serpentine Die Cut 11 Vert.
2014, Mar. 6

Coil Stamps
Self-Adhesive

4874	A3728	(49c) multicolored	1.50	.25
4875	A3729	(49c) multicolored	1.50	.25
4876	A3730	(49c) multicolored	1.50	.25
4877	A3731	(49c) multicolored	1.50	.25
4878	A3732	(49c) multicolored	1.50	.25
a.		Strip of 5, #4874-4878	7.50	
		Nos. 4874-4878 (5)	7.50	1.25

DISTINGUISHED AMERICANS

C. Alfred "Chief"
Anderson (1907-96),
Aviator — A3733

LITHOGRAPHED
Serpentine Die Cut 10¾x11
2014, Mar. 13

Self-Adhesive

4879	A3733	70c multicolored	1.40	.30
a.		Imperforate	2.25	—

MUSIC ICONS

Jimi Hendrix
(1942-70), Rock
Guitarist
A3734

PHOTOGRAVURE
2014, Mar. 13   **Tagged**

Self-Adhesive

4880	A3734	(49c) multicolored	1.00	.25
a.		Imperforate	1.50	—

Adjacent horizontal or vertical stamps have selvage between the stamps. Any stamp on the pane is rotated 90 degrees with respect to any adjacent stamp, so that any block of four has stamps oriented in each of the four directions.

Flowers and "Yes I Do" Type of 2013
LITHOGRAPHED
Serpentine Die Cut 10¾
2014, Mar. 21

Self-Adhesive

4881	A3639	70c multicolored	1.40	.30

SONGBIRDS

Western
Meadowlark
A3735

Mountain
Bluebird
A3736

Western Tanager
A3737

Painted Bunting
A3738

Baltimore Oriole
A3739

Evening
Grosbeak
A3740

Scarlet Tanager
A3741

Rose-breasted
Grosbeak
A3742

American
Goldfinch
A3743

White-throated
Sparrow
A3744

LITHOGRAPHED
Serpentine Die Cut 10¾ on 2 or 3 Sides
2014, Apr. 5

Booklet Stamps
Self-Adhesive

4882	A3735	(49c) multicolored	1.00	.40
4883	A3736	(49c) multicolored	1.00	.40
4884	A3737	(49c) multicolored	1.00	.40
4885	A3738	(49c) multicolored	1.00	.40
4886	A3739	(49c) multicolored	1.00	.40
4887	A3740	(49c) multicolored	1.00	.40
4888	A3741	(49c) multicolored	1.00	.40
4889	A3742	(49c) multicolored	1.00	.40
4890	A3743	(49c) multicolored	1.00	.40
4891	A3744	(49c) multicolored	1.00	.40
a.		Block of 10, #4882-4891	10.00	
b.		Booklet pane of 20, 2 each #4882-4891	20.00	
c.		Imperforate block of 10	17.50	—
d.		Imperforate booklet pane of 20	35.00	
		Nos. 4882-4891 (10)	10.00	4.00

No. 4891b is a double-sided booklet pane with 12 stamps on one side (Nos. 4883-4886, 4888-4891, 2 each Nos. 4882, 4887) and eight stamps (Nos. 4883-4886, 4888-4891) plus label (booklet cover) on the other side.

LEGENDS OF HOLLYWOOD

Charlton Heston
(1923-2008),
Actor — A3745

LITHOGRAPHED
Serpentine Die Cut 11
2014, Apr. 11

Self-Adhesive

4892	A3745	(49c) multicolored	1.00	.25
a.		Imperforate	1.50	—

Map of Sea
Surface
Temperatures
A3746

LITHOGRAPHED
2014, Apr. 22   *Serpentine Die Cut*
Self-Adhesive

4893	A3746	($1.15) multi	2.40	.50
a.		Imperforate	3.75	—

Unused values are for stamps with surrounding selvage. Adjacent stamps are separated by rouletting.

FLAGS

Flag With 5
Full and 3
Partial
Stars — A3747

Flag With 3
Full
Stars — A3748

Flag With 4
Full and 2
Partial
Stars — A3749

Flag With 2
Full and 2
Partial
Stars — A3750

PHOTOGRAVURE
Serpentine Die Cut 11 Vert.
2014, Apr. 25

Coil Stamps
Self-Adhesive

4894	A3747	(49c) blue & red	1.00	.25
4895	A3748	(49c) blue & red	1.00	.25
4896	A3749	(49c) blue & red	1.00	.25
4897	A3750	(49c) blue & red	1.00	.25
a.		Strip of 4, #4894-4897	4.00	
		Nos. 4894-4897 (4)	4.00	1.00

See note after No. 1549.

CIRCUS POSTERS

Barnum and Bailey Circus Poster With
Clown — A3751

Sells-Floto Circus
Poster — A3752

Ringling Bros. Barnum and Bailey
Circus Poster With Dainty Miss
Leitzel — A3753

Al G. Barnes Wild
Animal Circus
Poster — A3754

Ringling Bros. Shows Poster With
Hillary Long — A3755

Barnum and
Bailey Circus
Poster With
Tiger — A3756

Ringling Bros. Barnum and Bailey
Circus Poster With Elephant — A3757

Carl Hagenbeck-Wallace Circus
Poster — A3758

A3758a

LITHOGRAPHED, ENGRAVED (50c),
SHEET MARGIN (#4905b)

LITHOGRAPHED WITH FOIL APPLICATION

2014, May 5   *Serpentine Die Cut 11*
Self-Adhesive

4898	A3751	(49c) multicolored	1.00	.45
4899	A3752	(49c) multicolored	1.00	.45
4900	A3753	(49c) multicolored	1.00	.45
4901	A3754	(49c) multicolored	1.00	.45
4902	A3755	(49c) multicolored	1.00	.45
4903	A3756	(49c) multicolored	1.00	.45
4904	A3757	(49c) multicolored	1.00	.45
4905	A3758	(49c) multicolored	1.00	.45
a.		Block of 8, #4898-4905	8.00	
b.		Imperforate block of 8	15.00	
c.		A3758a Imperforate souvenir sheet of 3, #4905d, 2 #4905c	9.00	—
d.		A1811 50c red, imperforate	2.25	—
e.		$1 multicolored (57x48mm stamp similar to #4898), imperforate	4.50	—
f.		As "c," gold omitted in sheet margin	—	
		Nos. 4898-4905 (8)	8.00	3.60

No. 4905c was printed only in press sheets containing 12 souvenir sheets. No. 4905c has die cutting around the souvenir sheet margin, but values for unused examples are for souvenir sheets having the white press sheet margin surrounding the die cutting. Examples of No. 4905c with serpentine die cutting around the three stamps were sold only with the USPS 2014 Stamp Yearbook, which sold for $64.95. The souvenir sheets sold with the yearbook are punched out from the press sheets and lack the white press sheet margin.

HARVEY MILK

Harvey Milk (1930-78), Homosexual Rights Advocate and Politician — A3759

LITHOGRAPHED
Sheets of 240 in 12 panes of 20
Serpentine Die Cut 10¾
2014, May 22
Self-Adhesive

4906	A3759	(49c) multicolored	1.00	.25
a.		Imperforate	1.50	—

NEVADA STATEHOOD, 150th ANNIV.

Fire Canyon A3760

LITHOGRAPHED
Serpentine Die Cut 10¾
2014, May 29
Self-Adhesive

4907	A3760	(49c) multicolored	1.00	.25
a.		Imperforate	1.50	—

HOT RODS

Rear of 1932 Ford "Deuce" Roadster A3761

Front of 1932 Ford "Deuce" Roadster A3762

PHOTOGRAVURE
Serpentine Die Cut 11¾x11¼ on 2 or 3 Sides
2014, June 6
Booklet Stamps
Self-Adhesive

4908	A3761	(49c) multicolored	1.00	.25
4909	A3762	(49c) multicolored	1.00	.25
a.		Pair, #4908-4909	2.00	
b.		Booklet pane of 20, 10 each #4908-4909	20.00	
c.		Imperforate pair	3.25	—
d.		Imperforate booklet pane of 20	32.50	

No. 4909b is a double-sided booklet pane with 12 stamps on one side (6 each Nos. 4908-4909) and eight stamps (4 each Nos.

4908-4909) plus label (booklet cover) on the other side.

CIVIL WAR SESQUICENTENNIAL

Battle of Petersburg — A3763

Battle of Mobile Bay — A3764

LITHOGRAPHED
Serpentine Die Cut 11
2014, July 30
Self-Adhesive

4910	A3763	(49c) multicolored	1.00	.35
4911	A3764	(49c) multicolored	1.00	.35
a.		Pair, #4910-4911	2.00	
b.		Imperforate pair	5.00	—

FARMERS MARKETS

Breads A3765

Fruits and Vegetables A3766

Flowers A3767

Plants A3768

LITHOGRAPHED
Serpentine Die Cut 10¾
2014, Aug. 7
Self-Adhesive

4912	A3765	(49c) multicolored	1.00	.30
4913	A3766	(49c) multicolored	1.00	.30
4914	A3767	(49c) multicolored	1.00	.30
4915	A3768	(49c) multicolored	1.00	.30
a.		Horiz. strip of 4, #4912-4915	4.00	
b.		Imperf. horiz. strip of 4	7.50	—
		Nos. 4912-4915 (4)	4.00	1.20

MUSIC ICONS

Janis Joplin (1943-70), Rock Singer — A3769

LITHOGRAPHED
Serpentine Die Cut 10½
2014, Aug. 8
Self-Adhesive

4916	A3769	(49c) multicolored	1.00	.25
a.		Imperforate	1.50	—

HUDSON RIVER SCHOOL PAINTINGS

Grand Canyon, by Thomas Moran (1837-1926) — A3770

Summer Afternoon, by Asher B. Durand (1796-1886) A3771

Sunset, by Frederic Edwin Church (1826-1900) — A3772

Distant View of Niagara Falls, by Thomas Cole (1801-48) A3773

PHOTOGRAVURE
Serpentine Die Cut 10¾ on 2 or 3 Sides
2014, Aug. 21
Booklet Stamps
Self-Adhesive

4917	A3770	(49c) multicolored	1.00	.30
4918	A3771	(49c) multicolored	1.00	.30
4919	A3772	(49c) multicolored	1.00	.30
4920	A3773	(49c) multicolored	1.00	.30
a.		Block of 4, #4917-4920	4.00	
b.		Booklet pane of 20, 5 each #4917-4920	20.00	
c.		Imperforate block of 4	6.50	—
d.		Imperforate booklet pane of 20	32.50	
		Nos. 4917-4920 (4)	4.00	1.20

No. 4920b is a double-sided booklet pane with 12 stamps on one side (3 each #4917-4920), and eight stamps (2 each #4917-4920) plus label (booklet cover) on the other side.

WAR OF 1812 BICENTENNIAL

Bombardment of Fort McHenry — A3774

Designed by Greg Breeding. Printed by CCL Label, Inc.

PHOTOGRAVURE
Serpentine Die Cut 10¾x10½
2014, Sept. 13
Self-Adhesive

4921	A3774	(49c) multicolored	1.00	.25
a.		Pane of 20	20.00	
		Imperforate	1.50	—

CELEBRITY CHEFS

Edna Lewis (1916-2006) A3775

Felipe Rojas-Lombardi (1946-91) A3776

Joyce Chen (1917-94) A3777

James Beard (1903-85) A3778

Julia Child (1912-2004) A3779

Designed by Greg Breeding. Printed by Ashton-Potter (USA) Ltd.

LITHOGRAPHED
Sheets of 180 in nine panes of 20
Serpentine Die Cut 11x10¾
2014, Sept. 26
Self-Adhesive

4922	A3775	(49c) multicolored	1.00	.45
4923	A3776	(49c) multicolored	1.00	.45
4924	A3777	(49c) multicolored	1.00	.45
4925	A3778	(49c) multicolored	1.00	.45
4926	A3779	(49c) multicolored	1.00	.45
a.		Horiz. strip of 5, #4922-4926	5.00	
b.		Imperf. horiz. strip of 5	8.00	—
		Nos. 4922-4926 (5)	5.00	2.25

The gray shading of the inner curve of the dinner plate shown in the margin of the pane continues into the white frames surrounding some of the stamps in the pane's outer rows and columns.

AMERICAN LANDMARKS ISSUE

Glade Creek Grist Mill, West Virginia A3780

LITHOGRAPHED
Serpentine Die Cut 10¾x10½
2014, Sept. 29
Self-Adhesive

4927	A3780	$5.75 multi	11.50	6.50
a.		Imperforate	14.00	—

BATMAN

Bat Signal — A3781

Bat Signal — A3782

Bat
Signal — A3783

Bat
Signal — A3784

Batman
A3785

Batman and Bat
Signal
A3786

Batman and
Rope
A3787

Batman
A3788

LITHOGRAPHED
2014, Oct. 9   *Serpentine Die Cut*
Self-Adhesive

4928	A3781	(49c)	multicolored	1.00	.40
4929	A3782	(49c)	multicolored	1.00	.40
4930	A3783	(49c)	multicolored	1.00	.40
4931	A3784	(49c)	multicolored	1.00	.40

Serpentine Die Cut 11x10¾

4932	A3785	(49c)	multicolored	1.00	.40
4933	A3786	(49c)	multicolored	1.00	.40
4934	A3787	(49c)	multicolored	1.00	.40
4935	A3788	(49c)	multicolored	1.00	.40
a.	Vert. block of 8, #4928-4935		8.00	
b.	Imperf. vert. block of 8		18.00	—
	Nos. 4928-4935 (8)		8.00	3.20

Silver Bells
Wreath
A3789

LITHOGRAPHED
2014, Oct. 23   *Serpentine Die Cut*
Self-Adhesive

4936	A3789	($1.15)	multicolored	2.40	.50
a.	Imperforate		4.00	—

Unused values are for stamps with surrounding selvage. Adjacent stamps are separated by rouletting.

WINTER FUN

Skaters
A3790

Child Making
Snowman
A3791

Cardinal
A3792

Child Making
Snow Angel
A3793

Skaters
A3794

Cardinal
A3796

Child Making
Snowman
A3795

Child Making
Snow Angel
A3797

PHOTOGRAVURE (Nos. 4937-4940),
LITHOGRAPHED (Nos. 4941-4944)
*Serpentine Die Cut 10¾x11 on 2 or
3 Sides*
2014, Oct. 23
Booklet Stamps
Self-Adhesive

4937	A3790	(49c)	multicolored	1.00	.30
4938	A3791	(49c)	multicolored	1.00	.30
4939	A3792	(49c)	multicolored	1.00	.30
4940	A3793	(49c)	multicolored	1.00	.30
a.	Block of 4, #4937-4940		4.00	
b.	Booklet pane of 20, 5 each			
	#4937-4940		20.00	
c.	Imperforate block of 4		6.00	—
d.	Imperf. booklet pane of 20		30.00	—

*Serpentine Die Cut 11¼x11 on 2, 3
or 4 Sides*
Thin Paper

4941	A3794	(49c)	multicolored	1.00	.30
4942	A3795	(49c)	multicolored	1.00	.30
4943	A3796	(49c)	multicolored	1.00	.30
4944	A3797	(49c)	multicolored	1.00	.30
a.	Block of 4, #4941-4944		4.00	
b.	Booklet pane of 18, 5 each			
	#4941-4942, 4 each			
	#4943-4944		18.00	
	Nos. 4937-4944 (8)		8.00	2.40

CHRISTMAS

Magi — A3798

Rudolph, the Red-
Nosed
Reindeer — A3799

Hermey and
Rudolph — A3800

Santa
Claus — A3801

Bumble — A3802

LITHOGRAPHED (#4945),
PHOTOGRAVURE
*Serpentine Die Cut 10¾x11 on 2 or
3 Sides*
2014
Booklet Stamps
Self-Adhesive

4945	A3798	(49c)	multi	1.00	.25
a.	Booklet pane of 20		20.00	
b.	Imperforate		1.50	—
c.	Imperf. booklet pane of 20		30.00	

*Serpentine Die Cut 11x10¾ on 2 or
3 sides*

4946	A3799	(49c)	multi	1.00	.30
4947	A3800	(49c)	multi	1.00	.30
4948	A3801	(49c)	multi	1.00	.30
4949	A3802	(49c)	multi	1.00	.30
a.	Block of 4, #4946-4949		4.00	
b.	Booklet pane of 20, 5 each			
	#4946-4949		20.00	
c.	Imperf. block of 4		6.00	—
d.	Imperf. booklet pane of 20		30.00	—
	Nos. 4945-4949 (5)		5.00	1.45

Issued: No. 4945, 11/19; Nos. 4946-4949, 11/6.
Premiere of *Rudolph, the Red-Nosed Reindeer* animated television show, 50th anniv.
No. 4945a is a double-sided booklet with 12 stamps on one side and eight stamps plus a label that serves as a booklet cover on the other side. No. 4949b is a double-sided booklet with 12 stamps on one side (3 each of Nos. 4946-4949) and eight stamps (2 each of Nos. 4946-4949) plus a label that serves as a booklet cover on the other side.

WILT CHAMBERLAIN (1936-99),
BASKETBALL PLAYER

Chamberlain in
Philadelphia
Warriors Uniform
A3803

Chamberlain in
Los Angeles
Lakers Uniform
A3804

LITHOGRAPHED
Serpentine Die Cut 11x10¾
2014, Dec. 5
Self-Adhesive

4950	A3803	(49c)	multicolored	1.00	.25
4951	A3804	(49c)	multicolored	1.00	.25
a.	Pair, #4950-4951		2.00	
b.	Imperforate pair		3.00	—

WAR OF 1812 BICENTENNIAL

Battle of
New
Orleans
A3805

PHOTOGRAVURE
Serpentine Die Cut 10¾x10½
2015, Jan. 8
Self-Adhesive

4952	A3805	(49c)	multicolored	1.00	.25
a.	Imperforate		1.50	—

PATRIOTIC WAVES

A3806

A3807

Designed by Michael Dyer. Printed by Ashton-Potter (USA) Ltd.
LITHOGRAPHED
Sheets of 140 in 14 panes of 10
(#4953), Sheets of 100 in 10 panes of
10 (#4954)
Serpentine Die Cut 11
2015   **Tagged**
Self-Adhesive

4953	A3806	$1	multicolored	2.00	.50
a.	Imperforate		3.00	
4954	A3807	$2	multicolored	4.00	1.00
a.	Imperforate		5.00	

LOVE

A3808

A3809

Designed by Antonio Alcalá and Jessica Hische. Printed by CCL Label, Inc.
LITHOGRAPHED
Sheets of 120 in six panes of 20
Serpentine Die Cut 11
2015, Jan. 22   **Tagged**
Self-Adhesive

4955	A3808	(49c)	red	1.00	.25
4956	A3809	(49c)	red & gray	1.00	.25
a.	Pair, #4955-4956		2.00	
b.	Imperforate pair		3.00	—

CHINESE NEW YEAR

Year of the
Ram
A3810

LITHOGRAPHED
2015, Feb. 7   *Serpentine Die Cut 11*
Self-Adhesive

4957	A3810	(49c)	multicolored	1.00	.25
a.	Imperforate		1.75	—

BLACK HERITAGE

Robert Robinson
Taylor (1868-1942),
Architect — A3811

LITHOGRAPHED
Serpentine Die Cut 11
2015, Feb. 12
Self-Adhesive

4958	A3811	(49c)	multicolored	1.00	.25
a.	Imperforate		1.75	—

FLOWERS

Rose and
Heart — A3812

Tulip and
Heart — A3813

ENGRAVED
Serpentine Die Cut 10¾x 11
2015, Feb. 14
Self-Adhesive

4959	A3812	(49c)	red & black	1.00	.25
a.	Imperforate		1.50	—
4960	A3813	70c	black & red	1.50	.30
a.	Imperforate		2.50	—

FLAGS

Stripes at Left, Stars at Right
A3814

Stars and White Stripe
A3815

Stars at Left, Stripes at Right — A3816

LITHOGRAPHED
Serpentine Die Cut 11 Vert.
2015, Feb. 27
Coil Stamps
Self-Adhesive

4961	A3814	(10c) multicolored	.25	.25
4962	A3815	(10c) multicolored	.25	.25
4963	A3816	(10c) multicolored	.25	.25
a.		Strip of 3, #4961-4963	.75	
		Nos. 4961-4963 (3)	.75	.75

WATER LILIES

Pale Pink Water Lily — A3817

Red Water Lily — A3818

Purple Water Lily — A3819

White Water Lily — A3820

LITHOGRAPHED
Serpentine Die Cut 11x11¼ on 2 or 3 Sides
2015, Mar. 20
Booklet Stamps
Self-Adhesive

4964	A3817	(49c) multicolored	1.00	.25
4965	A3818	(49c) multicolored	1.00	.25
4966	A3819	(49c) multicolored	1.00	.25
4967	A3820	(49c) multicolored	1.00	.25
a.		Block of 4, #4964-4967	4.00	
b.		Booklet pane of 20, 5 each #4964-4967	20.00	
c.		Imperf. block of 4	6.00	—
d.		Imperf. booklet pane of 20	30.00	
		Nos. 4964-4967 (4)	4.00	1.00

No. 4967b is a double-sided booklet pane with 12 stamps on one side (3 each Nos. 4964-4967) and eight stamps (2 each Nos. 4964-4967) plus label (booklet cover) on the other side.

ART BY MARTIN RAMIREZ (1895-1963)

Untitled (Horse and Rider With Trees), 1954 — A3821

Untitled (Man Riding Donkey), c. 1960-63
A3822

Untitled (Trains on Inclined Tracks), c. 1960-63
A3823

Untitled (Deer), c. 1960-63
A3824

Untitled (Tunnel with Cars and Buses), 1954 — A3825

LITHOGRAPHED
Serpentine Die Cut 10¾
2015, Mar. 26
Self-Adhesive

4968	A3821	(49c) multicolored	1.00	.40
4969	A3822	(49c) multicolored	1.00	.40
4970	A3823	(49c) multicolored	1.00	.40
4971	A3824	(49c) multicolored	1.00	.40
4972	A3825	(49c) multicolored	1.00	.40
a.		Vert. strip of 5, #4968-4972	5.00	
b.		Imperf. vert. strip of 5	7.50	—

Ferns Type of 2014
LITHOGRAPHED
Serpentine Die Cut 11 Vert.
2015, Mar. 27
Coil Stamps
Self-Adhesive
With Microprinted "USPS" Dated "2014"

4973	A3729	(49c) multicolored	1.00	.25
a.		Dated "2015"	1.00	.25
4974	A3730	(49c) multicolored	1.00	.25
a.		Dated "2015"	1.00	.25
4975	A3731	(49c) multicolored	1.00	.25
a.		Dated "2015"	1.00	.25
4976	A3732	(49c) multicolored	1.00	.25
a.		Dated "2015"	1.00	.25
4977	A3728	(49c) multicolored	1.00	.25
a.		Dated "2015"	1.00	.25
b.		Strip of 5, #4973-4977	5.00	
c.		Strip of 5, #4973a-4977a	5.00	
		Nos. 4973-4977 (5)	5.00	1.25

Nos. 4973a-4977a are from coil rolls containing 3,000 stamps. Nos. 4973-4977 are from coil rolls containing 10,000 stamps. Microprinted "USPS" is near the end of the upper left fern branch on No. 4973 and near the base of the fern's stem on Nos. 4974-4977. Nos. 4973a-4977a have same microprinting locations as Nos. 4973-4977. Nos. 4874-4878 lack microprinted "USPS."

FROM ME TO YOU

A3826

LITHOGRAPHED
Sheets of 120 in six panes of 20
2015, Apr. 1 *Serpentine Die Cut 11*
Self-Adhesive

4978	A3826	(49c) multicolored	1.00	.25
a.		Imperforate	1.50	

MAYA ANGELOU (1928-2014), WRITER

Angelou and Quotation
A3827

LITHOGRAPHED
2015, Apr. 7 *Serpentine Die Cut 11*
Self-Adhesive

4979	A3827	(49c) multicolored	1.00	.25
a.		Imperforate	1.50	—

The quotation on the stamp is not Angelou's but is similar to a quote by Joan Walsh Anglund.

CIVIL WAR SESQUICENTENNIAL

Battle of Five Forks — A3828

Surrender at Appomattox Court House — A3829

LITHOGRAPHED
Double-sided sheets of 72 in six panes of 12 (60 on one side, 12 on other side)
2015, Apr. 9 *Serpentine Die Cut 11*
Self-Adhesive

4980	A3828	(49c) multicolored	1.00	.30
4981	A3829	(49c) multicolored	1.00	.30
a.		Pair, #4980-4981	2.00	
b.		Imperforate pair	25.00	—

GIFTS OF FRIENDSHIP

Lincoln Memorial and Cherry Blossoms
A3830

U.S. Capitol and Dogwood Blossoms
A3831

Japanese Diet, Tokyo, and Cherry Blossoms
A3832

Clock Tower, Tokyo, and Dogwood Blossoms
A3833

LITHOGRAPHED
Sheets of 72 in six panes of 12
Serpentine Die Cut 11
2015, Apr. 10
Self-Adhesive

4982	A3830	(49c) multicolored	1.00	.30
4983	A3831	(49c) multicolored	1.00	.30
a.		Horiz. pair, #4982-4983	2.00	
b.		Imperforate pair	4.50	
4984	A3832	(49c) multicolored	1.00	.30
4985	A3833	(49c) multicolored	1.00	.30
a.		Horiz. pair, #4984-4985	2.00	
b.		Imperforate pair	6.00	—
		Nos. 4982-4985 (4)	4.00	1.20

See Japan No. 3814.

SPECIAL OLYMPICS WORLD GAMES

Emblem — A3834

LITHOGRAPHED
Serpentine Die Cut 10¾
2015, May 9
Self-Adhesive

4986	A3834	(49c) multicolored	1.00	.25
a.		Imperforate	1.50	—

HELP FIND MISSING CHILDREN

Forget-me-nots — A3835

LITHOGRAPHED
Serpentine Die Cut 10¾
2015, May 18
Self-Adhesive

4987	A3835	(49c) multicolored	1.00	.25
a.		Imperforate	1.50	—

MEDAL OF HONOR

Air Force Medal of Honor — A3836

LITHOGRAPHED
2015, May 25 *Serpentine Die Cut 11*
Self-Adhesive

4988	A3836	(49c) multicolored	1.00	.25
a.		Horiz. strip of 3, #4822b, 4823b, 4988	3.00	
b.		Imperforate strip of 3	6.00	

WILDLIFE ISSUE

Emperor Penguins — A3837

LITHOGRAPHED
Serpentine Die Cut 10¾
2015, June 1
Self-Adhesive

4989	A3837	(22c) multicolored	.45	.25
a.		Imperforate	.75	—

Coil Stamp
Serpentine Die Cut 11 Vert.

4990	A3837	(22c) multicolored	.45	.25

COASTAL BIRDS

Red Knot — A3838

King Eider — A3839

Spoonbill
A3840

Frigatebird
A3841

LITHOGRAPHED
Serpentine Die Cut 11¼x11
2015, June 1
Self-Adhesive

4991	A3838	(35c) multicolored	.70	.25
4992	A3839	(35c) multicolored	.70	.25
4993	A3840	(35c) multicolored	.70	.25
4994	A3841	(35c) multicolored	.70	.25
a.		Block or vert. strip of 4, #4991-4994	2.80	
b.		Imperforate block or vert. strip of 4	5.00	—

Coil Stamps
Serpentine Die Cut 9½ Vert.

4995	A3840	(35c) multicolored	.70	.25
4996	A3841	(35c) multicolored	.70	.25
4997	A3838	(35c) multicolored	.70	.25
4998	A3839	(35c) multicolored	.70	.25
a.		Horiz. strip of 4, #4995-4998	2.80	

EASTERN TIGER SWALLOWTAIL BUTTERFLY

A3842

LITHOGRAPHED
Serpentine Die Cut 10½
2015, June 1
Self-Adhesive

4999	A3842	(71c) multicolored	1.50	.25
a.		Imperforate	2.50	

Wedding Cake — A3843

LITHOGRAPHED
Serpentine Die Cut 10¾
2015, June 1
Self-Adhesive

5000	A3843	(71c) multicolored	1.50	.25

Flowers and "Yes, I Do"
A3844

LITHOGRAPHED
Serpentine Die Cut 10¾
2015, June 1   **Tagged**
Self-Adhesive

5001	A3844	(71c) multicolored	1.50	.25

Tulip and Heart — A3845

ENGRAVED
2015, June 1   *Serpentine Die Cut 11*
Self-Adhesive

5002	A3845	(71c) black & red	1.50	.25

LITERARY ARTS

Flannery O'Connor (1925-64), Novelist
A3846

LITHOGRAPHED
Serpentine Die Cut 10¾
2015, June 5
Self-Adhesive

5003	A3846	(93c) multicolored	1.90	.30
a.		Imperforate	3.00	—

SUMMER HARVEST

Watermelon
A3847

Sweet Corn
A3848

Cantaloupes
A3849

Tomatoes
A3850

LITHOGRAPHED
Serpentine Die Cut 11¼x10¾ on 2 or 3 Sides
2015, July 11
Booklet Stamps
Self-Adhesive

5004	A3847	(49c) multicolored	1.00	.30
5005	A3848	(49c) multicolored	1.00	.30
5006	A3849	(49c) multicolored	1.00	.30
5007	A3850	(49c) multicolored	1.00	.30
a.		Block of 4, #5004-5007	4.00	
b.		Booklet pane of 20, 5 each #5004-5007	20.00	
c.		As "a," imperforate	6.00	
d.		As "b," imperforate	30.00	
		Nos. 5004-5007 (4)	4.00	1.20

No. 5007b is a double-sided booklet pane with 12 stamps on one side (3 each #5004-5007), and eight stamps (2 each #5004-5007) plus label (booklet cover) on the other side.

COAST GUARD

MH-65 Dolphin Helicopter and Cutter *Eagle*
A3851

LITHOGRAPHED
Serpentine Die Cut 10¾
2015, Aug. 4   **Tagged**
Self-Adhesive

5008	A3851	(49c) multicolored	1.00	.25
a.		Imperforate	1.50	—

MUSIC ICONS

Elvis Presley (1935-77), Singer — A3852

LITHOGRAPHED
Serpentine Die Cut 10½
2015, Aug. 12
Self-Adhesive

5009	A3852	(49c) multicolored	1.00	.25
a.		Imperforate	1.50	—

2016 WORLD STAMP SHOW, NEW YORK CITY

Star — A3853

LITHOGRAPHED
Serpentine Die Cut 11
2015, Aug. 20
Self-Adhesive

5010	A3853	(49c) red	1.00	.25
5011	A3853	(49c) blue	1.00	.25
a.		Pair, #5010-5011	2.00	
b.		As "a," imperforate	3.00	—

LEGENDS OF HOLLYWOOD

Ingrid Bergman (1915-82), Actress — A3854

LITHOGRAPHED
Serpentine Die Cut 11
2015, Aug. 20
Self-Adhesive

5012	A3854	(49c) multicolored	1.00	.25
a.		Imperforate	1.50	—

See Sweden Nos. 2756-2758.

Eagle Type of 2012
LITHOGRAPHED
Serpentine Die Cut 10¼ Vert.
2015, Sept. 2
Coil Stamps
Self-Adhesive
Color Behind "USA"

5013	A3504	(25c) green	.50	.25
5014	A3504	(25c) blue green	.50	.25
5015	A3504	(25c) blue	.50	.25
5016	A3504	(25c) red violet	.50	.25
5017	A3504	(25c) orange	.50	.25
5018	A3504	(25c) yellow orange	.50	.25
a.		Strip of 6, #5013-5018	3.00	
		Nos. 5013-5018 (6)	3.00	1.50

CELEBRATE

A3855

LITHOGRAPHED
Serpentine Die Cut 10¾
2015, Sept. 9
Self-Adhesive

5019	A3855	(49c) multicolored	1.00	.25

Compare with type A3441.

PAUL NEWMAN (1925-2008), ACTOR AND PHILANTHROPIST

A3856

LITHOGRAPHED
Serpentine Die Cut 10¾
2015, Sept. 18
Self-Adhesive

5020	A3856	(49c) multicolored	1.00	.25
a.		Imperforate	1.50	—

Die cut and imperforate uncut press sheets of No. 5020 were made available for sale. Values: horiz. pair with vert. gutter between, $3.75. See note after No. 4693.

CHRISTMAS

Charlie Brown Carrying Christmas Tree — A3857

Charlie Brown, Pigpen and Dirty Snowman A3858

Snoopy, Lucy, Violet, Sally and Schroeder Skating — A3859

Characters, Dog House and Christmas Tree — A3860

Linus and Christmas Tree — A3861

Charlie Brown Looking in Mailbox — A3862

Charlie Brown and Linus Behind Brick Wall — A3863

Charlie Brown, Linus and Christmas Tree — A3864

Charlie Brown Screaming, Snoopy Decorating Dog House — A3865

Charlie Brown Hanging Ornament on Christmas Tree — A3866

LITHOGRAPHED
Serpentine Die Cut 10¾ on 2 or 3 Sides
2015, Oct. 1
Booklet Stamps
Self-Adhesive

5021	A3857	(49c) multicolored	1.00	.40
5022	A3858	(49c) multicolored	1.00	.40
5023	A3859	(49c) multicolored	1.00	.40

5024	A3860	(49c) multicolored	1.00	.40
5025	A3861	(49c) multicolored	1.00	.40
5026	A3862	(49c) multicolored	1.00	.40
5027	A3863	(49c) multicolored	1.00	.40
5028	A3864	(49c) multicolored	1.00	.40
5029	A3865	(49c) multicolored	1.00	.40
5030	A3866	(49c) multicolored	1.00	.40
a.		Block of 10, #5021-5030	10.00	
b.		Booklet pane of 20, 2 each		
		#5021-5030	20.00	
c.		As "a," imperforate	17.50	
d.		As "b," imperforate	35.00	
		Nos. 5021-5030 (10)	10.00	4.00

Premiere of *A Charlie Brown Christmas* animated television show, 50th anniv.

No. 5030b is a double-sided booklet pane with 12 stamps on one side (Nos. 5023-5030, 2 each Nos. 5021-5022) and eight stamps (Nos. 5023-5030) plus label (booklet cover) on the other side.

GEOMETRIC SNOWFLAKES

 A3867   A3868

 A3869   A3870

LITHOGRAPHED
Serpentine Die Cut 11¼x10¾ on 2 or 3 Sides
2015, Oct. 23
Booklet Stamps
Self-Adhesive
Snowflake Colors

5031	A3867	(49c) purple & lilac	1.00	.30
5032	A3868	(49c) dark blue & blue	1.00	.30
5033	A3869	(49c) dark green & green	1.00	.30
5034	A3870	(49c) crimson & pink	1.00	.30
a.		Block of 4, #5031-5034	4.00	
b.		Booklet pane of 20, 5 each #5031-5034	20.00	
c.		As "a," imperforate	6.00	
d.		As "b," imperforate	30.00	
		Nos. 5031-5034 (4)	4.00	1.20

No. 5034b is a double-sided booklet pane with 12 stamps on one side (3 each Nos. 5031-5034), and eight stamps (2 each Nos. 5031-5034) plus label (booklet cover) on the other side.

Purple Heart and Ribbon Type of 2012
LITHOGRAPHED
2015, Oct. *Serpentine Die Cut 11*
Self-Adhesive
With "USPS" Microprinted At Left of Ribbon

5035	A3587	(49c) multicolored	1.00	.25

LOVE

Quilled Paper Heart — A3871

LITHOGRAPHED
Serpentine Die Cut 10¾
2016, Jan. 12
Self-Adhesive

5036	A3871	(49c) multicolored	1.00	.25
a.		Imperforate	1.50	
b.		Die cutting omitted, P#B11111 block of 4	—	

No. 5036b was printed from P#B11111 only and may also be collected in plate blocks of 6, half panes of 10 and full panes of 20. Pairs or other multiples without P#B11111 selvage attached cannot be distinguished from No. 5036a, which was printed only from P#S11111.

FRUIT

Albemarle Pippin Apples
A3872

Pinot Noir Grapes
A3873

Red Pears — A3874

LITHOGRAPHED
2016
Coil Stamps
Self-Adhesive

5037	A3872	1c multicolored	.25	.25
5038	A3873	5c multicolored	.25	.25

Serpentine Die Cut 10¾ Vert.

5039	A3874	10c multicolored	.25	.25

AMERICAN LANDMARKS ISSUE

La Cueva del Indio, Puerto Rico A3875

Columbia River Gorge A3876

LITHOGRAPHED
Serpentine Die Cut 10¾x10½
2016, Jan. 17
Self-Adhesive

5040	A3875	$6.45 multi	13.00	7.50
a.		Imperforate	17.50	
5041	A3876	$22.95 multi	45.00	24.00
a.		Imperforate	125.00	

Die cut and imperforate press sheets of No. 5040 were made available for sale. Value: cross gutter block of 4, $90; pairs with gutter between, $42.50.

Die cut and imperforate partial press sheets (containing 30 stamps) of No. 5041 were made available for sale. Value: vert. pair with horiz. gutter between, $150. See note after No. 4693.

See note after No. 1549.

BOTANICAL ART

Corn Lilies A3877

Tulips A3878

Tulips A3879

Dahlias A3880

Stocks A3881

Roses A3882

Japanese Irises — A3883

Tulips — A3884

Petunias A3885

Jonquils A3886

LITHOGRAPHED
Serpentine Die Cut 10¾ on 2 or 3 Sides
2016, Jan. 29
Booklet Stamps
Self-Adhesive

5042	A3877	(49c) multicolored	1.00	.40
5043	A3878	(49c) multicolored	1.00	.40
5044	A3879	(49c) multicolored	1.00	.40
5045	A3880	(49c) multicolored	1.00	.40
5046	A3881	(49c) multicolored	1.00	.40
5047	A3882	(49c) multicolored	1.00	.40
5048	A3883	(49c) multicolored	1.00	.40
5049	A3884	(49c) multicolored	1.00	.40
5050	A3885	(49c) multicolored	1.00	.40
5051	A3886	(49c) multicolored	1.00	.40
a.		Block of 10, #5042-5051	10.00	
b.		Booklet pane of 10, #5042-5051	10.00	
c.		Booklet pane of 20, 2 each #5042-5051	20.00	
d.		Imperforate block of 10	45.00	—
e.		Imperforate booklet pane of 20	90.00	—
		Nos. 5042-5051 (10)	10.00	4.00

No. 5051c is a double-sided booklet pane with 12 stamps on one side (Nos. 5042-5049, 2 each Nos. 5050-5051) and eight stamps (Nos. 5042-5049) plus label (booklet cover) on the other side.

Flag — A3887

LITHOGRAPHED
Serpentine Die Cut 11 Vert.
2016, Jan. 29
Coil Stamps
Self-Adhesive
Microprinted "USPS" To Right of Pole Under Flag

5052	A3887	(49c) multicolored	1.00	.25

Serpentine Die Cut 9½ Vert.
Microprinted "USPS" on Second White Flag Stripe

5053	A3887	(49c) multicolored	1.00	.25

Booklet Stamps
Microprinted "USPS" To Right of Pole Under Flag
Serpentine Die Cut 11¼x10¾ on 2 or 3 Sides

5054	A3887	(49c) multicolored	1.00	.25
a.		Booklet pane of 10	10.00	
b.		Booklet pane of 20	20.00	
c.		As "b," horiz. die cutting omitted on side with 12 stamps	—	

Microprinted "USPS" on Second White Flag Stripe

5055	A3887	(49c) multicolored	1.00	.25
a.		Booklet pane of 20	20.00	

Nos. 5054b and 5055a are double-sided booklets with 12 stamps on one side and eight stamps plus a label that serves as the booklet cover on the other side.

BLACK HERITAGE

Richard Allen (1760-1831), Founder of African Methodist Episcopal Church — A3888

LITHOGRAPHED
Serpentine Die Cut 10¾
2016, Feb. 2
Self-Adhesive

5056	A3888	(49c) multicolored	1.00	.25
a.		Imperforate	2.50	—

CHINESE NEW YEAR

Year of the Monkey A3889

LITHOGRAPHED
Serpentine Die Cut 10¾
2016, Feb. 5
Self-Adhesive

5057	A3889	(49c) multicolored	1.00	.25
a.		Imperforate	1.50	—

Moon A3890

LITHOGRAPHED
2016, Feb. 22 *Serpentine Die Cut*
Self-Adhesive

5058	A3890	($1.20) multicolored	2.40	.50

Unused values are for stamps with surrounding selvage. Adjacent stamps are separated by rouletting.

MUSIC ICONS

Sarah Vaughan (1924-90), Singer — A3891

LITHOGRAPHED
Serpentine Die Cut 10½
2016, Mar. 29
Self-Adhesive

5059	A3891	(49c) multicolored	1.00	.25

LEGENDS OF HOLLYWOOD

Shirley Temple (1928-2014), Actress and Diplomat — A3892

LITHOGRAPHED
Serpentine Die Cut 10¾
2016, Apr. 18
Self-Adhesive

5060 A3892 (47c) multicolored .95 .25

"USA" and
Star — A3893

LITHOGRAPHED
Serpentine Die Cut 10 Vert.
2016, Apr. 28
COIL STAMP
Self-Adhesive

5061 A3893 (5c) multicolored .25 .25
See note after No. 1549.

2016 WORLD STAMP SHOW, NEW YORK CITY

Star — A3894

ENGRAVED
Serpentine Die Cut 10¾
2016, May 28
Self-Adhesive

5062 A3894 (47c) blue .95 .25
5063 A3894 (47c) red .95 .25

REPEAL OF THE STAMP ACT, 250TH ANNIV.

Man Posting of
Notice of Repeal
on
Tree — A3895

LITHOGRAPHED
Serpentine Die Cut 10¾
2016, May 29
Self-Adhesive

5064 A3895 (47c) multicolored .95 .25

SERVICE CROSS MEDALS

Distinguished
Service
Cross — A3896

Navy
Cross — A3897

Air Force
Cross — A3898

Coast Guard
Cross — A3899

LITHOGRAPHED
Serpentine Die Cut 10¾
2016, May 30
Self-Adhesive

5065 A3896 (47c) multicolored .95 .30
5066 A3897 (47c) multicolored .95 .30
5067 A3898 (47c) multicolored .95 .30
5068 A3899 (47c) multicolored .95 .30
a. Block or horiz. strip of 4, #5065-5068 3.80
Nos. 5065-5068 (4) 3.80 1.20

VIEWS OF OUR PLANETS

Mercury
A3900

Venus — A3901

Earth — A3902

Mars — A3903

Jupiter — A3904

Saturn — A3905

Uranus — A3906

Neptune
A3907

LITHOGRAPHED
Serpentine Die Cut 10½
2016, May 31
Self-Adhesive

5069 A3900 (47c) multicolored .95 .40
5070 A3901 (47c) multicolored .95 .40
5071 A3902 (47c) multicolored .95 .40
5072 A3903 (47c) multicolored .95 .40
5073 A3904 (47c) multicolored .95 .40
5074 A3905 (47c) multicolored .95 .40
5075 A3906 (47c) multicolored .95 .40
5076 A3907 (47c) multicolored .95 .40
a. Block of 8, #5069-5076 7.60
Nos. 5069-5076 (8) 7.60 3.20

PLUTO EXPLORED

Pluto — A3908

New Horizons
Probe — A3909

LITHOGRAPHED
Serpentine Die Cut 10½
2016, May 31
Self-Adhesive

5077 A3908 (47c) multicolored .95 .25
5078 A3909 (47c) multicolored .95 .25
a. Pair, #5077-5078 1.90

CLASSICS FOREVER

A3910

No. 5079: a, George Washington (redrawn type A16). b, Benjamin Franklin (redrawn type A5). c, Washington (redrawn type A17). d, Washington (redrawn type A19). e, Abraham Lincoln (redrawn type A33). f, Franklin (redrawn type A24).

LITHOGRAPHED & ENGRAVED
Serpentine Die Cut 10¾
2016, June 1
Self-Adhesive

5079 A3910 Pane of 6 6.00
a. (47c) tan & black .95 .40
b. (47c) tan & blue .95 .40
c. (47c) tan & black .95 .40
d. (47c) tan & blue .95 .40
e. (47c) tan & black .95 .40
f. (47c) tan & blue .95 .40

NATIONAL PARK SERVICE, CENT.

A3911

No. 5080: a, Iceberg in Glacier Bay National Park and Preserve, Alaska (48x31mm). b, Mount Rainier National Park (48x31mm). c, *Scenery in the Grand Tetons,* painting by Albert Bierstadt, at Marsh-Billings-Rockefeller National Historic Park, Vermont (24x31mm). d, Bass Harbor Head Lighthouse, Acadia National Park, Maine (48x31mm). e, *The Grand Canyon of Arizona,* painting by Thomas Moran, at Grand Canyon National Park, Arizona (48x31mm). f, Horses at Assateague Island National Seashore, Virginia and Maryland (48x31mm). g, Ship *Balclutha,* at San Francisco Maritime National Historic Park, California (24x31mm). h, Stone arch at Arches National Park, Utah (24x31mm). i, Aerial view of Theodore Roosevelt National Park, North Dakota (24x31mm). j, Water lily at Kenilworth Park and Aquatic Gardens, Washington, D.C. (24x31mm). k, *Administration Building at Frijoles Canyon,* drawing by Helmuth Naumer, Sr., at Bandelier National Monument, New Mexico (48x31mm). l, Everglades National Park, Florida (48x31mm). m, Rainbow at Haleakala National Park, Hawaii (48x31mm). n, Bison at Yellowstone National Park, Idaho, Montana and Wyoming (48x31mm). o, Carlsbad Caverns National Park, New Mexico (48x31mm). p, Heron at Gulf Islands National Seashore, Florida and Mississippi (24x31mm).

LITHOGRAPHED
Serpentine Die Cut 10½x10¾
2016 June 2
Self-Adhesive

5080 A3911 Pane of 16 + label 15.50
a.-p. (47c) Any single .95 .50

COLORFUL CELEBRATIONS

Bird and
Flowers — A3912

Birds and
Flowers
A3913

Flowers — A3914

Flowers
A3915

Flowers — A3916

Flowers
A3917

Birds and
Flower — A3918

Bird and
Flower — A3919

Flowers — A3920

Birds and Flower — A3921

LITHOGRAPHED
Serpentine Die Cut 11 on 2 or 3 Sides
2016, June 3
Booklet Stamps
Self-Adhesive

5081	A3912	(47c)	lt blue	.95	.40
5082	A3913	(47c)	orange	.95	.40
5083	A3914	(47c)	violet	.95	.40
5084	A3915	(47c)	magneta	.95	.40
5085	A3916	(47c)	lt blue	.95	.40
5086	A3917	(47c)	orange	.95	.40
5087	A3918	(47c)	violet	.95	.40
5088	A3919	(47c)	magneta	.95	.40
5089	A3920	(47c)	magneta	.95	.40
5090	A3921	(47c)	violet	.95	.40
a.	Block of 10, #5081-5090			9.50	
b.	Booklet pane of 20, 2 each #5081-5090			19.00	
	Nos. 5081-5090 (10)			9.50	4.00

No. 5090b is a double-sided booklet pane with 12 stamps on one side (Nos. 5083-5090, 2 each Nos. 5081-5082) and eight stamps (Nos. 5083-5090) plus label (booklet cover) on the other side.

INDIANA STATEHOOD, 200th ANNIV.

Corn Field Near Milford A3922

LITHOGRAPHED
Serpentine Die Cut 10¾
2016, June 7
Self-Adhesive

5091	A3922	(47c)	multicolored	.95	.25

EID

"Eidukum Mubarak" A3923

LITHOGRAPHED
Serpentine Die Cut 11
2016, June 10
Self-Adhesive

5092	A3923	(47c)	multicolored	.95	.25

SODA FOUNTAIN FAVORITES

Ice Cream Cone A3924   Egg Cream A3925

Banana Split — A3926

Root Beer Float A3927   Hot Fudge Sundae A3928

LITHOGRAPHED
Serpentine Die Cut 10¾
2016, June 30
Booklet Stamps
Self-Adhesive

5093	A3924	(47c)	multicolored	.95	.40
5094	A3925	(47c)	multicolored	.95	.40
5095	A3926	(47c)	multicolored (long sloping die cut at bottom)	.95	.40
a.	Long sloping die cut at top			.95	.40
5096	A3927	(47c)	multicolored	.95	.40
5097	A3928	(47c)	multicolored	.95	.40
a.	Horiz. strip of 5, #5093-5097			4.75	
b.	Horiz. strip of 5, #5093-5094, 5095a, 5096-5097			4.75	
c.	Booklet pane of 20, 4 each #5093-5094, 5096-5097, 2 each #5095, 5095a			19.00	
	Nos. 5093-5097 (5)			4.75	2.00

STAR QUILTS

A3929   A3930

LITHOGRAPHED
Serpentine Die Cut 11 Vert.
2016, July 6
Coil Stamps
Self-Adhesive

5098	A3929	(25c)	multicolored	.50	.25
5099	A3930	(25c)	multicolored	.50	.25
a.	Pair, #5098-5099			1.00	

JAIME ESCALANTE

Jaime Escalante (1930-2010), High School Calculus Teacher — A3931

LITHOGRAPHED
Serpentine Die Cut 10¾
2016, July 13
Self-Adhesive

5100	A3931	(47c)	multicolored	.95	.25

Adjacent horizontal or vertical stamps have selvage between the stamps.

PICKUP TRUCKS

1938 International Harvester D-2 — A3932

1953 Chevrolet A3933

1948 Ford F-1 — A3934

1965 Ford F-100 — A3935

LITHOGRAPHED
Serpentine Die Cut 11 on 2 or 3 Sides
2016, July 15
Booklet Stamps
Self-Adhesive

5101	A3932	(47c)	multicolored	.95	.30
5102	A3933	(47c)	multicolored	.95	.30
5103	A3934	(47c)	multicolored	.95	.30
5104	A3935	(47c)	multicolored	.95	.30
a.	Block of 4, #5101-5104			3.80	
b.	Booklet pane of 20, 5 each #5101-5104			19.00	
	Nos. 5101-5104 (4)			3.80	1.20

No. 5104b is a double-sided booklet pane with 12 stamps on one side (3 each Nos. 5101-5104) and eight stamps (2 each Nos. 5101-5104) plus label (booklet cover) on the other side.

LITERARY ARTS

Henry James (1843-1916), Novelist — A3936

LITHOGRAPHED
Serpentine Die Cut 11
2016, July 31
Self-Adhesive

5105	A3936	(89c)	multicolored	1.90	.30

PETS

Puppy — A3937

Betta Fish — A3938

Iguana — A3939

Hamster A3940

Goldfish — A3941

Kitten — A3942

Rabbit — A3943

Tortoise — A3944

Guinea Pig — A3945

Parrot — A3946

Corn Snake — A3947

Mouse — A3948

Hermit Crab — A3949

Chinchilla A3950

Gerbil — A3951

Gecko — A3952

Cat — A3953

Horse — A3954

Parakeets
A3955

Dog — A3956

LITHOGRAPHED

Serpentine Die Cut 11 on 2 or 3 Sides

2016, Aug. 2

Booklet Stamps

Self-Adhesive

5106	A3937	(47c) multicolored	.95	.50
5107	A3938	(47c) multicolored	.95	.50
5108	A3939	(47c) multicolored	.95	.50
5109	A3940	(47c) multicolored	.95	.50
5110	A3941	(47c) multicolored	.95	.50
5111	A3942	(47c) multicolored	.95	.50
5112	A3943	(47c) multicolored	.95	.50
5113	A3944	(47c) multicolored	.95	.50
5114	A3945	(47c) multicolored	.95	.50
5115	A3946	(47c) multicolored	.95	.50
5116	A3947	(47c) multicolored	.95	.50
5117	A3948	(47c) multicolored	.95	.50
5118	A3949	(47c) multicolored	.95	.50
5119	A3950	(47c) multicolored	.95	.50
5120	A3951	(47c) multicolored	.95	.50
5121	A3952	(47c) multicolored	.95	.50
5122	A3953	(47c) multicolored	.95	.50
5123	A3954	(47c) multicolored	.95	.50
5124	A3955	(47c) multicolored	.95	.50
5125	A3956	(47c) multicolored	.95	.50
a.		Booklet pane of 20, #5106-5125	19.00	
		Nos. 5106-5125 (20)	19.00	10.00

No. 5125a is a double-sided booklet pane with 12 stamps on one side (Nos. 5106-5117) and eight stamps (Nos. 5118-5125) plus label (booklet cover) on the other side.

SONGBIRDS IN SNOW

Golden-crowned
Kinglets
A3957

Cedar Waxwing
A3958

Northern
Cardinal
A3959

Red-breasted
Nuthatches
A3960

LITHOGRAPHED

Serpentine Die Cut 10¾ on 2 or 3 Sides

2016, Aug. 4

Booklet Stamps

Self-Adhesive

5126	A3957	(47c) multicolored	.95	.30
5127	A3958	(47c) multicolored	.95	.30
5128	A3959	(47c) multicolored	.95	.30
5129	A3960	(47c) multicolored	.95	.30
a.		Block of 4, 5126-5129	3.80	
b.		Booklet pane of 20, 5 each #5126-5129	19.00	
		Nos. 5126-5129 (4)	3.80	1.20

No. 5129b is a double-sided booklet pane with 12 stamps on one side (3 each Nos. 5126-5129) and eight stamps (2 each Nos. 5126-5129) plus label (booklet cover) on the other side.

PATRIOTIC SPIRAL

Stars — A3961

LITHOGRAPHED

Serpentine Die Cut 10 Vert.

2016, Aug. 19

Coil Stamp

Self-Adhesive

5130	A3961	(47c) multicolored	.95	.25

Booklet Stamp

Serpentine Die Cut 11 on 2 or 3 Sides

5131	A3961	(47c) multicolored	.95	.25
a.		Booklet pane of 10	9.50	

STAR TREK TELEVISION SHOW, 50TH ANNIV

Starship
Enterprise and
Starfleet Insignia
A3962

Crewman in
Transporter
A3963

Starship
Enterprise and
Planet — A3964

Starship
Enterprise,
Planet, Vulcan
Hand
Salute — A3965

LITHOGRAPHED

2016, Sept. 2 *Serpentine Die Cut 11*

Self-Adhesive

5132	A3962	(47c) multicolored	.95	.30
5133	A3963	(47c) multicolored	.95	.30
5134	A3964	(47c) multicolored	.95	.30
5135	A3965	(47c) multicolored	.95	.30
a.		Block or vert. strip of 4, #5132-5135	3.80	
		Nos. 5132-5135 (4)	3.80	1.20

Die cut uncut press sheets of No. 5132-5135 were made available for sale. Values: cross gutter block of 8, $18; pairs with gutters between, $3.75 each. See note after No. 4693.

EASTERN TAILED-BLUE BUTTERFLY

A3966

LITHOGRAPHED

Serpentine Die Cut 10½

2016, Sept. 24

Self-Adhesive

5136	A3966	(68c) multicolored	1.40	.25

JACK-O'-LANTERNS

Four Teeth
A3967

Five Teeth
A3968

Three Teeth
A3969

Nine Teeth
A3970

LITHOGRAPHED

Serpentine Die Cut 11x10¾ on 2 or 3 Sides

2016, Sept. 29

Booklet Stamps

Self-Adhesive

5137	A3967	(47c) multicolored	.95	.30
5138	A3968	(47c) multicolored	.95	.30
5139	A3969	(47c) multicolored	.95	.30
5140	A3970	(47c) multicolored	.95	.30
a.		Block of 4, #5137-5140	3.80	
b.		Booklet pane of 20, 5 each #5137-5140	19.00	
		Nos. 5137-5140 (4)	3.80	1.20

No. 5140b is a double-sided booklet pane with 12 stamps on one side (3 each Nos. 5137-5140) and eight stamps (2 each Nos. 5137-5140) plus label (booklet cover) on the other side.

KWANZAA

Woman, Fruits and
Vegetables — A3971

LITHOGRAPHED

2016, Oct. 1 *Serpentine Die Cut 11*

Self-Adhesive

5141	A3971	(47c) multicolored	.95	.25

DIWALI

Diya — A3972

LITHOGRAPHED

2016, Oct. 5 *Serpentine Die Cut 11*

Self-Adhesive

5142	A3972	(47c) multicolored	.95	.25

CHRISTMAS

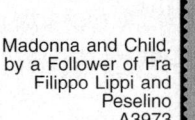

Madonna and Child,
by a Follower of Fra
Filippo Lippi and
Peselino
A3973

Nativity
A3974

Candle in
Window
A3975

Wreath in
Window
A3976

Star in Window
A3977

Christmas Tree
in Window
A3978

LITHOGRAPHED

Serpentine Die Cut 10¾x11 on 2 or 3 Sides

2016

Booklet Stamps

Self-Adhesive

5143	A3973	(47c) multicolored	.95	.25
a.		Booklet pane of 20	19.00	
5144	A3974	(47c) multicolored	.95	.25
a.		Booklet pane of 20	19.00	
5145	A3975	(47c) multicolored	.95	.25
5146	A3976	(47c) multicolored	.95	.25
5147	A3977	(47c) multicolored	.95	.25
5148	A3978	(47c) multicolored	.95	.25
a.		Block of 4, #5145-5148	3.60	
b.		Booklet pane of 20, 5 each #5145-5148	19.00	
		Nos. 5143-5148 (6)	5.70	1.50

Issued: No. 5143, 10/18; No. 5144, 11/3; Nos. 5145-5148, 10/6. Nos. 5143a and 5144a are double-sided booklet panes with 12 stamps on one side and eight stamps plus label (booklet cover) on the other side. No. 5148b is a double-sided booklet pane with 12 stamps on one side (3 each Nos. 5145-5148) and eight stamps (2 each Nos. 5145-5148) plus label (booklet cover) on the other side.

WONDER WOMAN, 75TH ANNIVERSARY

Modern Age Wonder Woman
A3979

Bronze Age Wonder Woman
A3980

Silver Age Wonder Woman
A3981

Golden Age Wonder Woman
A3982

LITHOGRAPHED

2016, Oct. 7   Serpentine Die Cut 11
Self-Adhesive

5149	A3979	(47c) multicolored	.95	.30
5150	A3980	(47c) multicolored	.95	.30
5151	A3981	(47c) multicolored	.95	.30
5152	A3982	(47c) multicolored	.95	.30
a.		Vert. strip of 4, #5149-5152	3.80	
		Nos. 5149-5152 (4)	3.80	1.20

HANUKKAH

Menorah
A3983

LITHOGRAPHED

2016, Nov. 1   Serpentine Die Cut 11
Self-Adhesive

5153	A3983	(47c) multicolored	.95	.25

CHINESE NEW YEAR

Year of the Rooster
A3984

LITHOGRAPHED

Serpentine Die Cut 10¾
2017, Jan. 5
Self-Adhesive

5154	A3984	(47c) multicolored	.95	.25

LOVE

Airplane and Skywriting
A3985

LITHOGRAPHED

Serpentine Die Cut 11x10¾
2017, Jan. 7
Self-Adhesive

5155	A3985	(47c) light blue	.95	.25

2016 Scott Supplements

Whether you're updating your album or decided to start collecting a new country, Scott supplements are the way to go. Heavy acid-free paper and the use of Scott numbers for easy identification makes collecting easy.

Country	Item No.	Retail	AA	Release Date
NATIONAL SERIES				
U.S. National	100S016	22.99	19.99	February
U.S. Minuteman	180S016	22.99	19.99	February
U.S. Pony Express	178S016	22.99	19.99	March
U.S. Platinum Hingeless	199S016	78.99	67.99	April
American (U.S. & U.N.)	170S016	34.99	29.99	March
U.S. Commemorative Singles	130S016	16.99	13.99	February
U.S. Commemorative & Air Plate Blocks	120S016	19.99	16.99	April
U.S. Regular & Air Plate Blocks	125S016	11.99	9.99	April
U.S. Small Panes	118S016	34.99	29.99	April
U.S. Booklet Panes	101S016	16.99	13.99	April
U.S. Plate Number Coils–Simplified	113S016	11.99	9.99	January
U.S. Plate Number Coils–Comprehensive	114S016	19.99	16.99	January
U.S. Plate Number Coil Singles	117S016	19.99	16.99	January
U.S. Federal & State Duck Stamps	115S016	22.99	19.99	October
U.S. Computer Vended Postage	103S016	11.99	9.99	March
U.N. Singles & Postal Stationery	551S016	25.99	21.99	March
U.N. Minuteman	181S016	25.99	21.99	March
U.N. Imprint Blocks	552S016	19.99	16.99	March
Republic of the Marshall Islands	111MA16	22.99	19.99	April
Republic of Palau	111PA16	34.99	29.99	April
Federated States of Micronesia	111MI16	34.99	29.99	April
SPECIALTY SERIES				
Argentina	642S016	19.99	16.99	September
Australia	210S016	22.99	19.99	September
Austria	300S016	19.99	16.99	May
Baltic States	361S016	19.99	16.99	August
Belgium	303S016	22.99	19.99	August
Brazil	644S016	19.99	16.99	September
Canada	240S016	25.99	21.99	May
Canada Master	245S016	28.99	24.99	May
Cyprus	203CY16	11.99	9.99	May
Czech Republic & Slovakia	307S016	22.99	19.99	August
Denmark	345DM16	16.99	13.99	June
Dependencies of Australia	211S016	22.99	19.99	September
Dependencies of New Zealand	221S016	34.99	29.99	September
Dominican Republic	648S016	16.99	13.99	September
Faroe Islands	345FI16	11.99	9.99	June
Finland & Aland	345FN16	22.99	19.99	June
France	310S016	34.99	29.99	May
French Polynesia	625S016	11.99	9.99	August
French Southern & Antarctic Territory	626S016	16.99	13.99	August

Country	Item No.	Retail	AA	Release Date
SPECIALTY SERIES				
Germany	315S316	16.99	13.99	May
Gibraltar	203GB16	16.99	13.99	May
Great Britain	200S016	22.99	19.99	May
Greece	320S016	22.99	19.99	June
Greenland	345GR16	16.99	13.99	June
Guernsey & Alderney	202GN16	22.99	19.99	May
Hong Kong	275HK16	22.99	19.99	May
Hungary	323S016	22.99	19.99	August
Iceland	345IC16	11.99	9.99	June
India	618S016	22.99	19.99	July
Ireland	201S016	16.99	13.99	May
Isle of Man	202IM16	22.99	19.99	May
Israel Singles	500S016	16.99	13.99	August
Israel Tab Singles	501S016	19.99	16.99	August
Italy	325S016	22.99	19.99	July
Japan	510S016	45.99	39.99	July
Jersey	202JR16	22.99	19.99	May
Liechtenstein	367S016	11.99	9.99	June
Luxembourg	330S016	11.99	9.99	August
Malta	203ML16	16.99	13.99	May
Mexico	430S016	19.99	16.99	September
Monaco & French Andorra	333S016	19.99	16.99	May
Netherlands	335S016	40.99	34.99	August
New Zealand	220S016	22.99	19.99	September
Norway	345NR16	11.99	9.99	June
People's Republic of China	520S016	22.99	19.99	July
Poland	338S016	19.99	16.99	August
Portugal/Azores/Maderia	340S016	22.99	19.99	July
Republic of China Taiwan	530S016	22.99	19.99	July
Russia	360S016	34.99	29.99	September
San Marino	328S016	11.99	9.99	July
Singapore	275SG16	22.99	19.99	May
South Africa	669S016	22.99	19.99	October
Spain & Spanish Andorra	355S016	22.99	19.99	July
Sri Lanka	622S016	19.99	16.99	July
Sweden	345SW16	16.99	13.99	September
Switzerland	365S016	16.99	13.99	June
Thailand	540S016	22.99	19.99	July
Turkey	505S016	22.99	19.99	July
Ukraine	362UK16	19.99	16.99	August
Vatican City	375S016	11.99	9.99	July
International Part A	852P116	160.99	140.00	December
International Part B	852P216	160.99	140.00	December

Visit AmosAdvantage.com
or Call 1-800-572-6885

Outside U.S. & Canada 937-498-0800 • Mail to: P.O. Box 4129, Sidney OH 45365

UNITED STATES

SEMI-POSTAL STAMPS

BREAST CANCER RESEARCH

SP1

PHOTOGRAVURE
Serpentine Die Cut 11
1998, July 29
Self-Adhesive

B1 SP1 (32c+8c) multicolored   1.00   .25

HEROES OF 2001

Firemen Atop
World Trade
Center
Rubble — SP2

LITHOGRAPHED
Serpentine Die Cut 11¼
2002, June 7
Self-Adhesive

B2 SP2 (34c+11c) multicolored   1.00   .35

STOP FAMILY VIOLENCE

SP3

PHOTOGRAVURE
2003, Oct. 8   *Serpentine Die Cut 11*
Self-Adhesive

B3 SP3 (37c+8c) multicolored   1.00   .45

SAVE VANISHING SPECIES

Amur Tiger
Cub — SP4

PHOTOGRAVURE
Serpentine Die Cut 10¾
2011, Sept. 20
Self-Adhesive

B4 SP4 (44c+11c) multicolored   1.25   .50

The 11c surtax was for the Multinational Species Conservation Funds of the U.S. Fish and Wildlife Service.

Breast Cancer Awareness Type of 1998

LITHOGRAPHED
Serpentine Die Cut 11x10¾
2014, Sept. 30
Design Size: 20x35mm
Dated 2014
Self-Adhesive

B5 SP1 (49c+11c) multicolored   1.25   .50
  a.   Imperforate   1.75   —

AIR POST STAMPS

Curtiss Jenny — AP1

FLAT PLATE PRINTINGS

1918   **Unwmk.**   **Engr.**   **Perf. 11**
C1   AP1   6c orange   60.   30.
   Never hinged   120.
C2   AP1   16c green   65.   35.
   Never hinged   130.
C3   AP1   24c car rose &
     blue   70.   35.
   Never hinged   140.
  a.   Center inverted   450,000.
   Never hinged   850,000.
   Nos. C1-C3 (3)   195.00   100.00
   Nos. C1-C3, never
   hinged   390.00

Wooden
Propeller and
Radiator — AP2

Emblem of Air
Service — AP3

De Havilland
Biplane — AP4

1923
C4   AP2   8c dark green   20.00   15.00
   Never hinged   40.00
C5   AP3   16c dark blue   65.00   30.00
   Never hinged   130.00
C6   AP4   24c carmine   70.00   30.00
   Never hinged   140.00
   Nos. C4-C6 (3)   155.00   75.00
   Nos. C4-C6, never hinged   310.00

Map of U.S. and Two Mail
Planes — AP5

1926-27
C7   AP5   10c dark blue   2.50   .35
   Never hinged   4.50
C8   AP5   15c olive brown   2.75   2.50
   Never hinged   5.25
C9   AP5   20c yellow green   7.00   2.00
   Never hinged   13.50
   Nos. C7-C9 (3)   12.25   4.85
   Nos. C7-C9, never hinged   23.25

Lindbergh's Airplane "Spirit of St.
Louis" — AP6

1927, June 18
C10   AP6   10c dark blue   7.50   2.50
   Never hinged   14.00
  a.   Booklet pane of 3   70.00   65.00
   Never hinged   120.00
  b.   Double impression   16,500.

Singles from No. C10a are imperf. at sides or imperf. at sides and bottom.
Only one example is recorded of No. C10b.

Beacon on
Rocky
Mountains
AP7

1928, July 25
C11   AP7   5c carmine and blue   5.50   .85
   Never hinged   10.00
  a.   Vert. pair, imperf. between   7,000.

No. C11a is unique. It is torn and valued thus.

Winged Globe — AP8

1930, Feb. 10
Stamp design: 46½x19mm
C12   AP8   5c violet   9.50   .50
  a.   Horiz. pair, imperf. between   4,500.

See Nos. C16-C17, C19.

GRAF ZEPPELIN ISSUE

Zeppelin over Atlantic Ocean — AP9

Zeppelin between Continents — AP10

Zeppelin Passing Globe — AP11

1930, Apr. 19
C13   AP9   65c green   190.   165.
   Never hinged   275.
C14   AP10 $1.30 brown   400.   375.
   Never hinged   625.
C15   AP11 $2.60 blue   575.   600.
   Never hinged   975.
   Nos. C13-C15 (3)   1,165.   1,140.
   Nos. C13-C15, never
   hinged   1,875.

ROTARY PRESS PRINTING

1931-32   **Perf. 10½x11**
Stamp design: 47½x19mm
C16   AP8   5c violet   5.00   .60
   Never hinged   8.75
C17   AP8   8c olive bister ('32)   2.25   .40
   Never hinged   4.00

CENTURY OF PROGRESS ISSUE

Airship "Graf Zeppelin" — AP12

FLAT PLATE PRINTING

1933, Oct. 2   **Perf. 11**
C18   AP12   50c green   47.50   47.50
   Never hinged   80.00

> Catalogue values for unused stamps in this section, from this point to the end, are for **Never Hinged** items.

Type of 1930 Issue
ROTARY PRESS PRINTING
1934, June 30   **Perf. 10½x11**
C19   AP8   6c dull orange   3.50   .25

TRANSPACIFIC ISSUES

The "China
Clipper"
over the
Pacific
AP13

FLAT PLATE PRINTING

1935, Nov. 22   **Perf. 11**
C20   AP13   25c blue   1.40   1.00

The "China
Clipper"
over the
Pacific
AP14

1937, Feb. 15
C21   AP14   20c green   11.00   1.75
C22   AP14   50c carmine   11.00   5.00

Eagle
Holding
Shield, Olive
Branch and
Arrows
AP15

1938, May 14
C23   AP15   6c dark blue &
     carmine   .70   .25
  a.   Vert. pair, imperf. horiz.   300.00
  b.   Horiz. pair, imperf. vert.   12,500.
  c.   6c ultra & car   160.00   1,500.
   On cover   1,750.

TRANSATLANTIC ISSUE

Winged Globe — AP16

1939, May 16
C24   AP16   30c dull blue   12.00   1.50

Twin-Motored Transport Plane — AP17

ROTARY PRESS PRINTING

1941-44   **Perf. 11x10½**
C25   AP17   6c carmine   .25   .25
  a.   Booklet pane of 3   3.50   1.50
  b.   Horiz. pair, imperf. between   1,500.

Singles from No. C25a are imperf. at sides or at sides and bottom.
Value of No. C25b is for pair without blue crayon P. O. rejection mark on front. Very fine pairs with crayon mark sell for about $1,500.

C26   AP17   8c olive green   .25   .25
  a.   All color omitted

No. C26a has an albino impression and exists as a pair of stamps within a double-paper spliced strip of six stamps.

C27   AP17   10c violet   1.10   .25
C28   AP17   15c brown carmine   2.10   .35
C29   AP17   20c bright green   2.10   .30
C30   AP17   30c blue   2.10   .35
C31   AP17   50c orange   11.00   3.25
   Nos. C25-C31 (7)   18.90   5.00

DC-4
Skymaster
AP18

1946, Sept. 25   **Perf. 11x10½**
C32   AP18   5c carmine   .25   .25

DC-4
Skymaster — AP19

1947, Mar. 26   *Perf. 10½x11*
C33 AP19 5c carmine   .25   .25

Pan American Union Building,
Washington, DC — AP20

Statue of
Liberty &
New York
Skyline
AP21

Plane over San Francisco-Oakland
Bay Bridge — AP22

1947   *Perf. 11x10½*
C34 AP20 10c black   .25   .25
 a.   Dry printing   .40   .25
C35 AP21 15c bright blue
        green   .35   .25
 a.   Horiz. pair, imperf. between 1,500.
 b.   Dry printing   .55   .25
C36 AP22 25c blue   .90   .25
 a.   Dry printing   1.20   .25
        Nos. C34-C36 (3)   1.50   .75

See note on wet and dry printings following
No. 1029.
No. C35a is valued in the grade of fine.

Type of 1947
ROTARY PRESS COIL STAMP
1948, Jan. 15 *Perf. 10 Horizontally*
C37 AP19 5c carmine   1.00   .80

NEW YORK CITY ISSUE

Map of Five Boroughs,
Circular Band &
Planes — AP23

50th anniv. of the consolidation of the five
boroughs of New York City.
ROTARY PRESS PRINTING
1948, July 31   *Perf. 11x10½*
C38 AP23 5c bright carmine   .25   .25

Type of 1947
1949   *Perf. 10½x11*
C39 AP19 6c carmine   .25   .25
 a.   Booklet pane of 6   12.00 5.00
 b.   Dry printing   .50   .25
 c.   As "a," dry printing   25.00   —

See note on wet and dry printings following
No. 1029.

**ALEXANDRIA BICENTENNIAL
ISSUE**

Home of John Carlyle, Alexandria Seal
& Gadsby's Tavern
AP24

200th anniv. of the founding of Alexandria,
Va.

1949, May 11   *Perf. 11x10½*
C40 AP24 6c carmine   .25   .25

Type of 1947
ROTARY PRESS COIL STAMP
1949, Aug. 25 *Perf. 10 Horizontally*
C41 AP19 6c carmine   3.00   .25

UNIVERSAL POSTAL UNION ISSUE

Post Office
Department
Building
AP25

Globe &
Doves
Carrying
Messages
AP26

Boeing Stratocruiser & Globe — AP27

ROTARY PRESS PRINTING
1949   *Perf. 11x10½*
C42 AP25 10c violet   .25   .25
C43 AP26 15c ultramarine   .30   .25
C44 AP27 25c rose carmine   .60   .40
        Nos. C42-C44 (3)   1.15   .90

WRIGHT BROTHERS ISSUE

Wilbur &
Orville
Wright and
their Plane
AP28

1949, Dec. 17
C45 AP28 6c magenta   .25   .25

Diamond
Head,
Honolulu,
Hawaii
AP29

1952, Mar. 26
C46 AP29 80c bright red violet 4.50 1.25

POWERED FLIGHT, 50th ANNIV.

First Plane
and Modern
Plane
AP30

1953, May 29
C47 AP30 6c carmine   .25   .25

Eagle in Flight — AP31

Issued primarily for use on domestic post
cards.
1954, Sept. 3
C48 AP31 4c bright blue   .25   .25

AIR FORCE, 50th ANNIV.

B-52 Stratofortress and F-104
Starfighters — AP32

1957, Aug. 1
C49 AP32 6c blue   .25   .25

Type of 1954
1958, July 31
C50 AP31 5c red   .25   .25

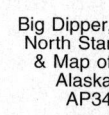

Silhouette of Jet
Airliner — AP33

1958, July 31   *Perf. 10½x11*
C51 AP33 7c blue   .25   .25
 a.   Booklet pane of 6   6.50 5.00
 b.   Vert. pair, imperf. between
        (from booklet pane)   4,000.

No. C51b resulted from a paper foldover
after perforating and before cutting into panes.
Two or three pairs are believed to exist.

ROTARY PRESS COIL STAMP
Perf. 10 Horizontally
C52 AP33 7c blue   2.00   .25

ALASKA STATEHOOD ISSUE

Big Dipper,
North Star
& Map of
Alaska
AP34

ROTARY PRESS PRINTING
1959, Jan. 3   *Perf. 11x10½*
C53 AP34 7c dark blue   .25   .25

BALLOON JUPITER ISSUE

Balloon &
Crowd — AP35

Centenary of the carrying of mail by the balloon Jupiter from Lafayette to Crawfordsville,
Ind.

GIORI PRESS PRINTING
1959, Aug. 17   *Perf. 11*
C54 AP35 7c dark blue & red   .30   .25

HAWAII STATEHOOD ISSUE

Alii Warrior,
Map of
Hawaii &
Star of
Statehood
AP36

ROTARY PRESS PRINTING
1959, Aug. 21   *Perf. 11x10½*
C55 AP36 7c rose red   .25   .25

PAN AMERICAN GAMES ISSUE

Runner Holding
Torch — AP37

3rd Pan American Games, Chicago, Aug.
27-Sept. 7, 1959.

GIORI PRESS PRINTING
1959, Aug. 27   *Perf. 11*
C56 AP37 10c red, white & blue   .25   .25

Liberty Bell
AP38

Statue of
Liberty
AP39

Abraham
Lincoln
AP40

1959-66
C57 AP38 10c black & green
        ('60)   1.00   .70
C58 AP39 15c black & orange   .35   .25
C59 AP40 25c black & maroon
        ('60)   .50   .25
 a.   Tagged ('66)   .60   .30
        Nos. C57-C59 (3)   1.85 1.20

Airmail stamps starting with No. C69
are tagged unless otherwise noted.

Type of 1958
ROTARY PRESS PRINTING
1960, Aug. 12   *Perf. 10½x11*
C60 AP33 7c carmine   .25   .25
 a.   Booklet pane of 6   7.00 6.00
 b.   Vert. pair, imperf between
        (from booklet pane)   5,500.

No. C60b resulted from a paper foldover
after perforating and before cutting into panes.
Two pairs are known.

Type of 1958
ROTARY PRESS COIL STAMP
1960, Oct. 22 *Perf. 10 Horizontally*
C61 AP33 7c carmine   4.00   .25

Type of 1959-60 and

Statue of
Liberty
AP41

GIORI PRESS PRINTING
1961-67   *Perf. 11*
C62 AP38 13c black & red   .40   .25
 a.   Tagged ('67)   .75   .50
C63 AP41 15c black & or-
        ange   .30   .25
 a.   Tagged ('67)   .35   .25
 b.   As "a," horiz. pair, imperf.
        vert.   15,000.
 c.   As "a," horiz. pair, imperf
        between and at left   2,750.
 d.   All color omitted   100.00

On No. C63d, there is a clear albino plate
impression.

Jet Airliner Over
Capitol — AP42

ROTARY PRESS PRINTING

1962, Dec. 5   *Perf. 10½x11*
C64 AP42 8c carmine   .25   .25
   a.   Tagged ('63)   .25   .25
   b.   Booklet pane of 5 + label   6.00   3.00
   c.   As "b," tagged ('64)   1.75   .75

Nos. C64a and C64c were made by overprinting Nos. C64 and C64b with phosphorescent ink. No. C64a was first issued at Dayton,
Ohio, for experiments in high speed mail sorting. The tagging is visible in shortwave ultraviolet light.

COIL STAMP; ROTARY PRESS
Perf. 10 Horizontally
C65 AP42 8c carmine   .40   .25
   a.   Tagged ('64)   .35   .25

MONTGOMERY BLAIR ISSUE

Montgomery Blair — AP43

Montgomery Blair (1813-83), Postmaster
General (1861-64), who called the 1st Intl.
Postal Conf., Paris, 1863, forerunner of the
UPU.

GIORI PRESS PRINTING

1963, May 3   *Perf. 11*
C66 AP43 15c dull red, dark
         brown & blue   .55   .50

Bald Eagle — AP44

Issued primarily for use on domestic post
cards.

ROTARY PRESS PRINTING

1963, July 12   *Perf. 11x10½*
C67 AP44 6c red   .25   .25
   a.   Tagged ('67)   4.00   3.00

AMELIA EARHART ISSUE

Amelia Earhart &
Lockheed
Electra — AP45

GIORI PRESS PRINTING

1963, July 24   *Perf. 11*
C68 AP45 8c carmine & maroon   .25   .25

ROBERT H. GODDARD ISSUE

Robert H. Goddard, Atlas Rocket &
Launching Tower, Cape Kennedy
AP46

1964, Oct. 5
C69 AP46 8c blue, red & bister   .35   .25

Luminescence
Air Post stamps issued after mid-
1964 are tagged.

ALASKA PURCHASE ISSUE

Tlingit Totem,
Southern
Alaska — AP47

1967, Mar. 30
C70 AP47 8c brown   .25   .25

"Columbia Jays," by
Audubon — AP48

1967, Apr. 26
C71 AP48 20c multicolored   .75   .25

See note over No. 1241.

50-Star
Runway — AP49

ROTARY PRESS PRINTING

1968, Jan. 5   *Perf. 11x10½*
C72 AP49 10c carmine   .25   .25
   b.   Booklet pane of 8   2.25   2.00
   c.   Booklet pane of 5 + label   3.50   1.25
   d.   Vert. pair, imperf. btwn., in
      #C72b with foldover   5,250.

No. C72d resulted from a paper foldover
after perforating and before cutting into panes.
Two pairs are recorded from different panes.

ROTARY PRESS COIL STAMP
Perf. 10 Vertically
C73 AP49 10c carmine   .30   .25
   a.   Imperf., pair   450.00

The $1 Airlift stamp is listed as No.
1341.

50th ANNIVERSARY OF AIR MAIL ISSUE

Curtiss
Jenny
AP50

50th anniv. of regularly scheduled air mail
service.

LITHOGRAPHED, ENGRAVED
(GIORI)

1968, May 15   *Perf. 11*
C74 AP50 10c blue, black & red   .25   .25

USA and
Jet — AP51

1968, Nov. 22
C75 AP51 20c red, blue & black   .35   .25

See No. C81.

MOON LANDING ISSUE

First
Man
on
the
Moon
AP52

1969, Sept. 9
C76 AP52 10c multicolored   .25   .25
   a.   Rose red (litho.) omitted   500.00   —

On No. C76a, the lithographed rose red is
missing from the entire vignette-the dots on
top of the yellow areas as well as the flag
shoulder patch.

Silhouette of
Delta Wing
Plane
AP53

Silhouette of
Jet Airliner
AP54

Winged Airmail
Envelope — AP55

Statue of
Liberty
AP56

ROTARY PRESS PRINTING

1971-73   *Perf. 10½x11*
C77 AP53 9c red   .25   .25

No. C77 issued primarily for use on domestic post cards.

Perf. 11x10½
C78 AP54 11c carmine   .25   .25
   a.   Booklet pane of 4 + 2 la-
      bels   1.25   1.00
   b.   Untagged (Bureau precan-
      celed)   .85   .85
C79 AP55 13c carmine ('73)   .25   .25
   a.   Booklet pane of 5 + label
      ('73)   1.50   1.00
   b.   Untagged (Bureau precan-
      celed)   .85   .85
   c.   Green instead of red tag-
      ging (single from booklet
      pane)   —

No. C78b Bureau precanceled "WASHING-
TON D.C." (or "DC" - more valuable thus), No.
C79b "WASHINGTON DC" only; both for use
of Congressmen, but available to any permit
holder.

GIORI PRESS PRINTING
Perf. 11
C80 AP56 17c bluish black,
         red, & dark
         green   .35   .25

"USA" & Jet Type of 1968
LITHOGRAPHED, ENGRAVED
(GIORI)

C81 AP51 21c red, blue &
         black   .40   .25
   b.   Black (engr.) missing (FO)   2,750.

The two recorded examples of No. C81b are
in a single full pane. Catalogue value is for
both errors.

COIL STAMPS
ROTARY PRESS PRINTING

1971-73   *Perf. 10 Vertically*
C82 AP54 11c carmine   .25   .25
   a.   Imperf., pair   225.00
C83 AP55 13c carmine ('73)   .30   .25
   a.   Imperf., pair   65.00

NATIONAL PARKS CENTENNIAL ISSUE
City of Refuge, Hawaii

Kii Statue & Temple,
City of Refuge,
Hawaii — AP57

LITHOGRAPHED, ENGRAVED
(GIORI)

1972, May 3   *Perf. 11*
C84 AP57 11c orange & mul-
         ticolored   .25   .25
   a.   Blue & green (litho.) omitted   650.00

OLYMPIC GAMES ISSUE

Skiing &
Olympic
Rings
AP58

11th Winter Olympic Games, Sapporo,
Japan, Feb. 3-13, and 20th Summer Olympic
Games, Munich, Germany, Aug. 26-Sept. 11.

PHOTOGRAVURE (Andreotti)

1972, Aug. 17   *Perf. 11x10½*
C85 AP58 11c black, blue, red,
         emerald & yellow   .25   .25

ELECTRONICS PROGRESS ISSUE

De Forest
Audions
AP59

LITHOGRAPHED, ENGRAVED
(GIORI)

1973, July 10   *Perf. 11*
C86 AP59 11c multicolored   .30   .25
   a.   Vermilion & olive (litho.) omit-
      ted   800.00
   c.   Olive omitted   1,000.

Statue of
Liberty
AP60

Mt.
Rushmore
National
Memorial
AP61

GIORI PRESS PRINTING

1974
C87 AP60 18c carmine, black &
         ultramarine   .35   .30
C88 AP61 26c ultramarine, black
         & carmine   .60   .25

Plane &
Globes
AP62

Plane,
Globes &
Flag
AP63

1976, Jan. 2
C89 AP62 25c red, blue & black   .50 .25
C90 AP63 31c red, blue & black   .60 .25
  b.   All colors omitted   —

On No. C90b, there is a colorless embossed image and a tagging ghost plane visible under UV light.

WRIGHT BROTHERS ISSUE

Orville and Wilbur Wright, Flyer A AP64

Wright Brothers, Flyer A and Shed AP65

LITHOGRAPHED, ENGRAVED (GIORI)

1978, Sept. 23
C91 AP64 31c ultra & multi   .65 .30
C92 AP65 31c ultra & multi   .65 .30
  a.   Vert. pair, #C91-C92   1.30 1.20
  b.   As "a," ultra. & black (engr.) omitted   500.00
  c.   As "a," black (engr.) omitted   2,000.
  d.   As "a," black, yellow, magenta, blue & brown (litho.) omitted   1,750.

OCTAVE CHANUTE ISSUE

Chanute & Biplane Hangglider AP66

Biplane Hanggliders & Chanute AP67

1979, Mar. 29
C93 AP66 21c blue & multi   .70 .35
C94 AP67 21c blue & multi   .70 .35
  a.   Vert. pair, #C93-C94   1.40 1.20
  b.   As "a," ultra & black (engr.) omitted   4,000.

WILEY POST ISSUE

Wiley Post & "Winnie Mae" AP68

NR-105 W, Post in Pressurized Suit, Portrait AP69

1979, Nov. 20
C95 AP68 25c blue &multi   .90 .45
C96 AP69 25c blue & multi   .90 .45
  a.   Vert. pair, #C95-C96   1.80 1.50

OLYMPIC GAMES ISSUE

High Jump AP70

PHOTOGRAVURE

1979, Nov. 1
C97 AP70 31c multicolored   .70 .30

PHILIP MAZZEI (1730-1816)

Philip Mazzei (1730-1816), Italian-born Political Writer — AP71

1980, Oct. 13
C98 AP71 40c multicolored   .80 .25
  b.   Imperf., pair   2,250.

1982   Perf. 10½x11¼
C98A AP71 40c multicolored   6.50 1.50
  c.   Horiz. pair, imperf. vert.   4,250.

BLANCHE STUART SCOTT

Blanche Stuart Scott (1886-1970) AP72

1980, Dec. 30   Perf. 11
C99 AP72 28c multicolored   .60 .25
  a.   Imperf., pair   2,000.

GLENN CURTISS

Glenn Curtiss (1878-1930) — AP73

1980, Dec. 30
C100 AP73 35c multicolored   .65 .25
  a.   Light blue (background) omitted   2,000.

SUMMER OLYMPICS 1984

Women's Gymnastics AP74

Hurdles AP75

Women's Basketball AP76

Soccer AP77

1983, June 17
C101 AP74 28c multicolored   1.00 .30
C102 AP75 28c multicolored   1.00 .30
C103 AP76 28c multicolored   1.00 .30
C104 AP77 28c multicolored   1.00 .30
  a.   Block of 4, #C101-C104   4.25 2.50
  b.   As "a," imperf. vert.   5,000.

Shot Put — AP78

Men's Gymnastics AP79

Women's Swimming AP80

Weight Lifting AP81

1983, Apr. 8   Perf. 11.2 Bullseye
C105 AP78 40c multicolored   .90 .40
C106 AP79 40c multicolored   .90 .40
C107 AP80 40c multicolored   .90 .40
C108 AP81 40c multicolored   .90 .40
  b.   Block of 4, #C105-C108   4.25 3.00
  d.   Block of 4, imperf.   700.00

Women's Fencing AP82

Cycling AP83

Women's Volleyball AP84

Pole Vaulting AP85

1983, Nov. 4   Perf. 11
C109 AP82 35c multicolored   .90 .55
C110 AP83 35c multicolored   .90 .55
C111 AP84 35c multicolored   .90 .55
C112 AP85 35c multicolored   .90 .55
  a.   Block of 4, #C109-C112   4.00 3.25

AVIATION PIONEERS

Alfred V. Verville AP86

Lawrence & Elmer Sperry AP87

1985, Feb. 13   Tagged   Perf. 11
C113 AP86 33c multicolored   .65 .25
  a.   Imperf., pair   600.00
C114 AP87 39c multicolored   .80 .25
  a.   Imperf., pair   1,250.

TRANSPACIFIC AIRMAIL
50th Anniversary

Transpacific Airmail AP88

1985, Feb. 15
C115 AP88 44c multicolored   .85 .25
  a.   Imperf., pair   600.00

FR. JUNIPERO SERRA (1713-1784)
California Missionary

Outline Map of Southern California, Portrait, San Gabriel Mission AP89

1985, Aug. 22
C116 AP89 44c multicolored   1.00 .35
  a.   Imperf., pair   900.00

SETTLING OF NEW SWEDEN, 350th ANNIV.

Settling of New Sweden, 350th Anniv. AP90

LITHOGRAPHED AND ENGRAVED

1988, Mar. 29
C117 AP90 44c multicolored   1.00 .25
See Sweden No. 1672 and Finland No. 768.

SAMUEL P. LANGLEY (1834-1906)

Langley and Unmanned Aerodrome No. 5 AP91

1988, May 14
C118 AP91 45c multicolored   1.00 .25

IGOR SIKORSKY (1889-1972)

Sikorsky and VS300 Helicopter, 1939 AP92

PHOTOGRAVURE AND ENGRAVED

1988, June 23
C119 AP92 36c multicolored   .70 .25
  a.   Red, dk blue & black (engraved) omitted   2,500.

Beware of examples with traces of engraved red offered as "red omitted" varieties.

FRENCH REVOLUTION BICENTENNIAL

Liberty, Equality and Fraternity — AP93

LITHOGRAPHED AND ENGRAVED

1989, July 14   Perf. 11½x11
C120 AP93 45c multicolored   .95 .25
See France Nos. 2143-2145a.

PRE-COLUMBIAN AMERICA ISSUE

UPAE Emblem &
*Key Marco
Cat* — AP94

PHOTOGRAVURE

1989, Oct. 12   *Perf. 11*
C121 AP94 45c multicolored   .90   .25

20th UPU CONGRESS
Futuristic Mail Delivery

Spacecraft
AP95

Air-suspended
Hover
Car — AP96

Moon
Rover — AP97

Space
Shuttle — AP98

LITHOGRAPHED & ENGRAVED
1989, Nov. 27
C122 AP95 45c multicolored   1.00   .50
C123 AP96 45c multicolored   1.00   .50
C124 AP97 45c multicolored   1.00   .50
C125 AP98 45c multicolored   1.00   .50
   a.   Block of 4, #C122-C125   4.00   3.00
   b.   As "a," light blue (engr.)
      omitted   575.00

Souvenir Sheet
LITHOGRAPHED & ENGRAVED
1989, Nov. 24   *Imperf.*
C126   Sheet of 4   5.00   4.00
   a.   AP95 45c multicolored   1.25   .50
   b.   AP96 45c multicolored   1.25   .50
   c.   AP97 45c multicolored   1.25   .50
   d.   AP98 45c multicolored   1.25   .50

PRE-COLUMBIAN AMERICA ISSUE

Tropical
Coast
AP99

PHOTOGRAVURE
1990, Oct. 12   *Perf. 11*
C127 AP99 45c multicolored   .90   .25

HARRIET QUIMBY, 1ST AMERICAN WOMAN PILOT

Harriet
Quimby,
Bleriot
Aircraft
AP100

1991, Apr. 27
C128 AP100 50c multicolored   1.00   .25
   a.   Vert. pair, imperf. horiz.   900.00
   b.   Perf. 11.2, prephosphored
     uncoated paper ('93)   1.20   .25

WILLIAM T. PIPER, AIRCRAFT MANUFACTURER

William T.
Piper, Piper
Cub
AP101

1991, May 17
C129 AP101 40c multicolored   .80   .25
Blue sky is plainly visible all the way across
stamp above Piper's head.
See No. C132.

ANTARCTIC TREATY, 30TH ANNIVERSARY

Antarctic
Treaty,
30th Anniv.
AP102

1991, June 21
C130 AP102 50c multicolored   1.00   .35

PRE-COLUMBIAN AMERICA ISSUE

First
Americans
Crossed
Over From
Asia
AP103

1991, Oct. 12
C131 AP103 50c multicolored   1.00   .35

Piper Type of 1991
1993   *Perf. 11.2*
C132 AP101 40c multicolored   3.50   .65
Piper's hair touches top edge of design. No
selvage inscriptions.
Bullseye perf.

"All LC (Letters and Cards) mail
receives First-Class Mail service in the
United States, is dispatched by the fastest transportation available, and travels
by airmail or priority service in the destination country. All LC mail should be
marked 'AIRMAIL' or 'PAR AVION.'"
(U.S. Postal Service, Pub. 51).
No. C133 listed below was issued to
meet the LC rate to Canada and Mexico
and is inscribed with the silhouette of a
jet plane next to the denomination indicating the need for airmail service. This
is unlike No. 2998, which met the LC
rate to other countries, but contained no
indication that it was intended for that
use.
Future issues that meet a specific
international airmail rate and contain
the airplane silhouette will be treated by
Scott as Air Post stamps. Stamps similar to No. 2998 will be listed in the Postage section.

SCENIC AMERICAN LANDSCAPES

Niagara
Falls
AP104

1999, May 12   *Serpentine Die Cut 11*
Self-Adhesive
C133 AP104 48c multicolored   .95   .25

Rio Grande
AP105

1999, July 30
Self-Adhesive
C134 AP105 40c multicolored   .80   .60

Grand
Canyon
AP106

LITHOGRAPHED
Serpentine Die Cut 11¼x11½
2000, Jan. 20
Self-Adhesive
C135 AP106 60c multi   1.25   .25
   a.   Die cutting omitted, pair   1,250.
   b.   Vert. pair, die cutting
     omitted horiz.   —
   c.   Horiz. pair, die cutting
     omitted between   —
   d.   Horiz. pair, die cutting
     omitted vert.   —

Nine-Mile
Prairie,
Nebraska
AP107

LITHOGRAPHED
2001, Mar. 6
Self-Adhesive
C136 AP107 70c multi   1.40   .30

Mt.
McKinley
AP108

PHOTOGRAVURE
Serpentine Die Cut 11
2001, Apr. 17
Self-Adhesive
C137 AP108 80c multi   1.60   .35

Acadia
National
Park
AP109

LITHOGRAPHED
Serpentine Die Cut 11.25x11.5
2001-05
Self-Adhesive
C138 AP109 60c multi   1.25   .25
   a.   Serpentine die cut
     11½x11¾   1.25   .25
   b.   As "a," with "2005" year
     date   1.25   .25
   c.   As "b," printed on back
     of backing paper   —

Bryce
Canyon
National
Park
AP110

Great
Smoky
Mountains
National
Park
AP111

LITHOGRAPHED
Serpentine Die Cut 10¾
2006, Feb. 24
Self-Adhesive
C139 AP110 63c multicolored   1.25   .25
   a.   Die cutting omitted, pair   450.00
C140 AP111 75c multicolored   1.50   .35
   a.   Die cutting omitted, pair   500.00

Yosemite
National
Park
AP112

PHOTOGRAVURE
Serpentine Die Cut 11
C141 AP112 84c multicolored   1.75   .35
   Nos. C139-C141 (3)   4.50   .95

Okefenokee
Swamp,
Georgia
and Florida
AP113

Hagatña
Bay, Guam
AP114

LITHOGRAPHED (#C142), PHOTOGRAVURE (#C143)
Serpentine Die Cut 10¾
2007, June 1
Self-Adhesive
C142 AP113 69c multicolored   1.40   .30
Serpentine Die Cut 11
C143 AP114 90c multicolored   1.80   .40

13-Mile
Woods,
New
Hampshire
AP115

Trunk Bay,
St. John,
Virgin
Islands
AP116

LITHOGRAPHED (#C144), PHOTOGRAVURE (#C145)
Serpentine Die Cut 10¾
2008, May 16
Self-Adhesive
C144 AP115 72c multicolored   1.50   .30
Serpentine Die Cut 11
C145 AP116 94c multicolored   1.90   .45

AP117

AP118

LITHOGRAPHED, PHOTOGRAVURE (#C147)

Serpentine Die Cut 10¾

2009, June 28
Self-Adhesive

C146 AP117 79c multicolored   1.75   .35

Serpentine Die Cut 11

C147 AP118 98c multicolored   2.00   .45

Voyageurs National Park, Minnesota AP119

LITHOGRAPHED

Serpentine Die Cut 10¾

2011, Apr. 11
Self-Adhesive

C148 AP119 80c multicolored   1.60   .25

See note after No. 1549.

Glacier National Park, Montana — AP120

Amish Horse and Buggy on Road, Lancaster County, Pennsylvania — AP121

LITHOGRAPHED

2012   *Serpentine Die Cut 10¾*
Self-Adhesive

C149 AP120 85c multicolored   1.75   .35
C150 AP121 $1.05 multicolored   2.10   .45
   a.   Die cutting omitted on front, pair   700.00
   b.   Silver (airplane silhouette) missing (PS)   —

Issued: 85c, 1/19; $1.05, 1/20.

AIR POST SPECIAL DELIVERY STAMPS

To provide for the payment of both the postage and the special delivery fee in one stamp.

Great Seal of United States APSD1

1934, Aug. 30   Unwmk.   *Perf. 11*
CE1 APSD1 16c dark blue   .70   .80
   Never hinged   .90

For imperforate variety see No. 771.

Great Seal of United States APSD2

1936, Feb. 10
CE2 APSD2 16c red & blue   .45   .35
   Never hinged   .65
   a.   Horiz. pair, imperf. vert.   4,250.
   Never hinged   5,250.

SPECIAL DELIVERY STAMPS

When affixed to any letter or article of mailable matter, secured immediate delivery, between 7 A. M. and midnight, at any post office.

Messenger Running — SD1

Flat Plate Printing

1885   Unwmk.   *Perf. 12*
E1 SD1 10c blue   575.00   80.00
   Never hinged   1,300.

Messenger Running SD2

1888, Sept. 6
E2 SD2 10c blue   475.00   45.00
   Never hinged   1,100.

COLUMBIAN EXPOSITION ISSUE

Though not issued expressly for the Exposition, No. E3 is considered to be part of that issue.

1893, Jan. 24
E3 SD2 10c orange   300.00   50.00
   Never hinged   675.00

Messenger Running SD3

1894, Oct. 10
Line under "TEN CENTS"
E4 SD3 10c blue   850.00   110.00
   Never hinged   2,100.

No. E5a

1895, Aug. 16   **Wmk. 191**
E5 SD3 10c blue   210.00   12.50
   Never hinged   500.00
   a.   Dots in curved frame above messenger (Pl. 882)   375.00   45.00
   Never hinged   750.00
   b.   Printed on both sides

Messenger on Bicycle SD4

1902, Dec. 9
E6 SD4 10c ultramarine   230.00   10.00
   Never hinged   525.00
   a.   10c blue   300.00   12.50
   Never hinged   800.00

Helmet of Mercury and Olive Branch — SD5

1908, Dec. 12
E7 SD5 10c green   65.00   50.00
   Never hinged   140.00

1911, Jan.   **Wmk. 190**   *Perf. 12*
E8 SD4 10c ultramarine   110.00   10.00
   Never hinged   240.00
   b.   10c violet blue   150.00   14.00
   Never hinged   325.00

1914, Sept.   *Perf. 10*
E9 SD4 10c ultramarine   190.00   12.00
   Never hinged   425.00
   a.   10c blue   250.00   15.00
   Never hinged   550.00

1916, Oct. 19   Unwmk.   *Perf. 10*
E10 SD4 10c pale ultramarine   320.00   50.00
   Never hinged   700.00
   a.   10c blue   375.00   50.00
   Never hinged   800.00

1917, May 2   *Perf. 11*
E11 SD4 10c ultramarine   20.00   .75
   Never hinged   45.00
   b.   10c gray violet   35.00   3.00
   Never hinged   75.00
   c.   10c blue   90.00   5.00
   Never hinged   190.00
   d.   Perf. 10 at left   —

Postman and Motorcycle SD6

1922, July 12
E12 SD6 10c gray violet   45.00   3.00
   Never hinged   95.00
   a.   10c deep ultramarine   55.00   3.50
   Never hinged   130.00

Post Office Truck SD7

1925
E13 SD6 15c deep orange   40.00   3.75
   Never hinged   75.00
E14 SD7 20c black   2.00   1.00
   Never hinged   4.00
   Nos. E12-E14 (3)   87.00   7.75

Motorcycle Type of 1922
ROTARY PRESS PRINTING

1927-31   *Perf. 11x10½*
E15 SD6 10c gray violet   1.00   .25
   Never hinged   1.75
   On cover   .50
   a.   10c red lilac   .80   .25
   Never hinged   1.40
   b.   10c gray lilac   .90   .25
   Never hinged   1.60
   c.   Horiz. pair, imperf. btwn., red lilac shade   300.00
   Never hinged   575.00
E16 SD6 15c orange ('31)   .60   .25
   Never hinged   .90

> **Catalogue values for unused stamps in this section, from this point to the end, are for Never Hinged items.**

1944-51
E17 SD6 13c blue   .60   .25
E18 SD6 17c orange yellow   3.50   2.50
E19 SD7 20c black ('51)   1.20   .25

Special Delivery Letter, Hand to Hand SD8

1954, Oct. 13   *Perf. 11x10½*
E20 SD8 20c deep blue   .40   .25

1957, Sept. 3
E21 SD8 30c lake   .50   .25

Arrows SD9

GIORI PRESS PRINTING

1969, Nov. 21   *Perf. 11*
E22 SD9 45c carmine & violet blue   1.20   .25

1971, May 10
E23 SD9 60c violet blue & carmine   1.25   .25

From 1885 to the present, special delivery stamps have not been and are not valid for the payment of postage of any description, nor for registry fees.

REGISTRATION STAMP

Issued for the prepayment of registry fees; not usable for postage.

Eagle — RS1

1911, Dec. 1   **Wmk. 190**   *Perf. 12*
F1 RS1 10c ultramarine   80.00   15.00
   Never hinged   175.00

CERTIFIED MAIL STAMP

For use on first-class mail for which no indemnity value is claimed, but for which proof of mailing and proof of delivery are available at less cost than registered mail.

> **Catalogue value for the unused stamp in this section is for a Never Hinged item.**

Letter Carrier — CM1

ROTARY PRESS PRINTING

1955, June 6   Unwmk.   *Perf. 10½x11*
FA1 CM1 15c red   .75   .75

POSTAGE DUE STAMPS

For affixing, by a postal clerk to any piece of mailable matter, to denote the amount to be collected from the addressee because of insufficient prepayment of postage.

D1

Printed by the American Bank Note Co.

Plates of 200 subjects in two panes of 100 each.

1879		Unwmk.	Engr.	Perf. 12
J1	D1	1c brown	90.00	14.00
		Never hinged	260.00	
J2	D1	2c brown	400.00	25.00
		Never hinged	1,050.	
J3	D1	3c brown	100.00	6.00
		Never hinged	280.00	
J4	D1	5c brown	775.00	70.00
		Never hinged	1,900.	
J5	D1	10c brown	900.00	70.00
		Never hinged	2,500.	
a.		Imperf., pair	2,500.	
J6	D1	30c brown	350.00	65.00
		Never hinged	800.00	
J7	D1	50c brown	600.00	90.00
		Never hinged	1,600.	
		Nos. J1-J7 (7)	3,215.	340.00

Special Printing

J8	D1	1c deep brown	16,000.	
		Never hinged	—	
J9	D1	2c deep brown	15,000.	
J10	D1	3c deep brown	20,000.	
J11	D1	5c deep brown	13,000.	
J12	D1	10c deep brown	7,000.	
J13	D1	30c deep brown	7,500.	
J14	D1	50c deep brown	7,500.	

1884				
J15	D1	1c red brown	70.00	7.00
		Never hinged	190.00	
J16	D1	2c red brown	80.00	6.00
		Never hinged	225.00	
J17	D1	3c red brown	1,050.	350.00
		Never hinged	2,500.	
J18	D1	5c red brown	600.00	50.00
		Never hinged	1,450.	
J19	D1	10c red brown	600.00	35.00
		Never hinged	1,450.	
J20	D1	30c red brown	200.00	70.00
		Never hinged	500.00	
J21	D1	50c red brown	1,750.	250.00
		Never hinged	3,750.	
		Nos. J15-J21 (7)	4,350.	768.00

1891				
J22	D1	1c bright claret	30.00	2.00
		Never hinged	85.00	
J23	D1	2c bright claret	32.50	2.00
		Never hinged	90.00	
J24	D1	3c bright claret	67.50	16.00
		Never hinged	180.00	
J25	D1	5c bright claret	100.00	16.00
		Never hinged	290.00	
J26	D1	10c bright claret	165.00	30.00
		Never hinged	500.00	
J27	D1	30c bright claret	575.00	225.00
		Never hinged	1,700.	
J28	D1	50c bright claret	600.00	225.00
		Never hinged	1,750.	
		Nos. J22-J28 (7)	1,570.	516.00

See Die and Plate Proofs in the Scott U.S. Specialized catalog for imperfs. on stamp paper.

The color on Nos. J29-J44 will run when immersed in water. Extreme caution is advised.

D2

Printed by the Bureau of Engraving and Printing.

1894				
J29	D2	1c vermilion	2,250.	725.
		Never hinged	5,750.	
J30	D2	2c vermilion	775.00	350.
		Never hinged	1,900.	

1894-95				
J31	D2	1c deep claret	72.50	12.00
		Never hinged	260.00	
b.		Vertical pair, imperf. horiz.	—	
J32	D2	2c deep claret	62.50	10.00
		Never hinged	240.00	
J33	D2	3c deep claret ('95)	200.00	50.00
		Never hinged	575.00	
J34	D2	5c deep claret ('95)	300.00	55.00
		Never hinged	850.00	
J35	D2	10c deep claret ('95)	350.00	40.00
		Never hinged	1,000.	
J36	D2	30c deep claret ('95)	550.00	250.00
		Never hinged	1,250.	
a.		30c carmine	675.00	275.00

		Never hinged	1,600.	
b.		30c pale rose	450.00	200.00
		Never hinged	1,100.	
J37	D2	50c deep claret ('95)	1,800.	800.00
		Never hinged	4,250.	
a.		50c pale rose	1,600.	725.00
		Never hinged	3,750.	
		Nos. J31-J37 (7)	3,335.	1,217.

Shades are numerous in the 1894 and later issues.
See Die and Plate Proofs in the Scott U.S. Specialized catalog for imperfs. on stamp paper.

1895-97			Wmk. 191	
J38	D2	1c deep claret	13.50	1.00
		Never hinged	40.00	
J39	D2	2c deep claret	13.50	1.00
		Never hinged	40.00	
J40	D2	3c deep claret	100.00	5.00
		Never hinged	225.00	
J41	D2	5c deep claret	110.00	5.00
		Never hinged	280.00	
J42	D2	10c deep claret	110.00	7.50
		Never hinged	280.00	
J43	D2	30c deep claret ('97)	600.00	75.00
		Never hinged	1,500.	
J44	D2	50c deep claret ('96)	375.00	60.00
		Never hinged	925.00	
		Nos. J38-J44 (7)	1,322.	154.50

1910-12			Wmk. 190	
J45	D2	1c deep claret	40.00	5.00
		Never hinged	115.00	
a.		1c rose carmine	35.00	5.00
		Never hinged	105.00	
J46	D2	2c deep claret	40.00	2.00
		Never hinged	115.00	
a.		2c rose carmine	35.00	2.00
		Never hinged	105.00	
J47	D2	3c deep claret	625.00	60.00
		Never hinged	1,600.	
J48	D2	5c deep claret	120.00	12.00
		Never hinged	275.00	
a.		5c rose carmine	120.00	12.00
		Never hinged	275.00	
J49	D2	10c deep claret	125.00	20.00
		Never hinged	280.00	
a.		10c rose carmine	125.00	20.00
		Never hinged	280.00	
J50	D2	50c deep claret ('12)	1,100.	175.00
		Never hinged	2,900.	
a.		50c rose carmine	1,150.	190.00
		Never hinged	3,000.	
		Nos. J45-J50 (6)	2,050.	274.00

1914			Perf. 10	
J52	D2	1c carmine lake	80.00	15.00
		Never hinged	220.00	
a.		1c dull rose	85.00	15.00
		Never hinged	230.00	
J53	D2	2c carmine lake	62.50	1.00
		Never hinged	170.00	
a.		2c dull rose	67.50	2.00
		Never hinged	180.00	
b.		2c vermilion	67.50	2.00
		Never hinged	180.00	
J54	D2	3c carmine lake	1,050.	75.00
		Never hinged	3,000.	
a.		3c dull rose	1,000.	75.00
		Never hinged	2,900.	
J55	D2	5c carmine lake	50.00	6.00
		Never hinged	140.00	
a.		5c dull rose	45.00	4.00
		Never hinged	130.00	
J56	D2	10c carmine lake	75.00	4.00
		Never hinged	200.00	
a.		10c dull rose	80.00	5.00
		Never hinged	210.00	
J57	D2	30c carmine lake	225.00	55.00
		Never hinged	525.00	
J58	D2	50c carmine lake	11,500.	1,600.
		Never hinged	21,000.	
		Nos. J52-J58 (7)	13,043.	1,756.

No. J58 unused is valued in the grade of fine to very fine.

1916		Unwmk.	Perf. 10	
J59	D2	1c rose	4,000.	750.00
		Never hinged	9,000.	
J60	D2	2c rose	225.00	75.00
		Never hinged	600.00	

1917			Perf. 11	
J61	D2	1c carmine rose	2.75	.25
		Never hinged	9.00	
		Never hinged	15.00	
a.		1c rose red	2.75	.25
		Never hinged	9.00	
b.		1c deep claret	2.75	.25
		Never hinged	9.00	
J62	D2	2c carmine rose	2.75	.25
		Never hinged	9.00	
a.		2c rose red	2.75	.25
		Never hinged	9.00	
b.		2c deep claret	2.75	.25
		Never hinged	9.00	
J63	D2	3c carmine rose	13.50	.80
		Never hinged	35.00	
a.		3c rose red	13.50	.80
		Never hinged	35.00	
b.		3c deep claret	13.50	.80
		Never hinged	35.00	
J64	D2	5c carmine	11.00	.80
		Never hinged	32.50	
a.		5c rose red	11.00	.80
		Never hinged	32.50	
b.		5c deep claret	11.00	.80
		Never hinged	32.50	
J65	D2	10c carmine rose	22.50	1.00
		Never hinged	65.00	
a.		10c rose red	22.50	1.00

WALTER KASELL STAMPS

Quality United States Stamps

Classics, U.S. Possessions & Plate Blocks

175 Richdale Ave., Cambridge, MA 02140 • (617) 694-9360
Email: wbkasell@yahoo.com

		Never hinged	65.00	
b.		10c deep claret	22.50	1.00
		Never hinged	65.00	
J66	D2	30c carmine rose	80.00	2.00
		Never hinged	220.00	
a.		30c deep claret	80.00	2.00
		Never hinged	220.00	
b.		As "a," perf 10 at top, precanceled		21,000.

No. J66b is valued with small faults and fine centering, as the two recorded examples are in this condition and grade.

J67	D2	50c carmine rose	140.00	1.00
		Never hinged	325.00	
a.		50c rose red	140.00	1.00
		Never hinged	325.00	
b.		50c deep claret	140.00	1.00
		Never hinged	325.00	
		Nos. J61-J67 (7)	272.50	6.10

1925				
J68	D2	½c dull red	1.00	.25
		Never hinged	1.75	

D3

D4

1930			Perf. 11	
J69	D3	½c carmine	4.25	1.90
		Never hinged	9.50	
J70	D3	1c carmine	2.75	.35
		Never hinged	6.25	
J71	D3	2c carmine	3.75	.35
		Never hinged	8.50	
J72	D3	3c carmine	20.00	2.75
		Never hinged	47.50	
J73	D3	5c carmine	18.00	5.00
		Never hinged	42.50	
J74	D3	10c carmine	42.50	2.00
		Never hinged	95.00	
J75	D3	30c carmine	125.00	4.00
		Never hinged	275.00	
J76	D3	50c carmine	175.00	2.00
		Never hinged	375.00	
J77	D4	$1 carmine	32.50	.35
		Never hinged	65.00	
a.		$1 scarlet	27.50	.35
		Never hinged	55.00	
J78	D4	$5 scarlet	37.50	.35
		Never hinged	85.00	
b.		carmine	37.50	.35
		Never hinged	70.00	
		Nos. J69-J78 (10)	461.25	19.05

Type of 1930-31 Issue
Rotary Press Printing

1931			Perf. 11x10½	
J79	D3	½c scarlet	.90	.25
		Never hinged	1.30	
a.		½c dull carmine	.90	.25
		Never hinged	1.30	
J80	D3	1c scarlet	.25	.25
		Never hinged	.30	
b.		dull carmine	.25	.25
		Never hinged	.30	
J81	D3	2c scarlet	.25	.25
		Never hinged	.30	
b.		dull carmine	.25	.25
		Never hinged	.30	
J82	D3	3c scarlet	.30	.25
		Never hinged	.45	
b.		dull carmine	.25	.25
		Never hinged	.40	
J83	D3	5c scarlet	.50	.25
		Never hinged	.75	
b.		dull carmine	.40	.25
		Never hinged	.60	

J84	D3	10c scarlet	1.25	.25
		Never hinged	1.90	
b.		dull carmine	1.10	.25
		Never hinged	1.80	
J85	D3	30c scarlet	7.50	.25
		Never hinged	11.50	
a.		30c dull carmine	7.50	.25
		Never hinged	11.50	
J86	D3	50c scarlet	9.00	.25
		Never hinged	15.00	
a.		50c dull carmine	9.00	.25
		Never hinged	15.00	

Design measures 22½x19mm

1956			Perf. 10½x11	
J87	D4	$1 scarlet	30.00	.25
		Never hinged	52.50	
		Nos. J79-J87 (9)	49.95	2.25

For listings of other color shades and printing varieties see the *Scott Specialized Catalogue of United States Stamps and Covers.*

Catalogue values for unused stamps in this section, from this point to the end, are for Never Hinged items.

D5

Denominations added in black by rubber plates in an operation similar to precanceling.

Rotary Press Printing
Perf. 11x10½

1959, June 19			Unwmk.	
		Denomination in Black		
J88	D5	½c carmine rose	1.50	1.10
J89	D5	1c carmine rose	.25	.25
a.		Denomination omitted	200.00	
b.		Pair, one without "1 CENT"	400.00	
J90	D5	2c carmine rose	.25	.25
J91	D5	3c carmine rose	.25	.25
a.		Pair, one without "3 CENTS"	600.00	
J92	D5	4c carmine rose	.25	.25
J93	D5	5c carmine rose	.25	.25
a.		Pair, one without "5 CENTS"	1,100.	
J94	D5	6c carmine rose	.25	.25
a.		Pair, one without "6 CENTS"	750.00	
J95	D5	7c carmine rose	.25	.25
J96	D5	8c carmine rose	.25	.25
a.		Pair, one without "8 CENTS"	750.00	
J97	D5	10c carmine rose	.25	.25
J98	D5	30c carmine rose	.70	.25
J99	D5	50c carmine rose	1.10	.25

Straight Numeral Outlined in Black

J100	D5	$1 carmine rose	2.00	.25
J101	D5	$5 carmine rose	9.00	.25
		Nos. J88-J101 (14)	16.55	4.35

All single stamps with denomination omitted are catalogued as No. J89a.

1978-85		Denomination in Black		
J102	D5	11c carmine rose	.25	.25
J103	D5	13c carmine rose	.25	.25
J104	D5	17c carmine rose ('85)	.40	.35

UNITED STATES OFFICES IN CHINA

Issued for sale by the postal agency at Shanghai, at their surcharged value in local currency. Valid to the amount of their original values for the prepayment of postage on mail dispatched from the U.S. postal agency at Shanghai to addresses in the U.S.

Nos. 498-499, 502-504, 506-510, 512, 514-518 Surcharged

1919		**Unwmk.**		**Perf. 11**
K1	A140	2c on 1c green	25.00	70.00
	Never hinged		70.00	
K2	A140	4c on 2c rose, type I	25.00	70.00
	Never hinged		70.00	
K3	A140	6c on 3c vio, type II	60.00	140.00
	Never hinged		150.00	
K4	A140	8c on 4c brown	60.00	140.00
	Never hinged		150.00	
K5	A140	10c on 5c blue	65.00	140.00
	Never hinged		170.00	
K6	A140	12c on 6c red org	85.00	210.00
	Never hinged		220.00	
K7	A140	14c on 7c black	87.50	210.00
	Never hinged		225.00	
K8	A148	16c on 8c ol bis	70.00	160.00
	Never hinged		180.00	
a.	16c on 8c ol grn		60.00	140.00
	Never hinged		160.00	
K9	A148	18c on 9c sal red	65.00	175.00
	Never hinged		170.00	
K10	A148	20c on 10c org yel	60.00	140.00
	Never hinged		160.00	
K11	A148	24c on 12c brn car	80.00	160.00
	Never hinged		200.00	
a.	24c on 12c cl brn		110.00	225.00
	Never hinged		275.00	
K12	A148	30c on 15c gray	87.50	230.00
	Never hinged		210.00	
K13	A148	40c on 20c deep ultra	130.00	325.00
	Never hinged		300.00	
K14	A148	60c on 30c org red	120.00	275.00
	Never hinged		280.00	
K15	A148	$1 on 50c lt vio	575.00	1,000.
	Never hinged		1,300.	
K16	A148	$2 on $1 vio brn	450.00	750.00
	Never hinged		1,000.	
a.	Double surcharge		10,500.	12,500.
	Never hinged		17,500.	
	Nos. K1-K16 (16)		2,045.	4,195.

Fake surcharges exist, but most are rather crudely made.

Nos. 498 and 528B Surcharged

1922, July 3				
K17	A140	2c on 1c green	110.00	225.00
	Never hinged		250.00	
K18	A140	4c on 2c car, type VII	100.00	200.00
	Never hinged		230.00	
a.	"SHANGHAI" omitted		7,500.	
b.	"CHINA" only		15,000.	

OFFICIAL STAMPS

The franking privilege having been abolished, as of July 1, 1873, these stamps were provided for each of the departments of Government for the prepayment of postage on official matter.

Penalty franks were first authorized in 1877, and their expanded use after 1879 reduced the need for official stamps, the use of which was finally abolished on July 5, 1884.

Designs, except Post Office, resemble those illustrated but are not identical. Each bears the name of Department. Portraits are as follows: 1c, Franklin; 2c, Jackson; 3c, Washington; 6c, Lincoln; 7c, Stanton; 10c, Jefferson;

12c, Clay; 15c, Webster; 24c, Scott; 30c, Hamilton; 90c, Perry.

Special printings overprinted "SPECIMEN" follow No. O120.

AGRICULTURE
Printed by the Continental Bank Note Co.

O1

Thin Hard Paper

1873	**Engr.**	**Unwmk.**		**Perf. 12**
O1	O1	1c yellow	300.00	200.00
	Never hinged		650.00	
	No gum		170.00	
O2	O1	2c yellow	275.00	100.00
	Never hinged		575.00	
	No gum		110.00	
O3	O1	3c yellow	225.00	17.50
	Never hinged		475.00	
	No gum		85.00	
O4	O1	6c yellow	275.00	60.00
	Never hinged		575.00	
	No gum		110.00	
O5	O1	10c yellow	525.00	200.00
	Never hinged		1,150.	
	No gum		220.00	
O6	O1	12c yellow	450.00	260.00
	Never hinged		950.00	
	No gum		250.00	
O7	O1	15c yellow	425.00	230.00
	Never hinged		950.00	
	No gum		225.00	
O8	O1	24c yellow	425.00	250.00
	Never hinged		950.00	
	No gum		225.00	
O9	O1	30c yellow	550.00	280.00
	Never hinged		1,200.	
	No gum		275.00	
	Nos. O1-O9 (9)		3,450.	1,598.

EXECUTIVE

Franklin—O2

1873				
O10	O2	1c carmine	900.00	550.00
	Never hinged		2,250.	
	No gum		450.00	
O11	O2	2c carmine	575.00	260.00
	Never hinged		1,250.	
	No gum		250.00	
O12	O2	3c carmine	700.00	225.00
	Never hinged		1,600.	
	No gum		270.00	
a.	3c violet rose		1,000.	275.00
	Never hinged		2,250.	
	No gum		375.00	
	On cover			—
O13	O2	6c carmine	900.00	600.00
	Never hinged			
	No gum		325.00	
O14	O2	10c carmine	1,200.	1,000.
	Never hinged		—	
	No gum		600.00	
	Nos. O10-O14 (5)		4,275.	2,635.

INTERIOR

O3

1873				
O15	O3	1c vermilion	75.00	10.00
	Never hinged		170.00	
	No gum		30.00	
O16	O3	2c vermilion	70.00	12.00
	Never hinged		160.00	
	No gum		30.00	
O17	O3	3c vermilion	80.00	6.00
	Never hinged		175.00	
	No gum		35.00	
O18	O3	6c vermilion	70.00	10.00
	Never hinged		160.00	
	No gum		27.50	
O19	O3	10c vermilion	70.00	20.00
	Never hinged		160.00	
	No gum		27.50	
O20	O3	12c vermilion	90.00	12.00
	Never hinged		200.00	
	No gum		35.00	

O21	O3	15c vermilion	200.00	25.00
	Never hinged		450.00	
	No gum		80.00	
O22	O3	24c vermilion	180.00	20.00
	Never hinged		400.00	
	No gum		60.00	
a.	Double impression			—
O23	O3	30c vermilion	290.00	20.00
	Never hinged		625.00	
	No gum		110.00	
O24	O3	90c vermilion	325.00	50.00
	Never hinged		700.00	
	No gum		120.00	
	Nos. O15-O24 (10)		1,450.	185.00

JUSTICE

O4

1873				
O25	O4	1c purple	250.00	100.00
	Never hinged		550.00	
	No gum		100.00	
O26	O4	2c purple	310.00	110.00
	Never hinged		700.00	
	No gum		120.00	
O27	O4	3c purple	320.00	35.00
	Never hinged		725.00	
	No gum		110.00	
O28	O4	6c purple	310.00	45.00
	Never hinged		700.00	
	No gum		110.00	
O29	O4	10c purple	310.00	100.00
	Never hinged		700.00	
	No gum		120.00	
O30	O4	12c purple	260.00	75.00
	Never hinged		575.00	
	No gum		95.00	
O31	O4	15c purple	500.00	200.00
	Never hinged		1,100.	
	No gum		220.00	
O32	O4	24c purple	1,250.	425.00
	Never hinged		—	
	No gum		550.00	
O33	O4	30c purple	1,300.	350.00
	Never hinged		—	
	No gum		550.00	
O34	O4	90c purple	1,900.	900.00
	Never hinged		—	
	No gum		800.00	
	Nos. O25-O34 (10)		6,710.	2,340.

NAVY

O5

1873				
O35	O5	1c ultramarine	160.00	50.00
	Never hinged		350.00	
	No gum		65.00	
a.	1c dull blue		175.00	50.00
	Never hinged		375.00	
	No gum		70.00	
O36	O5	2c ultramarine	160.00	25.00
	Never hinged		350.00	
	No gum		65.00	
a.	2c dull blue		175.00	25.00
	Never hinged		385.00	
	No gum		70.00	
O37	O5	3c ultramarine	170.00	15.00
	Never hinged		375.00	
	No gum		60.00	
a.	3c dull blue		175.00	15.00
	Never hinged		385.00	
	No gum		62.50	
O38	O5	6c ultramarine	150.00	25.00
	Never hinged		325.00	
	No gum		55.00	
a.	6c dull blue		175.00	25.00
	Never hinged		385.00	
	No gum		67.50	
O39	O5	7c ultramarine	700.00	230.00
	Never hinged		—	
	No gum		275.00	
a.	7c dull blue		750.00	230.00
	Never hinged		—	
	No gum		275.00	
O40	O5	10c ultramarine	210.00	45.00
	Never hinged		475.00	
	No gum		75.00	
a.	10c dull blue		225.00	45.00
	Never hinged		500.00	
	No gum		80.00	
O41	O5	12c ultramarine	240.00	45.00
	Never hinged		525.00	
	No gum		100.00	
O42	O5	15c ultramarine	425.00	75.00
	Never hinged		—	
	No gum		160.00	
O43	O5	24c ultramarine	425.00	85.00
	Never hinged		—	
	No gum		160.00	
a.	24c dull blue		425.00	80.00
	Never hinged		—	
	No gum		160.00	
O44	O5	30c ultramarine	350.00	50.00
	Never hinged		—	
	No gum		140.00	

O45	O5	90c ultramarine	1,050.	375.00
	Never hinged		—	
	No gum		450.00	
a.	Double impression			20,000.
	Nos. O35-O45 (11)		4,040.	1,020.

POST OFFICE

Stamps of the Post Office Department are often on paper with a gray surface. This is essentially a wiping problem, caused by an over-milled carbon black pigment that released acid and etched the plates. There is no premium for stamps on paper with a gray surface.

O6

1873				
O47	O6	1c black	25.00	12.00
	Never hinged		60.00	
	No gum		12.00	
O48	O6	2c black	30.00	10.00
	Never hinged		75.00	
	No gum		13.00	
a.	Double impression		700.00	400.00
O49	O6	3c black	10.00	2.00
	Never hinged		25.00	
	No gum		3.00	
a.	Printed on both sides			7,500.
O50	O6	6c black	30.00	8.00
	Never hinged		75.00	
	No gum		12.00	
a.	Diagonal half used as 3c on cover			5,000.
b.	Double impression			3,000.
O51	O6	10c black	140.00	55.00
	Never hinged		325.00	
	No gum		60.00	
O52	O6	12c black	120.00	12.00
	Never hinged		275.00	
	No gum		40.00	
O53	O6	15c black	140.00	20.00
	Never hinged		325.00	
	No gum		50.00	
O54	O6	24c black	225.00	25.00
	Never hinged		500.00	
	No gum		85.00	
O55	O6	30c black	200.00	25.00
	Never hinged		450.00	
	No gum		70.00	
O56	O6	90c black	220.00	25.00
	Never hinged		500.00	
	No gum		80.00	
	Nos. O47-O56 (10)		1,140.	194.00

STATE

Franklin — O7   Seward — O8

1873				
O57	O7	1c dark green	260.00	75.00
	Never hinged		575.00	
	No gum		110.00	
O58	O7	2c dark green	310.00	100.00
	Never hinged		—	
	No gum		120.00	
O59	O7	3c dark green	220.00	25.00
	Never hinged		500.00	
	No gum		85.00	
O60	O7	6c dark green	250.00	30.00
	Never hinged		550.00	
	No gum		110.00	
O61	O7	7c dark green	290.00	65.00
	Never hinged		650.00	
	No gum		95.00	
O62	O7	10c dark green	250.00	55.00
	Never hinged		575.00	
	No gum		110.00	
O63	O7	12c dark green	310.00	125.00
	Never hinged		700.00	
	No gum		140.00	
O64	O7	15c dark green	350.00	90.00
	Never hinged		775.00	
	No gum		150.00	
O65	O7	24c dark green	525.00	230.00
	Never hinged		—	
	No gum		275.00	
O66	O7	30c dark green	500.00	180.00
	Never hinged		—	
	No gum		240.00	
O67	O7	90c dark green	1,050.	325.00
	Never hinged		—	
	No gum		525.00	
O68	O8	$2 green & black	1,750.	3,000.
	Never hinged		3,750.	
	No gum		850.00	
O69	O8	$5 green & black	7,500.	13,000.
	Never hinged		—	
	No gum		3,500.	

O70	O8	$10 green & black	4,500.	7,500.
		Never hinged	10,500.	
		No gum	2,500.	
O71	O8	$20 green & black	5,000.	5,500.
		Never hinged	11,500.	
		No gum	2,250.	

No. O71 used is valued with a blue or red handstamp favor cancel. Nos. O68-O71 with pen cancels sell for approximately 25-40% of the values shown.

TREASURY

O9

1873

O72	O9	1c brown	120.00	10.00
		Never hinged	250.00	
		No gum	45.00	
O73	O9	2c brown	125.00	8.00
		Never hinged	275.00	
		No gum	45.00	
O74	O9	3c brown	110.00	2.00
		Never hinged	230.00	
		No gum	40.00	
a.		Double impression		5,000.
O75	O9	6c brown	120.00	4.00
		Never hinged	250.00	
		No gum	45.00	
O76	O9	7c brown	250.00	35.00
		Never hinged	550.00	
		No gum	95.00	
O77	O9	10c brown	240.00	12.00
		Never hinged	525.00	
		No gum	90.00	
O78	O9	12c brown	350.00	10.00
		Never hinged	750.00	
		No gum	125.00	
O79	O9	15c brown	300.00	12.00
		Never hinged	650.00	
		No gum	100.00	
O80	O9	24c brown	725.00	100.00
		No gum	290.00	
O81	O9	30c brown	400.00	12.00
		No gum	140.00	
O82	O9	90c brown	475.00	15.00
		No gum	160.00	
		Nos. O72-O82 (11)	3,215.	220.00

WAR

O10

1873

O83	O10	1c rose	240.00	15.00
		Never hinged	525.00	
		No gum	90.00	
O84	O10	2c rose	260.00	15.00
		Never hinged	600.00	
		No gum	110.00	
O85	O10	3c rose	275.00	5.00
		Never hinged	600.00	
		No gum	120.00	
O86	O10	6c rose	675.00	10.00
		Never hinged	1,450.	
		No gum	275.00	

Examples of Nos. O114-O117 which bear Continental Bank Note Co. imprints are often mistaken for/offered as Nos. O83-O86. If there are doubts, expert opinions should be requested.

O87	O10	7c rose	175.00	90.00
		Never hinged	375.00	
		No gum	90.00	
O88	O10	10c rose	140.00	25.00
		Never hinged	300.00	
		No gum	45.00	
O89	O10	12c rose	275.00	12.00
		Never hinged	600.00	
		No gum	110.00	
O90	O10	15c rose	85.00	15.00
		Never hinged	190.00	
		No gum	30.00	
O91	O10	24c rose	85.00	12.00
		Never hinged	190.00	
		No gum	30.00	
O92	O10	30c rose	130.00	12.00
		Never hinged	275.00	
		No gum	45.00	
O93	O10	90c rose	225.00	60.00
		Never hinged	500.00	
		No gum	80.00	
		Nos. O83-O93 (11)	2,565.	271.00

AGRICULTURE
Printed by the American Bank Note Co.

1879 — Soft Porous Paper

O94	O1	1c yel, no gum		6,000.
O95	O1	3c yellow	550.00	150.00
		Never hinged	1,250.	

		No gum	240.00	

INTERIOR

O96	O3	1c vermilion	300.00	400.00
		Never hinged	550.00	
		No gum	160.00	
O97	O3	2c vermilion	10.00	3.00
		Never hinged	17.50	
		No gum	3.00	
O98	O3	3c vermilion	10.00	3.00
		Never hinged	22.50	
		No gum	3.00	
O99	O3	6c vermilion	10.00	12.50
		Never hinged	17.50	
		No gum	3.00	
O100	O3	10c vermilion	110.00	75.00
		Never hinged	250.00	
		No gum	60.00	
O101	O3	12c vermilion	230.00	115.00
		Never hinged	525.00	
		No gum	130.00	
O102	O3	15c pale vermilion	400.00	500.00
		Never hinged	900.00	
		No gum	200.00	
O103	O3	24c pale vermilion	4,500.	6,250.
		Never hinged	10,000.	
		No gum	2,100.	
		Nos. O96-O103 (8)	5,570.	7,359.

JUSTICE

O106	O4	3c bluish pur	225.00	125.00
		Never hinged	525.00	
		No gum	110.00	
O107	O4	6c bluish pur	475.00	300.00
		Never hinged	1,050.	
		No gum	210.00	

POST OFFICE

O108	O6	3c black	30.00	10.00
		Never hinged	70.00	
		No gum	10.00	

TREASURY

O109	O9	3c brown	80.00	10.00
		Never hinged	175.00	
		No gum	35.00	
O110	O9	6c brown	200.00	50.00
		Never hinged	450.00	
		No gum	65.00	
O111	O9	10c brown	275.00	80.00
		Never hinged	650.00	
		No gum	120.00	
O112	O9	30c brown	2,400.	425.00
		No gum	875.00	
O113	O9	90c brown	9,000.	750.00
		No gum	3,000.	
		Nos. O109-O113 (5)	11,955.	1,315.

WAR

O114	O10	1c rose red	7.50	4.00
		Never hinged	15.00	
		No gum	2.75	
O115	O10	2c rose red	15.00	4.00
		Never hinged	30.00	
		No gum	5.00	
O116	O10	3c rose red	15.00	2.00
		Never hinged	30.00	
		No gum	5.00	
a.		Imperf., pair		5,000.
b.		Double impression		7,500.
O117	O10	6c rose red	12.50	3.00
		Never hinged	25.00	
		No gum	4.50	
O118	O10	10c rose red	75.00	50.00
		Never hinged	150.00	
		No gum	27.50	
O119	O10	12c rose red	70.00	14.00
		Never hinged	140.00	
		No gum	25.00	
O120	O10	30c rose red	225.00	100.00
		Never hinged	500.00	
		No gum	90.00	
		Nos. O114-O120 (7)	420.00	177.00

SPECIAL PRINTINGS

Special printings of Official stamps were made in 1875 at the time the other Reprints, Re-issues and Special Printings were printed. They are ungummed.

Although perforated, these stamps were sometimes (but not always) cut apart with scissors. As a result the perforations may be mutilated and the design damaged. Values are for very fine stamps with intact perforations.

All values exist imperforate.

Similar to Type D, without period, 11mm long
AGRICULTURE
Printed by the Continental Bank Note Co.

Overprinted in Block Letters

Thin, hard white paper
Carmine Overprint

1875 — *Perf. 12*

O1S	D	1c yellow	32.50	
a.		"Specimen" error	2,500.	
b.		Horiz. ribbed paper	37.50	
c.		As "b," small dotted "i" in "Specimen"	500.00	
O2S	D	2c yellow	55.00	
a.		"Specimen" error	3,000.	
		Block of 4, one stamp "Sepcimen" error	7,250.	
O3S	D	3c yellow	400.00	
a.		"Specimen" error	19,000.	
O4S	D	6c yellow	400.00	
a.		"Specimen" error	22,500.	
O5S	D	10c yellow	400.00	
a.		"Specimen" error	19,000.	
O6S	D	12c yellow	400.00	
a.		"Sepcimen" error	15,000.	
O7S	D	15c yellow	400.00	
a.		"Specimen" error	12,500.	
O8S	D	24c yellow	400.00	
a.		"Specimen" error	12,500.	
O9S	D	30c yellow	400.00	
a.		"Specimen" error	13,500.	
		Nos. O1S-O9S (9)	2,888.	

EXECUTIVE
Blue Overprint

O10S	D	1c carmine	32.50
a.		Horiz. ribbed paper	40.00
b.		As "a," small dotted "i" in "Specimen"	500.00
O11S	D	2c carmine	55.00
O12S	D	3c carmine	67.50
O13S	D	6c carmine	67.50
O14S	D	10c carmine	67.50
		Nos. O10S-O14S (5)	290.00

INTERIOR
Blue Overprint

O15S	D	1c vermilion	60.00
O16S	D	2c vermilion	140.00
a.		"Sepcimen" error	12,500.
O17S	D	3c vermilion	2,500.
O18S	D	6c vermilion	2,500.
O19S	D	10c vermilion	2,500.
O20S	D	12c vermilion	2,500.
O21S	D	15c vermilion	2,500.
O22S	D	24c vermilion	2,500.
O23S	D	30c vermilion	2,500.
O24S	D	90c vermilion	2,500.
		Nos. O15S-O24S (10)	20,200.

JUSTICE
Blue Overprint

O25S	D	1c purple	32.50
a.		"Sepcimen" error	1,900.
b.		Horiz. ribbed paper	35.00
c.		As "b," small dotted "i" in "Specimen"	500.00
O26S	D	2c purple	55.00
a.		"Sepcimen" error	3,500.
		Block of 4, one stamp "Sepcimen" error	8,250.
O27S	D	3c purple	1,250.
a.		"Specimen" error	11,000.
O28S	D	6c purple	1,250.
O29S	D	10c purple	1,250.
O30S	D	12c purple	1,250.
a.		"Specimen" error	19,000.
O31S	D	15c purple	1,250.
a.		"Specimen" error	25,000.
O32S	D	24c purple	1,250.
a.		"Specimen" error	20,000.
O33S	D	30c purple	1,250.
a.		"Specimen" error	15,000.
O34S	D	90c purple	1,250.
		Nos. O25S-O34S (10)	10,088.

NAVY
Carmine Overprint

O35S	D	1c ultramarine	35.00
a.		"Specimen" error	2,750.
		Block of 4, one stamp "Sepcimen" error	6,250.
b.		Double "Specimen" overprint	1,900.
O36S	D	2c ultramarine	75.00
a.		"Specimen" error	4,500.
		Block of 4, one stamp "Sepcimen" error	10,500.
O37S	D	3c ultramarine	1,750.
O38S	D	6c ultramarine	1,750.
O39S	D	7c ultramarine	550.00
a.		"Specimen" error	10,000.
		Block of 4, one stamp "Specimen" error	30,000.
O40S	D	10c ultramarine	1,750.
a.		"Specimen" error	17,500.
O41S	D	12c ultramarine	1,750.
a.		"Specimen" error	21,000.
O42S	D	15c ultramarine	1,750.
a.		"Specimen" error	16,000.
O43S	D	24c ultramarine	1,750.
a.		"Specimen" error	15,000.
O44S	D	30c ultramarine	1,750.
a.		"Specimen" error	17,500.
O45S	D	90c ultramarine	1,750.
		Nos. O35S-O45S (11)	14,660.

POST OFFICE
Carmine Overprint

O47S	D	1c black	45.00
a.		"Specimen" error	3,250.
b.		Inverted overprint	2,500.
O48S	D	2c black	325.00
a.		"Specimen" error	9,000.
O49S	D	3c black	1,600.
a.		"Specimen" error	37,500.
O50S	D	6c black	1,600.
O51S	D	10c black	1,000.
a.		"Specimen" error	15,000.
O52S	D	12c black	1,600.
O53S	D	15c black	1,600.
a.		"Sepcimen" error	26,000.

O54S	D	24c black	1,600.
a.		"Specimen" error	22,000.
O55S	D	30c black	1,600.
O56S	D	90c black	1,600.
a.		"Specimen" error	25,000.
		Nos. O47S-O56S (10)	12,570.

STATE
Carmine Overprint

O57S	D	1c bluish green	32.50
a.		"Specimen" error	1,900.
		Block of 4, one stamp "Specimen" error	4,500.
b.		Horiz. ribbed paper	35.00
c.		As "b," small dotted "i" in "Specimen"	650.00
d.		Double "Specimen" overprint	3,850.
O58S	D	2c bluish green	90.00
a.		"Specimen" error	2,500.
O59S	D	3c bluish green	140.00
a.		"Specimen" error	7,000.
O60S	D	6c bluish green	350.00
a.		"Specimen" error	12,500.
O61S	D	7c bluish green	140.00
a.		"Specimen" error	9,000.
		Block of 4, one stamp "Specimen" error	21,500.
O62S	D	10c bluish green	550.00
a.		"Specimen" error	27,500.
O63S	D	12c bluish green	550.00
a.		"Specimen" error	19,000.
O64S	D	15c bluish green	600.00
a.		"Specimen" error	25,000.
O65S	D	24c bluish green	600.00
a.		"Specimen" error	27,500.
O66S	D	30c bluish green	600.00
a.		"Specimen" error	27,500.
O67S	D	90c bluish green	600.00
a.		"Specimen" error	27,500.
O68S	D	$2 green & blk	19,000.
O69S	D	$5 green & blk	50,000.
O70S	D	$10 green & blk	110,000.
O71S	D	$20 green & blk	160,000.
		Nos. O57S-O67S (11)	4,253.

TREASURY
Blue Overprint

O72S	D	1c dark brown	80.00
O73S	D	2c dark brown	450.00
O74S	D	3c dark brown	1,600.
O75S	D	6c dark brown	1,600.
O76S	D	7c dark brown	950.00
O77S	D	10c dark brown	1,600.
O78S	D	12c dark brown	1,600.
O79S	D	15c dark brown	1,600.
O80S	D	24c dark brown	1,600.
O81S	D	30c dark brown	1,600.
O82S	D	90c dark brown	1,650.
		Nos. O72S-O82S (11)	14,330.

WAR
Blue Overprint

O83S	D	1c deep rose	35.00
a.		"Specimen" error	3,000.
O84S	D	2c deep rose	125.00
a.		"Specimen" error	3,500.
		Block of 4, one stamp "Specimen" error	9,750.
O85S	D	3c deep rose	1,400.
a.		"Specimen" error	30,000.
O86S	D	6c deep rose	1,400.
a.		"Specimen" error	32,000.
O87S	D	7c deep rose	425.00
a.		"Specimen" error	17,500.
O88S	D	10c deep rose	1,400.
a.		"Specimen" error	27,500.
O89S	D	12c deep rose	1,400.
a.		"Specimen" error	32,000.
O90S	D	15c deep rose	1,400.
a.		"Specimen" error	30,000.
O91S	D	24c deep rose	1,400.
a.		"Specimen" error	30,000.
O92S	D	30c deep rose	1,400.
a.		"Specimen" error	30,000.
O93S	D	90c deep rose	1,400.
a.		"Sepcimen" error	30,000.
		Nos. O83S-O93S (11)	11,785.

EXECUTIVE
Printed by the American Bank Note Co.
Soft Porous Paper

1881 — **Blue Overprint**

O10xS	D	1c violet rose	95.00

NAVY
Carmine Overprint

O35xS	D	1c gray blue	100.00
a.		Double overprint	1,200.

STATE

O57xS	D	1c yellow green	180.00

OFFICIAL POSTAL SAVINGS MAIL

These stamps were used to prepay postage on official correspondence of the Postal Savings Division of the POD. Discontinued Sept. 23, 1914.

O11

Printed by the Bureau of Engraving & Printing

1910-11		Engr.	Wmk. 191	
O121	O11	2c black	17.50	2.00
		Never hinged	40.00	
O122	O11	50c dark green	175.00	60.00
		Never hinged	425.00	
O123	O11	$1 ultramarine	200.00	15.00
		Never hinged	450.00	

		Wmk. 190		
O124	O11	1c dark violet	10.00	2.00
		Never hinged	22.50	
O125	O11	2c black	65.00	7.00
		Never hinged	150.00	
O126	O11	10c carmine	20.00	2.00
		Never hinged	50.00	
Nos. O121-O126 (6)			487.50	88.00

Catalogue values for unused stamps in this section, from this point to the end, are for Never Hinged items.

Catalogue values for used stamps are for regularly used examples, not for examples removed from first day covers.

From No. O127 onward, all official stamps are tagged unless noted.

OFFICIAL MAIL

O12

Engraved
Unwmk.

1983, Jan. 12-1985			Perf. 11	
O127	O12	1c red, blue & black	.25	.25
O128	O12	4c red, blue & black	.25	.25
O129	O12	13c red, blue & black	.50	15.00
O129A	O12	14c red, blue & black	.45	.50
O130	O12	17c red, blue & black	.55	.40
O132	O12	$1 red, blue & black	2.25	1.00
O133	O12	$5 red, blue & black	9.50	20.00
Nos. O127-O133 (7)			13.75	37.40

No. O129A does not have a "c" after the "14."

COIL STAMPS
Perf. 10 Vert.

O135	O12	20c red, blue & black	1.75	2.00
a.		Imperf., pair	1,000.	
O136	O12	22c red, blue & blk ('85)	1.00	2.00
a.		Tagging omitted		

Inscribed: Postal Card Rate D

1985, Feb. 4			Perf. 11	
O138	O12	(14c) red, blue & black	5.00	15.00

Frame line completely around blue design — O13

Inscribed: No. O139, Domestic Letter Rate D; No. O140, Domestic Mail E.

COIL STAMPS
Litho., Engr. (#O139)

1985-88			Perf. 10 Vert.	
O138A	O13	15c red, blue & blk	.50	.50
O138B	O13	20c red, blue & blk	.50	.30
O139	O12	(22c) red, blue & blk	5.25	20.00
O140	O13	(25c) red, blue & blk	.75	2.00

O141	O13	25c red, blue & blk	.65	.50
a.		Imperf., pair	1,000.	—
Nos. O138A-O141 (5)			7.65	23.30

Issue dates: 1985; E, Mar. 22, 1988; 15c, June 11; 20c, May 19; 25c, June 11.
See Nos. O143, O145-O151, O153-O156.

Plates of 400 in four panes of 100.

1989, July 5		Litho.	Perf. 11	
O143	O13	1c red, blue & black	.25	.25

On No. O143, the denomination is shown as "1". See No. O154.

Type of 1985 and

O14

COIL STAMPS

1991		Litho.	Perf. 10 Vert.	
O144	O14	(29c) red, blue & blk	.80	.50
O145	O13	29c red, blue & blk	.70	.30

Plates of 400 in four panes of 100.

1991-93		Litho.	Perf. 11	
O146	O13	4c red, blue & blk	.25	.30
O146A	O13	10c red, blue & blk	.30	.30
O147	O13	19c red, blue & blk	.40	.50
O148	O13	23c red, blue & blk	.50	.30

Perf. 11¼

O151	O13	$1 red, blue & blk	5.00	.75
Nos. O146-O151 (5)			6.45	2.15

Nos. O146A, O151 have a line of microscopic printing below eagle.
See No. O156 for 23c with microscopic text below eagle.
Imperfs of No. O148 are printer's waste.
Issued: No. O146, 4/6; Nos. O147-O148, 5/24; 10c, 10/19/93; No. O151, 9/1993.

COIL STAMPS

Inscribed: No. O152, For U.S. addresses only G.

Perf. 9.8 Vert.

O152	O14	(32c) red, blue & blk	.65	.50
O153	O13	32c red, blue & blk	1.50	.50

Nos. O146A, O151, O153 have a line of microscopic text below the eagle.

1995, May 9		Untagged	Perf. 11.2	
O154	O13	1c red, blue & black	.25	.50

Denomination on No. O154 has a cent sign. See No. O143.

O155	O13	20c red, blue & black	.55	.50
O156	O13	23c red, blue & black	.60	.50

COIL STAMP

1999, Oct. 8			Perf. 9¾ Vert.	
O157	O13	33c red, blue & black	2.25	—

Type of 1985
COIL STAMP

2001, Feb. 27			Perf. 9¾ Vert.	
O158	O13	34c red, blue & black	2.25	.50

Nos. O154-O158 have a line of microscopic text below the eagle.

Type of 1985
COIL STAMP

2002, Aug. 2		Photo.	Perf. 10 Vert.	
O159	O13	37c red, blue & black	.75	.50

Type of 1985
COIL STAMP

2006, Mar. 8			Perf. 10 Vert.	
O160	O13	39c red, blue & black	.80	.80

Type of 1988
LITHOGRAPHED

2006, Sept. 29			Perf. 11¼	
O161	O13	$1 red, blue & black	3.50	1.25

No. O161 has a solid blue background. No. O151 has a background of crosshatched lines.

Type of 1985
COIL STAMP

2007, June 25			Perf. 9¾	
O162	O13	41c red, blue & black	1.00	1.00

Nos. O159-O162 have solid blue backgrounds. Nos. O138A-O158 have a background of crosshatched lines.

Type of 1985
Serpentine Die Cut 11½x10¾

2009, Feb. 24			Untagged	
		Self-Adhesive		
O163	O13	1c red, blue & black	.25	.40

NEWSPAPER STAMPS

For the prepayment of postage on bulk shipments of newspapers and periodicals. From 1875 on, the stamps were affixed to pages of receipt books, sometimes canceled and retained by the post office. Discontinued on July 1, 1898.

Virtually all used stamps of Nos. PR1-PR4 are canceled by blue brush strokes. All are rare. Most used stamps of Nos. PR9-PR32, PR57-PR79 and PR81-PR89 are pen canceled (or uncanceled), with some of Nos. PR9-PR32 also known canceled by a thick blue brush stroke.

Handstamp cancellations on any of these issues are rare and sell for much more than catalogue values which are for pen-canceled examples.

Used values for Nos. PR90-PR125 are for stamps with handstamp cancellations.

Washington — N1

Franklin — N2

Lincoln — N3

Values for Nos. PR1-PR8 are for examples with perforations on all four sides. Examples with natural straight edges sell for somewhat less. Some panes were fully perforated, while others have natural straight edges either at top or bottom affecting five stamps in the pane of ten.

Printed by the National Bank Note Co.
Thin hard paper, without gum
Size of design: 51x95mm

Typographed and Embossed

1865			Unwmk.	Perf. 12	
			Colored Border		
PR1	N1	5c dark blue		750.00	2,000.
a.		5c light blue		1,350.	4,250.
PR2	N2	10c blue green		300.00	2,000.
a.		10c green		300.00	2,000.
b.		Pelure paper		400.00	2,000.
PR3	N3	25c orange red		400.00	2,500.
a.		25c carmine red		425.00	2,500.
b.		Pelure paper		450.00	

Nos. PR1-PR3 used are valued with faults.

White Border
Yellowish paper

PR4	N1	5c light blue		700.00	5,000.
a.		5c dark blue		700.00	—
b.		Pelure paper		800.00	—
Nos. PR1-PR4 (4)				2,150.	

No. PR4 used is valued with faults.

REPRINTS of 1865 ISSUE
Printed by the Continental Bank Note Co. using the original National Bank Note Co. plates
1875
Hard white paper, without gum
5c White Border, 10c and 25c Colored Border

PR5	N1	5c dull blue	225.00
a.		Printed on both sides	5,750.
PR6	N2	10c dark bluish green	250.00
a.		Printed on both sides	4,250.
PR7	N3	25c dark carmine	300.00
		Nos. PR5-PR7 (3)	775.00

The 5c has white border, 10c and 25c have colored borders.

Many fakes exist of Nos. PR1-PR7, some of high quality. Certification is highly recommended.

The Continental Bank Note Co. made another special printing from new plates, which did not have the colored border. These exist imperforate and perforated, but they were not regularly issued. Value, imperf. set $3,250.

Printed by the American Bank Note Co.
Soft porous paper, without gum
1881 — **White Border**

PR8	N1	5c dark blue	650.00

Statue of Freedom — N4

"Justice" — N5   Ceres — N6

"Victory" — N7   Clio — N8

Minerva — N9   Vesta — N10

"Peace" — N11   "Commerce" — N12

Hebe — N13   Indian Maiden — N14

Values for used examples of Nos. PR9-PR113 are for fine-very fine examples for denominations to $3, and fine for denominations of $5 or higher. Used examples of some Scott numbers might not exist without faults.

Printed by the Continental Bank Note Co.
Size of design: 24x35mm

1875, Jan. 1   **Engr.**

PR9	N4	2c black	300.00	40.00
		No gum	120.00	
PR10	N4	3c black	300.00	45.00
		No gum	120.00	
PR11	N4	4c black	300.00	40.00
		No gum	120.00	
PR12	N4	6c black	300.00	45.00
		No gum	120.00	
PR13	N4	8c black	350.00	65.00
		No gum	135.00	
PR14	N4	9c black	600.00	125.00
		No gum	225.00	
PR15	N4	10c black	375.00	60.00
		No gum	135.00	
PR16	N5	12c rose	800.00	100.00
		No gum	325.00	
PR17	N5	24c rose	850.00	125.00
		No gum	350.00	
PR18	N5	36c rose	850.00	150.00
		No gum	350.00	
PR19	N5	48c rose	1,250.	400.00
		No gum	450.00	
PR20	N5	60c rose	1,250.	115.00
		No gum	450.00	
PR21	N5	72c rose	1,500.	375.00
		No gum	550.00	
PR22	N5	84c rose	1,850.	375.00
		No gum	650.00	
PR23	N5	96c rose	2,000.	250.00
		No gum	775.00	
PR24	N6	$1.92 dk brn	1,750.	250.00
		No gum	700.00	
PR25	N7	$3 ver	2,500.	450.00
		No gum	975.00	
PR26	N8	$6 ultra	4,000.	550.00
		No gum	1,600.	
PR27	N9	$9 yel org	4,500.	2,000.
		No gum	1,750.	
PR28	N10	$12 bl grn	4,750.	1,100.
		No gum	1,850.	
PR29	N11	$24 dk gray vio	4,750.	1,200.
		No gum	1,850.	
PR30	N12	$36 brn rose	5,000.	1,400.
		No gum	2,000.	
PR31	N13	$48 red brn	7,000.	1,600.
		No gum	2,600.	
PR32	N14	$60 violet	6,500.	1,750.
		No gum	2,400.	

SPECIAL PRINTING of 1875 ISSUE
Printed by the Continental Bank Note Co.
Hard white paper, without gum

1875

PR33	N4	2c gray black	650.00
a.		Horiz. ribbed paper	500.00
PR34	N4	3c gray black	650.00
a.		Horiz. ribbed paper	500.00
PR35	N4	4c gray black	700.00
		Horiz. ribbed paper	1,000.
PR36	N4	6c gray black	900.00
PR37	N4	8c gray black	975.00
PR38	N4	9c gray black	1,050.
PR39	N4	10c gray black	1,400.
PR40	N5	12c pale rose	1,500.
PR41	N5	24c pale rose	2,100.
PR42	N5	36c pale rose	2,800.
PR43	N5	48c pale rose	3,750.
PR44	N5	60c pale rose	4,750.
PR45	N5	72c pale rose	4,500.
PR46	N5	84c pale rose	5,250.
PR47	N5	96c pale rose	8,500.
PR48	N6	$1.92 dk brn	20,000.
PR49	N7	$3 vermilion	45,000.
PR50	N8	$6 ultra	80,000.
PR51	N9	$9 yellow org	350,000.
PR52	N10	$12 blue green	175,000.
PR53	N11	$24 dk gray vio	500,000.
PR54	N12	$36 brn rose	250,000.
PR55	N13	$48 red brown	—
PR56	N14	$60 violet	—

Nos. PR50 and PR52 are valued in the grade of fine.

Although four examples of No. PR51 were sold, only one is currently documented.

No. PR54 is valued in the grade of fine. Although two stamps were sold, only one is currently documented.

All values of this issue, Nos. PR33 to PR56, exist imperforate but were not regularly issued thus. Value, set $60,000.

Printed by the American Bank Note Co.
Soft porous paper

1879

PR57	N4	2c black	75.00	15.00
		No gum	30.00	
PR58	N4	3c black	85.00	20.00
		No gum	35.00	
PR59	N4	4c black	85.00	20.00
		No gum	35.00	
a.		Double paper	—	
PR60	N4	6c black	125.00	35.00
		No gum	50.00	
PR61	N4	8c black	135.00	35.00
		No gum	55.00	
PR62	N4	10c black	135.00	35.00
		No gum	55.00	
PR63	N5	12c red	500.00	125.00
		No gum	210.00	
PR64	N5	24c red	500.00	125.00
		No gum	210.00	
PR65	N5	36c red	1,000.	325.00
		No gum	475.00	
PR66	N5	48c red	1,000.	300.00
		No gum	450.00	
PR67	N5	60c red	1,250.	275.00
		No gum	550.00	
a.		Imperf., pair	4,000.	
PR68	N5	72c red	1,500.	425.00
		No gum	700.00	
PR69	N5	84c red	1,250.	350.00
		No gum	575.00	
PR70	N5	96c red	1,200.	275.00
		No gum	525.00	
PR71	N6	$1.92 pale brn	550.00	175.00
		No gum	225.00	
PR72	N7	$3 red ver	625.00	200.00
		No gum	250.00	
PR73	N8	$6 blue	1,050.	300.00
		No gum	400.00	
PR74	N9	$9 orange	800.00	225.00
		No gum	325.00	
PR75	N10	$12 yel grn	850.00	250.00
		No gum	325.00	
PR76	N11	$24 dk vio	800.00	300.00
		No gum	300.00	
PR77	N12	$36 Indian red	850.00	350.00
		No gum	350.00	
PR78	N13	$48 yel brn	900.00	450.00
		No gum	350.00	
PR79	N14	$60 purple	850.00	400.00
		No gum	350.00	
		Nos. PR57-PR70 (14)	8,840.	2,360.

See the Scott U.S. Specialized Catalogue Die and Plate Proof section for imperforates.

SPECIAL PRINTING of 1879 ISSUE
Printed by the American Bank Note Co.
Without gum

1883

PR80	N4	2c intense black	1,700.

REGULAR ISSUE
With gum

1885

PR81	N4	1c black, *July 1, 1885*	95.00	12.50
		Never hinged	225.00	
		No gum	42.50	
PR82	N5	12c carmine	200.00	30.00
		Never hinged	450.00	
		No gum	85.00	
PR83	N5	24c carmine	225.00	32.50
		Never hinged	500.00	
		No gum	95.00	
PR84	N5	36c carmine	350.00	57.50
		Never hinged	800.00	
		No gum	145.00	
PR85	N5	48c carmine	425.00	75.00
		Never hinged	975.00	
		No gum	180.00	
PR86	N5	60c carmine	550.00	100.00
		No gum	240.00	
PR87	N5	72c carmine	550.00	110.00
		No gum	240.00	
PR88	N5	84c carmine	900.00	250.00
		No gum	350.00	
PR89	N5	96c carmine	750.00	190.00
		Never hinged	1,750.	
		No gum	300.00	
		Nos. PR81-PR89 (9)	4,045.	857.50

See the Scott U.S. Specialized Catalogue Die and Plate Proof section for imperforates.

Printed by the Bureau of Engraving and Printing

1894
Soft wove paper, with pale, whitish gum

PR90	N4	1c intense blk	400.00	5,000.
		Never hinged	900.00	
		No gum	160.00	

PR91	N4	2c intense blk	450.00	
		Never hinged	1,075.	
		No gum	190.00	
PR92	N4	4c intense blk	550.00	13,500.
		Never hinged	1,275.	
		No gum	210.00	
PR93	N4	6c intense blk	4,500.	
		Never hinged	11,500.	
		No gum	1,900.	
PR94	N4	10c intense blk	1,250.	
		Never hinged	2,250.	
		No gum	525.00	
PR95	N5	12c pink	2,600.	4,500.
		No gum	1,100.	
PR96	N5	24c pink	3,750.	8,000.
		No gum	1,850.	
PR97	N5	36c pink	50,000.	
PR98	N5	60c pink	40,000.	16,000.
PR99	N5	96c pink	50,000.	
PR100	N7	$3 scarlet	50,000.	
PR101	N8	$6 pale blue	50,000.	—
		No gum	25,000.	

Nos. PR90, PR95-PR98 used are valued with fine centering and small faults.

No. PR97 unused is valued in the grade of very good to fine. No. PR98 unused is valued in the grade of fine. Nos. PR99-PR100 unused are valued in the grade of fine-very fine.

Statue of Freedom N15   "Justice" N16

"Victory" — N17   Clio — N18

Vesta — N19   "Peace" — N20

"Commerce" N21   Indian Maiden N22

Size of designs: 1c-50c, 21x34mm; $2-$100, 24x35mm

1895, Feb. 1

PR102	N15	1c black	230.00	125.00
		Never hinged	500.00	
		No gum	90.00	
PR103	N15	2c black	230.00	125.00
		Never hinged	500.00	
		No gum	90.00	
PR104	N15	5c black	300.00	300.00
		Never hinged	650.00	
		No gum	125.00	
PR105	N15	10c black	600.00	400.00
		Never hinged	1,300.	
		No gum	240.00	
PR106	N16	25c car	750.00	500.00
		Never hinged	1,650.	
		No gum	300.00	
PR107	N16	50c car	2,750.	800.00
		Never hinged	6,250.	
		No gum	875.00	

PR108	N17	$2 scarlet	2,250.	1,100.
	Never hinged		5,000.	
	No gum		850.00	
PR109	N18	$5 ultra	2,100.	1,750.
	No gum		800.00	
PR110	N19	$10 green	2,500.	2,000.
	No gum		900.00	
PR111	N20	$20 slate	3,250.	2,500.
	No gum		1,200.	
PR112	N21	$50 dull rose	2,750.	950.00
	Never hinged		6,250.	
	No gum		1,050.	
PR113	N22	$100 purple	3,500.	7,000.
	No gum		1,400.	
	Nos. PR102-PR113 (12)		21,210.	17,550.

1895-97   Wmk. 191

PR114	N15	1c black	8.00	25.00
	Never hinged		20.00	
	No gum		2.75	
PR115	N15	2c black	8.00	25.00
	Never hinged		20.00	
	No gum		2.75	
PR116	N15	5c black	13.00	40.00
	Never hinged		27.50	
	No gum		4.25	
PR117	N15	10c black	13.00	25.00
	Never hinged		27.50	
	No gum		4.25	
PR118	N16	25c carmine	20.00	65.00
	Never hinged		45.00	
	No gum		7.00	
PR119	N16	50c carmine	25.00	75.00
	Never hinged		55.00	
	No gum		8.50	
PR120	N17	$2 scarlet	30.00	110.00
	Never hinged		75.00	
	No gum		10.00	
PR121	N18	$5 dark bl	40.00	175.00
	Never hinged		100.00	
	No gum		13.50	
a.	$5 light blue		200.00	500.00
	Never hinged		500.00	
	No gum		67.50	
PR122	N19	$10 green	42.50	175.00
	Never hinged		105.00	
	No gum		14.00	
PR123	N20	$20 slate	45.00	200.00
	Never hinged		110.00	
	No gum		15.00	
PR124	N21	$50 dull rose	75.00	300.00
	Never hinged		170.00	
	No gum		27.50	
PR125	N22	$100 purple	65.00	275.00
	Never hinged		150.00	
	No gum		22.50	
	Nos. PR114-PR125 (12)		384.50	1,490.
	Nos. PR114-PR125, never hinged		905.00	

In 1899 the Government sold 26,989 sets of these stamps, but, as the stock of high values was not sufficient to make up the required number, an additional printing was made of the $5, $10, $20, $50 and $100. These are virtually indistinguishable from earlier printings.

For overprints, see Nos. R159-R160.

PARCEL POST STAMPS

Issued for the prepayment of postage on parcel post packages only.

Post Office Clerk — PP1

City Carrier PP2

Railway Postal Clerk — PP3

Rural Carrier PP4

Mail Train — PP5

Steamship and Mail Tender PP6

Automobile Service PP7

Airplane Carrying Mail — PP8

Manufacturing — PP9

Dairying PP10

Harvesting PP11

Fruit Growing PP12

1913   Wmk. 190   Engr.   Perf. 12

Q1	PP1	1c carmine rose	5.00	1.75
	Never hinged		12.50	
Q2	PP2	2c carmine rose	5.25	1.40
	Never hinged		12.50	
a.	2c lake			1,750.
b.	2c carmine lake			350.00

No. Q2a is valued in the grade of fine to very fine.

Q3	PP3	3c carmine	9.50	6.50
	Never hinged		26.00	
Q4	PP4	4c carmine rose	30.00	3.50
	Never hinged		85.00	
Q5	PP5	5c carmine rose	25.00	2.50
	Never hinged		67.50	
Q6	PP6	10c carmine rose	42.50	3.50
	Never hinged		95.00	
Q7	PP7	15c carmine rose	62.50	15.00
	Never hinged		175.00	
Q8	PP8	20c carmine rose	120.00	30.00
	Never hinged		280.00	
Q9	PP9	25c carmine rose	57.50	8.50
	Never hinged		160.00	
Q10	PP10	50c carmine rose	235.00	50.00
	Never hinged		600.00	
Q11	PP11	75c carmine rose	85.00	40.00
	Never hinged		200.00	
Q12	PP12	$1 carmine rose	280.00	45.00
	Never hinged		650.00	
	Nos. Q1-Q12 (12)		957.25	207.65
	Nos. Q1-Q12, never hinged		2,468.	

PARCEL POST POSTAGE DUE STAMPS

For affixing by a postal clerk to any parcel post package, to denote the amount to be collected from the addressee because of insufficient prepayment of postage.

PPD1

1913   Wmk. 190   Engr.   Perf. 12

JQ1	PPD1	1c dark green	8.50	4.25
	Never hinged		21.00	
JQ2	PPD1	2c dark green	65.00	18.00
	Never hinged		160.00	
JQ3	PPD1	5c dark green	10.00	5.00
	Never hinged		25.00	
JQ4	PPD1	10c dark green	120.00	45.00
	Never hinged		300.00	
JQ5	PPD1	25c dark green	75.00	4.75
	Never hinged		190.00	
	Nos. JQ1-JQ5 (5)		278.50	77.00
	Nos. JQ1-JQ5, never hinged		696.00	

SPECIAL HANDLING STAMPS

For use on fourth-class mail to secure the same expeditious handling accorded to first-class mail matter.

PP13

1925-28   Engr.   Unwmk.   Perf. 11

QE1	PP13	10c yel grn ('28)	2.00	1.00
	Never hinged		4.25	
QE2	PP13	15c yel grn ('28)	2.25	.90
	Never hinged		4.75	
QE3	PP13	20c yel grn ('28)	3.75	1.50
	Never hinged		7.75	
QE4	PP13	25c dp grn ('25)	20.00	3.75
	Never hinged		37.50	
a.	yel grn ('28)		16.50	22.50
	Never hinged		32.50	
	Nos. QE1-QE4 (4)		28.00	7.15
	Nos. QE1-QE4, never hinged		54.25	

COMPUTER VENDED POSTAGE

CVP1

CVP2

1989, Aug. 23   Tagged   *Guillotined* Self-Adhesive
Washington, DC, Machine 82
Date Other Than First Day

CVP1	CVP1	25c First Class	6.00	—
a.	First day dated, serial Nos. 12501-15500		5.00	—
b.	First day dated, serial Nos. 00001-12500		5.00	—
c.	First day dated, over No. 27500		—	—
CVP2	CVP1	$1 Third Class	—	—
a.	First day dated, serial Nos. 24501-27500		—	—
b.	First day dated, over No. 27500		—	—

CVP3	CVP2	$1.69 Parcel Post	—	—
a.	First day dated, serial Nos. 21501-24500		—	—
b.	First day dated, over No. 27500		—	—
CVP4	CVP2	$2.40 Priority Mail	—	—
a.	First day dated, serial Nos. 18501-21500		—	—
b.	Priority Mail, with bar code (CVP2)		100.00	
c.	First day dated, over No. 27500		—	—
CVP5	CVP1	$8.75 Express Mail	—	—
a.	First day dated, serial Nos. 15501-18500		—	—
b.	First day dated, over No. 27500		—	—

Washington, DC, Machine 83
Date Other Than First Day

CVP6	CVP1	25c First Class	6.00	—
a.	First day dated, serial Nos. 12501-15500		5.00	—
b.	First day dated, serial Nos. 00001-12500		5.00	—
c.	First day dated, over No. 27500		—	—
CVP7	CVP1	$1 Third Class	—	—
a.	First day dated, serial Nos. 24501-27500		—	—
b.	First day dated, over No. 27500		—	—
CVP8	CVP2	$1.69 Parcel Post	—	—
a.	First day dated, serial Nos. 21501-24500		—	—
b.	First day dated, over No. 27500		—	—
CVP9	CVP1	$2.40 Priority Mail	—	—
a.	First day dated, serial Nos. 18501-21500		—	—
b.	First day dated, over No. 27500		—	—

A Priority Mail $3.25 value also exists unuses. A Priority Mail stamp exists on cover with error date 11/17/90 exists, and an unused stamp with error date 11/18/90 exists.

c.	Priority Mail, with bar code (CVP2)		100.00	

Error date 11/18/90 exists.

CVP10	CVP1	$8.75 Express Mail	—	—
a.	First day dated, serial Nos. 15501-18500		—	—
b.	First day dated, over No. 27500		—	—

Error date 11/17/90 exists.

1989, Sept. 1
Kensington, MD, Machine 82
Date Other Than First Day

CVP11	CVP1	25c First Class	6.00	—
a.	First day dated, serial Nos. 12501-15500		5.00	—
b.	First day dated, serial Nos. 00001-12500		5.00	—
c.	First day dated, over No. 27500		—	—
CVP12	CVP1	$1 Third Class	—	—
a.	First day dated, serial Nos. 24501-27500		—	—
b.	First day dated, over No. 27500		—	—
CVP13	CVP2	$1.69 Parcel Post	—	—
a.	First day dated, serial Nos. 21501-24500		—	—
b.	First day dated, over No. 27500		—	—
CVP14	CVP1	$2.40 Priority Mail	—	—
a.	First day dated, serial Nos. 18501-21500		—	—
b.	First day dated, over No. 27500		—	—
c.	Priority Mail, with bar code (CVP2)		100.00	
CVP15	CVP1	$8.75 Express Mail	—	—
a.	First day dated, serial Nos. 15501-18500		—	—
b.	First day dated, over No. 27500		—	—

Kensington, MD, Machine 83
Date Other Than First Day

CVP16	CVP1	25c First Class	6.00	—
a.	First day dated, serial Nos. 12501-15500		5.00	—
b.	First day dated, serial Nos. 00001-12500		5.00	—
c.	First day dated, over No. 27500		—	—
CVP17	CVP1	$1 Third Class	—	—
a.	First day dated, serial Nos. 24501-27500		—	—
b.	First day dated, over No. 27500		—	—
CVP18	CVP2	$1.69 Parcel Post	—	12.50
a.	First day dated, serial Nos. 21501-24500		—	—
b.	First day dated, over No. 27500		—	—
CVP19	CVP1	$2.40 Priority Mail	—	—
a.	First day dated, serial Nos. 18501-21500		—	—
b.	First day dated, over No. 27500		—	—
c.	Priority Mail, with bar code (CVP2)		100.00	

CVP20 CVP1 $8.75 Express Mail — —
 a. First day dated, serial Nos. 15501-18500 — —
 b. First day dated, over No. 27500 — —

1989, Nov.

Washington, DC, Machine 11

CVP21 CVP1 25c First Class *150.00*
 a. First Class, with bar code (CVP2)

Stamps in CVP1 design with $1.10 denominations exist (certified first class) dated 11/20/89. Value, unused, $650. A 45c denomination exists unused (dated 11/22/89) on cover to Europe and on Certificate of Mailing.

CVP22 CVP1 $1 Third Class *500.00*
CVP23 CVP2 $1.69 Parcel Post *500.00*
CVP24 CVP1 $2.40 Priority Mail *500.00*
 a. Priority Mail , with bar code (CVP2) —
CVP25 CVP1 $8.75 Express Mail *500.00*

Washington, DC, Machine 12

CVP26 CVP1 25c First Class *200.00*

No. CVP26, dated 12/13/89 is known on cover. $1.10 Certified First Class stamps dated 11/20/89 exist on covers.

CVP27 CVP1 $1 Third Class *600.00*

A $1.40 Third Class stamp of type CVP2, dated Dec. 1 is known on a Dec. 2 cover.

CVP28 CVP1 $1.65 Parcel Post *600.00*
CVP29 CVP1 $2.40 Priority Mail *600.00*
 a. Priority Mail , with bar code (CVP2) —
CVP30 CVP1 $8.75 Express Mail *600.00*

An $8.50 Express Mail stamp, dated Dec. 2, exists on cover.

CVP3 — Type 1   CVP3 — Type II

1992, Aug. 20 Engr. Perf. 10 Horiz.
Coil Stamp

CVP31 CVP3 29c red & blue, type I .75 .25
 c. 32c Type II ('94) 1.00 .40

No. CVP31 was available in all denominations from 1c to $99.99.
The listing is for the first class rate. Other denominations, se-tenant combinations, or "errors" are not listed.
Type II denomination has large sans-serif numerals preceded by an asterisk measuring 2mm across. No. CVP31 has small numerals with serifs preceded by an asterisk 1½mm across.

CVP4

1994, Feb. 19 Photo. Perf. 9.9 Vert.
CVP32 CVP4 29c dark red & dark blue .70 .35

No. CVP32 was available in all denominations from 19c to $99.99.
The listing is for the first class rate at time of issue. Other denominations, se-tenant combinations, or "errors" will not be listed.

1996, Jan. 26
CVP33 CVP4 32c brt red & blue, "1996" below design .70 .25

Letters in "USA" on No. CVP33 are thicker than on No. CVP32. Numerous other design differences exist in the moire pattern and in the bunting. No. CVP33 has "1996" in the lower left corner; No. CVP32 has no date.
For No. CVP33, the 32c value has been listed because it was the first class rate in effect at the time the stamp was issued.

CVP5

1999 Tagged Die Cut
Self-Adhesive
CVP34 CVP5 33c black *50.00*
 a. "Priority Mail" under encryption at LL —
 b. "Express Mail" under encryption at LL —

No. CVP34 was available from 15 NCR Automated Postal Center machines located in central Florida. Machines could produce values in any denomination required. The backing paper is taller and wider than the stamp.
Sales of No. CVP34 were discontinued in 2000 or 2001.

CVP6

1999, May 7 Tagged Die Cut
Self-Adhesive
Size: 77½x39mm
Microprinting Above Red Orange Line
CVP35 CVP6 33c blk & red org, control numbers only at LL, round corners *20.00* —
 a. "Priority Mail" at LL, square corners *150.00* —
 b. "Priority Mail AS" and text string at LL, square corners *150.00*

No Microprinting Above Red Orange Line
CVP36 CVP6 33c blk & red org, control numbers only at LL, round corners *10.00* —
 a. "Priority Mail" at LL, square corners *125.00* —
 b. "Priority Mail AS" and text string at LL, square corners *125.00*

Size: 73½x42mm
CVP37 CVP6 33c blk & pink, control numbers only at LL *3.75* —
 a. "Priority Mail" at LL *5.00* —
 b. "Priority Mail AS" and text string at LL *5.00*

Nos. CVP35-CVP37 were available from 18 IBM Neopost machines located in central Florida, and at least one machine in the Washington, DC area (Merrifield, VA Automated Postal Center). The backing paper is taller than the stamp. Any denomination could be printed up to $99.99.

Simplypostage.com — CVP8

Serpentine Die Cut 8 at Right
2001 Self-Adhesive
Eagle and Stars Background
CVP39 CVP8 34c blk, blue & org, *2001* —
CVP40 CVP8 34c blk, blue & org, with control number at UL, *2001* —

Flag Background
CVP41 CVP8 34c blk, blue & org, with control number at UL, *2001* —

CVP42 CVP8 34c blk, blue & org, with control number at LL, *2001* — *20.00*

Large Flag Design

The item shown was produced by Neopost. It was found that the large flag image hampered the barcode from being scanned. It is believed no examples were actually sold to the public. Five panes of four are believed to exist.

Neopostage.com — CVP9

Serpentine Die Cut 8¾ at Right
2002, June Self-Adhesive
CVP43 CVP9 21c blk, blue & org —
 a. Booklet pane of 10 —
CVP44 CVP9 23c blk, blue & org —
 a. Booklet pane of 10 *90.00*
CVP45 CVP9 34c blk, blue & org —
 a. Booklet pane of 10 —
CVP46 CVP9 37c blk, blue & org —
 a. Booklet pane of 10 *60.00*
CVP47 CVP9 50c blk, blue & org —
 a. Booklet pane of 10 *180.00*
CVP47B CVP9 57c blk, blue & org —
 a. Booklet pane of 10 —
CVP48 CVP9 60c blk, blue & org —
 a. Booklet pane of 10 *160.00*
CVP49 CVP9 70c blk, blue & org —
 a. Booklet pane of 10 *180.00*
CVP50 CVP9 80c blk, blue & org —
 a. Booklet pane of 10 *180.00*
CVP51 CVP9 $3.50 blk, blue & org —
 a. Booklet pane of 1 —
 b. Booklet pane of 2 —
 c. Booklet pane of 5 —
 d. Booklet pane of 10 —
CVP52 CVP9 $3.85 blk, blue & org —
 a. Booklet pane of 1 —
 b. Booklet pane of 2 —
 c. Booklet pane of 5 —
 d. Booklet pane of 10 —
CVP52E CVP9 $12.45 blk, blue & org —
 a. Booklet pane of 1 —
CVP53 CVP9 $13.65 blk, blue & org —
 a. Booklet pane of 1 —
 b. Booklet pane of 2 —
 c. Booklet pane of 5 —
 d. Booklet pane of 10 —

Nos. CVP43-CVP53 were printed only with the stated values.
Denominations of 34c, 57c, $3.50 and perhaps others exist with an ICNOVA kiosk location designation. These were produced during preissue testing at a location not publicly accessible and are not considered to be valid postage. Stamps from the ICNOVA location have much smaller 2-D bar code squares. The denominations listed above come from other publicly accessible kiosk locations from June 20, 2002, forward. Official sales of these stamps began on June 20, 2002, or later for some denominations.
The 21c, 34c, 57c, $3.50 and $12.45 denominations were only sold from June 21 to June 29, 2002. They are all scarce, and some

are rare. The 37c, $3.85 and $13.65 denominations were not sold until June 30, 2002, when the rate change took effect.
While the name on Nos. CVP39-CVP42 reads simplypostage.com and the name on Nos. CVP43-CVP53 reads neopostage.com, both were products of Neopost.
Issued: Nos. CVP43-CVP49, CVP51-CVP53, 6/2002; No. CVP50, 7/2002.

Earliest documented use: Nos. CVP43, CVP47, CVP51-CVP52, not known used; Nos. CVP44, CVP46, CVP48-CVP49, CVP53, 6/30; No. CVP45, 6/21; No. CVP50, 7/3.

CVP10

IBM Pitney Bowes — CVP11

2004, Apr. 14 Die Cut
Self-Adhesive
CVP54 CVP10 37c black & pink *5.75*
 a. "First Class Mail" under encryption at LL *2.50*
 b. "Priority Mail" under encryption at LL *2.50* —
 c. "Parcel Post" under encryption at LL *2.50* —
 d. "International" under encryption at LL *2.50* —
CVP55 CVP11 37c black, "US Postage" under encryption at LL *2.50* —
 a. "First Class Mail" under encryption at LL —
 b. "Priority Mail" under encryption at LL —
 c. "Parcel Post" under encryption at LL —
 d. "International" under encryption at LL —

Nos. CVP54-CVP55 could be printed in any denomination up to $99.99. Catalogue values for Nos. CVP54-CVP54d and CVP55 are for stamps with low denominations. Stamps with denominations appropriate to the service described are valued correspondingly higher.

CVP12

IBM Pitney Bowes — CVP13

2004, Nov. 19   *Die Cut*
Self-Adhesive
Serial Number Under Encryption
APC

CVP56	CVP12	37c black	2.50	.45
CVP57	CVP13	37c black &		
		pink	1.00	.45

Nos. CVP56-CVP57 could be printed in any denomination. No. CVP56 could be printed with three different rate inscriptions under the denomination. No. CVP57 could be printed with 18 different rate inscriptions and/or service indicators under the denomination, and with at least 27 different rate inscriptions and or/service indicators under the denomination on stamps with a four-digit code after the zip code.

Blank Under Denomination
"IM" and Numbers Under
Encryption

CVP58	CVP13	60c black &		
		pink	3.00	.50
CVP59	CVP13	80c black &		
		pink	3.75	.50

"PM" and Numbers Under
Encryption

CVP60	CVP13	$3.85 black &		
		pink	15.00	.50

"EM" and Numbers Under
Encryption

CVP61	CVP13	$13.65 black &		
		pink	42.50	1.00

"IB" and Numbers Under
Encryption

CVP62	CVP13	$1 black &		
		pink	4.00	.25

Nos. CVP58-CVP61 could only be printed in denominations listed. No. CVP62 could be printed in any denomination above 99c. As of May 12, 2008, it was possible to create stamps with "IB" and numbers under encryption in any denomination. The computer software was later changed to once again only permit stamps of certain denominations to be created with "IB" and numbers under the encryption.

IBM Pitney Bowes Type of 2004
2006   **Self-Adhesive**   *Die Cut*
Blank Under Denomination
"IM" and Numbers Under
Encryption

CVP63	CVP13	48c black &		
		pink	1.50	.40
CVP64	CVP13	63c black &		
		pink	1.75	.50
CVP65	CVP13	84c black &		
		pink	2.25	.50

"PM" and Numbers Under
Encryption

CVP66	CVP13	$4.05 black &		
		pink	11.00	.50
CVP66A	CVP13	$8.10 black &		
		pink	30.00	1.00

"EM" and Numbers Under
Encryption

CVP67	CVP13	$14.40 black &		
		pink	32.50	1.00

Nos. CVP63-CVP67 could only be printed in denominations listed.

IBM Pitney Bowes — CVP14

2006   **Self-Adhesive**   *Die Cut*
No Inscription Under Encryption
Serial Number to Right of "APC"
"Ship To:" Above Destination City

CVP69	CVP14	39c black	2.25	.25

Nos. CVP69 could be printed in any denomination, with 14 different rate inscriptions and/or service indicators under the denomination on stamps having "Ship To:" at the left and no code below the weight, and at least 29 different rate inscriptions and/or service indicators under the denomination on stamps having a four-digit code at the right that is even with the words "Ship To:" and below the weight.

IBM Pitney Bowes Type of 2004
2006(?)-07   **Self-Adhesive**   *Die Cut*
Blank Under Denomination
"IB" and Numbers Under
Encryption

CVP70	CVP13	39c black &		
		pink	1.00	.50
CVP71	CVP13	41c black &		
		pink	1.75	.50
CVP72	CVP13	69c black &		
		pink	2.50	.70

"IM" and Numbers Under
Encryption

CVP73	CVP13	61c black &		
		pink	2.25	.50
CVP74	CVP13	90c black &		
		pink	3.50	.95

Nos. CVP70-CVP74 could only be printed in the denominations listed.

Nos. CVP71-CVP74 issued May, 2007. No. CVP70 was issued before the May rate change. As of May 12, 2008, it was possible to create stamps with "IB" and numbers under encryption in any denomination. The computer software was later changed to once again only permit stamps of certain denominations to be created with "IB" and numbers under the encryption. No. CVP70 was available for sale from Nov. 2006 to May 13, 2007. Nos. CVP71-CVP72 were available for sale from May 14, 2007 to May 11, 2008.

Pitney Bowes With Eagle at
Right — CVP15

2006, Dec.   **Self-Adhesive**   *Die Cut*

CVP75	CVP15	41c black & pink, no inscription below sold date	—	—
a.		"Mailed From Zip Code …" on bottom line	—	—
b.		"Postcard" on bottom line	—	—
c.		"First-Class Mail" on bottom line	—	—
d.		"First-Class Mail Intl" on bottom line	—	—
e.		"Priority" on bottom line	—	—
f.		"Priority Envelope" on bottom line	—	—
g.		"Priority Box" on bottom line	—	—
h.		"Express Mail" on bottom line	—	—
i.		"Express Envelope" on bottom line	—	—
j.		"Parcel Post" on bottom line	—	—

No. CVP75 was put into service at large companies and universities in Dec. 2006, with the majority of the machines not being available to the general public. Information about this stamp was not made available until 2007. Other rates and inscriptions might be available.

Nos. CVP75a could be printed in any denomination. Nos. CVP75b-CVP75f could be printed only in pre-programmed denominations based on the current rates for the service, or in any denominations at or above the minimum rates for the service. Values are for stamps with low denominations. Stamps with "First Class," and "Priority - Irregular Shape" on the bottom lines have been reported to exist but have not been seen by the editors. No. CVP75 inscribed "First Class Tube" may theoretically exist in the CVP15 design as it does exist in the CVP22a design, but it has not been seen by the editors Inscriptions generated by the software may vary from machine to machine depending on when the software was installed.

Two distinctly different colors of phosphor stripes on labels used in Mail & Go machines are known, with many Mail & Go adhesives appearing in both versions.

IBM Pitney Bowes Type of 2004
2008, May   **Self-Adhesive**   *Die Cut*
Blank Under Denomination
"IM" and Numbers Under
Encryption

CVP76	CVP13	94c black &		
		pink	3.00	.60
CVP77	CVP13	$1.20 black &		
		pink	3.75	1.25

Nos. CVP76-CVP77 could only be printed in the denominations listed.

IBM — CVP16

Die Cut With Rounded Corners
2008, June 4   **Self-Adhesive**

CVP78	CVP16	42c black & pink	4.25	—

Die Cut With Perpendicular Corners

CVP79	CVP16	42c black & pink	4.25	—
a.		Pane of 6	—	
b.		Pane of 7	—	
c.		Pane of 8	—	
d.		Pane of 9	—	
e.		Pane of 10	—	

Nos. CVP78-CVP79 were made available during a pilot study to evaluate a new IBM kiosk at Schaumburg, IL. No. CVP78 could be printed in any denomination from 1c to $25. Because each kiosk transaction was limited to $100, No. CVP79e could only be bought with stamps denominated from 1c to $10. Individual panes with 6, 7, 8, 9 or 10 stamps could be purchased as long as the total face value of the pane did not exceed $100. Stamps denominated from $10.01 to $16.66 could only be purchased in panes containing fewer than 10 stamps. Stamps denominated from $16.67 to $25 could only be purchased as a single stamp.

No. CVP79e exists with the vertical pink tagging strip along the left side of the stamps.

IBM Pitney Bowes Type of 2004
2009   **Self-Adhesive**   *Die Cut*
Blank Under Denomination
"IM" and Numbers Under
Encryption

CVP80	CVP13	98c black &		
		pink	2.00	.60
CVP81	CVP13	$1.24 black &		
		pink	2.50	1.25

Nos. CVP80-CVP81 could only be printed in denominations listed.

IBM (Statue of Liberty) — CVP17

Illustration reduced.

Die Cut With Rounded Corners
2009, June 5   **Self-Adhesive**

CVP82	CVP17	44c black & pink	7.50	—

Die Cut With Perpendicular Corners

CVP83	CVP17	44c black & pink	7.50	—
a.		Pane of 6 (1c to $16.66)	—	
b.		Pane of 7 (1c to $14.28)	—	
c.		Pane of 8 (1c to $12.50)	—	
d.		Pane of 9 (1c to $11.11)	—	
e.		Pane of 10 (1c to $10)	—	

No. CVP82 could be printed in any denomination from 1c to $25. Nos. CVP82-CVP83 were made available during a pilot study to evaluate a new IBM kiosk at Schaumburg, IL. The machine study at Schaumburg was scheduled to end on July 31, 2009. No. CVP82 was created for purchases of one to five individual stamps or any extra stamps beyond multiples of 10 ending in numerals 1 to 5. Nos. CVP83a-CVP83e were created when stamps purchased ended in numerals 6 to 0.

Flag
CVP18

Serpentine Die Cut 13¼x12½
2011, Oct. 18   **Self-Adhesive**

CVP84	CVP18	44c multi, date sold only on bottom line	—	—
a.		Date sold and "Postcard" on bottom line	—	—
b.		Date sold and "First-Class" on bottom line	—	—

No. CVP84 was issued in panes of 10. It was made available at Mail & Go postal stations in Super Target stores in the Dallas, TX area. Panes could be printed in any denomination from 29c to $9.99. Serpentine die cut 9 examples of No. CVP84 with dates earlier than Oct. 18 were produced at Pitney Bowes facilities. This serpentine die cut 9 sticker stock is not known to have been sent out for use in machines that were available for use by the general public. No. CVP84 was made available in 2013 with dozens of images other than the flag shown. These optional images are for various holidays and events, as well as social causes, such as support for breast cancer, education and recycling. One image, for bridal showers, has been made available in two different types.

Thermal prints generated by vending machines with too little electrically generated heat tend to fade very quickly.

APC With Vertical Coding at Right of
Date — CVP19

Die Cut With Rounded Corners
2012, Apr. 12   **Self-Adhesive**

CVP85	CVP19	45c black & pink	1.50	—
a.		Die cut with perpendicular corners, colored bar at left, "Fold Here" at center, 100x38mm	—	—

No. CVP85 has "APC" reading upwards at right. No. CVP78 has "IBM" reading upwards at right. No. CVP85 was available during a nationwide test of machines, and could be printed in any denomination from 1c to $99.99. Only one to six examples of No. CVP85 could be purchased and printed at one time.

No. CVP85a was produced on label stock normally used for No. CVP87 when machines ran out of label stock to produce orders for No. CVP85.

APC With Vertical Coding At Left of Date — CVP19a

Die Cut With Rounded Corners
2012   **Self-Adhesive**

CVP85B CVP19a $2.05 black & pink   —

APC Variable Vignette Stamp — CVP20

Die Cut With Rounded Corners
2012, Apr. 12   **Self-Adhesive**

CVP86 CVP20 (45c) black & pink 2.50
a.   Die cut with perpendicular corners, colored bar at left, "Fold Here" at center, 100x38mm   4.00

No. CVP86 was available during a nationwide test of machines, and could be printed only as "Forever" stamps. The vignette portion of the stamp at left could be chosen from a gallery of six images (Mr. Zip, Heart, Flowers, Flag, Eagle, and Balloons and "Celebrate!", which is depicted). Values are for any vignette, or for any other vignette that may be programmed into the machine at a later date. Each vignette design could be purchased in a quantities ranging from 1 stamp to 100 stamps, but because a $1 minimum purchase was required, at least three examples of the first stamp chosen had to be purchased. A maximum of ten stamps could be printed on a sheet. Sales of stamps that are not in multiples of 10 were printed in strips, smaller-sized sheets containing an even number of stamps, or in sheets having one label inscribed "This Block Is Not Valid Postage" when the sheet contained an odd number of stamps.

No. CVP86a was produced on label stock normally used for No. CVP87 when machines ran out of stock to produce orders for No. CVP86.

Examples of No. CVP86 without a printed image at left are the result of machines having their image-printing capability shut off so preprinted label stock for producing No. CVP88 could be substituted for the blank label stock used for Nos. CVP85 and CVP86. See footnote under No. CVP86 for information about examples of No. CVP86 with date of purchase inscriptions to right of "Forever."

APC With Vertical Coding to Right of Date — CVP21

Die Cut With Perpendicular Corners
2012, Apr. 12   **Self-Adhesive**

CVP87 CVP21 45c black & pink   —

No. CVP87 was available during a nationwide test of machines, and could be printed in any denomination from 1c to $99.99. Stamps

can be inscribed with a variety of different service inscriptions.

APC With Vertical Coding to Left of Date — CVP21a

Die Cut With Perpendicular Corners
2012   **Self-Adhesive**

CVP87A CVP21a 45c black & pink   —

Labels of type CVP21a with postage indicia inscribed FCM LETTER below the denomination have only a bar code and the Zip code of the destination at the bottom third rather than a USPS TRACKING NUMBER. Labels for which a Certified Mail fee has been paid have a CERTIFIED MAIL bar code. Express Mail labels have POSTAL USE ONLY form at the bottom.

On Nov. 7, 2013, the USPS had distributed and had begun requiring the use of "signalling label" stock with a clear phosphor stripe. The clear stripe appears positioned vertically along the left margin of the labels. Labels with pink stripes along the right margin continued to be used until stocks were exhausted or labels with pre-printed vignettes were issued for use in some machines on Apr. 1, 2014 (CVP90-CVP91).

APC With Vertical Coding at Right of Date And Clear Phosphor Stripe Along Left Margin — CVP21b

Die Cut With Rounded Corners
2013, Nov. 7   **Self-Adhesive**

CVP87B CVP21b 46c black   5.00

The Scheduled Delivery and Expected Delivery inscriptions, date and times replaced "THIS BLOCK IS NOT VALID FOR POSTAGE" on labels normally found adjacent to Nos, CVP87B and CVP92A when sold for other than Priority Mail.

Mailbox CVP22

Die Cut With Rounded Corners
2013, Oct. 31   **Self-Adhesive**

CVP88 CVP22 (45c) multicolored 3.50

The mailbox vignette is preprinted on No. CVP88. This preprinted stock was placed in machines in November 2012 and is supposed to be removed from machines on December 31, 2012. The earliest known date of sale is Nov. 10, 2012.

Examples of No. CVP88 with the mailbox design covered by images used for Nos. CVP85 and CVP86 were the result of machines having their blank label stock replaced with the pre-printed label stock while

the machine's image-printing capability was not shut off to accommodate the preprinted stock.

On No. CVP88, the number of the month and last two digits of the year in which the stamp was purchased, separated by an asterisk, appear to the right of "Forever." Some examples of No. CVP86 might have the date included if the programming for this was done and the blank label stock was still in the machine.

Labels inscribed "This Block Is Not Valid For Postage" differ from similar labels created with No. CVP86. Various sizes of "Void" overprints on these labels exist.

USPS Emblem — CVP22a

Die Cut With Rounded Corners
2013, Nov. 2   **Self-Adhesive**

CVP88A CVP22a (46c) black & pink   3.50   —
b.   Die cut with perpendicular corners, colored bar at left, "Fold Here" at center, 100x38mm   8.50   —

This design was first placed in a few machines in the Washington, DC and Merrifield, VA area on Oct. 31, 2013. Stamps vended with encoded dates prior to Nov. 7, 2013 were test stamps. On Nov. 6, 2013, the USPS declared the test to be successful and the image was released for general use as a fall-back design.

No. CVP88Ab was produced on stock normally used to produce No. CVP87 when machines ran out of stock to produce orders for No. CVP88A. The earliest known sale date of No. CVP88Ab is Nov. 2, 2013.

Examples of CVP88A lacking the eagle vignette could be made if the machine had blank label stock in the feeder but was set to print on pre-printed labels such as No. CVP89. When the machine has pre-printed labels (starting with No. CVP89) in the feeder and is set to print on blank labels, the Eagle vignette will print on the labels.

Pitney Bowes With Eagle at Left — CVP22b

Pitney Bowes Without Eagle — CVP22c

Die Cut With Perpendicular Corners
2011, Oct. 18   **Self-Adhesive**

CVP88C CVP22b 46c black & pink, no inscription below sold date 5.00 —
d.   CVP22c 46c With eagle emblem omitted   —   —
e.   "Mailed From Zip Code ..." on bottom line   —   —
f.   "Postcard" on bottom line   —   —
g.   "First-Class Mail" on bottom line   —   —
h.   "First-Class Mail Intl" on bottom line   —   —
i.   "Priority Mail" on bottom line   —   —
j.   "Priority Envelope" on bottom line   —   —
k.   "Priority Box" on bottom line   —   —
l.   "Priority Tube" on bottom line   —   —
m.   "Priority - Irregular Shape" on bottom line   —   —
n.   "Express Mail" on bottom line   —   —

No. CVP88C was made available at Mail & Go postal stations in Super Target stores in the Dallas, TX area, and presumably could be printed in any denomination.

In 2013, twelve Mail & Go machines vending No. CVP88C and the holiday and social cause designs noted under No. CVP84 were installed and operated at thirteen Rite Aid drug stores in central California along the Highway 1 corridor. The machines were installed by the

LePages Company (a USPS-licensed manufacturer and wholesaler of USPS-brand mailing supplies). They were placed under the jurisdiction of the Oakland, CA region of the USPS throughout most of 2014-15. Postmasters in the towns supported the machines officially with Priority Mail containers, postal labels and daily mail collection. The locations were listed by the USPS in its online Internet database of self-service post office locations. The machines appear to have been removed between Oct. 2015 and Jan. 2016.

The stamps vended by these machines were officially approved by the USPS and are no different than stamps sold from the same models of machines installed at colleges and universities across the nation. Locations of about 40 other privately supported Mail & Go machines have been recorded. These other machines are installed and operated by Pitney Bowes employees who manage mail rooms the company operates under contracts. At those locations, the mail room staff takes the daily mail to the local post office, and there is no USPS logistical support.

The USPS regulation classify Mail & Go machines as "third party kiosks." No. CVP88Cd is an error that Pitney Bowes technicians could not explain. It appeared for a short time on a machine in Illinois and at the U.S. Department of Defense Medical HQ facility mailroom in Annandale, VA.

Reindeer — CVP23

Die Cut With Rounded Corners
2013

CVP89 CVP23 (46c) multicolored 3.50 2.00

The reindeer vignette is preprinted on No. CVP89. This preprinted stock was placed in machines in November 2013 and was supposed to be removed from machines sometime after Dec. 25, 2013.

USPS Emblem With Clear Phosphor Stripe Along Left Margin — CVP23a

Die Cut With Rounded Corners
2014, Jan.   **Self-Adhesive**

CVP89A CVP23a (46c) black   3.00   —

Examples of CVP89A lacking the eagle vignette could be made if the machine had blank label stock in the feeder but was set to print on pre-printed labels such as No. CVP89. When the machine has pre-printed labels (starting with No. CVP89) in the feeder and is set to print on blank labels, the Eagle vignette will print on the labels.

APC With Scheduled Delivery — CVP23b

Die Cut With Perpendicular Corners
2014, Jan.   **Self-Adhesive**

CVP89B CVP23b black & pink   —   —

No. CVP89B is generated when the mailer answers a machine-system prompt with a "no" answer when asked if the full-length label (Type CVP21) will fit on the mailer's item. This is vended only when pre-printed labels are installed in the machine or the small-label printer is defective.

APC With Expected Delivery — CVP23c

Die Cut With Perpendicular Corners
2014, Jan.   **Self-Adhesive**
CVP89C CVP23c   black & pink   — —

No. CVP89C is generated when the mailer answers a machine-system prompt with a "no" answer when asked if the full-length label (Type CVP21) will fit on the mailer's item. This is vended only when pre-printed labels are installed in the machine or the small-label printer is defective.

Spiderman — CVP24

Die Cut With Rounded Corners
2014, Apr. 1   **Self-Adhesive**
CVP90 CVP24 (49c) multicolored   2.50 2.00

The Spiderman vignette is preprinted on No. CVP90. This preprinted stock was placed only in machines that are able to sell ATM panes of 18 and labels.

Flag
CVP25

Die Cut With Rounded Corners
2014, Apr. 1
Self-Adhesive
CVP91 CVP25 (49c) multicolored   1.50 1.25
a.   "FOREVER" missing

The flag vignette is preprinted on No. CVP91.

Rudolph, the Red-Nosed
Reindeer — CVP26

Die Cut With Rounded Corners
2014, Nov. 6   **Self-Adhesive**
CVP92 CVP26 (49c) multicolored   2.50 1.75

The Rudolph vignette is preprinted on No. CVP92.

From Nov. 14, 2014, Automated Postal Centers (APC) vending machines were renamed by the USPS to be Self Service Kiosks (SSK), and the machines were changed to issue stamp inscribed "SSK" rather than "APC."

SSK
With
Vertical
Coding
at Left
of Date
CVP27

Die Cut With Rounded Corners
2014, Nov. 14   **Self-Adhesive**
CVP93 CVP27 1c black & pink   — —

No. CVP93 was available at machines that had not yet retired the pink-striped labels. It exists inscribed for all USPS self-service products (i.e., First Class and Priority Mail categories). Adjacent se-tenant labels exist inscribed "THIS BLOCK IS NOT VALID FOR POSTAGE," "Expected Delivery," and "Scheduled Delivery" with accompanying delivery dates. See illustration above No. CVP87B.

It was not intended by the USPS that indicia inscribed with SSK would be printed on pink-striped labels. The design was shifted to appear farther to the right, to insure the bar code would remain uncompromised and at a safe distance from the clear phosphor stripe on the newer labels. Almost all examples of this issue will have SSK appearing within the pink stripe.

SSK With Vertical Coding to Left of
Date — CVP28

Die Cut With Perpendicular Corners
2014, Nov. 14   **Self-Adhesive**
CVP94 CVP28 49c black & pink   — —

Like No. CVP87A, inscribed with various mail service inscritpions or with blackened square in place of letters such as "F," above, when generated for standard letter mail or standard parcel post and other non-priority mail.

SSK With Blank Area at Right of "Fold
Here"

Die Cut With Perpendicular Corners
2014, Nov. 14   **Self-Adhesive**
CVP95 CVP29 black & pink   — —

SSK With "Expected Delivery" at Right
of "Fold Here"

Die Cut With Perpendicular Corners
2014, Nov. 14   **Self-Adhesive**
CVP96 CVP30 black & pink   — —

SSK With "Scheduled Delivery" at
Right of "Fold Here" — CVP31

Die Cut With Perpendicular Corners
2014, Nov. 14   **Self-Adhesive**
CVP97 CVP31 black & pink   — —

Charlie Brown Looking in
Mailbox — CVP32

Die Cut With Rounded Corners
2015, Oct. 29   **Self-Adhesive**
CVP98 CVP32 (49c) multicolored   — —

The Charlie Brown vignette is preprinted on No. CVP98. Issue date is earliest recorded sale date. Post offices were authorized to place the labels in machines at the close of business on Oct. 20, which many did prior to the SSK system-wide date change that occurs daily prior to midnight.

---

mPOS — CVP33

Die Cut With Rounded Corners
2015   **Self-Adhesive**
CVP99 CVP33   black

No. CVP99 is generated by a mobile hand-held point-of-sale vending machine with integrated thermal postage printer and embedded credit/debit card acceptance processor. Possible denominations are limited to the postage prices applicable to each available pre-printed type of Priority and Express Mail flat rate envelopes and packages (rate determined by scanning the bar code on the package the customer needs). While this indicia is intended to be affixed to mail matter at the time it is presented, postage can be generated and sold in quantities to take away for later use. Labels are generated from vertical coils with blank labels.

Wreath in Window — CVP34

Die Cut With Rounded Corners
2016, Oct. 27   **Self-Adhesive**
CVP100 CVP34 (47c) multi   — —

The wreath in window vignette is preprinted on No. CVP100. Issue date is earliest recorded sale date.

———

PERSONAL COMPUTER POSTAGE

———

Personal computer postage, approved by the US Postal Service, was created by subscribing to Stamps.com, an Internet website. Customers ordered self-adhesive labels showing vignettes, but lacking any franking value. The franking value indicia of the stamps could be printed at the customer's convenience at any computer with an Internet connection, using the customer's access codes. Any postage printed would be charged against the customer's account.

Neopost

CVPA1

2000   *Serpentine Die Cut 8*
Self-Adhesive
1CVP1 CVPA1 33c black, yellow   — —
                            & pink

Stamps.com

Flag and Star
— CVPA1a

Serpentine Die Cut 5¾ at Left
2002, July
**"Stamps.com" in Lower Case
Letters
Identification Code Below Zip Code
No Mail Class Inscribed**
1CVP2 CVPA1a 37c black,
                 blue &
                 orange   7.00 3.00

**Identification Code Above Zip Code
Inscribed "US Postage" only**
1CVP2A CVPA1a 37c black,
                  blue &
                  orange   4.00 3.00
a.   "First Class" below "US
      Postage"   2.75 2.00
b.   "Priority" below "US
      Postage"   8.25 2.50
c.   "Express" below "US
      Postage"   25.00 5.00
d.   "Media Mail" below "US
      Postage"   7.75 2.50
e.   "Parcel Post" below
      "US Postage"   7.75 2.50
f.   "Bound Printed Matter"
      below "US Postage"   7.75 2.50
g.   "BPM" below "US Post-
      age"   7.75 2.50
See Nos. 1CVP9, 1CVP21.

No. 1CVP2 apparently could be printed in denominations up to and including 37c. The 37c denomination comes with "FIRST-CLASS" between the Zip code and the identification code.

Later versions of the Stamps.com software allow any denomination to be printed, as well as additional or different mail-class inscriptions, on any basic stamp except for No. 1CVP2.

Values for Nos. 1CVP2A and 1CVP3-1CVP42 are for items appropriate to the service described. Stamps with denominations far lower than those appropriate to the service are valued correspondingly lower.

The software changes allow Nos. 1CVP2A and 1CVP3-1CVP37 to be printed with the mail-class inscriptions described for Nos. 1CVP38f-1CVP38p.

Later software changes allow Nos. 1CVP2A, 1CVP3-1CVP42 and 1CVP51-1CVP58 to be printed with mail-class inscriptions "Library Mail," "Intl. First Class," "Intl Priority," "Intl Express," and "M-Bag" with any denomination.

Love — CVPA2

2002 *Serpentine Die Cut 5¾ at Left*
1CVP3 CVPA2 37c black, blue
                & orange   4.00 4.00
a.   "First Class" below "US
      Postage"   2.75 2.00
b.   "Priority" below "US Post-
      age"   8.25 2.50
c.   "Express" below "US Post-
      age"   25.00 5.00
d.   "Media Mail" below "US
      Postage"   7.75 2.50
e.   "Parcel Post" below "US
      Postage"   7.75 2.50
f.   "Bound Printed Matter"
      below "US Postage"   7.75 2.50
g.   "BPM" below "US Post-
      age"   7.75 2.50

Statue of
Liberty and
Flag — CVPA3

Liberty Bell and
Flag — CVPA4

Eagle and
Flag — CVPA5

George
Washington and
Flag — CVPA6

Capitol Building
and
Flag — CVPA7

Serpentine Die Cut 5¾ at Left
2003, June

1CVP4 CVPA3 37c black, blue
& orange 3.50 2.00
- a. "First Class" below "US Postage" .. 3.25 2.00
- b. "Priority" below "US Postage" ... 8.00 1.00
- c. "Express" below "US Postage" ... 25.00 3.00
- d. "Media Mail" below "US Postage" .. 7.50 1.00
- e. "Parcel Post" below "US Postage" . 7.50 1.00
- f. "Bound Printed Matter" below "US Postage" . 7.50 1.00
- g. "BPM" below "US Postage" ... 7.50 1.00

1CVP5 CVPA4 37c black, blue
& orange 3.50 2.00
- a. "First Class" below "US Postage" .. 3.25 2.00
- b. "Priority" below "US Postage" ... 8.00 1.00
- c. "Express" below "US Postage" ... 25.00 3.00
- d. "Media Mail" below "US Postage" .. 7.50 1.00
- e. "Parcel Post" below "US Postage" . 7.50 1.00
- f. "Bound Printed Matter" below "US Postage" . 7.50 1.00
- g. "BPM" below "US Postage" ... 7.50 1.00

1CVP6 CVPA5 37c black, blue
& orange 3.50 2.00
- a. "First Class" below "US Postage" .. 3.25 2.00
- b. "Priority" below "US Postage" ... 8.00 1.00
- c. "Express" below "US Postage" ... 25.00 3.00
- d. "Media Mail" below "US Postage" .. 7.50 1.00

- e. "Parcel Post" below "US Postage" . 7.50 1.00
- f. "Bound Printed Matter" below "US Postage" . 7.50 1.00
- g. "BPM" below "US Postage" ... 7.50 1.00

1CVP7 CVPA6 37c black, blue & orange .. 3.50 2.00
- a. "First Class" below "US Postage" .. 3.25 .25
- b. "Priority" below "US Postage" ... 8.00 1.00
- c. "Express" below "US Postage" ... 25.00 3.00
- d. "Media Mail" below "US Postage" .. 7.50 1.00
- e. "Parcel Post" below "US Postage" . 7.50 1.00
- f. "Bound Printed Matter" below "US Postage" . 7.50 1.00
- g. "BPM" below "US Postage" ... 7.50 1.00

1CVP8 CVPA7 37c black, blue & orange .. 3.50 2.00
- a. "First Class" below "US Postage" .. 3.25 .45
- b. "Priority" below "US Postage" ... 8.00 1.00
- c. "Express" below "US Postage" ... 25.00 3.00
- d. "Media Mail" below "US Postage" .. 7.50 1.00
- e. "Parcel Post" below "US Postage" . 7.50 1.00
- f. "Bound Printed Matter" below "US Postage" . 7.50 1.00
- g. "BPM" below "US Postage" ... 7.50 1.00
- h. Strip of 5, #1CVP4-1CVP8 .... 17.50

Flag and Star Type of 2002 Redrawn With "Stamps.com" in Upper Case Letters
Serpentine Die Cut 5¾ at Left
2003, June
Identification Code Above Zip Code

1CVP9 CVPA1a 37c black, blue & orange, "US Postage" only .. 3.00 1.50
- a. "First Class" below "US Postage" .. 2.00 .45
- b. "Priority" below "US Postage" ... 8.00 1.00
- c. "Express" below "US Postage" ... 25.00 3.00
- d. "Media Mail" below "US Postage" .. 7.50 1.00
- e. "Parcel Post" below "US Postage" . 7.50 1.00
- f. "Bound Printed Matter" below "US Postage" . 7.50 1.00
- g. "BPM" below "US Postage" ... 7.50 1.00

Snowman
CVPA8

Snowflakes
CVPA9

Holly
CVPA10

Dove
CVPA11

Gingerbread
Man and Candy
CVPA12

Serpentine Die Cut 4½ at Left
2003, Dec.

1CVP10 CVPA8 37c black, blue & orange .. 3.00 1.50
- a. "First Class" below "US Postage" .. 2.00 1.00
- b. "Priority" below "US Postage" ... 8.00 1.00
- c. "Express" below "US Postage" ... 25.00 3.00
- d. "Media Mail" below "US Postage" .. 7.50 1.00
- e. "Parcel Post" below "US Postage" . 7.50 1.00
- f. "Bound Printed Matter" below "US Postage" . 7.50 1.00
- g. "BPM" below "US Postage" ... 7.50 1.00

1CVP11 CVPA9 37c black, blue & orange .. 3.00 1.50
- a. "First Class" below "US Postage" .. 2.00 1.00
- b. "Priority" below "US Postage" ... 8.00 1.00
- c. "Express" below "US Postage" ... 25.00 3.00
- d. "Media Mail" below "US Postage" .. 7.50 1.00
- e. "Parcel Post" below "US Postage" . 7.50 1.00
- f. "Bound Printed Matter" below "US Postage" . 7.50 1.00
- g. "BPM" below "US Postage" ... 7.50 1.00

1CVP12 CVPA10 37c black, blue & orange .. 3.00 1.50
- a. "First Class" below "US Postage" .. 2.00 1.00
- b. "Priority" below "US Postage" ... 8.00 1.00
- c. "Express" below "US Postage" ... 25.00 3.00
- d. "Media Mail" below "US Postage" .. 7.50 1.00
- e. "Parcel Post" below "US Postage" . 7.50 1.00
- f. "Bound Printed Matter" below "US Postage" . 7.50 1.00
- g. "BPM" below "US Postage" ... 7.50 1.00

1CVP13 CVPA11 37c black, blue & orange .. 3.00 1.50
- a. "First Class" below "US Postage" .. 2.00 1.00
- b. "Priority" below "US Postage" ... 8.00 1.00
- c. "Express" below "US Postage" ... 25.00 3.00
- d. "Media Mail" below "US Postage" .. 7.50 1.00
- e. "Parcel Post" below "US Postage" . 7.50 1.00
- f. "Bound Printed Matter" below "US Postage" . 7.50 1.00
- g. "BPM" below "US Postage" ... 7.50 1.00

1CVP14 CVPA12 37c black, blue & orange .. 3.00 1.50
- a. "First Class" below "US Postage" .. 2.00 1.00
- b. "Priority" below "US Postage" ... 8.00 1.00
- c. "Express" below "US Postage" ... 25.00 3.00
- d. "Media Mail" below "US Postage" .. 7.50 1.00
- e. "Parcel Post" below "US Postage" . 7.50 1.00
- f. "Bound Printed Matter" below "US Postage" . 7.50 1.00
- g. "BPM" below "US Postage" ... 7.50 1.00
- h. Strip of 5, #1CVP10-1CVP14 ...... 12.50

Mailbox
CVPA13

Serpentine Die Cut 6½ at Left
2004, Mar.

1CVP15 CVPA13 37c black, blue & orange .. 25.00 15.00
- a. "First Class" below "US Postage" .. 25.00 15.00
- b. "Priority" below "US Postage" ... — —
- c. "Express" below "US Postage" ... — —
- d. "Media Mail" below "US Postage" .. — —
- e. "Parcel Post" below "US Postage" . — —
- f. "Bound Printed Matter" below "US Postage" . — —
- g. "BPM" below "US Postage" ... — —

Blank sheets of No. 1CVP15 were sent free of charge to those who responded to special Stamps.com promotions which offered a fixed amount of free postage as an enticement to new subscribers. The franking portion of the stamps could only be applied after subscribing.

George
Washington
CVPA14

Thomas
Jefferson
CVPA15

Abraham
Lincoln
CVPA16

Theodore
Roosevelt
CVPA17

John F.
Kennedy
CVPA18

Serpentine Die Cut 6½ at Left
2004, Apr.

1CVP16 CVPA14 37c black,
               blue &
               orange   2.00   1.00
a.   "First Class" below "US
        Postage"   1.10   .75
b.   "Priority" below "US
        Postage"   5.00   2.50
c.   "Express" below "US
        Postage"   20.00   5.00
d.   "Media Mail" below "US
        Postage"   5.00   2.50
e.   "Parcel Post" below "US
        Postage"   5.00   2.50
f.   "Bound Printed Matter"
        below "US Postage"   5.00   2.50
g.   "BPM" below "US Post-
        age"   5.00   2.50

1CVP17 CVPA15 37c black,
               blue &
               orange   2.00   1.00
a.   "First Class" below "US
        Postage"   1.10   .75
b.   "Priority" below "US
        Postage"   5.00   2.50
c.   "Express" below "US
        Postage"   20.00   5.00
d.   "Media Mail" below "US
        Postage"   5.00   2.50
e.   "Parcel Post" below "US
        Postage"   5.00   2.50
f.   "Bound Printed Matter"
        below "US Postage"   5.00   2.50
g.   "BPM" below "US Post-
        age"   5.00   2.50

1CVP18 CVPA16 37c black,
               blue &
               orange   2.00   1.00
a.   "First Class" below "US
        Postage"   1.10   .75
b.   "Priority" below "US
        Postage"   5.00   2.50
c.   "Express" below "US
        Postage"   20.00   5.00
d.   "Media Mail" below "US
        Postage"   5.00   2.50
e.   "Parcel Post" below "US
        Postage"   5.00   2.50
f.   "Bound Printed Matter"
        below "US Postage"   5.00   2.50
g.   "BPM" below "US Post-
        age"   5.00   2.50

1CVP19 CVPA17 37c black,
               blue &
               orange   2.00   1.00
a.   "First Class" below "US
        Postage"   1.10   .75
b.   "Priority" below "US
        Postage"   5.00   2.50
c.   "Express" below "US
        Postage"   20.00   5.00
d.   "Media Mail" below "US
        Postage"   5.00   2.50
e.   "Parcel Post" below "US
        Postage"   5.00   2.50
f.   "Bound Printed Matter"
        below "US Postage"   5.00   2.50
g.   "BPM" below "US Post-
        age"   5.00   2.50

1CVP20 CVPA18 37c black,
               blue &
               orange   2.00   1.00
a.   "First Class" below "US
        Postage"   1.10   .75
b.   "Priority" below "US
        Postage"   5.00   2.50
c.   "Express" below "US
        Postage"   20.00   5.00
d.   "Media Mail" below "US
        Postage"   5.00   2.50
e.   "Parcel Post" below "US
        Postage"   5.00   2.50
f.   "Bound Printed Matter"
        below "US Postage"   5.00   2.50
g.   "BPM" below "US Post-
        age"   5.00   2.50
h.   Horiz. strip of 5,
        #1CVP16-1CVP20   10.00

Flag and Star Type of 2002 Redrawn
With Orange Stars and Text at Left
Serpentine Die Cut 6½ at Left
2004, Apr.
"Stamps.com" in Upper Case
Letters
Identification Code Above Zip Code

1CVP21 CVPA1a 37c black,
               blue &
               orange   2.00   1.00
a.   "First Class" below "US
        Postage"   1.35   .75
b.   "Priority" below "US
        Postage"   6.00   2.50
c.   "Express" below "US
        Postage"   22.50   5.00
d.   "Media Mail" below "US
        Postage"   6.00   2.50
e.   "Parcel Post" below "US
        Postage"   6.00   2.50

---

f.   "Bound Printed Matter"
        below "US Postage"   6.00   2.50
g.   "BPM" below "US Post-
        age"   6.00   2.50

Bicycling
CVPA19

Running
CVPA20

Swimming
CVPA21

Boxing
CVPA22

Equestrian
CVPA23

Basketball
CVPA24

Judo
CVPA25

Soccer
CVPA26

Gymnastics
CVPA27

Tennis
CVPA28

Serpentine Die Cut 6½ at Left
2004, Apr.

1CVP22 CVPA19 37c black,
               blue &
               orange   3.00   2.00
a.   "First Class" below "US
        Postage"   2.50   1.50
b.   "Priority" below "US
        Postage"   8.00   1.00
c.   "Express" below "US
        Postage"   25.00   3.00
d.   "Media Mail" below "US
        Postage"   7.50   1.00
e.   "Parcel Post" below "US
        Postage"   7.50   1.00
f.   "Bound Printed Matter"
        below "US Postage"   7.50   1.00
g.   "BPM" below "US Post-
        age"   7.50   1.00

1CVP23 CVPA20 37c black,
               blue &
               orange   3.00   2.00
a.   "First Class" below "US
        Postage"   2.50   1.50
b.   "Priority" below "US
        Postage"   8.00   1.00
c.   "Express" below "US
        Postage"   25.00   3.00
d.   "Media Mail" below "US
        Postage"   7.50   1.00
e.   "Parcel Post" below "US
        Postage"   7.50   1.00
f.   "Bound Printed Matter"
        below "US Postage"   7.50   1.00
g.   "BPM" below "US Post-
        age"   7.50   1.00

1CVP24 CVPA21 37c black,
               blue &
               orange   3.00   2.00
a.   "First Class" below "US
        Postage"   2.50   1.50
b.   "Priority" below "US
        Postage"   8.00   1.00
c.   "Express" below "US
        Postage"   25.00   3.00
d.   "Media Mail" below "US
        Postage"   7.50   1.00
e.   "Parcel Post" below "US
        Postage"   7.50   1.00
f.   "Bound Printed Matter"
        below "US Postage"   7.50   1.00
g.   "BPM" below "US Post-
        age"   7.50   1.00

1CVP25 CVPA22 37c black,
               blue &
               orange   3.00   2.00
a.   "First Class" below "US
        Postage"   2.50   1.50
b.   "Priority" below "US
        Postage"   8.00   1.00
c.   "Express" below "US
        Postage"   25.00   3.00
d.   "Media Mail" below "US
        Postage"   7.50   1.00
e.   "Parcel Post" below "US
        Postage"   7.50   1.00
f.   "Bound Printed Matter"
        below "US Postage"   7.50   1.00
g.   "BPM" below "US Post-
        age"   7.50   1.00

1CVP26 CVPA23 37c black,
               blue &
               orange   3.00   2.00
a.   "First Class" below "US
        Postage"   2.50   1.50
b.   "Priority" below "US
        Postage"   8.00   1.00
c.   "Express" below "US
        Postage"   25.00   3.00

---

f.   "Bound Printed Matter"
        below "US Postage"   6.00   2.50
g.   "BPM" below "US Post-
        age"   6.00   2.50

d.   "Media Mail" below "US
        Postage"   7.50   1.00
e.   "Parcel Post" below "US
        Postage"   7.50   1.00
f.   "Bound Printed Matter"
        below "US Postage"   7.50   1.00
g.   "BPM" below "US Post-
        age"   7.50   1.00
h.   Horiz. strip of 5,
        #1CVP22-1CVP26   15.00

1CVP27 CVPA24 37c black,
               blue &
               orange   3.00   2.00
a.   "First Class" below "US
        Postage"   2.50   1.50
b.   "Priority" below "US
        Postage"   8.00   1.00
c.   "Express" below "US
        Postage"   25.00   3.00
d.   "Media Mail" below "US
        Postage"   7.50   1.00
e.   "Parcel Post" below "US
        Postage"   7.50   1.00
f.   "Bound Printed Matter"
        below "US Postage"   7.50   1.00
g.   "BPM" below "US Post-
        age"   7.50   1.00

1CVP28 CVPA25 37c black,
               blue &
               orange   3.00   2.00
a.   "First Class" below "US
        Postage"   2.50   1.50
b.   "Priority" below "US
        Postage"   8.00   1.00
c.   "Express" below "US
        Postage"   25.00   3.00
d.   "Media Mail" below "US
        Postage"   7.50   1.00
e.   "Parcel Post" below "US
        Postage"   7.50   1.00
f.   "Bound Printed Matter"
        below "US Postage"   7.50   1.00
g.   "BPM" below "US Post-
        age"   7.50   1.00

1CVP29 CVPA26 37c black,
               blue &
               orange   3.00   2.00
a.   "First Class" below "US
        Postage"   2.50   1.50
b.   "Priority" below "US
        Postage"   8.00   1.00
c.   "Express" below "US
        Postage"   25.00   3.00
d.   "Media Mail" below "US
        Postage"   7.50   1.00
e.   "Parcel Post" below "US
        Postage"   7.50   1.00
f.   "Bound Printed Matter"
        below "US Postage"   7.50   1.00
g.   "BPM" below "US Post-
        age"   7.50   1.00

1CVP30 CVPA27 37c black,
               blue &
               orange   3.00   2.00
a.   "First Class" below "US
        Postage"   2.50   1.50
b.   "Priority" below "US
        Postage"   8.00   1.00
c.   "Express" below "US
        Postage"   25.00   3.00
d.   "Media Mail" below "US
        Postage"   7.50   1.00
e.   "Parcel Post" below "US
        Postage"   7.50   1.00
f.   "Bound Printed Matter"
        below "US Postage"   7.50   1.00
g.   "BPM" below "US Post-
        age"   7.50   1.00

1CVP31 CVPA28 37c black,
               blue &
               orange   3.00   2.00
a.   "First Class" below "US
        Postage"   2.50   1.50
b.   "Priority" below "US
        Postage"   8.00   1.00
c.   "Express" below "US
        Postage"   25.00   3.00
d.   "Media Mail" below "US
        Postage"   7.50   1.00
e.   "Parcel Post" below "US
        Postage"   7.50   1.00
f.   "Bound Printed Matter"
        below "US Postage"   7.50   1.00
g.   "BPM" below "US Post-
        age"   7.50   1.00
h.   Horiz. strip of 5,
        #1CVP27-1CVP31   15.00

The item pictured above was produced by Stamps.com for a special promotional mailing of its own and was not
made available unused to customers.

Leaning Tower of Pisa — CVPA29

Sphinx and Pyramids CVPA30

Sydney Opera House CVPA31

Mayan Pyramid CVPA32

Asian Temple CVPA33

Serpentine Die Cut 6½ at Left
2004, July

1CVP32	CVPA29 37c black, blue & orange	3.00	2.00
a.	"First Class" below "US Postage"	2.30	1.50
b.	"Priority" below "US Postage"	8.00	1.00
c.	"Express" below "US Postage"	25.00	3.00
d.	"Media Mail" below "US Postage"	7.50	1.00
e.	"Parcel Post" below "US Postage"	7.50	1.00
f.	"Bound Printed Matter" below "US Postage"	7.50	1.00
g.	"BPM" below "US Postage"	7.50	1.00
1CVP33	CVPA30 37c black, blue & orange	3.00	2.00
a.	"First Class" below "US Postage"	2.30	1.50
b.	"Priority" below "US Postage"	8.00	1.00
c.	"Express" below "US Postage"	25.00	3.00
d.	"Media Mail" below "US Postage"	7.50	1.00
e.	"Parcel Post" below "US Postage"	7.50	1.00
f.	"Bound Printed Matter" below "US Postage"	7.50	1.00
g.	"BPM" below "US Postage"	7.50	1.00
1CVP34	CVPA31 37c black, blue & orange	3.00	2.00
a.	"First Class" below "US Postage"	2.30	1.50
b.	"Priority" below "US Postage"	8.00	1.00

c.	"Express" below "US Postage"	25.00	3.00
d.	"Media Mail" below "US Postage"	7.50	1.00
e.	"Parcel Post" below "US Postage"	7.50	1.00
f.	"Bound Printed Matter" below "US Postage"	7.50	1.00
g.	"BPM" below "US Postage"	7.50	1.00
1CVP35	CVPA32 37c black, blue & orange	3.00	2.00
a.	"First Class" below "US Postage"	2.30	1.50
b.	"Priority" below "US Postage"	8.00	1.00
c.	"Express" below "US Postage"	25.00	3.00
d.	"Media Mail" below "US Postage"	7.50	1.00
e.	"Parcel Post" below "US Postage"	7.50	1.00
f.	"Bound Printed Matter" below "US Postage"	7.50	1.00
g.	"BPM" below "US Postage"	7.50	1.00
1CVP36	CVPA33 37c black, blue & orange	3.00	2.00
a.	"First Class" below "US Postage"	2.30	1.50
b.	"Priority" below "US Postage"	8.00	1.00
c.	"Express" below "US Postage"	25.00	3.00
d.	"Media Mail" below "US Postage"	7.50	1.00
e.	"Parcel Post" below "US Postage"	7.50	1.00
f.	"Bound Printed Matter" below "US Postage"	7.50	1.00
g.	"BPM" below "US Postage"	7.50	1.00
h.	Strip of 5, #1CVP32-1CVP36	15.00	

Computer and Letters CVPA34

Serpentine Die Cut 6½ at Left
2005, Mar.

1CVP37	CVPA34 37c black, blue & orange	25.00	15.00
a.	"First Class" below "US Postage"	25.00	15.00
b.	"Priority" below "US Postage"	—	—
c.	"Express" below "US Postage"	—	—
d.	"Media Mail" below "US Postage"	—	—
e.	"Parcel Post" below "US Postage"	—	—
f.	"Bound Printed Matter" below "US Postage"	—	—
g.	"BPM" below "US Postage"	—	—

Blank sheets of No. 1CVP37 were sent free of charge to those who responded to special Stamps.com promotions which offered a fixed amount of free postage as an enticement to new subscribers. The franking portion of the stamps could only be applied after subscribing.

Logo CVPA35

2005, Aug.   Die Cut Perf. 6½ at Left

1CVP38	CVPA35 37c black, blue & orange	1.00	.45
a.	"Priority" below "US Postage"	8.00	1.00
b.	"Express" below "US Postage"	25.00	3.00
c.	"Media Mail" below "US Postage"	7.50	1.00
d.	"Parcel Post" below "US Postage"	7.50	1.00
e.	"BPM" below "US Postage"	7.50	1.00
f.	"Aerogramme" below "US Postage"	1.40	1.00
g.	"Intl Air Letter" below "US Postage"	1.25	1.00
h.	"Intl Eco Letter" (Economy Letter Mail) below "US Postage"	5.50	1.00
i.	"GXG" (Global Express Guaranteed) below "US Postage"	50.00	6.00

j.	"EMS" (Global Express Mail) below "US Postage"	32.50	4.00
k.	"GPM" (Global Priority Mail) below "US Postage"	8.00	1.00
l.	"Intl Air Parcel" (Air Parcel Post) below "US Postage"	26.00	3.00
m.	"Intl Eco Parcel" (Economy Parcel Post) below "US Postage"	32.50	4.00
n.	"M-Bag (Air)" below "US Postage"	35.00	5.00
o.	"M-Bag (Economy)" below "US Postage"	18.00	3.00
p.	"Mat for Blind" below "US Postage"	1.25	—

Values for lettered varieties on Nos. 1CVP38 are based on the prices set as the minimum values for each service classification in the software available at the time the stamps were issued. In mid-December 2005, the software was changed to allow for a 1c minimum value for any of these lettered varieties.

In 2006, No. 1CVP38 was made available on a coil roll. Value, $1.40.

Snowman — CVPA36

Candy Cane — CVPA37

Dove — CVPA38

Stylized Christmas Tree and Window — CVPA39

2005, Nov.   Die Cut Perf. 6 at Right

1CVP39	CVPA36 37c multi	1.60	.45
a.	"Priority" below "US Postage"	8.00	1.00
b.	"Express" below "US Postage"	25.00	3.00
c.	"Media Mail" below "US Postage"	7.50	1.00
d.	"Parcel Post" below "US Postage"	7.50	1.00
e.	"BPM" below "US Postage"	7.50	1.00
f.	"Aerogramme" below "US Postage"	1.40	1.00
g.	"Intl Air Letter" below "US Postage"	1.25	1.00
h.	"Intl Eco Letter" (Economy Letter Mail) below "US Postage"	5.50	1.00
i.	"GXG" (Global Express Guaranteed) below "US Postage"	50.00	6.00
j.	"EMS" (Global Express Mail) below "US Postage"	32.50	4.00
k.	"GPM" (Global Priority Mail) below "US Postage"	8.00	1.00
l.	"Intl Air Parcel" (Air Parcel Post) below "US Postage"	26.00	3.00
m.	"Intl Eco Parcel" (Economy Parcel Post) below "US Postage"	32.50	4.00
n.	"M-Bag (Air)" below "US Postage"	35.00	5.00
o.	"M-Bag (Economy)" below "US Postage"	18.00	3.00
p.	"Mat for Blind" below "US Postage"	.25	—
1CVP40	CVPA37 37c multi	1.60	.45
a.	"Priority" below "US Postage"	8.00	1.00
b.	"Express" below "US Postage"	25.00	3.00
c.	"Media Mail" below "US Postage"	7.50	1.00

d.	"Parcel Post" below "US Postage"	7.50	1.00
e.	"BPM" below "US Postage"	7.50	1.00
f.	"Aerogramme" below "US Postage"	1.40	1.00
g.	"Intl Air Letter" below "US Postage"	1.25	1.00
h.	"Intl Eco Letter" (Economy Letter Mail) below "US Postage"	5.50	1.00
i.	"GXG" (Global Express Guaranteed) below "US Postage"	50.00	6.00
j.	"EMS" (Global Express Mail) below "US Postage"	32.50	4.00
k.	"GPM" (Global Priority Mail) below "US Postage"	8.00	1.00
l.	"Intl Air Parcel" (Air Parcel Post) below "US Postage"	26.00	3.00
m.	"Intl Eco Parcel" (Economy Parcel Post) below "US Postage"	32.50	4.00
n.	"M-Bag (Air)" below "US Postage"	35.00	5.00
o.	"M-Bag (Economy)" below "US Postage"	18.00	3.00
p.	"Mat for Blind" below "US Postage"	.45	—
1CVP41	CVPA38 37c multi	1.60	.45
a.	"Priority" below "US Postage"	8.00	1.00
b.	"Express" below "US Postage"	25.00	3.00
c.	"Media Mail" below "US Postage"	7.50	1.00
d.	"Parcel Post" below "US Postage"	7.50	1.00
e.	"BPM" below "US Postage"	7.50	1.00
f.	"Aerogramme" below "US Postage"	1.40	1.00
g.	"Intl Air Letter" below "US Postage"	1.25	1.00
h.	"Intl Eco Letter" (Economy Letter Mail) below "US Postage"	5.50	1.00
i.	"GXG" (Global Express Guaranteed) below "US Postage"	50.00	6.00
j.	"EMS" (Global Express Mail) below "US Postage"	32.50	4.00
k.	"GPM" (Global Priority Mail) below "US Postage"	8.00	1.00
l.	"Intl Air Parcel" (Air Parcel Post) below "US Postage"	26.00	3.00
m.	"Intl Eco Parcel" (Economy Parcel Post) below "US Postage"	32.50	4.00
n.	"M-Bag (Air)" below "US Postage"	35.00	5.00
o.	"M-Bag (Economy)" below "US Postage"	18.00	3.00
p.	"Mat for Blind" below "US Postage"	.45	—
1CVP42	CVPA39 37c multi	1.60	.45
a.	"Priority" below "US Postage"	8.00	1.00
b.	"Express" below "US Postage"	25.00	3.00
c.	"Media Mail" below "US Postage"	7.50	1.00
d.	"Parcel Post" below "US Postage"	7.50	1.00
e.	"BPM" below "US Postage"	7.50	1.00
f.	"Aerogramme" below "US Postage"	1.40	1.00
g.	"Intl Air Letter" below "US Postage"	1.25	1.00
h.	"Intl Eco Letter" (Economy Letter Mail) below "US Postage"	5.50	1.00
i.	"GXG" (Global Express Guaranteed) below "US Postage"	50.00	6.00
j.	"EMS" (Global Express Mail) below "US Postage"	32.50	4.00
k.	"GPM" (Global Priority Mail) below "US Postage"	8.00	1.00
l.	"Intl Air Parcel" (Air Parcel Post) below "US Postage"	26.00	3.00
m.	"Intl Eco Parcel" (Economy Parcel Post) below "US Postage"	32.50	4.00
n.	"M-Bag (Air)" below "US Postage"	35.00	5.00
o.	"M-Bag (Economy)" below "US Postage"	18.00	3.00
p.	"Mat for Blind" below "US Postage"	.45	—
q.	Vert. strip, 2 each #1CVP39-1CVP42	6.00	

Values for lettered varieties on Nos. 1CVP39-1CVP42 are based on the prices set as the minimum values for each service classification in the software available at the time the stamps were issued. In mid-December 2005, the software was changed to allow for a 1c minimum value for any of these lettered varieties.

Endicia.com

$0.24⁰
US POSTAGE
POSTCARD
071V00566020
46860
000000105
endicia.com

CVPA40

$0.24⁰
US POSTAGE
POSTCARD
071V00566020
46860
000000146
endicia.com

CVPA41

2005-06 *Serpentine Die Cut 10¼*
1CVP43 CVPA40 24c black &
bright
rose 10.00 4.00
a. 39c "First Class" under
"US Postage" 2.00 .50
b. 63c "Intl. Mail" under
"US Postage" 3.25 2.50
c. $4.05 "Priority Mail"
under "US Postage" 12.00 2.50

Coil Stamps
Serpentine Die Cut 10½x10¼ on 2 Sides
1CVP44 CVPA41 24c black &
pink 11.00 4.00
a. 39c "First Class" under
"US Postage" 2.25 .50
b. 63c "Intl. Mail" under
"US Postage" 3.50 2.50
c. $4.05 "Priority Mail"
under "US Postage" 12.50 2.50

Issued: Nos. 1CVP43, Nov. 2005; Nos. 1CVP44, Jan. 2006.

Originally, face values of 2c, 52c, 63c, 87c, $1.11, $1.35, $1.59, $1.83, $2.07, $2.31, $2.55, $2.79, $3.03, and $3.27 could also be printed on stamps with the "First class" inscription. Additionally, an 84c face value could be printed on stamps with the "Intl. Mail" inscription, and a $8.10 face value could be printed on stamps with the "Priority Mail" inscription. Values for Nos. 1CVP43-1CVP44 are for stamps with the listed face values and mail-class inscription. Values for stamps with lower or higher face values are correspondingly lower or higher.

In 2007, software changes permitted Nos. 1CVP43 and 1CVP44 to be printed with mail class inscriptions "Media Mail," "BPM," "Parcel Post," "Library Mail," and "Express Mail," as well as any face value for any mail-class inscription.

Nos. 1CVP43 and 1CVP44 printed after the software changes are inscribed "First Class" under "US Postage" and sell for considerably less than the values shown. Stamps printed before the software changes are inscribed "Postcard" under "US Postage," as shown in the illustrations.

Stamps.com

Flag and Mount Rushmore — CVPA42

Flag and Eagle — CVPA43

Flag and Statue of Liberty — CVPA44

Flag and Liberty Bell — CVPA45

2006, Mar. *Die Cut Perf. 6 at Right*
1CVP51 CVPA42 39c multi .80 .45
1CVP52 CVPA43 39c multi .80 .45
1CVP53 CVPA44 39c multi .80 .45
1CVP54 CVPA45 39c multi .80 .45
a. Vert. strip of 8, 2 each
#1CVP51-1CVP54 8.00

Other service inscriptions with any possible face value can be printed on Nos. 1CVP51-1CVP54.

Stamps.com

Leaning Tower of Pisa — CVPA46

Taj Mahal — CVPA47

Eiffel Tower — CVPA48

Parthenon — CVPA49

2006 *Die Cut Perf 6 at Right*
1CVP55 CVPA46 39c multi .80 .45
1CVP56 CVPA47 39c multi .80 .45
1CVP57 CVPA48 39c multi .80 .45
1CVP58 CVPA49 39c multi .80 .45
a. Vert. strip, 2 each
#1CVP55-1CVP58 8.00

With the introduction of the new software in December 2005, any stamp could have any denomination 1c and above, and any service classification.

Pitney Bowes Stamp Expressions

U.S. POSTAGE $00.39
SCOTT
Serving collectors
since 1863
P800000004982
pitneybowes.com/se

CVPA50

2006 *Die Cut Perf. 6 Horiz.*
Inscribed "pitneybowes.com/se" at Right
1CVP59 CVPA50 39c black + label 1.35 .80

The stamp and label are separated by vertical roulettes. Users could create their own label images on the Pitney Bowes Stamp Expressions website (which required approval of the image from Pitney Bowes before it could be used), or download various pre-approved label images from the website into their personal computers. Stamps could be printed without label images. Stamps were printed on rolls of tagged thermal paper from a device that could be operated without a direct connection to the personal computer. See No. 1CVT1.

Stamps.com

39 FIRST-CLASS
US POSTAGE
SCOTT
Serving collectors
since 1863

CVPA51

39 cents US POSTAGE FIRST-CLASS
MEH 2006

Personalizable Images — CVPA52

2006, Sept. *Die Cut Perf. 6 at Right*
1CVP60 CVPA51 39c multi 1.50 .95
a. Numerals in denomination 2½mm high, thicker text 1.50 .95

Perf. Die Cut Perf. 6 at Top
1CVP61 CVPA52 39c multi 1.50 .95
a. Numerals in denomination 2½mm high, thicker text 1.50 .95

Users could requisition sheets of Nos. 1CVP60 and 1CVP61 with images of their choice from Stamps.com at $4.99 per sheet of 24. Priority and Express service classifications could also be printed on Nos. 1CVP60-1CVP61 with any denomination. Stamps exist with slightly larger die cutting (60x30mm and 30x60mm) in both squared and rounded corners. The denomination type shown on Nos. 1CVP60-1CVP61 can be placed on label types CVPA36-CVPA39, CVPA42-CVPA49, CVPA53-CVPA60 and any later stamps.com labels of this size.

Numerals in denomination are 3mm tall on Nos. 1CVP60-1CVP61. Serial numbers on Nos. 1CPVP60-1CVP61 lack periods and have small bank-check style numerals.

Autumn Leaves — CVPA53

Pumpkins — CVPA54

Basket of Apples, Sheaf of Wheat, Falling Leaves and Pumpkins — CVPA55

Leaves and Carved Pumpkin — CVPA56

2006 *Die Cut Perf. 6 at Right*
1CVP62 CVPA53 39c multi 1.25 .45
1CVP63 CVPA54 39c multi 1.25 .45
1CVP64 CVPA55 39c multi 1.25 .45
1CVP65 CVPA56 39c multi 1.25 .45
a. Vert. strip, 2 each
#1CVP62-1CVP65 10.00

See note after No. 1CVP58.

"Season's Greetings" — CVPA57

Christmas Trees — CVPA58

Snowman — CVPA59

Dove — CVPA60

2006 *Die Cut Perf. 6 at Right*
1CVP66 CVPA57 39c multi 1.25 .45
1CVP67 CVPA58 39c multi 1.25 .45
1CVP68 CVPA59 39c multi 1.25 .45
1CVP69 CVPA60 39c multi 1.25 .45
a. Vert. strip, 2 each
#1CVP66-1CVP69 10.00

See note after No. 1CVP58.

Flag — CVPA61

Statue of Liberty and Flag — CVPA62

Bald Eagle and Flag — CVPA63

Flag Painted on Building — CVPA64

2008   *Die Cut Perf. 5½ at Right*
Serial Number With Period, Large Letters and Numerals

1CVP70	CVPA61	42c multi	1.25	.45
1CVP71	CVPA62	42c multi	1.25	.45
1CVP72	CVPA63	42c multi	1.25	.45
1CVP73	CVPA64	42c multi	1.25	.45

On Nos. 1CVP70-1CVP105, and perhaps on other stamps, placement of the stamp serial number and the stamps.com logo might differ on various printings of the label stock. Descriptive text outside the frame might also vary or not be present on these various printings.

Autumn — CVPA65

Designs: No. 1CVP74, Oak leaves. No. 1CVP75, Pumpkin patch. No. 1CVP76, Autumn reflection. No. 1CVP77, Pumpkins and gourds.

2008
Serial Number With Period, Large Letters and Numerals

1CVP74	CVPA65	42c multi	1.25	.45
1CVP75	CVPA65	42c multi	1.25	.45
1CVP76	CVPA65	42c multi	1.25	.45
1CVP77	CVPA65	42c multi	1.25	.45

Flowers — CVPA66

Designs: No. 1CVP78, Sunflowers. No. 1CVP79, Daisies. No. 1CVP80, Sunflower sky. No. 1CVP81, Treasure flowers.

2008
Serial Number With Period, Large Letters and Numerals

1CVP78	CVPA66	42c multi	1.25	.45
1CVP79	CVPA66	42c multi	1.25	.45
1CVP80	CVPA66	42c multi	1.25	.45
1CVP81	CVPA66	42c multi	1.25	.45

Endangered Animals — CVPA67

Designs: No. 1CVP82, Bengal tiger. No. 1CVP83, Hawksbill turtle. No. 1CVP84, Panda. No. 1CVP85, African rhino.

2008
Serial Number With Period, Large Letters and Numerals

1CVP82	CVPA67	42c multi	1.25	.45
1CVP83	CVPA67	42c multi	1.25	.45
1CVP84	CVPA67	42c multi	1.25	.45
1CVP85	CVPA67	42c multi	1.25	.45

Parks — CVPA68

Designs: No. 1CVP86, Grand Canyon National Park, Arizona. No. 1CVP87, Yosemite National Park, California. No. 1CVP88, Niagara Falls. No. 1CVP89, Arches National Park, Utah.

2008
Serial Number With Period, Large Letters and Numerals

1CVP86	CVPA68	42c multi	1.25	.45
1CVP87	CVPA68	42c multi	1.25	.45
1CVP88	CVPA68	42c multi	1.25	.45
1CVP89	CVPA68	42c multi	1.25	.45

City Skylines — CVPA69

Designs: No. 1CVP90, New York City. No. 1CVP91, St. Louis. No. 1CVP92, Chicago. No. 1CVP93, San Francisco.

2008
Serial Number With Period, Large Letters and Numerals

1CVP90	CVPA69	42c multi	1.25	.45
1CVP91	CVPA69	42c multi	1.25	.45
1CVP92	CVPA69	42c multi	1.25	.45
1CVP93	CVPA69	42c multi	1.25	.45

Presidential Memorials — CVPA70

Designs: No. 1CVP94, Washington Monument. No. 1CVP95, Lincoln Memorial. No. 1CVP96, Jefferson Memorial. No. 1CVP97, Mount Rushmore.

2008
Serial Number With Period, Large Letters and Numerals

1CVP94	CVPA70	42c multi	1.25	.45
1CVP95	CVPA70	42c multi	1.25	.45
1CVP96	CVPA70	42c multi	1.25	.45
1CVP97	CVPA70	42c multi	1.25	.45

Christmas — CVPA71

Designs: No. 1CVP98, Ornament, "Happy Holidays." No. 1CVP99, Gingerbread men, "Season's Greetings." No. 1CVP100, Snowflake, "Happy Holidays." No. 1CVP101, Christmas tree, "Season's Greetings."

2008
Serial Number With Period, Large Letters and Numerals

Without Year or Text at Left

1CVP98	CVPA71	42c multi	1.25	.45
1CVP99	CVPA71	42c multi	1.25	.45
1CVP100	CVPA71	42c multi	1.25	.45
1CVP101	CVPA71	42c multi	1.25	.45

Love — CVPA72

"Love" and: No. 1CVP102, Rose. No. 1CVP103, Small hearts. No. 1CVP104, Large heart. No. 1CVP105, Hearts on curtain.

2009
Serial Number With Period, Large Letters and Numerals

Without Year or Text at Left

1CVP102	CVPA72	42c multi	1.25	.45
1CVP103	CVPA72	42c multi	1.25	.45
1CVP104	CVPA72	42c multi	1.25	.45
1CVP105	CVPA72	42c multi	1.25	.45

Wavy Lines
CVPA73

2009   *Die Cut Perf 6½ at Right*

1CVP106	CVPA73	44c multi	1.25	.45

Endicia .com

Globe
CVPA74

2009   *Serpentine Die Cut 10¼x10½*

1CVP107	CVPA74	44c orange & black	1.25	.45

Software allowed for six other inscriptions below "US Postage" (Priority Mail, Media Mail, Parcel Post, Library Mail, Express Mail and Intl Mail) and any face value for any mail-class inscription.

Stamps.com

Thank You For Your Business — CVPA75

Text: No. 1CVP108, On billboard. No. 1CVP109, And building. No. 1CVP110, On red background. No. 1CVP111, And two people shaking hands.

2009   *Die Cut Perf. 5½ at Right*
Serial Number With Period, Large Letters and Numerals

Without Year or Text at Left

1CVP108	CVPA75	44c multi	1.25	.45
1CVP109	CVPA75	44c multi	1.25	.45
1CVP110	CVPA75	44c multi	1.25	.45
1CVP111	CVPA75	44c multi	1.25	.45

We're Moving — CVPA76

Text: No. 1CVP112, Stack of three boxes, green background. No. 1CVP113, Eleven boxes, orange background. No. 1CVP114, Four boxes, green background. No. 1CVP115, Four boxes, red background.

2009
Serial Number With Period, Large Letters and Numerals

Without Year or Text at Left

1CVP112	CVPA76	44c multi	1.25	.45
1CVP113	CVPA76	44c multi	1.25	.45
1CVP114	CVPA76	44c multi	1.25	.45
1CVP115	CVPA76	44c multi	1.25	.45

Special Invitation — CVPA77

Text: No. 1CVP116, And pen nib. No. 1CVP117, And circled "15" on calendar. No. 1CVP118, On card on envelope. No. 1CVP119, On wax seal.

2009
Serial Number With Period, Large Letters and Numerals

Without Year or Text at Left

1CVP116	CVPA77	44c multi	1.25	.45
1CVP117	CVPA77	44c multi	1.25	.45
1CVP118	CVPA77	44c multi	1.25	.45
1CVP119	CVPA77	44c multi	1.25	.45

US Flag — CVPA78

Flag: No. 1CVP120, On flagpole. No. 1CVP121, Behind Statue of Liberty. No. 1CVP122, Behind bald eagle. No. 1CVP123, On United States map.

2009
Serial Number With Period, Large Letters and Numerals

Without Year or Text at Left

1CVP120	CVPA78	44c multi	1.25	.45
1CVP121	CVPA78	44c multi	1.25	.45
1CVP122	CVPA78	44c multi	1.25	.45
1CVP123	CVPA78	44c multi	1.25	.45

Patriotic Symbols — CVPA79

Designs: No. 1CVP124, Statue of Liberty. No. 1CVP125, Flag. No. 1CVP126, Bald eagle.

2010   *Die Cut Perf. 5½ Vert.*

1CVP124	CVPA79	44c multi	1.25	.45
1CVP125	CVPA79	44c multi	1.25	.45
1CVP126	CVPA79	44c multi	1.25	.45

Jewish Symbols — CVPA80

Designs: No. 1CVP127, Menorah. No. 1CVP125, Dreidel. No. 1CVP126, Star of David.

2010 *Die Cut Perf. 5½ Vert.*
1CVP127	CVPA80	44c multi	1.25	.45
1CVP128	CVPA80	44c multi	1.25	.45
1CVP129	CVPA80	44c multi	1.25	.45

Christmas — CVPA81

Designs: No. 1CVP130, Christmas stocking. No. 1CVP131, Christmas tree. No. 1CVP132, Santa Claus.

2010 *Die Cut Perf. 5½ Vert.*
1CVP130	CVPA81	44c multi	1.25	.45
1CVP131	CVPA81	44c multi	1.25	.45
1CVP132	CVPA81	44c multi	1.25	.45

Valentine's Day — CVPA82

Designs: No. 1CVP133, Hearts. No. 1CVP134, Rose. No. 1CVP135, Candy hearts.

2011 *Die Cut Perf. 5½ Vert.*
1CVP133	CVPA82	44c multi	1.25	.45
1CVP134	CVPA82	44c multi	1.25	.45
1CVP135	CVPA82	44c multi	1.25	.45

Christian Symbols — CVPA83

Designs: No. 1CVP136, Cross. No. 1CVP137, Fish. No. 1CVP138, Rosary beads.

2011 *Die Cut Perf. 5½ Vert.*
1CVP136	CVPA83	44c multi	1.25	.45
1CVP137	CVPA83	44c multi	1.25	.45
1CVP138	CVPA83	44c multi	1.25	.45

NON-PERSONALIZABLE POSTAGE

Stamps.com

These stamps, approved by the USPS, were non-personalizable stamps that could be purchased directly from private manufacturers, which shipped them to the customer. Other non-personalizable stamps have been created by a variety of companies, all sold at excessive amounts over face value as "collectibles". Such items are not listed here. Most items created that sold for excessive amounts over face value have vignettes that are licensed images, usually depicting sport team emblems or other sports-related themes, or celebrities.

Personalized postage stamps, first available in 2004, created by a variety of different companies, and heretofore listed with Scott numbers having a "2CVP" prefix, are no longer listed. Personalized stamps, though valid for postage, are not sold at any U.S. Postal Service post office. They are available only by on-line ordering through the company's website. Stamps are only available from the companies in full panes of 20. Each pane is sold at a significant premium above the stated face value to cover the costs of personalization, shipping and handling.

In recent years, there has been a steadily increasing number of private companies, either directly licensed by the USPS or created as spinoff companies of these licensees, creating distinctly different personalized stamps. None of the companies has issued fewer than seven stamps for each rate change, with one issuing as many as 42 different stamps. Because mailing rates set by the USPS are expected to change yearly, the collective output of distinctly different, rate-based stamps from these various companies likely will increase. There are no restrictions in place to prevent more firms from bringing personalized stamps to the marketplace, or to keep stamp producers from offering even more customer options. Some personalized stamps do not differ in any appreciable manner from some of the non-personalizable stamps sold as collectibles and not listed here.

CVPC1

PhotoStamps
your photo here
photostamps.com

CVPC2

2007, May *Die Cut*
Self-Adhesive
3CVP1	CVPC1	2c black & gray	.25	.25
a.		Inscribed "US Postag"		

Die Cut Perf. 5¼ at Right
3CVP2	CVPC2	2c multicolored	.25	.25
a.		Tagged	1.40	1.40

2008 *Die Cut*
3CVP3	CVPC1	1c black & gray	.25	.25

No. 3CVP1 was printed in sheets of 40 stamps. Stamps with serial numbers ending in "06" are No. 3CVP1a. Sheets were sold for face value plus a shipping charge and were obtainable through the stamps.com website.

No. 3CVP2 was printed in sheets of 20. Full sheets were given free of charge to first-time stamps.com customers, but the full sheets were available for sale to other customers at face value plus a shipping charge through the stamps.com website.

CARRIERS' STAMPS

GENERAL ISSUE CARRIER STAMPS

Issued by the U.S. Government to facilitate payment of fees for delivering and collecting letters.

Franklin — OC1

1851 Engr. Unwmk. Imperf.
LO1	OC1	(1c) dull blue, *rose*	7,000.	8,000.

U.S.P.O. Despatch

Eagle — OC2

1851
LO2	OC2	1c blue (shades)	50.00	*80.00*

1875 *Imperf.*
LO3	OC1	(1c) blue, *rose*	50.	

Perf. 12
LO4	OC1	(1c) blue	16,000.	

No. LO4 is valued in the grade of average to fine.

Eagle Reprints
Imperf.
LO5	OC2	1c blue	25.	

Perf. 12
LO6	OC2	1c blue	175.	

Reprints of the Franklin Carrier are printed in dark blue, instead of the dull blue or deep blue of the originals. Two reprintings of 10,000 each were made in 1875 on the same rose paper as the originals. A third reprinting of 5,000 in 1881 is on soft wove paper.

The first two reprintings of 10,000 each of the Eagle carrier are on hard white paper, ungummed and sometimes perforated. A third reprinting of 10,000 stamps in 1881 is on soft wove paper. Originals are on yellowish paper with brown gum.

No. LO6 is valued with the perfs cutting slightly into the design.

CITY CARRIER DEPARTMENT STAMPS

Issued by officials or employees of the U.S. Government for the purpose of securing or indicating payment of carriers' fees.

All are imperforate.
Baltimore, Md.

C1

1850-55 *Typo.*
Settings of 10 (2x5) varieties
1LB1	C1	1c red, *bluish*	180.	160.
1LB2	C1	1c blue, *bluish*	200.	150.
a.		Bluish laid paper		
1LB3	C1	1c blue	160.	100.
a.		Laid paper	200.	150.
b.		Block of 14 containing three tete-beche gutter pairs (unique)	6,250.	
1LB4	C1	1c green	—	1,000.
1LB5	C1	1c red	2,250.	1,750.

C2

1856 *Typo.*
1LB6	C2	1c blue (shades)	130.	90.
1LB7	C2	1c red (shades)	130.	90.

C3

The sheet consisted of at least four panes of 10 placed horizontally, the two center panes tete beche. This makes possible five horizontal tete beche gutter pairs.

Plate of 10 (2x5); 10 Varieties

1857
1LB8	C3	1c black (shades)	65.	50.
a.		"SENT"	100.	75.
b.		Short rays	100.	75.
1LB9	C3	1c red	100.	90.
a.		"SENT"	140.	110.
b.		Short rays	140.	110.
c.		As "b," double impression		800.

Boston, Mass.

C6

Several Varieties

1849-50 **Pelure Paper** **Typeset**
3LB1	C6	1c blue	375.	180.
a.		Wrong ornament at left		400.

C7

Several Varieties

1851
Wove Paper Colored Through
3LB2	C7	1c blue (shades), *slate*	190.	100.

Charleston, S. C.
Honour's City Express

C8

1849 **Typo.**
Wove Paper Colored Through
4LB1	C8	2c blk, *brn rose*	10,000.	
		Cut to shape	4,000.	4,000.
4LB2	C8	2c blk, *yel,* cut to shape	—	

No. 4LB1 unused is a unique uncanceled stamp on piece. The used cut-to-shape stamp is also unique. In addition two covers exist bearing No. 4LB1.

No. 4LB2 unused (uncanceled) off cover is unique; three known on cover.

See the Scott U.S. Specialized Catalogue.

4LB2A	C8	2c blk, *bl gray,* on cover, cut to shape	—	

No. 4LB2A is unique.

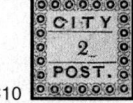

C10

1854 **Wove Paper** **Typeset**
4LB3	C10	2c black		1,500.

C11

Several Varieties

1849-50
Wove Paper Colored Through
4LB5	C11	2c black, *bluish,* pelure	750.	500.
a.		"Ceuts"	5,750.	
4LB7	C11	2c black, *yellow*	750.	1,000.
a.		"Ccnts," ms. tied on cover		14,500.

No. 4LB5a is unique. It is without gum and is valued thus. No. 4LB7a also is unique.

C13

C14

C15

Several varieties of each type

1851-58
Wove Paper Colored Through

4LB8	C13	2c black, *bluish*	350.	175.
a.		Period after "PAID"	500.	250.
b.		"Cens"	700.	900.
c.		"Conours" and "Bents"		

The No. 4LB8 with No. 2 combination cover is unique. It is a cover front only and is valued thus.

4LB9	C13	2c black, *bluish,* pelure	850.	950.
4LB10	C13	2c black, *pink,* pelure, on cover		7,000.
4LB11	C14	(2c) black, *bluish*	—	375.
4LB12	C14	(2c) black, *bluish* pelure	—	
4LB13	C15	(2c) black, *bluish* ('58)	750.	400.
a.		Comma after "PAID"	1,100.	
b.		No period after "Post"	1,400.	

Kingman's City Post

C16   C17

Several varieties of each
Wove Paper Colored Through

1851(?)-58(?)

4LB14	C16	2c black, *bluish*	1,400.	900.
a.		"Kingman's" erased	5,000.	
4LB15	C17	2c black, *bluish*	800.	800.
a.		"Kingman's" erased, on cover with 3c #11, tied by pen cancel (unique)		4,500.

Martin's City Post

C18

Several varieties

1858   Typeset
Wove Paper Colored Through

4LB16	C18	2c black, *bluish*	8,000.

Beckman's City Post
Same as C19, but inscribed:
"Beckmann's City Post."

1860

4LB17	C19	2c black, on cover	—

No. 4LB17 is unique.

Steinmeyer's City Post

C19   C20

Several varieties of Type C19
Type C20 printed from plate of 10 (2x5) varieties

1859   Typeset
Wove Paper Colored Through

4LB18	C19	2c black, *bluish*	21,000.
4LB19	C20	2c black, *bluish*	4,500.	—
4LB20	C20	2c black, *pink*	200.	—
4LB21	C20	2c black, *yellow*	200.	

Cincinnati, Ohio
Williams' City Post

C20a

1854   Wove Paper   Litho.

9LB1	C20a	2c brown	—	4,000.

Cleveland, Ohio
Bishop's City Post

C20b   C20c

1854   Wove Paper   Litho.

10LB1	C20b	blue	5,000.	4,000.

Vertically Laid Paper

10LB2	C20c	2c black, *bluish*	4,000.	6,000.

No. 10LB2 unused is unique. It is cut in at bottom and without gum, and is valued thus.

Louisville, Ky.
Wharton's U.S.P.O. Despatch

C21

1857   Lithographed

5LB1	C21	(2c) bluish green (shades)	125.

Brown & McGill's U. S. P. O. Despatch

C22

1858, Nov.-1860   Lithographed

5LB2	C22	(2c) blue (shades)	250.	750.

1858, Feb.-Aug.

5LB3	C22	(2c) black	4,500.	15,000.
		On cover, not tied, with 3c #26		17,500.

The value for No. 5LB3 used refers to the finer of the two known used (canceled) examples; it is extremely fine and on a piece with a 3c #26.

New York, N. Y.
United States City Despatch Post

C23

Wove Paper Colored Through

1842   Engr.

6LB1	C23	3c black, *grayish*	2,000.

Used examples are Carriers' stamps only when canceled with the regular government cancellation "U.S." in octagonal frame (see illustration), "U.S.CITY DESPATCH POST," or New York circular postmark.

When canceled "FREE" in frame they were used as local stamps. See No. 40L1 in the Scott Specialized Catalogue of United States Stamps.

C24

Wove Paper (unsurfaced) Colored Through

1842-45

6LB2	C24	3c black, *rosy buff*	5,000.	
6LB3	C24	3c black, *light blue*	1,500.	750.
6LB4	C24	3c black, *green*	11,500.	

Some authorities consider No. 6LB2 to be an essay, and No. 6LB4 a color changeling. No. 6LB2 unused is valued without gum.

Glazed Paper, Surface Colored

6LB5	C24	3c black, *blue green (shades)*	200.	175.
a.		Double impression		1,500.
b.		3c black, *blue*	650.	300.
c.		As "b," double impression		1,000.
d.		3c black, *green*	1,250.	750.
		black, *apple green*		2,000.
		Pair		2,750.
e.		As "d," double impression	—	
6LB6	C24	3c black, *pink,* on cover front		14,500.

No. 6LB6 is unique.

No. 6LB5 Surcharged in Red

1846

6LB7	C24	2c on 3c black, *bluish grn,* on cover		14,000.
		On cover, not tied, with certificate		70,000.

The City Despatch 2c red is listed in the Scott U.S. Specialized Catalogue as a Local stamp.

U.S. MAIL

C27

1849   Typo.
Wove Paper, Colored Through

6LB9	C27	1c black, *rose*	100.	100.

1849-50   Glazed Surface Paper

6LB10	C27	1c black, *yellow*	100.	100.
6LB11	C27	1c black, *buff*	100.	100.
a.		Pair, one stamp sideways		2,850.

Philadelphia, Pa.

C28

Several Varieties
Thick Wove Paper Colored Through

1849-50   Typeset

7LB1	C28	1c black, *rose* (with "L P")	450.	
7LB2	C28	1c black, *rose* (with "S")	3,000.	
7LB3	C28	1c black, *rose* (with "H")	275.	
7LB4	C28	1c black, *rose* (with "L S")	400.	500.
7LB5	C28	1c black, *rose* (with "J J")	7,500.	

The unique used No. 7LB5 is an uncanceled stamp on a cover front.

C29

Several Varieties

7LB6	C29	1c black, *rose*	300.	250.
7LB7	C29	1c black, *blue, glazed*	1,000.	
7LB8	C29	1c blk, *ver,* glazed	700.	
7LB9	C29	1c blk, *yel,* glazed	2,750.	2,250.

Cancellations on Nos. 7LB1-7LB9: Normally these stamps were left uncanceled on the letter, but occasionally were accidentally tied by

---

the Philadelphia town postmark which was normally struck in blue ink.

A 1c black on buff (unglazed) of type C29 is believed to be a color changeling.

C30

Settings of 25 (5x5) varieties (Five basic types)

1850-52   Litho.

7LB11	C30	1c gold, *black, glazed*	175.	110.
7LB12	C30	1c blue	400.	275.
7LB13	C30	1c black	750.	550.

25 varieties of C30.

C31

Handstamped

7LB14	C31	1c blue, *buff*	3,250.

1855(?)

7LB16	C31	1c black	5,000.

C32

1856(?)   Handstamped

7LB18	C32	1c black	1,250.	2,000.

Labels of these designs are believed by most specialists not to be carrier stamps. Those seen are uncanceled, either off cover or affixed to stampless covers of the early 1850s. Some students believe they should be given carrier status.

St. Louis, Mo.

C36   C37

Illustrations enlarged to show details of the two types (note upper corners especially). Sizes of actual designs are 17 1/2x22mm.

1849   White Wove Paper   Litho.
Two Types

8LB1	C36	2c black	7,000.	3,000.
8LB2	C37	2c black	6,000.	—

Cancellation on Nos. 8LB1-8LB2: Black town.

C38

1857   **Litho.**
8LB3 C38 2c blue   *22,500.*

The used example off cover is unique. Five covers are recorded.

Cancellations on No. 8LB3: Black boxed "1ct," "Paid" in arc, black pen.

STAMPED ENVELOPES & WRAPPERS

VALUES

Unless otherwise noted, values are for cut squares in a grade of very fine.

Very fine cut squares will have the design well centered within moderately large margins. Precanceled cut squares must include the entire precancellation.

Values for unused entires are for those without printed or manuscript address. Values for letter sheets are for folded entires. Unfolded examples sell for more. A "full corner" includes back and side flaps and commands a premium.

Entire envelopes and wrappers are listed in the Scott U.S. Specialized Catalogue.

Wrappers are listed with envelopes of corresponding designs, and indicated by prefix letter "W" instead of "U."

An ALBINO impression is where two or more envelope blanks are fed into the printing press. The one adjacent to the printing die receives the color and the embossing, while the others are embossed only. Albinos are printing errors and are sometimes worth more than normal, inked impressions. Because of the nature of the printing process, many albinos were produced, and most collectors will not pay much, or any, premium for most of them. Albinos of earlier issues, canceled while current, are scarce.

The papers of these issues vary greatly in texture, and in color from yellowish to bluish white and from amber to dark buff.

"+" Some authorities claim that Nos. U37, U48, U49, U110, U124, U125, U130, U133A, U137A, U137B, U137C, W138, U145, U162, U178A, U185, U220, U285, U286, U298, U299, UO3, UO32, UO38, UO45 and UO45A (each with "+" before number) were not regularly issued and are not known to have been used.

U1

"THREE" in short label with curved ends; 13mm wide at top. Twelve varieties.

Washington — U2

"THREE" in short label with straight ends; 15½mm wide at top. Three varieties.

U3

"THREE" in short label with octagonal ends. Two varieties.

U4

"THREE" in wide label with straight ends; 20mm wide at top.

U5

"THREE" in medium wide label with curved ends; 14½mm wide at top. Ten varieties. A sub-variety shows curved lines at either end of label omitted; both T's have longer cross stroke; R is smaller (20 varieties).

U6

Four varieties.

U7

"TEN" in short label; 15½mm wide at top.

U8

"TEN" in wide label; 20mm wide at top.

1853-55
On Diagonally Laid Paper (Early printings of No. U1 on Horizontally Laid Paper)

U1	U1	3c red	350.00	35.00
U2	U1	3c red, *buff*	90.00	30.00
U3	U2	3c red	950.00	50.00
U4	U2	3c red, *buff*	425.00	45.00
U5	U3	3c red ('54)	5,750.	500.00
U6	U3	3c red, *buff* ('54)	3,750.	100.00
U7	U4	3c red	5,000.	150.00
U8	U4	3c red, *buff*	8,250.	175.00
U9	U5	3c red ('54)	40.00	4.00
U10	U5	3c red, *buff* ('54)	20.00	4.00
U11	U6	3c red	300.00	90.00
U12	U6	3c red, *buff*	145.00	90.00
U13	U6	6c green	260.00	150.00
U14	U6	6c green, *buff*	200.00	125.00
U15	U7	10c green ('55)	400.00	100.00
U16	U7	10c green, *buff* ('55)	175.00	90.00
a.		10c pale green, *buff*	135.00	70.00
U17	U8	10c green ('55)	375.00	140.00
a.		10c pale green	275.00	125.00
U18	U8	10c green, *buff* ('55)	375.00	100.00
a.		10c pale green, *buff*	350.00	100.00

Nos. U9, U10, U11, U12, U13, U14, U17, and U18 have been reprinted on white and buff papers, wove or vertically laid, and are not known entire. The originals are on diagonally laid paper. Value, set of 8 reprints on laid, $225. Reprints on wove sell for more.

The first printings of Nos. U1, U2, U3, U4 and U7 have G.F. Nesbitt crests printed on the envelope flaps. These sell for a premium. Such examples of Nos. U1-U4 with 1853 year-dated cancels sell for a very large premium.

No. U1 with watermark having a space between lines and on horizontally laid paper sells for a substantial premium.

U9

Period after "POSTAGE." (Eleven varieties.)

Franklin, Period after "POSTAGE." — U10

Bust touches inner frame-line at front and back.

No period after "POSTAGE" — U11

No period after "POSTAGE." (Two varieties.)

Washington — U12

Nine varieties of type U12.

Envelopes are on diagonally laid paper.
Wrappers on vertically or horizontally laid paper, or on unwatermarked wove paper (Nos. U21A, W22, W25)

1860-61

W18B	U9	1c blue ('61)	5,500.	
U19	U9	1c blue, *buff*	35.00	12.50
W20	U9	1c bl, *buff* ('61)	65.00	50.00
W21	U9	1c bl, *man* ('61)	55.00	45.00
U21A	U9	1c bl, *org*		325.00
W22	U9	1c bl, *org* ('61)	3,000.	
U23	U10	1c bl, *org*	600.00	350.00
U24	U11	1c bl, *amb*	350.00	110.00
W25	U11	1c bl, *man* ('61)	6,750.	1,500.
U26	U12	3c red	25.00	17.50
U27	U12	3c red, *buff*	22.50	12.50
U28	U12+U9	3c +1c red & bl	250.00	225.00
U29	U12+U9	3c +1c red & bl, *buff*	250.00	250.00
U30	U12	6c red	1,800.	1,500.
U31	U12	6c red, *buff*	3,500.	1,450.
U32	U12	10c green	1,250.	450.00
U33	U12	10c green, *buff*	1,250.	400.00

Nos. U26, U27, U30 to U33 have been reprinted on the same vertically laid paper as the reprints of the 1853-55 issue, and are not known entire. Value, Nos. U26-U27, $75 each; Nos. U30-U33, $75 each.

U13

U14   U15

Washington
U16

Envelopes are on diagonally laid paper.

U36 and U45 come on vertically or horizontally laid paper.

1861

U34	U13	3c pink	27.50	5.00
U35	U13	3c pink, *buff*	32.50	6.00
U36	U13	3c pink, *blue* (Letter Sheet)	65.00	65.00
+U37	U13	3c pink, *orange*	2,750.	
U38	U14	6c pink	100.00	80.00
U39	U14	6c pink, *buff*	60.00	60.00
U40	U15	10c yellow green	40.00	30.00
a.		10c blue green	40.00	30.00
U41	U15	10c yel grn, *buff*	40.00	30.00
a.		10c blue green, *buff*	40.00	30.00
U42	U16	12c red & brn, *buff*	180.00	180.00
a.		12c lake & brown, *buff*	1,250.	
U43	U16	20c red & bl, *buff*	275.00	225.00
U44	U16	24c red & grn, *buff*	225.00	210.00
a.		24c lake & green, *salmon*	275.00	225.00
U45	U16	40c blk & red, *buff*	325.00	400.00

Nos. U38 and U39 have been reprinted on the same papers as the reprints of the 1853-55 issue, and are not known entire. Value, set of 2 reprints, $60.

Jackson — U17

"U.S. POSTAGE" above. Downstroke and tail of "2" unite near the point (seven varieties).

Jackson — U18

"U.S. POSTAGE" above. The downstroke and tail of the "2" touch but do not merge.

Jackson — U19

"U.S. POST" above. Stamp 24-25mm wide (Sixteen varieties).

Jackson — U20

"U.S. POST" above. Stamp 25½-26¼mm wide. (Twenty-five varieties.)

Envelopes are on diagonally laid paper. Wrappers on vertically or horizontally laid paper.

Envelopes are on diagonally laid paper.
Wrappers on vertically or horizontally laid paper.

1863-64

U46	U17	2c black, *buff*	50.00	24.00
W47	U17	2c black, *dark manila*	75.00	65.00
+U48	U18	2c black, *buff*	*2,250.*	
+U49	U18	2c black, *orange*	1,750.	
U50	U19	2c black, *buff* ('64)	17.50	11.00
W51	U19	2c black, *buff* ('64)	450.00	275.00
U52	U19	2c black, *orange* ('64)	20.00	11.00
W53	U19	2c black, *dark manila* ('64)	42.50	40.00
U54	U20	2c black, *buff* ('64)	17.50	9.50
W55	U20	2c black, *buff* ('64)	95.00	65.00
U56	U20	2c black, *orange* ('64)	20.00	10.00
W57	U20	2c black, *light manila* ('64)	22.50	14.00

Washington — U21

79 varieties for Nos. U58-U61; 2 varieties for Nos. U63-U65.

Washington U22

1864-65

U58	U21	3c pink	8.00	1.60
U59	U21	3c pink, *buff*	8.00	1.25
U60	U21	3c brown ('65)	65.00	40.00
U61	U21	3c brown, *buff* ('65)	50.00	30.00
U62	U21	6c pink	80.00	29.00
U63	U21	6c pink, *buff*	40.00	27.50
U64	U21	6c purple ('65)	50.00	26.00
U65	U21	6c purple, *buff* ('65)	40.00	20.00
U66	U22	9c lemon, *buff* ('65)	375.00	250.00
U67	U22	9c orange, *buff* ('65)	125.00	90.00
a.		9c orange yellow, *buff*	125.00	90.00
U68	U22	12c brown, *buff* ('65)	275.00	275.00
U69	U22	12c red brown, *buff* ('65)	125.00	55.00
U70	U22	18c red, *buff* ('65)	70.00	95.00
U71	U22	24c blue, *buff* ('65)	70.00	95.00
U72	U22	30c green, *buff* ('65)	90.00	80.00
a.		30c yellow green, *buff*	85.00	80.00
U73	U22	40c rose, *buff* ('65)	90.00	250.00

Printed by George H. Reay, Brooklyn, N. Y.
The engravings in this issue are finely executed.

Franklin — U23

Bust points to the end of the "N" of "ONE."

Jackson — U24

Bust narrow at back. Small, thick figures of value.

Washington — U25

Queue projects below bust.

Lincoln — U26

Neck very long at the back.

Stanton — U27

Bust pointed at the back; figures "7" are normal.

Jefferson — U28

Queue forms straight line with the bust.

Clay — U29

Ear partly concealed by hair, mouth large, chin prominent.

Webster — U30

Has side whiskers.

Scott — U31

Straggling locks of hair at top of head; ornaments around the inner oval end in squares.

Hamilton — U32

Back of bust very narrow, chin almost straight; labels containing figures of value are exactly parallel.

Perry — U33

Front of bust very narrow and pointed; inner lines of shields project very slightly beyond the oval.

1870-71

U74	U23	1c blue	37.50	30.00
a.		1c ultramarine	65.00	35.00
U75	U23	1c blue, *amber*	30.00	27.50
a.		1c ultramarine, *amber*	55.00	30.00
U76	U23	1c blue, *orange*	17.00	15.00
W77	U23	1c blue, *manila*	37.50	35.00
U78	U24	2c brown	35.00	16.00
U79	U24	2c brown, *amber*	15.00	10.00
U80	U24	2c brown, *orange*	10.00	6.50
W81	U24	2c brown, *manila*	25.00	20.00
U82	U25	3c green	7.00	1.00
a.		3c brown (error), *entire*	8,500.	
U83	U25	3c green, *amber*	6.00	2.00
U84	U25	3c green, *cream*	8.00	4.50
U85	U26	6c dark red	20.00	16.00
a.		6c vermilion	20.00	16.00
U86	U26	6c dark red, *amber*	35.00	20.00
a.		6c vermilion, *amber*	35.00	20.00
U87	U26	6c dark red, *cream*	35.00	25.00
a.		6c vermilion, *cream*	30.00	20.00
U88	U27	7c vermilion, *amber* ('71)	55.00	175.00
U89	U28	10c olive black	650.00	900.00
U90	U28	10c olive black, *amber*	650.00	800.00
U91	U28	10c brown	82.50	70.00
U92	U28	10c brown, *amber*	85.00	52.50
a.		10c dark brown, *amber*	85.00	75.00
U93	U29	12c plum	100.00	82.50
U94	U29	12c plum, *amber*	110.00	100.00
U95	U29	12c plum, *cream*	225.00	200.00
U96	U30	15c red orange	75.00	75.00
a.		15c orange	75.00	
U97	U30	15c red orange, *amber*	160.00	275.00
a.		15c orange, *amber*	170.00	
U98	U30	15c red orange, *cream*	300.00	375.00
a.		15c orange, *cream*	300.00	
U99	U31	24c purple	110.00	125.00
U100	U31	24c purple, *amber*	180.00	300.00
U101	U31	24c purple, *cream*	240.00	450.00
U102	U32	30c black	60.00	120.00
U103	U32	30c black, *amber*	180.00	450.00
U104	U32	30c black, *cream*	150.00	450.00
U105	U33	90c carmine	125.00	300.00
U106	U33	90c carmine, *amber*	350.00	900.00
U107	U33	90c carmine, *cream*	175.00	*2,250.*

Printed by Plimpton Manufacturing Co.
The profiles in this issue are inferior to the fine engraving of the Reay issue.

U34

Bust forms an angle at the back near the frame. Lettering poorly executed. Distinct circle in "O" of "Postage."

U35

Lower part of bust points to the end of the "E" in "ONE." Head inclined downward.

U36

Bust narrow at back. Thin numerals. Head of "P" narrow. Bust broad at front, ending in sharp corners.

U37

Bust broad. Figures of value in long ovals.

U38

Similar to U37 but the figure "2" at the left touches the oval.

U39

Similar to U37 but the "O" of "TWO" has the center netted instead of plain and the "G" of "POSTAGE" and the "C" of "CENTS" have diagonal crossline.

U40

Bust broad: numerals in ovals short and thick.

U41

Similar to U40 but the ovals containing the numerals are much heavier. A diagonal line runs from the upper part of the "U" to the white frame-line.

U42

Similar to U40 but the middle stroke of "N" in "CENTS" is as thin as the vertical strokes.

U43

Bottom of bust cut almost semi-circularly.

U44

Thin lettering, long thin figures of value.

U45

Thick lettering, well-formed figures of value, queue does not project below bust.

U46

Top of head egg-shaped; knot of queue well marked and projects triangularly.

Taylor — **U47**

Die 1- Figures of value with thick, curved tops | Die 2- Figures of value with long, thin tops

U48

Neck short at back.

U49

Figures of value turned up at the ends.

U50

Very large head.

U51

Knot of queue stands out prominently.

U52

Ear prominent, chin receding.

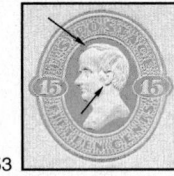

U53

No side whiskers, forelock projects above head.

U54

Hair does not project; ornaments around the inner oval end in points.

U55

Back of bust rather broad, chin slopes considerably; labels containing figures of value are not exactly parallel.

U56

Front of bust sloping; inner lines of shields project considerably into the inner oval.

1874-86   Design U34

U108	1c dark blue	175.00	70.00
a.	1c light blue	175.00	70.00
U109	1c dk bl, *amb*	150.00	75.00
+U110	1c dk blue, *cr*	1,000.	
U111	1c dk blue, *org*	15.00	17.50
a.	dk blue, *org*	12.50	12.50
W112	1c dk blue, *man*	62.50	40.00

Design U35

U113	1c light blue	2.25	1.00
a.	1c dark blue	8.00	7.00
U114	1c lt blue, *amb*	3.25	3.25
a.	dk blue, *amb*	17.50	10.00
U115	1c blue, *cr*	4.75	4.25
a.	dk blue, *cr*	17.50	8.50
U116	1c lt blue, *org*	.75	.40
a.	dk blue, *org*	4.00	2.50
I117	1c lt bl, *bl* ('80)	7.50	5.00
U118	1c lt bl, *fawn* ('79)	7.50	5.00
U119	1c lt bl, *man* ('86)	8.00	3.25
W120	1c lt bl, *man*	1.25	1.10
a.	dk bl, *man*	8.00	7.00
U121	1c lt bl, *amb man*	17.50	10.00

Design U36

U122	2c brown	140.00	65.00
U123	2c brown, *amb*	67.50	40.00
+U124	2c brn, *crm*	1,000.	
+U125	2c brn, *org*	18,000.	
W126	2c brn, *man*	140.00	85.00
W127	2c ver, *man*	2,500.	500.00

Design U37

U128	2c brown	60.00	35.00
U129	2c brn, *amb*	80.00	45.00
+U130	2c brn, *cr*	35,000.	
W131	2c brn, *man*	17.50	15.00

Design U38

U132	2c brown	70.00	27.50
U133	2c brn, *amb*	325.00	70.00
+U133A	2c brn, *cr*	70,000.	

Design U39

U134	2c brown	800.00	160.00
U135	2c brn, *amb*	425.00	150.00
U136	2c brn, *org*	50.00	27.50
W137	2c brn, *man*	75.00	40.00
+U137A	2c ver	32,500.	
+U137B	2c ver, *amb*	30,000.	
+U137C	2c ver, *org*	70,000.	
+W138	2c ver, *man*	25,000.	

Design U40

U139	2c brn ('75)	57.50	37.50
U140	2c brn, *amb* ('75)	85.00	62.50
+U140A	2c reddish brn, *org* ('75)	17,500.	
W141	2c brn, *man* ('75)	32.50	25.00
U142	2c ver ('75)	8.00	5.00
a.	2c pink	8.00	5.00
U143	2c ver, *amb* ('75)	9.00	5.00
U144	2c ver, *cr* ('75)	17.50	7.00
+U145	2c ver, *org* ('75)	35,000.	
U146	2c ver, *bl* ('80)	110.00	40.00
U147	2c ver, *fawn* ('75)	8.00	5.00
W148	2c ver, *man* ('75)	4.00	3.50

Design U41

U149	2c ver ('78)	45.00	25.00
a.	2c pink	52.50	27.00
U150	2c ver, *amb* ('78)	35.00	15.00
U151	2c ver, *bl* ('80)	10.00	8.00
a.	2c pink, *blue*	11.00	8.00
U152	2c ver, *fawn* ('78)	10.00	4.00

Design U42

U153	2c ver ('76)	75.00	30.00
U154	2c ver, *amb* ('76)	300.00	90.00
W155	2c ver, *man* ('76)	20.00	10.00

Design U43

U156	2c ver ('81)	1,250.	175.00
U157	2c ver, *amb* ('81)	42,500.	27,500.
W158	2c ver, *man* ('81)	90.00	55.00

Design U44

U159	3c green	35.00	10.00
U160	3c grn, *amb*	35.00	10.00
U161	3c grn, *cr*	35.00	12.00
+U162	3c grn, *bl*	75,000.	

Design U45

U163	3c green	1.40	.30
U164	3c grn, *amb*	1.50	.70
U165	3c grn, *cr*	8.50	6.50
U166	3c grn, *bl*	7.50	6.00
U167	3c grn, *fawn* ('75)	4.75	3.50

Design U46

U168	3c grn ('81)	1,000.	80.00
U169	3c grn, *amb*	450.00	140.00
U170	3c grn, *bl* ('81)	11,500.	2,750.
U171	3c grn, *fawn* ('81)	40,000.	2,750.

Design U47

U172	5c bl, die I ('75)	12.50	10.00
U173	5c bl, die I, *amb* ('75)	12.50	11.00
U174	5c bl, die I, *cr* ('75)	95.00	45.00
U175	5c bl, die I, *bl* ('75)	30.00	17.50
U176	5c bl, die I, *fawn* ('75)	160.00	65.00
U177	5c bl, die 2 ('75)	11.00	9.00
U178	5c bl, die 2, *amb* ('75)	9.00	8.00
+U178A	5c bl, die 2, *cr* ('76)	10,000.	
U179	5c bl, die 2, *bl* ('75)	25.00	12.50
U180	5c bl, die 2, *fawn* ('75)	125.00	50.00

Design U48

U181	6c red	8.00	6.50
a.	6c vermilion	8.00	6.50

U182		6c red, amber	12.50	6.50
	a.	6c ver, amb	12.50	6.50
U183		6c red, cream	50.00	17.50
	a.	6c ver, cr	45.00	15.00
U184		6c red, fawn ('75)	17.50	12.50

Design U49

+U185	7c vermilion	*1,200.*	
U186	7c ver, amb	125.00	75.00

Design U50

U187	10c brown	40.00	20.00
U188	10c brn, amb	75.00	35.00

Design U51

U189		10c choc ('75)	6.00	4.00
	a.	10c bister brown	7.00	5.00
	b.	10c yellow ocher	3,000.	
U190		10c choc, amb ('75)	7.00	6.00
	a.	10c bis brn, amb	7.00	6.00
	b.	10c yel ocher, amb	3,000.	
U191		10c brn, oriental buff ('86)	12.50	8.75
U192		10c brn, bl ('86)	12.50	8.00
	a.	10c gray blk, bl	12.50	7.50
	b.	10c red brn, bl	12.50	7.50
U193		10c brn, man ('86)	12.50	10.00
	a.	10c red brn, man	12.50	10.00
U194		10c brn, amb man ('86)	17.50	9.00
	a.	10c red brn, amb man	17.50	9.00

Design U52

U195	12c plum	250.00	100.00
U196	12c plum, amb	200.00	160.00
U197	12c plum, cr	180.00	130.00

Design U53

U198	15c orange	50.00	35.00
U199	15c org, amb	140.00	130.00
U200	15c org, cr	450.00	300.00

Design U54

U201	24c purple	175.00	150.00
U202	24c pur, amb	180.00	100.00
U203	24c pur, cr	170.00	100.00

Design U55

U204	30c black	60.00	25.00
U205	30c blk, amb	70.00	60.00
U206	30c blk, cr ('75)	325.00	325.00
U207	30c blk, oriental buff ('81)	100.00	80.00
U208	30c blk, bl ('81)	100.00	80.00
U209	30c blk, man ('81)	90.00	70.00
U210	30c blk, amb man ('86)	180.00	100.00

Design U56

U211	90c carmine ('75)	95.00	75.00
U212	90c car, amb	175.00	250.00
U213	90c car, cr ('75)	1,000.	
U214	90c car, oriental buff ('86)	140.00	250.00
U215	90c car, bl ('86)	175.00	250.00
U216	90c car, man ('86)	140.00	225.00
U217	90c car, amb man ('86)	160.00	*200.00*

Note: No. U206 has watermark #2; No. U207 watermark #6 or #7. No U213 has watermark #2; No. U214 watermark #7. These envelopes cannot be positively identified except by the watermark.

Single line under "POSTAGE" U57

Double line under "POSTAGE" U58

1876

U218	U57 3c red	35.00 25.00
U219	U57 3c green	35.00 17.50
+U220	U58 3c red	27,500.
U221	U58 3c green	35.00 25.00

Cent. of the U.S., and the World's Fair at Philadelphia.

Used examples of Nos. U218-U221 with exposition cancels and/or typed addresses sell for a premium. See No. U582.

Garfield — U59

1882-86

U222	U59 5c brown	5.00	3.00
U223	U59 5c brn, amb	5.25	3.50
+U224	U59 5c brn, oriental buff ('86)	140.00	
+U225	U59 5c brn, bl	75.00	
U226	U59 5c brn, fawn	300.00	

Washington — U60

1883, October

U227	U60 2c red	5.50	2.25
	a. 2c brown (error), entire	*4,000.*	
U228	U60 2c red, amb	6.50	2.75
U229	U60 2c red, blue	8.00	5.00
U230	U60 2c red, fawn	9.00	5.25

Wavy lines fine and clear — U61

1883, November
Four Wavy Lines in Oval

U231	U61 2c red	5.00	2.50
U232	U61 2c red, amber	6.00	3.75
U233	U61 2c red, blue	10.00	7.50
U234	U61 2c red, fawn	7.50	4.75
W235	U61 2c red, man	20.00	6.25

Wavy lines thick and blurred — U62

Retouched die.

1884, June

U236	U62 2c red	15.00	4.00
U237	U62 2c red, amber	20.00	10.00
U238	U62 2c red, blue	29.00	12.00
U239	U62 2c red, fawn	20.00	11.00

See Nos. U260-W269.

3 ½ links over left "2" — U63

U240	U63 2c red	90.00	45.00
U241	U63 2c red, amb	550.00	300.00
U242	U63 2c red, fawn		*25,000.*

2 links below right "2" — U64

U243	U64 2c red	125.00	75.00
U244	U64 2c red, amb	300.00	100.00
U245	U64 2c red, blue	350.00	210.00
U246	U64 2c red, fawn	350.00	200.00

Round "O" in "TWO." White lines above "WO" of "TWO" joined to form thick white dash. — U65

U247	U65 2c red	2,000.	400.00
U248	U65 2c red, amb	3,750.	750.00
U249	U65 2c red, fawn	1,100.	500.00

See Nos. U270-U276.

Jackson — U66

Die 1- Numeral at left is 2 ¾ mm wide | Die 2- Numeral at left is 3 ¼ mm wide

1883-86

U250	U66 4c green, die 1	4.00	3.50
U251	U66 4c grn, die 1, amb	5.00	3.50
U252	U66 4c grn, die 1, oriental buff ('86)	13.00	9.00
U253	U66 4c grn, die 1, blue ('86)	11.00	6.50
U254	U66 4c grn, die 1, man ('86)	16.00	7.50
U255	U66 4c grn, die 1, amb man ('86)	22.50	10.00
U256	U66 4c green, die 2	8.00	5.00
U257	U66 4c grn, die 2, amb	12.50	7.00
U258	U66 4c grn, die 2, man ('86)	12.50	7.50
U259	U66 4c grn, die 2, amb man ('86)	12.50	7.50

1884, May

U260	U61 2c brown	17.50	5.75
U261	U61 2c brown, amber	17.50	6.50
U262	U61 2c brown, blue	17.50	10.00
U263	U61 2c brown, fawn	15.00	9.25
W264	U61 2c brown, manila	15.00	11.50

1884, June
Retouched Die

U265	U62 2c brown	15.00	6.50
U266	U62 2c brn, amb	60.00	40.00
U267	U62 2c brown, blue	22.50	9.00
U268	U62 2c brown, fawn	15.00	11.00
W269	U62 2c brn, man	27.50	15.00

2 Links Below Right "2"

U270	U64 2c brown	130.00	50.00
U271	U64 2c brn, amb	425.00	125.00
U272	U64 2c brown, fawn	7,000.	2,000.

Round "O" in "Two"

U273	U65 2c brown	225.00	100.00
U274	U65 2c brn, amb	225.00	100.00
U275	U65 2c brown, blue		*10,000.*
U276	U65 2c brown, fawn	700.00	750.00

U67

Extremity of bust below the queue forms a point.

Washington — U68

Extremity of bust is rounded.

Similar to U61
Two wavy lines in oval

1884-86

U277		U67 2c brown	.50	.25
	a.	2c brown lake, die 1	22.50	21.00
U278		U67 2c brn, amb	.65	.50
	a.	2c brown lake, amber	35.00	25.00
U279		U67 2c brn, oriental buff ('86)	6.00	2.10
U280		U67 2c brown, blue	3.00	2.10
U281		U67 2c brown, fawn	3.75	2.40
U282		U67 2c brown, man ('86)	12.00	4.00
W283		U67 2c brn, man	8.00	5.00
U284		U67 2c brn, amb man ('86)	7.50	5.75
+U285		U67 2c red	600.00	
+U286		U67 2c red, blue	225.00	
W287		U67 2c red, manila	150.00	
U288		U68 2c brown	275.00	50.00
U289		U68 2c brn, amb	20.00	13.00
U290		U68 2c brown, blue	900.00	325.00
U291		U68 2c brown, fawn	30.00	25.00
W292		U68 2c brn, man	30.00	19.00

Gen. U.S. Grant — US1

Letter Sheet, 160x271mm

1886 **Creamy White Paper**
U293	US1 2c green, entire	30.00	20.00

See the Scott U.S. Specialized Catalogue for perforation and inscription varieties.

Franklin — U69 | Washington U70

Bust points between third and fourth notches of inner oval "G" of "POSTAGE" has no bar.

U71

Bust points between second and third notches of inner oval; "G" of "POSTAGE" has a bar; ear is indicated by one heavy line; one vertical line at corner of mouth.

U72

Frame same as U71; upper part of head more rounded; ear indicated by two curved lines with two locks of hair in front; two vertical lines at corner of mouth.

Jackson — U73   Grant — U74

There is a space between the beard and the collar of the coat. A button is on the collar.

U75

The collar touches the beard and there is no button.

1887-94   Design U69

U294	1c blue	.55	.25
U295	1c dk bl ('94)	6.50	2.50
U296	1c bl, amb	3.25	1.25
U297	1c dk bl, amb ('94)	40.00	22.50
+U298	1c bl, oriental buff	10,000.	
+U299	1c bl, bl	12,500.	
U300	1c bl, man	.65	.35
W301	1c bl, man	.45	.30
U302	1c dk bl, man ('94)	27.50	12.50
W303	1c DK bl, man ('94)	14.00	10.00
U304	1c bl, amb man	12.50	5.00

Design U70

U305	2c green	15.00	10.00
U306	2c grn, amb	40.00	17.50
U307	2c grn, oriental buff	90.00	40.00
U308	2c grn, bl	12,500.	4,250.
U309	2c grn, man	12,500.	1,000.
U310	2c grn, amb man	27,500.	2,250.

Design U71

U311	2c green	.30	.25
a.	2c dark green ('94)	.45	.30
b.	Double impression, entire	375.00	
U312	2c grn, amb	.40	.25
a.	Double impression	—	
b.	2c dk grn, amb ('94)	.55	.35
U313	2c grn, oriental buff	.55	.25
a.	2c dk grn, oriental buff ('94)	2.00	1.00
b.	Double impression	150.00	
U314	2c grn, bl	.60	.30
a.	2c dk grn, bl ('94)	.80	.40
U315	2c grn, man	2.00	.50
a.	2c dk grn, man ('94)	2.75	.75
W316	2c grn, man	3.50	2.50
U317	2c grn, amb man	2.50	1.90
a.	2c dk grn, amb man ('94)	3.50	3.00

Design U72

U318	2c green	110.00	12.50
U319	2c grn, amb	160.00	27.50
U320	2c grn, oriental buff	125.00	40.00
U321	2c grn, bl	150.00	70.00
U322	2c grn, man	240.00	70.00
U323	2c grn, amb man	400.00	100.00

Design U73

U324	4c carmine	3.25	2.00
a.	4c lake	3.50	2.00
b.	4c scarlet ('94)	3.50	2.00
U325	4c car, amb	3.50	3.50
a.	4c lake, amber	3.50	3.50
b.	4c scarlet, amber ('94)	4.00	3.75
U326	4c car, oriental buff	6.50	3.50
a.	4c lake, oriental buff	7.50	3.50
U327	4c car, bl	5.50	4.00
a.	4c lake, blue	6.00	4.00
U328	4c car, man	8.00	7.00
a.	4c lake, manila	8.00	6.00
b.	4c pink, manila	15.00	10.00
U329	4c car, amb man	6.00	3.25
a.	4c lake, amb man	6.00	3.25
b.	4c pink, amb man	15.00	10.00

Design U74

U330	5c blue	3.75	4.00
U331	5c bl, amb	5.00	2.50
a.	Double impression, entire	—	
U332	5c bl, oriental buff	5.50	4.00
U333	5c blue, blue	8.00	6.00

Design U75

U334	5c blue ('94)	20.00	12.50
U335	5c bl, amb ('94)	10.00	7.50

Design U55

U336	30c red brn	40.00	45.00
a.	30c yellow brown	40.00	45.00
b.	30c chocolate	40.00	45.00
U337	30c red brn, amb	40.00	45.00
a.	30c yel brn, amb	40.00	45.00
b.	30c choc, amb	40.00	45.00
U338	30c red brn, oriental buff	40.00	45.00
a.	30c yel brn, oriental buff	40.00	45.00

U339	30c red brn, bl	40.00	45.00
a.	30c yel brn, bl	40.00	45.00
U340	30c red brn, man	40.00	45.00
a.	30c brown, manila	40.00	45.00
U341	30c red brn, amb man	40.00	45.00
a.	30c yel brn, amb man	40.00	45.00

Design U56

U342	90c purple	62.50	85.00
U343	90c pur, amb	72.50	85.00
U344	90c pur, oriental buff	77.50	85.00
U345	90c pur, bl	77.50	85.00
U346	90c pur, man	80.00	85.00
U347	90c pur, amb man	80.00	85.00

Columbus and Liberty — U76

1893

U348	U76 1c deep blue	2.00	1.25
U349	U76 2c violet	1.50	.50
a.	2c dark slate (error)	2,250.	
U350	U76 5c chocolate	6.50	7.00
a.	5c slate brown (error)	750.00	950.00
U351	U76 10c slate brown	25.00	27.50
	Nos. U348-U351 (4)	35.00	36.25

Franklin U77   Washington U78

Bust points to first notch of inner oval and is only slightly concave below.

U79

Bust points to middle of second notch of inner oval and is quite hollow below. Queue has ribbon around it.

U80

Same as die 2, but hair flowing. No ribbon on queue.

Lincoln — U81

Bust pointed but not draped.

U82

Bust broad and draped.

U83

Head larger, inner oval has no notches.

Grant — U84

Similar to design of 1887-95 but smaller.

1899

U352	U77 1c green	2.00	.25
U353	U77 1c green, amber	5.50	1.50
U354	U77 1c green, oriental buff	8.00	2.75
U355	U77 1c green, blue	11.00	7.50
U356	U77 1c green, manila	2.50	.95
W357	U77 1c green, manila	2.75	1.10
U358	U78 2c carmine	3.00	1.75
U359	U78 2c car, amb	17.50	12.50
U360	U78 2c carmine, oriental buff	20.00	11.00
U361	U78 2c carmine, blue	60.00	35.00
U362	U79 2c carmine	.35	.25
a.	2c dark lake	30.00	30.00
U363	U79 2c car, amb	1.75	.25
U364	U79 2c carmine, oriental buff	1.20	.25
U365	U79 2c carmine, blue	1.50	.55
W366	U79 2c car, man	9.00	3.25
U367	U80 2c carmine	6.00	2.75
U368	U80 2c car, amb	10.00	6.50
U369	U80 2c carmine, oriental buff	20.00	12.50
U370	U80 2c carmine, blue	12.50	10.00
U371	U81 4c brown	15.00	12.50
U372	U81 4c brown, amber	15.00	12.50
U373	U82 4c brown	6,500.	1,100.
U374	U83 4c brown	10.00	8.00
U375	U83 4c brown, amber	60.00	25.00
W376	U83 4c brown, manila	15.00	12.50
U377	U84 5c blue	9.00	9.00
U378	U84 5c blue, amber	11.00	10.00

Franklin — U85

Washington — U86

"D" of "UNITED" contains vertical line at right that parallels the left vertical line. One short and two long vertical lines at the right of "CENTS."

Grant — U87

Lincoln — U88

1903

U379	U85 1c green	.75	.25
U380	U85 1c green, amber	10.00	2.00
U381	U85 1c green, oriental buff	15.00	2.50
U382	U85 1c green, blue	17.50	2.50
U383	U85 1c green, manila	4.00	.90
W384	U85 1c green, manila	2.50	.40
U385	U86 2c carmine	.40	.25
a.	2c pink	2.00	1.50
b.	2c red	2.00	1.50
U386	U86 2c carmine, amber	2.00	.50
a.	2c pink, amber	5.50	3.00
b.	2c red, amber	12.50	7.00
U387	U86 2c carmine, oriental buff	2.00	.30
a.	2c pink, oriental buff	3.50	2.00
b.	2c red, oriental buff	4.00	2.25
U388	U86 2c carmine, blue	1.75	.50
a.	2c pink, blue	17.50	14.00
b.	2c red, blue	17.50	14.00
W389	U86 2c carmine, manila	15.00	9.00
U390	U87 4c choc	17.50	11.00
U391	U87 4c choc, amber	17.50	11.00
W392	U87 4c choc, manila	20.00	12.50
U393	U88 5c blue	15.00	11.00
U394	U88 5c blue, amber	15.00	11.00

U89

Re-cut die — "D" of "UNITED" is well rounded at right. The three lines at the right of "CENTS" and at the left of "TWO" are usually all short; the lettering is heavier and the ends of the ribbons slightly changed.

1904   Re-cut Die

U395	U89 2c carmine	.75	.25
a.	2c pink	5.00	2.50
U396	U89 2c carmine, amber	7.50	1.00
a.	2c pink, amber	8.50	3.00
U397	U89 2c carmine, oriental buff	5.00	1.10
a.	2c pink, oriental buff	6.50	2.75
U398	U89 2c carmine, blue	3.75	.90
a.	2c pink, blue	5.00	2.50
W399	U89 2c carmine, manila	12.50	8.00
a.	2c pink, manila	25.00	17.50
b.	Double impression, entire	375.00	

Franklin — U90

Die 1   Die 2

Die 3   Die 4

Die 1 — Wide "D" in "UNITED."
Die 2 — Narrow "D" in "UNITED."
Die 3 — Wide "S-S" in "STATES" (1910).
Die 4 — Sharp angle at back of bust, "N" and "E" of "ONE" are parallel (1912).

1907-16   Die 1

U400	U90 1c green	.35	.25
a.	Die 2	.85	.25
b.	Die 3	.85	.55
c.	Die 4	.85	.25
U401	U90 1c green, amber	2.00	.40
a.	Die 2	2.50	1.00
b.	Die 3	3.25	3.00
c.	Die 4	2.00	1.00

U402 U90 1c green, *oriental buff* .75 .75
- a. Die 2 12.00 1.50
- b. Die 3 14.00 1.50
- c. Die 4 1.00 .75

U403 U90 1c green, *blue* .75 .75
- a. Die 2 12.00 3.00
- b. Die 3 11.50 3.00
- c. Die 4 .75 .65

U404 U90 1c green, *manila* 2.00 1.90
- a. Die 3 4.50 3.00

W405 U90 1c green, *manila* .65 .25
- a. Die 2 60.00 25.00
- b. Die 3 11.00 4.00
- c. Die 4 1,000. —

Washington — U91 — brown red

Die 1, Washington — U91 — carmine

Die 2

Die 3

Die 4

Die 5

Die 6

Die 7

Die 8

Die 1 — Oval "O" in "TWO" and "C" in "CENTS." Front of bust broad.
Die 2 — Similar to 1 but hair re-cut in two distinct locks at top of head.
Die 3 — Round "O" in "TWO" and "C" in "CENTS," coarse lettering.
Die 4 — Similar to 3 but lettering fine and clear, hair lines clearly embossed. Inner oval thin and clear.
Die 5 — All "S's" wide (1910).
Die 6 — Similar to 1 but front of bust narrow (1913).
Die 7 — Similar to 6 but upper corner of front of bust cut away (1916).
Die 8 — Similar to 7 but lower stroke of "S" in "CENTS" is a straight line. Hair as in Die 2 (1916).

Die 1

U406 U91 2c brown red .90 .25
- a. Die 2 40.00 7.00
- b. Die 3 .80 .25

U407 U91 2c brown red, *amber* 6.50 2.00
- a. Die 2 350.00 65.00
- b. Die 3 4.50 1.25

U408 U91 2c brown red, *oriental buff* 8.75 1.50
- a. Die 2 275.00 125.00
- b. Die 3 7.50 2.50

U409 U91 2c brn red, *blue* 5.75 2.00
- a. Die 2 375.00 200.00
- b. Die 3 5.75 1.75

W410 U91 2c brn red, *man* 35.00 35.00

U411 U91 2c carmine .35 .25
- a. Die 2 .75 .25
- b. Die 3 .75 .25
- c. Die 4 .65 .25
- d. Die 5 .65 .30
- e. Die 6 .60 .25
- f. Die 7 3.00 3.00
- g. Die 8 37.50 25.00
- h. #U411 with added impression of #U400, entire 475.00
- i. #U411 with added impression of #U416a, entire 475.00
- k. As No. U411, double impression, entire 175.00

U412 U91 2c carmine, *amb* .50 .25
- a. Die 2 1.00 .25
- b. Die 3 2.25 2.00
- c. Die 4 .55 .25
- d. Die 5 .90 .35
- e. Die 6 .70 .25
- f. Die 7 35.00 25.00

U413 U91 2c car, *oriental buff* .55 .25
- a. Die 2 2.00 .45
- b. Die 3 9.00 3.00
- c. Die 4 .55 1.00
- d. Die 5 3.50 1.25
- e. Die 6 1.00 .70
- f. Die 7 100.00 45.00
- g. Die 8 25.00 17.50

U414 U91 2c carmine, *blue* .55 .25
- a. Die 2 1.00 1.00
- b. Die 3 2.75 2.00
- c. Die 4 .50 .50
- d. Die 5 1.00 .45
- e. Die 6 .65 .30
- f. Die 7 37.50 25.00
- g. Die 8 37.50 25.00

W415 U91 2c car, *manila* 5.00 2.00
- a. Die 2 5.50 1.25
- b. Die 5 5.50 2.50
- c. Die 7 120.00 97.50

U90 4c Die 1   U90 4c Die 2

Die 1 — "F" close to (1mm) left "4."

Die 2 — "F" far from (1¾mm) left "4."

U416 U90 4c black, die 2, laid paper 2.00 1.50
- a. Die 1 1.50 2.00

U417 U90 4c black, *amb*, die 2 7.50 2.50
- a. Die 1 .75 2.00

Die 1 — Tall "F" in "FIVE"   Die 2 — Short "F" in "FIVE"

U418 U91 5c Die 2 1.50 1.50
- a. Die 1 7.00 2.25
- b. 5c blue, *buff*, die 2 (error) 3,250.
- c. 5c blue, *blue*, die 2 (error) 3,000.
- d. As "c," die 1 (error), entire 6,250.

U419 U91 5c blue, *amber*, die 2, laid paper 1.00 .75
- a. Die 1 15.00 12.00

Franklin — U92

Die 1   Die 2

Die 3   Die 4   Die 5

(The 1c and 4c dies are the same except for figures of value.)
Die 1 — UNITED nearer inner circle than outer circle.
Die 2 — Large U; large NT closely spaced.
Die 3 — Knob of hair at back of neck. Large NT widely spaced.
Die 4 — UNITED nearer outer circle than inner circle.
Die 5 — Narrow oval C, (also O and G).

1915-32   **Die 1**

U420 U92 1c green ('17) .25 .25
- a. Die 2 100.00 55.00
- b. Die 3 .35 .25
- c. Die 4 .55 .40
- d. Die 5 .45 .35

U421 U92 1c grn, *amber* ('17) .55 .30
- a. Die 2 400.00 175.00
- b. Die 3 1.40 .65
- c. Die 4 1.90 .85
- d. Die 5 1.10 .55

U422 U92 1c grn, *oriental buff* ('17) 2.40 .90
- a. Die 4 5.50 1.25

U423 U92 1c grn, *bl* ('17) .50 .35
- a. Die 3 .80 .45
- b. Die 4 1.40 .65
- c. Die 5 .85 .35

U424 U92 1c grn, *manila (unglazed)* ('16) 6.50 4.00

W425 U92 1c grn, *manila (unglazed)* ('16) .30 .25
- a. Die 3 175.00 125.00

U426 U92 1c grn, *brown (glazed)* ('20) 45.00 16.00

W427 U92 1c grn, *brown (glazed)* ('20) 65.00 35.00
- a. Printed on unglazed side 400.00
  - Entire 750.00
- b. Unglazed on both sides 150.00

U428 U92 1c grn, *brown (unglazed)* ('20) 12.50 7.50

W428A U92 1c grn, *brown (unglazed)* ('20) 3,000.

Washington — U93

Die 1

Die 2

Die 3

Die 4

Die 5

Die 6

Die 7

Die 8

Die 9

(The 1½c, 2c, 3c, 5c, and 6c dies are the same except for figures of value.)

Die 1 — Letters broad. Numerals vertical. Large head (9¼mm). from tip of nose to back of neck. E closer to inner circle than N of cents.

Die 2 — Similar to 1; but U far from left circle.

Die 3 — Similar to 2; but all inner circles very thin (Rejected die).

Die 4 — Large head as in Die 1. C of CENTS close to circle. Baseline of right numeral "2" slants downward to right. Left numeral "2" is larger.

Die 5 — Small head (8¾mm) from tip of nose to back of neck. T and S of CENTS close at bottom.

Die 6 — Similar to 5; but T and S of CENTS far apart at bottom. Left numeral slopes to right.

Die 7 — Large head. Both numerals slope to right. Clean cut lettering. All letters T have short top strokes.

Die 8 — Similar to 7; but all letters T have long top strokes.

Die 9 — Narrow oval C (also O and G).

1915-32			Die 1	
U429	U93 2c carmine		.25	.25
a.	Die 2	15.00	7.00
b.	Die 3	45.00	50.00
c.	Die 4	27.50	15.00
d.	Die 5	.55	.35
e.	Die 6	.65	.30
f.	Die 7	.70	.25
g.	Die 8	.50	.25
h.	Die 9	.50	.25
i.	2c green (error), die 1, entire	12,500.	
j.	#U429 with added impression of #U420	600.00	
k.	#U429 with added impression of #U416a, entire	3,500.	
l.	#U429 with added impression of #U400, entire	950.00	
m.	#U429, double impression, entire	1,500.	
n.	As "f," double impression, entire	750.00	
o.	As "e," triple impression		
p.	As "m," second impression on side flap, entire		250.00
U430	U93 2c car, amber ('16)	.30	.25
a.	Die 2	20.00	12.50
b.	Die 4	50.00	25.00
c.	Die 5	1.60	.35
d.	Die 6	1.25	.40
e.	Die 7	.75	.35
f.	Die 8	.70	.30
g.	Die 9	.65	.25
h.	As No. U430, with added impression of 4c black (#U416a), entire	600.00	
i.	As "g," with added impression of 2c car. die 1 on side flap, entire	—	
U431	U93 2c car, oriental buff ('16)	2.25	.65
a.	Die 2	180.00	75.00
b.	Die 4	75.00	60.00
c.	Die 5	3.50	2.00
d.	Die 6	3.50	2.00
e.	Die 7	3.50	2.00
U432	U93 2c car, blue ('16)	.30	.25
b.	Die 2	40.00	25.00
c.	Die 3	160.00	90.00
d.	Die 4	65.00	50.00
e.	Die 5	1.10	.30
f.	Die 6	1.10	.40
g.	Die 7	.85	.35
h.	Die 8	.65	.25
i.	Die 9	1.00	.30
j.	2c purple (error), die 9	—	
k.	Double impression	650.00	
U432A	U93 2c car, manila, die 7, entire	50,000.	
W433	U93 2c car, manila, ('16)	.25	.25
W434	U93 2c car, brn (glazed) ('20)	70.00	45.00
W435	U93 2c car, brn (unglazed) ('20)	90.00	60.00
U436	U93 3c purple ('32)	.30	.25
a.	3c dark violet, die 1 ('17)	.60	.25
b.	3c dark violet, die 5 ('17)	1.75	.75
c.	3c dark violet, die 6 ('17)	2.10	1.40
d.	3c dark violet, die 7 ('17)	1.50	.95

e.	3c, purple, die 7 ('32)	.70	.30
f.	3c purple, die 9 ('32)	.45	.25
g.	3c carmine (error), die 1	35.00	35.00
h.	3c carmine (error), die 5	30.00	—
i.	#U436 with added impression of #U420, entire	900.00	
j.	#U436 with added impression of #U429, entire	900.00	950.00
k.	As "f," double impression, preprinted, entire	600.00	
U437	U93 3c purple, amb ('32)	.35	.25
a.	3c dk vio, die 1 ('17)	5.50	1.25
b.	3c dk vio, die 5 ('17)	8.50	2.50
c.	3c dk vio, die 6 ('17)	8.50	2.50
d.	3c dk vio, die 7 ('17)	8.50	2.25
e.	3c pur, die 7 ('32)	.75	.25
f.	3c pur, die 9 ('32)	.55	.25
g.	3c carmine (error), die 5	375.00	400.00
h.	3c black (error), die 1	190.00	—
U438	U93 3c dk vio, oriental buff ('17)	22.50	5.50
a.	Die 5	22.50	5.50
b.	Die 6	30.00	8.00
c.	Die 7	30.00	10.00
U439	U93 3c purple, bl ('32)	.35	.25
a.	3c dark violet, die 1 ('17)	7.00	2.00
b.	3c dark violet, die 5 ('17)	7.50	6.00
c.	3c dark violet, die 6 ('17)	7.50	6.00
d.	3c dark violet, die 7 ('17)	10.00	6.00
e.	3c purple, die 7 ('32)	.75	.25
f.	3c purple, die 9 ('32)	.60	.25
g.	3c carmine (error), die 5	250.00	300.00
U440	U92 4c black ('18)	1.75	.60
a.	With added impression of 2c carmine (#U429), die 1, entire	450.00	
U441	U92 4c black, amb ('18)	3.00	.85
a.	4c black, amb, with added impression of 2c car (#U429), die 1	175.00	
U442	U92 4c blk, bl ('21)	3.25	.85
U443	U93 5c blue ('18)	3.25	2.75
U444	U93 5c blue, amber ('18)	4.00	1.60
U445	U93 5c bl, blue ('21)	3.75	3.25

For 1½c and 6c see Nos. U481-W485, U529-U531.

Double or triple surcharge listings of 1920-25 are for examples with surcharge directly or partly upon the stamp.

Surcharged on 1874-1920 Envelopes indicated by Numbers in Parentheses

Type 1

1920-21	Surcharged in Black
U446	U93 2c on 3c dark vio (U436a, die 1)	12.50	10.00
a.	On No. U436b (die 5)	12.50	10.00
b.	As "a," double surcharge	140.00	

Surcharged

Type 2

Rose Surcharge

U447	U93 2c on 3c dark vio (U436a, die 1)	8.00	7.50
b.	On No. U436c (die 6)	12.00	8.50

Black Surcharge

U447A	U92 2c on 1c green (U420, die 1) Entire	3,000.	
U447C	U93 2c on 2c carmine (U429, die 1)	—	
U447D	U93 2c on 2c car, amb (U430, die 1)	12,000.	
U448	U93 2c on 3c dark vio (U436a, die 1)	2.75	2.00
a.	On No. U436b (die 5)	2.75	2.00
b.	On No. U436c (die 6)	3.50	2.00
c.	On No. U436d (die 7)	2.75	2.00
U449	U93 2c on 3c dk vio, amb (U437a, die 1)	7.50	6.00
a.	On No. U437b (die 5)	13.00	7.50
b.	On No. U437c (die 6)	9.50	6.00
c.	On No. U437d (die 7)	8.50	6.50
U450	U93 2c on 3c dk vio, oriental buff (U438, die 1)	15.00	15.00
a.	On No. U438a (die 6)	15.00	15.00
b.	On No. U438b (die 6)	15.00	15.00
c.	On No. U438c (die 7)	130.00	90.00
U451	U93 2c on 3c dk vio, blue (U439a, die 1)	12.50	10.50
b.	On No. U439b (die 5)	12.50	10.50
c.	On No. U439c (die 6)	12.50	10.50
d.	On No. U439d (die 7)	25.00	22.50

Surcharged

Type 3

Bars 2mm apart, 25 to 26mm in length from outer edges of end bars

U451A	U90 2c on 1c green (U400, die 1)	25,000.	
U452	U92 2c on 1c green (U420, die 1)	1,750.	
a.	On No. U420b (die 3)	3,000.	
b.	As No. U452, double surcharge	3,750.	
U453	U91 2c on 2c car (U411b, die 3)	4,000.	
a.	On No. U411 (die 1)	3,750.	
U453B	U91 2c on 2c car, bl (U414e, die 6)	1,500.	750.00
U453C	U91 2c on 2c car, oriental buff (U413e, die 6)	1,400.	750.00
d.	On No. U413 (die 1)	1,400.	
U454	U93 2c on 2c car (U429e, die 6)	125.00	
a.	On No. U429 (die 1)	300.00	
b.	On No. U429d (die 5)	500.00	
c.	On No. U429f (die 7)	125.00	
U455	U93 2c on 2c car, amb (U430, die 1)	1,250.	
a.	On No. U430d (die 6)	1,500.	
b.	On No. U430e (die 7)	1,500.	
U456	U93 2c on 2c car, oriental buff (U431a, die 2)	225.00	
a.	On No. U431c (die 5)	225.00	
b.	On No. U431e (die 7)	800.00	
c.	As No. U456, double surcharge	700.00	
U457	U93 2c on 2c car, bl (U432f, die 6)	350.00	
a.	On No. U432e (die 5)	300.00	
b.	On No. U432g (die 7)	700.00	
U458	U93 2c on 3c dark vio (U436a, die 1)	.50	.35
a.	On No. U436b (die 5)	.50	.40
b.	On No. U436c (die 6)	.50	.35
c.	On No. U436d (die 7)	.50	.35
d.	As #U458, double surcharge	25.00	7.50
e.	As #U458, triple surcharge	90.00	
f.	As #U458, dbl. surch., 1 in magenta	90.00	

g.	As #U458, dbl. surch., types 2 & 3	140.00	
h.	As "a," double surcharge	27.50	15.00
i.	As "a," triple surcharge	110.00	
j.	As "a," double surch., both magenta	110.00	
k.	As "b," double surcharge	25.00	8.00
l.	As "c," double surcharge	25.00	8.00
m.	As "c," triple surcharge	110.00	
n.	Double impression of indicia, single surcharge, entire	450.00	
U459	U93 2c on 3c dk vio, amb (U437c, die 6)	3.00	1.00
a.	On No. U437a (die 5)	4.00	1.00
b.	On No. U437c (die 6)	4.00	1.00
c.	On No. U437d (die 7)	3.00	1.00
d.	As #U459, double surcharge	35.00	
e.	As "a," double surcharge	35.00	
f.	As "b," double surcharge	35.00	
g.	As "b," double surcharge, types 2 & 3	125.00	
h.	As "c," double surcharge	35.00	
U460	U93 2c on 3c dk vio, oriental buff (U438a, die 5)	3.50	2.00
a.	On No. U438 (die 1)	3.50	2.00
b.	On No. U438b (die 6)	4.00	2.00
c.	As #U460, double surcharge	20.00	
d.	As "a," double surcharge	20.00	
e.	As "b," double surcharge	20.00	
f.	As "b," triple surcharge	150.00	
U461	U93 2c on 3c dk vio, bl (U439a, die 1)	6.00	1.00
a.	On No. U439b (die 5)	6.00	1.00
b.	On No. U439c (die 6)	6.00	2.50
c.	On No. U439d (die 7)	12.50	7.50
d.	As #U461, double surcharge	17.50	
e.	As "a," double surcharge	17.50	
f.	As "b," double surcharge	17.50	
g.	As "c," double surcharge	17.50	
U462	U87 2c on 4c choc (U390)	475.00	260.00
U463	U87 2c on 4c choc, amb (U391)	750.00	350.00
U463A	U90 2c on 4c black (U416, die 2)	800.00	400.00
U464	U93 2c on 5c blue (U443)	850.00	

Surcharged

Type 4

Bars 1 mm apart, 21 to 23 mm in length from outer edges of end bars

U465	U92 2c on 1c green (U420, die 1)	900.00	
a.	On No. U420b (die 3)	1,100.	
U466	U91 2c on 2c car (U411e, die 6), entire	22,500.	
U466A	U93 2c on 2c carmine (U429, die 1)	700.00	
c.	On No. U429d (die 5)	900.00	
d.	On No. U429e (die 6)	900.00	
	On No. U429f (die 7)	750.00	
U466B	U93 2c on 2c car, amb (U430)	15,000.	
U466C	U93 2c on 2c car, oriental buff (U431), entire	15,000.	
U466D	U25 2c on 3c green, die 2 (U82)	7,500.	
U467	U45 2c on 3c green, die 2 (U163)	325.00	
U468	U93 2c on 3c dark vio (U436a, die 1)	.70	.45
a.	On No. U436b (die 5)	.70	.50
b.	On No. U436c (die 6)	.70	.50
c.	On No. U436d (die 7)	.70	.50
d.	As #U468, double surcharge	20.00	
e.	As #U468, triple surcharge	100.00	
f.	As #U468, dbl. surch., types 2 & 4	125.00	
g.	As "a," double surcharge	20.00	

h.	As "b," double surcharge	20.00	
i.	As "c," double surcharge	20.00	
j.	As "c," triple surcharge	100.00	
k.	As "c," inverted surcharge	75.00	
l.	2c on 3c carmine (error), (U436h).	600.00	
m.	As #U468, triple surcharge, one inverted, entire		700.00

U469 U93 2c on 3c dk vio, *amb* (U437a, die 1) — 3.75 2.25
a. On No. U437b (die 5) 3.75 2.25
b. On No. U437c (die 6) 3.75 2.25
c. On No. U437d (die 7) 3.75 2.25
d. As #U469, double surcharge 30.00
e. As "a," double surcharge 30.00
f. As "a," double surcharge, types 2 & 4 100.00
g. As "b," double surcharge 30.00
h. As "c," double surcharge 30.00

U470 U93 2c on 3c dk vio, *oriental buff* (U438, die 1) — 6.00 2.50
a. On No. U438a (die 5) 6.00 2.50
b. On No. U438b (die 6) 6.00 2.50
c. On No. U438c (die 7) 42.50 32.50
d. As #U470, double surch., types 2 & 4 25.00
e. As "a," double surcharge 85.00
f. As "a," double surcharge 25.00
g. As "b," double surcharge 25.00

U471 U93 2c on 3c dk vio, *bl* (U439a, die 1) — 6.00 1.75
a. On No. U439b (die 5) 7.00 1.75
b. On No. U439c (die 6) 7.00 1.75
c. On No. U439d (die 7) 10.00 10.00
d. As #U471, double surcharge 25.00
e. As #U471, double surch., types 2 & 4 160.00
f. As "a," double surcharge 25.00
g. As "b," double surcharge 25.00

U471A U83 2c on 4c brown, (U374), entire 625.00

U472 U87 2c on 4c choc (U390) 12.00 12.00
a. Double surcharge 150.00

U473 U87 2c on 4c choc, *amb* (U391) 17.00 10.00

Surcharged

Double Surcharge, Type 4 and 1c as above

U474 U93 2c on 1c on 3c dark violet (U436a, die 1) 200. 500.
a. On No. U436b (die 5) 200.
b. On No. U436d (die 7) 850.

U475 U93 2c on 1c on 3c dk vio, *amb* (U437a, die 1) 175.

Surcharged

Type 5

U476 U93 2c on 3c dk vio, *amb* (U437a, die 1) 200.
a. On No. U437c (die 6) 700.
b. As #U476, double surcharge —

Surcharged

Type 6

U477 U93 2c on 3c dark vio (U436a, die 1) 120.
a. On No. U436b (die 5) 250.
b. On No. U436c (die 6) 250.
c. On No. U436d (die 7) 250.
U478 U93 2c on 3c dk vio, *amb* (U437a, die 1) 250.

Handstamped Surcharge in Black or Violet — Type 7

U479 U93 2c on 3c dark violet (Bk) (U436a, die 1) 240. —
a. On No. U436b (die 5) 625.
b. On No. U436d (die 7) 425.
U480 U93 2c on 3c dark violet (V) (U436d, die 7) 4,500.
a. Double overprint —

Expertization by competent authorities is required for Nos. U476-U480.

Type of 1916-32 Issue

1925-34 **Die 1**
U481 U93 1½c brown .25 .25
a. Die 8 .70 .25
b. 1½c purple, die 1 (error) ('34) 60.00
U482 U93 1½c brown, *amber* .90 .40
a. Die 8 1.75 .75
U483 U93 1½c brown, *bl* 1.60 .95
a. Die 8 2.40 1.25
U484 U93 1½c brown, *manila* 5.00 3.00
W485 U93 1½c brown, *manila* .85 .25
a. With added impression of #W433 120.00 —

Surcharged Type 8

1925 **On Envelopes of 1887**
U486 U71 1½c on 2c grn (U311) 500.00
U487 U71 1½c on 2c green, *amb* (U312) 900.00
U488 U77 1½c on 1c green (U352) 400.00
U489 U77 1½c on 1c grn, *amb* (U353) 110.00 60.
U490 U90 1½c on 1c green (U400, die 1) 6.25 3.50
a. On No. U400a (die 2) 17.00 9.00
b. On No. U400b (die 3) 40.00 17.50
c. On No. U400c (die 4) 9.00 2.50
U491 U90 1½c on 1c grn, *amb* (U401c, die 4) 8.00 3.00
a. On No. U401 (die 1) 12.50 3.50
b. On No. U401a (die 2) 120.00 70.00
c. On No. U401b (die 3) 60.00 50.00
U492 U90 1½c on 1c grn, *oriental buff* (U402a, die 2) 500.00 150.00
a. On No. U402c (die 4) 750.00 250.00
U493 U90 1½c on 1c grn, *bl* (U403c, die 4) 100.00 65.00
a. On No. U403a (die 3) 100.00 67.50
U494 U90 1½c on 1c grn, *man* (U404, die 1) 300.00 100.00
a. On No. U404a (die 3) 1,000.
U495 U92 1½c on 1c green (U420, die 1) .80 .25
a. On No. U420a (die 2) 85.00 52.50
b. On No. U420b (die 3) 2.10 .70

c. On No. U420c (die 4) 2.10 .85
d. As #U495, double surcharge 10.00 3.00
e. As "b," double surcharge 10.00 3.00
f. As "c," double surcharge 10.00 3.00
U496 U92 1½c on 1c grn, *amb* (U421, die 1) 15.00 12.50
a. On No. U421b (die 3) 725.00
b. On No. U421c (die 4) 15.00 12.50
U497 U92 1½c on 1c grn, *oriental buff* (U422, die 1) 3.75 1.90
a. On No. U422b (die 4) 67.50
U498 U92 1½c on 1c grn, *bl* (U423c, die 4) 1.40 .75
a. On No. U423 (die 1) 2.40 1.50
b. On No. U423b (die 3) 1.75 1.50
U499 U92 1½c on 1c grn, *man* (U424) 10.00 6.00
U500 U92 1½c on 1c grn, *brn* (unglazed) (U428) 65.00 30.00
U501 U92 1½c on 1c grn, *brn* (glazed) (U426) 65.00 30.00
U502 U93 1½c on 2c car (U429, die 1) 200.00 —
a. On No. U429d (die 5) 250.00
b. On No. U429f (die 7) 250.00
c. On No. U429e (die 6) 325.00
d. On No. U429g (die 8) 450.00
U503 U93 1½c on 2c car, *oriental buff* (U431c, die 5) 200.00 —
a. Double surcharge 200.00
b. Double surcharge, one inverted 700.00
U504 U93 1½c on 2c car, *bl* (U432, die 1) 300.00 —
a. On No. U432g (die 7) 300.00
b. As "a," double surcharge, entire 350.00
c. On No. U432f (die 6), entire 400.00
U505 U93 1½c on 1½c brn (U481, die 1) 300.00 —
a. On No. U481a (die 8) 300.00
b. As No. U505, double surcharge, entire 2,000.
U506 U93 1½c on 1½c brn, *bl* (U483a, die 8) 200.00 —
a. On No. U483 (die 1) 300.00

The paper of No. U500 is not glazed and appears to be the same as that used for the wrappers of 1920.

Surcharged Type 9

Black Surcharge

U507 U69 1½c on 1c blue (U294) 1,750.
U507B U69 1½c on 1c blue, *manila* (U300) 4,750.
U508 U77 1½c on 1c grn, *amb* (U353) 55.00
U508A U85 1½c on 1c grn (U379) 3,000.
U509 U85 1½c on 1c grn, *amb* (U380) 12.50 10.00
a. Double surcharge 75.00
U509B U85 1½c on 1c green, *oriental buff* (U381) 40.00 40.00
U510 U90 1½c on 1c green (U400, die 1) 2.75 1.25
b. On No. U400a (die 2) 9.00 4.00
c. On No. U400b (die 3) 37.50 8.00
d. On No. U400c (die 4) 3.50 1.25
e. As No. U510, double surcharge 25.00
U511 U90 1½c on 1c grn, *amb* (U401, die 1) 200.00 100.00

U512 U90 1½c on 1c grn, *oriental buff* (U402, die 1) 8.00 4.00
a. On No. U402c (die 4) 21.00 14.00
U513 U90 1½c on 1c grn, *bl* (U403, die 1) 6.00 4.00
a. On No. U403c (die 4) 6.00 4.00
U514 U90 1½c on 1c grn, *man* (U404, die 1) 30.00 9.00
a. On No. U404a (die 3) 77.50 40.00
U515 U92 1½c on 1c green (U420, die 1) .40 .25
a. On No. U420a (die 2) 15.00 15.00
b. On No. U420b (die 3) .40 .25
c. On No. U420c (die 4) .40 .25
d. As #U515, double surcharge 10.00
e. As #U515, inverted surcharge 15.00
f. As #U515, triple surcharge 15.00
g. As #U515, dbl. surch., one invtd., entire —
h. As "b," double surcharge 10.00
i. As "b," inverted surcharge 15.00
j. As "b," triple surcharge 25.00
k. As "c," double surcharge 10.00
l. As "c," inverted surcharge 15.00
U516 U92 1½c on 1c grn, *amb* (U421c, die 4) 55.00 27.50
a. On No. U421 (die 1) 60.00 32.50
U517 U92 1½c on 1c grn, *oriental buff* (U422, die 1) 6.25 1.25
a. On No. U422a (die 4) 7.25 1.50
U518 U92 1½c on 1c grn, *bl* (U423b, die 4) 5.00 1.50
a. On No. U423 (die 1) 8.25 4.50
b. On No. U423a (die 3) 27.50 7.50
c. As "a," double surcharge 30.00
U519 U92 1½c on 1c grn, *man* (U424, die 1) 25.00 12.00
a. Double surcharge 100.00
U520 U93 1½c on 2c car (U429, die 1) 300.00 —
a. On No. U429d (die 5) 275.00
b. On No. U429e (die 6) 275.00
c. On No. U429f (die 7) 275.00
U520D U93 1½c on 2c car, *amber* (U430c, die 5), entire —
U520E U92 1½c on 4c black (U440, die 1), entire —

Magenta Surcharge

U521 U92 1½c on 1c grn (U420b, die 3) 4.25 3.50
a. Double surcharge 75.00

Sesquicentennial Exposition Issue

150th anniversary of the Declaration of Independence.

Liberty Bell — U94

Die 1. The center bar of "E" of "postage" is shorter than top bar.
Die 2. The center bar of "E" of "postage" is of same length as top bar.

1926, July 27
U522 U94 2c carmine, die 1 1.00 .50
a. Die 2 5.50 3.75

Washington Bicentennial Issue

200th anniversary of the birth of George Washington.

Mount Vernon — U95

2c Die 1 — "S" of "Postage" normal.
2c Die 2 — "S" of "Postage" raised.

1932

U523	U95	1c olive green	1.00	.80
U524	U95	1½c chocolate	2.00	1.50
U525	U95	2c car, die 1	.40	.25
a.		2c carmine, die 2	70.00	20.00
b.		2c carmine, *blue*, die 1		
		(error) entire	30,000.	
U526	U95	3c violet	1.75	.35
U527	U95	4c black	17.50	17.50
U528	U95	5c dark blue	3.50	3.50
		Nos. U523-U528 (6)	26.15	23.90

Type of 1916-32 Issue

1932, Aug. 18

U529	U93	6c orange, die 7	6.00	4.00
U530	U93	6c orange, *amber*, die 7	10.00	10.00
U531	U93	6c orange, *blue*, die 7	10.00	10.00

Franklin — U96

Die 1

Die 2

Die 3

Die 1 — Short (3½mm) and thick "I" in thick circle.

Die 2 — Tall (4½mm) and thin "1" in thin circle; upper and lower bars of E in ONE long and 1mm from circle.

Die 3 — As in Die 2, but E normal and 1½mm from circle.

1950

U532	U96	1c green, die 1	5.00	1.75
a.		Die 2	6.50	3.00
b.		Die 3	6.50	3.00
		Precanceled, die 3		1.25

Washington — U97

Die 1   Die 2

Die 3   Die 4

Die 1 — Thick "2" in thick circle; toe of "2" is acute angle.

Die 2 — Thin "2" in thin circle; toe of "2" is almost right angle; line through left stand of "N" in UNITED and stand of "E" in POSTAGE goes considerably below tip of chin; "N" of UNITED is tall; "O" of TWO is high.

Die 3 — Figure "2" as in Die 2. Short UN in UNITED thin crossbar in A of STATES.

Die 4 — Tall UN in UNITED; thick crossbar in A of STATES; otherwise like Die 3.

U533	U97	2c carmine, die 3	.70	.25
a.		Die 1	.80	.30
b.		Die 2	1.40	.85
c.		Die 4	1.30	.60

Die 1

Die 2

Die 3

Die 4

Die 5

Die 1 — Thick and tall (4½mm) "3" in thick circle; long top bars and short stems in T's of STATES.

Die 2 — Thin and tall (4½mm) "3" in medium circle; short top bars and long stems in T's of STATES.

Die 3 — Thin and short (4mm) "3" in thin circle; lettering wider than Dies 1 and 2; line from left stand of N to stand of E is distinctly below tip of chin.

Die 4 — Figure and letters as in Die 3. Line hits tip of chin; short N in UNITED and thin crossbar in A of STATES.

Die 5 — Figure, letter and chin line as in Die 4; but tall N in UNITED and thick crossbar in A of STATES.

U534	U97	3c dark violet, die 4	.35	.25
a.		Die 1	1.90	.70
b.		Die 2	.75	.50
c.		Die 3	.55	.25
d.		Die 5	.75	.45
e.		As "c," double impression	300.00	

Washington — U98

1952

U535	U98	1½c brown	4.50	3.50
		Precanceled		1.25

Die 1

Die 2

Die 3

Die 1 — Head high in oval (2mm below T of STATES). Circle near (1mm) bottom of colored oval.

Die 2 — Head low in oval (3mm). Circle 1½mm from edge of oval. Right leg of A in POSTAGE shorter than left. Short leg on P.

Die 3 — Head centered in oval (2½mm). Circle as in Die 2. Legs of A of POSTAGE about equal. Long leg on P.

1958

U536	U96	4c red violet, die 1	.75	.25
a.		Die 2	.90	.25
b.		Die 3	.90	.25

Nos. U429, U429f, U429h, U533, U533a-U533c Surcharged in Red at Left of Stamp

Nos. U429, U429f, U429h, U533, U533a-U533c Surcharged in Red

1958

U537	U93	2c + 2c carmine, die 1	3.25	1.50
a.		Die 7	10.00	7.00
b.		Die 9	4.75	5.00
U538	U97	2c + 2c carmine, die 1	.70	.80
a.		Die 2	.90	1.00
b.		Die 3	.70	.70
c.		Die 4	.70	1.00

Nos. U436a, U436e-U436f, U534, U534b-U534d Surcharged in Green at Left of Stamp

Nos. U436a, U436e-U436f, U534a-U534d Surcharged in Green

U539	U93	3c + 1c purple, die 1	12.50	9.00
a.		Die 7	11.00	7.50
b.		Die 9	20.00	15.00
U540	U97	3c + 1c dark violet, die 3	.40	1.00
a.		Die 2, entire	3,500.	—
b.		Die 4	.65	1.00
c.		Die 5	.70	1.00

Benjamin Franklin — U99

George Washington U100

Die 1

Die 2

Dies of 1¼c

Die 1 — The "4" is 3mm high. Upper leaf in left cluster is 2mm from "U."

Die 2 — The "4" is 3½mm high. Leaf clusters are larger. Upper leaf at left is 1mm from "U."

1960

U541	U99	1¼c turquoise, die 1	.65	.50
		Die 1, precanceled		.25
a.		Die 2, precanceled		1.25
U542	U100	2½c dull blue	.80	.50
		Precanceled		.25

Precanceled cut squares

Precanceled envelopes do not normally receive another cancellation. Since the lack of a cancellation makes it impossible to distinguish between cut squares from used and unused envelopes, they are valued here as used only.

Pony Express Centennial Issue

Pony Express Rider — U101

Envelope White Outside, Blue Inside.

1960

U543	U101	4c brown	.55	.30

Abraham Lincoln — U102

Die 1

Die 2

Die 3

Die 1 — Center bar of E of POSTAGE is above the middle. Center bar of E of STATES slants slightly upward. Nose sharper, more pointed. No offset ink specks inside envelope on back of die impression.
Die 2 — Center bar of E of POSTAGE in middle. P of POSTAGE has short stem. Ink specks on back of die impression.
Die 3 — FI of FIVE closer than Die 1 or 2. Second T of STATES seems taller than ES. Ink specks on back of die impression.

1962

U544	U102	5c dark blue, die 2	.80	.25
a.		Die 1	.80	.25
b.		Die 3	.85	.35
c.		Die 2 with albino impression of 4c (#U536)	60.00	
d.		Die 3 with albino impression of 4c (#U536), entire	140.00	—
e.		Die 3 on complete impression of 4c (#U536), cut square	125.00	

No. U536 Surcharged in Green at left of Stamp

Two types of surcharge:
Type I — "U.S. POSTAGE" 18½mm high. Serifs on cross of T both diagonal. Two lines of shading in C of CENT.
Type II — "U.S. POSTAGE" 17½mm high. Right serif on cross of T is vertical. Three shading lines in C.

1962

U545	U96	4c + 1c red vio, die 1, type I	1.25	1.10
a.		Type II	1.25	1.10

New York World's Fair Issue

Issued to publicize the New York World's Fair, 1964-65.

Globe with Satellite Orbit — U103

1964

U546	U103	5c maroon	.55	.40

Liberty Bell — U104

Old Ironsides U105

Eagle — U106

Head of Statue of Liberty — U107

1965-69

U547	U104	1¼c brown		.50
U548	U104	1⁴⁄₁₀c brown ('68)		.50
U548A	U104	1⁶⁄₁₀c orange ('69)		.50
b.		1⁶⁄₁₀c brown (error), entire	5,000.	

U549	U105	4c bright blue	.90	.25
U550	U106	5c bright purple	.75	.25
a.		Bar tagged ('67)	3.00	1.00

Tagged

U551	U107	6c lt green ('68)	.70	.25
a.		6c dark gray green, entire	200.00	—

Nos. U549-U550 Surcharged in Red or Green at Left of Stamp

1968, Feb. 5

U552	U105	4c + 2c bright blue (R)	3.25	2.00
U553	U106	5c + 1c bright purple (G)	3.00	2.75
a.		Tagged	3.00	2.75
b.		With 2c surcharge type "b" (error)	400.00	

Tagged

Envelopes from No. U554 onward are tagged, except for bulk-rate and non-profit envelopes, which are untagged. The tagging element is in the ink through No. 608 unless otherwise noted. From No. 611 on, envelopes have bar or block tagging unless otherwise noted.

Herman Melville Issue

Issued to honor Herman Melville (1819-1891), writer, and the whaling industry.

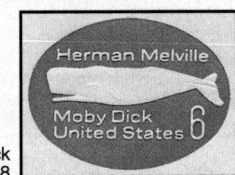

Moby Dick U108

1970, Mar. 7

U554	U108	6c blue	.50	.25

Youth Conference Issue

Issued to publicize the White House Conference on Youth, Estes Park, Colo., Apr. 18-22.

Youth Conference Emblem — U109

1971, Feb. 24

U555	U109	6c light blue	.70	1.00

Liberty Bell Type of 1965 and

Eagle — U110

1971

U556	U104	1⁷⁄₁₀c deep lilac, untagged		.35
U557	U110	8c ultramarine	.40	.25

Nos. U551 and U555 Surcharged in Green at Left of Stamp

1971, May 16

U561	U107	6c + (2c) light green	.90	1.25
a.		Inverted surcharge, entire	225.00	
U562	U109	6c + (2c) light blue	2.00	2.50
a.		Inverted surcharge printed on reverse, entire	—	

Bowling Issue

Issued as a salute to bowling and in connection with the 7th World Tournament of the International Bowling Federation, Milwaukee, Wis.

Bowling Ball and Pin U111

1971, Aug. 21

U563	U111	8c rose red	.60	.25

Aging Conference Issue

White House Conference on Aging, Washington, D.C., Nov. 28-Dec. 2, 1971.

Conference Symbol U112

1971, Nov. 15

U564	U112	8c light blue	.50	.25

International Transportation Exhibition Issue

U.S. International Transportation Exhibition, Dulles International Airport, Washington, D.C., May 27-June 4.

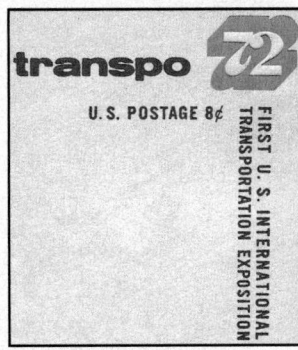

Transportation Exhibition Emblem — U113

1972, May 2

U565	U113	8c ultramarine & rose red	.50	.25

No. U557 Surcharged in Ultramarine at Left of Stamp

1973, Dec. 1

U566	U110	8c + 2c brt. ultramarine	.40	1.25

Liberty Bell — U114

1973, Dec. 5

U567	U114	10c emerald	.40	.25

"Volunteer Yourself" U115

1974, Aug. 23

Untagged

U568	U115	1⁸⁄₁₀c blue green		.25

Tennis Centenary Issue

Centenary of tennis in the United States.

Tennis Racquet — U116

1974, Aug. 31   **Block Tagged**

U569	U116	10c yellow, brt. blue & light green	.55	.25

Bicentennial Era Issue

The Seafaring Tradition — Compass Rose — U118

The American Homemaker — Quilt Pattern — U119

The American Farmer — Sheaf of Wheat — U120

The American Doctor — U121

The American Craftsman — Tools, c. 1750 — U122

Designs (in brown on left side of envelope): 10c, Norwegian sloop Restaurationen. No. U572, Spinning wheel. No. U573, Plow. No. U574, Colonial era medical instruments and bottle. No. U575, Shaker rocking chair.

1975-76   Embossed
Light Brown Diagonally Laid Paper
U571	U118	10c brown & blue	.30	.25
a.		Brown ("10c/USA," etc.) omitted, entire	100.00	
U572	U119	13c brown & blue green	.35	.25
a.		Brown ("13c/USA," etc.) omitted, entire	110.00	
U573	U120	13c brown & bright green	.35	.25
a.		Brown ("13c/USA," etc.) omitted, entire	110.00	
U574	U121	13c brown & orange	.35	.25
a.		Brown ("13c/USA," etc.) omitted, entire	110.00	
U575	U122	13c brown & carmine	.35	.25
a.		Brown ("13c/USA," etc.) omitted, entire	110.00	
		Nos. U571-U575 (5)	1.70	1.25

Liberty Tree, Boston, 1646 U123

1975, Nov. 8   Embossed
U576	U123	13c orange brown	.30	.25

Star and Pinweel U124

U125

U126

Eagle U127

"Uncle Sam" — U128

1976-78   Embossed
U577	U124	2c red, untagged		.25
U578	U125	2.1c green, untagged		.25
U579	U126	2.7c green, untagged		.25
U580	U127	(15c) orange	.40	.25
U581	U128	15c red, ink tagged	.40	.25
a.		Bar tagged	7.00	7.00

For No. U581 with surcharge, see No. U586b.

Bicentennial Issue

Centennial Envelope, 1876 — U129

1976, Oct. 15   Embossed
U582	U129	13c emerald	.35	.25

Golf Issue

Golf Club in Motion and Golf Ball — U130

Photogravure and Embossed
1977, Apr. 7
U583	U130	13c black, blue & yellow green	.65	.25
a.		Black omitted, entire	500.00	
b.		Black & blue omitted, entire	500.00	
c.		Black, blue & yellow green omitted, entire	500.00	

On No. U583c, the embossing is present.

Energy Issue
Conservation and development of national resources.

Energy Conservation U131

Energy Development U132

1977, Oct. 20   Photo.
Bar Tagged
U584	U131	13c black, red & yellow	.45	.25
a.		Red, yellow & tagging omitted, entire	190.00	
b.		Yellow & tagging omitted, entire	150.00	
c.		Black omitted, entire	135.00	
d.		Black & red omitted, entire	350.00	
U585	U132	13c black, red & yellow	.45	.25

Olive Branch and Star — U133

1978, July 28   Embossed
Black Surcharge
U586	U133	15c on 16c blue	.40	.25
a.		Surcharge omitted, entire	200.00	1,000.
b.		Surcharge on No. U581, entire	70.00	260.00
c.		As "a," with surcharge printed on envelope flap	175.00	—
d.		Surcharge inverted (in lower left corner), entire	200.00	

Auto Racing Issue

Indianapolis 500 Racing Car — U134

1978, Sept. 2   Embossed
U587	U134	15c red, blue & black	.45	.25
a.		Black omitted, entire	100.00	
b.		Black & blue omitted, entire	170.00	
c.		Red & tagging omitted, entire	100.00	
d.		Red, blue & tagging omitted, entire	170.00	

No. U576 Surcharged

1978, Nov. 28   Embossed
U588	U123	15c on 13c orange brown	.40	.25
a.		Surcharge inverted (in lower left corner), entire	—	

U135

Embossed
1979, May 18   Untagged
U589	U135	3.1c ultramarine	.35

Weaver Violins — U136

1980, June 23   Untagged
U590	U136	3.5c purple	.35
a.		3.5c violet, tagged (in ink), error of color and tagging using ink intended for No. U592, entire	300.00 500.00

U137

1982, Feb. 17   Untagged
U591	U137	5.9c brown	.35

Eagle — U138

1981, Mar. 15
U592	U138	(18c) violet	.45	.25

Star — U139

1981, Apr. 2
U593	U139	18c dark blue	.45	.25

Eagle U140

1981, Oct. 11
U594	U140	(20c) brown	.45	.25

Veterinary Medicine Issue

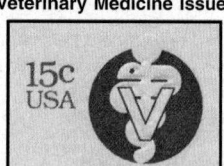
Seal of Veterinarians — U141

Design at left side of envelope shows 5 animals and bird in brown, "Veterinary Medicine" in gray.

1979, July 24
U595	U141	15c brown & gray	.50	.25
a.		Gray omitted, entire	425.00	
b.		Brown omitted, entire	500.00	
c.		Gray & brown omitted, entire	325.00	

On No. 595c, the embossing of the seal is present.

Olympic Games Issue
22nd Olympic Games, Moscow, July 19-Aug. 3, 1980.

U142

Design (multicolored on left side of envelope) shows two soccer players with ball.

1979, Dec. 10
U596	U142	15c red, green & black	.60	.25
a.		Red & green omitted, tagging omitted, entire	150.00	
b.		Black omitted, tagging omitted, entire	150.00	
c.		Black & green omitted, entire	150.00	
d.		Red omitted, tagging omitted, entire	325.00	
e.		All colors omitted	250.00	

No. U596c exists with a portion of the green present in the Olympics 1980 design at the lower left corner of the envelope.

On No. U596e, the blind embossing of "USA 15c" remains.

Highwheeler Bicycle — U143

Design (blue on left side of envelope) shows racing bicycle.

1980, May 16
U597 U143 15c blue & rose
claret .40 .25
a. Blue ("15c USA") omitted,
entire 100.00

Racing
Yacht — U144

1980, Sept. 15
U598 U144 15c blue & red .40 .25

Italian
Honeybee
and
Orange
Blossoms
U145

Bee and petals colorless embossed.

Photogravure and Embossed
1980, Oct. 10
U599 U145 15c brown, green
& yellow .35 .25
a. Brown ("USA 15c") omitted,
entire 100.00
b. Green omitted, entire 100.00

No. U599b also has almost all of the brown color missing.

Hand and braille colorless embossed.

1981, Aug. 13 **Embossed**
U600 U146 18c blue & red .45 .25
a. Blue omitted, entire 300.00
b. Red omitted, entire 210.00

Capitol Dome
U147

1981, Nov. 13
U601 U147 20c deep magenta,
ink tagged .45 .25
a. Bar tagged 4.50 1.50

U148

1982, June 15
U602 U148 20c dark blue,
black & magenta .45 .25
a. Dark blue omitted, entire 175.00
b. Dark blue & magenta omitted, entire 175.00
c. All colors omitted, entire 175.00

On No. 602c, the colorless embossed impression of the Great Seal is present.

U149

1982, Aug. 6
U603 U149 20c purple & black .75 .25
a. Black omitted, entire 80.00
b. Purple omitted, entire 200.00

U150

1983, Mar. 21 **Untagged**
U604 U150 5.2c orange .90

U151

1983, Aug. 3
U605 U151 20c red, blue &
black .45 .25
a. Red omitted, entire 260.00
b. Blue omitted, entire 260.00
c. Red & black omitted, entire 125.00
d. Blue & black omitted, entire 125.00
e. Black omitted, entire 260.00

U152

Design shows storefronts at lower left. Stamp and design continue on back of envelope.

1984, May 7 **Photo.**
U606 U152 20c multi .50 .25

U153

1985, Feb. 1 **Embossed**
U607 U153 (22c) deep green .55 .30

American
Buffalo
U154

1985, Feb. 25
U608 U154 22c violet brown, ink
tagged .55 .25
a. Untagged, 3 blue precancel
lines, unwmk'd ('86) .25
b. Bar tagged 2.00 1.00

Frigate U.S.S.
Constitution, "Old
Ironsides"
U155

1985, May 3 **Untagged**
U609 U155 6c green blue .35

Mayflower — U156

1986, Dec. 4 **Untagged**
Precanceled
U610 U156 8.5c black & gray .65

Stars
U157

1988, Mar. 26 **Typo. & Embossed**
U611 U157 25c dark red &
deep blue .60 .25
a. Dark red omitted, tagging
omitted 50.00 —
c. Dark red omitted, tagging not
omitted 60.00

Sea Gulls, Frigate USS
Constellation — U158

1988, Apr. 12 **Untagged**
Precanceled
U612 U158 8.4c black & bright
blue .65
a. Black omitted, entire 500.00

Snowflake — U159

"Holiday Greetings!" inscribed in lower left.

1988, Sept. 8 **Typo.**
U613 U159 25c dark red &
green 1.25 20.00

Stars and "*Philatelic Mail*"
Continuous in Dark Red Below
Vignette — U160

"Philatelic Mail" and asterisks in dark red below vignette; continuous across envelope face and partly on reverse.

1989, Mar. 10
U614 U160 25c dark red &
deep blue .50 .25
b. Red omitted, entire 125.00

"USA" and Stars — U161

1989, July 10 **Unwmk.**
U615 U161 25c dark red &
deep blue .50 .25
a. Dark red omitted, entire 425.00

Lined with a blue design to provide security for enclosures.

Love — U162

Litho. & Typo.
1989, Sept. 22 **Unwmk.**
U616 U162 25c dark red &
bright blue .50 .75
a. Dark red and bright blue
omitted, entire 150.00
b. Bright blue omitted, entire 150.00

No. U616 has light blue lines printed diagonally over the entire surface of the envelope.

Shuttle Docking at Space
Station — U163

1989, Dec. 3 **Typo.** **Unwmk.**
Die Cut
U617 U163 25c ultramarine .90 .60
a. Ultramarine omitted, entire 400.00

A hologram, visible through the die cut window to the right of "USA 25," is affixed to the inside of the envelope.
See Nos. U625, U639.

Vince Lombardi Trophy, Football
Players — U164

1990, Sept. 9 **Unwmk.** **Die Cut**
U618 U164 25c vermilion .90 .60

A hologram, visible through the die cut window to the right of "USA 25," is affixed to the inside of the envelope.

Star — U165

Typo. & Embossed
1991, Jan. 24 **Wmk.**
U619 U165 29c ultramarine &
rose .60 .30
a. Ultramarine omitted, entire 300.00
b. Rose omitted, tagged, entire 250.00
c. Rose omitted, tagging omitted, entire 275.00
See No. U623.

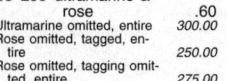
Birds — U166

Stamp and design continue on back of
envelope.

1991, May 3 **Typo.** **Wmk.**
Untagged, Precanceled
U620 U166 11.1c blue & red — .90
a. Blue omitted, entire

Love — U167

1991, May 9 **Litho.** **Unwmk.**
U621 U167 29c light blue, purple & bright
rose .60 .60
a. Bright rose omitted, entire 200.00
b. Purple omitted, entire 400.00

Magazine Industry, 250th
Anniv. — U168

Photo. & Typo.
1991, Oct. 7 **Unwmk.**
U622 U168 29c multicolored .70 1.00
The photogravure vignette, visible through
the die cut window to the right of "USA 29",
is affixed to the inside of the envelope.

Star
U169

Stamp and design continue on back of
envelope.

1991, July 20 **Typo.** **Unwmk.**
U623 U169 29c ultra & rose .60 .30
a. Ultra omitted, entire 500.00
b. Rose omitted, entire 200.00
Lined with a blue design to provide security
for enclosures.

Country
Geese
U170

1991, Nov. 8 **Litho. & Typo.** **Wmk.**
U624 U170 29c blue gray & yel-
low .60 .60

Space Shuttle Type of 1989
Unwmk.
1992, Jan. 21 **Typo.** **Die Cut**
U625 U163 29c yellow green .80 .50
A hologram, visible through the die cut window to the right of "USA 29," is affixed to the
inside of the envelope.

U171

Typo. & Litho.
1992, Apr. 10 **Die Cut**
U626 U171 29c multicolored .60 1.00
The lithographed vignette, visible through
the die cut window to the right of "USA 29," is
affixed to the inside of the envelope.

Hillebrandia — U172

1992, Apr. 22
U627 U172 29c multicolored .65 1.00
The lithographed vignette, visible through
the die cut window to the right of "29 USA," is
affixed to the inside of the envelope.

U173

Typo. & Embossed
1992, May 19 **Precanceled**
Untagged
U628 U173 19.8c red & blue .40

U174

1992, July 22 **Typo.**
U629 U174 29c red & blue .60 .30

U175

1993, Oct. 2 **Typo. & Litho.** **Die Cut**
U630 U175 29c multicolored 1.10 1.10
The lithographed vignette, visible through
the die cut window to the right of "USA 29," is
affixed to the inside of the envelope.

U176

Typo. & Embossed
1994, Sept. 17
U631 U176 29c brown &
black .70 1.25
a. Black ("29/USA") omitted,
entire 325.00

Liberty Bell — U177

1995, Jan. 3 **Typo. & Embossed**
U632 U177 32c greenish
blue &
blue .65 .30
a. Greenish blue omitted 100.00
b. Blue ("USA 32") omitted 90.00
c. All colors omitted, entire —
A colorless embossed design is present on
No. U632c.
See No. U638.

U178

Design sizes: 49x38mm (#U633), 53x44mm
(U634). Stamp and design continue on back of
envelope.

1995 **Typo.**
U633 U178 (32c) blue & red 1.25 2.00
U634 U178 (32c) blue & red 1.25 2.00
a. Red & tagging omitted,
entire 325.00
b. Blue omitted, entire 325.00
Originally, Nos. U633-U634 were only available through the Philatelic Fulfillment Center
after their announcement 1/12/95.

U179

Stamp and design continue on back of
envelope.

1995, Mar. 10
Precanceled, Untagged
U635 U179 (5c) green & red
brown .40

Graphic Eagle — U180

1995, Mar. 10
Precanceled, Untagged
U636 U180 (10c) dark carmine
& blue 1.50

Spiral Heart — U181

1995, May 12
U637 U181 32c red, light
blue .65 .30
a. Red omitted, entire 200.00

Liberty Bell Type of 1995
1995, May 16
U638 U177 32c greenish blue
& blue .70 .30
a. Greenish blue omitted, entire 175.00

Space Shuttle Type of 1989
1995, Sept. 22 **Die Cut**
U639 U163 32c carmine rose .75 .35
A hologram, visible through the die cut window to the right of "USA 32," is affixed to the
inside of the envelope.

U182

Typo. & Litho.
1996, Apr. 20 **Die Cut**
U640 U182 32c multicolored .70 .30
The lithographed vignette, visible through
the die cut window to the right of "USA 32c," is
affixed to the inside of the envelope.

U183

1996, May 2
U641 U183 32c multicolored .70 .30
a. Blue & red omitted, entire 260.00
b. Blue & gold omitted, entire 550.00
c. Red omitted, entire 260.00
d. Black & red omitted, entire 450.00
e. Blue omitted, entire 300.00

U184

U184a

1999, Jan. 11   **Typo. & Embossed**
U642 U184 33c yellow, blue
& red, tagging bar to left of design   1.00   .30

a.	Tagging bar to right of design	7.50	3.00
b.	As "a," blue omitted, entire		200.00
c.	As "a," yellow omitted, entire	175.00	
d.	As "a," yellow and blue omitted, entire	175.00	
e.	As "a," blue and red omitted, entire	175.00	
f.	As "a," all colors omitted, entire	175.00	
g.	As No. U642, red omitted, entire	—	
h.	As No. U642, yellow and red omitted, entire	—	
i.	As No. U642, blue and red omitted, entire	—	
j.	Tagging omitted	—	

On No. U642f, the distinctive tagging bar is present. Expertization is required.

1999, Jan. 11   **Typo.**
U643 U184a 33c blue & red   1.00   .30
  a.   Tagging bar to right of design   10.00   5.00

U185

1999, Jan. 28   **Litho.**
U644 U185 33c violet   .65   .30
  a.   Tagging bar to right of design   .65   .30

Lincoln — U186

1999, June 5   **Typo. & Litho.**
U645 U186 33c blue & black   .65   .30

Eagle
U187

2001, Jan. 7   **Typo.**
U646 U187 34c blue gray & gray   .70   .30
  a.   Blue gray omitted   175.00

Many color shades known.

Lovebirds — U188

2001, Feb. 14   **Litho.**
U647 U188 34c rose & dull violet   .70   .30

Community Colleges, Cent. — U189

2001, Feb. 20   **Typo.**
U648 U189 34c dark blue & orange brown   .70   .30

Ribbon Star — U190

2002, June 7
U649 U190 37c red, blue & gray   .75   .35
  a.   Gray omitted, entire   —
  b.   Blue and gray omitted, entire   —

All No. U649 were printed on recycled paper. It was also produced using a different blue-gray recycled paper starting in 2002.

Type of 1995 Inscribed "USA / Presorted / Standard"
2002, Aug. 8   **Untagged**
       Precanceled
U650 U180 (10c) dark carmine & blue   .25

Nurturing Love — U191

2003, Jan. 25
U651 U191 37c olive green & yellow orange   .80   .35

Jefferson Memorial Type
2003, Dec. 29
U652 A2818 $3.85 multicolored   11.00   6.25

On No. U652, the stamp indicia is printed on the flap of the envelope.

Disney Type of 2004
2004, June 23   **Letter Sheet**   **Litho.**
U653 A2949 37c multicolored   2.50   2.25
U654 A2950 37c multicolored   2.50   2.25
U655 A2951 37c multicolored   2.50   2.25
  a.   All color missing on reverse, entire
U656 A2952 37c multicolored   2.50   2.25
  a.   Booklet of 12 letter sheets, 3 each #U653-U656   30.00

No. U656a sold for $14.95.

White Lilacs and Pink Roses Type of 2004
2005, Mar. 3   **Letter Sheet**
U657 A2931 37c multicolored   2.50   2.50
No. U657 was sold in pads of 12 for $14.95.

Computer-generated Study of an X-Plane — U192

2006, Jan. 5   **Typo.**
U658 U192 $4.05 multicolored   8.25   7.50

Benjamin Franklin — U193

2006, Jan. 9
U659 U193 39c blue green & black   .80   .40
  a.   All color omitted, entire

On No. 659a, the tagging bar and the blue green printing on the reverse are present.

Air Force One
U194

2007, May 6
U660 U194 $4.60 multicolored   9.25   7.00

Marine One
U195

2007, May 6
U661 U195 $16.25 multicolored   33.00   17.00

Horses — U196

2007, May 12
U662 U196 41c reddish brown & black   .85   .40

Elk
U197

2008, May 2
U663 U197 42c green & black, tagging bar 20mm tall   .85   .40
  a.   Tagging bar 26mm tall   .85   .40
  b.   As No. U663, litho., tagging bar 19mm tall   .85   .40

No. U663 was printed by National Envelope for Ashton-Potter (USA) Ltd. No. U663a was printed by Westvaco.

No. U663b was printed by Ashton-Potter (USA) Ltd. The lithographed impressions of No. U663b are slightly sharper (some tree branches are slightly thinner and more distinct) than the typographed impressions on Nos. U663 and U663a, but because of the

nature of the design are nonetheless difficult to distinguish without measuring the tagging bar.

Mount Rushmore — U198

2008, May 12
U664 U198 $4.80 multicolored   9.75   7.00

Sunflower Type of 2008
Letter Sheet
2008, Aug. 15   **Litho.**
U665 A3309 42c multicolored   3.00   3.00
No. U665 was sold in packs of 10 for $14.95.

Redwood Forest Type of 2009
2009, Jan. 16   **Typo.**
U666 A3332 $4.95 multicolored   10.00   7.50

U199

2009-11
U667 U199 (44c) multicolored   .90   .90
  a.   As #U667, typographed   .90   .45
  b.   As #U667, dated "2011," "FOREVER" multicolored (with color dots)   .90   .90
  c.   As #U667b, "FOREVER" in brown (solid color)   .90   .90

Issued: No. U667, 5/11; No. U667a, 8/16; Nos. U667b, U667c, 1/3/11.

No. U667 had a franking value of 44c on the day of issue and will be valid for the one ounce first class postage rate after any new rates go into effect.

The typographed version (No. U667a) can be distinguished from No. U667 by the position of the recycle logo on the back. On the litho. version it is to the right of the recycle text; on the typo. version it is to the left of the text.

U200

2009, May 11
U668 U200 44c multicolored   .90   .45
  a.   As #U668, typographed   .90   .45
  b.   As No. U668, triple impression of black, entire   —

On No. U668a, the screened blue dots cover the entire area between the "S" and the "C" on No. U668, but appear more random on No. U668a. The pattern of blue dots running towards the shoulder under the head and neck of the horse is long and distinct on No. U668, but barely noticeable, with only a few dots showing, on No. U668a.

See second paragraph of No. U667 footnote, which also applies to Nos. U668 and U668a.

Gulf Coast Lighthouses Type of 2009
2009, July 23   **Litho.**
U669 A3354 44c multicolored   3.25   3.00
U670 A3355 44c multicolored   3.25   3.00
U671 A3356 44c multicolored   3.25   3.00
U672 A3357 44c multicolored   3.25   3.00
U673 A3358 44c multicolored   3.25   3.00
     Nos. U669-U673 (5)   16.25   15.00

Pack of ten, containing two of each letter sheet, sold for $15.95.

Mackinac Bridge
U201

Designed by Carl T. Herrman.

2010, Jan. 4   Typo.   Unwmk.
U674 U201 $4.90 multicolored   10.00   7.50
No. U674 was sold only in packs of 5.

New River Gorge Bridge, West Virginia
U202

Designed by Carl T. Herrman.

2011, Jan. 3   Typo.   Unwmk.
U675 U202 $4.95 multicolored   10.00   7.50
No. U675 was sold only in packs of 5.

Sunshine Skyway Bridge, Florida
U203

Designed by Carl T. Hermann.

2012, Jan. 3   Typo.   Unwmk.
U676 U203 $5.15 multicolored   10.50   7.50
No. U676 was sold only in packs of 5.

Purple Martin — U204

Designed by William J. Gicker.

2012, Jan. 23   Litho.   Unwmk.
Design Size: 48x33mm
U677 U204 (45c) multicolored   .95   .50

Design Size: 50x35mm
U678 U204 (45c) multicolored   .95   .50

No. U677 was from No. 6¾ size envelopes only. No. U678 was from No. 9 and No. 10 size envelopes.
No. U678 was reprinted in June 2012 without the 'Cradle to Cradle' recycling logo on the back.

Arlington Green Bridge Type of 2013

2013, Jan. 25   Typo.   Unwmk.
U679 A3612 $5.60 multicolored   11.00   8.00
No. U679 was sold only in packs of 5.

Bank Swallows
U205

Designed by William J. Gicker.

2013, Mar. 1   Litho.   Unwmk.
Design Size: 38x35mm
U680 U205 (46c) multicolored   .95   .50

Design Size: 41x38mm
U681 U205 (46c) multicolored   .95   .50

No. U680 is from No. 6¾ size envelopes only. No. U681 is from No. 9 and No. 10 size envelopes.

Eagle, Shield and Flags
U206

Designed by Richard Sheaff.

2013, Aug. 9   Litho.   Unwmk.
U682 U206 (46c) multicolored   .95   .50

Verrazano-Narrows Bridge Type of 2014

Designed by Phil Jordan.

2014, Mar. 4   Typo.   Unwmk.
U683 A3726 $5.60 multicolored   11.00   8.00
No. U683 was sold only in packs of 5, 10 or 25.

Poinsettia — U207

Snowflake
U208

Snowflake
U209

Cardinal
U210

Child Making Snowman
U211

2014, Oct. 1   Litho.   Unwmk.
U684 U207 (49c) multicolored   2.00   1.50
U685 U208 (49c) multicolored   2.00   1.50
U686 U209 (49c) multicolored   2.00   1.50
U687 U210 (49c) multicolored   2.00   1.50
U688 U211 (49c) multicolored   2.00   1.50
Nos. U684-U688 (5)   10.00   7.50

Packs of 10 No. U684 and 10 self-adhesive stickers sold for $9.95. Packs containing 5 each of Nos. U685 and U686 and 10 self-

adhesive stickers sold for $9.95. Packs containing 5 each of Nos. U687 and U688 and 10 self-adhesive stickers sold for $9.95. Nos. U684-U688 were available only as No. 10 size envelopes.

Glade Creek Grist Mill Type of 2014

Designed by Derry Noyes.

2015, Jan. 12   Typo.   Unwmk.
U689 A3780 $5.75 multicolored   11.50   8.25
No. U689 was sold only in packs of 5.

Red Water Lily — U212

White Water Lily — U213

2015, Apr. 17   Litho.   Unwmk.
U690 U212 (49c) multicolored   2.00   1.75
U691 U213 (49c) multicolored   2.00   1.75

Nos. U690 and U691 were only sold in packets of 10 containing five of each envelope and 10 stickers for $9.95. Nos. U690 and U691 were only available in #10 size with self-adhesive flap.

Forget-me-nots — U214

2015, May 18   Litho.   Unwmk.
U692 U214 (49c) multicolored   2.00   1.75

No. U692 was sold only in packets of 10 + 10 stickers for $9.95. It was only available in #10 size with self-adhesive flap.

La Cueva del Indio Type of 2016

2016, Jan. 17   Typo.   Unwmk.
U693 A3875 $6.45 multicolored   13.00   9.50
No. U693 was sold only in packs of 5.

Northern Cardinal
U215

Designed by Derry Noyes.

2016   Litho.   Unwmk.
U694 U215 (47c) multicolored   1.75   1.75

No. U694 was sold only in packets of 12 + 12 stickers for $9.95. It was only available in #10 size with self-adhesive flap. No. U694 was sold in post offices in Ohio and Puerto Rico (and perhaps elsewhere) in late December, prior to the envelope's existence being acknowledged by USPS Stamp Services. The packets were offered for sale by USPS Stamp Fulfillment Services on Jan. 4, 2017. The earliest documented use is postmarked Jan. 3, 2017. In late January, the packet was made available for direct order on the USPS Stamp Fulfillment Services website, which noted that the day of issue was Jan. 8, 2017, even though the packets could be ordered on Jan. 4.

AIR POST STAMPED ENVELOPES & AIR LETTER SHEETS

UC1

5c — Vertical rudder is not semi-circular but slopes down to the left. The tail of the plane projects into the G of POSTAGE.

UC2

Die 2 (5c and 8c): Vertical rudder is semi-circular. The tail of the plane touches but does not project into the G of POSTAGE.
Die 2 (6c) — Same as UC2 except three types of numeral.
2a — The numeral "6" is 6½mm wide.
2b — The numeral "6" is 6mm wide.
2c — The numeral "6" is 5½mm wide.
Die 3 (6c): Vertical rudder leans forward. S closer to O than to T of POSTAGE. E of POSTAGE has short center bar. Border types b and d, also without border.

1929-44
UC1 UC1 5c blue   3.25   2.00
  a.   Orange and blue border, type b   375.00   450.00
UC2 UC2 5c blue, die 2   10.00   5.00
UC3 UC2 6c orange, die 2a ('34)   1.25   .40
  a.   With added impression of 3c purple (#U436a), entire without border   4,000.
  b.   Double impression of indicium, entire, with bicolored border   —
UC4 UC2 6c orange, die 2b ('42)   3.00   2.00
UC5 UC2 6c orange, die 2c ('44)   .70   .30
UC6 UC2 6c orange, die 3 ('42)   1.00   .35
  a.   6c orange, *blue*, die 3 (error) Entire, without border   15,000.   10,000.
  b.   Double impression, entire   400.00
UC7 UC2 8c olive green, die 2 ('32)   12.50   3.50

Surcharged in Black on Envelopes Indicated by Number in Parenthesis

1945
UC8 U93 6c on 2c carmine (U429, die 1)   1.25   .65
  a.   On U429f, die 7   2.25   1.50
  b.   On U429g, die 8   1.90   1.10
  c.   On U429h, die 9   9.00   7.50
  d.   6c on 1c green (error) (U420)   1,750.
  e.   6c on 3c dk violet (error) (U436a)   2,000.
  f.   6c on 3c dk violet (error), *amber* (U437a)   3,000.
  g.   6c on 3c violet (error) (U526)   3,000.
UC9 U95 6c on 2c carmine (U525)   50.00   35.00

Surcharged in Black

REVALUED 5c

Surcharged on 6c orange air post envelopes without borders.

1946
UC10 UC2 5c on 6c orange, die 2a — 2.75 1.50
  a. Double surcharge — 75.00
UC11 UC2 5c on 6c orange, die 2b — 9.00 5.50
UC12 UC2 5c on 6c orange, die 2c — .75 .50
  a. Double surcharge — 75.00 900.00
UC13 UC2 5c on 6c orange, die 3 — .70 .60
  a. Double surcharge — 75.00 50.00
  c. Double surcharge, one on reverse
UC13B U93 5c on 6c (UC8a), entire — —

The 6c borderless envelopes and the revalued envelopes were issued primarily for use to and from members of the armed forces. The 5c rate came into effect Oct. 1, 1946.

DC-4 Skymaster UC3

Die 1 — The end of the wing at the right is a smooth curve. The juncture of the front end of the plane and the engine forms an acute angle. The first T of STATES and the E's of UNITED STATES lean to the left.
Die 2 — The end of the wing at the right is a straight line. The juncture of the front end of the plane and the engine is wide open. The first T of STATES and the E's of UNITED STATES lean to the right.

1946
UC14 UC3 5c carmine, die 1 — .75 .25
UC15 UC3 5c carmine, die 2 — .75 .25
  See Nos. UC18, UC26.

DC-4 Skymaster — UC4

1947-55   **Typo.**
Letter Sheets for Foreign Postage
UC16 UC4 10c brt red, *pale bl*, entire — 8.50 7.00
  e. Blue omitted, entire — 425.00
  f. Overlay omitted front & back, entire — 100.00
  g. Overlay omitted from front only, entire — 500.00
  a. "Air Letter" on face, 4-line inscription on back ('51), entire — 17.50 10.00
  b. As "a," 10c chocolate, *pale bl*, entire — 450.00
  c. "Air Letter" and "Aerogramme" on face, 4-line inscription on back ('53), entire — 45.00 12.50
  d. As "c," 3-line inscription on back ('55), entire — 9.00 8.00

Postage Stamp Centenary Issue
Centenary of the first postage stamps issued by the United States Government.

Washington & Franklin, Early and Modern Mail-carrying Vehicles UC5

Two dies: Rotary, design measures 22¼mm high; and flat bed press, design 21¾mm high.

Embossed, Rotary Press Printing
1947, May 21
For Domestic Postage
UC17 UC5 5c carmine (rotary) — .50 .30
  a. Flat plate printing — .50 .30

Type of 1946
Type I: 6's lean to right.
Type II: 6's upright.

1950 , Sept. 22
UC18 UC3 6c carmine, type I — .75 .25
  a. Type II — .90 .25
Several other types differ slightly from the two listed.

Nos. UC14, UC15, UC18 Surcharged in Red Left of Stamp

1951
UC19 UC3 6c on 5c carmine, die 1 — .85 1.50
  a. Surcharge inverted at lower left, entire — —
UC20 UC3 6c on 5c carmine, die 2 — .85 1.50
  a. 6c on 6c carmine (error) entire — 1,500.
  b. Double surcharge — 975.00
To qualify as No. UC20b, both surcharges must be to the left of the indicia.

Nos. UC14-UC15 Surcharged in Red at Left of Stamp

1952
UC21 UC3 6c on 5c carmine, die 1 — 25.00 20.00
  a. Double surcharge, entire — 600.00
UC22 UC3 6c on 5c carmine, die 2 — 3.75 2.50
  a. Double surcharge — 250.00
  b. Triple surcharge, entire — 275.00
To qualify as Nos. UC22a or UC22b, all surcharges must be to the left of the indicia.

No. UC17 Surcharged in Red

UC23 UC5 6c on 5c carmine — 1,000.
The 6c on 4c black (No. U440) is believed to be a favor printing.

Fifth International Philatelic Exhibition Issue
FIPEX, the Fifth International Philatelic Exhibition, New York, N.Y., Apr. 28-May 6, 1956.

Eagle in Flight — UC6

1956, May 2
UC25 UC6 6c red — .75 .50
Two types exist, differing slightly in the clouds at top.

Skymaster Type of 1946
1958, July 31
UC26 UC3 7c blue — .65 .50

Nos. UC3-UC5, UC18 and UC25 Surcharged in Green at Left of Stamp

1958
UC27 UC2 6c + 1c orange, die 2a — 275.00 *300.00*
UC28 UC2 6c + 1c orange, die 2b — 70.00 80.00
UC29 UC2 6c + 1c orange, die 2c — 35.00 55.00
UC30 UC3 6c + 1c carmine, type I — 1.00 .50
  a. Type II — 1.00 .50
UC31 UC6 6c + 1c red — 1.00 .50

Jet Airliner UC7

Type I: Back inscription in 3 lines.
Type II: Back inscription in 2 lines.

Letter Sheet for Foreign Postage
Typographed, Without Embossing
1958-59
UC32 UC7 10c blue & red, *blue*, II ('59), entire — 6.00 5.00
  a. Type I ('58), entire — 10.00 5.00
  b. Red omitted, II, entire — 825.00
  c. Blue omitted, II, entire — 850.00
  d. Red omitted, I, entire — 1,000.

Silhouette of Jet Airliner — UC8

1958, Nov. 21   **Embossed**
UC33 UC8 7c blue — .60 .25

1960, Aug. 18
UC34 UC8 7c carmine — .60 .25

Jet Plane and Globe UC9

Letter Sheet for Foreign Postage
Typographed, Without Embossing
1961, June 16
UC35 UC9 11c red & blue, *blue*, entire — 3.00 3.50
  a. Red omitted, entire — 900.00
  b. Blue omitted, entire — 1,000.

UC10

1962, Nov. 17   **Embossed**
UC36 UC10 8c red — .55 .25

UC11

1965-67
UC37 UC11 8c red — .45 .25
  a. Tagged — 4.50 .30
No. UC37a has a 8x24mm panel at left of stamp that glows orange red under ultraviolet light.

Pres. John F. Kennedy and Jet Plane UC12

Letter Sheets for Foreign Postage
Typographed, Without Embossing
1965, May 29
UC38 UC12 11c red & dark blue, *blue*, entire — 3.75 4.00

1967, May 29
UC39 UC12 13c red & dark blue, *blue*, entire — 3.25 4.00
  a. Red omitted, entire — 600.00
  b. Dark blue omitted, entire — 500.00

UC13

1968, Jan. 8   **Tagged**   **Embossed**
UC40 UC13 10c red — .50 .25

No. UC37 Surcharged in Red at Left of Stamp

1968, Feb. 5
UC41 UC11 8c + 2c red — .65 .25

Tagging
Envelopes and Letter Sheets from No. UC42 onward are tagged unless otherwise noted.

Human Rights Year Issue
Issued for International Human Rights Year, and to commemorate the 20th anniversary of the United Nations' Declaration of Human Rights.

Globes and Flock of Birds — UC14

Letter Sheet for Foreign Postage
1968, Dec. 3   **Photo.**
UC42 UC14 13c gray, brown, orange & black, *blue*, entire — 8.00 7.50
  a. Orange omitted, entire — 1,000.
  b. Brown omitted, entire — 375.00
  c. Black omitted, entire — 800.00
  d. Gray and black omitted, entire — —
No. UC42 has a luminescent panel ⅜x1 inch on the right globe. The panel glows orange red under ultraviolet light.

UC15

1971, May 6   **Embossed (Plane)**
UC43 UC15 11c red & blue — .50 *1.75*

Birds in Flight and "usa" — UC16

Letter Sheet for Foreign Postage

1971 **Photo.**
UC44 UC16 15c gray, red,
white & blue,
blue, entire   1.50 *7.50*
a.   "AEROGRAMME" added to
inscription, entire   1.50 *7.50*
b.   As #UC44, red omitted, entire   1.50 *7.50*
c.   As "a," red omitted, entire   300.00 —

Folding instructions (2 steps) in capitals on No. C44; (4 steps) in upper and lower case on No. UC44a.

On Nos. UC44-UC44a the white rhomboid background of "USA postage 15c" is luminescent. No. UC44 is inscribed: "VIA AIR MAIL-PAR AVION". "postage 15c" is in gray. See No. UC46.

No. UC40 Surcharged in Green at Left of Stamp

1971, June 28 **Embossed**
UC45 UC13 10c + (1c) red   1.50 *.75*

HOT AIR BALLOONING CHAMPIONSHIPS ISSUE

Hot Air Ballooning World Championships, Albuquerque, N.M., Feb. 10-17, 1973.

"usa" Type of 1971

Design: Three balloons and cloud at left in address section; no birds beside stamp. Inscribed "INTERNATIONAL HOT AIR BALLOONING." "postage 15c" in blue.

Letter Sheet for Foreign Postage

1973, Feb. 10
UC46 UC16 15c red, white &
blue, *blue,* en-
tire   1.00 *7.50*

Folding instructions as on No. UC44a. See notes after No. UC44.

Bird in
Flight — UC17

1973, Dec. 1 **Luminescent Ink**
UC47 UC17 13c rose red   .30 *.25*

Beginning with No. UC48, all listings are letter sheets for foreign postage.

UC18

1974, Jan. 4 **Photo.**
UC48 UC18 18c red & blue,
blue, entire   1.00 *6.00*
a.   Red omitted, entire   200.00

25TH ANNIVERSARY OF NATO ISSUE

UC19

Design: "NATO" and NATO emblem at left in address section.

1974, Apr. 4
UC49 UC19 18c red & blue,
blue, entire   1.00 *6.00*
Die cutting reversed, entire   100.00

UC20

1976, Jan. 16
UC50 UC20 22c red & blue, *blue,*
entire   1.00 *6.00*
a.   Red color missing due to
foldover and die cutting   —

UC21

1978, Nov. 3
UC51 UC21 22c blue, *blue,* entire 1.00 *3.00*

22nd OLYMPIC GAMES, MOSCOW, JULY 19-AUG. 3, 1980.

UC22

Design (multicolored in bottom left corner) shows discus thrower.

1979, Dec. 5
UC52 UC22 22c red, black &
green, *bluish,*
entire   1.50 *6.00*

UC23

Design (brown on No. UC53, green and brown on No. UC54): lower left, Statue of Liberty. Inscribed "Tour the United States." Folding area shows tourist attractions.

1980, Dec. 29
UC53 UC23 30c blue, red &
brown, *blue,*
entire   .85 *6.00*
a.   Red omitted, entire   70.00

1981, Sept. 21
UC54 UC23 30c yellow, magenta, blue &
black, *blue,*
entire   .65 *6.00*

UC24

Design: "Made in USA . . . world's best buys!" on flap, ship, tractor in lower left. Reverse folding area shows chemicals, jet silhouette, wheat, typewriter and computer tape disks.

1982, Sept. 16
UC55 UC24 30c multi, *blue,* entire   .80 *6.00*

WORLD COMMUNICATIONS YEAR

World Map Showing Locations of Satellite Tracking Stations — UC25

Design: Reverse folding area shows satellite, tracking station.

1983, Jan. 7
UC56 UC25 30c multi, *blue,* entire   .90 *8.00*

1984 OLYMPICS

UC26

Indicia in black, multicolor design of woman equestrian at lower left with montage of competitive events on reverse folding area.

1983, Oct. 14
UC57 UC26 30c black & multi,
light blue, en-
tire   .85 *8.00*

WEATHER SATELLITES, 25TH ANNIV.

UC27

Design: Landsat orbiting the earth at lower left with three Landsat photographs on reverse folding area. Inscribed: "Landsat views the Earth."

1985, Feb. 14
UC58 UC27 36c multi, *blue,* entire   1.25 *12.50*

NATIONAL TOURISM WEEK

Urban Skyline
UC28

Design: Inscribed "Celebrate America" at lower left and "Travel. . . the perfect freedom" on folding area. Skier, Indian chief, cowboy, jazz trumpeter and pilgrims on reverse folding area.

1985, May 21
UC59 UC28 36c multi, *blue,*
entire   1.25 *12.50*
a.   Black omitted, entire   600.00 —

MARK TWAIN AND HALLEY'S COMET

Comet Tail Viewed
from
Space — UC29

Design: Portrait of Twain at lower left and inscribed "I came in with Halley's Comet in 1835. It is coming again next year, and I expect to go out with it. It will be the greatest disappointment of my life if I don't go out with Halley's Comet." "1835 . Mark Twain . 1910 . Halley's Comet . 1985" and Twain, Huckleberry Finn, steamboat and comet on reverse folding areas.

1985, Dec. 4
UC60 UC29 36c multi, entire   2.00 *12.50*

UC30

1988, May 9 **Litho.**
UC61 UC30 39c multi, entire   1.25 *12.50*
a.   Tagging bar to left of design
('89)   1.25 *1.50*

On No. UC61, the tagging bar is between "USA" and "39."

MONTGOMERY BLAIR, POSTMASTER GENERAL 1861-64

Montgomery Blair and Pres.
Lincoln — UC31

Design: Mail bags and "Free city delivery," "Railway mail service" and "Money order system" at lower left. Globe, locomotive, bust of Blair, UPU emblem and "The Paris conference of 1863, initiated by Postmaster General Blair, led, in 1874, to the founding of the Universal Postal Union" contained on reverse folding area.

1989, Nov. 20
UC62 UC31 39c multicolored,
entire   1.40 *16.00*
a.   Double impression   —
b.   Triple impression   —
c.   Quadruple impression   —

UC32

1991, May 17
UC63 UC32 45c gray, red &
blue, *blue,* en-
tire   1.40 *16.00*
a.   White paper, entire   1.00 *16.00*

Thaddeus Lowe (1832-1913),
Balloonist — UC33

1995, Sept. 23
UC64 UC33 50c multicolored,
blue, entire   1.50 *20.00*

USA **60**

Voyageurs
Natl. Park,
Minnesota
UC34

1999, May 15
UC65 UC34 60c multicolored,
blue, entire   1.75 *12.50*

No. UC65 used is often found with additional postage affixed.

OFFICIAL STAMPED ENVELOPES

By the Act of Congress, January 31, 1873, the franking privilege of officials was abolished as of July 1, 1873 and the Postmaster General was authorized to prepare official envelopes. At the same time official stamps were prepared for all Departments. Department envelopes became obsolete July 5, 1884. After that, government offices began to use franked envelopes of varied design. These indicate no denomination and lie beyond the scope of this Catalogue.

Post Office Department

"2" 9mm high — UO1

"3" 9mm high — UO2

"6" 9½mm high — UO3

1873
UO1	UO1	2c black, *lemon*	22.50	10.00
UO2	UO2	3c black, *lemon*	17.50	6.50
+UO3	UO2	3c black	20,000.	
UO4	UO3	6c black, *lemon*	25.00	17.50

"2" 9¼mm high — UO4

"3" 9¼mm high — UO5

"6" 10½mm high — UO6

1874-79
UO5	UO4	2c black, *lemon*	10.00	4.25
UO6	UO4	2c black	140.00	37.50
UO7	UO5	3c black, *lemon*	2.75	.85
UO8	UO5	3c black	1,750.	1,200.
UO9	UO5	3c black, *amber*	140.00	40.00
UO10	UO5	3c black, *blue*	32,500.	
UO11	UO5	3c blue, *blue* ('75)	22,500.	
UO12	UO6	6c black, *lemon*	12.50	6.50
UO13	UO6	6c black	1,750.	2,100.

Fakes exist of Nos. UO3, UO8 and UO13.

Postal Service

UO7

1877
UO14	UO7	black	6.00	4.50
UO15	UO7	black, *amber*	180.00	50.00
UO16	UO7	blue, *amber*	180.00	40.00
UO17	UO7	blue, *blue*	8.50	6.75

War Department

Franklin — UO8

Bust points to the end of "N" of "ONE".

Jackson — UO9

Bust narrow at the back.

Washington — UO10

Queue projects below the bust.

Lincoln — UO11

Neck very long at the back.

Jefferson — UO12

Queue forms straight line with bust.

Clay — UO13

Ear partly concealed by hair, mouth large, chin prominent.

Webster — UO14

Has side whiskers.

Scott   Hamilton
UO15   UO16

Back of bust very narrow; chin almost straight; the labels containing the letters "U S" are exactly parallel.

Reay Issue

1873
UO18	UO8	1c dk red	500.00	300.00
WO18A	UO8	1c dk red, man, entire	—	
UO19	UO9	2c dk red	1,500.	400.00
UO20	UO10	3c dk red	25.00	42.50
UO21	UO10	3c dk red, amb	32,500.	
UO22	UO10	3c dk red, cr	600.00	300.00
UO23	UO11	6c dk red	250.00	100.00
UO24	UO11	6c dk red, cr	5,000.	425.00
UO25	UO12	10c dk red	10,000.	2,250.
UO26	UO13	12c dk red	150.00	60.00
UO27	UO14	15c dk red	125.00	55.00
UO28	UO15	24c dk red	150.00	50.00
UO29	UO16	30c dk red	250.00	150.00
UO30	UO8	1c ver	200.00	
WO31	UO8	1c ver, man	17.50	14.00
+UO32	UO9	2c ver	325.00	
WO33	UO9	2c ver, man	250.00	
UO34	UO10	3c ver	80.00	40.00
UO35	UO10	3c ver, amb	100.00	
UO36	UO10	3c ver, cr	12.50	12.50
UO37	UO11	6c ver	90.00	
+UO38	UO11	6c ver, cr	450.00	
UO39	UO12	10c ver	300.00	
UO40	UO13	12c ver	130.00	
UO41	UO14	15c ver	200.00	
UO42	UO15	24c ver	325.00	
UO43	UO16	30c ver	275.00	

UO17

Bottom serif on "S" is thick and short; bust at bottom below hair forms a sharp point.

UO18

Bottom serif on "S" is thick and short; front part of bust is rounded.

UO19

Bottom serif on "S" is short; queue does not project below bust.

UO20

Neck very short at the back.

UO21

Knot of queue stands out prominently.

UO22

Ear prominent, chin receding.

UO23

Has no side whiskers; forelock projects above head.

UO24

Back of bust rather broad; chin slopes considerably; the label containing letters "U S" are not exactly parallel.

Plimpton Issue

1875
UO44	UO17	1c red	175.00	85.00
+UO45	UO17	1c red, amb	800.00	
+UO45A	UO17	1c red, org	37,500.	
WO46	UO17	1c red, man	4.50	2.75
UO47	UO18	2c red	110.00	—
UO48	UO18	2c red, amber	15.00	17.50
UO49	UO18	2c red, orange	12.50	17.50
WO50	UO18	2c red, manila	120.00	50.00
UO51	UO19	3c red	12.50	10.00
UO52	UO19	3c red, amber	17.50	10.00
UO53	UO19	3c red, cream	6.50	3.75
UO54	UO19	3c red, blue	3.75	2.75
UO55	UO19	3c red, fawn	6.50	2.75
UO56	UO20	6c red	60.00	30.00
UO57	UO20	6c red, amber	75.00	40.00
UO58	UO20	6c red, cream	175.00	85.00
UO59	UO21	10c red	180.00	80.00

UO60	UO21	10c red, *amber*	750.00
UO61	UO22	12c red	50.00 40.00
UO62	UO22	12c red, *amber*	500.00
UO63	UO22	12c red, *cream*	450.00
UO64	UO23	15c red	225.00 140.00
UO65	UO23	15c red, *amber*	825.00
UO66	UO23	15c red, *cream*	525.00
UO67	UO24	30c red	160.00 140.00
UO68	UO24	30c red, *amber*	550.00
UO69	UO24	30c red, *cream*	675.00

POSTAL SAVINGS ENVELOPES

UO25

1911

UO70	UO25	1c green	85.00 25.00
UO71	UO25	1c green, *oriental buff*	210.00 85.00
UO72	UO25	2c carmine	13.00 4.00
a.		2c carmine, *manila* (error)	1,250. 1,000.

Used Values
Catalogue values for regularly used
entires. Those with first-day cancels
generally sell for much less.

Tagged
Envelopes from No. UO73 onward
are tagged unless otherwise noted.

OFFICIAL MAIL

UO26

1983, Jan. 12   Typo. & Embossed
UO73 UO26 20c blue, entire   1.10 30.00

UO27

1985, Feb. 26   Typo. & Embossed
UO74 UO27 22c blue, entire   .90 30.00

UO28

1987, Mar. 2   Typo.
UO75 UO28 22c blue, entire   1.50 35.00
Used exclusively to mail U.S. Savings Bonds.

UO29

1988, Mar. 22
UO76 UO29 (25c) black & blue,
                                entire   1.50 35.00
Used exclusively to mail U.S. Savings Bonds.

UO30

UO31

1988, Apr. 11   Typo. & Embossed
UO77 UO30 25c black & blue,
                                entire   .85 6.00
  a. Denomination & lettering as
       on No. UO78, entire   5.00 6.00

Nos. UO77 and UO77a used to mail U.S.
Savings Bonds and also used by the director
of admissions at the U.S. Air Force Academy
in 1990-91.

Typo.
UO78 UO31 25c black & blue,
                                entire   1.10 35.00
  a. Denomination & lettering as
       on No. UO77, entire   1.00 35.00

Used to mail U.S. Savings Bonds. Also used
by the Department of Agriculture.

Used Values
Postally used examples of Nos.
UO79-UO94 seldom appear in the marketplace and thus cannot be valued with
as much certainty as the editors would
like. They must show evidence of postal
usage. Clear cancels are valued even
higher. The editors would like to have
records of sales of examples of these
used envelopes. If a value exists, it is
based on a known transaction(s) or
consultation with experts.

1990, Mar. 17

Stars and "E Pluribus Unum" illegible. "Official" is 13mm, "USA" is 16mm long.

UO79 UO31 45c black & blue,
                                entire   1.25 200.00
UO80 UO31 65c black & blue,
                                entire   1.75 200.00

Used exclusively to mail U.S. passports.

UO32

Stars and "E Pluribus Unum" clear and
sharply printed. "Official" is 14½mm, "USA" is
17mm long.

1990, Aug. 10   Litho.
UO81 UO32 45c black & blue,
                                entire   1.25 —
UO82 UO32 65c black & blue,
                                entire   1.75 —
Used exclusively to mail U.S. passports.

UO33

1991, Jan. 22   Typo.   Wmk.
UO83 UO33 (29c) black & blue,
                                entire   1.10 35.00
Used exclusively to mail U.S. Savings Bonds.

UO34

Litho. & Embossed
1991, Apr. 6   Wmk.
UO84 UO34 29c black & blue,
                                entire   .80 20.00

UO35

1991, Apr. 17   Wmk.
UO85 UO35 29c black & blue,
                                entire   .80 20.00
Used exclusively to mail U.S. Savings Bonds.

Consular
Service, Bicent.
UO36

1992, July 10   Litho.   Unwmk.
UO86 UO36 52c blue & red,
                                entire   6.00 150.00
  a. 52c blue & red, *blue-white*, entire   1.50 150.00
UO87 UO36 75c blue & red,
                                entire   11.00 150.00
  a. 75c blue & red, *blue-white*, entire   2.50 150.00

Used exclusively to mail U.S. passports.
Available only in 4⅝ inch x 8⅞ inch size with
self-adhesive flap.

UO37

1995-99   Typo. & Embossed
UO88 UO37 32c blue & red,
                                entire   1.00 20.00
UO89 UO37 33c blue & red,
                                entire   1.00 20.00

Type of 1995
2001, Feb. 27
UO90 UO37 34c blue & red,
                                entire   1.00 20.00

Type of 1995
2002, Aug. 2
UO91 UO37 37c blue & red,
                         type I, entire   1.00 15.00
  a. Type II, entire   1.00 35.00

Type I has 29x28mm blue panel, top of
"USA" even with the bottom of the eagle's
neck and is made with "100% recycled paper"
as noted on reverse. Type II has a
27½x27½mm blue panel, top of "USA" even
with the highest arrow, and has no mention of
"100% recycled paper" on reverse.

Type of 1995
2006, Jan. 9
UO92 UO37 39c blue & red, en-
                                tire   2.00 25.00

Type of 1995
2007, May 12
UO93 UO37 41c blue & red, en-
                                tire   2.00 25.00

Type of 1995
2008, June 20   Typo.
UO94 UO37 42c blue & red, en-
                                tire   2.00 15.00

REVENUE STAMPS

Nos. R1-R102 were used to pay
taxes on documents and proprietary
articles including playing cards. Until
Dec. 25, 1862, the law stated that a
revenue stamp could be used only for
payment of the tax upon the particular
instrument or article specified on its
face. After that date stamps, except the
Proprietary, could be used
indiscriminately.

Values quoted are for pen-canceled
stamps. Stamps with handstamped
cancellations sell at higher prices.
Stamps canceled with cuts, punches or
holes sell for less. See the Scott U.S.
Specialized Catalogue.

General Issue
First Issue
Head of Washington in Oval. Various
Frames as Illustrated.

Nos. R1b to R42b, part perforate, occur perforated sometimes at sides only and sometimes at top and bottom only. The higher values, part perforate, are perforated at sides
only. Imperforate and part perforate revenues
often bring much more in pairs or blocks than
as single stamps. Part perforate revenues with
an asterisk (*) after the value exist imperforate
horizontally or vertically.

The experimental silk paper is a variety of
the old paper and has only a very few minute
fragments of fiber.

Some of the stamps were in use eight years
and were printed several times. Many color
variations occurred, particularly when unstable
pigments were used and the color was
intended to be purple or violet, such as the 4c
Proprietary, 30c and $2.50 stamps. Before
1868 dull colors predominate on these and the
early red stamps. In later printings of the 4c
Proprietary, 30c and $2.50 stamps, red pre-
dominates in the mixture, and on the dollar
values the red is brighter. The early $1.90
stamp is dull purple, imperf. or perforated. In a
later printing, perforated only, the purple is
darker.

R1

George
Washington — R2

Old Paper

1862-71	Engr.		*Perf. 12*
R1	R1	1c Express, red	
a.		Imperf.	75.00
b.		Part perf.	55.00*
c.		Perf.	1.50
d.		As No. R1c, silk paper	300.00
e.		As No. R1c, vertical pair, imperf. between	200.00
f.		As "c," foreign entry of 2c, pos. 210	—
R2	R1	1c Playing Cards, red	
a.		Imperf.	3,500.
b.		Part perf.	2,250.
c.		Perf.	210.00
R3	R1	1c Proprietary, red	
a.		Imperf.	1,250.
b.		Part perf.	275.00*
c.		Perf.	.50
d.		As No. R3c, silk paper	60.00
R4	R1	1c Telegraph, red	
a.		Imperf.	800.00
c.		Perf.	20.00
R5	R2	2c Bank Check, blue	
a.		Imperf.	1.50
b.		Part perf.	5.50*
c.		Perf.	.50
e.		As No. R5c, Double impression	800.00
f.		As No. R5c, pair imperf between	400.00
R6	R2	2c Bank Check, orange	
b.		Part perf.	60.00*
c.		Perf.	.45
d.		As No. R6c, silk paper	275.00
e.		As No. R6c, orange, *green*	700.00
R7	R2	2c Certificate, blue	
a.		Imperf.	17.50
c.		Perf.	32.50

R8	R2	2c Certificate, orange	
c.		Perf.	45.00
R9	R2	2c Express, blue	
a.		Imperf.	15.00
b.		Part perf.	35.00*
c.		Perf.	.40
R10	R2	2c Express, orange	
b.		Part perf.	800.00
c.		Perf.	14.00
d.		As No. R10c, silk paper	175.00
R11	R2	2c Playing Cards, blue	
a.		Imperf.	1,500.
b.		Part perf.	325.00
c.		Perf.	4.50
R12	R2	2c Playing Cards, org	
c.		Perf.	55.00
R13	R2	2c Proprietary, blue	
a.		Imperf.	1,200.
b.		Part perf.	350.
c.		Perf.	.40
d.		As No. R13c, silk paper	250.00
		Double transfer (T13a)	
e.		ultramarine	300.00
R14	R2	2c Proprietary, orange	
c.		Perf.	65.00
R15	R2	2c U.S. Internal Revenue, orange ('64)	
a.		Imperf	—
b.		Part perf.	—
c.		Perf.	.25
d.		As No. R15c, silk paper	1.00
e.		As No. R15c, orange, *green*	1,500.

R3

R16	R3	3c Foreign Exchange, green	
b.		Part perf.	950.00
c.		Perf.	5.00
d.		As No. R16c, silk paper	175.00
R17	R3	3c Playing Cards, green ('63)	
a.		Imperf.	40,000.
c.		Perf.	175.00
R18	R3	3c Proprietary, green	
b.		Part perf.	1,250.
c.		Perf.	9.00
d.		As No. R18c, silk paper	150.00
e.		As No. R18c, double impression	1,000.
f.		As No. R18c, printed on both sides	3,500.
R19	R3	3c Telegraph, green	
a.		Imperf.	100.00
b.		Part perf.	30.00
c.		Perf.	3.00
R20	R3	4c Inland Exchange, brown ('63)	
c.		Perf.	2.25
d.		As No. R20c, silk paper	175.00
R21	R3	4c Playing Cards, slate ('63)	
c.		Perf.	800.00
R22	R3	4c Proprietary, purple	
a.		Imperf.	—
b.		Part perf.	650.00
c.		Perf.	8.50
d.		As No. R22c, silk paper	250.00

There are shade and color variations of Nos. R21-R22.

R23	R3	5c Agreement, red	
c.		Perf.	.50
d.		As No. R23c, silk paper	4.50
R24	R3	5c Certificate, red	
a.		Imperf.	4.00
b.		Part perf.	15.00
c.		Perf.	.50
d.		As No. R24c, silk paper	1.10
f.		As No. R24d, impression of No. R3 on back	2,750.
R25	R3	5c Express, red	
a.		Imperf.	8.00
b.		Part perf.	8.00*
c.		Perf.	.40
R26	R3	5c Foreign Exchange, red	
b.		Part perf.	—
c.		Perf.	.50
d.		As No. R26c, silk paper	550.00
R27	R3	5c Inland Exchange, red	
a.		Imperf.	10.00
b.		Part perf.	6.75
c.		Perf.	.60
d.		As No. R27c, silk paper	17.50
e.		As No. R27c, double impression	—
R28	R3	5c Playing Cards, red ('63)	
c.		Perf.	40.00
e.		Double impression	1,200.
R29	R3	5c Proprietary, red ('64)	
c.		Perf.	30.00
d.		As No. R29c, silk paper	300.00
R30	R3	6c Inland Exchange, orange ('63)	
c.		Perf.	2.25
d.		As No. R30c, silk paper	250.00
R31	R3	6c Proprietary, orange ('71)	
c.		Perf.	1,750.

Nearly all examples of No. R31 are faulty or repaired and poorly centered. The catalogue value is for a fine centered stamp with minor faults which do not detract from its appearance.

R32	R3	10c Bill of Lading, blue	
a.		Imperf.	55.00
b.		Part perf.	500.00
c.		Perf.	1.75
R33	R3	10c Certificate, blue	
a.		Imperf.	400.00
b.		Part perf.	950.00*
c.		Perf.	.35
d.		As No. R33c, silk paper	6.00
R34	R3	10c Contract, blue	
a.		Imperf.	575.00
be.		As No. R34b, ultramarine	800.00
c.		Perf.	.50
ce.		As No. R34c, ultramarine	1.00
d.		As No. R34c, silk paper	4.25
R35	R3	10c Foreign Exchange, blue	
c.		Perf.	14.00
d.		As No. R35c, silk paper	—
e.		As No. R35c, ultramarine	20.00
R36	R3	10c Inland Exchange, blue	
a.		Imperf.	500.00
b.		Part perf.	4.50*
c.		Perf.	.30
d.		As No. R36c, silk paper	100.00
R37	R3	10c Power of Attorney, blue	
a.		Imperf.	1,100.
b.		Part perf.	30.00
c.		Perf.	1.00
R38	R3	10c Proprietary, blue ('64)	
c.		Perf.	19.00
R39	R3	15c Foreign Exchange, brown ('63)	
c.		Perf.	17.00
e.		Double impression	1,000.
R40	R3	15c Inland Exchange, brown	
a.		Imperf.	45.00
b.		Part perf.	14.00
c.		Perf.	2.00
e.		As No. R40b, double impression	1,900.
f.		As No. R40c, double impression	750.00
R41	R3	20c Foreign Exchange, red	
a.		Imperf.	95.00
c.		Perf.	80.00
d.		As No. R41c, silk paper	375.00
R42	R3	20c Inland Exchange, red	
a.		Imperf.	17.00
b.		Part perf.	22.50
c.		Perf.	.45
d.		As No. R42c, silk paper	—

R4

R5

R43	R4	25c Bond, red	
a.		Imperf.	300.00
b.		Part perf.	6.75
c.		Perf.	3.75
R44	R4	25c Certificate, red	
a.		Imperf.	11.00
b.		Part perf.	6.75*
c.		Perf.	.50
d.		As No. R44c, silk paper	2.75
e.		As No. R44c, printed on both sides	3,500.
f.		As No. R44c, impression of No. R48 on back	6,000.
R45	R4	25c Entry of Goods, red	
a.		Imperf.	22.50
b.		Part perf.	325.00
c.		Perf.	1.50
d.		As No. R45c, silk paper	100.00
R46	R4	25c Insurance, red	
a.		Imperf.	12.50
b.		Part perf.	19.00
c.		Perf.	.30
d.		As No. R46c, silk paper	7.00
e.		As No. R46c, double impression	500.00
R47	R4	25c Life Insurance, red	
a.		Imperf.	50.00
b.		Part perf.	1,000.
c.		Perf.	11.00
R48	R4	25c Power of Attorney, red	
a.		Imperf.	10.00
b.		Part perf.	45.00
c.		Perf.	1.00
d.		As No. R48c, silk paper	1,750.
R49	R4	25c Protest, red	
a.		Imperf.	35.00
b.		Part perf.	1,100.
c.		Perf.	10.00
R50	R4	25c Warehouse Receipt, red	
a.		Imperf.	55.00
b.		Part perf.	1,200.
c.		Perf.	45.00
R51	R4	30c Foreign Exchange, lilac	
a.		Imperf.	200.00
b.		Part perf.	7,500.
c.		Perf.	60.00
d.		As No. R51c, silk paper	600.00

R52	R4	30c Inland Exchange, lilac	
a.		Imperf.	72.50
b.		Part perf.	90.00
c.		Perf.	8.50
R53	R4	40c Inland Exchange, brown	
a.		Imperf.	2,500.
b.		Part perf.	9.00
c.		Perf.	8.00
d.		As No. R53c, silk paper	350.00
f.		As No. R53c, double impression	—
R54	R5	50c Conveyance, blue	
a.		Imperf.	20.00
b.		Part perf.	3.50
c.		Perf.	.35
ce.		As No. R54c, ultramarine	.50
d.		As No. R54c, silk paper, blue	.50
de.		As No. R54d, ultramarine	3.00
R55	R5	50c Entry of Goods, blue	
a.		Imperf.	17.50
c.		Perf.	.60
d.		As No. R55c, silk paper	125.00
R56	R5	50c Foreign Exchange, blue	
a.		Imperf.	75.00
b.		Part perf.	125.00
c.		Perf.	7.50
e.		As No. R56c, double impression	500.00
R57	R5	50c Lease, blue	
a.		Imperf.	35.00
b.		Part perf.	250.00
c.		Perf.	10.00
R58	R5	50c Life Insurance, blue	
a.		Imperf.	45.00
b.		Part perf.	200.00
c.		Perf.	1.75
e.		As No. R58c, double impression	800.00
R59	R5	50c Mortgage, blue	
a.		Imperf.	22.50
b.		Part perf.	5.00
c.		Perf.	.70
d.		As No. R59c, silk paper	—
e.		As No. R59a, double impression	—
f.		As No. R59c, double impression	—
R60	R5	50c Original Process, blue	
a.		Imperf.	5.50
b.		Part perf.	4,000.
c.		Perf.	1.00
d.		As No. R60c, silk paper	7.50
R61	R5	50c Passage Ticket, blue	
a.		Imperf.	140.00
b.		Part perf.	500.00
c.		Perf.	2.25
R62	R5	50c Probate of Will, blue	
a.		Imperf.	55.00
b.		Part perf.	250.00
c.		Perf.	22.50
R63	R5	50c Surety Bond, blue	
a.		Imperf.	400.00
b.		Part perf.	2.75
c.		Perf.	.30
e.		As No. R63c, ultramarine	.75
R64	R5	60c Inland Exchange, orange	
a.		Imperf.	110.00
b.		Part perf.	82.50
c.		Perf.	9.00
d.		As No. R64c, silk paper	75.00
R65	R5	70c Foreign Exchange, green	
a.		Imperf.	725.00
b.		Part perf.	200.00
c.		Perf.	14.00
d.		As No. R65c, silk paper	65.00

R6

R7

R66	R6	$1 Conveyance, red	
a.		Imperf.	27.50
b.		Part perf.	5,500.
c.		Perf.	27.50
d.		As No. R66c, silk paper	175.00
R67	R6	$1 Entry of Goods, red	
a.		Imperf.	50.00
c.		Perf.	2.75
d.		As No. R67c, silk paper	150.00
R68	R6	$1 Foreign Exchange, red	
a.		Imperf.	90.00
c.		Perf.	.75
d.		As No. R68c, silk paper	125.00
R69	R6	$1 Inland Exchange, red	
a.		Imperf.	17.00
b.		Part perf.	6,000.*
c.		Perf.	.70
d.		As No. R69c, silk paper	6.00
e.		As No. R69c, horiz. pair, imperf. vert.	

No. R69e is an error from a pane of stamps that was intended to be issued fully perforated. It can be differentiated from No. R69b by the

color, paper and date of cancel. Expertization is strongly recommended.

R70	R6	$1 Lease, red	
a.		Imperf.	50.00
c.		Perf.	4.50
R71	R6	$1 Life Insurance, red	
a.		Imperf.	300.00
c.		Perf.	10.00
d.		As No. R71c, silk paper	500.00
R72	R6	$1 Manifest, red	
a.		Imperf.	47.50
c.		Perf.	40.00
R73	R6	$1 Mortgage, red	
a.		Imperf.	27.50
c.		Perf.	300.00
R74	R6	$1 Passage Ticket, red	
a.		Imperf.	350.00
c.		Perf.	350.00
R75	R6	$1 Power of Attorney, red	
a.		Imperf.	100.00
c.		Perf.	2.75
R76	R6	$1 Probate of Will, red	
a.		Imperf.	100.00
c.		Perf.	55.00
R77	R7	$1.30 Foreign Exchange, orange ('63)	
a.		Imperf.	10,000.
c.		Perf.	85.00
R78	R7	$1.50 Inland Exchange, blue	
a.		Imperf.	32.50
c.		Perf.	7.00
R79	R7	$1.60 Foreign Exchange, green ('63)	
a.		Imperf.	1,500.
c.		Perf.	180.00
R80	R7	$1.90 Foreign Exchange, purple ('63)	
a.		Imperf.	12,500.
c.		Perf.	200.00
d.		As No. R80c, silk paper	300.00

R8

R81	R8	$2 Conveyance, red	
a.		Imperf.	250.00
b.		Part perf.	2,750.
c.		Perf.	4.00
d.		As No. R81c, silk paper	40.00
R82	R8	$2 Mortgage, red	
a.		Imperf.	150.00
c.		Perf.	7.00
d.		As No. R82c, silk paper	60.00
R83	R8	$2 Probate of Will, red ('63)	
a.		Imperf.	7,750.
c.		Perf.	90.00
R84	R8	$2.50 Inland Exchange, purple ('63)	
a.		Imperf.	10,000.
c.		Perf.	22.50
d.		As No. R84c, silk paper	40.00
e.		As No. R84c, double impression	1,400.

There are many shade and color variations of Nos. R84c and R84d.

R85	R8	$3 Charter Party, green	
a.		Imperf.	200.00
c.		Perf.	11.00
d.		As No. R85c, silk paper	175.00
e.		As No. R85c, printed on both sides	7,000.
g.		As No. R85c, impression of No. RS208 on back	17,000.
R86	R8	$3 Manifest, green	
a.		Imperf.	200.00
c.		Perf.	55.00
R87	R8	$3.50 Inland Exchange, blue ('63)	
a.		Imperf.	9,000.
c.		Perf.	70.00
e.		As No. R87c, printed on both sides	4,000.

The $3.50 has stars in upper corners.

R9

R10

R88	R9	$5 Charter Party, red	
a.		Imperf.	300.00
c.		Perf.	10.00
d.		As No. R88c, silk paper	100.00
R89	R9	$5 Conveyance, red	
a.		Imperf.	50.00
c.		Perf.	11.00
d.		As No. R89c, milky blue	140.00
R90	R9	$5 Manifest, red	
a.		Imperf.	250.00
c.		Perf.	120.00
R91	R9	$5 Mortgage, red	
a.		Imperf.	200.00
c.		Perf.	25.00
R92	R9	$5 Probate of Will, red	
a.		Imperf.	750.00
c.		Perf.	27.50
R93	R9	$10 Charter Party, green	
a.		Imperf.	900.00
c.		Perf.	37.50
R94	R9	$10 Conveyance, green	
a.		Imperf.	175.00
c.		Perf.	77.50
R95	R9	$10 Mortgage, green	
a.		Imperf.	900.00
c.		Perf.	40.00
R96	R9	$10 Probate of Will, green	
a.		Imperf.	3,500.
c.		Perf.	45.00
R97	R10	$15 Mortgage, blue	
a.		Imperf.	3,750.
c.		Perf.	300.00
e.		As No. R97c, ultramarine	350.00
f.		As No. R97c, milky blue	375.00
R98	R10	$20 Conveyance, orange	
a.		Imperf.	175.00
c.		Perf.	125.00
d.		As No. R98c, silk paper	175.00
R99	R10	$20 Probate of Will, orange	
a.		Imperf.	3,500.
c.		Perf.	3,000.
R100	R10	$25 Mortgage, red ('63)	
a.		Imperf.	2,700.
c.		Perf.	250.00
d.		As No. R100c, silk paper	275.00
e.		As No. R100c, horiz. pair, imperf. between	2,250.
R101	R10	$50 U.S. Internal Revenue, green ('63)	
a.		Imperf.	325.00
c.		Perf.	210.00

R11

R102	R11	$200 U.S. Int. Rev., green & red ('64)	
a.		Imperf.	2,750.
c.		Perf.	950.00

DOCUMENTARY STAMPS
Second Issue

After release of the First Issue revenue stamps, the Bureau of Internal Revenue received many reports of fraudulent cleaning and re-use. The Bureau ordered a Second Issue with new designs and colors, using a patented "chameleon" paper which is usually violet or pinkish, with silk fibers.

While designs are different from those of the first issue, stamp sizes and make up of the plates are the same as for corresponding denominations.

R12

R12a

George Washington
Various Frames and Numeral Arrangements

1871   **Perf. 12**

R103	R12	1c blue & black	90.00
		Cut cancel	35.00
a.		Inverted center	1,600.
R104	R12	2c blue & black	2.75
		Cut cancel	.30
a.		Inverted center	5,000.
R105	R12a	3c blue & black	50.00
		Cut cancel	20.00
R106	R12a	4c blue & black	125.00
		Cut cancel	45.00
R107	R12a	5c blue & black	2.00
		Cut cancel	.50
a.		Inverted center	4,000.
R108	R12a	6c blue & black	250.00
		Cut cancel	80.00
R109	R12a	10c blue & black	1.50
		Cut cancel	.30
a.		Inverted center	2,000.
b.		Double impression of center	—

No. R109a is valued in the grade of fine.

R110	R12a	15c blue & black	85.00
		Cut cancel	30.00
R111	R12a	20c blue & black	8.00
		Cut cancel	3.00
a.		Inverted center	7,000.

No. R111a is valued in the grade of fine and with small faults, as almost all examples have faults.

R13

R13a

R112	R13	25c blue & black	1.50
		Cut cancel	.30
a.		Inverted center	13,000.
b.		Sewing machine perf.	160.00
		Cut cancel	80.00
c.		Perf. 8	525.00
R113	R13	30c blue & black	160.00
		Cut cancel	60.00
R114	R13	40c blue & black	130.00
		Cut cancel	40.00
R115	R13a	50c blue & black	1.40
		Cut cancel	.35
a.		Sewing machine perf.	450.00
b.		Inverted center	1,150.
		Punch cancel	325.00
R116	R13a	60c blue & black	225.00
		Cut cancel	70.00
R117	R13a	70c blue & black	85.00
		Cut cancel	27.50
a.		Inverted center	4,000.
		Cut cancel	1,250.

R13b

R118	R13b	$1 blue & black	10.00
		Cut cancel	2.25
a.		Inverted center	6,000.
		Punch cancel	1,000.
R119	R13b	$1.30 blue & black	800.00
		Cut cancel	175.00
R120	R13b	$1.50 blue & black	22.50
		Cut cancel	9.00
a.		Sewing machine perf.	2,500.
R121	R13b	$1.60 blue & black	800.00
		Cut cancel	350.00
R122	R13b	$1.90 blue & black	550.00
		Cut cancel	150.00

R13c

R123	R13c	$2 blue & black	22.50
		Cut cancel	10.00
R124	R13c	$2.50 blue & black	50.00
		Cut cancel	25.00
R125	R13c	$3 blue & black	65.00
		Cut cancel	30.00
R126	R13c	$3.50 blue & black	500.00
		Cut cancel	130.00

R13d

R127	R13d	$5 blue & black	32.50
		Cut cancel	11.00
a.		Inverted center	3,000.
		Punch cancel	1,100.
R128	R13d	$10 blue & black	230.00
		Cut cancel	80.00

R13e

R129	R13e	$20 blue & black	1,150.
		Cut cancel	350.00
R130	R13e	$25 blue & black	1,100.
		Cut cancel	350.00
R131	R13e	$50 blue & black	1,400.
		Cut cancel	375.00

R13f

R132	R13f	$200 red, blue & black	9,000.
		Cut cancel	3,500.

Printed in sheets of one.

R13g

R133	R13g	$500 red org, grn & blk	17,500.

Printed in sheets of one.

Value for No. R133 is for a very fine appearing example with a light circular cut cancel or with minor flaws.

Inverted Centers: Fraudulently produced inverted centers exist, some excellently made.

Confusion resulting from the fact that all 1c through $50 denominations of the Second Issue were uniform in color, caused the ordering of a new printing with values in distinctive colors.

Plates used were those of the preceding issue.

Third Issue
Various Frames and Numeral Arrangements.
Violet "Chameleon" Paper with Silk Fibers.

1871-72   **Perf. 12**

R134	R12	1c claret & black ('72)	55.00
		Cut cancel	25.00
R135	R12	2c orange & black	.40
		Cut cancel	.25
a.		2c vermilion & black (error)	800.00
b.		Inverted center	475.00
c.		Imperf., pair	—
d.		As No. R135, double impression of frame	1,500.
e.		As No. R135, frame printed on both sides	1,600.
f.		As No. R135, double impression of center	150.00
R136	R12a	4c brown & black ('72)	95.00
		Cut cancel	35.00
R137	R12a	5c orange & black	.35
		Cut cancel	.25
a.		Inverted center	5,000.

No. R137a is valued in the grade of fine.

R138	R12a	6c orange & black ('72)	110.00
		Cut cancel	35.00

R139	R12a	15c brown & black ('72)	22.50	
		Cut cancel		6.75
a.		Inverted center	16,000.	
		Cut cancel		9,000.
R140	R13	30c orange & black ('72)	40.00	
		Cut cancel		10.00
a.		Inverted center	3,500.	
		Cut cancel		1,750.
R141	R13	40c brown & black ('72)	90.00	
		Cut cancel		25.00
R142	R13a	60c orange & black ('72)	125.00	
		Cut cancel		45.00
R143	R13a	70c green & black ('72)	90.00	
		Cut cancel		30.00
R144	R13b	$1 green & black ('72)	3.00	
		Cut cancel		.80
a.		Inverted center	15,000.	

No. R144a is valued in the grade of fine.

R145	R13c	$2 vermilion & black ('72)	45.00	
		Cut cancel		18.00
R146	R13c	$2.50 claret & black ('72)	90.00	
		Cut cancel		27.50
a.		Inverted center	22,500.	
R147	R13c	$3 green & black ('72)	85.00	
		Cut cancel		27.50
R148	R13d	$5 vermilion & black ('72)	42.50	
		Cut cancel		15.00
R149	R13d	$10 green & black ('72)	400.00	
		Cut cancel		85.00
R150	R13e	$20 orange & black ('72)	900.00	
		Cut cancel		350.00
a.		$20 vermilion & black (error)	1,250.	

See note on Inverted Centers after No. R133.

1874			**Perf. 12**	
R151	R12	2c orange & black, *green*		.25
		Cut cancel		.25
a.		Inverted center	800.00	
		Cut cancel		375.00

Liberty — R14

1875-78			**Perf. 12**	
R152	R14	2c blue, *blue*		.45
a.		silk paper		.35
b.		Wmk. 191R ('78)		32.50
c.		Wmk. 191R, rouletted 6		
d.		As "a," vert. pair, imperf. horiz.	525.00	
e.		As "b," imperf., pair	350.00	
f.		As "b," vert. pair, imperf. horiz.	350.00	

The watermarked paper came into use in 1878. The rouletted stamps probably were introduced in 1881.

Nos. 279, 267a, 267, 279Bg, 279B, 272-274 Overprinted in Red or Blue

a   b

1898			**Wmk. 191**	**Perf. 12**

For Nos. R153-R160, values in the first column are for unused examples, values in the second column are for used.

R153	A87 (a)	1c green (R)	5.00	2.75
R154	A87 (b)	1c green (R)	.35	.35
a.		Overprint inverted	35.00	22.50
b.		Overprint on back instead of face, inverted	4,000.	
c.		Pair, one without overprint	10,000.	
R155	A88 (b)	2c pink, III (Bl)	.30	.25
b.		2c carmine, type III (Bl)	.35	.25
c.		As No. R155, overprint inverted	6.50	4.50
d.		Vertical pair, one without overprint	1,750.	
e.		Horiz. pair, one without overprint	—	
f.		As No. R155, overprint on back instead of face, inverted	350.00	
i.		Double ovt., one split		750.00

R155A	A88 (b)	2c pink, IV (Bl)	.25	.25
g.		2c carmine, type IV (Bl)	.25	.25
h.		As No. R155A, overprint inverted	2.75	2.00

Handstamped Type "b" in Magenta

R156	A93	8c violet brown	5,500.	
R157	A94	10c dark green	4,250.	
R158	A95	15c dark blue	6,500.	

Nos. R156-R158 were emergency provisionals, privately prepared, not officially issued.

Privately Prepared Provisionals

No. 285 Overprinted in Red

1898			**Wmk. 191**	**Perf. 12**
R158A	A100	1c dark yellow green	12,500.	12,500.

No. 285 Ovptd. "I.R./P.I.D. & Son" in Red

R158B	A100	1c dark yellow green	30,000.	30,000.

No. R158B is valued with small faults as each of the four recorded examples have faults.

Nos. R158A-R158B were overprinted with federal government permission by the Purvis Printing Co. upon order of Capt. L. H. Chapman of the Chapman Steamboat Line. Both the Chapman Line and P. I. Daprix & Son operated freight-carrying steamboats on the Erie Canal. The Chapman Line touched at Syracuse, Utica, Little Falls and Fort Plain; the Daprix boat ran between Utica and Rome. Overprintings of 250 of each stamp were made.

Dr. Kilmer & Co. provisional overprints and St. Louis provisional proprietary stamps are listed under "Private Die Medicine Stamps" in the Scott U.S. Specialized Catalogue.

Newspaper Stamp No. PR121 Srchd. Vertically in Red

1898			**Perf. 12**	
R159	N18	$5 dark blue, surcharge reading down	550.00	325.00
R160	N18	$5 dark blue, surcharge reading up	150.00	140.00

Battleship — R15

Inscribed: "Series of 1898" and "Documentary."

There are 2 styles of rouletting for the 1898 proprietary and documentary stamps, an ordinary roulette 5½ and one where small rectangles of the paper are cut out, called hyphen hole perf. 7.

1898			**Wmk. 191R**	**Rouletted 5½**
R161	R15	½c orange	4.00	17.50
R162	R15	½c dark gray	.30	.25
a.		Vert. pair, imperf. horiz.	100.00	
R163	R15	1c pale blue	.25	.25
a.		Vert. pair, imperf. horiz.	8.00	
b.		Imperf., pair	500.00	
R164	R15	2c car rose	.30	.30
a.		Vert. pair, imperf. horiz.	100.00	
b.		Imperf., pair	300.00	
c.		Horiz. pair, imperf. vert.	325.00	
R165	R15	3c dark blue	3.50	.35
R166	R15	4c pale rose	2.50	.35
a.		Vert. pair, imperf. horiz.	175.00	
R167	R15	5c lilac	.65	.35
a.		Pair, imperf. horiz. or vert.	275.00	175.00
b.		Horiz. pair, imperf. btwn.		650.00

R168	R15	10c dark brown	2.00	.25
a.		Vert. pair, imperf. horiz.	40.00	35.00
b.		Horiz. pair, imperf. vert.	—	
R169	R15	25c pur brown	5.00	.50
R170	R15	40c blue lilac	125.00	1.50
		Cut cancellation		.35
R171	R15	50c slate violet	30.00	.25
a.		Imperf., pair	325.00	
b.		Horiz. pair, imperf. btwn.		375.00
R172	R15	80c bister	110.00	.50
				.25

No. R167b may not be genuine.

Hyphen Hole Perf. 7

R163p		1c	.30	.25
R164p		2c	.35	.25
R165p		3c	35.00	1.40
R166p		4c	13.00	1.60
R167p		5c	13.00	.35
R168p		10c	7.50	.25
R169p		25c	15.00	.50
R170p		40c	175.00	30.00
		Cut cancellation		12.50
R171p		50c	60.00	1.00
b.		Horiz. pair, imperf. btwn.		250.00
R172p		80c	210.00	50.00
		Cut cancellation		20.00

Commerce — R16

1898				**Rouletted 5½**
R173	R16	$1 dark green	25.00	.25
a.		Vert. pair, imperf. horiz.	800.00	
b.		Horiz. pair, imperf. vert.		325.00
p.		Hyphen hole perf. 7	37.50	2.00
		Cut cancel		.75
R174	R16	$3 dark brown	45.00	1.25
		Cut cancellation		.30
a.		Horiz. pair, imperf. vert.	500.00	
p.		Hyphen hole perf. 7	80.00	3.50
		Cut cancellation		.40
R175	R16	$5 orange red	75.00	2.00
				.30
R176	R16	$10 black	160.00	3.50
				.65
a.		Horiz. pair, imperf. vert.		
R177	R16	$30 red	500.00	160.00
		Cut cancellation		47.50
R178	R16	$50 gray brown	275.00	7.00
		Cut cancellation		2.50

See Nos. R182-R183.

John Marshall — R17

Alexander Hamilton — R18

James Madison — R19

1899				**Imperf.**

Without Gum

R179	R17	$100 yel brn & blk	300.00	40.00
		Cut cancel		22.50

R180	R18	$500 car lake & blk	2,100.	800.00
		Cut cancel		350.00
R181	R19	$1000 grn & blk	1,500.	400.00
		Cut cancel		160.00

1900   Hyphen-hole perf. 7
Allegorical Figure of Commerce

R182	R16	$1 carmine	45.00	.55
		Cut cancel		.30
R183	R16	$3 lake (fugitive ink)	300.00	60.00
		Cut cancel		10.00

Warning: The ink on No. R183 will run in water.

a

Surcharged type "a"

1900				
R184	R16	$1 gray	35.00	.40
		Cut cancel		.30
a.		Horiz. pair, imperf. vert	—	
b.		Surcharge omitted	140.00	
		As "b," cut cancel		82.50
R185	R16	$2 gray	35.00	.40
				.25
R186	R16	$3 gray	175.00	15.00
				6.00
R187	R16	$5 gray	85.00	11.00
				1.60
R188	R16	$10 gray	225.00	25.00
				4.50
R189	R16	$50 gray	2,000.	575.00
				140.00

b

Surcharged type "b"

Warning: If Nos. R190-R194 are soaked, the center part of the surcharged numeral may wash off. Before the surcharging, a square of soluble varnish was applied to the middle of some stamps.

1902				
R190	R16	$1 green	50.00	3.50
		Cut cancel		.30
a.		Inverted surcharge		190.00
R191	R16	$2 green	50.00	2.50
		Cut cancel		.45
a.		Surcharged as No. R185	150.00	90.00
b.		Surcharged as No. R185, in violet	2,000.	—
c.		As "a," double surcharge	150.00	
d.		As "a," triple surcharge	850.00	
e.		Pair, Nos. R191c and R191d	1,650.	
R192	R16	$5 green	240.00	42.50
		Cut cancel		5.00
a.		Surcharge omitted	300.00	
b.		Pair, one without surcharge	500.00	
R193	R16	$10 green	525.00	225.00
		Cut cancel		80.00
R194	R16	$50 green	2,750.	1,250.
		Cut cancel		350.00

R20

Inscribed "Series of 1914"

Offset Printing

1914			**Wmk. 190**	**Perf. 10**
R195	R20	½c rose	14.00	5.00
R196	R20	1c rose	2.75	.30
R197	R20	2c rose	4.00	.30
R198	R20	3c rose	100.00	40.00
R199	R20	4c rose	30.00	2.50
R200	R20	5c rose	10.00	.40
R201	R20	10c rose	8.00	.25
R202	R20	25c rose	50.00	.60
R203	R20	40c rose	32.50	3.00

Scott	Type	Description	Unused	Used
R204	R20	50c rose	13.00	.35
R205	R20	80c rose	210.00	17.00
		Nos. R195-R205 (11)	474.25	69.70

Wmk. 191R

Scott	Type	Description	Unused	Used
R206	R20	½c rose	1.60	.50
R207	R20	1c rose	.25	.25
R208	R20	2c rose	.30	.25
R209	R20	3c rose	1.50	.25
R210	R20	4c rose	4.50	.50
R211	R20	5c rose	2.00	.35
R212	R20	10c rose	.80	.25
R213	R20	25c rose	8.00	1.50
R214	R20	40c rose	125.00	15.00
		Cut cancel		.50
R215	R20	50c rose	27.50	.40
		Cut cancel		.25
R216	R20	80c rose	200.00	35.00
		Cut cancel		1.25
		Nos. R206-R216 (11)	371.45	54.25

Liberty — R21

Inscribed "Series 1914"

Engr.

Scott	Type	Description	Unused	Used
R217	R21	$1 green	75.00	.55
		Cut cancel		.25
a.		$1 yellow green	50.00	.25
R218	R21	$2 carmine	125.00	1.00
		Cut cancel		.25
R219	R21	$3 purple	150.00	5.00
		Cut cancel		.80
R220	R21	$5 blue	105.00	4.50
		Cut cancel		.65
R221	R21	$10 yel org	325.00	7.50
		Cut cancel		1.10
R222	R21	$30 vermilion	775.00	21.00
		Cut cancel		2.25
R223	R21	$50 violet	2,000.	1,200.
		Cut cancel		450.00

See Nos. R240-R245, R257-R259, R276-R281.

Portrait Types of 1899 Inscribed "Series of 1915" (#R224), or "Series of 1914"

1914-15 Without Gum Perf. 12

Scott	Type	Description	Unused	Used
R224	R19	$60 brown (Lincoln)	250.00	150.00
		Cut cancel		70.00
R225	R17	$100 green (Washington)	77.50	45.00
		Cut cancel		16.00
R226	R18	$500 blue (Hamilton)	—	700.00
		Cut cancel		275.00
R227	R19	$1000 orange (Madison)	—	800.00
		Cut cancel		325.00

The stamps of types R17, R18 and R19 in this and subsequent issues were issued in vertical strips of 4 which are imperforate at the top, bottom and right side; therefore, single stamps are always imperforate on one or two sides.

R22

Offset Printing

1917 Wmk. 191R Perf. 11

Scott	Type	Description	Unused	Used
R228	R22	1c carmine rose	.35	.25
R229	R22	2c carmine rose	.25	.25
R230	R22	3c carmine rose	1.75	.40
R231	R22	4c carmine rose	.75	.25
R232	R22	5c carmine rose	.30	.25
R233	R22	8c carmine rose	3.00	.35
R234	R22	10c carmine rose	.40	.25
R235	R22	20c carmine rose	.75	.25
R236	R22	25c carmine rose	1.75	.25
R237	R22	40c carmine rose	2.25	.50
R238	R22	50c carmine rose	2.50	.25
R239	R22	80c carmine rose	9.00	.35
		Nos. R228-R239 (12)	23.05	3.60

Liberty Type of 1914 without "Series 1914"

1917-33 Engr.

Scott	Type	Description	Unused	Used
R240	R21	$1 yellow green	10.00	.30
a.		$1 green	7.25	.25
R241	R21	$2 rose	17.50	.25
R242	R21	$3 violet	60.00	1.50
		Cut cancel		.30
R243	R21	$4 yellow brown ('33)	40.00	2.00
		Cut cancel		.30
R244	R21	$5 dark blue	27.50	.35
		Cut cancel		.25
R245	R21	$10 orange	60.00	1.40
		Cut cancel		.30

Portrait Types of 1899 without "Series of" and Date

Portraits: $30, Grant. $60, Lincoln. $100, Washington. $500, Hamilton. $1,000, Madison.

1917 Without Gum Perf. 12

Scott	Type	Description	Unused	Used
R246	R17	$30 dp org, green numerals	55.00	13.00
		Cut cancel		2.25
a.		As "b," imperf. pair	900.00	
b.		Numerals in blue	125.00	3.50
		Cut cancel		1.50
R247	R19	$60 brown	65.00	8.00
		Cut cancel		.85
R248	R17	$100 green	45.00	2.00
		Cut cancel		.50
R249	R18	$500 blue, red numerals	375.00	50.00
		Cut cancel		15.00
a.		Numerals in orange	425.00	65.00
R250	R19	$1000 orange	175.00	20.00
		Cut cancel		7.50
a.		imperf., pair	2,000.	

See note after No. R227.

1928-29 Offset Printing Perf. 10

Scott	Type	Description	Unused	Used
R251	R22	1c carmine rose	2.10	1.60
R252	R22	2c carmine rose	.60	.30
R253	R22	4c carmine rose	7.00	4.00
R254	R22	5c carmine rose	1.75	.55
R255	R22	10c carmine rose	2.75	1.25
R256	R22	20c carmine rose	6.00	4.50

Engr.

Scott	Type	Description	Unused	Used
R257	R21	$1 green	200.00	45.00
		Cut cancel		5.00
R258	R21	$2 rose	90.00	5.00
R259	R21	$10 orange	325.00	75.00
		Cut cancel		30.00

1929 Offset Printing Perf. 11x10

Scott	Type	Description	Unused	Used
R260	R22	2c carmine rose ('30)	3.00	2.75
R261	R22	5c carmine rose ('30)	2.00	1.90
R262	R22	10c carmine rose	9.25	6.75
R263	R22	20c carmine rose	15.00	8.25

Used values for Nos. R264-R734 are for stamps which are neither cut nor perforated with initials. Examples with cut cancellations or perforated initials are valued in the Scott U. S. Specialized Catalogue.

Types of 1917-33 Overprinted in Black

SERIES 1940

Offset Printing

1940 Wmk. 191R Perf. 11

Scott	Type	Description	Unused	Used
R264	R22	1c rose pink	3.75	2.40
R265	R22	2c rose pink	5.00	2.25
R266	R22	3c rose pink	11.00	5.00
R267	R22	4c rose pink	5.00	.80
R268	R22	5c rose pink	5.00	1.25
R269	R22	8c rose pink	22.50	17.00
R270	R22	10c rose pink	2.50	.65
R271	R22	20c rose pink	3.25	.80
R272	R22	25c rose pink	8.00	1.50
R273	R22	40c rose pink	6.75	.90
R274	R22	50c rose pink	11.00	.55
R275	R22	80c rose pink	14.00	1.75

Engr.

Scott	Type	Description	Unused	Used
R276	R21	$1 green	75.00	1.25
R277	R21	$2 rose	75.00	2.00
R278	R21	$3 violet	100.00	37.50
R279	R21	$4 yellow brown	190.00	35.00
R280	R21	$5 dark blue	85.00	20.00
R281	R21	$10 orange	240.00	50.00

Types of 1917 Handstamped "Series 1940" like R264-R281 in Blue (Nos. R282-R283), Green (Nos. R283-R284, R286) or Violet (No. R285)

1940 Wmk. 191R Perf. 12
Without Gum

Scott	Type	Description	Unused	Used
R282	R17	$30 vermilion		1,250.
a.		With black 2-line handstamp in larger type		25,000.
R283	R19	$60 brown		2,400.
a.		As #R282a, cut cancel		12,500.
R284	R17	$100 green		4,250.
R285	R18	$500 blue		3,000.
a.		As #R282a	3,250.	4,000.
b.		Blue handstamp; double transfer		—
R286	R19	$1000 orange		1,250.
a.		Double overprint, cut cancel		—

Alexander Hamilton R23   Levi Woodbury R24

Overprinted in Black   **SERIES 1940**

Various Portraits: 2c, Oliver Wolcott, Jr. 3c, Samuel Dexter. 4c, Albert Gallatin. 5c, G. W. Campbell. 8c, Alexander Dallas. 10c, William H. Crawford. 20c, Richard Rush. 25c, S. D. Ingham. 40c, Louis McLane. 50c, William J. Duane. 80c, Roger B. Taney. $2, Thomas Ewing. $3, Walter Forward. $4, J. C. Spencer. $5, G. M. Bibb. $10, R. J. Walker. $20, William M. Meredith.

1940 Engr. Wmk. 191R Perf. 11

Scott	Type	Description	Unused	Used
R288	R23	1c carmine	5.75	4.50
a.		Imperf, pair, without gum	250.00	
R289	R23	2c carmine	8.50	4.00
a.		Imperf, pair, without gum	250.00	
R290	R23	3c carmine	30.00	12.00
a.		Imperf, pair, without gum	250.00	
R291	R23	4c carmine	62.50	27.50
a.		Imperf, pair, without gum	250.00	
R292	R23	5c carmine	4.75	.80
a.		Imperf, pair, without gum	250.00	
R293	R23	8c carmine	85.00	60.00
a.		Imperf, pair, without gum	250.00	
R294	R23	10c carmine	4.25	.60
a.		Imperf, pair, without gum	250.00	
R295	R23	20c carmine	5.50	4.25
a.		Imperf, pair, without gum	250.00	
R296	R23	25c carmine	5.00	.75
a.		Imperf, pair, without gum	250.00	
R297	R23	40c carmine	75.00	30.00
a.		Imperf, pair, without gum	250.00	
R298	R23	50c carmine	8.00	.60
a.		Imperf, pair, without gum	250.00	
R299	R23	80c carmine	175.00	100.00
a.		Imperf, pair, without gum	475.00	
R300	R24	$1 carmine	42.50	.60
a.		Imperf, pair, without gum	250.00	
R301	R24	$2 carmine	80.00	.90
a.		Imperf, pair, without gum	1,400.	
R302	R24	$3 carmine	190.00	95.00
a.		Imperf, pair, without gum	1,400.	
R303	R24	$4 carmine	125.00	50.00
R304	R24	$5 carmine	70.00	3.00
R305	R24	$10 carmine	125.00	10.00
R305A	R24	$20 carmine	3,000.	1,100.
b.		Imperf, pair, without gum	700.00	

Thomas Corwin — R25

Various Frames and Portraits: $50, James Guthrie. $60, Howell Cobb. $100, P. F. Thomas. $500, J. A. Dix, $1,000, S. P. Chase.

Perf. 12
Without Gum

Scott	Type	Description	Unused	Used
R306	R25	$30 car	200.00	75.00
R306A	R25	$50 car	—	9,000.
R307	R25	$60 car	375.00	80.00
a.		Vert. pair, imperf. btwn.	2,750.	1,450.
R308	R25	$100 car	300.00	100.00
R309	R25	$500 car	—	5,000.
R310	R25	$1000 car	—	550.00

The $30 to $1,000 denominations in this and following similar issues, and the $2,500, $5,000 and $10,000 stamps of 1952-58 have straight edges on one or two sides. They were issued without gum through No. R723.

Nos. R288-R310 Overprinted

SERIES 1941

1941 Wmk. 191R Perf. 11

Scott	Type	Description	Unused	Used
R311	R23	1c carmine	5.00	2.75
R312	R23	2c carmine	5.25	1.10
R313	R23	3c carmine	10.00	4.25
R314	R23	4c carmine	7.50	1.75
R315	R23	5c carmine	1.50	.40
R316	R23	8c carmine	21.00	8.50
R317	R23	10c carmine	2.00	.35
R318	R23	20c carmine	4.75	.65
R319	R23	25c carmine	2.40	.65
R320	R23	40c carmine	16.00	3.25
R321	R23	50c carmine	3.50	.30
R322	R23	80c carmine	65.00	12.00
R323	R24	$1 carmine	15.00	.30
R324	R24	$2 carmine	20.00	.50
R325	R24	$3 carmine	32.50	3.50
R326	R24	$4 carmine	47.50	27.50
R327	R24	$5 carmine	60.00	1.10
R328	R24	$10 carmine	100.00	6.00
R329	R24	$20 carmine	850.00	400.00

Perf. 12
Without Gum

Scott	Type	Description	Unused	Used
R330	R25	$30 car	200.00	55.00
R331	R25	$50 car	1,100.	1,000.
R332	R25	$60 car	225.00	87.50
R333	R25	$100 car	110.00	37.50
R334	R25	$500 car	—	375.00
R335	R25	$1000 car	—	225.00

Nos. R288-R310 Overprinted

SERIES 1942

1942 Wmk. 191R Perf. 11

Scott	Type	Description	Unused	Used
R336	R23	1c carmine	.65	.60
R337	R23	2c carmine	.60	.60
R338	R23	3c carmine	.90	.80
R339	R23	4c carmine	1.75	1.10
R340	R23	5c carmine	.60	.35
R341	R23	8c carmine	9.50	4.75
R342	R23	10c carmine	1.75	.35
R343	R23	20c carmine	1.75	.60
R344	R23	25c carmine	3.00	.55
R345	R23	40c carmine	6.50	1.75
R346	R23	50c carmine	4.00	.35
R347	R23	80c carmine	27.50	13.00
R348	R24	$1 carmine	12.50	.25
R349	R24	$2 carmine	15.00	.30
R350	R24	$3 carmine	27.50	3.25
R351	R24	$4 carmine	35.00	7.50
R352	R24	$5 carmine	37.50	1.50
R353	R24	$10 carmine	85.00	3.75
R354	R24	$20 carmine	300.00	45.00
a.		Imperf., perf. initials		—

Perf. 12
Without Gum

Scott	Type	Description	Unused	Used
R355	R25	$30 carmine	100.00	42.50
R356	R25	$50 carmine	1,900.	1,400.
R357	R25	$60 carmine	5,000.	1,750.
R358	R25	$100 carmine	275.00	175.00
R359	R25	$500 carmine	1,600.	275.00
R360	R25	$1000 carmine	—	175.00

Nos. R288-R310 Overprinted

SERIES 1943

1943 Wmk. 191R Perf. 11

Scott	Type	Description	Unused	Used
R361	R23	1c carmine	.80	.65
R362	R23	2c carmine	.65	.55
R363	R23	3c carmine	3.75	3.50
R364	R23	4c carmine	1.60	1.50
R365	R23	5c carmine	.70	.45
R366	R23	8c carmine	6.00	4.00
R367	R23	10c carmine	.85	.30
R368	R23	20c carmine	2.50	.80
R369	R23	25c carmine	2.75	.50
R370	R23	40c carmine	7.50	4.00
R371	R23	50c carmine	2.00	.30
R372	R23	80c carmine	27.50	8.00
R373	R24	$1 carmine	9.00	.35
R374	R24	$2 carmine	18.00	.35
R375	R24	$3 carmine	30.00	3.00
R376	R24	$4 carmine	55.00	10.00
R377	R24	$5 carmine	52.50	.75
R378	R24	$10 carmine	85.00	5.00
R379	R24	$20 carmine	275.00	60.00

Perf. 12
Without Gum

Scott	Type	Description	Unused	Used
R380	R25	$30 carmine	125.00	25.00
R381	R25	$50 carmine	200.00	75.00
R382	R25	$60 carmine	325.00	125.00
R383	R25	$100 carmine	35.00	22.50
R384	R25	$500 carmine	375.00	325.00
R385	R25	$1000 carmine	350.00	200.00

Nos. R288-R310 Overprinted

Series 1944

1944 — Wmk. 191R — Perf. 11

R386	R23	1c carmine	.50	.45
R387	R23	2c carmine	.65	.55
R388	R23	3c carmine	.65	.40
R389	R23	4c carmine	.75	.65
R390	R23	5c carmine	.40	.25
R391	R23	8c carmine	2.25	1.75
R392	R23	10c carmine	.50	.25
R393	R23	20c carmine	1.10	.35
R394	R23	25c carmine	2.00	.30
R395	R23	40c carmine	3.75	.80
R396	R23	50c carmine	4.00	.35
R397	R23	80c carmine	21.00	5.50
R398	R24	$1 carmine	10.00	.30
R399	R24	$2 carmine	15.00	.45
R400	R24	$3 carmine	25.00	2.40
R401	R24	$4 carmine	32.50	11.50
R402	R24	$5 carmine	32.50	.50
R403	R24	$10 carmine	65.00	1.60
R404	R24	$20 carmine	275.00	19.00

Perf. 12 — Without Gum

R405	R25	$30 carmine	95.00	35.00
R406	R25	$50 carmine	42.50	22.50
R407	R25	$60 carmine	275.00	75.00
R408	R25	$100 carmine	52.50	12.50
R409	R25	$500 carmine	—	3,250.
R410	R25	$1000 carmine	4,000.	500.00

Nos. R288-R310 Overprinted
Series 1945

1945 — Wmk. 191R — Perf. 11

R411	R23	1c carmine	.40	.30
R412	R23	2c carmine	.40	.30
R413	R23	3c carmine	.75	.50
R414	R23	4c carmine	.45	.35
R415	R23	5c carmine	.45	.30
R416	R23	8c carmine	6.25	2.75
R417	R23	10c carmine	1.25	.25
R418	R23	20c carmine	8.00	1.50
R419	R23	25c carmine	1.75	.30
R420	R23	40c carmine	9.00	1.25
R421	R23	50c carmine	4.00	.25
R422	R23	80c carmine	26.00	14.00
R423	R24	$1 carmine	13.50	.30
R424	R24	$2 carmine	13.50	.40
R425	R24	$3 carmine	27.50	3.00
R426	R24	$4 carmine	35.00	4.25
R427	R24	$5 carmine	35.00	.50
R428	R24	$10 carmine	65.00	2.50
R429	R24	$20 carmine	200.00	16.00

Perf. 12 — Without Gum

R430	R25	$30 carmine	175.00	40.00
R431	R25	$50 carmine	200.00	45.00
R432	R25	$60 carmine	375.00	80.00
R433	R25	$100 carmine	40.00	20.00
R434	R25	$500 carmine	500.00	325.00
R435	R25	$1000 carmine	375.00	125.00

Nos. R288-R310 Overprinted
Series 1946

1946 — Wmk. 191R — Perf. 11

R436	R23	1c carmine	.30	.30
R437	R23	2c carmine	.45	.35
R438	R23	3c carmine	.55	.40
R439	R23	4c carmine	.80	.65
R440	R23	5c carmine	.45	.30
R441	R23	8c carmine	2.50	2.00
R442	R23	10c carmine	1.10	.30
R443	R23	20c carmine	1.75	.50
R444	R23	25c carmine	6.00	.35
R445	R23	40c carmine	4.50	.85
R446	R23	50c carmine	6.00	.30
R447	R23	80c carmine	17.50	5.00
R448	R24	$1 carmine	16.00	.30
R449	R24	$2 carmine	19.00	.30
R450	R24	$3 carmine	27.50	5.00
R451	R24	$4 carmine	60.00	20.00
R452	R24	$5 carmine	40.00	.50
R453	R24	$10 carmine	72.50	1.75
R454	R24	$20 carmine	200.00	16.00

Perf. 12 — Without Gum

R455	R25	$30 carmine	60.00	17.50
R456	R25	$50 carmine	50.00	12.50
R457	R25	$60 carmine	95.00	22.50
R458	R25	$100 carmine	70.00	12.50
R459	R25	$500 carmine	625.00	150.00
R460	R25	$1000 carmine	375.00	160.00

Nos. R288-R310 Overprinted
Series 1947

1947 — Wmk. 191R — Perf. 11

R461	R23	1c carmine	.85	.55
R462	R23	2c carmine	.75	.55
R463	R23	3c carmine	.85	.55
R464	R23	4c carmine	.90	.75
R465	R23	5c carmine	.55	.40
R466	R23	8c carmine	1.75	.80

R467	R23	10c carmine	1.40	.30
R468	R23	20c carmine	2.25	.55
R469	R23	25c carmine	3.00	.70
R470	R23	40c carmine	5.50	1.10
R471	R23	50c carmine	3.75	.40
R472	R23	80c carmine	12.00	8.00
R473	R24	$1 carmine	8.25	.35
R474	R24	$2 carmine	14.00	.65
R475	R24	$3 carmine	17.50	6.00
R476	R24	$4 carmine	19.00	5.00
R477	R24	$5 carmine	27.50	.40
R478	R24	$10 carmine	67.50	3.00
R479	R24	$20 carmine	110.00	14.00

Perf. 12 — Without Gum

R480	R25	$30 carmine	150.00	27.50
R481	R25	$50 carmine	72.50	17.50
R482	R25	$60 carmine	175.00	60.00
R483	R25	$100 carmine	65.00	15.00
R484	R25	$500 carmine	500.00	250.00
R485	R25	$1000 carmine	275.00	100.00

Nos. R288-R310 Overprinted
Series 1948

1948 — Wmk. 191R — Perf. 11

R486	R23	1c carmine	.35	.30
R487	R23	2c carmine	.50	.45
R488	R23	3c carmine	.60	.40
R489	R23	4c carmine	.55	.40
R490	R23	5c carmine	.50	.25
R491	R23	8c carmine	1.00	.50
R492	R23	10c carmine	1.00	.25
R493	R23	20c carmine	2.50	.40
R494	R23	25c carmine	2.25	.30
R495	R23	40c carmine	7.00	1.75
R496	R23	50c carmine	2.50	.30
R497	R23	80c carmine	12.00	8.00
R498	R24	$1 carmine	10.50	.30
R499	R24	$2 carmine	18.00	.40
R500	R24	$3 carmine	24.00	3.50
R501	R24	$4 carmine	35.00	4.00
R502	R24	$5 carmine	30.00	.50
R503	R24	$10 carmine	70.00	1.50
a.		Pair, one dated "1946"		—
R504	R24	$20 carmine	400.00	18.00

Perf. 12 — Without Gum

R505	R25	$30 carmine	125.00	35.00
R506	R25	$50 carmine	150.00	27.50
a.		Vert. pair, imperf. btwn.	2,500.	
R507	R25	$60 carmine	250.00	75.00
a.		Vert. pair, imperf. btwn.	2,500.	
R508	R25	$100 carmine	100.00	20.00
a.		Vert. pair, imperf. btwn.	2,000.	

No. R508a is known as four used singles, all four positions from a single pane of four, clearly imperf. horiz. before being separated.

R509	R25	$500 carmine	1,000.	200.00
R510	R25	$1000 carmine	300.00	125.00

Nos. R288-R310 Overprinted
Series 1949

1949 — Wmk. 191R — Perf. 11

R511	R23	1c carmine	.40	.35
R512	R23	2c carmine	.75	.45
R513	R23	3c carmine	.60	.50
R514	R23	4c carmine	.80	.60
R515	R23	5c carmine	.55	.30
R516	R23	8c carmine	1.00	.70
R517	R23	10c carmine	.60	.35
R518	R23	20c carmine	1.75	.75
R519	R23	25c carmine	2.25	.85
R520	R23	40c carmine	6.50	2.75
R521	R23	50c carmine	5.00	.40
R522	R23	80c carmine	15.00	7.50
R523	R24	$1 carmine	13.50	.85
R524	R24	$2 carmine	17.00	2.50
R525	R24	$3 carmine	27.50	8.00
R526	R24	$4 carmine	30.00	8.00
R527	R24	$5 carmine	32.50	4.25
R528	R24	$10 carmine	72.50	5.25
R529	R24	$20 carmine	150.00	15.00

Perf. 12 — Without Gum

R530	R25	$30 carmine	150.00	35.00
R531	R25	$50 carmine	160.00	60.00
R532	R25	$60 carmine	250.00	70.00
R533	R25	$100 carmine	80.00	21.00
R534	R25	$500 carmine	500.00	260.00
R535	R25	$1000 carmine	375.00	160.00

Nos. R288-R310 Overprinted
Series 1950

1950 — Wmk. 191R — Perf. 11

R536	R23	1c carmine	.40	.25
R537	R23	2c carmine	.40	.35
R538	R23	3c carmine	.50	.40
R539	R23	4c carmine	.70	.50
R540	R23	5c carmine	.45	.35
R541	R23	8c carmine	1.75	.80

R542	R23	10c carmine	.80	.30
R543	R23	20c carmine	1.40	.45
R544	R23	25c carmine	2.00	.45
R545	R23	40c carmine	6.00	2.10
R546	R23	50c carmine	8.00	.35
R547	R23	80c carmine	15.00	8.50
R548	R24	$1 carmine	15.00	.40
R549	R24	$2 carmine	17.50	2.75
R550	R24	$3 carmine	20.00	6.00
R551	R24	$4 carmine	27.50	7.50
R552	R24	$5 carmine	35.00	1.00
R553	R24	$10 carmine	70.00	10.00
R554	R24	$20 carmine	150.00	15.00

Perf. 12 — Without Gum

R555	R25	$30 carmine	125.00	70.00
R556	R25	$50 carmine	100.00	22.50
a.		Vert. pair, imperf. horiz.		
R557	R25	$60 carmine	210.00	75.00
R558	R25	$100 carmine	85.00	22.50
R559	R25	$500 carmine	300.00	125.00
R560	R25	$1000 carmine	300.00	95.00

Nos. R288-R310 Overprinted
Series 1951

1951 — Wmk. 191R — Perf. 11

R561	R23	1c carmine	.30	.25
R562	R23	2c carmine	.30	.35
R563	R23	3c carmine	.30	.35
R564	R23	4c carmine	.30	.35
R565	R23	5c carmine	.30	.35
R566	R23	8c carmine	1.25	.45
R567	R23	10c carmine	.30	.35
R568	R23	20c carmine	.30	.55
R569	R23	25c carmine	.30	.50
R570	R23	40c carmine	3.75	1.60
R571	R23	50c carmine	3.00	.60
R572	R23	80c carmine	10.00	3.25
R573	R24	$1 carmine	16.00	.30
R574	R24	$2 carmine	21.00	.55
R575	R24	$3 carmine	16.00	4.00
R576	R24	$4 carmine	20.00	12.50
R577	R24	$5 carmine	10.00	.70
R578	R24	$10 carmine	18.00	2.50
R579	R24	$20 carmine	55.00	16.00

Perf. 12 — Without Gum

R580	R25	$30 carmine	125.00	25.00
a.		Imperf., pair	2,500.	775.00
R581	R25	$50 carmine	200.00	45.00
R582	R25	$60 carmine	225.00	75.00
R583	R25	$100 carmine	70.00	25.00
R584	R25	$500 carmine	400.00	175.00
R585	R25	$1000 carmine	375.00	150.00

No. R583 is known imperf horizontally. It exists as a reconstructed used vertical strip of 4 that was separated into single stamps.

Documentary Stamps and Types of 1940 Overprinted in Black
Series 1952

Designs: 55c, $1.10, $1.65, $2.20, $2.75, $3.30, L. J. Gage; $2500, William Windom; $5000, C. J. Folger; $10,000, W. Q. Gresham.

1952 — Wmk. 191R — Perf. 11

R586	R23	1c carmine	.35	.30
R587	R23	2c carmine	.50	.35
R588	R23	3c carmine	.40	.35
R589	R23	4c carmine	.45	.30
R590	R23	5c carmine	.35	.30
R591	R23	8c carmine	.90	.60
R592	R23	10c carmine	.50	.30
R593	R23	20c carmine	1.25	.40
R594	R23	25c carmine	2.50	.45
R595	R23	40c carmine	6.00	1.75
R596	R23	50c carmine	3.50	.30
R597	R23	55c carmine	.60	15.00
R598	R23	80c carmine	19.00	4.00
R599	R24	$1 carmine	7.00	1.50
R600	R24	$1.10 carmine	25.00	30.00
R601	R24	$1.65 carmine	175.00	62.50
R602	R24	$2 carmine	17.00	.90
R603	R24	$2.20 carmine	160.00	70.00
R604	R24	$2.75 carmine	190.00	70.00
R605	R24	$3 carmine	32.50	6.00
a.		Horiz. pair, imperf. btwn.	1,300.	
R606	R24	$3.30 carmine	225.00	90.00
R607	R24	$4 carmine	37.50	6.00
R608	R24	$5 carmine	32.50	1.25
R609	R24	$10 carmine	60.00	1.25
R610	R24	$20 carmine	92.50	16.00

Perf. 12 — Without Gum

R611	R25	$30 carmine	70.00	27.50
R612	R25	$50 carmine	75.00	35.00
R613	R25	$60 carmine	475.00	70.00
R614	R25	$100 carmine	75.00	10.00
R615	R25	$500 carmine	750.00	160.00
R616	R25	$1000 carmine	250.00	75.00
R617	R25	$2500 carmine	375.00	275.00
R618	R25	$5000 carmine	—	5,500.
R619	R25	$10,000 carmine	—	1,400.

Documentary Stamps and Types of 1940 Overprinted in Black
Series 1953

1953 — Wmk. 191R — Perf. 11

R620	R23	1c carmine	.40	.35
R621	R23	2c carmine	.40	.30
R622	R23	3c carmine	.45	.35
R623	R23	4c carmine	.60	.45
R624	R23	5c carmine	.50	.30
a.		Vert. pair, imperf. horiz.		650.00
R625	R23	8c carmine	1.10	.85
R626	R23	10c carmine	.65	.35
R627	R23	20c carmine	1.50	.50
R628	R23	25c carmine	1.75	.65
R629	R23	40c carmine	2.50	.90
R630	R23	50c carmine	3.00	.35
R631	R23	55c carmine	7.00	2.00
a.		Horiz. pair, imperf. vert.	375.00	
R632	R23	80c carmine	10.00	2.10
R633	R24	$1 carmine	5.25	.35
R634	R24	$1.10 carmine	12.00	2.50
a.		Horiz. pair, imperf. vert.	700.00	
b.		Imperf. pair	600.00	
R635	R24	$1.65 carmine	12.00	4.50
R636	R24	$2 carmine	9.00	.75
R637	R24	$2.20 carmine	20.00	6.00
R638	R24	$2.75 carmine	1.75	7.00
R639	R24	$3 carmine	17.00	4.00
R640	R24	$3.30 carmine	50.00	17.50
R641	R24	$4 carmine	40.00	15.00
R642	R24	$5 carmine	27.50	1.25
R643	R24	$10 carmine	60.00	2.25
R644	R24	$20 carmine	140.00	22.50

Perf. 12 — Without Gum

R645	R25	$30 car	100.00	20.00
R646	R25	$50 car	160.00	42.50
R647	R25	$60 car	700.00	425.00
R648	R25	$100 car	55.00	15.00
R649	R25	$500 car	2,000.	175.00
R650	R25	$1000 car	600.00	80.00
R651	R25	$2500 car	2,000.	1,750.
R652	R25	$5000 car	—	6,000.
R653	R25	$10,000 car	—	3,500.

In 1955, the BEP began printing flat plate documentary stamps Nos. R654-R681 using the dry-printing method. This method used paper with a 5-10% moisture content versus the 15-35% moisture content for the wet printing. The dry-printed stamps from the same plates are .25-.75mm larger than the wet-printed examples. Four sub-varieties are known: (1) wet printing with ridged yellow gum, (2) wet printing with smooth yellow gum, (3) dry printing with smooth white gum, and (4) dry printing with smooth white gum.

Types of 1940
Without Overprint

1954 — Wmk. 191R — Perf. 11

R654	R23	1c carmine	.25	.25
a.		Horiz. pair, imperf. vert.	1,500.	
R655	R23	2c carmine	.25	.30
R656	R23	3c carmine	.25	.30
R657	R23	4c carmine	.25	.30
R658	R23	5c carmine	.25	.25
a.		Vert. pair, imperf. horiz.	—	
R659	R23	8c carmine	.25	.25
R660	R23	10c carmine	.25	.25
R661	R23	20c carmine	.30	.40
R662	R23	25c carmine	.35	.45
R663	R23	40c carmine	.75	.60
R664	R23	50c carmine	1.00	.25
a.		Horiz. pair, imperf. vert.	600.00	
R665	R23	55c carmine	.90	1.25
R666	R23	80c carmine	1.50	1.90
R667	R24	$1 carmine	.90	.35
R668	R24	$1.10 carmine	2.00	2.50
R669	R24	$1.65 carmine	25.00	7.50
R670	R24	$2 carmine	1.00	.45
R671	R24	$2.20 carmine	2.25	3.75
R672	R24	$2.75 carmine	25.00	55.00
R673	R24	$3 carmine	2.00	2.00
R674	R24	$3.30 carmine	3.50	5.00
R675	R24	$4 carmine	2.75	4.00
R676	R24	$5 carmine	3.25	.50
R677	R24	$10 carmine	5.00	1.50
R678	R24	$20 carmine	10.00	6.50

Documentary Stamps & Type of 1940 Ovptd. in Black

1954		**Wmk. 191R**		*Perf. 12*
Without Gum				

R679	R25	$30 car-		
		mine	55.00	17.50
a.	Booklet pane of 4		*225.00*	
R680	R25	$50 car-		
		mine	55.00	29.00
a.	Booklet pane of 4		*225.00*	
R681	R25	$60 car-		
		mine	55.00	30.00
a.	Booklet pane of 4		*225.00*	
R682	R25	$100 car-		
		mine	55.00	7.50
a.	Booklet pane of 4		*225.00*	
R683	R25	$500 car-		
		mine	150.00	87.50
a.	Booklet pane of 4		*600.00*	
R684	R25	$1000 car-		
		mine	300.00	90.00
a.	Booklet pane of 4		*1,200.*	
R685	R25	$2500 car-		
		mine	350.00	350.00
a.	Booklet pane of 4		*1,400.*	
R686	R25	$5000 car-		
		mine	1,750.	1,500.
a.	Booklet pane of 4		*7,000.*	
R687	R25	$10,000 car-		
		mine	1,750.	2,250.
a.	Booklet pane of 4		*7,000.*	

Documentary Stamps and Type of 1940 Overprinted in Black
Series 1955

1955		**Wmk. 191R**		*Perf. 12*
Without Gum				

R688	R25	$30 car-		
		mine	90.00	17.50
R689	R25	$50 car-		
		mine	100.00	30.00
R690	R25	$60 car-		
		mine	160.00	45.00
R691	R25	$100 car-		
		mine	125.00	20.00
R692	R25	$500 car-		
		mine	750.00	200.00
R693	R25	$1000 car-		
		mine	275.00	80.00
R694	R25	$2500 car-		
		mine	500.00	275.00
R695	R25	$5000 car-		
		mine	4,000.	2,000.
R696	R25	$10,000 car-		
		mine	—	1,250.

Documentary Stamps and Type of 1940 Overprinted "Series 1956"

1956		**Wmk. 191R**		*Perf. 12*
Without Gum				

R697	R25	$30 carmine	150.00	20.00
R698	R25	$50 carmine	250.00	27.50
R699	R25	$60 carmine	190.00	60.00
R700	R25	$100 carmine	110.00	15.00
R701	R25	$500 carmine	1,000.	150.00
R702	R25	$1000 carmine	1,000.	100.00
R703	R25	$2500 carmine	—	750.00
R704	R25	$5000 carmine	—	2,000.
R705	R25	$10,000 carmine	—	750.00

Documentary Stamps and Type of 1940 Overprinted "Series 1957"

1957		**Wmk. 191R**		*Perf. 12*
Without Gum				

R706	R25	$30 car-		
		mine	225.00	60.00
R707	R25	$50 car-		
		mine	125.00	47.50
R708	R25	$60 car-		
		mine	1,000.	400.00
R709	R25	$100 car-		
		mine	110.00	20.00
R710	R25	$500 car-		
		mine	450.00	200.00
R711	R25	$1000 car-		
		mine	300.00	100.00
R712	R25	$2500 car-		
		mine	—	1,200.
R713	R25	$5000 car-		
		mine	4,000.	1,800.
R714	R25	$10,000 car-		
		mine	—	650.00

Documentary Stamps and Type of 1940 Overprinted in Black "Series 1958"

1958		**Wmk. 191R**		*Perf. 12*
Without Gum				

R715	R25	$30 carmine	110.00	27.50
R716	R25	$50 carmine	150.00	35.00
R717	R25	$60 carmine	160.00	42.50
R718	R25	$100 carmine	175.00	15.00
R719	R25	$500 carmine	350.00	125.00
R720	R25	$1000 carmine	1,000.	90.00
R721	R25	$2500 carmine	—	1,500.
R722	R25	$5000 carmine	—	4,250.
R723	R25	$10,000 carmine	—	2,750.

Documentary Stamps and Type of 1940 Without Overprint

1958		**Wmk. 191R**		*Perf. 12*
With Gum				

R724	R25	$30 carmine	11.00	7.00
a.	Booklet pane of 4		*57.50*	
b.	Vert. pair, imperf. horiz.		*2,250.*	
R725	R25	$50 carmine	12.00	7.00
a.	Booklet pane of 4		*60.00*	
b.	Vert. pair, imperf. horiz.			*3,500.*
R726	R25	$60 carmine	17.50	21.00
a.	Booklet pane of 4		*90.00*	
R727	R25	$100 carmine	13.00	4.75
a.	Booklet pane of 4		*65.00*	
R728	R25	$500 carmine	17.50	26.00
a.	Booklet pane of 4		*90.00*	
R729	R25	$1000 carmine	16.00	21.00
a.	Booklet pane of 4		*80.00*	
b.	Vert. pair, imperf. horiz.			*1,750.*
R730	R25	$2500 carmine	175.00	175.00
a.	Booklet pane of 4		*800.00*	
R731	R25	$5000 carmine	275.00	175.00
a.	Booklet pane of 4		*1,200.*	
R732	R25	$10,000 carmine	275.00	140.00
a.	Booklet pane of 4		*1,200.*	

Internal Revenue Building,
Washington, DC — R26

Centenary of the Internal Revenue Service.

Giori Press Printing

1962, July 2		**Unwmk.**		*Perf. 11*
R733	R26	10c violet blue & bright		
		green	1.00	.40
		Never hinged	1.25	

1963
"Established 1862" Removed

R734	R26	10c violet blue & bright		
		green	3.00	.70
		Never hinged	5.00	

Documentary revenue stamps were no longer required after Dec. 31, 1967.

PROPRIETARY STAMPS

Stamps for use on proprietary articles were included in the first general issue of 1862-71. They are Nos. R3, R13-R14, R18, R22, R29, R31, R38.

Washington — RB1

RB1a

Various Frame Designs

1871-74		**Engr.**		*Perf. 12*
RB1	RB1	1c grn & blk		
a.	Violet paper ('71)		8.00	
b.	Green paper ('74)		14.00	
c.	As "a," Imperf.		80.00	
d.	As "a," Inverted center		*5,250.*	
RB2	RB1	2c grn & blk		
a.	Violet paper ('71)		8.75	
b.	Green paper ('74)		30.00	
c.	As "a," Invtd. center		45,000.	
d.	As "b," Invtd. center		8,000.	
e.	As "b," vert. half used as			
	1c on document		—	

Only two examples recorded of the inverted center on violet paper, No. RB2c. Value is for example with very good to fine centering and very small faults.

RB2d is valued with fine centering and small faults.

RB3	RB1a	3c grn & blk		
a.	Violet paper ('71)		32.50	
b.	Green paper ('74)		67.50	
c.	As "a," sewing machine			
	perf.		650.00	
d.	As "a," inverted center		14,000.	

No. RB3d is valued with small faults as 7 of the 8 recorded examples have faults.

RB4	RB1a	4c grn & blk		
a.	Violet paper ('71)		16.00	
b.	Green paper ('74)		25.00	
c.	As "a." inverted center		15,000.	
d.	As "b," vert. half used as			
	2c on document		—	

No. RB4c is valued with small faults as 6 of the 7 recorded examples have faults.

RB5	RB1a	5c grn & blk		
a.	Violet paper ('71)		175.00	
b.	Green paper ('74)		250.00	
c.	As "a," inverted center		130,000.	

No. RB5c is unique. Value represents price realized in 2000 auction sale.

RB6	RB1a	6c grn & blk		
a.	Violet paper ('71)		57.50	
b.	Green paper ('74)		140.00	
RB7	RB1a	10c grn & blk		
		('73)		
a.	Violet paper ('71)		300.00	
b.	Green paper ('74)		65.00	

RB1b

RB8	RB1b	50c grn & blk ('73)		
a.	Violet paper ('71)		1,000.	
b.	Green paper ('74)		850.00	
RB9	RB1a	$1 grn & blk ('73)		
a.	Violet paper ('71)		3,500.	
b.	Green paper ('74)		12,500.	

RB1c

RB10	RB1c	$5 grn & blk ('73)		
a.	Violet paper ('71)		11,000.	
b.	Green paper ('74)		85,000.	

No. RB10b is valued with small faults.

Washington — RB2

RB2a

Various Frame Designs
Green Paper

1875-81				*Perf.*
Unmwkd. (Silk Paper), Wmk. 191R				
RB11	RB2	1c green		
a.	Silk paper		2.25	
b.	Wmk 191R		.50	
c.	Rouletted 6		160.00	
d.	As No. RB11b, vert. pair, im-			
	perf. btwn.		300.00	
RB12	RB2	2c brown		
a.	Silk paper		3.25	
b.	Wmk 191R		2.00	
c.	Rouletted 6		175.00	
RB13	RB2a	3c orange		
a.	Silk paper		14.00	
b.	Wmk 191R		4.00	
c.	Rouletted 6		140.00	
d.	As No. RB13c, horiz. pair,			
	imperf. between		—	
e.	As No. RB13c, vert. pair, im-			
	perf. between		1,900.	
RB14	RB2a	4c red brown		
a.	Silk paper		10.00	
b.	Wmk 191R		9.00	
c.	Rouletted 6		22,000.	
RB15	RB2a	4c red		
b.	Wmk 191R		6.00	
c.	Rouletted 6		400.00	
RB16	RB2a	5c black		
a.	Silk paper		200.00	
b.	Wmk 191R		125.00	
c.	Rouletted 6		1,850.	
RB17	RB2a	6c violet blue		
a.	Silk paper		35.00	
b.	Wmk 191R		25.00	
c.	Rouletted 6		900.00	
RB18	RB2a	6c violet		
b.	Wmk 191R		35.00	
c.	Rouletted 6		2,000.	
RB19	RB2a	10c blue ('81)		
b.	Wmk 191R		400.00	

Many fraudulent roulettes exist.

Battleship — RB3

Inscribed "Series of 1898." and "Proprietary."
See note on rouletting preceding No. R161.

Rouletted 5½

1898		**Wmk. 191R**		**Engr.**
RB20	RB3	⅛c yel grn	.25	.25
a.	Vert. pair, imperf. horiz.			
b.	Vert. pair, imperf. btwn.	800.00	
RB21	RB3	¼c brown	.25	.25
a.	¼c red brown	.25	.25
b.	¼c yellow brown	.25	.25
c.	¼c orange brown	.25	.25
d.	¼c bister	.25	.25
f.	Vert. pair, imperf. horiz.		—	
g.	Printed on both sides		—	
RB22	RB3	⅜c dp org	.30	.30
a.	Horiz. pair, imperf. vert.	12.50	
b.	Vert. pair, imperf. horiz.	—	
RB23	RB3	⅝c deep ultra	.25	.25
a.	Vert. pair, imperf. horiz.	85.00	
b.	Horiz. pair, imperf. btwn.	350.00	200.00
RB24	RB3	1c dark green	2.25	.50
a.	Vert. pair, imperf. horiz.	325.00	
RB25	RB3	1 ¼c violet	.35	.25
a.	1 ¼c brown violet	.25	.25
b.	Vert. pair, imperf. btwn.	—	
RB26	RB3	1 ⅞c dull blue	15.00	2.00
RB27	RB3	2c violet		
		brown	1.40	.35
a.	Horiz. pair, imperf. vert.	60.00	
RB28	RB3	2 ½c lake	5.00	.35
a.	Vert. pair, imperf. horiz.	225.00	
RB29	RB3	3 ¾c olive gray	42.50	15.00
RB30	RB3	4c purple	16.00	1.50
RB31	RB3	5c brn org	15.00	1.50
a.	Vert. pair, imperf. horiz.	—	400.00
b.	Horiz. pair, imperf. vert.	—	425.00
Nos. RB20-RB31 (12)			98.55	22.50

Hyphen Hole Perf. 7

RB20p		⅛c	.30	.25
RB21p		¼c	.25	.25
b.	¼c yellow brown	.25	.25
c.	¼c orange brown	.25	.25
d.	¼c bister	.25	.25
RB22p		⅜c	.50	.35
RB23p		⅝c	.30	.25
RB24p		1c	30.00	15.00
RB25p		1 ¼c	.30	.30
a.	1 ¼c brown violet	.25	.25
RB26p		1 ⅞c	35.00	9.00
RB27p		2c	7.25	1.00
RB28p		2 ½c	6.00	.40
RB29p		3 ¾c	90.00	27.50
RB30p		4c	62.50	22.50
RB31p		5c	75.00	25.00

See note before No. R161.

RB4

Inscribed "Series of 1914"

Offset Printing
1914   Wmk. 190   Perf. 10

RB32	RB4	⅛c black	.25	.35
RB33	RB4	¼c black	4.00	1.50
RB34	RB4	⅜c black	.35	.35
RB35	RB4	⅝c black	7.75	3.00
RB36	RB4	1¼c black	5.00	1.75
RB37	RB4	1⅞c black	67.50	22.50
RB38	RB4	2½c black	16.00	3.50
RB39	RB4	3⅛c black	200.00	67.50
RB40	RB4	3¾c black	65.00	27.50
RB41	RB4	4c black	90.00	45.00
RB42	RB4	4⅜c black	3,000.	—
RB43	RB4	5c black	175.00	110.00
Nos. RB32-RB41,RB43 (11)			630.85	282.95

Wmk. 191R

RB44	RB4	⅛c black	.35	.30
RB45	RB4	¼c black	.25	.25
RB46	RB4	⅜c black	.75	.45
RB47	RB4	½c black	4.25	3.75
RB48	RB4	⅝c black	.30	.25
RB49	RB4	1c black	5.50	5.50
RB50	RB4	1¼c black	.65	.40
RB51	RB4	1½c black	4.25	3.00
RB52	RB4	1⅞c black	1.35	.90
RB53	RB4	2c black	7.50	6.00
RB54	RB4	2½c black	2.00	1.40
RB55	RB4	3c black	6.00	4.00
RB56	RB4	3⅛c black	8.00	5.00
RB57	RB4	3¾c black	17.50	11.00
RB58	RB4	4c black	.50	.30
RB59	RB4	4⅜c black	20.00	11.00
RB60	RB4	5c black	4.50	3.75
RB61	RB4	6c black	80.00	52.50
RB62	RB4	8c black	25.00	16.00
RB63	RB4	10c black	18.00	11.00
RB64	RB4	20c black	35.00	24.00
Nos. RB44-RB64 (21)			241.65	160.75

RB5

1919   Offset Printing   Perf. 11

RB65	RB5	1c dark blue	.25	.25
RB66	RB5	2c dark blue	.35	.25
RB67	RB5	3c dark blue	1.50	.75
RB68	RB5	4c dark blue	2.25	.75
RB69	RB5	5c dark blue	3.00	1.25
RB70	RB5	8c dark blue	22.50	16.00
RB71	RB5	10c dark blue	11.00	4.25
RB72	RB5	20c dark blue	17.50	6.00
RB73	RB5	40c dark blue	65.00	20.00
Nos. RB65-RB73 (9)			123.35	49.50

FUTURE DELIVERY STAMPS

Issued to facilitate the collection of a tax upon each sale, agreement of sale or agreement to sell any products or merchandise at any exchange or board of trade, or other similar place for future delivery.

Documentary Stamps of 1917 Overprinted in Black or Red

Documentary Stamps Nos. R228-R250 Overprinted in Black or Red

Offset Printing
1918-34   Wmk. 191R   Perf. 11
Overprint Horizontal (Lines 8mm apart)
Left Value — Unused
Right Value — Used

RC1	R22	2c carmine rose	8.75	.25
RC2	R22	3c carmine rose ('34)	47.50	37.50
a.		Cut cancel		20.00
RC3	R22	4c carmine rose	15.00	.25
b.		Double impression of stamp		10.00
RC3A	R22	5c carmine rose ('33)	90.00	7.50
RC4	R22	10c carmine rose	24.00	.35
a.		Double overprint		5.25
b.		"FUTURE" omitted	—	325.00
c.		"DELIVERY FUTURE"		37.50
RC5	R22	20c carmine rose	35.00	.35
a.		Double overprint		21.00
RC6	R22	25c carmine rose	75.00	.60
		Cut cancel		.30

RC7	R22	40c carmine rose	85.00	1.25
		Cut cancel		.35
RC8	R22	50c carmine rose	22.50	.35
a.		"DELIVERY" omitted	—	110.00
RC9	R22	80c carmine rose	175.00	15.00
		Cut cancel		4.00
a.		Double overprint		37.50

Engr.
Overprint Vertical, Reading Up (Lines 2mm apart)

RC10	R21	$1 green (R)	65.00	.35
		Cut cancel		.25
a.		Overprint reading down		300.00
b.		Black overprint		—
		Cut cancel		125.00
RC11	R21	$2 rose	75.00	.45
		Cut cancel		.25
RC12	R21	$3 violet (R)	225.00	3.50
		Cut cancel		.30
a.		Overprint reading down	—	52.50
RC13	R21	$5 dark blue (R)	125.00	.60
		Cut cancel		.25
RC14	R21	$10 orange	150.00	1.35
		Cut cancel		.30
a.		"DELIVERY FUTURE"		110.00
RC15	R21	$20 olive bister	400.00	9.00
		Cut cancel		.80

Overprint Horizontal (Lines 11⅝mm apart)
Perf. 12
Without Gum

RC16	R17	$30 vermilion, green numerals	125.00	5.50
		Cut cancel		1.75
a.		Numerals in blue	110.00	4.75
		Cut cancel		2.00
b.		Imperf., blue numerals	110.00	
RC17	R19	$50 olive green (Cleveland)	100.00	3.00
		Cut cancel		.90
a.		$50 olive bister	100.00	2.75
		Cut cancel		.25
RC18	R19	$60 brown	140.00	9.00
		Cut cancel		1.20
a.		Vert. pair, imperf. horiz.		550.00
RC19	R17	$100 yellow green ('34)	225.00	37.50
		Cut cancel		9.00
RC20	R18	$500 blue, red numerals (R)	275.00	25.00
		Cut cancel		9.00
a.		Numerals in orange	—	60.00
		Cut cancel		12.50
RC21	R19	$1000 orange	200.00	7.50
		Cut cancel		2.00
a.		Vert. pair, imperf. horiz.		1,350.

See note after No. R227.

1923-24   Offset Printing   Perf. 11
Overprint Horizontal (Lines 2mm apart)

RC22	R22	1c carmine rose	1.25	.25
RC23	R22	80c carmine rose	175.00	3.50
		Cut cancel		.70

Documentary Stamps of 1917 Overprinted in Black or Red

1925-34   Engr.

RC25	R21	$1 green (R)	85.00	2.00
		Cut cancel		.45
RC26	R21	$10 orange (Bk) ('34)	225.00	29.00
		Cut cancel		18.00

Overprint Type I
1928-29   Offset Printing   Perf. 10

RC27	R22	10c carmine rose	5,000.	
RC28	R22	20c carmine rose	5,000.	

Some specialists have questioned the status of No. RC28, believing known examples to be either fraudulently reperforated examples of No. RC5, or examples of No. R256 with fake overprints applied. The editors would like to see authenticated evidence of the existence of No. RC28.

STOCK TRANSFER STAMPS

Issued to facilitate the collection of a tax on all sales or agreements to sell, or memoranda of sales or delivery of, or transfers of legal title to shares or certificates of stock.

Documentary Stamps Nos. R228-R259 Overprinted in Black or Red

Offset Printing
1918-22   Wmk. 191R   Perf. 11
Overprint Horizontal (Lines 8mm apart)

RD1	R22	1c carmine rose	1.00	.25
a.		Double overprint	—	
RD2	R22	2c carmine rose	.25	.25
a.		Double overprint	—	15.00
		Double overprint, cut cancel		7.50
RD3	R22	4c carmine rose	.25	.25
a.		Double overprint		4.25
		Double overprint, cut cancel		2.10
b.		"STOCK" omitted	—	10.50
d.		Ovpt. lines 10mm apart	—	
RD4	R22	5c carmine rose	.30	.25
RD5	R22	10c carmine rose	.30	.25
a.		Double overprint	—	5.25
		Double overprint, cut cancel		2.75
b.		"STOCK" omitted	—	
RD6	R22	20c carmine rose	.55	.25
a.		Double overprint	—	6.25
b.		"STOCK" double	—	
RD7	R22	25c carmine rose	2.25	.30
		Cut cancel		.25
RD8	R22	40c carmine rose ('22)	2.25	.25
RD9	R22	50c carmine rose	.80	.25
a.		Double overprint	—	
RD10	R22	80c carmine rose	9.00	.45
		Cut cancel		.25

Engr.
Overprint Vertical, Reading Up (Lines 2mm apart)

RD11	R21	$1 green (R)	190.00	35.00
		Cut cancel		9.50
a.		Overprint reading down	225.00	35.00
		Overprint reading down, cut cancel		10.00
RD12	R21	$1 green (Bk)	3.00	.30
a.		Pair, one without overprint	—	160.00
b.		Overprinted on back instead of face, inverted	—	110.00
c.		Overprint reading down	—	7.50
d.		$1 yellow green	3.00	
RD13	R21	$2 rose	3.00	.25
a.		Overprint reading down	—	11.50
		Overprint reading down, cut cancel		1.50
b.		Vert. pair, imperf. horiz.	500.00	
RD14	R21	$3 violet (R)	27.50	6.00
		Cut cancel		.30
RD15	R21	$4 yellow brown	12.00	.30
		Cut cancel		.25
RD16	R21	$5 dark blue (R)	8.00	.30
		Cut cancel		.25
a.		Overprint reading down	42.50	1.35
		Overprint reading down, cut cancel		.25
RD17	R21	$10 orange	30.00	.45
		Cut cancel		.25
RD18	R21	$20 olive bister ('21)	130.00	18.00
		Cut cancel		4.50
a.		Overprint reading down	—	

Overprint Horizontal (Lines 11½mm apart)
1918   Without Gum   Perf. 12

RD19	R17	$30 ver, grn numerals	42.50	6.50
		Cut cancel		2.25
a.		Numerals in blue	175.00	75.00
RD20	R19	$50 ol grn, Cleveland	140.00	62.50
		Cut cancel		26.00
RD21	R19	$60 brown	300.00	25.00
		Cut cancel		10.50
RD22	R17	$100 green	45.00	7.50
		Cut cancel		3.00
RD23	R18	$500 blue (R)	425.00	150.00
		Cut cancel		75.00
a.		Numerals in orange		150.00
RD24	R19	$1,000 orange	375.00	95.00
		Cut cancel		32.50

See note after No. R227.

1928   Offset Printing   Perf. 10
Overprint Horizontal (Lines 8mm apart)

RD25	R22	2c carmine rose	5.50	.30
RD26	R22	4c carmine rose	5.50	.30
RD27	R22	10c carmine rose	5.50	.30
a.		Inverted overprint		1,400.
b.		Ovpt. lines 9½mm apart		
RD28	R22	20c carmine rose	6.50	.35

RD29	R22	50c carmine rose	10.00	.50

Engr.
Overprint Vertical, Reading Up (Lines 2mm apart)

RD30	R21	$1 green	50.00	.35
a.		$1 yellow green	50.00	.50
RD31	R21	$2 carmine rose	45.00	.35
a.		Pair, one without overprint	225.00	190.00
RD32	R21	$10 orange	45.00	.50

Overprinted Horiz. in Black

1920   Offset Printing   Perf. 11

RD33	R22	2c carmine rose	12.50	1.00
RD34	R22	10c carmine rose	3.00	.35
b.		Inverted overprint	1,500.	1,250.
RD35	R22	20c carmine rose	5.75	.25
a.		Horiz. pair, one without overprint	175.00	
d.		Inverted overprint (perf. initials)	—	
RD36	R22	50c carmine rose	5.00	.30

Engr.

RD37	R21	$1 green	70.00	13.50
RD38	R21	$2 rose	80.00	13.50

Offset Printing
Perf. 10

RD39	R22	2c carmine rose	13.00	1.10
RD40	R22	10c carmine rose	5.25	.55
RD41	R22	20c carmine rose	6.00	.25

Used values for Nos. RD42-RD372 are for stamps which are neither cut nor perforated with initials. Stamps with cut cancellations or perforated initials are valued in the Scott U.S. Specialized Catalogue.

Documentary Stamps of 1917-33 Overprinted in Black

1940   Perf. 11

RD42	R22	1c rose pink	4.50	.65
a.		"Series 1940" inverted (pos. 31LR)	600.00	450.00

No. RD42a always comes with a natural straight edge at left.

RD43	R22	2c rose pink	4.75	.65
RD45	R22	4c rose pink	5.50	.35
RD46	R22	5c rose pink	6.00	.25
RD48	R22	10c rose pink	11.00	.35
RD49	R22	20c rose pink	12.50	.35
RD50	R22	25c rose pink	12.50	1.10
RD51	R22	40c rose pink	9.25	1.00
RD52	R22	50c rose pink	10.50	.35
RD53	R22	80c rose pink	250.00	100.00

Engr.

RD54	R21	$1 green	42.50	.60
RD55	R21	$2 rose	47.50	1.00
RD56	R21	$3 violet	300.00	18.00
RD57	R21	$4 yellow brown	110.00	1.60
RD58	R21	$5 dark blue	85.00	2.00
RD59	R21	$10 orange	250.00	10.00
RD60	R21	$20 olive bister	500.00	150.00

Nos. RD19-RD24 Handstamped in Blue "Series 1940"

1940   Perf. 12
Without Gum

RD61	R17	$30 ver	1,500.	1,500.
RD62	R19	$50 ol grn	2,500.	2,500.
a.		Double ovpt., perf. initial		1,100.
RD63	R19	$60 brown	3,000.	3,000.
RD64	R17	$100 green	3,000.	850.00
RD65	R18	$500 blue		3,250.
RD66	R19	$1,000 orange		
		Cut cancel		5,000.

Alexander Hamilton ST1   Levi Woodbury ST2

Overprinted in Black   SERIES 1940

Same Portraits as Nos. R288-R310.

1940   Engr.   Perf. 11

No.	Type	Denom.	Unused	Used
RD67	ST1	1c brt grn	14.00	3.25
a.		Imperf., pair, without gum	250.00	
RD68	ST1	2c brt grn	9.00	1.75
a.		Imperf., pair, without gum	250.00	
RD70	ST1	4c brt grn	16.00	4.50
a.		Imperf., pair, without gum	250.00	
RD71	ST1	5c brt grn	10.00	1.75
a.		Imperf., pair, without gum	250.00	
b.		Without overprint, cut cancel		400.00
RD73	ST1	10c brt grn	14.00	2.10
a.		Imperf., pair, without gum	250.00	
RD74	ST1	20c brt grn	16.00	2.40
a.		Imperf., pair, without gum	250.00	
RD75	ST1	25c brt grn	55.00	10.50
a.		Imperf., pair, without gum	250.00	
RD76	ST1	40c brt grn	110.00	45.00
a.		Imperf., pair, without gum	250.00	
RD77	ST1	50c brt grn	14.00	2.10
a.		Imperf., pair, without gum	250.00	
RD78	ST1	80c brt grn	160.00	65.00
a.		Imperf., pair, without gum	250.00	
RD79	ST2	$1 brt grn	60.00	4.25
a.		Without overprint, perf. initial		400.00
RD80	ST2	$2 brt grn	65.00	12.00
a.		Imperf., pair, without gum	250.00	
RD81	ST2	$3 brt grn	90.00	15.00
a.		Imperf., pair, without gum	250.00	
RD82	ST2	$4 brt grn	500.00	275.00
a.		Imperf., pair, without gum	250.00	
RD83	ST2	$5 brt grn	90.00	16.00
a.		Imperf., pair, without gum	250.00	
RD84	ST2	$10 brt grn	225.00	60.00
a.		Imperf., pair, without gum	250.00	
RD85	ST2	$20 brt grn	1,250.	125.00
a.		Imperf., pair, without gum	250.00	

Nos. RD67-RD85 exist imperforate, without overprint. Value, set of pairs, $750.

Thomas Corwin — ST3

Overprinted "SERIES 1940"

Various frames and portraits as Nos. R306-R310.

Perf. 12
Without Gum

No.	Type	Denom.	Unused	Used
RD86	ST3	$30 brt grn	1,750.	175.00
RD87	ST3	$50 brt grn	800.00	500.00
RD88	ST3	$60 brt grn	5,000.	1,900.
RD89	ST3	$100 brt grn	600.00	375.00
RD90	ST3	$500 brt grn	—	3,750.
RD91	ST3	$1,000 brt grn	—	4,000.

Nos. RD86-RD91 exist as unfinished imperforates with complete receipt tabs, without overprints or serial numbers. Known in singles, pairs (Nos. RD86-RD88 and Nos. RD90-RD91, value $300 per pair; No. RD89, value $150 per pair), panes of four with plate number, uncut sheets of four panes (with two plate numbers), cross gutter blocks of eight, and blocks of four with vertical gutter between and plate number.

Stock Transfer Stamps and Type of 1940 Overprinted in Black
Nos. RD67-RD91   Overprinted Instead: SERIES 1941

1941   Perf. 11

No.	Type	Denom.	Unused	Used
RD92	ST1	1c brt grn	.80	.55
RD93	ST1	2c brt grn	.60	.30
RD95	ST1	4c brt grn	.65	.25
RD96	ST1	5c brt grn	.60	.25
RD98	ST1	10c brt grn	1.10	.25
RD99	ST1	20c brt grn	2.40	.30
RD100	ST1	25c brt grn	2.40	.45
RD101	ST1	40c brt grn	3.75	.75
RD102	ST1	50c brt grn	5.00	.35
RD103	ST1	80c brt grn	30.00	10.00
RD104	ST2	$1 brt grn	21.00	.25
RD105	ST2	$2 brt grn	22.50	.30
RD106	ST2	$3 brt grn	32.50	1.50
RD107	ST2	$4 brt grn	57.50	8.50
RD108	ST2	$5 brt grn	57.50	.65
RD109	ST2	$10 brt grn	125.00	5.50
RD110	ST2	$20 brt grn	350.00	90.00

Perf. 12
Without Gum

No.	Type	Denom.	Unused	Used
RD111	ST3	$30 brt grn	1,400.	325.00
RD112	ST3	$50 brt grn	1,000.	650.00
RD113	ST3	$60 brt grn	1,750.	350.00
RD114	ST3	$100 brt grn	400.00	190.00
RD115	ST3	$500 brt grn	2,750.	2,750.
RD116	ST3	$1,000 brt grn	—	2,750.

Stock Transfer Stamps and Type of 1940 Overprinted in Black
Nos. RD67-RD91   overprinted instead: SERIES 1942

1942   Perf. 11

No.	Type	Denom.	Unused	Used
RD117	ST1	1c brt grn	.75	.30
RD118	ST1	2c brt grn	.65	.35
RD119	ST1	4c brt grn	3.50	1.10
RD120	ST1	5c brt grn	.70	.25
a.		Overprint inverted		750.00
RD121	ST1	10c brt grn	2.25	.25
RD122	ST1	20c brt grn	2.75	.25
RD123	ST1	25c brt grn	2.50	.25
RD124	ST1	40c brt grn	5.75	.40
RD125	ST1	50c brt grn	6.50	.25
RD126	ST1	80c brt grn	27.50	6.00
RD127	ST2	$1 brt grn	24.00	.40
RD128	ST2	$2 brt grn	37.50	.40
RD129	ST2	$3 brt grn	42.50	1.10
RD130	ST2	$4 brt grn	57.50	24.00
RD131	ST2	$5 brt grn	50.00	.40
a.		Double overprint, perf. initial		1,250.
RD132	ST2	$10 brt grn	110.00	9.50
RD133	ST2	$20 brt grn	300.00	55.00

Perf. 12
Without Gum

No.	Type	Denom.	Unused	Used
RD134	ST3	$30 brt grn	425.00	100.00
RD135	ST3	$50 brt grn	750.00	175.00
RD136	ST3	$60 brt grn	500.00	240.00
RD137	ST3	$100 brt grn	625.00	100.00
RD138	ST3	$500 brt grn	—	15,000.
RD139	ST3	$1,000 brt grn	—	700.00

Stock Transfer Stamps and Type of 1940 Overprinted in Black
Nos. RD67-RD91   overprinted instead   SERIES 1943

1943   Perf. 11

No.	Type	Denom.	Unused	Used
RD140	ST1	1c brt grn	.55	.30
RD141	ST1	2c brt grn	.60	.40
RD142	ST1	4c brt grn	2.10	.25
RD143	ST1	5c brt grn	.60	.25
RD144	ST1	10c brt grn	1.50	.25
RD145	ST1	20c brt grn	2.25	.25
RD146	ST1	25c brt grn	6.75	.35
RD147	ST1	40c brt grn	6.25	.30
RD148	ST1	50c brt grn	5.75	.30
RD149	ST1	80c brt grn	30.00	7.50
RD150	ST2	$1 brt grn	22.50	.25
RD151	ST2	$2 brt grn	25.00	.50
RD152	ST2	$3 brt grn	30.00	2.50
RD153	ST2	$4 brt grn	75.00	27.50
RD154	ST2	$5 brt grn	80.00	.60
RD155	ST2	$10 brt grn	125.00	7.50
RD156	ST2	$20 brt grn	375.00	75.00

Perf. 12
Without Gum

No.	Type	Denom.	Unused	Used
RD157	ST3	$30 brt grn	750.00	300.00
RD158	ST3	$50 brt grn	2,500.	210.00
RD159	ST3	$60 brt grn	4,000.	1,900.
RD160	ST3	$100 brt grn	225.00	80.00
RD161	ST3	$500 brt grn	—	2,250.
RD162	ST3	$1,000 brt grn	1,000.	650.00

Stock Transfer Stamps and Type of 1940 Overprinted in Black
Series 1944

1944   Perf. 11

No.	Type	Denom.	Unused	Used
RD163	ST1	1c brt grn	.90	.75
RD164	ST1	2c brt grn	.70	.25
RD165	ST1	4c brt grn	.70	.35
RD166	ST1	5c brt grn	.65	.25
RD167	ST1	10c brt grn	1.00	.30
RD168	ST1	20c brt grn	2.25	.25
RD169	ST1	25c brt grn	3.25	.90
RD170	ST1	40c brt grn	15.00	8.00
RD171	ST1	50c brt grn	5.50	.30
RD172	ST1	80c brt grn	14.50	6.25
RD173	ST2	$1 brt grn	14.50	.50
RD174	ST2	$2 brt grn	50.00	.75
RD175	ST2	$3 brt grn	47.50	2.00
RD176	ST2	$4 brt grn	80.00	15.00
RD177	ST2	$5 brt grn	55.00	3.50
RD178	ST2	$10 brt grn	125.00	7.25
RD179	ST2	$20 brt grn	275.00	20.00

Perf. 12
Without Gum

Designs: $2,500, William Windom. $5,000, C. J. Folger. $10,000, W. Q. Gresham.

No.	Type	Denom.	Unused	Used
RD180	ST3	$30 brt grn	350.00	110.00
RD181	ST3	$50 brt grn	350.00	125.00
RD182	ST3	$60 brt grn	1,500.	325.00
RD183	ST3	$100 brt grn	1,000.	100.00
RD184	ST3	$500 brt grn	2,250.	1,750.
RD185	ST3	$1,000 brt grn	2,750.	1,900.
RD185A	ST3	$2,500 brt grn	—	
RD185B	ST3	$5,000 brt grn		75,000.
RD185C	ST3	$10,000 brt grn, cut cancel		45,000.

Stock Transfer Stamps and Type of 1940 Overprinted in Black
Series 1945

1945   Perf. 11

No.	Type	Denom.	Unused	Used
RD186	ST1	1c brt grn	.45	.25
RD187	ST1	2c brt grn	.45	.35
RD188	ST1	4c brt grn	.50	.35
RD189	ST1	5c brt grn	.45	.25
RD190	ST1	10c brt grn	1.25	.35
RD191	ST1	20c brt grn	2.25	.45
RD192	ST1	25c brt grn	3.50	.40
RD193	ST1	40c brt grn	5.00	.25
RD194	ST1	50c brt grn	10.00	.45
RD195	ST1	80c brt grn	15.00	4.75
RD196	ST2	$1 brt grn	17.50	.30
RD197	ST2	$2 brt grn	32.50	.90
RD198	ST2	$3 brt grn	55.00	1.75
RD199	ST2	$4 brt grn	55.00	4.25
RD200	ST2	$5 brt grn	35.00	1.00
RD201	ST2	$10 brt grn	85.00	12.00
RD202	ST2	$20 brt grn	300.00	20.00

Perf. 12
Without Gum

No.	Type	Denom.	Unused	Used
RD203	ST3	$30 brt grn	225.00	90.00
RD204	ST3	$50 brt grn	150.00	60.00
RD205	ST3	$60 brt grn	1,400.	350.00
RD206	ST3	$100 brt grn	250.00	65.00
RD207	ST3	$500 brt grn	—	1,400.
RD208	ST3	$1,000 brt grn	3,250.	1,400.
RD208A	ST3	$2,500 brt grn, perf. initial		20,000.
RD208B	ST3	$5,000 brt grn, cut cancel		45,000.
RD208C	ST3	$10,000 brt grn, cut cancel		45,000.

Stock Transfer Stamps and Type of 1940 Overprinted in Black
Series 1946

1946   Perf. 11

No.	Type	Denom.	Unused	Used
RD209	ST1	1c brt grn	.50	.35
a.		Pair, one dated "1945"	550.00	
RD210	ST1	2c brt grn	.50	.25
RD211	ST1	4c brt grn	.55	.25
RD212	ST1	5c brt grn	.55	.25
RD213	ST1	10c brt grn	1.25	.25
RD214	ST1	20c brt grn	2.50	.30
RD215	ST1	25c brt grn	3.00	.40
RD216	ST1	40c brt grn	6.50	1.25
RD217	ST1	50c brt grn	6.75	.25
RD218	ST1	80c brt grn	20.00	9.50
RD219	ST2	$1 brt grn	14.50	.90
RD220	ST2	$2 brt grn	16.00	1.00
RD221	ST2	$3 brt grn	30.00	2.25
RD222	ST2	$4 brt grn	30.00	9.00
RD223	ST2	$5 brt grn	50.00	2.25
RD224	ST2	$10 brt grn	87.50	4.25
RD225	ST2	$20 brt grn	450.00	62.50

Perf. 12
Without Gum

No.	Type	Denom.	Unused	Used
RD226	ST3	$30 brt grn	250.00	62.50
RD227	ST3	$50 brt grn	300.00	75.00
RD228	ST3	$60 brt grn	375.00	225.00
RD229	ST3	$100 brt grn	225.00	90.00
RD230	ST3	$500 brt grn	700.00	300.00
RD231	ST3	$1,000 brt grn	425.00	250.00
RD232	ST3	$2,500 brt grn		27,500.
RD233	ST3	$5,000 brt grn, cut cancel		17,500.
RD234	ST3	$10,000 brt grn, cut cancel		22,500.

Stock Transfer Stamps and Type of 1940 Overprinted in Black
Series 1947

1947   Perf. 11

No.	Type	Denom.	Unused	Used
RD235	ST1	1c bright green	2.75	.90
RD236	ST1	2c bright green	2.75	.90
RD237	ST1	4c bright green	2.00	.70
RD238	ST1	5c bright green	2.00	.60
RD239	ST1	10c bright green	2.00	.90
RD240	ST1	20c bright green	3.75	.90
RD241	ST1	25c bright green	5.00	.90
RD242	ST1	40c bright green	4.50	1.40
RD243	ST1	50c bright green	5.00	.35
RD244	ST1	80c bright green	27.50	14.00
RD245	ST2	$1 bright green	20.00	1.00
RD246	ST2	$2 bright green	32.50	1.25
RD247	ST2	$3 bright green	45.00	2.50
RD248	ST2	$4 bright green	62.50	9.50
RD249	ST2	$5 bright green	45.00	3.25
RD250	ST2	$10 bright green	200.00	11.00
RD251	ST2	$20 bright green	225.00	42.50

Perf. 12
Without Gum

No.	Type	Denom.	Unused	Used
RD252	ST3	$30 brt grn	600.00	75.00
RD253	ST3	$50 brt grn	700.00	250.00
RD254	ST3	$60 brt grn	1,150.	225.00
RD255	ST3	$100 brt grn	175.00	62.50
RD256	ST3	$500 brt grn	850.00	750.00
RD257	ST3	$1,000 brt grn	650.00	190.00
RD258	ST3	$2,500 brt grn, Cut cancel		350.00
RD259	ST3	$5,000 brt grn, Cut cancel	700.00	500.00
RD260	ST3	$10,000 brt grn, Cut cancel	—	75.00
a.		Vert. pair, imperf. horiz., cut cancel		

Stock Transfer Stamps and Type of 1940 Overprinted in Black
Series 1948

1948 — *Perf. 11*

RD261	ST1	1c bright green	.45	.35
RD262	ST1	2c bright green	.45	.35
RD263	ST1	4c bright green	.80	.45
RD264	ST1	5c bright green	.45	.25
RD265	ST1	10c bright green	.55	.35
RD266	ST1	20c bright green	1.60	.40
RD267	ST1	25c bright green	1.90	.55
RD268	ST1	40c bright green	3.50	1.00
RD269	ST1	50c bright green	5.75	.45
RD270	ST1	80c bright green	27.50	9.50
RD271	ST2	$1 bright green	14.00	.50
RD272	ST2	$2 bright green	27.50	1.00
RD273	ST2	$3 bright green	55.00	10.00
RD274	ST2	$4 bright green	60.00	20.00
RD275	ST2	$5 bright green	70.00	5.00
RD276	ST2	$10 bright green	80.00	7.25
RD277	ST2	$20 bright green	225.00	25.00

Perf. 12
Without Gum

RD278	ST3	$30 brt grn	275.00	90.00
RD279	ST3	$50 brt grn	175.00	85.00
RD280	ST3	$60 brt grn	350.00	225.00
RD281	ST3	$100 brt grn	140.00	30.00
RD282	ST3	$500 brt grn	600.00	325.00
RD283	ST3	$1,000 brt grn	425.00	200.00
RD284	ST3	$2,500 brt grn	850.00	500.00
RD285	ST3	$5,000 brt grn	650.00	425.00
RD286	ST3	$10,000 brt grn	—	

Stock Transfer Stamps and Type of 1940 Overprinted in Black
Series 1949

1949 — *Perf. 11*

RD287	ST1	1c bright green	2.25	.70
RD288	ST1	2c bright green	2.25	.75
RD289	ST1	4c bright green	2.50	.75
RD290	ST1	5c bright green	3.00	.75
RD291	ST1	10c bright green	6.00	1.00
RD292	ST1	20c bright green	10.00	1.00
RD293	ST1	25c bright green	11.00	1.25
RD294	ST1	40c bright green	25.00	3.25
RD295	ST1	50c bright green	30.00	.45
RD296	ST1	80c bright green	37.50	10.00
RD297	ST2	$1 bright green	27.50	1.00
RD298	ST2	$2 bright green	50.00	1.75
RD299	ST2	$3 bright green	85.00	10.00
RD300	ST2	$4 bright green	90.00	20.00
RD301	ST2	$5 bright green	72.50	3.00
RD302	ST2	$10 bright green	125.00	12.50
RD303	ST2	$20 bright green	250.00	22.50

Perf. 12
Without Gum

RD304	ST3	$30 brt grn	325.00	125.00
RD305	ST3	$50 brt grn	375.00	250.00
RD306	ST3	$60 brt grn	550.00	400.00
RD307	ST3	$100 brt grn	225.00	80.00
RD308	ST3	$500 brt grn	900.00	300.00
RD309	ST3	$1,000 brt grn	450.00	100.00
RD310	ST3	$2,500 brt grn	—	
RD311	ST3	$5,000 brt grn	—	
RD312	ST3	$10,000 brt grn	—	475.00
a.	Pair, one without ovpt., cut cancel			8,000.

No. RD312a is unique.

Stock Transfer Stamps and Type of 1940 Overprinted in Black
Series 1950

1950 — *Perf. 11*

RD313	ST1	1c bright green	.80	.40
RD314	ST1	2c bright green	.70	.35
RD315	ST1	4c bright green	.65	.40
RD316	ST1	5c bright green	.75	.25
RD317	ST1	10c bright green	3.25	.30
RD318	ST1	20c bright green	5.00	.80
RD319	ST1	25c bright green	8.00	1.00
RD320	ST1	40c bright green	12.00	1.50
RD321	ST1	50c bright green	15.00	.50
RD322	ST1	80c bright green	22.50	7.25
RD323	ST2	$1 bright green	22.50	.55
RD324	ST2	$2 bright green	35.00	1.25
RD325	ST2	$3 bright green	60.00	8.50
RD326	ST2	$4 bright green	75.00	20.00
RD327	ST2	$5 bright green	60.00	3.25
RD328	ST2	$10 bright green	190.00	12.50
RD329	ST2	$20 bright green	225.00	50.00

Perf. 12
Without Gum

RD330	ST3	$30 brt		
		grn	300.00	175.00
RD331	ST3	$50 brt		
		grn	350.00	200.00
a.	Booklet pane of 4	3,300.		
RD332	ST3	$60 brt		
		grn	325.00	225.00
a.	Booklet pane of 4	4,750.		
RD333	ST3	$100 brt		
		grn	125.00	55.00
a.	Vert. pair, imperf. btwn.	2,000.		1,750.
RD334	ST3	$500 brt		
		grn	650.00	300.00
RD335	ST3	$1,000 brt		
		grn	225.00	85.00
RD336	ST3	$2,500 brt		
		grn	—	2,000.
a.	Booklet pane of 4	10,000.		
RD337	ST3	$5,000 brt		
		grn	—	1,100.
a.	Booklet pane of 4	10,000.		
RD338	ST3	$10,000 brt		
		grn	—	1,500.
a.	Booklet pane of 4	10,000.		

Stock Transfer Stamps and Type of 1940 Overprinted in Black
Series 1951

1951 — *Perf. 11*

RD339	ST1	1c bright green	3.00	.75
RD340	ST1	2c bright green	2.50	.50
RD341	ST1	4c bright green	3.00	.75
RD342	ST1	5c bright green	2.25	.55
RD343	ST1	10c bright green	3.00	.35
RD344	ST1	20c bright green	7.50	1.25
RD345	ST1	25c bright green	10.00	1.50
RD346	ST1	40c bright green	45.00	12.50
RD347	ST1	50c bright green	17.00	1.50
RD348	ST1	80c bright green	35.00	14.00
RD349	ST2	$1 bright green	32.50	1.25
RD350	ST2	$2 bright green	45.00	1.75
RD351	ST2	$3 bright green	60.00	14.00
RD352	ST2	$4 bright green	300.00	25.00
RD353	ST2	$5 bright green	75.00	4.00
RD354	ST2	$10 bright green	150.00	11.00
RD355	ST2	$20 bright green	250.00	30.00

Perf. 12
Without Gum

RD356	ST3	$30 brt		
		grn	325.00	200.00
RD357	ST3	$50 brt		
		grn	325.00	125.00
RD358	ST3	$60 brt		
		grn	—	1,600.
RD359	ST3	$100 brt		
		grn	210.00	100.00
RD360	ST3	$500 brt		
		grn	750.00	450.00
RD361	ST3	$1,000 brt		
		grn	225.00	140.00
RD362	ST3	$2,500 brt		
		grn	—	4,750.
RD363	ST3	$5,000 brt		
		grn	—	2,000.
RD364	ST3	$10,000 brt		
		grn	2,000.	250.00

Stock Transfer Stamps and Type of 1940 Overprinted in Black
Series 1952

1952 — *Perf. 11*

RD365	ST1	1c brt grn	42.50	27.50
RD366	ST1	10c brt grn	45.00	27.50
RD367	ST1	20c brt grn	400.00	
RD368	ST1	25c brt grn	550.00	
RD369	ST1	40c brt grn	140.00	55.00
RD370	ST2	$4 brt grn	1,750.	800.00
RD371	ST2	$10 brt grn	4,500.	—
RD372	ST2	$20 brt grn	7,000.	

Stock Transfer Stamps were discontinued in 1952.

HUNTING PERMIT STAMPS

Catalogue values for all unused stamps in this section are for stamps with never-hinged original gum. Minor natural gum skips and bends are normal on Nos. RW1-RW20. No-gum stamps are without signature or other cancel.

Nos. RW1-RW12 were issued in panes of 28, of which 10 stamps have a straight edge on one or two sides. Such examples sell for 20%-30% less than the values shown.

Department of Agriculture
Various Designs Inscribed "U. S. Department of Agriculture"

Mallards Alighting — HP1

Engraved: Flat Plate Printing

1934 — **Unwmk.** — *Perf. 11*
Inscribed "Void after June 30, 1935"

RW1	HP1	$1 blue	725.	325.
		Hinged	350.	
		No gum	175.	
a.	Imperf., vertical pair	—		
b.	Vert. pair, imperf. horiz.	—		

Used value is for stamp with handstamp or manuscript cancel.

It is almost certain that No. RW1a is No. RW1b with vertical perfs trimmed off. No horizontal pairs of No. RW1a are known. All recorded pairs are vertical, with narrow side margins. Both varieties probably are printer's waste since examples exist with gum on front or without gum.

1935
Inscribed "Void after June 30, 1936"

RW2	HP2	$1 rose lake	700.00	160.00
		deep rose lake		
		Hinged	350.	
		No gum	165.	

1936
Inscribed "Void after June 30, 1937"

RW3	HP3	$1 brown black	325.	90.00
		Hinged	150.	
		No gum	90.	

1937
Inscribed "Void after June 30, 1938"

RW4	HP4	$1 light green	275.	65.00
		Hinged	125.	
		No gum	75.	

1938
Inscribed "Void after June 30, 1939"

RW5	HP5	$1 light violet	375.	75.00
		Hinged	175.	
		No gum	75.	

Department of the Interior
Various Designs Inscribed "U. S. Department of the Interior"

Green-Winged Teal — HP6

1939
Inscribed "Void after June 30, 1940"

RW6	HP6	$1 chocolate	225.	45.00
		Hinged	100.	
		No gum	55.	

1940
Inscribed "Void after June 30, 1941"

RW7	HP7	$1 sepia	225.	35.00
		Hinged	95.	
		No gum	45.	

1941
Inscribed "Void after June 30, 1942"

RW8	HP8	$1 brown carmine	225.	45.00
		Hinged	95.	
		No gum	45.	

1942
Inscribed "Void after June 30, 1943"

RW9	HP9	$1 violet brown	225.	45.00
		Hinged	95.	
		No gum	45.	

1943
Inscribed "Void After June 30, 1944"

RW10	HP10	$1 deep rose	120.00	35.00
		Hinged	55.00	
		No gum	35.00	

1944
Inscribed "Void after June 30, 1945"

RW11	HP11	$1 red orange	125.00	35.00
		Hinged	45.00	
		No gum	35.00	

1945
Inscribed "Void after June 30, 1946"

RW12	HP12	$1 black	95.00	22.50
		Hinged	40.00	
		No gum	30.00	

1946
Inscribed "Void after June 30, 1947"

RW13	HP13	$1 red brown	50.00	12.50
		No gum	15.00	

The previously listed No. RW13a in a bright rose pink shade has been determined to be a chemically induced changeling.

1947
Inscribed "Void after June 30, 1948"

RW14	HP14	$1 black	55.00	15.00
		No gum	18.00	

1948
Inscribed "Void after June 30, 1949"

RW15	HP15	$1 bright blue	60.00	12.00
		No gum	15.00	

Goldeneye Ducks — HP16

1949
Inscribed "Void after June 30, 1950"

RW16	HP16	$2 bright green	70.00	15.00
		No gum	20.00	

1950
Inscribed "Void after June 30, 1951"
RW17 HP17 $2 violet   90.00   12.00
  No gum   20.00

1951
Inscribed "Void after June 30, 1952"
RW18 HP18 $2 gray black   90.00   12.00
  No gum   20.00

1952
Inscribed "Void after June 30, 1953"
RW19 HP19 $2 dp ultra   90.00   12.00
  No gum   20.00

1953
Inscribed "Void after June 30, 1954"
RW20 HP20 $2 dp rose brn   90.00   12.00
  No gum   20.00

> No. RW21 and following issues are printed on dry, pregummed paper and the back inscription is printed on top of the gum, except for the self-adhesive stamp issues starting in 1998.

1954
Inscribed "Void after June 30, 1955"
RW21 HP21 $2 black   85.00   10.00
  No gum   20.00

1955
Inscribed "Void after June 30, 1956"
RW22 HP22 $2 dark blue   85.00   10.00
  No gum   20.00
  a. Back inscription invert-
    ed   5,500. 4,500.

1956
Inscribed "Void after June 30, 1957"
RW23 HP23 $2 black   85.00   10.00
  No gum   20.00

1957
Inscribed "Void after June 30, 1958"
RW24 HP24 $2 emerald   85.00   10.00
  No gum   20.00
  a. Back inscription inverted   5,000.

1958
Inscribed "Void after June 30, 1959"
RW25 HP25 $2 black   85.00   10.00
  No gum   20.00
  a. Back inscription inverted   —

Labrador Retriever Carrying Mallard Drake — HP26

Giori Press Printing

1959
Inscribed "Void after June 30, 1960"
RW26 HP26 $3 multi   120.00   12.00
  No gum   40.00
  a. Back inscription invert-
    ed   27,500.

Redhead Ducks — HP27

1960
Inscribed "Void after June 30, 1961"
RW27 HP27 $3 multi   90.00   10.00
  No gum   30.00

1961
Inscribed "Void after June 30, 1962"
RW28 HP28 $3 multicolored   95.00   10.00
  No gum   30.00

Pintail Drakes — HP29

1962
Inscribed "Void after June 30, 1963"
RW29 HP29 $3 multicolored   110.00   12.00
  No gum   35.00
  a. Back inscription omitted   —

1963
Inscribed "Void after June 30, 1964"
RW30 HP30 $3 multicolored   100.00   12.00
  No gum   35.00

1964
Inscribed "Void after June 30, 1965"
RW31 HP31 $3 multicolored   100.00   12.00
  No gum   35.00

1965
Inscribed "Void after June 30, 1966"
RW32 HP32 $3 multicolored   100.00   12.00
  No gum   40.00

Whistling Swans — HP33

1966
Inscribed "Void after June 30, 1967"
RW33 HP33 $3 multi   100.00   12.00
  No gum   40.00

1967
Inscribed "Void after June 30, 1968"
RW34 HP34 $3 multicolored   100.00   12.00
  No gum   40.00

1968
Inscribed "Void after June 30, 1969"
RW35 HP35 $3 multicolored   65.00   10.00
  No gum   20.00
  a. Back inscription omitted   —

White-winged Scoters — HP36

1969
Inscribed "Void after June 30, 1970"
RW36 HP36 $3 multi   65.00   7.00
  No gum   20.00

1970   Engraved & Lithographed
Inscribed "Void after June 30, 1971"
RW37 HP37 $3 multi   65.00   8.00
  No gum   20.00

1971
Inscribed "Void after June 30, 1972"
RW38 HP38 $3 multi   40.00   8.00
  No gum   15.00

1972
Inscribed "Void after June 30, 1973"
RW39 HP39 $5 multi   25.00   6.00
  No gum   8.00

1973
Inscribed "Void after June 30, 1974"
RW40 HP40 $5 multi   18.00   6.00
  No gum   7.00

1974
Inscribed "Void after June 30, 1975"
RW41 HP41 $5 multi   18.00   5.00
  No gum   6.00
  a. Back inscription missing,
    but printed vertically on
    face of stamp and
    selvage, from foldover   4,750.

1975
Inscribed "Void after June 30, 1976"
RW42 HP42 $5 multi   15.00   5.00
  No gum   7.00

1976   Engr.
Inscribed "Void after June 30, 1977"
RW43 HP43 $5 grn & blk   10.00   5.00
  No gum   7.00

1977   Litho. & Engr.
Inscribed "Void after June 30, 1978"
RW44 HP44 $5 multi   12.50   5.00
  No gum   7.00

Hooded Merganser — HP45

1978
Inscribed "Void after June 30, 1979"
RW45 HP45 $5 multicolored   10.00   5.00
  No gum   7.00

1979
Inscribed "Void after June 30, 1980"
RW46 HP46 $7.50 multi   12.50   6.00
  No gum   8.00

1980
Inscribed "Void after June 30, 1981"
RW47 HP47 $7.50 multi   12.50   6.00
  No gum   8.00

1981
Inscribed "Void after June 30, 1982"
RW48 HP48 $7.50 multi   12.50   6.00
  No gum   8.00

1982
Inscribed "Void after June 30, 1983"
RW49 HP49 $7.50 multi   12.50   7.00
  No gum   9.00
  a. Orange and violet omit-
    ted   10,000.

> A certificate from a recognized expertization committee is required for No. RW49a.

1983
Inscribed "Void after June 30, 1984"
RW50 HP50 $7.50 multi   12.50   7.00
  No gum   7.00

1984
Inscribed "Void after June 30, 1985"
RW51 HP51 $7.50 multi   12.50   7.00
  No gum   7.00

1985
Inscribed "Void after June 30, 1986"
RW52 HP52 $7.50 multi   12.50   8.00
  No gum   7.00
  a. Light blue (litho.)
    omitted   20,000.

> The omitted color on No. RW52a coincides with a double paper splice affecting the top row of five stamps from the sheet and top ⅓ of stamps in the second row. There is also a color changeling of the brownish red ducks and their reflections in the water to yellow and yellow orange, respectively, on the error stamps. This error currently exists as three vertical strips of 6 (top stamp the error) and a plate number block of 12 (2x6, top two stamps the error).

1986
Inscribed "Void after June 30, 1987"
RW53 HP53 $7.50 multi   12.50   7.00
  No gum   9.00
  a. Black omitted   1,900.

1987   Perf. 11½x11
Inscribed "Void after June 30, 1988"
RW54 HP54 $10 multi   15.00   7.00
  No gum   8.00

1988
Inscribed "Void after June 30, 1989"
RW55 HP55 $10 multicolored   15.00   7.00
  No gum   8.00

1989
Inscribed "Void after June 30, 1990"
RW56 HP56 $12.50 multi   21.50   8.00
  No gum   9.00

1990
Inscribed "Void after June 30, 1991"
RW57 HP57 $12.50 multi   20.00   8.00
  No gum   9.00
  a. Back inscription omitted   300.00
  b. Black inscription printed
    on the stamp paper
    rather than the gum   —

> The back inscription is normally on top of the gum so beware of examples with gum removed offered as No. RW57a. Full original gum must be intact on No. RW57a. Used examples of No. RW57a cannot exist.
>
> Some philatelic researchers have questioned the existence of No. RW57b as a genuine error. There appears to be evidence that the inscriptions printed on the gum on the back can leach through to the paper on one of the types of gums used on these stamps. Further research is ongoing.

King Eiders — HP58

1991
Inscribed "Void after June 30, 1992"
RW58 HP58 $15 multi   30.00   8.00
  No gum   15.00
  a. Black (engr.) omitted   20,000.

1992
Inscribed "Void after June 30, 1993"
RW59 HP59 $15 multi   30.00   8.00
  No gum   15.00

1993
Inscribed "Void after June 30, 1994"
RW60 HP60 $15 multi   27.50   8.00
  No gum   15.00
  a. Black (engr.) omitted   2,100.

1994   Perf. 11¼x11
Inscribed "Void after June 30, 1995"
RW61 HP61 $15 multi   27.50   12.00
  No gum   15.00

1995
Inscribed "Void after June 30, 1996"
RW62 HP62 $15 multi   32.50   12.00
  No gum   15.00

1996
Inscribed "Void after June 30, 1997"
RW63 HP63 $15 multi   32.50   12.00
  No gum   12.50

1997
Inscribed "Void after June 30, 1998"
RW64 HP64 $15 multi   27.50   12.00
  No gum   15.00

1998   Perf. 11¼
Inscribed "Void after June 30, 1999"
RW65 HP65 $15 multi   42.50   22.50
  No gum   21.00

Self-Adhesive
Die Cut Perf. 10

RW65A HP65 $15 *Barrow's
          Goldeneye*   35.00   17.50
  No gum   15.00

> Nos. RW65 and later issues were sold in panes of 30 (RW65 and RW66) or 20 (RW67 and later issues), with four plate numbers per pane. The self-adhesives starting with No. RW65A were sold in panes of 1. The self-adhesives are valued unused as complete panes and used as single stamps.

1999   *Perf. 11¼*
Inscribed "Void after June 30, 2000"
RW66   HP66 $15 multi   40.00 20.00
     No gum   22.50

Self-Adhesive
Die Cut Perf. 10

RW66A   HP66 $15 multi   25.00 12.00
     No gum   15.00

2000   *Perf. 11¼*
Inscribed "Void after June 30, 2001"
RW67   HP67 $15 multi   30.00 15.00
     No gum   17.50

Self-Adhesive
Die Cut Perf. 10

RW67A   HP67 $15 multi   25.00 14.00
     No gum   17.50

2001   *Perf. 11¼*
Inscribed "Void after June 30, 2002"
RW68   HP68 $15 multi   30.00 18.00
     No gum   17.50

Self-Adhesive
Die Cut Perf. 10

RW68A   HP68 $15 multi   25.00 14.00
     No gum   15.00

2002   *Perf. 11¼*
Inscribed "Void after June 30, 2003"
RW69   HP69 $15 multi   30.00 16.00
     No gum   17.50

Self-Adhesive
Serpentine Die Cut 11x10¾

RW69A   HP69 $15 multi   25.00 12.00
     No gum   15.00

2003   *Perf. 11*
Inscribed "Void after June 30, 2004"
RW70   HP70 $15 multi   30.00 16.00
     No gum   17.50
   b.   Imperf, pair   5,000.
   c.   Back inscription omit-
       ted   4,500.

Self-Adhesive
Serpentine Die Cut 11x10¾

RW70A   HP70 $15 multi   25.00 12.00
     No gum   15.00

2004   *Perf. 11*
Inscribed "Void after June 30, 2005"
RW71   HP71 $15 multicolored 25.00 16.00
     No gum   17.00

Self-Adhesive
Serpentine Die Cut 11x10¾

RW71A   HP71 $15 multicolored 25.00 12.00
     No gum   15.00

Printed by Banknote Corporation of America
for Sennett Security Products.

2005   **Litho. & Engr.**   *Perf. 11*
Inscribed "Void after June 30, 2006"
RW72   HP72 $15 multi,
             type I   25.00 16.00
     No gum   16.00
   b.   Souvenir sheet of 1   2,000.
   c.   Type II   22.50 16.00
     No gum   16.00
   d.   As "b," without art-
       ist's signature (er-
       ror)

There are two types of RW72: type I has no
frame lines; type II has gray frame lines at top,
right and bottom edges of design. No. RW72c,
the type II stamp, is any stamp from the right
two panes of the sheet of four panes. No.
RW72, the Type I stamp, is any stamp from the
left two panes.

No. RW72b sold for $20. 1,000 No. RW72b
were issued. Approximately 750 were signed
by the artist in black, value $2,000 as shown.
Approximately 150 were signed in blue ink,
value $2,500. Approximately 100 were signed
in gold ink, value $3,000. Most examples of
No. RW72b are in the grade of F-VF. Catalogue values are for Very Fine examples.

The Duck Stamp Office never announced
the existence of No. RW72b to the public
through a press release or a website
announcement during the time the sheet was
on sale, apparently because it was not clear
beforehand that the souvenir sheet could be
produced successfully and on time. No.
RW72b sold before a public announcement of the item's existence could be made.

Self-Adhesive
Litho. & Debossed
Serpentine Die Cut 11x10¾

RW72A   HP72 $15 multi   22.50 11.00
     No gum   15.00

Ross's Goose — HP73

2006   **Litho. & Engr.**   *Perf. 11*
Inscribed "Void after June 30, 2007"
RW73   HP73 $15 multi   25.00 11.00
     No gum   15.00
   b.   Souvenir sheet of 1   120.00   —
   c.   As "b," without art-
       ist's signature (er-
       ror)   2,500.

No. RW73b sold for $25. All examples of
No. RW73b have a black signature of the artist
on a designated line in the sheet margin. Ten
thousand were issued.

The sheet margin has a line designated for
the signature of the engraver, Piotr Naszarkowski, but no sheets were sold with his
signature. Naszarkowski signed approximately
2,500 sheets during three days at the Washington 2006 World Philatelic Exhibition, and he
signed another 2,500 or more after the conclusion of the exhibition. Value $160.

Self-Adhesive
Serpentine Die Cut 11x10¾

RW73A   HP73 $15 multi   22.50 11.00
     No gum   15.00

Ring-necked Ducks — HP74

2007   **Litho.**   *Perf. 11*
Inscribed "Void after June 30, 2008"
RW74   HP74 $15 multi   25.00 11.00
     No gum   15.00
   b.   Souvenir sheet of 1   125.00
   c.   As "b," without art-
       ist's signature (er-
       ror)   2,750.

No. RW74b sold for $25 plus a shipping fee.
The artist signed No. RW74b on a designated
line in the sheet margin. Ten thousand were
issued. There is no back inscription on No.
RW74b.

Self-Adhesive
Serpentine Die Cut 11x10¾

RW74A   HP74 $15 multi   22.50 11.00
     No gum   15.00

Northern Pintails — HP75

2008   **Litho.**   *Perf. 13¼*
Inscribed "Void after June 30, 2009"
RW75   HP75 $15 multi   25.00 11.00
     No gum   15.00
   b.   Souvenir sheet of 1   80.00   —
   c.   As "b," without artist's
       signature (error)   500.00

A sheet commemorating the 75th anniversary of Hunting Permit stamps containing one
example of No. RW75 and a label with the
vignette of No. RW1 sold for $50. Value, $90.

No. RW75b sold for $30 plus a shipping fee.
The artist signed No. RW75b on a designated
line in the sheet margin. Ten thousand were
prepared. There is no back inscription on No.
RW75b.

Self-Adhesive
Serpentine Die Cut 10¾

RW75A   HP75 $15 multi   22.50 11.00
     No gum   20.00

2009   **Litho.**   *Perf. 13¼*
Inscribed "Void after June 30, 2010"
RW76   HP76 $15 multi   25.00 11.00
     No gum   15.00
   b.   Souvenir sheet of 1   60.00
   c.   As "b," without artist's
       signature (error)   400.00

No. RW76b sold for $30 plus a shipping fee.
The artist signed No. RW76b on a designated
line in the sheet margin. Ten thousand were
prepared.

Self-Adhesive
Serpentine Die Cut 11x10¾

RW76A   HP76 $15 multi   22.50 11.00
     No gum   20.00

2010   **Litho.**   *Perf. 11¼x11*
Inscribed "Void after June 30, 2011"
RW77   HP77 $15 multi   25.00 11.00
     No gum   15.00
   b.   Souvenir sheet of 1,
       perf. 13¼   50.00
   c.   As "b," without artist's
       signature (error)   175.00

No. RW77b was sold for $30 plus a shipping
fee. The artist signed No. RW77b on a designated line in the sheet margin. Ten thousand
were prepared. There is no back inscription on
No. RW77b.

Self-Adhesive
Serpentine Die Cut 11x10¾

RW77A   HP77 $15 multi   22.50 11.00
     No gum   20.00

White-fronted Geese — HP78

2011   **Litho.**   *Perf. 13¼*
Inscribed "Void after June 30, 2012"
RW78   HP78 $15 multi   25.00 11.00
     No gum   15.00
   b.   Souvenir sheet of 1   65.00
   c.   As "b," without artist's
       signature (error)   175.00

No. RW78b was sold for $25 plus a shipping
fee. The artist signed No. RW78b on a designated line in the sheet margin. Ten thousand
were prepared.

Self-Adhesive
Serpentine Die Cut 11x10¾

RW78A   HP78 $15 multi   22.50 11.00
     No gum   20.00

Wood Duck — HP79

2012   **Litho.**   *Perf. 13¼*
Inscribed "Void after June 30, 2013"
RW79   HP79 $15 multi   25.00 11.00
     No gum   15.00
   b.   Souvenir sheet of 1   70.00
   c.   As "b," without artist's
       signature (error)   1,750.

No. RW79b was sold for $25 plus a shipping
fee. The artist signed No. RW79b on a designated line in the sheet margin. One No.
RW79b was signed in red ink as a "surprise"
for a random buyer. This was not authorized.

Self-Adhesive
Serpentine Die Cut 11x10¾

RW79A   HP79 $15 multi   22.50 11.00
     No gum   20.00

Common Goldeneye — HP80

2013   **Litho.**   *Perf. 13¼*
Inscribed "Void after June 30, 2014"
RW80   HP80 $15 multi   25.00 11.00
     No gum   15.00
   b.   Souvenir sheet of 1   60.00
   c.   As "b," without artist's
       signature (error)   —

No. RW80b was sold for $25 plus a shipping
fee. The artist signed No. RW80b on a designated line in the sheet margin.

Self-Adhesive
Serpentine Die Cut 11x10¾

RW80A   HP80 $15 multi   22.50 11.00
     No gum   20.00

Canvasbacks — HP81

2014   **Litho.**   *Perf. 13¼*
Inscribed "Void after June 30, 2015"
RW81   HP81 $15 multi   25.00 11.00
     No gum   15.00

Self-Adhesive
Serpentine Die Cut 11x10¾

RW81A   HP81 $15 multi   25.00 11.00
     No gum   20.00

Ruddy Ducks — HP82

2015   **Litho.**   *Perf. 13¼*
Inscribed "Void after June 30, 2016"
RW82   HP82 $25 multi   37.50 12.00
     No gum   25.00

Self-Adhesive
Serpentine Die Cut 11x10¾

RW82A   HP82 $25 multi   37.50 12.00
     No gum   32.50

Trumpeter Swans — HP83

2016   **Litho.**   *Perf. 13¼*
Inscribed "Void after June 30, 2017"
RW83   HP83 $25 multi   37.50 12.00
     No gum   25.00

Self-Adhesive
Serpentine Die Cut 11x10¾

RW83A   HP83 $25 multi   37.50 12.00
     No gum   32.50

CONFEDERATE STATES OF AMERICA

3¢ 1861 POSTMASTERS' PROVISIONALS

With the secession of South Carolina from the Union on Dec. 20, 1860, a new era began in U.S. history as well as its postal history. Other Southern states quickly followed South Carolina's lead, which in turn led to the formation of the provisional government of the Confederate States of America on Feb. 4, 1861.

President Jefferson Davis' cabinet was completed Mar. 6, 1861, with the acceptance of the position of Postmaster General by John H. Reagan of Texas. The provisional government had already passed regulations that required payment for postage in cash and that effectively carried over the U.S. 3c rate until the new Confederate Post Office Department took over control of the system.

Soon after entering on his duties, Reagan directed the postmasters in the Confederate States and in the newly seceded states to "continue the performance of their duties as such, and render all accounts and pay all moneys (sic) to the order of the Government of the U.S. as they have heretofore done, until the Government of the Confederate States shall be prepared to assume control of its postal affairs."

As coinage was becoming scarce, postal patrons began having problems buying individual stamps or paying for letters individually, especially as stamp stocks started to run short in certain areas. Even though the U.S. Post Office Department was technically in control of the postal system and southern postmasters were operating under Federal authority, the U.S.P.O. was hesitant in re-supplying seceded states with additional stamps and stamped envelopes.

The U.S. government had made the issuance of postmasters' provisionals illegal many years before, but the southern postmasters had to do what they felt was necessary to allow patrons to pay for postage and make the system work. Therefore, a few postmasters took it upon themselves to issue provisional stamps in the 3c rate then in effect.

Interestingly, these were stamps and envelopes that the U.S. government did not recognize as legal, but they did do postal duty unchallenged in the Confederate States. Yet the proceeds were to be remitted to the U.S. government in Washington! Six authenticated postmasters' provisionals in the 3c rate have been recorded.

On May 13, 1861, Postmaster General Reagan issued his proclamation "assuming control and direction of postal service within the limits of the Confederate States of America on and after the first day of June," with new postage rates and regulations.

The Federal government suspended operations in the Confederate States (except for western Virginia and the seceding state of Tennessee) by a proclamation issued by Postmaster General Montgomery Blair on May 27, 1861, effective from May 31, 1861, and June 10 for western and middle Tennessee.

As Tennessee did not join the Confederacy until July 2, 1861, the unissued 3c Nashville provisional was produced in a state that was in the process of seceding, while the other provisionals were used in the Confederacy before the June 1 assumption of control of postal service by the Confederate States of America.

Illustrations are reduced in size.
XU numbers are envelope entires.

FORT VALLEY, GA.

E1   E2

Handstamped Envelope

7AXU1 E1 3c black   —

HILLSBORO, N.C.

A1

Handstamped Adhesive

1AX1 A1 3c bluish black,
on cover   —

No. 1AX1 is unique. This is the same handstamp as used for No. 39X1. 3c usage is determined from the May 27, 1861 circular date stamp.

JACKSON, MISS.

E1

Handstamped Envelope

2AXU1 E1 3c black   3,500.
See Nos. 43XU1-43XU4.

MADISON COURT HOUSE, FLA.

A1   "CNETS"

Typeset Adhesive

3AX1 A1 3c gold   — 20,000.
   a.   "CNETS"   25,000.

No. 3AX1a is unique.

See No. 137XU1.

NASHVILLE, TENN.

A1

Typeset Adhesive (5 varieties)

4AX1   A1 3c carmine   400.

No. 4AX1 was prepared by Postmaster McNish with the U.S. rate, but the stamp was never issued.
See Nos. 61X2-61XU2.

SELMA, ALA.

E1

Handstamped Envelope

5AXU1 E1 3c black   1,950.
See Nos. 77XU1-77XU3.

TUSCUMBIA, ALA.

E1

Handstamped Envelope, impression at upper right

6AXU1 E1 3c dull red,
             buff   17,500.

Dangerous forgeries exist of No. 6AXU1.
See Nos. 84XU1-84XU3.

For later additions, listed out of numerical sequence, see:
#7AXU1, Fort Valley, Ga.

POSTMASTERS' PROVISIONAL ISSUES

These stamps and envelopes were issued by individual postmasters generally between June 1, 1861, when the use of U.S. stamps stopped in the Confederacy, and Oct. 16, 1861, when the 1st Confederate Government stamps were issued.

They were occasionally issued at later periods, especially in Texas, when regular issues of Government stamps were unavailable.

Canceling stamps of the post offices were often used to produce envelopes, some of which were supplied in advance by private citizens.

These envelopes and other stationery therefore may be found in a wide variety of papers, colors, sizes & shapes, including patriotic and semi-official types.

It is often difficult to determine whether the impression made by the canceling stamp indicates provisional usage or merely postage paid at the time the letter was deposited in the post office. Occasionally the same mark was used for both purposes.

The *press-printed* provisional envelopes are in a different category. They were produced in quantity, using envelopes procured in advance by the postmaster, such as those of Charleston, Lynchburg, Memphis, etc.

The press-printed envelopes are listed and valued on all known papers.

The handstamped provisional envelopes are listed and valued according to type and variety of handstamp, but not according to paper. Many exist on such a variety of papers that they defy accurate, complete listing.

The value of a handstamped provisional envelope is determined *primarily* by the clarity of the markings and its overall condition and attractiveness, rather than type of paper.

All handstamped provisional envelopes, when used, should also show the postmark of the town of issue.

Most handstamps are impressed at top right, although they exist from some towns in other positions.

Illustrations in this section are reduced in size.

XU numbers are envelope entires.

ABERDEEN, MISS.

E1

Handstamped Envelopes

1XU1	E1 5c black	7,000.
a.	10c (ms.) on 5c black	9,000.

No. 1XU1a is unique.

ABINGDON, VA.

E1

Handstamped Envelopes

2XU1	E1 2c black		12,500.
a.	5c (ms.) on 2c black		15,000.
2XU2	E1 5c black		1,750.
2XU3	E1 10c black	2,200.	3,500.

No. 2XU1 is unique. No. 2XU3 unused and used are each unique.

ALBANY, GA.

E1

E2

E3

E4

Handstamped Envelopes

3XU1	E1 5c greenish blue		1,000.
3XU2	E2 10c greenish blue		1,750.
a.	10c on 5c greenish blue		3,500.
3XU5	E3 5c greenish blue		—
3XU6	E4 10c greenish blue		3,500.

Only one example each recorded of Nos. 3XU2, 3XU2a and 3XU6. No. 3XU2 is a cover front only and is valued as such. No. 3XU2a is the unique Confederate example of one provisional marking revaluing another. No. 3XU5 is in question. The editors would like to see an authenticated example of this marking.

ANDERSON COURT HOUSE, S.C.

E1

E2

E3

Handstamped Envelopes

4XU1	E1 5c black	1,000.	2,750.
4XU2	E2 10c (ms.) black		2,500.
4XU3	E3 (2c) black, denomination omitted (circular rate)		2,250.

ATHENS, GA

A1 — Type I

A1 — Type II

E1

Typographed Adhesives
(from woodcuts of two types)

Pairs, both horizontal and vertical, always show one of each type.

5X1	A1 5c purple (shades)		1,000.	1,750.
a.	Tete beche pair (vertical)			7,500.
5X2	A1 5c red		5,750.	5,750.

The colorless ornaments in the four corners of No. 5X2 were recut making them wider than those in No. 5X1.

Dangerous fakes exist of Nos. 5X1 and 5X2. Certificates of authenticity from recognized committees are strongly recommended.

Handstamped Envelopes

5XU1	E1 10c black, on patriotic cover	2,500.

The markings on No. 5XU1 are the same as those used on stampless envelopes. On the unique listed example of No. 5XU1, there is a handwritten note on the inside of the flap: 'Andrew had these envelopes stamped & I am obliged to use them or loose the postage.' Two or more similar covers from the same correspondence are known, but without the note under the flap. While these also may be provisional use, it cannot be proven, and these covers are considered handstamp paid covers.

ATLANTA, GA.

E1

E2

E2

Handstamped Envelopes

6XU1	E1 5c red		5,000.
6XU2	E1 5c black	160.	1,000.
a.	10c on 5c black		2,500.

No. 6UX3 was probably used for drop letters and circulars.

6XU4	E3 2c black		3,000.
6XU5	E3 5c black		1,500.
a.	10c on 5c black		2,500.
6XU6	E3 10c black		550.

Only one example recorded of No. 6XU1.

E3

Handstamped Envelopes

6XU8	E3 5c black	3,500.
6XU9	E3 10c black ("10" upright)	3,250.

Only one example recorded of No. 6XU8.

AUSTIN, MISS.

E1

Press-printed Envelope (typeset)

8XU1	E1 5c red, *amber*	75,000.

One example recorded.

AUSTIN, TEX.

E1a

Handstamped Adhesive

9X1	E1a 10c black, *white or buff*	—

Handstamped Envelope

9XU1	E1a 10c black	2,500.

AUTAUGAVILLE, ALA.

E1

E2

Handstamped Envelopes

10XU1	E1 5c black	20,000.
10XU2	E2 5c black	20,000.

No. 10XU2 is unique.

BALCONY FALLS, VA.

E1

Handstamped Envelope

122XU1	E1 10c blue	2,000.

The use of No. 122XU1 as a provisional marking is in question. The editors would like to see authenticated evidence of its use as a provisional.

BARNWELL COURT HOUSE, S. C.

E1

Handstamped Envelope

123XU1	E1 5c black	3,000.

These are two separate handstamps. All recorded uses are on addressed covers without postmarks.

BATON ROUGE, LA.

A1   A2

Typeset Adhesives
Ten varieties of each
11X1	A1	2c green	8,250.	5,000.
a.		"McCcrmick"	40,000.	40,000.
11X2	A2	5c green &		
		carmine	1,500.	1,400.
a.		"McCcrmick"	10,000.	3,500.

Only one example each is recorded of No. 11X1a unused, used and on cover.

A3   A4

Ten varieties of each
11X3	A3	5c green &		
		carmine	10,000.	4,000.
a.		"McCcrmick"		32,500.
11X4	A4	10c blue		50,000.

BEAUMONT, TEX.

A1   A2

Typeset Adhesives
Several varieties of each
12X1	A1	10c black, *yellow*	—
12X2	A1	10c black, *pink*	20,000.

No. 12X1 is smaller than No. 12X2.
12X3	A2	10c black, *yellow,*	
		on cover	90,000.

One example recorded of No. 12X3.

BLUFFTON, S. C.

E1

Handstamped Envelope
124XU1	E1	5c black	4,250.

Only one example recorded of No. 124XU1.

BRIDGEVILLE, ALA.

A1

Handstamped Adhesive in black within red pen-ruled squares
13X1	A1	5c black & red,	
		pair on cover	20,000.

CAMDEN, S. C.

E1   E2

Handstamped Envelopes
125XU1	E1	5c black	2,500.
125XU2	E2	10c black	750.

No. 125XU2 unused was privately carried and is addressed but has no postal markings. No. 125XU2 is indistinguishable from a hand-stamp paid cover when used.

CANTON, MISS.

E1

"P" in star is initial of Postmaster William Priestly.

Handstamped Envelopes
14XU1	E1	5c black	4,000.
a.		10c (ms.) on 5c black	5,000.

CAROLINA CITY, N. C.

E1

Handstamped Envelope
118XU1	E1	5c black	5,000.

CARTERSVILLE, GA.

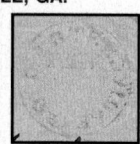

E1

Handstamped Envelope
126XU1	E1	(5c) red	1,500.

CHAPEL HILL, N. C.

E1

Handstamped Envelope
15XU1	E1	5c black	3,750.

CHARLESTON, S. C.

A1   E1

E2

Lithographed Adhesive
16X1	A1	5c blue	1,400.	800.

Values are for stamps showing parts of the outer frame lines on at least 3 sides. The vast majority of this stamp small faults and are valued thus. Completely sound examples are scarce and sell for more.

Press-printed Envelopes
(typographed from woodcut)
16XU1	E1	5c blue	1,250.	1,750.
16XU2	E1	5c blue, *amber*	1,250.	2,250.
16XU3	E1	5c blue, *orange*	1,250.	1,750.
16XU4	E1	5c blue, *buff*	1,250.	1,500.
16XU5	E1	5c blue, *blue*	1,250.	2,250.
16XU6	E2	10c blue, *orange*		80,000.

The No. 16XU6 used entire is unique; value based on 1997 auction sale.
Beware of fakes of the E1 design.

Handstamped Cut Square
16XU7	E2	10c black	2,000.

There is only one example of No. 16XU7. It is a cutout, not an entire. It may not have been mailed from Charleston, and it may not have paid postage.

CHARLOTTE, N. C.

E1

146XU1	E1	5c blue, "5" in	
		circle and	
		straight line	
		"PAID"	3,500.

CHARLOTTESVILLE, VA.

Control

E1

Handstamped Envelopes, Manuscript Initials
127XU1	E1	5c blue	—
127XU2	E1	10c blue	—

The control initials appear at the upper right on the front of the envelope.

CHATTANOOGA, TENN.

E1

E2

Handstamped Envelopes
17XU2	E1	5c black	1,750.
17XU3	E2	5c on 2c black	5,000.

No. 17XU3 is unique.

CHRISTIANSBURG, VA.

E1

Handstamped Envelopes
Impressed at top right
99XU1	E1	5c black	2,250.
99XU2	E1	5c blue	2,000.
99XU4	E1	5c green on U.S.	
		envelope No.	
		U27	4,500.
99XU5	E1	10c blue	3,500.

The absence of 5c and 10c handstamped paid markings from this town suggests that Nos. 99XU1-99XU5 were used as both provisional and handstamped paid markings.

COLAPARCHEE, GA.

E1

Control

Handstamped Envelope
119XU1	E1	5c black	3,500.

There are only two recorded examples of No. 119XU1, and both are used from Savannah with a general issue stamp.
The control appears on the front of the envelope.

COLUMBIA, S. C.

Oval Control   Circular Control

E1   E2

E3

E4

E5

E6

E7

E8

Handstamped Envelopes

18XU1	E1	5c blue	550.	900.
a.		10c on 5c blue		3,500.
18XU2	E1	5c black	600.	1,250.
18XU4	E2	5c blue, oval control on front		7,500.
a.		Oval control on back		1,250.
18XU7	E3	5c blue, oval control on back		1,000.
18XU8	E4	5c blue oval control on back		1,000.
a.		Circular control on back		2,000.
18XU9	E4	10c blue oval control on back		1,250.
18XU10	E5	10c blue oval control on back		1,250.
18XU11	E6	5c blue oval control on front		2,500.
18XU12	E6	10c blue oval control on back		1,250.
18XU13	E7	5c blue oval control on back		1,000.
a.		Circular control on back		1,500.
18XU14	E8	5c blue oval control on back		1,000.
a.		No control (unused)		—

COLUMBIA, TENN.

E1

Handstamped Envelope

113XU1	E1	5c red	6,000.

One example recorded.

COLUMBUS, GA.

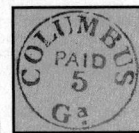

E1

Handstamped Envelopes

19XU1	E1	5c blue	900.
19XU2	E1	10c red	3,250.

COURTLAND, ALA.

E1

Handstamped Envelopes (from woodcut)

103XU1	E1	5c red	37,500.

CUTHBERT, GA

E1

Handstamped Envelope

95XU1	E1	10c black	750.

The unique example of No. 95XU1 was used by having a C.S.A. 10c #12c placed over it.

DALTON, GA

E1

Handstamped Envelopes

20XU1	E1	5c black	750.
a.		Denomination omitted (5c rate)	875.
b.		10c (ms.) on 5c black	1,500.
c.		20c (ms.) on 5c black	1,500.
20XU2	E1	10c black	1,250.

DANVILLE, VA.

A1

Design measures 60x37mm — E1

E2

E3

E4

E5

E6

Typeset Adhesive
Wove Paper

21X1	A1	5c red	7,500.

Two varieties known.

Laid Paper

21X2	A1	5c red	10,000.

No. 21X2 is unique.

Press-printed Envelopes
(typographed)

Two types: "SOUTHERN" in straight or curved line

Impressed (usually) at top left

21XU1	E1	5c black	9,000.
21XU2	E1	5c black, *amber*	—
21XU3	E1	5c black, *dark buff*	9,000.

The existence of No. 21XU2 is in question. The editors would like to see authenticated evidence of its existence.

Unissued 10c envelopes (type E1, in red) are known. All recorded examples are envelopes that show evidence of added stamps being torn off.

Dangerous forgeries exist of No. 21XU1.

Handstamped Envelopes

21XU3A	E2	5c black (ms "WBP" initials)	1,000.
21XU3B	E3	5c black (ms "WPB" initials)	8,500.
21XU4	E4	10c black	2,500.
21XU6	E5	10c black	2,750.
21XU7	E6	10c black (ms "WBP" initials)	

Types E4 and E5 both exist on one cover.
On No. 21XU3B, the "PAID 5 Cents" handstamp is to the left, and the "PAID" and ms. "5" are toward the right. It is unique.

DEMOPOLIS, ALA.

E1

Handstamped Envelopes, Signature in ms.

22XU1	E1	5c black ("Jno. Y. Hall")	3,500.
22XU2	E1	5c black ("J. Y. Hall")	3,500.
22XU3	E1	5c (ms.) black ("J. Y. Hall")	4,000.

EATONTON, GA.

E1

E2

Handstamped Envelopes

23XU1	E1	5c black	3,000.
a.		10 (ms) on 5c black	—
23XU2	E2	5c + 5c black	5,000.

EMORY, VA.

A1

Handstamped Adhesives ("PAID" and "5" in circle on selvage of U.S. 1c 1857 issue)
Perf. 15 on three sides

24X1	A1	5c blue, on cover, tied	27,500.

Also known with "5" above "PAID."

E1

E2

Handstamped Envelopes

24XU1	E1	5c blue	4,000.
24XU2	E2	10c blue	5,000.

One example each recorded of Nos. 24XU1 and 24XU2.

FINCASTLE, VA.

E1

Press-printed Envelope (typeset)
Impressed at top right

104XU1	E1	10c black	20,000.

One example recorded of No. 104XU1.

FORSYTH, GA.

E1   E2

Handstamped Envelope

120XU1	E1	10c black	2,000.
120XU2	E2	10c black	1,250.

Only one example each recorded of Nos. 120XU1 and 120XU2.

FORT VALLEY, GA.

E1

E2

Handstamped Envelope

148XU1	E1	5c on 3c black	3,250.

Black circle control on front of envelope. Unique.

FRANKLIN, N. C.

E1

E2

Press-printed Envelope (typeset)
(No. 25XU1)
Impressed at top right

25XU1	E1	5c blue, *buff*	30,000.
25XU2	E2	5c black, large "5" woodcut in 31mm circular town mark	2,500.

The one known No. 25XU1 envelope shows black circular Franklin postmark with manuscript date.

FRAZIERSVILLE, S. C.

E1

Handstamped Envelope, "5" manuscript

128XU1   E1   5c black   5,000.

Only one example recorded of No. 128XU1.

FREDERICKSBURG, VA.

A1

Sheets of 20, two panes of 10 varieties each

Typeset Adhesives
Thin bluish paper

26X1	A1	5c blue, *bluish*	900.	1,250.
26X2	A1	10c red (shades), *bluish*		2,250.

GAINESVILLE, ALA.

E1   E2

E3

Handstamped Envelopes

27XU1	E1	5c black	4,500.
27XU2	E2	5c black	5,000.
27XU3	E3	10c ("01") black	12,000.

GALVESTON, TEX.

E1

Handstamped Envelopes

98XU1	E1	5c black	500.	1,500.
98XU2	E1	10c black		2,000.

E2

E3

Handstamped Envelopes

98XU3	E2	10c black	550.	2,750.
98XU4	E2	20c black		3,500.
98XU5	E3	5c black		4,500.

GASTON, N. C.

E1

Handstamped Envelope

129XU1   E1   5c black   6,000.

Only one example recorded of No. 129XU1.

GEORGETOWN, S. C.

E1   Control

E2

Handstamped Envelopes

28XU1	E1	5c black	3,500.
28XU2	E2	5c black, separate "5" and straightline "PAID" handstamps, control on reverse	— 1,750.

GOLIAD, TEX.

A1   A2

Typeset Adhesives

29X1	A1	5c black	16,500.
29X2	A1	5c black, *gray*	11,500.
29X3	A1	5c black, *rose*	12,000.
29X4	A1	10c black	25,000.
29X5	A1	10c black, *rose*	12,000.

Type A1 stamps are signed "Clarke-P.M." vertically in black or red.

29X6	A2	5c black, *gray*	22,500.
a.		"GOILAD"	12,000.
29X7	A2	10c black, *buff*	12,000.
a.		"GOILAD"	15,000.
29X8	A2	5c black, *dark blue, on cover*	18,000.
29X9	A2	10c black, *dark blue*	27,500.

GONZALES, TEX.

Colman & Law were booksellers when John B. Law (of the firm) was appointed Postmaster. The firm used a small lithographed label on drugs and on the front or inside of books they sold.

A1

Lithographed Adhesives
on colored glazed paper

30X1	A1	(5c) gold, *dark blue*, pair on cover, 1861	15,000.
30X2	A1	(10c) gold, *garnet*, on cover, 1864	25,000.
30X3	A1	(10c) gold, *black*, on cover, 1865	50,000.

No. 30X1 must bear double-circle town cancel as validating control. The control was applied to the labels in the sheet before their sale as stamps. When used, the stamps bear an additional Gonzales double-circle postmark.

GREENSBORO, ALA.

E1

E2

E3

Handstamped Envelopes

31XU1	E1	5c black	3,000.
31XU2	E1	10c black	2,750.
31XU3	E2	10c black	6,000.
31XU4	E3	10c on 5c black, on cover	3,000.

GREENSBORO, N. C.

E1

Handstamped Envelope

32XU1   E1   10c red   1,250.

GREENVILLE, ALA.

A1   A2

Typeset Adhesives
On pinkish surface-colored glazed paper.

33X1	A1	5c blue & red	25,000.
33X2	A2	10c red & blue, on cover	47,500.

Two used examples each are known of Nos. 33X1-33X2, and all are on covers. Covers bear a postmark but it was not used to cancel the stamps.

The former No. 33X1a has been identified as a fake.

GREENVILLE, TENN.

E1

144XU1   E1   5c black   5,000.

Only one example of No. 144XU1 is recorded.

GREENVILLE COURT HOUSE, S. C.

E1

E2

Control A   Control B

Control C

Handstamped Envelopes (Several types)

34XU1	E1	5c black	2,000.
34XU2	E2	10c black	2,000.
a.		20c (ms.) on 10c black	3,000.

Envelopes must bear one of three different postmark controls on the back. When the control postmark is dated, the date must be the same or prior to the date of the postmark on the front of the envelope.

GREENWOOD DEPOT, VA.

A1

"PAID" Handstamped Adhesive ("PAID" with value and signature in ms.)
Laid Paper

35X1   A1   10c black, *gray blue, on cover*   22,500.

GRIFFIN, GA.

E1

Handstamped Envelopes

102XU1	E1	5c black	2,250.
102XU2	E1	10c black	5,000.

No. 102XU2 is on a large piece of an envelope with July 25 postmark at left. It is unique.

GROVE HILL, ALA.

A1

Handstamped Adhesive (from woodcut)

36X1 A1 5c black —

Two examples are recorded. One is on cover tied by the postmark. The other is canceled by magenta pen on a cover front.

HALLETTSVILLE, TEX.

A1

Handstamped Adhesive
Ruled Letter Paper

37X1 A1 10c black, *gray blue*, on cover   15,000.

One example known.

HAMBURGH, S. C.

E1

Handstamped Envelope

112XU1 E1 5c black   8,000.

HARRISBURGH (Harrisburg), TEX.

E1

E2

Handstamped Envelope

130XU1 E1 5c black   5,500.
130XU2 E2 10c black   —

The unused 5c entire is the only example recorded of No. 130XU1

HELENA, TEX.

A1

Typeset Adhesives
Several varieties

38X1 A1 5c black, *buff*   22,500. 20,000.
38X2 A1 10c black, *gray*   40,000.

On 10c "Helena" is in upper and lower case italics.
Used examples are valued with small faults or repairs, as all recorded have faults.

HILLSBORO, N. C.

A1

Handstamped Adhesive

39X1 A1 5c black, on cover   15,000.

See 3c 1861 Postmaster's Provisional No. 1AX1.

Ms./Handstamped Envelope

39XU1 E1 10c "paid 10" in manuscript with undated blue town cancel as control on face   2,400.

HOLLANDALE, TEX.

E1

Handstamped Envelope

132XU1 E1 5c black   —

HOUSTON, TEX.

E1

No. 40XU1a

Handstamped Envelopes

40XU1 E1 5c red   — 800.
  a. 10c (ms.) on 5c red   11,000.
40XU2 E1 10c red   — 2,000.
40XU3 E1 10c black   4,500.
40XU4 E1 5c +10c red   2,500.
40XU5 E1 10c +10c red   2,500.

Nos. 40XU2-40XU5 show "TEX" instead of "TXS."

HUNTSVILLE, TEX.

E1

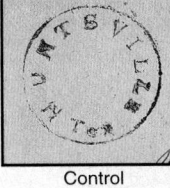

Control

Handstamped Envelope

92XU1 E1 5c black   5,000.

No. 92XU1 exists with "5" outside or within control circle.

INDEPENDENCE, TEX.

A1

A2

Handstamped Adhesives

41X1 A1 10c black, *buff*, on cover, uncanceled, cut to shape   20,000.
41X2 A1 10c black, *dull rose*, on cover   —

With small "10" and "Pd" in manuscript

41X3 A2 10c black, *buff*, on cover, uncanceled, cut to shape   32,500.

No. 41X1 is unique.
All known examples of Nos. 41X1-41X3 are uncanceled on covers with black "INDEPENDANCE TEX." (sic) postmark.
The existence of No. 41X2 has been questioned by specialists. The editors would like to see authenticated evidence of the existence of this item.

ISABELLA, GA.

E1

Handstamped Envelope, Manuscript "5"

133XU1 E1 5c black   5,000.

Only one example recorded of No. 133XU1.

IUKA, MISS.

E1

Handstamped Envelope

42XU1 E1 5c black   1,750.

JACKSON, MISS.

E1

Handstamped Envelopes
Two types of numeral

43XU1 E1 5c black   750.
  a. 10c on 5c black   2,750.
43XU2 E1 10c black   2,000.
  a. 5c on 10c black   3,750.
43XU4 E1 10c on 5c blue   2,750.

The 5c also exists on a lettersheet.
See 3c 1861 Postmaster's Provisional No. 2AXU1.

JACKSONVILLE, ALA.

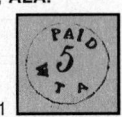

E1

Handstamped Envelope

110XU1 E1 5c black   — 3,000.

JACKSONVILLE, FLA.

E1

Control

Handstamped Envelope

134XU1 E1 5c black   —

Undated double circle postmark control on reverse.

JETERSVILLE, VA.

A1

Handstamped Adhesive
("5" with ms. "AHA." initials)
Laid Paper

44X1 A1 5c black, vertical pair on cover, uncanceled   16,000.

JONESBORO, TENN.

E1

Handstamped Envelopes

45XU1 E1 5c black   6,000.
45XU2 E1 5c dark blue   5,000.

KINGSTON, GA.

E1

E2

E3

E4

Typeset Envelopes
(design types E1-E2, E4 are handstamps; typeset design E3 probably impressed by hand but possibly press printed)

46XU1 E1 5c black   3,000.
46XU2 E2 5c black   3,250.
46XU4 E3 5c black   12,500.
46XU5 E4 5c black   2,000.

There is only one recorded example of No. 46XU4.

KNOXVILLE, TENN.

A1

Typographed Adhesives
(stereotype from woodcut)
Grayish Laid Paper

47X1	A1	5c brick red	1,750.	1,400.
47X2	A1	5c carmine	2,750.	2,250.
47X3	A1	10c green, on cover		57,750.

The #47X3 cover is unique. Value is based on 1997 auction sale.

E1

E2

Press-printed Envelopes
(typographed)

47XU1	E1	5c blue	2,500.
47XU2	E1	5c blue, orange	5,000.
47XU3	E1	10c red (cut to shape)	7,500.
47XU4	E1	10c red, orange (cut to shape)	7,500.

Only one example each recorded of Nos. 47XU3 and 47XU4.
Dangerous fakes exist of Nos. 47XU1 and 47XU2.

Handstamped Envelopes

47XU5	E2	5c black	1,400.
a.		10c on 5c black	3,500.

Type E2 exists with "5" above or below "PAID."

LA GRANGE, TEX.

E1

Handstamped Envelopes

48XU1	E1	5c black	—	3,250.
48XU2	E1	10c black		3,250.

LAKE CITY, FLA.

E1

Control Type A

Control Type B

Handstamped Envelope

96XU1	E1	10c black	3,000.

Envelopes have black circle control mark, or printed name of E. R. Ives, postmaster, on back.

LAURENS COURT HOUSE, S. C.

E1

E2

Control

Handstamped Envelopes

116XU1	E1	5c black	2,250.
116XU2	E2	5c black	2,250.

Envelopes have a 25mm undated control mark on reverse. No. 116XU1 is unique.

LENOIR, N. C.

A1

E1

Handstamped Adhesive (from woodcut)
White wove paper with cross-ruled orange lines

49X1	A1	5c blue & orange	7,250.	6,750.

Handstamped Envelopes

49XU1	A1	5c blue	4,000.
49XU2	A1	10c (5c+5c) blue	25,000.
49XU3	E1	5c blue	4,500.
49XU4	E1	5c black	4,500.

No. 49XU2 is unique.

LEXINGTON, MISS.

E1

Handstamped Envelopes

50XU1	E1	5c black	4,500.
50XU2	E1	10c black	6,000.

Only one example is recorded of No. 50XU2.

LEXINGTON, VA.

E1

Handstamped Envelopes

135XU1	E1	5c blue	350.
135XU2	E1	10c blue	350.

Nos. 135XU1-135XU2 by themselves are indistinguishable from stampless covers when used.

LIBERTY, VA. (and Salem, Va.)

A1

Typeset Adhesive (probably impressed by hand)
Laid Paper

74X1	A1	5c black, on cover, uncanceled	35,000.

Two known on covers with Liberty, Va. postmark; one cover known with the nearby Salem, Va. office postmark.

LIMESTONE SPRINGS, S. C.

A1

Handstamped Adhesive

121X1	A1	5c black, light blue, on cover	10,000.
121X2	A1	5c black, white, two on cover	32,500.

Stamps are cut round or rectangular. Covers are not postmarked. The No. 121X2 cover bears the only two recorded examples of this stamp.

LIVINGSTON, ALA.

A1

Lithographed Adhesive

51X1	A1	5c blue	15,000.

LYNCHBURG, VA.

A1

E1

Typographed Adhesive
(stereotype from woodcut)

52X1	A1	5c blue (shades)	1,800.	1,500.

Press-printed Envelopes
(typographed)
Impressed at top right or left

52XU1	E1	5c black	700.00	4,000.
52XU2	E1	5c black, amber		4,000.
52XU3	E1	5c black, buff		4,000.
52XU4	E1	5c black, brown		4,000.

MACON, GA.

A1

A2

A3

A4

Typeset Adhesives
Several varieties of type A1, 10 of A2, 5 of A3
Wove Paper

53X1	A1	5c black, light blue green (shades)	1,250.	1,000.

Warning: Dangerous forgeries exist of the normal variety and the Comma after "OFFICE"

variety. Certificates of authenticity from recognized committees are strongly recommended.

53X3	A2	5c black, yellow	2,500.	1,250.
53X4	A3	5c black, yellow (shades)	3,000.	2,250.
a.		Vertical tête bêche pair		
53X5	A4	2c black, gray green	—	

Laid Paper

53X6	A2	5c black, yellow	6,000.	6,000.
53X7	A3	5c black, yellow	6,000.	
53X8	A1	5c black, light blue green	1,750.	2,250.

No. 53X4a is unique.

E1

Handstamped Envelope

Two types: "PAID" over "5," "5" over "PAID"

53XU1	E1	5c black	250.	650.

Values are for "PAID" over "5" variety. "5" over "PAID" is much scarcer.

MADISON, GA.

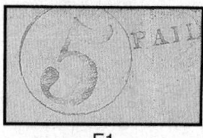
E1

Handstamped Envelope

136XU1	E1	5c red	600.

No. 136XU1 is indistinguishable from a handstamp paid cover when used.

MADISON COURT HOUSE, FLA.

E1

Typeset Envelope

137XU1	E1	5c black, yellow	25,000.

No. 137XU1 is unique.
See 3c 1861 Postmaster's Provisional No. 3AX1.

MARIETTA, GA.

E1

Control

E2

Handstamped Envelopes

54XU1	E1	5c black	500.
a.		10c on 5c black	1,750.

With Double Circle Control

54XU3	E1	10c black	
54XU4	E2	5c black	2,000.

The existence of No. 54XU3 has been questioned by specialists. The editors would like to see authenticated evidence that verifies this listing.

MARION, VA.

A1

Adhesives with Typeset frame and Handstamped numeral in center

55X1	A1	5c black		7,500.
55X2	A1	10c black	16,500.	10,000.
55X3	A1	5c black, bluish, laid paper		—

The 2c, 3c, 15c and 20c are believed to be bogus items printed later using the original typeset frame.

MARS BLUFF, S. C.

E1

145XU1	E1	5c black	2,000.

The No. 145XU1 marking is a provisional only when unused, used from another town or used under a general issue.

MEMPHIS, TENN.

A1

56X1a
Partial Print

A2

Typographed Adhesives (stereotyped from woodcut)

56X1	A1	2c blue (shades)	100.	1,250.
	a.	Partial print	250.	
56X2	A2	5c red (shades)	150.	250.
	a.	Tête bêche pair		1,500.
	b.	Pair, one sideways	2,500.	
	c.	Pelure paper	—	

Press-printed Envelopes (typographed)

56XU1	A2	5c red (shades)		3,000.
56XU2	A2	5c red, amber		3,500.
56XU3	A2	5c red, orange		2,500.
56XU4	A2	5c red, cream	5,750.	

Only one example of No. 56XU4 is recorded. It is on a cover on which a C.S.A. No. 11 affixed over the provisional to pay the postage.

MICANOPY, FLA.

E1

Handstamped Envelope

105XU1	E1	5c black	11,500.

One example recorded.

MILLEDGEVILLE, GA.

E1

E2

E3

Handstamped Envelopes

Two types of No. 57XU5: Type I, tall, thin "1" and "0" of "10"; Type II, short, fat "1" and "0" of "10."

57XU1	E1	5c black		500.
	a.	Wide spacing between "I" and "D" of "PAID"		600.
	b.	10c on 5c black		1,000.
57XU2	E1	5c blue		800.
57XU4	E2	10c black	375.	1,200.
	a.	Wide spacing between "I" and "D" of "PAID"		1,200.
57XU5	E3	10c black, type I	450.	800.
	a.	Type II		1,500.

On No. 57XU4, the "PAID/10" virtually always falls outside the Milledgeville control marking (as in illustration E1).

The existence of No. 57XU2 as a provisional has been questioned by specialists. The editors would like to see authenticated evidence of provisional use of this marking.

MILTON, N. C.

E1

Handstamped Envelope, "5" Manuscript

138XU1	E1	5c black	3,000.

MOBILE, ALA.

A1

Lithographed Adhesives

58X1	A1	2c black	2,250.	1,200.
58X2	A1	5c blue	350.	450.

MONTGOMERY, ALA.

E1

E1a

Handstamped Envelopes

59XU1	E1	5c red		1,100.
	a.	10c on 5c red		2,750.
59XU2	E1	5c blue	400.	1,000.
59XU3	E1a	10c red		900.
59XU4	E1a	10c blue		1,250.
59XU5	E1a	10c black		850.

MONTGOMERY, ALA.

E2

E3

59XU7	E2	2c red	2,500.
59XU7A	E2	2c blue	3,500.
59XU8	E2	5c black	2,000.
59XU9	E3	10c black	2,500.
59XU10	E3	10c red	1,750.

The existence of No. 59XU10 is in question. The editors would like to see an authenticated example of this marking.

MT. LEBANON, LA.

A1

Woodcut Adhesive (mirror image of design)

60X1	A1	5c red brown, on cover	255,000.

One example known. Value represents sale price at 2009 auction.

NASHVILLE, TENN.

A2   E1

Typographed Adhesives (stereotyped from woodcut)
Gray Blue Ribbed Paper

61X2	A2	5c carmine (shades)	1,000.	650.
	a.	Vertical tête bêche pair		4,000.
61X3	A2	5c brick red (shades)	1,000.	1,000.
61X4	A2	5c gray (shades)	1,250.	1,500.
61X5	A2	5c violet brown (shades)	1,250.	750.
	a.	Vertical tete bêche pair	5,000.	7,500.
61X6	A2	10c green	—	7,500.

Handstamped Envelopes

61XU1	E1	5c blue	900.
61XU2	E1	10c on 5c blue	2,750.

See 3c Postmaster's Provisional No. 4AX1.

NEW ORLEANS, LA.

A1

A2

Typographed Adhesives (stereotyped from woodcut)

62X1	A1	2c blue	225.	800.
	a.	Printed on both sides, on cover		10,500.
62X2	A1	2c red (shades)	190.	1,000.
62X3	A2	5c brown, white	300.	200.
	a.	Printed on both sides		3,750.
	b.	5c ocher	700.	625.
62X4	A2	5c red brn, bluish	325.	200.
	a.	Printed on both sides		3,250.
62X5	A2	5c yel brn, off-white	160.	250.
62X6	A2	5c red (shades)	—	14,000.

62X7	A2	5c red (shades), bluish	15,000.

E1

Handstamped Envelopes

62XU1	E1	5c black	4,500.
62XU2	E1	10c black	11,500.

"J. L. RIDDELL, P. M." omitted

62XU3	E1	2c black	9,500.

Some authorities question the use of No. 62XU3 as a provisional.

NEW SMYRNA, FLA.

A1

Handstamped Adhesive
On white paper with blue ruled lines

63X1	A1	10c ("O1") on 5c black	50,000.

One example known. It is uncanceled on a postmarked patriotic cover.

NORFOLK, VA.

E1

Manuscript Signature

Handstamped Envelopes
Ms Signature on Back

139XU1	E1	5c blue	1,000.	1,500.
139XU2	E1	10c blue		1,750.

OAKWAY, S. C.

A1

Handstamped Adhesive (from woodcut)

115X1	A1	5c black, on cover	60,000.

Two used examples of No. 115X1 are recorded, both on cover. Value represents 2012 auction realization for the cover on which the stamp is tied by manuscript "Paid."

PENSACOLA, FLA.

E1

Handstamped Envelopes

106XU1	E1	5c black	4,250.
	a.	10c (ms.) on 5c black	4,750.

PETERSBURG, VA.

A1

Typeset Adhesive
Ten varieties
65X1 A1 5c red
(shades)   2,250.   600.

PITTSYLVANIA COURT HOUSE, VA.

A1

Typeset Adhesives
66X1 A1 5c dull red,
      wove pa-
      per   7,500.   9,000.
66X2 A1 5c dull red, laid
      paper   5,500.

PLAINS OF DURA, GA.

E1

Handstamped Envelopes, Ms. Initials
140XU1 E1 5c black   —
140XU2 E1 10c black   5,000.
No. 140XU2 is unique.

PLEASANT SHADE, VA.

A1

Typeset Adhesive
Five varieties
67X1 A1 5c blue   8,000.   20,000.

PLUM CREEK, TEX.

E1

Manuscript Adhesive
141X1 E1 10c black, *blue*, on
      cover   —
The stamps have ruled lines with the value "10" in manuscript. Size and shape vary.

PORT GIBSON, MISS.

E1

Manuscript Signature

Handstamped Envelope, Ms Signature
142XU1 E1 5c black   —

PORT LAVACA, TEX.

A1

Typeset Adhesive
107X1 A1 10c black, on cover   25,000.
One example known. It is uncanceled on a postmarked cover.

RALEIGH, N. C.

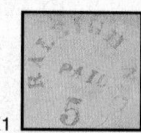

E1

Handstamped Envelopes
68XU1 E1 5c red   600.
68XU2 E1 5c blue   3,000.

RHEATOWN, TENN.

A1

Typeset Adhesive
Three varieties
69X1 A1 5c red   6,000.   6,500.

RICHMOND, TEX.

E1

Handstamped Envelopes or Letter Sheets
70XU1 E1 5c red   2,500.
    a. 10c on 5c red   5,000.
70XU2 E1 10c red   2,000.
    a. 15c (ms.) on 10c red   5,000.

RINGGOLD, GA.

E1

Handstamped Envelope
71XU1 E1 5c blue black   8,500.

RUTHERFORDTON, N. C.

A1

Handstamped Adhesive, Ms. "Paid 5cts"
72X1 A1 5c black, cut
      round, on
      cover (un-
      canceled)   60,000.
No. 72X1 is unique.

SALEM, N. C.

"Paid 5" in Ms.   "Paid 5"
— E1   Handstamped —
         E2

Handstamped Envelopes
73XU1 E1 5c black   1,750.
73XU2 E1 10c black   3,500.
73XU3 E2 5c black   2,250.
    a. 10c on 5c black   2,800.
Reprints exist on various papers. They either lack the "Paid" and value or have them counterfeited.

Salem, Va.
See No. 74X1 under Liberty, Va.

SALISBURY, N. C.

E1

Press-printed Envelope (typeset)
Impressed at top left
75XU1 E1 5c black,
         greenish   15,000.
One example known. Part of the envelope was torn away (now repaired), leaving part of design missing.

SAN ANTONIO, TEX.

E1

E2

Control

Handstamped Envelopes
76XU1 E1 10c black   500.   2,000.
76XU1A E2 5c black   1,500.
76XU2 E2 10c black   2,500.
Black circle control mark is on front or back.

SAVANNAH, GA.

E1

Control

SALEM, N. C.

E2

Handstamped Envelopes
101XU1 E1 5c black   400.
    a. 10c on 5c black   1,500.
101XU2 E2 5c black   600.
    a. 20c on 5c black   2,000.
101XU3 E1 10c black   750.
101XU4 E2 10c black   750.
Envelopes must have octagonal control mark. One example is known of No.101XU2a.

SELMA, ALA.

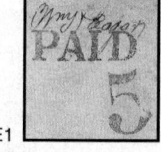

E1

Handstamped Envelopes; Signature in Ms.
77XU1 E1 5c black   1,250.
    a. 10c on 5c black   3,000.
77XU2 E1 10c black   2,500.
Signature is that of Postmaster William H. Eagar.
See 3c 1861 Postmaster's Provisional No. 5AX1.

SPARTA, GA.

E1

Handstamped Envelopes
93XU1 E1 5c red   —   2,250.
93XU2 E1 10c red   5,000.
Only one example recorded of No. 93XU2.

SPARTANBURG, S. C.

A1

A2

Handstamped Adhesives
(on ruled or plain wove paper)
78X1 A1 5c black, cut to
      shape   —
    a. "Paid" instead of denomi-
        nation, revalued to 5c
        with "PAID" and "5" in
        small circle handstamps   —
78X2 A2 5c black, *bluish*   4,000.
78X3 A2 5c black, *brown*   4,000.
Most examples of Nos. 78X1-78X3 are cut round. Cut square examples in sound condition are worth much more.

E1

Control

Handstamped Envelopes
78XU1 E1 10c black (control
on reverse) 5,000.

STATESVILLE, N. C.

E1

Handstamped Envelopes
79XU1 E1 5c black 1,500.
   a. 10c on 5c black 3,000.

Unused examples of No. 79XU1 are reprints.

SUMTER, S. C.

E1

Handstamped Envelopes
80XU1 E1 5c black 500.
   a. 10c on 5c black 900.
80XU2 E1 10c black 600.
   a. 2c (ms.) on 10c black 1,100.

Used examples of Nos. 80XU1-80XU2 are indistinguishable from handstamped "Paid" covers.

TALBOTTON, GA.

E1

Handstamped Envelopes
94XU1 E1 5c black 900.
   a. 10c on 5c black 2,000.
94XU2 E1 10c black 1,000.

TALLADEGA, ALA.

E1

Handstamped Envelopes
143XU1 E1 5c black 1,500. —
143XU2 E1 10c black 1,500. —

These same markings were used on hand-stamped "Paid" covers.

TELLICO PLAINS, TENN.

A1

Typeset Adhesives
Laid Paper
81X1 A1 5c red 2,500. —
81X2 A1 10c red 4,000.

THOMASVILLE, GA.

E1

Control

Handstamped Envelopes
82XU1 E1 5c black 750.

On No. 82XU1, the control is on the reverse of the cover. The dated control is known with four different dates, including June 18, June 21 and August 23. The patriotic cover use is unique.

E2

82XU2 E2 5c black 1,000.

TULLAHOMA, TENN.

E1 Control

Handstamped Envelope
111XU1 E1 10c black 6,000.

The control appears either on the front or the back of the envelope.

TUSCALOOSA, ALA.

E1

Handstamped Envelopes
83XU1 E1 5c black 250.
83XU2 E1 10c black 250.

Used examples of Nos. 83XU1-83XU2 are indistinguishable from handstamped "Paid" covers.

TUSCUMBIA, ALA.

E1

Handstamped Envelopes
84XU1 E1 5c black 4,000.
84XU2 E1 5c red 5,000.
84XU3 E1 10c black 5,250.

See 3c 1861 Postmaster's Provisional No. 6AXU1.

UNIONTOWN, ALA.

A1

Typeset Adhesives
(settings of 4 (2x2), 4 varieties of each value)
Laid Paper
86X1 A1 2c dark blue,
    gray blue,
    on cover —
86X2 A1 2c dark blue,
    sheet of 4 40,000.
86X3 A1 5c green, gray
    blue 4,000. 3,250.
86X4 A1 5c green, gray
    blue 4,000. 3,250.
86X5 A1 10c red, gray
    blue

Two examples known of No. 86X1, both on cover (drop letters), one uncanceled and one pen canceled.

The only recorded examples of No. 86X2 are in a unique sheet of 4.

The item listed as No. 86X5 used is an uncanceled stamp on a large piece with part of addressee's name in manuscript.

UNIONVILLE, S. C.

A1

Handstamped Adhesive
"PAID" and "5" applied separately
Paper with Blue Ruled Lines
87X1 A1 5c black, grayish —

VALDOSTA, GA.

E1 Control

E2

Handstamped Envelopes
100XU1 E1 10c black 9,000.
100XU2 E2 5c +5c black —

The black circle control must appear on front of the No. 100XU2 envelope and on the back of the No. 100XU1 envelope.

There is one recorded cover each of Nos. 100XU1-100XU2.

VICTORIA, TEX.

A1 A2

Typeset Adhesives
Surface colored paper
88X1 A1 5c red brown,
    green 20,000.
88X2 A1 10c red brown,
    green 22,500.
88X3 A2 10c red brown,
    green,
    pelure
    paper 32,500. 30,000.

WALTERBOROUGH, S. C.

E1

Handstamped Envelopes
108XU1 E1 10c black, buff —
108XU2 E1 10c carmine 4,000.

The existence of No. 108XU1 is in question. The editors would like to see authenticated evidence of its existence.

WARRENTON, GA.

E1

Handstamped Envelopes
89XU1 E1 5c black 2,100.
   a. 10c (ms.) on 5c black 1,000.

Fakes of the Warrenton provisional marking based on the illustration shown are known on addressed but postally unused covers.

WASHINGTON, GA.

 E1

Handstamped Envelope
117XU1 E1 10c black 2,000.

Envelopes must have black circle postmark control on the back. Examples with the undated control on the front are not considered provisional unless a dated postmark is also present.

WEATHERFORD, TEX.

E1

Handstamped Envelopes
(woodcut with "PAID" inserted in type)
109XU1 E1 5c black 2,000.
109XU2 E1 5c +5c black 11,000.

One example is known of No. 109XU2.

WILKESBORO, N. C.

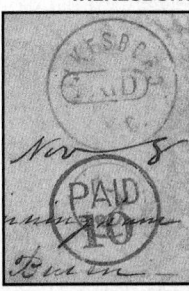

E1

Handstamped Envelope
147XU1 E1 5c black, revalued to
    10c —

No. 147XU1 is unique.

WINNSBOROUGH, S. C.

E1   Control

Handstamped Envelopes

97XU1	E1	5c black	2,000.
		On patriotic cover	3,750.
97XU2	E1	10c black	3,500.

Envelopes must have black circle control on front or back.

WYTHEVILLE, VA.

E1   Control

Handstamped Envelope

114XU1	E1	5c black	900.

For later additions, listed out of numerical sequence, see:

GENERAL ISSUES

Jefferson Davis — A1

1861   Unwmk.   Litho.   *Imperf.*

1	A1	5c green		
		(shades)	300.	175.
		No gum	175.	
a.		5c light green	275.	175.
		No gum	160.	
b.		5c dark green	375.	250.
		No gum	225.	
c.		5c olive green	400.	250.
		No gum	240.	

Thomas Jefferson — A2

1861-62

2	A2	10c blue	275.	180.
		No gum	150.	
a.		10c light blue	300.	200.
		No gum	175.	
b.		10c dark blue	700.	300.
		No gum	400.	
c.		10c indigo	5,000.	7,500.
		No gum	2,500.	
d.		Printed on both sides		1,750.
e.		light milky blue	1,250.	325.
		No gum	700.	

Specialists have questioned the existence of No. 2bd, the Hoyer & Ludwig printed on both sides. The editors would like to see authenticated evidence of its existence.

The earliest printings of No. 2 were made by Hoyer & Ludwig, the later ones by J. T. Paterson & Co.

Stamps of the later printings usually have a small colored dash below the lowest point of the upper left spandrel.

Andrew Jackson — A3

1862

3	A3	2c green	1,000.	750.
		No gum	575.	
a.		2c bright yellow green	2,000.	—
		No gum	1,300.	
4	A1	5c blue	225.	125.
		No gum	125.	
a.		5c dark blue	275.	175.
		No gum	150.	
b.		5c light milky blue	350.	200.
		No gum	190.	
5	A2	10c rose (shades)	2,400.	.450
		No gum	1,250.	
a.		10c carmine	3,750.	1,900.
		No gum	2,200.	

Jefferson Davis — A4

Typo.

6	A4	5c light blue	16.00	28.
		No gum	7.00	
7	A4	5c blue (De La Rue thin paper)	20.00	22.
		No gum	10.00	
a.		5c deep blue	27.50	30.
		No gum	13.50	
b.		Printed on both sides	2,500.	1,400.

No. 6 has fine, clear impression. No. 7 has coarser impression and the color is duller and often blurred.

Both 2c and 10c stamps, types A4 and A10, were privately printed in various colors.

Andrew Jackson — A5

1863   Engr.

8	A5	2c brown red	75.	350.
		No gum	40.	
a.		2c pale red	90.	450.
		No gum	45.	

A6

Thick or Thin Paper

9	A6	10c blue	950.	500.
		No gum	600.	
a.		10c milky blue (first printing)	1,000.	550.
		No gum	600.	
b.		10c gray blue	1,050.	600.
		No gum	650.	

Jefferson Davis — A6a

10	A6a	10c blue (with frame line)	5,750.	2,100.
		No gum	3,750.	
a.		10c milky blue	5,750.	2,100.
		No gum	3,750.	
b.		10c greenish blue	6,250.	2,100.
		No gum	4,250.	
c.		10c dark blue	6,250.	2,100.
		No gum	4,250.	

Values of Nos. 10, 10a, 10b and 10c are for examples showing parts of lines on at least three sides. Used stamps showing 4 complete lines sell for approximately 3 to 4 times the values given. Unused stamps showing 4 complete lines are exceedingly rare (only two recorded), and the one sound example is valued at $35,000.

A7

There are many slight differences between A7 and A8, the most noticeable being the additional line outside the ornaments at the four corners of A8.

1863-64

11	A7	10c blue	16.	20.
		No gum	7.	
a.		10c milky blue	55.	60.
		No gum	30.	
b.		10c dark blue	25.	30.
		No gum	12.	
c.		10c greenish blue	30.	50.
		No gum	17.	
d.		10c green	85.	80.
		No gum	55.	
e.		Officially perforated 12½ (Archer & Daly printing)	400.	350.

George Washington — A9

1863

13	A9	20c green	45.	400.
		No gum	27.	
a.		20c yellow green	80.	450.
		No gum	50.	
b.		20c dark green	65.	500.
		No gum	40.	
c.		20c bluish green	100.	—
		No gum	65.	
d.		Diagonal half used as 10c on cover		2,000.
e.		Horizontal half used as 10c on cover		3,500.

John C. Calhoun — A10

1862   Typo.

14	A10	1c orange	100.	
		No gum	60.	
a.		1c deep orange	140.	
		No gum	85.	

No. 14 was never put in use.

A8

12	A8	10c blue	20.	25.
		No gum	9.	
a.		10c milky blue	55.	60.
		No gum	30.	
b.		10c light blue	19.	22.
		No gum	9.	
c.		10c greenish blue	40.	50.
		No gum	20.	
d.		10c dark blue	22.	25.
		No gum	11.	
e.		10c green	150.	140.
		No gum	85.	
f.		Officially perforated 12½ (Archer & Daly printing)	400.	375.

The paper of Nos. 11 and 12 varies from thin hard to thick soft. The stamp that sometimes is offered as "laid paper" is actually normal paper with thick, streaky gum.

CANAL ZONE

kə-'nal 'zōn

LOCATION — A strip of land 10 miles wide, extending through the Republic of Panama, between the Atlantic and Pacific Oceans.

GOVT. — From 1904-79 a U.S. Government Reservation; from 1979-99 under joint control of the Republic of Panama and the U.S.

AREA — 552.8 sq. mi.

POP. — 41,800 (est. 1976)

The Canal Zone, site of the Panama Canal, was leased in perpetuity to the U.S. for a cash payment of $10,000,000 and a yearly rental. Treaties between the two countries provided for joint jurisdiction by the U.S. and Panama, 1979-1999, with Panama handling postal service. At the end of 1999, the canal, in its entirety, reverted to Panama.

100 Centavos = 1 Peso
100 Centesimos = 1 Balboa
100 Cents = 1 Dollar

Catalogue values for unused stamps in this country are for Never Hinged items, beginning with Scott 118 in the regular postage section and Scott C6 in the air post section.

Watermarks

Wmk. 190 — "USPS" in Single-lined Capitals

Wmk. 191 — Double-lined "USPS" in Capitals

Map of Panama — A1

Violet to Violet-Blue Handstamp on Panama Nos. 72, 72a-72c, 78, 79.

On the 2c "PANAMA" is normally 13mm long. On the 5c and 10c it measures about 15mm.

On the 2c, "PANAMA" reads up on the upper half of the sheet and down on the lower half. On the 5c and 10c, "PANAMA" reads up at left and down at right on each stamp.

On the 2c only, varieties exist with inverted "V" for "A," accent on "A," inverted "N," etc., in "PANAMA."

Unwmk.

1904, June 24	Engr.	Perf. 12	
1	A1	2c rose, both "PANAMA" reading up or down	650.	400.
a.	"CANAL ZONE" inverted	1,000.	850.
b.	"CANAL ZONE" double	4,250.	2,000.
c.	"CANAL ZONE" double, both inverted	20,000.	
d.	"PANAMA" reading down and up	750.	650.
e.	As "d," "CANAL ZONE" invtd.	9,000.	9,000.
f.	Vert. pair, "PANAMA" reading up on top 2c, down on other	2,100.	2,100.
g.	As "f," "CANAL ZONE" inverted	20,000.	
2	A1	5c blue	300.	190.
a.	"CANAL ZONE" inverted	775.	600.
b.	"CANAL ZONE" double	2,250.	1,500.
c.	Pair, one without "CANAL ZONE" overprint	5,000.	5,000.
d.	"CANAL ZONE" overprint diagonal, reading down to right	800.	700.
3	A1	10c yellow	400.	230.
a.	"CANAL ZONE" inverted	775.	600.
b.	"CANAL ZONE" double		14,000.

---

c.	Pair, one without "CANAL ZONE" overprint	6,000.	5,000.
	Nos. 1-3 (3)	1,350.	820.00

Cancellations consist of town and/or bars in magenta or black, or a mixture of both colors. Nos. 1-3 were withdrawn July 17, 1904. Forgeries of the "Canal Zone" overprint and cancellations are numerous.

United States Nos. 300, 319, 304, 306 & 307 Ovptd. in Black

1904, July 18			Wmk. 191	
4	A115	1c blue green	40.00	22.50
5	A129	2c carmine	35.00	25.00
a.		2c scarlet	35.00	30.00
6	A119	5c blue	95.00	65.00
7	A121	8c violet black	150.00	85.00
8	A122	10c pale red brown	140.00	90.00
		Nos. 4-8 (5)	460.00	287.50

Beware of fake overprints.

A2

A3

CANAL ZONE Regular Type	CANAL ZONE Antique Type

1904-06   **Unwmk.**

Black Overprint on Stamps of Panama

9	A2	1c green	2.75	2.00
a.	"CANAL" in antique type	100.00	100.00
b.	"ZONE" in antique type	70.00	70.00
c.	Inverted overprint	7,500.	6,000.
d.	Double overprint	2,750.	2,000.
10	A2	2c rose	4.50	2.75
a.	Inverted overprint	225.00	275.00
b.	"L" of "CANAL" sideways	2,000.	2,250.

"PANAMA" (15mm long) reading up at left, down at right

Overprint "CANAL ZONE" in Black, "PANAMA" and Bar in Red

11	A3	2c rose	7.00	5.00
a.	"ZONE" in antique type	200.00	200.00
b.	"PANAMA" overprint inverted, bar at bottom	600.00	675.00
12	A3	5c blue	8.00	3.25
a.	"CANAL" in antique type	75.00	65.00
b.	"ZONE" in antique type	75.00	65.00
c.	"CANAL ZONE" double	800.00	800.00
d.	"PANAMA" double	1,100.	1,000.
e.	"PANAMA" inverted, bar at bottom	1,000.	1,250.
f.	"PANAAM" at right	950.00	750.00
13	A3	10c yellow	18.00	12.00
a.	"CANAL" in antique type	190.00	200.00
b.	"ZONE" in antique type	175.00	160.00
c.	"PANAMA" ovpt. double	650.00	650.00
d.	"PANAMA" overprint in red brown	27.50	25.00
		Nos. 11-13 (3)	33.00	20.25

With Added Surcharge in Red

a

14	A3	8c on 50c bister brown	30.00	27.50
a.	"ZONE" in antique type	1,150.	1,150.
b.	"CANAL ZONE" inverted	450.00	425.00
c.	"PANAMA" overprint in rose brown	37.50	37.50
d.	As "c," "CANAL" in antique type	1,750.	850.00
e.	As "c," "ZONE" in antique type	1,750.	

---

f.	As "c," "8 cts" double	1,100.	
g.	As "c," "8" omitted	4,500.	
h.	As "c," "cts 8"		

Nos. 11-14 are overprinted or surcharged on Panama Nos. 77, 77e, 78, 78c, 78d, 78f, 78g, 78h, 79 79c, 79e, 79g and 81 respectively.

On No. 14 with original gum, the gum is almost always disturbed. Unused stamps are valued thus.

Panama No. 74a, 74b Overprinted "CANAL ZONE" in Regular Type in Black and Surcharged Type "a" in Red Both "PANAMA" (13mm long) Reading Up

15	A3(a)	8c on 50c bister brown	2,000.	4,750.
a.	"PANAMA" reading down and up	6,000.	—

On No. 15 with original gum, the gum is almost always disturbed. Unused stamps are valued thus.

Map of Panama — A4

Panama Nos. 19 and 21 Surcharged in Black

a

b

c

---

d

e

f

There were three printings of each denomination, differing principally in the relative position of the various parts of the surcharges. Varieties occur with inverted "V" for the final "A" in "PANAMA," "CA" spaced, "ZO" spaced, "2c" spaced, accents in various positions, and with bars shifted so that two bars appear on top or bottom of the stamp (either with or without the corresponding bar on top or bottom) and sometimes with only one bar at top or bottom.

1906				
16	A4	1c on 20c violet, type a	1.90	1.60
a.	Type b		1.90	1.60
b.	Type c		2.00	1.50
c.	As No. 16, double surcharge		2,000.	
17	A4	2c on 1p lake, type d	2.75	2.75
a.	Type e		2.75	2.75
b.	Type f		20.00	20.00

Panama Nos. 74, 74a and 74b Overprinted "CANAL ZONE" in Regular Type in Black and Surcharged in Red

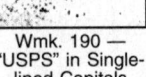

b

c

1905-06

Both "PANAMA" Reading Up

18	A3(b)	8c on 50c bister brown	50.00	50.00
a.		"ZONE" in antique type	200.00	180.00
b.		"PANAMA" reading down and up	175.00	160.00
19	A3(c)	8c on 50c bister brown	55.00	40.00
a.		"CANAL" in antique type	210.00	180.00
b.		"ZONE" in antique type	210.00	180.00
c.		"8 cts" double	1,100.	1,100.
d.		"PANAMA" reading down and up	110.00	90.00

On Nos. 18-19 with original gum, the gum is usually disturbed. Unused stamps are valued thus.

Panama No. 81 Overprinted "CANAL ZONE" in Regular Type in Black and Surcharged in Red Type "c" plus Period

"PANAMA" reading up and down

20	A3(c)	8c on 50c bister brown	35.00	37.50
a.		"CANAL" antique type	200.00	180.00
b.		"ZONE" in antique type	200.00	180.00
c.		"8 cts" omitted	800.00	800.00
d.		"8 cts" double	1,500.	
e.		"cts 8"		

Nos. 14 and 18-20 exist without CANAL ZONE overprint but were not regularly issued and are considered printer's waste. Forgeries of the overprint varieties of Nos. 9-15 and 18-20 are known.

On No. 20 with original gum, the gum is usually disturbed. Unused stamps are valued thus.

Francisco Hernandez de Cordoba — A5

Vasco Nunez de Balboa — A6

Fernández de Córdoba A7

Justo Arosemena A8

Manuel J. Hurtado — A9

Jose de Obaldia — A10

Stamps of Panama Overprinted in Black

1906-07   **Perf. 12**

Overprint Reading Up

21	A5	2c red & black	27.50	27.50
a.		"CANAL" only	4,000.	

Overprint Reading Down

22	A6	1c green & black	2.00	1.00
a.		Horiz. pair, imperf. btwn.	1,100.	1,100.
b.		Vert. pair, imperf. btwn.	2,000.	2,000.
c.		Vert. pair, imperf. horiz.	2,250.	1,750.
d.		Inverted overprint reading up	550.00	550.00
e.		Double overprint	275.00	275.00
f.		Double overprint, one inverted	1,750.	1,600.
g.		Invtd. center, ovpt. reading up	3,500.	4,750.
h.		Horiz. pair, imperf vert.	5,000.	
23	A7	2c red & black	3.00	1.10
a.		Horizontal pair, imperf. between	2,000.	2,000.
b.		Vertical pair, one without overprint	2,500.	2,500.
c.		Double overprint	600.00	650.00
d.		Double overprint, one diagonal	800.00	800.00
e.		Double overprint, one diagonal, in pair with normal	2,500.	
f.		2c carmine red & black	5.00	2.75
g.		As "f," inverted center and overprint reading up	14,000.	
h.		As "d," one "ZONE CANAL"	4,000.	
i.		"CANAL" double	6,250.	

24	A8	5c ultramarine & black	5.75	2.25
c.		Double overprint	500.00	400.00
d.		"CANAL" only	7,000.	
e.		"ZONE CANAL"	5,000.	
25	A9	8c purple & black	20.00	8.00
a.		Horizontal pair, imperf. between and at left margin	1,750.	4,000.
26	A10	10c violet & black	20.00	7.00
a.		Dbl. ovpt., one reading up	5,000.	
b.		Overprint reading up	5,500.	
		Nos. 22-26 (5)	50.75	19.35

Nos. 22-25 occur with "CA" of "CANAL" spaced ½mm further apart on position No. 50 of the setting.
The used pair of No. 25a is unique.

Cordoba A11

Arosemena A12

Hurtado — A13

Jose de Obaldia — A14

1909

Overprint Reading Down

27	A11	2c vermilion & black	12.00	5.00
a.		Horizontal pair, one without overprint	2,600.	
b.		Vert. pair, one without ovpt.	3,500.	
28	A12	5c deep blue & black	40.00	12.50
29	A13	8c violet & black	37.50	14.00
30	A14	10c violet & black	40.00	14.00
a.		Horizontal pair, one with "ZONE" omitted	3,000.	
b.		Vertical pair, one without overprint	4,000.	
		Nos. 27-30 (4)	129.50	45.50

Nos. 27-30 occur with "CA" spaced (position 50).
Do not confuse No. 27 with Nos. 39d or 53a. On No. 30a, the stamp with "ZONE" omitted is also missing most of "CANAL."
For designs A11-A14 with overprints reading up, see Nos. 32-35, 39-41, 47-48, 53-54, 56-57.

Black Overprint Reading Up

Vasco Nunez de Balboa — A15

Type I

Type I Overprint: "C" with serifs both top and bottom. "L," "Z" and "E" with slanting serifs.
Compare Type I overprint with Types II to V illustrated before Nos. 38, 46, 52 and 55.

1909-10

31	A15	1c dark green & black	4.25	1.25
a.		Inverted center and overprint reading down		22,500.
c.		Bklt. pane of 6, handmade, perf. margins	500.00	
32	A11	2c vermilion & black	4.50	1.25
a.		Vert. pair, imperf. horiz.	1,000.	1,000.
c.		Bklt. pane of 6, handmade, perf. margins	800.00	
d.		Double overprint (I)		6,000.
33	A12	5c deep blue & black	17.00	3.50
a.		Double overprint	375.00	375.00

34	A13	8c violet & black	11.00	5.00
a.		Vertical pair, one without overprint	1,750.	
35	A14	10c violet & black	47.50	20.00
		Nos. 31-35 (5)	84.25	31.00

No. 32d is unique and has small faults. See Nos. 38, 46, 52, 55.

A16

A17

Black Surcharge

1911, Jan. 14

36	A16	10c on 13c gray	6.00	2.00
a.		"10 cts" inverted	300.00	300.00
b.		"10 cts" omitted	300.00	

Many used stamps offered as No. 36b are merely No. 36 from which the surcharge has been chemically removed.

1914, Jan. 6

37	A17	10c gray	47.50	11.00

Black Overprint Reading Up

Type II: "C" with serif at top only. "L" and "E" with vertical serifs. "O" tilts to left

1912-16

38	A15	1c green & black	10.00	3.00
a.		Vertical pair, one without overprint	1,750.	1,750.
b.		Booklet pane of 6, imperf. margins	575.00	
c.		Booklet pane of 6, handmade, perf. margins	1,000.	
39	A11	2c vermilion & black	8.00	1.10
a.		Horiz. pair, right stamp without overprint	1,250.	
b.		Horiz. pair, left stamp without overprint	1,500.	
c.		Booklet pane of 6, imperf. margins	550.00	
d.		Overprint reading down	200.00	
e.		As "d," inverted center	600.00	750.00
f.		As "e," booklet pane of 6, handmade, perf. margins	8,000.	
g.		As "c," handmade, perf. margins	900.00	800.00
h.		As No. 39, "CANAL" only		1,100.
40	A12	5c deep blue & black	20.00	2.50
a.		With Cordoba portrait of 2c		12,500.
41	A14	10c violet & black	60.00	7.50
		Nos. 38-41 (4)	98.00	14.10

Map of Panama Canal A18

Balboa Takes Possession of the Pacific Ocean A19

Gatun Locks — A20

Culebra Cut — A21

1915, Mar. 1

Blue Overprint, Type II

42	A18	1c dark green & black	8.75	6.50
43	A19	2c carmine & black	12.00	4.25
44	A20	5c blue & black	10.00	5.75
45	A21	10c orange & black	19.00	11.00
		Nos. 42-45 (4)	49.75	27.50

Black Overprint Reading Up

Type III Overprint: Similar to Type I but letters appear thinner, particularly the lower bar of "L," "Z" and "E." Impressions are often light, rough and irregular, and not centered.

1915-20

46	A15	1c green & black	175.00	125.00
a.		Overprint reading down	375.00	
b.		Double overprint	225.00	
c.		"ZONE" omitted	6,500.	
d.		Double overprint, one reads "ZONE CANAL"	2,000.	
47	A11	2c orange vermilion & black	2,750.	60.00
48	A12	5c deep blue & black	450.00	130.00
		Nos. 46-48 (3)	3,375.	315.00

Spacing between words of overprint on Nos. 46-48 is 9¼mm; spacing varieties are not known. This should not be confused with a fairly common 9¼mm spacing of the 2c value of type I, nor with an uncommon 9¼mm spacing variety of the 5c of type I.

S.S. "Panama" in Culebra Cut — A22

S.S. "Panama" in Culebra Cut — A23

S.S. "Cristobal" in Gatun Locks — A24

1917, Jan. 23

Blue Overprint, Type II

49	A22	12c purple & black	17.50	5.25
50	A23	15c bright blue & black	50.00	17.50
51	A24	24c yellow brown & black	35.00	13.00
		Nos. 49-51 (3)	102.50	35.75

Black Overprint Reading Up

Type IV: "C" thick at bottom, "E" with center bar same length as top and bottom bars

1918-20

52	A15	1c green & black	32.50	10.00
a.		Overprint reading down	175.00	—
b.		Booklet pane of 6	600.00	
c.		Booklet pane of 6, left vertical row of 3 without overprint	7,500.	
d.		Booklet pane of 6, right vertical row of 3 without overprint	7,500.	
e.		Horiz. bklt. pair, left stamp without overprint	3,000.	
f.		Horiz. bklt. pair, right stamp with double overprint	3,000.	

g. Double overprint, booklet single ... 3,000.
53 A11 2c vermilion & black 110.00 6.00
a. Overprint reading down 150.00 150.00
b. Horiz. pair, right stamp without ovpt. (from misregistered overprints) 2,000.
c. Booklet pane of 6 1,050.
d. Booklet pane of 6, left vertical row of 3 without overprint 15,000.
e. Horiz. bklt. pair, left stamp without overprint 3,000.
f. Horiz. sheet pair, one without overprint (from foldover) 1,750.
54 A12 5c deep blue & black 150.00 32.50
Nos. 52-54 (3) 292.50 48.50

No. 53e used is unique and is on cover.

Black Overprint Reading Up

Type V: Smaller block type 1¾mm high. "A" with flat top

1920-21
55 A15 1c light green & black 22.50 3.25
a. Overprint reading down 300.00 225.00
b. Horiz. pair, right stamp without ovpt. 1,750.
c. Horiz. pair, left stamp without ovpt. 1,000.
d. "ZONE" only 4,000. —
e. Booklet pane of 6 2,250.
f. As No. 55, "CANAL" double 2,000.
56 A11 2c orange vermilion & black 8.50 1.75
a. Double overprint 500.00
b. Double overprint, one reading down 600.00
c. Horiz. pair, right stamp without overprint 1,400.
d. Horiz. pair, left stamp without overprint 1,000.
e. Vertical pair, one without overprint 1,500.
f. "ZONE" double 900.00
g. Booklet pane of 6 900.00
h. As No. 56, "CANAL" double 800.
57 A12 5c deep blue & black 300.00 45.00
a. Horiz. pair, right stamp without overprint 2,250.
b. Horiz. pair, left stamp without overprint 2,250.
Nos. 55-57 (3) 331.00 50.00

Drydock at Balboa A25

Ship in Pedro Miguel Locks — A26

1920, Sept.
Black Overprint Type V
58 A25 50c orange & black 250.00 160.00
59 A26 1b dark violet & black 175.00 50.00

Jose Vallarino — A27

The "Land Gate" — A28

Bolivar's Tribute — A29

Municipal Building in 1821 and 1921 — A30

Statue of Balboa — A31

Tomas Herrera — A32

Jose de Fabrega — A33

Type V overprint in black, reading up, on all values except the 5c which is overprinted with larger type in red

1921, Nov. 13
60 A27 1c green 3.75 1.50
a. "CANAL" double 1,900.
b. Booklet pane of 6 900.00
61 A28 2c carmine 2.75 1.00
a. Overprint reading down 200.00 225.00
b. Double overprint 900.00
c. Vertical pair, one without overprint 3,500.
d. "ZONE" double 1,900.
f. Booklet pane of 6 2,000.
62 A29 5c blue (R) 10.00 3.00
a. Overprint reading down (R) 60.00
63 A30 10c violet 18.00 7.50
a. Overprint, reading down 90.00
64 A31 15c light blue 47.50 17.50
65 A32 24c black brown 67.50 22.50
66 A33 50c black 145.00 85.00
Nos. 60-66 (7) 294.50 138.00

Experts question the status of the 5c with a small type V overprint in red or black.

Type III overprint in black, reading up

Coat of Arms — A34

1924, Jan. 28
67 A27 1c green 500. 200.
a. "ZONE CANAL" reading down 800.
b. "ZONE" only, reading down 1,900.
c. Se-tenant pair, #67a and 67b 2,750.

1924, Feb.
68 A34 1c dark green 10.00 4.50
69 A34 2c carmine 7.00 2.75

The 5c to 1b values were prepared but never issued. See listing in the Scott U.S. specialized catalogue.

United States Nos. 551-554, 557, 562, 564-566, 569, 570 and 571 Overprinted in Red (No. 70) or Black (all others)

Type A: Letters "A" with Flat Tops

1924-25 Unwmk. Perf. 11
70 A154 ½c olive brown .25 .70
Never hinged .40
71 A155 1c deep green 1.40 1.00
Never hinged 2.50
a. Inverted overprint 500.00 500.00
b. "ZONE" inverted 350.00 325.00
c. "CANAL" only 1,150.
d. "ZONE CANAL" 400.00
e. Booklet pane of 6 80.00 —
72 A156 1½c yellow brown 2.00 1.70
Never hinged 3.25
73 A157 2c carmine 6.75 1.70
Never hinged 10.50
a. Booklet pane of 6 175.00
74 A160 5c dark blue 16.00 7.00
Never hinged 25.00
75 A165 10c orange 40.00 20.00
Never hinged 65.00
76 A167 12c brown violet 32.50 30.00
Never hinged 62.50
a. "ZONE" inverted 3,750. 3,000.

77 A168 14c dark blue 27.50 22.50
Never hinged 45.00
78 A169 15c gray 45.00 37.50
Never hinged 70.00
79 A172 30c olive brown 32.50 20.00
Never hinged 52.50
80 A173 50c lilac 75.00 45.00
Never hinged 150.00
81 A174 $1 violet brown 225.00 95.00
Never hinged 400.00
Nos. 70-81 (12) 503.90 282.10

Normal spacing between words of the overprint is 9¼mm. Minor spacing variations are known.

All examples of Nos. 71b and 76a have a natural straight edge at right.

Type B: Letters "A" with Sharp Pointed Tops

1925-28
84 A157 2c carmine 27.50 8.00
Never hinged 45.00
a. "CANAL" only 2,250.
b. "ZONE CANAL" 425.00
c. Horizontal pair, one without overprint 3,500.
d. Booklet pane of 6 175.00
e. Vertical pair, "a" and "b" se-tenant 3,500.
85 A158 3c violet 3.75 3.00
Never hinged 6.00
a. "ZONE ZONE" 550.00 550.00
86 A160 5c dark blue 3.50 2.75
Never hinged 6.00
a. "ZONE ZONE" (LR18) 1,000.
b. "CANAL" inverted (LR7) 950.00
c. Inverted overprint 500.00
d. Horizontal pair, one without overprint 3,250.
e. Overprinted "ZONE CANAL" 350.00
f. "ZONE" only 2,000.
g. Vertical pair, one without overprint, other overprint inverted 2,250.
h. "CANAL" only 2,250.
87 A165 10c orange 35.00 12.00
Never hinged 52.50
a. "ZONE ZONE" (LR18) 3,000.
88 A167 12c brown violet 20.00 12.50
Never hinged 34.00
a. "ZONE ZONE" (LR18) 5,000.
89 A168 14c dark blue 27.50 15.00
Never hinged 42.50
90 A169 15c gray 7.50 4.50
Never hinged 12.00
a. "ZONE ZONE" (LR18) 5,500.
91 A187 17c black 4.50 2.75
Never hinged 7.50
a. "ZONE" only 1,000.
b. "CANAL" only 2,000.
c. "ZONE CANAL" 275.00
92 A170 20c carmine rose 7.25 3.25
Never hinged 12.00
a. "CANAL" inverted (UR48) 6,500.
b. "ZONE" inverted (LL76) 4,750.
c. "ZONE CANAL" (LL91) 4,750.
93 A172 30c olive brown 5.75 3.75
Never hinged 9.00
94 A173 50c lilac 230.00 165.00
Never hinged 400.00
95 A174 $1 violet brown 120.00 55.00
Never hinged 250.00
Nos. 84-95 (12) 492.25 287.50

Overprint Type B on U.S. Sesquicentennial Stamp No. 627

1926
96 A188 2c carmine rose 4.50 3.75
Never hinged 6.75

On this stamp there is a space of 5mm instead of 9mm between the two words of the overprint.

Overprint Type B in Black on U.S. Nos. 583, 584, 591

1926-27 Perf. 10
97 A157 2c carmine 45.00 11.00
Never hinged 75.00
a. Pair, one without overprint 2,500.
b. Booklet pane of 6 500.00
c. "CANAL" only 2,000.
d. "ZONE" only 2,750.
98 A158 3c violet 7.50 4.25
Never hinged 11.00
99 A165 10c orange 18.00 7.50
Never hinged 27.50
Nos. 97-99 (3) 70.50 22.75

No. 97d is valued in the grade of fine. Very fine examples are not known.

Overprint Type B in Black on U.S. Nos. 632, 634 (Type I), 635, 637, 642

1927-31 Perf. 11x10½
100 A155 1c green 1.75 1.40
Never hinged 2.60
a. Vertical pair, one without overprint 3,500.
101 A157 2c carmine 1.75 1.00
Never hinged 2.50
a. Booklet pane of 6 200.00

102 A158 3c violet 4.25 2.75
Never hinged 6.25
a. Booklet pane of 6, hand-made, perf. margins 6,500.
103 A160 5c dark blue 25.00 10.00
Never hinged 45.00
104 A165 10c orange 17.50 10.00
Never hinged 26.00
Nos. 100-104 (5) 50.25 25.15

Wet and Dry Printings
Canal Zone stamps printed by both the "wet" and "dry" process are Nos. 105, 108-109, 111-114, 117, 138-140, C21-C24, C26, J25, J27. Starting with Nos. 147 and C27, the Bureau of Engraving and Printing used the "dry" method exclusively. Late dry printings of Nos. 105, 108, 112-114, 117, 138 and 152 also exist with dull gum.

See note on Wet and Dry Printings following U.S. No. 1029.

Maj. Gen. William Crawford Gorgas A35

Maj. Gen. George Washington Goethals A36

Gaillard Cut — A37

Maj. Gen. Harry Foote Hodges A38

Lt. Col. David DuB. Gaillard A39

Maj. Gen. William L. Sibert — A40

Jackson Smith — A41

Rear Adm. Harry H. Rousseau A42

Col. Sydney B. Williamson A43

J.C.S. Blackburn — A44

1928-40 Perf. 11
105 A35 1c green .25 .25
Never hinged .25
106 A36 2c carmine .25 .25
Never hinged .30
a. Booklet pane of 6 15.00 20.00
Never hinged 22.50
107 A37 5c blue 1.00 .40
Never hinged 1.30
108 A38 10c orange .25 .25
Never hinged .25
109 A39 12c brown violet .75 .60
Never hinged 1.00
110 A40 14c blue .85 .85
Never hinged 1.20

111 A41 15c gray black	.40	.35
Never hinged	.55	
112 A42 20c dark brown	.60	.25
Never hinged	.80	
113 A43 30c black	.80	.70
Never hinged	1.10	
114 A44 50c rose lilac	1.50	.65
Never hinged	2.00	
Nos. 105-114 (10)	6.65	4.55

For surcharges and overprints, see Nos. J21-J24, O1-O8.
Coils are listed as Nos. 160-161.

United States Nos. 720 and 695 Overprinted type B

1933, Jan. 14 — **Perf. 11x10½**

115 A226 3c deep violet	2.75	.25
Never hinged	4.00	
b. "CANAL" only	2,600.	
c. Booklet pane of 6, hand-made, perf. margins	80.00	—
116 A168 14c dark blue	4.50	3.50
Never hinged	7.00	
a. "ZONE CANAL"	1,500.	

Gen. George Washington
Goethals — A45

20th anniversary of the opening of the Panama Canal.

1934 — **Perf. 11**

117 A45 3c red violet	.25	.25
Never hinged	.30	
a. Booklet pane of 6	12.50	32.50
b. As "a," handmade, perf. margins	160.00	—

Coil is listed as No. 153.

> **Catalogue values for unused stamps in this section, from this point to the end, are for Never Hinged items.**

United States Nos. 803 and 805 Overprinted in Black

1939, Sept. 1 — **Perf. 11x10½**

118 A275 ½c red orange	.25	.25
119 A277 1½c bister brown	.25	.25

Panama Canal Anniversary Issue

Balboa-Before — A46

Balboa-After — A47

Gaillard
Cut-Before
A48

Gaillard
Cut-After
A49

Bas Obispo-Before — A50

Bas Obispo-
After
A51

Gatun Locks-Before — A52

Gatun
Locks-After
A53

Canal
Channel-
Before
A54

Canal Channel-After — A55

Gamboa-
Before
A56

Gamboa-After — A57

Pedro Miguel Locks-Before — A58

Pedro
Miguel
Locks-After
A59

Gatun
Spillway-
Before
A60

Gatun Spillway-After — A61

25th anniversary of the opening of the Panama Canal.

1939, Aug. 15

120 A46 1c yellow green	.60	.30
121 A47 2c rose carmine	.70	.35
122 A48 3c purple	.70	.25
123 A49 5c dark blue	2.00	1.25
124 A50 6c red orange	4.50	3.00
125 A51 7c black	4.75	3.00
126 A52 8c green	7.00	3.25
127 A53 10c ultramarine	5.50	5.00
128 A54 11c blue green	11.00	8.00
129 A55 12c brown carmine	11.00	7.50
130 A56 14c dark violet	11.00	7.00
131 A57 15c olive green	14.00	5.75
132 A58 18c rose pink	15.00	8.50
133 A59 20c brown	17.50	7.00
134 A60 25c orange	27.50	17.50
135 A61 50c violet brown	30.00	6.00
Nos. 120-135 (16)	162.75	83.65

Maj. Gen.
George W.
Davis
A62

Gov. Charles
E. Magoon
A63

Theodore
Roosevelt
A64

John F.
Stevens
A65

John F.
Wallace — A66

1946-49

Size: 19x22mm

136 A62 ½c bright red	.40	.25
137 A63 1½c chocolate	.40	.25
138 A64 2c light rose carmine	.25	.25
139 A65 5c dark blue	.35	.25
140 A66 25c green	.85	.55
Nos. 136-140 (5)	2.25	1.55

See Nos. 155, 162, 164. For overprint, see No. O9.

Map of Biological Area and Coati-
Mundi — A67

25th anniversary of the establishment of the Canal Zone Biological Area on Barro Colorado Island.

1948, Apr. 17

141 A67 10c black	1.75	1.00

"Forty-niners"
Arriving at
Chagres
A68

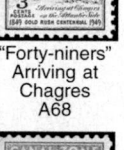

Journey by
"Bungo" to Las
Cruces
A69

Las Cruces
Trail to
Panama
A70

Departure for
San Francisco
A71

Centenary of the California Gold Rush.

1949, June 1

142 A68 3c blue	.65	.25
143 A69 6c violet	.65	.30
144 A70 12c bright blue green	1.75	.90
145 A71 18c deep red lilac	2.00	1.50
Nos. 142-145 (4)	5.05	2.95

Workers in Culebra
Cut — A72

Contribution of West Indian laborers in the construction of the Panama Canal.

1951, Aug. 15

146 A72 10c carmine	3.50	1.50

Centenary of the completion of the Panama Railroad and the first transcontinental railroad trip in the Americas.

Early Railroad
Scene — A73

1955, Jan. 28

147 A73 3c violet	1.00	.60

Gorgas
Hospital
and Ancon
Hill — A74

75th anniversary of Gorgas Hospital.

1957, Nov. 17

148 A74 3c black, *dull blue grn*	.45	.35

S.S. Ancon
A75

1958, Aug. 30

149 A75 4c greenish blue	.40	.30

Roosevelt
Medal and
Map — A76

Centenary of the birth of Theodore Roosevelt (1858-1919).

1958, Nov. 15

150 A76 4c brown .60 .30

Boy Scout Badge — A77

50th anniversary of the Boy Scouts of America.

1960, Feb. 8   Giori Press Printing

151 A77 4c dark blue, red & bister .55 .40

Administration Building — A78

1960, Nov. 1

152 A78 4c rose lilac .25 .25

Types of 1934, 1960 and 1946 Coil Stamps

1960-62 Unwmk. Perf. 10 Vertically

153 A45 3c deep violet .25 .25

Perf. 10 Horizontally

154 A78 4c dull rose lilac .25 .25

Perf. 10 Vertically

155 A65 5c deep blue .25 .25
Nos. 153-155 (3) .75 .75

Girl Scout Badge and Camp at Gatun Lake A79

50th anniversary of the Girl Scouts.

Giori Press Printing

1962, Mar. 12   Perf. 11

156 A79 4c blue, dark green & bister .40 .30

Thatcher Ferry Bridge and Map of Western Hemisphere A80

Opening of the Thatcher Ferry Bridge, spanning the Panama Canal.

Giori Press Printing

1962, Oct. 12

157 A80 4c black & silver .35 .25
a. Silver (bridge) omitted (50) 8,000.
Hinged 6,000.

Goethals Memorial, Balboa A81

Fort San Lorenzo A82

1968-71   Giori Press Printing

158 A81 6c green & ultra. .30 .30
159 A82 8c slate green, blue, dark brown & ocher .35 .25

Types of 1928, 1932 and 1948 Coil Stamps

1975, Feb. 14   Perf. 10 Vertically

160 A35 1c green .25 .25
161 A38 10c orange .70 .40
162 A66 25c yellow green 2.75 2.75
Nos. 160-162 (3) 3.70 3.40

Dredge Cascadas A83

Giori Press Printing

1976, Feb. 23

163 A83 13c multicolored .35 .25
a. Booklet pane of 4 3.00 —

No. 163a exists with and without staple holes in selvage tab.

Stevens Type of 1946

1977   Perf. 11x10½

Size: 19x22½mm

164 A65 5c deep blue .60 .85
a. Tagged, dull gum 12.00 15.00

No. 164 exists with both shiny gum and dull gum. Stamps with dull gum exist with and without tagging.

No. 164a exists even though there was no equipment in the Canal Zone to detect tagging.

Towing Locomotive, Ship in Lock — A84

1978, Oct. 25   Perf. 11

165 A84 15c dp grn & bl grn .35 .25

AIR POST STAMPS

Nos. 105-106 Surcharged in Dark Blue

Type I - Flag of "Five" pointing up

Type II - Flag of "5" curved

1929-31 Engr. Unwmk. Perf. 11

C1 A35 15c on 1c green, type I 7.50 4.75
Never hinged 11.50
C2 A35 15c on 1c yellow green, type II 60.00 47.50
Never hinged 110.00
C3 A36 25c on 2c carmine 3.50 2.00
Never hinged 5.25
Nos. C1-C3 (3) 71.00 54.25

AIR MAIL

Nos. 114 and 106 Surcharged

1929, Dec. 31

C4 A44 10c on 50c lilac 8.00 5.75
Never hinged 12.00

C5 A36 20c on 2c carmine 4.50 1.25
Never hinged 7.50
a. Dropped "2" in surcharge 85.00 60.00

Catalogue values for unused stamps in this section, from this point to the end, are for Never Hinged items.

Gaillard Cut — AP1

1931-49

C6 AP1 4c red violet .75 .65
C7 AP1 5c yellow green .60 .30
C8 AP1 6c yellow brown .75 .35
C9 AP1 10c orange 1.00 .35
C10 AP1 15c blue 1.25 .30
C11 AP1 20c red violet 2.00 .25
C12 AP1 30c rose lake 6.50 1.50
C13 AP1 40c yellow 3.50 1.10
C14 AP1 $1 black 10.00 1.60
Nos. C6-C14 (9) 26.35 6.40

For overprints, see Nos. CO1-CO14.

Douglas Plane over Sosa Hill — AP2

Planes and Map of Central America AP3

Pan American Clipper and Scene near Fort Amador AP4

Pan American Clipper at Cristobal Harbor AP5

Pan American Clipper over Gaillard Cut — AP6

Pan American Clipper Landing AP7

10th anniversary of Air Mail service and the 25th anniversary of the opening of the Panama Canal.

1939, July 15

C15 AP2 5c greenish black 3.75 2.25
C16 AP3 10c dull violet 3.50 3.00
C17 AP4 15c light brown 5.00 1.00
C18 AP5 25c blue 17.50 8.00
C19 AP6 30c rose carmine 17.50 6.00
C20 AP7 $1 green 45.00 27.50
Nos. C15-C20 (6) 92.25 47.75

Globe and Wing — AP8

1951, July 16

C21 AP8 4c lt red violet .75 .35
C22 AP8 6c lt brown .50 .25
C23 AP8 10c lt red orange .90 .35
C24 AP8 21c lt blue 8.00 4.00
C25 AP8 31c cerise 9.50 3.75
a. Horiz. pair, imperf. vert. 1,250.
C26 AP8 80c lt gray black 6.00 1.50
Nos. C21-C26 (6) 25.65 10.20

Flat Plate Printing

1958, Aug. 16 Unwmk. Perf. 11

C27 AP8 5c yellow green 1.00 .60
C28 AP8 7c olive 1.00 .45
C29 AP8 15c brown violet 4.50 2.75
C30 AP8 25c orange yellow 12.50 2.75
C31 AP8 35c dark blue 9.00 2.75
Nos. C27-C31 (5) 28.00 9.30
Nos. C21-C31 (11) 53.65 19.50

See No. C34.

Emblem of U.S. Army Caribbean School AP9

US Army Caribbean School for Latin America at Fort Gulick.

1961, Nov. 21

C32 AP9 15c red & blue 1.60 .75

Malaria Eradication Emblem and Mosquito AP10

World Health Organization drive to eradicate malaria.

1962, Sept. 24

C33 AP10 7c yellow & black .50 .40

Globe-Wing Type of 1951

1963, Jan. 7   Perf. 10½x11

C34 AP8 8c carmine .75 .30

Alliance Emblem AP11

2nd anniv. of the Alliance for Progress, which aims to stimulate economic growth and raise living standards in Latin America.

1963, Aug. 17   Perf. 11

C35 AP11 15c gray, grn & dk ultra 1.50 .85

Jet over Canal Zone Views AP12

50th anniversary of the opening of the Panama Canal.
Designs: 6c, Cristobal. 8c, Gatun Locks. 15c, Madden Dam. 20c, Gaillard Cut. 30c, Miraflores Locks. 80c, Balboa.

1964, Aug. 15

C36 AP12 6c green & black .60 .35
C37 AP12 8c rose red & black .60 .35
C38 AP12 15c blue & black 1.25 .75
C39 AP12 20c rose lilac & black 1.60 1.00
C40 AP12 30c reddish brown & black 2.75 2.25
C41 AP12 80c olive bister & black 4.75 3.00
Nos. C36-C41 (6) 11.55 7.70

Seal and
Jet Plane
AP13

1965, July 15

C42	AP13	6c green & black	.50	.30
C43	AP13	8c rose red & black	.45	.25
C44	AP13	15c blue & black	.75	.25
C45	AP13	20c lilac & black	.80	.30
C46	AP13	30c redsh brn & blk	1.10	.30
		On cover, single franking, to Australasia, Asia or sub-Sahara Africa		25.00
C47	AP13	80c bister & black	2.50	.75
		Nos. C42-C47 (6)	6.10	2.15

1968-76

C48	AP13	10c dull orange & black	.35	.25
a.		Booklet pane of 4	4.25	—
C49	AP13	11c olive & black	.35	.25
a.		Booklet pane of 4	3.50	
C50	AP13	13c emerald & black	.85	.25
a.		Booklet pane of 4	6.00	
C51	AP13	22c vio & blk	1.10	2.00
C52	AP13	25c pale yellow green & black	.80	.70
C53	AP13	35c salmon & black	1.25	2.00
		Nos. C48-C53 (6)	4.70	5.45

AIR POST OFFICIAL STAMPS

Beginning in March 1915, stamps for use on official mail were identified by a large "P" perforated through each stamp. These were replaced by overprinted issues in 1941. The use of official stamps was discontinued December 31, 1951. During their currency, they were not for sale in mint condition and were sold to the public only when canceled with a parcel post rotary canceler reading "Balboa Heights, Canal Zone" between two wavy lines.

After having been withdrawn from use, mint stamps (except Nos. CO8-CO12 and O3, O8) were made available to the public at face value for three months beginning Jan. 2, 1952. **Values for used examples of Nos. CO1-CO7, CO14, O1-O2, O4-O9, are for canceled-to-order stamps with original gum, postally used stamps being worth more.**

Nos. C7,
C9-C14
Overprinted
in Black

Two types of overprint
Type I — "PANAMA CANAL" 19-20mm long

1941-42   Unwmk.   Perf. 11

CO1	AP1	5c yellow green	6.50	1.50
CO2	AP1	10c orange	8.50	1.75
CO3	AP1	15c blue	11.00	1.75
CO4	AP1	20c red violet	13.00	4.00
CO5	AP1	30c rose lake	17.50	5.00
CO6	AP1	40c yellow	17.50	7.50
CO7	AP1	$1 black	20.00	10.00
		Nos. CO1-CO7 (7)	94.00	31.50

Overprint varieties occur on Nos. CO1-CO7 and CO14: "O" of "OFFICIAL" over "N" of "PANAMA" (entire third row). "O" of "OFFICIAL" broken at top (position 31). "O" of "OFFICIAL" over second "A" of "PANAMA" (position 45). First "F" of "OFFICIAL" over second "A" of "PANAMA" (position 50).

Type II — "PANAMA CANAL" 17mm long

1941, Sept. 22

CO8	AP1	5c yellow green	—	150.00
CO9	AP1	10c orange	—	260.00
CO10	AP1	20c red violet	—	160.00
CO11	AP1	30c rose lake	900.00	60.00
CO12	AP1	40c yellow	—	170.00
		Nos. CO8-CO12 (5)		800.00

Type I — "PANAMA CANAL" 19-20mm long

1947, Nov.

CO14	AP1	6c yellow brown	13.00	5.50
a.		Inverted overprint (50)		2,250.

POSTAGE DUE STAMPS

Prior to 1914, many of the postal issues were handstamped "Postage Due" and used as postage due stamps.

Postage Due Stamps of the U.S. Nos. J45a, J46a and J49a Overprinted in Black

Castle Gate
(See footnote) — D1

1914, Mar.   Wmk. 190   Perf. 12

J1	D2	1c rose carmine	85.00	15.00
J2	D2	2c rose carmine	220.00	42.50
J3	D2	10c rose carmine	1,000.	40.00
		Nos. J1-J3 (3)	1,335.	97.50

Statue of
Columbus
D2

Pedro J. Sosa
D3

1915, Mar.   Unwmk.
Blue Overprint, Type II, on Postage Due Stamps of Panama

J4	D1	1c olive brown	11.00	5.00
J5	D2	2c olive brown	225.00	17.50
J6	D3	10c olive brown	50.00	10.00
		Nos. J4-J6 (3)	286.00	32.50

Type D1 was intended to show a gate of San Lorenzo Castle, Chagres, and is so labeled. By error the stamp actually shows the main gate of San Geronimo Castle, Portobelo.

Surcharged in Red

1915, Nov.

J7	D1	1c on 1c olive brown	110.00	14.00
J8	D2	2c on 2c olive brown	22.50	7.50
J9	D3	10c on 10c olive brown	22.50	5.00
		Nos. J7-J9 (3)	155.00	26.50

Columbus
Statue — D4

Capitol, Panama
City — D5

1919, Dec.
Surcharged in Carmine by Panama Canal Press, Mount Hope, C. Z.
"Canal Zone" Type III

J10	D4	2c on 2c olive brown	30.00	11.00
J11	D5	4c on 4c olive brown	35.00	12.50
a.		"ZONE" omitted	9,250.	
b.		"4" omitted	8,500.	

Blue Overprint, Type V, on Postage Due Stamp of Panama

1922

J11C	D1	1c dark olive brown	—	5.00
d.		"CANAL ZONE" reading down	200.00	

United States Postage Due Stamps Nos. J61, J62b and J65b Overprinted

Type A
Letters "A" with Flat Tops

1924, July 1   Perf. 11

J12	D2	1c carmine rose	110.00	27.50
J13	D2	2c deep claret	55.00	15.00
J14	D2	10c deep claret	250.00	50.00
		Nos. J12-J14 (3)	415.00	92.50

U.S. Postage Stamps Nos. 552, 554 and 562 Overprinted Type A and additional Overprint in Red or Blue

1925, Feb.

J15	A155	1c deep green (R)	90.00	15.00
J16	A157	2c carmine (Bl)	22.50	7.00
J17	A165	10c orange (R)	55.00	11.00
a.		"POSTAGE DUE" double	800.00	
b.		"E" of "POSTAGE" omitted	750.00	
c.		As "b," "POSTAGE DUE" double	3,250.	
		Nos. J15-J17 (3)	167.50	33.00

Overprinted Type B
Letters "A" with Sharp Pointed Tops
On U.S. Postage Due Stamps Nos. J61, J62, J65, J65a

1925, June 24

J18	D2	1c carmine rose	8.00	2.75
a.		"ZONE ZONE" (LR18)	1,500.	
J19	D2	2c carmine rose	15.00	2.75
a.		"ZONE ZONE" (LR18)	1,500.	
J20	D2	10c carmine rose	150.00	20.00
a.		Vert. pair, one without ovpt.	3,000.	
b.		10c rose red	250.00	150.00
c.		As "b," double overprint	450.00	
		Nos. J18-J20 (3)	173.00	25.50

Regular Issue of 1928-29 Surcharged

1929-30

J21	A37	1c on 5c blue	3.75	1.75
		Never hinged	7.50	
a.		"POSTAGE DUE" missing	5,500.	
J22	A37	2c on 5c blue	6.50	2.50
		Never hinged	13.00	
J23	A37	5c on 5c blue	6.50	2.75
		Never hinged	13.00	
J24	A37	10c on 5c blue	6.50	2.75
		Never hinged	13.00	
		Nos. J21-J24 (4)	23.25	9.75

On No. J23 the three short horizontal bars in the lower corners of the surcharge are omitted.

Canal Zone Seal — D6

1932-41

J25	D6	1c claret	.25	.25
		Never hinged	.30	
J26	D6	2c claret	.25	.25
		Never hinged	.30	
J27	D6	5c claret	.35	.25
		Never hinged	.50	
J28	D6	10c claret	1.75	1.50
		Never hinged	2.25	
J29	D6	15c claret	1.25	1.00
		Never hinged	1.60	
		Nos. J25-J29 (5)	3.85	3.25

OFFICIAL STAMPS

See note at beginning of Air Post Official Stamps

Regular Issues of 1928-34 Overprinted in Black

Type 1

Type 2

Type 1 — "PANAMA" 10mm long
Type 2 — "PANAMA" 9mm long

Unwmk.

1941, Mar. 31   Engr.   Perf. 11

O1	A35	1c yellow green, type 1	2.00	.40
O2	A45	3c deep violet, type 1	3.75	.75
O3	A37	5c blue, type 2	1,000.	25.00
O4	A38	10c orange, type 1	7.50	1.90
O5	A41	15c gray black, type 1	15.00	2.25
O6	A42	20c olive brown, type 1	17.50	2.75
O7	A44	50c lilac, type 1	42.50	5.50
O8	A44	50c rose lilac, type 1a		525.00

No. 139 with Same Overprint in Black

1947, Feb.

O9	A65	5c deep blue, type 1	12.50	3.75

CUBA

'kyü-bə

LOCATION — The largest island of the West Indies; south of Florida.
GOVT. — socialist; under US military governor 1899-1902 and US provisional governor 1906-1909.
AREA — 44,206 sq. mi.
POP. — 9,710,000 (1981)
CAPITAL — Havana

Formerly a Spanish possession, Cuba's attempts to gain freedom led to US intervention in 1898. Under Treaty of Paris of that year, Spain relinquished the island to US trust. In 1902, a republic was established and Cuban Congress took over government from US military authorities.

100 Cents = 1 Dollar

Watermark

Wmk. 191 — Double-lined "USPS" in Capitals

Values for Nos. 176-220 are for stamps in the grade of fine and in sound condition where such exist. Values for Nos. 221-J4 are for very fine examples.

Issued under Administration of the United States
Puerto Principe Issue
Issues of Cuba of 1898 and 1896 Surcharged

a   b

Black Surcharge on Nos. 156-158, 160

1898-99

Types a, c, d, e, f, g and h are 17½mm high, the others are 19½mm high.

176	A19 (a)	1c on 1m		
		org brn	50.00	30.00
177	A19 (b)	1c on 1m		
		org brn	45.00	40.00
a.	Broken figure "1"		75.00	65.00
b.	Inverted surcharge		200.00	
d.	As "a," inverted		250.00	

c   d

178	A19 (c)	2c on 2m		
		org brn	28.00	21.50
a.	Inverted surcharge		250.00	50.00
179	A19 (d)	2c on 2m		
		org brn	40.00	35.00
a.	Inverted surcharge		350.00	100.00

k   l

179B	A19 (k)	3c on 1m		
		org brn	300.	175.
c.	Double surcharge		1,500.	750.

An unused example is known with "cents" omitted.

179D	A19 (l)	3c on 1m		
		org brn	1,500.	750.
e.	Double surcharge			

e   f

179F	A19 (e)	3c on 2m	
		org brn	1,500.

Value is for examples with minor faults.

179G	A19 (f)	3c on 2m	
		org brn	— 2,000.

Value is for examples with minor faults.

180	A19 (e)	3c on 3m		
		org brn	30.	30.
a.	Inverted surcharge			110.
181	A19 (f)	3c on 3m		
		org brn	75.	75.
a.	Inverted surcharge			200.

g   h

i   j

182	A19 (g)	5c on 1m		
		org brn	700.	250.
a.	Inverted surcharge			500.
183	A19 (h)	5c on 1m		
		org brn	1,300.	500.
a.	Inverted surcharge			700.
184	A19 (g)	5c on 2m		
		org brn	750.	275.
185	A19 (h)	5c on 2m		
		org brn	1,500.	500.
186	A19 (g)	5c on 3m		
		org brn	650.	175.
a.	Inverted surcharge		1,200.	700.
187	A19 (h)	5c on 3m		
		org brn		400.
a.	Inverted surcharge			1,000.
188	A19 (g)	5c on 5m		
		org brn	100.	80.
a.	Inverted surcharge		400.	200.
b.	Double surcharge		—	
189	A19 (h)	5c on 5m		
		org brn	350.	250.
a.	Inverted surcharge		—	425.
b.	Double surcharge		—	

The 2nd printing of Nos. 188-189 has shiny ink. Values are for the 1st printing.

189C	A19 (i)	5c on 5m	
		org brn	8,000.

No. 191

Black Surcharge on No. P25

190	N2 (g)	5c on ½m bl		
		grn	250.	75.
a.	Inverted surcharge		500.	150.
b.	Pair, one without surcharge			500.

Value for 190b is for pair with unsurcharged stamp at right. Also exists with unsurcharged stamp at left.

191	N2 (h)	5c on ½m bl		
		grn	300.	90.
a.	Inverted surcharge			200.
192	N2 (i)	5c on ½m bl		
		grn	550.	200.
a.	Dbl. surch., one diagonal			11,500.
193	N2 (j)	5c on ½m bl		
		grn	800.	300.

Red Surcharge on No. 161

196	A19 (k)	3c on 1c blk		
		vio	65.	35.
a.	Inverted surcharge			325.
197	A19 (l)	3c on 1c blk		
		vio	125.	55.
a.	Inverted surcharge			400.
198	A19 (i)	5c on 1c blk		
		vio	25.	30.
a.	Inverted surcharge			125.
b.	Surcharge vert. reading up			
c.	Double surcharge		400.	3,500.
d.	Double invtd. surch.			600.

Value for No. 198b is for surcharge reading up. One example is known with surcharge reading down.

199	A19 (j)	5c on 1c blk		
		vio	55.	55.
a.	Inverted surcharge			250.
b.	Vertical surcharge			2,000.
c.	Double surcharge		1,000.	700.

m

200	A19	10c on 1c blk		
	(m)	vio	20.	50.
a.	Broken figure "1"		40.	100.

Black Surcharge on Nos. P26-P30

201	N2 (k)	3c on 1m bl		
		grn	350.	350.
a.	Inverted surcharge			450.
b.	"EENTS"		550.	450.
c.	As "b," inverted			850.
202	N2 (l)	3c on 1m bl		
		grn	550.	400.
a.	Inverted surcharge			850.
203	N2 (k)	3c on 2m bl		
		grn	900.	400.
a.	"EENTS"		1,250.	500.
b.	Inverted surcharge			1,150.
c.	As "a," inverted			950.
204	N2 (l)	3c on 2m bl		
		grn	1,250.	875.
a.	Inverted surcharge			950.
205	N2 (k)	3c on 3m bl		
		grn	900.	400.
a.	Inverted surcharge			750.
b.	"EENTS"		1,250.	450.
c.	As "b," inverted			700.
206	N2 (l)	3c on 3m bl		
		grn	1,200.	550.
a.	Inverted surcharge			700.
211	N2 (i)	5c on 1m bl		
		grn		1,800.
a.	"EENTS"			2,500.
212	N2 (j)	5c on 1m bl		
		grn		2,250.
213	N2 (i)	5c on 2m bl		
		grn		1,800.
a.	"EENTS"			1,900.
214	N2 (j)	5c on 2m bl		
		grn		2,300.
215	N2 (i)	5c on 3m bl		
		grn		550.
a.	"EENTS"			1,000.
216	N2 (j)	5c on 3m bl		
		grn		1,000.
217	N2 (i)	5c on 4m bl		
		grn	2,500.	900.
a.	"EENTS"		3,000.	1,500.
b.	Inverted surcharge			2,500.
c.	As "a," inverted			2,000.
218	N2 (j)	5c on 4m bl		
		grn		1,500.
a.	Inverted surcharge			2,000.
219	N2 (i)	5c on 8m bl		
		grn	2,500.	1,250.
a.	Inverted surcharge			1,500.
b.	"EENTS"			1,800.
c.	As "b," inverted			2,500.
220	N2 (j)	5c on 8m bl		
		grn		2,000.
a.	Inverted surcharge			2,500.

Beware of forgeries of the Puerto Principe issue. Obtaining expert opinions is recommended.

United States Stamps Nos. 279, 267, 267b, 279Bf, 279Bh, 268, 281, 282C and 283 Surcharged in Black

1899   Wmk. 191   Perf. 12

221	A87	1c on 1c yel		
		grn	4.50	.40
		Never hinged	11.50	

222	A88	2c on 2c reddish car, III	10.00	.75
		Never hinged	25.00	
b.	2c on 2c vermilion, type III		10.00	.75
222A	A88	2c on 2c reddish car, IV	6.00	.40
		Never hinged	15.00	
c.	2c on 2c vermilion, IV		6.00	.40
d.	As No. 222A, inverted surcharge		5,500.	4,000.
223	A88	2½c on 2c reddish car, III	6.00	.80
		Never hinged	15.00	
b.	2½c on 2c vermilion, III		6.00	.80
223A	A88	2½c on 2c reddish car, IV	3.50	.50
		Never hinged	8.75	
c.	2½c on 2c vermilion, IV		3.50	.50
224	A89	3c on 3c purple	12.00	1.75
		Never hinged	30.00	
a.	Period between "B" and "A"		40.00	35.00
225	A91	5c on 5c blue	12.50	2.00
		Never hinged	30.00	
226	A94	10c on 10c brn, I	25.00	6.00
		Never hinged	70.00	
b.	"CUBA" omitted		7,000.	4,000.
226A	A94	10c on 10c brn, II	6,000.	
		Nos. 221-226 (8)	79.50	12.60

The 2½c was sold and used as a 2c stamp. Excellent counterfeits of this and the preceding issue exist, especially inverted and double surcharges.

Issues of the Republic under US Military Rule

Statue of Columbus A20

Royal Palms A21

"Cuba" — A22

Ocean Liner — A23

Cane Field — A24

1899   Wmk. US-C (191C)   Perf. 12

227	A20	1c yellow green	3.50	.25
		Never hinged	8.75	
228	A21	2c carmine	3.50	.25
		Never hinged	8.75	
a.	scarlet		3.50	.25
b.	Booklet pane of 6		5,500.	
229	A22	3c purple	3.50	.30
		Never hinged	8.75	
230	A23	5c blue	4.50	.30
		Never hinged	11.00	
231	A24	10c brown	11.00	.80
		Never hinged	27.50	
		Nos. 227-231 (5)	26.00	1.90

No. 228b was issued by the Republic. See Nos. 233-237 in Scott Standard Catalogue Vol 2. For surcharge see No. 232.

SPECIAL DELIVERY STAMPS

Issued under Administration of the United States

US No. E5 Surcharged in Red

1899   Wmk. 191   Perf. 12

E1	SD3 10c blue	130.	100.
	Never hinged	300.	
a.	No period after "CUBA"	575.	400.

Issue of the Republic under US Military Rule

Special Delivery Messenger SD2

Printed by the US Bureau of Engraving and Printing

1899   Wmk. US-C (191C)
Inscribed: "Immediata"

E2	SD2 10c orange	52.50	15.00
	Never hinged	120.00	

POSTAGE DUE STAMPS

Issued under Administration of the United States

Postage Due Stamps of the United States Nos. J38, J39, J41 and J42 Surcharged in Black Like Nos. 221-226A

D2

1899   Wmk. 191   Perf. 12

J1	D2 1c dp claret	45.00	5.25
	Never hinged	110.00	
J2	D2 2c dp claret	45.00	5.25
	Never hinged	110.00	
a.	Inverted surcharge		3,500.
J3	D2 5c dp claret	42.50	5.25
	Never hinged	105.00	
J4	D2 10c dp claret	25.00	2.50
	Never hinged	60.00	
	Nos. J1-J4 (4)	157.50	18.25

DANISH WEST INDIES AND UNITED STATES VIRGIN ISLANDS

'dā-nish 'west 'in-dēs

LOCATION — Group of islands in the West Indies, lying east of Puerto Rico
GOVT. — Danish colony
AREA — 132 sq. mi.
POP. — 27,086 (1911)
CAPITAL — Charlotte Amalie

The US bought these islands in 1917 and they became the US Virgin Islands, using US stamps and currency.

100 Cents = 1 Dollar
100 Bit = 1 Franc (1905)

Wmk. 111 —
Small Crown

Wmk. 112 —
Crown

Wmk. 113 —
Crown

Wmk. 114 —
Multiple Crosses

Coat of Arms — A1

Yellowish Paper
Yellow Wavy-line Burelage, UL to LR

1856   Typo.   Wmk. 111   Imperf.

1	A1 3c dark carmine, brown gum	200.	275.
a.	3c dark carmine, yellow gum	225.	275.
b.	3c carmine, white gum	4,250.	—

The brown and yellow gums were applied locally.

Reprint: 1981, carmine, back-printed across two stamps ("Reprint by Dansk Post og Telegrafmuseum 1978"), value, pair, $10.

White Paper

1866
Yellow Wavy-line Burelage UR to LL

2	A1 3c rose	40.	65.

No. 2 reprints, unwatermarked: 1930, carmine, value $100. 1942, rose carmine, back-printed across each row ("Nytryk 1942 G. A. Hagemann Danmark og Dansk Vestindiens Frimaerker Bind 2"), value $50.

1872   Perf. 12½

3	A1 3c rose	100.	275.

1873   Without Burelage

4	A1 4c dull blue	250.	475.
a.	Imperf., pair	775.	
b.	Horiz. pair, imperf. vert.	575.	

The 1930 reprint of No. 4 is ultramarine, unwatermarked and imperf., value $100.
The 1942 4c reprint is blue, unwatermarked, imperf. and has printing on back (see note below No. 2), value $60.

A2

Normal Frame

Inverted Frame

The arabesques in the corners have a main stem and a branch. When the frame is in normal position, in the upper left corner the branch leaves the main stem half way between two little leaflets. In the lower right corner the

branch starts at the foot of the second leaflet. When the frame is inverted the corner designs are, of course, transposed.

White Wove Paper
Varying from Thin to Thick

1874-79   Wmk. 112   Perf. 14x13½

Values for inverted frames, covers and blocks are for the cheapest variety.

5	A2 1c green & brown red	22.50	30.00
a.	1c green & rose lilac, thin paper	80.00	125.00
b.	1c green & red violet, medium paper	45.00	65.00
c.	1c green & claret, thick paper	20.00	30.00
e.	As "c," inverted frame	25.00	32.50
f.	As "a," inverted frame	475.00	—

No. 5 exists with a surcharge similar to the surcharge on No. 15, with 10 CENTS value and 1895 date. This stamp is an essay.

6	A2 3c blue & carmine	27.50	20.00
a.	3c light blue & rose carmine, thin paper	65.00	50.00
b.	3c deep blue & dark carmine, medium paper	40.00	17.00
c.	3c greenish blue & lake, thick paper	32.50	17.00
d.	Imperf., pair	375.00	—
e.	Inverted frame, thick paper	30.00	20.00
f.	As "a," inverted frame	350.00	
7	A2 4c brown & dull blue	16.00	19.00
b.	4c brown & ultramarine, thin paper	225.00	225.00
c.	Diagonal half used as 2c on cover		140.00
d.	As "b," inverted frame	900.00	1,400.
8	A2 5c grn & gray ('76)	30.00	20.00
a.	5c yellow green & dark gray, thin paper	55.00	32.50
b.	Inverted frame, thick paper	30.00	20.00
9	A2 7c lilac & orange	35.00	95.00
a.	7c lilac & yellow	90.00	100.00
b.	Inverted frame	65.00	150.00
10	A2 10c blue & brn ('76)	30.00	25.00
a.	10c dark blue & black brown, thin paper	70.00	40.00
b.	Period between "t" & "s" of "cents"	35.00	25.00
c.	Inverted frame	27.50	32.50
11	A2 12c red lil & yel grn ('77)	42.50	175.00
a.	12c lilac & deep green	160.00	200.00
12	A2 14c lilac & green	650.00	1,250.
a.	Inverted frame	2,500.	3,500.
13	A2 50c vio, thin paper ('79)	190.00	300.00
a.	50c gray violet, thick paper	250.00	375.00
	Nos. 5-13 (9)	1,044.	1,934.

The central element in the fan-shaped scrollwork at the outside of the lower left corner of Nos. 5a and 7b looks like an elongated diamond.

See Nos. 16-20. For surcharges see Nos. 14-15, 23-28, 40.

No. 9 Surcharged in Black

I CENT

a

1887

14	A2 (a) 1c on 7c lilac & orange	100.00	200.00
a.	1c on 7c lilac & yellow	120.00	225.00
b.	Double surcharge	250.00	500.00
c.	Inverted frame	110.00	350.00

No. 13 Surcharged in Black

10 CENTS 1895

b

1895

15	A2 (b) 10c on 50c violet, thin paper	42.50	67.50

The "b" surcharge also exists on No. 5, with "10" found in two sizes. These are essays.

Type of 1874-79

1896-1901   Perf. 13

16	A2 1c grn & red vio, inverted frame ('98)	15.00	22.50
a.	Normal frame	300.00	450.00
17	A2 3c blue & lake, inverted frame ('98)	12.00	17.50
a.	Normal frame	250.00	425.00
18	A2 4c bister & dull blue ('01)	17.50	11.00
a.	Diagonal half used as 2c on cover		100.00
b.	Inverted frame	60.00	80.00
c.	As "b," diagonal half used as 2c on cover		350.00
19	A2 5c green & gray, inverted frame	35.00	35.00
a.	Normal frame	800.00	1,200.
20	A2 10c blue & brn ('01)	80.00	150.00
a.	Inverted frame	1,000.	2,000.
b.	Period between "t" and "s" of "cents"	170.00	160.00
	Nos. 16-20 (5)	159.50	236.00

Arms — A5

1900

21	A5 1c light green	3.00	3.00
22	A5 5c light blue	17.50	25.00

See Nos. 29-30. For surcharges see Nos. 41-42.

Nos. 6, 17, 20 Surcharged

2 CENTS 1902

c

Surcharge "c" in Black

1902   Perf. 14x13½

23	A2 2c on 3c blue & carmine, inverted frame	700.00	900.00
a.	"2" in date with straight tail	750.00	950.00
b.	Normal frame	—	

Perf. 13

24	A2 2c on 3c blue & lake, inverted frame	10.00	27.50
a.	"2" in date with straight tail	12.00	32.50
b.	Dated "1901"	750.00	750.00
c.	Normal frame	175.00	300.00
d.	Dark green surcharge	2,750.	
e.	As "d" & "a"	—	—
f.	As "d" & "c"		

The overprint on No. 24b exists in two types: with "1901" measuring 2.5 mm or 2.2 mm high.
Only one example of No. 24f can exist.

25	A2 8c on 10c blue & brown	25.00	42.50
a.	"2" with straight tail	30.00	45.00
b.	On No. 20b	32.50	45.00
c.	Inverted frame	250.00	425.00

8 Cents 1902

d

Surcharge "d" in Black

1902   **Perf. 13**

27	A2	2c on 3c blue & lake, inverted frame	12.00	32.50
a.		Normal frame	240.00	425.00
28	A2	8c on 10c blue & brown	12.00	12.00
a.		On No. 20b	18.50	25.00
b.		Inverted frame	225.00	400.00
		Nos. 23-28 (5)	759.00	1,015.

1903   **Wmk. 113**

29	A5	2c carmine	8.00	22.50
30	A5	8c brown	27.50	35.00

King Christian IX — A8   St. Thomas Harbor — A9

1905   **Typo.**   **Perf. 13**

31	A8	5b green	3.75	3.25
32	A8	10b red	3.75	3.25
33	A8	20b green & blue	8.75	8.75
34	A8	25b ultramarine	8.75	10.50
35	A8	40b red & gray	8.25	9.50
36	A8	50b yellow & gray	10.00	10.00

Perf. 12

Wmk. Two Crowns (113)
Frame Typographed, Center Engraved

37	A9	1fr green & black	17.50	40.00
38	A9	2fr orange red & brown	30.00	55.00
39	A9	5fr yellow & brown	77.50	275.00
		Nos. 31-39 (9)	168.25	415.25

Favor cancels exist on Nos. 37-39. Value 25% less.

Nos. 18, 22 and 30 Surcharged in Black

1905   **Wmk. 112**

40	A2	5b on 4c bister & dull blue	16.00	50.00
a.		Inverted frame	45.00	90.00
41	A5	5b on 5c light blue	10.00	47.50

Wmk. 113

42	A5	5b on 8c brown	12.50	50.00
		Nos. 40-42 (3)	38.50	147.50

Favor cancels exist on Nos. 40-42. Value 25% less.

Frederik VIII — A10

Frame Typographed, Center Engraved

1908

43	A10	5b green	1.90	1.90
44	A10	10b red	1.90	1.90
45	A10	15b violet & brown	3.75	4.50
46	A10	20b green & blue	30.00	27.50
47	A10	25b blue & dark blue	1.90	2.50
48	A10	30b claret & slate	50.00	52.50
49	A10	40b vermilion & gray	5.75	9.50
50	A10	50b yellow & brown	5.75	14.00
		Nos. 43-50 (8)	100.95	114.30

Christian X — A11

1915   **Wmk. 114**   **Perf. 14x14½**

51	A11	5b yellow green	4.00	5.50
52	A11	10b red	4.00	55.00
53	A11	15b lilac & red brown	4.00	55.00
54	A11	20b green & blue	4.00	55.00

55	A11	25b blue & dark blue	4.00	17.50
56	A11	30b claret & black	4.00	100.00
57	A11	40b orange & black	4.00	100.00
58	A11	50b yellow & brown	3.75	100.00
		Nos. 51-58 (8)	31.75	488.00

Forged and favor cancellations exist.

POSTAGE DUE STAMPS

Royal Cipher, "Christian 9 Rex" D1

1902   **Litho.**   **Unwmk.**   **Perf. 11½**

J1	D1	1c dark blue	5.00	17.50
J2	D1	4c dark blue	12.50	22.50
J3	D1	6c dark blue	22.50	60.00
J4	D1	10c dark blue	20.00	65.00
		Nos. J1-J4 (4)	60.00	165.00

There are five types of each value. On the 4c they may be distinguished by differences in the figure "4"; on the other values differences are minute.

Used values of Nos. J1-J8 are for canceled stamps. Uncanceled stamps without gum have probably been used. Value 60% of unused.

Excellent counterfeits of Nos. J1-J4 exist.

Numeral of value — D2

1905-13   **Perf. 13**

J5	D2	5b red & gray	4.50	6.75
J6	D2	20b red & gray	7.50	14.00
J7	D2	30b red & gray	6.75	14.00
J8	D2	50b red & gray	6.00	30.00
a.		Perf. 14x14½ ('13)	37.50	140.00
b.		Perf. 11½	325.00	
		Nos. J5-J8 (4)	24.75	64.75

All values of this issue are known imperforate, but were not regularly issued.

Used values of Nos. J5-J8 are for canceled stamps. Uncanceled examples without gum have probably been used. Value 60% of unused.

Counterfeits of Nos. J5-J8 exist.

Danish West Indies stamps were replaced by those of the U.S. in 1917, after the U.S. bought the islands.

GUAM

'gwäm

LOCATION — One of the Mariana Islands in the Pacific Ocean, about 1450 miles east of the Philippines
GOVT. — United States Possession
AREA — 206 sq. mi.
POP. — 9,000 (est. 1899)
CAPITAL — Agaña

Formerly a Spanish possession, Guam was ceded to the United States in 1898 following the Spanish-American War. Stamps overprinted "Guam" were superseded by the regular postage stamps of the United States in 1901.

100 Cents = 1 Dollar

United States Nos. 279, 279B, 279Bc, 268, 280a, 281, 282, 272, 282C, 283, 284, 275, 275a, 276 and 276A Overprinted

GUAM

1899   **Wmk. 191**   **Perf. 12**
Black Overprint

1	A87	1c deep green	20.00	25.00
		Never hinged	40.00	

A bogus inverted overprint exists.

2	A88	2c red, type IV	17.50	25.00
		Never hinged	35.00	
a.		rose carmine, type IV	30.00	30.00
		Never hinged	60.00	
3	A89	3c purple	140.00	175.00
		Never hinged	275.00	
4	A90	4c lilac brown	125.00	175.00
		Never hinged	250.00	
5	A91	5c blue	32.50	45.00
		Never hinged	65.00	
6	A92	6c lake	125.00	190.00
		Never hinged	250.00	
7	A93	8c violet brown	125.00	160.00
		Never hinged	275.00	
8	A94	10c brown, type I	45.00	55.00
		Never hinged	90.00	
9	A94	10c brown, type II	2,750.	
		Never hinged	5,500.	
10	A95	15c olive green	150.00	140.00
		Never hinged	300.00	
11	A96	50c orange	350.00	400.00
		Never hinged	700.00	
a.		50c red orange	550.00	
		Never hinged	1,100.	

Red Overprint

12	A97	$1 black, type I	350.00	400.00
		Never hinged	700.00	
13	A97	$1 black, type II	3,750.	
		Nos. 1-8,10-12 (11)	1,480.	1,790.

Counterfeits of the overprint exist.
No. 13 exists only in the special printing.

SPECIAL DELIVERY STAMP

United States No. E5 Overprinted in Red

1899   **Wmk. 191**   **Perf. 12**

E1	SD3	10c blue	150.	200.00
		Never hinged	275.	
a.		Dots in curved frame above messenger (Plate 882)	200.	
		Never hinged	400.	

Counterfeits of the overprint exist.
The special stamps for Guam were replaced by the regular issues of the United States.
Guam Guard Mail stamps of 1930 are listed in the Scott U.S. specialized catalogue.

HAWAII

hə-'wä-yē

LOCATION — Group of 20 islands in the Pacific Ocean, about 2,000 miles southwest of San Francisco.
GOVT. — Former Kingdom and Republic
AREA — 6,435 sq. mi.
POP. — 150,000 (est. 1899)
CAPITAL — Honolulu

Until 1893 an independent kingdom, from 1893 to 1898 a republic, the Hawaiian Islands were annexed to the US in 1898. The Territory of Hawaii achieved statehood in 1959.

100 Cents = 1 Dollar

Values for Nos. 1-4 are for examples with minor damage that has been skillfully repaired.

Values of Hawaii stamps vary considerably according to condition. For Nos. 1-4, values are for examples with minor damage that has been skillfully repaired.

A1   A2

A3

1851-52   **Unwmk.**   **Typeset**   **Imperf.**
Pelure Paper

1	A1	2c blue	660,000.	250,000.
2	A1	5c blue	55,000.	35,000.
3	A2	13c blue	37,000.	29,000.
4	A3	13c blue	52,500.	35,000.

Nos. 1-4 are known as the "Missionaries."
Two varieties of each. Nos. 1-4, off cover, are almost invariably damaged.
No. 1 unused is unique.

Values for Nos. 5-82 are for very fine examples. Extremely fine to superb stamps sell at much higher prices, and inferior or poor stamps sell at reduced prices, depending on the condition of the individual example.

King Kamehameha III

A4   A5

Printed in Sheets of 20 (4x5)

1853   **Engr.**
Thick White Wove Paper

5	A4	5c blue	1,900.	1,900.
a.		Line through "Honolulu" (Pos. 2)	3,000.	3,000.
6	A5	13c dark red	875.	1,700.

See Nos. 8-11.

A6

1857

7	A6	5c on 13c dark red	7,000.	10,000.

Beware of fake manuscript surcharges. Expertization is strongly recommended.

1857   **Thin White Wove Paper**

8	A4	5c blue	700.	750.
a.		Line through "Honolulu" (Pos. 2)	1,350.	1,350.
b.		Double impression	3,500.	4,750.

1861   **Thin Bluish Wove Paper**

9	A4	5c blue	400.	400.
a.		Line through "Honolulu" (Pos. 2)	950.	1,000.

RE-ISSUE

1868   **Ordinary White Wove Paper**

10	A4	5c blue	27.50	
a.		Line through "Honolulu" (Pos. 2)	80.	
11	A5	13c dull rose	325.	

Remainders of Nos. 10 and 11 were overprinted "SPECIMEN." See Nos. 10S-11Sb in the Scott U.S. Specialized Catalogue.

Nos. 10 and 11 were never placed in use but stamps (both with and without overprint) were sold at face value at the Honolulu post office.

REPRINTS (Official Imitations)

Original   Reprint

Original   Reprint

5c — *Originals have two small dots near the left side of the square in the upper right corner. These dots are missing in the reprints.*

13c — *The bottom of the 3 of 13 in the upper left corner is flattened in the originals and rounded in the reprints. The "t" of "Cts" on the left side is as tall as the "C" in the reprints, but shorter in the originals.*

1889

10R	A4	5c blue	65.
11R	A5	13c orange red	300.

On August 19, 1892, the remaining supply of reprints was overprinted in black "REPRINT." The reprints (both with and without overprint) were sold at face value. See the Scott U.S. Specialized Catalogue.

Values for the Numeral stamps, Nos. 12-26, are for examples with four reasonably large margins. Unused values are for stamps without gum.

A7   A8

A9

1859-62   Typeset

12	A7	1c light blue, *bluish white*	15,000.	15,000.
a.		"1 Ce" omitted		22,500.
b.		"nt" omitted		

No. 12a is unique.

13	A7	2c light blue, *bluish white*	6,250.	5,000.
a.		2c dark blue, *grayish white*	6,750.	5,000.
b.		Comma after "Cents"	—	6,750.
c.		No period after "LETA"	—	—
14	A7	2c black, *greenish blue* ('62)	8,000.	6,000.
a.		"2-Cents."		

1859-63

15	A7	1c black, *grayish* ('63)	650.	2,750.
a.		Tête bêche pair	9,000.	
b.		"NTER"	—	—
c.		Period omitted after "Postage"	850.	
16	A7	2c black, *grayish*	1,000.	850.
a.		"2" at top of rectangle	3,750.	3,750.
b.		Printed on both sides	—	21,000.
c.		"NTER"	3,250.	6,500.
d.		2c black, *grayish white*	1,000.	850.
e.		Period omitted after "Cents"	—	—
f.		Overlapping impressions	—	—
g.		"TAGE"	—	—

17	A7	2c dark blue, *bluish* ('63)	12,000.	8,750.
a.		"ISL"		
18	A7	2c black, *blue gray* ('63)	3,250.	6,000.

1864-65

19	A7	1c black	600.	10,000.
20	A7	2c black	775.	1,500.
21	A8	5c blue, *blue* ('65)	900.	700.
a.		Tête bêche pair	10,500.	
b.		5c bluish black, *grayish white*	14,000.	3,750.

No. 21b unused is unique. No. 21b used is also unique but defective.

22	A9	5c blue, *blue* ('65)	575.	900.
a.		Tête bêche pair	18,000.	
b.		5c blue, *grayish white*		—
c.		Overlapping impressions		

1864   Laid Paper

23	A7	1c black	300.	2,500.
a.		"HA" instead of "HAWAIIAN"	3,500.	
b.		Tête bêche pair	6,000.	
c.		Tête bêche pair, Nos. 23, 23a	18,000.	
24	A7	2c black	350.	1,050.
a.		"NTER"	3,250.	
b.		"S" of "POSTAGE" omitted	1,500.	
c.		Tête bêche pair	7,000.	

A10

1865   Wove Paper

25	A10	1c dark blue	350.	—
a.		Double impression	—	
b.		With inverted impression of No. 21 on face	18,500.	
26	A10	2c dark blue	350.	—

Nos. 12 to 26 were typeset and were printed in settings of ten, each stamp differing from the others.

King Kamehameha
IV — A11

1861-63   Litho.
Horizontally Laid Paper

27	A11	2c pale rose	350.	350.
a.		2c carmine rose ('63)	3,000.	2,850.

Vertically Laid Paper

28	A11	2c pale rose	325.	325.
a.		2c carmine rose ('63)	400.	450.

RE-ISSUE

1869   Thin Wove Paper

29	A11	2c red	45.00

No. 29 was not issued for postal purposes although canceled examples are known. It was sold only at the Honolulu post office, at first without overprint and later with overprint "CANCELLED." See No. 29S in the Scott U.S. Specialized Catalogue.
See Nos. 50-51 and note following No. 51.

Princess Victoria
Kamamalu — A12

King   King
Kamehameha   Kamehameha
IV — A13   V — A14

King Kamehameha
V — A15

Mataio
Kekuanaoa — A16

1864-86   Engr.   Perf. 12
Wove Paper

30	A12	1c purple ('86)	11.00	8.00
		Never hinged	25.00	
a.		1c mauve ('71)	60.00	20.00
		Never hinged	95.00	
b.		1c violet ('78)	20.00	10.00
		Never hinged	45.00	
31	A13	2c rose vermilion	65.00	12.50
		Never hinged	150.00	
a.		2c vermilion ('86)	55.00	17.50
		Never hinged	130.00	
b.		Half used as 1c on cover with #32		8,500.
32	A14	5c blue ('66)	175.00	30.00
		Never hinged	375.00	
33	A15	6c yellow green ('71)	45.00	10.00
		Never hinged	100.00	
a.		6c bluish green ('78)	35.00	10.00
		Never hinged	85.00	
b.		As "a," horiz. pair, imperf.	2,250.	
34	A16	18c dull rose ('71)	100.00	42.50
		Never hinged	220.00	
		Nos. 30-34 (5)	396.00	103.00
		Set, never hinged	860.00	

No. 32 has traces of rectangular frame lines surrounding the design. Nos. 39 and 52C have no such frame lines.
For overprints see Nos. 53, 58-60, 65, 66C, 71.

King David   Prince William
Kalakaua   Pitt Leleiohoku
A17   A18

1875

35	A17	2c brown	9.00	3.00
		Never hinged	22.00	
36	A18	12c black	75.00	32.50
		Never hinged	165.00	

See Nos. 38, 43, 46. For overprints see Nos. 56, 62-63, 66, 69.

Princess   King David
Likelike   Kalakaua
A19   A20

Queen Kapiolani — A21

Statue of King   King William
Kamehameha   Lunalilo — A23
I — A22

Queen Emma Kaleleonalani — A24

1882

37	A19	1c blue	11.00	6.00
		Never hinged	27.50	
38	A17	2c lilac rose	125.00	47.50
		Never hinged	275.00	
39	A14	5c ultramarine	15.00	3.00
		Never hinged	35.00	
a.		Vert. pair, imperf. horiz.	5,000.	6,000.
40	A20	10c black	50.00	25.00
		Never hinged	115.00	
41	A21	15c red brown	70.00	27.50
		Never hinged	150.00	
		Nos. 37-41 (5)	271.00	109.00
		Set, never hinged	602.50	

1883-86

42	A19	1c green	3.00	2.00
		Never hinged	7.00	
43	A17	2c rose ('86)	5.00	1.00
		Never hinged	11.00	
a.		2c dull red	65.00	22.50
		Never hinged	140.00	
44	A20	10c red brown ('84)	40.00	11.00
		Never hinged	90.00	
45	A20	10c vermilion	45.00	14.00
		Never hinged	100.00	
46	A18	12c red lilac	90.00	40.00
		Never hinged	225.00	
47	A22	25c dark violet	160.00	65.00
		Never hinged	350.00	
48	A23	50c red	200.00	90.00
		Never hinged	425.00	
49	A24	$1 rose red	325.00	275.00
		Never hinged	675.00	8,000.
		Maltese cross cancellation		150.00
		Nos. 42-49 (8)	868.00	498.00
		Set, never hinged	1,833.	

Other fiscal cancellations exist on No. 49.
Nos. 48-49 are valued used with postal cancels. Canceled-to-order cancels exist and are worth less.

REPRODUCTION and REPRINT
Yellowish Wove Paper

1886-89   Engr.   Imperf.

50	A11	2c orange vermilion	170.00
		Never hinged	275.00
51	A11	2c carmine ('89)	35.00
		Never hinged	50.00

In 1885, the Postmaster General wished to have on sale complete sets of Hawaii's portrait stamps, but was unable to find either the stone from which Nos. 27 and 28 were printed, or the plate from which No. 29 was printed. He therefore sent an example of No. 29 to the American Bank Note Company, with an order to engrave a new plate like it and print 10,000 stamps therefrom, of which 5000 were overprinted "SPECIMEN" in blue.

The original No. 29 was printed in sheets of fifteen (5x3), but the plate of these "Official Imitations" was made up of fifty stamps (10x5). Later, in 1887, the original die for No. 29 was discovered, and, after retouching, a new plate was made and 37,500 stamps were printed (No. 51). These, like the originals, were printed in sheets of fifteen. They were delivered during 1889 and 1890. In 1892, all remaining unsold in the Post Office were overprinted "Reprint."

No. 29 is red in color, and printed on very thin white wove paper. No. 50 is orange vermilion in color, on medium, white to buff paper. In No. 50 the vertical line on the left side of the portrait touches the horizontal line over the label "Elua Keneta", while in the other two varieties, Nos. 29 and 51, it does not touch the horizontal line by half a millimeter. In No. 51 there are three parallel lines on the left side of the King's nose, while in No. 29 and No. 50 there are no such lines. No. 51 is carmine in color and printed on thick, yellowish to buff, wove paper.

It is claimed that both Nos. 50 and 51 were available for postage, although not made to fill a postal requirement. They exist with favor cancellation. No. 51 also is known postally used. See Nos. 50S-51S in the Scott U.S. specialized catalogue.

Queen
Liliuokalani — A25

HAWAII

1890-91   *Perf. 12*

52	A25	2c dull violet ('91)	15.00	1.50
		Never hinged	25.00	
a.		Vert. pair, imperf. horiz.	3,750.	
52C	A14	5c deep indigo	125.00	150.00
		Never hinged	280.00	

Stamps of 1864-91
Overprinted in Red

Three categories of double overprints:
I. Both overprints heavy.
II. One overprint heavy, one of moderate strength.
III. One overprint heavy, one of light or weak strength.

1893   **Overprinted in Red**

53	A12	1c purple	9.00	13.00
		Never hinged	20.00	
a.		"189" instead of "1893"	600.00	—
b.		No period after "GOVT"	275.00	275.00
f.		Double overprint (III)	600.00	
54	A19	1c blue	9.00	15.00
		Never hinged	21.00	
b.		No period after "GOVT"	140.00	150.00
e.		Double overprint (I)	1,500.	
f.		Double overprint (III)	400.00	
55	A19	1c green	2.00	3.00
		Never hinged	4.00	
d.		Double overprint (I)	650.00	650.00
f.		Double overprint (III)	250.00	250.00
j.		Pair, one without ovpt.	10,000.	
56	A17	2c brown	12.50	20.00
		Never hinged	27.50	
b.		No period after "GOVT"	325.00	—
57	A25	2c dull violet	2.00	1.50
		Never hinged	3.00	
a.		"18 3" instead of "1893"	900.00	900.00
d.		Double overprint (I)	1,300.	1,000.
f.		Double overprint (III)	190.00	190.00
g.		Inverted overprint	4,000.	4,750.
58	A14	5c deep indigo	15.00	30.00
		Never hinged	32.00	
b.		No period after "GOVT"	275.00	250.00
f.		Double overprint (III)	1,250.	675.00
59	A14	5c ultramarine	7.00	3.00
		Never hinged	15.00	
d.		Double overprint (I)	6,500.	
e.		Double overprint (II)	3,750.	3,750.
f.		Double overprint (III)		600.00
g.		Inverted overprint	1,500.	1,500.
60	A15	6c green	17.50	25.00
		Never hinged	40.00	
e.		Double overprint (II)	1,100.	
61	A20	10c black	14.00	20.00
		Never hinged	30.00	
e.		Double overprint (II)	1,000.	900.00
f.		Double overprint (III)	225.00	
61B	A20	10c red brown	15,000.	29,000.
		Never hinged	25,000.	
62	A18	12c black	14.00	20.00
		Never hinged	30.00	
d.		Double overprint (I)	2,000.	
e.		Double overprint (II)	1,750.	
63	A18	12c red lilac	175.00	250.00
		Never hinged	400.00	
64	A22	25c dark violet	35.00	45.00
		Never hinged	70.00	
b.		No period after "GOVT"	350.00	350.00
f.		Double overprint (III)	1,250.	
		Nos. 53-61,62-64 (12)	*312.00*	*445.50*
		Nos. 53-61, 62-64 never hinged	692.75	

Virtually all known examples of No. 61B are cut in at the top.

Overprinted in Black

65	A13	2c vermilion	85.00	90.00
		Never hinged	200.00	
b.		No period after "GOVT"	300.00	300.00
66	A17	2c rose	2.50	2.50
		Never hinged	3.75	
b.		No period after "GOVT"	70.00	70.00
d.		Double overprint (I)	4,000.	
e.		Double overprint (II)	2,750.	
f.		Double overprint (III)	300.00	
66C	A15	6c green	15,000.	29,000.
67	A20	10c vermilion	22.50	30.00
		Never hinged	45.00	
f.		Double overprint (III)	1,250.	
68	A20	10c red brown	12.00	13.00
		Never hinged	24.00	
f.		Double overprint (III)	4,000.	
69	A18	12c red lilac	350.00	500.00
		Never hinged	575.00	
70	A21	15c red brown	27.50	35.00
		Never hinged	55.00	
f.		Double overprint (III)	2,000.	
71	A16	18c dull rose	40.00	40.00
		Never hinged	80.00	
a.		"18 3" instead of "1893"	525.00	525.00
b.		No period after "GOVT"	350.00	350.00
d.		Double overprint (I)	650.00	
f.		Double overprint (III)	275.00	
g.		Pair, one without ovpt.	3,500.	
h.		As "b," double overprint (II)	1,750.	

72	A23	50c red	90.00	120.00
		Never hinged	180.00	
b.		No period after "GOVT"	500.00	500.00
f.		Double overprint (III)	775.00	
			1,000.	
73	A24	$1 rose red	160.00	190.00
		Never hinged	325.00	
b.		No period after "GOVT"	525.00	500.00
		Nos. 65-66,67-73 (9)	*789.50*	*1,021.*
		Nos. 65-66, 67-73 never hinged	1,485.	

Coat of Arms — A26

View of Honolulu — A27

Statue of Kamehameha I — A28

Stars and Palms — A29

S. S. "Arawa" — A30

Pres. Sanford Ballard Dole — A31

1894

74	A26	1c yellow	2.00	1.50
		Never hinged	4.00	
75	A27	2c brown	2.00	.60
		Never hinged	4.00	
76	A28	5c rose lake	5.00	2.00
		Never hinged	11.00	
77	A29	10c yellow green	8.00	5.00
		Never hinged	18.00	
78	A30	12c blue	17.50	20.00
		Never hinged	37.50	
79	A31	25c deep blue	22.50	17.50
		Never hinged	47.50	
		Nos. 74-79 (6)	*57.00*	*46.60*
		Set, never hinged	122.50	

Numerous double transfers exist on Nos. 75 and 81.

"CENTS" Added — A32

1899

80	A26	1c dark green	2.00	1.50
		Never hinged	4.50	
81	A27	2c rose	1.50	1.00
		Never hinged	3.50	
a.		2c salmon	1.50	1.50
		Never hinged	3.50	
b.		Vert. pair, imperf. horiz.	4,250.	
82	A32	5c blue	8.00	4.00
		Never hinged	20.00	
		Nos. 80-82 (3)	*11.50*	*6.50*
		Set, never hinged	28.00	

OFFICIAL STAMPS

Lorrin Andrews Thurston — O1

1896   **Engr.**   **Unwmk.**   *Perf. 12*

O1	O1	2c green	45.00	20.00
		Never hinged	110.00	
O2	O1	5c black brown	45.00	20.00
		Never hinged	110.00	
O3	O1	6c deep ultramarine	45.00	20.00
		Never hinged	110.00	
O4	O1	10c bright rose	45.00	20.00
		Never hinged	110.00	
O5	O1	12c orange	55.00	22.50
		Never hinged	135.00	
O6	O1	25c gray violet	65.00	22.50
		Never hinged	160.00	
		Nos. O1-O6 (6)	*300.00*	*125.00*
		Set, never hinged	735.00	

Used values for Nos. O1-O6 are for stamps canceled-to-order "FOREIGN OFFICE/HONOLULU H.I." in double circle without date. Values of postally used stamps: Nos. O1-O2, O4, $50 each; No. O3, $125; No. O5, $160; No. O6, $200.
The stamps of Hawaii were replaced by those of the United States.

PHILIPPINES

ˌfi-lə-ˈpēnz

LOCATION — Group of 7,100 islands and islets in the Malay Archipelago, north of Borneo, in the North Pacific Ocean
GOVT. — US Admin., 1898-1946
AREA — 115,748 sq. mi.
POP. — 16,971,100 (est. 1941)
CAPITAL — Quezon City

The islands were ceded to the US by Spain in 1898. On Nov. 15, 1935, they were given their independence, subject to a transition period which ended July 4, 1946. On that date the Commonwealth became the "Republic of the Philippines."

100 Cents = 1 Dollar (1899)

100 CENTAVOS = 1 PESO (1906)

Issued under U.S. Administration

Wmk. 191PI — Double-lined PIPS

Wmk. 190PI — Single-lined PIPS

Wmk. 257 — Curved Wavy Lines

Regular Issues of the United States Overprinted in Black

1899-1901   **Unwmk.**   *Perf. 12*
On U.S. Stamp No. 260

212	A96	50c orange	300.	225.
		Never hinged	775.	

On U.S. Stamps Nos. 279, 279B, 279Bd, 279Bj, 279Bf, 279Bc, 268, 281, 282C, 283, 284, 275, 275a
Wmk. Double-lined USPS (191)

213	A87	1c yellow green	3.50	.60
		Never hinged	10.00	
a.		Inverted overprint	77,500.	
214	A88	2c red, type IV	1.75	.60
		Never hinged	4.25	
a.		2c orange red, type IV, ('01)	1.75	.60
		Never hinged	4.25	
b.		Bklt. pane of 6, red, type IV ('00)	200.00	300.00
		Never hinged	450.00	
c.		2c reddish carmine, type IV	2.50	1.00
		Never hinged	6.00	

d.		2c rose carmine, type IV	3.00	1.10
		Never hinged	7.25	
215	A89	3c purple	9.00	1.25
		Never hinged	21.50	
216	A91	5c blue	9.00	1.00
		Never hinged	21.50	
a.		Inverted overprint		6,500.

No. 216a is valued in the grade of fine.

217	A94	10c brown, type I	35.00	4.00
		Never hinged	80.00	
217A	A94	10c orange brown, type II	125.00	27.50
		Never hinged	325.00	

No. 217A was overprinted on U.S. No. 283a, vertical watermark.

218	A95	15c olive green	40.00	8.00
		Never hinged	95.00	
219	A96	50c orange	125.00	37.50
		Never hinged	300.00	
a.		50c red orange	250.00	55.00
		Never hinged	600.00	
		Nos. 213-219 (8)	*348.25*	*80.45*

Regular Issue
Same Overprint in Black On U.S.
Stamps Nos. 280b, 282 and 272

1901, Aug. 30

220	A90	4c orange brown	35.00	5.00
		Never hinged	80.00	
221	A92	6c lake	40.00	7.00
		Never hinged	95.00	
222	A93	8c violet brown	40.00	7.50
		Never hinged	95.00	
		Nos. 220-222 (3)	*115.00*	*19.50*

Same Overprint in Red On U.S.
Stamps Nos. 276, 276A, 277a and 278

223	A97	$1 black, type I	300.00	200.00
		Never hinged	1,000.	
223A	A97	$1 black, type II	2,000.	750.00
		Never hinged	5,000.	
224	A98	$2 dark blue	350.00	325.00
		Never hinged	1,150.	
225	A99	$5 dark green	600.00	900.00
		Never hinged	1,600.	

Regular Issue
Same Overprint in Black On U.S.
Stamps Nos. 300 to 310 and Shades

1903-04

226	A115	1c blue green	7.00	.40
		Never hinged	15.50	
227	A116	2c carmine	9.00	1.10
		Never hinged	20.00	
228	A117	3c bright violet	67.50	12.50
		Never hinged	150.00	
229	A118	4c brown	80.00	22.50
		Never hinged	175.00	
a.		4c orange brown	80.00	20.00
		Never hinged	175.00	
230	A119	5c blue	17.50	1.00
		Never hinged	40.00	
231	A120	6c brownish lake	85.00	22.50
		Never hinged	190.00	
232	A121	8c violet black	50.00	15.00
		Never hinged	125.00	
233	A122	10c pale red brown	35.00	2.25
		Never hinged	80.00	
a.		10c red brown	35.00	3.00
		Never hinged	80.00	
b.		Pair, one without overprint		1,500.
234	A123	13c purple black	35.00	17.50
		Never hinged	80.00	
a.		13c brown violet	35.00	17.50
		Never hinged	80.00	
235	A124	15c olive green	60.00	15.00
		Never hinged	135.00	
236	A125	50c orange	125.00	35.00
		Never hinged	275.00	
		Nos. 226-236 (11)	*571.00*	*144.75*
		Set, never hinged	1,285.	

Same Overprint in Red On U.S.
Stamps Nos. 311, 312 and 313

237	A126	$1 black	300.00	200.00
		Never hinged	700.00	
238	A127	$2 dark blue	550.00	800.00
		Never hinged	1,500.	
239	A128	$5 dark green	800.00	2,750.
		Never hinged	2,000.	

Same Overprint in Black On U.S.
Stamp Nos. 319 and 319c

240	A129	2c carmine	8.00	2.25
		Never hinged	17.50	
a.		Booklet pane of 6	2,000.	
b.		2c scarlet	8.00	2.75
		Never hinged	19.00	
c.		As "b," booklet pane of 6	—	

José Rizal — A40

Designs: 4c, McKinley. 6c, Ferdinand Magellan. 8c, Miguel Lopez de Legaspi. 10c, Gen. Henry W. Lawton. 12c, Lincoln. 16c, Adm. William T. Sampson. 20c, Washington.

26c, Francisco Carriedo. 30c, Franklin. 1p-10p, Arms of City of Manila.

Wmk. Double-lined PIPS (191PI)
1906, Sept. 8   **Perf. 12**

241	A40	2c deep green	.40	.25
		Never hinged	1.00	
a.		2c yellow green ('10)	.60	.25
		Never hinged	1.50	
b.		Booklet pane of 6	750.00	800.00
			1,500.	
242	A40	4c carmine	.50	.25
		Never hinged	1.25	
a.		4c carmine lake ('10)	1.00	.25
		Never hinged	2.50	
b.		Booklet pane of 6	650.00	700.00
			1,250.	
243	A40	6c violet	2.50	.25
		Never hinged	6.25	
244	A40	8c brown	4.50	.90
		Never hinged	11.00	
245	A40	10c blue	3.50	.30
		Never hinged	8.75	
a.		10c dark blue	3.50	.30
		Never hinged	8.75	
246	A40	12c brown lake	9.00	2.50
		Never hinged	22.50	
247	A40	16c violet black	6.00	.35
		Never hinged	15.00	
248	A40	20c orange brown	7.00	.35
		Never hinged	17.50	
249	A40	26c vio brn	11.00	3.00
		Never hinged	27.50	
250	A40	30c olive green	6.50	1.75
		Never hinged	16.00	
251	A40	1p orange	55.00	17.50
		Never hinged	130.00	
252	A40	2p black	50.00	1.75
		Never hinged	130.00	
253	A40	4p dark blue	160.00	20.00
		Never hinged	375.00	
254	A40	10p dark green	225.00	80.00
		Never hinged	575.00	
		Nos. 241-254 (14)	540.90	129.15
		Set, never hinged	1,316.	

1909-13   **Change of Colors**

255	A40	12c red orange	11.00	3.00
		Never hinged	27.50	
256	A40	16c olive green	6.00	.75
		Never hinged	15.00	
257	A40	20c yellow	9.00	1.25
		Never hinged	22.50	
258	A40	26c blue green	3.50	1.25
		Never hinged	8.75	
259	A40	30c ultramarine	13.00	3.50
		Never hinged	32.50	
260	A40	1p pale violet	45.00	5.00
		Never hinged	110.00	
260A	A40	2p violet brown ('13)	100.00	12.00
		Never hinged	250.00	
		Nos. 255-260A (7)	187.50	26.75
		Set, never hinged	466.25	

Wmk. Single-lined PIPS (190PI)
1911

261	A40	2c green	.75	.25
		Never hinged	1.80	
a.		Booklet pane of 6	800.00	900.00
		Never hinged	1,400.	
262	A40	4c carmine lake	3.00	.25
		Never hinged	6.75	
a.		4c carmine	—	—
b.		Booklet pane of 6	600.00	700.00
			1,100.	
263	A40	6c deep violet	3.00	.25
		Never hinged	6.75	
264	A40	8c brown	9.50	.50
		Never hinged	21.50	
265	A40	10c blue	4.00	.25
		Never hinged	9.00	
266	A40	12c orange	4.00	.45
		Never hinged	9.00	
267	A40	16c olive green	4.50	.40
		Never hinged	10.00	
a.		16c pale olive green	4.50	.50
		Never hinged	10.00	
268	A40	20c yellow	3.50	.25
		Never hinged	7.75	
a.		20c orange	4.00	.30
		Never hinged	9.00	
269	A40	26c blue green	6.00	.30
		Never hinged	13.50	
270	A40	30c ultramarine	6.00	.50
		Never hinged	13.50	
271	A40	1p pale violet	27.50	.60
		Never hinged	62.50	
272	A40	2p violet brown	45.00	1.00
		Never hinged	100.00	
273	A40	4p deep blue	550.00	110.00
		Never hinged	1,100.	
274	A40	10p deep green	200.00	30.00
		Never hinged	400.00	
		Nos. 261-274 (14)	866.75	145.00
		Set, never hinged	1,862.	

1914

275	A40	30c gray	12.00	.50
		Never hinged	27.50	

1914   **Perf. 10**

276	A40	2c green	3.00	.25
		Never hinged	7.00	
a.		Booklet pane of 6	750.00	800.00
			1,250.	
277	A40	4c carmine	4.00	.30
		Never hinged	9.00	
a.		Booklet pane of 6	750.00	
			1,300.	
278	A40	6c light violet	45.00	9.50
		Never hinged	100.00	
a.		6c deep violet	50.00	6.25
		Never hinged	110.00	

279	A40	8c brown	55.00	10.50
		Never hinged	125.00	
280	A40	10c dark blue	30.00	.25
		Never hinged	67.50	
281	A40	16c olive green	100.00	5.00
		Never hinged	225.00	
282	A40	20c orange	40.00	1.00
		Never hinged	85.00	
283	A40	30c gray	60.00	4.50
		Never hinged	130.00	
284	A40	1p pale violet	150.00	3.75
		Never hinged	350.00	
		Nos. 276-284 (9)	487.00	35.05
		Set, never hinged	1,020.	

Wmk. Single-lined PIPS (190PI)
1918   **Perf. 11**

285	A40	2c green	21.00	4.25
		Never hinged	40.00	
a.		Booklet pane of 6	750.00	800.00
		Never hinged	1,300.	
286	A40	4c carmine	26.00	6.00
		Never hinged	55.00	
a.		Booklet pane of 6	1,350.	2,000.
287	A40	6c deep violet	40.00	6.00
		Never hinged	90.00	
287A	A40	8c light brown	220.00	25.00
		Never hinged	400.00	
288	A40	10c dark blue	60.00	3.00
		Never hinged	140.00	
289	A40	16c olive green	110.00	10.00
		Never hinged	250.00	
289A	A40	20c orange	175.00	12.00
		Never hinged	400.00	
289C	A40	30c gray	95.00	18.00
		Never hinged	215.00	
289D	A40	1p pale violet	100.00	25.00
		Never hinged	225.00	
		Nos. 285-289D (9)	847.00	109.25
		Set, never hinged	1,815.	

1917   **Unwmk.**   **Perf. 11**

290	A40	2c yellow green	.25	.25
		Never hinged	.55	
		Never hinged	25.00	
a.		2c dark green	.30	.25
		Never hinged	.65	
b.		Vert. pair, imperf. horiz.	2,000.	
c.		Horiz. pair, imperf. between	1,500.	—
d.		Vertical pair, imperf. btwn.	1,750.	1,000.
e.		Booklet pane of 6	27.50	30.00
		Never hinged	60.00	
291	A40	4c carmine	.30	.25
		Never hinged	.65	
a.		4c light rose	.30	.25
		Never hinged	.65	
b.		Booklet pane of 6	20.00	22.50
		Never hinged	35.00	
292	A40	6c deep violet	.35	.25
		Never hinged	.70	
a.		6c lilac	.40	.25
		Never hinged	.80	
b.		6c red violet	.40	.25
		Never hinged	.70	
c.		Booklet pane of 6	550.00	800.00
		Never hinged	900.00	
293	A40	8c yellow brown	.30	.25
		Never hinged	.50	
a.		8c orange brown	.30	.25
		Never hinged	.50	
294	A40	10c deep blue	.30	.25
		Never hinged	.65	
295	A40	12c red orange	.35	.25
		Never hinged	.75	
296	A40	16c light olive green	65.00	.25
		Never hinged	130.00	
a.		16c olive bister	65.00	.50
		Never hinged	130.00	
297	A40	20c orange yellow	.35	.25
		Never hinged	.75	
298	A40	26c green	.50	.45
		Never hinged	1.10	
a.		26c blue green	.60	.25
		Never hinged	1.35	
299	A40	30c gray	.55	.25
		Never hinged	1.35	
300	A40	1p pale violet	40.00	1.00
		Never hinged	90.00	
a.		1p red lilac	40.00	1.00
		Never hinged	90.00	
b.		1p pale rose lilac	40.00	1.10
		Never hinged	90.00	
301	A40	2p violet brown	35.00	1.00
		Never hinged	77.50	
302	A40	4p blue	32.50	.50
		Never hinged	72.50	
a.		4p dark blue	35.00	.55
		Never hinged	77.50	
		Nos. 290-302 (13)	175.75	5.20
		Set, never hinged	377.00	

1923-26

Design: 16c, Adm. George Dewey.

303	A40	16c olive bister	1.00	.25
		Never hinged	2.25	
a.		16c olive green	1.25	.25
		Never hinged	2.75	
304	A40	10p dp grn ('26)	50.00	20.00
		Never hinged	110.00	

gislative Palace A42

1926, Dec. 20   **Perf. 12**

319	A42	2c green & black	.50	.25
		Never hinged	1.25	
a.		Horiz. pair, imperf. between	300.00	
b.		Vert. pair, imperf. between	575.00	

320	A42	4c car & blk	.55	.40
		Never hinged	1.20	
a.		Horiz. pair, imperf. between	325.00	
b.		Vert. pair, imperf. between	600.00	
321	A42	16c ol grn & blk	1.00	.65
		Never hinged	2.25	
a.		Horiz. pair, imperf. between	350.00	
b.		Vert. pair, imperf. between	625.00	
c.		Double impression of center	675.00	
322	A42	18c lt brn & blk	1.10	.50
		Never hinged	2.50	
a.		Double impression of center	1,250.	
b.		Vertical pair, imperf. between	675.00	
323	A42	20c orange & black	2.00	1.00
		Never hinged	4.50	
a.		20c orange & brown	600.00	—
b.		As No. 323, imperf., pair	575.00	575.00
c.		As "a," imperf., pair	1,750.	
d.		Vert. pair, imperf. between	700.00	
324	A42	24c gray & black	1.00	.55
		Never hinged	2.25	
a.		Vert. pair, imperf. between	700.00	
325	A42	1p rose lil & blk	47.50	50.00
		Never hinged	70.00	
a.		Vert. pair, imperf. between	700.00	
		Nos. 319-325 (7)	53.65	53.35
		Set, never hinged	83.95	

Opening of the Legislative Palace.
No. 322a is valued in the grade of fine.
For overprints, see Nos. O1-O4.

Rizal Type of 1906
Coil Stamp
1928   **Perf. 11 Vertically**

326	A40	2c green	7.50	12.50
		Never hinged	19.00	

Types of 1906-1923
1925-31   **Imperf.**

340	A40	2c yel green ('31)	.50	.50
		Never hinged	.90	
a.		2c green ('25)	.80	.75
		Never hinged	1.80	
341	A40	4c car rose ('31)	.50	1.00
		Never hinged	1.00	
a.		4c carmine ('25)	1.20	1.00
		Never hinged	2.75	
342	A40	6c violet ('31)	3.00	3.75
		Never hinged	5.00	
a.		6c deep violet ('25)	12.00	8.00
		Never hinged	26.00	
343	A40	8c brown ('31)	2.00	5.00
		Never hinged	4.00	
a.		8c yellow brown ('25)	13.00	8.00
		Never hinged	26.00	
344	A40	10c blue ('31)	5.00	7.50
		Never hinged	12.00	
a.		10c deep blue ('25)	45.00	20.00
		Never hinged	100.00	
345	A40	12c dp orange ('31)	8.00	10.00
		Never hinged	15.00	
a.		12c red orange ('25)	60.00	35.00
		Never hinged	135.00	
346	A40	16c olive green ('31)	6.00	7.50
		Never hinged	11.00	
a.		16c bister green ('25)	42.50	18.00
		Never hinged	100.00	
347	A40	20c dp yel org ('31)	5.00	7.50
		Never hinged	11.00	
a.		20c yellow orange ('25)	45.00	20.00
		Never hinged	100.00	
348	A40	26c green ('31)	6.00	9.00
		Never hinged	11.00	
a.		26c blue green ('25)	45.00	25.00
		Never hinged	110.00	
349	A40	30c light gray ('31)	8.00	10.00
		Never hinged	16.00	
a.		30c gray ('25)	45.00	25.00
		Never hinged	110.00	
350	A40	1p light violet ('31)	10.00	15.00
		Never hinged	20.00	
a.		1p violet ('25)	200.00	100.00
		Never hinged	425.00	
351	A40	2p brn vio ('31)	30.00	45.00
		Never hinged	80.00	
a.		2p violet brown ('25)	400.00	400.00
		Never hinged	675.00	
352	A40	4p blue ('31)	80.00	90.00
		Never hinged	150.00	
a.		4p deep blue ('25)	2,200.	1,100.
		Never hinged	3,500.	
353	A40	10p green ('31)	175.00	225.00
		Never hinged	300.00	
a.		10p deep green ('25)	2,750.	2,950.
		Never hinged	4,250.	
		Nos. 340-353 (14)	339.00	436.75
		Set, never hinged	636.90	
		Nos. 340a-353a (14)	5,860.	4,711.

Nos. 340a-353a were the original post office issue. These were reprinted twice in 1931 for sale to collectors (Nos. 340-353).

Mount Mayon, Luzon A43

Post Office, Manila A44

Pier No. 7, Manila Bay — A45

(See footnote) — A46

Rice Planting A47

Rice Terraces A48

Baguio Zigzag A49

1932, May 3   **Perf. 11**

354	A43	2c yellow green	.75	.30
		Never hinged	1.25	
355	A44	4c rose carmine	.75	.30
		Never hinged	1.25	
356	A45	12c orange	1.00	.75
		Never hinged	1.25	
357	A46	18c red orange	50.00	15.00
		Never hinged	80.00	
358	A47	20c yellow	1.10	.75
		Never hinged	1.75	
359	A48	24c deep violet	1.75	1.00
		Never hinged	3.00	
360	A49	32c olive brown	1.75	1.00
		Never hinged	3.00	
		Nos. 354-360 (7)	57.10	19.10
		Set, never hinged	91.50	

The 18c vignette was intended to show Pagsanjan Falls in Laguna, central Luzon, and is so labeled. Through error the stamp pictures Vernal Falls in Yosemite National Park, California.

For overprints see #C29-C35, C47-C51, C63.

Nos. 302, 302a Surcharged in Orange or Red

1932

368	A40	1p on 4p blue (O)	7.50	1.00
		Never hinged	12.00	
a.		1p on 4p dark blue (O)	7.50	1.00
		Never hinged	12.00	
		P# block of 10, Impt.	140.00	
		Never hinged	175.00	
369	A40	2p on 4p dark blue (R)	10.00	1.50
		Never hinged	17.00	
		P# block of 10, Impt.	160.00	
		Never hinged	200.00	
a.		2p on 4p blue (R)	10.00	1.00
		Never hinged	17.00	

Far Eastern Championship
Issued in commemoration of the Tenth Far Eastern Championship Games.

Baseball Players A50

Tennis Player — A51

Basketball Players — A52

1934, Apr. 14   **Perf. 11½**
380	A50	2c yellow brown	1.50	.80
		Never hinged	2.25	
381	A51	6c ultramarine	.25	.25
		Never hinged	.30	
a.		Vertical pair, imperf. between	700.00	
		Never hinged	1,100.	
382	A52	16c violet brown	.50	.50
		Never hinged	.75	
a.		Vert. pair, imperf. horiz.	950.00	
		Never hinged	1,500.	
		Nos. 380-382 (3)	2.25	1.55
		Set, never hinged	3.30	

José Rizal — A53

Woman and Carabao A54

La Filipina — A55

Pearl Fishing A56

Fort Santiago A57

Salt Spring — A58

"Juan de la Cruz" — A60

Rice Terraces A61

"Blood Compact," 1565 — A62

Barasoain Church, Malolos A63

Battle of Manila Bay, 1898 A64

Montalban Gorge A65

George Washington A66

1935, Feb. 15   **Perf. 11**
383	A53	2c rose	.25	.25
		Never hinged	.25	
384	A54	4c yellow green	.25	.25
		Never hinged	.25	
385	A55	6c dark brown	.25	.25
		Never hinged	.35	
386	A56	8c violet	.25	.25
		Never hinged	.35	
387	A57	10c rose carmine	.30	.25
		Never hinged	.45	
388	A58	12c black	.35	.25
		Never hinged	.50	
389	A59	16c dark blue	.35	.25
		Never hinged	.55	
390	A60	20c light olive green	.35	.25
		Never hinged	.45	
391	A61	26c indigo	.40	.40
		Never hinged	.60	
392	A62	30c orange red	.40	.40
		Never hinged	.60	
393	A63	1p red org & blk	2.00	1.25
		Never hinged	3.00	
394	A64	2p bis brn & blk	12.00	2.00
		Never hinged	16.00	
395	A65	4p blue & black	12.00	4.00
		Never hinged	16.00	
396	A66	5p green & black	25.00	5.00
		Never hinged	50.00	
		Nos. 383-396 (14)	54.15	15.05
		Set, never hinged	74.45	

For overprints & surcharges see Nos. 411-424, 433-446, 449, 463-466, 468, 472-474, 478-484, 485-494, C52-C53, O15-O36, O38, O40-O43, N2-N9, N28, NO2-NO6.

Issues of the Commonwealth
Issued to commemorate the inauguration of the Philippine Commonwealth, Nov. 15, 1935.

The Temples of Human Progress — A67

1935, Nov. 15
397	A67	2c carmine rose	.25	.25
		Never hinged	.30	
398	A67	6c deep violet	.25	.25
		Never hinged	.30	
399	A67	16c blue	.25	.25
		Never hinged	.35	
400	A67	36c yellow green	.40	.30
		Never hinged	.60	
401	A67	50c brown	.60	.55
		Never hinged	.90	
		Nos. 397-401 (5)	1.75	1.60
		Set, never hinged	2.45	

Jose Rizal Issue
75th anniversary of the birth of Jose Rizal (1861-1896), national hero of the Filipinos.

Jose Rizal — A68

1936, June 19   **Perf. 12**
402	A68	2c yellow brown	.25	.25
		Never hinged	.25	
403	A68	6c slate blue	.25	.25
		Never hinged	.25	
a.		Imperf. vertically, pair	1,000.	
		Never hinged	1,500.	
404	A68	36c red brown	.50	.70
		Never hinged	.75	
		Nos. 402-404 (3)	1.00	1.20
		Set, never hinged	1.25	

Commonwealth Anniversary Issue
Issued in commemoration of the first anniversary of the Commonwealth.

President Manuel L. Quezon — A69

1936, Nov. 15   **Perf. 11**
408	A69	2c orange brown	.25	.25
		Never hinged	.30	
409	A69	6c yellow green	.25	.25
		Never hinged	.30	
410	A69	12c ultramarine	.25	.25
		Never hinged	.30	
		Nos. 408-410 (3)	.75	.75
		Set, never hinged	.90	

Stamps of 1935 Overprinted in Black

a

b

1936-37
411	A53(a)	2c rose	.25	.25
		Never hinged	.25	
a.		Bklt. pane of 6 ('37)	2.50	2.00
		Never hinged	4.00	
b.		Hyphen omitted	125.00	100.00

412	A54(b)	4c yel grn ('37)	.50	4.00
		Never hinged	.75	
		P# block of 6	35.00	
		Never hinged	45.00	
413	A55(a)	6c dark brown	.25	.25
		Never hinged	.25	
414	A56(b)	8c violet ('37)	.25	.25
		Never hinged	.35	
415	A57(b)	10c rose carmine	.25	.25
		Never hinged	.25	
a.		"COMMONWEALT"	20.00	—
		Never hinged	30.00	
416	A58(b)	12c black ('37)	.25	.25
		Never hinged	.30	
417	A59(b)	16c dark blue	.30	.25
		Never hinged	.45	
418	A60(a)	20c lt ol grn ('37)	1.00	.40
		Never hinged	1.60	
419	A61(b)	26c indigo ('37)	.90	.35
		Never hinged	1.50	
420	A62(b)	30c orange red	.50	.25
		Never hinged	.80	
421	A63(b)	1p red org & blk	1.00	.25
		Never hinged	1.60	
422	A64(b)	2p bis brn & blk ('37)	15.00	4.00
		Never hinged	25.00	
423	A65(b)	4p bl & blk ('37)	50.00	8.00
		Never hinged	80.00	
424	A66(b)	5p grn & blk ('37)	15.00	25.00
		Never hinged	25.00	
		Nos. 411-424 (14)	85.45	43.75
		Set, never hinged	110.75	

Eucharistic Congress Issue
Issued to commemorate the 33rd International Eucharistic Congress held at Manila, Feb. 3-7, 1937.

Map of Philippines — A70

1937, Feb. 3
425	A70	2c yellow green	.25	.25
		Never hinged	.25	
426	A70	6c light brown	.25	.25
		Never hinged	.25	
427	A70	12c sapphire	.25	.25
		Never hinged	.25	
428	A70	20c deep orange	.30	.25
		Never hinged	.50	
429	A70	36c deep violet	.55	.40
		Never hinged	.80	
430	A70	50c carmine	.70	.35
		Never hinged	1.10	
		Nos. 425-430 (6)	2.30	1.75
		Set, never hinged	3.15	

Arms of Manila — A71

1937, Aug. 27
431	A71	10p gray	6.00	2.00
		Never hinged	8.50	
		P# block of 6	67.50	
		Never hinged	85.00	
432	A71	20p henna brown	5.00	1.40
		Never hinged	8.00	

Stamps of 1935 Overprinted in Black

a

b

1938-40
433	A53(a)	2c rose ('39)	.25	.25
		Never hinged	.25	
		P# block of 6	8.00	
		Never hinged	10.00	
a.		Booklet pane of 6	3.50	3.50
		Never hinged	5.50	
b.		As "a," lower left-hand stamp overprinted "WEALTH COMMON-"	2,500.	
		Never hinged	4,000.	
c.		Hyphen omitted	100.00	50.00

434 A54(b)   4c yel grn ('40)   3.00   30.00
   Never hinged   4.75
   P# block of 6   35.00
   Never hinged   45.00
435 A55(a)   6c dk brn ('39)   .25   .25
   Never hinged   .40
    a.   6c golden brown   .25   .25
    Never hinged   .40
   P# block of 6   5.50
   Never hinged   7.00
436 A56(b)   8c violet ('39)   .25   1.75
   Never hinged   .25
   P# block of 6   8.00
   Never hinged   10.00
    a.   "COMMONWEALT" (LR 31)   90.00
    Never hinged   140.00
437 A57(b)   10c rose car ('39)   .25   .25
   Never hinged   .25
   P# block of 6   8.00
   Never hinged   10.00
    a.   "COMMONWEALT" (LR 31)   65.00   —
    Never hinged   100.00
438 A58(b)   12c black ('40)   .25   1.00
   Never hinged   .25
   P# block of 6   8.00
   Never hinged   10.00
439 A59(b)   16c dark blue ('39)   .25   .25
   Never hinged   .25
   P# block of 6   16.00
   Never hinged   20.00
440 A60(a)   20c lt ol grn ('39)   .25   .25
   Never hinged   .25
   P# block of 6   12.00
   Never hinged   15.00
441 A61(b)   26c indigo ('40)   1.00   2.50
   Never hinged   1.50
   P# block of 6   16.00
   Never hinged   20.00
442 A62(b)   30c org red ('39)   3.00   .70
   Never hinged   5.00
   P# block of 6   22.50
   Never hinged   35.00
443 A63(b)   1p red org & blk   .60   .25
   Never hinged   1.00
444 A64(b)   2p bis brn & blk ('39)   10.00   1.00
   Never hinged   15.00
   P# block of 4   87.50
   Never hinged   110.00
445 A65(b)   4p bl & blk ('40)   175.00   250.00
   Never hinged   350.00
446 A66(b)   5p grn & blk ('40)   20.00   8.00
   Never hinged   35.00
   P# block of 4   200.00
   Never hinged   250.00
   Nos. 433-446 (14)   214.35   *296.45*
   Set, never hinged   414.15

Overprint "b" measures 18½x1¾mm.
No. 433b occurs in booklet pane, No. 433a, position 5; all examples are straight-edged, left and bottom.

First Foreign Trade Week Issue
Nos. 384, 298a and 432 Surcharged in Red, Violet or Black

a

b   c

1939, July 5
449 A54(a)   2c on 4c yel grn (R)   .25   .25
   Never hinged   .35
450 A40(b)   6c on 26c blue grn (V)   .25   .50
   Never hinged   .35
    a.   6c on 26c green   3.00   1.00
    Never hinged   5.00
451 A71(c)   50c on 20p henna brn (Bk)   1.25   1.00
   Never hinged   2.00   5.00
   Nos. 449-451 (3)   1.75   1.75
   Set, never hinged   2.70

Commonwealth 4th Anniversary Issue (#452-460)

Triumphal Arch — A72

1939, Nov. 15
452 A72   2c yellow green   .25   .25
   Never hinged   .25
453 A72   6c carmine   .25   .25
   Never hinged   .25
454 A72   12c bright blue   .25   .25
   Never hinged   .25
   Nos. 452-454 (3)   .75   .75
   Set, never hinged   .75

For overprints see Nos. 469, 476.

Malacañan Palace A73

1939, Nov. 15
455 A73   2c green   .25   .25
   Never hinged   .25
456 A73   6c orange   .25   .25
   Never hinged   .25
457 A73   12c carmine   .25   .25
   Never hinged   .25
   Nos. 455-457 (3)   .75   .75
   Set, never hinged   .75

For overprint, see No. 470.

Pres. Quezon Taking Oath of Office — A74

1940, Feb. 8
458 A74   2c dark orange   .25   .25
   Never hinged   .25
459 A74   6c dark green   .25   .25
   Never hinged   .25
460 A74   12c purple   .25   .25
   Never hinged   .30
   Nos. 458-460 (3)   .75   .75
   Set, never hinged   .80

For overprints, see Nos. 471, 477.

José Rizal — A75

ROTARY PRESS PRINTING
1941, Apr. 14   **Perf. 11x10½**
    Size: 19x22½mm
461 A75   2c apple green   .25   *.50*
   Never hinged   .25

FLAT PLATE PRINTING
1941, Nov. 14   **Perf. 11**
    Size: 18¾x22¼mm
462 A75   2c pale apple green   1.00   —
   Never hinged   1.25
    a.   Booklet pane of 6   6.00   —
    Never hinged   7.50

No. 461 was issued only in sheets. No. 462 was issued only in booklet panes on Nov. 14, 1941, just before the war, and only a few used stamps and covers exist. All examples have one or two straight edges. Mint booklets reappeared after the war. In August 1942, the booklet pane was reprinted in a darker shade (apple green). However, the apple green panes were available only to U.S. collectors during the war years, so no war-period used stamps from the Philippines exist. Value of apple green booklet pane, never hinged, $6.
For type A75 overprinted, see Nos. 464, O37, O39, N1 and NO1.

Philippine Stamps of 1935-41, Handstamped in Violet

1944   **Perf. 11, 11x10½**
463 A53   2c rose (On 411)   1,250.   650.00
    a.   Booklet pane of 6   12,500.
463B A53   2c rose (On 433)   2,000.   1,750.
464 A75   2c apple grn (On 461)   12.50   10.00
    Never hinged   22.50
    a.   Pair, one without ovpt.   —   —

---

465 A54   4c yel grn (On 384)   47.50   50.00
   Never hinged   80.00
466 A55   6c dk brn (On 385)   3,250.   2,000.
467 A69   6c grn (On 409)   300.00   150.00
   Never hinged   525.00
468 A55   6c dk brn (On 413)   4,750.   825.00
469 A72   6c car (On 453)   350.00   125.00
470 A73   6c org (On 456)   1,750.   725.00
471 A74   6c dk grn (On 459)   275.00   225.00
472 A56   8c vio (On 436)   17.50   30.00
   Never hinged   30.00
473 A57   10c car rose (On 415)   350.00   150.00
474 A57   10c car rose (On 437)   275.00   200.00
   Never hinged   475.00
475 A69   12c ultra (On 410)   1,100.   400.00
476 A72   12c brt bl (On 454)   7,000.   2,500.
477 A74   12c pur (On 460)   500.00   275.00
478 A59   16c dk bl (On 389)   3,000.   —
479 A59   16c dk bl (On 417)   1,500.   1,000.
480 A59   16c dk bl (On 439)   500.00   200.00
481 A60   20c lt ol grn (On 440)   140.00   35.00
   Never hinged   230.00
482 A62   30c org red (On 420)   450.00   1,500.
483 A62   30c org red (On 442)   800.00   375.00
484 A63   1p red org & blk (On 443)   6,250.   4,500.

Nos. 463-484 are valued in the grade of fine to very fine.
No. 463 comes only from the booklet pane. All examples have one or two straight edges.

Types of 1935-37 Overprinted

a

b

Nos. 431-432 Overprinted in Black — c

1945   **Perf. 11**
485 A53(a)   2c rose   .25   .25
   Never hinged   .25
486 A54(b)   4c yellow green   .25   .25
   Never hinged   .25
487 A55(a)   6c golden brown   .25   .25
   Never hinged   .25
488 A56(b)   8c violet   .25   .25
   Never hinged   .25
489 A57(b)   10c rose carmine   .25   .25
   Never hinged   .25
490 A58(b)   12c black   .25   .25
   Never hinged   .25
491 A59(b)   16c dark blue   .25   .25
   Never hinged   .30
492 A60(a)   20c lt olive green   .30   .25
   Never hinged   .40
493 A62(b)   30c orange red   .50   .35
   Never hinged   .75
494 A63(b)   1p red orange & black   1.10   .25
   Never hinged   1.60
495 A71(c)   10p gray   55.00   13.50
   Never hinged   90.00
496 A71(c)   20p henna brown   50.00   15.00
   Never hinged   75.00
   Nos. 485-496 (12)   108.65   31.10
   Set, never hinged   169.55

José Rizal — A76

1946, May 28   **Perf. 11x10½**
497 A76   2c sepia   .25   .25
   Never hinged   .25

For overprints see Nos. 503, O44.

Later issues, released by the Philippine Republic on July 4, 1946, and thereafter, are listed in Scott's Standard Postage Stamp Catalogue, Vol. 5.

AIR POST STAMPS

Madrid-Manila Flight Issue
Issued to commemorate the flight of Spanish aviators Gallarza and Loriga from Madrid to Manila.

Regular Issue of 1917-26 Overprinted in Red or Violet

Designs: Nos. C7-C8, Adm. William T. Sampson. No. C9, Adm. George Dewey.

1926, May 13   **Unwmk.**   **Perf. 11**
C1 A40   2c green (R)   20.00   17.50
   Never hinged   45.00
C2 A40   4c carmine (V)   30.00   20.00
   Never hinged   55.00
    a.   Inverted overprint   4,000.
C3 A40   6c lilac (R)   75.00   75.00
   Never hinged   125.00
C4 A40   8c org brn (V)   75.00   60.00
   Never hinged   125.00
C5 A40   10c deep blue (R)   75.00   60.00
   Never hinged   140.00
C6 A40   12c red org (V)   80.00   65.00
   Never hinged   150.00
C7 A40   16c lt ol grn (R)   3,250.   3,250.
C8 A40   16c ol bister (R)   5,000.   5,000.
C9 A40   16c ol grn (V)   100.00   70.00
   Never hinged   160.00
C10 A40   20c org ye (V)   100.00   80.00
   Never hinged   160.00
C11 A40   26c blue grn (V)   100.00   80.00
   Never hinged   160.00
C12 A40   30c gray (V)   100.00   80.00
   Never hinged   160.00
C13 A40   2p vio brn (R)   600.00   600.00
   Never hinged   1,100.
C14 A40   4p dk blue (R)   750.00   750.00
   Never hinged   1,300.
C15 A40   10p dp grn (V)   1,350.   1,350.

Same Overprint on No. 269
Wmk. Single-lined PIPS (190)
Perf. 12
C16 A40   26c blue grn (V)   6,250.

Same Overprint on No. 284
Perf. 10
C17 A40   1p pale violet (V)   300.00   225.00
   Never hinged   450.00

London-Orient Flight Issue
Issued Nov. 9, 1928, to celebrate the arrival of a British squadron of hydroplanes.

Regular Issue of 1917-25 Overprinted in Red

1928, Nov. 9   **Perf. 11**
C18 A40   2c green   1.00   1.00
   Never hinged   2.00
C19 A40   4c carmine   1.25   1.50
   Never hinged   2.00
C20 A40   6c violet   5.00   3.00
   Never hinged   10.00
C21 A40   8c orange brown   5.00   3.00
   Never hinged   10.00
C22 A40   10c deep blue   5.00   3.00
   Never hinged   10.00
C23 A40   12c red orange   8.00   4.00
   Never hinged   12.00
C24 A40   16c ol grn (No. 303a)   8.00   4.00
   Never hinged   12.00
C25 A40   20c orange yellow   8.00   4.00
   Never hinged   12.00
C26 A40   26c blue green   20.00   8.00
   Never hinged   35.00
C27 A40   30c gray   20.00   8.00
   Never hinged   35.00

Same Overprint on No. 271
Wmk. Single-lined PIPS (190)
Perf. 12

C28	A40	1p pale violet	55.00	30.00
		Never hinged	90.00	
		Nos. C18-C28 (11)	136.25	69.50
		Set, never hinged	230.00	

Von Gronau Issue

Commemorating the visit of Capt. Wolfgang von Gronau's airplane on its round-the-world flight.

Nos. 354-360 Overprinted

1932, Sept. 27   Unwmk.   Perf. 11

C29	A43	2c yellow green	.90	.60
		Never hinged	1.40	
C30	A44	4c rose carmine	.90	.40
		Never hinged	1.40	
C31	A45	12c orange	1.25	.65
		Never hinged	2.00	
C32	A46	18c red orange	5.00	5.00
		Never hinged	8.00	
C33	A47	20c yellow	3.50	3.50
		Never hinged	5.75	
C34	A48	24c deep violet	3.50	4.00
		Never hinged	5.75	
C35	A49	32c olive brown	3.50	3.00
		Never hinged	5.75	
		Nos. C29-C35 (7)	18.55	17.15
		Set, never hinged	31.55	

Rein Issue

Commemorating the flight from Madrid to Manila of the Spanish aviator Fernando Rein y Loring.

Regular Issue of 1917-25 Overprinted

1933, Apr. 11

C36	A40	2c green	.75	.45
		Never hinged	1.10	
C37	A40	4c carmine	.90	.45
		Never hinged	1.40	
C38	A40	6c deep violet	1.10	.80
		Never hinged	1.75	
C39	A40	8c orange brown	3.75	2.00
		Never hinged	5.75	
		P# block of 6	120.00	
		Never hinged	150.00	
C40	A40	10c dark blue	3.75	2.25
		Never hinged	5.75	
		P# block of 6	120.00	
		Never hinged	150.00	
C41	A40	12c orange	3.75	2.00
		Never hinged	5.75	
		P# block of 6	120.00	
		Never hinged	150.00	
C42	A40	16c olive green	3.50	2.00
		Never hinged	5.25	
		P# block of 6	160.00	
		Never hinged	200.00	
C43	A40	20c yellow	3.75	2.00
		Never hinged	5.75	
		P# block of 6	160.00	
		Never hinged	200.00	
C44	A40	26c green	3.75	2.75
		Never hinged	5.75	
a.		26c blue green	4.00	2.00
		Never hinged	6.00	
C45	A40	30c gray	4.00	3.00
		Never hinged	6.00	
		Nos. C36-C45 (10)	29.00	17.70
		Set, never hinged	44.25	

No. 290a Overprinted

1933, May 26

C46	A40	2c green	.65	.40
		Never hinged	1.00	
		P# block of 6	12.00	
		Never hinged	15.00	

Regular Issue of 1932 Overprinted

C47	A44	4c rose carmine	.30	.25
		Never hinged	.45	
		P# block of 6	16.00	
		Never hinged	20.00	
C48	A45	12c orange	.60	.25
		Never hinged	.90	
		P# block of 6	20.00	
		Never hinged	25.00	
C49	A47	20c yellow	.60	.25
		Never hinged	.90	
		P# block of 6	20.00	
		Never hinged	25.00	
C50	A48	24c deep violet	.65	.25
		Never hinged	1.00	
		P# block of 6	24.00	
		Never hinged	30.00	
C51	A49	32c olive brown	.85	.35
		Never hinged	1.40	
		Nos. C46-C51 (6)	3.65	1.75
		Set, never hinged	5.65	

Transpacific Issue

Issued to commemorate the China Clipper flight from Manila to San Francisco, Dec. 2-5, 1935.

Nos. 387, 392 Overprinted in Gold

1935, Dec. 2

C52	A57	10c rose carmine	.40	.25
		Never hinged	.60	
C53	A62	30c orange red	.60	.35
		Never hinged	.90	

Manila-Madrid Flight Issue

Issued to commemorate the Manila-Madrid flight by aviators Antonio Arnaiz and Juan Calvo.

Regular Issue of 1917-25 Surcharged in Various Colors

1936, Sept. 6

C54	A40	2c on 4c carmine (Bl)	.25	.25
		Never hinged	.25	
C55	A40	6c on 12c red org (V)	.25	.25
		Never hinged	.30	
C56	A40	16c on 26c blue grn (Bk)	.25	.25
		Never hinged	.40	
a.		16c on 26c red	2.00	.70
		Never hinged	3.00	
		Nos. C54-C56 (3)	.75	.75
		Set, never hinged	.95	

Air Mail Exhibition Issue

Issued to commemorate the first Air Mail Exhibition, held Feb. 17-19, 1939.

Regular Issue of 1917-37 Surcharged in Black or Red

1939, Feb. 17

C57	A40	8c on 26c blue grn (Bk)	2.00	2.00
		Never hinged	4.00	
a.		8c on 26c green (Bk)	10.00	4.00
		Never hinged	16.00	
C58	A71	1p on 10p gray (R)	8.00	4.00
		Never hinged	12.00	

Moro Vinta and Clipper AP1

1941, June 30

C59	AP1	8c carmine	2.00	.60
		Never hinged	2.75	
C60	AP1	20c ultramarine	3.00	.50
		Never hinged	4.00	
C61	AP1	60c blue green	3.00	1.00
		Never hinged	4.00	

C62	AP1	1p sepia	.70	.50
		Never hinged	1.00	
		Nos. C59-C62 (4)	8.70	2.60
		Set, never hinged	11.75	

For overprint see No. NO7. For surcharges see Nos. N10-N11, N35-N36.

No. C47 Hstmpd. in Violet

1944, Dec. 3

C63	A44	4c rose carmine	3,750.	2,750.

SPECIAL DELIVERY STAMPS

United States No. E5 Overprinted in Red

Wmk. Double-lined USPS (191)

1901, Oct. 15   Perf. 12

E1	SD3	10c dark blue	100.	80.
		Never hinged	185.	
a.		Dots in curved frame above messenger (Pl. 882)	175.	160.

Special Delivery Messenger SD2

Wmk. Double-lined PIPS (191PI)

1906, Sept. 8

E2	SD2	20c deep ultra	45.00	8.00
		Never hinged	90.00	
b.		20c pale ultramarine	35.00	8.00
		Never hinged	70.00	

See Nos. E3-E6. For overprints see Nos. E7-E10, EO1.

SPECIAL PRINTING

U.S. No. E6 Overprinted in Red

Wmk. Double-lined USPS (191)

1907

E2A	SD4	10c ultramarine		2,750.

Wmk. Single-lined PIPS (190PI)

1911, Apr.

E3	SD2	20c deep ultra	22.00	1.75
		Never hinged	42.00	

1916   Perf. 10

E4	SD2	20c deep ultra	175.00	150.00
		Never hinged	275.00	

1919   Unwmk.   Perf. 11

E5	SD2	20c ultramarine	.60	.25
		Never hinged	.90	
a.		20c pale blue	.75	.25
		Never hinged	1.00	
b.		20c dull violet	.60	.25
		Never hinged	.90	

Type of 1906 Issue

1925-31   Imperf.

E6	SD2	20c dull violet ('31)	30.00	75.00
		Never hinged	45.00	
a.		20c violet blue ('25)	50.00	—
		Never hinged	80.00	

Type of 1919 Overprinted in Black

1939, Apr. 27   Perf. 11

E7	SD2	20c blue violet	.25	.25
		Never hinged	.40	

Nos. E5b and E7, Hstmpd. in Violet

1944

E8	SD2	20c dull violet (On E5b)	1,400.	550.00
		On cover		—
		Block of 4	6,000.	
E9	SD2	20c blue violet (On E7)	550.00	250.00

Type SD2 Overprinted

1945, May 1

E10	SD2	20c blue violet	.70	.55
		Never hinged	1.10	
a.		"IC" close together	3.25	2.75
		Never hinged	4.75	

SPECIAL DELIVERY OFFICIAL STAMP

Type of 1906 Issue Overprinted

1931   Unwmk.   Perf. 11

EO1	SD2	20c dull violet	3.00	75.00
		Never hinged	4.50	
		P# block of 6	150.00	
		Never hinged	190.00	
a.		No period after "B"	50.00	250.00
		Never hinged	75.00	
b.		Double overprint		

It is strongly recommended that expert opinion be acquired for Nos. EO1 and EO1a used.

POSTAGE DUE STAMPS

U.S. Nos. J38-J44 Overprinted in Black

Wmk. Double-lined USPS (191)

1899, Aug. 16   Perf. 12

J1	D2	1c deep claret	7.50	2.50
		Never hinged	15.00	
J2	D2	2c deep claret	7.50	2.50
		Never hinged	15.00	
J3	D2	5c deep claret	15.00	2.50
		Never hinged	30.00	
J4	D2	10c deep claret	19.00	5.50
		Never hinged	37.50	
J5	D2	50c deep claret	250.00	100.00
		Never hinged	425.00	

No. J1 was used to pay regular postage Sept. 5-19, 1902.

1901, Aug. 31

J6	D2	3c deep claret	17.50	7.00
		Never hinged	35.00	
J7	D2	30c deep claret	250.00	110.00
		Never hinged	415.00	
		Nos. J1-J7 (7)	566.50	230.00
		Set, never hinged	882.50	

Post Office Clerk — D3

1928, Aug. 21   Unwmk.   Perf. 11

J8	D3	4c brown red	.25	.25
		Never hinged	.25	
		P# block of 6	14.00	
		Never hinged	17.50	
J9	D3	6c brown red	.30	.75
		Never hinged	.45	
		P# block of 6	14.00	
		Never hinged	17.50	
J10	D3	8c brown red	.25	.75
		Never hinged	.35	
		P# block of 6	14.00	
		Never hinged	17.50	
J11	D3	10c brown red	.30	.75
		Never hinged	.45	
		P# block of 6	14.00	
		Never hinged	17.50	
J12	D3	12c brown red	.25	.75
		Never hinged	.35	
		P# block of 6	14.00	
		Never hinged	17.50	
J13	D3	16c brown red	.30	.75
		Never hinged	.45	
		P# block of 6	14.00	
		Never hinged	17.50	
J14	D3	20c brown red	.30	.75
		Never hinged	.45	
		P# block of 6	14.00	
		Never hinged	17.50	
		Nos. J8-J14 (7)	1.95	4.75
		Set, never hinged	2.75	

No. J8 Surcharged in Blue

1937, July 29   Unwmk.   Perf. 11

J15	D3	3c on 4c brown red	.25	.25
		Never hinged	.35	

See note after No. NJ1.

Nos. J8 to J14 Handstamped in Violet

1944, Dec. 3

J16	D3	4c brown red	150.00	—
J17	D3	6c brown red	100.00	—
J18	D3	8c brown red	110.00	350.00
J19	D3	10c brown red	100.00	—
J20	D3	12c brown red	100.00	—
J21	D3	16c brown red	100.00	350.00
a.		Pair, one without ovpt.	—	
J22	D3	20c brown red	110.00	—
		Nos. J16-J22 (7)	770.00	

OFFICIAL STAMPS

Official Handstamped Overprints

"Officers purchasing stamps for government business may, if they so desire, surcharge them with the letters O.B. either in writing with black ink or by rubber stamps but in such a manner as not to obliterate the stamp that postmasters will be unable to determine whether the stamps have been previously used." C.M. Cotterman, Director of Posts, December 26, 1905.

Beginning January 1, 1906, all branches of the Insular Government used postage stamps to prepay postage instead of franking them as before. Some officials used manuscript, some utilized the typewriting machines but by far the larger number provided themselves with rubber stamps. The majority of these read "O.B." but other forms were: "OFFICIAL BUSINESS" or "OFFICIAL MAIL" in two lines, with variations on many of these.

These "O.B." overprints are known on U.S. 1899-1901 stamps; on 1903-06 stamps in red and blue; on 1906 stamps in red, blue, black, yellow and green.

"O.B." overprints were also made on the centavo and peso stamps of the Philippines, per order of May 25, 1907.

Beginning in 1926 the Bureau of Posts issued press-printed official stamps, but many government offices continued to handstamp ordinary postage stamps "O.B." The press-printed "O.B." overprints are listed below.

During the Japanese occupation period 1942-45, the same system of handstamped official overprints prevailed, but the handstamp usually consisted of "K.P.", initials of the Tagalog words, "Kagamitang Pampamahalaan" (Official Business), and the two Japanese characters used in the printed overprint on Nos. NO1 to NO4.

Regular Issue of 1926 Ovptd. in Red

1926, Dec. 20   Unwmk.   Perf. 12

O1	A42	2c green & black	3.00	1.00
		Never hinged	4.50	
O2	A42	4c car & blk	3.00	1.25
		Never hinged	4.50	
a.		Vertical pair, imperf. between	750.00	
O3	A42	18c lt brn & blk	8.00	4.00
		Never hinged	12.00	
O4	A42	20c org & blk	7.75	1.75
		Never hinged	11.50	
		Nos. O1-O4 (4)	21.75	8.00
		Set, never hinged	32.50	

Opening of the Legislative Palace.

Regular Issue of 1917-26 Overprinted by the U.S. Bureau of Engraving and Printing

1931   Perf. 11

O5	A40	2c green	.40	.25
		Never hinged	.65	
		P# block of 6	20.00	
		Never hinged	25.00	
a.		No period after "B"	17.50	17.50
		Never hinged	27.50	
b.		No period after "O"	40.00	30.00
O6	A40	4c carmine	.45	.25
		Never hinged	.70	
		P# block of 6	20.00	
		Never hinged	25.00	
a.		No period after "B"	40.00	20.00
		Never hinged	60.00	
O7	A40	6c deep violet	.75	.25
		Never hinged	1.25	
		P# block of 10, Impt.	40.00	
		Never hinged	50.00	
O8	A40	8c yellow brown	.75	.25
		Never hinged	1.25	
		P# block of 6	32.00	
		Never hinged	40.00	
O9	A40	10c deep blue	1.20	.25
		Never hinged	1.90	
		P# block of 10, Impt.	32.00	
		Never hinged	40.00	
O10	A40	12c red orange	2.00	.25
		Never hinged	3.00	
		P# block of 6	65.00	
		Never hinged	80.00	
a.		No period after "B"	80.00	80.00
		Never hinged	120.00	
O11	A40	16c lt ol grn	1.00	.25
		Never hinged	1.50	
		P# block of 6	24.00	
		Never hinged	30.00	
a.		16c olive bister	2.00	.25
		Never hinged	3.00	
		P# block of 6	20.00	
		Never hinged	25.00	
O12	A40	20c orange yellow	1.25	.25
		Never hinged	1.90	
		P# block of 10, Impt.	75.00	
		Never hinged	95.00	
a.		No period after "B"	80.00	80.00
		Never hinged	120.00	
O13	A40	26c green	2.00	1.00
		Never hinged	3.25	
		P# block of 6	120.00	
		Never hinged	150.00	
		26c blue green	2.50	1.50
		Never hinged	4.00	
		P# block of 6	130.00	
		Never hinged	165.00	
O14	A40	30c gray	2.00	.25
		Never hinged	3.25	
		P# block of 10, Impt.	80.00	
		Never hinged	100.00	
		Nos. O5-O14 (10)	11.80	3.25
		Set, never hinged	18.65	

Many collectors prefer to collect the plate blocks of 6 of Nos. O5-O6, O8, O10-O11a and O14 as blocks of 10 so they fit aesthetically with the other plate blocks of 10 with imprints.

Overprinted on Nos. 383-392

1935

O15	A53	2c rose	.25	.25
		Never hinged	.30	
		P# block of 6	4.75	
		Never hinged	6.00	
a.		No period after "B"	15.00	10.00
		Never hinged	22.50	
b.		No period after "O"	—	—
O16	A54	4c yellow green	.25	.25
		Never hinged	.30	
		P# block of 6	4.00	
		Never hinged	5.00	
a.		No period after "B"	15.00	40.00
		Never hinged	22.50	

O17	A55	6c dark brown	.25	.25
		Never hinged	.40	
		P# block of 6	8.00	
		Never hinged	10.00	
a.		No period after "B"	35.00	35.00
		Never hinged	52.50	
O18	A56	8c violet	.30	.25
		Never hinged	.45	
		P# block of 6	9.50	
		Never hinged	12.00	
O19	A57	10c rose carmine	.30	.25
		Never hinged	.45	
		P# block of 6	8.00	
		Never hinged	10.00	
O20	A58	12c black	.75	.25
		Never hinged	1.10	
		P# block of 6	8.00	
		Never hinged	10.00	
O21	A59	16c dark blue	.55	.25
		Never hinged	.85	
		P# block of 6	8.00	
		Never hinged	10.00	
O22	A60	20c light olive green	.60	.25
		Never hinged	.90	
		P# block of 6	12.00	
		Never hinged	15.00	
O23	A61	26c indigo	.90	.25
		Never hinged	1.50	
		P# block of 6	20.00	
		Never hinged	25.00	
O24	A62	30c orange red	.80	.25
		Never hinged	1.20	
		P# block of 6	20.00	
		Never hinged	25.00	
		Nos. O15-O24 (10)	4.95	2.50
		Set, never hinged	7.40	

Nos. 411 and 418 with Additional Overprint in Black

1937-38

O25	A53	2c rose	.25	.25
		Never hinged	.30	
a.		No period after "B"	25.00	25.00
		Never hinged	45.00	
b.		Period after "B" raised (UL 4)	150.00	
O26	A60	20c lt ol grn ('38)	.70	.50
		Never hinged	1.10	
		P# block of 6	20.00	
		Never hinged	25.00	

Regular Issue of 1935 Overprinted In Black

a

b

1938-40

O27	A53(a)	2c rose	.25	.25
		Never hinged	.30	
		P# block of 6	4.75	
		Never hinged	6.00	
a.		Hyphen omitted	10.00	10.00
		Never hinged	15.00	
b.		No period after "B"	20.00	30.00
		Never hinged	30.00	
O28	A54(b)	4c yellow green	.75	1.00
		Never hinged	1.10	
		P# block of 6	24.00	
		Never hinged	30.00	
O29	A55(a)	6c dark brown	.30	.25
		Never hinged	.45	
		P# block of 6	12.00	
		Never hinged	15.00	
O30	A56(b)	8c violet	.75	.85
		Never hinged	1.10	
		P# block of 6	9.50	
		Never hinged	12.00	
O31	A57(b)	10c rose carmine	.25	.25
		Never hinged	.30	
		P# block of 6	16.00	
		Never hinged	20.00	
a.		No period after "O"	50.00	40.00
		Never hinged	75.00	
O32	A58(b)	12c black	.30	.25
		Never hinged	.45	
		P# block of 6	12.00	
		Never hinged	15.00	
O33	A59(b)	16c dark blue	.30	.25
		Never hinged	.45	
		P# block of 6	16.00	
		Never hinged	20.00	
O34	A60(a)	20c lt ol grn ('40)	.55	.85
		Never hinged	.85	
		P# block of 6	16.00	
		Never hinged	20.00	
O35	A61(b)	26c indigo	1.50	2.00
		Never hinged	2.25	
		P# block of 6	12.00	
		Never hinged	15.00	

O36	A62(b)	30c orange red	.75	.85
		Never hinged	1.10	
		P# block of 6	16.00	
		Never hinged	20.00	
		Nos. O27-O36 (10)	5.70	6.80
		Set, never hinged	8.25	

No. 461 Overprinted in Black — c

1941, Apr. 14   Perf. 11x10½

O37	A75(c)	2c apple green	.25	.40
		Never hinged	.30	

Official Stamps Handstamped in Violet

1944   Perf. 11, 11x10½

O38	A53	2c rose (On O27)	375.00	200.00
		Never hinged	750.00	
O39	A75	2c apple grn (On O37)	10.00	10.00
		Never hinged	15.00	
O40	A54	4c yel grn (On O16)	45.00	30.00
		Never hinged	80.00	
O40A	A55	6c dk brn (On O29)	8,000.	—
O41	A57	10c rose car (On O31)	500.00	
a.		No period after "O"	4,000.	
O42	A60	20c lt ol grn (On O22)	8,000.	
O43	A60	20c lt ol grn (On O26)	1,750.	

No. 497 Overprinted Type "c" in Black

1946, June 19   Perf. 11x10½

O44	A76	2c sepia	.25	.25
		Never hinged	.25	
a.		Vertical pair, bottom stamp without ovpt.	—	

OCCUPATION STAMPS

Issued Under Japanese Occupation

Nos. 461, 438 and 439 Overprinted in Black

1942-43   Unwmk.   Perf. 11x10½, 11

N1	A75	2c apple green	.25	1.00
		Never hinged	.30	
a.		Pair, one without overprint	—	
N2	A58	12c black ('43)	.25	2.00
		Never hinged	.40	
		P# block of 6	12.00	
		Never hinged	15.00	
N3	A59	16c dark blue	5.00	3.75
		Never hinged	7.50	
		P# block of 6	37.50	
		Never hinged	55.00	
		Nos. N1-N3 (3)	5.50	6.75
		Set, never hinged	8.20	

Nos. 435a, 435, 442, 443, and 423 Surcharged in Black

a

b

c

d

Type I

Type II

Two types of 50c surcharge
Type I: Center of "A" is a triangle.
Type II: Center of "A" is a pin hole.

1942-43   *Perf. 11*
N4	A55(a)	5(c) on 6c gold- en brown	.25	.75
	Never hinged		.35	
a.	Top bar shorter and thinner		.25	1.00
	Never hinged		.35	
	P# block of 6		40.00	
	Never hinged		50.00	
b.	5(c) on 6c dark brown		.25	.85
	Never hinged		.35	
c.	As "b," top bar shorter and thinner		.25	1.00
	Never hinged		.35	
d.	Double surcharge, on cover		—	
N5	A62(b)	16(c) on 30c org red ('43)	.25	.60
	Never hinged		.45	
N6	A63(c)	50c on 1p red org & blk ('43)	.75	1.25
	Never hinged		1.10	
	P# block of 4		16.00	
	Never hinged		20.00	
a.	Double surcharge			300.00
b.	Type I surcharge		100.00	90.00
	Never hinged		125.00	
	P# block of 4		500.00	
	Never hinged		600.00	
N7	A65(d)	1p on 4p bl & blk ('43)	100.00	150.00
	Never hinged		155.00	
	Nos. N4-N7 (4)		101.25	152.60
	Set, never hinged		156.90	

On Nos. N4 and N4b, the top bar measures 1½x22½mm. On Nos. N4a and N4c, the top bar measures 1x21mm and the "5" is smaller and thinner.

The used value for No. N7 is for postal cancellation. Used stamps exist with first day cancellations. They are worth somewhat less.

No. 384 Surcharged in Black

1942, May 18
N8	A54	2(c) on 4c yellow green	4.00	5.00
	Never hinged		8.75	

Issued to commemorate Japan's capture of Bataan and Corregidor. The American-Filipino forces finally surrendered May 7, 1942. No. N8 exists with "R" for "B" in BATAAN.

No. 384 Surcharged in Black

1942, Dec. 8
N9	A54	5(c) on 4c yellow green	.50	1.00
	Never hinged		.75	

1st anniversary of the "Greater East Asia War."

Nos. C59 and C62 Surcharged in Black

1943, Jan. 23
N10	AP1	2(c) on 8c carmine	.25	1.00
	Never hinged		.35	
	P# block of 6		20.00	
	Never hinged		25.00	
N11	AP1	5c on 1p sepia	.50	1.50
	Never hinged		.75	

1st anniv. of the Philippine Executive Commission.

Nipa Hut
OS1

Rice Planting
OS2

Mt. Mayon and
Mt. Fuji — OS3

Moro
Vinta — OS4

The "c" currency is indicated by four Japanese characters, "p" currency by two.

Engraved; Typographed (2c, 6c, 25c)

1943-44   **Wmk. 257**   *Perf. 13*
N12	OS1	1c dp orange	.25	.40
	Never hinged		.30	
	Margin block of 6, inscription		2.40	
			3.00	
N13	OS2	2c brt green	.25	.40
	Never hinged		.30	
	Margin block of 6, inscription		2.40	
			3.00	
N14	OS1	4c slate green	.25	.40
	Never hinged		.30	
	Margin block of 6, inscription		2.40	
			3.00	
N15	OS3	5c orange brown	.25	.40
	Never hinged		.30	
	Margin block of 6, inscription		2.40	
			3.00	
N16	OS2	6c red	.25	.60
	Never hinged		.30	
	Margin block of 6, inscription		2.40	
			3.00	
N17	OS3	10c blue green	.25	.40
	Never hinged		.30	
	Margin block of 6, inscription		2.40	
			3.00	
N18	OS4	12c steel blue	1.00	1.50
	Never hinged		1.50	
	Margin block of 6, inscription		11.00	
			14.00	
N19	OS4	16c dk brown	.25	.40
	Never hinged		.30	
	Margin block of 6, inscription		2.40	
			3.00	
N20	OS1	20c rose violet	1.25	1.75
	Never hinged		1.90	
	Margin block of 6, inscription		15.00	
			19.00	
N21	OS3	21c violet	.25	.40
	Never hinged		.35	
	Margin block of 6, inscription		2.40	
			3.00	
N22	OS2	25c pale brown	.25	.40
	Never hinged		.35	
	Margin block of 6, inscription		2.40	
			3.00	
N23	OS3	1p dp carmine	.75	1.25
	Never hinged		1.15	
	Margin block of 6, inscription		9.50	
			12.00	
N24	OS4	2p dull violet	6.50	6.50
	Never hinged		10.00	
N25	OS4	5p dark olive	16.00	18.00
	Never hinged		25.00	
	Nos. N12-N25 (14)		27.75	32.80
	Set, never hinged		42.00	

Issued: Nos. N13, N15, 4/1; Nos. N12, N14, N23, 6/7; Nos. N16-N19, 7/14; Nos. N20-N22, 8/16; No. N24, 9/16; No. N25, 4/1/44. For surcharges see Nos. NB5-NB7.

OS5

1943, May 7   **Photo.**   **Unwmk.**
N26	OS5	2c carmine red	.25	.75
	Never hinged		.30	
	Margin block of 6, inscription		4.00	
	Never hinged		5.00	
N27	OS5	5c bright green	.25	1.00
	Never hinged		.35	
	Margin block of 6, inscription		6.50	
			8.00	

1st anniversary of the fall of Bataan and Corregidor.

No. 440 Surcharged in
Black

1943, June 20   **Engr.**   *Perf. 11*
N28	A60	12(c) on 20c light olive green	.25	.75
	Never hinged		.35	
a.	Double surcharge			

350th anniversary of the printing press in the Philippines. "Limbagan" is Tagalog for "printing press."

Rizal
Monument,
Filipina and
Philippine
Flag — OS6

1943, Oct. 14   **Photo.**   *Perf. 12*
N29	OS6	5c light blue	.25	.90
	Never hinged		.30	
a.	Imperf.		.25	.90
N30	OS6	12c orange	.25	.90
	Never hinged		.30	
a.	Imperf.		.25	.90
N31	OS6	17c rose pink	.25	.90
	Never hinged		.30	
a.	Imperf.		.25	.90
	Nos. N29-N31 (3)		.75	2.70
	Set, never hinged		.90	

"Independence of the Philippines." Japan granted "independence" Oct. 14, 1943, when the puppet republic was founded.

The imperforate stamps were issued without gum.

José
Rizal — OS7

Rev. José
Burgos — OS8

Apolinario
Mabini — OS9

1944, Feb. 17   **Litho.**
N32	OS7	5c blue	.25	1.00
	Never hinged		.30	
a.	Imperf.		.25	2.00
	Never hinged		.35	
N33	OS8	12c carmine	.25	1.00
	Never hinged		.30	
a.	Imperf.		.25	2.00
	Never hinged		.35	
N34	OS9	17c deep orange	.25	1.00
	Never hinged		.30	
a.	Imperf.		.25	2.00
	Never hinged		.35	
	Nos. N32-N34 (3)		.75	3.00
	Set, never hinged		.90	

See No. NB8.

Nos. C60 and C61 Surcharged in Black

1944, May 7   *Perf. 11*
N35	AP1	5(c) on 20c ultra	.50	1.00
	Never hinged		.75	
	P# block of 6		32.50	
	Never hinged		40.00	
N36	AP1	12(c) on 60c blue green	1.75	1.75
	Never hinged		2.50	
	P# block of 6		42.50	
	Never hinged		52.50	

2nd anniversary of the fall of Bataan and Corregidor.

OS10

1945, Jan. 12   **Litho.**   *Imperf.*
Without Gum
N37	OS10	5c dull violet brown	.25	.50
	Never hinged		.30	
N38	OS10	7c blue green	.25	.50
	Never hinged		.30	
N39	OS10	20c chalky blue	.25	.50
	Never hinged		.30	
	Nos. N37-N39 (3)		.75	1.50
	Set, never hinged		.90	

Issued belatedly on Jan. 12, 1945, to commemorate the first anniversary of the puppet Philippine Republic, Oct. 14, 1944. "S" stands for "sentimos."

OCCUPATION SEMI-POSTAL STAMPS

Woman, Farming
and
Cannery — OSP1

Unwmk.
1942, Nov. 12   **Litho.**   *Perf. 12*
NB1	OSP1	2c + 1c pale violet	.25	.60
	Never hinged		.30	
NB2	OSP1	5c + 1c brt grn	.25	1.00
	Never hinged		.30	
NB3	OSP1	16c + 2c orange	25.00	32.50
	Never hinged		42.00	
	Nos. NB1-NB3 (3)		25.50	34.10
	Set, never hinged		42.60	

Issued to promote the campaign to produce and conserve food. The surtax aided the Red Cross.

Souvenir Sheet

OSP2

1943, Oct. 14 Without Gum Imperf.
NB4 OSP2 Sheet of 3 75.00 17.50

"Independence of the Philippines."
No. NB4 contains one each of Nos. N29a-N31a. Marginal inscription is from Rizal's "Last Farewell." Sold for 2.50p.
The value of No. NB4 used is for a sheet from a first day cover. Commercially used sheets are extremely scarce and worth much more.

Nos. N18, N20 and N21 Surcharged in Black

1943, Dec. 8 Wmk. 257 Perf. 13
NB5 OS4 12c + 21c steel blue .25 1.50
  Never hinged .30
  Margin block of 6, inscription 4.00
  Never hinged 5.00
NB6 OS1 20c + 36c rose violet .25 1.50
  Never hinged .30
  Margin block of 6, inscription 4.00
  Never hinged 5.00
NB7 OS3 21c + 40c violet .25 2.00
  Never hinged .30
  Margin block of 6, inscription 4.75
  Never hinged 6.00
  Nos. NB5-NB7 (3) .75 5.00
  Set, never hinged .90

The surtax was for the benefit of victims of a Luzon flood. "Baha" is Tagalog for "flood."

Souvenir Sheet

OSP3

Unwmk.
1944, Feb. 9 Litho. Imperf.
Without Gum
NB8 OSP3 Sheet of 3 6.50 3.50

No. NB8 contains 1 each of Nos. N32a-N34a.
Sheet sold for 1p, surtax going to a fund for the care of heroes' monuments.

The value for No. NB8 used is for a stamp from a first day cover. Commercially used examples are worth much more.

OCCUPATION POSTAGE DUE STAMP

No. J15 Overprinted in Blue

1942, Oct. 14 Unwmk. Perf. 11
NJ1 D3 3c on 4c brown red 25.00 35.00
  Never hinged 37.50

On examples of No. J15, two lines were drawn in India ink with a ruling pen across "United States of America" by employees of the Short Paid Section of the Manila Post Office to make a provisional 3c postage due stamp which was used from Sept. 1, 1942 (when the letter rate was raised from 2c to 5c) until Oct. 14 when No. NJ1 went on sale. Value on cover, $175.
Bottom plate blocks of 6 of No. NJ1 are much scarcer than the right side plate blocks. Value $325 hinged, $450 never hinged.

OCCUPATION OFFICIAL STAMPS

Nos. 461, 413, 435, 435a and 442 Ovptd. or Srchd. in Black with Bars and

1943-44 Unwmk. Perf. 11x10½, 11
NO1 A75 2c apple green .25 .75
  Never hinged .30
  a. Double overprint 400.00
    Never hinged 600.00
NO2 A55 5(c) on 6c dk brn
  (On No. 413)
  ('44) 40.00 45.00
  Never hinged 55.00
NO3 A55 5(c) on 6c golden brn (On No. 435a) .25 .90
  Never hinged .35
  P# block of 6 14.00
  Never hinged 17.50
  a. Narrower spacing between bars .25 .90
    Never hinged .35
  b. 5(c) on 6c dark brown (On No. 435) .25 .90
    Never hinged .35
  c. As "b," narrower spacing between bars .25 .90
    Never hinged .35
  d. Double overprint
NO4 A62 16(c) on 30c org red .30 1.25
  Never hinged .45
  P# block of 6 20.00
  Never hinged 25.00
  a. Wider spacing between bars .30 1.25
    Never hinged .45
  Nos. NO1-NO4 (4) 40.80 47.90
  Set, never hinged 56.10

On Nos. NO3 and NO3b the bar deleting "United States of America" is 9¾ to 10mm above the bar deleting "Common." On Nos. NO3a and NO3c, the spacing is 8 to 8½mm.
On No. NO4, the center bar is 19mm long, 3½mm below the top bar and 6mm above the Japanese characters. On No. NO4a, the center bar is 20½mm long, 9mm below the top bar and 1mm above the Japanese characters.
"K.P." stands for Kagamitang Pampamahalaan, "Official Business" in Tagalog.

Nos. 435 & 435a Surcharged in Black

1944, Aug. 28 Perf. 11
NO5 A55 (5c) on 6c gldn brn .30 .40
  Never hinged .45
  P# block of 6 20.00
  Never hinged 25.00

  a. 5(c) on 6c dark brown .30 .40
    Never hinged .45
    P# block of 6 20.00
    Never hinged 25.00

Nos. O34 and C62 Overprinted in Black

a

b

NO6 A60(a) 20c light olive green .40 .50
  Never hinged .60
  P# block of 6 12.00
  Never hinged 15.00
NO7 AP1(b) 1p sepia .90 1.00
  Never hinged 1.45
  P# block of 6 20.00
  Never hinged 25.00
  Nos. NO5-NO7 (3) 1.60 1.90
  Set, never hinged 2.05

PUERTO RICO

ˌpwer-tə-ˈrē-ˌkō

(Porto Rico)

LOCATION — Large island in the West Indies, east of Hispaniola
GOVT. — Former Spanish possession
AREA — 3,435 sq. mi.
POP. — 953,243 (1899)
CAPITAL — San Juan

The island was ceded to the US by the Treaty of 1898.
Spanish issues of 1855-73 used in both Puerto Rico and Cuba are listed as Cuba Nos. 1-4, 9-14, 18-21, 32-34, 35A-37, 39-41, 43-45, 47-49, 51-53, 55-57.
Spanish issues of 1873-1898 for Puerto Rico only are listed in Vol. 4 of this Catalogue.

100 Cents = 1 Dollar (1898)

Issued under U.S. Administration
PROVISIONAL ISSUES
Ponce Issue

A11

Handstamped
1898 Unwmk. Imperf.
200 A11 5c violet, yellowish 7,500. —

The only way No. 200 is known used is handstamped on envelopes. Unused stamps always have a violet control mark. Used envelopes do not have the control mark. The same handstamp used to prepare No. 200 also is known handstamped on an unused envelope, also without the control mark. Research into whether the envelopes represent prepaid postmaster provisional usage is ongoing.
Uses on 2c U.S. stamps on cover were strictly as a cancellation, not as provisional postage.
Dangerous forgeries exist.

Coamo Issue

A12

Typeset, setting of 10
1898, Aug.
201 A12 5c black 650. 1,250.

See the Scott U.S. Specialized Catalogue for more detailed listings.
The stamps bear the control mark "F. Santiago" in violet. About 500 were issued.
Dangerous forgeries exist.

Regular Issue

United States Nos. 279, 279Bf, 281, 272 and 282C Overprinted in Black at 36 degree angle

1899 Wmk. 191 Perf. 12
210 A87 1c yellow green 6.00 1.40
  Never hinged 13.00
  a. Overprint at 25 degree angle 8.00 2.25
    Never hinged 17.50
211 A88 2c redsh car, type IV 5.00 1.25
  Never hinged 11.00
  a. Overprint at 25 degree angle, Mar. 15 6.50 2.25
    Never hinged 14.00
212 A91 5c blue 12.50 2.50
  Never hinged 27.50
213 A93 8c violet brown 40.00 17.50
  Never hinged 90.00
  a. Overprint at 25 degree angle 45.00 19.00
    Never hinged 100.00
  c. "PORTO RIC" 150.00 110.00
214 A94 10c brown, type I 22.50 6.00
  Never hinged 50.00
  Nos. 210-214 (5) 86.00 28.65

Misspellings of the overprint on Nos. 210-214 (PORTO RICU, PORTU RICO, FORTO RICO) are actually broken letters.

United States Nos. 279 and 279B Overprinted Diagonally in Black

1900
215 A87 1c yellow green 7.50 1.40
  Never hinged 17.50
216 A88 2c red, type IV 5.50 2.00
  Never hinged 12.50
  b. Inverted overprint 12,500.

POSTAGE DUE STAMPS

United States Nos. J38, J39 and J42 Overprinted in Black at 36 degree angle

1899 Wmk. 191 Perf. 12
J1 D2 1c deep claret 22.50 5.50
  Never hinged 50.00
  a. Overprint at 25 degree angle 22.50 7.50
    Never hinged 50.00
J2 D2 2c deep claret 20.00 6.00
  Never hinged 45.00
  a. Overprint at 25 degree angle 20.00 7.00
    Never hinged 45.00
J3 D2 10c deep claret 180.00 55.00
  Never hinged 375.00
  a. Overprint at 25 degree angle 160.00 75.00
    Never hinged 330.00
  Nos. J1-J3 (3) 222.50 66.50

Stamps of Puerto Rico were replaced by those of the United States.

RYUKYU ISLANDS

rē-'yü-ṟ̣kyü 'i-lənds

LOCATION — Chain of 63 islands between Japan and Formosa, separating the East China Sea from the Pacific Ocean.

GOVT. — Semi-autonomous under United States administration.

AREA — 848 sq. mi.

POP. — 945,465 (1970)

CAPITAL — Naha, Okinawa

The Ryukyus were part of Japan until American forces occupied them in 1945. The islands reverted to Japan May 15, 1972.

Before the general issue of 1948, a number of provisional stamps were used. These included a mimeographed-handstamped adhesive for Kume Island, and various current stamps of Japan handstamped with chops by the postmasters of Okinawa, Amami, Miyako and Yaeyama. Although authorized by American authorities, these provisionals were local in nature, so are omitted in the listings that follow. They are listed in the *Scott United States Specialized Catalogue.*

100 Sen = 1 Yen

100 Cents = 1 Dollar (1958)

Catalogue values for unused stamps in this country are for Never Hinged items.

Wmk. 257

Cycad — A1

Lily — A2

Sailing Ship — A3

Farmer — A4

1948-49 Typo. Wmk. 257 *Perf. 13*
Second Printing, July 18, 1949

1	A1	5s magenta	2.00	2.00
2	A2	10s yellow green	5.00	5.00
3	A1	20s yellow green	3.00	3.00
4	A3	30s vermilion	1.25	1.25
5	A2	40s magenta	1.25	1.25
6	A3	50s ultramarine	5.00	4.00
7	A4	1y ultramarine	5.00	5.00
		Nos. 1-7 (7)	22.50	21.50

First Printing, July 1, 1948

1a	A1	5s magenta	3.00	3.50
2a	A2	10s yellow green	2.00	2.00
3a	A1	20s yellow green	2.00	2.00
4a	A3	30s vermilion	4.00	3.50
5a	A2	40s magenta	50.00	50.00
6a	A3	50s ultramarine	4.00	4.00
7a	A4	1y ultramarine	425.00	350.00
		Nos. 1a-7a (7)	490.00	415.00

First printing: thick yellow gum, dull colors, rough perforations, grayish paper. Second printing: white gum, sharp colors, cleancut perforations, white paper.

Tile Rooftop and Shishi — A5

Designs: 50s, Tile rooftop & Shishi. 1y, Ryukyu girl. 2y, Shuri Castle. 3y, Guardian dragon. 4y, Two women. 5y, Sea shells.

Perf. 13x13½
1950, Jan. 21 Photo. Unwmk. Off-white Paper

8	A5	50s dark carmine rose	.25	.25
a.		White paper, third printing, Sept. 6, 1958	.50	.50
b.		"White Sky" variety (pos. 76)	3.50	3.50
9	A5	1y deep blue	3.25	3.00
10	A5	2y rose violet	9.00	6.00
11	A5	3y carmine rose	22.50	11.00
12	A5	4y greenish gray	11.00	11.00
13	A5	5y blue green	6.50	6.00
		Nos. 8-13 (6)	52.50	37.25

The original first two printings (No. 8) were printed on off-white paper with yellowish gum and a 5-character imprint in the sheet margin. The first printing is a deep carmine red and the second printing a dark carmine rose. The first printing was issued Jan. 21, 1950; the second printing received in Naha Sept. 22, 1950; and the third printing (No. 8a) Sept. 6, 1958. Quantities: first printing: 300,000; second printing: 3,000,000; and third printing: 300,000. The first printing unused is much scarcer than the second printing because most of the first printing was used as postage.

No. 8a has colorless gum and an 8-character imprint in the sheet margin.

For No. 8b, a defect in position 76 of the plates used resulted in the sky above the roof being predominantly white in the second printing, whereas in the first printing the 'white sky' is not as pronounced. The master negative and plate were reworked for the third printing, so position 76 in this printing does not have the "white sky" variety.

For surcharges see Nos. 16-17.

Ryukyu University A6

1951, Feb. 12 *Perf. 13½x13*

14	A6	3y red brown	45.00	25.00

Opening of Ryukyu University, Feb. 12.

Pine Tree — A7

1951, Feb. 19 *Perf. 13*

15	A7	3y dark green	40.00	22.50

Reforestation Week, Feb. 18-24.

No. 8 surcharged in Black

Type I

Type II

Type III

There are three types of 10y surcharge:

Type I: narrow-spaced rules, "10" normal spacing, "Kai Tei" characters in 9-point type. First printing, Jan. 1, 1952.

Type II: wide-spaced rules, "10" normal spacing, "Kai Tei" characters in 9-point type. Second printing, June 5, 1952.

Type III: rules and "10" both wide-spaced, "Kai Tei" characters in 8-point type. Third printing, Dec. 8, 1952.

Both eight and nine point type were used in overprinting Nos. 16-17. In the varieties listed below, the first number indicates the size of the "Kai" character, and the second number is the size of the "Tei" character.

1952 *Perf. 13½x13*

16	A5	10y on 50s dark carmine rose (II)	8.00	8.00
c.		8/8 point Kai Tei	8.00	8.00
d.		9/8 point Kai Tei	80.00	80.00
e.		Surcharge transposed	900.00	
f.		Legend of surcharge only (no obliteration bars)	1,200.	
g.		Wrong font for "0" (pos. 59)	150.00	150.00
h.		Wrong font for "Yen" symbol (pos. 69)	150.00	150.00
i.		Surcharge on "white sky" variety (No. 8b) (pos. 76)	150.00	150.00

On No. 16e, the entire obliteration-bars portion of the surcharge normally under the 10 Yen must be visible at the top of the stamp. Ten examples of No. 16e exist (pos. 91-100) with the full obliteration bars also in the bottom selvage.

Forgeries to defraud the Postal Agency of revenue are known, used only, at the Gusikawa Post Office. Two types. Value, $500 each.

16A	A5	10y on 50s dark carmine rose (I)	30.00	30.00
a.		8/8 point Kai Tei	30.00	30.00
b.		Bottom two bars inverted (pos. 17)	150.00	150.00
c.		Wrong font for "0" (pos. 73)	250.00	250.00
d.		Surcharge on "white sky" variety (No. 8b) (pos. 76)	250.00	250.00
e.		Wide spaced obliterating bars (pos. 72)	150.00	150.00
f.		Wide spaced bottom obliterating bars (pos. 86, 95)	80.00	80.00
16B	A5	10y on 50s dark carmine rose (III)	45.00	35.00
a.		Wrong font for "Yen" symbol (pos. 25, 35, 85)	200.00	200.00
b.		Wrong font for "Tei" (pos. 26)	200.00	200.00
c.		Asterisk missing (pos. 54)	—	—
d.		"Kai Tei" 1.25mm above asterisk (pos. 54)	350.00	—
e.		"Kai" omitted (pos. 71)	350.00	—
f.		Narrow spaced "10" (pos. 96)	350.00	—
g.		Surcharge on "white sky" variety (No. 8b)	350.00	350.00
h.		Extra wide spaced "10" (pos. 60)	200.00	200.00
i.		Asterisk within 2.0mm of "Kai Tei" (pos. 87)	200.00	200.00

The Kai Tei of the third printing measures the same as the 8-point type in the earlier printings but has differing characteristics. The Top curved line of the Kai is shorter and the lower curved line is also much shorter.

No. 10 surcharged 100y in black

17	A5	100y on 2y rose violet, Kai Tei characters in 9/9-point type, June 16, 1952	2,000.	1,400.
a.		8/8 point Kai Tei	2,000.	1,400.
b.		9/8 point Kai Tei	3,250.	3,250.
c.		Center "0" in wrong font, stamp with 9/9 Kai Tei (pos. 42)	4,000.	4,000.
d.		Center "0" in wrong font, stamp with 8/8 Kai Tei (pos. 67, 86)	3,500.	3,500.
e.		Center "0" in wrong font, stamp with 9/8 Kai Tei (pos. 53)	5,000.	5,000.
f.		Wrong font for last "0" (pos. 59)	5,000.	5,000.
g.		Wrong font for "yen" symbol (pos. 69)	5,000.	5,000.

Varieties of shifted and damaged surcharge characters exist, most notably a damaged ("clipped") Kai.

See note after 16B to differentiate between 8-point and 9-point charaters.

Surcharge forgeries are known. Authentication by competant experts is recommended.

Dove, Bean Sprout and Map — A8

1952, Apr. 1 *Perf. 13½x13*

18	A8	3y deep plum	80.00	40.00

Establishment of the Government of the Ryukyu Islands (GRI), April 1, 1952.

Madanbashi Bridge — A9

Designs: 2y, Main Hall, Shuri Castle. 3y, Shurei Gate. 6y, Stone Gate, Soenji Temple, Naha. 10y, Benzaiten-do Temple. 30y, Sonohan Utaki (altar) at Shuri Castle. 50y, Tamaudun (royal mausoleum). Shuri. 100y, Stone Bridge, Hosho Pond, Enkaku Temple.

1952-53

19	A9	1y red	.30	.30
20	A9	2y green	.40	.40
21	A9	3y aquamarine	.50	.50
22	A9	6y blue	2.00	2.00
23	A9	10y crimson rose	2.50	1.00
24	A9	30y olive green	9.00	7.50
a.		30y light olive green, 1958	50.00	
25	A9	50y rose violet	12.50	9.00
26	A9	100y claret	15.00	5.00
		Nos. 19-26 (8)	42.20	25.70

Issued: 1y, 2y and 3y, 11/20/52. Others,1/20/53.

Reception at Shuri Castle — A10

Perry and American Fleet A11

1953, May 26 *Perf. 13½x13, 13x13½*

27	A10	3y deep magenta	12.00	6.50
28	A11	6y dull blue	1.25	1.50

Centenary of the arrival of Commodore Matthew Calbraith Perry at Naha, Okinawa.

Chofu Ota and Pencil-shaped Matrix — A12

1953, Oct. 1 *Perf. 13½x13*

29	A12	4y yellow brown	11.00	5.00

Third Newspaper Week.

Shigo Toma and Pen — A13

1954, Oct. 1
30   A13   4y blue   10.00   7.50
Fourth Newspaper Week.

Ryukyu Pottery — A14

Designs: 15y, Lacquerware. 20y, Textile design.

1954-55   Photo.   Perf. 13
31   A14   4y brown   .90   .50
32   A14   15y vermilion   3.50   3.50
33   A14   20y yellow orange 2.25   2.25
      Nos. 31-33 (3)   6.65   6.25
For surcharges see Nos. C19, C21, C23.

Noguni Shrine and
Sweet Potato
Plant — A15

1955, Nov. 26
34   A15   4y blue   10.00   7.00
350th anniv. of the introduction of the sweet potato to the Ryukyu Islands.

Stylized Trees — A16

1956, Feb. 18   Unwmk.
35   A16   4y bluish green   10.00   6.00
Arbor Week, Feb. 18-24.

Willow Dance — A17

8y, Straw hat dance. 14y, Dancer in warrior costume with fan.

1956, May 1   Perf. 13
36   A17   5y rose lilac   1.00   .60
37   A17   8y violet blue   2.00   2.00
38   A17   14y reddish brown 2.50   2.50
      Nos. 36-38 (3)   5.50   5.10
For surcharges see Nos. C20, C22.

Telephone — A18

1956, June 8
39   A18   4y violet blue   12.50   8.00
Establishment of dial telephone system.

Garland of Pine,
Bamboo and
Plum — A19

1956, Dec. 1   Perf. 13½x13
40   A19   2y multicolored   1.60   1.60
New Year, 1957.

Map of Okinawa and
Pencil Rocket — A20

1957, Oct. 1   Photo.   Perf. 13½x13
41   A20   4y deep violet
            blue   1.00   1.00
7th annual Newspaper Week, Oct. 1-7.

Phoenix — A21

1957, Dec. 1   Unwmk.   Perf. 13
42   A21   2y multicolored   .25   .25
New Year, 1958.

Ryukyu Stamps — A22

1958, July 1   Perf. 13½
43   A22   4y multicolored   .80   .80
10th anniv. of 1st Ryukyu stamps.

Yen Symbol and Dollar
Sign — A23

Perf. 10.3, 10.8, 11.1 & Compound
1958, Sept. 16   Typo.
Without Gum

44	A23	½c orange	.80	.80
a.		Imperf., pair	1,500.	
b.		Horiz. pair, imperf. between	225.00	
c.		Vert. pair, imperf. between	575.00	
d.		Vert. strip of 4, imperf. between	800.00	
45	A23	1c yellow green	1.25	1.25
a.		Horiz. pair, imperf. between	200.00	
b.		Vert. pair, imperf. between	150.00	
c.		Vert. strip of 3, imperf. between	650.00	
d.		Vert. strip of 4, imperf. between	800.00	
e.		Block of 4, imperf. btwn. vert. & horiz.	10,000.	
46	A23	2c dark blue	2.00	2.00
a.		Horiz. pair, imperf. between	200.00	
b.		Horiz. pair, imperf. between	2,200.	
c.		Horiz. strip of 3, imperf. between	450.00	
d.		Horiz. strip of 4, imperf. between	700.00	
47	A23	3c deep carmine	1.50	1.50
a.		Horiz. pair, imperf. between	200.00	
b.		Vert. pair, imperf. between	150.00	
c.		Vert. strip of 3, imperf. between	400.00	
d.		Vert. strip of 4, imperf. between	750.00	
e.		Block of 4, imperf. btwn. vert. & horiz.	10,000.	
48	A23	4c bright green	2.00	2.00
a.		Horiz. pair, imperf. between	400.00	
b.		Vert. pair, imperf. between	175.00	
49	A23	5c orange	4.00	3.75
a.		Horiz. pair, imperf. between	225.00	
b.		Vert. pair, imperf. between	850.00	
50	A23	10c aquamarine	5.25	4.75
a.		Horiz. pair, imperf. between	200.00	
b.		Vert. pair, imperf. between	150.00	
c.		Vert. strip of 3, imperf. between	750.00	
51	A23	25c bright violet blue	7.50	6.00
a.		Gummed paper, perf. 10.3 ('61)	15.00	15.00
b.		Horiz. pair, imperf. between	2,200.	
c.		Vert. pair, imperf. between	5,000.	
d.		Vert. strip of 3, imperf. between	900.00	
52	A23	50c gray	15.00	10.00
a.		Gummed paper, perf. 10.3 ('61)	15.00	15.00
b.		Horiz. pair, imperf. between	1,750.	
53	A23	$1 rose lilac	11.00	5.50
a.		Horiz. pair, imperf. between	500.00	
b.		Vert. pair, imperf. between	2,250.	
		Nos. 44-53 (10)	50.30	37.55

Printed locally. Perforation, paper and shade varieties exist. Nos. 51a and 52a are on off-white paper and perf 10.3.

Gate of Courtesy — A24

1958, Oct. 15   Photo.   Perf. 13½
54 A24 3c multicolored   1.25 1.25
Restoration of Shureimon, Gate of Courtesy, on road leading to Shuri City.
Imitations of this stamp were distributed in 1972 to discourage speculation in Ryukyuan stamps. The imitations were printed without gum and have a lengthy message in light blue printed on the back. A second type exists, with printed black perforations and three Japanese characters on the back ("Mozo Hin" — imitation) in black. Value, sheet of 10 $15.

Lion Dance — A25

1958, Dec. 10   Unwmk.   Perf. 13½
55 A25 1½c multicolored   .30   .30
New Year, 1959.

Trees and Mountains — A26

1959, Apr. 30   Litho.   Perf. 13½x13
56 A26 3c blue, yellow green,
              green & red   .70   .60
"Make the Ryukyus Green" movement.

Yonaguni Moth A27

1959, July 23   Photo.   Perf. 13
57 A27 3c multicolored   1.20 1.00
Meeting of the Japanese Biological Education Society in Okinawa.

Hibiscus — A28

琉球郵便 Inscribed

Designs: 3c, Fish (Moorish idol). 8c, Sea shell (Phalium bandatum). 13c, Butterfly (Kallinia Inachus Eucerca), denomination at left, butterfly going up. 17c, Jellyfish (Dactylometra pacifera Goette).

1959, Aug. 10   Perf. 13x13½
58 A28 ½c multicolored   .30   .25
59 A28 3c multicolored   .75   .40
60 A28 8c light ultramarine,
              black & ocher   10.00 5.50
61 A28 13c light blue, gray
              & orange   1.75 1.75
62 A28 17c violet blue, red
              & yellow   20.00 9.00
      Nos. 58-62 (5)   32.80 16.90
Four-character inscription measures 10x2mm on ½c; 12x3mm on 3c, 8c; 8½x2mm on 13c, 17c. See Nos. 76-80.

Toy (Yakaji) — A29

1959, Dec. 1   Litho.
63 A29 1½c gold & multi   .55   .45
New Year, 1960.

University Badge A30

1960, May 22   Photo.   Perf. 13
64 A30 3c multicolored   .95   .75
10th anniv. opening of Ryukyu University.

Dancer — A31

Designs: Various Ryukyu Dances.

1960, Nov. 1   Photo.   Perf. 13
Dark Gray Background
65 A31 1c yel, red & vio   2.00   .80
66 A31 2½c crim, blue & yel   3.00 1.00
67 A31 5c dk blue, yel & red   1.00   .50
68 A31 10c dk blue, yel & red   1.00   .70
      Nos. 65-68 (4)   7.00 3.00
See Nos. 81-87, 220.

Torch and Nago Bay A32

Runners at Starting Line A33

1960, Nov. 8
72 A32 3c lt blue, grn & red   5.00 3.00
73 A33 8c org & slate grn   1.00   .75
8th Kyushu Inter-Prefectural Athletic Meet, Nago, Northern Okinawa, Nov. 6-7.

Little Egret and Rising Sun A34

1960, Dec. 1   Unwmk.   Perf. 13
74 A34 3c reddish brown   5.00 3.50
National census.

Okinawa Bull Fight — A35

1960, Dec. 10   Perf. 13½
75 A35 1½c bister, dark blue &
              red brown   1.50 1.50
New Year, 1961.

**Type of 1959 With Japanese
Inscription Redrawn**

A28a

1960-61   Photo.   Perf. 13x13½
76 A28a ½c multicolored   .60   .45
77 A28a 3c multicolored   1.00   .35
78 A28a 8c lt ultra, blk &
               ocher   1.25   .80
79 A28a 13c blue, brown & red 1.50   .90
80 A28a 17c vio blue, red & yel 12.50 6.00
       Nos. 76-80 (5)   16.85 8.50
Size of Japanese inscription on Nos. 78-80 is 10½x1½mm. On No.79 the denomination is at right, butterfly going down.
Issued: Nos. 78-80, 7/1/60; No. 77, 8/23/61; No. 76, 10/61.

**Dancer Type of 1960 with
"RYUKYUS" Added in English**
1961-64   Perf. 13
81   A31 1c multicolored   .25   .25
82   A31 2½c multicolored   .25   .25
83   A31 5c multicolored   .25   .25
84   A31 10c multicolored   .45   .40
84A A31 20c multicolored   3.00 1.40
85   A31 25c multicolored   1.00   .90
86   A31 50c multicolored   2.50 1.40
87   A31 $1 multicolored   5.50   .25
       Nos. 81-87 (8)   13.20 5.10
Issued: Nos. 86-87, 9/1/61; No. 81, 12/5/61; No. 85, 2/1/62; Nos. 82-84, 6/20/62; No. 84A, 1/20/64.

Pine Tree — A36

1961, May 1   Photo.   Perf. 13
88 A36 3c yel grn & red   1.75 1.25
"Make the Ryukyus Green" movement.

Naha, Steamer and Sailboat A37

1961, May 20
89 A37 3c aquamarine   2.25 1.50
40th anniv. of Naha.

White Silver Temple — A38

Unwmk.
1961, Oct. 1   Typo.   Perf. 11
90 A38 3c red brown   2.50 2.00
  a. Horiz. pair, imperf. between   1,000.
  b. Vert. pair, imperf. between   700.00
Merger of townships Takamine, Kanegushiku and Miwa with Itoman.

A 3-cent stamp to commemorate the merger of two cities, Shimoji-cho and Hirara-shi of Miyako Island, was scheduled to be issued on Oct. 30, 1961. However, the merger was called off and the stamp never issued. It features a white chaplet on Kiyako linen on a blue background.

Books and Bird — A39

1961, Nov. 12   Litho.   Perf. 13
91 A39 3c multicolored   1.10   .90
Book Week.

Rising Sun and Eagles — A40

1961, Dec. 10   Photo.   Perf. 13½
92 A40 1½c gold, ver & blk   2.00 2.00
New Year, 1962.

Symbolic Steps, Trees and Government Building — A41

Design: 3c, Government Building.

1962, Apr. 1   Unwmk.   Perf. 13½
93 A41 1½c multicolored   .60   .60
94 A41 3c brt grn, red &
              gray   .80   .80
10th anniv. of the Government of the Ryukyu Islands (GRI).

Anopheles Hyrcanus Sinensis — A42

Design: 8c, Malaria eradication emblem and Shurei gate.

1962, Apr. 7   Perf. 13½x13
95 A42 3c multicolored   .60   .60
96 A42 8c multicolored   .90   .75
World Health Organization drive to eradicate malaria.

Dolls and Toys — A43

1962, May 5   Litho.   Perf. 13½
97 A43 3c red, black, blue
              & buff   1.10 1.00
Children's Day, 1962.

Linden or Sea Hibiscus — A44

Flowers: 3c, Indian coral tree. 8c, Iju (Schima liukiuensis Nakal). 13c, Touch-me-not (garden balsam). 17c, Shell flower (Alpinia speciosa).

1962, June 1 Photo.
98 A44 ½c multicolored .35 .25
99 A44 3c multicolored .30 .25
100 A44 8c multicolored .55 .45
101 A44 13c multicolored .75 .60
102 A44 17c multicolored 1.25 .80
Nos. 98-102 (5) 3.20 2.35
See Nos. 107 and 114 for 1½c and 15c flower stamps. For surcharge see No. 190.

Earthenware A45

1962, July 5 Perf. 13½x13
103 A45 3c multicolored 3.50 2.50
Philatelic Week.

Japanese Fencing (Kendo) A46

1962, July 25 Perf. 13
104 A46 3c multicolored 3.50 2.50
All-Japan Kendo Meeting in Okinawa, July 25, 1962.

Rabbit Playing near Water, Bingata Cloth Design — A47

1962, Dec. 10 Perf. 13x13½
105 A47 1½c gold & multi 1.00 .80
New Year, 1963.

Young Man and Woman, Stone Relief — A48

1963, Jan. 15 Photo. Perf. 13½
106 A48 3c gold, black & blue .90 .80

Gooseneck Cactus — A49

1963, Apr. 5 Perf. 13x13½
107 A49 1½c dark blue green, yellow & pink .25 .25

Trees and Wooded Hills — A50

1963, Mar. 25 Perf. 13½x13
108 A50 3c ultra, grn & red brn 1.00 .80
"Make the Ryukyus Green" movement.

Map of Okinawa — A51

1963, Apr. 30 Unwmk. Perf. 13½
109 A51 3c multicolored 1.25 1.00
Opening of the Round Road on Okinawa.

Hawks over Islands — A52

1963, May 10 Photo.
110 A52 3c multicolored 1.10 .95
Bird Day, May 10.

Shioya Bridge — A53

1963, June 5
111 A53 3c multicolored 1.10 .95
Opening of Shioya Bridge over Shioya Bay.

Tsuikin-wan Lacquerware Bowl — A54

1963, July 1 Unwmk. Perf. 13½
112 A54 3c multicolored 2.75 2.50

Map of Far East and JCI Emblem A55

1963, Sept. 16 Photo. Perf. 13½
113 A55 3c multicolored .70 .70
Meeting of the International Junior Chamber of Commerce (JCI), Naha, Okinawa, Sept. 16-19.

Mamaomoto — A56

1963, Oct. 15 Perf. 13x13½
114 A56 15c multicolored 1.25 .80

Site of Nakagusuku Castle — A57

1963, Nov. 1 Perf. 13½x13
115 A57 3c multicolored .60 .60
Protection of national cultural treasures.

Flame — A58

1963, Dec. 10 Perf. 13½
116 A58 3c red, dark blue & yellow .65 .60
15th anniv. of the Universal Declaration of Human Rights.

Dragon — A59

1963, Dec. 10 Photo.
117 A59 1½c multicolored .55 .50
New Year, 1964.

Carnation — A60

1964, May 10 Perf. 13½
118 A60 3c blue, yel, blk & car .40 .35
Mothers Day.

Pineapples and Sugar Cane — A61

1964, June 1
119 A61 3c multicolored .40 .35
Agricultural census.

Minsah Obi (Sash Woven of Kapok) — A62

1964, July 1 Unwmk. Perf. 13½
120 A62 3c deep blue, rose pink & ocher .50 .50
a. 3c deep blue, deep carmine & ocher .65 .65
Philatelic Week.

Girl Scout and Emblem A63

1964, Aug. 31 Photo.
121 A63 3c multicolored .40 .35
10th anniv. of Ryukyuan Girl Scouts.

Shuri Relay Station — A64

Parabolic Antenna and Map — A65

1964, Sept. 1 Unwmk. Perf. 13½
Black Overprint
122 A64 3c deep green .65 .65
a. Figure "1" inverted 30.00 30.00
b. Overprint inverted 1,500.
c. Overprint missing 3,500.
d. Overprint inverted and figure "1" inverted 5,000.
123 A65 8c ultramarine 1.25 1.25
a. Overprint missing 3,500.
Opening of the Ryukyu Islands-Japan microwave system carrying telephone and telegraph messages. The overprints indicate the system was not actually opened until 1964.
Many of the stamps with overprint errors listed above are damaged. The values listed here are for stamps in very fine condition.

Gate of Courtesy, Olympic Torch and Emblem — A66

1964, Sept. 7 Photo. Perf. 13½x13
124 A66 3c ultra, yel & red .30 .25
Relaying the Olympic torch on Okinawa en route to Tokyo.

"Naihanchi," Karate Stance — A67

"Makiwara," Strengthening Hands and Feet — A68

"Kumite," Simulated Combat — A69

1964-65 Photo. Perf. 13½
125 A67 3c dull clar, yel & blk .50 .45
126 A68 3c yel & multi .40 .40
127 A69 3c gray, red & blk .40 .40
Nos. 125-127 (3) 1.30 1.25
Karate, Ryukyuan self-defense sport. Issued: No. 125, 10/5/64; No. 126, 2/5/65; No. 127, 6/5/65.

Miyara
Dunchi — A70

1964, Nov. 1   **Perf. 13½**
128 A70 3c multicolored   .30   .25

Protection of national cultural treasures. Miyara Dunchi was built as a residence by Miyara-pechin Toen in 1819.

Snake and Iris
(Bingata) — A71

1964, Dec. 10   **Photo.**
129 A71 1½c multicolored   .30   .25

New Year, 1965.

Boy
Scouts — A72

1965, Feb. 6   **Perf. 13½**
130 A72 3c light blue & multi   .45   .40

10th anniv. of Ryukyuan Boy Scouts.

Main
Stadium,
Onoyama
A73

1965, July 1   **Perf. 13x13½**
131 A73 3c multicolored   .25   .25

Inauguration of the main stadium of the Onoyama athletic facilities.

Samisen of
King
Shoko — A74

1965, July 1   **Photo.**   **Perf. 13½**
132 A74 3c buff & multi   .45   .40

Philatelic Week.

Kin Power
Plant — A75

1965, July 1
133 A75 3c green & multi   .25   .25

Completion of Kin power plant.

ICY Emblem,
Ryukyu Map — A76

1965, Aug. 24   **Photo.**   **Perf. 13½**
134 A76 3c multicolored   .25   .25

20th anniv. of the UN and International Cooperation Year, 1964-65.

Naha City
Hall — A77

1965, Sept. 18   **Unwmk.**   **Perf. 13½**
135 A77 3c blue & multi   .35   .25

Completion of Naha City Hall.

Chinese Box
Turtle — A78

Turtles: No. 137, Hawksbill turtle (denomination at top, country name at bottom). No. 138, Asian terrapin (denomination and country name on top).

1965-66   **Photo.**   **Perf. 13½**
136 A78 3c golden brown & multi   .30   .30
137 A78 3c black, yel & brown   .30   .30
138 A78 3c gray & multicolored   .30   .30
     Nos. 136-138 (3)   .90   .90

Issued: No. 136, 10/20/65; No. 137, 1/20/66; No. 138, 4/20/66.

Horse
(Bingata) — A79

1965, Dec. 10   **Photo.**   **Perf. 13½**
139 A79 1½c multicolored   .25   .25
  a.   Gold omitted   2,000.   2,000.

New Year, 1966.
There are 92 unused and 2 used examples of No. 139a known.

Noguchi's
Okinawa
Woodpecker
A80

Sika Deer — A81

Design: No. 142, Dugong.

1966   **Photo.**   **Perf. 13½**
140 A80 3c blue green & multi   .25   .25
141 A81 3c bl, red, blk, brn & grn   .25   .25
142 A81 3c bl, yel grn, blk & red   .25   .25
     Nos. 140-142 (3)   .75   .75

Nature Conservation. Issued No. 140, 2/15; No. 141, 3/15; No. 142, 4/20.

Ryukyu Bungalow
Swallow — A82

1966, May 10   **Photo.**   **Perf. 13½**
143 A82 3c sky blue, black & brown   .25   .25

4th Bird Week, May 10-16.

Lilies and
Ruins
A83

1966, June 23   **Perf. 13x13½**
144 A83 3c multicolored   .25   .25

Memorial Day, end of the Battle of Okinawa, June 23, 1945.

University
of the
Ryukyus
A84

1966, July 1
145 A84 3c multicolored   .25   .25

Transfer of the University of the Ryukyus from U.S. authority to the Ryukyu Government.

Lacquerware, 18th
Century — A85

1966, Aug. 1   **Perf. 13½**
146 A85 3c gray & multicolored   .25   .25

Philatelic Week.

Tile-Roofed House
and UNESCO
Emblem — A86

1966, Sept. 20   **Photo.**   **Perf. 13½**
147 A86 3c multicolored   .25   .25

20th anniv. of UNESCO.

Government
Museum and
Dragon
Statue — A87

1966, Oct. 6
148 A87 3c multicolored   .25   .25

Completion of the GRI (Government of the Ryukyu Islands) Museum, Shuri.

Tomb of Nakasone-Tuimya Genga,
Ruler of Miyako — A88

1966, Nov. 1   **Photo.**   **Perf. 13½**
149 A88 3c multicolored   .25   .25

Protection of national cultural treasures.

Ram in Iris Wreath
(Bingata) — A89

1966, Dec. 10   **Photo.**   **Perf. 13½**
150 A89 1½c dark blue & multi   .25   .25

New Year, 1967.

Clown
Fish — A90

Fish: No. 152, Young boxfish (white numeral at lower left). No. 153, Forceps fish (pale buff numeral at lower right). No. 154, Spotted triggerfish (orange numeral). No. 155, Saddleback butterflyfish (carmine numeral, lower left).

1966-67
151 A90 3c orange red & multi   .25   .25
152 A90 3c org yel & multi   .25   .25
153 A90 3c multicolored   .40   .25
154 A90 3c multicolored   .35   .25
155 A90 3c multicolored   .30   .25
     Nos. 151-155 (5)   1.55   1.25

Issued No. 151, 12/20/66; No. 152, 1/10/67; No. 153, 4/10/67; No. 154, 5/25/67; No. 155, 6/10/67.

A 3-cent stamp to commemorate Japanese-American-Ryukyuan Joint Arbor Day was scheduled for release on March 16, 1967. However, it was not released. The stamp in light blue and white features American and Japanese flags joined by a shield containing a tree.

Tsuboya Urn — A91

1967, Apr. 20
156 A91 3c yellow & multicolored   .25   .25

Philatelic Week.

Episcopal
Miter — A92

Seashells: No. 158, Venus comb murex. No. 159, Chiragra spider. No. 160, Green truban. No. 161, Euprotomus bulla.

1967-68   Photo.   Perf. 13½
157 A92 3c light green & multi   .25   .25
158 A92 3c grnsh bl & multi   .25   .25
159 A92 3c emerald & multi   .25   .25
160 A92 3c light blue & multi   .30   .25
161 A92 3c bright blue & multi   .60   .50
Nos. 157-161 (5)   1.65   1.50

Issued: No. 157, 6/20/67; No. 159, 1/18/68; No. 160, 2/20/68; No. 161, 6/5/68; No. 158, 8/30/68.

Red-tiled Roofs and ITY Emblem A93

1967, Sept. 11   Photo.   Perf. 13½
162 A93 3c multicolored   .25   .25
International Tourist Year.

Mobile TB Clinic — A94

1967, Oct. 13   Photo.   Perf. 13½
163 A94 3c lilac & multicolored   .25   .25
15th anniv. of the Anti-Tuberculosis Society.

Hojo Bridge, Enkaku Temple, 1498 — A95

1967, Nov. 1
164 A95 3c blue green & multi   .25   .25
Protection of national cultural treasures.

Monkey (Bingata) — A96

1967, Dec. 11   Photo.   Perf. 13½
165 A96 1½c silver & multi   .25   .25
New Year, 1968.

TV Tower and Map — A97

1967, Dec. 22
166 A97 3c multicolored   .25   .25
Opening of Miyako and Yaeyama television stations.

Dr. Kijin Nakachi and Helper — A98

1968, Mar. 15   Photo.   Perf. 13½
167 A98 3c multicolored   .30   .25
120th anniv. of the first vaccination in the Ryukyu Islands, by Dr. Kijin Nakachi.

Pill Box (Inro) — A99

1968, Apr. 18
168 A99 3c gray & multicolored   .45   .45
Philatelic Week.

Young Man, Library, Book and Map of Ryukyu Islands A100

1968, May 13
169 A100 3c multicolored   .30   .25
10th International Library Week.

Mailmen's Uniforms and Stamp of 1948 A101

1968, July 1   Photo.   Perf. 13x13½
170 A101 3c multicolored   .30   .25
First Ryukyuan postage stamps, 20th anniv.

Main Gate, Enkaku Temple A102

Photo. & Engr.
1968, July 15   Perf. 13½
171 A102 3c multicolored   .30   .25
Restoration of the main gate Enkaku Temple, built 1492-1495, destroyed during World War II.

Old Man's Dance — A103

1968, Sept. 15   Photo.   Perf. 13½
172 A103 3c gold & multicolored   .30   .25
Old People's Day.

Mictyris Longicarpus A104

Crabs: No. 174, Uca dubia stimpson. No. 175, Baptozius vinosus. No. 176, Cardisoma carnifex. No. 177, Ocypode ceratophthalma pallas.

1968-69   Photo.   Perf. 13½
173 A104 3c blue, ocher & black   .30   .25
174 A104 3c lt bl grn & multi   .35   .30
175 A104 3c light green & multi   .35   .30
176 A104 3c light ultra & multi   .45   .40
177 A104 3c light ultra & multi   .45   .40
Nos. 173-177 (5)   1.90   1.65

Issued: No. 173, 10/10/68; No. 174, 2/5/69; No. 175, 3/5/69; No. 176, 5/15/69; No. 177, 6/2/69.

Saraswati Pavilion A105

1968, Nov. 1   Photo.   Perf. 13½
178 A105 3c multicolored   .30   .25
Restoration of the Saraswati Pavilion (in front of Enkaku Temple), destroyed during World War II.

Tennis Player — A106

1968, Nov. 23   Photo.   Perf. 13½
179 A106 3c green & multi   .40   .35
35th All-Japan East-West Men's Soft-ball Tennis Tournament, Naha City, Nov. 23-24.

Cock and Iris (Bingata) — A107

1968, Dec. 10
180 A107 1½c orange & multi   .25   .25
New Year, 1969.

Boxer — A108

1969, Jan. 3
181 A108 3c gray & multi   .40   .30
20th All-Japan Amateur Boxing Championships held at the University of the Ryukyus, Jan. 3-5.

Ink Slab Screen — A109

1969, Apr. 17   Photo.   Perf. 13½
182 A109 3c salmon, indigo & red   .40   .35
Philatelic Week.

Box Antennas and Map of Radio Link — A110

1969, July 1   Photo.   Perf. 13½
183 A110 3c multicolored   .30   .25
Opening of the UHF (radio) circuit system between Okinawa and the outlying Miyako-Yaeyama Islands.

Gate of Courtesy and Emblems — A111

1969, Aug. 1   Photo.   Perf. 13½
184 A111 3c Prussian blue, gold & vermilion   .30   .25
22nd All-Japan Formative Education Study Conf., Naha, Aug. 1-3.

Tug of War Festival A112

Hari Boat Race A113

Izaiho Ceremony, Kudaka Island A114

Mortardrum Dance — A115

Sea God Dance A116

1969-70   Photo.   Perf. 13
185 A112 3c multicolored   .30   .25
186 A113 3c multicolored   .35   .30
187 A114 3c multicolored   .35   .30
188 A115 3c multicolored   .50   .45
189 A116 3c multicolored   .50   .45
Nos. 185-189 (5)   2.00   1.75

Folklore. Issued, No. 185, 8/1/69; No. 186, 9/5/69; No. 187, 10/3/69; No. 188, 1/20/70; No. 189, 2/27/70.

No. 99 Surcharged

1969, Oct. 15   Photo.   Perf. 13½
190 A44 ½c on 3c multicolored   1.00   1.00
a. "1/2c" only surcharge   950.00

No. 190a are right margin stamps from a pane with a leftward misregistration of the surcharging plate.

Nakamura-ke Farm House, Built 1713-51
A117

1969, Nov. 1   Photo.   Perf. 13½
191   A117   3c multicolored   .25   .25
Protection of national cultural treasures.

Statue of Kyuzo Toyama, Maps of Hawaiian and Ryukyu Islands
A118

1969, Dec. 5   Photo.   Perf. 13½
192   A118   3c light ultra &
                multi   .50   .50
a.   Without overprint   3,000.
b.   Wide-spaced bars   700.00   500.00

70th anniv. of Ryukyu-Hawaii emigration led by Kyuzo Toyama.
The overprint "1969" at lower left and bars across "1970" at upper right was applied before No. 192 was issued.

Dog and Flowers (Bingata) — A119

1969, Dec. 10
193   A119   1½c pink & multi   .25   .25
          New Year, 1970.

Sake Flask Made from Coconut
A120

1970, Apr. 15   Photo.   Perf. 13½
194   A120   3c multicolored   .25   .25
          Philatelic Week, 1970.

"The Bell" (Shushin Kaneiri)
A121

Child and Kidnapper (Chu-nusudu)
A122

Robe of Feathers (Mekarushi)
A123

Vengeance of Two Young Sons (Nidotichiuchi)
A124

The Virgin and the Dragon (Kokonomaki)
A125

1970   Photo.   Perf. 13½
195   A121   3c dull blue & multi   .60   .40
a.   Souvenir sheet of 4   4.00   4.00
196   A122   3c light blue & multi   .60   .40
a.   Souvenir sheet of 4   4.00   4.00
197   A123   3c bluish grn & multi   .60   .40
a.   Souvenir sheet of 4   4.00   4.00
198   A124   3c dull bl grn & multi   .60   .40
a.   Souvenir sheet of 4   4.00   4.00
199   A125   3c multicolored   .60   .40
a.   Souvenir sheet of 4   4.00   4.00
        Nos. 195-199 (5)   3.00   2.00
        Nos. 195a-199a (5)   20.00   20.00

Classic Opera. Issued No. 195, 4/28; No. 196, 5/29; No. 197, 6/30; No. 198, 7/30; No. 199, 8/25.

Underwater Observatory and Tropical Fish — A126

1970, May 22
200   A126   3c blue green & multi   .30   .25
Completion of the underwater observatory of Busena-Misaki, Nago.

Noboru Jahana (1865-1908), Politician — A127

Portraits: No. 202, Saion Gushichan Bunjaku (1682-1761), statesman. No. 203, Choho Giwan (1823-1876), regent and poet.

1970-71   Engr.   Perf. 13½
201   A127   3c rose claret   .50   .45
202   A127   3c dull blue green   .75   .65
203   A127   3c black   .50   .45
        Nos. 201-203 (3)   1.75   1.55

Issued: No. 201, 9/25.70; No. 202, 12/22/70; No. 203, 1/22/71.

Map of Okinawa and People — A128

1970, Oct. 1   Photo.
204   A128   3c red & multicolored   .25   .25
          Oct. 1, 1970 census.

Great Cycad of Une — A129

1970, Nov. 2   Photo.   Perf. 13½
205   A129   3c gold & multicolored   .25   .25
Protection of national treasures.

Japanese Flag, Diet and Map of Ryukyu
A130

1970, Nov. 15   Photo.   Perf. 13½
206   A130   3c ultra & multi   .80   .75
Citizen's participation in national administration to Japanese law of Apr. 24, 1970.

Wild Boar and Cherry Blossoms (Bingata) — A131

1970, Dec. 10
207   A131   1½c multicolored   .25   .25
          New Year, 1971.

Low Hand Loom (Jibata) A132

Farmer Wearing Palm Bark Raincoat and Kuba Leaf Hat — A133

Fisherman's Wooden Box and Scoop A134

Designs: No. 209, Woman running a filature (reel). No. 211, Woman hulling rice with cylindrical "Shiri-ushi."

1971   Photo.   Perf. 13½
208   A132   3c light blue & multi   .30   .25
209   A132   3c pale grn & multi   .30   .25
210   A133   3c light blue & multi   .35   .30
211   A132   3c yellow & multi   .40   .35
212   A134   3c gray & multi   .35   .30
        Nos. 208-212 (5)   1.70   1.45

Issued: No. 208, 2/16; No. 209, 3/16; No. 210, 4/30; No. 211, 5/20; No. 212, 6/15.

Water Carrier (Taku) — A135

1971, Apr. 15   Photo.   Perf. 13½
213   A135   3c blue grn & multi   .35   .30
          Philatelic Week, 1971.

Old and New Naha, and City Emblem A136

1971, May 20   Perf. 13
214   A136   3c ultra & multi   .25   .25
50th anniv. of Naha as a municipality.

Caesalpinia Pulcherrima — A137

Design: 2c, Madder (Sandanka).

1971   Photo.   Perf. 13
215   A137   2c gray & multi   .25   .25
216   A137   3c gray & multi   .25   .25

Issued No. 216, 5/10; No. 215, 9/30.

View from Mabuni Hill — A138

Mt. Arashi from Haneji Sea — A139

Yabuchi Island from Yakena Port — A140

1971-72
217   A138   3c green & multi   .25   .25
218   A139   3c blue & multi   .25   .25
219   A140   4c multicolored   .25   .25
        Nos. 217-219 (3)   .75   .75
Government parks. Issued: No. 217, 7/30/71; No. 218, 8/31/71; No. 219, 1/20/72.

For the 4-cent unissued "stamp" picturing Iriomote Park, originally planned for issue in 1971 but never released, see the note after No. RQ8 in the Scott U.S. Specialized catalogue.

Dancer — A141

1971, Nov. 1   Photo.   Perf. 13
220   A141   4c Prussian blue &
                multicolored   .25   .25

Deva King, Torinji Temple — A142

1971, Dec. 1
221   A142   4c dp blue & multi   .25   .25
Protection of national cultural treasures.

Rat and Chrysanthemums A143

1971, Dec. 10

222	A143	2c brown orange & multi	.25	.25

New Year, 1972.

Student Nurse — A144

1971, Dec. 24

223	A144	4c lilac & multi	.25	.25

Nurses' training, 25th anniversary.

Birds on Seashore A145   Sun over Islands A147

Coral Reef — A146

1972   **Photo.**   **Perf. 13**

224	A145	5c brt blue & multi	.40	.35
225	A146	5c gray & multi	.40	.35
226	A147	5c ocher & multi	.40	.35
		Nos. 224-226 (3)	1.20	1.05

Issued: No. 226, 3/21; No. 225, 3/30; No. 224, 4/14.

Dove, US and Japanese Flags — A148

1972, Apr. 17   **Photo.**   **Perf. 13**

227	A148	5c bright blue & multi	.80	.80

Antique Sake Pot (Yushibin) — A149

1972, Apr. 20

228	A149	5c ultra & multi	.60	.60

Ryukyu stamps were replaced by those of Japan after May 15, 1972.

AIR POST STAMPS

Dove and Map of Ryukyus — AP1

Perf. 13x13½

1950, Feb. 15   **Photo.**   **Unwmk.**

C1	AP1	8y bright blue	110.00	40.00
C2	AP1	12y green	17.50	17.50
C3	AP1	16y rose carmine	9.00	9.00
		Nos. C1-C3 (3)	136.50	66.50

Heavenly Maiden AP2

1951-54

C4	AP2	13y blue	2.00	2.00
C5	AP2	18y green	3.00	3.00
C6	AP2	30y cerise	4.50	1.50
C7	AP2	40y red violet	6.50	6.50
C8	AP2	50y yellow orange	7.50	7.50
		Nos. C4-C8 (5)	23.50	20.50

Issued: Nos. C4-C6, 10/1/51; Nos. C7-C8, 8/16/54.

Heavenly Maiden Playing Flute — AP3

1957, Aug. 1   **Engr.**   **Perf. 13½**

C9	AP3	15y blue green	7.50	4.00
C10	AP3	20y rose carmine	9.00	7.00
C11	AP3	35y yellow green	10.00	8.00
a.		35y light yellow green, 1958	125.00	
C12	AP3	45y reddish brown	14.00	10.00
C13	AP3	60y gray	16.00	12.00
		Nos. C9-C13 (5)	56.50	41.00

On one printing of No. C10, position 49 shows an added spur on the right side of the second character from the left. Value unused, $175.

Same Surcharged in Brown Red or Light Ultramarine

1959, Dec. 20

C14	AP3	9c on 15y blue green (BrR)	2.50	2.00
a.		Inverted surcharge	850.00	
b.		Pair, one without surcharge		
C15	AP3	14c on 20y rose carmine (L.U.)	3.00	3.25
C16	AP3	19c on 35y light yellow green (BrR)	7.00	6.00
C17	AP3	27c on 45y reddish brown (L.U.)	12.50	6.00
C18	AP3	35c on 60y gray (BrR)	11.00	9.00
		Nos. C14-C18 (5)	36.00	26.25

No. C15 is found with the variety described below No. C13. Value unused, $125.

Nos. 31-33, 36 and 38 Surcharged in Black, Brown, Red, Blue or Green

1960, Aug. 3   **Photo.**   **Perf. 13**

C19	A14	9c on 4y brown	2.50	1.00
a.		Surcharge inverted and transposed	12,500.	12,500.
b.		Inverted surcharge (leg-end only)	10,000.	
c.		Surcharge transposed	800.00	
d.		Legend of surcharge only	3,500.	
e.		Vert. pair, one without surcharge	11,000.	

Nos. C19c and C19d are from a single sheet of 100 with surcharge shifted downward. Ten examples of No. C19c exist with "9c" also in bottom selvage. No. C19d is from the top row of the sheet.

No. C19e is unique, pos. 100, caused by paper foldover.

C20	A17	14c on 5y rose lilac (Br)	3.00	3.00
C21	A14	19c on 15y vermilion (R)	2.50	3.00

C22	A17	27c on 14y reddish brown (Bl)	7.00	2.50
C23	A14	35c on 20y yellow orange (G)	5.00	5.00
		Nos. C19-C23 (5)	20.00	14.50

Wind God — AP4

Designs: 9c, Heavenly Maiden (as on AP2). 14c, Heavenly Maiden (as on AP3). 27c, Wind God at right. 35c, Heavenly Maiden over treetops.

1961, Sept. 21   **Unwmk.**   **Perf. 13½**

C24	AP4	9c multicolored	.30	.25
C25	AP4	14c multicolored	.60	.75
C26	AP4	19c multicolored	.70	.85
C27	AP4	27c multicolored	3.00	.60
C28	AP4	35c multicolored	2.00	1.25
		Nos. C24-C28 (5)	6.60	3.70

Jet over Gate of Courtesy AP5   Jet Plane AP6

1963, Aug. 28   **Perf. 13x13½**

C29	AP5	5½c multicolored	.25	.25
C30	AP6	7c multicolored	.30	.30

SPECIAL DELIVERY STAMP

Sea Horse and Map of Ryukyus — SD1

Perf. 13x13½

1950, Feb. 15   **Unwmk.**   **Photo.**

E1	SD1	5y bright blue	25.00	17.50

UNITED NATIONS, OFFICES IN NEW YORK

yu-ˌnī-təd ˈnā-shənz

United Nations stamps are used on UN official mail sent from UN Headquarters in New York City, the UN European Office in Geneva, Switzerland, or from the Donaupark Vienna International Center or Atomic Energy Agency in Vienna, Austria to points throughout the world. They may be used on private correspondence sent through the UN post offices and are valid only at the individual UN post offices.

The UN stamps issued for use in Geneva and Vienna are listed in separate sections. Geneva issues were denominated in centimes and francs and Vienna issues in schillings (now cents and euros) and are valid only in Geneva or Vienna. The UN stamps issued for use in New York, denominated in cents and dollars, are valid only in New York.

Letters bearing Nos. 170-174 provide an exception as they were carried by the Canadian postal system.

See Switzerland Nos. 7O1-7O39 in Volume 6 of the Scott *Standard Postage Stamp Catalogue* for stamps issued by

---

the Swiss Government for official use of the UN European Office and other UN affiliated organizations. See France official stamp listings for stamps issued by the French Government for official use of UNESCO.

Stamps are inscribed in English, French, or Spanish or are multilingual.

Wmk. 309 — Wavy Lines

Peoples of the World — A1

UN Headquarters Building — A2   "Peace, Justice, Security" — A3

UN Flag — A4

UN Children's Fund — A5

World Unity — A6

Perf. 13x12½, 12½x13

1951   **Engr. and Photo.**   **Unwmk.**

1	A1	1c magenta	.25	.25
2	A2	1½c blue green	.25	.25
3	A3	2c purple	.25	.25
4	A4	3c magenta & blue	.25	.25
5	A5	5c blue	.25	.25
6	A1	10c chocolate	.25	.25
7	A4	15c violet & blue	.30	.25
8	A6	20c dark brown	.35	.25
9	A4	25c olive gray & blue	.40	.25
10	A2	50c indigo	4.00	1.75
11	A3	$1 red	1.60	1.00
		Nos. 1-11 (11)	8.15	5.00

Veteran's War Memorial Building, San Francisco A7

7th anniversary of the signing of the United Nations Charter.

1952, Oct. 24   *Perf. 12*
12 A7 5c blue   .65   .35

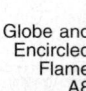

Globe and Encircled Flame A8

4th anniversary of the adoption of the Universal Declaration of Human Rights.

1952, Dec. 10   *Perf. 13½x14*
13 A8 3c deep green   .45   .35
14 A8 5c blue   .55   .40

Refugee Family — A9

Issued to publicize "Protection for Refugees."

1953, Apr. 24   *Perf. 12½x13*
15 A9 3c dark red brown & rose brown   .25   .25
16 A9 5c indigo & blue   .45   .40

Envelope, UN Emblem and Map — A10

Issued to honor the UPU.

1953, June 12   *Perf. 13*
17 A10 3c black brown   .40   .40
18 A10 5c dark blue   1.25   1.00

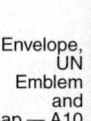

Gearwheels and UN Emblem — A11

UN activities in the field of technical assistance.

1953, Oct. 24   *Perf. 13x12½*
19 A11 3c dark gray   .25   .25
20 A11 5c dark green   .40   .45

Hands Reaching Toward Flame — A12

Human Rights Day.

1953, Dec. 10   *Perf. 12½x13*
21 A12 3c bright blue   .30   .30
22 A12 5c rose red   1.00   1.00

Ear of Wheat — A13

Issued to honor the FAO.

1954, Feb. 11   *Perf. 12½x13*
23 A13 3c dark green & yellow   .30   .25
24 A13 8c indigo & yellow   .75   .50

UN Emblem and Anvil — A14

Issued to honor the ILO.

1954, May 10   *Perf. 12½x13*
25 A14 3c brown   .25   .25
26 A14 8c magenta   1.00   .85

UN European Office, Geneva A15

Issued on the occasion of UN Day.

1954, Oct. 25   *Perf. 14*
27 A15 3c dark blue violet   1.25   1.00
28 A15 8c red   .35   .30

Mother and Child — A16

Human Rights Day.

1954, Dec. 10   *Perf. 14*
29 A16 3c red orange   8.00   2.50
30 A16 8c olive green   1.25   .35

Symbol of Flight A17

International Civil Aviation Organization.

1955, Feb. 9   *Perf. 13½x14*
31 A17 3c blue   1.00   .75
32 A17 8c rose carmine   .60   .50

UNESCO Emblem A18

Issued to honor the UN Educational, Scientific and Cultural Organization.

1955, May 11   *Perf. 13½x14*
33 A18 3c lilac rose   .35   .30
34 A18 8c light blue   .30   .30

UN Charter A19

10th anniversary of the United Nations.

1955, Oct. 24   *Perf. 13½x14*
35 A19 3c deep plum   .90   .55
36 A19 4c dull green   .50   .35
37 A19 8c bluish black   .35   .25
    Nos. 35-37 (3)   1.75   1.15

Souvenir Sheet

1955, Oct. 24   *Wmk. 309*   *Imperf.*
38 A19   Sheet of 3   75.00   30.00
  a.   3c deep plum   10.00   3.00
  b.   4c dull green   10.00   3.00
  c.   8c bluish black   10.00   3.00
  d.   As No. 38, corrected plates (see footnote)   85.00   35.00

Two printings were made of the sheet: No. 38 (200,000) and No. 38d (50,000). No. 38 may be distinguished by the broken lines in the background shading on the 8c. It leaves a small white spot below the left leg of the "n" of "Unies." On No. 38d, the broken line was retouched, eliminating the white spot. The 4c was also retouched.

Hand Holding Torch — A20

Issued in honor of Human Rights Day.

1955, Dec. 9   *Unwmk.*   *Perf. 14x13½*
39 A20 3c ultramarine   .30   .30
40 A20 8c green   .40   .30

Symbols of Telecommunication — A21

Honoring the International Telecommunication Union.

1956, Feb. 17   *Perf. 14*
41 A21 3c turquoise blue   .25   .25
42 A21 8c deep carmine   .30   .30

Globe & Caduceus — A22

Issued in honor of the World Health Organization.

1956, Apr. 6   *Perf. 14*
43 A22 3c bright greenish blue   .25   .25
44 A22 8c golden brown   .25   .25

General Assembly A23

Issued to commemorate UN Day.

1956, Oct. 24   *Perf. 14*
45 A23 3c dark blue   .25   .25
46 A23 8c gray olive   .25   .25

Flame and Globe A24

Issued to publicize Human Rights Day.

1956, Dec. 10   *Perf. 14*
47 A24 3c plum   .25   .25
48 A24 8c dark blue   .25   .25

Weather
Balloon — A25

Issued to honor the World Meterological
Organization.

1957, Jan. 28   **Perf. 14**
49 A25 3c violet blue   .25   .25
50 A25 8c dark carmine rose   .25   .25

Badge of UN
Emergency
Force — A26

Issued in honor of the UN Emergency
Force.

1957, Apr. 8   **Perf. 14x12½**
51 A26 3c light blue   .25   .25
52 A26 8c rose carmine   .25   .25

Nos. 51-52 Re-engraved
1957, Apr.-May   **Perf. 14x12½**
53 A26 3c blue   .25   .25
54 A26 8c rose carmine   .25   .35

On Nos. 53-54 the background within and
around the circles is shaded lightly, giving a
halo effect. The lettering is more distinct with a
line around each letter.

UN Emblem and
Globe — A27

Issued to honor the Security Council.

1957, Oct. 24   **Perf. 12½x13**
55 A27 3c orange brown   .25   .25
56 A27 8c dark blue green   .25   .25

Flaming Torch — A28

Issued in honor of Human Rights Day.

1957, Dec. 10   **Perf. 14**
57 A28 3c red brown   .25   .25
58 A28 8c black   .25   .25

Atom & UN
Emblem — A29

Issued in honor of the International Atomic
Energy Agency.

1958, Feb. 10   **Perf. 12**
59 A29 3c olive   .25   .25
60 A29 8c blue   .25   .25

Central Hall,
Westminster — A30

Central Hall, Westminster, London, was the
site of the first session of the United Nations
General Assembly, 1946.

1958, Apr. 14   **Perf. 12**
61 A30 3c violet blue   .25   .25
62 A30 8c rose claret   .25   .25

UN Seal — A31

Engraved and printed by Bradbury, Wilkinson & Co., Ltd., England. Panes of 50.
Designed by Herbert M. Sanborn.

1958, Oct. 24   **Perf. 13½x14**
63 A31 4c red orange   .25   .25

1958, June 2   **Perf. 13x14**
64 A31 8c bright blue   .25   .25

Issue dates: 4c, Oct. 24; 8c, June 2.

Gearwheels — A32

Issued to honor the Economic and Social
Council.

1958, Oct. 24   Unwmk.   **Perf. 12**
65 A32 4c dark blue green   .25   .25
66 A32 8c vermilion   .25   .25

Hands
Upholding
Globe — A33

Human Rights Day and to commemorate
the 10th anniversary of the signing of the Universal Declaration of Human Rights.

1958, Dec. 10   Unwmk.   **Perf. 12**
67 A33 4c yellow green   .25   .25
68 A33 8c red brown   .25   .25

New York
City
Building,
Flushing
Meadows
A34

Site of many General Assembly meetings,
1946-50.

1959, Mar. 30   Unwmk.   **Perf. 12**
69 A34 4c light lilac rose   .25   .25
70 A34 8c aquamarine   .25   .25

UN Emblems and
Symbols of
Agriculture, Industry
and Trade — A35

Issued to honor the Economic Commission
for Europe.

1959, May 18   Unwmk.   **Perf. 12**
71 A35 4c blue   .25   .25
72 A35 8c red orange   .25   .25

Figure Adapted
from Rodin's "Age
of Bronze" — A36

Issued to honor the Trusteeship Council.

1959, Oct. 23   Unwmk.   **Perf. 12**
73 A36 4c bright red   .25   .25
74 A36 8c dark olive green   .25   .25

World Refugee
Year
Emblem — A37

World Refugee Year, July 1, 1959-June 30,
1960.

1959, Dec. 10   Unwmk.   **Perf. 12**
75 A37 4c olive & red   .25   .25
76 A37 8c ol & brt greenish blue   .25   .25

Chaillot Palace,
Paris — A38

Chaillot Palace in Paris was the site of General Assembly meetings in 1948 and 1951.

1960, Feb. 29   Unwmk.   **Perf. 14**
77 A38 4c rose lilac & blue   .25   .25
78 A38 8c dull green & brown   .25   .25

Map of Far
East and
Steel Beam
A39

Honoring the Economic Commission for
Asia and the Far East (ECAFE).

**   Perf. 13x13½**
1960, Apr. 11   Photo.   Unwmk.
79 A39 4c dp clar, blue grn &
            dull yel   .25   .25
80 A39 8c ol grn, blue & rose   .25   .25

Tree, FAO and UN
Emblems — A40

Fifth World Forestry Congress, Seattle,
Washington, Aug. 29-Sept. 10.

**   Perf. 13½**
1960, Aug. 29   Photo.   Unwmk.
81 A40 4c dk blue, grn & org   .25   .25
82 A40 8c yel grn, blk & org   .25   .25

UN
Headquarters
and Preamble
to UN
Charter — A41

Issued to commemorate the 15th anniversary of the United Nations.

1960, Oct. 24   Unwmk.   **Perf. 11**
83 A41 4c blue   .25   .25
84 A41 8c gray   .25   .25

Souvenir Sheet
Imperf
85   Sheet of 2   1.25   1.25
  a.   A41 4c blue   .55   .55
  b.   A41 8c gray   .55   .55

Block and
Tackle — A42

Honoring the International Bank for Reconstruction and Development.

**   Perf. 13½x13**
1960, Dec. 9   Photo.   Unwmk.
86 A42 4c multicolored   .25   .25
87 A42 8c multicolored   .25   .25

Scales of
Justice — A43

Issued to honor the International Court of
Justice.

**   Perf. 13½x13**
1961, Feb. 13   Photo.   Unwmk.
88 A43 4c yel, org brn & blk   .25   .25
89 A43 8c yel, grn & blk   .25   .25

Seal of International Monetary
Fund — A44

Issued to honor the International Monetary
Fund.

**   Perf. 13x13½**
1961, Apr. 17   Photo.   Unwmk.
90 A44 4c bright bluish green   .25   .25
91 A44 7c terra cotta & yellow   .25   .25

Abstract
Group of
Flags — A45

**   Perf. 11½**
1961, June 5   Photo.   Unwmk.
92 A45 30c multicolored   .45   .30

See UN Offices in Geneva No. 10.

Cogwheel and Map of Latin America — A46

Issued to honor the Economic Commission for Latin America.

Perf. 13½

1961, Sept. 18   Photo.   Unwmk.
93	A46	4c blue, red & citron	.25	.25
94	A46	11c grn, lilac & org ver	.25	.25

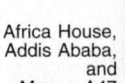

Africa House, Addis Ababa, and Map — A47

Issued to honor the Economic Commission for Africa.

Perf. 11½

1961, Oct. 24   Photo.   Unwmk.
95	A47	4c ultramarine, orange, yellow & brown	.25	.25
96	A47	11c emerald, orange, yellow & brown	.25	.25

Mother Bird Feeding Young and UNICEF Seal — A48

15th anniversary of the United Nations Children's Fund.

Perf. 11½

1961, Dec. 4   Photo.   Unwmk.
97	A48	3c brown, gold, orange & yellow	.25	.25
98	A48	4c brown, gold, blue & emerald	.25	.25
99	A48	13c deep green, gold, purple & pink	.25	.25
		Nos. 97-99 (3)	.75	.75

Family and Symbolic Buildings A49

UN program for housing and urban development,

Perf. 14½x14

1962, Feb. 28   Photo.   Unwmk.
Central design multicolored
100	A49	4c bright blue	.25	.25
a.		Black omitted	200.00	
b.		Yellow omitted	—	
c.		Brown omitted	—	
101	A49	7c orange brown	.25	.25
a.		Red omitted	—	
b.		Black omitted	—	
c.		Gold omitted	—	

"The World Against Malaria" — A50

Issued in honor of the WHO and to call attention to the international campaign to eradicate malaria from the world.

Perf. 14x14½

1962, Mar. 30   Photo.   Unwmk.
Word frame in gray
102	A50	4c orange, yellow, brown, green & black	.25	.25
103	A50	11c green, yellow, brown & indigo	.25	.25

"Peace" — A51

UN Flag — A52

Hands Combining "UN" and Globe — A53

UN Emblem over Globe A54

Photo.; Engr. (5c)
Perf. 14x14½

1962, May 25   Unwmk.
104	A51	1c vermilion, blue, black & gray	.25	.25
105	A52	3c light green, Prussian blue, yellow & gray	.25	.25

Perf. 12
106	A53	5c dark carmine rose	.25	.25

Perf. 12½
107	A54	11c dark & light blue & gold	.25	.25
		Nos. 104-107 (4)	1.00	1.00

See #167 and UN Offices in Geneva #2, 6. Compare A51 with A76.

Flag at Half-mast and UN Headquarters — A55

Issued on the 1st anniversary of the death of Dag Hammarskjold, Secretary General of the United Nations 1953-61, in memory of those who died in the service of the United Nations.

Perf. 11½

1962, Sept. 17   Photo.   Unwmk.
108	A55	5c black, light blue & blue	.25	.25
109	A55	15c black, gray olive & blue	.25	.25

World Map Showing Congo — A56

Issued to commemorate the United Nations Operation in the Congo.

Perf. 11½

1962, Oct. 24   Unwmk.
110	A56	4c olive, orange, black & yellow	.25	.25
111	A56	11c blue green, orange, black & yellow	.25	.25

Globe in Universe and Palm Frond — A57

Issued to honor the Committee on Peaceful Uses of Outer Space.

Perf. 14x13½

1962, Dec. 3   Engr.   Unwmk.
112	A57	4c violet blue	.25	.25
113	A57	11c rose claret	.25	.25

Development Decade Emblem — A58

UN Development Decade and UN Conference on the Application of Science and Technology for the Benefit of the Less Developed Areas, Geneva, Feb. 4-20.

Perf. 11½

1963, Feb. 4   Photo.   Unwmk.
114	A58	5c pale green, maroon, dark blue & Prussian blue	.25	.25
115	A58	11c yellow, maroon, dark blue & Prussian blue	.25	.25

Stalks of Wheat — A59

Issued for the "Freedom from Hunger" campaign of the Food and Agriculture Organization.

Perf. 11½

1963, Mar. 22   Photo.   Unwmk.
116	A59	5c vermilion, green & yellow	.25	.25
117	A59	11c vermilion, deep claret & yellow	.25	.25

Bridge over Map of New Guinea — A60

1st anniversary of the United Nations Temporary Executive Authority (UNTEA) in West New Guinea (West Irian).

Perf. 11½

1963, Oct. 1   Photo.   Unwmk.
118	A60	25c blue, green & gray	.50	.40

General Assembly Building, New York — A61

Since October 1955 all sessions of the General Assembly have been held in the General Assembly Hall, UN Headquarters, NY.

Unwmk.

1963, Nov. 4   Photo.   Perf. 13
119	A61	5c violet blue, blue, yellow green & red	.25	.25
120	A61	11c green, yellow green, blue, yellow & red	.25	.25

Flame — A62

15th anniversary of the signing of the Universal Declaration of Human Rights.

Unwmk.

1963, Dec. 10   Photo.   Perf. 13
121	A62	5c green, gold, red & yellow	.25	.25
122	A62	11c carmine, gold, blue & yellow	.25	.25

Ships at Sea and IMCO Emblem A63

Issued to honor the Intergovernmental Maritime Consultative Organization.

Perf. 11½

1964, Jan. 13   Photo.   Unwmk.
123	A63	5c blue, olive, ocher & yellow	.25	.25
124	A63	11c dark blue, dark green, emerald & yellow	.25	.25

Map of the World — A64

UN Emblem — A65

Three Men United Before Globe — A66

Stylized Globe and Weather Vane — A67

1964-71   Photo.   Unwmk.   Perf. 14
125	A64	2c light & dark blue, orange & yellow green	.25	.25
a.		Perf. 13x13½	.25	.25

Perf. 11½
126	A65	7c dark blue, orange brown & black	.25	.25
127	A66	10c blue green, olive green & black	.25	.25
128	A67	50c multicolored	.55	.45
		Nos. 125-128 (4)	1.30	1.20

Issued: 2c, 7c, May 29; 50c, Mar. 6.
See UN Offices in Geneva Nos. 3, 12.

Arrows Showing Global Flow of Trade A68

Issued to commemorate the UN Conference on Trade and Development, Geneva, Mar. 23-June 15.

Unwmk.

1964, June 15   Photo.   Perf. 13
129	A68	5c black, red & yellow	.25	.25
130	A68	11c black, olive & yellow	.25	.25

Poppy Capsule and Hands — A69

Honoring international efforts and achievements in the control of narcotics.

Unwmk.

1964, Sept. 21	**Engr.**		**Perf. 12**
131	A69	5c rose red & black	.25 .25
132	A69	11c emerald & black	.25 .25

Padlocked Atomic Blast — A70

Signing of the nuclear test ban treaty pledging an end to nuclear explosions in the atmosphere, outer space and under water.

Litho. and Engr.
Perf. 11x11½

1964, Oct. 23			**Unwmk.**
133	A70	5c dark red & dark brown	.25 .25

"Education for Progress" A71

Issued to publicize the UNESCO world campaign for universal literacy and for free compulsory primary education.

Perf. 12½

1964, Dec. 7	**Photo.**		**Unwmk.**
134	A71	4c orange, red, bister, green & blue	.25 .25
135	A71	5c bister, red, dark & light blue	.25 .25
136	A71	11c green, light blue, black & rose	.25 .25
		Nos. 134-136 (3)	.75 .75

Progress Chart, Key & Globe — A72

Issued to publicize the Special Fund program to speed economic growth and social advancement in low-income countries.

Perf. 13½x13

1965, Jan. 25	**Photo.**		**Unwmk.**
137	A72	5c dull blue, dark blue, yellow & red	.25 .25
138	A72	11c yellow green, dark blue, yellow & red	.25 .25
a.		Black omitted (UN emblem on key)	—

Leaves & View of Cyprus — A73

Issued to honor the United Nations Peacekeeping Force on Cyprus.

Perf. 11½

1965, Mar. 4	**Photo.**		**Unwmk.**
139	A73	5c orange, olive & black	.25 .25
140	A73	11c yellow green, blue green & black	.25 .25

"From Semaphore to Satellite" A74

Centenary of the International Telecommunication Union.

Perf. 11½

1965, May 17	**Photo.**		**Unwmk.**
141	A74	5c aquamarine, orange, blue & purple	.25 .25
142	A74	11c light violet, red orange, bister & bright green	.25 .25

ICY Emblem — A75

20th anniversary of the United Nations and International Cooperation Year.

Perf. 14x13½

1965, June 26	**Engr.**		**Unwmk.**
143	A75	5c dark blue	.25 .25
144	A75	15c lilac rose	.25 .25

Souvenir Sheet

145	A75	Sheet of two	.35 .35

"Peace" — A76

Opening Words, UN Charter — A77

UN Headquarters, Emblem — A78

UN Emblem — A79

UN Emblem A80

Perf. 13½x13

1965-66	**Photo.**		**Unwmk.**
146	A76	1c vermilion, blue, black & gray	.25 .25

Perf. 14

147	A77	15c olive bister, dull yellow, black & deep claret	.25 .25

Perf. 12

148	A78	20c dark blue, blue, red & yellow	.25 .25
a.		Yellow omitted	

Litho. and Embossed
Perf. 14

149	A79	25c light & dark blue	.30 .25
a.		25c light & dark blue, new dk blue plate/cylinder (see footnote)	.30 .25
b.		As "a," tagged	10.00 10.00

Photo.
Perf. 11½

150	A80	$1 aquamarine & sapphire	1.60 1.60
		Nos. 146-150 (5)	2.65 2.60

Issued: 1c, No. 149, 9/20/65; No. 149a, 11/5/65; 15c, 20c, 10/25/65; $1, 3/25/66.
On No. 149, the dark blue "halo" of the U.N. emblem is large, overlapping the "25c." On No. 149a, a new dark blue plate/cylinder was used, making the "halo" of the U.N. emblem smaller.
See UN Offices in Geneva Nos. 5, 9, 11.

Fields & People — A81

Design: 11c, French inscription.
Issued to emphasize the importance of the world's population growth and its problems and to call attention to population trends and development.

Unwmk.

1965, Nov. 29	**Photo.**		**Perf. 12**
151	A81	4c multicolored	.25 .25
152	A81	5c multicolored	.25 .25
153	A81	11c multicolored	.25 .25
		Nos. 151-153 (3)	.75 .75

Globe & Flags of UN Members — A82

Design: 11c, French inscription.
Issued to honor the World Federation of United Nations Associations.

Perf. 11½

1966, Jan. 31	**Photo.**		**Unwmk.**
154	A82	5c multicolored	.25 .25
155	A82	15c multicolored	.25 .25

WHO Headquarters, Geneva — A83

Design: 11c, French inscription.
Issued to commemorate the opening of the World Health Organization Headquarters, Geneva.

1966, May 26	**Photo.**		**Perf. 12½x12**

Granite Paper

156	A83	5c lt & dk orange, green & bister	.25 .25
157	A83	11c orange, lt & dark blue, green & bister	.25 .25

Coffee — A84

Design: 11c, Spanish inscription.
Issued to commemorate the International Coffee Agreement of 1962.

1966, Sept. 19	**Photo.**		**Perf. 13½x13**
158	A84	5c orange, lt blue, green, red & dk brown	.25 .25
159	A84	11c lt blue, yellow, green, red & dk brown	.25 .25

UN Observer — A85

Issued to honor the Peace Keeping United Nation Observers.
Printed by Courvoisier, S.A. Panes of 50.
Designed by Ole S. Hamann.

1966, Oct. 24	**Photo.**		**Perf. 11½**

Granite Paper

160	A85	15c steel blue, orange, black & green	.25 .25

Children of Various Races — A86

20th anniversary of the United Nations Children's Fund (UNICEF).

1966, Nov. 28	**Litho.**		**Perf. 13x13½**
161	A86	4c pink & multi	.25 .25
162	A86	5c pale green & multi	.25 .25
a.		Yellow omitted	
163	A86	11c light ultramarine & multi	.25 .25
b.		Dark blue omitted	
		Nos. 161-163 (3)	.75 .75

Hand Rolling up Sleeve & Chart Showing Progress A87

Design: 11c, French inscription.
United Nations Development Program.

1967, Jan. 23	**Photo.**		**Perf. 12½**
164	A87	5c green, yellow, purple & orange	.25 .25
165	A87	11c blue, chocolate, light green & orange	.25 .25

Type of 1962 and

UN Headquarters, New York & World Map — A88

1967	**Photo.**		**Perf. 11½**
166	A88	1½c ultramarine, black, orange & ocher	.25 .25

Size: 33x23mm

167	A53	5c red brown, brown & orange yellow	.25 .25

Issue dates: 1½c, Mar. 17; 5c, Jan. 23.
See UN Offices in Geneva No. 1.

Fireworks — A89

Design: 11c, French inscription.
Issued to honor all nations which gained independence since 1945.

1967, Mar. 17 Photo. Perf. 14x14½
168 A89 5c dark blue & multi   .25 .25
169 A89 11c brown lake & multi   .25 .25

"Peace" — A90

UN Pavilion, EXPO '67 — A91

EXPO '67, International Exhibition, Montreal, Apr. 28-Oct. 27, 1967.

Engr. & Litho.
1967, Apr. 28   Perf. 11
170 A90 4c red & red brown   .25 .25
171 A90 5c blue & red brown   .25 .25

Litho.
172 A91 8c multicolored   .25 .25

Engr. and Litho.
173 A90 10c green & red brown   .25 .25
174 A90 15c dark brown & red
              brown   .25 .25
       Nos. 170-174 (5)   1.25 1.25

Luggage Tags and UN Emblem A92

Issued to publicize International Tourist Year, 1967.

1967, June 19 Litho. Perf. 14
175 A92 5c reddish brown &
              multi   .25 .25
176 A92 15c ultramarine & multi .25 .25

Quotation from Isaiah 2:4 — A93

Design: 13c, French inscription.
Issued to publicize the UN General Assembly's resolutions on general and complete disarmament and for suspension of nuclear and thermonuclear tests.

1967, Oct. 24 Photo. Perf. 14
177 A93 6c ultramarine, yellow,
              gray & brown   .25 .25
178 A93 13c magenta, yellow,
              gray & brown   .25 .25

Art at UN Issue
Miniature Sheet

Memorial Window — A94

"The Kiss of Peace" — A95

1967, Nov. 17 Litho. Rouletted 9
179 A94 6c Sheet of 6, #a.-f.   .40 .40
                 Perf. 13x13½
180 A95 6c multicolored   .25 .25

No. 179 contains six 6c stamps, each rouletted on 3 sides, imperf. on fourth side. Size: 124x80mm. On Nos. 179a-179c, "United Nations 6c" appears at top; on Nos. 179d-179f, at bottom. No. 179f includes name "Marc Chagall."

Globe and Major UN Organs A96

Design: 13c, French inscription.
Issued to honor the United Nations Secretariat.

1968, Jan. 16 Photo. Perf. 11½
181 A96 6c multicolored   .25 .25
182 A96 13c multicolored   .25 .25

Art at UN Issue

Statue by Henrik Starcke — A97

1968, Mar. 1 Photo. Perf. 11½
183 A97 6c blue & multi   .25 .25
184 A97 75c rose lake & multi   1.10 .90

The 6c is part of the "Art at the UN" series. The 75c belongs to the regular definitive series. The teakwood Starcke statue, which stands in the Trusteeship Council Chamber, represents mankind's search for freedom and happiness.
See UN Offices in Geneva No. 13.

Factories and Chart — A98

Design: 13c, French inscription ("ONUDI," etc.).
Issued to publicize the UN Industrial Development Organization.

1968, Apr. 18 Litho. Perf. 12
185 A98 6c greenish blue, lt
              greenish blue,
              black & dull claret .25 .25
186 A98 13c dull red brown, light
              red brown, black &
              ultra   .25 .25

UN Headquarters A99

1968, May 31 Litho. Perf. 12x13½
187 A99 6c green, blue, black &
              gray   .25 .25

Radarscope and Globes A100

Design: 20c, French inscription.
Issued to publicize World Weather Watch, a new weather system directed by the World Meteorological Organization.

1968, Sept. 19 Photo. Perf. 13x13½
188 A100 6c green, black,
               ocher, red & blue   .25 .25
189 A100 20c lilac, black, ocher,
               red & blue   .30 .25

Human Rights Flame — A101

Design: 13c, French inscription.
Issued for International Human Rights Year, 1968.

Photo.; Foil Embossed
1968, Nov. 22   Perf. 12½
190 A101 6c bright blue, deep
               ultra & gold   .25 .25
191 A101 13c rose red, dark red
               & gold   .25 .25

Books and UN Emblem — A102

Design: 13c, French inscription in center, denomination panel at bottom.
United Nations Institute for Training and Research (UNITAR).

1969, Feb. 10 Litho. Perf. 13½
192 A102 6c yellow green &
               multi   .25 .25
193 A102 13c bluish lilac & multi .25 .25

UN Building, Santiago, Chile A103

Design: 15c, Spanish inscription.
The UN Building in Santiago, Chile, is the seat of the UN Economic Commission for Latin America and of the Latin American Institute for Economic and Social Planning.

1969, Mar. 14 Litho. Perf. 14
194 A103 6c light blue, violet
               blue & light green .25 .25
195 A103 15c pink, cream & red
               brown   .25 .25

"UN" and UN Emblem — A104

1969, Mar. 14 Photo. Perf. 13½
196 A104 13c bright blue, black
               & gold   .25 .25
       See UN Offices in Geneva No. 7.

UN Emblem and Scales of Justice — A105

Design: 13c, French inscription.
20th anniversary session of the UN International Law Commission.

Granite Paper
1969, Apr. 21 Photo. Perf. 11½
197 A105 6c bright green, ultra
               & gold   .25 .25
198 A105 13c crimson, lilac &
               gold   .25 .25

Allegory of Labor, Emblems of UN and ILO A106

Design: 20c, French inscription.
Issued to publicize "Labor and Development" and to commemorate the 50th anniversary of the International Labor Organization.

1969, June 5 Photo. Perf. 13
199 A106 6c blue, deep blue,
               yellow & gold   .25 .25
200 A106 20c orange vermilion,
               magenta, yellow
               & gold   .25 .25

Art at UN Issue

Ostrich, Tunisian Mosaic, 3rd Century — A107

Design: 13c, Pheasant; French inscription.

1969, Nov. 21 Photo. Perf. 14
201 A107 6c blue & multi   .25 .25
202 A107 13c red & multi   .25 .25

Art at UN Issue

Peace Bell, Gift of Japanese A108

Design: 25c, French inscription.
The Peace Bell was a gift of the people of Japan in 1954, cast from donated coins and metals. It is housed in a Japanese cypress structure at UN Headquarters, New York.

1970, Mar. 13 Photo. Perf. 13½x13
203 A108 6c violet blue & multi   .25 .25
204 A108 25c claret & multi   .30 .25

Mekong River, Power Lines and Map of Delta — A109

Design: 13c, French inscription.
Issued to publicize the Lower Mekong Basin Development project under UN auspices.

1970, Mar. 13   Perf. 14
205 A109 6c dark blue & multi   .25 .25
206 A109 13c deep plum & multi   .25 .25

"Fight Cancer"
A110

Design: 13c, French inscription.
Issued to publicize the fight against cancer in connection with the 10th International Cancer Congress of the International Union Against Cancer, Houston, Texas, May 22-29.

1970, May 22   Litho.   Perf. 14
207 A110 6c blue & black   .25 .25
208 A110 13c olive & black   .25 .25

UN Emblem and Olive Branch
A111

UN Emblem — A112

Design: 13c, French inscription.
25th anniv. of the UN. First day covers were postmarked at UN Headquarters, NY, and at San Francisco.

1970, June 26   Photo.   Perf. 11½
209 A111 6c red, gold, dark & light blue   .25 .25
210 A111 13c dark blue, gold, green & red   .25 .25

Perf. 12½
211 A112 25c dark blue, gold & light blue   .35 .25
Nos. 209-211 (3)   .85 .75

Souvenir Sheet
Imperf
212   Sheet of 3   .85 .85
a.   A111 6c red, gold & multicolored   .25 .25
b.   A111 13c violet blue, gold & multi   .25 .25
c.   A112 25c violet blue, gold & light blue   .35 .35

Scales, Olive Branch, Progress Symbol — A113

Design: 13c, French inscription.
Issued to publicize "Peace, Justice and Progress" in connection with the 25th anniversary of the United Nations.

1970, Nov. 20   Photo.   Perf. 13½
213 A113 6c gold & multi   .25 .25
214 A113 13c silver & multi   .25 .25

Sea Bed, Fish, Underwater Research — A114

Issued to publicize peaceful uses of the sea bed.

Photo. & Engr.
1971, Jan. 25   Perf. 13
215 A114 6c blue & multi   .25 .25
See UN Offices in Geneva No. 15.

Refugees, Sculpture by Kaare K. Nygaard
A115

International support for refugees.

1971, Mar. 2   Litho.   Perf. 13x12½
216 A115 6c brown, ocher & black   .25 .25
217 A115 13c ultramarine, greenish blue & black   .25 .25
See UN Offices in Geneva No. 16.

Wheat and Globe — A116

Publicizing the UN World Food Program.

1971, Apr. 13   Photo.   Perf. 14
218 A116 13c red & multicolored   .25 .25
See UN Offices in Geneva No. 17.

UPU Headquarters, Bern — A117

Opening of new Universal Postal Union Headquarters, Bern.

1971, May 28   Photo.   Perf. 11½
219 A117 20c brown orange & multi   .30 .25
See UN Offices in Geneva No. 18.

"Eliminate Racial Discrimination"
A118

A119

International Year Against Racial Discrimination.

1971, Sept. 21   Photo.   Perf. 13½
220 A118 8c yellow green & multi   .25 .25
221 A119 13c blue & multi   .25 .25
See UN Offices in Geneva Nos. 19-20.

UN Headquarters, New York — A120

UN Emblem and Symbolic Flags
A121

1971, Oct. 22   Photo.   Perf. 13½
222 A120 8c violet blue & multi   .25 .25

Perf. 13
223 A121 60c ultra & multi   .80 .80

Maia by Pablo Picasso — A122

To publicize the UN International School.

1971, Nov. 19   Photo.   Perf. 11½
224 A122 8c olive & multi   .25 .25
225 A122 21c ultra & multi   .25 .25

Letter Changing Hands
A123

1972, Jan. 5   Litho.   Perf. 14
226 A123 95c carmine & multi   1.30 1.10

"No More Nuclear Weapons"
A124

To promote non-proliferation of nuclear weapons.

1972, Feb. 14   Photo.   Perf. 13½x14
227 A124 8c dull rose, black, blue & gray   .25 .25
See UN Offices in Geneva No. 23.

Proportions of Man (c. 1509), by Leonardo da Vinci — A125

World Health Day, Apr. 7.

Litho. & Engr.
1972, Apr. 7   Perf. 13x13½
228 A125 15c black & multi   .25 .25
See UN Offices in Geneva No. 24.

"Human Environment"
A126

UN Conf. on Human Environment, Stockholm, June 5-16, 1972.

Litho. & Embossed
1972, June 5   Perf. 12½x14
229 A126 8c red, buff, green & blue   .25 .25
230 A126 15c blue green, buff, green & blue   .25 .25
See UN Offices in Geneva Nos. 25-26.

"Europe" and UN Emblem — A127

Economic Commission for Europe, 25th anniversary.

1972, Sept. 11   Litho.   Perf. 13x13½
231 A127 21c yellow brown & multi   .30 .30
See UN Offices in Geneva No. 27.

Art at UN Issue

The Five Continents, by José Maria Sert — A128

1972, Nov. 17   Photo.   Perf. 12x12½
232 A128 8c gold, brown & golden brown   .25 .25
233 A128 15c gold, blue green & brown   .25 .25
See UN Offices in Geneva Nos. 28-29.

Olive Branch and Broken Sword
A129

Disarmament Decade, 1970-79.

1973, Mar. 9   Litho.   Perf. 13½x13
234 A129 8c blue & multi   .25 .25
235 A129 15c lilac rose & multi   .25 .25
See UN Offices in Geneva Nos. 30-31.

Poppy Capsule and Skull — A130

Fight against drug abuse.

1973, Apr. 13   Photo.   Perf. 13½
236 A130 8c deep orange & multi   .25 .25
237 A130 15c pink & multi   .25 .25
See UN Offices in Geneva No. 32.

Honeycomb
A131

5th anniversary of the United Nations Volunteer Program.

1973, May 25   Photo.   Perf. 14
238 A131 8c olive bister & multi   .25 .25
239 A131 21c gray blue & multi   .30 .30
See UN Offices in Geneva No. 33.

Map of Africa
with Namibia
A132

To publicize Namibia (South-West Africa) for
which the UN General Assembly ended the
mandate of South Africa and established the
UN Council for Namibia to administer the territory until independence.

1973, Oct. 1   Photo.   Perf. 14
240   A132   8c emerald & multi   .25   .25
241   A132   15c bright rose & multi   .25   .25
See UN Offices in Geneva No. 34.

UN Emblem,
Human Rights
Flame
A133

25th anniversary of the adoption and proclamation of the Universal Declaration of Human
Rights.

1973, Nov. 16   Photo.   Perf. 13½
242   A133   8c deep carmine &
                   multi   .25   .25
243   A133   21c blue green & multi   .25   .25
See UN Offices in Geneva Nos. 35-36.

ILO
Headquarters,
Geneva
A134

New Headquarters of International Labor
Organization.

1974, Jan. 11   Photo.   Perf. 14
244   A134   10c ultra & multi   .25   .25
245   A134   21c blue green & multi   .30   .25
See UN Offices in Geneva Nos. 37-38.

Post Horn
Encircling
Globe
A135

Centenary of Universal Postal Union.

1974, Mar. 22   Litho.   Perf. 12½
246   A135   10c gold & multi   .25   .25
See UN Offices in Geneva Nos. 39-40.

Art at UN Issue

Peace Mural,
by Candido
Portinari
A136

The mural, a gift of Brazil, is in the Delegates' Lobby, General Assembly Building.

1974, May 6   Photo.   Perf. 14
247   A136   10c gold & multi   .25   .25
248   A136   18c ultra & multi   .35   .30
See UN Offices in Geneva Nos. 41-42.

Dove & UN
Emblem
A137

UN
Headquarters
A138

Globe, UN
Emblem, Flags
A139

1974, June 10   Photo.   Perf. 14
249   A137   2c dark & light blue   .25   .25
250   A138   10c multicolored   .25   .25
251   A139   18c multicolored   .25   .25
      Nos. 249-251 (3)   .75   .75

Children of the
World — A140

World Population Year.

1974, Oct. 18   Photo.   Perf. 14
252   A140   10c light blue & multi   .25   .25
253   A140   18c lilac & multi   .35   .25
See UN Offices in Geneva Nos. 43-44.

Law of the
Sea — A141

Declaration of UN General Assembly that
the sea bed is common heritage of mankind,
reserved for peaceful purposes.

1974, Nov. 22   Photo.   Perf. 14
254   A141   10c green & multi   .25   .25
255   A141   26c orange red & multi   .35   .30
See UN Offices in Geneva No. 45.

Satellite and
Globe — A142

Peaceful uses (meteorology, industry, fishing, communications) of outer space.

1975, Mar. 14   Litho.   Perf. 13
256   A142   10c multicolored   .25   .25
257   A142   26c multicolored   .35   .30
See UN Offices in Geneva Nos. 46-47.

Equality
Between Men
and
Women — A143

International Women's Year.

1975, May 9   Litho.   Perf. 15
258   A143   10c multicolored   .25   .25
259   A143   18c multicolored   .35   .30
See UN Offices in Geneva Nos. 48-49.

UN Flag and
"XXX" — A144

30th anniversary of the United Nations.

1975, June 26   Litho.   Perf. 13
260   A144   10c olive bister & multi   .25   .25
261   A144   26c purple & multi   .40   .35
Souvenir Sheet
Imperf
262   Sheet of 2   .60   .50
   a.   A144 10c olive bister & mul-
             ticolored   .25   .25
   b.   A144 26c purple & multicolored   .35   .25
See Offices in Geneva Nos. 50-52.

Hand Reaching up over Map of Africa
& Namibia — A145

"Namibia-United Nations direct responsibility." See note after No. 241.

1975, Sept. 22   Photo.   Perf. 13½
263   A145   10c multicolored   .25   .25
264   A145   18c multicolored   .30   .30
See UN Offices in Geneva Nos. 53-54.

Wild Rose Growing
from Barbed
Wire — A146

United Nations Peace-keeping Operations.

1975, Nov. 21   Engr.   Perf. 12½
265   A146   13c ultramarine   .25   .25
266   A146   26c rose carmine   .40   .40
See UN Offices in Geneva Nos. 55-56.

Symbolic Flags
Forming
Dove — A147

UN
Emblem — A149

People of
All Races
A148

UN Flag
A150

Dove and
Rainbow
A151

1976   Litho.   Perf. 13x13½, 13½x13
267   A147   3c multicolored   .25   .25
268   A148   4c multicolored   .25   .25
Photo.
Perf. 14
269   A149   9c multicolored   .25   .25
Litho.
Perf. 13x13½
270   A150   30c blue, emerald &
                   black   .35   .35
271   A151   50c yellow green &
                   multi   .65   .65
      Nos. 267-271 (5)   1.75 1.75
Issue dates: 3c, 4c, 30c, 50c, Jan. 6; 9c,
Nov. 19.
See UN Offices in Vienna No. 8.

Interlocking
Bands — A152

World Federation of United Nations
Associations.

1976, Mar. 12   Photo.   Perf. 14
272   A152   13c blue, green &
                   black   .25   .25
273   A152   26c green & multi   .35   .30
See UN Offices in Geneva No. 57.

Cargo, Globe and
Graph — A153

UN Conference on Trade and Development
(UNCTAD), Nairobi, Kenya, May 1976.

1976, Apr. 23   Photo.   Perf. 11½
274   A153   13c deep magenta &
                   multi   .25   .25
275   A153   31c dull blue & multi   .40   .30
See UN Offices in Geneva No. 58.

Houses Around
Globe — A154

Habitat, UN Conference on Human Settlements, Vancouver, Canada, May 31-June 11.

1976, May 28   Photo.   Perf. 14
276   A154   13c red brown & multi   .25   .25
277   A154   25c green & multi   .40   .30
See UN Offices in Geneva Nos. 59-60.

Magnifying Glass, Sheet of Stamps, UN Emblem A155

United Nations Postal Administration, 25th anniversary.

1976, Oct. 8   Photo.   Perf. 11½
278 A155 13c blue & multi   .25   .25
279 A155 31c green & multi   1.40 1.40
See UN Offices in Geneva Nos. 61-62.

Grain — A156

World Food Council.

1976, Nov. 19   Litho.   Perf. 14½
280 A156 13c multicolored   .25   .25
See UN Offices in Geneva No. 63.

WIPO Headquarters, Geneva — A157

World Intellectual Property Organization (WIPO).

1977, Mar. 11   Photo.   Perf. 14
281 A157 13c citron & multi   .25   .25
282 A157 31c bright green & multi .45   .35
See UN Offices in Geneva No. 64.

Drops of Water Falling into Funnel — A158

UN Water Conference, Mar del Plata, Argentina, Mar. 14-25.

1977, Apr. 22   Photo.   Perf. 13½x13
283 A158 13c yellow & multi   .25   .25
284 A158 25c salmon & multi   .40   .35
See UN Offices in Geneva Nos. 65-66.

Burning Fuse Severed A159

UN Security Council.

1977, May 27   Photo.   Perf. 14
285 A159 13c purple & multi   .25   .25
286 A159 31c dark blue & multi   .45   .30
See UN Offices in Geneva Nos. 67-68.

"Combat Racism" A160

Fight against racial discrimination.

1977, Sept. 19   Litho.   Perf. 13½x13
287 A160 13c black & yellow   .25   .25
288 A160 25c black & vermilion   .40   .30
See UN Offices in Geneva Nos. 60-70.

Atom, Grain, Fruit and Factory — A161

Peaceful uses of atomic energy.

1977, Nov. 18   Photo.   Perf. 14
289 A161 13c yellow bister & multi .25   .25
290 A161 18c dull green & multi   .30   .25
See UN Offices in Geneva Nos. 71-72.

Opening Words of UN Charter A162

"Live Together in Peace" A163

People of the World — A164

1978, Jan. 27   Litho.   Perf. 14½
291 A162 1c gold, brown & red   .25   .25
292 A163 25c multicolored   .35   .30
293 A164 $1 multicolored   1.25 1.25
     Nos. 291-293 (3)   1.85 1.80
See UN Offices in Geneva No. 73.

Smallpox Virus — A165

Global eradication of smallpox.

1978, Mar. 31   Photo.   Perf. 12x11½
294 A165 13c rose & black   .25   .25
295 A165 31c blue & black   .40   .40
See UN Offices in Geneva Nos. 74-75.

Open Handcuff — A166

Liberation, justice and cooperation for Namibia.

1978, May 5   Photo.   Perf. 12
296 A166 13c multicolored   .25   .25
297 A166 18c multicolored   .30   .25
See UN Offices in Geneva No. 76.

Multicolored Bands and Clouds — A167

International Civil Aviation Organization for "Safety in the Air."

1978, June 12   Photo.   Perf. 14
298 A167 13c multicolored   .25   .25
299 A167 25c multicolored   .35   .30
See UN Offices in Geneva Nos. 77-78.

General Assembly A168

1978, Sept. 15   Photo.   Perf. 13½
300 A168 13c multicolored   .25   .25
301 A168 18c multicolored   .35   .30
See UN Offices in Geneva Nos. 79-80.

Hemispheres as Cogwheels — A169

Technical Cooperation Among Developing Countries Conference, Buenos Aires, Argentina, Sept. 1978.

1978, Nov. 17   Photo.   Perf. 14
302 A169 13c multicolored   .25   .25
303 A169 31c multicolored   .50   .40
See UN Offices in Geneva No. 81.

Hand Holding Olive Branch — A170

Tree of Various Races — A171

Globe, Dove with Olive Branch — A172

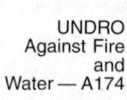

Birds and Globe — A173

1979, Jan. 19   Photo.   Perf. 14
304 A170 5c multicolored   .25   .25
305 A171 14c multicolored   .25   .25
306 A172 15c multicolored   .25   .25
307 A173 20c multicolored   .30   .25
     Nos. 304-307 (4)   1.05 1.00

UNDRO Against Fire and Water — A174

Office of the UN Disaster Relief Coordinator (UNDRO).

1979, Mar. 9   Photo.   Perf. 14
308 A174 15c multicolored   .25   .25
309 A174 20c multicolored   .35   .30
See UN Offices in Geneva Nos. 82-83.

Child and ICY Emblem A175

International Year of the Child.

1979, May 4   Photo.   Perf. 14
310 A175 15c multicolored   .25   .25
311 A175 31c multicolored   .35   .35
See UN Offices in Geneva Nos. 84-85.

Map of Namibia, Olive Branch — A176

For a free and independent Namibia.

1979, Oct. 5   Litho.   Perf. 13½
312 A176 15c multicolored   .25   .25
313 A176 31c multicolored   .30   .35
See UN Offices in Geneva No. 86.

Scales and Sword of Justice — A177

International Court of Justice, The Hague, Netherlands.

1979, Nov. 9   Litho.   Perf. 13x13½
314 A177 15c multicolored   .25   .25
315 A177 20c multicolored   .30   .35
See UN Offices in Geneva Nos. 87-88.

Graph of Economic Trends — A178

Key — A179

New International Economic Order.

1980, Jan. 11   Litho.   Perf. 15x14½
316 A178 15c multicolored   .25   .25
317 A179 31c multicolored   .45   .35
See UN Offices in Geneva No. 89; Vienna No. 7.

Women's Year Emblems A180

United Nations Decade for Women.

1980, Mar. 7   Litho.   Perf. 14½x15
318 A180 15c multicolored   .25   .25
319 A180 20c multicolored   .30   .25
See UN Offices in Geneva Nos. 90-91; Vienna Nos. 9-10.

UN Emblem
and "UN" on
Helmet
A181

Symbols of
Progress
A187

1980, Nov. 21 Litho. Perf. 13½x13
341 A186 15c multicolored .25 .25
342 A187 20c multicolored .40 .35
See UN Offices in Geneva, Nos. 96-97; Vienna Nos. 15-16.

Flag Type of 1980
1981, Sept. 25 Litho.
Granite Paper
350 A185 20c Djibouti .25 .25
351 A185 20c Sri Lanka .25 .25
352 A185 20c Bolivia .25 .25
353 A185 20c Equatorial Guinea .25 .25
a. Se-tenant block of 4, #350-353 1.50 1.50
354 A185 20c Malta .25 .25
355 A185 20c Czechoslovakia .25 .25
356 A185 20c Thailand .25 .25
357 A185 20c Trinidad & Tobago .25 .25
a. Se-tenant block of 4, #354-357 1.50 1.50
358 A185 20c Ukrainian SSR .25 .25
359 A185 20c Kuwait .25 .25
360 A185 20c Sudan .25 .25
361 A185 20c Egypt .25 .25
a. Se-tenant block of 4, #358-361 1.50 1.50
362 A185 20c US .40 .25
363 A185 20c Singapore .25 .25
364 A185 20c Panama .25 .25
365 A185 20c Costa Rica .25 .25
a. Se-tenant block of 4, #362-365 1.50 1.50
Nos. 350-365 (16) 4.15 4.00
See note after No. 340.

1982, Mar. 19 Litho. Perf. 13½x13
371 A199 20c multicolored .25 .25
372 A200 40c multicolored .65 .65
See UN Offices in Geneva Nos. 107-108; Vienna Nos. 25-26.

UN Emblem
and Olive
Branch in
Outer Space
A201

Exploration and Peaceful Uses of Outer Space.

1982, June 11 Litho. Perf. 13x13½
373 A201 20c multicolored .45 .45
See UN Offices in Geneva Nos. 109-110; Vienna No. 27.

Flag Type of 1980
1982, Sept. 24 Litho. **Perf. 12**
Granite Paper
374 A185 20c Austria .25 .25
375 A185 20c Malaysia .25 .25
376 A185 20c Seychelles .25 .25
377 A185 20c Ireland .25 .25
a. Se-tenant block of 4, #374-377 1.50 1.50
378 A185 20c Mozambique .25 .25
379 A185 20c Albania .25 .25
380 A185 20c Dominica .25 .25
381 A185 20c Solomon Islnads .25 .25
a. Se-tenant block of 4, #378-381 1.50 1.50
382 A185 20c Philippines .25 .25
383 A185 20c Swaziland .25 .25
384 A185 20c Nicaragua .25 .25
385 A185 20c Burma .25 .25
a. Se-tenant block of 4, #382-385 1.50 1.50
386 A185 20c Cape Verde .25 .25
387 A185 20c Guyana .25 .25
388 A185 20c Belgium .25 .25
389 A185 20c Nigeria .25 .25
a. Se-tenant block of 4, #386-389 1.50 1.50
Nos. 374-389 (16) 4.00 4.00
See note after No. 340.

Arrows and
UN Emblem
A182

United Nations Peace-keeping Operations.

1980, May 16 Litho. Perf. 14x13
320 A181 15c blue & black .25 .25
321 A182 31c multicolored .40 .40
See UN Offices in Geneva No. 92; Vienna No. 11.

"35" and
Flags — A183

Globe and
Laurel — A184

35th Anniversary of the United Nations.

1980, June 26 Litho. Perf. 13x13½
322 A183 15c multicolored .25 .25
323 A184 31c multicolored .40 .35

Souvenir Sheet
Imperf
324 Sheet of 2 .65 .65
a. A183 15c multicolored .25 .25
b. A184 31c multicolored .40 .40
See UN Offices in Geneva Nos. 93-95; Vienna Nos. 12-14.

Flag of
Turkey
A185

1980, Sept. 26 Litho. Perf. 12
Granite Paper
325 A185 15c shown .25 .25
326 A185 15c Luxembourg .25 .25
327 A185 15c Fiji .25 .25
328 A185 15c Viet Nam .25 .25
a. Se-tenant block of 4, #325-328 1.10 1.10
329 A185 15c Guinea .25 .25
330 A185 15c Surinam .25 .25
331 A185 15c Bangladesh .25 .25
332 A185 15c Mali .25 .25
a. Se-tenant block of 4, #329-332 1.10 1.10
333 A185 15c Yugoslavia .25 .25
334 A185 15c France .25 .25
335 A185 15c Venezuela .25 .25
336 A185 15c El Salvador .25 .25
a. Se-tenant block of 4, #333-336 1.10 1.10
337 A185 15c Madagascar .25 .25
338 A185 15c Cameroon .25 .25
339 A185 15c Rwanda .25 .25
340 A185 15c Hungary .25 .25
a. Se-tenant block of 4, #337-340 1.10 1.10
Nos. 325-340 (16) 4.00 4.00

Issued in 4 panes of 16. Each pane contains 4 blocks of 4 (Nos. 325-328, 329-332, 333-336, 337-340). A se-tenant block of 4 designs centers each pane.
See Nos. 350-365, 374-389, 399-414, 425-440, 450-465, 477-492, 499-514, 528-543, 554-569, 690-697, 719-726, 744-751, 795-802, 921-924, 1063-1066, 1083-1086.

Symbolic
Flowers
A186

Symbols of
Progress
A187

Inalienable
Rights of the
Palestinian
People
A188

1981, Jan. 30 Photo. Perf. 12x11½
343 A188 15c multicolored .30 .25
See UN Offices in Geneva No. 98; Vienna No. 17.

Interlocking
Puzzle
Pieces — A189

Stylized
Person — A190

International Year of the Disabled.

1981, Mar. 6 Photo. Perf. 14
344 A189 20c multicolored .25 .25
345 A190 35c black & orange .40 .45
See UN Offices in Geneva Nos. 99-100; Vienna Nos. 18-19.

Art at UN Issue

Divislava and
Sebastocrator
Kaloyan, Bulgarian
Mural, 1259,
Boyana Church,
Sofia — A191

1981, Apr. 15 Photo. Perf. 11½
Granite Paper
346 A191 20c multicolored .25 .25
347 A191 31c multicolored .40 .45
See UN Offices in Geneva No. 101; Vienna No. 20.

Solar Energy
A192

Conference
Emblem
A193

Conference on New and Renewable Sources of Energy, Nairobi, Aug. 10-21.

1981, May 29 Litho. Perf. 13
348 A192 20c multicolored .25 .25
349 A193 40c multicolored .50 .50
See UN Offices in Geneva No. 102; Vienna No. 21.

Seedling and
Tree Cross
Section
A194

"10" and
Symbols of
Progress
A195

United Nations Volunteers Program, 10th anniv.

1981, Nov. 13 Litho.
366 A194 18c multicolored .25 .25
367 A195 28c multicolored .55 .55
See UN Offices in Geneva Nos. 103-104; Vienna Nos. 22-23.

Respect for
Human
Rights — A196

Independence of
Colonial
Countries and
People — A197

Second
Disarmament
Decade — A198

1982, Jan. 22 Perf. 11½x12
368 A196 17c multicolored .25 .25
369 A197 28c multicolored .45 .40
370 A198 40c multicolored .75 .70
Nos. 368-370 (3) 1.45 1.35

A199   A200

10th Anniversary of United Nations Environment Program.

Conservation and
Protection of
Nature — A202

1982, Nov. 19 Photo. Perf. 14
390 A202 20c Leaf .30 .30
391 A202 28c Butterfly .55 .50
See UN Offices in Geneva Nos. 111-112; Vienna Nos. 28-29.

A203

World Communications Year — A204

World Communications Year.

1983, Jan. 28 Litho. Perf. 13
392 A203 20c multicolored .25 .25
393 A204 40c multicolored .65 .65
See UN Offices in Geneva No. 113; Vienna No. 30.

A205   Safety at Sea — A206

Safety at Sea.

1983, Mar. 18   **Litho.**   *Perf. 14½*
394 A205 20c multicolored   .25   .25
395 A206 37c multicolored   .60   .55
See UN Offices in Geneva Nos. 114-115; Vienna Nos. 31-32.

World Food Program A207

1983, Apr. 22   **Engr.**   *Perf. 13½*
396 A207 20c rose lake   .35   .35
See UN Offices in Geneva No. 116; Vienna Nos. 33-34.

A208

Trade and Development A209

UN Conference on Trade and Development.

1983, June 6   **Litho.**   *Perf. 14*
397 A208 20c multicolored   .25   .35
398 A209 28c multicolored   .70   .65
See UN Offices in Geneva Nos. 117-118; Vienna Nos. 35-36.

Flag Type of 1980
1983, Sept. 23   **Photo.**   *Perf. 12*
Granite Paper
399 A185 20c Great Britain   .25   .25
400 A185 20c Barbados   .25   .25
401 A185 20c Nepal   .25   .25
402 A185 20c Israel   .25   .25
  a.   Se-tenant block of 4, #399-402   1.80   1.50
403 A185 20c Malawi   .25   .25
404 A185 20c Byelorussian SSR   .25   .25
405 A185 20c Jamaica   .25   .25
406 A185 20c Kenya   .25   .25
  a.   Se-tenant block of 4, #403-406   1.80   1.80
407 A185 20c People's Republic of China   .25   .25
408 A185 20c Peru   .25   .25
409 A185 20c Bulgaria   .25   .25
410 A185 20c Canada   .25   .25
  a.   Se-tenant block of 4, #407-410   1.80   1.80
411 A185 20c Somalia   .25   .25
412 A185 20c Senegal   .25   .25
413 A185 20c Brazil   .25   .25
414 A185 20c Sweden   .25   .25
  a.   Se-tenant block of 4, #411-414   1.80   1.80
  Nos. 399-414 (16)   4.00   4.00
See note after No. 340.

A210

35th Anniv. of the Universal Declaration of Human Rights — A211

35th Anniversary of the Universal Declaration of Human Rights.

Photo. & Engr.
1983, Dec. 9   *Perf. 13½*
415 A210 20c multicolored   .30   .25
416 A211 40c multicolored   .70   .65
See UN Offices in Geneva Nos. 119-120; Vienna Nos. 37-38.

Intl. Population Conference A212

1984, Feb. 3   **Litho.**   *Perf. 14*
417 A212 20c multicolored   .25   .25
418 A212 40c multicolored   .65   .65
See UN Offices in Geneva No. 121; Vienna No. 39.

Tractor Plowing A213

Rice Paddy A214

World Food Day, Oct. 16.

1984, Mar. 15   **Litho.**   *Perf. 14½*
419 A213 20c multicolored   .30   .30
420 A214 40c multicolored   .60   .60
See UN Offices in Geneva Nos. 122-123; Vienna Nos. 40-41.

Grand Canyon A215

Ancient City of Polonnaruwa, Sri Lanka A216

World Heritage.

1984, Apr. 18   **Litho.**   *Perf. 14*
421 A215 20c multicolored   .25   .25
422 A216 50c multicolored   .75   .75
See Nos. 601-602, UN Offices in Geneva Nos. 124-125, 211-212; Vienna Nos. 42-43, 125-126.

A217   A218

Future for Refugees.

1984, May 29   **Photo.**   *Perf. 11½*
423 A217 20c multicolored   .30   .30
424 A218 50c multicolored   .90   .90
See UN Offices in Geneva Nos. 126-127; Vienna Nos. 44-45.

Flag Type of 1980
1984, Sept. 21   **Photo.**   *Perf. 12*
Granite Paper
425 A185 20c Burundi   .35   .35
426 A185 20c Pakistan   .35   .35
427 A185 20c Benin   .35   .35
428 A185 20c Italy   .35   .35
  a.   Se-tenant block of 4, #425-428   2.25   2.25
429 A185 20c Tanzania   .35   .35
430 A185 20c United Arab Emirates   .35   .35
431 A185 20c Ecuador   .35   .35
432 A185 20c Bahamas   .35   .35
  a.   Se-tenant block of 4, #429-432   2.25   2.25
433 A185 20c Poland   .35   .35
434 A185 20c Papua New Guinea   .35   .35
435 A185 20c Uruguay   .35   .35
436 A185 20c Chile   .35   .35
  a.   Se-tenant block of 4, #433-436   2.25   2.25
437 A185 20c Paraguay   .35   .35
438 A185 20c Bhutan   .35   .35
439 A185 20c Central African Republic   .35   .35
440 A185 20c Australia   .35   .35
  a.   Se-tenant block of 4, #437-440   2.25   2.25
  Nos. 425-440 (16)   5.60   5.60
See note after No. 340.

Intl. Youth Year — A219

1984, Nov. 15   **Litho.**   *Perf. 13½*
441 A219 20c multicolored   .35   .35
442 A219 35c multicolored   .85   .85
See UN Offices in Geneva No. 128; Vienna Nos. 46-47.

ILO Turin Center — A220

Printed by the Government Printing Bureau, Japan. Panes of 50. Engraved by Mamoru Iwakuni and Hiroshi Ozaki, Japan.

1985, Feb. 1   **Engr.**   *Perf. 13½*
443 A220 23c blue   .45   .45
See UN Offices in Geneva Nos. 129-130; Vienna No. 48.

UN University A221

50c, Farmer plowing, discussion group.

1985, Mar. 15   **Photo.**   *Perf. 11½*
444 A221 50c multi   .95   .95
See UN Offices in Geneva Nos. 131-132; Vienna No. 49.

Peoples of the World — A222

Painting UN Emblem A223

1985, May 10   **Litho.**   *Perf. 14*
445 A222 22c multicolored   .30   .30
446 A223 $3 multicolored   3.75   1.50
See UN Offices in Geneva Nos. 133-134; Vienna Nos. 50-51.

The Corner A224

Alvaro Raking Hay A225

UN 40th anniversary. Oil paintings (details) by American artist Andrew Wyeth (b. 1917).

       Perf. 12 x 11½
1985, June 26   **Photo.**
447 A224 22c multicolored   .35   .35
448 A225 45c multicolored   1.00   1.00
     Souvenir Sheet
       Imperf
449   Sheet of 2   1.30   1.30
  a.   A224 22c multicolored   .50   .50
  b.   A225 45c multicolored   .80   .80
See UN Offices in Geneva Nos. 135-137; Vienna Nos. 52-54.

Flag Type of 1980
1985, Sept. 20   **Photo.**   *Perf. 12*
Granite Paper
450 A185 22c Grenada   .30   .30
451 A185 22c Federal Republic of Germany   .30   .30
452 A185 22c Saudi Arabia   .30   .30
453 A185 22c Mexico   .30   .30
  a.   Se-tenant block of 4, #450-453   3.00   3.00
454 A185 22c Uganda   .30   .30
455 A185 22c St. Thomas & Prince   .30   .30
456 A185 22c USSR   .30   .30
457 A185 22c India   .30   .30
  a.   Se-tenant block of 4, #454-457   3.00   3.00
458 A185 22c Liberia   .30   .30
459 A185 22c Mauritius   .30   .30
460 A185 22c Chad   .30   .30
461 A185 22c Dominican Republic   .30   .30
  a.   Se-tenant block of 4, #458-461   3.00   3.00
462 A185 22c Sultanate of Oman   .30   .30
463 A185 22c Ghana   .30   .30
464 A185 22c Sierra Leone   .30   .30
465 A185 22c Finland   .30   .30
  a.   Se-tenant block of 4, #462-465   3.00   3.00
  Nos. 450-465 (16)   4.80   4.80
See note after 340.

A226

UNICEF Child Survival Campaign.

Photo. & Engr.
1985, Nov. 22   *Perf. 13½*
466 A226 22c Asian Toddler   .30   .30
467 A226 33c Breastfeeding   .65   .65

See UN Offices in Geneva Nos. 138-139; Vienna Nos. 55-56.

A227

Africa in Crisis, campaign against hunger.

1986, Jan. 31   Photo.   *Perf. 11½x12*
468 A227 22c multicolored   .40   .40

See UN Offices in Geneva No. 140; Vienna No. 57.

Water
Resources
A228

1986, Mar. 14   Photo.   *Perf. 13½*
469 A228 22c Dam   .60   .60
470 A228 22c Irrigation   .60   .60
471 A228 22c Hygiene   .60   .60
472 A228 22c Well   .60   .60
  a.   Block of 4, #469-472   2.75   2.75

UN Development Program. No. 472a has continuous design. See UN Offices in Geneva Nos. 141-144; Vienna Nos. 58-61.

Human Rights
Stamp of
1954 — A229

Stamp collecting: 44c, Engraver.

1986, May 22   Engr.   *Perf. 12½*
473 A229 22c dk vio & brt blue   .25   .25
474 A229 44c brn & emer grn   .75   .75

See UN Offices in Geneva Nos. 146-147; Vienna Nos. 62-63.

Birds Nest in
Tree — A230

Peace in
Seven
Languages
A231

Photo. & Embossed
1986, June 20   *Perf. 13½*
475 A230 22c multicolored   .50   .50
476 A231 33c multicolored   1.25   1.25

International Peace Year.
See UN Offices in Geneva Nos. 148-149; Vienna Nos. 64-65.

Flag Type of 1980
1986, Sept. 19   Photo.   *Perf. 12*
Granite Paper
477 A185 22c New Zealand   .30   .30
478 A185 22c Lao PDR   .30   .30
479 A185 22c Burkina Faso   .30   .30
480 A185 22c Gambia   .30   .30
  a.   Se-tenant block of 4, #477-480   3.00   3.00
481 A185 22c Maldives   .30   .30
482 A185 22c Ethiopia   .30   .30
483 A185 22c Jordan   .30   .30
484 A185 22c Zambia   .30   .30
  a.   Se-tenant block of 4, #481-484   3.00   3.00
485 A185 22c Iceland   .30   .30
486 A185 22c Antigua & Barbuda   .30   .30
487 A185 22c Angola   .30   .30
488 A185 22c Botswana   .30   .30
  a.   Se-tenant block of 4, #485-488   3.00   3.00
489 A185 22c Romania   .30   .30
490 A185 22c Togo   .30   .30
491 A185 22c Mauritania   .30   .30
492 A185 22c Colombia   .30   .30
  a.   Se-tenant block of 4, #489-492   3.00   3.00
      Nos. 477-492 (16)   4.80   4.80

See note after No. 340.

Souvenir Sheet

World Federation of UN Associations,
40th Anniv. — A232

22c, Mother Earth, by Edna Hibel, U.S. 33c, Watercolor by Salvador Dali (b. 1904), Spain. 39c, New Dawn, by Dong Kingman, U.S. 44c, Watercolor by Chaim Gross, U.S.

1986, Nov. 14   Litho.   *Perf. 13x13½*
493 A232   Sheet of 4   3.00   3.00
  a.   22c multicolored   .40   .40
  b.   33c multicolored   .50   .40
  c.   39c multicolored   .75   .50
  d.   44c multicolored   1.10   .75

See UN Offices in Geneva No. 150; Vienna No. 66.

Trygve Halvdan Lie
(1896-1968), 1st
Secretary-General
A233

Photo. & Engr.
1987, Jan. 30   *Perf. 13½*
494 A233 22c multicolored   .75   .75

See Offices in Geneva No. 151; Vienna No. 67.

Intl. Year
of Shelter
for the
Homeless
A234

22c, Surveying and blueprinting. 44c, Cutting lumber.

Perf. 13½x12½
1987, Mar. 13   Litho.
495 A234 22c multicolored   .35   .35
496 A234 44c multicolored   .90   .90

See Offices in Geneva Nos. 154-155; Vienna Nos. 68-69.

Fight Drug
Abuse
A235

22c, Construction. 33c, Education.

1987, June 12   Litho.   *Perf. 14½x15*
497 A235 22c multicolored   .45   .45
498 A235 33c multicolored   .90   .90

See Offices in Geneva Nos. 156-157; Vienna Nos. 70-71.

Flag Type of 1980
1987, Sept. 18   Photo.   *Perf. 12*
Granite Paper
499 A185 22c Comoros   .35   .35
500 A185 22c Yemen PDR   .35   .35
501 A185 22c Mongolia   .35   .35
502 A185 22c Vanuatu   .35   .35
  a.   Se-tenant block of 4, #499-502   3.25   3.25
503 A185 22c Japan   .35   .35
504 A185 22c Gabon   .35   .35
505 A185 22c Zimbabwe   .35   .35
506 A185 22c Iraq   .35   .35
  a.   Se-tenant block of 4, #503-506   3.25   3.25
507 A185 22c Argentina   .35   .35
508 A185 22c Congo   .35   .35
509 A185 22c Niger   .35   .35
510 A185 22c St. Lucia   .35   .35
  a.   Se-tenant block of 4, #507-510   3.25   3.25
511 A185 22c Bahrain   .35   .35
512 A185 22c Haiti   .35   .35
513 A185 22c Afghanistan   .35   .35
514 A185 22c Greece   .35   .35
  a.   Se-tenant block of 4, #511-514   3.25   3.25
      Nos. 499-514 (16)   5.60   5.60

See note after No. 340.

UN
Day — A236

Multinational people in various occupations.

1987, Oct. 23   Litho.   *Perf. 14½x15*
515 A236 22c multicolored   .35   .35
516 A236 39c multicolored   .55   .55

See Offices in Geneva Nos. 158-159; Vienna Nos. 74-75.

Immunize Every
Child — A237

22c, Measles. 44c, Tetanus.

1987, Nov. 20   Litho.   *Perf. 15x14½*
517 A237 22c multicolored   .75   .75
518 A237 44c multicolored   1.50   1.50

See Offices in Geneva Nos. 160-161; Vienna Nos. 76-77.

Intl. Fund for Agricultural Development
(IFAD) — A238

22c, Fishing. 33c, Farming.

1988, Jan. 29   Litho.   *Perf. 13½*
519 A238 22c multicolored   .35   .35
520 A238 33c multicolored   .75   .75

See Offices in Geneva Nos. 162-163; Vienna Nos. 78-79.

A239

1988, Jan. 29   Photo.   *Perf. 13½x14*
521 A239 3c multicolored   .25   .25

Survival of the
Forests
A240

Tropical rain forest: 25c, Treetops. 44c, Ground vegetation and tree trunks. Printed se-tenant in a continuous design.

1988, Mar. 18   Litho.   *Perf. 14x15*
522 A240 25c multicolored   .75   .75
523 A240 44c multicolored   1.00   1.00
  a.   Pair, #522-523   2.50   3.00

See Offices in Geneva Nos. 165-166; Vienna Nos. 80-81.

Intl. Volunteer
Day — A241

25c, Eduration. 50c, Vocational training, horiz.

Perf. 13x14, 14x13
1988, May 6   Litho.
524 A241 25c multicolored   .45   .45
525 A241 50c multicolored   .95   .95

See Offices in Geneva Nos. 167-168; Vienna Nos. 82-83.

Health in
Sports — A242

25c, Cycling, vert. 35c, Marathon.

Perf. 13½x13, 13x13½
1988, June 17   Litho.
526 A242 25c multicolored   .45   .45
527 A242 38c multicolored   1.00   1.00

See Offices in Geneva Nos. 169-170; Vienna Nos. 84-85.

Flag Type of 1980
1988, Sept. 15   Photo.   *Perf. 12*
Granite Paper
528 A185 25c Spain   .50   .50
529 A185 25c St. Vincent &
           Grenadines   .50   .50
530 A185 25c Ivory Coast   .50   .50
531 A185 25c Lebanon   .50   .50
  a.   Se-tenant block of 4, #528-531   3.25   3.25
532 A185 25c Yemen (Arab Re-
           public)   .50   .50
533 A185 25c Cuba   .50   .50
534 A185 25c Denmark   .50   .50
535 A185 25c Libya   .50   .50
  a.   Se-tenant block of 4, #532-535   3.25   3.25
536 A185 25c Qatar   .50   .50
537 A185 25c Zaire   .50   .50
538 A185 25c Norway   .50   .50
539 A185 25c German Democrat-
           ic Republic   .50   .50
  a.   Se-tenant block of 4, #536-539   3.25   3.25
540 A185 25c Iran   .50   .50
541 A185 25c Tunisia   .50   .50
542 A185 25c Samoa   .50   .50
543 A185 25c Belize   .50   .50
  a.   Se-tenant block of 4, #540-543   3.25   3.25
      Nos. 528-543 (16)   8.00   8.00

See note after No. 340.

A243

Photo. & Engr.

1988, Dec. 9   **Perf. 11x11½**
544 A243 25c multicolored   .45   .45

Souvenir Sheet

545 A243 $1 multicolored   1.25 1.25

Universal Declaration of Human Rights, 40th anniv.
See Offices in Geneva Nos. 171-172; Vienna Nos. 86-87.

A244

1989, Jan. 27   **Litho.**   **Perf. 13x14**
546 A244 25c Energy and nature .60 .60
547 A244 45c Agriculture   1.10 1.10

World Bank. See Offices in Geneva Nos. 173-174; Vienna Nos. 88-89.

UN Peace-Keeping Force, 1988 Nobel Peace Prize Winner — A245

UN Peace-Keeping Force, awarded 1988 Nobel Peace Prize.

1989, Mar. 17   **Litho.**   **Perf. 14x13½**
548 A245 25c multicolored   .45 .45

See Offices in Geneva No. 175; Vienna No. 90.

Aerial Photograph of New York Headquarters — A246

1989, Mar. 17   **Litho.**   **Perf. 14½x14**
549 A246 45c multicolored   .65 .65

World Weather Watch, 25th Anniv. (in 1988) — A247

Satellite photographs: 25c, Storm system off the U.S. east coast. 36c, Typhoon Abby in the north-west Pacific.

1989, Apr. 21   **Litho.**   **Perf. 13x14**
550 A247 25c multicolored   .50 .50
551 A247 36c multicolored   1.10 1.10

See Offices in Geneva Nos. 176-177; Vienna Nos. 91-92.

A248   A249

Photo. & Engr., Photo. (90c)

1989, Aug. 23   **Perf. 14**
552 A248 25c multicolored   1.25 1.25
553 A249 90c multicolored   2.50 2.50

See Offices in Geneva Nos. 178-179; Vienna Nos. 93-94.

Flag Type of 1980

1989, Sept. 22   **Photo.**   **Perf. 12**
Granite Paper
554 A185 25c Indonesia   .50 .50
555 A185 25c Lesotho   .50 .50
556 A185 25c Guatemala   .50 .50
557 A185 25c Netherlands   .50 .50
    a.   Se-tenant block of 4, #554-557   3.50 3.50
558 A185 25c South Africa   .50 .50
559 A185 25c Portugal   .50 .50
560 A185 25c Morocco   .50 .50
561 A185 25c Syrian Arab Republic   .50 .50
    a.   Se-tenant block of 4, #558-561   3.50 3.50
562 A185 25c Honduras   .50 .50
563 A185 25c Kampuchea   .50 .50
564 A185 25c Guinea-Bissau   .50 .50
565 A185 25c Cyprus   .50 .50
    a.   Se-tenant block of 4, #562-565   3.50 3.50
566 A185 25c Algeria   .50 .50
567 A185 25c Brunei   .50 .50
568 A185 25c St. Kitts and Nevis   .50 .50
569 A185 25c United Nations   .50 .50
    a.   Se-tenant block of 4, #566-569   3.50 3.50
    Nos. 554-569 (16)   8.00 8.00

See note after No. 340.

Declaration of Human Rights, 40th Anniv. (in 1988) — A250

Paintings: 25c, The Table of Universal Brotherhood, by Jose Clemente Orozco. 45c, Study for Composition II, by Vassily Kandinsky.

1989, Nov. 17   **Litho.**   **Perf. 13½**
570 A250 25c multicolored   .35 .35
571 A250 45c multicolored   .80 .80

Panes of 12+12 se-tenant labels containing Articles 1 (25c) or 2 (45c) inscribed in English, French or German.
See Nos. 582-583, 599-600, 616-617, 627-628; Offices in Geneva Nos. 180-181, 193-194, 209-210, 224-225, 234-235; Vienna Nos. 95-96, 108-109, 123-124, 139-140, 150-151.

Intl. Trade Center A251

1990, Feb. 2   **Litho.**   **Perf. 14½x15**
572 A251 25c multicolored   1.00 1.00

See Offices in Geneva No. 182; Vienna No. 97.

Fight AIDS Worldwide A252

40c, Shadow over crowd.

Perf. 13½x12½

1990, Mar. 16   **Litho.**
573 A252 25c multicolored   .35 .35
574 A252 40c multicolored   1.15 1.15

See Offices in Geneva Nos. 184-185, Vienna Nos. 99-100.

Medicinal Plants — A253

25c, Catharanthus roseus. 90c, Panax quinquefolium.

1990, May 4   **Photo.**   **Perf. 11½**
Granite Paper
575 A253 25c multi   .45 .45
576 A253 90c multi   1.40 1.40

See Offices in Geneva Nos. 186-187, Vienna Nos. 101-102.

United Nations, 45th Anniv. A254

45c, "45," emblem.

1990, June 26   **Litho.**   **Perf. 14½x13**
577 A254 25c multicolored   .50 .50
578 A254 45c multicolored   1.90 1.90

Souvenir Sheet
579   Sheet of 2, #577-578   3.50 3.50

See Offices in Geneva Nos. 188-190; Vienna Nos. 103-105.

Crime Prevention — A255

1990, Sept. 13   **Photo.**   **Perf. 14**
580 A255 25c Crimes of youth   .65 .65
581 A255 36c Organized crime   1.25 1.25

See Offices in Geneva Nos. 191-192; Vienna Nos. 106-107.

Human Rights Type of 1989

25c, Fragment from the sarcophagus of Plotinus, c. 270 A.D. 45c, Combined Chambers of the High Court of Appeal by Charles Paul Renouard.

1990, Nov. 16   **Litho.**   **Perf. 13½**
582 A250 25c black, gray & tan   .35 .35
583 A250 45c black & brown   .65 .65

See Offices in Geneva Nos. 193-194; Vienna Nos. 108-109.

Economic Commission for Europe A256

1991, Mar. 15   **Litho.**   **Perf. 14**
584 A256 30c Two storks   1.10 1.10
585 A256 30c Woodpecker, ibex   1.10 1.10
586 A256 30c Capercaille, plover   1.10 1.10
587 A256 30c Falcon, marmot   1.10 1.10
    a.   Block of 4, #584-587   4.50 4.50

See Offices in Geneva Nos. 195-198; Vienna Nos. 110-113.

Namibian Independence A257

1991, May 10   **Litho.**   **Perf. 14**
588 A257 30c Dunes, Namib Desert   .50 .50
589 A257 50c Savanna   1.10 1.00

See Offices in Geneva Nos. 199-200; Vienna Nos. 114-115.

A258

The Golden Rule by Norman Rockwell — A259   UN Headquarters, New York — A260

1991   **Litho.**   **Perf. 13½**
590 A258 30c multi   .60 .60

Photo.
Perf. 12x11½
591 A259 50c multi   1.00 1.00

Engr.
592 A260 $2 dark blue   2.75 2.75

Rights of the Child — A261

1991, June 14   **Litho.**   **Perf. 14½**
593 A261 30c Children, globe   1.00 1.00
594 A261 70c House, rainbow   2.00 2.00

See Offices in Geneva Nos. 203-204; Vienna Nos. 117-118.

Banning of Chemical Weapons A262

90c, Hand holding back chemical drums.

1991, Sept. 11   **Litho.**   **Perf. 13½**
595 A262 30c multicolored   .75 .75
596 A262 90c multicolored   2.25 2.25

See Offices in Geneva Nos. 205-206; Vienna Nos. 119-120.

UN Postal Administration, 40th Anniv. — A263

1991, Oct. 24   Litho.   *Perf. 14x15*
597 A263 30c No. 1   .65   .65
598 A263 40c No. 3   .85   .85

See Offices in Geneva Nos. 207-208;
Vienna Nos. 121-122.

Human Rights Type of 1989

30c, The Last of England, by Ford Madox
Brown. 40c, The Emigration to the East, by
Tito Salas.

1991, Nov. 20   Litho.   *Perf. 13½*
599 A250 30c multicolored   .40   .40
600 A250 50c multicolored   .80   1.00

See Offices in Geneva Nos. 209-210;
Vienna Nos. 123-124.

World Heritage Type of 1984

30c, Uluru Natl. Park, Australia. 50c, The
Great Wall of China.

1992, Jan. 24   Litho.   *Perf. 13*
Size: 35x28mm
601 A215 30c multicolored   .55   .55
602 A215 50c multicolored   .90   .90

See Offices in Geneva Nos. 211-212;
Vienna Nos. 125-126.

Clean Oceans — A264

1992, Mar. 13   Litho.   *Perf. 14*
603 A264 29c Ocean surface   .50   .50
604 A264 29c Ocean bottom   .50   .50
    a. Pair, #603-604   1.10   1.10

See Offices in Geneva Nos. 214-215,
Vienna Nos. 127-128.

Earth
Summit — A265

No. 605, Globe at LR. No. 606, Globe at LL.
No. 607, Globe at UR. No. 608, Globe at UL.

1992, May 22   Photo.   *Perf. 11½*
605 A265 29c multicolored   .65   .65
606 A265 29c multicolored   .65   .65
607 A265 29c multicolored   .65   .65
608 A265 29c multicolored   .65   .65
    a. Block of 4, #605-608   4.00   3.50

See Offices in Geneva Nos. 216-219,
Vienna Nos. 129-132.

Mission to Planet Earth — A266

No. 609, Satellites over city, sailboats, fishing boat. No. 610, Satellite over coast, passenger liner, dolphins, whale, volcano.

1992, Sept. 4   Photo.   *Rouletted 8*
Granite Paper
609 A266 29c multicolored   1.25   1.25
610 A266 29c multicolored   1.25   1.25
    a. Pair, #609-610   2.50   2.50

See Offices in Geneva Nos. 220-221,
Vienna Nos. 133-134.

Science and Technology for
Development — A267

50c, Animal, man drinking.

1992, Oct. 2   Litho.   *Perf. 14*
611 A267 29c multicolored   .40   .40
612 A267 50c multicolored   .70   .70

UN
University
Building,
Tokyo
A268

UN
Headquarters
A269

40c, UN University Building, Tokyo, diff.

Perf. 14, 13½x13 (29c)
1992, Oct. 2   Litho.
613 A268   4c multicolored   .25   .25
614 A269 29c multicolored   .50   .50
615 A268 40c multicolored   .65   .65
        Nos. 613-615 (3)   1.40   1.40

Human Rights Type of 1989

29c, Lady Writing a Letter with her Maid, by
Vermeer. 50c, The Meeting, by Ester Almqvist.

1992, Nov. 20   Litho.   *Perf. 13½*
616 A250 29c multicolored   .40   .40
617 A250 50c multicolored   .60   .60

See Offices in Geneva Nos. 224-225;
Vienna Nos. 139-140.

Aging With
Dignity — A270

29c, Elderly couple, family. 52c, Old man,
physician, woman holding fruit basket.

1993, Feb. 5   Litho.   *Perf. 13*
618 A270 29c multicolored   .45   .45
619 A270 52c multicolored   1.00   1.00

See Offices in Geneva Nos. 226-227;
Vienna Nos. 141-142.

Endangered
Species
A271

No. 620, Hairy-nosed wombat. No. 621,
Whooping crane. No. 622, Giant clam. No.
623, Giant sable antelope.

1993, Mar. 2   Litho.   *Perf. 13x12½*
620 A271 29c multicolored   .45   .45
621 A271 29c multicolored   .45   .45
622 A271 29c multicolored   .45   .45
623 A271 29c multicolored   .45   .45
    a. Block of 4, #620-623   2.00   2.00

See Nos. 639-642, 657-660, 674-677, 700-
703, 730-733, 757-760, 773-776; Offices in
Geneva Nos. 228-231, 246-249, 264-267,
280-283, 298-301, 318-321, 336-339, 352-
355; Vienna Nos. 143-146, 162-165, 180-183,
196-199, 214-217, 235-238, 253-256, 269-
272.

Healthy
Environment
A272

29c, Personal. 50c, Family.

1993, May 7   Litho.   *Perf. 15x14½*
624 A272 29c Man   .50   .50
625 A272 50c Family   .90   .90

See Offices in Geneva Nos. 232-233;
Vienna Nos. 147-148.

A273

1993, May 7   Litho.   *Perf. 15x14*
626 A273   5c multicolored   .25   .25

Human Rights Type of 1989

29c, Shocking Corn, by Thomas Hart Benton. 35c, The Library, by Jacob Lawrence.

1993, June 11   Litho.   *Perf. 13½*
627 A250 29c multicolored   .40   .40
628 A250 35c multicolored   .45   .45

See Offices in Geneva Nos. 234-235;
Vienna Nos. 150-151.

Intl. Peace Day — A274

Denomination at: #629, UL. #630, UR.
#631, LL. #632, LR.

Rouletted 12½
1993, Sept. 21   Litho. & Engr.
629 A274 29c blue & multi   1.00   1.00
630 A274 29c blue & multi   1.00   1.00
631 A274 29c blue & multi   1.00   1.00
632 A274 29c blue & multi   1.00   1.00
    a. Block of 4, #629-632   6.00   6.00

See Offices in Geneva Nos. 236-239;
Vienna Nos. 152-155.

Environment-Climate — A275

#633, Chameleon. #634, Palm trees, top of
funnel cloud. #635, Bottom of funnel cloud,
deer, antelope. #636, Bird of paradise.

1993, Oct. 29   Litho.   *Perf. 14½*
633 A275 29c multicolored   .75   .75
634 A275 29c multicolored   .75   .75
635 A275 29c multicolored   .75   .75
636 A275 29c multicolored   .75   .75
    a. Strip of 4, #633-636   4.00   4.00

See Offices in Geneva Nos. 240-243;
Vienna Nos. 156-159.

Intl. Year of the
Family — A276

29c, Mother holding child, two children,
woman. 45c, People tending crops.

1994, Feb. 4   Litho.   *Perf. 13.1*
637 A276 29c green & multi   .70   .70
638 A276 45c blue & multi   .90   .90

See Offices in Geneva Nos. 244-245;
Vienna Nos. 160-161.

Endangered Species Type of 1993

No. 639, Chimpanzee. No. 640, St. Lucia
Amazon. No. 641, American crocodile. No.
642, Dama gazelle.

1994, Mar. 18   Litho.   *Perf. 12.7*
639 A271 29c multicolored   .45   .45
640 A271 29c multicolored   .45   .45
641 A271 29c multicolored   .45   .45
642 A271 29c multicolored   .45   .45
    a. Block of 4, #639-642   2.00   2.00

See Offices in Geneva Nos. 246-249;
Vienna Nos. 162-165.

Protection for
Refugees — A277

1994, Apr. 29 Litho. *Perf. 14.3x14.8*
643 A277 50c multicolored   .90   .90

See Offices in Geneva No. 250; Vienna No.
166.

Dove of
Peace — A278

Sleeping Child,
by Stanislaw
Wyspianski
A279

Mourning Owl,
by Vanessa Isitt
A280

1994, Apr. 29   Litho.   *Perf. 12.9*
644 A278 10c multicolored   .25   .25
645 A279 19c multicolored   .30   .30

Engr.
Perf. 13.1
646 A280 $1 red brown   1.50   1.50
        Nos. 644-646 (3)   2.05   2.05

Intl. Decade for
Natural
Disaster
Reduction
A281

Earth seen from space, outline map of:
#647, North America. #648, Eurasia. #649,
South America, #650, Australia and South
Asia.

1994, May 27 Litho. *Perf. 13.9x14.2*
647 A281 29c multicolored   1.75   1.75
648 A281 29c multicolored   1.75   1.75
649 A281 29c multicolored   1.75   1.75
650 A281 29c multicolored   1.75   1.75
    a. Block of 4, #647-650   7.50   7.50

See Offices in Geneva Nos. 251-254;
Vienna Nos. 170-173.

Population and Development — A282

29c, Children playing. 52c, Family with house, car, other possessions.

1994, Sept. 1   Litho.   Perf. 13.2x13.6
651 A282 29c multicolored   .40   .40
652 A282 52c multicolored   .80   .80

See Offices in Geneva Nos. 258-259; Vienna Nos. 174-175.

UNCTAD, 30th Anniv. A283

1994, Oct. 28
653 A283 29c multicolored   .40   .40
654 A283 50c multi, diff.   .80   .80

See Offices in Geneva Nos. 260-261; Vienna Nos. 176-177.

UN, 50th Anniv. — A284

Litho. & Engr.
1995, Jan. 1   Perf. 13.4
655 A284 32c multicolored   .90   .90

See Offices in Geneva No. 262; Vienna No. 178.

Social Summit, Copenhagen A285

656 A285 50c multicolored   1.00   1.00

See Offices in Geneva No. 263; Vienna No. 179.

Endangered Species Type of 1993

No. 657, Giant armadillo. No. 658, American bald eagle. No. 659, Fijian/Tongan banded iguana. No. 660, Giant panda.

1995, Mar. 24   Litho.   Perf. 13x12½
657 A271 32c multicolored   .40   .40
658 A271 32c multicolored   .40   .40
659 A271 32c multicolored   .40   .40
660 A271 32c multicolored   .40   .40
    a.   Block of 4, 657-660   2.25   2.25

See Offices in Geneva Nos. 264-267; Vienna Nos. 180-183.

Intl. Youth Year, 10th Anniv. — A286

32c, Seated child. 55c, Children cycling.

1995, May 26   Litho.   Perf. 14.4x14.7
661 A286 32c multicolored   .55   .55
662 A286 55c multicolored   .95   .95

See Offices in Geneva Nos. 268-269; Vienna Nos. 184-185.

UN, 50th Anniv. — A287

32c, Hand with pen signing UN Charter, flags. 50c, Veterans' War Memorial, Opera House, San Francisco.

Perf. 13.3x13.6
1995, June 26   Engr.
663 A287 32c black   .55   .55
664 A287 50c maroon   1.00   1.00

Souvenir Sheet
Litho. & Engr.
Imperf
665   Sheet of 2, #663-664   2.75   2.75
    a.   A287 32c black   1.00   1.00
    b.   A287 50c maroon   1.25   1.25

No. 665 exists with gold China 1996 overprint. Value $20.

See Offices in Geneva Nos. 270-272; Vienna Nos. 186-188.

4th World Conference on Women, Beijing A288

32c, Mother and child. 40c, Seated woman, cranes flying above.

1995, Sept. 5   Photo.   Perf. 12
666 A288 32c multicolored   .50   .50

Size: 28x50mm
667 A288 40c multicolored   .85   .85

See Offices in Geneva Nos. 273-274; Vienna Nos. 189-190.

UN Headquarters — A289

1995, Sept. 5   Litho.   Perf. 15
668 A289 20c multicolored   .35   .35

Miniature Sheet

United Nations, 50th Anniv. — A290

1995, Oct. 24   Litho.   Perf. 14
669 A290 Sheet of 12   8.00   8.00
    a.-l. 32c any single   .65   .70
670   Souvenir booklet   8.00
    a.   A290 32c Booklet pane of 3,
          vert. strip of 3 from UL of
          sheet   2.00   2.00
    b.   A290 32c Booklet pane of 3,
          vert. strip of 3 from UR of
          sheet   2.00   2.00
    c.   A290 32c Booklet pane of 3,
          vert. strip of 3 from LL of
          sheet   2.00   2.00

---

    d.   A290 32c Booklet pane of 3,
          vert. strip of 3 from LR of
          sheet   2.00   2.00

See Offices in Geneva Nos. 275-276; Vienna Nos. 191-192.

WFUNA, 50th Anniv. — A291

1996, Feb. 2   Litho.   Perf. 13x13½
671 A291 32c multicolored   .50   .50

See Offices in Geneva No. 277; Vienna No. 193.

Mural, by Fernand Leger — A292

1996, Feb. 2   Litho.   Perf. 14½x15
672 A292 32c multicolored   .45   .45
673 A292 60c multi, diff.   .95   .95

Endangered Species Type of 1993

No. 674, Masdevallia veitchiana. No. 675, Saguaro cactus. No. 676, West Australian pitcher plant. No. 677, Encephalartos horridus.

1996, Mar. 14   Litho.   Perf. 12½
674 A271 32c multicolored   .45   .45
675 A271 32c multicolored   .45   .45
676 A271 32c multicolored   .45   .45
677 A271 32c multicolored   .45   .45
    a.   Block of 4, #674-677   2.25   2.25

See Offices in Geneva Nos. 280-283; Vienna Nos. 196-199.

City Summit (Habitat II) — A293

No. 678, Deer. No. 679, Man, child, dog sitting on hill, overlooking town. No. 680, People walking in park, city skyline. No. 681, Tropical park, Polynesian woman, boy. No. 682, Polynesian village, orchids, bird.

1996, June 3   Litho.   Perf. 14x13½
678 A293 32c multicolored   .80   .80
679 A293 32c multicolored   .80   .80
680 A293 32c multicolored   .80   .80
681 A293 32c multicolored   .80   .80
682 A293 32c multicolored   .80   .80
    a.   Strip of 5, #678-682   7.00   7.00

See Offices in Geneva Nos. 284-288; Vienna Nos. 200-204.

Sport and the Environment A294

32c, Men's basketball. 50c, Women's volleyball, horiz.

Perf. 14x14½, 14½x14
1996, July 19   Litho.
683 A294 32c multicolored   .65   .65
684 A294 50c multicolored   1.40   1.40

Souvenir Sheet
685 A294 Sheet of 2,
           #683-684   2.50   2.50

See Offices in Geneva Nos. 289-291; Vienna Nos. 205-207.
1996 Summer Olympic Games, Atlanta, GA.

Plea for Peace — A295

32c, Doves. 60c, Stylized dove.

1996, Sept. 17   Litho.   Perf. 14½x15
686 A295 32c multicolored   .50   .50
687 A295 60c multicolored   .90   .90

See Offices in Geneva Nos. 292-293; Vienna Nos. 208-209.

UNICEF, 50th Anniv. — A296

Fairy Tales: 32c, Yeh-Shen, China. 60c, The Ugly Duckling, by Hans Christian Andersen.

1996, Nov. 20   Litho.   Perf. 14½x15
688 A296 32c multicolored   .45   .45
689 A296 60c multicolored   1.10   1.10

See Offices in Geneva Nos. 294-295; Vienna Nos. 210-211.

Flag Type of 1980

1997, Feb. 12   Photo.   Perf. 12
Granite Paper
690 A185 32c Tadjikistan   1.00   1.00
691 A185 32c Georgia   1.00   1.00
692 A185 32c Armenia   1.00   1.00
693 A185 32c Namibia   1.00   1.00
    a.   Block of 4, #690-693   13.00 13.00
694 A185 32c Liechtenstein   1.00   1.00
695 A185 32c Republic of Korea 1.00   1.00
696 A185 32c Kazakhstan   1.00   1.00
697 A185 32c Latvia   1.00   1.00
    a.   Block of 4, #694-697   13.00 13.00

See note after No. 340.

Cherry Blossoms, UN Headquarters A297

Peace Rose — A298

1997, Feb. 12   Litho.   Perf. 14½
698 A297 8c multicolored   .25   .25
699 A298 55c multicolored   .90   .90

Endangered Species Type of 1993

No. 700, African elephant. No. 701, Major Mitchell's cockatoo. No. 702, Black-footed ferret. No. 703, Cougar.

1997, Mar. 13   Litho.   Perf. 12½
700 A271 32c multicolored   .40   .40
701 A271 32c multicolored   .40   .40
702 A271 32c multicolored   .40   .40
703 A271 32c multicolored   .40   .40
    a.   Block of 4, #700-703   2.25   2.25

See Offices in Geneva Nos. 298-301; Vienna Nos. 214-217.

Earth Summit,
5th Anniv.
A299

No. 704, Sailboat. No. 705, Three sailboats. No. 706, Two people watching sailboat, sun. No. 707, Person, sailboat.
$1, Combined design similar to Nos. 704-707.

1997, May 30   Photo.   Perf. 11.5
Granite Paper

704	A299	32c multicolored	.90	.90
705	A299	32c multicolored	.90	.90
706	A299	32c multicolored	.90	.90
707	A299	32c multicolored	.90	.90
a.		Block of 4, #704-707	5.00	5.00

Souvenir Sheet

708	A299	$1 multicolored	2.75	2.75
a.		Ovptd. in sheet margin	17.50	17.50

See Offices in Geneva Nos. 302-306; Vienna Nos. 218-222.
No. 708 contains one 60x43mm stamp. Overprint in sheet margin of No. 708a reads "PACIFIC 97 / World Philatelic Exhibition / San Francisco, California / 29 May - 8 June 1997".

Transportation
A300

Ships: No. 709, Clipper ship. No. 710, Paddle steamer. No. 711, Ocean liner. No. 712, Hovercraft. No. 713, Hydrofoil.

1997, Aug. 29   Litho.   Perf. 14x14½

709	A300	32c multicolored	.65	.65
710	A300	32c multicolored	.65	.65
711	A300	32c multicolored	.65	.65
712	A300	32c multicolored	.65	.65
713	A300	32c multicolored	.65	.65
a.		Strip of 5, #709-713	4.25	4.25

See Offices in Geneva Nos. 307-311; Vienna Nos. 223-227.
No. 713a has continuous design.

Philately — A301

32c, No. 473. 50c, No. 474.

1997, Oct. 14   Litho.   Perf. 13½x14

714	A301	32c multicolored	.60	.60
715	A301	50c multicolored	1.50	1.50

See Offices in Geneva Nos. 312-313; Vienna Nos. 228-229.

World Heritage
Convention, 25th
Anniv. — A302

Terracotta warriors of Xian: 32c, Single warrior. 60c, Massed warriors. No. 718a, like #716. No. 718b, like #717. No. 718c, like Geneva #314. No. 718d, like Geneva #315. No. 718e, like Vienna #230. No. 718f, like Vienna #231.

1997, Nov. 19   Litho.   Perf. 13½

716	A302	32c multicolored	.75	.75
717	A302	60c multicolored	1.25	1.25
718		Souvenir booklet	10.00	
a.-f.	A302	8c any single	.50	.50
g.		Booklet pane of 4 #718a	2.00	2.00
h.		Booklet pane of 4 #718b	2.00	2.00
i.		Booklet pane of 4 #718c	2.00	2.00
j.		Booklet pane of 4 #718d	2.00	2.00
k.		Booklet pane of 4 #718e	2.00	2.00
l.		Booklet pane of 4 #718f	2.00	2.00

See Offices in Geneva Nos. 314-316; Vienna Nos. 230-232.

Flag Type of 1980

No. 719, Micronesia. No. 720, Slovakia. No. 721, Democratic People's Republic of Korea. No. 722, Azerbaijan. No. 723, Uzbekistan. No. 724, Monaco. No. 725, Czech Republic. No. 726, Estonia.

1998, Feb. 13   Photo.   Perf. 12
Granite Paper

719	A185	32c multicolored	.80	.80
720	A185	32c multicolored	.80	.80
721	A185	32c multicolored	.80	.80
722	A185	32c multicolored	.80	.80
a.		Block of 4, #719-722	12.50	12.50
723	A185	32c multicolored	.80	.80
724	A185	32c multicolored	.80	.80
725	A185	32c multicolored	.80	.80
726	A185	32c multicolored	.80	.80
a.		Block of 4, #723-726	12.50	12.50
		Nos. 719-726 (8)	6.40	6.40

A303

A304

A305

Perf. 14½x15, 15x14½
1998, Feb. 13   Litho.

727	A303	1c multicolored	.25	.25
728	A304	2c multicolored	.25	.25
729	A305	21c multicolored	.40	.40
		Nos. 727-729 (3)	.90	.90

Endangered Species Type of 1993

No. 730, Lesser galago. No. 731, Hawaiian goose. No. 732, Golden birdwing. No. 733, Sun bear.

1998, Mar. 13   Litho.   Perf. 12½

730	A271	32c multicolored	.45	.45
731	A271	32c multicolored	.45	.45
732	A271	32c multicolored	.45	.45
733	A271	32c multicolored	.45	.45
a.		Block of 4, #730-733	2.25	2.25

See Offices in Geneva Nos. 318-321; Vienna Nos. 235-238.

Intl. Year of the Ocean — A306

1998, May 20   Litho.   Perf. 13x13½

734	A306	Sheet of 12	12.50	12.50
a.-l.		32c any single	1.00	1.00

See Offices in Geneva No. 322; Vienna No. 239.

Rain
Forests
A307

1998, June 19   Litho.   Perf. 13x13½

735	A307	32c Jaguar	.50	.50

Souvenir Sheet

736	A307	$2 like #735	3.00	3.00

See Offices in Geneva Nos. 323-324; Vienna Nos. 240-241.

U.N. Peacekeeping Forces, 50th
Anniv. — A308

33c, Commander with binoculars. 40c, Two soldiers on vehicle.

1998, Sept. 15   Photo.   Perf. 12

737	A308	33c multicolored	.50	.50
738	A308	40c multicolored	.75	.75

See Offices in Geneva Nos. 325-326; Vienna Nos. 242-243.

Universal
Declaration of
Human Rights,
50th
Anniv. — A309

Stylized people: 32c, Carrying flag. 55c, Carrying pens.

Litho. & Photo.
1998, Oct. 27   Perf. 13

739	A309	32c multicolored	.45	.45
740	A309	55c multicolored	.90	.90

See Offices in Geneva Nos. 327-328; Vienna Nos. 244-245.

Schönnbrun Palace, Vienna — A310

33c, #743f, The Gloriette. 60c, #743b, Wall painting on fabric (detail), by Johann Wenzl Bergl, vert. No. 743a, Blue porcelain vase, vert. No. 743c, Porcelain stove, vert. No. 743d, Palace. No. 743e, Great Palm House (conservatory).

1998, Dec. 4   Litho.   Perf. 14

741	A310	33c multicolored	.55	.55
742	A310	60c multicolored	1.25	1.00

Souvenir Booklet

743		Booklet	24.00	
a.-c.	A310	11c any single	.50	.50
d.-f.	A310	15c any single	1.60	1.60
g.		Booklet pane of 3 #743d	6.50	6.50
h.		Booklet pane of 3 #743a	1.50	1.50
i.		Booklet pane of 3 #743b	1.50	1.50
j.		Booklet pane of 3 #743c	1.50	1.50
k.		Booklet pane of 4 #743e	6.50	6.50
l.		Booklet pane of 4 #743f	6.50	6.50

See Offices in Geneva Nos. 329-331; Vienna Nos. 246-248.

Flag Type of 1980
1999, Feb. 5   Photo.   Perf. 12

744	A185	33c Lithuania	.85	.85
745	A185	33c San Marino	.85	.85
746	A185	33c Turkmenistan	.85	.85
747	A185	33c Marshall Islands	.85	.85
a.		Block of 4, #744-747	13.00	13.00
748	A185	33c Moldova	.85	.85
749	A185	33c Kyrgyzstan	.85	.85
750	A185	33c Bosnia & Herzegovina	.85	.85
751	A185	33c Eritrea	.85	.85
a.		Block of 4, #748-751	13.00	13.00
		Nos. 744-751 (8)	6.80	6.80

See note after No. 340.

Flags and
Globe — A311   Roses — A312

1999, Feb. 5   Litho.   Perf. 14x13½

752	A311	33c multicolored	.50	.50

Photo.
Granite Paper
Perf. 11½x12

753	A312	$5 multicolored	7.00	7.00

World
Heritage
Sites,
Australia
A313

33c, #756f, Willandra Lakes region. 60c, #756b, Wet tropics of Queensland. No. 756a, Tasmanian wilderness. No. 756c, Great Barrier Reef. No. 756d, Uluru-Kata Tjuta Natl. Park. No. 756e, Kakadu Natl. Park.

1999, Mar. 19   Litho.   Perf. 13

754	A313	33c multicolored	.60	.60
755	A313	60c multicolored	1.25	1.25

Souvenir Booklet

756		Booklet	20.00	
a.-c.	A313	5c any single	.45	.45
d.-f.	A313	15c any single	1.25	1.25
g.		Booklet pane of 4, #756d	1.80	1.80
h.		Booklet pane of 4, #756d	5.00	5.00
i.		Booklet pane of 4, #756b	1.80	1.80
j.		Booklet pane of 4, #756e	5.00	5.00
k.		Booklet pane of 4, #756c	1.80	1.80
l.		Booklet pane of 4, #756f	5.00	5.00

See Offices in Geneva Nos. 333-335; Vienna Nos. 250-252.

Endangered Species Type of 1993

No. 757, Tiger. No. 758, Secretary bird. No. 759, Green tree python. No. 760, Long-tailed chinchilla.

1999, Apr. 22   Litho.   Perf. 12½

757	A271	33c multicolored	.60	.60
758	A271	33c multicolored	.60	.60
759	A271	33c multicolored	.60	.60
760	A271	33c multicolored	.60	.60
a.		Block of 4, #757-760	2.40	2.40

See Offices in Geneva Nos. 336-339; Vienna Nos. 253-256.

UNISPACE III, Vienna — A314

No. 761, Probe on planet's surface. No. 762, Planetary rover. No. 763, Composite of #761-762.

1999, July 7   Photo.   Rouletted 8

761	A314	33c multicolored	.50	.50
762	A314	33c multicolored	.50	.50
a.		Pair, #761-762	1.75	1.75

Souvenir Sheet
Perf. 14½

763	A314	$2 multicolored	4.00	4.00
a.		Ovptd. in sheet margin	18.00	18.00

No. 763a was issued 7/7/00 and is overprinted in violet blue "WORLD STAMP EXPO 2000 / ANAHEIM, CALIFORNIA / U.S.A. / 7-16 JULY 2000."

See Offices in Geneva Nos. 340-342; Vienna Nos. 257-259.

UPU, 125th Anniv. — A315

Various people, 19th century methods of mail transportation, denomination at: No. 764, UL. No. 765, UR. No. 766, LL. No. 767, LR.

1999, Aug. 23   Photo.   Perf. 11¾

764	A315	33c multicolored	.45	.45
765	A315	33c multicolored	.45	.45
766	A315	33c multicolored	.45	.45
767	A315	33c multicolored	.45	.45
a.		Block of 4, #764-767	2.50	2.50

See Offices in Geneva Nos. 343-346; Vienna Nos. 260-263.

In Memoriam A316

Designs: 33c, $1, UN Headquarters. Size of $1 stamp: 34x63mm.

1999, Sept. 21   Litho.   Perf. 14½x14

768	A316	33c multicolored	.80	.80

Souvenir Sheet
Perf. 14

769	A316	$1 multicolored	2.00	2.00

Education, Keystone to the 21st Century — A317

Perf. 13½x13¾

1999, Nov. 18   Litho.

770	A317	Two readers	.50	.50
771	A317	60c Heart	1.00	1.00

See Offices in Geneva Nos. 349-350, Vienna Nos. 266-267.

International Year of Thanksgiving A318

2000, Jan. 1   Litho.   Perf. 13¼x13½

772	A318	33c multicolored	.75	.75

On No. 772 parts of the design were applied by a thermographic process producing a shiny, raised effect. See Offices in Geneva No. 351, Vienna No. 268.

Endangered Species Type of 1993

No. 773, Brown bear. No. 774, Black-bellied bustard. No. 775, Chinese crocodile lizard. No. 776, Pygmy chimpanzee.

2000, Apr. 6   Litho.   Perf. 12¾x12½

773	A271	33c multicolored	.50	.50
774	A271	33c multicolored	.50	.50
775	A271	33c multicolored	.50	.50
776	A271	33c multicolored	.50	.50
a.		Block of 4, #773-776	2.50	2.50

See Offices in Geneva Nos. 352-355; Vienna Nos. 269-272.

Our World 2000 A319

Winning artwork in Millennium painting competition: 33c, Crawling Toward the Millennium, by Sam Yeates, US. 60c, Crossing, by Masakazu Takahata, Japan, vert.

Perf. 13x13½, 13½x13

2000, May 30   Litho.

777	A319	33c multicolored	.60	.60
778	A319	60c multicolored	1.00	1.00

See Offices in Geneva No. 356-357, Vienna No. 273-274.

UN, 55th Anniv. — A320

33c, Workmen removing decorative discs in General Assembly Hall, 1956. 55c, UN Building in 1951.

2000, July 7   Litho.   Perf. 13¼x13

779	A320	33c multicolored	.55	.55
780	A320	55c multicolored	.95	.95

Souvenir Sheet

781	A320	Sheet of 2, #779-780	3.00	3.00

See Offices in Geneva Nos. 358-360, Vienna No. 275-277.

International Flag of Peace — A321

2000, Sept. 15   Litho.   Perf. 14½x14

782	A321	33c multicolored	.65	.65

The UN in the 21st Century — A322

No. 783: a, Farmers, animals in rice paddy. b, Vehicle chassis being lifted. c, People voting. d, Baby receiving inoculation. e, Woman, man at pump. f, Mason, construction workers.

2000, Sept. 15   Litho.   Perf. 14

783	A322	Sheet of 6	9.00	9.00
a.-f.		33c any single	1.25	1.25

See Offices in Geneva No. 361; Vienna No. 278.

World Heritage Sites, Spain — A323

Nos. 784, 786a, Alhambra, Generalife and Albayzin, Granada. Nos. 785, 786d, Amphitheater of Mérida. #786b, Walled Town of Cuenca. #786c, Aqueduct of Segovia. #786e, Toledo. #786f, Güell Park, Barcelona.

2000, Oct. 6   Litho.   Perf. 14¾x14½

784	A323	33c multicolored	.55	.55
785	A323	60c multicolored	1.10	1.10

Souvenir Booklet

786		Booklet	15.00	
a.-c.		A323 5c any single	.45	.45
d.-f.		A323 15c any single	.80	.80
g.		Booklet pane of 4, #786a	1.80	1.80
h.		Booklet pane of 4, #786d	3.20	3.20
i.		Booklet pane of 4, #786b	1.80	1.80
j.		Booklet pane of 4, #786e	3.20	3.20
k.		Booklet pane of 4, #786c	1.80	1.80
l.		Booklet pane of 4, #786f	3.20	3.20

See Offices in Geneva Nos. 362-364, Vienna Nos. 279-281.

Respect for Refugees A324

2000, Nov. 9   Litho.   Perf. 13¼x12¾

787	A324	33c multicolored	.75	.75

Souvenir Sheet

788	A324	$1 multicolored	2.00	2.00

See Offices in Geneva Nos. 365-366, Vienna Nos. 282-283.

Endangered Species Type of 1993

No. 789, Common spotted cuscus. No. 790, Resplendent quetzal. No. 791, Gila monster. No. 792, Guereza.

2001, Feb. 1   Litho.   Perf. 12¾x12½

789	A271	34c multicolored	.60	.60
790	A271	34c multicolored	.60	.60
791	A271	34c multicolored	.60	.60
792	A271	34c multicolored	.60	.60
a.		Block of 4, #789-792	2.40	2.40

See Offices in Geneva Nos. 367-370; Vienna Nos. 284-287.

Intl. Volunteers Year — A325

Paintings by: 34c, Jose Zaragoza, Brazil. 80c, John Terry, Australia.

2001, Mar. 29   Litho.   Perf. 13¼

793	A325	34c multicolored	.65	.65
794	A325	80c multicolored	1.60	1.60

See Offices in Geneva Nos. 371-372; Vienna Nos. 288-289.

Flag Type of 1980

No. 795, Slovenia. No. 796, Palau. No. 797, Tonga. No. 798, Croatia. No. 799, Former Yugoslav Republic of Macedonia. No. 800, Kiribati. No. 801, Andorra. No. 802, Nauru.

2001, May 25   Photo.   Perf. 12
Granite Paper

795	A185	34c multicolored	1.25	1.25
796	A185	34c multicolored	1.25	1.25
797	A185	34c multicolored	1.25	1.25
798	A185	34c multicolored	1.25	1.25
a.		Block of 4, #795-798	15.00	15.00
799	A185	34c multicolored	1.25	1.25
800	A185	34c multicolored	1.25	1.25
801	A185	34c multicolored	1.25	1.25
802	A185	34c multicolored	1.25	1.25
a.		Block of 4, #799-802	15.00	15.00
		Nos. 795-802 (8)	10.00	10.00

Sunflower — A326

Rose — A327

2001, May 25   Litho.   Perf. 13¼x13¾

803	A326	7c multicolored	.25	.25
804	A327	34c multicolored	.60	.60

World Heritage Sites, Japan — A328

34c, #807a, Kyoto. 70c, #807d, Shirakawa-Go and Gokayama. #807b, Nara. #807c, Himeji-Jo. #807e, Itsukushima Shinto Shrine. #807f, Nikko.

2001, Aug. 1   Litho.   Perf. 12¾x13¼

805	A328	34c multicolored	.60	.60
806	A328	70c multicolored	1.25	1.25

Souvenir Booklet

807		Booklet	16.00	
a.-c.		A328 5c any single	.50	.50
d.-f.		A328 20c any single	.80	.80
g.		Booklet pane of 4, #807a	2.00	2.00
h.		Booklet pane of 4, #807d	3.20	3.20
i.		Booklet pane of 4, #807b	2.00	2.00
j.		Booklet pane of 4, #807e	3.20	3.20
k.		Booklet pane of 4, #807c	2.00	2.00
l.		Booklet pane of 4, #807f	3.20	3.20

See Offices in Geneva Nos. 373-375, Vienna Nos. 290-292.

Dag Hammarskjöld (1905-61), UN Secretary General — A329

2001, Sept. 18   Engr.   Perf. 11x11¼

808	A329	80c blue	1.50	1.50

See Offices in Geneva No. 376, Vienna No. 293.

A330

UN Postal Administration, 50th
Anniv. — A331

2001, Oct. 18   Litho.   Perf. 13½
809 A330 34c Stamps, streamers   .55 .55
810 A330 80c Stamps, gifts   1.50 1.50

Souvenir Sheet
811 A331   Sheet of 2 #811a   8.00 8.00
a. $1 blue & light blue, 38mm di-
      ameter   4.00 4.00

See Offices in Geneva Nos. 377-379,
Vienna Nos. 294-296.

Climate
Change — A332

No. 812, Canada geese, greenhouses, butterfly, thistle. No. 813, Canada geese, iceberg,
penguins, tomato plant. No. 814, Palm tree,
solar collector. No. 815, Hand planting ginkgo
cutting.

2001, Nov. 16   Litho.   Perf. 13¼
812 A332 34c multicolored   1.00 1.00
813 A332 34c multicolored   1.00 1.00
814 A332 34c multicolored   1.00 1.00
815 A332 34c multicolored   1.00 1.00
a.   Horiz. strip, #812-815   4.00 4.00

See Offices in Geneva Nos. 380-383,
Vienna Nos. 297-300.

Awarding of Nobel Peace Prize to
Secretary General Kofi Annan and
UN — A333

2001, Dec. 10   Litho.   Perf. 13¼
816 A333 34c multicolored   .70 .70

See Offices in Geneva Nos. 384, Vienna
Nos. 301.

Children and
Stamps
A334

2002, Mar. 1   Litho.   Perf. 13¾
817 A334 80c multicolored   1.40 1.40

Endangered Species Type of 1993
No. 818, Hoffmann's two-toed sloth. No.
819, Bighorn sheep. No. 820, Cheetah. No.
821, San Esteban Island chuckwalla.

2002, Apr. 4   Litho.   Perf. 12¾x12½
818 A271 34c multicolored   .80 .80
819 A271 34c multicolored   .80 .80
820 A271 34c multicolored   .80 .80
821 A271 34c multicolored   .80 .80
a.   Block of 4, #818-821   3.25 3.25

See Offices in Geneva Nos. 386-389;
Vienna 308-311.

Independence of
East
Timor — A335

34c, Wooden ritual mask. 57c, Decorative
door panel.

2002, May 20   Litho.   Perf. 14x14½
822 A335 34c multicolored   .70 .70
823 A335 57c multicolored   1.20 1.20

See Offices in Geneva Nos. 390-391;
Vienna 312-313.

Intl. Year of
Mountains
A336

No. 824, Khan Tengri, Kyrgyzstan. No. 825,
Mt. Kilimanjaro, Tanzania. No. 826, Mt.
Foraker, US. No. 827, Paine Grande, Chile.

2002, May 24   Litho.   Perf. 13x13¼
824 A336 34c multicolored   1.00 1.00
825 A336 34c multicolored   1.00 1.00
826 A336 80c multicolored   2.00 2.00
827 A336 80c multicolored   2.00 2.00
a.   Vert. strip or block of four,
      #824-827   11.00 11.00

See Offices in Geneva Nos. 392-395;
Vienna Nos. 314-317.

World Summit on Sustainable
Development, Johannesburg — A337

No. 828, Sun, Earth, planets, stars. No. 829,
Three women. No. 830, Sailboat. No. 831,
Three faceless people.

2002, June 27   Litho.   Perf. 14½x14
828 A337 37c multicolored   1.00 1.00
829 A337 37c multicolored   1.00 1.00
830 A337 60c multicolored   1.75 1.75
831 A337 60c multicolored   1.75 1.75
a.   Vert. strip or block of four,
      #828-831   9.00 9.00

See Offices in Geneva Nos. 396-399;
Vienna Nos. 318-321.

World Heritage Sites, Italy — A338

37c, #834d, Florence. 70c, #834a, Amalfi
Coast. #834b, Aeolian Islands. #834c, Rome.
#834e, Pisa. #834f, Pompeii.

Perf. 13½x13¼
2002, Aug. 30   Litho.
832 A338 37c multicolored   .70 .70
833 A338 70c multicolored   1.40 1.40

Souvenir Booklet
834   Booklet   22.00
a.-c.   A338 5c any single   .50 .50
d.-f.   A338 15c any single   1.00 1.00
g.   Booklet pane of 4, #834d   4.00 4.00
h.   Booklet pane of 4, #834a   2.00 2.00
i.   Booklet pane of 4, #834e   4.00 4.00
j.   Booklet pane of 4, #834b   2.00 2.00
k.   Booklet pane of 4, #834f   4.00 4.00
l.   Booklet pane of 4, #834c   2.00 2.00

See Offices in Geneva Nos. 400-402,
Vienna Nos. 322-324.
See Italy Nos. 2506-2507.

AIDS Awareness
A339

2002, Oct. 24   Litho.   Perf. 13½
835 A339 70c multicolored   1.50 1.50

See No. B1, Offices in Geneva Nos. 403,
B1, Vienna Nos. 325, B1.

Indigenous Art — A340

No. 836: a, Detail of Paracas textile, Peru. b,
Sinu culture anthrozoo-morphic pendant,
Colombia. c, Hicholi Indian embroidery, Mex-
ico. d, Rigpaktsa back ornament, Brazil. e,
Wool crafts, Chile. f, Huari feathered woven
hat, Bolivia.

2003, Jan. 31   Litho.   Perf. 14¼
836   A340   Sheet of 6   9.00 9.00
a.-f.   37c Any single   1.50 1.50

See Offies in Geneva No. 405; Vienna No.
326.

Clasped
Hands — A341

UN Emblem
A342

UN
Headquarters
A343

2003, Mar. 28   Litho.   Perf. 14¼
837 A341 23c multicolored   .40 .40
Litho. with Foil Application
838 A342 37c gold & multicolored .60 .60
Litho. with Hologram
Perf. 13¼x12¾
839 A343 70c multicolored   1.40 1.40

Powered Flight, Cent. — A344

Perf. 13½x13¾
2003, Mar. 28   Litho.
840   23c multicolored   1.25 1.25
841   70c multicolored   2.75 2.75
a.   A344 Tete beche pair, #840-841 4.00 4.00

Endangered Species Type of 1993
No. 842, Great hornbill. No. 843, Scarlet
ibis. No. 844, Knob-billed goose. No. 845,
White-faced whistling duck.

2003, Apr. 3   Litho.   Perf. 12¾x12½
842 A271 37c multicolored   .80 .80
843 A271 37c multicolored   .80 .80
844 A271 37c multicolored   .80 .80
845 A271 37c multicolored   .80 .80
a.   Block of 4, #842-845   3.25 3.25

See Offices in Geneva Nos. 407-410;
Vienna 329-332.

Intl. Year of
Freshwater
A345

Perf. 14¼x14½
2003, June 20   Litho.
846 A345 23c Wildlife, garbage   1.50 1.50
847 A345 37c Trees, canoe   2.00 2.00
a.   Horiz. pair, #846-847   7.50 7.50

See Offices in Geneva, Nos. 411-412;
Vienna Nos. 333-334.

Ralph Bunche
(1903-71),
Diplomat — A346

Litho. With Foil Application

2003, Aug. 7   *Perf. 13½x14*
848   A346   37c blue & multi   .80   .80

See Offices in Geneva No. 413; Vienna No. 336.

In Memoriam of Victims of Aug. 19 Bombing of UN Complex in Baghdad, Iraq — A347

2003, Oct. 24   **Litho.**   *Perf. 13¼x13*
849   A347   60c multicolored   1.25   1.25

See Offices in Geneva No. 414, Vienna No. 337.

World Heritage Sites, United States A348

37c, #852a, Yosemite National Park. 60c, #852d, Hawaii Volcanoes National Park. #852b, Great Smoky Mountains National Park. #852c, Olympic National Park. #852e, Everglades National Park. #852f, Yellowstone National Park.

2003, Oct. 24   **Litho.**   *Perf. 14½x14¼*
850   A348   37c multicolored   .90   .90
851   A348   60c multicolored   1.50   1.50

Souvenir Booklet

852   Booklet   12.00
  a.-c.   A348 10c any single   .30   .30
  d.-f.   A348 20c any single   .60   .60
  g.   Booklet pane of 4 #852a   1.20   1.20
  h.   Booklet pane of 4 #852d   2.40   2.40
  i.   Booklet pane of 4 #852b   1.20   1.20
  j.   Booklet pane of 4 #852e   2.40   2.40
  k.   Booklet pane of 4 #852c   1.20   1.20
  l.   Booklet pane of 4 #852f   2.40   2.40

See Offices in Geneva Nos. 415-417, Vienna Nos. 338-340.

UN Security Council — A349

UN Emblem — A350

UN General Assembly — A351

Flags — A352

UN Headquarters — A353

2003, Nov. 26   **Litho.**   *Perf. 13¼*
853   A349   37c multi + label   10.00   10.00
854   A350   37c multi + label   10.00   10.00
855   A351   37c multi + label   10.00   10.00
856   A352   37c multi + label   10.00   10.00
857   A353   37c multi + label   10.00   10.00
  a.   Vert. strip of 5, #853-857, + 5 labels   50.00   50.00

The full sheet sold for $14.95 with or without personalized labels. The personalization of labels was available only at UN Headquarters, and not through mail order.

One thousand full sheets with sheet margins inscribed "Hong Kong Stamp Expo" were sold only at that venue. Value $125. Also exists with sheet margins inscribed "Essen." Value $115.

A sheet containing two strips of five stamps similar to Nos. 853-857 but dated "2005" and ten labels sold for $4.95. These sheets were only available canceled. Value $110. An imperforate error of this sheet is known.

Endangered Species Type of 1993

No. 858, American black bear. No. 859, Musk deer. No. 860, Golden snub-nosed monkey. No. 861, Wild yak.

2004, Jan. 29   Litho.   *Perf. 12¾x12½*
858   A271   37c multicolored   1.10   1.10
859   A271   37c multicolored   1.10   1.10
860   A271   37c multicolored   1.10   1.10
861   A271   37c multicolored   1.10   1.10
  a.   Block of 4, #858-861   4.50   4.50

See Offices in Geneva Nos. 418-421; Vienna Nos. 342-345.

Indigenous Art Type of 2003

No. 862: a, Viking wood carving depicting Saga of Sigurd Favnesbane, Norway. b, Stele, Italy. c, Detail of matador's suit, Spain. d, Amphora, Greece. e, Bronze figurine of bull, Czech Republic. f, Detail of lacquer box illustration depicting scene from "On the Seashore," by Alexander Pushkin, Russia.

2004, Mar. 4   Litho.   *Perf. 13¼*
862   A340   Sheet of 6   9.00   9.00
  a.-f.   37c Any single   1.25   1.25

See Offices in Geneva No. 422; Vienna No. 346.

Road Safety A354

Road map art with: 37c, Automobile with road signs, city skyline. 70c, Automobile, hand, vert.

Perf. 13x13¼, 13¼x13
2004, Apr. 7   **Litho.**
863   A354   37c multicolored   .85   .85
864   A354   70c multicolored   1.40   1.40

See Offices in Geneva Nos. 423-424, Vienna Nos. 347-348.

Japanese Peace Bell, 50th Anniv. — A355

Litho. & Engr.
2004, June 3   *Perf. 13¼x13*
865   A355   80c multicolored   1.50   1.50

See Offices in Geneva No. 425; Vienna No. 349.

World Heritage Sites, Greece — A356

No. 866, Acropolis, Athens. Nos. 867, 868e, Delos. No. 868a, Delphi. No. 868b, Pythagoreion and Heraion of Samos. No. 868c, Olympia. No. 868d, Mycenae and Tiryns.

2004, Aug. 12   Litho.   *Perf. 14x13¼*
866   A356   37c multicolored   .70   .70
  a.   Booklet pane of 4   3.00   —
867   A356   60c multicolored   1.10   1.10

Souvenir Booklet

868   Booklet, #866a, 868f-868j   15.00
  a.-d.   A356 23c any single   .55   .55
  e.   A356 37c multi   .90   .90
  f.   Booklet pane of 4 #868a   2.20   2.20
  g.   Booklet pane of 4 #868b   2.20   2.20
  h.   Booklet pane of 4 #868c   2.20   2.20
  i.   Booklet pane of 4 #868d   2.20   2.20
  j.   Booklet pane of 4 #868e   3.60   3.60

See Offices in Geneva Nos. 426-428, Vienna Nos. 350-352. No. 868 sold for $7.20.

My Dream for Peace — A357

Winning designs of Lions Club International children's global peace poster contest by: 37c, Sittichok Pariyaket, Thailand. 80c, Bayan Fais Abu Bial, Israel.

2004, Sept. 21   **Litho.**   *Perf. 14*
869   A357   37c multicolored   .60   .60
870   A357   80c multicolored   1.40   1.40

See Offices in Geneva Nos. 429-430, Vienna Nos. 353-354.

A358

Human Rights — A359

2004, Oct. 14   **Litho.**   *Perf. 11¼*
871   A358   37c multicolored   .75   .75
872   A359   70c multicolored   1.40   1.40

See Offices in Geneva Nos. 431-432, Vienna Nos. 355-356.

Disarmament A360

2004, Oct. 15   **Litho.**   *Perf. 13¾*
873   A360   37c multicolored   .80   .80

United Nations, 60th Anniv. — A361

Litho. & Engr.
2005, Feb. 4   *Perf. 11x11¼*
874   A361   80c multicolored   1.50   1.50

Souvenir Sheet
Litho.
Imperf
875   A361 $1 multicolored   15.00   15.00

See Offices in Geneva Nos. 434-435; Vienna Nos. 357-358.

Endangered Species Type of 1993

Designs: No. 876, Blue orchid. No. 877, Swan orchid. No. 878, Christmas orchid. No. 879, Aerangis modesta.

2005, Mar. 3   Litho.   *Perf. 12¾x12½*
876   A271   37c multicolored   1.10   1.10
877   A271   37c multicolored   1.10   1.10
878   A271   37c multicolored   1.10   1.10
879   A271   37c multicolored   1.10   1.10
  a.   Block of 4, #876-879   4.50   4.50

See Offices in Geneva Nos. 436-439; Vienna Nos. 360-363.

Non-Violence, Sculpture by Carl Fredrik Reuterswärd, New York — A362

Armillary Sphere, Sculpture by Paul Manship, Geneva — A363

Terra Cotta Warriors, Vienna — A364

Single Form, Sculpture by Barbara Hepworth, New York — A365

Sphere Within a Sphere, Sculpture by Arnaldo Pomodoro, New York — A366

2005, Mar. 3	Litho.	Perf. 13¼	
880	A362 80c multi + label	35.00	35.00
881	A363 80c multi + label	35.00	35.00
882	A364 80c multi + label	35.00	35.00
883	A365 80c multi + label	35.00	35.00
884	A366 80c multi + label	35.00	35.00
a.	Vert. strip of 5, #880-884, + 5 labels	175.00	175.00
b.	Sheet of 10, both #884 37c (error)	3,250.	
c.	Vert. strip of 5, #884 37c (error)	1,450.	

The full sheet sold for $14.95 with or without personalized labels. The personalization of labels was available only at UN Headquarters, and not through mail order.

The full sheet exists with sheet margins and labels commemorating the Riccione 2005 Philatelic Exhibition. This sheet went on sale 8/20/05 and was also sold for $14.95. Value $160.

Nature's Wisdom — A367

37c, Ice climber, Norway. 80c, Egret, Japan.

2005, Apr. 21 Litho.	Perf. 13½x13¼	
885	A367 37c multicolored	.65	.65
886	A367 80c multicolored	1.50	1.50

See Offices in Geneva Nos. 440-441, Vienna Nos. 364-365.

Intl. Year of Sport A368

2005, June 3 Litho.	Perf. 13x13¼	
887	A368 37c Sailing	.65	.65
888	A368 70c Running	1.25	1.25

See Offices in Geneva Nos. 442-443; Vienna Nos. 366-367.

World Heritage Sites, Egypt — A369

Nos. 889, 891a, Memphis and its Necropolis. Nos. 890, 891d, Ancient Thebes. No. 891b, Philae. No. 891c, Abu Mena. No. 891e, Islamic Cairo. No. 891f, St. Catherine area.

2005, Aug. 4 Litho.	Perf. 14x13¼	
889	A369 37c multicolored	.60	.60
890	A369 80c multicolored	1.40	1.40

Souvenir Booklet

891	Booklet, #891g-891l	15.00	
a.-c.	A369 23c any single	.50	.50
d.-f.	A369 37c any single	.75	.75
g.	Booklet pane of 4 #891a	2.00	2.00
h.	Booklet pane of 4 #891b	2.00	2.00
i.	Booklet pane of 4 #891c	2.00	2.00
j.	Booklet pane of 4 #891d	3.00	3.00
k.	Booklet pane of 4 #891e	3.00	3.00
l.	Booklet pane of 4 #891f	3.00	3.00

See Offices in Geneva Nos. 444-446, Vienna Nos. 368-370.

My Dream for Peace Type of 2004

Winning designs of Lions Club International children's global peace poster contest by: 37c, Vittoria Sansebastiano, Italy. 80c, Jordan Harris, US.

2005, Sept. 21 Litho.	Perf. 14	
892	A357 37c multicolored	.60	.60
893	A357 80c multicolored	1.40	1.40

See Offices in Geneva Nos. 447-448, Vienna Nos. 371-372.

Food for Life A370

37c, Oats, children and adults. 80c, Wheat, mothers breastfeeding babies.

2005, Oct. 20 Litho.	Perf. 13¾	
894	A370 37c multicolored	.60	.60
895	A370 80c multicolored	1.40	1.40

See Offices in Geneva Nos. 449-450; Vienna Nos. 373-374.

Stylized Flags in Heart and Hands A371

2006, Feb. 3 Litho.	Perf. 13x13¼	
896	A371 25c multicolored	.75	.75

Indigenous Art Type of 2003

No. 897 — Musical instruments: a, Drum, Ivory Coast. b, Drum, Tunisia. c, Stringed instruments, Morocco. d, Drums, Sudan. e, Instruments, Cameroun. f, Harp, Congo.

2006, Feb. 3 Litho.	Perf. 13¼	
897	A340 Sheet of 6	10.00	10.00
a.-f.	37c Any single	1.50	1.50

See Offices in Geneva No. 452; Vienna No. 375.

UN Symbols Type of 2003

2006, Mar. 6 Litho.	Perf. 13¼	
898	A349 39c multi + label	5.00	5.00
899	A350 39c multi + label	5.00	5.00
900	A351 39c multi + label	5.00	5.00
901	A352 39c multi + label	5.00	5.00
902	A353 39c multi + label	5.00	5.00
a.	Vert. strip of 5, #898-902, + 5 labels	25.00	25.00

The full sheet sold for $14.95 with or without personalized labels. The personalization of labels was available only at UN Headquarters, and not through mail order.

Sculpture Type of 2005

2006, Mar. 6 Litho.	Perf. 13¼	
903	A362 84c multi + label	12.00	12.00
a.	Perf. 14½x14 + label	16.00	16.00
904	A363 84c multi + label	12.00	12.00
a.	Perf. 14½x14 + label	16.00	16.00
905	A364 84c multi + label	12.00	12.00
a.	Perf. 14½x14 + label	16.00	16.00
906	A365 84c multi + label	12.00	12.00
a.	Perf. 14½x14 + label	16.00	16.00
907	A366 84c multi + label	12.00	12.00
a.	Perf. 14½x14 + label	16.00	16.00
b.	Vert. strip of 5, #903-907, + 5 labels	60.00	60.00
c.	Vert. strip of 5, #903a-907a, + 5 labels	80.00	80.00

The full sheet sold for $14.95 with or without personalized labels. The personalization of labels was available only at UN Headquarters, and not through mail order.

Nos. 903a-907a issued 9/21/06. Nos. 903a-907a were from sheet for 2006 Berlin Stamp Show. The year "2006" is slightly smaller on Nos. 903a-907a than on Nos. 903-907.

Full sheets with different margins were sold at the Washington 2006 World Philatelic Exhibition, where the labels could be personalized. These are worth slightly more than the generic No. 907b sheet.

Endangered Species Type of 1993

No. 908, Golden mantella. No. 909, Panther chameleon. No. 910, Peruvian rainbow boa. No. 911, Dyeing poison frog.

Perf. 12¾x12½

2006, Mar. 16	Litho.	
908	A271 39c multicolored	.90	.90
909	A271 39c multicolored	.90	.90
910	A271 39c multicolored	.90	.90
911	A271 39c multicolored	.90	.90
a.	Block of 4, #908-911	3.60	3.60

See Offices in Geneva Nos. 453-456; Vienna Nos. 376-379.

Dove Between War and Peace — A372

2006, Apr. 10 Litho.	Perf. 13¼	
912	A372 75c multi + label	6.50	5.00

The full sheet sold for $14.95 with or without personalized labels. The personalization of labels was available only at UN Headquarters, and not through mail order.

Intl. Day of Families A373

39c, Family harvesting grapes. 84c, Children playing with toy sailboats.

2006, May 27 Litho.	Perf. 14x13½	
913	A373 39c multicolored	.70	.70
914	A373 84c multicolored	1.50	1.50

See Offices in Geneva Nos. 457-458; Vienna Nos. 380-381.

World Heritage Sites, France — A374

Eiffel Tower and: Nos. 915, 917a, Banks of the Seine. Nos. 916, 917d, Roman Aqueduct. No. 917b, Provins. No. 917c, Carcasonne. No. 917e, Mont Saint-Michel. No. 917f, Chateau de Chambord.

Litho. & Embossed with Foil Application

2006, June 17	Perf. 13½x13¼	
915	A374 39c multicolored	.75	.75
916	A374 84c multicolored	1.75	1.75

Souvenir Booklet

917	Booklet, #917g-917l	16.00	
a.-c.	A374 24c any single	.50	.50
d.-f.	A374 39c any single	.80	.80
g.	Booklet pane of 4 #917a	2.00	2.00
h.	Booklet pane of 4 #917b	2.00	2.00
i.	Booklet pane of 4 #917c	2.00	2.00
j.	Booklet pane of 4 #917d	3.25	3.25
k.	Booklet pane of 4 #917e	3.25	3.25
l.	Booklet pane of 4 #917f	3.25	3.25

See Offices in Geneva Nos. 459-461, Vienna Nos. 382-384.

My Dream for Peace Type of 2004

Winning designs of Lions Club International children's global peace poster contest by: 39c, Cheuk Tat Li, Hong Kong. 84c, Kosshapan Paitoon, Thailand.

2006, Sept. 21 Litho.	Perf. 13½x13	
918	A357 39c multicolored	.80	.80
919	A357 84c multicolored	1.75	1.75

See Offices in Geneva Nos. 462-463; Vienna Nos. 385-386.

Flags and Coins — A375

No. 920 — Flag of: a, People's Republic of China, 1 yuan coin. b, Australia, 1 dollar coin. c, Ghana, 50 cedi coin. d, Israel, 10 agorot coin. e, Russia, 1 ruble coin. f, Mexico, 10 peso coin. g, Japan, 10 yen coin. h, Cambodia, 200 riel coin.

2006, Oct. 5 Litho.	Perf. 13¼x13	
920	Sheet of 8	10.00	10.00
a.-h.	A375 39c Any single	1.25	1.25

A column of rouletting in the middle of the sheet separates it into two parts. See Nos. 930, 953, 998, 1022, 1039, 1078, 1103; Offices in Geneva Nos. 464, 469, 484, 512, 532, 546, 576, 594; Vienna Nos. 387, 392, 421, 459, 483, 507, 539, 558.

Flag Type of 1980

2007, Feb. 2 Litho.	Perf. 14	
921	A185 39c Tuvalu	1.00	1.00
922	A185 39c Switzerland	1.00	1.00
923	A185 39c Timor-Leste	1.00	1.00
924	A185 39c Montenegro	1.00	1.00
a.	Block of 4, #921-924	12.00	12.00
	Nos. 921-924 (4)	4.00	4.00

Endangered Species Type of 1993

No. 925, Drill. No. 926, Common squirrel monkey. No. 927, Ring-tailed lemur. No. 928, Collared mangabey.

Perf. 12¾x12½

2007, Mar. 15	Litho.	
925	A271 39c multicolored	.85	.85
926	A271 39c multicolored	.85	.85
927	A271 39c multicolored	.85	.85
928	A271 39c multicolored	.85	.85
a.	Block of 4, #925-928	3.50	3.50

See Offices in Geneva Nos. 465-468; Vienna Nos. 388-391.

UN Emblem — A376

2007, Feb. 5 Litho.	Perf. 14½x14	
929	A376 84c dk blue + label	18.00	18.00

The full sheet sold for $14.95. The sheet has two each of five different labels that could not be personalized. The sheet was distributed to members of the Japanese mission on Sept. 21, 2006, but it was not sold to the public until 2007. The sheet's availability to the public was not announced through press releases or on the UNPA website prior to the day of issue or afterward. It was sent to standing order customers in May 2007.

Compare with Type A377.

Flags and Coins Type of 2006

No. 930 — Flag of: a, Brazil, 50 centavo coin. b, Thailand, 1 baht coin. c, Viet Nam, 5,000 dong coin. d, Ecuador, 10 centavo coin. e, India, 5 rupee coin. f, South Africa, 5 cent coin. g, Barbados, 25 cent coin. h, Republic of Korea, 500 won coin.

2007, May 3 Litho.	Perf. 13¼x13	
930	Sheet of 8	8.00	8.00
a.-h.	A375 39c Any single	1.00	1.00

A column of rouletting in the middle of the sheet separates it into two parts. See Offices in Geneva No. 469; Vienna No. 392.

UN Emblem — A377

2007, June 1   Litho.   Perf. 13¼
931 A377 84c blue + label   5.50 5.50

The full sheet sold for $14.95. The sheet has two each of five different labels that could not be personalized.
Compare with Type A376.

Peaceful Visions — A378

39c, "Nest." 84c, "Sisters Weave the Olive Branch."

2007, June 1   Litho.   Perf. 13x12½
932 A378 39c multicolored   .90   .90
933 A378 84c multicolored   1.80 1.80

See Offices in Geneva Nos. 470-471; Vienna Nos. 398-399.

UN Symbols Type of 2003
2007, May 14   Litho.   Perf. 13¼
934 A349 41c multi + label   3.25 3.25
935 A350 41c multi + label   3.25 3.25
936 A351 41c multi + label   3.25 3.25
937 A352 41c multi + label   3.25 3.25
938 A353 41c multi + label   3.25 3.25
  a.   Vert. strip of 5, #934-938, + 5
       labels   20.00 20.00

The full sheet sold for $14.95 with or without personalized labels. The personalization of labels was available only at UN Headquarters, and not through mail order.

UN Flag — A379

2007, May 14   Litho.   Perf. 13¼
939 A379 90c blue + label   9.00 9.00

The full sheet sold for $14.95. The sheet has two each of five different labels that could not be personalized.
A second printing of No. 939 has the "U" and "N" more closely spaced, and it has different labels and different pane borders. Value about the same.

Helmet of UN Peacekeeper A380

2007, Aug. 9   Litho.   Perf. 12½x13¼
940 A380 90c multicolored   1.90 1.90

World Heritage Sites, South America — A381

No. 941, Galapagos Islands, Ecuador. Nos. 942, 943a, Rapa Nui, Chile. No. 943b, Cueva de las Manos, Argentina. No. 943c, Machu Picchu, Peru. No. 943d, Tiwanaku, Bolivia. No. 943e, Iguaçu National Park, Brazil.

2007, Aug. 9   Litho.   Perf. 13¼x13
941 A381 41c multicolored   .85   .85
  a.   Booklet pane of 4   3.40   —
942 A381 90c multicolored   1.90 1.90

Souvenir Booklet
943   Booklet, #941a, 943f-
           943j   17.00
  a.-c. A381 26c Any single   .60   .60
  d.-e. A381 41c Either single   1.00 1.00
  f.   Booklet pane of 4 #943a   2.40 2.40
  g.   Booklet pane of 4 #943b   2.40 2.40
  h.   Booklet pane of 4 #943c   2.40 2.40
  i.   Booklet pane of 4 #943d   4.00 4.00
  j.   Booklet pane of 4 #943e   4.00 4.00

See Offices in Geneva Nos. 472-474, Vienna Nos. 400-402. No. 943 sold for $8.50.

Humanitarian Mail — A382

2007, Sept. 6   Litho.   Perf. 12½x13¼
944 A382 90c multicolored   1.90 1.90

See Offices in Geneva No. 475, Vienna No. 403, Switzerland No. 9O21.

Space for Humanity A383

41c, Space Shuttle. 90c, Astronauts spacewalking.
$1, International Space Station.

2007, Oct. 25   Litho.   Perf. 13½x14
945 A383 41c multicolored   .85   .85
946 A383 90c multicolored   1.90 1.90

Souvenir Sheet
947 A383 $1 multicolored   2.50 2.50
  a.   With World Space Week em-
       blem in margin   3.00 3.00

See Offices in Geneva Nos. 476-478, Vienna Nos. 409-411.

Intl. Holocaust Remembrance Day — A384

2008, Jan. 27   Litho.   Perf. 13
948 A384 41c multicolored   .85   .85

See Offices in Geneva No. 479, Vienna No. 412, Israel No. 1715.

Endangered Species Type of 1993

No. 949, South African fur seal. No. 950, Orange cup coral. No. 951, Longsnout seahorse. No. 952, Gray whale.

2008, Mar. 6   Litho.   Perf. 12¾x12½
949 A271 41c multicolored   1.00 1.00
950 A271 41c multicolored   1.00 1.00
941 A271 41c multicolored   1.00 1.00
952 A271 41c multicolored   1.00 1.00
  a.   Block of 4, #949-952   4.00 4.00

See Offices in Geneva Nos. 480-483; Vienna Nos. 417-420.

Flags and Coins Type of 2006

No. 953 — Flag of: a, United Kingdom, 2 pound coin. b, Singapore, 5 dollar coin. c, Colombia, 500 peso coin. d, Sri Lanka, 10 rupee coin. e, Philippines, 1 peso coin. f, Indonesia, 500 rupiah coin. g, United Arab Emirates, 1 dirham coin. h, Libya, 50 dinar coin.

2008, May 8   Litho.   Perf. 13¼x13
953   Sheet of 8   7.00 7.00
  a.-h. A375 41c Any single   .85   .85

A column of rouletting in the middle of the sheet separates it into two parts. See Offices in Geneva No. 484; Vienna No. 421.

Sculpture and Flags — A385

UN Flag — A386

UN General Assembly — A387

Flags — A388

UN Headquarters — A389

2008, May 12   Litho.   Perf. 13¼
954 A385 42c multi + label   4.00 4.00
955 A386 42c multi + label   4.00 4.00
956 A387 42c multi + label   4.00 4.00
957 A388 42c multi + label   4.00 4.00
958 A389 42c multi + label   4.00 4.00
  a.   Vert. strip of 5, #954-958, + 5
       labels   20.00 20.00

The full sheet sold for $14.95 with or without personalized labels. The personalization of labels was available only at UN Headquarters, and not through mail order.

UN Emblem — A390

2008, May 12   Litho.   Perf. 13¼
959 A390 94c blue + label   4.50 4.50

The full sheet sold for $14.95 with or without labels that could be personalized. There are five non-personalized labels. The personalization of labels was available only at UN Headquarters, and not through mail order.

Wheelchair Accessibility Symbol — A391

"UN" in Braille — A392

Litho. & Embossed
2008, June 6   Perf. 14x13¼
960 A391 42c blue & yellow   .85   .85
961 A392 94c yellow & blue   1.90 1.90

Convention on the Rights of Persons with Disabilities. See Offices in Geneva Nos. 485-486, Vienna Nos. 427-428.

Sport for Peace — A393

42c, $1.25, Sprinter. 94c, Hurdler.

2008, Aug. 8   Litho.   Perf. 14½
962 A393 42c multicolored   .85   .85
963 A393 94c multicolored   1.90 1.90

Souvenir Sheet
Perf. 12¾x13¼
964 A393 $1.25 multicolored   6.00 6.00

2008 Summer Olympics, Beijing. See Offices in Geneva Nos. 487-489, Vienna Nos. 429-431.

Sport for Peace — A394

2008, Aug. 8   Litho.   Perf. 13¼
965 A394 94c multi + label   3.75 3.75

2008 Summer Olympics, Beijing. The full pane sold for $14.95 with or without personalized labels. There are two non-personalized labels. The personalization of labels was available only at UN Headquarters, and not through mail order.
No. 965 is often collected as a single stamp with the two different labels attached; value thus $6.50.

"We Can End Poverty" — A395

Winning designs in children's art contest by: 42c, Grace Tsang, Hong Kong. 94c, Bryan Jevoncia, Indonesia, vert.

Perf. 12¾x12½

2008, Sept. 18   Litho.
966 A395 42c multicolored   .85   .85

Perf. 12½x12¾

967 A395 94c multicolored   1.90   1.90

See Offices in Geneva Nos. 490-491, Vienna Nos. 432-433.

Climate Change Types of Geneva and Vienna and

A396

Climate Change — A397

No. 968 — Parched ground and snail shell with quarter of Earth in: a, LR. b, LL. c, UR. d, UL.
No. 969 — Coral reef with quarter of Earth in: a, LR. b, LL. c, UR. d, UL.
No. 970: a, Like #969a. b, Like #969b. c, Like #969c. d, Like #969d. e, Like Geneva #493a. f, Like Geneva #493b. g, Like Geneva #493c. h, Like Geneva #493d. i, Like Vienna #434a. j, Like Vienna #434b. k, Like Vienna #434c. l, Like Vienna #434d. m, Like Geneva #492a. n, Like Geneva #492b. o, Like Geneva #492c. p, Like Geneva #492d. q, Like Vienna #435a. r, Like Vienna #435b. s, Like Vienna #435c. t, Like Vienna #435d.
All stamps have blue panels inscribed "Climate Change."

2008, Oct. 23   Litho.   **Perf. 13¼x13**
968   Sheet of 4   4.75   4.75
a.-d.   A396 42c Any single   1.10   1.10
e.   Booklet pane of 4, #968a-968d   6.00   6.00
969   Sheet of 4   10.00   10.00
a.-d.   A397 94c Any single   2.50   2.50

Souvenir Booklet
970   Booklet, #968e, 970u-970y   20.00
a.-d.   A397 27c Any single   .75   .75
e.-h.   G77 27c Any single   .75   .75
i.-l.   V72 27c Any single   .75   .75
m.-p.   G76 42c Any single   1.00   1.00
q.-t.   V73 42c Any single   1.00   1.00
u.   Booklet pane of 4, #970a-970d   3.00   3.00
v.   Booklet pane of 4, #970e-970h   3.00   3.00
w.   Booklet pane of 4, #970i-970l   3.00   3.00
x.   Booklet pane of 4, #970m-970p   4.00   4.00
y.   Booklet pane of 4, #970q-970t   4.00   4.00

No. 970 sold for $9. See Offices in Geneva Nos. 492-494, Vienna Nos. 434-436.

A398

Designs: 1c, Cielo rosado. 9c, Rosa de sangre. 10c, Espíritu de mujer.

2009, Feb. 6   Litho.   **Perf. 13¼**
971 A398 1c multicolored   .30   .30
972 A398 9c multicolored   .30   .30
973 A398 10c multicolored   .30   .30
   Nos. 971-973 (3)   .90   .90

A399

Litho. With Foil Application
2009, Feb. 6   **Perf. 14x13½**
974 A399 94c purple & multi   2.00   2.00

See Offices in Geneva No. 495, Vienna No. 437.

Endangered Species Type of 1993

No. 975, Emperor dragonfly. No. 976, Southern wood ant. No. 977, Rosalia longicorn. No. 978, Apollo butterfly.

2009, Apr. 16   Litho.   **Perf. 12¾x12½**
975 A271 42c multicolored   1.25   1.25
976 A271 42c multicolored   1.25   1.25
977 A271 42c multicolored   1.25   1.25
978 A271 42c multicolored   1.25   1.25
a.   Block of 4, #975-978   5.00   5.00
b.   Pane of 16, imperf.   5,000.

See Offices in Geneva Nos. 496-499; Vienna Nos. 438-441.

A400

Nos. 979, 981a, Town Hall and Roland on the Marketplace, Bremen. Nos. 980, 981d, Aachen Cathedral. No. 981b, Wartburg Castle. No. 981c, Palaces and Parks of Potsdam and Berlin. No. 981e, Luther Memorials in Eisleben and Wittenberg. No. 981f, Monastic Island of Reichenau.

2009, May 7   Litho.   **Perf. 14x13½**
979 A400 44c multicolored   .90   .90
980 A400 98c multicolored   2.00   2.00

Souvenir Booklet
981   Booklet, #981g-981l   17.50
a.-c.   A400 27c any single   .55   .55
d.-f.   A400 42c any single   .85   .85
g.   Booklet pane of 4 #981a   2.25   2.25
h.   Booklet pane of 4 #981b   2.25   2.25
i.   Booklet pane of 4 #981c   2.25   2.25
j.   Booklet pane of 4 #981d   3.50   3.50
k.   Booklet pane of 4 #981e   3.50   3.50
l.   Booklet pane of 4 #981f   3.50   3.50

See Offices in Geneva Nos. 500-502, Vienna Nos. 442-444.

UN Flag — A401

Let Us Beat Swords Into Plowshares, Sculpture by Evgeny Vuchetich — A402

Single Form, Sculpture by Barbara Hepworth — A403

Window Cleaner — A404

UN Headquarters — A405

2009, June 5   **Perf. 13¼**
982 A401 44c multi + label   2.00   2.00
a.   Perf. 11¼x11 + label   10.00   10.00
b.   Perf. 14¼x14½ + label   1.80   1.80
983 A402 44c multi + label   2.00   2.00
a.   Perf. 11¼x11 + label   10.00   10.00
b.   Perf. 14¼x14½ + label   1.80   1.80
984 A403 44c multi + label   2.00   2.00
a.   Perf. 11¼x11 + label   10.00   10.00
b.   Perf. 14¼x14½ + label   1.80   1.80
985 A404 44c multi + label   2.00   2.00
a.   Perf. 11¼x11 + label   10.00   10.00
b.   Perf. 14¼x14½ + label   1.80   1.80
986 A405 44c multi + label   2.00   2.00
a.   Perf. 11¼x11 + label   10.00   10.00
b.   Perf. 14¼x14½ + label   1.80   1.80
c.   Vert. strip of 5, #982-986, + 5 labels   10.00   10.00
d.   Vert. strip of 5, #982a-986a, + 5 labels   50.00   50.00
e.   Vert. strip of 5, #982b-986b, + 5 labels   9.00   7.50

The full sheets sold for $14.95 with or without personalized labels. The personalization of labels was available only at UN Headquarters, and not through mail order. The sheet of No. 986d has "ver. 2" in the lower right selvage. The sheet of No. 986e has "Ver. 3" in the lower right selvage.

Flags and UN Headquarters — A406

Single Form, Sculpture by Barbara Hepworth — A407

UN Flag — A408

Single Form, Sculpture by Barbara Hepworth — A403

Sphere Within a Sphere, Sculpture by Arnaldo Pomodoro — A409

UN Headquarters and Chrysler Building — A410

2009, June 5
987 A406 98c multi + label   3.50   3.50
a.   Perf. 11¼x11 + label   8.00   8.00
b.   Perf. 14¼x14½ + label   3.50   3.50
988 A407 98c multi + label   3.50   3.50
a.   Perf. 11¼x11 + label   8.00   8.00
b.   Perf. 14¼x14½ + label   3.50   3.50
989 A408 98c multi + label   3.50   3.50
a.   Perf. 11¼x11 + label   8.00   8.00
b.   Perf. 14¼x14½ + label   3.50   3.50
990 A409 98c multi + label   3.50   3.50
a.   Perf. 11¼x11 + label   8.00   8.00
b.   Perf. 14¼x14½ + label   3.50   3.50
991 A410 98c multi + label   3.50   3.50
a.   Perf. 11¼x11 + label   8.00   8.00
b.   Perf. 14¼x14½ + label   3.50   3.50
c.   Vert. strip of 5, #987-991, + 5 labels   17.50   17.50
d.   Vert. strip of 5, #987a-991a, + 5 labels   42.50   42.50
e.   Vert. strip of 5, #987b-991b, + 5 labels   17.50   17.50

The full sheets sold for $14.95 with or without personalized labels. The personalization of labels was available only at UN Headquarters, and not through mail order. The sheet of No. 991d has "ver. 2" in the lower right selvage. The sheet of No. 991e has "VER. 3" in the lower right selvage.

Economic and Social Council — A411

Designs: 44c, Water and sanitation. 98c, Traditional medicines.

2009, Aug. 6   **Perf. 12¾x12½**
992 A411 44c multicolored   2.00   .90
993 A411 98c multicolored   5.00   2.00

See Offices in Geneva Nos. 503-504, Vienna Nos. 450-451.

UN Emblem — A412

2009, Sept. 22   **Perf. 13¼**
994 A412 98c multi + label   5.50   5.50
a.   Perf. 11¼x11 + label   5.00   5.00

The full sheets sold for $14.95 with or without personalized labels. There are five different non-personalized labels. The personalization of labels was available only at UN Headquarters, and not through mail order. The sheet of No. 994a has "ver. 2" in the lower right selvage.

Miniature Sheet

Millennium Development
Goals — A413

No. 995: a, Bowl of hot food. b, Pencil. c,
Female symbol. d, Teddy bear. e, Pregnant
woman, heart. f, Medicine bottle. g, Stylized
tree. h, Conjoined people.

2009, Sept. 25
995 A413   Sheet of 8   10.00 10.00
a.-h.   44c Any single   1.20 1.20

See Offies in Geneva No. 505; Vienna No.
457.

Mohandas K.
Gandhi — A414

2009, Oct. 2
996 A414 $1 multicolored   2.25 2.25

Miniature Sheet

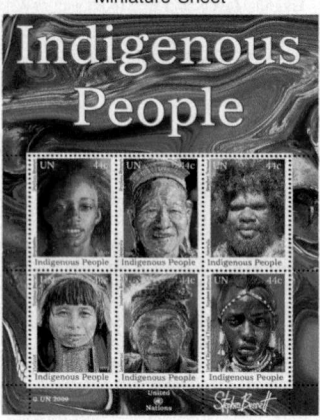

Indigenous People — A415

No. 997 — Portraits of person from: a, Seychelles. b, Malaysia. c, Australia. d, Thailand.
e, Indonesia. f, Tanzania.

2009, Oct. 8   Perf. 12½
997 A415   Sheet of 6   7.00 7.00
a.-f.   44c Any single   1.15 1.15

See Offices in Geneva No. 511, Vienna No.
458.

Flags and Coins Type of 2006

No. 998 — Flag of: a, Bahamas, 10 cent
coin. b, Jamaica, 20 dollar coin. c, Honduras,
50 centavo coin. d, Kuwait, 100 fils coin. e,
Panama, 1 cuarto de Balboa coin. f, Guatemala, 50 centavo coin. g, St. Lucia, 1 cent
coin. h, Yemen, 20 rial coin.

2010, Feb. 5   Litho.   Perf. 13¼x13
998   Sheet of 8   9.75 9.75
a.-h. A375 44c Any single   1.20 1.20

A column of rouletting in the middle of the
sheet separates it into two parts. See Offices
in Geneva No. 512; Vienna No. 459.

Endangered Species Type of 1993

No. 999, Monkey puzzle tree. No. 1000,
Quiver tree. No. 1001, Bristlecone pine tree.
No. 1002, Scarlet ball cactus.

2010, Apr. 15 Litho.   Perf. 12¾x12½
999   A271 44c multicolored   1.25 1.25
1000 A271 44c multicolored   1.25 1.25
1001 A271 44c multicolored   1.25 1.25
1002 A271 44c multicolored   1.25 1.25
a.   Block of 4, #999-1002   5.00 5.00

See Offices in Geneva Nos. 513-516;
Vienna Nos. 465-468.

The stamp pictured above was
printed in limited quantities and sold for
far more than face value. The label
attached to the stamp could not be personalized. Value for stamp and label,
$3. A similar stamp dated "2011" with a
different label attached exists.

**One Planet, One Ocean Types of
Geneva and Vienna and**

A416

One Planet, One Ocean — A417

No. 1003: a, Turtle at top, eel at left, fish at
LR. b, Fish at LL, turtle's flipper at bottom. c,
Fish at left, yellow sponge at LR, Lobster at
right. d, Lobster at left, turtle at right.
No. 1004: a, Octopus at left, fish at LR. b,
Fish at left and right, turtle's head at bottom. c,
Lobster at left. fish at LL and LR. d, Fish at LL
and LR, turtle's body at UR.
No. 1005: a, Like #1003a. b, Like #1003b, c,
Like #1003c, d, Like #1003d. e, Like Vienna
#471a. f, Like Vienna #471b. g, Like Vienna
#471c, h, Like Vienna #471d. i, Like Geneva
#519a. j, Like Geneva #519b, k, Like Geneva
#519c. l, Like Geneva #519d. m, Like #1004a.
n, Like #1004b. o, Like #1004c, p, Like
#1004d. q, Like Vienna #472a. r, Like Vienna
#472b. s, Like Vienna #472c. t, Like Vienna
#472d. u, Like Geneva #520a. v, Like Geneva
#520b. w, Like Geneva #520c. x, Like Geneva
#520d.

2010, May 6   Litho.   Perf. 14x13¼
1003 A416   Sheet of 4   3.60 3.60
a.-d.   44c Any single   .90   .90
1004 A417   Sheet of 4   8.00 8.00
a.-d.   98c Any single   2.00 2.00

Souvenir Booklet
Perf. 13¼x13
1005   Booklet, #1005y-
           1005z, 1005aa-
           1005ad   18.00
a.-d. A416 28c any single   .60   .60
e.-h. V91 28c any single   .60   .60
i.-l. G85 28c any single   .60   .60
m.-p. A417 44c any single   .90   .90
q.-t. V92 44c any single   .90   .90
u.-x. G86 44c any single   .90   .90
y.   Booklet pane of 4 #1005a-
           1005d   2.40 2.40
z.   Booklet pane of 4 #1005e-
           1005h   2.40 2.40
aa.   Booklet pane of 4 #1005i-
           1005l   2.40 2.40
ab.   Booklet pane of 4 #1005m-
           1005p   3.60 3.60
ac.   Booklet pane of 4 #1005q-
           1005t   3.60 3.60
ad.   Booklet pane of 4 #1005u-
           1005x   3.60 3.60

Intl. Oceanographic Commission, 50th
anniv. See Offices in Geneva Nos. 519-521,
Vienna Nos. 471-473.

People of
Different
Cultures — A418

People of
Different
Cultures as New
York Buildings
A419

2010, June 4   Litho.   Perf. 13
1006 A418 3c multicolored   .25   .25
1007 A419 4c multicolored   .25   .25

UN Headquarters and New York
Skyline — A420

Shanghai Skyline — A421

2010, June 4   Litho.   Perf. 13¼
1008 A420 98c multicolored   2.50 2.50
1009 A421 98c multicolored   2.50 2.50
a.   Horiz. pair, #1008-1009   5.00 5.00

Expo 2010, Shanghai. Nos. 1008-1009
were sold only in full panes for $14.95.

United Nations,
65th
Anniv. — A422

Litho. With Foil Application
2010, June 28   Perf. 13¼
1010 A422 98c light blue & gold 2.25 2.25

Souvenir Sheet
1011   Sheet of 2 #1011a   5.00 5.00
a.   A422 98c dark blue & gold   2.50 2.50

See Offices in Geneva No. 522, Vienna No.
474.

A423

A424

A425

A426

United Nations
Sea
Transport — A427

2010, Sept. 2   Litho.   Perf. 13¼x13
1012 A423 44c multicolored   .90   .90
1013 A424 44c multicolored   .90   .90
1014 A425 44c multicolored   .90   .90
1015 A426 44c multicolored   .90   .90
1016 A427 44c multicolored   .90   .90
a.   Horiz. strip of 5, #1012-1016 4.50 4.50

See Offices in Geneva Nos. 523-527,
Vienna Nos. 475-479.

Intl. Year of
Biodiversity
A428

Drawings from Art Forms from Nature, by
Ernst Heinrich: 15c, Hummingbird. $1.50,
Liverwort.

2010, Oct. 18   Litho.   Perf. 13
1017 A428 15c multicolored   .30   .30
1018 A428 $1.50 multicolored   3.00 3.00

See Offices in Geneva Nos. 517-518;
Vienna Nos. 469-470.

Miniature Sheet

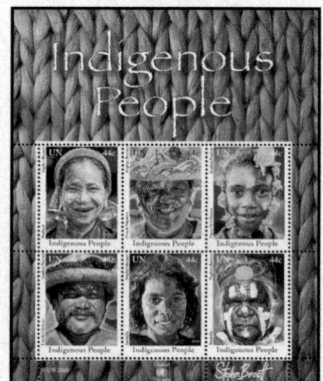

Indigenous People — A429

No. 1019 — Portraits of person from: a,
Thailand. b, French Polynesia (woman,
denomination in black). c, Papua New Guinea.
d, French Polynesia (man, denomination in
white). e, Australia (child). f, Australia (old man
with headband).

2010, Oct. 21   Litho.   Perf. 13
1019 A429   Sheet of 6   6.00 6.00
a.-f.   44c Any single   1.00 1.00

See Offices in Geneva No. 529; Vienna No.
480.

United Nations
Headquarters,
New
York — A430

United Nations Headquarters: 11c, Aerial view. $5, Ground-level view.

2011, Feb. 4   Litho.   Perf. 13
1020 A430 11c multicolored   .25   .25
1021 A430 $5 multicolored   10.00 10.00

See Offices in Geneva Nos. 530-531; Vienna Nos. 481-482.

Flags and Coins Type of 2006

No. 1022 — Flag of: a, Mauritius, 1 rupee coin. b, Guyana, 10 dollar coin. c, Timor, 5 cent coin. d, Iceland, 100 krónur coin. e, Chile, 1 peso coin. f, Norway, 20 kroner coin. g, Fiji, 50 cent coin. h, Comoro Islands, 100 franc coin.

2011, Mar. 3   Litho.   Perf. 13¼x13
1022   Sheet of 8   8.75   8.75
a.-h. A375 44c Any single   1.10   1.10

A column of rouletting in the middle of the sheet separates it into two parts. See Offices in Geneva No. 532; Vienna No. 483.

UN Emblem — A431

2011, Apr. 7   Litho.   Perf. 14¾
1023 A431 98c blue + label   5.00   5.00

Printed in sheets of 10 + 10 different labels which are not personalizable. The full sheet sold for $14.95

Human Space Flight, 50th
Anniv. — A432

No. 1024: Various parts of outer space scene.
No. 1025: a, Cosmonaut and rocket. b, Astronaut on ladder of Lunar Module.

2011, Apr. 12   Litho.   Perf. 13x13¼
1024 A432   Sheet of 16   16.00 16.00
a.-p. 44c any single   1.00   1.00

Souvenir Sheet
1025 A432   Sheet of 2   3.00   3.00
a.   44c multi   .90   .90
b.   98c multi   2.00   2.00

See Offices in Geneva Nos. 533-534; Vienna Nos. 484-485. No. 1024 contains two 40x48mm stamps that were printed as part of a larger sheet of six stamps, Vienna No. 485c, which was broken up into its component two-stamp souvenir sheets, and also sold as one unit.

UNESCO World Heritage Sites in
Nordic Countries — A433

Designs: 44c, Surtsey Volcanic Island, Iceland. 98c, Drottningholm Castle, Sweden.

2011, May 5   Litho.   Perf. 14x13½
1026 A433 44c multicolored   .90   .90
1027 A433 98c multicolored   2.00   2.00

See Offices in Geneva Nos. 535-536; Vienna Nos. 496-497.

AIDS Ribbon — A434

2011, June 3   Litho.   Die Cut
Self-Adhesive
1028 A434 44c red & blue   1.75   1.75

See Offices in Geneva No. 537; Vienna No. 498.

Economic and Social Council
(ECOSOC) — A435

2011, July 1   Litho.   Perf. 14¼
1029 A435 44c multicolored   1.50   1.50
1030 A435 98c multicolored   3.50   3.50

See Offices in Geneva Nos. 538-539; Vienna Nos. 499-500.

Endangered Species Type of 1993

Designs: No. 1031, Bali starling. No. 1032, California condor. No. 1033, Japanese crane. No. 1034, Black-fronted piping-guan.

2011, Sept. 7   Perf. 12¾x12½
1031 A271 44c multicolored   1.10   1.10
1032 A271 44c multicolored   1.10   1.10
1033 A271 44c multicolored   1.10   1.10
1034 A271 44c multicolored   1.10   1.10
a.   Block of 4, #1031-1034   4.40   4.40

See Offices in Geneva Nos. 540-543; Vienna Nos. 501-504.

Intl. Year of
Forests — A436

Designs: 44c, Tree with wildlife, man with mask. 98c, Tree roots.

Litho. With Foil Application
2011, Oct. 13   Perf. 12½
1035   44c multicolored   1.25   1.25
1036   98c multicolored   2.50   2.50
a.   A436 Vert. pair, #1035-1036 3.50   3.00

See Offices in Geneva Nos. 544-545; Vienna Nos. 505-506.

UN Emblem — A437

2012, Jan. 23   Litho.   Perf. 14¾
1037 A437 $1.05 blue + label   2.75   2.75
       Sheet of 10 + 10 labels   27.50

The full sheet sold for $14.95. The generic label exists as shown, and with dragon in yellow against red background. Labels could be personalized. The personalization of labels was available only at UN Headquarters, and not through mail order.

A438

No. 1038: a, Desk in lobby. b, Sculpture of Jesus holding lamb. c, Stained-glass window. d, Meeting room. e, Guided tour. f, Flags in front of United Nations buildings. g, United Nations Peacekeepers helmet in showcase. h, Gift shop. i, View of curved floors above lobby. j, Street signs.

2012, Jan. 23   Litho.   Perf. 14¾
1038 A438   Sheet of 10   30.00 30.00
a.-j. $1.05 Any single + label 3.00   3.00

The full sheet sold for $14.95. The generic labels are shown. Labels could be personalized. The personalization of labels was available only at UN Headquarters, and not through mail order.

Flags and Coins Type of 2006

No. 1039 — Flag of: a, Nepal, 1 rupee coin. b, Bahrain, 100 fils coin. c, Paraguay, 1000 guarani coin. d, Ethiopia, 25 cent coin. e, Peru, 1 sol coin. f, Solomon Islands, 20 cent coin. g, Dominican Republic, 1 peso coin. h, Canada, 1 dollar coin.

2012, Feb. 3   Litho.   Perf. 13¼x13
1039   Sheet of 8   7.25   7.25
a.-h. A375 45c Any single   .90   .90

A column of rouletting in the middle of the sheet separates it into two parts. See Offices in Geneva No. 546; Vienna No. 507.

A439

Autism
Awareness
A440

Drawings by autistic people: No. 1040, An Abstract Garden II, by Trent Altman, U.S. No. 1041, Crazy Love, by Hannah Kandel, U.S.

2012, Apr. 2   Litho.   Perf. 14x13½
1040 A439 $1.05 multicolored   2.10   2.10
1041 A440 $1.05 multicolored   2.10   2.10
a.   Pair, #1040-1041   4.20   4.20

See Offices in Geneva Nos. 547-548; Vienna Nos. 508-509.

Endangered Species Type of 1993

Designs: No. 1042, Giant panda. No. 1043, Short-horned chameleon. No. 1044, Oncilla. No. 1045, Cotton-headed tamarin.

2012, Apr. 19   Litho.   Perf. 12¾x12½
1042 A271 45c multicolored   1.10   1.10
1043 A271 45c multicolored   1.10   1.10
1044 A271 45c multicolored   1.10   1.10
1045 A271 45c multicolored   1.10   1.10
a.   Block of 4, #1042-1045   4.40   4.40

See Offices in Geneva Nos. 549-552; Vienna Nos. 511-514.

Tinker Bell — A441

Tinker Bell — A442

2012, June 1   Litho.   Perf. 14¾
1046 A441 $1.05 multi + label   3.00   3.00
1047 A442 $1.05 multi + label   3.00   3.00
a.   Vert. pair, #1046-1047, + 2 labels   6.00   6.00
       Sheet of 10, 5 each #1046-1047, + 10 labels   30.00 30.00

The full sheet sold for $14.95. The generic labels are shown. Labels could be personalized. The personalization of labels was available only at UN Headquarters, and not through mail order.

Rio + 20
Conference on
Sustainable
Development,
Rio de Janeiro
A443

2012, June 1   Litho.   Perf. 13x13¼
1048 A443 $1.05 multicolored   2.10   2.10

See Offices in Geneva No. 553; Vienna No. 515.

Sport for Peace — A444

2012 Paralympics events: 45c, Goalball. $1.05, Sitting volleyball.

Litho. With Foil Application
2012, Aug. 17   Perf. 14½
1049 A444 45c multicolored   .90   .90
1050 A444 $1.05 multicolored   2.10   2.10
a.   Souvenir sheet of 1   3.50   3.50

See Offices in Geneva Nos. 554-555; Vienna Nos. 516-517.

UNESCO World Heritage Sites in Africa — A445

Designs: 45c, Kilamanjaro National Park, Tanzania. $1.05, Old Towns of Djenné, Mali.

2012, Sept. 5   Litho.   Perf. 13¼
1051 A445 45c multicolored   .90   .90
1052 A445 $1.05 multicolored   2.10 2.10

See Offices in Geneva Nos. 556-557; Vienna Nos. 518-519.

Miniature Sheet

Indigenous People — A446

No. 1053 — Portrait of person from: a, Namibia. b, Japan. c, China. d, Ethiopia. e, Mongolia. f, Tanzania.

2012, Oct. 11   Litho.   Perf. 13¼x13
1053 A446 Sheet of 6   5.50 5.50
a.-f.   45c Any single   .90   .90

See Offices in Geneva No. 558; Vienna No. 520.

UN Emblem — A447

2013, Jan. 28   Litho.   Perf. 14¾
1054 A447 $1.10 multi + label   4.00 4.00
          Sheet of 10 + 10 labels 40.00

The full sheet sold for $14.95. The generic label exists as shown, and with snake against red background. Labels could be personalized. The personalization of labels was available only at UN Headquarters, and not through mail order.

A448

No. 1055: a, Flags in front of Secretariat Building, brown panel at right. b, Aerial view of headquarters and East River, yellow orange panel at left. c, Secretariat Building and wall of General Assembly building, yellow orange panel at left. d, Headquarters and East River, brown panel at right. e, General Assembly and Secretariat Buildings, flags at right, brown

panel at right. f, Sculpture and fountain at night, yellow orange panel at left. g, Secretariat Building and cherry blossoms, yellow orange panel at left. h, Secretariat Building, trees without leaves, flags at left, brown panel at right. i, Aerial view of headquarters at night, brown panel at right. j, Headquarters, yellow panel at left.

2013, Jan. 28   Litho.   Perf. 14¾
1055 A448 Sheet of 10   30.00 30.00
a.-j. $1.10 Any single + label 3.00 3.00

The full sheet sold for $14.95. The generic labels are shown. Labels could be personalized. The personalization of labels was available only at UN Headquarters, and not through mail order.

World Radio Day — A449

Designs: 46c, Radio antenna. $1.10, Audrey Hepburn at microphone.

2013, Feb. 13   Litho.   Perf. 13¼x13
1056 A449 46c multicolored   .95   .95
1057 A449 $1.10 multicolored 2.25 2.25

See Offices in Geneva Nos. 559-560; Vienna Nos. 521-522.

Circle of People A450

United Nations Headquarters A451

2013, Mar. 5   Litho.   Perf. 14x13½
1058 A450 $1.10 multicolored 2.25 2.25

Perf. 13½x14
1059 A451 $3 multicolored   6.00 6.00

See Offices in Geneva Nos. 561-562; Vienna Nos. 523-524.

World Heritage Sites, China — A452

Designs: Nos. 1060, 1062a, Mogao Caves. Nos. 1061, 1062d, Imperial Palace, Beijing. No. 1062b, Potala Palace, Lhasa. No. 1062c, Great Wall of China. No. 1062e, Mount Huangshan. No. 1062f, Mausoleum of the First Qing Emperor.

2013, Apr. 11   Litho.   Perf. 14x13½
1060 A452 46c multicolored   .95   .95
1061 A452 $1.10 multicolored 2.25 2.25

Souvenir Booklet
1062   Booklet, #1062g-
            1062l   20.00
a.-c.   A452 33c any single   .70   .70
d.-f.   A452 46c any single   .95   .95
g.   Booklet pane of 4 #1062a   2.80
h.   Booklet pane of 4 #1062b   2.80
i.   Booklet pane of 4 #1062c   2.80

j.   Booklet pane of 4 #1062d   3.80 —
k.   Booklet pane of 4 #1062e   3.80 —
l.   Booklet pane of 4 #1062f   3.80 —

See Offices in Geneva Nos. 563-565, Vienna Nos. 525-527.

Flag Type of 1980

No. 1063, Myanmar. No. 1064, Russian Federation. No. 1065, South Sudan. No. 1066, Cape Verde.

2013, May 2   Litho.   Perf. 13
1063 A185 $1.10 multicolored 2.25 2.25
1064 A185 $1.10 multicolored 2.25 2.25
1065 A185 $1.10 multicolored 2.25 2.25
1066 A185 $1.10 multicolored 2.25 2.25
a.   Block of 4, #1063-1066 9.00 9.00
        Nos. 1063-1066 (4)   9.00 9.00

World Oceans Day — A453

No. 1067 — Fish from One Fish, Two Fish, Red Fish, Blue Fish, by Dr. Seuss: a, Green fish, red fish, sign. b, Red fish facing right. c, Green fish facing left, sign. d, Yellow fish, sign. e, Blue fish. f, Red fish facing left, sign. g, Red fish facing right, water droplets, tail of yellow and red fish, sign. h, Yellow and red fish, green fish, side of blue fish. i, Head of blue fish, sign post. j, Sign and wave. k, Sign, red fish, side and tail of blue fish, wave. l, Side of blue fish, green fish, wave.

2013, May 31   Litho.   Perf. 13
1067 A453 Sheet of 12   11.50 11.50
a.-l.   46c any single   .95   .95

See Offices in Geneva No. 566; Vienna No. 528.

Nebulae — A454

Designs: No. 1068, V838 Mon. No. 1069, WR 25, Tr16-244. 46c, 30 Doradus.

2013, Aug. 9   Litho.   Perf. 13¼
1068 A454 $1.10 multicolored 2.25 2.25
1069 A454 $1.10 multicolored 2.25 2.25
a.   Pair, #1068-1069   4.50 4.50

Souvenir Sheet
1070 A454 46c multicolored   2.50 2.50

No. 1070 contains one 44x44mm stamp. See Offices in Geneva Nos. 567-569; Vienna Nos. 529-531.

World Humanitarian Day — A455

No. 1071 — "The World Needs More" in speech balloon in: a, Somali (Uduunku. . .). b, Thai. c, Arabic (people in background). d, Portuguese (O Mundo. . .). e, Russian. f, Korean.

g, Swahili (Mahitaji. . .). h, Chinese. i, Urdu (aerial view of village in background). j, English.

2013, Aug. 19   Litho.   Perf. 14¾
1071 A455 Sheet of 10   30.00 30.00
a.-j. $1.10 Any single + label 3.00 3.00

The full sheet sold for $14.95. The generic labels are shown. Labels could be personalized. The personalization of labels was available only at UN Headquarters, and not through mail order.

Works of Disabled Artists — A456

Designs: 46c, Self-portrait II by Chuck Close, U.S. $1.10, Tears and Laughter, by Josephine King, United Kingdom.

2013, Sept. 20   Litho.   Perf. 13¼x13
1072 A456 46c multicolored   .95   .95
1073 A456 $1.10 multicolored 2.25 2.25

See Offices in Geneva Nos. 570-571; Vienna Nos. 532-533.

Endangered Species Type of 1993

Designs: No. 1074, Asian tapir. No. 1075, Mongoose lemur. No. 1076, Flat-headed cat. No. 1077, Aye-aye.

2013, Oct. 10   Litho.   Perf. 12¾x12½
1074 A271 $1.10 multicolored 2.25 2.25
1075 A271 $1.10 multicolored 2.25 2.25
1076 A271 $1.10 multicolored 2.25 2.25
1077 A271 $1.10 multicolored 2.25 2.25
a.   Block of 4, #1074-1077 9.00 9.00

See Offices in Geneva Nos. 572-575; Vienna Nos. 534-537.

Flags and Coins Type of 2006

No. 1078 — Flag of: a, Montenegro, 20 cent coin. b, Grenada, 5 cent coin. c, United States, 25 cent coin. d, Gabon, 100 franc coin. e, Palau, 1 cent coin. f, Niger, 100 franc coin. g, Saint Kitts and Nevis, 5 cent coin. h, Venezuela, 1 bolivar coin.

2013, Nov. 6   Litho.   Perf. 13¼x13
1078   Sheet of 8   7.75 7.75
a.-h.   A375 46c Any single .95   .95

A column of rouletting in the middle of the sheet separates it into two parts. See Offices in Geneva No. 576; Vienna No. 539.

UN Emblem — A457

2014, Jan. 28   Litho.   Perf. 14¾
1079 A457 $1.15 multi + label   3.00 3.00

A458

No. 1080: a, The Golden Rule, mosaic by Norman Rockwell, dark green panel at right. b, Renovated Delegate's Lounge, yellow green panel at left. c, Renovated ECOSOC Chamber, red brown panel at left. d, Dag Hammarskjold Library, dark blue panel at right. e, Helmet of United Nations Peacekeeper and United Nations Flag, dark blue panel at right. f, United Nations Headquarters, dark green panel at left. g, Renovated Security Council Chamber, yellow green panel at left. h, Flags of member nations, red brown panel at right. i, Mankind's Struggle for Lasting Peace, by José Vela-Zanetti, dark blue panel at right. j, Relational Painting No. 90, by Fritz Glarner, yellow green panel at left.

2014, Jan. 28   Litho.   Perf. 14¾

1080	A458	Sheet of 10	30.00	30.00
a.-j.		$1.15 Any single + label	3.00	3.00

The full sheet sold for $14.95. The generic labels are shown. Labels could be personalized. The personalization of labels was available only at UN Headquarters, and not through mail order.

International Day of Happiness
A459

Designs: 47c, Woman smiling, photograph by Mario Castello, "Happy." $1.15, People kissing on beach, photograph by Henryk T. Kaiser, "Feliz."

2014, Mar. 17   Litho.   Perf. 13¼x13

1081	A459	47c multicolored	.95	.95
1082	A459	$1.15 multicolored	2.40	2.40

See Offices in Geneva Nos. 577-578; Vienna Nos. 540-541.

Flag Type of 1980

No. 1083, Afghanistan. No. 1084, Serbia. No. 1085, Cambodia. No. 1086, Democratic Republic of the Congo.

2014, Mar. 27   Litho.   Perf. 13x13¼

1083	A185	$1.15 multicolored	3.00	3.00
1084	A185	$1.15 multicolored	3.00	3.00
1085	A185	$1.15 multicolored	3.00	3.00
1086	A185	$1.15 multicolored	3.00	3.00
a.		Block of 4, #1083-1086	12.00	12.00
		Nos. 1083-1086 (4)	12.00	12.00

Miniature Sheet

International Year of Jazz — A460

No. 1087: a, Trumpeter with cap and mute in trumpet. b, Silhouette of trumpeter in tan. c, Saxophone. d, Trumpet. e, Silhouette of trumpeter in lilac. f, Saxophonist wearing hat. g, Man with hat holding trombone. h, Green saxophone. i, Saxophonist without hat. j, Trombone. k, Trumpeter wearing hat. l, Microphone.

2014, Apr. 30   Litho.   Perf. 13x13¼

1087	A460	Sheet of 12	12.00	12.00
		First day cover		15.00
a.-l.		49c Any single	1.00	1.00

See Offices in Geneva No. 579; Vienna No. 542.

A461

A462

Printed by Lowe-Martin Group, Canada. Panes of 20. Designed by Sergio Baradat, U.S.

2014, June 6   Litho.   Perf. 13¼x13

1088	A461	33c multicolored	.70	.70
1089	A462	$2 multicolored	4.00	4.00

See Offices in Geneva Nos. 580-581; Vienna Nos. 544-545.

Taj Mahal and Tourists — A463

Taj Mahal and Pink Sky — A464

Taj Mahal and Sun — A465

Taj Mahal and Reflecting Pool — A466

Taj Mahal and Camel — A467

Taj Mahal and Elephant — A468

2014, July 16   Engr.   Perf. 13¼x13

1090	A463	49c multicolored	1.00	1.00
1091	A464	$1.15 multicolored	2.40	2.40

Souvenir Booklet

1092		Booklet, #1092g-		
		1092l	20.50	
a.		A463 34c multi	.70	.70
b.		A465 34c multi	.70	.70
c.		A466 34c multi	.70	.70
d.		A467 49c multi	1.00	1.00
e.		A467 49c multi	1.00	1.00
f.		A468 49c multi	1.00	1.00
g.		Booklet pane of 4 #1092a	2.80	—
h.		Booklet pane of 4 #1092b	2.80	—
i.		Booklet pane of 4 #1092c	2.80	—
j.		Booklet pane of 4 #1092d	4.00	—
k.		Booklet pane of 4 #1092e	4.00	—
l.		Booklet pane of 4 #1092f	4.00	—

See Offices in Geneva Nos. 582-584; Vienna Nos. 546-548.

International Year of Family Farming — A469

2014, Aug. 21   Litho.   Perf. 13x13¼

1093	A469	49c multicolored	1.00	1.00
1094	A469	$1.15 multicolored	2.40	2.40

See Offices in Geneva Nos. 585-586; Vienna Nos. 549-550.

Global Education First Initiative A470

Designs: $1.15, Teacher and students in forest. $1.50, Chemistry teacher and student.

2014, Sept. 18   Litho.   Perf. 13x13¼

1095	A470	$1.15 multicolored	2.40	2.40

Souvenir Sheet
Perf. 12½

1096	A470	$1.50 multicolored	3.25	3.25

No. 1096 contains one 32x32mm stamp. See Offices in Geneva Nos. 588-589; Vienna Nos. 551-552.

Endangered Species A471

Maps and: No. 1097, Denise's pygmy seahorses. No. 1098, Whale shark. No. 1099, Scalloped hammerhead shark. No. 1100, Asian arowana.

2014, Oct. 23   Litho.   Perf. 12¾x12½

1097	A471	$1.15 multicolored	2.40	2.40
1098	A471	$1.15 multicolored	2.40	2.40
1099	A471	$1.15 multicolored	2.40	2.40
1100	A471	$1.15 multicolored	2.40	2.40
a.		Block of 4, #1097-1100	9.75	9.75

See Offices in Geneva Nos. 590-593; Vienna Nos. 553-556.

A472

No. 1101: a, United Nations emblem in gray, bottom panel in blue. b, Aerial view of United Nations Headquarters, bottom panel in red, year date at left. c, View of United Nations Headquarters from across East River, bottom

panel in red, year date at right. d, Interior balconies, bottom panel in blue. e, Crowd in lobby, bottom panel in blue. f, Sun reflecting off United Nations Building, street lights, bottom panel in red. g, United Nations emblem in brown, bottom panel in red. h, Woman and two men near General Assembly Building, bottom panel in blue. i, United Nations Building, flags, trees without leaves, bottom panel in blue. j, General Assembly and United Nations Buildings, bottom panel in red.

2014, Oct. 23   Litho.   Perf. 14¾

1101	A472	Sheet of 10	30.00	30.00
a.-j.		$1.15 Any single + label	3.00	3.00

The full sheet sold for $14.95. The generic labels are shown. Labels could be personalized. The personalization of labels was available only at UN Headquarters, and not through mail order.

UN Emblem — A473

2015, Jan. 23   Litho.   Perf. 14¾

1102	A473	$1.15 multi + label	3.00	3.00
		Sheet of 10 + 10 labels	30.00	

The full sheet sold for $14.95. The generic label exists as shown, with ram on deep bister background. Labels could be personalized. The personalization of labels was available only at UN Headquarters, and not through mail order.

Flags and Coins Type of 2006

No. 1103 — Flag of: a, Kiribati, 10 cent coin. b, Tonga, 2 seniti coin. c, Costa Rica, 10 centimos coin. d, Bhutan, 25 chetrum coin. e, Zimbabwe, 5 dollar coin. f, Angola, 1 kwanza coin. g, Congo Democratic Republic, 1 franc coin. h, Liberia, 25 cent coin.

2015, Feb. 6   Litho.   Perf. 13¼x13

1103		Sheet of 8	8.00	8.00
a.-h.		A375 49c Any single	1.00	1.00

A column of rouletting in the middle of the sheet separates it into two parts. See Offices in Geneva No. 594; Vienna No. 558.

Miniature Sheets

A474

World Poetry Day — A475

No. 1104: a, Black pen, denomination in red brown. b, William Wordsworth quotation in white, denomination in red. c, Wordsworth quotation in red brown, denomination in white. d, Gold pen, denomination in white. e, Black pen, denomination in white. f, Wordsworth quotation in black, denomination in red brown.
No. 1105: a, Gold pen, denomination in white, tree top and rose in background. b, José Martí quotation, denomination in lilac, tree tops in background. c, Martí quotation, denomination in white, tree top and rose in background. d, Gold pen, denomination in lilac, tree trunks and tree top in background. e, Gold pen, denomination in lilac, tree trunks and rose in background. f, Martí quotation, denomination in lilac, tree trunks in background.

Perf. 14½x14¼

2015, Mar. 20   Litho.
1104 A474   Sheet of 6   6.00   6.00
a.-f.   49c Any single   1.00   1.00
1105 A475   Sheet of 6   14.50   14.50
a.-f. $1.20 Any single   2.40   2.40

See Offices in Geneva Nos. 595-596;
Vienna Nos. 559-560.

Endangered
Species — A476

Designs: No. 1106, King bird-of-paradise.
No. 1107, Blue bird-of-paradise. No. 1108,
Princess Stephanie's bird-of-paradise. No.
1109, Carola's parotia.

2015, Apr. 16   Litho.   Perf. 12½x12¾
1106 A476 $1.20 multicolored   2.40   2.40
1107 A476 $1.20 multicolored   2.40   2.40
1108 A476 $1.20 multicolored   2.40   2.40
1109 A476 $1.20 multicolored   2.40   2.40
a.   Block of 4, #1106-1109   9.75   9.75
Nos. 1106-1109 (4)   9.60   9.60

See Offices in Geneva Nos. 597-600;
Vienna Nos. 561-564.

A477

A478

2015, May 7   Litho.   Perf. 13¼x13
1110 A477 35c multicolored   .70   .70
1111 A478 40c multicolored   .80   .80

See Offices in Vienna Nos. 565-566.

Miniature Sheet

A479

No. 1112: a, United Nations Headquarters
and flags, panel at right. b, Flags, panel at left.
c, Stairway and pillars, panel at left. d, Reflection of buildings in windows, panel at right. e,
Circular meeting room, panel at right. f, United
Nations Headquarters, panel at left. g, Trees
and United Nations Building, panel at left. h,
Let Us Beat Swords Into Plowshares statue,
panel at right. i, General Assembly Building,
flags and street, panel at right. j, Arrival sculpture, panel at left.

2015, May 7   Litho.   Perf. 14¾
1112 A479   Sheet of 10   30.00   30.00
a.-j. $1.20 Any single + label   3.00   3.00

The full sheet sold for $14.95. The generic
labels are shown. Labels could be personalized. The personalization of labels was available only at UN Headquarters, and not through
mail order.

World Heritage Sites, Southeast
Asia — A480

Designs: Nos. 1113, 1115a, Luang
Prabang, Laos. Nos. 1114, 1115d, Borobodur
Temple, Indonesia. No. 1115b, Angkor Wat,
Cambodia. No. 1115c, Ayutthaya, Thailand.
No. 1115e, Cordillera, Philippines. No. 1115f,
Hué Monuments, Viet Nam.

2015, June 5   Litho.   Perf. 14x13½
1113 A480   49c multicolored   1.00   1.00
1114 A480 $1.20 multicolored 2.40   2.40

Souvenir Booklet
1115   Booklet, #1115g-
          1115l   20.50
a.-c.   A480 35c any single   .70   .70
d.-f.   A480 49c any single   1.00   1.00
g.   Booklet pane of 4 #1115a   2.80   —
h.   Booklet pane of 4 #1115b   2.80   —
i.   Booklet pane of 4 #1115c   2.80   —
j.   Booklet pane of 4 #1115d   4.00   —
k.   Booklet pane of 4 #1115e   4.00   —
l.   Booklet pane of 4 #1115f   4.00   —

See Offices in Geneva Nos. 601-603,
Vienna Nos. 567-569.

End Violence Against Children — A481

Designs: 49c, Armed violence reduction.
$1.20, Sexual violence against children.

Perf. 14½x14¼
2015, Aug. 20   Litho.
1116 A481 49c multicolored   1.00   1.00
1117 A481 $1.20 multicolored   2.40   2.40

See Offices in Geneva Nos. 604-605;
Vienna Nos. 570-571.

United Nations, 70th Anniv. — A482

Designed by Sergio Baradat, U.S.

2015, Sept. 25   Litho.   Perf. 14¾
1118 A482 $1.20 multi + label   3.00   3.00
        Sheet of 10 + 10 labels   30.00

The full sheet sold for $14.95. The generic
label exists as shown, depicting Pope Francis.
Labels could be personalized. The personal-
ization of labels was available only at UN
Headquarters, and not through mail order. On
Sept. 27, No. 1118 was issued in a sheet of 10
+ 10 labels depicting Chinese characters.
See Vienna No. 577.

General
Assembly
Hall
A483

Visitors
Lobby
A484

Security
Council
A485

Woodrow Wilson Reading Room of
Dag Hammarskjöld Library — A486

General Assembly Hall — A487

Printed by Cartor Security Printing, France.
Panes of 6. Designed by Rorie Katz, U.S.

2015, Oct. 25   Litho.   Perf. 13¾
1119 A483 49c multicolored   1.00   1.00
1120 A484 49c multicolored   1.00   1.00
a.   Pair, #1119-1120   2.00   2.00
1121 A485 $1.20 multicolored   2.40   2.40
1122 A486 $1.20 multicolored   2.40   2.40
a.   Pair, #1121-1122   4.80   4.80
Nos. 1119-1122 (4)   6.80   6.80

Souvenir Sheet
Perf. 13½
1123 A487 $1.20 multicolored   2.40   2.40

United Nations, 70th anniv. See Offices in
Geneva Nos. 607-611; Vienna Nos. 572-576.

United Nations Educational, Scientific
and Cultural Organization (UNESCO),
70th Anniv. — A488

2015, Nov. 5   Litho.   Perf. 14¾
1124 A488 $1.20 multi + label   3.50   3.50
        Sheet of 10 + 10 labels   35.00

The full sheet sold for $14.95. Ten different
generic labels, one of which is shown, are on
the sheet. Labels could be personalized. The
personalization of labels was available only at
UN Headquarters, and not through mail order.

21st United
Nations
Climate
Chage
Conference,
Paris
A489

2015, Nov. 24   Litho.   Perf. 13¼
1125 A489 $1.20 multicolored   2.40   2.40

Values are for stamps with surrounding
selvage. See Offices in Geneva No. 612;
Vienna No. 578.

UN Emblem — A490

2016, Jan. 8   Litho.   Perf. 14¾
1126 A490 $1.20 multicolored +
              label   3.00   3.00
        Sheet of 10 + 10 labels   30.00

The full sheet sold for $14.95. The generic
label, with monkey on red background, is
shown. A sheet of 10 No. 1126 + 10 labels
depicting M. S. Subbulaskshmi was issued on
Oct. 2, 2016. Labels could be personalized.
The personalization of labels was available
only at UN Headquarters, and not through
mail order.

Free and
Equal — A491

Designs: 49c, Group of stylized people.
$1.20, Woman with butterfly wings.

2016, Feb. 5   Litho.   Perf. 13½x13¼
1127 A491 49c multicolored   1.00   1.00
1128 A491 $1.20 multicolored   2.40   2.40

See Offices in Geneva Nos. 613-614;
Vienna Nos. 579-580.

HeForShe
Movement
A492

Designs: 49c, Man, green background.
$1.20, Woman, yellow background.

2016, Mar. 8   Litho.   Perf. 12½x13
1129 A492 49c multicolored   1.00   1.00
1130 A492 $1.20 multicolored   2.40   2.40

See Offices in Geneva Nos. 615-616;
Vienna Nos. 581-582.

Miniature Sheet

Angry Birds — A493

No. 1131: a, Red, the Pigs, double-decker bus. b, Red with wing extended. c, Red and five Hatchlings. d, Red, New York City skyscrapers. e, Red, Eiffel Tower, recycling container. f, Red in jungle. g, Earth, Hatchlings, Chuck, Red, Bomb, Stella and Matilda. h, Red turning faucet, Pigs in tub. i, Red drinking from squirt bottle, Lower Manhattan skyline. j, Red with shovel, Pyramids.

2016, Apr. 22   Litho.   Perf. 14¾

| 1131 | A493 | Sheet of 10 | 30.00 | 30.00 |
| a.-j. | | $1.15 Any single + label | 3.00 | 3.00 |

The full sheet sold for $14.95. The generic labels are shown. Labels could be personalized. The personalization of labels was available only at UN Headquarters, and not through mail order.

Miniature Sheets

A494

International Dance Day — A495

No. 1132 — Illustration of Chinese dancers by Marcos Chin: a, Woman with arm extended upward. b, Two women, denomination in magenta. c, Woman facing left with arm extended outward. d, Two women, denomination in white. e, Woman with closed eyes. f, Woman with closed eyes with two pale yellow lines touching flower.

No. 1133 — Illustration of Thai dancers by Chin: a, Back of dancer's head, hand of another dancer. b, Dancer wearing mask, leg and arm of other dancers. c, Dancer with costume with blue shoulders, dancer with arm extended. d, Dancer with arm extended, leg and arm of other dancers. e, Two dancers with green and yellow costumes. f, Dancer with green and yellow costume.

2016, Apr. 29   Litho.   Perf. 13¼x13

1132	A494	Sheet of 6	5.75	5.75
a.-f.		47c Any single	.95	.95
1133	A495	Sheet of 6	14.50	14.50
a.-f.		$1.15 Any single	2.40	2.40

See Offices in Geneva Nos. 617-618; Vienna Nos. 583-584.

International Day of United Nations Peacekeepers A496

Designs: 47c, Peacekeeper saluting. $1.15, Man disabling landmine.

Litho. With Foil Application

2016, May 29   Perf. 13¼x13

| 1134 | A496 | 47c multicolored | .95 | .95 |
| 1135 | A496 | $1.15 multicolored | 2.40 | 2.40 |

See Offices in Geneva Nos. 619-620; Vienna Nos. 586-587.

Miniature Sheet

United Nations Postal Administration, 65th Anniv. — A497

No. 1136 — Old United Nations stamps: a, New York #1. b, New York #127. c, Vienna #86. d, New York #415. e, New York #301. f, New York #548. g, New York #474. h, Vienna #100. i, New York #476. j, Vienna #122.

2016, May 30   Litho.   Perf. 14¾

| 1136 | A497 | Sheet of 10 | 30.00 | 30.00 |
| a.-j. | | $1.15 Any single + label | 3.00 | 3.00 |

The full sheet sold for $14.95. The generic labels are shown. Labels could be personalized. The personalization of labels was available only at UN Headquarters, and not through mail order.

Sport for Peace — A498

Olympic rings and: No. 1137, Shot put, high jump. No. 1138, Runner, javelin. No. 1139, Dove facing left. No. 1140, Dove facing right.

2016, July 22   Litho.   Perf. 14¼

1137	A498	47c multicolored	.95	.95
1138	A498	47c multicolored	.95	.95
a.		Pair, #1137-1138	1.90	1.90
1139	A498	$1.15 multicolored	2.40	2.40
1140	A498	$1.15 multicolored	2.40	2.40
a.		Pair, #1139-1140	4.80	4.80
		Nos. 1137-1140 (4)	6.70	6.70

See Offices in Geneva Nos. 621-624; Vienna Nos. 588-591.

Souvenir Sheet

United Nations Economic and Social Commission for Asia and the Pacific Building, Bangkok — A499

No. 1141: a, Left third of building. b, Center third of building. c, Right third of building.

2016, Aug. 10   Litho.   Perf. 13¼x13

1141	A499	Sheet of 3	20.00	20.00
a.		$1.15 multi	4.00	4.00
b.		2fr multi	7.00	7.00
c.		€1.70 multi	6.75	6.75

32nd Asian International Stamp Exhibition. No. 1141 sold for $6.

World Heritage Sites, Czech Republic — A500

Designs: Nos. 1142, 1144a, Historic Center of Prague. Nos. 1143, 1144d, Holy Trinity Column, Olomouc. No. 1144b, Gardens and Castle at Kromeríz. No. 1144c, Historic Town Center of Kutná Hora. No. 1144e, Lednice-

Valtice Cultural Landscape. No. 1144f, Historic Center of Cesky Krumlov.

2016, Sept. 8   Litho.   Perf. 14¼

| 1142 | A500 | 47c multicolored | .95 | .95 |
| 1143 | A500 | $1.15 multicolored | 2.40 | 2.40 |

Souvenir Booklet

1144		Booklet, #1115g-		
		1115l	20.00	
a.-c.		A500 34c any single	.70	.70
d.-f.		A500 47c any single	.95	.95
g.		Booklet pane of 4 #1144a	2.80	—
h.		Booklet pane of 4 #1144b	2.80	—
i.		Booklet pane of 4 #1144c	2.80	—
j.		Booklet pane of 4 #1144d	3.80	—
k.		Booklet pane of 4 #1144e	3.80	—
l.		Booklet pane of 4 #1144f	3.80	—

See Offices in Geneva Nos. 625-627; Vienna Nos. 592-594, Czech Republic Nos. 3683-3684.

Miniature Sheet

World Wildlife Conference, Johannesburg — A501

No. 1145 — Part of map of Africa and: a, Addax. b, White rhinoceros. c, African lion. d, Disa uniflora.

2016, Sept. 24   Litho.   Perf. 13x13½

| 1145 | A501 | Sheet of 4 | 9.75 | 9.75 |
| a.-d. | | $1.15 Any single | 2.40 | 2.40 |

See Offices in Geneva No. 628; Vienna No. 596.

Miniature Sheet

World Post Day — A502

No. 1146 — Mail box from: a, Japan. b, Spain. c, Germany. d, Brazil. e, China. f, Denmark. g, India. h, Austria. i, England. j, United States.

2016, Oct. 6   Litho.   Perf. 14¾
1146 A502   Sheet of 10   30.00 30.00
a.-j. $1.15 single + label   3.00   3.00

The full sheet sold for $14.95. The generic labels are shown. Labels could be personalized. The personalization of labels was available only at UN Headquarters, and not through mail order.

Sustainable Development Goals — A503

No. 1147 — Inscription: a, 1 No poverty. b, 2 Zero hunger. c, 3 Good health and well-being. d, 4 Quality education. e, 5 Gender equality. f, 6 Clean water and sanitation. g, 7 Affordable and clean energy. h, 8 Decent work and economic growth. i, 9 Industry, innovation and infrastructure. j, 10 Reduced inequalities. k, 11 Sustainable cities and communities. l, 12 Responsible consumption and production. m, 13 Climate action. n, 14 Life below water. o, 15 Life on land. p, 16 Peace, justice and strong institutions. q, 17 Partnerships for the goals.

2016, Oct. 24   Litho.   Perf. 13¼
1147   Sheet of 17 + label   17.00 17.00
a.-q.   A503 47c Any single   1.00   1.00

See Offices in Geneva No. 629; Vienna No. 597.

Souvenir Sheet

Monkey King From Chinese Novel *Journey to the West* — A504

No. 1148 — Various depictions of Monkey King with inscriptions in: a, English. b, French. c, German.

Litho. With Foil Application
2016, Dec. 2   Perf. 12
1148 A504   Sheet of 3   20.00 20.00
a. $1.15 multi   4.00   4.00
b.   2fr multi   7.00   7.00
c.   €1.70 multi   6.75   6.75

33rd Asian International Stamp Exhibition, Nanning, People's Republic of China. No. 1148 sold for $6.

SEMI-POSTAL STAMPS

Souvenir Sheet

AIDS Awareness — SP1

2002, Oct. 24   Litho.   Perf. 14½
B1 SP1 37c + 6c multicolored   3.50 3.50
See Offices in Geneva No. B1, Vienna No. B1.

AIR POST STAMPS

Plane and Gull — AP1

Swallows and UN Emblem AP2

1951, Dec. 14   Unwmk.   Perf. 14
C1 AP1   6c henna brown   .25   .25
C2 AP1   10c brt blue grn   .30   .30
C3 AP2   15c deep ultra   .40   .40
a.   15c Prussian blue   65.00
C4 AP2   25c gray black   .85   .85
        Nos. C1-C4 (4)   1.80 1.80

Airplane Wing and Globe — AP3

1957, May 27   Perf. 12½x14
C5 AP3   4c maroon   .25   .25

Type of 1957 and

UN Flag and Plane AP4

Perf. 12½x13½
1959, Feb. 9   Unwmk.
C6 AP3   5c rose red   .25   .25

Perf. 13½x14
C7 AP4   7c ultramarine   .25   .25

Outer Space — AP5

UN Emblem — AP6

Bird of Laurel Leaves — AP7

Perf. 11½
1963, June 17   Photo.   Unwmk.
C8 AP5   6c blk, blue & yel grn   .25   .25
C9 AP6   8c yel, ol grn & red   .25   .25

Perf. 12½x12
C10 AP7   13c ultra, aquamarine, gray & carmine   .25   .25

"Flight Across Globe" — AP8

Jet Plane and Envelope AP9

Perf. 11½x12, 12x11½
1964, May 1   Photo.   Unwmk.
C11 AP8   15c vio, buff, gray & pale grn   .30   .30
a.   Gray omitted   225.00
C12 AP9   25c yel, org, gray, blue & red   .50   .50
        Nos. C8-C12 (5)   1.55 1.55

See UN Offices in Geneva No. 8.

Jet Plane and UN Emblem AP10

1968, Apr. 18   Litho.   Perf. 13
C13 AP10 20c multicolored   .35   .35

Wings, Envelopes and UN Emblem AP11

1969, Apr. 21   Litho.   Perf. 13
C14 AP11 10c org ver, org, yel & blk   .25   .25

UN Emblem and Stylized Wing — AP12

Birds in Flight — AP13

Clouds AP14

"UN" and Plane — AP15

1963, June 17   Photo.   Unwmk.

Litho. & Engr.
1972, May 1   Perf. 13x13½
C15 AP12 9c lt blue, dk red & vio blue   .25   .25

Photo.
Perf. 14x13½
C16 AP13 11c blue & multi   .25   .25

Perf. 13½x14
C17 AP14 17c yel, red & org   .25   .25

Perf. 13
C18 AP15 21c silver & multi   .25   .25
        Nos. C15-C18 (4)   1.00 1.00

Globe and Jet — AP16

Pathways Radiating from UN Emblem AP17

Bird in Flight, UN Headquarters AP18

Perf. 13, 12½x13 (18c)
1974, Sept. 16   Litho.
C19 AP16 13c multicolored   .25   .25
C20 AP17 18c gray olive & multi   .25   .25
C21 AP18 26c blue & multi   .35   .35
        Nos. C19-C21 (3)   .85   .85

Winged Airmail Letter — AP19

Symbolic Globe and Plane — AP20

1977, June 27   Photo.   Perf. 14
C22 AP19 25c greenish blue & multi   .35   .35
C23 AP20 31c magenta   .45   .45

OFFICES IN GENEVA, SWITZERLAND

For use only on mail posted at the Palais des Nations (UN European Office), Geneva. Inscribed in French unless otherwise stated.

100 Centimes = 1 Franc

Catalogue values for all unused stamps in this country are for Never Hinged items.

Types of United Nations Issues 1961-69 and

UN European Office, Geneva — G1

Designs: 5c, UN Headquarters, New York, and world map. 10c, UN flag. 20c, Three men united before globe. 50c, Opening words of UN Charter. 60c, UN emblem over globe. 70c, "un" and UN emblem. 75c, "Flight Across Globe." 80c, UN Headquarters and emblem. 90c, Abstract group of flags. 1fr, UN emblem. 2fr, Stylized globe and weather vane. 3fr, Statue by Henrik Starcke. 10fr, "Peace, Justice, Security."

The 20c, 80c and 90c are inscribed in French. The 75c and 10fr carry French inscription at top, English at bottom.

1969-70   Photo.   Unwmk.
Perf. 13 (5c, 70c, 90c); 12½x12 (10c);

1	A88	5c purple & multi	.25	.30
a.		Green omitted	.25	—
2	A52	10c salmon & multi	.25	.30

Perf. 11½ (20c-60c, 3fr)

3	A66	20c black & multi	.25	.30
4	G1	30c dark blue & multi	.25	.30
5	A77	50c ultra & multi	.25	.30
6	A54	60c dark brown, salmon & gold	.30	.35
7	A104	70c red, black & gold	.35	.40

Perf. 11½x12 (75c)

8	AP8	75c carmine rose & multi	.40	.45

Perf. 13½x14 (80c)

9	A78	80c blue green, red & yellow	.40	.45
10	A45	90c blue & multi	.45	.50

Litho. & Embossed
Perf. 14 (1fr)

11	A79	1fr light & dark green	.45	.50

Photo.
Perf. 12x11½ (2fr)

12	A67	2fr blue & multi	.90	1.00
13	A97	3fr olive & multi	1.10	1.25

Engr.
Perf. 12 (10fr)

14	A3	10fr dark blue	4.25	4.50
		Nos. 1-14 (14)	9.85	10.90

Sea Bed Type of UN
Photo. & Engr.
1971, Jan. 25   Perf. 13

15	A114	30c green & multi	.25	.30

Refugee Type of UN
1971, Mar. 12   Litho.   Perf. 13x12½

16	A115	50c deep carmine, deep orange & black	.25	.30

World Food Program Type of UN
1971, Apr. 13   Photo.   Perf. 14

17	A116	50c dark violet & multi	.25	.30

UPU Headquarters Type of UN
1971, May 28   Photo.   Perf. 11½

18	A117	75c green & multi	.35	.40

Eliminate Racial Discrimination Types of UN
1971, Sept. 21   Photo.   Perf. 13½

19	A118	30c blue & multi	.25	.30
20	A119	50c yellow green & multi	.25	.30

Picasso Type of UN
1971, Nov. 19   Photo.   Perf. 11½

21	A122	1.10fr multicolored	.75	.80

Palais des Nations, Geneva G2

1972, Jan. 5   Photo.   Perf. 11½

22	G2	40c olive, blue, salmon & dark green	.25	.30

Nuclear Weapons Type of UN
1972, Feb. 14   Photo.   Perf. 13½x14

23	A124	40c yellow, green, black, rose & gray	.25	.30

World Health Day Type of UN
Litho. & Engr.
1972, Apr. 7   Perf. 13x13½

24	A125	80c black & multi	.45	.50

Human Environment Type of UN
Lithographed & Embossed
1972, June 5   Perf. 12½x14

25	A126	40c olive, lemon, green & blue	.25	.30
26	A126	80c ultra, pink, green & blue	.45	.50

Economic Commission for Europe Type of UN
1972, Sept. 11   Litho.   Perf. 13x13½

27	A127	1.10fr red & multi	1.00	1.10

Art at UN (Sert) Type of UN
1972, Nov. 17   Photo.   Perf. 12x12½

28	A128	40c gold, red & brown	.30	.35
29	A128	80c gold, brown & olive	.60	.65

Disarmament Decade Type of UN
1973, Mar. 9   Litho.   Perf. 13½x13

30	A129	60c violet & multi	.40	.45
31	A129	1.10fr olive & multi	.85	.90

Drug Abuse Type of UN
1973, Apr. 13   Photo.   Perf. 13½

32	A130	60c blue & multi	.45	.50

Volunteers Type of UN
1973, May 25   Photo.   Perf. 14

33	A131	80c gray green & multi	.35	.40

Namibia Type of UN
1973, Oct. 1   Photo.   Perf. 13½

34	A132	60c red & multi	.35	.40

Human Rights Type of UN
1973, Nov. 16   Photo.   Perf. 13½

35	A133	40c ultramarine & multi	.30	.35
36	A133	80c olive & multi	.50	.55

ILO Headquarters Type of UN
1974, Jan. 11   Photo.   Perf. 14

37	A134	60c violet & multi	.45	.50
38	A134	80c brown & multi	.65	.70

Centenary of UPU Type of UN
1974, Mar. 22   Litho.   Perf. 12½

39	A135	30c gold & multi	.25	.30
40	A135	60c gold & multi	.60	.65

Art at UN (Portinari) Type of UN
1974, May 6   Photo.   Perf. 14

41	A136	60c dark red & multi	.40	.45
42	A136	1fr green & multi	.70	.75

World Population Year Type of UN
1974, Oct. 18   Photo.   Perf. 14

43	A140	60c bright green & multi	.50	.55
44	A140	80c brown & multi	.70	.75

Law of the Sea Type of UN
1974, Nov. 22   Photo.   Perf. 14

45	A141	1.30fr blue & multicolored	1.00	1.10

Outer Space Type of UN
1975, Mar. 14   Litho.   Perf. 13

46	A142	60c multicolored	.50	.55
47	A142	90c multicolored	.75	.80

International Women's Year Type of UN
1975, May 9   Litho.   Perf. 15

48	A143	60c multicolored	.40	.45
49	A143	90c multicolored	.70	.75

30th Anniversary Type of UN
1975, June 26   Litho.   Perf. 13

50	A144	60c green & multi	.40	.45
51	A144	90c violet & multi	.70	.75

Souvenir Sheet
Imperf

52		Sheet of 2	1.00	1.10
a.		A144 60c green & multicolored	.30	.35
b.		A144 90c violet & multicolored	.60	.65

Namibia Type of UN
1975, Sept. 22   Photo.   Perf. 13½

53	A145	50c multicolored	.30	.35
54	A145	1.30fr multicolored	.85	.90

Peace-keeping Operations Type of UN
1975, Nov. 21   Engr.   Perf. 12½

55	A146	60c greenish blue	.35	.40
56	A146	70c bright violet	.65	.65

WFUNA Type of UN
1976, Mar. 12   Photo.   Perf. 14

57	A152	90c multicolored	.90	.95

UNCTAD Type of UN
1976, Apr. 23   Photo.   Perf. 11½

58	A153	1.10fr sepia & multi	.90	.95

Habitat Type of UN
1976, May 28   Photo.   Perf. 14

59	A154	40c dull blue & multi	.25	.30
60	A154	1.50fr violet & multi	.75	.80

UN Emblem, Post Horn and Rainbow G3

UN Postal Administration, 25th anniversary.

1976, Oct. 8   Photo.   Perf. 11½

61	G3	80c tan & multicolored	.50	.55
62	A3	1.10fr light green & multi	1.60	1.75

World Food Council Type of UN
1976, Nov. 19   Litho.   Perf. 14½

63	A156	70c multicolored	.50	.55

WIPO Type of UN
1977, Mar. 11   Photo.   Perf. 14

64	A157	80c red & multi	.60	.65

Drop of Water and Globe — G4

UN Water Conference, Mar del Plata, Argentina, Mar. 14-25.

1977, Apr. 22   Photo.   Perf. 13½x13

65	G4	80c ultra & multi	.50	.55
66	G4	1.10fr dark carmine & multi	.80	.85

Hands Protecting UN Emblem — G5

UN Security Council.

1977, May 27   Photo.   Perf. 11

67	G5	80c blue & multi	.50	.55
68	G5	1.10fr emerald & multi	.80	.85

Colors of Five Races Spun into One Firm Rope — G6

Fight against racial discrimination.

1977, Sept. 19   Litho.   Perf. 13½x13

69	G6	40c multicolored	.25	.30
70	G6	1.10fr multicolored	.65	.70

Atomic Energy Turning Partly into Olive Branch — G7

Peaceful uses of atomic energy.

1977, Nov. 18   Photo.   Perf. 14

71	G7	80c dark carmine & multi	.55	.60
72	G7	1.10fr Prussian blue & multi	.75	.80

"Tree" of Doves — G8

1978, Jan. 27   Litho.   Perf. 14½

73	G8	35c multicolored	.25	.30

Globes with Smallpox Distribution G9

Global eradication of smallpox.

1978, Mar. 31   Photo.   Perf. 12x11½

74	G9	80c yellow & multi	.60	.65
75	G9	1.10fr light green & multi	.90	.95

Namibia Type of UN
1978, May 5   Photo.   Perf. 12

76	A166	80c multicolored	.85	.90

Jets and Flight Patterns — G10

International Civil Aviation Organization for "Safety in the Air."

1978, June 12   Photo.   Perf. 14

77	G10	70c multicolored	.40	.45
78	G10	80c multicolored	.70	.75

General Assembly, Flags and Globe — G11

1978, Sept. 15   Photo.   Perf. 13½

79	G11	70c multicolored	.45	.50
80	G11	1.10fr multicolored	.85	.90

Technical Cooperation Type of UN
1978, Nov. 17   **Photo.**   *Perf. 14*
81   A169   80c multicolored   .70   .75

Seismograph
Recording
Earthquake
G12

Office of the UN Disaster Relief Coordinator
(UNDRO).

1979, Mar. 9   **Photo.**   *Perf. 14*
82   G12   80c multicolored   .50   .55
83   G12   1.50fr multicolored   .80   .85

Children and
Rainbow
G13

International Year of the Child.

1979, May 4   **Photo.**   *Perf. 14*
84   G13   80c multicolored   .35   .40
85   G13   1.10fr multicolored   .65   .70

Namibia Type of UN
1979, Oct. 5   **Litho.**   *Perf. 13½*
86   A176   1.10fr multicolored   .60   .65

International Court
of Justice,
Scales — G14

International Court of Justice, The Hague,
Netherlands.

1979, Nov. 9   **Litho.**   *Perf. 13x13½*
87   G14   80c multicolored   .40   .45
88   G14   1.10fr multicolored   .60   .65

New Economic Order Type of UN
1980, Jan. 11   **Litho.**   *Perf. 15x14½*
89   A179   80c multicolored   .85   .90

Women's Year
Emblem
G15

United Nations Decade for Women.

1980, Mar. 7   **Litho.**   *Perf. 14½x15*
90   G15   40c multicolored   .30   .35
91   G15   70c multicolored   .70   .75

Peace-keeping Operations Type of UN
1980, May 16   **Litho.**   *Perf. 14x13*
92   A181   1.10fr blue & green   .85   .90

Dove and
"35" — G16

35th Anniversary of the United Nations.

1980, June 26   **Litho.**   *Perf. 13x13½*
93   G16   40c blue green & black   .35   .35
94   A183   70c multicolored   .65   .70

Souvenir Sheet
Imperf
95   Sheet of 2   1.10   1.20
   a.   G16 40c blue green & black   .30   .35
   b.   A183 70c multicolored   .80   .85

ECOSOC Type of UN and

Family
Climbing Line
Graph — G17

1980, Nov. 21   **Litho.**   *Perf. 13½x13*
96   A186   40c multicolored   .30   .35
97   G17   70c multicolored   .60   .65

Palestinian Rights
1981, Jan. 30   **Photo.**   *Perf. 12x11½*
98   A188   80c multicolored   .55   .60

International Year of the Disabled.
1981, Mar. 6   **Photo.**   *Perf. 14*
99   A190   40c black & blue   .25   .30
100   V4   1.50fr black & red   1.00   1.10

Art Type of UN
1981, Apr. 15   **Photo.**   *Perf. 11½*
Granite Paper
101   A191   80c multicolored   .80   .85

Energy Type of 1981
1981, May 29   **Litho.**   *Perf. 13*
102   A192   1.10fr multicolored   .75   .80

Volunteers Program Type and

Volunteers
Program Type
and Symbols
of Science,
Agriculture
and Industry
G18

1981, Nov. 13   **Litho.**
103   A194   40c multicolored   .45   .50
104   G18   70c multicolored   .90   .95

Fight Against   Flower of
Apartheid — G19   Flags — G20

1982, Jan. 22   *Perf. 11½x12*
105   G19   30c multicolored   .25   .30
106   G20   1fr multicolored   .80   .85

Human Environment Type of UN and:

Human
Environment — G21

10th Anniversary of United Nations Environment Program.

1982, Mar. 19   **Litho.**   *Perf. 13½x13*
107   G21   40c multicolored   .30   .35
108   A199   1.20fr multicolored   1.10   1.40

Outer Space Type of UN and

Satellite
Applications
of Space
Technology
G22

Exploration and Peaceful Uses of Outer
Space.

1982, June 11   **Litho.**   *Perf. 13x13½*
109   A201   80c multicolored   .60   .65
110   G22   1fr multicolored   .80   .85

Conservation & Protection of Nature
1982, Nov. 19   **Photo.**   *Perf. 14*
111   A202   40c Bird   .45   .50
112   A202   1.50fr Reptile   1.10   1.20

World Communications Year
1983, Jan. 28   **Litho.**   *Perf. 13*
113   A204   1.20fr multicolored   1.25   1.40

Safety at Sea Type of UN and

Life Preserver and
Radar — G23

1983, Mar. 18   **Litho.**   *Perf. 14½*
114   A205   40c multicolored   .40   .45
115   G23   80c multicolored   .80   .85

World Food Program
1983, Apr. 22   **Engr.**   *Perf. 13½*
116   A207   1.50fr blue   1.25   1.40

Trade Type of UN and

G24

1983, June 6   **Litho.**   *Perf. 14*
117   A208   80c multicolored   .50   .55
118   G24   1.10fr multicolored   .90   .95

G25

35th Anniv. of the
Universal
Declaration of
Human
Rights — G26

Photo. & Engr.
1983, Dec. 9   *Perf. 13½*
119   G25   40c multicolored   .45   .50
120   G26   1.20fr multicolored   .95   1.00

International Conference on Population Type
1984, Feb. 3   **Litho.**   *Perf. 14*
121   A212   1.20fr multicolored   .90   .95

Fishing
G27

Women
Farm
Workers,
Africa
G28

World Food Day, Oct. 16

1984, Mar. 15   **Litho.**   *Perf. 14½*
122   G27   50c multicolored   .30   .35
123   G28   80c multicolored   .60   .65

Valletta,
Malta — G29

Los Glaciares
Natl. Park,
Argentina
G30

World Heritage

1984, Apr. 18   **Litho.**   *Perf. 14*
124   G29   50c multicolored   .60   .65
125   G30   70c multicolored   .85   .90

G31   G32

Future for Refugees

1984, May 29   **Photo.**   *Perf. 11½*
126   G31   35c multicolored   .30   .35
127   G32   1.50fr multicolored   1.10   1.20

International Youth
Year — G33

1984, Nov. 15   **Litho.**   *Perf. 13½*
128   G33   1.20fr multicolored   1.25   1.40

ILO Type of UN and

Turin
Center — G34

1985, Feb. 1   **Engr.**   *Perf. 13½*
129   A220   80c dull red   .70   .75
130   G34   1.20fr U Thant Pavilion   1.10   1.20

UN University Type
50c,   Pastoral   scene,   advanced
communications.

1985, Mar. 15   **Photo.**   *Perf. 11½*
131   A221   50c multicolored   .60   .65
132   A221   80c like No. 131   1.00   1.10

Postman
G35

NATIONS UNIES **1.20** F.S.

Doves — G36

1985, May 10 Litho. _Perf. 14_
133 G35 20c multicolored .25 .30
134 G36 1.20fr multicolored 1.25 1.40

40th Anniversary Type
Perf. 12 x 11½
1985, June 26 Photo.
135 A224 50c multicolored .60 .65
136 A225 70c multicolored .90 .95

Souvenir Sheet
Imperf
137 Sheet of 2 2.25 2.40
  _a._ A224 50c multicolored .85 .90
  _b._ A225 70c multicolored 1.10 1.20

UNICEF Child Survival Campaign Type
Photo. & Engr.
1985, Nov. 22 _Perf. 13½_
138 A226 50c Three girls .40 .45
139 A226 1.20fr Infant drinking 1.10 1.20

Africa in Crisis Type
1986, Jan. 31 Photo. _Perf. 11½x12_
140 A227 1.40fr Mother, hungry
    children 1.25 1.40

UN Development Program Type
Forestry.
1986, Mar. 14 Photo. _Perf. 13½_
141 A228 35c Erosion control 1.60 1.75
142 A228 35c Logging 1.60 1.75
143 A228 35c Lumber transport 1.60 1.75
144 A228 35c Nursery 1.60 1.75
  _a._ Block of 4, #141-144 6.50 7.50

Doves and
Sun — G37

NATIONS UNIES **0,05** F.s

1986, Mar. 14 Litho. _Perf. 15x14½_
145 G37 5c multicolored .25 .30

Stamp Collecting Type
Designs: 50c, UN Human Rights stamp. 80c, UN stamps.
1986, May 22 Engr. _Perf. 12½_
146 A229 50c dark grn & hen brn .60 .65
147 A229 80c dark grn & yel org .90 .95

Flags and
Globe as
Dove — G38

nations unies **0,45** Fs

Peace in
French — G39

NATIONS UNIES **Paix** F.S.1,40

International Peace Year.
Photo. & Embossed
1986, June 20 _Perf. 13½_
148 G38 45c multicolored .60 .65
149 G39 1.40fr multicolored 1.25 1.40

WFUNA Anniversary Type
Souvenir Sheet
Designs: 35c, Abstract by Benigno Gomez, Honduras. 45c, Abstract by Alexander Calder (1898-1976), US. 50c, Abstract by Joan Miro (b. 1893), Spain. 70c, Sextet with Dove, by Ole Hamann, Denmark.

1986, Nov. 14 Litho. _Perf. 13x13½_
150 Sheet of 4 3.75 4.00
  _a._ A232 35c multicolored .50 .55
  _b._ A232 45c multicolored .70 .75
  _c._ A232 50c multicolored .90 1.00
  _d._ A232 70c multicolored 1.25 1.40
No. 150 has inscribed margin picturing UN and WFUNA emblems.

Trygve Lie Type
Photo. & Engr.
1987, Jan. 30 _Perf. 13½_
151 A233 1.40fr multicolored 1.10 1.20

NATIONS UNIES **F.s. 0,90**

Sheaf of Colored
Bands, by
Georges
Mathieu — G40

1,40 nations unies

Armillary Sphere,
Palais des
Nations — G41

Photo., Photo. & Engr. (#153)
1987, Jan. 30 _Perf. 11½x12, 13½_
152 G40 90c multicolored .65 .70
153 G41 1.40fr multicolored 1.25 1.40

Shelter for the Homeless Type
Designs: 50c, Cement-making and brick-making. 90c, Interior construction and decorating.
Perf. 13½x12½
1987, Mar. 13 Litho.
154 A234 50c multicolored .50 .55
155 A234 90c multicolored 1.00 1.10

Fight Drug Abuse Type
Designs: 80c, Mother and child. 1.20fr, Workers in rice paddy.
1987, June 12 Litho. _Perf. 14½x15_
156 A235 80c multicolored .50 .55
157 A235 1.20fr multicolored 1.00 1.10

UN Day Type
Designs: Multinational people in various occupations.
1987, Oct. 23 Litho. _Perf. 14½x15_
158 A236 35c multicolored .55 .60
159 A236 50c multicolored .80 .85

Immunize Every Child Type
Designs: 90c, Whooping cough. 1.70fr, Tuberculosis.
1987, Nov. 20 Litho. _Perf. 15x14½_
160 A237 90c multicolored 1.50 1.65
161 A237 1.70fr multicolored 2.75 3.00

IFAD Type
Designs: 35c, Flocks, dairy products. 1.40fr, Fruit.
1988, Jan. 29 Litho. _Perf. 13½_
162 A238 35c multicolored .35 .40
163 A238 1.40fr multicolored 1.40 1.50

NATIONS UNIES **F.s.0,50**

For A Better
World — G42

1988, Jan. 29 Photo. _Perf. 14_
164 G42 50c multicolored .80 .85

Survival of the Forests Type
Pine forest: 50c, Treetops, mountains. 1.10fr, Lake, tree trunks. Printed se-tenant in a continuous design.
1988, Mar. 18 Litho. _Perf. 14x15_
165 A240 50c multicolored 1.25 1.40
166 A240 1.10fr multicolored 3.50 3.75
  _a._ Pair, #165-166 5.50 6.00

Intl. Volunteer Day Type
Designs: 80c, Agriculture, vert. 90c, Veterinary medicine.
Perf. 13x14, 14x13
1988, May 6 Litho.
167 A241 80c multicolored .80 .85
168 A241 90c multicolored 1.00 1.10

Health in Sports Type
Paintings by LeRoy Neiman, American sports artist: 50c, Soccer, vert. 1.40fr, Swimming.
Perf. 13½x13, 13x13½
1988, June 17 Litho.
169 A242 50c multicolored .40 .45
170 A242 1.40fr multicolored 1.40 1.50

Universal Declaration of Human Rights 40th Anniv. Type
Photo. & Engr.
1988, Dec. 9 _Perf. 12_
171 A243 90c multicolored .70 .75
Souvenir Sheet
172 A243 2fr multicolored 2.75 3.00

World Bank Type
80c, Telecommunications. 1.40fr, Industry.
1989, Jan. 27 Litho. _Perf. 13x14_
173 A244 80c multicolored 1.00 1.10
174 A244 1.40fr multicolored 2.00 2.20

Peace-Keeping Force Type
1989, Mar. 17 _Perf. 14x13½_
175 A245 90c multicolored 1.25 1.40

World Weather Watch Type
Satellite photographs: 90c, Europe under the influence of Arctic air. 1.10fr, Surface temperatures of sea, ice and land surrounding the Kattegat between Denmark and Sweden.
1989, Apr. 21 Litho. _Perf. 13x14_
176 A247 90c multicolored 1.25 1.40
177 A247 1.10fr multicolored 2.00 2.20

Office des Nations Unies à Vienne
10° ANNIVERSAIRE
NATIONS UNIES **F.s.0,50**

G43

Office des
Nations Unies à Vienne
10°anniversaire
Nations Unies **2,00** F.s.

G44

Photo., Photo. & Engr. (2fr)
1989, Aug. 23 _Perf. 14_
178 G43 50c multicolored 1.00 1.10
179 G44 2fr multicolored 3.50 3.75
Offices in Vienna, 10th anniv.

Human Rights Type of 1989
Artwork: 35c, Young Mother Sewing, by Mary Cassatt. 80c, The Unknown Slave, sculpture by Albert Mangones.
1989, Nov. 17 Litho. _Perf. 13½_
180 A250 35c multicolored .35 .40
181 A250 80c multicolored 1.00 1.10
Printed in panes of 12+12 se-tenant labels containing Articles 3 (35c) or 4 (80c) inscribed in English, French or German.
See Nos. 193-194, 209-210,34-235.

Intl. Trade Center Type
1990, Feb. 2 Litho. _Perf. 14½x15_
182 A251 1.50fr multicolored 2.25 2.50

G45

1990, Feb. 2 Photo. _Perf. 14x13½_
183 G45 5fr multicolored 4.75 5.25

NATIONS UNIES **SIDA** F.s. 0,50
LUTTE MONDIALE CONTRE LE SIDA

G46

LUTTE MONDIALE CONTRE LE SIDA
NATIONS UNIES **F.S. 0,80**

Fight
AIDS
Worldwide
— G46a

Fight AIDS Type
Designs: 50c, "SIDA." 80c, Proportional drawing of man like the illustration by Leonardo da Vinci.
Perf. 13½x12½
1990, Mar. 16 Litho.
184 G46 50c multicolored 1.00 1.10
185 G46a 80c multicolored 1.75 1.90

Medicinal Plants Type
1990, May 4 Photo. _Perf. 11½_
Granite Paper
186 A253 90c Plumeria rubra 1.00 1.10
187 A253 1.40fr Cinchona of-
    ficinalis 2.00 2.20

UN 45th Anniv. Type
"45," emblem and: 90c, Symbols of clean environment, transportation and industry. 1.10fr, Dove in silhouette.
1990, June 26 Litho. _Perf. 14½x13_
188 A254 90c multicolored 1.10 1.20
189 A254 1.10fr multicolored 2.25 2.50
Souvenir Sheet
190 Sheet of 2, #188-189 6.00 6.50

Crime Prevention Type
1990, Sept. 13 Photo. _Perf. 14_
191 A255 50c Official corruption 1.25 1.40
192 A255 2fr Environmental
    crime 3.00 3.25

Human Rights Type of 1989
Artwork: 35c, The Prison Courtyard by Vincent Van Gogh. 90c, Katho's Son Redeems the Evil Doer From Execution by Albrecht Durer.
1990, Nov. 16 Litho. _Perf. 13½_
193 A250 35c multicolored .45 .50
194 A250 90c black & brown 1.25 1.40

Economic Commission for Europe Type
1991, Mar. 15 Litho. _Perf. 14_
195 A256 90c Owl, gull 1.25 1.40
196 A256 90c Bittern, otter 1.25 1.40
197 A256 90c Swan, lizard 1.25 1.40
198 A256 90c Great crested
    grebe 1.25 1.40
  _a._ Block of 4, #195-198 5.00 5.00

Namibian Independence Type
1991, May 10 Litho. _Perf. 14_
199 A257 70c Mountains 1.00 1.10
200 A257 90c Baobab tree 2.00 2.20

Nations Unies **0,80** Fs

Ballots Filling
Ballot
Box — G47

NATIONS UNIES **F.S.1,50**

UN
Emblem — G48

1991, May 10 Litho. _Perf. 15x14½_
201 G47 80c multicolored .75 .80
202 G48 1.50fr multicolored 2.00 2.20

DROITS DE L'ENFANT
NATIONS UNIES **F.S.0,80**

G49

Rights of
the Child
G50

1991, June 14   Litho.   *Perf. 14½*
203   G49   80c   Hands holding in-
            fant   1.00   1.10
204   G50   1.10fr   Children, flowers   2.00   2.20

G51

Banning of
Chemical
Weapons
G52

1991, Sept. 11   Litho.   *Perf. 13½*
205   G51   80c   multicolored   2.00   2.20
206   G52   1.40fr   multicolored   3.00   3.25

UN Postal Administration, 40th Anniv. Type

1991, Oct. 24   *Perf. 14x15*
207   A263   50c   UN NY No. 7   .80   .85
208   A263   1.60fr   UN NY No. 10   2.20   2.40

Human Rights Type of 1989

Artwork: 50c, Early Morning in Rio...1925,
by Paul Klee. 90c, Marriage of Giovanni (?)
Arnolfini and Giovanna Cenami (?), by Jan
Van Eyck.

1991, Nov. 20   Litho.   *Perf. 13½*
209   A250   50c   multicolored   .75   .80
210   A250   90c   multicolored   1.25   1.40

Panes of 12+12 se-tenant labels containing
Articles 15 (50c) or 16 (90c) inscribed in
French, German or English.

World Heritage Type of 1984

Designs: 50c, Sagarmatha Natl. Park,
Nepal. 1.10fr, Stonehenge, United Kingdom.

1992, Jan. 24   Litho.   *Perf. 13*
           Size: 35x28mm
211   G29   50c   multicolored   .80   .85
212   G29   1.10fr   multicolored   1.90   2.10

G53

1992, Jan. 24   Litho.   *Perf. 15x14½*
213   G53   3fr   multicolored   3.00   3.25

Clean Oceans Type

1992, Mar. 13   Litho.   *Perf. 14*
214   A264   80c   Ocean surface,
            diff.   .90   .95
215   A264   80c   Ocean bottom, diff.   .90   .95
   a.   Pair, #214-215   1.80   2.10

Earth Summit Type

Designs: No. 216, Rainbow. No. 217, Two
clouds shaped as faces. No. 218, Two sailboats. No. 219, Woman with parasol, boat,
flowers.

1992, May 22   Photo.   *Perf. 11½*
216   A265   75c   multicolored   1.50   1.60
217   A265   75c   multicolored   1.50   1.60
218   A265   75c   multicolored   1.50   1.60
219   A265   75c   multicolored   1.50   1.60
   a.   Block of 4, #216-219   6.00   6.50

Mission to Planet Earth Type

Designs: No. 220, Space station. No. 221,
Probes near Jupiter.

1992, Sept. 4   Photo.   *Rouletted 8*
           Granite Paper
220   A266   1.10fr   multicolored   2.00   2.20
221   A266   1.10fr   multicolored   2.00   2.20
   a.   Pair, #220-221   4.00   4.50

Science and Technology Type of 1992

Designs: 90c, Doctor, nurse. 1.60fr, Graduate seated before computer.

1992, Oct. 2   Litho.   *Perf. 14*
222   A267   90c   multicolored   1.25   1.40
223   A267   1.60fr   multicolored   3.00   3.25

Human Rights Type of 1989

Artwork: 50c, The Oath of the Tennis Court,
by Jacques Louis David. 90c, Rocking Chair I,
by Henry Moore.

1992, Nov. 20   Litho.   *Perf. 13½*
224   A250   50c   multicolored   .75   .80
225   A250   90c   multicolored   1.25   1.40

Panes of 12+12 se-tenant labels containing
Articles 21 (50c) and 22 (90c) inscribed in
French, German or English.

Aging With Dignity Type

Designs: 50c, Older man coaching soccer.
1.60fr, Older man working at computer
terminal.

1993, Feb. 5   Litho.   *Perf. 13*
226   A270   50c   multicolored   .50   .55
227   A270   1.60fr   multicolored   1.50   1.65

Endangered Species Type

Designs: No. 228, Pongidae (gorilla). No.
229, Falco peregrinus (peregrine falcon). No.
230, Trichechus inunguis (Amazonian manatee). No. 231, Panthera uncia (snow leopard).

1993, Mar. 2   Litho.   *Perf. 13x12½*
228   A271   80c   multicolored   1.10   1.20
229   A271   80c   multicolored   1.10   1.20
230   A271   80c   multicolored   1.10   1.20
231   A271   80c   multicolored   1.10   1.20
   a.   Block of 4, #228-231   4.50   4.80

Healthy Environment Type

1993, May 7   Litho.   *Perf. 15x14½*
232   A272   60c   Neighborhood   .75   .80
233   A272   1fr   Urban skyscrapers   1.75   1.90

Human Rights Type of 1989

Artwork: 50c, Three Musicians, by Pablo
Picasso. 90c, Voice of Space, by Rene
Magritte.

1993, June 11   Litho.   *Perf. 13½*
234   A250   50c   multicolored   .75   .80
235   A250   90c   multicolored   1.75   1.90

Printed in panes of 12 + 12 se-tenant labels
containing Article 27 (50c) and 28 (90c)
inscribed in French, German or English.

Intl. Peace Day Type

Denomination at: No. 236, UL. No. 237, UR.
No. 238, LL. No. 239, LR.

          Rouletted 12½
1993, Sept. 21   Litho. & Engr.
236   A274   60c   purple & multi   2.00   2.20
237   A274   60c   purple & multi   2.00   2.20
238   A274   60c   purple & multi   2.00   2.20
239   A274   60c   purple & multi   2.00   2.20
   a.   Block of 4, #236-239   8.00   9.00

Environment-Climate Type

1993, Oct. 29   Litho.   *Perf. 14½*
240   A275   1.10fr   Polar bears   2.00   2.20
241   A275   1.10fr   Whale sound-
            ing   2.00   2.20
242   A275   1.10fr   Elephant seal   2.00   2.20
243   A275   1.10fr   Penguins   2.00   2.20
   a.   Strip of 4, #240-243   8.00   9.00

Intl. Year of the Family Type of 1993

Designs: 80c, Parents teaching child to
walk. 1fr, Two women and child picking plants.

1994, Feb. 4   Litho.   *Perf. 13.1*
244   A276   80c   rose violet &
            multi   1.00   1.10
245   A276   1fr   brown & multi   1.40   1.50

Endangered Species Type of 1993

Designs: No. 246, Mexican prairie dog. No.
247, Jabiru. No. 248, Blue whale. No. 249,
Golden lion tamarin.

1994, Mar. 18   Litho.   *Perf. 12.7*
246   A271   80c   multicolored   1.10   1.20
247   A271   80c   multicolored   1.10   1.20
248   A271   80c   multicolored   1.10   1.20
249   A271   80c   multicolored   1.10   1.20
   a.   Block of 4, #246-249   4.50   5.00

Protection for Refugees Type of 1994

Design: 1.20fr, Hand lifting figure over
chasm.

1994, Apr. 29   Litho.   *Perf. 14.3x14.8*
250   A277   1.20fr   multicolored   2.25   2.40

Intl. Decade for Natural Disaster Reduction Type of 1994

Earth seen from space, outline map of: No.
251, North America. No. 252, Eurasia. No.
253, South America. No. 254, Australia and
South Pacific region.

1994, May 27   Litho.   *Perf. 13.9x14.2*
251   A281   60c   multicolored   1.75   1.90
252   A281   60c   multicolored   1.75   1.90
253   A281   60c   multicolored   1.75   1.90
254   A281   60c   multicolored   1.75   1.90
   a.   Block of 4, #251-254   7.00   7.75

Palais des
Nations,
Geneva
G54

Creation of
the World, by
Oili
Maki — G55

1994, Sept. 1   Litho.   *Perf. 14.3x14.6*
255   G54   60c   multicolored   .75   .80
256   G55   80c   multicolored   1.00   1.10
257   G54   1.80fr   multi, diff.   2.25   2.50
       Nos. 255-257 (3)   4.00   4.40

Population and Development Type of 1994

Designs: 60c, People shopping at open-air
market. 80c, People on vacation crossing
bridge.

1994, Sept. 1   Litho.   *Perf. 13.2x13.6*
258   A282   60c   multicolored   1.00   1.10
259   A282   80c   multicolored   1.25   1.40

UNCTAD Type of 1994

1994, Oct. 28
260   A283   80c   multi, diff.   1.10   1.20
261   A283   1fr   multi, diff.   1.50   1.65
   a.   Grayish green omitted   —

UN 50th Anniv. Type of 1995
Litho. & Engr.

1995, Jan. 1   *Perf. 13.4*
262   A284   80c   multicolored   1.10   1.20

Social Summit Type of 1995
Photo. & Engr.

1995, Feb. 3   *Perf. 13.6x13.9*
263   A285   1fr   multi, diff.   1.25   1.40

Endangered Species Type of 1993

Designs: No. 264, Crowned lemur, Lemur
coronatus. No. 265, Giant Scops owl, Otus
gurneyi. No. 266, Zetek's frog, Atelopus varius
zeteki. No. 267, Wood bison, Bison bison
athabascae.

1995, Mar. 24   Litho.   *Perf. 13x12½*
264   A271   80c   multicolored   1.10   1.20
265   A271   80c   multicolored   1.10   1.20
266   A271   80c   multicolored   1.10   1.20
267   A271   80c   multicolored   1.10   1.20
   a.   Block of 4, 264-267   4.50   5.00

Intl. Youth Year Type of 1995

Designs: 80c, Farmer on tractor, fields at
harvest time. 1fr, Couple standing by fields at
night.

1995, May 26   Litho.   *Perf. 14.4x14.7*
268   A286   80c   multicolored   1.25   1.40
269   A286   1fr   multicolored   2.00   2.20

UN, 50th Anniv. Type of 1995

Designs: 60c, Like No. 663. 1.80fr, Like No.
664.

        Perf. 13.3x13.6
1995, June 26   Engr.
270   A287   60c   maroon   .80   .85
271   A287   1.80fr   green   3.00   3.25
       Souvenir Sheet
       Litho. & Engr.
          Imperf
272   Sheet of 2, #270-271   3.75   4.00
   a.   A287 60c maroon   .75   .80
   b.   A287 1.80fr green   3.00   3.20

Conference on Women Type of 1995

Designs: 60c, Black woman, cranes flying
above. 1fr, Women, dove.

1995, Sept. 5   Photo.   *Perf. 12*
273   A288   60c   multicolored   1.00   1.10
          Size: 28x50mm
274   A288   1fr   multicolored   2.00   2.20

UN People, 50th Anniv. Type of 1995

1995, Oct. 24   Litho.   *Perf. 14*
275   Sheet of 12   14.00   15.00
   a.-l.   A290 30c each   1.20   1.20
276   Souvenir booklet   15.00
   a.   A290 30c Booklet pane of 3,
       vert. strip of 3 from UL of
       sheet   3.75   3.75
   b.   A290 30c Booklet pane of 3,
       vert. strip of 3 from UR of
       sheet   3.75   3.75
   c.   A290 30c Booklet pane of 3,
       vert. strip of 3 from LL of
       sheet   3.75   3.75
   d.   A290 30c Booklet pane of 3,
       vert. strip of 3 from LR of
       sheet   3.75   3.75

WFUNA, 50th Anniv. Type

Design: 80c, Fishing boat, fish in net.

1996, Feb. 2   Litho.   *Perf. 13x13½*
277   A291   80c   multicolored   1.25   1.40

The Galloping Horse Treading on a
Flying Swallow, Chinese Bronzework,
Eastern Han Dynasty (25-220
A.D.) — G56

Palais des
Nations,
Geneva
G57

1996, Feb. 2   Litho.   *Perf. 14½x15*
278   A292   40c   multicolored   .50   .55
279   G57   70c   multicolored   .90   .95

Endangered Species Type of 1993

Designs: No. 280, Paphiopedilum delenatii.
No. 281, Pachypodium baronii. No. 282,
Sternbergia lutea. No. 283, Darlingtonia
californica.

1996, Mar. 14   Litho.   *Perf. 12½*
280   A271   80c   multicolored   1.00   1.10
281   A271   80c   multicolored   1.00   1.10
282   A271   80c   multicolored   1.00   1.10
283   A271   80c   multicolored   1.00   1.10
   a.   Block of 4, #280-283   4.00   4.50

City Summit Type of 1996

Designs: No. 284, Asian family. No. 285,
Oriental garden. No. 286, Fruit, vegetable vendor, mosque. No. 287, Boys playing ball. No.
288, Couple reading newspaper.

1996, June 3   Litho.   *Perf. 14x13½*
284   A293   70c   multicolored   1.50   1.65
285   A293   70c   multicolored   1.50   1.65
286   A293   70c   multicolored   1.50   1.65
287   A293   70c   multicolored   1.50   1.65
288   A293   70c   multicolored   1.50   1.65
   a.   Strip of 5, #284-288   7.50   8.25

Sport and the Environment Type

Designs: 70c, Cycling, vert. 1.10fr, Sprinters.

Perf. 14x14½, 14½x14

1996, July 19			**Litho.**
289	A294	70c multicolored	1.00 1.10
290	A294	1.10fr multicolored	1.50 1.65

Souvenir Sheet

291	A294	Sheet of 2, #289-290	3.00 3.25

Plea for Peace Type

Designs: 90c, Tree filled with birds, vert. 1.10fr, Bouquet of flowers in rocket tail vase, vert.

1996, Sept. 17 Litho. Perf. 15x14½

292	A295	90c multicolored	1.25 1.40
293	A295	1.10fr multicolored	1.50 1.65

UNICEF Type

Fairy Tales: 70c, The Sun and the Moon, South America. 1.80fr, Ananse, Africa.

1996, Nov. 20 Litho. Perf. 14½x15

294	A296	70c multicolored	.80 .85
295	A296	1.80fr multicolored	2.00 2.20

UN Flag — G58

Palais des Nations Under Construction, by Massimo Campigli G59

1997, Feb. 12 Litho. Perf. 14½

296	G58	10c multicolored	.25 .30
297	G59	1.10fr multicolored	1.25 1.40

Endangered Species Type of 1993

Designs: No. 298, Ursus maritimus (polar bear). No. 299, Goura cristata (blue-crowned pigeon). No. 300, Amblyrhynchus cristatus (marine iguana). No. 301, Lama guanicoe (guanaco).

1997, Mar. 13 Litho. Perf. 12½

298	A271	80c multicolored	.90 .95
299	A271	80c multicolored	.90 .95
300	A271	80c multicolored	.90 .95
301	A271	80c multicolored	.90 .95
a.		Block of 4, #298-301	3.60 3.90

Earth Summit Anniv. Type

Designs: No. 302, Person flying over mountain. No. 303, Mountain, person's face. No. 304, Person standing on mountain, sailboats. No. 305, Person, mountain, trees. 1.10fr, Combined design similar to Nos. 302-305.

1997, May 30 Photo. Perf. 11½
Granite Paper

302	A299	45c multicolored	1.00 1.10
303	A299	45c multicolored	1.00 1.10
304	A299	45c multicolored	1.00 1.10
305	A299	45c multicolored	1.00 1.10
a.		Block of 4, #302-305	4.00 4.50

Souvenir Sheet

306	A299	1.10fr multicolored	3.50 3.50

Transportation Type of 1997

Air transportation: No. 307, Zeppelin, Fokker tri-motor. No. 308, Boeing 314 Clipper, Lockheed Constellation. No. 309, DeHavilland Comet. No. 310, Boeing 747, Illyushin jet. No. 311, Concorde.

1997, Aug. 29 Litho. Perf. 14x14½

307	A300	70c multicolored	1.00 1.10
308	A300	70c multicolored	1.00 1.10
309	A300	70c multicolored	1.00 1.10
310	A300	70c multicolored	1.00 1.10
311	A300	70c multicolored	1.00 1.10
a.		Strip of 5, #307-311	5.00 5.50

Philately Type

Designs: 70c, No. 146. 1.10fr, No. 147.

1997, Oct. 14 Litho. Perf. 13½x14

312	A301	70c multicolored	.80 .85
313	A301	1.10fr multicolored	1.50 1.65

World Heritage Convention Type

Terracotta warriors of Xian: 45c, Single warrior. 70c, Massed warriors. No. 316a, like NY No. 716. No. 316b, like NY No. 717. No. 316c, like Geneva No. 314. No. 316d, like Geneva No. 315. No. 316e, like Vienna No. 230. No. 316f, like Vienna No. 231.

1997, Nov. 19 Litho. Perf. 13½

314	A302	45c multicolored	1.25 1.40
315	A302	70c multicolored	2.25 2.50
316		Souvenir booklet	12.00
a.-f.	A302 10c any single		.45 .50
g.	Booklet pane of 4 #316a		2.00 2.00
h.	Booklet pane of 4 #316b		2.00 2.00
i.	Booklet pane of 4 #316c		2.00 2.00
j.	Booklet pane of 4 #316d		2.00 2.00
k.	Booklet pane of 4 #316e		2.00 2.00
l.	Booklet pane of 4 #316f		2.00 2.00

Palais des Nations, Geneva G60

1998, Feb. 13 Litho. Perf. 14½x15

317	G60	2fr multicolored	1.50 1.65

Endangered Species Type of 1993

Designs: No. 318, Macaca thibetana (short-tailed Tibetan macaque). No. 319, Phoenicopterus ruber (Caribbean flamingo). No. 320, Ornithoptera alexandrae (Queen Alexandra's birdwing). No. 321, Dama mesopotamica (Persian fallow deer).

1998, Mar. 13 Litho. Perf. 12½

318	A271	80c multicolored	1.00 1.10
319	A271	80c multicolored	1.00 1.10
320	A271	80c multicolored	1.00 1.10
321	A271	80c multicolored	1.00 1.10
a.		Block of 4, #318-321	4.00 4.50

Intl. Year of the Ocean — G61

1998, May 20 Litho. Perf. 13x13½

322	G61	Pane of 12	11.00 12.00
a.-l.	45c any single		.90 1.00

Rain Forests Type

1998, June 19 Litho. Perf. 13x13½

323	A307	70c Orangutans	.90 1.00

Souvenir Sheet

324	A307	3fr like #323	4.00 7.50

Peacekeeping Type

Designs: 70c, Soldier with two children. 90c, Two soldiers, children.

1998, Sept. 15 Photo. Perf. 12

325	A308	70c multicolored	.85 .90
326	A308	90c multicolored	1.40 1.50

Declaration of Human Rights Type of 1998

Designs: 90c, Stylized birds. 1.80fr, Stylized birds flying from hand.

Litho. & Photo.

1998, Oct. 27 Perf. 13

327	A309	90c multicolored	.95 1.05
328	A309	1.80fr multicolored	2.00 2.20

Schönbrunn Palace Type

Designs: 70c, No. 331b, Great Palm House. 1.10fr, No. 331d, Blue porcelain vase, vert. No. 331a, Palace. No. 331c, The Gloriette (archway). No. 331e, Wall painting on fabric (detail), by Johann Wenzl Bergl, vert. No. 331f, Porcelain stove, vert.

1998, Dec. 4 Litho. Perf. 14

329	A310	70c multicolored	.90 1.00
330	A310	1.10fr multicolored	1.20 1.30

Souvenir Booklet

331		Booklet	21.50
a.-c.	A310 10c any single		.55 .55
d.-f.	A310 30c any single		1.65 1.65
g.	Booklet pane of 4 #331a		2.20 2.20
h.	Booklet pane of 3 #331d		5.00 5.00
i.	Booklet pane of 3 #331e		5.00 5.00
k.	Booklet pane of 4 #331b		2.20 2.20
l.	Booklet pane of 4 #331c		2.20 2.20

Palais Wilson, Geneva G62

1999, Feb. 5 Photo. Perf. 11½
Granite Paper

332	G62	1.70fr brown red	1.75 1.90

World Heritage, Australia Type

Designs: 90c, No. 335e, Kakadu Natl. Park. 1.10fr, No. 335c, Great Barrier Reef. No. 335a, Tasmanian Wilderness. No. 335b, Wet tropics of Queensland. No. 335d, Uluru-Kata Tjuta Natl. Park. No. 335f, Willandra Lakes region.

1999, Mar. 19 Litho. Perf. 13

333	A313	90c multicolored	1.25 1.40
334	A313	1.10fr multicolored	1.50 1.65

Souvenir Booklet

335		Booklet	16.50
a.-c.	A313 10c any single		.45 .50
d.-f.	A313 20c any single		.90 1.00
g.	Booklet pane of 4, #335a		1.80 2.00
h.	Booklet pane of 4, #335d		3.60 4.00
i.	Booklet pane of 4, #335b		1.80 2.00
j.	Booklet pane of 4, #335e		3.60 4.00
k.	Booklet pane of 4, #335c		1.80 2.00
l.	Booklet pane of 4, #335f		3.60 4.00

Endangered Species Type of 1993

Designs: No. 336, Equus hemionus (Asiatic wild ass). No. 337, Anodorhynchus hyacinthinus (hyacinth macaw). No. 338, Epicrates subflavus (Jamaican boa). No. 339, Dendrolagus bennettianus (Bennetts' tree kangaroo).

1999, Apr. 22 Litho. Perf. 12½

336	A271	90c multicolored	1.00 1.10
337	A271	90c multicolored	1.00 1.10
338	A271	90c multicolored	1.00 1.10
339	A271	90c multicolored	1.00 1.10
a.		Block of 4, #336-339	4.00 4.50

UNISPACE III Type

Designs: No. 340, Farm, satellite dish. No. 341, City, satellite in orbit. No. 342, Composite of Nos. 340-341.

1999, July 7 Photo. Rouletted 8

340	A314	45c multicolored	.90 1.00
341	A314	45c multicolored	.90 1.00
a.		Pair, #340-341	2.00 2.20

Souvenir Sheet
Perf. 14½

342	A314	2fr multicolored	4.50 5.00
a.		Ovptd. in sheet margin	9.50 10.50

UPU Type

Various people, early 20th century methods of mail transportation, denomination at: No. 343, UL. No. 344, UR. No. 345, LL. No. 346, LR.

1999, Aug. 23 Photo. Perf. 11¾

343	A315	70c multicolored	.90 1.00
344	A315	70c multicolored	.90 1.00
345	A315	70c multicolored	.90 1.00
346	A315	70c multicolored	.90 1.00
a.		Block of 4, #343-346	3.60 4.00

In Memoriam Type

Designs: 1.10fr, 2fr, Armillary sphere, Palais de Nations. Size of 2fr stamp: 34x63mm.

1999, Sept. 21 Litho. Perf. 14½x14

347	A316	1.10fr multicolored	1.25 1.40

Souvenir Sheet
Perf. 14

348	A316	2fr multicolored	3.00 3.25

Education Type
Perf. 13½x13¾

1999, Nov. 18			**Litho.**
349	A317	90c Rainbow over globe	.75 .80
350	A317	1.80fr Fish, tree, globe, book	1.75 1.90

Intl. Year Of Thanksgiving Type

2000, Jan 1 Litho. Perf. 13¼x13½

351	A318	90c multicolored	1.00 1.10

On No. 351 portions of the design were applied by a thermographic process producing a shiny, raised effect.

Endangered Species Type of 1993

Designs: No. 352, Hippopotamus amphibius (hippopotamus). No. 353, Coscoroba coscoroba (Coscoroba swan). No. 354, Varanus prasinus (emerald monitor). No. 355, Enhydra lutris (sea otter).

2000, Apr. 6 Litho. Perf. 12¾x12½

352	A271	90c multicolored	1.25 1.40
353	A271	90c multicolored	1.25 1.40
354	A271	90c multicolored	1.25 1.40
355	A271	90c multicolored	1.25 1.40
a.		Block of 4, #352-355	5.00 5.75

Our World 2000 Type

Winning artwork in Millennium painting competition: 90c, The Embrace, by Rita Adaimy, Lebanon. 1.10fr, Living Single, by Richard Kimanthi, Kenya, vert.

Perf. 13x13½, 13½x13

2000, May 30			**Litho.**
356	A319	90c multicolored	1.00 1.10
357	A319	1.10fr multicolored	1.25 1.40

55th Anniversary Type

Designs: 90c, Trygve Lie, Harry S Truman, workers at cornerstone dedication ceremony, 1949. 1.40fr, Window cleaner on Secretariat Building, General Assembly Hall under construction, 1951.

2000, July 7 Litho. Perf. 13¼x13

358	A320	90c multicolored	1.00 1.10
359	A320	1.40fr multicolored	1.50 1.65

Souvenir Sheet

360	A320	Sheet of 2, #358-359	3.50 3.75

The UN in the 21st Century — G63

No. 361: a, Two people, terraced rice paddy. b, Man carrying bricks on head. c, UN Peacekeeper with binoculars. d, Dam, doves. e, Men with shovels. f, People working on irrigation system.

2000, Sept. 15 Litho. Perf. 14

361	G63	Pane of 6	9.00 10.00
a.-f.	50c any single		1.50 1.65

World Heritage, Spain Type

Designs: Nos. 362, 364b, Walled Town of Cuenca. Nos. 363, 364e, Toledo. No. 364a, Alhambra, Generalife and Albayzin, Granada. No. 364c, Aqueduct of Segovia. No. 364d, Amphitheater of Mérida. No. 364f, Güell Park, Barcelona.

2000, Oct. 6 Litho. Perf. 14¾x14½

362	A323	1fr multicolored	1.40 1.50
363	A323	1.20fr multicolored	1.60 1.75

Souvenir Booklet

364		Booklet	11.00
a.-c.	A323 10c any single		.30 .35
d.-f.	A323 20c any single		.60 .65
g.	Booklet pane of 4, #364a		1.20 1.40
h.	Booklet pane of 4, #364d		2.40 2.60
i.	Booklet pane of 4, #364b		1.20 1.40
j.	Booklet pane of 4, #364e		2.40 2.60
k.	Booklet pane of 4, #364c		1.20 1.40
l.	Booklet pane of 4, #364f		2.40 2.60

Respect for Refugees Type

Designs: 80c, 1.80fr, Refugee with cane, four other refugees.

2000, Nov. 9   Litho.   Perf. 13¼x12¾
365 A324 80c multicolored   1.25 1.40

Souvenir Sheet
366 A324 1.80fr multicolored   2.50 2.75

Endangered Species Type of 1993

Designs: No. 367, Felis lynx canadensis (North American lynx). No. 368, Pavo muticus (green peafowl). No. 369, Geochelone elephantopus (Galapagos giant tortoise). No. 370, Lepilemur spp. (sportive lemur).

2001, Feb. 1   Litho.   Perf. 12¾x12½
367 A271 90c multicolored   1.25 1.40
368 A271 90c multicolored   1.25 1.40
369 A271 90c multicolored   1.25 1.40
370 A271 90c multicolored   1.25 1.40
  a.   Block of 4, #367-370   5.00 5.75

Intl. Volunteers Year — G64

Paintings by: 90c, Ernest Pignon-Ernest, France. 1.30fr, Paul Siché, France.

2001, Mar. 29   Litho.   Perf. 13¼
371 G64 90c multicolored   1.10 1.20
372 G64 1.30fr multicolored   1.60 1.75

World Heritage, Japan Type

Designs: 1.10fr, No. 375b, Nara. 1.30fr, No. 375e, Itsukushima Shinto Shrine. No. 375a, Kyoto. No. 375c, Himeji-Jo. No. 375d, Shirakawa-Go and Gokayama. No. 375f, Nikko.

2001, Aug. 1   Litho.   Perf. 12¾x13¼
373 A328 1.10fr multicolored   1.30 1.40
374 A328 1.30fr multicolored   1.50 1.65

Souvenir Booklet
375   Booklet   15.00
  a.-c.   A328 10c any single   .50 .55
  d.-f.   A328 30c any single   .75 .80
  g.   Booklet pane of 4, #375a   2.00 2.20
  h.   Booklet pane of 4, #375d   3.00 3.20
  i.   Booklet pane of 4, #375b   2.00 2.20
  j.   Booklet pane of 4, #375e   3.00 3.20
  k.   Booklet pane of 4, #375c   2.00 2.20
  l.   Booklet pane of 4, #375f   3.00 3.20

Dag Hammarskjöld Type

2001, Sept. 18   Engr.   Perf. 11x11¼
376 A329 2fr carmine lake   2.50 2.75

UN Postal Administration, 50th Anniv. Types

2001, Oct. 18   Litho.   Perf. 13½
377 A330 90c Stamps, globe   1.00 1.10
378 A330 1.30fr Stamps, horns   1.75 1.90

Souvenir Sheet
379 A331 Sheet of 2   12.50 13.50
  a.   1.30fr red & light blue, 38mm diameter   5.00 5.50
  b.   1.80fr red & light blue, 38mm diameter   7.50 8.00

Climate Change Type

Designs: No. 380, Lizard, flowers, shoreline. No. 381, Windmills, construction workers. No. 382, Non-polluting factory. No. 383, Solar oven, city, village, picnickers.

2001, Nov. 16   Litho.   Perf. 13¼
380 A332 90c multicolored   1.10 1.20
381 A332 90c multicolored   1.10 1.20
382 A332 90c multicolored   1.10 1.20
383 A332 90c multicolored   1.10 1.20
  a.   Horiz. strip, #380-383   4.50 5.00

Nobel Peace Prize Type

2001, Dec. 10   Litho.   Perf. 13¼
384 A333 90c multicolored   1.10 1.20

Palais des Nations — G65

2002, Mar. 1   Litho.   Perf. 13¾
385 G65 1.30fr multicolored   1.40 1.50

Endangered Species Type of 1993

Designs: No. 386, Cacajao calvus (white uakari). No. 387, Mellivora capensis (honey badger). No. 388, Otocolobus manul (manul). No. 389, Varanus exantematicus (Bosc's monitor).

2002, Apr. 4   Litho.   Perf. 12¾x12½
386 A271 90c multicolored   1.50 1.65
387 A271 90c multicolored   1.50 1.65
388 A271 90c multicolored   1.50 1.65
389 A271 90c multicolored   1.50 1.65
  a.   Block of 4, #386-389   6.00 6.75

Independence of East Timor Type

Designs: 90c, Wooden statue of male figure. 1.30fr, Carved wooden container.

2002, May 20   Litho.   Perf. 14x14½
390 A335 90c multicolored   1.25 1.40
391 A335 1.30fr multicolored   1.75 1.90

Intl. Year of Mountains Type

Designs: No. 392, Weisshorn, Switzerland. No. 393, Mt. Fuji, Japan. No. 394, Vinson Massif, Antarctica. No. 395, Mt. Kamet, India.

2002, May 24   Litho.   Perf. 13x13¼
392 A336 70c multicolored   1.00 1.10
393 A336 70c multicolored   1.00 1.10
394 A336 1.20fr multicolored   1.75 1.90
395 A336 1.20fr multicolored   1.75 1.90
  a.   Vert. strip or block of four, #392-395   11.00 12.00

World Summit on Sustainable Development (Peter Max) Type

Designs: No. 396, Sun, birds, flowers, heart. No. 397, Three faceless people, diff. No. 398, Three women, diff. No. 399, Sailboat, mountain.

2002, June 27   Litho.   Perf. 14½x14
396 A337 90c multicolored   1.40 1.50
397 A337 90c multicolored   1.40 1.50
398 A337 1.80fr multicolored   2.75 3.00
399 A337 1.80fr multicolored   2.75 3.00
  a.   Vert. strip or block of four, #396-399   12.00 13.00

World Heritage, Italy Type

Designs: 90c, No. 402e, Pisa. 1.30fr, No. 402b, Aeolian Islands. No. 402a, Amalfi Coast. No. 402c, Rome. No. 402d, Florence. No. 402f, Pompeii.

Perf. 13½x13¼
2002, Aug. 30   Litho.
400 A338 90c multicolored   1.25 1.40
401 A338 1.30fr multicolored   2.00 2.20

Souvenir Booklet
402   Booklet   33.00 33.00
  a.-c.   A338 10c any single   .75 .80
  d.-f.   A338 20c any single   2.00 2.20
  g.   Booklet pane of 4, #402d   8.00 9.00
  h.   Booklet pane of 4, #402a   3.00 3.25
  i.   Booklet pane of 4, #402e   8.00 9.00
  j.   Booklet pane of 4, #402b   3.00 3.25
  k.   Booklet pane of 4, #402f   8.00 9.00
  l.   Booklet pane of 4, #402c   3.00 3.25

AIDS Awareness Type

2002, Oct. 24   Litho.   Perf. 13½
403 A339 1.30fr multicolored   2.00 2.20

Entry of Switzerland into United Nations — G66

2002, Oct. 24   Litho.   Perf. 14½x14¾
404 G66 3fr multicolored   3.50 3.75

Indigenous Art — G67

No. 405: a, Detail of Inca poncho, Peru. b, Bahia culture seated figure, Brazil. c, Blanket, Ecuador. d, Mayan stone sculpture, Belize. e, Embroidered fabric, Guatemala. f, Colima terra-cotta dog sculpture, Mexico.

New Inter-Parliamentary Union Headquarters, Geneva — G68

2003, Jan. 31   Litho.   Perf. 14¼
405 G67 Pane of 6   10.00 11.00
  a.-f.   90c Any single   1.50 1.65

2003, Feb. 20   Litho.   Perf. 14½x14
406 G68 90c multicolored   1.75 1.75

Endangered Species Type of 1993

Designs: No. 407, Branta ruficollis (red-breasted goose). No. 408, Geronticus calvus (bald ibis). No. 409, Dendrocygna bicolor (fulvous whistling duck). No. 410, Ramphastos vitellinus (channel-billed toucan).

2003, Apr. 3   Litho.   Perf. 12¾x12½
407 A271 90c multicolored   1.25 1.25
408 A271 90c multicolored   1.25 1.25
409 A271 90c multicolored   1.25 1.25
410 A271 90c multicolored   1.25 1.25
  a.   Block of 4, #407-410   5.00 5.00

International Year of Freshwater Type of 2003

Perf. 14¼x14½
2003, June 20   Litho.
411 A345 70c Waterfall   1.25 1.25
412 A345 1.30fr People, mountain   2.25 2.25
  a.   Horiz. pair, #411-412   5.00 5.00

Ralph Bunche Type

Litho. With Foil Application
2003, Aug. 7   Perf. 13½x14
413 A346 1.80fr brown red & multicolored   2.75 2.75

In Memoriam Type of 2003

2003, Oct. 24   Litho.   Perf. 13¼x13
414 A347 85c multicolored   1.50 1.50

World Heritage Sites, United States Type

Designs: 90c, No. 417b, Great Smoky Mountains National Park. 1.30fr, No. 417f, Yellowstone National Park. No. 417a, Yosemite National Park. No. 417c, Olympic National Park. No. 417d, Hawaii Volcanoes National Park. No. 417e, Everglades National Park.

2003, Oct. 24   Litho.   Perf. 14½x14¼
415 A348 90c multicolored   1.50 1.50
416 A348 1.30fr multicolored   2.25 2.25

Souvenir Booklet
417   Booklet   10.00
  a.-c.   A348 10c any single   .25 .25
  d.-f.   A348 30c any single   .55 .55
  g.   Booklet pane of 4 #417a   1.00 1.00
  h.   Booklet pane of 4 #417d   2.25 2.25
  i.   Booklet pane of 4 #417b   1.00 1.00
  j.   Booklet pane of 4 #417e   2.25 2.25
  k.   Booklet pane of 4 #417c   1.00 1.00
  l.   Booklet pane of 4 #417f   2.25 2.25

Endangered Species Type of 1993

Designs: No. 418, Ursus thibetanus (Asiatic black bear). No. 419, Hippocamelus antisensis (Northern Andean deer). No. 420, Macaca silenus (Lion-tailed macaque). No. 421, Bos gaurus (Gaur).

2004, Jan. 29   Litho.   Perf. 12¾x12½
418 A271 1fr multicolored   1.60 1.60
419 A271 1fr multicolored   1.60 1.60
420 A271 1fr multicolored   1.60 1.60
421 A271 1fr multicolored   1.60 1.60
  a.   Block of 4, #418-421   6.50 6.50

Indigenous Art Type of 2003

No. 422: a, Decoration for cows, Switzerland. b, Stone Age terra cotta sculpture of seated woman, Romania. c, Butter stamps, France. d, Detail of herald's tabard, United Kingdom. e, Woodcut print of medieval Cologne, Germany. f, Mesolithic era terra cotta sculpture of mother and child, Serbia and Montenegro.

2004, Mar. 4   Litho.   Perf. 13¼
422 G67 Sheet of 6   10.00 10.00
  a.-f.   1fr Any single   1.50 1.50

Road Safety Type

Road map art with: 85c, Man on hand. 1fr, Person, seat belt, vert.

Perf. 13x13¼, 13¼x13
2004, Apr. 7   Litho.
423 A354 85c multicolored   1.40 1.40
424 A354 1fr multicolored   1.75 1.75
  See France No. 3011.

Japanese Peace Bell, 50th Anniv. Type

Litho. & Engr.
2004, June 3   Perf. 13¼x13
425 A355 1.30fr multicolored   2.00 2.00

World Heritage Sites, Greece Type

Designs: 1fr, No. 428b, Delphi. 1.30fr, No. 428e, Pythagoreion and Heraion of Samos. No. 428a, Acropolis, Athens. No. 428c, Olympia. No. 428d, Delos. No. 428f, Mycenae and Tiryns.

2004, Aug. 12   Litho.   Perf. 14x13¼
426 A356 1fr multicolored   1.50 1.50
427 A356 1.30fr multicolored   2.00 2.00

Souvenir Booklet
428   Booklet   13.50
  a.-c.   A356 20c any single   .30 .30
  d.-f.   A356 50c any single   .80 .80
  g.   Booklet pane of 4 #428a   1.25 1.25
  h.   Booklet pane of 4 #428b   1.25 1.25
  i.   Booklet pane of 4 #428c   1.25 1.25
  j.   Booklet pane of 4 #428d   3.25 3.25
  k.   Booklet pane of 4 #428e   3.25 3.25
  l.   Booklet pane of 4 #428f   3.25 3.25

My Dream for Peace Type

Winning designs of Lions Club International children's global peace poster contest by: 85c, Anggun Sita Rustinya, Indonesia. 1.20fr, Amanda Nunez, Belize.

2004, Sept. 21   Litho.   Perf. 14
429 A357 85c multicolored   1.40 1.40
430 A357 1.20fr multicolored   2.00 2.00

Droits de l'homme — G69

Human Rights — G70

2004, Oct. 14   Litho.   Perf. 11¼
431 G69 85c multicolored   1.25 1.25
432 G70 1.30fr multicolored   2.25 2.25

Sports — G71

2004, Nov. 23   Litho.   Perf. 13x13½
433 G71 180c multicolored   3.25 3.25
  See Switzerland No. 1196.

United Nations, 60th Anniv. Type of 2005

Litho. & Engr.
2005, Feb. 1   Perf. 11x11¼
434 A361 1.30fr multicolored   2.50 2.50

Souvenir Sheet
Litho.
Imperf
435 A361 3fr multicolored   7.50 7.50

Endangered Species Type of 1993

Designs: No. 436, Laelia milleri. No. 437, Psygmorchis pusilla. No. 438, Dendrobium cruentum. No. 439, Orchis purpurea.

2005, Mar. 3   Litho.   Perf. 12¾x12½
436	A271	1fr multicolored	2.00	2.00
437	A271	1fr multicolored	2.00	2.00
438	A271	1fr multicolored	2.00	2.00
439	A271	1fr multicolored	2.00	2.00
a.		Block of 4, #436-439	8.00	8.00

Nature's Wisdom — G72

Designs: 1fr, Children collecting water, India. 80c, Ruby brittle star, Bahamas.

2005, Apr. 21   Litho.   Perf. 13½x13¼
| 440 | G72 | 1fr multicolored | 1.75 | 1.75 |
| 441 | G72 | 1.30fr multicolored | 2.00 | 2.00 |

Intl. Year of Sport Type

2005, June 3   Litho.   Perf. 13x13¼
| 442 | A368 | 1fr Wheelchair racing | 1.75 | 1.75 |
| 443 | A368 | 1.30fr Cycling | 2.25 | 2.25 |

World Heritage Sites, Egypt Type

Designs: Nos. 444, 446b, Philae. Nos. 445, 446e, Islamic Cairo. No. 446a, Memphis and its Necropolis. No. 446c, Abu Mena. No. 446d, Ancient Thebes. No. 446f, St. Catherine area.

2005, Aug. 4   Litho.   Perf. 14x13¼
| 444 | A369 | 1fr multicolored | 2.00 | 2.00 |
| 445 | A369 | 1.30fr multicolored | 2.50 | 2.50 |

Souvenir Booklet
446		Booklet, #446g-446l	16.50	
a.-c.		A369 20c any single	.40	.40
d.-f.		A369 50c any single	.90	.90
g.		Booklet pane of 4 #446a	1.60	1.60
h.		Booklet pane of 4 #446b	1.60	1.60
i.		Booklet pane of 4 #446c	1.60	1.60
j.		Booklet pane of 4 #446d	3.50	3.50
k.		Booklet pane of 4 #446e	3.50	3.50
l.		Booklet pane of 4 #446f	3.50	3.50

My Dream for Peace Type

Winning designs of Lions Club International children's global peace poster contest by: 1fr, Marisa Harun, Indonesia. 1.30fr, Carlos Javier Parramón Teixidó, Spain.

2005, Sept. 21   Litho.   Perf. 14
| 447 | A357 | 1fr multicolored | 1.75 | 1.75 |
| 448 | A357 | 1.30fr multicolored | 2.00 | 2.00 |

Food for Life Type

Designs: 1fr, Rye, airplane dropping parcels, camel caravan. 1.30fr, Sorghum, people carrying grain sacks, trucks.

2005, Oct. 20   Litho.   Perf. 13¾
| 449 | A370 | 1fr multicolored | 1.90 | 1.90 |
| 450 | A370 | 1.30fr multicolored | 2.40 | 2.40 |

Armillary
Sphere, Palais
des
Nations — G73

Litho. with Hologram

2006, Feb. 3   Perf. 13¼x13½
| 451 | G73 | 1.30fr multicolored | 2.25 | 2.25 |

Indigenous Art Type of 2003

No. 452 — Musical instruments: a, Bell, Benin. b, Drum, Swaziland. c, Sanza, Congo. d, Stringed instruments, Cape Verde. e, Caixixi, Ghana. f, Bells, Central Africa.

2006, Feb. 3   Litho.   Perf. 13¼
| 452 | G67 | Pane of 6 | 12.00 | 12.00 |
| a.-f. | | 1.20fr Any single | 2.00 | 2.00 |

Endangered Species Type of 1993

Designs: No. 453, Dyscophus antongilii. No. 454, Chamaeleo dilepsis. No. 455, Corallus caninus. No. 456, Phyllobates vittatus.

Perf. 12¾x12½
2006, Mar. 16   Litho.
453	A271	1fr multicolored	1.75	1.75
454	A271	1fr multicolored	1.75	1.75
455	A271	1fr multicolored	1.75	1.75
456	A271	1fr multicolored	1.75	1.75
a.		Block of 4, #453-456	7.00	7.00

Intl. Day of Families Type

Designs: 1fr, Family reading together. 1.30fr, Family on motorcycle.

2006, May 27   Litho.   Perf. 14x13½
| 457 | A373 | 1fr multicolored | 1.25 | 1.25 |
| 458 | A373 | 1.30fr multicolored | 1.75 | 1.75 |

World Heritage Sites, France Type

Eiffel Tower and: Nos. 459, 461b, Provins. Nos. 460, 461e, Mont Saint-Michel. No. 461a, Banks of the Seine. No. 461c, Carcassonne. No. 461d, Roman Aqueduct. No. 446f, Chateau de Chambord.

Litho. & Embossed with Foil Application

2006, June 17   Perf. 13½x13¼
| 459 | A374 | 1fr multicolored | 1.75 | 1.75 |
| 460 | A374 | 1.30fr multicolored | 2.25 | 2.25 |

Souvenir Booklet
461		Booklet, #461g-461l	15.00	
a.-c.		A374 20c any single	.35	.35
d.-f.		A374 50c any single	.85	.85
g.		Booklet pane of 4 #461a	1.40	1.40
h.		Booklet pane of 4 #461b	1.40	1.40
i.		Booklet pane of 4 #461c	1.40	1.40
j.		Booklet pane of 4 #461d	3.50	3.50
k.		Booklet pane of 4 #461e	3.50	3.50
l.		Booklet pane of 4 #461f	3.50	3.50

See France Nos. 3219-3220.

My Dream for Peace Type of 2004

Winning designs of Lions Club International children's global peace poster contest by: 85c, Ariam Boaglio, Italy. 1.20fr, Sierra Spicer, US.

2006, Sept. 21   Litho.   Perf. 13½x13
| 462 | A357 | 85c multicolored | 1.60 | 1.60 |
| 463 | A357 | 1.20fr multicolored | 2.25 | 2.25 |

Flags and Coins Type

No. 464 — Flag of: a, Uganda, 500 shilling coin. b, Luxembourg, 1 euro coin. c, Cape Verde, 20 escudo coin. d, Belgium, 1 euro coin. e, Italy, 1 euro coin. f, New Zealand, 1 dollar coin. g, Switzerland, 2 franc coin. h, Lebanon, 500 pound coin.

2006, Oct. 5   Litho.   Perf. 13¼x13
| 464 | | Pane of 8 | 15.00 | 15.00 |
| a.-h. | | A375 85c Any single | 1.50 | 1.50 |

A column of rouletting in the middle of the pane separates it into two parts.

Endangered Species Type of 1993

Designs: No. 465, Theropithecus gelada. No. 466, Cercopithecus neglectus. No. 467, Varecia variegata. No. 468, Hylobates moloch.

Perf. 12¾x12½
2007, Mar. 15   Litho.
465	A271	1fr multicolored	1.75	1.75
466	A271	1fr multicolored	1.75	1.75
467	A271	1fr multicolored	1.75	1.75
468	A271	1fr multicolored	1.75	1.75
a.		Block of 4, #465-468	7.00	7.00

Flags and Coins Type of 2006

No. 469 — Flag of: a, Burkina Faso, 500 franc coin. b, France, 50 cent coin. c, Moldova, 50 bani coin. d, Papua New Guinea, 1 kina coin. e, Bolivia, 1 boliviano coin. f, Myanmar, 100 kyat coin. g, Mali, 500 franc coin. h, Tunisia, 5 dinar coin.

2007, May 3   Litho.   Perf. 13¼x13
| 469 | | Sheet of 8 | 12.50 | 12.50 |
| a.-h. | | A375 85c Any single | 1.50 | 1.50 |

A column of rouletting in the middle of the sheet separates it into two parts.

Peaceful Visions Type of 2007

Designs: 1.20fr, "Harvest for All." 1.80fr, "This Dream Has Wings."

2007, June 1   Litho.   Perf. 13x12½
| 470 | A378 | 1.20fr multicolored | 2.25 | 2.25 |
| 471 | A378 | 1.80fr multicolored | 3.25 | 3.25 |

World Heritage Sites, South America Type

Designs: Nos. 472, 474a, Tiwanaku, Bolivia. Nos. 473, 474f, Machu Picchu, Peru. No.

474b, Iguaçu National Park, Brazil. No. 474c, Galapagos Islands, Ecuador. No. 474d, Rapa Nui, Chile. No. 474e, Cueva de las Manos, Argentina.

2007, Aug. 9   Litho.   Perf. 13¼x13
| 472 | A381 | 1fr multicolored | 1.90 | 1.90 |
| 473 | A381 | 1.80fr multicolored | 3.25 | 3.25 |

Souvenir Booklet
474		Booklet, #474g-474l	16.00	
a.-c.		A381 20c Any single	.40	.40
d.-f.		A381 50c Any single	.90	.90
g.		Booklet pane of 4 #474a	1.60	1.60
h.		Booklet pane of 4 #474b	1.60	1.60
i.		Booklet pane of 4 #474c	1.60	1.60
j.		Booklet pane of 4 #474d	3.60	3.60
k.		Booklet pane of 4 #474e	3.60	3.60
l.		Booklet pane of 4 #474f	3.60	3.60

Humanitarian Mail Type

2007, Sept. 6   Litho.   Perf. 12½x13¼
| 475 | A382 | 1.80fr multicolored | 3.00 | 3.00 |

Space for Humanity Type

Designs: 1fr, Astronaut spacewalking. 1.80fr, International Space Station, space probe, Jupiter. 3fr, Astronauts spacewalking.

2007, Oct. 25   Litho.   Perf. 13½x14
| 476 | A383 | 1fr multicolored | 1.90 | 1.90 |
| 477 | A383 | 1.80fr multicolored | 3.25 | 3.25 |

Souvenir Sheet
| 478 | A383 | 3fr multicolored | 7.50 | 7.50 |

Intl. Holocaust Remembrance Day Type

2008, Jan. 27   Litho.   Perf. 13
| 479 | A384 | 85c multicolored | 3.00 | 3.00 |

Endangered Species Type of 1993

Designs: No. 480, Odobenus rosmarus. No. 481, Platygyra daedalea. No. 482, Hippocampus bargibanti. No. 483, Delphinapterus leucas.

2008, Mar. 6   Litho.   Perf. 12¾x12½
480	A271	1fr multicolored	2.00	2.00
481	A271	1fr multicolored	2.00	2.00
482	A271	1fr multicolored	2.00	2.00
483	A271	1fr multicolored	2.00	2.00
a.		Block of 4, #480-483	8.00	8.00

Flags and Coins Type of 2006

No. 484 — Flag of: a, Madagascar, 1 ariary coin. b, Rwanda, 50 franc coin. c, Benin, 10 franc coin. d, Iran, 500 rial coin. e, Namibia, 5 dollar coin. f, Maldives, 1 rufiyaa coin. g, Albania, 10 lek coin. h, Turkey, 1 lira coin.

2008, May 8   Litho.   Perf. 13¼x13
| 484 | | Sheet of 8 | 15.00 | 15.00 |
| a.-h. | | A375 85c Any single | 1.75 | 1.75 |

A column of rouletting in the middle of the sheet separates it into two parts.

Handshake
G74

Sign
Language — G75

Litho. & Embossed

2008, June 6   Perf. 14x13¼
| 485 | G74 | 1fr orange & red | 2.25 | 2.25 |
| 486 | G75 | 1.80fr red & orange | 4.00 | 4.00 |

Convention on the Rights of Persons with Disabilities.

Sport for Peace Type of 2008

Designs: 1fr, 3fr, Gymnast. 1.80fr, Tennis player.

2008, Aug. 8   Litho.   Perf. 14½
| 487 | A393 | 1fr multicolored | 2.25 | 2.25 |

| 488 | A393 | 1.80fr multicolored | 4.00 | 4.00 |

Souvenir Sheet
Perf. 12¾x13¼
| 489 | A393 | 3fr multicolored | 9.00 | 9.00 |

2008 Summer Olympics, Beijing.

"We Can End Poverty" Type of 2008

Winning designs in children's art contest by: 1fr, Ranajoy Banerjee, India, vert. 1.80fr, Elizabeth Elaine Chun Nig Au, Hong Kong, vert.

Perf. 12½x12¾
2008, Sept. 18   Litho.
| 490 | A395 | 1fr multicolored | 2.25 | 2.25 |
| 491 | A395 | 1.80fr multicolored | 3.75 | 3.75 |

Climate Change Types of New York and Vienna and

Climate Change — G76

Climate Change — G77

No. 492 — Polar bear with quarter of Earth in: a, LR. b, LL. c, UR. d, UL.

No. 493 — Ship and sea ice with quarter of Earth in: a, LR. b, LL. c, UR. d, UL.

No. 494: a, Like New York #969a. b, Like New York #969b. c, Like New York #969c. d, Like New York #969d. e, Like Geneva #493a. f, Like Geneva #493b. g, Like Geneva #493c. h, Like Geneva #493d. i, Like Vienna #434a. j, Like Vienna #434b. k, Like Vienna #434c. l, Like Vienna #434d. m, Like New York #968a. n, Like New York #968b. o, Like New York #968c. p, Like New York #968d. q, Like Geneva #492a. r, Like Geneva #492b. s, Like Geneva #492c. t, Like Geneva #492d. u, Like Vienna #435a. v, Like Vienna #435b. w, Like Vienna #435c. x, Like Vienna #435d.

All stamps have red panels inscribed "Changement de climat."

2008, Oct. 23   Litho.   Perf. 13¼x13
492		Sheet of 4	10.50	10.50
a.-d.	G76	1.20fr any single	2.60	2.60
493		Sheet of 4	15.50	15.50
a.-d.	G77	1.80fr any single	3.75	3.75

Souvenir Booklet
494		Booklet, #494y-494ad	25.00	
a.-d.	A397	35c Any single	.75	.75
e.-h.	G77	35c Any single	.75	.75
i.-l.	V72	35c Any single	.75	.75
m.-p.	A396	50c Any single	1.00	1.00
q.-t.	G76	50c Any single	1.00	1.00
u.-x.	V73	50c Any single	1.00	1.00
y.		Booklet pane of 4, #494a-494d	3.00	3.00
z.		Booklet pane of 4, #494e-494h	3.00	3.00
aa.		Booklet pane of 4, #494i-494l	3.00	3.00
ab.		Booklet pane of 4, #494m-494p	4.25	4.25
ac.		Booklet pane of 4, #494q-494t	4.25	4.25
ad.		Booklet pane of 4, #494u-494x	4.25	4.25

U Thant Type of 2009
Litho. With Foil Application
2009, Feb. 6   Perf. 14x13½
| 495 | A399 | 1.30fr red & multi | 3.25 | 3.25 |

Endangered Species Type of 1993

No. 496, Maculinea arion. No. 497, Dolomedes plantarius. No. 498, Cerambyx cerdo. No. 499, Coenagrion mercuriale.

2009, Apr. 16   Litho.   Perf. 12¾x12½
496	A271	1fr multicolored	1.90	1.90
497	A271	1fr multicolored	1.90	1.90
498	A271	1fr multicolored	1.90	1.90
499	A271	1fr multicolored	1.90	1.90
a.		Block of 4, #496-499	7.75	7.75
b.		Pane of 16, imperf.	5,000.	

World Heritage Sites, Germany Type of 2009

Designs: Nos. 500, 502b, Wartburg Castle. Nos. 501, 502f, Monastic Island of Reichenau. No. 502a, Town Hall and Roland on the Marketplace, Bremen. No. 502c, Palaces and Parks of Potsdam and Berlin. No. 502d, Aachen Cathedral. No. 502e, Luther Memorials in Eisleben and Wittenberg.

2009, May 7   Litho.   Perf. 14x13½

500	A400	1fr multicolored	2.25	2.25
501	A400	1.30fr multicolored	2.75	2.75

Souvenir Booklet

502	Booklet, #502g-502l	18.00	
a.-c.	A400 30c any single	.55	.55
d.-f.	A400 50c any single	.90	.90
g.	Booklet pane of 4 #502a	2.25	2.25
h.	Booklet pane of 4 #502b	2.25	2.25
i.	Booklet pane of 4 #502c	2.25	2.25
j.	Booklet pane of 4 #502d	3.75	3.75
k.	Booklet pane of 4 #502e	3.75	3.75
l.	Booklet pane of 4 #502f	3.75	3.75

Economic and Social Council (ECOSOC) Type of 2009

Designs: 85c, Improving maternal health. 1.80fr, Access to essential medicines.

2009, Aug. 6   Perf. 12¾x12½

503	A411	85c multicolored	2.00	2.00
504	A411	1.80fr multicolored	4.00	4.00

Millennium Development Goals Type of 2009
Miniature Sheet

No. 505: a, Bowl of hot food. b, Pencil. c, Female symbol. d, Teddy bear. e, Pregnant woman, heart. f, Medicine bottle. g, Stylized tree. h, Conjoined people.

2009, Sept. 25   Perf. 13¼

505	A413	Sheet of 8	18.00	18.00
a.-h.		1.10fr Any single	2.25	2.25

Palais des Nations — G78

Palais des Nations — G79

Flags of United Nations and Switzerland — G80

Meeting Room — G81

Armillary Sphere — G82

2009, Oct. 2   Perf. 13¼

506	G78	1fr multi + label	6.00	6.00
a.		Perf. 11¼x11 + label	5.00	5.00

507	G79	1fr multi + label	6.00	6.00
a.		Perf. 11¼x11 + label	5.00	5.00
508	G80	1fr multi + label	6.00	6.00
a.		Perf. 11¼x11 + label	5.00	5.00
509	G81	1fr multi + label	6.00	6.00
a.		Perf. 11¼x11 + label	5.00	5.00
510	G82	1fr multi + label	6.00	6.00
a.		Perf. 11¼x11 + label	5.00	5.00
b.		Vert. strip of 5, #506-510, + 5 labels	30.00	30.00
c.		Vert. strip of 5, #506a-510a, + 5 labels	25.00	25.00

United Nations Postal Administration in Geneva, 40th anniv. The full sheets sold for €19.90 or $14.95. Labels could not be personalized. The sheet of No. 510c has "VER. 2" in the lower right selvage.

Miniature Sheet

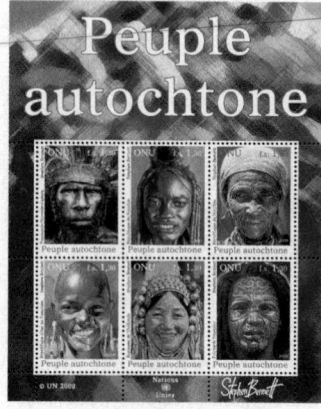

Indigenous People — G83

No. 511 — Portraits of person from: a, Papua New Guinea. b, Namibia (young woman). c, Namibia (old man). d, Tanzania. e, Thailand. f, French Polynesia.

2009, Oct. 8   Perf. 12½

511	G83	Sheet of 6	16.00	16.00
a.-f.		1.30fr Any single	2.60	2.60

Flags and Coins Type of 2006

No. 512 — Flag of: a, Equatorial Guinea, 100 franc coin. b, Laos, 20 kip coin. c, Seychelles, 5 rupee coin. d, Mauritania, 1 ougiya coin. e, Argentina, 1 peso coin. f, Morocco, 1 dirham coin. g, Sudan, 20 piaster coin. h, Brunei, 50 cent coin.

2010, Feb. 5   Litho.   Perf. 13¼x13

512		Sheet of 8	15.00	15.00
a.-h.	A375	85c Any single	1.75	1.75

A column of rouletting in the middle of the sheet separates it into two parts.

Endangered Species Type of 1993

No. 513, Fouquieria columnaris. No. 514, Aloe arborescens. No. 515, Galanthus krasnovii. No. 516, Dracaena draco.

2010, Apr. 15   Litho.   Perf. 12¾x12½

513	A271	1fr multicolored	2.25	2.25
514	A271	1fr multicolored	2.25	2.25
515	A271	1fr multicolored	2.25	2.25
516	A271	1fr multicolored	2.25	2.25
a.		Block of 4, #513-516	9.00	9.00

Intl. Year of Biodiversity G84

Drawings from Art Forms from Nature, by Ernst Heinrich: 1.60fr, Arachnid. 1.90fr, Starfish.

2010, Apr. 15   Litho.   Perf. 13

517	G84	1.60fr multicolored	3.75	3.75
518	G84	1.90fr multicolored	4.25	4.25

One Planet, One Ocean Types of New York and Vienna and

G85

G86

No. 519: a, Turtles at left and top, fish at bottom. b, Hammerhead shark. c, Fish at left and center, corals. d, Fish at left, coral.

No. 520: a, Dolphins. b, Shark, head of fish at right, small fish in background. c, Ray and fish. d, Fish at bottom, coral and sponges.

No. 521: a, Like New York #1003a. b, Like New York #1003b, c, Like New York #1003c, d, Like New York #1003d. e, Like Vienna #471a. f, Like Vienna #471b. g, Like Vienna #471c, h, Like Vienna #471d. i, Like #519a. j, Like #519b, k, Like #519c. l, Like #519d. m, Like New York #1004a. n, Like New York #1004b. o, Like New York #1004c, p, Like New York #1004d. q, Like Vienna #472a. r, Like Vienna #472b. s, Like Vienna #472c. t, Like Vienna #472d. u, Like #520a. v, Like #520b. w, Like #520c. x, Like #520d.

2010, May 6   Litho.   Perf. 14x13¼

519	G85	Sheet of 4	8.00	8.00
a.-d.		85c Any single	2.00	2.00
520	G86	Sheet of 4	10.00	10.00
a.-d.		1fr Any single	2.50	2.50

Souvenir Booklet
Perf. 13¼x13

521		Booklet, #521y-521z, 521aa-521ad	22.00	
a.-d.		A416 30c any single	.70	.70
e.-h.		V91 30c any single	.70	.70
i.-l.		G85 30c any single	.70	.70
m.-p.		A417 50c any single	1.10	1.10
q.-t.		V92 50c any single	1.10	1.10
u.-x.		G86 50c any single	1.10	1.10
y.		Booklet pane of 4 #521a-521d	2.80	2.80
z.		Booklet pane of 4 #521e-521h	2.80	2.80
aa.		Booklet pane of 4 #521i-521l	2.80	2.80
ab.		Booklet pane of 4 #521m-521p	4.40	4.40
ac.		Booklet pane of 4 #521q-521t	4.40	4.40
ad.		Booklet pane of 4 #521u-521x	4.40	4.40

Intl. Oceanographic Commission, 50th anniv.

United Nations, 65th Anniv. Type of 2010
Litho. With Foil Application

2010, June 28   Perf. 13¼

522	A422	1.90fr red & gold	4.00	4.00
a.		Souvenir sheet of 2 (40,500)+	8.00	8.00

TRANSPORTS de l'ONU

G87

TRANSPORTS de l'ONU

G88

TRANSPORTS de l'ONU

G89

TRANSPORTS de l'ONU

G90

TRANSPORTS de l'ONU

United Nations Land Transport — G91

2010, Sept. 2   Litho.   Perf. 13¼x13

523	G87	1fr multicolored	1.80	1.80
524	G88	1fr multicolored	1.80	1.80
525	G89	1fr multicolored	1.80	1.80
526	G90	1fr multicolored	1.80	1.80
527	G91	1fr multicolored	1.80	1.80
a.		Horiz. strip of 5, #523-527	9.00	9.00

Miniature Sheet

Campaign Against Child Labor — G92

No. 528: a, Child, buildings, road, burning can. b, Child with full basket on back, children playing in background. c, Child working, children on school bus. d, Child with mining helmet, three other children. e, Child near tubs, children working, child being beaten. f, Child with hoe. g, Marionette, traffic light. h, Child carrying basket on head. i, Children on rock field near hills. j, Child holding bags in road.

2010, Sept. 2   Litho.   Perf. 14¾

528	G92	Sheet of 10 + 10 labels	32.50	32.50
a.-j.		1.90fr Any single + label	3.25	3.25

No. 528 sold for $14.95, 15fr and €11.46, each of which was far lower than the level at which 19fr, the total face value of the stamps on the sheet, was worth on the day of issue. Labels could not be personalized.

Miniature Sheet

Indigenous People — G93

No. 529 — Portraits of person from: a, Australia. b, Brunei. c, Tanzania (girl with bald head). d, French Polynesia (man with headdress of leaves). e, Tanzania (man with headdress). f, French Polynesia (man with white headdress).

2010, Oct. 21	Litho.	Perf. 13		
529	G93	Pane of 6	16.50	16.50
a.-f.		1.30fr Any single	2.75	2.75

United Nations
Headquarters,
Geneva — G94

United Nations Headquarters, Geneva: 10c, Aerial view. 50c, Ground-level view.

2011, Feb. 4	Litho.	Perf. 13		
530	G94	10c multicolored	.35	.35
531	G94	50c multicolored	1.25	1.25

Flags and Coins Type of 2006

No. 532 — Flag of: a, Mongolia, 500 tugrik coin. b, Senegal, 500 franc coin. c, Egypt, 100 piaster coin. d, Congo, 100 franc coin. e, Nicaragua, 1 Córdoba coin. f, Central African Republic, 100 franc coin. g, Algeria, 5 dinar coin. h, Ukraine, 5 hryvnia coin.

2011, Mar. 3	Litho.	Perf. 13¼x13		
532		Sheet of 8	15.00	15.00
a.-h.		A375 85c Any single	1.75	1.75

A column of rouletting in the middle of the sheet separates it into two parts.

Human Space Flight, 50th
Anniv. — G95

No. 533: Various parts of outer space scene.
No. 534, vert.: a, International Space Station. b, International Space Station, diff.

2011, Apr. 12	Litho.	Perf. 13x13¼		
533	G95	Sheet of 16	18.00	18.00
a.-p.		50c any single	1.10	1.10

Souvenir Sheet

534	G95	Sheet of 2	9.00	9.00
a.		85c multi	4.00	4.00
b.		1fr multi	5.00	5.00

No. 534 contains two 40x48mm stamps that were printed as part of a larger sheet of six stamps, Vienna No. 485c, which was broken up into its component two-stamp souvenir sheets, and also sold as one unit.

UNESCO World Heritage Sites in Nordic Countries Type of 2011

Designs: 85c, Kronborg Castle, Denmark. 1fr, Suomenlinna Fortress, Finland.

2011, May 5	Litho.	Perf. 14x13½		
535	A433	85c multicolored	1.90	1.90
536	A433	1fr multicolored	2.25	2.25

AIDS Ribbon Type of 2011

2011, June 3	Litho.	Die Cut		

Self-Adhesive

537	A434	1.30fr red & orange	5.00	5.00

ECOSOC Type of 2011

2011, July 1	Litho.	Perf. 14¼		
538	A435	1fr multicolored	3.00	3.00
539	A435	1.30fr multicolored	4.00	4.00

Endangered Species Type of 1993

Designs: No. 540, Strigops habroptilus (Kakapo). No. 541, Lophophorus impejanus (Himalayan monal). No. 542, Ciconia nigra (Black stork). No. 543, Pithecophaga jeffreyi (Philippine eagle).

2011, Sept. 7	Litho.	Perf. 12¾x12½		
540	A271	1fr multicolored	2.60	2.60
541	A271	1fr multicolored	2.60	2.60
542	A271	1fr multicolored	2.60	2.60
543	A271	1fr multicolored	2.60	2.60
a.		Block of 4, #540-543	10.40	10.40

Intl. Year of Forests Type of 2011

Designs: 85c, Birds and butterflies, tree tops. 1.40fr, Fish and coral.

Litho. With Foil Application

2011, Oct. 13		Perf. 12½		
544		85c multicolored	2.25	2.25
545		1.40fr multicolored	3.75	3.75
a.		A436 Vert. pair, #544-545	6.00	6.00

Flags and Coins Type of 2006

No. 546 — Flag of: a, Saudi Arabia, 100 halala coin. b, Georgia, 2 lari coin. c, Democratic People's Republic of Korea, 50 won coin. d, Lesotho, 50 lisente coin. e, Serbia, 5 dinar coin. f, Djibouti, 20 franc coin. g, Belize, 1 dollar coin. h, Liechtenstein, 20 centime coin.

2012, Feb. 3	Litho.	Perf. 13¼x13		
546		Sheet of 8	16.50	16.50
a.-h.		A375 85c Any single	2.00	2.00

A column of rouletting in the middle of the sheet separates it into two parts.

G96

Autism
Awareness
G97

Drawings by autistic people: No. 547, Victory, by J.A Tan, Canada. No. 548, Untitled drawing, by Michael Augello, U.S.

2012, Apr. 2	Litho.	Perf. 14x13½		
547	G96	1.40fr multicolored	3.50	3.50
548	G97	1.40fr multicolored	3.50	3.50
a.		Pair, #547-548	7.00	7.00

Endangered Species Type of 1993

Designs: No. 549, Panthera tigris altaica. No. 550, Psitacella picta. No. 551, Iguana iguana. No. 552, Propithecus tattersalli.

2012, Apr. 19	Litho.	Perf. 12¾x12½		
549	A271	1fr multicolored	2.40	2.40
550	A271	1fr multicolored	2.40	2.40
551	A271	1fr multicolored	2.40	2.40
552	A271	1fr multicolored	2.40	2.40
a.		Block of 4, #549-552	9.75	9.75

Rio + 20 Type of 2012

2012, June 1	Litho.	Perf. 13x13¼		
553	A443	1.40fr multicolored	4.00	4.00

Sport for Peace Type of 2012

2012 Paralympics events: 1fr, Track. 1.40fr, Archery.

Litho. With Foil Application

2012, Aug. 17		Perf. 14½		
554	A444	1fr multicolored	2.40	2.40
555	A444	1.40fr multicolored	3.50	3.50
a.		Souvenir sheet of 1	3.50	3.50

UNESCO World Heritage Sites in Africa Type of 2012

Designs: 85c, Virunga National Park, Congo Democratic Republic. 1fr, Amphitheater of El Jem, Tunisia.

2012, Sept. 5	Litho.	Perf. 13¼		
556	A445	85c multicolored	2.00	2.00
557	A445	1fr multicolored	2.40	2.40

Miniature Sheet

Indigenous People — G98

No. 558 — Portrait of person from: a, China. b, Tibet, China. c, Mongolia. d, Mexico. e, Papua New Guinea. f, Haiti.

2012, Oct. 11	Litho.	Perf. 13¼x13		
558	G98	Sheet of 6	13.50	13.50
a.-f.		85c Any single	2.25	2.25

World Radio Day Type of 2013

Designs: 1.40fr, Reporter with microphone and tape recorder. 1.90fr, Engineers in studio.

2013, Feb. 13	Litho.	Perf. 13¼x13		
559	A448	1.40fr multicolored	3.50	3.50
560	A448	1.90fr multicolored	4.50	4.50

Person on
Leaf
G99

Dove and
People — G100

2013, Mar. 5	Litho.	Perf. 14x13½		
561	G99	1fr multicolored	2.40	2.40

		Perf. 13½x14		
562	G100	1.40fr multicolored	3.50	3.50

World Heritage Sites, China, Type of 2013

Designs: Nos. 563, 565b, Potala Palace, Lhasa. Nos. 564, 565e, Mount Huangshan. No. 565a, Mogao Caves. No. 565c, Great Wall of China. No. 565d, Imperial Palace, Beijing. No. 565f, Mausoleum of the First Qing Emperor.

2013, Apr. 11	Litho.	Perf. 14x13½		
563	A452	1.40fr multicolored	3.50	3.50
564	A452	1.90fr multicolored	4.50	4.50

Souvenir Booklet

565		Booklet, #565g-565l	24.00	
a.-c.		A452 30c any single	.75	.75
d.-f.		A452 50c any single	1.25	1.25
g.		Booklet pane of 4 #565a	3.00	—
h.		Booklet pane of 4 #565b	3.00	—
i.		Booklet pane of 4 #565c	3.00	—
j.		Booklet pane of 4 #565d	5.00	—
k.		Booklet pane of 4 #565e	5.00	—
l.		Booklet pane of 4 #565f	5.00	—

World Oceans Day — G101

No. 566 — Fish from One Fish, Two Fish, Red Fish, Blue Fish, by Dr. Seuss: a, Three red fish facing right. b, Green fish, tail of yellow fish. c, Three red fish facing right, part of tail of red fish. d, Two entire green fish facing left, tail of bottom fish ends above "n" in "océan." e, Red fish with eye open facing left. f, Tail of red fish, yellow and red fish facing left. g, Red fish facing right, water droplets. h, Yellow and red fish facing right. i, Two green fish facing left, tail of bottom fish ends to right of "océan." j, Red fish and wave. k, Two green fish, red fish, wave. l, Yellow fish in car, wave.

2013, May 31	Litho.	Perf. 13		
566	G101	Sheet of 12	22.50	22.50
a.-l.		85c any single	1.90	1.90

Nebulae Type of 2013

Designs: No. 567, NGC 2346. No. 568, Sh 2-106. 1fr, Messier 16.

2013, Aug. 9	Litho.	Perf. 13¼		
567	A454	1.40fr multicolored	3.50	3.50
568	A454	1.40fr multicolored	3.50	3.50
a.		Pair, #567-568	7.00	7.00

Souvenir Sheet

569	A454	1fr multicolored	2.40	2.40

No. 569 contains one 44x44mm stamp.

Works of Disabled Artists Type of 2013

Designs: 1.40fr, See the Girl with the Red Dress On, by Sargy Mann, United Kingdom. 1.90fr, Performers in China Disabled People's Performing Art Troupe, People's Republic of China.

2013, Sept. 20	Litho.	Perf. 13¼x13		
570	A456	1.40fr multicolored	3.50	3.50
571	A456	1.90fr multicolored	4.50	4.50

Endangered Species Type of 1993

Designs: No. 572, Smutsia temminckii. No. 573, Perodicticus potto. No. 574, Tarsius syrichta. No. 575, Pteropus livingstonii.

2013, Oct. 10	Litho.	Perf. 12¾x12½		
572	A271	1.40fr multicolored	3.25	3.25
573	A271	1.40fr multicolored	3.25	3.25
574	A271	1.40fr multicolored	3.25	3.25
575	A271	1.40fr multicolored	3.25	3.25
a.		Block of 4, #572-575	13.00	13.00

Flags and Coins Type of 2006

No. 576 — Flag of: a, Ivory Coast, 100 franc coin. b, Marshall Islands, 10 cent coin. c, Andorra, 20 cent coin. d, Guinea-Bissau, 100 franc coin. e, Kenya, 20 shilling coin. f, Antigua and Barbuda, 5 cent coin. g, Tajikistan, 50 diram coin. h, Micronesia, 5 cent coin.

2013, Nov. 6	Litho.	Perf. 13¼x13		
576		Sheet of 8	26.00	26.00
a.-h.		A375 1.40fr Any single	3.25	3.25

A column of rouletting in the middle of the sheet separates it into two parts.

International Day of Happiness Type of 2014

Designs: 1fr, A Sweet Dog's Muzzle, photograph by Jaymi Heimbuch, "Heureux." 1.40fr, Two women making heart with hands, photograph by Glow Images, Chinese characters for "Happy."

2014, Mar. 17   Litho.   Perf. 13¼x13
577	A459	1fr multicolored	2.50	2.50
578	A459	1.40fr multicolored	3.50	3.50

Miniature Sheet

International Year of Jazz — G102

No. 579: a, Woman behind microphone. b, Saxophone. c, Silhouette of pianist at grand piano. d, Cymbal and silhouette of man holding trumpet. e, Cymbal and clarinet. f, Clarinet and drum. g, Hi-hat. h, Silhouette of drummer and drum set. i, Trumpeter with hat. j, Microphone and cymbal stands. k, Clarinetist. l, Bass player.

2014, Apr. 30   Litho.   Perf. 13x13¼
579	G102	Sheet of 12	29.50	29.50
		First day cover		31.00
a.-l.		1fr Any single	2.40	2.40

G103

G104

2014, June 6   Litho.   Perf. 13¼x13
580	G103	2.20fr multicolored	5.50	5.50
581	G104	2.60fr multicolored	6.50	6.50

Taj Mahal Types of 2014

2014, July 16   Engr.   Perf. 13¼x13
582	A465	1.40fr multicolored	3.50	3.50
583	A467	1.90fr multicolored	4.75	4.75

Souvenir Booklet
584		Booklet, #584g-584l	24.00	
a.	A463 30c multi		.75	.75
b.	A465 30c multi		.75	.75
c.	A466 30c multi		.75	.75
d.	A464 50c multi		1.25	1.25
e.	A467 50c multi		1.25	1.25
f.	A468 50c multi		1.25	1.25
g.	Booklet pane of 4 #584a		3.00	—
h.	Booklet pane of 4 #584b		3.00	—
i.	Booklet pane of 4 #584c		3.00	—
j.	Booklet pane of 4 #584d		5.00	—
k.	Booklet pane of 4 #584e		5.00	—
l.	Booklet pane of 4 #584f		5.00	—

International Year of Family Farming — G105

2014, Aug. 21   Litho.   Perf. 13x13¼
585	G105	1.30fr multicolored	3.25	3.25
586	G105	1.60fr multicolored	4.00	4.00

G106

No. 587: a, Room with painted ceiling. b, Peacock with spread tail. c, Rows of flags, brown panel at bottom. d, Rows of flags near Palais des Nations, tan panel at top. e, Meeting hall with United nations emblem on rear wall. f, Armillary sphere and Palais des Nations. g, Meeting hall with movie screen on rear wall. h, Circular meeting hall. i, Farm animals on grass near buildings. j, Peacock with tail down.

2014, Sept. 12   Litho.   Perf. 14¾
587	G106	Sheet of 10	37.50	37.50
a.-j.		1.30fr Any single + label	3.75	3.75

The full sheet sold for 14.95fr. The generic labels are shown. Labels could be personalized.

Global Education First Initiative Type of 2014

Designs: No. 588, Students in art museum. No. 589, Student in library.

2014, Sept. 18   Litho.   Perf. 13x13¼
588	A470	1.90fr multicolored	4.75	4.75

Souvenir Sheet

Perf. 12½
589	A470	1.90fr multicolored	4.75	4.75

No. 589 contains one 32x32mm stamp.

Endangered Species Type of 2014

Maps and: No. 590, Arapaima gigas. No. 591, Cetorhinus maximus. No. 592, Pristis pristis. No. 593, Acipenser baerii.

2014, Oct. 23   Litho.   Perf. 12¾x12½
590	A471	1.40fr multicolored	3.50	3.50
591	A471	1.40fr multicolored	3.50	3.50
592	A471	1.40fr multicolored	3.50	3.50
593	A471	1.40fr multicolored	3.50	3.50
a.		Block of 4, #590-593	14.00	14.00

Flags and Coins Type of 2006

No. 594 — Flag of: a, Vanuatu, 20 vatu coin. b, Nauru, 1 dollar coin. c, Eritrea, 100 cent coin. d, El Salvador, 1 colon coin. e, Mozambique, 50 centavo coin. f, Burundi, 1 franc coin. g, Turkmenistan, 10 tenge coin. h, Guinea, 1 franc coin.

2015, Feb. 6   Litho.   Perf. 13¼x13
594		Sheet of 8	16.50	16.50
a.-h.	A375 90c Any single		2.00	2.00

A column of rouletting in the middle of the sheet separates it into two parts.

Miniature Sheets

G107

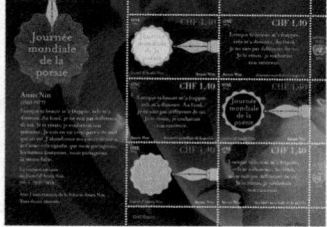

World Poetry Day — G108

No. 595: a, Pen and gray circle. b, Li Bai quotation in Chinese, denomination in light blue green. c, Li Bai quotation in Chinese, denomination in red. d, Pen and red circle. e, Pen and orange circle. f, Li Bai quotation in Chinese, denomination in white.
No. 596: a, Pen and light green circle. b, Anais Nin quotation, denomination and "Journée mondiale de poésie" in light blue. c, As "b," with "Journée mondiale de poésie" in white, dark blue area below and to left of date. d, Pen and black circle. e, Pen and lilac circle. f, As "c," with dark blue area below and to right of date.

Perf. 14½x14¼

2015, Mar. 20   Litho.
595	G107	Sheet of 6	14.00	14.00
a.-f.		1fr Any single	2.25	2.25
596	G108	Sheet of 6	19.50	19.50
a.-f.		1.40fr Any single	3.25	3.25

Endangered Species Type of 2015

Designs: No. 597, Diphyllodes respublica. No. 598, Ptiloris paradiseus. No. 599, Semioptera wallacii. No. 600, Paradisaea decora.

2015, Apr. 16   Litho.   Perf. 12½x12¾
597	A476	1.40fr multicolored	3.25	3.25
598	A476	1.40fr multicolored	3.25	3.25
599	A476	1.40fr multicolored	3.25	3.25
600	A476	1.40fr multicolored	3.25	3.25
a.		Block of 4, #597-600	13.00	13.00
		Nos. 597-600 (4)	13.00	13.00

World Heritage Sites, Southeast Asia, Type of 2015

Designs: Nos. 601, 603b, Angkor Wat, Cambodia. Nos. 602, 603e, Cordillera, Philippines. No. 603a, Luang Prabang, Laos. No. 603c, Ayutthaya, Thailand. No. 565d, Borobudur Temple, Indonesia. No. 603f, Hué Monuments, Viet Nam.

2015, June 5   Litho.   Perf. 14x13½
601	A480	1.40fr multicolored	3.25	3.25
602	A480	1.90fr multicolored	4.50	4.50

Souvenir Booklet
603		Booklet, #603g-603l	23.50	
a.-c.	A480 30c any single		.70	.70
d.-f.	A480 50c any single		1.25	1.25
g.	Booklet pane of 4 #603a		2.80	—
h.	Booklet pane of 4 #603b		2.80	—
i.	Booklet pane of 4 #603c		2.80	—
j.	Booklet pane of 4 #603d		5.00	—
k.	Booklet pane of 4 #603e		5.00	—
l.	Booklet pane of 4 #603f		5.00	—

End Violence Against Children Type of 2015

Designs: 1fr, Child marriage. 1.40fr, Child trafficking.

Perf. 14½x14¼

2015, Aug. 20   Litho.
604	A481	1fr multicolored	2.40	2.40
605	A481	1.40fr multicolored	3.25	3.25

Miniature Sheet

G109

No. 606: a, Balcony above auditorium seats. b, Flags. c, Spiral staircase. d, Stylized horned mammal. e, Painting of trees. f, Auditorium seats facing stage with dais. g, Side view of auditorium seats, painting on wall. h, United Nations emblem. i, Armillary Sphere. j, Palais des Nations and flowers.

2015, Sept. 3   Litho.   Perf. 14¾
606	G109	Sheet of 10 + 10 labels	37.00	37.00
a.-j.		1.40fr Any single + label	3.50	3.50

The full sheet sold for $18.39 or 14.95fr. The generic labels are shown. Labels could be personalized. The personalization of labels was available only at UN Headquarters, and not through mail order.

Visitors Lobby G110

ECOSOC Chamber G111

Façade of Secretariat — G112

Chairs in ECOSOC Chamber — G113

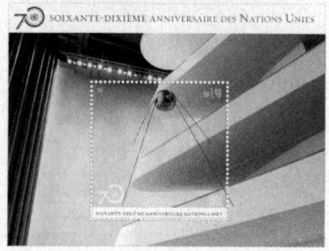

Visitors Lobby — G114

Printed by Cartor Security Printing, France. Panes of 6. Designed by Rorie Katz, U.S.

2015, Oct. 25   Litho.   Perf. 13¾
607	G110	1fr multicolored	2.40	2.40
608	G111	1fr multicolored	2.40	2.40
a.		Pair, #607-608	4.80	4.80
609	G112	1.90fr multicolored	4.50	4.50
610	G113	1.90fr multicolored	4.50	4.50
a.		Pair, #609-610	9.00	9.00
		Nos. 607-610 (4)	13.80	13.80

Souvenir Sheet

Perf. 13½
611	G114	1.40fr multicolored	3.25	3.25

United Nations, 70th anniv.

21st United
Nations
Climate
Chage
Conference,
Paris
G115

2015, Nov. 24   Litho.   Perf. 13¼
612 G115 1.40fr multicolored   3.25 3.25
Values are for stamps with surrounding
selvage.

Free and Equal Type of 2016
Designs: 1fr, Lesbians. 1.50fr, Gay family.

2016, Feb. 5   Litho.   Perf. 13½x13¼
613 A491 1fr multicolored   2.25 2.25
614 A491 1.50fr multicolored   3.50 3.50

HeForShe Type of 2016
Designs: 1fr, Man, blue background. 2fr,
Woman, mauve background.

2016, Mar. 8   Litho.   Perf. 12½x13
615 A492 1fr multicolored   2.25 2.25
616 A492 2fr multicolored   4.50 4.50

Miniature Sheets

G116

International Dance Day — G117

No. 617 — Illustration of Swedish dancers
by Karin Römark: a, Two male dancers. b,
Male dancer on one knee with female dancer.
c, Male dancer with yellow cap and female
dancer. d, Male dancer with red cap and vest
with female dancer. e, Three dancers, with
woman with red skirt at LR. f, Three dancers,
with woman with blue skirt at LR.
No. 618 — Illustration of African dancers by
Römark: a, Four dancers with sticks. b, Three
dancers with sticks. c, Dancers without sticks.
d, Dancer with blue and white mask. e, Two
masked dancers with sticks. f, Masked dancer
with two sticks.

2016, Apr. 29   Litho.   Perf. 13¼x13
617 G116 Sheet of 6   13.50 13.50
a.-f.   1fr Any single   2.25 2.25
618 G117 Sheet of 6   20.00 20.00
a.-f.   1.50fr Any single   3.25 3.25

International Day of United Nations Peacekeepers Type of 2016
Designs: 1fr, Helmeted peacekeepers.
1.50fr, Peacekeeper with African women.

Litho. With Foil Application
2016, May 29   Perf. 13¼x13
619 A496 1fr multicolored   2.25 2.25
620 A496 1.50fr multicolored   3.50 3.50

Sport for Peace Type of 2016
Olympic rings and: No. 621, Rowers,
denomination at UR. No. 622, Rowers,
denomination at UL. No. 623, Rhythmic gymnast facing forward, eyes open. No. 624,
Rhythmic gymnast facing left, eyes closed.

2016, July 22   Litho.   Perf. 14¼
621 A498 1fr multicolored   2.25 2.25
622 A498 1fr multicolored   2.25 2.25
a.   Pair, #621-622   4.50 4.50
623 A498 2fr multicolored   4.50 4.50
624 A498 2fr multicolored   4.50 4.50
a.   Pair, #623-624   9.00 9.00
           Nos. 621-624 (4)   13.50 13.50

World Heritage Sites, Czech Republic Type of 2016
Designs: Nos. 625, 627b, Gardens and
Castle at Kroměříz. Nos. 626, 627e, Lednice-
Valtice Cultural Landscape. No. 627a, Historic
Center of Prague. No. 627d, Holy Trinity Col-
umn, Olomouc. No. 627c, Historic Town
Center of Kutná Hora. No. 627f, Historic
Center of Cesky Krumlov.

2016, Sept. 8   Litho.   Perf. 14¼
625 A500 1fr multicolored   2.25 2.25
626 A500 1.50fr multicolored   3.50 3.50

Souvenir Booklet
627   Booklet, #1115g-
       1115l   22.00
a.-c. A500 30c any single   .65   .65
d.-f. A500 50c any single   1.10 1.10
g.   Booklet pane of 4 #627a   2.75   —
h.   Booklet pane of 4 #627b   2.75   —
i.   Booklet pane of 4 #627c   2.75   —
j.   Booklet pane of 4 #627d   4.50   —
k.   Booklet pane of 4 #627e   4.50   —
l.   Booklet pane of 4 #627f   4.50   —

Miniature Sheet

World Wildlife Conference,
Johannesburg — G118

No. 628 — Part of map of Africa and: a,
Grue royale (gray-crowned crane). b, Mantella
madagascariensis. c, Gorille des montagnes
(mountain gorilla). d, Avonia quinaria.

2016, Sept. 24   Litho.   Perf. 13x13½
628 G118 Sheet of 4   18.00 18.00
a.-d.   2fr Any single   4.50 4.50

Sustainable Development Goals Type of 2016
No. 629 — Inscription: a, 1 Pas de pauvreté.
b, 2 Faim "zéro". c, 3 Bonne santé et bien-être.
d, 4 Education de qualité. e, 5 Egalité entre les
sexes. f, 6 Eau propre et assainissement. g, 7
Energie propre et d'un coût abordable. h, 8
Travail décent et croissance écononmique. i, 9
Industrie, innovation et infrastructure. j, 10 Iné-
galités réduites. k, 11 Villes et communautés
durables. l, 12 Consommation et production
responsables. m, 13 Mesures relatives à la
lutte contre les changements climatiques. n,
14 Vie aquatique. o, 15 Vie terrestre. p, 16
Paix, justice et institutions efficaces. q, 17
Partneriats pour la réalisation des objectifs.

2016, Oct. 24   Litho.   Perf. 13¼
629   Sheet of 17 + label   39.00 39.00
a.-q.   A503 1fr Any single   2.25 2.25

SEMI-POSTAL STAMPS

AIDS Awareness Semi-postal Type
Souvenir Sheet

2002, Oct. 24   Litho.   Perf. 14½
B1 SP1 90c + 30c multicolored   4.00 4.00

OFFICES IN VIENNA, AUSTRIA

For use only on mail posted at the
Vienna International Center for the UN
and the International Atomic Energy
Agency.

100 Groschen = 1 Schilling
100 Cents = 1 Euro (2002)

> Catalogue values for all unused
> stamps in this country are for
> Never Hinged items.

Type of Geneva, 1978, UN Types of 1961-72 and

Donaupark,
Vienna — V1

Aerial View — V2

1979, Aug. 24   Photo.   Perf. 11½
Granite Paper
1 G8   50g multicolored   .25   .30
2 A52 1s multicolored   .25   .30
3 V1   4s multicolored   .25   .30
4 AP13 5s multicolored   .30   .35
5 V2   6s multicolored   .35   .35
6 A45 10s multicolored   .60   .70
       Nos. 1-6 (6)   2.00 2.30
No. 6 has no frame.

New Economic Order Type of UN
1980, Jan. 11   Litho.   Perf. 15x14½
7 A178 4s multicolored   .60   .70

Dove Type of UN
1980, Jan. 11   Litho.   Perf. 14x13½
8 A147 2.50s multicolored   .25   .30

Women's
Year Emblem
on World
Map — V3

United Nations Decade for Women.
1980, Mar. 7   Litho.   Perf. 14½x15
9   V3 4s light green & dark
        green   .40   .45
10 V3 6s bister brown   .75   .85

Peace-keeping Operations Type of UN
1980, May 16   Litho.   Perf. 14x13
11 A182 6s multicolored   .40   .45

35th Anniversary Types of Geneva and UN
1980, June 26   Litho.   Perf. 13x13½
12 G16   4s carmine rose &
          black   .35   .40
13 A184 6s multicolored   .60   .65
Souvenir Sheet
Imperf
14   Sheet of 2   .90 1.00
a.   G16 4s carmine rose & black .25 .30
b.   A184 6s multicolored   .65   .30

ECOSOC Types of UN and Geneva
1980, Nov. 21   Litho.   Perf. 13½x13
15 A187 4s multicolored   .30   .35
16 G17   6s multicolored   .60   .30

Palestinian Rights Type of UN
1981, Jan. 30   Photo.   Perf. 12x11½
17 A188 4s multicolored   .45   .50

Disabled Type of UN and

Interlocking
Stitches — V4

1981, Mar. 6   Photo.   Perf. 14
18 A189 4s multicolored   .40   .45
19 V4   6s black & orange   .60   .70

Art Type of UN
1981, Apr. 15   Photo.   Perf. 11½
Granite Paper
20 A191 6s multicolored   .75   .85

Energy Type of UN
1981, May 29   Litho.   Perf. 13
21 A193 7.50s multicolored   .70   .80

Volunteers Program Types
1981, Nov. 13   Litho.
22 A195 5s multicolored   .40   .45
23 G18   7s multicolored   .90 1.00

"For a Better
World" — V5

1982, Jan. 22   Perf. 11½x12
24 V5 3s multicolored   .35   .40

Human Environment Types of UN and Geneva
1982, Mar. 19   Litho.   Perf. 13½x13
25 A200 5s multicolored   .40   .45
26 G21   7s multicolored   .80   .90

Outer Space Type of Geneva
1982, June 11   Litho.   Perf. 13x13½
27 G22   5s multicolored   .60   .70

Conservation & Protection of Nature Type
1982, Nov. 16   Photo.   Perf. 14
28 A202 5s Fish   .50   .60
29 A202 7s Animal   .70   .80

World Communications Year Type
1983, Jan. 28   Litho.   Perf. 13
30 A203 4s multicolored   .40   .45

Safety at Sea Types of Geneva and UN
1983, Mar. 18   Litho.   Perf. 14½
31 G23   4s multicolored   .40   .45
32 A206 6s multicolored   .65   .75

World Food Program Type
1983, Apr. 22   Engr.   Perf. 13½
33 A207 5s green   .45   .50
34 A207 7s brown   .70   .80

UN Conference on Trade and Development Types of Geneva and UN
1983, June 6   Litho.   Perf. 14
35 G24   4s multicolored   .30   .35
36 A209 8.50s multicolored   .75   .85

V6

35th Anniv. of the Universal Declaration of Human Rights — V7

Photo. & Engr.

1983, Dec. 9			Perf. 13½
37	V6	5s multicolored	.45 .50
38	V7	7s multicolored	.70 .80

International Conference on Population Type

1984, Feb. 3		Litho.	Perf. 14
39	A212	7s multicolored	.65 .75

Field Irrigation V8

Harvesting Machine V9

World Food Day, Oct. 16

1984, Mar. 15		Litho.	Perf. 14½
40	V8	4.50s multicolored	.40 .45
41	V9	6s multicolored	.65 .75

Serengeti Park, Tanzania V10

Ancient City of Shiban, People's Democratic Rep. of Yemen — V11

World Heritage

1984, Mar. 15		Litho.	Perf. 14
42	V10	3.50s multicolored	.25 .30
43	V11	15s multicolored	1.25 1.40

V12　　　V13

Future for Refugees

1984, May 29		Photo.	Perf. 11½
44	V12	4.50s multicolored	.45 .50
45	V13	8.50s multicolored	1.25 1.40

International Youth Year — V14

1984, Nov. 15		Litho.	Perf. 13½
46	V14	3.50s multicolored	.45 .50
47	V14	6.50s multicolored	.70 .80

ILO Type of Geneva

1985, Feb. 1		Engr.	Perf. 13½
48	G34	7.50s U Thant Pavilion	.75 .85

UN University Type

1985, Mar. 15		Photo.	Perf. 11½
49	A221	8.50s Rural scene, lab researcher	.75 .85

Ship of Peace V15　　Sharing Umbrella V16

1985, May 10		Litho.	Perf. 14
50	V15	4.50s multicolored	.30 .35
51	V16	15s multicolored	2.00 2.25

40th Anniversary Type
Perf. 12 x 11½

1985, June 26			Photo.
52	A224	6.50s multicolored	.90 1.00
53	A225	8.50s multicolored	1.40 1.60

Souvenir Sheet
Imperf

54		Sheet of 2	2.50 2.75
a.		A224 6.50s multi	1.00 1.10
b.		A225 8.50s multi	1.40 1.50

UNICEF Child Survival Campaign Type

4s, Spoonfeeding children. 6s, Mother hugging infant.

Photo. & Engr.

1985, Nov. 22			Perf. 13½
55	A226	4s multicolored	.75 .85
56	A226	6s multicolored	1.40 1.60

Africa in Crisis Type

1986, Jan. 31		Photo.	Perf. 11½x12
57	A227	8s multicolored	.80 .90

UN Development Program Type

Agriculture: No. 58, Developing crop strains. No. 59, Animal husbandry. No. 60, Technical instruction. No. 61, Nutrition education.

1986, Mar. 14		Photo.	Perf. 13½
58	A228	4.50s multicolored	1.50 1.75
59	A228	4.50s multicolored	1.50 1.75
60	A228	4.50s multicolored	1.50 1.75
61	A228	4.50s multicolored	1.50 1.75
a.		Block of 4, #58-61	6.25 7.00

No. 61a has a continuous design.

Stamp Collecting Type

Designs: 3.50s, UN stamps. 6.50s, Engraver.

1986, May 22		Engr.	Perf. 12½
62	A229	3.50s dk ultra & dk brown	.40 .45
63	A229	6.50s int blue & brt rose	.90 1.00

Olive Branch, Rainbow, Earth — V17

Photogravure & Embossed

1986, June 20			Perf. 13½
64	V17	5s shown	.75 .85
65	V17	6s Doves, UN emblem	1.00 1.10

WFUNA Anniversary Type
Souvenir Sheet

Designs: 4s, White stallion by Elisabeth von Janota-Bzowski, Germany. 5s, Surrealistic landscape by Ernst Fuchs, Austria. 6s, Geometric abstract by Victor Vasarely (b. 1908), France. 7s, Mythological abstract by Wolfgang Hutter (b. 1928), Austria.

1986, Nov. 14		Litho.	Perf. 13x13½
66		Sheet of 4	4.00 4.25
a.		A232 4s multicolored	.75 .80
b.		A232 5s multicolored	.85 .90
c.		A232 6s multicolored	1.00 1.10
d.		A232 7s multicolored	1.25 1.40

No. 66 has inscribed margin picturing UN and WFUNA emblems.

Trygve Lie Type
Photogravure & Engraved

1987, Jan. 30			Perf. 13½
67	A233	8s multicolored	.70 .80

Shelter for the Homeless Type

Designs: 4s, Family and homes. 9.50s, Family entering home.

Perf. 13½x12½

1987, Mar. 13			Litho.
68	A234	4s multicolored	.50 .55
69	A234	9.50s multicolored	1.10 1.25

Fight Drug Abuse Type

Designs: 5s, Soccer players. 8s, Family.

1987, June 12		Litho.	Perf. 14½x12½
70	A235	5s multicolored	.40 .45
71	A235	8s multicolored	.90 1.00

Donaupark, Vienna V18

Peace Embracing the Earth — V19

1987, June 12		Litho.	Perf. 14½x15
72	V18	2s multicolored	.30 .35
73	V19	17s multicolored	1.60 1.75

UN Day Type

Designs: Multinational people in various occupations.

1987, Oct. 23		Litho.	Perf. 14½x15
74	A236	5s multicolored	.75 .85
75	A236	6s multicolored	.90 1.00

Immunize Every Child Type

Designs: 4s, Poliomyelitis. 9.50s, Diphtheria.

1987, Nov. 20		Litho.	Perf. 15x14½
76	A237	4s multicolored	.75 .85
77	A237	9.50s multicolored	2.00 2.25

IFAD Type

Designs: 4s, Grains. 6s, Vegetables.

1988, Jan. 29		Litho.	Perf. 13½
78	A238	4s multicolored	.40 .45
79	A238	6s multicolored	.90 1.00

Survival of the Forests Type

Deciduous forest in fall: 4s, Treetops, hills and dales. 5s, Tree trunks. Printed se-tenant in a continuous design.

1988, Mar. 18		Litho.	Perf. 14x15
80	A240	4s multicolored	2.25 2.40
81	A240	5s multicolored	3.00 3.25
a.		Pair, #80-81	5.25 5.75

Intl. Volunteer Day Type

Designs: 6s, Medical care, vert. 7.50s, Construction.

Perf. 13x14, 14x13

1988, May 6			Litho.
82	A241	6s multicolored	.75 .85
83	A241	7.50s multicolored	1.00 1.10

Health in Sports Type

Paintings by LeRoy Neiman, American Sports artist: 6s, Skiing, vert. 8s, Tennis.

Perf. 13½x13, 13x13½

1988, June 17			Litho.
84	A242	6s multicolored	.90 1.00
85	A242	8s multicolored	1.40 1.60

Universal Declaration of Human Rights 40th Anniv. Type
Photo. & Engr.

1988, Dec. 9			Perf. 11½
86	A243	5s multicolored	.50 .55

Souvenir Sheet

| 87 | A243 | 11s multicolored | 1.25 1.40 |

No. 87 has multicolored decorative margin inscribed with preamble to the human rights declaration in German.

World Bank Type

1989, Jan. 27		Litho.	Perf. 13x14
88	A244	5.50s Transportation	1.10 1.25
89	A244	8s Health care, education	1.75 1.90

Peace-Keeping Force Type

1989, Mar. 17			Perf. 14x13½
90	A245	6s multicolored	.85 .95

World Weather Watch Type

Satellite photograph and radar image: 4s, Helical cloud formation over Italy, the eastern Alps, and parts of Yugoslavia. 9.50s, Rainfall in Tokyo, Japan.

1989, Apr. 21		Litho.	Perf. 13x14
91	A247	4s multicolored	1.00 1.10
92	A247	9.50s multicolored	2.10 2.25

V20　　　V21

Photo. & Engr., Photo. (7.50s)

1989, Aug. 23			Perf. 14
93	V20	5s multicolored	1.50 1.75
94	V21	7.50s multicolored	1.50 1.75

Human Rights Type of 1989

Paintings: 4s, The Prisoners, by Kathe Kollwitz. 6s, Justice, by Raphael.

1989, Nov. 17		Litho.	Perf. 13½
95	A250	4s multicolored	.50 .55
96	A250	6s multicolored	.75 .85

See Nos. 108-109, 123-124, 150-151.

Intl. Trade Center Type

1990, Feb. 2		Litho.	Perf. 14½x15
97	A251	12s multicolored	1.25 1.40

Painting by Kurt Regschek V22

1990, Feb. 2		Litho.	Perf. 13x13½
98	V22	1.50s multicolored	.30 .35

V23

Designs: 5s, "SIDA." 11s, Stylized figures, ink blot.

Perf. 13½x12½

1990, Mar. 16			Litho.
99	V23	5s multicolored	1.00 1.10
100	V23	11s multicolored	2.25 2.40

Medicinal Plants Type

1990, May 4		Photo.	Perf. 11½

Granite Paper

| 101 | A253 | 4.50s Bixa orellana | 1.25 1.40 |
| 102 | A253 | 9.50s Momordica charantia | 2.50 2.75 |

UN 45th Anniv. Type

Designs: 7s, 9s, "45" and emblem.

1990, June 26   Litho.   Perf. 14½x13
103 A254 7s multicolored   1.40 1.60
104 A254 9s multicolored, diff.   2.40 2.75

Souvenir Sheet
105   Sheet of 2, #103-104   5.00 5.50

Crime Prevention Type

1990, Sept. 13   Photo.   Perf. 14
106 A255 6s Domestic violence   1.00 1.10
107 A255 8s Crimes against cul-
            tural heritage   2.25 2.50

Human Rights Type of 1989

Paintings: 4.50s, Before the Judge, by Sandor Bihari. 7s, Young Man Greeted by a Woman Writing a Poem, by Suzuki Harunobu.

1990, Nov. 16   Litho.   Perf. 13½
108 A250 4.50s multicolored   .30   .35
109 A250 7s multicolored   .90 1.00

Economic Commission for Europe Type

1991, Mar. 15   Litho.   Perf. 14
110 A256 5s Weasel, hoopoe   1.25 1.40
111 A256 5s Warbler, swans   1.25 1.40
112 A256 5s Badgers, squirrel   1.25 1.40
113 A256 5s Fish   1.25 1.40
a.   Block of 4, #110-113   5.00 5.50

Namibian Independence Type

1991, May 10   Litho.   Perf. 14
114 A257 6s Mountains,
            clouds   1.00 1.25
115 A257 9.50s Dune, Namib
            Desert   2.25 2.50

V24

1991, May 10   Litho.   Perf. 15x14½
116 V24 20s multicolored   1.75 2.00

V25

Rights of the Child — V26

1991, June 14   Litho.   Perf. 14½
117 V25 7s Stick drawings   1.00 1.25
118 V26 9s Child, clock, fruit   1.50 1.75

V27

Banning of Chemical Weapons V28

1991, Sept. 11   Litho.   Perf. 13½
119 V27 5s multicolored   .75   .90
120 V28 10s multicolored   1.75 2.00

UN Postal Administration, 40th Anniv. Type

1991, Oct. 24   Litho.   Perf. 14x15
121 A263 5s UN NY No. 8   .75   .90
122 A263 8s UN NY No. 5   1.50 1.75

Human Rights Type of 1989

Artwork: 4.50s, Pre-columbian Mexican pottery. 7s, Windows, by Robert Delaunay.

1991, Nov. 20   Litho.   Perf. 13½
123 A250 4.50s black & brown   .50   .55
124 A250 7s multicolored   .80   .90

World Heritage Type of 1984

Designs: 5s, Iguacu Natl. Park, Brazil. 9s, Abu Simbel, Egypt.

1992, Jan. 24   Litho.   Perf. 13
Size: 35x28mm
125 V10 5s multicolored   .75   .90
126 V10 9s multicolored   1.60 1.80

Clean Oceans Type

1992, Mar. 13   Litho.   Perf. 14
127 A264 7s Ocean surface, diff. 1.00 1.10
128 A264 7s Ocean bottom, diff.   1.00 1.10
a.   Pair, #127-128   2.25 2.50

Earth Summit Type

1992, May 22   Photo.   Perf. 11½
129 A265 5.50s Man in space   1.30 1.50
130 A265 5.50s Sun   1.30 1.50
131 A265 5.50s Man fishing   1.30 1.50
132 A265 5.50s Sailboat   1.30 1.50
a.   Block of 4, #129-132   5.50 6.00

Mission to Planet Earth Type

Designs: No. 133, Satellite, person's mouth. No. 134, Satellite, person's ear.

1992, Sept. 4   Photo.   Rouletted 8
Granite Paper
133 A266 10s multicolored   2.50 2.75
134 A266 10s multicolored   2.50 2.75
a.   Pair, #133-134   5.00 5.50

Science and Technology Type of 1992

Designs: 5.50s, Woman emerging from computer screen. 7s, Green thumb growing flowers.

1992, Oct. 2   Litho.   Perf. 14
135 A267 5.50s multicolored   .75   .85
136 A267 7s multicolored   1.40 1.60

V29

Intl. Center, Vienna — V30

1992, Oct. 2   Litho.   Perf. 13x13½
137 V29 5.50s multicolored   .90 1.00
Perf. 13½x13
138 V30 7s multicolored   1.25 1.40

Human Rights Type of 1989

Artwork: 6s, Les Constructeurs, by Fernand Leger. 10s, Sunday Afternoon on the Island of Le Grande Jatte, by Georges Seurat.

1992, Nov. 20   Litho.   Perf. 13½
139 A250 6s multicolored   .75   .85
140 A250 10s multicolored   1.25 1.40

Aging With Dignity Type

Designs: 5.50s, Elderly couple, family working in garden. 7s, Older woman teaching.

1993, Feb. 5   Litho.   Perf. 13
141 A270 5.50s multicolored   .75   .85
142 A270 7s multicolored   1.40 1.60

Endangered Species Type

Designs: No. 143, Equus grevyi (Grevy's zebra). No. 144, Spheniscus humboldti (Humboldt's penguins). No. 145, Varanus griseus (desert monitor). No. 146, Canis lupus (gray wolf).

1993, Mar. 2   Litho.   Perf. 13x12½
143 A271 7s multicolored   .90 1.00
144 A271 7s multicolored   .90 1.00
145 A271 7s multicolored   .90 1.00
146 A271 7s multicolored   .90 1.00
a.   Block of 4, #143-146   3.60 4.00

Healthy Environment Type

1993, May 7   Litho.   Perf. 15x14½
147 A272 6s Wave in ocean   1.25 1.40
148 A272 10s Globe   2.00 2.25

V31

1993, May 7   Photo.   Perf. 11½
Granite Paper
149 V31 13s multicolored   2.00 2.25

Human Rights Type of 1989

Artwork: 5s, Lower Austrian Peasants' Wedding, by Ferdinand G. Waldmuller. 6s, Outback, by Sally Morgan.

1993, June 11   Litho.   Perf. 13½
150 A250 5s multicolored   .80   .90
151 A250 6s multicolored   1.00 1.10

Intl. Peace Day Type

Denomination at: No. 152, UL. No. 153, UR. No. 154, LL. No. 155, LR.

Rouletted 12½
1993, Sept. 21   Litho. & Engr.
152 A274 5.50s green & multi   1.80 2.00
153 A274 5.50s green & multi   1.80 2.00
154 A274 5.50s green & multi   1.80 2.00
155 A274 5.50s green & multi   1.80 2.00
a.   Block of 4, #152-155   7.25 8.25

Environment-Climate Type

Designs: No. 156, Monkeys. No. 157, Bluebird, industrial pollution, volcano. No. 158, Volcano, nuclear power plant, tree stumps. No. 159, Cactus, tree stumps, owl.

1993, Oct. 29   Litho.   Perf. 14½
156 A275 7s multicolored   2.00 2.25
157 A275 7s multicolored   2.00 2.25
158 A275 7s multicolored   2.00 2.25
159 A275 7s multicolored   2.00 2.25
a.   Strip of 4, #156-159   8.00 9.00

Intl. Year of the Family Type of 1993

Designs: 5.50s, Adults, children holding hands. 8s, Two adults, child planting crops.

1994, Feb. 4   Litho.   Perf. 13.1
160 A276 5.50s blue green &
            multi   1.00 1.10
161 A276 8s red & multi   1.25 1.40

Endangered Species Type of 1993

Designs: No. 162, Ocelot. No. 163, White-breasted silver-eye. No. 164, Mediterranean monk seal. No. 165, Asian elephant.

1994, Mar. 18   Litho.   Perf. 12.7
162 A271 7s multicolored   1.00 1.10
163 A271 7s multicolored   1.00 1.10
164 A271 7s multicolored   1.00 1.10
165 A271 7s multicolored   1.00 1.10
a.   Block of 4, #162-165   4.00 4.40

Protection for Refugees Type

Design: 12s, Protective hands surround group of refugees.

1994, Apr. 29   Litho.   Perf. 14.3x14.8
166 A277 12s multicolored   1.50 1.75

V32   V33

V34

1994, Apr. 29   Litho.   Perf. 12.9
167 V32 50g multicolored   .25   .30
168 V33 4s multicolored   .40   .45
169 V34 30s multicolored   4.00 4.50
      Nos. 167-169 (3)   4.65 5.25

Intl. Decade for Natural Disaster Reduction Type

Earth seen from space, outline map of: No. 170, North America. No. 171, Eurasia. No. 172, South America. No. 173, Australia and South Asia.

1994, May 27   Litho.   Perf. 13.9x14.2
170 A281 6s multicolored   1.75 1.90
171 A281 6s multicolored   1.75 1.90
172 A281 6s multicolored   1.75 1.90
173 A281 6s multicolored   1.75 1.90
a.   Block of 4, #170-173   7.00 7.75

Population and Development Type

Designs: 5.50s, Women teaching, running machine tool, coming home to family. 7s, Family on tropical island.

1994, Sept. 1   Litho.   Perf. 13.2x13.6
174 A282 5.50s multicolored   .90 1.00
175 A282 7s multicolored   1.50 1.75

UNCTAD Type

1994, Oct. 28
176 A283 6s multi, diff.   .90 1.00
177 A283 7s multi, diff.   1.50 1.75

UN 50th Anniv. Type
Litho. & Engr.

1995, Jan. 1   Perf. 13.4
178 A284 7s multicolored   1.25 1.40

Social Summit Type
Photo. & Engr.

1995, Feb. 3   Perf. 13.6x13.9
179 A285 14s multi, diff.   2.00 2.25

Endangered Species Type of 1993

Designs: No. 180, Black rhinoceros, Diceros bicornis. No. 181, Golden conure, Aratinga guarouba. No. 182, Douc langur, Pygathrix nemaeus. No. 183, Arabian oryx, Oryx leucoryx.

1995, Mar. 24   Litho.   Perf. 13x12½
180 A271 7s multicolored   1.00 1.10
181 A271 7s multicolored   1.00 1.10
182 A271 7s multicolored   1.00 1.10
183 A271 7s multicolored   1.00 1.10
a.   Block of 4, 180-183   4.00 4.50

Intl. Youth Year Type

Designs: 6s, Village in winter. 7s, Teepees.

1995, May 26   Litho.   Perf. 14.4x14.7
184 A286 6s multicolored   .80   .90
185 A286 7s multicolored   1.00 1.10

UN, 50th Anniv. Type

Designs: 7s, Like No. 663. 10s, Like No. 664.

Perf. 13.3x13.6
1995, June 26   Engr.
186 A287 7s green   1.00 1.10
187 A287 10s black   1.50 1.70

Souvenir Sheet
Litho. & Engr.
Imperf
188   Sheet of 2, #186-187   2.50 2.80
a.   A287 7s green   1.00 1.10
b.   A287 10s black   1.50 1.70

Conference on Women Type

Designs: 5.50s, Women amid tropical plants. 6s, Woman reading, swans on lake.

1995, Sept. 5   Photo.   Perf. 12
189 A288 5.50s multicolored   .80   .90
Size: 28x50mm
190 A288 6s multicolored   1.20 1.30

UN People, 50th Anniv. Type

1995, Oct. 24   Litho.   Perf. 14
191   Sheet of 12   12.00 13.00
a.-l. A290 3s any single   1.00 1.10
192   Souvenir booklet   14.00
a.   A290 3s Booklet pane of 3,
       vert. strip of 3 from UL of
       sheet   3.50 4.00
b.   A290 3s Booklet pane of 3,
       vert. strip of 3 from UR of
       sheet   3.50 4.00
c.   A290 3s Booklet pane of 3,
       vert. strip of 3 from LL of
       sheet   3.50 4.00
d.   A290 3s Booklet pane of 3,
       vert. strip of 3 from LR of
       sheet   3.50 4.00

WFUNA, 50th Anniv. Type

Design: 7s, Harlequin holding dove.

1996, Feb. 2   Litho.   Perf. 13x13½
193 A291 7s multicolored   1.00 1.10

UN Flag — V35

Abstract, by Karl Korab — V36

1996, Feb. 2   Litho.   Perf. 15x14½
194	V35	1s multicolored	.25 .30
195	V36	10s multicolored	1.60 1.75

Endangered Species Type of 1993

Designs: No. 196, Cypripedium calceolus. No. 197, Aztekium ritteri. No. 198, Euphorbia cremersii. No. 199, Dracula bella.

1996, Mar. 14   Litho.   Perf. 12½
196	A271	7s multicolored	.75 .85
197	A271	7s multicolored	.75 .85
198	A271	7s multicolored	.75 .85
199	A271	7s multicolored	.75 .85
a.		Block of 4, #196-199	3.00 3.40

City Summit Type

Designs: No. 200, Arab family selling fruits, vegetables. No. 201, Women beside stream, camels. No. 202, Woman carrying bundle on head, city skyline. No. 203, Woman threshing grain, yoke of oxen in field. No. 204, Native village, elephant.

1996, June 3   Litho.   Perf. 14x13½
200	A293	6s multicolored	1.50 1.75
201	A293	6s multicolored	1.50 1.75
202	A293	6s multicolored	1.50 1.75
203	A293	6s multicolored	1.50 1.75
204	A293	6s multicolored	1.50 1.75
a.		Strip of 5, #200-204	7.50 9.00

Sport and the Environment Type

6s, Men's parallel bars (gymnastics), vert. 7s, Hurdles.

Perf. 14x14½, 14½x14
1996, July 19   Litho.
205	A294	6s multicolored	.80 .90
206	A294	7s multicolored	.90 1.00

Souvenir Sheet
207	A294	Sheet of 2, #205-206	1.75 1.90

Plea for Peace Type

Designs: 7s, Dove and butterflies. 10s, Stylized dove, diff.

1996, Sept. 17   Litho.   Perf. 14½x15
208	A295	7s multicolored	.80 .90
209	A295	10s multicolored	1.20 1.40

UNICEF Type

Fairy Tales: 5.50s, Hansel and Gretel, by the Brothers Grimm. 8s, How Maui Stole Fire from the Gods, South Pacific.

1996, Nov. 20   Litho.   Perf. 14½x15
210	A296	5.50s multicolored	.90 1.00
211	A296	8s multicolored	1.40 1.60

V37

Phoenixes Flying Down (Detail), by Sagenji Yoshida — V38

1997, Feb. 12   Litho.   Perf. 14½
212	V37	5s multicolored	.80 .90
213	V38	6s multicolored	.90 1.00

Endangered Species Type of 1993

Designs: No. 214, Macaca sylvanus (Barbary macaque). No. 215, Anthropoides paradisea (blue crane). No. 216, Equus przewalskii (Przewalski horse). No. 217, Myrmecophaga tridactyla (giant anteater).

1997, Mar. 13   Litho.   Perf. 12½
214	A271	7s multicolored	.75 .85
215	A271	7s multicolored	.75 .85
216	A271	7s multicolored	.75 .85
217	A271	7s multicolored	.75 .85
a.		Block of 4, #214-217	3.00 3.40

Earth Summit Anniv. Type

Designs: No. 218, Person running. No. 219, Hills, stream, trees. No. 220, Tree with orange leaves. No. 221, Tree with pink leaves.
11s, Combined design similar to Nos. 218-221.

1997, May 30   Photo.   Perf. 11.5
Granite Paper
218	A299	3.50s multicolored	1.50 1.75
219	A299	3.50s multicolored	1.50 1.75
220	A299	3.50s multicolored	1.50 1.75
221	A299	3.50s multicolored	1.50 1.75
a.		Block of 4, #218-221	6.00 7.00

Souvenir Sheet
222	A299	11s multicolored	2.00 2.25

Transportation Type

Ground transportation: No. 223, 1829 Rocket, 1901 Darraque. No. 224, Steam engine from Vladikawska Railway, trolley. No. 225, Double-decker bus. No. 226, 1950s diesel locomotive, semi-trailer. No. 227, High-speed train, electric car.

1997, Aug. 29   Litho.   Perf. 14x14½
223	A300	7s multicolored	1.25 1.40
224	A300	7s multicolored	1.25 1.40
225	A300	7s multicolored	1.25 1.40
226	A300	7s multicolored	1.25 1.40
227	A300	7s multicolored	1.25 1.40
a.		Strip of 5, #223-227	6.25 7.00

No. 227a has continuous design.

Philately Type

Designs: 6.50s, No. 62. 7s, No. 63.

1997, Oct. 14   Litho.   Perf. 13½x14
228	A301	6.50s multicolored	.80 .90
229	A301	7s multicolored	.90 1.00

World Heritage Convention Type

Terracotta warriors of Xian: 3s, Single warrior. 6s, Massed warriors. No. 232a, like No. 716. No. 232b, like No. 717. No. 232c, like Geneva No. 314. No. 232d, like Geneva No. 315. No. 232e, like Vienna No. 230. No. 232f, like Vienna No. 231.

1997, Nov. 19   Litho.   Perf. 13½
230	A302	3s multicolored	1.00 1.10
231	A302	6s multicolored	2.00 2.25
232		Souvenir booklet	12.00
a.-f.		A302 1s any single	.50 .55
g.		Booklet pane of 4 #232a	2.00 2.25
h.		Booklet pane of 4 #232b	2.00 2.25
i.		Booklet pane of 4 #232c	2.00 2.25
j.		Booklet pane of 4 #232d	2.00 2.25
k.		Booklet pane of 4 #232e	2.00 2.25
l.		Booklet pane of 4 #232f	2.00 2.25

Japanese Peace Bell, Vienna — V39

Vienna Subway, Vienna Intl. Center — V40

1998, Feb. 13   Litho.   Perf. 15x14½
233	V39	6.50s multicolored	.80 .90
234	V40	9s multicolored	1.00 1.10

Endangered Species Type of 1993

Designs: No. 235, Chelonia mydas (green turtle). No. 236, Speotyto cunicularia (burrowing owl). No. 237, Trogonoptera brookiana (Rajah Brooke's birdwing). No. 238, Ailurus fulgens (lesser panda).

1998, Mar. 13   Litho.   Perf. 12½
235	A271	7s multicolored	.75 .85
236	A271	7s multicolored	.75 .85
237	A271	7s multicolored	.75 .85
238	A271	7s multicolored	.75 .85
a.		Block of 4, #235-238	3.00 3.40

Intl. Year of the Ocean — V41

1998, May 20   Litho.   Perf. 13x13½
239	V41	Sheet of 12	11.00 12.00
a.-l.		3.50s any single	.90 1.00

Rain Forests Type

1998, June 19   Perf. 13x13½
240	A307	6.50s Ocelot	.90 1.00

Souvenir Sheet
241	A307	22s like #240	3.00 3.25

Peacekeeping Type of 1998

Designs: 4s, Soldier passing out relief supplies. 7.50s, UN supervised voting.

1998, Sept. 15   Photo.   Perf. 12
242	A308	4s multicolored	.50 .60
243	A308	7.50s multicolored	1.00 1.10

Declaration of Human Rights Type

Designs: 4.50s, Stylized person. 7s, Gears.

Litho. & Photo.
1998, Oct. 27   Perf. 13
244	A309	4.50s multicolored	.80 .90
245	A309	7s multicolored	1.25 1.40

Schönbrunn Palace Type

Designs: 3.50s, No. 248d, Palace. 7s, No. 248c, Porcelain stove, vert. No. 248a, Blue porcelain vase, vert. No. 248b, Wall painting on fabric (detail), by Johann Wenzl Bergl, vert. No. 248e, Great Palm House (conservatory). No. 248f, The Gloriette (archway).

1998, Dec. 4   Litho.   Perf. 14
246	A310	3.50s multicolored	.60 .70
247	A310	7s multicolored	1.10 1.25

Souvenir Booklet
248		Booklet	20.00
a.-c.		A310 1s any single	.60 .70
d.-f.		A310 2s any single	1.20 1.30
g.		Booklet pane of 4 #248d	4.80 5.25
h.		Booklet pane of 3 #248a	1.80 2.00
i.		Booklet pane of 3 #248b	1.80 2.00
j.		Booklet pane of 3 #248c	1.80 2.00
k.		Booklet pane of 4 #248e	4.80 5.25
l.		Booklet pane of 4 #248f	4.80 5.25

Volcanic Landscape — V42

1999, Feb. 5   Litho.   Perf. 13x13½
249	V42	8s multicolored	1.25 1.40

World Heritage, Australia Type

Designs: 4.50s, No. 252d, Uluru-Kata Tjuta Natl. Park. 6.50s, No. 252a, Tasmanian Wilderness. No. 252b, Wet tropics of Queensland. No. 252c, Great Barrier Reef. No. 252e, Kakadu Natl. Park. No. 252f, Willandra Lakes region.

1999, Mar. 19   Litho.   Perf. 13
250	A313	4.50s multicolored	.75 .85
251	A313	6.50s multicolored	1.10 1.25

Souvenir Booklet
252		Booklet	12.00
a.-c.		A313 1s any single	.35 .40
d.-f.		A313 2s any single	.65 .70
g.		Booklet pane of 4, #252a	1.40 1.60
h.		Booklet pane of 4, #252d	2.60 2.80
i.		Booklet pane of 4, #252b	1.40 1.60
j.		Booklet pane of 4, #252e	2.60 2.80
k.		Booklet pane of 4, #252c	1.40 1.60
l.		Booklet pane of 4, #252f	2.60 2.80

Endangered Species Type of 1993

Designs: No. 253, Pongo pygmaeus (oranutan). No. 254, Pelecanus crispus (Dalmatian pelican). No. 255, Eunectes notaeus (yellow anaconda). No. 256, Caracal.

1999, Apr. 22   Litho.   Perf. 12½
253	A271	7s multicolored	.75 .85
254	A271	7s multicolored	.75 .85
255	A271	7s multicolored	.75 .85
256	A271	7s multicolored	.75 .85
a.		Block of 4, #253-256	3.00 3.40

UNISPACE III Type

Designs: No. 257, Satellite over ships. No. 258, Satellite up close. No. 259, Composite of Nos. 257-258.

1999, July 7   Photo.   Rouletted 8
257	A314	3.50s multicolored	.75 .85
258	A314	3.50s multicolored	.75 .85
a.		Pair, #257-258	1.60 1.70

Souvenir Sheet
Perf. 14½
259	A314	13s multicolored	4.50 5.00

UPU Type

Various people, late 20th century methods of mail transportation, denomination at: No. 260, UL. No. 261, UR. No. 262, LL. No. 263, LR.

1999, Aug. 23   Photo.   Perf. 11¾
260	A315	6.50s multicolored	1.00 1.10
261	A315	6.50s multicolored	1.00 1.10
262	A315	6.50s multicolored	1.00 1.10
263	A315	6.50s multicolored	1.00 1.10
a.		Block of 4, #260-263	4.00 4.50

In Memoriam Type

Designs: 6.50s, 14s, Donaupark. Size of 14s stamp: 34x63mm.

1999, Sept. 21   Litho.   Perf. 14½x14
264	A316	6.50s multicolored	.90 1.00

Souvenir Sheet
Perf. 14
265	A316	14s multicolored	3.00 3.25

Education Type

Perf. 13½x13¾
1999, Nov. 18   Litho.
266	A317	7s Boy, girl, book	.75 .85
267	A317	13s Group reading	1.75 1.90

Intl. Year of Thanksgiving Type

2000, Jan. 1   Litho.   Perf. 13¼x13½
268	A318	7s multicolored	1.00 1.10

On No. 268 parts of the design were applied by a thermographic process producing a shiny, raised effect.

Endangered Species Type of 1993

Designs: No. 269, Panthera pardus (leopard). No. 270, Platalea leucorodia (white spoonbill). No. 271, Hippocamelus bisulcus (huemal). No. 272, Orcinus orca (killer whale).

2000, Apr. 6   Litho.   Perf. 12¾x12½
269	A271	7s multicolored	1.10 1.25
270	A271	7s multicolored	1.10 1.25
271	A271	7s multicolored	1.10 1.25
272	A271	7s multicolored	1.10 1.25
a.		Block of 4, #269-272	4.50 5.00

Our World 2000 Type

Winning artwork in Millennium painting competition: 7s, Tomorrow's Dream, by Voltaire Perez, Philippines. 8s, Remembrance, by Dimitris Nalbandis, Greece, vert.

Perf. 13x13½, 13½x13
2000, May 30   Litho.
273	A319	7s multicolored	.60 .70
274	A319	8s multicolored	.75 .85

55th Anniversary Type

Designs: 7s, Secretariat Building, unfinished dome of General Assembly Hall, 1951. 9s, Trygve Lie and Headquarters Advisory Committee at topping-out ceremony, 1949.

2000, July 7   Litho.   Perf. 13¼x13
275	A320	7s multicolored	.90 1.00
276	A320	9s multicolored	1.25 1.40

Souvenir Sheet
277	A320	Sheet of 2, #275-276	2.75 3.25

The UN in the 21st Century — V43

No. 278: a, Farm machinery. b, UN Peacekeepers and children. c, Oriental farm workers. d, Peacekeepers searching for mines. e, Medical research. f, Handicapped people.

2000, Sept. 15   Litho.   Perf. 14
278	V43	Sheet of 6	7.50	8.50
a.-f.		3.50s any single	1.25	1.40

World Heritage, Spain Type

Designs: Nos. 279, 281c, Aqueduct of Segovia. Nos. 280, 281f, Güell Park, Barcelona. No. 281a, Alhambra, Generalife and Albayzin, Granada. No. 281b, Walled Town of Cuenca. No. 281d, Amphitheater of Mérida. No. 281e, Toledo.

2000, Oct. 6   Litho.   Perf. 14¾x14½
279	A323	4.50s multicolored	.80	.90
280	A323	6.50s multicolored	1.20	1.40

Souvenir Booklet
281		Booklet	9.00	
a.-c.		A323 1s any single	.25	.30
d.-f.		A323 2s any single	.50	.55
g.		Booklet pane of 4, #281a	1.00	1.10
h.		Booklet pane of 4, #281b	2.00	2.25
i.		Booklet pane of 4, #281b	1.00	1.10
j.		Booklet pane of 4, #281e	2.00	2.25
k.		Booklet pane of 4, #281c	1.00	1.10
l.		Booklet pane of 4, #281f	2.00	2.25

Respect for Refugees Type

Designs: 7s, 25s, Refugee with hat, three other refugees.

2000, Nov. 9   Litho.   Perf. 13¼x12¾
282	A324	7s multicolored	1.10	1.25

Souvenir Sheet
283	A324	25s multicolored	3.75	4.25

Endangered Species Type of 1993

Designs: No. 284, Tremarctos ornatus (spectacled bear). No. 285, Anas laysanensis (Laysan duck). No. 286, Proteles cristatus (aardwolf). No. 287, Trachypithecus cristatus (silvered leaf monkey).

2001, Feb. 1   Litho.   Perf. 12¾x12½
284	A271	7s multicolored	1.10	1.25
285	A271	7s multicolored	1.10	1.25
286	A271	7s multicolored	1.10	1.25
287	A271	7s multicolored	1.10	1.25
a.		Block of 4, #284-287	4.50	5.00

Intl. Volunteers Year — V44

Paintings by: 10s, Nguyen Thanh Chuong, Viet Nam. 12s, Ikko Tanaka, Japan.

2001, Mar. 29   Litho.   Perf. 13¼
288	V44	10s multicolored	1.40	1.60
289	V44	12s multicolored	1.75	1.90

World Heritage, Japan Type

Designs: 7s, No. 290c, Himeji-Jo. 15s, No. 291f, Nikko. No. 292a, Kyoto. No. 292b, Nara. No. 292d, Shirakawa-Go and Gokayama. No. 292e, Itsukushima Shinto Shrine.

2001, Aug. 1   Litho.   Perf. 12¾x13¼
290	A328	7s multicolored	1.00	1.10
291	A328	15s multicolored	2.10	2.25

Souvenir Booklet
292		Booklet	11.50	
a.-c.		A328 1s any single	.30	.35
d.-f.		A328 2s any single	.60	.70
g.		Booklet pane of 4, #292a	1.20	1.40
h.		Booklet pane of 4, #292d	2.40	2.75
i.		Booklet pane of 4, #292b	1.20	1.40
j.		Booklet pane of 4, #292e	2.40	2.75
k.		Booklet pane of 4, #292c	1.20	1.40
l.		Booklet pane of 4, #292f	2.40	2.75

Dag Hammarskjöld Type

2001, Sept. 18   Engr.   Perf. 11x11¼
293	A329	7s green	1.00	1.10

UN Postal Administration, 50th Anniv. Types

2001, Oct. 18   Litho.   Perf. 13½
294	A330	7s Stamps, balloons	1.00	1.10
295	A330	8s Stamps, cake	1.10	1.25

Souvenir Sheet
296	A331	Sheet of 2	7.50	8.00
a.		7s green & light blue, 38mm diameter	2.50	2.75
b.		21s green & light blue, 38mm diameter	5.00	5.50

Climate Change Type

Designs: No. 297, Solar panels, automobile at pump. No. 298, Blimp, bicyclists, horse and rider. No. 299, Balloon, sailboat, lighthouse, train. No. 300, Bird, train, traffic signs.

2001, Nov. 16   Litho.   Perf. 13¼
297	A332	7s multicolored	1.00	1.10
298	A332	7s multicolored	1.00	1.10
299	A332	7s multicolored	1.00	1.10
300	A332	7s multicolored	1.00	1.10
a.		Horiz. strip, #297-300	5.00	5.50

Nobel Peace Prize Type

2001, Dec. 10   Litho.   Perf. 13¼
301	A333	7s multicolored	1.00	.55

100 Cents = 1 Euro (€)

Austrian Tourist Attractions V45

Designs: 7c, Semmering Railway. 51c, Pferdschwemme, Salzburg. 58c, Aggstein an der Donau Ruins. 73c, Hallstatt. 87c, Melk Abbey. €2.03, Kapitelschwemme, Salzburg.

2002, Mar. 1   Litho.   Perf. 14½x14
302	V45	7c multicolored	.25	.30
303	V45	51c multicolored	.90	1.25
304	V45	58c multicolored	1.00	1.10
305	V45	73c multicolored	1.25	1.40
306	V45	87c multicolored	1.75	2.00
307	V45	€2.03 multicolored	3.50	3.75
		Nos. 302-307 (6)	8.65	9.80

Endangered Species Type of 1993

Designs: No. 308, Hylobates syndactylus (siamang). No. 309, Spheniscus demersus (jackass penguin). No. 310, Prionodon linsang (banded linsang). No. 311, Bufo retiformis (Sonoran green toad).

2002, Apr. 4   Litho.   Perf. 12¾x12½
308	A271	51c multicolored	1.25	1.25
309	A271	51c multicolored	1.25	1.25
310	A271	51c multicolored	1.25	1.25
311	A271	51c multicolored	1.25	1.25
a.		Block of 4, #308-311	5.00	5.00

Independence of East Timor Type

Designs: 51c, Deer horn container with carved wooden stopper. €1.09, Carved wooden tai weaving loom.

2002, May 20   Litho.   Perf. 14x14½
312	A335	51c multicolored	1.00	1.00
313	A335	€1.09 multicolored	2.25	2.25

Intl. Year of Mountains Type

Designs: No. 314, Mt. Cook, New Zealand. No. 315, Mt. Robson, Canada. No. 316, Mt. Rakaposhi, Pakistan. No. 317, Mt. Everest (Sagarmatha), Nepal.

2002, May 24   Litho.   Perf. 13x13¼
314	A336	22c multicolored	.40	.40
315	A336	22c multicolored	.40	.40
316	A336	51c multicolored	1.00	1.00
317	A336	51c multicolored	1.00	1.00
a.		Vert. strip or block of four, #314-317	10.00	10.00

World Summit on Sustainable Development (Peter Max) Type

Designs: No. 318, Rainbow. No. 319, Three women, diff. No. 320, Three faceless people. No. 321, Birds, wave.

2002, June 27   Litho.   Perf. 14½x14
318	A337	51c multicolored	1.00	1.00
319	A337	51c multicolored	1.00	1.00
320	A337	58c multicolored	1.25	1.25
321	A337	58c multicolored	1.25	1.25
a.		Vert. strip or block of four, #318-321	8.50	8.50

World Heritage, Italy Type

Designs: 51c, No. 324f, Pompeii. 58c, No. 324c, Rome. No. 324a, Amalfi Coast. No. 324b, Aeolian Islands. No. 324d, Florence. No. 324e, Pisa.

Perf. 13½x13¼
2002, Aug. 30   Litho.
322	A338	51c multicolored	1.10	1.10
323	A338	58c multicolored	1.25	1.25

Souvenir Booklet
324		Booklet	15.00	
a.-c.		A338 7c any single	.40	.40
d.-f.		A338 15c any single	.85	.85
g.		Booklet pane of 4, #324d	3.40	3.40
h.		Booklet pane of 4, #324a	1.60	1.60
i.		Booklet pane of 4, #324e	3.40	3.40
j.		Booklet pane of 4, #324b	1.60	1.60
k.		Booklet pane of 4, #324f	3.40	3.40
l.		Booklet pane of 4, #324c	1.60	1.60

AIDS Awareness Type

2002, Oct. 24   Litho.   Perf. 13½
325	A339	€1.53 multicolored	2.50	2.75

Indigenous Art — V46

No. 326: a, Mola, Panama. b, Mochican llama-shaped spouted vessel, Peru. c, Tarabuco woven cloth, Bolivia. d, Masks, Cuba. e, Aztec priest's feather headdress, Mexico. f, Bird-shaped staff head, Colombia.

2003, Jan. 31   Litho.   Perf. 14¼
326	V46	Sheet of 6	10.00	10.00
a.-f.		51c Any single	1.60	1.60

Austrian Tourist Attractions Type of 2002

Designs: 25c, Kunsthistorisches Museum, Vienna. €1, Belvedere Palace, Vienna.

2003, Mar. 28   Litho.   Perf. 14½x14
327	V45	25c multicolored	.55	.55
328	V45	€1 multicolored	2.25	2.25

Endangered Species Type of 1993

Designs: No. 329, Anas formosa (Baikal teal). No. 330, Bostrychia hagedash (Hadada ibis). No. 331, Ramphastos toco (toco toucan). No. 332, Alopochen aegyptiacus (Egyptian goose).

2003, Apr. 3   Litho.   Perf. 12¾x12½
329	A271	51c multicolored	1.25	1.25
330	A271	51c multicolored	1.25	1.25
331	A271	51c multicolored	1.25	1.25
332	A271	51c multicolored	1.25	1.25
a.		Block of 4, #329-332	5.00	5.00

International Year of Freshwater Type of 2003

Perf. 14¼x14½
2003, June 20   Litho.
333	A345	55c Bridge, bird	3.00	3.00
334	A345	75c Horse, empty river	5.00	5.00
a.		Horiz. pair, #333-334	8.00	8.00

Austrian Tourist Attractions Type of 2002

Design: 4c, Schloss Eggenberg, Graz.

2003, Aug. 7   Litho.   Perf. 14x13¼
335	V45	4c multicolored	.45	.45

Ralph Bunche Type
Litho. With Foil Application
2003, Aug. 7   Perf. 13½x14
336	A346	€2.10 olive green & multicolored	3.50	3.50

In Memoriam Type of 2003

2003, Oct. 24   Litho.   Perf. 13¼x13
337	A347	€2.10 multicolored	5.00	5.00

World Heritage Sites, United States Type

Designs: 55c, No. 340c, Olympic National Park. 75c, No. 340e, Everglades National Park. No. 340a, Yosemite National Park. No. 340b, Great Smoky Mountains National Park. No. 340d, Hawaii Volcanoes National Park. No. 340f, Yellowstone National Park.

2003, Oct. 24   Litho.   Perf. 14½x14¼
338	A348	55c multicolored	1.50	.75
339	A348	75c multicolored	2.00	1.00

Souvenir Booklet
340		Booklet	12.00	
a.-c.		A348 15c any single	.45	.45
d.-f.		A348 20c any single	.55	.55
g.		Booklet pane of 4 #340a	1.80	1.80
h.		Booklet pane of 4 #340d	2.20	2.20
i.		Booklet pane of 4 #340b	1.80	1.80
j.		Booklet pane of 4 #340e	2.20	2.20
k.		Booklet pane of 4 #340c	1.80	1.80
l.		Booklet pane of 4 #340f	2.20	2.20

Austrian Tourist Attractions Type of 2002

Design: 55c, Schloss Schönbrunn, Vienna.

2004, Jan. 29   Litho.   Perf. 13x13¼
341	V45	55c multicolored	1.50	1.50

Endangered Species Type of 1993

Designs: No. 342, Melursus ursinus (Sloth bear). No. 343, Cervus eldi (Eld's deer). No. 344, Cercocebus torquatus (Cherry-crowned mangabey). No. 345, Bubalus arnee (Wild water buffalo).

2004, Jan. 29   Litho.   Perf. 12¾x12½
342	A271	55c multicolored	1.50	1.50
343	A271	55c multicolored	1.50	1.50
344	A271	55c multicolored	1.50	1.50
345	A271	55c multicolored	1.50	1.50
a.		Block of 4, #342-345	6.00	6.00

Indigenous Art Type of 2003

No. 346: a, Illuminated illustration from the Book of Kells, Ireland. b, Easter eggs, Ukraine. c, Venus of Willendorf, Paleolithic age limestone statue, Austria. d, Flatatunga panel, Iceland. e, Neolithic era idol, Hungary. f, Illuminated illustration from medical treatise, Portugal.

2004, Mar. 4   Litho.   Perf. 13¼
346	V46	Sheet of 6	12.00	12.00
a.-f.		55c Any single	2.00	2.00

Road Safety Type

Road map art with: 55c, Automobile, alcohol bottles. 75c, Road, clouds in traffic light colors, vert.

Perf. 13x13¼, 13¼x13
2004, Apr. 7   Litho.
347	A354	55c multicolored	1.25	1.25
348	A354	75c multicolored	1.75	1.75

Japanese Peace Bell, 50th Anniv. Type
Litho. & Engr.
2004, June 3   Perf. 13¼x13
349	A355	€2.10 multicolored	4.50	4.50

World Heritage Sites, Greece Type

Designs: 55c, No. 352f, Mycenae and Tiryns. 75c, No. 352e, Olympia. No. 352a, Acropolis, Athens. No. 352b, Delos. No. 352c, Delphi. No. 352d, Pythagoreion and Heraion of Samos.

2004, Aug. 12   Litho.   Perf. 14x13¼
350	A356	55c multicolored	1.75	1.75
351	A356	75c multicolored	2.25	2.25

Souvenir Booklet
352		Booklet	16.00	
a.-d.		A356 25c any single	.60	.60
e.-f.		A356 30c either single	.70	.70
g.		Booklet pane of 4 #352a	2.40	2.40
h.		Booklet pane of 4 #352b	2.40	2.40
i.		Booklet pane of 4 #352c	2.40	2.40
j.		Booklet pane of 4 #352d	2.40	2.40
k.		Booklet pane of 4 #352e	2.80	2.80
l.		Booklet pane of 4 #352f	2.80	2.80

My Dream for Peace Type

Winning designs of Lions Club International children's global peace poster contest by: 55c, Henry Ulfe Renteria, Peru. €1, Michelle Fortaliza, Philippines.

2004, Sept. 21	**Litho.**		**Perf. 14**	
353	A357	55c multicolored	1.40	1.40
354	A357	€1 multicolored	2.50	2.50

V47

Human Rights — V48

2004, Oct. 14	**Litho.**		**Perf. 11¼**	
355	V47	55c multicolored	1.00	1.00
356	V48	€1.25 multicolored	3.00	3.00

United Nations, 60th Anniv. Type of 2005

Litho. & Engr.

2005, Feb. 4			**Perf. 11x11¼**	
357	A361	55c multicolored	2.50	2.50

Souvenir Sheet

Litho.

Imperf

358	A361	€2.10 multicolored	6.50	6.50

International Center, Vienna — V49

Litho. with Hologram

2005, Feb. 4			**Perf. 13½x13¼**	
359	V49	75c multicolored	2.25	2.25

Endangered Species Type of 1993

Designs: No. 360, Ansellia africana. No. 361, Phragmipedium kovachii. No. 362, Cymbidium ensifolium. No. 363, Renanthera imschootiana.

2005, Mar. 3	**Litho.**		**Perf. 12¾x12½**	
360	A271	55c multicolored	1.40	1.40
361	A271	55c multicolored	1.40	1.40
362	A271	55c multicolored	1.40	1.40
363	A271	55c multicolored	1.40	1.40
a.		Block of 4, #360-363	6.00	6.00

Nature's Wisdom — V50

Designs: 55c, Desert landscape, China. 80c, Cheetah family, Africa.

2005, Apr. 21	**Litho.**		**Perf. 13½x13¼**	
364	V50	55c multicolored	1.60	1.60
365	V50	75c multicolored	2.25	2.25

Intl. Year of Sport Type

2005, June 3	**Litho.**		**Perf. 13x13¼**	
366	A368	55c Equestrian	1.60	1.60
367	A368	€1.10 Soccer	3.25	3.25

World Heritage Sites, Egypt Type

Designs: Nos. 368, 370c, Abu Mena. Nos. 369, 370f, St. Catherine area. No. 370a, Memphis and its Necropolis. No. 370b, Philae. No. 370d, Ancient Thebes. No. 370e, Islamic Cairo.

2005, Aug. 4	**Litho.**		**Perf. 14x13¼**	
368	A369	55c multicolored	1.60	1.60
369	A369	75c multicolored	2.25	2.25

Souvenir Booklet

370		Booklet, #370g-370l	19.50	
a.-c.		A369 25c any single	.75	.75
d.-f.		A369 30c any single	.85	.85
g.		Booklet pane of 4 #370a	3.00	3.00
h.		Booklet pane of 4 #370b	3.00	3.00
i.		Booklet pane of 4 #370c	3.00	3.00
j.		Booklet pane of 4 #370d	3.50	3.50
k.		Booklet pane of 4 #370e	3.50	3.50
l.		Booklet pane of 4 #370f	3.50	3.50

No. 370 sold for €6.80.

My Dream for Peace Type

Winning designs of Lions Club International children's global peace poster contest by: 55c, Lee Min Gi, Republic of Korea. €1, Natalie Chan, US.

2004, Sept. 21	**Litho.**		**Perf. 14**	
371	A357	55c multicolored	1.60	1.60
372	A357	€1 multicolored	2.75	2.75

Food for Life Type

Designs: 55c, Corn, people with food bowls, teacher and students. €1.25, Rice, helicopter dropping food, elephant caravan.

2005, Oct. 20	**Litho.**		**Perf. 13¾**	
373	A370	55c multicolored	1.60	1.60
374	A370	€1.25 multicolored	3.50	3.50

Indigenous Art Type of 2003

No. 375 — Musical instruments: a, Drum, Guinea. b, Whistle, Congo. c, Horn, Botswana. d, Drums, Burundi. e, Harp, Gabon. f, Bell, Nigeria.

2006, Feb. 3	**Litho.**		**Perf. 13¼**	
375	V46	Sheet of 6	12.00	12.00
a.-f.		55c Any single	2.00	2.00

Endangered Species Type of 1993

Designs: No. 376, Dendrobates pumilio. No. 377, Furcifer lateralis. No. 378, Corallus hortulanus. No. 379, Dendrobates leucomelas.

Perf. 12¾x12½

2006, Mar. 16			**Litho.**	
376	A271	55c multicolored	1.50	1.50
377	A271	55c multicolored	1.50	1.50
378	A271	55c multicolored	1.50	1.50
379	A271	55c multicolored	1.50	1.50
a.		Block of 4, #376-379	6.00	6.00

Intl. Day of Families Type

Designs: 55c, Family at water pump. €1.25, Family preparing food.

2006, May 27	**Litho.**		**Perf. 14x13½**	
380	A373	55c multicolored	1.25	1.25
381	A373	€1.25 multicolored	2.50	2.50

World Heritage Sites, France Type

Eiffel Tower and: Nos. 382, 384c, Carcasonne. Nos. 383, 384f, Chateau de Chambord. No. 384a, Banks of the Seine. No. 384b, Provins. No. 384d, Roman Aqueduct. No. 384e, Mont Saint-Michel.

Litho. & Embossed with Foil Application

2006, June 17			**Perf. 13½x13¼**	
382	A374	55c multicolored	1.50	1.50
383	A374	75c multicolored	2.00	2.00

Souvenir Booklet

384		Booklet, #384g-384l	18.00	
a.-c.		A374 25c any single	.65	.65
d.-f.		A374 30c any single	.80	.80
g.		Booklet pane of 4 #384a	2.60	2.60
h.		Booklet pane of 4 #384b	2.60	2.60
i.		Booklet pane of 4 #384c	2.60	2.60
j.		Booklet pane of 4 #384d	3.25	3.25
k.		Booklet pane of 4 #384e	3.25	3.25
l.		Booklet pane of 4 #384f	3.25	3.25

No. 384 sold for €6.80.

My Dream for Peace Type of 2004

Winning designs of Lions Club International children's global peace poster contest by: 55c, Klara Thein, Germany. €1, Laurensia Levina, Indonesia.

2006, Sept. 21	**Litho.**		**Perf. 13½x13**	
385	A357	55c multicolored	1.60	1.60
386	A357	€1 multicolored	3.00	3.00

Flags and Coins Type

No. 387 — Flag of: a, Gambia, 1 dalasi coin. b, Pakistan, 1 rupee coin. c, Afghanistan, 2 afghani coin. d, Austria, 1 euro coin. e, Germany, 50 cent coin. f, Haiti, 50 centimes coin. g, Denmark, 20 krone coin. h, Netherlands, 1 euro coin.

2006, Oct. 5	**Litho.**		**Perf. 13¼x13**	
387		Sheet of 8	14.00	14.00
a.-h.		A375 55c Any single	1.75	1.75

A column of rouletting in the middle of the sheet separates it into two parts.

Endangered Species Type of 1993

Designs: No. 388, Chlorocebus aethiops. No. 389, Nasalis larvatus. No. 390, Papio hamadryas. No. 391, Erythrocebus patas.

Perf. 12¾x12½

2007, Mar. 15			**Litho.**	
388	A271	55c multicolored	1.60	1.60
389	A271	55c multicolored	1.60	1.60
390	A271	55c multicolored	1.60	1.60
391	A271	55c multicolored	1.60	1.60
a.		Block of 4, #388-391	6.40	6.40

Flags and Coins Type of 2006

No. 392 — Flag of: a, Trinidad and Tobago, 50 cent coin. b, Sierra Leone, 10 cent coin. c, Hungary, 100 forint coin. d, San Marino, 2 euro coin. e, Croatia, 1 kuna coin. f, Spain, 1 euro coin. g, Kazakhstan, 100 tenge coin. h, Ireland, 5 cent coin.

2007, May 3	**Litho.**		**Perf. 13¼x13**	
392		Sheet of 8	13.00	13.00
a.-h.		A375 55c Any single	1.60	1.60

A column of rouletting in the middle of the sheet separates it into two parts.

Five 55c stamps depicting views of the Vienna International Center and the United Nations flag were released May 3, 2007. The editors have reason to believe that these stamps were not sold at the UN Post Office in Vienna. Value, strip of 5 with labels $45, sheet of 10 $90.

Peaceful Visions Type of 2007

Designs: 55c, "The Sowers." €1.25, "We All Thrive Under the Same Sky."

2007, June 1	**Litho.**		**Perf. 13x12½**	
398	A378	55c multicolored	1.60	1.60
399	A378	€1.25 multicolored	3.75	3.75

World Heritage Sites, South America Type

Designs: Nos. 400, 402e, Iguaçu National Park, Brazil. Nos. 401, 402b, Cueva de las Manos, Argentina. No. 402a, Rapa Nui, Chile. No. 402c, Machu Picchu, Peru. No. 402d, Tiwanaku, Bolivia. No. 474f, Galapagos Islands, Ecuador.

2007, Aug. 9	**Litho.**		**Perf. 13¼x13**	
400	A381	55c multicolored	2.00	2.00
401	A381	75c multicolored	2.75	2.75

Souvenir Booklet

402		Booklet, #402g-402l	20.00	
a.-c.		A381 25c Any single	.75	.75
d.-f.		A381 30c Any single	.90	.90
g.		Booklet pane of 4 #402a	3.00	3.00
h.		Booklet pane of 4 #402b	3.00	3.00
i.		Booklet pane of 4 #402c	3.00	3.00
j.		Booklet pane of 4 #402d	3.60	3.60
k.		Booklet pane of 4 #402e	3.60	3.60
l.		Booklet pane of 4 #402f	3.60	3.60

Humanitarian Mail Type

2007, Sept. 6	**Litho.**		**Perf. 12½x13¼**	
403	A382	75c multicolored	2.25	2.25

Five 65c stamps depicting the International Space Station, astronauts and planets were released Oct. 1, 2007. The editors have reason to believe that these stamps were not sold at the UN Post Office in Vienna. Value, strip of 5 with labels $60, sheet of 10 $120.

Space for Humanity Type

Designs: 65c, Space stations. €1.15, Space Station.

€2.10, Space probe, Jupiter.

2007, Oct. 25	**Litho.**		**Perf. 13½x14**	
409	A383	65c multicolored	2.00	2.00
410	A383	€1.15 multicolored	3.50	3.50

Souvenir Sheet

411	A383	€2.10 multicolored	8.00	8.00

Intl. Holocaust Remembrance Day Type

2008, Jan. 27	**Litho.**		**Perf. 13**	
412	A384	65c multicolored	3.00	3.00

Johann Strauss Memorial, Vienna — V61

Pallas Athene Fountain, Vienna V62

Pegasus Fountain, Salzburg V63

Statue, Belvedere Palace Gardens, Vienna V64

2008, Jan. 28	**Litho.**		**Perf. 13½x14**	
413	V61	10c black	.35	.35
			Perf. 14x13½	
414	V62	15c black	.50	.50
415	V63	65c black	2.25	2.25
416	V64	€1.40 black	4.75	4.75
		Nos. 413-416 (4)	7.85	7.85

Endangered Species Type of 1993

Designs: No. 4170, Mirounga angustirostris. No. 418, Millepora alcicornis. No. 419, Hippocampus histrix. No. 420, Physeter catodon.

2008, Mar. 6	**Litho.**		**Perf. 12¾x12½**	
417	A271	65c multicolored	2.50	2.50
418	A271	65c multicolored	2.50	2.50
419	A271	65c multicolored	2.50	2.50
420	A271	65c multicolored	2.50	2.50
a.		Block of 4, #417-420	10.00	10.00

Flags and Coins Type of 2006

No. 421 — Flag of: a, Poland, 5 zloty coin. b, Latvia, 1 lat coin. c, Portugal, 1 euro coin. d, Armenia, 500 dram coin. e, Sweden, 1 krona coin. f, Cyprus, 1 euro coin. g, Slovakia, 1 koruna coin. h, Qatar, 50 dirham coin.

2008, May 8	**Litho.**		**Perf. 13¼x13**	
421		Sheet of 8	18.00	18.00
a.-h.		A375 65c Any single	2.25	2.25

A column of rouletting in the middle of the sheet separates it into two parts.

Five 65c stamps depicting the Vienna International Center and its artwork were released May 12, 2008. The editors have reason to believe that these stamps were not sold at the UN Post Office in Vienna. Value, strip of 5 with labels $30, sheet of 10 $60.

Graduate — V70

Stylized Person,
Heart, Brain,
Hands — V71

Litho. & Embossed

2008, June 6   **Perf. 14x13¼**
427	V70	55c green & violet	2.00	2.00
428	V71	€1.40 violet & green	5.00	5.00

Convention on the Rights of Persons with Disabilities.

Sport for Peace Type of 2008

Designs: 65c, Man on rings. €1.30, €2.10, Swimmer.

2008, Aug. 8   **Litho.**   **Perf. 14½**
429	A393	65c multicolored	2.25	2.25
430	A393	€1.30 multicolored	4.50	4.50

Souvenir Sheet
Perf. 12¾x13¼
431	A393	€2.10 multicolored	9.00	9.00
a.		Overprinted in sheet margin	10.00	10.00

2008 Summer Olympics, Beijing. No. 431a is overprinted in black "Peking 2008" and medals with UN emblem.

"We Can End Poverty" Type of 2008

Winning designs in children's art contest: 65c, By Mariam Marukian, Armenia. 75c, By Rufaro Duri, Zimbabwe, vert.

Perf. 12¾x12½
2008, Sept. 18   **Litho.**
432	A395	65c multicolored	2.25	2.25

Perf. 12½x12¾
433	A395	75c multicolored	2.60	2.60

Five €1.40 stamps depicting views of the Vienna International Center and its artwork were released Sept. 18, 2008. The editors have reason to believe that these stamps were not sold at the UN Post Office in Vienna. Value, strip of 5 with labels $40, sheet of 10 $80.

Climate Change Types of New York and Geneva and

Climate Change — V73

No. 434 — Smokestacks with quarter of Earth in: a, LR. b, LL. c, UR. d, UL.
No. 435 — Cut trees with quarter of Earth in: a, LR. b, LL. c, UR. d, UL.
No. 436: a, Like New York #969a. b, Like New York #969b. c, Like New York #969c. d, New York #969d. e, Like Geneva #493a. f,

Like Geneva #493b. g, Like Geneva #493c. h, Like Geneva #493d. i, Like Vienna #434a. j, Like Vienna #434b. k, Like Vienna #434c. l, Like Vienna #434d. m, Like New York #968a. n, Like New York #968b, o, Like New York #968c, p, Like New York #968d. q, Like Geneva #492a. r, Like Geneva #492b. s, Like Geneva #492c. t, Like Geneva #492d. u, Like Vienna #435a. v, Like Vienna #435b. w, Like Vienna #435c. x, Like Vienna #435d.

All stamps have green panels inscribed "Klimawandel."

2008, Oct. 23   **Litho.**   **Perf. 13¼x13**
434		Sheet of 4	9.00	9.00
a.-d.		V72 65c Any single	2.25	2.25
435		Sheet of 4	16.00	16.00
a.-d.		V73 €1.15 Any single	4.00	4.00

Souvenir Booklet
436		Booklet, #436y-436ad	27.00	
a.-d.		A397 30c Any single	1.00	1.00
e.-h.		G77 30c Any single	1.00	1.00
i.-l.		V72 30c Any single	1.00	1.00
m.-p.		A396 35c Any single	1.10	1.10
q.-t.		G76 35c Any single	1.10	1.10
u.-x.		V73 35c Any single	1.10	1.10
y.		Booklet pane of 4, #436a-436d	4.25	4.25
z.		Booklet pane of 4, #436e-436h	4.25	4.25
aa.		Booklet pane of 4, #436i-436l	4.25	4.25
ab.		Booklet pane of 4, #436m-436p	4.75	4.75
ac.		Booklet pane of 4, #436q-436t	4.75	4.75
ad.		Booklet pane of 4, #436u-436x	4.75	4.75

U Thant Type of 2009
Litho. With Foil Application
2009, Feb. 6   **Perf. 14x13½**
437	A399	€1.15 green & multi	4.50	4.50

Endangered Species Type of 1993

Designs: No. 438, Trogonoptera brookiana. No. 439, Pandinus imperator. No. 440, Carabus intricatus. No. 441, Brachypelma smithi.

2009, Apr. 16   **Litho.**   **Perf. 12¾x12½**
438	A271	65c multicolored	2.00	2.00
439	A271	65c multicolored	2.00	2.00
440	A271	65c multicolored	2.00	2.00
441	A271	65c multicolored	2.00	2.00
a.		Block of 4, #438-441	8.00	8.00

World Heritage Sites, Germany Type of 2009

Designs: Nos. 442, 444c, Palaces and Parks of Potsdam and Berlin. Nos. 443, 444e, Luther Memorials in Eisleben and Wittenberg. No. 444a, Town Hall and Roland on the Marketplace, Bremen. No. 444b, Wartburg Castle. No. 444d, Aachen Cathedral. No. 444f, Monastic Island of Reichenau.

2009, May 7   **Litho.**   **Perf. 14x13½**
442	A400	65c multicolored	1.90	1.90
443	A400	€1.40 multicolored	4.00	4.00

Souvenir Booklet
444		Booklet, #444g-444l	22.50	
a.-c.		A400 30c any single	.85	.85
d.-f.		A400 35c any single	1.00	1.00
g.		Booklet pane of 4 #444a	3.50	3.50
h.		Booklet pane of 4 #444b	3.50	3.50
i.		Booklet pane of 4 #444c	3.50	3.50
j.		Booklet pane of 4 #444d	4.00	4.00
k.		Booklet pane of 4 #444e	4.00	4.00
l.		Booklet pane of 4 #444f	4.00	4.00

Memorial Plaza, Vienna International
Center — V74

The First Swallows, Sculpture by
Juozas Mikenas — V75

Conference Building, Vienna
International Center — V76

Butterfly Tree, by Rudolf
Hausner — V77

Flags in Memorial Plaza — V78

2009, May 7   **Perf. 13¼**
445	V74	65c multi + label	5.00	5.00
a.		Perf. 11¼x11	10.00	10.00
446	V75	65c multi + label	5.00	5.00
a.		Perf. 11¼x11	10.00	10.00
447	V76	65c multi + label	5.00	5.00
a.		Perf. 11¼x11	10.00	10.00
448	V77	65c multi + label	5.00	5.00
a.		Perf. 11¼x11	10.00	10.00
449	V78	65c multi + label	5.00	5.00
a.		Perf. 11¼x11	10.00	10.00
b.		Vert. strip of 5, #445-449, + 5 labels	25.00	25.00
c.		Vert. strip of 5, #445a-449a, + 5 labels	50.00	50.00

The sheet of No. 449c has "ver. 2" in the lower right selvage.

Economic and Social Council (ECOSOC) Type of 2009

Designs: 55c, Combat HIV/AIDS, malaria and other diseases. 65c, Reduce child mortality.

2009, Aug. 6   **Litho.**   **Perf. 12¾x12½**
450	A411	55c multicolored	2.25	2.25
451	A411	65c multicolored	3.50	3.50

V79

V80

V81

V82

Vienna International Center, 30th
Anniv. — V83

2009, Aug. 24   **Perf. 13¼**
452	V79	€1.40 multi + label	6.00	6.00
a.		Perf. 11¼x11	20.00	20.00
453	V80	€1.40 multi + label	6.00	6.00
a.		Perf. 11¼x11	20.00	20.00
454	V81	€1.40 multi + label	6.00	6.00
a.		Perf. 11¼x11	20.00	20.00
455	V82	€1.40 multi + label	6.00	6.00
a.		Perf. 11¼x11	20.00	20.00
456	V83	€1.40 multi + label	6.00	6.00
a.		Perf. 11¼x11	20.00	20.00
b.		Vert. strip of 5, #452-456, + 5 labels	30.00	30.00
c.		Vert. strip of 5, #452a-456a, + 5 labels	100.00	100.00

The sheet of No. 456c has "ver. 2" in the lower right selvage.

Millennium Development Goals Type of 2009
Miniature Sheet

No. 457: a, Bowl of hot food. b, Pencil. c, Female symbol. d, Teddy bear. e, Pregnant woman, heart. f, Medicine bottle. g, Stylized tree. h, Conjoined people.

2009, Sept. 25
457	A413	Sheet of 8	16.00	16.00
a.-h.		65c Any single	2.00	2.00

Miniature Sheet

Indigenous People — V84

No. 458 — Portraits of person from: a, Tanzania. b, Australia. c, Namibia (small child). d, Indonesia. e, Namibia (young girl). f, Untied Arab Emirates.

2009, Oct. 8   **Perf. 12½**
458	V84	Sheet of 6	12.00	12.00
a.-f.		65c Any single	2.00	2.00

Flags and Coins Type of 2006

No. 459 — Flag of: a, Romania, 1 ban coin. b, Slovenia, 5 cent coin. c, Azerbaijan, 10 giapik coin. d, Bangladesh, 5 taka coin. e, Belarus, 1 ruble coin. f, Malta, 1 euro coin. g, Swaziland, 1 lilangeni coin. h, Jordan, 10 piaster coin.

2010, Feb. 5   **Litho.**   **Perf. 13¼x13**
459		Sheet of 8	16.00	16.00
a.-h.		A375 65c Any single	2.00	2.00

A column of rouletting in the middle of the sheet separates it into two parts.

People Pulling Rope — V85

Person With Hands Over Eyes — V86

Woman Touching Her Shoulder — V87

Man With Wheelbarrow — V88

Blue Heart — V89

Designed by Rorie Katz, US.

2010, Feb. 5   Litho.   Perf. 11¼x11

460	V85	65c multi + label	4.50	4.50
461	V86	65c multi + label	4.50	4.50
462	V87	65c multi + label	4.50	4.50
463	V88	65c multi + label	4.50	4.50
464	V89	65c multi + label	4.50	4.50
a.		Vert. strip of 5, #460-464, + 5 labels	22.50	22.50

The full sheet sold for $14.95 or €19.90. The labels could not be personalized.

Endangered Species Type of 1993

Designs: No. 465, Mammillaria zeilmanniana. No. 466, Hoodia gordonii. No. 467, Welwitschia mirabilis. No. 468, Euphorbia milii.

2010, Apr. 15   Litho.   Perf. 12¾x12½

465	A271	65c multicolored	2.25	2.25
466	A271	65c multicolored	2.25	2.25
467	A271	65c multicolored	2.25	2.25
468	A271	65c multicolored	2.25	2.25
a.		Block of 4, #465-468	9.00	9.00

Intl. Year of Biodiversity V90

Drawings from Art Forms from Nature, by Ernst Heinrich: 5c, Colonial algae. 20c, Boxfish.

2010, Apr. 15   Litho.   Perf. 13

469	V90	5c multicolored	.25	.25
470	V90	20c multicolored	.70	.70

One Planet, One Ocean Types of New York and Geneva and

V91

V92

No. 471: a, Dolphin at left, fish at right. b, Fish at top, shark in center. c, Dolphin at left, fish at right and bottom. d, Fish at left, top and right.

No. 472: a, Dolphins. b, Shark and fish at center, ray at bottom. c, Fish at left, turtle at bottom. d, Fish and coral.

No. 473: a, Like New York #1003a. b, Like New York #1003b. c, Like New York #1003c. d, Like New York #1003d. e, Like #471a. f, Like #471b. g, Like #471c. h, Like #471d. i, Like Geneva #519a. j, Like Geneva #519b. k, Like Geneva #519c. l, Like Geneva #519d. m, Like New York #1004a. n, Like New York #1004b. o, Like New York #1004c. p, Like New York #1004d. q, Like #472a. r, Like #472b. s, Like #472c. t, Like #472d. u, Like Geneva #520a. v, Like Geneva #520b. w, Like Geneva #520c. x, Like Geneva #520d.

2010, May 6   Litho.   Perf. 14x13¼

471	V91	Sheet of 4	7.75	7.75
a.-d.		55c Any single	1.90	1.90
472	V92	Sheet of 4	9.00	9.00
a.-d.		65c Any single	2.25	2.25

Souvenir Booklet
Perf. 13¼x13

473		Booklet, #473y-473z, 473aa-473ad	27.00	
a.-d.		A416 30c any single	1.00	1.00
e.-h.		V91 30c any single	1.00	1.00
i.-l.		G85 30c any single	1.00	1.00
m.-p.		A417 35c any single	1.25	1.25
q.-t.		V92 35c any single	1.25	1.25
u.-x.		G86 35c any single	1.25	1.25
y.		Booklet pane of 4 #473a-473d	4.00	
z.		Booklet pane of 4 #473e-473h	4.00	4.00
aa.		Booklet pane of 4 #473i-473l	4.00	4.00
ab.		Booklet pane of 4 #473m-473p	5.00	5.00
ac.		Booklet pane of 4 #473q-473t	5.00	5.00
ad.		Booklet pane of 4 #473u-473x	5.00	5.00

Intl. Oceanographic Commission, 50th anniv.

United Nations, 65th Anniv. Type of 2010
Litho. With Foil Application

2010, June 28   Perf. 13¼

474	A422	75c green & gold	3.00	3.00
a.		Souvenir sheet of 2	6.00	6.00

V93

V94

V95

V96

V97

2010, Sept. 2   Litho.   Perf. 13¼x13

475	V93	65c multicolored	1.90	1.90
476	V94	65c multicolored	1.90	1.90
477	V95	65c multicolored	1.90	1.90
478	V96	65c multicolored	1.90	1.90
479	V97	65c multicolored	1.90	1.90
a.		Horiz. strip of 5, #475-479	9.50	9.50

Miniature Sheet

Indigenous People — V98

No. 480 — Portraits of person from: a, French Polynesia (denomination in white). b, Tanzania (child with cloth head covering). c, Malaysia. d, French Polynesia (denomination in white and green). e, Namibia. f, Tanzania (man with band around forehead).

2010, Oct. 21   Litho.   Perf. 13

480	V98	Pane of 6	11.50	11.50
a.-f.		65c Any single	1.90	1.90

United Nations Headquarters, Vienna — V99

United Nations Headquarters, Geneva — €1.25, Aerial view. €2.85, Ground-level view.

2011, Feb. 4   Litho.   Perf. 13

481	V99	€1.25 multicolored	3.75	3.75
482	V99	€2.85 multicolored	8.25	8.25

Flags and Coins Type of 2006

No. 483 — Flag of: a, Lithuania, 2 lita coin. b, Greece, 1 euro coin. c, Kyrgyzstan, 50 tyiyn coin. d, Oman, 100 baisa coin. e, Estonia, 2 euro coin. f, Czech Republic, 5 koruna coin. g, Uzbekistan, 100 som coin. h, Monaco, 1 euro coin.

2011, Mar. 3   Litho.   Perf. 13¼x13

483		Sheet of 8	15.00	15.00
a.-h.		A375 65c Any single	1.75	1.75

A column of rouletting in the middle of the sheet separates it into two parts.

Human Space Flight, 50th Anniv. — V100

No. 484: Various parts of outer space scene.

No. 485, vert.: a, Space Shuttle. b, Space Station.

2011, Apr. 12   Litho.   Perf. 13x13¼

484	V100	Sheet of 16	16.50	16.50
a.-p.		35c any single	1.00	1.00

Souvenir Sheet

485	V100	Sheet of 2	7.50	7.50
a.		55c multi	3.25	3.25
b.		65c multi	4.25	4.25
c.		Souvenir sheet of 6, New York #1024a-1024b, Geneva #534a-b, Vienna #485a-485b	22.50	22.50

No. 485 contains two 40x48mm stamps that were printed as part of a larger sheet of six stamps, No. 485c, which was broken up into its component two-stamp souvenir sheets, and also sold as one unit.

Vienna International Center and Flagpoles — V101

Fish-eye View of Vienna International Center and Flagpole — V102

Vienna International Center and Train — V103

Aerial View of Vienna International Center — V104

Vienna International Center and Water — V105

Detail From La Pioggia, Stadt Unter de Regen, by Friedensreich Hundertwasser — V106

Hand in Hand, by Hans Dietrich — V107

The Scholars Pavilion — V108

Detail From Grupo Expectante, by Alfredo Sosabravo — V109

Yes to Life, No to Drugs, by Sami Burhan — V110

2011, May 1	Litho.		Perf. 14¾	
486	V101	62c multi + label	2.50	2.50
487	V102	62c multi + label	2.50	2.50
488	V103	62c multi + label	2.50	2.50
489	V104	62c multi + label	2.50	2.50
490	V105	62c multi + label	2.50	2.50
a.		Vert. strip of 5, #486-490, + 5 labels	15.00	15.00
491	V106	70c multi + label	3.00	3.00
492	V107	70c multi + label	3.00	3.00
493	V108	70c multi + label	3.00	3.00
494	V109	70c multi + label	3.00	3.00
495	V110	70c multi + label	3.00	3.00
a.		Vert. strip of 5, #491-495, + 5 labels	17.50	17.50
		Nos. 486-495 (10)	25.50	25.50

The full sheet of Nos. 486-490 sold for $21.45 or €12.40. The full sheet of Nos. 491-495 sold for $14.26 or €9.90. The labels could be personalized.

UNESCO World Heritage Sites in Nordic Countries Type of 2011

Designs: 62c, Urnes Stave Church, Norway. 1fr, Struve Geodetic Arc, Norway, Finland and Sweden.

2011, May 5	Litho.		Perf. 14x13½	
496	A433	62c multicolored	1.90	1.90
497	A433	70c multicolored	2.10	2.10

AIDS Ribbon Type of 2011

2011, June 3	Litho.		Die Cut	
Self-Adhesive				
498	A434	70c red & green	2.40	2.40

ECOSOC Type of 2011

2011, July 1	Litho.		Perf. 14¼	
499	A435	62c multicolored	3.00	3.00
500	A435	70c multicolored	4.00	4.00

Endangered Species Type of 1993

Designs: No. 501, Cyanoramphus novaezelandiae (Red-fronted parakeet). No. 502, Haliaeetus albicilla (White-tailed eagle). No. 503, Probosciger aterrimus (Black palm cockatoo). No. 504, Caloenas nicobarica (Nicobar pigeon).

2011, Sept. 7	Litho.		Perf. 12¾x12½	
501	A271	70c multicolored	2.50	2.50
502	A271	70c multicolored	2.50	2.50
503	A271	70c multicolored	2.50	2.50
504	A271	70c multicolored	2.50	2.50
a.		Block of 4, #501-504	10.00	10.00

Intl. Year of Forests Type of 2011

Designs: 62c, Tree top, crosses, circles and ovals. 70c, Stylized people and trees.

Litho. With Foil Application

2011, Oct. 13			Perf. 12½	
505		62c multicolored	2.00	2.00
506		70c multicolored	2.25	2.25
a.		A436 Vert. pair, #505-506	4.25	4.25

Flags and Coins Type of 2006

No. 507 — Flag of: a, Cameroun, 100 franc coin. b, Samoa, 2 tala coin. c, Surinam, 5 cent coin. d, Macedonia, 50 denar coin. e, Bulgaria, 50 stotinka coin. f, Tanzania, 100 shilling coin. g, Finland, 1 euro coin. h, Cuba, 1 peso coin.

2012, Feb. 3	Litho.		Perf. 13¼x13	
507		Sheet of 8	16.50	16.50
a.-h.		A375 70c Any single	2.00	2.00

A column of rouletting in the middle of the sheet separates it into two parts.

AUTISMUS BESSER VERSTEHEN V111

Autism Awareness V112

Drawings by autistic people: No. 508, The Path, by Ryan Smoluk, Canada. No. 509, Untitled drawing, by Colm Isherwood, Ireland.

2012, Apr. 2	Litho.		Perf. 14x13½	
508	V111	70c multicolored	2.25	2.25
509	V112	70c multicolored	2.25	2.25
a.		Pair, #508-509	4.50	4.50

UN Emblem — V113

2012, Apr. 12	Litho.		Perf. 14½	
510	V113	70c pur, blk + label	3.50	3.50
		Sheet of 10 + 10 labels	35.00	35.00

The full sheet sold for $14.52 or €9.90. The labels could be personalized.

Endangered Species Type of 1993

Designs: No. 511, Panthera uncia. No. 512, Polyplectron schleiermacheri. No. 513, Tyto novaehollandiae. No. 514, Ambystoma mexicanum.

2012, Apr. 19	Litho.		Perf. 12¾x12½	
511	A271	70c multicolored	2.25	2.25
512	A271	70c multicolored	2.25	2.25
513	A271	70c multicolored	2.25	2.25
514	A271	70c multicolored	2.25	2.25
a.		Block of 4, #511-514	9.00	9.00

Rio + 20 Type of 2012

2012, June 1	Litho.		Perf. 13x13¼	
515	A443	70c multicolored	2.10	2.10

Sport for Peace Type of 2012

Litho. With Foil Application

2012, Aug. 17			Perf. 14½	
516	A444	62c multicolored	1.90	1.90
517	A444	70c multicolored	2.10	2.10
a.		Souvenir sheet of 1	2.10	2.10

UNESCO World Heritage Sites in Africa Type of 2012

Designs: 62c, Kenya Lake System, Kenya. 70c, Medina of Marrakesh, Morocco.

2012, Sept. 5	Litho.		Perf. 13¼	
518	A445	62c multicolored	1.75	1.75
519	A445	70c multicolored	2.00	2.00

Miniature Sheet

Indigenous People — V114

No. 520 — Portrait of person from: a, Chile. b, Malaysia. c, China (woman with black hair). d, China (woman with flower in hair). e, Tanzania. f, Mongolia.

2012, Oct. 11	Litho.		Perf. 13¼x13	
520	V114	Sheet of 6	11.50	11.50
a.-f.		70c Any single	1.90	1.90

World Radio Day Type of 2013

Designs: 70c, Microphone and scripts. €1.70, Boy with radio.

2013, Feb. 13	Litho.		Perf. 13¼x13	
521	A448	70c multicolored	2.00	2.00
522	A448	€1.70 multicolored	5.00	5.00

People in Handprint V115

People in Heart — V116

2013, Mar. 5	Litho.		Perf. 14x13½	
523	V115	62c multicolored	1.90	1.90
			Perf. 13½x14	
524	V116	€2.20 multicolored	6.50	6.50

World Heritage Sites, China, Type of 2013

Designs: Nos. 525, 527c, Great Wall of China. Nos. 526, 527f, Mausoleum of the First Qing Emperor. No. 527a, Mogao Caves. No. 527b, Potala Palace, Lhasa. No. 527d, Imperial Palace, Beijing. No. 527e, Mount Huangshan.

2013, Apr. 11	Litho.		Perf. 14x13½	
525	A452	70c multicolored	2.00	2.00
526	A452	€1.70 multicolored	5.00	5.00

Souvenir Booklet

527		Booklet, #527g-527l	25.00	
a.-c.	A452	30c any single	.85	.85
d.-f.	A452	40c any single	1.10	1.10
g.		Booklet pane of 4 #527a	3.50	—
h.		Booklet pane of 4 #527b	3.50	—
i.		Booklet pane of 4 #527c	3.50	—
j.		Booklet pane of 4 #527d	4.75	—
k.		Booklet pane of 4 #527e	4.75	—
l.		Booklet pane of 4 #527f	4.75	—

World Oceans Day — V117

No. 528 — Fish from One Fish, Two Fish, Red Fish, Blue Fish, by Dr. Seuss: a, Green fish facing left, wave. b, Red fish facing right. c, Three green fish on plate. d, Red fish, back half of red fish, wave. e, Red fish facing left, front half of red fish facing right. f, Two red fish facing left. g, Two green fish facing right, wave. h, Red fish facing right, head of blue fish wearing hat. i, Yellow fish with green star, wave. j, Yellow fish, back of blue fish, wave. k, Two red fish, body of blue fish. l, Tail of yellow fish, two green fish facing left, wave.

2013, May 31	Litho.		Perf. 13	
528	V117	Sheet of 12	24.00	24.00
a.-l.		70c any single	2.00	2.00

Nebulae Type of 2013

Designs: No. 567, NGC 2346. No. 568, Sh 2-106. 1fr, Messier 16.

2013, Aug. 9	Litho.		Perf. 13¼	
529	A454	€1.70 multicolored	5.00	5.00
530	A454	€1.70 multicolored	5.00	5.00
a.		Pair, #529-530	10.00	10.00

Souvenir Sheet

| 531 | A454 | 62c multicolored | 1.90 | 1.90 |

No. 531 contains one 44x44mm stamp.

Works of Disabled Artists Type of 2013

Designs: 70c, Electro Man, by Pete Eckert, U.S. €1.70, Dive Bomb, by Matt Sesow, U.S.

2013, Sept. 20	Litho.		Perf. 13¼x13	
532	A456	70c multicolored	2.00	2.00
533	A456	€1.70 multicolored	5.00	5.00

Endangered Species Type of 1993

Designs: No. 534, Hemigalus derbyanus. No. 535, Bubo ascalaphus. No. 536, Nycticebus coucang. No. 537, Zaglossus spp.

2013, Oct. 10	Litho.		Perf. 12¾x12½	
534	A271	70c multicolored	2.00	2.00
535	A271	70c multicolored	2.00	2.00
536	A271	70c multicolored	2.00	2.00
537	A271	70c multicolored	2.00	2.00
a.		Block of 4, #534-537	8.00	8.00

UN Emblem — V118

2013, Oct. 24   Litho.   Perf. 14½
538 V118 70c gray blue & blue
          + label   3.00 3.00
The full sheet sold for $14.20 or €9.90. The
labels could be personalized.

Flags and Coins Type of 2006

No. 539 — Flag of: a, Malaysia, 50 sen coin.
b, Nigeria, 1 naira coin. c, Zambia, 20 ngwee
coin. d, Togo, 100 franc coin. e, Dominica, 5
cent coin. f, Chad, 100 franc coin. g, St. Vincent and the Grenadines, 5 cent coin. h, Syria,
25 pound coin.

2013, Nov. 6   Litho.   Perf. 13¼x13
539   Sheet of 8   16.00 16.00
  a.-h.   A375 70c Any single   2.00   2.00
A column of rouletting in the middle of the
sheet separates it into two parts.

International Day of Happiness Type of 2014

Designs: 90c, Happy Asian Boy at the Park,
photograph by Alan Levenson, Russian word
for "Happy." €1.70, Barbary Macacque with
Baby, photograph by Gerhard Schulz, Arabic
word for "Happy."

2014, Mar. 17   Litho.   Perf. 13¼x13
540 A459 90c multicolored   2.75 2.75
541 A459 €1.70 multicolored   5.25 5.25

Miniature Sheet

International Year of Jazz — V119

No. 542: a, Silhouette of saxophonist in
blue. b, Woman singing. c, Silhouette of man
in red, neon lights. d, Bass player. e, Trombone in gold. f, Silhouette of saxophonist in
black, silhouette of man holding trombone. g,
"Cocktails" neon sign . h, Silhouette of bass
player in orange. i, Stack of record albums. j,
Cymbal. k, Trombone in silver. l, Silhouette of
clarinetist in black.

2014, Apr. 30   Litho.   Perf. 13x13¼
542 V119 Sheet of 12   25.50 25.50
        First day cover   27.00
  a.-l.   70c Any single   2.10   2.10

Vienna International Center, 35th
Anniv. — V120

No. 543: a, Vienna International Center
under construction (towers and shadows), red
panel. b, Vienna International Center, street
light at left, green panel. c, Vienna International Center, curved building at left, green
panel. d, Vienna International Center under
construction (arch in foreground, cranes at
right), red panel. e, Vienna International
Center under construction (cranes at left,
center and right), red panel. f, Doorway to
Vienna International Center, green panel. g,
View of curved buildings of Vienna International Center looking up from ground, green
panel. h, Vienna International Center under
construction (two cranes on central tower), red
panel. i, Completed Vienna International
Center, red panel. j, Flags in front of Vienna
International Center.

2014, May 8   Litho.   Perf. 14¾
543 V120 Sheet of 10   30.00 30.00
  a.-j.   70c Any single + label   3.00   3.00
The full sheet sold for $14.80 or €9.90. The
generic labels are shown. Labels could be
personalized.

V121

V122

Printed by Lowe-Martin Group, Canada.
Panes of 20. Designed by Sergio Baradat,
U.S.

2014, June 6   Litho.   Perf. 13¼x13
544 V121 70c multicolored   2.10 2.10
545 V122 €1.70 multicolored   5.25 5.25

Taj Mahal Types of 2014

2014, July 16   Engr.   Perf. 13¼x13
546 A466 90c multicolored   2.75 2.75
547 A468 €1.70 multicolored   5.25 5.25

Souvenir Booklet
548   Booklet, #548g-548l   26.00
  a.   A463 30c multi   .90   .90
  b.   A465 30c multi   .90   .90
  c.   A466 30c multi   .90   .90
  d.   A464 40c multi   1.25 1.25
  e.   A467 40c multi   1.25 1.25
  f.   A468 40c multi   1.25 1.25
  g.   Booklet pane of 4 #548a   3.60   —
  h.   Booklet pane of 4 #548b   3.60   —
  i.   Booklet pane of 4 #548c   3.60   —
  j.   Booklet pane of 4 #548d   5.00   —
  k.   Booklet pane of 4 #548e   5.00   —
  l.   Booklet pane of 4 #548f   5.00   —

International Year of Family
Farming — V123

2014, Aug. 21   Litho.   Perf. 13x13¼
549 V123 62c multi   1.90 1.90
550 V123 €1.70 multi   5.25 5.25

Global Education First Initiative Type of 2014

Designs: €1.70, Children boarding school
bus. €2, Tree growing from book held by
students.

2014, Sept. 18   Litho.   Perf. 13x13¼
551 A470 €1.70 multicolored   5.25 5.25

Souvenir Sheet
Perf. 12½
552 A470 €2 multicolored   6.00 6.00
No. 552 contains one 32x32mm stamp.

Endangered Species Type of 2014

Maps and: No. 553, Cheilinus undulatus.
No. 554, Carcharodon carcharias. No. 555,
Manta birostris. No. 556, Polyodon spathula.

2014, Oct. 23   Litho.   Perf. 12¾x12½
553 A471 70c multicolored   2.10 2.10
554 A471 70c multicolored   2.10 2.10
555 A471 70c multicolored   2.10 2.10
556 A471 70c multicolored   2.10 2.10
  a.   Block of 4, #553-556   8.50 8.50

Miniature Sheet

V124

No. 557: a, Flag on pole as seen from base
of pole. b, Vienna International Center, structure in shadow at bottom. c, Persian Scholars
Pavilion. d, Vienna International Center and
fountain. e, Sailboat and Vienna International
Center. f, Rowboat on water near Vienna International Center. g, Vienna International
Center, flags and sculpture. h, Entrance to
Vienna International Center. i, Woman Free
sculpture near Vienna International Center. j,
Aerial view of Vienna International Center.

2015, Jan. 23   Litho.   Perf. 14¾
557 V124 Sheet of 10   30.00 30.00
  a.-j.   80c Any single + label   3.00   3.00
The full sheet sold for $15 or €10.90. The
generic labels are shown. Labels could be
personalized.

Flags and Coins Type of 2006

No. 558 — Flag of: a, Tuvalu, 10 cent coin.
b, Malawi, 1 kwacha coin. c, Iraq, 50 dinar
coin. d, St. Thomas and Prince Islands, 250
dobra coin. e, Botswana, 10 thebe coin. f, Uruguay, 5 peso coin. g, Bosnia and Herzegovina,
20 pfennig coin. h, Somalia, 25 shilling coin.

2015, Feb. 6   Litho.   Perf. 13¼x13
558   Sheet of 8   18.00 18.00
  a.-h.   A375 80c Any single   2.25   2.25
A column of rouletting in the middle of the
sheet separates it into two parts.

Miniature Sheets

V125

World Poetry Day — V126

No. 559: a, Aleksey Tolstoy quotation in
Russian in red brown, date in purple, "Welttag
der Poesie" in red. b, Pen and circle, date in
black, "Frühling" in purple. c, Pen and circle,
date and "Frühling" in white, clouds above land
in background. d, Tolstoy quotation in Russian
in white, date in white, "Welttag der Poesie" in
red. e, Tolstoy quotation in white, date and
"Welttag der Poesie" in white. f, As "c," brown
background.
No. 560: a, Rumi quotation in Arabic in light
blue. b, Pen and red brown circle, denomination in red, purple jellyfish in background. c,
Pen and red brown circle, denomination in
white. d, Rumi quotation in orange, purple jellyfish tentacles in background. e, Rumi quotation in orange, red jellyfish tentacles in background. f, Pen and red brown circle, red
denomination, red and purple jellyfish tentacles in background.

Perf. 14½x14¼
2015, Mar. 20   Litho.
559 V125 Sheet of 6   11.50 11.50
  a.-f.   68c Any single   1.90   1.90
560 V126 Sheet of 6   13.50 13.50
  a.-f.   80c Any single   2.25   2.25

Endangered Species Type of 2015

Designs: No. 561, Pteridophora alberti. No.
562, Astrapia splendidissima. No. 563,
Paradisaea apoda. No. 564, Lophorina
superba.

2015, Apr. 16   Litho.   Perf. 12½x12¾
561 A476 80c multicolored   2.00 2.00
562 A476 80c multicolored   2.00 2.00
563 A476 80c multicolored   2.00 2.00
564 A476 80c multicolored   2.00 2.00
  a.   Block of 4, #561-564   8.00 8.00
      Nos. 561-564 (4)   8.00 8.00

V127

V128

2015, May 7   Litho.   Perf. 13¼x13
565 V127 68c multicolored   1.75 1.75
566 V128 80c multicolored   2.00 2.00

World Heritage Sites, Southeast Asia Type of 2015

Designs: Nos. 567, 569c, Ayutthaya, Thailand. Nos. 568, 569f, Hué Monuments, Viet
Nam. No. 569a, Luang Prabang, Laos. No.
569b, Angkor Wat, Cambodia. No. 569d,
Borobudur Temple, Indonesia. No. 569e, Cordillera, Philippines.

2015, June 5   Litho.   Perf. 14x13½
567 A480 80c multicolored   2.00 2.00
568 A480 €1.70 multicolored   4.25 4.25

Souvenir Booklet
569   Booklet, #569g-569l   21.00
  a.-c. A480 30c any single   .75   .75
  d.-f. A480 40c any single   1.00 1.00
  g.   Booklet pane of 4 #569a   3.00   —
  h.   Booklet pane of 4 #569b   3.00   —
  i.   Booklet pane of 4 #569c   3.00   —
  j.   Booklet pane of 4 #569d   4.00   —
  k.   Booklet pane of 4 #569e   4.00   —
  l.   Booklet pane of 4 #569f   4.00   —

End Violence Against Children Type of 2015

Designs: 68c, Gender-based violence. 80c,
Child labor.

Perf. 14½x14¼
2015, Aug. 20   Litho.
570 A481 68c multicolored   1.75 1.75
571 A481 80c multicolored   2.00 2.00

ECOSOC
Chamber
V129

Trusteeship Council — V130

Visitors Lobby V131

General Assembly Hall V132

Trusteeship Council — V133

Printed by Cartor Security Printing, France. Panes of 6. Designed by Rorie Katz, U.S.

2015, Oct. 25		**Litho.**	***Perf. 13¾***	
572	V129	80c multicolored	2.00	2.00
573	V130	80c multicolored	2.00	2.00
a.		Pair, #572-573	4.00	4.00
574	V131	€1.70 multicolored	4.25	4.25
575	V132	€1.70 multicolored	4.25	4.25
a.		Pair, #574-575	8.50	8.50
		Nos. 572-575 (4)	12.50	12.50

Souvenir Sheet
Perf. 13½

576	V133	€1.70 multicolored	4.25	4.25

United Nations, 70th anniv.

United Nations, 70th Anniv. Type of 2015

Designed by Sergio Baradat, U.S.

2015, Nov. 5		**Litho.**	***Perf. 14¾***	
577	A482	80c multi + label	2.50	2.50
		Sheet of 10 + 10 labels	27.00	—

The full sheet sold for $13.45 or €10.90. The sheet contains ten different generic labels. Labels could be personalized. The personalization of labels was available only at UN Headquarters, and not through mail order.

21st United Nations Climate Chage Conference, Paris V134

2015, Nov. 24		**Litho.**	***Perf. 13¼***	
578	V134	80c multicolored	2.00	2.00

Values are for stamps with surrounding selvage.

Free and Equal Type of 2016

Designs: 68c, Person coming out of closet. 80c, Gay men.

2016, Feb. 5		**Litho.**	***Perf. 13½x13¼***	
579	A491	68c multicolored	1.75	1.75
580	A491	80c multicolored	2.00	2.00

HeForShe Type of 2016

Designs: 1fr, Man, red background. 2fr, Woman, orange brown background.

2016, Mar. 8		**Litho.**	***Perf. 12½x13***	
581	A492	68c multicolored	1.75	1.75
582	A492	80c multicolored	2.00	2.00

Miniature Sheets

V135

International Dance Day — V136

No. 583 — Illustration of Spanish dancers by Allison Seiffer: a, Female dancer with fan. b, Male dancer with crossed arms. c, Red dress of dancer. d, Female dancer with male guitarist. e, Feet of dancer in ochre and green dress. f, Feet of male and female dancers, rose on floor.

No. 584 — Illustration of Middle Eastern dancers by Seiffer: a, Head of female dancer, "Welttanztag" in red, denomination in yellow. b, Head of female dancer, "Welttanztag" and denomination in red. c, Torso of dancer. d, Dancer, "Welttanztag" in black, denomination in yellow. e, Feet of dancer, "Welttanztag" in black. f, Feet of dancer and drum, "Welttanztag" in yellow.

2016, Apr. 29		**Litho.**	***Perf. 13¼x13***	
583	V135	Sheet of 6	10.00	10.00
a.-f.		68c Any single	1.60	1.60
584	V136	Sheet of 6	12.00	12.00
a.-f.		80c Any single	2.00	2.00

United Nations Industrial Development Organization, 50th Anniv. — V137

2016, May 12		**Litho.**	***Perf. 14¾***	
585	V137	80c multi + label	2.60	2.60
		Sheet of 10 + 10 labels	26.50	—

The full sheet sold for $13.12 and €10.90. One of the ten different generic labels is shown. Labels could be personalized. The personalization of labels was available only at UN Headquarters, and not through mail order.

International Day of United Nations Peacekeepers Type of 2016

Designs: 68c, Peacekeepers and African children. 80c, Peacekeepers in tank, Africans.

Litho. With Foil Application

2016, May 29			***Perf. 13¼x13***	
586	A496	68c multicolored	1.75	1.75
587	A496	80c multicolored	2.00	2.00

Sport for Peace Type of 2016

Olympic rings and: No. 588, Weight lifting, denomination at LR. No. 589, Weight lifting, denomination at LL. No. 590, Fencing, denomination at UR. No. 591, Fencing, denonomiation at UL.

2016, July 22		**Litho.**	***Perf. 14¼***	
588	A498	68c multicolored	1.75	1.75
589	A498	68c multicolored	1.75	1.75
a.		Pair, #588-589	3.50	3.50
590	A498	€1.70 multicolored	4.25	4.25
591	A498	€1.70 multicolored	4.25	4.25
a.		Pair, #590-591	8.50	8.50
		Nos. 588-591 (4)	12.00	12.00

World Heritage Sites, Czech Republic Type of 2016

Designs: Nos. 592, 594c, Historic Town Center of Kutná Hora. Nos. 593, 594f, Historic Center of Cesky Krumlov. No. 594a, Historic Center of Prague. No. 594b, Gardens and Castle at Kromeríz. No. 594d, Holy Trinity Column, Olomouc. Nos. 594e, Lednice-Valtice Cultural Landscape.

2016, Sept. 8		**Litho.**	***Perf. 14¼***	
592	A500	68c multicolored	1.75	1.75
593	A500	€1.70 multicolored	4.25	4.25

Souvenir Booklet

594		Booklet, #1115g-		
		1115l	20.50	
a.-c.		A500 30c any single	.65	.65
d.-f.		A500 40c any single	1.00	1.00
g.		Booklet pane of 4 #594a	2.75	—
h.		Booklet pane of 4 #594b	2.75	—
i.		Booklet pane of 4 #594c	2.75	—
j.		Booklet pane of 4 #594d	4.00	—
k.		Booklet pane of 4 #594e	4.00	—
l.		Booklet pane of 4 #594f	4.00	—

Comprehensive Nuclear Test-Ban Treaty Organization, 20th Anniv. — V138

2016, Sept. 23		**Litho.**	***Perf. 14¾***	
595	V138	80c multi + label	2.60	2.60

The full sheet sold for $13.27 and €10.90. One of the ten different generic labels is shown. Labels could be personalized. The personalization of labels was available only at UN Headquarters, and not through mail order.

Miniature Sheet

World Wildlife Conference, Johannesburg — V139

No. 596 — Part of map of Africa and: a, Nilkrokodil (Nile crocodile). b, Kapgeier (Cape vulture). c, Steppenschuppentier (Cape pangolin). d, Mystacidium capense.

2016, Sept. 24		**Litho.**	***Perf. 13x13½***	
596	V139	Sheet of 4	17.00	17.00
a.-d.		€1.70 Any single	4.25	4.25

Sustainable Development Goals Type of 2016

No. 597 — Inscription: a, 1 Keine armut. b, 2 Kein hunger. c, 3 Gesundheit und wohlergehen. d, 4 Hochwertige bildung. e, 5 Geschlechter-gleichheit. f, 6 Sauberes wasser und sanitär-einrichtungen. g, 7 Bezahlbare und saubere energie. h, 8 Menschenwürdige arbeit und wirtschafts-wachstum. i, 9 Industrie, innovation und infrastruktur. j, 10 Weniger ungleichheiten. k, 11 Nachhaltige städte und gemeinden. l, 12 Nachhaltige/r konsum und produktion. m, 13 Massnahmen zum klimaschutz. n, 14 Leben unter wasser. o, 15 Leben an land. p, 16 Frieden, gerechtigkeit und starke institutionen. q, 17 Partnerschaften zur erreichung der ziele.

2016, Oct. 24		**Litho.**	***Perf. 13¼***	
597		Sheet of 17 + label	28.50	28.50
a.-q.		A503 68c Any single	1.60	1.60

SEMI-POSTAL STAMPS

AIDS Awareness Semi-postal Type
Souvenir Sheet

2002, Oct. 24		**Litho.**	***Perf. 14½***	
B1	SP1	51c + 25c multicolored	3.50	3.50

U.N. TEMPORARY EXECUTIVE AUTHORITY, WEST NEW GUINEA

Temporary Executive Authority

LOCATION — Western half of New Guinea, southwest Pacific Ocean
GOVT. — Province of Indonesia
AREA — In 1958, the size was 151,789 sq. mi.
POP. — estimated at 730,000 in 1958
CAPITAL — Hollandia

The former Netherlands New Guinea became a territory under the administration of the United Nations Temporary Executive Authority on Oct. 1, 1962.

The territory came under Indonesian administration on May 1, 1963. For stamps issued by Indonesia see West Irian in Volume 3.

100 Cents = 1 Gulden
100 Cents = 1 Gulden

Catalogue values for all unused stamps in this country are for Never Hinged items.

First Printing (Hollandia)

Netherlands New Guinea Stamps of 1950-60 Overprinted

Overprint size: 17x3½mm. Top of "N" is slightly lower than the "U," and the base of the "T" is straight, or nearly so.

Photo.; Litho. (#4, 6, 8)
Perf. 12½x12, 12½x13½

1962				Unwmk.	
1	A4	1c vermilion & yellow	.25	.25
2	A1	2c deep orange	.25	.25
3	A4	5c chocolate & yellow	.25	.25
4	A5	7c org red, bl & brn vio	.25	.35
5	A4	10c aqua & red brown	.25	.35
6	A5	12c green, bl & brn vio	.25	.35
7	A4	15c deep yel & red brn	.45	.45
8	A5	17c brown violet & blue	.55	.70
9	A4	20c lt bl grn & red brn	.60	.75
10	A6	25c red	.40	.55
11	A6	30c deep blue	.75	.75
12	A6	40c deep orange	.75	.75
13	A6	45c dark olive	1.25	1.50
14	A6	55c slate blue	29.00	2.25
15	A6	80c dull gray violet	6.00	6.00
16	A6	85c dark violet brown	3.00	3.00
17	A6	1g plum	9.25	3.00

Engr.

18	A3	2g reddish brown	12.50	30.00
19	A3	5g green	9.00	8.00
		Nos. 1-19 (19)	75.00	59.50

Overprinted locally and sold in West New Guinea. Stamps of the second printing are used to complete sets sold to collectors.

Second Printing (Haarlen, Netherlands)

Overprint size: 17x3½mm. Top of the "N" is slightly higher than the "U," and the base of the "T" is concave.

Photo.; Litho. (#4a, 6a, 8a)
Perf. 12½x12, 12½x13½

1962				Unwmk.	
1a	A4	1c vermilion & yellow	.25	.25
2a	A1	2c deep orange	.25	.25
3a	A4	5c chocolate & yellow	.25	.25
4a	A5	7c org red, bl & brn vio	.25	.25
5a	A4	10c aqua & red brown	.25	.25
6a	A5	12c green, bl & brn vio	.25	.25
7a	A4	15c deep yel & red brn	.50	.25
8a	A5	17c brown violet & blue	.60	.40
9a	A4	20c lt blue grn & red brn	.60	.40
10a	A6	25c red	.35	.35
11a	A6	30c deep blue	.90	.40
12a	A6	40c deep orange	.90	.40
13a	A6	45c dark olive	1.75	.75
14a	A6	55c slate blue	5.00	1.00
15a	A6	80c dull gray violet	7.00	9.00
16a	A6	85c dark violet brown	3.75	4.75
17a	A6	1g plum	4.25	2.00

Engr.

18a	A3	2g reddish brown	16.00	27.50
19a	A3	5g green	8.00	6.50
		Nos. 1a-19a (19)	51.10	55.20

Third Printing

Overprint 14mm long.

Photo.; Litho. (#4b, 6b, 8b)
Perf. 12½x12

1963, Mar.		Photo.		Unwmk.	
1b	A4	1c vermilion & yellow	5.00	3.00
3b	A4	5c chocolate & yellow	6.00	4.00
4b	A5	7c org red, bl & brn vio	20.00	20.00
5b	A4	10c aqua & red brown	6.00	4.00
6b	A5	12c green, bl & brn vio	35.00	35.00
7b	A4	15c deep yel & red brn	130.00	130.00
8b	A5	17c brown violet & blue	15.00	12.00
9b	A4	20c lt blue grn & red brn	7.50	5.00
		Nos. 1b-9b (8)	224.50	213.00

The third printing was applied in West New Guinea and it is doubtful whether it was regularly issued. Used values are for canceled to order stamps.

Fourth Printing

Overprint 19mm long.

Photogravure

1963, Mar.		Unwmk.	*Perf. 12½x12*	
1c	A4	1c vermilion & yellow	50.00	50.00
5c	A4	10c aqua & red brown	150.00	150.00

The fourth printing was applied in West New Guinea and it is doubtful whether it was regularly issued. Used values are for canceled to order stamps.

U.N. TRANSITIONAL AUTHORITY IN EAST TIMOR

A30

2000, Apr. 29		Litho.	*Perf. 12x11¾*	
350	A30	Dom. red & multi	42.50	115.00
351	A30	Int. blue & multi	60.00	125.00

No. 350 sold for 10c and No. 351 sold for 50c on day of issue.

U.N. INTERIM ADMINISTRATION, KOSOVO

These stamps were issued by the United Nations Interim Administration Mission in Kosovo and the Post & Telecommunications of Kosovo. Service was local for the first two months, with international use to start in mid-May.

100 pfennigs = 1 mark
100 cents = €1 (2002)

Catalogue values for all unused stamps in this country are for Never Hinged items.

Peace in Kosovo — A1

Designs: 20pf, Mosaic depicting Orpheus, c. 5th-6th cent., Podujeve. 30pf, Dardinian idol, Museum of Kosovo. 50pf, Silver coin of Damastion from 4th cent. B.C. 1m, Statue of Mother Teresa, Prizren. 2m, Map of Kosovo.

Perf. 13½x13, 13½x13¼ (30pf)

2000, Mar. 14   Litho.   Unwmk.
1	A1	20pf multicolored	.50	.50
2	A1	30pf multicolored	1.00	1.00
3	A1	50pf multicolored	1.50	1.40
4	A1	1m multicolored	2.25	2.00
5	A1	2m multicolored	4.25	4.00
		Nos. 1-5 (5)	9.50	8.90

Beginning with No. 6, Kosovan stamps were not available to collectors through the United Nations Postal Administration.

Peace in Kosovo — A2

Designs: 20pf, Bird. 30pf, Street musician. 50pf, Butterfly and pear. 1m, Children and stars. 2m, Globe and handprints.

2001, Nov. 12   Litho.   Perf. 14
6	A2	20pf multicolored	1.00	1.00
7	A2	30pf multicolored	1.25	1.25
8	A2	50pf multicolored	2.25	2.25
9	A2	1m multicolored	5.00	5.00
10	A2	2m multicolored	9.00	9.00
		Nos. 6-10 (5)	18.50	18.50

Peace in Kosovo Type of 2001 With Denominations in Euros Only

2002, May 2   Litho.   Perf. 14
11	A2	10c Like #6	1.00	1.00
12	A2	15c Like #7	1.25	1.25
13	A2	26c Like #8	2.25	2.25
14	A2	51c Like #9	5.50	5.50
15	A2	€1.02 Like #10	10.00	10.00
		Nos. 11-15 (5)	20.00	20.00

Christmas — A3

Designs: 50c, Candles and garland. €1, Stylized men.

2003, Dec. 20   Litho.   Perf. 14
16	A3	50c multicolored	10.00	10.00
17	A3	€1 multicolored	20.00	20.00

Return of Refugees — A4

Five Years of Peace — A5

2004, June 29   Litho.   Perf. 13¼x13
18	A4	€1 multicolored	8.00	8.00
19	A5	€2 multicolored	18.00	18.00

Musical Instruments — A6

2004, Aug. 31   Litho.   Perf. 13¼x13
20	A6	20c Flute	7.00	7.00
21	A6	30c Ocarina	15.00	15.00

Aprons A7

Vests — A8

Designs: 20c, Apron from Prizren. 30c, Apron from Rugova. 50c, Three vests. €1, Two vests.

2004, Oct. 28   Litho.   Perf. 13x13¼
22	A7	20c multicolored	8.00	8.00
23	A7	30c multicolored	11.00	11.00
24	A8	50c multicolored	18.50	18.50
25	A8	€1 multicolored	37.50	37.50
		Nos. 22-25 (4)	75.00	75.00

Mirusha Waterfall A9

2004, Nov. 26   Litho.   Perf. 13x13¼
26	A9	€2 multicolored	10.00	10.00

House A10

2004, Dec. 14   Litho.   Perf. 13x13¼
27	A10	50c multicolored	6.00	6.00

Flowers — A11

2005, June 29   Litho.   Perf. 13½
28	A11	15c Peony	2.50	2.50
29	A11	20c Poppies	3.50	3.50
30	A11	30c Gentian	6.00	6.00
		Nos. 28-30 (3)	12.00	12.00

A12

Handicrafts A13

2005, July 20   Perf. 13¼x13
31	A12	20c shown	3.00	3.00
32	A12	30c Cradle	3.50	3.50
33	A13	50c shown	3.75	3.75
34	A12	€1 Necklace	4.75	4.75
		Nos. 31-34 (4)	15.00	15.00

Village A14

Town A15

City — A16

2005, Sept. 15   Perf. 13x13½
35	A14	20c multicolored	3.00	3.00
36	A15	50c multicolored	4.00	4.00
37	A16	€1 multicolored	8.00	8.00
		Nos. 35-37 (3)	15.00	15.00

Archaeological Artifacts — A17

2005, Nov. 2   Perf. 13½x13
38	A17	20c shown	2.00	2.00
39	A17	30c Statue	2.50	2.50
40	A17	50c Sculpture	4.00	4.00
41	A17	€1 Helmet	10.00	10.00
		Nos. 38-41 (4)	18.50	18.50

Minerals A18

2005, Dec. 10   Perf. 13x13½
42	A18	€2 multicolored	14.00	14.00

A19   Europa — A20

2006, July 20   Perf. 13¼x13
43	A19	50c multicolored	3.00	3.00
44	A20	€1 multicolored	5.00	5.00

Fauna A21

2006, May 23   Litho.   Perf. 13
45	A21	15c Wolf	1.00	1.00
46	A21	20c Cow	1.25	1.25
47	A21	30c Pigeon	1.50	1.50
48	A21	50c Swan	1.75	1.75
49	A21	€1 Dog	3.25	3.25
a.		Souvenir sheet, #45-49, + label	10.00	10.00
		Nos. 45-49 (5)	8.75	8.75

Children A22

Designs: 20c, Children in cradle. 30c, Children reading. 50c, Girls dancing. €1, Child in water.

2006, June 30   Litho.   Perf. 13
50	A22	20c multicolored	1.00	1.00
51	A22	30c multicolored	1.25	1.25
52	A22	50c multicolored	1.75	1.75
53	A22	€1 multicolored	4.00	4.00
a.		Souvenir sheet, #50-53	9.00	9.00
		Nos. 50-53 (4)	8.00	8.00

A23

A24

A25

Tourist Attractions — A26

2006, Sept. 1   **Litho.**   *Perf. 13*
54	A23	20c multicolored	1.00	1.00
55	A24	30c multicolored	1.25	1.25
56	A25	50c multicolored	1.75	1.75
57	A26	€1 multicolored	3.75	3.75
a.		Souvenir sheet, #54-57	11.00	11.00
		Nos. 54-57 (4)	7.75	7.75

Intl. Peace
Day — A27

2006, Sept. 21   **Litho.**   *Perf. 13*
58	A27	€2 multicolored	9.00	9.00

Ancient
Coins — A28

Various coins.

2006, Nov. 1   **Litho.**   *Perf. 13*
59	A28	20c multicolored	1.00	1.00
60	A28	30c multicolored	1.50	1.50
61	A28	50c multicolored	2.25	2.25
62	A28	€1 multicolored	4.00	4.00
a.		Souvenir sheet, #59-62	11.00	11.00
		Nos. 59-62 (4)	8.75	8.75

Sculpture — A29

2006, Dec. 1   **Litho.**   *Perf. 13*
63	A29	€2 multicolored	8.50	8.50
a.		Miniature sheet, #45-57, 59-63, + 2 labels	85.00	85.00

Convention on the
Rights of Persons
With
Disabilities — A30

Emblems of handicaps and: 20c, Children and butterfly. 50c, Handicapped women. 70c, Map of Kosovo. €1, Stylized flower.

2007, Apr. 23   **Litho.**   *Perf. 14x14¼*
64	A30	20c multicolored	1.25	1.25
65	A30	50c multicolored	2.50	2.50
66	A30	70c multicolored	3.50	3.50
67	A30	€1 multicolored	4.50	4.50
a.		Souvenir sheet, #64-67	12.50	12.50
		Nos. 64-67 (4)	11.75	11.75

Scouting,
Cent. — A31

Europa — A32

2007, May 12   **Litho.**   *Perf. 13¼*
68	A31	70c multicolored	4.50	4.50
69	A32	€1 multicolored	7.00	7.00
a.		Souvenir sheet, #68-69	110.00	110.00

A33

A34

A35

International
Children's
Day — A36

2007, June 1   **Litho.**   *Perf. 13¼*
70	A33	20c multicolored	1.25	1.25
71	A34	30c multicolored	1.50	1.50
72	A35	70c multicolored	3.00	3.00
73	A36	€1 multicolored	5.00	5.00
		Nos. 70-73 (4)	10.75	10.75

Nos. 70-73 exist imperf.

Native
Costumes — A37

Designs: 20c, Serbian woman. 30c, Prizren Region woman. 50c, Sword dancer. 70c, Drenica Region woman. €1, Shepherd, Rugova.

2007, July 6   **Litho.**   *Perf. 13½x13¼*
74	A37	20c multicolored	1.25	1.25
75	A37	30c multicolored	1.75	1.75
76	A37	50c multicolored	2.00	2.00
77	A37	70c multicolored	3.25	3.25
78	A37	€1 multicolored	4.25	4.25
a.		Souvenir sheet, #74-78, + label	16.00	16.00
		Nos. 74-78 (5)	12.50	12.50

Masks — A38

Various masks.

Perf. 13½x13¼

2007, Sept. 11   **Litho.**
79	A38	15c multicolored	.75	.75
80	A38	30c multicolored	1.00	1.00
81	A38	50c multicolored	1.75	1.75
82	A38	€1 multicolored	3.50	3.50
		Nos. 79-82 (4)	7.00	7.00

Sports — A39

Designs: 20c, Soccer ball, basketball, two people standing, person in wheelchair. 50c, Wrestlers. €1, Symbols of 24 sports.

2007, Oct. 2   **Litho.**   *Perf. 13¼x13½*
83	A39	20c multicolored	1.00	1.00
84	A39	50c multicolored	2.25	2.25
85	A39	€1 multicolored	4.50	4.50
		Nos. 83-85 (3)	7.75	7.75

Nos. 83-85 exist imperf.

Architecture
A40

Designs: 30c, Stone bridge, Vushtrri. 50c, Hamam, Prizren. 70c, Tower. €1, Tower, diff.

2007, Nov. 6   **Litho.**   *Perf. 13¼*
86	A40	30c multicolored	1.50	1.50
87	A40	50c multicolored	2.00	2.00
88	A40	70c multicolored	3.50	3.50
89	A40	€1 multicolored	4.50	4.50
		Nos. 86-89 (4)	11.50	11.50

Nos. 86-89 exist imperf.

Locomotives
A41

Designs: €1, Diesel locomotive. €2, Steam locomotive

2007, Dec. 7   **Litho.**   *Perf. 13¼*
90	A41	€1 multicolored	4.50	4.50
91	A41	€2 multicolored	8.50	8.50

Nos. 90-91 exist imperf.

Skanderbeg (1405-
68), Albanian
National
Hero — A42

2008, Jan. 17   **Litho.**   *Perf. 13¼*
92	A42	€2 multicolored	8.75	8.75

No. 92 exists imperf.

Kosovo declared its independence from Serbia on Feb. 17, 2008, ending the United Nations Interim Administration. Stamps issued after Feb. 17, 2008, by the Republic of Kosovo will be listed under Kosovo in the *Scott Standard Postage Stamp Catalogue.*

ABU DHABI

ˌä-bü-ˈthä-bē

LOCATION — Arabia, on Persian Gulf
GOVT. — Sheikdom under British protection
POP. — 25,000 (estimated)
CAPITAL — Abu Dhabi

Abu Dhabi is one of six Persian Gulf sheikdoms to join the United Arab Emirates, which proclaimed its independence Dec. 2, 1971. See United Arab Emirates.

100 Naye Paise = 1 Rupee
1000 Fils = 1 Dinar (1966)

Catalogue values for all unused stamps in this country are for Never Hinged items.

Sheik Shakbut bin Sultan — A1

Palace — A2

Designs: 40np, 50np, 75np, Gazelle. 5r, 10r, Oil rig and camels.

Perf. 14½

1964, Mar. 30   Photo.   Unwmk.

1	A1	5np brt yellow green	4.00	3.75
2	A1	15np brown	3.00	2.00
3	A1	20np brt ultra	3.25	1.75
a.		Perf 13x13½	575.00	
4	A1	30np red orange	3.25	1.25
5	A1	40np brt violet	6.00	1.00
6	A1	50np brown olive	6.50	2.25
7	A1	75np gray	9.00	6.75

Engr.   Perf. 13x13½

8	A2	1r light green	5.00	2.50
9	A2	2r black	9.00	5.00
10	A2	5r carmine rose	20.00	13.00
11	A2	10r dark blue	26.00	15.00
		Nos. 1-11 (11)	95.00	54.25

For surcharges see Nos. 15-25.

Falcon Perched on Wrist — A3

40np, Falcon facing left. 2r, Falcon facing right.

1965, Mar. 30   Photo.   Perf. 14½

12	A3	20np chlky blue & brn	13.50	2.75
13	A3	40np ultra & brown	17.00	3.50
14	A3	2r brt blue grn & gray brn	29.00	16.00
		Nos. 12-14 (3)	59.50	22.25

Nos. 1-11 Surcharged

a   b

c

1966, Oct. 1   Photo.   Perf. 14½

15	A1 (a)	5f on 5np	10.00	5.00
16	A1 (a)	15f on 15np	12.00	9.00
17	A1 (a)	20f on 20np, perf 13x13½	14.00	7.00
a.		Perf 14½ (#3a)	250.00	250.00
b.		As "a," inverted surcharge	600.00	850.00
18	A1 (a)	30f on 30np	14.00	16.50
a.		Double surcharge	400.00	
b.		Arabic surcharge "20f" instead of "30f"	9,000.	
19	A1 (b)	40f on 40np	13.00	1.50
20	A1 (b)	50f on 50np	35.00	32.50
21	A1 (b)	75f on 75np	35.00	32.50
a.		Double surcharge	400.00	

Engr.   Perf. 13x13½

22	A2 (c)	100f on 1r	17.00	4.00
23	A2 (c)	200f on 2r	17.50	13.00
24	A2 (c)	500f on 5r	42.50	47.50
25	A2 (c)	1d on 10r	62.50	72.50
		Nos. 15-25 (11)	272.50	241.00

Overprint on No. 25 has "1 Dinar" on 1 line and 3 bars through old denomination.

Sheik Zaid bin Sultan al Nahayan — A4

Dorcas Gazelle — A5

Designs: 5f, 15f, 20f, 35f, Crossed flags of Abu Dhabi. 200f, Falcon. 500f, 1d, Palace.

Engr.; Flags Litho.

1967, Apr. 1   Perf. 13x13½

26	A4	5f dull grn & red	.35	.25
27	A4	15f dk brown & red	.50	.25
28	A4	20f dk blue & red	.85	.25
29	A4	35f purple & red	1.00	.30

Engr.

30	A4	40f green	1.25	.30
31	A4	50f brown	1.50	.40
32	A4	60f blue	1.75	.45
33	A4	100f car rose	2.75	.65

Litho.

34	A5	125f green & brn ol	6.00	2.00
35	A5	200f sky blue & brn	26.00	9.50
36	A5	500f org & brt pur	19.00	8.00
37	A5	1d green & vio bl	47.50	17.50
		Nos. 26-37 (12)	108.45	39.85

For surcharge, see No. 55A.

Sheik Zaid bin Sultan al Nahayan — A6

1967, Aug. 6   Photo.   Perf. 14½x14

38	A6	40f Prussian green	4.00	2.50
39	A6	50f brown	5.00	2.00
40	A6	60f blue	17.50	4.00
41	A6	100f carmine rose	26.00	10.00
		Nos. 38-41 (4)	52.50	18.50

Human Rights Flame and Sheik Zaid — A6a

Perf. 14½x14

1968, Apr. 1   Photo.   Unwmk.
Emblem in Red and Green

42	A6a	35f peacock bl & gold	2.25	.90
43	A6a	60f dk blue & gold	3.50	1.25
44	A6a	150f dk brown & gold	9.00	3.00
		Nos. 42-44 (3)	14.75	5.15

International Human Rights Year.

Sheik Zaid and Coat of Arms A7

Perf. 14x14½

1968, Aug. 6   Photo.   Unwmk.

45	A7	5f multicolored	4.00	.60
46	A7	10f multicolored	4.00	.85
47	A7	100f multicolored	11.00	3.25
48	A7	125f multicolored	16.00	4.75
		Nos. 45-48 (4)	35.00	9.45

Accession of Sheik Zaid, 2nd anniversary.

Abu Dhabi Airport — A8

5f, Buildings under construction and earth-moving equipment. 35f, New bridge and falcon. Each stamp shows different portrait of Sheik Zaid.

Perf. 12, 12½x13 (10f)

1969, Mar. 28   Litho.
Size: 5f, 35f, 59x34mm

49	A8	5f multicolored	2.75	.55
50	A8	10f multicolored	7.75	1.00
51	A8	35f multicolored	30.00	8.00
		Nos. 49-51 (3)	40.50	9.55

Issued to publicize progress made in Abu Dhabi during preceding 2 years.

Sheik Zaid and Abu Dhabi Petroleum Co. — A9

Designs: 60f, Abu Dhabi Marine Areas drilling platform and helicopter. 125f, Zakum Field separator at night. 200f, Tank farm.

1969, Aug. 6   Litho.   Perf. 14x13½

52	A9	35f olive grn & multi	2.00	.85
53	A9	60f yel brown & multi	9.50	2.25
54	A9	125f multicolored	11.00	4.00
55	A9	200f red brown & multi	15.00	7.00
		Nos. 52-55 (4)	37.50	14.10

Accession of Sheik Zaid, 3rd anniversary.

No. 27 Surcharged "25" in Arabic

1969, Dec. 13

55A	A4	25f on 15f dk brown & red	300.00	160.00

Because of local demand for 25f stamps for mailing Christmas greeting cards abroad, the Director of Posts ordered that 20,000 examples of No. 27 be surcharged "25" in Arabic for emergency use. This surcharge was applied locally, using a hand numbering machine. All stamps were sold at post office counters

between Dec. 13 and Dec. 24, and the majority were used on mail during this period. Stamps remained valid and exist on covers into 1970. Double overprints exist.

Sheik Zaid — A10

Sheik Zaid and Stallion A11

5f, 25f, 60f, 90f, Oval frame around portrait. 150f, Gazelle and Sheik. 500f, Fort Jahili and Sheik. 1d, Grand Mosque and Sheik.

1970-71   Litho.   Perf. 14

56	A10	5f lt green & multi	1.00	.25
57	A10	10f bister & multi	1.25	.25
58	A10	25f lilac & multi	2.00	.25
59	A10	35f violet & multi	2.25	.25
60	A10	50f sepia & multi	3.25	.40
61	A10	60f violet & multi	3.75	.50
62	A10	70f rose red & multi	6.00	.65
63	A10	90f car rose & multi	8.25	1.00
64	A11	125f multi	12.00	2.00
65	A11	150f multi ('71)	15.00	2.50
66	A11	500f multi ('71)	50.00	11.00
67	A11	1d multi ('71)	85.00	22.50
		Nos. 56-67 (12)	189.75	41.55

For surcharge see No. 80.

Sheik Zaid and Mt. Fuji — A12

1970, Aug.   Litho.   Perf. 13½x13

68	A12	25f multicolored	5.00	1.25
69	A12	35f multicolored	7.00	2.00
70	A12	60f multicolored	12.50	4.00
		Nos. 68-70 (3)	24.50	7.25

Issued to publicize EXPO '70 International Exhibition, Osaka, Japan, Mar. 15-Sept. 13.

Abu Dhabi Airport A13

Designs: 60f, Airport entrance. 150f, Aerial view of Abu Dhabi Town, vert.

Perf. 14x13½, 13½x14

1970, Sept. 22   Litho.

71	A13	25f multicolored	5.25	.90
72	A13	60f multicolored	10.00	2.00
73	A13	150f multicolored	22.50	5.25
		Nos. 71-73 (3)	37.75	8.10

Accession of Sheik Zaid, 4th anniversary.

Gamal Abdel Nasser — A14

1971, May 3   Litho.   Perf. 14

74	A14	25f deep rose & blk	8.00	3.50
75	A14	35f rose violet & blk	11.00	5.25

In memory of Gamal Abdel Nasser (1918-1970), President of UAR.

Scout Cars A15

Designs: 60f, Patrol boat. 125f, Armored car in desert. 150f, Meteor jet fighters.

1971, Aug. 6   Litho.   Perf. 13

76	A15	35f multicolored	7.00	1.50
77	A15	60f multicolored	9.50	2.25
78	A15	125f multicolored	20.00	3.75
79	A15	150f multicolored	25.00	7.50
		Nos. 76-79 (4)	61.50	15.00

Accession of Sheik Zaid, 5th anniversary.

No. 60 Surcharged in Green

1971, Dec. 8   Perf. 14

80	A10	5f on 50f multi	120.00	120.00

Dome of the Rock, Jerusalem — A16

Different views of Dome of the Rock.

1972, June 3   Perf. 13

81	A16	35f lt violet & multi	30.00	5.75
82	A16	60f lt violet & multi	55.00	9.50
83	A16	125f lilac & multi	100.00	20.00
		Nos. 81-83 (3)	185.00	35.25

Nos. 80-83 were issued after Abu Dhabi joined the United Arab Emirates Dec. 2, 1971. Stamps of UAE replaced those of Abu Dhabi. UAE Nos. 1-12 were used only in Abu Dhabi except the 10f and 25f which were issued later in Dubai and Sharjah.

ADEN

ʾä-dən

LOCATION — Southern Arabia
GOVT. — British colony and protectorate
AREA — 112,075 sq. mi.
POP. — 220,000 (est. 1964)
CAPITAL — Aden

Aden used India stamps before 1937. In January, 1963, the colony of Aden (the port) and the sheikdoms and emirates of the Western Aden Protectorate formed the Federation of South Arabia. This did not include the Eastern Aden Protectorate with Kathiri and Qu'aiti States. Stamps of Aden, except those of Kathiri and Qu'aiti States, were replaced Apr. 1, 1965, by those of the Federation of South Arabia. See South

Arabia and People's Democratic Republic of Yemen, Vol. 6.

12 Pies = 1 Anna
16 Annas = 1 Rupee
100 Cents = 1 Shilling (1951)

Catalogue values for unused stamps in this country are for Never Hinged items.

ISSUES UNDER BRITISH ADMINISTRATION

Dhow — A1

Perf. 13x11½

1937, Apr. 1   Engr.   Wmk. 4

1	A1	½a lt green	4.50	2.75
2	A1	9p dark green	4.25	3.50
3	A1	1a black brown	4.25	2.00
4	A1	2a red	4.75	3.00
5	A1	2½a blue	6.75	2.25
6	A1	3a carmine rose	11.00	9.00
7	A1	3½a gray blue	10.00	6.00
8	A1	8a rose lilac	27.50	12.00
9	A1	1r brown	55.00	13.00
10	A1	2r orange yellow	110.00	40.00
11	A1	5r rose violet	300.00	125.00
12	A1	10r olive green	850.00	525.00
		Nos. 1-12 (12)	1,388.	743.50
		Set, hinged	675.00	

Common Design Types pictured following the introduction.

Coronation Issue
Common Design Type

1937, May 12   Perf. 13½x14

13	CD302	1a black brown	.80	1.25
14	CD302	2½a blue	.95	1.50
15	CD302	3½a gray blue	1.25	3.00
		Nos. 13-15 (3)	3.00	5.75
		Set, hinged	2.00	

Aidrus Mosque — A2

¾a, 5r, Camel Corpsman. 1a, 2r, Aden Harbor. 1½a, 1r, Adenese dhow. 2½a, 8a, Mukalla. 3a, 14a, 10r, Capture of Aden, 1839.

1939-48   Engr.   Wmk. 4   Perf. 12½

16	A2	½a green (7/42)	1.75	.50
17	A2	¾a red brn	2.50	1.40
18	A2	1a brt lt blue	1.25	.40
19	A2	1½a red	2.25	.65
20	A2	2a dark brown	1.50	.25
21	A2	2½a brt ultra	1.50	.30
22	A2	3a rose car & dk brn	1.50	.25
23	A2	8a orange	1.75	.40
23A	A2	14a lt bl & brn blk ('45)	3.50	1.00
24	A2	1r bright green	4.50	2.00
25	A2	2r dp mag & bl blk ('44)	11.00	2.75
26	A2	5r dp ol & lake brn (1/44)	30.00	11.00
27a	A2	10r dk pur & lake brn	40.00	16.00
		Nos. 16-27a (13)	103.00	36.90
		Set, hinged	37.50	

For shades, see the *Scott Classic Specialized Catalogue.*

Peace Issue
Common Design Type

Perf. 13½x14

1946, Oct. 15   Engr.   Wmk. 4

28	CD303	1½a carmine	.25	1.50
29	CD303	2½a deep blue	.70	1.00

Return to peace at end of World War II.

Silver Wedding Issue
Common Design Types

1949, Jan. 17   Photo.   Perf. 14x14½

30	CD304	1½a scarlet	.40	2.50

Engraved; Name Typographed
Perf. 11½x11

31	CD305	10r purple	37.50	42.50

25th anniv. of the marriage of King George VI and Queen Elizabeth.

UPU Issue
Common Design Types

Srchd. in Annas and Rupees

Engr.; Name typo. on Nos. 33-34

1949, Oct. 10   Perf. 13½, 11x11½

32	CD306	2½a on 20c dp ultra	.60	1.60
33	CD307	3a on 30c dp car	1.90	1.60
34	CD308	8a on 50c org	1.25	1.60
35	CD309	1r on 1sh blue	1.75	3.00
		Nos. 32-35 (4)	5.50	7.80

75th anniv. of the formation of the UPU.

Nos. 18 and 20-27 Surcharged in Black or Carmine

1951, Oct. 1   Wmk. 4   Perf. 12½

36	A2	5c on 1a #18a	.25	.40
37	A2	10c on 2a #20a	.25	.45
38	A2	15c on 2½a	.40	1.30
a.		Double surcharge	1,600.	
		Hinged	1,000.	
39	A2	20c on 3a	.50	.40
40	A2	30c on 8a #23b (C)	.60	.70
41	A2	50c on 8a #23b	1.25	.50
42	A2	70c on 14a (#23A)	2.25	1.60
43	A2	1sh on 1r #24a	2.75	.30
44	A2	2sh on 2r #25	15.00	3.50
45	A2	5sh on 5r #26	27.50	12.00
46	A2	10sh on 10r #27	37.50	14.00
		Nos. 36-46 (11)	88.25	35.15

Surcharge on No. 40 includes 2 bars.

Coronation Issue
Common Design Type

1953, June 2   Engr.   Perf. 13½x13

47	CD312	15c dk grn & blk	1.25	1.25

Minaret — A10   Camel Transport — A11

15c, Crater. 25c, Mosque. 35c, Dhow. 50c, Map. 70c, Salt works. 1sh, Dhow building. 1sh, 25c, Colony Badge. 2sh, Aden Protectorate levy. 5sh, Crater Pass. 10sh, Tribesman. 20sh, Aden in 1572.

Perf. 12, 12x13½ ('56)

1953-59   Engr.   Wmk. 4
Size: 29x23, 23x29mm

48	A10	5c grn, perf 12x13½ ('56)	.25	.25
a.		Perf. 12 ('55)	2.50	3.50
b.		5c bluish grn, perf 12x13½ ('56)	.25	.55
49	A11	10c orange	.45	.25
a.		10c vermilion ('55)	.25	.35
50	A11	15c blue green	1.25	.60
a.		15c grayish grn ('59)	8.00	6.00
51	A11	25c carmine	.85	.55
a.		25c deep rose red ('56)	4.50	1.50
52	A10	35c ultra, perf 12	2.50	1.50
a.		35c dp bl, perf 12x13½ ('58)	7.00	5.00
b.		35c vio bl, perf 12x13½ ('59)	14.00	4.25

53	A10	50c blue, perf 12	.30	.25
a.		As "b," perf 12x13½ ('56)	1.00	.25
b.		50c deep bl, perf 12 ('55)	3.25	1.50
54	A10	70c gray, perf 12	.30	.25
a.		As "b," perf 12x13½ ('56)	1.25	.25
b.		70c grayish blk, perf 12 ('54)	1.25	.35
55	A11	1sh pur & blk	.40	.25
55A	A11	1sh vio & blk ('55)	1.75	.25
56	A10	1sh25c blk & lt blue ('56)	12.00	.50
57	A10	2sh car rose & sep	1.75	.65
57A	A10	2sh car & blk ('56)	14.00	.60
58	A10	5sh blue & sepia	2.25	1.00
58A	A10	5sh dk blue & blk ('56)	16.00	1.75
59	A10	10sh olive & sepia	1.90	8.00
60	A10	10sh ol gray & blk ('54)	17.50	2.00

Size: 36½x27mm
Perf. 13½x13

61	A11	20sh rose vio & dk brn	7.00	15.00
61A	A11	20sh lt vio & blk ('57)	65.00	20.00
		Nos. 48-61A (18)	145.45	53.65

No. 60 has heavier shading on tribesman's lower garment than No. 59.
See Nos. 66-75. For overprints see Nos. 63-64.

Type of 1953
Inscribed: "Royal Visit 1954"

1954, Apr. 27   Perf. 12

62	A11	1sh purple & sepia	.65	2.00

Nos. 50 & 56 Overprinted in Red

No. 63

No. 64

1959, Jan. 26   Perf. 12, 12x13½

63	A11	15c dark blue green	.60	2.00
64	A10	1sh25c blk & light blue	1.25	3.00

Introduction of a revised constitution.

Freedom from Hunger Issue
Common Design Type

Perf. 14x14½

1963, June 4   Photo.   Wmk. 314

65	CD314	1sh25c green	1.75	1.75

Types of 1953-57
Perf. 12x13½, 12 (#67-69, 73)

1964-65   Engr.   Wmk. 314

66	A10	5c green ('65)	4.00	10.00
67	A11	10c orange	2.00	1.25
68	A11	15c Prus green	.95	5.00
69	A11	25c carmine	3.00	.45
70	A10	35c dk blue	7.00	6.00
71	A10	50c dull blue	.90	1.00
72	A10	70c gray	2.75	4.00
73	A11	1sh vio & black	12.00	5.00
74	A10	1sh25c blk & lt blue	18.50	3.00
75	A10	2sh car & blk ('65)	6.50	45.00
		Nos. 66-75 (10)	57.60	80.70

KATHIRI STATE OF SEIYUN

LOCATION — In Eastern Aden Protectorate
GOVT. — Sultanate
CAPITAL — Seiyun

The stamps of the Kathiri State of Seiyun were valid for use throughout Aden. Used stamps generally bear Aden GPO or Aden Camp cancels. Examples with cancels from offices in the Eastern Protectorate command a premium.

Sultan Ja'far
bin Mansur al
Kathiri — A1

Seiyun — A2

Minaret at
Tarim — A3

Designs: 2½a, Mosque at Seiyun. 3a, Palace at Tarim. 8a, Mosque at Seiyun, horiz. 1r, South Gate, Tarim. 2r, Kathiri House. 5r, Mosque at Tarim.

1942		Engr.	Wmk. 4	Perf. 13¾x14	
1	A1	½a dark green		.25	.75
2	A1	¾a copper brown		.40	1.60
3	A1	1a dark green		.75	.75
		Perf. 13x11½, 11½x13			
4	A2	1½a dark car rose		.75	1.00
5	A3	2a sepia brown		.40	.95
6	A3	2½a deep blue		1.30	1.00
7	A2	3a dk car rose & dull brn		1.85	3.50
8	A2	8a orange red		1.50	.90
9	A3	1r green		6.00	4.00
10	A2	2r rose vio & dk blue		14.00	22.50
11	A3	5r gray green & fawn		35.00	30.00
		Nos. 1-11 (11)		62.20	66.95

For surcharges see Nos. 20-27.

Nos. 4, 6 Ovptd. in Black or Red

a

b

		Perf. 13x11½, 11½x13			
1946, Oct. 15				Wmk. 4	
12	A2 (a)	1½a dark car rose		.25	.65
13	A3 (b)	2½a deep blue (R)		.25	.25
a.		Inverted overprint		900.00	
		Hinged		600.00	
b.		Double overprint		1,400.	
		Hinged		925.00	

Victory of the Allied Nations in WWII. All examples of No. 13b have the 2nd overprint almost directly over the 1st.

Silver Wedding Issue
Common Design Types

1949, Jan. 17		Photo.	Perf. 14x14½	
14	CD304	1½a scarlet	.35	2.50

Engraved; Name Typo.
Perf. 11½x11

| 15 | CD305 | 5r green | 18.50 | 15.00 |

25th anniv. of the marriage of King George VI and Queen Elizabeth.

UPU Issue
Common Design Types

Srchd. in
Annas and
Rupees

Engr.; Name Typo. on Nos. 17-18

1949, Oct. 10			Perf. 13½, 11x11½	
16	CD306	2½a on 20c dp ultra	.25	.50
17	CD307	3a on 30c dp car	1.30	1.00
18	CD308	8a on 50c orange	.55	1.00
19	CD309	1r on 1sh blue	1.00	1.10
		Nos. 16-19 (4)	3.10	3.60

75th anniv. of the formation of the UPU.

Nos. 3 and 5-11
Srchd. in Carmine
or Black

		Perf. 14, 13x11½, 11½x13			
1951, Oct. 1		Engr.		Wmk. 4	
20	A1	5c on 1a (C)		.25	1.75
21	A3	10c on 2a #5a		.30	1.50
22	A3	15c on 2½a		.30	2.00
23	A2	20c on 3a #7		.35	2.25
24	A2	50c on 8a		.60	1.25
25	A3	1sh on 1r		2.00	3.50
26	A2	2sh on 2r #10		12.50	32.50
27	A3	5sh on 5r		35.00	50.00
		Nos. 20-27 (8)		51.30	94.75

Coronation Issue
Common Design Type

1953, June 2			Perf. 13½x13	
28	CD312	15c dk green & blk	.40	1.50

Sultan
Hussein
A10

Seiyun Scene
A11

25c, Minaret at Tarim, vert. 35c, Mosque at Seiyun, vert. 50c, Palace at Tarim. 1sh, Mosque at Seiyun. 2sh, South Gate, Tarim, vert.. 5sh, Kathiri house. 10sh, Mosque entrance, Tarim, vert.

1954, Jan. 15		Engr.	Perf. 12½	
29	A10	5c dark brown	.25	.25
30	A10	10c deep blue	.25	.25
		Perf. 13x11½, 11½x13		
31	A11	15c dk blue green	.25	.25
32	A11	25c dk car rose	.25	.25
33	A11	35c deep blue	.25	.25
34	A11	50c dk car rose & dk brn	.25	.25
35	A11	1sh deep orange	.25	.25
36	A11	2sh gray green	4.25	2.25
37	A11	5sh vio & dk blue	10.00	11.00
38	A11	10sh vio & yel brn	11.00	11.50
		Nos. 29-38 (10)	27.00	26.50

Perf. 11½x13, 13x11½

1964, July 1			Wmk. 314	

Designs: 70c, Qarn Adh Dhabi. 1sh25c, Seiyun, horiz. 1sh50c, View of Gheil Omer, horiz.

39	A11	70c black	3.00	2.00
40	A11	1sh25c bright green	3.00	7.50
41	A11	1sh50c purple	3.00	8.00
		Nos. 39-41 (3)	9.00	17.50

QUAITI STATE OF SHIHR AND MUKALLA

LOCATION — In Eastern Aden Protectorate
GOVT. — Sultanate
CAPITAL — Mukalla

The stamps of the Quaiti State of Shihr and Mukalla were valid for use throughout Aden. Used stamps generally bear Aden GPO or Aden Camp cancels. Examples with cancels from offices in the Eastern Protectorate command a premium.

Sultan Sir
Saleh bin
Ghalib al
Qu'aiti — A1

Mukalla
Harbor — A2

Buildings at
Shibam — A3

Designs: 2a, Gateway of Shihr. 3a, Outpost of Mukalla. 8a, View of 'Einat. 1r, Governor's Castle, Du'an. 2r, Mosque in Hureidha. 5r, Meshhed.

1942		Engr.	Wmk. 4	Perf. 13¾x14	
1	A1	½a blue green		1.50	.55
2	A1	¾a copper brown		2.25	.30
3	A1	1a deep blue		1.00	1.00
		Perf. 13x11½, 11½x13			
4	A2	1½a dark car rose		1.75	.55
5	A2	2a black brown		1.75	1.90
6	A3	2½a deep blue		.50	.30
7	A2	3a dk car rose & dl brn		1.10	1.00
8	A3	8a orange red		1.10	.40
9	A2	1r green		6.75	4.50
a.		Missing "A" in "CA" of watermark		1,300.	1,200.
10	A3	2r rose vio & dk blue		17.50	13.00
11	A3	5r gray grn & fawn		35.00	19.00
		Nos. 1-11 (11)		70.20	42.50

For surcharges see Nos. 20-27.

Nos. 4, 6 Ovptd. in Black or Carmine like Kathiri Nos. 12-13

1946, Oct. 15		Perf. 11½x13, 13x11½		
12	A2 (b)	1½a dk car rose	.25	1.00
13	A3 (a)	2½a deep blue (C)	.25	.25

Victory of the Allied Nations in WWII.

Silver Wedding Issue
Common Design Types

1949, Jan. 17		Photo.	Perf. 14x14½	
14	CD304	1½a scarlet	.55	3.75

Engraved; Name Typo.
Perf. 11½x11

| 15 | CD305 | 5r green | 18.00 | 11.00 |

25th anniv. of the marriage of King George VI and Queen Elizabeth.

UPU Issue
Common Design Types
Surcharged with New Values in Annas and Rupees

Engr.; Name Typo. on Nos. 17 and 18

1949, Oct. 10			Perf. 13½, 11x11½	
16	CD306	2½a on 20c dp ultra	.25	.50
17	CD307	3a on 30c dp car	1.40	1.45
18	CD308	8a on 50c org	.40	1.10
19	CD309	1r on 1sh blue	.90	.90
a.		Surcharge omitted	3,000.	
		Hinged	2,000.	
		Nos. 16-19 (4)	2.95	3.95

Nos. 3, 5-11 &
Types Srchd.
in Carmine or
Black

		Perf. 14, 13x11½, 11½x13			
1951, Oct. 1		Engr.		Wmk. 4	
20	A1	5c on 1a (C)		.25	.25
21	A2	10c on 2a		.25	.25
22	A3	15c on 2½a		.25	.25
23	A2	20c on 3a #7		.30	.65
24	A2	50c on 8a org red		.55	2.50
25	A2	1sh on 1r		2.25	.55
26	A3	2sh on 2r		9.50	25.00
27	A3	5sh on 5r		17.50	37.50
		Nos. 20-27 (8)		30.85	66.75

Coronation Issue
Common Design Type

1953, June 2		Engr.	Perf. 13½x13	
28	CD312	15c dk blue & black	1.10	.60

Qu'aiti State in Hadhramaut

Metal Work — A10

Fisheries
A11

Designs: 10c, Mat making. 15c, Weaving. 25c, Pottery. 35c, Building. 50c, Date cultivation. 90c, Agriculture. 1sh25c, 10sh, Lime burning. 2sh, Dhow building. 5sh, Agriculture.

1955, Sept. 1		Engr.	Perf. 11½x13, 13½x14	Wmk. 4	
29	A10	5c greenish blue		.90	.25
30	A10	10c black		.90	.25
31	A10	15c dk green		.90	.35
32	A10	25c carmine		.50	.25
33	A10	35c ultra		1.00	.25
34	A10	50c red orange		.70	.30
35	A10	90c brown		.70	.25
36	A11	1sh purple & blk		.90	.25
37	A11	1sh25c red org & blk		.80	.65
38	A11	2sh dk blue & blk		4.00	.75
39	A11	5sh green & blk		5.00	2.00
40	A11	10sh car & black		15.00	8.00
		Nos. 29-40 (12)		31.30	13.55

Types of 1955 with Portrait of Sultan Awadh Bin Saleh El-Qu'aiti

Design: 70c, Agriculture. Others as before.

1963, Oct. 20			Wmk. 314	
41	A10	5c greenish blue	.25	1.75
42	A10	10c black	.25	1.50
43	A10	15c dark green	.25	2.00
44	A10	25c carmine	.25	.75
45	A10	35c ultra	.25	1.75
46	A10	50c red orange	.25	1.00
47	A10	70c brown	.30	.75
48	A11	1sh purple & blk	.35	.35
49	A11	1sh25c red org & blk	.75	6.00
50	A11	2sh dk blue & blk	3.25	2.25
51	A11	5sh green & blk	13.00	27.50
52	A11	10sh car & black	27.50	27.50
		Nos. 41-52 (12)	46.65	73.10

AFARS & ISSAS
French Territory of the

ˈä-ˌfärˌz and ēˈsäˌz

LOCATION — East Africa
GOVT. — French Overseas Territory
AREA — 8,880 sq. mi.
POP. — 150,000 (est. 1974)
CAPITAL — Djibouti (Jibuti)

The French overseas territory of Somali Coast was renamed the French Territory of the Afars and Issas in 1967. It became the Djibouti Republic on June 27, 1977.

100 Centimes = 1 Franc

> Catalogue values for all unused stamps in this country are for Never Hinged items.

Imperforates
Most stamps of Afars and Issas exist imperforate in issued and trial colors, and also in small presentation sheets in issued colors.

Grayheaded Kingfisher — A48

Xerus Rutilus — A48a

10fr, Halcyon leucocephala. 15fr, Haematopus ostralegus. 50fr, Tringa nebularia. 55fr, Coracias abyssinicus.

1967	Unwmk.	Engr.	Perf. 13	
310	A48	10fr multicolored	4.00	3.00
311	A48	15fr multicolored	5.00	3.75
312	A48	50fr multicolored	12.00	7.50
313	A48	55fr multicolored	17.50	10.00
314	A48a	60fr multicolored	24.00	17.00
	Nos. 310-314 (5)		62.50	41.25
	Nos. 310-314,C50 (6)		86.50	55.25

Issued: 10fr, 55fr, Aug. 21; 15fr, 50fr, 60fr, Sept. 25. See No. C50.

Soccer
A49

1967, Dec. 18	Engr.	Perf. 13	
315	A49	25fr shown	3.25	2.50
316	A49	30fr Basketball	3.75	2.75

Common Design Types
Pictured in section at front of book.

WHO Anniversary Issue
Common Design Type

1968, May 4	Engr.	Perf. 13	
317	CD126	15fr multicolored	3.00	3.00

20th anniv. of WHO.

Damerdjog Fortress
A50

Administration Buildings: 25fr, Ali Adde. 30fr, Dorra. 40fr, Assamo.

1968, May 17	Engr.	Perf. 13	
318	A50	20fr slate, brn & emer	1.25	1.00
319	A50	25fr brt grn, bl & brn	1.50	1.25
320	A50	30fr brn ol, brn org & sl	2.00	1.40
321	A50	40fr brn ol, sl & brt grn	3.25	2.75
	Nos. 318-321 (4)		8.00	6.40

Human Rights Year Issue
Common Design Type

1968, Aug. 10	Engr.	Perf. 13	
322	CD127	10fr purple, ver & org	2.25	1.60
323	CD127	70fr green, pur & org	4.25	2.10

International Human Rights Year.

Radio-television Station, Djibouti — A52

High Commission Palace, Djibouti — A53

Designs: 2fr, Justice Building. 5fr, Chamber of Deputies. 8fr, Great Mosque. 15fr, Monument of Free French Forces, vert. 40fr, Djibouti Post Office. 70fr, Residence of Gov. Léonce Lagarde at Obock. No. 332, Djibouti Harbormaster's Building. No. 333, Control tower, Djibouti Airport.

1968-70	Engr.	Perf. 13	
324	A52	1fr multicolored	.65	.65
325	A52	2fr multicolored	.90	.75
326	A52	5fr multicolored	1.25	1.00
327	A52	8fr multicolored	1.50	1.25
328	A52	15fr multicolored	4.00	3.75
329	A52	40fr multicolored	3.75	2.75
330	A53	60fr multicolored	3.25	2.25
331	A52	70fr multicolored	4.75	3.00
332	A52	85fr multicolored	6.25	3.75
333	A52	85fr multicolored	7.50	4.50
	Nos. 324-333 (10)		33.80	23.65

Issued: No. 330, 1968; Nos. 324-328, 331-332, 1969; Nos. 329, 333, 1970.
See Nos. C54-C55.

Locust
A54

Designs: 50fr, Pest control by helicopter. 55fr, Pest control by plane.

1969, Oct. 6	Engr.	Perf. 13	
334	A54	15fr brn, grn & slate	4.75	2.25
335	A54	50fr dk grn, bl & ol brn	2.75	2.25
336	A54	55fr red brn, bl & brn	3.50	2.25
	Nos. 334-336 (3)		11.00	6.75

Campaign against locusts.

ILO Issue
Common Design Type

1969, Nov. 24	Engr.	Perf. 13	
337	CD131	30fr org, gray & lil	2.75	2.00

Afar Dagger in Ornamental Scabbard
A56

1970, Apr. 3	Engr.	Perf. 13	
338	A56	10fr multicolored	1.40	.75
339	A56	15fr multicolored	1.60	.75
340	A56	20fr multicolored	2.00	1.00
341	A56	25fr multicolored	2.25	1.10
	Nos. 338-341 (4)		7.25	3.60

See No. 364.

UPU Headquarters Issue
Common Design Type

1970, May 20	Engr.	Perf. 13	
342	CD133	25fr brn, brt grn & choc	2.50	1.40

Trapshooting — A57

Motorboats
A58

Designs: 50fr, Steeplechase. 55fr, Sailboat, vert. 60fr, Equestrians.

1970	Engr.	Perf. 13	
343	A57	30fr dp brn, yel grn & brt bl	3.00	1.75
344	A58	48fr blue & multi	6.00	2.50
345	A58	50fr cop red, bl & pur	5.75	2.50
346	A58	55fr red brn, bl & ol	6.00	2.50
347	A58	60fr ol, blk & red brn	6.50	3.50
	Nos. 343-347 (5)		27.25	12.75

Issued: 30fr, 6/5; 48fr, 10/9; 50fr, 60fr, 11/6.

Automatic Ferry, Tadjourah
A59

1970, Nov. 25			
348	A59	48fr blue, brn & grn	4.25	2.75

Volcanic Geode
A60

Diabase and Chrysolite
A61

10fr, Doleritic basalt. 15fr, Olivine basalt.

1971	Photo.	Perf. 13	
349	A61	10fr black & multi	3.00	1.25
350	A61	15fr black & multi	4.00	1.75
351	A60	25fr black, crim & brn	8.25	3.25
352	A61	40fr black & multi	11.00	5.00
	Nos. 349-352 (4)		26.25	11.25

Issued: 10fr, 11/22; 15fr, 10/8; 25fr, 4/26; 40fr, 1/25.

A62

4fr, Manta birostris. 5fr, Coryphaena hippurus. 9fr, Pristis pectinatus.

1971, July 1	Photo.	Perf. 12x12½	
353	A62	4fr mulitcolored	2.75	1.25
354	A62	5fr multicolored	3.50	2.00
355	A62	9fr multicolored	4.75	2.40
	Nos. 353-355 (3)		11.00	5.65

See No. C60.

De Gaulle Issue
Common Design Type

Designs: 60fr, Gen. Charles de Gaulle, 1940. 85fr, Pres. de Gaulle, 1970.

1971, Nov. 9	Engr.	Perf. 13	
356	CD134	60fr dk vio bl & blk	7.00	4.25
357	CD134	85fr dk vio bl & blk	7.50	5.25

A63

Shells: 4fr, Strawberry Top. 9fr, Cypraea pantherina. 20fr, Bull-mouth helmet. 50fr, Ethiopian volute.

1972, Mar. 8	Photo.	Perf. 12½x13	
358	A63	4fr olive & multi	2.25	1.25
359	A63	9fr dk blue & multi	2.75	1.60
360	A63	20fr dp green & multi	4.50	2.50
361	A63	50fr dp claret & multi	8.00	4.25
	Nos. 358-361 (4)		17.50	9.60

Shepherd — A64

Design: 10fr, Dromedary breeding.

1973, Apr. 11	Photo.	Perf. 13	
362	A64	9fr blue & multi	2.00	.90
363	A64	10fr blue & multi	2.25	.90

Afar Dagger — A65

1974, Jan. 29	Engr.	Perf. 13	
364	A65	30fr slate grn & dk brn	1.90	1.00

For surcharge see No. 379.

Flamingos, Lake Abbe — A66

Flamingos and different views of Lake Abbe.

1974, Feb. 22   Photo.   *Perf. 13*
370 A66 5fr multicolored   4.00 1.50
371 A66 15fr multicolored   3.50 1.50
372 A66 50fr multicolored   5.25 2.25
Nos. 370-372 (3)   12.75 5.25

Soccer Ball — A67

1974, May 24   Engr.   *Perf. 13*
373 A67 25fr black & emerald   3.50 1.75
World Cup Soccer Championship, Munich,
June 13-July 7.

Letters Around
UPU
Emblem — A68

1974, Oct. 9   Engr.   *Perf. 13*
374 A68 20fr multicolored   1.60 .80
375 A68 100fr multicolored   4.25 2.50
Centenary of Universal Postal Union.

Oleo
Chrysophylla
A69

Designs: 15fr, Ficus species. 20fr, Solanum
adoense.

1974, Nov. 22   Photo.
376 A69 10fr shown   2.25 1.00
377 A69 15fr multicolored   2.50 1.25
378 A69 20fr multicolored   3.50 1.75
Nos. 376-378 (3)   8.25 4.00
Day Primary Forest.

No. 364 Surcharged
in Red

1975, Jan. 1   Engr.   *Perf. 13*
379 A65 40fr on 30fr multi   2.75 1.50

Treasury — A70

Design: 25fr, Government buildings.

1975, Jan. 7   Engr.   *Perf. 13*
380 A70 8fr blue, gray & red   .75 .50
381 A70 25fr red, blue & indigo   1.60 1.00

Darioconus Textile — A71

Sea Shells: No. 383, Murex palmarosa. 10fr,
Conus sumatrensis. 15fr, Cypraea pulchra.
No. 386, 45fr, Murex scolopax. No. 387,
Cypraea exhusta. 40fr, Ranella spinosa. 55fr,
Cypraea erythraensis. 60fr, Conus taeniatus.

1975-76   Engr.   *Perf. 13*
382 A71 5fr blue grn & brn   1.50 1.00
383 A71 5fr blue & multi ('76)   1.50 1.10
384 A71 10fr lilac, blk & brn   3.00 1.25
385 A71 15fr blue, ind & brn   4.25 1.75
386 A71 20fr purple & lt brn   6.50 3.50
387 A71 20fr brt grn & multi
          ('76)   3.00 1.50
388 A71 40fr green & brown   5.00 2.75
389 A71 45fr green, bl & bister   5.75 2.75
390 A71 55fr turq & multi ('76)   4.50 3.00
391 A71 60fr buff & sepia ('76)   8.00 3.50
Nos. 382-391 (10)   43.00 21.85

Hypolimnas
Misippus
A72

Butterflies: 40fr, Papilio nireus. 50fr, Acraea
anemosa. 65fr, Holocerina smilax menieri.
70fr, Papilio demodocus. No. 397, Papilio dar-
danus. No. 398, Balachowsky gonimbrasca.
150fr, Vanessa cardui.

1975-76   Photo.   *Perf. 13*
392 A72 25fr emerald & multi   4.75 2.25
393 A72 40fr yellow & multi   5.00 2.50
394 A72 50fr ultra & multi
          ('76)   6.25 3.25
395 A72 65fr ol & multi ('76)   6.00 3.25
396 A72 70fr violet & multi   7.00 4.00
397 A72 100fr blue & multi   8.50 4.75
398 A72 100fr Prus bl & multi
          ('76)   7.50 4.50
399 A72 150fr grn & multi ('76)   9.00 5.25
Nos. 392-399 (8)   54.00 29.75

A73

No. 400, Hyaena hyaena. No. 401,
Cercopithecus aethiops. No. 402, Equus
asinus somalicus. No. 403, Dorcatragus
megalotis. No. 404, Ichneumia albicauda. No.
405, Hystrix galeata. No. 406, Ictonyx striatus.
No. 407, Orycteropus afer.

Perf. 13x12½, 12½x13
1975-76   Photo.
400 A73 10fr multicolored   1.50 1.25
401 A73 15fr multicolored   2.75 1.75
402 A73 25fr multicolored   2.50 1.50
403 A73 30fr multicolored   3.25 2.25
404 A73 50fr multicolored   4.25 2.25
405 A73 60fr multicolored   6.00 2.75
406 A73 70fr multicolored   8.00 3.50
407 A73 200fr multicolored   11.00 6.25
Nos. 400-407 (8)   39.25 21.50

Nos. 401-402, 405 are vert.
Issued: 50fr, 60fr, 70fr, 2/21; No. 401, 200fr,
10/24; 10fr, No. 402, 30fr, 2/4/76.

A74

No. 413, Vidua macroura. No. 414, Psit-
tacula krameri. No. 415, Cinnyris venustus.
No. 416, Ardea goliath. No. 417, Scopus
umbretta. No. 418, Oena capensis. No. 419,
Platalea alba.

1975-76   Photo.   *Perf. 12½x13*
413 A74 20fr multicolored   3.25 1.75
414 A74 25fr multicolored   3.00 1.25
415 A74 50fr multicolored   6.00 3.00
416 A74 60fr multicolored   7.25 3.75
417 A74 100fr multicolored   13.00 6.00
418 A74 100fr multicolored   7.75 3.75
419 A74 300fr multicolored   15.00 8.50
Nos. 413-419 (7)   55.25 28.00

Issued: 300fr, 6/15/76; 25fr, No. 418,
10/13/76; others 11/21 and 12/19/75.

Palms — A75

1975, Dec. 19   Engr.   *Perf. 13*
421 A75 20fr multicolored   2.00 1.00

Satellite and Alexander Graham
Bell — A76

1976, Mar. 10   Engr.   *Perf. 13*
422 A76 200fr dp bl, org & sl grn   5.50 3.50
Centenary of the first telephone call by Alexander Graham Bell, Mar. 10, 1876.

Basketball
A77

1976, July 7   Litho.   *Perf. 12½*
423 A77 10fr shown   1.25 .55
424 A77 15fr Bicycling   1.25 .65
425 A77 40fr Soccer   2.00 1.10
426 A77 60fr Running   2.75 2.00
Nos. 423-426 (4)   7.25 4.30
21st Olympic Games, Montreal, Canada,
July 17-Aug. 1.

Pterois Radiata — A78

1976, Aug. 10   Photo.   *Perf. 13x13½*
428 A78 45fr blue & multi   4.00 2.50

Psammophis Elegans — A79

Design: 70fr, Naja nigricollis, vert.

Perf. 13x13½, 13½x13
1976, Sept. 27   Photo.
430 A79 70fr ocher & multi   5.75 3.00
431 A79 80fr emerald & multi   7.50 4.00

Motorcyclist
A80

1977, Jan. 27   Litho.   *Perf. 12x12½*
432 A80 200fr multicolored   8.50 5.00
Moto-Cross motorcycle race.

Conus Betulinus — A81

Sea Shells: 5fr, Cyprea tigris. 70fr, Conus
striatus. 85fr, Cyprea mauritiana.

1977   Engr.   *Perf. 13*
433 A81 5fr multicolored   3.00 1.50
434 A81 30fr multicolored   4.00 1.50
435 A81 70fr multicolored   9.50 4.50
436 A81 85fr multicolored   10.00 4.50
Nos. 433-436 (4)   26.50 12.00

Gaterin
Gaterinus
A82

1977, Apr. 15   Photo.   *Perf. 13x12½*
437 A82 15fr shown   2.00 1.25
438 A82 65fr Barracudas   5.00 2.25

AIR POST STAMPS

AP16

200fr, Aquila rapax belisarius.

Unwmk.
1967, Aug. 21   Engr.   Perf. 13
C50 AP16 200fr multicolored   24.00 14.00

AP17

48fr, Parachutists. 85fr, Water skier & skin diver.

1968   Engr.   Perf. 13
C51 AP17 48fr multicolored   5.50 2.00
C52 AP17 85fr multicolored   6.50 4.50

Issue dates: 48fr, Jan. 5; 85fr, Mar. 15.

Aerial Map of the Territory — AP18

1968, Nov. 15   Engr.   Perf. 13
C53 AP18 500fr bl, dk brn &
           ocher   22.50 15.00

Buildings Type of Regular Issue
100fr, Cathedral. 200fr, Sayed Hassan Mosque.

1969   Engr.   Perf. 13
C54 A53 100fr multi, vert.   5.50 2.50
C55 A53 200fr multi, vert.   8.50 5.50

Issue dates: 100fr, Apr. 4; 200fr, May 8.

Concorde Issue
Common Design Type
1969, Apr. 17
C56 CD129 100fr org red & ol   25.00 16.00

Arta Ionospheric
Station — AP19

1970, May 8   Engr.   Perf. 13
C57 AP19 70fr multicolored   4.50 3.00

Japanese Sword
Guard, Fish
Design — AP20

200fr, Japanese sword guard, horse design.

Gold embossed
1970, Oct. 26   Perf. 12½
C58 AP20 100fr multicolored   10.00 8.00
C59 AP20 200fr multicolored   13.50 10.00

EXPO '70 International Exposition, Osaka, Japan, Mar. 15-Sept. 13.

Scarus vetula — AP21

1971, July 1   Photo.   Perf. 12½
C60 AP21 30fr black & multi   6.00 3.75

Djibouti Harbor — AP22

1972, Feb. 3
C61 AP22 100fr blue & multi   5.50 3.00

New Djibouti harbor.

AP23

30fr, Pterocles lichtensteini. 49fr, Uppupa epops. 66fr, Capella media. 500fr, Francolinus ochropectus.

1972   Photo.   Perf. 12½x13
C62 AP23 30fr multi   4.00 2.75
C63 AP23 49fr multi   6.75 4.00
C64 AP23 66fr multi   9.00 6.25
C65 AP23 500fr multi   36.00 17.50
     Nos. C62-C65 (4)   55.75 30.50

Issue dates: No. C65, Nov. 3; others Apr. 21.

AP24

Olympic Rings and: 5fr, Running. 10fr, Basketball. 55fr, Swimming, horiz. 60fr, Olympic torch and Greek frieze, horiz.

1972, June 8   Engr.   Perf. 13
C66 AP24 5fr multicolored   1.10 .90
C67 AP24 10fr multicolored   1.25 .90
C68 AP24 55fr multicolored   2.75 1.75
C69 AP24 60fr multicolored   3.50 2.00
     Nos. C66-C69 (4)   8.60 5.55

20th Olympic Games, Munich, 8/26-9/11.

Louis Pasteur — AP25

100fr, Albert Calmette and C. Guérin.

1972, Oct. 5   Engr.   Perf. 13
C70 AP25 20fr multicolored   2.75 1.10
C71 AP25 100fr multicolored   5.50 4.00

Pasteur, Calmette, Guerin, chemists and bacteriologists, benefactors of mankind.

Map and Views of Territory — AP26

200fr, Woman and Mosque of Djibouti, vert.

1973, Jan. 15   Photo.   Perf. 13
C72 AP26 30fr brown & multi   6.50 4.25
C73 AP26 200fr multicolored   11.50 9.00

Visit of Pres. Georges Pompidou of France, Jan. 15-17.

AP27

30fr, Oryx beisa. 50fr, Madoqua saltiana. 66fr, Felis caracal.

1973, Feb. 26   Photo.   Perf. 13x12½
C74 AP27 30fr multicolored   3.25 1.50
C75 AP27 50fr multicolored   4.75 3.25
C76 AP27 66fr multicolored   6.50 3.50
     Nos. C74-C76 (3)   14.50 8.25

See Nos. C94-C96.

Celts — AP28

Various pre-historic flint tools. 40fr, 60fr, horiz.

1973   Perf. 13
C77 AP28 20fr yel grn, blk &
           brn   5.00 2.75
C78 AP28 40fr yellow & multi   5.25 3.50
C79 AP28 49fr lilac & multi   9.00 4.75
C80 AP28 60fr blue & multi   7.50 5.60
     Nos. C77-C80 (4)   26.75 16.60

Issued: 20fr, 49fr, 3/16; 40fr, 60fr, 9/7.

AP29

40fr, Octopus macropus. 60fr, Halicore dugong.

1973, Mar. 16
C81 AP29 40fr multicolored   4.50 2.25
C82 AP29 60fr multicolored   9.00 4.25

AP30

Copernicus: 8fr, Nicolaus Copernicus, Polish astronomer. 9fr, William C. Roentgen, physicist, X-ray discoverer. No. C85, Edward Jenner, physician, discoverer of vaccination. No. C86, Marie Curie, discoverer of radium and polonium. 49fr, Robert Koch, physician and bacteriologist. 50fr, Clement Ader (1841-1925), French aviation pioneer. 55fr, Guglielmo Marconi, Italian electrical engineer, inventor. 85fr, Moliere, French playwright. 100fr, Henri Farman (1874-1937), French aviation pioneer. 150fr, Andre-Marie Ampere (1775-1836), French physicist. 250fr, Michelangelo Buonarroti (1475-1564), Italian sculptor, painter and architect.

1973-75   Engr.   Perf. 13
C83 AP30 8fr multicolored   1.25 1.00
C84 AP30 9fr multicolored   2.00 1.25
C85 AP30 10fr multicolored   2.00 1.25
C86 AP30 10fr multicolored   1.75 1.25
C87 AP30 49fr multicolored   3.75 2.75
C88 AP30 50fr multicolored   3.75 2.75
C89 AP30 55fr multicolored   2.75 2.00
C90 AP30 85fr multicolored   6.75 2.75
C91 AP30 100fr multicolored   6.00 3.50
C92 AP30 150fr multicolored   6.00 3.50
C93 AP30 250fr multicolored   10.00 6.50
     Nos. C83-C93 (11)   46.00 28.50

Issued: 8fr, 85fr, 5/9/73; 9fr, No. C85, 49fr, 10/12/73; 100fr, 1/29/74; 55fr, 3/22/74; No. C86, 8/23/74; 150fr, 7/24/75; 250fr, 6/26/75; 50fr, 9/25/75.

AP31

20fr, Papio anubis. 50fr, Genetta tigrina, horiz. 66fr, Lapus habessinicus.

Perf. 12½x13, 13x12½
1973, Dec. 12   Photo.
C94 AP31 20fr multicolored   3.00 1.40
C95 AP31 50fr multicolored   4.50 2.00
C96 AP31 66fr multicolored   6.00 2.75
     Nos. C94-C96 (3)   13.50 6.15

Spearfishing — AP32

1974, Apr. 14   Engr.   *Perf. 13*
C97 AP32 200fr multicolored   12.00 8.00

No. C97 was prepared for release in Nov. 1972, for the 3rd Underwater Spearfishing Contest in the Red Sea. Dates were obliterated with a rectangle, and the stamp was not issued without this obliteration. Value without rectangle, $400.

Rock Carvings, Balho — AP33

1974, Apr. 26
C98 AP33 200fr carmine & slate 13.00 7.00

Lake Assal — AP34

Designs (Lake Assal): 50fr, Rock formations on shore. 85fr, Crystallized wood.

1974, Oct. 25   Photo.   *Perf. 13*
C99   AP34 49fr multicolored   2.75 1.75
C100 AP34 50fr multicolored   3.00 2.00
C101 AP34 85fr multicolored   6.00 4.00
   Nos. C99-C101 (3)   11.75 7.75

Columba Guinea — AP35

1975, May 23   Photo.   *Perf. 13*
C102 AP35 500fr multicolored 25.00 12.50

Djibouti Airport — AP36

1977, Mar. 1   Litho.   *Perf. 12*
C103 AP36 500fr multicolored 15.00 9.00
   Opening of new Djibouti Airport.

Thomas A. Edison and Phonograph — AP37

Design: 75fr, Alexander Volta, electric train, lines and light bulb.

1977, May 5   Engr.   *Perf. 13*
C104 AP37 55fr multicolored   5.50 3.00
C105 AP37 75fr multicolored   8.50 5.00

Famous inventors: Thomas Alva Edison and Alexander Volta (1745-1827).

POSTAGE DUE STAMPS

Nomad's Milk Jug — D3

Perf. 14x13
1969, Dec. 15   Engr.   Unwmk.
J49 D3 1fr red brn, red lil & sl   .60 1.00
J50 D3 2fr red brn, emer & sl   .70 1.00
J51 D3 5fr red brn, bl & slate   1.00 1.50
J52 D3 10fr red brn, brn & slate   1.75 2.25
   Nos. J49-J52 (4)   4.05 5.75

AFGHANISTAN

af-'ga-nə-,stan

LOCATION — Central Asia, bounded by Iran, Turkmenistan, Uzbekistan, Tajikistan, Pakistan, and China
GOVT. — Republic
AREA — 251,773 sq. mi.
POP. — 23,500,000 (1995 est.)
CAPITAL — Kabul

Afghanistan changed from a constitutional monarchy to a republic in July 1973.

12 Shahi = 6 Sanar = 3 Abasi =
2 Krans = 1 Rupee Kabuli
60 Paisas = 1 Rupee (1921)
100 Pouls = 1 Rupee Afghani (1927)

> **Catalogue values for unused stamps in this country are for Never Hinged items, beginning with Scott 364 in the regular postage section, Scott B1 in the semipostal section, Scott C7 in the airpost section, Scott O8 in officials section, and Scott RA6 in the postal tax section.**

From 1871 to 1892 and 1898, the Moslem year date appears on the stamp. Numerals as follows:

١ ٢ ٣ ٤ ٥
1 2 3 4 5

٦ ٧ ٨ ٩ ٠
6 7 8 9 0

Until 1891, cancellation consisted of cutting or tearing a piece from the stamps. Such examples should not be considered as damaged.
Values are for cut square examples of good color. Cut to shape or faded examples sell for much less, particularly Nos. 2-10.
Nos. 2-108 are on laid paper of varying thickness except where wove is noted.
Until 1907, all stamps were issued ungummed.
The tiger's head on types A1 to A11 symbolizes the name of the contemporary amir, Sher (Tiger) Ali.

Kingdom of Kabul

A1

Tiger's Head, Type I — A2

Tiger's Head, Type II — A2a

Both circles dotted. Outer circle measures 28mm in diameter. Type I: has well-defined inner and outer circles with evenly spaced dots.
Type II: has no well-defined inner and outer circles, and the dots are randomly spaced.

1871   Unwmk.   Litho.   *Imperf.*
Dated "1288"
1   A1   1sh black (30mm
              diameter)   1,350.   60.00
2   A2   1sh black   925.00 50.00
2A A2a 1sh black   525.00 35.00
3   A2   1sa black   650.00 32.50
3A A2a 1sa black   210.00 55.00
4   A2   1ab black   250.00 60.00
4A A2a 1ab black   100.00 60.00
   Nos. 1-4A (7)   4,010.   352.50

Thirty varieties of the shahi, 10 of the sanar and 5 of the abasi.
Similar designs without the tiger's head in the center are revenues.

A3

Outer circle dotted
Dated "1288"
5   A3   1sh black   525.00 35.00
6   A3   1sa black   300.00 50.00
7   A3   1ab black   200.00 32.50
   Nos. 5-7 (3)   1,025. 117.50

Five varieties of each.

A4

Toned Wove Paper

1872   Dated "1289"
8   A4   6sh violet   1,500.   900.
9   A4   1rup violet   1,750. 1,350.

Two varieties of each. Date varies in location. Printed in sheets of 4 (2x2) containing two of each denomination.
Most used examples are smeared with a greasy ink cancel.

A4a

White Laid Paper

1873 — Dated "1290"

No.	Type	Denom	Color		
10	A4a	1sh	black	25.00	12.00
a.		Corner ornament missing		550.00	500.00
b.		Corner ornament retouched		75.00	45.00

15 varieties. Nos. 10a, 10b are the sixth stamp on the sheet.

A5

1873

11	A5	1sh	black	22.50	11.00
11A	A5	1sh	violet	750.00	

Sixty varieties of each.

1874 — Dated "1291"

12	A5	1ab	black	90.00	55.00
13	A5	½rup	black	37.50	20.00
14	A5	1rup	black	40.00	24.00
		Nos. 12-14 (3)		167.50	99.00

Five varieties of each. Nos. 12-14 were printed on the same sheet. Se-tenant varieties exist.

A6

1875 — Dated "1292"

15	A6	1sa	black	375.00	350.00
a.		Wide outer circle		1,200.	750.00
16	A6	1ab	black	425.00	400.00
17	A6	1sa	brown violet	75.00	30.00
a.		Wide outer circle		300.00	190.00
18	A6	1ab	brown violet	80.00	60.00

Ten varieties of the sanar, five of the abasi. Nos. 15-16 and 17-18 were printed in the same sheets. Se-tenant pairs exist.

A7

1876 — Dated "1293"

19	A7	1sh	black	325.00	200.00
20	A7	1sa	black	375.00	200.00
21	A7	1ab	black	750.00	425.00
22	A7	½rup	black	450.00	275.00
23	A7	1rup	black	875.00	275.00
24	A7	1sh	violet	450.00	275.00
25	A7	1sa	violet	425.00	300.00
26	A7	1ab	violet	525.00	275.00
27	A7	½rup	violet	225.00	60.00
28	A7	1rup	violet	225.00	75.00

12 varieties of the shahi and 3 each of the other values.

A8

1876 — Dated "1293"

29	A8	1sh	gray	16.00	
29A	A8a	1sh	gray	65.00	30.00
30	A8	1sa	gray	20.00	8.00
31	A8	1ab	gray	42.50	20.00
32	A8	½rup	gray	50.00	25.00
33	A8	1rup	gray	50.00	17.50
34	A8	1sh	olive blk	140.00	80.00
35	A8	1sa	olive blk	190.00	100.00
36	A8	1ab	olive blk	400.00	250.00
37	A8	½rup	olive blk	275.00	275.00
38	A8	1rup	olive blk	375.00	400.00
39	A8	1sh	green	30.00	8.00
40	A8	1sa	green	40.00	25.00
41	A8	1ab	green	85.00	60.00
42	A8	½rup	green	125.00	80.00
43	A8	1rup	green	110.00	125.00
44	A8	1sh	ocher	32.50	15.00
45	A8	1sa	ocher	40.00	24.00
46	A8	1ab	ocher	80.00	50.00
47	A8	½rup	ocher	100.00	65.00
48	A8	1rup	ocher	140.00	125.00
49	A8	1sh	violet	37.50	15.00
50	A8	1sa	violet	37.50	15.00
51	A8	1ab	violet	50.00	15.00
52	A8	½rup	violet	70.00	27.50
53	A8	1rup	violet	100.00	40.00

24 varieties of the shahi, 4 of which show denomination written:

A8a

12 varieties of the sanar, 6 of the abasi and 3 each of the ½ rupee and rupee.

A9

1877 — Dated "1294"

54	A8a	1sh	gray	10.00	15.00
55	A9	1sa	gray	10.00	9.00
56	A9	1ab	gray	11.00	9.00
57	A9	½rup	gray	14.50	20.00
58	A9	1rup	gray	16.00	20.00
59	A9	1sh	black	14.50	20.00
60	A9	1sa	black	25.00	10.00
61	A9	1ab	black	42.50	15.00
62	A9	½rup	black	45.00	30.00
63	A9	1rup	black	45.00	30.00
64	A9	1sh	green	32.50	32.50
a.		Wove paper		40.00	40.00
65	A9	1sa	green	15.00	12.00
a.		Wove paper		20.00	20.00
66	A9	1ab	green	17.50	16.00
a.		Wove paper		30.00	30.00
67	A9	½rup	green	30.00	30.00
a.		Wove paper		32.50	42.50
68	A9	1rup	green	27.50	32.50
a.		Wove paper		32.50	42.50
69	A9	1sh	ocher	12.50	5.25
70	A9	1sa	ocher	12.50	7.25
71	A9	1ab	ocher	32.50	24.50
72	A9	½rup	ocher	40.00	35.00
73	A9	1rup	ocher	50.00	35.00
74	A9	1sh	violet	15.00	8.00
75	A9	1sa	violet	12.50	5.00
76	A9	1ab	violet	19.00	12.00
77	A9	½rup	violet	27.50	30.00
78	A9	1rup	violet	27.50	30.00

25 varieties of the shahi, 8 of the sanar, 3 of the abasi and 2 each of the ½ rupee and rupee.

Some examples of Nos. 54-78 show a "94" year date. These are valued less.

A10   A11

1878 — Dated "1295"

79	A10	1sh	gray	5.00	10.00
80	A10	1sa	gray	8.00	10.00
81	A10	1ab	gray	12.50	10.00
82	A10	½rup	gray	15.00	15.00
83	A10	1rup	gray	15.00	15.00
84	A10	1sh	black	10.00	
85	A10	1sa	black	10.00	
86	A10	1ab	black	37.50	
87	A10	½rup	black	35.00	
88	A10	1rup	black	35.00	
89	A10	1sh	green	32.50	55.00
90	A10	1sa	green	10.00	9.00
91	A10	1ab	green	35.00	30.00
92	A10	½rup	green	32.50	30.00
93	A10	1rup	green	60.00	40.00
94	A10	1sh	ocher	27.50	10.00
95	A10	1sa	ocher	12.00	15.00
96	A10	1ab	ocher	45.00	35.00
97	A10	½rup	ocher	65.00	45.00
98	A10	1rup	ocher	27.50	30.00
99	A11	1sh	violet	10.00	15.00
100	A10	1sa	violet	30.00	25.00
101	A10	1ab	violet	17.50	15.00
102	A10	½rup	violet	55.00	35.00
103	A10	1rup	violet	45.00	30.00
104	A11	1sh	gray	7.00	7.00
105	A11	1sh	black	100.00	50.00
106	A11	1sh	green	10.00	5.00
107	A11	1sh	ocher	10.00	9.00
108	A11	1sh	violet	8.00	8.00

40 varieties of the shahi, 30 of the sanar, 6 of the abasi and 2 each of the ½ rupee and 1 rupee.

Some examples of Nos. 79-108 show a "95" year date. These are valued less.

The 1876, 1877 and 1878 issues were printed in separate colors for each main post office on the Peshawar-Kabul-Khulm (Tashkurghan) postal route. Some specialists consider the black printings to be proofs or trial colors.

There are many shades of these colors.

1ab, Type I (26mm) — A12

1ab, Type II (28mm) — A13

A14

A15

Dated "1298", numerals scattered through design

Handstamped, in watercolor

1881-90

Thin White Laid Batonne Paper

109	A12	1ab	violet	5.00	3.00
109A	A13	1ab	violet	8.00	3.00
110	A12	1ab	black brn	8.00	3.00
a.		Ordinary thin wove paper		—	20.00
111	A12	1ab	rose	12.00	3.00
b.		Se-tenant with No. 111A		16.00	—
111A	A13	1ab	rose	9.00	3.00
112	A14	2ab	violet	10.00	3.00
113	A14	2ab	black brn	12.00	6.00
114	A14	2ab	rose	20.00	10.00
115	A15	1rup	violet	12.00	12.00
116	A15	1rup	black brn	14.00	10.00
117	A15	1rup	rose	12.50	7.50

Thin White Wove Batonne Paper

118	A12	1ab	violet	15.00	5.00
119	A12	1ab	vermilion	30.00	10.00
120	A12	1ab	rose	30.00	25.00
121	A14	2ab	violet	30.00	25.00
122	A14	2ab	vermilion	30.00	16.00
122A	A14	2ab	black brn		
123	A15	1rup	violet	15.00	8.00
124	A15	1rup	vermilion	14.00	7.50
125	A15	1rup	black brn	19.00	8.00

Thin White Laid Batonne Paper

126	A12	1ab	brown org	20.00	8.00
126A	A13	1ab	brn org (II)	22.50	9.00
127	A12	1ab	carmine lake	20.00	8.00
a.		Laid paper		22.50	10.00
128	A14	2ab	brown org	22.50	8.00
129	A14	2ab	carmine lake	20.00	8.00
130	A15	1rup	brown org	35.00	15.00
131	A15	1rup	car lake	60.00	40.00

Yellowish Laid Batonne Paper

132	A12	1ab	purple	10.00	10.00
133	A12	1ab	red	12.50	10.00

1884 — Colored Wove Paper

133A	A13	1ab	purple, yel (II)	17.50	17.50
134	A12	1ab	purple, grn		
135	A12	1ab	purple, blue	32.50	21.00
136	A12	1ab	red, grn	37.50	
137	A12	1ab	red, yel	30.00	
139	A12	1ab	red, rose	50.00	
140	A14	2ab	red, yel	30.00	
142	A14	2ab	red, rose	30.00	
143	A15	1rup	red, yel	55.00	20.00
145	A15	1rup	red, rose	65.00	25.00

Thin Colored Ribbed Paper

146	A14	2ab	red, yellow	40.00	
147	A15	1rup	red, yellow	80.00	
148	A12	1ab	lake, lilac	40.00	
149	A14	2ab	lake, lilac	40.00	
150	A15	1rup	lake, lilac	40.00	
151	A12	1ab	lake, green	40.00	
152	A14	2ab	lake, green	40.00	
153	A15	1rup	lake, green	40.00	

1886-88 — Colored Wove Paper

155	A12	1ab	black, magenta	60.00	
156	A12	1ab	claret brn, org	50.00	
156A	A12	1ab	red, org	40.00	
156B	A14	2ab	red, org	40.00	
156C	A15	1rup	red, org	40.00	

Laid Batonné Paper

157	A12	1ab	black, lavender	40.00	
158	A12	1ab	cl brn, grn	40.00	
159	A12	1ab	lake, pink	60.00	
160	A14	2ab	black, pink	100.00	
161	A15	1rup	black, pink	70.00	

Laid Paper

162	A12	1ab	black, pink	80.00	
163	A14	2ab	black, pink	80.00	
164	A15	1rup	black, pink	80.00	
165	A12	1ab	brown, yel	80.00	
166	A14	2ab	brown, yel	80.00	
167	A15	1rup	brown, yel	80.00	
168	A12	1ab	blue, grn	80.00	
169	A14	2ab	blue, grn	80.00	
170	A15	1rup	blue, grn	80.00	

1891 — Colored Wove Paper

175	A12	1ab	green, rose	100.00	
176	A15	1rup	pur, grn batonne	100.00	

Nos. 109-176 fall into three categories:

1. Those regularly issued and in normal postal use from 1881 on, handstamped on thin white laid or wove paper in strip sheets containing 12 or more impressions of the same denomination arranged in two irregular rows, with the impressions often touching or overlappng.

2. The 1884 postal issues provisionally printed on smooth or ribbed colored wove paper as needed to supplement low stocks of the normal white paper stamps.

3. The "special" printings made in a range of colors on several types of laid or wove colored papers, most of which were never used for normal printings. These were produced periodically from 1886 to 1891 to meet philatelic demands. Although nominally valid for postage, most of the special printings were exported directly to fill dealers' orders, and few were ever postally used. Many of the sheets contained all three denominations with impressions separated by ruled lines. Sometimes different colors were used, so se-tenant multiples of denomination or color exist. Many combinations of stamp and paper colors exist besides those listed.

Various shades of each color exist.

Type A12 is known dated "1297."

Counterfeits, lithographed or typographed, are plentiful.

Kingdom of Afghanistan

A16

A17

A18

Dated "1309"

1891 — Pelure Paper — Litho.

177	A16	1ab	slate blue	2.00	2.00
a.		Tete beche pair		19.00	
178	A17	2ab	slate blue	12.00	12.00
179	A18	1rup	slate blue	27.50	27.50
		Nos. 177-179 (3)		41.50	41.50

Revenue stamps of similar design exist in various colors.

Nos. 177-179 were printed in panes on the same sheet, so se-tenant gutter pairs exist. Examples in black or red are proofs.

A Mosque Gate and Crossed Cannons (National Seal) A19

Dated "1310" in Upper Right Corner

1892   **Flimsy Wove Paper**
180	A19	1ab black, *green*	3.50	3.00
181	A19	1ab black, *orange*	4.50	4.50
182	A19	1ab black, *yellow*	3.50	3.00
183	A19	1ab black, *pink*	4.00	3.25
184	A19	1ab black, *lil rose*	4.00	4.00
185	A19	1ab black, *blue*	6.00	5.50
186	A19	1ab black, *salmon*	4.50	3.75
187	A19	1ab black, *magenta*	4.00	4.00
188	A19	1ab black, *violet*	4.00	4.00
188A	A19	1ab black, *scarlet*	4.00	3.00

Many shades exist.

A20

A21

Undated

1894   **Flimsy Wove Paper**
189	A20	2ab black, *green*	12.00	8.00
190	A21	1rup black, *green*	14.50	13.00

24 varieties of the 2 abasi and 12 varieties of the rupee.
Nos. 189-190 and F3 were printed se-tenant in the same sheet. Pairs exist.

A21a

Dated "1316"

1898   **Flimsy Wove Paper**
191	A21a	2ab black, *pink*	3.00
192	A21a	2ab black, *magenta*	3.00
193	A21a	2ab black, *yellow*	1.40
193A	A21a	2ab black, *salmon*	3.50
194	A21a	2ab black, *green*	1.75
195	A21a	2ab black, *purple*	2.40
195A	A21a	2ab black, *blue*	22.50
		Nos. 191-195A (7)	37.55

Nos. 191-195A were not regularly issued. Genuinely used examples are scarce. No. 195A was found in remainder stocks and probably was never released.

A22

A23

A24

1907   **Engr.**   *Imperf.*
Medium Wove Paper
196	A22	1ab blue green	50.00	30.00
a.		1ab emerald	75.00	30.00
b.		Double impression	500.00	
c.		Printed on both sides		450.00
197	A22	1ab brt blue	45.00	25.00
198	A23	2ab deep blue	45.00	25.00
a.		Double impression	550.00	
199	A24	1rup green	100.00	50.00
a.		1rup blue green	100.00	75.00

Zigzag Roulette 10
200	A22	1ab green	*2,750.*	350.00
a.		Double impression		1,500.
b.		Printed on both sides		1,750.
c.		Double impression and printed on both sides		2,500.
d.		1ab blue green	*2,750.*	350.00
201	A23	2ab blue	*2,500.*	—

1908   *Serrate Roulette 13*
201A	A22	1ab green	—	—
b.		1ab emerald green, on cover		1,250.
201B	A23	2ab blue	*3,500.*	

Nos. 201A and 201Ab are only known used on cover.
No. 201B is known only unused.

Perf. 12 on 2, 3 or 4 Sides
202	A22	1ab green	—	65.00
203	A23	2ab deep blue	35.00	20.00
a.		Horiz. pair, imperf between	450.00	
204	A24	1rup blue green	125.00	65.00
c.		Pair, imperf. between	400.00	
		Nos. 202-204 (3)	160.00	150.00

Twelve varieties of the 1 abasi, 6 of the 2 abasi, 4 of the 1 rupee.
Nos. 196-204 were issued in small sheets containing 3 or 4 panes. Gutter pairs, normal and tete beche, exist.
Two plates were used for the 1 abasi: plate I, inner vert. lines extend into lower left panel; plate II, inner vert. lines do not extend into lower left panel.

A25   A26

A27

1909-19   **Typo.**   *Perf. 12*
205	A25	1ab ultra	5.00	2.00
a.		Imperf., pair	48.00	
206	A25	1ab red ('16)	1.60	1.25
a.		Imperf.	30.00	
207	A25	1ab rose ('18)	1.60	1.00
208	A26	2ab green	2.75	2.25
a.		Imperf., pair	48.00	
b.		Horiz. pair, imperf. btwn.		
208C	A26	2ab yellow ('16)	3.25	2.75
209	A26	2ab bis ('18-'19)	3.25	3.25
210	A27	1rup lilac brn	7.50	6.50
a.		1rup red brown	7.50	7.50
211	A27	1rup ol bis ('16)	10.00	8.00
		Nos. 205-211 (8)	34.95	27.00

A28

1913
212	A28	2pa drab brown	20.00	6.00
a.		2pa red brown	20.00	6.00

No. 212 is inscribed "Tiket waraq dak" (Postal card stamps). It was usable only on post-cards and not accepted for postage on letters.

Nos. 196-212 sometimes show letters of a papermaker's watermark, "Howard & Jones, London."

Royal Star — A29

1920, Aug. 24   *Perf. 12*
Size: 39x46mm
214	A29	10pa rose	175.00	100.00
215	A29	20pa red brown	275.00	175.00
216	A29	30pa green	375.00	250.00
		Nos. 214-216 (3)	825.00	525.00

2nd Independence Day. Issued to commemorate the first anniversary of the signing of the armistice that ended the war of independence (Third Afghan War).
Issued in sheets of two.
No. 214 exists in two sizes: 38.5mmx45mm, position 1 in sheet; 38.5mmx46mm, position 2.

1921, Mar.   **Size: 22½x28¼mm**
217	A29	10pa rose	2.50	1.25
a.		Perf. 11 ('27)	22.50	13.00
218	A29	20pa red brown	4.50	2.50
219	A29	30pa yel green	6.50	3.00
a.		Tete beche pair	55.00	32.50
b.		30pa green	6.50	3.00
c.		As "b," Tete beche pair	55.00	32.50
		Nos. 217-219 (3)	13.50	6.75

3rd Independence Day.
Two types of the 10pa, three of the 20pa.

Hstmpd. in black on Nos. 217-219

1923, Feb. 26
219D	A29a	10pa rose	—	125.00
219E	A29a	20pa red brown	—	125.00
219F	A29a	30pa yel green	400.00	—

5th Independence Day.
Two types of handstamp exist.
Forgeries exist.
See No. Q13B-Q13E.

These handstamps were used by the Kabul post office on incoming foreign mail from 1921 until Afghanistan joined the Universal Postal Union April 1, 1928. Afghan stamps were applied to foreign mail arriving in the country and were canceled with these postage-due handstamps to indicate that postage was to be collected from the addressee. The handstamps were applied primarily to Nos. 217-219, 227-235, 236, and

237-246. Values are the same as for stamps with postal cancellations. A third type of handstamp exists with no distinctive outer border.

A30

1924, Feb. 26   *Perf. 12*
220	A30	10pa chocolate	45.00	30.00
a.		Tete beche pair	150.00	100.00

6th Independence Day.
Printed in sheets of four consisting of two tete beche pairs, and in sheets of two. Two types exist.

Some authorities believe that Nos. Q15-Q16 were issued as regular postage stamps.

Crest of King Amanullah A32

Size: 29x37mm

1925, Feb. 26   *Perf. 12*
222	A32	10pa light brown	75.00	35.00

7th Independence Day.
Printed in sheets of 8 (two panes of 4).

Wove Paper

1926, Feb. 28   **Size: 26x33mm**
224	A32	10pa dark blue	8.00	8.00
a.		Imperf., pair	32.50	
b.		Horiz. pair, imperf. btwn.	75.00	
c.		Vert. pair, imperf. btwn.	75.00	
d.		Laid paper	40.00	13.00

7th anniv. of Independence. Printed in sheets of 4, and in sheets of 8 (two panes of 4). Tete beche gutter pairs exist.

Tughra and Crest of Amanullah A33

1927, Feb.
225	A33	10pa magenta	14.00	12.00
a.		Vertical pair, imperf. between	75.00	

Dotted Background
226	A33	10pa magenta	20.00	13.00
a.		Horiz. pair, imperf. between	75.00	

The surface of No. 226 is covered by a net of fine dots.
8th anniv. of Independence. Printed in sheets of 8 (two panes of 4).
Tete-beche gutter pairs exist. Value, pair $85.

National Seal — A34

A35

A36

1927, Oct. **Imperf.**
227 A34 15p pink 1.40 1.40
228 A35 30p Prus green 2.75 1.25
229 A36 60p light blue 3.75 3.25
Nos. 227-229 (3) 7.90 5.90

1927, Nov. **Perf. 11, 11¾**
230 A34 15p pink 1.75 1.40
231 A35 30p Prus green 3.25 1.40
232 A36 60p bright blue 3.50 2.00
a. Tete beche pair 17.50 17.50
Nos. 230-232 (3) 8.50 4.80

A37

A38   A39

A40

1928, Feb. **Perf. 11, 11¾**
233 A37 10p gray green 1.90 .40
a. Tete beche pair 14.00 6.50
b. Vert. pair, imperf. horiz. 11.00 11.00
c. Vertical pair, imperf. between
234 A38 25p car rose 2.25 .40
235 A39 40p ultra 3.00 .75
a. Tete beche pair 15.00 16.00
236 A40 50p red 3.75 1.00
Nos. 233-236 (4) 10.90 2.55

Nos. 230-232 are usually imperforate on one or two sides. The sheets of these stamps are often imperforate at the outer margin.

Tughra and Crest of Amanullah — A41

1928, Feb. 27
236D A41 15p pink 5.00 5.00
a. Tete beche pair 12.00 10.00
b. Horiz. pair, imperf. vert. 22.50 19.00
c. As "a," imperf. vert., block of 4 75.00

9th anniv. of Independence. This stamp is always imperforate on one or two sides.

A 15p blue of somewhat similar design was prepared for the 10th anniv., but was not issued due to Amanullah's dethronement. Value, $15.

Types of 1927 in New Colors

A42

1929-30
236E A34 15p ultra 1.75 1.40
236F A42 30p dp green ('30) 1.75 1.25
236G A36 60p black ('29) 4.00 2.25
Nos. 236E-236G (3) 7.50 4.90

No. 236F has been redrawn. A narrow border of pearls has been added and "30," in European and Arabic numerals, inserted in the upper spandrels.

A43

1928-30 **Perf. 11, 12**
237 A43 2p dull blue 7.75 4.50
a. Vertical pair, imperf. between 20.00
238 A43 2p lt rose ('30) .65 .55
240 A37 10p choc ('30) 3.00 1.25
a. 10p brown purple ('29) 8.50 4.00
242 A38 25p Prus green ('29) 4.00 1.25
244 A39 40p rose ('29) 3.50 1.25
a. Tete beche pair 14.50
b. Vert. pair, imperf. horiz. 11.00
246 A40 50p dk blue ('29) 5.00 1.50
Nos. 237-246 (10) 34.80 12.85

The sheets of these stamps are often imperforate at the outer margins.
Nos. 237-238 are newspaper stamps.

This handstamp was used for ten months by the Revolutionary Gov't in Kabul as a control mark on outgoing mail. It occasionally fell on the stamps but there is no evidence that it was officially used as an overprint. Unused examples were privately made.

Independence Monument A46

Laid Paper
Without Gum
Wmk. Large Seal in the Sheet
1931, Aug. **Litho.** **Perf. 12**
262 A46 20p red 2.50 1.25

13th Independence Day.

National Assembly Chamber A47

A48

National Assembly Building A49

A50

National Assembly Chamber A51

National Assembly Building A52

Wove Paper
1932 **Unwmk.** **Typo.** **Perf. 12**
263 A47 40p olive 1.15 .40
264 A48 60p violet 1.50 .80
265 A49 80p dark red 2.00 1.25
266 A50 1af black 16.00 7.50
267 A51 2af ultra 7.00 4.00
268 A52 3af gray green 7.50 3.50
Nos. 263-268 (6) 35.15 17.45

Formation of the Natl. Council. Imperforate or perforated examples on ungummed chalky paper are proofs.
See Nos. 304-305.

Mosque at Balkh — A53

Kabul Fortress A54

Parliament House, Darul Funun — A55

Parliament House, Darul Funun — A56

Arch of Qalai Bist — A57

Memorial Pillar of Knowledge and Ignorance A58

Independence Monument A59

Minaret at Herat — A60

Arch of Paghman A61

Ruins at Balkh — A62

Minarets of Herat — A63

Great Buddha at Bamian — A64

1932 **Typo.** **Perf. 12**
269 A53 10p brown .80 .25
270 A54 15p dk brown .60 .30
271 A55 20p red .95 .25
272 A56 25p dk green 1.35 .25
273 A57 30p red 1.35 .25
274 A58 40p orange 1.75 .50
275 A59 50p blue 2.40 1.40
a. Tete beche pair 12.00
276 A60 60p blue 2.25 .90
277 A61 80p violet 4.00 2.00
278 A62 1af dark blue 7.00 .80
279 A63 2af dk red violet 7.75 3.50
280 A64 3af claret 9.50 3.00
Nos. 269-280 (12) 39.70 12.15

Counterfeits of types A53-A65 exist.
See Nos. 290-295, 298-299, 302-303.

Entwined 2's — A65

Type I   Type II

Two types:
Type I — Numerals shaded. Size about 21x29mm.
Type II — Numerals unshaded. Size about 21¾x30mm.

1931-38   **Perf. 12, 11x12**
281 A65 2p red brn (I)   .40   .50
282 A65 2p olive blk (I) ('34)   .30   .80
283 A65 2p grnsh gray (I) ('34)   .40   .75
283A A65 2p black (I) ('36)   .25   .75
284 A65 2p salmon (II) ('38)   .50   .75
284A A65 2p rose (I) ('38)   .50   .90
   b.   Imperf., pair   10.00

Imperf
285 A65 2p black (II) ('37)   .75   .75
286 A65 2p salmon (II) ('38)   .75   .75
      Nos. 281-286 (8)   3.85 5.95

The newspaper rate was 2 pouls.

Independence Monument — A66

1932, Aug.   **Perf. 12**
287 A66 1af carmine   5.50 3.25
         14th Independence Day.

A67

1929 Liberation Monument, Kabul.

1932, Oct.   **Typo.**
288 A67 80p red brown   2.00 1.50

Arch of Paghman — A68

1933, Aug.
289 A68 50p light ultra   3.00 1.50
         15th Independence Day.
    No. 289 exists imperf. Value, $5.

Types of 1932 and

Royal Palace, Kabul A69

Darrah- Shikari Pass, Hindu Kush — A70

1934-38   **Typo.**   **Perf. 12**
290 A53 10p deep violet   .30   .25
291 A54 15p turq green   .50   .25
292 A55 20p magenta   .50   .25
293 A56 25p deep rose   .60   .25
294 A57 30p orange   .65   .30
295 A58 40p blue black   .75   .30
296 A69 45p dark blue   2.75 1.50
297 A69 45p red ('38)   .50   .25
298 A59 50p orange   .80   .25
299 A60 60p purple   1.00   .45
300 A70 75p red   4.00 2.00
301 A70 75p dk blue ('38)   1.00   .65
302 A61 80p brown vio   1.60   .80
303 A62 1af red violet   3.25 1.60
304 A51 2af gray black   5.25 2.40
305 A52 3af ultra   6.00 3.00
      Nos. 290-305 (16)   29.45 14.50

Nos. 290, 292, 300, 304, 305 exist imperf.

Independence Monument — A71

1934, Aug.   Litho.   Without Gum
306 A71 50p pale green   3.25 2.75
   a.   Tete beche pair   11.50 11.50

16th year of Independence. Each sheet of 40 (4x10) included 4 tete beche pairs as lower half of sheet was inverted.

Independence Monument — A74

1935, Aug. 15   **Laid Paper**
309 A74 50p dark blue   3.50 2.40
         17th year of Independence.

Fireworks Display A75

Wove Paper

1936, Aug. 15   **Perf. 12**
310 A75 50p red violet   3.25 2.50
         18th year of Independence.

Independence Monument and Nadir Shah — A76

1937
311 A76 50p vio & bis brn   2.75 2.10
   a.   Imperf., pair   9.50 9.50
         19th year of Independence.

Mohammed Nadir Shah — A77

1938   Without Gum   Perf. 11x12
315 A77 50p brt blue & sepia   2.75 2.40
   a.   Imperf. pair   24.00 19.00
         20th year of Independence.

Mohammed Nadir Shah — A78

1939   **Perf. 11, 12x11**
317 A78 50p deep salmon   2.40 1.50
         21st year of Independence.

National Arms A79

Parliament House, Darul Funun — A80

Royal Palace, Kabul A81

Independence Monument — A82

Independence Monument and Nadir Shah — A83

Mohammed Zahir Shah — A84

Mohammed Zahir Shah — A85

Perf. 11, 11x12, 12x11, 12
1939-61   **Typo.**
318 A79 2p intense blk   .30   .70
318A A79 2p brt pink ('61)   .30   .70
         Size: 36.5x24mm
319 A80 10p brt purple   .30   .25
         Size: 31.5x21mm
320 A80 15p brt green   .35   .25
         Size: 34x22.5mm
321 A80 20p red lilac   .50   .25
322 A81 25p rose red   .60   .30
322A A81 25p green ('41)   .35   .25
323 A81 30p orange   .50   .25
   a.   Vert. pair, imperf between   —
324 A81 40p dk gray   1.00   .50
325 A82 45p brt carmine   1.00   .40
326 A82 50p dp orange   .80   .25
327 A82 60p violet   1.00   .25
328 A83 75p ultra   3.00   .80
328A A83 75p red vio ('41)   2.25 1.60
328C A83 75p brt red ('44)   4.00 3.00
328D A83 75p chnt brn ('49)   4.00 3.00
329 A83 80p chocolate   2.00 1.00
   a.   80p dull red violet (error)
330 A84 1af brt red violet   2.25   .80
330A A85 1af brt red vio ('44) 2.25   .90
331 A85 2af copper red   3.00   .80
   a.   2af deep rose red   4.25 1.75
332 A84 3af deep blue   5.00 2.40
      Nos. 318-332 (21)   34.75 18.65

Many shades exist in this issue.
On No. 332, the King faces slightly left.
No. 318A issued with and without gum.
See Nos. 795A-795B. For similar design see No. 907A.

Mohammed Nadir Shah — A86

1940, Aug. 23   **Perf. 11**
333 A86 50p gray green   2.00 1.50
         22nd year of Independence.

Independence Monument — A87   Arch of Paghman — A88

1941, Aug. 23   **Perf. 12**
334 A87 15p gray green   25.00 5.75
335 A88 50p red brown   2.50 2.10
         23rd year of Independence.

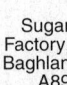

Sugar Factory, Baghlan A89

1942, Apr. **Perf. 12**
336 A89 1.25af blue (shades) 2.00 1.50
a. 1.25af ultra 2.50 1.75

In 1949, a 1.50af brown, type A89, was sold for 3af by the Philatelic Office, Kabul. It was not valid for postage. Value $6.

Independence Monument — A90

Mohammed Nadir Shah and Arch of Paghman A91

1942, Aug. 23 **Perf. 12**
337 A90 35p bright green 3.75 3.50
338 A91 125p chalky blue 3.00 2.00

24th year of Independence.

Independence Monument and Nadir Shah — A92

Mohammed Nadir Shah — A93

Perf. 11x12, 12x11
1943, Aug. 25 **Typo.** **Unwmk.**
339 A92 35p carmine 17.50 15.00
340 A93 1.25af dark blue 3.50 2.50

25th year of Independence.

Tomb of Gohar Shad, Herat — A94

Ruins of Qalai Bist — A95

1944, May 1 **Perf. 12, 11x12**
341 A94 35p orange 1.50 1.00
342 A95 70p violet 2.00 1.00
a. 70p rose lilac 2.00 1.00

A96

A97

1944, Aug. **Perf. 12**
343 A96 35p crimson 1.25 .65
344 A97 1.25af ultra 2.25 1.75

26th year of Independence.

> **Catalogue values for unused stamps in this section, from this point to the end of the section, are for Never Hinged items.**

A98

A99

1945, July
345 A98 35p deep red lilac 2.50 .80
346 A99 1.25af blue 4.00 2.00

27th year of Independence.

Mohammed Zahir Shah — A100

Independence Monument A101

Mohammed Nadir Shah A102

1946, July
347 A100 15p emerald 1.25 .70
348 A101 20p dp red lilac 2.00 .85
349 A102 125p blue 3.75 2.00
Nos. 347-349 (3) 7.00 3.55

28th year of Independence.

Zahir Shah and Ruins of Qalai Bist — A103

A104

A105

1947, Aug.
350 A103 15p yellow green .80 .55
351 A104 35p plum 1.00 .65
352 A105 125p deep blue 2.75 1.60
Nos. 350-352 (3) 4.55 2.80

29th year of Independence.

Begging Child A106

A107

1948, May Unwmk. Typo. Perf. 12
353 A106 35p yel green 4.75 4.00
354 A107 125p gray blue 4.75 4.00

Children's Day, May 29, 1948, and valid only on that day. Proceeds were used for Child Welfare.

A108

A109

A110

1948, Aug.
355 A108 15p green .65 .30
356 A109 20p magenta .80 .30
357 A110 125p dark blue 1.60 .80
Nos. 355-357 (3) 3.05 1.40

30th year of Independence.

United Nations Emblem — A111

1948, Oct. 24
358 A111 125p dk violet blue 9.50 8.00

UN, 3rd anniv. Valid one day only. Sheets of 9.

Maiwand Victory Column, Kandahar — A112

Zahir Shah and Ruins of Qalai Bist A113

Independence Monument and Nadir Shah — A114

1949, Aug. 24 **Typo.** **Perf. 12**
359 A112 25p green 1.25 .50
360 A113 35p magenta 1.50 .65
361 A114 1.25af blue 2.50 1.25
Nos. 359-361 (3) 5.25 2.40

31st year of Independence.

Nadir Shah — A117

1950, Aug.
364 A117 35p red brown .75 .30
365 A117 125p blue 2.00 .50

32nd year of Independence.

Medical School and Nadir Shah A119

Size: 38x25mm
1950, Dec. 22 **Typo.** **Perf. 12**
367 A119 35p emerald 1.25 .65

Size: 46x30mm
368 A119 1.25af deep blue 4.00 2.00
a. 1.25af black (error)

19th anniv. of the founding of Afghanistan's Faculty of Medicine. On sale and valid for use on Dec. 22-28, 1950.
See Nos. RA9-RA10.

Minaret, Herat
A120

Zahir Shah
A121

Mosque of
Khodja Abu
Parsar,
Balkh — A122

A123   A124

20p, Buddha at Bamian. 40p, Ruined arch. 45p, Maiwand Victory monument. 50p, View of Kandahar. 60p, Ancient tower. 70p, Afghanistan flag. 80p, 1af, Profile of Zahir Shah in uniform.

Imprint: "Waterlow & Sons Limited, London"

Photogravure, Engraved, Engraved and Lithographed
Perf. 12, 12½, 13x12½, 13½

			Unwmk.	
1951, Mar. 21				
369	A120	10p yellow & brn	.30	.25
370	A120	15p blue & brn	.55	.25
371	A120	20p black	10.00	5.50
372	A121	25p green	.50	.25
373	A122	30p cerise	.65	.25
374	A121	35p violet	.70	.25
375	A122	40p chestnut brn	.70	.25
376	A120	45p deep blue	.70	.25
377	A122	50p olive black	2.00	.25
378	A120	60p black	1.60	.30
379	A122	70p dk grn, blk, red & grn	.90	.25
380	A123	75p cerise	1.25	.50
381	A123	80p carmine & blk	2.10	.90
382	A123	1af dp grn & vio	1.60	.65
383	A124	1.25af rose lil & blk	1.90	1.00
384	A124	2af ultra	2.75	.80
385	A124	3af ultra & blk	6.00	1.25
		Nos. 369-385 (17)	34.20	13.15

Nos. 372, 374 and 381 to 385 are engraved, No. 379 is engraved and lithographed.
Imperfs. exist of the photogravure stamps.
See Nos. 445-451, 453, 552A-552D. For surcharges see Nos. B1-B2.

Arch of
Paghman
A125

Nadir Shah and Independence
Monument — A126

Overprint in
Violet

Perf. 13½x13, 13
1951, Aug. 25   **Engr.**
386   A125   35p dk green & blk   1.10   .65
387   A126   1.25af deep blue   3.00   1.40

Overprint reads "Sol 33 Istiqlal" or "33rd Year of Independence." Overprint measures about 11mm wide.
See Nos. 398-399B, 441-442.

Proposed Flag of
Pashtunistan — A127

Design: 125p, Flag and Pashtunistan warrior.

1951, Sept. 2   **Litho.**   *Perf. 11½*
388   A127   35p dull chocolate   1.50   .75
389   A127   125p blue   3.00   2.00

Issued to publicize "Free Pashtunistan" Day. Exist Imperf.

Imperforates

From 1951 to 1958, quantities of nearly all locally-printed stamps were left imperforate and sold by the government at double face. From 1959 until March, 1964, many of the imperforates were sold for more than face value.

Avicenna — A128

1951, Nov. 4   **Typo.**   *Perf. 11½*
390   A128   35p deep claret   7.50   1.50
391   A128   125p blue   3.00   4.00

20th anniv. of the founding of the national Graduate School of Medicine.
Exist imperf. Value $27.50.

A129

Dove and UN
Symbols
A130

1951, Oct. 24
392   A129   35p magenta   .90   .40
393   A130   125p blue   2.25   1.75

7th anniv. of the UN. Exist imperf.

Amir Sher Ali
Khan and
Tiger Head
Stamp
A131

Nos. 395, 397, Zahir Shah and stamp.

1951, Dec. 23   **Litho.**
394   A131   35p chocolate   .85   .40
395   A131   35p rose lilac   .85   .40
396   A131   125p ultra   1.25   .80
   a.   Cliche of 35p in plate of 125p   110.00   100.00
397   A131   125p aqua   1.25   .80
   Nos. 394-397 (4)   4.20   2.40

76th anniv. of the UPU. Exist imperf. Values: unused $9; used $17.50.

Stamps of 1951 Without Overprint
Perf. 13½x13, 13
1952, Aug. 24   **Engr.**
398   A125   35p dk green & blk   1.50   .55
399   A126   1.25af deep blue   3.25   1.25

For overprints see Nos. 399A-399B, 441-442.

Same
Overprinted in
Violet

399A   A125   35p dk grn & blk   4.00   2.25
399B   A126   1.25af deep blue   4.00   2.25

Nos. 398-399B issued for 34th Independence Day.

Globe — A132

Perf. 11½
1952, Oct. 25   **Unwmk.**   **Litho.**
400   A132   35p rose   .80   .65
401   A132   125p aqua   1.60   1.10

Issued to honor the United Nations. Exist Imperf. Values, set: unused $6; used $7.25.

Symbol of
Medicine
A134

1952, Nov.   *Perf. 11½*
403   A134   35p chocolate   .70   .50
404   A134   125p violet blue   2.00   1.40

21st anniv. of the natl. Graduate School of Medicine.
No. 404 is inscribed in French with white letters on a colored background.
Exist Imperf. Values: unused $3.50; used $4.50.

Tribal Warrior,
Natl.
Flag — A135

1952, Sept. 1   *Perf. 11*
405   A135   35p red   .80   .80
406   A135   125p dark blue   1.25   1.25

No. 406 is inscribed in French "Pashtunistan Day, 1952."
Exist imperf. Values, set, unused or used, $2.75.

Flags of
Afghanistan &
Pashtunistan
A139

Badge of
Pashtunistan
A140

Perf. 10½x11, 11
1953, Sept. 1   **Unwmk.**
411   A139   35p vermilion   .80   .80
412   A140   125p blue   1.25   1.25

Issued to publicize "Free Pashtunistan" Day.
Exist imperf. Values, set: unused, $3.50; used, $4.

Nadir Shah
and Flag
Bearer
A141

A142

Perf. 11
1953, Aug. 24
413   A141   35p green   .40   .25
414   A142   125p violet   .80   .55

35th anniv. of Independence.
Exist imperf. Values: unused, $3.50; used, $4.

United Nations
Emblem — A143

1953, Oct. 24
415   A143   35p lilac   1.00   .80
416   A143   125p violet blue   2.00   1.50

United Nations Day, 1953.
Exist imperf. Values, set, unused or used, $9.

A144

Nadir
Shah — A145

1953, Nov. 29
417   A144   35p orange   1.50   1.50
418   A145   125p chalky blue   3.00   3.00

22nd anniv. of the founding of the Natl. Graduate School of Medicine.
Exist imperf. Values: unused, $9; used, $12.50.

35p. Original — Right character in second line of Persian inscription

Redrawn — Persian character

Original

Redrawn

1953
419 A144 35p deep orange 9.50 9.50
420 A145 125p chalky blue 9.50 9.50
Exist imperf.

Nadir Shah and Symbols of Independence — A146

1954, Aug. Typo. Perf. 11
421 A146 35p carmine rose .70 .40
422 A146 125p violet blue 2.00 .80
36th year of Independence.
Exist imperf. Values, set: unused, $6; used, $7.

Raising Flag of Pashtunistan A147

1954, Sept. Perf. 11½
423 A147 35p chocolate .70 .40
424 A147 125p blue 2.00 .80
Issued to publicize "Free Pashtunistan" Day.
Exist imperf. Values, set: unused, $4.75; used, $6.50.

UN Flag and Map — A148

1954, Oct. 24 Perf. 11
425 A148 35p carmine rose 1.25 1.25
426 A148 125p dk violet blue 3.25 2.25
9th anniv. of the United Nations.
Exist imperf. Values, set: unused, $9; used, $10.

UN Symbols A149

Design: 125p, UN emblem & flags.
1955, June 26 Litho. Perf. 11
Size: 26½x36mm
427 A149 35p dark green 1.10 .55
Size: 28½x36mm
428 A149 125p aqua 2.00 1.00
10th anniv. of the UN charter.
Exist imperf. Values, set: unused, $12; used, $12.50.

Nadir Shah (center) and Brothers A150

1929 Civil War Scene and Zahir Shah — A151

1955, Aug. Unwmk. Perf. 11
429 A150 35p brt pink .65 .40
430 A150 35p violet blue .65 .40
431 A151 125p rose lilac 1.40 .90
432 A151 125p light violet 1.40 .90
Nos. 429-432 (4) 4.10 2.60
37th anniv. of Independence.
Exist imperf. Values, set: unused, $12; used, $13.50.

Tribal Elders' Council and Pashtun Flag — A152

1955, Sept. 5
433 A152 35p orange brown .60 .25
434 A152 125p yellow green 2.00 .55
Issued for "Free Pashtunistan" Day.
Exist imperf. Values, set: unused, $7; used, $9.

UN Flag — A153

1955, Oct. 24 Unwmk. Perf. 11
435 A153 35p orange brown 1.10 .60
436 A153 125p brt ultra 2.00 1.10
10th anniv. of the United Nations.
Exist imperf. Value for set: unused, $15; used, $17.50.

A154

1956, Aug. Litho.
437 A154 35p lt green .55 .30
438 A154 140p lt violet blue 2.25 .90
38th year of Independence.
Exist imperf. Value for set: unused, $3; used, $4.

Jesh'n Exhibition Hall A155

1956, Aug. 25
439 A155 50p chocolate .90 .40
440 A155 50p lt violet blue .90 .40
International Exposition at Kabul.
Of the 50p face value, only 35p paid postage. The remaining 15p went to the Exposition.
Exist imperf. Value for set: unused, $7; used, $8.

Nos. 398-399 Handstamped in Violet

a

b

1957, Aug. Engr. Perf. 13½x13, 13
441 A125 (a) 35p dk green & blk .65 .30
442 A126 (b) 1.25af deep blue 1.00 .70
Arabic overprint measures 19mm.
39th year of independence.

Pashtunistan Flag — A156

1957, Sept. 1 Litho. Perf. 11
443 A156 50p pale lilac rose 1.00 .55
444 A156 155p light violet 1.50 1.00
Issued for "Free Pashtunistan" Day. French inscription on No. 444. 15p of each stamp went to the Pashtunistan Fund.
Exist imperf. Values: set: unused, $4; used, $4.50.

Types of 1951 and

Game of Buzkashi A157

Perf. 12, 12½, 12½x13, 13, 13x12, 13x12½, 13½x14
Photo., Engr., Engr.& Litho.
1957, Nov. 23 Unwmk.
Imprint: "Waterlow & Sons Limited, London"

445 A122 30p brown .40 .25
446 A122 40p rose red .55 .25
447 A122 50p yellow .65 .25
448 A120 60p ultra .80 .25

449 A123 75p brt violet 1.00 .25
450 A123 80p violet & brn 1.10 .25
451 A123 1af carmine & ultra 1.75 .25
452 A157 140p olive & dp claret 2.75 .65
453 A124 3af orange & blk 2.75 .90
Nos. 445-453 (9) 11.75 3.30
No. 452 lacks imprint.

Nadir Shah and Flag-bearer A158

1958, Aug. 25 Perf. 13½x14
454 A158 35p dp yellow green .50 .25
455 A158 140p brown 1.25 1.00
40th year of Independence.

Exposition Buildings A159

1958, Aug. 23 Litho. Perf. 11
456 A159 35p brt blue green .50 .25
457 A159 140p vermilion 1.25 1.00
International Exposition at Kabul.
Exist imperf. Value set, unused or used, $4.

Pres. Celal Bayar of Turkey — A160

1958, Sept. 13 Unwmk.
458 A160 50p lt blue .30 .25
459 A160 100p brown .65 .30
Visit of President Celal Bayar of Turkey.
Exists Imperf. Values, set: unused, $2.25; used, $3.25.

Flags of UN and Afghanistan A161

1958, Oct. 24 Photo. Perf. 14x13½
Flags in Original Colors
460 A161 50p dark gray .65 .65
461 A161 100p green 1.40 1.10
United Nations Day, Oct. 24.
Exist imperf. Value set, unused or used, $4.50.

Atomic Energy Encircling the Hemispheres — A162

1958, Oct. 20 Perf. 13½x14
462 A162 50p blue .55 .50
463 A162 100p dp red lilac .90 .65
Issued to promote Atoms for Peace.
Exist imperf. Value set, unused or used, $3.50.

UNESCO Building, Paris A163

1958, Nov. 3
464 A163 50p dp yellow grn .80 .65
465 A163 100p brown olive .80 .80

UNESCO Headquarters in Paris opening, Nov. 3.
Exist imperf. Value set, unused or used, $6.

Globe and Torch A164

Perf. 13½x14
1958, Dec. 10   Unwmk.
466 A164 50p lilac rose .50 .50
467 A164 100p maroon 1.00 1.10

10th anniv. of the signing of the Universal Declaration of Human Rights.
Exist imperf. Value set, unused or used, $4.50.

Nadir Shah and Flags A165

1959, Aug.   Litho.   Perf. 11 Rough
468 A165 35p light vermilion .55 .50
469 A165 165p light violet 1.50 .65

41st year of Independence.
Exist imperf. Value set, unused or used, $2.50.

Uprooted Oak Emblem — A166

1960, Apr. 7   Perf. 11
470 A166 50p deep orange .25 .25
471 A166 165p blue .35 .25

World Refugee Year, 7/1/59-6/30/60.
Two imperf. souvenir sheets exist. Both contain a 50p and a 165p, type A166, with marginal inscriptions and WRY emblem in maroon. On one sheet the stamps are in the colors of Nos. 470-471 (size 108x81mm). Value $6. On the other, the 50p is blue and the 165p is deep orange (size 107x80mm). Value $7.
For surcharges see Nos. B35-B36.
Exist imperf. Value set, unused or used, $4.50.

Buzkashi A167

1960, May 4   Perf. 11, Imperf.
472 A167 25p rose red .55 .25
473 A167 50p bluish green 1.40 .55
   a. Cliche of 25p in plate of 50p 27.50 27.50

Exist imperf. Value set, unused or used, $2.75.
See Nos. 549-550A.

Independence Monument A168

1960, Aug.   Perf. 11, 12
474 A168 50p light blue .45 .25
475 A168 175p bright pink 1.25 .40

42nd Independence Day.
Exist imperf. Value set, unused or used, $1.75.

Globe and Flags A169

1960, Oct. 24   Litho.   Perf. 11, 12
476 A169 50p rose lilac .25 .25
477 A169 175p ultra 1.00 .65

UN Day.
Exist imperf. Value set, unused or used, $2.50.
An imperf. souvenir sheet contains one each of Nos. 476-477 with marginal inscriptions ("La Journée des Nations Unies 1960" in French and Persian) and UN emblem in light blue. Size: 127x85½mm. Value $6.
This sheet was surcharged "+20ps" in 1962. Value $5.50.

Teacher Pointing to Globe A170

1960, Oct. 23   Perf. 11
478 A170 50p brt pink .40 .30
479 A170 100p brt green 1.00 .50

Issued to publicize Teacher's Day.
Exist imperf. Value set, unused or used, $2.50.

Mohammed Zahir Shah — A171

1960, Oct. 15
480 A171 50p red brown .65 .25
481 A171 150p dk car rose 1.60 .55

Honoring the King on his 46th birthday.
Exist imperf. Value set, unused or used, $2.50.

Buzkashi A172

1960, Nov. 9   Perf. 11
482 A172 175p lt red brown 2.40 .50

Exists imperf. Value, unused or used, $3.
See Nos. 551-552.

No. 482 Overprinted in Bright Green

1960, Dec. 24
483 A172 175p red brown 2.00 2.00
   a. Souv. sheet of 1, imperf. 6.00 8.00

17th Olympic Games, Rome, 8/25-9/11.
Value, unused or used, $4.50.

Mir Wais — A173

1961, Jan. 5   Unwmk.   Perf. 10½
484 A173 50p brt rose lilac .70 .40
485 A173 175p ultra 1.25 .50
   a. Souv. sheet, #484-485, imperf. 3.75 3.75

Mir Wais (1665-1708), national leader.
Exist imperf. Value set, unused or used, $2.75.

No Postal Need
existed for the 1p-15p denominations issued with sets of 1961-63 (between Nos. 486 and 649, B37 and B65).
The lowest denomination actually used for non-philatelic postage in that period was 25p (except for the 2p newspaper rate for which separate stamps were provided).

Horse, Sheep and Camel A174

Designs: No. 487, 175p, Rock partridge. 10p, 100p, Afghan hound. 15p, 150p, Grain & grasshopper, vert.

1961, Mar. 29   Photo.   Perf. 13½x14
486 A174 2p maroon & buff .25 .25
487 A174 2p ultra & org .25 .25
488 A174 5p brown & yel .25 .25
489 A174 10p black & salmon .25 .25
490 A174 15p blue grn & yel .25 .25
491 A174 25p black & pink .25 .25
492 A174 50p black & citron .30 .30
493 A174 100p black & pink .45 .40
494 A174 150p green & yel .65 .65
495 A174 175p ultra & pink .80 .65
   Nos. 486-495 (10) 3.70 3.50

Two souvenir sheets, perf. and imperf., contain 2 stamps, 1 each of No. 492-493. Value $3 each.

Afghan Fencing A175

Designs: No. 497, 5p, 25p, 50p, Wrestlers. 10p, 100p, Man with Indian clubs. 15p, 150p, Afghan fencing. 175p, Children skating.

1961, July 6   Perf. 13½x14
496 A175 2p green & rose lil .25 .25
497 A175 2p brown & citron .25 .25
498 A175 5p gray & rose .25 .25
499 A175 10p blue & bister .25 .25
500 A175 15p sl bl & dl lil .25 .25
501 A175 25p black & dl bl .25 .25
502 A175 50p sl grn & bis brn .25 .25
503 A175 100p brown & bl grn .55 .55

504 A175 150p brown & org yel .90 .90
505 A175 175p black & blue .95 .95
   Nos. 496-505 (10) 4.15 4.15

Issued for Children's Day.
A souvenir sheet exists, perf. and imperf., containing one each of Nos. 502-503. Value $5 each.
For surcharges see Nos. B37-B41.

Bande Amir Lakes A176

1961, Aug. 7   Photo.   Perf. 13½x14
506 A176 3af brt blue .50 .25
507 A176 10af rose claret 1.40 1.25

Nadir Shah — A177

1961, Aug. 23   Perf. 14x13½
508 A177 50p rose red & blk .55 .50
509 A177 175p brt grn & org brn .95 .70

43rd Independence Day.
Exist imperf. Value set, unused or used, $2.50.
Two souvenir sheets, perf. and imperf., contain one each of Nos. 508-509. Value, each $3.00.

Girl Scout — A178

Perf. 14x13½
1961, July 23   Unwmk.
510 A178 50p dp car & dk gray .40 .25
511 A178 175p dp grn & rose brn 1.00 .50

Issued for Women's Day.
Exist imperf. Value set, unused or used, $4.50.
Two souvenir sheets exist, perf. and imperf., containing one each of Nos. 510-511. Value $5 each.

Exhibition Hall, Kabul A179

1961, Aug. 23   Perf. 13½x14
512 A179 50p yel brn & yel grn .25 .25
513 A179 175p blue & brn .70 .50

International Exhibition at Kabul.

Pathan with Pashtunistan Flag — A180

1961, Aug. 31   Photo.   Perf. 14x13½
514	A180	50p blk, lil & red	.30 .25
515	A180	175p brn, grnsh bl & red	.65 .55

Issued for "Free Pashtunistan Day."
Exist imperf. Value set, unused or used, $1.60.
Souvenir sheets exist perf. and imperf. containing one each of Nos. 514-515. Value $2.25 each.

Assembly Building A181

1961, Sept. 10   Perf. 12
516	A181	50p dk gray & brt grn	.25 .25
517	A181	175p ultra & brn	.65 .50

Anniv. of the founding of the Natl. Assembly.
Exist imperf. Value set, unused or used, $1.25.
Souvenir sheets exist, perf. and imperf., containing one each of Nos. 516-517. Value $1.50 each.

Exterminating Anopheles Mosquito — A182

1961, Oct. 5   Perf. 13½x14
518	A182	50p blk & brn lil	.75 .30
519	A182	175p maroon & brt grn	2.00 .90

Anti-Malaria campaign.
Exist imperf. Value set, unused or used, $4.
Souvenir sheets exist, perf. and imperf., containing one each of Nos. 518-519. Value $4.50 each.

Zahir Shah — A183

1961, Oct. 15   Perf. 13½
520	A183	50p rose lilac & grnish blue	.30 .25
521	A183	175p emerald & red brn	.90 .50

Issued to honor King Mohammed Zahir Shah on his 47th birthday.
See Nos. 609-612.

Pomegranates — A184

Fruit: No. 523, 5p, 25p, 50p, Grapes. 10p, 150p, Apples. 15p, 175p, Pomegranates. 100p, Melons.

1961, Oct. 16   Perf. 13½x14
Fruit in Natural Colors
522	A184	2p black	.25 .25
523	A184	2p green	.25 .25
524	A184	5p lilac rose	.25 .25
525	A184	10p lilac	.25 .25
526	A184	15p dk blue	.25 .25
527	A184	25p dull red	.25 .25
528	A184	50p purple	.25 .25
529	A184	100p brt blue	.55 .55

530	A184	150p brown	.90 .90
531	A184	175p olive gray	.95 .95
		Nos. 522-531 (10)	4.15 4.15

For Afghan Red Crescent Society.
Souvenir sheets exist, perf. and imperf., containing one each of Nos. 528-529. Value $2.25 each.
For surcharges see Nos. B42-B46.

UN Headquarters, NY — A185

1961, Oct. 24   Perf. 13½x14
Vertical Borders in Emerald, Red and Black
532	A185	1p rose lilac	.25 .25
533	A185	2p slate	.25 .25
534	A185	3p brown	.25 .25
535	A185	4p ultra	.25 .25
536	A185	50p rose red	.25 .25
537	A185	75p gray	.25 .25
538	A185	175p brt green	.55 .55
		Nos. 532-538 (7)	2.05 2.05

16th anniv. of the UN.
Nos. 536-538 exist imperf. Values, unused or used: 50p; 40c; 75p, 65c; 175p, $1.40.
Souvenir sheets exist, perf. and imperf., containing one each of Nos. 536-538. Value $2.50 each.

Children Giving Flowers to Teacher — A186

Designs: No. 540, 5p, 25p, 50p, Tulips. 10p, 100p, Narcissus. 15p, 150p, Children giving flowers to teacher. 175p, Teacher with children in front of school.

1961, Oct. 26   Photo.   Perf. 12
539	A186	2p multicolored	.25 .25
540	A186	2p multicolored	.25 .25
541	A186	5p multicolored	.25 .25
542	A186	10p multicolored	.25 .25
543	A186	15p multicolored	.25 .25
544	A186	25p multicolored	.25 .25
545	A186	50p multicolored	.25 .25
546	A186	100p multicolored	.50 .50
547	A186	150p multicolored	.80 .80
548	A186	175p multicolored	.90 .90
		Nos. 539-548 (10)	3.95 3.95

Issued for Teacher's Day.
Souvenir sheets exist, perf. and imperf. containing one each of Nos. 545-546. Value, 2 sheets, $4.50.
For surcharges see Nos. B47-B51.

Buzkashi Types of 1960
1961-72   Litho.   Perf. 10½, 11
549	A167	25p violet	1.40 .25
b.		25p brt vio, typo. ('72)	.25 .25
549A	A167	25p citron ('63)	2.50 .25
550	A167	50p blue	2.00 .25
550A	A167	50p yel org ('69)	.50 .30
551	A172	100p citron	.80 .25
551A	A172	150p orange ('64)	.65 .30
552	A172	2af lt green	1.50 1.00
		Nos. 549-552 (7)	9.35 2.60

Zahir Shah Types of 1951
Imprint: "Thomas De La Rue & Co. Ltd."

Photo., Engr., Engr. & Litho.
1962   Perf. 13x12, 13
552A	A123	75p brt purple	2.75 .25
552B	A123	1af car & ultra	3.50 .30
552C	A124	2af blue	7.25 .80
552D	A124	3af orange & blk	10.00 1.00
		Nos. 552A-552D (4)	23.50 2.35

People Raising UNESCO Symbol — A187

1962, July 2   Photo.   Perf. 14x13½
553	A187	2p rose lil & brn	.25 .25
554	A187	2p ol bis & brn	.25 .25
555	A187	5p dp org & dk grn	.25 .25
556	A187	10p gray & mag	.25 .25
557	A187	15p blue & brn	.25 .25
558	A187	25p org yel & pur	.25 .25
559	A187	50p lt grn & pur	.25 .25
560	A187	75p brt cit & brn	.25 .25
561	A187	100p dp org & brn	.30 .30
		Nos. 553-561 (9)	2.30 2.30

15th anniv. of UNESCO. Souvenir sheets exist, perf. and imperf. One contains Nos. 558-559; the other contains Nos. 560-561. Value, $3.25 each perforated, $2.40 each imperf.
For surcharges see Nos. B52-B60.

Ahmad Shah — A188

1962, Feb. 24   Photo.   Perf. 13½
562	A188	50p red brn & gray	.25 .25
563	A188	75p green & salmon	.30 .25
564	A188	100p claret & bister	.40 .30
		Nos. 562-564 (3)	.95 .80

Ahmad Shah (1724-73), founded the Afghan kingdom in 1747 and ruled until 1773.

Afghan Hound — A189

Designs: 5p, 75p, Afghan cock. 10p, 100p, Kondjid plant. 15p, 125p, Astrakhan skins.

1962, Apr. 21   Perf. 14x13½
565	A189	2p rose & brn	.25 .25
566	A189	2p lt green & brn	.25 .25
567	A189	5p dp rose & claret	.25 .25
568	A189	10p lt grn & sl grn	.25 .25
569	A189	15p blue grn & blk	.25 .25
570	A189	25p blue & brn	.25 .25
571	A189	50p gray & brn	.30 .25
572	A189	75p rose lil & lil	.50 .30
573	A189	100p gray & dl grn	.55 .40
574	A189	125p rose brn & blk	.65 .50
		Nos. 565-574 (10)	3.50 2.95

Agriculture Day. Perf. and imperf. souvenir sheets exist. Set of 4 sheets, value $11.00.

Athletes with Flag and Nadir Shah — A190

1962, Aug. 23   Perf. 12
575	A190	25p multicolored	.25 .25
576	A190	50p multicolored	.25 .25
577	A190	150p multicolored	.40 .30
		Nos. 575-577 (3)	.90 .80

44th Independence Day.

Woman in National Costume — A191

1962, Aug. 30   Perf. 11½x12
578	A191	25p lilac & brn	.25 .25
579	A191	50p green & brn	.25 .25
		Nos. 578-579,C15-C16 (4)	2.10 2.10

Issued for Women's Day. A souvenir sheet exists containing one each of Nos. 578-579, C15-C16. Value $4.50.

Man and Woman with Flag — A192

1962, Aug. 31   Photo.
580	A192	25p black, pale bl & red	.25 .25
581	A192	50p black, grn & red	.25 .25
582	A192	150p black, pink & red	.55 .40
		Nos. 580-582 (3)	1.05 .90

Issued for "Free Pashtunistan Day."

Malaria Eradication Emblem and Swamp — A193

1962, Sept. 5   Perf. 14x13½
583	A193	2p dk grn & ol gray	.25 .25
584	A193	2p dk green & sal	.25 .25
585	A193	5p red brn & ol	.25 .25
586	A193	10p red brn & brt grn	.25 .25
587	A193	15p red brn & gray	.25 .25
588	A193	25p brt bl & bluish grn	.25 .25
589	A193	50p brt bl & rose lil	.25 .25
590	A193	75p black & blue	.25 .25
591	A193	100p black & brt pink	.25 .25
592	A193	150p black & bis brn	.50 .40
593	A193	175p black & orange	.55 .50
		Nos. 583-593 (11)	3.35 3.15

WHO drive to eradicate malaria. Perf. and imperf. souvenir sheets exist. Set of 4 sheets, value $14.
For surcharges see Nos. B61-B71.

National Assembly Building — A194

Perf. 10½, 11 (100p)
1962, Sept. 10   Unwmk.   Litho.
594	A194	25p lt green	.25 .25
595	A194	50p blue	.45 .45
596	A194	75p rose	.60 .60
597	A194	100p violet	.75 .75
598	A194	125p ultra	1.00 1.00
		Nos. 594-598 (5)	3.05 3.05

Establishment of the National Assembly.

Horse Racing — A195

Designs: 2p, Horse racing. 3p, Wrestling. 4p, Weight lifting. 5p, Soccer.

1962, Sept. 22 Photo. Perf. 12
Black Inscriptions
599	A195	1p lt ol & red brn	.25	.25
600	A195	2p lt grn & red brn	.25	.25
601	A195	3p yellow & dk pur	.25	.25
602	A195	4p pale bl & grn	.25	.25
603	A195	5p bluish grn & dk brn	.25	.25
		Nos. 599-603,C17-C22 (11)	5.30	5.30

4th Asian Games, Djakarta, Indonesia.
Exist imperf. Value, set of 11, unused or used, $17.50.
Two souvenir sheets exist. A perforated one contains a 125p blue, dark blue and brown stamp in horse racing design. An imperf. one contains a 2af buff, purple and black stamp in soccer design. Value, $3.50 each.

Runners A196

1p, 2p, Diver, vert. 4p, Peaches. 5p, Iris, vert.

Perf. 11½x12, 12x11½
1962, Oct. 2 Unwmk.
604	A196	1p rose lil & brn	.25	.25
605	A196	2p blue & brn	.25	.25
606	A196	3p brt blue & lil	.25	.25
607	A196	4p ol gray & multi	.25	.25
608	A196	5p gray & multi	.25	.25
		Nos. 604-608,C23-C25 (8)	4.90	4.90

Issued for Children's Day.
Exist imperf. Value, set of 8, unused or used, $27.50.

Zahir Shah Type of 1961, Dated "1962"

1962, Oct. 15 Perf. 13½
Various Frames
609	A183	25p lilac rose & brn	.25	.25
610	A183	50p orange brn & grn	.30	.25
611	A183	75p blue & lake	.40	.25
612	A183	100p green & red brn	.55	.25
		Nos. 609-612 (4)	1.50	1.00

Issued to honor King Mohammed Zahir Shah on his 48th birthday.

Grapes A197

1962, Oct. 16 Perf. 12
613	A197	1p shown	.25	.25
614	A197	2p Grapes	.25	.25
615	A197	3p Pears	.25	.25
616	A197	4p Wistaria	.25	.25
617	A197	5p Blossoms	.25	.25
		Nos. 613-617,C26-C28 (8)	2.50	2.50

For the Afghan Red Crescent Society.
Exist imperf. Value, set of 8, unused or used, $20.

UN Headquarters, NY and Flags of UN and Afghanistan — A198

1962, Oct. 24 Unwmk.
618	A198	1p multicolored	.25	.25
619	A198	2p multicolored	.25	.25
620	A198	3p multicolored	.25	.25
621	A198	4p multicolored	.25	.25
622	A198	5p multicolored	.25	.25
		Nos. 618-622,C29-C31 (8)	2.70	2.70

UN Day.
Exist imperf. Value, set of 8, unused or used, $9.50.
Souvenir sheets exist. One contains a single 4af ultramarine stamp, perforated; the other, a 4af ocher stamp, imperf. Value, 2 sheets, $9.25.

Boy Scout — A199

1962, Oct. 18 Photo. Perf. 12
623	A199	1p yel, dk grn & sal	.25	.25
624	A199	2p dl yel, slate & sal	.25	.25
625	A199	3p rose, blk & sal	.25	.25
626	A199	4p multicolored	.25	.25
		Nos. 623-626,C32-C35 (8)	3.90	3.90

Issued to honor the Boy Scouts.
Exist imperf. Value, set of 8, unused or used, $27.50.

Pole Vault — A200

2p, Pole Vault. 3p, High jump. 4p, 5p, Different blossoms.

1962, Oct. 25 Unwmk. Perf. 12
627	A200	1p lilac & dk grn	.25	.25
628	A200	2p yellow grn & brn	.25	.25
629	A200	3p bister & vio	.25	.25
630	A200	4p sal pink, grn & ultra	.25	.25
631	A200	5p yellow, grn & bl	.25	.25
		Nos. 627-631,C36-C37 (7)	2.85	2.85

Issued for Teacher's Day.
Exist imperf. Value, set of 7, unused or used, $12.

Rockets A201

1962, Nov. 29
632	A201	50p pale lil & dk bl	.70	.70
633	A201	100p lt blue & red brn	1.50	1.50

UN World Meteorological Day.
Exist imperf. Value, set, unused or used, $27.50.
A souvenir sheet contains one 5af pink and green stamp. Value $6.

Ansari Mausoleum, Herat — A202

Perf. 13½
1963, Jan. 3 Unwmk. Photo.
634	A202	50p purple & green	.25	.25
635	A202	75p gray & magenta	.25	.25
636	A202	100p orange brn & brn	.40	.40
		Nos. 634-636 (3)	.90	.90

Khwaja Abdullah Ansari, Sufi, religious leader and poet, on the 900th anniv. of his death.

Sheep A203

Silkworm, Cocoons, Moth and Mulberry Branch A204

1963, Mar. 1 Perf. 12
637	A203	1p grnsh blue & blk	.25	.25
638	A203	2p yellow grn & blk	.25	.25
639	A203	3p lilac rose & blk	.25	.25
640	A204	4p gray, grn & brn	.25	.25
641	A204	5p red lil, grn & brn	.25	.25
		Nos. 637-641,C42-C44 (8)	3.25	3.25

Issued for the Day of Agriculture.
Exist imperf. Value, set of 8, unused or used, $12.

Rice — A205

Designs: 3p, Corn. 300p, Wheat emblem.

1963, Mar. 27 Unwmk. Perf. 14
642	A205	2p gray, claret & grn	.25	.25
643	A205	3p green, yel & ocher	.25	.25
644	A205	300p dk blue & yel	.75	.75
		Nos. 642-644,C45 (4)	2.65	2.65

FAO "Freedom from Hunger" campaign.

Meteorological Measuring Instrument — A206

Designs: 3p, 10p, Weather station. 4p, 5p, Rockets in space.

1963, May 23 Photo. Perf. 13½x14
645	A206	1p dp magenta & brn	.25	.25
646	A206	2p brt blue & brn	.25	.25
647	A206	3p red & brown	.25	.25
648	A206	4p orange & lilac	.25	.25
649	A206	5p green & dl vio	.25	.25

Imperf
650	A206	10p red brn & grn	.45	.40
		Nos. 645-650,C46-C50 (11)	12.30	12.25

3rd UN World Meteorological Day, Mar. 23.

Independence Monument A207

1963, Aug. 23 Litho. Perf. 10½
651	A207	25p lt green	.25	.25
652	A207	50p orange	.40	.25
653	A207	150p rose carmine	.65	.30
		Nos. 651-653 (3)	1.30	.80

45th Independence Day.

Pathans in Forest A208

1963, Aug. 31 Unwmk. Perf. 10½
654	A208	25p pale violet	.25	.25
655	A208	50p sky blue	.30	.25
655A	A208	150p dull red brn	.80	.40
		Nos. 654-655A (3)	1.35	.90

Issued for "Free Pashtunistan Day."

4th Asian Games, Djakarta — A208a

2p, 250p, 300p, Wrestling. 3p, 10p, Tennis. 4p, 500p, Javelin. 5p, 9af, Shot put.

1963, Sept. 3 Litho. Perf. 12
656	A208a	2p rose vio & brn	.25	.25
656A	A208a	3p olive grn & brn	.25	.25
656B	A208a	4p blue & brn	.25	.25
656C	A208a	5p yel grn & brn	.25	.25
656D	A208a	10p lt bl grn & brn	.25	.25
656E	A208a	300p yellow & vio	.50	.50
656F	A208a	500p lt yel bis & brn	.90	.90
656G	A208a	9af pale grn & vio	1.50	1.50
		Nos. 656-656G (8)	4.15	4.15

Souvenir Sheets
656H	A208a	250p lilac & vio	2.00	2.00
656I	A208a	300p blue & blk	2.00	2.00

Nos. 656E-656F are airmail. Nos. 656-656I exist imperf. Values, unused or used: set, $12; souvenir sheets, each $11.

National Assembly Building — A209

1963, Sept. 10 Perf. 11
657	A209	25p gray	.25	.25
658	A209	50p dull red	.25	.25
659	A209	75p brown	.25	.25
660	A209	100p olive	.25	.25
661	A209	125p lilac	.40	.25
		Nos. 657-661 (5)	1.40	1.25

Issued to honor the National Assembly.

Balkh Gate
A210

1963, Oct. 8
662 A210 3af choc (screened
margins) 1.00 .30
a. White margins 2.50 .55

In the original printing a halftone screen extended across the plate, covering the space between the stamps. A retouch removed the screen between the stamps (No. 662a).

Intl. Red
Cross,
Cent. —
A210a

4p, 5p, 200p, 3af, Nurse holding patient, vert. 10p, 4af, 6af, Crown Prince Ahmed Shah.

1963, Oct. 9 **Perf. 13½**
662B A210a 2p olive, blk &
red .25 .25
662C A210a 3p blue, blk &
red .25 .25
662D A210a 4p lt grn, blk &
red .25 .25
662E A210a 5p lt vio, blk &
red .25 .25
662F A210a 10p gray grn, red
& blk .25 .25
662G A210a 100p dull bl grn,
red & blk .25 .25
662H A210a 200p lt brn, blk &
blk .25 .25
662I A210a 4af brt bl grn, red
& blk .25 .25
m. Souvenir sheet of 1 1.75 1.60
662J A210a 6af lt brn, red &
blk .25 .25
Nos. 662B-662J (9) 2.25 2.25

Souvenir Sheet
662K A210a 3af dl blue, blk &
red 1.75

Nos. 662G-662K are airmail.
Nos. 662B-662K exist imperf. Values, unused or used: set, $12; souvenir sheets, each $11.

Zahir
Shah — A211

1963, Oct. 15 **Perf. 10½**
663 A211 25p green .25 .25
663A A211 50p gray .25 .25
663B A211 75p carmine rose .30 .25
663C A211 100p dull redsh brn .50 .25
Nos. 663-663C (4) 1.30 1.00

King Mohammed Zahir Shah, 49th birthday.

Kemal
Ataturk — A212

1963, Oct. 10 **Perf. 10½**
664 A212 1af blue .25 .25
665 A212 3af rose lilac .65 .50

25th anniv. of the death of Kemal Ataturk, president of Turkey.

Protection
of Nubian
Monuments
A213

Designs: 5af, 7.50af, 10af, Ruins, vert.

Perf. 12, Imperf. (150p, 250p, 10af)
1963, Nov. 16 **Photo.**
666 A213 100p lil rose & blk .25 .25
666A A213 150p rose lil & blk .25 .30
666B A213 200p brown & blk .40 .40
666C A213 250p ultra & blk .50 .50
666D A213 500p green & blk 1.00 1.00
666E A213 5af greenish blue
& gray bl 1.00 1.00
666F A213 7.50af red brn & gray
bl 1.75 1.75
666G A213 10af ver & gray bl 1.90 1.90
Nos. 666-666G (8) 7.05 7.10

Nos. 666E-666G are airmail. No. 666D exists imperf. Value, unused or used, 95¢.

Women's Day —
A213a

1964, Jan. 5 **Perf. 14x13½**
667 A213a 2p multicolored .25 .25
667A A213a 3p multicolored .25 .25
667B A213a 4p multicolored .25 .25
667C A213a 5p multicolored .25 .25
667D A213a 10p multicolored .25 .25
Nos. 667-667D (5) 1.25 1.25

Exist imperf. Value set, unused or used, $2.40.

A213b

Boy and Girl
Scouts — A213c

Nos. 668F-668G, 668K-668M, Girl with flag.

1964, Jan. 5 **Perf. 13½x14, 14x13½**
668 A213b 2p multi .25 .25
668A A213b 3p multi .25 .25
668B A213b 4p multi .25 .25
668C A213b 5p multi .25 .25
668D A213b 10p multi .25 .25
668E A213c 2af multi .25 .25
668F A213c 3af multi .25 .25
668G A213c 2.50af multi .25 .25
668H A213c 3af multi .30 .30
668I A213c 4af multi .40 .40
668J A213c 5af multi .50 .50
668K A213c 12af multi 1.25 1.25
Nos. 668-668K (12) 4.45 4.45

Souvenir Sheets
668L A213c 5af multi 1.25 1.25
668M A213c 5af multi 1.25 2.00
668N A213c 6af multi 2.50 2.50
668O A213c 6af multi 2.50 2.50

Nos. 668E-668O are airmail.
Nos 668-668K, 668N-668O exist imperf. Values, unused or used: set, $15; souvenir sheets, each $7.

Children — A213d

2p, Playing ball. 4p, Swinging, jumping rope, vert. 5p, Skiing, vert.

1964, Jan. 22 **Perf. 12**
669 A213d 2p multi .25 .25
669A A213d 3p like #669 .25 .25
669B A213d 4p multi .25 .25
669C A213d 5p multi .25 .25
669D A213d 10p like #669 .25 .25
669E A213d 200p like #669C .75 .75
669F A213d 300p like #669B 1.10 1.10
Nos. 669-669F (7) 3.10 3.10

Nos. 669E-669F are airmail.
Nos. 669-669F exist imperf. Value set, unused or used, $27.50.

Red Crescent Society — A213e

Designs: 100p, 200p, Pierre and Marie Curie, physicists. 2.50af, 7.50af Nurse examining child. 3.50af, 5af, Nurse and patients.

Perf. 14, Imperf. (#670A, 670C-670D)
1964, Feb. 8
670 A213e 100p multi .50 .50
670A A213e 100p multi .50 .50
670B A213e 200p multi .80 .80
670C A213e 2.50af multi 1.25 1.25
670D A213e 3.50af multi 1.90 1.90
670E A213e 5af multi 2.10 2.10
670F A213e 7.50af multi 3.00 3.00
Nos. 670-670F (7) 10.05 10.05

Nos. 670A and 670E-F are airmail.

Teachers' Day
— A213f

Flowers: 2p, 3p, 3af, 4af, Tulips. 4p, 5p, 3.50af, 6af, Flax. 10p, 1.50af, 2af, Iris.

Perf. 12, Imperf. (1.50af, 2af)
1964, Mar. 3
671 A213f 2p multicolored .25 .25
671A A213f 3p multicolored .25 .25
671B A213f 4p multicolored .25 .25
671C A213f 5p multicolored .25 .25
671D A213f 10p multicolored .25 .25
671E A213f 1.50af multicolored 2.25 2.25
671F A213f 2af multicolored 3.00 3.00
671G A213f 3af multicolored .90 .90
671H A213f 3.50af multicolored 1.10 1.10
Nos. 671-671H (9) 8.50 8.50

Souvenir Sheets
671I A213f 4af multi 2.40 2.40
671J A213f 6af multi, imperf 5.00 5.00

Nos. 671E-671J are airmail. Nos. 671-671D exist imperf. Value, each 20¢.

A213g

UN Day: 5p, 10p, 2af, 3af, 4af, Doctor and nurse, vert.

1964, Mar. 9 **Perf. 14**
672 A213g 2p multicolored .25 .25
672A A213g 3p multicolored .25 .25
672B A213g 4p multicolored .25 .25
672C A213g 5p multicolored .25 .25
672D A213g 10p multicolored .25 .25
672E A213g 100p multicolored .65 .65
672F A213g 2af multicolored 1.20 1.20
672G A213g 3af multicolored 1.75 1.75
Nos. 672-672G (8) 4.85 4.85

Souvenir Sheets
672H A213g 4af multi, imperf. 14.50 14.50
672I A213g 5af multi 3.25 3.25

Nos. 672E-672G are airmail.
Nos. 672-672G exist imperf. Value set, unused or used, $20.
For surcharges see Nos. B71A-B71J.

UNICEF
— A213h

Design: 5af, 7.50af, 10af, Children eating.

Perf. 14x13½, Imperf. (150p, 250p, 10af)
1964, Mar. 15
673 A213h 100p multi .30 .30
673A A213h 150p multi 1.75 1.75
673B A213h 200p multi .65 .65
673C A213h 250p multi 3.00 3.00
673D A213h 5af multi 1.50 1.50
673E A213h 7.50af multi 2.40 2.40
673F A213h 10af multi 12.50 12.50
Nos. 673-673F (7) 22.10 22.10

Nos. 673D-673F are airmail.

Eradication of Malaria — A213i

4p, 5p, 5af, 10af Spraying mosquitoes.

1964, Mar. 15 **Perf. 13½**
674 A213i 2p lt red brn &
yel grn .25 .25
674A A213i 3p olive grn &
buff .25 .25
674B A213i 4p dk vio & bl
grn .25 .25
674C A213i 5p brn & grn .25 .25
674D A213i 2af Prus bl & ver .65 .30
h. Souvenir sheet of 1 4.75 4.75
674E A213i 5af dk grn & lt
red brn, im-
perf. 5.25 5.25
i. Souv. sheet of 1, imperf. 14.50 14.50
674F A213i 10af red brn &
grnsh bl 2.75 1.75
Nos. 674-674F (7) 9.65 8.30

No. 674B Surcharged in Black

674G A213i 10p on 4p Prus bl &
rose .90 .25

No. 674G not issued without surcharge. Nos. 674D-674F are airmail.
Nos. 674-674C, 674G exist imperf. Values, each $2.75.

"Tiger's Head" of
1878 — A214

1964, Mar. 22   Photo.   Perf. 12
675 A214 1.25af gold, grn & blk   .25 .25
676 A214   5af gold, rose car &
               blk   .55 .35
Issued to honor philately.

Unisphere
and Flags
A215

1964, May 3   Perf. 13½x14
677 A215 6af crimson, gray & grn   .25 .25
New York World's Fair, 1964-65.

Hand Holding
Torch — A216

1964, May 12   Photo.   Perf. 14x13½
678 A216 3.75af multicolored   .25 .25
1st UN Seminar on Human Rights in Kabul,
May 1964. The denomination in Persian at
right erroneously reads "3.25" but the stamp
was sold and used as 3.75af.

Kandahar
Airport
A217

1964, Apr.   Litho.   Perf. 10½, 11
679 A217 7.75af dk red brown   .65 .40
680 A217 9.25af lt green   .90 .80
681 A217 10.50af lt green   1.10 .95
682 A217 13.75af carmine rose   1.40 1.00
     Nos. 679-682 (4)   4.05 3.15
Inauguration of Kandahar Airport.

Snow
Leopard
A218

50p, Ibex, vert. 75p, Head of argali. 5af, Yak.

1964, June 25   Photo.   Perf. 12
683 A218 25p yellow & blue   1.75 .25
684 A218 50p dl red & grn   2.00 .25
685 A218 75p Prus bl & lil   2.40 .25
686 A218 5af brt grn & dk brn   2.50 .90
     Nos. 683-686 (4)   8.65 1.65

View of
Herat
A219

Flag and
Map of
Afghanistan
A220

Tourist publicity: 75p, Tomb of Queen
Gowhar Shad, vert.

1964, July 12   Perf. 13½x14, 14x13½
687 A219 25p sepia & bl   .25 .25
688 A219 75p dp blue & buff   .30 .25
689 A220 3af red, blk & grn   .55 .25
     Nos. 687-689 (3)   1.10 .75

Wrestling
A221

25p, Hurdling, vert. 1af, Diving, vert. 5af,
Soccer.

1964, July 26   Perf. 12
690 A221   25p ol bis, blk & car   .25 .25
691 A221   1af bl grn, blk & car   .25 .25
692 A221   3.75af yel grn, blk &
                car   .40 .25
693 A221   5af brn, blk & car   .50 .30
  a. Souv. sheet, #690-693, imperf. 1.25 1.25
     Nos. 690-693 (4)   1.40 1.05
18th Olympic Games, Tokyo, Oct. 10-25,
1964. No. 693a sold for 15af. The additional
5af went to the Afghanistan Olympic
Committee.

Flag and
Outline of
Nadir Shah's
Tomb — A222

1964, Aug. 24   Photo.
695 A222 25p multicolored   .25 .25
696 A222 75p multicolored   .30 .25
Independence Day. The stamps were
printed with an erroneous inscription in upper
left corner: "33rd year of independence." This
was locally obliterated on all stamps with a
typographed gold bar.

Pashtunistan
Flag — A223

1964, Sept. 1   Unwmk.
697 A223 100p gold, blk, red, bl
               & grn   .55 .25
Issued for "Free Pashtunistan Day."

Zahir
Shah — A225

1964, Oct. 17   Perf. 14x13½
699 A225 1.25af gold & yel grn   .25 .25
700 A225 3.75af gold & rose   .40 .40
701 A225   50af gold & gray   3.50 2.25
     Nos. 699-701 (3)   4.15 2.90
King Mohammed Zahir Shah, 50th birthday.

Coat of
Arms of
Afghanistan
and UN
Emblem
A226

1964, Oct. 24   Perf. 13½x14
702 A226 5af gold, blk & dl bl   .25 .25
Issued for United Nations Day.

Emblem of
Afghanistan
Women's
Association
A227

1964, Nov. 9   Photo.   Unwmk.
703 A227 25p pink, dk bl & emer   .55 .30
704 A227 75p aqua, dk bl & em-
               er   .90 .40
705 A227 1af sil, dk bl & emer   1.25 .55
     Nos. 703-705 (3)   2.70 1.25
Issued for Women's Day.

Poet Mowlana
Nooruddin Abdul
Rahman Jami
(1414-1492)
A228

Perf. 11 Rough
1964, Nov. 23   Litho.
706 A228 1.50af blk, emer & yel   .95 .95
No. 706 also exists clean-cut perf 10½.

Woodpecker
A229

Birds: 3.75af, Black-throated jay, vert. 5af,
Impeyan pheasant, vert.

Perf. 13½x14, 14x13½
1965, Apr. 20   Photo.   Unwmk.
707 A229 1.25af multi   3.00 .40
708 A229 3.75af multi   5.25 .90
709 A229   5af multi   6.00 2.00
     Nos. 707-709 (3)   14.25 3.30

ITU Emblem, Old and New
Communication Equipment — A230

1965, May 17   Perf. 13½x14
710 A230 5af lt bl, blk & red   .50 .35
Cent. of the ITU.

"Red City,"
Bamian — A231

Designs: 3.75af, Ruins of ancient Bamian
city. 5af, Bande Amir, mountain lakes.

1965, May 30   Perf. 13x13½
711 A231 1.25af pink & multi   .40 .25
712 A231 3.75af lt blue & multi   .65 .25
713 A231   5af yellow & multi   .95 .25
     Nos. 711-713 (3)   2.00 .75
Issued for tourist publicity.

ICY Emblem
A232

1965, June 25   Perf. 13½x13
714 A232 5af multicolored   .50 .30
International Cooperation Year, 1965.

ARIANA Air
Lines
Emblem and
DC-3
A233

5af, DC-6 at right. 10af, DC-3 on top.

Perf. 13½x14
1965, July 15   Photo.   Unwmk.
715 A233 1.25af brt bl, gray & blk .30 .25
716 A233   5af red lil, blk & bl   .90 .25
717 A233 10af bis, blk, bl gray
               & grn   1.60 .55
  a. Souv. sheet, #715-717, imperf. 3.00 3.00
     Nos. 715-717 (3)   2.80 1.05
10th anniv. of Afghan Air Lines, ARIANA.

Nadir
Shah — A234

1965, Aug. 23   Perf. 14x13½
718 A234 1af dl grn, blk & red
               brn   .40 .25
For the 47th Independence Day.

Flag of Pashtunistan — A235

Perf. 13½x14
1965, Aug. 31   Photo.   Unwmk.
719 A235 1af multicolored   .40 .25
Issued for "Free Pashtunistan Day."

Zahir Shah Signing
Constitution — A236

1965, Sept. 11   Perf. 13x13½
720 A236 1.50af brt grn & blk   .40 .25
Promulgation of the new Constitution.

Zahir Shah and Oak Leaves — A237

1965, Oct. 14 *Perf. 14x13½*
721 A237 1.25af blk, ultra & salmon .25 .25
722 A237 6af blk, lt bl & rose lil .40 .35
King Mohammed Zahir Shah, 51st birthday.

Flags of UN and Afghanistan A238

1965, Oct. 24 *Perf. 13½x14*
723 A238 5af multicolored .25 .25
Issued for United Nations Day.

Dappled Ground Gecko A239

Designs: 4af, Caucasian agamid (lizard). 8af, Horsfield's tortoise.

Perf. 13½x14
1966, May 10 Photo. *Unwmk.*
724 A239 3af tan & multi 1.00 .25
725 A239 4af brt grn & multi 1.25 .30
726 A239 8af violet & multi 2.25 .65
Nos. 724-726 (3) 4.50 1.20

Soccer Player and Globe — A240

1966, July 31 Litho. *Perf. 14x13½*
727 A240 2af rose red & blk .70 .25
728 A240 6af violet bl & blk 1.25 .30
729 A240 12af bister brn & blk 2.50 .70
Nos. 727-729 (3) 4.45 1.25
World Cup Soccer Championship, Wembley, England, July 11-30.

Cotton Flower and Boll — A241

5af, Silkworm. 7af, Farmer plowing with oxen.

1966, July 31 *Perf. 13½x14*
730 A241 1af multicolored .90 .25
731 A241 5af multicolored 1.75 .30
732 A241 7af multicolored 2.50 .50
Nos. 730-732 (3) 5.15 1.05
Issued for the Day of Agriculture.

Independence Monument — A242

1966, Aug. 23 Photo. *Perf. 13½x14*
733 A242 1af multicolored .30 .25
734 A242 3af multicolored .90 .30
Issued to commemorate Independence Day.

Flag of Pashtunistan — A243

Perf. 11 Rough
1966, Aug. 31 *Litho.*
735 A243 1af bright blue .55 .25
"Free Pashtunistan Day."

Bagh-i-Bala Park Casino A244

Tourist publicity: 2af, Map of Afghanistan. 8af, Tomb of Abd-er-Rahman. The casino on 4af is the former summer palace of Abd-er-Rahman near Kabul.

1966, Oct. 3 Photo. *Perf. 13½x14*
736 A244 2af red & multi .40 .25
737 A244 4af multicolored .80 .35
738 A244 8af multicolored 1.20 .80
a. Souvenir sheet of 3, #736-738, imperf. 3.50 3.50
Nos. 736-738 (3) 2.40 1.40

Zahir Shah — A245

1966, Oct. 14 *Perf. 14x13½*
739 A245 1af dk slate grn .25 .25
740 A245 5af red brown .55 .30
King Mohammed Zahir Shah, 52nd birthday. See Nos. 760-761.

UNESCO Emblem — A246

1967, Mar. 6 *Litho.* *Perf. 12*
741 A246 2af multicolored .30 .25
742 A246 6af multicolored .50 .25
743 A246 12af multicolored 1.10 .25
Nos. 741-743 (3) 1.90 .75
20th anniv. of UNESCO.

Zahir Shah and UN Emblem A247

1967 *Photo.*
744 A247 5af multicolored .40 .25
745 A247 10af multicolored .80 .30
UN Intl. Org. for Refugees, 20th anniv.

New Power Station A248

5af, Carpet, vert. 8af, Cement factory.

1967, Jan. 7 Photo. *Perf. 13½x14*
746 A248 2af red lil & ol grn .30 .25
747 A248 5af multicolored .30 .25
748 A248 8af blk, dk bl & tan .60 .30
Nos. 746-748 (3) 1.20 .80
Issued to publicize industrial development.

International Tourist Year Emblem A249

Designs: 6af, International Tourist Year emblem and map of Afghanistan.

1967, May 11 Photo. *Perf. 12*
749 A249 2af yel, blk & lt bl .40 .25
750 A249 6af bis brn, blk & lt bl .65 .25
a. Souv. sheet, #749-750, imperf 2.00 1.25
Intl. Tourist Year, 1967. No. 750a sold for 10af.

Power Dam, Dorunta A250

6af, Sirobi Dam, vert. 8af, Reservoir at Jalalabad.

1967, July 2 Photo. *Perf. 12*
751 A250 1af dk green & lil .40 .25
752 A250 6af red brn & grnsh bl .80 .25
753 A250 8af plum & dk bl 1.20 .40
Nos. 751-753 (3) 2.40 .90
Progress in agriculture through electricity.

Macaque — A251

Designs: 6af, Striped hyena, horiz. 12af, Persian gazelles, horiz.

1967, July 28 Photo. *Perf. 12*
754 A251 2af dull yel & indigo .75 .25
755 A251 6af lt green & sepia 1.50 .30
756 A251 12af lt bl & red brn 2.25 .80
Nos. 754-756 (3) 4.50 1.35

Pashtun Dancers A252

1967, Sept. 1 Photo. *Perf. 12*
757 A252 2af magenta & violet .70 .25
Issued for "Free Pashtunistan Day."

Retreat of British at Maiwand A253

1967, Aug. 24
758 A253 1af dk brn & org ver .40 .25
759 A253 2af dk brn & brt pink .80 .25
Issued to commemorate Independence Day.

King Type of 1966
1967, Oct. 15 Photo. *Perf. 14x13½*
760 A245 2af brown red .25 .25
761 A245 8af dark blue .65 .30
Issued to honor King Mohammed Zahir Shah on his 53rd birthday.

Fireworks and UN Emblem — A254

1967, Oct. 24 Litho. *Perf. 12*
762 A254 10af violet bl & multi .70 .40
Issued for United Nations Day.

Greco-Roman Wrestlers A255

Design: 6af, Free style wrestlers.

1967, Nov. 20 *Photo.*
763 A255 4af ol grn & rose lil .50 .25
764 A255 6af dp carmine & brn .95 .25
a. Souv. sheet, #763-764, imperf 2.10 2.10
1968 Olympic Games.

Said Jamalluddin Afghan — A256

1967, Nov. 27
765 A256 1af magenta .25 .25
766 A256 5af brown .40 .25
Said Jamalluddin Afghan, politician (1839-97).

Bronze Vase, 11th-12th Centuries — A257

Design: 7af, Bronze vase, Ghasnavide era, 11th-12th centuries.

1967, Dec. 23 Photo. *Perf. 12*
767 A257 3af lt green & brn .65 .25
768 A257 7af yel & slate grn 1.20 .30
a. Souv. sheet, #767-768, imperf 3.00 3.00

WHO Emblem A258

1968, Apr. 7   Photo.   Perf. 12
769 A258 2af citron & brt bl   .25   .25
770 A258 7af rose & brt bl   .50   .30

20th anniv. of the WHO.

Karakul
A259

1968, May 20   Photo.   Perf. 12
771 A259 1af yellow & blk   .30   .30
772 A259 6af lt blue & blk   1.00   .30
773 A259 12af ultra & dk brn   1.75   .50
    Nos. 771-773 (3)   3.05   1.05

Issued for the Day of Agriculture.

Map of
Afghanistan
A260

Victory Tower,
Ghazni — A261

Design: 16af, Mausoleum, Ghazni.

1968, June 3   Perf. 13½x14, 12
774 A260   2af red, blk, lt bl &
         grn   .40   .25
775 A261   3af yel, dk brn & lt bl   .50   .25
776 A261 16af pink & multi   1.60   .55
    Nos. 774-776 (3)   2.50   1.05

Issued for tourist publicity.

Cinereous
Vulture — A262

6af, Eagle owl. 7af, Greater flamingoes.

1968, July 3   Perf. 12
777 A262 1af sky blue & multi   1.75   .65
778 A262 6af yellow & multi   4.00   2.00
779 A262 7af multicolored   6.00   2.25
    Nos. 777-779 (3)   11.75   4.90

Game of
"Pegsticking"
A263

2af, Olympic flame & rings, vert. 12af,
Buzkashi.

1968, July 20   Photo.   Perf. 12
780 A263 2af multicolored   .50   .25
781 A263 8af orange & multi   .85   .40
782 A263 12af multicolored   1.25   .65
    Nos. 780-782 (3)   2.60   1.30

19th Olympic Games, Mexico City, 10/12-27.

Flower-decked
Armored
Car — A264

1968, Aug. 23
783 A264 6af multicolored   .75   .25

Issued to commemorate Independence Day.

Flag of
Pashtunistan
A265

1968 Aug. 31   Photo.   Perf. 12
784 A265 3af multicolored   .30   .25

Issued for "Free Pashtunistan Day."

Zahir Shah — A266

1968, Oct. 14   Photo.   Perf. 12
785 A266 2af ultra   .25   .25
786 A266 8af brown   .55   .30

King Mohammed Zahir Shah, 54th birthday.

Human Rights
Flame — A267

1968, Oct. 24
787 A267 1af multicolored   .30   .25
788 A267 2af violet, bis & blk   .30   .25
789 A267 6af vio blk, bis & vio   .60   .25
    Nos. 787-789 (3)   1.20   .75

Souvenir Sheet
Imperf
790 A267 10af plum, bis & red
         org   1.75   1.75

International Human Rights Year.

Maolana Djalalodine
Balkhi — A268

1968, Nov. 26   Photo.   Perf. 12
791 A268 4af dk green & mag   .30   .25

Balkhi (1207-73), historian.

Kushan
Mural — A269

Design: 3af, Jug shaped like female torso.

1969, Jan. 2   Perf. 12
792 A269 1af dk grn, mar & yel   .55   .25
793 A269 3af violet, gray & mar   1.20   .25
  a.   Souv. sheet #792-793, imperf   2.40   1.75

Archaeological finds at Bagram, 1st cent.
B.C. to 2nd cent. A.D.

ILO
Emblem
A270

1969, Mar. 23   Photo.   Perf. 12
794 A270 5af lt yel, lemon & blk   .30   .25
795 A270 8af lt bl, grnsh bl & blk   .55   .30

50th anniv. of the ILO.

Arms Type of 1939
Rough Perf. 11
1969, May (?)   Typo.
795A A79 100p dark green   .40   .25
795B A79 150p deep brown   .55   .25

Nos. 795A-795B were normally used as
newspaper stamps.

Badakhshan
Scene
A271

Tourist Publicity: 2af, Map of Afghanistan.
7af, Three men on mules ascending the Pamir
Mountains.

1969, July 6   Photo.   Perf. 13½x14
796 A271 2af ocher & multi   .70   .25
797 A271 4af multicolored   .90   .30
798 A271 7af multicolored   1.40   .65
  a.   Souv. sheet #796-798, imperf   3.00   2.40
    Nos. 796-798 (3)   3.00   1.20

No. 798a sold for 15af.

Bust, from Hadda
Treasure, 3rd-5th
Centuries — A272

Designs: 5af, Vase and jug. 10af, Statue of
crowned woman. 5af and 10af from Bagram
treasure, 1st-2nd centuries.

1969, Aug. 3   Photo.   Perf. 14x13½
799 A272 1af olive grn & gold   .40   .25
800 A272 5af purple & gold   .70   .25
801 A272 10af dp blue & gold   1.10   .30
    Nos. 799-801 (3)   2.20   .80

Zahir Shah and
Queen
Humeira — A273

1969, Aug. 23   Perf. 12
802 A273   5af gold, dk bl & red
         brn   .40   .25
803 A273 10af gold, dp lil & bl
         grn   .70   .40

Issued to commemorate Independence Day.

Map of
Pashtunistan
and Rising
Sun — A274

1969, Aug. 31   Typo.   Perf. 10½
804 A274 2af lt blue & red   .40   .25

Issued for "Free Pashtunistan Day."

Zahir
Shah — A275

1969, Oct. 14   Photo.   Perf. 12
Portrait in Natural Colors
805 A275 2af dk brown & gold   .25   .25
806 A275 6af brown & gold   .55   .25

King Mohammed Zahir Shah, 55th birthday.

UN Emblem and Flag of
Afghanistan — A276

1969, Oct. 24   Litho.   Perf. 13½
807 A276 5af blue & multi   .30   .25

Issued for United Nations Day.

ITU
Emblem — A277

1969, Nov. 12
808 A277 6af ultra & multi   .30   .25
809 A277 12af rose & multi   .70   .40

Issued for World Telecommunications Day.

Crested
Porcupine
A278

1af, Long-tailed porcupine. 8af, Red deer.

1969, Dec. 7   Photo.   Perf. 12
810 A278 1af yellow & multi   .50   .30
811 A278 3af blue & multi   1.10   .50
812 A278 8af pink & multi   2.00   1.00
    Nos. 810-812 (3)   3.60   1.80

Man's First
Footprints on
Moon, and
Earth — A279

1969, Dec. 28   **Perf. 13½x14**
813 A279 1af yel grn & multi .25 .25
814 A279 3af yellow & multi .30 .25
815 A279 6af blue & multi .50 .25
816 A279 10af rose & multi .70 .40
    Nos. 813-816 (4) 1.75 1.15
Moon landing. See note after Algeria No. 427.

Anti-cancer
Symbol — A280

1970, Apr. 7   **Photo.**   **Perf. 14**
817 A280 2af dk grn & rose car .25 .25
818 A280 6af dk bl & rose claret .50 .25
Issued to publicize the fight against cancer.

Mirza Abdul
Quader
Bedel — A281

1970, May 6   **Perf. 14x13½**
819 A281 5af multicolored .40 .25
Mirza Abdul Quader Bedel (1643-1720), poet.

Education Year
Emblem — A282

1970, June 7   **Photo.**   **Perf. 12**
820 A282 1af black .25 .25
821 A282 6af deep rose .40 .25
822 A282 12af green .90 .40
    Nos. 820-822 (3) 1.55 .90
International Education Year 1970.

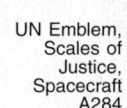

Mother and
Child — A283

1970, June 15   **Perf. 13½**
823 A283 6af yellow & multi .30 .25
Issued for Mother's Day.

UN Emblem,
Scales of
Justice,
Spacecraft
A284

1970, June 26
824 A284 4af yel, dk bl & dp bl .25 .25
825 A284 6af pink, dk bl & brt bl .40 .25
25th anniversary of United Nations.

Mosque of
the Amir of
the two
Swords,
Kabul
A285

2af, Map of Afghanistan. 7af, Arch of Paghman.

1970, July 6   **Perf. 12**
    Size: 30½x30½mm
826 A285 2af lt bl, blk & citron .30 .25
    Size: 36x26mm
827 A285 3af pink & multi .50 .25
828 A285 7af yellow & multi .95 .25
    Nos. 826-828 (3) 1.75 .75
Issued for tourist publicity.

Zahir Shah Reviewing Troops — A286

1970, Aug. 23   **Photo.**   **Perf. 13½**
829 A286 8af multicolored .40 .25
Issued to commemorate Independence Day.

Pathans — A287

1970, Aug. 31   **Typo.**   **Perf. 10½**
830 A287 2af ultra & red .40 .25
Issued for "Free Pashtunistan Day."

Quail — A288

4af, Golden eagle. 6af, Ringnecked pheasant.

1970, Sept.   **Photo.**   **Perf. 12**
831 A288 2af multicolored 2.10 .65
832 A288 4af multicolored 4.00 .95
833 A288 6af multicolored 5.25 1.60
    Nos. 831-833 (3) 11.35 3.20

Zahir
Shah — A289

1970, Oct. 14   **Photo.**   **Perf. 14x13½**
834 A289 3af green & vio .25 .25
835 A289 7af dk bl & vio brn .70 .30
King Mohammed Zahir Shah, 56th birthday.

Red Crescents
A290

1970, Oct. 16   **Typo.**   **Perf. 10½**
836 A290 2af black, gold & red .30 .25
Issued for the Red Crescent Society.

UN
Emblem
and
Charter
A291

1970, Oct. 24   **Photo.**   **Perf. 14**
837 A291 1af gold & multi .25 .25
838 A291 5af gold & multi .30 .25
United Nations Day.

Tiger Heads of
1871 — A292

1970, Nov. 10   **Perf. 12**
839 A292 1af sal, lt grnsh bl & blk .30 .25
840 A292 4af lt ultra, yel & blk .55 .25
841 A292 12af lilac, lt bl & blk .95 .40
    Nos. 839-841 (3) 1.80 .90
Cent. of the 1st Afghan postage stamps. The postal service was established in 1870, but the 1st stamps were issued in May, 1871.

Globe
and
Waves
A293

1971, May 17   **Photo.**   **Perf. 13½**
842 A293 12af green, blk & bl .65 .40
3rd World Telecommunications Day.

Callimorpha
Principalis
A294

Designs: 3af, Epizygaenella species. 5af, Parnassius autocrator.

1971, May 30   **Perf. 13½x14**
843 A294 1af vermilion & multi 1.25 .55
844 A294 3af yellow & multi 2.50 1.10
845 A294 5af ultra & multi 3.50 1.75
    Nos. 843-845 (3) 7.25 3.40

"UNESCO" and
Half of Ancient
Kushan
Statue — A295

1971, June 26   **Photo.**   **Perf. 13½**
846 A295 6af ocher & vio .50 .25
847 A295 10af lt blue & mar .80 .35
UNESCO-sponsored Intl. Kushani Seminar.

Tughra and Independence
Monument — A296

1971, Aug. 23
848 A296 7af rose red & multi .55 .25
849 A296 9af red orange & multi .90 .35
Independence Day.

Pashtunistan
Square,
Kabul — A297

1971, Aug. 31   **Typo.**   **Perf. 10½**
850 A297 5af deep rose lilac .50 .25
"Free Pashtunistan Day."

Zahir
Shah — A298

1971, Oct. 14   **Photo.**   **Perf. 12½x12**
851 A298 9af lt green & multi .55 .30
852 A298 17af yellow & multi 1.10 .65
King Mohammed Zahir Shah, 57th birthday.

A299

Design: Map of Afghanistan, red crescent, various activities.

1971, Oct. 16   **Perf. 14x13½**
853 A299 8af lt bl, red, grn & blk   .50   .30
For Afghan Red Crescent Society.

Equality
Year
Emblem
A300

1971, Oct. 24   **Perf. 12**
854 A300 24af brt blue   1.50   .80
International Year Against Racial Discrimination and United Nations Day.

"Your Heart is
your
Health" — A301

1972, Apr. 7   **Photo.**   **Perf. 14**
855 A301 9af pale yel & multi   .90   .30
856 A301 12af gray & multi   1.75   .40
World Health Day.

Tulip — A302

Designs: 10af, Rock partridge, horiz. 12af, Lynx, horiz. 18af, Allium stipitatum (flower).

1972, June 5   **Photo.**   **Perf. 14**
857 A302 7af green & multi   1.25   .70
858 A302 10af blue & multi   7.50   1.60
859 A302 12af lt green & multi   2.40   1.25
860 A302 18af blue grn & multi   2.40   1.40
Nos. 857-860 (4)   13.55   4.95

Buddhist
Shrine,
Hadda
A302a

Designs: 7af, Greco-Bactrian animal seal, 250 B.C. 9af, Greco-Oriental temple, Ai-Khanoum, 3rd-2nd centuries B.C.

1972, July 16   **Photo.**   **Perf. 12**
861 A302a 3af brown & dl bl   .65   .25
862 A302a 7af rose claret & dl
     grn   .95   .30
863 A302a 9af green & lilac   1.40   .40
Nos. 861-863 (3)   3.00   .95
Tourist publicity.

King and Queen Reviewing
Parade — A303

1972, Aug. 23   **Photo.**   **Perf. 13½**
864 A303 25af gold & multi   4.50   1.25
Independence Day.
Used as a provisional in 1978 with king and queen portion removed.

Wrestling
A304

10af, 19af, 21af, Wrestling, different hold.

1972, Aug. 26
865 A304 4af ol bis & multi   .30   .25
866 A304 8af lt blue & multi   .55   .25
867 A304 10af yel grn & multi   .70   .30
868 A304 19af multicolored   1.50   .50
869 A304 21af lilac & multi   1.60   .55
   a.   Souv. sheet, #865-869, imperf   3.25   3.25
Nos. 865-869 (5)   4.65   1.85

20th Olympic Games, Munich, Aug. 26-Sept. 11. No. 869a sold for 60af.

Pathan and
View of Tribal
Territory — A305

1972, Aug. 31   **Perf. 12½x12**
870 A305 5af ultra & multi   .55   .25
Pashtunistan day.

Zahir
Shah — A306

1972, Oct. 14   **Photo.**   **Perf. 14x13½**
871 A306 7af gold, blk & Prus bl   .70   .25
872 A306 14af gold, blk & lt brn   1.10   .40
58th birthday of King Mohammed Zahir Shah.

City Destroyed by Earthquake,
Refugees — A307

1972, Oct. 16   **Perf. 13½**
873 A307 7af lt bl, red & blk   .65   .25
For Afghan Red Crescent Society.

UN
Emblem
A308

1972, Oct. 24
874 A308 12af lt ultra & blk   .70   .30
UN Economic Commission for Asia and the Far East (ECAFE), 25th anniv.

Ceramics
A309

Designs: 9af, Leather coat, vert. 12af, Metal ware, vert. 16af, Inlaid artifacts.

1972, Dec. 10   **Photo.**   **Perf. 12**
875 A309 7af gold & multi   .50   .25
876 A309 9af gold & multi   .75   .35
877 A309 12af gold & multi   .90   .40
878 A309 16af gold & multi   1.50   .50
   a.   Souv. sheet, #875-878, imperf   4.00   4.00
Nos. 875-878 (4)   3.65   1.50

Handicraft industries. No. 878a sold for 45af.

WMO and National Emblems — A310

1973, Apr. 3   **Photo.**   **Perf. 14**
879 A310 7af lt lil & dk grn   .55   .25
880 A310 14af lt bl & dp claret   1.40   .40
Cent. of intl. meteorological cooperation.

Abu Rayhan al-
Biruni — A311

1973, June 16   **Photo.**   **Perf. 13½**
881 A311 10af multicolored   .65   .40
Millennium of birth (973-1048), philosopher and mathematician.

Family — A312

1973, June 30   **Photo.**   **Perf. 13½**
882 A312 9af orange & red lil   .75   .25
Intl. Family Planning Fed., 21st anniv.

Republic

Impeyan
Pheasant
A313

Birds: 9af, Great crested grebe. 12af, Himalayan snow cock.

1973, July 29   **Photo.**   **Perf. 12x12½**
883 A313 8af yellow & multi   3.00   2.00
884 A313 9af blue & multi   3.75   2.40
885 A313 12af multicolored   4.50   3.25
Nos. 883-885 (3)   11.25   7.65

Stylized
Buzkashi
Horseman
A314

1973, Aug.   **Perf. 13½**
886 A314 8af black   .55   .30
Tourist publicity.

Fireworks
A315

1973, Aug. 23   **Photo.**   **Perf. 12**
887 A315 12af multicolored   .65   .40
55th Independence Day.

Lake Abassine, Pashtunistan
Flag — A316

1973, Aug. 31   **Perf. 14x13½**
888 A316 9af multicolored   .65   .35
Pashtunistan Day.

Red Crescent
A317

1973, Oct. 16   **Perf. 13½**
889 A317 10af red, blk & gold   .95   .30
Red Crescent Society.

Kemal Ataturk A318

1973, Oct. 28   Litho.   *Perf. 10½*
890 A318 1af blue   .25   .25
891 A318 7af reddish brown   1.25   .25
50th anniversary of the Turkish Republic.

Human Rights Flame, Arms of Afghanistan A319

1973, Dec. 10   Photo.   *Perf. 12*
892 A319 12af sil, blk & lt bl   .55   .40
25th anniversary of the Universal Declaration of Human Rights.

Asiatic Black Bears A320

1974, Mar. 26   Litho.   *Perf. 12*
893 A320 5af shown   .65   .25
894 A320 7af Afghan hound   1.00   .40
895 A320 10af Persian goat   1.40   .50
896 A320 12af Leopard   1.75   .55
 a.   Souv. sheet, #893-896, imperf   10.00   10.00
       Nos. 893-896 (4)   4.80   1.70

Worker and Farmer A321

1974, May 1   Photo.   *Perf. 13½x12½*
897 A321 9af rose red & multi   .70   .30
International Labor Day, May 1.

Independence Monument and Arch — A322

1974, May 27   Photo.   *Perf. 12*
898 A322 4af blue & multi   .40   .25
899 A322 11af gold & multi   .55   .25
56th Independence Day.

Arms of Afghanistan and Symbol of Cooperation — A323

Pres. Mohammad Daoud Khan — A324

5af, Flag of Republic of Afghanistan. 15af, Soldiers, coat of arms of the Republic.

Sizes: 4af, 15af, 36x22mm; 5af, 7af, 36x26, 26x36mm

1974, July 25   *Perf. 13½x12½, 14*
900 A323 4af multicolored   .40   .25
901 A323 5af multicolored   .55   .25
902 A324 7af green, brn & blk   .65   .25
 a.   Souv. sheet, #901-902, imperf   1.75   1.75
903 A323 15af multicolored   1.25   .30
 a.   Souv. sheet, #900, 903, imperf   2.00   2.00
       Nos. 900-903 (4)   2.85   1.05
1st anniv. of the Republic of Afghanistan.

Lesser Spotted Eagle A325

Birds: 6af, White-fronted goose, ruddy shelduck and gray-lag goose. 11af, European coots and European crane.

1974, Aug. 6   Photo.   *Perf. 13½x13*
904 A325 1af car rose & multi   2.00   .50
905 A325 6af blue & multi   4.50   .80
906 A325 11af yellow & multi   7.00   1.40
 a.   Strip of 3, #904-906   14.00   14.00

Flags of Pashtunistan and Afghanistan — A326

1974, Aug. 31   Photo.   *Perf. 14*
907 A326 5af multicolored   .30   .25
Pashtunistan Day.

Natl. Arms A326a

1974, Aug.   Typo.   *Rough Perf. 11*
907A A326a 100p green   .80   .25

Coat of Arms A327

1974, Oct. 9
908 A327 7af gold, grn & blk   .30   .25
Centenary of Universal Postal Union.

"un" and UN Emblem A328

1974, Oct. 24   Photo.   *Perf. 14*
909 A328 5af lt ultra & dk bl   .40   .25
United Nations Day.

Minaret of Jam — A329

Buddha, Hadda — A330

14af, Lady riding griffin, 2nd century, Bagram.

1975, May 5   Photo.   *Perf. 13½*
910 A329 7af multicolored   .40   .25
911 A330 14af multicolored   .75   .40
912 A330 15af multicolored   .95   .40
 a.   Souv. sheet, #910-912, imperf.   3.50   3.50
       Nos. 910-912 (3)   2.10   1.05
South Asia Tourism Year 1975.

New Flag of Afghanistan A331

1975, May 27   Photo.   *Perf. 12*
913 A331 16af multicolored   .80   .25
57th Independence Day.

Celebrating Crowd — A332

1975, July 17   Photo.   *Perf. 13½*
914 A332 9af blue & multi   .50   .25
915 A332 12af carmine & multi .65   .30
Second anniversary of the Republic.

Women's Year Emblems A333

1975, Aug. 24   Photo.   *Perf. 12*
916 A333 9af car, lt bl & blk   .50   .25
International Women's Year 1975.

Pashtunistan Flag, Sun Rising Over Mountains — A334

1975, Aug. 31   *Perf. 13½*
917 A334 10af multicolored   .40   .25
Pashtunistan Day.

Mohammed Akbar Khan — A335

1976, Feb. 4   Photo.   *Perf. 14*
918 A335 15af lt brown & multi .55   .40
Mohammed Akbar Khan (1816-1846), warrior son of Amir Dost Mohammed Khan.

A336

Pres. Mohammad Daoud Khan — A337

1974-78   Photo.   *Perf. 14*
919 A336 10af multi   .65   .25
920 A336 16af multi ('78)   2.40   .90
921 A336 19af multi   .90   .50
922 A336 21af multi   1.40   .55
923 A336 22af multi ('78)   3.50   1.90
924 A336 30af multi ('78)   4.75   2.75
925 A337 50af multi ('75)   2.75   1.40
926 A337 100af multi ('75)   5.50   2.40
       Nos. 919-926 (8)   21.85   10.65

Arms of Republic, Independence Monument — A338

1976, June 1   Photo.   *Perf. 14*
927 A338 22af blue & multi   .70   .50
58th Independence Day.

Flag Raising — A339

1976, July 17   **Photo.**   *Perf. 14*
928   A339   30af multicolored   .80   .55
Republic Day.

Mountain Peaks and Flag of Pashtunistan A340

1976, Aug. 31   **Photo.**   *Perf. 14*
929   A340   16af multicolored   .65   .50
Pashtunistan Day.

Coat of Arms A340a

1976, Sept.   **Litho.**   *Perf. 11 Rough*
930   A340a   25p salmon   .50   .30
931   A340a   50p lt green   .55   .25
932   A340a   1af ultra   .55   .25
    Nos. 930-932 (3)   1.60   .80

Flag and Views on Open Book A341

1977, May 27   **Photo.**   *Perf. 14*
937   A341   20af green & multi   .70   .60
59th Independence Day.

Pres. Daoud and National Assembly — A342

President Taking Oath of Office A343

Designs: 10af, Inaugural address. 18af, Promulgation of Constitution.

1977, June 22
938   A342   7af multicolored   .80   .55
939   A343   8af multicolored   .90   .70
940   A343   10af multicolored   1.10   .90
941   A342   18af multicolored   1.90   1.50
  a.   Souvenir sheet of 4   3.50   3.50
    Nos. 938-941 (4)   4.70   3.65

Election of 1st Pres. and promulgation of Constitution. No. 941a contains 4 imperf. stamps similar to Nos. 938-941.

Jamalluddin Medal A344

1977, July 6   **Photo.**   *Perf. 14*
942   A344   12af blue, blk & gold   .40   .30
Sajo Jamalluddin Afghani, reformer, 80th death anniversary.

Afghanistan Flag over Crowd — A345

1977, July 17
943   A345   22af multicolored   .70   .55

Dancers, Fountain, Pashtunistan Flag — A346

1977, Aug. 31
944   A346   30af multicolored   1.10   .90
Pashtunistan Day.

Arms and Carrier Pigeon — A346a

1977, Oct. 30   **Litho.**   *Perf. 11*
944A   A346a   1af black & blue   .40   .25

Members of Parliament Congratulating Pres. Daoud — A347

1978, Feb. 5   **Litho.**   *Perf. 14*
945   A347   20af multicolored   2.00   1.10
Election of first president, first anniversary.

Map of Afghanistan, UPU Emblem — A348

1978, Apr. 1   **Photo.**   *Perf. 14*
946   A348   10af green, blk & gold   .40   .25
Afghanistan's UPU membership, 50th anniv.

Wall Telephone and Satellite Station A349

1978, Apr. 12
947   A349   8af multicolored   .40   .25
Afghanistan's ITU membership, 50th anniv.

Democratic Republic

Arrows Pointing to Crescent, Cross and Lion — A350

1978, July 6   **Litho.**   *Perf. 11 Rough*
948   A350   3af black   1.25   .65
50th anniv. of Afghani Red Crescent Soc.

Khalq Party Emblem — A350a

1978, Aug.   **Litho.**   *Perf. 11*
948A   A350a   1af rose red & gold   1.50   .65
948B   A350a   4af rose red & gold   2.10   .90

Qalai Bist Arch A351

Hazara Women — A351a

16af, Bamian Buddha.

1978, Aug. 19   *Perf. 14*
949   A351   16af multicolored   1.25   .50
949A   A351   22af shown   1.50   .65
949B   A351a   30af shown   2.10   1.10
    Nos. 949-949B (3)   4.85   2.25

Men with Pashtunistan Flag — A352

1978, Aug. 31   *Perf. 11 Rough*
950   A352   7af ultra & red   .50   .25
Pashtunistan Day.

Coat of Arms and Emblems A353

1978, Sept. 8   *Perf. 11*
951   A353   20af rose red   .90   .40
World Literacy Day.

A354

Perf. 11½ Rough
1978, Oct. 25   **Litho.**
952   A354   18af light green   .95   .40
Hero of Afghanistan.

Khalq Party Flag A355

1978, Oct. 19   **Photo.**   *Perf. 11½*
953   A355   8af black, red & gold   .65   .25
954   A355   9af black, red & gold   .95   .25
"The mail serving the people."

Nour Mohammad Taraki — A356

1979, Jan. 1   **Litho.**   *Perf. 12*
955   A356   12af multicolored   .70   .25
Nour Mohammad Taraki, founder of People's Democratic Party of Afghanistan, installation as president.

Woman Breaking Chain — A357

1979, Mar. 8   **Litho.**   *Perf. 11*
956   A357   14af red & ultra   1.25   .50
Women's Day. Inscribed "POSSTES."

Map of Afghanistan, Census Emblem — A358

1979, Mar. 25   Litho.   Perf. 12
957 A358 3af multicolored   .90 .70
First comprehensive population census.

Farmers A359

1979, Mar. 21
958 A359 1af multicolored   .65 .30
Agricultural advances.

Pres. Taraki Reading First Issue of Khalq — A360

1979, Apr. 11   Perf. 12½x12
959 A360 2af multicolored   .65 .25
Khalq, newspaper of People's Democratic Republic of Afghanistan.

Pres. Noor Mohammad Taraki A361

Plaza with Tank Monument and Fountain — A362

House where Revolution Started — A363

Designs: 50p, Taraki, tank. 12af, House where 1st Khalq Party Congress was held.

Perf. 12, 12½x12 (A362)
1979, Apr. 27   Litho.
959A A363 50p multicolored   .65 .25
960   A361 4af multicolored   .40 .25
961   A362 5af multicolored   .55 .25
962   A363 6af multicolored   .70 .25
963   A363 12af multicolored   .80 .25
   Nos. 959A-963 (5)   3.10 1.25
1st anniversary of revolution.

Carpenter and Blacksmith A364

1979, May 1   Perf. 12
964 A364 10af multicolored   1.10 .25
Int'l Labor Day.

Children, Flag and Map of Afghanistan — A366

1979, June 1   Litho.   Perf. 12½x12
966 A366 16af multicolored   2.00 .90
International Year of the Child.

Doves Circling Asia in Globe A366a

1979   Litho.   Perf. 11x10½
966A A366a 2af red & blue   1.25 .25

Armed Afghans, Kabul Memorial and Arch — A367

1979, Aug. 19   Litho.   Perf. 12
967 A367 30af multicolored   1.50 .90
60th independence day.

Pashtunistan Citizens, Flag — A368

1979, Aug. 31
968 A368 9af multicolored   .70 .25
Pashtunistan Day.

UPU Day A369

1979, Oct. 9   Litho.   Perf. 12
969 A369 15af multicolored   .65 .25

Tombstone — A369a

1979, Oct. 25   Litho.   Perf. 12½x12
969A A369a 22af multicolored   2.40 1.25

International Women's Day — A370

1980, Mar. 8   Litho.   Perf. 12
970 A370 8af multicolored   1.50 .50

Farmers' Day — A371

1980, Mar. 21   Litho.   Perf. 11½x12
971 A371 2af multicolored   2.25 .70

Non-smoker and Smoker A372

1980, Apr. 7   Perf. 11½
972 A372 5af multicolored   1.75 .70
Anti-smoking campaign; World Health Day.

Lenin, 110th Birth Anniversary A373

1980, Apr. 22   Perf. 12x12½
973 A373 12af multicolored   2.50 .85

People and Fist on Map of Afghanistan — A374

1980, Apr. 27   Litho.   Perf. 12½x12
974 A374 1af multicolored   .70 .25
Saur Revolution, 2nd anniversary.

International Workers' Solidarity Day — A375

1980, May 1
975 A375 9af multicolored   .50 .25

Wrestling, Moscow '80 Emblem A376

1980, July 19   Perf. 12x12½, 12½x12
976 A376 3af Soccer, vert.   .60 .25
977 A376 6af shown   .70 .25
978 A376 9af Buzkashi   .80 .25
979 A376 10af Pegsticking   .95 .25
   Nos. 976-979 (4)   3.05 1.00
22nd Summer Olympic Games, Moscow, July 19-Aug. 3.

61st Anniversary of Independence — A377

1980, Aug. 19   Litho.   Perf. 12½x12
980 A377 3af multicolored   .85 .25

Pashtunistan Day — A378

1980, Aug. 30
981 A378 25af multicolored   1.00 .45

Intl. UPU Day A379

1980, Oct. 9   Litho.   Perf. 12½x12
982 A379 20af multicolored   1.00 .45

The resistance group headed by Amin Wardak released some stamps in 1980. Some of these are inscribed "WARDAK AFGHANISTAN," others "Solidarite Internationale Avec la Resistance Afghane." The status of these labels is questionable.

International Women's Day — A381

1981, Mar. 9   Litho.   Perf. 12½x12
984 A381 15af multicolored   1.25 .35

Farmers' Day — A382

1981, Mar. 20   Litho.   Perf. 12½x12
985   A382   1af multicolored   1.00   .25

Bighorn Mountain Sheep (Protected Species) A383

1981, Apr. 4   Perf. 12x12½
986   A383   12af multicolored   2.40   .70

Saur Revolution, 3rd Anniversary A384

1981, Apr. 27   Perf. 11
987   A384   50p brown   .70   .25

Intl. Workers' Solidarity Day — A385

1981, May 1   Perf. 12½x12
988   A385   10af multicolored   .95   .35

13th World Telecommunications Day — A387

1981, May 17   Litho.   Perf. 12½x12
990   A387   9af multicolored   .70   .25

Intl. Children's Day — A388

1981, June 1   Perf. 12x12½
991   A388   15af multicolored   .95   .45

People's Independence Monument 62nd Anniv. of Independence — A389

1981, Aug. 19
992   A389   4af multicolored   1.10   .30

Pashtunistan Day — A390

1981, Aug. 31   Litho.   Perf. 12
992A   A390   2af multicolored   .70   .25

Intl. Tourism Day — A391

1981, Sept. 27   Perf. 12½x12
993   A391   5af multicolored   .70   .25

World Food Day — A392

1981, Oct. 16
995   A392   7af multicolored   .85   .25

Asia-Africa Solidarity Meeting — A393

1981, Nov. 18   Litho.   Perf. 11
996   A393   8af blue   .80   .25

Struggle Against Apartheid — A394

1981, Dec. 1   Perf. 12½x12
997   A394   4af multicolored   1.00   .25

1300th Anniv. of Bulgaria A395

1981, Dec. 9   Perf. 12x12½
998   A395   20af multicolored   1.75   .50

Buzkashi Game — A395a

1980   Photo.   Perf. 14
998A   A395a   50af multicolored   2.25   1.25
998B   A395a   100af multicolored   4.50   1.75

Intl. Women's Day A396

1982, Mar. 8   Litho.   Perf. 12
999   A396   6af multicolored   .60   .25

Farmers' Day — A397

1982, Mar. 21
1000   A397   4af multicolored   .70   .25

Judas Trees — A398

Designs: Various local plants.

1982, Apr. 9   Litho.   Perf. 12
1001   A398   3af shown   .40   .25
1002   A398   4af Rose of Sharon   .70   .25
1003   A398   16af Rhubarb plant   1.60   .35
       Nos. 1001-1003 (3)   2.70   .85

Saur Revolution, 4th Anniv. — A399

1982, Apr. 27
1004   A399   1af multicolored   1.50   .25

George Dimitrov (1882-1947), First Prime Minister of Bulgaria — A400

1982, Apr. 30
1005   A400   30af multicolored   2.40   .85

Intl. Workers' Solidarity Day A401

1982, May 1
1006   A401   10af multicolored   .85   .25

Storks — A402   Nightingales — A402a

1982, May 31
1007   A402   6af multicolored   1.75   .50
1008   A402a   11af multicolored   2.75   .60

Hedgehogs A403

1982, July 6   Litho.   Perf. 12
1009   A403   3af shown   .85   .25
1010   A403   14af Cobra   2.00   .25
       See Nos. 1020-1022.

63rd Anniv. of Independence — A404

1982, Aug. 19
1011   A404   20af multicolored   1.25   .50

Pashtunistan Day — A405

1982, Aug. 31
1012   A405   32af multicolored   2.50   .75

World Tourism Day A406

1982, Sept. 27   Litho.   Perf. 12
1013   A406   9af multicolored   .85   .35

UPU Day
A407

1982, Oct. 9
1014 A407 4af multicolored .95 .25

World Food
Day
A408

1982, Oct. 16
1015 A408 9af multicolored 1.50 .35

37th Anniv. of
UN — A409

1982, Oct. 24
1016 A409 15af multicolored 1.00 .45

ITU Plenipotentiaries Conference,
Nairobi, Sept. — A410

1982, Oct. 26
1017 A410 8af multicolored .80 .25

TB Bacillus
Centenary — A411

1982, Nov. 24 **Litho.** **Perf. 12**
1018 A411 7af multicolored .50 .25

Human Rights
Declaration, 34th
Anniv. — A412

1982, Dec. 10
1019 A412 5af multicolored .45 .25

Animal Type of 1982
1982, Dec. 16
1020 A403 2af Lions .50 .25
1021 A403 7af Donkeys 1.00 .35
1022 A403 12af Marmots, vert. 2.25 .50
 Nos. 1020-1022 (3) 3.75 1.10

Intl. Women's
Day — A413

1983, Mar. 8
1023 A413 3af multicolored .25 .25

Mir Alicher Nawai
Research
Decade — A414

1983, Mar. 19
1024 A414 22af multicolored .95 .35

Farmers'
Day
A415

1983, Mar. 21 **Litho.** **Perf. 12**
1025 A415 10af multicolored .85 .25

5th Anniv.
of Saur
Revolution
A416

1983, Apr. 27 **Litho.** **Perf. 12**
1026 A416 15af multicolored .70 .35

Intl. Workers'
Solidarity
Day — A417

1983, May 1
1027 A417 2af multicolored .70 .25

World Communications Year — A418

4af, Modes of communication. 11af,
Building.

1983, May 17
1028 A418 4af multicolored .45 .25
1029 A418 11af multicolored .75 .25

Intl.
Children's
Day — A419

1983, June 1 **Litho.** **Perf. 12**
1030 A419 25af multicolored .80 .35

2nd Anniv. of
National
Front — A420

1983, June 15
1031 A420 1af multicolored .35 .25

Local
Butterflies
A421

Various butterflies. 9af, 13af vert.

1983, July 6
1032 A421 9af multicolored 1.10 .80
1033 A421 13af multicolored 2.50 1.40
1034 A421 21af multicolored 3.25 1.75
 Nos. 1032-1034 (3) 6.85 3.95

Struggle Against
Apartheid — A422

1983, Aug. 1 **Litho.** **Perf. 12**
1035 A422 10af multicolored .55 .25

64th Anniv of Independence — A423

1983, Aug. 19
1036 A423 6af multicolored .45 .25

Parliament
House —
A423a

100af, Afghan Woman, Camel.

1983, Sept. **Litho.** **Perf. 12**
1036A A423a 50af shown 1.75 .35
1036B A423a 100af multi 4.25 .45

World Tourism
Day — A425

1983, Sept. 27 **Litho.** **Perf. 12**
1037 A424 5af shown .45 .25
1038 A425 7af shown .60 .25
1039 A424 12af Golden statues .95 .25
1040 A425 16af Stone carving 1.25 .25
 Nos. 1037-1040 (4) 3.25 1.00

World Communications Year — A426

14af, Dish antenna, dove. 15af, Building,
flag.

1983, Oct. 9 **Litho.** **Perf. 12**
1041 A426 14af multicolored .90 .25
1042 A426 15af multicolored .90 .25

World Food Day — A427

1983, Oct. 16 **Litho.** **Perf. 12**
1043 A427 14af multicolored .90 .25

Sports
A428

1983, Nov. 1 **Litho.** **Perf. 12**
1044 A428 1af Soccer .25 .25
1045 A428 18af Boxing 1.00 .35
1046 A428 21af Wrestling 1.25 .35
 Nos. 1044-1046 (3) 2.50 .95

Pashtunistan Day
— A428a

3af, Pathans Waving Flag.

1983, Nov. **Litho.** **Perf. 12**
1046A A428a 3af multicolored .45 .25

Handicrafts
A429

2af, Jewelry. 8af, Stone ashtrays, dishes.
19af, Furniture. 30af, Leather goods.

1983, Nov. 22
1047 A429 2af multicolored .25 .25
1048 A429 8af multicolored .35 .25
1049 A429 19af multicolored .60 .25
1050 A429 30af multicolored 1.50 .40
 Nos. 1047-1050 (4) 2.70 1.15

UN Declaration of Human Rights, 35th Anniv. A430

1983, Dec. 10 Litho. Perf. 12
1051 A430 20af multicolored .95 .25

Kabul Polytechnical Institute, 20th Anniv. — A431

1983, Dec. 28 Perf. 12½x12
1052 A431 30af multicolored 1.25 .35

1984 Winter Olympics A432

1984, Jan. Perf. 12
1053 A432 5af Figure skating .25 .25
1054 A432 9af Skiing .35 .25
1055 A432 11af Speed skating .50 .25
1056 A432 15af Hockey .60 .25
1057 A432 18af Biathlon .70 .25
1058 A432 20af Ski jumping .85 .25
1059 A432 22af Bobsledding 1.00 .25
Nos. 1053-1059 (7) 4.25 1.75

Intl. Women's Day — A433

1984, Mar. 8
1060 A433 4af multicolored .50 .25

Farmers' Day A434

Various agricultural scenes.

1984, Mar. 21 Litho. Perf. 12
1061 A434 2af multicolored .25 .25
1062 A434 4af multicolored .25 .25
1063 A434 7af multicolored .25 .25
1064 A434 9af multicolored .25 .25
1065 A434 15af multicolored .45 .25
1066 A434 18af multicolored .50 .25
1067 A434 20af multicolored .70 .25
Nos. 1061-1067 (7) 2.65 1.75

World Aviation Day A435

1984, Apr. 12
1068 A435 5af Luna 1 .35 .25
1069 A435 8af Luna 2 .45 .25
1070 A435 11af Luna 3 .55 .25
1071 A435 17af Apollo 11 .70 .25
1072 A435 22af Soyuz 6 .90 .35

1073 A435 28af Soyuz 7 .90 .35
1074 A435 34af Soyuz 6, 7, 8 1.10 .45
Nos. 1068-1074 (7) 4.95 2.15
Souvenir Sheet
Perf. 12x12½
1075 A435 25af S. Koroliov 1.50 .90
No. 1075 contains one 30x41mm stamp.

Saur Revolution, 6th Anniv. A436

1984, Apr. 27 Perf. 12
1076 A436 3af multicolored .45 .25

65th Anniv. of Independence — A437

1984, Aug. 19 Litho. Perf. 12
1077 A437 6af multicolored .65 .25

Pashto's and Balutchi's Day A438

3af, Symbolic sun, tribal terr.

1984, Aug. 31
1078 A438 3af multicolored .45 .25

Wildlife A439

1af, Cape hunting dog, vert. 2af, Argali sheep, vert. 6af, Przewalski's horse. 8af, Wild boar, vert. 17af, Snow leopard. 19af, Tiger. 22af, Indian elephant, vert.

Perf. 12½x12, 12x12½
1984, May 5 Litho.
1079 A439 1af multicolored .25 .25
1080 A439 2af multicolored .25 .25
1081 A439 6af multicolored .60 .25
1082 A439 8af multicolored .90 .25
1083 A439 17af multicolored 1.75 .25
1084 A439 19af multicolored 3.00 .25
1085 A439 22af multicolored 3.25 .25
Nos. 1079-1085 (7) 10.00 1.85

19th UPU Congress, Hamburg A440

25af, German postman, 17th cent. 35af, Postrider, 16th cent. 40af, Carrier pigeon, letter.
50af, Hamburg No. 3 in black.

1984, June 18 Perf. 12x12½
1086 A440 25af multicolored .95 .30
1087 A440 35af multicolored 1.50 .45
1088 A440 40af multicolored 1.90 .55
Nos. 1086-1088 (3) 4.35 1.30
Souvenir Sheet
1089 A440 50af multicolored 2.75 1.75
No. 1089 contains one 30x40mm stamp.

Natl. Aviation, 40th Anniv. A441

Soviet civil aircraft.

1984, June 29
1090 A441 1af Antonov AN-2 .25 .25
1091 A441 4af Ilyushin IL-12 .25 .25
1092 A441 9af Tupolev TU-104 .60 .25
1093 A441 10af Ilyushin IL-18 .90 .25
1094 A441 13af Tupolev TU-134 1.10 .25
1095 A441 17af Ilyushin IL-62 1.50 .30
1096 A441 21af Ilyushin IL-28 1.75 .40
Nos. 1090-1096 (7) 6.35 1.95

Ettore Bugatti (1881-1947), Type 43, Italy — A442

Classic automobiles and their designers: 5af, Henry Ford, 1903 Model A, US. 8af, Rene Panhard (1841-1908), 1899 Landau, France. 11af, Gottlieb Daimler (1834-1900), 1935 Daimler-Benz, Germany. 12af, Carl Benz (1844-1929), 1893 Victoris, Germany. 15af, Armand Peugeot (1848-1915), 1892 Vis-a-Vis, France. 22af, Louis Chevrolet (1879-1941), 1925 Sedan, US.

1984, June 30
1097 A442 2af multicolored .25 .25
1098 A442 5af multicolored .35 .25
1099 A442 8af multicolored .60 .25
1100 A442 11af multicolored .75 .25
1101 A442 12af multicolored 1.00 .25
1102 A442 15af multicolored 1.10 .25
1103 A442 22af multicolored 1.50 .35
Nos. 1097-1103 (7) 5.55 1.85

Qalai Bist Arch A443

World Tourism Day: 2af, Ornamental buck-led harness. 5af, Victory Monument and Memorial Arch, Kabul. 9af, Standing sculpture of Afghani ruler and attendants. 15af, Buffalo riders in snow. 19af, Camel driver, tent, camel in caparison. 21af, Horsemen playing buzkashi.

1984, Sept. 27
1104 A443 1af multicolored .25 .25
1105 A443 2af multicolored .25 .25
1106 A443 5af multicolored .25 .25
1107 A443 9af multicolored .25 .25
1108 A443 15af multicolored .45 .25
1109 A443 19af multicolored .90 .25
1110 A443 21af multicolored 1.00 .25
Nos. 1104-1110 (7) 3.35 1.75

UN World Food Day — A444

Fruit-bearing trees.

1984, Oct. 16
1111 A444 2af multicolored .25 .25
1112 A444 4af multicolored .25 .25
1113 A444 6af multicolored .35 .25
1114 A444 9af multicolored .50 .25
1115 A444 12af multicolored .60 .25
1116 A444 15af multicolored .75 .25
1117 A444 26af multicolored 1.25 .25
Nos. 1111-1117 (7) 3.95 1.75

People's Democratic Party, 20th Anniv. A445

1985, Jan. 1
1118 A445 25af multicolored 1.25 .45

Farmer's Day A446

1af, Oxen. 3af, Mare, foal. 7af, Brown horse. 8af, White horse, vert. 15af, Sheep, sheep-skins. 16af, Shepherd, cattle, sheep. 25af, Family, camels.

1985, Mar. 2
1119 A446 1af multicolored .35 .25
1120 A446 3af multicolored .35 .25
1121 A446 7af multicolored .35 .25
1122 A446 8af multicolored .60 .25
1123 A446 15af multicolored .95 .25
1124 A446 16af multicolored 1.10 .35
1125 A446 25af multicolored 1.60 .45
Nos. 1119-1125 (7) 5.30 2.05

Geologist's Day — A447

1985, Apr. 5
1126 A447 4af multicolored .35 .25

Lenin and Peasant Petitioners A448

Lenin and: 10af, Lenin and Peasant Petition-ers. 15af, Revolutionaries, 1917, Leningrad. 25af, Lenin leading Revolutionary Guards, 1917. 50af, Portrait.

1985, Apr. 21 Perf. 12x12½
1127 A448 10af multicolored .70 .25
1128 A448 15af multicolored .85 .25
1129 A448 25af multicolored 1.50 .40
Nos. 1127-1129 (3) 3.05 .90
Souvenir Sheet
1130 A448 50af multicolored 2.50 1.50

Saur Revolution, 7th Anniv. — A449

1985, Apr. 27
1131 A449 21af multicolored 1.00 .30

Berlin-Treptow Soviet War Memorial,
Red Army at Siege of Berlin,
1945 — A450

9af, Victorious Motherland monument, fireworks over Kremlin. 10af, Caecilienhof, site of Potsdam Treaty signing, Great Britain, USSR & US flags.

1985, May 9   *Perf. 12½x12*
1132	A450	6af multicolored	.60	.25
1133	A450	9af multicolored	.85	.25
1134	A450	10af multicolored	1.10	.25
	Nos. 1132-1134 (3)		2.55	.75

End of World War II, defeat of Nazi Germany, 40th anniv.

INTELSAT,
20th Anniv.
A451

Designs: 6af, INTELSAT I satellite orbiting Earth. 9af, INTELSAT VI. 10af, Delta D rocket launch, Cape Canaveral, vert.

1985, Apr. 6   *Perf. 12x12½, 12½x12*   **Litho.**
1135	A451	6af multicolored	.50	.25
1136	A451	9af multicolored	.70	.25
1137	A451	10af multicolored	.95	.25
	Nos. 1135-1137 (3)		2.15	.75

12th World Youth
Festival,
Moscow — A452

7af, Olympic stadium, Moscow. 12af, Festival emblem. 13af, Kremlin. 18af, Folk doll, emblem.

1985, May 5
1138	A452	7af multicolored	.25	.25
1139	A452	12af multicolored	.45	.25
1140	A452	13af multicolored	.55	.35
1141	A452	18af multicolored	.70	.60
	Nos. 1138-1141 (4)		1.95	1.45

Intl. Child
Survival
Campaign
A453

1985, June 1
1142	A453	1af Weighing child	.25	.25
1143	A453	2af Immunization	.25	.25
1144	A453	4af Breastfeeding	.35	.25
1145	A453	5af Mother, child	.40	.25
	Nos. 1142-1145 (4)		1.25	1.00

Flowers
A454

2af, Oenothera affinis. 4af, Erythrina crista-galli. 8af, Tillandsia aeranthos. 13af, Vinca major. 18af, Mirabilis jalapa. 25af, Cypella herbertii. 30af, Clytostoma callistegioides. 75af, Sesbania punicea, horiz.

1985, July 5
1146	A454	2af multicolored	.25	.25
1147	A454	4af multicolored	.35	.25
1148	A454	8af multicolored	.60	.25
1149	A454	13af multicolored	.95	.25
1150	A454	18af multicolored	1.40	.35
1151	A454	25af multicolored	1.90	.45
1152	A454	30af multicolored	2.50	.60
	Nos. 1146-1152 (7)		7.95	2.40

Souvenir Sheet
Perf. 12½x11½
1153	A454	75af multicolored	6.00	3.50

ARGENTINA '85.

Independence, 66th Anniv. — A455

1985, Aug. 19   *Perf. 12x12½*
1154	A455	33af Mosque	1.50	.45

Pashto's
and
Balutchi's
Day
A456

1985, Aug. 30
1155	A456	25af multicolored	1.50	.25

UN Decade
for Women
A457

1985, Sept. 22
1156	A457	10af Emblems	.70	.25

World
Tourism
Day, 10th
Anniv. —
A457a

1af, Guldara Stupa. 2af, Mirwais Tomb, vert. 10af, Statue of Bamyan, vert. 13af, No Gumbad Mosque, vert. 14af, Pule Kheshti Mosque. 15af, Bost Citadel. 20af, Ghazni Minaret, vert.

1985, Sept. 27   **Litho.**   *Perf. 12*
1156A	A457a	1af multi	.25	.25
1156B	A457a	2af multi	.25	.25
1156C	A457a	10af multi	.60	.25
1156D	A457a	13af multi	.85	.25
1156E	A457a	14af multi	.95	.25
1156F	A457a	15af multi	1.00	.25
1156G	A457a	20af multi	1.40	.25
	Nos. 1156A-1156G (7)		5.30	1.75

Sports —
A457b

Perf. 12x12½, 12½x12

1985, Oct. 3   **Litho.**
1156H	A457b	1af Boxing	.25	.25
1156I	A457b	2af Volleyball	.25	.25
1156J	A457b	3af Soccer, vert.	.50	.25
1156K	A457b	12af Buzkashi	.75	.25
1156L	A457b	14af Weight lifting	.95	.25
1156M	A457b	18af Wrestling	1.00	.25
1156N	A457b	25af Peg sticking	1.25	.25
	Nos. 1156H-1156N (7)		4.95	1.85

World Food
Day —
A457c

1985, Oct. 16
1156O	A457c	25af multicolored	.95	.30

UN 40th
Anniv. — A458

1985, Oct. 24   *Perf. 12½x12*
1157	A458	22af multicolored	1.10	.30

A459

A459a

A459b

A459c

Birds — A459d

2af, Jay. 4af, Plover, hummingbird. 8af, Pheasant. 13af, Hoopoe. 18af, Falcon. 25af, Partridge. 30af, Pelicans, horiz. 75af, Parakeets.

1985, Oct. 25   *Perf. 12½x12, 12x12½*
1158	A459	2af multicolored	.25	.25
1159	A459a	4af multicolored	1.00	.50
1160	A459b	8af multicolored	1.10	.50
1161	A459a	13af multicolored	1.75	.95
1162	A459	18af multicolored	2.00	1.00
1163	A459b	25af multicolored	3.00	1.60
1164	A459c	30af multicolored	4.00	1.90
	Nos. 1158-1164 (7)		13.10	6.70

Souvenir Sheet
Perf. 12x12½
1165	A459d	75af multicolored	7.50	5.00

Mushrooms
A460

3af, Tricholomopsis rutilans. 4af, Boletus miniatoporus. 7af, Amanita rubescens. 11af, Boletus scaber. 12af, Coprinus atramentarius. 18af, Hypholoma. 20af, Boletus aurantiacus.

1985, June 10   **Litho.**   *Perf. 12½x12*
1165A	A460	3af multicolored	.25	.25
1166	A460	4af multicolored	.45	.25
1167	A460	7af multicolored	.70	.35
1168	A460	11af multicolored	.95	.60
1169	A460	12af multicolored	1.25	.60
1170	A460	18af multicolored	1.75	.75
1171	A460	20af multicolored	2.00	.75
	Nos. 1165A-1171 (7)		7.35	3.55

World Wildlife Fund — A461

1985, Nov. 25
1172	A461	2af Leopard, cubs	1.00	.25
1173	A461	9af Adult's head	2.25	.50
1174	A461	11af Adult	3.00	1.00
1175	A461	15af Cub	4.50	1.50
	Nos. 1172-1175 (4)		10.75	3.25

Motorcycle, Cent. — A462

Designs: Different makes and landmarks.

1985, Dec. 16
1176	A462	2af multicolored	.25	.25
1177	A462	4af multicolored	.35	.25
1178	A462	8af multicolored	.60	.25
1179	A462	13af multicolored	.95	.25
1180	A462	18af multicolored	1.10	.25
1181	A462	25af multicolored	1.60	.35
1182	A462	30af multicolored	2.50	.40
		Nos. 1176-1182 (7)	7.35	2.00

Souvenir Sheet
Perf. 11½x12½

1183	A462	75af multicolored	6.50	1.00

People's Democratic Party, 21st
Anniv. — A463

1986, Jan. 1   *Perf. 12½x12*
1184	A463	2af multicolored	.35	.25

27th Soviet Communist Party
Congress — A464

1986, Mar. 31
1185	A464	25af Lenin	.85	.40

First Man in Space, 25th
Anniv. — A465

Designs: 3af, Spacecraft. 7af, Soviet space achievement medal, vert. 9af, Rocket lift-off, vert. 11af, Yuri Gagarin, military decorations, vert. 13af, Gagarin, cosmonaut. 15af, Gagarin, politician. 17af, Gagarin wearing flight suit, vert.

Perf. 12½x12, 12x12½

1986, Apr. 12   *Litho.*
1186	A465	3af multicolored	.25	.25
1187	A465	7af multicolored	.25	.25
1188	A465	9af multicolored	.40	.25
1189	A465	11af multicolored	.50	.25
1190	A465	13af multicolored	.60	.25
1191	A465	15af multicolored	.65	.25
1192	A465	17af multicolored	.75	.25
		Nos. 1186-1192 (7)	3.40	1.75

Loya Jirgah (Grand Assembly) of the
People's Democratic Republic, 1st
Anniv.
A465a

1986, Apr. 23   *Litho.*   *Perf. 12x12½*
1192A	A465a	3af multicolored	.40	.25

Intl. Day of Labor
Solidarity — A465b

1986, May 1   *Perf. 12½x12*
1192B	A465b	5af multicolored	.50	.25

Intl. Red
Crescent
Day
A465c

1986, May 8   *Perf. 12x12½*
1192C	A465c	7af multicolored	.50	.25

Intl.
Children's
Day
A466

1af, Mother, children, vert. 3af, Mother, child, vert. 9af, Children, map.

1986, June 1   *Perf. 12*
1193	A466	1af multicolored	.25	.25
1194	A466	3af multicolored	.25	.25
1195	A466	9af multicolored	.40	.25
		Nos. 1193-1195 (3)	.90	.75

World
Youth Day
A466a

1986, July 31   *Perf. 12x12½*
1195A	A466a	15af multicolored	.70	.45

Pashtos'
and
Baluchis'
Day
A467

1986, Aug. 31   *Perf. 12x12½*
1196	A467	4af multicolored	.25	.25

Intl. Peace
Year — A468

1986, Sept. 30 Photo.   *Perf. 12½x12*
1197	A468	12af black & Prus blue	.60	.25

A469

1986 World Cup Soccer
Championships, Mexico — A470

Various soccer plays.

1986, Apr. 15   *Litho.*   *Perf. 12*
1198	A469	3af multi, vert.	.25	.25
1199	A469	4af multicolored	.35	.25
1200	A469	7af multicolored	.40	.25
1201	A469	11af multi, vert.	.70	.25
1202	A469	12af multicolored	.85	.25
1203	A469	18af multi, vert.	1.25	.25
1204	A469	20af multi, vert.	1.50	.25
		Nos. 1198-1204 (7)	5.30	1.75

Souvenir Sheet
Perf. 12½x12

1205	A470	75af multicolored	4.75	3.00

A471

1986, Apr. 21   *Perf. 12½x12*
1206	A471	16af Lenin	.75	.45

A472

1986, Apr. 27   *Litho.*   *Perf. 12½x12*
1207	A472	8af multicolored	.60	.25

Saur revolution, 8th anniv.

Natl.
Independence,
67th
Anniv. — A473

1986, Aug. 19 Litho.   *Perf. 12½x12*
1208	A473	10af multicolored	.50	.25

Literacy
Day
A474

1986, Sept. 18   *Perf. 12x12½*
1209	A474	2af multicolored	.25	.25

Dogs — A475

5af, St. Bernard. 7af, Collie. 8af, Pointer.
9af, Golden retriever. 11af, German shepherd.
15af, Bulldog. 20af, Afghan hound.

1986, May 19 Litho.   *Perf. 12x12½*
1210	A475	5af multicolored	.25	.25
1211	A475	7af multicolored	.40	.25
1212	A475	8af multicolored	.50	.25
1213	A475	9af multicolored	.60	.25
1214	A475	11af multicolored	.70	.25
1215	A475	15af multicolored	.95	.25
1216	A475	20af multicolored	1.25	.30
		Nos. 1210-1216 (7)	4.65	1.80

Lizards — A476

1986, July 7   *Perf. 12x12½, 12½x12½*
1217	A476	3af Cobra	.25	.25
1218	A476	4af shown	.25	.25
1219	A476	5af Praying mantis	.35	.25
1220	A476	8af Beetle	.50	.25
1221	A476	9af Tarantula	.60	.30
1222	A476	10af Python	.70	.35
1223	A476	11af Scorpions	.85	.35
		Nos. 1217-1223 (7)	3.50	2.00

Nos. 1217, 1219, 1221-1223 horiz.

STOCKHOLMIA '86 — A477

Ships.

1986, Aug. 28   *Perf. 12½x12*
1224	A477	4af multicolored	.40	.25
1225	A477	5af multicolored	.60	.25
1226	A477	6af multicolored	.70	.25
1227	A477	7af multicolored	.85	.25
1228	A477	8af multicolored	1.00	.25
1229	A477	9af multicolored	1.10	.25
1230	A477	11af multicolored	1.40	.25
		Nos. 1224-1230 (7)	6.05	1.75

Souvenir Sheet

1231	A477	50af Galley	4.25	2.00

A479

1986, Sept. 14   *Perf. 12*
1232	A479	3af lt blue, blk & olive gray	.40	.25

Reunion of Afghan tribes under the
Supreme Girgah.

A480

1986, Oct. 25   *Perf. 12½x12*
1233 A480 3af black & brt ver   .40   .25
Natl. youth solidarity.

Locomotives — A481

1986, June 21   *Perf. 12½x12*
1234 A481 4af multicolored   .25   .25
1235 A481 5af multicolored   .35   .25
1236 A481 6af multicolored   .45   .25
1237 A481 7af multicolored   .50   .25
1238 A481 8af multicolored   .65   .25
1239 A481 9af multicolored   .85   .25
1240 A481 11af multicolored   1.25   .25
   Nos. 1234-1240 (7)   4.30 1.75

Fish
A482

Various fish.

1986, May 25
1241 A482 5af multicolored   .25   .25
1242 A482 7af multicolored   .40   .25
1243 A482 8af multicolored   .50   .25
1244 A482 9af multicolored   .60   .25
1245 A482 11af multicolored   .85   .25
1246 A482 15af multicolored   1.10   .35
1247 A482 20af multicolored   1.50   .35
   Nos. 1241-1247 (7)   5.20 1.95

Saur
Revolution,
9th Anniv.
A483

1987, Apr. 27   *Perf. 12*
1248 A483 3af multicolored   .25   .25

Natl. Reconciliation — A484

1987, May 27   *Perf. 12x12½*
1249 A484 3af multicolored   .25   .25

A485   A486

UN Child Survival
Campaign — A487

1987, June 1   *Perf. 12*
1250 A485 1af multicolored   .25   .25
1251 A486 5af multicolored   .25   .25
1252 A487 9af multicolored   .35   .25
   Nos. 1250-1252 (3)   .85   .75

Conference
of
Clergymen
and Ulema,
1st Anniv.
A488

1987, June 30
1253 A488 5af multicolored   .35   .25

Butterflies — A489

1987, July 3
1254 A489 7af multicolored   .60   .35
1255 A489 9af multi, diff.   .75   .35
1256 A489 10af multi, diff.   1.00   .50
1257 A489 12af multi, diff.   1.50   .50
1258 A489 15af multi, diff.   1.60   .70
1259 A489 22af multi, diff.   2.25   .95
1260 A489 25af multi, diff.   2.50   .95
   Nos. 1254-1260 (7)   10.20 4.30
10af, 15af and 22af horiz.

A490

1987, Aug. 11
1261 A490 1af multicolored   .25   .25
1st election of local representatives for State
Power and Administration.

Natl. Independence, 68th Anniv. —
A490a

1987, Aug. 19
1261A A490a 3af multicolored   .25   .25

1st Artificial
Satellite (Sputnik),
30th
Anniv. — A491

1987, Oct. 4   Litho.   *Perf. 12½x12*
1262 A491 10af Sputnik   .40   .25
1263 A491 15af Rocket launch   .60   .25
1264 A491 25af Soyuz   .85   .25
   Nos. 1262-1264 (3)   1.85   .75

World Post
Day
A492

1987, Oct. 9   *Perf. 12x12½*
1265 A492 22af multicolored   1.10   .60

Intl. Communications and Transport
Day — A493

1987, Oct. 24   *Perf. 12½x12*
1266 A493 42af multicolored   4.75 1.00

October Revolution
in Russia, 70th
Anniv. — A494

1987, Nov. 7
1267 A494 25af Lenin   1.25   .70

Mice — A495

Various mice. Nos. 1269-1272 horiz.

1987, Dec. 6   *Perf. 12½x12, 12x12½*
1268 A495 2af multicolored   .40   .25
1269 A495 4af multi, diff.   .50   .25
1270 A495 8af multi, diff.   .60   .25
1271 A495 16af multi, diff.   1.00   .25
1272 A495 20af multi, diff.   1.25   .25
   Nos. 1268-1272 (5)   3.75 1.25

Medicinal
Plants — A496

1987, Nov. 11   Litho.   *Perf. 12*
1273 A496 3af Castor bean   .25   .25
1274 A496 6af Licorice   .45   .25
1275 A496 9af Chamomile   .75   .25
1276 A496 14af Datura   1.00   .25
1277 A496 18af Dandelion   1.25   .30
   Nos. 1273-1277 (5)   3.70 1.30

Pashto's and
Baluchis'
Day — A497

1987, Aug. 30
1278 A497 4af multicolored   .25   .25

Dinosaurs
A498

3af, Mesosaurus. 5af, Styracosaurus. 10af,
Uinatherium. 15af, Protoceratops. 20af, Stegosaurus. 25af, Ceratosaurus. 30af, Dinornis
maximus.

Perf. 12½x12, 12x12½
1988, June 6   Litho.
1279 A498 3af multicolored   .25   .25
1280 A498 5af multicolored   .25   .25
1281 A498 10af multicolored   .50   .25
1282 A498 15af multicolored   .75   .25
1283 A498 20af multicolored   1.00   .30
1284 A498 25af multicolored   1.40   .35
1285 A498 30af multicolored   1.90   .60
   Nos. 1279-1285 (7)   6.05 2.25
Nos. 1280-1283 horiz.

Pashtos' and
Baluchis'
Day — A499

1988, Aug. 30   *Perf. 12½x12*
1286 A499 23af multicolored   .95   .60

Afghan-Soviet
Joint Space
Flight — A500

1988, Aug. 30
1287 A500 32af multicolored   1.25   .50

Valentina
Tereshkova, 1st
Woman in Space,
25th
Anniv. — A501

10af, Portrait, rocket, horiz. 15af, Lift-off,
dove. 25af, Spacecraft, Earth, horiz.

1988, Oct. 16   *Perf. 12x12½, 12½x12*
1288 A501 10af multicolored   .85   .35
1289 A501 15af multicolored   .85   .30
1290 A501 25af multicolored   1.00   .45
   Nos. 1288-1290 (3)   2.70 1.10

Traditional Crafts — A502

Perf. 12x12½, 12½x12

1988, Nov. 9　　　　　　**Litho.**
1291	A502	2af	Pitcher, bowls	.25 .25
1292	A502	4af	Vases	.25 .25
1293	A502	5af	Dress	.25 .25
1294	A502	9af	Mats, napkins	.35 .25
1295	A502	15af	Pocketbooks	.60 .25
1296	A502	23af	Jewelry	.95 .25
1297	A502	50af	Furniture	1.90 .25
		Nos. 1291-1297 (7)		4.55 1.75

Nos. 1291-1292, 1294-1297 horiz.

Precious and Semiprecious Gems — A503

1988, Dec. 5　　　　　　**Perf. 12½x12**
1298	A503	13af	Emeralds	1.00 .25
1299	A503	37af	Lapiz lazuli	2.25 .60
1300	A503	40af	Rubies	2.50 .75
		Nos. 1298-1300 (3)		5.75 1.60

1988 Winter Olympics, Calgary — A504

2af, Women's figure skating. 5af, Skiing. 9af, Bobsledding. 22af, Biathlon. 37af, Speed skating.

75af, Ice hockey.

1988, Dec. 25
1301	A504	2af	multicolored	.25 .25
1301A	A504	5af	multicolored	.25 .25
1301B	A504	9af	multicolored	.50 .25
1301C	A504	22af	multicolored	1.00 .35
1301D	A504	37af	multicolored	2.25 .65

Size: 80x60mm
1302	A504	75af	multicolored	4.50 3.50
		Nos. 1301-1302 (6)		8.75 5.25

A510

A511

A512

A513

A513a

Flowers — A514

Various flowering plants.

Perf. 12x12½, 12½x12

1988, Jan. 27　　　　　　**Litho.**
1303	A510	3af	multicolored	.25 .25
1304	A511	5af	multicolored	.35 .25
1305	A511	7af	multi, vert.	.50 .25
1306	A512	9af	multicolored	.70 .25
1307	A513	12af	multicolored	1.25 .35
1308	A513a	15af	multicolored	1.60 .35
1309	A514	24af	multicolored	2.25 .35
		Nos. 1303-1309 (7)		6.90 2.05

Traditional Musical Instruments A515

String and percussion instruments.

1988, Jan. 15　　　**Litho.**　　　**Perf. 12**
1310	A515	1af	shown	.25 .25
1311	A515	3af	drums	.25 .25
1312	A515	5af	multi, diff.	.30 .25
1313	A515	15af	multi, diff.	.70 .25
1314	A515	18af	multi, diff.	1.00 .30
1315	A515	25af	multi, diff.	1.40 .30
1316	A515	33af	multi, diff.	1.90 .30
		Nos. 1310-1316 (7)		5.80 1.90

Admission of Afghanistan to the ITU and UPU, 60th Anniv. — A516

1988, Apr. 13　　**Litho.**　　**Perf. 12**
1317	A516	20af	multicolored	.85 .50

Saur Revolution, 10th Anniv. A517

1988, Apr. 23
1318	A517	10af	multicolored	.50 .35

Fruit A518

2af, Baskets, compote. 4af, Four baskets. 7af, Basket. 8af, Grapes, vert. 16af, Market. 22af, Market, diff. 25af, Vendor, vert.

1988, July 18　　**Litho.**　　**Perf. 12**
1319	A518	2af	multicolored	.25 .25
1320	A518	4af	multicolored	.35 .25
1321	A518	7af	multicolored	.45 .25
1322	A518	8af	multicolored	.50 .25
1323	A518	16af	multicolored	.85 .35
1324	A518	22af	multicolored	1.25 .35
1325	A518	25af	multicolored	1.90 .35
		Nos. 1319-1325 (7)		5.55 2.05

Jawaharlal Nehru (1889-1964), 1st Prime Minister of Independent India — A519

1988, Nov. 14
1326	A519	40af	multicolored	2.25 .85

Natl. Independence, 69th Anniv. — A520

1988, Aug. 1
1327	A520	24af	multicolored	1.25 .70

Intl. Red Cross and Red Crescent Organizations, 125th Annivs. — A521

1988, Sept. 26
1328	A521	10af	multicolored	.85 .50

Natl. Reconciliation Institute, 2nd Anniv. — A522

1989, Jan. 4
1329	A522	4af	multicolored	.25 .25

Chess A523

Boards, early matches and hand-made chessmen.

1989, Feb. 2　　**Litho.**　　**Perf. 12x12½**
1330	A523	2af	Bishop	.25 .25
1331	A523	3af	Queen	.35 .25
1332	A523	4af	King (bust)	.45 .25
1333	A523	7af	King, diff.	.70 .25
1334	A523	16af	Knight	1.10 .25
1335	A523	24af	Pawn	1.60 .35
1336	A523	45af	Bishop, diff.	2.75 .45
		Nos. 1330-1336 (7)		7.20 2.05

Paintings by Picasso — A524

Designs: 4af, *The Old Jew.* 6af, *The Two Mountebanks.* 8af, *Portrait of Ambrouse Vollar.* 22af, *Woman of Majorca.* 35af, *Acrobat on the Ball.* 75af, *Usine a Horta de Ebro.*

1989, Feb. 13　　**Litho.**　　**Perf. 12½x12**
1341	A524	4af	multicolored	.35 .25
1342	A524	6af	multicolored	.45 .25
1343	A524	8af	multicolored	.55 .25
1344	A524	22af	multicolored	1.25 .25
1345	A524	35af	multicolored	2.50 .25

Size: 71x90mm

Imperf
1346	A524	75af	multicolored	4.75 1.25
		Nos. 1341-1346 (6)		9.85 2.50

Fauna — A525

3af, Allactaga euphratica. 4af, Equus hemionus. 14af, Felis lynx. 35af, Gypaetus barbatus. 44af, Capra falconeri.

100af, Naja oxiana.

1989, Feb. 20　　**Litho.**　　**Perf. 12½x12**
1347	A525	3af	multicolored	.35 .25
1348	A525	4af	multicolored	.35 .25
1349	A525	14af	multicolored	1.00 .35
1350	A525	35af	multicolored	3.75 1.60
1351	A525	44af	multicolored	2.50 1.25

Size: 71x91mm

Imperf
1352	A525	100af	multicolored	7.75 3.00
		Nos. 1347-1352 (6)		15.70 6.70

Intl. Women's
Day — A526

1989, Mar. 8   **Perf. 12½x12**
1353 A526 8af multicolored   .45   .25

Restoration and Development of
San'a, Yemen — A527

1988, Dec. 27   **Litho.**   **Perf. 12**
1354 A527 32af multicolored   1.60   1.10

Agriculture
Day
A528

1af, Cattle. 2af, Old and new plows. 3af,
Field workers.

1989, Mar. 21
1355 A528 1af multicolored   .25   .25
1356 A528 2af multicolored   .25   .25
1357 A528 3af multicolored   .25   .25
    Nos. 1355-1357 (3)   .75   .75

World Meteorology Day — A529

32af, Emblems. 40af, Weather station, balloon, vert.

1989, Mar. 23
1358 A529 27af shown   1.25   .25
1359 A529 32af multicolored   1.75   .25
1360 A529 40af multicolored   2.25   .25
    Nos. 1358-1360 (3)   5.25   .75

Saur
Revolution,
11th Anniv.
A530

1989, Apr. 27
1361 A530 20af multicolored   1.10   .25

Classic Automobiles — A531

5af, 1910 Duchs, Germany. 10af, 1911
Ford, US. 20af, 1911 Renault, France. 25af,
1911, Russo-Balte, Russia. 30af, 1926 Fiat,
Italy.

1989, Dec. 30   **Litho.**   **Perf. 12½x12**
1362 A531 5af multi   .45   .25
1363 A531 10af multi   .75   .25
1364 A531 20af multi   1.40   .25
1365 A531 25af multi   1.60   .35
1366 A531 30af multi   1.90   .35
    Nos. 1362-1366 (5)   6.10   1.45

Asia-Pacific Telecommunity, 10th
Anniv. — A532

27af, Emblem, satellite dish.

1989, Aug. 3   **Perf. 12**
1367 A532 3af shown   .25   .25
1368 A532 27af multicolored   1.10   .25

Teacher's
Day
A533

1989, May 30   **Litho.**   **Perf. 12**
1369 A533 42af multicolored   2.25   .35

French Revolution,
Bicent. — A534

1989, July   **Litho.**   **Perf. 12**
1370 A534 25af multicolored   1.60   .95

Natl. Independence, 70th
Anniv. — A535

1989, Aug. 18   **Litho.**   **Perf. 12**
1371 A535 25af multicolored   1.25   .35

A536

1989, Aug. 30
1372 A536 3af multicolored   .25   .25
Pashtos' and Baluchis' Day.

Birds — A537

3af, Platalea leucorodia. 5af, Porphyrio
porhyrio. 10af, Botaurus stellaris, horiz. 15af,
Pelecanus onocrotalus. 20af, Netta rufina.
25af, Cygnus olor. 30af, Phalacrocorax carbo,
horiz.

1989, Dec. 5   **Litho.**   **Perf. 12**
1373 A537 3af multicolored   .25   .25
1374 A537 5af multicolored   .50   .25
1375 A537 10af multicolored   .95   .45
1376 A537 15af multicolored   1.25   .55
1377 A537 20af multicolored   1.60   .60
1378 A537 25af multicolored   2.25   .70
1379 A537 30af multicolored   2.50   .95
    Nos. 1373-1379 (7)   9.30   3.75

Tourism — A538

1af, Mosque. 2af, Minaret. 3af, Buzkashi,
horiz. 4af, Jet over Hendo Kush, horiz.

1989, Dec.
1380 A538 1af multicolored   1.60   —
1381 A538 2af multicolored   3.25   —
1382 A538 3af multicolored   4.75   —
1383 A538 4af multicolored   6.50   —
    Nos. 1380-1383 (4)   16.10

Mavlavi Allahdad Balkhi, President of
Post of the Afghanistan Postal Administration, has declared that "the stamps
which have been printed after year
1989 are false stamps."

The following stamps have been con-
demned as unauthorized by the Afghan
Ministry of Communications:

Dated 1996: *Mushrooms,* 6 stamps +
souvenir sheet. *Bears,* 5 stamps + souvenir sheet. *1998 Word Soccer Cup
Championships,* 6 stamps + souvenir
sheet. *Silkworms,* 6 stamps + souvenir
sheet. *Domestic Cats,* 6 stamps + souvenir sheet. *Horses,* 5 stamps + souvenir sheet. *Islamic Revolution,* 6 stamps.
*Independence Anniv./Honoring Prophet
Mohammed,* 2 stamps.

Dated 1997: *Tulips,* 6 stamps + souvenir sheet. *Llamas & Camels,* 6
stamps + souvenir sheet. *Domestic
Cats,* 6 stamps + souvenir sheet. *Wildflowers,* 6 stamps + souvenir sheet.
Early Sailing Ships (triangles), 6 stamps
+ souvenir sheet. *1998 Word Soccer
Cup Championships,* 6 stamps + souvenir sheet. *Mushrooms,* 6 stamps +
souvenir sheet.

Dated 1998: *Mushrooms,* 6 stamps +
souvenir sheet. *Butterflies,* 6 stamps +
souvenir sheet. *Princess Diana,* 9
stamps in a miniature sheet. *WWF
(Wild Sheep),* strip of 4 stamps. *Wildlife,*
12 stamps. *Dogs,* 6 stamps + souvenir
sheet. *Locomotives,* 6 stamps + souvenir sheet. *Prehistoric Animals,* 6 stamps
+ souvenir sheet. *Antique Cars,* 6
stamps + souvenir sheet. *Fish,* 6
stamps + souvenir sheet. *Birds,* 6
stamps + souvenir sheet.

Dated 1999: *Chess,* 6 stamps + souvenir sheet. *Mushrooms,* 6 stamps +
souvenir sheet. *Locomotives,* 6 stamps
+ souvenir sheet. *Dogs,* 6 stamps +
souvenir sheet. *Minerals,* 6 stamps +
souvenir sheet. *Snails,* 6 stamps + souvenir sheet. *Vintage Race Cars,* 6
stamps + souvenir sheet. *China '99,* 12
stamps in a miniature sheet. *Cacti,* 6
stamps + souvenir sheet. *Horses,* 6
stamps + souvenir sheet. *Ferrari Automobiles,* 6 stamps + souvenir sheet.
Orchids, 6 stamps + souvenir sheet.
Parrots, 6 stamps + souvenir sheet.
Sailing Ships, 6 stamps + souvenir
sheet.

Dated 2000: *Cats,* 6 stamps + souvenir sheet. *WIPA 2000 (Birds),* 6 stamps
+ souvenir sheet.

Dated 2001: *Mushrooms,* 6 stamps +
souvenir sheet. *Locomotives,* 6 stamps
+ souvenir sheet.

In addition to these sets, a number of
bogus illegal issues have appeared.
These issues include:

Beetles: miniature sheet of 9 different
stamps.
Birds: 2 miniature sheets of 9 different stamps each.
Boats: 3 miniature sheets of 9 different stamps each.
Cars (Vintage): 3 miniature sheets of
9 different stamps each.
Cats: 3 miniature sheets of 9 different
stamps each.
Chess: 3 miniature sheets of 9 different stamps each.
Dinosaurs: 3 miniature sheets of 9
different stamps each.
Dogs: 3 miniature sheets of 9 different stamps each.
Eagles & Owls: miniature sheet of 9
different stamps.
Eagles: miniature sheet of 9 different
stamps.
Elvis Presley: 3 miniature sheets of 9
different stamps each.
Fauna of Afghanistan: miniature
sheet of 9 different stamps.
Fish: miniature sheet of 9 different
stamps.
Great People of the 20th Century:
miniature sheet of 9 different stamps.
Horses: 2 miniature sheets of 9 different stamps each.
Korea/Japan World Soccer Cup: 2
souvenir sheets.
Locomotives: 2 souvenir sheets
inscribed "Trains."
Locomotives: miniature sheet of 9 different stamps, inscribed "English
Trains."
Marilyn Monroe: 3 miniature sheets
of 9 different stamps each.
Marilyn Monroe: Block of 4 different
stamps.
Mother Teresa & Pope John Paul II: 3
miniature sheets of 6 different stamps
each + 3 souvenir sheets.
Osama Ben Laden Wanted Poster: 1
stamp in miniature sheet of 9.
Owls: 3 miniature sheets of 9 different stamps each + 2 souvenir sheets.
Paintings (Classic Posters): miniature
sheet of 9 different stamps.
Paintings (Impressionists): 3 miniature sheets of 6 different stamps each +
3 souvenir sheets.
Plants: miniature sheet of 9 different
stamps + souvenir sheet depicting
orchid.
Princess Diana: miniature sheet of 9
different stamps.
Sports: 4 miniature sheets of 9 different stamps each, inscribed "Formula
2000."

Transitional Islamic State

Ahmed Shah
Masood (1953?-
2001), Military
Leader — A539

2002   **Litho.**   **Perf. 13½x13**
1384 A539 14,000af multi   7.50   —

National Understanding — A540

2002, July 18   **Litho.**   **Perf. 13x13½**
1385 A540 11,000af multi   6.50   6.50

Destruction of Bamyan Buddha Statue by Taliban Government A541

2002, July 18   *Perf. 13½x13*
1386   A541   25,000af multi   7.50   7.50

Universal Declaration of Human Rights, 55th Anniv. — A542

2002, Dec. 10   *Litho.*   *Perf. 13x12¾*
1387   A542   4af multi   3.50   3.50

Farmer's Day A543

Designs: 3af, Tractor. 6af, Oxen pulling plow.

2003, Mar. 21   *Litho.*   *Perf. 12¾x13*
1388   A543   3af shown   5.00   —
1389   A453   6af multi   10.00   —

Miniature Sheet

Orchids — A544

No. 1390: a, 9af, Calanthe veitchii. b, 13af, Eulanthe sanderiana. c, 17af, Ordontioda vuylstekeae. d, 20af, Dendrobium infundibulum. e, 30af, Miltonsiopsis roezlii. f, 40af, Cattleya labiata. g, 100af, Vanda coerulea.

2003, Apr. 17   *Litho.*   *Perf. 13x12¾*
1390   A544   Sheet of 7, #a-g,
     + 2 labels   22.50   22.50

Birthday of Mohammed — A545

2003, May 14   *Litho.*   *Perf. 12¾x13*
1391   A545   10af multi   6.00   6.00

World Tuberculosis Day — A546

Designs: 1af, Boy and girl holding sign. 4af, Caricatures of doctors and patients, horiz. 9af, Caricatures of patients, horiz.

Perf. 13x12¾, 12¾x13
2003, May 18   *Litho.*
1392-1394   A546   Set of 3   6.00   6.00

Loya Jurga A547

2003, June 16   *Litho.*   *Perf. 12¾x13*
1395   A547   20af multi   4.00   4.00

Day Against Narcotics — A548

Designs: 1af, Map of Afghanistan, poppy. 2af, Poppy capsule, skulls, vert. 5af, Farmer and tractor in poppy field.
10af, Poppy capsule, skulls.

Perf. 12¾x13, 13x12¾
2003, June 25   *Litho.*
1396-1398   A548   Set of 3   3.50   3.50
Souvenir Sheet
1398A   A548   10af multi   2.75   2.75

Dogs — A549

Designs: 10af, Rottweiler. 20af, Cocker spaniel. 30af, Doberman pinscher. 40af, Afghan hound. 50af, Giant schnauzer. 60af, Boxer.
150af, Afghan hound, diff.

2003, July 4   *Litho.*   *Perf. 13x12¾*
1399-1404   A549   Set of 6   20.00   20.00
Souvenir Sheet
1405   A549   150af multi   14.50   14.50

Lighthouses A550

Designs: 10af, Bird Island, South Africa. 20af, Cordouan, France. 30af, Mahota Pagoda, China. 50af, Bay Canh, Viet Nam. 60af, Cap Roman Rock, South Africa. 100af, Mikomoto Shima, Japan.
150af, Bell Rock, Great Britain.

2003, Aug. 5
1406-1411   A550   Set of 6   22.50   22.50
Souvenir Sheet
1412   A550   150af multi   14.50   14.50

Independence, 84th Anniv. — A551

2003, Aug. 19   *Litho.*   *Perf. 12¾x13*
1413   A551   15af multi   3.50   3.50

Intl. Literacy Day A552

2003, Sept. 8   *Litho.*   *Perf. 12¾x13*
1414   A552   2af multi   1.00   1.00

Miniature Sheet

Heritage of Afghanistan — A553

No. 1415: a, 20af, Fragments of rock drawing depicting a woman, Bamiyan. b, 40af, Head of Buddha, Gandhara. c, 60af, Statue from Takht-i-Bahi Monastery, Gandhara. d, 100af, Hand of Buddha, Bamiyan.

2003, Oct. 10   *Litho.*   *Perf. 13x12¾*
1415   A553   Sheet of 4, #a-d   22.50   22.50

Revelation of the Koran to Mohammed — A554

2003, Nov. 23   *Litho.*   *Perf. 12¾x13*
1416   A554   9af multi   6.50   6.50

A555

Afghanistan Tourism Day—A555a

Designs: 8af, 25af, Fort. 12af, Bust, jar, historical artifacts.

2003, Dec. 16   *Litho.*   *Perf. 12¾x13*
1417   A555   4af shown   .75   .75
1418   A555a   8af ol grn & multi   1.00   1.00
1418A   A555   12af multi   1.25   1.25
    Nos. 1417-1418A (3)   3.00   3.00
Souvenir Sheet
1418B   A555a   25af lil & multi   3.00   3.00

Animals A556

Designs: 6af, Leopard. 11af, Jackal. 15af, Wild goat.
40af, Leopard facing left.

2003   *Litho.*   *Perf. 12¾*
1419-1421   A556   Set of 3   5.00   5.00
Souvenir Sheet
1422   A556   40af multi   8.25   8.25

World Post Day A557

2003, Oct. 9   *Litho.*   *Perf. 12¾x13*
1423   A557   8af multi   2.50   2.50

Int'l. Women's Day — A558

2004   *Litho.*   *Perf. 12¾x13*
1424   A558   6af multi   1.50   1.50

World Tuberculosis Day — A559

Designs: 1af, Woman, hands holding medicine and bloody tissue. 4af, Woman wearing mask, child. 9af, Eight men. 12af, Man, map of Afghanistan, vert. 15af, Doctor touching patient, people in white in background, vert.

Perf. 12¾x13, 13x12¾
2004, Mar. 23   *Litho.*
1425   A559   1af multi   .35   .35
1426   A559   4af multi   .75   .75
1427   A559   9af multi   1.50   1.50
1428   A559   12af multi   2.00   2.00
1429   A559   15af multi   2.50   2.50
    Nos. 1425-1429 (5)   7.10   7.10

Pres. Hamid
Karzai — A560

Karzai and Map
of Afghanistan
A561

2004, Oct. 7   *Perf. 13x12¾*
1430 A560 12af multi   3.00 3.00
1431 A561 12af multi   5.00 5.00

Oath of Pres. Karzai.

First Direct Presidential
Election — A562

Denominations: 15af, 25af.

2004, Oct. 9   Litho.   Perf. 12¾x13
1432-1433 A562   Set of 2   7.00 7.00

Two types of Arabic inscriptions exist on
each stamp. Values the same.

Afghanistan postal officials declared
a set of eight stamps depicting soccer
players and a set of eight stamps
depicting FIFA Presidents as "not
authorized."

The editors are seeking more information about the status of a set of four
Worldwide Fund for Nature stamps
depicting the Himalayan musk deer.

Souvenir Sheet

Inauguration of Pres. Karzai — A563

2004, Dec. 7   Litho.   Perf. 13½
1434 A563 100af multi   18.00 18.00

Diplomatic Relations Between
Afghanistan and People's Republic of
China, 50th Anniv. — A564

2005, Jan. 20   Litho.   Perf. 12
1435 A564 25af multi   3.00 3.00

**Souvenir Sheet
Printed On Cloth
Without Gum
Perf. 13¼x13**
1436 A564 150af multi   24.00 24.00
No. 1436 contains one 60x40mm stamp.

Mine
Clearance
Campaign
A565

Designs: 1af, Mine danger warning sign.
2af, Mine clearer with dog, vert. 3af. Mine
clearer with metal detector, vert.

2006, Apr. 4   Perf. 13¼x13, 13x13¼
1437-1439 A565   Set of 3   2.00 2.00

Independence,
87th
Anniv. — A566

2006, Aug. 19   Perf. 13x13¼
1440 A566 45af multi   8.00 8.00

World Literacy
Day — A567

2006, Sept. 8
1441 A567 12af multi   2.00 2.00

World Post
Day
A568

Color of "2006": No. 1442, 15af, Light green.
No. 1443, 15af, Black.

2006, Sept. 9   Perf. 13¼x13
1442-1443 A568   Set of 2   4.50 4.50

The length of the Arabic inscription on the
top of the stamp is longer on No. 1442 than on
No. 1443.

World
Tourism
Day
A569

Designs: 15af, Lamp, pitchers, bowl, building. 30af, Pitchers, cup, mountain.

2006, Sept. 27   Litho.   Perf. 13¼x13
1444 A569 15af multi   2.50 2.50
1445 A569 30af multi   4.50 4.50

Campaign for
Elimination of
Violence Against
Women — A570

Designs: 12af, Woman behind barbed wire,
chain, hands unlocking lock. 14af, Woman,
roots. 19af, Eyes of woman, needle and
thread closing eye hole of burqa, horiz.

Perf. 13x13¼, 13¼x13¼
2006, Nov. 25   **Litho.**
1446-1448 A570   Set of 3   6.75 6.75

Mevlana
Jalal ad-Din
ar-Rumi
(1207-73),
Islamic
Philosopher
A571

Designs: 65af, Birthplace at Balkh. 85af,
Mevlana and whirling dervishes, vert.
150af, Mevlana, whirling dervishes, birthplace at Balkh, horiz.

Perf. 13¼x13, 13x13¼
2006, Nov. 26
1449-1450 A571   Set of 2   15.00 15.00
Size: 106x78mm
Imperf
1451 A571 150af multi   30.00 30.00

No. 1451 contains two perforated labels
lacking country name or value. See Iran No.
2911, Syria No. 1574, Turkey No. 2971.

Successful
Completion
of Bonn
Process
A572

2007, Apr. 19   Perf. 13¼x13
1452 A572 25af multi   4.00 4.00

Dated 2006.

Mevlana
Jalal ad-Din
ar-Rumi
(1207-73),
Islamic
Philosopher
A573

2007, May 24
1453 A573 40af multi   6.00 6.00

Milli Attan
Dance
A574

2007, Aug. 19
1454 A574 38af multi   6.00 6.00

Natl. Day of Fine
Arts — A575

Singers: 20af, Ustad Awal Mir. 22af, Mirmun
Parwin.

2007, Sept. 25   Perf. 13x13¼
1455-1456 A575   Set of 2   7.50 7.50

Third Meeting of Economic
Cooperation Organization Postal
Authorities, Tehran — A576

2007, Dec. 22   Perf. 13¼x13
1457 A576 8af multi   2.00 2.00

National
Unity — A577

Emperors: 25af, Ahmad Shah Baba (c.
1723-73). 30af, Mirwais Nika. 34af, Sultan
Mahmood Ghaznawi (979-1030).

2007, Dec. 22   Perf. 13¼x13¼
1458-1460 A577   Set of 3   12.00 12.00

Red Crescent
Society — A578

2009, Jan. 21   Litho.   Perf. 13¼x13¼
1461 A578 17af multi   2.40 2.40

Rudaki (c. 859-
c.940),
Poet — A579

2009, Jan. 21
1462 A579 55af multi   6.50 6.50

World Enviornmental Protection
Day — A580

2010, Jan. 1   Litho.   Perf. 13½x12¾
1463 A580 5af multi   1.25 1.25

World
Literacy
Day
A581

2011, Jan. 1   Litho.   Perf. 14
1464 A581 22af multi   4.00 4.00

Emblem and Flags of Members of South Asian Association for Regional Cooperation
A583

2012, Feb. 1   Litho.   Perf. 13½x12¾
1466 A583 40af multi   6.50 6.50

World Peace Day — A584

2012, Feb. 1   Litho.   Perf. 13½x12¾
1467 A584 50af multi   6.50 6.50

Dated 2011.

SEMI-POSTAL STAMPS

Catalogue values for unused stamps in this section are for Never Hinged items.

No. 373 Surcharged in Violet

1952, July 12   Unwmk.   Perf. 12½
B1 A122 40p + 30p cerise   5.25 3.00
B2 A122 125p + 30p cerise   7.75 3.50

1000th anniv. of the birth of Avicenna.

Children at Play — SP1

1955, July 3   Typo.   Perf. 11
B3 SP1 35p + 15p dk green   1.25 .70
B4 SP1 125p + 25p purple   2.50 1.25

The surtax was for child welfare.
Exist imperf. Values: unused $6.50; used $7.

Amir Sher Ali Khan, Tiger Head Stamp and Zahir Shah — SP2

1955, July 2   Litho.
B5 SP2 35p + 15p carmine   1.00 .55
B6 SP2 125p + 25p pale vio bl 1.90 1.00

85th anniv. of the Afghan post.
Exist imperf. Values, set: unused $5; used $6.

Children at Play — SP3

1956, June 20   Typo.
B7 SP3 35p + 15p brt vio bl   .90 .40
B8 SP3 140p + 15p dk org brn 2.25 .85

Issued for Children's Day. The surtax was for child welfare. No. B8 inscribed in French.
Exist imperf. Values, set: unused $8; used $8.75.

Pashtunistan Monument, Kabul — SP4

1956, Sept. 1   Litho.
B9   SP4 35p + 15p dp violet   .40 .25
B10 SP4 140p + 15p dk brown   1.10 .75

"Free Pashtunistan" Day. The surtax aided the "Free Pashtunistan" movement.
No. B9 measures 30½x19½mm; No. B10, 29x19mm. On sale and valid for use only on Sept. 1-2.
Exist imperf. Values, set: unused $6; used $7.50.

Globe and Sun — SP5

1956, Oct. 24   Perf. 11
B11 SP5 35p + 15p ultra   1.25 1.10
B12 SP5 140p + 15p red brown 2.10 1.75

Afghanistan's UN admission, 10th anniv.
Exist imperf. Values, set: unused $14; used $17.50.

Children on Seesaw SP6

1957, June 20   Unwmk.
B13 SP6 35p + 15p brt rose   .85 .55
B14 SP6 140p + 15p ultra   1.60 1.40

Children's Day. Surtax for child welfare.
Exist imperf. Values, set: unused $3.25; used $4.

UN Headquarters and Emblems SP7

1957, Oct. 24   Perf. 11 Rough
B15 SP7 35p + 15p red brown   .60 .40
B16 SP7 140p + 15p lt ultra   1.10 1.10

United Nations Day.
Exist imperf. Values, set: unused $6; used $7.50.

Swimming Pool and Children SP8

1958, June 22   Perf. 11
B17 SP8 35p + 15p rose   .65 .40
B18 SP8 140p + 15p dl red brn .80 .65

Children's Day. Surtax for child welfare.
Exist imperf. Values, set: unused $5; used $6.

Pashtunistan Flag — SP9

1958, Aug. 31
B19 SP9 35p + 15p lt blue   .40 .25
B20 SP9 140p + 15p red brown 1.00 .65

Issued for "Free Pashtunistan Day."
Exist imperf. Values, set: unused $4; used $5.

Children Playing Tug of War — SP10

1959, June 23   Litho.   Perf. 11
B21 SP10 35p + 15p brown vio   .60 .35
B22 SP10 165p + 15p brt pink 1.25 .50

Children's Day. Surtax for child welfare.
Exist imperf. Value set, unused or used, $5.

Pathans in Tribal Dance SP11

Perf. 11 Rough
1959, Sept.   Unwmk.
B23 SP11 35p + 15p green   .60 .35
B24 SP11 165p + 15p orange   1.25 .75

Issued for "Free Pashtunistan Day."
Exist imperf. Value set, unused or used, $2.50.

Afghan Cavalryman with UN Flag — SP12

1959, Oct. 24   Perf. 11 Rough
B25 SP12 35p + 15p orange   .35 .25
B26 SP12 165p + 15p lt bl grn .75 .45

Issued for United Nations Day.
Exist imperf. Value set, unused or used, $2.50.

Children SP13

1960, Oct. 23   Litho.
B27 SP13 75p + 25p lt ultra   .90 .35
B28 SP13 175p + 25p lt green 1.75 .50

Children's Day. Surtax for child welfare.
Exist imperf. Value set, unused or used, $2.75.

Man with Spray Gun SP14

1960, Sept. 6   Perf. 11 Rough
B29 SP14 50p + 50p orange   1.40 1.25
B30 SP14 175p + 50p red brown 3.50 2.75

11th anniversary of the WHO malaria control program in Afghanistan.
Exist imperf. Value set, unused or used, $7.50.

SP15

1960, Sept. 1   Unwmk.
B31 SP15 50p + 50p rose   .60 .30
B32 SP15 175p + 50p dk blue   1.40 1.10

Issued for "Free Pashtunistan Day."
Exist imperf. Value set, unused or used, $3.25.

Ambulance — SP16

1960, Oct. 16   Perf. 11
Crescent in Red
B33 SP16 50p + 50p violet   .65 .50
B34 SP16 175p + 50p blue   1.75 1.00

Issued for the Red Crescent Society.
Exist imperf. Value set, unused or used, $3.25.

Nos. 470-471 Surcharged in Blue or Orange

1960, Dec. 31   Litho.   Perf. 11
B35 A166 50p + 25p dp org (Bl) 1.75 1.75
B36 A166 165p + 25p blue (O)   1.75 1.75

Exist imperf. Value set, unused or used, $11.
The souvenir sheets described after No. 471 were surcharged in carmine "+25 Ps" on each stamp. Values: normal colors, unused $6, used $6.50; reversed colors, unused $7.50, used $9.50.
See general note after No. 485.

Nos. 496-500 Surcharged

Perf. 13½x14
1961, July 6   Unwmk.   Photo.
B37 A175 2p + 25p green &
              rose lil   .50 .50
B38 A175 2p + 25p brown & cit .50 .50
B39 A175 5p + 25p gray & rose .50 .50
B40 A175 10p + 25p blue & bis .50 .50
B41 A175 15p + 25p sl bl & dl lil .50 .50
      Nos. B37-B41 (5)   2.50 2.50

UNICEF. The same surcharge was applied to an imperf. souvenir sheet like that noted after No. 505. Value $5.

Nos. 522-526 Surcharged "+25PS" and Crescent in Red

1961, Oct. 16 **Perf. 13½x14**
B42 A184 2p + 25p black .50 .50
B43 A184 2p + 25p green .50 .50
B44 A184 5p + 25p lilac rose .50 .50
B45 A184 10p + 25p lilac .50 .50
B46 A184 15p + 25p dk blue .50 .50
   Nos. B42-B46 (5) 2.50 2.50

Issued for the Red Crescent Society.

Nos. 539-543 Surcharged in Red: "UNESCO + 25PS"

1962 **Perf. 12**
B47 A186 2p + 25p multi .40 .40
B48 A186 2p + 25p multi .40 .40
B49 A186 5p + 25p multi .40 .40
B50 A186 10p + 25p multi .40 .40
B51 A186 15p + 25p multi .40 .40
   Nos. B47-B51 (5) 2.00 2.00

UNESCO. The same surcharge was applied to the souvenir sheets mentioned after No. 548. Value, 2 sheets, $10.

Nos. 553-561 Surcharged: "Dag Hammarskjöld +20PS"

1962, Sept. 17 **Perf. 14x13½**
B52 A187 2p + 20p .25 .25
B53 A187 2p + 20p .25 .25
B54 A187 5p + 20p .25 .25
B55 A187 10p + 20p .25 .25
B56 A187 15p + 20p .25 .25
B57 A187 25p + 20p .25 .25
B58 A187 50p + 20p .30 .30
B59 A187 75p + 20p .50 .50
B60 A187 100p + 20p .80 .80
   Nos. B52-B60 (9) 3.10 3.10

In memory of Dag Hammarskjold, Sec. Gen. of the UN, 1953-61. Perf. and imperf. souvenir sheets exist. Value, 2 sheets, $6.50.

Nos. 583-593 Surcharged "+15PS"

1963, Mar. 15 **Perf. 14x13½**
B61 A193 2p + 15p 1.00 1.00
B62 A193 2p + 15p 1.00 1.00
B63 A193 5p + 15p 1.00 1.00
B64 A193 10p + 15p 1.00 1.00
B65 A193 15p + 15p 1.00 1.00
B66 A193 25p + 15p 1.00 1.00
B67 A193 50p + 15p 1.00 1.00
B68 A193 75p + 15p 1.00 1.00
B69 A193 100p + 15p 1.00 1.00
B70 A193 150p + 15p 1.00 1.00
B71 A193 175p + 15p 1.00 1.00
   Nos. B61-B71 (11) 11.00 11.00

WHO drive to eradicate malaria.

Nos. 672-672G, 672I Surcharged in Various Positions

1964, Mar. 9
B71A A213g 2p + 50p .25 .25
B71B A213g 3p + 50p .25 .25
B71C A213g 4p + 50p .25 .25
B71D A213g 5p + 50p .25 .25
B71E A213g 10p + 50p .25 .25
B71F A213g 100p + 50p .70 .70
B71G A213g 2af + 50p 1.50 1.50
B71H A213g 3af + 50p 2.10 2.10
   Nos. B71A-B71H (8) 5.55 5.55

Souvenir Sheet
B71J A213g 5af + 50p 4.50 4.50

Nos. B71E-B71G are airmail semi-postals.

Blood Transfusion Kit — SP17

1964, Oct. 18 **Litho.** **Perf. 10½**
B72 SP17 1af + 50p black & rose .40 .30

Issued for the Red Crescent Society and Red Crescent Week, Oct. 18-24.

First Aid Station SP18

1965, Oct. 16 **Photo.** **Perf. 13½x14**
B73 SP18 1.50af + 50p multi .35 .25

Issued for the Red Crescent Society.

Children Playing SP19

1966, Nov. 28 **Photo.** **Perf. 13½x14**
B74 SP19 1af + 1af yel grn & cl .30 .25
B75 SP19 3af + 2af yel & brn .65 .25
B76 SP19 7af + 3af rose lil & grn .95 .50
   Nos. B74-B76 (3) 1.90 1.00

Children's Day.

Nadir Shah Presenting Society Charter SP20

1967, Feb. 15 **Photo.** **Perf. 13x14**
B77 SP20 2af + 1af red & dk grn .35 .25
B78 SP20 5af + 1af lil rose & brn .75 .35

Issued for the Red Crescent Society.

Vaccination SP21

1967, June 6 **Photo.** **Perf. 12**
B79 SP21 2af + 1af yellow & blk .25 .25
B80 SP21 5af + 2af pink & brn .65 .35

The surtax was for anti-tuberculosis work.

Red Crescent — SP22

1967, Oct. 18 **Photo.** **Perf. 12**
Crescent in Red
B81 SP22 3af + 1af gray ol & blk .25 .25
B82 SP22 5af + 1af dl bl & blk .40 .25

Issued for the Red Crescent Society.

Queen Humeira — SP23

1968, June 14 **Photo.** **Perf. 12**
B83 SP23 2af + 2af red brown .35 .25
B84 SP23 7af + 2af dull green .90 .60

Issued for Mother's Day.

Red Crescent — SP24

1968, Oct. 16 **Photo.** **Perf. 12**
B85 SP24 4af + 1af yel, blk & red .60 .25

Issued for the Red Crescent Society.

Red Cross, Crescent, Lion and Sun Emblems — SP25

1969, May 5 **Litho.** **Perf. 14x13½**
B86 SP25 3af + 1af multicolored .65 .35
B87 SP25 5af + 1af multicolored .80 .35

League of Red Cross Societies, 50th anniv.

Mother and Child — SP26

1969, June 14 **Photo.** **Perf. 12**
B88 SP26 1af + 1af yel org & brn .30 .25
B89 SP26 4af + 1af rose lil & pur .50 .35
   a.   Souvenir sheet of 2 2.50 2.50

Mother's Day. No. B89a contains 2 imperf. stamps similar to Nos. B88-B89. Sold for 10af.

Red Crescent — SP27

1969, Oct. 16 **Photo.** **Perf. 12**
B90 SP27 6af + 1af multi .80 .30

Issued for the Red Crescent Society.

UN and FAO Emblems, Farmer — SP28

1973, May 24 **Photo.** **Perf. 13½**
B91 SP28 14af + 7af grnsh bl & lil 1.40 .90

World Food Program, 10th anniversary.

Dome of the Rock, Jerusalem SP29

1977, Sept. 11 **Photo.** **Perf. 14**
B92 SP29 12af + 3af multi 2.10 .60

Surtax for Palestinian families and soldiers.

15 Cent. (lunar) of Islamic Pilgrimage (Hegira) — SP30

1981, Jan. 17 **Litho.** **Perf. 12½x12**
B93 SP30 13af + 2af multi 1.75 .30

Red Crescent Aid Programs SP31

1981, May 8 **Perf. 12x12½**
B94 SP31 1af + 4af multi .65 .80

Intl. Year of the Disabled SP32

1981, Oct. 12 **Perf. 12x12½**
B95 SP32 6af + 1af multi .90 .50

AIR POST STAMPS

Plane over Kabul AP1

Perf. 12, 12x11, 11
1939, Oct. 1 **Typo.** **Unwmk.**
C1 AP1 5af orange 6.00 4.50
   a.   Imperf., pair ('47) 29.00 29.00
   b.   Horiz. pair, imperf. vert. 32.50 32.50
C2 AP1 10af blue 6.50 4.50
   a.   10af lt bl 8.00 6.00
   b.   Imperf., pair ('47) 29.00
   c.   Horiz. pair, imperf. vert. 32.50
C3 AP1 20af emerald 12.00 7.50
   a.   Imperf., pair ('47) 29.00
   b.   Horiz. pair, imperf. vert. 32.50
   c.   Vert. pair, imperf. horiz. 35.00
   Nos. C1-C3 (3) 24.50 16.50

These stamps come with clean-cut or rough perforations. Counterfeits exist.

1948, June 14 **Perf. 12x11½**
C4 AP1 5af emerald 24.00 24.00
C5 AP1 10af red orange 24.00 24.00
C6 AP1 20af blue 24.00 24.00
   Nos. C4-C6 (3) 72.00 72.00

Imperforates exist.

Plane over Palace Grounds, Kabul
AP2

Imprint: "Waterlow & Sons, Limited, London"

1951-54		Engr.	Perf. 13½	
C7	AP2	5af henna brn	3.50	.70
C8	AP2	5af dp grn ('54)	2.00	.45
C9	AP2	10af gray	9.75	2.50
C10	AP2	20af dark blue	11.50	3.25

1957				
C11	AP2	5af ultra	2.10	.60
C12	AP2	10af dark vio	3.25	1.10
		Nos. C7-C12 (6)	32.10	8.60

See No. C38.

Ariana Plane over Hindu Kush
AP3

Perf. 11, Imperf.

1960-63		Litho.	Unwmk.	
C13	AP3	75p light vio	.65	.25
C14	AP3	125p blue	.80	.40

Perf. 10½, 11

C14A	AP3	5af citron ('63)	1.50	1.00
		Nos. C13-C14A (3)	2.95	1.65

Imperf examples of Nos. C13-C14 are valued at approx. 50 percent more than the values shown.

Girl Scout — AP4

1962, Aug. 30		Photo.	Perf. 11½x12	
C15	AP4	100p ocher & brn	.60	.60
C16	AP4	175p brt yel grn & brn	1.00	1.00

Women's Day. See Nos. 578-579 and note on souvenir sheet.

Sports Type of Regular Issue, 1962

25p, 50p, Horse racing. 75p, 100p, Wrestling. 150p, Weight lifting. 175p, Soccer.

1962, Sept. 25		Unwmk.	Perf. 12	
		Black Inscriptions		
C17	A195	25p rose & red brn	.25	.25
C18	A195	50p gray & red brn	.30	.30
C19	A195	75p pale vio & dk grn	.55	.55
C20	A195	100p gray ol & dk pur	.70	.70
C21	A195	150p rose lil & grn	1.00	1.00
C22	A195	175p sal & brn	1.25	1.25
		Nos. C17-C22 (6)	4.00	4.00

Children's Day Type of Regular Issue

Perf. 11½x12, 12x11½

1962, Oct. 14			Unwmk.	
C23	A196	75p Runners	.65	.65
C24	A196	150p Peaches	1.25	1.25
C25	A196	200p Iris, vert.	1.75	1.75
		Nos. C23-C25 (3)	3.65	3.65

A souvenir sheet contains one each of Nos. C23-C25. Value $4.00.

Red Crescent Type of Regular Issue

1962, Oct. 16			Perf. 12	
		Fruit and Flowers in Natural Colors; Carmine Crescent		
C26	A197	25p Grapes	.25	.25
C27	A197	50p Pears	.30	.30
C28	A197	100p Wistaria	.70	.70
		Nos. C26-C28 (3)	1.20	1.20

Two souvenir sheets exist. One contains a 150p gray brown stamp in blossom design, the other a 200p gray stamp in wistaria design, imperf. Value, each $5.00.

UN Type of Regular Issue

1962, Oct. 24			Photo.	
		Flags in Original Colors, Black Inscriptions		
C29	A198	75p blue	.30	.30
C30	A198	100p lt brn	.50	.50
C31	A198	125p brt grn	.65	.65
		Nos. C29-C31 (3)	1.45	1.45

Boy Scout Type of Regular Issue

1962, Oct. 25		Unwmk.	Perf. 12	
C32	A199	25p gray, blk, dl grn & sal	.30	.30
C33	A199	50p grn, brn & sal	.60	.60
C34	A199	75p bl grn, red brn & sal	.90	.90
C35	A199	100p bl, slate & sal	1.10	1.10
		Nos. C32-C35 (4)	2.90	2.90

Teacher's Day Type of Regular Issue

1962, Oct. 25				
C36	A200	100p Pole vault	.65	.65
C37	A200	150p High jump	.95	.95

A souvenir sheet contains one 250p pink and slate green stamp in design of 150p. Values: perf $3; imperf $24.

Type of 1951-54

Imprint: "Thomas De La Rue & Co. Ltd."

1962		Engr.	Perf. 13½	
C38	AP2	5af ultra	13.50	1.00

Agriculture Types of Regular Issue

Unwmk.

1963, Mar. 1		Photo.	Perf. 12	
C42	A204	100p dk car, grn & brn	.40	.40
C43	A203	150p ocher & blk	.65	.65
C44	A204	200p ultra, grn & brn	.95	.95
		Nos. C42-C44 (3)	2.00	2.00

Hands Holding Wheat Emblem
AP5

1963, Mar. 27		Photo.	Perf. 14	
C45	AP5	500p lil, lt brn & brn	1.40	1.40

FAO "Freedom from Hunger" campaign.

Two souvenir sheets exist. One contains a 1000p blue green, light brown and brown, type AP5, imperf. The other contains a 200p brown and green and 300p ultramarine, yellow and ocher in rice and corn designs, type A205. Values $6.50 and $4.50.

Meteorological Day Type of Regular Issue

Designs: 100p, 500p, Meteorological measuring instrument. 200p, 400p, Weather station. 300p, Rockets in space.

1963, May 23			Imperf.	
C46	A206	100p brn & bl	3.25	3.25

Perf. 13½x14

C47	A206	200p brt grn & lil	1.00	1.00
C48	A206	300p dk bl & rose	1.50	1.50
C49	A206	400p bl & dl red brn	2.10	2.10
C50	A206	500p car rose & gray grn	2.75	2.75
		Nos. C47-C50 (4)	7.35	7.35

Nos. C47 and C50 printed se-tenant.
Nos. C47 and C50 exist imperf. Values, unused or used: 200p, $6.75; 500p, $17.50.
Two souvenir sheets exist. One contains a 125p red and brown stamp in rocket design. The other contains a 100p blue and dull red brown in "rockets in space" design. Values $5 and $13.

Kabul International Airport — AP8

Perf. 12x11½

1964, Apr.		Unwmk.	Photo.	
C57	AP8	10af red lil & grn	.80	.25
C58	AP8	20af dk grn & red lil	1.00	.40
a.		Perf. 12 ('68)	5.00	3.00

C59	AP8	50af dk bl & grnsh bl	2.75	1.25
a.		Perf. 12 ('68)	8.00	5.00
		Nos. C57-C59 (3)	4.55	1.90

Inauguration of Kabul Airport Terminal. Nos. C58a-C59a are 36mm wide. Nos. C58-C59 are 35½mm wide.

Zahir Shah and Kabul Airport — AP9

100af, Zahir Shah and Ariana Plane.

1971		Photo.	Perf. 12½x13½	
C60	AP9	50af multi	4.50	4.50
C61	AP9	100af blk, red & grn	5.75	3.50

Remainders of No. C60 were used, summer in 1978, with king's portrait torn or cut off.

REGISTRATION STAMPS

R1

Dated "1309"
Pelure Paper

1891		Unwmk.	Litho.	Imperf.
F1	R1	1r slate blue		2.40
a.		Tete beche pair		13.50

Genuinely used examples of No. F1 are rare. Counterfeit cancellations exist.

R2

Dated "1311"

1893			Thin Wove Paper	
F2	R2	1r black, green		2.00

Genuinely used examples of No. F2 are rare. Counterfeit cancellations exist.

R3

1894			Undated	
F3	R3	2ab black, green	9.50	11.00

12 varieties. See note below Nos. 189-190.

R4

1898-1900				Undated
F4	R4	2ab black, deep rose	4.50	4.50
F5	R4	2ab black, lilac rose	6.50	5.00
F6	R4	2ab black, magenta	8.00	5.00
F7	R4	2ab black, salmon	4.50	4.50
F8	R4	2ab black, orange	4.50	4.50
F9	R4	2ab black, yellow	4.50	3.50
F10	R4	2ab black, green	4.50	3.50
		Nos. F4-F10 (7)	37.00	30.50

Many shades of paper.
Nos. F4-F10 come in two sizes, measured between outer frame lines: 52x36mm, 1st printing; 46x33mm, 2nd printing. The outer frame line (not pictured) is 3-6mm from inner frame line.
Used on P.O. receipts.

OFFICIAL STAMPS

(Used only on interior mail.)

Coat of Arms
O1

1909		Unwmk.	Typo.	Perf. 12
		Wove Paper		
O1	O1	red	1.25	1.25
a.		Carmine ('19?)	2.50	6.50

Later printings of No. O1 in scarlet, vermilion, claret, etc., on various types of paper, were issued until 1927.

Coat of Arms — O2

1939-68?		Typo.	Perf. 11, 12	
O3	O2	15p emerald	1.10	.80
O4	O2	30p ocher ('40)	1.50	1.50
O5	O2	45p dark carmine	1.25	1.25
O6	O2	50p brt car ('68)	.70	.70
a.		50p carmine rose ('55)	1.25	.70
O7	O2	1af brt red violet	2.00	1.75
		Nos. O3-O7 (5)	6.55	6.00

Size of 50p, 24x31mm, others 22½x28mm.

Catalogue values for unused stamps in this section, from this point to the end of the section, are for Never Hinged items.

1964-65		Litho.	Perf. 11	
O8	O2	50p rose	.90	.90
a.		50p salmon ('65)	2.00	2.00

Stamps of this type are revenues.

PARCEL POST STAMPS

Coat of Arms — PP1

PP2

PP3

PP4

1909   Unwmk.   Typo.   Perf. 12

Q1	PP1	3sh bister	1.25	2.25
a.		Imperf., pair	—	
Q2	PP2	1kr olive gray	3.50	3.50
a.		Imperf., pair	—	
Q3	PP3	1r orange	3.25	3.25
Q4	PP3	1r olive green	24.00	4.50
Q5	PP4	2r red	4.00	4.00
	Nos. Q1-Q5 (5)		36.00	17.50

Type I

Type II

A 1909 undenominated dull olive green Official parcel post stamp exists with two types. Type I has thinner and more rays below the crest; Type II has fewer and wider rays. Values: *$500* each. A pair, imperf between, exists. Value, $1,250. A complete sheet is known perforated on all sides.

1916-18

Q6	PP1	3sh green	1.75	3.50
Q7	PP2	1kr pale red	3.00	1.50
a.		1kr rose red ('18)	4.00	4.00
Q8	PP3	1r brown org	3.50	1.75
a.		1r deep brown ('18)	12.00	3.00
Q9	PP4	2r blue	6.25	6.50
	Nos. Q6-Q9 (4)		14.50	13.25

Nos. Q1-Q9 sometimes show letters of the papermaker's watermark "HOWARD & JONES LONDON."

Ungummed stamps are remainders. They sell for one-third the price of mint stamps.

Old Habibia College, Near Kabul — PP5

1921   Wove Paper

Q10	PP5	10pa chocolate	5.00	5.75
a.		Tete beche pair	22.50	22.50
Q11	PP5	15pa light brn	7.00	7.50
a.		Tete beche pair	27.50	27.50
Q12	PP5	30pa red violet	12.50	7.50
a.		Tete beche pair	40.00	40.00
b.		Laid paper	15.00	15.00
Q13	PP5	1r brt blue	14.00	14.00
a.		Tete beche pair	65.00	65.00
	Nos. Q10-Q13 (4)		38.50	34.75

Stamps of this issue are usually perforated on one or two sides only.
The laid paper of No. Q12b has a papermaker's watermark in the sheet.

Handstamped in black on Nos. Q10-Q13

PP5a

1923, Feb. 26

Q13B	PP5a	10pa chocolate	—	—
Q13C	PP5a	15pa light brn	—	—
Q13D	PP5a	30pa red violet	—	—
Q13E	PP5a	1r brt blue	—	—

5th Independence Day.
Two types of handstamp exist.
Forgeries exist.

PP6

1924-26   Wove Paper

Q15	PP6	5kr ultra ('26)	50.00	50.00
Q16	PP6	5r lilac	20.00	25.00

A 15r rose exists, but is not known to have been placed in use. Value, unused $350.

PP7

PP8

1928-29   Perf. 11, 11xImperf.

Q17	PP7	2r yellow orange	8.00	7.00
Q18	PP7	2r green ('29)	7.50	7.50
Q19	PP8	3r deep green	10.50	10.50
Q20	PP8	3r brown ('29)	9.50	10.50
	Nos. Q17-Q20 (4)		35.50	35.50

POSTAL TAX STAMPS

Aliabad Hospital near Kabul PT1

Pierre and Marie Curie PT2

Perf. 12x11½, 12

1938, Dec. 22   Typo.   Unwmk.

RA1	PT1	10p peacock grn	3.25	5.00
RA2	PT2	15p dull blue	3.25	5.00

Obligatory on all mail Dec. 22-28, 1938. The money was used for the Aliabad Hospital. See note with CD80.

> Catalogue values for unused stamps in this section, from this point to the end of the section, are for Never Hinged items.

PT3

Begging Child — PT4

1949, May 28   Typo.   Perf. 12

RA3	PT3	35p red orange	3.25	2.10
RA4	PT4	125p ultra	4.00	2.10

United Nations Children's Day, May 28. Obligatory on all foreign mail on that date. Proceeds were used for child welfare.

Paghman Arch and UN Emblem PT5

1949, Oct. 24

RA5	PT5	125p dk blue green	15.00	9.00

4th anniv. of the UN. Valid one day only. Issued in sheets of 9 (3x3).

Zahir Shah and Map of Afghanistan — PT6

1950, Mar. 30   Typo.

RA6	PT6	125p blue green	4.50	1.50

Return of Zahir Shah from a trip to Europe for his health. Valid for two weeks. The tax was used for public health purposes.

Hazara Youth — PT7

1950, May 28   Typo.   Perf. 11½

RA7	PT7	125p dk blue green	4.50	2.50

Tax for Child Welfare. Obligatory and valid only on May 28, 1950, on foreign mail.

Ruins of Qalai Bist and Globe — PT8

1950, Oct. 24
RA8 PT8 1.25af ultramarine   9.00 5.25
5th anniv. of the UN. Proceeds went to Afghanistan's UN Projects Committee.

Zahir Shah and Medical Center PT9

1950, Dec. 22   Typo.   *Perf. 11½*
Size: 38x25mm
RA9 PT9 35p carmine   1.25 .60
Size: 46x30mm
RA10 PT9 1.25af black   7.50 2.50
The tax was for the national Graduate School of Medicine.

Koochi Girl with Lamb PT10

Kohistani Boy and Sheep — PT11

1951, May 28
RA11 PT10 35p emerald   1.50 .90
RA12 PT11 1.25af ultramarine   1.50 .90
The tax was for Child Welfare.

Distributing Gifts to Children — PT12

Qandahari Boys Dancing the "Attan" PT13

1952, May 28   Litho.
RA13 PT12 35p chocolate   .80 .65
RA14 PT13 125p violet   1.60 .95
The tax was for Child Welfare.
Exist imperf. Values, set: unused $6; used $9.50.

Soldier Receiving First Aid — PT14

1952, Oct. 19
RA15 PT14 10p light green   .80 .65
Exist imperf. Value: unused $2.50; used $4.

Stretcher-bearers and Wounded — PT15

Soldier Assisting Wounded — PT16

1953, Oct.
RA16 PT15 10p yel grn & org red   .80 .80
RA17 PT16 10p vio brn & org red   .80 .80
Exist imperf. Values, set: unused $4; used $5.

Prince Mohammed Nadir — PT17

1953, May 28
RA18 PT17 35p orange yellow   .50 .25
RA19 PT17 125p chalky blue   .90 .55
No. RA19 is inscribed in French "Children's Day." The tax was for child welfare.
Exist imperf. Values: unused $4; used $5.

Map and Young Musicians PT18

1954, May 28   Unwmk.   *Perf. 11*
RA20 PT18 35p purple   .65 .40
RA21 PT18 125p ultra   1.90 1.25
No. RA21 is inscribed in French. The tax was for child welfare.
Exist imperf. Values, set: unused $4.50; used $6.50.

PT19

1954, Oct. 17   *Perf. 11½*
RA22 PT19 20p blue & red   .75 .35
Exists imperf. Values: unused $2; used $2.50.

Red Crescent PT20

1955, Oct. 18   *Perf. 11*
RA23 PT20 20p dull grn & car   .70 .35
Exists imperf. Values: unused $1.50; used $2.

Zahir Shah and Red Crescent PT21

1956, Oct. 18
RA24 PT21 20p lt grn & rose car   .40 .25
Exists imperf. Value, unused or used, $1.25.

Red Crescent Headquarters, Kabul — PT22

1957, Oct. 17
RA25 PT22 20p lt ultra & car   .90 .60
Exists imperf. Values: unused $2; used $2.50.

Map and Crescent PT23

1958, Oct.   Unwmk.   *Perf. 11*
RA26 PT23 25p yel grn & red   .40 .30
Exists imperf. Values: unused 50¢; used 80¢.

PT24

1959, Oct. 17   Litho.   *Perf. 11*
RA27 PT24 25p lt violet & red   .40 .25
The tax on Nos. RA15-RA17, RA22-RA27 was for the Red Crescent Society. Use of these stamps was required for one week.
Exists imperf. Values: unused 50¢; used 80¢.

AGÜERA, LA

ä-gwä'rä

LOCATION — An administrative district in southern Rio de Oro on the north-west coast of Africa.
GOVT. — Spanish possession
AREA — Because of indefinite political boundaries, figures for area and population are not available.

100 Centimos = 1 Peseta

Type of 1920 Issue of Rio de Oro Overprinted

1920, June   Typo.   Unwmk.   Perf. 13

1	A8	1c blue green	2.60	3.25
2	A8	2c olive brown	2.60	3.25
3	A8	5c deep green	2.60	3.25
4	A8	10c light red	2.60	3.25
5	A8	15c yellow	2.60	3.25
6	A8	20c lilac	2.60	3.25
7	A8	25c deep blue	2.60	3.25
8	A8	30c dark brown	2.60	3.25
9	A8	40c pink	2.60	3.25
10	A8	50c bright blue	8.50	10.00
11	A8	1p red brown	13.50	20.00
12	A8	4p dark violet	40.00	60.00
13	A8	10p orange	85.00	125.00
		Nos. 1-13 (13)	170.40	244.25
		Set, never hinged	400.00	

Very fine examples of Nos. 1-13 will be somewhat off center. Well-centered examples are uncommon and will sell for more.

King Alfonso XIII — A2

1922, June

14	A2	1c turquoise bl (I)	1.25	1.50
15	A2	2c dark green	1.40	1.50
16	A2	5c blue green	1.40	1.50
17	A2	10c red	1.40	1.50
18	A2	15c red brown	1.40	1.50
19	A2	20c yellow	1.40	1.50
20	A2	25c deep blue	1.40	1.50
21	A2	30c dark brown	1.40	1.50
22	A2	40c rose red	1.60	2.00
23	A2	50c red violet	5.50	5.75
24	A2	1p rose	13.00	15.00
25	A2	4p violet	35.00	37.50
26	A2	10p orange	50.00	55.00
		Nos. 14-26 (13)	116.15	127.25
		Set, never hinged	200.00	

For later issues, see Spanish Sahara.

AITUTAKI

ït-ə-'täk-ē

LOCATION — One of the larger Cook Islands, in the South Pacific Ocean northeast of New Zealand
GOVT. — A dependency of New Zealand
AREA — 7 sq. mi.
POP. — 2,335 (1981)

The Cook Islands were attached to New Zealand in 1901. Stamps of Cook Islands were used in 1892-1903 and 1932-72.
Aitutaki acquired its own postal service in August 1972, though remaining part of Cook Islands.

12 Pence = 1 Shilling
100 Cents = 1 Dollar (1972)

Catalogue values for unused stamps in this country are for Never Hinged items, beginning with Scott 37.

Watermark

Wmk. 61- Single-lined NZ and Star Close Together

Stamps of New Zealand Surcharged in Red or Blue

       a   b

1903   Engr.   Wmk. 61   Perf. 14

1	A18(a)	½p green (R)	4.75	7.00
2	A35(b)	1p rose (Bl)	5.00	6.25

c

       d   e

f

Perf. 11

3	A22(c)	2½p blue (R)	19.50	15.00
4	A23(d)	3p yel brn (Bl)	19.00	16.50
5	A26(e)	6p red (Bl)	32.50	27.50
6	A29(f)	1sh scar (Bl)	60.00	95.00
a.		1sh orange red (Bl)	72.50	105.00

1911, Sept.   Typo.   Perf. 14x15

7	A41(a)	½p yel grn (R)	1.00	8.75

Engr.   Perf. 14

9	A22(c)	2½p dp blue (R)	8.50	19.00

       g   h

1913-16   Typo.

10	A42(b)	1p rose (Bl)	3.25	13.50

Engr.

12	A41(g)	6p car brown (Bl) ('16)	50.00	145.00
13	A41(h)	1sh ver (Bl) ('14)	60.00	150.00

1916-17   Perf. 14x13½, 14x14½

17	A45(g)	6p car rose (Bl)	9.00	29.00
18	A45(h)	1sh ver (Bl) ('17)	14.00	95.00
		Nos. 1-18 (13)	286.50	627.50

New Zealand Stamps of 1909-19 Overprinted in Red or Dark Blue

---

1917-20   Typo.   Perf. 14x15

19	A43	½p yellow grn ('20)	1.00	6.25
20	A42	1p car (Bl) ('20)	5.00	35.00
21	A47	1½p gray black	4.50	32.50
22	A47	1½p brown org ('19)	.90	7.50
23	A43	3p choc (Bl) ('19)	3.75	22.00

Perf. 14x13½, 14x14½   Engr.

24	A44	2½p dull blue ('18)	1.90	16.00
25	A45	3p vio brn (Bl) ('18)	1.75	32.50
26	A45	6p car rose (Bl)	5.00	22.50
27	A45	1sh vermilion (Bl)	13.00	35.00
		Nos. 19-27 (9)	36.80	209.25

Landing of Capt. Cook A15   Avarua Waterfront A16

Capt. James Cook — A17   Palm — A18

Houses at Arorangi — A19

Avarua Harbor — A20

1920   Engr.   Unwmk.   Perf. 14

28	A15	½p green & black	3.75	26.00
29	A16	1p car & blk	3.75	18.00
30	A17	1½p brown & blk	6.25	13.00
31	A18	3p dp blue & blk	2.75	15.00
32	A19	6p slate & red		
33	A20	6p slate & red brn	6.25	15.00
33	A20	1sh claret & blk	10.00	22.50
		Nos. 28-33 (6)	32.75	109.50

Inverted centers, double frames, etc. are from printers waste.

Rarotongan Chief (Te Po) — A21

1924-27   Wmk. 61   Perf. 14

34	A15	½p green & blk ('27)	2.10	25.00
35	A16	1p carmine & blk	6.25	12.50
36	A21	2½p blue & blk ('27)	8.00	80.00
		Nos. 34-36 (3)	16.35	117.50

Catalogue values for unused stamps in this section, from this point to the end of the section, are for Never Hinged items.

Cook Islands Nos. 199-200, 202, 205-206, 210, 212-213, 215-217 Ovptd.

1972   Photo.   Unwmk.   Perf. 14x13½

37	A34	½c gold & multi	.40	.90
38	A34	1c gold & multi	.85	1.25
39	A34	2½c gold & multi	2.50	7.50
40	A34	4c gold & multi	.85	1.00
41	A34	5c gold & multi	3.00	8.50
42	A34	10c gold & multi	3.00	6.25
43	A34	20c gold & multi	3.75	1.10
44	A34	25c gold & multi	.90	1.25
45	A34	50c gold & multi	2.75	3.25
46	A35	$1 gold & multi	4.50	6.00
47	A35	$2 gold & multi	1.00	1.10
		Nos. 37-47 (11)	23.50	38.10

Overprint horizontal on Nos. 46-47. On $2, overprint is in capitals of different font; size: 21x3mm.
Issued: Nos. 37-46, Aug. 9; No. 47, Nov. 24.

Same Overprint Horizontal in Silver On Cook Islands Nos. 330-332

1972, Oct. 27   Perf. 13½

48	A53	1c gold & multi	.25	.25
49	A53	5c gold & multi	.25	.25
50	A53	10c gold & multi	.30	.30
		Nos. 48-50 (3)	.80	.80

Fluorescence

Starting in 1972, stamps carry a "fluorescent security underprinting" in a multiple pattern of New Zealand's coat of arms with "Aitutaki" above, "Cook Islands" below and two stars at each side.

Silver Wedding Type of Cook Islands

1972, Nov. 20   Photo.   Perf. 13½
Size: 29x40mm

51	A54	5c silver & multi	3.25	2.50

Size: 66x40mm

52	A54	15c silver & multi	1.25	1.25

25th anniversary of the marriage of Queen Elizabeth II and Prince Philip. Nos. 51-52 printed in sheets of 5 stamps and one label.

Flower Issue of Cook Islands Overprinted

1972, Dec. 11   Photo.   Perf. 14x13½

53	A34	½c on #199	.25	.25
54	A34	1c on #200	.25	.25
55	A34	2½c on #202	.25	.25
56	A34	4c on #205	.30	.25
57	A34	5c on #206	.30	.25
58	A34	10c on #210	.40	.35
59	A34	20c on #212	1.25	.45
60	A34	25c on #213	.55	.60
61	A34	50c on #215	.85	.90
62	A35	$1 on #216	1.25	1.75
		Nos. 53-62 (10)	5.65	5.30

See Nos. 73-76.

The Passion of Christ, by Mathias Grunewald — A22

Paintings: No. 63b, St. Veronica, by Rogier van der Weyden. No. 63c, Crucifixion, by Raphael. No. 63d, Resurrection, by della Francesca. No. 64a, Last Supper, by Master of Amiens. No. 64b, Condemnation of Christ, by Hans Holbein, the Elder. No. 64c, Crucifixion, by Rubens. No. 64d, Resurrection, by El Greco. No. 65a, Passion of Christ, by El Greco. No. 65b, St. Veronica, by Jakob Cornelisz. No. 65c, Crucifixion, by Rubens. No. 65d, Resurrection, by Dierik Bouts.

Perf. 13½

	1973, Apr. 6	Photo.	Unwmk.	
63	Block of 4		1.00	.40
a.-d.	A22 1c any single		.25	.25
64	Block of 4		1.25	1.00
a.-d.	A22 5c any single		.30	.25
65	Block of 4		1.40	1.75
a.-d.	A22 10c any single		.35	.25
	Nos. 63-65 (3)		3.65	3.15

Easter. Printed in blocks of 4 in sheets of 40. Design descriptions in top and bottom margins.

Coin Type of Cook Islands

Queen Elizabeth II Coins: 1c, Taro leaf. 2c, Pineapples. 5c, Hibiscus. 10c, Oranges. 20c, Fairy terns. 50c, Bonito. $1, Tangaroa, Polynesian god of creation, vert.

	1973, May 14		Perf. 13x13½	
		Size: 37x24mm		
66	A55 1c dp car & multi		.25	.25
67	A55 2c blue & multi		.25	.25
68	A55 5c green & multi		.25	.25
		Size: 46x30mm		
69	A55 10c vio blue & multi		.25	.25
70	A55 20c green & multi		.30	.25
71	A55 50c dp car & multi		.60	.40
		Size: 32x54½mm		
72	A55 $1 blue, blk & sil		.80	.50
	Nos. 66-72 (7)		2.70	2.20

Cook Islands coinage commemorating silver wedding anniv. of Queen Elizabeth II.
Printed in sheets of 20 stamps and label showing Westminster Abbey.

Cook Islands Nos. 208, 210, 212 and 215 Overprinted Like Nos. 53-62 and: "TENTH ANNIVERSARY/ CESSATION/ OF/ NUCLEAR TESTING/ TREATY"

	1973, July	Photo.	Perf. 14x13½	
73	A34 8c gold & multi		.25	.25
74	A34 10c gold & multi		.25	.25
75	A34 20c gold & multi		.35	.35
76	A34 50c gold & multi		.75	.75
	Nos. 73-76 (4)		1.60	1.60

Nuclear Test Ban Treaty, 10th anniv., protest against French nuclear testing on Mururoa Atoll.

Princess Anne, Hibiscus A23

Design: 30c, Mark Phillips and hibiscus.

	1973, Nov. 14	Photo.	Perf. 13½x14	
77	A23 25c gold & multi		.25	.25
78	A23 30c gold & multi		.30	.30
a.	Souvenir sheet of 2, #77-78		.65	.65

Wedding of Princess Anne and Capt. Mark Phillips.

Virgin and Child, by Il Perugino — A24

Paintings of the Virgin and Child by various masters — No. 79: a, Van Dyck. b, Bartolommeo Montagna. c, Carlo Crivelli. d, Il Perugino. No. 80: a, Cima da Conegliano. b, Memling. c, Veronese. d, Veronese. No. 81: a, Raphael. b, Lorenzo Lotto. c, Del Colle. d, Memling.

	1973, Dec.	Photo.	Perf. 13	
79	A24 1c Block of 4, #a.-d.		.50	.50
80	A24 5c Block of 4, #a.-d.		1.00	1.00
81	A24 10c Block of 4, #a.-d.		1.25	1.25
	Nos. 79-81 (3)		2.75	2.75

Christmas. Printed in blocks of 4 in sheets of 48. Design descriptions in margins.

Murex Ramosus A25

Terebra Maculata — A26

Pacific Shells: 1c, Nautilus macromphalus. 2c, Harpa major. 3c, Phalium strigatum. 4c, Cypraea talpa. 5c, Mitra stictica. 8c, Charonia tritonis. 10c, Murex triremis. 20c, Oliva sericea. 25c, Tritonalia rubeta. 60c, Strombus latissimus. $1, Biplex perca. $5, Cypraea hesitata.

	1974-75	Photo.	Perf. 13	
82	A25 ½c silver & multi		.95	.95
83	A25 1c silver & multi		.95	.95
84	A25 2c silver & multi		.95	.95
85	A25 3c silver & multi		.95	.95
86	A25 4c silver & multi		.95	.95
87	A25 5c silver & multi		.95	.95
88	A25 8c silver & multi		.95	.95
89	A25 10c silver & multi		.95	.85
90	A25 20c silver & multi		1.25	.85
91	A25 25c silver & multi		1.25	.85
92	A25 60c silver & multi		3.75	1.10
93	A25 $1 silver & multi		2.50	1.25
		Perf. 14		
94	A26 $2 silver & multi		6.00	6.00
95	A26 $5 silver & multi		27.50	9.50
	Nos. 82-95 (14)		49.85	27.05

Issued: Nos. 82-93, 1/31/74; $2, 1/20/75; $5, 2/28/75.
For overprints see Nos. O1-O16.

William Bligh and "Bounty" A27

No. 96, shown. No. 97, "Bounty" at sea. No. 98, Bligh and "Bounty" off Aitutaki. No. 99, Chart of Aitutaki, 1856. No. 100, James Cook and "Resolution". No. 101, Maps of Aitutaki and Pacific Ocean.

		Size: 38x22mm		
	1974, Apr. 11	Photo.	Perf. 13	
96	A27 1c multicolored		.45	.45
97	A27 1c multicolored		.45	.45
a.	Pair, #96-97		1.00	1.00
98	A27 5c multicolored		1.00	1.00
99	A27 5c multicolored		1.00	1.00
a.	Pair, #98-99		2.25	2.25
100	A27 8c multicolored		1.25	1.25
101	A27 8c multicolored		1.25	1.25
a.	Pair, #100-101		2.75	2.75
	Nos. 96-101,C1-C6 (12)		10.60	10.10

Capt. William Bligh (1754-1817), European discoverer of Aitutaki, Apr. 11, 1789.

Aitutaki Nos. 1 & 2 Map and UPU Emblem A28

Design: 50c, Aitutaki Nos. 4 and 28, map of Aitutaki and UPU emblem.

	1974, July 15	Photo.	Perf. 13½	
102	A28 25c blue & multi		.75	.75
103	A28 50c blue & multi		1.00	1.00
a.	Souvenir sheet of 2, #102-103		2.00	2.00

UPU, cent. Printed in sheets of 5 plus label showing UPU emblem.

A29

Designs: Paintings of the Virgin and Child by: 1c, Van der Goes. 5c, Giovanni Bellini. 8c, Gerard David. 10c, Antonello da Messina. 25c, Joos van Cleve. 30c, Maitre de St. Catherine.

	1974, Oct. 11	Photo.	Perf. 13½	
104	A29 1c multicolored		.25	.25
105	A29 5c multicolored		.25	.25
106	A29 8c multicolored		.25	.25
107	A29 10c multicolored		.25	.25
108	A29 25c multicolored		.35	.35
109	A29 30c multicolored		.75	.75
a.	Souvenir sheet of 6, #104-109		2.10	2.10

Christmas. Nos. 104-109 printed in sheets of 15 stamps and corner label. See Nos. B1-B6.

A30

Designs: Churchill portraits — 10c, Dublin, Age 5. 25c, As young man. 30c, Inspecting troops, WWII. 50c, Painting. $1, Giving V sign.

	1974, Nov. 29	Photo.	Perf. 14	
110	A30 10c multicolored		.25	.25
111	A30 25c multicolored		.25	.25
112	A30 30c multicolored		.30	.25
113	A30 50c multicolored		.50	.50
114	A30 $1 multicolored		.85	.85
a.	Souvenir sheet of 5, #110-114 + label, perf. 13½		4.50	4.50
	Nos. 110-114 (5)		2.15	2.10

Sir Winston Churchill (1874-1965). Nos. 110-114 printed in sheets of 5 stamps and corner label.

Emblem US & USSR Flags A31

50c, Icarus and Apollo Soyuz spacecraft.

	1975, July 24	Photo.	Perf. 13x14½	
115	A31 25c multicolored		.30	.30
116	A31 50c multicolored		.65	.65
a.	Souvenir sheet of 2		1.40	1.40

Apollo Soyuz space test project (Russo-American cooperation), launching July 15; link-up July 17. Nos. 115 and 116 each printed in sheets of 5 stamps and one label showing area of Apollo splash-downs. No. 116a contains one each of Nos. 115-116 with gold and black border and inscription.

Madonna and Child, by Pietro Lorenzetti — A32

Paintings: 7c, Adoration of the Kings, by Rogier van der Weyden. 15c, Madonna and Child, by Bartolommeo Montagna. 20c, Adoration of the Shepherds.

	1975, Nov. 24	Photo.	Perf. 14x13½	
117	A32 Strip of 3		.35	.35
a.	6c St. Francis		.25	.25
b.	6c Madonna and Child		.25	.25
c.	6c St. John the Evangelist		.25	.25
118	A32 Strip of 3		.40	.40
a.	7c One King		.25	.25
b.	7c Madonna and Child		.25	.25
c.	7c Two Kings		.25	.25
119	A32 Strip of 3		.75	.75
a.	15c St. Joseph		.25	.25
b.	15c Madonna and Child		.25	.25
c.	15c St. John the Baptist		.25	.25
120	A32 Strip of 3		1.10	1.10
a.	20c One Shepherd		.25	.25
b.	20c Madonna and Child		.25	.25
c.	20c Two Shepherds		.25	.25
d.	Souv. sheet of 12, #117-120, perf. 13½		2.75	2.75
	Nos. 117-120 (4)		2.60	2.60

Christmas. Nos. 117-120 printed in sheets of 30 (10 strips of 3).
For surcharges see Nos. B7-B10.

Descent from the Cross, detail — A33

Designs (Painting, Flemish School, 16th Century): 30c, Virgin Mary, disciple and body of Jesus. 35c, Mary Magdalene and disciple.

	1976, Apr. 5	Photo.	Perf. 13½	
121	A33 15c gold & multi		.25	.25
122	A33 30c gold & multi		.30	.30
123	A33 35c gold & multi		.45	.45
a.	Souvenir sheet of 3		1.25	1.25
	Nos. 121-123 (3)		1.00	1.00

Easter. No. 123a contains 3 stamps similar to Nos. 121-123, perf. 13, in continuous design without gold frames and white margins.

Declaration of Independence — A34

Paintings by John Trumbull: 35c, Surrender of Cornwallis at Yorktown. 50c, Washington's Farewell Address. a, "1976 BICENTENARY." b, "UNITED STATES." c, "INDEPENDENCE 1776."

	1976, June 1	Photo.	Perf. 13½	
124	A34 Strip of 3		1.25	1.25
a.-c.	30c any single		.30	.30
125	A34 Strip of 3		1.50	1.50
a.-c.	35c any single		.40	.40
126	A34 Strip of 3		2.00	2.00
a.-c.	50c any single		.55	.55
d.	Souvenir sheet of 9 (3x3)			
	Nos. 124-126 (3)		4.75	4.75

American Bicentennial. Nos. 124-126 printed in sheets of 5 strips of 3 and 3-part corner label showing portrait of John Trumbull, commemorative inscription and portraits of Washington (30c), John Adams (35c) and Jefferson (50c). No. 126d contains 3 strips similar to Nos. 124-126.

Bicycling
A35

Montreal Olympic Games Emblem and: 35c, Sailing. 60c, Field hockey. 70c, Running.

1976, July 15 Photo.   Perf. 13x14
127 A35 15c multicolored .30 .25
128 A35 35c multicolored .50 .45
129 A35 60c multicolored .75 .70
130 A35 70c multicolored 1.00 .90
  a.   Souvenir sheet of 4 3.00 3.00
     Nos. 127-130 (4) 2.55 2.30

21st Olympic Games, Montreal, Canada, July 17-Aug. 1. Nos. 127-130 printed in sheets of 5 stamps and label showing coat of Arms and Montreal Olympic Games emblem. No. 130a contains 4 stamps similar to Nos. 127-130 with gold margin around each stamp.

Nos. 127-130a Overprinted

1976, July 30
131 A35 15c multicolored .25 .25
132 A35 35c multicolored .40 .40
133 A35 60c multicolored .80 .80
134 A35 70c multicolored .80 .80
  a.   Souvenir sheet of 4 2.50 2.50
     Nos. 131-134 (4) 2.25 2.25

Visit of Queen Elizabeth II to Montreal and official opening of the Games. Each stamp of No. 134a has diagonal overprint. Sheet margin has additional overprint: "ROYAL VISIT OF H.M. QUEEN ELIZABETH II/OFFICIALLY OPENED 17 JULY 1976."

Annunciation — A36

Designs: Nos. 137-138, Angel appearing to the shepherds. Nos. 139-140, Nativity. Nos. 141-142, Three Kings.

1976, Oct. 18   Perf. 13½x13
135 6c dk green & gold .25 .25
136 6c dk green & gold .25 .25
  a. A36 Pair, #135-136 .25 .25
137 7c dk brown & gold .25 .25
138 7c dk brown & gold .25 .25
  a. A36 Pair, #137-138 .25 .25
139 15c dk blue & gold .25 .25
140 15c dk blue & gold .25 .25
  a. A36 Pair, #139-140 .30 .30
141 20c purple & gold .25 .25
142 20c purple & gold .25 .25
  a. A36 Pair, #141-142 .40 .40
  b. Souvenir sheet of 8 1.50 1.50
     Nos. 135-142 (8) 2.00 2.00

Christmas. No. 142b contains 8 stamps similar to Nos. 135-142 with white margin around each pair of stamps.
For overprints see Nos. B11-B18.

A. G. Bell and 1876 Telephone — A38

Design: 70c, Satellite and radar.

1977, Mar. 3 Photo.   Perf. 13½x13
143 A38 25c rose & multi .25 .25
144 A38 70c violet & multi .40 .40
  a.   Souvenir sheet of 2 1.50 1.50

Centenary of first telephone call by Alexander Graham Bell, Mar. 10, 1876. No. 144a contains a 25c in colors of 70c and 70c in colors of 25c.

Calvary (detail), by Rubens
A39

Paintings by Rubens: 20c, Lamentation. 35c, Descent from the Cross.

1977, Mar. 31 Photo.   Perf. 13½x14
145 A39 15c gold & multi .50 .50
146 A39 20c gold & multi .65 .65
147 A39 35c gold & multi .85 .85
  a.   Souv. sheet of 3, #145-147, perf. 13 2.25 2.25
     Nos. 145-147 (3) 2.00 2.00

Easter, and 400th birth anniv. of Peter Paul Rubens (1577-1640), Flemish painter.

Capt. Bligh, "Bounty" and George III — A40

Designs: 35c, Rev. John Williams, George IV, First Christian Church. 50c, British flag, map of Aitutaki, Queen Victoria. $1, Elizabeth II and family on balcony after coronation.

1977, Apr. 21   Perf. 13½
148 A40 25c gold & multi .25 .25
149 A40 35c gold & multi .30 .30
150 A40 50c gold & multi .50 .50
151 A40 $1 gold & multi 1.25 1.25
  a.   Souvenir sheet of 4, #148-151 2.25 2.25
     Nos. 148-151 (4) 2.30 2.30

Reign of Queen Elizabeth II, 25th anniv.
For overprint & surcharge see Nos. O11, O15.

Annunciation — A41

Designs: No. 154, Virgin, Child and ox. No. 155, Joseph and donkey (Nativity). No. 156, Three Kings. No. 157, Virgin and Child. No. 158, Joseph. No. 159, Virgin and donkey (Flight into Egypt).

1977, Oct. 14 Photo.   Perf. 13½x14
152 6c multicolored .25 .25
153 6c multicolored .25 .25
  a. A41 Pair, #152-153 .25 .25
154 7c multicolored .25 .25
155 7c multicolored .25 .25
  a. A41 Pair, #154-155 .25 .25
156 15c multicolored .25 .25
157 15c multicolored .25 .25
  a. A41 Pair, #156-157 .30 .30
158 20c multicolored .25 .25
159 20c multicolored .25 .25
  a. A41 Pair, #158-159 .40 .40
  b. Souvenir sheet of 8, #152-159 1.75 1.75
     Nos. 152-159 (8) 2.00 2.00

Christmas.
For surcharges see Nos. B19-B26a.

Hawaiian Wood Figurine — A43

Designs: 50c, Talbot hunting dog, figurehead of "Resolution", horiz. $1, Temple figure.

1978, Jan. 19 Litho.   Perf. 13½
160 A43 35c multicolored .45 .45
161 A43 50c multicolored .70 .70
162 A43 $1 multicolored 1.00 1.00
  a.   Souvenir sheet of 3, #160-162 2.75 2.75
     Nos. 160-162 (3) 2.15 2.15

Bicentenary of Capt. Cook's arrival in Hawaii. Nos. 160-162 issued in sheets of 6.

Jesus Carrying Cross, by Simone di Martini
A44

Paintings: 20c, Avignon Pietà, 15th Century. 35c, Christ at Emmaus, by Rembrandt.

1978, Mar. 17 Photo.   Perf. 13½x14
163 A44 15c gold & multi .25 .25
164 A44 20c gold & multi .25 .25
165 A44 35c gold & multi .30 .30
  a.   Souvenir sheet of 3 1.00 1.00
     Nos. 163-165 (3) .80 .80

Easter. No. 165a contains one each of Nos. 163-165, perf. 13 ½, and label showing Louvre, Paris. See Nos. B27-B29.

Souvenir Sheet

25th Anniv. of Coronation of Queen Elizabeth II. — A45

1978, June 15 Photo.   Perf. 13½x13
166 A45 Sheet of 6 2.50 2.50
  a. $1 Yale of Beaufort .35 .35
  b. $1 Elizabeth II .35 .35
  c. $1 Ancestral statue .35 .35
  d.   Souvenir sheet of 6 2.25 2.25

No. 166d contains 2 strips of Nos. 166a-166c separated by horizontal slate green gutter showing Royal family on balcony, silver marginal inscription.

Virgin and Child, by Dürer — A46

Designs: Various paintings of the Virgin and Child by Albrecht Dürer.

Capt. Cook, by Nathaniel Dance — A47

1978, Dec. 4 Photo.   Perf. 14½x13
167 A46 15c multicolored .35 .35
168 A46 17c multicolored .40 .40
169 A46 30c multicolored .55 .55
170 A46 35c multicolored .65 .65
     Nos. 167-170 (4) 1.95 1.95

Christmas; 450th death anniv. of Albrecht Dürer (1471-1528), German painter. Nos. 167-170 issued in sheets of 5 stamps and corner label. See No. B30.

Design: 75c, "Resolution" and "Adventure," by William Hodges.

1979, July 20 Photo.   Perf. 14x13½
171 A47 50c multicolored 1.50 1.00
172 A47 75c multicolored 2.00 1.50
  a.   Souvenir sheet of 2, #171-172 2.75 2.75

Capt. James Cook (1728-1779), explorer, death bicentenary.

Boy Holding Hibiscus, IYC Emblem — A48

IYC Emblem and: 35c, Boy playing guitar. 65c, Boys in outrigger canoe.

1979, Oct. 1 Photo.   Perf. 14x13½
173 A48 30c multicolored .25 .25
174 A48 35c multicolored .35 .35
175 A48 65c multicolored .45 .45
     Nos. 173-175 (3) 1.05 1.05

See No. B31.

Aitutaki No. 102, Hill, Penny Black
A49

Designs: Nos. 176, 178-179, 181, paintings of letter writers, Flemish School, 17th century.

1979, Nov. 14 Photo.   Perf. 13
176 A49 50c Gabriel Metsu .50 .50
177 A49 50c shown .50 .50
178 A49 50c Jan Vermeer .50 .50
179 A49 65c Gerard Terborch .60 .60
180 A49 65c (like No. 177) .60 .60
181 A49 65c Jan Vermeer .60 .60
  a.   Strip of 3, #179-181 2.00 2.00
     Nos. 176-181 (6) 3.30 3.30

Souvenir Sheet

182 Sheet of 6 2.75 2.75
  a.   A49 30c like No. 176 .40 .40
  b.   A49 30c like No. 177 .40 .40
  c.   A49 30c like No. 178 .40 .40
  d.   A49 30c like No. 179 .40 .40
  e.   A49 30c like No. 180 .40 .40
  f.   A49 30c like No. 181 .40 .40

Sir Rowland Hill (1795-1879), originator of penny postage. Nos. 176-178 and 179-181 printed in sheets of 9.

Descent from the Cross, Detail — A50

Easter: 30c, 35c, Descent from the Cross, by Quentin Metsys (details).

1980, Apr. 3   Photo.   Perf. 13x13½
183 A50 20c multicolored   .50   .40
184 A50 30c multicolored   .60   .50
185 A50 50c multicolored   .70   .60
    Nos. 183-185 (3)   1.80 1.50
    See No. B32.

Albert Einstein — A51

No. 187, Formula, atom structure. No. 188, Portrait, diff. No. 189, Atomic blast. No. 190, Portrait, diff. No. 191, Atomic blast, trees.

1980, July 21   Photo.   Perf. 14
186 A51 12c shown   .65   .65
187 A51 12c multicolored   .65   .65
 a.   Pair, #186-187   1.50 1.50
188 A51 15c multicolored   .70   .70
189 A51 15c multicolored   .70   .70
 a.   Pair, #188-189   1.60 1.60
190 A51 20c multicolored   .80   .80
191 A51 20c multicolored   .80   .80
 a.   Pair, #190-191   2.00 2.00
 b.   Souv. sheet of 6, #186-191, perf.
       13   5.00 5.00
    Nos. 186-191 (6)   4.30 4.30

Albert Einstein (1879-1955), theoretical physicist.

A52

No. 192, Ancestral Figure, Aitutaki. No. 193, God image staff, Rarotonga. No. 194, Trade adze, Mangaia. No. 195, Tangaroa carving, Rarotonga. No. 196, Wooden image, Aitutaki. No. 197, Hand club, Rarotonga. No. 198, Carved mace, Mangaia. No. 199, Fisherman's god, Rarotonga. No. 200, Ti'i image, Aitutaki. No. 201, Fisherman's god, diff. No. 202, Carved mace, Cook Islands. No. 203, Tangaroa, diff. No. 204, Chief's headdress, Aitutaki. No. 205, Carved mace, diff. No. 206, God image staff, diff.

1980, Sept. 26   Photo.   Perf. 14
192 A52 6c multicolored   .25   .25
193 A52 6c multicolored   .25   .25
194 A52 6c multicolored   .25   .25
195 A52 6c multicolored   .25   .25
 a.   Block of 4, #192-195   .60   .60
196 A52 12c multicolored   .25   .25
197 A52 12c multicolored   .25   .25
198 A52 12c multicolored   .25   .25
199 A52 12c multicolored   .25   .25
 a.   Block of 4, #196-199   .85   .85
200 A52 15c multicolored   .25   .25
201 A52 15c multicolored   .25   .25
202 A52 15c multicolored   .25   .25
203 A52 15c multicolored   .25   .25
 a.   Block of 4, #200-203   1.00 1.00
204 A52 20c multicolored   .40   .40
205 A52 20c multicolored   .40   .40
206 A52 20c multicolored   .40   .40
207 A52 20c like #195   .40   .40
 a.   Block of 4, #204-207   1.50 1.50
 b.   Souvenir sheet of 16, #192-207 4.00 4.00

Third South Pacific Arts Festival, Port Moresby, Papua New Guinea.

A53

Virgin and Child, Sculptures.

1980, Nov. 21   Photo.   Perf. 13x13½
208 A53 15c 13th cent.   .25   .25
209 A53 20c 14th cent.   .25   .25
210 A53 25c 15th cent.   .30   .30
211 A53 35c 15th cent., diff.   .40   .40
    Nos. 208-211 (4)   1.20 1.20

Christmas. See No. B33.

Mourning Virgin, by Pedro Roldan — A54

Easter (Roldan Sculptures): 40c, Christ. 50c, Mourning St. John.

1981, Mar. 31   Photo.   Perf. 14
212 A54 30c green & gold   .35   .35
213 A54 40c brt purple & gold   .40   .40
214 A54 50c dk blue & gold   .45   .45
    Nos. 212-214 (3)   1.20 1.20

    See No. B34.

Sturnus Vulgaris — A55

No. 216, Poephila gouldiae. No. 217, Petroica multicolor. No. 218, Pachycephala pectoralis. No. 219, Falco peregrinus. No. 220, Rhipidura rufifrons. No. 221, Tyto alba. No. 222, Padda oryzivora. No. 223, Artamus leucorhynchus. No. 224, Vini peruviana. No. 225, Columba livia. No. 226, Porphyrio porphyria. No. 227, Geopelia striata. No. 228, Lonchura castaneothorax. No. 229, Acridotheres tristis. No. 230, Egretta sacra. No. 231, Diomeda melanophris. No. 232, Numenius phaeopus. No. 233, Gygis alba. No. 234, Pluvialis dominica. No. 235, Sula leucogaster. No. 236, Anas superciliosa. No. 237, Anas acuta. No. 238, Fregata minor. No. 239, Stercorarius pomarinus. No. 240, Conopoderas caffra. No. 241, Lalage maculosa. No. 242, Gallirallus philippensis. No. 243, Vini stepheni. No. 244, Diomedea epomophora. No. 245, Ptilinopus victor. No. 246, Erythrura cyaneovirens. $1, Myiagra azureocapilla. $2, Myiagra vanikorensis. $4, Amandava amandava. $5, Halcyon recurvirostris.

1981-82   Perf. 14x13½, 13½x14
215 A55 1c shown   .40   .25
216 A55 1c multicolored   .40   .25
 a.   Pair, #215-216   1.00   .30
217 A55 2c multicolored   .45   .25
218 A55 2c multicolored   .45   .25
 a.   Pair, #217-218   1.10   .30
219 A55 3c multicolored   .55   .25
220 A55 3c multicolored   .55   .25
 a.   Pair, #219-220   1.25   .30
221 A55 4c multicolored   .65   .25
222 A55 4c multicolored   .65   .25
 a.   Pair, #221-222   1.50   .35
223 A55 5c multicolored   .70   .25
224 A55 5c multicolored   .70   .25
 a.   Pair, #223-224   1.60   .40
225 A55 6c multicolored   .75   .25
226 A55 6c multicolored   .75   .25
 a.   Pair, #225-226   1.75   .40
227 A55 10c multicolored   .85   .25
228 A55 10c multicolored   .85   .25
 a.   Pair, #227-228   2.00   .75

229 A55 12c multicolored   .90   .30
230 A55 12c multicolored   .90   .30
 a.   Pair, #229-230   2.10   .85
231 A55 15c multicolored   1.00   .40
232 A55 15c multicolored   1.00   .40
 a.   Pair, #231-232   2.75 1.25
233 A55 20c multicolored   1.25   .50
234 A55 20c multicolored   1.25   .50
 a.   Pair, #233-234   3.25 1.50
235 A55 25c multicolored   1.40   .60
236 A55 25c multicolored   1.40   .60
 a.   Pair, #235-236   3.75 1.60
237 A55 30c multicolored   1.50   .65
238 A55 30c multicolored   1.50   .65
 a.   Pair, #237-238   4.00 2.00
239 A55 35c multicolored   1.60   .75
240 A55 35c multicolored   1.60   .75
 a.   Pair, #239-240   4.25 3.00
241 A55 40c multicolored   1.75   .90
242 A55 40c multicolored   1.75   .90
 a.   Pair, #241-242   4.50 3.25
243 A55 50c multicolored   2.00 1.00
244 A55 50c multicolored   2.00 1.00
 a.   Pair, #243-244   5.00 3.50
245 A55 70c multicolored   4.25 2.00
246 A55 70c multicolored   4.25 2.00
 e.   Pair, #245-246   11.00 7.50

Size: 35x47mm

Photo.   Perf. 13½
246A A55 $1 multicolored   5.00 3.75
246B A55 $2 multicolored   5.50 7.50
246C A55 $4 multicolored   9.00 13.50
246D A55 $5 multicolored   11.00 17.50
    Nos. 215-246D (36)   70.50 59.95

Issued: Nos. 215-230, 4/6; Nos. 231-238, 5/8; Nos. 239-246, 1/14/82; Nos. 246A-246B, 2/15/82.
Nos. 231-246 horiz.
For surcharges and overprint see Nos. 293-306, 452-454, O40-O41.

Prince Charles and Lady Diana — A56

Perf. 13x13½, 13½x13
1981, June 10   Photo.
247 A56 60c Charles, vert.   .40   .40
248 A56 80c Lady Diana, vert.   .50   .50
    Complete booklet, one sheet of 4
      each #247-248   6.00
249 A56 $1.40 Shown   .60   .60
    Nos. 247-249 (3)   1.50 1.50

Royal Wedding. Issued in sheets of 4. For overprints and surcharges see Nos. 265-267, 307, 309, 355, 405-407, B35-B37.

1982 World Cup Soccer — A57

Designs: Various soccer players.

1981, Nov. 30   Photo.   Perf. 14
250 A57 12c Pair, #250a-250b   1.10 1.00
251 A57 15c Pair, #251a-251b   1.25 1.10
252 A57 20c Pair, #252a-252b   1.50 1.25
253 A57 25c Pair, #253a-253b   1.75 1.40
    Nos. 250-253 (4)   5.60 4.75

    See No. B38.

Christmas A58

Rembrandt Etchings: 15c, Holy Family, 1632, vert. 30c, Virgin with Child, 1634, vert. 40c, Adoration of the Shepherds, 1654. 50c, Holy Family with Cat, 1644.

1981, Dec. 10   Perf. 14
254 A58 15c gold & dk brown   .50   .50
255 A58 30c gold & dk brown   .65   .60
256 A58 40c gold & dk brown   .75   .75
257 A58 50c gold & dk brown   1.00 1.00
    Nos. 254-257 (4)   2.90 2.85

Souvenir Sheets
258 A58 80c + 5c like #254   .80   .75
259 A58 80c + 5c like #255   .80   .75
260 A58 80c + 5c like #256   .80   .75
261 A58 80c + 5c like #257   .80   .75

Nos. 258-261 have multicolored margins showing entire etching. Surtax on Nos. 258-261 was for local charities.

21st Birthday of Princess Diana — A59

1982, June 24   Photo.   Perf. 14
262 A59 70c shown   1.75   .75
263 A59 $1 Wedding portrait   1.75   .90
264 A59 $2 Diana, diff.   2.75 1.50
 a.   Souvenir sheet of 3, #262-264 6.00 6.00
    Nos. 262-264 (3)   6.25 3.15

See Nos. 268-270a. For surcharges see Nos. 308, 310.

Nos. 247-249 Overprinted

         a   b

1982, July 13   Perf. 13x13½, 13½x13
265 A56 60c Pair, #a.-b.   1.50 1.25
266 A56 80c Pair, #a.-b.   2.25 2.00
267 A56 $1.40 Pair, #a.-b.   3.75 3.25
    Nos. 265-267 (3)   7.50 6.50

Nos. 265-267 were overprinted with alternating inscriptions within the sheet.

Nos. 262-264a Inscribed: "Royal Birth 21 June 1982 Prince William Of Wales"

1982, Aug. 5   Perf. 14
268 A59 70c multicolored   .70   .70
269 A59 $1 multicolored   1.50 1.50
270 A59 $2 multicolored   2.00 2.00
 a.   Souvenir sheet of 3   5.00 5.00
    Nos. 268-270 (3)   4.20 4.20

Christmas — A60

Madonna and Child Sculptures, 12th-15th Cent.

1982, Dec. 10   Photo.   Perf. 13
271 A60 18c multicolored   .65   .65
272 A60 36c multicolored   .75   .75
273 A60 48c multicolored   .90   .90
274 A60 60c multicolored   1.25 1.25
    Nos. 271-274 (4)   3.55 3.55

Souvenir Sheet
275   Sheet of 4   4.50 4.50
 a.   A60 18c + 2c like 18c   .70   .70
 b.   A60 36c + 2c like 36c   .80   .80
 c.   A60 48c + 2c like 48c   1.00 1.00
 d.   A60 60c + 2c like 60c   1.25 1.25

Surtax was for children's charities.

Commonwealth Day — A61

1983, Mar. 14   Photo.   Perf. 13x13½
276 A61 48c Bananas   .95   .95
277 A61 48c Ti'i statuette   .95   .95
278 A61 48c Boys canoeing   .95   .95
279 A61 48c Capt. Bligh, Bounty   .95   .95
  a.   Block of 4, #276-279   4.75 4.75

Scouting
Year
A62

1983, Apr. 18   Photo.   Perf. 14
280 A62 36c Campfire   .50   .50
281 A62 48c Salute   .60   .60
282 A62 60c Hiking   .70   .70
     Nos. 280-282 (3)   1.80 1.80

Souvenir Sheet
Perf. 13½
283   Sheet of 3   2.50 2.50
  a.   A62 36c + 3c like #280   .60   .60
  b.   A62 48c + 3c like #281   .70   .70
  c.   A62 60c + 3c like #282   .90   .90

Surtax was for benefit of Scouting.

Nos. 280-283 Overprinted

1983, July 11   Photo.   Perf. 14
284 A62 36c multicolored   .85   .85
285 A62 48c multicolored   1.00 1.00
286 A62 60c multicolored   1.25 1.25
     Nos. 284-286 (3)   3.10 3.10

Souvenir Sheet
287   Sheet of 3   3.00 3.00
  a.   A62 36c + 3c like #284   .65   .65
  b.   A62 48c + 3c like #285   .80   .80
  c.   A62 60c + 3c like #286   1.00 1.00

A63

Manned Flight Bicentenary: Modern sport balloons.

1983, July 22   Photo.   Perf. 14x13
288 A63 18c multicolored   .60   .60
289 A63 36c multicolored   .75   .75
290 A63 48c multicolored   1.00 1.00
291 A63 60c multicolored   1.25 1.25
     Nos. 288-291 (4)   3.60 3.60

Souvenir Sheet
292 A63 $2.50 multicolored   3.25 3.25

Nos. 233-
246, 246D,
248-249
Surcharged
in Black

Nos. 263-264
Surcharged in Black
and Gold

1983, Sept. 22
293 A55 18c on 20c, #233   2.75 1.00
294 A55 18c on 20c, #234   2.75 1.00
  a.   Pair, #293-294   6.00 2.25
295 A55 36c on 25c, #235   3.25 1.25
296 A55 36c on 25c, #236   3.25 1.25
  a.   Pair, #295-296   7.25 3.00
297 A55 36c on 30c, #237   3.25 1.25
298 A55 36c on 30c, #238   3.25 1.25
  a.   Pair, #297-298   7.25 3.00
299 A55 36c on 35c, #239   3.50 1.40
300 A55 36c on 35c, #240   3.50 1.40
  a.   Pair, #299-300   7.50 3.25
301 A55 48c on 40c, #241   4.50 1.40
302 A55 48c on 40c, #242   4.50 1.40
  a.   Pair, #301-302   10.00 3.25
303 A55 48c on 50c, #243   4.50 1.40
304 A55 48c on 50c, #244   4.50 1.40
  a.   Pair, #303-304   10.00 3.25
305 A55 72c on 70c, #245   7.50 2.50
306 A55 72c on 70c, #246   7.50 2.50
  a.   Pair, #305-306   16.50 7.50
307 A56 96c on 80c, #248   3.00 2.25
308 A59 96c on $1, #263   2.75 2.00
309 A56 $1.20 on $1.40,
                     #249   3.00 2.25
310 A59 $1.20 on $2, #264   2.75 2.00

Size: 35x47mm
311 A55 $5.60 on $5, #246D   20.00 10.00
     Nos. 293-311 (19)   90.00 38.90
     Nos. 307-308, 310-311 vert.

A64

60, Global coverage. 96c, Communications satellite.

1983, Sept. 29   Photo.   Perf. 14
312 A64 48c shown   .80   .55
313 A64 60c multicolored   1.25   .70
314 A64 96c multicolored   1.50 1.25
  a.   Souvenir sheet of 3, #312-314 3.25 3.25
     Nos. 312-314 (3)   3.55 2.50

World Communications Year.

Christmas
A65

Raphael Paintings — 36c, Madonna of the Chair. 48c, Alba Madonna. 60c, Connestabile Madonna.

1983, Nov. 21   Photo.   Perf. 13½x14
315 A65 36c multicolored   .75   .40
316 A65 48c multicolored   1.00   .80
317 A65 60c multicolored   1.50 1.00
     Nos. 315-317 (3)   3.25 2.20

Souvenir Sheet
318   Sheet of 3   3.50 3.50
  a.   A65 36c + 3c like #315   1.00 1.00
  b.   A65 48c + 3c like #316   1.10 1.10
  c.   A65 60c + 3c like #317   1.25 1.25

1983, Dec. 15   Imperf.
Size: 46x46mm
319 A65 85c + 5c like #315   1.50 1.50
320 A65 85c + 5c like #316   1.50 1.50
321 A65 85c + 5c like #317   1.50 1.50
     Nos. 319-321 (3)   4.50 4.50

Surtax was for children's charities.

Local
Birds — A66

1984   Photo.   Perf. 14
322 A66   2c as No. 216   1.75   .90
323 A66   3c as No. 215   1.75   .90
324 A66   5c as No. 217   1.75 1.00
325 A66 10c as No. 218   2.50 1.00
326 A66 12c as No. 220   2.50 1.00
327 A66 18c as No. 219   2.50 1.25
328 A66 24c as No. 221   2.50 1.25
329 A66 30c as No. 222   2.50 1.25
330 A66 36c as No. 223   2.50 1.25
331 A66 48c as No. 224   2.50 1.25
332 A66 50c as No. 225   2.75 1.75
333 A66 60c as No. 226   2.75 1.75
334 A66 72c as No. 227   3.25 1.75
335 A66 96c as No. 228   3.25 1.75
336 A66 $1.20 as No. 229   3.25 2.50
337 A66 $2.10 as No. 230   3.75 3.50
338 A66 $3 as No. 246A   5.25 4.50
339 A66 $4.20 as No. 246B   4.00 5.75
340 A66 $5.60 as No. 246C   5.25 7.00
341 A66 $9.60 as No. 246D   8.00 10.00
     Nos. 322-341 (20)   64.25 51.30

For overprints and surcharges see Nos. O17-O39.

1984 Summer
Olympics — A67

1984, July 24   Photo.   Perf. 13x13½
342 A67 36c Javelin   .50   .50
343 A67 48c Shot put   .60   .60
344 A67 60c Hurdles   .70   .70
345 A67 $2   Handball   2.00 2.00
     Nos. 342-345 (4)   3.80 3.80

Souvenir Sheet
346   Sheet of 4   3.50 3.50
  a.   A67 36c + 5c like #342   .40   .40
  b.   A67 48c + 5c like #343   .55   .55
  c.   A67 60c + 5c like #344   .65   .65
  d.   A67 $2 + 5c like #345   1.50 1.50

Surtax was for benefit of local sports.

Nos. 342-345
Overprinted in
Gold and Black

1984, Aug. 21   Photo.   Perf. 13x13½
347 A67 36c multicolored   .40   .40
348 A67 48c multicolored   .50   .50
349 A67 60c multicolored   .60   .60
350 A67 $2   multicolored   1.75 1.75
     Nos. 347-350 (4)   3.25 3.25

Ausipex
'84 — A68

60c, William Bligh, map. 96c, Bounty, map. $1.40, Stamps, map.

1984, Sept. 14   Photo.   Perf. 14
351 A68 60c multicolored   4.50 4.50
352 A68 96c multicolored   4.50 4.50
353 A68 $1.40 multicolored   4.50 4.50
     Nos. 351-353 (3)   13.50 13.50

Souvenir Sheet
354   Sheet of 3   8.50 8.50
  a.   A68 60c + 5c like #351   1.75 1.75
  b.   A68 96c + 5c like #352   2.50 2.50
  c.   A68 $1.40 + 5c like #353   3.75 3.75

For overprint see No. 399.

No. 247 Surcharged

1984, Oct. 10   Photo.   Perf. 13x13½
355 A56 $3 on 60c multi   3.25 3.25

Issued in sheets of 4.

A69

1984, Nov. 16   Photo.   Perf. 13
356 A69 36c Annunciation   .55   .55
357 A69 48c Nativity   .65   .65
358 A69 60c Epiphany   .75   .75
359 A69 96c Flight into Egypt   1.00 1.00
     Nos. 356-359 (4)   2.95 2.95

Souvenir Sheets
Size: 45x53mm
Imperf
360 A69 90c + 7c like #356   1.25 1.25
361 A69 90c + 7c like #357   1.25 1.25
362 A69 90c + 7c like #358   1.25 1.25
363 A69 90c + 7c like #359   1.25 1.25

Christmas.

A70

1984, Dec. 10   Photo.   Perf. 13½x14
364 A70 48c Diana, Henry   2.75 2.75
365 A70 60c William, Henry   2.75 2.75
366 A70 $2.10 Family   3.50 3.50
     Nos. 364-366 (3)   9.00 9.00

Souvenir Sheet
367   Sheet of 3   8.00 8.00
  a.   A70 96c + 7c like #364   2.50 2.50
  b.   A70 96c + 7c like #365   2.50 2.50
  c.   A70 96c + 7c like #366   2.50 2.50

Christmas, Birth of Prince Henry, Sept. 15. Surtax was for benefit of local children's charities.

Audubon Birth
Bicentenary
A71

Illustrations of bird species by John J. Audubon — 55c, Gray kingbird. 65c, Bohemian waxwing. 75c, Summer tanager. 95c, Cardinal. $1.15, White-winged crossbill.

1985, Mar. 22 Litho. Perf. 13

368	A71	55c multicolored	1.25	1.25
369	A71	65c multicolored	1.50	1.50
370	A71	75c multicolored	1.75	1.75
371	A71	95c multicolored	2.00	2.00
372	A71	$1.15 multicolored	3.00	3.00
		Nos. 368-372 (5)	9.50	9.50

Queen Mother, 85th Birthday A72

Photographs: 55c, Lady Elizabeth Bowes-Lyon, age 7. 65c, Engaged to the Duke of York, 75c, Duchess of York with daughter, Elizabeth. $1.30, Holding the infant Prince Charles. $3, Portrait taken on 63rd birthday.

1985-86 Perf. 13½x13

373	A72	55c multicolored	.75	.75
374	A72	65c multicolored	.85	.85
375	A72	75c multicolored	1.00	1.00
376	A72	$1.30 multicolored	1.50	1.50
a.		Souvenir sheet of 4, #373-376	9.00	7.50
		Nos. 373-376 (4)	4.10	4.10

Souvenir Sheet

377	A72	$3 multicolored	5.00	5.00

Nos. 373-376 printed in sheets of 4. Issued: No. 376a, 8/4/86; others, 6/14/85. For overprint see No. 446.

Intl. Youth Year A73

Designs: 75c, The Calmady Children, by Thomas Lawrence (1769-1830). 90c, Madame Charpentier's Children, by Renoir (1841-1919). $1.40, Young Girls at Piano, by Renoir.

1985, Sept. 16 Photo. Perf. 13

378	A73	75c multicolored	3.00	3.00
379	A73	90c multicolored	3.00	3.00
380	A73	$1.40 multicolored	4.00	4.00
		Nos. 378-380 (3)	10.00	10.00

Souvenir Sheet

381		Sheet of 3	8.00	8.00
a.		A73 75c +10c like #378	2.00	2.00
b.		A73 90c +10c like #379	2.25	2.25
c.		A73 $1.40 +10c like #380	3.00	3.00

Surcharged for children's activities.

Adoration of the Magi, by Giotto di Bondone (1276-1337) — A74

Nos. 382, 384, Giotto probe. Nos. 383, 385, Planet A probe.

1985, Nov. 15 Photo. Perf. 13½x13

382	A74	95c multicolored	2.00	2.00
383	A74	95c multicolored	2.00	2.00
a.		Pair, #382-383	4.50	4.50
384	A74	$1.15 multicolored	2.00	2.00
385	A74	$1.15 multicolored	2.00	2.00
a.		Pair, #384-385	4.50	4.50
		Nos. 382-385 (4)	8.00	8.00

Souvenir Sheet
Imperf

386	A74	$6.40 multicolored	16.50	16.50

Christmas, return of Halley's Comet, 1985-86.

Halley's Comet A75

Designs: 90c, Halley's Comet, A.D. 684, wood engraving, Nuremberg Chronicles. $1.25, Sighting of 1066, Bayeux Tapestry, detail, c. 1092, France. $1.75, The Comet Inflicting Untold Disasters, 1456, Lucerne Chronicles, by Diebolt Schilling. $4.20, Melancolia I, engraving by Durer.

1986, Feb. 25 Photo. Perf. 13½x13

387	A75	90c multicolored	1.25	1.25
388	A75	$1.25 multicolored	1.75	1.75
389	A75	$1.75 multicolored	2.75	2.75
		Nos. 387-389 (3)	5.75	5.75

Souvenir Sheets

390		Sheet of 3 + label	7.50	7.50
a.		A75 95c, like #387	2.25	2.25
b.		A75 95c, like #388	2.25	2.25
c.		A75 95c, like #389	2.25	2.25

Imperf

391	A75	$4.20 multicolored	7.00	7.00

Elizabeth II, 60th Birthday — A76

1986, Apr. 21 Perf. 14

392	A76	95c Coronation portrait	1.25	1.25

Souvenir Sheet
Perf. 13½

393	A76	$4.20 Portrait, diff.	6.50	6.50

No. 392 printed in sheets of 5 with label picturing U.K. flag and Queen's flag for New Zealand.

Statue of Liberty, Cent. A77

1986, June 27 Photo. Perf. 14

394	A77	$1 Liberty head	1.75	1.75
395	A77	$2.75 Statue	3.50	3.50

Souvenir Sheet
Perf. 13½

396		Sheet of 2	3.50	3.50
a.		A77 $1.25 like $1	1.60	1.60
b.		A77 $1.25 like $2.75	1.60	1.60

For surcharges see Nos B45, B49.

Wedding of Prince Andrew and Sarah Ferguson — A78

1986, July 23 Perf. 14

397	A78	$2 multicolored	3.00	3.00

Souvenir Sheet
Perf. 13½

398	A78	$5 multicolored	7.00	7.00

No. 397 printed in sheets of 5 plus label picturing Westminster Abbey. For surcharge see No. B48.

No. 354 Overprinted

1986, Aug. 4 Photo. Perf. 14

399		Sheet of 3	14.50	14.50
a.		A68 60c + 5c like #351	3.50	3.50
b.		A68 96c + 5c like #352	4.00	4.00
c.		A68 $1.40 + 5c like #353	6.50	6.50

STAMPEX '86, Adelaide, Aug. 4-10.

Christmas A79

Paintings by Albrecht Durer: 75c, No. 404a, St. Anne with Virgin and Child. $1.35, No. 404b, Virgin and Child. $1.95, No. 404c, Adoration of the Magi. $2.75, No. 404d, Rosary Festivity.

1986, Nov. 21 Litho. Perf. 13½

400	A79	75c multicolored	1.50	1.50
401	A79	$1.35 multicolored	2.50	2.50
402	A79	$1.95 multicolored	3.50	3.50
403	A79	$2.75 multicolored	5.00	5.00
		Nos. 400-403 (4)	12.50	12.50

Souvenir Sheet

404		Sheet of 4	17.00	17.00
a.-d.		A79 $1.65 any single	4.00	4.00

For surcharges see Nos. B39-B44, B46-B47, B50-B54.

Nos. 247-249 Srchd. in Gold and Black

1987, Nov. 20 Photo. Perf. 13x12½

405	A56	$2.50 on 60c No. 247	2.75	2.75
406	A56	$2.50 on 80c No. 248	2.75	2.75
407	A56	$2.50 on $1.40 No. 249	2.75	2.75
		Nos. 405-407 (3)	8.25	8.25

Issued in sheets of 4 with margin inscriptions overprinted with gold bar and "40th Anniversary of the Royal Wedding / 1947-1987" in black; "OVERPRINTED BY NEW ZEALAND GOVERNMENT PRINTER, / WELLINGTON, NOVEMBER 1987" at left.

A80

The Virgin with Garland, by Rubens — A81

Painting details.

1987, Dec. 10 Photo. Perf. 13x13½

408	A80	70c UL	2.25	2.25
409	A80	85c UR	2.75	2.75
410	A80	$1.50 LL	3.25	3.25
411	A80	$1.85 LR	4.00	4.00
		Nos. 408-411 (4)	12.25	12.25

Souvenir Sheets

412		Sheet of 4	14.50	14.50
a.		A80 95c like No. 408	3.50	3.50
b.		A80 95c like No. 409	3.50	3.50
c.		A80 95c like No. 410	3.50	3.50
d.		A80 95c like No. 411	3.50	3.50

Perf. 13

413	A81	$6 multicolored	16.00	16.00

Christmas.

1988 Summer Olympics, Seoul — A82

Flags of Korea, Aitutaki, ancient and modern events, and Seoul Games emblem or $50 silver coin issued to commemorate the participation of Aitutaki athletes in the Olympics for the 1st time: 70c, No. 418a, Obverse of silver coin, chariot race, running. 85c, Emblem, running. 95c, Emblem, boxing, handball. $1.40, No. 418b, Reverse of coin, spearmen, women's tennis.

1988, Aug. 22 Photo. Perf. 14½x15

414	A82	70c multicolored	2.50	2.50
415	A82	85c multicolored	2.75	2.75
416	A82	95c multicolored	2.75	2.75
417	A82	$1.40 multicolored	3.50	3.50
		Nos. 414-417 (4)	11.50	11.50

Souvenir Sheet

418		Sheet of 2	9.00	9.00
a.-b.		A82 $2 any single	4.25	4.25

Nos. 414-417 Ovptd. with Names of 1988 Olympic Gold Medalists

a

GELINDO BORDIN ITALY MARATHON

b

HITOSHI SAITO JAPAN JUDO

c

STEFFI GRAF WEST GERMANY WOMEN'S TENNIS

d

1988, Oct. 10   Litho.   Perf. 14½x15

419	A82 (a)	70c on No. 414	2.00	2.00
420	A82 (b)	85c on No. 415	2.00	2.00
421	A82 (c)	95c on No. 416	2.00	2.00
422	A82 (d)	$1.40 on No. 417	4.25	4.25
		Nos. 419-422 (4)	10.25	10.25

Griffith is spelled incorrectly on No. 419.

Christmas A83

Paintings by Rembrandt: 55c, Adoration of the Shepherds (detail), National Gallery, London. 70c, Holy Family, Alte Pinakothek, Munich. 85c, Presentation in the Temple, Kunsthalle, Hamburg. 95c, The Holy Family, Louvre, Paris. $1.15, Presentation in the Temple, diff., Mauritshuis, The Hague. $4.50, Adoration of the Shepherds (entire painting).

1988, Nov. 2   Photo.   Perf. 13½

423	A83	55c multicolored	2.00	2.00
424	A83	70c multicolored	2.25	2.25
425	A83	85c multicolored	2.50	2.50
426	A83	95c multicolored	2.75	2.75
427	A83	$1.15 multicolored	3.25	3.25
		Nos. 423-427 (5)	12.75	12.75

Souvenir Sheet
Perf. 14

428	A83	$4.50 multicolored	9.50	9.50

No. 428 contains one 52x34mm stamp.

A84

Mutiny on the *Bounty*, 200th Anniv. — A85

55c, Ship, Capt. Bligh. 65c, Breadfruit. 75c, Bligh, chart. 95c, Bounty off Aitutaki. $1.65, Christian, Bligh. $4.20, Castaways.

1989, July 3   Photo.   Perf. 13½

429	A84	55c multicolored	2.25	2.25
430	A84	65c multicolored	2.75	2.75
431	A84	75c multicolored	3.00	3.00
432	A84	95c multicolored	3.50	3.50
433	A84	$1.65 multicolored	4.25	4.25
		Nos. 429-433 (5)	15.75	15.75

Souvenir Sheet

434	A85	$4.20 multicolored	13.50	13.50

Discovery of Aitutaki by William Bligh, bicent.

1st Moon Landing, 20th Anniv. — A86

Apollo 11 mission emblem, American flag, eagle, "The Eagle has landed" and: 75c, Astronaut standing on the lunar surface. $1.15, Conducting an experiment in front of the lunar module. $1.80, Carrying equipment. $6.40, Raising the flag.

1989, July 28   Photo.   Perf. 13½x13

435	A86	75c multicolored	3.00	3.00
436	A86	$1.15 multicolored	3.50	3.50
437	A86	$1.80 multicolored	4.50	4.50
		Nos. 435-437 (3)	11.00	11.00

Souvenir Sheet
Perf. 13½

438	A86	$6.40 multicolored	11.50	11.50

No. 438 contains one 42x31mm stamp.

Christmas — A87

Details from *Virgin in Glory*, by Titian: 70c, Virgin. 85c, Christ child. 95c, Angel. $1.25, Cherubs. $6, Entire painting.

1989, Nov. 20   Photo.   Perf. 13½x13

439	A87	70c multicolored	2.50	2.50
440	A87	85c multicolored	3.00	3.00
441	A87	95c multicolored	3.50	3.50
442	A87	$1.25 multicolored	4.25	4.25
		Nos. 439-442 (4)	13.25	13.25

Souvenir Sheet
Perf. 13½

443	A87	$6 multicolored	13.00	13.00

No. 443 contains one 45x60mm stamp.

World Environmental Protection — A88

Designs: a, Human comet, World Philatelic Programs emblem. b, Comet tail and "Protect The Endangered Earth!" $3, Human comet, emblem and inscription.

1990, Feb. 16   Photo.   Perf. 13½x13

444	A88	Pair	7.25	7.25
a.-b.		$1.75 any single	3.25	3.25

Souvenir Sheet

445	A88	$3 multicolored	8.00	8.00

No. 376a Overprinted

Designs: 55c, Lady Elizabeth Bowes-Lyon, 1907. 65c, Lady Elizabeth engaged to Duke of York. 75c, As Duchess of York with daughter Elizabeth. $1.30, As Queen Mother with grandson.

1990, July 16   Litho.   Perf. 13½x13

446		Sheet of 4	16.00	16.00
a.	A72	55c multicolored	2.50	2.50
b.	A72	65c multicolored	3.25	3.25
c.	A72	75c multicolored	4.00	4.00
d.	A72	$1.30 multicolored	6.25	6.25

Christmas — A89

Paintings: 70c, Madonna of the Basket by Correggio. 85c, Virgin and Child by Morando. 95c, Adoration of the Child by Tiepolo. $1.75, Mystic Marriage of St. Catherine by Memling. $6, Donne Triptych by Memling.

1990, Nov. 28   Litho.   Perf. 14

447	A89	70c multicolored	1.90	1.90
448	A89	85c multicolored	2.10	2.10
449	A89	95c multicolored	2.50	2.50
450	A89	$1.75 multicolored	3.50	3.50
		Nos. 447-450 (4)	10.00	10.00

Souvenir Sheet

451	A89	$6 multicolored	15.00	15.00

Nos. 246A-246B Overprinted

1990, Dec. 5   Photo.   Perf. 13½

452	A55	$1 multicolored	6.50	6.50
453	A55	$2 multicolored	7.50	7.50

Birdpex '90, 20 Intl. Ornithological Congress, New Zealand.

No. 246D Overprinted

COMMEMORATING 65th BIRTHDAY OF H.M. QUEEN ELIZABETH II

1991, Apr. 22   Photo.   Perf. 13

454	A55	$5 multicolored	13.00	13.00

Christmas — A90

Paintings: 80c, The Holy Family, by Mengs. 90c, Virgin and Child, by Fra Filippo Lippi. $1.05, Virgin and Child, by Durer. $1.75, Adoration of the Shepherds, by De La Tour. $6, The Holy Family, by Michelangelo.

1991, Nov. 13   Litho.   Perf. 14

455	A90	80c multicolored	1.90	1.90
456	A90	90c multicolored	2.10	2.10
457	A90	$1.05 multicolored	2.50	2.50
458	A90	$1.75 multicolored	3.50	3.50
		Nos. 455-458 (4)	10.00	10.00

Souvenir Sheet

459	A90	$6 multicolored	16.00	16.00

1992 Summer Olympics, Barcelona — A91

1992, July 29   Litho.   Perf. 14

460	A91	95c Hurdles	2.75	2.75
461	A91	$1.25 Weight lifting	3.00	3.00
462	A91	$1.50 Judo	3.50	3.50
463	A91	$1.95 Soccer	3.75	3.75
		Nos. 460-463 (4)	13.00	13.00

6th Festival of Pacific Arts, Rarotonga — A92

Canoes: 30c, Vaka Motu. 50c, Hamatafua. 95c, Alia Kalia Ndrua. $1.75, Hokule'a Hawaiian. $1.95, Tuamotu Pahi.

1992, Oct. 16   Litho.   Perf. 14x15

464	A92	30c multicolored	.90	.90
465	A92	50c multicolored	1.10	1.10
466	A92	95c multicolored	2.25	2.25
467	A92	$1.75 multicolored	3.25	2.75
468	A92	$1.95 multicolored	4.00	4.00
		Nos. 464-468 (5)	11.50	11.00

For overprints see Nos. 524-528.

Nos. 464-468 Overprinted

ROYAL VISIT

1992, Oct. 16

469	A92	30c on #464	1.25	1.25
470	A92	50c on #465	2.00	2.00
471	A92	95c on #466	3.25	3.25
472	A92	$1.75 on #467	4.50	4.50
473	A92	$1.95 on #468	5.50	5.50
		Nos. 469-473 (5)	16.50	16.50

Christmas A93

Designs: Different details from Virgin's Nativity, by Guido Reni.

1992, Nov. 19   Litho.   Perf. 13½
474	A93	80c multicolored	2.25	2.25
475	A93	90c multicolored	2.25	2.25
476	A93	$1.05 multicolored	2.40	2.40
477	A93	$1.75 multicolored	3.75	3.75
		Nos. 474-477 (4)	10.65	10.65

Souvenir Sheet
| 478 | A93 | $6 like #476 | 10.00 | 10.00 |

No. 478 contains one 39x50mm stamp.

Discovery of America, 500th Anniv. — A94

Designs: $1.25, Columbus being blessed as he departs from Spain. $1.75, Map of Columbus' four voyages. $1.95, Columbus landing in New World.

1992, Dec. 11   Perf. 14x15
479	A94	$1.25 multicolored	3.50	3.50
480	A94	$1.75 multicolored	4.25	4.25
481	A94	$1.95 multicolored	4.75	4.75
		Nos. 479-481 (3)	12.50	12.50

Coronation of Queen Elizabeth II, 40th Anniv. — A95

Designs: a, Victoria, Edward VII. b, George V, George VI. c, Elizabeth II.

1993, June 4   Litho.   Perf. 14
| 482 | A97 | $1.75 Strip of 3, #a.-c. | 12.50 | 12.50 |

Christmas — A96

Religious sculpture: 80c, Madonna and Child, by Nino Pisano. 90c, Virgin on Rosebush, by Luca Della Robbia. $1.15, Virgin with Child and St. John, by Juan Francisco Rustici. $1.95, Virgin with Child, by Michelangelo. $3, Madonna and Child, by Jacopo Della Quercia.

1993, Oct. 29   Litho.   Perf. 14
483	A96	80c multicolored	1.25	1.25
484	A96	90c multicolored	1.60	1.60
485	A96	$1.15 multicolored	2.00	2.00
486	A96	$1.95 multicolored	3.25	3.25

Size: 32x47mm
Perf. 13½
| 487 | A96 | $3 multicolored | 5.50 | 5.50 |
| | | Nos. 483-487 (5) | 13.60 | 13.60 |

1994 Winter Olympics, Lillehammer — A97

Designs: a, Ice hockey. b, Ski jumping. c, Cross-country skiing.

1994, Feb. 11   Litho.   Perf. 14
| 488 | A97 | $1.15 Strip of 3, #a.-c. | 13.50 | 13.50 |

Flowers — A98

Hibiscus A98a

1994-97   Litho.   Perf. 13½
489	A98	5c Prostrate morning glory	.25	.25
490	A98	10c White frangipani	.25	.25
491	A98	15c Red hibiscus	.35	.25
492	A98	20c Yellow allamanda	.45	.25
493	A98	25c Royal poinciana	.50	.25
494	A98	30c White gardenia	.75	.40
495	A98	50c Pink frangipani	1.10	.85
496	A98	80c Morning glory	1.40	1.25
497	A98	85c Yellow mallow	1.60	1.40
498	A98	90c Red coral tree	1.60	1.40
499	A98	$1 Cup of gold	2.00	1.50
500	A98	$2 Red cordia	2.75	2.75
501	A98a	$3 multicolored	4.50	4.50
502	A98a	$5 multicolored	6.50	6.50
503	A98a	$8 multicolored	10.00	10.00
		Nos. 489-503 (15)	34.00	31.80

Issued: 5c-90c, 2/17; $1, $2, 4/29; $3, $5, 11/18; $8, 11/21/97.

First Manned Moon Landing, 25th Anniv. A99

Designs: No. 506, Astronauts Collins, Armstrong, Aldrin. No. 507, Splash down in South Pacific.

1994, July 20   Litho.   Perf. 14
| 506 | A99 | $2 multicolored | 8.25 | 8.25 |
| 507 | A99 | $2 multicolored | 8.25 | 8.25 |

Christmas — A100

Paintings: No. 508a, The Madonna of the Basket, by Corregio. b, Virgin & Child with Saints, by Hans Memling. c, The Virgin & Child with Flowers, by Dolci. d, Virgin & Child with Angels, by Bergognone.
No. 509a, The Adoration of the Kings, by Dosso. b, The Virgin & Child, by Bellini. c, The Virgin & Child, by Schiavone. d, Adoration of the Kings, by Dolci.

1994, Nov. 30   Litho.   Perf. 14
| 508 | A100 | 85c Block of 4, #a.-d. | 6.25 | 6.25 |
| 509 | A100 | 90c Block of 4, #a.-d. | 6.75 | 6.75 |

End of World War II, 50th Anniv. — A101

Designs: a, Battle of Britain, 1940. b, Battle of Midway, June 1942.

1995, Sept. 4   Litho.   Perf. 13½x13
| 510 | A101 | $4 Pair, #a.-b. | 27.50 | 27.50 |

No. 510 issued in sheets of 4 stamps.

Queen Mother, 95th Birthday A102

1995, Sept. 14   Litho.   Perf. 13x13½
| 511 | A102 | $4 multicolored | 12.50 | 12.50 |

UN, 50th Anniv. — A103

1995, Oct. 18   Litho.   Perf. 13½
| 512 | A103 | $4.25 multicolored | 10.00 | 10.00 |

Year of the Sea Turtle A104

1995, Dec. 1   Litho.   Perf. 14x13½
513	A104	95c Green	3.50	3.50
514	A104	$1.15 Leatherback	3.75	3.75
515	A104	$1.50 Olive Ridley	4.00	4.00
516	A104	$1.75 Loggerhead	4.50	4.50
		Nos. 513-516 (4)	15.75	15.75

Queen Elizabeth II, 70th Birthday A105

1996, June 24   Litho.   Perf. 14
| 517 | A105 | $4.50 multicolored | 9.50 | 9.50 |

No. 517 was issued in sheets of 4.

Modern Olympic Games, Cent. A106

Designs: No. 518, Pierre de Coubertin, Olympic torch, parading athletes, 1896. No. 519, Modern sprinters, US flag, Atlanta, 1996.

1996, July 11   Litho.   Perf. 14
518	A106	$2 multicolored	6.00	6.00
519	A106	$2 multicolored	6.00	6.00
a.		Pair, #518-519	12.00	12.00

Queen Elizabeth II and Prince Philip, 50th Wedding Anniv. A107

Designs: $2.50, Queen Elizabeth II, Prince Philip, Queen Mother, and King George VI. $6, like No. 520, close-up.

1997, Nov. 20   Litho.   Perf. 14
| 520 | A107 | $2.50 multicolored | 4.50 | 4.50 |

Souvenir Sheet
| 521 | A107 | $6 multicolored | 10.00 | 10.00 |

No. 520 was issued in sheets of 4.

Diana, Princess of Wales (1961-97) — A108

1998, Apr. 15   Litho.   Perf. 14
| 522 | A108 | $1 multicolored | 1.25 | 1.25 |

Souvenir Sheet
| 523 | A108 | $4 like #522 | 6.00 | 6.00 |

No. 522 was issued in sheets of 5 + label. No. 523 is a continuous design. For surcharge see No. B55.

Nos. 464-468 Overprinted

1999, Dec. 31   **Litho.**   *Perf. 14x15*
524	A92	30c on #464	.40	.40
525	A92	50c on #465	.65	.65
526	A92	95c on #466	1.10	1.10
527	A92	$1.75 on #467	2.25	2.25
528	A92	$1.95 on #468	2.50	2.50
		Nos. 524-528 (5)	6.90	6.90

Queen Mother, 100th Birthday — A109

No. 529: a, Wearing crown, blue-toned photograph. b, Wearing crown, color photograph. c, Wearing hat. d, With King George VI.

2000, Oct. 20   **Litho.**   *Perf. 14*
529	A109	$3 Sheet of 4, #a-d	12.00	12.00

Souvenir Sheet
530	A109	$7.50 With flowers	8.00	8.00

2000 Summer Olympics, Sydney — A110

No. 531: a, Ancient wrestling. b, Wrestling. c, Ancient boxer. d, Boxing.

2000, Dec. 14   **Litho.**   *Perf. 14*
531	A110	$2 Sheet of 4, #a-d	8.75	8.75

Souvenir Sheet
532	A110	$2.75 Torch relay	3.50	3.50

Worldwide Fund for Nature (WWF) — A111

Various views of two blue lorikeets: 80c, 90c, $1.15, $1.95.

2002, Sept. 3   **Litho.**   *Perf. 14*
533-536	A111	Set of 4	6.50	6.50

United We Stand — A112

2003, Sept. 30   **Litho.**   *Perf. 14*
537	A112	$1.15 multi	2.10	2.10

Printed in sheets of 4.

Pope John Paul II (1920-2005) A113

2005, Nov. 11   **Litho.**   *Perf. 14*
538	A113	$1.95 multi	3.75	3.75

Printed in sheets of 5 + label.

Worldwide Fund for Nature (WWF) — A114

Blue moon butterfly: 80c, Caterpillar and chrysalis. 90c, Female. $1.15, Male. $1.95, Male, diff.

2008, Nov. 18   **Litho.**   *Perf. 13½*
539-542	A114	Set of 4	6.00	6.00

Nos. 539-542 were each printed in sheets of 4.

Worldwide Fund for Nature (WWF) — A115

Designs: 80c, Tomato grouper. 90c, Peacock grouper. $1.10, Pair of Tomato groupers. $1.20, Head of Peacock grouper.

2010, Dec. 9   **Litho.**   *Perf. 14*
543-546	A115	Set of 4	5.00	5.00

Tourism A116

Designs: 10c, Airplane, island. 20c, Bent palm tree, sun on horizon. 30c, Beach. 40c, Ship, islands. 50c, Road in forest. 60c, Islands and beach (at right) under dark skies. 70c, People fishing. 80c, Bent palm tree. 90c, Huts. $1, Islands and beach (at left). $1.10, Fence near beach. $1.20, Sun at horizon. $1.50, Moon above island. $2, Mountain on island. $3, Building and courtyard.

2010, Dec. 10
547	A116	10c multi	.25	.25
548	A116	20c multi	.30	.30
549	A116	30c multi	.45	.45
550	A116	40c multi	.60	.60
551	A116	50c multi	.75	.75
552	A116	60c multi	.90	.90
553	A116	70c multi	1.10	1.10
554	A116	80c multi	1.25	1.25
555	A116	90c multi	1.40	1.40
556	A116	$1 multi	1.50	1.50
557	A116	$1.10 multi	1.60	1.60
558	A116	$1.20 multi	1.75	1.75
559	A116	$1.50 multi	2.00	2.00
560	A116	$2 multi	2.75	2.75
561	A116	$3 multi	4.25	4.25
a.		Sheet of 15, #547-561	21.00	21.00
		Nos. 547-561 (15)	20.85	20.85

A117

Engagement of Prince William and Catherine Middleton — A118

Designs: Nos. 562, 565a, 567, 50c, Middleton. Nos. 563, 565b, 568, $5, Prince playing polo.
No. 564: a, Prince in military uniform. b, Prince playing polo. c, Middleton, fence. d, Prince, man and woman in background. e, Middleton, woman in background. f, Couple, Prince at left. g, Middleton with black hat. h, Prince. i, Couple, Middleton at left. j, Hands of couple, engagement ring.
$8.10, Couple, Prince in uniform at left.

2011, Jan. 14   *Perf. 14*
562	A117	50c multi	.75	.75
563	A117	$5 multi	7.75	7.75

Miniature Sheets
564	A118	$1 Sheet of 10, #a-j	15.50	15.50

Perf. 13¾x13½
565	A117	Sheet of 2, #a-b	8.50	8.50

Souvenir Sheets
Perf. 14¼
566	A117	$8.10 multi	12.50	12.50
567	A117	$11 multi	17.00	17.00
568	A117	$11 multi	17.00	17.00
		Nos. 566-568 (3)	46.50	46.50

No. 565 contains two 28x44mm stamps. Nos. 566-568 each contain one 38x50mm stamp.

Peonies A119

2011, Apr. 8   **Litho.**   *Perf. 13¼*
569	A119	90c multi	1.40	1.40

Souvenir Sheet
Perf. 14¾x14
570	A119	$6.60 Peonies in vase, horiz.	10.50	10.50

No. 569 was printed in sheets of 6. No. 570 contains one 48x42mm stamp.

Souvenir Sheet

Wedding of Prince William and Catherine Middleton — A120

No. 571 — Bride and groom: a, $1.10, Walking down aisle. b, $1.20, Kneeling.

2011, July 15   *Perf. 15x14¼*
571	A120	Sheet of 2, #a-b	4.00	4.00

Aitutaki Marine Research Center — A121

Designs: 10c, Suspended cages underwater. 20c, Station manager Richard Story. 80c, Tridacna maxima. 90c, Tridacna maxima, diff. $1.10, Tridacna derasa. $1.20, Tridacna derasa, diff.
No. 578, vert.: a, $2, Researcher underwater. b, $3, Researcher lifting cage on boat.

2011, July 25   *Perf. 14¼x14*
572-577	A121	Set of 6	7.25	7.25

Souvenir Sheet
Perf. 13¾
578	A121	Sheet of 2, #a-b	8.50	8.50

Nos. 572-577 each were printed in sheets of 4. No. 578 contains two 30x38mm stamps.

Christmas A122

No. 579 — Items from Christmas song "The Twelve Days of Christmas": a, Nine ladies dancing. b, Ten lords a leaping. c, Eleven pipers piping. d, Twelve drummers drumming.

2011, Dec. 24   **Litho.**   *Perf. 13¼*
579		Horiz. strip of 4	8.25	8.25
a.		A122 90c multi	1.50	1.50
b.		A122 $1 multi	1.60	1.60
c.		A122 $1.20 multi	1.90	1.90
d.		A122 $2 multi	3.25	3.25
e.		Souvenir sheet of 4, #579a-579d	8.25	8.25

No. 579 was printed in sheets containing three strips.

Beatification of Pope John Paul II — A123

No. 580: a, $1.10, Pope Benedict XVI. b, $5.10, Pope John Paul II.

2012, Jan. 10   **Perf. 13¾**
580 A123   Horiz. pair, #a-b   10.50 10.50

No. 580 was printed in sheets containing two pairs.

Cetaceans — A124

Designs: Nos. 581, 593a, 20c, Humpback whale. Nos. 582, 593b, 30c, Humpback whale tail. Nos. 583, 593c, 50c, Humpback whale, diff. Nos. 584, 593d, 80c, Striped dolphins. Nos. 585, 593e, 90c, Striped dolphins, diff. Nos. 586, 593f, $1, Striped dolphins, diff. Nos. 587, 593g, $1.10, Striped dolphin. Nos. 588, 593h, $1.20, Striped dolphins, diff. Nos. 589, 593i, $5, Striped dolphins, diff. Nos. 590, 593j, $6, Humpback whale tail, diff. Nos. 591, 593k, $7.50, Humpback whale, diff. Nos. 592, 593l, $10, Humpback whale, diff.

2012, June 22   **Perf. 14**
Stamps Without Dark Blue Frame Near Denomination
581-592 A124   Set of 12   55.00 55.00
Stamps With Dark Blue Frame All Around
593 A124   Sheet of 12, #a-l   55.00 55.00

Entombment of Christ, by Pietro Lorenzetti — A125

The Last Supper, by Lorenzetti A126

Madonna with St. Francis and St. John the Evangelist, by Lorenzetti A127

Deposition of Christ from the Cross, by Lorenzetti A128

The Flagellation of Christ, by Lorenzetti A129

Entry of Christ Into Jerusalem, by Lorenzetti A130

Perf. 14¾x14¼
2012, Nov. 16   **Litho.**
Stamps With White Frames
594   Horiz. pair   2.80 2.80
  a.   A125 80c multi   1.40 1.40
  b.   A126 80c multi   1.40 1.40
595   Horiz. pair   3.00 3.00
  a.   A127 90c multi   1.50 1.50
  b.   A128 90c multi   1.50 1.50
596   Horiz. pair   10.00 10.00
  a.   A129 $3 multi   5.00 5.00
  b.   A130 $3 multi   5.00 5.00
   Nos. 594-596 (3)   15.80 15.80
Miniature Sheet
Stamps Without White Frame
597   Sheet of 6   16.00 16.00
  a.   A125 80c multi   1.40 1.40
  b.   A126 80c multi   1.40 1.40
  c.   A127 90c multi   1.50 1.50
  d.   A128 90c multi   1.50 1.50
  e.   A129 $3 multi   5.00 5.00
  f.   A130 $3 multi   5.00 5.00

Christmas.

Personalizable Stamp — A131

2012, Dec. 21   **Litho.**   **Perf. 14x14¾**
598 A131 $4 multi   6.75 6.75

Miniature Sheet

New Year 2013 (Year of the Snake) — A132

No. 599 — Snake with background color of: a, Green. b, Yellow, c, Pink. d, Violet.

2013, Feb. 21   **Litho.**   **Perf. 14¾x14**
599 A132 $1.20 Sheet of 4, #a-d   8.00 8.00

Cetaceans — A133

Various boats and: Nos. 600, 612a, 10c, Humpback whale. Nos. 601, 612b, 40c, Humpback whale, diff. Nos. 602, 612c, 60c, Humpback whale, diff. Nos. 603, 612d, 70c, Striped dolphin. Nos. 604, 612e, $1.50, Striped dolphin, diff. Nos. 605, 612f, $1.80, Striped dolphin, diff. Nos. 606, 612g, $2, Striped dolphin, diff. Nos. 607, 612h, $2.25, Striped dolphin, diff. Nos. 608, 612i, $2.50, Striped dolphin, diff. Nos. 609, 612j, Humpback whale, diff. Nos. 610, 612k, $4, Humpback whale, diff. Nos. 611, 612l, $20, Humpback whale, diff.

2013, June 5   **Litho.**   **Perf. 14**
Stamps With White Frames
600-611 A133   Set of 12   62.50 62.50
Miniature Sheet
Stamps Without White Frames
612 A133   Sheet of 12, #a-l   62.50 62.50

Souvenir Sheet

TRH The Duke and Duchess of Cambridge

Birth of Prince George of Cambridge — A134

No. 613: a, $1.30, Duchess of Cambridge. b, $1.50, Duchess of Cambridge reviewing Scouts, Duchess and Duke of Cambridge kissing. c, $1.70, Duchess of Cambridge, diff.

2013, Aug. 1   **Litho.**   **Perf. 13½**
613 A134   Sheet of 3, #a-c   7.25 7.25

Souvenir Sheet

China International Collection Expo — A135

No. 614: a, $1.50, Painting by Paul Gauguin. b, $1.70, Beijing Exhibition Center.

2013, Sept. 26   **Litho.**   **Perf. 12**
614 A135   Sheet of 2, #a-b   5.50 5.50

Pres. John F. Kennedy (1917-63) A136

Designs: $2.50, Kennedy and quotation. $2.90, Kennedy.

2013, Nov. 8   **Litho.**   **Perf. 14¼**
615-616 A136   Set of 2   9.00 9.00

Christmas — A137

Religious paintings by: $1, William Brassey Hole. $1.30, Bernardino Luini.
No. 619 — Religious paintings by: a, $2, Gentile da Fabriano. b, $2.40, Marten de Vos. c, $2.60, Pietro Perugino.

2013, Nov. 18   **Litho.**   **Perf. 13¼**
617-618 A137   Set of 2   4.00 4.00
Souvenir Sheet
619 A137   Sheet of 3, #a-c   11.50 11.50

Miniature Sheet

New Year 2014 (Year of the Horse) — A138

No. 620 — Color of horse: a, $1, Purple. b, $1.30, White, horiz. c, $1.50, Dark blue. d, $1.70, Yellow, horiz.

2014, Jan. 10   **Litho.**   **Perf. 13¾**
620 A138   Sheet of 4, #a-d   9.00 9.00

Miniature Sheet

Easter — A139

No. 621 — Religious paintings by: a, 50c, Benvenuto Garofalo. b, $1, Tiziano Vecelli (Titian). c, $1.30, Piero della Francesca. d, $1.50, Peter Paul Rubens. e, $1.70, Ambrogio Borgognone.
$9.50, Painting by Paolo Veronese.

2014, Apr. 9   **Litho.**   **Perf. 13¼**
621 A139   Sheet of 5, #a-e, + label   10.50 10.50
Souvenir Sheet
622 A139 $9.50 multi   16.50 16.50

Worldwide Fund for Nature (WWF) A140

Various depictions of spotted reef crab: $1, $1.30, $1.70, $2.10.

2014, Nov. 28   **Litho.**   **Perf. 14**
623-626 A140   Set of 4   9.75 9.75
626a   Souvenir sheet of 4, #623-626   9.75 9.75

Nos. 623-626 were each printed in sheets of 4.

Souvenir Sheet

Christmas — A141

No. 627 — Religious paintings by: a, Fra Angelico. b, Pieter Breugel, the Elder. c, Paolo Schiavo.

Perf. 14¾x14¼
2014, Dec. 12   **Litho.**
627   A141 $1.50 Sheet of 3, #a-c   7.00 7.00

Souvenir Sheet

New Year 2015 (Year of the Sheep) — A142

No. 628 — Sheep with background color of: a, $3.80, Green. b, $4.10, Orange.

2015, Jan. 5   **Litho.**   **Perf. 13¼**
628   A142   Sheet of 2, #a-b   11.50 11.50

Miniature Sheet

Easter — A143

No. 629 — Paintings depicting Jesus Christ by: a, Bartolomé Esteban Murillo. b, Albrecht Altdorfer. c, John Singleton Copley. d, William Blake.

2015, Mar. 31   **Litho.**   **Perf. 14x14¼**
629   A143 $2 Sheet of 4, #a-d   12.50 12.50

Souvenir Sheet

Birth of Princess Charlotte of Cambridge — A144

No. 630: a, Duchess of Cambridge holding Princess Charlotte. b, Duke of Cambridge and Prince George.

Perf. 14¾x14¼
2015, June 23   **Litho.**
630   A144 $4.50 Sheet of 2, #a-b   12.00 12.00

New Year 2016 (Year of the Monkey) A145

Designs: $2.60, Monkey and red chop mark. $3, Monkey, diff.
No. 633: a, $3.80, Monkey and red chop mark. b, $4.10, Monkey, diff.

2015, Sept. 25   **Litho.**   **Perf. 13¼**
631-632 A145   Set of 2   7.25 7.25
Souvenir Sheet
633   A145   Sheet of 2, #a-b   10.50 10.50

No. 633 contains two 50x50mm diamond-shaped stamps.

Miniature Sheet

Queen Elizabeth II, Longest-Reigning British Monarch — A146

No. 634 — Various photographs of Queen Elizabeth II: a, $1.30. b, $1.50. c, $1.70. d, $2.

2015, Nov. 20   **Litho.**   **Perf. 14x14¼**
634   A146   Sheet of 4, #a-d   8.75 8.75

Souvenir Sheet

Christmas — A147

No. 635 — Details from *The Nativity*, by Lorenzo Monaco: a, Virgin Mary. b, Infant Jesus and farm animals, c, St. Joseph.

2015, Dec. 9   **Litho.**   **Perf. 13¼**
635   A147 $1 Sheet of 3, #a-c   4.00 4.00

SEMI-POSTAL STAMPS

Christmas Type of 1974

Designs: 1c+1c, like No. 104. 5c+1c, like No. 105. 8c+1c, like No. 106. 10c+1c, like No. 107. 25c+1c, like No. 108. 30c+1c, like No. 109.

1974, Dec. 2   **Photo.**   **Perf. 13½**
B1   A29   1c + 1c multicolored   .25 .25
B2   A29   5c + 1c multicolored   .25 .25
B3   A29   8c + 1c multicolored   .25 .25
B4   A29   10c + 1c multicolored   .25 .25
B5   A29   25c + 1c multicolored   .30 .30
B6   A29   30c + 1c multicolored   .30 .30
    Nos. B1-B6 (6)   1.60 1.60

Surtax was for child welfare.

Nos. 117-120
Surcharged in Silver

1975, Dec. 19   **Photo.**   **Perf. 14x13½**
B7   A32   Strip of 3   .45 .45
  a.-c.   6c+1c any single   .25 .25
B8   A32   Strip of 3   .50 .50
  a.-c.   7c+1c any single   .25 .25
B9   A32   Strip of 3   1.00 1.00
  a.-c.   15c+1c any single   .30 .30
B10   A32   Strip of 3   1.50 1.50
  a.-c.   20c+1c any single   .45 .45
    Nos. B7-B10 (4)   3.45 3.45

Christmas. The surtax was for children's activities during holiday season.

Nos. 135-142a
Surcharged in Silver

1976, Nov. 19   **Photo.**   **Perf. 13½x13**
B11   6c + 1c multicolored   .25 .25
B12   6c + 1c multicolored   .25 .25
  a.   A36   Pair, #B11-B12   .25 .25
B13   7c + 1c multicolored   .25 .25
B14   7c + 1c multicolored   .25 .25
  a.   A36   Pair, #B13-B14   .25 .25
B15   15c + 1c multicolored   .25 .25
B16   15c + 1c multicolored   .25 .25
  a.   A36   Pair, #B15-B16   .45 .45
B17   20c + 1c multicolored   .30 .30
B18   20c + 1c multicolored   .50 .50
  a.   A36   Pair, #B17-B18   1.00 1.00
  b.   Souvenir sheet of 8   2.00 2.00

Surtax was for child welfare. Stamps of No. B18b each surcharged 2c.

Nos. 152-159a
Surcharged in Black

1977, Nov. 15   **Perf. 13½x14**
B19   6c + 1c multicolored   .25 .25
B20   6c + 1c multicolored   .25 .25
  a.   A41   Pair, #B19-B20   .25 .25
B21   7c + 1c multicolored   .25 .25
B22   7c + 1c multicolored   .25 .25
  a.   A41   Pair, #B21-B22   .25 .25
B23   15c + 1c multicolored   .25 .25
B24   15c + 1c multicolored   .25 .25
  a.   A41   Pair, #B23-B24   .50 .50
B25   20c + 1c multicolored   .30 .30
B26   20c + 1c multicolored   .30 .30
  a.   A41   Pair, #B25-B26   .65 .65
  b.   Souvenir sheet of 8   2.50 2.50
    Nos. B19-B26 (8)   2.10 2.10

Surtax was for child welfare. Stamps of No. B26b each surcharged 2c.

Easter Type of 1978
Souvenir Sheets

Paintings: No. B27, like No. 163. No. B28, like No. 164. No. B29, like No. 165.

1978, Mar. 17   **Photo.**   **Perf. 14**
B27   A44   50c + 5c multicolored   .55 .55
B28   A44   50c + 5c multicolored   .55 .55
B29   A44   50c + 5c multicolored   .55 .55

Nos. B27-B29 contain one stamp 33x25mm.

Christmas Type of 1978
Souvenir Sheet

1978, Dec. 4   **Photo.**   **Perf. 14½x13**
B30   Sheet of 4   2.25 2.25
  a.   A46 15c + 2c like #167   .25 .25
  b.   A46 17c + 2c like #168   .30 .30
  c.   A46 30c + 2c like #169   .45 .45
  d.   A46 35c + 2c like #170   .60 .60

Year of the Child Type
Souvenir Sheet

1979, Oct. 1   **Photo.**   **Perf. 14x13½**
B31   Sheet of 3   1.25 1.25
  a.   A48 30c + 3c like #173   .30 .30
  b.   A48 35c + 3c like #174   .35 .35
  c.   A48 65c + 3c like #175   .45 .45

Easter Type of 1980
Souvenir Sheet

No. B32 shows entire painting in continuous design. Nos. B32a-B32c similar to Nos. 183-185. Size of Nos. B32a-B32c: 25x50mm.

1980, Apr. 3   **Photo.**   **Perf. 13x13½**
B32   Sheet of 3   1.90 1.90
  a.   A50 20c + 2c multicolored   .45 .45
  b.   A50 30c + 2c multicolored   .60 .60
  c.   A50 35c + 2c multicolored   .75 .75

Christmas Type of 1980
Souvenir Sheet

1980, Nov. 21   **Photo.**   **Perf. 13x13½**
B33   Sheet of 4   1.50 1.50
  a.   A53 15c + 2c like #208   .25 .25
  b.   A53 20c + 2c like #209   .30 .30
  c.   A53 25c + 2c like #210   .35 .35
  d.   A53 35c + 2c like #211   .45 .45

Easter Type of 1981
Souvenir Sheet

1981, Mar. 31   **Photo.**   **Perf. 13½**
B34   Sheet of 3   1.65 1.65
  a.   A54 30c + 2c like #212   .35 .35
  b.   A54 40c + 2c like #213   .50 .50
  c.   A54 50c + 2c like #214   .65 .65

Nos. 247-249
Surcharged

1981, Nov. 23   **Photo.**   **Perf. 13x13½**
B35   A56   60 + 5c multi   .65 .65
B36   A56   80 + 5c multi   .70 .70
B37   A56 $1.40 + 5c multi   .90 .90
    Nos. B35-B37 (3)   2.25 2.25

Intl. Year of the Disabled. Surtax was for the handicapped.

Soccer Type of 1981
Souvenir Sheet

a-b, 12c+2c. c-d, 15c+2c. e-f, 20c+2c. g-h, 25c+2c.

1981, Nov. 30   **Perf. 14**
B38   A57   Sheet of 8, multi   6.00 6.00

No. B38 contains stamps with 2c surtax similar to Nos. 250-253. Surtax was for local sports.

1986, Nov. 25   **Litho.**   **Perf. 13½**
B39   A79   75c + 10c multi   3.75 3.25
B40   A79 $1.35 + 10c multi   4.25 3.75
B41   A79 $1.95 + 10c multi   6.00 5.00
B42   A79 $2.75 + 10c multi   7.00 7.50
    Nos. B39-B42 (4)   21.00 19.50
Souvenir Sheet
B43   Sheet of 4   22.50 22.50
  a.-d.   A79 $1.65 +10c on #404a-404d, each   6.00 6.00

State visit of Pope John Paul II.
For surcharges see Nos. B51-B54.

Nos. 394-395, 397 and 400-403 Surcharged in Silver or Black

1987, Apr. 29 Litho. Perf. 13½, 14

B44	A79	75c + 50c #400	3.50	2.50
B45	A77	$1 + 50c #394 (B)	4.25	3.50
B46	A79	$1.35 + 50c #401	5.75	5.00
B47	A79	$1.95 + 50c #402	6.25	5.00
B48	A78	$2 + 50c #397	6.50	5.00
B49	A77	$2.75 + 50c #395 (B)	8.00	6.25
B50	A79	$2.75 + 50c #403	8.50	7.25
		Nos. B44-B50 (7)	42.75	34.50

Nos. B39-B42 Surcharged in Silver

1987, Apr. 29 Litho. Perf. 13½

B51	A79	75c + 50c No. B39	4.00	4.00
B52	A79	$1.35 + 50c No. B40	4.50	4.50
B53	A79	$1.95 + 50c No. B41	4.75	4.75
B54	A79	$2.75 + 50c No. B42	6.00	6.00
		Nos. B51-B54 (4)	19.25	19.25

No. 523 Surcharged in Silver

Souvenir Sheet

1998, Nov. 19 Litho. Perf. 14

B55	A108	$4 + $1 multicolored	6.25	6.25

AIR POST STAMPS

Capt. Bligh Type of 1974

1974, Sept. 9 Perf. 13
Size: 46x26mm

C1	A27	10c Bligh and "Bounty"	.75	.60
C2	A27	10c "Bounty" at sea	.75	.60
a.		Pair, #C1-C2	1.75	1.75
C3	A27	25c Bligh and "Bounty"	.85	.75
C4	A27	25c Chart, 1856	.85	.75
a.		Pair, #C3-C4	2.00	2.00
C5	A27	30c Cook and "Resolution"	1.00	1.00
C6	A27	30c Maps	1.00	1.00
a.		Pair, #C5-C6	2.75	2.75
		Nos. C1-C6 (6)	5.20	4.70

See note after No. 101.

OFFICIAL STAMPS

Nos. 83-90, 92-95, 150-151 Ovptd. or Srchd. in Black, Silver or Gold

1978-79 Photo. Perf. 13x13½

O1	A25	1c multi	1.10	.25
O2	A25	2c multi	1.75	.25
O3	A25	3c multi	1.75	.25
O4	A25	4c multi (G)	1.75	.25
O5	A25	5c multi	1.75	.25
O6	A25	8c multi	1.75	.25
O7	A25	10c multi	2.00	.25
O8	A25	15c on 60c multi	3.50	.25
O9	A25	16c on 60c multi	3.50	.25
O10	A25	20c multi (G)	3.50	.25
O11	A40	50c multi	1.50	.70
O12	A25	60c multi	12.00	.80
O13	A25	$1 multi	12.00	1.00
O14	A26	$2 multi	11.00	.80
O15	A40	$4 on $1 multi (S)	2.50	.80
O16	A26	$5 multi	13.00	1.50
		Nos. O1-O16 (16)	74.35	8.10

Overprint on 4c, 20c, $1 diagonal.
Issued: Nos. O14-O16, 2/20/79; others, 11/3/78.

Stamps of 1983-84 Ovptd. or Surcharged in Green

or Gold (#O29-O32)

1985, Aug. 9 Perf. 14, 13x13½

O17	A66	2c No. 322	2.10	2.10
O18	A66	5c No. 324	2.50	2.50
O19	A66	10c No. 325	3.00	3.00
O20	A66	12c No. 326	3.25	3.00
O21	A66	18c No. 327	4.00	3.50
O22	A66	20c on 24c No. 328	4.50	3.75
O23	A66	30c No. 329	3.50	2.50
O24	A66	40c on 36c No. 330	3.50	2.50
O25	A66	50c No. 332	3.50	2.50
O26	A66	55c on 48c No. 331	3.50	2.50
O27	A66	60c No. 333	4.00	2.75
O28	A66	65c on 72c No. 334	4.00	2.75
O29	A61	75c on 48c No. 276	2.50	2.10
O30	A61	75c on 48c No. 277	2.50	2.10
O31	A61	75c on 48c No. 278	2.50	2.10
O32	A61	75c on 48c No. 279	2.50	2.10
a.		Block of 4, Nos. O29-O32	11.00	11.00
O33	A66	80c on 96c No. 335	4.00	3.75
		Nos. O17-O33 (17)	55.35	45.50

Nos. 336-341 Overprinted Like Nos. O17-O21, O23, O25, O27 in Metallic Green

1986, Oct. 1 Perf. 14

O34	A66	$3 multi	8.50	6.50
O35	A66	$4.20 multi	11.00	8.50
O36	A66	$5.60 multi	12.00	10.00
O37	A66	$9.60 multi	15.00	12.00

1988-91 Perf. 14

O38	A66	$1.20 multi	5.00	2.50
O39	A66	$2.10 multi	7.50	4.00

Nos. 246C-246D Surcharged in Metallic Blue

O40	A55	$14 on $4 (B)	17.50	14.00
O41	A55	$18 on $5 (B)	22.50	19.00
		Nos. O34-O41 (8)	99.00	76.50

Issue dates: July 2, 1991; others, June 15.

AJMAN

äj-'man

LOCATION — Oman Peninsula, Arabia, on Persian Gulf
GOVT. — Sheikdom under British Protection
AREA — 100 sq. mi.
POP. — 4,400
CAPITAL — Ajman

Ajman is one of six Persian Gulf sheikdoms to join the United Arab Emirates, which proclaimed its independence Dec. 2, 1971. See United Arab Emirates.

100 Naye Paise = 1 Rupee

Catalogue values for all unused stamps in this country are for Never Hinged items.

Sheik Rashid bin Humaid al Naimi & Arab Stallion A1

Designs: 2np, 50np, Regal angelfish. 3np, 70np, Camel. 4np, 1r, Angelfish. 5np, 1.50r, Green turtle. 10np, 2r, Jewelfish. 15np, 3r, White storks. 20np, 5r, White-eyed gulls. 30np, 10r, Lanner falcon. 40np as 1np.

Photo. & Litho.

1964 Unwmk. Perf. 14
Size: 35x22mm

1	A1	1np gold & multi	.25	.25
2	A1	2np gold & multi	.25	.25
3	A1	3np gold & multi	.25	.25
4	A1	4np gold & multi	.25	.25
5	A1	5np gold & multi	.25	.25
6	A1	10np gold & multi	.25	.25
7	A1	15np gold & multi	.25	.25
8	A1	20np gold & multi	.25	.25
9	A1	30np gold & multi	.25	.25

Size: 42x27mm

10	A1	40np gold & multi	.25	.25
11	A1	50np gold & multi	.25	.25
12	A1	70np gold & multi	.25	.25
13	A1	1r gold & multi	.40	.25
14	A1	1.50r gold & multi	.50	.35
15	A1	2r gold & multi	.85	.50

Size: 53x33½mm

16	A1	3r gold & multi	1.50	.90
17	A1	5r gold & multi	4.00	2.00
18	A1	10r gold & multi	6.00	3.00
		Nos. 1-18 (18)	16.25	10.50

Issued: Nos. 1-9, 6/20; Nos. 10-15, 9/7; Nos. 16-18, 11/4. Exist imperf. Value, set $22.

Pres. and Mrs. John F. Kennedy with Caroline — A2

Pres. Kennedy: 10np, As a boy in football uniform. 15np, Diving. 50np, As navy lieutenant, receiving Navy and Marine Corps Medal from Capt. Frederic L. Conklin. 1r, Sailing with Jacqueline Kennedy. 2r, With Eleanor Roosevelt. 5r, With Lyndon B. Johnson and Hubert H. Humphrey. 10r, Portrait.

1964, Dec. 15 Photo. Perf. 13½x14

19	A2	10np grn & red lil	.25	.25
20	A2	15np Prus bl & vio	.25	.25
21	A2	50np org brn & dk bl	.25	.25
22	A2	1r brn & Prus grn	.50	.30
23	A2	2r red lil & dp ol	.75	.40
24	A2	3r grn & red brn	1.50	.50
25	A2	5r vio & brn	2.75	1.50
26	A2	10r dk bl & red brn	5.50	2.25
		Nos. 19-26 (8)	11.75	5.70

John F. Kennedy (1917-63). Exist imperf. Value, set $14. A souvenir sheet contains one each of Nos. 23-26. Value, perf or imperf, $14.

Runners at Start — A3

10np, 1.50r, Boxing. 25np, 2r, Judo. 50np, 5r, Gymnast on vaulting horse. 1r, 3r, Sailing yacht.

1965, Jan. 12 Photo. Perf. 13½x14

27	A3	5np red brn, brt pink & Prus grn	.25	.25
28	A3	10np dk ol grn, bl gray & red brn	.25	.25
29	A3	15np dk vio, grn & sep	.25	.25
30	A3	25np bl sal pink & blk	.25	.25
31	A3	50np mar, bl & ind	.25	.25
32	A3	1r dk grn, lil & ultra	.40	.25
33	A3	1.50r lil, grn & brn	.60	.40
34	A3	2r red org, bis & dk bl	1.00	.70
35	A3	3r dk brn, grnsh bl & lil	2.00	.95
36	A3	5r grn, yel & red brn	3.00	1.60
		Nos. 27-36 (10)	8.25	5.15

18th Olympic Games, Tokyo, Oct. 10-25, 1964. Exist imperf. Value, set $7.50. A souvenir sheet contains four stamps similar to Nos. 33-36 in changed colors. Values: perf $5; imperf $9.

Stanley Gibbons Catalogue, 1865, U.S. No. 1X2 — A4

Designs: 10np, Austria, Scarlet Mercury 1856. 15np, British Guiana 1c, 1856. 25np, Canada 12p, 1851. 50np, Hawaii 2c, 1851. 1r, Mauritius 2p, 1847. 3r, Switzerland, Geneva 10c, 1843. 5r, Tuscany 31, 1860. 5np, 15np, 50np and 3r show first edition of Stanley Gibbons Catalogue; 10np, 25np, 1r and 5r show 1965 Elizabethan Catalogue.

1965, May 6 Unwmk. Perf. 13

37	A4	5np multi	.25	.25
38	A4	10np multi	.25	.25
39	A4	15np multi	.25	.25
40	A4	25np multi	.25	.25
41	A4	50np multi	.25	.25
42	A4	1r multi	.45	.25
43	A4	3r multi	1.50	.50
a.		Souv. sheet of 4, #38-39, 42-43	4.25	
44	A4	3r multi	2.75	.95
a.		Souv. sheet of 4, #37, 40-41, 44	3.75	
		Nos. 37-44 (8)	5.95	2.95

Gibbons Catalogue Cent. Exhib., London, Feb. 17-20. Nos. 43a and 44a for 125th anniv. of 1st postage stamp. Exist imperf. Value, set

$6.50. Sheets exist imperf. Value for both sheets, $7.

Stamps of Ajman were replaced in 1972 by those of United Arab Emirates.

AIR POST STAMPS

Type of Regular Issue, 1964

Designs: 15np, Arab stallion. 25np, Regal angelfish. 35np, Camel. 50np, Angelfish. 75np, Green turtle. 1r, Jewelfish. 2r, White storks. 3r, White-eyed gulls. 5r, Lanner falcon.

Photo. & Litho.

		1965 Unwmk. Perf. 14		
		Size: 42x25½mm		
C1	A1	15np silver & multi	.25	.25
C2	A1	25np silver & multi	.25	.25
C3	A1	35np silver & multi	.25	.25
C4	Al	50np silver & multi	.30	.25
C5	A1	75np silver & multi	.55	.25
C6	A1	1r silver & multi	.40	.25
		Size: 53x33½mm		
C7	A1	2r silver & multi	1.25	.50
C8	A1	3r silver & multi	3.00	.75
C9	A1	5r silver & multi	4.50	1.00
		Nos. C1-C9 (9)	10.75	3.75

Issued: Nos. C1-C6, 11/15; Nos. C7-C9, 12/18. Exist imperf. Value, set $10.

AIR POST OFFICIAL STAMPS

Type of Regular Issue, 1964

Designs: 75np, Jewelfish. 2r, White storks. 3r, White-eyed gulls. 5r, Lanner falcon.

Photo. & Litho.

		1965, Dec. 18 Unwmk. Perf. 14		
		Size: 42x25½mm		
CO1	A1	75np gold & multi	.75	.35
		Size: 53x33½mm		
CO2	A1	2r gold & multi	2.25	.50
CO3	A1	3r gold & multi	3.00	1.00
CO4	A1	5r gold & multi	5.00	1.40
		Nos. CO1-CO4 (4)	11.00	3.25

OFFICIAL STAMPS

Type of Regular Issue, 1964

25np, Arab stallion. 40np, Regal angelfish. 50np, Camel. 75np, Angelfish. 1r, Green turtle.

Photo. & Litho.

		1965, Dec. 1 Unwmk. Perf. 14		
		Size: 42x25½mm		
O1	A1	25np gold & multi	.30	.25
O2	A1	40np gold & multi	.40	.25
O3	A1	50np gold & multi	.50	.30
O4	A1	75np gold & multi	.60	.35
O5	A1	1r gold & multi	.90	.40
		Nos. O1-O5 (5)	2.70	1.55

ALAOUITES

ˈal-au-ˌwītz

LOCATION — A division of Syria, in Western Asia
GOVT. — Under French Mandate
AREA — 2,500 sq. mi.
POP. — 278,000 (approx. 1930)
CAPITAL — Latakia

This territory became an independent state in 1924, although still administered under the French Mandate. In 1930, it was renamed Latakia, and Syrian stamps overprinted "Lattaquie" superseded the stamps of Alaouites. For these and subsequent issues, see Latakia and Syria.

100 Centimes = 1 Piaster

Issued under French Mandate

Stamps of France Surcharged

Nos. 1-6, 16-18 | Nos. 7-15, 19-21

		1925 Unwmk. Perf. 14x13½		
1	A16	10c on 2c vio brn	4.00	4.00
2	A22	25c on 5c orange	4.00	4.00
3	A20	75c on 15c gray grn	7.25	7.25
4	A22	1p on 20c red brn	4.00	4.00
5	A22	1.25p on 25c blue	4.50	4.50
6	A22	1.50p on 30c red	14.50	14.50
7	A22	2p on 35c violet	4.75	4.75
8	A18	2p on 40c red & pale bl	5.50	5.50
9	A18	2p on 45c grn & bl	19.00	19.00
10	A18	3p on 60c vio & ultra	8.75	8.75
11	A20	3p on 60c lt vio	14.00	14.00
b.		Double surcharge	165.00	165.00
12b	A20	4p on 85c vermilion	4.00	4.00
c.		As "b," inverted surcharge	50.00	50.00
13	A18	5p on 1fr cl & ol grn	8.50	8.50
14	A18	10p on 2fr org & pale bl	13.00	13.00
15	A18	25p on 5fr bl & buff	16.00	16.00
		Nos. 1-15 (15)	131.75	131.75

Two types of surcharge exist on the 4p and on the 5p-25p. For detailed listings, see Scott Classic Specialized Catalogue of Stamps and Covers 1840-1940.

For overprints, see Nos. C1-C4.

Same Surcharges on Pasteur Stamps of France

16	A23	50c on 10c green	3.00	3.00
17	A23	75c on 15c green	3.75	3.75
18	A23	1.50p on 30c red	3.00	3.00
19	A23	2p on 45c red	3.75	3.75
20	A23	2.50p on 50c blue	5.25	5.25
21	A23	4p on 75c blue	9.00	9.00
		Nos. 16-21 (6)	27.75	27.75

Two types of overprints exist on No. 21. For detailed listings, see Scott Classic Specialized Catalogue of Stamps and Covers 1840-1940.

Inverted Surcharges

1a	A16	10c on 2c vio brn	50.00
2a	A22	25c on 5c orange	50.00
3a	A20	75c on 15c gray grn	50.00
4a	A22	1p on 20c red brn	50.00
5a	A22	1.25p on 25c blue	50.00
6a	A22	1.50p on 30c red	50.00
7a	A22	2p on 35c violet	50.00
8a	A18	2p on 40c red & pale bl	50.00
9a	A18	2p on 45c grn & bl	60.00
10a	A18	3p on 60c vio & ultra	60.00
11a	A20	3p on 60c lt vio	60.00
12a	A20	4p on 85c vermilion	50.00
13a	A18	5p on 1fr cl & ol grn	60.00
14a	A18	10p on 2fr org & pale bl	70.00
15a	A18	25p on 5fr bl & buff	70.00
16a	A23	50c on 10c green	40.00
17a	A23	75c on 15c green	40.00
18a	A23	1.50p on 30c red	45.00
19a	A23	2p on 45c red	40.00
20a	A23	2.50p on 50c blue	40.00
21a	A23	4p on 75c blue	40.00

Stamps of Syria, 1925, Overprinted in Red, Black or Blue

On A3, A5

On A4

		1925, Mar. 1 Perf. 12½, 13½		
25	A3	10c dk violet (R)	1.50	2.25
a.		Double overprint	42.50	42.50
b.		Inverted overprint	35.00	
c.		Black overprint	37.50	37.50
e.		"ALAOUITE," instead of "ALAOUITES"	30.00	30.00
26	A4	25c olive black (R)	2.25	3.00
a.		Inverted overprint	40.00	
b.		Blue overprint	50.00	50.00
27	A4	50c yellow green	1.75	1.75
a.		Inverted overprint	40.00	40.00
b.		Blue overprint	50.00	50.00
c.		Red overprint	50.00	50.00
d.		"ALAOUITE," instead of "ALAOUITES"	50.00	50.00
e.		Double overprint	50.00	50.00
28	A4	75c brown orange	2.00	2.25
a.		Inverted overprint	45.00	60.00
b.		Double overprint	47.50	65.00
29	A5	1p magenta	2.75	2.75
a.		Inverted overprint	40.00	47.50
30	A4	1.25p deep green	3.25	3.50
a.		Red overprint	50.00	
b.		Double overprint		75.00
31	A4	1.50p rose red (Bl)	2.75	3.00
a.		Inverted overprint	45.00	45.00
b.		Black overprint	40.00	40.00
c.		As "b", inverted	80.00	
32	A4	2p dk brown (R)	2.75	3.50
a.		Blue overprint	65.00	65.00
b.		Inverted overprint	40.00	40.00
33	A4	2.50p pck blue (R)	4.25	4.50
a.		Black overprint	65.00	65.00
34	A4	3p orange brown	2.50	2.75
a.		Inverted overprint	40.00	40.00
b.		Blue overprint	70.00	70.00
c.		Double overprint		90.00
35	A4	5p violet	3.75	4.00
a.		Red overprint	70.00	70.00
b.		Inverted overprint	42.50	
36	A4	10p violet brown	5.50	6.00
37	A4	25p ultra (R)	9.00	10.00
		Nos. 25-37 (13)	44.00	49.25

For overprints see Nos. C5-C19.

Stamps of Syria, 1925, Surcharged in Black or Red

Nos. 38-42

Nos. 43-45

		1926		
38	A4	3.50p on 75c brn org	2.50	2.75
a.		Surcharged on face and back	22.50	22.50
39	A4	4p on 25c ol blk	2.50	2.50
40	A4	6p on 2.50p pck bl (R)	3.00	3.25
41	A4	12p on 1.25p dp grn	3.25	3.50
a.		Inverted surcharge	35.00	35.00
42	A4	20p on 1.25p dp grn	5.25	5.25
43	A4	4.50p on 75c brn org	5.25	3.25
a.		Inverted surcharge	60.00	60.00
b.		Double surcharge	55.00	55.00
44	A4	7.50p on 2.50p pck bl	4.75	3.25
45	A4	15p on 25p ultra	8.75	5.50
a.		Inverted surcharge	50.00	
		Nos. 38-45 (8)	35.25	29.25

Two types of overprints exist on No. 39. For detailed listings, see Scott Classic Specialized Catalogue of Stamps and Covers 1840-1940.

For overprint, see No. C21.

Syria No. 199 Ovptd. in Red like No. 25

		1928		
46	A3	5c on 10c dk violet	2.00	1.75
a.		Double surcharge	40.00	

Syria Nos. 178 and 174 Surcharged like Nos. 43-45 in Red

47	A4	2p on 1.25p dp green	16.00	8.00
a.		Double surcharge	60.00	
b.		Inverted surcharge	50.00	50.00
48	A4	4p on 25c olive black	11.00	6.50
a.		Double surcharge	50.00	50.00
b.		Inverted surcharge	50.00	50.00

For overprint see No. C20.

49	A4	4p on 25c olive black	82.50	50.00
a.		Double impression	150.00	
		Nos. 46-49 (4)	111.50	66.25

AIR POST STAMPS

Nos. 8, 10, 13 & 14 with Additional Ovpt. in Black

		1925, Jan. 1 Unwmk. Perf. 14x13½		
C1b	A18	2p on 40c	17.00	15.00
C2	A18	3p on 60c	22.50	20.00
a.		Inverted overprint	125.00	125.00
C3	A18	5p on 1fr	17.00	14.00
a.		Inverted overprint	37.50	37.50
C4	A18	10p on 2fr	22.00	15.00
a.		Inverted overprint	35.00	35.00
		Nos. C1-C4 (4)	78.50	64.00

Two types of overprints exist on Nos. C1-C4. For detailed listings, see Scott Classic Specialized Catalogue of Stamps and Covers 1840-1940.

Nos. 32, 34, 35 & 36 With Additional Ovpt. in Green

		1925, Mar. 1 Perf. 13½		
C5	A4	2p dark brown	7.50	6.00
a.		Inverted overprint	75.00	75.00
b.		Red overprint	125.00	
C6	A4	3p orange brown	7.50	6.00
a.		Inverted overprint	75.00	75.00
b.		Red overprint	100.00	
C7	A4	5p violet	7.50	6.00
a.		Inverted overprint	75.00	75.00
b.		Red overprint	100.00	
C8	A4	10p violet brown	7.50	6.00
a.		Inverted overprint	75.00	75.00
b.		Red overprint	100.00	
		Nos. C5-C8 (4)	30.00	24.00

Nos. 32, 34, 35 & 36 With Additional Ovpt. in Red

		1926, May 1		
C9	A4	2p dark brown	7.50	6.50
a.		Red overprint double	175.00	175.00
b.		Black overprint double	175.00	175.00
c.		Black overprint inverted	70.00	70.00
C10	A4	3p orange brown	7.50	6.50
a.		Black overprint inverted	70.00	70.00
C11	A4	5p violet	8.50	7.50
a.		Black overprint inverted	70.00	70.00
C12	A4	10p violet brown	8.50	7.50
a.		Black overprint inverted	70.00	70.00
		Nos. C9-C12 (4)	32.00	28.00

No. C9 has the original overprint in black.

Double or inverted overprints, original or plane, are known on most of Nos. C9-C12. Value, each $75. Value for example with both original and plane overprint inverted, each $150.

The red plane overprint was also applied to Nos. C5-C8. These are believed to have been essays, and were not regularly issued. Value, each $100.

Nos. 27c, 37 and Syria No. 177 With Addtl. Ovpt. of Airplane in Red or Black

1929, June-July

C17	A4	50c yel grn (R)	5.00	5.00
a.		Plane overprint double	250.00	
b.		Plane ovpt. on face and back	60.00	
c.		Pair with plane overprint Tête-bêche	325.00	
d.		Double overprint	225.00	225.00
e.		Overprint inverted	125.00	
f.		Plane only inverted	250.00	
C18	A5	1p magenta (Bk)	9.00	9.00
a.		Red overprint	50.00	
C19	A4	25p ultra (R)	52.50	40.00
a.		Plane overprint inverted	125.00	125.00
b.		Surcharge double	150.00	150.00
		Nos. C17-C19 (3)	66.50	54.00

Nos. 28 and 30 exist with additional overprint of airplane in red. These stamps were never issued. Value, each $100.

Nos. 47 and 45 With Additional Ovpt. of Airplane in Red

1929-30

C20	A4	2p on 1.25p ('30)	7.25	7.25
a.		Surcharge inverted	50.00	50.00
b.		Double surcharge	75.00	75.00
c.		Triple surcharge	175.00	
C21	A4	15p on 25p (Bk + R)	55.00	47.50
a.		Plane overprint inverted	225.00	225.00

POSTAGE DUE STAMPS

Postage Due Stamps of France, 1893-1920, Surcharged Like No. 1 (Nos. J1-J2) or No. 7 (Nos. J3-J5)

1925 Unwmk. Perf. 14x13½

J1	D2	50c on 10c choc	9.00	9.00
J2	D2	1p on 20c ol grn	9.00	9.00
J3	D2	2p on 30c red	9.50	9.50
J4	D2	3p on 50c vio brn	9.50	9.50
J5	D2	5p on 1fr red brn, straw	10.00	10.00
		Nos. J1-J5 (5)	47.00	47.00

Two types of overprints exist on No. J5. For detailed listings, see *Scott Classic Specialized Catalogue of Stamps and Covers 1840-1940.*

1925 Syria Postage Due Stamps Overprinted in Black, Blue or Red

1925 Perf. 13½

J6	D5	50c brown, yel	5.50	5.50
a.		Blue overprint	42.50	
b.		Red overprint	42.50	
c.		Overprint inverted	30.00	30.00
J7	D6	1p vio, rose (Bl)	5.00	5.00
a.		Black overprint	150.00	150.00
b.		Double overprint (Bk + Bl)	175.00	175.00
c.		Overprint inverted	40.00	40.00
J8	D5	2p blk, blue (R)	6.75	6.75
a.		Blue overprint	45.00	
J9	D5	3p blk, red org (Bl)	9.00	9.00
a.		Overprint inverted	30.00	
J10	D5	5p blk, bl grn (R)	11.00	11.00
a.		Overprint inverted	30.00	30.00
b.		Black overprint	45.00	
		Nos. J6-J10 (5)	37.25	37.25

The stamps of Alaouites were superseded in 1930 by those of Latakia.

ALBANIA

al-'bā-nē-ə

LOCATION — Southeastern Europe
GOVT. — Republic
AREA — 11,101 sq. mi.
POP. — 3,364,571 (1999 est.)
CAPITAL — Tirana

After the outbreak of World War I, the country fell into a state of anarchy when the Prince and all members of the International Commission left Albania. Subsequently General Ferrero in command of Italian troops declared Albania an independent country. A constitution was adopted and a republican form of government was instituted which continued until 1928 when, by constitutional amendment, Albania was declared to be a monarchy. The President of the republic, Ahmed Zogu, became king of the new state. Many unlisted varieties or surcharges and lithographed labels are said to have done postal duty in Albania and Epirus during this unsettled period.

On April 7, 1939, Italy invaded Albania. King Zog fled but did not abdicate. The King of Italy acquired the crown. Germany occupied Albania from September, 1943, until late 1944 when it became an independent state. The People's Republic began in January, 1946.

40 Paras = 1 Piaster = 1 Grossion
100 Centimes = 1 Franc (1917)
100 Qintar = 1 Franc
100 Qintar (Qindarka) = 1 Lek (1947)

> **Catalogue values for unused stamps in this country are for Never Hinged items, beginning with Scott 458 in the regular postage section, Scott B34 in the semipostal section, and Scott C67 in the airpost section.**

Watermarks

Wmk. 125 — Lozenges

Wmk. 220 — Double Headed Eagle

Issues of 1908 Turkey Stamps Handstamped

Perf. 12, 13½ and Compound

1913, June Unwmk.

1	A19	2½pi violet brown	750.00	900.00

With Additional Overprint in Carmine

2	A19	10pa blue green	675.00	650.00

Handstamped on Issue of 1909

4	A21	5pa ocher	450.00	450.00
5	A21	10pa blue green	350.00	225.00
6	A21	20pa car rose	350.00	250.00
7	A21	1pi ultra	325.00	250.00
8	A21	2pi blue black	500.00	450.00
10	A21	5pi dark violet	1,400.	1,500.
11	A21	10pi dull red	5,000.	4,750.

For surcharge see No. 19.
Additional values of 25pi dark green and 50pi red brown were overprinted and sold only to dealers. Values, 25pi $8,000; 50pi $16,000.

With Additional Overprint in Blue or Carmine

13A	A21	10pa blue green	900.00	850.00
14	A21	20pa car rose (Bl)	800.00	850.00
15	A21	1pi brt blue (C)	1,900.	1,750.

Handstamped on Newspaper Stamp of 1911

17	A21	2pa olive green	425.00	425.00

Handstamped on Postage Due Stamp of 1908

18	A19	1pi black, dp rose	3,000.	2,500.

No. 18 was used for regular postage.

No. 6 Surcharged With New Value

19	A21	10pa on 20pa car rose	1,250.	1,250.

The overprint on #1-19 was handstamped and is found inverted, double, etc.

Nos. 6, 7 and 8 exist with the handstamp in red, blue or violet, but these varieties are not known to have been regularly issued.

A 2pa on 5pa newspaper stamp and a 2pi Postage due stamp exist with the handstamp, but these are not known to have been regularly issued. Values, $1,800 and $725, respectively.

Excellent counterfeits exist of Nos. 1 to 19.

A1

Handstamped on White Laid Paper Without Eagle and Value Issued Without Gum

1913, July Imperf.

20	A1	(1pi) black	325.00	525.00
		Cut to shape	190.00	275.00
a.		Sewing machine perf.	575.00	725.00

Value Typewritten in Violet Issued Without Gum

1913, Aug. With Eagle

21	A1	10pa violet	12.00	12.00
a.		Double impression	—	—
22	A1	20pa red & black	16.00	13.50
a.		"2p para"	—	—
23	A1	1gr black	16.00	16.00
24	A1	2gr blue & violet	20.00	16.00
25	A1	5gr violet & blue	24.00	21.00
26	A1	10gr blue	24.00	21.00
		Nos. 21-26 (6)	112.00	99.50

Nos. 21-26 exist with the eagle inverted or omitted and with numerous errors in the figures of value and the spelling of the word "grosh."

A2

Handstamped on White Laid Paper Eagle and Value in Black Issued Without Gum

1913, Nov. Perf. 11½

27	A2	10pa green	4.00	3.25
b.		Eagle and value in green	1,750.	1,750.
c.		10pa red (error)	32.50	32.50
d.		10pa violet (error)	32.50	32.50
29	A2	20pa red	6.00	4.75
b.		20pa green (error)	42.50	32.50
30	A2	30pa violet	6.00	4.75
b.		30pa ultramarine (error)	32.50	32.50
c.		30pa red (error)	32.50	32.50
31	A2	1gr ultramarine	8.00	7.25
a.		1gr green (error)	32.50	32.50
b.		1gr black (error)	32.50	32.50
c.		1gr violet (error)	32.50	32.50
33	A2	2gr black	12.00	8.00
a.		2gr violet (error)	40.00	40.00
b.		2gr blue (error)	40.00	40.00
		Nos. 27-33 (5)	36.00	28.00

The stamps of this issue are known with eagle or value inverted or omitted.
1st anniv. of Albanian independence.
Counterfeits exist.

Skanderbeg (George Castriota) — A3

1913, Dec. Typo. Perf. 14

35	A3	2q orange brn & buff	3.50	1.75
36	A3	5q green & blue grn	3.50	1.75
37	A3	10q rose red	3.50	1.75
38	A3	25q dark blue	3.50	1.75
39	A3	50q violet & red	8.50	3.50
40	A3	1fr deep brown	20.00	10.50
		Nos. 35-40 (6)	42.50	21.00

For overprints and surcharges see Nos. 41-52, 105, J1-J9.

Nos. 35-40 Handstamped in Black or Violet

1914, Mar. 7

41	A3	2q orange brn & buff	50.00	65.00
42	A3	5q grn & bl grn (V)	50.00	65.00
43	A3	10q rose red	50.00	65.00
44	A3	25q dark blue (V)	50.00	65.00
45	A3	50q violet & red	50.00	65.00
46	A3	1fr deep brown	50.00	65.00
		Nos. 41-46 (6)	300.00	390.00

Issued to celebrate the arrival of Prince Wilhelm zu Wied on Mar. 7, 1914.

Nos. 35-40 Surcharged in Black

a   b

1914, Apr. 2

47	A3 (a)	5pa on 2q	2.10	2.10
48	A3 (a)	10pa on 5q	2.10	2.10
49	A3 (a)	20pa on 10q	3.50	2.75
50	A3 (b)	1gr on 25q	3.50	3.50
51	A3 (b)	2gr on 50q	3.50	3.50
52	A3 (b)	5gr on 1fr	14.00	10.50
		Nos. 47-52 (6)	28.70	24.45

For overprints see Nos. 105, J6-J9.

Inverted Surcharge

47a	A3 (a)	5pa on 2q	24.00	24.00
48a	A3 (a)	10pa on 5q	22.50	22.50
49a	A3 (a)	20pa on 10q	24.00	24.00
50a	A3 (b)	1gr on 25q	24.00	24.00
51a	A3 (b)	2gr on 50q	28.00	28.00
52b	A3 (b)	5gr on 1fr	90.00	90.00
		Nos. 47a-52b (6)	212.50	212.50

Korce (Korytsa) Issues

A4

1914   Handstamped   *Imperf.*
52A	A4	10pa violet & red	200.00	200.00
c.		10pa black & red	325.00	325.00
53	A4	25pa violet & red	200.00	200.00
a.		25pa black & red	425.00	425.00

Nos. 52A-53a were handstamped directly on the cover, so the paper varies. They were also produced in sheets; these are rarely found. Nos. 52A-53a were issued by Albanian military authorities.

Counterfeits exists of Nos. 52A and 53.

A5

1917   Typo. & Litho.   *Perf. 11½*
54	A5	1c dk brown & grn	17.50	12.00
55	A5	2c red & green	17.50	12.00
56	A5	3c gray grn & grn	17.50	12.00
57	A5	5c green & black	16.00	8.00
58	A5	10c rose red & black	16.00	8.00
59	A5	25c blue & black	16.00	8.00
60	A5	50c violet & black	16.00	10.00
61	A5	1fr brown & black	16.00	10.00
		Nos. 54-61 (8)	132.50	80.00

A6

1917-18
62	A6	1c dk brown & grn	2.75	2.40
63	A6	2c red brown & grn	2.75	2.40
a.		"CTM" for "CTS"	72.50	120.00
64	A6	3c black & green	2.75	2.40
a.		"CTM" for "CTS"	80.00	135.00
65	A6	5c green & black	4.00	4.00
66	A6	10c dull red & black	4.00	4.00
67	A6	50c violet & black	7.25	6.50
68	A6	1fr red brn & black	20.00	17.50
		Nos. 62-68 (7)	43.50	39.20

Counterfeits abound of Nos. 54-68, 80-81.

No. 65 Surcharged
in Red

1918
80	A6	25c on 5c green & blk	275.00	325.00

A7

1918
81	A7	25c blue & black	72.50	95.00

General Issue

A8

A9

Handstamped in
Rose or Blue   **XV I MCMXIX**

1919   *Perf. 12½*
84	A8	(2)q on 2h brown	7.50	7.50
85	A8	5q on 16h green	7.50	7.50
86	A8	10q on 8h rose (Bl)	7.50	7.50
87	A8	25q on 64h blue	8.50	8.50
88	A9	25q on 64h blue	300.00	300.00
89	A8	50q on 32h violet	7.50	7.50
90	A8	1fr on 1.28k org, bl	9.00	9.00
		Nos. 84-90 (7)	347.50	347.50

See Nos. J10-J13. Compare with types A10-A14. For overprints see Nos 91-104.

Handstamped in
Rose or Blue

1919, Jan. 16
91	A8	(2)q on 2h brown	14.00	14.00
92	A8	5q on 16h green	10.50	10.50
93	A8	10q on 8h rose (Bl)	10.50	10.50
94	A8	25q on 64h blue	140.00	140.00
95	A9	25q on 64h blue	45.00	60.00
96	A8	50q on 32h violet	14.00	14.00
97	A8	1fr on 1.28k org, bl	14.00	14.00
		Nos. 91-97 (7)	248.00	263.00

Handstamped in
Violet

1919
98	A8	(2)q on 2h brown	17.50	17.50
99	A8	5q on 16h green	17.50	17.50
100	A8	10q on 8h rose	17.50	17.50
101	A8	25q on 64h blue	17.50	17.50
102	A9	25q on 64h blue	140.00	140.00
103	A8	50q on 32h violet	17.50	17.50
104	A8	1fr on 1.28k org, bl	17.50	17.50
		Nos. 98-104 (7)	245.00	245.00

No. 50 Overprinted in
Violet

1919   *Perf. 14*
105	A3	1gr on 25q blue	32.50	25.00

A10

A11

1919, June 5   *Perf. 11½, 12½*
106	A10	10q on 2h brown	7.00	7.00
107	A11	15q on 8h rose	7.00	7.00
108	A11	20q on 16h green	7.00	7.00
109	A11	25q on 64h blue	7.00	7.00
110	A11	50q on 32h violet	7.00	7.00

111	A11	1fr on 96h orange	7.00	7.00
112	A10	2fr on 1.60k vio, buff	25.00	21.00
		Nos. 106-112 (7)	67.00	63.00

Nos. 106-108, 110 exist with inverted surcharge.

A12

A13

Surcharged in Black or Violet

1919
113	A12	10q on 8h car	7.00	7.00
114	A12	15q on 8h car (V)	7.00	7.00
115	A13	20q on 16h green	7.00	7.00
116	A13	25q on 32h violet	7.00	7.00
117	A13	50q on 64h blue	20.00	14.00
118	A13	1fr on 96h orange	8.50	7.00
119	A12	2fr on 1.60k vio, buff	14.00	10.50
		Nos. 113-119 (7)	70.50	59.50

A14

Overprinted in Blue or Black Without New Value

1920   *Perf. 12½*
120	A14	1q gray (Bl)	100.00	95.00
121	A14	10q rose (Bk)	14.00	32.50
a.		Double overprint	150.00	150.00
122	A14	20q brown (Bl)	45.00	40.00
123	A14	25q blue (Bk)	525.00	600.00
124	A14	50q brown vio (Bk)	60.00	80.00
		Nos. 120-124 (5)	744.00	847.50

Counterfeit overprints exist of Nos. 120-128.

Surcharged in Black with New Value

1920
125	A14	2q on 10q rose (R)	14.00	21.00
126	A14	5q on 10q rose (G)	14.00	17.50
127	A14	20q on 10q rose (Bl)	14.00	21.00
128	A14	50q on 10q rose (Br)	14.00	35.00
		Nos. 125-128 (4)	56.00	94.50

Stamps of type A14 (Portrait of the Prince zu Wied) were not placed in use without overprint or surcharge.

A15

Post Horn Overprinted in Black

1920   *Perf. 14x13*
129	A15	2q orange	10.50	8.50
130	A15	5q deep green	17.50	15.00
131	A15	10q red	32.50	32.50
132	A15	25q light blue	55.00	30.00
133	A15	50q gray green	12.50	10.50
134	A15	1fr claret	12.50	10.50
		Nos. 129-134 (6)	140.50	107.00

Type A15 was never placed in use without post horn or "Besa" overprint.

Stamps of Type A15
(No Post Horn)
Overprinted

1921
135	A15	2q orange	7.00	7.00
136	A15	5q deep green	7.00	7.00
137	A15	10q red	14.00	12.00
138	A15	25q light blue	25.00	21.00
139	A15	50q gray green	14.00	12.00
140	A15	1fr claret	14.00	12.00
		Nos. 135-140 (6)	81.00	71.00

For surcharge & overprints see Nos. 154, 156-157.

Stamps of these types, and with "TAKSE" overprint, were unauthorized and never placed in use. They are common.

Gjirokaster
A18

Korcha
A19

Designs: 5q, Kanina. 10q, Berati. 25q, Bridge at Vezirit. 50q, Rozafat. 2fr, Dursit.

1923   Typo.   *Perf. 12½, 11½*
147	A18	2q orange	.70	1.40
148	A18	5q yellow green	.70	1.10
149	A18	10q carmine	.70	1.10
150	A18	25q dark blue	.70	1.10
151	A18	50q dark green	.70	1.10
152	A19	1fr dark violet	.70	2.75
153	A19	2fr olive green	4.25	7.00
		Nos. 147-153 (7)	8.45	15.55

For overprints & surcharges see Nos. 158-185, B1-B8.

No. 135 Surcharged

1922   *Perf. 14x13*
154	A15	1q on 2q orange	3.25	8.50

Stamps of Type A15
(No Post Horn)
Overprinted

1922
156	A15	5q deep green	5.00	8.00
157	A15	10q red	5.00	8.00

Nos. 147-
151 Ovptd.
in Black and
Violet

1924, Jan.   *Perf. 12½*
158	A18	2q red orange	10.00	20.00
159	A18	5q yellow green	10.00	20.00
160	A18	10q carmine	7.50	14.50
161	A18	25q dark blue	7.50	14.50
162	A18	50q dark green	11.50	20.00
		Nos. 158-162 (5)	46.50	89.00

The words "Mbledhje Kushtetuese" are in taller letters on the 25q than on the other values. Opening of the Constituent Assembly.

Counterfeits of Nos. 158 and 161 are plentiful.

No. 147
Surcharged

1924

163	A18	1q on 2q red orange	3.00	*8.00*

Nos. 163,
147-152
Overprinted

1924

164	A18	1q on 2q orange	2.75	*7.25*
165	A18	2q orange	2.75	*7.25*
166	A18	5q yellow green	2.75	*7.25*
167	A18	10q carmine	2.75	*7.25*
168	A18	25q dark blue	2.75	*7.25*
169	A18	50q dark green	6.25	*14.00*
170	A19	1fr dark violet	6.25	*17.50*
		Nos. 164-170 (7)	26.25	*67.75*

Issued to celebrate the return of the Government to the Capital after a revolution.

Nos. 163,
147-152
Overprinted

1925

171	A18	1q on 2q orange	3.25	*8.00*
172	A18	2q orange	3.25	*8.00*
173	A18	5q yellow green	3.25	*8.00*
174	A18	10q carmine	3.25	*8.00*
175	A18	25q dark blue	3.25	*8.00*
176	A18	50q dark green	3.25	*12.00*
177	A19	1fr dark violet	6.25	*16.00*
		Nos. 171-177 (7)	25.75	*68.00*

Proclamation of the Republic, Jan. 21, 1925. The date "1921" instead of "1925" occurs once in each sheet of 50.
Counterfeits exist.

Nos. 163,
147-153
Overprinted

1925

178	A18	1q on 2q orange	1.10	*1.60*
a.		Inverted overprint	12.50	*12.50*
179	A18	2q orange	1.10	*1.60*
180	A18	5q yellow green	1.10	*1.60*
a.		Inverted overprint	12.50	*12.50*
181	A18	10q carmine	1.10	*1.60*
182	A18	25q dark blue	1.10	*1.60*
183	A18	50q dark green	1.10	*1.60*
184	A19	1fr dark violet	5.00	*4.00*
185	A19	2fr olive green	7.50	*4.00*
		Nos. 178-185 (8)	19.10	*17.60*

Counterfeits exist.

President Ahmed Zogu
A25   A26

1925   **Perf. 13½, 13½x13**

186	A25	1q orange	.25	*.25*
187	A25	2q red brown	.25	*2.00*
188	A25	5q green	.25	*.25*
189	A25	10q rose red	.25	*.25*
190	A25	15q gray brown	.75	*2.00*
191	A25	25q dark blue	.25	*.25*
192	A25	50q blue green	.85	*1.50*
193	A26	1fr red & ultra	1.75	*2.00*
194	A26	2fr green & orange	1.90	*2.00*

195	A26	3fr brown & violet	4.00	*5.00*
196	A26	5fr violet & black	4.50	*6.75*
		Nos. 186-196 (11)	15.00	*22.25*

No. 193 in ultramarine and brown, and No. 194 in green and brown were not regularly issued. Value, set $15.
For overprints & surcharges see Nos. 197-209, 238-248.

Nos. 186-196
Overprinted in Various
Colors

1927

197	A25	1q orange (V)	.60	*1.00*
198	A25	2q red brn (G)	.25	*.30*
199	A25	5q green (R)	1.25	*.50*
200	A25	10q rose red (Bl)	.25	*.30*
201	A25	15q gray brn (G)	7.00	*14.00*
202	A25	25q blue (R)	.50	*.40*
203	A25	50q blue grn (Bl)	.50	*.40*
204	A26	1fr red & ultra (Bk)	1.40	*.55*
205	A26	2fr green & org (Bk)	1.50	*.80*
206	A26	3fr brown & vio (Bk)	2.40	*1.60*
207	A26	5fr violet & blk (Bk)	3.50	*2.75*
		Nos. 197-207 (11)	19.15	*22.60*

No. 200 exists perf. 11.
For surcharges see Nos. 208-209, 238-240.

Nos. 200, 202
Surcharged in Black or
Red

1928

208	A25	1q on 10q rose red	.50	*.55*
a.		Inverted surcharge	4.00	*4.00*
209	A25	5q on 25q dk blue (R)	.50	*.55*
a.		Inverted surcharge	4.00	*4.00*

A27   King Zog
                I — A28

Black Overprint

1928   **Perf. 14x13½**

210	A27	1q orange brown	5.00	*9.50*
211	A27	2q slate	5.00	*9.50*
212	A27	5q blue green	5.00	*12.00*
213	A27	10q rose red	4.00	*12.00*
214	A27	15q bister	15.00	*47.50*
215	A27	25q deep blue	6.00	*12.00*
216	A27	50q lilac rose	10.00	*15.00*

Red Overprint

Perf. 13½x14

217	A28	1fr blue & slate	10.00	*12.00*
		Nos. 210-217 (8)	60.00	*129.50*

Compare with types A29-A32.

A29   A30

Black or Red Overprint

1928   **Perf. 14x13½**

218	A29	1q orange brown	12.50	*25.00*
219	A29	2q slate (R)	12.50	*25.00*
220	A29	5q blue green	10.00	*20.00*
221	A29	10q rose red	10.00	*16.00*
222	A29	15q bister	15.00	*27.50*
223	A29	25q deep blue (R)	10.00	*16.00*

224	A29	50q lilac rose	10.00	*16.00*
		Perf. 13½x14		
225	A30	1fr blue & slate (R)	12.50	*20.00*
226	A30	2fr green & slate (R)	12.50	*20.00*
		Nos. 218-226 (9)	105.00	*185.50*

Proclamation of Ahmed Zogu as King of Albania.

A31   A32

Black Overprint

1928   **Perf. 14x13½**

227	A31	1q orange brown	.40	*1.25*
228	A31	2q slate	.40	*1.25*
229	A31	5q blue green	2.75	*3.50*
230	A31	10q rose red	.40	*1.25*
231	A31	15q bister	15.00	*24.00*
232	A31	25q deep blue	.40	*1.25*
233	A31	50q lilac rose	.75	*2.00*

Perf. 13½x14

234	A32	1fr blue & slate	1.50	*2.50*
235	A32	2fr green & slate	1.50	*4.00*
236	A32	3fr dk red & ol bis	7.50	*12.00*
237	A32	5fr dull vio & gray	7.50	*16.00*
		Nos. 227-237 (11)	38.10	*69.00*

The overprint reads "Kingdom of Albania."

Nos. 203, 202, 200
Surcharged in Black

1929   **Perf. 13½x13, 11½**

238	A25	1q on 50q blue green	.40	*.55*
239	A25	5q on 25q dark blue	.40	*.55*
240	A25	15q on 10q rose red	.60	*1.00*
		Nos. 238-240 (3)	1.40	*2.10*

Nos. 186-189, 191-194
Overprinted in Black or
Red

1929   **Perf. 11½, 13½**

241	A25	1q orange	7.50	*20.00*
242	A25	2q red brown	7.50	*20.00*
243	A25	5q green	7.50	*20.00*
244	A25	10q rose red	7.50	*20.00*
245	A25	25q dark blue	7.50	*20.00*
246	A25	50q blue green (R)	10.00	*24.00*
247	A26	1fr red & ultra	14.00	*35.00*
248	A26	2fr green & orange	14.00	*35.00*
		Nos. 241-248 (8)	75.50	*194.00*

34th birthday of King Zog. The overprint reads "Long live the King."

Lake   King Zog
Butrinto — A33   I — A34

Zog Bridge   Ruin at Zog
A35   Manor
            A36

Perf. 14, 14½

1930, Sept. 1   Photo.   Wmk. 220

250	A33	1q slate	.25	*.25*
251	A33	2q orange red	.25	*.25*
252	A33	5q yellow green	.25	*.25*
253	A34	10q carmine	.25	*.25*
254	A34	15q dark brown	.25	*.25*
255	A34	25q dark ultra	.25	*.25*
256	A33	50q slate green	.70	*.55*
257	A35	1fr violet	1.10	*1.00*
258	A35	2fr indigo	1.50	*1.10*
259	A36	3fr gray green	3.50	*2.25*
260	A36	5fr orange brown	4.50	*3.50*
		Nos. 250-260 (11)	12.80	*9.90*

2nd anniversary of accession of King Zog I.
For overprints see Nos. 261-270, 299-309, J39. For surcharges see Nos. 354-360.

Nos. 250-259
Overprinted in Black

1934, Dec. 24

261	A33	1q slate	8.50	*12.00*
262	A33	2q orange red	8.50	*12.00*
263	A34	5q yellow green	8.50	*9.50*
264	A34	10q carmine	9.25	*12.00*
265	A34	15q dark brown	9.25	*12.00*
266	A34	25q dark ultra	9.25	*12.00*
267	A33	50q slate green	10.00	*16.00*
268	A35	1fr violet	11.00	*20.00*
269	A35	2fr indigo	12.00	*25.00*
270	A36	3fr gray green	15.00	*35.00*
		Nos. 261-270 (10)	101.25	*165.50*

Tenth anniversary of the Constitution.

Allegory of   Albanian Eagle
Death of   in Turkish
Skanderbeg   Shackles
A37   A38

5q, 25q, 40q, 2fr, Eagle with wings spread.

1937   Unwmk.   Perf. 14

271	A37	1q brown violet	.25	*.25*
272	A38	2q brown	.50	*.35*
273	A38	5q lt green	.50	*.50*
274	A37	10q olive brown	.50	*.80*
275	A38	15q rose red	.80	*1.00*
276	A38	25q blue	1.50	*2.00*
277	A37	50q deep green	3.75	*3.25*
278	A38	1fr violet	9.00	*6.00*
279	A38	2fr orange brown	12.00	*9.00*
		Nos. 271-279 (9)	28.80	*23.15*

Souvenir Sheet

280		Sheet of 3	17.50	*150.00*
a.	A37	20q red violet	3.50	*6.25*
b.	A38	30q olive brown	3.50	*6.25*
c.	A38	40q red	3.50	*6.25*

25th anniv. of independence from Turkey, proclaimed Nov. 26, 1912.

Queen
Geraldine
and King
Zog — A40

1938   Perf. 14

281	A40	1q slate violet	.30	*.40*
282	A40	2q red brown	.30	*.40*
283	A40	5q green	.30	*.40*
284	A40	10q olive brown	1.10	*.80*
285	A40	15q rose red	1.10	*.80*
286	A40	25q blue	2.75	*2.00*
287	A40	50q Prus green	5.75	*4.00*
288	A40	1fr purple	11.50	*8.00*
		Nos. 281-288 (8)	23.10	*16.80*

Souvenir Sheet

289		Sheet of 4	27.50	*125.00*
a.	A40	20q dark red violet	7.75	*9.75*
b.	A40	30q brown olive	7.75	*9.75*

Wedding of King Zog and Countess Geraldine Apponyi, Apr. 27, 1938.
No. 289 contains 2 each of Nos. 289a, 289b.

Queen Geraldine — A42 — National Emblems — A43

Designs: 10q, 25q, 30q, 1fr, King Zog.

1938

290	A42	1q dp red violet	.25	.55
291	A43	2q red orange	.25	.55
292	A42	5q deep green	.50	.50
293	A42	10q red brown	.50	1.00
294	A42	15q deep rose	1.00	1.25
295	A42	25q deep blue	1.40	1.40
296	A43	50q gray black	8.50	6.00
297	A42	1fr slate green	12.50	9.00
		Nos. 290-297 (8)	24.90	20.25

Souvenir Sheet

298		Sheet of 3	22.50	75.00
b.	A43	20q Prussian green	7.00	12.00
c.	A42	30q deep violet	7.00	12.00

10th anniv. of royal rule. They were on sale for 3 days (Aug. 30-31, Sept. 1) only, during which their use was required on all mail. No. 298 contains Nos. 294, 298b, 298c.

Issued under Italian Dominion

Nos. 250-260 Overprinted in Black

1939 Wmk. 220 Perf. 14

299	A33	1q slate	1.25	1.25
300	A33	2q orange red	1.25	1.25
301	A34	5q yellow green	1.25	1.25
302	A34	10q carmine	1.25	1.25
303	A34	15q dark brown	2.00	3.75
304	A34	25q dark ultra	2.00	3.75
305	A35	50q slate green	2.50	5.00
306	A35	1fr violet	2.50	5.00
307	A35	2fr indigo	3.25	9.50
308	A36	3fr gray green	7.75	22.50
309	A36	5fr orange brown	10.00	25.00
		Nos. 299-309 (11)	35.00	79.50

Resolution adopted by the Natl. Assembly, Apr. 12, 1939, offering the Albanian Crown to Italy.

A46 — A47

Native Costumes — A48

King Victor Emmanuel III
A49 — A50

Native Costume — A51

Monastery A52

Designs: 2fr, Bridge at Vezirit. 3fr, Ancient Columns. 5fr, Amphitheater.

1939 Unwmk. Photo. Perf. 14

310	A46	1q blue gray	1.25	.50
311	A47	2q olive green	1.25	.50
312	A48	3q golden brown	1.25	.50
313	A49	5q green	1.25	.25
314	A50	10q brown	1.25	.25
315	A50	15q crimson	1.25	.25
316	A50	25q sapphire	2.00	.80
317	A50	30q brt violet	2.50	1.40
318	A51	50q dull purple	3.25	3.25
319	A49	65q red brown	5.00	11.50
320	A52	1fr myrtle green	7.50	9.50
321	A52	2fr brown lake	11.50	19.00
322	A52	3fr brown black	19.00	35.00
323	A52	5fr gray violet	25.00	50.00
		Nos. 310-323 (14)	83.25	132.70

For overprints and surcharges see Nos. 331-353.

King Victor Emmanuel III — A56

1942 Photo.

324	A56	5q green	1.25	2.00
325	A56	10q brown	1.25	2.00
326	A56	15q rose red	1.25	2.00
327	A56	25q blue	1.25	2.00
328	A56	65q red brown	3.50	4.00
329	A56	1fr myrtle green	3.50	4.00
330	A56	2fr gray violet	3.50	4.00
		Nos. 324-330 (7)	15.50	20.00

Conquest of Albania by Italy, 3rd anniv.

No. 311 Surcharged in Black

331	A47	1q on 2q olive green	1.60	4.00

Issued under German Administration

Stamps of 1939 Overprinted in Carmine or Brown

1943

332	A47	2q olive green	1.00	4.00
333	A48	3q golden brown	1.00	4.00
334	A49	5q green	1.00	4.00
335	A50	10q brown	1.00	4.00
336	A50	15q crimson (Br)	1.00	4.00
337	A50	25q sapphire	1.00	4.00
338	A50	30q brt violet	1.00	4.00
339	A49	65q red brown	1.50	8.00
340	A52	1fr myrtle green	6.25	24.00
341	A52	2fr brown lake	7.75	80.00
342	A52	3fr brown black	60.00	200.00

Surcharged with New Values

343	A48	1q on 3q gldn brn	1.00	8.00
344	A49	50q on 65q red brn	1.50	12.00
		Nos. 332-344 (13)	85.00	360.00

Proclamation of Albanian independence. The overprint "14 Shtator 1943" on Nos. 324 to 328 is private and fraudulent.

Independent State

Nos. 312 to 317 and 319 to 321 Surcharged with New Value and Bars in Black or Carmine, and:

1945

345	A48	30q on 3q gldn brn	3.00	12.00
346	A49	40q on 5q green	3.00	12.00
347	A50	50q on 10q brown	3.00	12.00
348	A50	60q on 15q crimson	3.00	12.00
349	A50	80q on 25q saph (C)	3.00	12.00
350	A50	1fr on 30q brt violet	3.00	12.00
351	A49	2fr on 65q red brn	3.00	12.00
352	A52	3fr on 1fr myr green	3.00	12.00

353	A52	5fr on 2fr brown lake	3.00	12.00
		Nos. 345-353 (9)	27.00	108.00

"DEMOKRATIKE" is not abbreviated on Nos. 352 and 353.

Nos. 250, 251, 256 and 258 Surcharged in Black or Carmine, and

1945 Wmk. 220

354	A33	30q on 1q slate	2.00	6.00
355	A33	60q on 1q slate	2.00	6.00
356	A33	80q on 1q slate	2.00	6.00
357	A33	1fr on 1q slate	4.00	12.00
358	A33	2fr on 2q org red	5.00	13.50
359	A33	3fr on 50q sl grn	10.00	25.00
360	A33	5fr on 2fr indigo	12.50	40.00
		Nos. 354-360 (7)	37.50	108.50

Albanian Natl. Army of Liberation, 2nd anniv. The surcharge on No. 360 is condensed to fit the size of the stamp.

Country House, Labinot — A57

40q, 60q, Bridge at Berat. 1fr, 3fr, Permet.

1945, Nov. 28 Unwmk. Typo.

361	A57	20q bluish green	.30	1.20
362	A57	30q deep orange	.40	1.75
363	A57	40q brown	.40	1.75
364	A57	60q red violet	.60	2.50
365	A57	1fr rose red	1.50	5.00
366	A57	3fr dark blue	10.00	21.00
		Nos. 361-366 (6)	13.20	33.20

Counterfeits: lithographed; genuine: typographed.
For overprints and surcharges see Nos. 367-378, 418-423, B28-B33.

Nos. 361 to 366 Overprinted in Black

1946

367	A57	20q bluish green	.60	1.40
368	A57	30q deep orange	.80	1.75
369	A57	40q brown	1.00	2.10
370	A57	60q red violet	1.60	3.50
371	A57	1fr rose red	6.00	12.50
372	A57	3fr dark blue	10.00	21.00
		Nos. 367-372 (6)	20.00	42.25

Convocation of the Constitutional Assembly, Jan. 10, 1946.

People's Republic

#361-366 Overprinted in Black

1946 Perf. 11

373	A57	20q bluish green	.40	1.10
374	A57	30q deep orange	.60	1.40
375	A57	40q brown	1.00	2.75
376	A57	60q red violet	2.00	5.25
377	A57	1fr rose red	6.00	14.00
378	A57	3fr dark blue	10.00	21.00
		Nos. 373-378 (6)	20.00	45.50

Proclamation of the Albanian People's Republic.
Some values exist perf 11½.
For surcharges see Nos. 418-423.

Globe, Dove and Olive Branch — A60

Perf. 11½, Imperf.
1946, Mar. 8 Typo.
Denomination in Black

379	A60	20q lilac & dull red	.25	1.25
380	A60	40q dp lilac & dull red	.45	1.75
381	A60	50q violet & dull red	.90	2.50
382	A60	1fr lt blue & red	1.60	5.00
383	A60	2fr dk blue & red	2.00	8.00
		Nos. 379-383 (5)	5.20	18.50

International Women's Congress. Counterfeits exist.

Athletes with Shot and Indian Club A61

Perf. 11½
1946, Oct. 6 Litho. Unwmk.

384	A61	1q grnsh black	5.00	8.50
385	A61	2q green	5.00	8.50
386	A61	5q brown	5.00	8.50
387	A61	10q crimson	5.00	8.50
388	A61	20q ultra	5.00	8.50
389	A61	40q rose violet	5.00	8.50
390	A61	1fr deep orange	12.50	25.00
		Nos. 384-390 (7)	42.50	76.00

Balkan Games, Tirana, Oct. 6-13.

Qemal Stafa — A62

1947, May 5 Perf. 12½x11½

391	A62	20q brn & yel brn	5.00	11.00
392	A62	28q dk blue & blue	5.00	11.00
393	A62	40q brn blk & gray brn	5.00	11.00
a.		Souvenir sheet, #391-393	90.00	110.00
		Nos. 391-393 (3)	15.00	33.00

5th anniv. of the death of Qemal Stafa.

Young Railway Laborers A64

1947, May 16 Perf. 11½

395	A64	1q brn blk & gray brn	2.00	1.40
396	A64	4q dk green & green	2.00	1.40
397	A64	10q blk brn & bis brn	2.00	1.60
398	A64	15q dk red & red	2.00	1.60
399	A64	20q indigo & bl gray	4.00	3.00
400	A64	28q dk blue & blue	6.00	2.50
401	A64	40q brn vio & rose vio	12.50	14.50

Perf. 13x12½

402	A64	68q dk brn & org brn	15.00	25.00
		Nos. 395-402 (8)	45.50	51.00

Issued to publicize the construction of the Durres Elbasan Railway by Albanian youths. The 4q, 20q, 28q and 40q exist perf 13x12½.

Citizens Led by Hasim Zeneli A65

Enver Hoxha and Vasil Shanto — A66

Inauguration of Vithkuq Brigade — A67

Vojo Kushi — A68

1947, July 10   **Litho.**
403	A65	16q brn org & red brn	4.00	7.00
404	A66	20q org brn & dk brn	4.00	7.00
405	A67	28q blue & dk blue	4.00	7.00
406	A68	40q lilac & dk brn	4.00	7.00
		Nos. 403-406 (4)	16.00	28.00

4th anniv. of the formation of Albania's army, July 10, 1943.

Conference Building Ruins, Peza — A69

1947, Sept. 16
407	A69	2 l red violet	2.50	5.25
408	A69	2.50 l deep blue	2.50	5.25

Peza Conf., Sept. 16, 1942, 5th anniv.

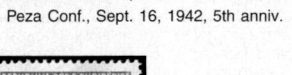

Disabled Soldiers — A70

1947, Nov. 17   **Perf. 12½x11½**
408A	A70	1 l red	7.00	11.00

Disabled War Veterans Cong., 11/14-20/47.

A71

A73

2 l, Banquet. 2.50 l, Peasants rejoicing.

Perf. 11½x12½, 12½x11½

1947, Nov. 17   **Unwmk.**
409	A71	1.50 l dull violet	3.50	7.00
410	A71	2 l brown	3.50	7.00
411	A71	2.50 l blue	3.50	7.00
412	A73	3 l rose red	3.50	7.00
		Nos. 409-412 (4)	14.00	28.00

Agrarian reform law of 11/17/46, 1st anniv.

Burning Farm Buildings A74

Designs: 2.50 l, Trench scene. 5 l, Firing line. 8 l, Winter advance. 12 l, Infantry column.

1947, Nov. 29   **Perf. 11½x12½**
413	A74	1.50 l red	2.00	3.00
414	A74	2.50 l rose brown	2.00	3.00
415	A74	5 l blue	4.00	6.00
416	A74	8 l purple	6.00	9.00
417	A74	12 l brown	10.00	14.00
		Nos. 413-417 (5)	24.00	35.00

3rd anniv. of Albania's liberation.

Nos. 373 to 378 Surcharged with New Value and Bars in Black

1948, Feb. 22   **Perf. 11**
418	A57	50q on 30q dp org	.25	.50
419	A57	1 l on 20q bluish grn	.40	.85
420	A57	2.50 l on 60q red vio	1.00	2.50
421	A57	3 l on 1fr rose red	1.40	3.25
422	A57	5 l on 3fr dk bl	3.00	5.25
423	A57	12 l on 40q brown	8.00	14.00
		Nos. 418-423 (6)	14.05	26.35

The two bars consist of four type squares each set close together.
Some values exist perf 11½.

Map, Train and Construction Workers — A75

1948, June 1   **Litho.**   **Perf. 11½**
424	A75	50q dk car rose	1.00	1.10
425	A75	1 l lt green & blk	1.00	1.10
426	A75	1.50 l deep rose	1.60	1.75
427	A75	2.50 l org brn & dk brn	2.50	2.25
428	A75	5 l dull blue	4.00	4.25
429	A75	8 l sal & dk brn	7.00	7.00
430	A75	12 l red vio & dk vio	12.00	8.50
431	A75	20 l olive gray	16.00	17.50
		Nos. 424-431 (8)	45.10	43.45

Issued to publicize the construction of the Durres-Tirana Railway.

Marching Soldiers A76

Design: 8 l, Battle scene.

1948, July 10
432	A76	2.50 l yellow brown	2.00	3.50
433	A76	5 l dark blue	2.75	5.00
434	A76	8 l violet gray	5.25	7.00
		Nos. 432-434 (3)	10.00	15.50

5th anniv. of the formation of Albania's army.

Bricklayer, Flag, Globe and "Industry" — A77

1949, May 1   **Photo.**   **Perf. 12½x12**
435	A77	2.50 l olive brown	.60	1.75
436	A77	5 l blue	1.20	1.75
437	A77	8 l violet brown	2.25	4.50
		Nos. 435-437 (3)	4.05	8.00

Issued to publicize Labor Day, May 1, 1949.

Map and Soldier — A78

1949, July 10   **Unwmk.**
438	A78	2.50 l brown	.60	1.75
439	A78	5 l light ultra	1.20	2.50
440	A78	8 l brown orange	2.25	5.25
		Nos. 438-440 (3)	4.05	9.75

6th anniv. of the formation of Albania's army.

Enver Hoxha — A79

1949, Oct. 16   **Engr.**   **Perf. 12½**
441	A79	50q purple	.25	.25
442	A79	1 l dull green	.25	.25
443	A79	1.50 l car lake	.25	.25
444	A79	2.50 l brown	.35	.25
445	A79	5 l violet blue	.80	.70
446	A79	8 l sepia	1.50	2.10
447	A79	12 l rose lilac	4.00	3.50
448	A79	20 l gray blue	4.75	5.25
		Nos. 441-448 (8)	12.15	12.55

Albanian Citizen and Spasski Tower, Kremlin — A80

1949, Sept. 10   **Photo.**   **Perf. 12½x12**
449	A80	2.50 l orange brown	.60	1.50
450	A80	5 l deep ultra	1.50	3.50

Albanian-Soviet friendship.

Albanian Soldier and Flag — A81

Battle Scene — A82

1949, Nov. 29   **Unwmk.**   **Perf. 12**
451	A81	2.50 l brown	.40	1.10
452	A82	3 l dark red	.40	2.10
453	A81	5 l violet	1.25	2.75
454	A82	8 l black	2.50	5.25
		Nos. 451-454 (4)	4.55	11.20

Fifth anniversary of Albania's liberation.

Joseph V. Stalin — A83

1949, Dec. 21
455	A83	2.50 l dark brown	.40	1.40
456	A83	5 l violet blue	1.00	2.50
457	A83	8 l rose brown	2.75	6.00
		Nos. 455-457 (3)	4.15	9.90

70th anniv. of the birth of Joseph V. Stalin.

Canceled to Order
Beginning in 1950, Albania sold some issues in sheets canceled to order. Values in second column, when much less than unused, are for "CTO" examples. Postally used stamps are valued at slightly less than, or the same as, unused.

Catalogue values for unused stamps in this section, from this point to the end of the section, are for Never Hinged items.

Symbols of UPU and Postal Transport A84

1950, July 1   **Photo.**   **Perf. 12x12½**
458	A84	5 l blue	2.00	1.40
459	A84	8 l rose brown	4.00	1.90
460	A84	12 l sepia	8.00	2.40
		Nos. 458-460 (3)	14.00	5.70

75th anniv. (in 1949) of the UPU.

Sami Frasheri — A85

Authors: 2.50 l, Andon Zako. 3 l, Naim Frasheri. 5 l, Kostandin Kristoforidhi.

1950, Nov. 5   **Perf. 14**
461	A85	2 l dark green	1.00	.40
462	A85	2.50 l red brown	1.40	.45
463	A85	3 l brown carmine	3.00	.65
464	A85	5 l deep blue	3.25	.80
		Nos. 461-464 (4)	8.65	2.30

"Jubilee of the Writers of the Renaissance."

Arms and Albanian Flags — A86

1951, Jan. 11   Engr.   Perf. 14x13½
465 A86 2.50 l brown carmine   1.60   .30
466 A86   5 l deep blue   3.25   .65
467 A86   8 l sepia   5.25 1.25
                                10.10 2.20
Nos. 465-467 (3)

5th anniv. of the formation of the Albanian People's Republic.

Skanderbeg — A87

1951, Mar. 1
468 A87 2.50 l brown   1.75   .30
469 A87   5 l violet   3.25   .55
470 A87   8 l olive bister   5.25 1.10
                                10.25 1.95
Nos. 468-470 (3)

483rd anniv. of the death of George Castriota (Skanderbeg).

Enver Hoxha and Congress of Permet — A88

1951, May 24   Photo.   Perf. 12
471 A88 2.50 l dark brown   .80   .25
472 A88   3 l rose brown   .80   .35
473 A88   5 l violet blue   2.00   .55
474 A88   8 l rose lilac   3.75   .85
                                 7.35 2.00
Nos. 471-474 (4)

Congress of Permet, 7th anniversary.

Child and Globe — A89

Weighing Baby — A90

1951, July 16
475 A89   2 l green   2.00   .80
476 A90 2.50 l brown   2.75   .95
477 A90   3 l red   3.75 1.25
478 A89   5 l blue   5.50 1.40
                               14.00 4.40
Nos. 475-478 (4)

Intl. Children's Day, June 1, 1951.

Enver Hoxha and Birthplace of Albanian Communist Party — A91

1951, Nov. 8   Photo.   Perf. 14
479 A91 2.50 l olive brown   .55   .25
480 A91   3 l rose brown   .55   .40
481 A91   5 l dark slate blue 1.25   .65
482 A91   8 l black   2.50   .90
                                 4.85 2.20
Nos. 479-482 (4)

Albanian Communist Party, 10th anniv.

Battle Scene A92

Designs: 5 l, Schoolgirl, "Agriculture and Industry." 8 l, Four portraits.

1951, Nov. 28   Perf. 12x12½
483 A92 2.50 l brown   .80   .25
484 A92   5 l blue   1.60   .50
485 A92   8 l brown carmine   3.60   .85
                                 6.00 1.60
Nos. 483-485 (3)

Albanian Communist Youth Org., 10th anniv.

Albanian Heroes (Haxhija, Lezha, Giylbegaj, Mazi and Deda) — A93

Designs: Nos. 486-489 each show 5 "Heroes of the People"; No. 490 shows 2 (Stafa and Shanto).

1950, Dec. 25   Unwmk.   Perf. 14
486 A93   2 l dark green   .75   .25
487 A93 2.50 l purple   1.10   .25
488 A93   3 l scarlet   2.25   .35
489 A93   5 l brt blue   3.75   .45
490 A93   8 l olive brown   7.50 1.25
                                15.35 2.55
Nos. 486-490 (5)

6th anniv. of Albania's liberation.

Tobacco Factory, Shkoder A94

Composite, Lenin Hydroelectric Plant — A95

Designs: 1 l, Canal. 2.50 l, Textile factory. 3 l, "8 November" Cannery. 5 l, Motion Picture Studio, Tirana. 8 l, Stalin Textile Mill, Tirana. 20 l, Central Hydroelectric Dam.

1953, Aug. 1   Perf. 12x12½, 12½x12
491 A94   50q red brown   .45   .25
492 A94   1 l dull green   .85   .25
493 A94 2.50 l brown   .85   .25
494 A94   3 l rose brown   1.25   .25
495 A94   5 l blue   2.10   .25
496 A94   8 l brown olive   2.50   .25
497 A95   12 l deep plum   4.25   .40
498 A94   20 l slate blue   6.00   .60
                               18.25 2.50
Nos. 491-498 (8)

Liberation Scene — A96

1954, Nov. 29   Perf. 12x12½
499 A96   50q brown violet   .25   .25
500 A96   1 l olive green   .55   .25
501 A96 2.50 l yellow brown   .80   .25
502 A96   3 l carmine rose   1.60   .25
503 A96   5 l gray blue   2.40   .25
504 A96   8 l rose brown   4.00   .65
                                 9.60 1.90
Nos. 499-504 (6)

10th anniversary of Albania's liberation.

School — A97

Pandeli Sotiri, Petro Nini Luarasi, Nuci Naci — A98

1956, Feb. 23   Unwmk.
505 A97   2 l rose violet   .40   .25
506 A98 2.50 l lt green   .55   .25
507 A98   5 l ultra   1.40   .40
508 A97   10 l brt grnsh blue 4.75   .75
                                7.10 1.65
Nos. 505-508 (4)

Opening of the 1st Albanian school, 70th anniv.

Flags — A99

Designs: 5 l, Labor Party headquarters, Tirana. 8 l, Marx and Lenin.

1957, June 1   Engr.   Perf. 11½x11
509 A99 2.50 l brown   .40   .25
510 A99   5 l lt violet blue 1.25   .25
511 A99   8 l rose lilac   1.60 1.00
                                3.25 1.50
Nos. 509-511 (3)

Albania's Labor Party, 15th anniv.

Congress Emblem A100

1957, Oct. 4   Unwmk.   Perf. 11½
512 A100 2.50 l gray brown   .50   .25
513 A100   3 l rose red   .50   .25
514 A100   5 l dark blue   .50   .25
515 A100   8 l green   2.50   .65
                                 4.00 1.40
Nos. 512-515 (4)

4th Intl. Trade Union Cong., Leipzig, 10/4-15.

Lenin and Cruiser "Aurora" A101

1957, Nov. 7   Litho.   Perf. 10½
516 A101 2.50 l violet brown   .50   .25
517 A101   5 l violet blue   1.50   .25
518 A101   8 l gray   1.50   .35
                                 3.50   .85
Nos. 516-518 (3)

40th anniv. of the Russian Revolution.

Albanian Fighter Holding Flag — A102

1957, Nov. 28   Perf. 10½
519 A102 1.50 l magenta   .50   .25
520 A102 2.50 l brown   1.00   .25
521 A102   5 l blue   1.50   .35
522 A102   8 l green   4.00   .65
                                 7.00 1.50
Nos. 519-522 (4)

Proclamation of independence, 45th anniv.

Naum Veqilharxhi — A103

1958, Feb. 1   Unwmk.
523 A103 2.50 l dark brown   .45   .25
524 A103   5 l violet blue   .90   .25
525 A103   8 l rose lilac   2.75   .60
                                 4.10 1.10
Nos. 523-525 (3)

160th anniv. of the birth of Naum Veqilharxhi, patriot and writer.

Luigj Gurakuqi (1879-1925), Writer & Politician — A104

1958, Apr. 15   Photo.   Perf. 10½
526 A104 1.50 l dark green   .45   .25
527 A104 2.50 l brown   .45   .25
528 A104   5 l blue   .45   .25
529 A104   8 l sepia   2.75   .50
                                 4.10 1.25
Nos. 526-529 (4)

Transfer of the ashes of Luigj Gurakuqi.

Soldiers A105

2.50 l, 11 l, Airman, sailor, soldier and tank.

1958, July 10   Litho.
530 A105 1.50 l blue green   .25   .25
531 A105 2.50 l dark red brown   .25   .25
532 A105   5 l rose red   .80   .30
533 A105   11 l bright blue   1.75   .50
                                 3.05 1.30
Nos. 530-533 (4)

15th anniversary of Albanian army.

Cerciz Topulli and Mihal Grameno A106

Buildings and Tree A107

1958, July 1
534 A106 2.50 l dk olive bister .45   .25
535 A107   3 l green   .45   .25
536 A106   5 l blue   1.40   .25
537 A107   8 l red brown   2.25   .40
                                 4.55 1.15
Nos. 534-537 (4)

50th anniversary, Battle of Mashkullore.

Ancient Amphitheater and Goddess of Butrinto A108

1959, Jan. 25   Litho.   Perf. 10½
538 A108 2.50 l redsh brown   .45   .25
539 A108 6.50 l lt blue green   1.40   .30
540 A108   11 l dark blue   2.75   .75
                                 4.60 1.30
Nos. 538-540 (3)

Cultural Monuments Week.

Frederic Joliot-Curie and World Peace Congress Emblem — A109

1959, July 1   Unwmk.
541 A109 1.50 l carmine rose   1.75   .25
542 A109 2.50 l rose violet   3.50   .30
543 A109   11 l blue   9.00   1.50
     Nos. 541-543 (3)   14.25 2.05

10th anniv. of the World Peace Movement.

Basketball — A110

Sports: 2.50 l, Soccer, 5 l, Runner. 11 l, Man and woman runners with torch and flags.

1959, Nov. 20   Perf. 10½
544 A110 1.50 l bright violet   .90   .25
545 A110 2.50 l emerald   .90   .25
546 A110   5 l carmine rose   1.75   .25
547 A110   .11 l ultra   5.50   1.75
     Nos. 544-547 (4)   9.05 2.50

1st Albanian Spartacist Games.

Fighter and Flags — A111

Designs: 2.50 l, Miner with drill standing guard. 3 l, Farm woman with sheaf of grain. 6.50 l, Man and woman in laboratory.

1959, Nov. 29
548 A111 1.50 l brt carmine   .90   .25
549 A111 2.50 l red brown   1.20   .25
550 A111   3 l brt blue green   1.75   .30
551 A111 6.50 l bright red   3.50   .50
  a.   Souvenir sheet   9.00 13.50
     Nos. 548-551 (4)   7.35 1.30

15th anniversary of Albania's liberation.
No. 551a contains one each of Nos. 548-551, imperf. and all in bright carmine. Inscribed ribbon frame of sheet and frame lines for each stamp are blue green.

Mother and Child, UN Emblem A112

1959, Dec. 5   Unwmk.
552 A112 5 l lt grnsh blue   4.50 1.00
  a.   Miniature sheet   6.50 9.50

10th anniv. (in 1958) of the signing of the Universal Declaration of Human Rights.
No. 552a contains one imperf. stamp similar to No. 552; ornamental border.

Woman with Olive Branch — A113

1960, Mar. 8   Litho.   Perf. 10½
553 A113 2.50 l chocolate   .90   .25
554 A113   11 l rose carmine   3.25   .50

50th anniv. of Intl. Women's Day, Mar. 8.

Alexander Moissi — A114

1960, Apr. 20
555 A114   3 l deep brown   .45   .25
556 A114   11 l Prus green   1.40   .35

80th anniversary of the birth of Alexander Moissi (Moisiu) (1880-1935), German actor.

Lenin — A115

1960, Apr. 22
557 A115   4 l Prus blue   1.40   .25
558 A115   11 l lake   3.50   .40

90th anniversary of birth of Lenin.

School Building — A116

1960, May 30   Litho.   Perf. 10½
559 A116   5 l green   1.75   .35
560 A116 6.50 l plum   1.75   .35

1st Albanian secondary school, 50th anniv.

Soldier on Guard Duty — A117

1960, May 12   Unwmk.   Perf. 10½
561 A117 1.50 l carmine rose   .45   .25
562 A117   11 l Prus blue   2.25   .40

15th anniversary of the Frontier Guards.

Liberation Monument, Tirana, Family and Policeman — A118

1960, May 14
563 A118 1.50 l green   .45   .25
564 A118 8.50 l brown   2.75   .40

15th anniversary of the People's Police.

Congress Site — A119

1960, Mar. 25
565 A119 2.50 l sepia   .45   .25
566 A119 7.50 l dull blue   1.40   .25

40th anniversary, Congress of Louchnia.

Pashko Vasa — A120

Designs: 1.50 l, Jani Vreto. 6.50 l, Sami Frasheri. 11 l, Page of statutes of association.

1960, May 5
567 A120   1 l gray olive   .45   .25
568 A120 1.50 l brown   .45   .25
569 A120 6.50 l blue   1.40   .25
570 A120   11 l rose red   4.00   .35
     Nos. 567-570 (4)   6.30 1.10

80th anniv. (in 1959) of the Association of Albanian Authors.

Albanian Fighter and Cannon — A121

1960, Aug. 2   Litho.   Perf. 10½
571 A121 1.50 l olive brown   .45   .25
572 A121 2.50 l maroon   .90   .35
573 A121   5 l dark blue   1.75   .45
     Nos. 571-573 (3)   3.10 1.05

Battle of Viona (against Italian troops), 40th anniv.

TU-104 Plane, Clock Tower, Tirana, and Kremlin, Moscow A122

1960, Aug. 18
574 A122   1 l redsh brown   .90   .25
575 A122 7.50 l brt grnsh blue   2.75   .35
576 A122 11.50 l gray   4.50   .60
     Nos. 574-576 (3)   8.15 1.20

TU-104 flights, Moscow-Tirana, 2nd anniv.

Rising Sun and Federation Emblem — A123

1960, Nov. 10   Unwmk.   Perf. 10½
577 A123 1.50 l ultra   .45   .25
578 A123 8.50 l red   1.75   .35

Intl. Youth Federation, 15th anniv.

Ali Kelmendi — A124

1960, Dec. 5   Litho.   Perf. 10½
579 A124 1.50 l pale gray grn   .45   .25
580 A124   11 l dull rose lake   1.75   .30

Ali Kelmendi, communist leader, 60th birthday.

Flags of Russia and Albania and Clasped Hands — A125

1961, Jan. 10   Unwmk.   Perf. 10½
581 A125 2 l violet   .45   .25
582 A125 8 l dull red brown   1.75   .35

15th anniv. of the Albanian-Soviet Friendship Society.

Marx and Lenin — A126

1961, Feb. 13   Litho.
583 A126 2 l rose red   .45   .25
584 A126 8 l violet blue   1.75   .25

Fourth Communist Party Congress.

Man from Shkoder — A127

Costumes: 1.50 l, Woman from Shkoder. 6.50 l, Man from Lume. 11 l, Woman from Mirdite.

1961, Apr. 28   Perf. 10½
585 A127   1 l slate   .90   .25
586 A127 1.50 l dull claret   .90   .25
587 A127 6.50 l ultra   3.50   .55
588 A127   11 l red   5.50   1.40
     Nos. 585-588 (4)   10.80 2.45

Otter — A128

Designs: 6.50 l, Badger. 11 l, Brown bear.

1961, June 25   Unwmk.   Perf. 10½
589 A128 2.50 l grayish blue   3.50   .25
590 A128 6.50 l blue green   7.25   .50
591 A128   11 l dark red brown   16.00   .85
     Nos. 589-591 (3)   26.75 1.60

Dalmatian Pelicans — A129

1961, Sept. 30   Perf. 14
592 A129 1.50 l shown   4.50   .25
593 A129 7.50 l Gray herons   6.25   .60
594 A129   11 l Little egret   11.50   .75
     Nos. 592-594 (3)   22.25 1.60

Cyclamen — A130

1961, Oct. 27   Litho.
595 A130 1.50 l shown   1.75   .25
596 A130 8 l Forsythia   6.00   .50
597 A130 11 l Lily   7.00   .60
   Nos. 595-597 (3)   14.75   1.35

Milosh G.
Nikolla — A131

1961, Oct. 30   Perf. 14
598 A131 50q violet brown   .45   .25
599 A131 8.50 l Prus green   1.40   .35

   50th anniv. of the birth of Milosh Gjergi Nikolla, poet.

Flag with Marx and Lenin — A132

1961, Nov. 8
600 A132 2.50 l vermilion   .55   .25
601 A132 7.50 l dull red brown   1.25   .35

   20th anniv. of the founding of Albania's Communist Party.

Worker, Farm
Woman and
Emblem — A133

1961, Nov. 23   Unwmk.   Perf. 14
602 A133 2.50 l violet blue   .45   .25
603 A133 7.50 l rose claret   1.75   .30

   20th anniv. of the Albanian Workers' Party.

Yuri Gagarin and
Vostok 1 — A134

1962, Feb. 15   Unwmk.   Perf. 14
604 A134 50q blue   .90   1.40
605 A134 4 l red lilac   3.50   3.50
606 A134 11 l dk slate grn   9.00   10.00
   Nos. 604-606 (3)   13.40   14.90

   1st manned space flight, made by Yuri A. Gagarin, Soviet astronaut, Apr. 12, 1961.
   Nos. 604-606 were overprinted with an overall yellow tint and with "POSTA AJRORE" (Air Mail) in maroon or black in 1962. Value: set, maroon ovpt., $90 mint, $130 used; set, black ovpt., $300 mint, $400 used.

Petro Nini
Luarasi — A135

1962, Feb. 28   Litho.
607 A135 50q Prus blue   .45   .25
608 A135 8.50 l olive gray   3.50   .25

   50th anniv. (in 1961) of the death of Petro Nini Luarasi, Albanian patriot.

Malaria Eradication
Emblem — A136

1962, Apr. 30   Unwmk.   Perf. 14
609 A136 1.50 l brt green   .45   .25
610 A136 2.50 l brown red   .45   .25
611 A136 10 l red lilac   .90   .25
612 A136 11 l blue   .90   .35
   Nos. 609-612 (4)   2.70   1.10

   WHO drive to eradicate malaria.
   Souvenir sheets, perf. and imperf., contain one each of Nos. 609-612. Value $30 each. Nos. 609-612 imperf., value, set $25.

Camomile — A137

   Medicinal plants.

1962, May 10
613 A137 50q shown   .45   .30
614 A137 8 l Linden   1.50   .60
615 A137 11.50 l Garden sage   2.50   .90
   Nos. 613-615 (3)   4.45   1.80

   Value, imperf. set $30 mint, $40 used.

Woman
Diver — A138

   2.50 l, Pole vault. 3 l, Mt. Fuji & torch, horiz. 9 l, Woman javelin thrower. 10 l, Shot putting.

1962, May 31   Perf. 14
616 A138 50q brt grnsh bl & blk   .25   .25
617 A138 2.50 l gldn brn & sepia   .25   .25
618 A138 3 l blue & gray   .35   .25
619 A138 9 l rose car & dk brn   1.75   .25
620 A138 10 l olive & blk   1.75   .30
   Nos. 616-620 (5)   4.35   1.30

   1964 Olympic Games, Tokyo. Value, imperf. set, $50 mint, $70 used. A 15 l (like 3 l) exists in souv. sheet, perf. and imperf. Value, each $35 mint, $50 used.

Globe and
Orbits — A139

Dog Laika and
Sputnik
2 — A140

   Designs: 1.50 l, Rocket to the sun. 20 l, 3 photographing far side of the moon.

1962, June   Unwmk.   Perf. 14
621 A139 50q violet & org   .45   .25
622 A140 1 l blue grn & brn   .90   .30
623 A140 1.50 l yellow & ver   1.25   .40
624 A139 20 l magenta & bl   9.00   5.50
   Nos. 621-624 (4)   11.60   6.45

   Russian space explorations.

   Nos. 621-624 exist imperf in changed colors. Value, mint $65, used $75.
   Two miniature sheets exist, containing one 14-lek picturing Sputnik 1. The perforated 14-lek is yellow and brown; the imperf. red and brown. Value, each mint $65, used $75.

Soccer Game,
Map of South
America
A141

   2.50 l, 15 l, Soccer game and globe as ball.

1962, July   Litho.
625 A141 1 l org & dk pur   .45   .25
626 A141 2.50 l emer & bluish grn   .90   .25
627 A141 6.50 l lt brn & pink   .90   .25
628 A141 15 l bluish grn & mar   2.25   .40
   Nos. 625-628 (4)   4.50   1.15

   World Soccer Championships, Chile, 5/30-6/17.
   Exist imperforate in changed colors. Value, mint $40, used $75.
   Two miniature sheets exist, each containing a single 20-lek in design similar to A141. The perf. sheet is brown and green; the imperf., brown and orange. Value, mint $40, used $75.

Map of Europe and
Albania — A142

   Designs: 1 l, 2.50 l, Map of Adriatic Sea and Albania and Roman statue.

1962, Aug.
630 A142 50q multicolored   .45   1.00
631 A142 1 l ultra & red   .90   2.75
632 A142 2.50 l blue & red   7.25   8.50
633 A142 11 l multicolored   10.00   17.50
   Nos. 630-633 (4)   18.60   29.75

   Tourist propaganda. Imperforates in changed colors exist. Value, mint $35, used $70.
   Miniature sheets containing a 7 l and 8 l stamp, perf. and imperf., exist. Value, mint $40, used $75.

Woman of
Dardhe — A143

   Regional Costumes: 1 l, Man from Devoll. 2.50 l, Woman from Lunxheri. 14 l, Man from Gjirokaster.

1962, Sept.
635 A143 50q car, bl & pur   .45   .25
636 A143 1 l red brn & ocher   .45   .25
637 A143 2.50 l vio, yel grn & blk   1.25   .60
638 A143 14 l red brn & pale grn   5.75   1.60
   Nos. 635-638 (4)   7.90   2.70

   Exist imperf. Value, set, mint $40, used $60.

Chamois — A144

   Animals: 1 l, Lynx, horiz. 1.50 l, Wild boar, horiz. 15 l, 20 l, Roe deer.

1962, Oct. 24   Unwmk.   Perf. 14
639 A144 50q sl grn & dk pur   .45   .25
640 A144 1 l orange & blk   1.75   .25
641 A144 1.50 l red brn & blk   2.25   .25
642 A144 15 l yel ol & red brn   17.50   1.00
   Nos. 639-642 (4)   21.95   1.75

Miniature Sheet
643 A144 20 l yel ol & red brn   135.00   145.00

   Imperfs. in changed colors, value Nos. 639-642 $75, No. 643 $125.

Ismail
Qemali — A145

   Designs: 1 l, Albania eagle. 16 l, Eagle over fortress formed by "RPSH."

1962, Dec. 28   Litho.
644 A145 1 l red & red brn   .45   .25
645 A145 3 l org brn & blk   3.00   .25
646 A145 16 l dk car rose & blk   5.25   .50
   Nos. 644-646 (3)   8.70   1.00

   50th anniv. of independence. Imperfs. in changed colors, value, set $40 mint, $60 used.

Monument of
October
Revolution — A146

1963, Jan. 5   Unwmk.   Perf. 14
647 A146 5 l shown   1.00   .25
648 A146 10 l Lenin statue   2.50   .35

   October Revolution (Russia, 1917), 45th anniv.

Henri Dunant,
Cross, Globe
and
Nurse — A147

1963, Jan 25   Unwmk.   Perf. 14
649 A147 1.50 l rose lake, red & blk   .45   .25
650 A147 2.50 l lt bl, red & blk   .90   .25
651 A147 6 l emerald, red & blk   1.75   .25
652 A147 10 l dull yel, red & blk   3.00   .60
   Nos. 649-652 (4)   6.10   1.35

   Cent. of the Geneva Conf., which led to the establishment of the Intl. Red Cross in 1864. Imperfs. in changed colors, value, set $60.

Stalin and
Battle of
Stalingrad
A148

1963, Feb. 2
653 A148 8 l dk green & slate   9.00   1.00

   Battle of Stalingrad, 20th anniv. See No. C67.

Andrian G.
Nikolayev — A149

Designs: 7.50 l, Vostoks 3 and 4 and globe, horiz. 20 l, Pavel R. Popovich. 25 l, Nikolayev, Popovich and globe with trajectories.

1963, Feb. 28   **Litho.**
654 A149 2.50 l vio bl & sepia   .45   .40
655 A149 7.50 l lt blue & blk   1.25   .80
656 A149 20 l violet & sepia   3.50   2.25
   Nos. 654-656 (3)   5.20   3.45

Miniature Sheet
657 A149 25 l vio bl & sepia   45.00   45.00

1st group space flight of Vostoks 3 and 4, Aug. 11-15, 1962. Imperfs in changed colors, value: Nos. 654-656 $45 mint or used; No. 657 perf, $45 mint or used; No. 657 imperf, $50 mint or used.

"Albania" Decorating Police
Officer — A150

1963, Mar. 20   **Unwmk.**   **Perf. 14**
658 A150 2.50 l crim, mag & blk   .90   .25
659 A150 7.50 l org ver, dk red &
   blk   3.00   .25

20th anniversary of the security police.

Polyphylla
Fullo — A151

Beetles: 1.50 l, Lucanus cervus. 8 l, Procerus gigas. 10 l, Cicindela albanica.

1963, Mar. 20
660 A151 50q ol grn & brn   1.00   .25
661 A151 1.50 l blue & brn   1.75   .25
662 A151 8 l dl rose & blk
   vio   7.50   1.25
663 A151 10 l brt citron & blk   9.75   1.40
   Nos. 660-663 (4)   20.00   3.15

1913 Stamp
and Postmark
A152

10 l, Stamps of 1913, 1937 and 1962.

1963, May 5
664 A152 5 l yel, buff, bl & blk   1.75   .25
665 A152 10 l car rose, grn & blk   3.00   .45

50th anniversary of Albanian stamps.

Boxer — A153

Designs: 3 l, Basketball baskets. 5 l, Volleyball. 6 l, Bicyclists. 9 l, Gymnast. 15 l, Hands holding torch, and map of Japan.

1963, May 25   **Perf. 13½**
666 A153 2 l yel, blk & red
   brn   .55   1.00
667 A153 3 l ocher, brn & bl   .60   2.00
668 A153 5 l gray bl, red brn
   & brn   1.00   2.75
669 A153 6 l gray, dk gray &
   grn   1.25   5.00
670 A153 9 l rose, red brn &
   bl   2.25   7.50
   Nos. 666-670 (5)   5.65   18.25

Miniature Sheet
671 A153 15 l lt bl, car, blk &
   brn   13.50   13.50

1964 Olympic Games in Tokyo. Value, imperfs. Nos. 666-670 $20, No. 671 $20.

Crested
Grebe — A154

Birds: 3 l, Golden eagle. 6.50 l, Gray partridges. 11 l, Capercaillie.

1963, Apr. 20   **Litho.**   **Perf. 14**
672 A154 50q multicolored   1.25   .25
673 A154 3 l multicolored   2.75   .50
674 A154 6.50 l multicolored   6.50   1.25
675 A154 11 l multicolored   9.00   2.00
   Nos. 672-675 (4)   19.50   4.00

Soldier
and
Building
A155

2.50 l, Soldier with pack, ship, plane. 5 l, Soldier in battle. 6 l, Soldier, bulldozer.

1963, July 10   **Unwmk.**   **Perf. 12**
676 A155 1.50 l brick red, yel &
   blk   .45   .25
677 A155 2.50 l bl, ocher & brn   .90   .25
678 A155 5 l bluish grn, gray
   & blk   1.25   .25
679 A155 6 l red brn, buff & bl   1.75   .25
   Nos. 676-679 (4)   4.35   1.00

Albanian army, 20th anniversary.

Maj. Yuri
A.
Gagarin
A156

Designs: 5 l, Maj. Gherman Titov. 7 l, Maj. Andrian G. Nikolayev. 11 l, Lt. Col. Pavel R. Popovich. 14 l, Lt. Col. Valeri Bykovski. 20 l, Lt. Valentina Tereshkova.

1963, July 30
Portraits in Yellow and Black
680 A156 3 l brt purple   .90   .25
681 A156 5 l dull blue   .90   .25
682 A156 7 l gray   1.25   .25
683 A156 11 l deep claret   2.75   .35
684 A156 14 l blue green   4.00   .60
685 A156 20 l ultra   6.25   1.10
   Nos. 680-685 (6)   16.05   2.80

Man's conquest of space. Value, imperf set $40.

Volleyball
A157

1963, Aug. 31   **Perf. 12x12½**
686 A157 2 l shown   .45   .25
687 A157 3 l Weight lifting   .45   .25
688 A157 5 l Soccer   .90   .25
689 A157 7 l Boxing   1.25   .25
690 A157 8 l Rowing   3.00   .30
   Nos. 686-690 (5)   6.05   1.30

European championships. Imperfs. in changed colors, value set $35.

Papilio
Podalirius
A158

1963, Sept. 29   **Litho.**
Various Butterflies and Moths in Natural Colors
691 A158 1 l red   .45   .25
692 A158 2 l blue   .90   .25
693 A158 4 l dull lilac   1.75   .60
694 A158 5 l pale green   2.25   .60
695 A158 8 l bister   4.50   1.25
696 A158 10 l light blue   5.75   1.75
   Nos. 691-696 (6)   15.60   4.70

Oil Refinery,
Cerrik — A159

2.50 l, Food processing plant, Tirana, horiz. 30 l, Fruit canning plant. 50 l, Tannery, horiz.

1963, Nov. 15   **Unwmk.**   **Perf. 14**
697 A159 2.50 l rose red, pnksh   .90   .25
698 A159 20 l slate grn, grnsh   3.50   .25
699 A159 30 l dull pur, grysh   9.00   .55
700 A159 50 l ocher, yel   9.00   .85
   Nos. 697-700 (4)   22.40   1.90

Industrial development in Albania. For surcharges see Nos. 841-846.

Flag and
Shield — A160

1963, Nov. 24   **Perf. 12½x12**
701 A160 2 l grnsh bl, blk, ocher
   & red   .45   .25
702 A160 8 l blue, blk, ocher &
   red   1.75   .50

1st Congress of Army Aid Assn.

Chinese, Caucasian and Negro
Men — A161

1963, Dec. 10   **Perf. 12x11½**
703 A161 3 l bister & blk   .45   .25
704 A161 5 l bister & ultra   .90   .25
705 A161 7 l bister & vio   2.25   .30
   Nos. 703-705 (3)   3.60   .80

15th anniv. of the Universal Declaration of Human Rights.

Slalom
Ascent — A162

Designs: 50q, Bobsled, horiz. 6.50 l, Ice hockey, horiz. 12.50 l, Women's figure skating. No. 709A, Ski jumper.

1963, Dec. 25   **Perf. 14**
706 A162 50q grnsh bl &
   blk   .45   .25
707 A162 2.50 l red, gray &
   blk   .60   .25
708 A162 6.50 l yel, blk &
   gray   1.20   .25
709 A162 12.50 l red, blk &
   yel grn   2.25   .55
   Nos. 706-709 (4)   4.50   1.30

Miniature Sheet
709A A162 12.50 l multi   25.00   25.00

9th Winter Olympic Games, Innsbruck, Jan. 29-Feb. 9, 1964. Imperfs. in changed colors, value Nos. 706-709 $75, No. 709A $50.

Lenin — A163

1964, Jan. 21   **Perf. 12½x12**
710 A163 5 l gray & bister   .90   .25
711 A163 10 l gray & ocher   2.00   .30

40th anniversary, death of Lenin.

Hurdling — A164

Designs: 3 l, Track, horiz. 6.50 l, Rifle shooting, horiz. 8 l, Basketball.

Perf. 12½x12, 12x12½
1964, Jan. 30   **Litho.**
712 A164 2.50 l pale vio & ultra   .45   .25
713 A164 3 l lt grn & red brn   .90   .35
714 A164 6.50 l blue & claret   1.25   1.00
715 A164 8 l lt blue & ocher   2.25   1.60
   Nos. 712-715 (4)   4.85   3.20

1st Games of the New Emerging Forces, GANEFO, Jakarta, Indonesia, Nov. 10-22, 1963.

Fish — A165

1964, Feb. 26   **Unwmk.**   **Perf. 14**
716 A165 50q Sturgeon   .45   .25
717 A165 1 l Gilthead   .90   .25
718 A165 1.50 l Striped mullet   1.25   .25
719 A165 2.50 l Carp   1.75   .25
720 A165 6.50 l Mackerel   2.75   .40
721 A165 10 l Lake Ohrid
   trout   4.50   .50
   Nos. 716-721 (6)   11.60   1.90

Wild Animals A166

1964, Mar. 28   **Perf. 12½x12**

722	A166	1 l	Red Squirrel	.45 .25
723	A166	1.50 l	Beech marten	.85 .25
724	A166	2 l	Red fox	.85 .40
725	A166	2.50 l	Hedgehog	1.25 .40
726	A166	3 l	Hare	1.75 .60
727	A166	5 l	Jackal	1.75 .60
728	A166	7 l	Wildcat	3.50 .60
729	A166	8 l	Wolf	4.50 .95
		Nos. 722-729 (8)		14.90 4.05

Lighting Olympic Torch — A167

5 l, Torch, globes. 7 l, 15 l, Olympic flag, Mt. Fuji. 10 l, National Stadium, Tokyo.

1964, May 18   **Perf. 12x12½**

730	A167	3 l	lt yel grn, yel & buff	.45 .70
731	A167	5 l	red & vio blue	.65 1.00
732	A167	7 l	lt bl, ultra & yel	.90 1.50
733	A167	10 l	orange, bl & vio	1.25 2.50
		Nos. 730-733 (4)		3.25 5.70

Miniature Sheet

734	A167	15 l	lt bl, ultra & org	22.50 22.50

18th Olympic Games, Tokyo, Oct. 10-25, 1964. No. 734 contains one 49x62mm stamp. Imperfs. in changed colors, value Nos. 730-733 $17.50; No. 734 $22.50. See No. 745.

Partisans — A168

5 l, Arms of Albania. 8 l, Enver Hoxha.

Perf. 12½x12
1964, May 24   **Litho.**   **Unwmk.**

735	A168	2 l	orange, red & blk	1.25 .25
736	A168	5 l	multicolored	3.00 .30
737	A168	8 l	red brn, blk & red	6.25 .90
		Nos. 735-737 (3)		10.50 1.45

20th anniv. of the Natl. Anti-Fascist Cong. of Liberation, Permet, May 24, 1944. The label attached to each stamp, without perforations between, carries a quotation from the 1944 Congress.

Albanian Flag and Revolutionists A169

Perf. 12½x12
1964, June 10   **Litho.**   **Unwmk.**

738	A169	2.50 l	red & gray	.45 .25
739	A169	7.50 l	lilac rose & gray	1.25 .25

Albanian revolution of 1924, 40th anniv.

Full Moon — A170

Designs: 5 l, New moon. 8 l, Half moon. 11 l, Waning moon. 15 l, Far side of moon.

1964, June 27   **Perf. 12x12½**

740	A170	1 l	purple & yel	.45 .25
741	A170	5 l	violet & yel	.60 .25
742	A170	8 l	blue & yel	.90 .30
743	A170	11 l	green & yel	3.50 .45
		Nos. 740-743 (4)		5.45 1.25

Miniature Sheet
Perf. 12 on 2 sides

744	A170	15 l	ultra & yel	15.00 15.00

No. 744 contains one stamp, size: 35x36mm, perforated at top and bottom. Imperfs. in changed colors, value Nos. 740-743 $16, No. 744 $15.

No. 733 with Added Inscription "Rimini 25-VI-64"

1964   **Perf. 12x12½**

745	A167	10 l	orange, bl & vio	7.00 7.00

"Toward Tokyo 1964" Phil. Exhib. at Rimini, Italy, June 25-July 6.

Wren — A171

Birds: 1 l, Penduline titmouse. 2.50 l, Green woodpecker. 3 l, Tree creeper. 4 l, Nuthatch. 5 l, Great titmouse. 6 l, Goldfinch. 18 l, Oriole.

1964, July 31   **Perf. 12x12½**

746	A171	50q	multi	.45 .25
747	A171	1 l	orange & multi	.90 .25
748	A171	2.50 l	multi	1.25 .40
749	A171	3 l	blue & multi	1.75 .40
750	A171	4 l	yellow & multi	2.25 .80
751	A171	5 l	blue & multi	2.75 .80
752	A171	6 l	lt vio & multi	3.00 1.25
753	A171	18 l	pink & multi	5.50 2.75
		Nos. 746-753 (8)		17.85 6.90

Running and Gymnastics A172

Sport: 2 l, Weight lifting, judo. 3 l, Equestrian, bicycling. 4 l, Soccer, water polo. 5 l, Wrestling, boxing. 6 l, Pentathlon, hockey. 7 l, Swimming, sailing. 8 l, Basketball, volleyball. 9 l, Rowing, canoeing. 10 l, Fencing, pistol shooting. 20 l, Three winners.

Perf. 12x12½
1964, Sept. 25   **Litho.**   **Unwmk.**

754	A172	1 l	lt bl, rose & emer	.25 .25
755	A172	2 l	bis brn, bluish grn & vio	.25 .25
756	A172	3 l	vio, red org & ol bis	.25 .25
757	A172	4 l	grnsh bl, ol & ultra	.45 .35
758	A172	5 l	grnsh bl, car & pale lil	.45 .35
759	A172	6 l	dk bl, org & lt bl	.70 .75
760	A172	7 l	dk bl, lt ol & org	.70 .75
761	A172	8 l	emer, gray & yel	.90 .75
762	A172	9 l	bl, yel & lil rose	.90 .75
763	A172	10 l	brt grn, org brn & yel grn	1.25 1.00
		Nos. 754-763 (10)		6.10 5.45

Miniature Sheet
Perf. 12

764	A172	20 l	violet & lemon	15.00 15.00

18th Olympic Games, Tokyo, Oct. 10-25. No. 764 contains one stamp, size: 41x68mm. Imperfs in changed colors, value: Nos. 754-763, $17.50 mint, $25 used; No. 764, $20 mint, $25 used.

Arms of People's Republic of China — A173

Mao Tse-tung and Flag A174

1964, Oct. 1   **Perf. 11½x12, 12x11½**

765	A173	7 l	black, red & yellow	10.00 4.50
766	A174	8 l	black, red & yellow	10.00 6.00

People's Republic of China, 15th anniv.

Karl Marx A175

Designs: 5 l, St. Martin's Hall, London. 8 l, Friedrich Engels.

1964, Nov. 5   **Perf. 12x11½**

767	A175	2 l	red, lt vio & blk	.90 .45
768	A175	5 l	gray blue	2.25 1.40
769	A175	8 l	ocher, blk & red	4.00 1.75
		Nos. 767-769 (3)		7.15 3.60

Centenary of First Socialist International.

Jeronim de Rada — A176

1964, Nov. 15   **Perf. 12½x11½**

770	A176	7 l	slate green	1.10 .35
771	A176	8 l	dull violet	1.90 .60

Birth of Jeronim de Rada, poet, 150th anniv.

Arms of Albania — A177

Factories A178

Designs: 3 l, Combine harvester. 4 l, Woman chemist. 10 l, Hands holding Communist Party book, hammer and sickle.

Perf. 11½x12, 12x11½
1964, Nov. 29

772	A177	1 l	multicolored	.45 .40
773	A178	2 l	red, yel & vio bl	.80 .80
774	A178	3 l	red, yel & brn	1.20 1.25
775	A178	4 l	red, yel & gray grn	1.50 1.60
776	A177	10 l	red, bl & blk	3.50 4.00
		Nos. 772-776 (5)		7.45 8.05

20th anniversary of liberation.

Planet Mercury — A179

Planets: 2 l, Venus and rocket. 3 l, Earth, moon and rocket. 4 l, Mars and rocket. 5 l, Jupiter. 6 l, Saturn. 7 l, Uranus. 8 l, Neptune. 9 l, Pluto. 15 l, Solar system and rocket.

1964, Dec. 15   **Perf. 12x12½**

777	A179	1 l	yellow & pur	.25 .25
778	A179	2 l	multicolored	.50 .25
779	A179	3 l	multicolored	.40 .40
780	A179	4 l	multicolored	.40 .40
781	A179	5 l	yel, dk pur & brn	.80 .60
782	A179	6 l	lt grn, vio brn & yel	1.20 .60
783	A179	7 l	yellow & grn	1.40 .90
784	A179	8 l	yellow & vio	1.60 1.00
785	A179	9 l	lt grn, yel & blk	1.75 1.25
		Nos. 777-785 (9)		8.30 5.65

Miniature Sheet
Perf. 12 on 2 sides

786	A179	15 l	car, bl, yel & grn	25.00 35.00

No. 786 contains one stamp, size: 62x51mm, perforated at top and bottom. Imperfs. in changed colors. Value Nos. 777-785, $30; No. 786, $25.

European Chestnut — A180

1965, Jan. 25   **Perf. 11½x12**

787	A180	1 l	shown	.25 .25
788	A180	2 l	Medlars	.35 .25
789	A180	3 l	Persimmon	.55 .25
790	A180	4 l	Pomegranate	.75 .40
791	A180	5 l	Quince	1.50 .50
792	A180	10 l	Orange	3.00 1.00
		Nos. 787-792 (6)		6.40 2.65

Symbols of Industry — A181

Designs: 5 l, Books, triangle and compass. 8 l, Beach, trees and hotel.

1965, Feb. 20

793	A181	2 l	blk, car rose & pink	7.50 7.00
794	A181	5 l	yel, gray & blk	12.00 10.50
795	A181	8 l	blk, vio bl & lt bl	15.00 13.00
		Nos. 793-795 (3)		34.50 30.50

Professional trade associations, 20th anniv.

Water Buffalo A182

Various designs: Water buffalo.

1965, Mar.   Perf. 12x11½

796	A182	1 l	lt yel grn, yel & brn blk	.75 .35
797	A182	2 l	lt bl, dk gray & blk	1.50 .65
798	A182	3 l	yellow, brn & grn	2.25 1.10
799	A182	7 l	brt grn, yel & brn blk	5.25 1.50
800	A182	12 l	pale lil, dk brn & ind	9.00 1.75
		Nos. 796-800 (5)		18.75 5.35

Mountain View, Valbona — A183

1.50 l, Seashore. 3 l, Glacier and peak. 4 l, Gorge. 5 l, Mountain peaks. 9 l, Lake and hills.

1965, Mar.   Litho.   Perf. 12

801	A183	1.50 l	multi	1.40 .35
802	A183	2.50 l	multi	3.00 .70
803	A183	3 l	multi, vert.	3.00 .70
804	A183	4 l	multi, vert.	3.75 1.25
805	A183	5 l	multi	4.75 1.50
806	A183	9 l	multi	12.50 3.00
		Nos. 801-806 (6)		28.40 7.50

Frontier Guard — A184

1965, Apr. 25   Unwmk.

807	A184	2.50 l	lt blue & multi	1.25 .25
808	A184	12.50 l	lt ultra & multi	7.25 .90

20th anniversary of the Frontier Guards.

Small-bore Rifle Shooting, Prone — A185

Designs: 2 l, Rifle shooting, standing. 3 l, Target over map of Europe, showing Bucharest. 4 l, Pistol shooting. 15 l, Rifle shooting, kneeling.

1965, May 10

809	A185	1 l	lil, car rose, blk & brn	.35 .25
810	A185	2 l	bl, blk, brn & vio bl	.35 .25
811	A185	3 l	pink & car rose	.70 .25
812	A185	4 l	bis, blk & vio brn	1.40 .25
813	A185	15 l	brt grn, brn & vio brn	4.25 .50
		Nos. 809-813 (5)		7.05 1.50

European Shooting Championships, Bucharest.

ITU Emblem, Old and New Communications Equipment A186

1965, May 17   Perf. 12½x12

814	A186	2.50 l	brt grn, blk & lil rose	.75 .25
815	A186	12.50 l	vio, blk & brt bl	4.25 .30

Centenary of the ITU.

Col. Pavel Belyayev — A187

Designs: 2 l, Voskhod II. 6.50 l, Lt. Col. Alexei Leonov. 20 l, Leonov floating in space.

1965, June 15   Perf. 12

816	A187	1.50 l	lt blue & brn	.25 .25
817	A187	2 l	dk bl, lt vio & lt ultra	.25 .25
818	A187	6.50 l	lilac & brn	.35 .25
819	A187	20 l	chlky bl, yel & blk	3.25 .40
		Nos. 816-819 (4)		4.10 1.15

Miniature Sheet
Perf. 12 on 2 sides

820	A187	20 l	brt bl, org & blk	11.00 11.00

Space flight of Voskhod II and 1st man walking in space, Lt. Col. Alexei Leonov. No. 820 contains one stamp, size: 51x59½mm, perforated at top and bottom. Imperf., brt grn background, value $12.

Marx and Lenin — A188

1965, June 21   Perf. 12

821	A188	2.50 l	dk brn, red & yel	.75 .25
822	A188	7.50 l	sl grn, org ver & blk	3.00 .25

6th Conf. of Postal Ministers of Communist Countries, Peking, June 21-July 15.

Mother and Child — A189

2 l, Pioneers. 3 l, Boy and girl at play, horiz. 4 l, Child on beach. 15 l, Girl with book.

Perf. 12½x12, 12x12½

1965, June 29   Litho.   Unwmk.

823	A189	1 l	brt bl, rose lil & blk	.25 .25
824	A189	2 l	salmon, vio & blk	.25 .25
825	A189	3 l	green, org & vio	.35 .25
826	A189	4 l	multicolored	.85 .25
827	A189	15 l	lil rose, brn & ocher	3.25 .50
		Nos. 823-827 (5)		4.95 1.50

Issued for International Children's Day.

Statue of Magistrate — A190

Designs: 1 l, Amphora. 2 l, Illyrian armor. 3 l, Mosaic, horiz. 15 l, Torso, Apollo statue.

1965, July 20   Perf. 12

828	A190	1 l	lt ol, org & brn	.25 .25
829	A190	2 l	gray grn, grn & brn	.55 .25
830	A190	3 l	tan, brn, car & lil	.75 .25
831	A190	4 l	green, bis & brn	1.60 .25
832	A190	15 l	gray & pale claret	4.00 .65
		Nos. 828-832 (5)		7.15 1.65

Flowers — A191

1965, Aug. 11   Perf. 12½x12

833	A191	1 l	Fuchsia	.25 .25
834	A191	2 l	Cyclamen	.75 .25
835	A191	3 l	Tiger lily	1.30 .25
836	A191	3.50 l	Iris	1.60 .25
837	A191	4 l	Dahlia	1.75 .25
838	A191	4.50 l	Hydrangea	2.25 .25
839	A191	5 l	Rose	2.40 .30
840	A191	7 l	Tulips	3.25 .35
		Nos. 833-840 (8)		13.55 2.15

Nos. 698-700 Surcharged New Value and Two Bars

1965, Aug. 16   Perf. 14

841	A159	5q on 30 l		.60 .60
842	A159	15q on 30 l		.60 .60
843	A159	25q on 50 l		1.00 1.00
844	A159	80q on 50 l		2.00 2.00
845	A159	1.10 l on 20 l		3.00 3.00
846	A159	2 l on 20 l		5.00 5.00
		Nos. 841-846 (6)		12.20 12.20

White Stork — A192

Migratory Birds: 20q, Cuckoo. 30q, Hoopoe. 40q, European bee-eater. 50q, European nightjar. 1.50 l, Quail.

1965, Aug. 31   Perf. 12

847	A192	10q	yel, blk & gray	.40 .40
848	A192	20q	brt pink, blk & dk bl	.80 .40
849	A192	30q	violet, blk & bis	1.20 .60
850	A192	40q	emer, blk yel & org	1.60 .80
851	A192	50q	ultra, brn & red brn	2.00 .95
852	A192	1.50 l	bis, red brn & dp org	6.00 2.75
		Nos. 847-852 (6)		12.00 5.90

"Homecoming," by Bukurosh Sejdini — A193

1965, Sept. 26   Litho.   Perf. 12x12½

853	A193	25q	olive black	1.75 .40
854	A193	65q	blue black	5.25 1.60
855	A193	1.10 l	black	7.50 3.25
		Nos. 853-855 (3)		14.50 5.25

Second war veterans' meeting.

Hunting — A194

1965, Oct. 6   Litho.   Unwmk.

856	A194	10q	Capercaillie	.35 .25
857	A194	20q	Deer	.65 .25
858	A194	30q	Pheasant	.75 .25
859	A194	40q	Mallards	1.25 .25
860	A194	50q	Boar	1.40 .25
861	A194	1 l	Rabbit	3.25 .55
		Nos. 856-861 (6)		7.65 1.80

Oleander — A195

Flowers: 20q, Forget-me-nots. 30q, Pink. 40q, White water lily. 50q, Bird's-foot. 1 l, Corn poppy.

1965, Oct. 26   Perf. 12½x12

862	A195	10q	brt bl, grn & car rose	.25 .25
863	A195	20q	org red, bl, brn & grn	.35 .25
864	A195	30q	vio, car rose & grn	.45 .25
865	A195	40q	emerald, yel & blk	.65 .30
866	A195	50q	org brn, yel & grn	1.10 .40
867	A195	1 l	yel grn, blk & rose red	2.50 1.60
		Nos. 862-867 (6)		5.30 3.05

Hotel Turizmi, Fier — A196

Buildings: 10q, Hotel, Peshkopi. 15q, Sanatorium, Tirana. 25q, Rest home, Pogradec. 65q, Partisan Sports Arena, Tirana. 80q, Rest home, Mali Dajt. 1.10 l, Culture House, Tirana. 1.60 l, Hotel Adriatik, Durres. 2 l, Migjeni Theater, Shkoder. 3 l, Alexander Moissi House of Culture, Durres.

1965, Oct. 27   Perf. 12x12½

868	A196	5q	blue & blk	.25 .25
869	A196	10q	ocher & blk	.25 .25
870	A196	15q	dull grn & blk	.25 .25
871	A196	25q	violet & blk	.25 .25
872	A196	65q	lt brn & blk	.70 .50
873	A196	80q	yel grn & blk	1.40 .50
874	A196	1.10 l	lilac & blk	2.00 .50
875	A196	1.60 l	lt vio bl & blk	2.75 1.40
876	A196	2 l	dull rose & blk	3.50 1.40
877	A196	3 l	gray & blk	6.25 2.50
		Nos. 868-877 (10)		17.60 7.80

Freighter "Teuta" — A197

Ships: 20q, Raft. 30q, Sailing ship, 19th cent. 40q, Sailing ship, 18th cent. 50q, Freighter "Vlora." 1 l, Illyric galleys.

1965, Nov. 16

878	A197	10q	brt grn & dk grn	.30 .25
879	A197	20q	ol bis & dk grn	.30 .25
880	A197	30q	lt & dp ultra	.40 .25
881	A197	40q	vio & dp vio	.50 .25
882	A197	50q	pink & dk red	1.50 .25
883	A197	1 l	bister & brn	3.50 .45
		Nos. 878-883 (6)		6.50 1.70

Brown Bear — A198

Various Albanian bears. 50q, 55q, 60q, horiz.

1965, Dec. 7   Perf. 11½x12

884	A198	10q	bister & dk brn	.45 .25
885	A198	20q	pale brn & dk brn	.55 .25
886	A198	30q	bis, dk brn & car	1.10 .25
887	A198	35q	pale brn & dk brn	1.30 .25
888	A198	40q	bister & dk brn	1.60 .25
889	A198	50q	bister & brn	2.75 .25
890	A198	55q	bister & dk brn	3.25 .30

891 A198 60q pale brn, dk brn
& car 6.00 .50
Nos. 884-891 (8) 17.00 2.30

Basketball and
Players — A199

10q, Games' emblem (map of Albania and basket). 30q, 50q, Players with ball (diff. designs). 1.40 l, Basketball medal on ribbon.

1965, Dec. 15 Litho. *Perf. 12½x12*
892 A199 10q blue, yel & car .25 .25
893 A199 20q rose lil, lt brn &
blk .25 .25
894 A199 30q bis, lt brn, red &
blk .30 .25
895 A199 50q lt grn, lt brn &
blk 1.20 .25
896 A199 1.40 l rose, blk, brn &
yel 2.40 .50
Nos. 892-896 (5) 4.40 1.50

7th Balkan Basketball Championships, Tirana, Dec. 15-19.

Arms of Republic
and Smokestacks
A200

Arms and: 10q, Book. 30q, Wheat. 60q, Book, hammer & sickle. 80q, Factories.

1966, Jan. 11 Litho. *Perf. 11½x12*
Coat of Arms in Gold
897 A200 10q crimson & brn .25 .25
898 A200 20q blue & vio bl .25 .25
899 A200 30q org yel & brn .50 .25
900 A200 60q yel grn & brt grn 1.20 .25
901 A200 80q crimson & brn 1.40 .25
Nos. 897-901 (5) 3.60 1.25

Albanian People's Republic, 20th anniv.

Cow
A201

1966, Feb. 25 *Perf. 12½x12, 12x12½*
902 A201 10q shown .25 .25
903 A201 20q Pig .40 .25
904 A201 30q Ewe & lamb .75 .30
905 A201 35q Ram 1.20 .30
906 A201 40q Dog 1.50 .30
907 A201 50q Cat, vert. 1.75 .30
908 A201 55q Horse, vert. 2.00 .40
909 A201 60q Ass, vert. 4.00 .60
Nos. 902-909 (8) 11.85 2.70

Soccer Player and
Map of
Uruguay — A202

5q, Globe in form of soccer ball. 15q, Player, map of Italy. 20q, Goalkeeper, map of France. 25q, Player, map of Brazil. 30q, Player, map of Switzerland. 35q, Player, map of Sweden. 40q, Player, map of Chile. 50q, Player, map of Great Britain. 70q, World Championship cup & ball.

1966, Mar. 20 Litho. *Perf. 12*
910 A202 5q gray & dp org .25 .25
911 A202 10q lt brn, bl & vio .25 .25
912 A202 15q cit, dk bl & brt bl .25 .25
913 A202 20q org, vio bl & brt bl .25 .25
914 A202 25q salmon & sepia .25 .25
915 A202 30q lt yel grn & brn .35 .25
916 A202 35q lt ultra & emer .50 .25
917 A202 40q pink & brown .55 .25
918 A202 50q pale grn, mag &
rose red .75 .25
919 A202 70q gray, brn, yel & blk 1.00 .30
Nos. 910-919 (10) 4.40 2.55

World Cup Soccer Championship, Wembley, England, July 11-30.

Andon Zako
Cajupi — A203

1966, Mar. 27 Unwmk.
920 A203 40q bluish blk .65 .25
921 A203 1.10 l dark green 2.00 .40

Andon Zako Cajupi, poet, birth centenary.

Painted
Lady — A204

Designs: 20q, Blue dragonfly. 30q, Cloudless sulphur butterfly. 35q, 40q, Splendid dragonfly. 50q, Machaon swallow-tail. 55q, Sulphur butterfly. 60q, Whitemarbled butterfly.

1966, Apr. 21 Litho. *Perf. 11½x12*
922 A204 10q multicolored .45 .25
923 A204 20q yellow & multi .55 .25
924 A204 30q yellow & multi .75 .25
925 A204 35q sky blue & multi 1.10 .25
926 A204 40q multicolored 1.60 .25
927 A204 50q rose & multi 2.25 .25
928 A204 55q multicolored 2.75 .25
929 A204 60q multicolored 7.00 .35
Nos. 922-929 (8) 16.45 2.10

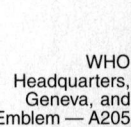

WHO
Headquarters,
Geneva, and
Emblem — A205

Designs (WHO Emblem and): 35q, Ambulance and stretcher bearers, vert. 60q, Albanian mother and nurse weighing infant, vert. 80q, X-ray machine and hospital.

Perf. 12x12½, 12½x12½
1966, May 3 Litho.
930 A205 25q lt blue & blk .40 .25
931 A205 35q salmon & ultra .75 .25
932 A205 60q lt grn, bl & red 1.20 .25
933 A205 80q yel, bl, grn & lt brn 1.50 .25
Nos. 930-933 (4) 3.85 1.00

Inauguration of the WHO Headquarters, Geneva.

Bird's Foot
Starfish
A206

Designs: 25q, Starfish. 35q, Brittle star. 45q, But-thorn starfish. 50q, Starfish. 60q, Sea cucumber. 70q, Sea urchin.

1966, May 10 *Perf. 12x12½*
934 A206 15q multicolored .25 .25
935 A206 25q multicolored .45 .30
936 A206 35q multicolored .75 .40
937 A206 45q multicolored 1.00 .45
938 A206 50q multicolored 1.10 .55
939 A206 60q multicolored 1.60 .90
940 A206 70q multicolored 2.00 1.90
Nos. 934-940 (7) 7.15 4.60

Luna
10 — A207

30q, 80q, Trajectory of Luna 10, earth & moon.

1966, June 10 *Perf. 12x12½*
941 A207 20q blue, yel & blk .35 .25
942 A207 30q yel grn, blk & bl .70 .25
943 A207 70q vio, yel & blk 1.40 .25
944 A207 80q yel, vio, grn & blk 2.50 .50
Nos. 941-944 (4) 4.95 1.25

Launching of the 1st artificial moon satellite, Luna 10, Apr. 3, 1966.

Jules
Rimet
Cup and
Soccer
A208

Designs: Various scenes of soccer play.

1966, July 12 Litho. *Perf. 12x12½*
Black Inscriptions
945 A208 10q ocher & lilac .30 .25
946 A208 20q lt blue & cit .35 .25
947 A208 30q brick red & Prus
bl .50 .25
948 A208 35q lt ultra & rose .70 .25
949 A208 40q yel grn & lt red
brn .70 .25
950 A208 50q lt red brn & yel
grn .85 .25
951 A208 55q rose lil & yel grn .85 .25
952 A208 60q dp rose & ocher 1.75 .25
Nos. 945-952 (8) 6.00 2.00

World Cup Soccer Championship, Wembley, England, July 11-30.

Water Level Map of
Albania — A209

30q, Water measure & fields. 70q, Turbine & pylon. 80q, Hydrological decade emblem.

1966, July *Perf. 12½x12½*
953 A209 20q brick red, blk & org .50 .25
954 A209 30q emer, blk & lt brn .50 .25
955 A209 70q brt violet & blk 1.50 .25
956 A209 80q brt bl, org, yel &
blk 2.50 .45
Nos. 953-956 (4) 5.00 1.20

Hydrological Decade (UNESCO), 1965-74.

Greek Turtle — A210

Designs: 15q, Grass snake. 25q, European pond turtle. 30q, Wall lizard. 35q, Wall gecko. 45q, Emerald lizard. 50q, Slowworm. 90q, Horned viper (or sand viper).

1966, Aug. 10 Litho. *Perf. 12½x12*
957 A210 10q gray & multi .25 .25
958 A210 15q yellow & multi .30 .25
959 A210 25q ultra & multi .35 .25
960 A210 30q multicolored .45 .25
961 A210 35q multicolored .70 .25
962 A210 45q multicolored .85 .25
963 A210 50q orange & multi 1.00 .30
964 A210 90q lilac & multi 1.75 .55
Nos. 957-964 (8) 5.65 2.35

Persian
Cat
A211

Cats: 10q, Siamese, vert. 15q, European tabby, vert. 25q, Black kitten. 60q, 65q, 80q, Various Persians.

Perf. 12x12½, 12½x12½
1966, Sept. 20 Litho.
965 A211 10q multicolored .35 .25
966 A211 15q blk, sepia & car .35 .25
967 A211 25q blk, dk & lt brn .70 .25
968 A211 45q blk, org & yel 1.00 .25
969 A211 60q blk, brn & yel 1.75 .30
970 A211 65q multicolored 1.75 .40
971 A211 80q blk, gray & yel 2.50 .50
Nos. 965-971 (7) 8.40 2.20

Pjeter Budi,
Writer — A212

1966, Oct. 5 *Perf. 12x12½*
972 A212 25q buff & slate grn .50 .25
973 A212 1.75 l gray & dull claret 1.50 .45

UNESCO
Emblem
A213

Designs (UNESCO Emblem and): 15q, Open book, rose and school. 25q, Male folk dancers. 1.55 l, Jug, column and old building.

1966, Oct. 20 Litho. *Perf. 12*
974 A213 5q lt gray & multi .25 .25
975 A213 15q dp blue & multi .30 .25
976 A213 25q gray & multi .30 .25
977 A213 1.55 l multi 2.25 .50
Nos. 974-977 (4) 3.05 1.25

20th anniv. of UNESCO.

A214

Designs: 15q, Hand holding book with pictures of Marx, Engels, Lenin and Stalin. 25q, Map of Albania, hammer and sickle, symbols of agriculture and industry. 65q, Symbolic grain and factories. 95q, Fists holding rifle, spade, axe, sickle and book.

1966, Nov. 1   Litho.   Perf. 11½x12
978	A214	15q vermilion & gold	.25	.25
979	A214	25q multicolored	.25	.25
980	A214	65q brn, brn org & gold	1.20	.30
981	A214	95q yellow & multi	1.50	.40
		Nos. 978-981 (4)	3.20	1.15

Albanian Communist Party, 5th Cong.

A215

Designs: 15q, Hammer and sickle, Party emblem in sunburst. 25q, Partisan and sunburst. 65q, Steel worker and blast furnace. 95q, Combine harvester, factories, and pylon.

1966, Nov. 8
982	A215	15q orange & multi	.40	.25
983	A215	25q red & multi	.40	.25
984	A215	65q multicolored	1.20	.25
985	A215	95q blue & multi	1.20	.40
		Nos. 982-985 (4)	3.20	1.15

25th anniv. of the founding of the Albanian Workers Party.

Russian Wolfhound — A216

Dogs: 15q, Sheep dog. 25q, English setter. 45q, English springer spaniel. 60q, Bulldog. 65q, Saint Bernard. 80q, Dachshund.

1966, Oct. 30   Litho.   Perf. 12½x12
986	A216	10q green & multi	.40	.25
987	A216	15q multicolored	.65	.25
988	A216	25q lilac & multi	.80	.25
989	A216	45q rose & multi	1.20	.35
990	A216	60q brown & multi	1.60	.40
991	A216	65q ultra & multi	1.75	.45
992	A216	80q blue grn & multi	3.25	.50
		Nos. 986-992 (7)	9.65	2.45

Ndre Mjeda — A217

1966   Perf. 12½x12
993	A217	25q brt bl & dk brn	.35	.25
994	A217	1.75 l brt grn & dk brn	2.40	.65

Birth Centenary of the priest Ndre Mjeda.

Proclamation A218

Designs: 10q, Banner, man and woman holding gun and axe, horiz. 1.85 l, man with axe and banner and partisan with gun.

1966, Dec. 25   Perf. 11½x12, 12x11½
995	A218	5q lt brn, red & blk	.25	.25
996	A218	10q red, blk, gray & bl	.40	.25

997	A218	1.85 l red, blk & salmon	2.40	.30
		Nos. 995-997 (3)	3.05	.80

Albanian Communist Party, 25th anniv.

Golden Eagle — A219

Birds of Prey: 15q, European sea eagle. 25q, Griffon vulture. 40q, Common sparrowhawk. 50q, Osprey. 70q, Egyptian vulture. 90q, Kestrel.

1966, Dec. 20   Litho.   Perf. 11½x12
998	A219	10q gray & multi	.35	.25
999	A219	15q multicolored	.35	.25
1000	A219	25q citron & multi	.70	.25
1001	A219	40q multicolored	1.00	.25
1002	A219	50q multicolored	1.40	.30
1003	A219	70q yellow & multi	2.00	.40
1004	A219	90q multicolored	3.00	.50
		Nos. 998-1004 (7)	8.80	2.20

Hake A220

Fish: 15q, Red mullet. 25q, Opah. 40q, Atlantic wolf fish. 65q, Lumpfish. 80q, Swordfish. 1.15 l, Shorthorn sculpin.

1967, Jan. 20   Photo.   Perf. 12x11½
Fish in Natural Colors
1005	A220	10q blue	.35	.25
1006	A220	15q lt yellow grn	.35	.25
1007	A220	25q Prus blue	.65	.25
1008	A220	40q emerald	.65	.25
1009	A220	65q brt blue grn	1.00	.30
1010	A220	80q blue	1.60	.40
1011	A220	1.15 l brt green	2.50	.65
		Nos. 1005-1011 (7)	7.10	2.35

White Pelican A221

Designs: Various groups of pelicans.

1967, Feb. 22   Litho.   Perf. 12
1012	A221	10q pink & multi	.25	.25
1013	A221	15q pink & multi	.25	.25
1014	A221	25q pink & multi	1.00	.25
1015	A221	50q pink & multi	2.00	.25
1016	A221	2 l pink & multi	5.00	.75
		Nos. 1012-1016 (5)	8.50	1.75

Camellia A222

Flowers: 10q, Chrysanthemum. 15q, Hollyhock. 25q, Flowering Maple. 35q, Peony. 65q, Gladiolus. 80q, Freesia. 1.15 l, Carnation.

Unwmk.
1967, Apr. 12   Litho.   Perf. 12
Flowers in Natural Colors
1017	A222	5q pale brown	.25	.25
1018	A222	10q lt lilac	.25	.25
1019	A222	15q gray	.25	.25
1020	A222	25q ultra	.45	.25
1021	A222	35q lt blue	.70	.25
1022	A222	65q lt blue grn	1.40	.25
1023	A222	80q lt bluish gray	1.75	.30
1024	A222	1.15 l dull yellow	2.10	.45
		Nos. 1017-1024 (8)	7.15	2.25

Congress Emblem and Power Station — A223

1967, Apr. 24   Litho.   Perf. 12
1025	A223	25q multi	.75	.25
1026	A223	1.75 l multi	2.25	.55

Cong. of the Union of Professional Workers, Tirana, Apr. 24.

Rose — A224

Various Roses in Natural Colors.

1967, May 15   Perf. 12x12½
1027	A224	5q blue gray	.35	.25
1028	A224	10q brt blue	.35	.25
1029	A224	15q rose violet	.35	.25
1030	A224	25q lemon	.35	.25
1031	A224	35q brt grnsh blue	.70	.25
1032	A224	65q gray	1.00	.25
1033	A224	80q brown	1.00	.30
1034	A224	1.65 l gray green	2.75	.50
		Nos. 1027-1034 (8)	6.85	2.30

Seashore, Bregdet Borsh — A225

Views: 15q, Buthrotum, vert. 25q, Shore, Fshati Piqeras. 45q, Shore, Bregdet. 50q, Shore, Bregdet Himare. 65q, Ship, Sarande (Santi Quaranta). 80q, Shore, Dhermi. 1 l, Sunset, Bregdet, vert.

Perf. 12x12½, 12½x12
1967, June 10
1035	A225	15q multicolored	.40	.25
1036	A225	25q multicolored	.40	.25
1037	A225	25q multicolored	.80	.35
1038	A225	45q multicolored	.80	.35
1039	A225	50q multicolored	.80	.35
1040	A225	65q multicolored	1.50	.50
1041	A225	80q multicolored	1.50	.70
1042	A225	1 l multicolored	2.40	1.00
		Nos. 1035-1042 (8)	8.60	3.75

Fawn A226

Roe Deer: 20q, Stag, vert. 25q, Doe, vert. 30q, Young stag and doe. 35q, Doe and fawn. 40q, Young stag, vert. 65q, Stag and doe, vert. 70q, Running stag and does.

Perf. 12½x12, 12x12½
1967, July 20   Litho.
1043	A226	15q multicolored	.35	.25
1044	A226	20q multicolored	.35	.25
1045	A226	25q multicolored	.70	.25
1046	A226	30q multicolored	.70	.25
1047	A226	35q multicolored	1.00	.25
1048	A226	40q multicolored	1.00	.25
1049	A226	50q multicolored	2.10	.35
1050	A226	70q multicolored	2.75	.55
		Nos. 1043-1050 (8)	8.95	2.40

Man and Woman from Madhe A227

Regional Costumes: 20q, Woman from Zadrimes. 25q, Dancer and drummer, Kukesit. 45q, Woman spinner, Dardhes. 50q, Farm couple, Myseqese. 65q, Dancer with tambourine, Tirana. 80q, Man and woman, Dropullit. 1 l, Piper, Laberise.

1967, Aug. 25   Perf. 12
1051	A227	15q tan & multi	.40	.25
1052	A227	20q lt yellow grn	.40	.25
1053	A227	25q multicolored	.40	.25
1054	A227	45q sky blue & multi	.80	.25
1055	A227	50q lemon & multi	.80	.30
1056	A227	65q pink & multi	.80	.40
1057	A227	80q multicolored	1.60	.45
1058	A227	1 l gray & multi	1.60	.60
		Nos. 1051-1058 (8)	6.80	2.75

Fighters and Newspaper — A228

75q, Printing plant, newspapers, microphone. 2 l, People holding newspaper.

1967, Aug. 25   Perf. 12½x12
1059	A228	25q multicolored	.35	.25
1060	A228	75q pink & multi	1.00	.50
1061	A228	2 l multicolored	2.75	1.25
		Nos. 1059-1061 (3)	4.10	2.00

Issued for the Day of the Press.

Street Scene, by Kole Idromeno — A229

Hakmarrja Battalion, by Sali Shijaku — A230

Designs: 20q, David, fresco by Onufri, 16th century, vert. 45q, Woman's head, ancient mosaic, vert. 50q, Men on horseback from 16th century icon, vert. 65q, Farm Women, by Zef Shoshi. 80q, Street Scene, by Vangjush Mio. 1 l, Bride, by Kolé Idromeno, vert.

Perf. 12, 12x12½, (A230)
1967, Oct. 25   Litho.
1062	A229	15q multicolored	.45	.25
1063	A229	20q multicolored	.45	.25
1064	A230	25q multicolored	1.00	.25
1065	A229	45q multicolored	1.00	.25
1066	A229	50q multicolored	1.00	.25
1067	A230	65q multicolored	1.75	.25
1068	A230	80q multicolored	1.75	.30
1069	A230	1 l multicolored	4.00	.35
		Nos. 1062-1069 (8)	11.40	2.15

Lenin at Storming of Winter Palace — A231

Designs: 15q, Lenin and Stalin, horiz. 50q, Lenin and Stalin addressing meeting. 1.10 l, Storming of the Winter Palace, horiz.

1967, Nov. 7   **Perf. 12**
1070	A231	15q red & multi	.30	.25
1071	A231	25q slate grn & blk	.70	.25
1072	A231	50q brn, blk & brn		
		vio	1.00	.25
1073	A231	1.10 l lilac, gray & blk	2.00	.30
		Nos. 1070-1073 (4)	4.00	1.05

50th anniv. of the Russian October Revolution.

Rabbit — A232

Designs: Various hares and rabbits. The 15q, 25q, 35q, 40q and 1 l are horizontal.

1967, Sept. 30
1074	A232	15q orange & multi	.25	.25
1075	A232	20q brt yel & multi	.35	.25
1076	A232	25q lt brn & multi	.35	.25
1077	A232	35q multicolored	.75	.25
1078	A232	40q yellow & multi	.75	.25
1079	A232	50q pink & multi	2.25	.35
1080	A232	65q multicolored	2.25	.35
1081	A232	1 l lilac & multi	3.00	.55
		Nos. 1074-1081 (8)	9.95	2.40

University, Torch and Book — A233

1967, Sept. 15   **Litho.**   **Perf. 12**
1082	A233	25q multi	.50	.25
1083	A233	1.75 l multi	3.00	.35

10th anniv. of the founding of the State University, Tirana.

Coat of Arms and Soldiers A234

65q, Arms, Factory, grain, flag, gun, radio tower. 1.20 l, Arms, hand holding torch.

1967, Sept. 16   **Perf. 12x11½**
1084	A234	15q multi	.30	.25
1085	A234	65q multi	1.00	.25
1086	A234	1.20 l multi	2.25	.25
		Nos. 1084-1086 (3)	3.55	.75

25th anniversary of the Democratic Front.

Turkey A235

Designs: 20q, Duck. 25q, Hen. 45q, Rooster. 50q, Guinea fowl. 65q, Goose, horiz. 80q, Mallard, horiz. 1 l, Chicks, horiz.

Perf. 12x12½, 12½x12
1967, Nov. 25   **Photo.**
1087	A235	15q gold & multi	.25	.25
1088	A235	20q gold & multi	.25	.25
1089	A235	25q gold & multi	.35	.25
1090	A235	45q gold & multi	1.00	.25
1091	A235	50q gold & multi	1.00	.25
1092	A235	65q gold & multi	1.00	.25
1093	A235	80q gold & multi	2.00	.35
1094	A235	1 l gold & multi	3.25	.45
		Nos. 1087-1094 (8)	9.10	2.30

Skanderbeg A236

Designs: 10q, Arms of Skanderbeg. 25q, Helmet and sword. 30q, Kruje Castle. 35q, Petreles Castle. 65q, Berati Castle. 80q, Skanderbeg addressing national chiefs. 90q, Battle of Albulenes.

1967, Dec. 10   **Litho.**   **Perf. 12x12½**
Medallion in Bister and Dark Brown
1095	A236	10q gold & violet	.25	.25
1096	A236	15q gold & rose car	.25	.25
1097	A236	25q gold & vio bl	.30	.25
1098	A236	30q gold & dk blue	.40	.25
1099	A236	35q gold & maroon	.50	.25
1100	A236	65q gold & green	.80	.25
1101	A236	80q gold & gray brn	1.60	.30
1102	A236	90q gold & ultra	1.60	.35
		Nos. 1095-1102 (8)	5.70	2.15

500th anniv. of the death of Skanderbeg (George Castriota), national hero.

10th Winter Olympic Games, Grenoble, France, Feb. 6-18 — A237

Designs: 15q, 2 l, Winter Olympics emblem. 25q, Ice hockey. 30q, Women's figure skating. 50q, Slalom. 80q, Downhill skiing. 1 l, Ski jump.

1967-68
1103	A237	15q multicolored	.25	.25
1104	A237	25q multicolored	.25	.25
1105	A237	30q multicolored	.25	.25
1106	A237	50q multicolored	.30	.25
1107	A237	80q multicolored	.75	.25
1108	A237	1 l multicolored	1.60	.25
		Nos. 1103-1108 (6)	3.40	1.50

Miniature Sheet
Imperf
1109	A237	2 l red, gray & brt bl		
		('68)	4.50	4.50

Nos. 1103-1108 issued Dec. 29, 1967.

Skanderbeg Monument, Kruje — A238

Designs: 10q, Skanderbeg monument, Tirana. 15q, Skanderbeg portrait, Uffizi Galleries, Florence. 25q, engraved portrait of Gen. Tanush Topia. 35q, Portrait of Gen. Gjergj Arianti, horiz. 65q, Portrait bust of Skanderbeg by O. Paskali. 80q, Title page of "The Life of Skanderbeg." 90q, Skanderbeg battling the Turks, painting by S. Rrota, horiz.

Perf. 12x12½, 12½x12
1968, Jan. 17   **Litho.**
1110	A238	10q multicolored	.35	.25
1111	A238	15q multicolored	.35	.25
1112	A238	25q blk, yel & lt bl	.75	.25
1113	A238	30q multicolored	.75	.25
1114	A238	35q lt vio, pink & blk	.75	.25
1115	A238	65q multicolored	1.50	.30
1116	A238	80q pink, blk & yel	2.25	.50
1117	A238	90q beige & multi	2.25	.65
		Nos. 1110-1117 (8)	8.95	2.70

500th anniv. of the death of Skanderbeg (George Castriota), national hero.

Carnation A239

1968, Feb. 15   **Perf. 12**
Various Carnations in Natural Colors
1118	A239	15q green	.25	.25
1119	A239	20q dk brown	.25	.25
1120	A239	25q brt blue	.25	.25
1121	A239	50q gray olice	.70	.25
1122	A239	80q bluish gray	.90	.25
1123	A239	1.10 l violet gray	1.50	.40
		Nos. 1118-1123 (6)	3.85	1.65

"Electrification" A240

65q, Farm tractor, horiz. 1.10 l, Cow & herd.

1968, Mar. 5   **Litho.**   **Perf. 12**
1124	A240	25q multi	.55	.25
1125	A240	65q multi	1.60	.30
1126	A240	1.10 l multi	2.25	.40
		Nos. 1124-1126 (3)	4.40	.95

Fifth Farm Cooperatives Congress.

Goat A241

Various goats. 15q, 20q, 25q are vertical.

1968, Mar. 25   **Perf. 12x12½, 12½x12**
1127	A241	15q multi	.25	.25
1128	A241	20q multi	.25	.25
1129	A241	25q multi	.35	.25
1130	A241	30q multi	.35	.25

1131	A241	40q multi	.50	.25
1132	A241	50q multi	.50	.25
1133	A241	80q multi	1.50	.25
1134	A241	1.40 l multi	2.25	.40
		Nos. 1127-1134 (8)	5.95	2.15

Zef N. Jubani — A242

1968, Mar. 30   **Perf. 12**
1135	A242	25q yellow & choc	.35	.25
1136	A242	1.75 l lt violet & blk	1.90	.50

Sesquicentennial of the birth of Zef N. Jubani, writer and scholar.

Physician and Hospital — A243

Designs (World Health Organization Emblem and): 65q, Hospital and microscope, horiz. 1.10 l, Mother feeding child.

Perf. 12½x12, 12x12½
1968, Apr. 7   **Litho.**
1137	A243	25q green & claret	.25	.25
1138	A243	65q black, yel & bl	.90	.30
1139	A243	1.10 l black & dp org	1.10	.40
		Nos. 1137-1139 (3)	2.25	.95

20th anniv. of WHO.

Scientist A244

Women: 15q, Militia member. 60q, Farm worker. 1 l, Factory worker.

1968, Apr. 14   **Perf. 12**
1140	A244	15q ver & dk red	.35	.25
1141	A244	25q blue grn & grn	.35	.25
1142	A244	60q dull yel & brn	1.10	.25
1143	A244	1 l lt vio & vio	1.90	.40
		Nos. 1140-1143 (4)	3.70	1.15

Albanian Women's Organization, 25th anniv.

Karl Marx A245

Designs: 25q, Marx lecturing to students. 65q, "Das Kapital," "Communist Manifesto" and marching crowd. 95q, Full-face portrait.

1968, May 5   **Litho.**   **Perf. 12**
1144	A245	15q gray, dk bl & bis	.45	.25
1145	A245	25q brn vio, dk brn &		
		dl yel	.60	.25
1146	A245	65q gray, blk, brn &		
		car	1.25	.25
1147	A245	95q gray, ocher & blk	3.00	.50
		Nos. 1144-1147 (4)	5.30	1.25

Karl Marx, 150th birth anniversary.

Heliopsis
A246

Flowers: 20q, Red flax. 25q, Orchid. 30q, Gloxinia. 40q, Turk's-cap lily. 80q, Amaryllis. 1.40 l, Red magnolia.

1968, May 10   **Perf. 12x12½**
1148	A246	15q gold & multi	.25	.25
1149	A246	20q gold & multi	.25	.25
1150	A246	25q gold & multi	.30	.25
1151	A246	30q gold & multi	.35	.25
1152	A246	40q gold & multi	.35	.25
1153	A246	80q gold & multi	1.10	.40
1154	A246	1.40 l gold & multi	1.90	.60
	Nos. 1148-1154 (7)		4.50	2.25

Proclamation of Prizren — A247

25q, Abdyl Frasheri. 40q, House in Prizren.

1968, June 10   **Litho.**   **Perf. 12**
1155	A247	25q emerald & blk	.40	.25
1156	A247	40q multicolored	.75	.25
1157	A247	85q yellow & multi	1.10	.30
	Nos. 1155-1157 (3)		2.25	.80

League of Prizren against the Turks, 90th anniv.

Shepherd, by
A.
Kushi — A248

Paintings from Tirana Art Gallery: 20q, View of Tirana, by V. Mio, horiz. 25q, Mountaineer, by G. Madhi. 40q, Refugees, by A. Buza. 80q, Guerrillas of Shahin Matrakut, by S. Xega. 1.50 l, Portrait of an Old Man, by S. Papadhimitri. 1.70 l, View of Scutari, by S. Rrota. 2.50 l, Woman in Scutari Costume, by Z. Colombi.

1968, June 20   **Perf. 12x12½**
1158	A248	15q gold & multi	.25	.25
1159	A248	20q gold & multi	.25	.25
1160	A248	25q gold & multi	.25	.25
1161	A248	40q gold & multi	.25	.25
1162	A248	80q gold & multi	.55	.25
1163	A248	1.50 l gold & multi	1.40	.30
1164	A248	1.70 l gold & multi	2.25	.55
	Nos. 1158-1164 (7)		5.20	2.10

Miniature Sheet
Perf. 12½xImperf.
1165	A248	2.50 l multi	2.50	2.50

No. 1165 contains one stamp, size: 50x71mm.

Soldier and Guns — A249

25q, Sailor, warships. 65q, Aviator, planes, vert. 95q, Militiamen, woman.

1968, July 10   **Litho.**   **Perf. 12**
1166	A249	15q multicolored	.35	.25
1167	A249	25q multicolored	.35	.25
1168	A249	65q multicolored	1.50	.25
1169	A249	95q multicolored	2.25	.25
	Nos. 1166-1169 (4)		4.45	1.00

25th anniversary of the People's Army.

Squid
A250

Designs: 20q, Crayfish. 25q, Whelk. 50q, Crab. 70q, Spiny lobster. 80q, Shore crab. 90q, Norway lobster.

1968, Aug. 20
1170	A250	15q multicolored	.35	.25
1171	A250	20q multicolored	.35	.25
1172	A250	25q multicolored	.35	.25
1173	A250	50q multicolored	.35	.25
1174	A250	70q multicolored	.75	.30
1175	A250	80q multicolored	1.90	.35
1176	A250	90q multicolored	1.90	.40
	Nos. 1170-1176 (7)		5.95	2.05

Women's Relay Race — A251

Sport: 20q, Running. 25q, Women's discus. 30q, Equestrian. 40q, High jump. 50q, Women's hurdling. 80q, Soccer. 1.40 l, Woman diver. 2 l, Olympic stadium.

1968, Sept. 23   **Photo.**   **Perf. 12**
1177	A251	15q multicolored	.25	.25
1178	A251	20q multicolored	.25	.25
1179	A251	25q multicolored	.25	.25
1180	A251	30q multicolored	.25	.25
1181	A251	40q multicolored	.30	.25
1182	A251	50q multicolored	.30	.25
1183	A251	80q multicolored	.75	.25
1184	A251	1.40 l multicolored	1.50	.35
	Nos. 1177-1184 (8)		3.85	2.10

Souvenir Sheet
Perf. 12½ Horizontally
1185	A251	2 l multicolored	2.50	2.50

19th Olympic Games, Mexico City, Oct. 12-27. No. 1185 contains one rectangular stamp, size: 64x54mm. Value of imperfs., Nos. 1177-1184 $10.50, No. 1185 $7.50.

Enver
Hoxha — A252

1968, Oct. 16   **Litho.**   **Perf. 12**
1186	A252	25q blue gray	.40	.25
1187	A252	35q rose brown	.40	.25
1188	A252	80q violet	.80	.25
1189	A252	1.10 l brown	1.20	.50
	Nos. 1186-1189 (4)		2.80	1.35

Souvenir Sheet
Imperf
1190	A252	1.50 l rose red, bl vio & gold	75.00	75.00

60th birthday of Enver Hoxha, First Secretary of the Central Committee of the Communist Party of Albania.

Book and
Pupils
A253

1968, Nov. 14   **Photo.**
1191	A253	15q mar & slate grn	.35	.25
1192	A253	85q gray olive & sepia	2.25	.25

60th anniv. of the Congress of Monastir, Nov. 14-22, 1908, which adopted a unified Albanian alphabet.

Waxwing — A254

Birds: 20q, Rose-colored starling. 25q, Kingfishers. 50q, Long-tailed tits. 80q, Wallcreeper. 1.10 l, Bearded tit.

1968, Nov. 15   **Litho.**
Birds in Natural Colors
1193	A254	15q lt blue & blk	.25	.25
1194	A254	20q bister & blk	.25	.25
1195	A254	25q pink & blk	.40	.25
1196	A254	50q lt yel grn & blk	1.00	.25
1197	A254	80q bis brn & blk	2.00	.35
1198	A254	1.10 l pale grn & blk	3.00	.55
	Nos. 1193-1198 (6)		6.90	1.90

Mao Tse-tung — A255

1968, Dec. 26   **Litho.**   **Perf. 12½x12**
1199	A255	25q gold, red & blk	1.00	.40
1200	A255	1.75 l gold, red & blk	6.50	3.50

75th birthday of Mao Tse-tung.

Adem Reka
and
Crane — A256

Portraits: 10q, Pjeter Lleshi and power lines. 15q, Mohammed Shehu and Myrteza Kepi. 25q, Shkurte Vata and women railroad workers. 65q, Agron Elezi, frontier guard. 80q, Ismet Bruçaj and mountain road. 1.30 l, Fuat Cela, blind revolutionary.

1969, Feb. 10   **Litho.**   **Perf. 12x12½**
1201	A256	5q multicolored	.35	.25
1202	A256	10q multicolored	.35	.25
1203	A256	15q multicolored	.70	.25
1204	A256	25q multicolored	1.00	.25
1205	A256	65q multicolored	1.40	.25
1206	A256	80q multicolored	1.40	.25
1207	A256	1.30 l multicolored	2.10	.25
	Nos. 1201-1207 (7)		7.30	1.75

Contemporary heroine and heroes.

Meteorological Instruments — A257

Designs: 25q, Water gauge. 1.60 l, Radar, balloon and isobars.

1969, Feb. 25   **Perf. 12**
1208	A257	15q multicolored	.40	.25
1209	A257	25q ultra, org & blk	.40	.25
1210	A257	1.60 l rose vio, yel & blk	2.60	.60
	Nos. 1208-1210 (3)		3.40	1.10

20th anniv. of Albanian hydrometeorology.

Partisans, 1944, by F. Haxmiu — A258

Paintings: 5q, Student Revolutionists, by P. Mele, vert. 65q, Steel Mill, by C. Ceka. 80q, Reconstruction, by V. Kilica. 1.10 l, Harvest, by N. Jonuzi. 1.15 l, Terraced Landscape, by S. Kaceli. 2 l, Partisans' Meeting.

Perf. 12x12½, 12½x12
1969, Apr. 25   **Litho.**
Size: 31½x41½mm
1211	A258	5q buff & multi	.25	.25

Size: 51½x30½mm
1212	A258	25q buff & multi	.25	.25

Size: 40½x32mm
1213	A258	65q buff & multi	.30	.25

Size: 51½x30½mm
1214	A258	80q buff & multi	.35	.25
1215	A258	1.10 l buff & multi	.75	.25
1216	A258	1.15 l buff & multi	.75	.25
	Nos. 1211-1216 (6)		2.65	1.50

Miniature Sheet
Imperf
Size: 111x90mm
1217	A258	2 l ocher & multi	1.50	1.50

Leonardo da
Vinci, Self-
portrait
A259

Designs (after Leonardo da Vinci): 35q, Lilies. 40q, Design for a flying machine, horiz. 1 l, Portrait of Beatrice. No. 1222, Portrait of a Noblewoman. No. 1223, Mona Lisa.

Perf. 12x12½, 12½x12
1969, May 2   **Litho.**
1218	A259	25q gold & sepia	.25	.25
1219	A259	35q gold & sepia	.35	.25
1220	A259	40q gold & sepia	.50	.25
1221	A259	1 l gold & multi	1.40	.25
1222	A259	2 l gold & sepia	2.75	.55
	Nos. 1218-1222 (5)		5.25	1.55

Miniature Sheet
Imperf
1223	A259	2 l gold & multi	3.50	2.50

Leonardo da Vinci (1452-1519), painter, sculptor, architect and engineer.

First Congress Meeting Place A260

Designs: 1 l, Albanian coat of arms. 2.25 l, Two partisans with guns and flag.

1969, May 24   **Perf. 12**

| 1224 | A260 | 25q lt grn, blk & red | .35 | .25 |
| 1225 | A260 | 2.25 l multi | 2.75 | 1.00 |

Souvenir Sheet

| 1226 | A260 | 1 l gold, bl, blk & red | 35.00 | 35.00 |

25th anniversary of the First Anti-Fascist Congress of Permet, May 24, 1944.

Albanian Violet — A261

Designs: Violets and Pansies.

1969, June 30   **Litho.**   **Perf. 12x12½**

1227	A261	5q gold & multi	.25	.25
1228	A261	10q gold & multi	.25	.25
1229	A261	15q gold & multi	.30	.25
1230	A261	20q gold & multi	.35	.25
1231	A261	25q gold & multi	.35	.25
1232	A261	80q gold & multi	1.10	.35
1233	A261	1.95 l gold & multi	1.90	.65
		Nos. 1227-1233 (7)	4.50	2.25

Plum, Fruit and Blossoms A262

Designs: Blossoms and Fruits.

1969, Aug. 10   **Litho.**   **Perf. 12**

1234	A262	10q shown	.25	.25
1235	A262	15q Lemon	.25	.25
1236	A262	25q Pomegranate	.30	.25
1237	A262	50q Cherry	.75	.25
1238	A262	80q Peach	1.10	.25
1239	A262	1.20 l Apple	1.90	.40
		Nos. 1234-1239 (6)	4.55	1.65

Basketball A263

Designs: 10q, 80q, 2.20 l, Various views of basketball game. 25q, Hand aiming ball at basket and map of Europe, horiz.

1969, Sept. 15   **Litho.**   **Perf. 12**

1240	A263	10q multi	.35	.25
1241	A263	15q buff & multi	.35	.25
1242	A263	25q blue & multi	.35	.25
1243	A263	80q multi	1.10	.25
1244	A263	2.20 l multi	2.00	.50
		Nos. 1240-1244 (5)	4.15	1.50

16th European Basketball Championships, Naples, Italy, Sept. 27-Oct. 5.

Runner A264

Designs: 5q, Games' emblem. 10q, Woman gymnast. 20q, Pistol shooting. 25q, Swimmer at start. 80q, Bicyclist. 95q, Soccer.

1969, Sept. 30

1245	A264	5q multicolored	.25	.25
1246	A264	10q multicolored	.25	.25
1247	A264	15q multicolored	.30	.25
1248	A264	20q multicolored	.35	.25
1249	A264	25q multicolored	.35	.25
1250	A264	80q multicolored	1.00	.25
1251	A264	95q multicolored	1.40	.25
		Nos. 1245-1251 (7)	3.90	1.75

Second National Spartakiad.

Electronic Technicians, Steel Ladle — A265

25q, Mao Tse-tung with microphones. 1.40 l, Children holding Mao's red book.

1969, Oct. 1   **Litho.**   **Perf. 12**

1252	A265	25q multi, vert.	2.50	.60
1253	A265	85q multi	7.50	2.25
1254	A265	1.40 l multi, vert.	12.00	4.00
		Nos. 1252-1254 (3)	22.00	6.85

People's Republic of China, 20th anniv.

Enver Hoxha A266

Designs: 80q, Pages from Berat resolution. 1.45 l, Partisans with flag.

1969, Oct. 20   **Litho.**   **Perf. 12**

1255	A266	25q multicolored	.25	.25
1256	A266	80q gray & multi	.55	.25
1257	A266	1.45 l ocher & multi	1.60	.45
		Nos. 1255-1257 (3)	2.40	.95

25th anniv. of the 2nd reunion of the Natl. Antifascist Liberation Council, Berat.

Soldiers — A267

Designs: 30q, Oil refinery. 35q, Combine harvester. 45q, Hydroelectric station and dam. 55q, Militia woman, man and soldier. 1.10 l, Dancers and musicians.

1969, Nov. 29

1258	A267	25q multi	.30	.25
1259	A267	30q multi	.35	.25
1260	A267	35q multi	.50	.25
1261	A267	45q multi	.85	.25
1262	A267	55q multi	1.20	.30
1263	A267	1.10 l multi	2.00	.45
		Nos. 1258-1263 (6)	5.20	1.75

25th anniv. of the socialist republic.

Joseph V. Stalin, (1879-1953), Russian Political Leader — A268

1969, Dec. 21   **Litho.**   **Perf. 12**

1264	A268	15q lilac	.25	.25
1265	A268	25q slate blue	.40	.25
1266	A268	1 l brown	1.40	.25
1267	A268	1.10 l violet blue	1.60	.25
		Nos. 1264-1267 (4)	3.65	1.00

Head of Woman A269

Greco-Roman Mosaics: 25q, Geometrical floor design, horiz. 80q, Bird and tree, horiz. 1.10 l, Floor with birds and grapes, horiz. 1.20 l, Fragment with corn within oval design.

1969, Dec. 25   **Perf. 12½x12**

1268	A269	15q gold & multi	.25	.25
1269	A269	25q gold & multi	.25	.25
1270	A269	80q gold & multi	.75	.25
1271	A269	1.10 l gold & multi	1.00	.25
1272	A269	1.20 l gold & multi	1.50	.35
		Nos. 1268-1272 (5)	3.75	1.35

Cancellation of 1920 — A270

25q, Proclamation and congress site.

1970, Jan. 21   **Litho.**   **Perf. 12**

| 1273 | A270 | 25q red, gray & blk | .35 | .25 |
| 1274 | A270 | 1.25 l dk grn, yel & blk | 2.25 | .25 |

Congress of Louchnia, 50th anniversary.

Worker, Student and Flag A271

1970, Feb. 11   **Perf. 12½x12**

| 1275 | A271 | 25q red & multi | .35 | .25 |
| 1276 | A271 | 1.75 l red & multi | 2.25 | .50 |

Vocational organizations in Albania, 25th anniv.

Turk's-cap Lily — A272

Lilies: 5q, Cernum, vert. 15q, Madonna, vert. 25q, Royal, vert. 1.10 l, Tiger. 1.15 l, Albanian.

Perf. 11½x12, 12x11½

1970, Mar. 10   **Litho.**

1277	A272	5q multi	.25	.25
1278	A272	15q multi	.25	.25
1279	A272	25q multi	.75	.25
1280	A272	80q multi	1.50	.25
1281	A272	1.10 l multi	2.25	.25
1282	A272	1.15 l multi	2.60	.30
		Nos. 1277-1282 (6)	7.60	1.55

Lenin A273

Designs (Lenin): 5q, Portrait, vert. 25q, As volunteer construction worker. 95q, Addressing crowd. 1.10 l, Saluting, vert.

1970, Apr. 22   **Litho.**   **Perf. 12**

1283	A273	5q multi	.25	.25
1284	A273	15q multi	.25	.25
1285	A273	25q multi	.35	.25
1286	A273	95q multi	.90	.25
1287	A273	1.10 l multi	1.60	.25
		Nos. 1283-1287 (5)	3.35	1.25

Centenary of birth of Lenin (1870-1924).

Frontier Guard A274

1970, Apr. 25

| 1288 | A274 | 25q multi | .35 | .25 |
| 1289 | A274 | 1.25 l multi | 1.75 | .50 |

25th anniversary of Frontier Guards.

Soccer Players — A275

Designs: 5q, Jules Rimet Cup and globes. 10q, Aztec Stadium, Mexico City. 25q, Defending goal. 65q, 80q, No. 1296, Two soccer players in various plays. No. 1297, Mexican horseman and volcano Popocatepetl.

1970, May 15   **Litho.**   **Perf. 12½x12**

1290	A275	5q multicolored	.25	.25
1291	A275	10q multicolored	.25	.25
1292	A275	15q multicolored	.25	.25
1293	A275	25q lt green & multi	.25	.25
1294	A275	65q pink & multi	.55	.25
1295	A275	80q lt blue & multi	.75	.40
1296	A275	2 l yellow & multi	1.50	.45
		Nos. 1290-1296 (7)	3.80	2.10

Souvenir Sheet

Perf 12 x Imperf

| 1297 | A275 | 2 l multicolored | 2.75 | 2.75 |

World Soccer Championships for the Jules Rimet Cup, Mexico City, May 31-June 21, 1970. No. 1297 contains one large horizontal stamp. Nos. 1290-1297 exist imperf. Value: Nos. 1290-1296, mint or used, $12; No. 1297, mint $10, used $5.

UPU Headquarters and Monument, Bern — A276

1970, May 30   Litho.   Perf. 12½x12
1298	A276	25q ultra, gray & blk	.25	.25
1299	A276	1.10 l	org, buff & blk	1.00	.25
1300	A276	1.15 l	grn, gray & blk	1.25	.30
		Nos. 1298-1300 (3)	2.50	.80

Inauguration of the new UPU Headquarters in Bern.

Bird and Grapes Mosaic A277

Mosaics, 5th-6th centuries, excavated near Pogradec: 10q, Waterfowl and grapes. 20q, Bird and tree stump. 25q, Bird and leaves. 65q, Fish. 2.25 l, Peacock, vert.

1970, July 10   Perf. 12½x12, 12x12½
1301	A277	5q multi	.25	.25
1302	A277	10q multi	.25	.25
1303	A277	20q multi	.30	.25
1304	A277	25q multi	.35	.25
1305	A277	65q multi	.75	.25
1306	A277	2.25 l multi	2.60	.35
		Nos. 1301-1306 (6)	4.50	1.60

Fruit Harvest and Dancers A278

Designs: 25q, Contour-plowed fields and conference table. 80q, Cattle and newspapers. 1.30 l, Wheat harvest.

1970, Aug. 28   Litho.   Perf. 12x11½
1307	A278	15q brt violet & blk	.35	.25
1308	A278	25q dp blue & blk	.35	.25
1309	A278	80q dp brown & blk	1.00	.25
1310	A278	1.30 l org brn & blk	1.40	.25
		Nos. 1307-1310 (4)	3.10	1.00

25th anniv. of the agrarian reform law.

Attacking Partisans — A279

Designs: 25q, Partisans with horses and flag. 1.60 l, Partisans.

1970, Sept. 3   Perf. 12
1311	A279	15q org brn & blk	.25	.25
1312	A279	25q brn, yel & blk	.50	.25
1313	A279	1.60 l dp grn & blk	1.50	.35
		Nos. 1311-1313 (3)	2.25	.85

50th anniversary of liberation of Vlona.

Miners, by Nexhmedin Zajmi — A280

Paintings from the National Gallery, Tirana: 5q, Bringing in the Harvest, by Isuf Sulovari, vert. 15q, The Activists, by Dhimitraq Trebicka, vert. 65q, Instruction of Partisans, by Hasan Nallbani. 95q, Architectural Planning, by Vilson Kilica. No. 1319, Woman Machinist, by Zef Shoshi, vert. No. 1320, Partisan Destroying Tank, by Sali Shijaku, vert.

Perf. 12½x12, 12x12½
1970, Sept. 25   Litho.
1314	A280	5q multicolored	.25	.25
1315	A280	15q multicolored	.25	.25
1316	A280	25q multicolored	.25	.25
1317	A280	65q multicolored	.25	.25
1318	A280	95q multicolored	.95	.25
1319	A280	2 l multicolored	1.75	.35
		Nos. 1314-1319 (6)	3.70	1.60

Miniature Sheet
Imperf
| 1320 | A280 | 2 l multicolored | 2.50 | 1.50 |

Electrification Map of Albania — A281

Designs: 25q, Light bulb, hammer and sickle emblem, map of Albania and power graph. 80q, Linemen at work. 1.10 l, Use of electricity on the farm, in home and business.

1970, Oct. 25   Litho.   Perf. 12
1321	A281	15q multi	.25	.25
1322	A281	25q multi	.35	.25
1323	A281	80q multi	1.00	.25
1324	A281	1.10 l multi	1.20	.25
		Nos. 1321-1324 (4)	2.80	1.00

Albanian village electrification completion.

Friedrich Engels A282

Designs: 1.10 l, Engels as young man. 1.15 l, Engels addressing crowd.

1970, Nov. 28   Litho.   Perf. 12x12½
1325	A282	25q bister & dk bl	.35	.25
1326	A282	1.10 l bis & dp claret	.95	.25
1327	A282	1.15 l bis & dk ol grn	1.20	.30
		Nos. 1325-1327 (3)	2.50	.80

150th anniv. of the birth of Friedrich Engels (1820-95), German socialist, collaborator with Karl Marx.

Factories — A282a

Designs: 10q, Tractor factory, Tirana, horiz. 15q, Fertilizer factory, Fier, horiz. 20q, Superphosphate factory, Lac. 25q, Cement factory, Elbasan, horiz. 80q, Coking plant, Qyteti Stalin, horiz.

1970-71   Litho.   Perf. 12
1327A	A282A	10q multi	250.00	160.00
1327B	A282A	15q multi	250.00	160.00
1327C	A282A	20q multi	250.00	160.00
1327D	A282A	25q multi	250.00	160.00
1327E	A282A	80q multi	250.00	160.00
		Nos. 1327A-1327E (5)	1,250.	800.00

Issue dates: 15q, 12/4/70. 10q, 20q, 25q, 80q, 1/20/71.

Ludwig van Beethoven A283

Designs: 5q, Birthplace, Bonn. 25q, 65q, 1.10 l, various portraits. 1.80 l, Scene from Fidelio, horiz.

1970, Dec. 16   Litho.   Perf. 12
1328	A283	5q dp plum & gold	.25	.25
1329	A283	15q brt rose lil & sil	.25	.25
1330	A283	25q green & gold	.35	.25
1331	A283	65q magenta & sil	.85	.25
1332	A283	1.10 l dk blue & gold	1.75	.30
1333	A283	1.80 l black & sil	2.75	.50
		Nos. 1328-1333 (6)	6.20	1.80

Ludwig van Beethoven (1770-1827), composer.

Coat of Arms A284

Designs: 25q, Proclamation. 80q, Enver Hoxha reading proclamation. 1.30 l, Young people and proclamation.

1971, Jan. 11   Litho.   Perf. 12
1334	A284	15q lt bl, gold, blk & red	.25	.25
1335	A284	25q rose lil, blk, gold & gray	.25	.25
1336	A284	80q emerald, blk & gold	.85	.25
1337	A284	1.30 l yel grn, blk & gold	1.20	.30
		Nos. 1334-1337 (4)	2.55	1.05

Declaration of the Republic, 25th anniv.

"Liberty" — A285

Designs: 50q, Women's brigade. 65q, Street battle, horiz. 1.10 l, Execution, horiz.

Perf. 12x11½, 11½x12
1971, Mar. 18   Litho.
1338	A285	25q dk bl & bl	.35	.25
1339	A285	50q slate green	.50	.25
1340	A285	65q dk brn & chest	.75	.25
1341	A285	1.10 l purple	1.25	.25
		Nos. 1338-1341 (4)	2.85	1.00

Centenary of the Paris Commune.

Black Men — A286

1.10 l, Men of 3 races. 1.15 l, Black protest.

1971, Mar. 21   Perf. 12x12½
1342	A286	25q blk & bis brn	.25	.25
1343	A286	1.10 l blk & rose car	.75	.25
1344	A286	1.15 l blk & ver	.90	.25
		Nos. 1342-1344 (3)	1.90	.75

Intl. year against racial discrimination.

Tulip — A287

Designs: Various tulips.

1971, Mar. 25
1345	A287	5q multi	.25	.25
1346	A287	10q yellow & multi	.25	.25
1347	A287	15q pink & multi	.30	.25
1348	A287	20q lt blue & multi	.35	.25
1349	A287	25q multi	.35	.25
1350	A287	80q multi	1.00	.25
1351	A287	1 l multi	1.75	.25
1352	A287	1.45 l citron & multi	2.10	.30
		Nos. 1345-1352 (8)	6.35	2.05

Horseman, by Dürer — A288

Art Works by Dürer: 15q, Three peasants. 25q, Dancing peasant couple. 45q, The bagpiper. 65q, View of Kalkebrut, horiz. 2.40 l, View of Trent, horiz. 2.50 l, Self-portrait.

Perf. 11½x12, 12x11½
1971, May 15   Litho.
1353	A288	10q blk & pale grn	.30	.25
1354	A288	15q black & pale lil	.30	.25
1355	A288	25q blk & pale bl	.35	.25
1356	A288	45q blk & pale rose	.90	.25
1357	A288	65q black & multi	1.75	.25
1358	A288	2.40 l black & multi	5.50	.40
		Nos. 1353-1358 (6)	9.10	1.65

Miniature Sheet
Imperf
| 1359 | A288 | 2.50 l multi | 3.50 | 2.50 |

Albrecht Dürer (1471-1528), German painter and engraver.

Satellite Orbiting Globe — A289

Designs: 1.20 l, Government Building, Tirana, and Red Star emblem. 2.20 l, like 60q, 2.50 l, Flag of People's Republic of China forming trajectory around globe.

1971, June 10   Litho.   Perf. 12x12½
1360	A289	60q purple & multi	.80	.25
1361	A289	1.20 l red & multi	1.60	.30
1362	A289	2.20 l green & multi	3.25	.30

Imperf
| 1363 | A289 | 2.50 l vio blk & multi | 5.00 | 2.75 |
| | | Nos. 1360-1363 (4) | 10.65 | 3.80 |

Space developments of People's Republic of China.

Mao Tse-tung
A290

Designs: 1.05 l, House where Communist Party was founded, horiz. 1.20 l, Peking crowd with placards, horiz.

1971, July 1   Perf. 12x12½, 12½x12
1364	A290	25q silver & multi	.85	.25
1365	A290	1.05 l silver & multi	2.25	2.00
1366	A290	1.20 l silver & multi	3.25	2.25
		Nos. 1364-1366 (3)	6.35	4.50

50th anniv. of Chinese Communist Party.

Crested Titmouse — A291

1971, Aug. 15   Litho.   Perf. 12½x12
1367	A291	5q shown	.25	.25
1368	A291	10q European serin	.30	.25
1369	A291	15q Linnet	.45	.25
1370	A291	25q Firecrest	.70	.25
1371	A291	45q Rock thrush	1.00	.25
1372	A291	60q Blue tit	1.75	.50
1373	A291	2.40 l Chaffinch	6.25	2.75
a.		Block of 7, #1367-1373 + label	17.50	15.00
		Nos. 1367-1373 (7)	10.70	4.50

Continuous design with bird's nest label at upper left.
Nos. 1367-1372 exist in blocks of 8, with two labels. Value: unused $55; used $25.

Olympic Rings and Running — A292

Designs (Olympic Rings and): 10q, Hurdles. 15q, Canoeing. 25q, Gymnastics. 80q, Fencing. 1.05 l, Soccer. 2 l, Runner at finish line. 3.60 l, Diving, women's.

1971, Sept. 15
1374	A292	5q green & multi	.25	.25
1375	A292	10q multicolored	.25	.25
1376	A292	15q blue & multi	.25	.25
1377	A292	25q violet & multi	.25	.25
1378	A292	80q lilac & multi	.75	.25
1379	A292	1.05 l multicolored	.95	.25
1380	A292	3.60 l multicolored	3.00	.50
		Nos. 1374-1380 (7)	5.70	2.00

Souvenir Sheet
Imperf
1381	A292	2 l brt blue & multi	2.50	1.50

20th Olympic Games, Munich, Aug. 26-Sept. 10, 1972.

Workers with Flags
A293

Designs: 1.05 l, Party Headquarters, Tirana, and Red Star. 1.20 l, Rifle, star, flag and "VI."

1971, Nov. 1   Perf. 12
1382	A293	25q multi	.35	.25
1383	A293	1.05 l multi	1.00	.25
1384	A293	1.20 l multi, vert.	1.40	.30
		Nos. 1382-1384 (3)	2.75	.80

6th Congress of Workers' Party.

Factories and Workers
A294

Designs: 80q, "XXX" and flag, vert. 1.55 l, Enver Hoxha and flags.

1971, Nov. 8
1385	A294	15q gold, sil, lil & yel	.25	.25
1386	A294	80q gold, sil & red	.90	.25
1387	A294	1.55 l gold, sil, red & brn	1.90	.30
		Nos. 1385-1387 (3)	3.05	.80

30th anniversary of Workers' Party.

Construction Work, by M. Fushekati — A295

Contemporary Albanian Paintings: 5q, Young Man, by R. Kuci, vert. 25q, Partisan, by D. Juknlu, vert. 80q, Fliers, by S. Kristo. 1.20 l, Girl in Forest, by A. Sadikaj. 1.55 l, Warriors with Spears and Shields, by S. Kamberi. 2 l, Freedom Fighter, by I. Lulani.

Perf. 12x12½, 12½x12
1971, Nov. 20
1388	A295	5q gold & multi	.25	.25
1389	A295	15q gold & multi	.25	.25
1390	A295	25q gold & multi	.25	.25
1391	A295	80q gold & multi	.75	.25
1392	A295	1.20 l gold & multi	.85	.25
1393	A295	1.55 l gold & multi	1.00	.30
		Nos. 1388-1393 (6)	3.35	1.55

Miniature Sheet
Imperf
1394	A295	2 l gold & multi	2.50	1.75

Young Workers' Emblem — A296

1971, Nov. 23   Perf. 12x12½
1395	A296	15q lt blue & multi	.25	.25
1396	A296	1.35 l grnsh gray & multi	1.25	.30

Albanian Young Workers' Union, 30th anniv.

"Halili and Hajria" Ballet — A297

Scenes from "Halili and Hajria" Ballet: 10q, Brother and sister. 15q, Hajria before Sultan Suleiman. 50q, Hajria and husband. 80q, Execution of Halili. 1.40 l, Hajria killing her husband.

1971, Dec. 27   Perf. 12½x12
1397	A297	5q silver & multi	.25	.25
1398	A297	10q silver & multi	.25	.25
1399	A297	15q silver & multi	.25	.25
1400	A297	50q silver & multi	.60	.25
1401	A297	80q silver & multi	1.00	.50
1402	A297	1.40 l silver & multi	2.00	.90
		Nos. 1397-1402 (6)	4.35	2.40

Albanian ballet Halili and Hajria after drama by Kol Jakova.

Biathlon and Olympic Rings — A298

Designs (Olympic Rings and): 10q, Sledding. 15q, Ice hockey. 20q, Bobsledding. 50q, Speed skating. 1 l, Slalom. 2 l, Ski jump. 2.50 l, Figure skating, pairs.

1972, Feb. 10
1403	A298	5q lt olive & multi	.25	.25
1404	A298	10q lt violet & multi	.25	.25
1405	A298	15q multicolored	.25	.25
1406	A298	20q pink & multi	.25	.25
1407	A298	50q lt blue & multi	.50	.25
1408	A298	1 l ocher & multi	.80	.25
1409	A298	2 l lilac & multi	1.75	.40
		Nos. 1403-1409 (7)	4.05	1.90

Souvenir Sheet
Imperf
1410	A298	2.50 l blue & multi	2.75	1.75

11th Winter Olympic Games, Sapporo, Japan, Feb. 3-13.

Wild Strawberries
A299

Wild Fruits and Nuts: 10q, Blackberries. 15q, Hazelnuts. 20q, Walnuts. 25q, Strawberry-tree fruit. 30q, Dogwood berries. 2.40 l, Rowan berries.

1972, Mar. 20   Litho.   Perf. 12
1411	A299	5q lt grn & multi	.25	.25
1412	A299	10q yellow & multi	.25	.25
1413	A299	15q lt vio & multi	.25	.25
1414	A299	20q pink & multi	.25	.25
1415	A299	25q multi	.25	.25
1416	A299	30q multi	.35	.25
1417	A299	2.40 l multi	3.00	.50
		Nos. 1411-1417 (7)	4.60	2.00

"Your Heart is Your Health"
A300

World Health Day: 1.20 l, Cardiac patient and electrocardiogram.

1972, Apr. 7   Perf. 12x12½
1418	A300	1.10 l multicolored	1.25	.40
1419	A300	1.20 l rose & multi	1.40	.85

Worker and Student — A301

7th Trade Union Cong., May 8: 2.05 l, Assembly Hall, dancers and emblem.

1972, Apr. 24   Litho.   Perf. 11½x12½
1420	A301	25q multi	.50	.25
1421	A301	2.05 l blue & multi	2.00	.40

Qemal Stafa
A302

Designs: 15q, Memorial flame. 25q, Monument "Spirit of Defiance," vert.

1972, May 5   Perf. 12½x12, 12x12½
1422	A302	15q gray & multi	.25	.25
1423	A302	25q sal rose, blk & gray	.30	.25
1424	A302	1.90 l dull yel & blk	1.75	.35
		Nos. 1422-1424 (3)	2.30	.85

30th anniversary of the murder of Qemal Stafa and of Martyrs' Day.

Camellia
A303

Designs: Various camellias.

1972, May 10   Perf. 12x12½
Flowers in Natural Colors
1425	A303	5q lt blue & blk	.25	.25
1426	A303	10q citron & blk	.25	.25
1427	A303	15q grnsh gray & blk	.25	.25
1428	A303	25q pale sal & blk	.25	.25
1429	A303	45q gray & blk	.45	.25
1430	A303	50q sal pink & blk	.85	.25
1431	A303	2.50 l bluish gray & blk	3.25	.90
		Nos. 1425-1431 (7)	5.55	2.40

High Jump — A304

Designs (Olympic and Motion Emblems and): 10q, Running. 15q, Shot put. 20q, Bicycling. 25q, Pole vault. 50q, Hurdles, women's. 75q, Hockey. 2 l, Swimming. 2.50 l, Diving, women's.

1972, June 30   Litho.   Perf. 12½x12
1432	A304	5q multicolored	.25	.25
1433	A304	10q lt brn & multi	.25	.25
1434	A304	15q lt lil & multi	.25	.25
1435	A304	20q multicolored	.30	.25
1436	A304	25q lt vio & multi	.30	.25
1437	A304	50q lt grn & multi	.50	.25
1438	A304	75q multicolored	1.00	.25
1439	A304	2 l multicolored	3.00	.35
		Nos. 1432-1439 (8)	5.85	2.10

Miniature Sheet
Imperf
1440	A304	2.50 l multi	3.50	2.50

20th Olympic Games, Munich, Aug. 26-Sept. 11. Nos. 1432-1439 each issued in sheets of 8 stamps and one label (3x3) showing Olympic rings in gold.

Autobus
A305

25q, Electric train. 80q, Ocean liner Tirana. 1.05 l, Automobile. 1.20 l, Trailer truck.

1972, July 25 Litho. Perf. 12
1441	A305	15q org brn & multi	.25	.25
1442	A305	25q gray & multi	.35	.25
1443	A305	80q dp grn & multi	.50	.25
1444	A305	1.05 l multi	.70	.25
1445	A305	1.20 l multi	1.40	.25
		Nos. 1441-1445 (5)	3.20	1.25

Arm
Wrestling
A306

Folk Games: 10q, Piggyback ball game. 15q, Women's jumping. 25q, Rope game (srum). 90q, Leapfrog. 2 l, Women throwing pitchers.

1972, Aug. 18
1446	A306	5q multi	.25	.25
1447	A306	10q lt bl & multi	.25	.25
1448	A306	15q rose & multi	.25	.25
1449	A306	25q lt bl & multi	.25	.25
1450	A306	90q ocher & multi	.90	.25
1451	A306	2 l lt grn & multi	1.75	.30
		Nos. 1446-1451 (6)	3.65	1.55

1st National Festival of People's Games.

Mastheads — A307

30th Press Day: 25q, Printing press. 1.90 l, Workers reading paper.

1972, Aug. 25
1452	A307	15q lt bl & blk	.25	.25
1453	A307	25q red, grn & blk	.25	.25
1454	A307	1.90 l lt vio & blk	1.40	.40
		Nos. 1452-1454 (3)	1.90	.90

Map of
Peza
Area,
Memorial
Tablet
A308

25q, Guerrillas with flag. 1.90 l, Peza Conference memorial.

1972, Sept. 16
1455	A308	15q shown	.25	.25
1456	A308	25q multicolored	.35	.25
1457	A308	1.90 l multicolored	1.90	.40
		Nos. 1455-1457 (3)	2.50	.90

30th anniversary, Conference of Peza.

Partisans, by Sotir Capo — A309

Paintings: 10q, Woman, by Ismail Lulani, vert. 15q, "Communists," by Lec Shkreli, vert. 20q, View of Nendorit, 1941, by Sali Shijaku, vert. 50q, Woman with Sheaf, by Zef Shoshi, vert. 1 l, Landscape with Children, by Dhimitraq Trebicka. 2 l, Women on Bicycles, by Vilson Kilica. 2.30 l, Folk Dance, by Abdurrahim Buza.

Perf. 12½x12, 12x12½
1972, Sept. 25 Litho.
1458	A309	5q gold & multi	.25	.25
1459	A309	10q gold & multi	.25	.25
1460	A309	15q gold & multi	.25	.25
1461	A309	20q gold & multi	.25	.25
1462	A309	50q gold & multi	.25	.25

1463	A309	1 l gold & multi	.70	.25
1464	A309	2 l gold & multi	1.75	.40
		Nos. 1458-1464 (7)	3.70	1.90

Miniature Sheet
Imperf
1465	A309	2.30 l gold & multi	2.50	1.75

No. 1465 contains one 41x68mm stamp.

Congress
Emblem — A310

Design: 2.05 l, Young worker with banner.

1972, Oct. 23 Litho. Perf. 12
1466	A310	25q silver, red & gold	.50	.25
1467	A310	2.05 l silver & multi	1.90	.50

Union of Working Youth, 6th Congress.

Hammer and
Sickle — A311

Design: 1.20 l, Lenin as orator.

1972, Nov. 7 Litho. Perf. 11½x12
1468	A311	1.10 l multi	1.00	.25
1469	A311	1.20 l multi	2.00	.30

Russian October Revolution, 55th anniv.

Ismail
Qemali — A312

Designs: 15q, Albanian fighters, horiz. 65q, Rally, horiz. 1.25 l, Coat of arms.

Perf. 12x11½, 11½x12
1972, Nov. 29
1470	A312	15q red, brt bl & blk	.25	.25
1471	A312	25q yel, blk & red	.25	.25
1472	A312	65q red, sal & blk	.55	.25
1473	A312	1.25 l dl red & blk	1.75	.25
		Nos. 1470-1473 (4)	2.80	1.00

60th anniv. of independence.

Cock,
Mosaic
A313

Mosaics, 2nd-5th centuries, excavated near Buthrotium and Apollonia: 10q, Bird, vert. 15q, Partridges, vert. 25q, Warrior's legs. 45q, Nymph riding dolphin, vert. 50q, Fish, vert. 2.50 l, Warrior with helmet.

1972, Dec. 10 Perf. 12½x12, 12x12½
1474	A313	5q silver & multi	.25	.25
1475	A313	10q silver & multi	.25	.25
1476	A313	15q silver & multi	.25	.25
1477	A313	25q silver & multi	.25	.25
1478	A313	45q silver & multi	.40	.25

1479	A313	50q silver & multi	.55	.25
1480	A313	2.50 l silver & multi	2.10	.80
		Nos. 1474-1480 (7)	4.05	2.30

Nicolaus
Copernicus
A314

Designs: 10q, 25q, 80q, 1.20 l, Various portraits of Copernicus. 1.60 l, Heliocentric solar system.

1973, Feb. 19 Litho. Perf. 12x12½
1481	A314	5q lil rose & multi	.25	.25
1482	A314	10q dull ol & multi	.25	.25
1483	A314	25q multicolored	.25	.25
1484	A314	80q lt violet & multi	.25	.25
1485	A314	1.20 l blue & multi	1.40	.30
1486	A314	1.60 l gray & multi	2.25	.40
		Nos. 1481-1486 (6)	4.65	1.70

500th anniversary of the birth of Nicolaus Copernicus (1473-1543), Polish astronomer.

Flowering Cactus — A315

Designs: Various flowering cacti.

1973, Mar. 25 Litho. Perf. 12
1487	A315	10q multicolored	.30	.25
1488	A315	15q multicolored	.30	.25
1489	A315	20q beige & multi	.30	.25
1490	A315	25q gray & multi	.30	.25
1491	A315	30q beige & multi	4.25	1.50
1492	A315	65q gray & multi	1.40	.25
1493	A315	80q multicolored	1.40	.25
1494	A315	2 l multicolored	1.75	.60
a.		Block of 8, #1487-1494	16.00	8.00
		Nos. 1487-1494 (8)	10.00	3.60

A block containing Nos. 1487-1490, 1492-1494 and a label exists.

Guard and Factories — A316

1.80 l, Guard and guards with prisoner.

1973, Mar. 20 Litho. Perf. 12½x12
1495	A316	25q ultra & blk	.35	.25
1496	A316	1.80 l dk red & multi	2.00	.40

30th anniv. of the State Security Branch.

Common Tern — A317

Sea Birds: 15q, White-winged black terns, vert. 25q, Black-headed gull, vert. 45q, Great black-headed gull. 80q, Slender-billed gull, vert. 2.40 l, Sandwich terns.

1973, Apr. 30 Perf. 12½x12, 12x12½
1497	A317	5q gold & multi	.25	.25
1498	A317	15q gold & multi	.25	.25
1499	A317	25q gold & multi	.30	.25
1500	A317	45q gold & multi	.70	.25
1501	A317	80q gold & multi	1.40	.25
1502	A317	2.40 l gold & multi	2.75	.55
		Nos. 1497-1502 (6)	5.65	1.80

Letters, 1913 Cancellation and Post Horn — A318

Design: 1.80 l, Mailman, 1913 cancel.

1973, May, 5 Litho. Perf. 12x11½
1503	A318	25q red & multi	.70	.25
1504	A318	1.80 l red & multi	2.75	.55

60th anniversary of Albanian stamps.

Farmer,
Worker,
Soldier
A319

Design: 25q, Woman and factory, vert.

1973, June 4 Perf. 12
1505	A319	25q carmine rose	.35	.25
1506	A319	1.80 l yel, dp org & blk	2.10	.50

7th Congress of Albanian Women's Union.

Creation of General Staff, by G. Madhi — A320

Designs: 40q, "August 1949," sculpture by Sh. Haderi, vert. 60q, "Generation after Generation," sculpture by H. Dule, vert. 80q, "Defend Revolutionary Victories," by M. Fushekati.

1973, July 10 Litho. Perf. 12½x12
1507	A320	25q gold & multi	7.00	10.00
1508	A320	40q gold & multi	7.00	10.00
1509	A320	60q gold & multi	7.00	10.00
1510	A320	80q gold & multi	7.00	10.00
		Nos. 1507-1510 (4)	28.00	40.00

30th anniversary of the People's Army.

"Electrification," by S. Hysa — A321

Albanian Paintings: 10q, Woman Textile Worker, by N. Nallbani. 15q, Gymnasts, by M. Fushekati. 50q, Aviator, by F. Stamo. 80q, Fascist Prisoner, by A. Lakuriqi. 1.20 l, Workers with Banner, by P. Mele. 1.30 l, Farm Woman, by Zef Shoshi. 2.05 l, Battle of Tenda, by F. Haxhiu. 10q, 50q, 80q, 1.20 l, 1.30 l, vertical.

Perf. 12½x12, 12x12½
1973, Aug. 10
1511	A321	5q gold & multi	.25	.25
1512	A321	10q gold & multi	.25	.25
1513	A321	15q gold & multi	.25	.25
1514	A321	50q gold & multi	.65	.25
1515	A321	80q gold & multi	.75	.25

1516	A321	1.20 l gold & multi	1.10	.25
1517	A321	1.30 l gold & multi	2.25	.25
		Nos. 1511-1517 (7)	5.50	1.75

Souvenir Sheet
Imperf

1518	A321	2.05 l multi	2.50	1.75

Mary
Magdalene,
by Caravaggio
A322

Paintings by Michelangelo da Caravaggio: 10q, The Lute Player, horiz. 15q, Self-portrait. 50q, Boy Carrying Fruit and Flowers. 80q, Still Life, horiz. 1.20 l, Narcissus. 1.30 l, Boy Peeling Apple. 2.05 l, Man with Feathered Hat.

Perf. 12x12½, 12½x12
1973, Sept. 28

1519	A322	5q gold & multi	.25	.25
1520	A322	10q gold & multi	.25	.25
1521	A322	15q gold, blk & gray	.25	.25
1522	A322	50q gold & multi	.25	.25
1523	A322	80q gold & multi	.55	.25
1524	A322	1.20 l gold & multi	.70	.30
1525	A322	1.30 l gold & multi	1.40	.30
		Nos. 1519-1525 (7)	3.65	1.85

Souvenir Sheet
Imperf

1526	A322	2.05 l multi	3.75	3.50

Michelangelo da Caravaggio (Merisi; 1573?-1609), Italian painter. No. 1526 contains one stamp, size: 63x73mm.

Soccer — A323

Designs: 5q-1.25 l, Various soccer scenes. 2.05 l, Ball in goal and list of cities where championships were held.

1973, Oct. 30   Litho.   Perf. 12½x12

1527	A323	5q multi	.25	.25
1528	A323	10q multi	.25	.25
1529	A323	15q multi	.25	.25
1530	A323	20q multi	.25	.25
1531	A323	25q multi	.25	.25
1532	A323	90q multi	.40	.25
1533	A323	1.20 l multi	.80	.25
1534	A323	1.25 l multi	1.25	.25
		Nos. 1527-1534 (8)	3.70	2.00

Minature Sheet
Imperf

1535	A323	2.05 l multi	2.75	2.00

World Soccer Cup, Munich 1974.

Weight
Lifter — A324

Designs: Various stages of weight lifting. 1.20 l, 1.60 l, horiz.

1973, Oct. 30   Litho.   Perf. 12

1536	A324	5q multi	.25	.25
1537	A324	10q multi	.25	.25
1538	A324	25q multi	.25	.25
1539	A324	90q multi	.25	.25

1540	A324	1.20 l multi	.65	.25
1541	A324	1.60 l multi	1.60	.25
		Nos. 1536-1541 (6)	3.25	1.50

Weight Lifting Championships, Havana, Cuba.

Cement Factory,
Kavaje — A325

Harvester
Combine
A326

Skiers and
Hotel — A326a

Mountain Lake —
A326b

Designs: 10q, Ali Kelmendi truck factory and tank cars, horiz. 15q, Ballet. 25q, "Communication." 60q, Resort, horiz. 1 l, Mao Tse-tung textile mill. 1.20 l, Steel workers. 2.40 l, Welder and pipe. 3 l, Skanderbeg Monument, Tirana. 5 l, Roman arches, Durres.

Perf. 12½x12, 12x12½
1973-74   Litho.

1543	A325	5q gold & multi	.25	.25
1544	A325	10q gold & multi	.25	.25
1545	A325	15q gold & multi	.40	.25
1545A	A326	20q gold & multi	.25	.25
1546	A325	25q gold & multi	.25	.25
1547	A326a	35q gold & multi	.30	.25
1548	A325	60q gold & multi	.80	.25
1549	A326b	80q gold & multi	1.40	.25
1549A	A325	1 l gold & multi	.25	.25
1549B	A325	1.20 l gold & multi	.95	.25
1549C	A326b	2.40 l gold & multi	1.90	.35
1550	A325	3 l gold & multi	3.50	.35
1551	A325	5 l gold & multi	3.50	.60
		Nos. 1543-1551 (13)	14.00	3.80

Issue dates: Nos. 1545-1546, 1549-1550, Dec. 5, 1973; others, 1974.

Mao Tse-
tung — A327

80th birthday of Mao Tse-tung: 1.20 l, Mao Tse-tung addressing crowd.

1973, Dec. 26   Perf. 12

1552	A327	85q multicolored	11.00	1.25
1553	A327	1.20 l multicolored	17.00	2.25

Old Man and
Dog, by
Gericault
A328

Paintings by Jean Louis André Theodore Gericault: 10q, Horse's Head. 15q, Male Model. 25q, Head of Black Man. 1.20 l, Self-portrait. 2.05 l, Raft of the Medusa, horiz. 2.20 l, Battle of the Giants.

Perf. 12x12½, 12½x12
1974, Jan. 18   Litho.

1554	A328	10q gold & multi	.25	.25
1555	A328	15q gold & multi	.25	.25
1556	A328	20q gold & multi	.25	.25
1557	A328	25q gold & blk	.25	.25
1558	A328	1.20 l gold & multi	1.40	.25
1559	A328	2.20 l gold & multi	2.60	.40
		Nos. 1554-1559 (6)	5.00	1.65

Souvenir Sheet
Imperf

1560	A328	2.05 l gold & multi	2.75	1.90

No. 1560 contains one 87x78mm stamp.

Lenin, by
Pandi
Mele — A329

Designs: 25q, Lenin with Sailors on Cruiser Aurora, by Dhimitraq Trebicka, horiz. 1.20 l, Lenin, by Vilson Kilica.

1974, Jan. 21   Perf. 12½x12, 12x12½

1561	A329	25q gold & multi	.90	.25
1562	A329	60q gold & multi	2.10	.25
1563	A329	1.20 l gold & multi	6.00	.55
		Nos. 1561-1563 (3)	9.00	1.05

50th anniv. of the death of Lenin.

Swimming Duck, Mosaic — A330

Designs: Mosaics from the 5th-6th Centuries A.D., excavated near Buthrotium, Pogradec and Apollonia.

1974, Feb. 20   Litho.   Perf. 12½x12

1564	A330	5q shown	.25	.25
1565	A330	10q Bird, flower	.25	.25
1566	A330	15q Vase, grapes	.25	.25
1567	A330	25q Duck	.25	.25
1568	A330	40q Donkey, bird	.25	.25
1569	A330	2.50 l Sea horse	1.25	.40
		Nos. 1564-1569 (6)	2.50	1.65

Soccer — A331

Various scenes from soccer. 2.05 l, World Soccer Cup & names of participating countries.

1974, Apr. 25   Litho.   Perf. 12½x12

1570	A331	10q gold & multi	.25	.25
1571	A331	15q gold & multi	.25	.25
1572	A331	20q gold & multi	.25	.25
1573	A331	25q gold & multi	.25	.25
1574	A331	40q gold & multi	.25	.25
1575	A331	80q gold & multi	.55	.25
1576	A331	1 l gold & multi	.70	.30
1577	A331	1.20 l gold & multi	1.20	.40
		Nos. 1570-1577 (8)	3.70	2.20

Souvenir Sheet
Imperf

1578	A331	2.05 l gold & multi	2.50	1.75

World Cup Soccer Championship, Munich, June 13-July 7. No. 1578 contains one stamp (60x60mm) with simulated perforations. Nos. 1570-1577 exist imperf, No. 1578 with simulated perfs omitted. Values $10 and $20, respectively.

Arms of Albania,
Soldier — A332

Design: 1.80 l, Soldier and front page of 1944 Congress Book.

1974, May 24   Litho.   Perf. 12

1579	A332	25q multicolored	.35	.25
1580	A332	1.80 l multicolored	1.40	.30

30th anniversary of the First Anti-Fascist Liberation Congress of Permet.

Medicinal
Plants
A333

10q, Bittersweet. 15q, Arbutus. 20q, Lilies of the valley. 25q, Autumn crocus. 40q, Borage, horiz. 80q, Soapwort, horiz. 2.20 l, Gentian, horiz.

1974, May 5   Perf. 12½x12

1581	A333	10q multicolored	.25	.25
1582	A333	15q multicolored	.25	.25
1583	A333	20q multicolored	.25	.25
1584	A333	25q multicolored	.25	.25
1585	A333	40q multicolored	.45	.25
1586	A333	80q multicolored	.85	.25
1587	A333	2.20 l multicolored	2.50	.45
		Nos. 1581-1587 (7)	4.80	1.95

Revolutionaries with Albanian
Flag — A334

1.80 l, Portraits of 5 revolutionaries, vert.

Perf. 12½x12, 12x12½
1974, June 10

1588	A334	25q red, blk & lil	.35	.25
1589	A334	1.80 l yel, red & blk	1.40	.45

50th anniversary Albanian Bourgeois Democratic Revolution.

European Redwing — A335

Designs: Songbirds; Nos. 1597-1600 vert.

Perf. 12½x12, 12x12½

1974, July 15				Litho.
1594	A335	10q shown	.25	.25
1595	A335	15q European robin	.25	.25
1596	A335	20q Greenfinch	.25	.25
1597	A335	25q Bullfinch	.25	.25
1598	A335	40q Hawfinch	.35	.25
1599	A335	80q Blackcap	1.40	.25
1600	A335	2.20 l Nightingale	2.75	.50
	Nos. 1594-1600 (7)		5.50	2.00

Globe — A336

Cent. of UPU: 1.20 l, UPU emblem. 2.05 l, Jet over globe.

1974, Aug. 25		Litho.	Perf. 12x12½	
1601	A336	85q grn & multi	1.20	.25
1602	A336	1.20 l vio & ol grn	1.75	.25

Miniature Sheet
Imperf

1603	A336	2.05 l blue & multi	15.00	25.00

Widows, by Sali Shijaku — A337

Albanian Paintings: 15q, Drillers, by Danish Jukniu, vert. 20q, Workers with Blueprints, by Clirim Ceka. 25q, Call to Action, by Spiro Kristo, vert. 40q, Winter Battle, by Sabaudin Xhaferi. 80q, Comrades, by Clirim Ceka, vert. 1 l, Aiding the Partisans, by Guri Madhi. 1.20 l, Teacher with Pupils, by Kleo Nini Brezat. 2.05 l, Comrades in Arms, by Guri Madhi.

Perf. 12½x12, 12x12½

1974, Sept. 25				
1604	A337	10q silver & multi	.25	.25
1605	A337	15q silver & multi	.25	.25
1606	A337	20q silver & multi	.25	.25
1607	A337	25q silver & multi	.25	.25
1608	A337	40q silver & multi	.30	.25
1609	A337	80q silver & multi	.70	.25
1610	A337	1 l silver & multi	1.00	.25
1611	A337	1.20 l silver & multi	1.40	.25
	Nos. 1604-1611 (8)		4.40	2.00

Miniature Sheet
Imperf

1612	A337	2.05 l silver & multi	2.50	1.75

Crowd on Tien An Men Square A338

Design: 1.20 l, Mao Tse-tung, vert.

1974, Oct. 1			Perf. 12	
1613	A338	85q gold & multi	6.00	1.50
1614	A338	1.20 l gold & multi	9.50	2.50

25th anniversary of the proclamation of the People's Republic of China.

Women's Volleyball A339

Spartakiad Medal and: 15q, Women hurdlers. 20q, Women gymnasts. 25q, Mass exercises in Stadium. 40q, Weight lifter. 80q, Wrestlers. 1 l, Military rifle drill. 1.20 l, Soccer.

1974, Oct. 9			Perf. 12x12½	
1615	A339	10q multi	.25	.25
1616	A339	15q multi	.25	.25
1617	A339	20q multi	.25	.25
1618	A339	25q gray & multi	.25	.25
1619	A339	40q multi	.25	.25
1620	A339	80q multi	.35	.25
1621	A339	1 l multi	.70	.25
1622	A339	1.20 l tan & multi	1.00	.25
	Nos. 1615-1622 (8)		3.30	2.00

National Spartakiad, Oct. 9-17.

View of Berat — A340

Designs: 80q, Enver Hoxha addressing Congress, bas-relief, horiz. 1 l, Hoxha and leaders leaving Congress Hall.

Perf. 12x12½, 12½x12

1974, Oct. 20				Litho.
1623	A340	25q rose car & blk	.35	.25
1624	A340	80q yel, brn & blk	1.00	.25
1625	A340	1 l dp lilac & blk	2.00	.30
	Nos. 1623-1625 (3)		3.35	.80

30th anniversary of 2nd Congress of Berat.

Anniversary Emblem, Factory Guards — A341

35q, Chemical industry. 50q, Agriculture. 80q, Arts. 1 l, Atomic diagram & computer. 1.20 l, Youth education. 2.05 l, Crowd & History Book.

1974, Nov. 29		Litho.	Perf. 12½x12	
1626	A341	25q green & multi	.25	.25
1627	A341	35q ultra & multi	.25	.25
1628	A341	50q brown & multi	.25	.25
1629	A341	80q multicolored	.35	.25
1630	A341	1 l violet & multi	.85	.25
1631	A341	1.20 l multicolored	1.00	.30
	Nos. 1626-1631 (6)		2.95	1.55

Miniature Sheet
Imperf

1632	A341	2.05 l gold & multi	1.75	1.50

30th anniv. of liberation from Fascism.

Artemis, from Apolloni A342

1974, Dec. 25		Photo.	Perf. 12x12½	
1633	A342	10q shown	.25	.25
1634	A342	15q Zeus statue	.25	.25
1635	A342	20q Poseidon statue	.30	.25
1636	A342	25q Illyrian helmet	.35	.25
1637	A342	40q Amphora	.70	.25
1638	A342	80q Agrippa	1.00	.25
1639	A342	1 l Demosthenes	1.40	.30
1640	A342	1.20 l Head of Bilia	2.00	.35
	Nos. 1633-1640 (8)		6.25	2.15

Miniature Sheet
Imperf

1641	A342	2.05 l Artemis & amphora	2.50	2.10

Archaeological discoveries in Albania.

Workers and Factories A343

25q, Handshake, tools and book, vert.

1975, Feb. 11		Litho.	Perf. 12	
1642	A343	25q brown & multi	.35	.25
1643	A343	1.80 l yellow & multi	1.40	.35

Albanian Trade Unions, 30th anniversary.

Chicory A344

1975, Feb. 15				
1644	A344	5q shown	.25	.25
1645	A344	10q Houseleek	.25	.25
1646	A344	15q Columbine	.25	.25
1647	A344	20q Anemone	.25	.25
1648	A344	25q Hibiscus	.25	.25
1649	A344	30q Gentian	.35	.25
1650	A344	35q Hollyhock	.35	.25
1651	A344	2.70 l Iris	1.10	.45
	Nos. 1644-1651 (8)		3.05	2.20

Protected flowers.

Jesus, from Doni Madonna A345

Works by Michelangelo: 10q, Slave, sculpture. 15q, Head of Dawn, sculpture. 20q, Awakening Giant, sculpture. 25q, Cumaenian Sybil, Sistine Chapel. 30q, Lorenzo di Medici, sculpture. 1.20 l, David, sculpture. 2.05 l, Self-portrait. 3.90 l, Delphic Sybil, Sistine Chapel.

1975, Mar. 20		Litho.	Perf. 12x12½	
1652	A345	5q gold & multi	.25	.25
1653	A345	10q gold & multi	.25	.25
1654	A345	15q gold & multi	.25	.25
1655	A345	20q gold & multi	.25	.25
1656	A345	25q gold & multi	.25	.25
1657	A345	30q gold & multi	.25	.25
1658	A345	1.20 l gold & multi	.55	.25
1659	A345	3.90 l gold & multi	1.60	.50
	Nos. 1652-1659 (8)		3.65	2.25

Miniature Sheet
Imperf

1660	A345	2.05 l gold & multi	3.25	2.00

Michelangelo Buonarroti (1475-1564), Italian sculptor, painter and architect.

Two-wheeled Cart — A346

Albanian Transportation of the Past: 5q, Horseback rider. 15q, Lake ferry. 20q, Coastal three-master. 25q, Phaeton. 3.35 l, Early automobile on bridge.

1975, Apr. 15		Litho.	Perf. 12½x12	
1661	A346	5q bl grn & multi	.25	.25
1662	A346	10q ol & multi	.25	.25
1663	A346	15q lil & multi	.25	.25
1664	A346	20q multi	.25	.25
1665	A346	25q multi	.25	.25
1666	A346	3.35 l ocher & multi	1.90	.50
	Nos. 1661-1666 (6)		3.15	1.75

Guard at Frontier Stone — A347

Guardsman and Militia — A348

1975, Apr. 25			Perf. 12	
1667	A347	25q multi	.35	.25
1668	A348	1.80 l multi	1.40	.35

30th anniversary of Frontier Guards.

Posting Illegal Poster — A349

Designs: 60q, Partisans in battle. 1.20 l, Partisan killing German soldier, and Albanian coat of arms.

1975, May 9			Perf. 12½x12	
1669	A349	25q multi	.25	.25
1670	A349	60q multi	.50	.25
1671	A349	1.20 l red & multi	1.00	.30
	Nos. 1669-1671 (3)		1.75	.80

30th anniversary of victory over Fascism.

European Widgeons — A350

Waterfowl: 5q, Anas penelope. 10q, Netta rufina. 15q, Anser albifrons. 20q, Anas acuta. 25q, Mergus serrator. 30q, Pata somateria. 35q, Cignus cygnus. 2.70 l, Spatula clypeata.

1975, June 15 **Litho.** **Perf. 12**
1672	A350	5q brt blue & multi	.25	.25
1673	A350	10q yel grn & multi	.25	.25
1674	A350	15q brt rose lil & multi	.25	.25
1675	A350	20q bl grn & multi	.25	.25
1676	A350	25q multicolored	.25	.25
1677	A350	30q multicolored	.30	.25
1678	A350	35q orange & multi	.45	.25
1679	A350	2.70 l multi	2.75	.90
	Nos. 1672-1679 (8)		4.75	2.65

Shyqyri Kanapari, by Musa Qarri — A351

Albanian Paintings: 10q, Woman Saving Children in Sea, by Agim Faja. 15q, "November 28, 1912" (revolution), by Petrit Ceno, horiz. 20q, "Workers Unite," by Sali Shijaku. 25q, The Partisan Shota Galica, by Ismail Lulani. 30q, Victorious Resistance Fighters, 1943, by Nestor Jonuzi. 80q, Partisan Couple in Front of Red Flag, by Vilson Halimi. 2.05 l, Dancing Procession, by Abdurahim Buza. 2.25 l, Republic Day Celebration, by Fatmir Haxhiu, horiz.

Perf. 12x12½, 12½x12
1975, July 15 **Litho.**
1680	A351	5q gold & multi	.25	.25
1681	A351	10q gold & multi	.25	.25
1682	A351	15q gold & multi	.25	.25
1683	A351	20q gold & multi	.25	.25
1684	A351	25q gold & multi	.25	.25
1685	A351	30q gold & multi	.25	.25
1686	A351	80q gold & multi	.30	.25
1687	A351	2.25 l gold & multi	1.40	.45
	Nos. 1680-1687 (8)		3.20	2.20

Miniature Sheet
Imperf
1688	A351	2.05 l gold & multi	2.25	2.25

Nos. 1680-1687 issued in sheets of 8 stamps and gold center label showing palette and easel.

Farmer Holding Reform Law — A352

Design: 2 l, Produce and farm machinery.

1975, Aug. 28 **Perf. 12**
1689	A352	15q multicolored	.35	.25
1690	A352	2 l multicolored	1.75	.50

Agrarian reform, 30th anniversary.

Alcynonium Palmatum A353

Corals: 10q, Paramuricea chamaeleon. 20q, Coralium rubrum. 25q, Eunicella covalini. 3.70 l, Cladocora cespitosa.

1975, Sept. 25 **Litho.** **Perf. 12**
1691	A353	5q blue, ol & blk	.30	.25
1692	A353	10q blue & multi	.30	.25
1693	A353	20q blue & multi	.30	.25
1694	A353	25q blue & blk	.30	.25
1695	A353	3.70 l blue & blk	3.00	.80
	Nos. 1691-1695 (5)		4.20	1.80

Bicycling A354

Designs (Montreal Olympic Games Emblem and): 10q, Canoeing. 15q, Fieldball. 20q, Basketball. 25q, Water polo. 30q, Hockey. 1.20 l, Pole vault. 2.05 l, Fencing. 2.15 l, Montreal Olympic Games emblem and various sports.

1975, Oct. 20 **Litho.** **Perf. 12½**
1696	A354	5q multi	.25	.25
1697	A354	10q multi	.25	.25
1698	A354	15q multi	.25	.25
1699	A354	20q multi	.40	.25
1700	A354	25q multi	.45	.25
1701	A354	30q multi	.55	.25
1702	A354	1.20 l multi	1.50	.30
1703	A354	2.05 l multi	2.75	.45
	Nos. 1696-1703 (8)		6.40	2.25

Miniature Sheet
Imperf
1704	A354	2.15 l org & multi	6.50	5.25

21st Olympic Games, Montreal, July 18-Aug. 8, 1976. Nos. 1696-1703 exist imperf. Value $10.

Power Lines Leading to Village A355

Designs: 25q, Transformers and insulators. 80q, Dam and power station. 85q, Television set, power lines, grain and cogwheel.

1975, Oct. 25 **Perf. 12x12½**
1705	A355	15q ultra & yel	.25	.25
1706	A355	25q brt vio & pink	.25	.25
1707	A355	80q lt grn & gray	.60	.25
1708	A355	85q ocher & brn	1.40	.45
	Nos. 1705-1708 (4)		2.50	1.20

General electrification, 5th anniversary.

Child, Rabbit and Teddy Bear Planting Tree — A356

Fairy Tales: 10q, Mother fox. 15q, Ducks in school. 20q, Little pigs building house. 25q, Animals watching television. 30q, Rabbit and bear at work. 35q, Working and playing ants. 2.70 l, Wolf in sheep's clothes.

1975, Dec. 25 **Litho.** **Perf. 12½x12**
1709	A356	5q black & multi	.25	.25
1710	A356	10q black & multi	.25	.25
1711	A356	15q black & multi	.25	.25
1712	A356	20q black & multi	.30	.25
1713	A356	25q black & multi	.40	.25
1714	A356	30q black & multi	.50	.25
1715	A356	35q black & multi	.55	.25
1716	A356	2.70 l black & multi	3.00	.75
	Nos. 1709-1716 (8)		5.50	2.50

Arms, People, Factories A357

Design: 1.90 l, Arms, government building, celebrating crowd.

1976, Jan. 11 **Litho.** **Perf. 12**
1717	A357	25q gold & multi	.35	.25
1718	A357	1.90 l gold & multi	2.25	.35

30th anniversary of proclamation of Albanian People's Republic.

Ice Hockey, Olympic Games' Emblem A358

Designs: 10q, Speed skating. 15q, Biathlon. 50q, Ski jump. 1.20 l, Slalom. 2.15 l, Figure skating, pairs. 2.30 l, One-man bobsled.

1976, Feb. 4
1719	A358	5q silver & multi	.25	.25
1720	A358	10q silver & multi	.25	.25
1721	A358	15q silver & multi	.25	.25
1722	A358	50q silver & multi	.35	.25
1723	A358	1.20 l silver & multi	1.10	.25
1724	A358	2.30 l silver & multi	2.00	.40
	Nos. 1719-1724 (6)		4.20	1.65

Miniature Sheet
Perf. 12 on 2 sides x Imperf.
1725	A358	2.15 l silver & multi	3.25	2.00

12th Winter Olympic Games, Innsbruck, Austria, Feb. 4-15.

Meadow Saffron A359

Medicinal Plants: 10q, Deadly night-shade. 15q, Yellow gentian. 20q, Horse chestnut. 70q, Shield fern. 80q, Marshmallow. 2.30 l, Thorn apple.

1976, Apr. 10 **Litho.** **Perf. 12x12½**
1726	A359	5q black & multi	.25	.25
1727	A359	10q black & multi	.25	.25
1728	A359	15q black & multi	.25	.25
1729	A359	20q black & multi	.25	.25
1730	A359	70q black & multi	.35	.25
1731	A359	80q black & multi	.60	.25
1732	A359	2.30 l black & multi	1.75	.35
	Nos. 1726-1732 (7)		3.70	1.85

Bowl and Spoon — A360

15q, Flask, vert. 20q, Carved handles, vert. 25q, Pistol and dagger. 80q, Wall hanging, vert. 1.20 l, Earrings and belt buckle. 1.40 l, Jugs, vert.

1976 **Litho.** **Perf. 12½x12, 12x12½**
1733	A360	10q lilac & multi	.25	.25
1734	A360	15q gray & multi	.25	.25
1735	A360	20q multi	.25	.25
1736	A360	25q car & multi	.25	.25
1737	A360	80q yellow & multi	.25	.25
1738	A360	1.20 l multi	.75	.30
1739	A360	1.40 l tan & multi	1.50	.40
	Nos. 1733-1739 (7)		3.50	1.95

Natl. Ethnographic Conf., Tirana, June 28. For surcharge see No. 1873.

Founding of Cooperatives, by Zef Shoshi — A361

Paintings: 10q, Going to Work, by Agim Zajmi, vert. 25q, Crowd Listening to Loudspeaker, by Vilson Kilica. 40q, Woman Welder, by Sabaudin Xhaferi, vert. 50q, Factory, by Isuf Sulovari, vert. 1.20 l, 1942 Revolt, by Lec Shkreli, vert. 1.60 l, Coming Home from Work, by Agron Dine. 2.05 l, Honoring a Young Pioneer, by Andon Lakuriqi.

Perf. 12½x12, 12x12½
1976, Aug. 8 **Litho.**
1740	A361	5q gold & multi	.25	.25
1741	A361	10q gold & multi	.25	.25
1742	A361	25q gold & multi	.25	.25
1743	A361	40q gold & multi	.25	.25
1744	A361	50q gold & multi	.25	.25
1745	A361	1.20 l gold & multi	.75	.55
1746	A361	1.60 l gold & multi	1.00	.85
	Nos. 1740-1746 (7)		3.00	2.65

Miniature Sheet
Perf. 12 on 2 sides x Imperf.
1747	A361	2.05 l gold & multi	2.00	1.50

Red Flag, Agricultural Symbols — A362

Design: 1.20 l, Red flag and raised pickax.

1976, Nov. 1
1748	A362	25q multi	.30	.25
1749	A362	1 l multi	1.75	.50

7th Workers Party Congress.

Enver Hoxha, Partisans and Albanian Flag — A363

1.90 l, Demonstrators with Albanian flag.

1976, Oct. 28   **Perf. 12x12½**
1750 A363   25q multi   .40 .25
1751 A363   1.90 l multi   1.60 .65

Anti-Fascist demonstrations, 35th anniv.

Attacking Partisans, Meeting House A364

Designs (Red Flag and): 25q, Partisans, pickax and gun. 80q, Workers, soldiers, pickax and gun. 1.20 l, Agriculture and industry. 1.70 l, Dancers, symbols of science and art.

1976, Nov. 8   **Litho.**   **Perf. 12x12½**
1752 A364   15q gold & multi   .25 .25
1753 A364   25q gold & multi   .25 .25
1754 A364   80q gold & multi   .70 .25
1755 A364   1.20 l gold & multi   1.00 .25
1756 A364   1.70 l gold & multi   1.40 .25
   Nos. 1752-1756 (5)   3.60 1.25

35th anniv. of 1st Workers Party Congress.

Young Workers and Track A365

1.25 l, Young soldiers and Albanian flag.

1976, Nov. 23   **Perf. 12**
1757 A365   80q yellow & multi   1.25 .35
1758 A365   1.25 l carmine & multi   2.25 .50

Union of Young Communists, 35th anniv.

"Cuca e Maleve" Ballet A366

Scenes from ballet "Mountain Girl."

1976, Dec. 14   **Perf. 12**
1759 A366   10q gold & multi   .25 .50
1760 A366   15q gold & multi   .25 .50
1761 A366   20q gold & multi   .25 1.00
1762 A366   25q gold & multi   .30 2.00
1763 A366   80q gold & multi   .85 3.00
1764 A366   1.20 l gold & multi   1.00 4.00
1765 A366   1.40 l gold & multi   1.40 4.00
   Nos. 1759-1765 (7)   4.30 15.00

Miniature Sheet
Perf. 12 on 2 sides x Imperf.
1766 A366   2.05 l gold & multi   2.75 2.75

Bashtove Castle A367

Albanian Castles: 15q, Gjirokastres. 20q, Ali Pash Tepelene. 25q, Petrele. 80q, Berat. 1.20 l, Durres. 1.40 l, Kruje.

1976, Dec. 30   **Litho.**   **Perf. 12**
1767 A367   10q black & dull bl   .25 .25
1768 A367   15q black & grn   .25 .25
1769 A367   20q black & gray   .25 .25
1770 A367   25q black & brn   .35 .25
1771 A367   80q black & rose   1.00 .35
1772 A367   1.20 l black & vio   1.60 .50
1773 A367   1.40 l black & brn red   1.75 .55
   Nos. 1767-1773 (7)   5.45 2.40

Skanderbeg's Shield and Spear — A368

Skanderbeg's Weapons: 80q, Helmet, sword and scabbard. 1 l, Halberd, quiver with arrows, crossbow and spear.

1977, Jan. 28   **Litho.**   **Perf. 12**
1774 A368   15q silver & multi   1.25 .40
1775 A368   80q silver & multi   4.25 2.50
1776 A368   1 l silver & multi   6.50 5.00
   Nos. 1774-1776 (3)   12.00 7.90

Skanderbeg (1403-1468), national hero.

Ilia Qiqi, Messenger in Storm — A369

Modern Heroes: 10q, Ilia Dashi, sailor in battle. 25q, Fran Ndue Ivanaj, fisherman in storm. 80q, Zeliha Allmetaj, woman rescuing child. 1 l, Ylli Zaimi, rescuing goats from flood. 1.90 l, Isuf Plloci, fighting forest fire.

1977, Feb. 28   **Litho.**   **Perf. 12x12½**
1777 A369   5q brown & multi   .25 .25
1778 A369   10q ultra & multi   .25 .25
1779 A369   25q blue & multi   .40 .25
1780 A369   80q ocher & multi   .90 .35
1781 A369   1 l brown & multi   1.25 .45
1782 A369   1.90 l brown & multi   2.60 1.40
   Nos. 1777-1782 (6)   5.65 2.95

Polyvinylchloride Plant, Vlore — A370

6th Five-year plan: 25q, Naphtha fractioning plant, Ballsh. 65q, Hydroelectric station and dam, Fjerzes. 1 l, Metallurgical plant and blast furnace, Elbasan.

1977, Mar. 29   **Litho.**   **Perf. 12½x12**
1783 A370   15q silver & multi   .35 .25
1784 A370   25q silver & multi   .40 .25
1785 A370   65q silver & multi   1.10 .35
1786 A370   1 l silver & multi   1.60 .65
   Nos. 1783-1786 (4)   3.45 1.50

Qerime Halil Galica — A371

Design: 1.25 l, Qerime Halil Galica "Shota" and father Azem Galica.

1977, Apr. 20   **Litho.**   **Perf. 12**
1787 A371   80q dark red   1.10 .30
1788 A371   1.25 l gray blue   1.60 .70

"Shota" Galica, communist fighter.

Victory Monument, Tirana — A372

Red Star and: 80q, Clenched fist, Albanian flag. 1.20 l, Bust of Qemal Stafa, poppies.

1977, May 5   **Litho.**   **Perf. 12**
1789 A372   25q multi   .35 .25
1790 A372   80q multi   1.25 .45
1791 A372   1.20 l multi   2.00 .85
   Nos. 1789-1791 (3)   3.60 1.55

35th anniversary of Martyrs' Day.

Physician Visiting Farm, Mobile Clinic — A373

10q, Cowherd, cattle ranch. 20q, Militia woman helping with harvest, rifle, combine. 80q, Modern village, highway, power lines. 2.95 l, Tractor, greenhouses.

1977, June 18
1792 A373   5q multi   .25 .25
1793 A373   10q multi   .25 .25
1794 A373   20q multi   .30 .25
1795 A373   80q multi   1.00 .25
1796 A373   2.95 l multi   3.50 .75
   Nos. 1792-1796 (5)   5.30 1.75

"Socialist transformation of the villages."

Armed Workers, Flag and Factory — A374

1.80 l, Workers with proclamation and flags.

1977, June 20
1797 A374   25q multi   1.00 .25
1798 A374   1.80 l multi   1.50 .80

9th Labor Unions Congress.

Kerchief Dance — A375

Designs: Various folk dances.

1977, Aug. 20   **Litho.**   **Perf. 12**
1799 A375   5q multi   .25 .25
1800 A375   10q multi   .25 .25
1801 A375   15q multi   .25 .25
1802 A375   25q multi   .25 .25
1803 A375   80q multi   .25 .25
1804 A375   1.20 l multi   .70 .35
1805 A375   1.55 l multi   1.00 .45
   Nos. 1799-1805 (7)   2.95 2.05

Miniature Sheet
Perf. 12 on 2 sides x Imperf.
1806 A375   2.05 l multi   2.25 2.00

See Nos. 1836-1840, 1884-1888.

Attack A376

Designs: 25q, Enver Hoxha addressing Army. 80q, Volunteers and riflemen. 1 l, Volunteers, hydrofoil patrolboat and MiG planes. 1.90 l, Volunteers and Albanian flag.

1977, July 10   **Litho.**   **Perf. 12**
1807 A376   25q gold & multi   .35 .25
1808 A376   25q gold & multi   .35 .25
1809 A376   80q gold & multi   1.00 .35
1810 A376   1 l gold & multi   1.75 .50
1811 A376   1.90 l gold & multi   2.75 .90
   Nos. 1807-1811 (5)   6.20 2.25

"One People-One Army."

Armed Workers, Article 3 of Constitution A377

Design: 1.20 l, Symbols of farming and fertilizer industry, Article 25 of Constitution.

1977, Oct.
1812 A377   25q red, gold & blk   .40 .25
1813 A377   1.20 l red, gold & blk   1.50 .50

New Constitution.

Picnic — A378

Film Frames: 15q, Telephone lineman in winter. 25q, Two men and a woman. 80q, Workers. 1.20 l, Boys playing in street. 1.60 l, Harvest.

1977, Oct. 25   **Litho.**   **Perf. 12½x12**
1814 A378   10q blue green   .35 .35
1815 A378   15q multi   .35 .35
1816 A378   25q black   .35 .35
1817 A378   80q multi   1.40 1.40
1818 A378   1.20 l deep claret   2.00 2.00
1819 A378   1.60 l multi   2.25 2.25
   Nos. 1814-1819 (6)   6.70 6.70

Albanian films.

Farm Workers in Field, by V. Mio A379

Paintings by V. Mio: 10q, Landscape in Snow. 15q, Grazing Sheep under Walnut Tree in Spring. 25q, Street in Korce. 80q, Horseback Riders on Mountain Pass. 1 l, Boats on Shore. 1.75 l, Tractors Plowing Fields. 2.05 l, Self-portrait.

1977, Dec. 25   **Litho.**   **Perf. 12½x12**
1820 A379   5q gold & multi   .25 .25
1821 A379   10q gold & multi   .25 .25
1822 A379   15q gold & multi   .25 .25
1823 A379   25q gold & multi   .25 .25
1824 A379   80q gold & multi   .35 .25
1825 A379   1 l gold & multi   .60 .25
1826 A379   1.75 l gold & multi   1.00 .25
   Nos. 1820-1826 (7)   2.95 1.75

Miniature Sheet
Imperf.; Perf. 12 Horiz. between Vignette and Value Panel
1827 A379   2.05 l gold & multi   2.50 2.25

Pan Flute — A380

Folk Musical Instruments: 25q, Single-string goat's-head fiddle. 80q, Woodwind. 1.20 l, Drum. 1.70 l, Bagpipe. Background shows various woven folk patterns.

1978, Jan. 20   **Perf. 12x12½**
1828	A380	15q multi	.40	.25
1829	A380	25q multi	.75	.25
1830	A380	80q multi	2.00	1.00
1831	A380	1.20 l multi	3.50	2.00
1832	A380	1.70 l multi	9.00	3.50
	Nos. 1828-1832 (5)		15.65	7.00

Albanian Flag, Monument and People — A381

25q, Ismail Qemali, fighters, horiz. 1.65 l, People dancing around Albanian flag, horiz.

Perf. 12½x12, 12x12½
1977, Nov. 28
1833	A381	15q multi	.25	.25
1834	A381	25q multi	.30	.25
1835	A381	1.65 l multi	2.40	2.00
	Nos. 1833-1835 (3)		2.95	2.50

65th anniversary of independence.

Folk Dancing Type of 1977

Designs: Various dances.

1978, Feb. 15   **Litho.**   **Perf. 12**
1836	A375	5q multi	.25	.25
1837	A375	25q multi	.25	.25
1838	A375	80q multi	.75	.30
1839	A375	1 l multi	.75	.40
1840	A375	2.30 l multi	1.75	1.40
	Nos. 1836-1840 (5)		3.75	2.60

Nos. 1836-1840 have white background around dancers, Nos. 1799-1805 have pinkish shadows.

Tractor Drivers, by Dhimitraq Trebicka A382

Working Class Paintings: 80q, Steeplejack, by Spiro Kristo. 85q, "A Point in the Discussion," by Skender Milori. 90q, Oil rig crew, by Anesti Cini, vert. 1.60 l, Metal workers, by Ramadan Karanxha. 2.20 l, Political discussion, by Sotiraq Sholla.

1978, Mar. 25   **Litho.**   **Perf. 12**
1841	A382	25q multi	.30	.25
1842	A382	80q multi	.50	.25
1843	A382	85q multi	.60	.25
1844	A382	90q multi	.70	.30
1845	A382	1.60 l multi	1.25	.90
	Nos. 1841-1845 (5)		3.35	1.95

Miniature Sheet
Perf. 12 on 2 sides x Imperf.
1846	A382	2.20 l multi	6.00	3.50

Woman with Rifle and Pickax A383

1.95 l, Farm & Militia women, industrial plant.

1978, June 1   **Litho.**   **Perf. 12**
1847	A383	25q gold & red	.35	.25
1848	A383	1.95 l gold & red	5.25	1.50

8th Congress of Women's Union.

Children and Flowers — A384

Designs: 10q, Children with rifle, ax, book and flags. 25q, Dancing children in folk costume. 1.80 l, Children in school.

1978, June 1   **Litho.**
1849	A384	5q multi	.25	.25
1850	A384	10q multi	.25	.25
1851	A384	25q multi	.45	.25
1852	A384	1.80 l multi	3.00	.90
	Nos. 1849-1852 (4)		3.95	1.65

International Children's Day.

Spirit of Skanderbeg as Conqueror A385

10q, Battle at Mostar Bridge. 80q, Marchers, Albanian flag. 1.20 l, Riflemen in winter battle. 1.65 l, Abdyl Frasheri (1839-92). 2.20 l, Rifles, scroll, pen, League building. 2.60 l, League headquarters, Prizren.

1978, June 10   **Litho.**   **Perf. 12**
1853	A385	10q multi	.25	.25
1854	A385	25q multi	.25	.30
1855	A385	80q multi	1.25	.75
1856	A385	1.20 l multi	1.75	1.00
1857	A385	1.65 l multi	2.75	1.50
1858	A385	2.60 l multi	4.50	4.50
	Nos. 1853-1858 (6)		10.75	8.30

Miniature Sheet
Perf. 12 on 2 sides x Imperf.
1859	A385	2.20 l multi	3.00	2.25

Centenary of League of Prizren.

Guerrillas and Flag, 1943 — A386

Designs: 25q, Soldier, sailor, airman, militiaman, horiz. 1.90 l, Members of armed forces, civil guards, and Young Pioneers.

1978, July 10   **Perf. 11½x12½**
1860	A386	5q multi	.75	.25
1861	A386	25q multi	1.25	.25
1862	A386	1.90 l multi	6.50	3.50
	Nos. 1860-1862 (3)		8.50	4.00

35th anniversary of People's Army.

Woman with Machine Carbine — A387

25q, Man with target rifle, horiz. 95q, Man shooting with telescopic sights, horiz. 2.40 l, Woman target shooting with pistol.

Perf. 12½x12, 12x12½
1978, Sept. 20   **Litho.**
1863	A387	25q black & yel	.25	.25
1864	A387	80q orange & blk	.50	.50
1865	A387	95q red & blk	.75	.50
1866	A387	2.40 l carmine & blk	1.90	1.50
	Nos. 1863-1866 (4)		3.40	2.60

32nd National Rifle-shooting Championships, Sept. 20.

Kerchief Dance — A388

15q, Musicians. 25q, Fiddler with single-stringed instrument. 80q, Dancers, men. 1.20 l, Saber dance. 1.90 l, Singers, women.

1978, Oct. 6   **Perf. 12**
1867	A388	10q multi	.25	.25
1868	A388	15q multi	.25	.25
1869	A388	25q multi	.25	.25
1870	A388	80q multi	.25	.25
1871	A388	1.20 l multi	1.00	.25
1872	A388	1.90 l multi	2.00	1.25
	Nos. 1867-1872 (6)		4.00	2.50

National Folklore Festival.
See Nos. 2082-2085, 2289-2290.

No. 1736 Surcharged with New Value, 2 Bars and "RICCIONE 78"
1978   **Litho.**   **Perf. 12½x12**
1873	A360	3.30 l on 25q multi	12.00	12.00

Riccione 78 Philatelic Exhibition.

Enver Hoxha A389

1978, Oct. 16   **Litho.**   **Perf. 12x12½**
1874	A389	80q red & multi	.40	.35
1875	A389	1.20 l red & multi	.75	.35
1876	A389	2.40 l red & multi	1.50	1.00
	Nos. 1874-1876 (3)		2.65	1.70

Miniature Sheet
Perf. 12½ on 2 sides x Imperf.
1877	A389	2.20 l multi	3.50	2.00

70th birthday of Enver Hoxha, First Secretary of Central Committee of the Communist Party of Albania.

Woman and Wheat — A390

25q, Woman with egg crates. 80q, Shepherd, sheep. 2.60 l, Milkmaid, cows.

1978, Dec. 15   **Perf. 12x12½**
1878	A390	15q multicolored	.40	.40
1879	A390	25q multicolored	.55	.40
1880	A390	80q multicolored	2.00	1.50
1881	A390	2.60 l multicolored	7.50	5.00
	Nos. 1878-1881 (4)		10.45	7.30

Dora d'Istria — A391

Design: 1.10 l, Full portrait of Dora d'Istria, author; birth sesquicentennial.

1979, Jan. 22   **Litho.**   **Perf. 12**
1882	A391	80q lt grn & blk	1.10	.75
1883	A391	1.10 l vio brn & blk	1.90	1.50

Folk Dancing Type of 1977

Designs: Various folk dances.

1979, Feb. 25
1884	A375	15q multi	.35	.25
1885	A375	25q multi	.35	.25
1886	A375	80q multi	1.50	.75
1887	A375	1.20 l multi	1.75	1.00
1888	A375	1.40 l multi	2.00	1.40
	Nos. 1884-1888 (5)		5.95	3.65

Nos. 1884-1888 have white background. Denomination in UL on No. 1885, in UR on No. 1802; LL on No.1886, UL on No. 1803.

Tower House — A392

Traditional Houses: 15q, Stone gallery house, horiz. 80q, House with wooden galleries, horiz. 1.20 l, Galleried tower house. 1.40 l, 1.90 l, Tower houses, diff.

1979, Mar. 20
1889	A392	15q multi	.25	.25
1890	A392	25q multi	.25	.25
1891	A392	80q multi	.75	.25
1892	A392	1.20 l multi	1.00	.45
1893	A392	1.40 l multi	1.50	.65
	Nos. 1889-1893 (5)		3.75	1.85

Miniature Sheet
Perf. 12 on 2 sides x Imperf.
1894	A392	1.90 l multi	5.25	3.75

See Nos. 2015-2018.

Soldier, Factories, Wheat A393

1.65 l, Soldiers, workers and coat of arms.

1979, May 14   **Litho.**   **Perf. 12**
1895	A393	25q multi	.75	.35
1896	A393	1.65 l multi	3.50	2.00

Congress of Permet, 35th anniversary.

Albanian Flag A394

1979, June 4
1897	A394	25q multi	.75	.35
1898	A394	1.65 l multi	3.50	2.25

5th Congress of Albanian Democratic Front.

Alexander Moissi, (1880-1935), Actor — A395

1979, Apr 2
1899	A395	80q multi	1.00	.35
1900	A395	1.10 l multi, diff.	1.50	1.00

Vasil Shanto, (1913-44)
A396

Design: 25q, 90q, Qemal Stafa (1921-42).

1979, May 5
1901	A396	15q multi	.25	.25
1902	A396	25q multi	.40	.25
1903	A396	60q multi	1.40	.60
1904	A396	90q multi	2.25	1.50
	Nos. 1901-1904 (4)		4.30	2.60

Shanto and Stafa, anti-Fascist fighters. For similar design see A410.

Winter Campaign, by Arben Basha — A397

Paintings of Military Scenes by: 25q, Ismail Lulani. 80q, Myrteza Fushekati. 1.20 l, Muhamet Deliu. 1.40 l, Jorgji Gjikopulli. 1.90 l, Fatmir Haxhiu.

1979, July 15   Litho.   Perf. 12½x12
1905	A397	15q multi	.25	.25
1906	A397	25q multi	.25	.25
1907	A397	80q multi	.75	.25
1908	A397	1.20 l multi	1.00	.45
1909	A397	1.40 l multi	1.50	.75
	Nos. 1905-1909 (5)		3.75	1.95

Miniature Sheet
Perf. 12 on 2 sides x Imperf.
1910	A397	1.90 l multi	2.75	2.00

Athletes Surrounding Flag — A398

1979, Oct. 1   Litho.   Perf. 12
1911	A398	15q shown	.25	.25
1912	A398	25q Shooting	.25	.25
1913	A398	80q Dancing	.70	.25
1914	A398	1.20 l Soccer	.85	.60
1915	A398	1.40 l High jump	1.20	.85
	Nos. 1911-1915 (5)		3.25	2.20

Liberation Spartakiad, 35th anniversary.

Literary Society Headquarters A399

Albanian Literary Society Centenary: 25q, Seal and charter. 80q, Founder. 1.55 l, 1879 Headquarters. 1.90 l, Founders.

1979, Oct. 12
1916	A399	25q multi	.25	.25
1917	A399	80q multi	.75	.35
1918	A399	1.20 l multi	1.00	.60
1919	A399	1.55 l multi	1.25	.75
	Nos. 1916-1919 (4)		3.25	1.95

Miniature Sheet
Perf. 12½ on 2 sides x Imperf.
1920	A399	1.90 l multi		2.50 2.00

Congress Statute, Coat of Arms — A400

1979, Oct. 20   Photo.   Perf. 12x12½
1921	A400	25q multi	.75	.75
1922	A400	1.65 l multi	3.00	2.50

2nd Congress of Berat, 35th anniversary.

Children Entering School, Books — A401

10q, Communications. 15q, Steel workers. 20q, Dancers, instruments. 25q, Newspapers, radio, television. 60q, Textile worker. 80q, Armed forces. 1.20 l, Industry. 1.60 l, Transportation. 2.40 l, Agriculture. 3 l, Medicine.

1979   Litho.   Perf. 12½x12
1923	A401	5q shown	.25	.25
1924	A401	10q multi	.25	.25
1925	A401	15q multi	.25	.25
1926	A401	20q multi	.25	.25
1927	A401	25q multi	.25	.25
1928	A401	60q multi	1.00	.25
1929	A401	80q multi	1.40	.25
1930	A401	1.20 l multi	2.40	.25
1931	A401	1.60 l multi	3.25	.40
1932	A401	2.40 l multi	5.00	.45
1932A	A401	3 l multi	6.75	.60
	Nos. 1923-1932A (11)		21.05	3.45

Workers and Factory A402

Worker, Red Flag and: 80q, Hand holding sickle and rifle. 1.20 l, Red star and open book. 1.55 l, Open book and cogwheel.

1979, Nov. 29
1933	A402	25q multi	.25	.25
1934	A402	80q multi	.75	.35
1935	A402	1.20 l multi	.90	.75
1936	A402	1.55 l multi	1.50	.90
	Nos. 1933-1936 (4)		3.40	2.25

35th anniversary of independence.

Joseph Stalin — A403

Design: 1.10 l, Stalin on dais, horiz.

1979, Dec. 21   Litho.   Perf. 12
1937	A403	80q red & dk bl	1.10	.75
1938	A403	1.10 l red & dk bl	1.50	1.50

Joseph Stalin (1879-1953), birth centenary.

Fireplace and Pottery, Korcar A404

Home Furnishings: 80q, Cupboard bed, dagger, pistol, ammunition pouch, Shkodar. 1.20 l, Stool, pot, chair, Mirdit. 1.35 l, Chimney, dagger, jacket, Gjirokaster.

1980, Feb. 27   Litho.   Perf. 12
1939	A404	25q multi	.25	.25
1940	A404	80q multi	.50	.50
1941	A404	1.20 l multi	1.10	.70
1942	A404	1.35 l multi	1.50	1.50
	Nos. 1939-1942 (4)		3.35	3.00

See Nos. 1985-1988.

Pipe, Painted Flask A405

80q, Leather handbags. 1.20 l, Carved eagle, embroidered rug. 1.35 l, Lace.

1980, Mar. 4
1943	A405	25q shown	.25	.25
1944	A405	80q multi	.50	.50
1945	A405	1.20 l multi	1.10	.75
1946	A405	1.35 l multi	1.50	1.50
	Nos. 1943-1946 (4)		3.35	3.00

Prof. Aleksander Xhuvanit Birth Centenary A406

1980, Mar. 14
1947	A406	80q multi	1.60	1.20
1948	A406	1 l multi	2.00	2.00

Revolutionaries on Horseback — A407

Insurrection at Kosove, 70th Anniversary: 1 l, Battle scene.

1980, Apr. 4
1949	A407	80q red & black	1.50	1.10
1950	A407	1 l red & black	2.25	1.90

Soldiers and Workers Laboring to Aid the Stricken Populations, by D. Jukniu and I. Lulani — A408

1980, Apr. 15   Litho.   Perf. 12½
1951	A408	80q lt blue & multi	1.50	1.10
1952	A408	1 l lt blue grn & multi	2.25	1.90

Lenin, 110th Birth Anniversary A409

1980, Apr. 22
1953	A409	80q multi	1.50	1.10
1954	A409	1 l multi	2.25	1.90

Misto Mame and Ali Demi, War Martyrs A410

War Martyrs: 80q, Sadik Staveleci, Vojo Kusji, Hoxhi Martini. 1.20 l, Bule Naipi, Persefoni Kokedhima. 1.35 l, Ndoc Deda, Hydajet Lezha, Naim Gyylbegu, Ndoc Mazi, Ahmed Haxha.

1980, May 5
1955	A410	25q multi	.25	.25
1956	A410	80q multi	.70	.50
1957	A410	1.20 l multi	1.20	.70
1958	A410	1.35 l multi	1.40	1.40
	Nos. 1955-1958 (4)		3.55	2.85

See Nos. 2012A-2012D, 2025-2028, 2064-2067, 2122-2125, 2171-2174, 2207-2209.

Scene from "Mirela" A411

1980, June 7
1959	A411	15q shown	.25	.25
1960	A411	25q The Scribbler	.25	.25
1961	A411	80q Circus Bears	.80	.80
1962	A411	2.40 l Waterdrops	2.75	2.75
	Nos. 1959-1962 (4)		4.05	4.05

Carrying Iron Castings in the Enver Hoxha Tractor Combine, by S. Shijaku and M. Fushekati — A412

Paintings (Gallery of Figurative Paintings, Tirana): 80q, The Welder, by Harilla Dhima. 1.20 l, Steel Erectors, by Petro Kokushta. 1.35 l, Pandeli Lena, 1.80 l Communists, by Vilson Kilica.

1980, July 22
1963	A412	25q multi	.25	.25
1964	A412	80q multi	.70	.70
1965	A412	1.20 l multi	1.20	1.20
1966	A412	1.35 l multi	1.40	1.40
	Nos. 1963-1966 (4)		3.55	3.55

Imperf
1967	A412	1.80 l multi	2.50	2.50

No. 1967 measures 66x82mm and has a row of perforations above and below the vignette.

Gate, Parchment Miniature, 11th Cent. — A413

Bas reliefs of the Middle Ages: 80q, Eagle, 13th cent. 1.20 l, Heraldic lion, 14th cent. 1.35 l, Pheasant, 14th cent.

1980, Sept. 27   Litho.   Perf. 12
1968	A413	25q gold & blk	.25	.25
1969	A413	80q gold & blk	.55	.55
1970	A413	1.20 l gold & blk	1.20	1.20
1971	A413	1.35 l gold & blk	1.20	1.20
	Nos. 1968-1971 (4)		3.20	3.20

Divjaka National Park A414

1980, Nov. 6   **Photo.**
1972 A414   80q shown   .75   .60
1973 A414   1.20 l Lura   1.10   1.10
1974 A414   1.60 l Thethi   1.90   1.60
    Nos. 1972-1974 (3)   3.75   3.30

Souvenir Sheet
Perf. 12½ Horiz.
1975 A414   1.80 l Llogara Park   3.50   3.50

Citizens, Flag and Arms of Albania A415

1 l, People's Party Headquarters, Tirana.

1981, Jan. 11   **Litho.**   **Perf. 12**
1976 A415   80q multicolored   1.00   .70
1977 A415   1 l multicolored   1.40   .70

35th anniversary of the Republic.

Child's Bed A416

80q, Wooden bucket, brass bottle. 1.20 l, Shoes. 1.35 l, Jugs.

1981, Mar. 20   **Litho.**   **Perf. 12**
1978 A416   25q multicolored   .25   .25
1979 A416   80q multicolored   .50   .40
1980 A416   1.20 l multicolored   .80   .70
1981 A416   1.35 l multicolored   1.00   .90
    Nos. 1978-1981 (4)   2.55   2.25

A417

80q, Soldiers. 1 l, Sword combat. 1.80 l, Soldier with pistol.

1981, Apr. 20
1982 A417   80q multicolored   .70   .70
1983 A417   1 l multicolored   .85   .70

Souvenir Sheet
Perf. 12½ Vert.
1984 A417   1.80 l multicolored   3.25   2.75

Battle of Shtimje centenary.

Home Furnishings Type of 1980

25q, House interior, Labara. 80q, Labara, diff. 1.20 l, Mat. 1.35 l, Dibres.

1981, Feb. 25   **Litho.**   **Perf. 12**
1985 A404   25q multicolored   .25   .25
1986 A404   80q multicolored   .35   .25
1987 A404   1.20 l multicolored   .85   .40
1988 A404   1.35 l multicolored   1.00   .90
    Nos. 1985-1988 (4)   2.45   1.80

A419

Designs: Children's circus.

1981, June   **Perf. 12**
1989 A419   15q multi   .25   .25
1990 A419   25q multi   .50   .40
1991 A419   80q multi   .80   .65
1992 A419   2.40 l multi   1.00   .90
    Nos. 1989-1992 (4)   2.55   2.20

Soccer Players A420

1982 World Cup Soccer Elimination Games: Various soccer players.

1981, Mar. 31   **Litho.**   **Perf. 12**
1993 A420   25q multi   .75   .35
1994 A420   80q multi   2.60   1.50
1995 A420   1.20 l multi   3.75   2.60
1996 A420   1.35 l multi   4.50   3.00
    Nos. 1993-1996 (4)   11.60   7.45

Allies, by S. Hysa A421

Paintings: 80q, Warriors, by A. Buza. 1.20 l, Rallying to the Flag, Dec. 1911, by A. Zajmi, vert. 1.35 l, My Flag is My Heart, by L. Cefa, vert. 1.80 l, Circling the Flag in a Common Cause, by N. Vasia.

1981, July 10   **Perf. 12½x12**
1997 A421   25q multi   .25   .25
1998 A421   80q multi   .75   .35
1999 A421   1.20 l multi   .85   .75
2000 A421   1.35 l multi   1.50   .85
    Nos. 1997-2000 (4)   3.35   2.20

Souvenir Sheet
Perf. 12½ Horiz.
2001 A421   1.80 l multi   3.50   2.50

No. 2001 contains one 55x55mm stamp.

Rifleman A422

1981, Aug. 30   **Perf. 12**
2002 A422   25q shown   .25   .25
2003 A422   80q Weight lifting   .50   .35
2004 A422   1.20 l Volleyball   .75   .65
2005 A422   1.35 l Soccer   1.00   .75
    Nos. 2002-2005 (4)   2.50   2.00

Albanian Workers' Party, 8th Congress A423

80q, Flag, star. 1 l, Flag, hammer & sickle.

1981, Nov. 1
2006 A423   80q multicolored   .60   .45
2007 A423   1 l multicolored   .85   .75

Albanian Workers' Party, 40th Anniv. — A424

80q, Symbols of industrialization. 2.80 l, Fist, emblem.
1.80 l, Enver Hoxha, Memoirs.

1981, Nov. 8
2008 A424   80q multicolored   .35   .35
2009 A424   2.80 l multicolored   1.75   1.40

Souvenir Sheet
Perf. 12 Horiz.
2010 A424   1.80 l multicolored   3.75   3.75

Communist Youth Org., 40th Anniv. — A425

1981, Nov. 23
2011 A425   80q Star, ax, map   .75   .75
2012 A425   1 l Flags, star   1.50   1.40

War Martyrs Type of 1980

25q, Perlat Rexhepi (1919-42) and Branko Kadia (1921-42). 80q, Xheladin Beqiri (1908-44) and Hajdar Dushi (1916-44). 1.20 l, Koci Bako (1905-41), Vasil Laci (1923-41) and Mujo Ulqinaku (1898-1939). 1.35 l, Mine Peza (1875-1942) and Zoja Cure (1920-44).

1981, May 5   **Litho.**   **Perf. 12**
2012A A410   25q silver & multi   .25   .25
2012B A410   80q gold & multi   1.00   .35
2012C A410   1.20 l silver & multi   1.25   .75
2012D A410   1.35 l gold & multi   2.00   .85
    Nos. 2012A-2012D (4)   4.50   2.20

Fan S. Noli, Writer, Birth Centenary A426

1982, Jan. 6   **Litho.**   **Perf. 12**
2013 A426   80q lt ol grn & gold   1.00   .50
2014 A426   1.10 l lt red brn & gold   1.25   .75

Traditional Houses Type of 1979
1982, Feb.   **Perf. 12½x12**
2015 A392   25q Bulqize   .25   .25
2016 A392   80q Lebush   1.00   .70
2017 A392   1.20 l Bicaj   1.50   1.00
2018 A392   1.55 l Klos   2.00   1.25
    Nos. 2015-2018 (4)   4.75   3.20

TB Bacillus Centenary A428

1982, Mar. 24   **Perf. 12**
2019 A428   80q Globe   3.75   1.50
2020 A428   1.10 l Koch   5.25   2.50

Albanian League House, Prizren, by K. Buza — A429

Kosova Landscapes: 25q, Castle at Prizrenit, by G. Madhi. 1.20 l, Mountain Gorge at Rogove, by K. Buza. 1.55 l, Street of the Hadhji at Zekes, by G. Madhi. 25q, 1.20 l, 1.55 l vert.

Perf. 12x12½, 12½x12
1982, Apr. 15   **Litho.**
2021 A429   25q multi   .45   .25
2022 A429   80q multi   1.40   1.00
2023 A429   1.20 l multi   2.25   1.25
2024 A429   1.55 l multi   3.25   1.50
    Nos. 2021-2024 (4)   7.35   4.00

War Martyrs Type of 1980

Designs: 25q, Hibe Palikuqi, Liri Gero. 80q, Mihal Duri, Kajo Karafili. 1.20 l, Fato Dudumi, Margarita Tutulani, Shejnaze Juka. 1.55 l, Memo Meto, Gjok Doci.

1982, May   **Perf. 12**
2025 A410   25q multi   .35   .25
2026 A410   80q multi   .85   .60
2027 A410   1.20 l multi   1.25   .75
2028 A410   1.55 l multi   2.25   1.00
    Nos. 2025-2028 (4)   4.70   2.60

Loading Freighter — A430

Children's Paintings.

1982, June 15   **Perf. 12½x12**
2029 A430   15q shown   .50   .25
2030 A430   80q Forest   1.00   .45
2031 A430   1.20 l City   1.50   .90
2032 A430   1.65 l Park   3.00   1.25
    Nos. 2029-2032 (4)   6.00   2.85

9th Congress of Trade Unions A431

80q, Workers, factories. 1.10 l, Emblem, flag.

1982, June 6   **Litho.**   **Perf. 12**
2033 A431   80q multicolored   2.00   1.25
2034 A431   1.10 l multicolored   2.75   1.50

Alpine Village Festival, by Danish Jukniu A432

Industrial Development Paintings: 80q, Hydroelectric Station Builders, by Ali Miruku. 1.20 l, Steel Workers, by Clirim Ceka. 1.55 l, Oil drillers, by Pandeli Lena. 1.90 l, Trapping the Furnace, by Jorgji Gjikopulli.

1982, July   **Perf. 12½**
2035 A432   25q multi   .50   .25
2036 A432   80q multi   1.50   1.40
2037 A432   1.20 l multi   2.25   1.60
2038 A432   1.55 l multi   3.00   1.90
    Nos. 2035-2038 (4)   7.25   5.15

Souvenir Sheet
Perf. 12 Horiz.
2039 A432 1.90 l multi   4.00 2.75

No. 2039 contains one 54x48mm stamp.

Communist Party Newspaper "Voice of the People," 40th Anniv. — A432a

80q, Newspapers. 1.10 l, Paper, press.

1982, Aug. 25   **Litho.**   **Perf. 12**
2039A A432a 80q multi   75.00 70.00
2039B A432a 1.10 l multi   75.00 70.00

40th Anniv. of Democratic Front A433

80q, Glory to the Heroes of Peza Monument. 1.10 l, Marchers.

1982, Sept. 16   **Perf. 12**
2040 A433 80q multi   7.50 2.50
2041 A433 1.10 l multi   11.00 3.50

8th Youth Congress — A434

1982, Oct. 4
2042 A434 80q multi   6.00 3.00
2043 A434 1.10 l multi   10.00 4.50

Handmade Shoulder Bags — A435

25q, Rug, horiz. 1.20 l, Wooden pots, bowls, horiz. 1.55 l, Jug.

1982, Nov.
2044 A435 25q multi   .45 .25
2045 A435 80q multi   1.00 .60
2046 A435 1.20 l multi   1.40 .85
2047 A435 1.55 l multi   2.25 1.10
  Nos. 2044-2047 (4)   5.10 2.80

70th Anniv. of Independence — A436

20q, Ishamil Qemali. 1.20 l, Partisans. 2.40 l, Partisans, diff. 1.90 l, Independence Monument, Tirana.

1982, Nov. 28
2048 A436 20q multicolored   .35 .25
2049 A436 1.20 l multicolored   1.75 .90
2050 A436 2.40 l multicolored   3.00 1.75
  Nos. 2048-2050 (3)   5.10 2.90

Souvenir Sheet
Perf. 12 Horiz.
2051 A436 1.90 l multicolored   5.00 3.50

Dhermi Beach A437

1982, Dec. 20
2052 A437 25q shown   .25 .25
2053 A437 80q Sarande   .75 .45
2054 A437 1.20 l Ksamil   1.00 .90
2055 A437 1.55 l Lukove   1.50 1.00
  Nos. 2052-2055 (4)   3.50 2.60

Handkerchief Dancers — A438

Folkdancers — 80q, With kerchief, drum. 1.20 l, With guitar, flute, tambourine. 1.55 l, Women.

1983, Feb. 20   **Litho.**   **Perf. 12**
2056 A438 25q multi   .25 .25
2057 A438 80q multi   .60 .25
2058 A438 1.20 l multi   1.10 .75
2059 A438 1.55 l multi   1.50 1.10
  Nos. 2056-2059 (4)   3.45 2.35

A439

1983, Mar. 14   **Litho.**   **Perf. 12**
2060 A439 80q multi   1.50 .75
2061 A439 1.10 l multi   1.90 1.00

Karl Marx (1818-83).

A440

80q, Electricity generation. 1.10 l, Gas & oil production.

1983, Apr. 20
2062 A440 80q multi   1.00 .60
2063 A440 1.10 l multi   1.25 .90

Energy development.

War Martyrs Type of 1980

Designs: 25q, Asim Zeneli (1916-43), Nazmi Rushiti (1919-42). 80q, Shyqyri Ishmi (1922-42), Shyqyri Alimerko (1923-43), Myzafer Asqeriu (1918-42). 1.20 l, Qybra Sokoli (1924-44), Qeriba Derri (1905-44), Ylbere Bilibashi (1928-44). 1.55 l, Themo Vasi (1915-43), Abaz Shehu (1905-42).

1983, May 5   **Litho.**   **Perf. 12**
2064 A410 25q multi   .25 .25
2065 A410 80q multi   .75 .30
2066 A410 1.20 l multi   1.25 .75
2067 A410 1.55 l multi   1.90 1.00
  Nos. 2064-2067 (4)   4.15 2.30

Women's Union, 9th Congress A441

1983, June 1   **Litho.**   **Perf. 12x12½**
2068 A441 80q red & gold   1.40 .75
2069 A441 1.10 l blue & gold   1.75 1.00

Bicycling A442

1983, June 20   **Perf. 12**
2070 A442 25q shown   .25 .25
2071 A442 80q Chess   .75 .25
2072 A442 1.20 l Gymnastics   1.25 .75
2073 A442 1.55 l Wrestling   1.50 1.00
  Nos. 2070-2073 (4)   3.75 2.25

40th Anniv. of People's Army — A443

20q, Armed services. 1.20 l, Soldier, gun barrels. 2.40 l, Factory guard, crowd.

1983, July 10
2074 A443 20q multicolored   .25 .25
2075 A443 1.20 l multicolored   1.50 .75
2076 A443 2.40 l multicolored   2.50 1.25
  Nos. 2074-2076 (3)   4.25 2.25

Sunny Day, by Myrteza Fushekati — A444

Paintings: 80q, Messenger of the Grasp, by Niko Progi. 1.20 l, 29 November 1944, by Harilla Dhimo. 1.55 l, Fireworks, by Pandi Mele. 1.90 l, Partisan Assault, by Sali Shijaku and M. Fushekati.

1983, Aug. 28   **Litho.**   **Perf. 12½x12**
2077 A444 25q multi   .25 .25
2078 A444 80q multi   .85 .40
2079 A444 1.20 l multi   1.00 .75
2080 A444 1.55 l multi   1.50 .85
  Nos. 2077-2080 (4)   3.60 2.25

Souvenir Sheet
Perf. 12
2081 A444 1.90 l multi   8.50 6.00

Folklore Festival Type of 1978

Gjirokaster Folklore Festival: folkdances: 25q, Sword dance. 80q, Kerchief dance. 1.20 l, Shepherd flautists. 1.55 l, Garland dance.

1983, Oct. 6   **Litho.**   **Perf. 12**
2082 A388 25q multicolored   .25 .25
2083 A388 80q multicolored   1.50 .75
2084 A388 1.20 l multicolored   1.50 .90
2085 A388 1.55 l multicolored   3.00 2.00
  Nos. 2082-2085 (4)   6.25 3.90

World Communications Year — A446

1983, Nov. 10
2086 A446 60q multicolored   .50 .35
2087 A446 1.20 l multicolored   1.40 1.10

75th Birthday of Enver Hoxha A447

1983, Oct. 16   **Litho.**   **Perf. 12½**
2088 A447 80q multi   .90 .75
2089 A447 1.20 l multi   1.50 1.25
2090 A447 1.80 l multi   2.00 1.75
  Nos. 2088-2090 (3)   4.40 3.75

Souvenir Sheet
Perf. 12 Horiz.
2091 A447 1.90 l multi   3.00 3.00

The Right to a Joint Triumph, by J. Keraj A448

Era of Skanderbeg in Figurative Art: 80q, The Heroic Center of the Battle of Krujes, by N. Bakalli. 1.20 l, The Rights of the Enemy after our Triumph, by N. Progri. 1.55 l, The Discussion at Lezhes, by B. Ahmeti. 1.90 l, Victory over the Turks, by G. Madhi.

1983, Dec. 10   **Perf. 12½x12**
2092 A448 25q multi   .35 .25
2093 A448 80q multi   1.10 .75
2094 A448 1.20 l multi   1.50 .90
2095 A448 1.55 l multi   2.25 1.10
  Nos. 2092-2095 (4)   5.20 3.00

Souvenir Sheet
Perf. 12 Horiz.
2096 A448 1.90 l multi   7.50 7.50

Greco-Roman Ruins of Illyria — A449

80q, Amphitheater, Buthroxtum. 1.20 l, Colonnade, Apollonium. 1.80 l, Vaulted gallery, amphitheater at Epidamnus.

1983, Dec. 28   **Perf. 12**
2097 A449 80q multicolored   1.50 1.10
2098 A449 1.20 l multicolored   2.25 1.50
2099 A449 1.80 l multicolored   2.25 1.75
  Nos. 2097-2099 (3)   6.00 4.35

Archeological Discoveries A450

Designs: Apollo, 3rd cent. 25q, Tombstone, Korce, 3rd cent. 80q, Apollo, diff. 1st cent. 1.10 l, Earthenware pot (child's head), Tren, 1st cent. 1.20 l, Man's head, Dyrrah, 2.20 l, Eros with Dolphin, statue Bronze Dyrrah, 3rd cent.

1984, Feb. 25			Perf. 12x12½	
2100	A450	15q multi	.25	.25
2101	A450	25q multi	.25	.25
2102	A450	80q multi	.80	.50
2103	A450	1.10 l multi	1.20	.75
2104	A450	1.20 l multi	1.60	.85
2105	A450	2.20 l multi	2.50	1.00
	Nos. 2100-2105 (6)		6.60	3.60

Clock Towers — A451

1984, Mar. 30		Litho.	Perf. 12	
2106	A451	15q Gjirokaster	.25	.25
2107	A451	25q Kavaje	.25	.25
2108	A451	80q Elbasan	.80	.50
2109	A451	1.10 l Tirana	1.00	.75
2110	A451	1.20 l Peqin	1.25	.90
2111	A451	2.20 l Kruje	2.25	1.50
	Nos. 2106-2111 (6)		5.80	4.15

40th Anniv. of Liberation A452

15q, Student & microscope. 25q, Guerrilla with flag. 80q, Children with flag. 1.10 l, Soldier. 1.20 l, Workers with flag. 2.20 l, Militia at dam.

1984, Apr. 20		Litho.	Perf. 12	
2112	A452	15q multi	.25	.25
2113	A452	25q multi	.25	.25
2114	A452	80q multi	.90	.45
2115	A452	1.10 l multi	1.20	.75
2116	A452	1.20 l multi	1.50	.90
2117	A452	2.20 l multi	2.25	1.10
	Nos. 2112-2117 (6)		6.35	3.70

Children — A453

15q, Children reading. 25q, Young pioneers. 60q, Gardening. 2.80 l, Kite flying.

1984, May		Litho.	Perf. 12	
2118	A453	15q multicolored	.45	.25
2119	A453	25q multicolored	1.00	.25
2120	A453	60q multicolored	1.75	.90
2121	A453	2.80 l multicolored	3.25	1.60
	Nos. 2118-2121 (4)		6.45	3.00

War Martyrs Type of 1980

Designs: 15q, Manush Almani, Mustafa Matohiti, Kastriot Muco. 25q, Zaho Koka, Reshit Collaku, Maliq Muco. 1.20 l, Lefter Talo, Tom Kola, Fuat Babani. 2.20 l, Myslysm Shyri, Dervish Hexali, Skender Caci.

1984, May 5		Litho.	Perf. 12	
2122	A410	15q multi	.50	.25
2123	A410	25q multi	1.10	.25
2124	A410	1.20 l multi	2.00	.90
2125	A410	2.20 l multi	3.50	2.00
	Nos. 2122-2125 (4)		7.10	3.40

A454

80q, Enver Hoxha. 1.10 l, Resistance fighter.

1984, May 24		Litho.	Perf. 12	
2126	A454	80q multicolored	2.50	1.50
2127	A454	1.10 l multicolored	3.00	1.75

40th anniv. of Permet Congress.

A455

15q, Goalkeeper. 25q, Referee. 1.20 l, Map of Europe. 2.20 l, Field diagram.

1984, June 12		Litho.	Perf. 12	
2128	A455	15q multicolored	1.20	.25
2129	A455	25q multicolored	1.20	.25
2130	A455	1.20 l multicolored	3.50	.75
2131	A455	2.20 l multicolored	4.25	1.50
	Nos. 2128-2131 (4)		10.15	2.75

European soccer championships.

Freedom Came, by Myrteza Fushekati — A456

Paintings, Tirana Gallery of Figurative Art: 25q, Morning, by Zamir Mati, vert. 80q, My Darling, by Agim Zajmi, vert. 2.60 l, For the Partisans, by Arben Basha. 1.90 l, Eagle, by Zamir Mati, vert.

1984, June 12			Perf. 12½	
2132	A456	15q multi	.40	.25
2133	A456	25q multi	.80	.35
2134	A456	80q multi	2.00	1.10
2135	A456	2.60 l multi	3.25	1.75
	Nos. 2132-2135 (4)		6.45	3.45

Souvenir Sheet
Perf. 12 Horiz.

2136	A456	1.90 l multi	8.00	3.50

Flora — A457

15q, Moraceae L. 25q, Plantaginaceae L. 1.20 l, Hypericaceae L. 2.20 l, Leontopodium alpinum.

1984, Aug. 20		Litho.	Perf. 12	
2137	A457	15q multicolored	2.25	.60
2138	A457	25q multicolored	3.00	1.10
2139	A457	1.20 l multicolored	8.25	3.50
2140	A457	2.20 l multicolored	17.00	6.50
	Nos. 2137-2140 (4)		30.50	11.70

AUSIPEX '84, Melbourne, Sept. 21-30 — A458

Perf. 12 Horiz.

1984, Sept. 21			Litho.	
2141	A458	1.90 l Sword dancers, emblem	4.00	4.00

A459

Forestry, logging, UNFAO emblem — 15q, Beech trees, transport. 25q, Pine forest, logging cable. 1.20 l, Firs, sawmill. 2.20 l, Forester clearing woods.

1984, Sept. 25			Perf. 12	
2142	A459	15q multi	.80	.45
2143	A459	25q multi	1.25	.75
2144	A459	1.20 l multi	4.00	2.50
2145	A459	2.20 l multi	6.00	3.25
	Nos. 2142-2145 (4)		12.05	6.95

View of Gjirokaster A460

1984, Oct. 13			Perf. 12½	
2146	A460	1.20 l multicolored	2.00	2.00

EURPHILA '84, Rome.

5th National Spartakiad A461

15q, Soccer. 25q, Women's track & field. 80q, Weight lifting. 2.20 l, Pistol shooting. 1.90 l, Opening ceremony, red flags.

1984, Oct. 19			Perf. 12	
2147	A461	15q multicolored	.25	.25
2148	A461	25q multicolored	.30	.25
2149	A461	80q multicolored	.75	.30
2150	A461	2.20 l multicolored	2.10	1.50
	Nos. 2147-2150 (4)		3.40	2.30

Souvenir Sheet
Perf. 12 Horiz.

2151	A461	1.90 l multicolored	3.00	2.25

November 29 Revolution, 40th Anniv. A462

80q, Industrial reconstruction. 1.10 l, Natl. flag, partisans. 1.90 l, Gen. Enver Hoxha reading 1944 declaration.

1984, Nov. 29			Perf. 12	
2152	A462	80q multicolored	2.00	.75
2153	A462	1.10 l multicolored	2.50	1.00

Souvenir Sheet
Perf. 12 Horiz.

2154	A462	1.90 l multicolored	4.00	4.00

Archaeological Discoveries from Illyria — A463

Designs: 15q, Iron Age water container. 80q, Terra-cotta woman's head, 6th-7th cent. B.C. 1.20 l, Aphrodite, bust, 3rd cent. B.C. 1.70 l, Nike, A.D. 1st-2nd cent. bronze statue.

1985, Feb. 25			Perf. 12x12½	
2155	A463	15q multi	.40	.25
2156	A463	80q multi	1.50	.75
2157	A463	1.20 l multi	2.00	.90
2158	A463	1.70 l multi	3.00	1.50
	Nos. 2155-2158 (4)		6.90	3.40

Hysni Kapo (1915-1980), Natl. Labor Party Leader — A464

1985, Mar. 4			Perf. 12	
2159	A464	90q red & blk	1.40	1.00
2160	A464	1.10 l chlky bl & blk	1.75	1.50

OLYMPHILEX '85, Lausanne — A465

25q, Women's track & field. 60q, Weight lifting. 1.20 l, Soccer. 1.50 l, Women's pistol shooting.

1985, Mar. 18				
2161	A465	25q multicolored	.25	.25
2162	A465	60q multicolored	.65	.35
2163	A465	1.20 l multicolored	1.10	.90
2164	A465	1.50 l multicolored	2.00	1.00
	Nos. 2161-2164 (4)		4.00	2.50

Johann Sebastian Bach — A466

80q, Portrait, manuscript. 1.20 l, Eisenach, birthplace.

1985, Mar. 31
2165	A466	80q multicolored	16.00	8.00
2166	A466	1.20 l multicolored	20.00	10.00

Gen. Enver Hoxha (1908-1985) A467

1985, Apr. 11   **Perf. 12½**
2167	A467	80q multicolored	2.00	1.90

Souvenir Sheet
Imperf
2168	A467	1.90 l multicolored	3.25	3.25

Natl. Frontier Guards, 40th Anniv. A468

25q, Guardsman, family. 80q, At frontier post.

1985, Apr. 25   **Perf. 12**
2169	A468	25q multicolored	1.25	.75
2170	A468	80q multicolored	3.00	2.25

War Martyrs Type of 1980

25q, Mitro Xhani (1916-44), Nimete Progonati (1929-44), Kozma Nushi (1909-44). 40q, Ajet Xhindoli (1922-43), Mustafa Kacaci (1903-44), Estref Caka Osaja (1919-44). 60q, Celo Sinani (1929-44), Lt. Ambro Andoni (1920-44), Meleq Gosnishti (1913-44). 1.20 l, Thodhori Mastora (1920-44), Fejzi Micoli (1919-45), Hysen Cino (1920-44).

1985, May 5
2171	A410	25q multi	.55	.35
2172	A410	40q multi	.85	.70
2173	A410	60q multi	1.40	.85
2174	A410	1.20 l multi	2.50	2.00
		Nos. 2171-2174 (4)	5.30	3.90

Victory over Fascism A469

25q, Rifle, red flag, inscribed May 9. 80q, Hand holding rifle, globe, broken swastika.

1985, May 9
2175	A469	25q multi	*22.50*	*35.00*
2176	A469	80q multi	*60.00*	*90.00*
		End of World War II, 40th anniv.		

Primary School, by Thoma Malo A470

Paintings, Tirana Gallery of Figurative Art: 80q, The Heroes, by Hysen Devolli, vert. 90q, In Our Days, by Angjelin Dodmasej, vert. 1.20 l, Going Off to Sow, by Ksenofon Dilo. 1.90 l, Foundry Workers, by Mikel Gurashi.

1985, June 25   **Perf. 12½**
2177	A470	25q multi	.25	.25
2178	A470	80q multi	1.00	.75
2179	A470	90q multi	1.25	1.00
2180	A470	1.20 l multi	1.60	1.25
		Nos. 2177-2180 (4)	4.10	3.25

Souvenir Sheet
Perf. 12 Horiz.
2181	A470	1.90 l multi	3.25	2.75

Basketball Championships, Spain — A471

Various plays.

1985, July 20   **Litho.**   **Perf. 12**
2182	A471	25q dull bl & blk	.30	.25
2183	A471	80q dull grn & blk	1.10	.35
2184	A471	1.20 l dl vio & blk	1.40	.90
2185	A471	1.60 l dl rose & blk	2.25	1.50
		Nos. 2182-2185 (4)	5.05	3.00

Fruits — A472

1985, Aug. 20
2186	A472	25q Oranges	.40	.25
2187	A472	80q Plums	2.00	1.10
2188	A472	1.20 l Apples	3.25	1.50
2189	A472	1.60 l Cherries	4.00	2.25
		Nos. 2186-2189 (4)	9.65	5.10

Architecture A473

1985, Sept. 20
2190	A473	25q Kruja	.50	.50
2191	A473	80q Gjirokastra	2.50	1.25
2192	A473	1.20 l Berati	2.75	1.50
2193	A473	1.60 l Shkodera	3.75	1.75
		Nos. 2190-2193 (4)	9.50	5.00

Natl. Folk Theater Festival — A474

Various scenes from folk plays.

1985, Oct. 6
2194	A474	25q multi	.50	.25
2195	A474	80q multi	1.50	.75
2196	A474	1.20 l multi	2.00	.90
2197	A474	1.60 l multi	2.50	1.40

Size: 56x82mm
Imperf
2198	A474	1.90 l multi	3.75	3.00
		Nos. 2194-2198 (5)	10.25	6.30

Socialist People's Republic, 40th Anniv. — A475

25q, Natl. crest, vert. 80q, Proclamation, 1946.

1986, Jan. 11   **Litho.**   **Perf. 12½**
2199	A475	25q multicolored	1.50	.75
2200	A475	80q multicolored	3.00	1.50

A476

Designs: 25q, Dam, River Drin, Melgun. 80q, Bust of Enver Hoxha, dam power house.

1986, Feb. 20   **Perf. 12**
2201	A476	25q multi	*5.50*	2.00
2202	A476	80q multi	*12.00*	7.00
		Enver Hoxha hydro-electric power station, Koman.		

A477

Flowers: 25q, Gymnospermium shqipetarum. 1.20 l, Leucojum valentinum.

1986, Mar. 20   **Litho.**   **Perf. 12**
2203	A477	25q multi	2.00	1.00
2204	A477	1.20 l multi	8.00	4.00
a.		Pair, #2203-2204	12.00	12.00

Nos. 2203-2204 exist imperf. Value, pair: mint $40, used $35.

A478

Famous Men — A479

Designs: 25q, Maxim Gorky, Russian author. 80q, Andre Marie Ampere, French physicist. 1.20 l, James Watt, English inventor of modern steam engine. 2.40 l, Franz Liszt, Hungarian composer.

1986, Apr. 20
2205		Strip of 4	*12.00*	8.00
a.	A478	25q dull red brown	.50	.50
b.	A478	80q dull violet	2.00	1.25
c.	A478	1.20 l blue green	3.50	2.00
d.	A478	2.40 l dull lilac rose	7.00	4.50

Size: 88x72mm
Imperf
2206	A479	1.90 l multi	*7.00*	4.00

No. 2206 has central area picturing Gorky, Ampere, Watt and Liszt, perf. 12½.

War Martyrs Type of 1980

25q, Ramiz Aranitasi (1923-43), Inajete Dumi (1924-44) and Laze Nuro Ferraj (1897-1944). 80q, Dine Kalenja (1919-44), Kozma Naska (1921-44), Met Hasa (1929-44) and Fahri Ramadani (1920-44). 1.20 l, Hiqmet Buzi (1927-44), Bajram Tusha (1922-42), Mumin Selami (1923-42) and Hajrfdin Bylyshi (1923-42).

1986, May 5   **Perf. 12**
2207	A410	25q multi	1.75	1.50
2208	A410	80q multi	4.50	2.50
2209	A410	1.20 l multi	7.25	5.00
		Nos. 2207-2209 (3)	13.50	9.00

A480

1986 World Cup Soccer Championships, Mexico — A481

25q, Globe, world cup. 1.20 l, Player, soccer ball.

1986, May 31   **Litho.**   **Perf. 12**
2210	A480	25q multicolored	.40	.30
2211	A480	1.20 l multicolored	2.00	1.50

Size: 97x64mm
Imperf
2212	A481	1.90 l multicolored	3.50	2.50
		Nos. 2210-2212 (3)	5.90	4.30

No. 2212 has central label, perf. 12½.

Transportation Workers' Day, 40th Anniv. — A482

1986, Aug. 10   **Litho.**   **Perf. 12**
2213	A482	1.20 l multi	11.00	6.50

Prominent Albanians A483

Designs: 30q, Naim Frasheri (1846-1900), poet. 60q, Ndre Mjeda (1866-1937), poet. 90q, Petro Nini Luarasi (1865-1911), poet, journalist. 1 l, Andon Zako Cajupi (1866-1930), poet. 1.20 l, Millosh Gjergj Nikolla Migjeni (1911-1938), novelist. 2.60 l, Urani Rumbo (1884-1936), educator.

1986, Sept. 20   **Litho.**   **Perf. 12**
2214	A483	30q multi	.70	.30
2215	A483	60q multi	1.25	1.60
2216	A483	90q multi	2.00	1.00
2217	A483	1 l multi	2.50	1.25

2218	A483	1.20 l multi	3.00	1.50
2219	A483	2.60 l multi	8.00	2.50
	Nos. 2214-2219 (6)		17.45	8.15

Albanian Workers' Party, 9th Congress, Tirana A484

1986, Nov. 3   Litho.   *Perf. 12*
2220   A484   30q multi   14.00   7.50

No. 2220 exists with country name misspelled "SHQIPERSIE." Value, mint, $150.

A485

Albanian Workers' Party, 45th Anniv.: 30q, Handstamp, signature of Hoxha. 1.20 l, Marx, Engels, Lenin and Stalin, party building.

1986, Nov. 8
2221	A485	30q multi	4.00	1.00
2222	A485	1.20 l multi	11.00	3.00

A486

Statue of Mother Albania.

1986, Nov. 29   *Perf. 12x12½*
2223	A486	10q peacock blue	.25	.25
2224	A486	20q henna brn	.25	.25
2225	A486	30q vermilion	.25	.25
2226	A486	50q dk olive bis	.25	.25
2227	A486	60q lt olive grn	.35	.25
2228	A486	80q rose	.25	.25
2229	A486	90q ultra	.50	.25
2230	A486	1.20 l green	1.00	.50
2231	A486	1.60 l red vio	1.25	.60
2232	A486	2.20 l myrtle grn	2.00	1.25
2233	A486	3 l brn org	2.50	1.75
2234	A486	6 l yel bister	5.00	3.25
	Nos. 2223-2234 (12)		13.85	9.10

For surcharges see Nos. 2435-2439.

Artifacts A487

Designs: 30q, Head of Aesoulapius, 5th cent. B.C. Byllis, marble. 80q, Aphrodite, 3rd cent. B.C., Fier, terracotta. 1 l, Pan, 3rd-2nd cent, B.C., Byllis, bronze. 1.20 l, Jupiter, A.D. 2nd cent., Tirana, limestone.

1987, Feb. 20
2235	A487	30q multi	1.00	.60
2236	A487	80q multi	2.00	1.00
2237	A487	1 l multi	3.00	1.40
2238	A487	1.20 l multi	4.00	2.50
	Nos. 2235-2238 (4)		10.00	5.50

A488

Gun, quill pen, book of the alphabet and: 30q, Monument, vert. 80q, School, Korca. 1.20 l, Students.

1987, Mar. 7   *Perf. 12*
2239	A488	30q multi	.40	.25
2240	A488	80q multi	1.25	.50
2241	A488	1.20 l multi	1.75	1.25
	Nos. 2239-2241 (3)		3.40	2.00

First Albanian school, cent.

A489

Famous Men: 30q, Victor Hugo, French author. 80q, Galileo Galilei, Italian mathematician, philosopher. 90q, Charles Darwin, British biologist. 1.30 l, Miguel Cervantes, Spanish novelist.

1987, Apr. 20
2242	A489	30q multi	.45	.25
2243	A489	80q multi	1.10	.50
2244	A489	90q multi	1.60	1.10
2245	A489	1.30 l multi	2.25	1.75
	Nos. 2242-2245 (4)		5.40	3.60

World Food Day — A490

30q, Forsythia europaea. 90q, Moltkia doerfleri. 2.10 l, Wulfenia baldacii.

1987, May 20
2246	A490	30q multicolored	.55	.30
2247	A490	90q multicolored	1.10	.75
2248	A490	2.10 l multicolored	2.40	2.10
	Nos. 2246-2248 (3)		4.05	3.15

10th Trade Unions Cong. — A491

1987, June 25
2249   A491   1.20 l multi   4.00   3.00

Sowing, by Bujar Asllani — A492

Paintings in the Eponymous Museum, Tirana: 30q, The Sustenance of Industry, by

Myrteza Fushekati, vert. 80q, The Gifted Partisan, by Skender Kokobobo, vert. 1.20 l, At the Forging Block, by Clirim Ceka.

Perf. 12x12½, 12½x12

1987, July 20   Litho.
2250	A492	30q multi	.50	.40
2251	A492	80q multi	.80	.80
2252	A492	1 l shown	1.20	1.00
2253	A492	1.20 l multi	1.60	1.40
	Nos. 2250-2253 (4)		4.10	3.60

A493

OLYMPHILEX '87, Rome, Aug. 29-Sept. 6 — A494

1987, Aug. 29   Litho.   *Perf. 12½*
2254	A493	30q Hammer throw	.40	.40
2255	A493	90q Running	1.25	.80
2256	A493	1.10 l Shot put	1.25	1.00

Size: 85x60mm
2257   A494   1.90 l Runner, globe   2.00   2.00
    Nos. 2254-2257 (4)   4.90   4.20

Famous Men A495

Designs: 30q, Themistokli Germenji (1871-1917), author, politician. 80q, Bajram Curri (1862-1925), founder of the Albanian League. 90q, Aleks Stavre Drenova (1872-1947), poet. 1.30 l, Gjerasim D. Qiriazi (1861-1894), teacher, journalist.

1987, Sept. 30   *Perf. 12*
2258	A495	30q multi	.25	.25
2259	A495	80q multi	.90	.30
2260	A495	90q multi	1.10	.75
2261	A495	1.30 l multi	1.90	1.50
	Nos. 2258-2261 (4)		4.15	2.80

Albanian Labor Party Congress, Tirana A496

1987, Oct. 22   Litho.   *Perf. 12*
2262   A496   1.20 l multi   5.00   3.50

Natl. Independence, 75th Anniv. — A497

1987, Nov. 27
2263   A497   1.20 l State flag   5.50   4.00

Postal Administration, 75th Anniv. — A498

1987, Dec. 5
2264	A498	90q P.O. emblem	5.00	3.50
2265	A498	1.20 l State seal	7.00	7.00

Art & Literature — A499

Portraits: 30q, Lord Byron (1788-1824), English Poet. 1.20 l, Eugene Delacroix (1798-1863), French painter.

1988, Mar. 10
2266	A499	30q org brn & blk	4.00	3.25
2267	A499	1.20 l pale vio & blk	16.00	12.50

WHO, 40th Anniv. — A500

1988, Apr. 7
2268	A500	90q multi	22.50	20.00
2269	A500	1.20 l multi	30.00	25.00

Flowers — A501

Designs: 30q, Sideritis raeseri. 90q, Lunaria telekiana. 2.10 l, Sanguisorba albanica.

1988, May 20   **Booklet Stamps**
2270	A501	30q multicolored	8.00	5.00
2271	A501	90q multicolored	16.00	11.00
2272	A501	2.10 l multicolored	24.00	16.00
a.		Bklt. pane of 3, plus label	50.00	50.00
	Nos. 2270-2272 (3)		48.00	32.00

10th Women's Federation Congress A502

1988, June 6
2273   A502   90q blk, red & dark org   21.00   19.00

European Soccer
Championships — A503

Various athletes.
1.90 l, Goalie designs of Nos. 2274-2276.

1988, June 10
2274	A503	30q multicolored	2.00	2.00
2275	A503	80q multicolored	3.00	3.00
2276	A503	1.20 l multicolored	5.00	5.00

Size: 79x68mm
Imperf
| 2277 | A503 | 1.90 l multicolored | 12.00 | 12.00 |
| | *Nos. 2274-2277 (4)* | | 22.00 | 22.00 |

League of
Prizren, 110th
Anniv. — A504

1988, June 10   Litho.   Perf. 12
| 2278 | A504 | 30q Hands | 40.00 | 40.00 |
| 2279 | A504 | 1.20 l House | 70.00 | 70.00 |

People's Army,
45th
Anniv. — A505

1988, July 10
| 2280 | A505 | 60q shown | 40.00 | 40.00 |
| 2281 | A505 | 90q Soldier statue | 70.00 | 70.00 |

Famous
Albanians
A506

Designs: 30q, Mihal Grameno (1871-1931),
author. 90q, Bajo Topulli (1868-1930), freedom fighter. 1 l, Murat Toptani (1868-1917),
poet. 1.20 l, Jul Variboba, poet.

1988, Aug. 15
2282	A506	30q multi	15.00	15.00
2283	A506	90q multi	25.00	25.00
2284	A506	1 l multi	30.00	30.00
2284A	A506	1.20 l multi	40.00	40.00
	Nos. 2282-2284A (4)		110.00	110.00

Migjeni (1911-1938), Poet — A507

1988, Aug. 26   Litho.   Perf. 12
| 2285 | A507 | 90q silver & brown | 16.00 | 16.00 |

Ballads
A508

1988, Sept. 5
2286	A508	30q Dede Skurra	10.00	8.00
2287	A508	90q Omeri Iri	25.00	21.00
2288	A508	1.20 l Gjergj Elez		
		Alia	30.00	25.00
	Nos. 2286-2288 (3)		65.00	54.00

Folklore Festival Type of 1978

30q, Kerchief Dance. 1.20 l, Dancers with
raised arm.

1988, Oct. 6
| 2289 | A388 | 30q multi | 30.00 | 30.00 |
| 2290 | A388 | 1.20 l multi | 110.00 | 90.00 |

Enver
Hoxha
Museum
A510

Perf. 12x12½, 12½x12
1988, Oct. 16   Litho.
| 2291 | A510 | 90q Portrait, vert. | 4.00 | 4.00 |
| 2292 | A510 | 1.20 l shown | 6.00 | 6.00 |

Hoxha (1908-85), Communist leader.

Monastir
Congress,
80th Anniv.
A511

1988, Nov. 14   Litho.   Perf. 12
| 2293 | A511 | 60q Scroll | 22.50 | 20.00 |
| 2294 | A511 | 90q Book, building | 35.00 | 30.00 |

Locomotives, Map Showing Rail
Network — A512

1989, Feb. 28   Litho.   Perf. 12½x12
2295	A512	30q 1947	.25	.25
2296	A512	90q 1949	.75	.35
2297	A512	1.20 l 1978	1.00	.60
2298	A512	1.80 l 1985	1.60	.75
2299	A512	2.40 l 1988	3.75	1.50
	Nos. 2295-2299 (5)		7.35	3.45

Archaeological Treasures — A513

30q, Illyrian grave. 90q, Warrior on
horseback.

1989, Mar. 10   Litho.   Perf. 12
2300	A513	30q blk & tan	.25	.25
2301	A513	90q blk & dl grn	.90	.75
2302	A513	2.10 l shown	1.50	1.25
	Nos. 2300-2302 (3)		2.65	2.25

Folklore
A514

1989, Apr. 5   Litho.   Perf. 12x12½
2303	A514	30q multicolored	.35	.25
2304	A514	80q multi, diff.	.75	.50
2305	A514	1 l multi, diff.	.75	.75
2306	A514	1.20 l multi, diff.	1.10	1.10
	Nos. 2303-2306 (4)		2.95	2.60

Flowers — A515

Designs: 30q, Aster albanicus. 90q, Orchis
x paparisti. 2.10 l, Orchis albanica.

1989, May 10   Perf. 12
2307	A515	30q multicolored	.75	.30
2308	A515	90q multicolored	3.25	1.10
2309	A515	2.10 l multicolored	5.25	1.75
	Nos. 2307-2309 (3)		9.25	3.15

Famous
People — A516

Designs: 30q, Johann Strauss the Younger
(1825-1899), composer. 80q, Marie Curie
(1867-1934), chemist. 1 l, Federico Garcia
Lorca (1898-1936), poet. 1.20 l, Albert Einstein (1879-1955), physicist.

1989, June 3
2310	A516	30q gold & blk brn	.35	.25
2311	A516	80q gold & blk brn	.75	.45
2312	A516	1 l gold & blk brn	1.10	.90
2313	A516	1.20 l gold & blk brn	1.50	1.25
a.	Block of 4, #2310-2313		5.50	4.75
	Nos. 2310-2313 (4)		3.70	2.85

6th
Congress
of Albanian
Democratic
Front
A517

1989, June 26
| 2314 | A517 | 1.20 l multicolored | 7.25 | 4.00 |

French Revolution, Bicent. — A518

90q, Storming of the Bastille. 1.20 l, Statue.

1989, July 7   Litho.   Perf. 12½
| 2315 | A518 | 90q multicolored | .65 | .45 |
| 2316 | A518 | 1.20 l shown | 1.20 | .75 |

Illyrian Ship
A519

80q, Caravel. 90q, 3-masted schooner.
1.30 l, Modern cargo ship.

1989, July 25   Perf. 12
2317	A519	30q shown	.35	.25
2318	A519	80q multicolored	.70	.70
2319	A519	90q multicolored	.70	.70
2320	A519	1.30 l multicolored	1.00	1.00
	Nos. 2317-2320 (4)		2.75	2.45

A520

Famous Men: 30q, Pjeter Bogdani (1625-
1689), writer. 80q, Gavril Dara (1826-1889),
poet. 90q, Thimi Mitko (1820-1890), writer.
1.30 l, Kole Idromeno (1860-1939), painter.

1989, Aug. 30   Litho.   Perf. 12
2321	A520	30q multicolored	.25	.25
2322	A520	80q multicolored	.50	.30
2323	A520	90q multicolored	.85	.60
2324	A520	1.30 l multicolored	1.25	.75
	Nos. 2321-2324 (4)		2.85	1.90

A521

1989, Sept. 29
| 2325 | A521 | 90q shown | .70 | .60 |
| 2326 | A521 | 1.20 l Workers | 1.00 | .50 |

First Communist International, 125th anniv.

Spartakiad
Games
A522

1989, Oct. 27   Perf. 12x12½
2327	A522	30q Gymnastics	.25	.25
2328	A522	80q Soccer	.50	.25
2329	A522	1 l Cycling	.55	.45
2330	A522	1.20 l Running	.85	.75
	Nos. 2327-2330 (4)		2.15	1.70

Miniature Sheet

45th Anniv. of Liberation — A523

1989, Nov. 29   Perf. 12x12½
2331	A523	Sheet of 4	4.25	4.25
a.	30q Revolutionary		.50	.25
b.	80q "45"		1.00	.30
c.	1 l Coat of arms		1.00	.50
d.	1.20 l Workers		1.00	.85

Rupicapra
Rupicapra
A524

1990, Mar. 15   **Perf. 12**
2332 A524 10q Two adults   .25   .25
2333 A524 30q Adult, kid   .55   .25
2334 A524 80q Adult   1.60   .75
2335 A524 90q Adult head   1.60 1.00
  a.   Block of 4, #2332-2335   5.00 5.00

World Wildlife Fund.

Tribal Masks
A525

1990, Apr. 4   **Perf. 12x12½**
2336 A525 30q shown   .30   .30
2337 A525 90q multi, diff.   .65   .40
2338 A525 1.20 l multi, diff.   .90   .55
2339 A525 1.80 l multi, diff.   1.40   .80
   Nos. 2336-2339 (4)   3.25 2.05

Mushrooms
A526

30q, Amanita caesarea. 90q, Lepiota procera. 1.20 l, Boletus edulis. 1.80 l, Clathrus cancelatus.

1990, Apr. 28   Litho.   Perf. 12
2340 A526 30q multicolored   .25   .25
2341 A526 90q multicolored   .50   .40
2342 A526 1.20 l multicolored   .85   .80
2343 A526 1.80 l multicolored   1.20 1.00
   Nos. 2340-2343 (4)   2.80 2.45

First
Postage
Stamp,
150th
Anniv.
A527

1990, May 6   **Perf. 12**
2344 A527 90q shown   .45   .45
2345 A527 1.20 l Post rider   .90   .90
2346 A527 1.80 l Carriage   1.75 1.25
  a.   Bklt. pane of 3, #2344-2346 +
         label   3.50
   Nos. 2344-2346 (3)   3.10 2.60

World Cup
Soccer,
Italy
A528

1990, June   Litho.   Perf. 12
2347 A528 30q multicolored   .30   .30
2348 A528 90q multi, diff.   .65   .65
2349 A528 1.20 l multi, diff.   1.10   .90

Size: 80x63mm
Imperf
2350 A528 3.30 l multi, diff.   3.25 3.25
   Nos. 2347-2350 (4)   5.30 5.10

Vincent
Van
Gogh,
Death
Cent.
A529

Self portraits and: 30q, Details from various paintings. 90q, Woman in field. 2.10 l, Asylum. 2.40 l, Self-portrait.

1990, July 27
2351 A529 30q multicolored   .40   .40
2352 A529 90q multicolored   .80   .80
2353 A529 2.10 l multicolored   1.75 1.75

Size: 87x73mm
Imperf
2354 A529 2.40 l multicolored   4.00 4.00
   Nos. 2351-2354 (4)   6.95 6.95

Albanian Folklore — A530

Scenes from medieval folktale of "Gjergj Elez Alia": 30q, Alia lying wounded. 90q, Alia being helped onto horse. 1.20 l, Alia fighting Bajloz. 1.80 l, Alia on horseback over severed head of Bajloz.

1990, Aug. 30   Perf. 12½x12
2355 A530 30q multicolored   .30   .30
2356 A530 90q multicolored   .70   .40
2357 A530 1.20 l multicolored   1.00   .80
2358 A530 1.80 l multicolored   1.50 1.00
   Nos. 2355-2358 (4)   3.50 2.50

Founding of
Berat, 2400th
Anniv. — A531

Designs: 30q, Xhamia E Plumbit. 90q, Kisha E Shen Triadhes. 1.20 l, Ura E Beratit. 1.80 l, Onufri-Piktor Mesjetar. 2.40 l, Nikolla-Piktor Mesjetar.

1990, Sept. 20   Perf. 12½
2359   Block of 5 + 4 labels   5.00 5.00
  a.   A531 30q multi   .25   .25
  b.   A531 90q multi   .25   .25
  c.   A531 1.20 l multi   .60   .60
  d.   A531 1.80 l multi   1.00 1.00
  e.   A531 2.40 l multi   1.25 1.25

No. 2359 was sold in souvenir folders for 9.90 l.

Illyrian
Heroes — A532

1990, Oct. 20   Perf. 12
2360 A532 30q Pirroja   .25   .25
2361 A532 90q Teuta   .50   .50
2362 A532 1.20 l Bato   .75   .75
2363 A532 1.80 l Bardhyli   1.00 1.00
   Nos. 2360-2363 (4)   2.50 2.50

Intl.
Literacy
Year
A533

1990, Oct. 30
2364 A533 90q lt bl & multi   .65   .60
2365 A533 1.20 l pink & multi   .90   .90

Albanian
Horseman by
Eugene
Delacroix
A534

Designs: 1.20 l, Albanian Woman by Camille Corot. 1.80 l, Skanderbeg by unknown artist.

1990, Nov. 30   Perf. 12x12½
2366 A534 30q multicolored   .30   .30
2367 A534 1.20 l multicolored   .90   .70
2368 A534 1.80 l multicolored   1.25 1.00
   Nos. 2366-2368 (3)   2.45 2.00

A535

1.20 l, Boletini standing.

1991, Jan. 23   Litho.   Perf. 12x12½
2369 A535 90q shown   .60   .50
2370 A535 1.20 l multicolored   .90   .70

Isa Boletini (1864-1916), freedom fighter.

A536

1991, Jan. 30   Litho.   Perf. 12
Background Color
2371 A536 90q pale yellow   .60   .50
2372 A536 90q pale gray   .90   .70

Arberi State, 800th anniv.

Pierre Auguste Renoir (1841-1919),
Painter — A537

Paintings: 30q, Girl Reading, 1876, vert. 90q, The Swing, 1876, vert. 1.20 l, Boating Party, 1868-1869. 1.80 l, Flowers and grapes, 1878. 3 l, Self-portrait.

1991, Feb. 25   Perf. 12½x12
2373 A537 30q multicolored   .50   .25
2374 A537 90q multicolored   .75   .50
2375 A537 1.20 l multicolored   1.10   .90
2376 A537 1.80 l multicolored   1.75 1.40

Size: 95x75mm
Imperf
2377 A537 3 l multicolored   4.00 4.00
   Nos. 2373-2377 (5)   8.10 7.05

Flowers — A538

30q, Cistus albanicus. 90q, Trifolium pilczii. 1.80 l, Lilium albanicum.

1991, Mar. 30   Perf. 12
2378 A538 30q multicolored   .30   .30
2379 A538 90q multicolored   .70   .70
2380 A538 1.80 l multicolored   1.40 1.00
   Nos. 2378-2380 (3)   2.40 2.00

Legend of
Rozafa
A539

Various scenes from legend.

1991, Sept. 30   Litho.   Perf. 12x12½
2381 A539 30q multicolored   .30   .30
2382 A539 90q multicolored   .50   .30
2383 A539 1.20 l multicolored   1.00   .70
2384 A539 1.80 l multicolored   1.40 1.20
   Nos. 2381-2384 (4)   3.20 2.50

For surcharges see Nos. 2586, 2604.

Wolfgang
Amadeus Mozart,
Death
Bicent. — A540

1991, Oct. 5   Litho.   Perf. 12
2385 A540 90q Conducting   .75   .45
2386 A540 1 l Portrait   1.00   .70
2387 A540 1.80 l Playing piano   1.60 1.20

Size: 89x70mm
Imperf
2388 A540 3 l Medal, score   5.00 5.00
   Nos. 2385-2388 (4)   8.35 7.35

Airplanes — A541

Designs: 30q, Glider, Otto Lilienthal, 1896. 80q, Avion III, Clement Ader, 1897. 90q, Flyer, Wright Brothers, 1903. 1.20 l, Concorde. 1.80 l, Tupolev 114. 2.40 l, Dornier 31 E.

1992, Jan. 27   Litho.   Perf. 12½x12
2389 A541 30q multicolored   .30   .30
2390 A541 80q multicolored   .45   .35
2391 A541 90q multicolored   .65   .55
2392 A541 1.20 l multicolored   .90   .65

2393	A541	1.80 l multicolored	.90 .65
2394	A541	2.40 l multicolored	1.40 1.20

Nos. 2389-2394 (6) 4.60 3.70

No. 2393 misidentifies a Tupolev 144.

Explorers — A542

1992, Jan. 10

2395	A542	30q Bering	.30 .30
2396	A542	90q Columbus	.70 .30
2397	A542	1.80 l Magellan	1.50 .90

Nos. 2395-2397 (3) 2.50 1.50

1992 Winter Olympics, Albertville A543

30q, Ski jumping. 90q, Cross country skiing. 1.20 l, Pairs figure skating. 1.80 l, Luge.

1992, Feb. 15   Litho.   Perf. 12½

2398	A543	30q multicolored	.30 .30
2399	A543	90q multicolored	.50 .45
2400	A543	1.20 l multicolored	.75 .60
2401	A543	1.80 l multicolored	1.10 1.00

Nos. 2398-2401 (4) 2.65 2.35

For surcharge see No. 2598.

Participation of Albania in Conference on Security and Cooperation in Europe, Berlin (1991) — A544

1992, Mar. 31   Litho.   Perf. 12½x12

2402	A544	90q shown	.85 .85
2403	A544	1.20 l Flags, map	1.00 1.00
a.		Pair, #2402-2403	3.50 3.50

Dated 1991. Issued in sheets containing 2 No. 2403a, 3 each Nos. 2402-2403 + 2 labels. No. 2402 was also issued in sheets of 16.

Albanian Admission to CEPT — A545

90q, Envelopes, CEPT emblem.

1992, Apr. 25   Litho.   Perf. 12½

2404	A545	90q blk, blue & red lil	.85 .85
2405	A545	1.20 l blk, pur & red lil	1.00 1.00
a.		Pair, #2404-2405	1.90 1.90

Issued in sheets containing 2 No. 2405a, 3 each Nos. 2404-2405 and 2 labels.

Martyrs' Day — A546

90q, Freedom flame, vert. 4.10 l, Flowers.

1992, May 5   Perf. 12x12½

2406	A546	90q multicolored	.50 .50

Perf. 12½x12

2407	A546	4.10 l multicolored	2.50 2.00

European Soccer Championships, Sweden'92 — A547

Various stylized designs of soccer plays.

1992, June 10   Litho.   Perf. 12

2408	A547	30q green & lt grn	.40 .25
2409	A547	90q blue & pink	.75 .50
2410	A547	10.80 l henna & tan	4.50 3.75

Size: 90x70mm

Imperf

2411	A547	5 l tan, lt green & pink	2.75 2.75

Nos. 2408-2411 (4) 8.40 7.25

1992 Summer Olympics, Barcelona A548

1992, June 14   Litho.   Perf. 12

2412	A548	30q Tennis	.35 .35
2413	A548	90q Baseball	1.00 .55
2414	A548	1.80 l Table tennis	2.00 1.50

Size: 90x70mm

Imperf

2415	A548	5 l Torch bearer	3.25 3.25

Nos. 2412-2415 (4) 6.60 5.65

United Europe A549

1992, July 10   Litho.   Perf. 12

2416	A549	1.20 l multicolored	1.00 .75

Horses A550

30q, Native. 90q, Nonius. 1.20 l, Arabian, vert. 10.60 l, Haflinger, vert.

1992, Aug. 10   Litho.   Perf. 12

2417	A550	30q multicolored	.25 .25
2418	A550	90q multicolored	.40 .40
2419	A550	1.20 l multicolored	.55 .55
2420	A550	10.60 l multicolored	4.25 4.25

Nos. 2417-2420 (4) 5.45 5.45

For surcharge, see No. 2781.

Discovery of America, 500th Anniv. A551

Map of North and South America and: 60q, Columbus, sailing ships. 3.20 l, Columbus meeting natives. 5 l, Map, Columbus.

1992, Aug. 20

2421	A551	60q blk, bl & gray	.50 .50
2422	A551	3.20 l blk, brn & gray	3.50 3.50

Size: 90x70mm

Imperf

2423	A551	5 l multi	70.00 70.00

Mother Theresa, Infant — A552

1992, Oct. 4   Litho.   Perf. 12x12½

2424	A552	40q fawn	.30 .30
2425	A552	60q brown	.30 .30
2426	A552	1 l violet	.30 .30
2427	A552	1.80 l gray	.30 .30
2428	A552	2 l red	.30 .30
2429	A552	2.40 l green	.30 .30
2430	A552	3.20 l blue	.40 .40
2431	A552	5.60 l rose violet	.60 .60
2432	A552	7.20 l olive	1.00 1.00
2433	A552	10 l org brn	1.25 1.25

Nos. 2424-2433 (10) 5.05 5.05

See Nos. 2472-2476.
For surcharge, see No. 2786.

A553

1993, Apr. 25   Litho.   Perf. 12

2434	A553	16 l multicolored	2.50 2.50

Visit of Pope John Paul II.

Nos. 2223-2226, 2229 Surcharged

1993, May 2   Litho.   Perf. 12x12½

2435	A486	3 l on 10q	.25 .25
2436	A486	6.50 l on 20q	.55 .55
2437	A486	13 l on 30q	1.50 1.50
2438	A486	20 l on 90q	2.25 2.25
2439	A486	30 l on 50q	3.00 3.00

Nos. 2435-2439 (5) 7.55 7.55

Lef Nosi (1873-1945), Minister of Posts A554

1993, May 5   Litho.   Perf. 12

2440	A554	6.50 l ol brn & bister	.90 .90

First Albanian postage stamps, 80th anniv.

Europa A555

Contemporary paintings by: 3 l, A. Zajmi, vert. 7 l, E. Hila. 20 l, B. Ahmeti-Peizazh.

1993, May 28   Litho.   Perf. 12

2441	A555	3 l multicolored	.90 .90
2442	A555	7 l multicolored	3.50 3.50

Size: 116x122mm

2443	A555	20 l multicolored	6.50 6.50

Nos. 2441-2443 (3) 10.90 10.90

1993 Mediterranean Games, France — A556

3 l, Running. 16 l, Kayaking. 21 l, Cycling. 20 l, Mediterranean map.

1993, June 20   Litho.   Perf. 12

2444	A556	3 l multicolored	.30 .30
2445	A556	16 l multicolored	1.75 1.75
2446	A556	21 l multicolored	2.40 2.40

Size: 111x78mm

Imperf

2447	A556	20 l multicolored	3.25 3.25

Nos. 2444-2447 (4) 7.70 7.70

For surcharge, see No. 2789.

Frang Bardhi, Author, 350th Death Anniv. A557

1993, Aug. 20   Litho.   Perf. 12x12½

2448	A557	6.50 l shown	1.10 1.10

Size: 89x101mm

Imperf

2449	A557	20 l Writing at desk	3.50 3.50

A558

68 l, Mascot, ball, US map.

1994, July 17   Litho.   Perf. 12

2450	A558	42 l shown	1.10 1.10
2451	A558	68 l multicolored	1.60 1.60

1994 World Cup Soccer Championships, US.

A559

European Inventors, Discoveries: 50 l, Gjovalin Gjadri, engineer. 100 l, Karl von Ghega, Austrian engineer. 150 l, Sketch of road project.

1994, Dec. 31	Litho.	Perf. 14		
2452	A559	50 l multicolored	1.50	1.50
2453	A559	100 l multicolored	2.25	2.25

Size: 50x70mm
Imperf

2454	A559	150 l multicolored	3.75	3.75
		Nos. 2452-2454 (3)	7.50	7.50

Europa (No. 2454).

Ali Pasa of Tepelene (Lion of Janina)
(1744-1822) — A560

1995, Jan. 28		Perf. 14		
2455	A560	60 l shown	1.40	1.40

Size: 70x50mm
Imperf

2456	A560	100 l Tepelene Palace	1.50	1.50

Intl. Olympic Committee,
Cent. — A561

1995, Feb. 2		Imperf.		
2457	A561	80 l multicolored	1.75	1.75

Karl Benz (1844-1929), Automobile
Pioneer — A562

Designs: 5 l, Automobile company emblem, Benz. 10 l, Modern Mercedes Benz automobile. 60 l, First four-wheel Benz 1886 motor car. 125 l, Pre-war Mercedes touring car.

1995, Jan. 21	Litho.	Perf. 14		
2458	A562	5 l multicolored	.30	.30
2459	A562	10 l multicolored	.30	.30
2460	A562	60 l multicolored	.90	.90
2461	A562	125 l multicolored	3.00	3.00
		Nos. 2458-2461 (4)	4.50	4.50

Liberation,
50th Anniv.
(in 1994)
A563

1995, Jan. 28	Litho.	Perf. 14		
2462	A563	50 l black, gray & red	1.25	1.25

Dated 1994.

Miniature Sheet

Albania '93 — A564

Composers: a, 3 l, Wagner. b, 6.50 l, Grieg. c, 11 l, Gounod. d, 20 l, Tchaikovsky.

1995, Jan. 26		Perf. 12		
2463	A564	Sheet of 4, #a.-d.	2.50	2.50

Voskopoja
Academy, 250th
Anniv. — A565

Buildings of Voskopoja.

1995, Feb. 2				
2464	A565	42 l multicolored	.90	.90
2465	A565	68 l multicolored	2.25	2.25
a.		Pair, #2464-2465	3.50	3.50

Bleta
Apricula — A566

5 l, On flower. 10 l, Honeycomb, bee. 25 l, Emerging from cell of honeycomb.

1995, Aug. 20	Litho.	Perf. 12		
2466	A566	5 l multicolored	.30	.30
2467	A566	10 l multicolored	.30	.30
2468	A566	25 l multicolored	1.25	1.25
		Nos. 2466-2468 (3)	1.85	1.85

Peace &
Freedom — A567

Stylized hands reaching for: 50 l, Olive branch. 100 l, Peace dove.
150 l, Stylized person.

1995, Aug. 10		Perf. 13½x14		
2469	A567	50 l multicolored	1.75	1.75
2470	A567	100 l multicolored	3.50	3.50

Size: 80x60mm
Imperf

2471	A567	150 l multicolored	5.00	5.00
		Nos. 2469-2471 (3)	10.25	10.25

Europa.
For surcharges, see Nos. B39-B40.

Mother Teresa Type of 1992

1994-95	Litho.	Perf. 12x12½		
2472	A552	5 l violet	.30	.30
2473	A552	18 l orange	1.10	1.10
2474	A552	20 l rose lilac	.45	.45
2475	A552	25 l green	1.75	1.75
2476	A552	60 l olive	1.75	1.75
		Nos. 2472-2476 (5)	5.35	5.35

Issued: 20 l, 1994; 60 l, 1995; others, 7/94.

Arctic Explorers — A568

Designs: a, Fridtjof Nansen (1861-1930), Norway. b, James Cook (1728-79), England. c, Roald Amundsen (1872-1928), Norway. d, Robert F. Scott (1872-1928), Great Britain.

1995, Sept. 14	Litho.	Perf. 13½x14		
2477	A568	25 l Block of 4, #a.-d.	3.50	3.50

For surcharges, see No. 2790.

UN, 50th
Anniv.
A569

100 l, Like #2478, flags streaming to right.

1995, Sept. 14	Litho.	Perf. 14x13½		
2478	A569	2 l shown	.25	.25
2479	A569	100 l multicolored	1.90	1.90

For surcharge, see No. 2782.

Poets — A570

1995		Perf. 13½x14		
2480	A570	25 l Paul Éluard	.65	.65
2481	A570	50 l Sergei Yesenin	1.25	1.25
a.		Pair, #2480-2481	2.00	2.00

Entry into
Council of
Europe
A571

Designs: 25 l, Doves flying from headquarters, Strasbourg. 85 l, Albanian eagle over map of Europe.

1995		Perf. 14x13½		
2482	A571	25 l multicolored	.90	.90
2483	A571	85 l multicolored	3.25	3.25

For surcharge see No. 2583

Jan Kukuzeli,
Composer
A572

Stylized figure: 18 l, Writing. 20 l, Holding hand to head. 100 l, Holding up scroll of paper.

1995, Oct. 17		Perf. 13½x14		
2484	A572	18 l multicolored	.50	.50
2485	A572	20 l multicolored	.50	.50

Size: 74x74mm

2486	A572	100 l multicolored	2.50	2.50
		Nos. 2484-2486 (3)	3.50	3.50

For surcharge, see No. 2787.

World Tourism
Organization, 20th
Anniv. — A573

Stylized designs: 18 l, Church, saint holding scroll. 20 l, City, older buildings. 42 l, City, modern buildings.

1995, Oct. 17				
2487	A573	18 l multicolored	.50	.50
2488	A573	20 l multicolored	.65	.65
2489	A573	42 l multicolored	1.40	1.40
		Nos. 2487-2489 (3)	2.55	2.55

For surcharge, see No. 2788.

Fables of
Jean de la
Fontaine
(1621-95)
A574

Designs: 2 l, Raptor, turtle, wolf, goose, mouse, lion, rats. 3 l, Crow, goose, dog, foxes. 25 l, Insect, doves, frogs. 60 l, Drawings of Da la Fontaine, animals, birds.

1995, Aug. 20	Litho.	Perf. 14x13½		
2490	A574	2 l multicolored	.25	.25
2491	A574	3 l multicolored	.25	.25
2492	A574	25 l multicolored	.50	.50

Imperf
Size: 73x56mm

2493	A574	60 l multicolored	2.00	2.00
		Nos. 2490-2493 (4)	3.00	3.00

For surcharges, see Nos. 2783, 2784, 2791.

Folklore Festival,
Berat — A575

Stylized designs: 5 l, Men's choir. 50 l, Costumed woman seated in chair.

1995, Oct. 17	Litho.	Perf. 13½x14		
2494	A575	5 l multicolored	.25	.25
2495	A575	50 l multicolored	1.20	1.20

Motion Pictures,
Cent. — A576

1995, Nov. 17
2496	A576	10 l	Louis Lumiere	.25 .25
2497	A576	85 l	Auguste Lumiere	1.50 1.50
a.		Pair, #2496-2497		2.00 2.00

Elvis
Presley
(1935-77)
A577

1995, Nov. 20 Litho. Perf. 14x13½
2498	A577	3 l	orange & multi	.30 .30
2499	A577	60 l	green & multi	1.75 1.75

For surcharge, see No. 2785.

A578

1995, Nov. 25 Perf. 13½x14
2500	A578	10 l	1925 Bank notes	.30 .30
2501	A578	25 l	1995 Bank notes	.80 .80

National Bank, 70th anniv.

A579

50 l, Maiden planting tree.

1995, Nov. 27 Litho. Perf. 13½x14
2502	A579	5 l	shown	.25 .25
2503	A579	50 l	multicolored	1.50 1.50

Democracy, 5th anniv.

A580

Designs: 25 l, Soccer ball, British flag, map
of Europe, stadium. 100 l, Soccer ball, player.

1996, June 4 Perf. 14
2504	A580	25 l	multicolored	.50 .50
2505	A580	100 l	multicolored	2.25 2.25

Euro '96, European Soccer Championships,
Great Britain.
For surcharge, see No. 2792.

Mother
Teresa — A581

150 l, Mother Teresa, diff.

1996, May 5 Perf. 13½x14
2506	A581	25 l	blue & multi	.90 .90
2507	A581	100 l	red & multi	2.25 2.25

Size: 52x74mm
Imperf
2508	A581	150 l	multi	6.25 6.25
		Nos. 2506-2508 (3)		9.40 9.40

Europa. For overprints see Nos. 2551, 2582.

GSM Cellular
Telephone
Transmission
A582

Designs: 10 l, Satellite transmitting signals.
60 l, Uses for cellular telephone, vert.

Perf. 13x13½, 13½x13
1996, Aug. 1 Litho.
2509	A582	10 l	multicolored	.25 .25
2510	A582	60 l	multicolored	1.50 1.50

1996 Summer
Olympic Games,
Atlanta — A583

Stylized designs: 5 l, Runners. 25 l, Throw-
ers. 60 l, Jumpers. 100 l, Emblem, US flag.

1996, Aug. 3 Litho. Perf. 13x14
2511	A583	5 l	multicolored	.25 .25
2512	A583	25 l	multicolored	.55 .55
2513	A583	60 l	multicolored	1.50 1.50

Size: 52x37mm
Imperf
2514	A583	100 l	multicolored	2.25 2.25
		Nos. 2511-2514 (4)		4.55 4.55

Gottfried Wilhelm Leibniz (1646-1716),
Mathematician — A584

85 l, René Descartes (1596-1650),
mathematician.

1996, Sept. 20 Litho. Perf. 14
2515	A584	10 l	multicolored	.40 .40
2516	A584	85 l	multicolored	2.00 2.00

Paintings by
Francisco
Goya
(1746-1828)
A585

Designs: 10 l, The Naked Maja. 60 l, Dona
Isabel Cobos de Porcel. 100 l, Self portrait.

1996, Sept. 25 Perf. 14x13½
2517	A585	10 l	multicolored	.30 .30
2518	A585	60 l	multicolored	1.40 1.40

Souvenir Sheet
2519	A585	100 l	multicolored	2.00 2.00

Religious Engravings — A586

Designs: a, 5 l, Book cover showing crucifixion, angels. b, 25 l, Medallion of crucifixion. c,
85 l, Book cover depicting life of Christ.

1996, Nov. 5 Perf. 13x13½
2520	A586	Block of 3, #a.-c. + label		2.50 2.50

UNICEF, 50th
Anniv. — A587

Children's paintings: 5 l, Fairy princess. 10 l,
Doll, sun. 25 l, Sea life. 50 l, House, people.

1996, Nov. 11 Perf. 13½
2521	A587	5 l	multicolored	.25 .25
2522	A587	10 l	multicolored	.25 .25
2523	A587	25 l	multicolored	.80 .80
2524	A587	50 l	multicolored	1.20 1.20
		Nos. 2521-2524 (4)		2.50 2.50

Gjergj Fishta
(1871-1940),
Writer,
Priest — A588

60 l, Battle scene, portrait.

1996, Dec. 20 Perf. 13½x14
2525	A588	10 l	shown	.25 .25
2526	A588	60 l	multicolored	1.40 1.40

Omar
Khayyam — A589

1997, Mar. 6 Perf. 14
2527	A589	20 l	shown	.40 .40
2528	A589	50 l	Portrait, diff.	1.00 1.00

A590

1997, Mar. 20 Perf. 14x14½
2529	A590	20 l	Portrait	.40 .40
2530	A590	60 l	Printing press	1.20 1.20
a.		Pair, #2529-2530		1.75 1.75

Johannes Gutenberg (1397?-1468).

A591

The Azure Eye (Stories and Legends): 30 l,
Dragon on rock looking at warrior, donkey.
100 l, Dragon drinking water from pond,
warrior.

1997, May 5 Litho. Perf. 13x14
2531	A591	30 l	multicolored	.70 .70
2532	A591	100 l	multicolored	2.25 2.25

Europa.

A592

1997, Apr. 10 Perf. 14
2533		10 l	Pelicanus crispus	.25 .25
2534		80 l	Pelicans, diff.	1.40 1.40
a.		A592 Pair, #2533-2534		1.75 1.75

No. 2534a is a continuous design.

A593

1997, June 25 Litho. Perf. 14
2535	A593	10 l	blk & dark brn	.25 .25
2536	A593	25 l	blk & blue blk	.75 .75

Souvenir Sheet
2537	A593	80 l	gray brown	2.00 2.00

Faik Konica (1875-1942), writer and
politician.
No. 2537 contains one 22x26mm stamp.

A594

1997 Mediterranean Games, Bari: 20 l, Man
running. 30 l, Woman running, 3-man canoe.

100 l, Man breaking finish line, silhouettes of man and woman.

1997, June 13
2538	A594	20 l multicolored	.40	.40
2539	A594	30 l multicolored	.80	.80

Size: 52x74mm
Imperf
2540	A594	100 l multicolored	2.00	2.00

Skanderbeg — A595

1997, Aug. 25   Litho.   *Perf. 13*
2541	A595	5 l red brn & red	.25	.25
2542	A595	10 l dp ol & ol	.25	.25
2543	A595	20 l dp grn & grn	.40	.40
2544	A595	25 l dp mag & red lil	.50	.50
2545	A595	30 l dk vio & vio	.55	.55
2546	A595	50 l black	.80	.80
2547	A595	60 l brn & lt brn	1.00	1.00
2548	A595	80 l dk brown & brn	1.50	1.50
2549	A595	100 l dk red brown & red brn	1.75	1.75
2550	A595	110 l dark blue	1.90	1.90
		Nos. 2541-2550 (10)	8.90	8.90

No. 2507 Ovptd. in Silver "HOMAZH / 1910-1997"

1997   *Perf. 13½x14*
2551	A581	100 l red & multi	2.50	2.50

Religious Manuscripts — A596

Albanian Codex: a, 10 l, 11th cent. b, 25 l, 6th cent. c, 60 l, 6th cent., diff.

1997, Nov. 15   Litho.   *Perf. 13x14*
2552	A596	Block of 3, #a.-c. + label	2.25	2.25

See No. 2575.

Post and Telecommunications Administration, 85th Anniv. — A597

1997, Dec. 4   *Perf. 13½*
2553	A597	10 l multi	.25	.25
2554	A597	30 l multi, diff.	.75	.75

A598

1998, Mar. 25   Litho.   *Perf. 14*
2555	A598	30 l red brn & multi	.60	.60
2556	A598	100 l tan & multi	1.90	1.90
a.		Pair, #2555-2556	2.50	2.50

Nikete Dardani, musician.

A599

Legends of Pogradecit: a, 30 l, Old man seated at table. b, 50 l, Three Graces. c, 60 l, Two women, fountain. d, 80 l, Iceman.

1998, Apr. 15
2557	A599	Block of 4, #a.-d.	3.50	3.50

A600

1998, May 5   Litho.   *Perf. 13x14*
2558	A600	60 l shown	1.50	1.50
2559	A600	100 l multi, diff.	2.00	2.00

Size: 50x72mm
Imperf
2560	A600	150 l multi, diff.	3.50	3.50

Europa (folk festivals).

A601

Albanian League of Prizren, 120th anniv.: a, 30 l, Abdyl Frasheri. b, 50 l, Sulejman Vokshi. c, 60 l, Iljaz Pashe Dibra. d, 80 l, Ymer Prizreni.

1998, June 10   Litho.   *Perf. 13½x13*
2561	A601	Block of 4, #a.-d.	2.75	2.75

1998 World Cup Soccer Championships, France — A602

Stylized soccer players.

1998, June 10   *Perf. 13½*
2562	A602	60 l multicolored	.90	.90
2563	A602	100 l multicolored	1.60	1.60

Size: 50x73mm
Imperf
2564	A602	120 l Mascot	2.25	2.25

European Youth Greco-Roman Wrestling Championships, Albania — A603

1998, July 5   *Perf. 13½*
2565	A603	30 l shown	.50	.50
2566	A603	60 l Wrestlers, diff.	1.00	1.00
a.		Pair, #2565-2566	1.60	1.60

Eqerem Cabej (1908-1980), Albanian Etymologist — A604

1998, Aug. 7   *Perf. 14*
2567	A604	60 l yel brn & multi	.80	.80
2568	A604	80 l brn red & multi	1.20	1.20
a.		Pair, #2567-2568	2.25	2.25

Paul Gauguin (1848-1903) A605

Paintings (details): 60 l, The Vision after the Sermon. 80 l, Ea Haere Ia Oe.

120 l, Stylized design to resemble self-portrait.

1998, Sept. 10   *Perf. 13½*
2569	A605	60 l multicolored	.90	.90
2570	A605	80 l multicolored	1.25	1.25
a.		Pair, #2569-2570	2.25	2.25

Size: 50x73mm
Imperf
2571	A605	120 l multicolored	2.25	2.25

Epitaph of Gllavenica, 14th Cent. Depiction of Christ — A606

Designs: 30 l, Entire cloth showing artwork. 80 l, Closer view. 100 l, Upper portion of cloth, vert.

1998, Oct. 5   *Perf. 14½x14*
2572	A606	30 l multicolored	.50	.50
2573	A606	80 l multicolored	1.50	1.50

Souvenir Sheet
Perf. 13
2574	A606	100 l multicolored	1.75	1.75

No. 2574 contains one 25x29mm stamp.

Religious Manuscripts Type of 1997

Illustrations from Purple Codex, Gold Codex: a, 30 l, Manuscript, columns on sides, arched top. b, 50 l, Manuscript cover with embossed pictures of icons. c, 80 l, Manuscript picturing cathedral, birds.

1998, Oct. 15   *Perf. 13x14*
2575	A596	Block of 3, #a.-c. + label	3.00	3.00

Mikel Koliqi (1902-97), First Albanian Cardinal — A607

1998, Nov. 28   *Perf. 14*
2576	A607	30 l shown	.50	.50
2577	A607	100 l Portrait, facing	1.75	1.75
a.		Pair, #2576-2577	2.50	2.50

Mother Teresa (1910-97) — A608

60 l, With child, horiz.

Perf. 14x13½, 13½x14
1998, Sept. 5   Photo.
2578	A608	60 l multicolored	1.50	1.50
2579	A608	100 l shown	2.50	2.50

See Italy Nos. 2254-2255.

Diana, Princess of Wales (1961-97) — A609

100 l, With Mother Teresa.

1998, Aug. 31   Litho.   *Perf. 13½*
2580	A609	60 l shown	2.00	2.00
2581	A609	100 l multicolored	3.00	3.00

No. 2508 Overprinted in Blue

1998, Oct. 23   **Litho.**   *Imperf.*
2582   A581   150 l multicolored   8.00   8.00

No. 2482 Surcharged

1999, Apr. 20   **Litho.**   *Perf. 14x13½*
2583   A571   150 l on 25 l multi   4.00   4.00

Famous Americans — A610

a, Washington. b, Lincoln. c. Martin Luther King, Jr.

1999, Mar. 15   *Perf. 14*
2584   A610   150 l Block of 3,
      #a.-c. + la-
      bel   9.00   9.00

Monachus Albiventer — A611

Seals: a, 110 l, One looking left, one looking right. b, 150 l, Both looking right. c, 110 l, Mirror image of No. 2585b. d, 150 l, Mirror image of No. 2585a.

1999, Apr. 10
2585   A611   Sheet of 4, #a.-d.   10.00   10.00

No. 2382
Surcharged

1999, Apr. 24   **Litho.**   *Perf. 12x12¼*
2586   A539   150 l on 90 l multi   3.25   3.25
     IBRA '99, Nuremburg.

A612

1999, Apr. 25   **Litho.**   *Perf. 13½x13¾*
2587   A612   10 l blue & multi   .75   .75
2588   A612   100 l green & multi   4.00   4.00

Souvenir Sheet
Perf. 13
2589   A612   250 l green & multi   5.00   5.00
     NATO, 50th anniv. No. 2589 contains one 30x50mm stamp.

A613

Cartoon mouse: a, 80 l, Writing. b, 110 l, Holding chin. c, 150 l, Wearing bow tie. d, 60 l, Pointing.

1999, Apr. 30   **Litho.**   *Perf. 13x13¾*
2590   A613   Strip of 4, #a.-d.   8.50   8.50
     Animated films.

Europa
A614

1999, May 1   **Litho.**   *Perf. 13¾x13*
2591   A614   90 l Thethi Park   2.00   2.00
2592   A614   310 l Lura Park   4.50   4.50

Imperf
Size: 80x60mm
2592A   A614   350 l Kombetare
      Park   9.00   9.00
     Nos. 2591-2592A (3)   15.50   15.50

Illyrian Coins
A615

Designs: a, 200 l, Kings of Illyria — Monumiou c. 300-280 BC cow suckling calf, square containing double stellate pattern, and Epidamos-Dyrrachium c. 623 BC, square with double stellate. b, 20 l, Damastion c. 395-380 BC siver drachm portable ingot, Byllis c. 238-168 BC AE13 serpent entwined around cornucopia, Skodra after 168 BC, AE17 war galley, and other war galley coin. c, 10l, Epirote Republic before 238 BC silver tetraobol with jugate busts of Zeus and Dione on obverse and thunderbolt within oak wreath reverse.
310 l, Kings of Illyria — Genthos c. 197-168 BC head wearing kausia.

1999, June 1   **Litho.**   *Perf. 13¾x13¼*
2593   A615   Strip of 3, #a.-c.   5.00   5.00
Souvenir Sheet
Perf. 13
2594   A615   310 l multicolored   6.50   6.50

Charlie
Chaplin — A616

Designs: 30 l, Holding cigarette. 50 l, Tipping hat. 250 l, Dancing.

1999, June 20   **Litho.**   *Perf. 14x14¼*
2595   A616   30 l multicolored   .75   .75
2596   A616   50 l multicolored   1.50   1.50
2597   A616   250 l multicolored   6.00   6.00
   a.   Booklet pane, 2 each
      #2595-2597, perf. 14¼
      vert.   70.00
      Complete booklet   70.00
      Nos. 2595-2597 (3)   8.25   8.25
In No. 2597a, the 30 l stamps are in the ends of the pane and the 250 l stamps are in the middle.

No. 2398
Surcharged

1999, July 2   **Litho.**   *Perf. 12½*
2598   A543   150 l on 30q multi   3.00   3.00
     PhilexFrance 99.

Holocaust — A617

1999, July 6   **Litho.**   *Perf. 14x14¼*
2599   A617   30 l brown & multi   .60   .60
2600   A617   150 l gray & multi   3.25   3.25

First Manned Moon Landing, 30th
Anniv. — A618

No. 2601: a, 30 l, Astronaut, earth. b, 150 l, Lunar Module. c, 300 l, Astronaut, flag. 280 l, Lift-off.

1999, July 25   **Litho.**   *Perf. 13¼x14*
2601   A618   Strip of 3, #a.-c   10.00   10.00
Souvenir Sheet
Perf. 13
2602   A618   280 l multicolored   6.00   6.00
     No. 2602 contains one 25x29mm stamp.

UPU, 125th Anniv. — A619

Background colors: a, 20 l, aquamarine and brown. b, 60 l, bister and dark blue.

1999, Aug. 1   **Litho.**   *Perf. 14x14¼*
2603   A619   Pair, #a.-b.   2.00   2.00

No. 2383
Surcharged in
Brown, Symbol
in Red and
Green

1999   **Method & Perf. as Before**
2604   A539   150 l on 1.20 l multi   3.00   3.00
     China 1999 World Philatelic Exhibition.

A620

Background colors: a, 10 l, Yellow. b, 20 l, Orange. c, 200 l, Green.

1999, Sept. 2   **Litho.**   *Perf. 14x14¼*
2605   A620   Strip of 3, #a.-c.   5.00   5.00
     First Natl. Track & Field Championships, 70th anniv.

A621

30 l, Madonna and Child.

1999, Oct. 30   **Perf. 14**
2606 A621 30 l multicolored   .50   .50
2607 A621 300 l shown   6.00   6.00
   a.   Souv. sheet, 2 ea #2606-
     2607   12.00   12.00

Art by Onufri of Elbasan.

Famous Albanians — A622

Designs: a, 10 l, Bilal Golemi (1899-1955), veterinarian. b, 20 l, Azem Galica (1889-1924), freedom fighter. c, 50 l, Viktor Eftimiu (1889-1972), writer. d, 300 l, Lasgush Poradeci (1900-87), poet.

1999, Nov. 28   **Litho.**   **Perf. 14¼x14**
2608 A622 Block of 4, #a.-d.   8.00   8.00

Carnival Masks — A623

1999, Dec. 1   **Perf. 13¾**
2609 A623 30 l shown   .50   .50
2610 A623 300 l Turkey head   6.50   6.50

Millennium
A624

2000, Mar. 27   **Litho.**   **Perf. 13½x14**
2611 A624 40 l red & multi   .75   .75
2612 A624 90 l blue & multi   2.00   2.00

Native Costumes — A625

a, 5 l, Librazhdi. b, 10 l, Malesia e Madhe woman. c, 15 l, Malesia e Madhe man. d, 20 l, Tropoje. e, 30 l, Dumrea. f, 35 l, Tirana man. g, 40 l, Tirana woman. h, 45 l, Arbereshe. i, 50 l, Gjirokaster. j, 55 l, Lunxheri. k, 70 l, Cameria. l, 90 l, Laberia.

2000, Mar. 28   **Perf. 13x13¾**
2613 A625 Booklet pane of 12   9.00   9.00
    Booklet, #2613   12.00

Gustave Mayer (1850-1900), Student of Albanian Culture — A626

Colors: a, 50 l, olive green. b, 130 l, carmine lake.

2000, Mar. 30   **Perf. 13½x14**
2614 A626 Pair, #a-b   3.50   3.50

Cartoon Duck — A627

Duck with: a, 250 l, Top hat. b, 10 l, Ten-gallon hat. c, 30 l, Cap. d, 90 l, Bow.

2000, Apr. 6   **Litho.**   **Perf. 13x13¾**
2615 A627 Strip of 4, #a-d   7.50   7.50

Grand Prix Race Cars — A628

Various cars.

2000, Apr. 10   **Litho.**   **Perf. 14¼x14**
2616   Bklt. pane of 10 + 2 labels   12.50   12.50
   a.-j.   A628 30 l any single   1.25   1.25
     Booklet, #2616   15.00

Holy Year 2000
A629

Designs: 15 l, Church with bell tower. 40 l, Church with conical roof. 90 l, Ruins. 250 l, Aerial view of ruins.

2000, Apr. 22   **Litho.**   **Perf. 13¾x14**
2617-2619 A629 Set of 3   4.00   4.00
    Souvenir Sheet
    Perf. 13¾
2620 A629 250 l multi   4.50   4.50

No. 2620 contains one 38x38mm stamp.

Europa, 2000
Common Design Type
2000, May 9   **Perf. 13x13¾**
2621 CD17 130 l multi   3.00   3.00
    Souvenir Sheet
    Perf. 13
2622 CD17 300 l Detail of #2621   8.00   8.00

No. 2622 contains one 25x29mm stamp.

Miniature Sheet

Wild Animals — A630

No. 2623: a, 10 l, Canis lupus. b, 40 l, Ursus arctos. c, 90 l, Sus scrofa. d, 220 l, Vulpes vulpes.

2000, May 17   **Perf. 14¼x13¾**
2623 A630 Sheet of 4, #a-d   7.50   7.50

Gustav Mahler (1860-1911), Composer A631

2000, May 30   **Perf. 13½x14**
2624 A631 130 l multi   2.50   2.50

WIPA 2000 Stamp Exhibition, Vienna.

European Soccer Championships — A632

10 l, Goalie. 120 l, Player heading ball. 260 l, Player kicking ball.

2000, June 1   **Perf. 13¾x13¼**
2625-2626 A632 Set of 2   2.50   2.50
    Imperf
    Size: 81x60mm
2627 A632 260 l multi   5.00   5.00

Paintings by Pablo Picasso — A633

Various unnamed paintings or self-portraits: 30 l, Brown panel. 40 l, Green panel. 130 l, Self-portrait, with Espana 2000 philatelic exhibition emblem, vert. 250 l, Blue panel.

2000   **Litho.**   **Perf. 13¾**
2628-2631 A633 Set of 4   6.50   6.50
    Souvenir Sheet
    Perf. 13
2632 A633 400 l Self-portrait   8.00   8.00

No. 2632 contains one 25x29mm stamp. Issued: 130 l, 10/6; others 6/7.

2000 Summer Olympics, Sydney — A634

No. 2633: a, 10 l, Basketball. b, 40 l, Soccer. c, 90 l, Runner. d, 250 l, Cycling.

2000, July 1   **Perf. 14x14¼**
2633 A634 Block of 4, #a-d   8.00   8.00

First Zeppelin Flight, Cent. — A635

No. 2634: a, 15 l, LZ-1 over Friedrichshafen. b, 30 l, Airship over Paris. c, 300 l, R34 over New York.
No. 2635, Ferdinand von Zeppelin.

2000, July 2   **Perf. 13¾x13**
2634 A635 Sheet of 3,
    #a-c   7.50   7.50
    Souvenir Sheet
    Perf. 13
2635 A635 300 l multi   6.50   6.50

No. 2634 contains three 40x28mm stamps.

Flowers — A636

No. 2636: a, 50 l, Gentiana lutea. b, 70 l, Gentiana cruciata.

2000, Oct. 10   **Perf. 13¼x14**
2636 A636 Pair, #a-b   2.75   2.75

Famous Albanians — A637

a, 30 l, Naim Frasheri, writer (1845-1900). b, 50 l, Bajram Curri, politician (1862-1925).

2000, Nov. 28   **Perf. 14¼x13¾**
2637 A637 Pair, #a-b   2.00   2.00

UN High Commissioner on Refugees, 50th Anniv. — A638

50 l, Mother & child. 90 l, Mother & child, diff.

2000, Dec. 14   **Perf. 13¾x14¼**
2638-2639 A638 Set of 2   3.00 3.00

Famous Albanians — A639

No. 2640: a, Ahmed Myftar Dede. b, Sali Njazi Dede.

2001, Feb. 22 Litho. Perf. 14¼x14
2640 A639 90 l Horiz. pair, #a-b   4.50 4.50

Native Costumes — A640

No. 2641: a, Man from Tropoje. b, Woman from Lume. c, Woman from Mirdite. d, Man from Lume. e, Woman from Zadrime. f, Woman from Shpati. g, Man from Kruje. h, Woman from Macukulli. i, Woman from Dardhe. j, Man from Lushnje. k, Woman from Dropulli. l, Woman from Shmili.

2001, Mar. 15   **Perf. 13x13¾**
2641 A640 20 l Sheet of 12, #a-l   5.00 5.00
    Booklet, #2641   7.00 7.00

See Nos. 2669, 2701, 2760, 2770.

Flowers — A641

No. 2642: a, 10 l, Magnolia grandiflora. b, 20 l, Rosa virginiana. c, 90 l, Dianthus barbatus. d, 140 l, Syringa vulgaris.

2001, Mar. 30   **Perf. 14x14¼**
2642 A641 Block of 4, #a-d   5.00 5.00

Cartoon Dog — A642

Denominations: a, 50 l. b, 90 l. c, 140 l, d, 20 l.

2001, Apr. 6   **Perf. 13x13¾**
2643 A642 Strip of 4, #a-d   5.00 5.00

Opera Composers — A643

Designs: No. 2644, 90 l, Vincenzo Bellini (1801-35). No. 2645, 90 l, Giuseppe Verdi (1813-1901). 300 l, Bellini and Verdi.

2001, Apr. 20   **Perf. 13¾x13**
2644-2645 A643 Set of 2   3.50 3.50
    Souvenir Sheet
    Perf. 13¾
2646 A643 300 l multi   5.00 5.00

Europa A644

Designs: 40 l, Waterfall, cliffs. 110 l, Waterfall, boulders. 200 l, Water, shoreline. 350 l, Ripples in water, vert.

2001, Apr. 29   **Perf. 13¾x14**
2647-2649 A644 Set of 3   6.50 6.50
    Souvenir Sheet
    Perf. 12¾x13
2650 A644 350 l multi   8.00 8.00

No. 2650 contains one 25x29mm stamp.

Domestic Animals — A645

No. 2651: a, 10 l, Horse. b, 15 l, Donkey. c, 80 l, Cat. d, 90 l, Dog. 300 l, Cat.

2001, May 17   **Perf. 14¼x14**
2651 A645 Sheet of 4, #a-d   4.00 4.00
    Souvenir Sheet
    Perf. 12¾x13
2652 A645 300 l shown   5.00 5.00

No. 2651 contains four 42x26mm stamps.

2001 Mediterranean Games, Tunis, Tunisia — A646

No. 2653: a, 10 l, Swimmer. b, 90 l, Runners. c, 140 l, Cyclists. 260 l, Discus thrower.

2001, June 1   **Perf. 14¼x14**
2653 A646 Vert. strip of 3, #a-c 5.00 5.00
    Souvenir Sheet
    Perf. 13x12¾
2654 A646 260 l multi   5.25 5.25

No. 2654 contains one 29x25mm stamp.

History of Aviation — A647

No. 2655: a, Clement Ader's flight of Eole, Oct. 9, 1890. b, Louis Blériot's flight of Blériot IX over English Channel, July 25, 1909. c, Charles Lindbergh's solo transatlantic flight of Spirit of St. Louis, May, 1927. d, Flight over Tirana, May 30, 1925. e, Antonov AN-10, 1956. f, First Concorde flight, Feb. 9, 1969. g, First Boeing 747 flight, Jan. 22, 1970. h, First flight of Space Shuttle Columbia, Apr. 12, 1981.

2001, June 20   **Perf. 13¾x13**
2655 A647 40 l Sheet of 8, #a-h   8.00 8.00

Bridges — A648

No. 2656: a, 10 l, Tabakeve. b, 20 l, Kamares. c, 40 l, Golikut. d, 90 l, Mesit. 250 l, Tabakeve.

2001, July 20   **Perf. 13¾x13¼**
2656 A648 Sheet of 4, #a-d   3.25 3.25
    Souvenir Sheet
    Perf. 12¾x13
2657 A648 250 l shown   5.00 5.00

No. 2656 contains four 38x30mm stamps.

Coats of Arms — A649

Arms of: 20 l, Dimitri of Arber. 45 l, Balsha. 50 l, Muzaka. 90 l, George Castrioti (Skanderbeg).

2001, Sept. 12   **Perf. 12¾x13**
2658 A649 20 l multi   .50 .50
   a.   Booklet pane of 4   2.00
2659 A649 45 l multi   1.00 1.00
   a.   Booklet pane of 4   9.00
2660 A649 50 l multi   1.10 1.10
   a.   Booklet pane of 4   4.50
2661 A649 90 l multi   2.00 2.00
   a.   Booklet pane of 4   8.00
    Booklet, #2658a-2661a   24.00
    Nos. 2658-2661 (4)   4.60 4.60

See Nos. 2681-2684, 2709-2712, 2775, 2797-2800, 2801-2804.

Year of Dialogue Among Civilizations A650

Colors of denomination: 45 l, Green. 50 l, Black. 120 l, White.

2001, Oct. 6   **Perf. 13½x14**
2662-2664 A650 Set of 3   5.00 5.00

Nobel Prizes, Cent. A651

Laureates: 10 l, Doctors Without Borders, Peace, 1999. 20 l, Wilhelm C. Roentgen, Physics, 1901. 90 l, Ferid Murad, Physiology or Medicine, 1988. 200 l, Mother Teresa, Peace, 1979.

2001, Dec. 1   **Perf. 13¾x13¼**
2665-2668 A651 Set of 4   7.50 7.50

Costumes Type of 2001

No. 2669: a, Man from Gjakova. b, Woman from Prizren. c, Man from Shkoder. d, Woman from Shkoder. e, Man from Berat. f, Woman from Berat. g, Woman from Elbasan. h, Man from Elbasan. i, Woman from Vlore. j, Man from Vlore. k, Woman from Gjirokaster. l, Woman from Delvina.

2002, Mar. 20 Litho. Perf. 13x13¾
2669 A640 30 l Sheet of 12, #a-l   8.75 8.75
    Complete booklet, #2669   9.75

Cartoon Deer — A652

No. 2670: a, 50 l, Deer. b, 90 l, Deer and rabbit. c, 140 l, Deer, diff. d, 20 l, Deer and rabbit, diff.

2002, Apr. 8   **Perf. 13x13¾**
2670 A652 Horiz. strip of 4, #a-d   5.50 5.50

Fireplaces — A653

Fireplace color: a, 30 l, Deep brown. b, 40 l, Henna brown. 50 l, Orange brown. 90 l, Chestnut.

2002, Apr. 15   Litho.   Perf. 14
2671 A653   Sheet of 4, #a-d   4.00 4.00

Europa — A654

Designs: 40 l, High wire act. 90 l, Acrobats. 220 l, Contortionist.
350 l, Trained horse act.

2002, May 1   Litho.   Perf. 13x13¾
2672-2674 A654   Set of 3   7.50 7.50
Souvenir Sheet
Perf. 13¾
2675 A654   350 l multi   7.50 7.50
No. 2675 contains one 37x37mm stamp.

2002 World Cup Soccer Championships, Japan and Korea — A655

Emblem, soccer ball and stylized players: 20 l, 30 l, 90 l, 120 l
360 l, Stylized player and emblem.

2002, May 6   Litho.   Perf. 13¾x13¼
2676-2679 A655   Set of 4   5.00 5.00
Souvenir Sheet
Perf. 13
2680 A655   360 l multi   7.00 7.00
No. 2680 contains one 50x29mm stamp.

Arms Type of 2001
2002, May 12   Perf. 13
2681 A649   20 l Gropa   .40 .40
a.   Booklet pane of 4   1.75
2682 A649   45 l Skurra   .90 .40
a.   Booklet pane of 4   4.00
2683 A649   50 l Bua   1.00 1.00
a.   Booklet pane of 4   4.50
2684 A649   90 l Topia   2.00 2.00
a.   Booklet pane of 4   9.00   —
    Complete booklet, #2681a-
    2684a   20.00
    Nos. 2681-2684 (4)   4.30 3.80

Cacti — A656

No. 2685: a, Opuntia catingola. b, Neoporteria pseudoreicheana. c, Lobivia shaferi. d, Hylocereus undatus. e, Borzicactus madisoniorum.

2002, May 17   Perf. 14
2685 A656   50 l Sheet of 5, #a-e   5.00 5.00

Blood Donation — A657

Letters "A," "B," and "O" with: No. 2686, 90 l, Stylized people. No. 2687, 90 l, Wings.

2002, June 16   Perf. 13¾x14¼
2686-2687 A657   Set of 2   4.00 4.00

Sportsmen A658

No. 2688: a, Naim Kryeziu, soccer player. b, Riza Lushta, soccer player. c, Ymer Pampuri, weight lifter.
300 l, Loro Borici, soccer player, vert.

2002, July 3   Perf. 14¼x14
2688   Horiz. strip of 3   3.50 3.50
a.-c.   A658 50 l Any single   1.10 1.10
Size: 60x80mm
Imperf
2689 A658   300 l multi   6.00 6.00

Intl. Federation of Stamp Dealers Associations, 50th Anniv. A659

Designs: 50 l, Man, #2471. 100 l, Map of Albania, Europe, cube of blue spheres.

2002, Sept. 1   Litho.   Perf. 13¾x13¼
2690-2691 A659   Set of 2   3.00 3.00

Anti-Terrorism — A660

Designs: 100 l, Statue of Liberty. 150 l, World Trade Center on fire.
350 l, Statue of Liberty and World Trade Center, vert.

2002, Sept. 11   Perf. 13¾x13
2692-2693 A660   Set of 2   5.00 5.00
Souvenir Sheet
Perf. 13
2694 A660   350 l multi   7.00 7.00
No. 2694 contains one 29x50mm stamp.

Mediterranean Sealife — A661

No. 2695: a, Caretta caretta. b, Delphinus delphis. c, Prionace glauca. d, Balaenoptera physalus. e, Torpedo torpedo. f, Octopus vulgaris.

Perf. 14¼x14¾
2002, Sept. 12   Litho.
2695 A661   50 l Sheet of 6, #a-
    f   6.00 6.00

Famous Albanians — A662

No. 2696: a, Tefta Tashko Koço (1910-47), singer. b, Naim Frasheri (1923-75), actor. c, Kristaq Antoniu (1909-79), singer. d, Panajot Kanaçi (1923-96), choreographer.

2002, Oct. 6   Perf. 13¾
2696 A662   50 l Block of 4, #a-d   4.00 4.00

Independence, 90th Anniv. — A663

Designs: 20 l, Flags of Albania and other nations. 90 l, People, Albanian flag.

2002, Nov. 28   Litho.   Perf. 13½x14
2697-2698 A663   Set of 2   2.00 2.00

Post and Telecommunications Administration, 90th Anniv. — A664

Designs: 20 l, Satellite dish. 90 l, Telegraph, air mail envelope.

2002, Dec. 4
2699-2700 A664   Set of 2   2.00 2.00

Costumes Type of 2001
No. 2701: a, Woman from Kelmendi. b, Man from Zadrime. c, Woman from Zerqani. d, Man from Peshkopi. e, Man from Malesia e Tiranes. f, Woman from Malesia e Tiranes. g, Woman from Fushe Kruje. h, Man from Shpati. i, Woman from Myzeqe. j, Woman from Labinoti. k, Man from Korce. l, Woman from Laberi.

2003, Apr. 1   Litho.   Perf. 13¼
2701 A640   30 l Sheet of 12,
    #a-l   8.00 8.00
    Booklet, #2701   10.00 10.00

Characterizations of Popeye — A665

No. 2702: a, 80 l, Popeye and Olive Oyl. b, 150 l, Popeye smoking pipe. c, 40 l, Popeye and Brutus. d, 50 l, Popeye walking.

2003, Apr. 6
2702 A665   Strip of 4, #a-d   7.00 7.00

Castles — A666

No. 2703: a, 10 l, Porto Palermo. b, 20 l, Petrela. c, 50 l, Kruja. d, 120 l, Preza.

2003, Apr. 15   Litho.   Perf. 13¼
2703 A666   Sheet of 4, #a-d   4.50 4.50

Europa — A667

Poster art: 150 l, Onufri. 200 l, Various posters.
350 l, Face from Onufri poster.

2003, Apr. 30   Perf. 14
2704-2705 A667   Set of 2   6.00 6.00
Souvenir Sheet
2706 A667   350 l multi   8.00 8.00

First Albanian Stamps, 90th Anniv. — A668

Designs: 50 l, Stamped envelopes, sheets of stamps. 1000 l, Seal of Post, Telegraph and Telephone Ministry.

2003, May 12   Perf. 13¼
2707-2708 A668   Set of 2   22.50 22.50

Arms Type of 2001
Family arms: 10 l, Arianiti. 20 l, Jonima. 70 l, Dukagjini. 120 l, Kopili.

2003, May 12
2709 A649   10 l multi   .30 .30
a.   Booklet pane of 4   1.25
2710 A649   20 l multi   .50 .50
a.   Booklet pane of 4   2.25
2711 A649   70 l multi   1.50 1.50
a.   Booklet pane of 4   7.00
2712 A649   120 l multi   2.50 2.50
a.   Booklet pane of 4   11.00   —
    Complete booklet, #2709a,
    2710a, 27111a, 2712a   24.00
    Nos. 2709-2712 (4)   4.80 4.80

Fruit — A669

No. 2713: a, 50 l, Punica gramatunil. b, 60 l, Citrus medica. c, 70 l, Cucumis melo. d, 80 l, Ficus.

Serpentine Die Cut 6¼

2003, May 17   **Self-Adhesive**
2713 A669   Sheet of 4, #a-d   5.50 5.50

Roman Emperors from Illyria and Coins Depicting Them — A670

No. 2714: a, Diocletian (c. 245-c. 313). b, Justinian I (483-565). c, Claudius II (214-70). d, Constantine I (the Great) (d. 337).

2003, June 20   **Litho.**   **Perf. 13¼**
2714 A670 70 l   Block of 4, #a-d   6.00 6.00

Birds — A671

No. 2715: a, Ciconia ciconia. b, Aquilia chrysaetos. c, Bubo bubo. d, Tetrao urogallos.

2003, Aug. 20   **Perf. 14½x14¼**
2715 A671 70 l   Sheet of 4, #a-d   6.00 6.00

First International Soccer Match in Albania, 90th Anniv. — A672

No. 2716: a, Denomination at right. b, Denomination at left.

2003, Sept. 2
2716 A672 80 l   Horiz. pair, #a-b   3.50 3.50

Paintings by Edouard Manet — A673

Designs: 40 l, Lunch in the Workshop (detail). 100 l, The Fifer.
250 l, Manet, horiz.

2003, Sept. 20   **Perf. 14½x14¼**
2717-2718 A673   Set of 2   3.00 3.00
Souvenir Sheet
Perf. 14¼x14½
2719 A673 250 l multi   4.50 4.50

Sculptors — A674

No. 2720: a, Odhise Paskali. b, Janaq Paco. c, Llazar Nikolla. d, Murat Toptani.

2003, Oct. 6   **Perf. 13¼**
2720 A674 50 l   Block of 4, #a-d   4.00 4.00

Beatification of Mother Teresa — A675

Sculptures of Mother Teresa: 40 l, Profile. 250 l, Front view.
350 l, Mother Teresa praying.

2003, Oct. 19   **Perf. 13¼**
2721-2722 A675   Set of 2   6.00 6.00
Souvenir Sheet
Perf.
2723 A675 350 l multi   7.00 7.00
   No. 2723 contains one 40mm diameter stamp.

Natural Monuments — A676

Designs: 20 l, Divjaka Forest Park. 30 l, Fir trees, Hotova. 200 l, Fir tree, Drenova.

2003, Oct. 20   **Perf. 13¼**
2724-2726 A676   Set of 3   5.00 5.00

Tour de France Bicycle Race, Cent. A677

Designs: 50 l, Cyclist, "100," map of France. 100 l, Cyclists, French flag.

2003, Nov. 1   **Perf. 14¼x14½**
2727-2728 A677   Set of 2   3.00 3.00

Europa — A678

Various vacation spots with country name in: No. 2729, 200 l, White. No. 2730, 200 l, Light blue.
350 l, Orange.

2004, June 23   **Litho.**   **Perf. 13½**
2729-2730 A678   Set of 2   9.00 9.00
   a. Booklet pane, 4 each #2729-
     2730, perf. 13½ on 3 sides   46.00   —
     Complete booklet, #2730a   46.00
Souvenir Sheet
Perf. 14¼x13½
2731 A678 350 l multi   9.00 9.00
   No. 2731 contains one 29x37mm stamp. In No. 2730a, the two columns in the middle are tete-beche pairs of Nos. 2729-2730.

European Soccer Championships, Portugal — A679

Various players: 20 l, 40 l, 50 l, 200 l. 350 l, Player (37mm diameter stamp).

2004, June 24   **Perf. 14**
2732-2735 A679   Set of 4   7.00 7.00
Souvenir Sheet
Perf.
2736 A679 350 l multi   8.00 8.00

2004 Summer Olympics, Athens — A680

Designs: 10 l, Statue of discus thrower. 200 l, Bust.
350 l, Torch bearer.

2004, Aug. 12   **Perf. 13½**
2737-2738 A680   Set of 2   4.50 4.50
Souvenir Sheet
Perf. 13½x13¾
2739 A680 350 l multi   8.00 8.00
   No. 2739 contains one 38x54mm stamp.

Prince Wilhelm zu Wied (1876-1945), Appointed Ruler of Albania A681

Designs: 40 l, With hat. 150 l, Without hat.

2004, Aug. 30   **Litho.**   **Perf. 13½**
2740-2741 A681   Set of 2   4.00 4.00

Characterizations of Bugs Bunny — A682

No. 2742 — Background color: a, 40 l, Orange. b, 50 l, Light blue. c, 80 l, Purple. d, 150 l, Green.

2004, Sept. 15
2742 A682   Horiz. strip of 4, #a-d   7.00 7.00

Icons Painted by Nikolla Onufri A683

Various saints: 10 l, 20 l, 1000 l.

2004, Oct. 3   **Perf. 14**
2743-2745 A683   Set of 3   22.50 22.50
Souvenir Sheet
Perf. 13½x14¼
2746 A683 400 l Saint, diff.   9.00 9.00

Souvenir Sheet

Ladybugs — A684

No. 2747: a, With 12 spots, on flower. b, With 5 spots, on flower. c, With wings extended. d, On leaves.

2004, Oct. 10   **Perf. 14**
2747 A684 80 l   Sheet of 4, #a-d   7.00 7.00

Entertainment Personalities — A685

No. 2748: a, Ndrek Luca (1924-93), actor. b, Jorgjia Truja (1909-94), singer, film director. c, Maria Kraja (1911-99), opera singer. d, Zina Andri (1924-80), actress, theater director.

2004, Oct. 12   **Perf. 13¾x13½**
2748 A685 50 l   Block of 4, #a-d   4.50 4.50

Coats of Arms — A686

Designs: 20 l, Spani. 40 l, Gjuraj. 80 l, Zaharaj. 150 l, Dushmani.

2004, Oct. 25   **Perf. 13¾x14**
2749 A686 20 l multi   .50 .50
   a.   Booklet pane of 4   2.00
2750 A686 40 l multi   .80 .80
   a.   Booklet pane of 4   3.50

2751	A686	80 l multi	2.00	2.00
a.		Booklet pane of 4	8.00	
2752	A686	150 l multi	3.25	3.25
a.		Booklet pane of 4	14.00	
		Complete booklet, #2749a-2752a	29.00	
		Nos. 2749-2752 (4)	6.55	6.55

Souvenir Sheet

Dahlias — A687

No. 2753: a, Pink flower with small petals, large bud in front. b, Bud in back. c, Small flower at right. d, Red flower with large petals, small bud in front.

2004, Nov. 1   **Perf. 14**
2753 A687   80 l Sheet of 4, #a-d   7.00   7.00

Art in National Gallery — A688

No. 2745 — Art by: a, Unknown artist (Madonna and Child). b, Mihal Anagnosti. c, Onufer Qiprioti. d, Cetiret. e, Onuferi. f, Kel Kodheli. g, Vangjush Mio. h, Abdurahim Buza. i, Mustafa Arapi. j, Guri Madhi. k, Janaq Paço. l, Zef Kolombi. m, Hasan Reçi. n, Vladimir Jani. o, Halim Beqiri. p, Edison Gjergo. q, Naxhi Bakalli. r, Agron Bregu. s, Edi Hila. t, Artur Muharremi. u, Rembrandt. v, Gazmend Leka. w, Damien Hirst. x, Edvin Rama. y, Ibrahim Kodra.

2004, Nov. 20   **Perf. 14**
2754		Sheet of 25	12.50	12.50
a.-y.	A688	20 l Any single	.50	.50

NATO in Kosovo, 5th Anniv. — A689

NATO emblem and: 100 l, Pennants and stars. 200 l, Doves, UN flag. 350 l, Buildings, Albanian flag.

2004, Nov. 28   **Perf. 14¼x13½**
2755-2756 A689   Set of 2   7.00   7.00

Souvenir Sheet
2757 A689 350 l multi   8.00   8.00

Liberation From Nazi Occupation, 60th Anniv. — A690

Designs: 50 l, Two doves. 200 l, One dove.

2004, Nov. 29   **Perf. 13¾x13½**
2758-2759 A690   Set of 2   6.00   6.00

Native Costumes Type of 2001

No. 2760: a, Woman from Gramshi (showing back). b, Woman from Gramshi (showing front). c, Woman from Korça with blue skirt. d, Man from Kolonja. e, Woman from Korça with red dress. f, Woman from Librazhdi. g, Woman from Permeti. h, Woman from Pogradeci. i, Man from Skrapari. j, Woman from Skrapari. k, Woman from Tepelena. l, Woman from Vlora.

2004, Dec. 4   **Perf. 13½**
2760	A640	30 l Sheet of 12, #a-l	10.00	10.00
		Complete booklet, #2760	11.50	

Europa Stamps, 50th Anniv. (in 2006) — A691

Vignettes similar to: 200 l, #2558. 250 l, #2471, horiz. 500 l, #2675.

2005, Oct. 1   **Litho.**   **Perf. 13¾**
2761-2762 A691   Set of 2   10.00   10.00

Souvenir Sheet
2763 A691 500 l multi   12.00   12.00

No. 2763 contains one 38x38mm stamp.

A692

Europa — A693

2005, Oct. 5   **Perf. 14x13¾**
2764	A692	200 l multi	5.00	5.00
a.		Perf. 13¼x13¾ on 2 or 3 sides	5.00	5.00
2765	A693	200 l multi	5.00	5.00
a.		Perf. 13¼x13¾ on 2 or 3 sides	5.00	5.00

Souvenir Sheet
Perf. 12¾x13
2766	A633	350 l Stuffed cabbage	9.00	9.00
a.		Booklet pane, 3 each 2764a, 2765a	40.00	—
		Complete booklet, #2766a	55.00	

No. 2766 contains one 25x30mm stamp. Serial number is at top right of sheet margin on No. 2766, and on binding stub on No. 2766a. No. 2766a sold for 1650 l.

Admission to the United Nations, 50th Anniv. — A694

2005, Oct. 19   **Perf. 12¾**
2767 A694 40 l multi   .80   .80

Cartoon Characters: — A695

No. 2768 — Tom & Jerry: a, 150 l, Tom. b, 40 l, Tom & Jerry. c, 50 l, Tom & Jerry, diff. d, 80 l, Jerry.

2005, Oct. 20   **Perf. 14**
2768 A695   Horiz. strip of 4, #a-d   6.00   6.00

Paintings A696

Various unattributed paintings: a, Mountain, town and river. b, Castle and aqueduct. c, Crowd, minaret. d, Castle on mountain, people near river.

2005, Oct. 21   **Perf. 14**
2769		Horiz. strip of 4	20.00	20.00
a.	A696	10 l multi	.30	.30
b.	A696	20 l multi	.30	.30
c.	A696	30 l multi	.60	.60
d.	A696	1000 l multi	17.50	17.50

Costumes Type of 2001

No. 2770: a, Man, Tirana. b, Woman, Bende Tirana. c, Woman, Zall Dajt. d, Man, Kavaje-Durres. e, Woman, Has. f, Man, Mat. g, Woman, Liqenas. h, Woman, Klenje. i, Woman, Maleshove. j, Woman, German. k, Woman, Kruje. l, Man, Reç.

2005, Oct. 24   **Perf. 14x13¾**
2770	A640	30 l Sheet of 12, #a-l	8.00	8.00
		Complete booklet, #2770	13.00	

Complete booklet sold for 460 l.

2005 Mediterranean Games, Almería, Spain — A697

2005, Oct. 25   **Perf. 14¼x13¾**
2771		Horiz. strip of 3	3.50	3.50
a.	A697	20 l Runner in blocks	.40	.40
b.	A697	60 l Gymnastics	1.00	1.00
c.	A697	120 l Relay race	2.00	2.00

Souvenir Sheet
Perf. 12¾x13
2772 A697 300 l Diver   7.50   7.50

No. 2772 contains one 50x30mm stamp.

Rotary International, Cent. — A698

Rotary International emblem and: 30 l, Map of North America. 150 l, Rays and "100 Vjet," vert.

2005, Nov. 11   **Perf. 13¾**
2773-2774 A698   Set of 2   4.00   4.00

Arms Type of 2001

No. 2775 — Arms of: a, Bua Despots. b, Karl Topia. c, Dukagjini II. d, Engjej.

2005, Nov. 14   **Perf. 12¾**
2775		Horiz. strip of 4	5.00	5.00
a.	A649	10 l multi	.30	.30
b.	A649	30 l multi	.50	.50
c.	A649	100 l multi	1.50	1.50
d.	A649	150 l multi	2.50	2.50
e.		Booklet pane, 4 #2775a	1.30	—
f.		Booklet pane, 4 #2775b	2.50	—
g.		Booklet pane, 4 #2775c	7.00	—
h.		Booklet pane, 4 #2775d	11.00	—
		Complete booklet, #2775e-2775h	25.00	

Souvenir Sheet

Portulaca Flowers — A699

No. 2776: a, Yellow flowers. b, Three white flowers. c, Red and bright yellow flowers. d, Pink flower. e, Red flower.

2005, Nov. 17   **Perf. 14**
2776 A699 70 l Sheet of 5, #a-e   9.00   9.00

Cycling in Albania, 80th Anniv. — A700

2005, Nov. 20   **Perf. 13¼x13¾**
2777		Strip of 3	6.00	6.00
a.	A700	50 l blue & multi	1.25	1.25
b.	A700	60 l red & multi	1.75	1.75
c.	A700	120 l bright red & multi	3.25	3.25

Souvenir Sheet

Skanderbeg (1405-68), National Hero — A701

No. 2778 — Various scenes of warriors in battle: a, 40 l (50x30mm). b, 50 l (50x30mm). c, 60 l (50x30mm). d, 70 l (50x30mm). e, 80 l (30mm diameter). f, 90 l (30mm diameter).

2005, Nov. 28   **Perf. 13**
2778 A701   Sheet of 6, #a-f   10.00   10.00

End of World War II, 60th Anniv. — A702

No. 2779: a, 50 l, Doves, roses, army helmet. b, 200 l, Statues, flags, dove.

2005, Nov. 29   **Perf. 14x13¾**
2779 A702   Horiz. pair, #a-b   5.25   5.25

Marubi Family Artists A703

No. 2780: a, Matia Kodheli-Marubi. b, Gege Marubi. c, Pjeter Marubi. d, Kel Marubi.

2005, Dec. 4
2780		Horiz. strip of 4	7.50	7.50
a.	A703	10 l multi	.30	.30
b.	A703	20 l multi	.50	.50
c.	A703	70 l multi	1.75	1.75
d.	A703	200 l multi	5.00	5.00

Nos. 2417, 2433, 2446, 2477, 2478, 2484, 2487, 2490-2492, 2498 and 2504 Surcharged

Methods and Perfs as Before
2006
2781	A550	on 30q #2417	2.00	2.00
2782	A569	on 2 l #2478	2.00	2.00
2783	A574	on 2 l #2490		

2784	A574	on 3 l #2491	2.00	2.00
2785	A577	on 3 l #2498	2.00	2.00
2786	A552	on 10 l #2433	2.00	2.00
2787	A572	on 18 l #2484	2.00	2.00
2788	A573	on 18 l #2487	2.00	2.00
2789	A556	on 21 l #2446	2.00	2.00
2790	A568	on 25 l #2477		
		(block of 4, #a-d)	150.00	150.00
2791	A574	on 25 l #2492	2.00	2.00
2792	A580	on 25 l #2504	2.00	2.00
		Nos. 2781-2789,2791-2792		
		(11)	22.00	22.00

Location of surcharge varies.

Visit of Pres. George W. Bush to Albania — A704

No. 2793 — Photograph of Bush in: a, 20 l, Blue. b, 40 l, Green. c, 80 l, Full color. 200 l, Statue of Liberty, flags of US and Albania, horiz.

Perf. 13¼x13½

2007, June 10   **Litho.**
2793 A704   Horiz. strip of 3,
   #a-c   3.50   3.50

Souvenir Sheet
Perf. 13½x13¼
2794 A704   200 l multi   4.00   4.00

Italian Delegation of Experts in Albania, 10th Anniv. — A705

Perf. 13¼x13½
2007, Sept. 15   **Litho.**
Granite Paper
2795 A705   40 l multi   1.25   1.25

Miniature Sheet

Albanian Flag — A706

No. 2796 — Various depictions of Albanian flag blowing in wind: a, 5 l. b, 10 l. c, 20 l. d, 30 l. e, 40 l. f, 50 l. g, 60 l. h, 70 l. i, 80 l. j, 100 l. k, 1000 l. l, 2000 l.

2007, Oct. 5   **Litho.**   **Perf. 13¼x13**
2796 A706   Sheet of 12,
   #a-l   100.00 100.00

Arms Type of 2001

Arms of: 20 l, Despot Andrea II Muzaka. 40 l, Matrenga family. 80 l, Leke Dukagjini. 150 l, Konstantin Kastrioti.

2007, Oct. 15   **Litho.**   **Perf. 12¾x13¼**
2797	A649	20 l multi	1.50	1.50
2798	A649	40 l multi	3.00	3.00
2799	A649	80 l multi	5.50	5.50
2800	A649	150 l multi	10.00	10.00
a.		Vert. strip of 4, #2797-2800		
		Nos. 2797-2800 (4)	20.00	20.00

Nos. 2797-2800 are dated 2006.

Arms Type of 2001

Arms of: 10 l, Lança family. 20 l, Riki family. 60 l, Kokini family. 100 l, Zako family.

2007, Oct. 17   **Litho.**   **Perf. 12¾x13¼**
2801	A649	10 l multi	.50	.50
2802	A649	20 l multi	1.00	1.00
2803	A649	60 l multi	3.00	3.00

2804	A649	100 l multi	5.50	5.50
a.		Vert. strip of 4, #2801-2804		
		Nos. 2801-2804 (4)	10.00	10.00

Europa — A707

Men and women and: No. 2805, 200 l, Flag of European Union, map of Europe. No. 2806, 200 l, Flag and map of Albania. 350 l, Men, women, flags of Albania and European Union, horiz.

2007, Oct. 23   **Litho.**   **Perf. 13x13¼**
2805-2806 A707   Set of 2   10.00 10.00

Souvenir Sheet
Perf. 13¼x13
2807 A707   350 l multi   9.00   9.00

No. 2807 contains one 30x25mm stamp. Dated 2006.

Europa — A708

Designs: 100 l, Scouts, flags, mountain. 150 l, Scouts, flags, mountain, diff. 250 l, Knot, horiz.

2007, Oct. 24   **Perf. 13¼x13**
2808-2809 A708   Set of 2   6.50   6.50

Souvenir Sheet
2810 A708   250 l multi   6.50   6.50

Scouting, cent. No. 2810 contains one 30x25mm stamp.

Pink Panther — A709

No. 2811 — Pink Panther: a, 150 l, Wearing uniform. b, 40 l, Wearing bowtie. c, 50 l, With inspector. d, 80 l, With elbow resting on orange panel.

2007, Oct. 25   **Perf. 13**
2811 A709   Horiz. strip of 4,
   #a-d   7.00   7.00

Children's Art — A710

No. 2812 — Art by: a, 10 l, Arkida Lema. b, 40 l, Amarilda Prifti. c, 50 l, Iliaz Kasa. d, 80 l, Klaudia Mezini, horiz.

2007, Oct. 29   **Perf. 13**
2812 A710   Horiz. strip of 4, #a-d   7.00   7.00

Frescoes — A712

Designs: 70 l, sower, by David Selenices. 110 l, Floral mural, Et'hem Bey Mosque, Tirana.

2007, Oct. 31   **Litho.**   **Perf. 13**
2814-2815 A712   Set of 2   4.50   4.50

Miniature Sheet

Native Costumes — A713

No. 2816: a, German woman. b, Kurbin man. c, Golloborde woman. d, Kerrabe Malesi man. e, Gur i Bardhe woman. f, Martanesh woman. g, Puke woman. h, Serice Labinot woman. i, Shen Gjergj woman. j, Tirane Qytet woman. k, Zalle Dajt man. l, Zaranike Godolesh woman.

2008, Nov. 1   **Litho.**   **Perf. 13**
2816 A713   40 l Sheet of 12,
   #a-l   12.00 12.00

Dated 2006. A sheet of 20 l stamps depicting native costumes with country name at left was issued on Nov. 2 in limited quantities to those with reservations to purchase the sheet, and later was sold at an inflated price. Value, $100.

Tourism A714

No. 2817: a, Thethi National Park (Parku Kombetar Thethit). b, Lures Lake (Liqenet e Lures). c, Kanina Castle (Kalaja e Kanines). d, Karavasta Lagoon (Laguna e Karavastase).

2007, Nov. 5
2817   Horiz. strip of 4   7.00   7.00
   a. A714 40 l green & multi   1.00   1.00
   b. A714 50 l red violet & multi   1.25   1.25
   c. A714 60 l red & multi   1.50   1.50
   d. A714 70 l blue violet & multi   2.25   2.25

Trees of Elbasan A715

Designs: 70 l, Tree and pond. 90 l, Hollowed-out tree.

2007, Nov. 8   **Perf. 13x13¼**
2818-2819 A715   Set of 2   4.50   4.50

Dated 2006.

Pope Clement XI (1649-1721) A716

No. 2820: a, 30 l, Red background. b, 120 l, Blue background.

2007, Nov. 9   **Perf. 13¼x13**
2820 A716   Vert. pair, #a-b   4.50   4.50

Dated 2006.

Léopold Sédar Senghor (1906-2001), First President of Senegal — A717

Color of photograph: 40 l, Sepia. 80 l, Black.

2007, Nov. 10
2821-2822 A717   Set of 2   4.00   4.00

Dated 2006.

Albania as Balkan Soccer Champions, 60th Anniv. (in 2006) — A718

Background colors: 10 l, Buff and red. 80 l, Light and dark blue.

2007, Nov. 11   **Perf. 13x13¼**
2823-2824 A718   Set of 2   7.00   7.00

Dated 2006.

Miniature Sheet

Gjirokaster UNESCO World Heritage Site — A719

No. 2825: a, 10 l, Cannons. b, 20 l, Wall decoration. c, 30 l, Building. d, 60 l, Bridge. e, 80 l, Aerial view of town. f, 90 l, Castle atop cliff.

2007, Nov. 12   **Perf. 13¼x13**
2825 A719   Sheet of 6, #a-f   9.00   9.00

Dated 2006.

Participation of Albanian Military in International Missions, 10th Anniv. (in 2006) — A720

Designs: 10 l, Soldier in gas mask. 100 l, Soldiers in raft.

2008, Nov. 13
2826-2827 A720 Set of 2 3.00 3.00
Dated 2006.

Mother Teresa (1910-97), 1978 Nobel Peace Laureate — A721

Background color: 60 l, Orange yellow. 130 l, Brown.

2007, Nov. 15 *Perf. 13¼x13*
2828-2829 A721 Set of 2 7.50 7.50

Statue of Gaia Found Near Durres — A722

No. 2831: a, 30 l, Small image of statue. b, 120 l, Large image of statue.

2007, Nov. 16 Litho. *Perf. 13¼x13*
2831 A722 Vert. pair, #a-b 10.00 10.00

A 200 l souvenir sheet issued with this set was sold in limited quantities to those with reservations to purchase the sheet, and later was sold at an inflated price. Value, $100.

Prehistoric Cave and Rock Drawings A723

Designs: 20 l, Rock drawings, Lepenice. 100 l, Rock drawing, Tren. 300 l, Cave drawing, Tren.

2007, Nov. 19 *Perf. 13¼x13*
2832-2833 A723 Set of 2 3.00 3.00
Souvenir Sheet
Perf. 13x13¼
2834 A723 300 l multi 6.00 6.00
Dated 2006.

Famous Men A724

No. 2835: a, Osman Kazazi (1917-99), resistance leader. b, Pjeter Arbnori (1935-2006), politician. c, Lasgush Poradeci (1899-1987), writer. d, Cesk Zadeja (1927-97), musician.

2007, Nov. 22 *Perf. 13¼x13*
2835 Horiz. strip of 4 5.50 5.50
a. A724 10 l multi .30 .30
b. A724 20 l multi .30 .30
c. A724 60 l multi 1.25 1.25
d. A724 100 l multi 2.00 2.00

Famous Men — A725

No. 2836: a, Abdurrahim Buza (1905-87), painter. b, Aleks Buda (1911-93), historian. c, Thimi Mitko (1820-90), writer. d, Martin Camaj (1925-94), writer.

2007, Nov. 22 *Perf. 13x13¼*
2836 Horiz. strip of 4 5.75 5.75
a.-d. A725 50 l Any single 1.25 1.25
Dated 2006.

2006 World Cup Soccer Championships, Germany — A726

Stylized soccer players with background colors of: 30 l, Yellow. 60 l, Red. 120 l, Black. 350 l, Emblem of 2006 World Cup.

2007, Nov. 26
2837-2839 A726 Set of 3 10.00 10.00
Souvenir Sheet
2840 A726 350 l multi 15.00 15.00
Dated 2006.

Independence, 95th Anniv. — A727

Ismail Qemali (1844-1919), first Albanian Prime Minister and: 50 l, Heraldic eagle and years. 110 l, Text.

2007, Nov. 28 *Perf. 13x13¼*
2841-2842 A727 Set of 2 5.50 5.50

Vegetables A728

No. 2843: a, Garlic. b, Onions. c, Peppers. d, Tomatoes.

2007, Dec. 3 Litho. *Perf. 12¾*
2843 Horiz. strip of 4 + 3 labels 12.50 12.50
a.-d. A728 80 l Any single 3.00 3.00

Wulfenia Baldacci A729

2007, Dec. 4 Litho. *Perf. 13*
2844 Horiz. pair + central label 10.00 10.00
a. A729 70 l lilac & multi 3.75 3.75
b. A729 100 l buff & multi 5.25 5.25

Albanian Post and Telecommunications Department, 95th Anniv. — A730

Denomination in: 80 l, Red. 90 l, Black.

2007, Dec. 5 *Perf. 13¼x13*
2845-2846 A730 Set of 2 5.50 5.50

Miniature Sheet

Infrastructure Development — A731

No. 2847: a, 10 l, Trans-Balkan Road. b, 20 l, Port of Durres. c, 30 l, Road, Tirana. d, 40 l, Mother Teresa Terminal. e, 50 l, Road, Shkoder. f, 60 l, Tepelene-Gjirokaster Road. g, 70 l, Fier-Lushnje Road. h, 80 l, Kalimash-Morine Road.
150 l, Mother Teresa Air Terminal, Tirana.

2007, Dec. 7 *Perf. 13¼x12¾*
2847 A731 Sheet of 8, #a-h 11.00 11.00
Souvenir Sheet
2848 A731 150 l multi 4.50 4.50

Invitation to Join NATO — A732

No. 2849 — NATO emblem and: a, 40 l, Flags of member nations. b, 60 l, Heraldic eagles.

2008, Apr. 12 Litho. *Perf. 13x13¼*
2849 A732 Horiz. pair, #a-b 2.00 2.00

Children's Drawings — A733

No. 2850 — Dove and: a, 40 l, Black doves and flowers. b, 70 l, Boat on water.

2008, June 1 Litho. *Perf. 13x13¼*
2850 A733 Horiz. pair, #a-b 3.00 3.00

UEFA Euro 2008 Soccer Championships, Austria and Switzerland — A734

No. 2851: a, 50 l, Map of Switzerland. b, 250 l, Map of Austria
200 l, Mascots, vert.

2008, June 16 *Perf. 13x13¼*
2851 A734 Horiz. pair, #a-b 10.00 10.00
Souvenir Sheet
Perf. 13¼x13
2852 A734 200 l multi 5.00 5.00

Prizren League, 130th Anniv. — A735

No. 2853: a, 100 l, Handwritten document. b, 150 l, Building, Albanian flag.

2008, June 27 *Perf. 13¼x13*
Granite Paper
2853 A735 Vert. pair, #a-b 7.50 7.50

First Albanian Postage Stamps, 95th Anniv. — A736

2008, June 30 *Litho.*
2854 A736 40 l multi 1.00 1.00

Famous People of Albanian Heritage A737

No. 2855: a, John Belushi (1949-82), actor. b, Gjon Mili (1904-84), photographer. c, Mimar Sinan (1489-1588), architect. d, Ibrahim Kodra (1918-2006), artist.

2008, July 9 *Perf. 13¼x13¼*
2855 Horiz. strip of 4 5.50 5.50
a. A737 5 l multi .30 .30
b. A737 10 l multi .30 .30
c. A737 20 l multi .30 .30
d. A737 200 l multi 4.00 4.00

A738

Europa — A739

Hand holding quill pen and: 100 l, Map of Europe. 150 l, Map of Albania and Adriatic region.

2008, July 15   *Perf. 13¼x13*
Granite Paper (#2856-2857)
2856-2857 A738   Set of 2   6.50   6.50

Souvenir Sheet
Perf. 13x13¼
2858 A739 250 l multi   6.50   6.50

Poppies — A740

No. 2859: a, 50 l, Two poppies. b, 150 l, One poppy.

2008, July 30   *Perf. 13¼x13*
Granite Paper
2859 A740   Vert. pair, #a-b   5.00   5.00

2008 Summer Olympics, Beijing — A741

No. 2860: a, Soccer. b, Water polo. c, Running. d, Cycling.

2008, Aug. 8   *Perf. 13x13¼*
2860   Horiz. strip of 4   4.00   4.00
   a. A741 20 l multi   .60   .60
   b. A741 30 l multi   .80   .80
   c. A741 40 l multi   1.00   1.00
   d. A741 50 l multi   1.40   1.40

Landscapes — A742

No. 2861: a, 60 l, Osumit Canyon. b, 250 l, Komanit Lake.

2008, Aug. 25   *Perf. 13*
2861 A742   Horiz. pair, #a-b   9.00   9.00

King Zog (1895-1961) — A743

No. 2862 — Denomination color: a, 40 l, Black. b, 100 l, Red.

2008, Sept. 1   *Perf. 13x13¼*
2862 A743   Horiz. pair, #a-b   4.25   4.25

Freedom Fighters — A744

No. 2863: a, 40 l, Azem Hajdari (1963-98), assassinated politician. b, 200 l, Adem Jashari (1955-98), Kosovar independence leader.

2008, Sept. 12
2863 A744   Horiz. pair, #a-b   7.00   7.00

Independence of Kosovo — A745

No. 2864: a, 20 l, Ymer Prizreni (1820-87), political leader. b, 30 l, Isa Boletini (1864-1916), military leader. c, 40 l, Ibrahim Rugova (1944-2006), President of Kosovo. d, 50 l, Azem Galica (1889-1924), military leader. e, 70 l, Adem Jashari (1955-98), independence leader.

2008, Sept. 20   *Perf. 13¼x13*
2864 A745   Block of 5, #a-e, +   4 labels   6.00   6.00

Roman Emperors of Illyrian Origin — A746

No. 2865: a, 30 l, Decius (201-51). b, 200 l, Maximinus Thrax (173-238).

2008, Oct. 3   *Perf. 13*
2865 A746   Vert. pair, #a-b   6.50   6.50

Harry Potter — A747

No. 2866 — Harry Potter and: a, 20 l, Professor Dumbledore. b, 30 l, Kreacher. c, 50 l, Hermione Granger and friends. d, 100 l, Kreacher.

2008, Oct. 15   *Perf. 13x13¼*
2866 A747   Block of 4, #a-d   7.50   7.50

A booklet containing a pane of Nos. 2866a-2866d sold for 550 l.

Monastir Congress, Cent. — A748

No. 2867: a, 40 l, Building. b, 100 l, Pages with handwritten Albanian alphabet.

2008, Nov. 14   *Perf. 13*
2867 A748   Horiz. pair, #a-b   4.50   4.50

Archaeology — A749

No. 2868: a, Ruins of synagogue, Sarande. b, Site at Orikumit. c, Site at Antigonese.

2008, Dec. 5   *Perf. 13*
2868   Horiz. strip of 3   4.50   4.50
   a. A749 10 l multi   .30   .30
   b. A749 50 l multi   1.75   1.75
   c. A749 80 l multi   2.25   2.25

Universal Postal Union, 135th Anniv. — A750

No. 2869 — Emblems of Albania Post and UPU, world map and background color of: a, 100 l, Yellow bister. b, 200 l, Light blue, vert.

Perf. 13x13¼ (#2869a), 13¼x13 (#2869b)
2009, Oct. 9   Litho.
2869 A750   Pair, #a-b   6.50   6.50

Stan Laurel (1890-1965) and Oliver Hardy (1892-1957), Comedians A751

No. 2870 — Laurel and Hardy: a, 150 l, Holdings hats. b, 200 l, Wearing hats. 300 l, Laurel and Hardy wearing mortarboards, horiz.

2009, Oct. 16   Litho.   *Perf. 13¼x13*
2870 A751   Vert. pair, #a-b   10.00   10.00

Souvenir Sheet
Perf. 13x13¼
2871 A751 300 l multi   8.00   8.00

Weight Lifting — A752

No. 2872 — Various weight lifters and: a, 10 l, Oval with latitudinal and longitudinal lines. b, 60 l, Olympic rings. c, 120 l, Circles and stars. d, 150 l, Double-headed eagle of Albanian arms.

2009, Oct. 21   *Perf. 13¼x13*
2872 A752   Block of 4, #a-d   10.00   10.00

European Court of Human Rights, 50th Anniv. A753

2009, Oct. 30   *Perf. 13*
2873 A753 200 l multi   5.50   5.50

Council of Europe, 60th Anniv. A754

2009, Nov. 2
2874 A754 150 l multi 4.00 4.00

Albanian Painters — A755

No. 2875: a, 40 l, Abidin Dino (1913-93). b, 50 l, Lin Delija (1926-94). c, 60 l, Lika Janko (1928-2001). d, 150 l, Artur Tashko (1901-94).

2009, Nov. 11
2875 A755 Block of 4, #a-d 9.00 9.00

Traffic Safety — A756

No. 2876 — Traffic officer: a, 5 l, Holding matador's red cape. 1000 l, Stopping traffic.

2009, Nov. 16 *Perf. 13¼x13*
2876 A756 Horiz. pair, #a-b 20.00 20.00

Diplomatic Relations Between Albania and People's Republic of China, 60th Anniv. — A757

2009, Nov. 23 *Perf. 13*
2877 A757 20 l multi .50 .50

Albanian Iso-polyphonic Singers, UNESCO Intangible Cultural Heritage — A758

No. 2878: a, 40 l, Singers. b, 250 l, Musicians.

2009, Nov. 25 *Perf. 13¼x13*
2878 A758 Horiz. pair, #a-b 6.00 6.00

End of World War II, 65th Anniv. — A759

No. 2879 — Double-headed eagle and: a, 70 l, Soldier. b, 200 l, Bombers.

2009, Nov. 29 *Perf. 13x13¼*
2879 A759 Horiz. pair, #a-b 6.00 6.00

Legend of Mujit and Halitit — A760

No. 2880: a, 30 l, Man being held against giant's breasts. b, 200 l, Man and woman on horse.

2009, Dec. 5
2880 A760 Horiz. pair, #a-b 6.00 6.00

Religious Art and Buildings — A761

No. 2881: a, Mosque, Berat. b, Church, Korçe. c, Church, Lezhe.

2009, Dec. 9 *Perf. 13¼x13*
2881 Horiz. strip of 3 8.00 8.00
a. A761 90 l multi 1.75 1.75
b. A761 100 l multi 2.00 2.00
c. A761 120 l multi 2.50 2.50

Europa A762

Designs: 200 l, Planets, dish antenna. 250 l, Spacecraft and exploration vehicle on Mars. 350 l, Satellite above planet.

2009, Dec. 11 *Perf. 13x13¼*
2882 A762 200 l multi 5.00 5.00
2883 A762 250 l multi 6.00 6.00
Souvenir Sheet
Perf. 13¼x13
2884 A762 350 l multi 9.00 9.00
a. Booklet pane, #2882-2884 22.50 —
Complete booklet, #2884a 22.50

Intl. Year of Astronomy. No. 2884 contains one 30x25mm stamp.

Archaeological Sites — A763

No. 2885: a, 30 l, Fort, Tirana. b, 250 l, Tomb, Kamenica.

2009, Dec. 16 *Perf. 13*
2885 A763 Horiz. pair, #a-b 6.00 6.00

National Theater A764

No. 2886 — Scenes from plays: a, Shi ne Plazh. b, Pallati 176. c, Apologjia e Vertete e Sokratit.

2009, Dec. 21
2886 Horiz. strip of 3 8.00 8.00
a. A764 20 l multi .40 .40
b. A764 80 l multi 1.60 1.60
c. A764 200 l multi 4.00 4.00

Central State Archives, 60th Anniv. — A765

No. 2887: a, 40 l, Book, handwritten manuscript. b, 60 l, Scroll.

2009, Dec. 28
2887 A765 Horiz. pair, #a-b 2.50 2.50

Albanian-Italian Friendship — A766

2010, Apr. 12 *Litho.* *Perf. 13*
2888 A766 40 l multi .80 .80

Mother Teresa (1910-97), Humanitarian A767

2010, Aug. 26
2889 A767 100 l multi 1.90 1.90
See Kosovo No. 154, Macedonia No. 529.

Visaless Entry Into Europe for Albanians A768

2010, Nov. 8 *Perf. 13x13¼*
2890 A768 40 l multi .80 .80

National Library. 50th Anniv. — A769

No. 2891: a, 10 l, Man reading book. b, 1000 l, Man at computer.

2011, Feb. 18
2891 A769 Horiz. pair, #a-b 20.00 20.00
Dated 2010.

Student's Protest Movement, 20th Anniv. — A770

No. 2892: a, 40 l, Protestors, man at microphone. b, 60 l, Toppling of Enver Hoxha statue.
200 l, Students giving "V" for victory hand sign, vert.

2011, Feb. 20 *Perf. 13*
2892 A770 Horiz. pair, #a-b 2.00 2.00
Souvenir Sheet
2893 A770 200 l multi 4.00 4.00
Dated 2010.

Europa — A771

No. 2894 — Characters from children's stories: a, 100 l, Sun, donkey and rooster. b, 150 l, Bird and cat in balloons, girl. 250 l, Girl, stack of books, horiz.

2011, Feb. 25 *Perf. 13¼x13*
2894 A771 Vert. pair, #a-b 4.50 4.50
Souvenir Sheet
Perf. 13x13¼
2895 A771 250 l multi 4.50 4.50
Dated 2010.

Underwater Archaeology — A772

No. 2896: a, 50 l, Close-up of underwater artifact. b, 250 l, Items on seabed.

2011, Mar. 2 *Perf. 13¼x13*
2896 A772 Horiz. pair, #a-b 6.00 6.00
Dated 2010.

2010 World Cup Soccer Championships, South Africa — A773

No. 2897 — Emblem, ball and players: a, 80 l. b, 120 l.
200 l, Two players.

2011, Mar. 10 *Perf. 13¼x13*
2897 A773 Horiz. pair, #a-b 4.00 4.00
Souvenir Sheet
2898 A773 200 l multi 4.00 4.00
Dated 2010.

Albanian Peacekeeping Force — A774

No. 2899: a, 50 l, Helicopter, soldiers. b, 200 l, Soldier, tank.

2011, Mar. 21
2899 A774   Horiz. pair, #a-b   5.25 5.25
Dated 2010.

Lushnja Congress, 90th
Anniv. — A775

No. 2900: a, 70 l, Document and seal. b, 150 l, Building.

2011, Mar. 23
2900 A775   Horiz. pair, #a-b   4.50 4.50
Dated 2010.

National
Cultural
Heritage
Day — A776

No. 2901: a, House, Gjirokaster. b, Apron, Dumre. c, Fortress, Tirana. d, Lute, Shkoder. 200 l, Woman, Zadrime.

2011, Mar. 31   **Perf. 13x13¼**
2901   Horiz. strip of 4   5.75 5.75
  a. A776 10 l multi   .25   .25
  b. A776 70 l multi   1.40 1.40
  c. A776 80 l multi   1.60 1.60
  d. A776 120 l multi   2.50 2.50
Souvenir Sheet
2902 A776 200 l multi   4.25 4.25
Dated 2010.

Items Made of Silver — A777

No. 2903: a, Pendant. b, Purse. c, Butterfly. d, Decorated case and cylinder with tip. 200 l, Open case and cylinder.

2011, Apr. 6   **Perf. 13**
2903 A777   Block of 4, #a-d   4.25 4.25
Souvenir Sheet
2904 A777 200 l multi   4.25 4.25
Dated 2010.

Durres-Kukes Road — A778

No. 2905 — Road design and: a, 40 l, Hills. b, 60 l, Construction equipment. c, 90 l, Tunnel. d, 150 l, Bridge.

2011, Apr. 11   **Perf. 13x13¼**
2905 A778   Block of 4, #a-d   7.00 7.00
Dated 2010.

Miniature Sheet

Historic Center of Berati UNESCO
World Heritage Site — A779

No. 2906: a, 10 l, Building. b, 20 l, Buildings on hillside, street light. c, 30 l, Bridge. d, 50 l, Archway, fence on wall, buildings. e, 60 l, Buildings on hillside. 80 l, Church.

2011, Apr. 11   **Perf. 13x13¼**
2906 A779   Sheet of 6, #a-f   5.25 5.25

Europa — A780

Map of Europe with tree trunks and hills in: 200 l, Brown. 250 l, Green.

2011, July 30   **Perf. 13¼x13**
2907 A780 200 l multi   4.25 4.25
Souvenir Sheet
2908 A780 250 l multi   5.25 5.25
Intl. Year of Forests.

Boxing — A781

No. 2909: a, 50 l, Boxers, boxer with red shirt at left. b, 100 l, Boxers, boxer with red shirt at right. 250 l, Boxer throwing punch.

2011, Aug. 26
2909 A781   Horiz. pair, #a-b   3.00 3.00
Souvenir Sheet
2910 A781 250 l multi   5.00 5.00

Multi-party
Elections, 20h
Anniv. — A782

2011, Sept. 1   **Perf. 13x13¼**
2911 A782 150 l multi   3.00 3.00

Ismail
Kadare,
Writer
A783

2011, Sept. 12   **Perf. 13**
2912 A783 40 l multi   .80   .80

Tourism — A784

No. 2913: a, 80 l, Valbona River and mountains. b, 120 l, Rocks in Valbona River.

2011, Sept. 27
2913 A784   Horiz. pair, #a-b   4.00 4.00

Albanian Red Cross, 90th
Anniv. — A785

No. 2914 — Emblem and: a, 70 l + 10 l, Aid to pregnant woman, first aid. b, 120 l, Woman receiving two bags.

2011, Oct. 4
2914 A785   Horiz. pair, #a-b   4.00 4.00

Carrier Pigeons — A786

No. 2915 — Globe and: a, 10 l, Pigeon with mail bag. b, 1000 l, Pigeon without mail bag.

2011, Oct. 9
2915 A786   Horiz. pair, #a-b   19.50 19.50

Mosaics — A787

No. 2916 — Mosaic from: a, 20 l, St. Michael's Basilica, Arapaj. b, 60 l, Church, Antigone. c, 120 l, Mesaplikut Basilica.

2011, Oct. 14   **Litho.**
2916 A787   Horiz. strip of 3,
             #a-c   4.00 4.00

Forum of
States on
Adriatic
and Ionian
Seas
A788

2011, Nov. 18   **Perf. 13x13¼**
2917 A788 90 l multi   1.75 1.75

Flowers — A789

No. 2918: a, 30 l, Gymnospermium shqipetarum. b, 70 l, Viola kosaninii. c, 100 l, Aster albanicus subsp. paparisoi.

2011, Dec. 5   **Perf. 13¼x13**
2918 A789   Horiz. strip of 3,
             #a-c   4.00 4.00

Academy of
Arts, 45th
Anniv. — A790

2011, Dec. 15   **Perf. 13**
2919 A790 250 l multi   4.75 4.75

Nudes — A791

No. 2920 — Nude: a, 10 l, Painting by Vangjush Mio. b, 90 l, Painting by Abdurrahim Buza. c, 100 l, Sculpture by Janaq Paço. 250 l, Nude sculpture by Paço, diff.

2011, Dec. 22   **Perf. 13x13¼**
2920 A791   Horiz. strip of 3, #a-
             c   3.75 3.75
Souvenir Sheet
2921 A791 250 l multi   4.75 4.75

Democracy in Albania, 20th
Anniv. — A792

2012, Mar. 22   **Perf. 13**
2922 A792 100 l multi   1.90 1.90

Europa — A793

No. 2923 — Various tourist attractions: a, 30 l. b, 250 l.

2012, Sept. 21   **Perf. 13x13¼**
2923 A793   Horiz. pair, #a-b   5.25 5.25

2012 European Soccer Championships, Poland and Ukraine — A794

No. 2924 — Emblem, soccer ball, flags of European nations and large flag of: a, 100 l, Poland. b, 200 l, Ukraine.

2012, Sept. 28 **Perf. 13**
2924 A794 Horiz. pair, #a-b 5.75 5.75

Kin Dushi (1922-94), Writer A795

2012, Oct. 3 **Perf. 13x13¼**
2925 A795 150 l multi 2.75 2.75

Albanian Membership in Universal Postal Union, 90th Anniv. — A796

2012, Oct. 9 **Perf. 13¼x12¾**
2926 A796 250 l multi 4.75 4.75

Revolts Against Ottoman Rule, Cent. — A797

No. 2927: a, 10 l, Rebel leader, row of rebels. b, 1000 l, Rebels.

2012, Oct. 19 **Perf. 13**
2927 A797 Horiz. pair, #a-b 18.50 18.50

Souvenir Sheet

Rock Art — A798

No. 2928 — Rock art at: a, 20 l, Rubik. b, 60 l, Boville. c, 150 l, Lepenice.

2012, Oct. 29 **Perf. 13¼x13**
2928 A798 Sheet of 3, #a-c 4.25 4.25

Linguists Who Have Studied Albanian Language A799

No. 2929: a, Eric Hamp. b, Norbert Jokl (1877-1942). c, Holger Pedersen (1867-1953).

2012, Nov. 16 **Perf. 13**
2929 Horiz. strip of 3 3.50 3.50
  a. A799 50 l multi .95 .95
  b. A799 60 l multi 1.10 1.10
  c. A799 70 l multi 1.40 1.40
See No. 2947.

Dancers A800

No. 2930 — Dancers from: a, Tropoje. b, Tirana. c, Cameri. d, Lushnje.

2012, Nov. 23 **Perf. 13x13¼**
2930 Horiz. strip of 4 6.25 6.25
  a. A800 20 l multi .40 .40
  b. A800 40 l multi .75 .75
  c. A800 120 l multi 2.25 2.25
  d. A800 150 l multi 2.75 2.75

Independence, Cent. — A801

2012, Nov. 23 **Perf. 13¼x13**
2931 A801 40 l black & red .75 .75

Declaration of Independence, Cent. — A802

No. 2932: a, People, Albanian flag. b, People, Albanian flag, diff. c, Flags, United Nations Headquarters. d, Flags, NATO emblem.

2012, Nov. 28 **Perf. 13x13¼**
2932 Horiz. strip of 4 5.50 5.50
  a. A802 50 l multi .95 .95
  b. A802 60 l multi 1.10 1.10
  c. A802 70 l multi 1.40 1.40
  d. A802 100 l multi 1.90 1.90
  e. Booklet pane of 4, #2932a-2932d 5.50
    Complete booklet, #2932e 5.50

Albanian Army, Cent. — A803

No. 2933: a, 90 l, Soldiers in traditional costumes. b, 150 l, Soldiers wearing helmets.

2012, Dec. 4 **Litho.**
2933 A803 Horiz. pair, #a-b 4.50 4.50

Albanian Post, Telegraph and Telephone Administration, Cent. — A804

No. 2934 — Telephone, poles, wires, and: a, 80 l, Envelopes, mailbox. b, 200 l, Letter in open envelope.

2012, Dec. 5 **Perf. 13**
2934 A804 Horiz. pair, #a-b 5.25 5.25
  c. Booklet pane of 2, #2934a-2934b, + 2 labels 5.25 —
    Complete booklet, #2934c 5.25

Marine Life and Plants — A805

No. 2935: a, 10 l, Fish, sea grasses, diver. b, 250 l, Fish, sea grasses, coral.

2012, Dec. 14 **Perf. 13x12¾**
2935 A805 Horiz. pair, #a-b 5.00 5.00
  c. Booklet pane of 2, #2935a-2935b 5.00 —
    Complete booklet, #2935c 5.00

First Handstamped Envelope of Albania, Cent. — A806

No. 2936: a, 120 l, Front of addressed handstamped envelope. b, 150 l, Back of envelope, handstamp.

2013, May 5 **Perf. 13**
2936 A806 Horiz. pair, #a-b 5.25 5.25
  c. Booklet pane of 2, #2936a-2936b 5.25 —
    Complete booklet, #2936c 5.25

World Track and Field Championships, Moscow — A807

No. 2937: a, 30 l, Runner. b, 200 l, High jumper. 250 l, Pole vaulter.

2013, Aug. 27 **Litho.** **Perf. 13**
2937 A807 Horiz. pair, #a-b 4.50 4.50
Souvenir Sheet
2938 A807 250 l multi 4.75 4.75

Vedat Kokona (1913-98), Lexicographer — A808

2013, Aug. 30 **Litho.** **Perf. 13**
2939 A808 150 l multi 3.00 3.00

Europa — A809

No. 2940 — Globe, parcels, envelopes and: a, 80 l, Postal van and truck. b, 200 l, Airplane, train and ship.

2013, Oct. 4 **Litho.** **Perf. 13¼x13**
2940 A809 Horiz. pair, #a-b 5.50 5.50
  c. Booklet pane of 2, #2940a-2940b 5.50 —
    Complete booklet, #2940c 5.50

Albanian Police, Cent. — A810

No. 2941 — Flag and: a, 10 l, Policewoman. b, 250 l, Policeman.

2013, Oct. 18 **Litho.** **Perf. 13¼x13**
2941 A810 Horiz. pair, #a-b 5.00 5.00

Flowers A811

No. 2942: a, Scilla albanica. b, Gymnospermium maloi. c, Tulipa albanica.

2013, Oct. 30 **Litho.** **Perf. 13x13¼**
2942 Horiz. strip of 3 5.00 5.00
  a. A811 20 l multi .40 .40
  b. A811 90 l multi 1.75 1.75
  c. A811 175 l multi 2.75 2.75

17th Mediterranean Games, Mersin, Turkey — A812

No. 2943: a, 40 l, Diving, swimming, synchronized swimming. b, 150 l, Volleyball, weight lifting, cycling. 200 l, Rowing, horiz.

2013, Nov. 6 **Litho.** **Perf. 13¼x13**
2943 A812 Horiz. pair, #a-b 4.75 4.75
Souvenir Sheet
Perf. 13x13¼
2944 A812 200 l multi 4.00 4.00

International Red Cross, 150th Anniv. — A813

No. 2945 — Red cross and: a, 40 l, Aid workers helping injured man, feeding woman. b, 150 l, Worker giving bags of goods to man. 250 l, Aid workers assisting injured man.

2013, Nov. 15   Litho.   Perf. 13
2945 A813   Horiz. pair, #a-b   3.75 3.75
Souvenir Sheet
2946 A813 250 l multi   5.00 5.00

Linguists Type of 2012

No. 2947 — Historians: a, Milan Sufflay (1879-1931). b, Konstantin Jiracek (1854-1918). c, Ludwig von Thallóczy (1854-1916).

2013, Nov. 25   Litho.   Perf. 13
2947   Horiz. strip of 3   5.25 5.25
a. A799 10 l multi   .25 .25
b. A799 100 l multi   2.00 2.00
c. A799 150 l multi   3.00 3.00

Recent Archaeological Finds — A814

No. 2948: a, Bronze foot, 2nd-3rd cent. b, Bronze fibula with horse design, 7th-8th cent. c, Marble statue of an aristocrat, 2nd cent. d, Relief of Heraclius and Apollo, 2nd cent.

2013, Dec. 3   Litho.   Perf. 13
2948   Horiz. strip of 4   6.50 6.50
a. A814 20 l multi   .35 .35
b. A814 90 l multi   1.75 1.75
c. A814 100 l multi   2.00 2.00
d. A814 120 l multi   2.40 2.40

Nikolla Naço (1843-1913), Newspaper Editor — A815

2013, Dec. 18   Litho.   Perf. 13¼x13
2949 A815 200 l multi   4.00 4.00

2014 World Cup Soccer Championships, Brazil — A816

No. 2950: a, Mascot. b, Mascot holding soccer ball. c, Mascot dribbling soccer ball. 140 l, Emblem, vert.

2014, July 9   Litho.   Perf. 13
2950   Horiz. strip of 3   3.25 3.25
a. A816 10 l multi   .25 .25
b. A816 50 l multi   1.00 1.00
c. A816 100 l multi   2.00 2.00
Souvenir Sheet
2951 A816 140 l multi   2.75 2.75

Visit to Albania of Pope Francis — A817

2014, Sept. 21   Litho.   Perf. 13
2952 A817 100 l multi   1.90 1.90

Europa — A818

No. 2953: a, 100 l, Gajdja (bagpipes). b, 150 l, Lodra (drum).

2014, Oct. 9   Litho.   Perf. 13¼x13
2953 A818   Horiz. pair, #a-b   4.50 4.50
c.   Souvenir sheet of 2, #2953a-2953b + central label   4.50 4.50
    Complete booklet, #2953c   4.50

Kuçi Assembly, 400th Anniv. — A819

No. 2954: a, 80 l, Participants examining document. b, 150 l, Participants. 200 l, Participants, diff.

2014, Oct. 14   Litho.   Perf. 13x13¼
2954 A819   Horiz. pair, #a-b   4.25 4.25
Souvenir Sheet
2955 A819 200 l multi   3.75 3.75

Souvenir Sheet

Relations Between Albania and Kuwait — A820

No. 2956: a, 100 l, Shiekh Sabah, emir of Kuwait. b, Handshake, flags of Albania and Kuwait.

2014, Nov. 11   Litho.   Perf. 13¼x13
2956 A820 100 l Sheet of 2, #a-b 3.50 3.50

Sulejman Pashe Delvina (1884-1933), Prime Minister — A821

2014, Nov. 18   Litho.   Perf. 13¼x13
2957 A821 150 l multi   2.75 2.75

Reptiles and Amphibians — A822

No. 2958: a, 80 l, Caretta caretta. b, 170 l, Hyla arborea.

2014, Nov. 22   Litho.   Perf. 13
2958 A822   Horiz. pair, #a-b   4.50 4.50

Miniature Sheet

Coronation of Prince William of Wied, Cent. — A823

No. 2959: a, 60 l, Princess Sophie (1885-1936), wife of Prince William. b, 70 l, Crown, arms of Albania. c, 80 l, Star with eagle in circle. d, 90 l, Prince William of Wied (1876-1945).

2014, Nov. 26   Litho.   Perf. 13¼x13
2959 A823   Sheet of 4, #a-d   5.50 5.50

World War II Liberation of Albania, 70th Anniv. — A824

2014, Nov. 29   Litho.   Perf. 13
2960 A824 40 l multi   .70 .70

Archaeological Items From Dyrrachium (Dürres) — A825

No. 2961 — Depictions of Artemis: a, 50 l, Statue, 4th cent. B.C. b, 60 l, Bust, 4th cent. B.C. c, 70 l, Marble bust, 4th cent. B.C. d, 90 l, Bronze statue, 3rd cent. B.C.

2014, Dec. 5   Litho.   Perf. 13
2961   Horiz. strip of 4   4.75 4.75
a. A825 50 l multi   .90 .90
b. A825 60 l multi   1.00 1.00
c. A825 70 l multi   1.25 1.25
d. A825 90 l multi   1.60 1.60

Albanian Candidacy for European Union Membership — A826

2014, Dec. 8   Litho.   Perf. 13x13¼
2962 A826 40 l multi   .70 .70

William Shakespeare (1564-1616), Writer — A827

2014, Dec. 12   Litho.   Perf. 13
2963 A827 150 l multi   2.60 2.60

Wooden Handicrafts — A828

No. 2964: a, 40 l, Chair, Mirdite. b, 50 l, Cradle, Rreshen. c, 60 l, Shepherd's crook, Laberi. d, 70 l, Spoons, Tirana. 180 l, Ceiling decorations, Leuse.

2014, Dec. 19   Litho.   Perf. 13
2964 A828   Block of 4, #a-d   4.00 4.00
Souvenir Sheet
2965 A828 180 l multi   3.25 3.25

Icons in Museums — A829

No. 2966 — Icon from: a, 10 l, Himare. b, 30 l, Dhermi. c, 40 l, Dhermi, diff. d, 70 l, Vuno. e, 90 l, Deme. f, 100 l, Vuno, diff.

2014, Dec. 24   Litho.   Perf. 13¼x13
2966 A829   Sheet of 6, #a-f   6.00 6.00
g.   Booklet pane of 6, #2966a-2966f   6.00 —
    Complete booklet, #2966g   6.00

No. 2966g has a decorative, curved pane margin.

Elez Isufi (1861-1924), Guerrilla Leader — A830

2014, Dec. 29   Litho.   Perf. 13¼x13
2967 A830 1000 l multi   17.50 17.50

Europa — A831

2015, Sept. 2   Litho.   Perf. 13¼x13
2968 A831 130 l multi   2.10 2.10
Souvenir Sheet
2969 A831 250 l multi   4.00 4.00
a.   Booklet pane of 2, #2968-2969   6.25
    Complete booklet, #2969a   6.25

National Parks A832

No. 2970: a, Shebenik-Jabllanice National Park. b, Bredhi i Hotoves National Park. c, Dajti National Park.

2015, Sept. 16 Litho. Perf. 13¼x13
2970   Horiz. strip of 3   5.00 5.00
  a. A832 50 l multi   .80 .80
  b. A832 100 l multi   1.60 1.60
  c. A832 150 l multi   2.50 2.50

Early Locomotives and Their Inventors — A833

No. 2971: a, 50 l, New Castle, Richard Trevithick (1771-1833). b, 60 l, Salamanca, Matthew Murray (1765-1826). c, 90 l, Rocket, Robert Stephenson (1803-59). d, 100 l, Locomotion, George Stephenson (1781-1848).

Perf. 13¼x12¾
2015, Sept. 27   Litho.
2971 A833   Block of 4, #a-d   5.00 5.00
Locomotives, 190th anniv.

Famous Men — A834

No. 2972: a, 40 l, Dhimiter Shuteriqi (1915-2003), writer. b, 50 l, Zef Skiroi (1865-1927), poet. c, 60 l, Mahir Domi (1915-2000), linguist. d, 100 l, Gaqo Avrazi (1915-85), composer.

2015, Sept. 28 Litho. Perf. 13¼x13
2972 A834   Block of 4, #a-d   4.00 4.00

Albanian Soccer Federation, 85th Anniv. — A835

No. 2973 — Federation emblem and: a, 5 l, Soccer ball, goaltender and net. b, 10 l, Grass. c, 1000 l, Soccer ball and player making scissor kick.

2015, Oct. 8 Litho. Perf. 13¼x13
2973 A835   Horiz. strip of 3,
               #a-c   16.00 16.00

Famous Men — A836

No. 2974: a, Nicéphore Niépce (1765-1833), inventor of photography. b, Carl Patsch (1865-1945), historian. c, Boris Pasternak (1890-1960), 1958 Nobel laureate in Literature. d, Norman Wisdom (1915-2010), comedian and actor.

2015, Oct. 9 Litho. Perf. 13
2974   Horiz. strip of 4   4.25 4.25
  a. A836 10 l multi   .25 .25
  b. A836 60 l multi   .95 .95
  c. A836 80 l multi   1.25 1.25
  d. A836 100 l multi   1.60 1.60

United Nations, 70th Anniv. A837

2015, Oct. 24 Litho. Perf. 13¼x13
2975 A837 180 l multi   3.00 3.00

Ceramic Vessels — A838

No. 2976 — Various vessels: a, 50 l. b, 60 l. c, 70 l. d, 120 l.
200 l, Various ceramic vessels, diff.

2015, Nov. 6   Perf. 13
2976 A838   Block of 4, #a-d   4.75 4.75
         Souvenir Sheet
2977 A838 200 l multi   3.25 3.25

Recent Archaeological Discoveries — A839

No. 2978: a, 10 l, Ivory mirror handle, 4th-5th cent. B.C. b, 30 l, Marble statue of officer, 1st cent. B.C. c, 60 l, Bronze utensil handle, 6th-7th cent. B.C. d, 150 l, Bronze statue of Hermes, 1st cent. B.C.

2015, Nov. 16   Litho.   Perf. 13
2978 A839   Block of 4, #a-d   4.00 4.00

International Telecommunication Union, 150th Anniv. — A840

2015, Dec. 5   Litho.   Perf. 13
2979 A840 2500 l multi   40.00 40.00

Marine Life — A841

No. 2980: a, 5 l, Sabella spallanzanii. b, 150 l, Antedon mediterranea. 250 l, Cotylorhiza tuberculata.

2015, Dec. 23 Litho. Perf. 13¼x13
2980 A841   Horiz. pair, #a-b   2.50 2.50
         Souvenir Sheet
2981 A841 250 l multi   4.00 4.00

2016 European Soccer Championships, France — A842

No. 2982 — Emblem and player with denomination at: a, 70 l, UL. b, 100 l, UR.

2016, June 10 Litho. Perf. 13x13¼
2982 A842   Horiz. pair, #a-b   2.75 2.75

Europa A843

2016, July 9 Litho. Perf. 13x13¼
2983 A843 200 l multi   3.25 3.25
Think Green Issue.

Flowers — A844

No. 2984: a, Tulipa kosovarica. b, Campanula comosiformis. c, Solenanthus albanicus.

2016, July 27 Litho. Perf. 13¼x13
2984   Horiz. strip of 3   4.00 4.00
  a. A844 20 l multi   .35 .35
  b. A844 30 l multi   .50 .50
  c. A844 190 l multi   3.00 3.00

Balkanfila 2016 Intl. Stamp Exhibition, Tirana — A845

2016, Aug. 9 Litho. Perf. 13x13¼
2985 A845 250 l multi   4.25 4.25

Famous Men — A846

No. 2986: a, Ndre Mjeda (1866-1937), poet. b, Kole Jakova (1916-2002), writer. c, Jusuf Vrioni (1916-2001), diplomat and translator.

2016, Aug. 17 Litho. Perf. 13x13¼
2986   Horiz. strip of 3   3.50 3.50
  a. A846 10 l multi   .25 .25
  b. A846 50 l multi   .80 .80
  c. A846 150 l multi   2.40 2.40

Albania, 2015-17 Member of United Nations Human Rights Council A847

2016, Aug. 29 Litho. Perf. 13x13¼
2987 A847 1000 l multi   16.50 16.50

Albanian Literary Commission, Cent. — A848

2016, Sept. 1   Litho.   Perf. 13
2988 A848 60 l multi   1.00 1.00

Canonization of St. Teresa of Calcutta (Mother Teresa) — A849

2016, Sept. 4 Litho. Perf. 13x13¼
2989 A849 120 l multi   2.00 2.00

SEMI-POSTAL STAMPS

Nos. 148-151 Surcharged in Red and Black

1924, Nov. 1
B1 A18 5q + 5q yel grn   11.00 *30.00*
B2 A18 10q + 5q carmine   11.00 *30.00*
B3 A18 25q + 5q dark blue   11.00 *30.00*
B4 A18 50q + 5q dark grn   11.00 *30.00*
    Nos. B1-B4 (4)   44.00 *120.00*

Nos. B1 to B4 with Additional Surcharge in Red and Black

1924

B5	A18	5q + 5q + 5q yel grn	11.00	26.00
B6	A18	10q + 5q + 5q car	11.00	26.00
B7	A18	25q + 5q + 5q dk bl	11.00	26.00
B8	A18	50q + 5q + 5q dk	11.00	26.00
		grn		
	Nos. B5-B8 (4)		44.00	104.00

Issued under Italian Dominion

Nurse and Child — SP1

Unwmk.

1943, Apr. 1   Photo.   Perf. 14

B9	SP1	5q + 5q dark grn	.75	1.50
B10	SP1	10q + 10q olive brn	.75	1.50
B11	SP1	15q + 10q rose red	.75	1.50
B12	SP1	25q + 15q saphire	.75	2.75
B13	SP1	30q + 20q violet	.75	2.75
B14	SP1	50q + 25q dk org	1.00	2.75
B15	SP1	65q + 30q grnsh blk	1.40	4.00
B16	SP1	1fr + 40q chestnut	.75	5.25
	Nos. B9-B16 (8)		9.15	22.00

The surtax was for the control of tuberculosis.
For surcharges see Nos. B24-B27.

Issued under German Administration

War Victims SP2

1944, Sept. 22

B17	SP2	5g + 5(q) dp grn	2.50	17.00
B18	SP2	10g + 5(q) dp brn	2.50	17.00
B19	SP2	15g + 5(q) car lake	2.50	17.00
B20	SP2	25g + 10(q) dp blue	2.50	17.00
B21	SP2	1fr + 50q dk olive	2.50	17.00
B22	SP2	2fr + 1(fr) purple	2.50	17.00
B23	SP2	3fr + 1.50(fr) dk org	2.50	17.00
	Nos. B17-B23 (7)		17.50	119.00

Surtax for victims of World War II.

Independent State

Nos. B9 to B12 Surcharged in Carmine

1945, May 4   Unwmk.   Perf. 14

B24	SP1	30q +15q on 5q+5q	8.25	13.00
B25	SP1	50q +25q on 10q+10q	8.25	13.00
B26	SP1	1fr +50q on 15q+15q	21.00	27.50
B27	SP1	2fr +1fr on 25q+15q	29.00	37.50
	Nos. B24-B27 (4)		66.50	91.00

The surtax was for the Albanian Red Cross.

People's Republic

Nos. 361 to 366 Overprinted in Red (cross) and Surcharged in Black

1946, July 16   Perf. 11

B28	A57	20q + 10q bluish grn	17.50	30.00
B29	A57	30q + 15q dp org	17.50	30.00
B30	A57	40q + 20q brown	17.50	30.00
B31	A57	60q + 30q red vio	17.50	30.00
B32	A57	1fr + 50q rose red	17.50	30.00
B33	A57	3fr + 1.50fr dk bl	17.50	30.00
	Nos. B28-B33 (6)		105.00	180.00

To honor and benefit the Congress of the Albanian Red Cross.
Counterfeits: lithographed; genuine: typographed.

> **Catalogue values for unused stamps in this section, from this point to the end of the section, are for Never Hinged items.**

SP3

First Aid and Red Cross: 25q+5q, Nurse carrying child on stretcher. 65q+25q, Symbolic blood transfusion. 80q+40q, Mother and child.

1967, Dec. 1   Litho.   Perf. 11½x12

B34	SP3	15q + 5q blk, red & brn	.80	.35
B35	SP3	25q + 5q multi	1.60	.80
B36	SP3	65q + 25q multi	5.50	2.75
B37	SP3	80q + 40q multi	8.00	4.00
	Nos. B34-B37 (4)		15.90	7.90

6th congress of the Albanian Red Cross.

SP4

1996, Aug. 5   Litho.   Perf. 13½x13

B38	SP4	50 l +10 l multi	1.50	1.50

Albanian Red Cross, 75th anniv.

Nos. 2469-2470 Surcharged

Methods and Perfs as Before

2001, Mar. 12

B39	A567	80 l +10 l on 50 l multi	4.50	4.50
B40	A567	130 l +20 l on 100 l multi	7.50	7.50

AIR POST STAMPS

Airplane Crossing Mountains AP1

Wmk. 125

1925, May 30   Typo.   Perf. 14

C1	AP1	5q green	2.25	3.50
C2	AP1	10q rose red	2.25	3.50
C3	AP1	25q deep blue	2.25	3.50
C4	AP1	50q dark green	3.50	6.00
C5	AP1	1fr dk vio & blk	6.25	10.50
C6	AP1	2fr ol grn & vio	10.50	17.50
C7	AP1	3fr brn org & dk grn	12.50	17.50
	Nos. C1-C7 (7)		39.50	62.00

Nos. C1-C7 exist imperf. Value $3,000.
For overprint see Nos. C8-C28.

Nos. C1-C7 Overprinted

1927, Jan. 18

C8	AP1	5q green	5.25	10.50
a.		Dbl. overprint, one invtd.	50.00	
C9	AP1	10q rose red	5.25	10.50
a.		Inverted overprint	45.00	
b.		Dbl. overprint, one invtd.	50.00	
C10	AP1	25q deep blue	4.75	9.50
C11	AP1	50q dark grn	3.25	6.50
a.		Inverted overprint	45.00	
C12	AP1	1fr dk vio & blk	3.25	6.50
a.		Inverted overprint	45.00	
b.		Double overprint	45.00	
C13	AP1	2fr ol grn & vio	7.50	10.50
C14	AP1	3fr brn org & dk grn	10.50	15.00
	Nos. C8-C14 (7)		39.75	69.00

Nos. C1-C7 Overprinted

1928, Apr. 21

C15	AP1	5q green	5.25	10.50
a.		Inverted overprint	70.00	
C16	AP1	10q rose red	5.25	10.50
C17	AP1	25q deep blue	5.25	10.50
C18	AP1	50q dark green	10.00	21.00
C19	AP1	1fr dk vio & blk	55.00	110.00
C20	AP1	2fr ol grn & vio	55.00	110.00
C21	AP1	3fr brn org & dk grn	55.00	110.00
	Nos. C15-C21 (7)		190.75	382.50

First flight across the Adriatic, Valona to Brindisi, Apr. 21, 1928.
The variety "SHQYRTARE" occurs once in the sheet for each value. Value 3 times normal.

Nos. C1-C7 Overprinted in Red Brown

1929, Dec. 1

C22	AP1	5q green	6.00	8.75
C23	AP1	10q rose red	6.00	8.75
C24	AP1	25q deep blue	6.00	8.75
C25	AP1	50q dk grn	125.00	175.00
C26	AP1	1fr dk vio & blk	225.00	350.00
C27	AP1	2fr ol grn	225.00	350.00
C28	AP1	3fr brn org & dk grn	225.00	350.00
	Nos. C22-C28 (7)		818.00	1,251.

Excellent counterfeits exist.

King Zog and Airplane over Tirana AP2

AP3

1930, Oct. 8   Photo.   Unwmk.

C29	AP2	5q yellow green	1.00	1.75
C30	AP2	15q rose red	1.00	1.75
C31	AP2	20q slate blue	1.00	1.75
C32	AP2	50q olive green	2.00	2.75
C33	AP3	1fr dark blue	3.00	5.25
C34	AP3	2fr olive brown	10.00	17.50
C35	AP3	3fr purple	22.50	17.50
	Nos. C29-C35 (7)		40.50	48.25

For overprints and surcharges see Nos. C36-C45.

Nos. C29-C35 Overprinted

1931, July 6

C36	AP2	5q yellow grn	5.25	10.50
a.		Double overprint	140.00	
C37	AP2	15q rose red	5.25	10.50
C38	AP2	20q slate blue	5.25	10.50
C39	AP2	50q olive grn	5.25	10.50
C40	AP3	1fr dark blue	30.00	60.00
C41	AP3	2fr olive brn	30.00	60.00
C42	AP3	3fr purple	30.00	60.00
a.		Inverted overprint	275.00	
	Nos. C36-C42 (7)		111.00	222.00

1st air post flight from Tirana to Rome.
Only a very small part of this issue was sold to the public. Most of the stamps were given to the Aviation Company to help provide funds for conducting the service.

Issued under Italian Dominion

Nos. C29-C30 Overprinted in Black

1939, Apr. 19   Unwmk.   Perf. 14

C43	AP2	5q yel green	2.50	7.00
C44	AP2	15q rose red	2.50	7.00

No. C32 With Additional Surcharge

C45	AP2	20q on 50q ol grn	5.00	11.50
a.		Inverted overprint	—	—
	Nos. C43-C45 (3)		10.00	25.50

See note after No. 309.

King Victor Emmanuel III and Plane over Mountains AP4

1939, Aug. 4   Photo.

C46	AP4	20q brown	32.50	15.00

Shepherds AP5

Map of Albania
Showing Air
Routes — AP6

Designs: 20q, Victor Emmanuel III and harbor view. 50q, Woman and river valley. 1fr, Bridge at Vezirit. 2fr, Ruins. 3fr, Women waving to plane.

1940, Mar. 20   Unwmk.

C47	AP5	5q green	1.25	1.25
C48	AP6	15q rose red	1.25	1.90
C49	AP5	20q deep blue	2.50	3.25
C50	AP6	50q brown	3.25	9.50
C51	AP5	1fr myrtle green	6.50	12.50
C52	AP6	2fr brown black	9.50	19.00
C53	AP6	3fr rose violet	16.00	25.00
		Nos. C47-C53 (7)	40.25	72.40

People's Republic

Vuno-Himare
AP12

Albanian Towns: 1 l, 10 l, Rozafat-Shkoder. 2 l, 20 l, Keshtjelle-Butrinto.

1950, Dec. 15   Engr.   Perf. 12½x12

C54	AP12	50q gray black	.25	.80
C55	AP12	1 l red brown	.25	.80
C56	AP12	2 l ultra	.50	1.60
C57	AP12	5 l deep green	1.75	3.25
C58	AP12	10 l deep blue	4.50	5.50
C59	AP12	20 l purple	9.00	8.00
		Nos. C54-C59 (6)	16.25	19.95

Nos. C56-C58 Surcharged with New Value and Bars in Red or Black

1952-53

C60	AP12	50q on 2 l (R)	90.00	150.00
C61	AP12	50q on 5 l	22.50	30.00
C62	AP12	2.50 l on 5 l (R)	150.00	175.00
C63	AP12	2.50 l on 10 l	25.00	45.00
		Nos. C60-C63 (4)	287.50	400.00

Issued: Nos. C60, C62, 12/26/52; Nos. C61, C63, 3/14/53.

> Catalogue values for unused stamps in this section, from this point to the end of the section, are for Never Hinged items.

Banner with
Lenin, Map of
Stalingrad and
Tanks — AP13

1963, Feb. 2   Litho.   Perf. 14

C67	AP13	7 l grn & dp car	9.00	3.50

20th anniversary, Battle of Stalingrad.

Sputnik
and Sun
AP14

Designs: 3 l, Lunik 4. 5 l, Lunik 3 photographing far side of the Moon. 8 l, Venus space probe. 12 l, Mars 1.

1963, Oct. 31   Unwmk.   Perf. 12

C68	AP14	2 l org, yel & blk	.35	.35
C69	AP14	3 l multi	.70	.35
C70	AP14	5 l rose lil, yel & blk	1.00	.35
C71	AP14	8 l multi	1.75	.70
C72	AP14	12 l blue & org	3.50	2.75
		Nos. C68-C72 (5)	7.30	4.50

Russian interplanetary explorations.

Nos. C68 and C71 Overprinted "Riccione 23-8-1964"

1964, Aug. 23

C73	AP14	2 l org, yel & blk	7.00	14.00
C74	AP14	8 l multicolored	14.00	21.00

Intl. Space Exhib. in Riccione, Italy.

Plane
over
Berat
AP15

1975, Nov. 25   Litho.   Perf. 12

C75	AP15	20q multi	.25	.25
C76	AP15	40q Gjirokaster	.30	.25
C77	AP15	60q Sarande	.55	.30
C78	AP15	90q Durres	1.10	.35
C79	AP15	1.20 l Kruje	1.40	.70
C80	AP15	2.40 l Boga	2.75	1.40
C81	AP15	4.05 l Tirana	4.25	2.10
		Nos. C75-C81 (7)	10.60	5.35

SPECIAL DELIVERY STAMPS

Issued under Italian Dominion

King Victor
Emmanuel
III — SD1

1940   Unwmk.   Photo.   Perf. 14

E1	SD1	25q bright violet	4.75	7.50
E2	SD1	50q red orange	11.50	18.00

Issued under German Administration

No. E1
Overprinted
in Carmine

1943

E3	SD1	25q bright violet	12.50	24.00

Proclamation of Albanian independence.

POSTAGE DUE STAMPS

Nos. 35-39
Handstamped in
Various Colors

1914, Feb. 23   Unwmk.   Perf. 14

J1	A3	2q org brn & buff (Bl)	10.50	4.50
J2	A3	5q green (R)	10.50	4.50
J3	A3	10q rose red (Bl)	15.00	4.50
J4	A3	25q dark blue (R)	17.50	4.50
J5	A3	50q vio & red (Bk)	26.00	14.00
		Nos. J1-J5 (5)	79.50	32.00

The two parts of the overprint are handstamped separately. Stamps exist with one or both handstamps inverted, double, omitted or in wrong color.

Nos. 48-51
Overprinted in Black

1914, Apr. 16

J6	A3 (a)	10pa on 5q green	5.25	4.50
J7	A3 (a)	20pa on 10q rose red	5.25	4.50
J8	A3 (b)	1gr on 25q blue	5.25	4.50

J9	A3 (b)	2gr on 50q vio & red	5.25	4.50
		Nos. J6-J9 (4)	21.00	18.00

Same Design as
Regular Issue of
1919, Overprinted

1919, Feb. 10   Perf. 11½, 12½

J10	A8	(4)q on 4h rose	13.00	10.50
J11	A8	(10)q on 10k red, grn	13.00	10.50
J12	A8	20q on 2k org, gray	13.00	10.50
J13	A8	50q on 5k brn, yel	13.00	10.50
		Nos. J10-J13 (4)	52.00	42.00

Fortress at
Scutari — D3

Post Horn Overprinted in Black

1920, Apr. 1   Perf. 14x13

J14	D3	4q olive green	.75	4.50
J15	D3	10q rose red	1.50	6.50
J16	D3	20q bister brn	1.50	6.50
J17	D3	50q black	4.00	17.50
		Nos. J14-J17 (4)	7.75	35.00

D5

Background of Red Wavy Lines

1922   Perf. 12½, 11½

J23	D5	4q black, red	1.10	4.50
J24	D5	10q black, red	1.10	4.50
J25	D5	20q black, red	1.10	4.50
J26	D5	50q black, red	1.10	4.50
		Nos. J23-J26 (4)	4.40	18.00

Nos. J23-J26
Overprinted in White

1925

J27	D5	4q black, red	1.90	4.50
J28	D5	10q black, red	1.90	4.50
J29	D5	20q black, red	1.90	4.50
J30	D5	50q black, red	1.90	4.50
		Nos. J27-J30 (4)	7.60	18.00

The 10q with overprint in gold was a trial printing. It was not put in use.

D7

Overprinted "QIND. AR" in Red

1926, Dec. 24   Perf. 13½x13

J31	D7	10q dark blue	.75	3.50
J32	D7	20q green	.75	3.50
J33	D7	30q red brown	1.50	7.00
J34	D7	50q dark brown	2.75	13.00
		Nos. J31-J34 (4)	5.75	27.00

Coat of Arms — D8

Wmk. Double Headed Eagle (220)

1930, Sept. 1   Photo.   Perf. 14, 14½

J35	D8	10q dark blue	6.75	21.00
J36	D8	20q rose red	2.75	13.00
J37	D8	30q violet	2.75	13.00
J38	D8	50q dark green	2.75	13.00
		Nos. J35-J38 (4)	15.00	60.00

Nos. J36-J38 exist with overprint "14 Shtator 1943" (see Nos. 332-344) which is private and fraudulent on these stamps.

No. 253 Overprinted

1936   Perf. 14

J39	A34	10q carmine	15.00	45.00
a.		Hyphens on each side of "Takse" ('39)	100.00	200.00

Issued under Italian Dominion

Coat of Arms — D9

1940   Unwmk.   Photo.   Perf. 14

J40	D9	4q red orange	37.50	75.00
J41	D9	10q bright violet	37.50	75.00
J42	D9	20q brown	37.50	75.00
J43	D9	30q dark blue	37.50	75.00
J44	D9	50q carmine rose	37.50	75.00
		Nos. J40-J44 (5)	187.50	375.00

ALEXANDRETTA

ˌa-lig-ˌzan-ˈdre-tə

LOCATION — A political territory in northern Syria, bordering on Turkey
GOVT. — French mandate
AREA — 10,000 sq. mi. (approx.)
POP. — 270,000 (approx.)

Included in the Syrian territory mandated to France under the Versailles Treaty, the name was changed to Hatay in 1938. The following year France returned the territory to Turkey in exchange for certain concessions. See Hatay.

100 Centimes = 1 Piaster

Stamps of Syria, 1930-36, Overprinted or Surcharged in Black or Red

a

b

c

d

e

		1938	Unwmk.	Perf. 12x12½	
1	A6 (a)	10c vio brn		3.50	3.50
2	A6 (a)	20c brn org		3.50	3.00
			Perf. 13½		
3	A9 (b)	50c vio (R)		4.50	3.50
4	A10 (b)	1p bis brn		4.50	3.00
5	A9 (b)	2p dk vio (R)		5.75	3.50
6	A13 (b)	3p yel grn (R)		9.00	7.00
7	A10 (b)	4p yel org		10.00	7.00
8	A16 (b)	6p grnsh blk (R)		12.00	8.00
9	A18 (b)	25p vio brn		25.00	25.00
10	A15 (c)	75c org red		9.00	9.00
11	A10 (d)	2.50p on 4p yel		7.50	4.00
12	AP2 (e)	12.50p on 15p org red		20.00	15.00
		Nos. 1-12 (12)		114.25	91.50
		Set, never hinged		275.00	

Issue dates: Nos. 1-9, Apr. 14, Nos. 10-12, Sept. 2.

Nos. 4, 7, 10-12 Ovptd. in Black

1938, Nov. 10

13	A15	75c		60.00	60.00
a.	Overprint inverted			500.00	

14	A10	1p		37.50	37.50
a.	"Sandjah d'Alexandrette" omitted			300.00	
15	A10	2.50p on 4p		32.50	32.50
16	A10	4p		37.50	37.50
a.	"Sandjah d'Alexandrette" omitted			300.00	
17	AP2	12.50p on 15p		90.00	90.00
a.	"Sandjah d'Alexandrette" omitted			1,500.	
		Nos. 13-17 (5)		257.50	257.50
		Set, never hinged		450.00	

Death of Kemal Ataturk, pres. of Turkey.

AIR POST STAMPS

Air Post Stamps of Syria, 1937, Overprinted Type "b" in Red or Black

		1938, Apr. 14	Unwmk.	Perf. 13	
C1	AP14	½p dark vio (R)		4.00	4.75
C2	AP15	1p black (R)		4.00	5.00
C3	AP14	2p blue grn (R)		5.50	7.00
C4	AP14	3p deep ultra		6.00	7.50
C5	AP14	5p rose lake		11.00	17.50
C6	AP15	10p red brown		11.50	19.00
C7	AP14	15p lake brown		14.50	22.50
C8	AP15	25p dk blue (R)		20.00	30.00
		Nos. C1-C8 (8)		76.50	113.25
		Set, never hinged		225.00	

POSTAGE DUE STAMPS

Postage Due Stamps of Syria, 1925-31, Ovptd. Type "b" in Black or Red

		1938, Apr. 14	Unwmk.	Perf. 13½	
J1	D5	50c brown, yel		6.00	5.50
J2	D6	1p violet, rose		7.00	6.00
J3	D5	2p blk, blue (R)		8.00	7.50
J4	D5	3p blk, red org		10.00	9.00
J5	D5	5p blk, bl grn (R)		16.00	14.50
J6	D7	8p blk, gray bl (R)		22.50	20.00
		Nos. J1-J6 (6)		69.50	62.50
		Set, never hinged		225.00	

On No. J2, the overprint is vertical, reading up, other denominations, horizontal.

Stamps of Alexandretta were discontinued in 1938 and replaced by those of Hatay.

ALGERIA

al-ˈjir-ē-ə

LOCATION — North Africa
GOVT. — Republic
AREA — 919,595 sq. mi.
POP. — 29,300,000 (1998 est.)
CAPITAL — Algiers

The former French colony of Algeria became an integral part of France on Sept. 1, 1958, when French stamps replaced Algerian stamps. Algeria became an independent country July 3, 1962.

100 Centimes = 1 Franc
100 Centimes = 1 Dinar (1964)

> **Catalogue values for unused stamps in this country are for Never Hinged items, beginning with Scott 109 in the regular postage section, Scott B27 in the semipostal section, Scott C1 in the airpost section, Scott CB1 in the airpost semi-postal section, and Scott J25 in the postage due section.**

Stamps of France Overprinted in Red, Blue or Black

a

b

c

d

		1924-26	Unwmk.	Perf. 14x13½	
1	A16(a)	1c dk gray (R)		.40	.40
2	A16(a)	2c violet		.40	.40
3	A16(a)	3c orange	brn	.40	.40
4	A16(a)	4c yel brn (Bl)		.40	.40
5	A22(a)	5c orange (Bl)		.40	.40
6	A16(a)	5c green		.40	.40
7	A23(a)	10c green ('25)		.80	.40
b.	Booklet pane of 10				
	Complete booklet, 2 #7b			300.00	
8	A22(a)	10c green ('25)		.80	.40
a.	Pair, one without overprint			1,600.	
9	A20(a)	15c slate grn		.40	.40
10	A23(a)	15c green ('25)		1.20	.40
11	A22(a)	15c red brn (Bl) ('26)		.40	.40
12	A22(a)	20c red brn (Bl)		.40	.40
a.	Pair, one without overprint			1,600.	
13	A22(a)	25c blue (R)		.80	.40
a.	Booklet pane of 10			—	
	Complete booklet, 2 #13a			1,450.	
b.	Pair, one without overprint			1,900.	
14	A23(a)	30c red (Bl)		2.40	.80
15	A22(a)	30c cerise ('25)		.80	.80
a.	"ALGERIE" double			225.00	150.00
16	A22(a)	30c lt bl (R) ('25)		.80	.80
a.	Booklet pane of 10			—	
	Complete booklet, 2 #16a			550.00	
17	A22(a)	35c violet		.80	.80
18	A18(b)	40c red & pale bl		1.20	.80
19	A22(a)	40c ol brn (R) ('25)		1.20	.80
20	A18(b)	45c grn & bl (R)		1.20	.80
a.	Double overprint			325.00	
21	A23(a)	45c red (Bl) ('25)		1.25	.80
22	A23(a)	50c blue (R)		1.20	.80
23	A20(a)	60c lt violet		1.20	.80
a.	Inverted overprint			3,250.	
24	A20(a)	65c rose (Bl)		1.20	.80
25	A23(a)	75c blue (R)		1.25	.75
a.	Double overprint			325.00	325.00
26	A20(a)	80c ver ('26)		2.00	1.20
27	A20(a)	85c ver (Bl)		1.20	1.20
28	A18(b)	1fr cl & ol grn		2.00	1.20
a.	Olive green omitted			325.00	325.00
29	A22(a)	1.05fr ver ('26)		1.60	1.60
30	A18(c)	2fr org & pale bl ('26)		2.40	1.60
31	A18(b)	3fr vio & bl ('26)		5.50	2.40
a.	Blue omitted			325.00	
32	A18(d)	5fr bl & buff (R)		16.00	12.00
		Nos. 1-32 (32)		52.80	36.35

No. 15 was issued precanceled only. Values for precanceled stamps in first column are for those which have not been through the post and have original gum. Values in second column are for postally used, gumless stamps.
For surcharges see Nos. 75, P1.

Street in Kasbah, Algiers
A1

Mosque of Sidi Abd-er-Rahman
A2

La Pêcherie Mosque — A3

Marabout of Sidi Yacoub
A4

		1926-39	Typo.	Perf. 14x13½	
33	A1	1c olive		.25	.25
a.	Imperforate			110.00	
34	A1	2c red brown		.25	.25
35	A1	3c orange		.25	.25
36	A1	5c blue green		.25	.25
37	A1	10c brt violet		.40	.25
a.	Booklet pane of 10				
	Complete booklet, 2 #37a			400.00	
38	A2	15c orange brn		.40	.25
a.	Imperforate			110.00	
b.	Booklet pane of 10				
	Complete booklet, 2 #38b			350.00	
39	A2	20c green		.40	
40	A2	20c deep rose		.25	.25
a.	Imperforate			120.00	
41	A2	25c blue grn		.40	.25
42	A2	25c blue ('27)		.80	.40
a.	Imperforate			120.00	
43	A2	25c vio bl ('39)		.25	.25
44	A2	30c blue		.40	.25
a.	Imperforate			120.00	
45	A2	30c bl grn ('27)		1.25	.80
46	A2	35c dp violet		1.60	1.20
47	A2	40c olive green		.40	.25
a.	Booklet pane of 10				
	Complete booklet, 2 #47a			325.00	
b.	Imperforate			120.00	
48	A3	45c violet brn		.80	.40
49	A3	50c blue		.40	.40
a.	Booklet pane of 10				
	Complete booklet, 2 #49a			400.00	
b.	Imperforate			125.00	
c.	Vert. pair, #49 and 49b			225.00	
50	A3	50c dk red ('30)		.40	.25
a.	Booklet pane of 10				
	Complete booklet, 2 #50a			450.00	
b.	Imperforate			120.00	
51	A3	60c yellow grn		.40	.40
52	A3	65c blk brn ('27)		3.25	2.40
53	A1	65c ultra ('38)		.40	.40
a.	Booklet pane of 10				
	Complete booklet, 2 #53a			160.00	
54	A3	75c carmine		1.20	.80
a.	Imperforate			125.00	
b.	Vert. pair, #54 and 54a			225.00	
55	A3	75c blue ('29)		4.75	.80
56	A3	80c orange red		1.20	.80
57	A3	90c red ('27)		8.00	4.00
a.	Imperforate			120.00	
58	A4	1fr gray grn & red brn		1.20	.80
a.	Imperforate			175.00	
59	A3	1.05fr lt brown		1.20	.80
60	A3	1.10fr mag ('27)		8.00	4.00
61	A4	1.25fr dk bl & ultra		1.60	1.20
62	A4	1.50fr dk bl & ultra ('27)		5.50	.80
a.	Imperforate			400.00	
63	A4	2fr prus bl & blk brn		4.75	1.20
a.	Imperforate			125.00	
64	A4	3fr violet & org		8.00	1.60
65	A4	5fr red & violet		16.00	4.75
66	A4	10fr ol brn & rose ('27)		80.00	47.50
a.	Imperforate			800.00	
67	A4	20fr vio & grn ('27)		8.00	8.00
		Nos. 33-67 (35)		162.60	86.85

A 90c red, design A1, was prepared but not issued. Values: unused $950, never hinged $1,350.

Type A4, 50c blue and rose red, inscribed "CENTENAIRE-ALGERIE" is France No. 255.

See design A24. For stamps and types surcharged see Nos. 68-74, 131, 136, 187, B1-B13, J27, P2.

Stamps of 1926 Surcharged

1927

68	A2	10c on 35c dp violet	.25	.25
69	A2	25c on 30c blue	.25	.25
70	A2	30c on 25c blue grn	.40	.40
71	A3	65c on 60c yel grn	1.60	1.20
72	A3	90c on 80c org red	1.40	.95
73	A3	1.10fr on 1.05fr lt brn	1.00	1.00
74	A4	1.50fr on 1.25fr dk bl & ultra	3.25	1.50
		Nos. 68-74 (7)	8.15	4.90

Bars cancel the old value on Nos. 68, 69, 73, 74.

No. 4 Surcharged

1927

75	A16	5c on 4c yellow brown	.40	.40
a.		Blue surcharge	1,250.	1,400.

Bay of Algiers
A5

1930, May 4   Engr.   Perf. 12½

78	A5	10fr red brown	21.00	21.00
a.		Imperf., pair	150.00	

Cent. of Algeria and for Intl. Phil. Exhib. of North Africa, May, 1930.

One example of No. 78 was sold with each 10fr admission.

Travel across the Sahara
A6

Arch of Triumph, Lambese
A7

Admiralty Building, Algiers
A8

Kings' Tombs near Touggourt
A9

El-Kebir Mosque, Algiers
A10

Oued River at Colomb-Bechar
A11

Sidi Bon Medine Cemetery at Tlemcen
A13

View of Ghardaia
A12

1936-41   Engr.   Perf. 13

79	A6	1c ultra	.25	.40
80	A11	2c dk violet	.25	.25
81	A7	3c dk blue grn	.25	.40
82	A12	5c red violet	.40	.25
83	A8	10c emerald	.25	.40
84	A9	15c red	.25	.40
85	A13	20c dk blue grn	.40	.40
86	A10	25c rose vio	1.20	.80
87	A12	30c yellow grn	.80	.40
88	A9	40c brown vio	.40	.40
89	A13	45c deep ultra	2.00	1.20
		On cover		4.50
90	A8	50c red	1.20	.40
91	A6	65c red brn	8.00	4.00
92	A6	65c rose car ('37)	.80	.40
93	A6	70c red brn ('39)	.80	.40
94	A11	75c slate bl	.80	.40
95	A7	90c henna brn	2.40	1.60
96	A10	1fr brown	.80	.40
97	A8	1.25fr lt violet	1.20	.80
98	A8	1.25fr car rose ('39)	.80	.40
99	A11	1.50fr turq blue	2.40	.80
99A	A11	1.50fr rose ('40)	.80	.80
100	A12	1.75fr henna brn	.40	.40
101	A7	2fr dk brown	.80	.40
102	A6	2.25fr yellow grn	20.00	13.50
103	A12	2.50fr dk ultra ('41)	.80	.80
104	A13	3fr magenta	1.20	.80
105	A10	3.50fr pck blue	6.50	4.00
106	A8	5fr slate blue	1.60	.80
107	A11	10fr brown	1.20	.80
108	A9	20fr turq blue	1.60	1.20
		Nos. 79-108 (31)	60.15	38.95

See Nos. 124-125, 162.

Nos. 82 and 100 with surcharge "E. F. M. 30frs" (Emergency Field Message) were used in 1943 to pay cable tolls for US and Canadian servicemen.

For other surcharges see Nos. 122, B27.

> Catalogue values for unused stamps in this section, from this point to the end of the section, are for Never Hinged items.

Algerian Pavilion — A14

1937   Perf. 13

109	A14	40c brt green	2.00	1.20
110	A14	50c rose carmine	2.00	.80
111	A14	1.50fr blue	2.75	1.20
112	A14	1.75fr brown black	2.75	1.60
		Nos. 109-112 (4)	9.50	4.80

Paris International Exposition.

Constantine in 1837 — A15

1937

113	A15	65c deep rose	1.20	.80
114	A15	1fr brown	12.00	1.60
115	A15	1.75fr blue green	1.60	.80
116	A15	2.15fr red violet	1.60	.80
		Nos. 113-116 (4)	16.40	4.00

Taking of Constantine by the French, cent.

Ruins of a Roman Villa — A16

1938

117	A16	30c green	2.00	.80
118	A16	65c ultra	.80	.80
119	A16	75c rose violet	2.00	.80
120	A16	3fr carmine rose	5.50	4.00
121	A16	5fr yellow brown	8.00	5.50
		Nos. 117-121 (5)	18.30	11.90

Centenary of Philippeville.

No. 90 Surcharged in Black

1938

122	A8	25c on 50c red	.80	.40
a.		Double surcharge	100.00	60.00
b.		Inverted surcharge	72.50	47.50
c.		Pair, one without surcharge	400.00	

Types of 1936 Numerals of Value on Colorless Background

1939

124	A7	90c henna brown	1.20	.40
125	A10	2.25fr blue green	1.20	.80

For surcharge see No. B38.

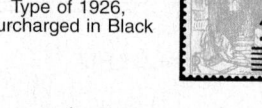

American Export Liner Unloading Cargo
A17

1939

126	A17	20c green	4.00	1.60
127	A17	40c red violet	4.00	1.60
128	A17	90c brown black	2.40	.80
129	A17	1.25fr rose	9.50	4.00
130	A17	2.25fr ultra	4.00	2.40
		Nos. 126-130 (5)	23.90	10.40

New York World's Fair.

Type of 1926, Surcharged in Black

Two types of surcharge:
I — Bars 6mm
II — Bars 7mm

1939-40   Perf. 14x13½

131	A1	1fr on 90c crimson (I)	.80	.40
a.		Booklet pane of 10 Complete booklet, 2 #131a	625.00	
b.		Double surcharge (I)	175.00	
c.		Inverted surcharge (I)	87.50	
d.		Pair, one without surch. (I)	2,000.	
e.		Type II ('40)	8.00	1.60
f.		Inverted surcharge (II)	95.00	
g.		Pair, one without surch. (II)	2,000.	

View of Algiers — A18

1941   Typo.

132	A18	30c ultra	.50	.30
133	A18	70c sepia	.50	.30
134	A18	1fr carmine rose	.50	.30
		Nos. 132-134 (3)	1.50	.90

See No. 163.

Marshal Pétain — A19

1941   Engr.   Perf. 13

135	A19	1fr dark blue	.50	.30

For stamp and type surcharged see Nos. B36-B37.

No. 53 Surcharged in Black

1941   Perf. 14x13½

136	A1	50c on 65c ultra	.70	.25
a.		Booklet pane of 10 Complete booklet, 2 #136a	120.00	
b.		Inverted surcharge	90.00	
c.		Pair, one without surch.	225.00	

Marshal Pétain — A20

1942   Perf. 14x13

137	A20	1.50fr orange red	.30	.25

Four other denominations of type A20 exist but were not placed in use. Values: 4fr, $1,300; 5fr, $1,100; 10fr, 20fr, each $600.

Constantine
A21

Oran
A22

Arms of Algiers — A23

Engraver's Name at Lower Left

1942-43   Photo.   Perf. 12

138	A21	40c dark vio ('43)	.70	.40
139	A22	60c rose ('43)	.55	.25
140	A21	1.20fr yel grn ('43)	.30	.25
141	A23	1.50fr car rose	.30	.25
142	A22	2fr sapphire	.80	.25
143	A21	2.40fr rose ('43)	.55	.25
144	A23	3fr sapphire	.90	.25
145	A21	4fr blue ('43)	.70	.25
146	A22	5fr yel grn ('43)	.65	.30
		Nos. 138-146 (9)	5.45	2.45

For type surcharged see No. 166.
No. 142 exists in green and violet. Value, each $60.

Imperforates

Nearly all of Algeria Nos. 138-285, B39-B96, C1-C12 and CB1-CB3 exist imperforate. See note after France No. 395.

Without Engraver's Name

1942-45   Typo.   Perf. 14x13½

147	A23	10c dull brn vio ('45)	.30	.25
148	A22	30c dp bl grn ('45)	.30	.25
149	A21	40c dull brn vio ('45)	.30	.25
150	A22	60c rose ('45)	.30	.25
151	A21	70c deep bl ('45)	.30	.25
152	A23	80c dk bl grn ('43)	1.20	.90
153	A21	1.20fr dp bl ('45)	.50	.30
154	A23	1.50fr brt rose ('43)	.30	.25
155	A22	2fr dp blue ('45)	.30	.25
156	A21	2.40fr rose ('45)	.80	.65

157	A23	3fr dp blue ('45)	.55	.40
158	A22	4.50fr brown vio	.30	.25

Nos. 147-158 (12) 5.45 4.25

For surcharge see No. 190.

La Pêcherie
Mosque — A24

1942   **Typo.**
159	A24	50c dull red	.55	.25
a.		Booklet pane of 10	—	
		Complete booklet, 2 #159a	325.00	

1942   **Photo.**   **Perf. 12**
160	A24	40c gray green	.55	.25
161	A24	50c red	.55	.25

Types of 1936-41, Without "RF"

1942   **Engr.**   **Perf. 13**
162	A11	1.50fr rose	.55	.25

      Typo.   **Perf. 14x13½**
163	A18	30c ultra	.55	.25

"One Aim Alone —
Victory"
A25   A26

1943   **Litho.**   **Perf. 12**
164	A25	1.50fr deep rose	.55	.25
165	A26	1.50fr dark blue	.55	.25

**Type of 1942-3 Surcharged with
New Value in Black**

1943   **Photo.**
166	A22	2fr on 5fr red orange	.30	.25
a.		Surcharge omitted	325.00	

Summer
Palace,
Algiers
A27

1944, Dec. 1   **Litho.**
167	A27	15fr slate	2.00	1.75
168	A27	20fr lt blue grn	2.00	.80
169	A27	50fr dk carmine	1.60	.80
170	A27	100fr deep blue	4.00	2.50
171	A27	200fr dull bis brn	5.50	2.75

Nos. 167-171 (5) 15.10 8.60

Marianne   Gallic Cock
A28   A29

1944-45
172	A28	10c gray	.55	.30
173	A28	30c red violet	.30	.25
174	A29	40c rose car ('45)	.50	.30
175	A28	50c red	.50	.25
176	A28	80c emerald	.30	.25
177	A28	1fr red ('45)	.30	.25
178	A28	1.20fr rose lilac	.30	.25
179	A28	1.50fr dark blue	.30	.25
a.		Double impression	65.00	
180	A29	2fr red	.30	.25
a.		Double impression	80.00	
181	A28	2fr dk brown ('45)	.30	.25
182	A28	2.40fr rose red	.55	.25
183	A28	3fr purple	.55	.40
184	A29	4fr ultra ('45)	.30	.25
185	A28	4.50fr olive blk	.95	.70
186	A29	10fr grnsh blk ('45)	1.90	.95

Nos. 172-186 (15) 7.90 5.20

No. 38 Surcharged in
Black

1944   **Perf. 14x13½**
187	A2	30c on 15c orange brn	1.20	.50
a.		Inverted surcharge	65.00	

This stamp exists precanceled only. See
note below No. 32.

No. 154 Surcharged

1945
190	A23	50c on 1.50fr brt rose	.55	.40
a.		Inverted surcharge	67.50	

**Stamps of France, 1944,
Overprinted Type "a" of 1924 in
Black**

1945-46
191	A99	80c yellow grn	.65	.25
192	A99	1fr grnsh blue	.50	.25
193	A99	1.20fr violet	.70	.25
194	A99	2fr violet brown	.90	.25
195	A99	2.40fr carmine rose	1.20	.40
196	A99	3fr orange	1.00	.30

Nos. 191-196 (6) 4.95 1.70

Stamps of France,
1945-47, Overprinted in
Black, Red or Carmine

1945-47
197	A145	40c lilac rose	.30	.25
198	A145	50c violet bl (R)	.30	.25
199	A146	60c brt ultra (R)	.95	.25
200	A146	1fr rose red ('47)	.50	.25
201	A146	1.50fr rose lilac ('47)	.50	.25
202	A147	2fr myr grn (R) ('46)	.30	.25
203	A147	3fr deep rose	.70	.25
204	A147	4.50fr ultra (C) ('47)	2.00	.25
205	A147	5fr lt green ('46)	.50	.25
206	A147	10fr ultra	1.75	.50

Nos. 197-206 (10) 7.80 2.75

France No. 383
Surcharged and
Overprinted in Black

1946
207	A99	2fr on 1.50fr henna brn	.50	.25
a.		Without "2F"	525.00	

France Nos. 562 and
564 Overprinted in
Carmine or Blue

1947
208	A153	10c dp ultra & blk (C)	.30	.25
209	A155	50c brown, yel & red (Bl)	.80	.30

Constantine   Algiers
A30   A31

Arms of Oran — A32

Perf. 14x13½

1947-49   **Unwmk.**   **Typo.**
210	A30	10c dk grn & brt red	.30	.25
211	A31	50c black & orange	.30	.25
212	A32	1fr ultra & yellow	.30	.25
213	A30	1.30fr blk & grnsh bl	1.90	1.25
214	A31	1.50fr pur & org yel	.50	.25
215	A32	2fr blk & brt grn	.30	.25
216	A31	2.50fr blk & brt red	1.20	.80
217	A31	3fr vio brn & grn	.55	.25
218	A32	3.50fr lt grn & rose lil	.55	.25
219	A30	4fr dk brn & brt grn	.45	.25
220	A31	4.50fr ultra & scar	.55	.25
221	A31	5fr blk & grnsh bl	.30	.25
222	A32	6fr brown & scarlet	1.00	.30
223	A32	8fr choc & ultra ('48)	.65	.25
224	A30	10fr car & choc ('48)	1.00	.40
225	A31	15fr black & red ('49)	1.10	.25

Nos. 210-225 (16) 10.95 5.75

See Nos. 274-280, 285.

Peoples of
the World
A33

1949, Oct. 24   **Engr.**   **Perf. 13**
226	A33	5fr green	2.75	2.00
227	A33	15fr scarlet	3.50	2.00
228	A33	25fr ultra	6.00	5.25

Nos. 226-228 (3) 12.25 9.25

75th anniv. of the UPU.

Grapes — A34

25fr, Dates. 40fr, Oranges and lemons.

1950, Feb. 25
229	A34	20fr multicolored	2.75	.80
230	A34	25fr multicolored	3.25	1.25
231	A34	40fr multicolored	7.25	1.60

Nos. 229-231 (3) 13.25 3.65

Apollo of
Cherchell — A35

Designs: 12fr, 18fr, Isis statue, Cherchell.
15fr, 20fr, Child with eagle.

1952   **Unwmk.**   **Perf. 13**
240	A35	10fr gray black	.65	.25
241	A35	12fr orange brn	1.25	.40
242	A35	15fr deep blue	1.10	.25
243	A35	18fr rose red	1.10	.40
244	A35	20fr deep green	1.60	.25
245	A35	30fr deep blue	1.90	.95

Nos. 240-245 (6) 7.60 2.50

War Memorial,
Algiers — A38

1952, Apr. 11
246	A38	12fr dark green	2.00	.80

Issued to honor the French Africa Army.

Fossilized
Nautilus — A39

Phonolite
Dike
A40

1952, Aug. 11
247	A39	15fr brt crimson	6.50	2.75
248	A40	30fr deep ultra	3.50	1.60

19th Intl. Geological Cong., Algiers, 9/8-15.

French and Algerian
Soldiers and
Camel — A41

1952, Nov. 30
249	A41	12fr chestnut brown	2.50	1.75

50th anniv. of the establishment of the
Sahara Companies.

Eugène
Millon
A42

François C.
Maillot — A43

Portrait: 50fr, Alphonse Laveran.

      Unwmk.

1954, Jan. 4   **Engr.**   **Perf. 13**
250	A42	25fr dk grn & choc	2.00	.80
251	A43	40fr org brn & brn car	3.00	1.20
252	A42	50fr ultra & indigo	3.00	.80

Nos. 250-252 (3) 8.00 2.80

Military Health Service.

Oranges — A44

1954, May 8
253 A44 15fr indigo & blue　2.00 1.20
3rd Intl. Cong. on Agronomy, Algiers, 1954.

Type of France, 1954 Overprinted type "a" in Black
Unwmk.
1954, June 6　Engr.　Perf. 13
254 A240 15fr rose carmine　2.00 1.20
Liberation of France, 10th anniversary.

Darguinah Hydroelectric Works — A45

1954, June 19
255 A45 15fr lilac rose　1.60 1.20
Opening of Darguinah hydroelectric works.

Patio of Bardo Museum — A46

1954　Typo.　Perf. 14x13½
257 A46 12fr red brn & brn org　.80 .30
258 A46 15fr dk blue & blue　.70 .25
See Nos. 267-271.

Type of France, 1954, Overprinted type "a" in Carmine
1954　Engr.　Perf. 13
260 A247 12fr dark green　2.00 1.00
150th anniv. of the 1st Legion of Honor awards at Camp de Boulogne.

St. Augustine — A47

1954, Nov. 11
261 A47 15fr chocolate　1.60 1.25
1600th anniv. of the birth of St. Augustine.

Aesculapius Statue and El Kattar Hospital, Algiers A48

1955, Apr. 3　Unwmk.　Perf. 13
262 A48 15fr red　1.60 .80
Issued to publicize the 30th French Congress of Medicine, Algiers, April 3-6, 1955.

Chenua Mountain and View of Tipasa A49

1955, May 31
263 A49 50fr brown carmine　1.50 .95
2000th anniv. of the founding of Tipasa.

Type of France, 1955 Overprinted type "a" in Red
1955, June 13
264 A251 30fr deep ultra　2.00 1.20
Rotary Intl., 50th anniv.

Marianne — A50

Perf. 14x13½
1955, Oct. 3　Typo.　Unwmk.
265 A50 15fr carmine　.80 .25
See No. 284.

Great Kabylia Mountains A51

1955, Dec. 17　Engr.　Perf. 13
266 A51 100fr indigo & ultra　6.50 .80

Bardo Type of 1954, "Postes" and "Algerie" in White
Perf. 14x13½
1955-57　Unwmk.　Typo.
267 A46 10fr dk brn & lt brn　.80 .25
268 A46 12fr red brn & brn org ('56)　.40 .20
269 A46 18fr crimson & ver ('57)　1.00 .30
270 A46 20fr grn & yel grn ('57)　.90 .50
271 A46 25fr purple & brt purple　1.00 1.00
Nos. 267-271 (5)　4.10 1.55

Marshal Franchet d'Esperey A52

1956, May 25　Engr.　Perf. 13
272 A52 15fr sapphire & indigo　2.00 1.20
Birth cent. of Marshal Franchet d'Esperey.

Marshal Jacques Leclerc A53

1956, Nov. 29
273 A53 15fr red brown & sepia　2.00 1.60
Death of Marshal Leclerc.
For design surcharged see No. B90.

Type of 1947-49 and

Arms of Bône — A54

Arms: 2fr, Tizi-Quzou. 3fr, Mostaganem. 5fr, Tlemcen. 10fr, Setif. 12fr, Orleansville.

1956-58　Typo.　Perf. 14x13½
274 A54 1fr green & ver　.30 .25
275 A54 2fr ver & ultra ('58)　1.00 .55
276 A54 3fr ultra & emer ('58)　1.40 .30
277 A54 5fr ultra & yellow　.80 .25
278 A31 6fr red & grn ('57)　1.40 .80
279 A54 6fr dp cl & emer ('58)　1.50 .90
280 A54 12fr ultra & red ('58)　1.75 .90
Nos. 274-280 (7)　8.15 3.95
Nos. 275 and 279 are inscribed "Republique Francaise." See No. 285.

View of Oran — A55

1956-58　Engr.　Perf. 13
281 A55 30fr dull purple　1.20 .40
282 A55 35fr car rose ('58)　2.40 .80

Electric Train Crossing Bridge A56

1957, Mar. 25
283 A56 40fr dk blue grn & emer　2.40 .55

Marianne Type of 1955 Inscribed "Algerie" Vertically
Perf. 14x13½
1957, Dec. 2　Typo.　Unwmk.
284 A50 20fr ultra　.95 .25

Arms Type of 1947-49 Inscribed "Republique Francaise"
1958, July
285 A31 6fr red & green　37.50 28.00

Independent State
France Nos. 939, 968, 945-946 & 1013 Ovptd. in Black or Red

No. 286　No. 287

No. 288　No. 289

No. 290

1962, July 2
Typographed Overprint
286 A336 10c brt green　.75 .45
287 A349 25c lake & gray　.75 .45
288 A339 45c brt vio & ol gray　7.00 3.75
289 A339 50c sl grn & lt claret　7.00 3.75
290 A372 1fr dk bl, sl & bis　4.25 1.75
Nos. 286-290 (5)　19.75 10.15

Handstamped Overprint
286a A336 10c bright green　.75 .45
287a A349 25c lake & gray　.75 .45
288a A339 45c brt vio & ol gray　29.00 22.50
289a A339 50c sl grn & lt claret　29.00 22.50
290a A372 1fr dk bl, sl & bis　6.00 3.00
Nos. 286a-290a (5)　65.50 48.90

Post offices were authorized to overprint their stock of these 5 French stamps. The size of the letters was specified as 3x6mm each, but various sizes were used. The post offices

had permission to make their own rubber stamps. Typography, pen or pencil were also used. Many types exist. Colors of handstamped overprints include black, red, blue, violet. "EA" stands for Etat Algérien.

Mosque, Tlemcen — A57

Roman Gates of Lodi, Médéa A58

5c, Kerrata Gorge. 10c, Dam at Foum el Gherza. 95c, Oil field, Hassi Messaoud.

1962, Nov. 1　Engr.　Perf. 13
291 A57 5c Prus grn, grn & choc　.25 .25
292 A58 10c ol blk & dk bl　.25 .25
293 A57 25c sl grn, brn & ver　.50 .25
294 A57 95c dk bl, blk & bis　2.75 .95
295 A58 1fr green & blk　2.40 1.50
Nos. 291-295 (5)　6.15 3.20

The designs of Nos. 291-295 are similar to French issues of 1959-61 with "Republique Algerienne" replacing "Republique Francaise."

Flag, Rifle, Olive Branch — A59

Design: Nos. 300-303, Broken chain and rifle added to design A59.

1963, Jan. 6　Litho.　Perf. 12½
Flag in Green and Red
296 A59 5c bister brown　.25 .25
297 A59 10c blue　.25 .25
298 A59 25c vermilion　1.75 .25
299 A59 95c violet　1.35 .75
300 A59 1fr green　1.20 .35
301 A59 2fr brown　3.00 .75
302 A59 5fr lilac　5.25 3.00
303 A59 10fr gray　20.00 14.00
Nos. 296-303 (8)　33.05 19.60

Nos. 296-299 for the successful revolution and Nos. 300-303 the return of peace.

Men of Various Races, Wheat Emblem and Globe A60

1963, Mar. 21　Engr.　Perf. 13
304 A60 25c maroon, dl grn & yel　.65 .25
FAO "Freedom from Hunger" campaign.

Map of Algeria and Emblems — A61

1963, July 5　Unwmk.　Perf. 13
305 A61 25c bl, dk brn, grn & red　.65 .25
1st anniv. of Algeria's independence.

Physicians from 13th Century Manuscript — A62

1963, July 29 **Engr.**
306 A62 25c brn red, grn & bis 2.00 .55
2nd Congress of the Union of Arab physicians.

Orange and Blossom — A63

1963 **Perf. 14x13**
307 A63 8c gray grn & org .25 .25
308 A63 20c slate & org red .25 .25
309 A63 40c grnsh bl & org .70 .30
310 A63 55c ol grn & org red 1.00 .55
Nos. 307-310 (4) 2.20 1.35

Nos. 307-310 issued precanceled only. See note below No. 32.

Scales and Scroll A64

1963, Oct. 13 **Unwmk.** **Perf. 13**
311 A64 25c blk, grn & rose red .65 .35
Issued to honor the new constitution.

Guerrillas — A65

1963, Nov. 1
312 A65 25c dk brn, yel grn & car .65 .35
9th anniversary of Algerian revolution.

Centenary Emblem — A66

1963, Dec. 8 **Photo.** **Perf. 12**
313 A66 25c lt vio bl, yel & dk red .90 .60
Centenary of International Red Cross.

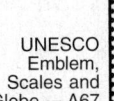

UNESCO Emblem, Scales and Globe — A67

1963, Dec. 16 **Unwmk.** **Perf. 12**
314 A67 25c lt blue & blk .65 .25
15th anniv. of the Universal Declaration of Human Rights.

Workers — A68

1964, May 1 **Engr.** **Perf. 13**
315 A68 50c dull red, red org & bl 1.25 .40
Issued for the Labor Festival.

Map of Africa and Flags A69

1964, May 25 **Unwmk.** **Perf. 13**
316 A69 45c blue, orange & car 1.00 .35
Africa Day on the 1st anniv. of the Addis Ababa charter on African unity.

Ramses II Battling the Hittites (from Abu Simbel) — A70

Design: 30c, Two statues of Ramses II.

1964, June 28 **Engr.** **Perf. 13**
317 A70 20c choc, red & vio bl .90 .40
318 A70 30c brn, red & grnsh bl 1.05 .55
UNESCO world campaign to save historic monuments in Nubia.

A71

5c, 25c, 85c, Tractors. 10c, 30c, 65c, Men working with lathe. 12c, 15c, 45c, Electronics center & atom symbol. 20c, 50c, 95c, Draftsman & bricklayer.

1964-65 **Typo.** **Perf. 14x13½**
319 A71 5c red lilac .25 .25
320 A71 10c brown .25 .25
321 A71 12c emerald ('65) .45 .25
322 A71 15c dk blue ('65) .30 .25
323 A71 20c yellow .45 .25
324 A71 25c red .45 .25
325 A71 30c purple ('65) .35 .25
326 A71 45c rose car .65 .25
327 A71 50c ultra .65 .25
328 A71 65c orange .70 .25
329 A71 85c green 1.40 .25
330 A71 95c car rose 1.75 .35
Nos. 319-330 (12) 7.65 3.10

For surcharges see Nos. 389, 424.

A72

1964, Aug. 30 **Engr.** **Perf. 13**
331 A72 85c Communications tower 1.90 .75
Inauguration of the Hertzian cable telephone line Algiers-Annaba.

Industrial & Agricultural Symbols — A73

1964, Sept. 26 **Typo.** **Perf. 13½x14**
332 A73 25c lt ultra, yel & red .60 1.25
1st Intl. Fair at Algiers, Sept. 26-Oct. 11.

Gas Flames and Pipes — A74

1964, Sept. 27
333 A74 30c violet, blue & yel .85 .50
Arzew natural gas liquification plant opening.

Planting Trees — A75

1964, Nov. 29 **Unwmk.**
334 A75 25c slate grn, yel & car .50 .25
National reforestation campaign.

Children and UNICEF Emblem — A76

1964, Dec. 13 **Perf. 13½x14**
335 A76 15c pink, vio bl & lt grn .50 .25
Issued for Children's Day.

Decorated Camel Saddle — A77

1965, May 29 **Typo.** **Perf. 13½x14**
336 A77 20c blk, red, emer & brn .70 .25
Handicrafts of Sahara.

ICY Emblem A78

1965, Aug. 29 **Engr.** **Perf. 13**
337 A78 30c blk, mar & bl grn .90 .40
338 A78 60c blk, brt bl & bl grn 1.25 .50
International Cooperation Year, 1965.

ITU Emblem A79

1965, Sept. 19
339 A79 60c purple, emer & buff .90 .50
340 A79 95c dk brn, mar & buff 1.25 .55
Cent. of the ITU.

Musicians A80

Miniatures by Mohammed Racim: 60c, Two female musicians. 5d, Algerian princess and antelope.

1965, Dec. 27 **Photo.** **Perf. 11½**
341 A80 30c multicolored 1.75 .65
342 A80 60c multicolored 2.50 1.25
343 A80 5d multicolored 14.00 7.50
Nos. 341-343 (3) 18.25 9.40

Bulls, Painted in 6000 B.C. — A81

Wall Paintings from Tassili-N-Ajjer, c. 6000 B.C.: No. 345, Shepherd, vert. 2d, Fleeing ostriches. 3d, Two girls, vert.

1966, Jan. 29 **Photo.** **Perf. 11½**
344 A81 1d brn, bis & red brn 4.50 2.75
345 A81 1d gray, blk & ocher & dk brn 4.50 2.75
346 A81 2d brn, ocher & red brn 10.00 4.75
347 A81 3d buff, blk, ocher & brn red 10.00 4.75
Nos. 344-347 (4) 29.00 15.00

See Nos. 365-368.

Pottery — A82

Handicrafts from Great Kabylia: 50c, Weaving, woman at loom, horiz. 70c, Jewelry.

1966, Feb. 26 **Engr.** **Perf. 13**
348 A82 40c Prus bl, brn red & blk .50 .35
349 A82 50c dk red, ol & ocher .75 .40
350 A82 70c vio bl, blk & red 1.25 .55
Nos. 348-350 (3) 2.50 1.30

Weather Balloon, Compass Rose and Anemometer — A83

1966, Mar. 23   Engr.   Unwmk.
351 A83 1d claret, brt bl & grn   1.25   .50
World Meteorological Day.

Book, Grain, Cogwheel and UNESCO Emblem — A84

Design: 60c, Grain, cogwheel, book and UNESCO emblem.

1966, May 2   Typo.   Perf. 13x14
352 A84 30c yellow bis & blk   .45   .25
353 A84 60c dk red, gray & blk   .70   .40
Literacy as basis for development.

WHO Headquarters, Geneva — A85

1966, May 30   Engr.   Perf. 13
354 A85 30c multicolored   .45   .35
355 A85 60c multicolored   .85   .40
Inauguration of the WHO Headquarters, Geneva.

Algerian Scout Emblem — A86   Arab Jamboree Emblem — A87

1966, July 23   Photo.   Perf. 12x12½
356 A86 30c multicolored   1.25   .60
357 A87 1d multicolored   1.75   .65

No. 356 commemorates the 30th anniv. of the Algerian Mohammedan Boy Scouts. No. 357, the 7th Arab Boy Scout Jamboree, held at Good Daim, Libya, Aug. 12.

Map of Palestine and Victims — A88

1966, Sept. 26   Typo.   Perf. 10½
358 A88 30c red & black   .60   .25
Deir Yassin Massacre, Apr. 9, 1948.

Abd-el-Kader — A89

1966, Nov. 2   Photo.   Perf. 11½
359 A89 30c multicolored   .25   .25
360 A89 95c multicolored   1.05   .40

Transfer from Damascus to Algiers of the ashes of Abd-el-Kader (1807?-1883), Emir of Mascara. See Nos. 382-387.

UNESCO Emblem — A90

1966, Nov. 19   Typo.   Perf. 10½
361 A90 1d multicolored   1.05   .40
20th anniv. of UNESCO.

Horseman A91

Miniatures by Mohammed Racim: 1.50d, Woman at her toilette. 2d, The pirate Barbarossa in front of the Admiralty.

1966, Dec. 17   Photo.   Perf. 11½
Granite Paper
362 A91 1d multicolored   3.25   1.50
363 A91 1.50d multicolored   5.25   1.75
364 A91 2d multicolored   6.50   3.50
Nos. 362-364 (3)   15.00   6.75

Wall Paintings Type of 1966
Wall Paintings from Tassili-N-Ajjer, c. 6000 B.C.: 1d, Cow. No. 366, Antelope. No. 367, Archers. 3d, Warrior, vert.

1967, Jan. 28   Photo.   Perf. 11½
365 A81 1d brn, bis & dl vio   3.25   1.90
366 A81 2d brn, ocher & red brn   5.00   3.75
367 A81 2d brn, yel & red brn   5.00   3.75
368 A81 3d blk, gray, yel & red brn   7.00   5.25
Nos. 365-368 (4)   20.25   14.65

Bardo Museum A92

La Kalaa Minaret — A93

Design: 1.30d, Ruins at Sedrata.

1967, Feb. 27   Photo.   Perf. 13
369 A92 35c multicolored   .40   .25
370 A93 95c multicolored   .90   .50
371 A92 1.30d multicolored   1.50   .65
Nos. 369-371 (3)   2.80   1.40

Moretti and International Tourist Year Emblem A94

Design: 70c, Tuareg riding camel, Tassili, and Tourist Year Emblem, vert.

1967, Apr. 29   Litho.   Perf. 14
372 A94 40c multi   .70   .40
373 A94 70c multi   1.40   .60
International Tourist Year, 1967.

Spiny-tailed Agamid A95

Designs: 20c, Ostrich, vert. 40c, Slender-horned gazelle, vert. 70c, Fennec.

1967, June 24   Photo.   Perf. 11½
374 A95 5c bister & blk   .70   .70
375 A95 20c ocher, blk & pink   1.40   .70
376 A95 40c ol bis, blk & red brn   2.10   1.00
377 A95 70c gray, blk & dp org   2.75   1.75
Nos. 374-377 (4)   6.95   4.15

Dancers — A96

Typographed and Engraved
1967, July 4   Perf. 10½
378 A96 50c gray vio, yel & blk   .90   .40
National Youth Festival.

Map of the Mediterranean and Sport Scenes — A97

1967, Sept. 2   Typo.   Perf. 10½
379 A97 30c black, red & blue   .65   .40
Issued to publicize the 5th Mediterranean Games, Tunis, Sept. 8-17.

Skiers — A98

Olympic Emblem and Sports A99

1967, Oct. 21   Engr.   Perf. 13
380 A98 30c brt blue & ultra   .90   .40
381 A99 95c brn org, pur & brt grn   1.65   .75
Issued to publicize the 10th Winter Olympic Games, Grenoble, Feb. 6-18, 1968.

Abd-el-Kader Type of 1966
Lithographed, Photogravure
1967-71   Perf. 13½, 11½
382 A89 5c dull pur ('68)   .25   .25
383 A89 10c green   .25   .25
383A A89 10c sl grn (litho., '69)   .25   .25
383B A89 25c orange ('71)   .30   .25
384 A89 30c black ('68)   .35   .25
385 A89 30c lt violet ('68)   .45   .25
386 A89 50c rose claret   .75   .25
387 A89 70c violet blue   .85   .30
Nos. 382-387 (8)   3.45   2.05

No. 383, 50c and 70c, issued Nov. 13, 1967, are on granite paper, photo. The 5c, No.383A, 25c and 30c are litho., perf. 13½; others, perf. 11½.

The three 1967 stamps (No. 383, 50c, 70c) have numerals thin, narrow and close together; the Arabic inscription at lower right is 2mm high. The 5 litho. stamps are redrawn, with numerals thicker and spaced more widely; Arabic at lower right 3mm high.

Boy Scouts Holding Jamboree Emblem A100

1967, Dec. 23   Engr.   Perf. 13
388 A100 1d multicolored   1.90   .70

12th Boy Scout World Jamboree, Farragut State Park, Idaho, Aug. 1-9.

No. 324 Surcharged
1967   Typo.   Perf. 14x13½
389 A71 30c on 25c red   .65   .25

Mandolin — A101

1968, Feb. 17   Photo.   Perf. 12½x13
390 A101 30c shown   .55   .25
391 A101 40c Lute   .75   .40
392 A101 1.30d Rebec   2.75   1.10
Nos. 390-392 (3)   4.05   1.75

Nememcha Rug — A102

Algerian Rugs: 70c, Guergour. 95c, Djebel-Amour. 1.30d, Kalaa.

1968, Apr. 13   Photo.   Perf. 11½
393 A102 30c multi   .95   .60
394 A102 70c multi   1.75   .95
395 A102 95c multi   3.00   2.00
396 A102 1.30d multi   3.50   1.50
Nos. 393-396 (4)   9.20   5.05

Human Rights Flame A103

1968, May 18 Typo. Perf. 10½
397 A103 40c blue, red & yel .65 .80
International Human Rights Year, 1968.

WHO Emblem A104

1968, May 18
398 A104 70c blk, lt bl & yel .80 .40
20th anniv. of the WHO.

Welder — A105

1968, June 15 Engr. Perf. 13
399 A105 30c gray, brn & ultra .45 .25
Algerian emigration to Europe.

Athletes, Olympic Flame and Rings — A106

50c, Soccer player. 1d, Mexican pyramid, emblem, Olympic flame, rings & athletes, horiz.

Perf. 12½x13, 13x12½
1968, July 4 Photo.
400 A106 30c green, red & yel .65 .50
401 A106 50c rose car & multi .95 .60
402 A106 1d dk grn, org, brn & red 1.60 .95
Nos. 400-402 (3) 3.20 2.05
19th Olympic Games, Mexico City, 10/12-27.

Scouts and Emblem — A107

1968, July 4 Perf. 13
403 A107 30c multicolored .65 .25
8th Arab Boy Scout Jamboree, Algiers, 1968.

Barbary Sheep — A108

1968, Oct. 19 Photo. Perf. 11½
404 A108 40c shown .90 .40
405 A108 1d Red deer 2.10 .65

Hunting Scenes, Djemila — A109

Design: 95c, Neptune's chariot, Timgad, horiz. Both designs are from Roman mosaics.

Perf. 12½x13, 13x12½
1968, Nov. 23 Photo.
406 A109 40c gray & multi .60 .25
407 A109 95c gray & multi 1.35 .55

"Industry" — A110

Designs: No. 409, Miner with drill. 95c, "Energy" (circle and rays).

1968, Dec. 14 Perf. 11½
408 A110 30c dp orange & sil .45 .25
409 A110 30c brown & multi .45 .25
410 A110 95c silver, red & blk 1.25 .40
Nos. 408-410 (3) 2.15 .90
Issued to publicize industrial development.

ALGERIE

Opuntia Ficus Indica — A111

Flowers: 40c, Carnations. 70c, Roses. 95c, Bird-of-paradise flower.

1969, Jan. Photo. Perf. 11½
Flowers in Natural Colors
411 A111 25c pink & blk .65 .45
412 A111 40c yellow & blk 1.10 .60
413 A111 70c gray & blk 1.65 .75
414 A111 95c brt blue & blk 2.90 1.10
Nos. 411-414 (4) 6.30 2.90
See Nos. 496-499.

Irrigation Dam at Djorf Torba-Oued Guir — A112

Design: 1.50d, Truck on Highway No. 51 and camel caravan.

1969, Feb. 22 Photo. Perf. 11½
415 A112 30c multi .55 .25
416 A112 1.50d multi 1.90 .75
Public works in the Sahara.

Mail Coach A113

1969, Mar. 22 Photo. Perf. 11½
417 A113 1d multicolored 2.60 .75
Issued for Stamp Day, 1969.

Capitol, Timgad — A114

1d, Septimius Temple, Djemila, horiz.

1969, Apr. 5 Photo. Perf. 13x12½
418 A114 30c gray & multi .55 .25
419 A114 1d gray & multi 1.35 .50
Second Timgad Festival, Apr. 4-8.

ILO Emblem A115

1969, May 24 Photo. Perf. 11½
420 A115 95c dp car, yel & blk 1.15 .45
50th anniv. of the ILO.

Arabian Saddle — A116

Algerian Handicrafts: 30c, Bookcase. 60c, Decorated copper plate.

1969, June 28 Photo. Perf. 12x12½
Granite Paper
421 A116 30c multicolored .45 .25
422 A116 60c multicolored .85 .35
423 A116 1d multicolored 1.50 .65
Nos. 421-423 (3) 2.80 1.25

No. 321 Surcharged

1969 Typo. Perf. 14x13½
424 A71 20c on 12c emerald .50 .25

Pan-African Culture Festival Emblem — A117

1969, July 19 Photo. Perf. 12½
425 A117 30c multicolored .60 .25
1st Pan-African Culture Festival, Algiers, 7/21-8/1.

African Development Bank Emblem — A118

1969, Aug. 23 Typo. Perf. 10½
426 A118 30c dull blue, yel & blk .60 .25
5th anniv. of the African Development Bank.

Astronauts and Landing Module on Moon — A119

Perf. 12½x11½
1969, Aug. 23 Photo.
427 A119 50c gold & multi 1.10 .50
Man's 1st landing on the moon, July 20, 1969. US astronauts Neil A. Armstrong and Col. Edwin E. Aldrin, Jr., with Lieut. Col. Michael Collins piloting Apollo 11.

Algerian Women, by Dinet — A120

1.50d, The Watchmen, by Etienne Dinet.

1969, Nov. 29 Photo. Perf. 14½
428 A120 1d multi 2.00 .80
429 A120 1.50d multi 2.50 1.25

Mother and Child — A121

1969, Dec. 27 Photo. Perf. 11½
430 A121 30c multicolored .65 .40
Issued to promote mother and child protection.

Agricultural Growth Chart, Tractor and Dam A122

30c, Transportation and development. 50c, Abstract symbols of industrialization.

1970, Jan. 31 Photo. Perf. 12½
Size: 37x23mm
431 A122 25c dk brn, yel & org .30 .25

Litho. Perf. 14
Size: 49x23mm
432 A122 30c blue & multi 1.00 .25

Photo. **Perf. 12½**
Size: 37x23mm
433 A122 50c rose lilac & blk .60 .25
Nos. 431-433 (3) 1.90 .75
Four-Year Development Plan.

Old and New Mail
Delivery — A123

1970, Feb. 28 **Photo.** **Perf. 11½**
Granite Paper
434 A123 30c multicolored .70 .25
Issued for Stamp Day.

Spiny
Lobster — A124

Designs: 40c, Mollusks. 75c, Retepora cellulosa. 1d, Red coral.

1970, Mar. 28
435 A124 30c ocher & multi .55 .25
436 A124 40c multicolored .80 .40
437 A124 75c ultra & multi 1.35 .55
438 A124 1d lt blue & multi 2.10 .80
Nos. 435-438 (4) 4.80 2.00

Oranges,
EXPO '70
Emblem
A125

Designs (EXPO '70 Emblem and): 60c, Algerian pavilion. 70c, Grapes.

1970, Apr. 25 **Photo.** **Perf. 12½x12**
439 A125 30c lt blue, grn & org .65 .25
440 A125 60c multicolored .65 .40
441 A125 70c multicolored 1.30 .60
Nos. 439-441 (3) 2.60 1.25

EXPO '70 International Exhibition, Osaka, Japan, Mar. 15-Sept. 13, 1970.

Olives, Oil
Bottle — A126

1970, May 16 **Photo.** **Perf. 12½x12**
442 A126 1d yellow & multi 2.00 .80
Olive Year, 1969-1970.

Common Design Types
pictured following the introduction.

UPU Headquarters Issue
Common Design Type
1970, May 30 **Perf. 13**
Size: 36x26mm
443 CD133 75c multicolored 1.10 .40

Saber — A127

Designs: 40c, Guns, 18th century, horiz. 1d, Pistol, 18th century, horiz.

1970, June 27 **Photo.** **Perf. 12½**
444 A127 40c yellow & multi 1.10 .60
445 A127 75c red & multi 1.50 .80
446 A127 1d multicolored 2.10 1.10
Nos. 444-446 (3) 4.70 2.50

Map of
Arab
Countries
and Arab
League
Flag
A128

Typographed and Engraved
1970, July 25 **Perf. 10½**
447 A128 30c grn, ocher & lt bl .55 .25
25th anniversary of the Arab League.

Lenin — A129

1970, Aug. 29 **Litho.** **Perf. 11½x12**
448 A129 30c brown & buff 2.50 .40
Lenin (1870-1924), Russian communist leader.

Exhibition Hall and Algiers Fair
Emblem — A130

1970, Sept. 11 **Engr.** **Perf. 14x13½**
449 A130 60c lt olive green .65 .30
New Exhibition Hall for Algiers Intl. Fair.

Education Year Emblem, Blackboard,
Atom Symbol — A131

Koran
Page — A132

1970, Oct. 24 **Photo.** **Perf. 14**
450 A131 30c pink, blk, gold & lt bl .50 .25
451 A132 3d multicolored 4.00 1.75
Issued for International Education Year.

Great
Mosque,
Tlemcen
A133

Design: 40c, Ketchaoua Mosque, Algiers, vert. 1d, Mosque, Sidi-Okba, vert.

1970-71 **Litho.** **Perf. 14**
456 A133 30c multicolored .40 .25
457 A133 40c sepia & lemon
('71) .50 .25
458 A133 1d multicolored 1.00 .40
Nos. 456-458 (3) 1.90 .90

Symbols of
the Arts
A134

1970, Dec. 26 **Photo.** **Perf. 13x12½**
459 A134 1d grn, lt grn & org 1.00 .50

Main Post
Office,
Algiers
A135

1971, Jan. 23 **Perf. 11½**
460 A135 30c multicolored 1.00 .40
Stamp Day, 1971.

Hurdling
A136

40c, Vaulting, vert. 75c, Basketball, vert.

1971, Mar. 7 **Photo.** **Perf. 11½**
461 A136 20c lt blue & slate .45 .25
462 A136 40c lt ol grn & slate .55 .40
463 A136 75c salmon pink &
slate .95 .60
Nos. 461-463 (3) 1.95 1.25
Mediterranean Games, Izmir, Turkey, Oct. 1971.

Symbolic
Head — A137

1971, Mar. 27 **Perf. 12½**
464 A137 60c car rose, blk & sil .65 .30
Intl. year against racial discrimination.

Emblem
and
Technicians
A138

1971, Apr. 24 **Photo.** **Perf. 12½x12**
465 A138 70c cl, org & bluish blk .75 .30
Founding of the Institute of Technology.

Woman from
Aurès — A139

Regional Costumes: 70c, Man from Oran. 80c, Man from Algiers. 90c, Woman from Amour Mountains.

1971, Oct. 16 **Perf. 11½**
466 A139 50c gold & multi 1.10 .50
467 A139 70c gold & multi 1.40 .80
468 A139 80c gold & multi 1.75 .95
469 A139 90c gold & multi 2.10 1.00
Nos. 466-469 (4) 6.35 3.25

See Nos. 485-488, 534-537.

UNICEF Emblem,
Birds and
Plants — A140

1971, Dec. 6 **Perf. 11½**
470 A140 60c multicolored .75 .50
25th anniv. of UNICEF.

Lion
of St.
Mark
A141

1.15d, Bridge of Sighs, Venice, vert.

1972, Jan. 24 **Litho.** **Perf. 12**
471 A141 80c multi 1.10 .55
472 A141 1.15d multi 2.25 .95
UNESCO campaign to save Venice.

Javelin — A142

Designs: 25c, Bicycling, horiz. 60c, Wrestling. 1d, Gymnast on rings.

1972, Mar. 25   Photo.   Perf. 11½
473 A142 25c maroon & multi   .40   .25
474 A142 40c ocher & multi   .50   .25
475 A142 60c ultra & multi   1.10   .50
476 A142 1d rose & multi   1.50   .55
    Nos. 473-476 (4)   3.50   1.55

20th Olympic Games, Munich, 8/26-9/11.

Book and Book Year Emblem — A143

1972, Apr. 15
477 A143 1.15d bister, brn & red   .80   .50

International Book Year 1972.

Mailmen — A144

1972, Apr. 22
478 A144 40c gray & multi   .70   .25

Stamp Day 1972.

Flowers — A145

1972, May 27
479 A145 50c Jasmine   .65   .40
480 A145 60c Violets   .65   .50
481 A145 1.15d Tuberose   1.75   .65
    Nos. 479-481 (3)   3.05   1.55

Olympic Stadium, Chéraga A146

1972, June 10
482 A146 50c gray, choc & grn   .70   .40

New Day, Algerian Flag — A147

1972, July 5
483 A147 1d green & multi   1.15   .60

10th anniversary of independence.

Festival Emblem — A148

1972, July 5   Litho.   Perf. 10½
484 A148 40c grn, dk brn & org   .60   .25

1st Arab Youth Festival, Algiers, July 5-11.

Costume Type of 1971

Regional Costumes: 50c, Woman from Hoggar. 60c, Kabyle woman. 70c, Man from Mzab. 90c, Woman from Tlemcen.

1972, Nov. 18   Photo.   Perf. 11½
485 A139 50c gold & multi   1.40   .65
486 A139 60c gold & multi   1.75   .65
487 A139 70c gold & multi   1.90   .95
488 A139 90c gold & multi   2.25   1.10
    Nos. 485-488 (4)   7.30   3.35

Mailing a Letter — A149

1973, Jan. 20   Photo.   Perf. 11
489 A149 40c orange & multi   .60   .25

Stamp Day.

Ho Chi Minh, Map of Viet Nam — A150

1973, Feb. 17   Photo.   Perf. 11½
490 A150 40c multicolored   .90   .35

To honor the people of Viet Nam.

Embroidery from Annaba A151

Designs: 60c, Tree of Life pattern from Algiers. 80c, Constantine embroidery.

1973, Feb. 24
491 A151 40c gray & multi   .55   .30
492 A151 60c blue and multi   .80   .50
493 A151 80c dk red, gold & blk 1.25   .65
    Nos. 491-493 (3)   2.60   1.45

Stylized Globe and Wheat — A152

1973, Mar. 26   Photo.   Perf. 11½
494 A152 1.15d brt rose lil, org & grn   .80   .35

World Food Program, 10th anniversary.

Soldier and Flag A153

1973, Apr. 23   Photo.   Perf. 14x13½
495 A153 40c multicolored   .60   .25

Honoring the National Service.

Flower Type of 1969

30c, Opuntia ficus indica. 40c, Roses. 1d, Carnations. 1.15d, Bird-of-paradise flower.

1973, May 21   Photo.   Perf. 11½
Flowers in Natural Colors
496 A111 30c pink & blk   .75   .25
497 A111 40c gray & blk   .90   .40
498 A111 1d yellow & multi   2.00   .65
499 A111 1.15d multi   3.25   .95
    Nos. 496-499 (4)   6.90   2.25

For overprints and surcharges see Nos. 518-519, 531.

OAU Emblem — A154

1973, May 28   Photo.   Perf. 12½x13
500 A154 40c multicolored   .60   .25

Org. for African Unity, 10th anniv.

Desert and Fruitful Land, Farmer and Family A155

1973, June 18   Perf. 11½
501 A155 40c gold & multi   .70   .25

Agricultural revolution.

Map of Africa, Scout Emblem — A156

1973, July 16   Litho.   Perf. 10½
502 A156 80c purple   .80   .40

24th Boy Scout World Conference (1st in Africa), Nairobi, Kenya, July 16-21.

Algerian PTT Emblem A157

1973, Aug. 6   Perf. 14
503 A157 40c blue & orange   .60   .25

Adoption of new emblem for Post, Telegraph and Telephone System.

Conference Emblem — A158

Perf. 13½x12½
1973, Sept. 5   Photo.
504 A158 40c dp rose & multi   .40   .30
505 A158 80c blue grn & multi   .75   .40

4th Summit Conference of Non-aligned Nations, Algiers, Sept. 5-9.

Port of Skikda A159

1973, Sept. 29   Photo.   Perf. 11½
506 A159 80c ocher, blk & ultra .70   .40

New port of Skikda.

Young Workers — A160

1973, Oct. 22   Photo.   Perf. 13
507 A160 40c multicolored   .60   .25

Voluntary work service.

Arms of Algiers A161

1973, Dec. 22   Photo.   Perf. 13
508 A161 2d gold & multi   2.75 1.40
Millennium of Algiers.

Infant — A162

1974, Jan. 7   Litho.   Perf. 10½x11
509 A162 80c orange & multi   .70 .50
Fight against tuberculosis.
No. 509 exists with 1973 year date. Value $60.

Man and Woman, Industry and Transportation — A163

1974, Feb. 18   Photo.   Perf. 11½
510 A163 80c multicolored   .85 .40
Four-year plan.

A164

1974, Feb. 25   Photo.   Perf. 11½
511 A164 1.50d multi   2.75 1.40
Millennium of the birth of abu-al-Rayhan al-Biruni (973-1048), philosopher and mathematician.

Map and Colors of Algeria, Tunisia, Morocco A165

1974, Mar. 4   Photo.   Perf. 13
512 A165 40c gold & multi   .60 .25
Maghreb Committee for Coordination of Posts and Telecommunications.

Hand Holding Rifle — A166

1974, Mar. 25   Perf. 11½
513 A166 80c red & black   .70 .25
Solidarity with the struggle of the people of South Africa.

Mother and Children — A167

1974, Apr. 8   Perf. 13½
514 A167 85c multicolored   .70 .25
Honoring Algerian mothers.

Village A168

Designs: 80c, Harvest. 90c, Tractor and sun. Designs after children's drawings.

1974, June 15   Size: 45x26mm
515 A168 70c multicolored   .65 .25
Size: 48x33mm
516 A168 80c multicolored   .85 .40
517 A168 90c multicolored   1.05 .60
Nos. 515-517 (3)   2.55 1.25

Nos. 498-499 Overprinted

1974, June 22   Photo.   Perf. 11½
518 A111 1d multi   1.65 .80
519 A111 1.15d multi   2.25 1.25
1974 Flower Show.

Stamp Vending Machine — A169

1974, Oct. 7   Photo.   Perf. 13
520 A169 80c multicolored   .85 .25
Stamp Day 1974.

UPU Emblem and Globe A170

1974, Oct. 14   Perf. 14
521 A170 80c multicolored   1.00 .40
Centenary of Universal Postal Union.

"Revolution" — A171

Soldiers and Mountains A172

Raising New Flag — A173

Design: 1d, Algerian struggle for independence (people, sun and fields).

1974, Nov. 4   Photo.   Perf. 14
522 A171 40c multicolored   .50 .25
523 A172 70c multicolored   .70 .25
524 A173 95c multicolored   .90 .35
525 A171 1d multicolored   1.15 .40
Nos. 522-525 (4)   3.25 1.25
20th anniv. of the start of the revolution.

"Horizon 1980" — A174

1974, Nov. 23   Photo.   Perf. 13
526 A174 95c ocher, dk red & blk   .70 .40
10-year development plan, 1971-1980.

Ewer and Basin — A175

1974, Dec. 21   Perf. 11½
527 A175 50c shown   .45 .30
528 A175 60c Coffee pot   .75 .40
529 A175 95c Sugar bowl   1.00 .55
530 A175 1d Bath tub   1.40 .65
Nos. 527-530 (4)   3.70 1.90
17th century Algerian copperware.

No. 497 Surcharged in Black

1975, Jan. 4
531 A111 50c on 40c multi   2.50 .55

Mediterranean Games' Emblem — A176

1975, Jan. 27   Perf. 13½
532 A176 50c purple, yel & grn   .45 .25
533 A176 1d orange, bl & mar   .80 .35
Mediterranean Games, Algiers, 1975.

Costume Type of 1971

Regional Costumes: No. 534, Woman from Hoggar. No. 535, Woman from Algiers. No. 536, Woman from Oran. No. 537, Man from Tlemcen.

1975, Feb. 22   Photo.   Perf. 11½
534 A139 1d gold & multi   1.50 .75
535 A139 1d gold & multi   1.50 .75
536 A139 1d gold & multi   1.50 .75
537 A139 1d gold & multi   1.50 .75
Nos. 534-537 (4)   6.00 3.00

Map of Arab Countries, ALO Emblem A177

1975, Mar. 10   Litho.   Perf. 10½x11
538 A177 50c red brown   .60 .30
Arab Labor Organization, 10th anniversary.

Blood Transfusion A178

1975, Mar. 15   Perf. 14
539 A178 50c car rose & multi   .75 .40
Blood donation and transfusions.

Post Office, Al-Kantara — A179

1975, May 10   Photo.   Perf. 11½
Granite Paper
540 A179 50c multicolored   .65 .25
Stamp Day 1975.

Policeman and Map of Algeria — A180

1975, June 1   Photo.   Perf. 13
541 A180 50c multicolored   1.00 .40

Natl. Security and 10th Natl. Police Day.

Ground Receiving Station A181

Designs: 1d, Map of Algeria with locations of radar sites, transmission mast and satellite. 1.20d, Main and subsidiary stations.

1975, June 28   Photo.   Perf. 13
542 A181 50c blue & multi   .50 .25
543 A181 1d blue & multi   .85 .25
544 A181 1.20d blue & multi   1.10 .40
    Nos. 542-544 (3)   2.45 .90

National satellite telecommunications network.

Revolutionary with Flag — A182

1975, Aug. 20   Photo.   Perf. 11½
545 A182 1d multicolored   .65 .35

August 20th Revolutionary Movement (Skikda), 20th anniversary.

Swimming and Games' Emblem A183

Perf. 13x13½, 13½x13
1975, Aug. 23   Photo.
546 A183 25c shown   .25 .25
547 A183 50c Judo, map   .40 .25
548 A183 70c Soccer, vert.   .60 .30
549 A183 1d Running, vert.   .80 .40
550 A183 1.20d Handball, vert.   1.00 .60
 a. Souv. sheet, #546-550, perf 13   6.75 6.75
    Nos. 546-550 (5)   3.05 1.80

7th Mediterranean Games, Algiers, 8/23-9/46.
No. 550a sold for 4.50d. Exists imperf., same value.

Setif, Guelma, Kherrata — A184

1975   Litho.   Perf. 13½x14
551 A184 5c orange & blk   .25 .25
552 A184 10c emerald & brn   .25 .25
553 A184 25c dl blue & blk   .25 .25
554 A184 30c lemon & blk   .40 .25
555 A184 50c brt grn & blk   .40 .25

556 A184 70c fawn & blk   .45 .25
557 A184 1d vermilion & blk   .75 .35
    Nos. 551-557 (7)   2.75 1.85

30th anniv. of victory in World War II. Issued: 50c, 1d, Nov. 3; others, Dec. 17. For surcharge see No. 611.

Map of Maghreb and APU Emblem A185

1975, Nov. 20   Photo.   Perf. 11½
558 A185 1d multicolored   .70 .40

10th Cong. of Arab Postal Union, Algiers.

Mosaic, Bey Constantine's Palace A186

Dey-Alger Palace — A187

Famous buildings: 2d, Prayer niche, Medersa Sidi-Boumediene, Tlemcen.

1975, Dec. 22
559 A186 1d lt blue & multi   1.05 .40
560 A186 2d buff & multi   2.10 .95
561 A187 2.50d buff & blk   2.75 1.40
    Nos. 559-561 (3)   5.90 2.75

Al-Azhar University A188

Perf. 11½x12½
1975, Dec. 29   Litho.
562 A188 2d multicolored   2.10 .80

Millennium of Al-Azhar University.

Red-billed Firefinch — A189

Birds: 1.40d, Black-headed bush shrike, horiz. 2d, Blue tit. 2.50d, Blackbellied sandgrouse, horiz.

1976, Jan. 24   Photo.   Perf. 11½
563 A189 50c multi   1.75 .70
564 A189 1.40d multi   3.00 1.25
565 A189 2d multi   3.50 1.40
566 A189 2.50d multi   4.00 2.00
    Nos. 563-566 (4)   12.25 5.35

See Nos. 595-598.

Telephones 1876 and 1976 — A190

1976, Feb. 23   Photo.   Perf. 13½x13
567 A190 1.40d rose, dk & lt bl   1.00 .55

Centenary of first telephone call by Alexander Graham Bell, Mar. 10, 1876.

Map of Africa with Angola and its Flag — A191

1976, Feb. 23   Perf. 11½
568 A191 50c brown & multi   .60 .25

Algeria's solidarity with the People's Republic of Angola.

A192

Sahraoui flag and child, map of former Spanish Sahara.

1976, Mar. 15   Photo.   Perf. 11½
569 A192 50c multicolored   .55 .25

Algeria's solidarity with Sahraoui Arab Democratic Republic, former Spanish Sahara.

Stamp Day — A193

1976, Mar. 22
570 A193 1.40d Mailman   1.25 .40

Microscope, Slide with TB Bacilli, Patients A194

1976, Apr. 26   Perf. 13x13½
571 A194 50c multicolored   1.05 .30

Fight against tuberculosis.

"Setif, Guelma, Kherrata" — A195

1976, May 24   Photo.   Perf. 13½x13
572 A195 50c blue & yellow   .60 .25
 a. Booklet pane of 6   8.00
 b. Booklet pane of 10   12.00

No. 572 was issued in booklets only.

Ram's Head over Landscape A196

1976, June 17   Photo.   Perf. 11½
573 A196 50c multicolored   .70 .25

Livestock breeding.

People Holding Torch, Map of Algeria — A197

1976, June 29   Photo.   Perf. 14x13½
574 A197 50c multicolored   .60 .25

National Charter.

Palestine Map and Flag — A198

1976, July 12   Perf. 11½
Granite Paper
575 A198 50c multicolored   .65 .25

Solidarity with the Palestinians.

Map of Africa — A199

1976, Oct. 3   Litho.   Perf. 10½x11
576 A199 2d dk blue & multi   1.50 .65

2nd Pan-African Commercial Fair, Algiers.

Blind Brushmaker A200

The Blind, by Dinet A201

1976, Oct. 23 Photo. **Perf. 14½**
577 A200 1.20d blue & multi .95 .50
578 A201 1.40d gold & multi .95 .65
Rehabilitation of the blind.

"Constitution 1976" — A202

1976, Nov. 19 Photo. **Perf. 11½**
579 A202 2d multicolored 1.50 .65
New Constitution.

Soldiers Planting Seedlings A203

1976, Nov. 25 Litho. **Perf. 12**
580 A203 1.40d multicolored 1.50 .55
Green barrier against the Sahara.

Ornamental Border and Inscription — A204

1976, Dec. 18 Photo. **Perf. 11½**
Granite Paper
581 A204 2d multicolored 1.50 .65
Re-election of Pres. Houari Boumediene. See No. 627.

Map with Charge Zones and Dials — A205

1977, Jan. 22 **Perf. 13**
582 A205 40c silver & multi .50 .25
Inauguration of automatic national and international telephone service.

People and Buildings — A206

1977, Jan. 29 Photo. **Perf. 11½**
583 A206 60c on 50c multi .60 .25
2nd General Population and Buildings Census. No. 583 was not issued without the typographed red brown surcharge, date, and bars.

Sahara Museum, Uargla A207

1977, Feb. 12 Litho. **Perf. 14**
584 A207 60c multicolored .60 .40

El-Kantara Gorge — A208

Perf. 12½x13½
1977, Feb. 19 Photo.
585 A208 20c green & yellow .25 .25
a. Bklt. pane, 3 #585, 4 #586 + label 6.00
b. Bklt. pane, 5 #585, 2 #587 + label 7.00
586 A208 60c brt lilac & yel .25 .25
587 A208 1d brown & yellow .65 .25
Nos. 585-587 (3) 1.15 .75

National Assembly — A209

1977, Feb. 27 **Perf. 11½**
588 A209 2d multicolored 1.30 .55

People and Flag — A210

Soldier and Flag — A211

Perf. 13½, 11½ (3d)
1977, Mar. 12 Photo.
589 A210 2d multicolored 1.30 .55
590 A211 3d multicolored 2.10 .80
Solidarity with the peoples of Zimbabwe (Rhodesia), 2d; Namibia, 3d.

Winter, Roman Mosaic A212

The Seasons from Roman Villa, 2nd century A.D.: 1.40d, Fall. 2d, Summer. 3d, Spring.

1977, Apr. 21 Photo. **Perf. 11½**
Granite Paper
591 A212 1.20d multi 1.50 .75
592 A212 1.40d multi 1.50 .75
593 A212 2d multi 2.40 1.15
594 A212 3d multi 3.25 1.50
a. Souv. sheet, #591-594 12.00 12.00
Nos. 591-594 (4) 8.65 4.15
No. 594a sold for 8d and exists imperf.

Bird Type of 1976

Birds: 60c, Tristram's warbler. 1.40d, Moussier's redstart, horiz. 2d, Temminck's horned lark, horiz. 3d, Eurasian hoopoe.

1977, May 21 Photo. **Perf. 11½**
595 A189 60c multi 1.30 .65
596 A189 1.40d multi 1.90 .90
597 A189 2d multi 3.00 1.30
598 A189 3d multi 4.25 1.90
Nos. 595-598 (4) 10.45 4.75

Horseman — A213

Design: 5d, Attacking horsemen, horiz.

1977, June 25 Photo. **Perf. 11½**
599 A213 2d multicolored 2.00 .80
600 A213 5d multicolored 5.00 2.00

Flag Colors, Games Emblem — A214

Wall Painting, Games Emblem A215

1977, Sept. 24 Photo. **Perf. 11½**
601 A214 60c multi .55 .25
602 A215 1.40d multi 1.30 .60
3rd African Games, Algiers 1978.

Village and Tractor A216

1977, Nov. 12 **Perf. 14x13**
603 A216 1.40d multi 1.00 .40
Socialist agricultural village.

Almohades Dirham, 12th Century — A217

Ancient Coins: 1.40d, Almohades coin, 12th century. 2d, Almoravides dinar, 11th century.

1977, Dec. 17 Photo. **Perf. 11½**
604 A217 60c ultra, sil & blk .55 .40
605 A217 1.40d grn, gold & brn 1.30 .60
606 A217 2d red brn, gold & brn 1.75 .90
Nos. 604-606 (3) 3.60 1.90

Flowering Trees — A218

1978, Feb. 11 Photo. **Perf. 11½**
607 A218 60c Cherry .55 .25
608 A218 1.20d Peach 1.05 .70
609 A218 1.30d Almond 1.20 .75
610 A218 1.40d Apple 1.45 .80
Nos. 607-610 (4) 4.25 2.50

No. 555 Surcharged in Black

1978, Feb. 11 Litho. **Perf. 13½x14**
611 A184 60c on 50c .80 .25

Children with Traffic Signs and Car — A219

1978, Apr. 29 Photo. **Perf. 11½**
612 A219 60c multicolored .80 .25
Road safety and protection of children.

Sports and Games Emblems A220

Designs (Games Emblem and): 40c, Volleyball. 60c, Rowing, vert. 1.20d, Basketball. 1.30d, Hammer throwing, vert. 1.40d, Map of Africa and boxers, vert.

1978, July 13 Photo. **Perf. 11½**
613 A220 40c multi .25 .25
614 A220 60c multi .45 .25
615 A220 1.20d multi 1.00 .40

616 A220 1.30d multi 1.00 .50
617 A220 1.40d multi 1.40 .60
Nos. 613-617 (5) 4.10 2.00

3rd African Games, Algiers, July 13-28.

TB Patient Returning to Family — A221

1978, Oct. 5 Photo. Perf. 13½x14
618 A221 60c multicolored .70 .25

Anti-tuberculosis campaign.

Holy Kaaba — A222

1978, Oct. 28 Photo. Perf. 11½
619 A222 60c multicolored .80 .25

Pilgrimage to Mecca.

National Servicemen Building Road — A223

1978, Nov. 4
620 A223 60c multicolored .80 .25

African Unity Road from El Goleah to In Salah, inauguration.

Fibula — A224

Jewelry: 1.35d, Pendant. 1.40d, Ankle ring.

1978, Dec. 21 Photo. Perf. 12x11½
621 A224 1.20d multi 1.20 .50
622 A224 1.35d multi 1.45 .60
623 A224 1.40d multi 1.75 .75
Nos. 621-623 (3) 4.40 1.85

Pres. Boumediene A225

1979, Jan. 7 Photo. Perf. 12x11½
624 A225 60c green, red & brown .55 .25

Houari Boumediene, pres. of Algeria 1965-1978.

Torch and Books A226

1979, Jan. 27 Photo. Perf. 11½
625 A226 60c multicolored .55 .25

Natl. Front of Liberation Party Cong.

Pres. Boumediene — A227

1979, Feb. 4 Photo. Perf. 11½
626 A227 1.40d multi 1.25 .55

40 days after death of Pres. Houari Boumediene.

Ornamental Type of 1976

Proclamation of new President.

1979, Feb. 10
627 A204 2d multicolored 1.50 .40

Election of Pres. Chadli Bendjedid.

A229

1979, Apr. 18 Photo. Perf. 11½
628 A229 60c multicolored .50 .25

Sheik Abdul-Hamid Ben Badis (1889-1940).

A230

Designs: 1.20d, Telephone dial, map of Africa. 1.40d, Symbolic Morse key and waves.

1979, May 19 Photo. Perf. 13½x14
629 A230 1.20d multi .85 .30
630 A230 1.40d multi 1.05 .50

Telecom '79 Exhib., Geneva, Sept. 20-26.

Harvest, IYC Emblem A231

1.40d, Dancers and IYC emblem, vert.

Perf. 11½x11, 11x11½
1979, June 21
631 A231 60c multi .55 .25
632 A231 1.40d multi 1.10 .50

International Year of the Child.

Nuthatch — A232

1979, Oct. 20 Photo. Perf. 11½
633 A232 1.40d multicolored 2.40 1.25

A233

Designs: 1.40d, Flag, soldiers and workers. 3d, Revolutionaries and emblem.

1979, Nov. 1 Photo. Perf. 12½
634 A233 1.40d multi 1.00 .30

Size: 37x48mm
Perf. 11½
635 A233 3d multi 1.90 .85

November 1 revolution, 25th anniversary.

Hegira, 1500 Anniv. A234

1979, Dec. 2 Photo. Perf. 11½
636 A234 3d multicolored 2.00 .75

Camels, Lion, Men and Slave — A235

Dionysian Procession (Setif Mosaic): 1.35d, Elephants, tigers and women. 1.40d, Men in tiger-drawn cart. No. 639a has continuous design.

Granite Paper

1980, Feb. 16 Photo. Perf. 11½
637 A235 1.20d multi 1.50 .40
638 A235 1.35d multi 1.50 .55
639 A235 1.40d multi 1.75 .80
a. Strip of 3, #637-639 5.75 5.75

Science Day — A236

1980, Apr. 19 Photo. Perf. 12
640 A236 60c multicolored .65 .25

Dam and Workers A237

1980, June 17 Photo. Perf. 11½
641 A237 60c multicolored .60 .25

Extraordinary Congress of the National Liberation Front Party.

Olympic Sports, Moscow '80 Emblem A238

50c, Flame, rings, vert.

1980, June 28
642 A238 50c multicolored .45 .25
643 A238 1.40d shown .90 .50

22nd Summer Olympic Games, Moscow, July 19-Aug. 3.

20th Anniversary of OPEC — A239

60c, Men holding OPEC emblem, vert.

Perf. 11x10½, 10½x11
1980, Sept. 15 Engr.
644 A239 60c multicolored .60 .25
645 A239 1.40d shown 1.40 .50

Aures Valley A240

1980, Sept. 25 Litho. Perf. 13½x14
646 A240 50c shown .45 .25
647 A240 1d El Oued Oasis .85 .25
648 A240 1.40d Tassili Rocks 1.25 .40
649 A240 2d View of Algiers 2.10 .70
Nos. 646-649 (4) 4.65 1.60

World Tourism Conf., Manila, Sept. 27.

Avicenna (980-1037), Philosopher and Physician
A241

1980, Oct. 25 Photo. *Perf. 12*
650 A241 2d multicolored 2.25 .80

Ruins of El Asnam
A242

1980, Nov. 13 Photo. *Perf. 12*
651 A242 3d multicolored 2.10 .55

Earthquake relief.

Crown
A243

No. 652, Necklace, vert. No. 653, Earrings, bracelet, vert. No. 654, Crown.

Granite Paper
1980, Dec. 20 Photo. *Perf. 12*
652 A243 60c multi .60 .25
653 A243 1.40d multi 1.00 .50
654 A243 2d multi 1.50 .65
Nos. 652-654 (3) 3.10 1.40

See Nos. 705-707.

1980-1984 Five-Year Plan — A244

1981, Jan. 29 Litho. *Perf. 14*
655 A244 60c multicolored .60 .25

Basket Weaving — A245

Granite Paper
1981, Feb. 19 Photo. *Perf. 12½*
656 A245 40c shown .40 .25
657 A245 60c Rug weaving .50 .25
658 A245 1d Coppersmith .80 .25
659 A245 1.40d Jeweler 1.10 .45
Nos. 656-659 (4) 2.80 1.20

Cedar Tree
A246

Arbor Day: 1.40d, Cypress tree, vert.

Granite Paper
1981, Mar. 19 Photo. *Perf. 12*
660 A246 60c multi .40 .25
661 A246 1.40d multi 1.10 .60

Mohamed Bachir el Ibrahimi (1869-1965)
A247

Children Going to School
A248

1981, Apr. 16 Granite Paper
662 A247 60c multicolored .60 .25
663 A248 60c multicolored .60 .25

Science Day.

12th International Hydatidological Congress, Algiers — A249

1981, Apr. 23 *Perf. 14x13½*
664 A249 2d multicolored 2.00 .50

13th World Telecommunications Day — A250

1981, May 14 Photo. *Perf. 14x13½*
665 A250 1.40d multi 1.25 .25

Disabled People and Hand Offering Flower — A251

1.20d, Symbolic globe, vert.

Perf. 12½x13, 13x12½
1981, June 20 Litho.
666 A251 1.20d multicolored .95 .25
667 A251 1.40d shown 1.10 .30

Intl. Year of the Disabled.

Papilio Machaon
A252

1.20d, Rhodocera rhamni. 1.40d, Charaxes jasius. 2d, Papilio podalirius.

1981, Aug. 20 Photo. *Perf. 11½*
Granite Paper
668 A252 60c shown .90 .35
669 A252 1.20d multicolored 1.60 .50
670 A252 1.40d multicolored 2.00 .90
671 A252 2d multicolored 2.50 .90
Nos. 668-671 (4) 7.00 2.65

Monk Seal — A253

1981, Sept. 17 *Perf. 14x13½*
672 A253 60c shown .90 .40
673 A253 1.40d Macaque 1.90 .80

World Food Day — A254

1981, Oct. 16 Photo. *Perf. 14x14½*
674 A254 2d multicolored 1.25 .50

Cave Drawings of Tassili — A255

Various cave drawings. 1.60d, 2d horiz.

1981, Nov. 21 *Perf. 11½*
675 A255 60c multi .60 .25
676 A255 1d multi 1.20 .40
677 A255 1.60d multi 1.65 .55
678 A255 2d multi 2.25 .80
Nos. 675-678 (4) 5.70 2.00

Galley, 17-18th Cent.
A256

1981, Dec. 17 Photo. *Perf. 11½*
679 A256 60c shown .70 .50
680 A256 1.60d Ship, diff. 1.90 .95

1982 World Cup Soccer
A257

Designs: Various soccer players.

Perf. 13x12½x 12½x13
1982, Feb. 25 Litho.
681 A257 80c multi, vert. .65 .25
682 A257 2.80d multi 2.00 .80

TB Bacillus Centenary
A258

1982, Mar. 20 Photo. *Perf. 14½x14*
683 A258 80c multi .60 .25

Painted Stand
A259

1982, Apr. 24 Photo. *Perf. 11½*
Granite Paper
684 A259 80c Mirror, vert. .50 .25
685 A259 2d shown 1.25 .45

Size: 48x33mm
686 A259 2.40d Chest 1.75 .60
Nos. 684-686 (3) 3.50 1.30

Djamaael Djadid Mosque, Algiers
A260

No. 688, Sidi Boumediene Mosque, Tlemcen. No. 689, Garden of Dey, Algiers.

1982, May 15 Litho. *Perf. 14*
Size: 32x22mm
687 A260 80c brown .50 .25
a. Size: 30½x21mm 3.50 .75
688 A260 2.40d purple 1.50 .50
689 A260 3d slate 2.00 .60
a. Size: 30½x21mm 5.00 1.25
Nos. 687-689 (3) 4.00 1.35

See Nos. 731-734, 745-747, 774, 778-783.

A261

Medicinal plants: No. 690, Callitris articulata. No 691, Artemisia herba-alba. No. 692, Ricinus communis. No. 693, Thymus fontanesii.

1982, May 27 Photo. *Perf. 11½*
Granite Paper
690 A261 50c multi .40 .25
691 A261 80c multi .60 .25
692 A261 1d multi .90 .40
693 A261 2.40d multi 1.75 .75
Nos. 690-693 (4) 3.65 1.65

A262

No. 694, Riflemen. No. 695, Soldiers, horiz. No. 696, Symbols, citizens, horiz. No. 697, Emblem.

1982, July 5 — Granite Paper

694	A262	50c multi	.45	.25
695	A262	80c multi	.55	.25
696	A262	2d multi	1.40	.75
		Nos. 694-696 (3)	2.40	1.25

Souvenir Sheet

697	A262	5d multi	5.50	5.50

Independence, 20th anniv.
No. 697 contains one 32x39mm stamp.

Soummam Congress A263

1982, Aug. 20 — Litho.

698	A263	80c Congress building	.60	.25

Scouting Year — A264

1982, Oct. 21 — Photo. Granite Paper

699	A264	2.80d multi	2.00	.60

Palestinian Child — A265

1982, Nov. 25 — Litho. Perf. 10½

700	A265	1.60d multi	.95	.30

Chlamydotis Undulata — A266

Protected birds: No. 701, Geronticus eremita, horiz. No. 702, Chlamydotis Undulata. No. 703, Aguila rapax, horiz. No. 704, Gypaetus barbatus.

Perf. 15x14, 14x15

1982, Dec. 23 — Photo.

701	A266	50c mutli	.75	.55
702	A266	80c multi	1.15	.75
703	A266	2d multi	2.10	1.50
704	A266	2.40d multi	2.75	1.90
		Nos. 701-704 (4)	6.75	4.70

Jewelry Type of 1980

1983, Feb. 10 — Perf. 11½ Granite Paper

705	A243	50c Picture frame	.35	.25
706	A243	1d Flaska	.60	.40
707	A243	2d Brooch, horiz.	1.25	.65
		Nos. 705-707 (3)	2.20	1.30

A267

80c, Abies numidica, vert. 2.80d, Acacia raddiana.

1983, Mar. 17 — Photo. Granite Paper

708	A267	80c multicolored	.70	.25
709	A267	2.80d multicolored	2.25	.80

Intl. Arbor Day.

Various Minerals — A268

1.20d, 2.40d horiz.

Granite Paper

Perf. 12x12½, 12½x12

1983, Apr. 21 — Photo.

710	A268	70c multi	1.25	.35
711	A268	80c multi	1.40	.50
712	A268	1.20d multi	1.60	.65
713	A268	2.40d multi	2.50	1.25
		Nos. 710-713 (4)	6.75	2.75

30th Anniv. of Intl. Customs Cooperation Council A269

1983, May 14 — Photo. Perf. 11½ Granite Paper

714	A269	80c multi	.70	.25

Emir Abdelkader Death Centenary — A270

1983, May 22 — Photo. Perf. 12 Granite Paper

715	A270	4d multi	2.40	.90

Local Mushrooms A271

No. 716, Amanita muscaria. No. 717, Amanita phalloides. No. 718, Pleurotus eryngii. No. 719, Tefezia leonis.

1983, July 21 — Perf. 14x15

716	A271	50c multi	1.00	.35
717	A271	80c multi	1.45	.75
718	A271	1.40d multi	3.00	1.10
719	A271	2.80d multi	4.50	2.10
		Nos. 716-719 (4)	9.95	4.30

A272

1983, Sept. 1 — Photo. Perf. 11½

720	A272	80c multi	.70	.25

ibn-Khaldun, historian, philosopher.

World Communications Year — A273

80c, Post Office, Algiers. 2.40d, Telephone, circuit box.

Perf. 11½x12½

1983, Sept. 22 — Litho.

721	A273	80c multicolored	.55	.25
722	A273	2.40d multicolored	1.40	.60

Goat and Tassili Mountains A274

80c, Tuaregs in native costume. 2.40d, Animals, rock painting. 2.80d, Rock formation.

1983, Oct. 20 — Litho. Perf. 12½x13

723	A274	50c shown	.40	.25
724	A274	80c multicolored	.50	.25
725	A274	2.40d multicolored	1.40	.55
726	A274	2.80d multicolored	1.75	.75
		Nos. 723-726 (4)	4.05	1.80

Sloughi Dog — A275

Perf. 14x14½, 14½x14

1983, Nov. 24 — Photo.

727	A275	80c shown	1.10	.35
728	A275	2.40d Sloughi, horiz.	2.75	.95

Natl. Liberation Party, 5th Congress — A276

80c, Symbols of development. 5d, Emblem.

1983, Dec. 19 — Photo. Perf. 11½

729	A276	80c multicolored	.80	.40

Souvenir Sheet

730	A276	5d multicolored	5.00	5.00

No. 730 contains one 32x38mm stamp.

View Type of 1982

10c, View of Oran, 1830. 1d, Sidi Abderahman and Taalibi Mosques. 2d, Bejaia, 1830. 4d, Constantine, 1830.

1984, Jan. 26 — Litho. Perf. 14
Size: 32x22mm

731	A260	10c multicolored	.25	.25
a.		Size: 30½x21mm	.80	.40
732	A260	1d multicolored	.50	.25
a.		Size: 30½x21mm	1.50	.80
733	A260	2d multicolored	1.00	.50
a.		Size: 30½x21mm	3.00	1.50
734	A260	4d multicolored	2.50	.65
a.		Size: 30½x21mm	6.00	1.50
		Nos. 731-734 (4)	4.25	1.65

Pottery A278

Perf. 11½x12, 12x11½

1984, Feb. 23 — Photo. Granite Paper

735	A278	80c Jug, vert.	.50	.25
736	A278	1d Platter	.65	.40
737	A278	2d Oil lamp, vert.	1.40	.60
738	A278	2.40d Pitcher	1.75	.75
		Nos. 735-738 (4)	4.30	2.00

Fountains of Old Algiers — A279

Various fountains.

1984, Mar. 22 — Photo. Perf. 11½
Granite Paper

739	A279	50c multi	.25	.25
740	A279	80c multi	.55	.40
741	A279	2.40d multi	1.40	.65
		Nos. 739-741 (3)	2.20	1.30

1984 Summer Olympics — A280

1984, May 19 — Photo. Perf. 11½
Granite Paper

742	A280	1d multi	1.25	.40

Brown Stallion A281

1984, June 14 — Photo. Perf. 11½
Granite Paper

743	A281	80c shown	.80	.40
744	A281	2.40d White mare	2.10	.95

View Type of 1982

1984 — Litho. Perf. 14
Size: 32x22mm

745	A260	5c Mustapha Pacha	.50	.25
a.		Size: 30½x21mm	.80	.40
746	A260	20c Bab Azzoun	.50	.25
d.		Size: 30½x21mm	1.00	.60
746A	A260	30c Algiers	.50	.25
		Size: 30½x21mm	1.50	.50
746B	A260	40c Kolea	.50	.25
746C	A260	50c Algiers	.50	.25
e.		Size: 30½x21mm	1.50	.50
747	A260	70c Mostaganem	.60	.25
a.		Size: 30½x21mm	2.00	1.00
		Nos. 745-747 (6)	3.10	1.50

Issued: Nos. 745, 746, 747, 7/19; Nos. 746A-746C, 10/20.

Lute A282

Native musical instruments.

1984, Sept. 22   Litho.   Perf. 15x14
748 A282   80c shown   .60   .25
749 A282   1d Drum   .90   .40
750 A282   2.40d Fiddle   1.75   .75
751 A282   2.80d Bagpipe   2.00   .95
      Nos. 748-751 (4)   5.25   2.35

30th Anniv. of Algerian
Revolution — A284

80c, Partisans. 5d, Algerian flags, vert.

1984, Nov. 3   Photo.   Perf. 11½x12
757 A284   80c multicolored   .85   .25

Souvenir Sheet
758 A284   5d multicolored   5.50   5.50

M'Zab
Valley
A285

80c, Map of valley. 2.40d, Town of M'Zab,
vert.

1984, Dec. 15   Perf. 15x14, 14x15
759 A285   80c multicolored   .75   .25
760 A285   2.40d multicolored 1.75   .60

18th and 19th
Century
Metalware — A286

1985, Jan. 26   Photo.   Perf. 11½
761 A286   80c Coffee pot   .60   .25
762 A286   2d Bowl, horiz.   1.25   .65
763 A286   2.40d Covered bowl 1.75   .85
      Nos. 761-763 (3)   3.60   1.75

Fish
A287

50c, Thunnus thynnus. 80c, Sparus aurata.
2.40d, Epinephelus guaza. 2.80d, Mustelus
mustelus.

1985, Feb. 23   Photo.   Perf. 15x14
764 A287   50c multicolored   .50   .25
765 A287   80c multicolored   .90   .40
766 A287   2.40d multicolored 2.25   1.10
767 A287   2.80d multicolored 2.75   1.15
      Nos. 764-767 (4)   6.40   3.00

National
Games
A288

1985, Mar. 28   Perf. 11½x12
Granite Paper
768 A288   80c Doves, emblem   .80   .25

Environmental Conservation — A289

1985, Apr. 25   Perf. 13½
769 A289   80c Stylized trees   .70   .25
770 A289   1.40d Stylized waves 1.00   .40

View Type of 1982 and

The Casbah — A290

View of
Constantine
A290a

Street Scene
in Algiers
A290b

Designs: 2.50d, Djamaael Djadid Mosque,
Algiers. 2.90d, like No. 746. 5d, like No. 746A.
1.50d, like No. 746B. 4.20d, like No. 764.

Perf. 13½x12½, 13 (#774, 4.20d),
Perf. 13½x14 (#775)
Perf. 14½x14 (2d)

Photo., Litho. (2d, 6,20d, 7.50d,
#775)

1985-94
771 A290   20c dk blue & buff   .25   .25
772 A290   80c sage grn &
                buff   .60   .25
773 A290a   1d dk olive grn   .50   .25
  a. Bklt. pane of 5 + label   4.00
774 A260   1.50d dull red   .55   .25
775 A290b   1.50d red brn & brn .40   .25
  a. Booklet pane of 6   2.75
776 A290b   2d dk bl & lt bl   .40   .25
  a. Booklet pane of 5 + label 3.00
777 A290   2.40d chestnut &
                buff   1.75   .25
  a. Bklt. pane of 5 (20c, 3 80c,
         2.40d) + label   5.75
778 A260   2.50d bluish green 1.00   .25
779 A260   2.90d slate   1.25   .25
780 A260   4.20d gray green   1.40   .35
781 A260   5d dp bis & blk   2.10   .40

Perf. 14
782 A260   6.20d like #731   1.10   .30
783 A260   7.50d like #745   1.75   .30
      Nos. 771-783 (13)   13.05 3.60

Nos. 771-772, 777 issued only in booklet
panes.
Issued: 20c, 80c, 2.40d, 6/1/85; 1d, 1/26/89;
2.50d, 2.90d, 5d, 2/23/89; No. 774, 4.20d,
3/21/91; No. 775, 5/20/92; 6.20d, 7.50d,
4/22/92; 2d, 10/21/93; No. 776a, 10/21/94.
See No. 1010.

UN, 40th
Anniv. — A291

1985, June 26   Photo.   Perf. 14
784 A291   1d Dove, emblem, 40   .90   .25

Natl. Youth
Festival — A292

1985, July 5   Litho.   Perf. 13½
785 A292   80c multicolored   .70   .25

Intl. Youth
Year
A293

80c, Silhouette, globe, emblem, vert. 1.40d,
Doves, globe.

1985, July 5
786 A293   80c multicolored   .60   .25
787 A293   1.40d multicolored .90   .40

World Map,
OPEC — A294

1985, Sept. 14   Photo.   Perf. 12½x13
788 A294   80c multicolored   .80   .25

Organization of Petroleum Exporting Countries, 25th anniv.

Family
Planning — A295

1985, Oct. 3   Litho.   Perf. 14
789 A295   80c Mother and sons .60   .25
790 A295   1.40d Weighing infant .90   .40
791 A295   1.70d Breast-feeding 1.30   .50
      Nos. 789-791 (3)   2.80   1.15

El-Meniaa
Township — A296

80c, Chetaibi Bay, horiz. 2.40d, Bou Noura
Town, horiz.

1985, Oct. 24   Engr.   Perf. 13
792 A296   80c multicolored   .50   .25
793 A296   2d shown   1.40   .40
794 A296   2.40d multicolored 1.60   .60
      Nos. 792-794 (3)   3.50   1.25

The Palm
Grove, by N.
Dinet — A297

1985, Nov. 21   Photo.   Perf. 11½x12
Granite Paper
795 A297   2d multicolored   1.50   .75
796 A297   3d multi, diff.   2.10   1.10

Tapestries
A298

Various designs.

1985, Dec. 19   Granite Paper
797 A298   80c multi   .70   .50
798 A298   1.40d multi   1.40   .75
799 A298   2.40d multi   2.00   1.25
800 A298   2.80d multi   2.50   1.75
      Nos. 797-800 (4)   6.60   4.25

Wildcats
A299

80c, Felis margarita. 1d, Felis caracal. 2d,
Felis sylvestris. 2.40d, Felis serval, vert.

1986, Jan. 23   Perf. 12x11½, 11½x12
Granite Paper
801 A299   80c multicolored   1.40   .60
802 A299   1d multicolored   1.75   .70
803 A299   2d multicolored   2.50   .90
804 A299   2.40d multicolored 3.50   1.60
      Nos. 801-804 (4)   9.15   3.80

UN Child Survival
Campaign
A300

80c, Oral vaccine. 1.40d, Mother, child, sun.
1.70d, Three children.

1986, Feb. 13   Litho.   Perf. 13½
805 A300   80c multicolored   .55   .25
806 A300   1.40d multicolored 1.10   .65
807 A300   1.70d multicolored 1.60   .85
      Nos. 805-807 (3)   3.25   1.75

Algerian General
Worker's Union,
30th Anniv. — A301

1986, Feb. 24   Perf. 12½
Granite Paper
808 A301   2d multicolored   1.50   .60

National Charter — A302

Granite Paper

1986, Mar. 6   Photo.   Perf. 11½
809 A302 4d multicolored   3.00 1.25

Natl. Day of the Disabled — A303

1986, Mar. 15   Perf. 12½x13
810 A303 80c multicolored   .70 .30

A304

1986, Apr. 17   Litho.   Perf. 14x15
811 A304 80c multicolored   .75 .40

Anti-Tuberculosis campaign.

A305

2d, Soccer ball, sombrero. 2.40d, Soccer players.

1986, Apr. 24   Perf. 14
812 A305 2d multicolored   1.50 .55
813 A305 2.40d multicolored   1.75 .65

1986 World Cup Soccer Championships, Mexico.

Inner Courtyards — A306

Granite Paper

1986, May 15   Photo.   Perf. 11½
814 A306 80c multicolored   .70 .30
815 A306 2.40d multi, diff.   1.90 .95
816 A306 3d multi, diff.   2.40 1.25
   Nos. 814-816 (3)   5.00 2.50

Blood Donation Campaign A307

1986, June 26   Litho.   Perf. 13½
817 A307 80c multicolored   1.40 .40

Southern District Radio Communication Inauguration A308

1986, July   Perf. 13
818 A308 60c multicolored   .50 .25

Mosque Gateways A309

2d, Door. 2.40d, Ornamental arch.

Granite Paper

1986, Sept. 27   Photo.   Perf. 12x11½
819 A309   2d multicolored   1.40 .60
820 A309 2.40d multicolored   1.60 .85

Intl. Peace Year A310

Perf. 13½x14½
1986, Oct. 16   Photo.
821 A310 2.40d multi   1.60 .60

Folk Dancing A311

1986, Nov. 22   Litho.   Perf. 14x13½
822 A311   80c Woman, scarf   .70 .25
823 A311 2.40d Woman, diff.   1.75 .70
824 A311 2.80d Man, sword   1.90 .80
   Nos. 822-824 (3)   4.35 1.75

Flowers — A312

80c, Narcissus tazetta. 1.40d, Iris unguicularis. 2.40d, Capparis spinosa. 2.80d, Gladiolus segetum.

1986, Dec. 18   Photo.   Perf. 14
825 A312   80c multicolored   .70 .30
826 A312 1.40d multicolored   1.25 .60
827 A312 2.40d multicolored   1.75 1.00
828 A312 2.80d multicolored   2.10 1.25
   Nos. 825-828 (4)   5.80 3.15

See Nos. 936-938.

Abstract Paintings by Mohammed Issia Khem — A313

2d, Man and woman, vert. 5d, Man and books.

Perf. 11½x12, 12x11½
1987, Jan. 29   Litho.
829 A313 2d multicolored   1.50 .85
830 A313 5d multicolored   3.25 2.00

Jewelry from Aures A314

Granite Paper

1987, Feb. 27   Photo.   Perf. 12
831 A314 1d Earrings   .75 .45
832 A314 1.80d Bracelets   1.20 .70
833 A314 2.90d Nose rings   1.75 1.10
834 A314 3.30d Necklace   2.10 1.25
   Nos. 831-834 (4)   5.80 3.50

Nos. 831-833 vert.

Petroglyphs, Atlas — A315

1987, Mar. 26   Litho.   Perf. 12x11½
Granite Paper
835 A315   1d Man and woman   1.10 .70
836 A315 2.90d Goat   2.50 1.40
837 A315 3.30d Horse, bull   2.75 1.40
   Nos. 835-837 (3)   6.35 3.50

Syringe as an Umbrella — A316

Granite Paper

1987, Apr. 7   Perf. 11½
838 A316 1d multicolored   .80 .25

Child Immunization Campaign, World Health Day.

Volunteers A317

1987, Apr. 23   Perf. 10½
839 A317 1d multicolored   .55 .30

Third General Census — A318

1987, May 21   Perf. 13½
840 A318 1d multicolored   .70 .30

Algerian Postage, 25th Anniv. — A319

War Orphans' Fund label (1fr + 9fr) of 1962.

Granite Paper

1987, July 5   Photo.   Perf. 11½x12
841 A319 1.80d multicolored   2.75 .70

A320

A321

1987, July 5   Granite Paper
842 A320 1d multicolored   .60 .25
Souvenir Sheet
843 A321 5d multicolored   5.50 5.50

Natl. independence, 25th anniv.

Amateur Theater Festival, Mostaganem A322

Granite Paper

1987, July 20   **Perf. 12x11½**
844 A322   1d Actors on stage   .55   .25
845 A322   1.80d Theater   .95   .60
a.   Pair, #844-845   1.50   1.50

No. 845a has continuous design.

Mediterranean Games,
Latakia — A323

1987, Aug. 6   **Perf. 13x12½, 12½x13**
846 A323   1d Discus   .60   .30
847 A323   2.90d Tennis, vert.   1.50   .85
848 A323   3.30d Team handball   1.75   1.00
    Nos. 846-848 (3)   3.85   2.15

Birds — A324

1d, Phoenicopterus ruber roseus. 1.80d,
Porphyrio porphyrio. 2.50d, Elanus caeruleus.
2.90d, Milvus milvus.

1987   **Litho.**   **Perf. 13½**
849 A324   1d multicolored   .85   .50
850 A324   1.80d multicolored   1.40   1.00
851 A324   2.50d multicolored   2.25   1.25
852 A324   2.90d multicolored   2.50   1.50
    Nos. 849-852 (4)   7.00   4.25

Agriculture
A325

No. 853, Planting. No. 854, Reservoir. No.
855, Harvesting crop, vert. No. 856, Produce,
vert.

   Perf. 10½x11, 11x10½
1987, Nov. 26   **Litho.**
853 A325   1d multicolored   .65   .25
854 A325   1d multicolored   .65   .25
855 A325   1d multicolored   .65   .25
856 A325   1d multicolored   .65   .25
    Nos. 853-856 (4)   2.60   1.00

African Telecommunications
Day — A326

1987, Dec. 7   **Perf. 10½**
857 A326 1d multicolored   .90   .25

Transportation — A327

1987, Dec. 18   **Litho.**   **Perf. 10½x11**
858 A327   2.90d shown   1.50   .70
859 A327   3.30d Diesel train   3.00   1.50

Algerian
Universities
A328

Various campuses.

1987, Dec. 26   **Perf. 10½x11, 11x10½**
860 A328   1d shown   .50   .25
861 A328   2.50d multi, diff.   1.30   .50
862 A328   2.90d multi, diff.   1.50   .60
863 A328   3.30d multi, diff., vert.   1.75   .70
    Nos. 860-863 (4)   5.05   2.05

Intl. Rural Development Fund, 10th
Anniv. — A329

1988, Jan. 27   **Perf. 10½x11**
864 A329 1d multicolored   .80   .25

Autonomy of
State-owned
Utilities — A330

1988, Feb. 27   **Litho.**   **Perf. 11x10½**
865 A330 1d multicolored   .60   .25

Intl. Women's
Day — A331

1988, Mar. 10   **Litho.**   **Perf. 11x10½**
866 A331 1d multicolored   .70   .25

Arab Scouts, 75th
Anniv. — A332

1988, Apr. 7   **Litho.**   **Perf. 10½**
867 A332 2d multicolored   1.20   .50

1988 Summer
Olympics,
Seoul — A333

1988, July 23   **Litho.**   **Perf. 10½**
868 A333 2.90d multicolored   1.60   .85

Hot
Springs — A334

2.90d, Caverns, horiz. 3.30d, Gazebo, fountain, horiz.

1988, July 16
869 A334   1d shown   .45   .25
870 A334   2.90d multicolored   1.50   .60
871 A334   3.30d multicolored   1.75   .90
    Nos. 869-871 (3)   3.70   1.55

World
Wildlife
Fund
A335

Barbary apes, Macaca sylvanus: 50c, Adult.
90c, Family. 1d, Close-up, vert. 1.80d, Seated
on branch, vert.

1988, Sept. 17   **Litho.**   **Perf. 10½**
872 A335   50c multicolored   1.00   .45
873 A335   90c multicolored   1.25   .65
874 A335   1d multicolored   1.75   .90
875 A335   1.80d multicolored   3.00   1.60
    Nos. 872-875 (4)   7.00   3.60

Intl. Literacy
Day — A336

1988, Sept. 10   **Photo.**   **Perf. 10½**
876 A336 2.90d multicolored   1.50   .85

WHO, 40th
Anniv. — A337

1988, Oct. 15
877 A337 2.90d multicolored   1.50   .70

Fight
Apartheid
A338

1988, Nov. 19   **Litho.**   **Perf. 10½x11**
878 A338 2.50d multicolored   1.25   .50

Natl. Front
Congress — A339

1988, Nov. 29   **Perf. 11x10½**
879 A339 1d multicolored   .60   .25

Agriculture
A340

No. 880, Irrigation. No. 881, Orchard, fields,
livestock.

1988, Dec. 24   **Perf. 10½**
880 A340 1d multicolored   .55   .25
881 A340 1d multicolored   .55   .25

Natl. Goals — A342

No. 887, Ancient fort. No. 888, Telecommunications. No. 889, Modern buildings.

1989, Mar. 9   **Litho.**   **Perf. 11½**
         Granite Paper
886 A342   1d shown   .50   .25
887 A342   1d multicolored   .50   .25
888 A342   1d multicolored   .50   .25
889 A342   1d multicolored   .50   .25
    Nos. 886-889 (4)   2.00   1.00

Nos. 887-889 horiz.

Airports — A343

2.90d, Oran Es Senia, horiz. 3.30d,
Tebessa, horiz.

1989, Mar. 23   **Perf. 10½x11, 11x10½**
890 A343   2.90d multicolored   1.20   .55
891 A343   3.30d multicolored   1.40   .70
892 A343   5d shown   2.10   1.25
    Nos. 890-892 (3)   4.70   2.50

Development of the South — A344

1d, Irrigation. 1.80d, Building. 2.50d, Fossil
fuel extraction, vert.

1989, Apr. 24   **Litho.**   **Perf. 13½**
893 A344   1d multicolored   .50   .25
894 A344   1.80d multicolored   .70   .40
895 A344   2.50d multicolored   1.05   .55
    Nos. 893-895 (3)   2.25   1.20

Eradicate
Locusts
A345

1989, May 25   **Perf. 10½**
896 A345 1d multicolored   .50   .25

National
Service — A346

1989, May 11   Litho.   Perf. 13½
897 A346 2d multicolored   1.40   .70

1st Moon
Landing,
20th Anniv.
A347

4d, Astronaut, lunar module, Moon's
surface.

1989, July 23   Litho.   Perf. 13½
898 A347 2.90d shown   1.25   .60
899 A347 4d multi, vert.   1.60   .90

Interparliamentary Union,
Cent. — A348

1989, Sept. 4   Perf. 10½
900 A348 2.90d gold, brt rose lil
& blk   1.20   .40

Produce
A349

1989, Sept. 23   Litho.   Perf. 11½
Granite Paper
901   Strip of 3   4.00   4.00
  a. A349 2d multi, diff.   .75   .50
  b. A349 3d multi, diff.   1.20   .65
  c. A349 5d shown   1.90   1.20

Fish — A350

1d, Sarda sarda. 1.80d, Zeus faber. 2.90d,
Pagellus bogaraveo. 3.30d, Xiphias gladius.

1989, Oct. 27   Litho.   Perf. 13½
902 A350 1d multicolored   .70   .30
903 A350 1.80d multicolored   1.25   .50
904 A350 2.90d multicolored   1.90   .70
905 A350 3.30d multicolored   2.25   .90
  Nos. 902-905 (4)   6.10   2.40

Algerian
Revolution, 35th
Anniv. — A351

1989, Nov. 4   Litho.   Perf. 13½
906 A351 1d multicolored   .50   .25

African
Development
Bank, 25th
Anniv. — A352

1989, Nov. 18   Perf. 10½
907 A352 1d multicolored   .50   .25

Mushrooms
A353

No. 908, Boletus satanas. No. 909, Psalliota
xanthoderma. No. 910, Lepiota procera. No.
911, Lactarius deliciosus.

1989, Dec. 16   Perf. 13½
908 A353 1d mutli   1.00   .30
909 A353 1.80d multi   1.50   .75
910 A353 2.90d multi   2.40   1.00
911 A353 3.30d multi   3.25   1.25
  Nos. 908-911 (4)   8.15   3.30

A354

1990, Jan. 18   Litho.   Perf. 10½
912 A354 1d multicolored   .50   .25
Pan-African Postal Union, 10th anniv.

Energy
Conservation
A355

1990, Feb. 22   Litho.   Perf. 14
913 A355 1d multicolored   .60   .25

A356

1990, Mar. 2   Photo.   Perf. 11½
914 A356 3d multicolored   1.30   .60
African Soccer Championships.

A357

1990, May 17   Litho.   Perf. 13½
917 A357 2.90d shown   1.10   .60
918 A357 5d Trophy   2.00   1.10
World Cup Soccer Championships, Italy.

Rural Electrification — A358

1990, June 21
919 A358 2d multicolored   .90   .30

Youth
A359

Youth Holding
Rainbow — A360

1990, July 6   Perf. 13½
920 A359 2d multicolored   .85   .30
921 A360 3d multicolored   1.25   .50

Maghreb Arab
Union — A361

1990   Perf. 14x13½
922 A361 1d multicolored   .50   .25

Vocations
A362

1990, Apr. 26   Litho.   Perf. 12½
923 A362 2d Craftsmen   .75   .40
924 A362 2.90d Auto mechanics 1.00   .60
925 A362 3.30d Deep sea fishing 1.75 .75
  Nos. 923-925 (3)   3.50   1.75

Organization of Petroleum Exporting
Countries (OPEC), 30th
Anniv. — A363

1990   Perf. 13½
926 A363 2d multicolored   1.50   .30

Savings
Promotion
A364

1990, Oct. 31   Litho.   Perf. 14
927 A364 1d multicolored   .50   .25

Namibian Independence — A365

1990, Nov. 8
928 A365 3d multicolored   1.00   .30

A366

Farm animals.

1990, Nov. 29   Perf. 13½
929 A366 1d Duck   .50   .25
930 A366 2d Rabbit, horiz.   1.00   .40
931 A366 2.90d Turkey   1.30   .65
932 A366 3.30d Rooster, horiz. 1.60 .85
  Nos. 929-932 (4)   4.40   2.15

A367

1990, Dec. 11
933 A367 1d multicolored   .65   .25
Anti-French Riots, 30th anniv.

A368

1990, Dec. 20 *Perf. 14*
934 A368 1d multicolored .40 .25

Fight against respiratory diseases.

A369

1991, Feb. 24 **Litho.** *Perf. 13½*
935 A369 1d multicolored .55 .25

Constitution, 2nd anniv.

Flower Type of 1986

2d, Jasminum fruticans. 4d, Dianthus crinitus. 5d, Cyclamen africanum.

1991, May 23 **Litho.** *Perf. 13½*
Size: 26x36mm
936 A312 2d multicolored .80 .30
937 A312 4d multicolored 1.90 .70
938 A312 5d multicolored 2.25 1.00
Nos. 936-938 (3) 4.95 2.00

Children's
Drawings
A370

1991, June 3 **Litho.** *Perf. 13½*
939 A370 3d shown 1.20 .50
940 A370 4d Children playing 1.20 .50

Maghreb Arab
Union
Summit — A371

1991, June 10
941 A371 1d multicolored .45 .25

Geneva Convention on Refugees, 40th
Anniv. — A372

1991, July 28 **Litho.** *Perf. 14½x13½*
942 A372 3d multicolored 1.00 .35

Postal
Service
A373

4.20d, Expo emblem, vert.

1991, Oct. 12 *Perf. 14*
943 A373 1.50d shown .60 .25
944 A373 4.20d multicolored 1.25 .50

Telecom '91, 6th World Forum and Exposition on Telecommunications, Geneva, Switzerland (No. 944).

Butterflies
A374

2d, Zerynthia rumina. 4d, Melitaea didyma. 6d, Vanessa atalanta. 7d, Nymphalis polychloros.

Granite Paper

1991, Nov. 21 **Litho.** *Perf. 11½*
945 A374 2d multicolored .85 .35
946 A374 4d multicolored 1.20 .50
947 A374 6d multicolored 1.65 .55
948 A374 7d multicolored 2.00 1.10
Nos. 945-948 (4) 5.70 2.70

A375

3d, Necklace. 4d, Jewelry of Southern Tuaregs. 5d, Brooch. 7d, Rings, horiz.

Granite Paper

1991, Dec. 21 *Perf. 12*
949 A375 3d multicolored .75 .30
950 A375 4d multicolored .85 .45
951 A375 5d multicolored 1.00 .70
952 A375 7d multicolored 1.75 1.10
Nos. 949-952 (4) 4.35 2.55

Algerian
Women — A376

1992, Mar. 8 **Litho.** *Perf. 14*
953 A376 1.50d multicolored .50 .25

Gazelles
A377

Designs: 1.50d, Gazella dorcas. 6.20d, Gazella cuvieri. 8.60d, Gazella dama.

1992, May 13 *Perf. 14½x13*
954 A377 1.50d multicolored .50 .35
955 A377 6.20d multicolored 1.10 .75
956 A377 8.60d multicolored 1.75 1.10
Nos. 954-956 (3) 3.35 2.20

1992
Summer
Olympics,
Barcelona
A379

1992, June 24 **Litho.** *Perf. 14*
958 A379 6.20d Runners 1.25 .50

A381

1992, July 7 **Litho.** *Perf. 14*
960 A381 5d multicolored 1.00 .30

Independence, 30th anniv.

Medicinal
Plants — A382

No. 961, Ajuga iva. No. 962, Rhamnus alaternus. No. 963, Silybum marianum. No. 964, Lavandula stoechas.

1992, Sept. 23 **Litho.** *Perf. 14*
961 A382 1.50d multi .50 .25
962 A382 5.10d multi 1.20 .50
963 A382 6.20d multi 1.30 .60
964 A382 8.60d multi 1.60 .85
Nos. 961-964 (4) 4.60 2.20

Post Office
Modernization
A383

1992, Oct. 10 **Litho.** *Perf. 14*
965 A383 1.50d multicolored .40 .25

Marine
Life — A384

Designs: 1.50d, Hippocampus hippocampus. 2.70d, Caretta caretta. 6.20d, Muraena helena. 7.50d, Palinurus elephas.

1992, Dec. 23
966 A384 1.50d multicolored .60 .25
967 A384 2.70d multicolored .90 .25
968 A384 6.20d multicolored 1.90 .65
969 A384 7.50d multicolored 2.10 .85
Nos. 966-969 (4) 5.50 2.00

Pres. Mohammad Boudiaf (1919-
92) — A385

Granite Paper

1992, Nov. 3 **Litho.** *Perf. 11½*
970 A385 2d green & multi .35 .25
971 A385 8.60d blue & multi 1.60 .85

Coins
A386

1.50d, Numidia, 2nd cent. BC. 2d, Dinar, 14th cent. 5.10d, Dinar, 11th cent. 6.20d, Abdelkader, 19th cent.

Granite Paper

1992, Dec. 16 **Litho.** *Perf. 11½*
972 A386 1.50d multicolored .30 .25
973 A386 2d multicolored .40 .25
974 A386 5.10d multicolored .90 .35
975 A386 6.20d multicolored 1.15 .50
Nos. 972-975 (4) 2.75 1.35

Door
Knockers — A387

1993, Feb. 17 **Litho.** *Perf. 14*
976 A387 2d Algiers .30 .25
977 A387 5.60d Constantine .80 .40
978 A387 8.60d Tlemcen 1.50 .65
Nos. 976-978 (3) 2.60 1.30

Flowering
Trees — A388

4.50d, Neflier (medlar), horiz. 8.60d, Cognassier (quince). 11d, Abricotier (apricot).

Granite Paper

1993, Mar. 17 *Perf. 12x11½, 11½x12*
979 A388 4.50d multicolored .85 .40
980 A388 8.60d multicolored 1.75 .75
981 A388 11d multicolored 2.25 1.00
Nos. 979-981 (3) 4.85 2.15

Natl. Coast
Guard
Service,
20th Anniv.
A389

1993, Apr. 3 **Litho.** *Perf. 14*
982 A389 2d multicolored 1.10 .30

Traditional Grain
Processing
A390

1993, May 19   Litho.   Perf. 14
983 A390 2d Container   .45   .25
984 A390 5.60d Millstone   .90   .50
985 A390 8.60d Press   1.40   .65
    Nos. 983-985 (3)   2.75 1.40

Royal Mausoleums — A391

1993, June 16   Litho.   Perf. 14
986 A391 8.60d Mauretania   1.25   .60
987 A391 12d El Khroub   2.00   .85

Ports
A392

1993, Oct. 20   Litho.   Perf. 14x13½
988 A392 2d Annaba   .35   .25
989 A392 8.60d Arzew   1.50   .55

Varanus
Griseus
A393

Design: 2d, Chamaeleo vulgaris, vert.

Perf. 13½x14, 14x13½
1993, Nov. 20
990 A393 2d multicolored   .50   .25
991 A393 8.60d multicolored   1.75   .80

Tourism
A394

1993, Dec. 18   Litho.   Perf. 14x13½
992 A394 2d Tipaza   .35   .25
993 A394 8.60d Kerzaz   1.10   .50

A395

1994, Jan. 2   Perf. 13½x14
994 A395 2d multicolored   .60   .25

SONATRACH (Natl. Society for Research,
Transformation, and Commercialization of
Hydrocarbons), 30th anniv.

Chahid
Day — A396

1994, Feb. 18   Litho.   Perf. 13½x14
995 A396 2d multicolored   .60   .25

1994 World Cup Soccer
Championships, US — A397

1994, Mar. 16   Perf. 14x13½
996 A397 8.60d multicolored   2.25   .85

Orchids — A398

5.60d, Orchis simia lam. 8.60d, Ophrys
lutea cavan. 11d, Ophrys apifera huds.

1994, Apr. 20   Litho.   Perf. 11½
      Granite Paper
997 A398 5.60d multicolored   1.50   .60
998 A398 8.60d multicolored   1.75   .85
999 A398 11d multicolored   2.75 1.25
    Nos. 997-999 (3)   6.00 2.70

Ancient
Petroglyphs
A399

3d, Inscriptions. 10d, Man on horse.

1994, May 21   Litho.   Perf. 13x14
1000 A399 3d multicolored   .95   .25
1001 A399 10d multicolored   2.10   .75

A400

1994, June 25
1002 A400 12d multicolored   1.90   .65
Intl. Olympic Committee, cent.

World Population
Day — A401

1994, July 13
1003 A401 3d multicolored   .50   .25

Views of Algiers Type of 1992
Design: 3d, like No. 775.

1994, July 13   Litho.   Perf. 14
1010 A290b 3d dk blue & lt blue .75 .25

Jewelry
from
Saharan
Atlas
Region
A402

Perf. 13½x14, 14x13½
1994, Oct. 18   Litho.
1019 A402 3d Fibules, vert.   .60   .25
1020 A402 5d Belt   .90   .30
1021 A402 12d Bracelets   2.40   .85
    Nos. 1019-1021 (3)   3.90 1.40

Algerian
Revolution, 40th
Anniv. — A403

1994, Nov. 3   Litho.   Perf. 13½x14
1022 A403 3d multicolored   .40   .25

A404

1994, Nov. 16   Litho.   Perf. 13½x14
1023 A404 3d Ladybugs   .50   .25
1024 A404 12d Beetles   2.00   .75

Fight
Against
AIDS
A405

1994, Dec. 1   Litho.   Perf. 14x13½
1025 A405 3d multicolored   1.00   .25

Folk
Dances — A406

1994, Dec. 17   Litho.   Perf. 13½x14
1026 A406 3d Algeroise   .40   .30
1027 A406 10d Constantinoise 1.20   .75
1028 A406 14d Alaoui   1.40   .90
    Nos. 1026-1028 (3)   3.00 1.95
    See Nos. 1170-1172.

Minerals — A407

1994, Sept. 21
1029 A407 3d Gres lite-erode .60   .25
1030 A407 5d Cipolin   1.00   .50
1031 A407 10d Marne a turitella 2.40 .95
    Nos. 1029-1031 (3)   4.00 1.70

World Tourism Organization, 20th
Anniv. — A408

1995, Jan. 28   Litho.   Perf. 14x13½
1032 A408 3d multicolored   .40   .25

Honey
Bees — A409

1995, Feb. 22   Perf. 13½x14, 14x13½
1033 A409 3d shown   .40   .30
1034 A409 13d On flower, horiz. 1.60 .90

Flowers — A410

Granite Paper
1995, Mar. 29   Photo.   Perf. 11½
1035 A410 3d Dahlias   .50   .30
1036 A410 10d Zinnias   1.50   .80
1037 A410 13d Lilacs   1.75   .90
    Nos. 1035-1037 (3)   3.75 2.00

Decorative
Stonework — A411

Various patterns.

1995, Apr. 19   Perf. 14
1039 A411 3d brown   .60   .30
1040 A411 4d green   .75   .30
1041 A411 5d deep claret   .90   .30
    Nos. 1039-1041 (3)   2.25   .90

End of World War II, 50th Anniv. A413

1995, May 3   *Perf. 14x13½*
1048 A413 3d multicolored   .70   .30

Souvenir Sheet

VE Day, 50th Anniv. — A414

1995, May 10   **Litho.**   *Perf. 13½x14*
1049 A414 13d multicolored   7.00   7.00

Volleyball, Cent. — A415

1995, June 14
1050 A415 3d multicolored   .65   .30

Environmental Protection — A416

3d, Air, water pollution. 13d, Air pollution.

1995, June 5
1051 A416 3d multicolored   .40   .30
1052 A416 13d multicolored   1.60   .85

General Electrification A417

1995, July 5   **Litho.**   *Perf. 13½x14*
1053 A417 3d multicolored   .65   .30

UN, 50th Anniv. A418

1995, Oct. 24   *Perf. 14x13½*
1054 A418 13d multicolored   2.50   1.00

Pottery — A419

10d, Pot, Lakhdaria. 20d, Pitcher, Aokas. 21d, Jar, Larbaa Nath Iraten. 30d, Vase, Ouadhia.

1995, Nov. 14   **Litho.**   *Perf. 14*
1055 A419 10d dark brown   1.00   .50
1056 A419 20d dull maroon   2.10   1.00
1057 A419 21d golden brown   2.10   1.00
1058 A419 30d dark rose brown   3.25   1.25
     Nos. 1055-1058 (4)   8.45   3.75

Aquatic Birds A420

1995, Dec. 20   **Litho.**   *Perf. 14x13½*
1059 A420 3d Tadorna tadorna   .70   .25
1060 A420 5d Gallinago gallinago   1.20   .40

1996 Summer Olympics, Atlanta A421

1996, Jan. 24   **Litho.**   *Perf. 14x13½*
1061 A421 20d multicolored   2.10   1.00

Touareg Leather Crafts A422

Perf. 14x13½, 13½x14
1996, Feb. 14   **Litho.**
1062 A422 5d shown   1.00   .30
1063 A422 16d Saddle bag, vert.   1.50   1.00

Pasteur Institute of Algeria — A423

1996, Mar. 20   **Litho.**   *Perf. 13½x14*
1064 A423 5d multicolored   .75   .25

Youm El Ilm — A424

Designs: 16d, Dove, stylus, vert. 23d, Open book showing pencil, stylus, compass, satellite in earth orbit, vert.

Perf. 14x13½, 13½x14
1996, Apr. 16   **Litho.**
1065 A424 5d multicolored   .55   .30
1066 A424 16d multicolored   1.40   .80
1067 A424 23d multicolored   2.50   1.25
     Nos. 1065-1067 (3)   4.45   2.35

Minerals A425

Mineral, region: 10d, Iron, Djebel-Ouenza. 20d, Gold, Tirek-Amesmessa.

1996, May 6   **Litho.**   *Perf. 14x13½*
1068 A425 10d multicolored   1.15   .55
1069 A425 20d multicolored   2.10   1.00

Butterflies A426

Designs: 5d, Pandoriana pandora. 10d, Coenonympha pamphilus. 20d, Cynthia cardui. 23d, Melanargia galathea.

1996, June 12   **Litho.**   *Perf. 11½*
       Granite Paper
1070 A426 5d multicolored   .75   .30
1071 A426 10d multicolored   1.25   .60
1072 A426 20d multicolored   2.75   1.00
1073 A426 23d multicolored   3.00   1.50
     Nos. 1070-1073 (4)   7.75   3.40

Civil Protection A427

5d, Giving medical aid, ambulance. 23d, Prevention of natural disasters, vert.

Perf. 14x13½, 13½x14
1996, Oct. 9   **Litho.**
1074 A427 5d multicolored   .60   .30
1075 A427 23d multicolored   2.75   1.25

World Day Against Use of Illegal Drugs A428

1996, June 26   **Litho.**   *Perf. 14x13½*
1076 A428 5d multicolored   .70   .30

UNICEF, 50th Anniv. — A429

Stylized designs: 5d, Two children, wreath, pencils, flowers. 10d, Five children, pencil, key, flower, flag, hypodermic.

1996, Nov. 20   **Litho.**   *Perf. 13½x14*
1077 A429 5d multicolored   .40   .30
1078 A429 10d multicolored   .80   .45

4th General Census A430

1997, Feb. 12   **Litho.**   *Perf. 14x13½*
1079 A430 5d multicolored   .50   .30

Protest at Ouargla, 35th Anniv. — A431

1997, Feb. 27   *Perf. 13½x14*
1080 A431 5d multicolored   .50   .30

Interior Courts of Algerian Dwellings A432

Designs: 5d, Palace of Hassan Pasha. 10d, Khedaouj El-Amia, Algiers. 20d, Palace of Light. 30d, Abdellatif Villa.

1996, Dec. 18   **Litho.**   *Perf. 13½x14*
1081 A432 5d multicolored   .40   .25
1082 A432 10d multicolored   .80   .45
1083 A432 20d multicolored   1.75   1.00
1084 A432 30d multicolored   2.50   1.40
     Nos. 1081-1084 (4)   5.45   3.10

Paintings by Ismail Samsom (1934-88) A433

20d, Woman with Pigeons. 30d, Interrogation.

1996, Dec. 25   *Perf. 14*
1085 A433 20d multicolored   1.25   1.00
1086 A433 30d multicolored   1.75   1.50

Victory Day, 35th Anniv. A434

1997, Mar. 19 *Perf. 14x13½*
1087 A434 5d multicolored .50 .25

Flowers — A435

Designs: 5d, Ficaria verna. 16d, Lonicera arborea. 23d, Papaver rhoeas.

1997, Apr. 23 Litho. *Perf. 13½x14*
1088 A435 5d multicolored .50 .30
1089 A435 16d multicolored 1.40 .90
1090 A435 23d multicolored 2.00 1.50
Nos. 1088-1090 (3) 3.90 2.70

World Day to Stop Smoking — A436

1997, May 31 Litho. *Perf. 13½x14*
1091 A436 5d multicolored .65 .25

Legislative Elections — A437

1997, June 4
1092 A437 5d multicolored .45 .25

Scorpions A438

Designs: 5d, Buthus occitanus tunetanus. 10d, Androctonus australis hector.

1997, June 18 *Perf. 14x13½*
1093 A438 5d multicolored .55 .30
1094 A438 10d multicolored .95 .60

Natl. Independence, 35th Anniv. — A439

Designs: 5d, Crowd celebrating, flags. 10d, Doves, broken chain, "35," flag.

1997, July 5 Litho. *Perf. 14x13½*
1095 A439 5d multicolored .50 .25

Souvenir Sheet
Perf. 14
1096 A439 10d multicolored 2.75 2.75
No. 1096 contains one 30x40mm stamp.

Wood Carvings — A440

Designs: 5d, Inscription, Nedroma Mosque. 23d, Door, Ketchaoua Mosque.

1997, Jan. 15 Litho. *Perf. 13½x14*
1097 A440 5d multicolored .50 .30
1098 A440 23d multicolored 1.75 1.10

Moufdi Zakaria (1908-77), poet.— A441

1997, Aug. 17 Litho. *Perf. 13½x14*
1099 A441 5d multicolored .50 .25

Textile Patterns A442

1997, Sept. 17 Litho. *Perf. 14*
1100 A442 3d Dokkali .40 .30
1101 A442 5d Tellis .50 .30
1102 A442 10d Bou-Taleb .90 .60
1103 A442 20d Ddil 1.75 1.25
Nos. 1100-1103 (4) 3.55 2.45

Natl. Police Force, 25th Anniv. A443

1997, Oct. 6 *Perf. 14x13½*
1104 A443 5d multicolored .60 .25

Express Mail Service A444

1997, Oct. 9
1105 A444 5d multicolored .60 .25

Local Elections — A445

1997, Oct. 23 *Perf. 13½x14*
1106 A445 5d multicolored .50 .25

Lighthouses A446

5d, Tenes. 10d, Cape Caxine, vert.

Perf. 14x13½, 13½x14
1997, Nov. 5 *Litho.*
1107 A446 5d multicolored .65 .25
1108 A446 10d multicolored 1.50 .70

New Airpost Service, 1st Anniv. A447

1997, Nov. 17 *Perf. 14x13½*
1109 A447 5d multicolored .60 .25

Shells A448

Designs: 5d, Chlamys varia. 10d, Bolinus brandaris. 20d, Hinia reticulata, vert.

Perf. 14x13½, 13½x14
1997, Dec. 17 *Litho.*
1110 A448 5d multicolored .90 .25
1111 A448 10d multicolored 1.50 .60
1112 A448 20d multicolored 3.00 1.20
Nos. 1110-1112 (3) 5.40 2.05

A449

1997, Dec. 25 *Perf. 13½x14*
1113 A449 5d multicolored .60 .25
Election of the Natl. Council.

A450

Completion of Government Reforms: a, Natl. flag, people, book, ballot box. b, People, open book, torch. c, Ballot box. d, Flag, rising sun, flower. e, Ballots, building, flag.

1997, Dec. 30 Litho. *Perf. 13½x14*
1114 A450 5d Strip of 5, #a.-e. 2.50 2.50

Bombing of Sakiet Sidi Youcef, 40th Anniv. A451

1998, Feb. 8 Litho. *Perf. 14x13½*
1115 A451 5d multicolored .70 .25

National Archives A452

1998, Feb. 16
1116 A452 5d multicolored .50 .25

Intl. Women's Day A453

1998, Mar. 8 Litho. *Perf. 14x13½*
1117 A453 5d multicolored .50 .25

Expo '98, Lisbon A454

1998, Jan. 21 Litho. *Perf. 14x13½*
1118 A454 5d shown .50 .25
Size: 80x75mm
Imperf
1119 A454 24d Mosaic 3.25 3.25

1998 World Cup Soccer Championships, Paris — A455

1998, Apr. 15 Litho. *Perf. 13½x14*
1120 A455 24d multi 2.40 1.25

Algiers Casbah A456

Designs: 5d, Aerial view, vert. 10d, Buildings, vert. 24d, Aerial view, diff.

1998, Apr. 22 Perf. 13½x14, 14x13½
1121 A456 5d multi .40 .25
1122 A456 10d multi .75 .60
1123 A456 24d multi 1.75 1.25
Nos. 1121-1123 (3) 2.90 2.10

Zaatcha Resistance — A457

1998, May 20   **Perf. 13¼x13**
1124 A457 5d multi   .50   .25

Tourism
A458

5d, Mountains, farm, desert, vert. 10d, Youths, modes of transportation. 24d, Taghit.

Perf. 13½x14, 14x13½
1998, June 4   **Litho.**
1125 A458 5d multi   .40   .25
1126 A458 10d multi   .80   .50
1127 A458 24d multi   1.75   1.25
    Nos. 1125-1127 (3)   2.95   2.00

Arab Post
Day
A459

1998, Aug. 3   **Litho.**   **Perf. 14x13½**
1128 A459 5d multi   .75   .25

Interpol,
75th Anniv.
A460

1998, Sept. 7   **Litho.**   **Perf. 14x13½**
1129 A460 5d multi   .60   .25

Creation of Provisional Government,
40th Anniv. — A461

1998, Sept. 19   **Perf. 13¼x13**
1130 A461 5d multi   .50   .25

Natl.
Diplomacy
Day
A462

1998, Oct. 8   **Perf. 14**
1131 A462 5d multi   .50   .25

Algerian
Olympic
Committee,
35th Anniv.
A463

1998, Oct. 18   **Perf. 14x13½**
1132 A463 5d multi   .60   .25

Birds
A464

Designs: 5d, Pandion haliaetus. 10d, Larus audouinii. 24d, Phalacrocorax aristotelis, vert. 30d, Phalacrocorax carbo, vert.

Perf. 14x13½, 13½x14
1998, Nov. 11
1133 A464   5d multi   .70   .25
1134 A464 10d multi   1.40   .60
1135 A464 24d multi   2.75   1.25
1136 A464 30d multi   3.50   1.75
    Nos. 1133-1136 (4)   8.35   3.85
    See Nos. 1204-1207, 1325-1326.

Universal
Declaration
of Human
Rights, 50th
Anniv.
A465

1998, Dec. 10   **Litho.**   **Perf. 14x13½**
1137 A465 5d Profiles, emblem   .60   .25
1138 A465 24d shown   2.25   1.00

Spinning
and
Weaving
Tools
A466

Designs: 5d, Comb, vert. 10d, Cards. 20d, Spindle, vert. 24d, Loom, vert.

1999, Jan. 20   **Perf. 13½x14, 14x13½**
1139 A466   5d multi   .55   .25
1140 A466 10d multi   1.00   .50
1141 A466 20d multi   2.10   1.00
1142 A466 24d multi   2.50   1.25
    Nos. 1139-1142 (4)   6.15   3.00

Natl. Chahid
Day — A467

1999, Feb. 18   **Perf. 13x13¼**
1143 A467 5d multi   .50   .25

Flowering
Trees
A468

1999, Mar. 17   **Perf. 14x13½, 13½x14**
1144 A468   5d Pear   .50   .25
1145 A468 10d Plum   .90   .50
1146 A468 24d Orange, vert.   2.10   1.25
    Nos. 1144-1146 (3)   3.50   2.00

Presidential
Elections
A469

1999, Apr. 15   **Perf. 13x13¼**
1147 A469 5d multi   .50   .25

Handicrafts
A470

Designs: 5d, Tlemcen mosaic, 14th cent., vert. 10d, Mosaic, Al Qal'a of Beni Hammad, 11th cent, vert. 20d, Cradle. 24d, Table.

1999, Apr. 18   **Perf. 13¼x14, 14x13¼**
1148 A470   5d multi   .55   .25
1149 A470 10d multi   .90   .60
1150 A470 20d multi   1.75   1.00
1151 A470 24d multi   2.10   1.25
    Nos. 1148-1151 (4)   5.30   3.10

7th African Games,
Johannesburg — A471

Stylized athletes and: 5d, Map of Africa, vert. 10d, South African flag.

1999, May 12   **Perf. 13¼x14, 14x13¼**
1152 A471   5d multi   .45   .25
1153 A471 10d multi   .80   .50

Rocks — A472

1999, June 6   **Perf. 13¼x14**
1154 A472   5d Gneiss   .45   .25
1155 A472 20d Granite   1.60   1.00
1156 A472 24d Schist   2.00   1.25
    Nos. 1154-1156 (3)   4.05   2.50

A473

1999, July 12   **Perf. 13x13¼**
1157 A473 5d multi   .50   .25
Organization of African Unity, 35th summit.

A474

1999, July 12   **Perf. 13¼x14**
1158 A474 5d multi   .50   .25
Organization of African Unity Convention on
Refugees.

Police
Day — A475

1999, July 22   **Perf. 13x13¼**
1159 A475 5d multicolored   1.00   .25

Intl. Year of
Culture and
Peace (in
2000)
A476

1999, Sept. 14   **Litho.**   **Perf. 14**
1160 A476 5d multi   .50   .25

Fish
A477

Designs: 5d, Dentex dentex. 10d, Mullus surmuletus. 20d, Dentex gibbosus. 24d, Diplodus sargus.

1999, Sept. 15   **Perf. 14x13¼**
1161 A477   5d multi   .65   .25
1162 A477 10d multi   1.25   .50
1163 A477 20d multi   2.25   1.00
1164 A477 24d multi   3.25   1.25
    Nos. 1161-1164 (4)   7.40   3.00

Civil Peace
Referendum
A478

1999, Sept. 16   **Perf. 13¼x14**
1165 A478 5d multi   .50   .25

UPU, 125th
Anniv.
A479

1999, Oct. 9   **Perf. 14x13¼**
1166 A479 5d multi   .55   .25

World Post Day
A480

1999, Oct. 9   Litho.   Perf. 14x13½
1167 A480 5d multi   .55 .25

Intl. Rural Women's Day
A481

1999, Oct. 14   Litho.   Perf. 14x13¼
1168 A481 5d multi   .55 .25

Algerian Revolution, 45th
Anniv. — A482

Soldiers and: a, Helicopters, burning flag. b, Burning flag.

1999, Nov. 1   Perf. 13x13¼
1169 A482 5d Pair, #a.-b.   1.25 1.25

Folk Dances Type of 1994

1999, Dec. 15   Perf. 13¼x14
1170 A406 5d Chaoui   .60   .25
1171 A406 10d Targuie   1.10   .50
1172 A406 24d Mzab   2.25 1.25
   Nos. 1170-1172 (3)   3.95 2.00

Millennium — A483

No. 1173: a, Doves, UN emblem. b, Sun, plant, trees. c, Umbrella over wheat and corn plants. d, Microscope and flasks. e, Crane, ship, truck. f, Train, Concorde, satellite dish, satellite, Moon. g, Windmills. h, Globe, ballot box. i, Apollo 15 astronauts on Moon. j, Film, inkwell, musical instrument and notes.
No. 1174: a, Dove with olive branch. b, Hand, flora, fauna. c, Satellites, computer, map of Africa and Europe. d, Heart, staff of Aesculapius, Red Cross, Red Crescent. e, Stylized globe and arrows. f, Animals, film, violin, painting, book. g, Flame, sun, water. h, Hand holding plant. i, symbols of democracy. j, Satellite, planets, space shuttle, astronaut.

Sawtooth Die Cut 6¼ Vert.
2000, Jan. 19   Self-Adhesive
Booklet Stamps
1173   Bklt. pane of 10 + 2 labels   10.00
 a.-j. A483 5d any single   .50   .50
1174   Bklt. pane of 10 + 2 labels   10.00
 a.-j. A483 5d any single   .50   .50

Birds
A484

Designs: No. 1175, 5d, Canary (serin cini). No. 1176, 5d, Finch (pinson), vert. 10d, Bullfinch (bouvreuil). 24d, Goldfinch (chardonneret), vert.

Perf. 14x13¼, 13¼x14
2000, Jan. 19   Litho.
1175-1178 A484 Set of 4   5.50 5.50

Expo 2000, Hanover
A485

2000, Feb. 16   Litho.   Perf. 14x13¼
1179 A485 5d multi   .60   .30

2000 Summer Olympics, Sydney
A486

2000, Mar. 22
1180 A486 24d multi   2.50 1.25

Telethon 2000 — A487

2000, Apr. 8   Perf. 13¼x14
1181 A487 5d multi   .75   .25

Civil Concord
A488

Designs: 5d, Dove, handshake, crowd, vert. 10d, Handshake, hands releasing dove. 20d, Handshake, doves, flowers. 24d, Doves, flowers, handshake, vert.

Perf. 11½x11¾, 11¾x11½
2000, Apr. 15
1182-1185 A488 Set of 4   6.50 3.25

National Library — A489

2000, Apr. 16   Perf. 13½x13
1186 A489 5d multi   .60   .25

Blood Donation — A490

2000, May 2   Perf. 13¼x14
1187 A490 5d multi   .60   .25

Tuareg Handicrafts
A491

Background colors: 5d, Rose. 10d, Buff, vert.

2000, May 17   Perf. 14
1188-1189 A491 Set of 2   1.60   .75

Famous Men — A492

No. 1190, Mohammed Dib (b. 1920), writer. No. 1191, Mustapha Kateb (1920-89), actor. No. 1192, Ali Maachi (1927-58), musician. No. 1193, Mohamed Racim (1896-1975), artist.

2000, June 8   Perf. 13¼x13
1190-1193 A492 10d Set of 4   4.25 2.00

Insects — A493

No. 1194, 5d, Hanneton. No. 1195, 5d, Anthrene. 10d, Vrillete du pain. 24d, Carabe.

2000, Sept. 20   Perf. 13¼x14
1194-1197 A493 Set of 4   5.25 2.50

Roman Cinerary Urns Found at Tipasa — A494

2000, Oct. 18   Litho.   Perf. 14
1198-1200 A494 Set of 3, 5d, 10d, 24d   4.25 2.25

Orchids — A495

Designs: 5d, Limodorum abortivum. 10d, Orchis papilionacea. 24d, Orchis provincialis.

2000, Dec. 13   Litho.   Perf. 14
1201-1203 A495 Set of 3   4.50 2.50

Bird Type of 1998
Designs: No. 1204, 5d, Anser anser. No. 1205, 5d, Recurvirostra avosetta, vert. 10d, Botaurus stellaris, vert. 24d, Numenius arquata.

2001, Jan. 24
1204-1207 A464 Set of 4   5.00 2.75

Handicrafts — A496

Designs: 5d, Skampla, vert. 10d, Etagere. 24d, Mirror, vert.

2001, Feb. 21
1208-1210 A496 Set of 3   4.50 2.50

National Parks
A497

Designs: 5d, Belezma, vert. 10d, Gouraya. 20d, Théniet el Had. 24d, El Kala, vert.

2001, Mar. 21   Perf. 13¼x14, 14x13¼
1211-1214 A497 Set of 4   7.00 3.25

1st Intl. Colloquium on St. Augustine of Hippo — A498

Designs: 5d, Statue of St. Augustine (25x37mm). 24d, Mosaic.

Perf. 13¼x14, 13¼x13 (24d)
2001, Mar. 31
1215-1216 A498 Set of 2   3.50 1.60

Silver Coins — A499

Designs: 5d, 1830 Ryal boudjou. 10d, 1826 Double boudjou. 24d, 1771 Ryal drahem.

2001, Apr. 25   Litho.   Perf. 13½x13
1217-1219 A499 Set of 3   4.50 2.25

Natl. Scouting Day — A500

2001, May 27   Litho.   Perf. 14
1220 A500 5d multi   .60   .25

Palestinian Intifada — A501

2001, June 2
1221 A501 5d multi   .60   .25

Children's Games
A502

Designs: No. 1222, 5d, Jacks. No. 1223, 5d, Hopscotch. No. 1224, 5d, Top spinning. No. 1225, 5d, Marbles.

2001, June 2
1222-1225 A502 Set of 4   2.50   .90

Natl. Asthma Day — A503

2001, June 9
1226 A503 5d multi   .50   .25

14th Mediterranean Games, Tunis, Tunisia — A504

Designs: No. 1227, 5d, Map, "50." No. 1228, 5d, Runners, emblem.

2001, July 25   Litho.   Perf. 14
1227-1228 A504 Set of 2   1.00   .50

15th World Festival of Youth and Students — A505

2001, Aug. 8
1229 A505 5d multi   .50   .25

Natl. Mujahedeen Day — A506

2001, Aug. 20   Perf. 13¼x14
1230 A506 5d multi   .50   .25

Intl. Teachers' Day — A507

2001, Oct. 6   Litho.   Perf. 13¼x14
1231 A507 5d multi   .50   .25

Year of Dialogue Among Civilizations A508

2001, Oct. 9
1232 A508 5d multi   .75   .30

Natl. Emigration Day — A509

2001, Oct. 17   Perf. 14x13¼
1233 A509 5d multi   .50   .25

19th Cent. Revolt Leaders — A510

Designs: No. 1234, 5d, Sheik El-Mokrani, 1871-73. No. 1235, 5d, Sheik Bouamama, 1881-1908.

2001, Nov. 1   Perf. 13¼x14
1234-1235 A510 Set of 2   1.10   .50

Jewelry From Aurès Region — A511

Designs: No. 1236, 5d, Fibula. No. 1237, 5d, Earring. 24d, Pendant.

2002, Jan. 23
1236-1238 A511 Set of 3   3.00   3.00

2002 World Cup Soccer Championships, Japan and Korea — A512

Designs: 5d, Goalie, ball, net, pagoda. 24d, Oriental man, ball, vert.

2002, Feb. 27   Perf. 14x13¼, 13¼x14
1239-1240 A512 Set of 2   2.75   2.00

Ceasefire With French Forces, 40th Anniv. — A513

2002, Mar. 19   Perf. 13x13½
1241 A513 5d multi   .70   .40

Villages A514

Designs: No. 1242, 5d, Sidi-Ouali. No. 1243, 5d, Casbah of Ighzar.

2002, Apr. 17   Litho.   Perf. 14x13¼
1242-1243 A514 Set of 2   1.00   .80

World Basketball Championships, Indianapolis A515

2002, May 15   Perf. 13¼x14
1244 A515 5d multi   .75   .45

Children's Day — A516

Children's art: No. 1245, 5d, Shown. No. 1246, 5d, Two girls, one waving.

2002, June 1   Perf. 14x13¼
1245-1246 A516 Set of 2   1.00   .80

Mohamed Temmam (1915-88), Artist — A517

Designs: No. 1247, 10d, Self-portrait. No. 1248, 10d, Tailor.

2002, June 8   Perf. 13x13¼
1247-1248 A517 Set of 2   2.00   1.50

Independence, 40th Anniv. — A518

Designs: 5d, Emblem. 24d, People with flag.

2002, July 5   Litho.   Perf. 14
1249-1250 A518 Set of 2   2.50   2.00

Rocks and Minerals A519

Designs: No. 1251, 5d, Conglomerate rock. No. 1252, 5d, Galena. No. 1253, 5d, Calcite, vert. No. 1254, 5d, Feldspar, vert.

2002, July 24
1251-1254 A519 Set of 4   2.00   2.00

Lighthouses A520

Designs: 5d, Cherchell. 10d, Cap de Fer. 24d, Ile de Rachgoun.

2002, Sept. 11
1255-1257 A520 Set of 3   3.25   3.25

Reorganization of Postal Service — A521

2002, Oct. 9
1258 A521 5d multi   .50   .50

Pottery — A522

Designs: No. 1259, 5d, Oil lamp. No. 1260, 5d, Jar with handles, Iraten. No. 1261, 5d, Jar, Miliana. No. 1262, 5d, Cooking pot and cous-cousier, Lakhdaria.

2002, Oct. 23
1259-1262 A522 Set of 4   2.00   2.00

Intl. Day for Tolerance A523

2002, Nov. 16   Litho.   Perf. 14
1263 A523 24d multi   2.00   2.00

Shells A524

Designs: No. 1264, 5d, Acanthocardia aculeata. No. 1265, 5d, Venus verrucosa. No. 1266, 5d, Epitonium commune. No. 1267, 5d, Xenophora crispa.

2002, Dec. 4   Litho.   Perf. 14
1264-1267 A524 Set of 4   2.50   2.50

Medicinal Plants — A525

Designs: 5d, Eucalyptus globulus. 10d, Malva sylvestris. 24d, Laurus nobilis.

2002, Dec. 21
1268-1270 A525   Set of 3   3.25 3.25

Algeria — France Year A526

Designs: 5d, Eiffel Tower, Paris and Martyr's Monument, Algiers, vert. 24d, Flags of Algeria and France.

2003, Feb. 19
1271-1272 A526   Set of 2   2.50 2.50

10th Arab Games A527

2003, Feb. 26
1273 A527 5d multi   .40 .40

Intl. Year of Water A528

Designs: 5d, El Maadjen, Relizane. 10d, Well, M'zab Valley. 24d, Kesria, Timimoun.

2003, Mar. 22   Litho.   Perf. 14
1274-1276 A528   Set of 3   3.50 3.50

Vandal Tablets A529

Designs: 10d, Slave sale document, 494. 24d, Tablet for calculations, 493, vert.

Perf. 13x13¼, 13¼x13
2003, Apr. 23   Litho.
1277-1278 A529   Set of 2   3.00 3.00

Portions of the designs were applied by a thermographic process producing a shiny, raised effect.

Natl. Students Day — A530

2003, May 19   Litho.   Perf. 14
1279 A530 5d multi   .40 .40

Snails — A531

Designs: 5d, Rumina decollata. 24d, Heix aspersa.

2003, May 21   Litho.   Perf. 14
1280-1281 A531   Set of 2   2.50 2.50

African Union, 1st Anniv. — A532

2003, July 9   Perf. 13¼x14
1282 A532 5d multi   .50 .50

Seaweeds — A533

Designs: 5d, Ulva lactuca. 24d, Gymnogongrus crenulatus.

2003, July 30   Litho.   Perf. 14
1283-1284 A533   Set of 2   2.50 2.50

Roman Mosaics — A534

Designs: 5d, Farm Work. 10d, Ulysses and the Sirens. 24d, Hunting Scene.

2003, Sept. 17   Perf. 13½x14
1285-1287 A534   Set of 3   3.00 3.00

Algerian Olympic Committee, 40th Anniv. A535

2003, Oct. 18   Litho.   Perf. 14x13½
1288 A535 5d multi   .50 .50

World Diabetes Prevention Day — A536

2003, Nov. 14   Perf. 13½x14
1289 A536 5d multi   .50 .50

Architectural Decorations A537

Designs: 5d, Door, Hassan Pacha Palace, Algiers. 10d, Window, Hassan Pacha Palace. 24d, Ceiling, Djamaa Edjedid, Algiers.

2003, Dec. 17   Litho.   Perf. 13x13¼
1290-1292 A537   Set of 3   3.00 3.00

Algeria — People's Republic of China Diplomatic Relations, 45th Anniv. A538

2003, Dec. 22   Perf. 12
1293 A538 5d multi   .50 .50

2004 Summer Olympics, Athens — A539

Olympic rings, Parthenon and: 5d, Hurdler. 10d, Torch bearer.

2004, Feb. 29   Perf. 13¼x14
1294-1295 A539   Set of 2   1.25 1.25

Intl. Women's Day — A540

2004, Mar. 8
1296 A540 5d multi   .50 .50

Arbor Day A541

Trees: 5d, Olive. 10d, Date palm, vert.

Perf. 14x13¼, 13¼x14
2004, Mar. 21   Litho.
1297-1298 A541   Set of 2   1.25 1.25

Numidian Kings — A542

Designs: No. 1299, 5d, Massinissa (r. 203 BC-148 BC). No. 1300, 5d, Micipsa (r. 148 BC-118 BC). No. 1301, 5d, Jugurtha (r. 118 BC-105 BC). No. 1302, 5d, Juba I (r. 63 BC-50 to 46 BC). No. 1303, 5d, Juba II (r. 29 BC- 25 BC).

2004, Mar. 31   Litho.   Perf. 13¼x14
1299-1303 A542   Set of 5   2.25 2.25

2004 Presidential Elections — A543

Litho. & Embossed
2004, Apr. 8   Perf. 13¼x13
1304 A543 24d multi   2.25 2.25

FIFA (Fédération Internationale de Football Association), Cent. — A544

"100" and: 5d, Goalie. 24d, Soccer balls, world map.

Perf. 14, 14x13¼ (24d)
2004, May 21   Litho.
1305-1306 A544   Set of 2   2.50 2.50

Dromedary A545

2004, June 9   Litho.   Perf. 14x13¼
1307 A545 24d multi   2.25 2.25

Blood Donation Day — A546

2004, June 14   Perf. 14
1308 A546 5d multi   .50 .50

Professional Training — A547

2004, June 23
1309 A547 5d multi   .50 .50

Intl. Chess
Federation
(FIDE), 80th
Anniv. — A548

2004, July 21　　Litho.　　Perf. 14
1310 A548 5d multi　　　　　1.20　.50

CNEP
Bank, 40th
Anniv.
A549

Bank emblems and: 5d, Bank notes. 24d,
Algiers.

2004, Aug. 10　　Litho.　　Perf. 14
1311-1312 A549　Set of 2　　2.50 2.50

Roses — A550

2004, Oct. 20　　Litho.　　Perf. 14
Color of Rose
1313 A550 15d yellow　　　　1.00　1.00
1314 A550 20d yellow, diff.　　2.00　2.00
1315 A550 30d red　　　　　3.00　3.00
1316 A550 50d pink　　　　　4.00　4.00
　Nos. 1313-1316 (4)　　　10.00 10.00

Sixth Pan-African Conference of Red
Cross and Red Crescent,
Algiers — A551

2004, Sept. 8　　Litho.　　Perf. 14
1317 A551 24d multi　　　　2.25 2.25

Sahara
Desert
Landmarks
A552

Designs: 5d, In Téhaq. 24d, Ekanassay,
vert.

Perf. 14, 14¼x14 (24d)
2004, Sept. 15
1318-1319 A552　Set of 2　　2.50 2.50

Revolutionary Committee of Unity and
Action, 50th Anniv. — A553

2004, Nov. 1　　Litho.　　Perf. 13¼x13
1320 A553 15d multi　　　　1.75 1.75

Souvenir Sheet

Start of Algerian Revolution, 50th
Anniv. — A554

2004, Nov. 1　　Litho.　　Perf. 13½x13
1321 A554 30d multi　　　　2.50 2.50

Launch of
ALSAT 1
Satellite,
2nd Anniv.
A555

2004, Nov. 28　　Litho.　　Perf. 14x13½
1322 A555 30d multi　　　　2.50 2.50

Environmental Protection — A556

2004, Dec. 22
1323 A556 15d multi　　　　1.25 1.25

Rabah Bitat (1925-2000),
Politician — A557

2004, Dec. 29　　Litho.　　Perf. 14x13½
1324 A557 15d multi　　　　1.25 1.25

Bird Type of 1998

Designs: 10d, Columba palumbus. 15d,
Columba livia.

2005, Jan. 26　　Litho.　　Perf. 14x13½
1325-1326 A464　Set of 2　　2.25 2.25

Flowers — A559

Designs: 15d, Echium australis. 30d,
Borago officinalis.

2005, Feb. 23　　Litho.　　Perf. 13½x14
1327-1328 A559　Set of 2　　3.50 3.50

Day of the Handicapped — A560

2005, Mar. 14　　　　Perf. 14x13½
1329 A560 15d multi　　　　1.10 1.10

Arab
League
Emblem
and
Algerian
Flag
A561

Inscription commemorating: 15d, 17th Arab
Summit, Algiers. 30d, Arab League, 60th
anniv., vert.

2005, Mar. 22　Perf. 14x13½, 13½x14
1330-1331 A561　Set of 2　　3.50 3.50

National Reconciliation — A562

2005, Apr. 8　　　　Perf. 14x13½
1332 A562 15d multi　　　　1.25 1.25

Madrases
A563

Madras in: 10d, Algiers. 15d, Constantine.
30d, Tlemcen.

2005, Apr. 16
1333-1335 A563　Set of 3　　4.50 4.50
　Science Day.

Intl. Day of
Intellectual
Property
A564

2005, Apr. 26
1336 A564 15d multi　　　　1.25 1.25

Intl. Day of Work
Safety and
Health — A565

2005, Apr. 28　　　　Perf. 13½x14
1337 A565 15d multi　　　　1.25 1.25

Massacres
of May 8,
1945, 60th
Anniv.
A566

2005, May 8　　Litho.　　Perf. 14x13¼
1338 A566 15d multi　　　　1.25 1.25

15th
Mediterranean
Games, Almeria,
Spain — A567

Games emblem and: 15d, Medal, stylized
athletes. 30d, Mediterranean Sea and "2005,"
horiz.

2005, May 28　　Perf. 13¼x14, 14x13¼
1339-1340 A567　Set of 2　　3.50 3.50

Poets — A568

Designs: 10d, Lakhdar Ben Khlouf. 15d,
Mohamed Ben M'sayeb. 20d, Si Mohand-Ou-
M'hand. 30d, Aissa El-Djermouni.

2005, June 8　　Litho.　　Perf. 13x13½
1341-1344 A568　Set of 4　　6.50 6.50

World Day
Against
Drug
Abuse
A569

2005, June 26　　　　Perf. 14x13½
1345 A569 15d multi　　　　1.50 1.50

General Algerian
Muslim Student's
Union, 50th
Anniv. — A570

2005, July 9　　Litho.　　Perf. 13½x14
1346 A570 15d multi　　　　1.25 1.25

Leopards
A571

Leopard: 15d, Sitting. 30d, Standing.

2005, July 21　　　　Perf. 14x13½
1347-1348 A571　Set of 2　　3.50 3.50

World Summit on the Information Society, Tunis — A572

2005, July 27 *Perf. 13½x14*
1349 A572 15d multi 1.75 1.75

Moudjahid Day — A573

2005, Aug. 20
1350 A573 15d multi 1.25 1.25

Uprising at Constantine and Philippeville, 50th anniv.

Intl. Year of Sports and Physical Education A574

2005, Sept. 7 Litho. *Perf. 13¼x14*
1351 A574 30d multi 2.40 2.40

Forts A575

Designs: 10d, Lighthouse Fort, Algiers. 15d, Cap Matifou Fort, Algiers. 30d, Santa Cruz Fort, Oran.

2005, Sept. 15 *Perf. 14x13¼*
1352-1354 A575 Set of 3 4.50 4.50

September 29, 2005 Referendum — A576

2005 Litho. *Perf. 14x13½*
1355 A576 15d multi 1.15 1.15

Acquisition of Control of Broadcasting, 43rd Anniv. — A577

2005, Oct. 28
1356 A577 30d multi 2.25 2.25

Personal Effects of Emir Abdelkader (1808-83) A578

Designs: 15d, Saddle. 30d, Boots. 40d, Vest, vert. 50d, Signet, vert.

2005, Nov. 1 *Perf. 14x13½, 13½x14*
1357-1360 A578 Set of 4 10.50 10.50

Miguel de Cervantes (1547-1616), Writer — A579

2005, Nov. 16 Litho. *Perf. 13½x14*
1361 A579 30d multi 2.25 2.25

Public Destruction of Mines — A580

2005, Nov. Litho. *Perf. 13½x14*
1362 A580 30d multi 2.25 2.25

World AIDS Day — A581

2005, Dec. 1 Litho. *Perf. 13½x14*
1363 A581 30d multi 2.50 2.50

Numidian Kings — A582

Designs: 15d, Ptolemy of Mauretania, ruler from 23-40 A.D. 30d, Syphax, ruler from 220-203 B.C.

2005, Dec. 14 Litho. *Perf. 13¼x14*
1364-1365 A582 Set of 2 3.25 3.25

Emblem and Headquarters of Algeria Post — A583

2006, Jan. 14 *Perf. 14x13¼*
1366 A583 30d multi 2.25 2.25

Birds — A584

Designs: 10d, Ciconia ciconia. 15d, Ciconia nigra. 20d, Platalea leucorodia. 30d, Grus grus.

2006, Jan. 25 *Perf. 13x13½*
1367-1370 A584 Set of 4 5.50 5.50

2006 Winter Olympics, Turin A585

2006, Feb. 1 *Perf. 14x13¼*
1371 A585 15d multi 1.10 1.10

General Union of Algerian Workers, 50th Anniv. — A586

2006, Feb. 24 *Perf. 13¼x14*
1372 A586 15d multi 1.10 1.10

2006 World Cup Soccer Championships, Germany A587

2006, Mar. 22
1373 A587 30d multi 2.25 2.25

Opening of New Algiers Airport A588

2006, Apr. 8 *Perf. 14x13¼*
1374 A588 30d multi 2.25 2.25

Student's Day, 50th Anniv. — A589

2006, May 19 *Perf. 13x13½*
1375 A589 20d multi 1.40 1.40

World Environment Day — A590

2006, June 5 *Perf. 14*
1376 A590 30d multi 2.25 2.25

Soummam Congress, 50th Anniv. — A591

2006, Aug. 20 *Perf. 13x13½*
1377 A591 20d multi 1.50 1.50

16th Arab Scholars' Games — A592

2006, Sept. 2 *Perf. 13¼x14*
1378 A592 30d multi 2.25 2.25

Intl. Year of Deserts and Desertifcation — A593

Designs: No. 1379, 15d, Oasis. No. 1380, 15d, Oasis, sand dunes and water.

2006, Sept. 20 Litho. *Perf. 14*
1379-1380 A593 Set of 2 2.25 2.25

World Teachers Day A594

2006, Oct. 5
1381 A594 20d multi 1.40 1.40

Arbor Day — A595

Trees: 20d, Atlas pistachio. 30d, Pomagranate.

2006, Oct. 25
1382-1383 A595 Set of 2 3.75 3.75

Sino-African Cooperation Summit, Beijing — A596

2006, Nov. 4 *Perf. 12*
1384 A596 30d multi 2.25 2.25

19th Century Powder Flasks — A597

Background color: 15d, Pink. 20d, Pale green.

2006, Nov. 22 **Litho.** *Perf. 13½x14*
1385-1386 A597 Set of 2 3.00 3.00

Transitory Arab Parliament, 1st Anniv. — A598

2006, Dec. 17 *Perf. 13½x13*
1387 A598 15d multi 1.10 1.10

El Moudjahid Newspaper, 50th Anniv. — A599

2006, Dec. 18 *Perf. 14*
1388 A599 30d multi 2.25 2.25

Desalinization of Sea Water — A600

2006, Dec. 20
1389 A600 20d multi 1.50 1.50

A601

Algiers, 2007 Arab Cultural Capital — A602

2007, Jan. 12 **Litho.** *Perf. 13½x13*
1390 A601 15d multi 1.25 1.25
1391 A602 30d multi 2.25 2.25

Lighthouses — A603

Lighthouse at: 15d, Ilot d'Arzew. 20d, Cap Sigli. 38d, Ras-afia.

2007, Feb. 14 **Litho.** *Perf. 14*
1392-1394 A603 Set of 3 5.25 5.25

Employment of Women — A604

2007, Mar. 8 **Litho.** *Perf. 14*
1395 A604 15d multi 1.25 1.25

Sheikh Mohamed Ameziane Belhaddad (1790-1873), Leader of 1871 Rebellion A605

2007, Apr. 8 *Perf. 13x13¼*
1396 A605 15d multi 1.25 1.25

Ksars A606

Village scenes: No. 1397, 15d, Kenadsa. No. 1398, 15d, Temacine, vert.

2007, Apr. 21 *Perf. 13¼x13, 13x13¼*
1397-1398 A606 Set of 2 2.25 2.25

2nd Afro-Asiatic Games, Algiers A607

2007, May 18 **Litho.** *Perf. 14*
1399 A607 15d multi 1.10 1.10

9th All-African Games, Algiers — A608

2007, May 18
1400 A608 15d multi 1.10 1.10

Gardens — A609

Designs: 15d, Landon Gardens, Biskra. 20d, Ibn Badis Gardens, Oran. 38d, Essai du Hamma Gardens, Algiers.

2007, June 5 *Perf. 13½x13*
1401-1403 A609 Set of 3 5.50 5.50

National Gendarmerie, 45th Anniv. — A610

Designs: 15d, Gendarmerie emblem. 38d, Gendarmerie emblem, gendarme and automobile.

2007, June 25 **Litho.** *Perf. 14*
1404-1405 A610 Set of 2 4.00 4.00

Independence, 45th Anniv. — A611

Designs: 15d, People, flags and dove. 20d, Anniversary emblem, vert.

2007, July 5 *Perf. 13¼x13*
1406 A611 15d multi 1.25 1.25

Imperf
Size: 60x77mm
1407 A611 20d multi 3.00 3.00

Ceramics A612

Designs: No. 1408, 15d, Jar with handles. No. 1409, 15d, Glazed jar without handles. 20d, Censer. 38d, Lamp, horiz.

2007, Aug. 5 **Litho.** *Perf. 14*
1408-1411 A612 Set of 4 6.00 6.00

Endangered Animals — A613

Designs: 15d, Striped hyena. 38d, White-tailed fox.

2007, Sept. 12 *Perf. 13¼x13*
1412-1413 A613 Set of 2 3.25 3.25

Theaters A614

Theater in: No. 1414, 15d, Setif. No. 1415, 15d, Oran. 20d, Annaba, horiz. 38d, Algiers.

Perf. 13x13¼, 13¼x13
2007, Oct. 24 **Litho.**
1414-1417 A614 Set of 4 5.75 5.75

Encyclopedia of Algerian Postage Stamps A615

2007, Nov. 1 *Perf. 13x13¼*
1418 A615 15d multi 1.40 1.40

Bey Ahmed of Constantine (1784-1850), Leader of 1836-48 Resistance Against French A616

2007, Nov. 7
1419 A616 15d multi 1.25 1.25

National Artisan's Day — A617

2007, Nov. 9 *Perf. 13¼x14*
1420 A617 15d multi 1.40 1.40

Tilapia
A618

2007, Dec. 12   Litho.   *Perf. 14*
1421   A618   15d multi   1.50 1.50

Miniature Sheet

Emir Abdelkader (1808-83) — A619

No. 1422: a, Abdelkader seated. b, Abdelkader standing. c, Abdelkader, diff.

2007, Dec. 15
1422   A619   Sheet of 3   5.00 5.00
a.-b.   15d Either single   1.10 1.10
c.   38d multi   2.75 2.75

Fifth
General
Census
A620

2008, Jan. 16   *Perf. 14x13¼*
1423   A620   15d multi   1.25 1.25

French Air
Raid on Sakiet
Sidi Youssef,
Tunisia, 50th
Anniv. — A621

2008, Feb. 8   Litho.   *Perf. 13x13¼*
1424   A621   15d multi   1.25 1.25

Miniature Sheet

Fountains — A621a

2008, Feb. 23   *Perf. 14*
1425   A621a   Sheet of 4   5.50 5.50
a.   10d Ain de la Grande Rue   .65   .65
b.   15d Ain Bir Djebbah   1.00 1.00
c.   20d Ain Sidi Abdellah   1.35 1.35
d.   38d Ain Bir Chebana   2.60 2.60

Miniature Sheet

Water and Sustainable
Development — A622

No. 1428: a, Issakarssen Wetlands. b, Reghaia Wetlands. c, Guerbes Wetlands. d, Emblem of Expo Zaragoza 2008.

2008, Mar. 22   Litho.   *Perf. 14*
1428   A622   Sheet of 4, #a-d   5.50 5.50
a.   10d multi   .65   .65
b.   15d multi   1.00 1.00
c.   20d multi   1.35 1.35
d.   38d multi   2.60 2.60

Souvenir Sheet

National Liberation Front Soccer Team,
50th Anniv. — A623

2008, Apr. 12   Litho.   *Perf.*
1429   A623   38d multi   2.75 2.75
No. 1429 contains one 36mm diameter stamp.

Writers
A624

No. 1430: a, Redha Houhou (1911-56). b, Abdelhamid Benhadouga (1925-96). c, Malek Bennabi (1905-73). d, Kateb Yacine (1929-89).

2008, Apr. 16   Litho.   *Perf. 14x13½*
1430   Horiz. strip of 4   4.25 4.25
a.-d.   A624 15d Any single   1.00 1.00

Children and New
Technologies
A625

2008, June 1   *Perf. 13½x14*
1431   A625   15d multi   1.05 1.05

Souvenir Sheet

Baya Mahieddine (1931-98),
Artist — A626

No. 1432: a, 15d, Mahieddine. b, 38d, Painting by Mahieddine.

2008, June 8   *Perf. 14*
1432   A626   Sheet of 2, #a-b   4.00 4.00

Kassamen,
Algerian
National
Anthem, by
Moufdi Zakaria
A627

2008, July 3   *Perf. 13x13¼*
1433   A627   15d multi   1.05 1.05

Railway
Stations
A628

Station in: 10d, Algiers. 15d, Constantine. 20d, Oran. 38d, Skikda.

2008, July 9   *Perf. 14x13½*
1434-1437 A628   Set of 4   5.00 5.00

Ferhat Abbas
(1899-1985),
President of
First Algerian
Temporary
Government
A629

2008, Sept. 19   *Perf. 13x13¼*
1438   A629   15d multi   1.10 1.10

2008
Summer
Olympics,
Beijing
A630

Designs: No. 1439, 15d, Fencing. No. 1440, 15d, Wrestling.

2008, July 23   Litho.   *Perf. 14x13½*
1439-1440 A630   Set of 2   2.10 2.10

National
Popular
Army
A631

2008, Nov. 1
1441   A631   15d multi   1.05 1.05

12th Session of
Government
Postage Stamp
Printers
Assoc.,
Algiers — A632

2008, Nov. 5   *Perf. 13x13¼*
1442   A632   15d multi   1.05 1.05

Miniature Sheet

Bridges in Constantine — A633

No. 1443: a, 10d, Sidi M'Cid Bridge. b, 15d, Sidi Rached Bridge. c, 20d, El Kantara Bridge. d, 38d, La Medersa Bridge.

2008, Nov. 26   *Perf. 14*
1443   A633   Sheet of 4, #a-d   5.00 5.00

Universal
Declaration
of Human
Rights,
60th Anniv.
A634

2008, Dec. 10   *Perf. 14x13½*
1444   A634   15d multi   1.05 1.05

Cities
A635

Designs: 10d, Tebessa. 15d, Saida. 20d, Miliana. 38d, Biskra.

2008, Dec. 18   *Perf. 13¼x13*
1445-1448 A635   Set of 4   5.00 5.00

Diplomatic
Relations
Between
Algeria and
People's
Republic of
China, 50th
Anniv.
A636

2008, Dec. 20   *Perf. 12*
1449   A636   15d multi   1.10 1.10

Louis Braille (1809-52), Educator of the Blind — A637

2009, Jan. 4   *Perf. 13½x14*
1450 A637 15d multi   1.10 1.10

Mausoleums A638

Mausoleum of: 15d, Sidi Abderrahmane, Algiers. 20d, Sidi Ibrahim El Atteuf, Ghardaia, horiz.

2009, Feb. 25   *Perf. 13½x14, 14x13½*
1451-1452 A638   Set of 2   2.25 2.25

Natl. Day of the Handicapped A639

Designs: 15d, Silhouettes of man with raised arm and man in wheelchair. 20d, Athlete in wheelchair, hand prints.

2009, Mar. 14   *Perf. 13½x14*
1453-1454 A639 Set of 2   2.25 2.25

Protection of Polar Regions and Glaciers — A640

2009, Mar. 28   Litho.
1455 A640 38d multi   2.75 2.75

Presidential Elections A641

2009, Apr. 9   *Perf. 13x13¼*
1456 A641 15d multi   1.00 1.00

Items in National Museum A642

Designs: 15d, Wooden sandals. 20d, Fragment of silver brooch. 30d, Vest.

2009, Apr. 18   *Perf. 14x13½*
1457-1459 A642   Set of 3   4.50 4.50

University of Algiers, Cent. A643

2009, May 11
1460 A643 15d multi   1.00 1.00

Jewelry of Southern Algeria — A644

Designs: 1d, Silver fibulas. 5d, Amulet necklace. 9d, Pectoral jewelry and chain. 10d, Circular fibula.

2009, May 13   *Perf. 13¾*
1461-1464 A644   Set of 4   1.75 1.75

Protection of Children From Cyberspace Dangers — A645

2009, May 17   *Perf. 14x13½*
1465 A645 15d multi   1.10 1.10

16th Mediterranean Games, Pescara, Italy — A646

Designs: 15d, Sailboarding. 20d, Equestrian, horiz.

      Perf. 13½x14, 14x13½
2009, June 3   Litho.
1466-1467 A646   Set of 2   2.40 2.40

Roman Era Archaeological Sites — A647

Designs: 15d, Madaure archaeological site. 20d, Khemissa archaeological site. 30d, Old Theater, Guelma.

2009, June 14   *Perf. 13½x14*
1468-1470 A647   Set of 3   4.25 4.25

Second Panafrican Cultural Festival of Algiers — A648

Designs: 15d, Shown. 20d, Map of Africa, antelope, geometric designs.

2009, July 4   *Perf. 13¼x13*
1471-1472 A648   Set of 2   2.25 2.25

"The Child of Today, the Man of Tomorrow" A649

"I Love My Country" — A650

2009, June 26   *Perf. 13½x14*
1473 A649 15d multi   1.00 1.00
1474 A650 20d multi   1.25 1.25

Algerian Electricity and Gas Company, 40th Anniv. — A651

2009, July 28
1475 A651 15d multi   1.00 1.00

Traffic Safety — A652

2009, Aug. 6
1476 A652 15d multi   1.00 1.00

Fishing Ports — A653

Designs: 15d, Bouharoun. 20d, Béni Saf. 30d, Stora.

2009, Sept. 2   Litho.   *Perf. 13½x13*
1477-1479 A653   Set of 3   4.25 4.25

Protection of the Aged — A654

2009, Oct. 10   *Perf. 13½x14*
1480 A654 15d multi   1.00 1.00

National Armed Forces — A655

2009, Nov. 1   Litho.   *Perf. 13x13¼*
1481 A655 15d multi   1.00 1.00

Olive Oil Production — A656

Designs: 15d, Picking olives. 20d, Pressing olives, vert.

    Perf. 13¼x13, 13x13¼
2009, Nov. 25
1482-1483 A656   Set of 2   2.40 2.40

Folktales A657

No. 1484: a, Loundja, la Fille de l'Ogre. b, Badra. c, La Fée Colombe. d, La Rose Rouge.

2009, Dec. 7   Litho.   *Perf. 13x13¼*
1484   Block or strip of 4   4.25 4.25
a.-d.   A657 15d Any single   .95 .95

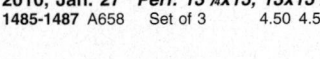

Birds of Prey A658

Designs: 15d, Aquila chrysaetos. 20d, Falco biarmicus, vert. 30d, Falco peregrinus, vert.

2010, Jan. 27   *Perf. 13¼x13, 13x13¼*
1485-1487 A658   Set of 3   4.50 4.50

Victims of French Nuclear Testing in
Algeria — A659

2010, Feb. 10   *Perf. 13¼x13*
1488 A659 15d multi   1.60 1.60

Forts
A660

Designs: 15d, Fort de l'Empereur, Bordj
Moulay Hassan, Algiers. 20d, Gouraya Fort,
Béjaia.

2010, Feb. 15
1489-1490 A660   Set of 2   2.50 2.50

Expo 2010, Shanghai — A661

Designs: 15d, Stylized people, flowers,
buildings. 38d, Algeria Pavilion.

2010, Mar. 24   **Litho.**   *Perf. 13¼x13*
1491-1492 A661   Set of 2   3.75 3.75

16th Intl.
Conference on
Liquified Gas,
Oran — A662

Conference emblem, world map and: 15d,
Gas plant. 20d, Port, horiz.

2010, Apr. 18   *Perf. 13x13½, 13½x13*
1493-1494 A662   Set of 2   2.50 2.50

May 8, 1945
Massacres, 65th
Anniv. — A663

2010, May 8   *Perf. 13¼*
1495 A663 15d multi   1.00 1.00

2010 World Cup Soccer
Championships, South Africa — A664

Designs: No. 1496, 15d, World Cup trophy,
flags of participating countries. No. 1497, 15d,
Player, crowd holding Algerian flags.
No. 1498: a, Fox playing soccer. b, Player,
soccer ball.

2010, May 8   *Perf. 13x13¼*
1496-1497 A664   Set of 2   2.00 2.00
    Souvenir Sheet
    Imperf
1498 A664 15d Sheet of 2, #a-b   2.00 2.00

Ahellil of Gourara UNESCO World
Intangible Cultural Heritage — A665

2010, June 2   *Perf. 13¼x13*
1499 A665 15d multi   1.15 1.15

Martyr's
Sanctuary,
Algiers — A666

2010, June 20
1500 A666 (15d) multi   1.10 1.10

African Year of
Peace and
Security
A667

2010, July 19   *Perf. 13x13¼*
1501 A667 15d multi   1.10 1.10

Caves
A668

Designs: No. 1502, 15d, Béni Add Cave,
Ain Fezza. No. 1503, 15d, Ziama Cave,
Mansouriah.

2010, July 25   *Perf. 13¼x13*
1502-1503 A668   Set of 2   2.10 2.10

Organization of the Petroleum
Exporting Countries, 50th
Anniv. — A669

Designs: 15d, Emblem. 38d, Emblem, world
map, oil tanker.

2010, Sept. 14   **Litho.**   *Perf. 13¼x13*
1504-1505 A669   Set of 2   3.75 3.75

Mosques
A670

Designs: 15d, El Hanafi Mosque, Blida. 20d,
Sidi Ali Dib Mosque, Skikda. 30d, Grand
Mosque, Nedroma.

2010, Sept. 15   *Perf. 13x13¼*
1506-1508 A670   Set of 3   4.50 4.50

Dates
A671

Date varieties: No. 1509, 15d, Degla Beida.
No. 1510, 15d, Akerbuch. No. 1511, 15d,
Ghars, vert. No. 1512, 15d, Deglet Nour, vert.

2010, Oct. 6   *Perf. 13¼x13, 13x13¼*
1509-1512 A671   Set of 4   4.50 4.50

Handcrafted
Items — A672

Designs: 15d, Candlestick holder. 20d, Qua-
noun (musical instrument). 30d, Leather-cov-
ered chest with handles, horiz.

    Perf. 13¼x14, 14x13¼
2010, Nov. 30   **Litho.**
1513-1515 A672   Set of 3   4.50 4.50

Trees
A673

Designs: 15d, Cork oak. 20d, Carob tree.
30d, Soapberry tree. 38d, Argan tree.

2011, Jan. 29   *Perf. 13¼x13*
1516-1519 A673   Set of 4   6.25 6.25

Tlemcen, 2011
Capital of
Islamic Culture
A674

Designs: 15d, Minaret of Mansoura. 20d,
Door knocker, Side Boumedienne Mosque.

2011, Feb. 15   **Litho.**   *Perf. 13x13¼*
1520-1521 A674   Set of 2   2.10 2.10

Snakes
A675

Designs: No. 1522, 15d, Couleuvre a
diademe (diadem snake). No. 1523, 15d,
Vipere a cornes (Saharan horned viper).

2011, Mar. 13
1522-1523 A675   Set of 2   2.00 2.00

First Economic
Census — A676

2011, Apr. 12   *Perf. 13½x14*
1524 A676 15d multi   .90 .90

18th Cent. Tableware From
Algiers — A677

Designs: 15d, Couscous dish. 30d, Butter
dish.

2011, Apr. 19   *Perf. 13¼x13*
1525-1526 A677   Set of 2   2.75 2.75

Telecenters — A678

2011, May 17   *Perf. 14x13½*
1527 A678 15d multi   1.10 1.10

Campaign Against Human
Immunodeficiency Virus — A679

2011, June 30   *Perf. 13½x14*
1528 A679 15d multi   1.10 1.10

Benyoucef
Benkhedda
(1920-2003),
Politician
A680

2011, Sept. 19   *Perf. 13x13¼*
1529 A680 15d multi   .90 .90

A681

Comic
Strips — A682

2011, Sept. 25   *Perf. 13¼x14*
1530 A681 15d multi   .90 .90
1531 A682 15d multi   .90 .90

World Post
Day
A683

Main post office in: No. 1532, 15d, Constantine. No. 1533, 15d, Oran.

2011, Oct. 9   *Perf. 14x13¼*
1532-1533 A683   Set of 2   1.90 1.90

Paris
Massacre of
Algerian
Protestors,
50th
Anniv. — A684

2011, Oct. 17   *Perf. 13x13¼*
1534 A684 15d multi   .90 .90

Algerian
Press
Service,
50th Anniv.
A685

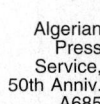

2011, Oct. 25   *Perf. 14x13¼*
1535 A685 15d multi   .90 .90

Army Museum — A686

2011, Nov. 1   *Perf. 13¼x13*
1536 A686 15d multi   .90 .90

Souvenir Sheet

Algiers Metro — A687

No. 1537: a, Train at station, people on platform. b, Train in tunnel.

2011, Nov. 14   *Perf. 14*
1537 A687 15d Sheet of 2, #a-b   2.00 2.00

Sheep — A688

Sheep breeds: No. 1538, 15d, Ouled Djallal. No. 1539, 15d, El Hamra.

2011, Nov. 16   *Perf. 13¼x13*
1538-1539 A688   Set of 2   2.00 2.00

Ornamental
Plants — A689

Designs: 15d, Bougainvillea. 20d, Glycine (wisteria). 30d, Mimosa, horiz. 38d, Galant de nuit (night-blooming cestrum), horiz.

2011, Dec. 26   *Perf. 13x13¼, 13¼x13*
1540-1543 A689   Set of 4   6.25 6.25

Ceasefire
Between
Algeria and
France, 50th
Anniv. — A690

2012, Mar. 19   *Litho.*   *Perf. 13x13¼*
1544 A690 15d multi   .90 .90

Expo 2012, Yeosu, South
Korea — A691

2012, Mar. 21   *Perf. 13¼x13*
1545 A691 15d multi   .90 .90

Wainscoting
A692

Designs: 15d, Door, Dar Aziza, Algiers. 20d, Ceiling, Dar Aziza. 30d, Window, Hassen Pacha Palace, Algiers.

2012, Mar. 26   *Perf. 13x13¼*
1546-1548 A692   Set of 3   3.75 3.75

Snails — A693

Designs: 15d, Theba pisana. 20d, Eobania vermiculata.

2012, Mar. 28
1549-1550 A693   Set of 2   2.10 2.10

Ulemas
A694

Designs: 15d, Sheikh Larbi Djedri Tebessi (1895-1957). 20d, Sheikh Embarek El-Mili (1898-1945). 30d, Sheikh Ahmed Hamani (1915-98).

2012, Apr. 16   *Litho.*   *Perf. 13x13¼*
1551-1553 A694   Set of 3   3.75 3.75

City Scenes
A695

Designs: 15d, Casbah of Dellys. 20d, Saracen Gate, Bejaia. 30d, Casbah of Constantine.

2012, June 26
1554-1556 A695   Set of 3   3.75 3.75

2012
Summer
Olympics,
London
A696

Designs: 15d, Judo, London Eye. 38d, Rowing, Tower Bridge, vert.

Perf. 14x13¼, 13¼x14
2012, June 27
1557-1558 A696   Set of 2   1.40 1.40

Algerian
Armed
Forces, 50th
Anniv.
A697

Designs: No. 1559, 15d, Gendarme on motorcycle. No. 1560, 15d, Tank. No. 1561, 15d, Missiles. No. 1562, 15d, Airplane in flight. No. 1563, 15d, Member of Republican Guard on horse. No. 1564, 15d, Naval vessel.

2012, July 5   *Perf. 14*
Stamps With Year and Inscriptions At Bottom
1559-1564 A697   Set of 6   2.25 2.25
1561a   Souvenir sheet of 3, #1559-1561, with year and inscriptions at bottom of stamp removed   1.10 1.10
1564a   Souvenir sheet of 3, #1562-1564, with year and inscriptions at bottom of stamp removed   1.10 1.10

Souvenir Sheet

Algerian Independence, 50th
Anniv. — A698

2012, July 5   *Imperf.*
1565 A698 15d multi   .40 .40

Wheat Varieties
A699

Designs: 15d, Bousselam. 20d, Mohamed Ben Bachir. 30d, Hedba 03.

2012, Sept. 29   *Perf. 13x13¼*
1566-1568 A699   Set of 3   1.75 1.75

Algerian Radio and Television, 50th Anniv. — A700

2012, Oct. 28   *Perf. 13¼x13*
1569 A700 15d multi   .40 .40

Postage Stamps of Independent Algeria, 50th Anniv. — A701

2012, Nov. 1
1570 A701 15d multi   .40 .40

Medicinal Plants — A702

Designs: 15d, Globularia vulgaris. 20d, Glycyrrhiza glabra. 30d, Menyanthes trifoliata.

2012, Dec. 11   **Litho.**   *Perf. 13x13¼*
1571-1573 A702   Set of 3   1.75 1.75

Diplomatic Relations Between Algeria and Russia, 50th Anniv. — A703

2012, Dec. 18   **Litho.**   *Perf. 13¼x13*
1574 A703 15d multi   .40 .40

Roman Mosaics A704

Mosaic depicting: 15d, Muse. 20d, Hunting scene.

2012, Dec. 18   **Litho.**   *Perf. 13x13¼*
1575-1576 A704   Set of 2   .90 .90

Yennayer Festival (Berber New Year) — A705

2013, Jan. 12   **Litho.**   *Perf. 13x13¼*
1577 A705 15d multi   .40 .40

Lighthouses — A706

Designs: 15d, Srigina Island Lighthouse. 20d, Cap Bougaroun Lighthouse. 30d, Cap Ivi Lighthouse.

2013, Feb. 27   **Litho.**   *Perf. 13¼x13*
1578-1580 A706   Set of 3   3.75 3.75

Fruit and Blossoms — A707

Designs: 15d, Apricots. 20d, Cherries.

2013, Mar. 3   **Litho.**   *Perf. 13¼x13*
1581-1582 A707   Set of 2   1.90 1.90

First Chinese Medical Team in Algeria, 50th Anniv. — A708

2013, Apr. 16   **Litho.**   *Perf. 12*
1583 A708 15d multi   .40 .40

National Copyright Office, 40th Anniv. — A709

2013, Apr. 26   **Litho.**   *Perf. 13x13¼*
1585 A709 15d multi   .40 .40

National Administration School — A710

2013, Apr. 29   **Litho.**   *Perf. 13¼x13*
1586 A710 15d multi   .40 .40

Roman Pottery — A711

Designs: No. 1587, 15d, Two-handled urn with lid, denomination at LL (shown). No. 1588, 15d, Two-handled urn without lid, denomination at LL. No. 1589, 15d, Single-handled urn without lid, denomination at LR.

2013, May 5   **Litho.**   *Perf. 13x13¼*
1587-1589 A711   Set of 3   1.25 1.25

Improvements in Road Safety With Global Positioning Satellite Technology A712

2013, May 17   **Litho.**   *Perf. 13x13¼*
1590 A712 15d multi   .40 .40

Algerian Insurance and Re-insurance Company, 50th Anniv. — A713

2013, June 8   **Litho.**   *Perf. 13x13¼*
1591 A713 15d multi   .40 .40

Police Day — A714

2013, July 22   **Litho.**   *Perf. 13x13¼*
1592 A714 15d multi   .40 .40

Marine Life — A715

Designs: No. 1593, 15d, Paracentrotus lividus. No. 1594, 15d, Bathynectes maravigna. No. 1595, 15d, Haliotis tuberculata.

2013, Aug. 3   **Litho.**   *Perf. 13¼x13*
1593-1595 A715   Set of 3   1.25 1.25

Flowers A716

Designs: No. 1596, 15d, Carnations. No. 1597, 15d, Petunias.

2013, Aug. 5   **Litho.**   *Perf. 13x13¼*
1596-1597 A716   Set of 2   .75 .75

22nd African Regional Conference of Interpol, Oran — A717

2013, Sept. 10   **Litho.**   *Perf. 13¼x13*
1598 A717 38d multi   .95 .95

Algerian Olympic Committee, 50th Anniv. A718

Olympic rings, "50," and: 15d, Stylized bird. 30d, Stylized bird and torch, vert.

2013, Oct. 28   **Litho.**   *Perf. 14*
1599-1600 A718   Set of 2   1.10 1.10

Transportation — A719

Designs: 15d, Cable cars, Constantine. 20d, Tram, Oran.

2013, Oct. 30 Litho. *Perf. 13¼x13*
1601-1602 A719 Set of 2 .90 .90

Diplomatic Relations Between Algeria and People's Republic of China, 55th Anniv. — A720

2013, Dec. 20 Litho. *Perf. 12*
1603 A720 15d multi .40 .40

Fish Farming A721

Designs: 15d, Floating cages. 20d, Clenopharyngodon idella.

2013, Dec. 24 Litho. *Perf. 14*
1604-1605 A721 Set of 2 .90 .90

Sonatrach (State-owned Oil and Gas Corporation), 50th Anniv. — A722

2013, Dec. 31 Litho. *Perf. 13x13¼*
1606 A722 15d multi .40 .40

Souvenir Sheet

1607 A722 50d multi 1.40 1.40

No. 1607 contains one 35x48mm stamp.

Flowers — A723

Designs: 15d, Ornithogalum arabicum. 20d, Bellis sylvestris. 30d, Calendula arvensis.

2014, Jan. 29 Litho. *Perf. 14*
1608-1610 A723 Set of 3 1.75 1.75

Constitutional Council Building, Algiers, 25th Anniv. — A724

2014, Feb. 23 Litho. *Perf. 13¼x13*
1611 A724 15d multi .40 .40

Coins A725

Obverse and reverse of Almohad dinar from: 15d, 524-58. 20d, 580-95.

2014, Feb. 26 Litho. *Perf. 13¼x13*
1612-1613 A725 Set of 2 .90 .90

Supreme Court, 50th Anniv. — A726

2014, Mar. 2 Litho. *Perf. 14*
1614 A726 15d multi .40 .40

National Day of Handicapped Persons A727

2014, Mar. 14 Litho. *Perf. 13x13¼*
1615 A727 15d multi .40 .40

Intl. Day of Anti-Personnel Mine Victims — A728

2014, Apr. 4 Litho. *Perf. 13x13¼*
1616 A728 15d multi .40 .40

2014 Presidential Election — A729

2014, Apr. 16 Litho. *Perf. 13¼x13*
1617 A729 15d multi .40 .40

19th Century Kitchen Tools — A730

Designs: 15d, Coffee mill, Algiers. 20d, Tuareg sugar hammer, horiz. 30d, Tuareg sugar shears, horiz.

Perf. 13x13¼, 13¼x13
2014, Apr. 28 Litho.
1618-1620 A730 Set of 3 1.75 1.75

Amazigh High Commission, 19th Anniv. — A731

2014, May 27 Litho. *Perf. 13¼x14*
1621 A731 15d multi .40 .40

17th Ministerial Conference of the Non-Aligned Movement, Algiers — A732

Designs: No. 1622, 15d, Stylized dove with olive branch, globe with Algeria highlighted. No. 1623, 15d, Conference emblem.

2014, May 28 Litho. *Perf. 13x13¼*
1622-1623 A732 Set of 2 .75 .75

2014 World Cup Soccer Championships, Brazil — A733

Algerian soccer player dribbling ball with country name in: 15d, White. 38d, Green.

2014, June 26 Litho. *Perf. 13x13¼*
1624-1625 A733 Set of 2 1.40 1.40

Olympic Complex, Oran — A734

2014, July 5 Litho. *Perf. 13¼x13*
1626 A734 15d multi .40 .40

Traditional Women's Veils — A735

Designs: 15d, Haik. 30d, M'laya.

2014, Aug. 27 Litho. *Perf. 13x13¼*
1627-1628 A735 Set of 2 1.10 1.10

Prehistoric Art — A736

Designs: 15d, Painting on rock of horse-drawn chariot. 20d, Head of ram. 30d, Baetulus, vert.

2014, Sept. 1 Litho. *Perf. 14*
1629-1631 A736 Set of 3 1.60 1.60

Souvenir Sheet

Rugs — A737

No. 1632: a, Rug from Serbia ("Radomir Bojanic" inscribed at LR). b, Rug from Algeria (Arabic script at LR).

2014, Oct. 7 Litho. *Perf. 13¼x14*
1632 A737 15d Sheet of 2, #a-b .75 .75

See Serbia No. 647.

World Post Day — A738

2014, Oct. 9 Litho. *Perf. 13¼x14*
1633 A738 15d multi .35 .35

Algerian War of Independence, 60th Anniv. — A739

2014, Nov. 1 Litho. Perf. 13x13¼
1634 A739 15d multi .35 .35

Sheikh Abdelkrim Dali (1914-78), Musician A740

2014, Nov. 16 Litho. Perf. 13x13¼
1635 A740 15d multi .35 .35

Bridges — A741

Designs: No. 1636, 15d, Saleh Bey Viaduct, Constantine. No. 1637, 15d, Highway bridge and Algerian flag, vert.

Perf. 13¼x13, 13x13¼
2014, Nov. 19 Litho.
1636-1637 A741 Set of 2 .70 .70

Intl. Year of Solidarity With the Palestinian People — A742

2014, Dec. 13 Litho. Perf. 13¼x13
1638 A742 15d multi .35 .35

Expo 2015, Milan — A743

Designs: 15d, Globe, hand holding wheat stalks, silhouettes of people. 38d, Stylized fish and fruit, horiz.

2014, Dec. 22 Litho. Perf. 14
1639-1640 A743 Set of 2 1.25 1.25

Bordj el Kifan, Algiers — A744

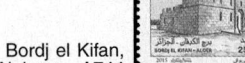

2015 Litho. Perf. 14x13¾
1641 A744 4d pale orange .25 .25
1642 A744 10d lt blue .25 .25
1643 A744 25d green .55 .55
Issued: 4d, 10d, 8/5; 25d, 1/4.

Algerian Customs — A745

2015, Jan. 26 Litho. Perf. 13¼x13
1644 A745 25d multi .55 .55

Intl. Day of the Fight Against Cancer A746

2015, Feb. 4 Litho. Perf. 14
1645 A746 25d multi .55 .55

World Consumer Rights Day — A747

World map, bar code and: 25d, Shopping cart. 30d, Umbrella.

2015, Mar. 15 Litho. Perf. 13½x14
1646-1647 A747 Set of 2 1.25 1.25

A748

A749

Constantine, 2015 Capital of Arab Culture — A750

Perf. 13x13¼, 13¼x13
2015, Apr. 16 Litho.
1648 A748 10d multi .25 .25
1649 A749 25d multi .55 .55

Souvenir Sheet
1650 A750 60d purple & blk 1.25 1.25

Diplomatic Relations Between Algeria and Mexico, 50th Anniv. — A751

2015, Apr. 23 Litho. Perf. 13x13¼
1651 A751 25d multi .55 .55

Mosques A752

El Aatiq Mosque in: No. 1652, 25d, Ghardaia. No. 1653, 25d, Metlili, vert.

Perf. 14x13½, 13½x14
2015, May 28 Litho.
1652-1653 A752 Set of 2 1.00 1.00

World Refugee Day — A753

2015, June 20 Litho. Perf. 13½x14
1654 A753 25d multi .50 .50

Traditional Costumes A754

Man and woman from: 25d, Algiers. 30d, Kabylie.

2015, July 15 Litho. Perf. 13x13¼
1655-1656 A754 Set of 2 1.10 1.10

Famous Men A755

Designs: No. 1657, 25d, Abdelhamid Benhadouga (1925-96), writer. No. 1658, 25d, M'hamed Issiakhem (1928-85), painter. No. 1659, 25d, Ismail Samsom (1934-88), painter, vert. No. 1660, 25d, Mouloud Feraoun (1913-62), writer, vert.

Perf. 14x13½, 13½x14
2015, Sept. 21 Litho.
1657-1660 A755 Set of 4 1.90 1.90

Day of Algerian Diplomacy — A756

2015, Oct. 8 Litho. Perf. 13¼x13
1661 A756 25d multi .50 .50

United Nations, 70th Anniv. A757

2015, Oct. 24 Litho. Perf. 14x13½
1662 A757 25d multi .50 .50

Algerian Revolution, 61st Anniv. — A758

2015, Nov. 1 Litho. Perf. 13½x14
1663 A758 25d multi .50 .50

A759

Energy A760

2015, Nov. 11 Litho. Perf. 14x13½
1664 A759 10d multi .25 .25
1665 A760 25d multi .50 .50

A761

Arab Family
Day
A762

2015, Dec. 7   Litho.   Perf. 13½x14
1666 A761 25d multi   .50   .50

Perf. 14x13½
1667 A762 30d multi   .60   .60

International Year
of Light — A763

2015, Dec. 20   Litho.   Perf. 13½x14
1668 A763 25d multi   .50   .50

International Telecommunication
Union, 150th Anniv. — A764

2015, Dec. 22   Litho.   Perf. 14x13½
1669 A764 25d multi   .50   .50

SEMI-POSTAL STAMPS

Regular Issue of 1926
Surcharged in Black or
Red

1927   Unwmk.   Perf. 14x13½
B1   A1   5c +5c bl grn   1.60   1.60
B2   A1   10c +10c lilac   1.60   1.60
B3   A2   15c +15c org brn   1.60   1.60
B4   A2   20c +20c car rose   1.60   1.60
B5   A2   25c +25c bl grn   1.60   1.60
B6   A2   30c +30c lt bl   1.60   1.60
B7   A2   35c +35c dp vio   1.60   1.60
B8   A2   40c +40c ol grn   1.60   1.60
B9   A3   50c +50c dp bl (R)   1.60   1.60
  a.   Double surcharge   460.00 475.00
B10 A3   80c +80c red org   1.60   1.60
B11 A4   1fr +1fr gray grn &
           red brn   1.60   1.60
B12 A4   2fr +2fr Prus bl &
           blk brn   32.50 32.50
B13 A4   5fr +5fr red & vio   40.00 40.00
  Nos. B1-B13 (13)   90.10 90.10

The surtax was for the benefit of wounded
soldiers. Government officials speculated in
this issue.

Railroad
Terminal,
Oran
SP1

Ruins at Djemila
SP2

Mosque of Sidi
Abd-er-Rahman
SP3

Designs: 10c+10c, Rummel Gorge, Constantine. 15c+15c, Admiralty Buildings,
Algiers. 25c+25c, View of Algiers. 30c+30c,
Trajan's Arch, Timgad. 40c+40c, Temple of
the North, Djemila. 75c+75c Mansourah Minaret,
Tlemcen.   1f+1f,   View   of   Ghardaia.
1.50f+1.50f, View of Tolga. 2f+2f, Tuareg warriors. 3f+3f, Kasbah, Algiers.

1930   Engr.   Perf. 12½
B14 SP1 5c +5c orange   12.00 12.00
B15 SP1 10c +10c ol grn   12.00 12.00
B16 SP1 15c +15c dk brn   12.00 12.00
B17 SP1 25c +25c black   12.00 12.00
B18 SP1 30c +30c dk red   12.00 12.00
B19 SP1 40c +40c ap grn   12.00 12.00
B20 SP2 50c +50c ultra   9.50   9.50
B21 SP2 75c +75c red pur   9.50   9.50
B22 SP2 1fr +1fr org red   9.50   9.50
B23 SP2 1.50fr +1.50fr deep
           ultra   9.50   9.50
B24 SP2 2fr +2fr dk car   9.50   9.50
B25 SP2 3fr +3fr dk grn   9.50   9.50
B26 SP3 5fr +5fr grn &
           car   24.00 24.00
  a.   Center inverted   750.00
  Nos. B14-B26 (13)   153.00 153.00

Centenary of the French occupation of Algeria. The surtax on the stamps was given to the
funds for the celebration.
Nos. B14-B26 exist imperf. Value, set in
pairs, $800.

┌─────────────────────────────────┐
│ Catalogue values for unused   │
│ stamps in this section, from   │
│ this point to the end of the   │
│ section, are for Never Hinged   │
│ items.   │
└─────────────────────────────────┘

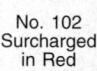

No. 102
Surcharged
in Red

1938   Perf. 13
B27 A6 65c +35c on 2.25fr
          yel grn   1.60   1.20
  a.   Inverted surcharge   350.00
  b.   Pair, one without surcharge 1,875.

20th anniversary of Armistice.
No. 79 with surcharge is considered an
essay. Values: unused $260, never hinged
$350.

René
Caillié,
Charles
Lavigerie
and Henri
Duveyrier
SP14

1939   Engr.
B28 SP14 30c +20c dk bl
            grn   2.40   2.40
B29 SP14 90c +60c car rose   2.40   2.40
B30 SP14 2.25fr +75c ultra   20.00 16.00
B31 SP14 5fr +5fr brn blk   40.00 32.50
  Nos. B28-B31 (4)   64.80 53.30

Pioneers of the Sahara.

French and
Algerian
Soldiers
SP15

1940   Photo.   Perf. 12
B32 SP15 1fr +1fr bl & car   1.60   1.20
  a.   Double surcharge   260.00

B33 SP15 1fr +2fr brn rose &
            blk   1.60   1.20
B34 SP15 1fr +4fr dp grn &
            red   2.40   2.00
B35 SP15 1fr +9fr brn & car   4.00   2.75
  Nos. B32-B35 (4)   9.60   7.15

The surtax was used to assist the families of
mobilized men.
Nos. B32-B35 exist without surcharge.
Value set, $325.

Type of Regular
Issue, 1941
Surcharged in
Carmine

1941   Engr.   Perf. 13
B36 A19 1fr +4fr black   .65   .30

No. 135 Surcharged
in Carmine

B37 A19 1fr +4fr dark blue   .65   .30

The surtax was for National Relief.

No. 124
Surcharged
in Black

1942
B38 A7 90c +60c henna brn   .55   .25
  a.   Double surcharge   175.00

The surtax was used for National Relief.
The stamp could also be used as 1.50 francs
for postage.

Mother and
Child — SP16

1943, Dec. 1   Litho.   Perf. 12
B39 SP16 50c +4.50fr brt pink   1.00   1.30
B40 SP16 1.50fr +8.50fr lt grn 1.00   1.30
B41 SP16 3fr +12fr dp bl   1.00   1.30
B42 SP16 5fr +15fr vio brn   1.00   1.40
  Nos. B39-B42 (4)   4.00   5.30

The surtax was for the benefit of soldiers
and prisoners of war.

Planes
over Fields
SP17

Unwmk.
1945, July 2   Engr.   Perf. 13
B43 SP17 1.50fr +3.50fr lt ultra,
            red org & blk   1.10   .85

The surtax was for the benefit of Algerian
airmen and their families.

**France No. B192 Overprinted Type
"a" of 1924 in Black**
1945
B44 SP146 4fr +6fr dk vio brn   1.10   .85

The surtax was for war victims of the P.T.T.

**Overprinted in Blue on Type of
France, 1945**
1945, Oct. 15
B45 SP150 2fr +3fr dk brn   1.10   .85

For Stamp Day.

**Overprinted in Blue on Type of
France, 1946**
1946, June 29
B46 SP160 3fr +2fr red   1.60   1.25

For Stamp Day.

Children
Playing by
Stream
SP18

Girl — SP19   Athlete — SP20

Repatriated
Prisoner
and Bay of
Algiers
SP21

1946, Oct. 2   Engr.   Perf. 13
B47 SP18 3fr +17fr dark grn   2.75   2.25
B48 SP19 4fr +21fr red   2.75   2.25
B49 SP20 8fr +27fr rose lilac   7.25   6.25
B50 SP21 10fr +35fr dark blue   3.25   2.50
  Nos. B47-B50 (4)   16.00 13.25

**Type of France, 1947, Overprinted
type "a" of 1924 in Carmine**
1947, Mar. 15
B51 SP172 4.50fr +5.50fr dp ultra 1.75 1.25

For Stamp Day.

**Same on Type of France, 1947,
Surcharged Like No. B36 in
Carmine**
1947, Nov. 13
B52 A173 5fr +10fr dk Prus grn 1.60   1.25

Type of France,
1948, Overprinted in
Dark Green — f

1948, Mar. 6
B53 SP176 6fr +4fr dk grn   1.75   1.25

For Stamp Day.

Type of France, 1948, Overprinted in Blue

1948, May
B54 A176 6fr +4fr red   1.60 1.25

Battleship Richelieu and the Admiralty, Algiers SP22

Aircraft Carrier Arromanches — SP23

Unwmk.
1949, Jan. 15   Engr.   Perf. 13
B55 SP22 10fr +15fr dp blue   10.00 8.00
B56 SP23 18fr +22fr red   10.00 8.00
The surtax was for naval charities.

Type of France, 1949, Overprinted in Blue — g

1949, Mar. 26
B57 SP180 15fr +5fr lilac rose   3.25 2.25
For Stamp Day, Mar. 26-27.

Type of France, 1950, Overprinted type "f" in Green

1950, Mar. 11
B58 SP183 12fr +3fr blk brn   3.25 2.75
For Stamp Day, Mar. 11-12.

Foreign Legionary — SP24

1950, Apr. 30
B59 SP24 15fr +5fr dk grn   3.00 2.40

Charles de Foucauld and Gen. J. F. H. Laperrine SP25

1950, Aug. 21   Unwmk.   Perf. 13
B60 SP25 25fr +5fr brn ol & brn   blk   8.00 6.25
50th anniversary of the presence of the French in the Sahara.

Emir Abd-el-Kader and Marshal T. R. Bugeaud — SP26

1950, Aug. 21
B61 SP26 40fr +10fr dk brn & blk brn   8.00 6.25
Unveiling of a monument to Emir Abd-el-Kader at Cacheron.

Col. Colonna d'Ornano and Fine Arts Museum, Algiers SP27

1951, Jan. 11
B62 SP27 15fr +5fr blk brn, vio brn & red brn   1.40 1.25
Death of Col. Colonna d'Ornano, 10th anniv.

Type of France, 1951, Overprinted type "a" of 1924 in Black

1951, Mar. 10
B63 SP186 12fr +3fr brown   2.75 2.50
For Stamp Day.

Type of France, 1952, Overprinted type "g" in Dark Blue

1952, Mar. 8   Unwmk.   Perf. 13
B64 SP190 12fr +3fr dk bl   2.75 2.50
For Stamp Day.

French Military Medal — SP28

Unwmk.
1952, July 5   Engr.   Perf. 13
B65 SP28 15fr +5fr grn, yel & brn   3.50 2.75
Centenary of the creation of the French Military Medal.

Type of France 1952, Surcharged type "g" and Surtax in Black

1952, Sept. 15
B66 A222 30fr +5fr dp ultra   4.00 3.25
10th anniv. of the defense of Bir-Hakeim.

View of El Oued SP29

Design: 12fr+3fr, View of Bou-Noura.

1952, Nov. 15   Engr.
B67 SP29 8fr +2fr ultra & red   3.25 3.00
B68 SP29 12fr +3fr red   6.50 4.75
The surtax was for the Red Cross.

Type of France, 1953, Overprinted type "a" of 1924 in Black

1953, Mar. 14   Engr.
B69 SP193 12fr +3fr purple   2.50 2.40
For Stamp Day. Surtax for Red Cross.

Victory of Cythera — SP30

Unwmk.
1953, Dec. 18   Engr.   Perf. 13
B70 SP30 15fr +5fr blk brn & brn   1.60 1.25
The surtax was for army welfare work.

Type of France, 1954, Overprinted type "a" of 1924 in Black

1954, Mar. 20   Unwmk.   Perf. 13
B71 SP196 12fr +3fr scarlet   2.25 2.00
For Stamp Day.

Soldiers and Flags — SP31

1954, Mar. 27
B72 SP31 15fr +5fr dk brn   2.00 1.25
The surtax was for old soldiers.

Foreign Legionary — SP32

1954, Apr. 30
B73 SP32 15fr +5fr dk grn   3.00 2.50
The surtax was for the welfare fund of the Foreign Legion.

Nurses and Verdun Hospital, Algiers SP33

15fr+5fr, J. H. Dunant & ruins at Djemila.

1954, Oct. 30
B74 SP33 12fr +3fr indigo & red   6.50 5.50
B75 SP33 15fr +5fr pur & red   7.50 6.25
The surtax was for the Red Cross.

Earthquake Victims and Ruins — SP34

First Aid — SP35

Design: Nos. B80-B81, Removing wounded.

1954, Dec. 5
B76 SP34 12fr +4fr dk vio brn   3.50 2.75
B77 SP34 15fr +5fr dp bl   3.50 2.75
B78 SP35 18fr +6fr lil rose   4.50 3.50
B79 SP35 20fr +7fr violet   4.50 3.50
B80 SP35 25fr +8fr rose brn   4.50 3.50
B81 SP35 30fr +10fr brt bl grn   4.50 3.50
   Nos. B76-B81 (6)   25.00 19.50
The surtax was for victims of the Orleansville earthquake disaster of September 1954.

Type of France, 1955, Overprinted type "a" of 1924 in Black

1955, Mar. 19
B82 SP199 12fr +3fr dp ultra   2.75 2.25
For Stamp Day, Mar. 19-20.

Women and Children — SP36

1955, Nov. 5
B83 SP36 15fr +5fr blue & indigo 1.40 1.25
The tax was for war victims.

Cancer Victim — SP37

1956, Mar. 3   Unwmk.   Perf. 13
B84 SP37 15fr +5fr dk brn   2.00 1.60
The surtax was for the Algerian Cancer Society. The male figure in the design is Rodin's "Age of Bronze."

Type of France, 1956, Overprinted type "a" of 1924 in Black

1956, Mar.
B85 SP202 12fr +3fr red   2.50 2.00
For Stamp Day, Mar. 17-18.

Foreign Legion Rest Home SP38

1956, Apr. 29
B86 SP38 15fr +5fr dk bl grn   2.50 2.00
Honoring the French Foreign Legion.

Type of France, 1957, Overprinted type "f" in Black

1957, Mar. 16   Engr.   Perf. 13
B87 SP204 12fr +3fr dull purple   2.00 1.60
For Stamp Day and to honor the Maritime Postal Service.

Fennec SP39

Design: 15fr+5fr, Stork flying over roofs.

1957, Apr. 6
B88 SP39 12fr +3fr red brn & red   9.00 7.25
B89 SP39 15fr +5fr sepia & red   9.00 7.25
The surtax was for the Red Cross.

Regular
Issue of
1956
Srchd. in
Dark Blue

1957, June 18
B90 A53 15fr +5fr scar & rose
     red   2.50   1.60
    17th anniv. of General de Gaulle's appeal
for a Free France.

The Giaour, by
Delacroix — SP40

On the
Banks of
the Oued,
by
Fromentin
SP41

Design: 35fr+10fr, Dancer, by Chasseriau.

Unwmk.
1957, Nov. 30   Engr.   Perf. 13
B91 SP40 15fr +5fr dk car   8.00   7.00
B92 SP41 20fr +5fr grn   8.00   7.00
B93 SP40 35fr +10fr dk bl   9.00   7.25
   Nos. B91-B93 (3)   25.00   21.25
Surtax for army welfare organizations.

**Type of France Overprinted type "f"
in Blue**
1958, Mar. 15   Unwmk.   Perf. 13
B94 SP206 15fr +5fr org brn   2.00   1.60
      For Stamp Day.

Bird-of-Paradise
Flower — SP42

1958, June 14   Engr.   Perf. 13
B95 SP42 20fr +5fr grn, org & vio 5.50 4.00
   The surtax was for Child Welfare.

Arms & Marshal's
Baton — SP43

1958, July 20
B96 SP43 20fr +5fr ultra, car &
     grn   2.50   2.00
   Marshal de Lattre Foundation.

Independent State

Clasped Hands,
Wheat, Olive
Branch — SP44

1963, May 27   Unwmk.   Perf. 13
B97 SP44 50c +20c sl grn, brt
     grn & car   1.10   .65
   Surtax for the Natl. Solidarity Fund.

Burning
Books — SP45

1965, June 7   Engr.   Perf. 13
B98 SP45 20c +5c ol grn, red &
     blk   .50   .40
   Burning of the Library of Algiers, 6/7/62.

Soldiers and Woman
Comforting Wounded
Soldier — SP46

1966, Aug. 20   Photo.   Perf. 11½
B99   SP46 30c +10c multi   1.25   .70
B100 SP46 95c +10c multi   1.75   1.25
   Day of the Moudjahid (Moslem volunteers).

Red Crescent,
Boy and
Girl — SP47

1967, May 27   Litho.   Perf. 14
B101 SP47 30c +10c brt grn, brn
     & car   .85   .50
   Algerian Red Crescent Society.

Flood
Victims — SP48

Design: 95c+25c, Rescuing flood victims.

1969, Nov. 15   Typo.   Perf. 10½
B102 SP48 30c +10c multi   .70   .50
Litho.
B103 SP48 95c +25c multi   1.60   .95

Red
Crescent
Flag
SP49

1971, May 17   Engr.   Perf. 10½
B104 SP49 30c +10c slate grn &
     car   .70   .40
   Algerian Red Crescent Society.

Intl. Children's
Day — SP50

1989, June 1   Litho.   Perf. 10½x11
B105 SP50 1d +30c multi   .70   .55
   Surtax for child welfare.

Solidarity with
Palestinians
SP51

1990, Dec. 9   Litho.   Perf. 10½x11
B106 SP51 1d +30c multi   .70   .45

Natl. Solidarity
with Education
SP52

1995, Sept. 20   Litho.   Perf. 13x14
B107 SP52 3d +50c multi   .60   .30

Red Crescent
Society
SP53

1998, May 2   Litho.   Perf. 13x13¼
B108 SP53 5d +1d multi   .50   .30

World
Children's
Day
SP54

No. B110, Flower, child, adult, vert.

1998, June 1   Perf. 14x13½, 13½x14
B109 SP54 5d +1d shown   .50   .25
B110 SP54 5d +1d multi   .50   .25

Flood Victim
Relief — SP55

2001, Dec. 24   Litho.   Perf. 13¼x14
B111 SP55 5d +5d multi   1.00   .75

Earthquake
Relief — SP56

2003, Dec. 3   Litho.   Perf. 13¼x14
B112 SP56 5d +5d multi   .90   .90

TeleFood
SP57

Children's drawings with: No. B113, 5d+1d,
Blue frame. No. B114, 5d+1d, Pink frame.

     Perf. 14, 14x13½ (#B114)
2004, Oct. 16   Litho.
B113-B114 SP57   Set of 2   1.00 1.00

AIR POST STAMPS

Catalogue values for unused
stamps in this section are for
Never Hinged items.

Plane over
Algiers
Harbor
AP1

Two types of 20fr:
   Type I — Monogram "F" without serifs.
"POSTE" indented 3mm.
   Type II — Monogram "F" with serifs.
"POSTE" indented 4½mm.

       Unwmk.
1946, June 20   Engr.   Perf. 13
C1   AP1   5fr red   .30   .25
C2   AP1 10fr deep blue   .30   .25
C3   AP1 15fr deep green   1.20   .40
C4   AP1 20fr brown (II)   1.10   .25
C4A AP1 20fr brown (I)   225.00 140.00
C5   AP1 25fr violet   1.40   .25
C6   AP1 40fr gray black   1.60   .65
   Nos. C1-C4,C5-C6 (6)   5.90   2.05
   For surcharges see Nos. C7, CB1-CB2.

No. C1
Surcharged
in Black

1947, Jan. 18
C7   AP1 (4.50fr) on 5fr red   .35   .25
   a.   Inverted surcharge   800.00 600.00
   b.   Double surcharge   1,000. 700.00
   c.   Pair, one without surcharge 1,200.

Storks over Mosque — AP2

Plane over Village AP3

1949-53
C8	AP2 50fr green	4.50	.90
C9	AP3 100fr brown	3.50	.65
C10	AP2 200fr bright red	10.50	5.25
C11	AP3 500fr ultra ('53)	32.50	20.00
	Nos. C8-C11 (4)	51.00	26.80

Beni Bahdel Dam — AP4

1957, July 1   Unwmk.   Perf. 13
C12	AP4 200fr dark red	9.50	2.00

Independent State

Caravelle over Ghardaia — AP5

Designs: 2d, Caravelle over El Oued. 5d, Caravelle over Tipasa.

1967-68   Engr.   Perf. 13
C13	AP5 1d lil, org brn & emer	1.40	.60
C14	AP5 2d brt bl, org brn & emer	3.25	1.40
C15	AP5 5d brt bl, grn & org brn ('68)	8.50	3.25
	Nos. C13-C15 (3)	13.15	5.25

Plane over Casbah, Algiers — AP6

Designs: 3d, Plane over Oran. 4d, Plane over Rhumel Gorge.

1971-72   Photo.   Perf. 12½
C16	AP6 2d grysh blk & multi	2.50	1.00
C17	AP6 3d violet & blk	3.75	1.60
C18	AP6 4d blk & multi	4.25	2.00
	Nos. C16-C18 (3)	10.50	4.60

Issued: 2d, 6/12/71; 3d, 4d, 2/28/72.

Storks and Plane — AP7

1979, Mar. 24   Photo.   Perf. 11½
C19	AP7 10d multi	6.50	2.50

Plane Approaching Coastal City — AP8

1991, Apr. 26   Litho.   Perf. 13½
C20	AP8 10d shown	3.00	1.50
C21	AP8 20d Plane over city	6.00	3.00

Plane Over Djidjelli Corniche — AP9

1993, Sept. 25   Engr.   Perf. 13½x14
C22	AP9 50d blue, grn & brn	6.75	3.25

AIR POST SEMI-POSTAL STAMPS

> Catalogue values for unused stamps in this section are for Never Hinged items.

No. C2 Surcharged in Carmine

1947, June 18   Perf. 13
CB1	AP1 10fr +10fr deep blue	2.50	1.75

7th anniv. of Gen. Charles de Gaulle's speech in London, June 18, 1940.

No. C1 Surcharged in Blue

1948, June 18
CB2	AP1 5fr +10fr red	2.50	1.75

8th anniv. of Gen. Charles de Gaulle's speech in London, June 18, 1940.

Monument, Clock Tower and Plane — SPAP1

1949, Nov. 10   Engr.   Unwmk.
CB3	SPAP1 15fr +20fr dk brn	7.00	5.25

25th anniv. of Algeria's 1st postage stamps.

POSTAGE DUE STAMPS

D1

Perf. 14x13½
1926-27   Typo.   Unwmk.
J1	D1 5c light blue	.40	.30
J2	D1 10c dk brn	.40	.30
J3	D1 20c olive grn	.80	.30
J4	D1 25c car rose	.80	.65
J5	D1 30c rose red	1.20	.50
J6	D1 45c blue grn	1.60	.65
J7	D1 50c brn vio	.80	.25
J8	D1 60c green ('27)	3.25	.90
J9	D1 1fr red brn, *straw*	.40	.30
J10	D1 2fr lil rose ('27)	.80	.30
J11	D1 3fr deep blue ('27)	.80	.30
	Nos. J1-J11 (11)	11.25	4.75

See Nos. J25-J26, J28-J32. For surcharges, see Nos. J18-J20.

D2

1926-27
J12	D2 1c olive grn	.40	.40
J13	D2 10c violet	1.60	.80
J14	D2 30c bister	1.60	.80
J15	D2 60c dull red	1.20	.80
J16	D2 1fr brt vio ('27)	20.00	4.00
J17	D2 2fr lt bl ('27)	16.00	1.60
	Nos. J12-J17 (6)	40.80	8.40

See note below France No. J51.
For surcharges, see Nos. J21-J24.

Stamps of 1926 Surcharged

1927
J18	D1 60c on 20c olive grn	2.00	.80
J19	D1 2fr on 45c blue grn	2.75	1.60
J20	D1 3fr on 25c car rose	1.60	.80
	Nos. J18-J20 (3)	6.35	3.20

Recouvrement Stamps of 1926 Surcharged

1927-32
J21	D2 10c on 30c bis ('32)	5.50	4.00
J22	D2 1fr on 1c olive grn	4.00	1.60
J23	D2 1fr on 60c dl red ('32)	24.00	.80
J24	D2 2fr on 10c violet	16.00	12.00
	Nos. J21-J24 (4)	49.50	18.40

> Catalogue values for unused stamps in this section, from this point to the end of the section, are for Never Hinged items.

Type of 1926, Without "R F"
1942   Typo.   Perf. 14x13½
J25	D1 30c dark red	1.25	1.25
J26	D1 2fr magenta	1.75	2.75

Type of 1926 Surcharged in Red

1944   Perf. 14x13½
J27	A2 50c on 20c yel grn	1.00	.70
a.	Inverted surcharge	27.50	
b.	Double surcharge	70.00	

No. J27 was issued precanceled only. See note after No. 32.

Type of 1926
1944   Litho.   Perf. 12
J28	D1 1.50fr brt rose lilac	1.00	.50
J29	D1 2fr greenish blue	1.25	.90
J30	D1 5fr rose carmine	1.25	1.10
	Nos. J28-J30 (3)	3.50	2.50

Type of 1926
1947   Typo.   Perf. 14x13½
J32	D1 5fr green	2.50	1.25

France Nos. J80-J81 Overprinted in Carmine or Black

1947
J33	D5 10c sepia (C)	.50	.25
J34	D5 30c bright red violet	.65	.25

D3

Perf. 14x13
1947-55   Unwmk.   Engr.
J35	D3 20c red	.70	.35
J36	D3 60c ultra	1.00	.45
J37	D3 1fr dk org brn	.50	.35
J38	D3 1.50fr dull green	1.50	1.10
J39	D3 2fr red	.70	.35
J40	D3 3fr violet	.75	.45
J41	D3 5fr ultra ('49)	1.10	.35
J42	D3 6fr black	.85	.45
J43	D3 10fr lil rose	1.40	.45
J44	D3 15fr ol grn ('55)	1.40	1.25
J45	D3 20fr brt grn	1.10	.85
J46	D3 30fr red org ('55)	2.50	1.50
J47	D3 50fr indigo ('51)	4.75	2.75
J48	D3 100fr brt bl ('53)	17.50	8.50
	Nos. J35-J48 (14)	35.75	19.15

Independent State

France Nos. J93-J97 Overprinted in Black

Perf. 14x13½
1962, July 2   Typo.   Unwmk.
Handstamped Overprint
J49	D6 5c bright pink	7.00	7.00
J50	D6 10c red orange	7.00	7.00
J51	D6 20c olive bister	7.00	7.00
J52	D6 50c dark green	10.00	10.00
J53	D6 1fr deep green	14.00	14.00
	Nos. J49-J53 (5)	45.00	45.00

Typographed Overprint
J49a	D6 5c bright pink	23.00	17.00
J50a	D6 10c red orange	23.00	17.00
J51a	D6 20c olive bister	23.00	17.00
J52a	D6 50c dark green	50.00	35.00
J53a	D6 1fr deep green	70.00	55.00
	Nos. J49a-J53a (5)	189.00	141.00

See note after No. 290.

Scales — D4

1963, June 25   Perf. 14x13½
J54	D4 5c car rose & blk	.25	.25
J55	D4 10c olive & car	.25	.25
J56	D4 20c ultra & blk	.55	.30
J57	D4 50c bister brn & grn	1.25	.80
J58	D4 1fr lilac & org	2.25	2.00
	Nos. J54-J58 (5)	4.55	3.60

No. J58 Surcharged with New Value & 3 Bars

1968, Mar. 28   Typo.   Perf. 14x13½

J59	D4	60c on 1fr lilac & org	1.25	1.00

Grain — D5

1972-93   Litho.   **Perf. 13½x14**

J60	D5	10c bister	.25	.25
J61	D5	20c deep brown	.25	.25
J62	D5	40c orange	.25	.25
J63	D5	50c dk vio blue	.30	.25
J64	D5	80c dk olive gray	.75	.30
J65	D5	1d green	.90	.55
a.		yel green, perf. 14¼x14	.25	.25
J66	D5	2d blue	1.75	1.00
a.		Prus bl, perf. 14¼x14	.25	.25
J67	D5	3d violet	.50	.25
J68	D5	4d lilac rose	.65	.35
		Nos. J60-J68 (9)	5.60	3.45

Issued: 3d, 4d, 1/21/93; others, 10/21/72.
Nos. J65a is inscribed "B ALGERIE" at bottom right. No. J66a is inscribed "B ALGERIE" or "BC ALGERIE."

Main Post Office, Algiers — D6

2006, Mar. 28   Litho.   **Perf. 13¾x14**

J69	D6	5d green	.90	.90
J70	D6	10d blue	1.60	1.60

NEWSPAPER STAMPS

Nos. 1 and 33
Surcharged in Red

1924-26   Unwmk.   **Perf. 14x13½**

P1	A16	½c on 1c dk gray	.40	.40
a.		Triple surcharge	300.00	
P2	A1	½c on 1c olive ('26)	.40	.40

ALLENSTEIN

'a-lən-ˌshtin

LOCATION — In East Prussia
AREA — 4,457 sq. mi.
POP. — 540,000 (estimated 1920)
CAPITAL — Allenstein

Allenstein, a district of East Prussia, held a plebiscite in 1920 under the Versailles Treaty, voting to join Germany rather than Poland. Later that year, Allenstein became part of the German Republic.

100 Pfennig = 1 Mark

Stamps of Germany, 1906-20, Overprinted

Perf. 14, 14½, 14x14½, 14½x14
1920   **Wmk. 125**

1	A16	5pf green	.40	1.15
2	A16	10pf carmine	.40	1.15
3	A22	15pf dk vio	.40	1.15
4	A22	15pf vio brn	5.50	11.50
5	A16	20pf bl vio	.40	1.50
6	A16	30pf org & blk, buff	.40	1.50
7	A16	40pf lake & blk	.40	1.15
8	A16	50pf pur & blk, buff	.40	1.15
9	A16	75pf grn & blk	.40	1.15
10	A17	1m car rose	1.60	5.00
a.		Double overprint	275.00	1,100.
11	A17	1.25m green	1.60	5.25
a.		Double overprint	—	
12	A17	1.50m yel brn	.95	4.00
13	A21	2.50m lilac rose	2.40	10.50
14	A19	3m blk vio	2.40	5.25
a.		Double overprint	325.00	1,150.
		Never hinged	650.00	
b.		Inverted overprint	—	
		Nos. 1-14 (14)	17.65	51.40
		Set, never hinged	50.00	

Overprinted

15	A16	5pf green	.40	1.00
16	A16	10pf carmine	.40	1.00
17	A22	15pf dark vio	.40	1.00
18	A22	15pf vio brn	20.00	40.00
19	A16	20pf blue vio	.65	1.50
20	A16	30pf org & blk, buff	.40	1.00
21	A16	40pf lake & blk	.40	1.00
22	A16	50pf pur & blk, buff	.40	1.00
23	A16	75pf grn & blk	.65	1.50
24	A17	1m car rose	1.60	3.00
a.		Inverted overprint	600.00	800.00
		Never hinged	800.00	
25	A17	1.25m green	1.60	3.00
26	A17	1.50m yel brn	1.25	3.00
27	A21	2.50m lilac rose	2.75	7.50
28	A19	3m blk vio	1.75	3.00
a.		Inverted overprint	400.00	975.00
		Never hinged	725.00	
b.		Double overprint	200.00	600.00
		Never hinged	600.00	
		Nos. 15-28 (14)	32.65	68.50
		Set, never hinged	75.00	

The 40pf carmine rose (Germany No. 124) exists with this oval overprint, but it is doubtful whether it was regularly issued. Value $105 hinged, $210 never hinged.

ANDORRA, SPANISH ADMINISTRATION

an-'dor-ə

LOCATION — On the southern slope of the Pyrenees Mountains between France and Spain.
GOVT. — Co-principality
AREA — 179 sq. mi.
POP. — 72,766 (July 1, 1996)
CAPITAL — Andorra la Vella

Andorra was subject to the joint control of France and the Spanish Bishop of Urgel and paid annual tribute to both. In 1993, Andorra became a constitutional coprincipality, governed by its own parliament.

100 Centimos = 1 Peseta
100 Centimes = 1 Franc
100 Cents = 1 Euro (2002)

Catalogue values for unused stamps in the Spanish Administration for this country are for Never Hinged items, beginning with Scott 50 in the regular postage section and Scott C2 in the airpost section; for the French Administration of this country, Never Hinged items begin at Scott 78 for regular postage, Scott B1 for the semi-postal section, Scott C1 for the airpost section, and Scott J21 for the postage due section.

A majority of the Spanish Andorra stamps issued to about 1950 are poorly centered. The fine examples that are valued will be somewhat off center. Very poorly centered examples (perfs cutting design) sell for less. Well centered very fine stamps are scarce and sell for approximately twice the values shown (Nos. 1-24, E1-E3), or 50% more (Nos. 25-49, E4-E5).

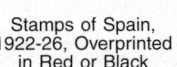

Stamps of Spain, 1922-26, Overprinted in Red or Black

Perf. 13½x12½, 12½x11½, 14

1928   **Unwmk.**

1	A49	2c olive green	.55	.55

Control Numbers on Back

2	A49	5c car rose (Bk)	.80	.80
3	A49	10c green	.80	.80
4	A49	15c slate blue	3.25	3.25
5	A49	20c violet	3.25	3.50
6	A49	25c rose red (Bk)	3.25	3.50
b.		Inverted ovpt., perf 14	160.00	—
7	A49	30c black brown	18.00	16.50
b.		Inverted ovpt., perf 12½x11½	160.00	50.00
8	A49	40c deep blue	18.00	11.00
9	A49	50c orange (Bk)	18.00	14.50
c.		Inverted ovpt., perf 14	160.00	
10	A49a	1p blue blk	23.00	23.50
11	A49a	4p lake	150.00	175.00
12	A49a	10p brown (Bk)	275.00	275.00
a.		Double overprint	1,000.	
		Nos. 1-12 (12)	513.90	527.90
		Set, never hinged	1,200.	

Counterfeit overprints exist.
Nos. 1-12 perf 14 are worth much more. See the *Scott Classic Specialized Catalogue.*

La Vall
A1

St. Juan de Caselles
A2

St. Julia de Loria — A3

St. Coloma — A4

General Council — A5

1929, Nov. 25   **Engr.**   **Perf. 14**

13	A1	2c olive green	1.10	.60

Control Numbers on Back

14	A2	5c carmine lake	3.50	1.25
15	A3	10c yellow green	3.50	4.50
16	A3	15c slate green	3.50	4.50
17	A3	20c violet	3.50	4.50
18	A4	25c carmine rose	7.75	6.25
19	A3	30c olive brown	115.00	175.00
20	A2	40c dark blue	4.50	3.00
21	A3	50c deep orange	5.50	4.50
22	A5	1p slate	12.50	14.50
23	A5	4p deep rose	90.00	110.00
24	A5	10p bister brown	100.00	140.00
		Nos. 13-24 (12)	350.35	468.60
		Set, never hinged	800.00	

Nos. 13-24 exist imperforate. Value, $950.

1931-38   **Perf. 11½**

13a	A1	2c	6.25	.80

Control Numbers on Back

14a	A2	5c	10.00	2.25
15a	A3	10c	10.00	2.00
16a	A4	15c	30.00	25.00
17a	A3	20c	10.00	6.00
18a	A4	25c	10.00	6.00
19a	A1	30c ('33)	175.00	65.00
20a	A2	40c ('35)	17.00	13.00
22a	A5	1p ('38)	40.00	25.00
		Nos. 13a-22a (9)	308.25	145.05
		Set, never hinged	500.00	

Without Control Numbers

1936-43   **Perf. 11½x11**

25	A1	2c red brown ('37)	2.00	1.60
26	A2	5c dark brown	2.00	1.60
27	A3	10c blue green	13.00	3.25
a.		10c yellow green	120.00	62.50
		Never hinged	165.00	
28	A4	15c blue green ('37)	7.50	3.50
a.		15c yellow green	8.00	5.75
29	A3	20c violet	7.00	3.50
30	A4	25c deep rose ('37)	3.25	3.25
31	A1	30c carmine	5.50	3.25
31A	A2	40c dark blue	700.00	—
		Never hinged	1,200.	
32	A1	45c rose red ('37)	2.00	1.60
33	A3	50c deep orange	10.00	5.75
34	A1	60c deep blue ('37)	7.00	3.50
34A	A5	1p slate	800.00	
		Never hinged	1,500.	
35	A5	4p deep rose ('43)	40.00	47.50
36	A5	10p bister brn ('43)	57.50	57.50
		Nos. 25-31,32-34,35-36 (12)	151.75	135.80
		Set, never hinged	325.00	

Exist imperforate. Value hinged, $290.
Beware of counterfeits of Nos. 31A and 34A. Purchase of stamps with certificates is strongly advised.

Edelweiss — A6

Provost — A7

Coat of Arms — A8

Plaza of Ordino — A9

Chapel of Meritxell — A10

Map — A11

1948-53   **Unwmk. Photo.**   **Perf. 12½**

37	A6	2c dark ol grn ('51)	.35	.35
38	A6	5c deep org ('53)	.35	.35
39	A6	10c deep blue ('53)	.35	.35

		Engr.	**Perf. 9½x10**	
40	A7	20c brown vio	4.25	2.75
41	A7	25c org, perf. 12½ ('53)	3.00	2.10
42	A8	30c dk slate grn	4.25	3.25
43	A9	50c deep green	5.00	4.75
44	A10	75c dark blue	6.50	4.75
45	A9	90c dp car rose	3.50	3.50
46	A11	1p brt orange ver	5.00	4.25
47	A8	1.35p dk blue vio	3.50	3.50

			Perf. 10	
48	A11	4p ultra ('53)	4.75	8.50
49	A11	10p dk vio brn ('51)	11.00	11.00
		Nos. 37-49 (13)	51.80	49.40
		Set, never hinged	120.00	

Catalogue values for unused stamps in this section, from this point to the end of the section, are for Never Hinged items.

Bridge of St. Anthony — A12

Madonna of Meritxell, 8th Century — A13

Designs: 70c, Aynos pasture. 1p, View of Canillo. 2p, St. Coloma. 2.50p, Arms of Andorra. 3p, Old Andorra, horiz. 5p, View of Ordino, horiz.

1963-64   **Unwmk. Engr.**   **Perf. 13**

50	A12	25c dk gray & sepia	.25	.25
51	A12	70c dk sl grn & brn blk	.35	.35
52	A12	1p slate & dull pur	.45	.45
53	A12	2p violet & dull pur	.50	.50
54	A12	2.50p rose claret	.70	.70
55	A12	3p blk & grnsh gray	1.10	.80
56	A12	5p dk brn & choc	2.00	1.25
57	A13	6p sepia & car	2.75	2.75
		Nos. 50-57 (8)	8.10	7.05

Issued: 25c-2p, 7/20/63; 2.50p-6p, 2/29/64.

Narcissus — A14

1966, June 10   **Engr.**   **Perf. 13**

58	A14	50c shown	.50	.50
59	A14	1p Pinks	.50	.50
60	A14	5p Jonquils	1.50	1.50
61	A14	10p Hellebore	1.00	1.00
		Nos. 58-61 (4)	3.50	3.50

Common Design Types pictured following the introduction.

Europa Issue 1972
Common Design Type

1972, May 2   **Photo.**   **Perf. 13**
Size: 25½x38mm

62	CD15	8p multicolored	45.00	45.00

Encamp Valley — A15

Tourist publicity: 1.50p, Massana (village). 2p, Skiing on De La Casa Pass. 5p, Pessons Lake, horiz.

1972, July 4   **Photo.**   **Perf. 13**

63	A15	1p multicolored	.35	.35
64	A15	1.50p multicolored	.45	.40
65	A15	2p multicolored	1.30	1.00
66	A15	5p multicolored	1.75	1.10
		Nos. 63-66 (4)	3.85	2.85

Butterfly Stroke A16

Design: 2p, Volleyball, vert.

1972, Oct.   **Photo.**   **Perf. 13**

67	A16	2p lt blue & multi	.40	.40
68	A16	5p multicolored	.60	.60

20th Olympic Games, Munich, 8/26-9/11.

St. Anthony Singers A17

1.50p, Les Caramelles (boys' choir). 2p, Nativity scene. 5p, Man holding giant cigar, vert. 8p, Hermit of Meritxell, vert. 15p, Marratxa dancers.

1972, Dec. 5   **Photo.**   **Perf. 13**

69	A17	1p multicolored	.25	.25
70	A17	1.50p multicolored	.25	.25
71	A17	2p multicolored	.35	.35
72	A17	5p multicolored	.45	.45
73	A17	8p multicolored	.65	.50
74	A17	15p multicolored	1.35	1.10
		Nos. 69-74 (6)	3.30	2.90

Andorran customs. No. 71 is for Christmas.

Europa Issue 1973
Common Design Type and

Symbol of Unity A18

1973, Apr. 30   **Photo.**   **Perf. 13**

75	A18	2p ultra, red & blk	.30	.25

Size: 37x25mm

76	CD16	8p tan, red & blk	.65	.55

Nativity — A19

Christmas: 5p, Adoration of the Kings. Designs are from altar panels of Meritxell Parish Church.

1973, Dec. 14   **Photo.**   **Perf. 13**

77	A19	2p multicolored	.30	.30
78	A19	5p multicolored	1.00	1.00

Virgin of Ordino — A20

Europa: 8p, Les Banyes Cross.

1974, Apr. 29　　Photo.　　Perf. 13
79　A20　2p multicolored　　　　.90　.70
80　A20　8p slate & brt blue　　2.75　1.75

Cupboard — A21　　Crowns of Virgin and Child of Roser — A22

1974, July 30　　Photo.　　Perf. 13
81　A21　10p multicolored　　　1.75　1.60
82　A22　25p dark red & multi　3.75　3.25

UPU Monument, Bern A23

1974, Oct. 9　　Photo.　　Perf. 13
83　A23　15p multicolored　　　1.40　1.40
Centenary of Universal Postal Union.

Nativity A24

Christmas: 5p, Adoration of the Kings.

1974, Dec. 4　　Photo.　　Perf. 13
84　A24　2p multicolored　　　　.90　.80
85　A24　5p multicolored　　　2.10　1.75

Mail Delivery, Andorra, 19th Century — A25

1975, Apr. 4　　Photo.　　Perf. 13
86　A25　3p multicolored　　　　.45　.45
Espana 75 Intl. Philatelic Exhibition, Madrid, 4/4-13.

12th Century Painting, Ordino Church — A26

Design: 12p, Christ in Glory, 12th century Romanesque painting, Ordino church.

1975, Apr. 28　　Photo.　　Perf. 13
87　A26　3p multicolored　　　1.25　.70
88　A26　12p multicolored　　2.25　1.40

Urgel Cathedral and Document — A27

1975, Oct. 4　　Photo.　　Perf. 13
89　A27　7p multicolored　　　1.35　1.10
Millennium of consecration of Urgel Cathedral, and Literary Festival 1975.

Nativity, Ordino A28

Christmas: 7p, Adoration of the Kings, Ordino.

1975, Dec. 3　　Photo.　　Perf. 13
90　A28　3p multicolored　　　　.40　.40
91　A28　7p multicolored　　　　.85　.85

Caldron and CEPT Emblem — A29

Europa: 12p, Chest and CEPT emblem.

1976, May 3　　Photo.　　Perf. 13
92　A29　3p bister & multi　　　　.30　.25
93　A29　12p yel & multi, horiz.　.90　.30

Slalom and Montreal Olympic Emblem — A30

Design: 15p, One-man canoe and Montreal Olympic emblem, horiz.

1976, July 9　　Photo.　　Perf. 13
94　A30　7p multicolored　　　　.45　.25
95　A30　15p multicolored　　　　.90　.35
21st Olympic Games, Montreal, Canada, July 17-Aug. 1.

Nativity A31

Christmas: 25p, Adoration of the Kings. Wall paintings in La Massana Church.

1976, Dec. 7　　Photo.　　Perf. 13
96　A31　3p multicolored　　　　.55　.25
97　A31　25p multicolored　　　1.10　.35

View of Ansalonge — A32

Europa: 12p, Xuclar, valley, mountains.

1977, May 2　　Litho.　　Perf. 13
98　A32　3p multicolored　　　　.35　.25
99　A32　12p multicolored　　　　.90　.25

Cross of Terme — A33

Christmas: 12p, Church of St. Miguel d'Engolasters.

1977, Dec. 2　　Photo.　　Perf. 13x12½
100　A33　5p multicolored　　　　.45　.35
101　A33　12p multicolored　　　1.10　.65

Souvenir Sheet

A34

Designs: 5p, Map of Post Offices. 10p, Mail delivery. 20p, Post Office, 1928. 25p, Andorran coat of arms.

1978, Mar. 31　　Photo.　　Perf. 13x13½
102　A34　Sheet of 4　　　　　1.40　1.40
　a.　5p multicolored　　　　　.30　.30
　b.　10p multicolored　　　　　.30　.30
　c.　20p multicolored　　　　　.30　.30
　d.　25p multicolored　　　　　.30　.30
Spanish postal service in Andorra, 50th anniv.

La Vall — A35

Europa: 12p, St. Juan de Caselles.

1978, May 2　　　　　　　　Perf. 13
103　A35　5p multicolored　　　　.25　.25
104　A35　12p multicolored　　　　.80　.25

Crown, Bishop's Mitre and Staff A36

1978, Sept. 24　　Photo.　　Perf. 13
105　A36　5p brown, car & yel　　.65　.30
700th anniversary of the signing of treaty establishing Co-Principality of Andorra.

Holy Family — A37

Christmas: 25p, Adoration of the Kings. Both designs after frescoes in the Church of St. Mary d'Encamp.

1978, Dec. 5　　Photo.　　Perf. 13
106　A37　5p multicolored　　　　.25　.25
107　A37　25p multicolored　　　　.60　.30

Young Woman — A38

Designs: 5p, Young man. 12p, Bridegroom and bride riding mule.

1979, Feb. 14　　Photo.　　Perf. 13
108　A38　3p multicolored　　　　.25　.25
109　A38　5p multicolored　　　　.25　.25
110　A38　12p multicolored　　　　.25　.25
　　Nos. 108-110 (3)　　　　　.75　.75

Old Mail Truck A39

Europa: 12p, Stampless covers of 1846 & 1854.

1979, Apr. 30　　Engr.　　Perf. 13
111　A39　5p yel grn & dk blue　　.30　.25
112　A39　12p dk red & violet　　　.60　.25

Children Holding Hands A40

1979, Oct. 18　　Photo.　　Perf. 13
113　A40　19p multicolored　　　　.80　.30
International Year of the Child.

St. Coloma's Church — A41

Christmas: 25p, Agnus Dei roundel, St. Coloma's Church.

1979, Nov. 28   Photo.   Perf. 13½
114 A41 8p multicolored   .25 .25
115 A41 25p multicolored   .35 .25

Bishop Pere d'Arg A42

Bishops of Urgel: 5p, Josep Caixal. 13p, Joan Benlloch.

1979, Dec. 27   Engr.
116 A42 1p dk blue & brown   .25 .25
117 A42 5p rose lake & purple   .25 .25
118 A42 13p brown & dk green   .25 .25
        Nos. 116-118 (3)   .75 .75

See Nos. 132-133, 159, 175, C4.

Antoni Fiter, Magistrate — A43

Europa: 19p, Francesc Cairat, magistrate.

1980, Apr. 28   Photo.   Perf. 13x13½
119 A43 8p bister, blk & brn   .35 .25
120 A43 19p lt green & blk   .70 .25

Boxing, Moscow '80 Emblem A44

1980, July 23   Photo.   Perf. 13½x13
121 A44 5p Downhill skiing   .25 .25
122 A44 8p shown   .25 .25
123 A44 50p Target shooting   .80 .35
        Nos. 121-123 (3)   1.30 .85

12th Winter Olympic Games, Lake Placid, NY, Feb. 12-24 (5p); 22nd Summer Olympic Games, Moscow, July 19-Aug. 3.

Nativity A45

1980, Dec. 12   Litho.   Perf. 13
124 A45 10p Nativity, vert.   .25 .25
125 A45 22p shown   .50 .25

Christmas 1980.

Children Dancing at Santa Anna Feast A46

Europa: 30p, Going to church on Aplec de la Verge de Canolich Day.

1981, May 7   Photo.   Perf. 13
126 A46 12p multicolored   .25 .25
127 A46 30p multicolored   .65 .30

50th Anniv. of Police Force A47

1981, July 2   Photo.   Perf. 13½x13
128 A47 30p multicolored   .80 .25

Intl. Year of the Disabled A48

1981, Oct. 8   Photo.   Perf. 13½
129 A48 50p multicolored   1.10 .40

Christmas 1981 A49

Designs: Encamp Church retable.

1981, Dec. 3   Photo.   Perf. 13½
130 A49 12p Nativity   .30 .25
131 A49 30p Adoration   .50 .45

Bishops of Urgel Type of 1979

1981, Dec. 12   Engr.
132 A42 7p Salvador Casanas   .30 .25
133 A42 20p Josep de Boltas   .55 .25

Natl. Arms — A51

1982, Feb. 17   Photo.   Perf. 13x13½
134 A51 1p bright pink   .25 .25
135 A51 3p bister brown   .25 .25
136 A51 7p red orange   .25 .25
137 A51 12p lake   .25 .25
138 A51 15p ultra   .30 .25
139 A51 20p blue green   .35 .25
140 A51 30p crimson rose   .45 .25

Perf. 13½x12½
1982, Sept. 30   Engr.
Size: 25½x30½mm
141 A51 50p dark green   .90 .25
142 A51 100p dark blue   1.50 .60
        Nos. 134-142 (9)   4.50 2.60

For type A51 without "PTA" see Nos. 192-198.

Europa 1982 A52

14p, New Reforms, 1866, vert. 33p, Reform of Institutions, 1981.

1982, May 12   Photo.   Perf. 13
143 A52 14p multicolored   .30 .25
144 A52 33p multicolored   .80 .25

1982 World Cup — A53

Designs: Various soccer players.

1982, June 13   Photo.   Perf. 13x13½
145 A53 14p multicolored   .90 .90
146 A53 33p multicolored   1.60 1.60
    a. Pair, #145-146 + label   2.75 2.75

A54

Anniversaries: 9p, Permanent Spanish and French delegations, cent. 14p, 50th anniv. of Andorran stamps, horiz. 23p, St. Francis of Assisi (1182-1226). 33p, Anyos Pro-Vicarial District membership centenary (Relacio sobre la Vall de Andorra titlepage).

1982, Sept. 7   Engr.   Perf. 13
147 A54 9p dk blue & brown   .25 .25
148 A54 14p black & green   .45 .25
149 A54 23p dk blue & brown   .30 .25
150 A54 33p black & olive grn   .50 .35
        Nos. 147-150 (4)   1.50 1.10

A55

A55a

Christmas: 14p, Madonna and Child, Andorra la Vieille Church, vert. 33p, El Tio de Nadal (children in traditional costumes striking hollow tree).

Perf. 13x13½, 13½x13
1982, Dec. 9   Photo.
151 A55 14p multicolored   .35 .25
152 A55a 33p multicolored   .60 .30

Europa 1983 A56

16, La Cortinada Church, architect, 12th cent. 38p, Water mill, 16th cent.

1983, June 7   Photo.   Perf. 13
153 A56 16p multicolored   .40 .25
154 A56 38p multicolored   .80 .35

Local Mushrooms — A57

16p, Lactarius sanguifluus.

1983, July 20   Photo.   Perf. 13x12½
155 A57 16p multicolored   .80 .60

See Nos. 165, 169, 172.

Universal Suffrage, 50th Anniv. A58

Photogravure and Engraved
1983, Sept. 6   Perf. 13
156 A58 10p multicolored   .30 .25

Visit of Monsignor Jacinto Verdaguer Bishop and Co-Prince A59

1983, Sept. 6
157 A59 50p multicolored   .85 .55

Christmas 1983 — A60

Saint Cerni de Nagol, Romanesque fresco, Church of San Cerni de Nagol.

1983, Nov. 24   Photo.   Perf. 13½
158 A60 16p multicolored   .45 .25

Bishops of Urgel Type of 1979

26p, Joan J. Laguarda Fenollera.

1983, Dec. 7   Engr.   Perf. 13
159 A42 26p multicolored   .45 .25

1984 Winter Olympics A62

1984, Feb. 17   Litho.   Perf. 13½x14
160 A62 16p Ski jumping   .80 .25

ESPANA '84 — A63

1984, Apr. 27   Photo.   Perf. 13
161 A63 26p Emblems   .50 .25

Europa
(1959-84)
A64

1984, May 5   **Engr.**
162 A64 16p brown   .55 .25
163 A64 38p blue   .80 .35

1984
Summer
Olympics
A65

1984, Aug. 9   **Litho.**   **Perf. 13½x14**
164 A65 40p Running   .85 .40

Mushroom Type of 1983

11p, Morchella esculenta.

1984, Sept. 27   **Photo.**   **Perf. 13x12½**
165 A57 11p multicolored   7.25 2.00

Christmas
1984
A66

1984, Dec. 6   **Photo.**   **Perf. 13½**
166 A66 17p Nativity carving   .50 .25

Europa
1985
A67

18p, Mossen Enric Arfany, composer, natl. hymn score. 45p, Musician Playing Viol, Romanesque fresco detail, La Cortinada Church, vert.

1985, May 3   **Engr.**   **Perf. 13½**
167 A67 18p dk vio, grn & choco-
     late   .45 .25
168 A67 45p green & chocolate   1.40 .35

Mushroom Type of 1983
Perf. 13½x12½
1985, Sept. 19   **Photo.**
169 A57 30p Gyromitra esculenta 1.10 .25

Pal Village — A68

1985, Nov. 7   **Engr.**   **Perf. 13½**
170 A68 17p brt ultra & dk blue   .50 .25

Christmas
1985
A69

Fresco: Angels Playing Trumpet and Psaltery, St. Bartholomew Chapel.

1985, Dec. 11   **Photo.**   **Perf. 13½x13**
171 A69 17p multicolored   .50 .25

Mushroom Type of 1983
Perf. 13½x12½
1986, Apr. 10   **Photo.**
172 A57 30p Marasmius oreades   .70 .25

Europa
1986 — A70

1986, May 5   **Engr.**   **Perf. 13**
173 A70 17p Water   .35 .25
174 A70 45p Soil and air   1.50 .25

Bishops of Urgel Type of 1979
1986, Sept. 11   **Engr.**   **Perf. 13½**
175 A42 35p Justi Guitart   .55 .25

Christmas — A72

Santa Roma de Les Bons Church bell.

1986, Dec. 11   **Litho.**   **Perf. 14**
176 A72 19p multicolored   .50 .25

A73

Contemporary Natl. Coat of Arms.

1987, Mar. 27   **Photo.**   **Perf. 14**
177 A73 48p multicolored   .90 .30

Visit of the co-princes: the Bishop of Urgel and president of France, September 26, 1986.

Europa
1987
A74

Modern architecture: 19p, Meritxell Sanctuary interior. 48p, Sanctuary exterior, vert.

1987, May 15   **Engr.**   **Perf. 14x13½**
178 A74 19p dark blue & brown   .35 .25
179 A74 48p dark blue & brown   1.60 .25

Souvenir Sheet

1992 Summer Olympics,
Barcelona — A75

20p, House of the Valleys. 50p, Bell tower, Chapel of the Archangel Michael, and torch-bearer.

1987, July 20   **Photo.**   **Perf. 14**
180 A75   Sheet of 2   3.00 3.00
   a.   20p multicolored   .90 .90
   b.   50p multicolored   1.75 1.75

Local
Mushrooms — A76

1987, Sept. 11   **Perf. 13½x12½**
181 A76 100p Boletus edulis   2.25 .60

Christmas
A77

Design: Detail from a Catalan manuscript, De Nativitat, by R. Llull.

1987, Nov. 18   **Litho.**   **Perf. 14**
182 A77 20p multicolored   .50 .25

Lance and
Arrowhead
(Bronze
Age)
A78

1988, Mar. 25   **Photo.**   **Perf. 14**
183 A78 50p multicolored   .90 .30

Europa
1988 — A79

Transport and communications: 20p, Les Bons, a medieval road. 45p, Trader and pack mules, early 20th cent.

1988, May 5   **Engr.**   **Perf. 14x13½**
184 A79 20p dark bl & dark red   .45 .25
185 A79 45p dark bl & dark red   1.50 .25

Pyrenean
Mastiff — A80

1988, July 26   **Litho.**   **Perf. 14x13½**
186 A80 20p multicolored   .80 .25

Bishop of Urgel
and Seigneur of
Caboet Confirming
Co-Principality,
700th
Anniv. — A81

1988, Oct. 24   **Litho.**   **Perf. 14x13½**
187 A81 20p gold, blk & int blue   .50 .25

Christmas
1988
A82

1988, Nov. 30   **Litho.**   **Perf. 14x13½**
188 A82 20p multicolored   .30 .25

Arms Type of 1982 Without "PTA"
1988, Dec. 2   **Photo.**   **Perf. 13x13½**
192 A51 20p brt blue green   .45 .25
Size: 25x30½mm
Perf. 13½x12½
Engr.
194 A51 50p grnsh black   .90 .25
196 A51 100p dark blue   1.90 .40
198 A51 500p dark brown   7.75 2.00
   Nos. 192-198 (4)   11.00 2.90

Europa
1989
A83

Perf. 14x13½, 13½x14
1989, May 8   **Litho. & Engr.**
200 A83 20p Leapfrog, vert.   .55 .25
201 A83 45p Tug of war   1.50 .25

Santa
Roma
Church,
Les Bons
A84

Litho. & Engr.
1989, June 20   **Perf. 13½x14**
202 A84 50p blk, dp bl & grn bl   1.10 .25

Anniv.
Emblem — A85

1989, Oct. 26   **Litho.**   **Perf. 14x13½**
203 A85 20p multicolored   .70 .25

Intl. Red Cross and Red Crescent societies, 125th annivs.; Year for the Protection of Human Life.

Christmas — A86

The Immaculate Conception.

1989, Dec. 1
204 A86 20p multicolored   .50 .25

Europa
1990
A87

Post offices.

Perf. 13½x14, 14x13½
1990, May 17 **Photo.**
205 A87 20p shown .55 .25
206 A87 50p Post office, vert. 1.40 .25

Gomphidius
Rutilus — A88

1990, June 21 **Litho.** **Perf. 13x13½**
207 A88 45p multicolored 1.10 .35

Plandolit
House — A89

Litho. & Engr.
1990, Oct. 17 **Perf. 13x12½**
208 A89 20p brown & org yel .50 .25

Christmas — A90

1990, Nov. 26 **Litho.** **Perf. 14x13½**
209 A90 25p lake, brn & bister .50 .25

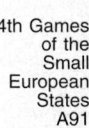

4th Games
of the
Small
European
States
A91

1991, Apr. 29 **Photo.** **Perf. 13½x14**
210 A91 25p Discus .55 .25
211 A91 45p High jump, runner .90 .30

Europa — A92

Perf. 14x13½, 13½x14
1991, May 10 **Litho.**
212 A92 25p Olympus-1 satellite .70 .25
213 A92 55p Olympus-1, horiz. 2.50 .35

Macrolepiota
Procera — A93

1991, Sept. 20 **Litho.** **Perf. 13x12½**
214 A93 45p multicolored 1.10 .30

Christmas — A94

1991, Nov. 29 **Photo.** **Perf. 14x13½**
215 A94 25p multicolored .75 .25

Woman
Carrying
Water Pails
A95

1992, Feb. 14 **Photo.** **Perf. 13½x14**
216 A95 25p multicolored .50 .25

European
Discovery
of America,
500th
Anniv.
A96

Perf. 14x13½, 13½x14
1992, May 8 **Photo.**
217 A96 27p Santa Maria, vert. .65 .25
218 A96 45p King Ferdinand 2.25 .30

Europa.

1992
Summer
Olympics,
Barcelona
A97

1992, July 22 **Photo.** **Perf. 13½x14**
219 A97 27p Kayak .80 .25

Nativity Scene, by
Fra
Angelico — A98

1992, Nov. 18 **Photo.** **Perf. 14**
220 A98 27p multicolored .50 .25

Natl.
Automobile
Museum
A99

Litho. & Engr.
1992, Sept. 10 **Perf. 13½x14**
221 A99 27p 1894 Benz 1.00 .25

Cantharellus Cibarius — A100

1993, Mar. 25 **Photo.** **Perf. 13½x14**
222 A100 28p multicolored .75 .40

Contemporary Paintings — A101

Europa: 28p, Upstream, by John Alan Morrison. 45p, Rhythm, by Angel Calvente, vert.

Perf. 13½x14, 14x13½
1993, May 20 **Litho.**
223 A101 28p multicolored .55 .25
224 A101 45p multicolored 1.10 .35

Art and Literature
Society, 25th
Anniv. — A102

1993, Sept. 23 **Litho.** **Perf. 14**
225 A102 28p multicolored .75 .25

Christmas — A103

Litho. & Engr.
1993, Nov. 25 **Perf. 14x13½**
226 A103 28p multicolored .55 .25

Souvenir Sheet

Constitution, 1st Anniv. — A104

1994, Mar. 14 **Photo.** **Perf. 14**
227 A104 29p multicolored .75 .50

Sir Alexander Fleming (1881-1955),
Co-discoverer of Penicillin — A105

1994, May 6 **Photo.** **Perf. 13½x14**
228 A105 29p Portrait .50 .30
229 A105 55p AIDS virus 1.40 .60

Europa.

Hygrophorus Gliocyclus — A106

1994, Sept. 27 **Photo.** **Perf. 14**
230 A106 29p multicolored .75 .50

Christmas — A107

1994, Nov. 29 **Photo.** **Perf. 14x13½**
231 A107 29p multicolored .75 .50

Nature Conservation in
Europe — A108

1995, Mar. 23 **Photo.** **Perf. 14**
232 A108 30p Farm in valley .70 .45
233 A108 60p Stone fence, valley 1.35 .75

Europa
A109

1995, May 8 **Photo.** **Perf. 14**
234 A109 60p multicolored 1.60 .70

Christmas — A110

1995, Nov. 8 **Photo.** **Perf. 14**
235 A110 30p Flight to Egypt .65 .35

Entrance
Into
Council of
Europe
A111

1995, Nov. 10
236 A111 30p multicolored 1.10 .35

Mushrooms — A112

30p, Ramaria aurea. 60p, Tuber melanosporum.

1996, Apr. 30   **Photo.**   *Perf. 14*
237 A112 30p multicolored   .90   .35
238 A112 60p multicolored   1.60   .80

Isabelle Sandy (1884-1975), Writer — A113

1996, May 7
239 A113 60p brown & violet   1.50   .65

Europa.

Intl. Museum Day A114

Design: Antique coal-heated iron.

1996, Sept. 12   **Photo.**   *Perf. 14*
240 A114 60p multicolored   .90   .55

Christmas A115

The Annunciation, by Andrew Martin, 1753, St. Eulalia d'Encamp Church.

1996, Nov. 26   **Photo.**   *Perf. 14*
241 A115 30p multicolored   .75   .35

Museums of Andorra A116

Early bicycles designed by: 32p, Karl Drais, 1818. 65p, Pierre Michaux, 1861.

1997, Apr. 28   **Photo.**   *Perf. 14*
242 A116 32p multicolored   .45   .35
243 A116 65p multicolored   .90   .70

See Nos. 248-249.

A117

Europa (Stories and Legends): Hikers watching family of bears crossing over river on fallen tree.

1997, May 6   **Photo.**   *Perf. 14*
244 A117 65p multicolored   1.25   .50

UNESCO — A118

1997, Sept. 30   **Photo.**   *Perf. 14*
245 A118 32p multicolored   .70   .35

Christmas — A119

1997, Nov. 25   **Photo.**   *Perf. 14*
246 A119 32p multicolored   .60   .35

1998 Winter Olympic Games, Nagano A120

1998, Feb. 23   **Photo.**   *Perf. 14*
247 A120 35p Slalom skier   .60   .35

Museums of Andorra Type of 1997

Early bicycles: 35p, Kangaroo, 1878. 70p, Hirondelle, 1889.

1998, Apr. 24   **Photo.**   *Perf. 13½x14*
248 A116 35p multicolored   .55   .35
249 A116 70p multicolored   1.10   .70

Harlequins, Canillas Carnival A121

1998, May 22   **Photo.**   *Perf. 14*
250 A121 70p multicolored   1.35   .70

Europa.

Manual Digest, 250th Anniv. — A122

1998, Sept. 30   **Photo.**   *Perf. 14*
251 A122 35p multicolored   .60   .40

Inauguration of the Postal Museum of Andorra — A123

1998, Nov. 19   **Photo.**   *Perf. 14*
252 A123 70p multicolored   1.10   .75

Christmas A124

1998, Nov. 26
253 A124 35p multicolored   .75   .40

Museums of Andorra A125

Early bicycles designed by: 35p, Salvo, 1878, vert. 70p, Rudge, 1883.

1999, Jan. 29   **Photo.**   *Perf. 14*
254 A125 35p multicolored   .70   .40
255 A125 70p multicolored   1.10   .75

Council of Europe, 50th Anniv. A126

1999, Apr. 29   **Photo.**   *Perf. 14*
256 A126 35p multicolored   .70   .35

Incles Valley A127

1999, May 6
257 A127 70p multicolored   1.60   .80

Europa.

Transporting Mail on Horseback — A128

1999, Feb. 18   **Photo.**   *Perf. 14*
258 A128 35p black & sepia   .60   .40

Restoration of Casa Rull, Sispony, La Massana A129

1999, Sept. 22   **Photo.**   *Perf. 13½x14*
259 A129 35p multicolored   .45   .35

Christmas — A130

1999, Nov. 10   **Engr.**   *Perf. 14x13½*
260 A130 35p orange brn & brn   .60   .35

St. Coloma's Church — A131

1999, Nov. 12   **Photo.**
261 A131 35p multicolored   .60   .35

European heritage.

Europa, 2000
Common Design Type

2000, May 11   **Photo.**   *Perf. 13¾*
262 CD17 70p multicolored   1.60   .70

Angonella Lakes A132

2000, June 29   **Photo.**   *Perf. 13¾x14*
263 A132 35p multicolored   .65   .35

Casa Lacruz A133

2000, July 20   **Photo.**   *Perf. 13¾x14*
264 A133 35p multicolored   .65   .35

China, Areny-Plandolit Museum — A134

2000, July 27   *Perf. 14x13¾*
265 A134 70p multicolored   1.35   .70

2000 Summer Olympics, Sydney — A135

2000, Sept. 29   **Photo.**   *Perf. 14x13½*
266 A135 70p multicolored   1.35   .65

European Convention on Human Rights, 50th Anniv. A136

2000, Nov. 3 *Perf. 13½x14*
267 A136 70p multicolored 1.35 .65

Natl. Archives, 25th Anniv. — A137

2000, Nov. 14 *Perf. 14x13½*
268 A137 35p multicolored .60 .30

Christmas — A138

2000, Nov. 22
269 A138 35p multicolored .75 .30

Rec de Solà — A139

2001, Mar. 30 Photo. *Perf. 14x13¾*
270 A139 40p multicolored .60 .60

Europa A140

2001, May 16 *Perf. 13¾x14*
271 A140 75p multicolored 1.35 .85

Casa Palau, Sant Julià de Lòria — A141

2001, June 20 Photo. *Perf. 14x13¾*
272 A141 75p multi 1.00 1.10

Chapel of the Virgin of Meritxell, 25th Anniv. of Rebuilding — A142

2001, Sept. 7 Photo. *Perf. 14x13¾*
273 A142 40p multi .65 .60

Natl. Auditorium, 10th Anniv. A143

2001, Sept. 20 *Perf. 13¾x14*
274 A143 75p multi 1.35 1.00

Christmas A144

2001, Nov. 20 Photo. *Perf. 13¾x14*
275 A144 40p multi .70 .55

100 Cents = 1 Euro (€)

Coat of Arms — A145

2002, Jan. 2 Photo. *Perf. 12¾x13¼*
276 A145 25c brown orange .75 .60
277 A145 50c claret 1.25 1.10

Birds A146

Designs: 25c, Prunella collaris. 50c, Montifringilla nivalis.

2002, Mar. 27 *Perf. 13¾x14*
278-279 A146 Set of 2 2.25 2.00

Intl. Year of Mountains A147

2002, Apr. 5
280 A147 50c multi 1.60 1.10

Europa A148

2002, May 9
281 A148 50c multi 11.50 1.75

Architectural Heritage — A149

Designs: €1.80, Casa Fusilé, Escaldes-Engordany. €2.10, Farga Rossell Centre, La Massana.

2002, June 14 Photo. *Perf. 14x13¾*
282-283 A149 Set of 2 10.00 9.00

Historic Automobiles A150

Designs: 25c, Pinette. 50c, Rolls-Royce, horiz.

2002, Oct. 8 *Perf. 14x13¾, 13¾x14*
284-285 A150 Set of 2 2.25 2.00

Christmas A151

2002, Nov. 26 *Perf. 13¾x14*
286 A151 25c multi .80 .70

Artistic Heritage — A152

Various religious murals from Santa Coloma Church: a, 25c. b, 75c. c, 50c.

2002, Nov. 28 *Perf. 14x13¾*
287 A152 Horiz. strip of 3, #a-c 4.00 3.50

Sassanat Bridge A153

Perf. 13½x13¾
2003, Feb. 27 Photo.
288 A153 26c multi .70 .60

Constitution, 10th Anniv. — A154

2003, Mar. 14 Photo. *Perf. 13¾x14*
289 A154 76c multi 2.00 1.75

Europa — A155

2003, Apr. 24 *Perf. 14x13¾*
290 A155 76c multi 2.00 1.10

Oenanthe Oenanthe — A156

2003, June 11 Photo. *Perf. 14x13¾*
291 A156 26c multi .70 .60

Admission to United Nations, 10th Anniv. A157

2003, July 28 Photo. *Perf. 13¾x14*
292 A157 76c multi 2.00 1.75

Automobiles — A158

Designs: 51c, 1908 Carter, vert. 76c, 1928 Peugeot.

2003, Oct. 15 *Perf. 14x13¾, 13¾x14*
293-294 A158 Set of 2 7.75 7.75

Christmas A159

2003, Nov. 20 *Perf. 13¾x14*
295 A159 26c multi .70 .60

Coat of Arms — A160

2004, Jan. 2 *Perf. 12¾x13¼*
296 A160 27c bright blue .70 .60
297 A160 52c olive green 1.40 1.25
298 A160 77c red orange 2.00 1.75
Nos. 296-298 (3) 4.10 3.60

See Nos. 308-310, 319-320, 327-328.

Art by Joaquim Mir
A161

Designs: 27c, Fira del Bestiar. 52c, L'Escorxador, vert.

2004 *Perf. 13¾x14, 14x13¾*
299-300 A161　Set of 2　2.00 1.75
Issued: 27c, 2/20; 52c, 3/18.

Europa — A162

2004, Apr. 29　Photo.　Perf. 14x13¾
301 A162 77c black　2.00 1.60

Fringilla Coelebs
A163

2004, June 15　Photo.　Perf. 13¾x14
302 A163 27c multi　.70 .60

Automobiles — A164

Designs: €1.90, 1939 Simca 508-C. €2.19, 1955 Messerschmitt KR-1.

2004, Oct. 15　Photo.　Perf. 13¾x14
303-304 A164　Set of 2　11.00 9.50

Postal Code — A165

2004, Oct. 25　Perf. 14x13¾
305 A165 52c multi　1.40 1.25

Admission to Council of Europe, 10th Anniv.
A166

2004, Nov. 10　Perf. 13¾x14
306 A166 52c multi　1.40 1.25

Christmas
A167

2004, Nov. 22
307 A167 27c multi　.75 .75

Arms Type of 2004
2005, Jan. 28　Litho.　Perf. 12¾x13¼
308 A160 28c blue　.70 .65
309 A160 53c yel green　1.35 1.25
310 A160 78c brt pink　2.00 1.75
　　Nos. 308-310 (3)　4.05 3.65

Selection of Madriu-Peralita-Claror Valley as UNESCO World Heritage Site — A168

2005, Mar. 7　Photo.　Perf. 14x13¾
311 A168 28c multi　.70 .70

Endless, Sculpture by Mark Brusse
A169

2005, Mar. 14　Perf. 13¾x14
312 A169 53c multi　1.35 1.35

Europa
A170

2005, Apr. 15　Photo.　Perf. 13¾x14
313 A170 78c multi　2.00 1.60

9th Games of Small European States — A171

2005, May 20　Photo.　Perf. 14x13¾
314 A171 €1.95 multi　5.00 4.25

Caritas Andorra, 25th Anniv. — A172

2005, June 15
315 A172 28c multi　.70 .70

Cinclus Cinclus
A173

2005, July 11　Photo.　Perf. 13¾x14
316 A173 €2.21 multi　5.75 5.75

Christmas
A174

2005, Nov. 2　Photo.　Perf. 13¾x14
317 A174 28c blk & org　.75 .65

2006 Winter Olympics, Turin
A175

2006, Feb. 6
318 A175 29c multi　.75 .70

Arms Type of 2004
2006, Mar. 1　Litho.　Perf. 12¾x13¼
319 A160 29c yel brown　.75 .65
320 A160 57c blue　1.50 1.25

Earth, Fire, Water and Wind, Sculpture by Satoru Sato — A176

2006, Apr. 10　Photo.　Perf. 14x13¾
321 A176 78c multi　2.00 1.75

Europa
A177

2006, May 16　Perf. 13¾x14
322 A177 57c multi　1.45 1.35

Perdix Perdix
A178

2006, June 6
323 A178 €2.39 multi　6.75 6.75

Fulbright Scholarships — A179

2006, Aug. 8　Photo.　Perf. 13¾x14
324 A179 57c multi　1.45 1.45

UNESCO, 60th Anniv., Andorran National UNESCO Committee, 10th Anniv. — A180

2006, Oct. 2　Perf. 14x13¾
325 A180 €2.33 multi　6.75 6.75

Christmas
A181

2006, Nov. 2　Photo.　Perf. 13¾x14
326 A181 29c multi　.75 .75

Arms Type of 2004
2007, Jan. 19　Litho.　Perf. 12¾x13¼
327 A160 30c red　.75 .75
328 A160 58c gray　1.50 1.50

Santa Eulalia d'Encamp Church, by Francesc Galobardes
A182

2007, Feb. 12　Photo.　Perf. 14x13¾
329 A182 30c multi　.75 .75

Europa — A183

2007, Apr. 23　Photo.　Perf. 14x13¾
330 A183 58c multi　1.50 1.50
　Scouting, cent.

Jordino Family, Sculptures by Rachid Khimoune — A184

2007, May 21
331 A184 €2.43 multi　6.25 6.25

Tetrao Urogallus
A185

2007, July 4　Photo.　Perf. 13¾x14
332 A185 €2.49 multi　6.50 6.50

Casa de la Vall, by Francesc
Galobardes — A186

2007, Sept. 10
333 A186 78c multi   2.00 2.00

Andorran
Red Cross,
25th Anniv.
A187

2007, Oct. 15 Photo. *Perf. 13¾x14*
334 A187 30c black & red   .80 .80

Christmas
A188

2007, Nov. 2
335 A188 30c multi   .80 .80

Gypaetus
Barbatus
A189

2008, Jan. 24 Photo. *Perf. 13¾*
336 A189 31c multi   .80 .80

Carro Votiu,
Sculpture by
Jordi
Casamajor
A190

2008, Jan. 24 *Perf. 12¾x13*
337 A190 60c multi   1.60 1.60

Constitution, 15th
Anniv. — A191

2008, Mar. 12 Photo. *Perf. 14x13¾*
338 A191 31c multi   .90 .90

Europa — A192

2008, Apr. 23
339 A192 60c black & deep blue   1.75 1.75

Andorran Science
Society, 25th
Anniv. — A193

2008, May 14
340 A193 78c blue & black   2.25 2.25

Souvenir Sheet

Expo Zaragoza 2008 — A194

2008, June 13 Photo. *Perf. 13¾*
341 A194 €2.60 multi   7.50 7.50

2008 Summer
Olympics,
Beijing — A195

2008, July 8 Litho. *Perf. 14x13¾*
342 A195 60c multi   1.90 1.90

Vall del
Comapedrosa
A196

2008, Sept. 15
343 A196 €2.44 multi   6.25 6.25

Sispony, by Carme Massana — A197

2008, Oct. 13 Photo. *Perf. 12¾*
344 A197 31c multi   .80 .80

La Missa del
Gallo, by Sergi
Mas — A198

2008, Nov. 11
345 A198 31c multi   .80 .80
Christmas.

Narcissus
A199

Die Cut Perf. 13
2009, Jan. 17 Litho.
Self-Adhesive
346 A199 32c multi   .85 .85

Andorran School,
25th
Anniv. — A200

2009, Feb. 9 *Perf. 14x13¾*
347 A200 62c multi   1.60 1.60

Mercè Rodoreda
(1908-83),
Writer — A201

2009, Mar. 6
348 A201 78c black   2.00 2.00

Council of Europe,
60th
Anniv. — A202

2009, Apr. 6 Litho. *Perf. 14x13¾*
349 A202 32c multi   .90 .90

Europa — A203

2009, Apr. 23
350 A203 62c multi   1.75 1.75
Intl. Year of Astronomy.

Souvenir Sheet

Madrid Bridge — A204

2009, May 18 Photo.
351 A204 €2.70 multi   7.00 7.00

Eurasian
Sparrowhawk
A205

2009, Sept. 10 Photo. *Perf. 14x13¾*
352 A205 €2.47 multi   6.75 6.75

Paintings
A206

Designs: 62c, El Tarter, by Francesc
Galobardes. 78c, Contrallum a Canillo, by
Carme Massana.

2009, Oct. 8 Photo. *Perf. 13¾x14*
353-354 A206   Set of 2   4.00 4.00

Christmas
A207

2009, Nov. 2 Litho.
355 A207 32c multi   .95 .95

Pyrenees
Iris
A208

Die Cut Perf. 13
2010, Jan. 12 Litho.
Self-Adhesive
356 A208 34c multi   .95 .95

Jacint Verdaguer
(1845-1902),
Poet — A209

Litho. & Engr.
2010, Feb. 8 *Perf. 14x13¾*
357 A209 64c black & red   1.75 1.75

Paris Bridge, Andorra la Vella — A210

2010, Mar. 5   **Litho.**
358 A210 €2.75 multi   7.50 7.50

Europa — A211

2010, May 6 Photo. *Perf. 13¼x13¾*
359 A211 64c multi   1.75 1.75

Bonfire
A212

2010, June 1 *Perf. 13¾x13¼*
360 A212 64c multi   1.60 1.60

2010 World Cup Soccer Championships, South Africa — A213

2010, June 1
361 A213 78c multi   1.90 1.90

Recycling
A214

Perf. 13¾x13¼
2010, Sept. 6   **Photo.**
362 A214 €2.49 multi   6.50 6.50

Churches — A215

Nos. 363: a, Sant Joan de Caselles Church.
b, Sant Romà de Les Bons Church, horiz.

Perf. 13¼x13, 13x13¼
2010, Oct. 6   **Engr.**
363 A215 78c Sheet of 2, #a-b   4.50 4.50
See Andorra, French Administration No. 679.

Christmas
A216

2010, Nov. 2 Photo. *Perf. 13¾x13¼*
364 A216 34c multi   .95 .95

Escaldes-Engordany Parish, 2011 Capital of Catalan Culture — A217

Die Cut Perf. 13
2011, Jan. 12   **Litho.**
Self-Adhesive
365 A217 35c multi   .95 .95

Miquel Marti i Pol (1929-2003), Writer — A218

2011, Feb. 7 *Perf. 14x13¾*
366 A218 65c black & gray   1.75 1.75

Europa — A219

2011, Apr. 4
367 A219 65c multi   1.90 1.90
Intl. Year of Forests.

Casa Farràs
A220

2011, May 3 *Perf. 13¾x14*
368 A220 80c multi   2.40 2.40

Painted Keystone, Sant Esteve Church
A221

2011, June 1
369 A221 €2.55 multi   7.50 7.50

Venice Biennale
A222

Artwork by: 80c, Helena Guàrdia. €2.55, Francisco Sánchez.

2011, July 1
370-371 A222   Set of 2   9.50 9.50

Equality of the Sexes — A223

2011, Sept. 8 *Perf. 14x13¾*
372 A223 80c multi   2.25 2.25

America Issue, Mailbox
A224

2011, Oct. 11 *Perf. 13¾x14*
373 A224 80c multi   2.25 2.25

Christmas
A225

2011, Nov. 3
374 A225 35c multi   1.00 1.00
a.   Tete-beche pair   2.00 2.00

Rossell Forge Interpretive Center, La Massana, 10th Anniv, — A226

2012, Jan. 9 Litho. *Die Cut Perf. 13*
Self-Adhesive
375 A226 36c multi   .95 .95

Agustí Bartra (1908-82), Poet — A227

2012, Feb. 27 *Perf. 14x13¾*
376 A227 51c black   1.40 1.40

Europa
A228

2012, Apr. 4 *Perf. 13¾x14*
377 A228 70c multi   1.90 1.90

CIAM Building, Escaldes-Engordany — A229

2012, May 3
378 A229 85c multi   2.25 2.25

Wood Carving, Sant Marti de la Cortinada Church, Ordino — A230

2012, June 1 *Perf. 14x13¾*
379 A230 85c multi   2.25 2.25

A231

Art — A232

2012, July 2 *Perf. 13¾x14*
380 A231 €2.90 multi   7.25 7.25
Perf. 14x13¾
381 A232 €2.90 multi   7.25 7.25

Civic Values — A233

2012, Sept. 10 *Perf. 14x13¾*
382 A233 85c multi   2.25 2.25

America Issue,
Cosmological
Legend — A234

2012, Oct. 11
383 A234 85c multi   2.25 2.25

Christmas — A235

2012, Nov. 5
384 A235 36c multi   .95 .95

Salvador Espriu
(1913-85),
Poet — A236

2013, Jan. 10   *Die Cut Perf. 13*
Self-Adhesive
385 A236 37c multi   1.00 1.00

Road Between Andorra and La Seu
d'Urgell, Spain, Cent.
A237

2013, Feb. 21   *Perf. 13¾x14*
386 A237 75c multi   2.00 2.00

Areny-Plandolit
Museum,
Ordino — A238

2013, Mar. 4   *Perf. 14x13¾*
387 A238 52c multi   1.40 1.40

Winter Jazz Festival — A239

2013, Apr. 1   *Perf. 13¼x13¾*
388 A239 €2.72 multi   7.00 7.00

Europa
A240

2013, Apr. 23   *Perf. 13¾x13¼*
389 A240 75c multi   2.00 2.00

Women in Portuguese
Costumes — A241

2013, May 6   *Perf. 13½x13¼*
390 A241 90c multi   2.40 2.40

Casa dels
Russos
A242

2013, June 3
391 A242 75c multi   2.00 2.00

Souvenir Sheet

School Correspondence — A243

Perf. 13¼x13¾
2013, Sept. 16   *Litho.*
392 A243 €2.72 multi   7.50 7.50

Diversity and Anti-
Discrimination — A244

2013, Oct. 3   *Litho.*   *Perf. 13¾x13¼*
393 A244 90c multi   2.50 2.50

A245

Christmas — A246

2013, Nov. 4   *Litho.*   *Perf. 13¼x13¾*
394 A245 37c multi   1.00 1.00
395 A246 75c multi   2.00 2.00

14th Intl. Winter
Road Conference,
Andorra — A247

2014, Jan. 13   *Litho.*   *Perf. 13¼x13¾*
396 A247 38c multi   1.10 1.10

Coat of
Arms — A248

2014, Feb. 3   *Litho.*   *Perf. 13¼x13¾*
397   Vert. strip of 5   4.50 4.50
  a.   A248 1c gray   .25 .25
  b.   A248 2c brown   .25 .25
  c.   A248 5c blue   .25 .25
  d.   A248 50c dull green   1.40 1.40
  e.   A248 €1 red   2.75 2.75

Sculpture by
Samantha
Bosque — A249

2014, Mar. 3   *Litho.*   *Perf. 13¼x13¾*
398 A249 54c multi   1.50 1.50

Closure of
Radio
Andorra,
30th
Anniv.
A250

2014, Apr. 7   *Litho.*   *Perf. 13¾x13¼*
399 A250 92c multi   2.60 2.60

Accordion — A251

2014, Apr. 23   *Litho.*   *Perf. 13¼x13¾*
400 A251 76c multi   2.10 2.10

Europa.

Andorra
Ultra Trail,
Vallnord
A252

2014, June 9   *Litho.*   *Perf. 13¾x13¼*
401 A252 76c red & black   2.10 2.10

Filipinos in
Andorra
A253

2014, July 7   *Litho.*   *Perf. 13¾x13¼*
402 A253 92c multi   2.50 2.50

Intl. Year
of Family
Farming
A254

Perf. 13¾x13¼
2014, Sept. 15   *Litho.*
403 A254 76c multi   2.00 2.00

Souvenir Sheet

Mural in Sant Martí de la Cortinada
Church — A255

2014, Oct. 6   *Litho.*   *Perf. 13¼x13¾*
404 A255 €2.72 multi   6.75 6.75

Christmas
A256

2014, Nov. 5 Litho. Perf. 13¾x13¼
405 A256 38c multi   .95 .95

Casa
Felipó — A257

Perf. 13¼x13¾
2014, Nov. 10   Litho.
406 A257 €2.72 multi   6.75 6.75

Virgin of
Meritxell — A258

2015, Jan. 13 Litho. Perf. 14x13¾
407 A258 A multi   .95 .95
No. 407 sold for 42c on day of issue.

Chamois
A259

2015, Feb. 9 Litho. Perf. 13¾x14
408 A259 €1 multi   2.25 2.25

Higher
Education
in
Andorra,
25th
Anniv.
A260

2015, Mar. 2 Litho. Perf. 13¾x13¼
409 A260 55c multi   1.25 1.25

Europa
A261

2015, Apr. 23 Litho. Perf. 13¾x13¼
410 A261 90c multi   2.10 2.10

Between,
Sculpture
by Agusti
Roqué
A262

2015, May 1 Litho. Perf. 13¾x13¼
411 A262 €2.84 multi   6.50 6.50
Venice Biennale.

2015 World Motorcycling Trial Grand
Prix, Andorra — A263

Perf. 13¾x13¼
2015, June 10   Litho.
412 A263 €1 multi   2.25 2.25

English
Community
in
Andorra — A264

2015, July 8 Litho. Perf. 13¼x13¾
413 A264 90c multi   2.00 2.00

Joan Martí Alanis
(1929-2009),
Bishop of Urgell
and Co-
Prince — A265

2015, Sept. 8 Litho. Perf. 13¼x13¾
414 A265 42c multi   .95 .95

Age of Majority at
18, 30th
Anniv. — A266

2015, Sept. 8 Litho. Perf. 13¾
415 A266 €1 multi   2.25 2.25

Souvenir Sheet

Hotel Rosaleda, Encamp — A267

2015, Oct. 15 Litho. Perf. 13¼x13¾
416 A267 €2.84 multi   6.25 6.25

Christmas
A268

2015, Nov. 2 Litho. Perf. 13¾x13¼
417 A268 42c multi   .95 .95

Dolors Parella i
Fivaller (d. 1855),
Murdered
Baroness — A269

2015, Nov. 4 Litho. Perf. 13¼x13¾
418 A269 90c multi   1.90 1.90

Coat of
Arms — A270

2016, Jan. 13 Litho. Perf. 14x13½
419 A270 A magenta & black   1.00 1.00
No. 419 sold for 45c on day of issue.

Dog from Retable
in Church of Sant
Cristòfol,
d'Anyós — A271

2016, Feb. 9 Litho. Perf. 14x13½
420 A271 €1.30 multi   3.00 3.00

Interpretive Center
for Romanesque
Art, Pal, 10th
Anniv. — A272

2016, Mar. 2 Litho. Perf. 13¼x13¾
421 A272 57c multi   1.25 1.25
No. 421 has two die cut openings in the
interior of the arches.

Europa
A273

2016, Apr. 22 Litho. Perf. 13¾x13¼
422 A273 €1.15 multi   2.75 2.75
Think Green Issue.

Anima Compartida, by Joan
Xandri — A274

2016, May 11 Litho. Perf. 13¾x13¼
423 A274 €2.95 multi   6.75 6.75
2015 Venice Biennale.

Andorra la Vella, 2016 Ibero-American
Capital of Culture — A275

Perf. 13¾x13¼
2016, June 10   Litho.
424 A275 €1.30 multi   3.00 3.00

French
Community in
Andorra — A276

2016, July 8 Litho. Perf. 13¼x13¾
425 A276 €1.15 multi   2.60 2.60

Tree of
Science
A277

2016, Sept. 8 Litho. Perf. 13¾x13¼
426 A277 45c blk & brn   1.00 1.00
Ramon Llull (c. 1232-c. 1315), philosopher.

Reforms of 1866,
150th
Anniv. — A278

2016, Sept. 8 Litho. Perf. 13¼x13¾
427 A278 €1.30 multi   3.00 3.00

AIR POST STAMPS

A set of 12 stamps, inscribed
"CORREU AER / SOBRETAXA" was
authorized in 1932 for a proposed
private air service between Andorra
and Barcelona. These stamps were
prepared but not issued. Value, set
$40. The stamps were also over-
printed "FRANQUICIA DEL CON-
SELL" for official use. Value, set
$140.

**Catalogue values for unused
stamps in this section are for
Never Hinged items.**

AP1

Unwmk.
1951, June 27   Engr.   Perf. 11
C1 AP1 1p dark violet brown   17.50 4.25

AP2

Litho. & Engr.
1983, Oct. 20   *Perf. 13*
C2 AP2 20p brown & bis brn   .30 .25
Jaime Sansa Nequi, Episcopal Church official.

AP3

1984, Oct. 25   Photo.   *Perf. 13*
C3 AP3 20p multicolored   .30 .25
Pyrenees Art Center.

Bishops of Urgel Type of 1979
1985, June 13   Engr.   *Perf. 13½*
C4 A42 20p Ramon Iglesias   .30 .25

SPECIAL DELIVERY STAMPS

Special Delivery Stamp of Spain,
1905 Overprinted

1928   Unwmk.   *Perf. 14*
Without Control Number on Back
E1 SD1 20c red   80.00 95.00
      Never hinged   150.00

With Control Number on Back
E2 SD1 20c pale red   50.00 50.00
      Never hinged   90.00

Eagle over Mountain Pass — SD2

1929   *Perf. 14*
With Control Number on Back
E3 SD2 20c scarlet   25.00 20.00
      Never hinged   35.00

Perf 11½ examples are numbered A000.000 and are specimens. Value, $400.

1937   *Perf. 11½x11*
Without Control Number on Back
E4 SD2 20c red   7.75 9.50
      Never hinged   8.75

Arms and Squirrel — SD3

1949   Unwmk.   Engr.   *Perf. 10x9½*
E5 SD3 25c red   5.75 4.50
      Never hinged   8.25

ANDORRA, FRENCH ADMINISTRATION

Stamps and Types of France, 1900-1929, Overprinted

Perf. 14x13½

1931, June 16   Unwmk.
1   A16   1c gray   1.25   1.25
  a.   Double overprint   2,000. 2,000.
2   A16   2c red brown   1.60   1.60
3   A16   3c orange   1.60   1.60
4   A16   5c green   2.40   2.40
5   A16   10c lilac   4.00   4.75
6   A22   15c red brown   5.50   5.50
7   A22   20c red violet   8.75   9.50
8   A22   25c yellow brn   9.50 10.00
9   A22   30c green   9.50 10.00
10 A22   40c ultra   10.00 12.00
11 A20   45c lt violet   20.00 21.50
12 A20   50c vermilion   13.50 15.00
  a.   Pair, one without over-
       print   525.00
13 A20   65c gray green   28.00 28.00
14 A20   75c rose lilac   32.50 28.00
15 A22   90c red   40.00 45.00
16 A20   1fr dull blue   40.00 45.00
17 A22   1.50fr light blue 45.00 47.50

Overprinted

18 A18   2fr org & pale
            bl   87.50 95.00
19 A18   3fr brt vio &
            rose   115.00 125.00
20 A18   5fr dk bl & buff 140.00 145.00
21 A18   10fr grn & red 300.00 350.00
22 A18   20fr mag & grn 400.00 575.00
      Nos. 1-22 (22)   1,316. 1,579.
    See No. P1 for ½c on 1c gray.
    Nos. 9, 15 and 17 were not issued in France without overprint.

Chapel of Meritxell A50

Bridge of St. Anthony A51

St. Miguel d'Engolasters A52

Gorge of St. Julia A53

Old Andorra A54

1932-43   Engr.   *Perf. 13*
23 A50   1c gray blk   .55   .65
24 A50   2c violet   .90   .90
25 A50   3c brown   .90   .95
26 A50   5c blue green   .90   .95
27 A51   10c dull lilac 1.40   1.40
28 A50   15c deep red   2.00   2.00
29 A51   20c lt rose   13.50 11.00
30 A52   25c brown   6.50   5.50
31 A51   25c brn car ('37) 11.00 14.00
32 A51   30c emerald   4.75   4.75
33 A51   40c ultra   13.50 11.00
34 A51   40c brn blk ('39) 1.25   1.25
35 A51   45c lt red   13.50 11.00
36 A51   45c bl grn ('39) 6.00   5.25
37 A52   50c lilac rose 14.50 13.00
38 A51   50c lt vio ('39) 6.00   5.50
38A A51   50c grn ('40)   2.40   2.40
39 A51   55c lt vio ('39) 24.00 16.00
40 A51   60c yel brn ('38) 1.60   1.60
41 A52   65c yel grn   65.00 52.50
42 A51   65c blue ('38) 18.50 14.50
43 A51   70c red ('39)   2.40   2.40
44 A52   75c violet   11.00   8.75
45 A51   75c ultra ('39) 4.50   4.75
46 A51   80c green ('38) 27.50 23.00
46A A53   80c bl grn ('40) .40   .40
47 A53   90c deep rose   6.50   6.50
48 A53   90c dk grn ('39) 3.50   3.50
49 A53   1fr blue grn   20.00 14.50
50 A53   1fr scarlet ('38) 32.50 24.00
51 A53   1fr dp ultra ('39) .40   .40
51A A53   1.20fr brt vio ('42) .40 .40
52 A50   1.25fr rose car
            ('33)   60.00 45.00
52A A50   1.25fr rose ('38) 5.50   4.00
52B A53   1.30fr sepia ('40) .40   .40
53 A54   1.50fr ultra   24.00 19.50
53A A53   1.50fr crim ('40) .40   .40
54 A53   1.75fr violet ('33) 120.00 120.00
55 A53   1.75fr dk bl ('38) 47.50 40.00
56 A53   2fr red violet 13.00 11.50
56A A50   2fr rose red
            ('40)   1.60   1.60
56B A50   2fr dk bl grn
            ('42)   .40   .40
57 A50   2.15fr dk vio ('38) 65.00 52.50
58 A50   2.25fr ultra ('39) 8.75   8.75
58A A50   2.40fr red ('42) .80   .40
59 A50   2.50fr gray blk ('39) 8.00 8.00
59A A50   2.50fr dp ultra ('40) 2.75 2.75
60 A53   3fr orange brn 13.50 10.50
60A A50   3fr red brn ('40) .40   .40
60B A50   4fr sl bl ('42) .40   .40
60C A50   4.50fr dp vio ('42) 2.00 2.00
61 A54   5fr brown   .90   .80
62 A54   10fr violet   1.00   .80
62B A54   15fr dp ultra ('42) 1.20 1.20
63 A54   20fr rose lake 1.20   .80
63A A51   50fr turq bl ('43) 1.60 1.20
      Nos. 23-63A (56)   698.05 598.00

A 20c ultra exists but was not issued. Value: unused, $27,500; never hinged $42,500.

No. 37 Surcharged in Black

1935, Sept. 18
64 A52   20c on 50c lil rose 18.50 17.00
  a.   Double surcharge   7,000.

Coat of Arms — A55

1936-42   *Perf. 14x13*
65 A55   1c black ('37)   .25   .25
66 A55   2c blue   .25   .25
67 A55   3c brown   .25   .25
68 A55   5c rose lilac   .25   .25
69 A55   10c ultra ('37) .25   .25
70 A55   15c red violet 2.75   2.25
71 A55   20c emerald ('37) .25   .25
72 A55   30c cop red ('38) .80   .80
72A A55   30c blk brn ('42) .40   .40
73 A55   35c Prus grn ('38) 70.00 70.00
74 A55   40c cop red ('42) .80   .80
75 A55   50c Prus grn ('42) .80   .80

---

76 A55   60c turq bl ('42) .80   .80
77 A55   70c vio ('42)   .80   .80
      Nos. 65-77 (14)   78.65 78.15
      Set, never hinged   135.00

> Catalogue values for unused stamps in this section, from this point to the end of the section, are for Never Hinged items.

Coat of Arms — A56

1944
78 A56   10c violet   .30   .30
79 A56   30c deep magenta .30   .30
80 A56   40c dull blue   .30   .30
81 A56   50c orange red   .30   .30
82 A56   60c black   .30   .30
83 A56   70c brt red violet .30   .30
84 A56   80c blue green   .30   .30
      Nos. 78-84 (7)   2.10   2.10
      See No. 114.

St. Jean de Caselles A57

La Maison des Vallees A58

Old Andorra A59

Provost A60

1944-47   *Perf. 13*
85 A57   1fr brown violet .25   .25
86 A57   1.20fr blue   .25   .25
87 A57   1.50fr red   .25   .25
88 A57   2fr dk blue grn   .25   .25
89 A58   2.40fr rose red   .25   .25
90 A58   2.50fr rose red ('46) 7.25 .80
91 A58   3fr sepia   .25   .25
92 A58   4fr ultra   .40   .25
93 A59   4.50fr brown blk .40   .25
94 A58   4.50fr dk bl grn ('47) 9.50 5.50
95 A59   5fr ultra   .35   .25
96 A59   5fr Prus grn ('46) 1.40   .50
97 A59   6fr rose car ('45) .35   .25
98 A59   10fr Prus green   .35   .25
99 A59   10fr ultra ('46) 2.40   .40
100 A60   15fr rose lilac   .95   .40
101 A60   20fr deep blue   .95   .40
102 A60   25fr lt rose red ('46) 5.50 1.90
103 A60   40fr dk green ('46) 5.50 2.00
104 A60   50fr sepia   1.75   1.40
      Nos. 85-104 (20)   38.55 16.05

1948-49
105 A58   4fr lt blue grn 1.60   .80
106 A59   6fr violet brn   .80   .40
107 A59   8fr indigo   1.25   1.20
108 A59   12fr bright red 1.25   1.20
109 A59   12fr blue grn ('49) 1.50 .75
110 A59   15fr crimson ('49) 1.00   .55
111 A60   18fr deep blue   5.00   2.40
112 A60   20fr dark violet 3.50   2.00
113 A60   25fr ultra ('49) 2.50   1.20
      Nos. 105-113 (9)   18.40 10.50

1949-51   *Perf. 14x13, 13*
114 A56   1fr deep blue   .95   .65
115 A57   3fr red ('51)   7.25   4.75
116 A57   4fr sepia   2.50   2.25
117 A58   5fr emerald   3.75   2.75
118 A58   5fr purple ('51) 13.50 4.75

119	A58	6fr blue grn ('51)	7.25	3.25
120	A58	8fr brown	.95	.75
121	A59	15fr blk brn ('51)	16.00	3.00
122	A59	18fr rose red ('51)	30.00	15.00
123	A60	30fr ultra ('51)	40.00	22.50
		Nos. 114-123 (10)	122.15	59.65

Les Escaldres
Spa — A61

St. Coloma
Belfry
A62

Designs: 15fr-25fr, Gothic cross. 30fr-75fr,
Village of Les Bons.

1955-58   Unwmk.   Engr.   *Perf. 13*

124	A61	1fr dk gray bl	.25	.25
125	A61	2fr dp green	.35	.25
126	A61	3fr red	.35	.25
127	A61	5fr chocolate	.35	.25
128	A62	6fr dk bl grn	.80	.80
129	A62	8fr rose brown	.80	.80
130	A62	10fr brt violet	1.25	.80
131	A62	12fr indigo	1.60	.80
132	A61	15fr red	1.60	.85
133	A61	18fr blue grn	2.00	.85
134	A61	20fr dp purple	3.50	2.00
135	A61	25fr sepia	3.50	2.00
136	A62	30fr deep blue	40.00	19.50
137	A62	35fr Prus bl ('57)	12.00	7.25
138	A62	40fr dk green	47.50	28.00
139	A62	50fr cerise	4.50	3.25
140	A62	65fr purple ('58)	12.00	6.50
141	A62	70fr chestnut ('57)	7.25	6.50
142	A62	75fr violet blue	65.00	45.00
		Nos. 124-142 (19)	204.60	125.90

Issued: 35fr, 70fr, 8/19; 65fr, 2/10; others,
2/15.

Coat of Arms — A63

Gothic
Cross,
Meritxell
A64

65c, 85c, 1fr, Engolasters Lake.

1961, June 19   Typo.   *Perf. 14x13*

143	A63	5c brt green & blk	.25	.25
144	A63	10c red, pink & blk	.25	.25
145	A63	15c blue & black	.25	.25
146	A63	20c yellow & brown	.40	.30

      Engr.   *Perf. 13*

147	A64	25c violet, bl & grn	.60	.30
148	A64	30c mar, ol grn & brn	.70	.50
149	A64	45c indigo, bl & grn	17.50	16.00
150	A64	50c pur, lt brn & ol grn	1.50	1.25
151	A64	65c bl, ol & brn	22.00	18.50
152	A64	85c rose lil, vio bl & brn	22.00	18.50
153	A64	1fr grnsh bl, ind & brn	1.50	1.25
		Nos. 143-153 (11)	66.95	57.35

See Nos. 161-166A.

Imperforates

Most stamps of Andorra, French
Administration, from 1961 onward exist
imperforate in issued and trial colors,
and also in small presentation sheets in
issued colors.

Common Design Types
pictured following the introduction.

Telstar Issue
Common Design Type

1962, Sept. 29   Engr.

154	CD111	50c ultra & purple	2.00 1.60

1st television connection of the US and
Europe through the Telstar satellite, 7/11-12.

"La
Sardane"
A66

Charlemagne Crossing Andorra — A67

1fr, Louis le Debonnaire giving founding
charter.

1963, June 22   Unwmk.   *Perf. 13*

155	A66	20c lil rose, cl & ol grn	5.00	5.00
156	A67	50c sl grn & dk car rose	8.50	8.50
157	A67	1fr red brn, ultra & dk grn	14.00	14.00
		Nos. 155-157 (3)	27.50	27.50

Old Andorra Church and Champs-
Elysées Palace — A68

1964, Jan. 20   Engr.

158	A68	25c vio brn, grn & blk	2.00 1.60

"PHILATEC," Intl. Philatelic and Postal Techniques Exhib., Paris, June 5-21, 1964.

Bishop of Urgel and Seigneur of
Caboet Confirming Co-Principality,
1288 — A69

Design: 60c, Napoleon re-establishing Co-
principality, 1806.

1964, Apr. 25   Engr.   *Perf. 13*

159	A69	60c dk brn, red brn & sl grn	22.50 22.50
160	A69	1fr brt bl, org brn & blk	22.50 22.50

Arms Type of 1961

1964, May 16   Typo.   *Perf. 14x13*

161	A63	1c dk blue & gray	.25	.25
162	A63	2c black & orange	.25	.25
163	A63	12c purple, emer & yel	.90	.90
164	A63	18c black, lil & pink	1.00	1.00
		Nos. 161-164 (4)	2.40	2.40

Scenic Type of 1961

Designs: 40c, 45c, Gothic Cross, Meritxell.
60c, 90c, Pond of Engolasters.

1965-71   Engr.   *Perf. 13*

165	A64	40c dk brn, org brn & sl grn	1.00	.80
165A	A64	45c vio bl, ol bis & slate	1.10	.80
166	A64	60c org brn & dk brn	1.60	1.25
166A	A64	90c ultra, bl grn & bis-ter	2.00	1.00
		Nos. 165-166A (4)	5.70	3.85

Issued: 40c, 60c, Apr. 25, 1965. 45c, June
13, 1970. 90c, Aug. 28, 1971.

Syncom Satellite
over Pleumeur-
Bodou
Station — A70

1965, May 17   Unwmk.

167	A70	60c dp car, lil & bl	6.50 4.75

Cent. of the ITU.

Andorra House,
Paris — A71

1965, June 5

168	A71	25c dk bl, org brn & ol gray	1.25 .80

Ski
Lift — A72

Design: 25c, Chair lift, vert.

1966, Apr. 2   Engr.   *Perf. 13*

169	A72	25c brt bl, grn & dk brn	1.60 1.25
170	A72	40c mag, brt ultra & sep	2.40 1.60

Winter sports in Andorra.

FR-1 Satellite — A73

1966, May 7   *Perf. 13*

171	A73	60c brt bl, grn & dk grn	2.10 1.60

Issued to commemorate the launching of
the scientific satellite FR-1, Dec. 6, 1965.

Europa Issue, 1966
Common Design Type

1966, Sept. 24   Engr.   *Perf. 13*
Size: 21½x35½mm

172	CD9	60c brown	3.00 3.00

Folk Dancers,
Sculpture by Josep
Viladomat — A74

1967, Apr. 29   Engr.   *Perf. 13*

173	A74	30c ol grn, dp grn & slate	1.25 .80

Cent. (in 1966) of the New Reform, which
reaffirmed and strengthened political freedom
in Andorra.

Europa Issue, 1967
Common Design Type

1967, Apr. 29
Size: 22x36mm

174	CD10	30c bluish blk & lt bl	4.25 1.75
175	CD10	60c dk red & brt pink	6.50 4.50

Telephone
Encircling the
Globe — A75

1967, Apr. 29

176	A75	60c dk car, vio & blk	2.00 1.25

Automatic telephone service.

Injured
Father at
Home
A76

1967, Sept. 23   Engr.   *Perf. 13*

177	A76	2.30fr ocher, dk red brn & brn red	9.75 7.50

Introduction of Social Security System.

Jesus in Garden of
Gethsemane — A77

Designs (from 16th century frescoes in La
Maison des Vallees): 30c, The Kiss of Judas.
60c, The Descent from the Cross (Pieta).

1967, Sept. 23

178	A77	25c black & red brn	.80	.80
179	A77	30c purple & red lilac	.80	.80
180	A77	60c indigo & Prus blue	1.60	1.25
		Nos. 178-180 (3)	3.20	2.85

See Nos. 185-187.

Downhill
Skier — A78

1968, Jan. 27   Engr.   *Perf. 13*

181	A78	40c org, ver & red lil	1.60 1.25

10th Winter Olympic Games, Grenoble,
France, Feb. 6-18.

Europa Issue, 1968
Common Design Type

1968, Apr. 27   Engr.   *Perf. 13*
Size: 36x22mm

182	CD11	30c gray & brt bl	6.50 3.00
183	CD11	60c brown & lilac	10.00 7.00

High Jump A79

1968, Oct. 12   Engr.   Perf. 13
184 A79 40c brt blue & brn   1.50 1.25
19th Olympic Games, Mexico City, Oct. 12-27.

Fresco Type of 1967

Designs (from 16th century frescoes in La Maison des Vallees): 25c, The Scourging of Christ. 30c, Christ Carrying the Cross. 60c, The Crucifixion. (All horiz.)

1968, Oct. 12
185 A77 25c dk grn & gray grn   .85 .80
186 A77 30c dk brown & lilac   .85 .80
187 A77 60c dk car & vio brn   1.75 1.25
       Nos. 185-187 (3)   3.45 2.85

Europa Issue, 1969
Common Design Type

1969, Apr. 26   Engr.   Perf. 13
188 CD12 40c rose car, gray &
       dl bl   7.50 3.50
189 CD12 70c indigo, dl red &
       ol   11.00 8.50
10th anniv. of the Conf. of European Postal and Telecommunications Administrations.

Kayak on Isere River — A80

1969, Aug. 2   Engr.   Perf. 13
190 A80 70c dk sl grn, ultra & ind 2.50 2.75
Intl. Canoe & Kayak Championships, Bourg-Saint-Maurice, Savoy, July 31-Aug. 6.

Drops of Water & Diamond — A80a

1969, Sept. 27   Engr.   Perf. 13
191 A80a 70c blk, dp ultra &
       grnsh bl   3.25 4.00
European Water Charter.

St. John, the Woman and the Dragon A81

The Revelation (From the Altar of St. John, Caselles): 40c, St. John Hearing Voice from Heaven on Patmos. 70c, St. John and the Seven Candlesticks.

1969, Oct. 18
192 A81 30c brn, dp pur & brn
       red   .75 .75
193 A81 40c gray, dk brn & brn
       ol   1.10 1.10

194 A81 70c dk red, maroon &
       brt rose lilac   1.40 1.40
       Nos. 192-194 (3)   3.25 3.25
See Nos. 199-201, 207-209, 214-216.

Field Ball — A82

1970, Feb. 21   Engr.   Perf. 13
195 A82 80c multi   2.00 2.00
Issued to publicize the 7th International Field Ball Games, France, Feb. 26-Mar. 8.

Europa Issue, 1970
Common Design Type

1970, May 2   Engr.   Perf. 13
       Size: 36x22mm
196 CD13 40c orange   6.00 2.50
197 CD13 80c violet blue   14.00 6.00

Shot Put — A83

1970, Sept. 11   Engr.   Perf. 13
198 A83 80c bl & dk brn   2.00 2.00
1st European Junior Athletic Championships, Colombes, France, Sept. 11-13.

Altar Type of 1969

The Revelation (from the Altar of St. John, Caselles): 30c, St. John recording angel's message. 40c, Angel erecting column symbolizing faithful in heaven. 80c, St. John's trial in kettle of boiling oil.

1970, Oct. 24
199 A81 30c dp car, dk brn & brt
       pur   .90 .90
200 A81 40c violet & slate grn   1.10 1.10
201 A81 80c ol, dk bl & car rose   1.90 1.90
       Nos. 199-201 (3)   3.90 3.90

Ice Skating A84

1971, Feb. 20   Engr.   Perf. 13
202 A84 80c dk red, red lil & pur 2.00 2.00
World Figure Skating Championships, Lyons, France, Feb. 23-28.

Capercaillie — A85

Nature protection: No. 204, Brown bear.

1971, Apr. 24   Photo.   Perf. 13
203 A85 80c multicolored   3.25 3.25
       Engr.
204 A85 80c blue, grn & brn   2.40 2.40

Europa Issue, 1971
Common Design Type

1971, May 8   Engr.   Perf. 13
       Size: 35½x22mm
205 CD14 50c rose red   8.00 2.25
206 CD14 80c lt blue green   12.00 5.50

Altar Type of 1969

The Revelation (from the Altar of St. John, Caselles): 30c, St. John preaching, Rev. 1:3. 50c, "The Sign of the Beast . . ." Rev. 16:1-2. 90c, The Woman, Rev. 17:1.

1971, Sept. 18
207 A81 30c dl grn, ol & brt grn 1.25 1.00
208 A81 50c rose car, org & ol
       brn   1.60 1.25
209 A81 90c blk, dk pur & bl   2.40 2.00
       Nos. 207-209 (3)   5.25 4.25

Europa Issue 1972
Common Design Type

1972, Apr. 29   Photo.   Perf. 13
       Size: 21½x37mm
210 CD15 50c brt mag & multi   7.50 2.50
211 CD15 90c multicolored   13.50 4.50

Golden Eagle A86

1972, May 27   Engr.
212 A86 60c dk grn, olive & plum 5.00 3.25
Nature protection.

Shooting A87

1972, July 8
213 A87 1fr dk purple   3.75 2.00
20th Olympic Games, Munich, 8/26-9/11.

Altar Type of 1969

The Revelation (from the Altar of St. John, Caselles): 30c, St. John, bishop and servant. 50c, Resurrection of Lazarus. 90c, Angel with lance and nails.

1972, Sept. 16   Engr.   Perf. 13
214 A81 30c dk ol, gray & red lil 1.25 .85
215 A81 50c vio blue & slate   1.50 1.25
216 A81 90c dk Prus bl & sl grn   2.40 2.40
       Nos. 214-216 (3)   5.15 4.50

De Gaulle as Coprince of Andorra — A88

90c, De Gaulle in front of Maison des Vallées.

1972, Oct. 23   Engr.   Perf. 13
217 A88 50c violet blue   2.00 2.00
218 A88 90c dk carmine   3.00 3.00
   a. Pair, #217-218 + label   6.00 6.00
Visit of Charles de Gaulle to Andorra, 5th anniv.
See Nos. 399-400.

Europa Issue 1973
Common Design Type

1973, Apr. 28   Photo.   Perf. 13
       Size: 36x22mm
219 CD16 50c violet & multi   9.00 3.00
220 CD16 90c dk red & multi   11.00 8.00

Virgin of Canolich A89

1973, June 16   Engr.   Perf. 13
221 A89 1fr ol, Prus bl & vio   2.25 1.60

Lily — A90

45c, Iris. 50c, Columbine. 65c, Tobacco. No. 226, Pinks. No. 227, Narcissuses.

1973-74   Photo.   Perf. 13
222 A90 30c car rose & multi   .80 .80
223 A90 45c yel grn & multi   .40 .40
224 A90 50c buff & multi   1.75 1.75
225 A90 65c gray & multi   .40 .40
226 A90 90c ultra & multi   1.50 1.50
227 A90 90c grnsh bl & multi   1.25 1.25
       Nos. 222-227 (6)   6.10 6.10
Issued: 30c, 50c, No. 226, 7/7/73. 45c, 65c, No. 227, 4/6/74.
See Nos. 238-240.

Blue Titmouse — A91

Nature protection: 60c, Citril finch and mistletoe. 80c, Eurasian bullfinch. 1fr, Lesser spotted woodpecker.

1973-74   Photo.   Perf. 13
228 A91 60c buff & multi   4.00 1.75
229 A91 80c gray & multi   4.00 2.25
230 A91 90c gray & multi   2.75 1.25
231 A91 1fr yel grn & multi   2.75 1.60
       Nos. 228-231 (4)   13.50 6.85
Issued: 90c, 1fr, 10/27/73. 60c, 80c, 9/21/74.

Europa Issue

Virgin of Pal — A92

90c, Virgin of Santa Coloma. Statues are polychrome 12th cent. carvings by rural artists.

1974, Apr. 27   Engr.   Perf. 13
232 A92 50c multicolored   9.00 3.00
233 A92 90c multicolored   12.50 7.00

Arms of Andorra and Cahors Bridge — A93

1974, Aug. 24   **Engr.**   **Perf. 13**
234 A93 1fr blue, vio & org   1.00 .80

First anniv. of meeting of the co-princes of Andorra: Pres. Georges Pompidou of France and Msgr. Juan Marti Alanis, Bishop of Urgel.

Mail Box, Chutes and Globe — A94

1974, Oct. 5   **Engr.**   **Perf. 13**
235 A94 1.20fr multi   1.25 1.25

Centenary of Universal Postal Union.

Coronation of St. Marti, 16th Century — A95

Europa: 80c, Crucifixion, 16th cent., vert.

Perf. 11½x13, 13x11½
1975, Apr. 26   **Photo.**
236 A95   80c gold & multi   4.50 3.00
237 A95 1.20fr gold & multi   6.50 4.00

Flower Type of 1973

Designs: 60c, Gentian. 80c, Anemone. 1.20fr, Autumn crocus.

1975, May 10   **Photo.**   **Perf. 13**
238 A90   60c olive & multi   .50 .40
239 A90   80c brt rose & multi   1.25 .80
240 A90 1.20fr green & multi   1.25 .80
   Nos. 238-240 (3)   3.00 2.00

Abstract Design — A96

1975, June 7   **Engr.**   **Perf. 13**
241 A96 2fr bl, magenta & emer   1.75 1.50

ARPHILA 75 International Philatelic Exhibition, Paris, June 6-16.

A97

1975, Aug. 23   **Engr.**   **Perf. 13**
242 A97 80c violet bl & blk   1.00 1.00

Georges Pompidou (1911-74), pres. of France and co-prince of Andorra (1969-74).

A98

1975, Nov. 8   **Engr.**   **Perf. 13**
243 A98 1.20fr Costume, IWY Emblem   1.25 1.00

International Women's Year.

Skier and Snowflake A99

1976, Jan. 31   **Engr.**   **Perf. 13**
244 A99 1.20fr multicolored   1.50 1.10

12th Winter Olympic Games, Innsbruck, Austria, Feb. 4-15.

Telephone and Satellite — A100

1976, Mar. 20   **Engr.**   **Perf. 13**
245 A100 1fr multicolored   1.00 1.00

Centenary of first telephone call by Alexander Graham Bell, Mar. 10, 1976.

Catalan Forge A101

Europa: 1.20fr, Woolen worker.

1976, May 8   **Engr.**   **Perf. 13**
246 A101   80c multi   3.25 1.00
247 A101 1.20fr multi   4.75 1.75

Thomas Jefferson — A102

1976, July 3   **Engr.**   **Perf. 13**
248 A102 1.20fr multi   1.25 1.00

American Bicentennial.

Trapshooting A103

1976, July 17   **Engr.**   **Perf. 13**
249 A103 2fr multi   1.75 1.40

21st Olympic Games, Montreal, Canada, July 17-Aug. 1.

Meritxell Sanctuary and Old Chapel — A104

1976, Sept. 4   **Engr.**   **Perf. 13**
250 A104 1fr multi   1.00 1.00

Dedication of rebuilt Meritxell Church, Sept. 8, 1976.

Apollo — A105

Design: 1.40fr, Morio butterfly.

1976, Oct. 16   **Photo.**   **Perf. 13**
251 A105   80c black & multi   1.90 1.25
252 A105 1.40fr salmon & multi   3.25 2.00

Nature protection.

Ermine — A106

1977, Apr. 2   **Photo.**   **Perf. 13**
253 A106 1fr vio bl, gray & blk   1.60 1.25

Nature protection.

St. Jean de Caselles — A107

Europa: 1.40fr, Sant Vicens Castle.

1977, Apr. 30   **Engr.**   **Perf. 13**
254 A107   1fr multi   3.00 1.25
255 A107 1.40fr multi   4.75 2.00

Manual Digest, 1748, Arms of Andorra — A108

1977, June 11   **Engr.**   **Perf. 13**
256 A108 80c grn, bl & brn   .90 .90

Establishment of Institute of Andorran Studies.

St. Romanus of Caesarea A109

1977, July 23   **Engr.**   **Perf. 12½x13**
257 A109 2fr multi   1.75 1.50

Design from altarpiece in Church of St. Roma de les Bons.

General Council Chamber A110

Guillem d'Arény Plandolit — A111

1977, Sept. 24   **Engr.**   **Perf. 13**
258 A110 1.10fr multi   1.40 1.00
259 A111   2fr car & dk brn   1.40 1.00

Andorran heritage. Guillem d'Arény Plandolit started Andorran reform movement in 1866.

Squirrel — A112

1978, Mar. 18   **Engr.**   **Perf. 13**
260 A112 1fr multi   .90 .75

Flag and Valira River Bridge — A113

1978, Apr. 8
261 A113 80c multi .65 .65
Signing of the treaty establishing the Co-Principality of Andorra, 700th anniv.

Pal Church A114

Europa: 1.40fr, Charlemagne's Castle, Charlemagne on horseback, vert.

1978, Apr. 29   Engr.   Perf. 13
262 A114   1fr multi   3.00 1.50
263 A114 1.40fr multi   5.50 2.75

Virgin of Sispony A115

1978, May 20   Engr.   Perf. 12x13
264 A115 2fr multi   1.50 1.25

Visura Tribunal A116

1978, June 24   Engr.   Perf. 13
265 A116 1.20fr multi   1.00 .50

Preamble of 1278 Treaty — A117

1978, Sept. 2   Engr.   Perf. 13x12½
266 A117 1.70fr multi   1.00 .75
700th anniversary of the signing of treaty establishing Co-Principality of Andorra.

Pyrenean Chamois — A118

1979, Mar. 26   Engr.   Perf. 13
267 A118 1fr multi   .65 .65

White Partridges — A119

1979, Apr. 7   Photo.   Perf. 13
268 A119 1.20fr multi   1.50 .75
Nature protection. See Nos. 288-289.

French Mailman, 1900 — A120

Europa: 1.70fr, 1st French p.o. in Andorra.

1979, Apr. 28   Engr.   Perf. 13
269 A120 1.20fr multi   2.00 .75
270 A120 1.70fr multi   4.00 1.25

Falcon, Pre-Roman Painting A121

1979, June 2   Engr.   Perf. 12½x13
271 A121 2fr multi   1.10 .90

Child with Lambs, Church, IYC Emblem. — A122

1979, July 7   Photo.   Perf. 13
272 A122 1.70fr multi   1.20 .85
International Year of the Child.

Trobada Monument A123

1979, Sept. 29   Engr.   Perf. 13
273 A123 2fr multi   1.25 1.00
Co-Principality of Andorra, 700th anniv

Judo Hold — A124

1979, Nov. 24   Engr.   Perf. 13
274 A124 1.30fr multi   .90 .75
World Judo Championships, Paris, Dec. 1979.

Farm House, Cortinada — A125

1980, Jan. 26   Engr.   Perf. 13
275 A125 1.10fr multi   .75 .60

Cross-Country Skiing — A126

1980, Feb. 9
276 A126 1.80fr ultra & lil rose   1.50 1.10
13th Winter Olympic Games, Lake Placid, NY, Feb. 12-24.

A128

1980, Aug. 30   Engr.   Perf. 13
278 A128 1.20fr multi   .75 .75
World Bicycling championships.

A129

Europa: 1.30fr, Charlemagne (742-814). 1.80fr, Napoleon I (1769-1821).

1980, Apr. 26   Engr.   Perf. 13
279 A129 1.30fr multi   1.75 .60
280 A129 1.80fr gray grn & brn   2.00 1.00

Pyrenees Lily — A130

1.10fr, Dog-toothed violet.

1980   Photo.
281 A130 1.10fr multicolored   .75 .55
282 A130 1.30fr shown   .75 .65
Nature protection. Issue dates: 1.10fr, June 21; 1.30fr, May 17.

De La Vall House, 400th Anniversary of Restoration A131

1980, Sept. 6   Engr.
283 A131 1.40fr multi   .75 .65

Angel, Church of St. Cerni de Nagol, Pre-Romanesque Fresco — A132

1980, Oct. 25   Perf. 13x12½
284 A132 2fr multi   1.25 1.25

Bordes de Mereig Mountain Village A133

1981, Mar. 21   Engr.   Perf. 13
285 A133 1.40fr bl gray & dk brn   .80 .80

Europa Issue

Ball de l'Ossa, Winter Game A134

2fr, El Contrapas dance.

1981, May 16   Engr.
286 A134 1.40fr shown   1.50 .50
287 A134   2fr multicolored   1.75 1.00

Bird Type of 1979

1.20fr, Phylloscopus bonelli. 1.40fr, Tichodroma muraria.

1981, June 20   Photo.
288 A119 1.20fr multicolored   .65 .65
289 A119 1.40fr multicolored   1.00 .65

World Fencing Championship,
Clermont-Ferrand, July 2-13 — A135

1981, July 4   **Engr.**
290 A135 2fr bl & blk   .90   .80

St. Martin,
12th Cent.
Tapestry
A136

1981, Sept. 5   **Engr.**   *Perf. 12x13*
291 A136 3fr multi   1.25 1.00

Intl. Drinking Water
Decade — A137

1981, Oct. 17   *Perf. 13*
292 A137 1.60fr multi   .75   .50

Intl. Year of the
Disabled — A138

1981, Nov. 7
293 A138 2.30fr multi   1.00   .65

Europa
1982
A139

1.60fr, Creation of Andorran govt., 1982.
2.30fr, Land Council, 1419.

1982, May 8   **Engr.**   *Perf. 13*
294 A139 1.60fr multi   1.50   .70
295 A139 2.30fr multi   2.00   .70

1982 World Cup — A140

Various soccer players.

1982, June 12   **Engr.**   *Perf. 13*
296   1.60fr red & dk brn   .80   .65
297   2.60fr red & dk brn   1.10   .95
  a. A140 Pair, #296-297 + label   2.25 2.25

Souvenir Sheet

No. 52 — A141

1982, Aug. 21   **Engr.**
298 A141 5fr blk & rose car   2.40 2.40
1st Andorran Stamp Exhib., 8/21-9/19.

Horse, Roman Wall Painting — A142

1982, Sept. 4   **Photo.**   *Perf. 13x12½*
299 A142 3fr multi   1.25 1.00

Wild
Cat — A143

1982, Oct. 9   **Engr.**   *Perf. 13*
300 A143 1.80fr shown   1.10   .85
301 A143 2.60fr Pine trees   .90   .75

TB Bacillus
Centenary — A144

1982, Nov. 13
302 A144 2.10fr Koch, lungs   .85   .65

St. Thomas Aquinas
(1225-74) — A145

1982, Dec. 4
303 A145 2fr multi   .85   .65

Manned
Flight
Bicentenary
A146

1983, Feb. 26   **Engr.**
304 A146 2fr multi   .90   .75

Nature
Protection
A147

1983, Apr. 16   **Engr.**   *Perf. 13*
305 A147   1fr Birch trees   .40   .30
306 A147 1.50fr Trout   .75   .55
See Nos. 325-326.

Catalane
Gold Works
A148

1983, May 7   **Engr.**   *Perf. 13*
307 A148 1.80fr Exterior   1.00   .50
308 A148 2.60fr Interior   1.60   .80
Europa.

30th Anniv. of Customs Cooperation
Council — A149

3fr, Letter of King Louis XIII.

1983, May 14
309 A149 3fr multicolored   1.25 1.00

First Arms
of Valleys of
Andorra
A150

1983, Sept. 3   **Engr.**   *Perf. 13*
310 A150   5c olive grn & red   .25   .25
311 A150 10c grn & olive grn   .25   .25
312 A150 20c brt pur & red   .25   .25
313 A150 30c brn vio & red   .35   .35
314 A150 40c dk bl & vio   .35   .35
315 A150 50c gray & red   .25   .25
316 A150   1fr deep magenta   .25   .25
317 A150   2fr org red & red brn   .90   .40
318 A150   5fr dk brn & red   1.25   .80
    Nos. 310-318 (9)   4.10 3.15
See Nos. 329-335, 380-385, 464-465.

Painting,
Cortinada
Church
A151

1983, Sept. 24   *Perf. 12x13*
319 A151 4fr multi   1.75 1.00

Plandolit
House — A152

1983, Oct. 15   **Photo.**   *Perf. 13*
320 A152 1.60fr dp ultra & brn   .75   .55

1984 Winter
Olympics
A153

1984, Feb. 18   **Engr.**
321 A153 2.80fr multicolored   1.25   .90

Pyrenees
Region
Work
Community
(Labor
Org.)
A154

1984, Apr. 28   **Engr.**   *Perf. 13*
322 A154 3fr brt blue & sepia   1.20   .90

Europa
(1959-84)
A155

1984, May 5   **Engr.**
323 A155   2fr brt grn   1.60   .80
324 A155 2.80fr rose car   2.75 1.40

Nature Protection Type of 1983
1984, July 7   **Engr.**   *Perf. 13*
325 A147 1.70fr Chestnut tree   .80   .40
326 A147 2.10fr Walnut tree   1.20   .65

Pyrenees
Art Center
— A155a

1984, Sept. 7   **Engr.**
327 A155a 3fr multi   1.40 1.00

Romanesque Fresco, Church of St.
Cerni de Nagol — A156

1984, Nov. 17   *Perf. 12x13*
328 A156 5fr multi   2.25 1.90

First Arms Type of 1983
1984-87   **Engr.**   *Perf. 13*
329 A150 1.90fr emerald   3.25   .80
330 A150 2.20fr red orange   1.25   .40
  a.   Bklt. pane, 2 #329, 6 #330   15.00
331 A150   3fr bl grn & red
               brn   1.50 1.00
332 A150   4fr brt org & brn   3.50 1.25
333 A150 10fr brn org & blk   3.50 1.60
334 A150 15fr grn & dk grn   5.00 2.40

335 A150 20fr brt bl & red
          brn   7.00 2.75
Nos. 329-335 (7)   25.00 10.20

Nos. 329-330 issued in booklets only.
Issued: 3fr, 20fr, 12/1/84; 10fr, 2/9/85; 4fr, 15fr, 4/19/86; 1.90fr, 2.20fr, 3/28/87.

Saint Julia Valley A157

1985, Apr. 13   **Engr.**
336 A157 2fr multi   1.00 .60

Europa 1985 — A158

2.10fr, Le Val D'Andorre. 3fr, Instruments.

1985, May 4   **Engr.**
337 A158 2.10fr multicolored 1.75 .75
338 A158 3fr multicolored   4.00 1.25

Intl. Youth Year — A159

1985, June 8   **Engr.**
339 A159 3fr multicolored 1.25 .90

Wildlife Conservation — A160

1.80fr, Anas platyrhynchos. 2.20fr, Carduelis carduelis.

1985, Aug. 3   **Photo.**
340 A160 1.80fr multicolored 1.00 .65
341 A160 2.20fr multicolored 1.40 .85

Two Saints, Medieval Fresco in St. Cerni de Nagol Church A161

1985, Sept. 14 **Engr.** *Perf. 12½x13*
342 A161 5fr multicolored   2.00 1.75

Postal Museum Inauguration A162

1986, Mar. 22 **Engr.** *Perf. 13*
343 A162 2.20fr like No. 269 1.00 .65

Europa 1986 A163

1986, May 3   **Engr.** *Perf. 13*
344 A163 2.20fr Ansalonga 2.50 .90
345 A163 3.20fr Isard   5.00 1.60

1986 World Cup Soccer Championships, Mexico — A164

1986, June 14
346 A164 3fr multi   1.50 1.00

Angonella Lake A165

1986, June 28
347 A165 2.20fr multi   1.00 .70

Manual Digest Frontispiece, 1748 — A166

1986, Sept. 6   **Engr.**
348 A166 5fr chnt brn, gray ol & blk   2.25 1.40

Intl. Peace Year A167

1986, Sept. 27
349 A167 1.90fr bl gray & grnsh bl   1.00 .65

St. Vincenc d'Enclar — A168

1986, Oct. 18 **Engr.** *Perf. 13½x13*
350 A168 1.90fr multicolored .95 .65

Contemporary Natl. Coat of Arms — A169

1987, Mar. 27 **Litho.** *Perf. 12½x13*
351 A169 2.20fr multi   1.60 1.60

Visit of the French co-prince.

Europa 1987 A170

2.20fr, Meritxell Sanctuary. 3.40fr, Pleta D'Ordino.

1987, May 2   **Engr.** *Perf. 13*
352 A170 2.20fr multicolored 2.00 .80
353 A170 3.40fr multicolored 4.50 2.00

Ransol Village — A171

1987, June 13   **Photo.**
354 A171 1.90fr multicolored 1.25 1.00

Nature A172

1.90fr, Cavall rogenc. 2.20fr, Graellsia isabellae.

1987, July 4
355 A172 1.90fr multicolored 1.25 .80
356 A172 2.20fr multicolored 1.60 1.25

Aryalsu, Romanesque Painting, La Cortinada Church — A173

Litho. & Engr.
1987, Sept. 5   *Perf. 12½x13*
357 A173 5fr multi   2.50 1.60

Hiker Looking at Map A174

1987, Sept. 19 **Engr.** *Perf. 13*
358 A174 2fr olive, grn & dark brn vio   1.00 .60

Medieval Iron Key, La Cortinada A175

1987, Oct. 17   **Litho.**
359 A175 3fr multi   1.25 1.00

Andorran Coat of Arms — A176

Booklet Stamp
1988, Feb. 6 **Engr.** *Perf. 13*
360 A176 2.20fr red   1.00 .50
 a. Bklt. pane of 5 5.00
    Complete bklt., 2 #360a 10.00
   See Nos. 386-388.

Shoemaker's Last from Roc de l'Oral — A177

1988, Feb. 13   **Photo.**
361 A177 3fr multi   1.50 1.10

Rugby A178

1988, Mar. 19 **Engr.** *Perf. 13½x13*
362 A178 2.20fr blk, org, turq grn 1.20 .95

Europa 1988 — A179

Transport and communication: 2.20fr, Broadcast tower. 3.60fr, Computer graphics.

1988, Apr. 30 **Engr.** *Perf. 13*
363 A179 2.20fr multicolored 1.75 .90
364 A179 3.60fr multicolored 3.75 1.10

Hot Springs, Escaldes — A180

1988, May 14   **Engr.**
365 A180 2.20fr Prus blue, org
      brn & emer   1.25 .80

Tor D'Ansalonga Farmhouse, Ansalonga Pass — A181

1988, June 11   **Engr.**
366 A181 2fr multi   1.10 .65

Sheepdog — A182

1988, July 2   **Photo.**
367 A182   2fr shown   1.50 .60
368 A182 2.20fr Hare   1.50 .60

Roman Fresco, 8th Cent., St. Steven's Church, Andorre-La-Vieille — A183

1988, Sept. 3   **Engr.**   *Perf. 13x12½*
369 A183 5fr multicolored   2.25 1.50

French Revolution, Bicent. — A184

1989, Jan. 1   **Litho.**   *Perf. 13*
370 A184 2.20fr red & vio bl   1.00 1.00

Poble de Pal Village A185

1989, Mar. 4   **Engr.**   *Perf. 13*
371 A185 2.20fr indigo & lilac   1.00 .65

Europa 1989 A186

1989, Apr. 29   **Engr.**   *Perf. 13*
372 A186 2.20fr multi   2.00 .80
373 A186 3.60fr multi   2.50 1.75

Children's games: 2.20fr, Human tower. 3.60fr, The handkerchief.

Red Cross A187

1989, May 6
374 A187 3.60fr multi   1.75 1.25

Visigothic — Merovingian Age Cincture from a Column, St. Vicenc D'Anclar — A188

1989, June 3   **Photo.**
375 A188 3fr multi   1.40 1.10

Wildlife A189

1989, Sept. 16   **Engr.**   *Perf. 13*
376 A189 2.20fr Wild boar   1.25 .90
377 A189 3.60fr Newt   2.00 1.25

Scene of Salome from the Retable of St. Michael of Mosquera, Encamp — A190

1989, Oct. 14   *Perf. 13x13½*
378 A190 5fr multi   2.50 1.25

La Margineda Bridge A191

1990, Feb. 26   **Engr.**   *Perf. 13*
379 A191 2.30fr multi   1.25 .60

Tourism.

Arms Types of 1983 and 1988

1990-93   **Engr.**   *Perf. 13*
380 A150 2.10fr green   1.00 .40
381 A150 2.20fr green   1.25 .40
382 A150 2.30fr vermilion   1.00 .40
383 A150 2.40fr green   1.40 .80
384 A150 2.50fr vermilion   1.25 .40
385 A150 2.80fr vermilion   1.60 .40
    Nos. 380-385 (6)   7.50 2.80

Booklet Stamps
Perf. 13
386 A176 2.30fr red   1.00 .40
  a.   Booklet pane of 5   5.00
387 A176 2.50fr vermilion   1.25 .40
  a.   Booklet pane of 5   6.25
388 A176 2.80fr red   1.25 .40
  c.   Booklet pane of 5   6.25
    Nos. 386-388 (3)   3.50 1.20

Issued: 2.20fr, #384, 10/26/91; #387, 10/21/91; 2.40fr, 2.80fr, 8/9/93; 2.10fr, 2.30fr, 1990.

Llorts Mines A193

1990, Apr. 21   **Engr.**   *Perf. 12½x13*
390 A193 3.20fr multicolored   1.75 1.00

Europa A194

Designs: 2.30fr, Early post office. 3.20fr, Modern post office.

1990, May 5   *Perf. 13*
391 A194 2.30fr blk & scar   2.00 .75
392 A194 3.20fr scar & vio   3.00 1.50

Otter A195

1990, May 25   *Perf. 12x13*
393 A195 2.30fr Roses, vert.   1.10 .55
394 A195 3.20fr shown   1.75 1.00

Censer of St. Roma of Les Bons A196

1990, June 25   *Perf. 12½x13*
395 A196 3fr multicolored   1.25 .65

Tobacco Drying Sheds, Les Bons A197

1990, Sept. 15   **Engr.**   *Perf. 12½x13*
396 A197 2.30fr multi   1.00 .65

St. Coloma (Detail) A198

1990, Oct. 8   *Perf. 12½x13*
397 A198 5fr multi   2.50 1.50

Coin from Church of St. Eulalia d'Encamp A199

1990, Oct. 27   **Litho.**   *Perf. 13*
398 A199 3.20fr multi   1.40 .75

De Gaulle Type of 1972 Dated 1990

1990, Oct. 23   **Engr.**   *Perf. 13*
399 A88 2.30fr vio bl   1.00 .65
400 A88 3.20fr dk car   1.25 1.10
  a.   Pair, #399-400 + label   2.50 2.50
    Birth centenary of De Gaulle.

4th Games of the Small European States — A200

1991, Apr. 8   **Photo.**   *Perf. 13*
401 A200 2.50fr multicolored   1.00 .60

Chapel of St. Roma Dels Vilars A201

1991, Mar. 9   **Engr.**   *Perf. 13*
402 A201 2.50fr multicolored   1.10 .65

Europa — A202

2.50fr, TV satellite. 3.50fr, Telescope, horiz.

1991, Apr. 27   *Perf. 13x12½, 12½x13*
403 A202 2.50fr multicolored   2.75 1.75
404 A202 3.50fr multicolored   4.50 2.25

Bottles from Tombs of St. Vincenc d'Enclar A203

1991, May 11   **Photo.**   *Perf. 13*
405 A203 3.20fr multicolored   1.50 1.00

Farm Animals A204

1991, June 22   **Engr.**   *Perf. 13*
406 A204 2.50fr Sheep   1.25 .80
407 A204 3.50fr Cow   2.00 1.25

Petanque World
Championships — A205

1991, Sept. 14   **Engr.**   **Perf. 13**
408   A205   2.50fr multicolored   1.25   .95

Wolfgang
Amadeus
Mozart,
Death
Bicent.
A206

1991, Oct. 5
409   A206   3.40fr multicolored   1.75   1.10

Virgin and
Child of St.
Julia and
St. Germa
A207

1991, Nov. 16   **Engr.**   **Perf. 12½x13**
410   A207   5fr multicolored   2.00   1.00

1992 Winter
Olympics,
Albertville — A208

1992, Feb. 10   **Litho.**   **Perf. 13**
411   A208   2.50fr Slalom skiing   1.25   1.00
412   A208   3.40fr Figure skating   1.25   1.00
   a.   Pair, #411-412 + label   2.75   2.75

Church of
St. Andrew
of Arinsal
A209

1992, Mar. 21   **Engr.**   **Perf. 12x13**
413   A209   2.50fr black & tan   .75   .50

Discovery
of America,
500th
Anniv.
A210

2.50fr, Columbus' fleet. 3.40fr, Landing in
New World.

1992, Apr. 25   **Perf. 13**
414   A210   2.50fr multicolored   *2.50 1.00*
415   A210   3.40fr multicolored   *5.00 2.00*
Europa.

1992 Summer
Olympics,
Barcelona — A211

1992, June 8   **Litho.**   **Perf. 13**
416   A211   2.50fr Kayaking   1.25   1.00
417   A211   3.40fr Shooting   1.25   1.00
   a.   Pair, #416-417 + label   2.75   2.75

European
Globeflower — A212

Design: 3.40fr, Vulture, horiz.

1992, July 6
418   A212   2.50fr multicolored   1.25   .65
419   A212   3.40fr multicolored   1.75   1.00

Martyrdom
of St.
Eulalia
A213

1992, Sept. 14   **Photo.**   **Perf. 13**
420   A213   4fr multicolored   1.50   .95

Sculpture
by Mauro
Staccioli
A214

1992, Oct. 5   **Engr.**   **Perf. 12½x13**
421   A214   5fr multicolored   2.00   1.00
Ordino Arcalis '91.

Tempest in a Tea Cup, by Dennis
Oppenheim — A215

1992, Nov. 14   **Engr.**   **Perf. 13x12½**
422   A215   5fr multicolored   2.00   1.00

Skiing in Andorra — A216

Ski resorts: No. 423: a, 2.50fr, Soldeu El
Tarter. b, 3.40fr, Arinsal.

No. 424: a, 2.50fr, Pas de la Casa-Grau
Roig. b, 2.50fr, Ordino Arcalis. c, 3.40fr, Pal.

1993, Mar. 13   **Litho.**   **Perf. 13**
423   A216   Pair, #a.-b. + label   2.60   2.60
424   A216   Strip of 3, #a.-c.   3.75   3.75

Sculptures — A217

Europa: 2.50fr, "Estructures Autogener-
adores," by Jorge du Bon, vert. 3.40fr, Sculpture, "Fisicromia per Andorra," by Carlos Cruz-
Diez.

1993, May 15   **Engr.**   **Perf. 12½x13**
425   A217   2.50fr multicolored   1.60   1.25
       Litho.
       Perf. 14x13½
426   A217   3.40fr multicolored   2.00   1.50

Butterflies
A218

2.50fr, Polymmatus icarus. 4.20fr,
Nymphalidae.

1993, June 28   **Litho.**   **Perf. 13**
427   A218   2.50fr multicolored   1.20   .65
428   A218   4.20fr multicolored   1.90   1.40

Tour de France
Bicycle
Race — A219

1993, July 20   **Litho.**   **Perf. 13**
429   A219   2.50fr multicolored   1.25   .65

Andorra
School,
10th Anniv.
A220

1993, Sept. 20   **Litho.**   **Perf. 13**
430   A220   2.80fr multicolored   1.25   1.00

Un Lloc
Paga, by
Michael
Warren
A221

1993, Oct. 18   **Engr.**   **Perf. 12½x13**
431   A221   5fr blue & black   2.00   1.50

Sculpture,
by Erik
Dietman
A222

1993, Nov. 8   **Engr.**   **Perf. 12½x13**
432   A222   5fr multicolored   2.00   1.50

1994 Winter
Olympics,
Lillehammer
A223

1994, Feb. 21   **Litho.**   **Perf. 13**
433   A223   3.70fr multicolored   2.25   1.50

1st Anniversary of
the
Constitution — A224

Designs: 2.80fr, Monument, by Emili
Armengol. 3.70fr, Stone tablet with inscription.

1994, Mar. 15   **Litho.**   **Perf. 13**
434   A224   2.80fr multicolored   1.25   1.00
435   A224   3.70fr multicolored   1.25   1.00
   a.   Pair, #434-435 + label   2.75   2.75

European
Discoveries
A225

Europa: 2.80fr, Discovery of AIDS virus.
3.70fr, Radio diffusion.

1994, May 7   **Litho.**   **Perf. 13**
436   A225   2.80fr multicolored   1.75   .90
437   A225   3.70fr multicolored   2.75   1.25

1994 World Cup Soccer
Championships, US — A226

1994, June 20
438   A226   3.70fr multicolored   2.00   1.25

Tourist
Sports — A227

Designs: No. 439, Mountain climbing. No.
440, Fishing. No. 441, Horseback riding. No.
442, Mountain biking.

1994, July 11
439 A227 2.80fr multicolored   1.20 1.00
440 A227 2.80fr multicolored   1.20 1.00
  a.   Pair, #439-440 + label   2.50 2.50
441 A227 2.80fr multicolored   1.20 1.00
442 A227 2.80fr multicolored   1.20 1.00
  a.   Pair, #441-442 + label   2.50 2.50
   Nos. 439-442 (4)   4.80 4.00

Butterflies
A228

2.80fr, Iphiclides podalirus. 4.40fr, Aglais urticae.

1994, Sept. 5   **Litho.**   *Perf. 13*
443 A228 2.80fr multicolored   1.60 .65
444 A228 4.40fr multicolored   2.25 .95

A229

1994, Oct. 22   **Litho.**   *Perf. 13*
445 A229 2.80fr multicolored   1.10 .65
Meeting of the Co-Princes, 1st anniv.

A230

1995, Feb. 27   **Litho.**   *Perf. 13*
446 A230 2.80fr multicolored   1.50 .50
European Nature Conservation Year

1995 World Cup Rugby
Championships — A231

1995, Apr. 24   **Litho.**   *Perf. 13*
447 A231 2.80fr multicolored   1.50 .75

Peace &
Freedom
A232

Europa: 2.80fr, Dove with olive branch. 3.70fr, Flock of doves.

1995, Apr. 29
448 A232 2.80fr multicolored   1.90 .75
449 A232 3.70fr multicolored   3.00 1.00

Caritas in
Andorra,
15th Anniv.
A233

1995, May 15   **Litho.**   *Perf. 13*
450 A233 2.80fr multicolored   1.40 .65

Caldea Health
Spa — A234

1995, June 26   **Litho.**   *Perf. 13*
451 A234 2.80fr multicolored   1.20 .65

Ordino Natl.
Auditorium
A235

1995, July 10   **Litho. & Engr.**
452 A235 3.70fr black & buff   1.50 1.00

Virgin of Meritxell — A236

1995, Sept. 11   **Litho.**   *Perf. 14*
453 A236 4.40fr multicolored   1.75 .95

Protection
of Nature
A237

Butterflies: 2.80fr, Papallona llimonera, vert. 3.70fr, Papallona melanargia galathea.

1995, Sept. 25   *Perf. 13*
454 A237 2.80fr multicolored   1.50 1.00
455 A237 3.70fr multicolored   1.75 1.25

UN, 50th
Anniv. — A238

2.80fr, Flag, emblem. 3.70fr, Emblem, "50," flag.

1995, Oct. 21   **Litho.**   *Perf. 13*
456 A238 2.80fr multicolored   1.25 1.00
457 A238 3.70fr multicolored   1.25 1.00
  a.   Pair, #456-457 + label   2.75 2.75

Andorra's
Entrance
into Council
of Europe
A239

1995, Nov. 4
458 A239 2.80fr multicolored   1.40 .65

World Skiing Championships, Ordino
Arcalis — A240

1996, Jan. 29   **Litho.**   *Perf. 13*
459 A240 2.80fr multicolored   1.10 .65

Basketball in
Andorra — A241

1996, Jan. 29   **Litho.**   *Perf. 13*
460 A241 3.70fr multicolored   1.50 .95

Our Lady of
Meritxell
Special
School,
25th Anniv.
A242

1996, Feb. 17   **Litho.**   *Perf. 13*
461 A242 2.80fr multicolored   1.10 .65

Songbirds
A243

3fr, Pit riog. 3.80fr, Mallarenga carbonera.

1996, Mar. 25
462 A243   3fr multicolored   1.25 .65
463 A243   3.80fr multicolored   1.75 1.40

First Arms Type of 1983
1996, Apr. 17   **Engr.**   *Perf. 13*
464 A150 2.70fr green   .95 .65
465 A150   3fr red   1.20 .35

Cross of St. James
d'Engordany
A244

1996, Apr. 20   **Litho.**
466 A244 3fr multicolored   1.25 .65

Censer of
St. Eulalia
d'Encamp
A245

1996, Apr. 20
467 A245 3.80fr multicolored   1.50 1.20

Europa — A246

3fr, Ermessenda de Castellbo.

1996, May 6
468 A246 3fr multicolored   *1.90 1.00*

Chess — A247

1996, June 8   **Litho.**   *Perf. 13*
469 A247 4.50fr multicolored   1.90 1.00

1996
Summer
Olympic
Games,
Atlanta
A248

1996, June 29   **Litho.**   *Perf. 13*
470 A248 3fr multicolored   1.50 .70

Arms of the Community
of Canillo — A249

Serpentine Die Cut 7 Vert.
1996, June 10   **Litho.**
Self-Adhesive
471 A249 (3fr) multicolored   1.20 .45
  a.   Booklet of 10   12.00

Natl.
Children's
Choir, 5th
Anniv.
A250

1996, Sept. 14   *Perf. 13*
472 A250 3fr multicolored   1.20 .60

Livestock
Fair
A251

1996, Oct. 26   **Engr.**   *Perf. 12x13*
473 A251 3fr multicolored   1.20 .60

Churches
A252

Designs: No. 474, St. Romá de Les Bons. No. 475, St. Coloma.

1996, Nov. 16   Litho.   Perf. 13
474 A252 6.70fr multicolored   2.75 1.40
475 A252 6.70fr multicolored   2.75 1.40

A253

1997, Jan. 7   Litho.   Perf. 13
476 A253 3fr multicolored   1.20 .60
Pres. Francois Mitterrand (1916-96).

A254

Sawtooth Die Cut 7 Vert. x Straight Die Cut
1997, Feb. 24   Litho.
Self-Adhesive
477 A254 (3fr) Arms of Encamp   1.50 .45
a.   Booklet pane of 10   15.00

By its nature, No. 477a is a complete booklet. The peelable paper backing serves as a booklet cover.

A255

1997, Mar. 22   Perf. 13
478 A255 3fr Volleyball   1.25 .60

"The White Lady" — A256

1997, June 10   Litho.   Perf. 13
479 A256 3fr multicolored   1.75 .90
Europa (Stories and Legends).

Oreneta Cuablanca A257

1997, May 31   Litho.   Perf. 13
480 A257 3.80fr multicolored   2.40 1.25

Paintings of Mills A258

1997, Sept. 15   Litho.   Perf. 13
481 A258   3fr Cal Pal, vert.   1.25 .60
482 A258 4.50fr Mas d'en Sole   2.00 1.00

Religious Artifacts A259

Designs: 3fr, Monstrance of St. Iscle and St. Victoria. 15.50fr, Altar piece of St. Pierre d'Alxirivall.

1997, Oct. 27
483 A259   3fr multicolored   1.40 .60
484 A259 15.50fr multicolored   5.50 2.75
a.   Pair, #483-484 + label   7.50 7.50

Legends — A260

Designs: No. 485, Legend of Meritxell. No. 486, The cross of seven arms. 3.80fr, The fountain of Esmelicat.

1997, Nov. 22   Litho.   Perf. 13
485 A260   3fr multicolored   1.40 .60
486 A260   3fr multicolored   1.40 .60
487 A260 3.80fr multicolored   2.00 1.00
a.   Strip of 3, #485-487   5.00 5.00

Chapel of St. Miguel d'Engolasters — A261

1997, Nov. 28   Litho.   Perf. 13
488 A261 3fr multicolored   1.20 .60
Monaco Intl. Philatelic Exhibition.

Happy Anniversary — A262

1998, Jan. 3   Litho.   Perf. 13
489 A262 3fr Juggling candles   1.20 .60

1998 Winter Olympic Games, Nagano — A263

1998, Feb. 14
490 A263 4.40fr multicolored   2.00 1.00

Arms of Ordino — A264

Serpentine Die Cut Vert.
1998, Mar. 7   Self-Adhesive   Litho.
Booklet Stamp
491 A264 (3fr) multicolored   1.25 .30
a.   Booklet pane of 10   12.50
     Complete booklet, #491a   12.50
See Nos. 504, 518, 531.

Mesa de Vila Church — A265

1998, Mar. 28   Perf. 13
492 A265 4.50fr multicolored   2.25 2.00

Rotary Club of Andorra, 20th Anniv. — A265a

1998, Apr. 11
493 A265a 3fr multicolored   1.20 .60

Finch A266

1998   Litho.   Perf. 13
494 A266 3.80fr multicolored   2.00 1.00

1998 World Cup Soccer Championships, France — A267

1998, June 6   Litho.   Perf. 13
495 A267 3fr multicolored   1.60 1.25
For overprint see No. 499.

Music Festival A268

1998, June 20   Litho.   Perf. 13
496 A268 3fr multicolored   1.50 .90
Europa.

Expo '98, Lisbon A269

1998, July 6
497 A269 5fr multicolored   2.25 1.40

Chalice, House of the Valleys — A270

1998, Sept. 19   Litho.   Perf. 13
498 A270 4.50fr multicolored   2.25 1.00

No. 495 Overprinted

1998, Nov. 16
499 A267 3fr multicolored   2.75 1.50

Early Maps of Andorra A271

1998, Nov. 16
500 A271   3fr 1717, vert.   2.00 1.25
501 A271 15.50fr 1777   8.00 3.50

Inauguration of the Postal Museum — A272

1998, Nov. 19   Litho.   Perf. 13
502 A272 3fr multicolored   1.20 .60

Manual Digest, 250th Anniv. A273

1998, Dec. 7
503 A273 3.80fr multicolored   1.50 1.00

Arms Type of 1998
Self-Adhesive
Serpentine Die Cut Vert.
1999, Jan. 18   Booklet Stamp
504 A264 (3fr) La Massana   1.25 .55
a.   Booklet pane of 10   12.50
No. 504a is a complete booklet.

Recycling
A274

1999, Mar. 13   Litho.   Perf. 13
505 A274 5fr multicolored   2.25 1.40

Sorteny Valley — A275

1999, Apr. 10
506 A275 3fr multicolored   2.00 1.25

Europa.

Council of
Europe,
50th Anniv.
A276

1999, May 5   Litho.   Perf. 13
507 A276 3.80fr multicolored   1.60 1.00

First Stage
Coach — A277

1999, May 15
508 A277 2.70fr multi   1.60 1.25

1999 European National Soccer
Championships — A278

1999, June 10   Photo.   Perf. 13
509 A278 4.50fr multicolored   2.25 1.50

PhilexFrance 99 — A279

1999, July 2   Litho.   Perf. 13x13¼
510 A279 3fr multicolored   1.20 .60

Historic
View of
Pal — A280

Perf. 13x13¼, 13¼x13
1999, July 10   Litho.
511 A280 3fr shown   1.20 .60
512 A280 3fr Different view, vert. 1.40 .60

International Federation of
Photographic Art, 50th Anniv. — A281

1999, July 24   Litho.   Perf. 13
513 A281 4.40fr multicolored   2.25 1.00

Casa Rull,
Sispony
A282

1999, Sept. 6   Litho.   Perf. 13x13¼
514 A282 15.50fr multicolored   6.00 3.50

Chest With Six Locks — A283

1999, Oct. 9   Litho.   Perf. 13x13¼
515 A283 6.70fr multicolored   2.75 1.50

Christmas
A284

1999, Nov. 27   Litho.   Perf. 13
516 A284 3fr multicolored   1.20 .60

Year 2000
A285

2000, Jan. 5   Litho.   Perf. 13x13¼
517 A285 3fr multicolored   1.20 .60

Arms Type of 1998
Self-Adhesive
Serpentine Die Cut 6½ Vert.
2000, Feb. 26   Booklet Stamp
518 A264 (3fr) Andorra-la-Vielle   1.25 .40
 a.   Booklet pane of 10   12.50

No. 518a is a complete booklet.

Snowboarding
A286

2000, Mar. 17   Litho.   Perf. 13
519 A286 4.50fr multi   2.00 1.00

Montserrat
Caballé
Chant
Competition
A287

2000, Apr. 3   Perf. 13x13¼
520 A287 3.80fr multi   2.00 1.00

Campanula
Cochlearifolia
A288

2000, Apr. 17   Litho.   Perf. 13
521 A288 2.70fr multi   1.20 .60

Europa, 2000
Common Design Type
2000, May 9   Perf. 13½x13
522 CD17 3fr multi   2.00 1.00

Festivals
A289

No. 523: a, Canòlic. b, Meritxell.

2000, May 27   Litho.   Perf. 13
523   Pair + central label   3.00 3.00
 a.-b.   A289 3fr Any single   1.25 .60

Pardal
Comú — A290

2000, July 7   Litho.   Perf. 13
524 A290 4.40fr multi   2.00 1.00

A291

2000, Sept. 11   Litho.   Perf. 13
525 A291 5fr multi   2.00 1.00

2000 Summer Olympics, Sydney.

World Tourism
Day — A292

2000, Sept. 28
526 A292 3fr multi   1.20 .60

Expo 2000,
Hanover
A293

2000, Oct. 6   Litho.   Perf. 13
527 A293 3fr multi   1.20 .60

"Europe, A
Common
Heritage"
A294

2000, Nov. 4   Litho.   Perf. 13½x13
528 A294 3.80fr multi   1.60 1.00

Prehistoric Pottery of Prats — A295

2000, Dec. 16   Perf. 13x13¼
529 A295 6.70fr multi   3.00 1.50

National Archives,
25th Anniv. — A296

2000, Dec. 22   Perf. 13
530 A296 15.50fr multi   7.50 4.50

Arms Type of 1998
Serpentine Die Cut 6½ Vert.
2001, Feb. 19   Litho.
Booklet Stamp
Self-Adhesive
531 A264 (3fr) Sant Julià de
            Lòria   1.25 .40
 a.   Booklet, 10 #531   12.50

Canillo Aliga Mountain Station — A297

2001, Feb. 10   Litho.   **Perf. 13**
532 A297 4.50fr multi   2.00 1.00

Casa Cristo Museum A298

2001, Feb. 17   **Perf. 13¼x13**
533 A298 6.70fr multi   2.75 1.50

Andorran Heritage — A299

No. 534: a, Legend of Engolasters Lake. b, Foundation of Andorra.

2001, Mar. 23   **Perf. 13**
534 A299 3fr Pair, #a-b, with central label   3.00 3.00

Intl. Book Day — A300

2001, Apr. 23   Litho.   **Perf. 13**
535 A300 3.80fr multi   1.75 1.00

Europa — A301

2001, Apr. 28
536 A301 3fr multi   2.00 1.00

A302

3fr, Raspberries, vert.

2001, May 12
537 A302   3fr multicolored   1.20 .60
538 A302 4.40fr shown   2.00 1.00

European Language Year A303

2001, June 16   Litho.   **Perf. 13**
539 A303 3.80fr multi   1.75 1.00

Escaldes-Engordany Jazz Festival — A304

2001, July 7
540 A304 3fr multi   1.60 .70

General Council's Kitchen A305

2001, Aug. 10
541 A305 5fr multi   2.50 1.50

Chapel of the Virgin of Meritxell, 25th Anniv. of Rebuilding — A306

2001, Sept. 7   Litho.   **Perf. 13**
542 A306 3fr multi   1.60 .80

Hotel Pla — A307

2001, Oct. 12
543 A307 15.50fr multi   6.50 3.00

Cross of Terme — A308

2001, Nov. 17   Litho.   **Perf. 13½x13**
544 A308 2.70fr multi   1.25 .75

100 Cents = 1 Euro (€)

National Arms — A309

Legends
A310   A311

Designs: 10c, Legend of Meritxell. 20c, Fountain of Esmelicat. 50c, The Cross with Seven Arms. €1, The Founding of Andorra. €2, Legend of Engolasters Lake. €5, The White Lady.

Perf. 13¼ (A309), 13¼x13
2002, Jan. 2   Photo. (A309), Litho.
545 A309   1c yel & multi   .25 .25
546 A309   2c tan & multi   .25 .25
547 A309   5c bl & multi   .25 .25
548 A310   10c multi   .25 .25
549 A310   20c multi   .50 .40
550 A309 (46c) red & multi   1.00 .40
551 A310   50c multi   2.25 .80
552 A311   €1 multi   2.50 1.00
553 A311   €2 multi   4.50 1.50
554 A311   €5 multi   12.00 5.00
   Nos. 545-554 (10)   23.75 10.10

See Nos. 577, 618, 635, 661-666, 680.

Traffic Safety Education in Schools — A312

2002, Jan. 25   Litho.   **Perf. 13½x13**
555 A312 69c multi   2.25 1.00

2002 Winter Olympics, Salt Lake City — A313

2002, Feb. 2   Litho.   **Perf. 13**
556 A313 58c multi   1.50 .75

Hotel Rosaleda A314

2002, Mar. 16   Litho.   **Perf. 13**
557 A314 46c multi   2.25 1.00

World Day for Water — A315

2002, Mar. 22   Litho.   **Perf. 13**
558 A315 67c multi   1.60 1.00

Europa — A316

2002, May 10   Litho.   **Perf. 13**
559 A316 46c multi   2.00 .40

Bilberries — A317

2002, July 6   Litho.   **Perf. 13**
560 A317 46c multi   1.60 .80

Seated Nude, Sculpture by Josep Viladomat — A318

2002, Aug. 24   Litho.   **Perf. 13¼x13**
561 A318 €2.36 multi   6.50 3.25

Envalira Tunnel A319

2002, Sept. 2   **Perf. 13**
562 A319 46c multi   1.75 .80

Piper of Ordino — A320

2002, Sept. 27
563 A320 41c multi   1.75 .80

See No. 578.

Detail of Santa Coloma Wall Painting — A321

2002, Nov. 16   Litho.   **Perf. 13**
564 A321 €1.02 multi   3.00 1.75

Comú d'Escaldes — Engordany Coat of Arms — A322

Serpentine Die Cut 6¾ Vert.
2003, Jan. 20   **Photo.**
Booklet Stamp
Self-Adhesive
565   A322   (46c) multi   1.40   .50
a.   Booklet pane of 10   14.00

Legend of the Margineda Pine — A323

2003, Feb. 10   **Litho.**   *Perf. 13*
566   A323   69c multi   2.00   1.00
      See No. 579.

Constitution, 10th Anniv. A324

2003, Mar. 14   **Litho.**   *Perf. 13x13½*
567   A324   €2.36 multi   6.50   3.50

Buildings, Les Bons — A325

2003, Mar. 31   *Perf. 13*
568   A325   67c multi   2.25   1.25

Hotel Mirador A326

2003, Apr. 12   **Litho.**   *Perf. 13*
569   A326   €1.02 multi   3.00   2.00

Europa — A327

2003, May 17
570   A327   46c multi   1.75   .80

Falles de San Joan A328

2003, June 23   **Litho.**   *Perf. 13*
571   A328   50c multi   1.60   .80

A329

2003, July 5
572   A329   50c multi   1.75   .80
      Tour de France bicycle race, cent.

A330

2003, Aug. 8
573   A330   90c multi   2.50   1.50
      World Track and Field Championships, Paris.

Sparassis Crispa A331

Currants A332

2003, Sept. 15   **Litho.**   *Perf. 13*
574   A331   45c multi   1.50   1.00
575   A332   75c multi   2.25   1.00

Telephones in Andorra, Cent. A333

2003, Oct. 30   **Litho.**   *Perf. 13*
576   A333   50c multi   1.75   .65

Types of 2002-03 Inscribed "Postes"
2003, Nov. 29   **Photo.**   *Perf. 13x13¼*
577   A309   (45c) green & multi   1.30   .80
      Litho.
      Perf. 13
578   A320   75c multi   3.25   2.00
579   A323   90c multi   3.25   2.25
      Nos. 577-579 (3)   7.80   5.05

Maternity, by Paul Gauguin A334

2003, Nov. 29   **Litho.**   *Perf. 13¼x13*
580   A334   75c multi   3.00   1.75

St. Anthony's Auction — A335

2004, Jan. 17   **Litho.**   *Perf. 13*
581   A335   50c multi   1.25   .60

Children of the World — A336

2004, Mar. 20   **Litho.**   *Perf. 13*
582   A336   50c multi   1.25   .60

Hotel Valira A337

2004, Apr. 17   **Litho.**   *Perf. 13*
583   A337   €1.11 multi   3.00   2.50

Europa — A338

2004, May 7   **Litho.**   *Perf. 13*
584   A338   50c multi   1.40   .60

A339

2004, May 15
585   A339   45c multi   1.25   .65
      Legend of the Castle of St. Vincent.

A340

2004, June 26
586   A340   75c multi   1.75   .90
      Madriu-Peralita-Claror Valley, UNESCO World Heritage Site candidate.

Poblet de Fontenada A341

2004, July 3
587   A341   50c multi   1.40   .60

2004 Summer Olympics, Athens A342

2004, Aug. 7   **Litho.**   *Perf. 13*
588   A342   90c multi   2.50   1.75

Margineda Bridge — A343

No. 589: a, €1, Black and white sketch. b, €2, Full color painting.

2004, Oct. 2
589   A343   Horiz. pair, #a-b, + central label   8.00   8.00

Postal Code — A344

2004, Oct. 23   *Perf. 13¼x13*
590   A344   50c multi   1.40   .60

Admission to Council of Europe, 10th Anniv. — A345

2004, Nov. 6
591   A345   €2.50 multi   6.50   4.00

Christmas — A346

2004, Dec. 4   **Perf. 13**
592 A346 50c multi   1.40 .60

The Magi
A347

2005, Jan. 5
593 A347 50c multi   1.50 .65

Selection of Madriu-Peralita-Claror
Valley as UNESCO World Heritage
Site — A348

2005, Jan. 22
594 A348 50c multi   1.40 .60

Legend of
Rat Pass
A349

2005, Feb. 12
595 A349 48c multi   1.50 .65

Aegolius
Funereus — A350

2005, Apr. 6   **Litho.**   **Perf. 13**
596 A350 90c multi   2.50 2.25

Europa
A351

2005, May 7   **Litho.**   **Perf. 13x13¼**
597 A351 55c multi   1.60 1.40

Souvenir Sheet

9th Games of Small European
States — A352

No. 598: a, 53c, Shooting. b, 55c, Track and
field. c, 82c, Swimming. d, €1, Basketball.

2005, May 28   **Perf. 13¼x13**
598 A352 Sheet of 4, #a-d   8.00 8.00

Bordes
d'Ensegur — A353

2005, June 11   **Litho.**   **Perf. 13**
599 A353 €2.50 multi   6.50 5.00

Police
Motorcycle — A354

2005, July 2
600 A354 53c multi   1.50 1.20

Prats de Santa Coloma, by J.
Mir — A355

2005, Aug. 10   **Perf. 13x13¼**
601 A355 82c multi   2.25 1.75

Calones
Hostel
A356

2005, Sept. 10   **Litho.**   **Perf. 13**
602 A356 €1.98 multi   6.00 4.50

Josep Alsina
Photography
Business — A357

2005, Oct. 8   **Litho.**   **Perf. 13¼x13**
603 A357 53c multi   1.40 .65

Rotary International, Cent. — A358

2005, Nov. 5   **Perf. 13**
604 A358 55c multi   1.40 .65

Adoration of the Shepherds, by Antoni
Viladomat — A359

2005, Dec. 7   **Litho.**   **Perf. 13**
605 A359 €1.22 multi   3.50 3.00

Animals
A360

Designs: No. 606, 53c, Ursus arctos. No.
607, 53c, Rupicapra pyrenaica, vert.

2006, Jan. 16
606-607 A360   Set of 2   3.00 2.50
    See Nos. 619-620, 633-634, 648-649, 670-
671.

2006 Winter Olympics, Turin — A361

No. 608: a, 55c, Alpine skiing. b, 75c,
Cross-country skiing.

2006, Feb. 4
608 A361   Horiz. pair, #a-b, +
       central label   3.50 3.50

Tobacco
Museum — A362

2006, Mar. 4   **Litho.**   **Perf. 13**
609 A362 82c multi   2.00 1.50

Decree of Napoleon I, Bicent. — A363

2006, Mar. 27
610 A363 53c multi   1.40 .65

Legend of the Bear
Cave — A364

2006, Apr. 10   **Litho.**   **Perf. 13**
611 A364 48c multi   2.00 1.00

Europa
A365

2006, May 9   **Litho.**   **Perf. 13x13¼**
612 A365 53c multi   1.40 .65

Sorteny Valley
Nature
Park — A366

2006, June 10   **Perf. 13**
613 A366 55c multi   1.40 .65

Pablo Casals (1876-
1973),
Cellist — A367

2006, July 31   **Litho.**   **Perf. 13**
614 A367 90c multi   2.25 2.10

Ford
Model
T — A368

2006, Sept. 2   **Litho.**   **Perf. 13**
615 A368 85c multi   2.25 2.10

Montserrat Procession, by Josp
Borrell — A369

2006, Nov. 4   **Litho.**   **Perf. 13¼x13**
616 A369 €1.30 multi   3.25 3.00

Retable, St. Martin's Church, Cortinada A370

2006, Dec. 2   **Perf. 13**
617 A370 54c multi   1.40 .65

Arms Type of 2002 Inscribed "Postes"

2007, Jan. 13   **Perf. 13x13¼**
618 A309 60c multi   1.50 .75

Animals Type of 2006

Designs: 54c, Marmota marmota, vert. 60c, Sciurus vulgaris.

2007, Jan. 20   **Perf. 13**
619-620 A360   Set of 2   3.00 2.50

Legend of the Wolf's Testament — A371

2007, Feb. 24
621 A371 49c multi   1.40 .65

Predelle, Prats A372

2007, Mar. 17   Litho.   Perf. 13¼x13
622 A372 €1.30 multi   3.50 3.25

Compare with types A383, A396, A414 and A420.

National Arms — A373

Serpentine Die Cut 11
2007, Apr. 2   **Litho.**
Booklet Stamp
Self-Adhesive
623 A373 (54c) multi   1.60 1.60
   a.   Booklet pane of 10   16.00
   b.   Booklet pane of 12   21.00

Issued: No. 623b, 3/1/16. Stamps in No. 623b sold for 80c on day of issue.

Rose A374

2007, Apr. 23   Photo.   Perf. 13¼
624 A374 86c multi   2.25 2.00
Values are for stamps with surrounding selvage.

Europa — A375

2007, May 5   Litho.   Perf. 13¼x13
625 A375 54c multi   1.75 1.60
Scouting, cent.

Joining of Meritxell and Sabart — A376

No. 626: a, Madonna and Child. b, Priest.

2007, June 2   Litho.   Perf. 13
626 A376 54c Horiz. pair, #a-b, +   3.00 3.00
     central label

Engine A377

2007, July 10
627 A377 60c multi   1.50 1.25

2007 Rugby World Cup, France A378

2007, Sept. 1   Litho.   Perf. 13¼
628 A378 85c multi   2.00 1.50
Values are for stamps with surrounding selvage.

Comapedrosa Valley — A379

2007, Oct. 6   Litho.   Perf. 13¼x13
629 A379 €3.04 multi   7.50 6.50

Prehistoric People — A380

Prehistoric people at: 60c, Margineda Grotto. 85c, Cedre.

2007, Nov. 10
630-631 A380   Set of 2   4.00 3.50

Retable, St. Martin's Church, Cortinada A381

2007, Dec. 3   Litho.   Perf. 13
632 A381 54c multi   1.40 .65

Animals Type of 2006

Designs: 54c, Vulpes vulpes. 60c, Sus scrofa, vert.

2008, Jan. 28
633-634 A360   Set of 2   3.50 3.00

Arms Type of 2002 Inscribed "Postes"
2008, Mar. 1   Photo.   Perf. 13x13¼
635 A309 65c blue & multi   1.50 1.00

Legend of the Treasure of the Fountain of Manegó — A382

2008, Mar. 8   Litho.   Perf. 13
636 A382 50c multi   1.25 .75

Predelle, Prats A383

2008, Apr. 12   Perf. 13¼x13
637 A383 €1.33 multi   3.50 3.50
Compare with Types A372, A396, A414 and A420.

Cartercar Automobile A384

2008, May 3   Litho.   Perf. 13
638 A384 65c multi   1.75 1.50

Europa A385

2008, May 17
639 A385 55c multi   1.50 .75

Miniature Sheet

2008 Summer Olympics, Beijing — A386

No. 640: a, Kayaking. b, Running. c, Swimming. d, Judo.

2008, June 16   Litho.   Perf. 13x13½
640 A386 55c Sheet of 4, #a-d   6.00 6.00
Olympex 2008 Philatelic Exhibition, Beijing (#640d).

Narcissus Poeticus — A387

2008, June 18   Perf. 13¼x13
641 A387 55c multi   1.50 .75
No. 641 is impregnated with a narcissus scent.

Vall d'Incles A388

2008, July 5   Perf. 13
642 A388 €2.80 multi   7.50 7.50

Universal Male Suffrage, 75th Anniv. A389

2008, Aug. 30   Litho.   Perf. 13
643 A389 55c multi   1.40 .75

Sustainable Development — A390

2008, Oct. 4   Litho.   Perf. 13
644 A390 88c multi   2.00 1.25

Roc d'Enclar — A391

2008, Nov. 8   Perf. 13¼
645 A391 85c multi   2.00 1.25

Retable of St. Mark and St. Mary — A392

2008, Dec. 13   *Perf. 13*
646   A392   55c multi   1.40   .75

Louis Braille (1809-52), Educator of the Blind — A393

2009, Jan. 24   *Engr.*
647   A393   88c multi   2.00   1.25

Animals Type of 2006

Designs: 55c, Equus mulus, vert. 65c, Bos taurus.

2009, Feb. 14   *Litho.*   *Perf. 13*
648-649   A360   Set of 2   2.75   2.00

Legend of the Devils of Aixirvall — A394

2009, Mar. 7
650   A394   51c multi   1.40   .75

Souvenir Sheet

Protection of Polar Regions and Glaciers — A395

No. 651: a, 56c, Emperor penguins. b, 85c, Boat off shore in polar regions, vert.

Perf. 13x13¼, 13¼x13 (85c)
2009, Mar. 27   *Litho. & Engr.*
651   A395   Sheet of 2, #a-b, + label   3.50   3.50

Predelle, Prats A396

2009, Apr. 18   *Litho.*   *Perf. 13¼x13*
652   A396   €1.35 multi   3.50   3.50

Compare with types A372, A383, A414 and A420.

Europa A397

2009, May 2   *Perf. 13*
653   A397   56c multi   1.40   .75

Intl. Year of Astronomy.

Early Renault Automobile A398

2009, May 16
654   A398   70c multi   1.75   1.00

St. Joan de Caselles, by Maurice Utrillo — A399

2009, May 23   *Perf. 13x13¼*
655   A399   90c multi   2.25   1.50

Cercle des Pessons A400

2009, June 13   *Litho.*   *Perf. 13*
656   A400   €2.80 multi   7.50   6.00

Tour de France Bicycle Race — A401

2009, July 11
657   A401   56c multi   1.40   .75

Arts and Letters Circle, 40th Anniv. — A402

2009, Oct. 3   *Litho.*   *Perf. 13*
658   A402   51c multi   1.40   .75

Romanesque Art — A403

2009, Nov. 7   *Perf. 13¼x13*
659   A403   85c multi   2.00   1.50

Epiphany — A404

2009, Dec. 12   *Perf. 13*
660   A404   56c multi   1.40   .75

Arms Type of 2002 Inscribed "POSTES"

2010, Jan. 4   *Photo.*   *Perf. 13x13¼*
661   A309   1c yel & multi   .25   .25
662   A309   5c lt bl & multi   .25   .25
663   A309   10c org & multi   .25   .25
664   A309   20c lilac & multi   .45   .45
665   A309   50c ol grn & multi   1.25   1.25
666   A309   (70c) dk bl & multi   1.60   1.60
    Nos. 661-666 (6)   4.05   4.05

2010 Winter Olympics, Vancouver A405

2010, Jan. 23   *Photo.*   *Perf. 13x13¼*
667   A405   85c multi   2.00   1.50

Casamanya Peak — A406

2010, Feb. 15   *Litho.*   *Perf. 13*
668   A406   €2.80 multi   6.50   5.00

Rights of the Child Convention, 20th Anniv. — A407

2010, Mar. 2   *Photo.*
669   A407   56c multi   1.40   .75

Animals Type of 2006

Designs: 56c, Gyps fulvus, vert. 90c, Ovis aries.

2010, Mar. 8   *Litho.*   *Perf. 13*
670-671   A360   Set of 2   3.00   2.25

Andorran Embassy, Brussels — A408

2010, Apr. 12   *Engr.*   *Perf. 13*
672   A408   70c multi + label   1.75   1.75

Legend of Charlemagne's Chair — A409

2010, Apr. 26   *Litho.*   *Perf. 13*
673   A409   51c multi   1.25   .65

Europa A410

Litho. & Embossed with Foil Application

2010, May 10   *Perf. 13¼*
674   A410   56c multi   1.40   1.00

Radio Andorra Building A411

2010, May 25   *Litho.*   *Perf. 13*
675   A411   56c multi   1.40   1.00

1985 Ferrari 328 GTS A412

2010, June 21   *Litho.*   *Perf. 13*
676   A412   70c multi   1.75   1.75

Still Life, by Carme Massana
A413

2010, July 12   *Perf. 13¼x13*
677 A413 95c multi   2.50 2.50

Predelle, Prats
A414

2010, Sept. 6   Litho.   *Perf. 13¼x13*
678 A414 €1.40 multi   3.75 3.75
Compare with types A372, A383, A396 and A420.

Souvenir Sheet

Churches — A415

No. 679: a, Sant Joan de Caselles Church. b, Sant Romà de Les Bons Church, horiz.

Perf. 13¼x13, 13x13¼
2010, Oct. 4   Engr.
679 A415 58c Sheet of 2, #a-b   3.25 3.25
See Andorra, Spanish Administration No. 363.

Arms Type of 2002 Inscribed "POSTES"
2010, Oct. 18   Photo.   *Perf. 13x13¼*
680 A309 (58c) red & multi   1.75 1.75

Feudal Andorra — A416

681 A416 87c multi   2.40 2.40

Christmas — A417

2010, Nov. 29   *Perf. 13*
682 A417 58c multi   1.60 1.60

Legend of St. Joan de Caselles — A418

2011, Feb. 12   Litho.   *Perf. 13*
683 A418 €2.80 multi   8.00 8.00

Francophonia — A419

2011, Mar. 19   *Perf. 13x13¼*
684 A419 87c multi   2.50 2.50

Predelle, Prats
A420

2011, Apr. 9   *Perf. 13¼x13*
685 A420 €1.40 multi   4.00 4.00
Compare with types A372, A383, A386 and A414.

Europa — A421

Silk-Screened on Wood Veneer
2011, May 7   *Serpentine Die Cut 11*
Self-Adhesive
686 A421 58c black & white   1.75 1.75
Intl. Year of Forests.

Councilor, by Francesc Borràs (1891-1968) — A422

2011, May 21   Litho.   *Perf. 13*
687 A422 95c multi   2.75 2.75

Placeta de Sant Esteve — A423

2011, June 4   Engr.
688 A423 58c multi   1.75 1.75

Soriano-Pedroso Automobile — A424

2011, June 18   Litho.
689 A424 75c multi   2.10 2.10

Rugby
A425

2011, July 9   Photo.   *Perf. 13*
690 A425 89c multi   2.40 2.40
Values are for stamps with surrounding selvage.

Souvenir Sheet

Dance of the Seven Parishes, Plaza Benlloch — A426

2011, July 16   Litho. & Engr.
691 A426 €1.45 multi   4.25 4.25

Flora — A427

Designs: 60c, Rhododendron ferrugineum. €1, Rosa sempervirens, horiz.

2011, Sept. 4   Litho.   *Perf. 13*
692-693 A427   Set of 2   4.50 4.50
See Nos. 706-707, 720-721, 751.

Council of the Land
A428

2011, Sept. 24   *Perf. 13x13¼*
694 A428 89c multi   2.50 2.50

Leaf and Coat of Arms — A429

2011, Oct. 1   Photo.   *Perf. 13x13¼*
695 A429 (57c) multi   1.60 1.60

Angel From Santa Eulalia d'Encamp Retable — A430

2011, Nov. 26   Litho.   *Perf. 13*
696 A430 60c multi   1.60 1.60

Legend of the Shop of the Sorceresses
A431

2012, Jan. 14
697 A431 €2.78 multi   7.50 7.50

Women's World Cup Alpine Skiing Races, Soldeu
A432

2012, Feb. 11   *Perf. 13x13¼*
698 A432 89c multi   2.40 2.40

Massana Valley, by Joaquim Mir (1873-1940) — A433

2012, Mar. 3
699 A433 €1 multi   2.60 2.60

Souvenir Sheet

Restoration of Casa de la Vall, 50th Anniv. — A434

No. 700 — Casa de la Vall in: a, 1962. b, 2012.

2012, Mar. 10   **Litho. & Engr.**
700 A434 60c Sheet of 2, #a-b   3.25 3.25

Bugatti 37 Race Car A435

2012, Apr. 14   **Litho.**   *Perf. 13*
701 A435 77c multi   2.10 2.10

Souvenir Sheet

Europa — A436

2012, May 5   **Litho.**   *Perf. 13¼x13*
702 A436 77c multi   2.00 2.00
   Noi. 702 has die cut opening in center of stamp.

Placeta de la Consòrcia, Andorra la Vella — A437

2012, June 8   **Engr.**   *Perf. 13x12¾*
703 A437 60c multi   1.50 1.50

Judo — A438

2012, July 6   **Litho.**   *Perf. 13*
704 A438 77c multi   1.90 1.90

Souvenir Sheet

Marratxa Dance — A439

Litho. & Engr.
2012, July 20   *Perf. 13x13¼*
705 A439 €1.45 multi   3.75 3.75

Flora Type of 2011
   Designs: 60c, Sempervivum montanum. €1, Eryngium bourgatii.

2012, Sept. 14   **Litho.**   *Perf. 13*
706-707 A427   Set of 2   4.25 4.25

Woman Suffrage, 42nd Anniv. — A440

2012, Oct. 5   *Perf. 13¼x13*
708 A440 89c multi   2.25 2.25

Andorran Presidency of the Council of Europe — A441

2012, Oct. 26
709 A441 €1 multi   2.60 2.60

King Henri IV of France (1553-1610), Co-Prince of Andorra — A442

2012, Nov. 8   **Engr.**   *Perf. 13x13¼*
710 A442 60c multi   1.60 1.60
   a.   Sheet of 10, 5 each #710,
       France #4297,   16.00 16.00

   See France No. 4297.

Angel From Roser d'Ordino Retable — A443

2012, Nov. 23   **Litho.**   *Perf. 13*
711 A443 57c multi   1.50 1.50

Legend of Moixella — A444

2013, Jan. 12
712 A444 €2.78 multi   7.50 7.50

Souvenir Sheet

Bear Ball, Encamp — A445

Litho. & Engr.
2013, Feb. 23   *Perf. 13x13¼*
713 A445 €1.55 multi   4.00 4.00

Constitution, 20th Anniv. — A446

2013, Mar. 16   **Litho.**   *Perf. 13*
714 A446 63c multi   1.60 1.60

Cord 810 Phaeton A447

2013, Apr. 13
715 A447 95c multi   2.50 2.50

Plaça Rebés, Andorra la Vella — A448

2013, May 11   **Engr.**   *Perf. 12¾*
716 A448 63c multi   1.75 1.75

Europa A449

2013, May 18   **Litho.**   *Perf. 13¼*
717 A449 80c multi   2.25 2.25

Retable, Church of Sant Miquel, Prats A450

2013, July 6   **Litho.**   *Perf. 13¼x13*
718 A450 €1.05 multi   2.75 2.75

Andorran School, 30th Anniv. A451

2013, July 27   **Litho.**   *Perf. 13*
719 A451 63c multi   1.75 1.75

Flora Type of 2011
   Designs: 58c, Papaver rhoeas. €1.05, Paeonia mascula, horiz.

2013, Sept. 7   **Litho.**   *Perf. 13*
720-721 A427   Set of 2   4.50 4.50

First French School in Canillo, Cent. — A452

2013, Oct. 2   **Litho.**   *Perf. 13¼*
722 A452 63c multi   1.75 1.75

Andorran Presidency of the Working Community of the Pyrenees — A453

2013, Oct. 5   **Litho.**   *Perf. 13¼*
723 A453 95c multi   2.60 2.60

El Pas de la Casa, Painting by Véronique Bandry A454

2013, Oct. 26   **Litho.**   *Perf. 13¼x13*
724 A454 €1.55 multi   4.25 4.25

Angel, Saint Joan de Sispony Church — A455

2013, Nov. 12   Litho.   *Perf. 13*
725 A455 58c multi   1.60 1.60
Christmas.

Legend of the Canòlich Sanctuary — A456

2014, Jan. 11   Litho.   *Perf. 13*
726 A456 €3.50 multi   9.50 9.50

Schools in Partnership With UNESCO — A457

2014, Feb. 15   Litho.   *Perf. 13¼*
727 A457 66c multi   1.90 1.90

1917 Hispano Guadalajara Automobile — A458

2014, Mar. 29   Litho.   *Perf. 13*
728 A458 98c multi   2.75 2.75

Cyanistes Caeruleus A459

2014, May 3   Engr.   *Perf. 13¼*
729 A459 66c multi   1.90 1.90

Bagpipes A460

2014, May 24   Litho.   *Perf. 13¼*
730 A460 83c multi   2.25 2.25
Europa.

Madriu-Perafita-Claror Valley — A461

2014, June 16   Litho.   *Perf. 13*
731 A461 98c multi   2.75 2.75

Buildings in Engordany — A462

2014, June 16   Engr.   *Perf. 13x12¾*
732 A462 66c multi   1.90 1.90

Fixats en la Contemporaneïtat, by Javier Balmaseda — A463

2014, July 11   Litho.   *Perf. 13x13¼*
733 A463 €1.65 multi   4.50 4.50

Souvenir Sheet

Santa Anna Ball — A464

Litho. & Engr.
2014, July 25   *Perf. 13x13¼*
734 A464 €1.65 multi   4.50 4.50

Electricity Museum, Encamp A465

2014, July 25   Litho.   *Perf. 13x13¼*
735 A465 €1.10 multi   3.00 3.00

Pitavola Butterfly A466

2014, Sept. 6   Litho.   *Perf. 13*
736 A466 83c multi   2.10 2.10

Detail From Sant Miquel de Prats Retable A467

2014, Sept. 27   Litho.   *Perf. 13¼x13*
737 A467 €1.10 multi   2.75 2.75

Skis and Ski Poles — A468

2014, Oct. 18   Litho.   *Perf. 13¼*
738 A468 83c multi   2.10 2.10

Esteve Albert (1914-95), Writer — A469

2014, Nov. 9   Engr.   *Perf. 13¼*
739 A469 66c ochre & blk   1.75 1.75

Christmas A470

2014, Nov. 29   Litho.   *Perf. 13*
740 A470 66c multi   1.75 1.75

Instinct of Conservation, by Javier Balmaseda — A471

2015, Jan. 3   Litho.   *Perf. 13x13¼*
741 A471 €1.90 multi   4.50 4.50

Legend of the First Snow — A472

2015, Feb. 7   Litho.   *Perf. 13*
742 A472 €3.67 multi   8.25 8.25

Citroen DS 21 — A473

2015, Mar. 20   Litho.   *Perf. 13*
743 A473 €1.20 multi   2.75 2.75

Departure of French Gendarmes Led by Col. René Baulard, 75th Anniv. A474

2015, Apr. 11   Litho.   *Perf. 13*
744 A474 76c multi   1.75 1.75

Europa — A475

2015, May 9   Litho.   *Perf. 13¼*
745 A475 95c multi   2.10 2.10

Trobada Monument A476

2015, June 13   Engr.   *Perf. 13¼*
746 A476 €1.25 multi   2.75 2.75

Comapedrosa, Highest Peak in Andorra — A477

2015, June 20   Litho.   *Perf. 13¼*
747 A477 76c multi   1.75 1.75

Inside, by Agustí Roqué — A478

2015, July 4   Litho.   *Perf. 13x13¼*
748 A478 €3.05 multi   6.75 6.75
Venice Biennale.

Souvenir Sheet

Contrapas Dance — A479

Litho. & Engr.

2015, July 18		Perf. 13x13¼
749	A479 €1.90 multi	4.25 4.25

UCI Mountain
Bike and Trials
World
Championships,
Vallnord — A480

2015, Aug. 29	Litho.	Perf. 13¼x13
750	A480 €1.20 multi	2.75 2.75

Flora Type of 2011 and

Parnassius
Apollo
A481

Design: 76c, Thymus vulgaris, vert.

2015, Oct. 2	Engr.	Perf. 13
751	A427 76c multi	1.60 1.60
752	A481 95c multi	2.25 2.25

Ramon d'Areny-Plandolit, Philatelist,
and Maximum Cards — A482

2015, Nov. 7	Engr.	Perf. 13x12½
753	A482 €1.25 multi	2.75 2.75

Live
Nativity
Scene,
Engordany
A483

2015, Nov. 27	Litho.	Perf. 13
754	A483 76c multi	1.60 1.60

Christmas.

2014 Andorran Coinage — A484

No. 755: a, 1-cent, 2-cent, 5-cent and 2-
euro coins. b, 10-cent, 20-cent, 50-cent and 1-
euro coins.

2016, Jan. 8	Litho.	Perf. 13
755	A484 80c Horiz. pair, #a-b	3.50 3.50

Women's
Alpine
Skiing
World Cup
Race at
Soldeu-El
Tarter
A485

2016, Feb. 27	Litho.	Perf. 13¼
756	A485 €1.25 multi	2.75 2.75

Donzella Cremada
Rock
Carving — A486

2016, Mar. 19	Litho.	Perf. 13
757	A486 €3.77 multi	8.75 8.75

Reforms of 1866,
150th
Anniv. — A487

2016, Apr. 23	Litho.	Perf. 13¼
758	A487 €1 multi	2.40 2.40

The Republic, Statue by Josep
Viladomat (1899-1989) and Escaldes-
Engordany Art Center — A488

2016, Apr. 6	Engr.	Perf. 13¼
759	A488 80c multi	1.90 1.90

Europa
A489

2016, May 8	Litho.	Perf. 13¼
760	A489 €1 multi	2.25 2.25

Think Green Issue.

Dancing Giants
of Andorra
Festival — A490

2016, June 10	Litho.	Perf. 13¼
761	A490 80c multi	1.90 1.90

Souvenir Sheet

Sardana Dance — A491

Litho. & Engr.

2016, July 15		Perf. 13x13¼
762	A491 €1.60 multi	3.75 3.75

Intimitat Compartida, by Joan
Xandri — A492

2016, July 29	Litho.	Perf. 13x13¼
763	A492 €3.20 multi	7.25 7.25

2015 Venice Biennale.

Clipol Bus
A493

2016, Sept. 2	Litho.	Perf. 13
764	A493 €1.25 multi	2.75 2.75

Isabelle Sandy (1884-1975),
Writer — A494

2016, Oct. 7	Engr.	Perf. 13¼
765	A494 €1.60 multi	3.50 3.50

SEMI-POSTAL STAMP

> Catalogue values for unused
> stamps in this section are for
> Never Hinged items.

Virgin of St.
Coloma — SP1

Unwmk.

1964, July 25	Engr.	Perf. 13
B1	SP1 25c + 10c multi	24.00 24.00

The surtax was for the Red Cross.

AIR POST STAMPS

> Catalogue values for unused
> stamps in this section are for
> Never Hinged items.

Chamois
AP1

Unwmk.

1950, Feb. 20	Engr.	Perf. 13
C1	AP1 100fr indigo	87.50 60.00

East Branch of
Valira River — AP2

1955-57

C2	AP2 100fr dark green	16.00 10.50
C3	AP2 200fr cerise	32.50 16.00
C4	AP2 500fr dp bl ('57)	120.00 65.00
	Nos. C2-C4 (3)	168.50 91.50

No. C3 in dark green was not regularly
issued. Value, $3,500.

D'Inclès
Valley
AP3

1961-64	Unwmk.	Perf. 13
C5	AP3 2fr red, ol gray & cl	1.25 1.25
C6	AP3 3fr bl, mar & slate grn	1.60 1.60
C7	AP3 5fr rose lil & red org	3.25 2.40
C8	AP3 10fr bl grn & slate grn	4.75 4.50
	Nos. C5-C8 (4)	10.85 9.75

Issued: 10fr, 4/25/64; others, 6/19/61.

POSTAGE DUE STAMPS

Postage Due Stamps of
France, 1893-1931,
Overprinted

On Stamps of 1893-1926

1931-33	Unwmk.	Perf. 14x13½
J1	D2 5c blue	2.40 2.40
J2	D2 10c brown	2.40 2.40
J3	D2 30c rose red	1.60 1.60
J4	D2 50c violet brn	2.40 2.40
J5	D2 60c green	34.00 34.00
J6	D2 1fr red brn, straw	2.40 2.40
J7	D2 2fr brt violet	16.00 16.00
J8	D2 3fr magenta	3.25 3.25
	Nos. J1-J8 (8)	64.45 64.45

On Stamps of 1927-31

J9	D4 1c olive grn	3.25 3.25
J10	D4 10c rose	5.50 6.50
J11	D4 60c red	27.50 26.50
J12	D4 1fr Prus grn ('32)	110.00 120.00
J13	D4 1.20fr on 2fr bl	80.00 80.00
J14	D4 2fr ol brn ('33)	200.00 225.00
J15	D4 5fr on 1fr vio	120.00 120.00
	Nos. J9-J15 (7)	546.25 581.25

D5   D6

1935-41   Typo.

J16	D5	1c gray green	3.25	3.25
J17	D6	5c light blue ('37)	6.75	6.75
J18	D6	10c brown ('41)	4.00	5.50
J19	D6	2fr violet ('41)	11.00	8.75
J20	D6	5fr red orange ('41)	19.00	11.00
		Nos. J16-J20 (5)	44.00	35.25

> Catalogue values for unused stamps in this section, from this point to the end of the section, are for Never Hinged items.

Wheat Sheaves — D7

1943-46   Perf. 14x13½

J21	D7	10c sepia	.80	.70
J22	D7	30c brt red vio	.90	.70
J23	D7	50c blue grn	1.25	1.10
J24	D7	1fr brt ultra	1.10	.90
J25	D7	1.50fr rose red	6.75	5.50
J26	D7	2fr turq blue	1.75	1.60
J27	D7	3fr brown org	2.00	1.90
J28	D7	4fr dp vio ('45)	6.25	5.50
J29	D7	5fr brt pink	4.25	3.75
J30	D7	10fr red org ('45)	6.50	5.50
J31	D7	20fr olive brn ('46)	7.75	6.50
		Nos. J21-J31 (11)	39.30	33.65

Inscribed: "Timbre Taxe"

1946-53

J32	D7	10c sepia ('46)	1.60	1.60
J33	D7	1fr ultra	.80	.80
J34	D7	2fr turq blue	1.25	1.25
J35	D7	3fr orange brn	2.75	2.75
J36	D7	4fr violet	3.50	3.50
J37	D7	5fr brt pink	2.75	2.75
J38	D7	10fr red orange	4.75	4.75
J39	D7	20fr olive brn	8.00	8.00
J40	D7	50fr dk green ('50)	47.50	47.50
J41	D7	100fr dp green ('53)	120.00	120.00
		Nos. J32-J41 (10)	192.90	192.90

Inscribed: "Timbre Taxe"

1961, June 19   Perf. 14x13½

J42	D7	5c rose pink	4.00	4.00
J43	D7	10c red orange	8.00	8.00
J44	D7	20c olive	12.00	12.00
J45	D7	50c dark slate green	24.00	24.00
		Nos. J42-J45 (4)	48.00	48.00

D8

1964-71   Typo.   Perf. 14x13½

J46	D8	5c Centaury ('65)	.25	.25
J47	D8	10c Gentian ('65)	.25	.25
J48	D8	15c Corn poppy	.25	.25
J49	D8	20c Violets ('71)	.30	.25
J50	D8	30c Forget-me-not	.40	.30
J51	D8	40c Columbine ('71)	.55	.40
J52	D8	50c Clover ('65)	.65	.55
		Nos. J46-J52 (7)	2.65	2.25

D9

1985, Oct. 21   Engr.   Perf. 13

J53	D9	10c Holly	.25	.25
J54	D9	20c Blueberries	.25	.25
J55	D9	30c Raspberries	.25	.25
J56	D9	40c Bilberries	.25	.25
J57	D9	50c Blackberries	.25	.25
J58	D9	1fr Broom	.40	.40
J59	D9	2fr Rosehips	.95	.65
J60	D9	3fr Nightshade	1.25	.95
J61	D9	4fr Nabiu	1.50	1.25
J62	D9	5fr Strawberries	1.90	1.50
		Nos. J53-J62 (10)	7.25	6.00

NEWSPAPER STAMP

France No. P7
Overprinted

1931   Unwmk.   Perf. 14x13½

P1	A16	½c on 1c gray	1.25	1.25
a.		Double overprint	3,000.	
		Never Hinged	4,000.	

ANGOLA

aŋˈgō-lə

LOCATION — S.W. Africa between Zaire and Namibia.
GOVT. — Republic
AREA — 481,351 sq. mi.
POP. — 11,177,537 (1999 est.)
CAPITAL — Luanda

Angola was a Portuguese overseas territory until it became independent November 11, 1975, as the People's Republic of Angola.

1000 Reis = 1 Milreis
100 Centavos = 1 Escudo (1913, 1954)
100 Centavos = 1 Angolar (1932)
10 Lweys = 1 Kwanza (1977)

> Catalogue values for unused stamps in this country are for Never Hinged items, beginning with Scott 328 in the regular postage section, Scott C26 in the airpost section, Scott J31 in the postage due section, and Scott RA7 in the postal tax section.

Watermark

Wmk. 232 — Maltese Cross

Portuguese Crown — A1

Perf. 12½, 13½
1870-77   Typo.   Unwmk.
Thin to Medium Paper

1	A1	5r gray black	3.25	2.00
2	A1	10r yellow	30.00	20.00
3	A1	20r bister	3.00	2.25
4	A1	25r red	15.00	10.00

5	A1	40r blue ('77)	275.00	175.00
6	A1	50r green	70.00	15.00
7	A1	100r lilac	15.00	5.00
8	A1	200r orange ('77)	7.00	3.25
9	A1	300r choc ('77)	20.00	12.00

1881-85   Perf. 12½, 13½

10	A1	10r green ('83)	8.50	4.75
11	A1	20r carmine rose ('85)	21.00	14.00
12	A1	25r violet ('85)	12.50	5.00
13	A1	40r buff ('82)	13.00	4.75
15	A1	50r blue	45.00	10.00
		Nos. 10-15 (5)	100.00	38.50

Two types of numerals are found on #2, 11, 13, 15.

The cliche of 40r in plate of 20r error, was discovered before the stamps were issued. All examples were defaced by a blue pencil mark. Values, $2,100 unused; in pair with 20r, $2,400.

In perf. 12½, Nos. 1-4, 4a and 6, as well as 7a, were printed in 1870 on thicker paper and 1875 on normal paper. Stamps of the earlier printing sell for 2 to 5 times more than those of the 1875 printing.

Some reprints of the 1870-85 issues are on a smooth white chalky paper, ungummed and perf. 13½.

Other reprints of these issues are on thin ivory paper with shiny white gum and clear-cut perf. 13½.

King Luiz — A2

1886   Embossed   Perf. 12½

16	A2	5r black	14.00	6.50
17	A2	10r green	14.00	6.50
18	A2	20r rose	19.00	12.50
19	A2	25r red violet	15.00	4.00
20	A2	40r chocolate	17.50	7.50
21	A2	50r blue	21.00	4.00
22	A2	100r yellow brn	30.00	10.00
23	A2	200r gray violet	40.00	13.00
24	A2	300r orange	40.00	14.00
		Nos. 16-24 (9)	210.50	78.00

For surcharges see Nos. 61-69, 172-174, 208-210.

Reprints of 5r, 20r & 100r have cleancut perf. 13½.

King Carlos — A3

1893-94   Typo.   Perf. 11½, 12½, 13½

25	A3	5r yellow	3.75	1.50
26	A3	10r redsh violet	5.00	3.00
27a	A3	15r chocolate	7.00	3.00
28	A3	20r lavender	7.00	3.00
29c	A3	25r green	7.00	3.75
30b	A3	50r light blue	10.00	4.00
31	A3	75r carmine	20.00	12.00
32	A3	80r lt green	20.00	9.00
33	A3	100r brown, *buff*	20.00	9.00
34	A3	150r car, *rose*	30.00	17.50
35	A3	200r dk blue, *lt bl*	30.00	17.50
36	A3	300r dk blue, *sal*	35.00	17.50

For surcharges see Nos. 70-81, 175-179, 213-216, 234.

No. P1 Surcharged in Blue

1894, Aug.

37	N1	25r on 2½r brown	75.00	60.00

King Carlos — A5

1898-1903   Perf. 11½
Name and Value in Black except 500r

38	A5	2½r gray	.65	.50
39	A5	5r orange	.65	.50
40	A5	10r yellow grn	.65	.50
41	A5	15r violet brn	3.25	1.60
42	A5	15r violet green ('03)	1.60	1.40
43	A5	20r gray violet	.70	.50
44	A5	25r sea green	1.60	.75
45	A5	25r car ('03)	.85	.45
46	A5	50r blue	2.75	1.00
47	A5	50r brown ('03)	8.00	3.75
48	A5	65r dull blue ('03)	8.50	5.75
49	A5	75r rose	11.00	6.00
50	A5	75r red violet ('03)	3.00	2.00
51	A5	80r violet	10.00	3.00
52	A5	100r dk blue, *blue*	2.00	1.40
53	A5	115r org brn, *pink* ('03)	11.00	7.50
54	A5	130r brn, *straw* ('03)	11.00	7.50
55	A5	150r brn, *straw*	11.00	6.00
56	A5	200r red vio, *pink*	7.00	1.75
57	A5	300r dk blue, *rose*	6.50	5.00
58	A5	400r dull bl, *straw* ('03)	12.50	3.50
59	A5	500r blk & red, *bl* ('01)	16.00	5.00
60	A5	700r vio, *yelsh* ('01)	35.00	17.00
		Nos. 38-60 (23)	165.20	82.35

For surcharges and overprints see Nos. 83-102, 113-117, 159-171, 181-183, 217-218, 221-225.

Stamps of 1886-94 Surcharged in Black or Red

Two types of surcharge:
I — 3mm between numeral and REIS.
II — 4½mm spacing.

1902   Perf. 12½

61	A2	65r on 40r choc	12.00	6.50
62	A2	65r on 300r org, I	12.00	6.50
a.		Type II	12.00	6.50
63	A2	115r on 10r green	10.00	5.00
a.		Inverted surcharge	90.00	50.00
b.		Perf. 13½	75.00	45.00
64	A2	115r on 200r gray vio	10.00	5.00
65	A2	130r on 50r blue	13.00	5.00
66	A2	130r on 100r brown	8.50	5.00
67	A2	400r on 20r rose	110.00	65.00
a.		Perf. 13½	175.00	92.50
68	A2	400r on 25r violet	22.50	12.00
69	A2	400r on 5r black (R)	20.00	13.00
a.		Double surcharge	75.00	50.00
		Nos. 61-69 (9)	218.00	123.00

For surcharges see Nos. 172-174, 208-210.

Perf. 11½, 12½, 13½

70	A3	65r on 5r yel, I, perf. 11½	11.00	6.50
a.		Type II	11.00	7.00
71	A3	65r on 10r red vio, I, perf. 12½	7.25	5.50
a.		Type II	7.25	5.50
b.		Perf. 11½, I	12.00	7.00
c.		Perf. 11½, I	12.00	7.00
72	A3	65r on 20r lav, perf. 11½	11.00	6.50
73	A3	65r on 25r green, perf. 12½	15.00	9.00
b.		Perf. 13½	7.00	5.00
74	A3	115r on 80r lt grn, perf. 12½	15.00	9.00
75	A3	115r on 100r brn, buff, perf. 12½	15.00	7.25
b.		Perf. 13½	80.00	40.00
76	A3	115r on 150r car, rose, perf. 11½	17.50	13.00
a.		Perf. 13½	25.00	15.00
b.		Perf. 12½	24.00	15.00
77	A3	130r on 15r choc, perf. 12½	6.50	5.50
b.		Type II	8.00	4.50
78	A3	130r on 75r carmine, perf. 11½	60.00	50.00
a.		Perf. 13½	70.00	55.00
b.		Perf. 12½	15.00	11.00
79	A3	130r on 300r dk bl, sal, perf. 12½	20.00	15.00
a.		Perf. 13½	35.00	12.50
80	A3	400r on 50r lt bl, I, perf. 12½	11.00	5.50
a.		Perf. 11½	32.50	15.00
c.		Type II	9.00	6.00
81	A3	400r on 200r bl, bl, perf. 12½	11.00	8.00
a.		Perf. 13½	375.00	225.00
82	N1	400r on 2½r brn, I, perf. 12½	1.75	1.60
a.		Type II	1.75	1.60
		Nos. 70-82 (13)	202.00	142.35

For surcharges see Nos. 175-180, 211-216, 234-235.

Reprints of Nos. 65, 67, 68 and 69 have clean-cut perforation 13½.

For detailed listings of perforation and paper varieties, see *Scott Classic Specialized Catalogue of Stamps and Covers 1840-1940.*

Stamps of 1898 Overprinted — a

1902			**Perf. 11½**	
83	A5	15r brown	2.50	1.75
84	A5	25r sea green	2.00	1.00
85	A5	50r blue	4.50	2.00
86	A5	75r rose	7.00	5.25
		Nos. 83-86 (4)	16.00	10.00

For surcharge see No. 116.

No. 48 Surcharged in Black

1905				
87	A5	50r on 65r dull blue	6.00	3.00

For surcharge see No. 183.

Stamps of 1898-1903 Overprinted in Carmine or Green — b

1911				
88	A5	2½r gray	.60	.50
89	A5	5r orange yel	.60	.50
90	A5	10r light green	.60	.50
91	A5	15r gray green	.85	.70
92	A5	20r gray violet	.90	.75
93	A5	25r car (G)	.90	.75
94	A5	50r brown	3.25	1.75
95	A5	75r lilac	6.75	3.25
96	A5	100r dk blue, *bl*	6.75	3.50
97	A5	115r org brn, *pink*	3.75	1.75
98	A5	130r brn, *straw*	3.75	1.75
99	A5	200r red lil, *pnksh*	4.50	2.40
100	A5	400r dull bl, *straw*	4.50	1.75
101	A5	500r blk & red, *bl*	4.50	2.25
102	A5	700r violet, *yelsh*	4.50	2.50
		Nos. 88-102 (15)	46.70	24.60

Inverted and double overprints of Nos. 88-102 were made intentionally.
For surcharges see Nos. 217-218, 221-222, 224.

King Manuel II — A6

Overprinted in Carmine or Green

1912			**Perf. 11½x12**	
103	A6	2½r violet	.75	.50
104	A6	5r black	.75	.50
105	A6	10r gray green	.75	.50
106	A6	20r carmine (G)	.75	.50
107	A6	25r violet brown	.75	.50
108	A6	50r dk blue	1.75	1.40
109	A6	75r bister brown	2.00	1.75
110	A6	100r brown, *lt green*	3.75	2.25
111	A6	200r dk green, *salmon*	3.75	2.40
112	A6	300r black, *azure*	3.75	2.40
		Nos. 103-112 (10)	18.75	12.70

For surcharges see Nos. 219-220, 226-227.

No. 91 Surcharged in Black

1912, June			**Perf. 11½**	
113	A5	2½r on 15r gray green	6.00	3.75
114	A5	5r on 15r gray green	6.75	3.75
115	A5	10r on 15r gray green	5.25	3.75
		Nos. 113-115 (3)	18.00	11.25

Inverted and double surcharges of Nos. 113-115 were made intentionally.

Nos. 86 and 50 Surcharged in Black and Overprinted in Violet — c

1912				
116	A5	25r on 75r rose	110.00	60.00
117	A5	25r on 75r red violet	7.50	6.00
a.		"REUPBLICA"	135.00	70.00
b.		"25" omitted	135.00	70.00
c.		"REPUBLICA" omitted	135.00	70.00

Ceres — A7

With Imprint

1914		**Chalky Paper**	**Perf. 15x14**	
		Name and Value in Black		
118	A7	¼c olive brown	2.00	.90
119	A7	½c black	2.00	.90
120	A7	1c blue green	2.00	.90
121	A7	1½c lilac brown	4.00	2.25
122	A7	2c carmine	7.00	3.25
123	A7	2½c violet	1.40	.60
124	A7	5c blue	3.00	1.60
125	A7	7½c yellow brn	4.00	2.40
126	A7	8c slate	4.00	2.40
127	A7	10c orange brn	4.00	2.40
128	A7	15c brown rose	6.00	2.50
129	A7	20c yel green	3.00	1.60
130	A7	30c brown, *green*	3.00	2.40
131	A7	40c brown, *pink*	3.00	2.40
132	A7	50c orange, *sal*	11.00	8.25
133	A7	1e green, *blue*	8.00	4.75
		Nos. 118-133 (16)	67.40	39.50

1915-22			**Ordinary Paper**	
134	A7	¼c olive brown	.45	.45
135	A7	½c black	.45	.45
136	A7	1c blue green	.45	.45
137	A7	1c yellow green ('18)	.45	.45
138	A7	1½c lilac brown	.45	.45
139	A7	2c carmine	.55	.45
140	A7	2½c dark violet	.45	.45
141	A7	3c orange	27.50	24.00
142	A7	4c dull rose ('21)	.45	.45
143	A7	5c blue	1.75	1.40
144	A7	6c lilac ('21)	.45	.45
145	A7	7c ultra ('21)	.45	.45
146	A7	7½c yellow brn ('20)	.55	.45
147	A7	8c slate	.60	.45
148	A7	10c orange brn ('18)	.55	.45
149	A7	12c olive brown ('21)	1.50	1.00
150	A7	15c plum ('20)	.55	.45
151	A7	15c brown rose ('21)	.55	.45
152	A7	20c yel green ('18)	6.75	5.00
153	A7	30c gray green ('21)	1.00	.65
154	A7	80c pink ('21)	1.75	1.00
155	A7	2e dark violet ('22)	3.50	3.00
		Nos. 134-155 (22)	51.25	42.80

1921-26			**Perf. 12x11½**	
156	A7	¼c olive brown ('24)	.45	.45
157	A7	½c black	.45	.45
158	A7	1c blue green ('24)	.45	.45
158C	A7	1½c lilac brown ('24)	.45	.45
158D	A7	2c carmine ('24)	.45	.45
158E	A7	2c gray ('25)	.75	.55
158F	A7	2½c lt violet ('24)	.45	.45
158G	A7	3c orange	.45	.45
158H	A7	4c dull rose	.45	.45
158I	A7	4½c gray	.45	.45
158J	A7	5c blue ('24)	.45	.45
158K	A7	6c lilac	.45	.45
158L	A7	7c ultra	.45	.45
158M	A7	7½c yellow brown ('24)	.55	.45
158N	A7	8c slate ('24)	.55	.45
158O	A7	10c orange brn ('24)	.45	.40
158P	A7	12c olive brn	.75	.60
158Q	A7	12c dp green ('25)	.75	.50
158R	A7	15c plum ('24)	.45	.35
158S	A7	20c yel green	1.75	1.60
158T	A7	24c ultra ('25)	1.60	1.20
158U	A7	25c choc ('25)	1.60	1.20
158V	A7	30c gray grn	.75	.60
158W	A7	40c turq blue	1.20	.70
158X	A7	50c lt violet ('25)	1.40	.70
158Y	A7	60c dk blue ('22)	1.50	1.00
158Z	A7	60c dp rose ('26)	75.00	47.50

159A	A7	80c pink ('22)	1.75	1.00
159B	A7	1e rose ('22)	1.75	1.00
		Nos. 156-159B (29)	97.95	65.20

Glazed Paper

1921-25			**Perf. 12x11½**	
159C	A7	1e rose	1.75	1.75
159D	A7	1e deep blue ('25)	3.25	1.60
159E	A7	2e dark violet ('22)	2.25	1.25
159F	A7	5e buff ('25)	14.00	11.50
159G	A7	10e pink ('25)	40.00	25.00
159H	A7	20e pale turq ('25)	120.00	80.00
		Nos. 159C-159H (6)	181.25	121.10

For surcharges see Nos. 228-229, 236-239.

Stamps of 1898-1903 Overprinted type "c" in Red or Green

1914			**Perf. 11½, 12**	
159	A5	10r yel green (R)	7.50	5.50
160	A5	15r gray green (R)	6.75	5.50
161	A5	20r gray violet (G)	2.75	2.00
163	A5	75r red violet (G)	2.00	1.40
164	A5	100r blue, *blue* (R)	4.50	3.75
165	A5	115r org brn, *pink* (R)	150.00	
167	A5	200r red vio, *pnksh* (G)	2.75	1.75
169	A5	400r dl bl, *straw* (R)	50.00	50.00
170	A5	500r blk & red, *bl* (R)	6.75	6.25
171	A5	700r vio, *yelsh* (G)	35.00	27.00

Inverted and double overprints were made intentionally. No. 165 was not regularly issued. Red overprints on the 20r, 75r, 200r were not regularly issued. The 130r was not regularly issued without surcharge (No. 225).

On Nos. 63-65, 74-76, 78-79, 82

			Perf. 11½, 12½, 13½	
172	A2	115r on 10r (R)	17.00	17.00
a.		Perf. 13½	17.00	17.00
173	A2	115r on 200r (R)	22.50	22.50
174	A2	130r on 50r (R)	110.00	110.00
175	A3	115r on 80r (R)	210.00	200.00
176	A3	115r on 100r (R)	250.00	200.00
a.		Perf. 11½	300.00	300.00
b.		Perf. 13½	900.00	850.00
177	A3	115r on 150r (G)	250.00	200.00
a.		Perf. 13½	250.00	200.00
b.		Perf. 12½	750.00	700.00
178	A3	130r on 75r (G)	8.25	7.50
a.		Perf. 12½	9.00	7.50
179	A3	130r on 300r (R)	10.50	8.25
a.		Perf. 12½	17.50	16.00
180	N1	400r on 2½r (R)	1.10	.85
a.		Perf. 11½	5.25	4.00
		Nos. 172-180 (9)	879.35	766.10

Nos. 85-87 Overprinted in Red or Green

On Stamps of 1902

			Perf. 11½, 12	
181	A5	50r blue (R)	2.50	2.25
182	A5	75r rose (G)	6.00	4.50

On No. 87

183	A5	50r on 65r dull blue (R)	5.50	4.00
		Nos. 181-183 (3)	14.00	10.75

Inverted and double surcharges of Nos. 181-183 were made intentionally.

Common Design Types pictured following the introduction.

Vasco da Gama Issue of Various Portuguese Colonies

Common Design Types CD20-CD27 Srchd.

On Stamps of Macao

1913			**Perf. 12½ to 16**	
184		¼c on ½a blue grn	2.25	1.75
185		½c on 1a red	2.25	1.75
186		1c on 2a red violet	2.40	1.75
187		2½c on 4a yel green	1.75	1.25
188		5c on 8a dk blue	1.75	1.25
189		7½c on 12a vio brn	8.00	5.50
190		10c on 16a bister brn	2.75	2.00
191		15c on 24a bister	3.75	2.00
		Nos. 184-191 (8)	24.90	17.25

On Stamps of Portuguese Africa

Perf. 14 to 15

192		¼c on 2½r blue grn	1.25	.85
193		½c on 5r red	1.25	.85
194		1c on 10r red violet	1.25	.85
195		2½c on 25r yel grn	1.25	.85
196		5c on 50r dk blue	1.25	.85
197		7½c on 75r vio brn	7.50	6.75
198		10c on 100r bister brn	3.00	2.00
199		15c on 150r bister	3.50	2.25
		Nos. 192-199 (8)	20.25	15.25

On Stamps of Timor

200		¼c on ½a blue grn	2.25	1.75
201		½c on 1a red	2.25	1.75
202		1c on 2a red vio	2.40	1.75
203		2½c on 4a yel grn	1.75	1.25
204		5c on 8a dk blue	1.75	1.25
205		7½c on 12a vio brn	8.00	5.50
206		10c on 16a bis brn	2.75	2.00
207		15c on 24a bister	3.75	2.00
		Nos. 200-207 (8)	24.90	17.25
		Nos. 184-207 (24)	70.05	49.75

Provisional Issue of 1902 Overprinted in Carmine

1915			**Perf. 11½, 12½, 13½**	
208	A2	115r on 10r green	2.00	2.00
a.		Perf. 12½	2.50	2.25
209	A2	115r on 200r gray vio	2.25	1.90
210	A3	115r on 100r brown	1.90	1.60
211	A3	115r on 80r lt green	2.50	2.25
212	A3	115r on 100r brn, *buff*	2.25	2.00
a.		Perf. 11½	100.00	90.00
b.		Perf. 13½	16.00	13.50
213	A3	115r on 150r car, *rose*	1.60	1.60
a.		Perf. 12½	3.75	3.25
b.		Perf. 13½	2.60	2.25
214	A3	130r on 15r choc	1.60	1.60
a.		Perf. 12½	8.25	6.75
215	A3	130r on 75r carmine	3.25	2.00
a.		Perf. 12½	5.00	4.25
b.		Perf. 12½	3.25	2.00
216	A3	130r on 300r dk bl, *sal*	2.00	2.00
a.		Perf. 13½	3.75	2.00
		Nos. 208-216 (9)	19.35	16.95

Stamps of 1911-14 Surcharged in Black

d   e

On Stamps of 1911

1919			**Perf. 11½**	
217	A5 (d)	½c on 75r red lilac	3.25	2.60
218	A5 (d)	2½c on 100r blue, *grysh*	3.50	2.60

On Stamps of 1912

			Perf. 11½x12	
219	A6 (e)	½c on 75r bis brn	2.00	1.50
220	A6 (e)	2½c on 100r brn, *lt grn*	3.50	2.60

On Stamps of 1914

221	A5 (d)	½c on 75r red lil	2.25	1.90
222	A5 (d)	2½c on 100r bl, *grysh*	2.60	2.25
		Nos. 217-222 (6)	17.10	13.45

Inverted and double surcharges were made for sale to collectors.

Nos. 163, 98 and Type of 1914 Surcharged in Black

1921				
223	A5 (c)	00.5c on 75r	400.00	350.00
224	A5 (b)	4c on 115r (#98)	3.00	3.00
225	A5 (c)	4c on 130r brn, *straw*	7.50	7.50
a.		Without surcharge	240.00	

Nos. 109 and 108 Surcharged with New Values and Bars in Black

226	A6	00.5c on 75r	2.25	1.90
227	A6	1c on 50r	2.50	2.50

Nos. 133 and 138 Surcharged with New Values and Bars in Black

228	A7	00.5c on 7½c	2.50	2.25
229	A7	04c on 15c	3.00	3.00
		Nos. 224-229 (6)	20.75	20.15
		Nos. 223-229 (7)	420.75	370.15

The 04c surcharge exists on the 15c brown rose, perf 12x11½, No. 139.

Some authorities question the status of No. 223.

Nos. 81-82 Surcharged

1925   **Perf. 12½**

234	A3	40c on 400r on 200r bl, bl	1.50	1.10
a.		Perf. 13½	11.00	7.50
235	N1	40c on 400r on 2½r brn	1.10	1.10
a.		Perf. 13½	1.10	1.10

Nos. 150-151, 154-155 Surcharged

1931   **Perf. 12x 11½**

236	A7	50c on 60c deep rose	2.25	2.00
237	A7	70c on 80c pink	4.50	3.00
238	A7	70c on 1e deep blue	4.00	3.00
239	A7	1.40e on 2e dark violet	2.50	2.00
		Nos. 236-239 (4)	13.25	10.00

Ceres — A14

Perf. 12x11½

1932-46		Typo.	Wmk. 232	
243	A14	1c bister brn	.30	.25
244	A14	5c dk brown	.35	.30
245	A14	10c dp violet	.35	.30
246	A14	15c black	.35	.30
247	A14	20c gray	.40	.30
248	A14	30c myrtle grn	.40	.30
249	A14	35c yel grn ('46)	7.50	4.50
250	A14	40c dp orange	.40	.30
251	A14	45c lt blue	1.75	1.25
252	A14	50c lt brown	.30	.25
253	A14	60c olive grn	1.00	.30
254	A14	70c orange brn	1.10	.30
255	A14	80c emerald	.75	.25
256	A14	85c rose	5.50	2.00
257	A14	1a claret	1.10	.30
258	A14	1.40a dk blue	11.50	1.75
258A	A14	1.75a dk blue ('46)	16.00	5.25
259	A14	2a dull vio	5.25	.55
260	A14	5a pale yel grn	10.50	1.75
261	A14	10a olive bis	20.00	5.25
262	A14	20a orange	52.50	5.25
		Nos. 243-262 (21)	137.30	31.00
		Set, never hinged	175.00	

For surcharges see Nos. 263-267, 271-273, 294A-300, J31-J36.

Surcharged in Black

5½mm between bars and new value.

1934

263	A14	10c on 45c lt bl	3.50	2.50
264	A14	20c on 85c rose	3.50	2.50
265	A14	30c on 1.40a dk bl	3.50	2.50
266	A14	70c on 2a dl vio	4.50	3.25

267	A14	80c on 5a pale yel grn	7.00	2.75
		Nos. 263-267 (5)	22.00	13.50
		Set, never hinged	37.50	

See Nos. 294A-300.

Nos. J26, J30 Surcharged in Black

1935   **Unwmk.**   **Perf. 11½**

268	D2	5c on 6c lt brown	2.50	1.60
269	D2	30c on 50c gray	2.50	1.60
270	D2	40c on 50c gray	2.50	1.60
		Nos. 268-270 (3)	7.50	4.80
		Set, never hinged	14.00	

No. 255 Surcharged in Black

1938   **Wmk. 232**   **Perf. 12x11½**

271	A14	5c on 80c emerald	1.10	.55
272	A14	10c on 80c emerald	1.60	.75
273	A14	15c on 80c emerald	2.25	.75
		Nos. 271-273 (3)	4.95	2.05
		Set, never hinged	8.25	

Vasco da Gama Issue
Common Design Types
Engr.; Name & Value Typo. in Black
Perf. 13½x13

1938, July 26			Unwmk.
274	CD34	1c gray green	.25	.25
275	CD34	5c orange brn	.30	.30
276	CD34	10c dk carmine	.40	.30
277	CD34	15c dk violet brn	.40	.30
278	CD34	20c slate	.40	.30
279	CD35	30c rose violet	.55	.40
280	CD35	35c brt green	1.00	.75
281	CD35	40c brown	.40	.25
282	CD35	50c brt red vio	.55	.25
283	CD36	60c gray black	1.10	.30
284	CD36	70c brown vio	1.10	.30
285	CD36	80c orange	1.10	.30
286	CD36	1a brown	1.10	.30
287	CD37	1.75a blue	2.10	1.00
288	CD37	2a brown car	3.25	1.50
289	CD37	5a olive grn	13.50	1.50
290	CD38	10a blue vio	29.00	1.90
291	CD38	20a red brown	42.50	4.25
		Nos. 274-291 (18)	99.00	14.45
		Set, never hinged	150.00	

For surcharges see Nos. 301-304.

Marble Column and Portuguese Arms with Cross — A20

1938, July 29   **Perf. 12½**

292	A20	80c blue green	3.75	2.25
293	A20	1.75a deep blue	20.00	6.00
294	A20	20a dk red brown	60.00	27.00
		Nos. 292-294 (3)	83.75	35.25
		Set, never hinged	140.00	

Visit of the President of Portugal to this colony in 1938.

Stamps of 1932 Surcharged with New Value and Bars

8mm between bars and new value.

1941-45		Wmk. 232	Perf. 12x11½	
294A	A14	5c on 80c emer ('45)	.85	.55
295	A14	10c on 45c lt blue	1.75	1.25
296	A14	15c on 45c lt blue	1.75	1.25
297	A14	20c on 85c rose	1.75	1.25
298	A14	35c on 85c rose	1.75	1.25
299	A14	50c on 1.40a dk blue	1.75	1.25
300	A14	60c on 1a claret	9.00	7.50
		Nos. 294A-300 (7)	18.60	14.30
		Set, never hinged	32.50	

Nos. 285 to 287 Surcharged with New Values and Bars in Black or Red

1945		Unwmk.	Perf. 13½x13	
301	CD36	5c on 80c org	.85	.55
302	CD36	50c on 1a red	.85	.55
303	CD37	50c on 1.75a bl (R)	.85	.55
304	CD37	50c on 1.75a bl	.85	.55
		Nos. 301-304 (4)	3.40	2.20
		Set, never hinged	5.00	

Sao Miguel Fort, Luanda — A21

John IV — A22

Designs: 10c, Our Lady of Nazareth Church, Luanda. 50c, Salvador Correia de Sa e Bene vides. 1a, Surrender of Luanda. 1.75a, Diogo Cao. 2a, Manuel Cerveira Pereira. 5a, Stone Cliffs, Yelala. 10a, Paulo Dias de Novais. 20a, Massangano Fort.

Perf. 14½

1948, May			Unwmk.	Litho.
305	A21	5c dk violet	.30	.30
306	A21	10c dk brown	.75	.30
307	A22	30c blue grn	.30	.30
308	A22	50c vio brown	.30	.30
309	A21	1a carmine	.70	.30
310	A22	1.75a slate blue	1.00	.45
311	A22	2a green	1.00	.55
312	A21	5a gray black	2.50	1.10
313	A22	10a rose lilac	8.25	1.50
314	A21	20a gray blue	17.50	5.25
a.		Sheet of 10, #305-314	140.00	100.00
		Never hinged	200.00	
		Nos. 305-314 (10)	32.60	10.35
		Set, never hinged	50.00	

300th anniv. of the restoration of Angola to Portugal. No. 314a sold for 42.50a.

Lady of Fatima Issue
Common Design Type

1948, Dec.

315	CD40	50c carmine	1.50	.75
316	CD40	3a ultra	6.00	2.25
317	CD40	6a red orange	18.00	5.25
318	CD40	9a dp claret	42.50	9.00
		Nos. 315-318 (4)	68.00	17.25
		Set, never hinged	110.00	

Our Lady of the Rosary at Fatima, Portugal.

Chiumbe River — A24

Black Rocks — A25

Designs: 50c, View of Luanda. 2.50a, Sa da Bandeira. 3.50a, Mocamedes. 15a, Cubal River. 50a, Duke of Bragança Falls.

1949		Unwmk.	Perf. 13½	
319	A24	20c dk slate blue	.55	.30
320	A25	40c black brown	.55	.30
321	A24	50c rose brown	.55	.30
322	A24	2.50a blue violet	3.00	.75
323	A24	3.50a slate gray	3.00	.90
323A	A24	15a dk green	18.00	2.75
324	A24	50a dp green	110.00	7.50
		Nos. 319-324 (7)	135.65	12.80
		Set, never hinged	225.00	

Sailing Vessel — A26

1949, Aug.				Perf. 14
325	A26	1a chocolate	6.75	.75
326	A26	4a dk Prus green	17.50	2.75
		Set, never hinged	37.50	

Centenary of founding of Mocamedes.

UPU Symbols — A27

1949, Oct.

327	A27	4a dk grn & lt grn	10.50	3.00
		Never hinged	16.00	

75th anniv. of the UPU.

> **Catalogue values for unused stamps in this section, from this point to the end of the section, are for Never Hinged items.**

Stamp of 1870 — A28

1950, Apr. 2				Perf. 11½x12
328	A28	50c yellow green	1.75	.55
329	A28	1a fawn	1.75	.85
330	A28	4a black	6.25	1.25
a.		Sheet of 3, #328-330	40.00	40.00
		Nos. 328-330 (3)	9.75	2.65

Angola's first philatelic exhibition, marking the 80th anniversary of Angola's first stamps. No. 330a contains Nos. 328, 329 (inverted), 330, perf. 11½ and sold for 6.50a. All copies carry an oval exhibition cancellation in the margin but the stamps were valid for postage.

Holy Year Issue
Common Design Types

1950, May				Perf. 13x13½
331	CD41	1a dull rose vio	1.60	.35
332	CD42	4a black	6.00	1.00

Dark Chanting Goshawk — A31

European Bee Eater — A32

10c, Racquet-tailed roller. 15c, Bateleur eagle. 50c, Giant kingfisher. 1a, Yellow-fronted barbet. 1.50a, Openbill (stork). 2a, Southern ground hornbill. 2.50a, African skimmer. 3a, Shikra. 3.50a, Denham's bustard. 4a, African golden oriole. 4.50a, Long-tailed shrike. 5a, Red-shouldered glossy starling. 6a, Sharp-tailed glossy starling. 7a, Red-shouldered widow bird. 10a, Half-colored kingfisher.

12.50a, White-crowned shrike. 15a, White-winged babbling starling. 20a, Yellow-billed hornbill. 25a, Amethyst starling. 30a, Orange-breasted shrike. 40a, Secretary bird. 50a, Rosy-faced lovebird.

Photogravure and Lithographed

1951		Unwmk.		Perf. 11½
Birds in Natural Colors				
333	A31	5c lt blue	.55	.25
334	A32	10c aqua	.55	.25
335	A32	15c salmon pink	.75	.25
336	A32	20c pale yellow	.75	.40
337	A31	50c gray blue	.75	.25
338	A31	1a lilac	.75	.25
339	A31	1.50a gray buff	.75	.25
340	A31	2a cream	4.00	.25
341	A32	2.50a gray	1.50	.25
342	A32	3a lemon yel	1.10	.25
343	A31	3.50a lt gray	1.50	.25
344	A31	4a rose buff	1.75	.25
345	A32	4.50a rose lilac	1.75	.25
346	A31	5a green	7.50	.55
347	A31	6a blue	10.50	1.50
348	A31	7a orange	11.50	2.00
349	A31	10a lilac rose	45.00	2.75
350	A32	12.50a slate gray	13.00	3.75
351	A31	15a pale olive	11.50	3.75
352	A31	20a pale bis brn	110.00	9.00
353	A31	25a lilac rose	40.00	6.75
354	A32	30a pale salmon	40.00	9.00
355	A31	40a yellow	57.50	11.50
356	A31	50a turquoise	140.00	22.50
	Nos. 333-356 (24)		502.95	76.45
	Set, hinged		225.00	

Holy Year Extension Issue
Common Design Type

1951, Oct.	Litho.		Perf. 14
357 CD43	4a orange + label	5.25	1.50

Sheets contain alternate vertical rows of stamps and labels bearing quotations from Pope Pius XII or the Patriarch Cardinal of Lisbon. Stamp without label attached sells for less.

Medical Congress Issue
Common Design Type

Design: Medical examination

1952, June		Perf. 13½
358 CD44	1a vio blue & brn blk	1.50 .50

Head of Christ — A35

1952, Oct.		Unwmk.		Perf. 13
359	A35	10c dk blue & buff	.25	.25
360	A35	50c dk ol grn & ol gray	1.00	.30
361	A35	2a rose vio & cream	1.25	.95
	Nos. 359-361 (3)		2.50	1.50

Exhibition of Sacred Missionary Art, Lisbon, 1951.

Leopard — A36   Sable Antelope — A37

Animals: 20c, Elephant. 30c, Eland. 40c, African crocodile. 50c, Impala. 1a, Mountain zebra. 1.50a, Sitatunga. 2a, Black rhinoceros. 2.30a, Gemsbok. 2.50a, Lion. 3a, Buffalo. 3.50a, Springbok. 4a, Brindled gnu. 5a, Hartebeest. 7a, Wart hog. 10a, Defassa waterbuck. 12.50a, Hippopotamus. 15a, Greater kudu. 20a, Giraffe.

1953, Aug. 15			Perf. 12½
362	A36	5c multicolored	.25	.25
363	A37	10c multicolored	.25	.25
364	A37	20c multicolored	.25	.25
365	A37	30c multicolored	.25	.25
366	A36	40c multicolored	.25	.25
367	A37	50c multicolored	.25	.25
368	A37	1a multicolored	.35	.25
369	A37	1.50a multicolored	.40	.25
370	A36	2a multicolored	.40	.25
371	A37	2.30a multicolored	.45	.25
372	A37	2.50a multicolored	.50	.25
373	A36	3a multicolored	.55	.25
374	A37	3.50a multicolored	.55	.25

375	A37	4a multicolored	20.00	.40
376	A37	5a multicolored	1.00	.35
377	A37	7a multicolored	1.50	.35
378	A37	10a multicolored	3.00	.35
379	A37	12.50a multicolored	7.50	6.00
380	A37	15a multicolored	10.00	6.00
381	A37	20a multicolored	13.00	1.10
	Nos. 362-381 (20)		60.70	17.80
	Set, hinged		20.00	

Stamp of Portugal and Arms of Colonies — A38

1953, Nov.	Photo.		Perf. 13
Stamp and Arms Multicolored			
382 A38	50c gray & dark gray	1.25	.60

Cent. of Portugal's 1st postage stamps.

Map and Plane — A39

Typographed and Lithographed

1954, May 27		Perf. 13½
383 A39	35c multicolored	.25 .25
384 A39	4.50c multicolored	1.10 .65

Visit of Pres. Francisco H C. Lopes.

Sao Paulo Issue
Common Design Type

1954		Litho.
385 CD46	1e bister & gray	.80 .50

Map of Angola — A41

1955, Aug.		Unwmk.		Perf. 13½
386	A41	5c multicolored	.25	.25
387	A41	20c multicolored	.25	.25
388	A41	50c multicolored	.25	.25
389	A41	1e multicolored	.25	.25
390	A41	2.30e multicolored	.50	.35
391	A41	4e multicolored	2.50	.25
392	A41	10e multicolored	2.50	.25
393	A41	20e multicolored	4.00	.45
	Nos. 386-393 (8)		10.50	2.30

For overprints see Nos. 593, 598, 604.

Artur de Paiva — A42

1956, Oct. 9		Perf. 13½x12½
394 A42	1e blk, dk bl & ocher	.50 .30

Cent. of the birth of Col. Artur de Paiva.

Man of Malange — A43

Various Costumes in Multicolor; Inscriptions in Black Brown

1957, Jan. 1	Photo.		Perf. 11½
Granite Paper			
395	A43	5c gray	.25	.25
396	A43	10c orange yel	.25	.25
397	A43	15c lt blue grn	.25	.25
398	A43	20c pale rose vio	.25	.25
399	A43	30c brt rose	.25	.25
400	A43	40c blue gray	.25	.25
401	A43	50c pale olive	.25	.25
402	A43	80c lt violet	.45	.40
403	A43	1.50e buff	2.50	.40
404	A43	2.50e lt yel grn	3.25	.25
405	A43	4e salmon	2.00	.25
406	A43	10e salmon pink	3.00	.50
	Nos. 395-406 (12)		12.95	3.55

Jose M. Antunes — A44

1957, Apr.		Perf. 13½
407 A44	1e aqua & brown	.90 .45

Birth cent. of Father Jose Maria Antunes.

Fair Emblem, Globe and Arms — A45

1958, July	Litho.		Perf. 12x11½
408 A45	1.50e multicolored	.75 .35

World's Fair, Brussels, Apr. 17-Oct. 19.

Tropical Medicine Congress Issue
Common Design Type

Design: Securidaca longipedunculata.

1958, Dec. 15		Perf. 13½
409 CD47	2.50e multicolored	3.50 1.10

Medicine Man — A47

Designs: 1.50e, Early government doctor. 2.50e, Modern medical team.

1958, Dec. 18		Perf. 11½x12
410	A47	1e blue blk & brown	.45	.25
411	A47	1.50e gray, blk & brown	1.40	.50
412	A47	2.50e multicolored	2.25	1.10
	Nos. 410-412 (3)		4.10	1.85

75th anniversary of the Maria Pia Hospital, Luanda.

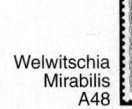

Welwitschia Mirabilis A48

1959, Oct. 1	Litho.		Perf. 14½
Various Views of Plant and Various Frames			
413	A48	1.50e lt brn, grn & blk	1.10	.65
414	A48	2.50e multicolored	1.75	.85
415	A48	5e multicolored	3.00	1.00
416	A48	10e multicolored	4.50	2.10
	Nos. 413-416 (4)		10.35	4.60

Centenary of discovery of Welwitschia mirabilis, desert plant.

Map of West Africa, c. 1540, by Jorge Reinel — A49

1960, June 25		Perf. 13½
417 A49	2.50e multicolored	.55 .25

500th anniv. of the death of Prince Henry the Navigator.

Distributing Medicines A50

1960, Oct.	Litho.		Perf. 14½
418 A50	2.50e multicolored	.65 .35

10th anniv. of the Commission for Technical Co-operation in Africa South of the Sahara (C.C.T.A.).

Girl of Angola — A51

Various portraits.

1961, Nov. 30		Unwmk.		Perf. 13
419	A51	10c multicolored	.25	.25
420	A51	15c multicolored	.25	.25
421	A51	30c multicolored	.25	.25
422	A51	40c multicolored	.25	.25
423	A51	60c multicolored	.25	.25
424	A51	1.50e multicolored	.25	.25
425	A51	2e multicolored	1.00	.25
426	A51	2.50e multicolored	1.00	.25
427	A51	3e multicolored	3.50	.30
428	A51	4e multicolored	1.50	.25
429	A51	5e multicolored	1.10	.30
430	A51	7.50e multicolored	1.50	.90
431	A51	10e multicolored	1.20	.70
432	A51	15e multicolored	2.00	.90
432A	A51	25e multicolored	2.40	1.25
432B	A51	50e multicolored	3.75	2.75
	Nos. 419-432B (16)		20.45	9.35

Sports Issue
Common Design Type

Sports: 50c, Flying. 1e, Rowing. 1.50e, Water polo. 2.50e, Hammer throwing. 4.50e, High jump. 15e, Weight lifting.

1962, Jan. 18		Perf. 13½
Multicolored Design		
433	CD48	50c lt blue	.25	.25
434	CD48	1e olive bister	1.10	.25
435	CD48	1.50e salmon	.75	.30
436	CD48	2.50e lt green	.90	.30
437	CD48	4.50e pale blue	.75	.60
438	CD48	15e yellow	1.75	1.50
	Nos. 433-438 (6)		5.50	3.20

For overprint see No. 608.

Anti-Malaria Issue
Common Design Type

Design: Anopheles funestus.

1962, April	Litho.		Perf. 13½
439 CD49	2.50e multicolored	1.75 .90

Gen. Norton de Matos — A54

1962, Aug. 8	Unwmk.		Perf. 14½
440 A54	2.50e multicolored	.65 .40

50th anniv. of the founding of Nova Lisboa.

Locusts — A56

1963, June 2   Litho.   Perf. 14
447 A56 2.50e multicolored   1.60 .95
15th anniv. of the Intl. Anti-Locust Organ.

Arms of
Luanda
A57

Vila de Santo
Antonio do
Zaire — A58

Coats of Arms (Provinces and Cities): 10c,
Massangano. 15c, Sanza-Pombo. 25c,
Ambriz. 30c, Muxima. 40c, Ambrizete. 50c,
Carmona. 60c, Catete. 70c, Quibaxe. No. 458,
Salazar. No. 459, Maquela do Zombo. 1.20e,
Bembe. No. 461, Malanje. No. 462, Caxito.
1.80e, Dondo. 2e, Henrique de Carvalho. No.
465, Moçamedes. No. 466, Damba. 3e, Novo
Redondo. 3.50e, S. Salvador do Congo. 4e,
Cuimba. 5e, Luso. 6.50e, Negage. 7e,
Quitexe. 7.50e, S. Filipe de Benguela. 8e,
Mucaba. 9e, 31 de Janeiro. 10e, Lobito. 11e,
Nova Caipemba. 12.50e, Gabela. 14e, Songo.
15e Sá da Bandeira. 17e, Quimbele. 17.50e,
Silva Porto. 20e, Nova Lisboa. 22.50e,
Cabinda. 25e, Noqui. 30e, Serpa Pinto. 35e,
Santa Cruz. 50e, General Freire.

1963   Perf. 13½
Arms in Original Colors; Red and
Violet Blue Inscriptions
448 A57   5c tan   .25   .25
449 A57   10c lt blue   .25   .25
450 A57   15c salmon   .25   .25
451 A58   20c olive   .25   .25
452 A57   25c lt blue   .25   .25
453 A57   30c buff   .25   .25
454 A57   40c gray   .25   .25
455 A57   50c lt green   .25   .25
456 A58   60c brt yellow   .25   .25
457 A57   70c dull rose   .25   .25
458 A57   1e pale lilac   .65   .25
459 A58   1e dull yellow   .30   .25
460 A58   1.20e rose   .30   .25
461 A57   1.50e pale salmon   .90   .25
462 A58   1.50e lt green   .75   .25
463 A58   1.80e yel olive   .75   .55
464 A57   2e lt yel green   .65   .25
465 A57   2.50e lt gray   2.50   .30
466 A58   2.50e dull blue   2.25   .25
467 A57   3e yel olive   .75   .25
468 A57   3.50e gray   .90   .25
469 A58   4e citron   .60   .30
470 A57   5e citron   .75   .30
471 A58   6.50e tan   .65   .40
472 A58   7e rose lilac   .90   .75
473 A58   7.50e pale lilac   1.00   .75
474 A58   8e lt aqua   .90   .75
475 A57   9e yellow   1.10 1.00
476 A57   10e dp salmon   1.20   .80
477 A58   11e dull yel grn   1.25 1.25
478 A57 12.50e pale blue   1.50 1.25
479 A58   14e lt gray   1.50 1.25
480 A58   15e lt blue   1.50 1.25
481 A58   17e pale blue   1.60 1.50
482 A57 17.50e dull yellow   2.40 2.25
483 A57   20e lt aqua   2.40 1.75
484 A58 22.50e gray   2.50 2.40
485 A57   25e citron   2.10 1.50
486 A57   30e yellow   3.00 2.50
487 A58   35e grysh blue   3.25 3.00
488 A58   50e dp yellow   4.50 2.25
       Nos. 448-488 (41)   47.80 32.80

Pres. Américo
Rodrigues
Thomaz — A59

1963, Sept. 16   Litho.
489 A59 2.50e multicolored   .65 .30
Visit of the President of Portugal.

Airline Anniversary Issue
Common Design Type
1963, Oct. 5   Unwmk.   Perf. 14½
490 CD50 1e lt blue & multi   1.00 .35

Cathedral of Sá da
Bandeira — A61

Malange
Cathedral
A62

Churches: 20c, Landana. 30c, Luanda
Cathedral. 40c, Gabela. 50c, St. Martin's
Chapel, Baia dos Tigres. 1.50e, St. Peter,
Chibia. 2e, Church of Our Lady, Benguela.
2.50e, Church of Jesus, Luanda. 3e, Cama-
batela. 3.50e, Mission, Cabinda. 4e, Vila Fol-
gares. 4.50e, Church of Our Lady, Lobito. 5e,
Church of Cabinda. 7.50e, Cacuso Church,
Malange. 10e, Lubango Mission. 12.50e, Huila
Mission. 15e, Church of Our Lady, Luanda
Island.

1963, Nov. 1   Litho.
Multicolored Design and Inscription
491 A61   10c gray blue   .25   .25
492 A61   20c pink   .25   .25
493 A61   30c lt blue   .25   .25
494 A61   40c tan   .25   .25
495 A61   50c lt green   .25   .25
496 A62   1e buff   .25   .25
497 A61   1.50e lt vio blue   .25   .25
498 A62   2e pale rose   .35   .25
499 A61   2.50e gray   .35   .25
500 A62   3e buff   .35   .25
501 A61   3.50e olive   .55   .25
502 A62   4e buff   .55   .25
503 A62   4.50e pale blue   .75   .30
504 A61   5e tan   .75   .30
505 A62   7.50e gray   1.00   .55
506 A61   10e dull yellow   1.40   .75
507 A62 12.50e bister   1.60 1.25
508 A62   15e pale gray vio   2.40 1.40
       Nos. 491-508 (18)   11.80 7.55

National Overseas Bank Issue
Common Design Type
Design: Antonio Teixeira de Sousa.

1964, May 16   Perf. 13½
509 CD51 2.50e multicolored   .90 .30

Commerce
Building
and Arms
of Chamber
of
Commerce
A64

1964, Nov.   Litho.   Perf. 12
510 A64 1e multicolored   .45 .25
Luanda Chamber of Commerce centenary.

ITU Issue
Common Design Type
1965, May 17   Unwmk.   Perf. 14½
511 CD52 2.50e gray & multi   1.25 .65

Plane over Luanda
Airport — A65

1965, Dec. 3   Litho.   Perf. 13
512 A65 2.50e multicolored   1.25 .60
25th anniv. of DTA, Direccao dos Transportes Aereos.

Harquebusier,
1539 — A66

50c, Harquebusier, 1539. 1e, Harquebusier,
1640. 1.50e, Infantry officer, 1777. 2e, Standard bearer, infantry, 1777. 2.50e, Infantry soldier, 1777. 3e, Cavalry officer, 1783. 4e, Cavalry soldier, 1783. 4.50e, Infantry officer, 1807.
5e, Infantry soldier, 1807. 6e, Cavalry officer,
1807. 8e, Cavalry soldier, 1807. 9e, Infantry
soldier, 1873.

1966, Feb. 25   Litho.   Perf. 14½
513 A66   50c multicolored   .25   .25
514 A66   1e multicolored   .25   .25
515 A66   1.50e multicolored   .25   .25
516 A66   2e multicolored   .25   .25
517 A66   2.50e multicolored   .40   .25
518 A66   3e multicolored   .40   .25
519 A66   4e multicolored   .60   .25
520 A66   4.50e multicolored   .65   .25
521 A66   5e multicolored   .65   .30
522 A66   6e multicolored   1.10   .65
523 A66   8e multicolored   1.50 1.10
524 A66   9e multicolored   1.60 1.25
       Nos. 513-524 (12)   7.90 5.30

National Revolution Issue
Common Design Type
Design: St. Paul's Hospital and Commercial
and Industrial School.

1966, May 28   Litho.   Perf. 12
525 CD53 1e multicolored   .50 .25

Emblem of Holy
Ghost Society — A68

1966   Litho.   Perf. 13
526 A68 1e blue & multi   .50 .25
Centenary of the Holy Ghost Society.

Navy Club Issue
Common Design Type
Designs: 1e, Mendes Barata and cruiser
Dom Carlos I. 2.50e, Capt. Augusto de Cas-
tilho and corvette Mindelo.

1967, Jan. 31   Litho.   Perf. 13
527 CD54 1e multicolored   .75 .25
528 CD54 2.50e multicolored   1.00 .50

Fatima
Basilica — A70

1967, May 13 Litho. Perf. 12½x13
529 A70 50c multicolored   .45 .25
50th anniv. of the apparition of the Virgin
Mary to 3 shepherd children at Fatima.

Angola Map, Manuel
Cerveira
Pereira — A71

1967, Aug. 15 Litho. Perf. 12½x13
530 A71 50c multicolored   .45 .25
350th anniv. of the founding of Benguela.

Administration Building,
Carmona — A72

1967   Litho.   Perf. 12
531 A72 1e multicolored   .45 .25
50th anniv. of the founding of Carmona.

Military Order of
Valor — A73

50c, Ribbon of the Three Orders. 1.50e, Military Order of Avis. 2e, Military Order of Christ.
2.50e, Military Order of St. John of Espada.
3e, Order of the Empire. 4e, Order of Prince
Henry. 5e, Order of Benemerencia. 10e, Order
of Public Instruction. 20e, Order for Industrial
& Agricultural Merit.

1967, Oct. 31   Perf. 14
532 A73   50c lt gray & multi   .25   .25
533 A73   1e lt green & multi   .25   .25
534 A73   1.50e yellow & multi   .25   .25
535 A73   2e multicolored   .25   .25
536 A73   2.50e multicolored   .25   .25
537 A73   3e lt olive & multi   .35   .25
538 A73   4e gray & multi   .50   .25
539 A73   5e multicolored   .60   .25
540 A73   10e lilac & multi   1.00   .50
541 A73   20e lt blue & multi   2.25 1.20
       Nos. 532-541 (10)   5.95 3.70

Our Lady of
Hope — A74

1e, Belmonte Castle, horiz. 1.50e, St.
Jerome's Convent. 2.50e, Cabral's Armada.

1968, Apr. 22   Litho.   Perf. 14
542 A74   50c yellow & multi   .25   .25
543 A74   1e gray & multi   .50   .25
544 A74   1.50e lt blue & multi   .60   .25
545 A74   2.50e buff & multi   1.00   .35
       Nos. 542-545 (4)   2.35 1.10

500th anniv. of the birth of Pedro Alvares
Cabral, navigator who took possession of Brazil for Portugal.

Francisco Inocencio
de Souza
Coutinho — A75

1969, Jan. 7   Litho.   Perf. 14
546 A75 2e multicolored   .45 .25
Founding of Novo Redondo, 200th anniv.

Admiral Coutinho Issue
Common Design Type

Design: Adm. Gago Coutinho and his first ship.

1969, Feb. 17   Litho.   Perf. 14
547 CD55 2.50e multicolored   .85   .35

Compass Rose — A77

1969, Aug. 29   Litho.   Perf. 14
548 A77 1e multicolored   .45   .25

500th anniv. of the birth of Vasco da Gama (1469-1524), navigator.

Administration Reform Issue
Common Design Type

1969, Sept. 25   Litho.   Perf. 14
549 CD56 1.50e multicolored   .35   .25

Portal of St. Jeronimo's Monastery — A79

1969, Dec. 1   Litho.   Perf. 14
550 A79 3e multicolored   .45   .25

500th anniv. of the birth of King Manuel I.

Angolasaurus Bocagei — A80

Fossils and Minerals: 1e, Ferrometeorite. 1.50e, Dioptase crystals. 2e, Gondwanidium. 2.50e, Diamonds. 3e, Estromatolite. 3.50e, Procarcharodon megalodon. 4e, Microceratodus angolensis. 4.50e, Moscovite. 5e, Barite. 6e, Nostoceras. 10e, Rotula orbiculus angolensis.

1970, Oct. 31   Litho.   Perf. 13
551 A80 50c tan & multi   .25   .25
552 A80 1e multicolored   .25   .25
553 A80 1.50e multicolored   .30   .25
554 A80 2e multicolored   .30   .25
555 A80 2.50e lt gray & multi   .30   .25
556 A80 3e multicolored   .35   .25
557 A80 3.50e blue & multi   .50   .30
558 A80 4e lt gray & multi   .50   .30
559 A80 4.50e gray & multi   .50   .30
560 A80 5e gray & multi   .75   .30
561 A80 6e pink & multi   1.50   .90
562 A80 10e lt blue & multi   2.10   1.20
Nos. 551-562 (12)   7.60   4.80

Marshal Carmona Issue
Common Design Type

1970, Nov. 15   Perf. 14
563 CD57 2.50e multicolored   .45   .25

Arms of Malanje, Cotton Boll and Field — A82

1970, Nov. 20   Perf. 13
564 A82 2.50e multicolored   .55   .35

Centenary of the municipality of Malanje.

Mail Ships and Angola No. 1 A83

4.50e, Steam locomotive and Angola No. 4.

1970, Dec. 1   Perf. 13½
565 A83 1.50e multicolored   .40   .30
566 A83 4.50e multicolored   1.75   .75

Cent. of stamps of Angola. See No. C36. For overprint see No. 616B.

Map of Africa, Diagram of Seismic Tests — A84

1971, Aug. 22   Litho.   Perf. 13
567 A84 2.50e multicolored   .45   .25

5th Regional Conference of Soil and Foundation Engineers, Luanda, Aug. 22-Sept. 5.

Galleon on Congo River — A85

1972, May 25   Litho.   Perf. 13
568 A85 1e brt grn & multi   .65   .25

4th centenary of the publication of The Lusiads by Luiz Camoens.

Olympic Games Issue
Common Design Type

1972, June 20   Perf. 14x13½
569 CD59 50c multicolored   .65   .25

Lisbon-Rio de Janeiro Flight Issue
Common Design Type

1972, Sept. 20   Litho.   Perf. 13½
570 CD60 1e multicolored   .35   .25

WMO Centenary Issue
Common Design Type

1973, Dec. 15   Litho.   Perf. 13
571 CD61 1e dk gray & multi   .45   .25

Radar Station A89

1974, June 25   Litho.   Perf. 13
572 A89 2e multicolored   .45   .25

Establishment of satellite communications network via Intelsat among Portugal, Angola and Mozambique.
For overprint see No. 616A.

Harpa Doris — A90

Designs: Sea shells: 30c, Murex melanamathos. 50c, Venus foliaceo lamellosa. 70c, Lathyrus filosus. 1e, Cymbium cisium. 1.50e, Cassis tesselata. 2e, Cypraea stercoraria. 2.50e, Conus prometheus. 3e, Strombus latus. 3.50e, Tympanotonus fuscatus. 4e, Cardium costatum. 5e, Natica fulminea. 6e, Lyropecten nodosus. 7e, Tonna galea. 10e, Donax rugosus. 25e, Cymatium trigonum. 30e, Olivancilaria acuminata. 35e,

Semifusus morio. 40e, Clavatula lineata. 50e, Solarium granulatum.

1974, Oct. 25   Litho.   Perf. 12x12½
573 A90 25c shown   .25   .25
574 A90 30c multicolored   .25   .25
575 A90 50c multicolored   .30   .25
576 A90 70c multicolored   .35   .25
577 A90 1e multicolored   .35   .25
578 A90 1.50e multicolored   .40   .25
579 A90 2e multicolored   .40   .25
580 A90 2.50e multicolored   .45   .25
581 A90 3e multicolored   .65   .25
582 A90 3.50e multicolored   .65   .45
583 A90 4e multicolored   .65   .45
584 A90 5e multicolored   .75   .45
585 A90 6e multicolored   1.25   .45
586 A90 7e multicolored   1.25   .45
587 A90 10e multicolored   1.00   .45
588 A90 25e multicolored   2.25   .90
589 A90 30e multicolored   2.50   .90
590 A90 35e multicolored   3.00   .90
591 A90 40e multicolored   3.50   1.10
592 A90 50e multicolored   5.00   1.75
Nos. 573-592 (20)   25.20   10.50

For overprints see Nos. 605-607, 617-630.

No. 386 Overprinted in Blue

1974, Dec. 21   Litho.   Perf. 13½
593 A41 5c multicolored   .30   .25

Youth philately.

Republic

Star and Hand Holding Rifle — A91

1975, Nov. 11   Litho.   Perf. 13x13½
594 A91 1.50e red & multi   .50   .25

Independence in 1975.

Diquiche Mask — A92

Design: 3e, Bui ou Congolo mask.

1976, Feb. 6   Perf. 13½
595 A92 50c lt blue & multi   .25   .25
596 A92 3e multicolored   .55   .25

Workers — A93

1976, May 1   Litho.   Perf. 12
597 A93 1e red & multi   .35   .25

International Workers' Day.

No. 392 Overprinted

1976, June 15   Litho.   Perf. 13½
598 A41 10e multicolored   1.10   .75

Stamp Day.

President Agostinho Neto — A94

1976, Nov. 11   Litho.   Perf. 13
599 A94 50c yel & dk brown   .25   .25
600 A94 2e lt gray & plum   .25   .25
601 A94 3e gray & indigo   .40   .25
602 A94 5e buff & brown   .40   .25
603 A94 10e tan & sepia   .55   .25
  a.   Souv. sheet of 1, imperf.   4.00   4.00
Nos. 599-603 (5)   1.85   1.25

First anniversary of independence.

Nos. 393, 588-589, 592 Overprinted

1977, Feb. 9   Perf. 13½, 12x12½
604 A41 20e multicolored   1.75   .50
605 A90 25e multicolored   2.25   .60
606 A90 30e multicolored   2.60   .75
607 A90 50e multicolored   4.25   1.25
Nos. 604-607 (4)   10.85   3.10

Overprint in 3 lines on No. 604, in 2 lines on others.

No. 438 Overprinted

1976, Dec. 31   Perf. 13½
608 CD48 15e multicolored   2.00   .65

Child and WHO Emblem — A95

1977   Litho.   Perf. 10½
609 A95 2.50k blk & lt blue   .65   .25

Campaign for vaccination against poliomyelitis.

Map of Africa,
Flag of
Angola — A96

1977   **Photo.**
610 A96 6k blk, red & blue   .60 .35
    First Congress of Popular Movement for the
Liberation of Angola.

Anti-Apartheid
Emblem — A97

1979, June 20   **Litho.**   **Perf. 13½**
611 A97 1k multicolored   .25 .25
      Anti-Apartheid Year.

Human Rights
Emblem — A98

1979, June 15   **Litho.**   **Perf. 13½**
612 A98 2.50k multicolored   .35 .25
    Declaration of Human Rights, 30th anniv. (in
1975).

Child Flowers,
Globe, IYC
Emblem — A99

1980, May 1   **Litho.**   **Perf. 14x14½**
613 A99 3.50k multicolored   .45 .25
    International Year of the Child (1979).

Running, Moscow
'80 Emblem — A100

1980, Dec. 15   **Litho.**   **Perf. 13½**
614 A100 9k shown   .70 .25
615 A100 12k Swimming, horiz.   .80 .25
    22nd Summer Olympic Games, Moscow,
July 19-Aug. 3.

5th Anniv. of
Independence
A101

1980, Nov. 11
616 A101 5.50k multicolored   .45 .25

Nos. 572,
566
Overprinted

1980-81   **Litho.**   **Perf. 13½x13**
616A A89   2e multi (bar only)   1.25 .25
616B A83 4.50e multicolored   2.75 1.50
    Issued: 2e, 5/17/81; 4.50e, 6/15/80.
See No. C37.

Nos. 577-
580, 582-591
Overprinted

1981, June 15   **Litho.**   **Perf. 12x12½**
617 A90   1e multicolored   .25 .25
618 A90 1.50e multicolored   .25 .25
619 A90   2e multicolored   .25 .25
620 A90 2.50e multicolored   .25 .25
621 A90 3.50e multicolored   .25 .25
622 A90   4e multicolored   .30 .25
623 A90   5e multicolored   .35 .25
624 A90   6e multicolored   .40 .25
625 A90   7e multicolored   .55 .25
626 A90   10e multicolored   .65 .30
627 A90   25e multicolored   1.40 .50
628 A90   30e multicolored   1.75 .75
629 A90   35e multicolored   2.00 .90
630 A90   40e multicolored   2.50 1.25
     Nos. 617-630 (14)   11.15 5.95

Man Walking with
Canes, Tchibinda
Ilunga
Statue — A102

1981, Sept. 5   **Litho.**   **Perf. 13½**
631 A102 9k multicolored   .50 .30
    Turipex '81 tourism exhibition.

M.P.L.A.
Workers' Party
Congress
A103

1980, Dec. 23   **Litho.**   **Perf. 14**
632 A103   50 l Millet   .25 .25
633 A103   5k Coffee   .35 .25
634 A103 7.50k Sunflowers   .40 .25
635 A103 13.50k Cotton   .65 .30
636 A103   14k Oil   .80 .35
637 A103   16k Diamonds   .95 .45
     Nos. 632-637 (6)   3.40 1.85

People's
Power — A104

1980, Nov. 11
638 A104 40k lt blue & blk   1.75 .65

Natl. Heroes'
Day — A105

4.50k, Former Pres. Neto. 50k, Neto, diff.

1980, Sept. 17   **Perf. 14x13½**
639 A105 4.50k multicolored   .25 .25
640 A105 50k multicolored   2.75 .75

Soweto
Uprising,
5th Anniv.
A106

1981
641 A106 4.50k multicolored   .35 .25

2nd
Central
African
Games
A107

    50 l, Bicycling, tennis. 5k, Judo, boxing. 6k,
Basketball, volleyball. 10k, Handball, soccer.

1981, Sept. 3   **Litho.**   **Perf. 13½**
642 A107   50 l multicolored   .25 .25
643 A107   5k multicolored   .65 .25
644 A107   6k multicolored   .85 .25
645 A107   10k multicolored   1.40 .35
     Nos. 642-645 (4)   3.15 1.10

Souvenir Sheet
Imperf
646 A107 15k multicolored   3.00 3.00

Charaxes
Kahldeni
A108

    1k, Abantis zambesiaca. 5k, Catacroptera
cloanthe. 9k, Myrina ficedula, vert. 10k,
Colotis danae. 15k, Acraea acrita. 100k, Precis hierta.

1982, Feb. 26   **Litho.**   **Perf. 13½**
647 A108   50 l shown   .25 .25
648 A108   1k multicolored   .25 .25
649 A108   5k multicolored   .40 .25
650 A108   9k multicolored   1.00 .25
651 A108   10k multicolored   1.00 .25
652 A108   15k multicolored   1.25 .40
653 A108 100k multicolored   8.00 3.00
   a.   Souvenir sheet   12.00 12.00
     Nos. 647-653 (7)   12.15 4.65

    No. 653a contains Nos. 647-653, imperf.,
and sold for 30k (stamps probably not valid
individually).

5th Anniv. of UN Membership — A109

    5.50k, The Silence of the Night, by Mus-
seque Catambor. 7.50k, Cotton picking,
Catete.

1982, Sept. 22   **Litho.**
654 A109 5.50k multicolored   .40 .25
655 A109 7.50k multicolored   .55 .25

20th Anniv.
of
Engineering
Laboratory
A110

1982, Dec. 21   **Litho.**   **Perf. 14**
656 A110   9k Lab   .65 .30
657 A110   13k Worker, vert.   .65 .40
658 A110 100k Equipment, vert.   6.75 3.50
     Nos. 656-658 (3)   8.05 4.20

Local Flowers — A111

    5k, Dichrostachys glomerata. 12k, Amblygo-
nocarpus obtusangulus. 50k, Albizzia
versicolor.

1983, Feb. 18   **Perf. 13½**
659 A111   5k multicolored   .40 .25
660 A111 12k multicolored   .75 .30
661 A111 50k multicolored   3.50 1.40
     Nos. 659-661 (3)   4.65 1.95

Women's Org.,
First Congress
A112

1983   **Litho.**   **Perf. 13½**
662 A112 20k multicolored   1.25 .50

Africa
Day — A113

1983, June 30   **Perf. 13**
663 A113 6.5k multicolored   .65 .35

World Communications Year — A114

1983, June 30   **Litho.**   **Perf. 13½**
664 A114 6.5k M'pungi   .75 .35
665 A114 12k Mondu   1.25 .55

BRASILIANA '83 Stamp Exhibition,
Rio de Janeiro, July 29-Aug. 7 — A115

    Crop-eating insects: 4.50k, Antestiopsis
lineaticollis. 6.5k, Stephanoderes hampei ferr.
10k, Zonocerus variegatus.

1983, July 29   **Litho.**   **Perf. 13**
666 A115 4.5k multicolored   .50 .25
667 A115 6.5k multicolored   .55 .35
668 A115 10k multicolored   1.00 .60
     Nos. 666-668 (3)   2.05 1.20

25th Anniv. of Economic Commission
for Africa — A116

1983, Aug. 2
669 A116 10k Map, emblem .70 .50

185th
Anniv. of
Post Office
A117

50 l, Mail collection, vert. 3.5k, Unloading
mail plane. 5k, Sorting mail. 15k, Mailing letter, vert. 30k, Post office box delivery.

1983, Dec. 7   Litho.   Perf. 13½
670 A117 50 l multicolored .25 .25
671 A117 3.5k multicolored .35 .25
672 A117 5k multicolored .55 .40
673 A117 15k multicolored 1.50 .90
674 A117 30k multicolored 2.90 1.60
 a. Min. sheet of 3, #671-672,
    674 8.00 8.00
   Nos. 670-674 (5) 5.55 3.40
  No. 674a sold for 100k.

Local
Butterflies
A118

50 l, Parasa karschi. 1k, Diaphone angolensis. 3.5k, Choeropasis jucunda. 6.5k, Hespa-
garista rendalli. 15k, Euchromia guineensis.
17.5k, Mazuca roseistriga. 20k, Utetheisa
callima.

1984, Jan. 20   Litho.   Perf. 13½
675 A118 50 l multicolored .25 .25
676 A118 1k multicolored .30 .25
677 A118 3.5k multicolored .55 .25
678 A118 6.5k multicolored .95 .35
679 A118 15k multicolored 1.60 .90
680 A118 17.5k multicolored 1.90 1.00
681 A118 20k multicolored 2.75 1.25
   Nos. 675-681 (7) 8.30 4.25

A119

1984, Apr. 11   Litho.   Perf. 13½
682 A119 30k multicolored 2.50 1.75
  First Natl. Worker's Union Congress, Apr.
11-16.

Local
Birds — A120

10.50k, Bucorvus leadbeateri. 14k,
Gypohierax angolensis. 16k, Ardea goliath.
19.50k, Pelecanus onocrotalus. 22k, Platalea
alba. 26k, Balearica pavonnia.

1984, Oct. 24   Litho.   Perf. 13½
683 A120 10.50k multicolored .80 .40
684 A120 14k multicolored 1.00 .50
685 A120 16k multicolored 1.20 .65
686 A120 19.50k multicolored 1.60 .65
687 A120 22k multicolored 1.75 .75
688 A120 26k multicolored 2.50 1.00
   Nos. 683-688 (6) 8.85 3.95

Local
Animals
A121

1k, Tragelaphus strepsiceros. 4k, Antidorcas
marsupialis angolensis. 5k, Pan troglodytes.
10k, Syncerus caffer. 15k, Hippotragus niger
variani. 20k, Orycteropus afer. 25k, Crocuta
crocuta.

1984, Nov. 12
689 A121 1k multicolored .35 .25
690 A121 4k multicolored .45 .25
691 A121 5k multicolored .60 .25
692 A121 10k multicolored 1.75 .30
693 A121 15k multicolored 2.10 .45
694 A121 20k multicolored 2.50 .60
695 A121 25k multicolored 3.00 .65
   Nos. 689-695 (7) 10.75 2.75

Angolese
Monuments
A122

5k, San Pedro da Barra. 12.5k, Nova
Oeiras. 18k, M'Banza Kongo. 26k, Massangano. 39k, Escravatura Museum.

1985, Feb. 21   Litho.   Perf. 13½
696 A122 5k multicolored .35 .25
697 A122 12.5k multicolored .90 .50
698 A122 18k multicolored 1.20 .75
699 A122 26k multicolored 1.90 .90
700 A122 39k multicolored 2.60 1.50
   Nos. 696-700 (5) 6.95 3.90

United
Workers'
Party, 25th
Anniv.
A123

1985, May   Litho.   Perf. 12
701 A123 77k XXV, red flags 7.00 4.00
  Printed in sheets of 5.

A124

1k, Flags. 11k, Oil drilling platform, Cabinda.
57k, Conference.

1985, May
702 A124 1k multicolored .25 .25
703 A124 11k multicolored 1.00 .80
704 A124 57k multicolored 2.60 1.25
 a. Strip of 3, #702-704 4.50 4.50
  Southern African Development Council, 5th
anniv.

Medicinal
plants — A125

No. 705, Lonchocarpus sericeus. No. 706,
Gossypium. No. 707, Cassia occidentalis. No.
708, Gloriosa superba. No. 709, Cochlospermum angolensis.

Lithographed and Typographed
1985, July 5   Perf. 11
705 A125 1k multi .30 .25
706 A125 4k multi .40 .30
707 A125 11k multi 1.00 .70
708 A125 25.50k multi 2.00 1.00
709 A125 55k multi 3.50 2.50
   Nos. 705-709 (5) 7.20 4.75
  ARGENTINA '85 exhibition.

5th Natl.
Heroes Day
A126

Natl. flag and: 10.50k, Portrait of Agostinho
Neto, party leader. 36.50k, Neto working.

1985   Litho.   Perf. 13½
710 A126 10.50k multicolored 12.00 7.50
711 A126 36.50k multicolored 16.00 10.00

Ministerial Conference of Non-Aligned
Countries, Luanda — A127

1985, Sept. 4   Photo.   Perf. 11
712 A127 35k multicolored 2.50 1.75

UN, 40th
Anniv.
A128

1985, Oct. 29   Litho.   Perf. 11
713 A128 12.50k multicolored 1.25 .75

Industry and Natural
Resources — A129

1985, Nov. 11
714 A129 50 l Cement Factory .25 .25
715 A129 5k Logging .35 .25
716 A129 7k Quartz .50 .40
717 A129 10k Iron mine .85 .50
 a. Souvenir sheet of 4, #714-717,
    imperf. 3.50 3.50
   Nos. 714-717 (4) 1.95 1.40
  Natl. independence, 10th anniv.

2nd Natl. Workers' Party Congress
(MPLA) — A130

1985, Nov. 28   Perf. 13½
718 A130 20k multicolored 1.50 1.00

Demostenes de Almeida Clington
Races, 30th Anniv. — A131

Various runners.

1985, Dec. 13
719 A131 50 l multicolored .25 .25
720 A131 5k multicolored .40 .25
721 A131 6.50k multicolored .60 .25
722 A131 10k multicolored .80 .30
   Nos. 719-722 (4) 2.05 1.05

1986 World Cup
Soccer
Championships,
Mexico — A132

Map, soccer field and various plays.

1986, May 6   Litho.   Perf. 11½x11
723 A132 50 l multi .25 .25
724 A132 3.50k multi .40 .25
725 A132 5k multi .65 .25
726 A132 7k multi .80 .25
727 A132 10k multi 1.25 .40
728 A132 18k multi 2.10 .60
   Nos. 723-728 (6) 5.45 2.00

Struggle
Against
Portugal,
25th Anniv.
A133

1986, May 6   Perf. 11x11½
729 A133 15k multicolored 1.40 .50

First Man in
Space, 25th
Anniv.
A134

50 l, Skylab, US. 1k, Spacecraft. 5k, A. Leonov space-walking. 10k, Lunokhod on Moon.
13k, Apollo-Soyuz link-up.

1986, Aug. 21   Litho.   Perf. 11x11½
730 A134 50 l multicolored .25 .25
731 A134 1k multicolored .25 .25
732 A134 5k multicolored .40 .25
733 A134 10k multicolored .90 .35
734 A134 13k multicolored .95 .40
   Nos. 730-734 (5) 2.75 1.50

Admission of Angola to UN, 10th Anniv. A135

1986, Dec. 1   Litho.   Perf. 11x11½
735 A135 22k multi   1.60 1.10

Liberation Movement, 30th Anniv. — A136

Angolese at work, fighting and: No. 736a, "1956." No. 736b, Congress emblem, "1980." No. 736c, Labor Party emblem, "1985."

1986, Dec. 3   Perf. 11½x11
736 A136   Strip of 3   1.50 1.50
a.-c.   5k any single   .45   .25

Agostinho Neto University, 10th Anniv. A137

1986, Dec. 30   Litho.   Perf. 11x11½
737 A137   50 l Mathematics   .25   .25
738 A137   1k   Law   .50   .35
739 A137   10k   Medicine   .85   .60
   Nos. 737-739 (3)   1.60 1.20

Tribal Hairstyles — A138

1987, Apr. 15   Litho.   Perf. 11½x11
740 A138   1k   Ouioca   .25   .25
741 A138   1.50k Luanda   .35   .25
742 A138   5k   Humbe   .65   .25
743 A138   7k   Muila   .80   .25
744 A138   20k   Muila, diff.   2.00   .45
745 A138   30k   Dilolo   3.75   .80
   Nos. 740-745 (6)   7.80 2.25

Landscapes A139

Perf. 11½x12, 12x11½
1987, July 7   Litho.
746 A139   50 l   Pambala Shore   .25   .25
747 A139   1.50k Dala Waterfalls   .25   .25
748 A139   3.50k Black Stones   .25   .25
749 A139   5k   Cuango River   .45   .25
750 A139   10k   Luanda coast   .95   .35
751 A139   20k   Hills of Leba   1.90   .45
   Nos. 746-751 (6)   4.05 1.80

Nos. 746-747, 749 and 751 horiz.

Lenin — A140

1987, Nov. 25   Perf. 12x12½
752 A140 15k multi   1.25   .45

October Revolution, Russia, 70th anniv.

2nd Congress of the Organization of Angolan Women (OMA) — A141

10k, Soldier, nurse, technician, student.

1988, May 30   Litho.   Perf. 13x13½
753 A141   2k shown   .25   .25
754 A141   10k multicolored   .65   .25

Victory Carnival, 10th Anniv. A142

Various carnival scenes.

1988, June 15   Litho.   Perf. 13½x13
755 A142   5k shown   .40   .25
756 A142   10k multi, diff.   .70   .30

Augusto N'Gangula (1956-1968), Youth Pioneer Killed by Portuguese Colonial Army — A143

Agostinho Neto Pioneers' Organization (OPA), 25th Anniv. — A144

1989, Oct. 2   Litho.   Perf. 12x11½
757 A143   12k multicolored   1.10   .65
758 A144   15k multicolored   1.40   .80

Pioneer Day.

0th Natl. Soccer Championships, Benguela, May 1 — A145

1989, Oct. 16
759 A145 5k shown   .50   .40
760 A145 5k Luanda, 3 years   .50   .40
761 A145 5k Luanda, 5 years   .50   .40
a.   Strip of 3, #759-761   1.60 1.60
   Nos. 759-761 (3)   1.50 1.20

Intl. Fund for Agricultural Development, 10th Anniv. — A146

1990, Feb. 15   Litho.   Perf. 11½x12
762 A146 10k multicolored   1.10   .45

Ingombotas' Houses — A147

Architecture: 2k, Alta Train Station. 5k, National Museum of Anthropology. 15k, Ana Joaquina Palace. 23k, Iron Palace. 36k, Meteorological observatory, vert. 50k, People's Palace.

1990, Feb. 20   Perf. 12x11½, 11½x12
763 A147   1k shown   .25   .25
764 A147   2k multicolored   .25   .25
765 A147   5k multicolored   .40   .25
766 A147   15k multicolored   1.10   .60
767 A147   23k multicolored   1.90   .90
768 A147   36k multicolored   3.00 1.25
769 A147   50k multicolored   4.00 1.75
   Nos. 763-769 (7)   10.90 5.25

Luanda and Benguela Railways A148

Various maps and locomotives.

1990, Mar. 1   Perf. 12x11½
770 A148   5k shown   .40   .25
771 A148   12k Garrat T (left)   1.25   .45
772 A148   12k Garrat T (right)   1.25   .45
a.   Pair, #771-772   2.75 2.75
773 A148   14k Mikado   1.25   .75
   Nos. 770-773 (4)   4.15 1.90

Souvenir Sheet
774 A148   25k Diesel electric   3.00 3.00

No. 772a has a continuous design.

Southern Africa Development Coordinating Conf. (SADCC), 10th Anniv. — A149

1990, Apr. 1   Litho.   Perf. 14
775 A149 5k shown   .40   .25
776 A149 9k Floating oil rig   1.00   .45

Pan-African Postal Union (PAPU), 10th Anniv. A150

10k, Simulated stamp, map.

1990, Apr. 6
777 A150   4k shown   .45   .25
778 A150   10k multicolored   1.00   .65

Paintings by Raul Indipwo A151

6k, Tres Gracas. 9k, Muxima, vert.

1990, Apr. 24
779 A151 6k multicolored   .45   .25
780 A151 9k multicolored   1.00   .35

Stamp World London 90.

Hippotragus Niger Variani, Adult Male and Female — A152

1990, May 9   Perf. 14x13½
781 A152 5k Adult male   1.50 1.50
782 A152 5k shown   1.50 1.50
783 A152 5k Adult female   1.50 1.50
784 A152 5k Female, calf   1.50 1.50
   Nos. 781-784 (4)   6.00 6.00

World Wildlife Fund. Various combinations available in blocks or strips of four.

Rosa de Porcelana A153

1990, June 2   Litho.   Perf. 14
785 A153 5k shown   .40   .25
786 A153 8k Cravo burro   .80   .35
787 A153 10k Alamandra   .95   .45
   Nos. 785-787 (3)   2.15 1.05

Souvenir Sheet
788 A153 40k Hibiscus   5.00 5.00

Belgica '90.

Miniature Sheet

Intl. Literacy Year — A154

Various animals and forest scenes.

1990, July 26   Litho.   Perf. 14
789   A154   Sheet of 30   10.00 10.00
a.-ad. 1k any single   .30   .30
790   A154   5k Zebra   1.00 1.00
791   A154   5k Butterfly   1.00 1.00
792   A154   5k Horse   1.00 1.00
a.   Block of 3, #790-792 + label 4.00 4.00

People's
Assembly,
10th Anniv.
A155

1990, Nov. 11 **Perf. 14**
793 A155 10k multicolored .90 .90

3rd Natl. Labor
Congress
A156

1990 **Litho.** **Perf. 13½**
794 A156 14k multicolored 1.00 .50

War of Independence, 30th
Anniv. — A157

Uniforms: No. 795, Machete, 1961. No. 796,
Rifle, 1962-63. No. 797, Rifle, 1968. No. 798,
Automatic rifle, 1972.

1991, Feb. 28 **Litho.** **Perf. 14**
795 A157 6k multicolored .65 .25
  a. Perf. 13½ vert. 1.20 .75
796 A157 6k multicolored .65 .25
  a. Perf. 13½ vert. 1.20 .75
797 A157 6k multicolored .65 .25
  a. Perf. 13½ vert. 1.20 .75
798 A157 6k multicolored .65 .25
  a. Perf. 13½ vert. 1.20 .75
  b. Bklt. pane of 4, #795a-798a 6.00
    Nos. 795-798 (4) 2.60 1.00

Musical Instruments — A158

Designs: a, Marimba. b, Mucupela. c,
Ngoma la Txina. d, Kissange.

1991, Apr. 5 **Litho.** **Perf. 14**
799 A158 6k Block or strip of 4,
    #799a-799d 2.50 2.50

Tourism
A159

Designs: 3k, Iona National Park. 7k,
Kalandula Waterfalls. 35k, Lobito Bay. 60k,
Weltwitschia Mirabilis plant.

1991, June 25 **Litho.** **Perf. 14**
800 A159 3k multi .25 .25
801 A159 7k multi .40 .40
802 A159 35k multi 1.90 .80
803 A159 60k multi 3.25 1.50
    Nos. 800-803 (4) 5.80 2.95
Souvenir Sheet
Design: 30k, Map details.

1991, June 25 **Litho.** **Perf. 13¼**
803A A159 30k multi 4.00 4.00

Dogs
A160

1991, July 5 **Litho.** **Perf. 14**
804 A160 5k Kabir of dembos .50 .50
805 A160 7k Ombua .55 .55
806 A160 11k Kabir massongo .90 .40
807 A160 12k Kawa tchowe .90 .50
    Nos. 804-807. (4) 2.85 1.95

1992
Summer
Olympics,
Barcelona
A161

1991, July 26 **Perf. 13**
808 A161 4k Judo .25 .25
809 A161 6k Sailing .25 .25
810 A161 10k Running .45 .25
811 A161 100k Swimming 3.50 2.25
    Nos. 808-811 (4) 4.45 3.00

Navigation
Aids
A162

1991, Nov. 8 **Litho.** **Perf. 12**
812 A162 5k Quadrant .25 .25
813 A162 15k Astrolabe .55 .55
814 A162 20k Cross-staff .75 .40
815 A162 50k Portolano 1.75 1.00
    Nos. 812-815 (4) 3.30 2.20

Iberex '91.

Rays
A163

1992, Mar. 30 **Litho.** **Perf. 14**
816 A163 40k Myliobatis aquila .90 .30
817 A163 50k Aetobatus narinari .90 .40
818 A163 66k Manta birostris 1.10 .50
819 A163 80k Raja miraletus 1.50 .65
    Nos. 816-819 (4) 4.40 1.85
Souvenir Sheet
Perf. 13½
820 A163 25k Manta birostris,
    diff. 5.00 5.00

Quioca
Masks — A164

1992, Apr. 30 **Litho.** **Perf. 13½**
821 A164 60k Kalelwa .25 .25
822 A164 100k Mukixe Wa Kino .45 .35
823 A164 150k Cikunza .75 .55

824 A164 250k Mukixi Wa
    Mbwesu 1.20 .70
    Nos. 821-824 (4) 2.65 1.85
See Nos. 854-857, 868-871, 883-886, 895-
898.

Lubrapex
'92 — A165

Medicinal Plants: 200k, Ptaeroxylon obli-
quum. 300k, Spondias mombin. 500k, Parinari
curatellifolia. 600k, Cochlospermum
angolense.

1992, May 8 **Perf. 14**
825 A165 200k brown & pale yel .75 .55
826 A165 300k brown & pale yel 1.10 .90
827 A165 500k brown & pale yel 2.00 1.60
828 A165 600k brown & pale yel 2.10 1.75
  a. Block or strip of 4, #825-828 6.00 6.00

Evangelization of Angola, 500th
Anniv. — A166

150k, King, missionaries. 420k, Ruins of
M'banza Congo. 470k, Maxima Church. 500k,
Faces of people.

1992, May 10 **Perf. 13½**
829 A166 150k multicolored .55 .45
830 A166 420k multicolored 1.60 1.25
831 A166 470k multicolored 1.75 1.40
832 A166 500k multicolored 2.00 1.60
    Nos. 829-832 (4) 5.90 4.70

Traditional
Houses — A167

150k, Dimbas. 330k, Cokwe. 360k, Mbali.
420k, Ambwelas. 500k, Upper Zambezi.

Perf. 14, 13½ Vert. (#832A)
1992, May 22
832A A167 150k multi 1.25 1.00
  b. Bklt. pane of 4, #832A,
    833a-835a 7.50
833 A167 330k multi 1.40 1.10
  a. Perf. 13½ vert. 1.60 1.60
834 A167 360k multi 1.60 1.25
  a. Perf. 13½ vert. 1.60 1.60
835 A167 420k multi 2.00 1.60
  a. Perf. 13½ vert. 2.00 2.00
836 A167 500k multi 2.00 1.60
    Nos. 832A-836 (5) 8.25 6.55

Expo '92, Seville.

Agapornis
Roseicollis
A168

150k, Two birds on branch. 200k, Birds
feeding. 250k, Hand holding bird. 300k, Bird
on perch.

1992, June 2 **Perf. 12x11½**
837 A168 150k multicolored 1.00 .50
838 A168 200k multicolored 1.40 .65
839 A168 250k multicolored 1.75 .80
840 A168 300k multicolored 2.10 1.00
  a. Strip of 4, #837-840 6.50 6.50
Expo '92, Seville.

Souvenir Sheet

Visit of Pope John Paul II to
Angola — A169

Abstract paintings: a, 340k, The Crucifixion.
b, 370k, The Resurrection.

1992, June 4 **Litho.** **Perf. 13½**
841 A169 Sheet of 2, #a.-b. + 2
    labels 4.00 4.00

1992
Summer
Olympics,
Barcelona
A170

1992, July 30 **Perf. 14**
842 A170 120k Hurdles .55 .40
843 A170 180k Cycling .80 .55
844 A170 240k Roller hockey .95 .75
845 A170 360k Basketball 1.50 1.10
    Nos. 842-845 (4) 3.80 2.80

Native
Fishing — A171

1992, Aug. 5 **Perf. 11½x12**
846 A171 65k Building traps .50 .25
847 A171 90k Using nets .65 .35
848 A171 100k Laying traps .80 .40
849 A171 120k Fisherman in
    boats .95 .50
    Nos. 846-849 (4) 2.90 1.50

Souvenir Sheet

Discovery of America, 500th
Anniv. — A172

1992, Sept. 18 **Litho.** **Perf. 12**
850 A172 500k multicolored 4.00 4.00
Genoa '92.

First Free
Elections in
Angola — A173

Designs: 120k, People voting. 150k, Map, ballot box, peace doves. 200k, People, dove, hand dropping ballot into ballot box.

1992, Oct. 27   **Litho.**   **Perf. 11½x12**
851	A173	120k multicolored	.35	.25
852	A173	150k multicolored	.40	.30
853	A173	200k multicolored	.55	.40
		Nos. 851-853 (3)	1.30	.95

Quioca Mask Type of 1992

1992, Nov. 6   **Perf. 13½**
854	A164	72k Cihongo	.25	.25
855	A164	80k Mbwasu	.35	.25
856	A164	120k Cinhanga	.40	.35
857	A164	210k Kalewa	.75	.65
		Nos. 854-857 (4)	1.75	1.50

Inauguration of Express Mail
Service — A174

1992, Dec. 14   **Litho.**   **Perf. 12x11½**
858	A174	450k Truck	1.40	1.20
859	A174	550k Airplane	1.75	1.40

Meteorological
Instruments
A175

1993, Mar. 23   **Litho.**   **Perf. 11½x12**
860	A175	250k Weather balloon	.95	.80
861	A175	470k Actinometer	1.90	1.40
862	A175	500k Rain gauge	1.90	1.60
		Nos. 860-862 (3)	4.75	3.80

Seashells
A176

210k, Trochita trochiformis. 330k, Strombus latus. 400k, Aporrhais pesgallinae. 500k, Fusos aff. albinus.
1000k, Pusionella nifat.

1993, Apr. 6   **Perf. 12x11½**
863	A176	210k multicolored	.75	.75
864	A176	330k multicolored	1.10	1.10
865	A176	400k multicolored	1.50	1.50
866	A176	500k multicolored	1.75	1.75
		Nos. 863-866 (4)	5.10	5.10

Souvenir Sheet
867	A176	1000k multicolored	4.00	4.00

Quioca Art Type of 1992

1993, June 7   **Litho.**   **Perf. 12**
868	A164	72k Men with vehicles	.25	.25
869	A164	210k Cavalier	.75	.50
870	A164	420k Airplane	1.50	.90
871	A164	600k Men carrying stretcher	2.00	1.25
		Nos. 868-871 (4)	4.50	2.90

Flowering
Plants — A177

360k, Sansevieria cylindrica. 400k, Euphorbia tirucalli. 500k, Opuntia ficus-indica. 600k, Dracaena aubryana.

1993, June 28   **Perf. 11½x12**
872	A177	360k multicolored	1.20	.90
873	A177	400k multicolored	1.40	1.00
874	A177	500k multicolored	1.50	1.00
875	A177	600k multicolored	2.00	1.40
		Nos. 872-875 (4)	6.10	4.30

Souvenir Sheet

Africa Day — A178

1993, May 31   **Perf. 12**
876	A178	1500k Leopard	6.00	6.00

Tribal
Pipes — A179

1993, Aug. 16   **Litho.**   **Perf. 11½x12**
877	A179	72k Vimbundi	.25	.25
878	A179	200k Vimbundi, diff.	.75	.40
879	A179	420k Mutopa	1.40	.90
880	A179	600k Pexi	2.00	1.25
		Nos. 877-880 (4)	4.40	2.80

Souvenir Sheet

Union of Portuguese Speaking
Capitals — A180

1993, July 30   **Perf. 12x11½**
881	A180	1500k multicolored	5.50	5.50

Turtles — A181

Designs: a, 180k, Chelonia mydas (b). b, 450k, Eretmochelys imbricata. c, 550k, Dermochelys coriacea. d, 630k, Caretta caretta.

1993, July 9   **Litho.**   **Perf. 12½x12**
882	A181	Block of 4, #a.-d.	7.00	7.00

Quioca Art Type of 1992

1993, Sept. 1   **Litho.**   **Perf. 12**
883	A164	300k Leopard	.95	.65
884	A164	600k Malhado	1.90	1.25
885	A164	800k Birds	2.50	1.75
886	A164	1000k Chickens	3.25	2.10
		Nos. 883-886 (4)	8.60	5.75

Mushrooms
A182

300k, Tricholoma georgii. 500k, Amanita phalloides. 600k, Amanita vaginata. 1000k, Macrolepiota procera.

1993, Dec. 5   **Litho.**   **Perf. 12**
887	A182	300k multicolored	.95	.55
a.		Perf. 11½ vert.	1.60	1.60
888	A182	500k multicolored	1.60	.95
a.		Perf. 11½ vert.	2.40	2.40
889	A182	600k multicolored	1.90	1.20
a.		Perf. 11½ vert.	3.25	3.25
890	A182	1000k multicolored	3.25	2.00
a.		Perf. 11½ vert.	4.75	4.75
b.		Booklet pane of 4, #887a-890a	12.00	
		Nos. 887-890 (4)	7.70	4.70

A183

Natl. Culture Day: 500k, Cinganji, wood carving of dancer. 1000k, Ohunya yo soma, staff with woman's face. 1200k, Ongende, sculpture of man on donkey. 2200k, Upi, corn pestle.

1994, Jan. 10   **Litho.**   **Perf. 12**
891	A183	500k multicolored	.80	.50
892	A183	1000k multicolored	1.50	.95
893	A183	1200k multicolored	2.00	1.25
894	A183	2200k multicolored	3.50	2.25
		Nos. 891-894 (4)	7.80	4.95

Hong Kong '94.

Quioca Art Type of 1992

1994, Feb. 21   **Litho.**   **Perf. 12**
895	A164	500k Bird on flower	.50	.40
896	A164	2000k Plant with roots	2.25	1.60
897	A164	2500k Feto	2.75	2.00
898	A164	3000k Plant	3.50	2.40
		Nos. 895-898 (4)	9.00	6.40

Social
Responsibilities of
AIDS — A184

500k, Mass of people. 1000k, Witchdoctor receiving AIDS through needle, people being educated. 3000k, Stylized man, woman.

1994, May 5   **Litho.**   **Perf. 12**
899	A184	500k multicolored	.55	.40
900	A184	1000k multicolored	1.10	.55
901	A184	3000k multicolored	3.50	2.40
		Nos. 899-901 (3)	5.15	3.35

1994 World Cup Soccer
Championships, US — A185

500k, Large arrows, small ball. 700k, Small arrows, large ball. 2200k, Ball in goal. 2500k, Ball, foot.

1994, June 17   **Perf. 14**
902	A185	500k multicolored	.55	.40
903	A185	700k multicolored	.80	.55
904	A185	2200k multicolored	2.50	1.75
905	A185	2500k multicolored	3.00	2.00
		Nos. 902-905 (4)	6.85	4.70

Dinosaurs
A186

1000k, Brachiosaurus. 3000k, Spinosaurus. 5000k, Ouranosaurus. 10,000k, Lesothosaurus.
19,000k, Lesothosaurus, map of Africa.

1994, Aug. 16   **Litho.**   **Perf. 12**
906	A186	1000k multi	.25	.25
907	A186	3000k multi	.75	.55
908	A186	5000k multi	1.25	.95
909	A186	10,000k multi	2.50	2.00
		Nos. 906-909 (4)	4.75	3.75

Souvenir Sheet
910	A186	19,000k multi	7.50	7.50

PHILAKOREA '94, SINGPEX '94. No. 910 contains one 44x34mm stamp.

Tourism
A187

2000k, Birds. 4000k, Wild animals. 8000k, Native women. 10,000k, Native men.

1994, Sept. 27   **Litho.**   **Perf. 12x11½**
911	A187	2000k multi	.50	.40
912	A187	4000k multi	.95	.80
913	A187	8000k albinus	2.00	1.60
914	A187	10,000k multi	2.50	2.00
		Nos. 911-914 (4)	5.95	4.80

Post
Boxes — A188

Designs: 5000k, Letters, bundled mail wall box. 7500k, Wall box for letters. 10,000k, Pillar box. 21,000k, Multi-function units.

1994, Oct. 7   **Perf. 14½**
915	A188	5000k multicolored	.75	.40
916	A188	7500k multicolored	1.00	.55
917	A188	10,000k multicolored	1.40	.80
918	A188	21,000k multicolored	3.00	1.75
		Nos. 915-918 (4)	6.15	3.50

Cotton
Pests — A189

Insects: 5000k, Heliothis armigera. 6000k, Bemisia tabasi. 10,000k, Dysdercus. 27,000k, Spodoptera exigua.

1994, Nov. 11   **Litho.**   *Perf. 14*
919	A189	5000k multicolored	.80	.40
920	A189	6000k multicolored	1.00	.50
921	A189	10,000k multicolored	1.60	.90
922	A189	27,000k multicolored	4.00	2.10
		Nos. 919-922 (4)	7.40	3.90

Intl. Olympic Committee, Cent. A190

1994, Dec. 15
923	A190	27,000k multicolored	4.50	4.50

Tribal Culture A191

Designs: 10,000k. Rubbing sticks to start fire. 15,000k, Extracting sap from tree. 20,000k, Smoking tribal pipe. 25,000k, Shooting bow & arrow. 28,000k, Mothers, children. 30,000k, Cave art.

1995, Jan. 6   **Litho.**   *Perf. 14*
924	A191	10,000k multicolored	.50	.35
925	A191	15,000k multicolored	.75	.50
926	A191	20,000k multicolored	1.00	.65
927	A191	25,000k multicolored	1.25	.80
928	A191	28,000k multicolored	1.25	.90
929	A191	30,000k multicolored	1.50	1.20
		Nos. 924-929 (6)	6.25	4.40

Traditional Ceramics A192

Designs: No. 930, Pitcher with bust of a woman as stopper. No. 931, Cone-shaped vase. No. 932, Bird-shaped vase. No. 933, Pitcher with bust of a man as stopper.

1995, Jan. 2   **Litho.**   *Perf. 14½*
930	A192	(2) 2nd class natl.	.55	.25
931	A192	(1) 1st class natl.	.80	.35
932	A192	(2) 2nd class intl.	1.10	.55
933	A192	(1) 1st class intl.	1.50	1.25
		Nos. 930-933 (4)	3.95	2.40

Rotary Intl., 90th Anniv. A193

a, Immunizing boy against polio. b, Medical examination. c, Immunizing girl against polio. No. 936, Dove over map.

1995, Feb. 23   **Litho.**   *Perf. 14*
934		Strip of 3	6.00	6.00
a.-c.		A193 27,000k any single	2.00	1.25
935		Strip of 3	6.00	6.00
a.-c.		A193 27,000k any single	2.00	1.25

Souvenir Sheet
936	A193	81,000k multicolored	7.50	7.50
a.		English inscription	7.50	7.50

No. 934 has Portuguese inscriptions. No. 935 has English inscriptions. Both were issued in sheets of 9 stamps.

No. 936 contains Portuguese inscription in sheet margin.

Rotary Intl., 90th Anniv. — A194

Litho. & Embossed
1995, Feb. 23   *Perf. 11½x12*
937	A194	81,000k gold	50.00

World Telecommunications Day — A195

Designs: No. 938, 1957 Sputnik 1. No. 939, Shuttle, Intelsat satellite.

1995   **Litho.**   *Perf. 14*
938	A195	27,000k multicolored	2.00	2.00
939	A195	27,000k multicolored	2.00	2.00
a.		Souvenir sheet, #938-939	4.50	4.50

Independence, 20th Anniv. — A196

1995, Nov. 11   **Litho.**   *Perf. 14*
940	A196	2900k multicolored	1.60	1.60

4th World Conference on Women, Beijing — A197

Designs: 375k, Women working in fields. 1106k, Woman teaching, girls with book. 1265k, Woman in industry, career woman. 2900k, Woman in native headdress, vert. 1500k, Native mother, children, vert.

1996, Jan. 29   **Litho.**   *Perf. 14*
941	A197	375k multicolored	.25	.25
942	A197	1106k multicolored	.80	.80
943	A197	1265k multicolored	1.50	1.50
944	A197	2900k multicolored	3.00	3.00
		Nos. 941-944 (4)	5.55	5.55

Souvenir Sheet
945	A197	1500k multicolored	2.75	2.75

UN Assistance Programs — A198

Designs: 200k, Boy, highlift moving supplies. 1265k, Supply ship arriving. No. 948, Two high lifts. No. 949, Tractor-trailer traveling past vultures, native girl. No. 950, Man, ship.

1996   **Litho.**   *Perf. 14*
946	A198	200k multicolored	.25	.25
947	A198	1265k multicolored	1.00	1.00
948	A198	2583k multicolored	2.25	2.25
949	A198	2583k multicolored	2.50	2.50
		Nos. 946-949 (4)	6.00	6.00

Souvenir Sheet
950	A198	1265k multicolored	*6.50*	*6.50*

Flora and Fauna A199

1500k, Verdant hawkmoth. 4400k, Water lily. 5100k, Panther toad. 6000k, African wild dog.
1500k: a, Western honey buzzard. b, Bateleuer. c, Common kestrel.
4400k; d, Red-crested turaco. e, Giraffe. f, Elephant.
5100k: g, Hippopotamus. h, Cattle egret. i, Lion.
6000k: j, Helmeted turtle. k, African pygmy goose. l, Egyptian plover.
12,000k, Spotted hyena.

1996, Apr. 20   **Litho.**   *Perf. 14*
951-954	A199	Set of 4	5.00	5.00
955	A199	Sheet of 12, #a.-l.	10.00	10.00

Souvenir Sheet
956	A199	12,000k multicolored	3.00	3.00

Sheets of 12, #a-i.

Birds — A200

Fowl, each 5500k: No. 957a, California quail. b, Greater prairie chicken. c, Painted quail. d, Golden pheasant. e, Roulroul partridge. f, Ceylon sourfowl. g, Himalayan snowcock. h, Temmincks tragopan. i, Lady Amherst's pheasant. j, Great curassow. k, Red-legged partridge. l, Impeyan pheasant.
Hummingbirds, each 5500k: No. 958a, Anna's. b, Blue-throated. c, Broad-tailed. d, Costa's. e, White-eared. f, Calliope. g, Violet-crowned. h, Rufous. i, Crimson topaz. j, Broad-billed. k, Frilled coquette. l, Ruby-throated.
No. 959, 12,000k, Ring-necked pheasant. No. 960, 12,000k, Racquet-tail hummingbird.

1996, Apr. 20
957-958	A200	Set of 2	20.00	20.00

Souvenir Sheets
959-960	A200	Set of 2	5.50	5.50

Lubrapex '96 — A201

Wild animals: a, 180k, Lions attacking zebra. b, 450k, Zebras, lions, diff. c, 180k, Zebras grazing, lions stalking. d, 450k, Panthera leo. e, 550k, Cheetah. f, 630k, Cheetah running. g, 550k, Cheetah chasing antelope. h, 630k, Cheetah attacking antelope. i, 180k, Antilope (gnu) being attacked by wild dogs. j, 450k, Antelope, wild dogs. k, 180k, Pack of wild dogs. l, 450k, Licaon pictus. m, 550k, Panthera pardus. n, 630k, Oryx. o, 550k, Oryx, diff. p, 630k, Leopard attacking oryx.

1996, Apr. 27
961	A201	Sheet of 16, #a.-p.	9.00	9.00

Ships — A202

Designs, each 6000k: No. 962a, Styrbjorn, Sweden, 1789. b, Constellation, US, 1797. c, Taureau, France, 1865. d, Bomb Ketch, France, 1682. e, Sardegna, Italy, 1881. f, HMS Glasgow, England, 1867.
No. 963a, Essex, US, 1812. b, HMS Inflexible, England, 1881. c, HMS Minotaur, England, 1863. d, Napoleon, France, 1854. e, Sophia Amalia, Denmark, 1650. f, Massena, France, 1887.
No. 964, 12,000k, HMS Tremendous, England, 1806, vert. No. 965, 12,000k, Royal Prince, England, 1666.

1996, May 4
962-963	A202	Set of 2	12.00	12.00

Souvenir Sheets
964-965	A202	Set of 2	10.00	10.00

UN, 50th Anniv. (in 1995) A203

Designs: No. 966, Boys pumping water. No. 967, Man, woman with girl. 8000k, Unloading supplies from ship.

1996, Apr. 27   **Litho.**   *Perf. 14*
966	A203	3500k multicolored	1.25	1.25
967	A203	3500k multicolored	1.25	1.25

Souvenir Sheet
968	A203	8000k multicolored	2.75	2.75

Sonangol, 20th Anniv. A204

Face in traditional mask, costume, native birds, and: No. 969, Oil derricks. No. 970, Oil storage tanks, ship. 2500k, Refinery equipment. 5000k, Cargo shipment, jet.

1996, May 12
969	A204	1000k multicolored	.25	.25
970	A204	1000k multicolored	.25	.25
971	A204	2500k multicolored	1.60	1.60
972	A204	5000k multicolored	2.75	2.75
		Nos. 969-972 (4)	4.85	4.85

Brapex '96 — A205

Designs: No. 973, Slaves in hold. No. 974, Slaves fleeing ship as it's overturned. No. 975, Slave boats approaching ship. No. 976, Slaves talking with captain. 50,000k, like No. 975.

1996, Oct. 19   **Litho.**   *Perf. 14*
973	A205	20,000k multicolored	2.25	2.25
974	A205	20,000k multicolored	2.25	2.25
975	A205	30,000k multicolored	3.00	3.00
976	A205	30,000k multicolored	3.00	3.00
		Nos. 973-976 (4)	10.50	10.50

Souvenir Sheet
977	A205	50,000k multicolored	8.00	8.00

Churches — A206

Designs: 5,000k, Mission, Huila. No. 979, Church of the Nazarene. No. 980, Church of Our Lady of Pó Pulo. 25,000k, St. Adriáo Church.

1996, Dec. 6 Litho. Perf. 14
978 A206 5,000k multicolored .40 .40
979 A206 10,000k multicolored .90 .90
980 A206 10,000k multicolored .90 .90
981 A206 25,000k multicolored 2.10 2.10
Nos. 978-981 (4) 4.30 4.30

1996 Summer Olympic Games, Atlanta A207

5,000k, Handball, vert. 10,000k, Swimming. 25,000k, Track & field, vert. 35,000k, Shooting. 65,000k, Basketball.

1996, Dec. 9
982 A207 5,000k multi .60 .60
983 A207 10,000k multi 1.25 1.25
984 A207 25,000k multi 3.25 3.25
985 A207 35,000k multi 4.50 4.50
Nos. 982-985 (4) 9.60 9.60

Souvenir Sheet
986 A207 65,000k multi 6.00 6.00

MPLA (Liberation Movement), 40th Anniv. — A208

1996, Dec. 10 Litho. Perf. 14
987 A208 30,000k Dolphins, map 3.50 3.50

Trains — A209

Trains — A209a

No. 988: a, AVE, Spain. b, Bullet Train, Japan. c, GM F7 Warbonnet, US. d, Deltic, Great Britain. e, Eurostar, France/Great Britain. f, ETR 450, Italy.
No. 989: a, Class E1300, Morocco. b, ICE, Germany. c, X2000, Sweden. d, TGV Duplex, France.
No. 989E, each 250,000k: f, Steam engine. g, Garrat. h, General Electric.
No. 990, 110,000k, Canadian Pacific 4-4-0, Canada. No. 991, 110,000k, Via Rail Canadian, Canada.

1997, May 29 Litho. Perf. 14
Sheets of 6, 4 or 3
988 A209 100,000k #a.-f. 8.00 8.00
989 A209 140,000k #a.-d. 8.00 8.00
989E A209a Sheet of 3, #f.-h. 14.00 14.00

Souvenir Sheets
Perf. 13½
990-991 A209 Set of 2 8.00 8.00
Nos. 990-991 contain one 38x50 or 50x38mm stamp, respectively.
PACIFIC 97.

Horses — A210

No. 992: a, Thoroughbred. b, Palomino, appaloosa. c, Arabians. d, Arabian colt. e, Thoroughbred colt. f, Mustang. g, Mustang, diff. h, Furioso.
No. 993: a, Thoroughbred. b, Arabian, palomino. c, Arabian, chincoteague. d, Pintos. e, Przewalski's horse. f, Thoroughbred colt. g, Arabians. h, New forest pony.
No. 994: a, Selle Francais. b, Fjord. c, Percheron. d, Italian heavy draft. e, Shagya Arab. f, Avelignese. g, Czechoslovakian warmblood. h, New forest pony.
215,000k, Thoroughbreds. 220,000k, Thoroughbreds, diff.

1997, July 5 Litho. Perf. 14
Sheets of 8
992 A210 100,000k #a.-h. 8.50 8.50
993 A210 120,000k #a.-h. 10.00 10.00
994 A210 140,000k #a.-h. 12.50 12.50

Souvenir Sheets
995 A210 215,000k multi 6.00 6.00
996 A210 220,000k multi 6.00 6.00
PACIFIC 97.

1998 World Cup Soccer Championships, France — A211

Winners holding World Cup trophy: No. 997: a, Uruguay, 1930. b, Germany, 1954. c, Brazil, 1970. d, Argentina, 1986. e, Brazil, 1994.
Winning team pictures: No. 998a, Germany, 1954. b, Uruguay, 1958. c, Italy, 1938. d, Brazil, 1962. e, Brazil, 1970. f, Uruguay, 1930.
220,000k, Angolan team members standing. 250,000k, 1997 Angolan team picture.

1997, July 5 Litho. Perf. 14
Sheets of 5 or 6
997 A211 100,000k #a.-e. + label 9.00 9.00
998 A211 100,000k #a.-f. 10.00 10.00

Souvenir Sheets
999 A211 220,000k multi 5.50 5.50
1000 A211 250,000k multi 5.50 5.50

ENSA (Security System), 20th Anniv. — A212

"Star" emblem, and stylized protection of "egg," each 240,000k: No. 1001, Industry. No. 1002, Recreation. No. 1003, Homes, shelters. No. 1004, Accident prevention.
350,000k, Emblem.

1998 Litho. Perf. 13½
1001-1004 A212 Set of 4 8.00 8.00

Souvenir Sheet
Perf. 13½x13
1005 A212 350,000k multi 4.00 4.00
No. 1005 contains one 60x40mm stamp.

GURN (Natl. Unity & Reconciliation Government), 1st Anniv. — A213

Emblem, portion of country map and: 100,000k, a, Sea, swordfish, ships, oil derrick. b, Sea, ships, swordfish. c, Sea, swordfish, ships, mining car on railroad track. d, Sea, power lines.
200,000k: e, Train on track, antelope. f, Mining cars on track, tractor pulling cart. g, Railroad track across rivers, tractor plowing. h, Power lines. i, UR corner of map, crystals. j, Train on track. k, Elephant, tree. l, Trunk of tree, bottom edge of map.

1998
1006 A213 Sheet of 12, #a.-l. 18.00 18.00

Education in Angola — A214

1998
1007 A214 400,000k multi 6.00 6.00

Diana, Princess of Wales (1961-97) — A215

Various portraits, each 100,000k, color of sheet margin: No. 1008, pale green. No. 1009, pale yellow.
400,000k, Wearing protective clothing.

1998, May 21 Litho. Perf. 14
Sheets of 6, #a.-f.
1008-1009 A215 Set of 2 20.00 20.00

Souvenir Sheet
1010 A215 400,000k multi 5.00 5.00
See No. 1028.

Expo '98, Lisbon A216

Marine life: No. 1011, 100,000k, Anemones. No. 1012, 100,000k, Sea urchin. No. 1013, 100,000k, Sea horses. No. 1014, 100,000k, Coral (Caravela). No. 1015, 240,000k, Sea slug. No. 1016, 240,000k, Worms (Tunicados).

1998, May 21 Perf. 13½
1011-1016 A216 Set of 6 10.00 10.00

Butterflies — A217

No. 1017, each 120,000k: a, Metamorpha stelene. b, Papilio glaucus. c, Danaus plexippus. d, Catonephele numili. e, Plebejus argus. f, Hypolimnas bolina.
No. 1018, each 120,000k: a, Terinos terpander. b, Bematistes aganice. c, Hebomoia glaucippe. d, Colias eurytheme. e, Pereute leucodrosime. f, Lycaena dispar.
No. 1019, each 120,000k, horiz.: a, Dynastor napolean. b, Zeuxidia amethystus. c, Battus philenor. d, Phoebis philea. e, Danaus chrysippus. f, Glaucopsyche alexis.

Each 250,000k: No. 1020, Euphaedra neophron. No. 1021, Thecla betulae, horiz. No. 1022, Uraneis ucubis, armillaria staminea.

1998, May 21   *Perf. 14*
Sheets of 6, #a.-f.
1017-1019   A217   Set of 3   20.00   20.00
Souvenir Sheets
1020-1022   A217   Set of 3   16.00   16.00

Cats and Dogs — A218

Cats, each 140,000k: No. 1023a, British tortoiseshell. b, Chinchilla. c, Russian blue. d, Black Persian (longhair). e, British red tabby. f, Birman.

Dogs, each 140,000k: No. 1024a, West Highland terrier. b, Irish setter. c, Dachshund. d, St. John water dog. e, Shetland sheep dog. f, Dalmatian.

Each 500,000k: No. 1025, Turkish van (swimming cat). No. 1026, Labrador retriever.

1998, May 21   Litho.   *Perf. 14x13½*
Sheets of 6, #a.-f.
1023-1024   A218   Set of 2   15.00   15.00
Souvenir Sheets
1025-1026   A218   Set of 2   12.00   12.00

Wild Animals — A219

100,000k: a, Panthera leo. b, Hippopotamus amphibius. c, Loxodonta africana. d, Giraffa camelopardalis.

220,000k: e, Syncerus caffer-caffer. f, Gorilla gorilla. g, Ceratotherim simum. h, Oryx gazella.

1998, July 24   Litho.   *Perf. 14*
1027   A219   Sheet of 8, #a.-h.   12.00   12.00

Diana, Princes of Wales Type of 1998

Pictures showing Diana's campaign to ban land mines, each 150,000k: a, With girl. b, With two boys. c, Wearing protective clothing.

1998, Aug. 31   Litho.   *Perf. 14*
1028   A215   Strip of 3, #a.-c.   7.00   7.00
No. 1028 was issued in sheets of 6 stamps.

Intl. Year of the Ocean — A220

Marine life: No. 1029a, Pagurites. b, Callinectes marginatus. c, Thais forbesi. d, Ostrea tulipa. e, Balanus amohitrite. f, Uca tangeri.

No. 1030: a, Littorina angulifera. b, Semifusus morio. c, Thais coronata. d, Cerithium atratum (red branch). e, Ostrea tulipa. f, Cerithium atratum (green branch).

Each 300,000k: No. 1031, Goniopsis, horiz. No. 1032, Unidentified shell.

1998, Sept. 4   **Sheets of 6**
1029   A220   100,000k #a.-f.   5.00   5.00
1030   A220   170,000k #a.-f.   7.00   7.00
Souvenir Sheets
1031-1032   A220   Set of 2   11.00   11.00

Souvenir Sheet

Battle Against Polio in Angola — A221

1998, Aug. 28   Litho.   *Perf. 13½*
1033   A221   500,000k multicolored   3.75   3.75

Traditional Boats A222

Designs: No. 1034, 250,000k, Boat, Bimba. No. 1035, 250,000k, Canoe with sail, Ndongo. 500,000k, Constructing boat, Ndongo.

1998, Sept. 4   *Perf. 14*
1034-1036   A222   Set of 3   7.50   7.50

Titanic — A223

Views of Titanic, each 350,000k: a, Under tow. b, Stern. c, Starboard side at night. d, At dock.

1998, Sept. 4
1037   A223   Sheet of 4, #a.-d.   9.00   9.00
No. 1037c is 76x30mm, No. 1037d is 38x61mm.

Angolan Food A224

Various vegetables, fruits: No. 1038, 100,000k, 4 fruits. No. 1039, 100,000k, Squash sliced in half. No. 1040, 120,000k, Ears of corn. No. 1041, 120,000k, Green beans. No. 1042, 140,000k, Fruit with red seeds sliced in half. No. 1043, 140,000k, Sliced bananas.

1998
1038-1043   A224   Set of 6   7.00   7.00
Portugal '98.

Airplanes A225

No. 1044, IL-62 M. No. 1045, B737 100.
No. 1046: a, Ultralight. b, Gyroplane. c, Business jet. d, onvertible plane (e). e, Chuterplane (a, b, d). f, Twin rotors (e). g, Skycrane. h, Aerospatiale Concorde (i). i, Flying boat.

No. 1047: a, Pedal power (b). b, Sail plane (a, e). c, Aerobatic (f). d, Hang gliding (g). e, Balloon (h). f, Glidercraft (e, i). g, Model airplane. h, Air racing (i). i, Solar cells.

No. 1048, 1,000,000k, Boeing 777. No. 1049, 1,000,000k, Columbia Space Shuttle, vert. No. 1049A, 1,000,000k, Boeing 737-200. No. 1049B, 1,000,000k, Boeing 747-300.

1998-99   Litho.   *Perf. 14*
1044   A225   200,000k multi   1.75   1.75
1045   A225   200,000k multi   1.75   1.75
Sheets of 9
1046   A225   150,000k #a.-i.   5.00   5.00
1047   A225   250,000k #a.-i.   8.00   8.00
Souvenir Sheets
1048-1049B   A225   Set of 4   26.00   26.00

Nos. 1048-1049B each contain one 85x28mm stamp.
Issued: Nos. 1049A-1049B, 3/25/99; others 12/24/98.

Dinosaurs — A226

Designs, vert., each 120,000k: No. 1050, Parasaurolophus. No. 1051, Maiasaura. No. 1052, Iguanodon. No. 1053, Elaphosaurus.

No. 1054, vert, 120,000k: a, Brontosaurus. b, Plateosaurus. c, Brachiosaurus. d, Anatosaurus. e, Tyrannosaurus. f, Carnotaurus. g, Corythosaurus. h, Stegosaurus. i, Iguanodon, diff.

No. 1055, 120,000k: a, Hadrosaurus. b, Ouranosaurus. c, Hypsilophodon. d, Brachiosaurus. e, Shunosaurus. f, Amargasaurus. g, Tuojiangosaurus. h, Monoclonius. i, Struthiosaurus.

Each 550,000k: No. 1056, Triceratops, vert. No. 1057, Tyrannosaurus, vert.

1998, Dec. 28
1050-1053   A226   Set of 4   7.00   6.00
Sheets of 9, #a.-i.
1054-1055   A226   Set of 2   17.00   17.00
Souvenir Sheets
1056-1057   A226   Set of 2   8.00   8.00

World Wildlife Fund — A227

Lesser flamingo: a, Facing left. b, Body facing forward. c, Head and neck. d, With wings spread.

Strip of 4
1999   Litho.   *Perf. 14*
1058   A227   300,000k #a.-d.   5.00   5.00
No. 1058 was issued in sheets of 16 stamps.

Fauna A228

Designs, each 300,000k: No. 1059, Equis caballus przewalski. No. 1060, Sphenisciformes, vert. No. 1061, Haliaeetus leucocephalus, vert. No. 1062, Anodorhynchus hyacinthinus.

No. 1063, 300,000k: a, Vulpes velox hebes. b, Odocoileus. c, Pongo pygmaeus. d, Leontopitecus rosalia. e, Panthera tigris. f, Tragelaphus eurycerus.

No. 1064, 300,000k: a, Tremarctos ornatus. b, Aphelocoma. c, Otus insularis. d, Balaeniceps rex. e, Lepidochelys kempii. f, Lutra canadensis.

Each 1,000,000k: No. 1065, Ailuropoda melanoleuca, vert. No. 1066, Ursus arctos horribilis.

1999
1059-1062   A228   Set of 4   5.00   5.00
Sheets of 6, #a.-f.
1063-1064   A228   Set of 2   15.00   15.00
Souvenir Sheets
1065-1066   A228   Set of 2   12.00   12.00

These Flora and Fauna stamps, formerly Nos. 1067-1078, were not authorized by Angola postal authorities.

Other items inscribed "Angola" that were not authorized but which have appeared on the market include sheets with the themes of Disney and History of Animation, Millennium, Animals, Trains, Flora, Muhammad Ali & Lennox Lewis, Bruce Lee, Albert Einstein / Moon Landing, Elvis Presley and other entertainers, Great Personalities, John Kennedy and Marilyn Monroe, Martin Luther King, Jr., Payne Stewart, Colin Montgomerie, Babe Ruth, Cardinal John O'Connor, Pope John Paul II / Mother Teresa and Queen Elizabeth II / Winston Churchill.

World Telecommunications Day — A230

1999, May 17   Litho.   *Perf. 14*
1079   A230   500,000k multi   .75   .75

Souvenir Sheet

Waterfalls — A231

a, Andulo. b, Chiumbo. c, Ruacaná. d, Coemba.

1999, June 5   **Sheet of 4**
1080 A231 500,000k #a.-d.   3.00 3.00

A232

African Men's Basketball Championships — No. 1081: a, Poster. b, Basketball, hoop, tan background. c, Basketball, hoop, green background. d, Welwitschia plant holding basketball.

2,500,000k, Similar to No. 1081c.

1999, July 29 Sheet of 4 Perf. 13½
1081 A232 1,500,000k #a.-d.   4.00 4.00
Souvenir Sheet
Perf. 13x13½
1082 A232 2,500,000k multi   2.50 2.50

No. 1082 contains one 40x30mm stamp. Stamps have one "0" too many in the denominations. Correct denominations would be 1.500.000.00

A233

1999, Aug. 17   **Perf. 14**
1083 A233 1,000,000k multi   1.25 1.25

Southern African Development Community. Issued in sheets of 4. Value $5.

Tribal Kings — A234

No. 782: a, Ekuikui II. b, Mvemba Nzinga. c, Mwata Yamvu Naweji II. d, Njinga Mbande. 1,000,000k, Mandume Ndemufayo.

1999, Sept. 17   **Sheet of 4**
1084 A234 500,000k #a.-d.   7.50 7.50
Souvenir Sheet
1085 A234 1,000,000k multi   4.00 4.00

A235

Queen Mother (b. 1900) — No. 1086: a, With King George VI. b, Wearing brooch. c, Wearing tiara. d, Wearing hat. 500,000k, Wearing academic gown.

Sheet of 4
1999, Sept. 17   Litho.   Perf. 14
1086 A235 200,000k #a.-d.   8.00 8.00
Souvenir Sheet
Perf. 13¾
1087 A235 500,000k multi   5.50 5.50

No. 1087 contains one 38x51mm stamp.

Ships — A236

No. 1088, each 950,000k: a, Egyptian bark, 1300 B.C. b, Flemish carrack, 1480. c, Beagle, 1830. d, North Star, 1852. e, Fram, 1892. f, Unyon Maru, 1909. g, Juan Sebastian de Elcano, 1927. h, Tovarishch, 1933.

No. 1089, each 950,000k: a, Bucentauro, 1728. b, Clermont, 1807. c, Savannah, 1819. d, Dromedary, 1844. e, Iberia, 1881. f, S.S. Gluckauf, 1886. g, City of Paris, 1888. h, Mauretania, 1906.

No. 1090, each 950,000k: a, Gloire, 1859. b, L'Ocean, 1868. c, Dandalo, 1876, stern of HMS Dreadnought, 1906. d, Bow of Dreadnought. e, Bismarck, 1939, stern of USS Cleveland, 1946. f, Bow of Cleveland. g, USS Boston, 1942, stern of USS Long Beach, 1959. h, Bow of Long Beach.

Each 5,000,000k: No. 1091, Chinese junk. No. 1092, Madre de Deus, 1609. No. 1093, Catamaran, 1861. No. 1094, Natchez, 1870.

1999, Sept. 23   Litho.   Perf. 14
Sheets of 8
1088-1090 A236 Set of 3   27.00 27.00
Souvenir Sheets
1091-1094 A236 Set of 4   22.00 22.00

Mushrooms
A237

No. 1095, Amanita caesarea. No. 1096, Psalliota xanthoderma. No. 1097, Hygrocybe conica. No. 1098, Boletus chrysenteron. No. 1099, Coprinus comatus. No. 1100, Boletus luteus.

No. 1101: a, Morchella crassipes. b, Boletus rufescens. c, Amanita phalloides. d, Collybia iocephala. e, Tricholoma aurantium. f, Cortinarius violaceus. g, Mycena polygramma. h, Psalliota augusta.

No. 1102: a, Amanita muscaria. b, Boletus aereus. c, Coprinus comatus. d, Amanita

---

rubescens. e, Cortinarius collinitus. f, Boletus satanas. g, Lepiota procera. h, Clitocybe geotropa.

No. 1103: a, Russula nigricans. b, Boletus granulatus. c, Mycena strobilinoides. d, Amanita caesarea. e, Amanita muscaria. f, Boletus, crocipodius. g, Russula virescens. h, Lactarius deliciosus.

No. 1104, Psalliota haemorrhoidaria.
No. 1105, Mycena lilacifolia.

1999, Sept. 23   Litho.   Perf. 14
1095 A237 1,250,000k multi   1.25 1.00
1096 A237 1,250,000k multi   1.25 1.00
1097 A237 1,250,000k multi   1.25 1.00
1098 A237 1,250,000k multi   1.25 1.00
1099 A237 1,250,000k multi   1.25 1.00
1100 A237 1,250,000k multi   1.25 1.00
   Nos. 1095-1100 (6)   7.50 6.00
Sheets of 8
1101 A237 1,000,000k #a-h   8.00 8.00
1102 A237 1,000,000k #a-h   8.00 8.00
1103 A237 1,000,000k #a-h   8.00 8.00
Souvenir Sheets
1104 A237 5,000,000k multi   5.50 5.50
1105 A237 5,000,000k multi   5.50 5.50

A238

First Manned Moon Landing, 30th Anniv. A239

No. 1107: a, Astronaut spacewalking. b, Mariner 8. c, Viking 10. d, GINGA satellite. e, Soyuz 19. f, Voyager.

No. 1108, vert.: a, Space telescope. b, Space shuttle Atlantis. c, Uhuru satellite. d, Mir space station. e, Gemini 7. f, Venera 7.

No. 1109: a, Mercury, Venus. b, Jupiter. c, Neptune, Pluto. d, Earth, Mars. e, Saturn. f, Uranus.

No. 1110: a, Explorer 17. b, Intelsat 4A. c, GOES-D Satellite. d, Intelsat 2. e, Navstar. f, S.M.S.

No. 1111, 6,000,000k, Lunar rover, vert. No. 1112, 6,000,000k, Apollo 17 astronaut on moon, vert. No. 1113, 12,000,000k, Neil Armstrong, vert. No. 1114, 12,000,000k, Space shuttle Columbia. No. 1115, 12,000,000k, SBS-4, vert.

Perf. 13¾ (A238), 14 (A239)
1999, Nov. 15   Litho.
Sheets of 6, #a.-f.
1107-1108 A238 3,500,000k   10.00 10.00
1109-1110 A239 3,500,000k   10.00 10.00
Souvenir Sheets
1111-1112 A238 Set of 2   8.00 8.00
1113-1115 A239 Set of 3   16.00 16.00

Hokusai Paintings — A240

No. 1116, each 3,500,000k: a, Night attack. b, Usigafuchi No Kudan. c, Drawing of man and bowl. d, Wildlife. e, Pheasant. f, People on bridge.

No. 1117, each 3,500,000k: a, Tree and shoreline. b, Kabuki theater. c, Hen. d, Cooper. e, Trip to Enoshima. f, Sumida River landscape.

Each 12,000,000k: No. 1118, Yama-uba and Kintori, vert. No. 1119, Woman, vert.

1999, Dec. 13   Litho.   Perf. 13¾
Sheets of 6, #a.-f.
1116-1117 A240 Set of 2   18.00 18.00
Souvenir Sheets
1118-1119 A240 Set of 2   12.00 12.00

On Dec. 13, the date of issue of these stamps, Angola devalued its currency, with approximately 1,000,000k being the equivalent of 1k after the devaluation.

Souvenir Sheets

PhilexFrance 99 — A241

No. 1120, 4-8-4 Linder Compound express. No. 1121, Hovertrain prototype.

2000, Mar. 13   Litho.   Perf. 13¾
1120-1121 A241 12k Set of 2   11.00 11.00

A242

Wildlife — A243

1.50k, Zebra. 2k, Fruit bat. 3k, California condor. 5.50k, Lion.

No. 1126, horiz.: a, Equus zebra. b, Ploceus xanthops. c, Lycaon protus. d, Acinonyx jubatus. e, Oryx gazella. f, Nursing Otocyon megalotis. g, Giraffa camelopardalis. h, Canis adustus. i, Perodicticus potto. j, Panthera leo. k, Coracius caudata. l, Pair of Otocyon megalotis.

No. 1127, horiz.: a, Struthio camelus. b, Felis lybica. c, Aepyceros melampus. d, Cercopithecus aethiops. e, Diceros bicornis. f, Papio sp. g, Felis caracal. h, Sagittarius serpentarius. i, Phacochoerus aethiopicus. j, Arctocephalus pusillus. k, Alcedo cristata. l, Hippopotamus amphibius.

No. 1128, 3.50k: a, Deer. b, Turkey. c, Beaver. d, Frog. e, Manatee. f, Trout.

No. 1129, 3.50k: a, Macaque. b, Toucan. c, Bothriopsis bilineata. d, Hyla leucopyliata. e, Tamarin. f, Eagle.

No. 1130, 3.50k, vert.: a, Mountain gorilla. b, Rhinoceros. c, Water buffalo. d, Chameleon. e, Cobra. f, Meerkats.

No. 1131, 3.50k, vert.: a, Kangaroo. b, Koala. c, Kingfishers. d, Frog on tree root. e, Three fish. f, Turtle.

No. 1132, 12k, Sloth. No. 1133, 12k, Lemur, vert. No. 1134, 12k, Cheetah, vert. No. 1135, 12k, Orangutan, vert. No. 1136, 12k, Cercopithecus aethiops, diff. No. 1137, 12k, Loxodonta africana.

2000, Apr. 7   Perf. 14
1122-1125 A242 Set of 4   6.00 6.00
1126 A243 1.50k Sheet of 12,
                        #a-l   9.00 9.00
1127 A243 2k Sheet of 12,
                        #a-l   13.00 13.00

Sheets of 6, #a-f

1128-1131	A242	Set of 4	40.00	40.00

Souvenir Sheets

1132-1135	A242	Set of 4	24.00	24.00
1136-1137	A243	Set of 2	12.00	12.00

Birds of Prey
A244

1.50k, Harpy eagle. 2k, Unidentified bird. 3k, Vulture, vert. 5.50k, King vulture, vert.

No. 1142, 3.50k: a, Accipiter gentilis. b, Surnia ulula. c, Falco peregrinus. d, Otus asio. e, Haliaetus vocifer. f, Herpetotheres cachinnans.

No. 1143, 3.50k: a, Falco sparverius. b, Pulsetrix perspicillata. c, Elemus leucurus. d, Ninox novaseelandiae. e, Polemaetus bellicosus. f, Polyborus plancus.

No. 1144, 6.50k: a, Verreaux's eagle. b, Aguia gigante. c, Aguia peixe.

No. 1145, 6.50k, vert.: a, Aguia despeida. b, Aguia dourada. c, Aguia devoradora de macacos.

No. 1146, 12k, King vulture, diff. No. 1147, 12k, Falcon, vert. No. 1148, 15k, Sagittarius serpentarius. No. 1149, 15k, Aquila chrysaetos.

2000, Apr. 10

1138-1141	A244	Set of 4	5.50	5.50

Sheets of 6, #a-f

1142-1143	A244	Set of 2	19.00	19.00

Sheets of 3, #a-c

1144-1145	A244	Set of 2	18.00	18.00

Souvenir Sheets

1146-1147	A244	Set of 2	12.00	12.00
1148-1149	A244	Set of 2	13.00	13.00

Millennium — A245

Highlights of the 16th Century: a, Paintings by Lai-Ji. b, The Last Judgment, by Luca Signorelli. c, Garden of Earthly Delights by Hieronymus Bosch. d, The Prince, written by Niccolò Machiavelli. e, Utopia, written by Sir Thomas More. f, Martin Luther. g, Charles I of Spain becomes Holy Roman Emperor Charles V. h, The School of Athens, by Raphael. i, Juan Sebastián de Elcano circumnavigates globe. j, Henry VIII of England. k, Spanish conquest of Aztecs and Incas. l, Placentia Cathedral. m, Potatoes introduced to Europe. n, Heliocentric theory of Copernicus. o, Portuguese reach Japan. p, Death of Albrecht Dürer (60x40mm). q, Bartolomé de Las Casas promotes rights for Indians.

2000, Oct. 2   Litho.   Perf. 12¾x12½

1150	A245	2.50k Sheet of 17, #a-q, + label	24.00	24.00

War Damage in Angola
A246

Designs: No. 1151, 3k, B.N.A. Building, Kuito. No. 1152, 3k, Kunje St., Kuito. No. 1153, 4k, Post office. No. 1154, 4k, Police headquarters. No. 1155, 5k, Apartment house. No. 1156, 5k, Independence Square. No. 1157, 6k, Child waving from upper floor of apartment house. No. 1158, 6k, Building, man carrying pack.

2000, Sept. 29   Litho.   Perf. 14

1151-1158	A246	Set of 8	18.00	18.00

Popes — A247

No. 1159, 3k: a, Nicholas II, 1059-61. b, Paschal II, 1099-1118. c, Sergius IV, 1009-1012. d, Victor II, 1055-57. e, Victor III, 1086-87. f, Urban III, 1185-87.

No. 1160, 3k: a, Innocent II, 1130-43. b, John XIII, 965-72. c, Agapetus II, 946-55. d, John XV, 985-96. e, John XVIII, 1003-09. f, Lucius II, 1144-45.

No. 1161, 3k: a, Celestine II, 1143-44. b, Clement II, 1046-47. c, Clement III, 1187-91. d, Gelasius II, 1118-19. e, Benedict VII, 974-83. f, Gregory V, 996-99.

No. 1162, 12k, Leo IX, 1049-54. No. 1163, 12k, Gregory VII, 1073-85. No. 1164, 12k, Leo XIII, 1878-1903.

2000, Oct. 2   Perf. 12x12¼

Sheets of 6, #a-f

1159-1161	A247	Set of 3	27.00	27.00

Souvenir Sheets

1162-1164	A247	Set of 3	18.00	18.00

Monarchs — A248

No. 1165, 3k: a, Henry II, King of Germany and Holy Roman Emperor, 1002-24. b, Marina Mniszek, wife of false Russian czar Dmitri, 1605-06. c, Ivan IV of Russia, 1533-84. d, Ivan III of Russia, 1462-1505.

No. 1166, 3k: a, Charles II of Great Britain, 1660-85. b, Lady Jane Grey of England, 1533. c, Leopold III of Belgium, 1934-51. d, Louis XV of France, 1715-74.

No. 1167, 3k: a, James I of Great Britain, 1603-25. b, James II of Great Britain, 1685-88. c, James IV of Scotland, 1567-1625. d, Brian Boru of Ireland, 1002-14. e, Wilhelm I, King of Prussia and German Emperor, 1861-88. f, Edward VI of England, 1547-53.

No. 1168, 12k, Feodor I of Russia, 1584-98. No. 1169, 12k, False Russian czar Dmitri, 1605-06. No. 1170, 12k, William IV of Great Britain, 1830-37.

2000, Oct. 2   Sheets of 4, #a-d

1165-1166	A248	Set of 2	12.50	12.50
1167	A248	Sheet of 6, #a-f	9.50	9.50

Souvenir Sheets

1168-1170	A248	Set of 3	18.00	18.00

Children's Drawings
A249

Various designs. Denominations: 3k, 4k, 5k.

2000, Nov. 7   Perf. 14

1171-1173	A249	Set of 3	4.75	4.75

Post Office Buildings
A250

Designs: No. 1174, 5k, Former Secretary of Communications Building, Luanda. No. 1175, 5k, Mbanza Congo Post Office. No. 1176, 5k, Namibe Post Office. No. 1177, 8k, Facade of Luanda Post Office. No. 1178, 8k, Luanda Post Office, diff. No. 1179, 8k, Lobito Post Office.

2000, Sept. 29   Litho.   Perf. 14

1174-1179	A250	Set of 6	8.50	8.50

National Radio and Television, 25th Anniv. — A251

No. 1180, 9.50k: a, Woman at computer in newsroom. b, Reporter with tape recorder reporting on tank battle. c, Rescuing victims from airplane crash.

No. 1181, 9.50k: a, People and equipment in newsroom. b, Cameraman filming tank battle. c, Refugees.

No. 1182, 20k, Reporter with tape recorder. No. 1183, 20k, Cameraman, vert.

Perf. 13¼x13½, 13½x13¼

2000, Dec. 7   Sheets of 3, #a-c

1180-1181	A251	Set of 2	12.00	12.00

Souvenir Sheets

1182-1183	A251	Set of 2	8.00	8.00

Souvenir Sheet

Independence, 25th Anniv. — A252

No. 1184: a, Tank, rifle, dove. b, Dove, hoe, tractor.

2001, Feb. 13   Litho.   Perf. 14¼x14

1184	A252	12k Sheet of 2, #a-b	5.00	5.00

Africa Day
A253

Designs: No. 1185, 10k, Shown. No. 1186, 10k, Xylophone.

30k, Map, musical instruments, native with mask, elephant, satellite dishes and computer.

2001, May 25   Perf. 13x13¼

1185-1186	A253	Set of 2	4.00	4.00

Souvenir Sheet

1187	A253	30k multi	6.00	6.00

Flowers
A254

Butterfly and: 8k, Nicolaia speciosa. 9k, Allamanda cathartica. No. 1190, 10k, Welwitschia mirabilis. No. 1191, 10k, Tagetes patula. 30k, Welwitschia mirabilis.

2001, June 9

1188-1191	A254	Set of 4	7.75	7.75

Souvenir Sheet

1192	A254	30k multi	6.50	6.50

Belgica 2001 Intl. Stamp Exhibition, Brussels (No. 1192).

Souvenir Sheet

Total Solar Eclipse, June 21 — A255

2001, June 21

1193	A255	30k multi	6.50	6.50

Fish
A256

Designs: 11k, Protopterus annectens. 17k, Protopterus amphibius. 18k, Tilapia ruweti. 36k, Tilapia rendalli.

Perf. 13½x13¼

2001, Sept. 28   Litho.

1194-1196	A256	Set of 3	7.75	7.75

Souvenir Sheet

Perf. 13x13¼

1197	A256	36k multi	6.00	6.00

Traditional Dances and Costumes
A257

Designs: No. 1198, 11k, Massemba. No. 1199, 11k, Ovambo Efundula. 17k, Macolo Batuque. No. 1201, 18k, Humbi Puberty. No. 1202, 18k, Mukixi. 36k, Carneval.

2001, Nov. 12   Perf. 13x13¼

1198-1202	A257	Set of 5	11.00	11.00

Souvenir Sheet

1203	A257	36k multi	5.50	5.50

Souvenir Sheet

Handmade Weaving — A258

No. 1204: a, 17k, Banda. b, 18k, Kijinga.

2001, Dec. 7

1204	A258	Sheet of 2, #a-b	5.25	5.25

Minerals
A259

Designs: No. 1205, 11k, Hematite. No. 1206, 11k, Malachite. No. 1207, 18k, Psilomelane. No. 1208, 18k, Diamond.

2001, Dec. 14   **Perf. 13½x13¼**
1205-1208 A259   Set of 4   8.50 8.50

Masks — A260

Designs: 10k, Mwana Mpwevo. No. 1210, 11k, Mukixi. No. 1211, 11k, Mbunda. 17k, Mwana Pwo. 18k, Likisi-Cinganji. 36k, Ndemba, horiz.

2002, Jan. 8   **Perf. 13¼x13½**
1209-1213 A260   Set of 5   10.00 10.00
Souvenir Sheet
Perf. 13x13¼
1214 A260 36k multi   5.50 5.50

2002 World Cup Soccer Championships, Japan and Korea — A261

Two players and: 35k, Ball in air. 37k, Ball on ground.

2002, June 28   **Perf. 13x13¼**
1215-1216 A261   Set of 2   11.00 11.00
1216a   Souvenir sheet, #1215-1216   10.00 10.00

Meeting of African Committee of International Socialists A262

Designs: No. 1217, 10k, Fight against poverty (red and orange map of Africa). No. 1218, 10k, Abolition of the death penalty (man with target on chest). No. 1219, 10k, End to violence against women (stylized woman). No. 1220, 10k, Fight against poverty (masks). No. 1221, 10k, Annulment of foreign debt (map of Africa with dollar sign)

2002, July 12
1217-1221 A262   Set of 5   7.50 7.50
1221a   Souvenir sheet, #1218-1221   6.00 6.00

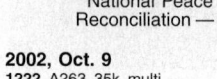

National Peace and Reconciliation — A263

2002, Oct. 9
1222 A263 35k multi   2.75 2.75

Reptiles
A264

Designs: 21k, Pithon anchietae. 35k, Lacerta sp. 37k, Naja nigricollis. 40k, Crocodylus niloticus.

2002, Oct. 15   **Perf. 13x13¼**
1223-1226 A264   Set of 4   10.00 10.00

Lighthouses and Buoys A265

Designs: No. 1227, 45k, Tafe. No. 1228, 45k, Red buoy, Luanda Bay. No. 1229, 45k, Green buoy, Luanda Bay. No. 1230, 45k, Cabeça da Cobra. No. 1231, 45k, Barra do Dande. No. 1232, 45k, Moita Seca.

2002, Nov. 22
1227-1232 A265   Set of 6   20.00 20.00

Souvenir Sheet

Dec. 4, 2002 Total Solar Eclipse — A266

No. 1233: a, 21k, Sun partially eclipsed. b, 35k, Sun mostly eclipsed. c, 37k, Sun totally eclipsed.

2002, Dec. 4
1233 A266   Sheet of 3, #a-c   7.00 7.00

Angola - Italy Friendship A267

António Manuel, Prince of N'Funta and Ambassador of Congo to Rome (d. 1608), and: 35k, Lion. 45k, Plaque with Italian inscription.

2002, Dec. 6
1234-1235 A267   Set of 2   6.00 6.00
1235a   Souvenir sheet, #1234-1235   6.00 6.00

Pottery A268

Designs: 27k, Omolingui. 45k, Mulondo. 47k, Ombya yo Tuma. 51k, Sanga.

2002, Dec. 7   **Litho.**
1236-1238 A268   Set of 3   8.50 8.50
Souvenir Sheet
1239 A268 51k multi   4.00 4.00

United Nations 3rd Meeting on Science, Technology and Development — A269

2003, May 30   **Perf. 13x13¼**
1240 A269 50k multi   3.75 3.75

Powered Flight, Cent. A270

2003, Aug. 21   **Litho.**   **Perf. 13x13½**
1241 A270 25k multi   1.90 1.90
Printed in sheets of 3 stamps + label.

Poets
A271

Designs: No. 1242, 27k, António Jacinto (1924-91) and poem. No. 1243, 45k, Agostinho Neto (1922-79) and poem.
No. 1244: a, 27k, Jacinto. b, 45k, Neto.

2003, Sept. 18   **Litho.**   **Perf. 13x13¼**
1242-1243 A271   Set of 2   5.00 5.00
Souvenir Sheet
1244 A271   Sheet of 2, #a-b   5.00 5.00

Hippotragus Niger A272

Designs: 27k, Pair with curved horns. 45k, Pair with straight horns. 47k, With herd in background.

2003, Oct. 9
1245-1247 A272   Set of 3   8.50 8.50

Women's Hairstyles — A273

No. 1248: a, Mbunda. b, Soyo. c, Huila. d, Humbi. e, Cabinda. f, Quipungu.

2003, Nov. 10   **Perf. 13¼x13**
1248 A273 25k Sheet of 6, #a-f   10.00 10.00

Whales
A274

Designs: 27k, Balaenoptera edeni. 45k, Cephalorhynchus heavisidii.
No. 1251: a, 47k, Giobiocephaia melaena.

2003, Dec. 5   **Perf. 14¾x14¼**
1249-1250 A274   Set of 2   5.00 5.00
Souvenir Sheet
1251 A274   Sheet, #1249, 1251a   5.50 5.50

Christmas — A275

No. 1252, 27k: a, The Ascension, attributed to Jorge Afonso. b, Adoration of the Shepherds, by André Reinoso.
No. 1253, 45k: a, Adoration of the Shepherds, detail showing Holy Family, by Josefa de Obidos. b, Adoration of the Shepherds, detail showing angels, by de Obidos.

2003, Dec. 5   **Perf. 13¼x13¾**
Horiz. Pairs, #a-b
1252-1253 A275   Set of 2   10.00 10.00
1253c   Souvenir sheet, #1252a-1252b, 1253a-1253b   10.00 10.00

Chess — A276

No. 1254: a, Chess pieces. b, Chess pieces and board.

2003, Dec. 10
1254 A276 45k Horiz. pair, #a-b   6.50 6.50

Eagles
A277

Designs: No. 1255, 20k, Aquila rapax. No. 1256, 20k, Polemaetus bellicosus. No. 1257, 25k, Haliaeetus vocifer. No. 1258, 25k, Terathopius ecaudatus.
45k, Aquila verreauxi.

2003, Dec. 10   **Perf. 14¾x14¼**
1255-1258 A277   Set of 4   6.50 6.50
Souvenir Sheet
1259 A277 45k multi   3.25 3.25

Election of Pope John Paul II, 25th Anniv. — A278

No. 1260: a, Portrait. b, Pope waving.

2003, Dec. 15   **Perf. 13¼x13¾**
1260 A278 27k Horiz. pair, #a-b, + central label   4.00 4.00

Flora
A279

Designs: No. 1261, 27k, Psidium guayava. No. 1262, 27k, Adansonia digitata. No. 1263, 45k, Cymbopogon citratus. No. 1264, 45k, Carica papaya.

2004, Aug. 17   **Litho.**   **Perf. 14x13½**
1261-1264 A279   Set of 4   6.00 6.00
1264a   Souvenir sheet, #1261-1264   6.00 6.00

2004 Summer Olympics, Athens — A280

Designs: No. 1265, 27k, Handball. No. 1266, 27k, Basketball. No. 1267, 45k, Track. No. 1268, 45k, Volleyball.

2004, Sept. 30   **Perf. 13¾**
1265-1268 A280   Set of 4   6.00 6.00

Marine Mammals A281

No. 1269: a, Megaptera novaeangliae. b, Cephalorhynchus heavisidii. c, Tursiops truncatus.
99k, Megaptera novaeangliae, diff.

2004, Oct. 9   **Perf. 14x13½**
1269   Horiz. strip of 3   4.00 4.00
a.-b.   A281 27k Either single   1.10 1.10
c.   A281 45k multi   1.75 1.75

Souvenir Sheet
1270 A281 99k multi   4.00 4.00

A sheetlet of eight hexagonal 15k depicting the national birds of South African Postal Operators Association (SAPOA) countries was produced in extremely limited quantities. Shee inscribed Angola, value $300.

Trains A282

Designs: No. 1271, 27k, shown. No. 1272, 27k, Benguela Locomotive 225. No. 1273, 27k, Moçamedes locomotive.

2004, Nov. 30   **Perf. 13¾**
1271-1273 A282   Set of 3   3.25 3.25

Fire Fighting A283

Telephone, emergency number and: No. 1274, 27k, Fire fighter with hose. No. 1275, 27k, Fire truck. 45k, Fire truck, diff.

2004, Nov. 30
1274-1276 A283   Set of 3   4.00 4.00
1276a   Souvenir sheet, #1274-1276   4.00 4.00

FIFA (Fédération Internationale de Football Association), Cent. — A284

2004, Dec. 7
1277 A284 45k multi   1.90 1.90

Christmas — A285

No. 1278: a, 27k, Magi. b, 45k Holy Family.

2004, Dec. 14   **Perf. 13¾**
1278 A285   Horiz. pair, #a-b   3.00 3.00

Worldwide Fund for Nature (WWF) — A286

No. 1279 — Colobus angolensis: a, Pair of adults. b, Adult and juvenile. c, Close-up of adult's face. d, Adult on rock.

2004, Dec. 29   **Perf. 13¾**
1279 A286 27k Block of 4, #a-d   4.00 4.00

Rotary International, Cent. — A287

Woman and: 45k, City. 51k, Ostriches.

2005, Feb. 23   **Litho.**   **Perf. 13x13¼**
1280-1281 A287   Set of 2   4.00 4.00
1281a   Souvenir sheet, #1280-1281   4.00 4.00

Basketry A288

Designs: No. 1282, 27k, Kinda Kya Kuzambuila. No. 1283, 27k, Ngyendu. No. 1284, 45k, Ngombo Ya Cisuka. No. 1285, 45k, Silo.
90k, Kinda Kya Kuzambuila, diff.

2005, Sept. 6   **Litho.**   **Perf. 12x12½**
1282-1285 A288   Set of 4   12.00 12.00

Souvenir Sheet
1286 A288 90k multi   20.00 20.00

Expo 2005, Aichi, Japan.

Independence, 30th Anniv. — A289

Designs: 27k, Capanda Hydroelectric Dam. 45k, Presidents Agostinho Neto and José Eduardo dos Santos, Angolan flag and dove.

2005, Nov. 8   **Litho.**   **Perf. 12x12½**
1287-1288 A289   Set of 2   5.50 5.50

Souvenir Sheet

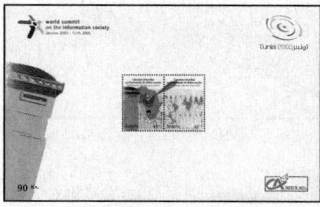

World Summit on the Information Society, Tunis — A290

No. 1289: a, Mail box, map of Africa, dish antenna, Angolan. b, Computer, world map, dish antenna.

2005, Nov. 14   **Litho.**   **Perf. 12**
1289 A290 45k Sheet of 2, #a-b   20.00 20.00

Souvenir Sheet

23rd Ministerial Conference of the African Oil Producing Countries — A291

Design: 51p, Off-shore oil rig.

2006, Apr. 24   **Litho.**   **Perf. 12x12½**
1294 A291 51k multi   — —

Four additional stamps were issued in this set. The editors would like to examine any examples.

A292

2006 World Cup Soccer Championships, Germany — A293

2006, Aug. 30   **Perf. 12x11¾**
1295 A292 45k shown   3.00 3.00
1296 A293 45k shown   3.00 3.00

Souvenir Sheet
1297 A293 90k Player dribbling   4.50 4.50

Nos. 1295-1297 lack country name.

Community of Portuguese Language Nations, 10th Anniv. — A294

Anniversary emblem, emblem of 2006 Lubrapex Intl. Stamp Exhibition and: 27k,

Dogs. No. 1299, 45k, Vultures. No. 1300, 45k, Parrots.

2006, Oct. 30   **Litho.**   **Perf. 12x11¾**
1298-1300 A294   Set of 3   6.00 6.00

Nos. 1298-1300 lack country name.

National Bank of Angola, 30th Anniv. A295

Designs: No. 1301, 27k, Bird in flight, people in boat, ship, Katanga cross currency. No. 1302, 27k, Men, cowrie shells. No. 1303, 45k, Early automobile, coins. No. 1304, 45k, Building, banknotes.
90k, Dome, luggage

2006, Nov. 7
1301-1304 A295   Set of 4   7.50 7.50

Souvenir Sheet
1305 A295 90k multi   7.00 7.00

José Sayovo, First Angolan Paralympian Gold Medalist — A296

2006, Dec. 29   **Litho.**   **Perf. 12x11¾**
1306 A296 45k multi   1.10 1.10

Peace, 5th Anniv. A297

2007, Apr. 20   **Litho.**   **Perf. 13x13½**
1307 A297 51k multi   1.75 1.75

52nd Venice Art Biennale A298

Designs: 65k, Entire painting. 155k, Painting detail.

2007, Apr. 20   **Perf. 13x13½**
1308 A298 65k multi   1.90 1.90

Souvenir Sheet
   Perf. 13½x13
1309 A298 155k multi   4.50 4.50

No. 1309 contains one 60x40mm stamp.

Souvenir Sheet

Africa Day — A299

2007, Apr. 20   **Perf. 13½x13**
1310 A299 130k multi   3.75 3.75

Scouting, Cent. — A300

No. 1311: a, 30k, Scouts sitting in fleur-de-lis pattern. b, 30k, Scouts sitting at desks. c, 55k, Scouts sitting on ground. d, 65k, Scouts saluting.
130k, Group of scouts standing on steps.

2007, June 1   *Perf. 13x13½*
1311 A300   Sheet of 4, #a-d   5.50 5.50
Souvenir Sheet
Perf. 13½x13
1312 A300 130k multi   4.00 4.00
No. 1312 contains one 60x40mm stamp.

Souvenir Sheet

Southern African Development
Community, 27th Anniv. — A301

2007, Aug. 17   *Perf. 12½x13*
1313 A301 150k multi   8.00 8.00

Souvenir Sheet

Sports — A302

Perf. 13¼ Syncopated
2007, Sept. 20
1314 A302 130k multi   4.00 4.00

Souvenir Sheet

World Post Day — A303

No. 1315 — Post office at: a, Malange. b, Huamba.

2007, Oct. 9   *Perf. 12¾x13½*
1315 A303 45k Sheet of 2, #a-b   2.75 2.75

Sea Turtles — A304

No. 1316: a, 27k, Caretta caretta. b, 27k, Chelonia mydas. c, 45k, Eretmochelys imbricata. d, 45k, Lepidochelys olivacea.
130k, Dermochelys coriacea, vert.

2007, Nov. 11   *Perf. 13x13¼*
1316 A304   Sheet of 4, #a-d   4.50 4.50
Souvenir Sheet
Perf. 13¼ Syncopated
1317 A304 130k multi   4.00 4.00
No. 1317 contains one 38x39mm stamp.

Angolan
Cuisine
A305

Various unnamed Angolan dishes: 37k, 40k, 59k, 153k.

2008, May 30   *Perf. 13x13½*
1318-1320 A305 Set of 3   7.00 7.00
Souvenir Sheet
1321 A305 153k multi   13.00 13.00

Water
Resources
A306

Designs: No. 1322, 37k, Kuebe River. No. 1323, 37k, Kuanza Rapids. No. 1324, 40k, Kuanza River. No. 1325, 40k, Mouth of Mbridge River.
153k, Kalandula Waterfalls.

2008, June 30   *Perf. 13x13½*
1322-1325 A306 Set of 4   8.00 8.00
Souvenir Sheet
1326 A306 153k multi   8.00 8.00

Miniature Sheet

Lwini Fund, 10th Anniv. — A307

No. 1327: a, 37k, Land mine removal, vert. b, 40k, Wooden box and books. c, 40k, Princess Diana and Angolan woman. d, 59k, Children in wheelchairs. e, 59k, Men making baskets.

Perf. 13½x13, 13x13½ (37k)
2008, June 30
1327 A307   Sheet of 5, #a-e,
    + label   10.00 10.00

Water
Jugs — A308

Designs: No. 1328, 37k, Jug with head on top. No. 1329, 37k, Two-handled jug. No. 1330, 40k, Jug with handle and spout. No. 1331, 40k, Jug with woman on top.

2008, July 30   *Perf. 13½x13*
1328-1331 A308 Set of 4   8.50 8.50

Mangroves
on
Chiloango
River
A309

Designs: No. 1332, 37k, Roots. No. 1333, 37k, Trees along river. 59k, Roots, diff.

2008, Aug. 30   *Perf. 13x13½*
1332-1334 A309 Set of 3   7.00 7.00

Miniature Sheet

2008 Summer Olympics,
Beijing — A310

No. 1335: a, Basketball. b, Handball. c, Running. d, Canoeing.

2008, Sept. 20   *Perf. 12¾x13½*
1335 A310 30k Sheet of 4, #a-d   5.00 5.00

Coffee — A311

Designs: 37k, Coffee berries. No. 1337, 45k, Woman picking berries, horiz. No. 1338, 45k, Tree with berries.

Perf. 13¼x13, 13x13¼
2009, Dec. 7   Litho.
Granite Paper
1336-1338 A311 Set of 3   4.00 4.00

Pres. Antonio
Agostinho Neto
(1922-79) — A312

Pres. Neto: 40k, Behind lectern. 50k, In army uniform.
150k, Pres. Neto with school children, horiz.

2009, Dec. 7   **Granite Paper**
1339-1340 A312 Set of 2   2.75 2.75
Souvenir Sheet
1341 A312 150k multi   4.25 4.25

Souvenir Sheet

Pope Benedict XVI — A313

2009, Dec. 7   *Perf. 13¼x13*
Granite Paper
1342 A313 100k multi + label   4.00 4.00

2010 Africa Cup of Nations Soccer
Tournament, Angola — A314

Stadiums in: No. 1343, 40k, Benguela. No. 1344, 40k, Cabinda. No. 1345, 50k, Luanda. No. 1346, 50k, Huilá.

2010, Jan. 8   *Perf. 13x13¼*
Granite Paper
1343-1346 A314 Set of 4   5.00 5.00

Africa Day
A315

Designs: 40k, People from Uige and Zaire Provinces. 60k, People from Lunda and Moxico Provinces.
120k, People from Luanda Province.

2010   *Perf. 13x13¼*
1348-1349 A315 Set of 2   2.75 2.75
Souvenir Sheet
Perf. 13¼ Syncopated
1350 A315 120k multi   3.75 3.75
Expo 2010, Shanghai. No. 1350 contains one 50x39mm stamp.

African Women's
Day — A316

Designs: No. 1351, 60k, Kwanhama woman. No. 1352, 60k, Quipungo woman. 150k, Mucubal woman.

2010   *Perf. 13¼x13*
1351-1352 A316 Set of 2   3.25 3.25
Souvenir Sheet
Perf. 13¼ Syncopated
1353 A316 150k multi   4.00 4.00
Expo 2010, Shanghai. No. 1353 contains one 39x50mm stamp.

Intl. Children's Day A317

Children, flowers and wildlife with background color of: No. 1354, 40k, Green. No. 1355, 40k, Orange. No. 1356, 60k, Blue. No. 1357, 60k, Green.
150k, Orange.

2010 *Perf. 13x13¼*
1354-1357 A317 Set of 4 ... 5.00 5.00
Souvenir Sheet
Perf. 13¼ Syncopated
1358 A317 150k multi ... 4.25 4.25
Expo 2010, Shanghai. No. 1358 contains one 50x39mm stamp.

Organization of Petroleum Exporting Countries, 50th Anniv. — A318

50th anniversary emblem with Angolan flag and: 40k, Antelope. 50k, Statue. 60k, Offshore oil drilling platform.
150k, Off-shore oil drilling platform and other equipment.

2010, Oct. *Perf. 13x13¼*
1359-1361 A318 Set of 3 ... 3.25 3.25
Souvenir Sheet
Perf. 13½ Syncopated
1362 A318 150k multi ... 3.25 3.25
No. 1362 contains one 50x39mm stamp.

Portuguese Agency for External Investment and Commerce, 20th Anniv. — A319

2010, Nov. *Perf. 13x13¼*
1363 A319 60k multi ... 1.40 1.40

Worldwide Fund for Nature (WWF) A320

No. 1364: a, Two Cercopithecus cephus, one on rock at left. b, Three Cercopithecus ascanius. c, Two Cercopithecus ascanius. d, Two Cercopithecus cephus, one on branch at right.
350k, Cercopithecus cephus and Cercopithecus ascanius, vert.

2011, Aug. 31 *Perf. 13x13¼*
1364 Strip of 4, #a-d ... 9.00 9.00
a.-d. A320 100k Any single ... 2.25 2.25
e. Souvenir sheet of 8, 2 each #1364a-1364d ... 18.00 18.00
Souvenir Sheet
Perf. 13¼
1365 A320 350k multi ... 7.50 7.50
No. 1365 contains one 39x45mm stamp.

A321

A322

A323

Southern African Development Community, 31st Anniv. — A324

Design: 150k, Emblem and map of Africa, diff.

2011, Aug. 12 *Perf. 13x13¼*
1366 A321 50k multi ... 1.10 1.10
1367 A322 50k multi ... 1.10 1.10
1368 A323 50k multi ... 1.10 1.10
1369 A324 50k multi ... 1.10 1.10
Nos. 1366-1369 (4) ... 4.40 4.40
Souvenir Sheet
Perf. 13½
1370 A324 150k multi ... 3.25 3.25

Peonies — A325

No. 1371: a, Paeonia daurica. b, Paeonia mlokosewitschii. c, Paeonia veitchii. d, Paeonia broteri.
350k, Paeonia officinalis salmonea.

2011, Apr. 31 *Perf. 13¼x13*
1371 Horiz. strip of 4 ... 9.00 9.00
a.-d. A325 100k Any single ... 2.25 2.25
e. Souvenir sheet of 4, #1371a-1371d ... 9.00 9.00
Souvenir Sheet
Perf. 13½
1372 A325 350k multi ... 7.50 7.50
China 2011 International Stamp Exhibition, Wuxi. No. 1372 contains one 39x45mm stamp.

National Bank of Angola, 35th Anniv. A326

Emblem and: 40k, Ornamental planter. 50k, Crest on exterior wall. No. 1375, 60k, Roof ornament. No. 1376, 60k, Windows near corner of building.
150k, Aerial view of building.

2011, Nov. 4 *Perf. 13x13¼*
1373-1376 A326 Set of 4 ... 4.50 4.50
Souvenir Sheet
Perf. 13x13¼ Syncopated
1377 A326 150k multi ... 3.25 3.25
No. 1377 contains one 50x39mm stamp.

SEMI-POSTAL STAMPS

Angolan Red Cross — SP1

No. B1, Mother and child. No. B2, Zebra and foal.

1991, Sept. 19 *Litho.* *Perf. 14*
B1 SP1 20k +5k multi ... 1.25 1.25
B2 SP1 40k +5k multi ... 2.25 2.25

AIR POST STAMPS

Plane Over Globe
Common Design Type
Perf. 13½x13
1938, July 26 *Engr.* *Unwmk.*
Name and Value in Black
C1 CD39 10c red orange ... .60 .40
C2 CD39 20c purple ... .60 .40
C3 CD39 50c orange ... .60 .40
C4 CD39 1a ultra ... .60 .40
C5 CD39 2a lilac brn ... 1.25 .40
C6 CD39 3a dk green ... 2.50 .60
C7 CD39 5a red brown ... 6.00 .90
C8 CD39 9a rose carmine ... 9.25 1.90
C9 CD39 10a magenta ... 12.50 3.00
Nos. C1-C9 (9) ... 33.90 8.40
Set, Never Hinged ... 47.50

No. C7 exists with overprint "Exposicao Internacional de Nova York, 1939-1940" and Trylon and Perisphere. Value; used & unused $110., never hinged, $160.

AP2

1947, Aug. *Litho.* *Rough Perf. 10½*
C10 AP2 1a red brown ... 16.00 5.25
C11 AP2 2a yellow grn ... 18.00 6.75
C12 AP2 3a orange ... 18.00 6.75
C13 AP2 3.50a orange ... 32.50 6.75
C14 AP2 5a olive grn ... 110.00 30.00
C15 AP2 6a rose ... 110.00 22.50
C16 AP2 9a red ... 375.00 275.00
C17 AP2 10a green ... 250.00 110.00
C18 AP2 20a blue ... 350.00 120.00
C19 AP2 50a black ... 450.00 290.00
C20 AP2 100a yellow ... 625.00 550.00
Nos. C10-C20 (11) ... 2,355. 1,423.

Planes Circling Globe — AP3

1949, May 1 *Photo.* *Perf. 11½*
C21 AP3 1a henna brown ... .75 .25
C22 AP3 2a red brown ... 1.50 .25
C23 AP3 3a plum ... 2.00 .25

C24 AP3 6a dull green ... 4.00 .85
C25 AP3 9a violet brown ... 5.50 2.25
Nos. C21-C25 (5) ... 13.75 3.85
Set, Never Hinged ... 21.00

> Catalogue values for unused stamps in this section, from this point to the end of the section, are for Never Hinged items.

Cambambe Dam AP4

Designs: 1.50e, Oil refinery, vert. 3e, Salazar Dam. 4e, Capt. Teófilo Duarte Dam. 4.50e, Craveiro Lopes Dam. 5e, Cuango Dam. 6e, Quanza River Bridge. 7e, Capt. Teófilo Duarte Bridge. 8.50e, Oliveira Salazar Bridge. 12.50e, Capt. Silva Carvalho Bridge.

Perf. 11½x12, 12x11½
1965, July 12 *Litho.* *Unwmk.*
C26 AP4 1.50e multicolored ... 2.50 .25
C27 AP4 2.50e multicolored ... 1.50 .25
C28 AP4 3e multicolored ... 2.50 .25
C29 AP4 4e multicolored ... 1.00 .25
C30 AP4 4.50e multicolored ... 1.00 .25
C31 AP4 5e multicolored ... 1.60 .25
C32 AP4 6e multicolored ... 1.60 .25
C33 AP4 7e multicolored ... 2.50 .25
C34 AP4 8.50e multicolored ... 3.25 1.40
C35 AP4 12.50e multicolored ... 3.75 1.60
Nos. C26-C35 (10) ... 21.20 5.00

Stamp Centenary Type
Design: 2.50e, Boeing 707 jet & Angola #2.
1970, Dec. 1 *Litho.* *Perf. 13½*
C36 A83 2.50e multicolored ... 1.40 .35
a. Souv. sheet of 3, #565-566, C36 ... 13.00 13.00
No. C36a sold for 15e.

No. C36 Ovptd.

1980, June 15 *Litho.* *Perf. 13½*
C37 A83 2.50e multicolored ... 1.40 .45

POSTAGE DUE STAMPS

D1

1904 *Unwmk.* *Typo.* *Perf. 11½x12*
J1 D1 5r yellow grn ... .55 .45
J2 D1 10r slate ... .55 .45
J3 D1 20r yellow brn ... 1.00 .55
J4 D1 30r orange ... 1.00 .55
J5 D1 50r gray brown ... 1.25 .90
J6 D1 60r red brown ... 11.50 5.50
J7 D1 100r lilac ... 4.75 3.00
J8 D1 130r dull blue ... 4.75 3.00
J9 D1 200r carmine ... 14.00 7.50
J10 D1 500r gray violet ... 12.00 6.00
Nos. J1-J10 (10) ... 51.35 27.90

Postage Due Stamps of 1904 Overprinted in Carmine or Green

1911
J11 D1 5r yellow grn ... .40 .30
J12 D1 10r slate ... .40 .30
J13 D1 20r yellow brn ... .40 .30
J14 D1 30r orange ... .55 .30
J15 D1 50r gray brown ... .55 .30
J16 D1 60r red brown ... 1.50 1.00

J17	D1 100r lilac	1.50	1.00
J18	D1 130r dull blue	1.75	1.25
J19	D1 200r carmine (G)	2.25	1.25
J20	D1 500r gray violet	2.50	2.50
	Nos. J11-J20 (10)	11.80	8.50
	Set, Never Hinged	19.00	

D2

1921   **Perf. 11½**

J21	D2 ½c yellow green	.40	.30
J22	D2 1c slate	.40	.30
J23	D2 2c orange brown	.40	.30
J24	D2 3c orange	.40	.30
J25	D2 5c gray brown	.40	.30
J26	D2 6c lt brown	.40	.30
J27	D2 10c red violet	.60	.45
J28	D2 13c dull blue	1.10	.85
J29	D2 20c carmine	1.10	.85
J30	D2 50c gray	1.10	.85
	Nos. J21-J30 (10)	6.30	4.80

For surcharges see Nos. 268-270.

> **Catalogue values for unused stamps in this section, from this point to the end of the section, are for Never Hinged items.**

Stamps of 1932
Surcharged in Black

1948   **Wmk. 232**   **Perf. 12x11½**

J31	A14 10c on 20c gray	.45	.30
J32	A14 20c on 30c myrtle grn	.80	.55
J33	A14 30c on 50c lt brown	1.20	.85
J34	A14 40c on 1a claret	1.75	1.25
J35	A14 50c on 2a dull vio	2.90	2.10
J36	A14 1a on 5a pale yel grn	3.50	2.50
	Nos. J31-J36 (6)	10.60	7.55

Common Design Type

Photogravure and Typographed

1952   **Unwmk.**   **Perf. 14**

Numeral in Red, Frame Multicolored

J37	CD45 10c red brown	.35	.25
J38	CD45 30c olive green	.35	.25
J39	CD45 50c chocolate	.35	.25
J40	CD45 1a dk vio blue	.80	.70
J41	CD45 2a red brown	1.10	.85
J42	CD45 5a black brown	1.10	.85
	Nos. J37-J42 (6)	4.05	3.15

NEWSPAPER STAMP

N1

1893   **Typo.**   **Unwmk.**   **Perf. 11½**

P1	N1 2½r brown	4.00	1.60
a.	Perf. 12½	4.00	1.40
b.	Perf. 13½	3.50	1.40

No. P1 was also used for ordinary postage.
For surcharges see Nos. 37, 82, 180, 235.

POSTAL TAX STAMPS

Pombal Issue
Common Design Types

1925, May 8   **Unwmk.**   **Perf. 12½**

RA1	CD28 15c lilac & black	1.10	1.10
RA2	CD29 15c lilac & black	1.10	1.10
RA3	CD30 15c lilac & black	1.10	1.10
	Nos. RA1-RA3 (3)	3.30	3.30

"Charity" — PT1

1929   **Litho.**   **Perf. 11**
Without Gum

RA4	PT1 50c dark blue	8.25	2.25

Coat of Arms — PT2

1939   **Without Gum**   **Perf. 10½**

RA5	PT2 50c turq green	3.50	.35
RA6	PT2 1a red	5.50	2.25

A 1.50a, type PT2, was issued for fiscal use.
Value, $7.50.

> **Catalogue values for unused stamps in this section, from this point to the end of the section, are for Never Hinged items.**

Old Man — PT3

Designs: 1e, Boy. 1.50e, Girl.

Imprint: "Foto-Lito-E.G.A.-Luanda"
Heads in dark brown

1955   **Unwmk.**   **Perf. 13**

RA7	PT3 50c dk ocher	.50	.25
RA8	PT3 1e orange ver	.75	.60
RA9	PT3 1.50e brt yel grn	1.00	.60
	Nos. RA7-RA9 (3)	2.25	1.45

A 2.50e, type PT3 showing an old woman, was issued for revenue use. Value $2.
See Nos. RA16, RA19-RA21, RA25-RA27.

No. RA7 Surcharged in
Red or Black

1957-58   **Head in dark brown**

RA11	PT3 10c on 50c dk ocher (R)	.35	.30
RA12	PT3 10c on 50c dk ocher ('58)	.35	.30
RA13	PT3 30c on 50c dk ocher	.35	.30
	Nos. RA11-RA13 (3)	1.05	.90

Mother and Child — PT4

Design: 30c, Boy and girl.

1959   **Litho.**   **Perf. 13**

RA14	PT4 10c orange & blk	.30	.25
RA15	PT4 30c slate & blk	.30	.25

Type of 1955 Redrawn
Design: 1e, Boy.

1961, Nov.   **Perf. 13**

RA16	PT3 1e salmon pink & dk brn	.35	.30

Denomination in italics.

Yellow, White and Black Men — PT5

1962, July 1   **Typo.**   **Perf. 10½**
Without Gum

RA17	PT5 50c multicolored	.35	.25
RA18	PT5 1e multicolored	.50	.25

Issued for the Provincial Settlement Committee (Junta Provincial do Povoamento). The tax was used to promote Portuguese settlement in Angola, and to raise educational and living standards of recent immigrants.
Denominations higher than 1e were used for revenue purposes.

Head Type of 1955

Designs: 50c, Old man. 1e, Boy. 1.50e, Girl.

Without Imprint
Heads in dark brown

1964-65   **Litho.**   **Perf. 11½**

RA19	PT3 50c orange	.35	.25
RA20	PT3 1e dull red org ('65)	.35	.25
RA21	PT3 1.50e yel grn ('65)	.35	.35
	Nos. RA19-RA21 (3)	1.05	.85

No. RA20 is the second redrawing of 1e, with bolder lettering. Space between "Assistencia" and denomination on RA20-RA21 is ½mm; on the 1955 issue space is 2¼mm and 1¾mm, respectively.

Map of Angola, Industrial and Farm Workers — PT6

1965, Sept. 1   **Litho.**   **Perf. 13**

RA22	PT6 50c multicolored	.25	.25
RA23	PT6 1e multicolored	.30	.25

The 2e was used for revenue purposes. Value 50c.

Head Type of 1955

Designs: 50c, Old man. 1e, Boy. 1.50e, Girl.

Imprint: "I.N.A." or "INA" (1e)

1966   **Heads in dark brown**

RA25	PT3 50c dull orange	.30	.25
RA26	PT3 1e dull brick red	.30	.25
RA27	PT3 1.50e lt yel grn	.35	.35
	Nos. RA25-RA27 (3)	.95	.85

Woman Planting Tree — PT7

1972   **Litho.**   **Perf. 13**

RA28	PT7 50c shown	.25	.25
RA29	PT7 1e Workers	.30	.25
RA30	PT7 2e Produce	.30	.25
	Nos. RA28-RA30 (3)	.85	.75

POSTAL TAX DUE STAMPS

Pombal Issue
Common Design Types

1925, May 8   **Unwmk.**   **Perf. 12½**

RAJ1	CD28 30c lilac & black	1.10	1.10
RAJ2	CD29 30c lilac & black	1.10	1.10
RAJ3	CD30 30c lilac & black	1.10	1.10
	Nos. RAJ1-RAJ3 (3)	3.30	3.30

See note after Portugal No. RAJ4.

ANGRA

ˈaŋ-grə

LOCATION — An administrative district of the Azores, consisting of the islands of Terceira, Sao Jorge and Graciosa.
GOVT. — A district of Portugal
AREA — 275 sq. mi.
POP. — 70,000 (approx.)
CAPITAL — Angra do Heroismo

1000 Reis = 1 Milreis

King Carlos — A1

1892-93   **Typo.**   **Unwmk.**   **Perf. 12½**

1	A1	5r yellow	5.00	2.75
a.		Perf 11½	14.00	7.00
b.		Perf 13½	4.00	2.75
2	A1	10r redsh violet	5.00	2.75
a.		Perf 13½	5.75	4.00
3	A1	15r chocolate	7.00	4.00
a.		Perf 13½	7.00	4.00
4	A1	20r lavender	9.0	3.00
a.		Perf 13½	9.00	3.25
5	A1	25r green	5.00	.80
a.		Perf 13½	10.00	6.00
b.		Perf 11½	6.00	1.25
7	A1	50r blue	12.00	4.50
a.		Perf 13½	14.00	7.00
8	A1	75r carmine	12.00	6.00
9	A1	80r yellow green	15.00	11.50
10	A1	100r brown, yel, perf 13½ ('93)	60.00	16.00
a.		Perf 12½	175.00	150.00
11	A1	150r car, rose ('93)	80.00	45.00
a.		Perf 13½	75.00	60.00
12	A1	200r dk blue, bl ('93)	80.00	45.00
		Never hinged	100.00	
a.		Perf 13½	75.00	60.00
13	A1	300r dk blue, sal ('93)	90.00	45.00
		Never hinged	100.00	
a.		Perf 13½	80.00	60.00
		Nos. 1-13 (12)	380.00	186.30

Reprints of 50r, 150r, 200r and 300r, made in 1900, are perf. 11½ and ungummed. Value, each $50. Reprints of all values, made in 1905, have shiny white gum and clean-cut perf. Value, each $22.50.

King Carlos — A2

Name and Value in Black except
Nos. 26 and 35

1897-1905   **Perf. 11½**

14	A2	2½r gray	.75	.50
15	A2	5r orange	.75	.50
a.		Diagonal half used as 2½r on newspaper or circular		32.50
16	A2	10r yellow grn	.75	.50
17	A2	15r brown	10.00	7.00
18	A2	15r gray grn ('99)	1.00	.70
19	A2	20r gray violet	2.00	1.50
20	A2	25r sea green	3.25	1.40
21	A2	25r car rose ('99)	.75	.70
22	A2	50r dark blue	6.00	2.00
23	A2	50r ultra ('05)	25.00	12.50
24	A2	65r slate bl ('98)	1.40	.70
25	A2	75r rose	4.00	1.90
26	A2	75r gray brn & car, straw ('05)	30.00	12.50
27	A2	80r violet	1.60	1.40
28	A2	100r dk blue, bl	3.50	2.00
29	A2	115r org brn, pink ('98)	4.00	2.25
30	A2	130r gray brn, straw ('98)	4.00	2.25
31	A2	150r lt brn, straw	3.50	2.00
32	A2	180r sl, pnksh ('98)	5.00	3.25
33	A2	200r red vio, pnksh	6.00	5.50
34	A2	300r blue, rose	18.00	8.00
35	A2	500r blk & red, bl	24.00	16.00
a.		Perf. 12½	40.00	20.00
		Nos. 14-35 (22)	155.25	85.05

Azores stamps were used in Angra from 1906 to 1931, when they were superseded by those of Portugal.

ANGUILLA

aŋˌgwi-lə

LOCATION — In the West Indies southeast of Puerto Rico
GOVT. — British territory
AREA — 60 sq. mi.
POP. — 10,663 (est. 1997)
CAPITAL — The Valley

Anguilla separated unilaterally from the Associated State of St. Kitts-Nevis-Anguilla in 1967, formalized in 1980 following direct United Kingdom intervention some years before. A British Commissioner exercises executive authority.

100 Cents = 1 Eastern Caribbean Dollar

Catalogue values for all unused stamps in this country are for Never Hinged items.

St. Kitts-Nevis Nos. 145-160 Overprinted

On Type A14

On Type A15

Wmk. 314

1967, Sept. 4		**Photo.**		**Perf. 14**
1	A14	½c blue & dk brn	85.00	32.50
2	A15	1c multicolored	100.00	11.00
3	A14	2c multicolored	85.00	2.75
4	A14	3c multicolored	85.00	7.25
5	A14	4c multicolored	100.00	9.00
6	A15	5c multicolored	375.00	35.00
7	A15	6c multicolored	160.00	14.50
8	A15	10c multicolored	90.00	11.00
9	A14	15c multicolored	180.00	22.50
10	A15	20c multicolored	425.00	40.00
11	A14	25c multicolored	300.00	75.00
12	A15	50c multicolored	5,500	800.00
13	A14	60c multicolored	6,500.	1,500.
14	A14	$1 multicolored	5,000	750.00
15	A15	$2.50 multicolored	3,750.	475.00
16	A14	$5 multicolored	4,200.	500.00
		Nos. 1-16 (16)	26,935.	4,286.

Counterfeit overprints exist.

Mahogany Tree, The Quarter A1

Designs: 2c, Sombrero Lighthouse. 3c, St. Mary's Church. 4c, Valley Police Station. 5c, Old Plantation House, Mt. Fortune. 6c, Valley Post Office. 10c, Methodist Church, West End. 15c, Wall-Blake Airport. 20c, Plane over Sandy Ground. 25c, Island Harbor. 40c, Map of Anguilla. 60c, Hermit crab and starfish. $1, Hibiscus. $2.50, Coconut harvest. $5, Spiny lobster.

		Perf. 12½x13		
1967-68		**Litho.**		**Unwmk.**
17	A1	1c orange & multi	.25	.80
18	A1	2c gray green & blk	.25	1.00
19	A1	3c emerald & blk	.25	.25
20	A1	4c brt blue & blk	.25	.25
21	A1	5c lt blue & multi	.25	.25
22	A1	6c ver & black	.25	.25
23	A1	10c multicolored	.25	.25
24	A1	15c multicolored	2.10	.25
25	A1	20c multicolored	1.25	1.75

26	A1	25c multicolored	.60	.25
27	A1	40c blue & multi	1.00	.50
28	A1	60c yellow & multi	4.50	4.00
29	A1	$1 lt green & multi	1.75	3.00
30	A1	$2.50 multicolored	2.25	5.50
31	A1	$5 multicolored	3.00	3.50
		Nos. 17-31 (15)	18.20	21.80

Issued: 1c, 5c, 10c, 20c, 25c, 40c, 11/27/67; 3c, 4c, 15c, 60c, $1, $5, 2/10/68; 2c, 6c, $2.50, 3/21/68.
For overprints see Nos. 53-67, 78-82.

Sailboats A2

Designs: 15c, Boat building. 25c, Schooner Warspite. 40c, Yacht Atlantic Star.

1968, May 11				**Perf. 14**
32	A2	10c rose & multi	.35	.25
33	A2	15c olive & multi	.40	.25
34	A2	25c lilac rose & multi	.60	.25
35	A2	40c dull blue & multi	.65	.35
		Nos. 32-35 (4)	2.00	1.10

Purple-throated Carib — A3

Anguillan Birds: 15c, Bananaquit. 25c, Black-necked stilt, horiz. 40c, Royal tern, horiz.

1968, July 8				
36	A3	10c dull yel & multi	.90	.25
37	A3	15c yel green & multi	1.10	.25
38	A3	25c multicolored	1.50	.25
39	A3	40c multicolored	2.00	.35
		Nos. 36-39 (4)	5.50	1.10

Girl Guide Badge — A4

10c, Girl Guide badge, horiz. 25c, Badge and Headquarters, horiz. 40c, Merit Badges.

1968, Oct. 14		**Perf. 13x13½, 13½x13**		
40	A4	10c lt green & multi	.25	.25
41	A4	15c lt blue & multi	.25	.25
42	A4	25c multicolored	.25	.25
43	A4	40c multicolored	.30	.25
		Nos. 40-43 (4)	1.05	1.00

Anguillan Girl Guides, 35th anniversary.

Three Kings A5

Christmas: 10c, Three Kings seeing Star, vert. 15c, Holy Family, vert. 40c, Shepherds seeing Star. 50c, Holy Family and donkey.

1968, Nov. 18				
44	A5	1c lilac rose & black	.25	.25
45	A5	10c blue & black	.25	.25
46	A5	15c brown & black	.25	.25
47	A5	40c brt ultra & black	.25	.25
48	A5	50c green & black	.30	.25
		Nos. 44-48 (5)	1.30	1.25

Bagging Salt — A6

Salt Industry: 15c, Packing salt. 40c, Salt pond. 50c, Loading salt.

1969, Jan. 4				**Perf. 13**
49	A6	10c red & multi	.25	.25
50	A6	15c lt blue & multi	.30	.25
51	A6	40c emerald & multi	.30	.25
52	A6	50c purple & multi	.35	.25
		Nos. 49-52 (4)	1.20	1.00

Nos. 17-31 Overprinted

1969, Jan. 9				**Perf. 12½x13**
53	A1	1c orange & multi	.25	.25
54	A1	2c gray green & blk	.25	.25
55	A1	3c emerald & blk	.25	.25
56	A1	4c brt blue & blk	.25	.25
57	A1	5c lt blue & multi	.25	.25
58	A1	6c vermilion & blk	.25	.25
59	A1	10c multicolored	.25	.25
60	A1	15c multicolored	.25	.30
61	A1	20c multicolored	.30	.35
62	A1	25c multicolored	.40	.50
63	A1	40c blue & multi	.70	.70
64	A1	60c yellow & multi	.80	.80
65	A1	$1 lt green & multi	1.25	1.50
66	A1	$2.50 multicolored	3.75	4.50
67	A1	$5 multicolored	8.25	9.50
		Nos. 53-67 (15)	17.45	19.90

Crucifixion, School of Quentin Massys A7

Easter: 40c, The Last Supper, ascribed to Roberti.

1969, Mar. 31		**Litho.**		**Perf. 13½**
68	A7	25c multicolored	.30	.25
69	A7	40c multicolored	.40	.25

Amaryllis A8

1969, June 10				**Perf. 14**
70	A8	10c shown	.25	.25
71	A8	15c Bougainvillea	.40	.35
72	A8	40c Hibiscus	.60	.60
73	A8	50c Cattleya orchid	2.00	1.40
		Nos. 70-73 (4)	3.25	2.60

Turban and Star Shells A9

Sea Shells: 15c, Spiny oysters. 40c, Scotch, royal and smooth bonnets. 50c, Triton trumpet.

1969, Sept. 22				
74	A9	10c multicolored	.30	.25
75	A9	15c multicolored	.40	.30
76	A9	40c multicolored	.75	.35
77	A9	50c multicolored	.90	.40
		Nos. 74-77 (4)	2.35	1.30

No. 17 Ovptd.

No. 25 Ovptd.

No. 26 Ovptd.

No. 27 Ovptd.

No. 28 Ovptd.

1969, Oct. 27				***Perf. 12½x13***
78	A1	1c orange & multi	.25	.25
79	A1	20c multicolored	.25	.25
80	A1	25c multicolored	.25	.25
81	A1	40c blue & multi	.50	.25
82	A1	60c yellow & multi	1.05	.30
		Nos. 78-82 (5)	2.30	1.30

Red Goatfish A10

Designs: 15c, Blue-striped grunts. 40c, Mutton grouper. 50c, Banded butterfly-fish.

1969, Dec. 1				***Perf. 14***
83	A10	10c multicolored	.30	.25
84	A10	15c multicolored	.40	.25
85	A10	40c multicolored	1.35	.55
86	A10	50c multicolored	1.75	.80
		Nos. 83-86 (4)	3.80	1.85

Morning Glory — A11

1970, Feb. 23				
87	A11	10c shown	.50	.25
88	A11	15c Blue petrea	.70	.25
89	A11	40c Hibiscus	.90	.30
90	A11	50c Flamboyant	1.10	.35
		Nos. 87-90 (4)	3.20	1.15

The Way to Calvary, by Tiepolo — A12

Easter: 20c, Crucifixion, by Masaccio, vert. 40c, Descent from the Cross, by Rosso Fiorentino, vert. 60c, Jesus Carrying the Cross, by Murillo.

1970, Mar. 26   **Perf. 13½**
91	A12	10c multicolored	.25	.25
92	A12	20c multicolored	.25	.25
93	A12	40c multicolored	.30	.25
94	A12	60c multicolored	.45	.35
		Nos. 91-94 (4)	1.25	1.10

Anguilla Map, Scout Badge A13

Designs: 15c, Cub Scouts practicing first aid. 40c, Monkey bridge. 50c, Scout Headquarters, The Valley, and Lord Baden-Powell.

1970, Aug. 10   **Perf. 13**
95	A13	10c multicolored	.25	.25
96	A13	15c multicolored	.25	.25
97	A13	40c multicolored	.30	.30
98	A13	50c multicolored	.45	.35
		Nos. 95-98 (4)	1.25	1.15

Anguilla Boy Scouts, 40th anniversary.

Boat Building A14

Designs: 2c, Road construction. 3c, Blowing Point dock. 4c, Radio announcer. 5c, Cottage Hospital extension. 6c, Valley secondary school. 10c, Hotel extension. 15c, Sandy Ground. 20c, Supermarket and movie house. 25c, Bananas and mangoes. 40c, Wall-Blake airport. 60c, Sandy Ground jetty. $1, Administration building. $2.50, Cow and calf. $5, Sandy Hill Bay.

1970, Nov. 23   **Litho.**   **Perf. 14**
99	A14	1c multicolored	.35	.40
100	A14	2c multicolored	.35	.40
101	A14	3c multicolored	.35	.25
102	A14	4c multicolored	.35	.55
103	A14	5c multicolored	.65	.55
104	A14	6c multicolored	.45	.55
105	A14	10c multicolored	.45	.30
106	A14	15c multicolored	.45	.30
107	A14	20c multicolored	.80	.30
108	A14	25c multicolored	.50	1.10
109	A14	40c multicolored	4.50	3.25
110	A14	60c multicolored	.75	3.50
111	A14	$1 multicolored	1.50	1.25
112	A14	$2.50 multicolored	2.00	4.00
113	A14	$5 multicolored	4.25	4.00
		Nos. 99-113 (15)	17.70	20.70

Adoration of the Shepherds, by Guido Reni — A15

Christmas: 20c, Virgin and Child, by Benozzo Gozzoli. 25c, Nativity, by Botticelli. 40c, Santa Margherita Madonna, by Mazzola. 50c, Adoration of the Kings, by Tiepolo.

1970, Dec. 11   **Perf. 13½**
114	A15	1c multicolored	.25	.25
115	A15	20c multicolored	.25	.25
116	A15	25c multicolored	.30	.25
117	A15	40c multicolored	.45	.35
118	A15	50c multicolored	.50	.40
		Nos. 114-118 (5)	1.75	1.50

Angels Weeping over the Dead Christ, by Guercino — A16

Easter: 10c, Ecce Homo, by Correggio, vert. 15c, Christ Appearing to St. Peter, by Carracci, vert. 50c, The Supper at Emmaus, by Caravaggio.

1971, Mar. 29
119	A16	10c pink & multi	.25	.25
120	A16	15c lt blue & multi	.25	.25
121	A16	40c yel green & multi	.45	.25
122	A16	50c violet & multi	.55	.25
		Nos. 119-122 (4)	1.50	1.00

Hypolimnas Misippus — A17

Butterflies: 15c, Junonia lavinia. 40c, Agraulis vanillae. 50c, Danaus plexippus.

1971, June 21   **Perf. 14x14½**
123	A17	10c multicolored	2.25	1.00
124	A17	15c multicolored	2.25	1.25
125	A17	40c multicolored	2.75	1.50
126	A17	50c multicolored	2.75	2.00
		Nos. 123-126 (4)	10.00	5.75

Magnanime and Aimable in Battle — A18

Ships: 15c, HMS Duke and Agamemnon against Glorieux. 25c, HMS Formidable and Namur against Ville de Paris. 40c, HMS Canada. 50c, HMS St. Albans and wreck of Hector.

1971, Aug. 30   **Litho.**   **Perf. 14**
127	A18	10c multicolored	1.10	1.10
128	A18	15c multicolored	1.40	1.40
129	A18	25c multicolored	1.50	1.50
130	A18	40c multicolored	1.60	1.60
131	A18	50c multicolored	1.75	1.75
a.		Strip of 5, #127-131	8.50	8.50

West Indies sea battles.

Ansidei Madonna, by Raphael — A19

Christmas: 25c, Mystic Nativity, by Botticelli. 40c, Virgin and Child, School of Seville, inscribed Murillo. 50c, Madonna of the Iris, ascribed to Dürer.

1971, Nov. 29   **Perf. 14x13½**
132	A19	20c green & multi	.25	.30
133	A19	25c blue & multi	.25	.30
134	A19	40c lilac rose & multi	.35	.40
135	A19	50c violet & multi	.40	.50
		Nos. 132-135 (4)	1.25	1.50

Map of Anguilla and St. Maarten, by Jefferys, 1775 — A20

Maps of Anguilla by: 15c, Samuel Fahlberg, 1814. 40c, Thomas Jefferys, 1775, horiz. 50c, Capt. E. Barnett, 1847, horiz.

1972, Jan. 24   **Perf. 14x13½, 13½x14**
136	A20	10c lt blue & multi	.25	.25
137	A20	15c lt green & multi	.40	.30
138	A20	40c lt green & multi	.60	.50
139	A20	50c lt ultra & multi	.85	.50
		Nos. 136-139 (4)	2.10	1.55

Jesus Buffeted, Stained-glass Window — A21

Easter (19th cent. Stained-glass Windows, Bray Church): 15c, Jesus Carrying the Cross. 25c, Crucifixion. 40c, Descent from the Cross. 50c, Burial.

1972, Mar. 14   **Perf. 14x13½**
140	A21	10c multicolored	.30	.30
141	A21	15c multicolored	.35	.35
142	A21	25c multicolored	.35	.35
143	A21	40c multicolored	.40	.40
144	A21	50c multicolored	.50	.50
a.		Strip of 5, #140-144	2.50	2.50

Spear Fishing — A22

Sandy Ground — A23

2c, Loblolly tree, vert. 4c, Ferry, Blowing Point, vert. 5c, Agriculture. 6c, St. Mary's Church, vert. 10c, St. Gerard's Church. 15c, Cottage Hospital. 20c, Public Library. 25c, Sunset, Blowing Point. 40c, Boat building. 60c, Hibiscus. $1, Man-o-war bird. $2.50, Frangipani. $5, Brown pelican. $10, Green-back turtle.

1972-75   **Perf. 13½**
145	A22	1c shown	.25	.50
146	A22	2c multicolored	.25	.50
147	A23	3c shown	.25	.50
148	A23	4c multicolored	1.75	.25
149	A23	5c multicolored		1.25
150	A23	6c multicolored	.35	.25
151	A23	10c multicolored	.35	.50
152	A22	15c multicolored	.35	.40
153	A23	20c multicolored	.35	.45
154	A23	25c multicolored	.50	2.00
155	A22	40c multicolored	5.00	1.25
156	A22	60c multicolored	4.25	4.25
157	A23	$1 multicolored	10.00	8.50
158	A23	$2.50 multicolored	6.00	11.00
159	A23	$5 multicolored	18.00	19.00
160	A22	$10 multicolored	17.00	20.00
		Nos. 145-160 (16)	64.90	70.60

Issued: $10, 5/20/75; others 10/30/72.
For overprints see Nos. 229-246.

Common Design Types pictured following the introduction.

Silver Wedding Issue, 1972
Common Design Type

Design: Queen Elizabeth II, Prince Philip, schooner and dolphin.

Perf. 14x14½
1972, Nov. 20   **Photo.**   **Wmk. 314**
161	CD324	25c olive & multi	.65	.75
162	CD324	40c maroon & multi	.65	.75

Flight into Egypt — A24

20c, Star of Bethlehem. 25c, Nativity. 40c, Three Kings. 50c, Adoration of the Kings.

Perf. 13½
1972, Dec. 4   **Litho.**   **Unwmk.**
163	A24	1c shown	.25	.25
164	A24	20c multicolored	.25	.25
165	A24	25c multicolored	.25	.25
166	A24	40c multicolored	.25	.25
167	A24	50c multicolored	.25	.30
a.		Vert. strip of 4, #164-167	1.00	1.00
		Nos. 163-167 (5)	1.25	1.30

Christmas.

Betrayal of Jesus — A25

10c, Man of Sorrow. 20c, Jesus Carrying Cross. 25c, Crucifixion. 40c, Descent from Cross. 50c, Resurrection.

1973, Mar. 26
168	A25	1c shown	.25	.25
169	A25	10c multicolored	.25	.25
170	A25	20c multicolored	.25	.25
171	A25	25c multicolored	.25	.25
172	A25	40c multicolored	.25	.25
173	A25	50c multicolored	.25	.35
a.		Souvenir sheet of 6	1.25	1.50
b.		Vert. strip of 5, #169-173	1.00	1.00
		Nos. 168-173 (6)	1.50	1.60

Easter. No. 173a contains 6 stamps similar to Nos. 168-173 with bottom panel in lilac rose.

Santa Maria A26

20c, Old West Indies map. 40c, Map of voyages. 70c, Sighting land. $1.20, Columbus landing.

1973, Sept. 10
174	A26	1c multicolored	.25	.25
175	A26	20c multicolored	1.60	1.60
176	A26	40c multicolored	1.90	1.90
177	A26	70c multicolored	2.00	2.00

178	A26	$1.20 multicolored	2.75	2.75
a.		Souvenir sheet of 5, #174-178	8.75	8.75
b.		Horiz. strip of 4, #175-178	8.00	8.00
		Nos. 174-178 (5)	8.50	8.50

Discovery of West Indies by Columbus.

Princess Anne's Wedding Issue
Common Design Type
1973, Nov. 14   Wmk. 314   Perf. 13½

179	CD325	60c blue grn & multi	.25	.25
180	CD325	$1.20 lilac & multi	.30	.30

Wedding of Princess Anne and Capt. Mark Phillips, Nov. 14, 1973.

Adoration of the Shepherds, by Guido Reni — A27

Paintings: 10c, Virgin and Child, by Filippino Lippi. 20c, Nativity, by Meester Van de Brunswijkse Diptiek. 25c, Madonna of the Meadow, by Bellini. 40c, Virgin and Child, by Cima. 50c, Adoration of the Kings, by Geertgen Tot Sint Jans.

1973, Dec. 2   Unwmk.

181	A27	1c multicolored	.25	.25
182	A27	10c multicolored	.25	.25
183	A27	20c multicolored	.25	.25
184	A27	25c multicolored	.25	.25
185	A27	40c multicolored	.25	.25
186	A27	50c multicolored	.25	.25
a.		Souvenir sheet of 6, #181-186	1.50	1.50
b.		Horiz. strip of 5, #182-186	1.00	1.00
		Nos. 181-186 (6)	1.50	1.50

Christmas.

Crucifixion, by Raphael — A28

Easter (Details from Crucifixion by Raphael): 15c, Virgin Mary and St. John. 20c, The Two Marys. 25c, Left Angel. 40c, Right Angel. $1, Christ on the Cross.

1974, Mar. 30

187	A28	1c lilac & multi	.25	.25
188	A28	15c gray & multi	.25	.25
189	A28	20c salmon & multi	.25	.25
190	A28	25c yel green & multi	.25	.25
191	A28	40c orange & multi	.25	.25
192	A28	$1 lt blue & multi	.25	.25
a.		Souvenir sheet of 6, #187-192	1.50	1.75
b.		Vert. strip of 5, #188-192	1.00	1.00
		Nos. 187-192 (6)	1.50	1.50

Churchill Making Victory Sign — A29

20c, Roosevelt, Churchill, US, British flags. 25c, Churchill broadcasting during the war. 40c, Blenheim Palace. 60c, Churchill Statue & Parliament. $1.20, Chartwell.

1974, June 24

193	A29	1c multicolored	.25	.25
194	A29	20c multicolored	.25	.25
195	A29	25c multicolored	.25	.25
196	A29	40c multicolored	.30	.30
197	A29	60c multicolored	.35	.35
198	A29	$1.20 multicolored	.50	.50
a.		Souvenir sheet of 6, #193-198	2.00	2.00
b.		Horiz. strip of 5, #194-198	2.00	2.00
		Nos. 193-198 (6)	1.90	1.90

Sir Winston Spencer Churchill (1874-1965).

UPU Emblem, Map of Anguilla — A30

1974, Aug. 27

199	A30	1c black & ultra	.25	.25
200	A30	20c black & orange	.25	.25
201	A30	25c black & yellow	.25	.25
202	A30	40c black & brt lilac	.25	.25
203	A30	60c black & lt green	.30	.30
204	A30	$1.20 black & blue	.45	.45
a.		Souvenir sheet of 6	1.60	2.00
b.		Horiz. strip of 5, #200-204	1.50	1.50
		Nos. 199-204 (6)	1.75	1.75

UPU, centenary. No. 204a contains one each of Nos. 199-204 with second row (40c, 60c, $1.20) perf. 15 at bottom.

Fishermen Seeing Star — A31

Christmas: 20c, Nativity. 25c, King offering gift. 40c, Star over map of Anguilla. 60c, Family looking at star. $1.20, Two angels with star and "Peace."

1974, Dec. 16   Litho.   Perf. 14½

205	A31	1c brt blue & multi	.25	.25
206	A31	20c dull grn & multi	.25	.25
207	A31	25c gray & multi	.25	.25
208	A31	40c car & multi	.25	.25
209	A31	60c dp blue & multi	.25	.25
210	A31	$1.20 ultra & multi	.25	.25
a.		Souvenir sheet of 6, #205-210	2.00	2.25
b.		Horiz. strip of 5, #206-210	1.25	1.25
		Nos. 205-210 (6)	1.50	1.50

Virgin Mary, St. John, Mary Magdalene A32

Paintings from Isenheim Altar, by Matthias Grunewald: 10c, Crucifixion. 15c, John the Baptist. 20c, St. Sebastian and Angels. $1, Burial of Christ, horiz. $1.50, St. Anthony, the Hermit.

1975, Mar. 25   Perf. 13½

211	A32	1c multicolored	.25	.25
212	A32	10c multicolored	.25	.25
213	A32	15c multicolored	.25	.25
214	A32	20c multicolored	.25	.25
215	A32	$1 multicolored	.25	.35
216	A32	$1.50 multicolored	.30	.45
a.		Souvenir sheet of 6	1.75	2.00
b.		Horiz. strip of 5, #212-216	1.25	1.25
		Nos. 211-216 (6)	1.55	1.80

Easter. No. 216a contains 6 stamps similar to Nos. 211-216 with simulated perforations.

Statue of Liberty, N.Y. Skyline — A33

10c, Capitol, Washington, DC. 15c, Congress voting independence. 20c, Washington, map & his battles. $1, Boston Tea Party. $1.50, Bicentennial emblem, historic US flags.

1975, Nov. 10

217	A33	1c multicolored	.25	.25
218	A33	10c multicolored	.25	.25
219	A33	15c multicolored	.25	.25
220	A33	20c multicolored	.25	.25
221	A33	$1 multicolored	.50	.40
222	A33	$1.50 multicolored	.60	.60
a.		Souvenir sheet of 6	1.90	2.50
b.		Horiz. strip of 5, #218-222	2.00	2.00
		Nos. 217-222 (6)	2.10	2.00

American Bicentennial. No. 222a contains one each of Nos. 217-222 with second row (20c, $1, $1.50) perf. 15 at bottom.

Virgin and Child with St. John, by Raphael — A34

Paintings, Virgin and Child by: 10c, Cima. 15c, Dolci. 20c, Durer. $1, Bellini. $1.50, Botticelli.

1975, Dec. 8   Perf. 14x13½

223	A34	1c ultra & multi	.25	.25
224	A34	10c Prus blue & multi	.25	.25
225	A34	15c plum & multi	.25	.25
226	A34	20c car rose & multi	.25	.25
227	A34	$1 brt grn & multi	.30	.25
228	A34	$1.50 blue grn & multi	.45	.40
a.		Souvenir sheet of 6, #223-228	2.75	2.75
b.		Horiz. strip of 5, #224-228	1.75	1.50
		Nos. 223-228 (6)	1.75	1.65

Christmas.

Nos. 145-146, 148, 150-160 Surcharged and/or Overprinted

(a)

(b)

1976   Litho.   Perf. 13½

229	A22 (a)	1c #145	.35	.50
230	A22 (b)	2c on 1c #145	.35	.50
231	A23 (b)	2c #146	7.75	1.75
232	A22 (b)	3c on 40c #155	.90	.75
233	A22 (a)	4c #148	1.10	1.25
234	A22 (b)	5c on 40c #155	.35	.65
235	A22 (a)	6c #150	.35	.65
236	A23 (b)	10c on 20c #153	.35	.65
237	A22 (a)	10c #151	8.25	5.50
238	A22 (a)	15c #152	.35	1.25
239	A22 (a)	20c #153	.35	.60
240	A23 (a)	25c #154	.35	.60
241	A22 (a)	40c #155	1.10	.80
242	A23 (a)	60c #156	.75	.80
243	A23 (a)	$1 #157	6.75	2.50
244	A23 (a)	$2.50 #158	2.25	2.50
245	A23 (a)	$5 #159	8.50	10.00
246	A22 (a)	$10 #160	3.25	7.00
		Nos. 229-246 (18)	43.40	38.25

Flowering Trees — A35

1976, Feb. 16   Perf. 13½x14

247	A35	1c Almond	.25	.25
248	A35	10c Clusia rosea	.25	.25
249	A35	15c Calabash	.25	.25
250	A35	20c Cordia	.25	.25
251	A35	$1 Papaya	.50	.40
252	A35	$1.50 Flamboyant	.70	.55
a.		Souvenir sheet of 6, #247-252	2.50	2.50
b.		Horiz. strip of 5, #248-252	2.50	2.50
		Nos. 247-252 (6)	2.20	1.95

The Three Marys — A36

Designs: 10c, Crucifixion. 15c, Two soldiers. 20c, Annunciation. $1, Altar tapestry, 1470, Monastery of Rheinau, Switzerland, horiz. $1.50, "Noli me Tangere" (Jesus and Mary Magdalene). Designs of vertical stamps show details from tapestry shown on $1 stamp.

1976, Apr. 5   Perf. 14x13½, 13½x14

253	A36	1c multicolored	.25	.25
254	A36	10c multicolored	.25	.25
255	A36	15c multicolored	.25	.25
256	A36	20c multicolored	.25	.25
257	A36	$1 multicolored	.55	.55
258	A36	$1.50 multicolored	.75	.75
a.		Souvenir sheet of 6	2.25	2.25
b.		Horiz. strip of 5, #254-258	2.25	2.25
		Nos. 253-258 (6)	2.30	2.30

Easter. No. 258a contains 6 stamps similar to Nos. 253-258 with simulated perforations.

Le Desius and La Vaillante Approaching Anguilla — A37

Sailing Ships: 3c, Sailboat leaving Anguilla for Antigua to get help. 15c, HMS Lapwing in battle with frigate Le Desius and brig La Vaillante. 25c, La Vaillante aground off St. Maarten. $1, Lapwing. $1.50, Le Desius burning.

1976, Nov. 8   Litho.   Perf. 13½x14

259	A37	1c multicolored	.25	.25
260	A37	3c multicolored	1.40	.50
261	A37	15c multicolored	1.50	.70
262	A37	25c multicolored	1.50	.95
263	A37	$1 multicolored	2.00	1.40
264	A37	$1.50 multicolored	2.25	1.90
a.		Souvenir sheet of 6, #259-264	8.50	8.50
b.		Strip of 5, #260-264	9.50	9.50
		Nos. 259-264 (6)	8.90	5.70

Bicentenary of Battle of Anguilla between French and British ships.

Christmas Carnival — A38

Children's Paintings: 3c, 3 children dreaming of Christmas gifts. 15c, Caroling. 25c, Candlelight procession. $1, Going to Church on Christmas Eve. $1.50, Airport, coming home for Christmas.

1976, Nov. 22

265	A38	1c multicolored	.25	.25
266	A38	3c multicolored	.25	.25
267	A38	15c multicolored	.25	.25
268	A38	25c multicolored	.25	.25
269	A38	$1 multicolored	.35	.35
270	A38	$1.50 multicolored	.50	.50
a.		Souvenir sheet of 6, #265-270	2.75	2.75
b.		Strip of 5, #265-270	1.70	1.50
		Nos. 265-270 (6)	1.85	1.85

Christmas. For overprints and surcharges see Nos. 305-310a.

Prince Charles and HMS Minerva, 1973 — A39

Designs: 40c, Prince Philip landing at Road Bay, 1964. $1.20, Homage to Queen at Coronation. $2.50, Coronation regalia and map of Anguilla.

1977, Feb. 9

271	A39	25c multicolored	.25	.25
272	A39	40c multicolored	.25	.25
273	A39	$1.20 multicolored	.25	.25
274	A39	$2.50 multicolored	.35	.30
a.		Souvenir sheet of 4, #271-274	1.00	1.50
		Complete booklet, 2 each #271-274	3.00	
		Complete booklet, 2 each #271-274 with thin vert. selvage at right	5.00	
		Nos. 271-274 (4)	1.10	1.05

25th anniv. of reign of Queen Elizabeth II. The booklets with thin vert. selvage at right were from a separate printing.
For overprints see Nos. 297-300.

Yellow-crowned Night Heron — A40

Designs: 2c, Great barracuda. 3c, Queen conch. 4c, Spanish bayonet (Yucca). 5c, Trunkfish. 6c, Cable and telegraph building. 10c, American sparrow hawk. 15c, Ground orchids. 20c, Parlorfish. 22c, Lobster fishing boat. 35c, Boat race. 50c Sea bean (flowers). $1, Sandy Island with palms. $2.50, Manchineel (fruit). $5, Ground lizard. $10, Red-billed tropic bird.

1977-78   Litho.   Perf. 13½x14

275	A40	1c multicolored	.35	1.00
276	A40	2c multicolored	.35	2.50
277	A40	3c multicolored	2.10	3.50
278	A40	4c multicolored	.45	.70
279	A40	5c multicolored	1.75	.45
280	A40	6c multicolored	.35	.45
281	A40	10c multicolored	5.75	4.50
282	A40	15c multicolored	3.75	1.00
283	A40	20c multicolored	4.00	1.00
284	A40	22c multicolored	.65	1.00
285	A40	35c multicolored	1.50	1.00
286	A40	50c multicolored	1.00	.90
287	A40	$1 multicolored	.75	.90
288	A40	$2.50 multicolored	1.25	1.00
289	A40	$5 multicolored	2.50	2.25
290	A40	$10 multicolored	10.00	7.50
		Nos. 275-290 (16)	36.50	30.65

Issued: Nos. 275-280, 290, 4/18/77; others 2/20/78.
For overprints and surcharges see Nos. 319-324, 337-342, 387-390, 402-404, 407-415, 417-423.

Crucifixion, by Quentin Massys — A41

Easter (Paintings): 3c, Betrayal of Christ, by Ugolino. 22c, Way to Calvary, by Ugolino. 30c, The Deposition, by Ugolino. $1, Resurrection, by Ugolino. $1.50, Crucifixion, by Andrea del Castagno.

1977, Apr. 25

291	A41	1c multicolored	.25	.25
292	A41	3c multicolored	.25	.25
293	A41	22c multicolored	.25	.25
294	A41	30c multicolored	.35	.30
295	A41	$1 multicolored	.60	.55
296	A41	$1.50 multicolored	.90	.80
a.		Souvenir sheet of 6, #291-296	2.75	2.75
b.		Strip of 5, #292-296	2.50	2.50
		Nos. 291-296 (6)	2.60	2.40

Nos. 271-274, 274a Overprinted

1977, Oct. 26   Litho.   Perf. 13½x14

297	A39	25c multicolored	.25	.25
298	A39	40c multicolored	.25	.25
299	A39	$1.20 multicolored	.50	.60
300	A39	$2.50 multicolored	1.00	1.25
a.		Souvenir sheet of 4	1.75	2.00
		Nos. 297-300 (4)	2.00	2.35

Visit of Queen Elizabeth II to West Indies.

Suzanne Fourment in Velvet Hat, by Rubens — A42

Rubens Paintings: 40c, Helena Fourment with her Children. $1.20, Rubens with his wife. $2.50, Marchesa Brigida Spinola-Doria.

1977, Nov. 1   Perf. 14x13½

301	A42	25c black & multi	.25	.25
302	A42	40c black & multi	.30	.30
303	A42	$1.20 multicolored	.90	.90
304	A42	$2.50 black & multi	1.25	1.35
a.		Souvenir sheet of 4, #301-304	2.75	2.75
		Nos. 301-304 (4)	2.70	2.80

Peter Paul Rubens, 400th birth anniv. Nos. 301-304 printed in sheets of 5 stamps and blue label with Rubens' portrait.
For overprint, see Nos. 311-314.

Nos. 265-270b Ovptd. & Srchd.

1977, Nov. 7   Perf. 13½x14

305	A38	1c multicolored	.25	.25
306	A38	5c on 3c multi	.25	.25
307	A38	12c on 15c multi	.25	.25
308	A38	18c on 25c multi	.30	.30
309	A38	$1 multicolored	.60	.60
310	A38	$2.50 on $1.50 multi	1.25	1.25
a.		Souvenir sheet of 6, #305-310	3.75	3.75
b.		Strip of 6, #306-310	3.00	3.00
		Nos. 305-310 (6)	2.90	2.90

Christmas. Stamps and souvenir sheets have "1976" and old denomination obliterated with variously shaped rectangles.

Nos. 301-304a Ovptd. in Gold

1978, Mar. 6   Perf. 14x13½

311	A42	25c black & multi	.25	.25
312	A42	40c black & multi	.25	.25
313	A42	$1.20 black & multi	.65	.65
314	A42	$2.50 black & multi	.75	.75
a.		Souvenir sheet of 4, #311-314	2.50	2.50
		Nos. 311-314 (4)	1.90	1.90

Buckingham Palace — A43

Designs: 50c, Coronation procession. $1.50, Royal family on balcony. $2.50, Royal coat of arms.

1978, Apr. 6   Perf. 14

315	A43	22c multicolored	.25	.25
316	A43	50c multicolored	.25	.25
317	A43	$1.50 multicolored	.40	.40
318	A43	$2.50 multicolored	.60	.60
a.		Souvenir sheet of 4, #315-318	2.00	2.00
		Complete booklet, 2 each #315-318	3.50	
		Complete booklet, 2 each #315-318 with thin vert. selvage at right	3.50	
		Nos. 315-318 (4)	1.50	1.50

25th anniv. of coronation of Queen Elizabeth II.
The booklets with thin vert. selvage at right were from a separate printing.

Nos. 284-285 and 288 Ovptd. and Surcharged

1978, Aug. 14   Litho.   Perf. 13½x14

319	A40	22c multicolored	.50	.50
320	A40	35c multicolored	.70	.70
321	A40	$1.50 on $2.50 multi	1.50	1.50
		Nos. 319-321 (3)	2.70	2.70

Valley Secondary School, 25th anniv. Surcharge on No. 321 includes heavy bar over old denomination.

Nos. 286-287, 289 Ovptd. and Surcharged

1978, Aug. 14

322	A40	50c multicolored	1.00	1.00
323	A40	$1 multicolored	1.25	1.25
324	A40	$1.20 on $5 multi	2.00	2.00
		Nos. 322-324 (3)	4.25	4.25

Road Methodist Church, centenary. Surcharge on No. 324 includes heavy bar over old denomination.

Mother and Child — A44

Christmas: 12c, Christmas masquerade. 18c, Christmas dinner. 22c, Serenade. $1, Star over manger. $2.50, Family going to church.

1978, Dec. 11   Litho.   Perf. 13½

325	A44	5c multicolored	.25	.25
326	A44	12c multicolored	.25	.25
327	A44	18c multicolored	.25	.25
328	A44	22c multicolored	.25	.25
329	A44	$1 multicolored	.35	.35
330	A44	$2.50 multicolored	.65	.65
a.		Souvenir sheet of 6, #325-330	2.00	2.25
		Nos. 325-330 (6)	2.00	2.00

Type A44 in Changed Colors with IYC Emblem and Inscription

1979, Jan. 15   Litho.   Perf. 13½

331	A44	5c multicolored	.25	.25
332	A44	12c multicolored	.25	.25
333	A44	18c multicolored	.25	.25
334	A44	22c multicolored	.25	.25
335	A44	$1 multicolored	.35	.35
336	A44	$2.50 multicolored	.60	.60
a.		Souvenir sheet of 6, #331-336	3.00	3.25
		Nos. 331-336 (6)	1.95	1.95

Intl. Year of the Child. For overprint see No. 416.

Nos. 275-278, 280-281 Surcharged

1979, Feb. 8   Litho.   Perf. 13½x14

337	A40	12c on 2c multi	.60	.50
338	A40	14c on 4c multi	.50	.60
339	A40	18c on 3c multi	1.10	.90
340	A40	25c on 6c multi	.70	.55
341	A40	38c on 10c multi	2.75	1.10
342	A40	$2.50 on 5c multi	3.00	1.10
		Nos. 337-342 (6)	8.65	4.75

Valley Methodist Church A45

Church Interiors: 12c, St. Mary's Anglican Church, The Valley. 18c, St. Gerard's Roman Catholic Church, The Valley. 22c, Road Methodist Church. $1.50, St. Augustine's Anglican Church, East End. $2.50, West End Methodist Church.

1979, Mar. 30   Litho.   Perf. 14

343	A45	5c multicolored	.25	.25
344	A45	12c multicolored	.25	.25
345	A45	18c multicolored	.25	.25
346	A45	22c multicolored	.25	.25
347	A45	$1.50 multicolored	.40	.40
348	A45	$2.50 multicolored	.60	.60
a.		Souvenir sheet of 6	2.25	2.25
b.		Strip of 6, #343-348	2.00	2.00
		Nos. 343-348 (6)	2.00	2.00

Easter. No. 348a contains Nos. 343-348 in 2 horizontal rows of 3.

US No. C3a A46

No. 350, Cape of Good Hope #1. No. 351, Penny Black. No. 352, Germany #C36. No. 353, US #245. No. 354, Great Britain #93.

1979, Apr. 23   Litho.   Perf. 14

349	A46	1c multicolored	.25	.25
350	A46	1c multicolored	.25	.25
351	A46	22c multicolored	.25	.25
352	A46	35c multicolored	.25	.25
353	A46	$1.50 multicolored	.50	.50
354	A46	$2.50 multicolored	.75	.75
a.		Souvenir sheet of 6, #349-353	2.25	2.75
		Complete booklet, 2 each #349-354	4.00	
		Nos. 349-354 (6)	2.25	2.25

Sir Rowland Hill (1795-1879), originator of penny postage.

Wright's Flyer
A — A47

History of Aviation: 12c, Louis Bleriot landing at Dover, 1909. 18c, Vickers Vimy, 1919. 22c, Spirit of St. Louis, 1927. $1.50, LZ127 Graf Zeppelin, 1928. $2.50, Concorde, 1979.

1979, May 21   Litho.   Perf. 14

355	A47	5c multicolored	.25	.25
356	A47	12c multicolored	.30	.25
357	A47	18c multicolored	.35	.25
358	A47	22c multicolored	.40	.30
359	A47	$1.50 multicolored	.95	.95
360	A47	$2.50 multicolored	3.50	1.50
a.		Souvenir sheet of 6, #355-360	6.50	6.50
		Nos. 355-360 (6)	5.75	3.50

Map of Anguilla, Map and View of Sombrero Island
A48

Map of Anguilla, Map and View of: 12c, Anguillita Island. 18c, Sandy Island. 25c, Prickly Pear Cays. $1, Dog Island. $2.50, Scrub Island.

1979   Litho.   Perf. 14

361	A48	5c multicolored	.25	.25
362	A48	12c multicolored	.25	.25
363	A48	18c multicolored	.25	.25
364	A48	25c multicolored	.25	.25
365	A48	$1 multicolored	.50	.55
366	A48	$2.50 multicolored	.80	.95
a.		Souvenir sheet of 6, #361-366	3.25	3.25
		Nos. 361-366 (6)	2.30	2.50

Anguilla's Outer Islands.

Red Poinsettia — A49

35c, Kalanchoe. $1.50, Cream poinsettia. $2.50, White poinsettia.

1979, Oct. 22   Litho.   Perf. 14½

367	A49	22c shown	.25	.25
368	A49	35c multicolored	.25	.25
369	A49	$1.50 multicolored	.45	.45
370	A49	$2.50 multicolored	.70	.70
a.		Souvenir sheet of 4, #367-370	2.50	2.50
		Nos. 367-370 (4)	1.65	1.65

Christmas.

Booths and Frames
A50

Designs: 50c, Earls Court Exhibition Hall. $1.50, Penny Black, Great Britain #2. $2.50, Exhibition emblem.

1979, Dec. 10   Litho.   Perf. 13

371	A50	35c multicolored	.25	.25
372	A50	50c multicolored	.25	.25
373	A50	$1.50 multicolored	.40	.40

374	A50	$2.50 multicolored	.70	.70
b.		Souvenir sheet of 4, #371-374	2.00	2.00
		Complete booklet, 2 each #371-374	4.00	
		Nos. 371-374 (4)	1.60	1.60

Perf. 14½

371a	A50	35c	.25	.25
372a	A50	50c	.25	.25
373a	A50	$1.50	.45	.45
374a	A50	$2.50	.80	.80
c.		Souvenir sheet of 4, #371-374	2.25	2.25
		Nos. 371a-374a (4)	1.75	1.75

London 1980 Intl. Stamp Exhibition, May 6-14, 1980.

Lake Placid and Olympic Rings — A51

Olympic Rings and: 18c, Ice Hockey. 35c, Figure skating. 50c, Bobsledding. $1, Downhill skiing. $2.50, Luge.

1980, Jan.   Litho.   Perf. 13½, 14½

375	A51	5c multicolored	.25	.25
376	A51	18c multicolored	.25	.25
377	A51	35c multicolored	.25	.25
378	A51	50c multicolored	.30	.25
379	A51	$1 multicolored	.45	.65
380	A51	$2.50 multicolored	.80	1.10
a.		Souvenir sheet of 6, #375-380	2.25	3.00
		Nos. 375-380 (6)	2.30	2.75

13th Winter Olympic Games, Lake Placid, NY, Feb. 12-24.

Salt Field
A52

12c, Tallying salt. 18c, Unloading salt flats. 22c, Storage pile. $1, Bagging and grinding. $2.50, Loading onto boats.

1980, Apr. 14   Litho.   Perf. 14

381	A52	5c multicolored	.25	.25
382	A52	12c multicolored	.25	.25
383	A52	18c multicolored	.25	.25
384	A52	22c multicolored	.25	.25
385	A52	$1 multicolored	.40	.40
386	A52	$2.50 multicolored	.85	.85
a.		Souvenir sheet of 6, #381-386	2.25	2.25
		Nos. 381-386 (6)	2.25	2.25

Salt industry.

Nos. 281, 288 Overprinted

1980, Apr. 16   Perf. 13½x14

387	A40	10c multicolored	3.50	.30
388	A40	$2.50 multicolored	3.50	1.60

Nos. 283, 289 Overprinted

1980, Apr. 16   Perf. 13½x14

389	A40	20c multicolored	3.00	.30
390	A40	$5 multicolored	5.50	2.40

Rotary International, 75th anniversary.

Big Ben, Great Britain #643, London 1980 Emblem — A53

Designs: $1.50, Canada #756. $2.50, Statue of Liberty, US #1632.

1980, May

391	A53	50c multicolored	.40	.40
392	A53	$1.50 multicolored	.60	.60
393	A53	$2.50 multicolored	1.00	1.00
a.		Souvenir sheet of 3, #391-393	2.25	2.25
		Nos. 391-393 (3)	2.00	2.00

London 1980 International Stamp Exhibition, May 6-14.

Queen Mother Elizabeth, 80th Birthday — A54

1980, Aug. 4   Litho.   Perf. 14

394	A54	35c multicolored	.55	.35
395	A54	50c multicolored	.70	.40
396	A54	$1.50 multicolored	1.25	1.00
397	A54	$2.50 multicolored	1.50	1.50
a.		Souvenir sheet of 4, #394-397	5.00	4.25
		Nos. 394-397 (4)	4.00	3.25

Pelicans — A55

22c, Great gray herons. $1.50, Swallows. $3, Hummingbirds.

1980, Nov. 10   Litho.   Perf. 14

398	A55	5c multicolored	.40	.25
399	A55	22c multicolored	1.10	.30
400	A55	$1.50 multicolored	2.40	.95
401	A55	$3 multicolored	3.00	2.10
a.		Souvenir sheet of 4, #398-401	12.50	12.50
		Nos. 398-401 (4)	6.90	3.60

Christmas. For overprints see Nos. 405-406.

Nos. 275, 278, 280-290, 334, 400-401 Overprinted

Perf. 13½x14, 14 (A55)

1980, Dec. 18   Litho.

402	A40	1c #275	.25	.80
403	A40	2c on 4c #278	.25	.80
404	A40	5c on 15c #280	1.25	.80
405	A55	5c on $1.50 #400	1.25	.80
406	A55	5c on $3 #401	1.25	.80
407	A40	10c #281	1.90	.80
408	A40	14c on $1 #287	.30	.80
409	A40	14c on $2.50 #288	.30	.80
410	A40	15c #282	1.50	.80
411	A40	18c on $5 #289	.35	.80
412	A40	20c #283	.35	.80
413	A40	22c #284	.35	.80
414	A40	25c on 15c #282	1.50	.95

415	A40	35c #285	.40	.95
416	A44	38c on 22c #334	.40	.95
417	A40	40c on 1c #275	.40	.95
418	A40	50c #286	.45	1.10
419	A40	$1 #287	.60	1.40
420	A40	$2.50 #288	1.50	3.50
421	A40	$5 #289	2.75	4.50
422	A40	$10 #290	6.25	6.50
423	A40	$10 on 6c #280	6.25	6.50
		Nos. 402-423 (22)	29.80	36.90

Petition for Separation, 1825 — A56

22c, Referendum ballot, 1967. 35c, Airport blockade, 1967. 50c, Anguilla flag. $1, Separation celebration, 1980.

1980, Dec. 18   Perf. 14

424	A56	18c multicolored	.25	.25
425	A56	22c multicolored	.25	.25
426	A56	35c multicolored	.30	.30
427	A56	50c multicolored	.40	.35
428	A56	$1 multicolored	.70	.80
a.		Souvenir sheet of 5, #424-428	1.90	2.00
		Nos. 424-428 (5)	1.90	1.95

Separation from St. Kitts-Nevis.

Nelson's Dockyard, by R. Granger Barrett
A57

Ship Paintings: 35c, Agamemnon, Vanguard, Elephant, Captain and Victory, by Nicholas Pocock. 50c, Victory, by Monamy Swaine. $3, Battle of Trafalgar, by Clarkson Stanfield. $5, Lord Nelson, by L.F. Abbott and Nelson's arms.

1981, Mar. 2   Litho.   Perf. 14

429	A57	22c multicolored	2.10	.90
430	A57	35c multicolored	2.40	1.25
431	A57	50c multicolored	2.75	1.50
432	A57	$3 multicolored	3.75	5.50
		Nos. 429-432 (4)	11.00	9.15

Souvenir Sheet

433	A57	$5 multicolored	5.00	5.00

Lord Horatio Nelson (1758-1805), 175th death anniversary (1980).

Minnie Mouse
A58

Easter: Various Disney characters in Easter outfits.

1981, Mar. 30   Litho.   Perf. 13½

434	A58	1c multicolored	.25	.25
435	A58	2c multicolored	.25	.25
436	A58	3c multicolored	.25	.25
437	A58	5c multicolored	.25	.25
438	A58	7c multicolored	.25	.25
439	A58	9c multicolored	.25	.25
440	A58	10c multicolored	.25	.25
441	A58	$2 multicolored	1.50	1.50
442	A58	$3 multicolored	2.25	2.25
		Nos. 434-442 (9)	5.50	5.50

Souvenir Sheet

443	A58	$5 multicolored	5.50	5.50

Prince Charles, Lady Diana, St. Paul's Cathedral
A59

$2.50, Althorp. $3, Windsor Castle. $5, Buckingham Palace.

1981, June 15		**Litho.**	**Perf. 14**
444 A59	50c shown	.25	.25
a.	Souvenir sheet of 2	.30	.30
b.	Wmk. 380	.30	.30
c.	Booklet pane of 4 #444b	1.25	1.25
445 A59	$2.50 multicolored	.45	.60
a.	Souvenir sheet of 2	1.60	1.60
446 A59	$3 multicolored	.55	.75
a.	Souvenir sheet of 2	2.00	2.00
b.	Wmk. 380	2.00	2.00
c.	Booklet pane of 4 #446b	8.00	8.00
	Complete booklet, #444c, 446c	9.50	
	Nos. 444-446 (3)	1.25	1.60

Souvenir Sheet

447 A59	$5 multicolored	1.75	1.75

Royal Wedding. Nos. 444a-446a contain stamps in different colors.

Boys Climbing Tree A60

10c, Boys sailing boats. 15c, Children playing instruments. $3, Children with animals. $4, Boys playing soccer, vert.

1981		**Litho.**	**Perf. 14**
448 A60	5c multicolored	.25	.25
449 A60	10c multicolored	.30	.30
450 A60	15c multicolored	.40	.45
451 A60	$3 multicolored	2.75	3.50
	Nos. 448-451 (4)	3.70	4.50

Souvenir Sheet

452 A60	$4 multicolored	5.00	5.00

UNICEF, 35th anniv.
Issued: 5c-15c, July 31; $3-$4, Sept. 30.

"The Children were Nestled all Snug in their Beds" — A61

Christmas: Scenes from Walt Disney's The Night Before Christmas.

1981, Nov. 2		**Litho.**	**Perf. 13½**
453 A61	1c multicolored	.25	.25
454 A61	2c multicolored	.25	.25
455 A61	3c multicolored	.25	.25
456 A61	5c multicolored	.30	.25
457 A61	7c multicolored	.30	.25
458 A61	10c multicolored	.30	.25
459 A61	12c multicolored	.30	.25
460 A61	$2 multicolored	4.00	2.10
461 A61	$3 multicolored	4.00	2.50
	Nos. 453-461 (9)	9.95	6.35

Souvenir Sheet

462 A61	$5 multicolored	8.00	8.00

Red Grouper — A62

No. 473

5c, Ferries, Blowing Point. 10c, Racing boats. 15c, Majorettes. 20c, Launching boat, Sandy Hill. 25c, Coral. 30c, Little Bay cliffs. 35c, Fountain Cave. 40c, Sandy Isld. 45c, Landing, Sombrero. 60c, Seine fishing. 75c,

Boat race, Sandy Ground. $1, Bagging lobster, Island Harbor. $5, Pelicans. $7.50, Hibiscus. $10, Queen triggerfish.

1982, Jan. 1		**Litho.**	**Perf. 14**
463 A62	1c multi	.25	.90
464 A62	5c multi	.35	.90
465 A62	10c multi	.25	.90
466 A62	15c multi	.25	.90
467 A62	20c multi	.45	.90
468 A62	25c multi	1.75	.90
469 A62	30c multi	.35	1.10
470 A62	35c multi	1.75	1.25
471 A62	40c multi	.35	1.10
472 A62	45c multi	.55	1.25
473 A62	50c on 45c, #472	.60	.55
474 A62	60c multi	3.50	3.75
475 A62	75c multi	1.10	3.00
476 A62	$1 multi	2.50	3.00
477 A62	$5 multi	18.00	18.00
478 A62	$7.50 multi	14.00	20.00
479 A62	$10 multi	18.00	24.00
	Nos. 463-479 (17)	64.00	82.40

For overprints & surcharges see Nos. 507-510, 546A-546D, 578-582, 606-608, 640-647.

Easter — A63

Butterflies on flowers: 10c, Zebra, anthurium. 35c, Caribbean buckeye. 75c, Monarch, allamanda. $3, Red rim, orchid. $5, Flambeau, amaryllis.

1982, Apr. 5			
480 A63	10c multicolored	1.25	.25
481 A63	35c multicolored	2.00	.55
482 A63	75c multicolored	2.25	.80
483 A63	$3 multicolored	3.75	2.40
	Nos. 480-483 (4)	9.25	4.00

Souvenir Sheet

484 A63	$5 multicolored	6.50	7.00

Princess Diana, 21st Birthday — A64

Designs: Portraits, 1961-1981.

1982, May 17			
485 A64	10c 1961	.65	.25
486 A64	30c 1968	1.50	.25
487 A64	40c 1970	.80	.30
488 A64	60c 1974	.80	.40
489 A64	$2 1981	1.25	1.50
490 A64	$3 1981	5.50	2.10
a.	Souvenir sheet of 6, #485-490	11.00	11.00
	Complete booklet, 4 each #485, 487-489	10.00	
	Nos. 485-490 (6)	10.50	4.80

Souvenir Sheet

491 A64	$5 1981	11.00	11.00

For overprints see Nos. 639A-639G.

1982 World Cup — A65

Various Disney characters playing soccer.

1982, Aug. 3		**Litho.**	**Perf. 11**
492 A65	1c multicolored	.25	.25
493 A65	3c multicolored	.25	.25
494 A65	4c multicolored	.25	.25
495 A65	5c multicolored	.25	.25
496 A65	7c multicolored	.25	.25
497 A65	9c multicolored	.25	.25

498 A65	10c multicolored	.25	.25
499 A65	$2.50 multicolored	3.00	2.40
500 A65	$3 multicolored	3.00	2.40
	Nos. 492-500 (9)	7.75	6.55

Souvenir Sheet
Perf. 14

501 A65	$5 multicolored	8.50	8.50

Scouting Year A66

1982, July 5			
502 A66	10c Pitching tent	.65	.55
503 A66	35c Marching band	1.10	.80
504 A66	75c Sailing	1.60	1.40
505 A66	$3 Flag bearers	4.25	3.25
	Nos. 502-505 (4)	7.60	6.00

Souvenir Sheet

506 A66	$5 Camping	7.00	7.00

Nos. 465, 474-475, 477 Overprinted

1982, Oct. 18		**Litho.**	**Perf. 14**
507 A62	10c multicolored	.30	.30
508 A62	60c multicolored	.75	.75
509 A62	75c multicolored	1.00	1.00
510 A62	$5 multicolored	5.50	5.50
	Nos. 507-510 (4)	7.55	7.55

12th Commonwealth Games, Brisbane, Australia, Sept. 30-Oct. 9.

Christmas — A67

Scenes from Walt Disney's Winnie the Pooh.

1982, Nov. 29			
511 A67	1c multicolored	.25	.25
512 A67	2c multicolored	.25	.25
513 A67	3c multicolored	.25	.25
514 A67	5c multicolored	.45	.25
515 A67	7c multicolored	.45	.25
516 A67	10c multicolored	.55	.25
517 A67	12c multicolored	.70	.30
518 A67	20c multicolored	1.50	.35
519 A67	55c multicolored	9.50	9.50
	Nos. 511-519 (9)	13.90	11.65

Souvenir Sheet

520 A67	$5 multicolored	13.00	13.00

Commonwealth Day (Mar. 14) — A68

10c, Carnival procession. 35c, Flags. 75c, Economic cooperation. $2.50, Salt pond. $5, Map showing Commonwealth.

1983, Feb. 28		**Litho.**	**Perf. 14**
521 A68	10c multicolored	.25	.25
522 A68	35c multicolored	.45	.50
523 A68	75c multicolored	.85	1.00
524 A68	$2.50 multicolored	6.00	4.75
	Nos. 521-524 (4)	7.55	6.50

Souvenir Sheet

525 A68	$5 multicolored	7.50	7.50

Easter — A69

Ten Commandments.

1983, Mar. 31		**Litho.**	**Perf. 14**
526 A69	1c multicolored	.25	.25
527 A69	2c multicolored	.25	.25
528 A69	3c multicolored	.25	.25
529 A69	10c multicolored	.25	.25
530 A69	35c multicolored	.55	.30
531 A69	60c multicolored	1.00	.50
532 A69	75c multicolored	1.10	.55
533 A69	$2 multicolored	2.75	2.10
534 A69	$2.50 multicolored	3.00	2.10
535 A69	$5 multicolored	4.75	3.25
	Nos. 526-535 (10)	14.15	9.80

Souvenir Sheet

536 A69	$5 Moses Taking Tablets	5.00	5.00

Local Turtles and World Wildlife Fund Emblem — A70

1983, Aug. 10		**Litho.**	**Perf. 13½**
537 A70	10c Leatherback	5.00	2.10
538 A70	35c Hawksbill	8.25	3.25
539 A70	75c Green	12.00	4.75
540 A70	$1 Loggerhead	13.50	6.50
	Nos. 537-540 (4)	38.75	16.60

Souvenir Sheet

541 A70	$5 Leatherback, diff.	30.00	8.25

1983, Aug. 10		**Litho.**	**Perf. 12**
537a A70	10c Leatherback	3.50	2.40
538a A70	35c Hawksbill	11.00	4.75
539a A70	75c Green	14.50	10.50
540a A70	$1 Loggerhead	22.00	13.00
	Nos. 537a-540a (4)	51.00	30.65

Manned Flight Bicentenary A71

10c, Montgolfiere, 1783. 60c, Blanchard & Jeffries, 1785. $1, Giffard's airship, 1852. $2.50, Lilienthal's glider, 1890. $5, Wright Brothers' plane, 1909.

1983, Aug. 22			**Perf. 14**
542 A71	10c multicolored	.65	.40
543 A71	60c multicolored	2.00	.90
544 A71	$1 multicolored	2.25	1.10
545 A71	$2.50 multicolored	3.00	3.00
	Nos. 542-545 (4)	7.90	5.40

Souvenir Sheet

546 A71	$5 multicolored	7.00	8.25

Nos. 465, 471, 476-477 Overprinted

10c, Racing boats. 40c, Sandy Isld. $1, Bagging lobster, Island Harbor. $5, Pelicans.

1983, Oct. 24   Litho.   Perf. 14

546A	A62	10c multicolored	.30	.25
546B	A62	40c multicolored	.45	.35
546C	A62	$1 multicolored	1.10	.65
546D	A62	$5 multicolored	8.50	3.75
		Nos. 546A-546D (4)	10.35	5.00

Jiminy Cricket
A72

Various Disney productions: 2c, Jiminy Cricket, kettle. 3c, Jiminy Cricket, toys. 4c, Mickey and Morty. 5c, Scrooge McDuck. 6c, Minnie and Goofy. 10c, Goofy and Elf. $2, Scrooge McDuck, diff. $3, Disney characters. $5, Scrooge McDuck.

1983, Nov. 14   Perf. 13½

547	A72	1c shown	.25	.25
548	A72	2c multicolored	.25	.25
549	A72	3c multicolored	.25	.25
550	A72	4c multicolored	.25	.25
551	A72	5c multicolored	.25	.25
552	A72	6c multicolored	.25	.25
553	A72	10c multicolored	.25	.25
554	A72	$2 multicolored	4.75	3.50
555	A72	$3 multicolored	5.50	3.25
		Nos. 547-555 (9)	12.00	8.50

Souvenir Sheet

556	A72	$5 multicolored	8.00	8.00

Boys' Brigade Centenary — A73

10c, Anguilla company, banner. $5, Marching with drummer.

1983, Sept. 12   Litho.   Perf. 14

557	A73	10c multicolored	.50	.50
558	A73	$5 multicolored	4.00	3.25
a.		Souvenir sheet of 2, #557-558	5.00	5.00

1984 Olympics, Los Angeles — A74

Mickey Mouse Competing in Decathlon.

1984, Feb. 20   Litho.   Perf. 14

559	A74	1c 100-meter run	.25	.25
560	A74	2c Long jump	.25	.25
561	A74	3c Shot put	.25	.25
562	A74	4c High jump	.25	.25
563	A74	5c 400-meter run	.25	.25
564	A74	6c Hurdles	.25	.25
565	A74	10c Discus	.25	.25
566	A74	$1 Pole vault	3.75	3.00
567	A74	$4 Javelin	7.50	4.75
		Nos. 559-567 (9)	13.00	9.50

Souvenir Sheet

568	A74	$5 1500-meter run	14.00	14.00

1984, Apr. 24   Perf. 12½x12

559a	A74	1c	.25	.25
560a	A74	2c	.25	.25
561a	A74	3c	.25	.25
562a	A74	4c	.25	.25
563a	A74	5c	.25	.25
564a	A74	6c	.25	.25
565a	A74	10c	.25	.25
566a	A74	$1	5.25	3.75
567a	A74	$4	7.00	10.50
		Nos. 559a-567a (9)	14.00	16.00

Souvenir Sheet

568a	A74	$5 With Olympic rings emblem	12.00	12.00

Nos. 559a-567a inscribed with Olympic rings emblem. Printed in sheets of 5 plus label.

Easter
A75

Ceiling and Wall Frescoes, La Stanze della Segnatura, by Raphael (details).

1984, Apr. 19   Litho.   Perf. 13½x14

569	A75	10c Justice	.25	.25
570	A75	25c Poetry	.30	.30
571	A75	35c Philosophy	.40	.40
572	A75	40c Theology	.40	.40
573	A75	$1 Abraham & Paul	1.00	1.00
574	A75	$2 Moses & Matthew	2.00	2.00
575	A75	$3 John & David	2.75	2.75
576	A75	$4 Peter & Adam	3.25	3.25
		Nos. 569-576 (8)	10.35	10.35

Souvenir Sheet

577	A75	$5 Astronomy	5.75	5.75

Nos. 463, 469, 477-479 Surcharged

1984   Litho.   Perf. 14

578	A62	25c on $7.50 #478	.85	.45
579	A62	35c on 30c #469	.70	.55
580	A62	60c on 1c #463	.75	.60
581	A62	$2.50 on $5 #477	4.00	1.90
582	A62	$2.50 on $10 #479	3.00	1.90
		Nos. 578-582 (5)	9.30	5.40

Issue dates: 25c, May 17, others, Apr. 24.

Ausipex '84 — A76

Australian stamps.

1984, July 16   Litho.   Perf. 13½

583	A76	10c No. 2	.60	.45
584	A76	75c No. 18	1.90	1.40
585	A76	$1 No. 130	2.50	1.90
586	A76	$2.50 No. 178	3.50	3.50
		Nos. 583-586 (4)	8.50	7.25

Souvenir Sheet

587	A76	$5 Nos. 378, 379	7.00	7.00

Slavery Abolition
Sesquicentennial — A77

Abolitionists and Vignettes: 10c, Thomas Fowell Buxton, planting sugar cane. 25c, Abraham Lincoln, cotton field. 35c, Henri Christophe, armed slave revolt. 60c, Thomas Clarkson, addressing Anti-Slavery Society. 75c, William Wilberforce, Slave auction. $1, Olaudah Equiano, slave raid on Benin coast. $2.50, General Gordon, slave convoy in Sudan. $5, Granville Sharp, restraining ship captain from boarding slave.

1984, Aug. 1   Perf. 12

588	A77	10c multicolored	.25	.25
589	A77	25c multicolored	.45	.45
590	A77	35c multicolored	.55	.55
591	A77	60c multicolored	.70	.70
592	A77	75c multicolored	.90	.90
593	A77	$1 multicolored	1.00	1.00
594	A77	$2.50 multicolored	1.90	1.90

595	A77	$5 multicolored	4.25	4.25
a.		Miniature sheet of 8, #588-595	10.00	12.00
		Nos. 588-595 (8)	10.00	10.00

For overprints see Nos. 688-695a.

Christmas — A78

Various Disney characters and celebrations.

Perf. 14, 12½x12 ($2)

1984, Nov. 12   Litho.

596	A78	1c multicolored	.25	.25
597	A78	2c multicolored	.25	.25
598	A78	3c multicolored	.25	.25
599	A78	4c multicolored	.25	.25
600	A78	5c multicolored	.25	.25
601	A78	10c multicolored	.25	.25
602	A78	$1 multicolored	4.00	3.00
603	A78	$2 multicolored	5.00	5.00
604	A78	$4 multicolored	7.00	9.50
		Nos. 596-604 (9)	17.50	19.00

Souvenir Sheet

605	A78	$5 multicolored	9.00	9.00

Nos. 464-465, 477 Ovptd. or Srchd.

1984, Aug. 13

606	A62	5c #464	.35	.25
607	A62	20c on 10c #465	.50	.30
608	A62	$5 #477	7.50	4.50
		Nos. 606-608 (3)	8.35	4.80

Intl. Civil Aviation Org., 40th Anniv.
A79

60c, Icarus, by Hans Erni. 75c, Sun Princess, by Sadiou Diouf. $2.50, Anniv. emblem, vert. $5, Map of the Caribbean.

1984, Dec. 3   Litho.   Perf. 14

609	A79	60c multicolored	1.00	1.10
610	A79	75c multicolored	1.60	1.75
611	A79	$2.50 multicolored	4.50	4.75
		Nos. 609-611 (3)	7.10	7.60

Souvenir Sheet

612	A79	$5 multicolored	6.50	7.50

Audubon Birth Bicent. — A80

Illustrations by artist and naturalist J. J. Audubon (1785-1851) — 10c, Hirundo rustica. 60c, Mycteria americana. 75c, Sterna dougallii. $5, Pandion haliaetus.

No. 617, Vireo solitarus, horiz. No. 618, Piranga ludoviciana, horiz.

1985, Apr. 30   Litho.   Perf. 14

613	A80	10c multicolored	1.40	1.10
614	A80	60c multicolored	2.40	2.40
615	A80	75c multicolored	2.40	2.40
616	A80	$5 multicolored	8.50	8.50
		Nos. 613-616 (4)	14.70	14.40

Souvenir Sheets

617	A80	$4 multicolored	7.50	7.50
618	A80	$4 multicolored	7.50	7.50

Queen Mother 85th Birthday — A81

Photographs: 10c, Visiting the children's ward at King's College Hospital. $2, Inspecting Royal Marine Volunteer Cadets at Deal. $3, Outside Clarence House in London. $5, In an open carriage at Ascot.

1985, July 2

619	A81	10c multicolored	.25	.25
620	A81	$2 multicolored	1.40	1.40
621	A81	$3 multicolored	2.25	2.25
		Nos. 619-621 (3)	3.90	3.90

Souvenir Sheet

622	A81	$5 multicolored	3.00	3.00

Nos. 619-621 printed in sheetlets of 5.

Birds
A82

5c, Brown pelican. 10c, Turtle dove. 15c, Man-o-war. 20c, Antillean crested hummingbird. 25c, White-tailed tropicbird. 30c, Caribbean elaenia. No. 629, 35c, Black-whiskered vireo. No. 629A, 35c, Lesser Antillean bullfinch ('86). 40c, Yellow-crowned night heron. 45c, Pearly-eyed thrasher. 50c, Laughing bird. 65c, Brown booby. 80c, Gray kingbird. $1, Audubon's shearwater. $1.35, Roseate tern. $2.50, Bananaquit. $5, Belted kingfisher. $10, Green heron.

1985-86   Litho.   Perf. 13½x14

623	A82	5c multi	3.00	2.00
624	A82	10c multi	3.00	2.00
625	A82	15c multi	3.00	2.00
626	A82	20c multi	3.00	2.50
627	A82	25c multi	3.00	2.50
628	A82	30c multi	3.00	2.50
629	A82	35c multi	13.00	10.00
629A	A82	35c multi	3.00	2.50
630	A82	40c multi	3.00	2.50
631	A82	45c multi	3.00	2.50
632	A82	50c multi	3.00	2.50
633	A82	65c multi	3.00	2.50
634	A82	80c multi	4.00	5.00
635	A82	$1 multi	4.00	5.00
636	A82	$1.35 multi	3.00	5.00
637	A82	$2.50 multi	10.00	11.00
638	A82	$5 multi	7.75	13.50
639	A82	$10 multi	13.00	17.50
		Nos. 623-639 (18)	87.75	92.50

Issued: 25c, 65c, $1.35, $5, 7/22; 45c, 50c, 80c, $1, $10, 9/30; 5c-20c, 30c, No. 629, 40c, $2.50, 11/11; No. 629A, 3/10.

For overprints & surcharges see Nos. 678-682, 713-716, 723-739, 750-753, 764-767, 783-786.

Nos. 485-491 Overprinted

1985, Oct. 31   Litho.   Perf. 14

639A	A64	10c multicolored	.25	.25
639B	A64	30c multicolored	.25	.25
639C	A64	40c multicolored	.30	.30
639D	A64	60c multicolored	.45	.45
639E	A64	$2 multicolored	1.50	1.50
639F	A64	$3 multicolored	4.25	4.25
h.		Souv. sheet of 6, #639A-639F	4.80	4.80

Complete booklet, 4 each
#639A, 639C-639E 11.00
Nos. 639A-639F (6) 7.00 7.00

Souvenir Sheet

639G A64 $5 multicolored 5.00 5.00

Nos. 464, 469, 475 and 477 Ovptd.

1985, Oct. 14 Litho. Perf. 14
640 A62 5c multicolored .45 .25
641 A62 30c multicolored .75 .55
642 A62 75c multicolored 1.10 .90
643 A62 $5 multicolored 11.75 11.75
Nos. 640-643 (4) 14.05 13.45

Nos. 465 and 469 Ovptd. or Srchd.

1985, Nov. 18
644 A62 10c multicolored .65 .25
645 A62 35c on 30c multi 1.40 .50

Nos. 476, 469 Srchd. or Ovptd.

1985, Nov. 18
646 A62 $1 multicolored 2.25 1.25
647 A62 $5 on 30c multi 7.25 7.25

Brothers Grimm — A83

Christmas: Disney characters in Hansel and Gretel.

1985, Nov. 11 Litho. Perf. 14
648 A83 5c multicolored .55 .55
649 A83 50c multicolored 1.75 .80
650 A83 90c multicolored 2.25 1.25
651 A83 $4 multicolored 4.50 4.50
Nos. 648-651 (4) 9.05 7.10

Souvenir Sheet

652 A83 $5 multicolored 8.00 8.00

Mark Twain (1835-1910), Author — A84

Disney characters in Huckleberry Finn.

1985, Nov. 11
653 A84 10c multicolored .70 .35
654 A84 60c multicolored 2.25 1.25
654A A84 $1 multicolored 3.00 1.90
655 A84 $3 multicolored 4.25 4.25
Nos. 653-655 (4) 10.20 7.75

Souvenir Sheet

656 A84 $5 multicolored 9.00 9.00

Christmas. No. 654A printed in sheets of 8.

Statue of Liberty Centennial A85

10c, Danmark, Denmark. 20c, Eagle, USA. 60c, Amerigo Vespucci, Italy. 75c, Sir Winston Churchill, G.B. $2, Nippon Maru, Japan. $2.50, Gorch, Germany. $5, Statue of Liberty, vert.

1985, Nov. 25
657 A85 10c multicolored .85 .70
658 A85 20c multicolored 1.25 .95
659 A85 60c multicolored 1.75 1.60
660 A85 75c multicolored 1.75 1.50
661 A85 $2 multicolored 1.75 2.40
662 A85 $2.50 multicolored 2.10 2.75
Nos. 657-662 (6) 9.45 9.90

Souvenir Sheet

663 A85 $5 multicolored 9.00 9.00

Easter — A86

Stained glass windows.

1986, Mar. 27 Litho. Perf. 14
664 A86 10c multicolored .25 .25
665 A86 25c multicolored .50 .50
666 A86 45c multicolored .90 .90
667 A86 $4 multicolored 5.25 5.25
Nos. 664-667 (4) 6.90 6.90

Souvenir Sheet

668 A86 $5 multi, horiz. 7.25 7.25

Halley's Comet A87

A88

Designs: 5c, Johannes Hevelius (1611-1687), Mayan temple observatory. 10c, US Viking probe landing on Mars, 1976. 60c, Theatri Cosmicum (detail), 1668. $4, Sighting, 1835. $5, Comet over Anguilla.

1986, Mar. 24
669 A87 5c multicolored .45 .45
670 A87 10c multicolored .50 .50
671 A87 60c multicolored 1.50 1.10
672 A87 $4 multicolored 6.25 6.25
Nos. 669-672 (4) 8.70 8.30

Souvenir Sheet

673 A88 $5 multicolored 5.25 7.25

Queen Elizabeth II, 60th Birthday
Common Design Type

20c, Inspecting guards, 1946. $2, Garter Ceremony, 1985. $3, Trooping the color. $5, Christening, 1926.

1986, Apr. 21
674 CD339 20c multicolored .25 .25
675 CD339 $2 multicolored 1.50 1.50
676 CD339 $3 multicolored 2.25 2.25
Nos. 674-676 (3) 4.00 4.00

Souvenir Sheet

677 CD339 $5 multicolored 4.00 4.00

Nos. 623, 631, 635, 637 and 639 Ovptd.

1986, May 22 Perf. 13½x14
678 A82 5c multicolored 1.00 1.10
679 A82 45c multicolored 2.25 .90
680 A82 $1 multicolored 4.00 1.90
681 A82 $2.50 multicolored 5.00 5.00
682 A82 $10 multicolored 11.00 12.00
Nos. 678-682 (5) 23.25 20.90

Wedding of Prince Andrew and Sarah Ferguson — A89

1986, July 23 Litho. Perf. 14
683 A89 10c Couple .25 .25
684 A89 35c Andrew .30 .35
685 A89 $2 Sarah 1.25 1.90
686 A89 $3 Couple, diff. 2.00 3.00
Nos. 683-686 (4) 3.80 5.50

Souvenir Sheet

687 A89 $6 Westminster Abbey 6.00 6.00

Perf. 12
683a A89 10c Couple .40 .25
684a A89 35c Andrew .65 .30
685a A89 $2 Sarah 1.60 1.25
686a A89 $3 Couple, diff. 2.00 1.90
Nos. 683a-686a (4) 4.65 3.70

Souvenir Sheet

687a A89 $6 Westminster Abbey 6.00 6.00

Nos. 588-595 Overprinted

1986, Sept. 29 Litho. Perf. 12
688 A77 10c multicolored .65 .35
689 A77 25c multicolored 1.00 .55
690 A77 35c multicolored 1.25 .65
691 A77 60c multicolored 2.00 .95
692 A77 75c multicolored 2.00 1.25
693 A77 $1 multicolored 2.00 1.40
694 A77 $2.50 multicolored 3.50 5.00
695 A77 $5 multicolored 4.75 6.50
a. Miniature sheet, #688-695 20.00 21.00
Nos. 688-695 (8) 17.15 16.65

Ships A90

1986, Nov. 29 Litho. Perf. 14
696 A90 10c Trading Sloop 1.75 .45
697 A90 45c Lady Rodney 3.25 .60
698 A90 80c West Derby 4.50 3.00
699 A90 $3 Warspite 7.75 6.00
Nos. 696-699 (4) 17.25 10.05

Souvenir Sheet

700 A90 $6 Boat Race Day, vert. 21.00 21.00

Christmas.

Discovery of America, 500th Anniv. (in 1992) — A91

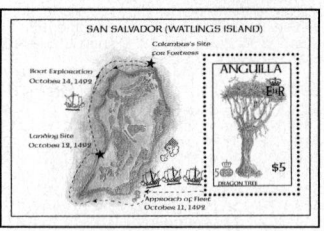

Dragon Tree — A92

5c, Christopher Columbus, astrolabe. 10c, Aboard ship. 35c, Santa Maria. 80c, Ferdinand, Isabella. $4, Indians. No. 707, Caribbean manatee.

1986, Dec. 22
701 A91 5c multi .90 .90
702 A91 10c multi 1.50 .90
703 A91 35c multi 3.00 1.60
704 A91 80c multi, horiz. 2.25 2.25
705 A91 $4 multi 5.00 5.00
Nos. 701-705 (5) 12.65 10.65

Souvenir Sheets

706 A92 $5 shown 9.00 9.00
707 A92 $5 multi, horiz. 9.00 9.00

Butterflies A93

10c, Monarch. 80c, White peacock. $1, Zebra. $2, Caribbean buckeye. $6, Flambeau.

1987, Apr. 14 Litho. Perf. 14
708 A93 10c multicolored 2.00 .90
709 A93 80c multicolored 5.50 2.75
710 A93 $1 multicolored 6.50 3.25
711 A93 $2 multicolored 10.00 11.00
Nos. 708-711 (4) 24.00 17.90

Souvenir Sheet

712 A93 $6 multicolored 20.00 20.00

Easter.

Nos. 629A, 631, 634 and 639 Ovptd in Red

1987, May 25 Litho. Perf. 13½x14
713 A82 35c on No. 629A 2.25 1.00
714 A82 45c on No. 631 2.25 1.10
715 A82 80c on No. 634 3.25 1.60
716 A82 $10 on No. 639 12.00 16.00
Nos. 713-716 (4) 19.75 19.70

Separation from St. Kitts and Nevis,
20th Anniv. — A94

10c, Old goose iron, electric iron. 35c, Old East End School, Albena Lake-Hodge Comprehensive College. 45c, Old market place, People's Market. 80c, Old ferries & modern ferry at Blowing Point. $1, Old & new cable & wireless offices. $2, Public meeting at Burrowes Park, House of Assembly.

1987, May 25   **Perf. 14**

717	A94	10c multicolored	.75	.50
718	A94	35c multicolored	.85	.65
719	A94	45c multicolored	1.00	.80
720	A94	80c multicolored	2.25	1.00
721	A94	$1 multicolored	1.75	1.25
722	A94	$2 multicolored	2.50	2.75
a.		Souvenir sheet of 6, #717-722	12.50	12.50
		Nos. 717-722 (6)	9.10	6.95

**Nos. 623, 625-628, 629A-639 Ovptd.
in Red or Srchd. in Red & Black**

1987, Sept. 4   **Litho.**   **Perf. 13½x14**

723	A82	5c No. 623	3.00	2.50
724	A82	10c on 15c No. 625	3.00	2.50
725	A82	15c No. 625	3.50	3.00
726	A82	20c No. 626	3.50	3.00
727	A82	25c No. 627	3.50	3.00
728	A82	30c No. 628	3.50	3.00
729	A82	35c No. 629A	3.50	3.00
730	A82	40c No. 630	3.50	3.00
731	A82	45c No. 631	3.50	3.00
732	A82	50c No. 632	3.50	3.00
733	A82	65c No. 633	3.50	3.00
734	A82	80c No. 634	3.50	3.00
735	A82	$1 No. 635	4.00	4.00
736	A82	$1.35 No. 636	4.75	4.75
737	A82	$2.50 No. 637	5.25	6.00
738	A82	$5 No. 638	7.25	8.25
739	A82	$10 No. 639	11.00	13.50
		Nos. 723-739 (17)	73.25	71.50

Cricket World Cup — A95

Various action scenes.

1987, Oct. 5   **Perf. 14**

740	A95	10c multicolored	1.75	.90
741	A95	35c multicolored	2.50	.90
742	A95	45c multicolored	2.50	.95
743	A95	$2.50 multicolored	5.00	6.00
		Nos. 740-743 (4)	11.75	8.75

Souvenir Sheet

744	A95	$6 multicolored	14.50	14.50

Sea Shells, Crabs A96

10c, West Indian top shell. 35c, Ghost crab. 50c, Spiny Caribbean vase. $2, Great land crab.
$6, Queen conch.

1987, Nov. 2

745	A96	10c multicolored	1.75	.70
746	A96	35c multicolored	2.25	1.10
747	A96	50c multicolored	4.00	2.10
748	A96	$2 multicolored	5.75	10.50
		Nos. 745-748 (4)	13.75	14.40

Souvenir Sheet

749	A96	$6 multicolored	13.00	13.00

Christmas.

**Nos. 629A, 635-636 and 639 Ovptd.
in Scarlet**

1987, Dec. 14   **Litho.**   **Perf. 13½x14**

750	A82	35c multicolored	.30	.30
751	A82	$1 multicolored	.70	.75
752	A82	$1.35 multicolored	1.00	1.00
753	A82	$10 multicolored	7.00	7.50
		Nos. 750-753 (4)	9.00	9.55

Easter (Lilies) — A97

30c, Crinum erubescens. 45c, Hymenocallis caribaea. $1, Crinum macowanii. $2.50, Hemerocallis fulva.
$6, Lilium longiflorum.

1988, Mar. 28   **Litho.**   **Perf. 14**

754	A97	30c multicolored	.65	.35
755	A97	45c multicolored	.85	.35
756	A97	$1 multicolored	2.25	1.00
757	A97	$2.50 multicolored	2.75	4.00
		Nos. 754-757 (4)	6.50	5.70

Souvenir Sheet

758	A97	$6 multicolored	6.00	7.25

1988 Summer Olympics, Seoul — A98

1988, July 25   **Litho.**   **Perf. 14**

759	A98	35c 4x100-Meter relay	.70	.35
760	A98	45c Windsurfing	.80	.50
761	A98	50c Tennis	2.25	1.60
762	A98	80c Basketball	5.50	4.25
		Nos. 759-762 (4)	9.25	6.70

Souvenir Sheet

763	A98	$6 Women's 200 meters	5.75	5.75

Nos. 629A, 634-635 and 637 Ovptd.

1988, Dec. 14   **Litho.**   **Perf. 13½x14**

764	A82	35c multicolored	2.10	.85
765	A82	80c multicolored	3.00	1.75
766	A82	$1 multicolored	3.00	2.10
767	A82	$2.50 multicolored	5.25	5.75
		Nos. 764-767 (4)	13.35	10.45

Marine Life — A99

35c, Common sea fan. 80c, Coral crab. $1, Grooved brain coral. $1.60, Old wife.
$6, West Indies spiny lobster.

1988, Dec. 5   **Litho.**   **Perf. 14**

768	A99	35c multicolored	1.50	.45
769	A99	80c multicolored	2.25	.95
770	A99	$1 multicolored	3.25	1.60
771	A99	$1.60 multicolored	3.75	4.50
		Nos. 768-771 (4)	10.75	7.50

Souvenir Sheet

772	A99	$6 multicolored	6.75	6.75

Christmas.

Lizards — A100

1989, Feb. 20   **Litho.**   **Perf. 13½x14**

773	A100	45c Wood slave	1.50	.70
774	A100	80c Slippery back	2.40	1.25
775	A100	$2.50 Iguana	5.50	7.00
		Nos. 773-775 (3)	9.40	8.95

Souvenir Sheet

776	A100	$6 Tree lizard	16.00	16.00

Easter — A101

Paintings: 35c, Christ Crowned with Thorns, by Hieronymous Bosch (c. 1450-1516. 80c, Christ Bearing the Cross, by David. $1, The Deposition, by David. $1.60, Pieta, by Rogier van der Weyden (1400-1464). $6, Crucified Christ with the Virgin Mary and Saints, by Raphael.

1989, Mar. 23   **Litho.**   **Perf. 14x13½**

777	A101	35c multicolored	.50	.35
778	A101	80c multicolored	.90	.75
779	A101	$1 multicolored	1.00	.80
780	A101	$1.60 multicolored	1.60	2.00
		Nos. 777-780 (4)	4.00	3.90

Souvenir Sheet

781	A101	$6 multicolored	4.00	5.00

University of the West Indies, 40th Anniv. — A102

1989, Apr. 24   **Litho.**   **Perf. 14x13½**

782	A102	$5 Coat of arms	3.50	4.50

Nos. 634-636 and 638 Ovptd.

1989, July 3   **Litho.**   **Perf. 13½X14**

783	A82	80c multicolored	2.75	1.25
784	A82	$1 multicolored	2.75	1.60
785	A82	$1.35 multicolored	3.25	2.50
786	A82	$5 multicolored	9.25	12.00
		Nos. 783-786 (4)	18.00	17.35

Christmas — A103

Well-known and historic houses: 5c, Lone Star, 1930. 35c, Whitehouse, 1906. 45c, Hodges House. 80c, Warden's Place.
$6, Wallblake House, 1787.

1989, Dec. 4   **Litho.**   **Perf. 13½x14**

787	A103	5c multicolored	.45	.75
788	A103	35c multicolored	.80	.55
789	A103	45c multicolored	.95	.65
790	A103	80c multicolored	1.75	2.10
		Nos. 787-790 (4)	3.95	4.05

Souvenir Sheet

791	A103	$6 multicolored	5.00	5.00

Fish A104

5c, Blear eye. 10c, Redman. 15c, Speckletail. 25c, Grunt. 30c, Amber jack. 35c, Red hind. 40c, Goatfish. 45c, Old wife. 50c, Butter fish. 65c, Shell fish. 80c, Yellowtail snapper. $1, Katy. $1.35, Mutton grouper. $2.50, Doctor fish. $5, Angelfish. $10, Barracuda.

1990, Apr. 2   **Litho.**   **Perf. 13½x14**

792	A104	5c multicolored	1.10	1.00
793	A104	10c multicolored	1.10	1.00
794	A104	15c multicolored	1.10	.90
795	A104	25c multicolored	1.25	1.10
796	A104	30c multicolored	1.25	1.10
797	A104	35c multicolored	1.25	1.10
798	A104	40c multicolored	1.50	1.10
799	A104	45c multicolored	1.50	.80
800	A104	50c multicolored	1.75	1.25
801	A104	65c multicolored	2.25	1.25
802	A104	80c multicolored	2.10	1.50
803	A104	$1 multicolored	2.25	1.50
804	A104	$1.35 multicolored	2.50	2.25
805	A104	$2.50 multicolored	4.00	4.75
806	A104	$5 multicolored	5.75	7.75
807	A104	$10 multicolored	9.25	12.00
		Nos. 792-807 (16)	39.90	40.35

Inscribed "1992"

792a	A104	5c Blear eye	.90	.90
793a	A104	10c Redman	.90	.90
797a	A104	35c Red hind	1.00	1.00
		Nos. 792a-797a (3)	2.80	2.80

For overprints and surcharge see Nos. 821-824, 849. For booklet see No. 890.

Easter — A105

35c, Last Supper. 45c, Trial. $1.35, Calvary. $2.50, Empty tomb.
$6, The Resurrection.

1990, Apr. 2			**Perf. 14x13½**	
811	A105	35c multicolored	1.25	.25
812	A105	45c multicolored	1.25	.35
813	A105	$1.35 multicolored	3.00	3.00
814	A105	$2.50 multicolored	3.75	3.75
		Nos. 811-814 (4)	9.25	7.35
		Souvenir Sheet		
815	A105	$6 multicolored	11.50	11.50

See Nos. 834-838.

Cape of Good Hope #7
A106

Stamps of Great Britain and exhibition emblem: 25c, #1, vert. 50c, #2, vert. $2.50, #93. $6, #1-2.

1990, Apr. 30			**Perf. 14**	
816	A106	25c multicolored	1.00	.40
817	A106	50c multicolored	1.75	.70
818	A106	$1.50 shown	3.00	3.00
819	A106	$2.50 multicolored	4.00	4.75
		Nos. 816-819 (4)	9.75	8.85
		Souvenir Sheet		
820	A106	$6 multicolored	13.00	14.00

Stamp World London '90, Penny Black 150th anniv.

Nos. 803-806 Overprinted

a

b

c

d

$1, Katy. $1.35, Mutton grouper. $2.50, Doctor fish. $5, Angelfish.

1990, Sept. 24		**Litho.**	**Perf. 13½x14**	
821	A104(a)	$1 multi	2.25	1.40
822	A104(b)	$1.35 multi	2.50	1.60
823	A104(c)	$2.50 multi	6.00	6.00
824	A104(d)	$5 multi	11.50	11.50
		Nos. 821-824 (4)	22.25	20.50

Christmas — A107

Birds.

1990, Dec. 3			**Perf. 14**	
825	A107	10c Laughing gull	.95	.55
826	A107	35c Brown booby	1.60	.55
827	A107	$1.50 Bridled tern	2.25	2.75
828	A107	$3.50 Brown pelican	5.00	5.00
		Nos. 825-828 (4)	9.80	8.85
		Souvenir Sheet		
829	A107	$6 Least tern	10.00	10.00

Flags
A108

50c, Mermaid. 80c, New Anguilla official. $1, Three dolphins. $5, Governor's official.

1990, Nov. 5		**Litho.**	**Perf. 13½x14**	
830	A108	50c multicolored	1.75	1.25
831	A108	80c multicolored	2.75	1.25
832	A108	$1 multicolored	2.90	1.50
833	A108	$5 multicolored	8.25	7.75
		Nos. 830-833 (4)	15.65	11.15

Nos. 811-815 Inscribed or Overprinted

1991, Apr. 30		**Litho.**	**Perf. 14x13½**	
834	A105	35c like #811	1.25	.75
835	A105	45c like #812	1.50	.75
836	A105	$1.35 like #813	3.00	3.00
837	A105	$2.50 like #814	5.25	5.25
		Nos. 834-837 (4)	11.00	9.75
		Souvenir Sheet		
838	A105	$6 like #815	14.00	14.00

Easter. "1990" obliterated by black bar in souvenir sheet margin.

Christmas — A109

5c, Angel, vert. 35c, Santa, vert. $1, Palm trees, poinsettias.
$5, Homes, holly.

Perf. 14x13½, 13½x14			
1991, Dec.			**Litho.**
839	A109	5c multicolored	.75 .90
840	A109	35c multicolored	2.00 .75
841	A109	80c shown	3.00 2.75
842	A109	$1 multicolored	3.00 2.75
		Nos. 839-842 (4)	8.75 7.15
		Souvenir Sheet	
843	A109	$5 multicolored	11.00 11.00

Easter
A110

Designs: 35c, Church, angels holding palms, vert. 45c, Church, angels singing, vert. 80c, Village. $1, People going to church, vert. $5, People at beach, sailboats.

1992		**Litho.**	**Perf. 14**	
844	A110	35c multicolored	1.00	.65
845	A110	45c multicolored	1.25	.65
846	A110	80c multicolored	2.25	1.10
847	A110	$1 multicolored	2.25	1.60
848	A110	$5 multicolored	6.25	12.00
		Nos. 844-848 (5)	13.00	16.00

No. 796 Surcharged

1992, June 10		**Litho.**	**Perf. 13½x14**	
849	A104	$1.60 on 30c #796	3.75	2.75

No. 849 inscribed "1992."

Independence, 25th Anniv. — A111

80c, Official seal, flag. $1, Official seal. $1.60, Flags, airport. $2, First seal.
$10, #1, 8-11, 15-16.

1992, Aug. 10		**Litho.**	**Perf. 14**	
850	A111	80c multicolored	2.50	1.50
851	A111	$1 multicolored	2.50	1.50
852	A111	$1.60 multicolored	4.75	4.75
853	A111	$2 multicolored	4.75	4.75
		Nos. 850-853 (4)	14.50	12.50
		Souvenir Sheet		
854	A111	$10 multicolored	15.00	15.00

No. 854 contains one 85x85mm stamp. For booklet see No. 970.

Sailboat Racing — A112

Designs: 20c, On course. 35c, Stylized boat poster. 45c, Start of race. No. 858, Blue Bird, 1971, vert. No. 859, Construction plans for Blue Bird, vert. $1, Stylized boat poster, diff. $6, Like Nos. 855 & 857.

Perf. 13½x14, 14x13½				
1992, Oct. 12			**Litho.**	
855	A112	20c multicolored	1.90	.60
856	A112	35c multicolored	2.40	.60
857	A112	45c multicolored	2.75	.50
858	A112	80c multicolored	3.75	4.00
859	A112	80c multicolored	3.75	4.00
a.		*Pair, #858-859*	8.00	10.00
860	A112	$1 multicolored	3.75	2.50
		Nos. 855-860 (6)	18.30	12.10
		Souvenir Sheet		
861	A112	$6 multicolored	11.00	11.00

No. 861 contains one 96x31mm stamp.

Discovery of America, 500th Anniv.
A113

80c, Landfall. $1, Columbus, vert. $2, Fleet. $3, Pinta.
$6, Map of voyage, vert.

1992, Dec. 15		**Litho.**	**Perf. 14**	
862	A113	80c multicolored	3.25	1.75
863	A113	$1 multicolored	3.25	1.75
864	A113	$2 multicolored	5.25	5.50
865	A113	$3 multicolored	6.00	7.00
		Nos. 862-865 (4)	17.75	16.00
		Souvenir Sheet		
866	A113	$6 multicolored	15.50	15.50

Christmas
A114

Various Christmas trees and: 20c, Mucka Jumbie on stilts. 70c, Masquerading house to house. $1.05, Christmas baking, old oven style. $2.40, $5, Collecting presents.

1992, Dec. 7				
867	A114	20c multicolored	.90	.65
868	A114	70c multicolored	2.00	.95
869	A114	$1.05 multicolored	2.25	1.75
870	A114	$2.40 multicolored	4.25	6.00
		Nos. 867-870 (4)	9.40	9.35
		Souvenir Sheet		
871	A114	$5 Sheet of 1 + 3 labels	7.50	7.50

Labels on No. 871 are similar to Nos. 867-869, but without denomination.

Easter — A115

Children's drawings: 20c, Kite flying. 45c, Cliff top village service. 80c, Morning devotion on Sombrero. $1.50, Hilltop church service. $5, Good Friday kites.

1993, Mar. 29		**Litho.**	**Perf. 14**	
872	A115	20c multicolored	1.75	.90
873	A115	45c multicolored	2.75	.90
874	A115	80c multicolored	4.00	2.10
875	A115	$1.50 multicolored	5.50	7.00
		Nos. 872-875 (4)	14.00	10.90
		Souvenir Sheet		
876	A115	$5 multicolored	9.00	9.00

No. 876 contains one 42x56mm stamp.

Native Industries
A116

1993, June 23		**Litho.**	**Perf. 14**	
877	A116	20c Salt	3.25	1.10
878	A116	80c Tobacco	3.25	1.75
879	A116	$1 Cotton	3.25	1.75
880	A116	$2 Sugar cane	4.75	6.50
		Nos. 877-880 (4)	14.50	11.10
		Souvenir Sheet		
881	A116	$6 Fishing	14.50	14.50

Coronation of Queen Elizabeth II, 40th Anniv. — A117

Designs: 80c, Lord Great Chamberlain presents the spurs of chivalry. $1, The benediction. $2, Queen Elizabeth II, coronation photograph. $3, St. Edward's Crown. $6, Queen, Prince Philip in Gold State Coach.

1993, Aug. 16   Litho.   *Perf. 14*
882	A117	80c multicolored	2.25	1.00
883	A117	$1 multicolored	2.50	1.10
884	A117	$2 multicolored	3.25	3.25
885	A117	$3 multicolored	3.75	4.75
		Nos. 882-885 (4)	11.75	10.10

Souvenir Sheet
886	A117	$6 multicolored	15.00	16.00

Anguilla Carnival — A118

20c, Pan musician. 45c, Pirates. 80c, Stars. $1, Playing mas. $2, Masqueraders. $3, Commandos. $5, Carnival fantasy.

1993, Aug. 23   Litho.   *Perf. 14*
887	A118	20c multicolored	.70	.50
888	A118	45c multicolored	1.25	.50
889	A118	80c multicolored	2.40	1.10
890	A118	$1 multicolored	2.40	1.25
		Booklet, 5 ea #796, 890	13.75	
891	A118	$2 multicolored	3.75	5.50
892	A118	$3 multicolored	4.50	6.25
		Nos. 887-892 (6)	15.00	15.10

Souvenir Sheet
893	A118	$5 multicolored	15.00	15.00

Christmas A119

Traditional Christmas customs: 20c, Mucka Jumbies. 35c, Serenaders. 45c, Baking. $3, Five-fingers Christmas tree. $4, Mucka Jumbies and serenaders.

1993, Dec. 7   Litho.   *Perf. 14x13½*
894	A119	20c multicolored	1.10	.90
895	A119	35c multicolored	1.50	.90
896	A119	45c multicolored	1.75	.90
897	A119	$3 multicolored	6.25	8.00
		Nos. 894-897 (4)	10.60	10.70

Souvenir Sheet
Perf. 14
898	A119	$4 multicolored	5.25	5.25

No. 898 contains one 54x42mm stamp.

Mail Delivery — A120

Designs: 20c, Traveling Branch mail van, Sandy Ground, horiz. 45c, Mail boat, Betsy R, The Forest. 80c, Old post office, horiz. $1, Mail by jeep, Island Harbor. $4, New post office, 1993, horiz.

1994, Feb. 11   Litho.   *Perf. 14*
899	A120	20c multicolored	2.00	.95
900	A120	45c multicolored	2.75	.95
901	A120	80c multicolored	3.50	1.90
902	A120	$1 multicolored	3.50	1.90
903	A120	$4 multicolored	5.50	8.75
		Nos. 899-903 (5)	17.25	14.45

Royal Visits — A121

45c, Princess Alexandra. 50c, Princess Alice. 80c, Prince Philip. $1, Prince Charles. $2, Queen Elizabeth II.

1994, Feb. 18
904	A121	45c multicolored	2.00	.80
905	A121	50c multicolored	2.25	.80
906	A121	80c multicolored	3.00	1.75
907	A121	$1 multicolored	3.50	1.75
908	A121	$2 multicolored	4.75	5.50
a.		Souvenir sheet of 4, #904-908	15.00	15.00
		Nos. 904-908 (5)	15.50	10.60

Easter — A122

Stained glass windows: 20c, Crucifixion. 45c, Empty tomb. 80c, Resurrection. $3, Risen Christ with disciples.

1994, Apr. 6   Litho.   *Perf. 14x15*
909	A122	20c multicolored	.90	.65
910	A122	45c multicolored	1.10	.80
911	A122	80c multicolored	2.10	1.10
912	A122	$3 multicolored	5.50	6.25
		Nos. 909-912 (4)	9.60	8.80

Christmas — A123

Designs: 20c, Adoration of the shepherds. 30c, Magi, shepherds. 35c, The Annunciation. 45c, Nativity Scene. $2.40, Flight into Egypt.

1994, Nov. 22   Litho.   *Perf. 14*
913	A123	20c multicolored	1.00	.80
914	A123	30c multicolored	1.25	.80
915	A123	35c multicolored	1.25	.80
916	A123	45c multicolored	1.50	.80
917	A123	$2.40 multicolored	4.50	5.50
		Nos. 913-917 (5)	9.50	8.70

1994 World Cup Soccer Championships, US — A124

Soccer player and: 20c, Pontiac Silverdome, Detroit. 70c, Foxboro Stadium, Boston. $1.80, RFK Memorial Stadium, Washington. $2.40, Soldier Field, Chicago. $6, Two players.

1994, Oct. 3   Litho.   *Perf. 13½x14*
918	A124	20c multicolored	1.00	.50
919	A124	70c multicolored	1.50	1.10
920	A124	$1.80 multicolored	3.00	3.25
921	A124	$2.40 multicolored	3.50	4.00
		Nos. 918-921 (4)	9.00	8.85

Souvenir Sheet
922	A124	$6 multicolored	14.00	14.00

Easter A125

Turtle dove: 45c, One on tree branch. 50c, One on nest, one on branch. $5, Mother with young.

1995, Apr. 10   Litho.   *Perf. 14*
923	A125	20c multicolored	.70	.60
924	A125	45c multicolored	1.10	.90
925	A125	50c multicolored	1.25	1.10
926	A125	$5 multicolored	8.00	11.00
		Nos. 923-926 (4)	11.05	13.60

UN, 50th Anniv. A126

Secretaries general and: 20c, Trygve Lie (1946-53), general assembly. 80c, UN flag, UN headquarters with "50" (no portrait). $1, Dag Hammarskjold (1953-61), charter, U Thant (1961-71). $5, UN complex, New York, vert. (no portrait).

Perf. 13½x14, 14x13½
1995, June 26   Litho.
927	A126	20c multicolored	.40	.40
928	A126	80c multicolored	.80	.80
929	A126	$1 multicolored	1.00	1.00
930	A126	$5 multicolored	5.25	5.25
		Nos. 927-930 (4)	7.45	7.45

Caribbean Development Bank, 25th Anniv. — A127

Designs: 45c, Emblem, map of Anguilla. $5, Local headquarters along waterfront.

1995, Aug. 15   Litho.   *Perf. 13½x14*
931	A127	45c multicolored	2.50	2.50
932	A127	$5 multicolored	5.25	5.25
a.		Pair, #931-932	8.00	8.00

Whales — A128

20c, Blue whale. 45c, Right whale, vert. $1, Sperm whale. $5, Humpback whale.

Perf. 13½x14, 14x13½
1995, Nov. 24   Litho.
933	A128	20c multicolored	2.75	.95
934	A128	45c multicolored	3.00	.80
935	A128	$1 multicolored	3.75	2.10
936	A128	$5 multicolored	9.50	11.50
		Nos. 933-936 (4)	19.00	15.35

Christmas A129

1995, Dec. 12   *Perf. 14½*
937	A129	10c Palm tree	.80	.80
938	A129	25c Fish net floats	1.10	.65
939	A129	45c Sea shells	1.25	.65
940	A129	$5 Fish	9.50	12.00
		Nos. 937-940 (4)	12.65	14.10

Corals A130

20c, Deep water gorgonia. 80c, Common sea fan. $5, Venus sea fern.

1996, June 21   Litho.   *Perf. 14x14½*
941	A130	20c multicolored	2.00	.95
942	A130	80c multicolored	3.25	1.40
943	A130	$5 multicolored	9.50	11.25
		Nos. 941-943 (3)	14.75	13.60

A131

1996 Summer Olympic Games, Atlanta: 20c, Running. 80c, Javelin, wheelchair basketball. $1, High jump. $3.50, Olympic torch, Greek, US flags.

1996, Dec. 12   Litho.   *Perf. 14*
944	A131	20c multicolored	.95	.75
945	A131	80c multicolored	3.25	1.50
946	A131	$1 multicolored	2.25	1.50
947	A131	$3.50 multicolored	6.00	7.00
		Nos. 944-947 (4)	12.45	10.75

A132

Battle for Anguilla, bicent.: 60c, Sandy Hill Fort, HMS Lapwing. 75c, French troops destroy church, horiz. $1.50, HMS Lapwing defeats Valiant, Decius, horiz. $4, French troops land, Rendezvous Bay.

1996, Dec. 12
948	A132	60c multicolored	1.25	1.25
949	A132	75c multicolored	1.25	1.25
950	A132	$1.50 multicolored	2.50	2.50
951	A132	$4 multicolored	4.25	4.25
		Nos. 948-951 (4)	9.25	9.25

Fruits and Nuts A133

10c, Gooseberry. 20c, West Indian cherry. 40c, Tamarind. 50c, Pomme-surette. 60c, Sea almond. 75c, Sea grape. 80c, Banana. $1, Genip. $1.10, Coco plum. $1.25, Pope. $1.50, Papaya. $2, Sugar apple. $3, Soursop. $4, Pomegrante. $5, Cashew. $10, Mango.

1997, Apr. 30   Litho.   Perf. 14
952	A133	10c multicolored	.25	.50
953	A133	20c multicolored	.25	.40
954	A133	40c multicolored	.35	.40
955	A133	50c multicolored	.55	.50
956	A133	60c multicolored	.65	.60
957	A133	75c multicolored	.90	.80
958	A133	80c multicolored	.95	.90
959	A133	$1 multicolored	1.25	1.25
960	A133	$1.10 multicolored	1.50	1.75
961	A133	$1.25 multicolored	1.75	1.90
962	A133	$1.50 multicolored	1.90	1.90
963	A133	$2 multicolored	2.50	2.50
964	A133	$3 multicolored	4.00	4.00
965	A133	$4 multicolored	5.25	5.50
966	A133	$5 multicolored	6.25	6.00
967	A133	$10 multicolored	10.00	10.50
		Nos. 952-967 (16)	38.30	39.40

Iguanas — A134

World Wildlife Fund: a, 20c, Baby iguanas emerging from eggs, juvenile iguana. b, 50c, Adult on rock. c, 75c, Two iguanas on tree limbs. d, $3, Adult up close, adult on tree branch.

1997, Oct. 13   Litho.   Perf. 13½x14
968	A134	Strip of 4, #a.-d.	10.00	9.75

Diana, Princess of Wales (1961-97) — A135

Designs: a, 15c, In red & white. b, $1, In yellow. c, $1.90, Wearing tiara. d, $2.25, Wearing blouse with Red Cross emblem.

1998, Apr. 14   Litho.   Perf. 14
969	A135	Strip of 4, #a.-d.	11.00	11.00

No. 969 was issued in sheets of 16 stamps.

Fountain Cavern Carvings A136

30c, Rainbow Deity (Juluca). $1.25, Lizard. $2.25, Solar Chieftan. $2.75, Creator.

1997, Nov. 17   Litho.   Perf. 14x14½
970	A136	30c multicolored	.55	.55
		Booklet, 5 ea #851, 970	12.00	
971	A136	$1.25 multicolored	1.25	1.25
972	A136	$2.25 multicolored	2.10	2.10
973	A136	$2.75 multicolored	2.75	2.75
		Nos. 970-973 (4)	6.65	6.65

1998 Intl. Arts Festival A137

Paintings: 15c, "Treasure Island." 30c, "Posing in the Light." $1, "Pescadores de Anguilla." $1.50, "Fresh Catch." $1.90, "The Bell Tower of St. Mary's."

1998, Aug. 24   Litho.   Perf. 14
974	A137	15c multi	.65	.65
975	A137	30c multi, vert.	.80	.80
976	A137	$1 multi, vert.	1.40	1.40
		Booklet, 5 ea #975-976	10.00	
977	A137	$1.50 multi	1.60	1.60
978	A137	$1.90 multi, vert.	2.00	2.00
		Nos. 974-978 (5)	6.45	6.45

Christmas A138

Paintings of "Hidden beauty of Anguilla": 15c, Woman cooking over open fire, girl seated on steps. $1, Person looking over fruits and vegetables. $1.50, Underwater scene. $3, Cacti growing along shore.

1998
979	A138	15c multicolored	.50	.50
980	A138	$1 multicolored	1.00	1.00
981	A138	$1.50 multicolored	1.40	1.40
982	A138	$3 multicolored	2.10	2.10
		Nos. 979-982 (4)	5.00	5.00

Royal Air Force, 80th Anniv. A139

Designs: 30c, Sopwith Camel, Bristol F2B. $1, Supermarine Spitfire II, Hawker Hurricane Mk1. $1.50, Avro Lancaster. $1.90, Harrier GR7, Panavia Tornado F3.

1998   Litho.   Perf. 13½
Granite Paper (No. 983)
983	A139	30c multicolored	1.25	.60
984	A139	$1 multicolored	2.00	1.00
985	A139	$1.50 multicolored	2.50	2.25
986	A139	$1.90 multicolored	4.00	3.25
		Booklet, 5 ea #983-984	16.50	
		Nos. 983-986 (4)	9.75	7.10

University of the West Indies, 50th Anniv. — A140

Designs: $1.50, Anguilla campus. $1.90, Anguilla campus, torchbearer, University arms.

1998   Litho.   Perf. 13¼
Granite Paper (#988)
987-988	A140	Set of 2	2.75	3.25

First Manned Moon Landing, 30th Anniv. — A141

Designs: 30c, Lift-off of Apollo 11, Command and Service Modules in lunar orbit. $1, Buzz Aldrin on Moon, footprint. $1.50, Lunar Module leaving Moon. $1.90, Splashdown.

1999, May 6   Litho.   Perf. 13¾
989	A141	30c multi	.80	.50
990	A141	$1 multi	1.40	.90
991	A141	$1.50 multi	1.50	1.75
992	A141	$1.90 multi	2.50	3.25
		Nos. 989-992 (4)	6.20	6.40

Heroes of Anguilla's Revolution A142

Designs: 30c, Albena Lake Hodge (1920-85). $1, Collins O. Hodge (1926-78). $1.50, Edwin W. Rey (1906-80). $1.90, Walter G. Hodge (1920-89).

1999, July 5   Perf. 14½x14¼
993	A142	30c multi	.50	.30
994	A142	$1 multi	.90	.60
995	A142	$1.50 multi	1.25	1.25
996	A142	$1.90 multi	1.90	2.00
		Nos. 993-996 (4)	4.55	4.15

Modern Architecture A143

Designs: No. 997, 30c, Library and resource center. No. 998, 65c, Parliamentary building and court house. No. 999, $1, Caribbean Commercial Bank. No. 999A, $1.50, Police headquarters. No. 1000, $1.90, Post office.

1999   Litho.   Perf. 14x14½
997-1000	A143	Set of 5	7.50	7.75

Christmas and Millennium Celebrations — A144

Designs: 30c, Fireworks display and barbecue. $1, Globe, musicians. $1.50, Family dinner. $1.90, Decorated tree.

1999   Litho.   Perf. 13¼
1001	A144	30c multi	.55	.50
1002	A144	$1 multi	1.40	.90
1003	A144	$1.50 multi	2.10	2.10
1004	A144	$1.90 multi	2.25	3.75
		Nos. 1001-1004 (4)	6.30	7.25

Beaches — A145

1005, 15c, Shoal Bay. 1006, 30c, Maundys Bay. 1007, $1, Rendezvous Bay. 1008, $1.50, Meads Bay. 1009, $1.90, Little Bay. 1010, $2, Sandy Ground.

1999   Perf. 12
1005-1010	A145	Set of 6	8.75	8.75
a.		Sheet of 6, #1005-1010	8.75	8.75
b.		As "a," with show emblem in margin	8.00	8.25

The Stamp Show 2000, London (No. 1010b). Issued: No. 1010b, 5/22/00.

Easter A146

Toys: 25c, Banjo. 30c, Top. $1.50, Slingshot. $1.90, Roller. $2.50, Killy ban.
No. 1016: a, 75c, Rag doll. b, $1, Kite. c, $1.25, Cricket ball. d, $4, Pond boat.

2000   Perf. 13¼
1011	A146	25c multi	.25	.25
1012	A146	30c multi	.35	.35
1013	A146	$1.50 multi	1.25	1.25
1014	A146	$1.90 multi	1.75	2.25
1015	A146	$2.50 multi	2.40	3.00
		Nos. 1011-1015 (5)	6.00	7.10
		Souvenir Sheet		
1016	A146	Sheet of 4, #a-d	6.25	6.25

100th Test Match at Lord's Ground — A147

$2, Lanville Harrigan. $4, Cardigan Connor. $6, Lord's Ground, horiz.

2000, May 5   Litho.   Perf. 13¾x13¼
1017-1018	A147	Set of 2	7.75	7.75
		Souvenir Sheet		
1018A	A147	$6 multi	12.00	12.00

Prince William, 18th Birthday — A148

Prince William and: 30c, Queen Elizabeth II, Princes Philip and Charles. $1, Princess Diana, Princes Harry and Charles. $1.90, Princes Harry and Charles. $2.25, Princes Charles and Harry, in winter wear. $8, Prince William, vert.

2000, July 20   Perf. 13¼
1019-1022	A148	Set of 4	9.25	9.25
		Souvenir Sheet		
1023	A148	$8 multicolored	9.75	10.00

Queen Mother, 100th Birthday — A149

Queen Mother and: 30c, Prince William. $1.50, Anguilla shoreline. $1.90, Clarence House. $5, Castle of Mey.

2000, Aug. 4
1024-1027	A149	Set of 4	9.00	9.00

Intl. Arts Festival A150

Artwork: 15c, Anguilla Montage, by Weme Caster. 30c, Serenity, by Damien Carty. 65c, Inter-island Cargo, by Paula Walden. $1.50, Rainbow City Where Spirits Find Form, by

Fiona Percy. $1.90, Sailing Silver Seas, by Valerie Carpenter.
$7, Historic Anguilla, by Melsadis Fleming.

2000, Sept. 21   *Perf. 14¼x14½*
1028-1032 A150 Set of 5   5.25 5.25
Souvenir Sheet
Perf. 14¼
1033 A150 $7 multi   6.75 6.75

No. 1033 contains one 43x28mm stamp.

Christmas
A151

Flower and Garden Show flower arrangements by: 15c, Rowena Carty. 25c, Yvonda Hodge. 30c, Carty, diff. $1, Simon Rogers. $1.50, Lady Josephine Gumbs. $1.90, Carty, diff.

2000, Nov. 22   *Perf. 13¼*
1034-1039 A151 Set of 6   7.25 8.00

Natl. Bank of Anguilla, 15th
Anniv. — A152

Designs: 30c, Soccer team in annual primary school tournament. $1, Sponsored sailboat, De Chan, vert. $1.50, Bank's crest, vert. $1.90, New bank building.

2000, Nov. 27   *Perf. 13¼*
1040-1043 A152 Set of 4   5.50 6.00

Ebenezer Methodist Church, 170th
Anniv. — A153

Church in: 30c, Sepia tones. $1.90, Full color.

2000, Dec. 4
1044-1045 A153 Set of 2   2.75 3.25

UN Women's Human Rights
Campaign — A154

Designs: 25c, Soroptimist Day Care Center. 30c, Britannia Idalia Gumbs, vert. $2.25, Woman, vert.

2001   *Litho.*   *Perf. 13¼*
1046-1048 A154 Set of 3   3.50 4.00

American Revolution, 225th
Anniv. — A155

Designs: 30c, John Paul Jones, USS Ranger. $1, George Washington, Battle of Yorktown. $1.50, Thomas Jefferson, Submission of Declaration of Independence. $1.90, John Adams, Adams and Benjamin Franklin signing peace treaty.

2001, July 4   *Litho.*   *Perf. 13¼*
1049-1052 A155 Set of 4   7.75 8.00

Birds
A156

Designs: 30c, White-cheeked pintail. $1, Black-faced grassquits, vert. $1.50, Brown noddy. $2, Black-necked stilts, vert. $3, Snowy plovers.
No. 1058: a, 25c, Snowy egret. b, 65c, Red-billed tropicbird. $1.35, Greater yellowlegs. $2.25, Sooty tern.

2001, Aug. 7
1053-1057 A156 Set of 5   13.00 13.00
Souvenir Sheet
1058 A156 Sheet of 4, #a-d   10.00 10.00

Year of Dialogue Among Civilizations
A157

2001, Oct. 9   *Perf. 13¼x13*
1059 A157 $1.90 multi   2.50 2.75

Christmas — A158

Musical instruments: 15c, Triangle. 25c, Maracas. 30c, Guiro, vert. $1.50, Marimba. $1.90, Tambu, vert. $2.50, Bath pan, vert.
No. 1066, vert.: a, 75c, Banjo. b, $1, Quatro. c, $1.25, Ukulele. d, $3, Cello.

2001, Nov. 5   *Litho.*   *Perf. 13¼*
1060-1065 A158 Set of 6   8.75 8.75
Souvenir Sheet
1066 A158 Sheet of 4, #a-d   7.75 8.25

Sombrero Lighthouse — A159

Designs: 30c, Lighhouse in 1960s, vert. $1.50, Comparison of old and new lighthouses. $1.90, New lighthouse, 2001, vert.

2002, Apr. 2   *Litho.*   *Perf. 13¼*
1067-1069 A159 Set of 3   6.50 6.50

Social Security Board, 20th
Anniv. — A160

Social Security: 30c, Community service, vert. 75c, Benefits all ages, vert. $2.50, Benefits employees.

2002, May 28   *Litho.*   *Perf. 13¼*
1070-1072 A160 Set of 3   5.00 5.00

Royal Navy Ships
A161

Designs: 30c, HMS Antrim, 1967. 50c, HMS Formidable, 1939. $1.50, HMS Dreadnought, 1906. $2, HMS Warrior, 1860.
$7, HMS Ark Royal, 1981, vert.

2002, June 24   *Litho.*   *Perf. 13¼*
1073-1076 A161 Set of 4   6.25 6.25
Souvenir Sheet
1077 A161 $7 multi   10.00 10.00

Reign of Queen Elizabeth II, 50th
Anniv. — A162

Designs: 30c, Holding baby. $1.50, Wearing white dress. $1.90, Wearing tiara. $5, Wearing yellow hat.
$8, At desk.

2002, Oct. 14   *Litho.*   *Perf. 13¼*
1078-1081 A162 Set of 4   8.50 8.50
Souvenir Sheet
1082 A162 $8 multi   9.00 10.50

Pan-American Health Organization,
Cent. — A163

Designs: 30c, The Valley Health Center. $1.50, Emblem, "100."

2002, Nov. 11
1083-1084 A163 Set of 2   2.50 2.50

Ships
A164

15c, Finance. 30c, Tiny Gull. 65c, Lady Laurel. 75c, Spitfire. $1, Liberator. $1.35, Excelsior. $1.50, Rose Millicent. $1.90, Betsy R. $2, Sunbeam R. $2.25, New London. $3, Ismay. $10, Warspite.

2003, June 10   *Litho.*   *Perf. 14*
1085 A164 15c multi   .25 .25
1086 A164 30c multi   .25 .25
1087 A164 65c multi   .65 .65
1088 A164 75c multi   .85 .75
1089 A164 $1 multi   1.00 1.00
1090 A164 $1.35 multi   1.50 1.50
1091 A164 $1.50 multi   1.75 1.60
1092 A164 $1.90 multi   2.00 1.90
1093 A164 $2 multi   2.25 2.00
1094 A164 $2.25 multi   3.00 2.50
1095 A164 $3 multi   3.25 3.25
1096 A164 $10 multi   10.00 11.00
Nos. 1085-1096 (12)   26.75 26.65

Artifacts — A165

Designs: 30c, Stone pestle. $1, Frog-shaped shell ornament. $1.50, Pottery. $1.90, Mask.

2003, Aug. 18   *Litho.*   *Perf. 13¼*
1097-1100 A165 Set of 4   5.25 5.25

Hotels
A166

Designs: 75c, Frangipani Beach Club. $1, Pimms, Cap Juluca. $1.35, Cocoloba Beach Resort. $1.50, Malliouhana Hotel. $1.90, Carimar Beach Club. $3, Covecastles.

2003   *Litho.*   *Perf. 13¼*
1101-1106 A166 Set of 6   8.50 8.50

2002 International Arts
Festival — A167

Paintings: 15c, Eudice's Garden, by Eunice Summer. 30c, Hammocks, by Lisa Davenport. $1, Conched Out, by Richard Shaffett. $1.50, Island Rhythms, by Carol Gavin. $1.90, Party at the Beach, by Jean-Pierre Ballagny. $3, Shoal Bay Before Luis, by Jacqueline Mariethoz, vert.

Perf. 13½x13¼, 13¼x13½
2004, Aug. 23   *Litho.*
1107-1112 A167 Set of 6   11.00 11.00

2004 Summer Olympics,
Athens — A168

2004 Athens Olympics emblem and: 30c, Runners. $1, Yachting. $1.50, Gymnastics. $1.90, Acropolis, Pierre de Coubertin, Dimitrios Vikelas, horiz.

Perf. 13½x13¼, 13¼x13½
2004, Sept. 20   *Litho.*
1113-1116 A168 Set of 4   6.25 6.25

Goats
A169

Various goats: 30c, 50c, $1, $1.50, $1.90, $2.25. $1, $1.90 are vert.

Perf. 13¼x13½, 13½x13¼
2004, Oct. 4
1117-1122 A169 Set of 6   9.50 9.50

Development of
the Telephone
A170

Types of telephones: 30c, Cordless. $1, Touch-tone. $1.50, Cellular. $1.90, Rotary dial, horiz. $3.80, Magneto.

Perf. 13¼x13, 13x13¼
2004, Nov. 8   **Litho.**
1123-1127 A170 Set of 5   8.00 8.00

Christmas
A171

Santa Claus: 30c, Baking with rock oven. $1.50, Climbing coconut tree. $1.90, With string band. $3.80, Delivering gifts by donkey. $8, Delivering gifts by boat.

2004, Nov. 15   **Perf. 13x13¼**
1128-1131 A171 Set of 4   6.75 6.75
Souvenir Sheet
1132 A171 $8 multi   7.00 7.00

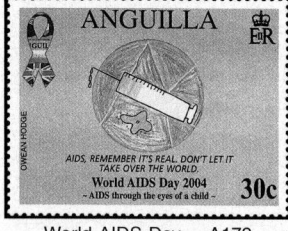

World AIDS Day — A172

Children's drawings by: 30c, Owean Hodge. $1.50, Lydia Fleming. $1.90, Nina Rodriguez. No. 1136: a, 15c, Kenswick Richardson. b, 75c, Toniquewah Ruan. c, $1, Elizabeth Anne Orchard. d, $2, Tricia Watty-Beard.

2004, Dec. 1   **Perf. 13**
1133-1135 A172 Set of 3   4.00 4.00
Souvenir Sheet
1136 A172 Sheet of 4, #a-d   4.00 4.00

Rotary
International,
Cent. — A173

Designs: 30c, Emblem of Anguilla Rotary Club. $1, Pelican and palm tree. $1.50, Rotary

International founder Paul Harris. $1.90, Children at playground.

2005   **Litho.**   **Perf. 14¾x14¼**
1137-1140 A173 Set of 4   4.25 4.25

Dogs
A174

Designs: 30c, Dog in field. $1.50, Two dogs sitting, vert. $1.90, Dog sitting, vert. $2.25, Dog.

2005   **Perf. 14¼x14¾, 14¾x14¼**
1141-1144 A174 Set of 4   5.00 5.00

Commercial Airplanes — A175

Designs: 30c, Air Anguilla Cessna 402. 40c, LIAT DHC Dash 8. 60c, Winair Foxtrot-DHC Twin Otter. $1, Anguilla Airways Piper Aztec. $1.50, St. Thomas Air Transport Piper Aztec. $1.90, Carib Air Service Piper Aztec.

2006, Mar. 13   **Litho.**   **Perf. 13¼**
1145-1150 A175 Set of 6   6.50 6.50

Butterflies — A176

Designs: 30c, Appias drusillia. $1.50, Danaus plexippus megalippe. $1.90, Phoebis sennae. $2.75, Papilio demoleus.
No. 1155: a, 40c, Aphrissa statira. b, 60c, Eurema elathea. c, $1, Danaus plexippus megalippe, diff. d, $3, Agraulis vanillae.

2006, Oct. 9   **Litho.**   **Perf. 13¼**
1151-1154 A176 Set of 4   6.75 6.75
Miniature Sheet
1155 A176 Sheet of 4, #a-d   5.25 5.25

Anguilla
Soroptomist
Club, 25th
Anniv. — A177

Designs: $1.90, Soroptomist International emblem. $2.75, Alecia Ballin.

2007, Jan. 29
1156-1157 A177 Set of 2   4.75 4.75

Bronze
Devotional
Medallions From
El Buen
Consuelo
Shipwreck
A178

Medallions depicting: 30c, St. Bruno. $1.50, Our Lady of Sorrows. $1.90, Five Wounds of Jesus. $2.75, Virgin and Child.

2007, Mar. 19   **Litho.**   **Perf. 13¼**
1158-1161 A178 Set of 4   5.75 5.75

Anguilla
Revolution, 40th
Anniv. — A179

Participants: 30c, Hyacinth Carty. $1, Edward Duncan. $1.50, Connell Harrigan. $1.90, Rev. Leonard Carty. $2.25, Jeremiah Gumbs. $3.75, Atlin Harrigan.

2007, July 18   **Litho.**   **Perf. 13¼**
1162-1167 A179 Set of 6   9.25 9.25

Historical Architecture — A180

Designs: 30c, Building with lean-to and gabled roof, by Melsadis Fleming. $1, Building with lean-to and gabled roof, by Daryl Thompson. $1.25, Building with double-hipped roof, by Fleming. $1.50, Building with hipped roof, by Susan Croft. $1.90, Building with double-gabled roof, by Fleming. $2.40, Building with double-hipped roof, by Fleming, diff. $2.75, Building with hipped roof, by Fleming. $3.75, Building with gabled roof, by Fleming.

2008, Oct. 6   **Perf. 14x14¾**
1168-1175 A180 Set of 8   9.00 9.00

Traditional Household Items — A181

Designs: 30c, Three-legged pot. $1, Mortar and pestle. $1.50, Gas and coal irons. $1.90, Oil and gas lamps. $2, Coal pots. $2.25, Enamel and aluminum utensils.

2009, June 18   **Perf. 13¼**
1176-1181 A181 Set of 6   6.75 6.75

Wild
Flowers — A182

Designs: 30c, Tabebulia heterophylla. $1, Argemone mexicana. $1.50, Catharanthus roseus. $1.90, Datura stramonium. $2, Centrosena virginiatum. $2.25, Tetramicra canaliculata.

2009, Sept. 12
1182-1187 A182 Set of 6   6.75 6.75

Endemic Flora and Fauna — A183

Designs: $1.50, Sombrero Island ground lizard. $2, Little Scrub Island ground lizard. $2.25, Anguilla bush.

2010, Aug. 10   **Perf. 13¼**
1188-1190 A183 Set of 3   4.50 4.50

Wedding of
Prince William
and Catherine
Middleton
A184

Designs: $4, Couple. $5, Couple, horiz. $6, Couple, diff. $10, Couple and royal arms, horiz.

2011, June 20   **Litho.**   **Perf. 13¼**
1191-1194 A184 Set of 4   18.50 18.50

Anguilla Revolutionary Coins — A185

Designs: 15c, 1967 Liberty dollar counterstruck on Panamanian balboa. 40c, 1967 Liberty dollar counterstruck on Mexican peso. $2.50, Obverse and reverse of 1968 silver $25 coin commemorating first year of Independence. $5, Ship, reverse of 1969 $4 coin.

2012, Feb. 28   **Perf. 13½x13¼**
1195-1198 A185 Set of 4   6.00 6.00

Royal Anguilla Police Force, 40th
Anniv. — A186

Designs: 30c, Old Valley Police Station. $1, Police on parade. $1.50, Police headquarters. $1.90, Past and present police crests. $5, Lt. Col. Claudius M. Roberts, first Chief of Police, vert.

2012, Nov. 26   **Perf. 13¼**
1199-1203 A186 Set of 5   7.25 7.25

Methodism on Anguilla, 200th
Anniv. — A187

Designs: 40c, Old Methodist Manse, Sandy Ground. 65c, Map of Anguilla, 200th anniversary emblem. $10, Montage of Ebenezer and Bethel Churches, by Aileen Lamond-Smith.

2013, Nov. 11   **Litho.**   **Perf. 13¼**
1204-1206 A187 Set of 3   8.25 8.25

Ship
Captains — A188

Captains: 15c, George Richardson (1919-2003). 50c, James Woods (1908-98). 75c, Fritz Ericson Hughes (1891-1970). $1.35, Christopher John Connor (1925-94). $2, Herchel Gumbs (1884-1965). $2.25, Zilphus Fleming (1915-92). $2.50, Walter Hodge (1920-89). $5, John Franklin (1912-98).

2013, Nov. 25   Litho.   Perf. 13¼
1207-1214 A188   Set of 8   11.00 11.00
1214a   Sheet of 8, #1207-1214   11.00 11.00
           See Nos. 1219-1226.

Secondary
Education , 60th
Anniv. — A189

Designs: 15c, Boy's shirt and tie, 1950s. $1.35, Girl's uniform, 1950s. $2, James T. Thom, first principal of Valley Secondary School. $2.50, Valley Secondary School crest.

2013, Dec. 31   Litho.   Perf. 13¼
1215-1218 A189   Set of 4   4.50 4.50

Ship Captains Type of 2013

Designs: 50c, Harry S. Franklin (1926-2006). 65c, John A. Edwards (1910-75). 75c, Amos Richardson (1924-2004). 80c, George Joshua Gumbs (1926-2012). $2, Ivan Richardson (1917-67). $2.50, Edward Camile Connor (1910-2000). $3, Henry E. Richardson (1890-1990). $6, Malcolm C. Wathey (1905-84).

2014, July 7   Litho.   Perf. 13¼
1219-1226 A188   Set of 8   12.00 12.00
1226a   Souvenir sheet of 8,
           #1219-1226   12.00 12.00

Day Around the
Island Boat Race
Winning
Sailboats — A190

Designs: 50c, Real Deal, champion in 2011, 2012. 60c, Superstar, champion in 2004, 2007, 2009, horiz. 80c, Nathalie, champion in 1993, 1994, 1995. $1.35, UFO, champion in 1997, 1998, 2003, 2005, horiz. $3, De Tree, champion in 2001, 2006, 2008, 2010, 2013, horiz. $10, De Chan, champion in 1982-84, 1986, 1991-92, 1996, 2002.
No. 1233: a, 15c, Sonic, champion in 2014. b, 40c, Satellite, champion in 2000. c, 65c, Viagra, champion in 1999. d, 75c, Saga Boy, champion in 1990. e, $4, Wasp, champion in 1987.

2015, May 29   Litho.   Perf. 13¼
1227-1232 A190   Set of 6   12.00 12.00
           Souvenir Sheet
1233 A190   Sheet of 5, #a-e   4.50 4.50

Summer
Festival — A191

Designs: 50c, Calypso Show. $1, August Monday Beach Party, horiz. $1.40, Jouvert, horiz. $1.80, Woman in butterfly costume, horiz. $2.10, Parade, horiz. $3, Queen Show.

2016, Aug. 2   Litho.   Perf. 13¼
1234-1239 A191   Set of 6   7.25 7.25

ANJOUAN

'an-jü-wän

LOCATION — One of the Comoro Islands in the Mozambique Channel between Madagascar and Mozambique.
GOVT. — French colony.
AREA — 89 sq. mi.
POP. — 20,000 (approx. 1912)
CAPITAL — Mossamondu
        See Comoro Islands.

100 Centimes = 1 Franc

Navigation and
Commerce — A1

Perf. 14x13½
1892-1907   Typo.   Unwmk.
Name of Colony in Blue or Carmine
1   A1 1c black, *blue*   1.75   1.75
2   A1 2c brown, *buff*   2.75   1.75
3   A1 4c claret, *lav*   5.50   4.00
4   A1 5c green, *grnsh*   9.50   6.25
5   A1 10c blk, *lavender*   11.50   6.75
6   A1 10c red ('00)   37.50 30.00
7   A1 15c blue, quadrille
        paper   17.00 11.50
8   A1 15c gray, *lt
        gray*('00)   27.50 22.50
9   A1 20c red, *green*   17.50 11.00
10 A1 25c black, *rose*   17.50 14.00
11 A1 25c blue ('00)   30.00 22.50
12 A1 30c brn, *bister*   35.00 22.50
13 A1 35c blk, *yel* ('06)   18.00 10.00
14 A1 40c red, *straw*   37.50 32.50
15 A1 45c blk, *gray grn*
        ('07)   140.00 115.00
16 A1 50c car, *rose*   42.50 32.50
17 A1 50c brn, *az* ('00)   32.50 32.50
18 A1 75c vio, *orange*   37.50 27.50
19 A1 1fr brnz grn, *straw*   85.00 77.50
        Nos. 1-19 (19)   606.00 482.00

Perf. 13½x14 stamps are counterfeits.

**Issues of 1892-1907 Surcharged in
Black or Carmine**

1912
20 A1 5c on 2c brn,
        buff   1.25   1.25
21 A1 5c on 4c cl, *lav*
        (C)   1.40   1.50
a.   Pair, one without
       surcharge   1,000. 1,100.
22 A1 5c on 15c blue
        (C)   1.40   1.40
a.   Pair, one without
       surcharge   1,100. 1,000.
23 A1 5c on 20c red,
        green   1.40   1.40
a.   Pair, one without
       surcharge   1,100. 1,100.
24 A1 5c on 25c blk,
        rose (C)   1.50   1.75

25 A1 5c on 30c brn,
        bis (C)   2.00   2.10
26 A1 10c on 40c red,
        straw   2.00   2.25
27 A1 10c on 45c black,
        gray green
        (C)   2.40   2.40
28 A1 10c on 50c car,
        rose   5.75   6.50
29 A1 10c on 75c vio,
        org   4.00   4.50
30 A1 10c on 1fr brnz
        grn, *straw*   5.25   5.75
a.   Pair, one without
       surcharge   1,250. 1,200.
        Nos. 20-30 (11)   28.35 30.80

Two spacings between the surcharged numerals are found on Nos. 20-30. See the *Scott Classic Specialized Catalogue of Stamps and Covers* for detailed listings.
Nos. 20-30 were available for use in Madagascar and the Comoro archipelago.
The stamps of Anjouan were superseded by those of Madagascar, and in 1950 by those of Comoro Islands.

ANNAM & TONKIN

a-'nam and 'tän-'kin

LOCATION — In French Indo-China bordering on the China Sea on the east and Siam on the west.
GOVT. — French Protectorate
AREA — 97,503 sq. mi.
POP. — 14,124,000 (approx. 1890)
CAPITAL — Annam: Hue; Tonkin: Hanoi

For administrative purposes, the Protectorates of Annam, Tonkin, Cambodia, Laos and the Colony of Cochin-China were grouped together and were known as French Indo-China.

100 Centimes = 1 Franc

Catalogue values for unused stamps are for examples without gum as most stamps were issued in that condition.

**Stamps of French Colonies, 1881-86
Handstamped Surcharged in Black**

Perf. 14x13½
1888, Jan. 21   Unwmk.
1   A9 1c on 2c brn, *buff*   47.50 50.00
a.   Inverted surcharge   200.00 200.00
b.   Sideways surcharge   200.00 210.00
2   A9 1c on 4c claret, *lav* 37.50 35.00
a.   Inverted surcharge   200.00 210.00
b.   Double surcharge   275.00 225.00
c.   Sideways surcharge   200.00 210.00
3   A9 5c on 10c blk, *lav*   47.50 37.50
a.   Inverted surcharge   200.00 200.00
b.   Double surcharge   225.00 225.00
       Hyphen between "A" and "T"
7   A9 1c on 2c brn, *buff*   350.00 400.00
a.   Inverted surcharge   750.00 775.00
b.   Sideways surcharge   750.00 775.00
c.   Pair, Nos. 1, 7   9,000.
8   A9 1c on 4c claret, *lav* 525.00 625.00
9   A9 5c on 10c blk, *lav*   220.00 240.00

A 5c on 2c was prepared but not issued. Value $8,500.
In these surcharges there are different types of numerals and letters.
There are numerous other errors in the placing of the surcharges, including double one inverted, double both inverted, double one sideways, and pair one without surcharge. Such varieties command substantial premiums.
These stamps were superseded in 1892 by those of Indo-China.

ANTIGUA

an-'tēg-ẉə

LOCATION — In the West Indies, southeast of Puerto Rico
GOVT. — Independent state
AREA — 171 sq. mi.
POP. — 64,246 (est. 1999)
CAPITAL — St. John's

Antigua was one of the presidencies of the former Leeward Islands colony until becoming a Crown Colony in 1956. It became an Associated State of the United Kingdom in 1967 and an independent nation on November 1, 1981, taking the name of Antigua and Barbuda.

Antigua stamps were discontinued in 1890 and resumed in 1903. In the interim, stamps of Leeward Islands were used. Between 1903-1956, stamps of Antigua and Leeward Islands were used concurrently.

12 Pence = 1 Shilling
20 Shillings = 1 Pound
100 Cents = 1 Dollar (1951)

> **Catalogue values for unused stamps in this country are for Never Hinged items, beginning with Scott 96.**

Watermark

Wmk. 5 — Star

Values for unused stamps are for examples with original gum as defined in the catalogue introduction. Any exceptions will be noted. Very fine examples of Nos. 1-8, 11, 18-20 will have perforations touching the design on at least one frameline due to the narrow spacing of the stamps on the plates. Stamps with perfs clear of the framelines on all four sides are extremely scarce and will command higher prices.

Queen Victoria — A1

Rough Perf. 14-16

1862		Engr.		Unwmk.
1	A1	6p blue green	950.00	600.00
a.		Perf. 11-13	8,500.	
b.		Perf. 11-13x14-16	3,750.	
c.		Perf. 11-13 compound with 14-16	3,750.	

There is a question whether Nos. 1a-1c ever did postal duty.
Values for No. 1 are for stamps with perfs. cutting into the design. Values for No. 1b are for examples without gum.

1863-67				Wmk. 5
2	A1	1p dull rose	135.00	60.00
a.		Vert. pair, imperf. btwn.	37,500.	
b.		Imperf., pair		2,750.
c.		1p lilac rose	150.00	82.50
3	A1	1p vermilion ('67)	275.00	32.50
a.		Horiz. pair, imperf. btwn.	37,500.	
4	A1	6p green	775.00	30.00
a.		6p yellow green	4,750.	110.00
b.		Pair, imperf. btwn.		—

1872		Wmk. 1		Perf. 12½
5	A1	1p lake	220.00	22.50
6	A1	1p vermilion	225.00	26.50
7	A1	6p blue green	600.00	12.50

Queen Victoria — A2

1873-79				Perf. 14
8	A1	1p lake	250.00	12.50
a.		Half used as ½p on cover		9,500.

Typo.

9	A2	2½p red brown ('79)	700.00	210.00
10	A2	4p blue ('79)	290.00	18.00

Engr.

11	A1	6p blue green ('76)	450.00	22.50

1882-86		Typo.		Wmk. 2
12	A2	½p green	5.00	20.00
13	A2	2½p red brown	225.00	67.50
14	A2	2½p ultra ('86)	8.50	17.00
15	A2	4p blue	350.00	19.00
16	A2	4p brown org ('86)	2.50	3.75
17	A2	1sh violet ('86)	190.00	175.00

Engr.

18	A1	1p carmine ('84)	2.60	4.50
19	A1	6p deep green	77.50	150.00

No. 18 was used for a time in St. Christopher and is identified by the "A12" cancellation.

1884				Perf. 12
20	A1	1p rose red	65.00	19.00

Seal of the Colony — A3   King Edward VII — A4

1903	Typo.	Wmk. 1		Perf. 14
21	A3	½p blue grn & blk	4.00	7.50
a.		Bluish paper ('09)	100.00	100.00
22	A3	1p car & black	13.50	1.50
a.		Bluish paper ('09)	92.50	92.50
23	A3	2p org brn & vio	8.25	27.50
24	A3	2½p ultra & black	17.50	25.00
25	A3	3p ocher & gray green	12.00	24.00
26	A3	6p black & red vio	35.00	60.00
27	A3	1sh violet & ultra	55.00	65.00
28	A3	2sh pur & gray green	90.00	120.00
29	A3	2sh6p red vio & blk	27.50	70.00
30	A3	5sh pur & gray green	110.00	160.00
		Nos. 21-30 (10)	372.75	560.50

The 2½p, 1sh and 5sh exist on both ordinary and chalky paper.

1908-20				Wmk. 3
31	A3	½p green	4.75	5.25
32	A3	1p carmine	12.00	2.75
33	A3	2p org brn & dull vio ('12)	5.25	35.00
34	A3	2½p ultra	24.00	19.00
35	A3	3p ocher & grn ('12)	7.00	21.00
36	A3	6p blk & red vio ('11)	8.25	47.50
37	A3	1sh vio & ultra	27.50	80.00
38	A3	2sh vio & green ('12)	110.00	130.00
		Nos. 31-38 (8)	198.75	340.50

Nos. 33, 35 to 38 are on chalky paper.
For overprints see Nos. MR1-MR3.

George V — A6

1913				
41	A6	5sh violet & green	100.00	160.00

St. John's Harbor — A7

1921-29				Wmk. 4
42	A7	½p green	3.25	.60
43	A7	1p rose red	4.50	.60
44	A7	1p dp violet ('23)	8.75	1.75
45	A7	1½p orange ('22)	6.50	8.00
46	A7	1½p rose red ('26)	10.00	2.00
47	A7	1½p fawn ('29)	3.25	.75
48	A7	2p gray	4.50	.90
49	A7	2½p ultra	17.00	5.00
50	A7	2½p orange ('23)	2.75	20.00

Chalky Paper

51	A7	3p violet, yel ('25)	16.00	10.00
52	A7	6p vio & red vio	8.50	7.50
53	A7	1sh black, emer ('29)	6.50	9.00
54	A7	2sh vio & ultra, blue ('27)	12.00	65.00
55	A7	2sh6p blk & red, blue ('27)	50.00	47.50
56	A7	3sh grn & vio ('22)	52.50	105.00
57	A7	4sh blk & red ('22)	52.50	77.50
		Nos. 42-57 (16)	258.50	361.10

				Wmk. 3
				Chalky Paper
58	A7	3p violet, yel	5.00	13.00
59	A7	4p black & red, yel ('22)	2.50	6.50
60	A7	1sh black, emerald	4.75	10.50
61	A7	2sh vio & ultra, bl	14.50	35.00
62	A7	2sh6p blk & red, bl	19.00	65.00
63	A7	5sh grn & red, yel ('22)	9.25	60.00
64	A7	£1 vio & black, red	275.00	425.00
		Nos. 58-64 (7)	330.00	615.00

Old Dockyard, English Harbour — A8

Govt. House, St. John's — A9

Nelson's "Victory," 1805 — A10

Sir Thomas Warner's Ship, 1632 — A11

Perf. 12½

1932, Jan. 27		Engr.		Wmk. 4
67	A8	½p green	4.75	8.75
68	A8	1p scarlet	6.50	9.00
69	A8	1½p lt brown	4.75	5.50
70	A9	2p gray	9.00	27.50

71	A9	2½p ultra	8.75	9.75
72	A9	3p orange	8.75	14.00
73	A10	6p violet	16.00	14.00
74	A10	1sh olive green	21.00	32.50
75	A10	2sh6p claret	55.00	82.50
76	A11	5sh red brown & black	120.00	150.00
		Nos. 67-76 (10)	254.50	353.50
		Set, never hinged	650.00	

Tercentenary of the colony.
Forged cancellations abound, especially dated "MY 18 1932."

Common Design Types pictured following the introduction.

Silver Jubilee Issue
Common Design Type

1935, May 6				Perf. 13½x14
77	CD301	1p car & blue	2.25	3.75
78	CD301	1½p gray blk & ultra	2.50	1.00
79	CD301	2½p blue & brn	6.50	1.75
80	CD301	1sh brt vio & ind	9.00	14.00
		Nos. 77-80 (4)	20.25	20.50
		Set, never hinged	32.50	

Coronation Issue
Common Design Type

1937, May 12				Perf. 11x11½
81	CD302	1p carmine	.50	1.00
82	CD302	1½p brown	.35	1.00
83	CD302	2½p deep ultra	1.00	1.75
		Nos. 81-83 (3)	1.85	3.75
		Set, never hinged	2.75	

English Harbour — A14   Nelson's Dockyard — A15

Fort James — A16   St. John's Harbor — A17

1938-51		Engr.		Perf. 12½
84	A14	½p yel green	.30	1.50
85	A15	1p scarlet	2.25	2.50
86	A15	1½p red brown ('43)	1.80	2.75
87	A14	2p gray	.70	1.00
88	A15	2½p ultra ('43)	.75	.90
89	A16	3p pale orange ('44)	.75	1.10
90	A17	6p purple	2.75	1.25
91	A17	1sh brown & blk	3.50	2.00
92	A16	2sh6p dp claret ('42)	16.00	18.00
93	A17	5sh grayish olive green ('44)	9.00	10.00
94	A15	10sh red vio ('48)	11.00	35.00
95	A16	£1 Prussian blue ('48)	22.50	55.00
		Nos. 84-95 (12)	71.30	131.00
		Set, never hinged	105.00	

See Nos. 107-113, 115-116, 118-121, 136-142, 144-145.
For overprint see Nos. 125-126.

> **Catalogue values for unused stamps in this section, from this point to the end of the section, are for Never Hinged items.**

Peace Issue
Common Design Type

1946, Nov. 1		Wmk. 4		Perf. 13½x14
96	CD303	1½p brown	.25	.25
97	CD303	3p dp orange	.25	.55

Silver Wedding Issue
Common Design Types

1949, Jan. 3		Photo.		Perf. 14x14½
98	CD304	2½p bright ultra	.55	2.75

Engraved; Name Typographed
Perf. 11½x11
99 CD305 5sh dk brown olive 12.00 10.00

UPU Issue
Common Design Types
Perf. 13½, 11x11½
1949, Oct. 10   **Wmk. 4**
Engr.; Name Typo. on 3p and 6p
100	CD306	2½p deep ultra	.45	.60
101	CD307	3p orange	1.90	2.75
102	CD308	6p purple	.90	2.00
103	CD309	1sh red brown	.90	1.50
		Nos. 100-103 (4)	4.15	6.85

University Issue
Common Design Types
Perf. 14x14½
1951, Feb. 16   Engr.   Wmk. 4
| 104 | CD310 | 3c chocolate & blk | .45 | 1.50 |
| 105 | CD311 | 12c purple & blk | .90 | 1.75 |

Coronation Issue
Common Design Type
1953, June 2   Perf. 13½x13
106 CD312 2c dk green & blk .50 .75

Types of 1938 with Portrait of Queen Elizabeth II

Martello Tower — A24

Perf. 13x13½, 13½x13
1953-56   Wmk. 4
107	A16	½c dk red brn ('56)	.35	.35
108	A14	1c gray	.30	1.25
109	A15	2c deep green	.30	.25
110	A15	3c yellow & blk	.50	.25
111	A14	4c rose red (shades)	1.25	.25
112	A15	5c dull vio & blk	2.25	.45
113	A16	6c orange	2.25	.25
114	A24	8c deep blue	2.50	.25
115	A17	12c violet	2.50	.25
116	A17	24c chocolate & blk	4.25	.25
117	A24	48c dp bl & rose lil	9.00	2.75
118	A16	60c claret	8.00	.75
119	A17	$1.20 olive green	3.50	.90
120	A15	$2.40 magenta	16.00	11.50
121	A16	$4.80 greenish blue	21.00	24.50
		Nos. 107-121 (15)	73.95	44.20

See No. 143. For overprint see No. 125-126.

West Indies Federation
Common Design Type
Perf. 11½x11
1958, Apr. 22   Engr.   Wmk. 314
122	CD313	3c green	1.50	.30
123	CD313	6c blue	1.90	2.75
124	CD313	12c carmine rose	2.40	.75
		Nos. 122-124 (3)	5.80	3.80

Nos. 110 and 115 Overprinted in Red or Black: "Commemoration Antigua Constitution 1960"
Perf. 13x13½, 13½x13
1960, Jan. 1   Wmk. 4
| 125 | A15 | 3c yellow & black | .25 | .25 |
| 126 | A17 | 12c violet (Blk) | .25 | .25 |

Constitutional reforms effective Jan. 1, 1960.

Lord Nelson and Nelson's Dockyard A26

Perf. 11½x11
1961, Nov. 14   Wmk. 314
| 127 | A26 | 20c brown & lilac | 1.60 | 1.60 |
| 128 | A26 | 30c dk blue & green | 1.75 | 2.00 |

Completion of the restoration of Lord Nelson's headquarters, English Harbour.

Stamp of 1862 and Royal Mail Steam Packet in English Harbour A27

1962, Aug. 1   Engr.   Perf. 13
129	A27	3c dull green & pur	.70	.25
130	A27	10c dull green & ultra	.80	.25
131	A27	12c dull green & blk	.90	.25
132	A27	50c dull grn & brn org	1.50	2.00
		Nos. 129-132 (4)	3.90	2.75

Centenary of first Antigua postage stamp.

Freedom from Hunger Issue
Common Design Type
Perf. 14x14½
1963, June 4   Photo.   Wmk. 314
133 CD314 12c green .35 .35

Red Cross Centenary Issue
Common Design Type
1963, Sept. 2   Litho.   Perf. 13
| 134 | CD315 | 3c black & red | .25 | .25 |
| 135 | CD315 | 12c ultra & red | .85 | 1.25 |

Types of 1938-53 with Portrait of Queen Elizabeth II
Perf. 13x13½, 13½x13
1963-65   Engr.   Wmk. 314
136	A16	½c brown ('65)	2.50	.75
137	A14	1c gray ('65)	1.25	1.00
138	A15	2c deep green	.70	.30
139	A15	3c orange yel & blk	.40	.30
140	A14	4c brown red	.35	2.00
141	A15	5c dull vio & black	.30	.25
142	A16	6c orange	.60	.35
143	A24	8c deep blue	.35	.25
144	A17	12c violet	1.00	.25
145	A17	24c choc & black	5.00	.90
		Nos. 136-145 (10)	12.45	6.35

For surcharge see No. 152.

Shakespeare Issue
Common Design Type
Perf. 14x14½
1964, Apr. 23   Photo.   Wmk. 314
151 CD316 12c red brown .40 .25

No. 144 Surcharged with New Value and Bars
Perf. 13½x13
1965, Apr. 1   Engr.   Wmk. 314
152 A17 15c on 12c violet .30 .30

ITU Issue
Common Design Type
Perf. 11x11½
1965, May 17   Litho.   Wmk. 314
| 153 | CD317 | 2c blue & ver | .25 | .25 |
| 154 | CD317 | 50c orange & vio bl | 1.40 | 1.10 |

Intl. Cooperation Year Issue
Common Design Type
1965, Oct. 25   Perf. 14½
| 155 | CD318 | 4c blue grn & claret | .25 | .25 |
| 156 | CD318 | 15c lt vio & green | .35 | .25 |

Churchill Memorial Issue
Common Design Type
1966, Jan. 24   Photo.   Perf. 14
Design in Black, Gold and Carmine Rose
157	CD319	½c bright blue	.25	1.50
158	CD319	4c orange	.30	.25
159	CD319	25c brown	1.25	.30
160	CD319	35c violet	1.25	.50
		Nos. 157-160 (4)	3.05	2.55

Royal Visit Issue
Common Design Type
1966, Feb. 4   Litho.   Perf. 11x12
Portraits in Black
| 161 | CD320 | 6c violet blue | 1.90 | 1.10 |
| 162 | CD320 | 15c dark car rose | 1.90 | 1.50 |

World Cup Soccer Issue
Common Design Type
1966, July 1   Wmk. 314   Perf. 14
| 163 | CD321 | 6c multicolored | .25 | .25 |
| 164 | CD321 | 35c multicolored | .60 | .25 |

WHO Headquarters Issue
Common Design Type
1966, Sept. 20   Perf. 14
| 165 | CD322 | 2c multicolored | .25 | .25 |
| 166 | CD322 | 15c multicolored | .80 | .30 |

Nelson's Dockyard A35

Designs: 1c, Old post office, St. John's. 2c, Health Center. 3c, Teachers' Training College. 4c, Martello Tower, Barbuda. 5c, Ruins of officers quarters, Shirley Heights. 6c, Government House, Barbuda. 10c, Princess Margaret School. 15c, Air terminal. 25c, General post office. 35c, Clarence House. 50c, Government House. 75c, Administration building. $1, Court House, St. John's. $2.50, Magistrates' Court. $5, St. John's Cathedral.

Perf. 11½x11
1966, Nov. 1   Engr.   Wmk. 314
167	A35	½c green & blue	.25	1.00
168	A35	1c purple & rose	.25	.30
169	A35	2c slate & org	.25	.30
170	A35	3c rose red & blk	.30	.30
171	A35	4c dull vio & brn	1.00	.25
172	A35	5c vio bl & olive	.25	.25
173	A35	6c dp org & pur	1.00	.30
174	A35	10c brt grn & rose red	.25	.25
175	A35	15c brn & blue	1.50	.25
		Complete booklet, 4 ea. #172, 174, 175	11.00	
176	A35	25c slate & brn	.55	.25
177	A35	35c dp rose & sep	1.50	.55
178	A35	50c green & black	2.00	2.00
179	A35	75c Prus bl & vio blue	3.50	2.25
180	A35	$1 dp rose & olive	8.00	2.50
181	A35	$2.50 black & rose	6.50	6.75
182	A35	$5 ol grn & dl vio	9.00	6.50
		Nos. 167-182 (16)	36.10	23.95

For surcharge see No. 231.

1969   Perf. 13½
167a	A35	½c	.25	2.00
168a	A35	1c	.25	1.00
169a	A35	2c	.25	.65
170a	A35	3c	.25	.25
171a	A35	4c	.25	.25
172b	A35	5c	.25	.80
173a	A35	6c	.25	.25
174b	A35	10c	.55	.25
175b	A35	15c	.45	.25
176a	A35	25c	.60	1.00
177a	A35	35c	.75	2.25
178a	A35	50c	1.25	5.00
180a	A35	$1	1.50	8.00
181a	A35	$2.50	11.50	24.00
182a	A35	$5	18.60	46.20
		Nos. 167a-182a (15)		

The ½c, 3c, 6c are on ordinary paper. The 15c through $5 on glazed paper. The others exist on both papers.

UNESCO Anniversary Issue
Common Design Type
1966, Dec. 1   Litho.   Perf. 14
183	CD323	4c "Education"	.25	.25
184	CD323	25c "Science"	.40	.25
185	CD323	$1 "Culture"	1.25	2.00
		Nos. 183-185 (3)	1.90	2.50

Independent State

Flag of Antigua, Spiny Lobster, Maps of Antigua and Barbuda A37

Designs: 15c, 35c, Flag of Antigua. 25c, Flag and Premier's Office Building.

1967, Feb. 27   Photo.   Perf. 14
186	A37	4c multicolored	.25	.25
187	A37	15c multicolored	.25	.25
188	A37	25c multicolored	.25	.25
189	A37	35c multicolored	.25	.25
		Nos. 186-189 (4)	1.00	1.00

Antigua's independence, Feb. 27, 1967.

Gilbert Memorial Church, Antigua — A38

25c, Nathaniel Gilbert's House. 35c, Map of the Caribbean and Central America.

Perf. 14x13½
1967, May 18   Photo.   Wmk. 314
190	A38	4c brt red & black	.25	.25
191	A38	25c emerald & black	.25	.25
192	A38	35c ultra & black	.25	.25
		Nos. 190-192 (3)	.75	.75

Attainment of autonomy by the Methodist Church in the Caribbean and the Americas, and the opening of headquarters near St. John's, Antigua, May 1967.

Antiguan and British Royal Arms — A39

1967, July 21   Perf. 14½x14
| 193 | A39 | 15c dark green & multi | .25 | .25 |
| 194 | A39 | 35c deep blue & multi | .25 | .25 |

Granting of a new coat of arms to the State of Antigua; 300th anniv. of the Treaty of Breda.

Sailing Ship, 17th Century A40

Design: 6c, 35c, Map of Barbuda from Jan Blaeu's Atlas, 1665.

Perf. 11½x11
1967, Dec. 14   Engr.   Wmk. 314
195	A40	4c dark blue	.35	.25
196	A40	6c deep plum	.35	.90
197	A40	25c green	.50	.25
198	A40	35c black	.50	.30
		Nos. 195-198 (4)	1.70	1.70

Resettlement of Barbuda, 300th anniv.

Dow Hill Antenna — A41

Designs: 15c, Antenna and rocket blasting off. 25c, Nose cone orbiting moon. 50c, Reentry of space capsule.

Perf. 14½x14
1968, Mar. 29   Photo.   Wmk. 314
199	A41	4c dk blue, org & black	.25	.25
200	A41	15c dk blue, org & black	.25	.25
201	A41	25c dk blue, org & black	.25	.25
202	A41	50c dk blue, org & black	.25	.25
		Nos. 199-202 (4)	1.00	1.00

Dedication of the Dow Hill tracking station in Antigua for the NASA Apollo project.

Beach and Sailfish A42

Designs: ½c, 50c, Limbo dancer, flames and dancing girls. 15c, Three girls on a beach and water skier. 35c, Woman scuba diver, corals and fish.

1968, July 1   Photo.   Perf. 14
203	A42	½c red & multi	.25	.25
204	A42	15c sky blue & multi	.25	.25
205	A42	25c blue & multi	.35	.25
206	A42	35c brt blue & multi	.35	.25
207	A42	50c multicolored	.60	.90
	Nos. 203-207 (5)		1.80	1.90

Issued for tourist publicity.

St. John's Harbor, 1768 A43

St. John's Harbor: 15c, 1829. 25c, Map of deep-sea harbor, 1968. 35c, Dock, 1968. 2c, Like $1.

Engr. & Litho.; Engr. ($1)
1968, Oct. 31   Wmk. 314   Perf. 13
208	A43	2c dp car & lt blue	.25	.30
209	A43	15c sepia & yel grn	.40	.25
210	A43	25c dk blue & yel	.50	.25
211	A43	35c dp green & sal	.55	.25
212	A43	$1 black	.95	1.50
	Nos. 208-212 (5)		2.65	2.55

Opening of St. John's deep-sea harbor.

Mace and Parliament A44

Mace and: 15c, Mace bearer. 25c, House of Representatives, interior. 50c, Antigua coat of arms and great seal.

1969, Feb. 3   Photo.   Perf. 12½
213	A44	4c crimson & multi	.25	.25
214	A44	15c crimson & multi	.25	.25
215	A44	25c crimson & multi	.25	.25
216	A44	50c crimson & multi	.30	1.00
	Nos. 213-216 (4)		1.05	1.75

300th anniversary of Antigua Parliament.

CARIFTA Cargo — A45

4c, 15c, Ship, plane and trucks, horiz.

Perf. 13½x13, 13x13½
1969, Apr. 14   Litho.   Wmk. 314
217	A45	4c blk & brt lilac rose	.25	.25
218	A45	15c blk & brt grnsh blue	.25	.25
219	A45	25c bister & black	.25	.25
220	A45	35c tan & black	.25	.25
	Nos. 217-220 (4)		1.00	1.00

1st anniv. of CARIFTA (Caribbean Free Trade Area).

Map of Redonda Island A46

25c, View of Redonda from the sea & seagulls.

1969, Aug. 1   Photo.   Perf. 13x13½
221	A46	15c ultra & multi	.25	.25
222	A46	25c multicolored	.25	.25
223	A46	50c salmon & multi	.40	.50
	Nos. 221-223 (3)		.90	1.00

Centenary of Redonda phosphate industry.

Adoration of the Kings, by Gugliemo Marcillat A47

Christmas: 10c, 50c, Holy Family, by anonymous German artist, 15th century.

1969, Oct. 15   Litho.   Perf. 13x14
224	A47	6c bister brn & multi	.25	.25
225	A47	10c fawn & multi	.25	.25
226	A47	35c gray olive & multi	.25	.25
227	A47	50c gray blue & multi	.30	.25
	Nos. 224-227 (4)		1.05	1.00

Arms of Antigua — A48

Coil Stamps
Wmk. 314 upright
1970, Jan. 30   Photo.   Perf. 14½x14
228	A48	5c bright blue	.25	.25
a.	Wmk. 373 ('77)		7.00	
229	A48	10c bright green	.25	.25
a.	Wmk. 373, invtd. ('77)		—	2.00
230	A48	25c deep magenta	.25	.25
a.	Wmk. 373 ('77)		12.50	
	Nos. 228-230 (3)		.75	.75

Glazed Paper
1973, Mar. 5   Wmk. 314 sideways
228b	A48	5c bright blue	1.00	1.00
229b	A48	10c bright green	1.00	1.00
230b	A48	25c deep magenta	1.25	1.25
	Nos. 228b-230b (3)		3.25	3.25

No. 176 Surcharged

1970, Jan. 2   Engr.   Perf. 11½x11
231	A35	20c on 25c slate & brown	.35	.25

Sikorsky S-38 A49

Aircraft: 20c, Dornier DO-X. 35c, Hawker Siddeley 748. 50c, Douglas C-124C Globemaster II. 75c, Vickers VC 10.

1970, Feb. 16   Litho.   Perf. 14½
232	A49	5c brt green & multi	.75	.25
233	A49	20c ultra & multi	1.25	.25
234	A49	35c blue grn & multi	1.50	.25
235	A49	50c blue & multi	1.50	1.50
236	A49	75c vio blue & multi	2.00	2.00
	Nos. 232-236 (5)		7.00	4.25

40th anniversary of air service.

Dickens and Scene from "Pickwick Papers" A50

Charles Dickens (1812-1870), English novelist and Scene from: 5c, "Nicholas Nickleby." 35c, "Oliver Twist." $1, "David Copperfield."

Wmk. 314
1970, May 19   Litho.   Perf. 14
237	A50	5c olive & sepia	.25	.25
238	A50	20c aqua & sepia	.25	.25
239	A50	35c violet & sepia	.30	.25
240	A50	$1 scarlet & sepia	.75	.60
	Nos. 237-240 (4)		1.55	1.35

Carib Indian and War Canoe A51

Ships: 1c, Columbus and "Nina." 2c, Sir Thomas Warner's arms and sailing ship. 3c, Viscount Hood and "Barfleur." 4c, Sir George Rodney and "Formidable." 5c, Capt. Horatio Nelson and "Boreas." 6c, King William IV and "Pegasus." 10c, Blackbeard (Edward Teach) and pirate ketch. 15c, Capt. Cuthbert Collingwood and "Pelican." 20c, Admiral Nelson and "Victoria." 25c, Paddle steamer "Solent" and Steam Packet Company emblem. 35c, King George V and corvette "Canada." 50c, Cruiser "Renown" and royal badge. 75c, S.S. "Federal Maple" and maple leaf. $1, Racing yacht "Sol-Quest" and Gallant 53 class emblem. $2.50, Missile destroyer "London" and her emblem. $5, Tug "Pathfinder" and arms of Antigua.

Wmk. 314 Sideways
1970, Aug. 19   Litho.   Perf. 14
241	A51	½c ocher & multi	.25	1.25
242	A51	1c Prus bl & multi	.30	1.25
243	A51	2c yel grn & multi	.35	3.00
244	A51	3c ol bis & multi	.35	2.50
245	A51	4c bl gray & multi	.40	2.75
246	A51	5c fawn & multi	.50	.40
247	A51	6c rose lil & multi	1.50	3.50
248	A51	10c brn org & multi	.80	.25
249	A51	15c ultra & multi	7.50	1.00
250	A51	20c ol grn & multi	1.25	.40
251	A51	25c olive & multi	1.25	.40
252	A51	35c dull red brn & multi	1.75	.80
253	A51	50c lt brn & multi	3.75	5.25
254	A51	75c beige & multi	5.00	5.25
255	A51	$1 Prus green & multi	5.00	1.75
256	A51	$2.50 gray & multi	7.00	7.00
257	A51	$5 yel & multi	3.00	6.00
	Nos. 241-257 (17)		39.95	42.75

1972-74   Wmk. 314 Upright
241a	A51	½c	.30	.45
242a	A51	1c	.40	1.00
244a	A51	3c	.80	1.00
245a	A51	4c	.55	1.75
246a	A51	5c	.60	.40
247a	A51	6c	.90	2.75
248a	A51	10c	.60	.60
249a	A51	15c	7.00	.90
254a	A51	75c	7.00	3.00
255a	A51	$1	3.00	1.75
256a	A51	$2.50	2.75	6.50
257a	A51	$5	4.00	10.00
	Nos. 241a-257a (12)		27.90	30.10

For surcharge see No. 368.

1975, Jan. 21   Wmk. 373
257b	A51	$5 yellow & multi	4.50	12.00

Nativity, by Albrecht Dürer — A52

Christmas: 10c, 50c, Adoration of the Magi, by Albrecht Dürer.

Engr. & Litho.
1970, Oct. 28   Perf. 13½x14
258	A52	3c brt grnsh blue & blk	.25	.25
259	A52	10c pink & plum	.25	.25
260	A52	35c brick red & black	.25	.25
261	A52	50c lilac & violet	.35	.25
	Nos. 258-261 (4)		1.10	1.00

Private, 4th West India Regiment, 1804 — A53

Military Uniforms: ½c, Drummer Boy, 4th King's Own Regiment, 1759. 20c, Grenadier Company Officer, 60th Regiment, The Royal American, 1809. 35c, Light Company Officer, 93rd Regiment, The Sutherland Highlanders, 1826-1834. 75c, Private, 3rd West India Regiment, 1851.

Perf. 14x13½
1970, Dec. 1   Litho.   Wmk. 314
262	A53	½c lake & multi	.25	.25
263	A53	10c brn org & multi	.50	.25
264	A53	20c Prus grn & multi	1.00	.25
265	A53	35c dl pur & multi	1.25	.25
266	A53	75c dk ol grn & multi	2.50	2.00
a.	Souv. sheet. #262-266 + label		8.00	8.00
	Nos. 262-266 (5)		5.50	3.00

See Nos. 274-278, 283-287, 307-311, 329-333.

Market Woman Voting — A54

Voting by: 20c, Businessman. 35c, Mother (and child). 50c, Workman.

Perf. 14½x14
1971, Feb. 1   Photo.   Wmk. 314
267	A54	5c brown	.25	.25
268	A54	20c olive black	.25	.25
269	A54	35c rose magenta	.25	.25
270	A54	50c violet blue	.25	.25
	Nos. 267-270 (4)		1.00	1.00

Adult suffrage, 20th anniversary.

Last Supper, from The Small Passion, by Dürer — A55

Woodcuts by Albrecht Dürer: 35c, Crucifixion from Eichstatt Missal. 75c, Resurrection from The Great Passion.

Perf. 14x13½
1971, Apr. 7   Litho.   Wmk. 314
271	A55	5c gray, red & black	.25	.25
272	A55	35c gray, violet & black	.25	.25
273	A55	75c gray, gold & black	.25	.25
	Nos. 271-273 (3)		.75	.75

Easter.

Uniform Type of 1970

Military Uniforms: ½c, Private, Suffolk Regiment, 1704. 10c, Grenadier, South Staffordshire, 1751. 20c, Fusilier, Royal Northumberland, 1778. 35c, Private, Northamptonshire. 1793, 75c, Private, East Yorkshire, 1805.

1971, July 12   Litho.   Wmk. 314

274	A53	½c gray grn & multi	.25	.25
275	A53	10c bluish blk & multi	.50	.25
276	A53	20c dk pur & multi	1.25	.25
277	A53	35c dk ol & multi	1.50	.25
278	A53	75c brown & multi	2.00	2.75
a.		Souv. sheet, #274-278 + label	8.00	8.00
		Nos. 274-278 (5)	5.50	3.75

Virgin and Child, by Veronese — A56

Christmas: 5c, 50c, Adoration of the Shepherds, by Bonifazio Veronese.

1971, Oct. 4   Perf. 14x13½

279	A56	3c multicolored	.25	.25
280	A56	5c multicolored	.25	.25
281	A56	35c multicolored	.25	.25
282	A56	50c multicolored	.40	.30
		Nos. 279-282 (4)	1.15	1.05

Uniform Type of 1970

Military Uniforms: ½c, Officer, King's Own Borderers Regiment, 1815. 10c, Sergeant, Buckinghamshire Regiment, 1837. 20c, Private, South Hampshire Regiment, 1853. 35c, Officer, Royal Artillery, 1854. 75c, Private, Worcestershire Regiment, 1870.

1972, July 1

283	A53	½c ol brn & multi	.25	.25
284	A53	10c dp grn & multi	.70	.25
285	A53	20c brt vio & multi	1.25	.25
286	A53	35c mar & multi	1.50	.30
287	A53	75c dk vio bl & multi	2.00	3.00
a.		Souvenir sheet of 5, #283-287 + label	8.75	8.75
		Nos. 283-287 (5)	5.70	4.05

Reticulated Helmet Cowrie — A57

Sea Shells: 5c, Measled cowrie. 35c, West Indian fighting conch. 50c, Hawkwing conch.

1972, Aug. 1   Perf. 14½x14

288	A57	3c multicolored	.60	.25
289	A57	5c ver & multi	.60	.25
290	A57	35c lt vio & multi	1.75	.25
291	A57	50c rose red & multi	2.00	2.50
		Nos. 288-291 (4)	4.95	3.25

St. John's Cathedral, 1745-1843 — A58

Christmas: 50c, Interior of St. John's. 75c, St. John's rebuilt.

1972, Nov. 6   Litho.   Perf. 14

292	A58	35c org brn & multi	.25	.25
293	A58	50c vio & multi	.30	.30
294	A58	75c multicolored	.50	.50
a.		Souv. sheet #292-294, perf 15	1.00	1.25
		Nos. 292-294 (3)	1.05	1.05

Silver Wedding Issue, 1972
Common Design Type

1972, Nov. 20   Photo.   Perf. 14x14½

295	CD324	20c ultra & multi	.25	.25
296	CD324	35c steel blue & multi	.25	.25

Map of Antigua, Batsman Driving Ball — A60

Designs: 35c, Batsman and wicketkeeper. $1, Emblem of Rising Sun Cricket Club.

1972, Dec. 15   Perf. 13½x14

297	A60	5c multicolored	.25	.25
298	A60	35c multicolored	.75	.30
299	A60	$1 multicolored	2.25	2.50
a.		Souvenir sheet of 3, #297-299	5.75	5.75
		Nos. 297-299 (3)	3.25	3.05

Rising Sun Cricket Club, St. John's, 50th anniv.

Map of Antigua and Yacht — A61

1972, Dec. 29   Perf. 14½

300	A61	35c shown	.25	.25
301	A61	50c Racing yachts	.25	.25
302	A61	75c St. John's G.P.O.	.40	.25
303	A61	$1 Statue of Liberty	.35	.25
a.		Souvenir sheet of 2, #301, 303	1.25	1.25
		Nos. 300-303 (4)	1.25	1.00

Opening of Antigua and Barbuda Information Office in New York City.

Window with Episcopal Coat of Arms — A62

Stained glass windows from Cathedral of St. John: 35c, Crucifixion. 75c, Arm of Rt. Rev. D.G. Davis, 1st bishop of Antigua.

1973, Apr. 16   Litho.   Perf. 13½

304	A62	5c yellow & multi	.25	.25
305	A62	35c brt lilac & multi	.25	.25
306	A62	75c blue & multi	.35	.25
		Nos. 304-306 (3)	.85	.75

Easter.

Uniform Type of 1970

Military Uniforms: ½c, Private, Col. Zacharia Tiffin's Regiment, 1701. 10c, Private, 63rd Regiment, 1759. 20c, Officer, 35th Sussex Regiment, 1828. 35c, Private, 2nd West India Regiment, 1853. 75c, Sergeant, Princess of Wales Regiment, Hertfordshire, 1858.

Perf. 14x13½

1973, July 1   Wmk. 314

307	A53	½c dp ultra & multi	.25	.25
308	A53	10c rose lilac & multi	.35	.25
309	A53	20c gray & multi	.50	.25
310	A53	35c multicolored	.70	.25
311	A53	75c multicolored	1.50	1.25
a.		Souv. sheet, #307-311 + label	4.50	4.25
		Nos. 307-311 (5)	3.30	2.25

Butterfly Costumes — A63

Designs: 20c, Carnival revelers. 35c, Costumed group. 75c, Carnival Queen.

Perf. 13½x14

1973, July 30   Unwmk.

312	A63	5c multicolored	.25	.25
313	A63	20c multicolored	.25	.25
314	A63	35c multicolored	.25	.25
315	A63	75c multicolored	.30	.25
a.		Souvenir sheet of 4, #312-315	1.10	1.25
		Nos. 312-315 (4)	1.05	1.00

Carnival, July 29-Aug. 7.

Virgin of the Porridge, by David — A64

Christmas: 5c, Adoration of the Kings, by Stomer. 20c, Virgin of the Grand Duke, by Raphael. 35c, Nativity with God the Father and Holy Ghost, by Tiepolo. $1, Madonna and Child, by Murillo.

Perf. 14½

1973, Oct. 15   Photo.   Unwmk.

316	A64	3c brt blue & multi	.25	.25
317	A64	5c emerald & multi	.25	.25
318	A64	20c gold & multi	.25	.25
319	A64	35c violet & multi	.25	.25
320	A64	$1 red & multi	.35	.40
a.		Souvenir sheet of 5, #316-320	1.50	1.50
		Nos. 316-320 (5)	1.35	1.40

Princess Anne and Mark Phillips — A65

Design: $2, different border.

1973, Nov. 14   Litho.   Perf. 13½

321	A65	35c dull ultra & multi	.25	.25
322	A65	$2 yel grn & multi	.25	.25
a.		Souvenir sheet of 2, #321-322	.75	.75

Wedding of Princess Anne and Capt. Mark Phillips.
Nos. 321-322 were issued in sheets of 5 plus label.

Nos. 321-322 and 322a Ovptd.

1973, Dec. 15   Litho.   Perf. 13½

323	A65	35c multicolored	.25	.25
324	A65	$2 multicolored	.50	.50
a.		Souvenir sheet of 2, #323-324	.75	.75

Visit of Princess Anne and Mark Phillips to Antigua, Dec. 16. Same overprint in sheet margins of Nos. 323-324 and 324a.
Overprint lithographed. Also exists typographed.

Arms of Antigua and U.W.I. A66

Designs: 20c, Dancers. 35c, Antigua campus. 75c, Chancellor Sir Hugh Wooding.

1974, Feb. 18   Wmk. 314

325	A66	5c multicolored	.25	.25
326	A66	20c multicolored	.25	.25
327	A66	35c multicolored	.25	.25
328	A66	75c multicolored	.25	.25
		Nos. 325-328 (4)	1.00	1.00

University of the West Indies, 24th anniv.

Uniform Type of 1970

Military Uniforms: ½c, Officer, 59th Foot, 1797. 10c, Gunner, Royal Artillery, 1800. 20c, Private, 1st West India Regiment, 1830. 35c, Officer, Gordon Highlanders, 1843. 75c, Private, Royal Welsh Fusiliers, 1846.

1974, May 1   Perf. 14x13½

329	A53	½c dull grn & multi	.25	.25
330	A53	10c ocher & multi	.40	.25
331	A53	20c multicolored	.75	.25
332	A53	35c gray bl & multi	.90	.25
333	A53	75c dk gray & multi	1.25	1.75
a.		Souvenir sheet of 5, #329-333	3.75	3.00
		Nos. 329-333 (5)	3.55	2.75

English Mailman and Coach, Helicopter — A67

UPU, Cent.: 1c, English bellman, 1846; Orinoco mailboat, 1851; telecommunications satellite. 2c, English mailtrain guard, 1852; Swiss post passenger bus, 1906; Italian hydrofoil. 5c, Swiss messenger, 16th century; Wells Fargo coach, 1800; Concorde. 20c, German position, 1820; Japanese mailmen, 19th century; carrier pigeon. 35c, Contemporary Antiguan mailman; radar station; aquaplane. $1, Medieval French courier; American train, 1884; British Airways jet.

1974, July 15   Litho.   Perf. 14½

334	A67	½c multicolored	.25	.25
335	A67	1c multicolored	.25	.25
336	A67	2c multicolored	.25	.25
337	A67	5c multicolored	.60	.40
338	A67	20c multicolored	.35	.25
339	A67	35c multicolored	.45	.25
340	A67	$1 multicolored	1.75	1.75
a.		Souvenir sheet of 7, #334-340 + label, perf. 13	4.50	3.50
		Nos. 334-340 (7)	3.90	3.40

For surcharges see Nos. 365-367.

Traditional Steel Band — A68

Carnival 1974 (Steel Bands): 5c, Traditional players, vert. 35c, Modern steel band. 75c, Modern players, vert.

1974, Aug. 1,   Wmk. 314   Perf. 14

341	A68	5c rose red, dk red & blk	.25	.25
342	A68	20c ocher, brn & blk	.25	.25
343	A68	35c yel grn, grn & blk	.25	.25
344	A68	75c dl bl, dk bl & blk	.25	.50
a.		Souvenir sheet of 4, #341-344	.75	.75
		Nos. 341-344 (4)	1.00	1.25

For surcharge see No. 364.

Soccer — A69

Designs: Games' emblem and soccer.

1974, Sept. 23   Unwmk.   Perf. 14½

345	A69	5c multicolored	.25	.25
346	A69	35c multicolored	.25	.25
347	A69	75c multicolored	.25	.25

348 A69 $1 multicolored .... .35 .35
    a.   Souvenir sheet of 4 .... 1.25 1.25
    Nos. 345-348 (4) 1.10 1.10

World Cup Soccer Championship, Munich, June 13-July 7. Nos. 345-348 issued in sheets of 5 plus label showing Soccer Cup. No. 348a contains one each of Nos. 345-348, perf. 13½, and 2 labels.

For overprints and surcharges see Nos. 361-363.

Winston Churchill (1874-1965) at
Harrow — A70

Designs: 35c, St. Paul's during bombing and Churchill portrait. 75c, Churchill's coat of arms and catafalque. $1, Churchill during Boer war, warrant for arrest and map of his escape route.

1974, Oct. 20   **Unwmk.**   **Perf. 14½**
349 A70 5c multicolored .... .25 .25
350 A70 35c multicolored .... .25 .25
351 A70 75c multicolored .... .25 .30
352 A70 $1 multicolored .... .35 .50
    a.   Souvenir sheet of 4, #349-352 .... 1.25 1.75
    Nos. 349-352 (4) 1.10 1.30

Virgin and Child,
by Giovanni
Bellini — A71

Christmas — Paintings of the Virgin and Child: 1c, Raphael. 2c, Van der Weyden. 3c, Giorgione. 5c, Andrea Mantegna. 20c, Alvise Vivarini. 35c, Bartolommeo Montagna. 75c, Lorenzo Costa.

1974, Nov. 18   **Litho.**   **Perf. 14½**
353 A71 ½c shown .... .25 .25
354 A71 1c multicolored .... .25 .25
355 A71 2c multicolored .... .25 .25
356 A71 3c multicolored .... .25 .25
357 A71 5c multicolored .... .25 .25
358 A71 20c multicolored .... .25 .25
359 A71 35c multicolored .... .25 .25
360 A71 75c multicolored .... .35 .60
    a.   Souv. sheet of 4, #357-360, perf 13½ 1.25 1.50
    Nos. 353-360 (8) 2.10 2.35

Nos. 346-348   No. 344
Overprinted   Surcharged and
                      Overprinted

1974, Oct. 16   **Litho.**   **Perf. 14½, 14**
361 A69 35c multicolored .... .35 .30
362 A69 75c multicolored .... .50 .35
363 A69 $1 multicolored .... .60 .45
364 A68 $5 on 75c multi 2.00 2.00
    Nos. 361-364 (4) 3.45 3.10

Earthquake of Oct. 8, 1974.

Nos. 338-340 and 254a Surcharged

1974-75   **Wmk. 314**   **Perf. 14½**
365 A67 50c on 20c 1.40 2.10
366 A67 $2.50 on 35c 3.00 6.25
367 A67 $5 on $1 .... 6.50 8.00

Perf. 14
368 A51 $10 on 75c 3.00 8.75
    Nos. 365-368 (4) 13.90 25.10

Carib War
Canoe,
English
Harbour
A72

Designs (Nelson's Dockyard): 15c, Raising ship, 1770. 35c, Lord Nelson and "Boreas." 50c, Yachts arriving for Sailing Week, 1974. $1, "Anchorage" in Old Dockyard, 1970.

1975, Mar. 17   **Unwmk.**   **Perf. 14½**
369 A72 5c multicolored .... .30 .25
370 A72 15c multicolored .... 1.00 .25
371 A72 35c multicolored .... 1.50 .25
372 A72 50c multicolored 1.75 1.75
373 A72 $1 multicolored 2.00 2.00
    Nos. 369-373 (5) 6.55 4.50

Souvenir Sheet
Perf. 13½
373A A72 Sheet of 5, #369-373 .... 7.00 7.00

Stamps in No. 373A are 43x28mm.

Lady of
the Valley
Church
A73

Churches of Antigua: 20c, Gilbert Memorial. 35c, Grace Hill Moravian. 50c, St. Phillip's. $1, Ebenezer Methodist.

1975, May 19   **Litho.**   **Perf. 14½**
374 A73 5c multicolored .... .25 .25
375 A73 20c multicolored .... .25 .25
376 A73 35c multicolored .... .25 .25
377 A73 50c multicolored .... .25 .25
378 A73 $1 multicolored .... .25 .25
    a.   Souvenir sheet of 3, #376-378, perf. 13½ 1.00 1.50
    Nos. 374-378 (5) 1.25 1.25

Antigua, Senex's Atlas, 1721, and
Hevelius Sextant, 1640
A74

Maps of Antigua: 20c, Jeffery's Atlas, 1775, and 18th century engraving of ship. 35c, Barbuda and Antigua, 1775 and 1975. $1, St. John's and English Harbour, 1973.

1975, July 21   **Wmk. 314**
379 A74 5c multicolored .... .40 .25
380 A74 20c multicolored .... .75 .25
381 A74 35c multicolored .... .95 .25
382 A74 $1 multicolored 1.90 1.90
    a.   Souvenir sheet of 4, #379-382 .... 5.25 3.50
    Nos. 379-382 (4) 4.00 2.65

Bugler
and
Sunset
A75

Nordjamb 75 Emblem and: 20c, Black and white Scouts, tents and flags. 35c, Lord Baden-Powell and tents. $2, Dahomey dancers.

Unwmk.
1975, Aug. 26   **Litho.**   **Perf. 14**
383 A75 15c multicolored .... .30 .25
384 A75 20c multicolored .... .40 .25
385 A75 35c multicolored .... .60 .30

---

386 A75 $2 multicolored 2.25 2.10
    a.   Souvenir sheet of 4, #383-386 .... 4.75 4.75
    Nos. 383-386 (4) 3.55 2.90

Nordjamb 75, 14th Boy Scout Jamboree, Lillehammer, Norway, July 29-Aug. 7.

Eurema
Elathea
A76

Butterflies: 1c, Danaus plexippus. 2c, Phoebis philea. 5c, Marpesia petreus thetys. 20c, Eurema proterpia. 35c, Papilio polydamas. $2, Vanessa cardui.

1975, Oct. 30   **Litho.**   **Perf. 14**
387 A76 ½c multicolored .... .25 .25
388 A76 1c multicolored .... .25 .25
389 A76 2c multicolored .... .25 .25
390 A76 5c multicolored .... .30 .25
391 A76 20c multicolored .... 1.25 .50
392 A76 35c multicolored .... 1.75 .90
393 A76 $2 multicolored 5.00 5.00
    a.   Miniature sheet of 4, #390-393 .... 9.50 9.50
    Nos. 387-393 (7) 9.05 7.40

Virgin and Child,
by
Correggio — A77

Christmas: Virgin and Child paintings.

1975, Nov. 17   **Unwmk.**
394 A77 ½c shown .... .25 .25
395 A77 1c El Greco .... .25 .25
396 A77 2c Durer .... .25 .25
397 A77 3c Antonello .... .25 .25
398 A77 5c Bellini .... .25 .25
399 A77 10c Durer .... .25 .25
400 A77 35c Bellini .... .40 .25
401 A77 $2 Durer .... .75 .60
    a.   Souvenir sheet of 4, #398-401 .... 2.25 2.25
    Nos. 394-401 (8) 2.65 2.35

West
Indies
Team
A78

Designs: 5c, Batsman I.V.A. Richards and cup, vert. 35c, Bowler A.M.E. Roberts and cup, vert.

1975, Dec. 15   **Litho.**   **Perf. 14**
402 A78 5c multicolored .... 1.25 .25
403 A78 35c multicolored .... 2.25 .55
404 A78 $2 multicolored 4.75 7.25
    Nos. 402-404 (3) 8.25 8.05

World Cricket Cup, victory of West Indies team.

A number of unissued items, imperfs., part perfs., missing color varieties, etc., were made available when the Format International inventory was liquidated. Imperfs of some or all of the Antigua stamps in the following sets are included: #405-422, 503-507, 515-517, 703-707, 745-749, 755-759, 808-816, 819-826, 905-909, 934-937.

See footnote after #962.

Antillean Crested Hummingbird — A79

Irrigation System, Diamond
Estate — A80

Designs: 1c, Imperial parrot. 2c, Zenaida dove. 3c, Loggerhead kingbird. 4c, Red-necked pigeon. 5c, Rufous-throated solitaire. 6c, Orchid tree. 10c, Bougainvillea. 15c, Geiger tree. 20c, Flamboyant. 25c, Hibiscus. 35c, Flame of the Woods. 50c, Cannon at Fort James. 75c, Premier's Office. $1, Potworks Dam. $5, Government House. $10, Coolidge International Airport.

1976, Jan. 19   **Litho.**   **Perf. 15**
405 A79 ½c multicolored .... .35 .50
406 A79 1c multicolored .... 1.00 .50
407 A79 2c multicolored .... 1.00 .50
408 A79 3c multicolored .... 1.00 .55
409 A79 4c multicolored 1.10 1.25
410 A79 5c multicolored .... 1.50 .25
411 A79 6c multicolored .... .30 1.25
412 A79 10c multicolored .... .30 .25
413 A79 15c multicolored .... .35 .25
414 A79 20c multicolored .... .30 .25
415 A79 25c multicolored .... .35 .25
416 A79 35c multicolored .... .35 .35
417 A79 50c multicolored .... .50 .50
418 A79 75c multicolored .... .60 1.25
419 A79 $1 multicolored .... .75 .85

Perf. 13½x14
420 A80 $2.50 rose & multi 1.50 3.75
421 A80 $5 lilac & multi 2.50 5.00
422 A80 $10 multicolored 4.25 6.50
    Nos. 405-422 (18) 18.05 24.10

Inscribed "1978"
1978
405a A79 ½c multicolored .... .55 .75
406a A79 1c multicolored 1.25 1.00
407a A79 2c multicolored 1.25 1.00
408a A79 3c multicolored 1.25 1.00
409a A79 4c multicolored 1.40 1.00
410a A79 5c multicolored .... 1.50 .60
411a A79 6c multicolored .... .35 1.25
412a A79 10c multicolored .... .35 .35
413a A79 15c multicolored .... .30 .35
414a A79 20c multicolored .... .30 1.00
415a A79 25c multicolored .... .35 .55
416a A79 35c multicolored .... .35 .55
417a A79 50c multicolored .... .55 1.00
418a A79 75c multicolored .... .55 1.10
419a A79 $1 multicolored .... .75 1.25

Perf. 13½x14
420a A80 $2.50 rose & multi 1.75 6.50
421a A80 $5 lilac & multi 1.90 6.50
422a A80 $10 multicolored 6.50 8.50
    Nos. 405-422a (18) 21.20 33.25

For overprints see Nos. 607-617.

Some Antigua issues from the 1970s were overprinted "Redonda." Other stamps inscribed "Redonda," but lacking any mention of Antigua, were also created in the 1970s and 1980s. These stamps are not listed because Redonda is uninhabited and has no need for stamps of its own.

Privates, Clark's
Illinois
Regiment — A81

1c, Riflemen, Pennsylvania Militia. 2c, Decorated American powder horn. 5c, Water bottle of Maryland troops. 35c, "Liberty Tree" and "Rattlesnake" flags. $1, American privateer Montgomery. $2.50, Congress Flag. $5, Continental Navy sloop Ranger.

1976, Mar. 17   **Litho.**   **Perf. 14½**
423 A81 ½c multicolored .... .25 .25
424 A81 1c multicolored .... .25 .25
425 A81 2c multicolored .... .25 .25
426 A81 5c multicolored .... .25 .25
427 A81 35c multicolored .... .55 .25
428 A81 $1 multicolored .... 1.50 .30
429 A81 $5 multicolored 2.75 2.75
    Nos. 423-429 (7) 5.80 4.30

Souvenir Sheet
Perf. 13
430 A81 $2.50 multicolored   2.10   2.10
American Bicentennial.

High Jump, Olympic Rings A82

Olympic Rings and: 1c, Boxing. 2c, Pole vault. 15c, Swimming. 30c, Running. $1, Bicycling. $2, Shot put.

1976, July 12   Litho.   **Perf. 14½**
431	A82	½c yellow & multi	.25	.25
432	A82	1c purple & multi	.25	.25
433	A82	2c emerald & multi	.25	.25
434	A82	15c brt blue & multi	.25	.25
435	A82	30c olive & multi	.30	.25
436	A82	$1 orange & multi	.50	.25
437	A82	$2 red & multi	1.50	1.50
a.		Souvenir sheet of 4	2.50	3.25
		Nos. 431-437 (7)	3.30	3.00

21st Olympic Games, Montreal, Canada, July 17-Aug. 1. No. 437a contains one each of Nos. 434-437, perf. 13½.

Water Skiing A83

Water Sports: 1c, Sailfish sailing. 2c, Snorkeling. 20c, Deep-sea fishing. 50c, Scuba diving. $2, Swimming.

1976, Aug. 26   **Perf. 14**
438	A83	½c yel grn & multi	.25	.25
439	A83	1c sepia & multi	.25	.25
440	A83	2c gray & multi	.25	.25
441	A83	20c multicolored	.25	.25
442	A83	50c brt vio & multi	.45	.50
443	A83	$2 lt gray & multi	1.25	1.40
a.		Souvenir sheet of 3, #441-443	2.25	2.25
		Nos. 438-443 (6)	2.70	2.90

French Angelfish — A84

1976, Oct. 4   Litho.   **Perf. 13½x14**
444	A84	15c shown	.50	.25
445	A84	30c Yellowfish grouper	.85	.25
446	A84	50c Yellowtail snappers	1.00	.45
447	A84	90c Shy hamlet	1.50	.75
		Nos. 444-447 (4)	3.85	1.70

The Annunciation A85

Christmas: 10c, Flight into Egypt. 15c, Three Kings. 50c, Shepherds and star. $1, Kings presenting gifts to Christ Child.

1976, Nov. 15   Litho.   **Perf. 14**
448	A85	8c multicolored	.25	.25
449	A85	10c multicolored	.25	.25
450	A85	15c multicolored	.25	.25
451	A85	50c multicolored	.25	.25
452	A85	$1 multi	.25	.25
		Nos. 448-452 (5)	1.25	1.25

Mercury and UPU Emblem A86

Designs: 1c, Alfred Nobel, symbols of prize categories. 10c, Viking spacecraft. 50c, Vivi Richards (batsman) and Andy Roberts (bowler). $1, Alexander G. Bell, telephones, 1876 and 1976. $2, Schooner Freelance.

1976, Dec. 28   Litho.   **Perf. 14**
453	A86	½c multicolored	.25	.25
454	A86	1c multicolored	.25	.25
455	A86	10c multicolored	.35	.25
456	A86	50c multicolored	3.75	1.75
457	A86	$1 multicolored	1.00	1.25
458	A86	$2 multicolored	2.25	3.00
a.		Souvenir sheet of 4, #455-458	8.25	8.25
		Nos. 453-458 (6)	7.85	6.75

Special 1976 Events: UN Postal Admin., 25th anniv. (½c); Nobel Prize, 75th anniv. (1c); Viking Space Mission to Mars (10c); World Cricket Cup victory (50c); Telephone cent. ($1); Operation Sail, American Bicent. ($2).

Royal Family — A87

Designs: 10c, Queen Elizabeth, Prince Philip and their children. 30c, Elizabeth II and Prince Philip touring Antigua. 50c, Queen enthroned. 90c, Queen wearing crown. $2.50, Queen and Prince Charles. $5, Queen and Prince Philip.

1977, Feb. 7   **Perf. 13½x14**
459	A87	10c multicolored	.25	.25
460	A87	30c multicolored	.25	.25
461	A87	50c multicolored	.25	.25
462	A87	90c multicolored	.25	.25
463	A87	$2.50 multicolored	.25	.40
		Nos. 459-463 (5)	1.25	1.40

Souvenir Sheet
464	A87	$5 multicolored	.80	1.00
		Complete booklet, 6 #461 var., 1 #464 var., self-adhesive and in changed colors		4.50

Reign of Queen Elizabeth II, 25th anniv. Nos. 459-463 were printed in sheets of 40. Sheets of 5 plus label, perf. 12, probably were not sold by the Antigua Post Office. For overprints see Nos. 477-482.

Scouts Camping A88

Boy Scout Emblem and: 1c, Scouts on hike. 2c, Rock climbing. 10c, Cutting logs. 30c, Map and compass reading. 50c, First aid. $2, Scouts on raft.

1977, May 23   Litho.   **Perf. 14**
465	A88	½c multicolored	.25	.25
466	A88	1c multicolored	.25	.25
467	A88	2c multicolored	.25	.25
468	A88	10c multicolored	.25	.25
469	A88	30c multicolored	.35	.25
470	A88	50c multicolored	.60	.35
471	A88	$2 multicolored	1.25	1.25
a.		Souvenir sheet of 3, #469-471	3.50	3.50
		Nos. 465-471 (7)	3.20	2.85

Caribbean Boy Scout Jamboree, Jamaica.

Carnival Queen Holding Horseshoe — A89

30c, Carnival Queen in feather costume. 50c, Butterfly costume. 90c, Carnival Queen with ornaments. $1, Carnival King, Queen.

1977, July 18   Litho.   **Perf. 14**
472	A89	10c multicolored	.25	.25
473	A89	30c multicolored	.25	.25
474	A89	50c multicolored	.25	.25
475	A89	90c multicolored	.45	.40
476	A89	$1 multicolored	.50	.50
a.		Souvenir sheet of 4, #473-476	1.75	1.75
		Nos. 472-476 (5)	1.70	1.65

21st Summer Carnival.

Nos. 459-464 Overprinted

Perf. 13½x14, 12
1977, Oct. 17   Litho.
477	A87	10c multicolored	.25	.25
478	A87	30c multicolored	.25	.25
479	A87	50c multicolored	.25	.25
480	A87	90c multicolored	.35	.30
481	A87	$2.50 multicolored	.50	.40
		Nos. 477-481 (5)	1.60	1.45

Souvenir Sheet
482	A87	$5 multicolored	1.75	1.75

Visit of Queen Elizabeth II, Oct. 28.

Virgin and Child, by Cosimo Tura — A90

Virgin and Child by: 1c, $2, Carlo Crivelli (different). 2c, 25c, Lorenzo Lotto (different). 8c, Jacopo da Pontormo. 10c, Tura.

1977, Nov. 15   Litho.   **Perf. 14**
483	A90	½c multicolored	.25	.25
484	A90	1c multicolored	.25	.25
485	A90	2c multicolored	.25	.25
486	A90	8c multicolored	.25	.25
487	A90	10c multicolored	.25	.25
488	A90	25c multicolored	.25	.25
489	A90	$2 multicolored	.85	.80
a.		Souvenir sheet of 4, #486-489	1.50	2.00
		Nos. 483-489 (7)	2.35	2.30

Christmas.

Pineapple A91

10th anniv. of Statehood: 15c, Flag of Antigua. 50c, Police band. 90c, Prime Minister V. C. Bird. $2, Coat of Arms.

1977, Dec. 28   Litho.   **Perf. 13x13½**
490	A91	10c multicolored	.25	.25
491	A91	15c multicolored	.50	.25
492	A91	50c multicolored	2.50	.75
493	A91	90c multicolored	.50	.75

494	A91	$2 multicolored	.90	1.50
a.		Souv. sheet, #491-494, perf 14	3.50	3.50
		Nos. 490-494 (5)	4.65	3.50

Wright Glider III, 1902 A92

1c, Flyer I in air, 1903. 2c, Weight and derrick launch system and Wright engine, 1903. 10c, Orville Wright, vert. 50c, Flyer III, 1905. 90c, Wilbur Wright, vert. $2, Wright Model B, 1910. $2.50, Flyer I, 1903, on ground.

1978, Mar. 28   **Perf. 14**
495	A92	½c multicolored	.25	.25
496	A92	1c multicolored	.25	.25
497	A92	2c multicolored	.25	.25
498	A92	10c multicolored	.35	.25
499	A92	50c multicolored	.55	.25
500	A92	90c multicolored	.80	.30
501	A92	$2 multicolored	1.10	.80
		Nos. 495-501 (7)	3.55	2.35

Souvenir Sheet
502	A92	$2.50 multicolored	2.25	2.75

1st powered flight by Wright brothers, 75th anniv.

Sunfish Regatta A93

Sailing Week 1978: 50c, Fishing and work boat race. 90c, Curtain Bluff race. $2, Powerboat rally. $2.50, Guadeloupe-Antigua race.

1978, Apr. 29   Litho.   **Perf. 14½**
503	A93	10c multicolored	.30	.25
504	A93	50c multicolored	.40	.25
505	A93	90c multicolored	.75	.40
506	A93	$2 multicolored	1.50	.75
		Nos. 503-506 (4)	2.95	1.65

Souvenir Sheet
507	A93	$2.50 multicolored	2.25	2.25

25th Anniv. of the Coronation of Queen Elizabeth II — A94

Designs: 10c, Elizabeth II and Prince Philip. 30c, Coronation. 50c, State coach. 90c, Elizabeth II and Archbishop. $2.50, Elizabeth II. $5, Elizabeth II, Prince Philip, Prince Charles and Princess Anne as children.

1978, June 2   Litho.   **Perf. 14, 12**
508	A94	10c multicolored	.25	.25
509	A94	30c multicolored	.25	.25
510	A94	50c multicolored	.25	.25
511	A94	90c multicolored	.25	.25
512	A94	$2 multicolored	.40	.40
		Nos. 508-512 (5)	1.40	1.40

Souvenir Sheet
513	A94	$5 multicolored	1.40	1.40

25th anniv. of coronation of Queen Elizabeth II.
Nos. 508-512 were printed in sheets of 50 (2 panes of 25), perf. 14, and in sheets of 3 plus label, perf. 12, with frames in changed colors.

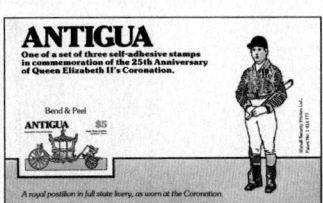

Glass Coach — A95

Royal Coaches: 50c, Irish state coach. $5, Coronation coach.

1978, June 2   Litho.   *Imperf.*
Self-adhesive

514		Souvenir booklet	2.50	
	a.	A95 Bklt. pane, 3 each 25c, 50c	1.00	
	b.	A95 Bklt. pane, 1 $5	1.40	

25th anniversary of coronation of Queen Elizabeth II. No. 514 contains 2 booklet panes printed on peelable paper backing showing royal processions.

Soccer — A96

Designs: Various soccer scenes. Stamps in souvenir sheet horizontal.

1978, Aug. 18   Litho.   Perf. 15

515	A96	10c multicolored	.25	.25
516	A96	15c multicolored	.25	.25
517	A96	$3 multicolored	1.75	1.75
		Nos. 515-517 (3)	2.25	2.25

Souvenir Sheet

518		Sheet of 4	4.25	4.25
	a.	A96 25c multicolored	.30	.30
	b.	A96 30c multicolored	.45	.45
	c.	A96 50c multicolored	.80	.80
	d.	A96 $2 multicolored	2.25	2.25

11th World Cup Soccer Championship, Argentina, June 1-25.

Purple Wreath — A97

1978, Oct.   Litho.   Perf. 14

519	A97	25c shown	.30	.25
520	A97	50c Sunflowers	.45	.25
521	A97	90c Frangipani	.75	.30
522	A97	$2 Passionflower	1.60	1.50
		Nos. 519-522 (4)	3.10	2.30

Souvenir Sheet

| 523 | A97 | $2.50 Red hibiscus | 2.00 | 2.00 |

St. Ildefonso Receiving Chasuble, by Rubens A98

Christmas: 25c, Flight of St. Barbara, by Rubens. $2, Madonna and Child with Ss. Joseph and John and a Dono, by Sebastiano del Piombo. $4, Annunciation, by Rubens.

1978, Oct. 30   Litho.   Perf. 14

524	A98	8c multicolored	.25	.25
525	A98	25c multicolored	.25	.25
526	A98	$2 multicolored	.65	.55
		Nos. 524-526 (3)	1.15	1.05

Souvenir Sheet

| 527 | A98 | $4 multicolored | 2.10 | 2.10 |

No. 526 is incorrectly attributed to Rubens.

Antigua #2 — A99

Designs: 50c, Great Britain Penny Black, 1840. $1, Woman posting letter in pillar box, and coach. $2, Mail train, ship, plane and Concorde. $2.50, Rowland Hill.

1979, Aug. 27   Litho.   Perf. 14

528	A99	25c multicolored	.25	.25
529	A99	50c multicolored	.25	.25
530	A99	$1 multicolored	.35	.25
531	A99	$2 multicolored	.85	.50
		Nos. 528-531 (4)	1.70	1.25

Souvenir Sheet

| 532 | A99 | $2.50 multicolored | 1.25 | 1.40 |

Sir Rowland Hill (1795-1879), originator of penny postage.

Nos. 528-531 were printed in sheets of 50 (2 panes of 25), perf. 14, and in sheets of 5 plus label, perf. 12, with frames in changed colors.

For overprints, see Nos. 571A-571D.

Crucifixion, by Durer — A100

Designs (after Dürer): 10c, Deposition. $2.50, Crucifixion. $4, Man of Sorrows.

1979, Mar. 15

533	A100	10c multicolored	.25	.25
534	A100	50c multicolored	.50	.25
535	A100	$4 multicolored	1.25	1.10
		Nos. 533-535 (3)	2.00	1.60

Souvenir Sheet

| 536 | A100 | $2.50 multicolored | 1.25 | 1.25 |

Easter.

Child Playing with Sailboat — A101

IYC emblem, child's hand holding toy: 50c, Rocket. 90c, Automobile. $2, Train. $5, Plane.

1979, Apr. 9   Litho.   Perf. 14

537	A101	25c multicolored	.25	.25
538	A101	50c multicolored	.25	.25
539	A101	90c multicolored	.40	.30
540	A101	$2 multicolored	1.10	1.00
		Nos. 537-540 (4)	2.00	1.80

Souvenir Sheet

| 541 | A101 | $5 multicolored | 2.10 | 2.10 |

International Year of the Child.

Yellowjacks — A102

Sport Fish: 50c, Bluefin tunas. 90c, Sailfish. $2.50, Barracuda. $3, Wahoos.

1979, May   Litho.   Perf. 14½

542	A102	30c multicolored	.35	.25
543	A102	50c multicolored	.50	.30
544	A102	90c multicolored	1.00	.40
545	A102	$3 multicolored	3.00	2.00
		Nos. 542-545 (4)	4.85	2.95

Souvenir Sheet

| 546 | A102 | $2.50 multicolored | 2.25 | 2.25 |

Capt. Cook and his Birthplace at Marton — A103

Capt. James Cook (1728-1779) and: 50c, HMS Endeavour. 90c, Marine timekeeper. $2.50, HMS Resolution. $3, Landing at Botany Bay.

1979, July 2   Litho.   Perf. 14

547	A103	25c multicolored	.60	.30
548	A103	50c multicolored	.95	.40
549	A103	90c multicolored	.70	.40
550	A103	$3 multicolored	1.60	2.50
		Nos. 547-550 (4)	3.85	3.90

Souvenir Sheet

| 551 | A103 | $2.50 multicolored | 2.75 | 2.75 |

Holy Family — A104

Stained-glass Windows: 25c, Flight into Egypt. 50c, Shepherd and star. $3, Angel with trumpet. $4, Three Kings offering gifts.

1979, Oct. 1   Litho.   Perf. 14

552	A104	8c multicolored	.25	.25
553	A104	25c multicolored	.25	.25
554	A104	50c multicolored	.30	.30
555	A104	$4 multicolored	.90	2.00
		Nos. 552-555 (4)	1.70	2.80

Souvenir Sheet
Perf. 12x12½

| 556 | A104 | $3 multicolored | 1.25 | 2.00 |

Christmas.

Javelin, Olympic Rings — A105

1980, Feb. 7   Litho.   Perf. 14

557	A105	10c shown	.25	.25
558	A105	25c Running	.30	.30
559	A105	$1 Pole vault	.60	.60
560	A105	$2 Hurdles	.70	.70
		Nos. 557-560 (4)	1.85	1.85

Souvenir Sheet

| 561 | A105 | $3 Boxing, horiz. | 1.40 | 1.40 |

22nd Summer Olympic Games, Moscow, July 19-Aug. 3.

Disney Characters and IYC Emblem A106

Transportation scenes: ½c, Mickey, plane. 1c, Donald, car. 2c, Goofy driving taxi. 3c, Mickey, Minnie in sidecar. 4c, Huey, Dewey and Louie. 5c, Grandma Duck. 10c, Mickey in

jeep. $1, Chip and Dale sailing. $4, Donald on train.
$2.50, Goofy in glider.
½c, 2c, 3c, 4c, 5c, $1, $2.50, horiz.

1980, Mar. 24   Litho.   Perf. 11

562	A106	½c multicolored	.25	.25
563	A106	1c multicolored	.25	.25
564	A106	2c multicolored	.25	.25
565	A106	3c multicolored	.25	.25
566	A106	4c multicolored	.25	.25
567	A106	5c multicolored	.25	.25
568	A106	10c multicolored	.25	.25
569	A106	$1 multicolored	1.50	1.50
570	A106	$4 multicolored	3.75	4.00
		Nos. 562-570 (9)	7.00	7.25

Souvenir Sheet

| 571 | A106 | $2.50 multicolored | 7.50 | 7.50 |

Nos. 528-531 in Changed Colors & Overprinted

1980, May 6   Litho.   Perf. 12

571A	A99	25c multicolored	.35	.35
571B	A99	50c multicolored	.45	.45
571C	A99	$1 multicolored	.75	.75
571D	A99	$2 multicolored	3.25	3.25
		Nos. 571A-571D (4)	4.80	4.80

London '80 Intl. Stamp Exhib., May 6-14.
For overprints see Barbuda Nos. 423-426.

Birth of Venus, by Botticelli — A106a

10c, David, by Donatello. 50c, Reclining Couple, sarcophagus, Cerveteri. 90c, The Garden of Earthly Delights, by Hieronymus Bosch. $1, Portinari Altarpiece, by Hugo van der Goes. $4, Eleanora of Toledo and her Son Giovanni de Medici, by Bronzino. $5, The Holy Family, by Rembrandt.

Perf. 13½x14, 14x13½

1980, June 23   Litho.

572	A106a	10c multi, vert.	.25	.25
573	A106a	30c multi	.40	.25
574	A106a	50c multi	.55	.40
575	A106a	90c multi	.75	.75
576	A106a	$1 multi	.85	.85
577	A106a	$4 multi, vert.	2.25	3.00
		Nos. 572-577 (6)	5.05	5.50

Souvenir Sheet
Perf. 14

| 578 | A106a | $5 multicolored | 3.25 | 3.25 |

Anniversary Emblem, Intl. Headquarters, Evanston, IL — A107

50c, Antigua club banner. 90c, Map of Antigua. $3, Paul P. Harris, emblem. $5, Emblems, Antigua flags.

1980, July 21   Litho.   Perf. 14

579	A107	30c shown	.35	.25
580	A107	50c multicolored	.40	.40
581	A107	90c multicolored	.60	.60
582	A107	$3 multicolored	2.00	2.50
		Nos. 579-582 (4)	3.35	3.75

Souvenir Sheet

| 583 | A107 | $5 multicolored | 2.00 | 2.00 |

Rotary International, 75th anniv.

A108

1980, Sept. 15

584	A108	10c multicolored	.25	.25
585	A108	$2.50 multicolored	1.25	1.75

Souvenir Sheet
Perf. 12

586	A108	$3 multicolored	1.50	2.00

Queen Mother Elizabeth, 80th birthday.

A109

No. 587, Ringed Kingfisher. No. 588, Plain pigeon. No. 889, Green-throated carib. No. 890, Black-necked stilt.
No. 591, Roseate tern.

1980, Nov. 3   Litho.   Perf. 14

587	A109	10c multicolored	.90	.30
588	A109	30c multicolored	1.25	1.50
589	A109	$1 multicolored	1.75	1.75
590	A109	$2 multicolored	2.50	3.50
		Nos. 587-590 (4)	6.40	6.05

Souvenir Sheet

591	A109	$2.50 multicolored	7.50	7.50

Sleeping Beauty and the Prince — A110

Christmas: Various scenes from Walt Disney's Sleeping Beauty. $4 vert.

1980, Dec. 23   Perf. 11, 13½x14 ($4)

592	A110	½c multicolored	.25	.25
593	A110	1c multicolored	.25	.25
594	A110	2c multicolored	.25	.25
595	A110	4c multicolored	.25	.25
596	A110	8c multicolored	.25	.25
597	A110	10c multicolored	.25	.25
598	A110	25c multicolored	.30	.30
599	A110	$2 multicolored	2.50	2.50
600	A110	$2.50 multicolored	2.75	2.75
		Nos. 592-600 (9)	7.05	7.05

Souvenir Sheet

601	A110	$4 multicolored	7.25	7.25

Sugar-cane Railway Diesel Locomotive No. 15 — A111

50c, Narrow-gauge steam locomotive. 90c, Diesels #1, #10. $3, Hauling sugar-cane. $2.50, Sugar factory, train yard.

1981, Jan. 12   Perf. 14

602	A111	25c shown	.25	.25
603	A111	50c multicolored	.40	.40
604	A111	90c multicolored	.75	.75
605	A111	$3 multicolored	2.75	2.75
		Nos. 602-605 (4)	4.15	4.15

Souvenir Sheet

606	A111	$2.50 multicolored	3.00	3.00

Nos. 411-412, 414-422 Overprinted

1981, Mar. 31   Litho.

607	A79	6c multicolored	.25	.25
608	A79	10c multicolored	.25	.25
609	A79	20c multicolored	.25	.25
610	A79	25c multicolored	.25	.25
611	A79	35c multicolored	.30	.30
612	A79	50c multicolored	.55	.55
613	A79	75c multicolored	.65	.65
614	A79	$1 multicolored	.95	1.25
615	A80	$2.50 Couple	1.60	2.25
616	A80	$5 multicolored	2.75	3.75
617	A80	$10 multicolored	5.75	8.00
		Nos. 607-617 (11)	13.55	17.75

Pipes of Pan, by Picasso — A112

Paintings by Pablo Picasso (1881-1973): 50c, Seated Harlequin. 90c, Paulo as Harlequin. $4, Mother and Child. $5, Three Musicians.

1981, May 5   Litho.   Perf. 14

618	A112	10c multicolored	.25	.25
619	A112	50c multicolored	.40	.40
620	A112	90c multicolored	.75	.75
621	A112	$4 multicolored	2.75	2.75
		Nos. 618-621 (4)	4.15	4.15

Souvenir Sheet
Perf. 14x14½

622	A112	$5 multicolored	2.75	2.75

Royal Wedding Issue
Common Design Type

1981, June 16   Litho.   Perf. 14

623	CD331a	25c Couple	.25	.25
624	CD331a	50c Glamis Castle	.25	.25
625	CD331a	$4 Charles	.80	.80
		Nos. 623-625 (3)	1.30	1.30

Souvenir Sheet

626	CD331	$5 Glass coach	1.25	1.25
627	CD331	Booklet	5.00	
a.		Pane of 6 (2x25c, 2x$1, 2x$2), Charles	3.00	
b.		Pane of 1, $5, Couple	2.00	

No. 627 contains imperf., self-adhesive stamps.
Nos. 623-625 also printed in sheets of 5 plus label, perf. 12 in changed colors.
For surcharges see Nos. 792, 795, 802, 805.

Campfire Sing A113

1981, Oct. 28   Litho.   Perf. 15

628	A113	10c Irene Joshua	.25	.25
629	A113	50c shown	.45	.25
630	A113	90c Sailing	.75	.55
631	A113	$2.50 Milking cow	1.75	1.75
		Nos. 628-631 (4)	3.20	2.80

Souvenir Sheet

632	A113	$5 Flag raising	6.25	6.25

Girl Guides, 50th anniv.

A114

10c, Arms. 50c, Flag. 90c, Prime Minister Bird. $2.50, St. John's Cathedral, horiz. $5, Map.

1981, Nov. 1   Litho.   Perf. 15

633	A114	10c multicolored	.30	.25
634	A114	50c multicolored	1.00	.50
635	A114	90c multicolored	.60	.60
636	A114	$2.50 multicolored	1.60	2.25
		Nos. 633-636 (4)	3.50	3.60

Souvenir Sheet

637	A114	$5 multicolored	4.75	4.75

Independence.
No. 637 contains one 41x41mm stamp.

A115

Christmas (Virgin and Child Paintings by): 8c, Holy Night, by Jacques Stella (1596-1657). 30c Julius Schnorr von Carolsfeld (1794-1872). $1, Alonso Cano (1601-1667). $3, Lorenzo de Credi (1459-1537). $5, Holy Family, by Pieter von Avont (1600-1652).

1981, Nov. 16

638	A115	8c multicolored	.30	.25
639	A115	30c multicolored	.60	.25
640	A115	$1 multicolored	1.40	1.40
641	A115	$3 multicolored	2.00	3.50
		Nos. 638-641 (4)	4.30	5.40

Souvenir Sheet

642	A115	$5 multicolored	4.25	4.50

On No. 639, the artist's name is misspelled as "Carolfeld."

Intl. Year of the Disabled A116

1981, Dec. 1   Litho.   Perf. 15

643	A116	10c Swimming	.25	.25
644	A116	50c Discus	.30	.30
645	A116	90c Archery	.45	.50
646	A116	$2 Baseball	1.25	1.40
		Nos. 643-646 (4)	2.25	2.45

Souvenir Sheet

647	A116	$4 Basketball	5.00	5.00

1982 World Cup Soccer A117

Designs: Various soccer players.

1982, Apr. 15   Litho.   Perf. 14

648	A117	10c multicolored	.30	.25
649	A117	50c multicolored	.55	.30
650	A117	90c multicolored	1.10	.65
651	A117	$4 multicolored	3.50	3.50
		Nos. 648-651 (4)	5.45	4.70

Souvenir Sheet

652	A117	$5 multicolored	7.75	7.75

Also issued in sheetlets of 5 + label in changed colors, perf. 12.

A118

No. 653, A-300 Airbus. No. 654, Hawker-Siddeley 748. No. 655, De Havilland Twin Otter DCH6. No. 656, Britten-Norman Islander.
No. 657, Jet, horiz.

1982, June 17   Litho.   Perf. 14½

653	A118	10c multicolored	.25	.25
654	A118	50c multicolored	.35	.35
655	A118	90c multicolored	.75	.75
656	A118	$2.50 multicolored	2.25	2.25
		Nos. 653-656 (4)	3.60	3.60

Souvenir Sheet

657	A118	$5 multicolored	4.25	4.25

Coolidge Intl. Airport opening.

A119

No. 658, Cordia, vert. No. 659, Golden spotted mongoose. No. 660, Corallita, vert. No. 661, Bulldog bats.
No. 662, Caribbean monk seals.

1982, June 28   Litho.   Perf. 14½

658	A119	10c multicolored	.35	.25
659	A119	50c multicolored	.70	.40
660	A119	90c multicolored	1.10	.75
661	A119	$3 multicolored	2.50	3.25
		Nos. 658-661 (4)	4.65	4.65

Souvenir Sheet

662	A119	$5 multicolored	7.75	7.75

Charles Darwin's death centenary.

Princess Diana Issue
Common Design Type

90c, Greenwich Palace. $1, Wedding. $4, Diana.
$5, Diana, diff.

1982, July 1   Litho.   Perf. 14½x14

663	CD332	90c multicolored	.80	.80
664	CD332	$1 multicolored	.90	.90
665	CD332	$4 multicolored	3.50	3.50
		Nos. 663-665 (3)	5.20	5.20

Souvenir Sheet

666	CD332	$5 multicolored	4.50	4.50

For overprints and surcharges see Nos. 672-675, 797, 799, 803, 806.

Scouting Year A120

Independence Day celebration: 10c, Decorating buildings. 50c, Helping woman. 90c, Princess Margaret. $2.20, Cub Scout giving directions.
$5, Baden-Powell.

1982, July 15   Perf. 14

667	A120	10c multicolored	.30	.25
668	A120	50c multicolored	.60	.45
669	A120	90c multicolored	.95	.65
670	A120	$2.20 multicolored	1.75	2.25
		Nos. 667-670 (4)	3.60	3.60

Souvenir Sheet

671	A120	$5 multicolored	6.75	6.75

Nos. 663-666
Overprinted

1982, Aug. 30   Litho.   Perf. 14½x14
672	CD332	90c multicolored	.45	.45
673	CD332	$1 multicolored	.55	.55
674	CD332	$4 multicolored	2.25	1.90

Nos. 672-674 (3)   3.25   2.90

Souvenir Sheet
675	CD332	$5 multicolored	3.00	3.00

For surcharges see Nos. 798, 800, 804, 807.

Roosevelt
Driving by
"The Little
White
House"
A121

25c, Washington as blacksmith. 45c, Churchill, Roosevelt, Stalin. 60c, Washington crossing Delaware, vert. $1, Roosevelt on train, vert. $3, Roosevelt, vert.
No. 682, Washington, vert. No. 683, Eleanor and Franklin.

1982, Sept. 20   Perf. 15
676	A121	10c shown	.25	.25
677	A121	25c multicolored	.40	.25
678	A121	45c multicolored	1.50	.35
679	A121	60c multicolored	1.00	.35
680	A121	$1 multicolored	1.25	.90
681	A121	$3 multicolored	1.40	2.50

Nos. 676-681 (6)   5.80   4.60

Souvenir Sheets
682	A121	$4 multicolored	3.75	3.75
683	A121	$4 multicolored	3.75	3.75

George Washington's 250th birth anniv. and Franklin D. Roosevelt's birth centenary.

Christmas — A122

Raphael Paintings: 10c, Annunciation. 30c, Adoration of the Magi. $1, Presentation at the Temple. $4, Coronation of the Virgin.
$5, Marriage of the Virgin.

1982, Nov.   Litho.   Perf. 14
684	A122	10c multicolored	.25	.25
685	A122	30c multicolored	.25	.25
686	A122	$1 multicolored	.50	.50
687	A122	$4 multicolored	2.50	2.50

Nos. 684-687 (4)   3.50   3.50

Souvenir Sheet
688	A122	$5 multicolored	3.50	3.25

500th Birth Anniv. of Raphael — A123

45c, Galatea taking Reins of Dolphins, vert. 50c, Sea Nymphs carried by Tritons, vert. 60c, Winged Angel Steering Dolphins. $4, Cupids Shooting Arrows.
$5, Galatea.

1983, Jan. 28.   Litho.   Perf. 14½
689	A123	45c multicolored	.30	.30
690	A123	50c multicolored	.40	.40
691	A123	60c multicolored	.45	.45
692	A123	$4 multicolored	2.50	2.50

Nos. 689-692 (4)   3.65   3.65

Souvenir Sheet
693	A123	$5 multicolored	4.50	4.50

A124

1983, Mar. 14   Perf. 14
694	A124	25c Pineapple crop	.25	.25
695	A124	45c Carnival	.25	.25
696	A124	60c Tourists, sailboat	.35	.35
697	A124	$3 Control Tower	1.10	1.10

Nos. 694-697 (4)   1.95   1.95

Commonwealth Day.

World Communications Year — A125

15c, TV screen, camera. 50c, Police radio, car. 60c, Long distance phone call. $3, Dish antenna, planets.
$5, Comsat satellite.

1983, Apr. 5   Litho.   Perf. 14
698	A125	15c multicolored	.50	.25
699	A125	50c multicolored	2.10	1.25
700	A125	60c multicolored	2.25	1.40
701	A125	$3 multicolored	4.25	5.00

Nos. 698-701 (4)   9.10   7.90

Souvenir Sheet
702	A125	$5 multicolored	3.50	3.50

Imperforates
See note following No. 404.

Bottlenose
Dolphin
A126

50c, Finback whale. 60c, Bowhead whale. $3, Spectacled porpoise.
$5, Unicorn whale.

1983, May 9   Litho.   Perf. 15
703	A126	15c shown	.85	.25
704	A126	50c multicolored	1.75	1.25
705	A126	60c multicolored	2.00	1.25
706	A126	$3 multicolored	3.75	4.25

Nos. 703-706 (4)   8.35   7.00

Souvenir Sheet
707	A126	$5 multicolored	8.75	8.75

Cashew
Nut
A127

1983, July 11   Perf. 14
708	A127	1c shown	.25	.90
709	A127	2c Passion fruit	.25	.90
710	A127	3c Mango	.25	.90
711	A127	5c Grapefruit	.25	.50
712	A127	10c Pawpaw	.40	.25
713	A127	15c Breadfruit	.75	.25
714	A127	20c Coconut	.45	.25
715	A127	25c Oleander	.75	.35
716	A127	30c Banana	.55	.40
717	A127	40c Pineapple	.75	.40
718	A127	45c Cordia	.85	.55
719	A127	50c Cassia	.90	.60
720	A127	60c Poui	1.75	.90
721	A127	$1 Frangipani	2.25	1.25
722	A127	$2 Flamboyant	3.50	3.50
723	A127	$2.50 Lemon	3.75	5.00
724	A127	$5 Lignum vitae	6.00	11.00
725	A127	$10 Arms	9.00	16.00

Nos. 708-725 (18)   32.65   43.90

1985   Perf. 12½x12
708a	A127	1c	.25	.55
709a	A127	2c	.25	.55
710a	A127	3c	.25	.55
711a	A127	5c	.30	.45
712a	A127	10c	.35	.25
713a	A127	15c	.50	.25
714a	A127	20c	.60	.25
715a	A127	25c	.60	.25
716a	A127	30c	.70	.30
717a	A127	40c	.75	.30
718a	A127	45c	.80	.45
719a	A127	50c	1.20	.45
720a	A127	60c	1.75	1.10
721a	A127	$1	2.00	1.25
722a	A127	$2	3.75	3.75
723a	A127	$2.50	4.25	5.00
724a	A127	$5	6.75	10.00
725a	A127	$10	11.00	16.00

Nos. 708a-725a (18)   36.05   41.70

Issue dates: $2-$5, Dec; others Mar.

Manned Flight Bicentenary — A128

30c, Dornier DoX. 50c, Supermarine S-6B. 60c, Curtiss F9C, USS Akron. $4, Pro Juventute balloon.
$5, Graf Zeppelin.

1983, Aug. 15   Perf. 15
726	A128	30c multicolored	1.00	.30
727	A128	50c multicolored	1.25	.60
728	A128	60c multicolored	1.50	.75
729	A128	$4 multicolored	3.75	5.00

Nos. 726-729 (4)   7.50   6.65

Souvenir Sheet
730	A128	$5 multicolored	4.00	4.00

Christmas — A129

Raphael Paintings: 10c, Angel flying with scroll. 30c, Angel, diff. $1, Inscribing tablet. $4, Angel showing tablet.
$5, Vision of Ezekiel.
10c, 30c, $1, $4, Sybils and Angels details.

1983, Oct. 4   Litho.   Perf. 14
731	A129	10c multicolored	.40	.25
732	A129	30c multicolored	.75	.40
733	A129	$1 multicolored	1.60	1.25
734	A129	$4 multicolored	3.25	4.50

Nos. 731-734 (4)   6.00   6.40

Souvenir Sheet
735	A129	$5 multicolored	1.90	1.90

Methodist Church,
Anniv. — A130

Designs: 15c, John Wesley founder of Methodism. 50c, Nathaniel Gilbert, Antiguan founder. 60c, St. John's Methodist Church Steeple. $3, Ebenezer Methodist Church.

1983, Nov.   Litho.   Perf. 14
736	A130	15c multicolored	.35	.25
737	A130	50c multicolored	.95	.45
738	A130	60c multicolored	1.00	.60
739	A130	$3 multicolored	2.75	3.75

Nos. 736-739 (4)   5.05   5.05

1984 Olympics,
Los
Angeles — A131

1984, Jan.   Litho.   Perf. 15
740	A131	25c Discus	.25	.25
741	A131	50c Gymnastics	.30	.25
742	A131	90c Hurdling	.60	.60
743	A131	$3 Bicycling	2.40	3.00

Nos. 740-743 (4)   3.55   4.10

Souvenir Sheet
744	A131	$5 Volleyball, horiz.	3.50	4.00

Booker
Vanguard
A132

1984, June 4   Litho.   Perf. 15
745	A132	45c shown	1.25	.45
746	A132	50c Canberra	1.50	.70
747	A132	60c Yachts	1.75	.85
748	A132	$4 Fairwind	3.50	6.00

Nos. 745-748 (4)   8.00   8.00

Souvenir Sheet
749	A132	$5 Man-of-war, vert.	3.00	4.00

Local
Flowers — A133

1984, June 25   Litho.   Perf. 15
755	A133	15c multicolored	.50	.25
756	A133	50c multicolored	1.00	.75
757	A133	60c multicolored	1.00	1.00
758	A133	$3 multicolored	3.50	5.50

Nos. 755-758 (4)   6.00   7.50

Souvenir Sheet
759	A133	$5 multicolored	4.25	4.25

US
Presidents — A134

1984, July 18   Litho.   Perf. 14
760	A134	10c Lincoln	.25	.25
761	A134	20c Truman	.25	.25
762	A134	30c Eisenhower	.30	.25
763	A134	40c Reagan	.50	.45
764	A134	90c Lincoln, diff.	1.00	.80
765	A134	$1.10 Truman, diff.	1.25	1.10
766	A134	$1.50 Eisenhower, diff.	1.75	1.50
767	A134	$2 Reagan, diff.	2.00	1.75

Nos. 760-767 (8)   7.30   6.35

Slavery Abolition
Sesquicentennial — A135

40c, Moravian Mission. 50c, Antigua Courthouse, 1823. 60c, Sugar cane planting. $3, Boiling House, Delaps' Estate.

$5, Willoughby Bay.

1984, Aug. 1
768	A135	40c multicolored	.95	.45
769	A135	50c multicolored	1.00	.60
770	A135	60c multicolored	1.10	.70
771	A135	$3 multicolored	4.25	4.25
		Nos. 768-771 (4)	7.30	6.00

Souvenir Sheet
772	A135	$5 multicolored	7.25	7.25

Song Birds — A136

40c, Rufous-sided towhee. 50c, Parula warbler. 60c, House wren. $2, Ruby-crowned kinglet. $3, Yellow-shafted flicker.
$5, Yellow-breasted chat.

1984, Aug. 15 **Perf. 15**
773	A136	40c multicolored	1.50	.70
774	A136	50c multicolored	1.75	.90
775	A136	60c multicolored	2.00	1.90
776	A136	$2 multicolored	2.25	1.50
777	A136	$3 multicolored	2.50	4.00
		Nos. 773-777 (5)	10.00	9.00

Souvenir Sheet
778	A136	$5 multicolored	5.25	5.25

AUSIPEX '84 — A137

$1, Grass skiing. No. 780, $5, Australian rules football. No. 781, $5, Boomerang.

1984, Sept. 21 **Perf. 15**
779	A137	$1 multicolored	1.40	1.40
780	A137	$5 multicolored	4.50	4.50

Souvenir Sheet
781	A137	$5 multicolored	3.75	3.75

The Blue Dancers, by Degas — A137a

Paintings by Correggio: 25c, Virgin and Infant with Angels and Cherubs. 60c, The Four Saints. 90c, Saint Catherine. $3, The Campori Madonna. No. 790, St. John the Baptist.
Paintings by Degas: 50c, The Pink Dancers. 70c, Two Dancers. $4, Dancers at the Bar. No. 791, Folk Dancers.

1984, Oct. **Litho.** **Perf. 15**
782	A137a	15c multicolored	.40	.25
783	A137a	25c multicolored	.45	.25
784	A137a	50c multicolored	1.00	.50
785	A137a	60c multicolored	1.00	.40
786	A137a	70c multicolored	1.25	.70
787	A137a	90c multicolored	1.25	.75
788	A137a	$3 multicolored	2.75	3.50
789	A137a	$4 multicolored	3.00	4.00
		Nos. 782-789 (8)	11.10	10.35

Souvenir Sheets
790	A137a	$5 multicolored	3.75	3.75
791	A137a	$5 multi, horiz.	3.75	3.75

Nos. 623-626, 663-666, 672-675, 694-697 Surcharged in Black or Gold

(CD331)

(A124)

(CD332)

1984, June **Perf. 14, 14½x14**
792	CD331	$2 on 25c #623	3.50	3.50
793	A124	$2 on 25c #694	2.75	1.50
794	A124	$2 on 45c #695	2.75	1.50
795	CD331	$2 on 50c #624	3.50	3.50
796	A124	$2 on 60c #696	2.75	1.50
797	CD332	$2 on 90c #663 (G)	3.00	2.75
798	CD332	$2 on 90c #672 (G)	3.00	2.75
799	CD332	$2 on $1 #664 (G)	3.00	2.75
800	CD332	$2 on $1 #664 (G)	3.00	2.75
801	A124	$2 on $3 #697	2.75	1.50
802	CD331	$2 on $4 #625	3.50	3.50
803	CD332	$2 on $4 #665 (G)	3.00	2.75
804	CD332	$2 on $4 #674 (G)	3.00	2.75
		Nos. 792-804 (13)	39.50	34.25

Souvenir Sheets
805	CD331	$2 on $5 #626	9.50	9.50
806	CD332	$2 on $5 #666	8.25	8.25
807	CD332	$2 on $5 #675	8.25	8.25

Nos. 797-800, 803-804 exist with silver surcharge.

Christmas 1984 and 50th Anniv. of Donald Duck A138

Scenes from various Donald Duck comics.

1984, Nov. **Litho.** **Perf. 11**
808	A138	1c multicolored	.25	.25
809	A138	2c multicolored	.25	.25
810	A138	3c multicolored	.25	.25
811	A138	4c multicolored	.25	.25
812	A138	5c multicolored	.25	.25
813	A138	10c multicolored	.25	.25
814	A138	$1 multicolored	2.00	1.00
815	A138	$3 multicolored	2.25	2.25
816	A138	$5 multicolored	4.25	4.25
		Nos. 808-816 (9)	10.00	9.00

Souvenir Sheets
Perf. 14
817	A138	$5 multi, horiz.	6.50	6.50
818	A138	$5 Donald on beach	6.50	6.50

20th Century Leaders A139

No. 819, John F. Kennedy (1917-1963), vert. No. 820, Winston Churchill (1874-1965), vert. No. 821, Mahatma Gandhi (1869-1948), vert. No. 822, Mao Tse-Tung (1883-1976), vert. No. 823, Kennedy in Berlin. No. 824, Churchill in Paris. No. 825, Gandhi in Great Britain. No. 826, Mao in Peking.
No. 827, Flags of Great Britain, India, China, USA.

1984, Nov. 19 **Litho.** **Perf. 15**
819	A139	60c multicolored	1.30	1.30
820	A139	60c multicolored	1.30	1.30
821	A139	60c multicolored	1.30	1.30
822	A139	60c multicolored	1.30	1.30
823	A139	$1 multicolored	1.40	1.40
824	A139	$1 multicolored	1.40	1.40
825	A139	$1 multicolored	1.40	1.40
826	A139	$1 multicolored	1.40	1.40
		Nos. 819-826 (8)	10.80	10.80

Souvenir Sheet
827	A139	$5 multicolored	9.25	9.25

Statue of Liberty Centennial A140

25c, Torch on display, 1885. 30c, Restoration, 1984-1986, vert. 50c, Bartholdi supervising construction, 1876. 90c, Statue on Liberty Island. $1, Dedication Ceremony, 1886, vert. $3, Operation Sail, 1976, vert.
$5, Port of New York.

1985, Jan. 7
828	A140	25c multicolored	.25	.25
829	A140	30c multicolored	.25	.25
830	A140	50c multicolored	.40	.30
831	A140	90c multicolored	.80	.50
832	A140	$1 multicolored	1.60	1.10
833	A140	$3 multicolored	2.25	2.25
		Nos. 828-833 (6)	5.55	4.65

Souvenir Sheet
834	A140	$5 multicolored	5.00	5.00

Traditional Scenes A141

15c, Ceramics, Arawak pot shard. 50c, Tatooing, body design. 60c, Harvesting Manioc, god Yocahu. $3, Caribs in battle, war club. $5, Tainos worshiping.

1985, Jan. 21
835	A141	15c multicolored	.30	.25
836	A141	50c multicolored	.50	.40
837	A141	60c multicolored	.65	.50
838	A141	$3 multicolored	2.00	2.50
		Nos. 835-838 (4)	3.45	3.65

Souvenir Sheet
839	A141	$5 multicolored	3.50	3.50

Invention of the Motorcycle, Cent. — A142

10c, Triumph 2HP Jap, 1903. 30c, Indian Arrow, 1949. 60c, BMW R100RS, 1976. $4, Harley Davidson Model II, 1916.
$5, Laverda Jota, 1975.

1985, Mar. 7 **Perf. 14**
840	A142	10c multicolored	.70	.40
841	A142	30c multicolored	1.25	.50
842	A142	60c multicolored	1.60	1.25
843	A142	$4 multicolored	6.00	6.00
		Nos. 840-843 (4)	9.55	8.15

Souvenir Sheet
844	A142	$5 multicolored	7.00	7.00

John J. Audubon, 200th Birth Anniv. A143

90c, Horned grebe. $1, Least petrel. $1.50, Great blue heron. $3, Double-crested cormorant.
$5, White-tailed tropic bird, vert.

1985, Mar. 25 **Perf. 14**
845	A143	90c multicolored	1.75	1.10
846	A143	$1 multicolored	2.00	1.10
847	A143	$1.50 multicolored	2.75	2.75
848	A143	$3 multicolored	4.50	5.25
		Nos. 845-848 (4)	11.00	10.20

Souvenir Sheet
849	A143	$5 multicolored	9.50	9.50

See Nos.910-914.

Butterflies A144

25c, Polygrapha cyanea. 60c, Leodonta dysoni. 90c, Junea doraete. $4, Prepona xenagoras.
$5, Caerois gerdrudtus.

1985, Apr. 16 **Perf. 14**
850	A144	25c multicolored	1.40	.25
851	A144	60c multicolored	2.50	1.00
852	A144	90c multicolored	3.25	1.10
853	A144	$4 multicolored	8.00	9.00
		Nos. 850-853 (4)	15.15	11.35

Souvenir Sheet
854	A144	$5 multicolored	7.25	7.25

Cessna 172 A145

90c, Fokker DVII. $1.50, Spad VII. $3, Boeing 747.
$5, Twin Otter, Coolidge Intl. Airport.

1985, Apr. 30
855	A145	30c shown	1.25	.25
856	A145	90c multicolored	2.50	1.25
857	A145	$1.50 multicolored	3.50	3.25
858	A145	$3 multicolored	5.25	6.00
		Nos. 855-858 (4)	12.50	10.75

Souvenir Sheet
859	A145	$5 multicolored	5.75	5.75

40th anniv. of the ICAO. Nos. 855, 858-859 show the ICAO and UN emblems.

Maimonides (1135-1204), Judaic Philosopher and Physician — A146

1985, June 17 **Litho.** **Perf. 14**
860	A146	$2 yellow green	4.00	3.25

Souvenir Sheet
861	A146	$5 deep brown	7.25	6.00

Intl. Youth Year A147

25c, Agriculture. 50c, Hotel management. 60c, Environmental studies. $3, Windsurfing. $5, Youths, national flag.

1985, July 1
862	A147	25c multicolored	.25	.25
863	A147	50c multicolored	.35	.30
864	A147	60c multicolored	1.00	.75
865	A147	$3 multicolored	2.25	3.25
		Nos. 862-865 (4)	3.85	4.55

Souvenir Sheet
866	A147	$5 multicolored	3.75	3.75

Queen Mother, 85th Birthday — A148

Designs: 90c, $1, Attending a church service. No. 867A, $1.50, Touring the London Gardens, children in a sandpit. $2.50, $3, Photograph (1979). $5, With Prince Edward at the wedding of Prince Charles and Lady Diana Spencer.

Perf. 14, 12x12½ (90c, $1, $3)
1985, July 15
866A	A148	90c multi ('86)	.65	.65
867	A148	$1 multi	.75	.75
867A	A148	$1 multi ('86)	.75	.75
868	A148	$1.50 multi	1.10	1.10
869	A148	$2.50 multi	1.75	1.75
869A	A148	$3 multi ('86)	2.00	2.00
		Nos. 866A-869A (6)	7.00	7.00

Souvenir Sheet
870	A148	$5 multicolored	4.50	4.50

Nos. 866A, 867A, 869A issued in sheets of 5 plus label on Jan. 13, 1986.

Marine Life — A149

15c, Fregata magnificens. 45c, Diploria labyrinthi-formis. 60c, Oreaster reticulatus. $3, Gymnothorax moringa. $5, Acropora palmata.

1985, Aug. 1   **Perf. 14**
871	A149	15c multicolored	1.00	.25
872	A149	45c multicolored	2.00	.75
873	A149	60c multicolored	2.25	1.50
874	A149	$3 multicolored	7.00	7.50
		Nos. 871-874 (4)	12.25	10.00

Souvenir Sheet
875	A149	$5 multicolored	8.75	8.75

Johann Sebastian Bach — A150

1985, Aug. 26   **Litho.**   **Perf. 14**
876	A150	25c Bass trombone	1.10	.40
877	A150	50c English horn	1.40	.90
878	A150	$1 Violino piccolo	2.75	1.50
879	A150	$3 Bass rackett	6.50	6.50
		Nos. 876-879 (4)	11.75	9.30

Souvenir Sheet
880	A150	$5 Portrait	6.25	6.25

Girl Guides, 75th Anniv. A151

Public service and growth-oriented activities: 15c, Public service. 45c, Guides meeting. 60c, Lord and Lady Baden-Powell. $3, Nature study.
$5, Barn swallow.

1985, Sept. 10
881	A151	15c multicolored	.75	.25
882	A151	45c multicolored	1.40	.40
883	A151	60c multicolored	1.75	.60
884	A151	$3 multicolored	4.50	4.50
		Nos. 881-884 (4)	8.40	5.75

Souvenir Sheet
885	A151	$5 multicolored	5.75	5.75

State Visit of Elizabeth II, Oct. 24 — A152

1985, Oct. 24   **Litho.**   **Perf. 14½**
886	A152	60c National flags	1.00	.45
887	A152	$1 Elizabeth II, vert.	1.50	.90
888	A152	$4 HMY Britannia	3.50	5.00
		Nos. 886-888 (3)	6.00	6.35

Souvenir Sheet
889	A152	$5 Map of Antigua	4.00	4.00

Mark Twain — A153

Disney characters in Roughing It: 25c, Cowboys and Indians. 50c, Canoeing. $1.10, Pony Express. $1.50, Buffalo hunt in Missouri. $2, Nevada silver mine.
$5, Stagecoach on Kansas plains.

1985, Nov. 4   **Perf. 14**
890	A153	25c multicolored	1.00	.25
891	A153	50c multicolored	1.25	.40
892	A153	$1.10 multicolored	2.00	1.25
893	A153	$1.50 multicolored	2.50	2.50
894	A153	$2 multicolored	3.25	3.25
		Nos. 890-894 (5)	10.00	7.65

Souvenir Sheet
895	A153	$5 multicolored	8.75	8.75

Jacob and Wilhelm Grimm, Fabulists and Philologists — A154

Disney characters in Spindle, Shuttle and Needle.

1985, Nov. 11
896	A154	30c multicolored	1.00	.30
897	A154	60c multicolored	1.50	.55
898	A154	70c multicolored	1.75	.90
899	A154	$1 multicolored	2.00	1.40
900	A154	$3 multicolored	4.50	5.00
		Nos. 896-900 (5)	10.75	8.15

Souvenir Sheet
900A	A154	$5 multicolored	8.75	8.75

UN 40th Anniv. A155

Stamps of UN and portraits: 40c, No. 18 and Benjamin Franklin. $1, No. 391 and George Washington Carver, agricultural chemist. $3, No. 299 and Charles Lindbergh. $5, Marc Chagall, artist, vert.

1985, Nov. 18   **Perf. 13½x14**
901	A155	40c multicolored	.90	.50
902	A155	$1 multicolored	1.75	1.25
903	A155	$3 multicolored	4.75	5.75
		Nos. 901-903 (3)	7.40	7.50

Souvenir Sheet
Perf. 14x13½
904	A155	$5 multicolored	7.25	7.25

Christmas — A156

Religious paintings: 10c, Madonna and Child, by De Landi. 25c, Madonna and Child, by Bonaventura Berlingheiri (d. 1244). 60c, The Nativity, by Fra Angelico (1400-1455). $4, Presentation at the Temple, by Giovanni di Paolo Grazia (c.1403-1482). $5, The Nativity, by Antoniazzo Romano.

1985, Dec. 30   **Perf. 15**
905	A156	10c multicolored	.35	.25
906	A156	25c multicolored	.75	.25
907	A156	60c multicolored	1.00	.45
908	A156	$4 multicolored	2.25	3.25
		Nos. 905-908 (4)	4.35	4.20

Souvenir Sheet
909	A156	$5 multicolored	3.75	3.75

Audubon Type of 1985

Illustrations of North American ducks: 60c, Mallard. 90c, Dusky duck. $1.50, Common pintail. $3, Widgeon.
$5, Common eider.

1986, Jan. 6   **Perf. 12½x12**
910	A143	60c multicolored	2.25	1.00
911	A143	90c multicolored	2.75	1.50
912	A143	$1.50 multicolored	3.50	3.50
913	A143	$3 multicolored	4.75	5.25
		Nos. 910-913 (4)	13.25	11.25

Souvenir Sheet
Perf. 14
914	A143	$5 multicolored	7.75	7.75

1986 World Cup Soccer Championships, Mexico — A157

1986, Mar. 17   **Litho.**   **Perf. 14**
915	A157	30c shown	1.50	.25
916	A157	60c Heading the ball	1.75	.60
917	A157	$1 Referee	2.25	1.40
918	A157	$4 Goal	6.00	6.00
		Nos. 915-918 (4)	11.50	8.25

Souvenir Sheet
919	A157	$5 Action	8.50	7.50

Nos. 916-917 vert.
For overprints see Nos. 963-967.

A158

Halley's Comet — A159

Designs: 5c, Edmond Halley, Greenwich Observatory. 10c, Me 163B Komet. German WWII fighter plane. 60c, Montezuma sighting comet, 1517. $4, Pocahontas saving Capt. John Smith's life, 1607 sighting as sign for Powhatan Indians to raid Jamestown. $5, Comet over Antigua.

1986, Mar. 24
920	A158	5c multicolored	.35	.25
921	A158	10c multicolored	.40	.25
922	A158	60c multicolored	1.75	.50
923	A158	$4 multicolored	5.25	5.25
		Nos. 920-923 (4)	7.75	6.25

Souvenir Sheet
924	A159	$5 multicolored	5.00	5.00

For overprints see Nos. 973-977.

Queen Elizabeth II, 60th Birthday
Common Design Type

60c, Wedding, 1947. $1, Trooping the color. $4, Visiting Scotland.
$5, Held by Queen Mary, 1927.

1986, Apr. 21
925	CD339	60c multicolored	.45	.45
926	CD339	$1 multicolored	.70	.70
927	CD339	$4 multicolored	2.10	2.10
		Nos. 925-927 (3)	3.25	3.25

Souvenir Sheet
928	CD339	$5 multicolored	3.50	3.50

Boats — A160

30c, Tugboat. 60c, Fishing boat. $1, Sailboat 2056. $4, Lateen-rigged sailboat. $5, Boatbuilding.

1986, May 15
929	A160	30c multicolored	.30	.25
930	A160	60c multicolored	.55	.30
931	A160	$1 multicolored	1.00	.50
932	A160	$4 multicolored	3.75	3.75
		Nos. 929-932 (4)	5.60	4.80

Souvenir Sheet
933	A160	$5 multicolored	3.75	4.00

A number of unissued items, imperfs., part perfs., missing color varieties, etc., were made available when the Format International inventory was liquidated. Imperfs of some or all of the Antigua stamps in the following sets are included: Nos. 405-422, 503-507, 515-517, 703-707, 745-749, 755-759, 808-816, 819-826, 905-909, 934-937.
See footnote after No. 962.

AMERIPEX '86 — A161

American trains.

1986, May 22			**Perf. 15**	
934	A161	25c Hiawatha	1.25	.30
935	A161	50c Grand Canyon	1.50	.60
936	A161	$1 Powhattan Arrow	2.00	1.75
937	A161	$3 Empire State	3.25	5.00
		Nos. 934-937 (4)	8.00	7.65

Souvenir Sheet

938	A161	$5 Daylight	8.00	8.00

Wedding of Prince Andrew and Sarah Ferguson
Common Design Type

1986, July 23			**Perf. 14**	
939	CD340	45c Couple	.30	.30
940	CD340	60c Prince Andrew	.45	.45
941	CD340	$4 Princes Andrew, Philip	3.75	3.75
		Nos. 939-941 (3)	4.50	4.50

Souvenir Sheet

942	CD340	$5 Couple, diff.	3.75	3.75

Conch Shells — A162

15c, Say fly-specked cerith. 45c, Gmelin smooth scotch bonnet. 60c, Linne West Indian crown conch. $3, Murex ciboney. $5, Atlantic natica.

1986, Aug. 6		Litho.	**Perf. 15**	
943	A162	15c multicolored	.90	.35
944	A162	45c multicolored	2.10	1.25
945	A162	60c multicolored	2.25	2.25
946	A162	$3 multicolored	6.75	8.00
		Nos. 943-946 (4)	12.00	11.85

Souvenir Sheet

947	A162	$5 multicolored	7.50	7.50

Flowers A163

10c, Water lily. 15c, Queen of the night. 50c, Cup of gold. 60c, Beach morning glory. 70c, Golden trumpet. $1, Air plant. $3, Purple wreath. $4, Zephyr lily.
No. 956, Dozakie. No. 957, Four o'clock.

1986, Aug. 25		Litho.	**Perf. 15**	
948	A163	10c multicolored	.30	.25
949	A163	15c multicolored	.30	.25
950	A163	50c multicolored	.60	.45
951	A163	60c multicolored	.75	.55
952	A163	70c multicolored	.85	.65
953	A163	$1 multicolored	1.00	1.00
954	A163	$3 multicolored	2.25	2.50
955	A163	$4 multicolored	2.75	3.50
		Nos. 948-955 (8)	8.80	9.15

Souvenir Sheets

956	A163	$4 multicolored	3.00	3.25
957	A163	$5 multicolored	3.75	4.00

Fungi — A164

10c, Hygrocybe occidentalis scarletina. 50c, Trogia buccinalis. $1, Collybia subpruinosa. $4, Leucocoprinus brebissonii. $5, Pyrrhoglossum pyrrhum.

1986, Sept. 15				
958	A164	10c multicolored	.35	.25
959	A164	50c multicolored	.75	.55
960	A164	$1 multicolored	1.50	1.25
961	A164	$4 multicolored	3.75	4.50
		Nos. 958-961 (4)	6.35	6.55

Souvenir Sheet

962	A164	$5 multicolored	11.00	11.00

An unissued $3 stamp and No. 961 inscribed "4$" were made available when the Format International inventory was liquidated.

Nos. 915-919 Ovptd. in Gold in 2 or 3 lines

1986, Sept. 15			**Perf. 14**	
963	A157	30c multicolored	1.10	.35
964	A157	60c multicolored	1.60	.70
965	A157	$1 multicolored	2.25	1.10
966	A157	$4 multicolored	5.50	4.50
		Nos. 963-966 (4)	10.45	6.65

Souvenir Sheet

967	A157	$5 multicolored	6.00	6.00

Automobile, Cent. — A165

Carl Benz and classic automobiles: 10c, 1933 Auburn Speedster. 15c, 1986 Mercury Sable. 50c, 1959 Cadillac. 60c, 1950 Studebaker. 70c, 1939 Lagonda V-12. $1, 1930 Adler Standard. $3, 1956 DKW. $4, 1936 Mercedes 500K.
No. 972, 1921 Mercedes Knight. No. 972A, 1896 Daimler.

1986, Oct. 20				
968	A165	10c multicolored	.25	.25
968A	A165	15c multicolored	.30	.25
969	A165	50c multicolored	.65	.25
970	A165	60c multicolored	.80	.30
970A	A165	70c multicolored	.90	.40
970B	A165	$1 multicolored	1.25	.55
970C	A165	$3 multicolored	3.00	3.00
971	A165	$4 multicolored	3.50	3.50
		Nos. 968-971 (8)	10.65	8.50

Souvenir Sheets

972	A165	$5 multicolored	4.50	4.00
972A	A165	$5 multicolored	4.50	4.00

Nos. 920-924 Ovptd. in Black or Silver

1986, Oct. 22		Litho.	**Perf. 14**	
973	A158	5c multicolored	.25	.25
974	A158	10c multicolored	.25	.25
975	A158	60c multicolored	1.25	.60
976	A158	$4 multicolored	5.50	4.00
		Nos. 973-976 (4)	7.25	5.10

Souvenir Sheet

977	A159	$5 multicolored (S)	6.50	6.50

Christmas — A166

Disney characters as children: 25c, Mickey. 30c, Mickey, Minnie. 40c, Aunt Matilda, Goofy. 60c, Goofy, Pluto. 70c, Pluto, Donald, Daisy. $1.50, Stringing popcorn. $3, Grandma Duck, Minnie. $4, Donald, Pete. No. 986, Playing with presents. No. 987, Reindeer.

1986, Nov. 4			**Perf. 11**	
978	A166	25c multicolored	.60	.25
979	A166	30c multicolored	.75	.30
980	A166	40c multicolored	.85	.35
981	A166	60c multicolored	1.00	.65
982	A166	70c multicolored	1.25	1.00
983	A166	$1.50 multicolored	2.00	2.00
984	A166	$3 multicolored	3.00	3.75
985	A166	$4 multicolored	3.50	4.00
		Nos. 978-985 (8)	12.95	12.30

Souvenir Sheets
Perf. 14

986	A166	$5 multicolored	7.00	7.00
987	A166	$5 multicolored	7.00	7.00

Nos. 985 printed in sheets of 8.

Coat of Arms A167

Natl. Flag A168

1986, Nov. 25	Litho.	**Perf. 14x14½**		
988	A167	10c bright blue	1.00	.90
989	A168	25c orange	1.75	1.25

Marc Chagall (1887-1985), Artist A169

Designs: No. 990, The Profile, 1957. No. 991, Portrait of the Artist's Sister, 1910. No. 992, Bride with Fan, 1911. No. 993, David in Profile, 1914. No. 994, Fiancee with Bouquet, 1977. No. 995, Self-portrait with Brushes, 1909. No. 996, The Walk, 1973. No. 997, Candles, 1938. No. 998, Fall of Icarus, 1975. No. 999, Myth of Orpheus, 1977.

1987, Mar. 30	Litho.	**Perf. 13½x14**		
990	A169	10c multicolored	.45	.25
991	A169	30c multicolored	.60	.30
992	A169	40c multicolored	.80	.35
993	A169	60c multicolored	.90	.40
994	A169	90c multicolored	1.00	.55
995	A169	$1 multicolored	1.00	.60
996	A169	$3 multicolored	2.50	2.50
997	A169	$4 multicolored	2.75	2.75

Size: 110x95mm
Imperf

998	A169	$5 multicolored	5.75	5.75
999	A169	$5 multicolored	5.75	5.75
		Nos. 990-999 (10)	21.50	19.20

A170

America's Cup — A171

30c, Canada I, 1981. 60c, Gretel II, 1970. $1, Sceptre, 1958. $3, Vigilant, 1893. $5, Australia II, Liberty, 1983.

1987, Feb. 5			**Perf. 15**	
1000	A170	30c multicolored	.55	.25
1001	A170	60c multicolored	.70	.35
1002	A170	$1 multicolored	1.25	1.00
1003	A170	$3 multicolored	2.75	3.00
		Nos. 1000-1003 (4)	5.25	4.60

Souvenir Sheet

1004	A171	$5 multicolored	6.25	6.25

Fish, World Wildlife Fund A172

Marine Birds A173

15c, Bridled burrfish. 30c, Brown noddy. 40c, Nassau grouper. 50c, Laughing gull. 60c, French angelfish. $1, Porkfish. $2, Royal tern. $3, Sooty tern.
No. 1013, Banded butterfly fish. No. 1014, Brown booby.

1987, Feb. 23		Litho.	**Perf. 14**	
1005	A172	15c multicolored	3.00	.40
1006	A173	30c multicolored	6.00	.45
1007	A172	40c multicolored	3.75	.55
1008	A173	50c multicolored	6.75	1.25
1009	A172	60c multicolored	4.00	1.25
1010	A172	$1 multicolored	4.00	1.50
1011	A173	$2 multicolored	9.00	4.75
1012	A173	$3 multicolored	9.00	7.00
		Nos. 1005-1012 (8)	45.50	17.15

Souvenir Sheets

1013	A172	$5 multicolored	11.00	11.00
1014	A173	$5 multicolored	11.00	11.00

The 30c, 50c, $2, $3 and Nos. 1013-1014 do not picture the WWF emblem.
For overprints see Nos. 1137-1139A.

Statue of Liberty, Cent. A174

Photographs by Peter B. Kaplan: 15c, Lee Iacocca. 30c, Statue at dusk. 45c, Crown, head. 50c, Iacocca, torch. 60c, Crown observatory. 90c, Interior restoration. $1, Head. $2, Statue at sunset. $3, Men on scaffold, flag. $5, Statue at night.

1987, Apr. 20			**Perf. 14**	
1015	A174	15c multicolored	.25	.25
1016	A174	30c multicolored	.25	.25
1017	A174	45c multicolored	.40	.40
1018	A174	50c multicolored	.45	.45
1019	A174	60c multicolored	.45	.45
1020	A174	90c multicolored	.65	.65
1021	A174	$1 multicolored	.75	.75
1022	A174	$2 multicolored	1.50	1.50
1023	A174	$3 multicolored	1.60	2.00
1024	A174	$5 multicolored	2.75	3.50
		Nos. 1015-1024 (10)	9.05	10.20

Nos. 1015-1018, 1021-1022, 1024 vert.

A175

Transportation Innovations — A175a

10c, Spirit of Australia, 1978. 15c, Siemens' Electric locomotive, 1879. 30c, USS Triton, 1960. 50c, Trevithick, 1801. 60c, USS New Jersey, 1942. 70c, Draisine bicycle, 1818. 90c, SS United States, 1952. $1.50, Cierva C-4, 1923. $2, Curtiss NC-4, 1919. $3, Queen Elizabeth II, 1969.

1987, Apr. 19   *Perf. 15*

1025	A175	10c multi	.85	.25
1026	A175a	15c multi	1.10	.30
1027	A175	30c multi	1.10	.35
1028	A175a	50c multi	1.25	.45
1029	A175	60c multi	1.25	.50
1030	A175a	70c multi	1.25	.65
1031	A175	90c multi	1.25	.75
1032	A175a	$1.50 multi	1.90	*1.90*
1033	A175	$2 multi	2.10	2.10
1034	A175	$3 multi	3.25	3.25
	Nos. 1025-1034 (10)		15.30	10.50

Reptiles and Amphibians — A176

30c, Eleutherodactylus martinicensis. 60c, Thecadactylus rapicauda. $1, Anolis bimaculatus leachi. $3, Geochelone carbonaria. $5, Ameiva griswoldi.

1987, June 15   *Perf. 14*

1035	A176	30c multicolored	.55	.25
1036	A176	60c multicolored	.85	.35
1037	A176	$1 multicolored	1.10	.65
1038	A176	$3 multicolored	2.25	*2.75*
	Nos. 1035-1038 (4)		4.75	4.00

Souvenir Sheet

1039	A176	$5 multicolored	5.50	5.50

Entertainers
A177

1987, May 11

1040	A177	15c Grace Kelly	1.00	.30
1041	A177	30c Marilyn Monroe	2.75	.60
1042	A177	45c Orson Welles	1.00	.40
1043	A177	50c Judy Garland	1.00	.45
1044	A177	60c John Lennon	4.00	1.00
1045	A177	$1 Rock Hudson	1.50	.90
1046	A177	$2 John Wayne	2.75	1.50
1047	A177	$3 Elvis Presley	9.00	4.00
	Nos. 1040-1047 (8)		23.00	9.15

No. 1047
Overprinted

1987, Sept. 9   **Litho.**   *Perf. 14*
1047A	A177	$3 multicolored	8.50	8.50

1988
Summer
Olympics,
Seoul
A178

10c, Basketball. 60c, Fencing. $1, Women's gymnastics. $3, Soccer. $5, Boxing glove.

1987, Mar. 23

1048	A178	10c multicolored	.60	.30
1049	A178	60c multicolored	.90	.40
1050	A178	$1 multicolored	1.25	1.00
1051	A178	$3 multicolored	3.00	*4.00*
	Nos. 1048-1051 (4)		5.75	5.70

Souvenir Sheet

1052	A178	$5 multicolored	4.75	*4.75*

16th World
Scout
Jamboree,
Australia,
1987-88
A179

10c, Campfire, red kangaroo. 60c, Kayaking, blue-winged kookaburra. $1, Obstacle course, ring-tailed rock wallaby. $3, Field kitchen, koalas. $5, Flags.

1987, Nov. 2   **Litho.**   *Perf. 15*

1053	A179	10c multicolored	.75	.25
1054	A179	60c multicolored	1.50	.65
1055	A179	$1 multicolored	1.25	.75
1056	A179	$3 multicolored	2.00	*3.50*
	Nos. 1053-1056 (4)		5.50	*5.15*

Souvenir Sheet

1057	A179	$5 multicolored	4.00	4.00

US Constitution Bicent. — A180

Designs: 15c, Virginia House of Burgesses exercising right of freedom of speech. 45c, Connecticut state seal. 60c, Delaware state seal. $4, Gouverneur Morris (1752-1816), principal writer of the Constitution, vert. $5, Roger Sherman (1721-1793), jurist and statesman, vert.

1987, Nov. 16   **Litho.**   *Perf. 14*

1058	A180	15c multicolored	.25	.25
1059	A180	45c multicolored	.30	.30
1060	A180	60c multicolored	.35	.35
1061	A180	$4 multicolored	2.75	*3.00*
	Nos. 1058-1061 (4)		3.65	*3.90*

Souvenir Sheet

1062	A180	$5 multicolored	4.00	4.00

A181

Christmas (Paintings): 45c, Madonna and Child, by Bernardo Daddi (1290-1355). 60c, Joseph, detail from The Nativity, by Sano Di Pietro (1406-1481). $1, Mary, detail from Di Pietro's The Nativity. $4, Music-making Angel, by Melozzo Da Forli (1438-1494). $5, The Flight into Egypt, by Di Pietro.

1987, Dec. 1

1063	A181	45c multicolored	.35	.25
1064	A181	60c multicolored	.45	.35
1065	A181	$1 multicolored	.75	.55
1066	A181	$4 multicolored	2.10	*3.00*
	Nos. 1063-1066 (4)		3.65	*4.15*

Souvenir Sheet

1067	A181	$5 multicolored	3.75	3.75

A182

No. 1068, Wedding portrait. No. 1069, Elizabeth II, c. 1970. No. 1070, Christening of Charles, 1948. No. 1071, Elizabeth II, c. 1980. No. 1072, Royal family, c. 1951.

1988, Feb. 8   **Litho.**   *Perf. 14*

1068	A182	25c multi	.25	.25
1069	A182	60c multi	.50	.40
1070	A182	$2 multi	1.10	1.10
1071	A182	$3 multi	1.75	1.75
	Nos. 1068-1071 (4)		3.60	3.50

Souvenir Sheet

1072	A182	$5 multi	3.25	3.25

40th wedding anniv. of Queen Elizabeth II and Prince Philip.

Tropical
Birds
A183

10c, Great blue heron, vert. 15c, Ringed kingfisher. 50c, Bananaquit. 60c, Purple gallinule. 70c, Blue-hooded euphonia. $1, Caribbean parakeet, vert. $3, Troupial. $4, Hummingbird. No. 1081, Roseate flamingo, vert. No. 1082, Brown pelicans, vert.

1988, Mar. 1

1073	A183	10c multicolored	.55	.35
1074	A183	15c multicolored	.60	.30
1075	A183	50c multicolored	1.10	.40
1076	A183	60c multicolored	1.10	.40
1077	A183	70c multicolored	1.25	.50
1078	A183	$1 multicolored	1.50	.60
1079	A183	$3 multicolored	3.00	*3.50*
1080	A183	$4 multicolored	3.00	*3.50*
	Nos. 1073-1080 (8)		12.10	9.55

Souvenir Sheets

1081	A183	$5 multicolored	4.75	4.75
1082	A183	$5 multicolored	4.75	4.75

Salvation Army — A184

25c, Day-care, Antigua. 30c, Penicillin inoculation, Indonesia. 40c, Day-care Center, Bolivia. 45c, Rehabilitation, India. 50c, Training the blind, Kenya. 60c, Infant care, Ghana. $1, Job training, Zambia. $2, Food distribution, Sri Lanka. $5, General Eva Burrows.

1988, Mar. 7

1083	A184	25c multicolored	.90	.45
1084	A184	30c multicolored	.90	.45
1085	A184	40c multicolored	1.00	.55
1086	A184	45c multicolored	1.00	.55
1087	A184	50c multicolored	1.25	1.10
1088	A184	60c multicolored	1.40	1.25
1089	A184	$1 multicolored	1.75	1.50
1090	A184	$2 multicolored	2.50	*3.00*
	Nos. 1083-1090 (8)		10.70	*8.85*

Souvenir Sheet

1091	A184	$5 multicolored	5.50	5.50

A185

Discovery of America, 500th Anniv. (in 1992) — A186

Anniv. emblem and: 10c, Fleet. 30c, View of fleet in harbor from Paino Indian village. 45c, Caravel anchored in harbor, Paino village. 60c, Columbus, 3 Indians in canoe. 90c, Indian, parrot, Columbus. $1, Columbus in longboat. $3, Spanish guard, fleet in harbor. $4, Ships under full sail. No. 1100, Stone cross given to Columbus by Queen Isabella. No. 1101, Gold excelente.

1988, Mar. 14   **Litho.**   *Perf. 14*

1092	A185	10c multicolored	.75	.30
1093	A185	30c multicolored	.75	.35
1094	A185	45c multicolored	.85	.35
1095	A185	60c multicolored	.85	.35
1096	A185	90c multicolored	1.50	.80
1097	A185	$1 multicolored	1.50	.80
1098	A185	$3 multicolored	2.50	3.00
1099	A185	$4 multicolored	2.75	*3.25*
	Nos. 1092-1099 (8)		11.45	9.20

Souvenir Sheets

1100	A186	$4 multicolored	4.50	4.50
1101	A186	$5 multicolored	4.50	4.50

Paintings by
Titian
A187

Details: 30c, Bust of Christ. 40c, Scourging of Christ. 45c, Madonna in Glory with Saints. 50c, The Averoldi Polyptych. $1, Christ Crowned with Thorns. $2, Christ Mocked. $3, Christ and Simon of Cyrene. $4, Crucifixion with Virgin and Saints. No. 1110, Ecce Homo. No. 1111, Noli Me Tangere.

1988, Apr. 11   **Litho.**   *Perf. 13½x14*

1102	A187	30c shown	.55	.25
1103	A187	40c multicolored	.65	.30
1104	A187	45c multicolored	.65	.30
1105	A187	50c multicolored	.65	.45
1106	A187	$1 multicolored	1.00	.65
1107	A187	$2 multicolored	1.25	1.25
1108	A187	$3 multicolored	2.00	2.00
1109	A187	$4 multicolored	2.50	*2.75*
	Nos. 1102-1109 (8)		9.25	*7.95*

Souvenir Sheets

1110	A187	$5 multicolored	4.25	4.25
1111	A187	$5 multicolored	4.25	4.25

Sailing
Week
A188

30c, Canada I, 1980. 60c, Gretel II, Australia, 1970. $1, Sceptre, GB, 1958. $3, Vigilant, US, 1893. $5, Australia II, 1983.

1988, Apr. 18   *Perf. 15*

1112	A188	30c multicolored	.25	.25
1113	A188	60c multicolored	.50	.45
1114	A188	$1 multicolored	.70	.60
1115	A188	$3 multicolored	1.50	*2.25*
	Nos. 1112-1115 (4)		2.95	*3.55*

Souvenir Sheet

1116	A188	$5 multicolored	3.50	3.50

Walt Disney Animated Characters and Epcot Center, Walt Disney World — A189

25c, The Living Seas. 30c, World of Motion. 40c, Spaceship Earth. 60c, Universe of Energy. 70c, Journey to Imagination. $1.50, The Land. $3, Communicore. $4, Horizons. No. 1125, Epcot Center. No. 1126, The Contemporary Resort Hotel.

1988, May 3   Perf. 14x13½, 13½x14

1116A	A189	1c like 25c	.25	.25
1116B	A189	2c like 30c	.25	.25
1116C	A189	3c like 40c	.25	.25
1116D	A189	4c like 60c	.25	.25
1116E	A189	5c like 70c	.25	.25
1116F	A189	10c like $1.50	.25	.25
1117	A189	25c multi	.50	.25
1118	A189	30c multi	.50	.25
1119	A189	40c multi	.60	.25
1120	A189	60c multi	.85	.35
1121	A189	70c multi	.95	.40
1122	A189	$1.50 multi	1.75	1.75
1123	A189	$3 multi	2.50	2.50
1124	A189	$4 multi	2.50	2.50
		Nos. 1116A-1124 (14)	11.65	9.75

Souvenir Sheets

1125	A189	$5 multi	4.50	4.50
1126	A189	$5 multi	4.50	4.50

30c, 40c, $1.50, $3 and No. 1126 are vert.

Flowering Trees — A190

1988, May 16   Perf. 14

1127	A190	10c Jacaranda	.30	.25
1128	A190	30c Cordia	.35	.25
1129	A190	50c Orchid tree	.50	.40
1130	A190	90c Flamboyant	.60	.50
1131	A190	$1 African tulip tree	.75	.60
1132	A190	$2 Potato tree	1.40	1.40
1133	A190	$3 Crepe myrtle	1.75	2.00
1134	A190	$4 Pitch apple	2.00	2.50
		Nos. 1127-1134 (8)	7.65	7.90

Souvenir Sheets

1135	A190	$5 Cassia	3.75	4.00
1136	A190	$5 Chinaberry	3.75	4.00

Nos. 1135-1136 are continuous designs.

Nos. 1011-1012, 1014 and 1013 Ovptd. in Black for Philatelic Exhibitions

a

b

c

d

1988, May 9   Litho.   Perf. 14

1137	A173 (a)	$2 multi	8.50	8.50
1138	A173 (b)	$3 multi	9.00	9.00

Souvenir Sheets

1139	A173 (c)	$5 multi	15.00	15.00
1139A	A172 (d)	$5 multi	15.00	15.00

1988 Summer Olympics, Seoul A192

40c, Gymnastic rings, vert. 60c, Weight lifting, vert. $1, Water polo. $3, Boxing. $5, Torch-bearer, vert.

1988, June 10

1140	A192	40c multicolored	.40	.30
1141	A192	60c multicolored	.45	.30
1142	A192	$1 multicolored	.90	.45
1143	A192	$3 multicolored	1.75	2.25
		Nos. 1140-1143 (4)	3.50	3.30

Souvenir Sheet

1144	A192	$5 multicolored	3.75	3.75

Butterflies A193

1c, Monarch. 2c, Jamaican clearwing. 3c, Yellow-barred ringlet. 5c, Cracker. 10c, Jamaican mestra. 15c, Mimic. 20c, Silver spot. 25c, Zebra. 30c, Fiery sulphur. 40c, Androgeus swallowtail. 45c, Giant brimstone. 50c, Orbed sulphur. 60c, Blue-backed skipper. $1, Common white skipper. $2, Baracoa skipper. $2.50, Mangrove skipper. $5, Silver king. $10, Pygmy skipper. $20, Parides lycimenes.

1988-90   Litho.   Perf. 14

1145	A193	1c multi	.50	.90
1146	A193	2c multi	.65	.90
1147	A193	3c multi	.65	.90
1148	A193	5c multi	.80	.90
1149	A193	10c multi	.95	.35
1150	A193	15c multi	1.25	.35
1151	A193	20c multi	1.40	.35
1152	A193	25c multi	1.40	.35
1153	A193	30c multi	1.40	.35
1154	A193	40c multi	1.40	.35
1155	A193	45c multi	1.40	.35
1156	A193	50c multi	1.50	.45
1157	A193	60c multi	1.60	.60
1158	A193	$1 multi	2.00	1.00
1159	A193	$2 multi	3.00	3.00
1160	A193	$2.50 multi	4.00	4.00
1161	A193	$5 multi	5.00	5.00
1161A	A193	$10 multi	7.00	11.00
1162	A193	$20 multi	18.00	20.00
		Nos. 1145-1162 (19)	53.90	51.10

Issued: $20, Feb. 19, 1990; others, Aug. 29.

John F. Kennedy A194

30c, First family. 60c, Motorcade, Mexico. $1, Funeral procession. $4, Aboard PT109.

$5, Taking Oath of Office.

1988, Nov. 22   Litho.   Perf. 14

1162A	A194	1c like 30c	.25	.25
1162B	A194	2c like $4	.25	.25
1162C	A194	3c like $1	.25	.25
1162D	A194	4c like 60c	.25	.25
1163	A194	30c multi	.40	.25
1164	A194	60c multi	.80	.40
1165	A194	$1 multi	.90	.65
1166	A194	$4 multi	2.50	2.50
		Nos. 1162A-1166 (8)	5.60	4.80

Souvenir Sheet

1167	A194	$5 multi	4.25	4.25

Miniature Sheet

Christmas, Mickey Mouse 60th Anniv. — A195

Walt Disney characters: No. 1168: a, Morty and Ferdie. b, Goofy. c, Chip-n-Dale. d, Huey and Dewey. e, Minnie Mouse. f, Pluto. g, Mickey Mouse. h, Donald Duck and Louie. No. 1169, Goofy driving Mickey and Minnie in a horse-drawn carriage. No. 1170, Characters on roller skates, caroling.

1988, Dec. 1   Perf. 13½x14, 14x13½

1168	A195	Sheet of 8	9.50	9.50
a.-h.		$1 any single	1.00	1.00

Souvenir Sheets

1169	A195	$7 multicolored	5.75	5.75
1170	A195	$7 multi, horiz.	5.75	5.75

1988, Dec. 1   Litho.   Perf. 14

1171	A195	10c like No. 1168e	.25	.25
1172	A195	25c like No. 1168f	.25	.25
1173	A195	30c like No. 1168g	.30	.30
1174	A195	70c like No. 1168h	.70	.70
		Nos. 1171-1174 (4)	1.50	1.50

Arawak Indian Whip Dance — A196

UPAE and discovery of America emblems and: a, Five adults. b, Eight adults. c, Seven adults. d, Three adults, three children.

1989, May 16   Litho.   Perf. 14

1175		Strip of 4	5.50	5.50
a.-d.	A196	$1.50 any single	1.00	1.00

Souvenir Sheet

1176	A196	$6 Arawak chief	4.50	4.50

Discovery of America 500th anniv. (in 1992), pre-Columbian societies and customs.

Jet Flight, 50th Anniv. A197

Various jet aircraft: 10c, DeHavilland Comet 4. 30c, Messerschmitt Me262. 40c, Boeing 707. 60c, Canadair F-86 Sabre. $1, Lockheed F-104 Starfighter. $2, McDonnell Douglas DC-10. $3, Boeing 747. $4, McDonnell F-4 Phantom. No. 1185, Grumman F-14 Tomcat. No. 1186, Concorde.

1989, May 29   Litho.   Perf. 14x13½

1177	A197	10c multicolored	1.00	.35
1178	A197	30c multicolored	1.50	.35
1179	A197	40c multicolored	1.50	.35
1180	A197	60c multicolored	1.75	.50
1181	A197	$1 multicolored	1.90	.75

1182	A197	$2 multicolored	2.75	2.75
1183	A197	$3 multicolored	3.00	3.25
1184	A197	$4 multicolored	3.00	3.25
		Nos. 1177-1184 (8)	16.40	11.55

Souvenir Sheets

1185	A197	$7 multicolored	6.00	6.00
1186	A197	$7 multicolored	6.00	6.00

Caribbean Cruise Ships A198

25c, TSS Festivale. 45c, M.S. Southward. 50c, M.S. Sagafjord. 60c, MTS Daphne. 75c, M.V. Cunard Countess. 90c, M.S. Song of America. $3, M.S. Island Princess. $4, S.S. Galileo. No. 1195, S.S. Norway. No. 1196, S.S. Oceanic.

1989, June 20   Litho.   Perf. 14

1187	A198	25c multi	1.30	.35
1188	A198	45c multi	1.50	.35
1189	A198	50c multi	1.50	.35
1190	A198	60c multi	1.50	.40
1191	A198	75c multi	1.75	.90
1192	A198	90c multi	2.00	1.00
1193	A198	$3 multi	4.00	5.00
1194	A198	$4 multi	4.00	5.50
		Nos. 1187-1194 (8)	17.55	13.85

Souvenir Sheets

1195	A198	$6 multi	5.00	5.50
1196	A198	$6 multi	5.00	5.50

Paintings by Hiroshige — A199

Designs: 25c, Fish Swimming by Duck Half-submerged in Stream. 45c, Crane and Wave. 50c, Sparrows and Morning Glories. 60c, Crested Blackbird and Flowering Cherry. $1, Great Knot Sitting among Water Grass. $2, Goose on a Bank of Water. $3, Black Paradise Flycatcher and Blossoms. $4, Sleepy Owl Perched on a Pine Branch. No. 1205, Bullfinch Flying Near a Clematis Branch. No. 1206, Titmouse on a Cherry Branch.

1989, July 3   Perf. 14x13½

1197	A199	25c multicolored	.90	.30
1198	A199	45c multicolored	1.10	.40
1199	A199	50c multicolored	1.25	.40
1200	A199	60c multicolored	1.25	.50
1201	A199	$1 multicolored	1.60	.65
1202	A199	$2 multicolored	2.50	2.50
1203	A199	$3 multicolored	3.00	3.00
1204	A199	$4 multicolored	3.00	3.00
		Nos. 1197-1204 (8)	14.60	10.75

Souvenir Sheets

1205	A199	$6 multicolored	6.00	6.00
1206	A199	$5 multicolored	6.00	6.00

Hirohito (1901-1989) and enthronement of Akihito as emperor of Japan.

PHILEXFRANCE '89 — A200

Walt Disney characters, French landmarks: 1c, Helicopter over the Seine. 2c, Arc de Triomphe. 3c, Painting Notre Dame Cathedral. 4c, Entrance to the Metro. 5c, Fashion show. 10c, Follies. No. 1213, Shopping stalls on the Seine. $6, Sidewalk cafe, Left Bank. No. 1215, Hot air balloon Ear Force One. No. 1216, Dining.

1989, July 7   Perf. 14x13½

1207	A200	1c multicolored	.25	.25
1208	A200	2c multicolored	.25	.25
1209	A200	3c multicolored	.25	.25

1210	A200	4c multicolored	.25	.25
1211	A200	5c multicolored	.25	.25
1212	A200	10c multicolored	.25	.25
1213	A200	5c multicolored	8.50	8.50
1214	A200	$6 multicolored	8.50	8.50
		Nos. 1207-1214 (8)	18.50	18.50

Souvenir Sheets

1215	A200	$5 multicolored	7.00	7.00
1216	A200	$5 multicolored	7.00	7.00

1990 World Cup Soccer Championships, Italy — A201

Natl. flag, various actions of a defending goalie.

1989, Aug. 21   **Perf. 14**

1217	A201	15c multicolored	.90	.25
1218	A201	25c multicolored	1.00	.25
1219	A201	$1 multicolored	1.50	1.00
1220	A201	$4 multicolored	2.50	4.25
		Nos. 1217-1220 (4)	5.90	5.75

Souvenir Sheets

1221	A201	$5 2 players, horiz.	4.25	4.25
1222	A201	$5 3 players, horiz.	4.25	4.25

For overprints see Nos. 1344-1349.

Mushrooms — A202

10c, Lilac fairy helmet. 25c, Rough psathyrella, vert. 50c, Golden tops. 60c, Blue cap, vert. 75c, Brown cap, vert. $1, Green gill, vert. $3, Red pinwheel. $4, Red chanterelle. No. 1231, Slender stalk. No. 1232, Paddy straw mushroom.

1989, Oct. 12   **Litho.**   **Perf. 14**

1223	A202	10c multi	.85	.35
1224	A202	25c multi	1.25	.30
1225	A202	50c multi	1.75	.50
1226	A202	60c multi	1.75	.60
1227	A202	75c multi	2.00	1.10
1228	A202	$1 multi	2.00	1.25
1229	A202	$3 multi	3.25	3.75
1230	A202	$4 multi	3.25	3.75
		Nos. 1223-1230 (8)	16.10	11.60

Souvenir Sheets

1231	A202	$6 multi	8.50	8.50
1232	A202	$6 multi	8.50	8.50

Nos. 1224, 1226-1228, 1231 vert.

Wildlife A203

25c, Hutia. 45c, Caribbean monk seal. 60c, Mustache bat, vert. $4, Manatee, vert. $5, West Indies giant rice rat.

1989, Oct. 19   **Litho.**   **Perf. 14**

1233	A203	25c multi	.80	.35
1234	A203	45c multi	2.50	.75
1235	A203	60c multi	1.50	.75
1236	A203	$4 multi	3.50	4.25
		Nos. 1233-1236 (4)	8.30	6.10

Souvenir Sheet

1237	A203	$5 multi	8.50	8.50

American Philatelic Soc. Emblem, Stamps on Stamps and Walt Disney Characters Promoting Philately A204

Designs: 1c, Israel #150, printing press. 2c, Italy #1238, first day cancel. 3c, US #143L4, Pony Express recruits. 4c, Denmark #566, early radio broadcast. 5c, German Democratic Republic #702, television. 10c, Great Britain #1, stamp collector. $4, Japan #1414, integrated circuits. $6, Germany #B667, boom box. No. 1246, US #1355, C3a, and Jenny biplane over Disneyland, horiz. No. 1247, US #940, 1421 and stamps for the wounded.

1989, Nov. 2   **Perf. 13½x14, 14x13½**

1238	A204	1c multicolored	.25	.25
1239	A204	2c multicolored	.25	.25
1240	A204	3c multicolored	.25	.25
1241	A204	4c multicolored	.25	.25
1242	A204	5c multicolored	.25	.25
1243	A204	10c multicolored	.25	.25
1244	A204	$4 multicolored	4.50	4.50
1245	A204	$6 multicolored	5.50	5.50
		Nos. 1238-1245 (8)	11.50	11.50

Souvenir Sheets

1246	A204	$5 multicolored	6.50	6.50
1247	A204	$5 multicolored	6.50	6.50

Locomotives and Walt Disney Characters — A205

25c, John Bull, 1831. 45c, Atlantic, 1832. 50c, William Crook's, 1861. 60c, Minnetonka, 1869. $1, Thatcher Perkins, 1863. $2, Pioneer, 1848. $3, Peppersass, 1869. $4, Gimbels Flyer. No. 1256, #6100 Class S-1 & 1835 Thomas Jefferson. No. 1257, Jupiter & #119.

Perf. 14x13½, 13½x14

1989, Nov. 17

1248	A205	25c multi	1.00	.40
1249	A205	45c multi	1.10	.40
1250	A205	50c multi	1.10	.40
1251	A205	60c multi	1.10	.60
1252	A205	$1 multi	1.40	.75
1253	A205	$2 multi	2.00	2.00
1254	A205	$3 multi	2.50	3.00
1255	A205	$4 multicolored	2.75	3.00
		Nos. 1248-1255 (8)	12.95	10.55

Souvenir Sheets

1256	A205	$6 multi	6.50	6.50
1257	A205	$6 multi	6.50	6.50

New York World's Fair, 50th anniv., and World Stamp Expo '89, Washington, DC.

1st Moon Landing, 20th Anniv. A206

10c, Apollo 11 liftoff. 45c, Aldrin walking on Moon. $1, Eagle ascending from Moon. $4, Recovery after splashdown. $5, Armstrong.

1989, Nov. 24   **Litho.**   **Perf. 14**

1258	A206	10c multicolored	.60	.25
1259	A206	45c multicolored	1.50	.25
1260	A206	$1 multicolored	1.75	.85
1261	A206	$4 multicolored	2.75	3.75
		Nos. 1258-1261 (4)	6.60	5.10

Souvenir Sheet

1262	A206	$5 multicolored	6.25	6.25

Nos. 1258-1259 and 1262, vert.

Souvenir Sheet

Smithsonian Institution, Washington, DC — A207

1989, Nov. 17   **Litho.**   **Perf. 14**

1263	A207	$4 multicolored	3.75	3.75

World Stamp Expo '89.

Christmas — A208

Religious paintings: 10c, The Small Cowper Madonna. 25c, Madonna of the Goldfinch. 30c, The Alba Madonna. 50c, Bologna Altarpiece (attendant). 60c, Bologna Altarpiece (heralding angel). 70c, Bologna Altarpiece (archangel). $4, Bologna Altarpiece (saint holding ledger). No. 1271, Madonna of Foligno. No. 1272, The Marriage of the Virgin. No. 1273, Bologna Altarpiece (Madonna and Child).

Bologna Altarpiece by Giotto. Other paintings by Raphael.

1989, Dec. 11   **Litho.**   **Perf. 14**

1264	A208	10c multicolored	.35	.25
1265	A208	25c multicolored	.45	.25
1266	A208	30c multicolored	.45	.25
1267	A208	50c multicolored	.70	.40
1268	A208	60c multicolored	.75	.45
1269	A208	70c multicolored	.85	.50
1270	A208	$4 multicolored	3.00	3.50
1271	A208	$6 multicolored	3.00	4.25
		Nos. 1264-1271 (8)	9.55	9.85

Souvenir Sheets

1272	A208	$5 multicolored	5.50	5.50
1273	A208	$5 multicolored	5.50	5.50

America Issue — A210

UPAE, discovery of America 500th anniv. emblems and marine life: 10c, Star-eyed hermit crab. 20c, Spiny lobster. 25c, Magnificent banded fanworm. 45c, Cannonball jellyfish. 60c, Red-spiny sea star. $2, Peppermint shrimp. $3, Coral crab. $4, Branching fire coral. No. 1283, Common sea fan. No. 1284, Portuguese man-of-war.

1990, Mar. 26   **Litho.**   **Perf. 14**

1275	A210	10c multicolored	.50	.25
1276	A210	20c multicolored	.75	.25
1277	A210	25c multicolored	.80	.25
1278	A210	45c multicolored	1.00	.30
1279	A210	60c multicolored	1.25	.50
1280	A210	$2 multicolored	2.00	2.00
1281	A210	$3 multicolored	2.25	3.00
1282	A210	$4 multicolored	2.25	3.00
		Nos. 1275-1282 (8)	10.80	9.55

Souvenir Sheets

1283	A210	$5 multicolored	4.75	4.75
1284	A210	$5 multicolored	4.75	4.75

Orchids — A211

No. 1285, Vanilla mexicana. No. 1286, Epidendrum ibaguense. No. 1287, Epidendrum secundum. No. 1288, Maxillaria conferta. No. 1289, Oncidium altissimum. No. 1290, Spiranthes lanceolata. No. 1291, Tonopsis utricularioides. No. 1292, Epidendrum nocturnum.

No. 1293, Octomeria graminifolia. No. 1294, Rodriguezia lanceolata.

1990, Apr. 17   **Perf. 14**

1285	A211	15c multicolored	.90	.35
1286	A211	45c multicolored	1.25	.35
1287	A211	50c multicolored	1.40	.40
1288	A211	60c multicolored	1.50	.40
1289	A211	$1 multicolored	1.60	.85
1290	A211	$2 multicolored	2.00	2.00
1291	A211	$3 multicolored	2.50	2.50
1292	A211	$5 multicolored	3.25	3.75
		Nos. 1285-1292 (8)	14.40	10.60

Souvenir Sheets

1293	A211	$6 multicolored	4.50	4.50
1294	A211	$6 multicolored	4.50	4.50

EXPO '90, Osaka.

Fish A212

10c, Flamefish. 15c, Coney. 50c, Squirrelfish. 60c, Sergeant major. $1, Yellowtail snapper. $2, Rock beauty. $3, Spanish hogfish. $4, Striped parrotfish. No. 1303, Blackbar soldierfish. No. 1304, Foureye butterflyfish.

1990, May 21   **Perf. 14**

1295	A212	10c multicolored	.80	.45
1296	A212	15c multicolored	1.10	.45
1297	A212	50c multicolored	1.50	.55
1298	A212	60c multicolored	1.60	.55
1299	A212	$1 multicolored	1.75	.75
1300	A212	$2 multicolored	2.50	2.50
1301	A212	$3 multicolored	3.00	3.00
1302	A212	$4 multicolored	3.25	3.25
		Nos. 1295-1302 (8)	15.50	11.50

Souvenir sheets

1303	A212	$5 multicolored	6.75	6.75
1304	A212	$5 multicolored	6.75	6.75

Victoria and Elizabeth II — A213

1990, May 3   **Litho.**   **Perf. 15x14**

1305	A213	45c green	1.00	.30
1306	A213	60c bright rose	1.40	.50
1307	A213	$5 bright ultra	4.25	4.75
		Nos. 1305-1307 (3)	6.65	5.55

Souvenir Sheet

1308	A213	$6 black	5.50	5.50

Penny Black, 150th anniv.

Royal Mail Transport A214

Designs: 50c, Steam packet Britannia, 1840. 75c, Railway mail car, 1892. $4, Centaurus seaplane, 1938. $6, Subway, 1927.

1990, May 3   **Perf. 13½**
1309 A214 50c red & deep green 1.25 .30
1310 A214 75c red & vio brn 1.50 1.00
1311 A214 $4 red & brt ultra 4.00 5.00
Nos. 1309-1311 (3) 6.75 6.30

Souvenir Sheet
1312 A214 $6 red & black 5.50 5.50
Stamp World London '90.

Miniature Sheet

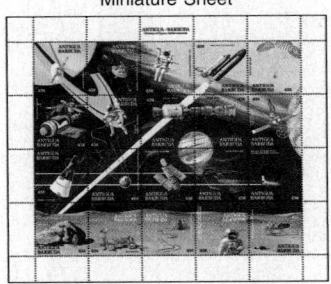

Space Achievements — A215

Designs: a, *Voyager 2* passing Saturn. b, *Pioneer 11* photographing Saturn. c, Manned maneuvering unit. d, *Columbia* space shuttle. e, Splashdown of Apollo 10 command module. f, *Skylab*. g, Ed White space walking, Gemini 4 mission. h, Apollo module, Apollo-Soyuz mission. i, Soyuz module, Apollo-Soyuz mission. j, *Mariner 1* passing Venus. k, Gemini 4 module. l, *Sputnik*. m, Hubble Space Telescope. n, X-15 rocket plane. o, Bell X-1 breaking sound barrier. p, Astronaut, Apollo 17 mission. r, American lunar rover. r, Lunar module, Apollo 14 mission. s, First men on the Moon, Apollo 11 mission. t, Lunokhod, Soviet lunar rover.

1990, June 11   **Litho.**   **Perf. 14**
1313 A215 Sheet of 20 16.00 16.00
a.-t. 45c any single .75 .75

Mickey Production Studios — A216

Walt Disney characters in Hollywood: 45c, Minnie Mouse reading script. 50c, Director Mickey Mouse, take 1 of Minnie. 60c, Make-up artist Daisy Duck. $1, Clarabelle as Cleopatra. $2, Mickey, Goofy, Donald Duck. $3, Goofy destroying set. $4, Mickey, Donald editing film. No. 1322, Mickey directs surfing film. No. 1323, Minnie, Daisy, Clarabelle in musical.

1990, Sept. 3   **Litho.**   **Perf. 14x13½**
1314 A216 25c shown .80 .25
1315 A216 45c multicolored .90 .25
1316 A216 50c multicolored 1.00 .25
1317 A216 60c multicolored 1.25 .30
1318 A216 $1 multicolored 1.40 .60
1319 A216 $2 multicolored 1.75 1.75
1320 A216 $3 multicolored 2.25 2.25
1321 A216 $4 multicolored 2.25 2.25
Nos. 1314-1321 (8) 11.60 7.90

Souvenir Sheets
1322 A216 $5 multicolored 4.75 4.75
1323 A216 $5 multicolored 4.75 4.75

A217

1990, Aug. 27   **Litho.**   **Perf. 14**
1324 A217 15c multicolored .50 .25
1325 A217 35c multi, diff. .75 .25
1326 A217 75c multi, diff. 1.25 .65
1327 A217 $3 multi, diff. 2.25 3.00
Nos. 1324-1327 (4) 4.75 4.15

Souvenir Sheet
1328 A217 $6 multi, diff. 5.50 5.50
Queen Mother, 90th birthday.

A218

No. 1329, 20-Kilometer Walk. No. 1330, Triple jump. No. 1331, 10,000 meter run. No. 1332, Javelin.
No. 1333, Opening ceremony, Los Angeles, 1984.

1990, Oct. 1   **Litho.**   **Perf. 14**
1329 A218 50c multicolored 1.00 .30
1330 A218 75c multicolored 1.25 .60
1331 A218 $1 multicolored 1.50 .70
1332 A218 $5 multicolored 3.75 4.50
Nos. 1329-1332 (4) 7.50 6.10

Souvenir Sheet
1333 A218 $6 multicolored 6.50 6.50
1992 Summer Olympics, Barcelona.

Intl. Literacy Year — A219

Walt Disney characters in scenes from books by Charles Dickens: 15c, Huey and Dewey, Christmas Stories. 25c, Donald Duck, Bleak House. 50c, Dewey, Bad Pete, Oliver Twist. 60c, Daisy Duck, Old Curiosity Shop. $1, Little Nell. $2, Scrooge McDuck, Pickwick Papers. $3, Mickey and Minnie Mouse, Dombey and Son. $5, Minnie, Our Mutual Friend. No. 1342, Mickey and friends, David Copperfield. No. 1343, Pinocchio, Oliver Twist.

1990, Oct. 15   **Litho.**   **Perf. 14**
1334 A219 15c multicolored .75 .25
1335 A219 45c multicolored 1.00 .35
1336 A219 50c multicolored 1.10 .40
1337 A219 60c multicolored 1.25 .45
1338 A219 $1 multicolored 1.50 .70
1339 A219 $2 multicolored 2.00 2.00
1340 A219 $3 multicolored 2.25 2.25
1341 A219 $5 multicolored 3.00 3.50
Nos. 1334-1341 (8) 12.85 9.90

Souvenir Sheets
1342 A219 $6 multicolored 6.50 6.50
1343 A219 $6 multicolored 6.50 6.50

Nos. 1217-1222 Overprinted

1990, Nov. 11
1344 A201 15c multicolored .85 .30
1345 A201 25c multicolored .85 .30
1346 A201 $1 multicolored 2.00 1.50
1347 A201 $4 multicolored 3.75 4.25
Nos. 1344-1347 (4) 7.45 6.35

Souvenir Sheets
1348 A201 $5 on #1221 6.00 6.00
1349 A201 $5 on #1222 6.00 6.00
Overprint on Nos. 1348-1349 is 32x13mm.

Birds A220

10c, Pearly-eyed thrasher. 25c, Purple-throated carib. 50c, Common yellowthroat. 60c, American kestrel. $1, Yellow-bellied sapsucker. $2, Purple gallinule. $3, Yellow-crowned night heron. $4, Blue-hooded euphonia.
No. 1358, Brown pelican. No. 1359, Frigate bird.

1990, Nov. 19
1350 A220 10c multicolored .50 .35
1351 A220 25c multicolored .60 .40
1352 A220 50c multicolored .70 .45
1353 A220 60c multicolored 1.10 .75
1354 A220 $1 multicolored 1.25 .80
1355 A220 $2 multicolored 2.25 2.25
1356 A220 $3 multicolored 2.50 2.50
1357 A220 $4 multicolored 2.75 2.75
Nos. 1350-1357 (8) 11.65 10.25

Souvenir Sheets
1358 A220 $6 multicolored 8.00 8.00
1359 A220 $6 multicolored 8.00 8.00

Christmas — A221

Paintings: 25c, Madonna and Child with Saints by del Piombo. 30c, Virgin and Child with Angels by Grunewald, vert. 40c, Holy Family and a Shepherd by Titian. 60c, Virgin and Child by Fra Filippo Lippi, vert. $1, Jesus, St. John and Two Angels by Rubens. $4, Adoration of the Shepherds by Catena. $5, Virgin and Child Adored by a Warrior by Catena. No. 1368, Allegory of the Blessings of Jacob by Rubens, vert. No. 1369, Adoration of the Magi by Fra Angelico, vert.

Perf. 14x13½, 13½x14
1990, Dec. 10   **Litho.**
1360 A221 25c multicolored .85 .40
1361 A221 30c multicolored .85 .40
1362 A221 40c multicolored 1.00 .45
1363 A221 60c multicolored 1.25 .50
1364 A221 $1 multicolored 1.50 1.00
1365 A221 $2 multicolored 2.25 2.25
1366 A221 $4 multicolored 3.50 3.50
1367 A221 $4 multicolored 3.50 3.50
Nos. 1360-1367 (8) 14.70 12.00

Souvenir Sheets
1368 A221 $6 multicolored 4.50 4.50
1369 A221 $6 multicolored 4.50 4.50

Peter Paul Rubens (1577-1640), Painter — A222

Entire paintings or different details from: 25c, Rape of the Daughters of Leucippus. 45c, $2, $4, Bacchanal. 50c, $1, $3, Rape of the Sabine Women. 60c, Battle of the Amazons. No. 1378, Rape of Hippodameia. No. 1379, Battle of the Amazons.

1991, Jan. 21   **Litho.**   **Perf. 14**
1370 A222 25c multicolored 1.00 .30
1371 A222 45c multicolored 1.25 .45
1372 A222 50c multicolored 1.25 .50
1373 A222 60c multicolored 1.50 .65

1374 A222 $1 multicolored 1.75 1.00
1375 A222 $2 multicolored 2.00 2.25
1376 A222 $3 multicolored 2.50 3.00
1377 A222 $4 multicolored 2.75 3.50
Nos. 1370-1377 (8) 14.00 11.65

Souvenir Sheets
1378 A222 $6 multicolored 4.75 4.75
1379 A222 $6 multicolored 4.75 4.75

World War II Milestones A223

Designs: 10c, US troops enter Germany, Sept. 11, 1944. 15c, All axis forces surrender in North Africa, May 12, 1943. 25c, US troops invade Kwajalein, Jan. 31, 1944. 45c, Roosevelt and Churchill meet in Casablanca, Jan. 14, 1943. 50c, Marshal Badoglio signs agreement with allies, Sept. 1, 1943. $1, Mountbatten appointed Supreme Allied Commander, Southeast Asia Command, Aug. 25, 1943. $2, Major Greek tactical victory, Koritza, Nov. 22, 1940. $4, Britain and USSR sign mutual assistance pact, July 12, 1941. $5, Operation Torch, Nov. 8, 1942. No. 1389, Japanese attack on Pearl Harbor, Dec. 7, 1941. No. 1390, American bombing attack on Schweinfurt, Oct. 14, 1943.

1991, Mar. 11   **Litho.**   **Perf. 14**
1380 A223 10c multicolored 1.10 .60
1381 A223 15c multicolored 1.25 .50
1382 A223 25c multicolored 1.25 .50
1383 A223 45c multicolored 2.50 .65
1384 A223 50c multicolored 1.50 .65
1385 A223 $1 multicolored 2.75 1.50
1386 A223 $2 multicolored 3.00 2.75
1387 A223 $4 multicolored 3.00 3.00
1388 A223 $5 multicolored 3.25 3.25
Nos. 1380-1388 (9) 19.60 13.40

Souvenir Sheets
1389 A223 $6 multicolored 6.75 6.75
1390 A223 $6 multicolored 6.75 6.75

Cog Railways of the World A224

Designs: 25c, Prince Regent, Middleton Colliery, 1812. 30c, Snowdon Mountain Railway, Wales. 40c, 1st Railcar at Hell Gate, Manitou and Pike's Peak Railway. 60c, PNKA Rack Railway, Amberawa, Java. $1, Green Mountain Railway, Mt. Desert Island, Maine, 1883. $2, Cog locomotive, Pike's Peak, 1891. $4, Vitznau-Rigi Cog Railway, Lake Lucerne. $5, Leopoldina Railway, Brazil. No. 1399, Electric Cog Donkey Engines, Panama Canal. No. 1400, Gornergratbahn, 1st electric cog railway in Switzerland, vert.

1991, Mar. 18   **Litho.**   **Perf. 14**
1391 A224 25c multicolored 1.10 .35
1392 A224 30c multicolored 1.25 .35
1393 A224 40c multicolored 1.25 .45
1394 A224 60c multicolored 1.50 .50
1395 A224 $1 multicolored 2.00 .75
1396 A224 $2 multicolored 2.75 2.75
1397 A224 $4 multicolored 3.25 3.25
1398 A224 $5 multicolored 3.25 3.25
Nos. 1391-1398 (8) 16.35 11.65

Souvenir Sheets
1399 A224 $6 multicolored 7.50 7.50
1400 A224 $6 multicolored 7.50 7.50

Butterflies A225

10c, Zebra. 35c, Southern daggertail. 50c, Red anartia. 75c, Malachite. $1, Polydamas swallowtail. $2, Orion. $4, Mimic. $5, Cracker. Caterpillars: No. 1409, Monarch, vert. No. 1410, Painted lady, vert.

1991, Apr. 15   **Litho.**   **Perf. 14**
1401 A225 10c multicolored .70 .35
1402 A225 15c multicolored 1.10 .35
1403 A225 50c multicolored 1.25 .45
1404 A225 75c multicolored 1.50 .85
1405 A225 $1 multicolored 1.75 1.00

1406	A225	$2 multicolored	2.25	2.25
1407	A225	$4 multicolored	3.00	3.00
1408	A225	$5 multicolored	3.00	3.75
		Nos. 1401-1408 (8)	14.55	12.00

Souvenir Sheets

1409	A225	$6 multicolored	8.00	8.00
1410	A225	$6 multicolored	8.00	8.00

Voyages
of
Discovery
A226

Designs: 10c, Hanno, Phoenicia, c. 450 B.C. 15c, Pytheas, Greece, 325 B.C. 45c, Eric the Red, Viking, A.D. 985. 60c, Leif Erikson, Viking, A.D. 1000. $1, Scylax, Greece, A.D. 518. $2, Marco Polo, A.D. 1259. $4, Queen Hatsheput, Egypt, 1493 B.C. $5, St. Brendan, Ireland, 500 A.D. No. 1419, Columbus, bareheaded. No. 1420, Columbus, wearing hat.

1991, Apr. 22

1411	A226	10c multicolored	.85	.35
1412	A226	15c multicolored	.95	.35
1413	A226	45c multicolored	1.25	.40
1414	A226	60c multicolored	1.50	.55
1415	A226	$1 multicolored	2.00	.90
1416	A226	$2 multicolored	2.25	2.25
1417	A226	$4 multicolored	3.00	3.00
1418	A226	$5 multicolored	3.00	4.00
		Nos. 1411-1418 (8)	14.80	11.80

Souvenir Sheets

1419	A226	$6 multicolored	4.75	4.75
1420	A226	$6 multicolored	4.75	4.75

Discovery of America, 500th anniv. (in 1992).

Paintings by
Vincent Van
Gogh
A227

Designs: 5c, Portrait of Camille Roulin. 10c, Portrait of Armand Roulin. 15c, Young Peasant Woman with Straw Hat Sitting in the Wheat. 25c, Portrait of Adeline Ravoux. 30c, The Schoolboy (Camille Roulin). 40c, Portrait of Doctor Gachet. 50c, Portrait of a Man. 75c, Two Children. $2, Portrait of Postman Joseph Roulin. $3, The Seated Zouave. $4, L'arlesienne: Madame Ginoux with Books. No. 1432, Self Portrait, November/December 1888. No. 1433, Flowering Garden. No. 1434, Farmhouse in Provence. $6, The Bridge at Trinquetaille.

1991, May 13   *Perf. 13½*

1421	A227	5c multicolored	.60	.75
1422	A227	10c multicolored	.60	.55
1423	A227	15c multicolored	.70	.45
1424	A227	25c multicolored	.80	.45
1425	A227	30c multicolored	.80	.45
1426	A227	40c multicolored	.90	.45
1427	A227	50c multicolored	1.00	.45
1428	A227	75c multicolored	1.60	.75
1429	A227	$2 multicolored	2.50	2.50
1430	A227	$3 multicolored	3.00	2.75
1431	A227	$4 multicolored	3.50	3.50
1432	A227	$5 multicolored	3.50	3.50
		Nos. 1421-1432 (12)	19.50	16.55

Size: 102x76mm
Imperf

1433	A227	$5 multicolored	5.00	5.00
1434	A227	$5 multicolored	5.00	5.00
1435	A227	$6 multicolored	6.00	6.00

Phila Nippon '91 — A228

Walt Disney characters demonstrating Japanese martial arts: 10c, Mickey as champion sumo wrestler, vert. 15c, Goofy using tonfa. 45c, Ninja Donald in full field dress. 60c, Mickey using weapon in kung fu, vert. $1, Goofy tries kendo, vert. $2, Mickey, Donald demonstrating special technique of aikido. $4, Mickey flips Donald with judo throw. $5, Mickey demonstrates yabusame (target shooting from running horse), vert. No. 1444, Mickey using karate. No. 1445, Mickey demonstrating tamashiwara (powerbreaking), vert.

Perf. 13½x14, 14x13½
1991, June 29   Litho.

1436	A228	10c multicolored	.75	.25
1437	A228	15c multicolored	.85	.25
1438	A228	45c multicolored	1.50	.45
1439	A228	60c multicolored	2.00	.60
1440	A228	$1 multicolored	2.50	1.25
1441	A228	$2 multicolored	3.00	3.00
1442	A228	$4 multicolored	4.00	4.00
1443	A228	$5 multicolored	4.00	4.00
		Nos. 1436-1443 (8)	18.60	13.80

Souvenir Sheets

1444	A228	$6 multicolored	6.50	6.50
1445	A228	$6 multicolored	6.50	6.50

Royal Family Birthday, Anniversary
Common Design Type

1991, July 8   Litho.   *Perf. 14*

1446	CD347	10c multicolored	.50	.25
1447	CD347	15c multicolored	.35	.25
1448	CD347	20c multicolored	.35	.25
1449	CD347	40c multicolored	1.00	.30
1450	CD347	$1 multicolored	1.25	.75
1451	CD347	$2 multicolored	1.75	1.75
1452	CD347	$4 multicolored	2.75	2.75
1453	CD347	$5 multicolored	4.50	4.50
		Nos. 1446-1453 (8)	12.45	10.80

Souvenir Sheets

1454	CD347	$4 Elizabeth, Philip	3.75	3.75
1455	CD347	$4 Charles, Diana, sons	5.75	5.75

10c, 40c, $1, $5, No. 1455, Charles and Diana, 10th wedding anniversary. Others, Queen Elizabeth II, 65th birthday.

Walt Disney
Characters
Playing
Golf — A229

Designs: 10c, Daisy Duck teeing off. 15c, Goofy using 3-Wood. 45c, Mickey using 3-Iron. 60c, Mickey missing ball using 6-Iron. $1, Donald trying 8-Iron to get out of pond. $2, Minnie using 9-Iron. $4, Donald digging hole with sand wedge. $5, Goofy trying new approach with putter. No. 1464, Grandma Duck using pitching wedge. No. 1465, Mickey cheering Minnie as she uses her 5-Wood, horiz.

Perf. 13½x14, 14x13½
1991, Aug. 7   Litho.

1456	A229	10c multicolored	.75	.40
1457	A229	15c multicolored	.85	.40
1458	A229	45c multicolored	1.25	.40
1459	A229	60c multicolored	1.75	.50
1460	A229	$1 multicolored	2.00	1.10
1461	A229	$2 multicolored	2.50	2.50
1462	A229	$4 multicolored	3.25	3.25
1463	A229	$5 multicolored	3.50	4.00
		Nos. 1456-1463 (8)	15.85	12.55

Souvenir Sheets

1464	A229	$6 multicolored	6.50	6.50
1465	A229	$6 multicolored	6.50	6.50

1992
Summer
Olympics,
Barcelona
A230

Archie Comics, 50th anniv.: 10c, Moose receiving gold medal. 25c, Archie, Veronica, Mr. Lodge, polo match, horiz. 40c, Archie & Betty, fencing. 60c, Archie, women's volleyball. $1, Archie, tennis. $2, Archie, marathon race. $4, Archie, judging women's gymnastics, horiz. $5, Archie, Betty, Veronica, basketball. No. 1474, Archie, soccer. No. 1475, Archie, Betty, baseball, horiz.

Perf. 13½x14, 14x13½
1991, Aug. 19

1466	A230	10c multicolored	.65	.30
1467	A230	25c multicolored	1.00	.30
1468	A230	40c multicolored	1.25	.35
1469	A230	60c multicolored	1.50	.45
1470	A230	$1 multicolored	1.75	1.00
1471	A230	$2 multicolored	2.50	2.50
1472	A230	$4 multicolored	3.75	3.75
1473	A230	$5 multicolored	4.00	5.00
		Nos. 1466-1473 (8)	16.40	13.65

Souvenir Sheets

1474	A230	$6 multicolored	6.25	6.25
1475	A230	$6 multicolored	6.25	6.25

Charles
de Gaulle,
Birth
Cent.
A231

Charles de Gaulle: 10c, and Pres. Kennedy, families, 1961. 15c, and Pres. Roosevelt, 1945, vert. 45c, and Chancellor Adenauer, 1962, vert. 60c, Liberation of Paris, 1944, vert. $1, Crossing the Rhine, 1945. $2, In Algiers, 1944. $4, and Pres. Eisenhower, 1960. $5, Returning from Germany, 1968, vert. No. 1484, and Churchill at Casablanca, 1943. No. 1485, and Citizens.

1991, Sept. 11   Litho.   *Perf. 14*

1476	A231	10c multicolored	.90	.35
1477	A231	15c multicolored	1.00	.35
1478	A231	45c multicolored	1.40	.40
1479	A231	60c multicolored	1.50	.50
1480	A231	$1 multicolored	1.75	.90
1481	A231	$2 multicolored	2.75	2.75
1482	A231	$4 multicolored	3.25	3.25
1483	A231	$5 multicolored	3.50	4.00
		Nos. 1476-1483 (8)	16.05	12.50

Souvenir Sheets

1484	A231	$6 multicolored	6.50	6.50
1485	A231	$6 multicolored	6.50	6.50

Independence, 10th Anniv. — A232

Designs: 10c, Island maps, government building. $6, Old P. O., St. Johns, #1 & #635.

1991, Oct. 28

1486	A232	10c multicolored	.85	.50

Souvenir Sheet

1487	A232	$6 multicolored	7.50	7.50

No. 1487 contains one 50x38mm stamp.

Miniature Sheet

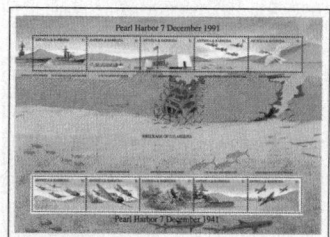

Attack on Pearl Harbor, 50th
Anniv. — A233

Designs: No. 1488a, Bow of Nimitz class carrier, Ticonderoga class cruiser. b, Tourist boat to Arizona Memorial. c, USS Arizona Memorial. d, Aircraft salute to missing men. e, White tern. f, Japanese Kate torpedo bombers. g, Japanese Zero fighters. h, Battleship row in flames. i, USS Nevada breaking out. j, Zeros returning to carriers.

1991, Dec. 9   *Perf. 14½x15*

1488	A233	$1 Sheet of 10, #a.-j.	22.50	22.50

Inscription for No. 1488f incorrectly describes torpedo bombers as Zekes.

3rd
Antigua
Methodist
Cub Scout
Pack, 60th
Anniv.
A234

Designs: $2, Lord Robert Baden-Powell, scouts, vert. $3.50, Scouts around campfire. $5, Antigua & Barbuda flag, Jamboree emblem, vert.

1991, Dec. 9   *Perf. 14*

1489	A234	75c multicolored	1.75	.90
1490	A234	$2 multicolored	6.50	5.50
1491	A234	$3.50 multicolored	5.50	5.50
		Nos. 1489-1491 (3)	13.75	11.90

Souvenir Sheet

1492	A234	$5 multicolored	5.25	5.25

17th World Scout Jamboree, Korea.

Wolfgang
Amadeus
Mozart,
Death
Bicent.
A235

Portrait of Mozart and: $1.50, Scene from opera, Don Giovanni. $4, St. Peter's Cathedral, Salzburg.

1991, Dec. 9

1493	A235	$1.50 multicolored	4.00	2.75
1494	A235	$4 multicolored	7.50	6.50

Anniversaries and Events — A236

Designs: $2, Otto Lilienthal's glider No. 5. $2.50, Locomotive cab, vert.

1991, Dec. 9   Litho.   *Perf. 14*

1495	A236	$2 multicolored	4.00	2.75
1496	A236	$2.50 multicolored	7.25	4.00

First glider flight, cent. (No. 1495). Trans-Siberian Railway, cent. (No. 1496). Numbers have been reserved for additional values in this set.

Brandenburg Gate, Bicent. — A237

25c, Demonstrators in autos, German flag. $2, Statue. $3, Portions of decorative frieze.

1991, Dec. 9   Litho.   *Perf. 14*

1499	A237	25c multicolored	.25	.25
1500	A237	$2 multicolored	1.25	1.50
1501	A237	$3 multicolored	2.25	2.25
		Nos. 1499-1501 (3)	3.75	4.00

Souvenir Sheet

1502	A237	$4 multicolored	5.25	5.25

Antigua & Barbuda 10c
Christmas 1991

Christmas A238

Paintings by Fra Angelico: 10c, The Annunciation. 30c, Nativity. 40c, Adoration of the Magi. 60c, Presentation in the Temple. $1, Circumcision. $3, Flight into Egypt. $4, Massacre of the Innocents. $5, Christ Teaching in the Temple. No. 1511, Adoration of the Magi, diff. No. 1512, Adoration of the Magi (Cook Tondo).

			Perf. 12	
1991, Dec. 12				
1503	A238	10c multicolored	.40	.25
1504	A238	30c multicolored	.65	.25
1505	A238	40c multicolored	.80	.30
1506	A238	60c multicolored	1.00	.45
1507	A238	$1 multicolored	1.25	.75
1508	A238	$3 multicolored	2.50	2.50
1509	A238	$4 multicolored	2.75	2.75
1510	A238	$5 multicolored	3.00	3.75
		Nos. 1503-1510 (8)	12.35	11.00

Souvenir Sheets

1511	A238	$6 multicolored	7.00	7.00
1512	A238	$6 multicolored	7.00	7.00

Queen Elizabeth II's Accession to the Throne, 40th Anniv.
Common Design Type

Queen Elizabeth II and various island scenes.

		Litho.	Perf. 14	
1992, Feb. 6				
1513	CD348	10c multicolored	.90	.30
1514	CD348	30c multicolored	1.10	.30
1515	CD348	$1 multicolored	1.25	.75
1516	CD348	$5 multicolored	2.75	2.75
		Nos. 1513-1516 (4)	6.00	4.10

Souvenir Sheets

1517	CD348	$6 Beach	5.00	5.00
1518	CD348	$6 Flora	5.00	5.00

Antigua & Barbuda 15¢
Collybia fusipes
edible mushrooms

Mushrooms A239

10c, Amanita caesarea. 15c, Collybia fusipes. 30c, Boletus aereus. 40c, Laccaria amethystina. $1, Russula virescens. $2, Tricholoma auratum. $4, Calocybe gambosa. $5, Panus tigrinus.
No. 1527, Auricularia auricula. No. 1528, Clavariadelphus truncatus.

		Litho.	Perf. 14	
1992				
1519	A239	10c multicolored	.75	.35
1520	A239	15c multicolored	.90	.35
1521	A239	30c multicolored	1.25	.35
1522	A239	40c multicolored	1.25	.45
1523	A239	$1 multicolored	2.25	1.00
1524	A239	$2 multicolored	3.00	3.00
1525	A239	$4 multicolored	3.75	3.75
1526	A239	$5 multicolored	3.75	4.25
		Nos. 1519-1526 (8)	16.90	13.50

Souvenir Sheet

1527	A239	$6 multicolored	7.50	7.50
1528	A239	$6 multicolored	7.50	7.50

Issued: 10c, 30c, $1, $5, No. 1528, May 18; others, Mar.

Antigua & Barbuda – 15¢
KAYAKING Barcelona'92

Disney Characters at Summer Olympics, Barcelona A240

Designs: 10c, Mickey presenting gold medal to mermaid for swimming. 15c, Dewey and Huey watching Louie in kayak. 30c, Uncle McScrooge, Donald yachting. 50c, Donald, horse trying water polo. $1, Big Pete weight lifting. $2, Donald, Goofy fencing. $4, Mickey, Donald playing volleyball. $5, Goofy vaulting over horse.
No. 1537, $6, Mickey playing basketball, horiz. No. 1538, $6, Minnie Mouse on uneven parallel bars, horiz. No. 1539, $6, Mickey, Goofy, and Donald judging Minnie's floor exercise, horiz. No. 1540, $6, Mickey running after soccer ball.

			Perf. 13	
1992, Mar. 16				
1529	A240	10c multicolored	.65	.25
1530	A240	15c multicolored	.75	.25
1531	A240	30c multicolored	.95	.30
1532	A240	50c multicolored	1.50	.50
1533	A240	$1 multicolored	1.75	.85
1534	A240	$2 multicolored	2.75	2.75
1535	A240	$4 multicolored	3.50	3.50
1536	A240	$5 multicolored	3.50	3.50
		Nos. 1529-1536 (8)	15.35	11.90

Souvenir Sheets

1537-1540	A240	Set of 4	17.50	17.50

Antigua & Barbuda $2

Dinosaurs A241

10c, Pteranodon. 15c, Brachiosaurus. 30c, Tyrannosaurus rex. 50c, Parasaurolophus. $1, Deinonychus. $2, Triceratops. $4, Protoceratops. $5, Stegosaurus.
No. 1549, Apatosaurus. No. 1550, Allosaurus.

			Perf. 14	
1992, Apr. 6				
1541	A241	10c multicolored	.70	.35
1542	A241	15c multicolored	.75	.35
1543	A241	30c multicolored	.95	.35
1544	A241	50c multicolored	1.10	.45
1545	A241	$1 multicolored	1.50	.80
1546	A241	$2 multicolored	2.25	2.25
1547	A241	$4 multicolored	2.50	2.50
1548	A241	$5 multicolored	2.50	4.00
		Nos. 1541-1548 (8)	12.25	11.05

Souvenir Sheets

1549	A241	$6 multicolored	5.50	5.50
1550	A241	$6 multicolored	5.50	5.50

Nos. 1541-1544 are vert.

EASTER 1992
SUPPER AT EMMAUS · CARAVAGGIO 1573-1609
ANTIGUA & BARBUDA 10c

Easter — A242

Paintings: 10c, Supper at Emmaus, by Caravaggio. 15c, The Vision of St. Peter, by Francisco de Zurbaran. 30c, $1, Christ Driving the Money Changers from the Temple, by Tiepolo (detail on $1). 40c, Martyrdom of St. Bartholomew (detail), by Jusepe de Ribera. $2, Crucifixion (detail), by Albrecht Altdorfer. $4, $5, The Deposition (diff. detail), by Fra Angelico. No. 1559, Crucifixion, by Albrecht Altdorfer, vert. No. 1560, The Last Supper, by Vicente Juan Masip.

			Perf. 14x13½	
1992				
1551	A242	10c multicolored	.55	.25
1552	A242	15c multicolored	.75	.25
1553	A242	30c multicolored	1.00	.35
1554	A242	40c multicolored	1.25	.50
1555	A242	$1 multicolored	2.25	1.00
1556	A242	$2 multicolored	3.25	3.25
1557	A242	$4 multicolored	4.25	4.25
1558	A242	$5 multicolored	4.25	4.25
		Nos. 1551-1558 (8)	17.55	14.10

Souvenir Sheet
Perf. 13½x14

1559	A242	$6 multicolored	6.00	6.00
1560	A242	$6 multicolored	6.00	6.00

Antigua & Barbuda 10¢
The Miracle at the Well
Alonso Cano GRANADA 1992

Spanish Art — A243

Designs: 10c, The Miracle at the Well, by Alonso Cano. 15c, The Poet Luis de Gongora y Argote, by Velazquez. 30c, The Painter Francisco Goya, by Vincente Lopez Portana. 40c, Maria de Las Nieves Michaela Fourdiniere, by Luis Paret y Alcazar. $1, Charles III Eating before His Court, by Paret y Alcazar, horiz. $2, A Rain Shower in Granada, by Antonio Munoz Degrain, horiz. $4, Sarah Bernhardt, by Santiago Rusinol y Prats. $5, The Hermitage Garden, by Joaquin Mir Trinxet. No. 1569, Olympus: Battle with the Giants, by Francisco Bayeu y Subias. No. 1570, The Ascent of Monsieur Boucle's Montgolfier Balloon in the Gardens of Aranjuez, by Antonio Carnicero.

1992, May 11				
1561	A243	10c multicolored	.45	.25
1562	A243	15c multicolored	.65	.30
1563	A243	30c multicolored	.90	.35
1564	A243	40c multicolored	1.00	.50
1565	A243	$1 multicolored	1.60	.90
1566	A243	$2 multicolored	2.50	2.50
1567	A243	$4 multicolored	3.75	3.75
1568	A243	$5 multicolored	4.25	4.50

Size: 120x95mm
Imperf

1569	A243	$6 multicolored	7.50	7.50
1570	A243	$6 multicolored	7.50	7.50
		Nos. 1561-1570 (10)	30.10	28.05

Granada '92.

15¢ ANTIGUA & BARBUDA
San Salvador
Where Columbus is said to have first landed.

Discovery of America, 500th Anniv. A244

Designs: 15c, San Salvador Island. 30c, Martin Alonzo Pinzon, captain of Pinta. 40c, Columbus, signature, coat of arms. $1, Pinta. $2, Nina. $4, Santa Maria. No. 1577, Sea monster. No. 1578, Map, sailing ship.

		Litho.	Perf. 14	
1992, May 25				
1571	A244	15c multicolored	.35	.25
1572	A244	30c multicolored	.45	.25
1573	A244	40c multicolored	.60	.35
1574	A244	$1 multicolored	2.25	2.25
1575	A244	$2 multicolored	2.50	2.50
1576	A244	$4 multicolored	3.00	3.50
		Nos. 1571-1576 (6)	9.15	9.10

Souvenir Sheets

1577	A244	$6 multicolored	6.00	6.00
1578	A244	$6 multicolored	6.00	6.00

World Columbian Stamp Expo '92, Chicago.

M.J.Hummel 15¢
ANTIGUA & BARBUDA

Hummel Figurines — A245

Designs 15c, No. 1587a, $1.50, Boy sitting on rock pointing to flower in cap. 30c, No. 1587b, $1.50, Girl sitting on fence. 40c, No. 1587c, $1.50, Boy holding binoculars. 50c, No. 1587d, $1.50, Boy carrying umbrella. $1, No. 1588a, $1.50, Two boys looking up at direction marker. $2, No. 1588b, $1.50, Boy carrying basket on back, walking with stick. $4, No. 1588c, $1.50, Two girls, goat. $5, No. 1588d, $1.50, Boy carrying walking stick.

1993, Jan. 6				
1579	A245	15c multicolored	.40	.25
1580	A245	30c multicolored	.65	.25
1581	A245	40c multicolored	.80	.30
1582	A245	50c multicolored	.90	.40
1583	A245	$1 multicolored	1.50	.75
1584	A245	$2 multicolored	1.75	1.75
1585	A245	$4 multicolored	2.75	2.75
1586	A245	$5 multicolored	2.75	3.75
		Nos. 1579-1586 (8)	11.50	10.20

Souvenir Sheets

1587	A245	$1.50 Sheet of 4, #a.-d.	8.50	8.50
1588	A245	$1.50 Sheet of 4, #a.-d.	8.50	8.50

25¢ Antigua and Barbuda
Green Mango
Parrot's Plantain

Hummingbirds and Flowers — A246

Designs: 10c, Antillean crested, wild plantain. 25c, Green mango, parrot's plantain. 45c, Purple-throated carib, lobster claws. 60c, Antillean mango, coral plant. $1, Vervain, cardinal's guard. $2, Rufous breasted hermit, heliconia. $4, Blue-headed, red ginger. $5, Green-throated carib, ornamental banana. No. 1597, Bee, jungle flame. No. 1598, Western streamertails, bignonia.

		Litho.	Perf. 14	
1992, Aug. 10				
1589	A246	10c multicolored	.45	.45
1590	A246	25c multicolored	.60	.30
1591	A246	45c multicolored	.80	.35
1592	A246	60c multicolored	.90	.45
1593	A246	$1 multicolored	1.25	1.25
1594	A246	$2 multicolored	2.00	2.00
1595	A246	$4 multicolored	3.25	3.25
1596	A246	$5 multicolored	3.50	3.50
		Nos. 1589-1596 (8)	12.75	11.05

Souvenir Sheets

1597	A246	$6 multicolored	6.50	6.50
1598	A246	$6 multicolored	6.50	6.50

Genoa '92.

1492 CHRISTOPHER COLUMBUS 1992
ANTIGUA & BARBUDA $1

Discovery of America, 500th Anniv. — A247

		Litho.	Perf. 14½	
1992				
1599	A247	$1 Coming ashore	1.10	.75
1600	A247	$2 Natives, ships	1.90	1.90

Organization of East Caribbean States.

Souvenir Sheet

Postage Stamp Mega-Event
$6 ANTIGUA AND BARBUDA

Madison Square Garden, NYC — A248

		Litho.	Perf. 14	
1992				
1601	A248	$6 multicolored	5.50	5.50

Postage Stamp Mega-Event, Jacob Javits Center, New York City.

ELVIS PRESLEY – ROCK AND ROLL LEGEND

15TH ANNIVERSARY OF HIS DEATH

Elvis Presley (1935-1977) — A249

Various pictures of Elvis Presley.

1992   **Perf. 13½x14**
1602 A249 $1 Sheet of 9, #a.- |
    i.   15.00 15.00

Inventors and Pioneers A250

Designs: 10c, Ts'ai Lun, paper. 25c, Igor I. Sikorsky, 4-engine airplane. 30c, Alexander Graham Bell, telephone. 40c, Johannes Gutenberg, printing press. 60c, James Watt, steam engine. $1, Anton van Leeuwenhoek, microscope. $4, Louis Braille, Braille printing. $5, Galileo, telescope. No. 1607, Phonograph. No. 1608, Steamboat.

1992, Oct. 19		**Litho.**	**Perf. 14**	
1603	A250	10c multicolored	.25	.25
1604	A250	25c multicolored	1.50	.35
1605	A250	30c multicolored	.60	.40
1605A	A250	40c multicolored	.60	.40
1605B	A250	60c multicolored	3.75	1.00
1605C	A250	$1 multicolored	2.00	1.25
1605D	A250	$4 multicolored	4.50	4.50
1606	A250	$5 multicolored	4.75	4.50
		Nos. 1603-1606 (8)	17.95	12.65

Souvenir Sheet

1607	A250	$6 multicolored	6.00	6.00
1608	A250	$6 multicolored	6.00	6.00

ANTIGUA and BARBUDA
CHRISTMAS 1992

VIRGIN AND CHILD WITH ANGELS
School of Piero Della Francesca

Christmas A251

Details from Paintings: 10c, Virgin and Child with Angels, by School of Piero Della Francesca. 25c, Madonna Degli Alberelli, by Giovanni Bellini. 30c, Madonna and Child with St. Anthony Abbot and St. Sigismund, by Neroccio di Landi. 40c, Madonna and the Grand Duke, by Raphael. 60c, The Nativity, by George de la Tour. $1, Holy Family, by Jacob Jordaens. $4, Madonna and Child Enthroned, by Margaritone. $5, Madonna and Child on a Curved Throne, by Byzantine artist. No. 1617, Madonna and Child, by Domenico Ghirlandaio (both names misspelled). No. 1618, The Holy Family, by Pontormo.

1992			**Perf. 13½x14**	
1609	A251	10c multicolored	.65	.25
1610	A251	25c multicolored	1.00	.25
1611	A251	30c multicolored	1.10	.25
1612	A251	40c multicolored	1.25	.30
1613	A251	60c multicolored	1.75	.60
1614	A251	$1 multicolored	2.00	1.00
1615	A251	$4 multicolored	4.00	4.00
1616	A251	$5 multicolored	4.00	4.00
		Nos. 1609-1616 (8)	15.75	10.65

Souvenir Sheet

1617	A251	$6 multicolored	6.50	6.50
1618	A251	$6 multicolored	6.50	6.50

Year of Space C.I.S. Commonwealth
10c
ANTIGUA BARBUDA
A252

$2
50th Anniversary Inter-American Institute for Cooperation on Agriculture 1942-1992
IICA
ANTIGUA BARBUDA
A253

Anniversaries and Events: 10c, Cosmonauts. 40c, Graf Zeppelin, Goodyear blimp. 45c, Right Rev. Daniel C. Davis, St. John's Cathedral. 75c, Konrad Adenauer. $1, Bus Mosbacher, Weatherly. $1.50, Rain forest. No. 1625, Felis tigris. No. 1626, Flag, emblems, plant. No. 1627, Women acting on stage. $2.25, Women carrying baskets of food on their heads. $3, Lions Club emblem, club member. No. 1630, West German, NATO flags. No. 1631, China's Long March Booster Rocket. No. 1632, Dr. Hugo Eckener. No. 1633, $6, The Hindenburg. No. 1634, $6, Brandenburg Gate, German flag. No. 1635, $6, Monarch butterfly. No. 1636, $6, Hermes Shuttle, Columbus Space Station.

1992		**Litho.**	**Perf. 14**	
1619	A252	10c multicolored	.80	.50
1620	A252	40c multicolored	1.75	.55
1621	A252	45c multicolored	.75	.35
1622	A252	75c multicolored	.90	.60
1623	A252	$1 multicolored	1.25	.75
1624	A252	$1.50 multicolored	1.75	1.10
1625	A252	$2 multicolored	4.25	2.00
1626	A253	$2 multicolored	2.75	1.50
1627	A253	$2 multicolored	2.50	1.75
1628	A252	$2.25 multicolored	2.50	2.50
1629	A252	$3 multicolored	3.75	3.75
1630	A252	$4 multicolored	3.75	3.75
1631	A252	$4 multicolored	4.25	4.25
1632	A252	$6 multicolored	4.00	4.00
		Nos. 1619-1632 (14)	34.95	27.35

Souvenir Sheets

1633-1636	A252	Set of 4	22.00	22.00

Intl. Space Year (Nos. 1619, 1631, 1636). Count Zeppelin, 75th anniv. of death (Nos. 1620, 1632-1633). Diocese of Northeast Caribbean and Aruba District, 150th anniv. (No. 1621). Konrad Adenauer, 25th anniv. of death (Nos. 1622, 1630, 1634). 1962 winner of America's Cup (No. 1623). Earth Summit, Rio (Nos. 1624-1625, 1635). Inter-American Institute for Cooperation on Agriculture, 50th anniv. (No. 1626). Cultural Development, 40th anniv. (No. 1627). WHO Intl. Conf. on Nutrition, Rome (No. 1628). Lions Club, 75th anniv. (No. 1629).
Issued: Nos. 1619, 1621-1623, 1626-1631, 1634, 1636, Nov.; Nos. 1624-1625, 1635, Dec. 14.

10¢ ANTIGUA and BARBUDA
LE GOLF D'EURO DISNEY
EuroDisney RESORT PARIS

Euro Disney, Paris — A254

Disney characters: 10c, Golf course. 25c, Davy Crockett Campground. 30c, Cheyenne Hotel. 40c, Santa Fe Hotel. $1, New York Hotel. $2, In car, map showing location. $4, Pirates of the Caribbean. $5, Adventureland.
No. 1645, $6, Mickey Mouse on map with star, vert. No. 1646, $6, Roof turret at entrance, Mickey Mouse in uniform. No. 1646A, $6, Mickey Mouse, colored spots on poster, vert. No. 1646B, $6, Mickey on poster, vert., diff.

1992-93		**Litho.**	**Perf. 14x13½**	
1637	A254	10c multicolored	.70	.25
1638	A254	25c multicolored	.90	.25
1639	A254	30c multicolored	.90	.25
1640	A254	40c multicolored	1.00	.30
1641	A254	$1 multicolored	2.00	.75
1642	A254	$2 multicolored	2.75	2.75

1643	A254	$4 multicolored	3.75	3.00
1644	A254	$5 multicolored	3.75	3.75
		Nos. 1637-1644 (8)	15.75	11.30

Souvenir Sheets
Perf. 13½x14

1645-1646B	A254	Set of 4	19.00	19.00

Issued: Nos. 1638-1639, 1642-1643, 1646-1646B, 2/22/93; others, 12/1992.

Miniature Sheets

PAINTINGS FROM THE LOUVRE
ANTIGUA & BARBUDA
BICENTENNIAL 1793 – 1993

Louvre Museum, Bicent. — A255

Details or entire paintings, by Peter Paul Rubens: No. 1647a, Destiny of Marie de' Medici. b, Birth of Marie de'Medici. c, Marie's Education. d, Destiny of Marie de'Medici, diff. e, Henry IV Receives the Portrait. f, The Meeting at Lyons. g, The Marriage. h, The Birth of Louis XIII.
No. 1648a, The Capture of Juliers. b, The Exchange of Princesses. c, The Happiness of the Regency. d, The Majority of Louis XIII. e, The Flight from Blois. f, The Treaty of Angouleme. g, The Peace of Angers. h, The Queen's Reconciliation with Her Son.
$6, Helene Fourment Au Carosse.

1993, Mar. 22		**Litho.**	**Perf. 12**	
1647	A255	$1 Sheet of 8, #a.-h., + label	7.50	7.50
1648	A255	$1 Sheet of 8, #a.-h., + label	7.50	7.50

Souvenir Sheet
Perf. 14½

1649	A255	$6 multicolored	7.75	7.75

No. 1649 contains one 55x88mm stamp.
Nos. 1647-1649 exist imperf. Values about double those of normal sheets.

ANTIGUA BARBUDA
CARDINAL'S GUARD Pachystachys coccinea
15c

Flowers — A256

15c, Cardinal's guard. 25c, Giant granadilla. 30c, Spider flower. 40c, Gold vine. $1, Frangipani. $2, Bougainvillea. $4, Yellow oleander. $5, Spicy jatropha.
No. 1658, Bird lime tree. No. 1659, Fairy lily.

1993, Mar. 15		**Litho.**	**Perf. 14**	
1650	A256	15c multicolored	.95	.30
1651	A256	25c multicolored	1.10	.35
1652	A256	30c multicolored	1.10	.35
1653	A256	40c multicolored	1.10	.35
1654	A256	$1 multicolored	2.10	.90
1655	A256	$2 multicolored	2.75	2.75
1656	A256	$4 multicolored	4.00	4.00
1657	A256	$5 multicolored	4.00	4.50
		Nos. 1650-1657 (8)	17.10	13.45

Souvenir Sheets

1658	A256	$6 multicolored	6.00	6.00
1659	A256	$6 multicolored	6.00	6.00

"ENDANGERED SPECIES"
ANTIGUA & BARBUDA

Endangered Species — A257

Designs: No. 1660a, St. Lucia parrot. b, Cahow. c, Swallow-tailed kite. d, Everglades kite. e, Imperial parrot. f, Humpback whale. g, Puerto Rican plain pigeon. h, St. Vincent parrot. i, Puerto Rican parrot. j, Leatherback turtle. k, American crocodile. l, Hawksbill turtle.
No. 1662, West Indian manatee.

1993, Apr. 5				
1660	A257	$1 Sheet of 12, #a.-l.	13.00	13.00

Souvenir Sheets

1661	A257	$6 like #1660f	5.25	5.25
1662	A257	$6 multicolored	5.25	5.25

Antigua & Barbuda $1.50

Philatelic Publishing Personalities — A258

Portrait, stamp: No. 1663, J. Walter Scott (1842-1919), US "#C3a," Antigua #1. No. 1664, Theodore Champion, France #8, Antigua #1. No. 1665, E. Stanley Gibbons (1856-1913), cover of his first price list and catalogue, Antigua #1. No. 1666, Hugo Michel (1866-1944), Bavaria #1, Antigua #1. No. 1667, Alberto (1877-1944) and Giulio (1902-1987) Bolaffi, Sardinia #1, Great Britain #3. No. 1668, Richard Borek (1874-1947), Brunswick #24, Bavaria #1.
Front pages, Mekeel's Weekly Stamp News: No. 1669a, Jan. 7, 1890. b, Feb. 12, 1993.

1993, June 14				
1663	A258	$1.50 multicolored	2.10	2.10
1664	A258	$1.50 multicolored	2.10	2.10
1665	A258	$1.50 multicolored	2.10	2.10
1666	A258	$1.50 multicolored	2.10	2.10
1667	A258	$1.50 multicolored	2.10	2.10
1668	A258	$1.50 multicolored	2.10	2.10
		Nos. 1663-1668 (6)	12.60	12.60

Souvenir Sheet

1669	A258	$3 Sheet of 2, #a.-b.	7.50	7.50

Mekeel's Weekly Stamp News, cent. (in 1891; No. 1669).

Miniature Sheets

The 40th Anniversary of the Coronation of HM Queen Elizabeth II
1953 1993

Coronation of Queen Elizabeth II, 40th Anniv. — A259

No. 1670 — Coronation: a, 30c, Official photograph. b, 40c, Crown of Queen Elizabeth, the Queen Mother. c, $2, Dignataries attending ceremony. d, $4, Queen, Prince Edward.
No. 1671, $1 — First decade, 1953-1963: a, Wedding photograph of Princess Margaret and Antony Armstrong-Jones. b, Queen opening Parliament, Prince Philip. c, Queen holding infant. d, Royal family. e, Queen Elizabeth II, formal portrait. f, Queen, Charles de Gaulle. g, Queen, Pope John XXIII. h, Queen inspecting troops.
No. 1672, $1 — Second decade, 1963-1973: a, Investiture of Charles as Prince of Wales. b, Queen opening Parliament, Prince Philip, diff. c, Queen holding infant, diff. d, Queen, Prince Philip, children. e, Wearing blue robe, diadem. f, Prince Philip, Queen

seated. g, Prince Charles, Queen at microphone. h, Queen conversing, model airplane.

No. 1673, $1 — Third decade, 1973-1983: a, Wedding photograph of Prince Charles and Princess Diana. b, Queen opening Parliament, Prince Philip, diff. c, Princess Diana with infant. d, Princess Anne with infant. e, Portrait of Queen. f, Queen waving, Prince Philip. g, Queen, Pope John Paul II. h, Wedding portrait of Mark Phillips and Princess Anne.

No. 1674, $1 — Fourth decade, 1983-1993: a, Wedding photograph of Sarah Ferguson and Prince Andrew. b, Queen opening Parliament, Prince Philip, diff. c, Princess Diana holding infant, diff. d, Sarah Ferguson, infant. e, Queen wearing blue dress. f, Queen waving from carriage, Prince Philip. g, Queen wearing military uniform. h, Queen Mother.

$6, Portrait, by Denis Fildes.

1993, June 2   Litho.   Perf. 13½x14
1670 A259   Sheet, 2 each
      #a.-d.   11.50 11.50
Sheets of 8, #a-h
1671-1674 A259   Set of 4   37.50 37.50
Souvenir Sheet
Perf. 14
1675 A259 $6 multicolored   5.75   5.75

No. 1675 contains one 28x42mm stamp.

Wedding of Japan's Crown Prince Naruhito and Masako Owada
A260

Cameo photos of couple and: 40c, Crown Prince. $3, Princess.
$6, Princess wearing white coat, vert.

1993, Aug. 16   Litho.   Perf. 14
1676 A260   40c multicolored   .75   .40
1677 A260 $3 multicolored   2.50   2.25
Souvenir Sheet
1678 A260 $6 multicolored   6.00   6.00

Picasso (1881-1973) — A261

Paintings: 30c, Cat and Bird, 1939. 40c, Fish on a Newspaper, 1957. $5, Dying Bull, 1934.
$6, Woman with a Dog, 1953.

1993, Aug. 16   Litho.   Perf. 14
1679 A261   30c multicolored   1.00   .40
1680 A261   40c multicolored   1.00   .40
1681 A261 $5 multicolored   4.00   4.00
      Nos. 1679-1681 (3)   6.00   4.80
Souvenir Sheet
1682 A261 $6 multicolored   6.50   6.50

Copernicus (1473-1543)
A262

Designs: 40c, Astronomical devices. $4, Photograph of supernova.
$5, Copernicus.

1993, Aug. 16
1683 A262   40c multicolored   .75   .50
1684 A262 $4 multicolored   3.50   3.50
Souvenir Sheet
1685 A262 $5 multicolored   6.00   6.00

Willy Brandt (1913-1992), German Chancellor — A263

Designs: 30c, Helmut Schmidt, George Leber, Brandt. $4, Brandt, newspaper headlines.
$6, Brandt at Warsaw Ghetto Memorial, 1970.

1993, Aug. 16
1686 A263   30c multicolored   1.00   .35
1687 A263 $4 multicolored   4.25   4.25
Souvenir Sheet
1688 A263 $6 multicolored   6.25   6.25

Polska '93
A264

Paintings: $1, Study of a Woman Combing Her Hair, by Wladyslaw Slewinski, 1897. $3, Artist's Wife with Cat, by Konrad Krzyzanowski, 1912.
$6, General Confusion, by S. I. Witkiewicz, 1930, vert.

1993, Aug. 16
1689 A264 $1 multicolored   1.00   1.00
1690 A264 $3 multicolored   2.50   2.50
Souvenir Sheet
1691 A264 $6 multicolored   6.00   6.00

Inauguration of Pres. William J. Clinton — A265

Designs: $5, Pres. Clinton driving car. $6, Pres. Clinton, inauguration ceremony, vert.

1993, Aug. 16
1692 A265 $5 multicolored   3.75   3.75
Souvenir Sheet
1693 A265 $6 multicolored   6.00   6.00

No. 1693 contains one 43x57mm stamp.

1994 Winter Olympics, Lillehammer, Norway — A266

15c, Irina Rodnina, Alexei Ulanov, gold medalists, pairs figure skating, 1972. $5, Alberto Tomba, gold medal, giant slalom, 1988, 1992.
$6, Yvonne van Gennip, Andrea Ehrig, gold, bronze medalists, speedskating, 1988.

1993, Aug. 16
1694 A266   15c multicolored   1.10   .30
1695 A266 $5 multicolored   3.50   3.50
Souvenir Sheet
1696 A266 $6 multicolored   6.00   6.00

1994 World Cup Soccer Championships, US — A267

English soccer players: No. 1697, $2, Gordon Banks. Nos. 1698, $2, Bobby Moore. No. 1699, $2, Peter Shilton. No. 1700, $2, Nobby Stiles. No. 1701, $2, Bryan Robson. No. 1702, $2, Geoff Hurst. No. 1703, $2, Gary Lineker. No. 1704, $2, Bobby Charlton. No. 1705, $2, Martin Peters. No. 1706, $2, John Barnes. No. 1707, $2, David Platt. No. 1708, $2, Paul Gascoigne.
No. 1709, $6, Bobby Moore. No. 1710, $6, Player holding 1990 Fair Play Winners Trophy.

1993, July 30   Litho.   Perf. 14
1697-1708 A267   Set of 12   19.00 19.00
Souvenir Sheets
1709-1710 A267   Set of 2   11.50 11.50

Nos. 1697-1708 issued in sheets of five plus label identifying player.

Aviation Anniversaries — A268

Designs: 30c, Dr. Hugo Eckener, Dr. Wm. Beckers, zeppelin over Lake George, NY. No. 1712, Chicago Century of Progress Exhibition seen from zeppelin. No. 1713, George Washington, Blanchard's balloon, vert. No. 1714, Gloster E.28/39, first British jet plane. $4, Pres. Wilson watching take-off of first scheduled air mail plane. No. 1716, Hindenburg over Ebbets Field, Brooklyn, NY, 1937. No. 1717, Gloster Meteor in combat.
No. 1718, Eckener, vert. No. 1719, Alexander Hamilton, Pres. Washington, John Jay, gondola of Blanchard's balloon. No. 1720, PBY-5.

1993, Oct. 11
1711 A268   30c multicolored   1.00   .60
1712 A268   40c multicolored   1.00   1.00
1713 A268   40c multicolored   1.00   1.00
1714 A268   40c multicolored   1.00   1.00
1715 A268 $4 multicolored   4.00   4.00
1716 A268 $5 multicolored   4.00   4.00
1717 A268 $5 multicolored   5.75   5.75
      Nos. 1711-1717 (7)   17.75 17.35
Souvenir Sheets
1718 A268 $6 multicolored   5.50   5.50
1719 A268 $6 multicolored   6.25   6.25
1720 A268 $6 multicolored   6.25   6.25

Dr. Hugo Eckener, 125th anniv. of birth (Nos. 1711-1712, 1716, 1718). First US balloon flight, bicent. (Nos. 1713, 1715, 1719). Royal Air Force, 75th anniv. (Nos. 1714, 1717, 1720).
No. 1720 contains one 57x43mm stamp.

Mickey Mouse Movie Posters
A269

Nos. 1721-1729: 10c, The Musical Farmer, 1932. 15c, Little Whirlwind, 1941. 30c, Pluto's Dream House, 1940. 40c, Gulliver Mickey, 1934. 50c, Alpine Climbers, 1936. $1, Mr. Mouse Takes a Trip, 1940. $2, The Nifty Nineties, 1941. $4, Mickey Down Under, 1948. $5, The Pointer, 1939.
No. 1730, $6, The Simple Things, 1953. No. 1731, $6,The Prince and the Pauper, 1990.

1993, Oct. 25   Litho.   Perf. 13½x14
1721-1729 A269   Set of 9   15.50 15.50
Souvenir Sheets
1730-1731 A269   Set of 2   15.00 15.00

St. John's Lodge #492, 150th Anniv.
A270

Designs: 10c, W.K. Heath, Grand Inspector 1961-82, vert. 30c, Present Masonic Hall. 40c, 1st Masonic Hall. 60c, J.L.E. Jeffery, Grand Inspector 1953-61, vert.

1993, Aug. 16   Litho.   Perf. 14
1732-1735 A270   Set of 4   11.00 11.00

First Ford Engine and Benz's First 4-Wheel Car, Cent.
A271

30c, Lincoln Continental. 40c, 1914 Mercedes racing car. $4, 1966 Ford GT40. $5, 1954 Mercedes Benz gull wing coupe, street version.
No. 1740, $6, Mustang emblem. No. 1741, $6, US #1286A, Germany #471.

1993, Oct. 11   Litho.   Perf. 14
1736-1739 A271   Set of 4   10.00 10.00
Souvenir Sheets
1740-1741 A271   Set of 2   12.50 12.50

Christmas — A272

Nos. 1742-1750, Disney characters in The Nutcracker: 10c, 15c, 20c, 30c, 40c, 50c, 60c, $3, $6.
No. 1751, $6, Minnie and Mickey. No. 1752, $6, Mickey, vert.

1993, Nov. 8   Perf. 14x13½, 13½x14
1742-1750 A272   Set of 9   14.50 14.50
Souvenir Sheets
1751-1752 A272   Set of 2   13.00 13.00

Fine Art — A273

Paintings by Rembrandt: No. 1753, 15c, Hannah and Samuel. No. 1755, 30c, Isaac & Rebecca (The Jewish Bride). No. 1756, 40c, Jacob Wrestling with the Angel. No. 1760, $5, Moses with the Tablets of the Law.
Paintings by Matisse: No. 1754, 15c, Guitarist. No. 1757, 60c, Interior with a Goldfish Bowl. No. 1758, $1, Portrait of Mlle. Yvonne Landsberg. No. 1759, $4, The Toboggan, Plate XX from Jazz.
No. 1761, $6, The Blinding of Samson by the Philistines, by Rembrandt. No. 1762, $6, The Three Sisters, by Matisse.

1993, Nov. 22   Perf. 13½x14
1753-1760 A273   Set of 8   11.50 11.50
Souvenir Sheets
1761-1762 A273   Set of 2   13.00 13.00

A274

Hong Kong '94 — A275

Stamps, fishing boats at Shau Kei Wan: No. 1763, Hong Kong #370, bow of boat. No. 1764, Stern of boat, #1300.

Museum of Qin figures, Shaanxi Province, Tomb of Qin First Emperor: No. 1765a, Inside museum. b, Cavalryman, horse. c, Warriors in battle formation. d, Painted bronze horses, chariot. e, Pekingese dog (not antiquity). f, Chin warrior figures, horses.

1994, Feb. 18   Litho.   Perf. 14
1763 A274 40c multicolored   .80   .80
1764 A274 40c multicolored   .80   .80
   a.   Pair, #1763-1764   1.75   1.75
            Miniature Sheet
1765 A275 40c Sheet of 6, #a.-f.   5.75   5.75

Nos. 1763-1764 issued in sheets of 5 pairs. No. 1764a is a continuous design.
New Year 1994 (Year of the Dog) (No. 1765e).

Hong Kong '94 — A276

Disney characters: 10c, Mickey's "Pleasure Junk." 15c, Mandarin Minnie. 30c, Donald, Daisy journey by house boat. 50c, Mickey, Birdman of Mongkok. $1, Pluto encounters a good-luck dog. $2, Minnie, Daisy celebrate Bun Festival. $4, Goofy, the noodle maker. $5, Goofy pulls Mickey in a rickshaw.

No. 1774, $5, Mickey celebrating New Year with Dragon Dance, horiz. No. 1775, $5, View of Hong Kong Harbor, horiz.

1994, Feb. 18   Litho.   Perf. 13½x14
1766-1773 A276 Set of 8   15.00 15.00
            Souvenir Sheets
               Perf. 14x13½
1774-1775 A276 $5 Set of 2   10.00 10.00

Sierra Club, Cent. — A277

No. 1776: a, Bactrian camel, emblem UR. b, Bactrian camel, emblem UL. c, African elephant, emblem UL. d, African elephant, emblem UR. e, Leopard, blue background. f,

Leopard, emblem UR. g, Leopard, emblem UL. h, Club emblem.

No. 1777: a, Sumatran rhinoceros, lying on ground. b, Sumatran rhinoceros, looking straight ahead. c, Ring-tailed lemur standing. d, Ring-tailed lemur sitting on branch. e, Red-fronted brown lemur on branch. f, Red-fronted brown lemur, g, Red-fronted brown lemur, diff.

No. 1778, $1.50, Sumatran rhinoceros, horiz. No. 1779, $1.50, Ring-tailed lemur, horiz. No. 1780, $1.50, Bactrian camel, horiz. No. 1781, $1.50, African elephant, horiz.

1994, Mar. 1   Litho.   Perf. 14
1776 A277 $1.50 Sheet of 8,
               #a.-h.   12.00 12.00
1777 A277 $1.50 Sheet of 8,
               #a.-g,
               #1776h   12.00 12.00
            Souvenir Sheets
1778-1781 A277 Set of 4   7.00   7.00

New Year 1994 (Year of the Dog) — A278

Small breeds of dogs: No. 1782a, West highland white terrier. b, Beagle. c, Scottish terrier. d, Pekingese. e, Dachshund. f, Yorkshire terrier. g, Pomeranian. h, Poodle. i, Shetland sheepdog. j, Pug. k, Shih tzu. l, Chihuahua.

Large breeds of dogs: No. 1783a, Mastiff. b, Border collie. c, Samoyed. d, Airedale terrier. e, English setter. f, Rough collie. g, Newfoundland. h, Weimaraner. i, English springer spaniel. j, Dalmatian. k, Boxer. l, Old English sheepdog.

No. 1784, $6, Welsh corgi. No. 1785, $6, Labrador retriever.

1994, Apr. 5   Perf. 14
1782 A278 50c Sheet of 12,
               #a.-l.   7.50   7.50
1783 A278 75c Sheet of 12,
               #a.-l.   11.00 11.00
            Souvenir Sheets
1784-1785 A278 Set of 2   11.00 11.00

Orchids — A279

Designs: 10c, Spiranthes lanceolata. 20c, Ionopsis utricularioides. 30c, Tetramicra canaliculata. 50c, Oncidium picturatum. $1, Epidendrum difforme. $2, Epidendrum ciliare. $4, Epidendrum ibaguense. $5, Epidendrum nocturnum.

No. 1794, $6, Encyclia cochleata. No. 1795, $6, Rodriguezia lanceolata.

1994, Apr. 11   Perf. 14
1786-1793 A279 Set of 8   17.50 17.50
            Souvenir Sheets
1794-1795 A279 Set of 2   12.50 12.50

Butterflies — A280

Designs: 10c, Monarch. 15c, Florida white. 30c, Little sulphur. 40c, Troglodyte. $1, Common long-tail skipper. $2, Caribbean buckeye. $4, Polydamas swallowtail. $5, Zebra.

No. 1804, $6, Cloudless sulphur. No. 1805, $6, Hanno blue.

1994, June 27   Perf. 14
1796-1803 A280 Set of 8   18.50 18.50
            Souvenir Sheets
1804-1805 A280 Set of 2   12.50 12.50

Marine Life — A281

No. 1806: a, Bottlenose dolphin. b, Killer whale (a). c, Spinner dolphin (b). d, Ocean sunfish (a). e, Caribbean reef shark, short fin pilot whale (d, f). f, Butterfly fish. g, Moray eel. h, Trigger fish. i, Red lobster (h).

No. 1807, $6, Blue marlin, horiz. No. 1808, $6, Sea horse.

1994, July 21   Litho.   Perf. 14
1806 A281 50c Sheet of 9, #a.-i. 7.75   7.75
            Souvenir Sheets
1807-1808 A281 Set of 2   13.00 13.00

Intl. Year of the Family A282

1994, Aug. 4
1809 A282 90c multicolored   1.10   1.10

D-Day, 50th Anniv. A283

Designs: 40c, Short Sunderland attacks U-boat. $2, Lockheed P-38 Lightning attacks train. $3, B-26 Marauders of 9th Air Force. $6, Hawker Typhoon Fighter Bombers.

1994, Aug. 4
1810-1812 A283 Set of 3   7.00   7.00
            Souvenir Sheet
1813 A283 $6 multicolored   6.75   6.75

A284

Intl. Olympic Committee, Cent. — A285

Designs: 50c, Edwin Moses, US, hurdles, 1984. $1.50, Steffi Graf, Germany, tennis, 1988. $6, Johann Olav Koss, Norway, speed skating, 1994.

1994, Aug. 4
1814 A284 50c multicolored   .40   .30
1815 A284 $1.50 multicolored   2.00   2.00
            Souvenir Sheet
1816 A285 $6 multicolored   6.25   6.25

English Touring Cricket, Cent. A286

35c, M.A. Atherton, England, Wisden Trophy. 75c, I.V.A. Richards, Leeward Islands, vert. $1.20, R.B. Richardson, Leeward Islands, Wisden Trophy. $3, First English team, 1895.

1994, Aug. 4
1817-1819 A286 Set of 3   6.00   6.00
            Souvenir Sheet
1820 A286 $3 multicolored   3.25   3.25

First Manned Moon Landing, 25th Anniv. — A287

No. 1821, $1.50: a, Edwin E. Aldrin, Jr. b, First footprint on Moon. c, Neil A. Armstrong. d, Aldrin descending to lunar surface. e, Aldrin deploys ALSEP (spelled ALSET in error on stamp). f, Aldrin, US flag, Tranquility Base.

No. 1822, $1.50: a, Scientific research, Tranquility Base. b, Plaque on Moon. c, Eagle ascending to docking. d, Command module in lunar orbit. e, US No. C76 made from die carried to Moon. f, Pres. Nixon, Apollo 11 crew.

$6, Armstrong, Aldrin, Postmaster General Blount.

1994, Aug. 4   Sheets of 6, #a-f
1821-1822 A287 Set of 2   22.50 22.50
            Souvenir Sheet
1823 A287 $6 multicolored   5.75   5.75

A288

PHILAKOREA '94 — A289

40c, Entrance bridge, Songgwangsa Temple. 90c, Song-op Folk Village, Cheju. $3, Panoramic view, Port Sogwip'o.

Ceramics, Koryo & Choson Dynasties: No. 1827a, Long-necked bottle. b, Jar. c, Jar, diff. d, Ewer in form of bamboo shoot. e, Jar, diff. f, Pear-shaped bottle. g, Porcelain jar with dragon design. h, Porcelain jar with bonsai design.

$4, Ox, ox herder, vert.

1994, Aug. 4   Perf. 14, 13½ (#1827)
| 1824-1826 | A288 | Set of 3 | 3.25 | 3.25 |
| 1827 | A289 | 75c Sheet of 8, #a.-h. | 6.50 | 6.50 |

Souvenir Sheet
| 1828 | A288 | $4 multicolored | 4.75 | 4.75 |

Stars of Country & Western Music — A290

No. 1829, 75c: a, Patsy Cline. b, Tanya Tucker. c, Dolly Parton. d, Anne Murray. e, Tammy Wynette. f, Loretta Lynn. g, Reba McEntire. h, Skeeter Davis.

No. 1830, 75c: a, Travis Tritt. b, Dwight Yoakam. c, Billy Ray Cyrus. d, Alan Jackson. e, Garth Brooks. f, Vince Gill. g, Clint Black. h, Eddie Rabbit.

No. 1831, 75c: a, Hank Snow. b, Gene Autry. c, Jimmie Rogers. d, Ernest Tubb. e, Eddy Arnold. f, Willie Nelson. g, Johnny Cash. h, George Jones.

No. 1832, $6, Kitty Wells, horiz. No. 1833, $6, Hank Williams, Sr. No. 1834, $6, Hank Williams, Jr.

1994, Aug. 18   Litho.   Perf. 14
Sheets of 8, #a-h
| 1829-1831 | A290 | Set of 3 | 16.50 | 16.50 |

Souvenir Sheets
| 1832-1834 | A290 | Set of 3 | 16.50 | 16.50 |

1994 World Cup Soccer Championships, US — A291

Designs: 15c, Hugo Sanchez, Mexico. 35c, Juergen Klinsmann, Germany. 65c, Antigua player. $1.20, Cobi Jones, US. $4, Roberto Baggio, Italy. $5, Bwalya Kalusha, Zambia.

No. 1841, $6, FIFA World Cup Trophy, vert. No. 1842, $6, Maldive Islands player, vert.

1994, Sept. 19
| 1835-1840 | A291 | Set of 6 | 14.50 | 14.50 |

Souvenir Sheets
| 1841-1842 | A291 | Set of 2 | 9.75 | 9.75 |

Order of the Caribbean Community — A292

First award recipients: 65c, Sir Shridath Ramphal, statesman, Guyana. 90c, William Demas, economist, Trinidad & Tobago. $1.20, Derek Walcott, writer, St. Lucia.

1994, Sept. 26
| 1843-1845 | A292 | Set of 3 | 3.50 | 3.50 |

Herman E. Sieger (1902-54) A293

Germany #C35, Graf Zeppelin, Sieger.

1994   Litho.   Perf. 14
| 1846 | A293 | $1.50 multicolored | 4.25 | 4.25 |

Birds A294

Designs: 10c, Magnificent frigate birds. 15c, Bridled quail dove. 30c, Magnificent frigate bird hatchling. 40c, Purple-throated carib, vert. No. 1851, $1, Antigua broad-wing hawk, vert. No. 1852, $1, Magnificent frigate bird, vert. $3, Magnificent frigate bird, white head. $4, Yellow warbler.

No. 1855, $6, West Indian Whistling duck. No. 1856, $6, Magnificent frigate bird, diff., vert.

1994, Dec. 12   Litho.   Perf. 14
| 1847-1854 | A294 | Set of 8 | 11.00 | 11.00 |

Souvenir Sheets
| 1855-1856 | A294 | Set of 2 | 9.25 | 9.25 |

World Wildlife Fund (Nos. 1847, 1849, 1852-1853).

Christmas A295

Paintings of Madonnas: 15c, The Virgin and Child by the Fireside, by Robert Campin. 35c, The Reading Madonna, by Giorgione. 40c, Madonna and Child, by Giovanni Bellini. 45c, The Litta Madonna, by da Vinci. 65c, The Virgin and Child Under the Apple Tree, by Lucas Cranach the Elder. 75c, Madonna and Child, by Master of the Female Half-Lengths. $1.20, An Allegory of the Church, by Alessandro Allori. $5, Madonna and Child Wreathed with Flowers, by Jacob Jordaens.

No. 1865, $6, The Virgin Enthroned with Child, by Bohemian Master. No. 1866, $6, Madonna and Child with (painting's) Commissioners, by Palma Vecchio.

1994, Dec. 12   Perf. 13½x14
| 1857-1864 | A295 | Set of 8 | 15.00 | 15.00 |

Souvenir Sheets
| 1865-1866 | A295 | Set of 2 | 10.00 | 10.00 |

Birds — A296

Designs: 15c, Magnificent frigate bird. 25c, Blue-hooded euphonia. 35c, Meadowlark. 40c, Red-billed tropic bird. 45c, Greater flamingo. 60c, Yellow-faced grassquit. 65c, Yellow-billed cuckoo. 70c, Purple-throated carib. 75c, Bananaquit. 90c, Painted bunting. $1.20, Red-legged honeycreeper. $2, Jacana. $5, Greater antillean bullfinch. $10, Caribbean elaenia. $20, Trembler.

1995, Feb. 6   Perf. 14½x14
1867	A296	15c multicolored	.25	.25
1868	A296	25c multicolored	.25	.25
1869	A296	35c multicolored	.25	.25
1870	A296	40c multicolored	.30	.30
1871	A296	45c multicolored	.40	.40
1872	A296	60c multicolored	.45	.45
1873	A296	65c multicolored	.60	.60
1874	A296	70c multicolored	.60	.60
1875	A296	75c multicolored	.65	.65
1876	A296	90c multicolored	.80	.80
1877	A296	$1.20 multicolored	1.00	1.00
1878	A296	$2 multicolored	1.75	1.75
1879	A296	$5 multicolored	4.75	4.75
1880	A296	$10 multicolored	9.50	9.50
1881	A296	$20 multicolored	19.00	19.00
		Nos. 1867-1881 (15)	40.55	40.55

See Nos. 2693-2694.

Prehistoric Animals A297

Designs, vert.: 15c, Pachycephalosaurus. 20c, Afrovenator. 65c, Centrosaurus. 90c, Pentaceratops. $1.20, Tarbosaurus. $5, Styracosaur.

No. 1888: a, Kronosaur. b, Ichthyosaur. c, Plesiosaur. d, Archelon. e, Two tyrannosaurs. f, One tyrannosaur. g, One parasaurolophus. h, Two parasaurolophuses. i, Oviraptor. j, Protoceratops with eggs. k, Pteranodon, protoceratops. l, Protoceratops.

No. 1889, $6, Carnotaurus. No. 1890, $6, Corythosaurus.

1995, May 15   Litho.   Perf. 14
| 1882-1887 | A297 | Set of 6 | 7.50 | 7.50 |
| 1888 | A297 | 75c Sheet of 12, #a.-l. | 8.50 | 8.50 |

Souvenir Sheets
| 1889-1890 | A297 | Set of 2 | 14.50 | 14.50 |

1996 Summer Olympics, Atlanta A298

Gold medalists: 15c, Al Oerter, US, discus. 20c, Greg Louganis, US, diving. 65c, Naim Suleymanoglu, Turkey, weight lifting. 90c, Louise Ritter, US, high jump. $1.20, Nadia Comaneci, Romania, gymnastics. $5, Olga Bondarenko, USSR, 10,000-meter run.

No. 1897, $6, Lutz Hessilch, Germany, 1000-meter sprint cycling, vert. No. 1898, $6, US team, eight-oared shell, 800-, 1500-meters.

1995, June 6   Litho.   Perf. 14
| 1891-1896 | A298 | Set of 6 | 7.25 | 7.25 |

Souvenir Sheets
| 1897-1898 | A298 | Set of 2 | 13.50 | 13.50 |

End of World War II, 50th Anniv. A299

No. 1899: a, Chiang Kai-Shek. b, Gen. MacArthur. c, Gen. Chennault. d, Brigadier Orde C. Wingate. e, Gen. Stilwell. f, Field Marshall William Slim.

No. 1900: a, Map of Germany showing battle plan. b, Tanks, infantry advance. c, Red Army at gates of Berlin. d, German defenses smashed. e, Airstrikes on Berlin. f, German soldiers give up. g, Berlin falls to Russians. h, Germany surrenders.

$3, Plane, ship, Adm. Chester Nimitz. $6, Gen. Konev at command post outside Berlin, vert.

1995, July 20
| 1899 | A299 | $1.20 Sheet of 6, #a.-f. + label | 7.00 | 7.00 |
| 1900 | A299 | $1.20 Sheet of 8, #a.-h. + label | 10.50 | 10.50 |

Souvenir Sheets
| 1901 | A299 | $3 multicolored | 4.00 | 4.00 |
| 1902 | A299 | $6 multicolored | 6.00 | 6.00 |

UN, 50th Anniv. — A300

No. 1903: a, 75c, Earl of Halifax, signatures. b, 90c, Virginia Gildersleeve. c, $1.20, Harold Stassen.

$6, Franklin D. Roosevelt.

1995, July 20   Litho.   Perf. 14
| 1903 | A300 | Strip of 3, #a.-c. | 2.50 | 2.50 |

Souvenir Sheet
| 1904 | A300 | $6 multicolored | 4.75 | 4.75 |

No. 1903 is a continuous design.

FAO, 50th Anniv. — A301

No. 1905 — Street market scene: a, 75c, Two women, bananas. b, 90c, Women, crates, produce. c, $1.20, Women talking, one with box of food on head.

$6, Tractor.

1995, July 20
| 1905 | A301 | Strip of 3, #a.-c. | 2.50 | 2.50 |

Souvenir Sheet
| 1906 | A301 | $6 multicolored | 4.75 | 4.75 |

No. 1905 is a continuous design.

Rotary Intl., 90th Anniv. — A302

1995, July 20
| 1907 | A302 | $5 shown | 5.00 | 5.00 |

Souvenir Sheet
| 1908 | A302 | $6 Natl. flag, Rotary emblem | 5.00 | 5.00 |

Queen Mother, 95th Birthday — A303

No. 1909: a, Drawing. b, White & dark pink hat. c, Formal portrait. d, Blue green hat, dress.

$6, Light blue dress, pearls.

1995, July 20   **Perf. 13½x14**
1909 A303 $1.50 Strip or block of
4, #a.-d.   5.75 5.75

Souvenir Sheet
1910 A303 $6 multicolored   6.00 6.00

No. 1909 was issued in sheets of 2 each.
Sheets of 1909-1910 exist with black frame
overprinted in margin, with text "In
Memoriam/1900-2002."

Ducks — A304

No. 1911: a, Ring-necked duck. b, Ruddy
duck. c, Green-winged teal (d). d, Wood duck.
e, Hooded merganser (f). f, Lesser scaup (g).
g, West Indian tree duck (h, k, l). h, Fulvous
whistling duck (l). i, Bahama pintail. j, Shoveler
(i). k, Masked duck (l). l, American widgeon.
$6, Blue-winged teal.

1995, Aug. 31   **Litho.**   **Perf. 14**
1911 A304 75c Sheet of 12,
#a.-l.   11.00 11.00

Souvenir Sheet
1912 A304 $6 multicolored   7.50 7.50

Bees
A305

Designs: 90c, Mining bee. $1.20, Solitary
bee. $1.65, Leaf-cutter. $1.75, Honey bee.
$6, Solitary mining bee.

1995, Sept. 7
1913-1916 A305   Set of 4   6.75 6.75
Souvenir Sheet
1917 A305 $6 multicolored   6.00 6.00

Domestic Cats — A306

Designs: a, Somali. b, Persian. c, Devon
rex. d, Turkish angora. e, Himalayan. f, Maine
coon. g, Nonpedigree. h, American wirehair. i,
British shorthair. j, American curl. k, Black
nonpedigree. l, Birman.
$6, Siberian, vert.

1995, Sept. 7
1918 A306 45c Sheet of 12,
#a.-l.   9.50 9.50
Souvenir Sheet
1919 A306 $6 multicolored   6.75 6.75

Tourism
A307

Stylized paintings depicting: a, Caring. b,
Marketing. c, Working. d, Enjoying life.

1995, July 31   **Litho.**   **Perf. 14**
1920 A307 $2 Sheet of 4, #a.-d.   7.25 7.25

Date of issue is in question. First day cover
of Aug. 10, 1995, has been seen.

Greenbay
Moravian Church,
150th
Anniv. — A308

Designs: 20c, 1st structure, wood & stone.
60c, 1st stone, concrete building, 3/67. 75c,
$2, Present structure. 90c, John A. Buckley,
1st minister of African descent. $1.20, John
Ephraim Knight, longest serving minister. $6,
Front of present structure.

1995, Sept. 4
1921-1926 A308   Set of 6   9.00 9.00
Souvenir Sheet
1927 A308 $6 multicolored   6.00 6.00

Flowers — A309

No. 1928: a, Narcissus. b, Camellia. c, Iris.
d, Tulip. e, Poppy. f, Peony. g, Magnolia. h,
Oriental lily. i, Rose. j, Pansy. k, Hydrangea. l,
Azaleas.
$6, Bird of paradise, calla lily.

1995, Sept. 7
1928 A309 75c Sheet of 12,
#a.-l.   9.50 9.50
Souvenir Sheet
1929 A309 $6 multicolored   6.00 6.00

1995 Boy Scout Jamboree,
Netherlands — A310

No. 1930, $1.20: a, Explorer tent. b, Camper
tent. c, Wall tent.
No. 1931, $1.20: a, Trail tarp. b, Miner's. c,
Voyager.
No. 1932, $6, Scout with camping equip-
ment, vert. No. 1933, $6, Scout making camp
fire.

1995, Oct. 5   **Strips of 3, #a-c**
1930-1931 A310   Set of 2   9.50 9.50
Souvenir Sheets
1932-1933 A310   Set of 2   11.00 11.00

For overprints see Nos. 1963-1966.

Trains
A311

Designs: 35c, Gabon. 65c, Canadian. 75c,
US. 90c, British high-speed. No. 1938, $1.20,
French high-speed. No. 1939, $6, American
high-speed (Amtrak).
No. 1940: a, Australian diesel. b, Italian
high-speed. c, Thai diesel. d, US steam. e,

South African steam. f, Natal steam. g, US war
train. h, British steam. i, British steam, diff.
No. 1941, $6, Australian diesel, vert. No.
1942, $6, Asian steam, vert.

1995, Oct. 23   **Litho.**   **Perf. 14**
1934-1939 A311   Set of 6   11.50 11.50
1940 A311 $1.20 Sheet of 9,
#a.-i.   13.50 13.50
Souvenir Sheets
1941-1942 A311   Set of 2   15.00 15.00

Birds — A312

No. 1943: a, Purple-thoated carib. b, Antillean crested hummingbird. c, Bananaquit (d).
d, Mangrove cuckoo. e, Troupial. f, Green-
throated carib (e, g). g, Yellow warbler (h). h,
Blue-hooded Euphonia. i, Scally-breasted
thrasher. j, Burrowing owl (i). k, Caribbean
crackle (k). l, Adelaide's warbler.
$6, Purple gallinule.

1995
1943 A312 75c Sheet of 12,
#a.-l.   10.00 10.00
Souvenir Sheet
1944 A312 $6 multicolored   7.50 7.50

Miniature Sheets of 9

Establishment of Nobel Prize Fund,
Cent. — A313

No. 1945, $1: a, S.Y. Agnon, literature,
1966. b, Kipling, literature, 1907. c, Aleksandr
Solzhenitsyn, literature, 1970. d, Jack Stein-
berger, physics, 1988. e, Andrei Sakharov,
peace, 1975. f, Otto Stern, physics, 1943. g,
Steinbeck, literature, 1962. h, Nadine
Gordimer, literature, 1991. i, Faulkner, literature, 1949.
No. 1946, $1: a, Hammarskjold, peace,
1961. b, Georg Wittig, chemistry, 1979. c, Wilhelm Ostwald, chemistry, 1909. d, Koch, physiology or medicine, 1945. e, Karl Ziegler,
chemistry, 1963. f, Fleming, physiology or
medicine, 1945. g, Hermann Staudinger,
chemistry, 1953. h, Manfred Eigen, chemistry,
1967. i, Arno Penzias, physics, 1978.
No. 1947, $6, Elie Wiesel, peace, 1986,
vert. No. 1948, $6, Dalai Lama, peace, 1989,
vert.

Sheets of 9, #a-i, + label
1995, Nov. 8
1945-1946 A313   Set of 2   22.00 22.00
Souvenir Sheets
1947-1948 A313   Set of 2   11.00 11.00

Christmas
A314

Details or entire paintings: 15c, Rest on the
Flight into Egypt, by Veronese. 35c, Madonna
with The Child, by Van Dyck. 65c, Sacred
Conversation Piece, by Veronese. 75c, Vision
of Saint Anthony, by Van Dyck. 90c, The Virgin
and the Infant, by Van Eyck. No. 1954, The
Immaculate Conception, by Tiepolo.
$5, Christ Appearing to His Mother, by Van
Der Weyden. $6, Infant Jesus and the Young
St. John, by Murillo.

1995, Dec. 18   **Litho.**   **Perf. 13½x14**
1949-1954 A314   Set of 6   8.00 8.00
Souvenir Sheets
1955 A314 $5 multicolored   4.50 4.50
1956 A314 $6 multicolored   6.00 6.00

Elvis Presley
(1935-77)
A315

Nos. 1957-1958, Various portraits depicting
Presley's life.

1995, Dec. 8   **Perf. 14**
1957 A315 $1 Sheet of 9, #a.-
i.   11.50 11.50
Souvenir Sheet
1958 A315 $6 multicolored   7.50 7.50

John Lennon
(1940-80),
Entertainer — A316

45c, 50c, 65c, 75c, Various portraits of
Lennon.

1995, Dec. 8
1959-1962 A316   Set of 4   3.25 3.25
Souvenir Sheet
1962A A316 $6 like 75c   7.25 7.25

Nos. 1959-1962 were each issued in miniature sheets of 16.
No. 1962A has a continuous design.

Nos. 1930-1933 Ovptd.

1995, Dec. 14
1963 A310 $1.20 Strip of 3, #a-c
(#1930)   3.75 3.75
1964 A310 $1.20 Strip of 3, #a-c
(#1931)   3.75 3.75
Souvenir Sheets
1965 A310 $6 multi (#1932)   7.00 7.00
1966 A310 $6 multi (#1933)   7.00 7.00

Size and location of overprint varies.

Mushrooms — A317

No. 1967, 75c: a, Hygrophoropsis aurantiaca. b, Hygrophorus bakerensis. c,
Hygrophorus conicus. d, Hygrophorus
miniatus.

No. 1968, 75c: a, Suillus brevipes. b, Suillus luteus. c, Suillus granulatus. d, Suillus caerulescens.
No. 1969, $6, Conocybe filaris. No. 1970, $6, Hygrocybe flavescens.

1996, Apr. 22   Litho.   Perf. 14
Strips of 4, #a-d
1967-1968 A317   Set of 2   6.75   6.75
Souvenir Sheets
1969-1970 A317   Set of 2   10.00   10.00
Nos. 1967-1968 were each issued in sheets of 12 stamps.

Sailing Ships A318

Designs: 15c, Resolution. 25c, Mayflower. 45c, Santa Maria. No. 1970D, 75c, Aemilia, Holland, 1630. No. 1970E, 75c, Sovereign of the Seas, England, 1637. 90c, HMS Victory, England, 1765.
No. 1971 — Battleships: a, Aemila, Holland, 1630. b, Sovereign of the Seas, England, 1637. c, Royal Louis, France, 1692. d, HMS Royal George, England, 1715. e, Le Protecteur, France, 1761. f, HMS Victory, England, 1765.
No. 1972 — Ships of exploration: a, Santa Maria. b, Victoria. c, Golden Hinde. d, Mayflower. e, Griffin. f, Resolution.
No. 1973, $6, Grande Hermine. No. 1974, $6 USS Constitution, 1797.

1996, Apr. 25
1970A-1970F A318   Set of 6   3.50   3.50
1971 A318 $1.20 Sheet of 6, #a.-f.   8.50   8.50
1972 A318 $1.50 Sheet of 6, #a.-f.   10.00   10.00
Souvenir Sheets
1973-1974 A318   Set of 2   12.50   12.50

1996 Summer Olympics, Atlanta A319

Designs: 65c, Florence Griffith Joyner, women's track, vert. 75c, Olympic Stadium, Seoul, 1988. 90c, Allison Jolly, yachting. $1.20, 2000m Tandem cycling.
No. 1979, 90c — Medalists: a, Wolfgang Nordwig, pole vault. b, Shirley Strong, women's 100m hurdles. c, Sergei Bubka, pole vault. d, Filbert Bayi, 3000m steeplechase. e, Victor Saneyev, triple jump. f, Silke Renk, women's javelin. g, Daley Thompson, decathlon. h, Bob Richards, pole vault. i, Parry O'Brien, shot put.
No. 1980, 90c — Diving medalists: a, Ingrid Kramer, women's platform. b, Kelly McCormick, women's springboard. c, Gary Tobian, men's springboard. d, Greg Louganis, men's diving. e, Michelle Mitchell, women's platform. f, Zhou Jihong, women's platform. g, Wendy Wyland, women's platform. h, Xu Yanmei, women's platform. i, Fu Mingxia, women's platform.
$5, Bill Toomey, decathlon. $6, Mark Lenzi, men's springboard.

1996, May 6
1975-1978 A319   Set of 4   2.75   2.75
Sheets of 9, #a-i
1979-1980 A319 90c Set of 2   14.00   14.00
Souvenir Sheets
1981 A319 $5 multicolored   5.00   5.00
1982 A319 $6 multicolored   6.00   6.00

Sea Birds A320

No. 1983, 75c: a, Black skimmer. b, Black-capped petrel. c, Sooty tern. d, Royal tern.
No. 1984, 75c: a, Pomarina jaegger. b, White-tailed tropicbird. c, Northern gannet. d, Laughing gull.
$5, Great frigatebird. $6, Brown pelican.

1996, May 13
Vertical Strips of 4, #a-d
1983-1984 A320   Set of 2   6.00   6.00
Souvenir Sheets
1985 A320 $5 multicolored   5.00   5.00
1986 A320 $6 multicolored   6.00   6.00
Nos. 1983-1984 were each issued in sheets of 12 stamps with each strip in sheet having a different order.

Disney Characters In Scenes from Jules Verne's Science Fiction Novels — A321

Designs: 1c, Around the World in Eighty Days. 2c, Journey to the Center of the Earth. 5c, Michel Strogoff. 10c, From the Earth to the Moon. 15c, Five Weeks in a Balloon. 20c, Around the World in Eighty Days, diff. $1, The Mysterious Island. $2, From the Earth to the Moon, diff. $3, Captain Grant's Children. $5, Twenty Thousand Leagues Under the Sea.
No. 1997, $6, Twenty Thousand Leagues Under the Sea, diff. No. 1998, $6, Journey to the Center of the Earth, diff.

1996, June 6   Litho.   Perf. 14x13½
1987-1996 A321   Set of 10   14.00   14.00
Souvenir Sheets
1997-1998 A321   Set of 2   14.00   14.00

Bruce Lee (1940-73), Martial Arts Expert — A322

Various portraits.

Queen Elizabeth II, 70th Birthday — A323

1996, June 13   Perf. 14
1999 A322 75c Sheet of 9, #a.-i.   7.25   7.25
Souvenir Sheet
2000 A322 $5 multicolored   6.25   6.25
China '96 (No. 1999).

Designs: a, In blue dress, pearls. b, Carrying bouquet of flowers. c, In uniform. $6, Painting as younger woman.

1996, July 17   Perf. 13½x14
2001 A323 $2 Strip of 3, #a.-c.   4.25   4.25
Souvenir Sheet
2002 A323 $6 multicolored   5.25   5.25
No. 2001 was issued in sheets of 9 stamps.

Traditional Cavalry — A324

No. 2003: a, Ancient Egyptian. b, 13th cent. English. c, 16th cent. Spanish. d, 18th cent. Chinese.
$6, 19th cent. French.

1996, July 24   Litho.   Perf. 14
2003 A324 60c Block of 4, #a.-d.   2.75   2.75
Souvenir Sheet
2004 A324 $6 multicolored   5.25   5.25
No. 2003 was issued in sheets of 16 stamps.

UNICEF, 50th Anniv. — A325

Designs: 75c, Girl. 90c, Children. $1.20, Woman holding baby. $6, Girl, diff.

1996, July 30
2005-2007 A325   Set of 3   3.25   3.25
Souvenir Sheet
2008 A325 $6 multicolored   4.75   4.75

Jerusalem, 3000th Anniv. — A326

Site, flower: 75c, Tomb of Zachariah, verbascum sinuatum. 90c, Pool of Siloam, hyacinthus orientalis. $1.20, Hurva Synagogue, ranunculus asiaticus.
$6, Model of Herod's Temple.

1996, July 30
2009-2011 A326   Set of 3   2.50   2.50
Souvenir Sheet
2012 A326 $6 multicolored   7.00   7.00

Radio, Cent. A327

Entertainers: 65c, Kate Smith. 75c, Dinah Shore. 90c, Rudy Vallee. $1.20, Bing Crosby. $6, Jo Stafford.

1996, July 30
2013-2016 A327   Set of 4   3.75   3.75
Souvenir Sheet
2017 A327 $6 multicolored   4.75   4.75

Christmas A328

Details or entire paintings, by Filippo Lippi: 60c, Madonna Enthroned. 90c, Adoration of the Child and Saints. $1, Annunciation. $1.20, Birth of the Virgin. $1.60, Adoration of the Child. $1.75, Madonna and Child.
No. 2024, $6, Madonna and Child, diff. No. 2025, $6, Circumcision.

1996, Nov. 25   Perf. 13½x14
2018-2023 A328   Set of 6   8.00   8.00
Souvenir Sheets
2024-2025 A328   Set of 2   11.50   11.50

Disney Pals — A329

Designs: 1c, Goofy, Wilbur. 2c, Donald, Goofy. 5c, Donald, Panchito, Jose Carioca. 10c, Mickey, Goofy. 15c, Dale, Chip. 20c, Pluto, Mickey. $1, Daisy, Minnie at ice cream shop. $2, Daisy, Minnie. $3, Gus Goose, Donald.
No. 2035, $6, Donald, vert. No. 2036, $6, Goofy.

1997, Feb. 17   Litho.   Perf. 14x13½
2026-2034 A329   Set of 9   6.00   6.00
Souvenir Sheets
Perf. 13½x14, 14x13½
2035-2036 A329   Set of 2   10.00   10.00

Salute to Broadway A330

No. 2037 — Stars, show: a, Robert Preston, The Music Man. b, Michael Crawford, Phantom of the Opera. c, Zero Mostel, Fiddler on the Roof. d, Patti Lupone, Evita. e, Raul Julia,

Threepenny Opera. f, Mary Martin, South Pacific. g, Carol Channing, Hello Dolly. h, Yul Brynner, The King and I. i, Julie Andrews, My Fair Lady.

$6, Mickey Rooney, Sugar Babies.

1997   *Perf. 14*
2037 A330 $1 Sheet of 9, #a.-i.   8.75 8.75
Souvenir Sheet
2038 A330 $6 multicolored   6.00 6.00

Butterflies — A331

Designs: 90c, Charaxes porthos. $1.20, Aethiopana honorius. $1.60, Charaxes hadrianus. $1.75, Precis westermanni.

No. 2043, $1.10: a, Charaxes protoclea. b, Byblia ilithyia. c, Black-headed tchagra (bird). d, Charaxes nobilis. e, Pseudacraea boisduvali. f, Charaxes smaragdalis. g, Charaxes lasti. h, Pseudacraea poggei. i, Graphium colonna.

No. 2044, $1.10: a, Carmine bee-eater (bird). b, Pseudacraea eurytus. c, Hypolimnas monteironis. d, Charaxes anticlea. e, Graphium leonidas. f, Graphium illyris. g, Nepheronia argia. h, Graphium policenes. i, Papilio dardanus.

No. 2045, $6, Euxanthe tiberius, horiz. No. 2046, $6, Charaxes lactitinctus, horiz. No. 2047, $6, Euphaedra neophron.

1997, Mar. 10
2039-2042 A331 Set of 4   5.75 5.75
Sheets of 9, #a-i
2043-2044 A331 Set of 2   18.50 18.50
Souvenir Sheets
2045-2047 A331 Set of 3   14.50 14.50

UNESCO, 50th Anniv. — A332

World Heritage Sites: 60c, Convent of the Companions of Jesus, Morelia, Mexico. 90c, Fortress, San Lorenzo, Panama, vert. $1, Canaima Natl. Park, Venezuela, vert. $1.20, Huascarán Natl. Park, Peru, vert. $1.60, Church of San Francisco, Guatemala, vert. $1.75, Santo Domingo, Dominican Republic, vert.

No. 2054, vert, each $1.10: a-c, Guanajuato, Mexico. d, Jesuit missions of the Chiquitos, Bolivia. e, Huascarán Natl. Park, Peru. f, Jesuit missions, La Santisima, Paraguay. g, Cartagena, Colombia. h, Old Havana fortification, Cuba.

No. 2055, each $1.65: a, Tikal Natl. Park, Guatemala. b, Rio Platano Reserve, Honduras. c, Ruins of Copán, Honduras. d, Church of El Carmen, Antigua, Guatemala. e, Teotihuacán, Mexico.

No. 2056, $6, Teotihuacán, Mexico, diff. No. 2057, $6, Tikal Natl. Park, Guatemala, diff.

1997, Apr. 10   *Litho.*   *Perf. 14*
2048-2053 A332 Set of 6   5.00 5.00
2054 A332 Sheet of 8, #a.-h. + label   8.50 8.50
2055 A332 Sheet of 5, #a.-e. + label   8.00 8.00
Souvenir Sheets
2056-2057 A332 Set of 2   10.50 10.50

Fauna — A333

No. 2058, each $1.20: a, Red bishop. b, Yellow baboon. c, Superb starling. d, Ratel. e, Hunting dog. f, Serval.

No. 2059, each $1.65: a, Okapi. b, Giant forest squirrel. c, Masked weaver. d, Common genet. e, Yellow-billed stork. f, Red-headed agama.

No. 2060, $6, Malachite kingfisher. No. 2061, $6, Gray crowned crane. No. 2062, $6, Bat-eared fox.

1997, Apr. 24
2058 A333 Sheet of 6, #a.-f.   8.00 8.00
2059 A333 Sheet of 6, #a.-f.   10.00 10.00
Souvenir Sheets
2060-2062 A333 Set of 3   17.50 17.50

Charlie Chaplin (1889-1977), Comedian, Actor — A334

Various portraits.

1997, Feb. 24   *Litho.*   *Perf. 14*
2063 A334 $1 Sheet of 9, #a.-i.   7.25 7.25
Souvenir Sheet
2064 A334 $6 multicolored   5.75 5.75

Paul P. Harris (1868-1947), Founder of Rotary, Intl. — A335

Designs: $1.75, Service above self, James Grant, Ivory Coast, 1994, portrait of Harris. $6, Group study exchange, New Zealand.

1997, June 12   *Litho.*   *Perf. 14*
2065 A335 $1.75 multicolored   1.75 1.75
Souvenir Sheet
2066 A335 $6 multicolored   5.00 5.00

Heinrich von Stephan (1831-97) A336

No. 2067, each $1.75, Portrait of Von Stephan and: a, Kaiser Wilhelm I. b, UPU emblem. c, Pigeon Post.

$6, Von Stephan, Basel messenger, 1400's.

1997, June 12
2067 A336 Sheet of 3, #a.-c.   4.00 4.00
Souvenir Sheet
2068 A336 $6 multicolored   5.50 5.50

PACIFIC 97.

Queen Elizabeth II, Prince Philip, 50th Wedding Anniv. A337

No. 2069: a, Queen. b, Royal arms. c, Queen, Prince in royal attire. d, Queen, King riding in open carriage. e, Balmoral Castle. f, Prince Philip.

$6, Early portrait of Queen, King in royal attire.

1997, June 12
2069 A337 $1 Sheet of 6, #a.-f.   6.75 6.75
Souvenir Sheet
2070 A337 $6 multicolored   5.75 5.75

Grimm's Fairy Tales A338

Scenes from "Cinderella", each $1.75: No. 2071: a, Mother, stepsisters. b, Cinderella, fairy godmother. c, Cinderella, Prince Charming.

$6, Prince trying shoe on Cinderella.

1997, June 13   *Perf. 13½x14*
2071 A338 Sheet of 3, #a.-c.   5.00 5.00
Souvenir Sheet
2072 A338 $6 multicolored   5.75 5.75

Chernobyl Disaster, 10th Anniv. A339

Designs: $1.65, UNESCO. $2, Chabad's Children of Chernobyl.

1997, June 12
2073 A339 $1.65 multicolored   1.60 1.60
2074 A339 $2 multicolored   1.90 1.90

Mushrooms — A340

Designs: 45c, Marasmius rotula. 65c, Cantharellus cibarius. 70c, Lepiota cristata. 90c, Auricularia mesenterica. $1, Pholiota alnicola. $1.65, Leccinum aurantiacum.

No. 2081, each $1.75: a, Entoloma serrulatum. b, Panaeolus sphinctrinus. c, Volvariella bombycina. d, Conocybe percincta. e, Pluteus cervinus. f, Russula foetens.

No. 2082, $6, Panellus serotinus. No. 2083, $6, Amanita cothurnata.

1997, Aug. 12   *Litho.*   *Perf. 14*
2075-2080 A340 Set of 6   4.50 4.50

2081 A340 Sheet of 6, #a.-f.   8.75 8.75
Souvenir Sheets
2082-2083 A340 Set of 2   11.00 11.00

Orchids — A341

Designs: 45c, Odontoglossum cervantesii. 65c, Medford star. 75c, Motes resplendent. 90c, Debutante. $1, Apple blossom. $2, Dendrobium.

No. 2090, $1.65: a, Angel lace. b, Precious stones. c, Orange theope butterfly. d, Promenaea xanthina. e, Lycaste macrobulbon. f, Amesiella philippinensis. g, Machu Picchu. h, Zuma urchin.

No. 2091, $1.65: a, Sophia Martin. b, Dogface butterfly. c, Mini purple. d, Showgirl. e, Mem. Dorothy Bertsch. f, Black II. g, Leeanum. h, Paphiopedilum macranthum.

No. 2092, Seine. No. 2093, $6, Paphiopedilum gratrixianum.

1997, Aug. 19   *Litho.*   *Perf. 14*
2084-2089 A341 Set of 6   6.25 6.25
Sheets of 8, #a-h
2090-2091 A341 Set of 2   19.00 19.00
Souvenir Sheets
2092-2093 A341 Set of 2   11.00 11.00

1998 World Cup Soccer Championships, France — A342

Designs: 60c, Maradona, Argentina, 1986. 75c, Fritz Walter, W. Germany, 1954. 90c, Zoff, Italy, 1982. $1.20, Moore, England, 1966. $1.65, Alberto, Brazil, 1970. $1.75, Matthäus, W. Germany.

No. 2100, vert: a, Ademir, Brazil, 1950. b, Eusebio, Portugal, 1966. c, Fontaine, France, 1958. d, Schillaci, Italy, 1990. e, Leonidas, Brazil, 1938. f, Stabile, Argentina, 1930. g, Nejedly, Czechoslovakia, 1934. h, Muller, W. Germany, 1970.

No. 2101, $6, Players, W. Germany, 1990. No. 2102, $6, Bebeto, Brazil, vert.

1997, Oct. 6   *Litho.*   *Perf. 14*
2094-2099 A342 Set of 6   5.75 5.75
2100 A342 $1 Sheet of 8, #a.-h., + label   5.75 5.75
Souvenir Sheets
2101-2102 A342 Set of 2   9.25 9.25

Domestic Animals A343

No. 2103, $1.65 — Dogs: a, Dachshund. b, Staffordshire terrier. c, Sharpei. d, Beagle. e, Norfolk terrier. f, Golden retriever.

No. 2104, $1.65 — Cats: a, Scottish fold. b, Japanese bobtail. c, Tabby manx. d, Bicolor American shorthair. e, Sorrel abyssinian. f, Himalayan blue point.

No. 2105, $6, Siberian husky, vert. No. 2106, $6, Red tabby American shorthair kitten, vert.

1997, Oct. 27   *Litho.*   *Perf. 14*
Sheets of 6, #a-f
2103-2104 A343 Set of 2   19.50 19.50
Souvenir Sheets
2105-2106 A343 Set of 2   11.00 11.00

Early Trains A344

No. 2107, $1.65: a, Original Trevithick drawing, 1804. b, "Puffing Billy," William Hedley, 1860. c, Crampton locomotive, Northern Railway, France, 1858. d, Twenty-five ton locomotive, Lawrence Machine Shop, 1860's. e, First locomotive, "Mississippi," built in England. f, "Coppernob," locomotive by Edward Bury, Furness Railway.

No. 2108, $1.65: a, "Jenny Lind," by David Joy for E.B. Wilson. b, "Atlantic" type locomotive, by Schenectady Locomotive Works, 1899. c, British built tank engine, Japan, by Kisons of Leeds, 1881. d, Express freight locomotive, 4-8-2 type, Pennsylvania Railroad. e, Four-cylinder locomotive, by Karl Golsdorf, Austria. f, "E" series 0-10-0 locomotive, produced by Lugansk Works, Russia, 1930.

No. 2109, $6, "Patente" George Stephenson, 1843. No. 2110, $6, Brunel's Trestle, Lynher River.

1997, Nov. 10   **Sheets of 6, #a-f**
2107-2108 A344 Set of 2 20.00 20.00
Souvenir Sheets
2109-2110 A344 Set of 2 11.00 11.00

Christmas A345

Entire paintings or details: 15c, The Angel Leaving Tobias and His Family, by Rembrandt. 25c, The Resurrection, by Martin Knoller. 60c, Astronomy, by Raphael. 75c, Music-making Angel, by Melozzo da Forli. 90c, Amor, by Parmigianino. $1.20, Madonna and Child with Saints John the Baptist, Anthony, Stephen and Jerome, by Rosso Fiorentino.

No. 2117, $6, The Portinari Altarpiece, by Hugo Van Der Goes. No. 2118, $6, The Wedding of Tobiolo, by Gianantonio and Francesco Guardi.

1997, Dec. 2 **Litho.** **Perf. 14**
2111-2116 A345 $6 Set of 6 4.00 4.00
Souvenir Sheets
2117-2118 A345 $6 Set of 2 10.00 10.00

Diana, Princess of Wales (1961-97) — A346

Various portraits, color of sheet margin: No. 2119, $1.65, Pale green. No. 2120, $1.65, Pale pink.
No. 2121, $6,With her sons (in margin). No. 2122, $6, With Pope John Paul II (in margin).

1998, Jan. 19 **Litho.** **Perf. 14**
Sheets of 6, #a-f
2119-2120 A346 Set of 2 13.50 13.50
Souvenir Sheets
2121-2122 A346 Set of 2 9.75 9.75

Fish A347

Designs: 75c, Yellow damselfish. 90c, Barred hamlet. $1, Jewelfish. $1.20, Bluehead wrasse. $1.50, Queen angelfish. $1.75, Queen triggerfish.
No. 2129, $1.65: a, Jack-knife fish. b, Cuban hogfish. c, Sergeant major. d, Neon goby. e, Jawfish. f, Flamefish.
No. 2130, $1.65: a, Rock beauty. b, Yellowtail snapper. c, Creole wrasse. d, Slender filefish. e, Squirrel fish. f, Fairy basslet.
No. 2131, $6, Black-capped gramma. No. 2132, $6, Porkfish.

1998, Feb. 19
2123-2128 A347 Set of 6 4.75 4.75
Sheets of 6, #a-f
2129-2130 A347 Set of 2 14.00 14.00
Souvenir Sheets
2131-2132 A347 Set of 2 11.00 11.00

Cedar Hall Moravian Church, 175th Anniv. A348

Designs: 20c, First church, manse, 1822-40. 45c, Cedar Hall School, 1840. 75c, Hugh A. King, former minister. 90c, Present structure. $1.20, Water tank, 1822. $2, Former manse demolished, 1978.
$6, Present structure, diff.

1998, Mar. 16 **Litho.** **Perf. 14**
2133-2138 A348 Set of 6 4.25 4.25
Souvenir Sheet
2139 A348 $6 multicolored 5.00 5.00
No. 2139 contains one 50x37mm stamp.

Lighthouses — A349

Lighthouse, location: 45c, Trinity, Europa Point, Gibraltar, vert. 65c, Tierra Del Fuego, Argentina. 75c, Point Loma, California, US. 90c, Groenpoint, South Africa, vert. $1, Youghal, County Cork, Ireland, vert. $1.20, Launceston, Tasmania, Australia, vert. $1.65, Point Abino, Ontario, Canada. $1.75, Great Inagua, Bahamas.
$6, Capa Hatteras, North Carolina, US.

1998, Apr. 20
2140-2147 A349 Set of 8 8.25 8.25
Souvenir Sheet
2148 A349 $6 multi, vert. 8.00 8.00

Thomas Oliver Robinson Memorial High School, Cent. A351

Designs: 20c, $6, Nellie Robinson (1880-1972), founder. vert. 45c, School picture, 1985. 65c, Former building, 1930-49. 75c, Students with present headmistress, Natalie Hurst. 90c, Ina Loving (1908-96), educator, vert. $1.20, Present building, 1950.

1998, July 23 **Litho.** **Perf. 14**
2155-2160 A351 Set of 6 4.00 4.00
Souvenir Sheet
2161 A351 $6 multicolored 4.25 4.25
No. 2161 is a continuous design.

Intl. Year of the Ocean A352

No. 2162 — Marine life, "20,000 Leagues Under the Sea": a, Spotted eagle ray. b, Manta ray. c, Hawksbill turtle. d, Jellyfish. e, Queen angelfish. f, Octopus. g, Emperor angelfish. h, Regal angelfish. i, Porkfish. j, Raccoon butterfly fish. k, Atlantic barracuda. l, Sea horse. m, Nautilus. n, Trumpet fish. o, White tip shark. p, Spanish galleon. q, Black tip shark. r, Long-nosed butterfly fish. s, Green moray eel. t, Captain Nemo. u, Treasure chest. v, Hammerhead shark. w, Divers. x, Lion fish. y, Clown fish.

No. 2163 — Wildlife and birds: a, Maroon tailed conure. b, Cocoi heron. c, Common tern. d, Rainbow lorikeet. e, Saddleback butterfly fish. f, Goatfish, cat shark. g, Blue shark, stingray. h, Majestic snapper. i, Nassau grouper. j, Black-cap gramma, blue tang. k, Stingrays. l, Stingrays, giant starfish.

No. 2164, $6, Fiddler ray. No. 2165, $6, Humpback whale.

1998, Aug. 17
2162 A352 40c Sheet of 25, #a.- y. 8.75 8.75
2163 A352 75c Sheet of 12, #a.-l. 8.25 8.25
Souvenir Sheets
2164-2165 A352 Set of 2 10.00 10.00

Ships A353

No. 2166, each $1.75: a, Savannah. b, Viking ship. c, Greek warship.
No. 2167, each $1.75: a, Clipper. b, Dhow. c, Fishing cat.
No. 2168, $6, Dory, vert. No. 2169, $6, Baltimore clipper. No. 2170, $6, English warship, 13th cent.

1998, Aug. 18 **Perf. 14x14½**
Sheets of 3, #a-c
2166-2167 A353 Set of 2 7.50 7.50
Souvenir Sheets
Perf. 14
2168-2170 A353 $6 Set of 3 16.50 16.50

CARICOM, 25th Anniv. — A354

1998, Aug. 20 **Litho.** **Perf. 13½**
2171 A354 $1 multicolored 1.50 1.50

Antique Automobiles — A355

No. 2172 $1.65: a, 1911 Torpedo. b, 1913 Mercedes 22. c, 1920 Rover. d, 1956 Mercedes Benz. e, 1934 Packard V12. f, 1924 Opel.
No. 2173, $1.65 — Fords: a, 1896. b, 1903 Model A. c, 1928 Model T. d, 1922 Model T. e, 1929 Blackhawk. f, 1934 Sedan.
No. 2174, $6, 1908 Ford. No. 2175, $6, 1929 Ford.

1998, Sept. 1 **Perf. 14**
Sheets of 6, #a-f
2172-2173 A355 Set of 2 15.50 15.50
Souvenir Sheets
2174-2175 A355 Set of 2 9.50 9.50
Nos. 2174-2175 each contain one 60x40mm stamp.

Aircraft A356

No. 2176, $1.65: a, NASA Space Shuttle. b, Saab Grippen. c, Eurofighter EF2000. d, Sukhoi SU 27. e, Northrop B-2. f, Lockheed F-117 Nighthawk.
No. 2177, $1.65: a, Lockheed-Boeing General Dynamics Yf-22. b, Dassault-Breguet Rafale BO 1. c, MiG 29. d, Dassault-Breguet Mirage 2000D. e, Rockwell B-1B Lancer. f, McDonnell-Douglas C-17A.
No. 2178, $6, Sukhoi SU 35. No. 2179, $6, F-18 Hornet.

1998, Sept. 21 **Sheets of 6, #a-f**
2176-2177 A356 Set of 2 15.50 15.50
Souvenir Sheets
2178-2179 A356 Set of 2 11.00 11.00

Inventors and Inventions — A357

No. 2180 $1: a, Rudolf Diesel (1858-1913). b, Internal combustion, diesel engines. c, Zeppelin war balloon, Intrepid. d, Ferdinand von Zeppelin (1838-1917). e, Wilhelm Conrad Röntgen (1845-1923). f, X-ray machine. g, Saturn rocket. h, Wernher von Braun (1912-77).
No. 2181, $1: a, Carl Benz (1844-1929). b, Internal combustion engine, automobile. c, Atomic bomb. d, Albert Einstein. e, Leopold Godowsky, Jr. (1901-83) and Leopold Damrosch Mannes (1899-1964). f, Kodachrome film. g, First turbo jet airplane. h, Hans Pabst von Ohain (1911-98).
No. 2182, $6, Hans Geiger (1882-1945), inventor of the Geiger counter. No. 2183, $6, William Shockley (1910-89), developer of transistors.

1998, Nov. 10 **Litho.** **Perf. 14**
Sheets of 8, #a-h
2180-2181 A357 Set of 2 17.00 17.00
Souvenir Sheets
2182-2183 A357 Set of 2 10.50 10.50
Nos. 2180b-2180c, 2180f-2180g, 2181b-2181c, 2181f-2181g are 53x38mm.

1998, May 11 **Litho.** **Perf. 13½x14**
Sheets of 6, #a-f
2149-2150 A350 Set of 2 13.50 13.50
Souvenir Sheet
2151-2154 A350 Set of 4 20.00 20.00

Winnie the Pooh A350

No. 2149, $1: a, Pooh, Tigger in January. b, Pooh, Piglet in February. c, Piglet in March. d, Tigger, Pooh, Piglet in April. e, Kanga, Roo in May. f, Pooh, Owl in June.
No. 2150, $1,: a, Pooh, Eeyore, Tigger, Piglet in July. b, Pooh, Piglet in August. c, Christopher Robin in September. d, Eeyore in October. e, Pooh, Rabbit in November. f, Pooh, Piglet in December.
No. 2151, $6, Pooh, Rabbit holding blanket, Spring. No. 2152, $6, Pooh holding hand to mouth, Summer. No. 2153, $6, Pooh holding rake, Fall. No. 2154, $6, Eeyore, Pooh, Winter.

Diana, Princess
of Wales (1961-
97)
A358

1998, Nov. 18
2184 A358 $1.20 multicolored 1.25 1.25
No. 2184 was issued in sheets of 6.

Gandhi — A359

Portraits: 90c, Up close, later years. $1,
Seated with hands clasped. $1.20, Up close,
early years. $1.65, Primary school, Rajkot,
age 7. $6, With stick, walking with boy (in
margin).

1998, Nov. 18
2185-2188 A359 Set of 4 6.00 6.00
Souvenir Sheet
2189 A359 $6 multicolored 5.25 5.25

Picasso — A360

Paintings: $1.20, Figures on the Seashore,
1931, horiz. $1.65, Three Figures Under a
Tree, 1907. $1.75, Two Women Running on
the Beach, 1922, horiz.
$6, Bullfight, 1900, horiz.

1998, Nov. 18
2190-2192 A360 Set of 3 3.25 3.25
Souvenir Sheet
2193 A360 $6 multicolored 5.00 5.00

1998
World
Scouting
Jamboree,
Chile
A361

90c, Handshake. $1, Scouts hiking. $1.20,
Sign.
$6, Lord Baden-Powell.

1998, Oct. 8 Litho. Perf. 14
2194-2196 A361 Set of 3 2.50 2.50
Souvenir Sheet
2197 A361 $6 multicolored 4.75 4.75

Organization
of American
States, 50th
Anniv.
A362

1998, Nov. 18 Perf. 13½
2198 A362 $1 multicolored .85 .85

Enzo Ferrari (1898-1988), Automobile
Manufacturer — A363

No. 2199, each $1.75: a, Top view of Dino
246 GT-GTS. b, Front view of Dino 246 GT-
GTS. c, 1977 365 GT4 BB.
$6, Dino 246 GT-GTS.

1998, Nov. 18 Perf. 14
2199 A363 Sheet of 3, #a.-c. 8.00 8.00
Souvenir Sheet
2200 A363 $6 multicolored 8.00 8.00
No. 2200 contains one 92x35mm stamp.

Royal Air
Force,
80th
Anniv.
A364

No. 2201, each $1.75: a, McDonnell Doug-
las Phantom FGR1. b, Sepecat Jaguar GR1A.
c, Panavia Tornado F3. d, McDonnell Douglas
Phantom FGR2.
No. 2202, $6, Eurofighter 2000, Hurricane.
No. 2203, $6, Hawk, biplane.

1998, Nov. 18
2201 A364 Sheet of 4, #a.-d. 6.25 6.25
Souvenir Sheets
2202-2203 A364 Set of 2 11.50 11.50

Sea Birds
A365

Designs: 15c, Brown pelican. 25c, Dunlin.
45c, Atlantic puffin. 90c, Pied cormorant.
No. 2208: a, King eider. b, Inca tern. c,
Dovekie. d, Ross's bull. e, Brown noddy. f,
Marbled murrelet. g, Northern gannet. h,
Razorbill. i, Long-tailed jaeger. j, Black guille-
mot. k, Whimbrel. l, Oystercatcher.
No. 2209, $6, Rhynchops niger. No. 2210,
$6, Diomedea exulans.

1998, Nov. 24
2204-2207 A365 Set of 4 2.00 2.00
2208 A365 75c Sheet of 12, #a.-l. 9.00 9.00
Souvenir Sheets
2209-2210 A365 Set of 2 11.50 11.50

Christmas
A366

Dogs with Christmas decorations: 15c, Border collie. 25c, Dalmatian. 65c, Weimaraner.

75c, Scottish terrier. 90c, Long-haired dachs-
hund. $1.20, Golden retriever. $2, Pekingese.
No. 2218, $6, Dalmatian, diff. No. 2219, $6,
Jack Russell terrier.

1998, Dec. 10
2211-2217 A366 Set of 7 7.25 7.25
Souvenir Sheet
2218-2219 A366 Set of 2 9.50 9.50

Disney
Characters
in Water
Sports
A367

No. 2220, $1 — Water skiing: a, Goofy,
maroon skis. b, Mickey. c, Goofy, Mickey. d,
Donald. e, Goofy, blue skis. f, Minnie.
No. 2221, $1 — Surfing: a, Goofy running
with board. b, Mickey. c, Donald holding
board. d, Donald, riding board. e, Minnie. f,
Goofy in water.
No. 2221G, Sailing & sailboarding: h,
Mickey wearing cap. i, Mickey, Goofy, counter-
balancing boat. j, Goofy sailboarding. k,
Mickey, seagull overhead. l, Goofy puffing at
sail. m, Mickey sailboarding.
No. 2222, Mickey. No. 2223, Minnie. No.
2224, Goofy. No. 2225, Donald.

1999, Jan. 11 Litho. Perf. 13½x14
Sheets of 6, #a-f
2220-2221 A367 Set of 2 11.00 11.00
2221G A367 $1 Sheet of 6,
#h.-m. 5.50 5.50
Souvenir Sheets
2222-2225 A367 Set of 4 19.50 19.50
Mickey Mouse, 70th anniv.

Hell's
Gate
Steel
Orchestra,
50th
Anniv.
A368

Designs: 20c, Nelson's Dockyard, 1996.
60c, Holiday Inn, Rochester, New York, 1992.
75c, Early years, 1950. 90c, World's Fair,
1964, Eustace Henry (AKA Manning). $1.20,
Alston Henry playing double tenor.
No. 2231, $4, Like #2229, vert. No. 2232,
$4, The early years, vert.

1999, Feb. 1 Litho. Perf. 14
2226-2230 A368 Set of 5 3.25 3.25
Souvenir Sheets
2231-2232 A368 Set of 2 6.75 6.75

Flowers
A369

Designs, vert.: 60c, Tulip. 75c, Fuschia.
$1.20, Calla lily. $1.65, Sweet pea.
No. 2237: a, Morning glory. b, Geranium. c,
Blue hibiscus. d, Marigolds. e, Sunflower. f,
Impatiens. g, Petunia. h, Pansy. i, Saucer
magnolia.
No. 2238: a, Primrose. b, Bleeding heart. c,
Pink dogwood. d, Peony. e, Rose. f, Helle-
bores. g, Lily. h, Violet. i, Cherry blossoms.
No. 2239, $6, Lily, vert. No. 2240, $6, Zin-
nias, vert.

1999, Apr. 19 Litho. Perf. 14
2233-2236 A369 Set of 4 3.25 3.25
2237 A369 90c Sheet of 9, #a.-i. 6.50 6.50
2238 A369 $1 Sheet of 9, #a.-i. 7.50 7.50
Souvenir Sheets
2239-2240 A369 Set of 2 9.25 9.25

Elle Macpherson,
Model — A370

Various portraits, each $1.20.

1999, Apr. 26 Perf. 13½
2241 A370 Sheet of 8, #a.-h. 8.50 8.50
Australia '99 World Stamp Expo.

John Glenn's
Space
Flight — A371

Space Exploration — A372

No. 2242 — John Glenn, 1962, each $1.75:
a, Climbing into Mercury Capsule. b, Formal
portrait. c, Having helmet adjusted. d, Entering
pressure chamber.
No. 2243, $1.65: a, Luna 2. b, Mariner 2. c,
Giotto space probe. d, Rosat. e, Intl. Ultravio-
let Explorer. f, Ulysses Space Probe.
No. 2244, $1.65: a, Mariner 10. b, Luna 9. c,
Advanced X-ray Astrophysics Facility. d,
Magellan Spacecraft. e, Pioneer-Venus 2. f,
Infra-red Astronomy Satellite.
No. 2245, $6, Salyut 1, horiz. No. 2246, $6,
MIR, horiz.

1999, May 6 Litho. Perf. 14
2242 A371 Sheet of 4, #a.-d. 6.50 6.50
Sheets of 6, #a-f
2243-2244 A372 Set of 2 15.00 15.00
Souvenir Sheets
2245-2246 A372 Set of 2 9.00 9.00
Nos. 2245-2246 are incorrectly inscribed.

Prehistoric
Animals
A373

Designs: 65c, Brachiosaurus. 75c,
Oviraptor, vert. $1, Homotherium. $1.20,
Macrauchenia, vert.
No. 2251, each $1.65: a, Leptictidium. b,
Ictitherium. c, Plesictis. d, Hemicyon. e,
Diacodexis. f, Stylinodon. g, Kanuites. h,
Chriacus. i, Argyrolagus.
No. 2252, each $1.65: a, Struthiomimus. b,
Corythosaurus. c, Dsungaripterus. d, Com-
pognathus. e, Prosaurolophus. f, Montanocer-
atops. g, Stegosaurus. h, Deinonychus. i,
Ouranosaurus.
No. 2253, each $6, Pteranodon. No. 2254,
$6, Eurhinodelphus.

1999, May 26
2247-2250 A373 Set of 4   3.50   3.50
Sheets of 9, #a-i
2251-2252 A373 Set of 2   23.00 23.00
Souvenir Sheets
2253-2254 A373 Set of 2   9.25   9.25
Illustrations on Nos. 2247-2248 are switched.

IBRA'99, World Stamp Exhibition,
Nuremberg — A374

Exhibition emblem, Leipzig-Dresden Railway and: No. 2255, $1, Caroline Islands #19. No. 2257, $1.65, Caroline Islands #4.
Emblem, Gölsdorf 4-4-0 and: No. 2256, $1.20, Caroline Islands #16. No. 2258, $1.90, Caroline Islands #8, #10.
$6, Registered label on cover.

1999, June 24   Litho.   *Perf. 14*
2255-2258 A374 Set of 4   5.00 5.00
Souvenir Sheet
2259 A374 $6 multicolored   4.75 4.75

Paintings by Hokusai (1760-
1849) — A375

No. 2260, $1.65 — Details or entire paintings: a, Asakusa Honganji. b, Dawn at Isawa in Kai Province. c, Samurai with Bow and Arrow (bows level). d, Samurai with Bow and Arrow (bows at different angles). e, Kajikazawa in Kai Province. f, A Great Wave.
No. 2261, $1.65: a, People on the Balcony of the Sazaido. b, Nakahara in Sagami Province. c, Defensive Positions (2 men). d, Defensive Positions (3 men). e, Mount Fuji in Clear Weather. f, Nihonbashi in Edo.
No. 2262, $6, Gotenyama At Shinagawa on Tokaido Highway, vert. No. 2263, $6, A Netsuke Workshop, vert.

1999, June 24   Sheets of 6, #a-f
2260-2261 A375 Set of 2   15.00 15.00
Souvenir Sheets
2262-2263 A375 Set of 2   9.25   9.25

Johann Wolfgang von Goethe (1749-
1832), Poet — A376

No. 2264, each $1.75: a, Three archangels in "Faust." b, Portraits of Goethe and Friedrich von Schiller (1759-1805). c, Faust reclining in landscape with spirits.
$6, Profile portrait of Goethe.

1999, June 24   Litho.   *Perf. 14*
2264 A376 Sheet of 3, #a.-c.   4.50 4.50
Souvenir Sheet
2265 A376 $6 multicolored   4.50 4.50

Souvenir Sheets

Philexfrance '99, World Philatelic
Exhibition — A377

Locomotives: No. 2266, Crampton 1855-69. No. 2267, 232-U1 4-Cylinder Compound 4-6-4, 1949.

1999, June 24   *Perf. 13¾*
2266 A377 $6 multicolored   5.00 5.00
2267 A377 $6 multicolored   5.00 5.00

Wedding of Prince Edward and Sophie
Rhys-Jones — A378

No. 2268: a, Sophie. b, Sophie, Edward. c, Edward.
$6, Horse and carriage, couple.

1999, June 24   *Perf. 13½*
2268 A378 $3 Sheet of 3, #a.-c.   6.75 6.75
Souvenir Sheet
2269 A378 $6 multicolored   5.00 5.00

A379

Various white kittens: 35c, 45c, 60c, 75c, 90c, $1.
No. 2276, $1.65: a, One holding paw on another. b, Black & white. c, White kitten, black kitten. d, One with yarn. e, Two in basket. f, One looking up.
No. 2277, $1.65: a, One playing with red yarn. b, Two long-haired. c, Yellow tabby. d, One with mouse. e, Yellow tabby on pillow. f, Black & gray tabby.
No. 2278, $6, Tabby cat carrying kitten. No. 2279, $6, Yellow kitten in tree.

1999, May 25   Litho.   *Perf. 14½x14*
2270-2275 A379 Set of 6   3.00 3.00
Sheets of 6
2276-2277 A379 Set of 2   15.00 15.00
Souvenir Sheets
2278-2279 A379 Set of 2   9.25 9.25
Australia '99, World Stamp Expo (Nos. 2276-2279).

A380

UN Rights of the Child Convention, 10th Anniv. — No. 2280: a, Three children. b, Adult hand taking child's hand, silhouette of mother holding infant. c, UN Building, member flags, dove.
$6, Dove.

1999, June 22   *Perf. 14*
2280 A380 $3 Sheet of 3, #a.-c.   6.75 6.75
Souvenir Sheet
2281 A380 $6 multicolored   5.00 5.00

Boats — A381

Designs: 25c, Missa Ferdie. 45c, Sailboats. 60c, Jolly Roger Pirate Ship. 90c, $4, Freewinds. $1.20, Monarch of the Seas.

1999, June 24   Litho.   *Perf. 13x11*
2282-2286 A381 Set of 5   3.25 3.25
2286a   Souvenir sheet, #2282-2286   3.75 3.75
Souvenir Sheet
Perf. 13¾
2287 A381 $4 multicolored   3.75 3.75
No. 2287 contains one 51x38mm stamp.

A382

Butterflies: 65c, Fiery jewel. 75c, Hewitson's blue hairstreak. $1.20, Scarce bamboo page, horiz. $1.65, Paris peacock, horiz.
No. 2292, horiz.: a, California dog face. b, Small copper. c, Zebra swallowtail. d, White M hairstreak. e, Old world swallowtail. f, Buckeye. g, Apollo. h, Sonoran blue. i, Purple emperor.
No. 2293, $6, Monarch. No. 2294, $6, Cairns birdwing, horiz.

1999, Aug. 16   *Perf. 14*
2288-2291 A382 Set of 4   3.75 3.75
2292 A382 $1 Sheet of 9, #a.-
    i.   8.50 8.50
Souvenir Sheets
2293-2294 A382 Set of 2   11.00 11.00

Christmas
A383

15c, Madonna and child in a Wreath of Flowers by Peter Paul Rubens. 25c, Shroud of Christ Held by Two Angels, by Albrecht Dürer. 45c, Madonna and Child Enthroned Between Two Saints, by Raphael. 60c, Holy Family with the Lamb, by Raphael. $2, The Transfiguration, by Raphael. $4, Three Putti Holding a Coat of Arms, by Dürer.
$6, The Coronation of the Holy St. Catherine, by Rubens.

1999, Nov. 22   Litho.   *Perf. 13¾*
2295-2300 A383 Set of 6   6.50 6.50
Souvenir Sheet
2301 A383 $6 multicolored   5.50 5.50

Famous
Elderly
People
A384

Designs: a, Katharine Hepburn. b, Martha Graham. c, Eubie Blake. d, Agatha Christie. e, Eudora Welty. f, Helen Hayes. g, Vladimir Horowitz. h, Katharine Graham. i, Pablo Casals. j, Pete Seeger. k, Andres Segovia. l, Frank Lloyd Wright.

2000, Jan. 18   Litho.   *Perf. 14*
2302 A384 90c Sheet of 12, #a-l   8.00 8.00

Charlie
Chaplin
A385

Designs: a, "Modern Times," street scene. b, "The Gold Rush," with other actor. c, Unidentified film. d, "Modern Times," on gears. e, "The Gold Rush," arms akimbo. f, "The Gold Rush," with cane.

2000, Jan. 18   *Perf. 13¾*
2303 A385 $1.65 Sheet of 6, #a-f 7.25 7.25

Sir Cliff
Richard,
Rock
Musician
A386

2000, Jan. 18   *Perf. 13¼*
2304 A386 $1.65 multi   1.25 1.25
Issued in sheets of 6.

Birds
A387

Designs: 75c, Streamertail. 90c, Yellow-bellied sapsucker. $1.20, Rufous-tailed jacamar. $2, Spectacled owl.

No. 2309, $1.20: a, Ground dove. b, Wood stork. c, Saffron finch. d, Green-backed heron. e, Lovely cotinga. f, St. Vincent parrot. g, Cuban grassquit. h, Red-winged blackbird.

No. 2310, $1.20: a, Scarlet macaw. b, Yellow-fronted amazon. c, Queen-of-Bavaria. d, Nanday conure. e, Jamaican tody. f, Smooth-billed ani. g, Puerto Rican woodpecker. h, Ruby-throated hummingbird.

No. 2311, $6, Vermilion flycatcher. No. 2312, $6, Red-capped manakin, vert.

2000, Apr. 17   Litho.   Perf. 14
2305-2308 A387 Set of 4   4.00 4.00
Sheets of 8, #a-h
Perf. 13¾x14
2309-2310 A387 Set of 2   15.00 15.00
Souvenir Sheets
Perf. 13¾
2311-2312 A387 Set of 2   9.25 9.25

The Stamp Show 2000, London (Nos. 2309-2312). Size of stamps: Nos. 2309-2310, 48x31mm; No. 2311, 50x38mm; No. 2312, 38x50mm.

Paintings of Anthony Van Dyck — A388

No. 2313, $1.20: a, Arthur Goodwin. b, Sir Thomas Wharton. c, Mary Villers (as Venus), Daughter of the Duke of Buckingham. e, Christina Bruce, Countess of Devonshire. e, James Hamilton, 3rd Marquis and 1st Duke of Hamilton. f, Henry Danvers, Earl of Danby.

No. 2314, $1.20: a, Charles I in Robes of State. b, Henrietta Maria. c, Queen Henrietta Maria with Her Dwarf Sir Jeffrey Hudson. d, Charles I in Armor. e, Henrietta Maria in Profile, facing right. f. Queen Henrietta Maria.

No. 2315, $1.20: a, Marie de Raet, Wife of Philippe le Roy. b, Jacomo de Cachiopin. c, Princess Henrietta of Lorraine Attended by a Page. d, Portrait of a Man. e, Portrait of a Woman. f, Philippe le Roy, Seigneur de Ravels.

No. 2316, $5, Charles I on Horseback with Monsieur de St. Antoine. No. 2317, $5, Le Roi a La Chasse (Charles I hunting). No. 2318, $5, Charles I in Three Positions. No. 2319, $5, Charles I and Queen Henrietta.

No. 2320, $6, Portrait of Two Young English Gentlemen, Sons of the Duke of Lenox. No. 2321, $6, George, Lord Digby, and William, Lord Russell.
Illustration reduced.

2000, May 15   Perf. 13¾
Sheets of 6, #a-f
2313-2315 A388 Set of 3   15.00 15.00
Souvenir Sheets
2316-2319 A388 Set of 4   15.50 15.50
2320-2321 A388 Set of 2   9.25 9.25

Butterflies — A389

No. 2322, $1.65: a, Orange theope. b, Sloane's urania. c, Gold-drop helicopis. d, Papilio velovis. e, Graphium androcles. f, Cramer's mesene.

No. 2323, $1.65, horiz.: a, Euploea miniszeki. b, Doris. c, Evenus coronata. d, Anchisiades swallowtail. e, White-spotted tadpole. f, Morpho patroclus.

No. 2324, $1.65, horiz.: a, Mesosemia loruhama. b, Bia actorion. c, Ghost brimstone. d, Blue tharops. e, Catasticta manco. f, White-tailed page.

No. 2325, $6, Reakirt's blue. No. 2326, $6, Graphium encelados, horiz. No. 2327, $6, Graphium milon, horiz.
Illustration reduced.

2000, May 29   Perf. 14
Sheets of 6, #a-f
2322-2324 A389 Set of 3   22.50 22.50
Souvenir Sheets
2325-2327 A389 Set of 3   14.00 14.00

Prince William, 18th Birthday — A390

Prince William — No. 2328: a, With checked shirt, waving. b, In jacket and white shirt. c, With arms clasped. d, In striped shirt, waving. $6, With Prince Harry, Princess Diana and unidentified man.

2000, June 21   Perf. 14
2328 A390 $1.65 Sheet of 4, #a-d   4.75 4.75
Souvenir Sheet
Perf. 13¾
2329 A390 $6 multi   4.25 4.25

100th Test Cricket Match at Lord's Ground — A391

90c, Richie Richardson. $5, Viv Richard. $6, Lord's Ground, horiz.

2000, June 26   Perf. 14
2330-2331 A391 Set of 2   4.50 4.50
Souvenir Sheet
2332 A391 $6 multi   4.50 4.50

2000 Summer Olympics, Sydney — A392

Designs: a, Cyclist. b, Diver. c, Italian flag, Flaminio Stadium, Rome. d, Ancient Greek javelin thrower.

2000, June 26
2333 A392 $2 Sheet of 4, #a-d   6.00 6.00

First Zeppelin Flight, Cent. — A393

No. 2334: a, LZ-1. b, LZ-2. c, LZ-3. $6, LZ-7.

2000, June 26   Perf. 13½
2334 A393 $3 Sheet of 3, #a-c   6.75 6.75
Souvenir Sheet
Perf. 14¼
2335 A393 $6 multi   4.25 4.25
No. 2334 contains three 45x27mm stamps.

Cats — A394

No. 2336: a, Long-haired blue & white. b, Snow shoe. c, Persian. d, Chocolate lynx point. e, Brown & white sphynx. f, White tortoiseshell.
$6, Lavender tortie.

2000, May 29   Litho.   Perf. 14
2336 A394 $1.65 Sheet of 6, #a-f 7.50 7.50
Souvenir Sheet
2337 A394 $6 multi   4.50 4.50

Public Railways, 175th Anniv. — A395

No. 2338: a, Locomotion No. 1, George Stephenson. b, John Bull.

2000, June 26
2338 A395 $3 Sheet of 2, #a-b   4.50 4.50
The Stamp Show 2000, London.

Johann Sebastian Bach (1685-1750) — A396

2000, June 26
2339 A396 $6 multi   4.25 4.25

Berlin Film Festival, 50th Anniv. — A397

No. 2340: a, Une Femme Est Une Femme. b, Carmen Jones. c, Die Ratten. d, Die Vier im Jeep. e, Lilies of the Field. f, Invitation to the Dance.
$6, Sense and Sensibility.

2000, June 26
2340 A397 $1.65 Sheet of 6, #a-f 7.25 7.25
Souvenir Sheet
2341 A397 $6 multi   4.50 4.50

Flowers — A398

Designs: 45c, Epidendrum pseudepidn-drum. 65c, Odontoglossum cervantesii. 75c, Cattleya dowiana. 90c, Beloperone guttata. $1, Colliandra haematocephala. $1.20, Brassavola nodosa.
No. 2348, $1.65: a, Masdevallia coccinea. b, Paphinia cristata. c, Vanilla planifolia. d, Cattleya forbesii. e, Lycaste skinneri. f, Cattleya percivaliana.
No. 2349, $1.65: a, Anthurium andreanum. b, Doxantha unguiscati. c, Hibiscus rosa-sinensis. d, Canna indica. e, Heliconius umilis. f, Strelitzia reginae.
No. 2350, $1.65: a, Pseudocalymna alliaceum. b, Datura candida. c, Ipomoea tuberosa. d, Allamanda cathartica. e, Aspasia epidendroides. f, Maxillaria cucullata.
No. 2351, $6, Strelitzia reginae. No. 2352, $6, Cattleya leopoldii. No. 2353, $6, Rossi-oglossum grande.

2000, May 29   Litho.   Perf. 14
2342-2347 A398 Set of 6   3.50 3.50
   Sheets of 6, #a-f
2348-2350 A398 Set of 3   22.50 22.50
   Souvenir Sheets
2351-2353 A398 Set of 3   13.00 13.00

Dogs — A399

Designs: 90c, Boxer. $1, Wire-haired pointer (inscribed Alaskan malamute). $2, Alaskan malamute (inscribed Wire-haired pointer). $4, Saluki.
No. 2358: a, Bearded collie. b, Cardigan Welsh corgi. c, Saluki. d, Basset hound. e, Standard poodle. f, Boston terrier.
$6, Cavalier King Charles Spaniel.

2000, May 29
2354-2357 A399 Set of 4   5.50 5.50
2358 A399 $1.65 Sheet of 6, #a-f 7.00 7.00
   Souvenir Sheet
2359 A399 $6 multi   4.50 4.50

Space Achievements — A400

No. 2360, $1.65: a, Sputnik 1. b, Explorer 1. c, Mars Express. d, Luna 1. e, Ranger 7. f, Mariner 4.
No. 2361, $1.65: a, Mariner 10. b, Soho. c, Mariner 2. d, Giotto. e, Exosat. f, Pioneer.
No. 2362, $6, Hubble Space Telescope. No. 2363, $6, Vostok 1.

2000, June 26   Sheets of 6, #a-f
2360-2361 A400 Set of 2   14.00 14.00
   Souvenir Sheets
2362-2363 A400 Set of 2   9.00 9.00
World Stamp Expo 2000, Anaheim.

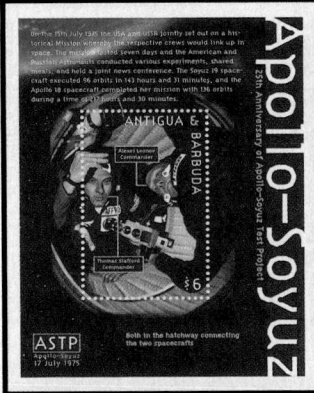

Apollo-Soyuz Mission, 25th Anniv. — A401

No. 2364: a, Alexei Leonov. b, Soyuz 19. c, Valeri Kubasov.
$6, Leonov and Thomas Stafford.

2000, June 26
2364 A401 $3 Sheet of 3, #a-c   6.50 6.50
   Souvenir Sheet
2365 A401 $6 multi   4.25 4.25

Souvenir Sheet

Albert Einstein (1879-1955) — A402

2000, June 26   Perf. 14¼
2366 A402 $6 multi   4.25 4.25

Girls' Brigade A403

Designs: 20c, Outreach program to Sunshine Home for Girls. 60c, Ullida Rawlins Gill, Intl. vice-president, vert. 75c, Officers and girls. 90c, Raising the flag, vert. $1.20, Members with 8th Antigua Company flag.
$5, Emblem, vert.

2000, July 13   Perf. 14
2367-2371 A403 Set of 5   2.75 2.75
   Souvenir Sheet
2372 A403 $5 multi   3.75 3.75

A404

Queen Mother, 100th Birthday — A405

No. 2373: a, As child. b, In 1940. c, With Princess Anne, 1951. d, In Canada, 1989.
$6, Inspecting the troops. $20, In gardens.

Litho., Margin Embossed
2000, Aug. 4   Perf. 14
2373 A404 $2 Sheet of 4, #a-d,
         + label   6.00 6.00
   Souvenir Sheet
      Perf. 13¾
2374 A404 $6 multi   4.50 4.50
   Without Gum
   Litho. & Embossed
   Die Cut 8¾x9
2375 A405 $20 gold & multi
No. 2374 contains one 38x51mm stamp. See Nos. 2536-2537.

Popes — A406

No. 2376, $1.65: a, Alexander VI, 1492-1503, hands clasped. b, Benedict XIII, 1724-30. c, Boniface IX, 1389-1404. d, Alexander VI, no hands. e, Clement VIII, 1592-1605. f, Clement VI, 1342-52.
No. 2377, $1.65: a, John Paul II, 1978-present. b, Benedict XV, 1914-22. c, John XXIII, 1958-63. d, Pius XI, 1922-39. e, Pius XII, 1939-58. f, Paul VI, 1963-78.
No. 2378, $6, Pius II, 1458-1464. No. 2379, $6, Pius VII, 1800-23.

2000, Aug. 21   Litho.   Perf. 13¾
   Sheets of 6, #a-f
2376-2377 A406 Set of 2   15.00 15.00
   Souvenir Sheets
2378-2379 A406 Set of 2   9.25 9.25

Monarchs — A407

No. 2380, $1.65: a, Donaldbane of Scotland, 1093-97. b, Duncan I of Scotland, 1034-40. c, Duncan II of Scotland, 1094. d, Macbeth of Scotland, 1040-57. e, Malcolm III of Scotland, 1057-93. f, Edgar of Scotland, 1097-1107.
No. 2381, $1.65: a, Charles I of Great Britain, 1625-49. b, Charles II of Great Britain, 1660-85. c, Charles Edward Stuart, the "Young Pretender," 1720-1788. d, James II of Great Britain, 1685-89. e, James II of Scotland, 1437-60. f, James III of Scotland, 1460-88.
No. 2382, $6, Robert I of Scotland, 1306-29. No. 2383, $6, Anne of Great Britain, 1702-14. Illustration reduced.

2000, Aug. 21
   Sheets of 6, #a-f
2380-2381 A407 Set of 2   15.00 15.00
   Souvenir Sheets
2382-2383 A407 Set of 2   9.25 9.25

Millennium (#2385) — A408

No. 2384 — Chinese paintings: a, Admonitions of the Instructress to the Court Ladies, attributed to Ku K'ai-chih. b, Ink drawing on silk, 3rd cent. B.C. c, Ink and color drawing on silk, 2nd cent. B.C. d, Scholars of the Northern Qi Collating Texts (detail), attributed to Yang Zihua. e, Spring Outing (detail), attributed to Zhan Ziqian. f, Portrait of the Emperors (detail), attributed to Yen Liben. g, Sailing Boats and a Riverside Mansion, attributed to Li Sixun. h, Two Horses and a Groom (detail), by Han Kan. i, King's Portrait (detail), attributed to Wu Daozi. j, Court Ladies Wearing Flowered Headdresses (detail), attributed to Zhou Fang. k, Wintry Groves and Layered Banks, by Dong Yuan. l, Mount Kuanglu, by Jing Hao. m, Pheasant and Small Birds by a Jujube Shrub, by Huang Jucai. n, Deer Among Red Maples, by anonymous painter. o, Wintry Groves and Layered Banks, diff., by Dong Yuan. p, Literary Gathering, by Han Huang (60x40mm). q, Sketches of Birds and Insects (detail), by Huang Quan.

   Perf. 12¾x12½
2000, Aug. 21   Litho.
2384 A408 25c Sheet of 17, #a-
         q, + label   5.00 5.00

Highlights of 1250-1300: a, Expansion of the Inquisition. b, Chartres Cathedral. c, Sculptures in Naumburg Cathedral. d, 1st English Parliament. e, The Madonna in Majesty (Maestà), by Cimabue. f, Marco Polo. g

Divine wind. h, Death of St. Thomas Aquinas. i, Arezzo Cathedral. j, Margaret, Queen of Scotland. k, Jewish exodus from England. l, Fall of Acre to Muslims. m, Moses de León writes much of The Zohar. n, German Civil War. o, Death of Kublai Khan. p, Dante writes La Vita Nuova (60x40mm). q, Chao Meng-fu paints Autumn Colors on the Quiao and Hua Mountains.

2000, Aug. 21
2385 A408 60c Sheet of 17, #a-q
+ label 9.00 9.00

Battle of Britain, 60th Anniv. — A409

No. 2386, $1.20: a, Bristol Blenheim. b, Winston Churchill. c, Bristol Blenheim and barrage balloon. d, Heinkel. e, Spitfire. f, German rescue vessel. g, Messerschmitt 109. h, RAF air and sea rescue launch.

No. 2387, $1.20: a, German lookout. b, Children being evacuated. c, Youngsters evacuated from hospitals. d, Hurricane. e, Rescue workers. f, British political cartoon. g, King George VI and Queen Elizabeth inspect wreckage. h, Barrage balloon over Tower Bridge.

No. 2388, $6, Spitfires. No. 2389, $6, Junkers 87B.

2000, Oct. 16 Litho. Perf. 14
Sheets of 8, #a-h
2386-2387 A409 Set of 2 14.50 14.50
Souvenir Sheets
2388-2389 A409 Set of 2 9.25 9.25

Rainforest Fauna — A410

Designs: 75c, Agouti. 90c, Capybara. $1.20, Basilisk lizard. $2, Heliconid butterfly.

No. 2394, $1.65: a, Green violet-ear hummingbird. b, Harpy eagle. c, Three-toed sloth. d, White uakari monkey. e, Anteater. f, Coati.

No. 2395, $1.75: a, Red-eyed tree frog. b, Black spider monkey. c, Emerald toucanet. d, Kinkajou. e, Spectacled bear. f, Tapir.

No. 2396, $6, Keel-billed toucan, horiz. No. 2397, $6, Scarlet macaw, horiz.

2000, Sept. 25 Litho. Perf. 14
2390-2393 A410 Set of 4 3.75 3.75
Sheets of 6, #a-f
2394-2395 A410 Set of 2 15.00 15.00
Souvenir Sheets
2396-2397 A410 Set of 2 9.25 9.25

Submarines — A411

Designs: 65c, Sea Cliff. 75c, Beaver Mark IV. 90c, Reef Ranger. $1, Cubmarine. $1.20, Alvin. $3, Argus.

No. 2404, $2: a, Revenge. b, Walrus. c, Los Angeles. d, Daphne. e, USS Ohio. f, USS Skipjack.

No. 2405, $6, Trieste. No. 2406, $6, German Type 209.

2000, Oct. 2
2398-2403 A411 Set of 6 5.50 5.50
2404 A411 $2 Sheet of 6, #a-f 8.75 8.75
Souvenir Sheets
2405-2406 A411 Set of 2 9.00 9.00

Paintings from the Prado — A412

No. 2407, $1.65: a, Three men. b, Man's head. c, Three women. d, Man on white horse. e, Man on brown horse. f, Man leading horse. a-c from Family Portrait, by Adriaen Thomasz Key. d-f from The Devotion of Rudolf I, by Peter Paul Rubens and Jan Wildens.

No. 2408, $1.65: a, Seated man. b, Man with sash. c, Group of men. d, Laureated figure. e, Men working at anvil. f, Two workers. a-c from The Defense of Cadiz Against the English by Francisco de Zurbaran. d-f from Vulcan's Forge, by Diego Velázquez.

No. 2409, $1.65: a, Mandolin player. b, Woman with fan. c, Two men. d, Bald man. e, Two Magi. f, Jesus, Mary and Joseph. a-c from The Concert, by Vicente Palmaroli y Gonzalez. d-f from The Adoration of the Magi, by Juan Bautista Maino

No. 2410, $6, The Seller of Fans, by José del Castillo. No. 2411, $6, Portrati of a Family in a Garden, by Jan van Kessel, the Younger. No. 2412, $6, The Deliverance of St. Peter, by José de Ribera, horiz.

Illustration reduced.

2000, Oct. 6 Perf. 12x12¼, 12¼x12
Sheets of 6, #a-f
2407-2409 A412 Set of 3 20.00 20.00
Souvenir Sheets
2410-2412 A412 Set of 3 13.00 13.00
España 2000 Intl. Philatelic Exhibition.

Christmas — A413

Designs (background): 25c, No. 2417a, Angels, full body (blue). 45c, No. 2417b, Angel's heads (orange). 90c, No. 2417c, Angel's heads (blue). $5, No. 2417d, Angels, full body (yellow).

2000, Dec. 4 Perf. 14
2413-2416 A413 Set of 4 4.50 4.50
2417 A413 $1.75 Sheet of 4, #a-d 5.25 5.25
Souvenir Sheet
2418 A413 $6 Jesus 4.50 4.50

Rijksmuseum, Amsterdam, Bicent. (in 2000) — A414

No. 2419, $1: a, Dr. Ephraim Bueno, by Rembrandt. b, Woman Writing a Letter, by Frans van Mieris, the Elder. c, Mary Magdalene, by Jan van Scorel. d, Portrait of a Woman (inscribed Anna Coddle) by Maarten van Heemskerck. e, Cleopatra's Banquet, by Gerard Lairesse. f, Titus van Rijn in Friar's Habit, by Rembrandt.

No. 2420, $1.20: a, Saskia van Uylenburgh, by Rembrandt. b, In the Month of July, by Paul Joseph Constantin Gabriel. c, Maria Trip, by Rembrandt. d, Still Life with Flowers, by Jan van Huysum. e, Hesje van Cleyburgh, by Rembrandt. f, Girl in a White Kimono, by George Hendrik Breitner.

No. 2421, $1.65: a, Man and woman at spinning wheel, by Rembrandt. b, Self-portrait, by Rembrandt. c, Jeremiah Lamenting the Destruction of Jerusalem, by Rembrandt. d, The Jewish Bride, by Rembrandt. e, Tobit and Anna with a Kid, by Rembrandt. f, The Prophetess Anna, by Rembrandt.

No. 2422, $6, Doubting Thomas, by Hendrick ter Brugghen. No. 2423, $6, Still Life with Cheeses, by Floris van Dijck. No. 2424, $6, Isaac Blessing Jacob, by Govert Flinck.

2001, Jan. 15 Litho. Perf. 13¾
Sheets of 6, #a-f
2419-2421 A414 Set of 3 17.00 17.00
Souvenir Sheets
2422-2424 A414 Set of 3 13.50 13.50

Pokémon — A415

No. 2425: a, Starmie. b, Misty. c, Brock. d, Geodude. e, Krabby. f, Ash.

2001, Feb. 13
2425 A415 $1.75 Sheet of 6, #a-f 7.25 7.25
Souvenir Sheet
2426 A415 $6 Charizard 4.25 4.25

Mushrooms A416

Designs: 25c, Blue-toothed entoloma. 90c, Common morel. $1, Red cage fungus. $1.75, Fawn shield-cap.

No. 2431, $1.65: a, Lilac bonnet. b, Silky volvar. c, Poplar field cap. d, St. George's mushroom. e, Red-stemmed tough shank. f, Fly agaric.

No. 2432, $1.65: a, Copper trumpet. b, Meadow mushroom. c, Green-gilled parasol. d, Panther. e, Death cap. f, King bolete.

No. 2433, $6, Yellow parasol. No. 2434, Mutagen milk cap.

2001, Mar. 26 Perf. 13¾x13¼
2427-2430 A416 Set of 4 3.00 3.00
Sheets of 6, #a-f
2431-2432 A416 Set of 2 15.00 15.00
Souvenir Sheets
2433-2434 A416 Set of 2 9.25 9.25
Hong Kong 2001 Stamp Exhibition (2431-2434).

Population and Housing Census — A417

Map of Antigua with various graphs. Denominations: 15c, 25c, 65c, 90c.

2001, Apr. 2 Perf. 13¾
2435-2438 A417 Set of 4 1.50 1.50
Souvenir Sheet
2439 A417 $6 Map, emblem 4.50 4.50

Phila Nippon '01, Japan — A418

Designs: 45c Two women facing right, from Yuna (Bath-house Women). 60c, Woman facing left, from Yuna. 65c, Two women, from Yuna. 75c, Man with stringed instrument at top, from Hikone Screen. $1, Woman with stringed instrument at bottom, from Hikone Screen. $1.20, Two people, from Hikone Screen.

No. 2446 — Namban Screen, by Naizen Kano, each $1.65: a, Ship's stern. b, Ship's bow. c, Man with closed umbrella. d, Man with open umbrella.

No. 2447 — Merry Making Under the Cherry Blossoms, by Naganobu Kano, each $1.65: a, Steps. b, Tree. c, Four people near building. d, Four people, mountains. e, Three people. f, One person.

No. 2448, $6, Visiting a Shrine on a Rainy Night, by Harunobu Suzuki. No. 2449, $6, Courtesan on a Veranda Upstairs, by Kokan Shiba. No. 2450, $6, Daruma, by Tsujo Kano.

2001, May 28 Litho. Perf. 14¼x14
2440-2445 A418 Set of 6 3.50 3.50
2446 A418 Sheet of 4, #a-d 5.00 5.00
2447 A418 Sheet of 6, #a-f 7.50 7.50
Souvenir Sheets
Perf. 13¾
2448-2450 A418 Set of 3 12.50 12.50

Nos. 2448-2450 each contain one 38x51mm stamp.

No. 2449 is incorrectly inscribed. It actually depicts "Courtesan on a Veranda Upstairs," by Kokan.

Orchids A419

Designs: 45c, Hintleya burtii. 75c, Neomoovea irrovata. 90c, Comparettia speciosa. $1, Cypripedium crapeanum.

No. 2455, $1.20, vert.: a, Trichoceuos muralis. b, Dracula rampira. c, Psychopsis papilio. d, Lycaste clenningiana. e, Telipogon nevuosus. f, Masclecallia ayahbacana.

No. 2456, $1.65, vert.: a, Rhyncholaelia glanca. b, Oncidium barbatum. c, Phaius tankervillege. d, Ghies brechtiana. e, Angraecum leonis. f, Cychnoches loddigesti.

No. 2457, $1.65, vert.: a, Cattleya dowiana. b, Dendrobium cruentum. c, Bulbophyllum lobbi. d, Chysis laevis. e, Ancistrochilus rothschildicanus. f, Angraecum sororium.

No. 2458, $6, Trichopilia fragrans, vert. No. 2459, $6, Symphalossum sanguinem, vert.

2001, June 11 Perf. 14
2451-2454 A419 Set of 4 2.40 2.40
Sheets of 6, #a-f
2455-2457 A419 Set of 3 19.00 19.00
Souvenir Sheets
2458-2459 A419 Set of 2 9.00 9.00

Souvenir Sheets

I Love Lucy — A420

Designs: No. 2460, $6, Fred and Ricky. No. 2461, $6, Lucy and Ethel. No. 2462, $6, Lucy and fireplace. No. 2463, $6, Lucy and open door.

2001, Mar. 5   Litho.   Perf. 13¾
2460-2463 A420 Set of 4   18.00 18.00
See Nos. 2522-2525.

Marine Life and Birds A421

Designs: 25c, Yellowtail damselfish. 45c, Indigo hamlet. 65c, Great white shark. No. 2467, 90c, Bottlenose dolphin. No. 2468, 90c, Palette surgeonfish. $1, Octopus.
No. 2470, $1.20: a, Common dolphin. b, Franklin's gull. c, Rock beauty. d, Bicolor angelfish. e, Beaugregory. f, Banded butterflyfish.
No. 2471, $1.20: a, Common tern. b, Flying fish. c, Queen angelfish. d, Blue-striped grunt. e, Porkfish. f, Blue tang.
No. 2472, $1.65: a, Dugong. b, White-tailed tropicbird. c, Bull shark and Spanish grunt. d, Manta ray. e, Green turtle. f, Spanish grunt.
No. 2473, $1.65: a, Red-footed booby. b, Bottlenose dolphin. c, Hawksbill turtle. d, Monk seal. e, Bull shark and coral. f, Lemon shark.
No. 2474, $5, Sailfish. No. 2475, $5, Beaugregory and brown pelican, vert. No. 2476, $6, Hawksbill turtle. No. 2477, $6, Queen triggerfish.

2001, June 11   Perf. 14
2464-2469 A421 Set of 6   3.25 3.25
Sheets of 6, #a-f
2470-2473 A421 Set of 6   24.00 24.00
Souvenir Sheets
2474-2477 A421 Set of 4   16.00 16.00

Ship Freewinds — A422

Designs: 30c, Maiden voyage anniversary in Antigua. 45c, In St. Barthelemy. 75c, In Caribbean at sunset. 90c, In Bonaire. $1.50, In Bequia.
No. 2483, $4, With lights on during eclipse. No. 2484, $4, In Curacao.

2001, June 15
2478-2482 A422 Set of 5   3.00 3.00
Souvenir Sheets
2483-2484 A422 Set of 2   6.00 6.00

Toulouse-Lautrec Paintings — A423

No. 2485: a, Monsieur Georges-Henri Manuel Standing. b, Monsieur Louis Pascal. c, Roman Coolus. d, Monsieur Fourcade.
$5, Dancing at the Moulin de la Galette.

2001, July 3   Perf. 13¾
2485 A423 $2 Sheet of 4, #a-d   6.00 6.00
Souvenir Sheet
2486 A423 $5 multi   3.75 3.75

Giuseppe Verdi (1813-1901), Opera Composer — A424

No. 2487: a, Verdi in hat. b, Character and score from Don Carlos. c, Conductor and score for Aida. d, Musicians and score for Rigoletto.

2001, July 3   Perf. 14
2487 A424 $2 Sheet of 4, #a-d   6.00 6.00
Souvenir Sheet
2488 A424 $5 Verdi, score   3.75 3.75

Marlene Dietrich — A425

No. 2489: a, With cigarette. b, On sofa. c, Color photograph. d, With piano.

2001, July 3   Perf. 13¾
2489 A425 $2 Sheet of 4, #a-d   6.00 6.00

Queen Victoria (1819-1901) — A426

No. 2490: a, Blue dress. b, Red hat. c, Crown. d, Crown and blue sash.

2001, July 3   Perf. 14
2490 A426 $2 Sheet of 4, #a-d   6.00 6.00
Souvenir Sheet
2491 A426 $5 As old woman   3.75 3.75

Queen Elizabeth II, 75th Birthday — A427

No. 2492: a, At birth, 1926. b, In 1938. c, In 1939. d, At coronation, 1953. e, In 1956. f, In 1985.

2001, July 3
2492 A427 $1 Sheet of 6, #a-f   3.75 3.75
Souvenir Sheet
2493 A427 $6 In 1940   4.50 4.50

Photomosaic of Queen Elizabeth II — A428

2001, July 3   Litho.   Perf. 14
2494 A428 $1 multi   .75 .75
Queen Elizabeth II, 75th birthday. Issued in sheets of 8.

Monet Paintings — A429

No. 2495, horiz.: a, Water Lilies. b, Rose Portals, Giverny. c, The Water Lily Pond, Harmony in Green. d, The Artist's Garden, Irises. $5, Jerusalem Artichokes.

2001, July 3   Perf. 13¾
2495 A429 $2 Sheet of 4, #a-d   6.00 6.00
Souvenir Sheet
2496 A429 $5 multi   3.75 3.75

Endangered Animals — A430

Designs: 25c, Collared peccary. 30c, Baird's tapir. 45c, Agouti. 75c, Bananaquit. 90c, Six-banded armadillo. $1, Roseate spoonbill.
No. 2503, each $1.80: a, Mouse opossum. b, Magnificent black frigatebird. c, Northern jacana. d, Painted bunting. e, Haitian solenodon. f, St. Lucia iguana.
No. 2504, each $2.50: a, West Indian iguana. b, Scarlet macaw. c, Cotton-topped tamarin. d, Kinkajou.
No. 2505, $6, Ocelot, vert. No. 2506, $6, King vulture, vert.

2001, Sept. 10   Perf. 14
2497-2502 A430 Set of 6   2.50 2.50
2503 A430 Sheet of 6, #a-f   8.00 8.00
2504 A430 Sheet of 4, #a-d   7.00 7.00
Souvenir Sheets
2505-2506 A430 Set of 2   9.00 9.00

Rudolph Valentino (1895-1926), Actor — A431

No. 2507, $1: a, Blood and Sand. b, Eyes of Youth. c, All Night. d, Last known photo of Valentino. e, Camille. f, Cobra.
No. 2508, $1: a, The Son of the Sheik. b, The Young Rajah. c, The Eagle. d, The Sheik. e, A Sainted Devil. f, Monsieur Beaucaire.
No. 2509, $6, The Four Horsemen of the Apocalypse. No. 2510, $6, Valentino with Natasha Rambova.

2001, Oct. 2   Perf. 13¾
Sheets of 6, #a-f
2507-2508 A431 Set of 2   9.00 9.00
Souvenir Sheets
2509-2510 A431 Set of 2   9.00 9.00

Scenes From Shirley Temple Movies — A432

No. 2511, $1.65 — Scenes from Baby, Take a Bow, with Temple: a, In polka-dot dress. b, With man on steps. c, With man holding gun. d, With woman.
No. 2512, $1.80 — Scenes from The Little Princess, with Temple: a, With man. b, Washing floor. c, With woman and child. d, With old woman.
No. 2513, $1.50 — Scenes from The Little Princess, with Temple: a, With woman. b, In pink dress. c, Holding doll. d, On throne. e, With man. f, With birthday cake.
No. 2514, $1.65, horiz. — Scenes from Baby, Take a Bow, with Temple: a, With woman and five children. b, With arms around

man. c, Being tucked in bed. d, With man. e, Standing with man and woman. f, Looking in cradle.

No. 2515, $6, In polka-dot dress, from Baby, Take a Bow. No. 2516, With soldiers, from The Little Princess.

2001, Oct. 2   **Sheets of 4, #a-d**
2511-2512 A432   Set of 2   10.50 10.50
       Sheets of 6, #a-f
2513-2514 A432   Set of 2   14.00 14.00
       Souvenir Sheets
2515-2516 A432   Set of 2   8.00 8.00

Nobel Prizes, Cent. — A433

No. 2517, $1.50 — Chemistry laureates: a, Melvin Calvin, 1961. b, Linus C. Pauling, 1954. c, Vincent du Vigneaud, 1955. d, Richard Synge, 1952. e, Archer Martin, 1952. f, Alfred Werner, 1913.

No. 2518, $1.50 — Chemistry laureates: a, Robert F. Curl, Jr., 1996. b, Alan J. Heeger, 2000. c, Michael Smith, 1993. d, Sidney Altman, 1989. e, Elias James Corey, 1990. f, William Francis Giauque, 1949.

No. 2519, $6, Ernest Rutherford, Chemistry, 1908. No. 2520, $6, International Red Cross, Peace, 1944. No. 2521, $6, Ernst Otto Fischer, Chemistry, 1973.

2001, Nov. 29   **Perf. 14**
       Sheets of 6, #a-f
2517-2518 A433   Set of 2   13.50 13.50
       Souvenir Sheets
2519-2521 A433   Set of 3   13.50 13.50

I Love Lucy Type of 2001

Designs: No. 2522, $6, Fred at desk. No. 2523, $6, Lucy and Fred. No. 2524, $6, Lucy, closed door. No. 2525, $6, Fred and Ricky at desk, horiz.

2001   **Perf. 13¾**
2522-2525 A420   Set of 4   18.00 18.00

Christmas — A434

Paintings: 25c, Madonna and Child with Angels, by Filippo Lippi. 45c, Madonna of Corneto Tarquinia, by Lippi. 50c, Madonna and Child, by Domenico Ghirlandaio. 75c, Madonna and Child, by Lippi. $4, Madonna del Ceppo, by Lippi.

$6, Madonna Enthroned with Angels and Saints, by Lippi.

2001, Dec. 4   **Litho.**   **Perf. 14**
2526-2530 A434   Set of 5   4.50 4.50
       Souvenir Sheet
2531 A434 $6 multi   4.50 4.50

2002 World Cup Soccer Championships, Japan and Korea — A435

No. 2532, $1.50: a, Scene from final game, 1950. b, Ferenc Puskas, 1954. c, Raymond Kopa, 1958. d, Mauro, 1962. e, Gordon Banks, 1966. f, Pelé, 1970.

No. 2533, $1.50: a, Daniel Passarella, 1978. b, Karl-Heinz Rummenigge, 1982. c, World Cup trophy, 1986. d, Diego Maradona, 1990. e, Roger Milla, 1994. f, Zinedine Zidane, 1998.

No. 2534, $6, Head from Jules Rimet Cup, 1930. No. 2535, $6, Head and globe from World Cup trophy, 2002.

2001, Dec. 17   **Perf. 13¾x14¼**
       Sheets of 6, #a-f
2532-2533 A435   Set of 2   12.00 12.00
       Souvenir Sheets
       Perf. 14¼
2534-2535 A435   Set of 2   8.00 8.00

Queen Mother Type of 2000 Redrawn

No. 2536, each $2: a, As child. b, In 1940. c, With Princess Anne, 1951. d, In Canada, 1989.
$6, Inspecting the troops.

2001, Dec.   **Perf. 14**
       Yellow Orange Frames
2536 A404   Sheet of 4, #a-d, +   label   6.00 6.00
       Souvenir Sheet
       Perf. 13¾
2537 A404 $6 multi   4.50 4.50

Queen Mother's 101st birthday. No. 2537 contains one 38x51mm stamp with a darker appearance than that found on No. 2374. Sheet margins of Nos. 2536-2537 lack embossing and gold arms found on Nos. 2373-2374.

US Civil War — A436

No. 2538: a, Battle of Nashville. b, Battle of Atlanta. c, Battle of Spotsylvania. d, Battle of the Wilderness. e, Battle of Chickamauga Creek. f, Battle of Gettysburg. g, Battle of Chancellorsville. h, Battle of Fredericksburg. i, Battle of Antietam. j, Second Battle of Bull Run. k, Battle of Five Forks. l, Seven Days' Battle. m, Battle of Bull Run. n, Battle of Shiloh. o, Battle of Seven Pines. p, Battle of Fort Sumter. q, Battle of Chattanooga. r, Surrender at Appomattox.

No. 2539, vert.: a, Gen. Ulysses S. Grant. b, Pres. Abraham Lincoln. c, Confederate Pres. Jefferson Davis. d, Gen. Robert E. Lee. e, Gen. George A. Custer. f, Adm. Andrew Hull Foote. g, General Thomas "Stonewall" Jackson. h, Gen. J.E.B. Stuart. i, Gen. George G. Meade. j, Gen. Philip H. Sheridan. k, Gen. James Longstreet. l, Gen. John S. Mosby.

No. 2540, $6, Monitor. No. 2541, $6, Merrimack.

2002, Jan. 28   **Perf. 14¾**
2538 A436   45c Sheet of 18,   #a-r   10.00 10.00
2539 A436   50c Sheet of 12,   #a-l   8.00 8.00
       Souvenir Sheets
       Perf. 14½x14¾ (#2540), 13¾
2540-2541 A436   Set of 2   11.00 11.00

No. 2541 contains one 50x38mm stamp.

GOLDEN JUBILEE - 6th February, 2002
50th Anniversary of Her Majesty Queen Elizabeth II's Accession

Reign of Queen Elizabeth II, 50th Anniv. — A437

No. 2542: a, Striped dress. b, Green patterned dress. c, Orange patterned dress. d, White jacket.
$6, Queen with Princess Margaret.

2002, Feb. 6   **Perf. 14¼**
2542 A437 $2 Sheet of 4, #a-d   7.00 7.00
       Souvenir Sheet
2543 A437 $6 multi   4.50 4.50

United We Stand — A438

2002, Feb. 11   **Perf. 13½x13¼**
2544 A438 $2 multi   1.50 1.50
   Printed in sheets of 4.

Cricket Player Sir Vivian Richards, 50th Birthday — A439

Designs: 25c, Raising bat. 30c, Receiving gift. 50c, With arms raised. 75c, At bat. $1.50, Wearing sash, with woman. $1.80, Standing next to photograph of himself.

No. 2551, $6, Holding sword. No. 2552, $6, With Antigua color guard.

2002, Mar. 7   **Perf. 13½x13¼**
2545-2550 A439   Set of 6   4.00 4.00
       Souvenir Sheets
2551-2552 A439   Set of 2   9.00 9.00

Flora and Fauna — A440

Designs: 50c, Thick-billed parrot. 75c, Lesser long-nosed bat. $1.50, Montserrat oriole. $1.80, Miss Perkin's blue butterfly.

No. 2557, 90c: a, Quetzals. b, Two-toed sloth. c, Lovely cotinga. d, Giant hairstrak butterfly. e, Magenta-throated woodstar. f, Bull's-eye silk moth. g, Golden toads. h, Collared peccaries. i, Tamandua anteater.

No. 2558, $1: a, St. Lucia parrot. b, Cuban kite. c, West Indian whistling duck. d, Poey's sulphur butterfly. e, Scarlet ibis. f, Black-capped petrel. g, St. Lucia whiptail. h, Cuban

---

Solenodon. i, False androgeus swallowtail butterfly.
No. 2559, $6, Margay. No. 2560, $6, Olive Ridley turtle.

2002, Apr. 8   **Perf. 14**
2553-2556 A440   Set of 4   3.50 3.50
       Sheets of 9, #a-i
2557-2558 A440   Set of 2   14.00 14.00
       Souvenir Sheets
2559-2560 A440   Set of 2   9.00 9.00

Antigua Community Players, 50th Anniv. — A441

Various photos: 20c, 25c, 30c, 75c, 90c, $1.50, $1.80.
No. 2568, $4, Former Pres. Edie Hill-Thibou, vert. No. 2569, $4, Acting Pres. and Music Director Yvonne Maginley, vert.

       Perf. 13½x13¾
2002, June 11   **Litho.**
2561-2567 A441   Set of 7   4.25 4.25
       Souvenir Sheets
       Perf. 14
2568-2569 A441   Set of 2   6.00 6.00

Endangered Animals — A442

No. 2570, each $1.50: a, Red-billed tropic-bird. b, Brown pelican. c, Magnificent frigatebird. d, Ground lizard. e, West Indian whistling duck. f, Antiguan racer snake. g, Spiny lobster. h, Hawksbill turtle. i, Queen conch.

2002, July 12   **Perf. 14**
2570 A442 Sheet of 9, #a-i   9.00 9.00

2002 Winter Olympics, Salt Lake City — A443

Designs: No. 2571, $2, Cross-country skiing. No. 2572, $2, Pairs figure skating.

2002, July 15   **Perf. 13½x13¼**
2571-2572 A443   Set of 2   3.00 3.00
2572a   Souvenir sheet, #2571-   2572   3.00 3.00

First Solo Transatlantic Flight, 75th Anniv. — A444

No. 2573, each $2.50: a, Charles Lindbergh and The Spirit of St. Louis. b, Arrival at Le Bourget Airport, Paris. c, Lindbergh receiving hero's welcome, New York.
$6, Lindbergh in airplane.

2002, July 15   *Perf. 13¼x13½*
2573 A444 Sheet of 3, #a-c   5.75 5.75
Souvenir Sheet
2574 A444 $6 multi   4.50 4.50

Intl. Year of Mountains — A445

No. 2575: a, Mt. Fuji. b, Machu Picchu. c, Matterhorn.

2002, July 15   *Perf. 13½x13¼*
2575 A445 $2 Sheet of 3, #a-c   4.50 4.50

Amerigo Vespucci (1454-1512), Explorer — A446

No. 2576, horiz., each $2.50: a, Vespucci with gray head covering. b, Vespucci with red head covering. c, Hands and map.
$6, Vespucci and compass.

Perf. 13¼x13½, 13½x13¼
2002, July 15
2576 A446 Sheet of 3, #a-c   6.00 6.00
Souvenir Sheet
2577 A446 $6 multi   4.50 4.50

Princess Diana (1961-97) — A447

No. 2578: a, Wearing seven-strand pearl necklace. b, Wearing tiara and white dress. c, Wearing hat. d, Wearing earrings and black dress. e, Wearing tiara, no dress seen. f, Wearing earrings, no dress seen.
$6, Wearing white dress.

2002, July 29   *Perf. 14*
2578 A447 $1.80 Sheet of 6, #a-f 7.50 7.50
Souvenir Sheet
2579 A447 $6 multi   4.50 4.50

Presidents John F. Kennedy and Ronald Reagan — A448

No. 2580, $1.50, horiz.: a, John, Robert and Edward Kennedy. b, Kennedy with Danny Kaye. c, Kennedy addressing nation. d, With wife, Jacqueline. e, Shaking hands with young Bill Clinton. f, Family members at funeral.
No. 2581, $1.50, horiz.: a, Reagan with wife, Nancy, and Pope John Paul II. b, As George Gipp in movie *Knute Rockne, All American.* c, With Gen. Matthew Ridgeway at Bitburg Cemetery. d, With Vice-president George H. W. Bush and Mikhail Gorbachev. e, With Presidents Ford, Carter, and Nixon. f, On horseback, with Queen Elizabeth II.
No. 2582, $6, Kennedy and flag. No. 2583, $6, Reagan.

2002, July 29   *Litho.*
Sheets of 6, #a-f
2580-2581 A448 Set of 2   13.50 13.50
Souvenir Sheets
2582-2583 A448 Set of 2   9.00 9.00

Elvis Presley (1935-77) A449

2002, Aug. 20   *Perf. 13¾*
2584 A449 $1 multi   .90 .90
Printed in sheets of 9.

Teddy Bears, Cent. — A450

No. 2585: a, Cheerleader bear. b, Figure skater bear. c, Ballet dancer bear. d, Aerobics instructor bear.

2002, Aug. 26
2585 A450 $2 Sheet of 4, #a-d   6.00 6.00

Pokémon — A451

No. 2586: a, Croconau. b, Mantine. c, Feraligatr. d, Quilfish. e, Remoraid. f, Quagsire.
$6, Chinchou.

2002, Aug. 26
2586 A451 $1.50 Sheet of 6, #a-f 6.75 6.75
Souvenir Sheet
2587 A451 $6 multi   4.50 4.50

Lee Strasberg (1901-82), Movie Actor and Director — A452

2002, Sept. 16   *Perf. 14*
2588 A452 $1 multi   .75 .75
Printed in sheets of 9.

Charlie Chaplin (1889-1977), Actor — A453

No. 2589: a, Wearing bowler hat, facing forward. b, Wearing suit and vest. c, Wearing top hat. d, Wearing bowler hat, profile. e, Wearing bow tie and suit. f, With hand at chin.
$6, Wearing bowler hat, diff.

2002, Sept. 16
2589 A453 $1.80 Sheet of 6, #a-f 8.25 8.25
Souvenir Sheet
2590 A453 $6 multi   4.50 4.50

Marlene Dietrich (1901-92), Actress — A454

No. 2591: a, With hands at side of face. b, Wearing top hat. c, Faciing forward. d, With hand on chin. e, Wearing black hat. f, Wearing gloves.
$6, Facing forward, diff.

2002, Sept. 16
2591 A454 $1.50 Sheet of 6, #a-f 6.75 6.75
Souvenir Sheet
2592 A454 $6 multi   4.50 4.50

Bob Hope — A455

No. 2593: a, Wearing red cap. b, Wearing hat with strap. c, Wearing top hat. d, Wearing black cap. e, Wearing camouflage. f, Wearing white cap.

2002, Sept. 16
2593 A455 $1.50 Sheet of 6, #a-f 7.50 7.50

Ferrari
Race Cars
A456

Designs: 20c, 1957 801. 25c, 1959 256 F1. 30c, 1960 246P F1. 90c, 1966 246 F1. $1, 1971 312 B2. $1.50, 1969 312 F1. $2, 1997 F310B. $4, 2002 F2002.

2002, Oct. 14 Litho.
2594-2601 A456 Set of 8 7.75 7.75

Independence, 21st Anniv. — A457

Designs: 25c, Flag. 30c, Arms, vert. $1.50, Mt. St. John's Hospital nearing completion. $1.80, Parliament Building.
No. 2606, $6, Prime Minister Lester B. Bird, vert. No. 2607, $6, Sir Vere C. Bird, vert.

2002, Oct. 31 Perf. 14
2602-2605 A457 Set of 4 3.50 3.50
Souvenir Sheets
2606-2607 A457 Set of 2 9.00 9.00

Nos. 2606-2607 each contain one 38x50mm stamp.

Second Round of World Cup Soccer Championships — A458

No. 2608, $1.65: a, Pyo Lee. b, Ji Sung Park. c, Jung Hwan Ahn. d, Filippo Inzaghi. e, Paolo Maldini. f, Damiano Tommasi.
No. 2609, $1.65: a, Juan Valeron. b, Iker Casillas. c, Fernando Hierro. d, Gary Kelly. e, Damien Duff. f, Matt Holland.
No. 2610, $3: a, South Korean coach Guus Hiddink. b, Chul Sang Yoo.
No. 2611, $3: a, Francesco Totti. b, Italy coach Giovanni Trapattoni.
No. 2612, $3: a, Spain coach Jose Antonio Camacho. b, Carlos Gamarra.
No. 2613, $3: a, Robbie Keane. b, Ireland coach Mick McCarthy.

2002, Nov. 4 Perf. 13½x13¼
Sheets of 6, #a-f
2608-2609 A458 Set of 2 15.00 15.00
Souvenir Sheets, #a-b
2610-2613 A458 Set of 4 18.00 18.00

Christmas A459

Designs: 25c, Coronation of the Virgin, by Domenico Ghirlandaio. 45c, Adoration of the Magi (detail), by Ghirlandaio. 75c, Annunciation (detail), by Simone Martini, vert. 90c, Adoration of the Magi (detail, diff.) by Ghirlandaio. $5, Madonna and Child, by Giovanni Bellini. $6, Madonna and Child, by Martini.

2002, Nov. 18 Perf. 14
2614-2618 A459 Set of 5 5.50 5.50
Souvenir Sheet
2619 A459 $6 multi 4.50 4.50

Worldwide Fund for Nature (WWF) A460

Antiguan racer snake: a, Head. b, Snake with head near tail. c, Snake and dried leaves. d, Snake on rocks.

2002, Nov. 25
2620 Strip of 4 3.75 3.75
a.-d. A460 $1 Any single .90 .90

Printed in sheets of 4 strips.

Flora & Fauna — A461

No. 2621, $1.50: a, Magnificent frigatebird. b, Sooty tern. c, Bananaquit. d, Yellow-crowned night heron. e, Greater flamingo. f, Belted kingfisher.
No. 2622, $1.50: a, Killer whale. b, Sperm whale. c, Minke whale. d, Blainville's beaked whale. e, Blue whale. f, Cuvier's beaked whale.
No. 2623, $1.80: a, Hieroglyphic moth. b, Hypocrita dejanira. c, Snowy eupseudosoma moth. d, Composia credula. e, Giant silkworm moth. f, Diva moth.
No. 2624, $1.80: a, Epidendrum fragrans. b, Dombeya. c, Yellow poui. d, Milky wave plant. e, Cinderella plant. f, Coral orchid.
No. 2625, $5, Snowy egret. No. 2626, $5, Rothschildia orizaba. No. 2627, $6, Humpback whale. No. 2628, $6, Ionopsis utricularoides.

2002, Nov. 25 Litho.
Sheets of 6, #a-f
2621-2624 A461 Set of 4 30.00 30.00
Souvenir Sheets
2625-2628 A461 Set of 4 17.50 17.50

Souvenir Sheet

Pan-American Health Organization, Cent. — A462

No. 2629: a, Dr. Margaret O'Garro. b, Nurse Ineta Wallace. c, Public Health Worker Vincent Edwards.

2002, Dec. 2
2629 A462 $1.50 Sheet of 3, #a-c 3.50 3.50

Science Fiction — A463

No. 2630, $6, Writings of Nostradamus. No. 2631, $6, 2001: A Space Odyssey, by Arthur C. Clarke. No. 2632, $6, Are We Alone?

2002, Dec. 12 Perf. 13¾
2630-2632 A463 Set of 3 13.50 13.50

A464

20th World Scout Jamboree, Thailand — A465

No. 2633, horiz.: a, Lord Robert Baden-Powell. b, Ernest Thompson Seton, first Chief Scout. c, First black troop.
No. 2634: a, Brownie with broad neckerchief "X." b, Brownie with narrow neckerchief "X." c, Brownie with incomplete neckerchief "X."
No. 2635, Seton. No. 2636, Scout salute.

2002, Dec. 12 Litho. Perf. 14
2633 A464 $3 Sheet of 3, #a-c 7.00 7.00
2634 A465 $3 Sheet of 3, #a-c 7.00 7.00
Souvenir Sheet
2635 A464 $6 multi 4.50 4.50
2636 A465 $6 multi 4.50 4.50

Ram, by Liu Jiyou — A466

2003, Feb. 10 Perf. 13¾
2637 A466 $1.80 multi 1.40 1.40

New Year 2003 (Year of the Ram). Issued in sheets of 4.

A467

Coronation of Queen Elizabeth II, 50th Anniv. — A468

No. 2638, each $3: a, In uniform. b, With tan jacket. c, With white dress and hat.
$6, With white dress.

2003 Litho. Perf. 14
2638 A467 Sheet of 3, #a-c 6.75 6.75
Souvenir Sheet
2639 A467 $6 multi 4.50 4.50
Miniature Sheet
Litho. & Embossed
Perf. 13¼x13
2640 A468 $20 gold & multi 17.50 17.50

Issued: Nos. 2638-2639, 5/14; No. 2640, 2/10.

Paintings of Lucas Cranach the Elder (1472-1553) A469

Designs: 75c, Lucretia. 90c, Venus and Cupid. $1, Judith with the Head of Holofernes, c. 1530. $1.50, Portrait of a Young Lady.
No. 2645: a, Portrait of the Wife of a Jurist. b, Portrait of a Jurist. c, Johannes Cuspinian. d, Portrait of Anna Cuspinian.

$6, Judith with the Head of Holofernes, c. 1532.

2003, Apr. 30   **Litho.**   **Perf. 14¼**
2641-2644 A469   Set of 4   3.25 3.25
2645 A469 $2 Sheet of 4, #a-d   6.00 6.00
Souvenir Sheet
2646 A469 $6 multi   4.50 4.50

Paintings of Yoshitoshi Taiso (1839-92) A470

Designs: 25c, A High Class Maid Training in a Samurai Household. 50c, A Castle-Toppler Known as "Keisei": A Beautiful Woman Able to Seduce a Ruler So That He Forgets the Affairs of the State. $1, Stylish Young Geisha Battling a Snowstorm on Her Way to Work. $5, A Lady in Distress Being Treated With Moxa.

No. 2651: a, A Lady of the Imperial Court Wearing Four Layers of Robes. b, Young Mother Adoring Her Infant Son. c, Lady-in-waiting Looking Amused Over a Veranda in the Household of a Great Lord. d, A High-ranking Courtesan Known as "Oiran" Waiting For a Private Assignation.

$6, A Girl Teasing Her Cat.

2003, Apr. 30
2647-2650 A470   Set of 4   5.00 5.00
2651 A470 $2 Sheet of 4, #a-d   6.00 6.00
Souvenir Sheet
2652 A470 $6 multi   4.50 4.50

Paintings of Raoul Dufy (1877-1953) — A471

Designs: 90c, Boats at Martigues. $1, Harvesting. $1.80, Sailboats in the Port of Le Havre. $5, The Big Bather, vert.

No. 2657: a, The Beach and the Pier at Trouville. b, Port With Sailing Ships. c, Black Cargo. d, Nice, the Bay of Anges.

No. 2658, $6, The Interior With an Open Window. No. 2659, $6, Vence.

2003, Apr. 30
2653-2656 A471   Set of 4   6.50 6.50
2657 A471 $2 Sheet of 4, #a-d   6.00 6.00
Size: 96x76mm
Imperf
2658-2659 A471   Set of 2   9.00 9.00

Prince William, 21st Birthday — A472

No. 2660: a, With yellow and black shirt. b, With polo helmet. c, With blue shirt.
$6, In suit.

2003, May 14   **Perf. 14**
2660 A472 $3 Sheet of 3, #a-c   7.00 7.00
Souvenir Sheet
2661 A472 $6 multi   4.50 4.50

Salvation Army in Antigua, Cent. — A473

Designs: 30c, Emblem, Tamarind tree, Parham, vert. 90c, Salvation Army Pre-school, vert. $1, Meals on Wheels. $1.50, St. John's Citadel Band. $1.80, Salvation Army Citadel. $6, Tamarind tree, Parham, vert.

2003, May 19   **Perf. 14¼**
2662-2666 A473   Set of 5   4.25 4.25
Souvenir Sheet
2667 A473 $6 multi   4.50 4.50

Antigua & Barbuda Scouts Association, 90th Anniv. — A474

Designs: 30c, First Anglican Scout troop, 1931. $1, National Scout Camp, 2002. $1.50, Woodbadge Training Course, 2000, horiz. $1.80, Men visiting National Scout Camp, 1986, horiz.

No. 2672: a, Edris George. b, Theodore George. c, Edris James.
$6, Scout with semaphore flags.

2003, June 9   **Perf. 14**
2668-2671 A474   Set of 4   3.75 3.75
2672 A474 90c Sheet of 3, #a-c   2.25 2.25
Souvenir Sheet
2673 A474 $6 multi   4.75 4.75

Tour de France Bicycle Race, Cent. — A475

No. 2674, $2: a, Cesar Garin, 1903. b, Henri Cornet, 1904. c, Louis Trousselier, 1905. d, René Pottier, 1906.

No. 2675, $2: a, Lucien Petit-Breton, 1907. b, Petit-Breton, 1908. c, François Faber, 1909. d, Octave Lapize, 1910.

No. 2676, $2: a, Gustave Garrigou, 1911. b, Odile Defraye, 1912. c, Philippe Thys, 1913. d, Thys, 1914.

No. 2677, $6, Pierre Giffard. No. 2678, $6, Henri Desgrange. No. 2679, $6, Comte de Dion.

2003, June 9   **Perf. 13¼**
Sheets of 4, #a-d
2674-2676 A475   Set of 3   18.00 18.00
Souvenir Sheets
2677-2679 A475   Set of 3   13.50 13.50

Caribbean Community, 30th Anniv. — A476

2003, July 4   **Perf. 14**
2680 A476 $1 multi   .80 .80

Intl. Year of Fresh Water — A477

No. 2681, horiz.: a, Chutes de Carbet and rocks. b, Chutes de Carbet and foliage at left and right. c, Rocks at base of Chutes de Carbet.
$6, Ocho Rios Waterfall.

2003, July 14   **Perf. 13¼**
2681 A477 $2 Sheet of 3, #a-c   5.25 5.25
Souvenir Sheet
2682 A477 $6 multi   5.00 5.00

General Motors Automobiles — A478

No. 2683, $2 — Cadillacs: a, 1955 Eldorado convertible. b, 1937 Series 60. c, 1959 Eldorado. d, 2002 Eldorado.

No. 2684, $2 — Chevrolet Corvettes: a, 1954 convertible. b, 1964 Sting Ray. c, 1964 Sting Ray convertible. d, 1998 convertible.

No. 2685, $6, 1953 Cadillac Eldorado. No. 2686, $6, 1956 Corvette convertible.

2003, July 14   **Perf. 13¼x13½**
Sheets of 4, #a-d
2683-2684 A478   Set of 2   12.00 12.00
Souvenir Sheets
2685-2686 A478   Set of 2   9.00 9.00
Cadillac, cent.; Corvette, 50th anniv.

History of Aviation — A479

No. 2687, $2: a, First Wright Brothers flight, 1903. b, First free flight in helicopter by Paul Cornu, 1907. c, First landing on ship, by E. B. Ely. d, Curtiss A-1, first hydroplane, 1911.

No. 2688, $2: a, Bell X-5, 1951. b, Convair XFY-1, 1954. c, North American X-15, 1959 . d, Alexei Leonov, first man to walk in space, 1965.

No. 2689, $2: a, Concorde, 1969. b, Martin X-24, 1969. c, Apollo-Soyuz space mission, 1975. d, Mars probe Viking, 1976.

No. 2690, $6, Boeing Model 200 Monomail, 1930. No. 2691, $6, Breaking of sound barrier by Bell X-1, 1947. No. 2692, $6, Grumman X-29, 1984.

2003, July 28   **Perf. 14**
Sheets of 4, #a-d
2687-2689 A479   Set of 3   20.00 20.00
Souvenir Sheets
2690-2692 A479   Set of 3   13.50 13.50

Bird Type of 1995

Designs: $5, Montezuma oropendola. $10, Green jay.

2003, Aug. 11   **Litho.**   **Perf. 15x14**
2693 A296 $5 multi   3.75 3.75
2694 A296 $10 multi   7.50 7.50

Circus Performers — A480

No. 2695, $1.80 — Clowns: a, Apes. b, Mo Lite. c, Gigi. d, "Buttons" McBride.

No. 2696, $1.80 — Performers: a, Chun Group. b, Casselly Sisters. c, Oliver Groszer. d, Keith Nelson.

2003, Sept. 1   **Perf. 14**
Sheets of 4, #a-d
2695-2696 A480   Set of 2   11.00 11.00

Christmas A481

Designs: 25c, Madonna and Child, by Bartolomeo Vivarini. 30c, Holy Family, by Pompeo Girolamo Batoni. 45c, Madonna and Child, by Benozzo Gozzoli. 50c, Madonna and Child (Calci Parish Church), by Gozzoli. 75c, Madonna and Child Giving Blessings, by Gozzoli. 90c, Madonna and Child, by Master of the Female Half-figures. $2.50, Benois Madonna, by Leonardo da Vinci.

$6, The Virgin and Child with Angels, by Rosso Fiorentino.

2003, Nov. 10   **Litho.**   **Perf. 14¼**
2697-2703 A481   Set of 7   4.25 4.25
Souvenir Sheet
2704 A481 $6 multi   4.50 4.50

Orchids — A482

No. 2705, $2.50, vert.: a, Psychopsis papilio. b, Amesiella philippinensis. c, Maclellanara Pagan Dove Song. d, Phalaenopsis Little Hal.

No. 2706, $2.50: a, Daeliocattleya Amber Glow. b, Hygrochilus parishii. c, Dendrobium crystallinum. d, Disa hybrid.

$5, Cattleya deckeri.

2003, Dec. 8   **Perf. 13½**
Sheets of 4, #a-d
2705-2706 A482   Set of 2   15.00 15.00
Souvenir Sheet
2707 A482 $5 multi   4.00 4.00

Birds — A483

No. 2708, $2.50, vert.: a, Blue and gold macaw. b, Green-winged macaw. c, Greennaped lorikeet. d, Lesser sulfur-crested cockatoo.

No. 2709, $2.50: a, Severe macaw. b, Blueheaded parrot. c, Budgerigar. d, Sun conure.

$5, Bald ibis.

2003, Dec. 8   **Sheets of 4, #a-d**
2708-2709 A483   Set of 2   17.00 17.00
Souvenir Sheet
2710 A483 $5 multi   4.00 4.00

Butterflies — A484

No. 2711, $2: a, Esmerelda. b, Tiger pierid. c, Blue night. d, Charaxes nobilis.

No. 2712, $2.50: a, Orange-barred sulphur. b, Scarce bamboo page. c, Charaxes latona. d, Hewitson's blue hairstreak.

$5, Diaethia meridionalis.

2003, Dec. 8   **Sheets of 4, #a-d**
2711-2712 A484   Set of 2   14.50 14.50
Souvenir Sheet
2713 A484 $5 multi   4.00 4.00

Sharks — A485

No. 2714: a, Bull. b, Gray reef. c, Black tip. d, Leopard.

$5, Great white.

2003, Dec. 8
2714 A485 $2 Sheet of 4, #a-d   6.50 6.50
Souvenir Sheet
2715 A485 $5 multi   3.75 3.75

New Year 2004 (Year of the Monkey) — A486

No. 2716, each $1.50: a, Monkey with black face and white chest. b, Monkey with brown face and white chest. c, Monkey with black, gray and yellow face. d, Red brown monkey on branch.

2004, Jan. 19   **Perf. 14**
2716 A486   Sheet of 4, #a-d   5.00 5.00

Arthur and Friends — A487

No. 2717, each $1.50: a, Binky. b, Buster. c, Francine. d, D.W. e, Sue Ellen. f, Muffy.

No. 2718, each $1.80: a, Binky. b, Muffy. c, Francine. d, Buster.

No. 2719, each $2.50: a, Arthur hitting baseball. b, Sue Ellen. c, Binky. d, Arthur with foot on home plate.

2004, Feb. 16   **Perf. 13¼**
2717 A487   Sheet of 6, #a-f   6.75 6.75
Sheets of 4, #a-d
2718-2719 A487   Set of 2   13.00 13.00

Paintings by Ren Xiong (1820-57) — A488

No. 2720, each $1.50: a, Purple hills. b, Cliffside waves. c, Hills at left, trees, Chinese text at right. d, House and tree.

No. 2721, each $1.50: a, Rocky pinnacles. b, Rocks at left and right. c, Hills, trees and bridge, Chinese text top right. d, Waterfall at right, Chinese text at top left. e, Waterfalls, Chinese text at left. f, Rocks and flowers, Chinese text at top left.

No. 2722, each $1.50: a, Bird on flowering tree. b, Bird in tree.

2004, Feb. 16
2720 A488   Sheet of 4, #a-d   4.50 4.50
2721 A488   Sheet of 6, #a-f   6.75 6.75
2722 A488   Sheet of 2, #a-b   4.00 4.00

Paintings by Pablo Picasso — A489

No. 2723: a, Woman with a Flower. b, Marie-Thérèse Seated. c, The Red Armchair (Marie-Thérèse). d, The Dream (Marie-Thérèse) Seated.

$5, Bust of a Girl (Marie-Thérèse).

2004, Mar. 8   **Perf. 14¼**
2723 A489 $2 Sheet of 4, #a-d   6.50 6.50
Imperf
2724 A489 $5 shown   4.00 4.00
No. 2723 contains four 38x50mm stamps.

Paintings by Norman Rockwell — A490

No. 2725: a, Freedom of Speech. b, Freedom to Worship. c, Freedom from Want. d, Freedom from Fear.

$5, Painting for cover of Apr. 1, 1961 Saturday Evening Post.

2004, Mar. 8
2725 A490 $2 Sheet of 4, #a-d   6.00 6.00
Imperf
2726 A490 $6 shown   4.50 4.50
No. 2725 contains four 38x50mm stamps.

Paintings by Paul Gauguin (1848-1903) — A491

Designs: 25c, Vaite Goupil, vert. 30c, Autoportrait prés de Golgotha, vert. 75c, Le Moulin David à Pont-Aver. $2.50, Moisson en Bretagne, vert.

$4, Cavaliers sur la Plage.

2004, Mar. 8   **Litho.**   **Perf. 14¼**
2727-2730 A491   Set of 4   3.00 3.00
Imperf
Size: 77x63mm
2731 A491 $4 multi   4.75 4.75

Paintings by Joan Miró (1893-1983) — A492

Designs: 75c, The Smile of Flaming Wings. 90c, The Bird's Song in the Dew of the Moon. $1, Dancer II, vert. $4, Painting, 1954, vert.

No. 2736, $2 — Painting Based on a Collage, description in: a, LL. b, LR. c, UL. d, UR.

$5, Bather. $6, Flame in Space and Nude Woman, vert.

2004, Mar. 8   **Litho.**   **Perf. 14¼**
2732-2735 A492   Set of 4   5.50 5.50
2736 A492 $2 Sheet of 4, #a-d   6.50 6.50
Imperf
Size: 102x83mm
2737 A492 $5 multi   4.00 4.00
Size: 83x102mm
2738 A492 $6 multi   5.00 5.00

Wedding of Prince Felipe de Borbón of Spain and Letizia Ortiz A493

Designs: 30c, Couple. 50c, Couple, diff. 75c, Letizia. 90c, Prince Felipe. $1, Couple, diff. No. 2744, $5, Couple, diff.

No. 2745: a, Spanish royal family. b, Flags and Prince Felipe in uniform. c, Prince Felipe, his grandfather, Juan de Borbón y Battenberg, and his father, King Juan Carlos. d, Letizia, Prince Felipe, King Juan Carlos and Queen Sophia, horiz. e, Similar to 75c. f, Similar to 90c.

No. 2746, $5, Couple, diff. No. 2747, $5, Similar to #2745a. No. 2748, $5, Similar to #2745c. No. 2749, $6, Letizia, map of Europe. No. 2750, $6, Similar to #2745b. No. 2751, $6, Similar to #2745d, horiz.

2004, May 21   **Perf. 13¼**
2739-2744 A493   Set of 6   6.50 6.50
2745 A493 $1.80 Sheet of 6, #a-f   8.50 8.50
Souvenir Sheets
2746-2751 A493   Set of 6   25.00 25.00

Election of Pope John Paul II, 25th Anniv. (in 2003) — A494

No. 2752: a, Pope with Mother Teresa. b, Pope in the Holy Land. c, Pope meeting with Pres. George W. Bush. d, Pope waving, dark background. e, Pope waving, light background.

2004, June 17   **Perf. 14**
2752 A494 $1.80 Sheet of 5, #a-e   7.25 7.25
Inscription of "2000" on No. 2752a is incorrect.

Intl. Year of Peace — A495

No. 2753 Dove and: a, Intl. Year of Peace emblem. b, Earth. c, UN emblem.

2004, June 17
2753 A495 $3 Sheet of 3, #a-c   6.75 6.75

2004 Summer Olympics, Athens A496

Designs: $1, Poster for 1964 Tokyo Olympics. $1.65, Commemorative medal for 1964 Tokyo Olympics. $1.80, Fencing, horiz. $2, Wrestlers, horiz.

2004, June 17   **Perf. 14¼**
2754-2757 A496   Set of 4   5.00 5.00

European Soccer Championships, Portugal — A497

No. 2758: a, Milan Galic. b, Slava Metreveli. c, Igor Netto. d, Parc des Princes. $6, 1960 USSR team.

2004, June 17   **Perf. 14**
2758 A497 $2 Sheet of 4, #a-d   7.50 7.50
     Souvenir Sheet
     Perf. 14¼
2759 A497 $6 multi   5.00 5.00
No. 2758 contains four 28x42mm stamps.

Locomotives, Signals and Stations — A498

No. 2760, $1: a, Evening Star. b, Indian Railways XC Pacific. c, German Kreigslokomotive. d, Bulleid Light Pacific. e, G. W. R. copper cap chimney. f, Tallylyn Railway. g, Preservation volunteers. h, N. E. R. Y7 0-4-0T. h, Breda 0-4-0 WT, locomotive shed, Asmara, Eritrea.

No. 2761, $1, vert.: a, King Class 4-6-0. b, Argentinian 11B Class 2-8-0. c, Baldwin Mikado. d, Round trackside signal with red horizontal band. e, Wooden box with button signal. f, Signal house, signals with red and yellow arms. g, Signal house, signal with two red arms. h, Window of signal house. i, Signal lights.

No. 2762, $1, vert.: a, 2-4-0T on Douglas to Port Erin line, Isle of Man. b, South African Railways 4-8-2S. c, China Railways SY Class 2-8-2. d, St. Pancras Station. e, Ulverston Station, f, Bolton Station. g, Liverpool St. Station. h, Cannon St. Station. i, Malvern Station.

No. 2763, $5, Settle-Carlisle line. No. 2764, $6, Douro Valley Railway. No. 2765, $6, Train over Lake Egridir, Turkey.

2004, June 17   **Perf. 14**
     Sheets of 9, #a-i
2760-2762 A498 Set of 3   21.00 21.00
     Souvenir Sheets
2763-2765 A498 Set of 3   14.00 14.00

D-Day, 60th Anniv. A499

Designs: 30c, Derrick Tysoe. 45c, Lt. Gen. Walter Bedell Smith. $1.50, Les Perry. $3, Maj. Gen. Percy Hobart.

No. 2770, $2: a, Tiger II tank. b, Standartenfuhrer Kurt Meyer. c, Canadian infantry. d, British infantry.

No. 2771, $2: a, Hamilcar disgorges Tetrarch tank. b, Horsa glider unloads cargo. c, Beachheads established. d, Liberation begins.

No. 2772, $6, Sherman tank. No. 2773, $6, Mulberry Harbor.

2004, July 26   **Perf. 14¼**
     Stamp + Label (#2766-2769)
2766-2769 A499 Set of 4   4.00 4.00
     Sheets of 4, #a-d
2770-2771 A499 Set of 2   12.00 12.00
     Souvenir Sheets
2772-2773 A499 Set of 2   9.00 9.00

     Miniature Sheet

Queen Juliana of the Netherlands (1909-2004) — A500

No. 2774 — Netherlands flag and: a, Juliana. b, Juliana and Prince Bernhard. c, Juliana and Princess Beatrix. d, Juliana and Princess Irene. e, Juliana and Princess Margriet. f, Juliana and Princess Christina.

2004, June 17   **Litho.**   **Perf. 13¼**
2774 A500 $2 Sheet of 6, #a-f   9.00 9.00
     Miniature Sheet

National Basketball Association Players — A501

No. 2775: a, Mike Bibby, Sacramento Kings. b, Jim Jackson, Houston Rockets. c, Tracy McGrady, Houston Rockets. d, Chris Webber, Sacramento Kings. e, Peja Stojakovic, Sacramento Kings. f, Yao Ming, Houston Rockets.

2004, Nov. 8   **Perf. 12**
2775 A501 $1.50 Sheet of 6, #a-f 6.75 6.75

FIFA (Fédération Internationale de Football Association), Cent. — A502

No. 2776: a, Zinedine Zidane. b, Roberto Baggio. c, Franz Beckenbauer. d, Ossie Ardiles.
$6, Jimmy Greaves.

2004, Nov. 8   **Perf. 12¾x12½**
2776 A502 $2 Sheet of 4, #a-d   6.00 6.00
     Souvenir Sheet
2777 A502 $6 multi   4.50 4.50

     Miniature Sheet

John Denver (1943-97), Singer — A503

No. 2778, each $1.50: a, At microphone. b, Tuning guitar. c, With arm extended. d, Facing left, playing guitar.

2004, Nov. 22   **Perf. 14**
2778 A503 Sheet of 4, #a-d   4.50 4.50

     Miniature Sheet

George Herman "Babe" Ruth (1895-1948), Baseball Player — A504

No. 2779, each $1.80: a, Wearing blue cap. b, Wearing crown. c, Wearing pinstriped cap. d, Holding bat.

2004, Nov. 22
2779 A504 Sheet of 4, #a-d   5.50 5.50

The Family Circus, Comic Strip by Bil and Jeff Keane — A505

No. 2780, $2: a, "Billy attackled me too hard," blue panel. b, "His ears came from where his eyes are." c, "Tennessee!" d, "One candy or one bowl?"

No. 2781, $2: a, "If you had wider shoulders, Daddy, you could be a two-seater." b, "Billy attackled me too hard," red panel. c, "Who tee-peed the mummies?" d, "Looking out there makes me realize it's indeed the little things that count."

No. 2782, $2: a, "Someday I might travel to another planet, but I'm not sure why." b, "Adam and Eve were lucky. They didn't have any history to learn." c, "My backpack is too full. Will somebody help me stand up?" d, "I tripped because one foot tried to hug the other foot."

No. 2783, $2: a, "If you don't put enough stamps on it the mailman will only take it part way." b, "Gee, Grandma, you have a lot of thoughts on your wall." c, "Shall I play for you pa-rum-pa-pum-pummm. . .?" d, "You have to do that when you're married."

No. 2784, $2: a, Billy. b, Jeffy. c, PJ. d, Dolly.

     Perf. 13¼, 14¼(#2784)
2004, Nov. 22   **Sheets of 4, #a-d**
2780-2784 A505 Set of 5   30.00 30.00

World AIDS Day A506

2004, Dec. 1   **Perf. 14**
2785 A506 $2 multi   1.75 1.75

Christmas A507

Designs: 20c, Madonna in Floral Wreath, by Jan Breughel the Elder and Peter Paul Rubens. 25c, Madonna and Child, by Jan Gossaert. 30c, Santa Claus on skis. 45c, Santa Claus with raised arms. 50c, Santa Claus, reindeer on roof. $1, Floral Wreath with Virgin and Child, by Daniel Seghers. $1.80, Madonna and Child, by Andrea Mantegna. $6, Madonna in a Floral Wreath, by Seghers.

2004, Dec. 13   **Perf. 12¼x12**
2786-2792 A507 Set of 7   3.50 3.50
     Souvenir Sheet
2793 A507 $6 multi   5.00 5.00

Dogs — A508

Designs: 30c, American pit bull terrier. 90c, Maltese. $1.50, Rottweiler. $3, Australian terrier.
$6, German shepherd, horiz.

2005, May 23   **Litho.**   *Perf. 12¾*
2794-2797 A508   Set of 4   7.00 7.00
Souvenir Sheet
2798 A508 $6 multi   5.50 5.50

Cats — A509

Designs: 75c, Golden Persian. $1, Calico shorthair. $1.50, Siamese. $3, Tabby Persian. $5, Turkish.

2005, May 23
2799-2802 A509   Set of 4   5.00 5.00
Souvenir Sheet
2803 A509 $5 multi   4.00 4.00

Insects — A510

No. 2804, horiz.: a, Figure-of-eight butterfly. b, Honeybee. c, Migratory grasshopper. d, Hercules beetle.
$5, Cramer's Mesene butterfly.

2005, May 23
2804 A510 $2 Sheet of 4, #a-d   6.50 6.50
Souvenir Sheet
2805 A510 $5 multi   3.75 3.75

Marine Life — A511

No. 2806: a, Yellowtail damselfish. b, French angelfish. c, Horseshoe crab. d, Emerald mithrax crab.
$6, Spanish hogfish.

2005, May 23
2806 A511 $2 Sheet of 4, #a-d   6.00 6.00
Souvenir Sheet
2807 A511 $6 multi   4.75 4.75

Prehistoric Animals — A512

No. 2808, $2: a, Mammuthus imperator. b, Brontops. c, Hyracotherium. d, Propaleotherium.
No. 2809, $2.50: a, Ceratosaur. b, Coelurosaurs. c, Ornitholestes. d, Baryonyx.
No. 2810, $3: a, Plateosaurus. b, Yangchuanosaurus. c, Ceolophysis. d, Lystrosaurus.
No. 2811, $4, Triceratops. No. 2812, $5, Stegoasurus, vert. No. 2813, $6, Coelodonta.

2005, May 23
Sheets of 4, #a-d
2808-2810 A512   Set of 3   25.00 25.00
Souvenir Sheets
2811-2813 A512   Set of 3   12.00 12.00

Miniature Sheet

Pres. Ronald Reagan (1911-2004) — A513

No. 2814 — Background colors: a, Gray blue. b, Gray brown. c, Pink. d, White. e, Gray green. f, Buff.

2005, June 15   *Perf. 14*
2814 A513 $1.50 Sheet of 6, #a-f 7.50 7.50

New Year 2005 (Year of the Rooster) A514

Mother Hen and Her Brood, by Wang Ning: $1, Detail. $4, Entire painting.

2005, June 15   *Perf. 14¼*
2815 A514 $1 multi   .75 .75
Souvenir Sheet
2816 A514 $4 multi   4.00 4.00
No. 2815 printed in sheets of 4.

Friedrich von Schiller (1759-1805), Writer — A515

No. 2817: a, Bust of Schiller, by C. L. Richter, Central Park, New York. b, Actors in "Kabale und Liebe." c, Schiller's birthplace, Marbach, Germany.
$6, Sculpture of Schiller, by Ernst Rau, Lincoln Park, Chicago.

2005, June 15   *Perf. 14*
2817 A515 $3 Sheet of 3, #a-c   6.75 6.75
Souvenir Sheet
2818 A515 $6 multi   5.25 5.25

Jules Verne (1828-1905), Writer — A516

No. 2819, vert. — Movie posters for Verne works: a, Monster Island, 1961. b, Journey to the Center of the Earth, 1961. c, From the Earth to the Moon, 1956. d, Sea Devils, 1961.
$5, Michael Strogoff, 1956.

2005, June 15
2819 A516 $2 Sheet of 4, #a-d   6.00 6.00
Souvenir Sheet
2820 A516 $5 multi   3.75 3.75
No. 2819 contains four 28x42mm stamps.

World Cup Soccer Championships, 75th Anniv. — A517

No. 2821, each $1.50 — Uruguayan flag, first place medal and: a, 1930 Uruguay team. b, Hector Castro scoring goal against Argentina. c, Crowd in Estadio Centenario. d, Hector Castro.
$6, Uruguay team celebrating 1930 victory.

2005, June 15   *Perf. 14¼*
2821 A517   Sheet of 4, #a-d   8.00 8.00
Souvenir Sheet
2822 A517 $6 multi   4.50 4.50

End of World War II, 60th Anniv. — A518

No. 2823, $1.50: a, Soldiers in Red Square, Moscow, May 9, 1945. b, Gen. Bernard Law Montgomery. c, Marshal Georgi K. Zhukov. d, Gen. Omar N. Bradley.
No. 2824, $2, horiz.: a, Winston Churchill, Franklin D. Roosevelt and Joseph Stalin at Yalta Summit. b, Raising of US flag on Mount Suribachi. c, Gen. Douglas MacArthur signing Japanese surrender documents. d, Japanese officials at surrender ceremony.

2005, June 15   *Perf. 14*
Sheets of 4, #a-d
2823-2824 A518   Set of 2   10.50 10.50

Battle of Trafalgar, Bicent. — A519

Various ships in battle: 90c, $1, $1.50, $1.80.
$6, The Victory firing during the Battle of Trafalgar.

2005, June 15   *Perf. 14¼*
2825-2828 A519   Set of 4   6.75 6.75
Souvenir Sheet
2829 A519 $6 multi   7.75 7.75

National Basketball Association Players — A520

Designs: No. 2830, 75c, Ray Allen, Seattle Supersonics. No. 2831, 75c, Lucious Harris, Cleveland Cavaliers. No. 2832, 75c, Dwight Howard, Orlando Magic. No. 2833, 75c, Antonio McDyess, Detroit Pistons. No. 2834, 75c, Emeka Okafor, Charlotte Bobcats.

2005   *Perf. 14*
2830-2834 A520   Set of 5   3.00 3.00

Pope John Paul II (1920-2005) and Meir Lau, Chief Rabbi of Israel — A521

2005, Oct. 10   *Perf. 13½x13¼*
2835 A521 $3 multi   4.25 4.25
Printed in sheets of 6.

Albert Einstein (1879-1955),
Physicist — A522

No. 2836 — Photograph of Einstein in: a,
Brown. b, Olive green. c, Black.

2005, Oct. 10   Litho.   Perf. 13¼x13½
2836 A522 $3 Sheet of 3, #a-c   6.75 6.75

Hans Christian Andersen (1805-75),
Author — A523

No. 2837: a, Portrait of Andersen. b, Statue
of Andersen, Central Park, New York City. c,
Andersen's gravesite.
$6, Andersen seated.

2005, Oct. 10   Perf. 13½x13¼
2837 A523 $3 Sheet of 3, #a-c   6.75 6.75
Souvenir Sheet
2838 A523 $6 multi   5.25 5.25

Rotary International, Cent. — A524

No. 2839, vert.: a, Italy #1372. b, Paul Harris
Medallion. c, Paul P. Harris, first Rotary
President.
$6, Children.

2005, Oct. 10   Perf. 13½x13¼
2839 A524 $3 Sheet of 3, #a-c   7.25 7.25
Souvenir Sheet
Perf. 13¼x13½
2840 A524 $6 multi   6.00 6.00

Pope Benedict
XVI — A525

2005, Nov. 21   Perf. 13½x13¼
2841 A525 $2 multi   1.75 1.75

Christmas — A526

Churches: 25c, Gilbert's Memorial Methodist Church. No. 2843, 30c, People's Church,
Barbuda. No. 2844, 30c, Tyrell's Roman Catholic Church. 45c, St. Barnabas Anglican
Church. 50c, St. Peter's Anglican Church. No.
2847, 75c, Spring Gardens Moravian Church.
No. 2848, 75c, St. Steven's Anglican Church.
No. 2849, 90c, Holy Family Catholic Cathedral. No. 2850, 90c, Pilgrim Holiness Church,
vert. $1, Ebenezer Methodist Church.
No. 2852, $5, St. John's Cathedral. No.
2853, $5, Worship service, Spring Gardens
Moravian Church, vert.

2005, Dec. 19   Perf. 12¾
2842-2851 A526 Set of 10   6.75 6.75
Souvenir Sheets
2852-2853 A526 Set of 2   8.00 8.00

Elvis Presley (1935-77) — A527

Serpentine Die Cut 8¾x9
2005   Litho. & Embossed
2854 A527 $20 gold & multi   16.00 16.00

National
Parks
A528

Designs: No. 2855, 20c, Joiner's Loft, Nelson's Dockyard Natl. Park. No. 2856, 20c, Pay
Office, Nelson's Dockyard Natl. Park, vert. No.
2857, 30c, Admiral's House Museum, Nel-
son's Dockyard Natl. Park. No. 2858, 30c,
Bakery, Nelson's Dockyard Natl. Park. No.
2859, 75c, Devil's Bridge Natl. Park. No. 2860,
75c, View from Shirley Heights Lookout, Nel-
son's Dockyard Natl. Park. No. 2861, 90c,
Green Castle Hill Natl. Park. No. 2862, 90c,
Fort Berkeley, Nelson's Dockyard Natl. Park.
No. 2863, $1.50, Pigeon Point Beach, Nel-
son's Dockyard Natl. Park. No. 2864, $1.50,
Half Moon Bay Natl. Park. $1.80, Cannon at
Ft. Berkeley.
No. 2866, $5, Codrington Lagoon Natl.
Park. No. 2867, $5, Museum, Nelson's Dock-
yard Natl. Park, vert.

2006, Jan. 9   Perf. 14
2855-2865 A528 Set of 11   7.00 7.00
Souvenir Sheets
2866-2867 A528 Set of 2   9.50 9.50

National Parks of the United
States — A529

No. 2868: a, Yellowstone. b, Olympic. c,
Glacier. d, Grand Canyon. e, Yosemite. f,
Great Smoky Mountains.
$6, Mount Rainier.

2006, Jan. 6   Perf. 14¼
2868 A529 $1.50 Sheet of 6, #a-f 7.50 7.50
Souvenir Sheet
Perf. 14
2869 A529 $6 multi   4.75 4.75
No. 2868 contains six 50x38mm stamps.

Moravian Church
Antigua
Conference, 250th
Anniv. — A530

Designs: 30c, Bishop John Ephraim Knight.
$1, John Andrew Buckley. $1.50, Old Spring
Gardens Moravian Church, horiz.
No. 2873, $5, Sandbox tree. No. 2874, $5,
Westerby Memorial. No. 2875, $5, Spring Gar-
dens Teachers College, horiz.

2006, Apr. 3   Perf. 12¾
2870-2872 A530 Set of 3   2.25 2.25
Souvenir Sheets
2873-2875 A530 Set of 3   13.00 13.00

Marilyn Monroe
(1926-62),
Actress — A531

2006, Apr. 10   Perf. 13¼
2876 A531 $3 multi   2.25 2.25
Printed in sheets of 4.

Queen Elizabeth II, 80th
Birthday — A532

No. 2877: a, As young woman (black and
white photo). b, Wearing pearl necklace. c,
Wearing white blouse. d, Wearing crown.
$6, Wearing crown, diff.

2006, Apr. 10
2877 A532 $2 Sheet of 4, #a-d   6.50 6.50
Souvenir Sheet
2878 A532 $6 multi   4.75 4.75

2006 Winter Olympics, Turin — A533

Designs: No. 2879, 75c, Austria #715. No.
2880, 75c, Poster for 1972 Sapporo Winter
Olympics, vert. No. 2881, 90c, Austria #714.
No. 2882, 90c, Japan #1103, vert. $2, Austria
#717. $3, Poster for 1964 Innsbruck Winter
Olympics, vert.

2006, May 11   Litho.   Perf. 14¼
2879-2884 A533 Set of 6   7.00 7.00

A534

Washington 2006 World Philatelic
Exhibition — A535

No. 2885: a, Framed circular portrait of Benjamin Franklin wearing red jacket with fur collar. b, Framed circular portrait of Franklin
seated. c, Framed circular portrait of Franklin
wearing gray jacket.
No. 2886: a, Unframed portrait of Franklin
wearing jacket with fur collar. b, US #1. c,
Unframed portrait of Franklin wearing black
coat. d, Framed oval portrait like #2885a
(73x87mm).

2006, May 29   Perf. 11½
2885 A534 $3 Sheet of 3, #a-c   7.50 7.50
Perf. 11½, Imperf. (#2886d)
2886 A535 $3 Sheet of 4, #a-d   9.50 9.50

Miniature Sheet

Wolfgang Amadeus Mozart (1756-91),
Composer — A536

No. 2887: a, Mozart's viola. b, Mozart at age
11. c, Young Mozart. d, Mozart in Verona,
1770.

2006, July 3   Perf. 12¾
2887 A536 $3 Sheet of 4, #a-d   11.00 11.00

Miniature Sheet

Posters of Elvis Presley
Movies — A537

No. 2888: a, Charro! b, Follow That Dream. c, G.I. Blues. d, Blue Hawaii.

2006, July 12　　　　　**Perf. 13¼**
2888 A537 $3 Sheet of 4, #a-d　10.00 10.00

Antigua and Barbuda Girl Guides, 75th Anniv. — A538

Designs: 25c, Leaders after garbage collection race, 2002. 30c, Girl Guides color party, horiz. 45c, Uniformed and non-uniformed members. 50c, Girl Guides marching band, horiz. $1, Leeward Islands leaders training camp, 1946.
No. 2894, $5, Assistant Commissioner Lisa Simon. No. 2895, $5, Girl Guides gathering at Fort James, 1935, horiz. No. 2896, $5, Enrollment ceremony, 2006, horiz.

2006, July 17　　　　　**Perf. 12¾**
2889-2893 A538　Set of 5　2.75 2.75
Souvenir Sheets
2894-2896 A538　Set of 3　12.50 12.50

Leeward Islands Air Transport, 50th Anniv. A539

Designs: 30c, HS-748 Hawker Siddely Avro. No. 2898, 50c, BN2 Islanders. No. 2899, 50c, BN2 Norman Islander. No. 2900, 50c, Beechcraft Twin Bonanza, vert. $1.50, BAC 111, HS-748. $2.50, DH8-300 de Havilland.
$5, Sir Frank Delisle, LIAT founder, and Beechcraft Twin Bonanza, vert.

2006, Oct. 2　**Litho.**　**Perf. 14¼**
2897-2902 A539　Set of 6　6.25 6.25
Souvenir Sheet
2903 A539 $5 multi　5.25 5.25

Independence, 25th Anniv. — A540

Designs: 30c, Pineapple. $1, Flag. $1.50, Coat of arms.
No. 2907: a, One magnificent frigatebird. b, Two fallow deer. c, One fallow deer. d, Two magnificent frigatebirds.
$5, New Parliament Building, vert.

2006, Oct. 30　　　　　**Perf. 12¾**
2904-2906 A540　Set of 3　2.50 2.50
2907 A540 25c Sheet of 4, #a-d　1.50 1.50
Souvenir Sheet
2908 A540 $5 multi　5.50 5.50
No. 2908 contains one 38x50mm stamp.

Civil Rights Leaders — A541

No. 2909, $2: a, Dalai Lama. b, Pres. Abraham Lincoln. c, Susan B. Anthony. d, Harriet Tubman.
No. 2910, $2: a, Mahatma Gandhi. b, Nelson Mandela. c, Rosa Parks.
$5, Dr. Martin Luther King, Jr.

2006, Nov. 20　**Perf. 12, 12½ (#2910)**
2909　　Horiz. strip of 4　8.00 8.00
　a.-d. A541 $2 Any single　1.75 1.75

2910 A541 $2 Sheet of 3, #a-c　5.00 5.00
Souvenir Sheet
2911 A541 $5 multi　5.50 5.50

Detail: Landscape with the Baptism of the Eunuch, 1636

Antigua & Barbuda 50c
Rembrandt Harmensz van Rijn (1606 - 1669)

Rembrandt (1606-69), Painter A542

Designs: 50c, Landscape with the Baptism of the Eunuch. 75c, Landscape with a Coach. $1, River Landscape with Ruins. $2, Landscape with a Castle.
No. 2916, $2: a, The Holy Family (Joseph at table). b, The Good Samaritan Arriving at the Inn. c, Rebecca Taking Leave of Her Family. d, The Holy Family (Madonna and Child).
No. 2917, $2 — Samson Posting the Riddle to the Wedding Guests: a, Woman with beads in hair. b, Three men. c, Two men. d, Woman holding glass.
No. 2918, $5, Self-portrait. No. 2919, $5, Rembrandt's Mother.

2006, Dec. 20　　　　　**Perf. 12¼x12**
2912-2915 A542　Set of 4　5.00 5.00
Sheets of 4, #a-d
2916-2917 A542　Set of 2　13.50 13.50
Imperf
Size: 70x100mm
2918-2919 A542　Set of 2　9.00 9.00

©2006 King Features Syndicate, Inc./Fleischer Studios Inc. TM Hearst Holdings, Inc./Fleischer Studios

Betty Boop — A543

No. 2920, vert. — Background color: a, Yellow. b, Green. c, Red violet. d, Orange. e, Blue green. f, Purple.
No. 2921: a, Text, "Betty Boop" and stars. b, Betty Boop and cat.

2006, Dec. 20　　　　　**Perf. 14¼**
2920 A543 $1.50 Sheet of 6, #a-f 7.50 7.50
Souvenir Sheet
2921 A543　$3 Sheet of 2　5.00 5.00

Back to the Moon

Space Achievements — A544

No. 2922: a, JSC Shuttle mission simulator. b, STS-1 prime crew in classroom. c, STS-1 Columbia on launch pad. d, Launch of Columbia. e, Columbia landing at Edwards Air Force Base. f, Columbia on runway.
No. 2923, $3: a, Molniya 8K78M launch vehicle. b, Luna 9 flight apparatus. c, Moon

images transmitted by Luna 9. d, Luna 9 capsule.
No. 2924, $3: a, Apollo crew boards transfer van. b, Handshake after Apollo-Soyuz linkup. c, Display of Apollo-Soyuz plaque. d, Recovery of Apollo command module.
No. 2925, $6, Artist's conception of NASA spaceship to orbit Moon. No. 2926, $6, Calipso Satellite. No. 2927, $6, Space Station Mir.

2006　　　　　**Perf. 12¾**
2922 A544 $2 Sheet of 6, #a-f　10.00 10.00
Sheets of 4, #a-d
2923-2924 A544　Set of 2　21.00 21.00
Souvenir Sheets
2925-2927 A544　Set of 3　16.00 16.00

Christmas — A545

Ornaments: 30c, Ball. 90c, Star. $1, Bell. $1.50, Christmas tree.
No. 2932: a, Ball. b, Star. c, Bell. d, Christmas tree.
$6, Santa Claus at beach.

2006　　　　　**Perf. 13½**
2928-2931 A545　Set of 4　3.00 3.00
2932 A545 $2 Sheet of 4, #a-d　6.75 6.75
Souvenir Sheet
2933 A545 $6 multi　6.00 6.00

WORLD SCOUTING 1907-2007

ANTIGUA & BARBUDA $4

Scouting, Cent. — A546

Scout emblem at: $4, UL. $6, LR.

2007, Jan. 18　　　　　**Perf. 13½**
2934 A546 $4 multi　4.00 4.00
Souvenir Sheet
2935 A546 $6 multi　6.00 6.00
No. 2934 was printed in sheets of 3.

Antigua & Barbuda

Christopher Columbus (1451-1506), Explorer — A547

Designs: 75c, Map of North and South America, Columbus on bended knee. 90c, Portrait of Columbus. $2, Portrait, diff. $3, Portrait, diff.
$6, Columbus and ships.

2007, Jan. 18　　　　　**Perf. 13¼**
2936-2939 A547　Set of 4　7.00 7.00
Souvenir Sheet
2940 A547 $6 multi　6.00 6.00

Miniature Sheets

John F. Kennedy Joins the Navy (1941-1945)
USN

Pres. John F. Kennedy (1917-63) — A548

No. 2941, $3: a, Wearing naval ensign dress uniform. b, With crew. c, On PT-109. d, Wearing light jacket in South Pacific.
No. 2942, $3: a, Campaigning on crutches. b, Wearing t-shirt. c, With John F. Fitzgerald and Joseph P. Kennedy. d, Celebrating victory with sister.

Sheets of 4, #a-d
2007, Jan. 18　　　　　**Litho.**
2941-2942 A548　Set of 2　22.00 22.00

Guridoma sp.

Mushrooms of the Caribbean
$6
Antigua & Barbuda

Mushrooms — A549

No. 2943: a, Cantharellus cibarius. b, Auricularia auricula-judae. c, Mycena acicula. d, Peziza vesiculosa.
$6, Pleurotus djamor.

2007, Apr. 2　**Litho.**　**Perf. 14¼**
2943 A549 $2 Sheet of 4, #a-d　8.00 8.00
Souvenir Sheet
2944 A549 $6 multi　6.00 6.00

Butterflies — A550

Designs: 75c, Figure-of-eight. 90c, Tiger pierid. $1, Purple mort bleu. $4, Mosaic.
No. 2949: a, Small lacewing. b, Clorinde. c, Common morpho. d, White peacock.
$5, Grecian shoemaker.

2007, Apr. 2
2945-2948 A550　Set of 4　7.00 7.00
2949 A550 $2 Sheet of 4, #a-d　6.00 6.00
Souvenir Sheet
2950 A550 $5 multi　5.75 5.75

Alamanda

Antigua & Barbuda 75c

Flowers — A551

Designs: 75c, Allamanda. 90c, Bidens sulphurea. $1, Alstromeria caryophyflacea. $4, Bougainvillea.
No. 2955, $2, horiz.: a, Canna limbata. b, Gazania rigens. c, Gloriosa rothschildiana. d, Hibiscus sinensis.

No. 2956, $3, horiz.: a, Oncidium flexuosum. b, Paphiopedilum pinocchio. c, Cattleyopsis lindenii. d, Cattleyopsis cubensis.
No. 2957, $6, Caesalpinia pulcherrima. No. 2958, $6, Osmoglossum pulchellum.

2007, Apr. 2
2951-2954	A551	Set of 4	7.00	7.00

Sheets of 4, #a-d
2955-2956	A551	Set of 2	19.00	19.00

Souvenir Sheets
2957-2958	A551	Set of 2	11.00	11.00

Cricket Players — A552

Designs: 25c, Kenneth Benjamin. 30c, Anderson Roberts. 90c, Ridley Jacobs. $1, Curtly Ambrose. $1.50, Richard Richardson. $5, Sir Vivian Richards.

2007, Apr. 5   **Perf. 12¾**
2959-2963	A552	Set of 5	3.75	3.75

Souvenir Sheet
2964	A552	$5 multi	6.00	6.00

Wedding of Queen Elizabeth II and Prince Philip, 60th Anniv. A553

No. 2965: a, Couple. b, Wedding sandals. $6, Couple, vert.

2007, May 1   **Perf. 14**
2965	A553	$1.50 Pair, #a-b	3.00	3.00

Souvenir Sheet
2966	A553	$6 multi	6.00	6.00

No. 2965 was printed in sheets containing three of each stamp.

Painted Fans by Qi Baishi (1864-1957) — A554

No. 2967, horiz.: a, Camellias and butterfly. b, Two Shrimp and Arrowhead Leaves. c, Gourd and Ladybug. d, Bird. e, Landscape. f, Five Shrimp.
No. 2968: a, Chrysanthemums. b, Maple Leaves.
$6, Wisteria.

2007, May 1   **Perf. 14¼**
2967	A554	$1.50 Sheet of 6, #a-f	7.50	7.50
2968	A554	$3 Sheet of 2, #a-b	6.00	6.00

Souvenir Sheet
2969	A554	$6 multi	6.00	6.00

Miniature Sheet

Ferrari Automobiles — A555

No. 2970: a, 1969 365 GTS4. b, 2005 Superamerica. c, 1990 F1 90. d, 1976 400 Automatic. e, 1954 250 GT Coupe. f, 1960 156 F2. g, 1972 312 P. h, 1956 D 50.

2007, June 4   **Perf. 13¼**
2970	A555	$1.40 Sheet of 8, #a-h	10.00	10.00

Concorde — A556

No. 2971, $1.50 — Concorde O1: a, On ground, red frame. b, In air, green frame. c, On ground, blue violet frame. d, In air, red frame. e, On ground, green frame. f, In air, blue violet frame.
No. 2972, $1.50 — Concorde in flight and: a, Millennium Wheel, green denomination. b, Sydney Opera House, black denomination. c, Millennium Wheel, red violet denomination. d, Sydney Opera House, red orange denomination. e, Millennium Wheel, black denomination. f, Sydney Opera House, blue denomination.

2007, June 20   **Perf. 12¾**
Sheets of 6, #a-f
2971-2972	A556	Set of 2	17.50	17.50

First Helicopter Flight, Cent. — A557

No. 2973, horiz.: a, NH 90. b, BO 105, black denomination at LR. c, NH 90. d, AS-61 over water. e, BO 105, black denomination at LL. f, AS-61 from below.
$6, UH-1 Iroquois.

2007, June 20   **Perf. 12¾**
2973	A557	$1.50 Sheet of 6, #a-f	9.25	9.25

Souvenir Sheet
2974	A557	$6 multi	6.75	6.75

Pope Benedict XVI — A558

2007, July 30   **Perf. 13¾**
2975	A558	$1.40 multi	1.50	1.50

Printed in sheets of 8.

Miniature Sheet

Elvis Presley (1935-77) — A559

No. 2967 — Presley: a, Wearing black jacket. b, Facing left, wearing striped shirt, brown background. c, Wearing jacket and holding guitar. d, Facing forward, wearing striped shirt, brown background. e, Wearing red shirt. f, Holding guitar, purple background.

2007, July 30   **Perf. 13¼**
2976	A559	$1.50 Sheet of 6, #a-f	11.00	11.00

Princess Diana (1961-97) — A560

No. 2977 — Princess Diana wearing: a, Beige suit. b, Lilac dress. c, Purple jacket with black-edged collar. d, Hat.
$6, White robe.

2007, July 30
2977	A560	$2 Sheet of 4, #a-d	7.50	7.50

Souvenir Sheet
2978	A560	$6 multi	5.75	5.75

Flora — A561

Designs: 15c, Bird of paradise. 20c, Seaside mahoe. 30c, Hibiscus. 50c, Agave. 70c, Barringtonia tree. 75c, Coconut tree. 90c, Mesquite tree, horiz. $1, Tamarind tree. $1.50, Black willow flowers, horiz. $1.80, Baobab tree, horiz. $2, Petrea volubilis. $2.50, Opuntia cochenillifera, horiz. $5, Locust fruit, horiz. $10, Barbuda black warri. $20, Castor oil plant.

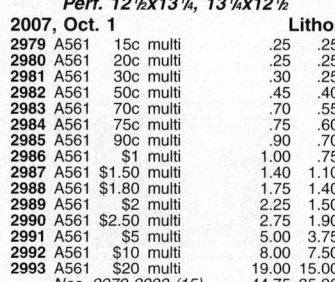

Perf. 12½x13¼, 13¼x12½
2007, Oct. 1   **Litho.**
2979	A561	15c multi	.25	.25
2980	A561	20c multi	.25	.25
2981	A561	30c multi	.30	.25
2982	A561	50c multi	.45	.40
2983	A561	70c multi	.70	.55
2984	A561	75c multi	.75	.60
2985	A561	90c multi	.90	.70
2986	A561	$1 multi	1.00	.75
2987	A561	$1.50 multi	1.40	1.10
2988	A561	$1.80 multi	1.75	1.40
2989	A561	$2 multi	2.25	1.50
2990	A561	$2.50 multi	2.75	1.90
2991	A561	$5 multi	5.00	3.75
2992	A561	$10 multi	8.00	7.50
2993	A561	$20 multi	19.00	15.00
		Nos. 2979-2993 (15)	44.75	35.90

Miniature Sheet

Intl. Holocaust Remembrance Day — A562

No. 2994 — United Nations delegates, each $1.40: a, John W. Ashe, Antigua & Barbuda. b, Alfred Capelle, Marshall Islands. c, Masao Nakayama, Micronesia. d, Gilles Noghes, Monaco. e, Baatar Choisuren, Mongolia. f, Filipe Chidumo, Mozambique. g, Marlene Moses, Nauru. h, Franciscus Majoor, Netherlands.

2007, Oct. 25   **Perf. 13¼**
2994	A562	Sheet of 8, #a-h	10.00	10.00

Christmas A563

Designs: 30c, Stylized map of Antigua & Barbuda, sailboat, candy canes. 90c, Dancers, sailboat, decorated palm tree. $1, Decorated cake. $1.50, Woman in costume.

2007, Nov. 5   **Perf. 14¾x14**
2995-2998	A563	Set of 4	2.75	2.75

Hospice and Palliative Care A564

Emblem of Hospice Antigua & Barbuda and: No. 2999, 30c, Clock. No. 3000, 30c, Hands.

2007, Dec. 27   **Perf. 13¼**
2999-3000	A564	Set of 2	.85	.85

National Heroes — A565

Designs: No. 3001, 90c, King Court (1691-1736), slave rebellion leader. No. 3002, 90c, Dame Georgianna E. (Nellie) Robinson (1880-1972), educator. $1, Sir Vivian Richards, cricket player. $1.50, Sir Vere Cornwall Bird, Sr. (1909-99), first Prime Minister.

2008, Mar. 7   Litho.   Perf. 12¾
3001-3004 A565   Set of 4   4.00 4.00

World Glaucoma Day — A566

Designs: 30c, Person applying glaucoma eyedrops. 50c, Normal and glaucomatous optic nerves. $1, Braille writing.

2008, Mar. 7   Perf. 13¼
3005-3007 A566   Set of 3   2.25 2.25

32nd America's Cup Yacht Races, Off Valencia, Spain — A567

No. 3008 — Various yachts with text "32nd America's Cup" in: a, $1.20, Yellow. b, $1.80, White. c, $3, Blue. d, $5, Orange.

2008, Mar. 25   Perf. 12½
3008 A567   Block of 4, #a-d   8.25 8.25

Miniature Sheet

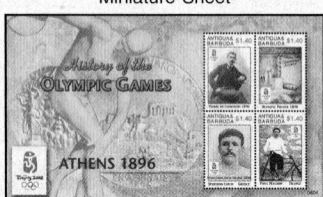

2008 Summer Olympics, Beijing — A568

No. 3009, each $1.40: a, Pierre de Coubertin. b, Poster for 1896 Athens Olympic Games. c, Spiridon Louis, 1896 marathon gold medalist. d, Paul Masson, 1896 cycling gold medalist.

2008, Mar. 25   Perf. 12¾
3009 A568   Sheet of 4, #a-d   4.25 4.25

2008 World Stamp Championship, Israel — A569

2008, May 14   Imperf.
3010 A569 $6 multi   4.75 4.75

Visit of Pope Benedict XVI to United States A570

2008, June 18   Perf. 13¼
3011 A570 $2 multi   1.75 1.75
   Printed in sheets of 4.

Miniature Sheet

Army Induction of Elvis Presley, 50th Anniv. — A571

No. 3012 — Presley wearing: a, Dress uniform and cap. b, Dress uniform, no cap. c, Army fatigues and cap. d, Dress uniform with shoulder insignia and cap.

2008, June 18
3012 A571 $2 Sheet of 4, #a-d   6.50 6.50

Space Achievements — A572

No. 3013, $1.50, vert. — Vanguard I: a, Against black background, with five rods showing. b, Against white and green background. c, Against black background, with six rods showing.
No. 3014, $1.50: a, Explorer III and equipment, vert. b, Explorer III and Earth, vert. c, Diagram of Van Allen radiation belts.
No. 3015, $2, vert. — Vanguard I and: a, Black background. b, Multicolored background.
No. 3016, $2, vert. — Explorer III and: a, Red and green background. b, Black background.
No. 3017, $6, Vanguard I. No. 3018, $6, Explorer III.

2008, July 29   Perf. 13¼
   Horiz. Strips of 3, #a-c
3013-3014 A572   Set of 2   9.00 9.00
   Pairs, #a-b
3015-3016 A572   Set of 2   8.00 8.00
   Souvenir Sheets
3017-3018 A572   Set of 2   12.00 12.00
   Nos. 3013-3014 were each printed in sheets containing two strips. Nos. 3015-3016 were each printed in sheets containing two pairs.

Miniature Sheets

Muhammad Ali, Boxer — A573

No. 3019 — Ali with words or letters in background: a, "ws" at UR. b, "learned" above denomination. c, "is so ugly" at UR. d, "should donate" at UR. e, "greates" at UR. f, "hat" at UR.
No. 3020 — Ali, each $2: a, Hitting punching bag. b, Wearing robe. c, With bare shoulders. d, Wearing protective headgear.

2008, Sept. 29   Perf. 11½
3019 A573 $1.50 Sheet of 6, #a-f 7.50 7.50
                           Perf. 13¼
3020 A573   Sheet of 4, #a-d   6.50 6.50
   No. 3020 contains four 37x50mm stamps.

Star Trek — A574

No. 3021: a, Capt. James Kirk and Mr. Spock. b, Chief Engineer Scott, Dr. Leonard McCoy, Kirk and Spock. c, Lt. Uhura, Spock. d, Actors on planetary city set. e, Uhura. f, Scott.
No. 3022: a, McCoy. b, Spock. c, Kirk. d, Hikaru Sulu.

2008, Sept. 29   Perf. 11½
3021 A574 $1.50 Sheet of 6, #a-f 8.00 8.00
                           Perf. 13¼
3022 A574 $2 Sheet of 4, #a-
                             d   7.50 7.50
   No. 3022 contains four 50x37mm stamps.

Miniature Sheet

Pres. John F. Kennedy (1917-63) — A575

No. 3023 — Kennedy: a, Looking right. b, Looking forward, curtains in background. c, Looking forward, smiling with teeth showing. d, Looking right with hand at chin.

2008, Dec. 18   Perf. 13¼
3023 A575 $2 Sheet of 4, #a-d   6.75 6.75

Miniature Sheet

Marilyn Monroe (1926-62), Actress — A576

No. 3024 — Monroe wearing: a, Orange sweater, with arm raised. b, Orange sweater, arms at side. c, Pink sweater. d, Purple sweater.

2008, Dec. 18
3024 A576 $2 Sheet of 4, #a-d   8.50 8.50

Christmas A577

Stained-glass windows: 30c, Holy Family. 90c, Infant Jesus in manger. $1, Madonna and Child, vert. $1.50, Sts. Elizabeth and John the Baptist, vert.

2009, Jan. 2   Perf. 14¾x14, 14x14¾
3025-3028 A577   Set of 4   3.00 3.00

Miniature Sheet

China 2009 World Stamp Exhibition — A578

No. 3029: a, Baseball. b, Beach volleyball. c, Artistic gymnastics. d, Judo.

2009, Jan. 5   Perf. 11¼x11½
3029 A578 $1.40 Sheet of 4, #a-
                             d   4.50 4.50

Miniature Sheet

Pres. Abraham Lincoln (1809-65) — A579

No. 3030: a, Lincoln's first inaugural address, 1861. b, Lincoln, flag. c, Lincoln's second inaugural address, 1865. d, Lincoln at right, crowd at second inaugural.

2009, Jan. 5   Perf. 11½x11¼
3030 A579 $2 Sheet of 4, #a-d   7.25 7.25

Inauguration of US Pres. Barack Obama — A580

Pres. Obama facing: $2.75, Right. $10, Left.

2009, Jan. 20   **Perf. 12¼x11¾**
3031 A580 $2.75 multi   2.75 .275
Souvenir Sheet
Perf. 13¼x13½
3032 A580 $10 multi   7.75 7.75

No. 3031 was printed in sheets of 4. No. 3032 contains one 37x51mm stamp.

New Year 2009 (Year of the Ox) A581

2009, Jan. 26   **Perf. 11½x12**
3033 A581 $1 multi   1.25 1.25
Printed in sheets of 4.

A582

A583

2009, Apr. 10   **Perf. 13½x13¼**
3034 A582 $1 multi   1.10 1.10
Souvenir Sheet
Perf. 13
3035 A583 $5 multi   4.75 4.75

No. 3034 was printed in sheets of 8.

Miniature Sheet

Elvis Presley (1935-77) — A584

No. 3036 — Presley wearing: a, Hat. b, Suit with handkerchief in pocket. c, Black shirt and pants. d, Pink, white and black windbreaker. e, Blue shirt and lei. f, Suit without handkerchief.

2009, Apr. 14   **Perf. 14x14¼**
3036 A584 $1.50 Sheet of 6, #a-f 7.75 7.75

Miniature Sheets

A585

China 2009 World Stamp Exhibition — A586

No. 3037 — Landmarks in China: a, Bell Tower, Xian. b, St. Sophia Church, Harbin. c, Great Hall of the People, Chongqing. d, Fenghua Bridge, Tianjin.
No. 3038 — First emperor of China: a, Qin Shi Huang (259-210 B.C.). b, Horses of Terracotta Army. c, Soldiers of Terracotta Army. d, Excavated Terracotta Army.

2009, June 29   **Litho.**   **Perf. 12**
3037 A585 $1.40 Sheet of 4, #a-d   5.50 5.50
Perf. 12½x12¾
3038 A586 $1.40 Sheet of 4, #a-d   5.50 5.50

A587

2009, July 9   **Perf. 14x15**
3039 A587 $4 multi   3.50 3.50

Miniature Sheets

Dogs — A588

No. 3040, $2.50 — Labrador retrievers: a, Puppy in canoe. b, Two puppies at window. c, Two puppies with stick. d, Puppy in bucket.
No. 3041, $2.50 — Dachshunds: a, Dog and carrying case. b, Dog and flowers. c, Two dogs in flower box. d, Dog near flower pot.

2009, Aug. 13   **Perf. 12**
Sheets of 4, #a-d
3040-3041 A588   Set of 2   19.00 19.00

Michael Jackson (1958-2009), Singer — A590

No. 3042 — Jackson: a, Holding microphone, wearing black coat with gold trim. b, Wearing black coat with gold trim, not holding microphone. c, Wearing red and black shirt. d, Wearing jacket with eagle and shield.
No. 3043 — Jackson: a, Wearing black pants, white above red orange frame at top of stamp. b, Wearing pants with buckles along leg, white above red orange frame at top of stamp. c, As "b," with black above red orange frame. d, As "a," with black above red orange frame.
$6, Jackson singing.

2009   **Litho.**   **Perf. 11¼x11½**
3042 A589 $2.50 Sheet of 4, #a-d   9.50 9.50
Perf. 12x11½
3043 A590 $2.50 Sheet of 4, #a-d   9.50 9.50
Souvenir Sheet
Perf. 13¼
3044 A590 $6 multi   4.75 4.75
Issued: Nos. 3042-3043, 9/30; No. 3044, 12/3. No. 3044 contains one 37x50mm stamp.

Meeting of US Pres. Barack Obama and Pope Benedict XVI — A591

No. 3045, vert.: a, Pres. Obama. b, Pope Benedict XVI. c, Michelle Obama.
$6, Pope Benedict XVI and Pres. Obama.

2009, Nov. 4   **Perf. 11¼x11½**
3045 A591 $2.75 Sheet of 3, #a-c   7.50 7.50
Souvenir Sheet
Perf. 11½x12
3046 A591 $6 multi   5.75 5.75

Chinese Aviation, Cent. — A592

No. 3047 — Aerobatic team: a, Six airplanes with blue, white and red contrails. b, Six airplanes flying right in double triangle formation. c, Six airplanes flying left in diagonal line formation. d, Five airplanes.
$6, J-7GB.

2009, Nov. 12   **Perf. 14**
3047 A592 $2 Sheet of 4, #a-d   6.75 6.75
Souvenir Sheet
Perf. 14¼
3048 A592 $6 multi   5.00 5.00

Aeropex 2009 Intl. Philatelic Exhibition, Biejing. No. 3048 contains one 50x37mm stamp.

First Man on the Moon, 40th Anniv. — A593

No. 3049: a, Apollo 11 patch, US flag on Moon. b, Lunar Module on Moon. c, Passive seismic experiment package. d, Apollo 11 on launch pad.
$6, Apollo 11 Command and Service Modules.

2009, Nov. 13   **Perf. 12¾x12½**
3049 A593 $2.50 Sheet of 4, #a-d   9.50 9.50
Souvenir Sheet
Perf. 12¾x13
3050 A593 $6 multi   5.50 5.50
Intl. Year of Astronomy.

Souvenir Sheets

A594

A595

A596

Elvis Presley (1935-77) — A597

2009, Nov. 26   *Perf. 13¼*
3051 A594 $6 multi   5.50   5.50
3052 A595 $6 multi   5.50   5.50
3053 A596 $6 multi   5.50   5.50
3054 A597 $6 multi   5.50   5.50
    Nos. 3051-3054 (4)   22.00 22.00

Worldwide Fund for Nature
(WWF) — A598

No. 3055 — Caribbean coots: a, Pair in water. b, Pair taking off. c, Pair and chick. d, Adult and chick.

2009, Dec. 3   *Perf. 13¼*
3055   Strip of 4   8.50   8.50
a.-d.   A598 $2.65 Any single   2.00   2.00
e.   Miniature sheet, 2 each
    #3055a-3055d   20.00 20.00

Christmas
A599

Christmas light displays: 90c, Candles. $1, Palm tree and reindeer. $1.80, Bells. $3, Nativity scene, horiz.

2009, Dec. 3   *Perf. 14x14¾, 14¾x14*
3056-3059 A599   Set of 4   5.00   5.00

Sir Vere Cornwall Bird, Sr. (1909-99), First Chief Minister, Premier and Prime Minister — A600

Bird: 30c, In chair. 75c, With blue, white and red stripes in background. 90c, Wearing red hat. $1.50, With building in background.
No. 3064: a, Like 75c. b, Like 30c. c, Like 90c. d, Like $1.50.
$6, Bird, map of Antigua with flag.

2009, Dec. 8   *Perf. 11¼x11½*
3060-3063 A600   Set of 4   3.00   3.00
3064 A600 $2.50 Sheet of 4, #a-
    d   8.00   8.00

Souvenir Sheet
Perf. 12x11½
3065 A600 $6 multi   5.00   5.00

Birds
A601

Designs: $1.20, Glossy ibis. $1.80, Green-winged teal. No. 3068, $3, California clapper rail. $5, Cattle egret, vert.
No. 3070: a, Green heron. b, Common ground dove. c, White-tailed hawk. d, Black-faced grassquit.
No. 3071, $3: a, Bananaquit. b, Osprey.

Perf. 11½x11¼, 11¼x11½
2009, Dec. 8
3066-3069 A601   Set of 4   8.75   8.75
Perf. 11½x12
3070 A601 $2.50 Sheet of 4, #a-
    d   8.00   8.00
Souvenir Sheet
3071 A601 $3 Sheet of 2, #a-
    b   5.00   5.00

Souvenir Sheet

New Year 2010 (Year of the Tiger) — A602

No. 3072 — Chinese bronze tigers of: a, Western Han Dynasty. b, Shang Dynasty.

2010, Jan. 4   *Perf. 11½x12*
3072 A602 $5 Sheet of 2, #a-b   7.75 7.75

Ferrari Automobiles and Their Parts — A603

No. 3073, $1.25: a, Engine of 1960 246 P F1. b, 1960 246 P F1.
No. 3074, $1.25: a, Engine of 1964 158 F1. b, 1964 158 F1.
No. 3075, $1.25: a, Interior of 1966 365P Speciale. b, 1966 365P Speciale.
No. 3076, $1.25: a, Air foil and rear wheel of 1968 312 F1-68. b, 1968 312 F1-68.

2010, Feb. 22   *Perf. 12*
Vert. Pairs, #a-b
3073-3076 A603   Set of 4   8.25 8.25
Nos. 3073-3076 exist imperf. Value, set of pairs $25.

Whales and Dolphins
A604

Designs: $1.20, Risso's dolphin. $1.80, Common dolphin. $3, Humpback whale. $5, Sperm whale.
No. 3081: a, Shortsnout dolphin. b, Spotted dolphin. c, Cuvier's beaked whale. d, Shortfin pilot whale. e, Gulf Stream beaked whale. f, Rough-toothed dolphin.

2010, Feb. 23   *Litho.*
3077-3080 A604   Set of 4   9.00   9.00
3081 A604 $2 Sheet of 6, #a-f   10.00 10.00

Miniature Sheets

A605

A606

No. 3072 — Chinese bronze tigers of: a,

Princess Diana (1961-97) — A607

No. 3082 — Diana wearing: a, White dress. b, Pink dress. c, Lilac suit. d, White dress, holding flowers.
No. 3083 — Diana wearing tiara and: a, White dress, two earrings visible. b, Red dress, earring with black stone. c, Red dress, pearl earring. d, White dress with high collar.
No. 3084 — Diana wearing: a, Lei. b, Lilac dress. c, Blue and white dress and hat. d, Red orange hat and dress.

2010   *Litho.*   *Perf. 12x11½*
3082 A605 $2 Sheet of 4,
    #a-d   6.50   6.50
3083 A606 $2.75 Sheet of 4,
    #a-d   8.25   8.25
3084 A607 $2.75 Sheet of 4,
    #a-d   8.25   8.25
    Nos. 3082-3084 (3)   23.00 23.00
Issued: No. 3082, 2/23; Nos. 3083-3084, 5/10.

Butterflies
A608

Designs: $1.20, Common buckeye. $1.80, Red postman. $3, Red admiral. $5, Zebra longwing.
No. 3089: a, Orange sulfur. b, Blue morpho. c, Queen butterfly. d, Zebra swallowtail. e, Malachite. f, Gatekeeper butterfly.

2010, Apr. 14   *Perf. 14*
3085-3088 A608   Set of 4   9.00   9.00
Perf. 14¾x14
3089 A608 $2 Sheet of 6, #a-f   9.50 9.50
No. 3089 contains six 40x30mm stamps.

Sharks
A609

Designs: $1.20, Nurse shark. $1.80, Caribbean reef shark. $3, Tiger shark. $5, Whale shark.
No. 3094: a, Caribbean sharpnose shark. b, Blacktip shark. c, Oceanic whitetip shark. d, Bull shark.

2010, Apr. 14   *Perf. 14*
3090-3093 A609   Set of 4   9.25   9.25
Perf. 14¾x14
3094 A609 $2.75 Sheet of 4, #a-
    d   9.00   9.00
No. 3094 contains four 40x30mm stamps.

Pope John Paul II (1920-2005) A610

2010, May 10   *Perf. 11¼x11½*
3095 A610 $2.75 multi   2.10 2.10
Printed in sheets of 4, with each stamp having slight differences in background.

Boy Scouts of America, Cent. — A611

No. 3096, $2.50: a, Scout at lectern. b, Scouts canoeing.
No. 3097, $2.50: a, Statue of Liberty giving Scout salute. b, Scouts using map and compass.

2010, May 10   **Perf. 13¼**
Pairs, #a-b
3096-3097 A611   Set of 2   7.50 7.50
Nos. 3096 and 3097 each were printed in sheets containing two pairs.

Girl Guides, Cent. — A612

No. 3098: a, Rainbows. b, Brownies. c, Guides. d, Senior Section.
$6, Girl Guides, diff.

2010, May 10   **Perf. 11½x12**
3098 A612 $2.75 Sheet of 4, #a-d   8.50 8.50
Souvenir Sheet
Perf. 11½
3099 A612 $6 multi   4.75 4.75

Miniature Sheet

Expo 2010, Shanghai — A613

No. 3100: a, Dancers, Shanghai Intl. Culture and Art Festival. b, China National Grand Theater, Beijing. c, Rice terraces, Guangxi Province, China. d, Dance performance, Beijing.

2010, May 10   **Perf. 11½**
3100 A613 $1.50 Sheet of 4, #a-d   4.50 4.50

Miniature Sheet

Mother Teresa (1910-97), Humanitarian — A614

No. 3101 — Mother Teresa and: a, Princess Diana. b, Queen Elizabeth II. c, Pres. Ronald Reagan. d, Pope John Paul II.

2010, May 10   **Perf. 11½x12**
3101 A614 $2.50 Sheet of 4, #a-d   7.50 7.50

Miniature Sheet

Pres. John F. Kennedy (1917-63) — A615

No. 3102: a, Sitting in limousine. b, Standing. c, Sitting in rocking chair. d, Behind microphones.

2010, May 10   **Perf. 11¼x11½**
3102 A615 $2.75 Sheet of 4, #a-d   8.25 8.25

Miniature Sheet

Awarding of Nobel Peace Prize to Pres. Barack Obama — A616

No. 3103 — Pres. Obama: a, Holding diploma and medal, blue curtain in background. b, At lectern, with hand closed. c, At lectern, with hand open. d, Holding diploma and medal.

2010, May 10   **Perf. 12x11½**
3103 A616 $2.75 Sheet of 4, #a-d   8.25 8.25

Miniature Sheets

A617

Pres. Abraham Lincoln (1809-65) — A618

Various photographs of Lincoln.

2010, May 10   **Perf. 11¼x11½**
3104 A617 $2.75 Sheet of 4, #a-d   8.25 8.25
3105 A618 $2.75 Sheet of 4, #a-d   8.25 8.25

Miniature Sheets

A619

Elvis Presley (1935-77) — A620

No. 3106: a, Wearing rhinestone-studded jacket, microphone in front of mouth. b, Wearing black open-neck shirt. c, Two portraits. d, Wearing white jacket with lapels and pockets with dark trim.
No. 3107: a, Presley holding guitar, parts of "E" and "L" in background. b, Presley holding guitar, parts of "L" and "V" in background. c, Presley holding guitar, parts of "V" and "7" in background. d, Three portraits.

2010, May 10   **Perf. 13¼**
3106 A619 $2.75 Sheet of 4, #a-d   8.25 8.25
3107 A620 $2.75 Sheet of 4, #a-d   8.25 8.25

Miniature Sheet

Chinese Zodiac Animals — A621

No. 3108: a, Rat. b, Ox. c, Tiger. d, Rabbit. e, Dragon. f, Snake. g, Horse. h, Goat. i, Monkey. j, Cock. k, Dog. l, Pig.

2010, Jan. 4   **Litho.**   **Perf. 12¼**
3108 A621 60c Sheet of 12, #a-l   5.50 5.50

Miniature Sheet

The Three Stooges — A622

No. 3109: a, Moe and Larry with cowboy hats, Curly with pick. b, Moe, Larry and Curly in painter's coveralls. c, Moe and Larry in surgical garb examining Curly. d, Moe and Larry squeezing Curly's neck in giant nutcracker.

2010, Sept. 27   **Litho.**   **Perf. 11½x12**
3109 A622 $2.50 Sheet of 4, #a-d   7.50 7.50

2010 World Cup Soccer Championships, South Africa — A623

No. 3110: a, Maximiliano Pereira. b, John Heitinga. c, Edinson Cavani. d, Mark Van Bommel. e, Martin Caceres. f, Giovanni van Bronckhorst.
No. 3111, $3.50: a, Netherlands Coach Bert van Marwijk. b, Netherlands flag on soccer ball.
No. 3112, $3.50: a, Uruguay Coach Oscar Tabarez. b, Uruguay flag on soccer ball.

2010, Oct. 18   **Perf. 12**
3110 A623 $1.50 Sheet of 6, #a-f   7.75 7.75
Souvenir Sheets of 2, #a-b
3111-3112 A623   Set of 2   11.00 11.00

Henri Dunant (1828-1910), Founder of Red Cross — A624

No. 3113 — Red Cross, scenes from Battle of Solferino and portrait of Dunant in: a, Blue green. b, Brown. c, Lilac. d, Blue gray.
$6, Red Cross, Battle of Solferino, Dunant in lilac.

2010, Dec. 20
3113 A624 $2.50 Sheet of 4, #a-d   8.00 8.00
Souvenir Sheet
3114 A624 $6 multi   4.75 4.75

Cats — A625

No. 3115: a, California spangled cat. b, Siamese cat. c, British shorthair cat. d, Norwegian forest cat. e, Egyptian Mau cat. f, American curl longhair cat.
$6, Manx cat.

2010, Dec. 20
3115 A625 $2.50 Sheet of 6,
　　　　#a-f　　　　12.00 12.00

Souvenir Sheet
3116 A625　$6 multi　　4.50 4.50

No. 3115 contains six 30x40mm stamps.

A626

Pope Benedict XVI — A627

No. 3118 — Pope Benedict XVI and: a, Buff area below "G" in "Antigua," brown area below "U" in "Antigua." b, Red brown area below "IG" of "Antigua," buff area below first "A" in "Antigua." c, Dark brown areas below "ANTIG" of "Antigua." d, Buff areas below first and second "A" of "Antigua."

2010, Dec. 20　Litho.　Perf. 12
3117 A626 $2.75 multi　　2.10 2.10
3118 A627 $2.75 Sheet of 4,
　　　　#a-d　　　　8.50 8.50

No. 3117 issued in sheets of 4.

Souvenir Sheet

New Year 2011 (Year of the Rabbit) — A628

No. 3119: a, Rabbit. b, Chinese character for "rabbit."

2011, Jan. 3
3119 A628 $4 Sheet of 2, #a-b　6.00 6.00

Pandas — A629

No. 3120: a, Panda with mouth open. b, Head of panda. c, Panda eating, large leaf partially covering head. d, Panda eating, diff. $5, Panda, diff.

2011, Jan. 3
3120 A629 $2 Sheet of 4, #a-d　7.00 7.00

Souvenir Sheet
3121 A629　$5 multi　　4.25 4.25

Beijing 2010 Intl. Philatelic Exhibition.

Christmas 2010 — A630

Designs: 30c, Casini Madonna, by Tommaso Masaccio. 75c, Madonna of the Stars, by Tintoretto. 90c, Wall mosaic, Basilica of Sant'Apollinaire Nuovo, Ravenna, Italy. $1.50, The Annunciation, by Fra Angelico.

2011, Jan. 17　Perf. 12¾x12½
3122-3125 A630　Set of 4　2.60 2.60

Engagement of Prince William and Catherine Middleton — A631

Design: No. 3126, Couple.
No. 3127: a, Prince William. b, Middleton.
No. 3128, $6, Prince William wearing striped shirt and necktie, vert. No. 3129, $6, Prince William wearing white shirt and bow tie, vert.

2011, Feb. 14　Perf. 13 Syncopated
3126 A631 $2.50 multi　　1.90 1.90
3127 A631 $2.50 Horiz. pair,
　　　　#a-b　　　　3.75 3.75

Souvenir Sheets
3128-3129 A631　Set of 2　9.00 9.00

No. 3126 printed in sheets of 4. No. 3127 printed in sheets of 2 pairs.

Miniature Sheets

A632

Mohandas K. Gandhi (1869-1948), Indian Nationalist — A633

No. 3130 — Gandhi and: a, Qutub Minar Tower, Delhi. b, Asoka pillar. c, Hyderabad Mosque. d, Taj Mahal.
No. 3131 — Crowd and: a, Profile of Gandhi, robe visible. b, Gandhi looking forward. c, Profile of Gandhi, robe not visible. d, Gandhi looking right.

2011, Mar. 1　Perf. 12
3130 A632 $2.75 Sheet of 4,
　　　　#a-d　　　　8.25 8.25
3131 A633 $2.75 Sheet of 4,
　　　　#a-d　　　　8.25 8.25

2011 Indipex Intl. Philatelic Exhibition, New Delhi

Beatification of Pope John Paul II — A634

No. 3132 — Pope John Paul II: a, Holding crucifix. b, Wearing red stole.
$6, Head of Pope John Paul II.

2011, Apr. 4　Perf. 13 Syncopated
3132 A634 $2 Pair, #a-b　3.00 3.00

Souvenir Sheet
Perf. 12
3133 A634　$6 multi　　4.50 4.50

Miniature Sheets

United States Civil War, 150th Anniv. — A635

No. 3134, $2.50 — Eagle, shield, flags, Generals Henry R. Jackson and Joseph J. Reynolds of Battle of Greenbrier River, Oct. 3, 1861, and: a, Battle map by A. T. McRae, Quitman Guards. b, Skirmish along the Greenbrier river. c, Union forces assembling near Greenbrier River. d, Battle scene.
No. 3135, $2.50 — Eagle, shield, flags, Confederate Secretary of the navy Stephen Mallory, Union Lt. Commander Alexander Murray of Battle of Cockle Creek, Oct. 5, 1861, and: a, Warships of the Atlantic Blockading Squadron. b, Flotilla of Union warships. c, Confederate privateers near Delaware Bay. d, USS Minnesota.
No. 3136, $2.50 — Eagle, shield, flags, Confederate Brigadier General Richard H. Anderson, Union Colonel Harvey Brown of Battle of Santa Rosa Island, Oct. 9, 1861, and: a, Fort Pickens. b, Drawing of Fight at Santa Rosa Island, by John Volck. c, Boats cutting off confederate dispatch galley. d, Col. Brown commanding 3rd U.S. Infantry.

Sheets of 4, #a-d
2011, Apr. 4　Perf. 12
3134-3136 A635　Set of 3　22.50 22.50

Mushrooms — A636

No. 3137: a, Tylopilus potamogeton. b, Amanita campinaranae. c, Cantharellus altratus. d, Tylopilus orsonianus. e, Boletellus ananas. f, Amanita craseoderma.

No. 3138: a, Amanita cyanopus. b, Phyllobolites miniatus. c, Chroogomphus jamaicensis. d, Coltricia cf. montagnei.
No. 3139, $6, Austroboletus rostrupii. No. 3140, $6, Austroboletus festivus.

2011, May 9　　　　Litho.
3137 A636　$2 Sheet of 6,
　　　　#a-f　　　　10.00 10.00
3138 A636 $2.50 Sheet of 4,
　　　　#a-d　　　　7.50 7.50

Souvenir Sheets
3139-3140 A636　Set of 2　9.00 9.00

1997 Visit of Princess Diana To Barbuda — A637

Designs: No. 3141, $10, Princess Diana, her sons, family friend and airplane. No. 3142, $10, Princess Diana.
$50, Princess Diana, horiz.

2011, July 12　　Perf. 12
3141-3142 A637　Set of 2　17.00 17.00

Souvenir Sheet
3143 A637　$50 multi　　37.50 37.50

Nos. 3141-3142 each were issued in sheets of 5.

Wedding of Prince William and Catherine Middleton — A638

No. 3144: a, Prince William wearing cap. b, Middleton, name at left in line. c, Couple.
No. 3145: a, Prince William waving. b, Middleton, name at top in two lines. c, Couple kissing.
$6, Couple, diff.

2011, Aug. 15　　Perf. 13x13¼
3144 A638 $2.50 Sheet of 4,
　　　　#3144a-
　　　　3144b, 2
　　　　#3144c　　7.50 7.50
3145 A638 $2.50 Sheet of 4,
　　　　#3145a-
　　　　3145b, 2
　　　　#3145c　　7.50 7.50

Souvenir Sheet
Perf. 12
3146 A638　$6 multi　　4.50 4.50

Shells — A639

No. 3147: a, Bleeding tooth nerite. b, Pen shell. c, Banded tulip shell. d, Chank shell. e, Flame helmet. f, Atlantic partridge tun.

No. 3148: a, Pink conch. b, Sunrise tellin. c, Flamingo tongue. d, Queen's helmet.

No. 3149, $6, King's helmet. No. 3150, $6, Triton's trumpet, horiz.

Perf. 13¼x13, 13x13¼
2011, Aug. 15
3147 A639 $2 Sheet of 6, #a-f 9.00 9.00
3148 A639 $2.75 Sheet of 4, #a-d 8.25 8.25

Souvenir Sheets
3149-3150 A639 Set of 2 9.00 9.00

Pres. John F. Kennedy (1917-63) — A640

No. 3151, vert. — Pres. Kennedy: a, Inspecting Mercury capsule, Feb. 22, 1962. b, On Cape Canaveral tour, Nov. 16, 1963. c, At Saturn rocket briefing, Nov. 16, 1963. d, At Cape Canaveral, pointing, Nov. 16, 1963.

$6, Kennedy and flag.

2011, Sept. 9   Perf. 12
3151 A640 $2.75 Sheet of 4, #a-d 8.25 8.25

Souvenir Sheet
Perf. 12¾
3152 A640 $6 multi 4.50 4.50

No. 3151 contains four 30x40mm stamps.

Pres. Barack Obama, 50th Birthday — A641

No. 3153 — Pres. Obama: a, Looking right, wearing dark tie and flag lapel pin. b, Wearing light patterned tie, standing in front of microphone. c, Wearing dark patterned tie, standing in front of microphones. d, Looking left.

$6, Pres. Obama, diff.

2011, Sept. 9   Perf. 13 Syncopated
3153 A641 $2.75 Sheet of 4, #a-d 8.25 8.25

Souvenir Sheet
3154 A641 $6 multi 5.00 5.00

Princess Diana (1961-97) — A642

No. 3155 — Princess Diana: a, Seated on sofa. b, Wearing beige and white dress. c, Wearing white dress. d, With Prince Charles. $6, Princess Diana, horiz.

2011, Sept. 9   Perf. 12
3155 A642 $2.75 Sheet of 4, #a-d 8.25 8.25

Souvenir Sheet
Perf. 12¾
3156 A642 $6 multi 4.50 4.50

No. 3156 contains one 51x38mm stamp.

First Man in Space, 50th Anniv. — A643

No. 3157, $2.75: a, Liftoff of Vostok 1. b, Russian tracking ship named after Yuri Gagarin. c, Vostok 1 mission emblem. d, Alan Shepard, first American astronaut.

No. 3158, $2.75: a, Map of Gagarin's flightpath. b, Vostok 8K72K rocket. c, Gagarin, first cosmonaut. d, Virgil "Gus" Grissom, American astronaut, and rocket.

No. 3159, $6, Gagarin, diff. No. 3160, $6, Vostok spacecraft and Earth.

Sheets of 4, #a-d
2011, Sept. 9   Perf. 12
3157-3158 A643 Set of 2 16.50 16.50

Souvenir Sheets
3159-3160 A643 Set of 2 9.00 9.00

A644

A645

A646

Elvis Presley (1935-77) — A647

No. 3161 — Presley: a, With building in background. b, On train steps. c, On motorcycle.

No. 3162 — Presley wearing: a, Army dress uniform. b, Dress uniform, standing next to railing. c, Battle fatigues. d, Battle fatigues, reading letter.

No. 3163 — Presley wearing: a, Glasses and red shirt. b, Suit, facing right. c, Sequined suit, facing forward. d, Suit, facing left.

No. 3164 — Presley: a, On stage. b, Wearing sweater.

2011, Sept. 9   Perf. 13 Syncopated
3161 A644 $2 Sheet of 3, #a-c 4.50 4.50
3162 A645 $2.75 Sheet of 4, #a-d 8.25 8.25
3163 A646 $2.75 Sheet of 4, #a-d 8.25 8.25
Nos. 3161-3163 (3) 21.00 21.00

Souvenir Sheet
3164 A647 $3 Sheet of 2, #a-b 4.50 4.50

Miniature Sheets

A648

Visit of Pope Benedict XVI to Germany — A649

No. 3165 — Pope Benedict XVI: a, With church spires behind head. b, With arm extended, crucifix visible, hand in front of church steeple. c, With mountain behind head, chuch steeple and building with flowers at right.

No. 3166 — Pope Benedict XVI: a, Facing right, church with red roof at right. b, With arm extended, no crucifix visible, chuch at right. c, With Brandenburg Gate at left.

2011, Aug. 3   Litho.   Perf. 12
3165 A648 $3 Sheet of 3, #a-c 6.75 6.75
3166 A649 $3 Sheet of 3, #a-c 6.75 6.75

Fish — A650

No. 3167, $3.50: a, Queen angelfish. b, Ocean surgeonfish. c, Rock beauty. d, Gray angelfish.

No. 3168, $3.50: a, Foureye butterflyfish. b, French grunt. c, French angelfish. d, Spotfin butterflyfish.

No. 3169, $9, Great barracuda (80x30mm). No. 3170, $9, Banded butterflyfish (40x40mm).

Sheets of 4, #a-d
2011, Sept. 30   Perf. 12
3167-3168 A650 Set of 2 21.00 21.00

Souvenir Sheets
3169-3170 A650 Set of 2 13.50 13.50

Hu Jintao, President of People's Republic of China — A651

Pres. Hu and flag of People's Republic of China: $3, At lower left. $6, In background.

2011, Oct. 24
3171 A651 $3 multi 2.25 2.25

Souvenir Sheet
3172 A651 $6 multi 4.50 4.50

China 2011 Intl. Philatelic Exhibition, Wuxi (No. 3172).

Christmas
A652

Paintings: 30c, Madonna and Child with Angels, by Giottino. 75c, The Annunciation and Two Saints, by Simone Martini. $1.50, Paradise, by Giusto de' Menabuoi. $3, Madonna, by Vitale da Bologna.

2011, Nov. 15   Perf. 14
3173-3176 A652 Set of 4 4.25 4.25

Miniature Sheet

Chinese Zodiac Animals — A653

No. 3177: a, Rat. b, Ox. c, Tiger. d, Rabbit. e, Dragon. f, Snake. g, Horse. h, Sheep. i, Monkey. j, Rooster. k, Dog. l, Boar.

Litho. With Foil Application
2011, Nov. 15   Perf. 13 Syncopated
3177 A653 65c Sheet of 12, #a-l   5.75 5.75

Pres. Abraham Lincoln (1809-65) — A654

No. 3178: a, Lincoln without beard. b, Campaign poster for Lincoln and Hannibal Hamlin. c, Eyes and nose of Lincoln. d, Linoln with beard.
$6, Lincoln, vert.

2011, Dec. 19   Litho.   Perf. 12
3178 A654 $2.75 Sheet of 4,
               #a-d   8.25 8.25
Souvenir Sheet
3179 A654 $6 multi   4.50 4.50

No. 3179 contains one 30x50mm stamp.

Sinking of the Titanic, Cent. — A655

No. 3180 — Titanic passengers: a, Joseph Bruce Ismay (1862-1937), chairman of White Star Line. b, William Stead (1849-1912), journalist. c, Benjamin Guggenheim (1865-1912), businessman. d, Thomas Andrews (1873-1912), naval architect of Titanic.
$9, Titanic, horiz.

2012, Jan. 25
3180 A655 $3.50 Sheet of 4,
               #a-d   10.50 10.50
Souvenir Sheet
3181 A655 $9 multi   6.75 6.75

No. 3181 contains one 50x30mm stamp.

Reign of Queen Elizabeth II, 60th Anniv. — A656

No. 3182 — Queen Elizabeth II as young girl: a, At piano. b, Color photograph, looking left. c, In meadow, looking right. d, Near house and flowers.
$9, Queen Elizabeth II and flowers, vert.

2012, Mar. 26
3182 A656 $3.50 Sheet of 4,
               #a-d   10.50 10.50
Souvenir Sheet
3183 A656 $9 multi   6.75 6.75

First Wedding Anniversary of the Duke and Duchess of Cambridge — A657

No. 3184 — Duke and Duchess, rose and background color of: a, Dark red violet. b, Red. c, Rose. d, Pink.
No. 3185: a, Rose and Duke of Cambridge. b, Rose and Duchess of Cambridge.

2012, May 3   Perf. 13 Syncopated
3184 A657 $3.50 Sheet of 4,
               #a-d   10.50 10.50
Souvenir Sheet
3185 A657 $4.50 Sheet of 2,
               #a-b   6.75 6.75

Miniature Sheet

2012 Summer Olympics, London — A658

No. 3186: a, Rhythmic gymnastics. b, Hurdles. c, Judo. d, Three runners.

2012, June 18   Perf. 12
3186 A658 $2.20 Sheet of 4, #a-d   6.50 6.50

Charles Dickens (1812-70), Writer — A659

No. 3187: a, Illustration from *Great Expectations*. b, Illustration from *Oliver Twist*. c, Sketch of Dickens. d, Photograph of Dickens. e, Illustration from *David Copperfield*. f, Illustration from *A Christmas Carol*.
$9, Illustration from *A Tale of Two Cities*, horiz.

2012, July 30   Perf. 14
3187 A659 $2.75 Sheet of 6,
               #a-f   12.50 12.50
Souvenir Sheet
Perf. 12
3188 A659 $9 multi   6.75 6.75

Princess Diana (1961-97) — A660

No. 3189 — Princess Diana wearing: a, White gown, denomination at UL. b, White jacket, denomination at UL. c, Red dress. d, White dress and necklace, denomination at UR.
$9, Princess Diana and school children.

2012, July 30   Perf. 14
3189 A660 $3.50 Sheet of 4,
                                       10.50 10.50
Souvenir Sheet
3190 A660 $9 multi   6.75 6.75

Miniature Sheet

Seahorses — A661

Various seahorses.

2012, Sept. 24   Perf. 14
3191 A661 $3 Sheet of 5, #a-e 11.50 11.50

War of 1812 — A662

No. 3192: a, HMS Shannon Leading Her Prize The American Frigate Chesapeake into Halifax Harbor, by Louis Haghe. b, Action Between USS Constitution and HMS Guerriere, by Michele F. Corne. c, Portrait of Pres. James Madison, by John Vanderlyn. d, Portrait of Pres. Andrew Jackson, by Ralph E. W. Earl. e, The U.S. Capitol After Burning by the British, by George Munger. f, Battle of Lake Erie, by William H. Powerll.
$9, A View of the Bombardment of Fort McHenry, Near Baltimore, by John Bower.

2012, Nov. 12   Perf. 12
3192 A662 $2.75 Sheet of 6,
               #a-f   12.50 12.50
Souvenir Sheet
3193 A662 $9 multi   6.75 6.75

Christmas A663

Paintings: 30c, Adoration of the Child, by Antonio da Correggio. 75c, Madonna and Child with Two Angels, by Fra Filippo Lippi. $1.50, Virgin and Child, by Peter Paul Rubens. $2, Madonna and Child, by Parmigianino. $3, The Grand Duke's Madonna, by Raphael. $3.25, Adoration of the Magi, by Sandro Botticelli.

2012, Nov. 19   Perf. 12¾
3194-3199 A663   Set of 6   8.00 8.00

Miniature Sheet

Marine Life — A664

No. 3200: a, Copperband butterflyfish. b, Butterfly fish. c, Moon jellyfish, tentacles at bottom. d, Moon jellyfish, tentacles at top. e, Masked butterflyfish. f, Head of Green sea turtle. g, Rear of Green sea turtle, Ocellaris clownfish. h, Forbes sea star. i, Fan coral, red coral at left. j, Fan coral at left. k, Ocellaris clownfish and sea anemone. l, Sea anemone.

2012, Dec. 3   Perf. 13 Syncopated
3200 A664 $1.25 Sheet of 12,
               #a-l   11.50 11.50

Stingrays and Skates — A665

No. 3201: a, Dipturus batis. b, Dipturus oxyrhynchus without long appendages near tail. c, Dipturus oxyrhynchus with long appendages near tail. d, Raja microocellata.
$9, Leucoraja naevus, vert.

2012, Dec. 3   Perf. 13¾
3201 A665 $3 Sheet of 4, #a-d   9.00 9.00
Souvenir Sheet
Perf. 12¾
3202 A665 $9 multi   6.75 6.75

No. 3202 contains one 38x51mm stamp.

Turtles — A666

No. 3203: a, Chelonia mydas. b, Trachemys decorata. c, Dermochelys coriacea. d, Chelonoidis carbonaria.
$9, Chelus fimbriatus.

2012, Dec. 3   Perf. 14
3203 A666 $3.50 Sheet of 4,
               #a-d   10.50 10.50
Souvenir Sheet
Perf. 12
3204 A666 $9 multi   6.75 6.75

RAPHAEL

Paintings by Raphael — A667

No. 3205: a, Andrea Navagero. b, La Muta. c, Self-portrait. d, La Fornarina. $9, Portrait of a Cardinal.

2013, Feb. 20   *Perf. 12½*
3205 A667 $3.25 Sheet of 4, #a-
d   9.75 9.75
Souvenir Sheet
3206 A667 $9 multi   6.75 6.75

Souvenir Sheets

Elvis Presley (1935-77) — A668

Presley: No. 3207, $9, Standing in front of sign depicting him playing guitar, purple frame. No. 3208, $9, Wearing suit and tie, black frame. No. 3209, $9, Holding microphone, red frame. No. 3210, $9, With guitar on back, looking at music stand, red frame. No. 3211, $9, With Pres. Richard M. Nixon, gray frame.

2013, Feb. 20
3207-3211 A668 Set of 5   34.00 34.00

Coronation of Queen Elizabeth II, 60th Anniv. — A669

No. 3212 — Queen Elizabeth II: a, As young woman in field. b, As young woman at piano. c, With Prince Philip. d, Behind microphone. e, Wearing tiara. f, Boarding airplane. $9, Queen Eliazbeth II wearing hat, vert.

2013, May 13   **Litho.**   *Perf. 13¾*
3212 A669 $2.50 Sheet of 6,
#a-f   11.50 11.50
Souvenir Sheet
Perf. 12½
3213 A669 $9 multi   6.75 6.75
No. 3213 contains one 38x51mm stamp.

CONSTELLATIONS

Constellations — A670

No. 3214: a, Ursa Major. b, Ursa Minor. c, Sagittarius. d, Orion. e, Gemini. f, Cassiopeia. $9, Canis Major, vert.

2013, May 13   **Litho.**   *Perf. 13¾*
3214 A670 $2.50 Sheet of 6,
#a-f   11.50 11.50
Souvenir Sheet
Perf. 12½
3215 A670 $9 multi   6.75 6.75
No. 3215 contains one 38x51mm stamp.

Election of Pope Francis — A671

No. 3216 — Pope Francis: a, Waving, orange background. b, Behind microphone, cardinal in background. c, Waving, behind lectern and microphone. d, Facing right, waving, cardinals in background. $9, Pope Francis waving, diff.

Perf. 13¼x12½
2013, June 19   **Litho.**
3216 A671 $3.25 Sheet of 4, #a-
d   9.75 9.75
Souvenir Sheet
Perf. 13½
3217 A671 $9 multi   6.75 6.75
No. 3217 contains one 38x51mm stamp.

Dolphins — A672

No. 3218: a, Bottlenose dolphins. b, Spotted dolphins. c, Striped dolphins. d, Fraser's dolphins. $9, Pygmy killer whale.

Perf. 12½x13¼
2013, June 19   **Litho.**
3218 A672 $3.25 Sheet of 4, #a-
d   9.75 9.75
Souvenir Sheet
Perf. 12½x12
3219 A672 $9 multi   6.75 6.75

Mythological Beings of Asia — A673

No. 3220: a, Rakshasa. b, Indra. c, Vayu.

$9, Garuda.

2013, Oct. 28   **Litho.**   *Perf. 12½*
3220 A673 $3.75 Sheet of 3, #a-
c   8.50 8.50
Souvenir Sheet
3221 A673 $9 multi   6.75 6.75
Thailand 2013 World Stamp Exhibition, Bangkok.

Tourist Attractions in China — A674

No. 3222: a, Dazu Rock Carvings. b, Terracotta warriors. c, Seventeen-arch bridge at Summer Palace. d, Temple of Heaven.
No. 3223: a, Forbidden City. b, Potala Palace.

2013, Oct. 28   **Litho.**   *Perf. 14*
3222 A674 $3.25 Sheet of 4, #a-
d   9.75 9.75
Souvenir Sheet
3223 A674 $4.75 Sheet of 2, #a-
b   7.00 7.00
2013 China International Collection Expo, Beijing.

Dogs — A675

No. 3224: a, Chow chow. b, Japanese chin. c, Poodle. d, French bulldog. $9, Toy spaniel.

2013, Oct. 28   **Litho.**   *Perf. 14*
3224 A675 $3.25 Sheet of 4, #a-
d   9.75 9.75
Souvenir Sheet
Perf. 12
3225 A675 $9 multi   6.75 6.75

Birth of Prince George of Cambridge — A676

No. 3226 — Duke and Duchess of Cambridge with Prince George: a, Duke holding Prince. b, Duchess holding Prince, Duke waving. c, Duke holding Prince, head of prince visible. d, Duchess holding Prince, shoulder of Duke visible. $9, Duke and Duchess of Cambridge with Prince George, diff.

2013, Oct. 28   **Litho.**   *Perf. 13¾*
3226 A676 $3.25 Sheet of 4, #a-
d   9.75 9.75
Souvenir Sheet
3227 A676 $9 multi   6.75 6.75

ANIMALS OF SOUTH AMERICA

Animals of South America — A677

No. 3228: a, Black howler. b, South American tapir. c, Spectacled bear, d, Maned wolf. $9, Toco toucan.

2013, Nov. 18   **Litho.**   *Perf. 12½x12*
3228 A677 $3.25 Sheet of 4, #a-
d   9.75 9.75
Souvenir Sheet
3229 A677 $9 multi   6.75 6.75
2013 Brasiliana World Stamp Exhibition, Rio de Janeiro.

Christmas
A678

Paintings: 30c, Holy Family, by Alessandro Buonvicino. 75c, Christ Blessing, by Girolamo Romani (Il Romanino). 90c, Madonna, by Correggio. $1.50, The Adoration of the Shepherds, by Girolamo Savoldo. $3, Madonna and Child, by Giovanni da Pordenone.

2013, Dec. 2   **Litho.**   *Perf. 12½*
3230-3234 A678 Set of 5   4.75 4.75

New Year 2014 (Year of the Horse) — A679

No. 3235 — Various paintings of horses, by Liu Jiyu (1918-83), with: a, Artist's name at UL, "Year of the Horse" in red at LL. b, Artist's name at LL, "Year of the Horse" in red at UR. c, Artist's name at LL, no "Year of the Horse" inscription. d, Artist's name at UL, "Year of the Horse" in tan at LL.
No. 3236, horiz. — Various paintings of horses, by Liu Jiyu, with "Year of the Horse" at: a, LR. b, LL.

2013, Dec. 2　Litho.　Perf. 14
3235　A679　$3.25　Sheet of 4, #a-
　　　　　　　d　　　　　　　9.75　9.75
　　　　　Souvenir Sheet
　　　　　　　Perf. 12
3236　A679　$3.50　Sheet of 2, #a-
　　　　　　　b　　　　　　　5.25　5.25

A680

A681

Nelson Mandela (1918-2013),
President of South Africa — A682

No. 3237 — Mandela: a, Behind
microphone. b, Wearing blue shirt with circular
designs. c, Sitting in chair. d, With cap lifted. e,
Wearing black shirt. f, Wearing sunglasses.
No. 3238 — Mandela: a, Wearing black-
and-white patterned shirt, with red ribbon near
collar. b, Wearing black-and-white patterned
shirt, no red ribbon. c, Wearing white shirt and
jacket with leopard-skin pattern. d, Waving. e,
Wearing black, white and red patterned shirt,
with red ribbon near collar. f, Wearing tasseled
cap.
$9, Mandela with people in background.
$13.50, Mandela, diff.

2013, Dec. 15　Litho.　Perf. 13¾
3237　A680　$2.50　Sheet of 6,
　　　　　　　#a-f　　　　　11.00　11.00
3238　A681　$2.50　Sheet of 6,
　　　　　　　#a-f　　　　　11.00　11.00
　　　　　Souvenir Sheets
3239　A681　$9　multi　　　6.75　6.75
**Litho.; Margin Embossed With Foil
Application**
　　　　　　　Imperf
3240　A682　$13.50　multi　10.00　10.00

Characters From *Downton Abbey*
Television Series — A683

No. 3241: a, Mrs. Hughes. b, Miss O'Brein.
c, Thomas Barrow. d, William Mason.
$9, Mrs. Patmore and Daisy, horiz.

2014, Mar. 24　Litho.　Perf. 14
3241　A683　$3.25　Sheet of 4, #a-
　　　　　　　d　　　　　　　9.75　9.75
　　　　　Souvenir Sheet
3242　A683　$9　multi　　　6.75　6.75

Parrots — A684

No. 3243, $4.75: a, Eclectus parrot. b, Blue-
and-yellow macaw. c, Black-capped lory. d,
Sun parakeet.
No. 3244, $4.75: a, Blue-and-yellow macaw,
leg near beak. b, Lilac-crowned Amazon. c,
Saint Vincent Amazon. d, Indian ring-necked
parakeet.
No. 3245, $9.50: a, Scarlet macaw. b, Yel-
low-headed Amazon.
No. 3246, $9.50: a, Rainbow lorikeet. b,
Hyacinth macaw.

2014, June 23　Litho.　Perf. 14
　　　　Sheets of 4, #a-d
3243-3244　A684　Set of 2　28.00　28.00
　　Souvenir Sheets of 2, #a-b
3245-3246　A684　Set of 2　28.00　28.00

A685

A686

A687

Aloe Vera — A688

No. 3247: a, Plant in pot. b, Plant (no pot
and plus signs). c, Close-up of plant.
No. 3248: a, Plant and roots. b, Plant diago-
nally. c, Close-up of plant, diff.
No. 3249: a, Plant (no plus signs). b, Plant
and plus signs.
No. 3250: a, Plant (no plus signs), diff. b,
Plant cut into pieces and plus signs.

2014, June 23　Litho.　Perf. 13¾
3247　A685　$4.75　Sheet of 4,
　　　　　　　#3247a-
　　　　　　　3247b, 2
　　　　　　　#3247c　　14.00　14.00
3248　A686　$4.75　Sheet of 4,
　　　　　　　#3248a-
　　　　　　　3248b, 2
　　　　　　　#3248c　　14.00　14.00
　　　　　Souvenir Sheets
3249　A687　$9.50　Sheet of 2,
　　　　　　　#a-b　　　14.00　14.00
3250　A688　$9.50　Sheet of 2,
　　　　　　　#a-b　　　14.00　14.00

Christmas
A689

Paintings by Raphael: $2.25, Holy Family
Below the Oak. $3.50, Madonna with the Blue
Diadem. No. 3253, $5, Incoronazione della
Vergine, detta Pala Oddi. No. 3254, $5,
Aldobrandini Madonna.

2014, Dec. 29　Litho.　Perf. 14¼
3251-3254　A689　Set of 4　12.00　12.00

New Year 2015 (Year of the
Ram) — A690

No. 3255 — Ram with: a, Orange horns (at
right). b, Red horns (at left). c, Green horns (at
left). d, Olive horns at right.
$10, Ram with red horns at right.

2015, Jan. 2　Litho.　Perf. 14
3255　A690　$3.25　Sheet of 4,
　　　　　　　#a-d　　　9.75　9.75
　　　　　Souvenir Sheet
　　　　　　　Perf.
3256　A690　$10　multi　7.50　7.50
No. 3256 contains one 38mm diameter
stamp.

Rare Stamps — A691

No. 3257: a, Canada #3. b, Livingston, Alabama #51X1. c, Belgium #123B.
$10, Canada #387a, horiz.

2015, Jan. 2　Litho.　Perf. 13¼x12½
3257　A691　$3.50　Sheet of 3, #a-
　　　　　　　c　　　　　　7.75　7.75
　　　　　Souvenir Sheet
　　　　　Perf. 12½x13¼
3258　A691　$10　multi　7.50　7.50

Hummingbirds — A692

No. 3259, $3.25: a, Broad-tailed humming-
bird, flower at LL. b, Broad-billed hummingbird, beak at right. c, Rufous-tailed hummingbird. d, Allen's hummingbird in flight.
No. 3260, $3.25: a, Allen's hummingbird on
perch. b, Broad-tailed hummingbird, flower at
UR. c, Broad-billed hummingbird, beak and
flower at left. d, Ruby-throated hummingbird.
No. 3261, $5: a, Ruby-throated humming-
bird on branch. b, Buff-bellied hummingbird.
No. 3262, $5: a, Anna's hummingbird. b,
Calliope hummingbird.

Perf. 14, 12 (#3262)
2015, Jan. 2　　　　　　Litho.
　　Sheets of 4, #a-d
3259-3260　A692　Set of 2　19.50　19.50
　Souvenir Sheets of 2, #a-b
3261-3262　A692　Set of 2　15.00　15.00

Macaws — A693

No. 3263, $3.25: a, Red-shouldered macaw. b, Hyacinth macaw. c, Blue-and-yellow macaw. d, Military macaw.
No. 3264, $3.25, vert.: a, Blue-headed macaw. b, Blue-throated macaw. c, Catalina macaw. d, Miligold macaw.
No. 3265, $5, vert.: a, Harlequin macaw. b, Scarlet macaw.
No. 3266, $5, vert.: a, Great green macaw. b, Green-winged macaw.

Perf. 14, 12 (#3264)
2015, Jan. 2   **Litho.**
Sheets of 4, #a-d
3263-3264 A693   Set of 2   19.50 19.50
Souvenir Sheets of 2, #a-b
3265-3266 A693   Set of 2   15.00 15.00

Ducks and Geese — A694

No. 3267, $3.25: a, Hartlaub's ducks. b, Wood ducks. c, Common shelducks. d, Mallards.
No. 3268, $3.25: a, Ruddy shelducks. b, White-backed duck and eggs in nest. c, Knob-billed ducks. d, Fulvous whistling ducks.
No. 3269, $5: a, Egyptian geese. b, Chiloé wigeons.
No. 3270, $5: a, White-face whistling ducks. b, Red-billed teals.

2015, Jan. 2   **Litho.**   **Perf. 14**
Sheets of 4, #a-d
3267-3268 A694   Set of 2   19.50 19.50
Souvenir Sheets of 2, #a-b
3269-3270 A694   Set of 2   15.00 15.00

Corals — A695

No. 3271, $3.25: a, Purple wide-mesh sea fans. b, Orange wide-mesh sea fan. c, Brain coral with green spots. d, Brain coral with red spots.
No. 3272, $3.25: a, Solitary disk coral. b, Antler coral. c, Common mushroom coral. d, Common lettuce coral.
No. 3273: a, Elkhorn coral. b, Orage cup coral.
$10, Great star coral, vert.

2015, Jan. 2   **Litho.**   **Perf. 14**
Sheets of 4, #a-d
3271-3272 A695   Set of 2   19.50 19.50
3273 A695 $5 Sheet of 2, #a-b   7.50 7.50
Souvenir Sheet
Perf. 12½
3274 A695 $10 multi   7.50 7.50
No. 3274 contains oner 38x51mm stamp.

Prince George of Cambridge — A696

No. 3275 — Prince George in hands of: a, Duchess of Cambridge. b, Duke of Cambridge.
No. 3276, $9.50, Prince George, black panel at bottom. No. 3277, $9.50, Prince George, Duchess of Cambridge, red panel at bottom.

Perf. 13 Syncopated
2015, Jan. 2   **Litho.**
3275 A696 $3.25 Pair, #a-b   5.00 5.00
Souvenir Sheets
3276-3277 A696   Set of 2   14.00 14.00
No. 3275 was printed in sheets containing three pairs.

Julie Mango Tree — A697

2015, Jan. 16   **Litho.**   **Perf. 13¾**
3278 A697   25c multi   .25 .25

Pink Desert Roses — A698

2015, Feb. 24   **Litho.**   **Perf. 14**
3279 A698 $2.20 multi   1.75 1.75
Souvenir Sheet
Perf. 12
3280 A698 $10 Pink desert roses, diff.   7.50 7.50
No. 3279 was printed in sheets of 8 + central label.

Valentina Tereshkova, First Woman in Space — A699

No. 3281: a, Space capsule and Earth, conical section of capsule at left. b, Space capsule and Earth, conical section of capsule at bottom. c, Tereshkova. d, Rocket lift-off.
$10, Capsule, diff.

2015, Mar. 24   **Litho.**   **Perf. 14**
3281 A699 $3.25 Sheet of 4, #a-d   9.75 9.75
Souvenir Sheet
Perf. 12¾
3282 A699 $10 multi   7.50 7.50
No. 3282 contains one 51x38mm stamp.

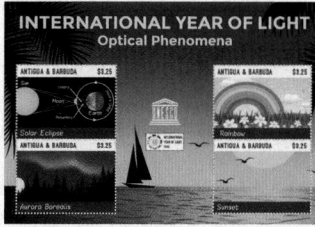

International Year of Light — A700

No. 3283: a, Solar eclipse. b, Rainbow. c, Aurora Borealis. d, Sunset.
$10, Sunlight.

2015, Mar. 24   **Litho.**   **Perf. 12¾**
3283 A700 $3.25 Sheet of 4, #a-d   9.75 9.75
Souvenir Sheet
Perf.
3284 A700 $10 multi   7.50 7.50
No. 3284 contains one 38mm diameter stamp.

Paintings by Vincent van Gogh (1853-90) — A701

No. 3285: a, Cafén Terrace at Night, 1888. b, Self-portrait, 1889. c, Vincent's Bedroom in Arles, 1888. d, Starry Night, 1889. e, Vase with 12 Sunflowers, 1888. f, Interior of a Restaurant, 1887.
$10, Postman Joseph Roulin, 1888.

2015, Mar. 24   **Litho.**   **Perf. 12¾**
3285 A701 $3.15 Sheet of 6, #a-f   14.00 14.00
Souvenir Sheet
3286 A701 $10 multi   7.50 7.50

A702

Horses in Art — A703

No. 3287 — Various unattributed paintings depicting: a, Roundup of wild horses. b, Rider on horse, woman tending to two horses. c, Brown horse facing left. d, White horse and attendant facing left. e, Horse and colt. f, White horse facing right.
No. 3288 — Various unattributed paintings depicting: a, Horses and jockeys at race track.

b, Horses and riders at seashore. c, Horse and jockey with race track grandstand in background. d, Horse and fence. No. 3289, $10, Black horse with clipped tail facing left. No. 3290, $10, Rider on galloping horse beside running dogs.

2015, Mar. 24   **Litho.**   **Perf. 12¾**
3287 A702 $3.15 Sheet of 6, #a-f   14.00 14.00
3288 A703 $3.25 Sheet of 4,   9.75 9.75
Souvenir Sheets
3289-3290 A703   Set of 2   15.00 15.00

Landscapes A704

Designs: 30c, White sand beach, Barbuda. 75c, Aerial view of St. John's, Antigua. 90c, English Harbor, Antigua. $1, Pink sand beach, Barbuda. $1.50, Green Island.

2015, Apr. 20   **Litho.**   **Perf. 13¼x12½**
3291-3295 A704   Set of 5   3.50 3.50

Flag of Antigua and Barbuda — A705

Coat of Arms of Antigua and Barbuda — A706

2015, Apr. 20   **Litho.**   **Perf. 13¼x12½**
3296 A705 $50 multi   37.50 37.50
3297 A706 $100 multi   75.00 75.00

Queen Elizabeth II, Longest-Reigning British Monarch — A707

No. 3298 — Queen Elizabeth II: a, As young woman. b, Wearing tiara. c, Wearing hat. d, Wearing blue dress. e, Wearing green dress. f, Wearing pink jacket.
No. 3299 — Queen Elizabeth II: a, As child. b, As older woman wearing white hat.

2015, July 8   **Litho.**   **Perf. 14**
3298 A707 $3.15 Sheet of 6, #a-f   14.00 14.00
Souvenir Sheet
Perf. 12
3299 A707 $5 Sheet of 2, #a-b   7.50 7.50

Souvenir Sheets

$10

Elvis Presley (1935-77) — A708

Various photographs of Presley with panel at bottom of stamp in: No. 3300, $10, Dull green. No. 3301, $10, Purple. No. 3302, $10, Orange. No. 3303, $10, Salmon.

2015, Aug. 31　　Litho.　　Perf. 14
3300-3303　A708　Set of 4　　30.00　30.00

Battle of Waterloo, 200th Anniv. — A709

No. 3304: a, King William II of the Netherlands. b, Portrait of the Duke of Wellington. c, Emperor Napoleon in His Study at the Tuileries. d, Gebhard Lebrecht von Blücher. $10, The Battle of Waterloo, horiz.

2015, Dec. 1　　Litho.　　Perf. 12x12½
3304　A709　$3.25　Sheet of 4, #a-
　　　　　　　d　　　　　　9.75　9.75
Souvenir Sheet
Perf. 13½
3305　A709　$10 multi　　　　7.50　7.50

No. 3305 contains one 51x38mm stamp.

Gemstones — A711

No. 3310: a, Diamond. b, Sapphire. c, Aquamarine. d, Topaz. e, Turquoise. f, Emerald. $10, Opal.

2015, Dec. 28　　Litho.　　Perf. 13¾
3310　A711　$3.15　Sheet of 6,
　　　　　　　#a-f　　　　14.00　14.00
Souvenir Sheet
3311　A711　$10 multi　　　　7.50　7.50

World War I Events of 1915 — A712

No. 3312: a, Zeppelins. b, Sinking of British steamer Andex. c, Diagrams of torpedoed RMS Lusitania. d, Fokker airplane. e, Serbian refugees. f, Evacuation of Gallipoli. $10, Soldier wearing gas mask.

2015, Dec. 28　　Litho.　　Perf. 12
3312　A712　$3.15　Sheet of 6,
　　　　　　　#a-f　　　　14.00　14.00
Souvenir Sheet
3313　A712　$10 multi　　　　7.50　7.50

WAR TAX STAMPS

No. 31 and Type A3 Overprinted in Black or Red

1916-18　　Wmk. 3　　Perf. 14
MR1　A3　½p green　　　　　2.40　2.90
MR2　A3　½p green (R) ('17)　1.60　2.90
MR3　A3　1½p orange ('18)　1.10　1.45
　　　　Nos. MR1-MR3 (3)　　5.10　7.25

ARGENTINA

¡är-jən-'tē-nə

LOCATION — In South America
GOVT. — Republic
AREA — 1,084,120 sq. mi.
POP. — 36,737,664 (est. 1999)
CAPITAL — Buenos Aires

100 Centavos = 1 Peso (1858, 1992)
100 Centavos = 1 Austral (1985)

> Catalogue values for unused stamps in this country are for Never Hinged items, beginning with Scott 587 in the regular postage section, Scott B12 in the semipostal section, Scott C59 in the airpost section, Scott CB1 in the airpost semi-postal section and Scott O79 in the officials section.

Watermarks

Wmk. 84 — Italic RA

Wmk. 85 — Small Sun, 4½mm

Wmk. 86 — Large Sun, 6mm

Wmk. 87 — Honeycomb

Wmk. 88 — Multiple Suns

Wmk. 89 — Large Sun

In this watermark the face of the sun is 7mm in diameter, the rays are heavier than in the large sun watermark of 1896-1911 and the watermarks are placed close together, so that parts of several frequently appear on one stamp. This paper was intended to be used for fiscal stamps and is usually referred to as "fiscal sun paper."

Wmk. 90 — RA in Sun

In 1928 watermark 90 was slightly modified, making the diameter of the Sun 9mm instead of 10mm. Several types of this watermark exist.

Wmk. 205 — AP in Oval

The letters "AP" are the initials of "AHORRO POSTAL." This paper was formerly used exclusively for Postal Savings stamps.

Wmk. 287 — Double Circle and Letters in Sheet

Wmk. 288 — RA in Sun with Straight Rays

Wmk. 365 — Argentine Arms, "Casa de Moneda de la Nacion" & "RA" Multiple

> **Values for Unused**
> Unused values for Nos. 5-17 are for examples without gum. Examples with original gum command higher prices. Unused values of Nos. 1-4B and stamps after No. 17 are for examples with original gum as defined in the catalogue introduction.

Argentine Confederation

Symbolical of the Argentine Confederation — A1

Unwmk.
1858, May 1　　Litho.　　Imperf.
1　　A1　5c red　　　　　　1.50　40.00
　a.　Colon after "5"　　　1.75　35.00
　b.　Colon after "V"　　　1.75　35.00
2　　A1　10c green　　　　2.50　90.00
　f.　Diagonal half used as 5c
　　　on cover　　　　　　　　725.00
3　　A1　15c blue　　　　18.00　250.00
　c.　Horiz. third used as 5c on
　　　cover　　　　　　　　　10,000.
　　　Nos. 1-3 (3)　　　22.00　380.00

There are nine varieties of Nos. 1, 2 and 3. Counterfeits and forged cancellations of Nos. 1-3 are plentiful.

Symbolical of the Argentine Confederation — A2

1860, Jan.
4　　A2　5c red　　　　　3.25　100.00
4A　A2　10c green　　　7.00
4B　A2　15c blue　　　30.00
　　　Nos. 4-4B (3)　　40.25

Nos. 4A and 4B were never placed in use. Some compositions of Nos. 4-4B contain 8 different types across the sheet. Other settings exist with minor variations. Counterfeits and forged cancellations of Nos. 4-4B are plentiful.

Argentine Republic

Seal of the Republic — A3

Broad "C" in "CENTAVOS," Accent on "U" of "REPUBLICA"

1862, Jan. 11

5	A3	5c rose	49.00	37.50
6	A3	10c green	175.00	80.00
	b.	Diagonal half used as 5c on cover		7,000.
7	A3	15c blue	350.00	225.00
	a.	Without accent on "U"	8,000.	5,000.
	b.	Tete beche pair	150,000.	120,000.
	i.	15c ultramarine	500.00	350.00
	j.	Diagonal third used as 5c on cover		12,000.

Only one used example of No. 7b is known. It has faults. Two unused examples are known. One is sound with original gum, the other is in a block, without gum, and has tiny faults.

Broad "C" in "CENTAVOS," No Accent on "U"

1863

7C	A3	5c rose	20.00	21.00
	d.	5c rose lilac	200.00	250.00
	m.	Worn plate (rose)	500.00	52.50
7F	A3	10c yellow green	1,000.	250.00
	g.	10c olive green	1,500.	400.00
	q.	10c green, ribbed paper	1,200.	350.00
	r.	Worn plate (green)	1,200.	375.00
	s.	Worn plate (olive green)	650.00	500.00

Narrow "C" in "CENTAVOS," No Accent on "U"

1864

7H	A3	5c rose red	225.00	32.50

The so-called reprints of 10c and 15c are counterfeits. They have narrow "C" and straight lines in shield. Nos. 7C and 7H have been extensively counterfeited.

Rivadavia Issue

Bernardino Rivadavia
A4   A5

Rivadavia — A6

1864-67   Engr.   Wmk. 84   Imperf.
Clear Impressions

8	A4	5c brown rose	2,500.	250.
	a.	5c orange red ('67)	2,500.	250.
9	A5	10c green	3,000.	1,750.
10	A6	15c blue	13,500.	6,500.

Perf. 11½
Dull to Worn Impressions

11	A4	5c brown rose ('65)	40.00	16.00
11B	A4	5c lake	100.00	22.50
12	A5	10c green	150.00	70.00
	a.	Diagonal half used as 5c on cover		2,000.
	b.	Vert. half used as 5c on cover		3,000.
	c.	Horiz. pair, imperf vert.		5,000.
13	A6	15c blue	450.00	150.00

1867-72   Unwmk.   Imperf.

14	A4	5c carmine ('72)	350.	100.
15	A4	5c rose	350.	100.
15A	A5	10c green	3,000.	3,200.
16	A6	15c blue	3,000.	2,700.

Nos. 15A-16 issued without gum.

1867   Perf. 11½

17	A4	5c carmine	1,000.	200.00

Nos. 14, 15 and 17 exist with part of papermaker's wmk. Unused values, $1,200, $2,000 and $2,000, respectively.

Rivadavia   Manuel
A7   Belgrano
          A8

Jose de San
Martin — A9

Groundwork of Horizontal Lines

1867-68   Perf. 12

18	A7	5c vermilion	225.00	17.50
18A	A8	10c green	50.00	7.50
	b.	Diag. half used as 5c on cover		2,500.
19	A9	15c blue	100.00	22.50

Groundwork of Crossed Lines

20	A7	5c vermilion	15.00	1.25
21	A9	15c blue	120.00	15.00

See Nos. 27, 33-34, 39 and types A19, A33, A34, A37. For surcharges and overprints see Nos. 30-32, 41-42, 47-51, O6-O7, O26.

Gen. Antonio   Mariano
G. Balcarce   Moreno
A10   A11

Carlos Maria   Gervasio
de Alvear   Antonio
A12   Posadas
          A13

Cornelio
Saavedra — A14

1873

22	A10	1c purple	6.00	2.25
	a.	1c gray violet	10.00	2.25
23	A11	4c brown	6.00	.75
	a.	4c red brown	15.00	2.00
24	A12	30c orange	140.00	25.00
	a.	Vert. pair, imperf horiz.	4,000.	
25	A13	60c black	160.00	5.00
26	A14	90c blue	60.00	3.00
		Nos. 22-26 (5)	372.00	36.00

For overprints see Nos. O5, O12-O14, O19-O21, O25, O29.
Four examples of No. 24a are known. Three examples of No. 26 are known on cover.

1873   Laid Paper

27	A8	10c green	325.00	32.50

Nos. 18, 18A Surcharged in Black

Nos. 30-31   No. 32

1877, Feb.   Wove Paper

30	A7	1c on 5c vermilion	75.00	25.00
	a.	Inverted surcharge	1,000.	300.00
31	A7	2c on 5c vermilion	125.00	75.00
	a.	Inverted surcharge	1,200.	750.00
32	A8	8c on 10c green	160.00	40.00
	b.	Inverted surcharge	2,500.	1,000.
		Nos. 30-32 (3)	360.00	140.00

Varieties also exist with double and triple surcharges, surcharge on reverse, 8c on No. 27, all made clandestinely from the original cliches of the surcharges.
Forgeries of these surcharges include the inverted and double varieties.

1876-77   Rouletted

33	A7	5c vermilion	200.00	85.00
34	A7	8c lake ('77)	35.00	.65

Belgrano   Dalmacio
A17   Vélez Sarsfield
          A18

San Martín — A19

1878   Rouletted

35	A17	16c green	12.00	1.10
36	A18	20c blue	20.00	2.25
37	A19	24c blue	30.00	3.50
		Nos. 35-37 (3)	62.00	6.85

See No. 56. For overprints see Nos. O9-O10, O15-O17, O22, O28.

Vicente   Alvear — A21
Lopez — A20

1877-80   Perf. 12

38	A20	2c yellow green	5.00	.75
39	A7	8c lake ('80)	4.50	.75
	a.	8c brown lake	52.50	.75
40	A21	25c lake ('78)	30.00	6.00
		Nos. 38-40 (3)	39.50	7.50

For overprints see Nos. O4, O11, O18, O24.

No. 18 Surcharged in Black

Large "P"   Small "P"

1882

41	A7	½c on 5c ver	2.75	2.75
	a.	Double surcharge	100.00	100.00
	b.	Inverted surcharge	50.00	50.00
	c.	"PROVISORIO" omitted	110.00	110.00
	d.	Fraction omitted	100.00	
	e.	"PROVISOBIO"	50.00	50.00
	f.	Pair, one without surcharge	250.00	
	g.	Small "P" in "PROVISORIO"	2.75	2.75
	h.	As "a," small "P" in "PROVISORIO"	50.00	50.00
	i.	As "b," small "P" in "PROVISORIO"	75.00	75.00
	j.	As "d," small "P" in "PROVISORIO"	30.00	30.00

Perforated across Middle of Stamp

42	A7	½c on 5c ver	6.00	6.00
	a.	"PROVISORIO"	50.00	50.00
	b.	Large "P" in "PROVISORIO"	40.00	30.00

A23

1882   Typo.   Perf. 12½

43	A23	½c brown	2.25	1.50
	a.	Imperf., pair	100.00	80.00
44	A23	1c red	15.00	6.00
45	A23	12c ultra	90.00	14.00

Perf. 14¼

44A	A23	1c red	3.50	1.50
45A	A23	12c ultra	65.00	12.00

Engr.

46	A23	12c grnsh blue	225.00	16.00
		Nos. 43-46 (6)	400.75	51.00

See type A29. For overprints see Nos. O2, O8, O23, O27.

No. 21 Surcharged in Red

a   b

c

1884   Engr.   Perf. 12

47	A9 (a)	½c on 15c blue	3.00	2.00
	a.	Groundwork of horiz. lines	150.00	90.00
	b.	Inverted surcharge	35.00	25.00
48	A9 (b)	1c on 15c blue	22.50	16.50
	a.	Groundwork of horiz. lines	13.00	11.50
	b.	Inverted surcharge	100.00	62.50
	c.	Double surcharge	50.00	40.00
	d.	Triple surcharge	400.00	

Nos. 20-21 Surcharged in Black

49	A7 (a)	½c on 5c ver	5.00	4.50
	a.	Inverted surcharge	200.00	150.00
	b.	Date omitted	200.00	—
	c.	Pair, one without surcharge	500.00	
	d.	Double surcharge	550.00	
50	A9 (a)	½c on 15c blue	15.00	12.00
	a.	Groundwork of horiz. lines	50.00	35.00
	b.	Inverted surcharge	90.00	70.00
	c.	Pair, one without surcharge	400.00	
51	A7 (c)	4c on 5c ver	12.00	9.00
	a.	Inverted surcharge	35.00	28.00
	b.	Double surcharge	700.00	350.00
	c.	Pair, one without surcharge but with "4" in manuscript	750.00	650.00
	d.	Pair, one without surcharge	400.00	
		Nos. 47-51 (5)	57.50	44.00

A29

1884-85   Engr.   Perf. 12

52	A29	½c red brown	1.50	.65
	a.	Horiz. pair, imperf vert.		1,200.
53	A29	1c rose red	7.00	.65
	a.	Horiz. pair, imperf vert.	300.00	250.00
54	A29	12c deep blue	35.00	1.50
	a.	12c grnsh blue ('85)	50.00	1.50
	b.	Horiz. pair, imperf vert.	300.00	250.00
		Nos. 52-54 (3)	43.50	2.80

For overprints see Nos. O1, O3, O9.

San Martin Type of 1878

1887   Engr.

56	A19	24c blue	20.00	1.40

Justo Jose de   Lopez — A31
Urquiza — A30

Miguel Juarez
Celman — A32

Rivadavia
(Large
head) — A33

Rivadavia (Small
head)
A34

Domingo F.
Sarmiento
A35

Nicolas
Avellaneda — A36

San Martin —
A37

Julio A.
Roca — A37a

Belgrano —
A37b

Manuel
Dorrego — A38

Moreno — A39

Bartolome
Mitre — A40

CINCO CENTAVOS.
A33 — Shows collar on left side only.
A34 — Shows collar on both sides. Lozenges in background larger and clearer than in A33.

1888-90   **Litho.**   **Perf. 11½**

57	A30	½c blue	1.75	.75
b.		Vert. pair, imperf. horiz.	200.00	200.00
c.		Horiz. pair, imperf. vert.	200.00	200.00
58	A31	2c yel grn	20.00	10.00
b.		Vert. pair, imperf. horiz.	130.00	
c.		Horiz. pair, imperf. vert.	250.00	
59	A32	3c blue green	3.50	1.50
b.		Horiz. pair, imperf. horiz.	60.00	
c.		Horiz. pair, imperf. vert.	130.00	
d.		Vert. pair, imperf. btwn.	25.00	25.00
60	A33	5c carmine	18.00	.75
b.		Horiz. pair, imperf. horiz.	175.00	
61	A34	5c carmine	26.00	2.25
b.		Vert. pair, imperf. btwn.	200.00	
c.		Horiz. pair, imperf. horiz.		400.00
62	A35	6c red	50.00	20.00
b.		Vert. pair, imperf. btwn.	150.00	
c.		Perf. 12	100.00	50.00
63	A36	10c brown	26.00	1.50
64	A37	15c orange	27.50	2.25
b.		Vert. pair, imperf. btwn.		600.00
64A	A37a	20c green	25.00	1.50
64B	A37b	25c purple	45.00	4.00
65	A38	30c brown	40.00	4.00
b.		30c reddish chocolate brown	400.00	80.00
c.		Horiz. pair, imperf. btwn.	700.00	500.00

66	A39	40c slate, perf. 12	150.00	3.00
a.		Perf. 11½	300.00	4.00
b.		Horiz. pair, imperf. btwn. (#66)		800.00
67	A40	50c blue	350.00	20.00
		Nos. 57-67 (13)	782.75	71.50

In this issue there are several varieties of each value, the difference between them being in the relative position of the head to the frame.

Imperf., Pairs

57a	A30	½c	85.00	67.50
58a	A31	2c	100.00	
59a	A32	3c	45.00	27.50
61a	A34	5c		100.00
62a	A35	6c	150.00	150.00
63a	A36	10c	55.00	
64c	A37	15c		200.00
65a	A38	30c blue	325.00	225.00

Urquiza
A41

Velez
Sarsfield
A42

Miguel Juarez
Celman
A43

Rivadavia
(Large head)
A44

Sarmiento
A45

Juan Bautista
Alberdi
A46

1888-89   **Engr.**   **Perf. 11½, 11½x12**

68	A41	½c ultra	.75	.45
a.		Vert. pair, imperf. horiz.	30.00	—
b.		Imperf., pair	30.00	—
69	A42	1c brown	1.50	.75
a.		Vert. pair, imperf. horiz.	65.00	
b.		Vert. pair, imperf. btwn.		
c.		Imperf., pair	30.00	
d.		Horiz. pair, imperf. btwn.	100.00	
70	A43	3c blue green	6.00	1.75
71	A44	5c rose	4.50	.75
a.		Imperf., pair	50.00	—
72	A45	6c blue black	3.00	.90
b.		Perf. 11½x12	15.00	4.50
73	A46	12c blue	8.75	3.75
a.		Imperf., pair	45.00	
b.		bluish paper	9.50	3.75
c.		Perf. 11½	14.00	3.00
		Nos. 68-73 (6)	24.50	8.35

Nos. 69-70 exist with papermakers' watermarks.
See No. 77, types A50, A61. For surcharges see Nos. 83-84.

Jose Maria
Paz — A48

Santiago
Derqui — A49

Rivadavia
(Small head)
A50

Avellaneda
A51

Moreno
A53

Mitre
A54

Posadas — A55

1890   **Engr.**   **Perf. 11½**

75	A48	¼c green	.65	.45
76	A49	2c violet	1.50	.75
a.		2c purple	2.00	.75
b.		2c slate	2.00	.75
c.		Horiz. pair, imperf. btwn.	30.00	25.00
d.		Imperf., pair	37.50	
e.		Perf. 11½x12	9.00	.75
77	A50	5c carmine	3.50	.45
a.		Imperf., pair	70.00	32.50
b.		Perf. 11½x12	10.00	1.25
c.		Vert. pair, imperf. btwn.	75.00	60.00
d.		Horiz. pair, imperf. btwn.	75.00	60.00
78	A51	10c brown	4.50	.75
b.		Imperf., pair	150.00	
a.		Vert. pair, imperf. btwn.	225.00	
80	A53	40c olive green	8.00	1.50
a.		Imperf., pair	55.00	
b.		Horiz. pair, imperf. btwn.		250.00
81	A54	50c orange	9.00	1.50
a.		Imperf., pair	80.00	
b.		Perf. 11½x12	40.00	3.00
82	A55	60c black	20.00	4.50
a.		Imperf., pair	—	
b.		Vert. pair, imperf. btwn.	125.00	100.00
		Nos. 75-82 (7)	47.15	9.90

Type A50 differs from type A44 in having the head smaller, the letters of "Cinco Centavos" not as tall, and the curved ornaments at sides close to the first and last letters of "Republica Argentina."

**Lithographed Surcharge
on No. 73 in Black or
Red**

1890   **Perf. 11½x12**

83	A46	¼c on 12c blue	.75	.75
a.		Perf. 11½	50.00	40.00
b.		Double surcharge	75.00	47.50
c.		Inverted surcharge	100.00	
84	A46	¼c on 12c blue (R)	.75	.75
a.		Double surcharge	55.00	50.00
b.		Perf. 11½	8.00	6.00

Surcharge is different on Nos. 83 and 84. Nos. 83-84 exist as pairs, one without surcharge. These were privately produced.

Rivadavia
A57

Jose de San
Martin
A58

Gregorio
Araoz de
Lamadrid
A59

Admiral
Guillermo
Brown
A60

1891   **Engr.**   **Perf. 11½**

85	A57	8c carmine rose	1.50	.65
a.		Imperf., pair	130.00	

86	A58	1p deep blue	50.00	12.00
87	A59	5p ultra	325.00	45.00
88	A60	20p green	500.00	100.00
		Nos. 85-88 (4)	876.50	157.65

A 10p brown and a 50p red were prepared but not issued. Values: 10p $1,500 for fine, 50p $1,200 with rough or somewhat damaged perfs.

Velez Sarsfield — A61

1890   **Perf. 11½**

89	A61	1c brown	1.25	.65
b.		Horiz. pair, imperf. btwn.		550.00

Type A61 is a re-engraving of A42. The figure "1" in each upper corner has a short horizontal serif instead of a long one pointing downward. In type A61 the first and last letters of "Correos y Telegrafos" are closer to the curved ornaments below than in type A42. Background is of horizontal lines (cross-hatching on No. 69).

"Santa Maria,"
"Nina" and
"Pinta" — A62

1892, Oct. 12   **Wmk. 85**   **Perf. 11½**

90	A62	2c light blue	8.50	3.00
a.		Double impression	225.00	
91	A62	5c dark blue	9.50	4.00

Discovery of America, 400th anniv. Counterfeits of Nos. 90-91 are litho.

Rivadavia
A63

Belgrano
A64

San Martin — A65

1892-95   **Wmk. 85**   **Perf. 11½**

92	A63	½c dull blue	1.00	.35
a.		½c bright ultra	80.00	40.00
93	A63	1c brown	.65	.50
94	A63	2c green	1.00	.35
95	A63	3c org ('95)	1.75	.35
96	A63	5c carmine	1.75	.35
b.		5c green (error)	700.00	700.00
98	A64	10c car rose	13.50	.60
99	A64	12c dp bl ('93)	10.00	.60
100	A64	16c gray	16.50	.60
101	A64	24c gray brown	16.50	.65
102	A64	50c blue green	27.50	.75
103	A65	1p lake ('93)	12.00	1.00
a.		1p red brown	20.00	5.00
104	A65	2p dark green	27.50	3.50
105	A65	5p dark blue	37.50	3.50
		Nos. 92-105 (13)	167.15	13.15

Perf. 12

92E	A63	½c dull blue	6.00	1.00
93E	A63	1c brown	10.00	2.00
94E	A63	2c green	10.00	3.00
95E	A63	3c org ('95)	30.00	5.00
96E	A63	5c carmine	35.00	1.00
98E	A64	10c car rose	21.00	3.50
99E	A64	12c dp bl ('93)	40.00	4.00
100E	A64	16c gray	40.00	4.00
101E	A64	24c gray brown	30.00	17.00
102E	A64	50c blue green	30.00	6.00
104E	A65	2p dark green	125.00	40.00
		Nos. 92E-104E (11)	377.00	86.50

Perf. 11½x12

92F	A63	½c dull blue	18.00	10.00
93F	A63	1c brown	15.00	8.00
94F	A63	2c green	40.00	15.00
95F	A63	3c org ('95)	55.00	22.50
96F	A63	5c carmine	20.00	4.00
98F	A64	10c car rose	30.00	7.50
99F	A64	12c dp bl ('93)	60.00	27.50
100F	A64	16c gray	60.00	27.50
102F	A64	50c blue green	60.00	10.00

103F	A64	1p red brown	60.00	10.00
104F	A65	2p dark green	175.00	75.00
		Nos. 92F-104F (11)	593.00	217.00

The high values of this and succeeding issues are frequently punched with the word "INUTILIZADO," parts of the letters showing on each stamp. These punched stamps sell for only a small fraction of the catalogue values.

Examples of No. 95 in yellow shades are changelings.

Reprints of No. 96b have white gum. The original stamp has yellowish gum. Value $125.

Imperf., Pairs

92b	A63	½c	60.00
93a	A63	1c	60.00
94a	A63	2c	30.00
96a	A63	5c	60.00
98a	A64	10c	60.00
99a	A64	12c	60.00
100a	A64	16c	60.00
101a	A64	24c	60.00
102a	A65	50c	60.00
103b	A65	1p	60.00
105a	A65	5p	150.00

Nos. 102a, 103b and 105a exist only without gum; the other imperfs are found with or without gum, and values are the same for either condition.

Vertical Pairs, Imperf. Between

92c	A63	½c	125.00
93b	A63	1c	100.00
94b	A63	2c	50.00
95a	A63	3c	250.00
96c	A63	5c	45.00 —
98b	A64	10c	100.00
99b	A64	12c	100.00

Horizontal Pairs, Imperf. Between

93c	A63	1c	110.00
94c	A63	2c	55.00
96d	A63	5c	55.00 45.00
98c	A64	10c	110.00

1896-97   Wmk. 86   Perf. 11½

106	A63	½c slate	.65	.30
a.		½c gray blue	.65	.30
b.		½c indigo	.65	.30
107	A63	1c brown	.65	.30
108	A63	2c yellow green	.65	.30
109	A63	3c orange	.65	.30
110	A63	5c carmine	.65	.30
a.		Imperf., pair	100.00	
111	A64	10c carmine rose	10.00	.30
112	A64	12c deep blue	5.00	.30
a.		Imperf., pair	—	
113	A64	16c gray	13.50	.90
114	A64	24c gray brown	13.50	1.25
a.		Imperf., pair	100.00	—
115	A64	30c orange ('97)	13.50	.70
116	A64	50c blue green	13.50	.70
117	A64	80c dull violet	20.00	.90
118	A65	1p lake	30.00	1.60
119	A65	1p20c black ('97)	13.50	3.50
120	A65	2p dark green	20.00	10.00
121	A65	5p dark blue	135.00	13.50
		Nos. 106-121 (16)	290.75	35.15

Perf. 12

106E	A63	½c slate	2.00	1.00
a.		½c gray blue	10.00	4.00
b.		½c indigo	10.00	4.00
107E	A63	1c brown	1.75	1.00
108E	A63	2c yellow green	2.50	1.00
109E	A63	3c orange	45.00	2.00
110E	A63	5c carmine	3.50	1.00
111E	A64	10c car rose	15.00	1.00
112E	A64	12c deep blue	11.00	2.00
113E	A64	16c gray	35.00	5.50
114E	A64	24c gray brown	52.50	11.00
115E	A64	30c orange ('97)	52.50	2.50
116E	A64	50c blue green	65.00	.80
117E	A64	80c dull violet	65.00	22.50
118E	A65	1p lake	65.00	3.50
119E	A65	1p20c black ('97)	65.00	22.50
121E	A65	5p dark blue	800.00	20.00
		Nos. 106E-121E (15)	1,281.	97.30

Perf. 11½x12

106F	A63	½c slate	20.00	11.00
107F	A63	1c brown	30.00	25.00
108F	A63	2c yellow green	20.00	11.00
109F	A63	3c orange	13.00	8.00
110F	A63	5c carmine	26.00	4.50
111F	A64	10c car rose	45.00	18.00
112F	A64	12c deep blue	47.50	15.00
113F	A64	16c gray	60.00	20.00
115F	A64	30c org ('97)	—	75.00
116F	A64	50c blue green	—	75.00
117F	A64	80c dull violet	—	75.00
119F	A65	1p20c black ('97)	100.00	60.00
		Nos. 106F-119F (12)	361.50	397.50

Vertical Pairs, Imperf. Between

106c	A63	½c	200.00
107a	A63	1c	125.00
108a	A63	2c	125.00
109a	A63	3c	200.00
110b	A63	5c	125.00 125.00
112b	A64	12c	125.00 100.00

Horizontal Pairs, Imperf. Between

107b	A63	1c	125.00
108b	A63	2c	125.00
110c	A63	5c	125.00 80.00
111a	A64	10c	125.00
112c	A64	12c	125.00

A66

Allegory, Liberty Seated — A67

1899-1903   Perf. 11½

122	A66	½c yel brn	.40	.30
123	A66	1c green	.60	.30
124	A66	2c slate	.60	.30
125	A66	3c org ('01)	.80	.50
126	A66	4c yel ('03)	1.40	.60
127	A66	5c car rose	.60	.30
128	A66	6c blk ('03)	.90	.60
129	A66	10c dk grn	1.40	.40
130	A66	12c dull blue	.95	.60
131	A66	12c ol grn ('01)	.95	.60
132	A66	15c sea grn ('01)	2.50	.60
132B	A66	15c dl blue ('01)	2.50	.60
133	A66	16c orange	8.00	8.00
134	A66	20c claret	1.90	.30
135	A66	24c violet	4.00	1.00
136	A66	30c rose	7.25	.60
137	A66	30c ver ('01)	4.00	.50
a.		30c scarlet	47.50	3.00
138	A66	50c brt blue	4.50	.50
139	A67	1p bl & blk	15.00	1.25
a.		Center inverted	2,000.	1,000.
b.		Perf. 12	500.00	160.00
140	A67	5p org & blk	57.50	11.00
		Punch cancellation		3.00
a.		Center inverted	2,750.	2,500.
141	A67	10p grn & blk	70.00	18.00
		Punch cancellation		3.00
a.		Center inverted	5,000.	
		Punch cancellation		675.00
142	A67	20p red & blk	200.00	35.00
		Punch cancellation		5.00
a.		Center invtd. (punch cancel)		4,000.
		Nos. 122-142 (22)	385.75	81.85

Nos. 139-142 used are valued with violet oval or black boxed parcel cancels. Examples with letter cancels are worth ⅓rd more.

Perf. 12

122E	A66	½c yellow brown	1.50	1.20
123E	A66	1c green	2.00	.60
124E	A66	2c slate	1.50	.60
125E	A66	3c orange ('01)	3.50	1.75
126E	A66	4c yellow ('03)	10.00	3.50
127E	A66	5c carmine rose	5.25	.60
128E	A66	6c black ('03)	8.50	2.00
129E	A66	10c dark green	8.50	1.75
130E	A66	12c dull blue	8.50	2.00
131E	A66	12c ol grn ('01)	8.50	2.00
132E	A66	15c sea grn ('01)	17.00	1.75
133E	A66	16c orange	10.00	9.50
134E	A66	20c claret	12.00	9.50
135E	A66	24c violet	11.00	8.50
136E	A66	30c rose	28.00	3.50
137E	A66	30c ver ('01)	60.00	4.00
a.		30c scarlet	47.50	3.00
138E	A66	50c brt blue	27.50	3.50
139E	A67	1p bl & blk	500.00	160.00
		Nos. 122E-139E (18)	723.25	216.25

Perf. 11½x12

122F	A66	½c yellow brown	25.00	15.00
		Never hinged	37.50	
		On cover, single franking		20.00
123F	A66	1c green	25.00	15.00
		Never hinged	37.50	
		On cover		1.00
124F	A66	2c slate	12.00	3.00
		Never hinged	18.00	
		On cover		1.00
125F	A66	3c orange ('01)	47.50	18.00
		Never hinged	72.50	
		On cover		1.50
127F	A66	5c carmine rose	12.00	6.00
		Never hinged	18.00	
		On cover		1.00
128F	A66	6c black ('03)	32.50	20.00
		Never hinged	13.00	
		On cover		2.00
129F	A66	10c dark green	30.00	6.50
		Never hinged	45.00	
		On cover		1.50
130F	A66	12c dull blue	50.00	15.00
		Never hinged	75.00	
		On cover		2.00
131F	A66	12c ol grn ('01)	50.00	10.00
		Never hinged	75.00	
		On cover		2.00
132F	A66	15c sea grn ('01)	50.00	8.00
		Never hinged	75.00	
		On cover		2.50
134F	A66	20c claret	60.00	12.00
		Never hinged	90.00	
		On cover		1.00

135F	A66	24c violet	50.00	10.00
		Never hinged	75.00	
		On cover		5.00
136F	A66	30c rose	120.00	20.00
		Never hinged	175.00	
		On cover		5.00
137F	A66	30c ver ('01)	140.00	25.00
		Never hinged	210.00	
		On cover		5.00
138F	A66	50c brt blue	120.00	20.00
		Never hinged	175.00	
		On cover		10.00
		Nos. 122F-138F (15)	824.00	203.50

Imperf., Pairs

122a	A66	½c	35.00
123a	A66	1c	50.00
124a	A66	2c	17.50
125a	A66	3c	325.00
127a	A66	5c	17.50
128a	A66	6c	60.00
129a	A66	10c	50.00
132a	A66	15c	50.00

Vertical Pairs, Imperf. Between

122b	A66	½c	10.00 9.50
123b	A66	1c	10.00 9.50
124b	A66	2c	5.00 4.50
125b	A66	3c	325.00 200.00
126a	A66	4c	400.00 275.00
127b	A66	5c	4.50 2.50
128b	A66	6c	13.50 10.00
129b	A66	10c	85.00
132c	A66	15c	15.00 10.00

Horizontal Pairs, Imperf. Between

122c	A66	½c	30.00 19.00
123c	A66	1c	47.50 27.50
124c	A66	2c	10.00 5.00
125c	A66	3c	325.00 200.00
126b	A66	4c	400.00
127c	A66	5c	10.00 5.00
128c	A66	6c	17.00 10.00
129c	A66	10c	17.00 10.00
132d	A66	15c	40.00 23.00
138a	A66	50c	165.00

River Port of Rosario A68

1902, Oct. 26   Perf. 11½, 11½x12

143	A68	5c deep blue	4.75	2.00
a.		Imperf., pair	95.00	
b.		Vert. pair, imperf. btwn.	60.00	
c.		Horiz. pair, imperf. btwn.	90.00	

Completion of port facilities at Rosario.

San Martin
A69   A70

1908-09   Typo.   Perf. 13½x12½

144	A69	½c violet	.50	.30
145	A69	1c brnsh buff	.50	.30
146	A69	2c chocolate	.60	.30
147	A69	3c green	.65	.40
148	A69	4c redsh violet	1.25	.40
149	A69	5c carmine	.60	.40
150	A69	6c olive bister	.75	.40
151	A69	10c gray green	1.75	.30
152	A69	12c yellow buff	1.00	.60
153	A69	12c dk blue ('09)	1.75	.30
155	A69	20c ultra	1.25	.30
156	A69	24c red brown	3.50	.60
157	A69	30c dull rose	6.00	.60
158	A69	50c black	6.00	.50
159	A70	1p sl bl & pink	18.00	2.50
		Nos. 144-159 (15)	44.10	8.10

The 1c blue was not issued. Value $500.

Wmk. 86 appears on ½, 1, 6, 20, 24 and 50c. Other values have similar wmk. with wavy rays.

Stamps lacking wmk. are from outer rows printed on sheet margin.

Perf. 13½

146A	A69	2c chocolate	1.20	.25
147A	A69	3c green	2.00	1.00
148A	A69	4c redsh violet	1.30	.50
149A	A69	5c carmine	1.00	.30
151A	A69	10c gray green	6.25	2.25
152A	A69	12c yellow buff	1.20	.70
153A	A69	12c dk blue ('09)	4.25	1.00
154A	A69	15c apple green	.60	.50
156A	A69	24c red brown	4.75	1.30
157A	A69	30c dull rose	9.50	1.30
159A	A70	1p sl bl & pink	20.00	3.00

Pyramid of May — A71

Nicolas Rodriguez Pena and Hipolito Vieytes — A72

Meeting at Pena's Home — A73

Designs: 3c, Miguel de Azcuenaga (1754-1833) and Father Manuel M. Alberti (1763-1811). 4c, Viceroy's house and Fort Buenos Aires. 5c, Cornelio Saavedra (1759-1829). 10c, Antonio Luis Beruti (1772-1842) and French distributing badges. 12c, Congress building. 20c, Juan Jose Castelli (1764-1812) and Domingo Matheu (1765-1831). 24c, First council. 30c, Manuel Belgrano (1770-1820) and Juan Larrea (1782-1847). 50c, First meeting of republican government, May 25, 1810. 1p, Mariano Moreno (1778-1811) and Juan Jose Paso (1758-1833). 5p, Oath of the Junta. 10p, Centenary Monument. 20p, Jose Francisco de San Martin (1778-1850).

Inscribed "1810 1910"
Various Frames

1910, May 1   Engr.   Perf. 11½

160	A71	½c bl & gray bl	.30	.25
161	A72	1c bl grn & blk	.30	.30
b.		Horiz. pair, imperf. btwn.	65.00	
162	A73	2c olive & gray	.25	.30
163	A72	3c green	.70	.40
164	A73	4c dk blue & grn	.70	.40
165	A71	5c carmine	.40	.25
166	A73	10c yel brn & blk	1.10	.50
167	A73	12c brt blue	1.10	.50
168	A72	20c gray brn & blk	3.25	.60
169	A73	24c org brn & bl	1.75	1.25
170	A72	30c lilac & blk	1.75	1.00
171	A71	50c car & blk	4.50	1.25
172	A72	1p brt blue	9.50	3.25
173	A73	5p orange & vio	72.50	35.00
		Punch cancel		5.00
174	A71	10p orange & blk	90.00	62.50
		Punch cancel		10.00
175	A71	20p dp blue & ind	150.00	100.00
		Punch cancel		15.00
		Nos. 160-175 (16)	338.10	207.75

Centenary of the republic.

Center Inverted

160a	A71	½c	1,000.
161a	A72	1c	1,000.
162a	A73	2c	800.00
164a	A73	4c	650.00
167a	A73	12c	1,000.
171a	A71	50c	1,000.
173a	A73	5p	750.00

Domingo F. Sarmiento — A87

1911, May 15   Typo.   Perf. 13½

176	A87	5c gray brn & blk	.80	.40

Domingo Faustino Sarmiento (1811-88), pres. of Argentina, 1868-74.

Agriculture — A88

Size: 19x25mm

Wmk. 86, without Face

1911	**Engr.**	**Perf. 12**	
177	A88	5c vermilion	.40 .25
178	A88	12c deep blue	5.00 .50

Size: 18x23mm

Wmk. 86, with Face

1911	**Typo.**	**Perf. 13½x12½**	
179	A88	½c violet	.50 .30
180	A88	1c brown ocher	.30 .30
181	A88	2c chocolate	.30 .25
a.		Perf. 13½	15.00 4.00
b.		Imperf., pair	40.00
182	A88	3c green	.50 .50
183	A88	4c brown violet	.50 .50
184	A88	10c gray green	.50 .30
185	A88	20c ultra	4.00 .95
186	A88	24c red brown	6.00 3.75
187	A88	30c claret	3.00 .50
188	A88	50c black	6.00 .80
		Nos. 179-188 (10)	21.60 7.95

The 5c dull red is a proof. In this issue Wmk. 86 comes: straight rays (4c, 20c, 24c) and wavy rays (2c). All other values exist with both forms.

Wmk. 87 (Horiz. or Vert.)

1912-14		**Perf. 13½x12½**	
189	A88	½c violet	.30 .30
190	A88	1c ocher	.30 .30
191	A88	2c chocolate	.50 .30
192	A88	3c green	.50 .50
193	A88	4c brown violet	.50 .60
194	A88	5c red	.40 .30
195	A88	10c deep green	1.75 .30
196	A88	12c deep blue	.60 .30
197	A88	20c ultra	3.00 .50
198	A88	24c red brown	6.00 2.00
199	A88	30c claret	5.00 7.00
200	A88	50c black	9.00 .90
		Nos. 189-200 (12)	27.85 13.30

See Nos. 208-212. For overprints see Nos. OD1-OD8, OD47-OD54, OD102-OD108, OD146-OD152, OD183-OD190, OD235-OD241, OD281-OD284, OD318-OD323.

Perf. 13½

189a	A88	½c	1.00 .30
190a	A88	1c	1.00 .30
191a	A88	2c	1.00 .30
192a	A88	3c	150.00 30.00
193a	A88	4c	2.50 1.25
194a	A88	5c	.90 .30
196a	A88	12c	3.50 1.50
197a	A88	20c	9.00 .90
		Nos. 189a-197a (8)	168.90 34.85

A89

1912-13		**Perf. 13½**	
201	A89	1p dull bl & rose	10.00 1.10
		Punch cancel	.30
202	A89	5p slate & ol grn	19.00 7.00
		Punch cancel	1.00
203	A89	10p violet & blue	75.00 17.50
		Punch cancel	1.40
204	A89	20p blue & claret	210.00 80.00
		Punch cancel	2.00
		Nos. 201-204 (4)	314.00 105.60

1915	**Unwmk.**	**Perf. 13½x12½**	
208	A88	1c ocher	.50 .30
209	A88	2c chocolate	.90 .30
212	A88	5c red	.50 .30
		Nos. 208-212 (3)	1.90 .90

Only these denominations were printed on paper without watermark.

Other stamps of the series are known unwatermarked but they are from the outer rows of sheets the other parts of which are watermarked.

Francisco Narciso de Laprida
A90

Declaration of Independence
A91

A92   A92a

Jose de San Martin

Perf. 13½, 13½x12½

1916, July 9	**Litho.**	**Wmk. 87**	
215	A90	½c violet	.60 .30
216	A90	1c buff	.50 .30

Perf. 13½x12½

217	A90	2c chocolate	.60 .30
218	A90	3c green	.60 .60
219	A90	4c red violet	.60 .60

Perf. 13½

220	A91	5c red	.50 .30
a.		Imperf., pair	40.00
221	A91	10c gray green	1.50 .30
222	A92	12c blue	.90 .35
223	A92	20c ultra	.70 .70
224	A92	24c red brown	2.75 1.40
225	A92	30c claret	2.75 1.60
226	A92	50c gray black	6.75 1.60
227	A92a	1p slate bl & red	10.00 10.00
		Punch cancel	.50
a.		Imperf., pair	325.00
228	A92a	5p black & gray grn	100.00 80.00
		Punch cancel	15.00
229	A92a	10p violet & blue	150.00 135.00
		Punch cancel	9.00
230	A92a	20p dull blue & cl	150.00 100.00
		Punch cancel	7.00
a.		Imperf., pair	650.00
		Nos. 215-230 (16)	428.75 333.35

Cent. of Argentina's declaration of independence of Spain, July 9, 1816.

The watermark is either vert. or horiz. on Nos. 215-220, 222; only vert. on No. 221, and only horiz. on Nos. 223-230.

For overprints see Nos. OD9, OD55-OD56, OD109, OD153, OD191-OD192, OD285, OD324.

A93   A94

A94a

1917		**Perf. 13½**	
231	A93	½c violet	.30 .30
a.		Imperf., pair	70.00
232	A93	1c buff	.30 .30
a.		Imperf., pair	70.00
233	A93	2c brown	.30 .30
a.		Imperf., pair	70.00
234	A93	3c lt green	.70 .30
a.		Imperf., pair	70.00
235	A93	4c red violet	.70 .30
a.		Imperf., pair	70.00
236	A93	5c red	.30 .30
		Never hinged	.45
a.		Imperf., pair	15.00
237	A93	10c gray green	.30 .30
a.		Imperf., pair	70.00
		Nos. 231-237 (7)	2.90 2.10

Perf. 13½x12½

231B	A93	½c violet	.30 .30
232B	A93	1c buff	.40 .40
233B	A93	2c brown	.40 .40
234B	A93	3c lt green	.70 .30
235B	A93	4c red violet	.70 .30
236B	A93	5c red	.30 .30
237B	A93	10c gray green	.30 .30
		Nos. 231B-237B (7)	3.10 2.30

Perf. 13½

238	A94	12c blue	1.00 .25
239	A94	20c ultra	2.50 .30
240	A94	24c red brown	6.00 3.00
241	A94	30c claret	6.00 1.50
242	A94	50c gray black	6.00 .60
243	A94a	1p slate bl & red	6.00 1.00
244	A94a	5p blk & gray grn	19.00 3.00
		Punch cancel	1.50
245	A94a	10p violet & blue	47.50 12.00
		Punch cancel	1.50

246	A94a	20p dull blue & cl	90.00 50.00
		Punch cancel	1.00
a.		Center inverted	1,500. 1,500.
		Nos. 231-246 (16)	186.90 73.35

The watermark is either vert. or horiz. on Nos. 231-236, 238 and 231B-236B, 238B; only vert. on No. 237 and 237B, and only horiz. on Nos. 239-246.

All known examples of No. 246a are off-center to the right.

Juan Gregorio Pujol — A95

1918, June 15	**Litho.**	**Perf. 13½**	
247	A95	5c bister & gray	.60 .30

Cent. of the birth of Juan G. Pujol (1817-61), lawyer and legislator.

1918-19	**Unwmk.**	**Perf. 13½**	
248	A93	½c violet	.30 .25
249	A93	1c buff	.30 .25
a.		Imperf., pair	14.00
250	A93	2c brown	.30 .25
251	A93	3c lt green	.50 .25
252	A93	4c red violet	.50 .25
253	A93	5c red	.30 .25
254	A93	10c gray green	.80 .25
255	A94	12c blue	1.25 .25
256	A94	20c ultra	1.40 .25
257	A94	24c red brown	2.40 .25
258	A94	30c claret	3.00 .30
259	A94	50c gray black	6.00 .50
		Nos. 248-259 (12)	17.05 3.30

Perf. 13½x12½

248B	A93	½c violet	.30 .25
249B	A93	1c buff	.30 .25
250B	A93	2c brown	.30 .25
251B	A93	3c lt green	.50 .25
252B	A93	4c red violet	.50 .25
253B	A93	5c red	.30 .25
254B	A93	10c gray green	1.10 .25
		Nos. 248B-254B (7)	3.30 1.75

The stamps of this issue sometimes show letters of papermakers' watermarks.

There were two printings, in 1918 and 1923, using different ink and paper.

1920		**Wmk. 88**	
264	A93	½c violet	.50 .25
265	A93	1c buff	.50 .25
266	A93	2c brown	.50 .25
267	A93	3c green	1.50 1.00
268	A93	4c red violet	2.00 1.50
269	A93	5c red	.50 .25
270	A93	10c gray green	4.50 .25

Perf. 13½

264A	A93	½c violet	.80 .30
265A	A93	1c buff	.80 .30
266A	A93	2c brown	1.00 .30
267A	A93	3c green	2.00 1.00
269A	A93	5c red	4.00 .30
270A	A93	10c gray green	55.00 15.00
271	A94	12c blue	3.00 .30
272	A94	20c ultra	4.25 .40
274	A94	30c claret	15.00 3.00
275	A94	50c gray black	10.00 3.00
		Nos. 264-275 (17)	105.85 27.65

See Nos. 292-300, 304-307A, 310-314, 318, 322.

For overprints see Nos. OD10-OD20, OD57-OD71, OD74, OD110-OD121, OD154-OD159, OD161-OD162, OD193-OD207, OD209-OD211, OD242-OD252, OD254-OD255, OD286-OD290, OD325-OD328, OD330.

Belgrano's Mausoleum
A96

Creation of Argentine Flag
A97

Gen. Manuel Belgrano — A98

1920, June 18			
280	A96	2c red	1.00 .30
a.		Perf. 13½x12½	2.00 .50
281	A97	5c rose & blue	1.00 .30
282	A98	12c green & blue	2.00 1.00
		Nos. 280-282 (3)	4.00 1.60

Belgrano (1770-1820), Argentine general, patriot and diplomat.

Gen. Justo Jose de Urquiza — A99

1920, Nov. 11			
283	A99	5c gray blue	.60 .30

Gen. Justo Jose de Urquiza (1801-70), pres. of Argentina, 1854-60. See No. 303.

Bartolome Mitre — A100

1921, June 26		**Unwmk.**	
284	A100	2c violet brown	.50 .30
285	A100	5c light blue	.50 .30

Bartolome Mitre (1821-1906), pres. of Argentina, 1862-65.

Allegory, Pan-America — A101

1921, Aug. 25		**Perf. 13½**	
286	A101	3c violet	.55 .30
287	A101	5c blue	2.00 .30
288	A101	10c vio brown	2.50 .50
289	A101	12c rose	3.00 1.00
		Nos. 286-289 (4)	8.05 2.10

Inscribed "Buenos Aires-Agosto de 1921"
A102

Inscribed "Republica Argentina"
A103

1921, Oct.		**Perf. 13½x12½**	
290	A102	5c rose	.60 .30
291	A103	5c rose	2.50 .30

Perf. 13½

290A	A102	5c rose	6.00 .50
291A	A103	5c rose	2.50 .30

1st Pan-American Postal Cong., Buenos Aires, Aug., 1921.

See Nos. 308-309, 319. For overprints see Nos. OD72, OD160, OD208, OD253, OD329.

1920	**Wmk. 89**	**Perf. 13½x12½**	
292	A93	½c violet	1.60 .80
293	A93	1c buff	4.50 1.50
294	A93	2c brown	3.50 .25
297	A93	5c red	4.50 .35
298	A93	10c gray green	4.50 .35

Perf. 13½

294A	A93	2c brown	7.00	1.50
297A	A93	5c red	52.50	9.00
298A	A93	10c gray green	40.00	2.00
299	A94	12c blue	*3,000.*	200.00
300	A94	20c ultra	12.00	1.00

1920

303	A99	5c gray blue	450.00	300.00

1922-23   Wmk. 90   Perf. 13½

304	A93	½c violet	.60	.25
305	A93	1c buff	1.00	.30
306	A93	2c brown	1.00	.30
307	A93	3c green	.60	.40
307A	A93	4c red violet	1.50	1.00
308	A102	5c rose	10.00	3.00
309	A103	5c red	5.00	.80
310	A93	10c gray green	9.00	1.00
311	A94	12c blue	1.00	.40
312	A94	20c ultra	2.00	.50
313	A94	24c red brown	20.00	10.00
314	A94	30c claret	10.00	1.00

Perf. 13½x12½

304B	A93	½c violet	.50	.30
305B	A93	1c buff	.50	.30
306B	A93	2c brown	.50	.30
307B	A93	3c green	1.00	.80
307C	A93	4c red violet	22.50	10.00
308B	A102	5c rose	3.00	.60
309B	A103	5c red	.50	.25
310B	A93	10c gray green	2.25	.25
		Nos. 304-310B (20)	92.45	31.75

Paper with Gray Overprint RA in Sun

1922-23   Unwmk.   Perf. 13½

318	A93	2c brown	3.00	1.00
319	A103	5c red	10.00	1.00
322	A94	20c ultra	30.00	1.50

Perf. 13½x12½

318A	A93	2c brown	3.00	1.00
319A	A103	5c red	3.00	.30

A104

San Martín — A105

With Period after Value

Perf. 13½x12½

1923, May   Litho.   Wmk. 90

323	A104	½c red violet	.50	.30
324	A104	1c buff	.50	.30
325	A104	2c dark brown	.50	.30
326	A104	3c lt green	.50	.40
327	A104	4c red brown	.50	.40
328	A104	5c red	.50	.30
329	A104	10c dull green	3.50	.30
330	A104	12c deep blue	.50	.30
331	A104	20c ultra	1.50	.30
332	A104	24c lt brown	3.50	3.00
333	A104	30c claret	15.00	.30
334	A104	50c black	7.50	.50

Perf. 13½

323A	A104	½c red violet	.50	.30
324A	A104	1c buff	.50	.30
325A	A104	2c dark brown	.50	.30
326A	A104	3c lt green	.50	.40
327A	A104	4c red brown	.50	.40
328A	A104	5c red	.50	.30
329A	A104	10c dull green	3.50	.30
330A	A104	12c deep blue	.50	.30
331A	A104	20c ultra	1.50	.30
332A	A104	24c lt brown	3.50	3.00
333A	A104	30c claret	15.00	.50
334A	A104	50c black	7.50	.50

Without Period after Value

Perf. 13½

Wmk. 87

335	A105	1p blue & red	10.00	.50
336	A105	5p gray lil & grn	30.00	6.00
		Punch cancel		1.00
337	A105	10p clar & blue	90.00	15.00
		Punch cancel		2.00
338	A105	20p sl & brn lake	120.00	45.00
		Punch cancel		1.25
a.		Center inverted		
		Nos. 323-338 (28)	319.00	80.30

Nos. 335-338 and 353-356 canceled with round or oval killers in purple (revenue cancellations) sell for one-fifth to one-half as much as postally used copies.

For overprints see Nos. 399-404.

Design of 1923
Without Period after Value

Perf. 13½x12½

1923-24   Litho.   Wmk. 90

340	A104	½c red violet	.50	.30
341	A104	1c buff	.50	.30
342	A104	2c dk brown	.50	.30
343	A104	3c green	.60	.30
a.		Imperf., pair	8.00	
344	A104	4c red brown	.60	.30
345	A104	5c red	.50	.30
346	A104	10c dull green	.50	.30
347	A104	12c deep blue	.60	.30
348	A104	20c ultra	.90	.30
349	A104	24c lt brown	2.50	1.25
350	A104	25c purple	1.25	.30
351	A104	30c claret	2.50	.30
352	A104	50c black	6.00	.30

Perf. 13½

340B	A104	½c red violet	125.00	40.00
345B	A104	5c red	55.00	22.50
346B	A104	10c dull green	55.00	22.50
349B	A104	24c lt brown	92.50	30.00
353	A105	1p blue & red	6.00	.30
354	A105	5p dk vio & grn	30.00	1.50
355	A105	10p claret & blue	75.00	6.00
356	A105	20p slate & lake	105.00	15.00
		Nos. 340-356 (21)	560.95	142.65

1931-33   Typo.

343b	A104	3c	3.00	.50
345a	A104	5c	4.50	.50
346a	A104	10c	7.50	.50
347a	A104	12c	15.00	3.00
348a	A104	20c	50.00	2.50
350a	A104	25c	40.00	1.75
351a	A104	30c	21.00	1.25
		Nos. 343b-351a (7)	141.00	10.00

The typographed stamps were issued only in coils and have a rough impression with heavy shading about the eyes and nose. Nos. 343 and 346 are known without watermark.

Nos. 341-345, 347-349, 351a may be found in pairs, one with period.

See note after No. 338. See Nos. 362-368. For overprints see Nos. OD21-OD33, OD75-OD87, OD122-OD133, OD163-OD175, OD212-OD226, OD256-OD268, OD291-OD304, OD331-OD345.

Rivadavia — A106

1926, Feb. 8   Perf. 13½

357	A106	5c rose	.60	.30

Presidency of Bernardino Rivadavia, cent.

Rivadavia
A108

San Martin
A109

General Post Office, 1926 — A110

General Post Office, 1826 — A111

1926, July 1   Perf. 13½x12½

358	A108	3c gray green	.40	.30
359	A109	5c red	.40	.30

Perf. 13½

360	A110	12c deep blue	1.25	.40
361	A111	25c chocolate	1.60	.25
a.		"1326" for "1826"	15.00	5.00
		Nos. 358-361 (4)	3.65	1.25

Centenary of the Post Office.

For overprints see Nos. OD34, OD88, OD134, OD227-OD228, OD269, OD305, OD346.

Type of 1923-31 Issue
Without Period after Value

1927   Wmk. 205   Perf. 13½x12½

362	A104	½c red violet	.50	.50
a.		Pelure paper	2.50	2.50
363	A104	1c buff	.50	.50
364	A104	2c dark brown	.50	.50
a.		Pelure paper	.70	.70
365	A104	5c red	.50	.30
a.		Period after value	9.00	6.00
b.		Pelure paper	.70	.70
366	A104	10c dull green	5.00	3.00
367	A104	20c ultra	47.50	4.75

Perf. 13½

368	A105	1p blue & red	36.00	6.00
		Nos. 362-368 (7)	90.50	15.35

Arms of Argentina and Brazil A112

Wmk. RA in Sun (90)

1928, Aug. 27   Perf. 12½x13

369	A112	5c rose red	1.50	.40
370	A112	12c deep blue	2.50	.70

Cent. of peace between the Empire of Brazil and the United Provinces of the Rio de la Plata.

Allegory, Discovery of the New World — A113

"Spain" and "Argentina" — A114

"America" Offering Laurels to Columbus A115

1929, Oct. 12   Litho.   Perf. 13½

371	A113	2c lilac brown	2.00	.40
372	A114	5c light red	2.00	.40
373	A115	12c dull blue	6.00	1.00
		Nos. 371-373 (3)	10.00	1.80

Discovery of America by Columbus, 437th anniv.

Spirit of Victory Attending Insurgents — A116

March of the Victorious Insurgents A117

Perf. 13½x12½ (A116), 12½x13 (A117)

1930

374	A116	½c violet gray	1.00	.50
375	A116	1c myrtle green	1.00	.50
376	A117	2c dull violet	1.00	.50
377	A116	3c green	.50	.50
378	A116	4c violet	.80	.70
379	A116	5c rose red	.70	.30
380	A116	10c gray black	1.00	.70
381	A117	12c dull blue	1.50	.70
382	A117	20c ocher	1.50	.80
383	A117	24c red brown	5.00	2.00
384	A117	25c green	6.00	2.00
385	A117	30c deep violet	8.00	3.00
386	A117	50c black	10.00	4.00
387	A117	1p sl bl & red	24.00	8.00
388	A117	2p black & org	30.00	12.00
389	A117	5p dull grn & blk	92.50	35.00
390	A117	10p dp red brn & dull blue	120.00	40.00

391	A117	20p yel grn & dl bl	210.00	90.00
392	A117	50p dk grn & vio	750.00	650.00
		Nos. 374-390 (17)	304.50	111.20

Revolution of 1930.

Nos. 387-392 with oval (parcel post) cancellation sell for less.

For overprint see No. 405.

1931   Perf. 12½x13

393	A117	½c red violet	.50	.50
394	A117	1c gray black	1.50	1.00
395	A117	3c green	1.50	.70
396	A117	4c red brown	.80	.50
397	A117	5c red	.70	.50
a.		Plane omitted, top left corner	3.00	1.50
398	A117	10c dull green	1.50	.70
		Nos. 393-398 (6)	6.50	3.90

Revolution of 1930.

Stamps of 1924-25 Overprinted in Red or Green

1931, Sept. 6   Perf. 13½, 13½x12½

399	A104	3c green	.40	.40
400	A104	10c dull green	.60	.60
401	A104	30c claret (G)	4.50	2.50
402	A104	50c black	4.50	3.00

Overprinted in Blue

403	A105	1p blue & red	5.50	3.00
404	A105	5p dk violet & grn	60.00	20.00

No. 388 Overprinted in Blue

Perf. 12½x13

405	A117	2p black & orange	10.00	7.50
		Nos. 399-405 (7)	85.50	37.00

1st anniv. of the Revolution of 1930.
See Nos. C30-C34.

Refrigeration Compressor — A118

Perf. 13½x12½

1932, Aug. 29   Litho.

406	A118	3c green	1.00	.50
407	A118	10c scarlet	2.00	.40
408	A118	12c gray blue	7.00	1.10
		Nos. 406-408 (3)	10.00	2.00

6th Intl. Refrigeration Congress.

Port of La Plata A119

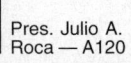

Pres. Julio A. Roca — A120

Municipal
Palace
A121

Cathedral of
La
Plata — A122

Dardo Rocha
A123

Perf. 13½x13, 13x13½ (10c)
1933, Jan.

409	A119	3c green & dk brn	.40	.30
410	A120	10c orange & dk vio	.60	.30
411	A121	15c dk bl & dp bl	2.50	1.50
412	A122	20c violet & yel brn	1.75	.90
413	A123	30c dk grn & vio brn	13.00	6.00
		Nos. 409-413 (5)	18.25	9.00

50th anniv. of the founding of the city of La Plata, Nov. 19th, 1882.

Christ of the
Andes — A124

Buenos Aires
Cathedral
A125

1934, Oct. 1   Perf. 13x13½, 13½x13

414	A124	10c rose & brown	1.00	.30
415	A125	15c dark blue	3.00	.60

32nd Intl. Eucharistic Cong., Oct. 10-14.

"Liberty" with
Arms of Brazil
and Argentina
A126

Symbolical of
"Peace" and
"Friendship"
A127

1935, May 15   Perf. 13x13½

416	A126	10c red	1.00	.30
417	A127	15c blue	2.00	.60

Visit of Pres. Getulio Vargas of Brazil.

Belgrano
A128

Sarmiento
A129

Urquiza — A130

Louis
Braille — A131

San
Martin — A132

Brown — A133

Moreno
A134

Alberdi
A135

Nicolas
Avellaneda
A136

Rivadavia
A137

Mitre
A138

Bull (Cattle
Breeding)
A139

Martin Güemes
A140

Agriculture
A141

Merino
Sheep (Wool)
A142

Sugar Cane
A143

Two types of A140:
Type I — Inscribed Juan Martin Guemes.
Type II — Inscribed Martin Güemes.

Perf. 13, 13½x13, 13x13½

1935-51		Litho.	Wmk. 90	
418	A128	½c red violet	.30	.25
419	A129	1c buff	.30	.25
a.		Typo.	.80	.25
420	A130	2c dark brown	.50	.25
421	A131	2½c black ('39)	.30	.25
422	A132	3c green	.50	.25
423	A132	3c lt gray ('39)	.50	.25
424	A134	3c lt gray ('46)	.50	.25
425	A133	4c lt gray	.50	.25
426	A133	4c sage grn ('39)	.40	.25
427	A134	5c yel brn, typo.	.25	.25
a.		Tete beche pair, typo.	20.00	10.00
b.		Booklet pane of 8, typo.		
c.		Booklet pane of 4, typo.		
d.		Litho.	5.00	.50
428	A135	6c olive green	.40	.25
429	A136	8c orange ('39)	.40	.25
430	A137	10c car, perf. 13½ (typo.)	.25	.25
a.		Perf. 13½x13	2.00	.25
431	A137	10c brown ('42)	.25	.25
432	A138	12c brown	1.00	.25
433	A138	12c red ('39)	.25	.25
434	A139	15c slate bl ('36)	1.50	.25
435	A139	15c pale ultra ('39)	1.00	.25
436	A140	15c lt gray bl (II) ('42)	45.00	2.00
437	A140	20c lt ultra (I)	1.00	.25
438	A140	20c lt ultra (II) ('36)	1.00	.25
439	A140	20c bl gray (II) ('39)	.35	.25
439A	A139	20c dk bl & pale bl, ('42) 22x33mm	1.00	.25
440	A139	20c blue ('51)	.25	.25
a.		Typo.	.25	.25

Oil Well
(Petroleum) — A144

Map of South America
A145   A146

Fruit — A147

Iguacu Falls
(Scenic
Wonders)
A148

Grapes
(Vineyards)
A149

Cotton — A150

441	A141	25c car & pink ('36)	.50	.25
442	A142	30c org brn & yel brown ('36)	.80	.25
443	A143	40c dk vio ('36)	.70	.25
444	A144	50c red & org ('36)	.70	.25
445	A145	1p brn blk & lt bl	25.00	1.00
446	A146	1p brn blk & lt bl ('37)	15.00	.30
a.		Chalky paper	100.00	2.00
447	A147	2p brn lake & dk ultra ('36)	1.00	.25
448	A148	5p ind & ol grn ('36)	3.00	.25
449	A149	10p brn lake & blk	15.00	1.00
450	A150	20p bl grn & brn ('36)	25.00	3.00
		Nos. 418-450 (34)	144.40	14.55

See Nos. 485-500, 523-540, 659, 668. For overprints see Nos. O37-O41, O43-O51, O53-O56, O58-O78, O108, O112, OD35-OD46, OD89-OD101, OD135-OD145, OD176-OD182C, OD229-OD234F, OD270-OD280, OD306-OD317, OD347-OD357.

No. 439A exists with attached label showing medallion. Value $42.50 unused, $22.50 used.

Souvenir Sheet

A151

Without Period after Value
1935, Oct. 17   Litho.   Imperf.

452	A151	Sheet of 4	75.00	35.00
a.		10c dull green	16.50	7.50

Phil. Exhib. at Buenos Aires, Oct. 17-24, 1935. The stamps were on sale during the 8 days of the exhibition only. Sheets measure 83x101mm.

Plaque — A152

1936, Dec. 1   Perf. 13x13½

453	A152	10c rose	.80	.40

Inter-American Conference for Peace.

Domingo Faustino
Sarmiento — A153

1938, Sept. 5

454	A153	3c sage green	.50	.50
455	A153	5c red	.50	.50
456	A153	15c deep blue	1.00	.50
457	A153	50c orange	4.00	1.00
		Nos. 454-457 (4)	6.00	2.50

50th anniv. of the death of Domingo Faustino Sarmiento, pres., educator and author.

"Presidente Sarmiento" — A154

1939, Mar. 16
458 A154 5c greenish blue .50 .30

Final voyage of the training ship "Presidente Sarmiento."

Allegory of the UPU — A155

Coat of Arms — A157

Post Office, Buenos Aires — A156

Iguacu Falls — A158

Bonete Hill, Nahuel Huapi Park — A159

Allegory of Modern Communications A160

Argentina, Land of Promise A161

Lake Frias, Nahuel Huapi Park — A162

Perf. 13x13½, 13½x13
1939, Apr. 1 **Photo.**
459 A155 5c rose carmine .70 .25
460 A156 15c grnsh black .70 .40
461 A157 20c brt blue .70 .25
462 A158 25c dp blue grn 1.10 .40
463 A159 50c brown 1.60 .90
464 A160 1p brown violet 4.25 2.40
465 A161 2p magenta 18.50 15.00
466 A162 5p purple 42.50 30.00
Nos. 459-466 (8) 70.05 49.60

Universal Postal Union, 11th Congress.

Souvenir Sheets

A163

A164

1939, May 12 **Wmk. 90** *Imperf.*
467 A163 Sheet of 4 6.50 5.00
  a. 5c rose carmine (A155) 1.40 1.00
  b. 20c bright blue (A157) 1.40 1.00
  c. 25c deep blue green (A158) 1.40 1.00
  d. 50c brown (A159) 1.40 1.00
468 A164 Sheet of 4 6.50 5.00

Issued in four forms:
  a. Unsevered horizontal pair of sheets, type A163 at left, A164 at right 27.50 16.00
  b. Unsevered vertical pair of sheets, type A163 at top, A164 at bottom 27.50 16.00
  c. Unsevered block of 4 sheets, type A163 at left, A164 at right 55.00 55.00
  d. Unsevered block of 4 sheets, type A163 at top, A164 at bottom 55.00 55.00

11th Cong. of the UPU and the Argentina Intl. Phil. Exposition (C.Y.T.R.A.). No. 468 contains Nos. 467a-467d.

Family and New House A165

Perf. 13½x13
1939, Oct. 2 **Litho.** **Wmk. 90**
469 A165 5c bluish green .50 .25

1st Pan-American Housing Congress.

Bird Carrying Record A166

Head of Liberty and Arms of Argentina A167

Record and Winged Letter A168

Perf. 13x13½, 13½x13 (#472)
1939, Dec. 11 **Photo.**
470 A166 1.18p indigo 14.00 10.00
471 A167 1.32p bright blue 14.00 10.00
472 A168 1.50p dark brown 52.50 35.00
Nos. 470-472 (3) 80.50 55.00

These stamps were issued for the recording and mailing of flexible phonograph records.

Map of the Americas — A169

1940, Apr. 14 **Perf. 13x13½**
473 A169 15c ultramarine .50 .25

50th anniv. of the Pan American Union.

Souvenir Sheet

Reproductions of Early Argentine Stamps — A170

Wmk. RA in Sun (90)
1940, May 25 **Litho.** *Imperf.*
474 A170 Sheet of 5 11.00 8.00
  a. 5c dark blue (Corrientes A2) 1.75 1.50
  b. 5c red (Argentina A1) 1.75 1.50
  c. 5c dark blue (Cordoba #1) 1.75 1.50
  d. 5c red (Argentina A3) 1.75 1.50
  e. 10c dark blue (Buenos Aires A1) 1.75 1.50

100th anniv. of the first postage stamp.

General Domingo French and Colonel Antonio Beruti A171

1941, Feb. 20 **Perf. 13½x13**
475 A171 5c dk gray blue & lt blue .35 .25

Issued in honor of General French and Colonel Beruti, patriots.

Marco M. de Avellaneda — A172

1941, Oct. 3 **Perf. 13x13½**
476 A172 5c dull slate blue .35 .25

Avellaneda, (1814-41), army leader and martyr.

Statue of Gen. Julio Roca — A173

1941, Oct. 19 **Photo.** **Wmk. 90**
477 A173 5c dark olive green .35 .25

Dedication of a monument to Lt. Gen. Julio Argentino Roca (1843-1914).

Carlos Pellegrini and Bank of the Nation A174

1941, Oct. 26 **Perf. 13½x13**
478 A174 5c brown carmine .35 .25

Founding of the Bank of the Nation, 50th anniv.

Gen. Juan Lavalle — A175

1941, Dec. 5 **Perf. 13x13½**
479 A175 5c bright blue .35 .25

Gen. Juan Galo de Lavalle (1797-1841).

National Postal Savings Bank A176

1942, Apr. 5 **Litho.** **Perf. 13½x13**
480 A176 1c pale olive .35 .25

Jose Manuel Estrada — A177

1942, July 13 **Perf. 13x13½**
481 A177 5c brown violet .45 .25

Jose Estrada (1842-1894), writer and diplomat.
Exists imperf. Value, pair $45.
No. 481 exists with label, showing medallion, attached. Value, pair $11.

Types of 1935-51
Perf. 13, 13x13½, 13½x13
1942-50 **Litho.** **Wmk. 288**
485 A128 ½c brown violet 9.00 1.50
486 A129 1c buff ('50) .30 .30
487 A130 2c dk brown ('50) .40 .25
488 A132 3c lt gray 16.00 1.25
489 A134 3c lt gray ('49) .25 .25
490 A137 10c red brn ('49) .25 .25
491 A138 12c red .25 .25
492 A140 15c lt gray blue (II) .30 .25
493 A139 20c dk sl bl & pale bl 4.00 .30
494 A141 25c dull rose ('49) 1.00 .25
495 A142 30c org brn ('49) 1.50 .25
496 A143 40c violet ('49) 10.00 1.00
497 A144 50c red & org ('49) 10.00 .40
498 A146 1p brn blk & lt bl 10.00 .30
499 A147 2p brn lake & bl ('49) 20.00 2.00

500 A148   5p ind & ol grn
                    ('49)   60.00   3.00
       Nos. 485-500 (16)   143.25   11.80
       No. 493 measures 22x33mm.

Post Office,
Buenos
Aires — A178

Inscribed: "Correos y Telegrafos."

1942, Oct. 5   Litho.   Perf. 13
503 A178   35c lt ultra   4.25   .25
              See Nos. 541-543.

Proposed
Columbus
Lighthouse
A179

1942, Oct. 12   Wmk. 288
504 A179   15c dull blue   3.00   .50
                    Wmk. 90
505 A179   15c dull blue   65.00   8.00
       450th anniv. of the discovery of America by
Columbus.

Jose C. Paz — A180

1942, Dec. 15   Wmk. 288
506 A180   5c dark gray   .35   .25
       Cent. of the birth of Jose C. Paz, stateman
and founder of the newspaper La Prensa.

Books and Argentine
Flag — A181

1943, Apr. 1   Litho.   Perf. 13
507 A181   5c dull blue   .30   .25
       1st Book Fair of Argentina.

Arms of Argentina
Inscribed "Honesty,
Justice,
Duty" — A182

1943-50   Wmk. 288   Perf. 13
              Size: 20x26mm
508 A182   5c red ('50)   4.50   .25
                    Wmk. 90
509 A182   5c red   .30   .25
  a.   5c dull red, unsurfaced paper   5.00   .25
510 A182   15c green   .60   .25
              Perf. 13x13½
              Size: 22x33mm
511 A182   20c dark blue   .95   .25
       Nos. 508-511 (4)   6.35   1.00
       Change of political organization, 64/43.

Independence House,
Tucuman — A183

1943-51   Wmk. 90   Perf. 13
512 A183   5c blue green   .95   .25
                    Wmk. 288
513 A183   5c blue green ('51) .45   .25
       Restoration of Independence House.

Liberty Head and
Savings
Bank — A184

1943, Oct. 25   Wmk. 90
514 A184   5c violet brown   .45   .25
                    Wmk. 288
515 A184   5c violet brown   47.50   6.00
       1st conference of National Postal Savings.

Port of Buenos
Aires in
1800 — A185

1943, Dec. 11   Wmk. 90
516 A185   5c gray black   .45   .25
       Day of Exports.

Warship, Merchant
Ship and
Sailboat — A186

1944, Jan. 31   Perf. 13
517 A186   5c blue   .45   .25
       Issued to commemorate Sea Week.

Arms of Argentine
Republic — A187

1944, June 4
518 A187   5c dull blue   .45   .35
       1st anniv. of the change of political organi-
zation in Argentina.

St. Gabriel   Cross at
A188   Palermo
                     A189

1944, Oct. 11
519 A188   3c yellow green   .45   .25
520 A189   5c deep rose   .45   .25
       Fourth national Eucharistic Congress.

Allegory of
Savings — A190

1944, Oct. 24
521 A190   5c gray   .25   .25
       20th anniv. of the National Savings Bank.

Reservists
A191

1944, Dec. 1
522 A191   5c blue   .25   .25
       Day of the Reservists.

Types of 1935-51
Perf. 13x13½, 13½x13

1945-47   Litho.   Unwmk.
523 A128   ½c brown vio ('46)   .25   .25
524 A129   1c yellow brown   .25   .25
525 A130   2c sepia   .25   .25
526 A132   3c lt gray (San
                    Martin)   .60   .25
527 A134   3c lt gray (More-
                    no) ('46)   .25   .25
528 A135   6c olive grn ('47)   .35   .35
529 A137   10c brown ('46)   1.60   .30
530 A140   15c lt gray bl (II) .70   .25
531 A139   20c dk sl bl & pale
                    bl   1.60   .25
532 A141   25c dull rose   .75   .25
533 A142   30c orange brown   .70   .25
534 A143   40c violet   1.75   .35
535 A144   50c red & orange   2.00   .25
536 A146   1p brn blk & lt bl   2.75   .25
537 A147   2p brown lake &
                    bl   27.50   1.00
538 A148   5p ind & ol grn
                    ('46)   40.00   4.00
539 A149   10p dp cl & int blk 10.00   2.00
540 A150   20p bl grn & brn
                    ('46)   9.00   2.00
       Nos. 523-540 (18)   100.30   12.75
       No. 531 measures 22x33mm.

**Post Office Type Inscribed:
"Correos y Telecommunicaciones"**

1945   Unwmk.   Perf. 13x13½
541 A178   35c lt ultra   1.75   .25
                    Wmk. 90
542 A178   35c lt ultra   1.00   .25
                    Wmk. 288
543 A178   35c lt ultra   .35   .25
       Nos. 541-543 (3)   3.10   .75
       Nos. 541 and 543 exist imperf. Value, each,
pair $10.

Bernardino Rivadavia
A192   A193

Mausoleum
of Rivadavia
A194

Perf. 13½x13
1945, Sept. 1   Litho.   Unwmk.
544 A192   3c blue green   .25   .25
545 A193   5c rose   .25   .25
546 A194   20c blue   .35   .25
       Nos. 544-546 (3)   .85   .75
       Cent. of the death of Bernardino Rivadavia,
Argentina's first president.
       No. 546 exists imperf. Value, pair $20.
       No. 546 exists with mute label attached.
Value, pair, $4.50.

San Martin — A195

1945-46   Wmk. 90   Typo. or Litho.
547 A195   5c carmine   .25   .25
  a.   Litho. ('46)   .25   .25
                    Wmk. 288
548 A195   5c carmine, litho. 100.00   30.00
                    Unwmk.
549 A195   5c carmine ('46)   .65   .25
  a.   Litho. ('46)   .25   .25
       Nos. 547 and 547a exist imperf. Values,
pairs: No. 547, $17.50; No. 547a, $10.
       For overprints see Nos. O42, O57.

Monument to Army of
the Andes,
Mendoza — A196

1946, Jan. 14   Litho.   Perf. 13½x13
550 A196   5c violet brown   .25   .25
       Issued to honor the Unknown Soldier of the
War for Independence.

Franklin D.
Roosevelt — A197

1946, Apr. 12
551 A197   5c dark blue   .25   .25

A198

Liberty Administering Presidential Oath.

1946, June 4   Perf. 13x13½
552 A198   5c blue   .25   .25
       Inauguration of Pres. Juan D. Perón, 6/4/46.

Argentina
Receiving
Popular
Acclaim
A199

1946, Oct. 17   Perf. 13½x13
553 A199   5c rose violet   .35   .30
554 A199   10c blue green   .40   .40
555 A199   15c dark blue   .55   .55
556 A199   50c red brown   .40   .50
557 A199   1p carmine rose   1.00   1.20
       Nos. 553-557 (5)   2.70   3.00
       First anniversary of the political organization
change of Oct. 17, 1945.

Coin Bank and World Map — A200

1946, Oct. 31 **Unwmk.**
558 A200 30c dk rose car & pink .45 .30
Universal Day of Savings, October 31, 1946.

Argentine Industry — A201

1946, Dec. 6 **Perf. 13x13½**
559 A201 5c violet brown .25 .25
Day of Argentine Industry, Dec. 6.

International Bridge Connecting Argentina and Brazil A202

1947, May 21 Litho. **Perf. 13½x13**
560 A202 5c green .25 .25
Opening of the Argentina-Brazil International Bridge, May 21, 1947.

Map of Argentine Antarctic Claims — A203

1947-49 **Unwmk.** **Perf. 13x13½**
561 A203 5c violet & lilac .35 .25
562 A203 20c dk car rose & rose .70 .25
Wmk. 90
563 A203 20c dk car rose & rose 1.40 .30
Wmk. 288
564 A203 20c dk car rose & rose
('49) 4.25 .50
Nos. 561-564 (4) 6.70 1.30
1st Argentine Antarctic mail, 43rd anniv. Nos. 561 and 563 exist imperf. Values, pairs: No. 561, $13.50; No. 563, $27.50.

Justice — A204

1947, June 4 **Unwmk.**
565 A204 5c brn vio & pale yel .25 .25
1st anniversary of the Peron government.

Icarus Falling A205

1947, Sept. 25 **Perf. 13½x13**
566 A205 15c red violet .25 .25
Aviation Week.

Training Ship Presidente Sarmiento — A206

1947, Oct. 5 **Perf. 13x13½**
567 A206 5c blue .25 .25
50th anniv. of the launching of the Argentine training frigate "Presidente Sarmiento."

Cervantes and Characters from Don Quixote A207

Perf. 13½x13
1947, Oct. 12 Photo. Wmk. 90
568 A207 5c olive green .25 .25
400th anniv. of the birth of Miguel de Cervantes Saavedra, playwright and poet. Exists imperf. Value, pair $10.

Gen. Jose de San Martin A208

Perf. 13½x13
1947-49 **Unwmk.** **Litho.**
569 A208 5c dull green .25 .25
Wmk. 288
570 A208 5c dull green ('49) .35 .25
Transfer of the remains of Gen. Jose de San Martin's parents. Nos. 569 and 570 exist imperf. Value for pair, each $10.

School Children — A209

1947-49 **Unwmk.** **Perf. 13x13½**
571 A209 5c green .25 .25
Wmk. 90
574 A209 20c brown .35 .25
Wmk. 288
575 A209 5c green ('49) .30 .25
Nos. 571-575 (3) .90 .75
Argentine School Crusade for World Peace. Nos. 571 and 574 exist imperf. Value for pair, each $10.

Statue of Araucanian Indian — A210

1948, May 21 **Wmk. 90**
576 A210 25c yellow brown .25 .25
American Indian Day, Apr. 19. No. 576 exists imperf. Value, pair $10.

Cap of Liberty — A211

1948, July 16
577 A211 5c ultra .25 .25
Revolution of June 4, 1943, 5th anniv.

Manual Stop Signal — A212

1948, July 22
578 A212 5c chocolate & yellow .25 .25
Traffic Safety Day, June 10. No. 578 exists imperf. Value, pair $10.

Post Horn and Oak Leaves — A213

1948, July 22 **Unwmk.**
579 A213 5c lilac rose .25 .25
200th anniversary of the establishment of regular postal service on the Plata River. No. 579 exists imperf. Value, pair $10.

Argentine Farmers — A214

Perf. 13x13½
1948, Sept. 20 **Wmk. 288**
580 A214 10c red brown .25 .25
Agriculture Day, Sept. 8, 1948.

Liberty and Symbols of Progress — A215

Perf. 13x13½
1948, Nov. 23 Photo. Wmk. 287
581 A215 25c red brown .30 .25
3rd anniversary of President Juan D. Peron's return to power, October 17, 1945. No. 581 exists imperf. Value, pair $10.

Souvenir Sheets

A216

15c, Mail coach. 45c, Buenos Aires in 18th cent. 55c, 1st train, 1857. 85c, Sailing ship, 1767.

1948, Dec. 21 Unwmk. Imperf.
582 A216 Sheet of 4 5.50 4.50
a. 15c dark green 1.00 .75
b. 45c orange brown 1.00 .75
c. 55c lilac brown 1.00 .75
d. 85c ultramarine 1.00 .75

A217

Designs: 85c, Domingo de Basavilbaso (1709-75). 1.05p, Postrider. 1.20p, Sailing ship, 1798. 1.90p, Courier in the Andes, 1772.

583 A217 Sheet of 4 26.50 15.00
a. 85c brown 4.75 3.25
b. 1.05p dark green 4.75 3.25
c. 1.20p dark blue 4.75 3.25
d. 1.90p red brown 4.75 3.25
200th anniversary of the establishment of regular postal service on the Plata River.

Winged Wheel — A218

Perf. 13½x13
1949, Mar. 1 **Wmk. 288**
584 A218 10c blue .25 .25
Railroad nationalization, 1st anniv.

Liberty A219

1949, June 20 Engr. Wmk. 90
585 A219 1p red & red violet .70 .30
Ratification of the Constitution of 1949.

Allegory of the UPU A220

1949, Nov. 19
586 A220 25c dk grn & yel grn   .25   .25
    75th anniv. of the UPU.

> Catalogue values for unused stamps in this section, from this point to the end of the section, are for Never Hinged items.

Gen. Jose de San Martin — A221

San Martin at Boulogne sur Mer — A222

Mausoleum of San Martin — A223

20c, 50c, 75c, Different portraits of San Martin. 1p, House where San Martin died.

Engr., Photo. (25c, 1p, 2p)
1950, Aug. 17   Wmk. 90   Perf. 13½
587 A221 10c indigo & dk pur   .35   .25
588 A221 20c red brn & dk brn   .35   .25
589 A222 25c brown   .35   .30
590 A221 50c dk green & ind   .60   .30
591 A221 75c choc & dk grn   .90   .30
   a.   Souv. sheet of 4, #587, 588,
       590, 591, imperf.   4.00   2.50
592 A222 1p dark green   2.00   .40
593 A223 2p dp red lilac   2.50   .50
    Nos. 587-593 (7)   7.05   2.30

Death cent. of General Jose de San Martin.

Map Showing Antarctic Claims — A224

1951, May 21   Litho.   Perf. 13x13½
594 A224 1p choc & lt blue   .75   .25
    For overprint see No. O52.
    No. 594 exists imperf. Value, pair $25.

Pegasus and Train A225

Communications Symbols — A226

Design: 25c, Ship and dolphin.

1951, Oct. 17   Photo.   Perf. 13½
595 A225 5c dark brown   1.50   .25
596 A225 25c Prus green   3.00   .30
597 A226 40c rose brown   3.50   .30
    Nos. 595-597 (3)   8.00   .85

    Close of Argentine Five Year Plan.

Woman Voter and "Argentina" A227

1951, Dec. 14   Perf. 13½x13
598 A227 10c brown violet   .35   .25
    Granting of women's suffrage.

Eva Peron
A228   A229
Litho. or Engraved (#605)
1952, Aug. 26   Wmk. 90   Perf. 13
599 A228 1c orange brown   .35   .25
600 A228 5c gray   .35   .25
601 A228 10c rose lilac   .35   .25
602 A228 20c rose pink   .35   .25
603 A228 25c dull green   .40   .25
604 A228 40c dull violet   .50   .25
605 A228 45c deep blue   .50   .25
606 A228 50c dull brown   .75   .25

Photo.
607 A229 1p dark brown   .90   .30
608 A229 1.50p deep green   4.00   .30
609 A229 2p brt carmine   .90   .30
610 A229 3p indigo   1.60   .30
    Nos. 599-610 (12)   10.95   3.20

    For overprints see Nos. O79-O85.
    Nos. 599, 601-604 and 606 exist imperf. Value for set of 6 pairs, $235.

Inscribed: "Eva Peron"
1952-53   Perf. 13x13½
611 A229 1p dark brown   .90   .35
612 A229 1.50p deep green   2.00   .35
613 A229 2p brt car ('53)   2.00   .40
614 A229 3p indigo   4.00   .90

Engr.
Perf. 13½x13
Size: 30x40mm
615 A229 5p red brown   4.75   1.75
616 A229 10p red   8.00   3.75
617 A229 20p green   17.50   8.50
618 A228 50p ultra   40.00   17.50
    Nos. 611-618 (8)   79.15   33.50

    For overprints see Nos. O86-O93.

Indian Funeral Urn — A230

1953, Aug. 28   Photo.   Perf. 13x13½
619 A230 50c blue green   .35   .25
    Founding of Santiago del Estero, 400th anniv.

Rescue Ship "Uruguay" — A231

1953, Oct. 8   Perf. 13½
620 A231 50c ultra   1.75   .50
    50th anniv. of the rescue of the Antarctic expedition of Otto C. Nordenskjold.

Planting Argentine Flag in the Antarctic A232

1954, Jan. 20   Engr.   Perf. 13½x13
621 A232 1.45p blue   1.40   .50

    50th anniv. of Argentina's 1st antarctic p.o. and the establishing of the La Hoy radio p.o. in the South Orkneys.

Wired Communications A233

Television A234

Perf. 13x13½, 13½x13
1954, Apr.   Photo.   Wmk. 90
622 A233 1.50p shown   .50   .30
623 A233 3p Radio   2.00   .30
624 A234 5p shown   3.00   .40
    Nos. 622-624 (3)   5.50   1.00

    Intl. Plenipotentiary Conf. of Telecommunications, Buenos Aires, 1952.

Pediment, Buenos Aires Stock Exchange A235

1954, July 13   Perf. 13½x13
625 A235 1p dark green   .50   .25
    Cent. of the establishment of the Buenos Aires Stock Exchange.

Eva Peron — A236

1954   Wmk. 90
626 A236 3p dp car rose   3.00   .50
Wmk. 288
627 A236 3p dp car rose   250.00   50.00
    2nd anniv. of the death of Eva Peron.

Jose de San Martin — A237

Wheat — A238

Industry — A238a

Eva Peron Foundation Building A239

Cliffs of Humahuaca — A240

Gen. Jose de San Martin — A241

    Designs: 50c, Buenos Aires harbor. 1p, Cattle ranch (Ganaderia). 3p, Nihuil Dam. 5p, Iguacu Falls, vert. 20p, Mt. Fitz Roy, vert.

Engraved (#632, 638-642),
Photogravure (#634-637)
Perf. 13½, 13x13½ (80c), 13½x13
(#639, 641-642)
1954-59   Wmk. 90
628 A237 20c brt red, typo.   .25   .25
629 A237 20c red, litho. ('55)   1.00   .25
630 A237 40c red, litho. ('56)   .25   .25
631 A237 40c brt red, typo.
               ('55)   .25   .25
632 A239 50c blue ('56)   .30   .25
633 A239 50c bl, litho. ('59)   .60   .25
634 A238 80c brown   .40   .25
635 A239 1p brown ('58)   .40   .25
636 A238a 1.50p ultra ('58)   .40   .25
637 A239 2p dk rose lake   .50   .25
638 A239 3p violet brn ('56)   .50   .25

639	A240	5p gray grn ('55)	8.00	.25
a.		Perf. 13½	10.00	.25
640	A240	10p yel grn ('55)	8.00	.25
641	A240	20p dull vio ('55)	11.00	.50
a.		Perf. 13½	14.00	1.50
642	A241	50p ultra & ind ('55)	12.00	1.50
a.		Perf. 13½	15.00	1.00
		Nos. 628-642 (15)	43.85	5.25

See Nos. 699-700. For similar designs inscribed "Republica Argentina" see Nos. 823-827, 890, 935, 937, 940, 990, 995, 1039, 1044, 1048.

For overprints see Nos. O94-O106, O142, O153-O157.

Allegory A242

1954, Aug. 26   Typo.   Perf. 13½
| 643 | A242 | 1.50p slate black | .80 | .25 |

Cent. of the establishment of the Buenos Aires Grain Exchange.

Clasped Hands and Congress Medal — A243

1955, Mar. 21   Photo.   Perf. 13½x13
| 644 | A243 | 3p red brown | 1.50 | .30 |

Issued to publicize the National Productivity and Social Welfare Congress.

Allegory of Aviation — A244

1955, June 18   Wmk. 90   Perf. 13½
| 645 | A244 | 1.50p olive gray | 1.00 | .25 |

Commercial aviation in Argentina, 25th anniv.

Argentina Breaking Chains — A245

1955, Oct. 16   Litho.
| 647 | A245 | 1.50p olive green | .70 | .25 |

Liberation Revolution of Sept. 16, 1955.

Army Navy and Air Force Emblems A246

Perf. 13½x13
1955, Dec. 31   Photo.   Wmk. 90
| 648 | A246 | 3p blue | .50 | .25 |

"Brotherhood of the Armed Forces."

Justo Jose de Urquiza — A247

1956, Feb. 3   Perf. 13½
| 649 | A247 | 1.50p dk grn, lt grn | .70 | .25 |

Battle of Caseros, 104th anniversary. No. 649 exists imperf. Value, pair $30.

Coin and Die — A248

1956, July 28   Engr.   Perf. 13½x13
| 650 | A248 | 2p multicolored | .40 | .25 |

75th anniversary of the Argentine Mint.

1856 Stamp of Corrientes A249

Juan G. Pujol — A250

Design: 2.40p, Stamp of 1860-78.

1956, Aug. 21
| 651 | A249 | 40c dk grn & blue | .30 | .25 |
| 652 | A249 | 2.40p brn & lil rose | .40 | .25 |

Photo.
653	A250	4.40p brt blue	.90	.30
a.		Souv. sheet, #651-653, imperf.	6.00	6.00
		Nos. 651-653 (3)	1.60	.80

Centenary of Argentine postage stamps. No. 653a for the Argentine stamp cent. and Philatelic Exhib. for the Cent. of Corrientes Stamps, Oct. 12-21. The 4.40p is photo., the other two stamps and border litho. Colors of 40c and 2.40p differ slightly from engraved stamps.

Felling Trees, La Pampa A251

Maté Herb and Gourd, Misiones — A252

1p, Cotton plant and harvest, Chaco.

1956, Sept. 1   Perf. 13½
654	A251	50c ultra	.55	.25
655	A251	1p magenta	.55	.25
656	A252	1.50p green	.55	.25
		Nos. 654-656 (3)	1.65	.75

Elevation of the territories of La Pampa, Chaco and Misiones to provinces.

"Liberty" — A253

Perf. 13½
1956, Sept. 15   Wmk. 90   Photo.
| 657 | A253 | 2.40p lilac rose | .75 | .25 |

1st anniv. of the Revolution of Liberation.

Florentino Ameghino — A254

1956, Nov. 30
| 658 | A254 | 2.40p brown | .40 | .25 |

Issued to honor Florentino Ameghino (1854-1911), anthropologist.
For overprint see No. O110.

Adm. Brown Type of 1935-51

Two types:
I.   Bust touches upper frame line of name panel at bottom.
II. White line separates bust from frame line.

Size: 19½-20½x26-27mm
1956   Litho.   Perf. 13
659	A133	20c dull purple (I)	.25	.25
a.		Type II	.25	.25
b.		Size 19½x25¼mm (I)	.25	.25

For overprint see No. O108.

Benjamin Franklin A255

1956, Dec. 22   Photo.   Perf. 13½
| 660 | A255 | 40c intense blue | .40 | .25 |

250th anniv. of the birth of Benjamin Franklin.

Frigate "Hercules" A256

Guillermo Brown A257

1957, Mar. 2
661	A256	40c brt blue	.25	.25
662	A257	2.40p gray black	.40	.25
		Nos. 661-662,C63-C65 (5)	1.50	1.25

Admiral Guillermo (William) Brown (1777-1857), founder of the Argentine navy.

Roque Saenz Pena (1851-1914) A258

1957, Apr. 1
| 663 | A258 | 4.40p grnsh gray | .45 | .25 |

Roque Saenz Pena, pres. 1910-14.
For overprint see No. O111.

Church of Santo Domingo, 1807 — A259

1957, July 6   Wmk. 90
| 664 | A259 | 40c brt blue green | .30 | .25 |

150th anniv. of the defense of Buenos Aires.

"La Portena" A260

1957, Aug. 31   Wmk. 90   Perf. 13½
| 665 | A260 | 40c pale brown | .50 | .25 |

Centenary of Argentine railroads.

Esteban Echeverria — A261

1957, Sept. 2   Perf. 13x13½
| 666 | A261 | 2p claret | .30 | .25 |

Esteban Echeverria (1805-1851), poet.
For overprint see No. O109.

"Liberty" — A262

1957, Sept. 28   Perf. 13½
| 667 | A262 | 40c carmine rose | .40 | .25 |

Constitutional reform convention.

Portrait Type of 1935-51
1957, Oct. 28   Litho.   Perf. 13½
Size: 16½x22mm
| 668 | A128 | 5c Jose Hernandez | .25 | .25 |

For overprint see No. O112.

Oil Derrick and Hands Holding Oil — A263

Perf. 13½
1957, Dec. 21   Wmk. 90   Photo.
669 A263 40c bright blue   .65   .25
50th anniv. of the national oil industry.
No. 669 exists imperf. Value, pair $30.

Museum, La Plata — A264

1958, Jan. 11
670 A264 40c dark gray   .30   .25
City of La Plata, 75th anniversary.

A265   A266

40c, Locomotive & arms of Argentina & Bolivia. 1p, Map of Argentine-Bolivian boundary & plane.

1958, Apr. 19   Wmk. 90   Perf. 13½
671 A265 40c slate & dp car   .55   .25
672 A266 1p dark brown   .55   .25
Argentine-Bolivian friendship. No. 671 for the opening of the Jacuiba-Santa Cruz railroad; No. 672, the exchange of presidential visits.

Symbols of the Republic A267

1958, Apr. 30   Photo. & Engr.
673 A267 40c multicolored   .25   .25
674 A267 1p multicolored   .30   .25
675 A267 2p multicolored   .50   .25
Nos. 673-675 (3)   1.05   .75
Transmission of Presidential power.

Flag Monument — A268

1958, June 21   Litho.   Wmk. 90
676 A268 40c blue & violet bl   .30   .25
1st anniv. of the Flag Monument of Rosario.
Exists imperf. Value, pair $40.

Map of Antarctica — A269

1958, July 12   Perf. 13½
677 A269 40c car rose & blk   .70   .40
International Geophysical Year, 1957-58.
Exists imperf. Value, pair $80.

Stamp of Cordoba and Mail Coach A270

1958, Oct. 18
678 A270 40c pale blue & slate   .30   .25
Nos. 678,C72-C73 (3)   .80   .75
Centenary of Cordoba postage stamps.

"Slave" by Michelangelo and UN Emblem — A271

Engraved and Lithographed
1959, Mar. 14   Wmk. 90   Perf. 13½
679 A271 40c violet brn & gray   .30   .25
10th anniv. (in 1958) of the signing of the Universal Declaration of Human Rights. No UN Emblem (error) Value, $200.
Exists imperf. Value, pair $50.

Orchids and Globe — A272

1959, May 23   Photo.   Perf. 13½
680 A272 1p dull claret   .30   .25
1st International Horticulture Exposition.
Exists imperf. Value, pair $50.

Pope Pius XII — A273

1959, June 20   Engr.   Perf. 13½
681 A273 1p yellow & black   .40   .25
Pope Pius XII, 1876-1958.
Exists imperf. Value, pair $50.

William Harvey — A274

1p, Claude Bernard. 1.50p, Ivan P. Pavlov.

1959, Aug. 8   Litho.   Wmk. 90
682 A274 50c green   .25   .25
683 A274 1p dark red   .25   .25
684 A274 1.50p brown   .30   .25
Nos. 682-684 (3)   .80   .75
21st Intl. Cong. of Physiological Sciences, Buenos Aires.

Type of 1958 and

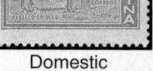

Domestic Horse — A275   Jose de San Martin — A276

Tierra del Fuego A277

Inca Bridge, Mendoza — A278

Ski Jumper A279

Mar del Plata A280

Designs: 10c, Cayman. 20c, Llama. 50c, Puma. No. 690, Sunflower. 3p, Zapata Slope, Catamarca. 12p, 23p, 25p, Red Quebracho tree. 20p, Nahuel Huapi Lake. 22p, "Industry" (cogwheel and factory).
Two overall paper sizes for 1p, 5p:
I — 27x37½mm or 37½x27mm.
II — 27x39mm or 39x27mm.

Perf. 13x13½
1959-70   Litho.   Wmk. 90
685 A275 10c slate green   .35   .25
686 A275 20c dl red brn ('61)   .35   .25
687 A275 50c bister ('60)   .35   .25
688 A275 50c bis, typo. ('60)   .35   .25
689 A275 1p rose red   .35   .25

Perf. 13½
690 A278 1p brn, photo., I ('61)   .25   .25
a.   Paper II ('69)   1.00   .25
690B A278 1p brown, I   .80   .25
691 A276 2p rose red ('61)   .40   .25

692 A276 2p red, typo.
(19½ x 26mm) ('61)   .50   .25
a.   Redrawn (19½ x 25mm)   4.00   .25
693 A277 3p dk bl, photo. ('60)   .25   .25
694 A276 4p red, typo ('62)   1.00   .25
694A A276 4p red ('62)   .60   .25
695 A277 5p gray brn, photo., I   .30   .25
e.   5p dark brown, paper II ('70)   8.00   4.00
695A A276 8p ver ('65)   1.75   .25
695B A276 8p red, typo. ('65)   .30   .25
695C A276 10p ver ('66)   .50   .25
695D A276 10p red, typo. ('66)   .50   .25

Photo.
696 A278 10p lt red brn ('60)   .50   .25
697 A278 12p dk brn vio ('62)   1.00   .25
697A A278 12p dk brn, litho. ('64)   12.00   .30
698 A278 20p Prus grn ('60)   3.00   .25
698A A276 20p red, typo. ('67)   .30   .25
699 A238a 22p ultra ('62)   1.75   .25
700 A238a 22p ultra, litho. ('62)   25.00   .30
701 A278 23p green ('65)   5.00   .25
702 A278 25p dp vio ('66)   1.50   .25
703 A278 25p pur, litho. ('66)   6.00   .25
704 A279 100p blue ('61)   8.00   .25
705 A280 300p dp vio ('62)   4.00   .25
Nos. 685-705 (29)   76.95   7.35

Imperf. and imperf. between examples of some numbers exist.
See Nos. 882-887, 889, 892, 923-925, 928-930, 938, 987-989, 991.
For overprints and surcharges see Nos. 1076, C82-C83, O113-O118, O122-O124, O126-O141, O143-O145, O163.
The 300p remained on sale as a 3p stamp after the 1970 currency exchange.

Symbolic Sailboat — A281

1959, Oct. 3   Litho.   Perf. 13½
706 A281 1p blk, red & bl   .30   .25
Red Cross sanitary education campaign.

Child Playing with Doll — A282

1959, Oct. 17
707 A282 1p red & blk   .30   .25
Issued for Mother's Day, 1959.

Buenos Aires 1p Stamp of 1859 — A283

1959, Nov. 21   Wmk. 90   Perf. 13½
708 A283 1p gray & dk bl   .30   .25
Issued for the Day of Philately.

Bartolomé Mitre and Justo José de Urquiza — A284

1959, Dec. 12   Photo.   Perf. 13½
709 A284 1p purple   .30   .25
Treaty of San Jose de Flores, centenary.
Exists imperf. Value, pair $40.

WRY Emblem — A285

1960, Apr. 7   Litho.   Wmk. 90
710 A285   1p bister & car   .35   .25
711 A285   4.20p apple grn & dp
            claret   .35   .25
World Refugee Year, July 1, 1959-June 30, 1960. See No. B25.

Abraham Lincoln — A286

1960, Apr. 14   Photo.   Perf. 13½
712 A286 5p ultra   .45   .25
Sesquicentennial (in 1959) of the birth of Abraham Lincoln.
Exists imperf. Value, pair $70.

Cornelio Saavedra and Cabildo, Buenos Aires — A287

"Cabildo" and: 2p, Juan José Paso. 4.20p, Manuel Alberti and Miguel Azcuénaga. 10.70p, Juan Larrea and Domingo Matheu.

Perf. 13½
1960, May 28   Wmk. 90   Photo.
713 A287   1p rose lilac   .25   .25
714 A287   2p bluish grn   .25   .25
715 A287   4.20p gray & grn   .30   .25
716 A287   10.70p gray & ultra   .45   .25
   Nos. 713-716,C75-C76 (6)   1.85 1.50
150th anniversary of the May Revolution. Souvenir sheets are Nos. C75a and C76a.

Luis Maria Drago — A288

1960, July 8
717 A288 4.20p brown   .30   .25
Centenary of the birth of Dr. Luis Maria Drago, statesman and jurist.
Exists imperf. Value, pair $40.

Juan Bautista Alberdi — A289

1960, Sept. 10   Wmk. 90   Perf. 13½
718 A289 1p green   .30   .25
150th anniversary of the birth of Juan Bautista Alberdi, statesman and philosopher.
Exists imperf. Value, pair $40.

Map of Argentina and Antarctic Sector — A290

1960, Sept. 24   Litho.   Perf. 13½
719 A290 5p violet   .75   .25
National census of 1960.
Exists imperf. Value, pair $70.

Caravel and Emblem A291

1960, Oct. 1   Photo.
720 A291 1p dk olive grn   .40   .25
721 A291 5p brown   .65   .25
   Nos. 720-721,C78-C79 (4)   2.25 1.10
8th Congress of the Postal Union of the Americas and Spain.

Virgin of Luján, Patroness of Argentina — A292

1960, Nov. 12   Wmk. 90   Perf. 13½
722 A292 1p dark blue   .60   .25
First Inter-American Marian Congress.
Exists imperf. Value, pair $30.

Argentine Boy Scout Emblem — A293

1961, Jan. 17   Litho.
723 A293 1p car rose & blk   .30   .25
International Patrol Encampment of the Boy Scouts, Buenos Aires.
Exists imperf. Value, pair $70.

"Shipment of Cereals," by Quinquela Martin — A294

1961, Feb. 11   Photo.   Perf. 13½
724 A294 1p red brown   .30   .25
Export drive: "To export is to advance."
Exists imperf. Value, pair $40.

Naval Battle of San Nicolás — A295

1961, Mar. 2   Perf. 13½
725 A295 2p gray   .30   .25
Naval battle of San Nicolas, 150th anniv.
Exists imperf. Value, pair $67.50.

Mariano Moreno by Juan de Dios Rivera A296

1961, Mar. 25   Perf. 13½
726 A296 2p blue   .30   .25
Mariano Moreno (1778-1811), writer, politician, member of the 1810 Junta.
Exists imperf. Value, pair $40.

Emperor Trajan Statue — A297

1961, Apr. 11
727 A297 2p slate green   .30   .25
Visit of Pres. Giovanni Gronchi of Italy to Argentina, April 1961.
Exists imperf. Value, pair $40.

Rabindranath Tagore — A298

1961, May 13   Photo.   Perf. 13½
728 A298 2p purple, grysh   .65   .25
Centenary of the birth of Rabindranath Tagore, Indian poet.

San Martin Statue, Madrid A299

1961, May 24   Wmk. 90
729 A299 1p olive gray   .30   .25
Unveiling of a statue of General José de San Martin in Madrid.
Exists imperf. Value, $40.

Manuel Belgrano A300

1961, June 17   Perf. 13½
730 A300 2p violet blue   .60   .25
Erection of a monument by Hector Rocha, to General Manuel Belgrano in Buenos Aires.
Exists imperf. Value, pair $40.

Explorers, Sledge and Dog Team A301

1961, Aug. 19   Photo.   Wmk. 90
731 A301 2p black   .60   .30
10th anniversary of the General San Martin Base, Argentine Antarctic.
Exists imperf. Value, pair $75.

Spanish Conquistador and Sword — A302

1961, Aug. 19   Litho.
732 A302 2p red & blk   .30   .25
First city of Jujuy, 400th anniversary.
Exists imperf. Value, pair $40.

Sarmiento Statue by Rodin, Buenos Aires — A303

1961, Sept. 9   Photo.
733 A303 2p violet   .30   .25
Domingo Faustino Sarmiento (1811-88), political leader and writer.
Exists imperf. Value, pair $40.

Symbol of World Town Planning A304

1961, Nov. 25   Litho.   Perf. 13½
734 A304 2p ultra & yel   .30   .25
World Town Planning Day, Nov. 8.

Manuel Belgrano Statue, Buenos Aires — A305

1962, Feb. 24 **Photo.**
735 A305 2p Prus blue .30 .25
150th anniversary of the Argentine flag.
Exists imperf. Value, pair $40.

Grenadier, Flag and Regimental Emblem — A306

1962, Mar. 31 **Wmk. 90** **Perf. 13½**
736 A306 2p carmine rose .60 .25
150th anniversary of the San Martin Grenadier Guards regiment.
Exists imperf. Value, pair $40.

Mosquito and Malaria Eradication Emblem A307

1962, Apr. 7 **Litho.**
737 A307 2p vermilion & blk .35 .25
WHO drive to eradicate malaria.

Church of the Virgin of Lujàn — A308

1962, May 12 **Perf. 13½**
738 A308 2p org brn & blk .30 .25
75th anniversary of the pontifical coronation of the Virgin of Lujan.

Bust of Juan Jufrè — A309

1962, June 23 **Photo.**
739 A309 2p Prus blue .30 .25
Founding of San Juan, 4th cent.
Exists imperf. Value, pair $40.

"Soaring into Space" — A310

1962, Aug. 18 **Litho.** **Perf. 13½**
740 A310 2p maroon, blk & bl .30 .25
Argentine Air Force, 50th anniversary.
Exists imperf. Value, pair $40.

Juan Vucetich — A311

1962, Oct. 6 **Photo.** **Wmk. 90**
741 A311 2p green .30 .25
Juan Vucetich (1864-1925), inventor of the Argentine system of fingerprinting.
Exists imperf. Value, pair $40.

Domingo F. Sarmiento — A312

Design: 4p, Jose Hernandez.

1962-66 **Photo.** **Perf. 13½**
742 A312 2p deep green .50 .25
Litho.
742A A312 2p lt green ('64) .50 .25
Photo.
742B A312 4p dull red ('65) .50 .25
Litho.
742C A312 4p rose red ('66) 1.25 .25
Nos. 742-742C (4) 2.75 1.00
No. 742A exists imperf. Value, pair $40.
See No. 817-819. For overprints see Nos. O119-O121, O125, O149.

February 20th Monument, Salta — A313

1963, Feb. 23 **Photo.** **Wmk. 90**
743 A313 2p dark green .60 .25
150th anniversary of the Battle of Salta, War of Independence.
Exists imperf. Value, pair $40.

Gear Wheels A314

1963, Mar. 16 **Litho.** **Perf. 13½**
744 A314 4p gray, blk & brt rose .60 .25
Argentine Industrial Union, 75th anniv.
Exists imperf. Value, pair $40.

National College, Buenos Aires — A315

1963, Mar. 16 **Wmk. 90**
745 A315 4p dull org & blk .65 .25
National College of Buenos Aires, cent.
Exists imperf. Value, pair $40.

Child Draining Cup — A316

1963, Apr. 6
746 A316 4p multicolored .30 .25
FAO "Freedom from Hunger" campaign.
Exists imperf. Value, pair $40.

Frigate "La Argentina," 1817, by Emilio Biggeri A317

1963, May 18 **Photo.**
747 A317 4p bluish green .90 .25
Issued for Navy Day, May 17.
Exists imperf. Value, pair $40.

Seat of 1813 Assembly and Official Seal — A318

1963, July 13 **Litho.** **Perf. 13½**
748 A318 4p lt blue & blk .60 .25
150th anniversary of the 1813 Assembly.
Exists imperf. Value, pair $40.

Battle of San Lorenzo, 1813 A319

1963, Aug. 24
749 A319 4p grn & blk, grnsh .60 .25
Sesquicentennial of the Battle of San Lorenzo.

Queen Nefertari Offering Papyrus Flowers, Abu Simbel A320

1963, Sept. 14 **Perf. 13½**
750 A320 4p ocher, blk & bl grn .60 .25
Campaign to save the historic monuments in Nubia.
Exists imperf. Value, pair $40.

Government House, Buenos Aires — A321

1963, Oct. 12 **Wmk. 90** **Perf. 13½**
751 A321 5p rose & brown .60 .25
Inauguration of President Arturo Illia.
Exists imperf. Value, pair $40.

"Science" — A322

1963, Oct. 16 **Litho.**
752 A322 4p org brn, bl & blk .65 .25
10th Latin-American Neurosurgery Congress.
Exists imperf. Value, pair $40.

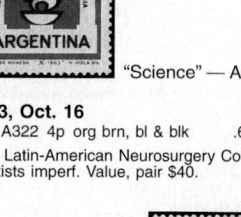

Francisco de las Carreras, Supreme Court Justice — A323

1963, Nov. 23 **Photo.** **Perf. 13½**
753 A323 5p bluish green .30 .25
Centenary of judicial power.
Exists imperf. Value, pair $40.

Blackboards A324

1963, Nov. 23 **Litho.**
754 A324 5p red, blk & bl .30 .25
Issued to publicize "Teachers for America" through the Alliance for Progress program.
Exists imperf. Value, pair $40.

Kemal Atatürk — A325

1963, Dec. 28 **Photo.** **Perf. 13½**
755 A325 12p dark gray .60 .25
25th anniversary of the death of Kemal Atatürk, president of Turkey.
Exists imperf. Value, pair $40.

"Payador" by Juan Carlos Castagnino — A326

1964, Jan. 25   **Litho.**
756 A326 4p ultra, blk & lt bl   .60   .25
Fourth National Folklore Festival.
Exists imperf. Value, pair $40.

Maps of South Georgia, South Orkney and South Sandwich Islands A327

4p, Map of Argentina & Antarctic claims, vert.

1964, Feb. 22   **Wmk. 90**   **Perf. 13½**
    Size: 33x22mm
757 A327 2p lt & dk bl & bister   1.40   .30
    Size: 30x40mm
758 A327 4p lt & dk bl & ol grn   2.10   .30
   Nos. 757-758,C92 (3)   6.25   1.35
Argentina's claim to Antarctic territories, 60th anniv.
Exist imperf. Value, set of 3 pairs, $150.

Jorge Newbery in Cockpit A328

1964, Feb. 23   **Photo.**
759 A328 4p deep green   .65   .25
Newbery, aviator, 50th death anniv.
Exists imperf. Value, pair $40.

John F. Kennedy A329

1964, Apr. 14   **Engr.**   **Wmk. 90**
760 A329 4p claret & dk bl   .50   .25
President John F. Kennedy (1917-63).
Exists imperf. Value, pair $100.

José Brochero by José Cuello — A330

1964, May 9   **Photo.**   **Perf. 13½**
761 A330 4p light sepia   .60   .25
50th anniversary of the death of Father Jose Gabriel Brochero.
Exists imperf. Value, pair $50.

Soldier of Patricios Regiment A331

1964, May 29   **Litho.**   **Wmk. 90**
762 A331 4p blk, ultra & red   .60   .25
Issued for Army Day. Later Army Day stamps, inscribed "Republica Argentina," are of type A340a.
Exists imperf. Value, pair $40.

Pope John XXIII — A332

1964, June 27   **Engr.**
763 A332 4p orange & blk   .30   .25
Issued in memory of Pope John XXIII.
Exists imperf. Value, pair $50.

University of Cordoba Arms — A333

1964, Aug. 22   **Litho.**   **Wmk. 90**
764 A333 4p blk, ultra & yel   .30   .25
350th anniv. of the University of Cordoba.

Pigeons and UN Building, NYC — A334

1964, Oct. 24   **Perf. 13½**
765 A334 4p dk blue & lt blue   .35   .25
Issued for United Nations Day.
Exists imperf. Value, pair $40.

Joaquin V. Gonzalez — A335

1964, Nov. 14   **Photo.**
766 A335 4p dk rose carmine   .60   .25
Centenary (in 1963) of the birth of Joaquin V. Gonzalez, writer.
Exists imperf. Value, pair $40.

Julio Argentino Roca — A336

1964, Dec. 12   **Perf. 13½**
767 A336 4p violet blue   .30   .25
General Julio A. Roca, (1843-1914), president of Argentina, (1880-86, 1898-1904).
Exists imperf. Value, pair $40.

Market at Montserrat Square, by Carlos Morel — A337

1964, Dec. 19   **Photo.**
768 A337 4p sepia   .35   .25
19th century Argentine painter Carlos Morel.
Exists imperf. Value, pair $40.

Icebreaker General San Martin A338

2p, General Belgrano Base, Antarctica.

1965   **Perf. 13½**
769 A338 2p dull purple   .60   .25
770 A338 4p ultra   1.20   .25
Issued to publicize the natl. territory of Tierra del Fuego, Antarctic and South Atlantic Isles.
Issue dates: 4p, Feb. 27; 2p, June 5.
No. 769 exists imperf. Value, pair $50.

Girl with Piggy Bank — A339

1965, Apr. 3   **Litho.**
771 A339 4p red org & blk   .30   .25
National Postal Savings Bank, 50th anniv.
Exists imperf. Value, pair $40.

Sun and Globe A340

1965, May 29
772 A340 4p blk, org & dl bl   .60   .30
   Nos. 772,C98-C99 (3)   2.55   1.15
International Quiet Sun Year, 1964-65.
Exists imperf. Value, pair $40.

Hussar of Pueyrredon Regiment — A340a

1965, June 5   **Wmk. 90**   **Perf. 13½**
773 A340a 8p dp ultra, blk & red   .50   .25
Issued for Army Day. See Nos. 796, 838, 857, 893, 944, 958, 974, 1145.
Exists imperf. Value, pair $50.

Ricardo Rojas (1882-1957) A341

Portraits: No. 775, Ricardo Guiraldes (1886-1927). No. 776, Enrique Larreta (1873-1961). No. 777, Leopoldo Lugones (1874-1938). No. 778, Roberto J. Payro (1867-1927).

1965, June 26   **Photo.**
774 A341 8p brown   .35   .25
775 A341 8p brown   .35   .30
776 A341 8p brown   .35   .25
777 A341 8p brown   .35   .25
778 A341 8p brown   .35   .25
   Nos. 774-778 (5)   1.75   1.30
Issued to honor Argentine writers. Printed se-tenant in sheets of 100 (10x10); 2 horizontal rows of each design with Guiraldes in top rows and Rojas in bottom rows.
Nos. imperf. Value, strip of 5, $250.

Hipolito Yrigoyen A342

1965, July 3   **Litho.**
779 A342 8p pink & black   .30   .25
Hipolito Yrigoyen (1852-1933), president of Argentina 1916-22, 1928-30.

Children Looking Through Window A343

1965, July 24   **Photo.**
780 A343 8p salmon & blk   .60   .25
International Seminar on Mental Health.
Exists imperf. Value, pair $40.

Child's Funerary Urn and 16th Century Map A344

1965, Aug. 7   **Litho.**
781 A344 8p lt grn, dk red, brn & ocher   .35   .25
City of San Miguel de Tucuman, 400th anniv.
Exists imperf. Value, pair $40.

Cardinal
Cagliero — A345

1965, Aug. 21   **Photo.**
782 A345 8p violet   .30   .25
Juan Cardinal Cagliero (1839-1926), missionary to Argentina and Bishop of Magida. Exists imperf. Value, pair $40.

Dante
Alighieri — A346

1965, Sept. 16   Wmk. 90   Perf. 13½
783 A346 8p light ultra   .60   .25
Dante Alighieri (1265-1321), Italian poet. Exists imperf. Value, pair $40.

Clipper
"Mimosa" and
Map of
Patagonia
A347

1965, Sept. 25   **Litho.**
784 A347 8p red & black   .35   .25
Centenary of Welsh colonization of Chubut, and the founding of the city of Rawson. Exists imperf. Value, pair $40.

Map of Buenos Aires, Cock and
Compass Emblem of Federal Police
A348

1965, Oct. 30   Photo.   Perf. 13½
785 A348 8p carmine rose   .35   .25
Issued for Federal Police Day. Exists imperf. Value, pair $40.

Child's
Drawing of
Children
A349

1965, Nov. 6   Litho.   Wmk. 90
786 A349 8p lt yel grn & blk   .35   .25
Public education law, 81st anniversary. Exists imperf. Value, pair $40.

Church of St.
Francis,
Catamarca — A350

1965, Dec. 8
787 A350 8p org yel & red brn   .30   .25
Brother Mamerto de la Asuncion Esquiu, preacher, teacher and official of 1885 Provincial Constitutional Convention.

Ruben
Dario — A351

Litho. and Photo.
1965, Dec. 22   **Perf. 13½**
788 A351 15p bl vio, *gray*   .30   .25
Ruben Dario (pen name of Felix Ruben Garcia Sarmiento, 1867-1916), Nicaraguan poet, newspaper correspondent and diplomat. Exists imperf. Value, pair $40.

"The
Orange
Seller"
A352

Pueyrredon Paintings: No. 790, "Stop at the Grocery Store." No. 791, "Landscape at San Fernando" (sailboats). No. 792, "Bathing Horses at River Plata."

1966, Jan. 29   Photo.   Perf. 13½
789 A352 8p bluish green   .70   .50
790 A352 8p bluish green   .70   .50
791 A352 8p bluish green   .70   .50
792 A352 8p bluish green   .70   .50
 a.   Block of 4, #789-792 + 2 labels 3.50 3.50
Prilidiano Pueyrredon (1823-1870), painter.

Sun Yat-sen, Flags
of Argentina and
China — A353

1966, Mar. 12   Wmk. 90   Perf. 13½
793 A353 8p dk red brown   .70   .30
Dr. Sun Yat-sen (1866-1925), founder of the Republic of China. Exists imperf. Value, pair $100.

Souvenir Sheet

Rivadavia Issue of 1864 — A354

Wmk. 90
1966, Apr. 20   Litho.   Imperf.
794 A354   Sheet of 3   1.10   1.10
 a.   4p gray & red brown   .25   .25
 b.   5p gray & green   .25   .25
 c.   8p gray & dark blue   .25   .25
2nd Rio de la Plata Stamp Show, Buenos Aires, Mar. 16-24. Exists with flags omitted (error). Value, $150.

People
of
Various
Races
and
WHO
Emblem
A355

1966, Apr. 23   **Perf. 13½**
795 A355 8p brown & black   .30   .25
Opening of the WHO Headquarters, Geneva. Exists imperf. Value, pair $40.

Soldier Type of 1965
Army Day: 8p, Cavalryman, Guemes Infernal Regiment.

1966, May 28   **Litho.**
796 A340a 8p multicolored   .60   .30
Exists imperf. Value, pair $40.

Coat of
Arms — A356

Arms: a, National. b, Buenos Aires. c, La Rioja. d, Catamarca. e, Cordoba. f, Corrientes. g, Chaco. h, Chubut. i, Entre Rios. j, Formosa. k, Jujuy. l, La Pampa. m, Federal Capital. n, Mendoza. o, Misiones. p, Neuquen. q, Salta. r, San Juan. s, San Luis. t, Santa Cruz. u, Santa Fe. v, Santiago del Estero. w, Tucuman. x, map of Rio Negro. y, Map of Tierra del Fuego, Antarctica, South Atlantic Islands.

1966, July 30   Wmk. 90   Perf. 13½
797   Sheet of 25   35.00
 a.-y. A356 10p black & multi   1.00   1.00
150th anniv. of Argentina's Declaration of Independence. Exists imperf. Value, sheet $2,000.

Three
Crosses,
Caritas
Emblem
A357

1966, Sept. 10   Litho.   Perf. 13½
798 A357 10p ol grn, blk & lt bl   .30   .25
Caritas, charity organization.

Hilario Ascasubi
(1807-75) — A358

Portraits: No. 800, Estanislao del Campo (1834-80). No. 801, Miguel Cane (1851-1905). No. 802, Lucio V. Lopez (1848-94). No. 803, Rafael Obligado (1851-1920). No. 804, Luis Agote (1868-1954), M.D. No. 805, Juan B. Ambrosetti (1865-1917), naturalist and archaeologist. No. 806, Miguel Lillo (1862-1931), botanist and chemist. No. 807, Francisco P. Moreno (1852-1919), naturalist and paleontologist. No. 808, Francisco J. Muñiz (1795-1871), physician.

1966   Photo.   Wmk. 90
799 A358 10p dk blue green   .40   .30
800 A358 10p dk blue green   .40   .30
801 A358 10p dk blue green   .40   .30
802 A358 10p dk blue green   .40   .30
803 A358 10p dk blue green   .40   .30
804 A358 10p deep violet   .40   .30
805 A358 10p deep violet   .40   .30
806 A358 10p deep violet   .40   .30
807 A358 10p deep violet   .40   .30
808 A358 10p deep violet   .40   .30
     Nos. 799-808 (10)   4.00   3.00
Nos. 799-803 issued Sept. 17 to honor Argentine writers. Printed se-tenant in sheets of 100 (10x10); 2 horizontal rows of each portrait. Nos. 804-808 issued Oct. 22 to honor Argentine scientists; 2 horizontal rows of each portrait. Scientists set has value at upper left, frame line with rounded corners.

Anchor
A359

1966, Oct. 8   **Litho.**
809 A359 4p multicolored   .30   .25
Argentine merchant marine. Exists imperf. Value, pair $40.

Flags and
Map of the
Americas
A360

1966, Oct. 29   **Perf. 13½**
810 A360 10p gray & multi   .30   .25
7th Conference of American Armies.

Argentine National
Bank — A361

1966, Nov. 5   **Photo.**
811 A361 10p brt blue green   .30   .25
75th anniv. of the Argentine National Bank. Exists imperf. Value, pair $40.

La Salle
Monument
and College,
Buenos
Aires — A362

1966, Nov. 26   Litho.   Perf. 13½
812 A362 10p brown org & blk   .30   .25
75th anniv. of the Colegio de la Salle, Buenos Aires, and to honor Saint Jean Baptiste de la Salle (1651-1719), educator. Exists imperf. Value, pair $125.

Map of
Argentine
Antarctica and
Expedition
Route — A363

1966, Dec. 10   **Wmk. 90**
813 A363 10p multicolored   .75   .35
1965 Argentine Antarctic expedition, which planted the Argentine flag on the South Pole. Exists imperf. Value, pair $70.
See No. 851.

Juan Martin de Pueyrredon — A364

1966, Dec. 17   Photo.   Perf. 13½
814 A364 10p dull red brn   .30   .25

Issued to honor Juan Martin de Pueyrredon (1777-1850), Governor of Cordoba and of the United Provinces of the River Plata.

Gen. Juan de Las Heras — A365

1966, Dec. 17   Engr.
815 A365 10p black   .30   .25

Issued to honor Gen. Juan Gregorio de Las Heras (1780-1866), Peruvian field marshal and aide-de-camp to San Martin.

**Inscribed "Republica Argentina"
Types of 1955-61 and**

Jose Hernandez — A366

Trout Leaping in National Park — A366a

Designs: 50p, Gen. Jose de San Martin. 90p, Guillermo Brown. 500p, Red deer in forest.

Two overall paper sizes for 6p, 50p (No. 827) and 90p:
I — 27x37½mm
II — 27x39mm

Perf. 13½

1965-68		**Wmk. 90**		**Photo.**
817	A366	6p rose red, litho, I		
		('67)	1.50	.25
818	A366	6p rose red ('67), II	5.50	.25
819	A366	6p brn, 15x22mm		
		('68)	.30	.25
823	A238a	43p dk car rose	7.00	.25
824	A238a	45p brn ('66)	3.50	.25
825	A238a	45p brn, litho ('67)	7.00	.25
826	A241	50p dk bl, 29x40mm	7.00	.40
827	A241	50p dk bl, 22x31½mm, I		
		('67)	4.00	.25
a.		Paper II	2.25	.25
828	A366	90p ol bis, I ('67)	2.25	.25
a.		Paper II	14.00	3.75

Engr.
829	A495	500p yellow grn		
		('66)	2.50	.30
829A	A366a	1,000p vio bl ('68)	7.00	.25
		Nos. 817-829A (11)	47.55	2.95

The 500p and 1,000p remained on sale as 5p and 10p stamps after the 1970 currency exchange.

See Nos. 888, 891, 939, 992, 1031, 1045-1047. For surcharge and overprints see Nos. 1077, O153-O158, O162.

Pre-Columbian Pottery — A367

1967, Feb. 18   Litho.   Perf. 13½
830 A367 10p multicolored   .35   .25

20th anniv. of UNESCO. Exists imperf. Value, pair $40.

"The Meal" by Fernando Fader — A368

1967, Feb. 25   Photo.   Wmk. 90
831 A368 10p red brown   .35   .25

Issued in memory of the Argentine painter Fernando Fader (1882-1935). Exists imperf. Value, pair $40.

Col. Juana Azurduy de Padilla (1781-1862), Soldier — A369

Famous Argentine Women: No. 833, Juana Manuela Gorriti, writer. No. 834, Cecilia Grierson (1858-1934), physician. No. 835, Juana Paula Manso (1819-75), writer and educator. No. 836, Alfonsina Storni (1892-1938), writer and educator.

1967, May 13   Photo.   Perf. 13½
832	A369	6p dark brown	.40	.25
833	A369	6p dark brown	.40	.25
834	A369	6p dark brown	.40	.25
835	A369	6p dark brown	.40	.25
836	A369	6p dark brown	.40	.25
		Nos. 832-836 (5)	2.00	1.25

Printed se-tenant in sheets of 100 (10x10); 2 horizontal rows of each portrait.

Schooner "Invencible," 1811 — A370

1967, May 20   Litho.
837 A370 20p multicolored   1.00   .35

Issued for Navy Day. Exists imperf. Value, pair $50.

Soldier Type of 1965

Army Day: 20p, Highlander (Arribeños Corps).

1967, May 27
838 A340a 20p multicolored   .65   .30

Exists imperf. Value, pair $50.

Manuel Belgrano and José Artigas — A371

1967, June 22   Imperf.
839 A371 Sheet of 2   .85   .55
  a.   6p gray & brown   .25   .25
  b.   22p brown & gray   .25   .25

Third Rio de la Plata Stamp Show, Montevideo, Uruguay, June 18-25.

Peace Dove and Valise — A372

1967, Aug. 5   Litho.   Perf. 13½
840 A372 20p multicolored   .35   .25

Issued for International Tourist Year 1967.

PADELAI Emblem — A373

1967, Aug. 12   Litho.
841 A373 20p multicolored   .30   .25

75th anniv. of the Children's Welfare Association (Patronato de la Infancia-PADELAI).

Stagecoach and Modern City — A374

1967, Sept. 23   Wmk. 90   Perf. 13½
842 A374 20p rose, yel & blk   .30   .25

Centenary of Villa Maria, Cordoba.

San Martin by Ibarra — A375

"Battle of Chacabuco" by P. Subercaseaux — A376

1967, Sept. 30   Litho.
843 A375 20p blk brn & pale yel   .50   .25

Engr.
844 A376 40p blue black   .80   .30

Battle of Chacabuco, 150th anniversary.

Exhibition Rooms — A377

1967, Oct. 11   Photo.
845 A377 20p blue gray   .30   .25

Government House Museum, 10th anniv.

Pedro L. Zanni, Fokker and 1924 Flight Route A378

1967, Oct. 21   Litho.   Perf. 13½
846 A378 20p multicolored   .35   .25

Issued for Aviation Week and to commemorate the 1924 flight of the Fokker seaplane "Province of Buenos Aires" from Amsterdam, Netherlands, to Osaka, Japan.

Training Ship General Brown, by Emilio Biggeri A379

1967, Oct. 28   Wmk. 90
847 A379 20p multicolored   1.00   .35

Issued to honor the Military Naval School.

Ovidio Lagos and Front Page — A380

1967, Nov. 11   Photo.
848 A380 20p sepia   .30   .25

Centenary of La Capital, Rosario newspaper. Imperf pair $40.

St. Barbara
A381

1967, Dec. 2　　　*Perf. 13½*
849 A381 20p rose red　　　.35 .25
St. Barbara, patron saint of artillerymen.

Portrait of his
Wife, by
Eduardo
Sivori — A382

1968, Jan. 27　Photo.　*Perf. 13½*
850 A382 20p blue green　　　.35 .25
Eduardo Sivori (1847-1918), painter.

Antarctic Type of 1966 and

Admiral
Brown
Scientific
Station
A383

Planes over Map of Antarctica — A384

6p, Map showing radio-postal stations 1966-67.

1968, Feb. 17　Litho.　Wmk. 90
851 A363 6p multicolored　　.50 .25
852 A383 20p multicolored　　.70 .25
853 A384 40p multicolored　1.20 .50
　　Nos. 851-853 (3)　　2.40 1.00
Issued to publicize Argentine research projects in Argentine Antarctica.

The Annunciation,
by Leonardo da
Vinci — A385

1968, Mar. 23　Photo.　*Perf. 13½*
854 A385 20p lilac rose　　　.30 .25
Issued for the Day of the Army Communications System and its patron saint, Gabriel. Exists imperf. Value, pair $40.

Man in Wheelchair
and
Factory — A386

1968, Mar. 23　　　　　　**Litho.**
855 A386 20p green & black　　.30 .25
Day of Rehabilitation of the Handicapped.

Children and WHO
Emblem — A387

1968, May 11　Wmk. 90　*Perf. 13½*
856 A387 20p dk vio bl & ver　.30 .25
20th anniv. of WHO.

Soldier Type of 1965

Army Day: 20p, Uniform of First Artillery Regiment "General Iriarte."

1968, June 8　　　　　　**Litho.**
857 A340a 20p multicolored　　.75 .30

Frigate "Libertad," Painting by Emilio
Biggeri — A388

1968, June 15　　　　　**Wmk. 90**
858 A388 20p multicolored　　1.20 .30
Issued for Navy Day. Exists imperf. Value, pair $40.

Guillermo
Rawson and
Old Hospital
A389

1968, July 20　Photo.　*Perf. 13½*
859 A389 6p olive bister　　　.35 .25
Cent. of Rawson Hospital, Buenos Aires.

Student
Directing
Traffic for
Schoolmates
A390

1968, Aug. 10　Litho.　*Perf. 13½*
860 A390 20p lt bl, blk, buff & car　.55 .25
Traffic safety and education.

O'Higgins Joining San Martin at Battle
of Maipu, by P. Subercaseaux — A391

1968, Aug. 15　　　　　　**Engr.**
861 A391 40p bluish black　　.65 .30
Sesquicentennial of the Battle of Maipu.

Osvaldo Magnasco
(1864-1920),
Lawyer, Professor
of Law and Minister
of Justice — A392

1968, Sept. 7　Photo.　*Perf. 13½*
862 A392 20p brown　　　　.40 .25

Grandmother's Birthday, by Patricia
Lynch — A393

The Sea, by
Edgardo
Gomez — A394

1968, Sept. 21　　　　　　**Litho.**
863 A393 20p multicolored　　.30 .25
864 A394 20p multicolored　　.30 .25
The designs were chosen in a competition among kindergarten and elementary school children.

Mar del
Plata at
Night
A395

1968, Oct. 19　Litho.　*Perf. 13½*
865 A395 20p black, ocher & bl　.30 .25
　　Nos. 865,C113-C114 (3)　2.30 1.05
4th Plenary Assembly of the Intl. Telegraph and Telephone Consultative Committee, Mar del Plata, Sept. 23-Oct. 25.

Frontier
Gendarme
A396

Patrol Boat
A397

1968, Oct. 26
866 A396 20p multicolored　　.30 .25
867 A397 20p blue, vio bl & blk　.30 .25
No. 866 honors the Gendarmery; No. 867 the Coast Guard.

Aaron de
Anchorena
and
Pampero
Balloon
A398

1968, Nov. 2　　　　　　　**Photo.**
868 A398 20p blue & multi　　.30 .25
22nd Aeronautics and Space Week.

St. Martin of Tours,
by Alfredo
Guido — A399

1968, Nov. 9　　　　　　　**Litho.**
869 A399 20p lilac & dk brn　　.30 .25
St. Martin of Tours, patron saint of Buenos Aires.

Municipal
Bank
Emblem
A400

1968, Nov. 16
870 A400 20p multicolored　　.30 .25
Buenos Aires Municipal Bank, 90th anniv.

Anniversary
Emblem
A401

1968, Dec. 14　Wmk. 90　*Perf. 13½*
871 A401 20p car rose & dk grn　.30 .25
ALPI (Fight Against Polio Assoc.), 25th anniv.

Shovel and State
Coal Fields
Emblem — A402

Pouring Ladle
and Army
Manufacturing
Emblem — A403

1968, Dec. 21　　　　　　**Litho.**
872 A402 20p orange, bl & blk　.30 .25
873 A403 20p dl vio, dl yel & blk　.30 .25
Issued to publicize the National Coal and Steel industry at the Rio Turbio coal fields and the Zapla blast furnaces.

Woman Potter, by Ramon Gomez Cornet — A404

1968, Dec. 21 Photo. Perf. 13½
874 A404 20p carmine rose .50 .40
Centenary of the Witcomb Gallery.

View of Buenos Aires and Rio de la Plata by Ulrico Schmidl A405

1969, Feb. 8 Litho. Wmk. 90
875 A405 20p yellow, blk & ver .50 .35
Ulrico Schmidl (c. 1462-1554) who wrote "Journey to the Rio de la Plata and Paraguay."

Types of 1955-67

Designs: 50c, Puma. 1p, Sunflower. 3p, Zapata Slope, Catamarca. 5p, Tierra del Fuego. 6p, José Hernandez. 10p, Inca Bridge, Mendoza. 50p, José de San Martin. 90p, Guillermo Brown. 100p, Ski jumper.

Photo.; Litho. (50c, 3p, 10p)
1969-70 Wmk. 365 Perf. 13½
882 A275 50c bister ('70) 1.00 .60
883 A277 5p brown 1.40 .90
884 A279 100p blue 26.00 8.00

Unwmk.
885 A278 1p brown ('70) .40 .25
886 A277 3p dk blue ('70) .65 .25
  a. Wmk. 90 10.00 3.00
887 A277 5p brown ('70) .75 .25
888 A366 6p red brn, 15x22mm ('70) .90 .25
889 A278 10p dull red ('70) .50 .25
  a. Wmk. 90 475.00 60.00
890 A241 50p dk bl, 22x31½mm ('70) 1.25 .25
891 A366 90p ol brn, 22x32mm ('70) 3.50 .50
892 A279 100p blue ('70) 11.00 1.00
  Nos. 882-892 (11) 47.35 12.50

For surcharges see Nos. 1076-1077.

Soldier Type of 1965

Army Day: 20p, Sapper (gastador) of Buenos Aires Province, 1856.

Wmk. 365
1969, May 31 Litho. Perf. 13½
893 A340a 20p multicolored .85 .35

Frigate Hercules, by Emilio Biggeri — A406

1969, May 31
894 A406 20p multicolored 1.50 .30
Issued for Navy Day.

"All Men are Equal" — A407

1969, June 28 Wmk. 90
895 A407 20p black & ocher .30 .25
International Human Rights Year.

ILO Emblem — A408

1969, June 28 Litho. Wmk. 365
896 A408 20p lt green & multi .30 .25
50th anniv. of the ILO. Exists imperf. Value, pair $100.

Pedro N. Arata (1849-1922), Chemist — A409

Portraits: No. 898, Miguel Fernandez (1883-1950), zoologist. No. 899, Angel P. Gallardo (1867-1934), biologist. No. 900, Cristobal M. Hicken (1875-1933), botanist. No. 901, Eduardo Ladislao Holmberg, M.D. (1852-1937), natural scientist.

1969, Aug. 9 Wmk. 365 Perf. 13½
897 A409 6p Arata .45 .30
898 A409 6p Fernandez .45 .30
899 A409 6p Gallardo .45 .30
900 A409 6p Hicken .45 .30
901 A409 6p Holmberg .45 .30
  Nos. 897-901 (5) 2.25 1.50

Argentine scientists. See No. 778 note.

Radar Antenna, Balcarce Station and Satellite — A410

1969, Aug. 23 Wmk. 99
902 A410 20p yellow & blk .30 .25
Communications by satellite through Intl. Telecommunications Satellite Consortium (INTELSAT). Exists imperf. Value, pair $40. See No. C115.

Military College Gate and Emblem A412

1969, Oct. 4 Wmk. 365 Perf. 13½
904 A412 20p multicolored .30 .25
Cent. of the National Military College, El Palomar (Greater Buenos Aires).

Gen. Angel Pacheco — A413

1969, Nov. 8 Photo. Wmk. 365
905 A413 20p deep green .30 .25
Gen. Angel Pacheco (1795-1869).

La Farola, Logotype of La Prensa — A414

Design: No. 907, Bartolomé Mitre & La Nacion logotype.

1969, Nov. 8 Litho. Perf. 13½
906 A414 20p orange, yel & blk .70 .30
907 A414 20p brt green & blk .70 .30
Cent. of newspapers La Prensa and La Nacion.

Julian Aguirre — A415

Musicians: No. 909, Felipe Boero. No. 910, Constantino Gaito. No. 911, Carlos Lopez Buchardo. No. 912, Alberto Williams.

Wmk. 365
1969, Dec. 6 Photo. Perf. 13½
908 A415 6p Aguirre .65 .30
909 A415 6p Boero .65 .30
910 A415 6p Gaito .65 .30
911 A415 6p Buchardo .65 .30
912 A415 6p Williams .65 .30
  Nos. 908-912 (5) 3.25 1.50

Argentine musicians. See No. 778 note.

Lt. Benjamin Matienzo and Nieuport Plane — A416

1969, Dec. 13 Litho.
913 A416 20p multicolored .50 .35
23rd Aeronautics and Space Week.

High Power Lines and Map A417

Design: 20p, Map of Santa Fe Province and schematic view of tunnel.

1969, Dec. 13
914 A417 6p multicolored .50 .25
915 A417 20p multicolored 1.00 .25

Completion of development projects: 6p for the hydroelectric dams on the Limay and Neuquen Rivers, the 20p the tunnel under Rio Grande from Sante Fe to Parana. Set exists imperf.©

Lions Emblem A418

1969, Dec. 20 Wmk. 365 Perf. 13½
916 A418 20p black, emer & org .70 .25
Argentine Lions Intl. Club, 50th anniv.

Madonna and Child, by Raul Soldi — A419

1969, Dec. 27 Litho.
917 A419 20p multicolored .65 .30
Christmas 1969.

Manuel Belgrano, by Jean Gericault A420

The Creation of the Flag, Bas-relief by Jose Fioravanti — A421

Perf. 13½

1970, July 4   **Unwmk.**   **Photo.**
918 A420 20c deep brown   .40   .25

Litho.   **Perf. 12½**
919 A421 50c bister, blk & bl   .75   .50

Gen. Manuel Belgrano (1770-1820), Argentine patriot.

San Jose Palace A422

1970, Aug. 9   **Litho.**   **Perf. 13½**
920 A422 20c yellow grn & multi   .30   .25

Gen. Justo Jose de Urquiza (1801-70), pres. of Argentina, 1854-60.

Schooner "Juliet" — A423

1970, Aug. 8   **Unwmk.**
921 A423 20c multicolored   1.10   .40

Issued for Navy Day.

Receiver of 1920 and Waves A424

1970, Aug. 29
922 A424 20c lt blue & multi   .45   .30

50th anniv. of Argentine broadcasting.

Types of 1955-67 Inscribed "Republica Argentina" and

Belgrano A425   Lujan Basilica A426

Designs: 1c, Sunflower. 3c, Zapata Slope, Catamarca. 5c, Tierra del Fuego. 8c, No. 931, Belgrano. 10c, Inca Bridge, Mendoza. 25c, 50c, 70c, Jose de San Martin. 65c, 90c, 1.20p, San Martin. 1p, Ski jumper. 1.15p, 1.80p, Adm. Brown.

1970-73   **Photo.**   **Unwmk.**   **Perf. 13½**
923 A278   1c dk green ('71)   .25   .25
924 A277   3c car rose ('71)   .25   .25
925 A277   5c blue ('71)   .25   .25
926 A425   6c deep blue   .25   .25
927 A425   8c green ('72)   .25   .25
928 A278   10c dull red ('71)   .30   .25
929 A278   10c brn, litho. ('71)   .60   .25
930 A278   10c org brn ('72)   .25   .25
931 A425   10c brown ('73)   .25   .25
932 A426   18c yel & dk brn, litho ('73)   .25   .25
933 A425   25c brown ('71)   .35   .25
934 A425   50c scarlet ('72)   .90   .25
935 A241   65c brn, 22x31½mm, paper II ('71)   .85   .25
936 A425   70c dk blue ('73)   .25   .25
937 A241   90c emer, 22x31½mm ('72)   2.25   .25

938 A279   1p brn, 22½x29½mm ('71)   4.00   .25
939 A366   1.15p dk bl, 22½x32mm ('71)   .85   .25
940 A241   1.20p org, 22x31½mm ('73)   .90   .25
941 A366   1.80p brown ('73)   .30   .25
     Nos. 923-941 (19)   13.55   4.75

The imprint "Casa de Moneda de la Nacion" (in capitals) appears on 3c, 5c, Nos. 928-929; 65c, 90c, 1p, 1.20p.

On type A425 only the 6c is inscribed "Ley 18.188" below denomination.

Fluorescent paper was used in printing the 25c, 50c, and 70c. The 3c, 5c, 8c, No. 931 and 65c were issued on both ordinary and fluorescent paper.

See Nos. 987-996, 1032-1038, 1042-1043, 1089-1107. For overprint and surcharge see Nos. 1010, 1078.

Soldier Type of 1965

Galloping messenger of Field Army, 1879.

1970, Oct. 17   **Litho.**   **Perf. 13½**
944 A340a 20c multicolored   .85   .30

Dome of Cathedral of Cordoba A430

1970, Nov. 7   **Unwmk.**
945 A430 50c gray & blk   .80   .25

Bishopric of Tucuman, 400th anniv. See No. C131.

People Around UN Emblem A431

1970, Nov. 7
946 A431 20c tan & multi   .30   .25

25th anniversary of the United Nations.

State Mint and Medal A432

1970, Nov. 28   **Unwmk.**   **Perf. 13½**
947 A432 20c gold, grn & blk   .30   .25

Inauguration of the State Mint Building, 25th anniversary.

St. John Bosco and Dean Funes College A433

1970, Dec. 19   **Litho.**
948 A433 20c olive & blk   .30   .25

Honoring the work of the Salesian Order in Patagonia.

Nativity, by Horacio Gramajo Gutierrez — A434

1970, Dec. 19
949 A434 20c multicolored   .55   .35

Christmas 1970.

Argentine Flag, Map of Argentine Antarctica A435

1971, Feb. 20   **Litho.**   **Perf. 13½**
950 A435 20c multicolored   1.25   .25

Argentine South Pole Expedition, 5th anniv.

Phosphorescent Sorting Code and Albert Einstein — A436

1971, Apr. 30   **Unwmk.**   **Perf. 13½**
951 A436 25c multicolored   .45   .30

Electronics in postal development.

Symbolic Road Crossing A437

1971, May 29   **Litho.**
952 A437 25c blue & blk   .25   .25

Inter-American Regional Meeting of the Intl. Federation of Roads, Buenos Aires, 3/28-31.

Elias Alippi — A438

Actors: No. 954, Juan Aurelio Casacuberta. No. 955, Angelina Pagano. No. 956, Roberto Casaux. No. 957, Florencio Parravicini. See No. 778 note.

1971, May 29   **Litho.**
953 A438 15c Alippi   .30   .25
954 A438 15c Casacuberta   .30   .25
955 A438 15c Pagano   .30   .30
956 A438 15c Casaux   .30   .25
957 A438 15c Parravicini   .30   .25
     Nos. 953-957 (5)   1.50   1.30

Soldier Type of 1965

Army Day, May 29: Artilleryman, 1826.

1971, July 3   **Unwmk.**   **Perf. 13½**
958 A340a 25c multicolored   1.25   .25

Bilander "Carmen," by Emilio Biggeri — A439

1971, July 3
959 A439 25c multicolored   1.25   .25

Navy Day

Peruvian Order of the Sun A440

1971, Aug. 28
960 A440 31c multicolored   .60   .25

Sesquicentennial of Peru's independence.

Güemes in Battle, by Lorenzo Gigli A441

Design: No. 962, Death of Güemes, by Antonio Alice.

1971, Aug. 28   **Size: 39x29mm**
961 A441 25c multicolored   .50   .25

Size: 84x29mm
962 A441 25c multicolored   .50   .25

Sesquicentennial of the death of Martin Miguel de Güemes, leader in Gaucho War, Governor and Captain General of Salta Province.

Stylized Tulip — A442

1971, Sept. 18
963 A442 25c tan & multi   .35   .25

3rd Intl. and 8th Natl. Horticultural Exhib.

Father Antonio Saenz, by Juan Gut — A443

1971, Sept. 18
964 A433 25c gray & multi   .35   .25

Sesquicentennial of University of Buenos Aires, and to honor Father Antonio Saenz, first Chancellor and Rector.

Fabricaciones Militares Emblem — A444

1971, Oct. 16 **Unwmk.** *Perf. 13½*
965 A444 25c brn, gold, bl & blk .25 .25
30th anniv. of military armament works.

Cars and Trucks A445

Design: 65c, Tree converted into paper.

1971, Oct. 16
966 A445 25c dull bl & multi .50 .25
967 A445 65c green & multi 1.25 .30
Nos. 966-967,C134 (3) 2.55 .85
Nationalized industries.

Luis C. Candelaria and his Plane, 1918 — A446

1971, Nov. 27
968 A446 25c multicolored .35 .25
25th Aeronautics and Space Week.

Observatory and Nebula of Magellan — A447

1971, Nov. 27
969 A447 25c multicolored .65 .25
Cordoba Astronomical Observatory, cent.

Christ in Majesty A448

1971, Dec. 18 **Litho.**
970 A448 25c blk & multi .30 .25
Christmas 1971. Design is from a tapestry by Horacio Butler in Basilica of St. Francis, Buenos Aires.

Mother and Child, by J. C. Castagnino A449

1972, May 6 **Unwmk.** *Perf. 13½*
971 A449 25c fawn & black .40 .25
25th anniv. (in 1971) of UNICEF.

Mailman's Bag — A450

1972, Sept. 2 **Litho.** *Perf. 13½*
972 A450 25c lemon & multi .30 .25
Bicentenary of appointment of first Argentine mailman.

Adm. Brown Station, Map of Antarctica — A451

1972, Sept. 2
973 A451 25c blue & multi .65 .30
10th anniv. (in 1971) of Antarctic Treaty.

Soldier Type of 1965
Army Day: 25c, Sergeant, Negro and Mulatto Corps, 1806-1807.

1972, Sept. 23
974 A340a 25c multicolored .65 .35

Brigantine "Santisima Trinidad" — A452

1972, Sept. 23
975 A452 25c multicolored .90 .35
Navy Day. See No. 1006.

Oil Pump — A453

1972, Sept. 30 **Litho.** *Perf. 13½*
976 A453 45c multicolored .75 .25
50th anniv. of the organ. of the state oil fields (Yacimientos Petroliferos Fiscales).

Sounding Balloon — A454

1972, Sept. 30
977 A454 25c multicolored .25 .25
Cent. of Natl. Meteorological Service.

Trees and Globe — A455

1972, Oct. 14 *Perf. 13x13½*
978 A455 25c bl, blk & lt bl .60 .25
7th World Forestry Congress, Buenos Aires, Oct. 4-18.

Arms of Naval School, Frigate "Presidente Sarmiento" — A456

1972, Oct. 14
979 A456 25c gold & multi .70 .25
Centenary of Military Naval School.

Early Balloon and Plane, Antonio de Marchi — A457

1972, Nov. 4 *Perf. 13½*
980 A457 25c multicolored .45 .30
Aeronautics and Space Week, and in honor of Baron Antonio de Marchi (1875-1934), aviation pioneer.

Bartolomé Mitre — A458

1972, Nov. 4 **Engr.**
981 A458 25c dark blue .45 .30
Pres. Bartolome Mitre (1821-1906), writer, historian, soldier.

Flower and Heart — A459

1972, Dec. 2 **Litho.** *Perf. 13½*
982 A459 90c lt bl, ultra & blk .50 .30
"Your heart is your health," World Health Day.

"Martin Fierro," by Juan C. Castagnino A460

"Spirit of the Gaucho," by Vicente Forte — A461

1972, Dec. 2 **Litho.** *Perf. 13½*
983 A460 50c multicolored .30 .25
984 A461 90c multicolored .45 .30
Intl. Book Year 1972, and cent. of publication of the poem, Martin Fierro, by Jose Hernandez (1834-86).

Iguacu Falls and Tourist Year Emblem — A462

1972, Dec. 16 *Perf. 13x13½*
985 A462 45c multicolored .30 .25
Tourism Year of the Americas.

King, Wood Carving, 18th Century A463

1972, Dec. 16 *Perf. 13½*
986 A463 50c multicolored .45 .25
Christmas 1972.

Types of 1955-73 Inscribed "Republica Argentina" and

Moon Valley, San Juan Province — A463a

Designs: 1c, Sunflower. 5c, Tierra del Fuego. 10c, Inca Bridge, Mendoza. 50c, Lujan Basilica. 65c, 22.50p, San Martin. 1p, Ski jumper. 1.15p, 4.50p, Guillermo Brown. 1.80p, Manuel Belgrano.

Litho.; Photo. (1c, 65c, 1p)
Perf. 13½, 12½ (1.80p)

1972-75			Wmk. 365	
987	A278	1c dk green	.25	.25
988	A277	5c dark blue	.25	.25
989	A278	10c bister brn	.30	.25
989A	A426	50c dull pur ('75)	.25	.25
990	A241	65c gray brown	3.25	.25
991	A279	1p brown	4.00	.25
992	A366	1.15p dk gray bl	1.50	.45
993	A425	1.80p blue ('75)	.30	.25
994	A366	4.50p green ('75)	.45	.25
995	A241	22.50p vio bl ('75)	1.50	.30
996	A463a	50p multi ('75)	1.40	.25
	Nos. 987-996 (11)		13.45	3.00

Paper size of 1c is 27½x39mm; others of 1972, 37x27, 27x37mm.
Size of 22.50p, 50p: 26½x38½mm.
See Nos. 1050, 1108.

Cock (Symbolic of Police) — A464

1973, Feb. 3   Litho.   Unwmk.
997 A464 50c lt green & multi   .30 .25
Sesqui. of Federal Police of Argentina.

First Coin of Bank of Buenos Aires — A465

1973, Feb. 3   Perf. 13½
998 A465 50c purple, yel & brn   .25 .25
Sesquicentennial of the Bank of Buenos Aires Province.

DC-3 Planes Over Antarctica — A466

1973, Apr. 28   Litho.   Perf. 13½
999 A466 50c lt blue & multi   1.40 .50
10th anniversary of Argentina's first flight to the South Pole.

Rivadavia's Chair, Argentine Arms and Colors — A467

1973, May 19   Litho.   Perf. 13½
1000 A467 50c multicolored   .25 .25
Inauguration of Pres. Hector J. Campora, May 25, 1973.

San Martin, by Gil de Castro — A468

San Martin and Bolivar A469

1973, July 7   Litho.   Perf. 13½
1001 A468 50c lt green & multi   .35 .25
1002 A469 50c yellow & multi   .35 .25
Gen. San Martin's farewell to the people of Peru and his meeting with Simon Bolivar at Guayaquil July 26-27, 1822.

Eva Peron A470

1973, July 26   Litho.   Perf. 13½
1003 A470 70c black, org & bl   .30 .25
Maria Eva Duarte de Peron (1919-1952), political leader.

House of Viceroy Sobremonte, by Hortensia de Virgilion — A471

1973, July 28   Perf. 13x13½
1004 A471 50c blue & multi   .35 .25
400th anniversary of the city of Cordoba.

Woman, by Lino Spilimbergo A472

1973, Aug. 28   Litho.   Perf. 13½
1005 A472 70c multicolored   .70 .25
Philatelists' Day. See Nos. B60-B61.

Ship Type of 1972

Navy Day: 70c, Frigate "La Argentina."

1973, Oct. 27   Litho.   Perf. 13½
1006 A452 70c multicolored   .55 .25

New and Old Telephones — A473

1973, Oct. 27
1007 A473 70c brt blue & multi   .35 .25
Natl. telecommunications system, 25th anniv.

Plume Made of Flags of Participants A474

1973, Nov. 3   Perf. 13½
1008 A474 70c yellow bis & multi   .30 .25
12th Cong. of Latin Notaries, Buenos Aires.

No. 940 Overprinted

1973, Nov. 30   Photo.
1010 A241 1.20p orange   .85 .30
Assumption of presidency by Juan Peron, Oct. 12.

Virgin and Child, Window, La Plata Cathedral A476

Christmas: 1.20p, Nativity, by Bruno Venier, b. 1914.

1973, Dec. 15   Litho.   Perf. 13½
1011 A476 70c gray & multi   .35 .25
1012 A476 1.20p black & multi   .65 .35

The Lama, by Juan Battle Planas — A477

Paintings: 50c, Houses in Boca District, by Eugenio Daneri, horiz. 90c, The Blue Grotto, by Emilio Pettoruti, horiz.

1974, Feb. 9   Litho.   Perf. 13½
1013 A477 50c multicolored   .45 .25
1014 A477 70c multicolored   .45 .25
1015 A477 90c multicolored   .45 .30
Nos. 1013-1015,B64 (4)   1.70 1.05
Argentine painters.

Mar del Plata A478

1974, Feb. 9
1016 A478 70c multicolored   .35 .25
Centenary of Mar del Plata.

Weather Symbols — A479

1974, Mar. 23   Litho.   Perf. 13½
1017 A479 1.20p multicolored   .30 .25
Cent. of intl. meteorological cooperation.

Justo Santa Maria de Oro — A480

1974, Mar. 23
1018 A480 70c multicolored   .30 .25
Bicentenary of the birth of Brother Justo Santa Maria de Oro (1772-1836), theologian, patriot, first Argentine bishop.

Belisario Roldan (1873-1922), Writer — A481

1974, June 29   Photo.   Unwmk.
1019 A481 70c bl & brn   .30 .25

Poster with Names of OAS Members — A482

1974, June 29 Litho.
1020 A482 1.38p multicolored .30 .25
Organization of American States, 25th anniv.

ENCOTEL Emblem — A483

1974, Aug. 10 Litho. *Perf. 13*
1021 A483 1.20p blue, gold & blk .45 .25
ENCOTEL, Natl. Post and Telegraph Press.

Flags of Argentina, Bolivia, Brazil, Paraguay, Uruguay A484

1974, Aug. 16 *Perf. 13½*
1022 A484 1.38p multicolored .30 .25
6th Meeting of Foreign Ministers of Rio de la Plata Basin Countries.

El Chocon Hydroelectric Complex, Limay River — A485

Somisa Steel Mill, San Nicolas A486

Gen. Belgrano Bridge, Chaco-Corrientes — A487

Perf. 13½, 13x13½ (4.50p)
1974, Sept. 14
1023 A485 70c multicolored .35 .25
1024 A486 1.20p multicolored .60 .30
1025 A487 4.50p multicolored 1.75 .45
  Nos. 1023-1025 (3) 2.70 1.00
Development projects.

Brigantine Belgrano, by Emilio Biggeri — A488

1974, Oct. 26 Litho. *Perf. 13½*
1026 A488 1.20p multicolored 1.00 .30
Departure into exile in Chile of General San Martin, Sept. 22, 1822.

Alberto R. Mascias and Bleriot Plane — A489

1974, Oct. 26 Unwmk.
1027 A489 1.20p multicolored .55 .25
  a. Wmk 365
Air Force Day, Aug. 10, and to honor Alberto Roque Garcias (1878-1951), aviation pioneer.

Hussar, 1812, by Eleodoro Marenco A490

1974, Oct. 26
1028 A490 1.20p multicolored .55 .25
Army Day.

Post Horn and Flags A491

1974, Nov. 23 Unwmk. *Perf. 13½*
1029 A491 2.65p multicolored .75 .25
  a. Wmk 365 45.00 22.50
Centenary of Universal Postal Union.

Franciscan Monastery — A492

1974, Nov. 23 Litho.
1030 A492 1.20p multicolored .35 .25
400th anniversary, city of Santa Fe.

Trout Type of 1968
1974 Engr. Unwmk.
1031 A366a 1000p vio bl 1.40 .25
Due to a shortage of 10p stamps a quantity of this 1,000p was released for use as 10p.

Types of 1954-73 Inscribed "Republica Argentina" and

Red Deer in Forest — A495

Congress Building — A497

Designs: 30c, 60c, 1.80p, Manuel Belgrano. 50c, Lujan Basilica. 1.20p, 2p, 6p, San Martin (16x22½mm). 2.70p, 7.50p, 22.50p, San Martin (22x31½mm). 4.50p, 13.50p, Guillermo Brown. 10p, Leaping trout.

1974-76 Unwmk. Photo. *Perf. 13½*
1032 A425 30c brown vio .30 .25
1033 A426 50c blk & brn
  red .30 .25
1034 A426 50c bister & bl .25 .25
1035 A425 60c ocher .30 .25
1036 A425 1.20p red .30 .25
1037 A425 1.80p deep blue .30 .25
1038 A425 2p dark purple .40 .30
1039 A241 2.70p dk bl,
  22x31½mm .30 .25
1040 A366 4.50p green 1.50 .25
1041 A495 5p yel green .40 .25
1042 A425 6p red orange .30 .25
1043 A425 6p emerald .30 .25
1044 A241 7.50p grn,
  22x31½mm .90 .25
1045 A366a 10p violet blue 2.00 .25
1046 A366 13.50p scar,
  16x22½mm .45 .25
1047 A366 13.50p scar,
  22x31½mm .90 .35
1048 A241 22.50p dp bl,
  22x31½mm .90 .45
1049 A497 30p yel & dk red
  brn 3.50 .25
1050 A463a 50p multicolored 1.40 .25
  Nos. 1032-1050 (19) 15.00 5.10

Issued: 10p, 5/74; 30c, 1.20p, 2.70p, 5/15/74; 5p, 11/20/74; 30p, 12/10/74; 2p, 3/1/75; 60c, 7.50p, 4/30/75; 4.50p, 7/21/75; 1.80p, Nos. 1042, 1047, 22.50p, 8/14/75; No. 1046, 10/10/75; No. 1034, 10/30/75; No. 1043, 11/6/75; 50p, 2/76.
Fluorescent paper was used in printing No. 1036, 2p, Nos. 1044 and 1047. The 30p was issued on both ordinary and fluorescent paper.
See No. 829. For type of A495 overprinted see No. 1144.

Miniature Sheet

A498

1974, Dec. 7 Litho. *Perf. 13½*
1052 A498 Sheet of 6 3.00 3.00
  a. 1p Mariano Necochea .35 .25
  b. 1.20p Jose de San Martin .35 .25
  c. 1.70p Manuel Isidoro Suarez .35 .25
  d. 1.90p Juan Pascual Pringles .35 .25
  e. 2.70p Latin American flags .35 .25
  f. 4.50p Jose Felix Bogado .35 .25
Sesqui. of Battles of Junin and Ayacucho.

Dove, by Vito Campanella — A499

St. Anne, by Raul Soldi — A500

1974, Dec. 21 Litho. *Perf. 13½*
1053 A499 1.20p multicolored .65 .25
1054 A500 2.65p multicolored .65 .30
Christmas 1974.

Boy Looking at Stamp — A501

1974, Dec. 21
1055 A501 1.70p black & yel .35 .25
World Youth Philately Year.

Space Monsters, by Raquel Forner — A502

Argentine modern art: 4.50p, Dream, by Emilio Centurion.

1975, Feb. 22 Litho. *Perf. 13½*
1056 A502 2.70p multi .85 .25
1057 A502 4.50p multi 1.60 .35

Indian Woman and Cathedral, Catamarca — A503

Tourist Publicity: No. 1059, Carved chancel and street scene. No. 1060, Logging operations and monastery yard. No. 1061, Painted pottery and power station. No. 1062, Farm cart and colonial mansion. No. 1063, Perito Moreno glacier and spinning mill. No. 1064, Lake Lapataia and scientific surveyor. No. 1065, Los Alerces National Park and oil derrick.

1975 Litho. *Perf. 13½*
Unwmk., Wmk 365 (6p)
1058 A503 1.20p shown .30 .25
1059 A503 1.20p Jujuy .30 .25
1060 A503 1.20p Salta .30 .25
1061 A503 1.20p Santiago del
  Estero .30 .25
1062 A503 1.20p Tucuman .30 .25
1063 A503 6p Santa Cruz .55 .25

1064	A503	6p	Tierra del		
			Fuego	.55	.25
1065	A503	6p	Chubut	.55	.25

Nos. 1058-1065 (8) 3.15 2.00

Issue dates: 1.20p, Mar. 8; 6p, Dec. 20.

"We Have
Been
Inoculated"
A504

1975, Apr. 26 Unwmk. Perf. 13½
1066 A504 2p multi .45 .25

Children's inoculation campaign (child's painting).

Hugo A. Acuña and South Orkney
Station — A505

Designs: No. 1068, Francisco P. Moreno and Lake Nahuel Huapi. No. 1069, Lt. Col. Luis Piedra Buena and cutter, Luisito. No. 1070, Ensign José M. Sobral and Snow Hill House. No. 1071, Capt. Carlos M. Moyano and Cerro del Toro (mountain).

1975, June 28 Litho. Perf. 13
1067	A505	2p grnsh bl & multi	.30	.25
1068	A505	2p yel grn & multi	.30	.25
1069	A505	2p lt vio & multi	.30	.25
1070	A505	2p gray bl & multi	.30	.25
1071	A505	2p pale grn & multi	.30	.25

Nos. 1067-1071 (5) 1.50 1.25

Pioneers of Antarctica.

Frigate
"25 de
Mayo"
A506

1975, Sept. 27 Unwmk. Perf. 13½
1072 A506 6p multi .85 .25

Navy Day 1975.

Eduardo
Bradley and
Balloon
A507

1975, Sept. 27 Wmk. 365
1073 A507 6p multi .45 .25

Air Force Day.

Declaration of Independence, by Juan
M. Blanes — A508

1975, Oct. 25
1074 A508 6p multi .70 .25

Sesquicentennial of Uruguay's declaration of independence.

Flame
A509

1975, Oct. 17 Unwmk.
1075 A509 6p gray & multi .35 .25

Loyalty Day, 30th anniversary of Pres. Peron's accession to power.

No. 886
Surcharged

No. 891
Surcharged

No. 932
Surcharged

1975 Lithographed, Photogravure
1076	A277	6c on 3p	.25	.25
1077	A366	30c on 90p	.30	.25
1078	A426	5p on 18c	.35	.25

Nos. 1076-1078 (3) .90 .75

Issued: 6c, 10/30; 30c, 11/20; 5p, 10/24.
The 6c also exists on No. 886a. Value, $50.

International Bridge, Flags of
Argentina & Uruguay — A510

1975, Oct. 25 Litho. Wmk. 365
1081 A510 6p multi .35 .25

Post Horn,
Surcharged
A511

1975, Nov. 8
1082 A511 10p on 20c multi .50 .25

Introduction of postal code. Not issued without surcharge.

Nurse
Holding
Infant
A512

1975, Dec. 13 Litho. Perf. 13½
1083 A512 6p multi .70 .25

Children's Hospital, centenary.

Nativity, Nueva
Pompeya
Church — A513

1975, Dec. 13 Litho. Unwmk.
1084 A513 6p multicolored .45 .25

Christmas 1975.

Types of 1970-75 and

Church of St.
Francis,
Salta — A515

Designs: 3p, No. 1099, 60p, 90p, Manuel Belgrano. 12p, 15p, 20p, 30p, No. 1100, 100p, 110p, 120p, 130p, San Martin. 15p, 70p, Guillermo Brown. 300p, Moon Valley (lower inscriptions italic). 500p, Adm. Brown Station, Antarctica.

1976-78 Photo. Unwmk. Perf. 13½
1089	A425	3p slate	.30	.25
1090	A425	12p rose red	.25	.25

Perf. 12½x13
Litho. Wmk. 365
1091	A425	12p rose red	.35	.25
1092	A425	12p emerald	.35	.25

Perf. 13½
Photo. Unwmk.
1093	A425	12p emer ('77)	.35	.25
1094	A425	15p rose red	.30	.25
1095	A425	15p vio bl ('77)	.35	.25
1097	A425	20p rose red ('77)	.35	.25
1098	A425	30p rose red ('77)	.35	.25
1099	A425	40p dp grn	1.00	.25
1100	A425	40p rose red ('77)	.35	.25
1101	A425	60p dk bl ('77)	1.50	.25
1102	A425	70p dk bl ('77)	1.50	.30
1103	A425	90p emer ('77)	.75	.25
1104	A425	100p red	1.00	.25
1105	A425	110p rose red ('78)	.35	.25
1106	A425	120p rose red ('78)	.35	.25
1107	A425	130p rose red ('78)	.50	.25

Litho.
1108	A463a	300p multi	3.00	.30
a.		Wmk. 365	17.50	5.00
1109	A515	500p multi ('77)	5.00	.30
a.		Wmk. 365	120.00	14.00
1110	A515	1000p multi ('77)	4.00	8.00

Nos. 1089-1110 (21) 22.25 13.15

Fluorescent paper was used in printing 12p rose red, 15p rose red, 20p, 30p, 40p rose red, 100p, 110p, 120p, 130p.
No. 1099 and the 300p were issued on both ordinary and fluorescent paper.
Nos. 1108 and 1109 exist imperf. Values, pairs: No. 1108 $250; No. 1109 $120.
See Nos. B73-B74.

A516

1976 Photo. Unwmk. Perf. 13½
1112	A516	12c gray & blk	.25	.25
1113	A516	50c gray & grn	.25	.25
1114	A516	1p red & blk	.25	.25
1115	A516	4p bl & blk	.25	.25
1116	A516	5p org & blk	.30	.25
1117	A516	6p dp brn & blk	.30	.25
1118	A516	10p gray & vio bl	.50	.25
1119	A516	27p lt grn & blk	.35	.25
1120	A516	30p lt bl & blk	1.75	.25
1121	A516	45p yel & blk	1.00	.25
1122	A516	50p dl grn & blk	1.00	.25
1123	A516	100p brt grn & red	1.00	.25

Perf. 13x12½
1976 Litho. Wmk. 365
1124	A516	5p grn & blk	.30	.25
1125	A516	27p lt grn & blk	.75	.25
1126	A516	45p yel & blk	1.00	.25

Nos. 1112-1126 (15) 9.25 3.75

The 1p, 6p, 10p, 50p and No. 1116 were issued on both ordinary and fluorescent paper.

Jet and Airlines Emblem — A517

Perf. 13x13½
1976, Apr. 24 Litho. Unwmk.
1130 A517 30p bl, lt bl & dk bl 1.10 .25

Argentine Airlines, 25th anniversary.

Frigate Heroina & Map of Falkland
Islands — A518

1976, Apr. 26
1131 A518 6p multi 3.00 .40

Argentina's claim to Falkland Islands.

Louis
Braille — A519

Wmk. 365
1976, May 22 Engr. Perf. 13½
1132 A519 19.70 deep blue .30 .25

Sesquicentennial of the invention of the Braille system of writing for the blind by Louis Braille (1809-1852).

Private, 7th
Infantry
Regiment
A520

1976, May 29 Litho. Unwmk.
1133 A520 12p multi .45 .25

Army Day.

Schooner Rio de la Plata, by Emilio Biggeri — A521

1976, June 19
1134 A521 12p multi .45 .25
Navy Day.

Dr. Bernardo Houssay — A522

Argentine Nobel Prize Winners:
10p, Bernardo Houssay, medicine and physiology, 1947. 15p, Luis F. Leloir, chemistry, 1970. 20p, Carlos Saavedra Lamas, peace, 1936.

1976, Aug. 14   Litho.   Perf. 13½
1135 A522 10p org & blk .30 .25
1136 A522 15p yel & blk .30 .25
1137 A522 20p ocher & blk .30 .25
    Nos. 1135-1137 (3) .90 .75

Rio de la Plata International Bridge — A523

1976, Sept. 18   Litho.   Perf. 13½
1138 A523 12p multi .70 .25
Inauguration of International Bridge connecting Puerte Unzue, Argentina, and Fray Bentos, Uruguay.

Pipelines & Cooling Tower, Gen. Mosconi Plant A524

1976, Nov. 20   Litho.   Perf. 13½
1139 A524 28p multi .45 .25

Pablo Teodoro Fels & Bleriot Monoplane, 1910 — A525

1976, Nov. 20
1140 A525 15p multi .35 .25
Air Force Day.

Nativity A526

1976, Dec. 18   Litho.   Perf. 13½
1141 A526 20p multi .65 .30
Christmas. Painting by Edith Chiapetto.

Water Conference Emblem — A527

1977, Mar. 19   Litho.   Perf. 13½
1142 A527 70p multi .65 .25
UN Water Conf., Mar del Plata, Mar. 14-25.

Dalmacio Velez Sarsfield — A528

1977, Mar. 19   Engr.
1143 A528 50p blk & red brn .70 .30
Dalmacio Velez Sarsfield (1800-1875), author of Argentine civil code.

Red Deer Type of 1974 Surcharged

1977, July 30   Photo.   Perf. 13½
1144 A495 100p on 5p brn 1.40 .30
Sesquicentennial of Uruguayan postal service. Not issued without surcharge.

Soldier, 16th Lancers A529

1977, July 30
1145 A529 30p multi .85 .25
Army Day.

Schooner Sarandi, by Emilio Biggeri — A530

1977, July 30
1146 A530 30p multi .85 .25
Navy Day.

Soccer Games' Emblem A531

70p, Argentina '78 emblem, flags & soccer field.

1977, May 14
1147 A531 30p multi .45 .25
1148 A531 70p multi .75 .25
11th World Cup Soccer Championship, Argentina, June 1-25, 1978.

The Visit, by Horacio Butler A532

Consecration, by Miguel P. Caride — A533

1977, Mar. 26   Litho.
1149 A532 50p multi .50 .25
1150 A533 70p multi .75 .30
Argentine artists.

Sierra de la Ventana — A534

Views: No. 1152, Civic Center, Santa Rosa. No. 1153, Skiers, San Martin de los Andes. No. 1154, Boat on Lake Fonck, Rio Negro.

1977, Oct. 8   Litho.   Perf. 13x13½
1151 A534 30p multi .35 .25
1152 A534 30p multi .35 .25
1153 A534 30p multi .35 .25
1154 A534 30p multi .35 .25
    Nos. 1151-1154 (4) 1.40 1.00

Guillermo Brown, by R. del Villar — A535

1977, Oct. 8   Perf. 13½
1155 A535 30p multi .35 .25
Adm. Guillermo Brown (1777-1857), leader in fight for independence, bicentenary of birth.

Jet A536

Double-decker, 1926 — A537

1977   Litho.   Perf. 13½
1156 A536 30p multi .25 .25
1157 A537 40p multi .30 .25
50th anniversary of military plane production (30p); Air Force Day (40p).
Issue dates: 30p, Dec. 3; 40p, Nov. 26.

Adoration of the Kings — A538

1977, Dec. 17
1158 A538 100p multi .90 .25
Christmas 1977.

Historic City Hall, Buenos Aires — A539

Chapel of Rio Grande Museum, Tierra del Fuego A540

5p, 20p, La Plata Museum. 10p, Independence Hall, Tucuman. 40p, City Hall, Salta. No. 1165, City Hall, Buenos Aires. 100p, Columbus Theater, Buenos Aires. 200p, flag Monument, Rosario. 280p, 300p, Chapel of Rio Grande Museum, Tierra del Fuego. 480p, 520p, 800, Ruins of Jesuit Mission Church of San Ignacio, Misiones. 500p, Candonga Chapel, Cordoba. 1000p, G.P.O., Buenos Aires. 2000p, Civic Center, Bariloche, Rio Negro.

Three types of 10p: I. Nine vertical window bars; small imprint "E. MILIAVACA Dib." II. Nine bars; large imprint "E. MILIAVACA DIB." III. Redrawn; 5 bars; large imprint.

1977-81 Photo. Unwmk. Perf. 13½
Size: 32x21mm, 21x32mm

1159	A540	5p gray & blk	.25	.25
1160	A540	10p lt ultra & blk, I	.25	.25
a.		Type II	.30	.25
1161	A540	10p lt bl & blk, III	.25	.25
1162	A540	20p citron & blk, litho.	.25	.25
1163	A539	40p gray bl & blk	.30	.25
1164	A539	50p yel & blk	.35	.25
1165	A540	50p citron & blk	.50	.25
1166	A540	100p org & blk, litho.	.30	.25
a.		Wmk. 365	100.00	18.00
1167	A540	100p red org & blk	.30	.25
1168	A540	100p turq & blk	.25	.25
1169	A539	200p lt bl & blk	.50	.25
1170	A540	280p rose & blk	6.50	.80
1171	A540	300p lemon & blk	.80	.25
1172	A540	480p org & blk	1.00	.25
1173	A540	500p yel grn & blk	.35	.25
1174	A540	520p org & blk	.70	.30
1175	A540	800p rose lil & blk	1.25	.30
1176	A540	1000p lem bis & blk	1.00	.40
1177	A540	1000p gold & blk, 40x29mm	1.75	.25
1178	A540	2000p multi	.80	.40
		Nos. 1159-1178 (20)	17.65	5.95

Nos. 1161, 1163, 1165, 1167, 1169, 1171, 1173, 1177 were issued on both ordinary and fluorescent paper. No. 1174 was issued only on fluorescent paper. All others were issued only on ordinary paper.

Issued: No. 1164, 5/30/77; 280p, 12/15/77; No. 1160, 3/14/78; 480p, 5/22/78; 5p, 7/25/78; 20p, 500p, 9/8/78; No. 1166, 9/20/78; No. 1177, 9/28/78; 520p, 9/30/78; 300p, 10/5/78; 40p, 12/1/78; No. 1161, 1979; No. 1165, 1/8/79; 800p, 3/20/79; No. 1167, 4/25/79; 200p, 6/23/79; No. 1176, 12/15/79; 2000p, 6/25/80; No. 1168, 5/26/81.

For overprints see Nos. 1253, 1315.

Soccer Games' Emblem A544

1978, Feb. 10 Photo. Perf. 13½
1179	A544	200p yel grn & bl	.85	.30
a.		Wmk 365	100.00	75.00

11th World Cup Soccer Championship, Argentina, June 1-25.

View of El Rio, Rosario — A545

Designs (Argentina '78 Emblem and): 100p, Rio Tercero Dam, Cordoba. 150p, Cordillera Mountains, Mendoza. 200p, City Center, Mar del Plata. 300p, View of Buenos Aires.

1978, May 6 Litho. Perf. 13
1180	A545	50p multi	.30	.25
1181	A545	100p multi	.30	.25
1182	A545	150p multi	.50	.25
1183	A545	200p multi	.50	.25
1184	A545	300p multi	.90	.30
		Nos. 1180-1184 (5)	2.50	1.30

Sites of 11th World Cup Soccer Championship, June 1-25.

Children — A546

1978, May 20
1185	A546	100p multi	.35	.25

50th anniversary of Children's Institute.

Labor Day, by B. Quinquela Martin — A547

Design: No. 1187, Woman's torso, sculpture by Orlando Pierri.

1978, May 20 Perf. 13½
1186	A547	100p multi	.50	.25
1187	A547	100p multi	.50	.25

Argentina, Hungary, France, Italy and Emblem — A548

Stadium — A549

Teams and Argentina '78 Emblem: 200p, Poland, Fed. Rep. of Germany, Tunisia, Mexico. 300p, Austria, Spain, Sweden, Brazil. 400p, Netherlands, Iran, Peru, Scotland.

1978 Litho. Perf. 13
1188	A548	100p multi	.30	.25
1189	A548	200p multi	.70	.25
1190	A548	300p multi	1.00	.30
1191	A548	400p multi	1.25	.30
		Nos. 1188-1191 (4)	3.25	1.10

Souvenir Sheet
Lithographed and Engraved
Perf. 13½
1192	A549	700p buff & blk	2.75	2.75

11th World Cup Soccer Championship, Argentina, June 1-25. Issued: Nos. 1188-1191, 6/6; No. 1192, 6/3.

Stadium Type of 1978 Inscribed in Red

Lithographed and Engraved
1978, Sept. 2 Perf. 13½
1193	A549	1000p buff, blk & red	4.25	4.25

Argentina's victory in 1978 Soccer Championship. No. 1193 has margin similar to No.

1192 with Rimet Cup emblem and text added in red.

Young Tree Nourished by Old Trunk, UN Emblem — A550

1978 Sept. 2 Litho.
1194	A550	100p multi	.35	.25

Technical Cooperation among Developing Countries Conf., Buenos Aires, Sept. 1978.

Emblems of Buenos Aires & Bank — A551

1978, Sept. 16
1195	A551	100p multi	.35	.25

Bank of City of Buenos Aires, centenary.

General Savio & Steel Production — A552

1978, Sept. 16
1196	A552	100p multi	.35	.25

Gen. Manuel N. Savio (1892-1948), general manager of military heavy industry.

San Martin — A553

1978, Oct. Engr.
1197	A553	2000p grnsh blk	4.00	.30

1979 Wmk. 365
1198	A553	2000p grnsh blk	5.50	1.00

Gen Jose de San Martin (1778-1850), soldier and statesman. See No. 1292.

Globe & Argentine Flag — A554

1978, Oct. 7 Litho. Perf. 13½
1199	A554	200p multi	.80	.25

12th Intl. Cancer Cong., Buenos Aires, Oct. 5-11.

Chessboard, Queen & Pawn — A555

1978, Oct. 7
1200	A555	200p multi	4.25	.65

23rd National Chess Olympics, Buenos Aires, Oct. 25-Nov. 12.

Correct Positioning of Stamps A557

50p, Use correct postal code number.

1978 Photo. Perf. 13½
1201	A557	20p ultra	.25	.25
1203	A557	50p carmine	.25	.25

No. 1201 issued on both ordinary and fluorescent paper.

A558   A559

1978-82 Photo. Perf. 13½
1204	A558	150p bl & ultra	.35	.25
1205	A558	180p bl & ultra	.35	.25
1206	A558	200p bl & ultra	.50	.25
1207	A559	240p ol bis & bl ('79)	.35	.25
1208	A559	260p blk & lt bl ('79)	.35	.25
1209	A559	290p brn & lt bl ('79)	.45	.25
1210	A559	310p mag & bl ('79)	.45	.25
1211	A559	350p ver & bl ('79)	.55	.25
1212	A559	450p ultra & bl	.50	.25
1213	A559	600p grn & bl ('80)	1.10	.25
1214	A559	700p blk & bl ('80)	.65	.25
1215	A559	800p red & bl ('81)	.45	.25
1216	A559	1100p gray & bl ('81)	.90	.25
1217	A559	1500p blk & bl ('81)	.50	.25
1218	A559	1700p grn & bl ('82)	.50	.25
		Nos. 1204-1218 (15)	7.95	3.75

No. 1204 issued on fluorescent and ordinary paper. No. 1206 issued only on fluorescent paper.

For overprint see No. 1338.

Balsa "24" A561

Ships: 200p, Tug Legador. 300p, River Parana tug No. 34. 400p, Passenger ship Ciudad de Parana.

1978, Nov. 4 Litho. Perf. 13½
1220	A561	100p multi	.30	.25
1221	A561	200p multi	.50	.25
1222	A561	300p multi	.70	.25
a.		Pair, #1221-1222	1.50	
1223	A561	400p multi	.95	.50
a.		Pair, #1220, 1223	1.50	
		Nos. 1220-1223 (4)	2.45	1.25

20th anniversary of national river fleet. Issued on fluorescent paper.

View and Arms of Bahia Blanca A562

1978, Nov. 25   Litho.   Perf. 13½
1224 A562 20p multi   .50 .25
Sesquicentennial of Bahia Blanca.

"Spain," (Queen Isabella and Columbus) by Arturo Dresco — A563

1978, Nov. 25
1225 A563 300p multi   2.75 .35
Visit of King Juan Carlos and Queen Sofia of Spain to Argentina, Nov. 26.

Virgin and Child, San Isidro Cathedral A564

1978, Dec. 16
1226 A564 200p gold & multi   .65 .25
Christmas 1978.

Slope at Chacabuco, by Pedro Subercaseaux — A565

Painting: 1000p, The Embrace of Maipu (San Martin and O'Higgins), by Pedro Subercaseaux, vert.

1978, Dec. 16   Litho.   Perf. 13½
1227 A565 500p multi   2.00 .30
1228 A565 1000p multi   3.50 .35
José de San Martin, 200th birth anniversary.

Adolfo Alsina A566

Design: No. 1230, Mariano Moreno.

1979, Jan. 20
1229 A566 200p lt bl & blk   .50 .25
1230 A566 200p yel red & blk   .50 .25
Adolfo Alsina (1828-1877), political leader, vice-president; Mariano Moreno (1778-1811), lawyer, educator, political leader.

Argentina No. 37 and UPU Emblem — A567

1979, Jan. 20
1231 A567 200p multi   .50 .25
Centenary of Argentina's UPU membership.

Still-life, by Carcova A568

Painting: 300p, The Laundresses, by Faustino Brughetti.

1979, Mar. 3
1232 A568 200p multi   .45 .25
1233 A568 300p multi   .85 .30
Ernesto de la Carcova (1866-1927) and Faustino Brughetti (1877-1956), Argentine painters.

Balcarce Earth Station — A569

1979, Mar. 3
1234 A569 200p multicolored   .65 .25
Third Inter-American Telecommunications Conference, Buenos Aires, March 5-9.

Stamp Collecting — A570

1979
1235 A570 30p multicolored   .25 .25
Printed on ordinary and fluorescent paper.

European Olive — A571

1979, June 2   Litho.   Perf. 13½
1236 A571 100p shown   .65 .35
1237 A571 200p Tea   .65 .35
1238 A571 300p Sorghum   1.25 .45
1239 A571 400p Common flax   1.25 .55
   Nos. 1236-1239 (4)   3.80 1.70

Laurel and Regimental Emblem A572

1979, June 9
1240 A572 200p gold & multi   .45 .25
Founding of Subteniente Berdina Village in memory of Sub-lieutenant Rodolfo Hernan Berdina, killed by terrorists in 1975.

"75" and Automobile Club Emblem — A573

1979, June 9
1241 A573 200p gold & multi   .35 .25
Argentine Automobile Club, 75th anniv.

Exchange Building and Emblem — A574

1979, June 9
1242 A574 200p bl, blk & gold   .35 .25
Grain Exchange, 125th anniversary.

Cavalry Officer, 1817 — A575

1979, July 7   Litho.   Perf. 13½
1243 A575 200p multi   1.00 .30
Army Day.

Corvette Uruguay and Navy Emblem — A576

Design: No. 1245, Hydrographic service ship & emblem.

1979   Perf. 13
1244 A576 250p multi   1.00 .35
1245 A576 250p multi   1.00 .35
Navy Day; Cent. of Naval Hydrographic Service. Issued: No. 1244, July 28; No. 1245, July 7.

Tree and Man — A577

1979, July 28   Perf. 13½
1246 A577 250p multi   .60 .25
Protection of the Environment Day, June 5.

"Spad" Flying over Andes, and Vicente Almandos Almonacid — A578

1979, Aug. 4
1247 A578 250p multi   .75 .25
Air Force Day.

Gen. Julio A. Roca Occupying Rio Negro, by Juan M. Blanes — A579

1979, Aug. 4
1248 A579 250p multi   .75 .25
Conquest of Rio Negro Desert, centenary.

Rowland Hill — A580

1979, Sept. 29   Litho.   Perf. 13½
1249 A580 300p gray red & blk   .65 .25
Sir Rowland Hill (1795-1879), originator of penny postage.

Viedma Navarez Monument A581

1979, Sept. 29
1250 A581 300p multi   .85 .25
Viedma and Carmen de Patagones towns, bicentenary.

Pope Paul
VI — A582

Design: No. 1252, Pope John Paul I.

1979, Oct. 27   Engr.   Perf. 13½
1251 A582 500p black   1.00   .30
1252 A582 500p sepia   1.00   .30

No. 1169
Overprinted in Red

1979, Nov. 10   Photo.   Perf. 13½
1253 A539 200p lt blue & blk   .65   .25
Rosario Philatelic Society, 75th anniversary.

A583

1979, Nov. 10   Litho.
1254 A583 300p multi   .75   .30
Frontier resettlement.

A584

1979, Dec. 1   Litho.   Perf. 13½
1255 A584 300p multi   .75   .30
Military Geographic Institute centenary.

Christmas 1979 — A585

1979, Dec. 1
1256 A585 300p multi   .65   .25

General Mosconi Birth
Centenary — A586

1979, Dec. 15   Engr.   Perf. 13½
1257 A586 1000p blk & bl   1.50   .50

Rotary
Emblem
and
Globe
A587

1979, Dec. 29   Litho.
1258 A587 300p multi   1.75   .35
Rotary International, 75th anniversary.

Child and IYC
Emblem
A588

Family, by Pablo Menicucci — A589

1979, Dec. 29
1259 A588 500p lt bl & sepia   .75   .35
1260 A589 1000p multi   1.50   .25
International Year of the Child.

Microphone, Waves, ITU
Emblem — A590

1980, Mar. 22   Litho.   Perf. 13x13½
1261 A590 500p multi   1.40   .25
Regional Administrative Conference on
Broadcasting by Hectometric Waves for Area
2, Buenos Aires, Mar. 10-29.

Guillermo
Brown — A591

1980   Engr.   Perf. 13½
1262 A591 5000p black   5.00   .25
See No. 1372.

Argentine Red Cross
Centenary — A592

1980, Apr. 19   Litho.   Perf. 13½
1263 A592 500p multi   .55   .25

OAS Emblem
A593

1980, Apr. 19
1264 A593 500p multi   .55   .25
Day of the Americas, Apr. 14.

Dish Antennae, Balcarce — A594

No. 1266, Hydroelectric Station, Salto
Grande. No. 1267, Bridge, Zarate-Brazo
Largo.

1980, Apr. 26   Litho. & Engr.
1265 A594 300p shown   .45   .25
1266 A594 300p multicolored   .45   .25
1267 A594 300p multicolored   .45   .25
    Nos. 1265-1267 (3)   1.35   .75

Capt. Hipolito Bouchard, Frigate
"Argentina" — A595

1980, May 31   Litho.   Perf. 13x13½
1268 A595 500p multicolored   .85   .30
Navy Day.

"Villarino," San Martin, by Theodore
Gericault — A596

1980, May 31
1269 A596 500p multicolored   .85   .30
Return of the remains of Gen. Jose de San
Martin to Argentina, centenary.

Buenos Aires Gazette, 1810,
Signature — A597

1980, June 7   Perf. 13½
1270 A597 500p multicolored   .55   .25
Journalism Day.

Miniature Sheet

Coaches in Victoria Square — A598

1980 June 14
1271 A598   Sheet of 14   12.50 12.50
  a.-n.   500p any single   .75   .50
Buenos Aires, 400th anniv. No. 1271 shows
ceramic mural of Victoria Square by Rodolfo
Franco in continuous design. See No. 1285.

Gen. Pedro
Aramburu
A599

1980, July 12   Litho.   Perf. 13½
1272 A599 500p yel & blk   .65   .25
Gen. Pedro Eugenio Aramburu (1903-
1970), provisional president, 1955.

Army
Day
A600

1980, July 12
1273 A600 500p multicolored   .85   .30

Gen. Juan Gregorio de Las Heras
(1780-1866), Hero of 1817 War of
Independence — A601

Grandees of Argentina Bicentenary: No.
1275, Rivadavia. No. 1276, Brig. Gen Jose
Matias Zapiola (1780-1874), naval commander and statesman.

1980, Aug. 2   Litho.   Perf. 13½
1274 A601 500p tan & blk   .55   .25
1275 A601 500p multicolored   .55   .25
1276 A601 500p lt lilac & blk   .55   .25
    Nos. 1274-1276 (3)   1.65   .75

Avro "Gosport" Biplane, Maj. Francisco de Artega — A602

1980, Aug. 16   **Perf. 13**
1277 A602 500p multicolored   .60 .25

Air Force Day. Artega (1882-1930) was first director of Military Aircraft Factory where Avro "Gosport" was built (1927).

University of La Plata, 75th Anniversary — A603

1980, Aug. 16   **Perf. 13½**
1278 A603 500p multi   .55 .25

Souvenir Sheets

A604

A605

No. 1279: a, King penguin. b, Bearded penguin. c, Adelie penguins. d, Papua penguins. e, Sea elephants. f, Puerto Soledad, 1829. g, Puerto Soledad harbor, 1829. h, Fur seals. i, Giant petrels. j, Blue-eyed cororants. k, Stormy petrels. l, Antarctic doves.

No. 1280: Letters a-e and h-l are the same as No. 1279. f, South Orkneys Argentine Base, towers and buildings. g, South Orkneys Argentine Base, buildings and mountains.

1980, Sept. 27   **Litho.**   **Perf. 13½**
1279 A604 Sheet of 12   12.50 12.50
   a.-l.   500p, any single   .75 .60
1280 A605 Sheet of 12   12.50 12.50
   f.-g.   500p, any single   .75 .60

75th anniv. of Argentina's presence in the South Orkneys and 150th anniv. of political and military command in the Falkland Islands. Nos. 1279-1280 each contain 12 stamps (4x3) with landscape designs in center of sheets. Silhouettes of Argentine exploration ships in margins. No. 1280 contains Nos. 1279a-1279e, 1279h-1279m, 1280a-1280b.

Anti-smoking Campaign A608

1980, Oct. 11
1282 A608 700p multi   .90 .25

National Census — A609

1980, Sept.
1283 A609 500p blk & bl   1.10 .25

Madonna and Child (Congress Emblem) — A610

1980, Oct. 1   **Litho.**
1284 A610 700p multi   .85 .25

National Marian Cong., Mendoza, Oct. 8-12

Mural Type of 1980
Miniature Sheet
1980, Oct. 25
1285   Sheet of 14   10.00 10.00
   a.-n.   A598 500p, any single   .65 .50

Buenos Aires, 400th anniv./Buenos Aires '80 Stamp Exhib., Oct. 24-Nov. 2. No. 1285 shows ceramic mural Arte bajo la Ciudad by Alfredo Guido in continuous design.

Technical Military Academy, 50th Anniversary A611

1980, Nov. 1
1286 A611 700p multi   .75 .25

Amateur Radio Operation A612

1980, Nov. 1
1287 A612 700p multi   .75 .25

Medal — A613

Lujan Cathedral Floor Plan — A614

1980, Nov. 29   **Litho.**   **Perf. 13½**
1288 A613 700p multi   .75 .30
1289 A614 700p olive & brn   .75 .30

Christmas 1980. 150th anniv. of apparition of Holy Virgin to St. Catherine Laboure, Paris (No. 1288), 350th anniv. of apparition at Lujan.

150th Death Anniversary of Simon Bolivar — A615

1980, Dec. 13
1290 A615 700p multi   .75 .25

Soccer Gold Cup Championship, Montevideo, 1980 — A616

1981, Jan. 3   **Litho.**
1291 A616 1000p multi   1.10 .25

San Martin Type of 1978
1981, Jan. 20   **Engr.**   **Perf. 13½**
1292 A553 10,000p dark blue   7.50 .25

Landscape in Lujan, by Marcos Tiglio — A617

Paintings: No. 1304, Expansion of Light along a Straight Line, by Miguel Angel Vidal, vert.

1981, Apr. 11   **Litho.**
1303 A617 1000p multi   .90 .35
1304 A617 1000p multi   .90 .35

Intl. Sports Medicine Congress, June 7-12 — A618

1981, June 6   **Litho.**   **Perf. 13½**
1305 A618 1000p bl & dk brn   .75 .25

Esperanza Base, Antarctica — A619

Cargo Plane, Map of Vice-Commodore Marambio Island — A620

Perf. 13½, 13x13½ (No. 1308)
1981, June 13
1306 A619 1000p shown   1.40 .45
1307 A619 2000p Almirante Irizar   2.50 .50
1308 A620 2000p shown   2.40 .80
   Nos. 1306-1308 (3)   6.30 1.75

Antarctic Treaty 20th anniv.

Antique Pistols (Military Club Centenary) — A621

1981, June 27   **Perf. 13½**
1309 A621 1000p Club building   .80 .25
1310 A621 2000p shown   .80 .25

Gen. Juan A. Alvarez de Arenales (1770-1831) A622

Famous Men: No. 1312, Felix G. Frias (1816-1881), writer. No. 1313, Jose E. Uriburu (1831-1914), statesman.

1981, Aug. 8   **Litho.**   **Perf. 13½**
1311 A622 1000p multi   .70 .25
1312 A622 1000p multi   .70 .25
1313 A622 1000p multi   .70 .25
   Nos. 1311-1313 (3)   2.10 .75

Naval Observatory Centenary — A623

1981, Aug. 15 Litho. *Perf. 13x13½*
1314 A623 1000p multi   1.00 .30

No. 1176
Overprinted
in Red

1981, Aug. 15 Photo. *Perf. 13½*
1315 A540 1000p lem & blk   1.75 .35
50th anniv. of Bahia Blanca Philatelic and Numismatic Society.

St. Cayetano, Stained-glass Window, Buenos Aires — A624

1981, Sept. 5 Litho. *Perf. 13½*
1316 A624 1000p multi   .70 .25
St. Cayetano, founder of Teatino Order, 500th birth anniv.

Pablo Castaibert (1883-1909) and his Monoplane (Air Force Day) — A625

1981, Sept. 5 *Perf. 13x13½*
1317 A625 1000p multi   1.10 .30

Intl. Year
of the
Disabled
A626

1981, Sept. 10 *Perf. 13½*
1318 A626 1000p multi   .75 .25

22nd Latin-American Steelmakers' Congress, Buenos Aires, Sept. 21-23 — A627

1981, Sept. 19
1319 A627 1000p multi   .60 .25

Army Regiment No. 1 (Patricios), 175th Anniv. — A628

1981, Oct. 10 Litho. *Perf. 13½*
1320 1500p Natl. arms   .45 .25
1321 1500p shown   .45 .25
  a. A628 Pair, #1320-1321   1.10 1.10

A629

San Martin as artillery Captain in Battle of Bailen, 1808.

1981, Oct. 5
1322   Sheet of 8 + 4 labels   4.75 4.75
  a. A629 1000p multi   .35 .30
  b. A629 1500p multi   .50 .35
Espamer '81 Intl. Stamp Exhib. (Americas, Spain, Portugal), Buenos Aires, Nov. 13-22. No. 1322 contains 2 each se-tenant pairs with label between.

A630

1981, Oct. 5
1323 A630 1000p multi   6.75 .40
Anti-indiscriminate whaling.

Espamer '81
Emblem and
Ship
A631

1981
1324 A631 1300p multi   1.00 .40

No. 1324
Overprinted
in Blue

1981, Nov. 7 Photo. *Perf. 13½*
1325 A631 1300p multi   1.50 .25
Postal Administration philatelic training course.

Soccer Players
A632

Designs: Soccer players.

1981, Nov. 13 Litho.
1326   Sheet of 4 + 2 labels   8.00 8.00
  a. A632 2000p multi   1.50 1.25
  b. A632 3000p multi   1.75 1.50
  c. A632 5000p multi   2.00 1.75
  d. A632 15,000p multi   2.25 2.00
Espamer '81.

"Peso" Coin Centenary — A633

2000p, Patacon, 1881. 3000p, Argentine Oro, 1881.

1981, Nov. 21
1327 A633 2000p multicolored   .55 .25
1328 A633 3000p multicolored   .55 .25

Christmas
1981 — A634

1981, Dec. 12
1329 A634 1500p multi   2.40 .50

Traffic
Safety
A635

1000p, Observe traffic lights, vert. 2000p, Drive carefully, vert. 3000p, Cross at white lines. 4000p, Don't shine headlights.

1981, Dec. 19 Litho.
1330 A635 1000p multicolored   1.50 .40
1331 A635 2000p multicolored   .80 .50
1332 A635 3000p multicolored   1.25 .45
1333 A635 4000p multicolored   1.25 .65
  Nos. 1330-1333 (4)   4.80 2.00

Francisco Luis
Bernardez,
Ciuda
Laura — A636

Writers and title pages from their works: 2000p, Lucio V. Mansilla, Excursion a los indios ranqueles. 3000p, Conrado Nale Roxlo, El Grillo. 4000p, Victoria Ocampo, Sur.

1982, Mar. 20 Litho.
1334 A636 1000p shown   1.50 .40
1335 A636 2000p multi   .80 .40
1336 A636 3000p multi   .80 .50
1337 A636 4000p multi   1.50 .30
  Nos. 1334-1337 (4)   4.60 1.60

No. 1218 Overprinted

1982, Apr. 17 Photo. *Perf. 13½*
1338 A559 1700p green & blue   .70 .25
Argentina's claim on Falkland Islands.

Robert
Koch — A637

1982, Apr. 17 Litho. Wmk. 365
1339 A637 2000p multi   1.10 .25
TB bacillus centenary and 25th Intl. Tuberculosis Conference.

American
Airforces
Commanders'
22nd
Conf. — A638

1982, Apr. 17
1340 A638 2000p multi   1.25 .30

Stone Carving, City Founder's Signature (Don Hernando de Lerma) — A639

1982, Apr. 17
1341 A639 2000p multi   1.50 .30
Souvenir Sheet
1342 A639 5000p multi   3.00 3.00
City of Salta, 400th anniv. No. 1342 contains one 43x30mm stamp.

Naval Center Centenary — A640

1982, Apr. 24 *Perf. 13x13½*
1343 A640 2000p multi   .80 .30

Chorisia
Speciosa — A641

200p, Zinnia peruviana. 300p, Ipomoea purpurea. 400p, Tillandsia aeranthos. 800p, Oncidium bifolium. 1000p, Erythrina crista-galli. 2000p, Jacaranda mimosi-folia. 3000p, Bauhinia candicans. 5000p, Tecoma stans. 10,000p, Tabebuia ipe. 20,000p, Passiflora coerulea. 30,000p, Aristolochia littoralis. 50,000p, Oxalis enneaphylla.

1982	Unwmk.	Photo.	Perf. 13½	
1344	A641	200p multi	.30	.25
1345	A641	300p multi	.30	.25
1346	A641	400p multi	.25	.25
1347	A641	500p shown	.25	.25
1348	A641	800p multi	.25	.25
1349	A641	1000p multi	.30	.25
1350	A641	2000p multi	.30	.25
1351	A641	3000p multi	.65	.25
1352	A641	5000p multi	.60	.25
1353	A641	10,000p multi	1.00	.25
1354	A641	20,000p multi	1.25	.35
1355	A641	30,000p multi	1.75	.40
1356	A641	50,000p multi	3.50	.65
	Nos. 1344-1356 (13)		10.70	3.90

Nos. 1344-1346, 1348-1350 issued on fluo-rescent paper. Nos. 1353-1356 issued on ordi-nary paper. Others issued on both fluorescent and ordinary paper.
Issued: 500p, 2000p, 5000p, 10,000p, 5/22; 200p, 300p, 1000p, 20,000p, 9/25; 400p, 800p, 30,000p, 50,000p, 12/4; 3000p, 12/18.
See Nos. 1429-1443A, 1515-1527, 1683-1691. For overprint see No. 1382.

10th Death Anniv. of Gen. Juan C. Sanchez — A641a

1982, May 29	Litho.	Wmk. 365	
1364	A641a	5000p grn & blk	.90	.25

Luis Vernet, First Commander — A641b

1982, June 12			
1365	A641b	5000p org & blk	1.75	.55
	Size: 83x28mm		
1366	A641b	5000p Map	1.00	.40
a.	Pair, Nos. 1365-1366	2.75	2.00

153rd Anniv. of Malvinas Political and Mili-tary Command District. Compare with No. 1411.

Visit of Pope John Paul II — A641c

1982, June 12			
1367	A641c	5000p multi	2.00	.55

Organ Grinder, by Aldo Severi (b. 1928) — A641d

3000p, Still Life, by Santiago Cogorno (b. 1915).

1982, July 3		Wmk. 365	
1368	A641d	2000p shown	.80	.35
1369	A641d	3000p multi	.80	.35

Guillermo Brown Type of 1980 and

Jose de San Martin — A641e

Litho. and Engr.			
1982	**Unwmk.**		**Perf. 13½**
1372	A591	30,000p blk & bl	3.75	.70
1376	A641e	50,000p sepia & car	7.50	1.00

Issue dates: 30,000p, June; 50,000p, July.

Scouting Year — A641f

1982, Aug. 7	Litho.	Wmk. 365	Perf. 13½	
1380	A641f	5000p multi	2.40	.40

Alconafta Fuel Campaign — A641g

1982, Aug. 7		Wmk. 365	
1381	A641g	2000p multi	.85	.25

No. 1352 Overprinted

1982, Aug. 7	Photo.	Unwmk.	
1382	A641	5000p multi	2.40	1.00

Rio III Central Nuclear Power Plant, Cordoba A642

	Wmk. 365		
1982, Sept. 4	**Litho.**	**Perf. 13½**	
1383	A642	2000p shown	.45	.25
1384	A642	2000p Control room	.45	.25

Namibia Day — A643

1982, Sept. 4			
1385	A643	5000p Map	.95	.25

Formosa Cathedral — A644

Churches and Cathedrals of the Northeast: 2000p, Our Lady of Itati, Corrientes, vert. 3000p, Resistencia Cathedral, Chaco, vert. 10,000p, St. Ignatius Church ruins, Misiones.

1982, Sept. 18		Litho. & Engr.	
1386	A644	2000p dk grn & blk	.55	.55
1387	A644	3000p dk brn & brn	.55	.55
1388	A644	5000p dk bl & brn	1.00	.55
1389	A644	10,000p dp org & blk	1.50	.55
	Nos. 1386-1389 (4)		3.60	2.20

Tension Sideral, by Mario Alberto Agatiello A645

Sculpture (Espamer '81 and Juvenex '82 Exhibitions): 3000p, Sugerencia II, by Eduardo Mac Entyre. 5000p, Storm, by Carlos Silva.

1982, Oct. 2	Litho.	Perf. 13½	
1390	A645	2000p multi	1.00	.40
1391	A645	3000p multi	1.00	.40
1392	A645	5000p multi	1.50	.45
	Nos. 1390-1392 (3)		3.50	1.25

Santa Fe Bridge A646

1982, Oct. 16		Litho. & Engr.	
1393	A646	2000p bl & blk	1.00	.25

2nd Southern Cross Games, Santa Fe and Rosario, Nov. 26-Dec. 5.

10th World Men's Volleyball Championship — A647

1982, Oct. 16	Litho.	Wmk. 365	
1394	A647	2000p multi	.35	.25
1395	A647	5000p multi	.50	.25

Los Andes Newspaper Centenary — A648

Design: Army of the Andes Monument, Hill of Glory, Mendoza.

1982, Oct. 30			
1396	A648	5000p multi	.60	.30

A649

1982, Oct. 30		Wmk. 365	
1397	A649	5000p Signs	.65	.25

50th Anniv. of Natl. Roads, Administration.

A650

A650a

La Plata City Cent., each 2500p: No. 1400: a, Cathedral, diff. b, Head, top. c, Observatory. d, City Hall, diff. e, Head, bottom. f, University.

1982, Nov. 20		Litho.	
1398	A650	5000p Cathedral	.85	.25
1399	A650	5000p City Hall	.85	.25
1400	A650a	Sheet of 6	2.50	2.50
a.-f.	2500p Any single		.35	.25

Well, Natl. Hydrocarbon Congress
Emblem — A651

1982, Nov. 20
1401 A651 5000p multi 1.20 .25
Oil Discovery, Comodoro Rivadavia, 75th
anniv.

Jockey Club of
Buenos Aires
Centenary
A652

Design: No. 1403, Carlos Pellegrini, first
president.

1982, Dec. 4 **Litho.**
1402 A652 5000p Emblem 1.00 .25
1403 A652 5000p multi 1.00 .25

Christmas
A653

3000p, St. Vincent de Paul. 5000p, St. Francis of Assisi.

1982, Dec. 18 **Perf. 13½**
1404 A653 3000p multi 2.00 .40
Size: 29x38mm
1405 A653 5000p multi 1.40 .25

Pedro B.
Palacios (1854-
1917),
Writer — A654

Writers: 2000p, Leopoldo Marechal (1900-
1970). 3000p, Delfina Bunge de Galvez (1881-
1952). 4000p, Manuel Galvez (1882-1962).
5000p, Evaristo Carriego (1883-1912).

1983, Mar. 26 **Litho.** **Perf. 13½**
1406 A654 1000p multi .50 .30
1407 A654 2000p multi .50 .30
1408 A654 3000p multi .50 .30
1409 A654 4000p multi .50 .30
1410 A654 5000p multi .50 .30
a. Strip of 5, #1406-1410 2.60 2.60

Recovery of the Malvinas (Falkland
Islands) — A655

20,000p, Map, flag.

1983, Apr. 9 **Litho.** **Perf. 13½**
1411 A655 20,000p multi 1.75 .60
Compare No. 1411 with No. 1366.

Telecommunications Systems — A656

No. 1412, SITRAM, No. 1413, ARPAC
network.

1983, Apr. 16 **Wmk. 365**
1412 A656 5000p multi 1.25 .65
1413 A656 5000p multi 1.25 .65

Naval League
Emblem
A657

1983, May 14 **Litho.** **Perf. 13½**
1414 A657 5000p multi .65 .25
Navy Day and 50th anniv. of Naval League.

Allegory, by
Victor Rebuffo
A658

1983, May 14
1415 A658 5000p multi .65 .30
Natl. Arts Fund, 25th Anniv.

75th Anniv. of
Colon Opera
House, Buenos
Aires — A659

1983, May 28 **Wmk. 365**
1416 A659 5000p Main hall .75 .40
1417 A659 10000p Stage 1.00 .40

Protected Species — A660

1p, Chrysocyon brachyurus. 1.50p,
Ozotocerus bezoarticus. 2p, Myrmecophaga
tridactyla. 2.50p, Leo onca.

1983, July 2 **Litho.** **Perf. 13½**
1418 A660 1p multicolored 1.00 .40
1419 A660 1.50p multicolored 1.50 .40
1420 A660 2p multicolored 1.60 .40
1421 A660 2.50p multicolored 1.90 .40
Nos. 1418-1421 (4) 6.00 1.60

City of
Catamarca,
300th
Anniv. — A661

Foundation of the City of Catamarca, by
Luis Varela Lezana (1900-1982).

1983, July 16 **Litho.** **Perf. 13½**
1422 A661 1p multi .50 .40

Mamerto
Esquiu (1826-
1883)
A662

1983, July 16
1423 A662 1p multi .50 .40

Bolivar, by
Herrera
Toro — A663

Bolivar,
Engraving by
Kepper — A664

Perf. 13 (A663), 13½ (A664)
1983 **Unwmk.**
1424 A663 1p multi .45 .35
1425 A664 2p blk & maroon .65 .40
1426 A664 10p San Martin 3.50 .45
Nos. 1424-1426 (3) 4.60 1.20
Issue dates: 1p, 2p, July 23. 10p, Aug. 20.
See Nos. 1457-1462B.

Gen. Toribio de
Luzuriaga
(1782-1842)
A665

1983, Aug. 20 **Litho.** **Perf. 13½**
1427 A665 1p multi .60 .40

50th
Anniv. of
San
Martin
National
Institute
A666

1983, Aug. 20 **Engr.** **Unwmk.**
1428 A666 2p sepia .60 .40

**Flower Type of 1982 in New
Currency**

1983-85 **Photo.** **Perf. 13½**
1429 A641 5c like #1347 .50 .25
1430 A641 10c like #1349 .25 .25
1431 A641 20c like #1350 .25 .25
1432 A641 30c like #1351 .40 .25
1433 A641 40c Eichhornia
crassipes .25 .25
1434 A641 50c like #1352 .25 .25
1435 A641 1p like #1353 .30 .25
1435A A641 1.80p Mutisia
retusa .30 .25
1436 A641 2p like #1354 .35 .25
1437 A641 3p like #1355 .40 .25
1438 A641 5p like #1356 .40 .25
1439 A641 10p Alstroemeria
aurantiaca 1.10 .80
1440 A641 20p like #1345 .40 .25
1441 A641 30p Embothrium
coccineum 2.00 .25
1442 A641 50p like #1346 .60 .40
1443 A641 100p like #1348 1.75 .25
1443A A641 300p Cassia
carnaval 2.00 .50
Nos. 1429-1443A (17) 11.50 5.20
Issued: 20p, 8/27/84; 50p, 10/19/84; 100p,
12/84; 300p, 6/15/85.
Nos. 1429, 1433, 1435A issued on fluorescent paper. Nos. 1443, 1443A issued on ordinary paper. Others issued on both ordinary
and fluorescent paper.
No. 1440 has denomination at UL.
For overprint and surcharge see Nos. 1489,
1530.

Intl. Rotary
South
American
Regional
Conference,
Buenos Aires,
Sept. 25-
28 — A667

1983, Sept. 24 **Litho.**
1444 A667 1p multi .65 .25

9th Pan American Games, Caracas,
Aug. 13-28 — A668

1983, Sept. 24
1445 A668 1p Track .45 .25
1446 A668 2p Emblem .60 .25

World Communications Year — A669

1983, Oct. 8   **Perf. 13½**
1447 A669 2p multi   .60 .25

Squash
Peddler by
Antonio Berni
(1905-1981)
A670

2p, Figure in Yellow by Luis Seoane (1910-79).

1983, Oct. 15   **Perf. 13½**
1448 A670 1p multi   .50 .25
1449 A670 2p multi   .60 .25

World Communications Year — A671

Designs: 1p, Wagon, 18th cent. 2p, Post chaise, 19th cent. 4p, Steam locomotive, 1857. 5p, Tramway, 1910.

1983, Nov. 19   **Litho.**   **Perf. 13½**
1450 A671 1p multi   .60 .35
1451 A671 2p multi   .60 .35
1452 A671 4p multi   .85 .35
1453 A671 5p multi   .85 .35
    Nos. 1450-1453 (4)   2.90 1.40

World
Communications
Year — A672

2p, General Post Office.

1983, Nov. 26   **Litho.**   **Perf. 12½x12**
1454 A672 2p multicolored   .40 .30

Return to
Elected
Government
A673

1983, Dec. 10   **Photo.**   **Perf. 13½**
1455 A673 2p Coin, 1813   .65 .25

Eudyptes
Crestatus
A674

Designs: b, Diomedea exulans. c, Diomedea melanophris. d, Eudyptes chrysolophus. e, Luis Piedra Buena. f, Carlos Maria Moyano. g, Luis Py. h, Augusto Lasserre. i, Phoebetria palpebrata. j, Hydrurga leptonyx. k, Lobodon carcinophagus. l, Leptonychotes weddelli.

1983, Dec. 10   **Litho.**
1456   Sheet of 12   11.00 11.00
   a.-l. A674 2p any single   .40 .25

Southern pioneers and fauna. Margin depicts various airplanes and emblems.

Bolivar Type of 1983

Famous men: 10p, Angel J. Carranza (1834-99), historian. No. 1458, 500p, Guillermo Brown. No. 1459, Estanislao del Campo (1834-80), poet. 30p, Jose Hernandez (1834-86), author. 40p, Vicente Lopez y Planes (1784-1856), poet and patriot. 50p, San Martin. 200p, Belgrano.

1983-85   **Litho. & Engr.**   **Perf. 13½**
1457   A664   10p pale bl & dk
                  bl   .50 .40
1458   A664   20p dk bl & blk   .50 .40
1459   A664   20p dl brn ol & ol
                  blk   .50 .40
1460   A664   30p pale bl & blu-
                  ish blk   .60 .40
1461   A664   40p lt bl grn & blk   1.00 .40
1462   A664   50p Prus grn &
                  choc   2.40 1.50
1462A A664   200p int bl & blk   2.10 1.00
1462B A664   500p brn & int bl   2.00 .50
    Nos. 1457-1462B (8)   9.60 5.00

Issued: No. 1458, 10/6; 10p, No. 1459, 30p, 40p, 3/23/85; 50p, 4/23/85; 200p, 11/2/85; 500p, 5/2/85.

Christmas 1983 — A675

Nativity Scenes: 2p, Tapestry, by Silke. 3p, Stained-glass window, San Carlos de Bariloche's Wayn Church, vert.

1983, Dec. 17   **Litho.**   **Perf. 13½**
1463 A675 2p multi   .45 .25
1464 A675 3p multi   .90 .30

Centenary of El
Dia Newspaper
A676

4p, Masthead, printing roll.

1984, Mar. 24   **Litho.**
1465 A676 4p multicolored   .45 .25

Alejandro Carbo Teachers' College
Centenary — A677

1984, June 2   **Litho.**   **Perf. 13½**
1466 A677 10p Building   .45 .30

1984
Olympics
A678

Designs: No. 1468, Weightlifting, discus, shot put. No. 1469, Javelin, fencing. No. 1470, Bicycling, swimming.

1984, July 28   **Litho.**   **Perf. 13½**
1467 A678 5p shown   .30 .25
1468 A678 5p multicolored   .30 .25
1469 A678 10p multicolored   .50 .30
1470 A678 10p multicolored   .50 .30
    Nos. 1467-1470 (4)   1.60 1.10

Rosario Stock
Exchange
Centenary
A679

1984, Aug. 11
1471 A679 10p multicolored   .50 .30

Wheat
A680

1984, Aug. 11
1472 A680 10p shown   .60 .30
1473 A680 10p Corn   .60 .30
1474 A680 10p Sunflower   .60 .30
    Nos. 1472-1474 (3)   1.80 .90

18th FAO Regional Conference for Latin America and Caribbean (No. 1472); 3rd Natl. Corn Congress (No. 1473); World Food Day (No. 1474).

Wildlife Protection — A681

No. 1475, Hippocamelus bisulcus. No. 1476, Vicugna vicugna. No. 1477, Aburria jacutinga. No. 1478, Mergus octosetaceus. No. 1479, Podiceps gallardoi.

1984, Sept. 22   **Perf. 13½**
1475 A681 20p multicolored   1.00 .30
1476 A681 20p multicolored   1.00 .30
1477 A681 20p multicolored   1.00 .30
1478 A681 20p multicolored   1.00 .30
1479 A681 20p multicolored   1.00 .30
    Nos. 1475-1479 (5)   5.00 1.50

First Latin
American
Theater
Festival,
Cordoba,
Oct. — A682

1984, Oct. 13   **Litho.**   **Perf. 13½**
1480 A682 20p Mask   .40 .30

Intl. Eucharistic Congress, 50th
Anniv. — A683

Apostles' Communion, by Fra Angelico.

1984, Oct. 13
1481 A683 20p multicolored   .45 .30

Glaciares Natl. Park (UNESCO World
Heritage List) — A684

1984, Nov. 17   **Litho.**
1482 A684 20p Sea   .70 .25
1483 A684 30p Glacier   1.10 .25

City of Puerto Deseado
Centenary — A685

No. 1485, Ushuaia centenary.

1984, Nov. 17   **Perf. 13½**
1484 A685 20p shown   .70 .30
1485 A685 20p multicolored   .70 .30

Childrens' Paintings, Christmas
1984 — A686

1984, Dec. 1   **Litho.**   **Perf. 13½**
1486 A686 20p Diego Aguero   .60 .30
1487 A686 30p Leandro Ruiz   .75 .30
1488 A686 50p Maria Castillo,
                vert.   .80 .30
    Nos. 1486-1488 (3)   2.15 .90

No. 1439
Overprinted

1984, Dec. 1 Photo. Perf. 13½
1489 A641 10p multicolored .45 .45
Buenos Aires Philatelic Center, 50th anniv.

Vista Del Jardin Zoologico, by Fermin
Eguia — A687

Paintings: No. 1491, El Congreso Iluminado,
by Francisco Travieso. No. 1492, Galpones
(La Boca), by Marcos Borio.

1984, Dec. 15 Perf. 13½
1490 A687 20p multi .50 .30
1491 A687 20p multi, vert. .50 .30
1492 A687 20p multi, vert. .50 .30
Nos. 1490-1492 (3) 1.50 .90

Gen. Martin Miguel de Guemes (1785-
1821) — A688

1985, Mar. 23 Litho. Perf. 13½
1493 A688 30p multicolored .30 .30

ARGENTINA '85 Exhibition — A689

First airmail service from: 20p, Buenos
Aires to Montevideo, 1917. 40p, Cordoba to
Villa Dolores, 1925. 60p, Bahia Blanca to
Comodoro Rivadavia, 1929. 80p, Argentina to
Germany, 1934. 100p, naval service to the
Antarctic, 1952.

1985, Apr. 27
1494 A689 20p Bleriot Gnome .25 .25
1495 A689 40p Junker F-13L .40 .25
1496 A689 60p Latte 25 .60 .25
1497 A689 80p L.Z. 127 Graf
Zeppelin .75 .40
1498 A689 100p Consolidated
PBY Catalina 1.00 .45
Nos. 1494-1498 (5) 3.00 1.60

Central
Bank,
50th
Anniv.
A690

80p, Bank Building, Buenos Aires.

1985, June 1
1499 A690 80p multicolored .70 .25

Jose A. Ferreyra (1889-1943), Director
of Munequitas Portenas — A691

Famous directors and their films: No. 1501,
Leopoldo Torre Nilsson (1924-1978), scene
from Martin Fierro.

1985, June 1
1500 A691 100p shown .75 .35
1501 A691 100p multi .75 .35

Carlos Gardel
(1890-1935),
Entertainer
A692

Paintings: No. 1502, Gardel playing the guitar on stage, by Carlos Alonso (b. 1929). No.
1503, Gardel in a wide-brimmed hat, by
Hermenegildo Sabat (b. 1933). No. 1504,
Portrait of Gardel in an ornamental frame, by
Aldo Severi (b. 1928) and Martiniano Arce (b.
1939).

1985, June 15
1502 A692 200p multi 1.50 .45
1503 A692 200p multi 1.50 .45
1504 A692 200p multi 1.50 .45
Nos. 1502-1504 (3) 4.50 1.35

The
Arrival,
by Pedro
Figari
A693

1985, July 6 Litho. Perf. 13½
1505 A693 20c multi 1.00 .40
1506 A693 30c multi 1.40 .40

Souvenir Sheet
Perf. 12
1507 A693a Sheet of 2 3.75 3.75
a. 20c Pilgrims, vert. .40 .40
b. 30c Wagon .45 .45

ARGENTINA '85. No. 1507 contains 2
30x40mm stamps. See No. 1542.

Buenos Aires to Montevideo, 1917
Teodoro Fels Flight — A694

Historic flight covers: No. 1509, Villa
Dolores to Cordoba, 1925. No. 1510, Buenos
Aires to France, 1929 St. Exupery flight. No.
1511, Buenos Aires to Bremerhaven, 1934

Graf Zeppelin flight. No. 1512, 1st Antarctic
flight, 1952.

1985, July 13 Perf. 12x12½
1508 A694 10c emer & multi .45 .25
1509 A694 10c ultra & multi .45 .25
1510 A694 10c lt choc & multi .45 .25
1511 A694 10c chnt & multi .45 .25
1512 A694 10c ap grn & multi .45 .25
Nos. 1508-1512 (5) 2.25 1.25

ARGENTINA '85.

Illuminated Fruit, by Fortunato
Lacamera (1887-1951) — A695

Paintings: 20c, Woman with Bird, by Juan
del Prete, vert.

1985, Sept. 7 Perf. 13½
1513 A695 20c multi .90 .40
1514 A695 30c multi 1.00 .40

Flower Types of 1982-85

Designs: 1a, Begonia micranthera var. hier-
onymi. 5a, Gymnocalycium bruchii.

1985-88 Photo. Perf. 13½
1515 A641 ½c like #1356 .50 .25
1516 A641 1c like #1439 .30 .25
1517 A641 2c like #1345 .30 .25
1518 A641 3c like #1441 .30 .25
1519 A641 5c like #1346 .30 .25
1520 A641 10c like #1348 .50 .25
1521 A641 20c like #1347 .30 .25
1522 A641 30c like #1443A .80 .30
1523 A641 50c like #1344 1.10 .30
1524 A641 1a multi 1.50 .35
1525 A641 2a like #1351 .60 .25
1526 A641 5a multi 3.50 2.50

Size: 15x23mm

1527 A641 8½c like #1349 .30 .25
Nos. 1515-1527 (13) 10.40 5.70

Issued: ½c, 1c, 12/16; 2c, 8½c, 30c, 9/18;
3c, 5c, 10c, 50c, 1a, 9/7; 20c, 10/17; 5a,
3/21/87; 2a, 12/5/88.

No. 1435 Surcharged
1986, Nov. 4 Photo. Perf. 13½
1530 A641 10c on 1p No. 1435 1.00 .50

Folk Musical
Instruments
A699

1985, Sept. 14 Litho. Perf. 13½
1531 A699 20c Frame drum .60 .40
1532 A699 20c Long flute .60 .40
1533 A699 20c Jew's harp .60 .40
1534 A699 20c Pan flutes .60 .40
1535 A699 20c Musical bow .60 .40
Nos. 1531-1535 (5) 3.00 2.00

Juan Bautista
Alberdi (1810-
1884),
Historian,
Politician
A700

Famous men: 20c, Nicolas Avellaneda
(1836-1885), President in 1874. 30c, Fr. Luis
Beltran (1784-1827), military and naval engineer. 40c, Ricardo Levene (1885-1959), historian, author.

Skaters
A701

Type of 1985 and

Deception, by J. H. Rivoira — A702

1985, Oct. 5
1536 A700 10c multi .25 .25
1537 A700 20c multi .45 .25
1538 A700 30c multi .65 .40
1539 A700 40c multi 1.20 .45
Nos. 1536-1539 (4) 2.55 1.35

1985, Oct. 19 Litho. Perf. 13½
1540 A701 20c multi .60 .40
1541 A702 30c multi .65 .40

Size: 147x75mm
Imperf
1542 A693a 1a multi 3.50 3.50

IYY. No. 1542 is inscribed in silver with the
UN 40th anniversary and IYY emblems.

Provincial
Views — A703

Designs: No. 1543, Rock Window, Buenos
Aires. No. 1544, Forclaz Windmill, Entre Rios.
No. 1545, Lake Potrero de los Funes, San
Luis. No. 1546, Mission church, north-east
province. No. 1547, Penguin colony, Punta
Tombo, Chubut. No. 1548, Water Mirrors,
Cordoba.

1985, Nov. 23 Perf. 13½
1543 A703 10c multi .45 .25
1544 A703 10c multi .45 .25
1545 A703 10c multi .45 .25
1546 A703 10c multi .45 .25
1547 A703 10c multi .45 .25
1548 A703 10c multi .45 .25
Nos. 1543-1548 (6) 2.70 1.50

Christmas
1985 — A704

Designs: 10c, Birth of Our Lord, by Carlos
Cortes. 20c, Christmas, by Hector Viola.

1985, Dec. 7
1549 A704 10c multi .40 .25
1550 A704 20c multi .85 .50

Natl. Campaign for the Prevention of Blindness — A705

1985, Dec. 7
1551 A705 10c multi .40 .25

Rio Gallegos City, Cent. — A716

1985, Dec. 21 Litho. Perf. 13½
1552 A716 10c Church 1.50 .40

Natl. Grape Harvest Festival, 50th Anniv. A717

1986, Mar. 15
1553 A717 10c multi .45 .30

Exists with Wmk. 265, Value $20.

Historical Architecture in Buenos Aires — A718

Designs: No. 1554, Valentin Alsina House, Italian Period, 1860-70. No. 1555, House on Cerrito Street, French influence, 1880-1900. No. 1556, House on the Avenida de Mayo y Santiago del Estero, Art Nouveau, 1900-10. No. 1557, Customs Building, academic architecture, 1900-15. No. 1558, Isaac Fernandez Blanco Museum, house of architect Martin Noel, natl. restoration, 1910-30. Nos. 1554-1556 vert.

1986, Apr. 19
1554 A718 20c multi .60 .40
1555 A718 20c multi .60 .40
1556 A718 20c multi .60 .40
1557 A718 20c multi .60 .40
1558 A718 20c multi .60 .40
Nos. 1554-1558 (5) 3.00 2.00

Antarctic Bases, Pioneers and Fauna — A719

Designs: a, Base, Jubany. b, Arctocephalus gazella. c, Otaria byronia. d, Gen. Belgrano Base. e, Daption capensis. f, Diomedia melanophris. g, Apterodytes patagonica. h, Macronectes giganteus. i, Hugo Alberto Acuna (1885-1953). j, Spheniscus magellanicus. k, Gallinago gallinage. l, Capt. Agustin del Castillo (1855-89).

Famous People — A720

Designs: No. 1560, Dr. Alicia Moreau de Justo, human rights activist. No. 1561, Dr. Emilio Ravignani (1886-1954), historian. No. 1562, Indira Gandhi.

1986, July 5 Litho. Perf. 13½
1560 A720 10c multi .45 .40
1561 A720 10c multi .45 .40
1562 A720 30c multi 1.40 .75
Nos. 1560-1562 (3) 2.30 1.55

Statuary, Buenos Aires — A721

20c, Fountain of the Nereids, by Dolores Lola Mora (1866-1936). 30c, Lamenting at Work, by Rogelio Yrurtia (1879-1950), horiz.

1986, July 5
1563 A721 20c multi .90 .30
1564 A721 30c multi .90 .30

Famous Men — A722

Designs: No. 1565, Francisco N. Laprida (1786-1829), politician. No. 1566, Estanislao Lopez (1786-1838), brigadier general. No. 1567, Francisco Ramirez (1786-1821), general.

1986, Aug. 9 Litho. Perf. 13
1565 A722 20c dl yel, brn & blk .50 .40
1566 A722 20c dl yel, brn & blk .50 .40
1567 A722 20c dl yel, brn & blk .50 .40
Nos. 1565-1567 (3) 1.50 1.20

Fr. Ceferino Namuncura (1886-1905) A723

1986, Aug. 30 Perf. 13½
1568 A723 20c multi .60 .40

Miniature Sheets

Natl. Team Victory, 1986 World Cup Soccer Championships, Mexico — A724

Designs: No. 1569a-1569d, Team. Nos. 1569e-1569h, Shot on goal. Nos. 1570a-1570d, Action close-up. Nos. 1570e-1570h, Diego Maradona holding soccer cup.

1986, Nov. 8 Litho. Perf. 13½
1569 A724 Sheet of 8 11.00 11.00
a.-h. 75c any single 1.25 1.25
1570 A724 Sheet of 8 11.00 11.00
a.-h. 75c any single 1.25 1.25

San Francisco (Cordoba), Cent. — A725

20c, Municipal Building.

1986, Nov. 8
1571 A725 20c multicolored .50 .35

Trelew City (Chubut), Cent. — A726

20c, Old railroad station, 1865.

1986, Nov. 22 Litho. Perf. 13½
1572 A726 20c multicolored .50 .35

Mutualism Day — A727

1986, Nov. 22
1573 A727 20c multicolored .75 .40

Christmas — A728

Designs: 20c, Naif retable, by Aniko Szabo (b. 1945). 30c, Everyone's Tree, by Franca Delacqua (b. 1947).

1986, Dec. 13 Litho. Perf. 13½
1574 A728 20c multicolored 1.00 .45
1575 A728 30c multicolored 1.10 .45

Santa Rosa de Lima, 400th Birth Anniv. — A729

1986, Dec. 13
1576 A729 50c multicolored 1.90 .75

Rio Cuarto Municipal Building A730

No. 1578, Court Building, Cordoba.

1986, Dec. 20
1577 A730 20c shown .90 .30
1578 A730 20c multicolored .90 .30

Rio Cuarto City, bicent. Court Building, Cordoba, 50th anniv.

Antarctic Treaty, 25th Anniv. — A731

1987, Mar. 7 Litho. Perf. 13½
1579 A731 20c Marine biologist 1.00 .45
1580 A731 30c Ornithologist 1.25 .45
Souvenir Sheet
Perf. 12
1581 Sheet of 2 5.50 5.50
a. A731 20c like No. 1579 2.00 1.50
b. A731 30c like No. 1580 3.00 2.00

No. 1581 contains 2 stamps, size: 40x50mm. Exist imperf. Value $500.

Natl. Mortgage Bank, Cent. — A732

1987, Mar. 21 Perf. 13½
1582 A732 20c multicolored .80 .40

Natl. Cooperative Associations
Movement — A733

1987, Mar. 21
1583   A733   20c multicolored   .80   .40

Second State
Visit of Pope
John
Paul II — A734

Engr., Litho. (No. 1585)
1987, Apr. 4   **Perf. 13½**
1584   A734   20c shown   .40   .25
1585   A734   80c Papal blessing   1.50   .70

Souvenir Sheet
Perf. 12
1586   A734   1a like 20c   3.50   2.50
No. 1586 contains one 40x50mm stamp.

Intl.
Peace
Year
A735

30c, Pigeon, abstract sculpture by Victor
Kaniuka.

1987, Apr. 11   **Litho.**
1587   A735   20c multicolored   .70   .30
1588   A735   30c multicolored   .70   .30

Low Handicap
World Polo
Championships
A736

Polo Players, painting by Alejandro Moy.

1987, Apr. 11
1589   A736   20c multicolored   .90   .25

Miniature Sheet

ICOM '86 — A737

Designs: a, Emblem. b, Family crest,
National History Museum, Buenos Aires. c, St.
Bartholomew, Enrique Larreta Museum of
Spanish Art, Buenos Aires. d, Zoomorphic
club, Patagonian Museum, San Carlos de
Bariloche. e, Supplication, anthropomorphic
sculpture, Natural Sciences Museum, La
Plata. f, Wrought iron lattice from the house of

J. Urquiza, president of the Confederation of
Argentina, Entre Rios History Museum,
Parana. g, St. Joseph, 18th cent. wood figu-
rine, Northern History Museum, Salta. h,
Funerary urn, Provincial Archaeological
Museum, Santiago del Estero.

1987, May 30
1590   A737   Sheet of 8   3.75   3.75
   a.-h.   25c any single   .45   .45
Intl. Council of Museums, 14th general conf.

Natl. College of Monserrat, Cordoba,
300th Anniv. — A738

1987, July 4   **Imperf.**
1591   A738   1a multicolored   1.50   1.50
Monserrat '87 Philatelic Exposition.

Fight
Drug
Abuse
A739

The Proportions of Man, by da Vinci.

1987, Aug. 15   **Perf. 13½**
1592   A739   30c multicolored   1.10   .30

Famous
Men
A740

Portraits and quotations: 20c, Jorge Luis
Borges (1899-1986), writer. 30c, Armando
Discepolo (1887-1971), playwright. 50c, Car-
los A. Pueyrredon (1887-1962), professor,
Legion of Honor laureate.

1987, Aug. 15
1593   A740   20c multicolored   .50   .45
1594   A740   30c multicolored   .50   .45
1595   A740   50c multicolored   .50   .45
   Nos. 1593-1595 (3)   1.50 1.35

Pillar Boxes
A741   A742

1987   **Photo.**   **Perf. 13½**
1596   A741   (30c) yel, blk & dark
                 red   .90   .30
   Booklet with 10 stamps   9.00
1597   A742   (33c) lt blue grn, blk
                 & yel   .90   .35
   Complete booklet, 10 #1597   9.00
Issue dates: (30c), June 8; (33c), July 13.

The
Sower,
by Julio
Vanzo
A743

1987, Sept. 12
1598   A743   30c multicolored   .75   .30
Argentine Agrarian Federation, 75th anniv.

10th Pan
American
Games,
Indianapolis,
Aug. 7-
25 — A744

1987, Sept. 26
1599   A744   20c Basketball   .45   .25
1600   A744   30c Rowing   .50   .25
1601   A744   50c Yachting   .50   .25
   Nos. 1599-1601 (3)   1.45   .75

Children
Playing
Doctor,
WHO
Emblem
A745

1987, Oct. 7
1602   A745   30c multi   .50   .30
Vaccinate every child campaign.

Heroes of the
Revolution
A746

Signing
of the
San
Nicolas
Accord,
1852, by
Rafael
del Villar
A747

Independence anniversaries and historic
events: No. 1603, Maj.-Col. Ignacio Alvarez
Thomas (1787-1857). No. 1604, Col. Manuel
Crispulo Bernabe Dorrego (1787-1829). No.
1606, 18th cent. Spanish map of the Falkland
Isls., administered by Jacinto de Altolaguirre.

1987, Oct. 17
1603   A746   25c shown   .50   .25
1604   A746   25c multi   .50   .25
1605   A747   50c shown   1.00   .35
1606   A747   50c multi   1.00   .35
   Nos. 1603-1606 (4)   3.00 1.20

Museum established in the House of the
San Nicholas Accord, 50th anniv. (No. 1605);
Jacinto de Altolaguirre (1754-1787), governor
of the Malvinas Isls. for the King of Spain (No.
1606).

Celedonio Galvan Moreno, 1st
Director — A748

1987, Nov. 21
1607   A748   50c multicolored   .80   .45
Postas Argentinas magazine, 50th anniv.

LRA National
Radio, Buenos
Aires, 50th
Anniv. — A749

1987, Nov. 21
1608   A749   50c multicolored   .80   .45

Natl.
Philatelic
Society,
Cent.
A750

1987, Nov. 21
1609   A750   1a Jose Marco del
                 Pont   1.60   .50

Christmas
A751

Tapestries: 50c, Navidad, by Alisia Frega.
1a, Vitral, by Silvina Trigos.

1987, Dec. 5
1610   A751   50c multicolored   .60   .30
1611   A751   1a multicolored   1.25   .45

Natl. Parks — A752

1987, Dec. 19   **Perf. 13x13½**
1612   A752   50c Baritu   1.25   .35
1613   A752   50c Nahuel Huapi 1.25   .35
1614   A752   50c Rio Pilcomayo 1.25   .35
1615   A752   50c Tierra del Fuego 1.25 .35
1616   A752   50c Iguacu   1.25   .35
   Nos. 1612-1616 (5)   6.25 1.75
See Nos. 1647-1651, 1715-1719, 1742-1746.

Landscapes in Buenos Aires Painted by Jose Cannella — A753

No. 1617, Caminito. No. 1618, Viejo Almacen.

1988-89   Litho.   Perf. 13½
1617	A753	5a multi	2.40	1.25
1618	A753	10a multi	4.75	2.50
1618A	A753	10a like No. 1618	1.25	.60
1618B	A753	50a like No. 1617	1.25	.60
c.		Wmk 365	125.00	20.00
		Nos. 1617-1618B (4)	9.65	4.95

No. 1618 inscribed "Viejo Almacen"; No. 1618A inscribed "El Viejo Almacen."
Issue dates: 5a, No. 1618, 3/15; No. 1618A, 10/20; 50a, 5/30/89.
For overprint see No. 1635.

Minstrel in a Tavern, by Carlos Morel A754

Paintings: No. 1620, Interior of Curuzu, by Candido Lopez.

1988, Mar. 19   Litho.   Perf. 13½
| 1619 | A754 | 1a shown | 1.00 | .35 |
| 1620 | A754 | 1a multicolored | 1.00 | .35 |

See Nos. 1640-1641.

Argentine-Brazilian Economic Cooperation and Integration Program for Mutual Growth — A755

1988, Mar. 19
| 1621 | A755 | 1a multicolored | .65 | .35 |

Cities of Alta Gracia and Corrientes, 400th Anniv. — A756

No. 1622, Alta Gracia Church. No. 1623, Chapel of St. Anne, Corrientes.

1988, Apr. 9   Litho.   Perf. 13½
| 1622 | A756 | 1a multicolored | 1.00 | .45 |
| 1623 | A756 | 1a multicolored | 1.00 | .45 |

Labor Day — A757

Grain Carriers, a tile mosaic by Alfredo Guido, Line D of Nueve de Julio station, Buenos Aires subway: a, (UL). b, (UR). c, (LL). d, (LR).

1988, May 21
| 1624 | A757 | Block of 4 | 2.25 | 2.25 |
| a.-d. | | 50c any single | .55 | .55 |

1988 Summer Olympics, Seoul — A758

1988, July 16   Litho.   Perf. 13½
1625	A758	1a Running	.50	.30
1626	A758	2a Soccer	1.10	.30
1627	A758	3a Field hockey	1.60	.50
1628	A758	4a Tennis	2.00	.65
		Nos. 1625-1628 (4)	5.20	1.75

Mendoza Bank, Cent. — A759

Natl. Gendarmerie, Cent. — A760

1988, Aug. 13
| 1629 | A759 | 2a multicolored | 1.20 | .50 |
| 1630 | A760 | 2a multicolored | 1.20 | .50 |

Sarmiento and Cathedral School to the North, Buenos Aires — A761

1988, Sept. 10   Litho.   Perf. 13½
| 1631 | A761 | 3a multicolored | 1.25 | .35 |

Domingo Faustino Sarmiento (1811-1888), educator, politician.

St. Cayetano, Patron of Workers A762

El Amor, by Antonio Berni, Pacific Gallery, Buenos Aires — A763

3a, Our Lady of Carmen, Cuyo.

1988, Sept. 10   Litho.
| 1632 | A762 | 2a multicolored | .55 | .45 |
| 1633 | A762 | 3a multicolored | .85 | .85 |

Souvenir Sheet
Perf. 12
| 1634 | A763 | 5a multicolored | 2.75 | 2.75 |

Liniers Philatelic Circle and the Argentine Western Philatelic Institution (IFADO), 50th anniv.
No. 1634 contains one 40x30mm stamp.

No. 1617 Ovptd.

1988, Oct. 29   Litho.   Perf. 13½
| 1635 | A753 | 5a multicolored | 6.75 | 2.00 |

21st Congress of the Intl. Urology Soc.

Tourism — A763a

3a, Purmamarca, Jujuy. 20a, Ushuaia.

1988, Nov. 1   Litho.   Perf. 13½
| 1635A | A763a | 3a multi | .70 | .30 |

Size: 28½x38mm
| 1635B | A763a | 20a multi | 4.50 | 2.00 |

Buenos Aires Subway, 75th Anniv. A764

5a, Train, c. 1913.

1988, Dec. 17   Litho.   Perf. 13½
| 1636 | A764 | 5a multicolored | 1.40 | .60 |

Christmas A765

Frescoes in Ucrania Cathedral, Buenos Aires: No. 1637, Virgin Patron. No. 1638, Virgin of Tenderness.

1988, Dec. 17
| 1637 | A765 | 5a multicolored | 2.25 | .60 |
| 1638 | A765 | 5a multicolored | 2.25 | .60 |

St. John Bosco (1815-1888), Educator, and Church in Ushuaia — A766

1989, Apr. 8   Litho.   Perf. 13½
| 1639 | A766 | 5a multicolored | .90 | .25 |

Dated 1988.

Art Type of 1988

Paintings: No. 1640, Blancos, by Fernando Fader (1882-1935). No. 1641, Rincon de los Areneros, by Justo Lynch (1870-1953).

1989, Apr. 8
| 1640 | A754 | 5a multicolored | 1.75 | .30 |
| 1641 | A754 | 5a multicolored | 1.75 | .30 |

Holy Week A767

Sculpture and churches: No. 1642, The Crown of Thorns, Calvary of Tandil, and Church of Our Lady Carmelite, Tandil. No. 1643, Jesus the Nazarene and Metropolitan Cathedral, Buenos Aires. No. 1644, Jesus Encounters His Mother (scene of the crucifixion), La Quebrada Village, San Luis. No. 1645, Our Lady of Sorrow and Church of Humahuaca, Jujuy.

1989, Apr. 22   Litho.   Perf. 13½
1642	A767	2a multicolored	.30	.25
1643	A767	2a multicolored	.30	.25
1644	A767	3a multicolored	.40	.25
1645	A767	3a multicolored	.40	.25
a.		Block of 4 + 2 labels	1.50	1.25
		Nos. 1642-1645 (4)	1.40	1.00

Printed in sheets of 16+4 labels containing blocks of 4 of each design. Labels picture Jesus's arrival in Jerusalem (Palm Sunday).

Prevent Alcoholism — A768

1989, Apr. 22
| 1646 | A768 | 5a multicolored | .75 | .30 |

Natl. Park Type of 1987
1989, May 6   Perf. 13x13½
1647	A752	5a Lihue Calel	.85	.30
1648	A752	5a El Palmar	.85	.30
1649	A752	5a Calilegua	.85	.30
1650	A752	5a Chaco	.85	.30
1651	A752	5a Los Glaciares	.85	.30
		Nos. 1647-1651 (5)	4.25	1.50

Admission of Argentina to the ITU, Cent. — A769

1989, May 6   **Perf. 13½**
1652 A769 10a multicolored   1.75   .30

World Model Aircraft Championships — A770

No. 1653, F1A glider. No. 1654, F1B rubber band motor. No. 1655, F1C gas motor.

1989, May 27   **Litho.**   **Perf. 13½**
1653 A770 5a multi   .60   .25
1654 A770 5a multi   .60   .25
1655 A770 10a multi   1.10   .30
   Nos. 1653-1655 (3)   2.30   .80

French Revolution, Bicent. — A771

Designs: 10a, "All men are born free and equal." 15a, French flag and *La Marianne,* by Gandon. 25a, *Liberty Guiding the People,* by Delacroix.

1989, July 1   **Litho.**   **Perf. 13½**
1656 A771 10a shown   .60   .30
1657 A771 15a multicolored   .60   .30
     Souvenir Sheet
        Perf. 12
1658 A771 25a multicolored   1.50 1.50
No. 1658 contains one 40x30mm stamp.

The Republic, a Bronze Bust in the Congreso de la Nacion, Buenos Aires — A772

1989, Aug. 12   **Litho.**   **Perf. 13½**
1659 A772 300a on 50a multi   1.75 .50

Peaceful transition of power (presidential office). Not issued without surcharge.

Immigration to Argentina — A773

150a, S.S. Weser, 1889. 200a, Immigrant hotel, 1889.

1989, Aug. 19   **Perf. 13½**
1660 A773 150a multi   1.75   .50
1661 A773 200a multi   1.75   .60
     Souvenir Sheet
        Perf. 12
1662   Sheet of 2   2.75 2.75
  a.   A773 150a like No. 1660   1.25 1.25
  b.   A773 200a like No. 1661   1.25 1.25
No. 1662 contains 40c30mm stamps.

Famous Men A774

Designs: No. 1663, Fr. Guillermo Furlong (1889-1974), historian, and title page of *The Jesuits.* No. 1664, Dr. Gregorio Alvarez (1889-1986), physician, and title page of *Canto a Chos Malal.* 200a, Brig.-Gen. Enrique Martinez (1789-1870) and lithograph *La Batalla de Maipu,* by Teodoro Gericault.

1989, Oct. 7   **Litho.**   **Perf. 13½**
1663 A774 150a multicolored   .55   .35
1664 A774 150a multicolored   .55   .35
1665 A774 200a multicolored   .55   .35
   Nos. 1663-1665 (3)   1.65 1.05

America Issue — A775

Emblem of the Postal Union of the Americas and Spain (PUAS) and pre-Columbian art from Catamarca Province: 200a, Wooden mask from Atajo, Loma Morada. 300a, Urn of the Santa Maria Culture (Phase 3) from Punta de Balastro, Santa Maria Department.

1989, Oct. 14
1666 A775 200a multicolored   1.25   .50
1667 A775 300a multicolored   1.90   .60

Federal Police Week — A776

Children's drawings: No. 1668, Diego Molinari, age 13. No. 1669, Carlos Alberto Sarago, age 8. No. 1670, Roxana Andrea Osuna, age 7. No. 1671, Pablo Javier Quaglia, age 9.

1989, Oct. 28   **Litho.**   **Perf. 13½**
1668 A776 100a multi   .65   .25
1669 A776 100a multi   .65   .25
1670 A776 150a multi   1.10   .35
1671 A776 150a multi   1.10   .35
   Nos. 1668-1671 (4)   3.50 1.20

Battle of Vuelta de Obligado, 1845 — A777

1989, Dec. 2   **Litho.**   **Perf. 13x13½**
1672 A777 300a multicolored   1.50   .30

Paintings — A778

Cristo de los Cerros, Sculpture by Chipo Cespedes A779

No. 1673, Gato Frias. No. 1674, Maria Carballido.

1989, Dec. 2   **Perf. 13½**
1673 A778 200a multi   1.10   .30
1674 A778 200a multi   1.10   .30
1675 A779 300a shown   1.10   .30
   Nos. 1673-1675 (3)   3.30   .90
       Christmas.

Buenos Aires Port, Cent. — A780

1990, Mar. 3   **Litho.**   **Perf. 13½**
1676 A780 Strip of 4   8.50 8.50
  a.-d.   200a any single   1.50   .75

Aconcagua Intl. Fair, Mendoza — A781

Design: Aconcagua mountain, Los Horcones Lagoon and fair emblem.

1990, Mar. 3
1677 A781 Pair, #a.-b.   2.00 1.25

Natl. Savings and Insurance Fund, 75th Anniv. — A782

1990, May 5   **Litho.**   **Perf. 13½**
1678 A782 1000a multicolored   .60   .30

         Miniature Sheet

1990 World Cup Soccer Championships, Italy — A783

Designs: a, Athlete's torso (striped jersey). b, Athlete's torso (solid jersey). c, Players' feet, soccer ball. d, Player (knee to waist).

1990, May 5
1679 A783 Sheet of 4   6.00 6.00
  a.-d.   2500a multicolored   1.50 1.00

Carlos Pellegrini, Commercial High School Founder, Cent. — A784

1990, June 2   **Litho.**   **Perf. 13½**
1680 A784 2000a multicolored   1.10   .60

Youth Against Drugs A785

1990, June 2
1681 A785 2000a multicolored   1.50   .60

Intl. Literacy Year A786

1990, July 14   **Litho.**   **Perf. 13½**
1682 A786 2000a multicolored   .90   .60

Flower Type of 1982 in New Currency

1989-90   **Photo.**   **Perf. 13½**
1683 A641 10a like #1433   .30   .25
1684 A641 20a like #1440   .25   .25
1685 A641 50a like #1354   .30   .25
1686 A641 100a like #1439   .35   .25
1687 A641 300a like #1345   1.25   .50
1688 A641 500a like #1441   2.00   .75
1689 A641 1000a like #1355   .60   .35
1690 A641 5000a like #1349   .30   .35
1691 A641 10,000a like #1350   4.75 3.25
   Nos. 1683-1691 (9)   12.80 6.20

Issued: 20a, 100a, 300a, 500a, 10a, 8/24/89; 50a, 8/30/89; 1000, 3/8/90; 5000a, 4/6/90; 10,000a, 7/2/90.

World Basketball Championships A787

1990, Aug. 11   Litho.   Perf. 13½
1703 A787 2000a multicolored   2.00 1.50

Souvenir Sheet
Perf. 12
1704 A787 5000a Jump ball   4.75 4.00

Postal Union of the Americas and Spain, 14th Congress — A788

No. 1705, Arms, seal. No. 1706, Sailing ships. No. 1707, Modern freighter. No. 1708, Van, cargo plane.

1990, Sept. 15   Litho.   Perf. 13½
1705 A788 3000a multi   1.50 .75
1706 A788 3000a multi   1.50 .75
1707 A788 3000a multi   1.50 .75
1708 A788 3000a multi   1.50 .75
    Nos. 1705-1708 (4)   6.00 3.00

America Issue A789

No. 1709, Iguacu Falls, hamelia erecta. No. 1710, Puerto Deseado, elephant seal.

1990, Oct. 13
1709 A789 3000a multicolored   2.00 1.25
1710 A789 3000a multicolored   2.00 1.25

Natl. Park Type of 1987
1990, Oct. 27   Perf. 13x13½
1715 A752 3000a Lanin   1.25 .90
1716 A752 3000a Laguna Blanca   1.25 .90
1717 A752 3000a Perito Moreno   1.25 .90
1718 A752 3000a Puelo   1.25 .90
1719 A752 3000a El Rey   1.25 .90
    Nos. 1715-1719 (5)   6.25 4.50

Stamp Day A790

1990, Oct. 27   Perf. 13½
1720 A790 3000a multicolored   1.50 .55

Salvation Army, Cent. — A793

Designs: No. 1722, Natl. University of the Littoral, Santa Fe, cent.

1990, Dec. 1   Litho.   Perf. 13½
1721 A793 3000a multicolored   1.75 .90
1722 A793 3000a multicolored   1.75 .90
    a.   Pair, #1721-1722 + label   7.50 6.50

Miniature Sheets

Christmas — A794

Stained glass windows: No. 1723, The Immaculate Conception. No. 1724, The Nativity. No. 1725, Presentation of Jesus at the Temple.

1990, Dec. 1   Perf. 13½x13
Sheets of 4
1723 A794 3000a #a.-d.   6.75 6.75
1724 A794 3000a #a.-d.   6.75 6.75
1725 A794 3000a #a.-d.   6.75 6.75

Landscapes — A795

Paintings: No. 1726, Los Sauces, by Atilio Malinverno. No. 1727, Paisaje, by Pio Collivadino, vert.

1991, May 4   Litho.   Perf. 13½
1726 A795 4000a multicolored   1.10 .90
1727 A795 4000a multicolored   1.10 .90

Return of Remains of Juan Manuel de Rosas (1793-1877) A796

1991, June 1   Litho.   Perf. 13½
1728 A796 4000a multicolored   1.10 .75

Swiss Confederation, 700th Anniv. — A797

1991, Aug. 3   Litho.   Perf. 13½
1729 A797 4000a multicolored   1.25 .75

Miniature Sheet

Cartoons — A798

Designs: a, Hernan, the Corsair by Jose Luis Salinas. b, Don Fulgencio by Lino Palacio. c, Medical Rules of Salerno by Oscar Esteban Conti. d, Buenos Aires Undershirt by Alejandro del Prado. e, Girls! by Jose A.G. Divito. f, Langostino by Eduardo Carlos Ferro. g, Mafalda by Joaquin Salvador Lavoro. h, Mort Cinder by Alberto Breccia.

1991, Aug. 3
1730 A798 4000a Sheet of 8,
        #a.-h.   12.00 12.00

City of La Rioja, 400th Anniv. — A799

1991, Sept. 14   Litho.   Perf. 13½
1731 A799 4000a multicolored   1.25 .75

First Balloon Flight over the Andes, 75th Anniv. — A800

1991, Sept. 14
1732 A800 4000a multicolored   1.25 .75

America Issue A801

Designs: No. 1733, Magellan's caravel, Our Lady of Victory. No. 1734, Ships of Juan Diaz de Solis.

1991, Nov. 9   Litho.   Perf. 13½
1733 A801 4000a multicolored   1.75 .75
1734 A801 4000a multicolored   1.75 .75

Anniversaries — A802

Designs: a, Johann Heinrich Pestalozzi, Swiss pedagogue and educational reformer, whose Argentine school, the Colegio Pestalozzi, was associated with the anti-fascist newspaper Argentinisches Tageblatt. b, Leandro N. Alem, founder of Radical People's Party. c, Man with rifle, emblem of Argentine Federal Shooting Club. d, Dr. Nicasio Etcheparaborda, emblem of College of Odontology. e, Dalmiro Huergo, emblem of Graduate School of Economics.

1991, Nov. 30
1735 A802 4000a Strip of 5,
        #a.-e.   5.25 5.25

Christmas — A803

Stained glass windows from Our Lady of Lourdes Basilica, Buenos Aires: Nos. 1736a-1736b, Top and bottom portions of Virgin of the Valley, Catamarca. Nos. 1736c-1736d, Top and bottom portions of Virgin of the Rosary of the Miracle, Cordoba.

1991, Nov. 30
1736 A803 4000a Block of 4,
        #a.-d.   7.00 7.00
    a.   Sheet of 16, 4 ea #a-d, + 4
         labels   30.00 30.00

The four labels of No. 1736a form a nativity scene across the middle of the sheet.

Famous Men — A804

Designs: a, Gen. Juan de Lavalle (1797-1841), Peruvian medal of honor. b, Brig. Gen. Jose Maria del Rosario Ciriaco Paz (1791-1854), medal. c, Marco Manuel de Avellaneda (1813-1841), lawyer. d, Guillermo Enrique Hudson (1841-1922), author.

1991, Dec. 14   Litho.   Perf. 13½
1737 A804 4000a Block of 4, #a.-
        d.   5.00 5.00

Birds — A805

No. 1738, Pterocnemia pennata. No. 1739, Morphnus guianensis. No. 1740, Ara chloroptera.

1991, Dec. 28
1738 A805 4000a multicolored   1.50 1.00
1739 A805 4000a multicolored   1.50 1.00
1740 A805 4000a multicolored   1.50 1.00
    Nos. 1738-1740 (3)   4.50 3.00

Miniature Sheet

Arbrafex '92, Argentina-Brazil Philatelic Exhibition — A806

Traditional costumes: a, Gaucho, woman. b, Gaucho, horse. c, Gaucho in store. d, Gaucho holding lariat.

1992, Mar. 14　Litho.　Perf. 13½
1741　A806　38c Sheet of 4, #a.-d.　5.00　5.00

Natl. Park Type of 1987

No. 1742, Alerces. No. 1743, Formosa Nature Reserve. No. 1744, Petrified Forest. No. 1745, Arrayanes. No. 1746, Laguna de los Pozuelos.

1992, Apr. 4　Litho.　Perf. 13x13½
1742　A752　38c multicolored　1.00　.50
1743　A752　38c multicolored　1.00　.50
1744　A752　38c multicolored　1.00　.70
1745　A752　38c multicolored　1.00　.50
1746　A752　38c multicolored　1.00　.50
　Nos. 1742-1746 (5)　5.00　2.70

Mushrooms — A807

10c, Psilocybe cubensis. 25c, Coprinus atramentarius. 50c, Suillus granulatus. 51c, Morchella esculenta. 61c, Amanita muscaria. 68c, Coprinus comatus. 1.77p, Stropharia oeruginosa.

1992-94　Photo.　Perf. 13½
1748　A807　10c multi　　.70　.30
1749　A807　25c multi　　.80　.30
　a.　　Wmk. 365　　12.50　4.00
1750　A807　38c like #1748　.80　.30
1751　A807　48c like #1749　1.00　.60
1752　A807　50c multi　　1.50　.50
1753　A807　51c multi　　1.00　.60
1754　A807　61c multi　　1.25　.75
1755　A807　68c multi　　2.00　.50
1756　A807　1p like #1754　3.00　.80
1757　A807　1.25p like #1752　3.00　.50
1758　A807　1.77p multi　　5.50　2.75
1759　A807　2p like #1753　6.50　2.25
　Nos. 1748-1759 (12)　27.05　9.95

No. 1758 not issued without overprint "Centro Filatelico de Neuquen y Rio Negro 50th Aniversario."

Issued: 38c, 4/4/92; 48c, 51c, 61c, 8/1/92; 1.77p, 11/7/92; 25c, 50c, 8/17/93; 1p, 2p, 8/26/93; 10c, 1/11/94; 68c, 1.25p, 10/10/92; No. 1749a, 1997.

See design A838.

Falkland Islands War, 10th Anniv. A808

No. 1767, Pucara 1A-58. No. 1768, Cruiser Gen. Belgrano. No. 1769, Soldier and truck.

1992, May 2　Litho.　Perf. 13½
1767　A808　38c multicolored　1.10　.50
1768　A808　38c multicolored　1.10　.50
1769　A808　38c multicolored　1.10　.50
　Nos. 1767-1769 (3)　3.30　1.50

Miniature Sheet

Preserve the Environment — A809

a, Deer. b, Geese. c, Butterflies. d, Whale.

1992, June 6　Litho.　Perf. 12
1770　A809　38c Sheet of 4, #a.-d.　7.00　7.00

Paintings by Florencio Molina Campos — A810

No. 1771, A La Sombra. No. 1772, Tileforo Areco, vert.

1992, June 6　　Perf. 13½
1771　A810　38c multicolored　1.00　.60
1772　A810　38c multicolored　1.00　.60

Famous Men A811

Designs: No. 1773, Gen. Lucio N. Mansilla (1792-1871). No. 1774, Jose Manuel Estrada (1842-1894), writer. No. 1775, Brig. Gen. Jose I. Garmendia (1842-1915).

1992, July 4　Litho.　Perf. 13½
1773　A811　38c multicolored　1.00　.60
1774　A811　38c multicolored　1.00　.60
1775　A811　38c multicolored　1.00　.60
　Nos. 1773-1775 (3)　3.00　1.80

Fight Against Drugs — A812

1992, Aug. 1　　Perf. 13½x13
1776　A812　38c multicolored　1.25　.60

Col. Jose M. Calaza, 140th Birth Anniv. A813

1992, Sept. 5　Litho.　Perf. 13½
1777　A813　38c multicolored　1.25　.70

Discovery of America, 500th Anniv. — A814

Designs: a, Columbus, castle, ship. b, Native drawings, Columbus.

1992, Oct. 10　Litho.　Perf. 13½
1778　A814　38c Pair, #a.-b.　3.50　3.50

Argentine Film Posters A815

No. 1779, Dios Se Lo Pague, 1948. No. 1780, Las Aguas Bajan Turbias, 1952. No. 1781, Un Guapo Del 900, 1960. No. 1782, La Tregua, 1974. No. 1783, La Historia Oficial, 1984.

1992, Nov. 7　Litho.　Perf. 13½
1779　A815　38c multicolored　1.25　.50
1780　A815　38c multicolored　1.25　.50
1781　A815　38c multicolored　1.25　.50
1782　A815　38c multicolored　1.25　.50
1783　A815　38c multicolored　1.25　.50
　Nos. 1779-1783 (5)　6.25　2.50

Christmas A816

1992, Nov. 28
1784　A816　38c multicolored　1.25　.60

Miniature Sheet

Iberoprenfil '92 — A817

Lighthouses: a, Punta Mogotes. b, Rio Negro. c, San Antonio. d, Cabo Blanco.

1992, Dec. 5
1785　A817　38c Sheet of 4, #a.-d.　5.50　4.00

A818

Fight Against AIDS — A819

1992, Dec. 12　Litho.　Perf. 13½
1786　A818　10c multicolored　2.50　.30
1787　A819　26c multicolored　5.00　.30

Intl. Space Year A820

1992, Dec. 19
1788　A820　38c multicolored　1.25　.50

Souvenir Sheet

Miraculous Lord Crucifix, 400th Anniv. of Arrival in America — A821

1992, Dec. 26　　Perf. 12
1789　A821　76c multicolored　4.50　4.50

Jujuy City, 400th Anniv. — A822

1993, Apr. 24　Litho.　Perf. 13½
1790　A822　38c multicolored　1.25　.60

Argentina Soccer Assoc., Cent. — A823

1993, Mar. 27
1791 A823 38c multicolored   1.25   .60

Souvenir Sheet

Intl. Philatelic Exhibitions — A824

Designs: a, 38c, City Hall, Poznan, Poland. b, 48c, Statue of Christ the Redeemer, Rio de Janeiro, Brazil. c, 76c, Royal Palace, Bangkok, Thailand.

1993, May 8   Litho.   Perf. 12
1792 A824   Sheet of 3, #a.-c.   5.00 5.00
   Polska '93 (No. 1792a), Brasiliana '93 (No. 1792b), Bangkok '92 (No. 1792c).

Luis C. Candelaria's Flight Over Andes Mountains, 75th Anniv. — A825

1993, June 26   Litho.   Perf. 13x13½
1793 A825 38c multicolored   1.50   .60

Order of San Martin, 50th Anniv. — A826

National History Academy, Cent. — A827

1993, May 29   Perf. 13½
1794 A826 38c multicolored   1.50   .60
1795 A827 38c multicolored   1.50   .60

Armed Forces Memorial Day — A828

No. 1796, Natl. Gendarmerie. No. 1797, Coast Guard.

1993, June 12
1796 A828 38c multicolored   1.50   .60
1797 A828 38c multicolored   1.50   .60

Paintings — A829

Designs: No. 1798, Old House, by Norberto Russo. No. 1799, Pa'las Casas, by Adriana Zaefferer.

1993, Aug. 14   Litho.   Perf. 13½
1798 A829 38c multicolored   1.50   .60
1799 A829 38c multicolored   1.50   .60

Pato — A830

1993, Aug. 28   Litho.   Perf. 12
1800 A830 1p multicolored   3.25 1.25

Nut-Bearing Trees — A831

Designs: No. 1801, Enterolobium contortisiliquum. No. 1802, Prosopis alba. No. 1803, Magnolia grandiflora. No. 1804, Erythrina falcata.

1993, Sept. 25   Litho.   Perf. 13x13½
1801 A831   75c multicolored   2.50 1.00
1802 A831   75c multicolored   2.50 1.00
1803 A831 1.50p multicolored   5.00 2.00
1804 A831 1.50p multicolored   5.00 2.00
   Nos. 1801-1804 (4)   15.00 6.00

America Issue A832

Whales: 50c, Eubalaena australis. 75c, Cephalorhynchus commersonii.

1993, Oct. 9   Perf. 13½
1805 A832 50c multicolored   1.75   .80
1806 A832 75c multicolored   2.75 1.25

Miniature Sheet

Christmas, New Year — A833

Denomination at: a, UL. b, UR. c, LL. d, LR.

1993, Dec. 4   Litho.   Perf. 13½
1807 A833 75c Sheet of 4, #a.-d.   9.00 8.00

Cave of the Hands, Santa Cruz — A834

1993, Dec. 18
1808 A834 1p multicolored   3.00 1.25

New Emblem, Argentine Postal Service — A835

1994, Jan. 8   Perf. 11½
1809 A835 75c multicolored   4.00 1.25

A836

Players from: 25c, Germany, 1990. 50c, Brazil, 1970. 75c, 1.50p, Argentina, 1986. 1p, Italy, 1982.

1994, June 11   Litho.   Perf. 13½
1810 A836   25c multicolored   .75   .45
1811 A836   50c multicolored   1.50   .90
1812 A836   75c multicolored   2.25 1.40
1813 A836   1p multicolored   3.50 2.00
   Nos. 1810-1813 (4)   8.00 4.75

Souvenir Sheet
Perf. 12
1814 A836 1.50p multicolored   5.00 5.00
   No. 1814 contains one 40x50mm stamp with continuous design.

1994 World Cup Soccer Championships, US — A837

Drawings of championships by: No. 1815, Julian Lisenberg. No. 1816, Matias Taylor, vert. No. 1817, Torcuato S. Gonzalez Agote, vert. No. 1818, Maria Paula Palma.

1994, July 23   Perf. 13½
1815 A837 75c multicolored   3.00 1.00
1816 A837 75c multicolored   3.00 1.00
1817 A837 75c multicolored   3.00 1.00
1818 A837 75c multicolored   3.00 1.00
   Nos. 1815-1818 (4)   12.00 4.00
   Issued in sheet containing a block of 4 of each stamp + 4 labels.

A838

Molothrus Badius — A838a

1994-95   Litho.   Perf. 13½
1819 A838   10c like #1748   .25   .25
1820 A838   25c like #1749   .60   .35
1823 A838   50c like #1752   1.25   .60
1828 A838   1p like #1754   2.50 1.25
1832 A838   2p like #1753   5.00 2.50
1835 A838a 9.40p multicolored   25.00 25.00
   Nos. 1819-1835 (6)   34.60 29.95

   See designs A807, A849.
   Issued: 10c, 25c, 50c, 1p, 2p, 6/14/94; 9.40p, 4/12/95.

Wildlife of Falkland Islands A839

Designs: 25c, Melanodera melanodera. 50c, Pygoscelis papua. 75c, Tachyeres brachypterus. 1p, Mirounga leonina.

1994, Aug 6
1839 A839 25c multicolored   .80   .55
1840 A839 50c multicolored   1.25   .75
1841 A839 75c multicolored   2.50 1.50
1842 A839 1p multicolored   3.50 2.00
   Nos. 1839-1842 (4)   8.05 4.80

City of San Luis, 400th Anniv. — A840

1994, Aug. 20
1843 A840 75c multicolored   4.00 1.50

Province of Tierra del Fuego, Antarctica and South Atlantic Islands
A841

1994, Aug. 20
1844 A841 75c multicolored   2.25 1.50

Argentine Inventors — A842

Designs: No. 1845, Ladislao Jose Biro (1899-1985), ball point pen. No. 1846, Raul Pateras de Pescara (1890-1966), helicopter. No. 1847, Quirino Cristiani (1896-1984), animated drawings. No. 1848, Enrique Finochietto (1881-1948), surgical instruments.

1994, Oct. 1
1845 A842 75c multicolored   2.25 2.25
1846 A842 75c multicolored   2.25 2.25
1847 A842 75c multicolored   2.25 2.25
1848 A842 75c multicolored   2.25 2.25
   a.   Block of 4, #1845-1848   9.00 9.00
Issued in sheets containing 4 No. 1848a + 4 labels.

UNICEF Christmas A843

75c, Bell, red ornament, star.

1994, Nov. 26   Litho.   Perf. 11½
1849 A843 50c shown   1.50 1.00
1850 A843 75c multicolored   2.25 1.50

Take Care of Our Planet A844

Children's paintings: No. 1851, Boy, girl holding earth, vert. No. 1852, Children outdoors, vert. No. 1853, World as house. No. 1854, People around "world" table.

1994, Dec. 3   Perf. 13½
1851 A844 25c multicolored   .75 .50
1852 A844 25c multicolored   .75 .50
1853 A844 50c multicolored   1.25 .80
1854 A844 50c multicolored   1.25 .80
      Nos. 1851-1854 (4)   4.00 2.60

Christmas — A845

1994, Dec. 10
1855 A845 50c Annunciation   1.50 1.00
1856 A845 75c Madonna & Child   2.25 1.00

Nos. 1855-1856 each issued in sheets of 20 + 5 labels.

12th Pan American Games, Mar del Plata — A846

1995   Litho.   Perf. 13½
1857 A846 75c Running   2.25 .65
1858 A846 75c Cycling   2.25 .65
1859 A846 75c Diving   2.25 .65
1860 A846 1.25p Gymnastics, vert. 3.50 .75
1861 A846 1.25p Soccer, vert.   3.50 .75
      Nos. 1857-1861 (5)   13.75 3.45
Issued: No. 1857, 2/18; others, 3/11.

Natl. Constitution — A847

Design: 75c, Natl. Congress Dome, woman from statue The Republic Triumphant.

1995, Apr. 8
1862 A847 75c multicolored   2.25 .70

21st Intl. Book Fair — A848

1995, Apr. 8
1863 A848 75c multicolored   2.25 .70

Birds A849

5p, Carduelis magellanica. 10p, Zonotrichia capensis.

1995   Litho.   Perf. 13½
1876 A849 5p multicolored   15.00 15.00
1880 A849 10p multicolored   30.00 30.00
Issued: 5p, 10p, 5/23/95.

A850

1995, Mar. 25   Litho.   Die Cut
Self-Adhesive
1883A A850 25c multicolored   10.00 .50
1884 A850 75c multicolored   3.00 .50
   a.   Booklet pane, 2 #1883A, 6 #1884 40.00
         Complete booklet, #1884a   50.00
   b.   Booklet pane, 4 #1883A, 12 #1884 77.50
         Complete booklet, #1884b   85.00
See Nos. 1921A-1921B.

Argentine Engineers' Center, Cent. — A851

1995, June 3   Perf. 13½
1885 A851 75c multicolored   2.25 .60

Jose Marti (1853-95) — A852

No. 1887, Antonio Jose de Sucre (1795-1830).

1995, Aug. 12   Litho.   Perf. 13½
1886 A852 1p multicolored   3.00 .75
1887 A852 1p multicolored   3.00 .75

Fauna — A853

1995, Sept. 1   Litho.   Perf. 13½
1888 A853 5c Ostrich   .25 .25
1889 A853 25c Penguin   .65 .35
1890 A853 50c Toucan   1.25 .35
1891 A853 75c Condor   1.75 .35
1892 A853 1p Owl   3.50 .35
1893 A853 2p Bigua   5.00 .35
1894 A853 2.75p Tero   8.50 .35

Booklet Stamps
Perf. 13½ on 2 or 3 Sides
1895 A853 25c Alligator   .65 .40
1896 A853 50c Fox   1.25 .70
1897 A853 75c Anteater   1.75 1.00
1898 A853 75c Deer   1.75 1.00
1899 A853 75c Whale   1.75 1.00
   a.   Booklet pane, 1 each Nos. 1889-1891, 1895-1899 10.00 10.00
         Complete booklet, #1899a   11.00
      Nos. 1888-1899 (12)   28.05 6.45
See Nos. 1958, 2004-2004A.

Native Heritage — A854

a, Cave drawings, shifting sands. b, Stone mask. c, Anthropomorphous vessel. d, Woven textile.

1995, Sept. 9
1900 A854 75c Block of 4, #a.-d. 9.00 9.00

Sunflower, Postal Service Emblem — A855

1995, Oct. 7
1901 A855 75c multicolored   8.00 1.00

Juan D. Peron (1895-1974) — A856

1995, Oct. 7
1902 A856 75c lt ol bis & dk bl   2.00 .60

Miniature Sheet

Anniversaries — A857

Annivs: a, UN, 50th. b, ICAO, 50th (in 1994). c, FAO, 50th. d, ILO, 75th (in 1994).

1995, Oct. 14   Perf. 12
1903 A857 75c Sheet of 4, #a.-d. 9.00 9.00

Christmas and New Year — A858

Designs: Nos. 1904, 1908, Christmas tree, presents. No. 1905, "1996." No. 1906, Champagne glasses. No. 1907, Present.

1995, Nov. 25   Litho.   Perf. 13½
1904 A858 75c multicolored   2.00 .45
Booklet Stamps
Perf. 13½ on 1 or 2 Sides
1905 A858 75c multicolored   2.00 .75
1906 A858 75c multicolored   2.00 .75
1907 A858 75c multicolored   2.00 .75
1908 A858 75c multicolored   2.00 .75
   a.   Booklet pane, #1905-1908 + label 8.00
         Complete booklet, #1908a   16.00
      Nos. 1904-1908 (5)   10.00 3.45

No. 1908a is a continuous design. Ribbon extends from edge to edge on No. 1908 and stops at edge of package on No. 1905.

Miniature Sheet

Motion Pictures, Cent. — A859

Black and white film clips, director: a, The Battleship Potemkin, Sergei Eisenstein (Soviet Union). b, Casablanca, Michael Curtiz (US). c, Bicycle Thief, Vittorio De Sica (Italy). d, Limelights, Charles Chaplin (England). e, The 400 Blows, Francois Truffaut (France). f, Chronicle of the Lonely Child, Leonardo Favio (Argentina).

1995, Dec. 2   **Perf. 13½**
1909   A859   75c Sheet of 6,
     #a.-f.   25.00   25.00

The Sky — A860

1995, Dec. 16   **Perf. 13½ on 3 Sides**
Booklet Stamps
1910	A860	25c Dirigible	.70	.35
1911	A860	25c Kite	.70	.35
1912	A860	25c Hot air balloon	.70	.35
1913	A860	50c Balloons	1.50	.35
1914	A860	50c Paper airplane	1.50	.35
1915	A860	75c Airplane	2.25	.35
1916	A860	75c Helicopter	2.25	.35
1917	A860	75c Parachute	2.25	.35

a.   Booklet pane, #1910-1917 +
    label   13.00
    Complete booklet, No. 1917a   25.00

Nos. 1910-1917 do not appear in Scott number order in No. 1917a, which has a continuous design.

America
Issue
A861

Postal vehicles from Postal &Telegraph Museum: No. 1918, Horse & carriage. No. 1919, Truck.

1995, Dec. 16   **Perf. 13½**
1918	A861	75c multicolored	2.50	.75
1919	A861	75c multicolored	2.50	.75

Olympic
Games,
Cent.
A862

1996, Mar. 30   **Litho.**   **Perf. 13½**
1920	A862	75c Running	2.50	.75
1921	A862	1p Discus	3.00	.90

Type of 1995
Self-Adhesive
Coil Stamps
Country Name and Denomination in Blue
1996		**Litho.**	**Die Cut**	
1921A	A850	25c multi	2.00	2.00
1921B	A850	75c multi	3.50	3.00

Physicians
A863

Designs: a, Francisco J. Muniz (1795-1871). b, Ricardo Gutierrez (1838-96). c, Ignacio Pirovano (1844-95). d, Esteban L. Maradona (1895-1995).

1996, Apr. 20   **Litho.**   **Perf. 12**
1922	A863	50c Sheet of 4	6.00	6.00
a.-d.		Any single	1.00	1.00

Jerusalem, 3000th Anniv. — A864

7th cent. mosaic maps of city, denomination at: No. 1923, LL. No. 1924, LR.

1996, May 18   **Litho.**   **Perf. 13½**
1923	A864	75c multicolored	1.50	.75
1924	A864	75c multicolored	1.50	.75
a.		Pair, #1923-1924	6.00	4.00

No. 1924a is a continuous design and was issued in sheets of 8 + 4 labels.

Endangered Fauna — A865

1996, June 15   **Litho.**   **Perf. 13½**
1925	A865	75c Capybara	2.00	.75
1926	A865	75c Guanaco	2.00	.75
a.		Pair, #1925-1926	5.00	5.00

America Issue.

Summer
Olympic
Games
A866

Designs: 75c, Torch bearer, Buenos Aires, candidate for 2004 Games. 1p, Men's eight with coxswain, Atlanta, 1996.

1996, July 6
1927	A866	75c multicolored	2.00	.70
1928	A866	1p multicolored	2.50	.90

National Parks — A867

Wildlife, national park: No. 1929, Mountain turkey, Diamante. No. 1930, Parrot, San Antonio Nature Reserve. No. 1931, Deer, Otamendi Natl. Reserve. No. 1932, Rabbit, El Leoncito Nature Reserve.

1996, Aug. 24   **Litho.**   **Perf. 13x13½**
1929	A867	75c multicolored	2.00	.70
1930	A867	75c multicolored	2.00	.70
1931	A867	75c multicolored	2.00	.70
1932	A867	75c multicolored	2.00	.70
		Nos. 1929-1932 (4)	8.00	2.80

Central Post
Office, Buenos
Aires — A868

1996, Oct. 5   **Litho.**   **Die Cut**
Self-Adhesive
Size: 25x35mm
1933	A868	75c multicolored	8.50	1.00

Vignette of No. 1933 is broken by circular and rectangular die cut areas to guard against reuse.
See Nos. 1983-1984.

Carousel Figures — A869

Designs: No. 1934, Hand-carved decorative ornaments. No. 1935, Child on carousel horse. No. 1936, Carousel. No. 1937, Heads of horses. No. 1938, Child in airplane. No. 1939, Carousel pig. No. 1940, Boy in car.

1996, Oct. 5   **Perf. 13½ Horiz.**
Booklet Stamps
1934	A869	25c multicolored	.50	.30
1935	A869	25c multicolored	.50	.30
1936	A869	25c multicolored	.50	.30
1937	A869	50c multicolored	1.00	.60
1938	A869	50c multicolored	1.00	.60
1939	A869	50c multicolored	1.00	.60
1940	A869	75c multicolored	1.50	.70
a.		Booklet pane, #1934-1940	7.00	
		Complete booklet, #1940a	14.00	

Sequence of stamps in No. 1940a: No. 1940, 1934, 1937, 1935, 1938, 1936, 1939.

Port Belgrano Naval Base,
Cent. — A870

Designs: 25c, LST "San Antonio." 50c, Corvette *Rosales.* 75c, Destroyer *Hercules.* 1p, Aircraft carrier, "25th of May."

1996-97   **Litho.**   **Perf. 13½**
1941	A870	25c multicolored	1.00	.50
1942	A870	50c multicolored	1.50	.50
1943	A870	75c multicolored	2.25	.75
1944	A870	1p multicolored	2.75	1.00
		Nos. 1941-1944 (4)	7.50	2.75

Issued: 25c, 1p, 10/5/96; 50c, 75c, 2/1/97.

Christmas — A871

Tapestries: 75c, Nativity, by Gladys Angelica Rinaldi, vert. 1p, Candles, by Norma Bonet de Maekawa.

1996, Nov. 30   **Litho.**   **Perf. 13½**
1945	A871	75c multicolored	1.50	.75
1946	A871	1p multicolored	2.25	1.00

Exploration of Antarctica — A872

Designs: 75c, Melchior Base. 1.25p, Icebreaker ARA Alte. Irizar.

1996, Nov. 30
1947	A872	75c multicolored	2.00	.75
1948	A872	1.25p multicolored	3.00	1.25

National
Gallery,
Cent.
A873

Paintings of women by: 75c, Paul Gauguin, vert. No. 1950, Edouard Manet, vert. No. 1951, Amedeo Modigiliani, vert. 1.25p, Pablo Picasso.

1996, Dec. 14
1949	A873	75c multicolored	1.75	.60
1950	A873	1p multicolored	2.25	.90
1951	A873	1p multicolored	2.25	.90
1952	A873	1.25p multicolored	3.50	1.10
		Nos. 1949-1952 (4)	9.75	3.50

Mining Industry — A874

1997, Feb. 1   **Litho.**   **Perf. 13½**
1953	A874	75c Granite	1.75	.75
1954	A874	1.25p Borax	3.25	1.10

Traditional Costumes — A875

1997, Feb. 22   **Litho.**   **Perf. 13½**
1955	A875	75c multicolored	2.25	.75

America issue.

Repatriation of the Curved Sword of
Gen. San Martin, Cent. — A876

1997, Mar. 15   **Litho.**   **Perf. 13½**
1956	A876	75c multicolored	2.25	.60

29th Youth Rugby World Championships — A877

1997, Mar. 22
1957 A877 75c multicolored   2.25 .75

Fauna Type of 1995

1997, Feb. 22   Litho.   Perf. 13½
1958 A853 10c Reddish sandpiper   1.40 .25

Buenos Aires-Rio de Janeiro Regatta, 50th Anniv. — A879

1997, Apr. 5   Litho.   Perf. 13½
1960 A879 75c Fortuna II   2.25 .75

Natl. History Museum, Cent. — A880

1997, May 17
1961 A880 75c multicolored   2.25 .75

La Plata Natl. University, Cent. — A881

1997, May 17
1962 A881 75c multicolored   2.25 .75

Lighthouses A882

a, Cabo Virgenes. b, Isla Pingüino. c, San Juan de Salvamento. d, Punta Delgada.

1997, May 31
1963 A882 75c Sheet of 4, #a.-d.   9.50 7.50

Ramón J. Cárcano (1860-1946), Developer of Postal and Telegraph System A883

1997, May 31
1964 A883 75c multicolored   2.25 .75

Buenos Aires, Candidate for 2004 Summer Olympics — A884

1997, June 21
1965 A884 75c multicolored   2.25 .50

First Electric Tram in Buenos Aires, Cent. A885

Designs: a, Lacroze Suburban Service Tram Co., 1912. b, Lacroze Urban Service Tram Co., 1907. c, Anglo Argentina Tram Co., 1930. d, Buenos Aires City Transportation Corp., 1942. e, Military Manufacture Tram, 1956. f, South Electric Tram, 1908.

1997, July 12   Sheet of 6
1966 A885 75c #a.-f. + 2 labels   12.50 12.50

Monument to Joaquín V. González (1863-1923), La Rioja — A886

1997, Aug. 9
1967 A886 75c multicolored   2.25 .75

Musicians and Composers A887

Paintings: No. 1968, Alberto Ginastera (1916-83), by Carlos Nine. No. 1969, Astor Piazzolla (1921-92), by Carlos Alonso. No. 1970, Anibal Troilo (1914-75), by Hermenegildo Sabat. No. 1971, Atahualpa Yupanqui (b. 1908), by Luis Scafati.

1997, Aug. 9
1968 A887 75c multicolored   2.25 .70
1969 A887 75c multicolored   2.25 .70
1970 A887 75c multicolored   2.25 .70
1971 A887 75c multicolored   2.25 .70
      Nos. 1968-1971 (4)   9.00 2.80

Argentine Authors — A888

Designs: No. 1972, Jorge Luis Borges (1899-1986), maze. No. 1973, Julio Cortázar (1914-84), hop scotch game.

1997, Aug. 30   Litho.   Perf. 13
1972 A888 1p multicolored   2.60 1.00
1973 A888 1p multicolored   2.60 1.00

Women's Political Rights Law, 50th Anniv. A889

1997, Sept. 6   Litho.   Perf. 13½
1974 A889 75c Eva Perón   2.50 1.00

Mercosur (Common Market of Latin America) A890

1997, Sept. 27   Litho.   Perf. 13½
1975 A890 75c multicolored   2.25 .60
   See Bolivia No. 1019, Brazil No. 2646, Paraguay No. 2564, Uruguay No. 1681.

Launching of Frigate President Sarmiento, Cent. — A891

Designs: No. 1976, Painting of ship by Hugo Leban.
No. 1977: a, Ship. b, Ship's figurehead, vert.

1997, Oct. 4
1976 A891 75c multicolored   2.50 .75

Souvenir Sheet
Perf. 12
1977 A891 75c Sheet of 2, #a.-b. 5.00 4.00
   No. 1977 contains two 40x30mm stamps.

Ernesto "Che" Guevara (1928-67) A892

1997, Oct. 18
1978 A892 75c multicolored   5.00 .75

Ecology on Stamps — A893

Children's drawings: No. 1979, Animal, by J. Chiapparo, vert. No. 1980, Vicuna, by L.L. Portal, vert. No. 1981, Seal, by A. Lloren. No. 1982, Bird in flight, by J. Saccone.

1997, Nov. 8   Litho.   Perf. 13½
1979 A893 50c multicolored   1.50 .50
1980 A893 50c multicolored   1.50 .50
1981 A893 75c multicolored   2.00 .75
1982 A893 75c multicolored   2.00 .75
      Nos. 1979-1982 (4)   7.00 2.50

Central Post Office, Buenos Aires, Type of 1996
1997, July 24   Litho.   Die Cut
Self-Adhesive
Size: 23x35mm
1983 A868 25c multicolored   12.00 .75
1984 A868 75c multicolored   5.00 .75
   a.   Bklt. pane, 2 #1983, 6 #1984 55.00
        Complete booklet, #1984a   60.00
   Nos. 1983-1984 are broken at both the top and bottom of each stamp by three lines of wavy die cutting.

Christmas — A893a

Nativity scene tapestries by: Nos. 1984B, 1984G, Mary José. No. 1984C, Elena Aguilar. No. 1984D, Silvia Pettachi. No. 1984E, Ana Escobar. No. 1984F, Alejandra Martinez. No. 1984H, Nidia Martinez.

1997, Nov. 22   Litho.   Perf. 13½
1984B A893a 75c multicolored 2.25 .75

Booklet Stamps
Self-Adhesive
Size: 44x27mm
Die Cut
1984C A893a 25c multicolored .75 .50
1984D A893a 25c multicolored 1.00 .50
1984E A893a 50c multicolored 1.50 .75
1984F A893a 50c multicolored 1.50 .75
1984G A893a 75c multicolored 2.00 .75
1984H A893a 75c multicolored 2.00 .75
   i.   Booklet pane, #1984C-1984H   10.00

   Nos. 1984C-1984H are broken at upper right by three die cut chevrons. By its nature, No. 1984Hi is a complete booklet.

Mother Teresa (1910-97) — A893b

1997, Dec. 27
1984J A893b 75c multicolored 2.25 .75

Dr. Bernardo A. Houssay (1887-1971), 1947 Nobel Prize Winner in Medicine — A894

1998, Jan. 31   Litho.   *Perf. 13½*
1985 A894 75c multicolored   2.25 .60

First Ascension of Mount Aconcagua, Cent. — A895

1998, Feb. 14   *Perf. 12*
1986 A895 1.25p multicolored   3.50 1.10

Founding of San Martin de los Andes, Cent. — A896

1998, Mar. 14   Litho.   *Perf. 13½*
1987 A896 75c multicolored   2.25 .75

Regimental Quarters of Gen. San Martin's Mounted Grenadiers A897

Designs: a, Statue. b, Large jar with painting of San Martin. c, Regimental seal. d, Regimental quarters.

1998, Mar. 21   Litho.   *Perf. 13½*
1988 A897 75c Block of 4, #a.-d. 8.00 6.00

Protection of the Ozone — A898

1998, Mar. 28   Litho.   *Perf. 13½*
1989 A898 75c multicolored   2.25 .75

America Issue — A899

Letter carriers: No. 1990, Wearing white uniform. No. 1991, Carrying letter bag with shoulder strap.

1998, Apr. 4
1990 A899 75c multicolored   2.25 .75
1991 A899 75c multicolored   2.25 .75

Characters from Stories by Maria Elena Walsh — A900

Designs: No. 1992, El Reino Del Reves. No. 1993, Zoo Loco. No. 1994, Dailan Kifki. No. 1995, Manuelita.

1998, Apr. 17   Litho.   *Die Cut*
Booklet Stamps
Self-Adhesive
1992 A900 75c multicolored   3.75 3.00
1993 A900 75c multicolored   3.75 3.00
1994 A900 75c multicolored   3.75 3.00
1995 A900 75c multicolored   3.75 3.00
a.   Complete booklet, #1992-1995   20.00

Historic Chapels A901

Designs: No. 1996, San Pedro de Fiambalá, Catamarca. No. 1997, Huacalera, Jujuy. No. 1998, Santo Domingo, La Rioja. No. 1999, Tumbaya, Jujuy.

1998, Apr. 25   Litho.   *Perf. 13x13½*
1996 A901 75c multicolored   2.00 .75
1997 A901 75c multicolored   2.00 .75
1998 A901 75c multicolored   2.00 .75
1999 A901 75c multicolored   2.00 .75
Nos. 1996-1999 (4)   8.00 3.00

White Helmets, A Commitment to Humanity — A902

1998, May 23   Litho.   *Perf. 13½*
2000 A902 1p multicolored   2.75 1.00

Beginning with No. 2001, many Argentine stamps are inscribed "Correo Oficial," but these are not Official stamps (i.e., for government use only). The addition of "Correo Oficial" distinguishes these stamps, which are products of the Argentine Postal Service, from other stamps from a private post, OCA, which are also inscribed "Republica Argentina."

1998 World Cup Soccer Championships, France — A903

Stylized players representing: a, Argentina. b, Croatia. c, Jamaica. d, Japan.

1998, May 30
2001 A903 75c Block of 4, #a.-d. 6.50 6.50

Journalist's Day — A904

1998, June 20
2002 A904 75c multicolored   2.25 .75

Creation of Argentine Postal System, 250th Anniv. — A905

a, Corrientes design A2, peso coin. b, Building, post box.

1998, June 27
2003 A905 75c Pair, #a.-b.   4.50 3.25

Fauna Type of 1995
1998   Litho.   *Die Cut*
Self-Adhesive (#2004)
2004   A853   60c Picaflor   1.75 .50
Perf. 13½
2004A   A853   3.25p Tero   10.00 .50

No. 2004 is broken at bottom right by 3 or 5 lines of wavy die cutting.
Issued: 60c, 12/12; 3.25p, 7/22.

Ruins, Mission St. Ignacio A906

1998, July 25   Litho.   *Perf. 13½*
2005 A906 75c multicolored   2.25 .75
Mercosur.

Cattle A907

1998, Aug. 1
2006 A907 25c Brahman   .65 .50
2007 A907 25c Aberdeen-Angus   .65 .50
2008 A907 50c Hereford   1.25 .50

2009 A907 50c Criolla   1.25 .50
2010 A907 75c Holland-Argentina   1.75 1.00
2011 A907 75c Shorthorn   1.75 1.00
Nos. 2006-2011 (6)   7.30 4.00

Deception Island Base, Antarctica, 50th Anniv. — A908

1998, Aug. 15   Litho.   *Perf. 14½*
2012 A908 75c multicolored   2.40 1.00

State of Israel, 50th Anniv. A909

1998, Sept. 5   Litho.   *Perf. 13½*
2013 A909 75c multicolored   2.25 .75

Argentina-Japan Friendship Treaty, Cent. — A910

1998, Oct. 3
2014 A910 75c multicolored   2.25 .75

Post Office Building, Buenos Aires, 70th Anniv. A911

Designs: No. 2015, Building, clock, tile. No. 2016, Column ornamentation, tile, bench.

1998, Oct. 3
2015 A911 75c multicolored   1.75 .75
2016 A911 75c multicolored   1.75 .75
a.   Pair, #2015-2016   4.25 4.25

Cartoons — A912

Designs: a, Patoruzu, by Quinterno. b, Matias, by Sendra. c, Clemente, by Caloi. d, El Eternauta, by Oesterheld and López. e, Loco Chavez, by Trillo and Altuna. f, Inodoro Pereyra, by Fontanarrosa. g, Tia Vicenta, by Landrú. h, Gaturro, by Nik.

1998, Oct. 17   Litho.   *Perf. 13¾x13¼*
2017 A912 75c Sheet of 8,
#a.-h.   16.00 16.00

Dr. Pedro de Elizalde's Children's Hospital, 220th Anniv. — A913

1998, Oct. 24   **Litho.**   *Perf. 13½*
2025 A913 75c multicolored   2.40   .75

Raoul Wallenberg (1912-47), Humanitarian — A914

1998, Nov. 21
2026 A914 75c multicolored   2.25   .75

Espamer '98 — A915

25c, Spanish flags, arms. 75c, 18th cent. schooner. 75c+75c, Brigantine, gray sails. 1.25p+1.25p, Brigantine, white sails.

1998, Nov. 21   *Die Cut*
Booklet Stamps
Self-Adhesive
2027 A915 25c multicolored   .75   .75
2028 A915 25c multicolored   2.25   2.00
2029 A915 75c +75c multi   4.50   4.00
2030 A915 1.25p +1.25p multi   7.50   3.25
   a.   Booklet pane, #2027-2030   14.00

Nos. 2027-2030 are broken at top right of each stamp by four lines of wavy die cutting. No. 2030a is a complete booklet.

Organization of American States, 50th Anniv. — A916

1998, Nov. 28   *Perf. 13½*
2031 A916 75c multicolored   2.25   .75

Dinosaurs of Argentina — A917

Designs: a, Eoraptor. b, Gasparinisaura. c, Giganotosaurus. d, Patagosaurus.

1998, Nov. 28
2032 A917 75c Sheet of 4, #a.-d.   10.00   9.00

Christmas A918

1998, Dec. 5
2033 A918 75c multicolored   2.25   .75

Newspaper El Liberal, Cent. A919

1998, Dec. 5
2034 A919 75c Juan A. Figueroa   2.25   .75

La Nueva Provincia, Daily Newspaper, Cent. A920

1998, Dec. 12
2035 A920 75c Enrique Julio   2.25   .75

Universal Declaration of Human Rights, 50th Anniv. — A921

1998, Dec. 12
2036 A921 75c multicolored   2.25   .75

Holocaust Memorial, Cathedral of Buenos Aires — A922

1998, Dec. 12
2037 A922 75c multicolored   2.25   1.00

Southern Cross — A923

Inscriptions: 8.75p, Sur postal express. 17.50p, Sur postal 24.

1999-2000   **Litho.**   *Die Cut*
Self-Adhesive
2038 A923 8.75p bl & silver   17.50   15.00
2039 A923 17.50p bl & gold   35.00   30.00

Issued: 8.75p, 7/1/99; 17.50p, 3/2/00. Nos. 2038-2039 are broken at right by five wavy lines of die cutting.

National Fund for the Arts, 40th Anniv. A925

1999, Mar. 6   **Litho.**   *Perf. 13½*
2042 A925 75c multicolored   1.75   .75

Intl. Year of the Ocean (in 1998) A926

1999, Mar. 6
2043 A926 50c Penguin, vert.   1.50   1.00
2044 A926 75c Dolphins   1.60   1.00

Postmen — A927

Designs: 25c, Early postman, city scene. 50c, Early postman, people on bicycles, factory. 75c, Modern postman, city buildings.

1998-2001   **Litho.**   *Die Cut*
Self-Adhesive
2045 A927 25c multicolored   30.00   .75
2046 A927 75c multicolored   15.00   .50
   a.   Strip of 4, 1 #2045, 3 #2046   75.00

Booklet Stamps
Serpentine Die Cut 6
2047 A927 25c multicolored   27.00   1.00
2048 A927 75c multicolored   10.00   1.00
   a.   Bklt. pane, 2 #2047, 6 #2048   115.00
     Complete booklet, #2048a   120.00

Serpentine Die Cut 11
2048B A927 25c multi   1.00   .25
2048C A927 75c multi   3.00   .50
   d.   Booklet pane, 2 #2048B, 6 #2048C   22.00
     Complete booklet, 2 #2048Cd   44.00
     Complete booklet, 4 #2048Cd   88.00

Size: 21x27mm
Die Cut
2049 A927 25c multicolored   3.50   .50
2050 A927 50c multicolored   3.50   1.00
2051 A927 75c multicolored   3.50   1.75
   a.   Bklt. pane, 2 ea #2049-2051   21.00
     Complete booklet, #2051a   30.00

Nos. 2045-2048C are broken at lower right by five lines of wavy die cutting. Nos. 2049-2051 are broken in center by five wavy lines of die cutting. Nos. 2045-2046 have darker vignettes than Nos. 2047-2048.
Issued: Nos. 2045-2048, 12/9/98. Nos. 2049-2051, 2/2/99. Nos. 2048B-2048C, Feb. 2001.

25th Book Fair A928

Designs: a, Book. b, Obelisk, readers.

1999, Apr. 17   **Litho.**   *Perf. 13¾x13½*
2052 A928 75c Pair, a.-b.   3.50   3.50

Argentine Rugby Union, Cent. — A929

75c, Player, balls. 1.50p, Old, modern players.

1999, Apr. 24   **Litho.**   *Perf. 13¾x13½*
2054 A929 75c multicolored   1.75   1.00
Souvenir Sheet
2055 A929 1.50p multi + 3 labels   3.50   3.50

Cafes of Buenos Aires — A930

Designs: a, Mug, Giralda Dairy. b, Two glasses, Homero Manzi Cafe. c, Hat hanging on rack, Ideal Sweet Shop. d, Cup and saucer, Tortoni Cafe.

Serpentine Die Cut
1999, Apr. 30   **Litho.**
Self-Adhesive
2056   Booklet pane of 4   8.00   8.00
   a.   A930 25c multicolored   .50   .50
   b.-c.   A930 75c multi, each   1.50   1.00
   d.   A930 1.25p multicolored   2.50   1.25
     Complete booklet, #2056   10.00

Argentine Olympic Committee, 75th Anniv. — A931

1999, May 15   *Perf. 14x13¼*
2057 A931 75c Pierre de Coubertin   1.75   .70

Enrico Caruso (1873-1921), Opera Singer — A932

Designs: a, Portrait of Caruso. b, Singer, various musical instruments. c, Outside of Colon Theatre, Buenos Aires. d, Scene from opera, "El Matrero."

1999, May 15   *Perf. 13½*
2058 A932 75c Sheet of 4, #a.-d.   7.75   7.75

Famous Women A933

Designs: a, Rosario Vera Penaloza (1873-1950), educator. b, Julieta Lanteri (1862-1932), physician.

1999, June 5   **Perf. 14x13¼**
2059 A933 75c Pair, #a.-b.   3.50 2.00

Souvenir Sheets

Paintings from Natl. Museum of Art, Buenos Aires — A934

No. 2060: a, Anarchy of Year 20, by Luis Felipe Noé. b, Retrato de L.E.S., by Carlos Alonso.
No. 2061: a, Typical Orchestra, by Antonio Berni. b, Untitled, (Woman seated), by Aída Carballo.

1999, June 5   **Perf. 14**
Sheets of 2
2060 A934 75c #a.-b.   4.00 3.25
2061 A934 75c #a.-b.   4.00 3.25

No. 2060b is 40x40mm, No. 2061a, 70x50mm, No. 2061b, 40x50mm.

Carrier Pigeon A935

1999, June 12   **Perf. 13¾x13½**
2062 A935 75c multicolored   2.25 .75

Maps — A936

1999, June 12   **Die Cut**
Self-Adhesive
2063 A936 35c Local highway   1.00 .50
2064 A936 40c City street   1.10 .50
2065 A936 50c Regional highway   1.40 .50
    Nos. 2063-2065 (3)   3.50 1.50

Nos. 2063-2065 are broken at lower left by five wavy lines of die cutting.

Dogs A937

Designs: a, 25c, Boxer. b, 25c, English sheepdog. c, 50c, Collie. d, 50c, St. Bernard. e, 75c, German shepherd. f, 75c, Siberian husky.

1999, July 24   **Litho.**   **Perf. 13½**
2066 A937   Sheet of 6, #a.-f.   7.00 7.00

Natl. Telecommunications Day — A938

1999, July 24   **Perf. 13½x13¾**
2067 A938 75c multicolored   1.75 .75

Justo José de Urquiza School, Concepcion del Uruguay, 150th Anniv. — A939

1999, Aug. 7   **Perf. 13¾x13½**
2068 A939 75c multicolored   1.75 .75

Otto Krause Technical School, Buenos Aires, Cent. — A940

1999, Aug. 7   **Perf. 13½x13¾**
2069 A940 75c multicolored   1.75 .75

Bethlehem 2000 Project — A941

1999, Aug. 21   **Perf. 13½**
2070 A941 75c multicolored   1.75 .75

America Issue, A New Millennium Without Arms — A942

No. 2072, Tree of hands, vert.

    Perf. 13½x13¾, 13¾x13½
1999, Aug. 21
2071 A942 75c shown   1.75 .75
2072 A942 75c multicolored   1.75 .75

National Parks — A943

Parks and animals: No. 2073, Mburucuyá, coypu. No. 2074, Quebrada de Los Condoritos, condor. No. 2075, San Guillermo, vicuna. No. 2076, Sierra de las Quijadas, puma. No. 2077, Talampaya, gray fox.

1999, Sept. 25   **Litho.**   **Perf. 14x13½**
2073 A943 50c multicolored   1.25 .60
2074 A943 50c multicolored   1.25 .60
2075 A943 50c multicolored   1.25 .60
2076 A943 75c multicolored   1.75 .75
2077 A943 75c multicolored   1.75 .75
    Nos. 2073-2077 (5)   7.25 3.30

Inter-American Development Bank, 40th Anniv. — A944

1999, Oct. 9   **Litho.**   **Perf. 13½x13¾**
2078 A944 75c multi   1.75 1.00

UPU, 125th Anniv. A945

1999, Oct. 9   **Perf. 13¾x13½**
2079 A945 1.50p multi   3.50 1.50

Trees — A946

a, Nothofagus pumilio. b, Prosopis caldenia. c, Schinopsis balansae. d, Cordia trichotoma.

1999, Oct. 16   **Perf. 13½x13¾**
2080 A946 75c Strip of 4, #a-d   7.00 7.00

Sinking of A.R.A. Fournier, 50th Anniv. A947

1999, Oct. 16   **Perf. 13¾x13½**
2081 A947 75c multi   1.75 .75

Aviation Anniversaries — A948

Designs: No. 2082, Late 25 airplane. No. 2083, Parachutists.

1999, Oct. 30   **Perf. 13¾x13½**
2082 A948 75c multi   1.75 .75
2083 A948 75c multi   1.75 .75

First Argentine airmail flight, 70th anniv. (No. 2082), Hundred consecutive jumps by Argentine Parachute Club, 50th anniv.

Souvenir Sheets

Millennium — A949

No. 2084: a, 75c, Head of soccer player. b, 50c, Machine as soccer player.
No. 2085: a, 50c, Cane, vert. b, 75c, Head of Jorge Luis Borges (1899-1986), writer.
No. 2086: a, 50c, Accordion player on bed, vert. b, 75c, Stylized tango dancers.

1999, Oct. 30   **Perf. 14**
2084 A949   Sheet of 2, #a.-b.   2.75 2.75
2085 A949   Sheet of 2, #a.-b.   2.75 2.75
2086 A949   Sheet of 2, #a.-b.   2.75 2.75

Size of 75c stamps: 40x40mm.

Argentine Soccer Teams — A950

Designs: No. 2087, Banner and flags of River Plate team. No. 2088, Banner of Boca Juniors team, balloons.
River Plate team (red and white team colors) — No. 2089: a, Stadium, emblem, soccer balls. b, Team on field. c, Fans. d, Emblem. e, Trophy. f, Banner in stadium. g, Player, ball.
Boca Juniors team (blue and yellow team colors) — No. 2090: a, Two players, ball. b, Emblem. c, Four players celebrating. d, Fans, balloons. e, Banner in stadium. f, Blurred shot of players in action. g, Blurred shot of players, diff.

1999   **Perf. 13½x13¼**
2087 A950 75c multi   1.60 .50
2088 A950 75c multi   1.60 .50
Self-Adhesive
Die Cut
2089   Pane of 7   37.50
   a. A950 25c multi   2.50 2.00
   b.-c. A950 50c any single   2.50 2.00
   d.-f. A950 75c any single   5.50 5.50
   g. A950 1.50p multi   11.00 10.00
2090   Pane of 7   37.50
   a. A950 25c multi   2.50 2.00
   b.-c. A950 50c any single   3.50 3.50
   d.-f. A950 75c any single   5.50 5.00
   g. A950 1.50p multi   11.00 10.00

Issued: Nos. 2087-2088, 11/13; Nos. 2089-2090, 11/15.
Sizes: Nos. 2089a-2089f, 2090a-2090f, 37x27mm; No. 2089g, 2090g, 37x37mm.

Canonization of Brother Héctor Valdivielso Sáez — A951

1999, Nov. 20   **Perf. 13¾x13½**
2091 A951 75c multi   1.75 .75

Manuel Belgrano National Naval School, Bicent. A952

1999, Nov. 27
2092 A952 75c multi   1.75 .75

Souvenir Sheet

Launch of Corvette Uruguay, 125th
Anniv. — A953

1999, Nov. 27 **Litho.** *Perf. 14*
2093 A953 1.50p multi 3.50 3.50

A954

Christmas
A955

No. 2094, Figurines of Holy Family.
No. 2095: a, Magus. b, Bell. c, Two Magi,
camels. d, Leaf. e, Angel with star. f, Nativity
scene. g, Star. h, Ornaments.

1999, Dec. 4 *Perf. 13¾x13½*
2094 A954 75c multi 1.25 .60

Perf. 14
2095 Sheet of 8 10.00 10.00
a.-b. A955 25c any single .75 .50
c.-d. A955 50c any single 1.25 1.00
e.-h. A955 75c any single 1.50 1.25

Sizes: Nos. 2095a, 2095b, 2095g, 2095h,
30x30mm.

Viticulture — A956

Designs: a, 25c, Grape on vine. b, 50c, Bottoms of wine bottles. c, 50c, Cork and corkscrew. d, 25c, Glass of wine, wine bottle.

2000, Feb. 26 **Litho.** *Perf. 13¼*
2096 A956 Block of 4, #a-d 4.50 4.50

World Mathematics Year — A957

2000, Mar. 18 *Perf. 13¾x13½*
2097 A957 75c multi 1.50 .60

Birds
A958

a, Leptotila verrauxi. b, Columba picazuro.
c, Columbina picni. d, Zenaida auriculata.

2000, Mar. 18 *Die Cut*
Self-Adhesive
2098 Booklet of 4 8.00
a.-d. A958 75c any single 2.00 1.50

Souvenir Sheet

Bangkok 2000 Stamp
Exhibition — A959

Designs: a, 25c, Vanda coerulea. b, 75c,
Erythrina crista-galli.

2000, Mar. 25 *Perf. 14*
2099 A959 Sheet of 2, #a-b 3.50 2.50

Miniature Sheet

Libraries — A960

Designs: a, 25c, National Public Library Protection Commission. b, 50c, Jujuy Public Library. c, 75c, Argentine Library for the Blind. d, 1p, Argentine National Library.

Litho., Litho. & Embossed (#2100c)
2000, Apr. 15 *Perf. 13½*
2100 A960 Sheet of 4, #a-d 6.75 5.50

Gen.
Luis
Maria
Campos
Military
School,
Cent.
A961

2000, Apr. 29 *Perf. 13¾x13½*
2101 A961 75c multi 1.75 1.00

Discovery of Brazil, 500th
Anniv. — A962

a, 75c, Pedro Cabral, 1558 map of Brazil
coastline. b, 25c, Compass rose and ship.

2000, Apr. 29
2102 A962 Pair, #a-b 2.75 2.50

Souvenir Sheet

The Stamp Show 2000,
London — A963

Designs: a, 25c, Great Britain #1 and design
A1, La Porteña, 1st locomotive in Argentina. b,
75c, Argentina No. 7, mail box.

2000, May 20 *Perf. 14*
2103 A963 Sheet of 2, #a-b 3.00 3.00

91st Intl.
Convention of
Rotary
International,
Buenos
Aires — A964

2000, June 3 **Litho.** *Perf. 13½x13¾*
2104 A964 75c multi 1.75 1.00

Stampin' the Future — A965

Children's Stamp Design Contest Winners:
25c, Rocío Casado. 50c, Carolina Cáceres,
vert. 75c, Valeria A. Pizarro. 1p, Cristina Ayala
Castro, vert.

Perf. 13½x13¼, 13¼x13½
2000, June 24
2105-2108 A965 Set of 4 6.00 4.00

America
Issue
A966

AIDS Prevention: No. 2109, Handshake.
No. 2110, Heart and hands.

2000, July 8 *Perf. 13¾x13½*
2109-2110 A966 75c Set of 2 3.50 2.00

Antoine de Saint-Exupéry (1900-44),
Pilot, Writer — A967

Designs: Nos. 2111, 2115, Potez 25. Nos.
2112, 2116, Late 28. No. 2113, Saint-Exupéry.
No. 2114, Henri Guillaumet, Vicente A.
Almonacid and Jean Mermoz. No. 2117, Map
of southern Argentina, tail of Late 25 plane.
1p, Nose of Late 25 plane, cover from 1st airmail flight to Trelew.

2000, July 29 *Perf. 13½*
2111 A967 25c multi .50 .40

2112 A967 50c multi 1.10 .80

Booklet Stamps
Perf. 14
Size: 30x30mm
2113 A967 25c multi 1.00 .50
2114 A967 50c multi 1.50 1.10
Size: 60x20mm
2115 A967 25c multi 1.00 .50
2116 A967 50c multi 1.50 1.10
a. Booklet pane, #2113-2116 5.50
Size: 40x30mm
2117 A967 50c multi 1.50 1.10
2118 A967 1p multi 2.10 1.75
a. Booklet pane, #2117-2118 4.00
Booklet, #2116a, 2118a 10.00
Nos. 2111-2118 (8) 10.20 7.25

Argentine airmail service, 73rd anniv., Aerofila 2000 Philatelic Exhibition, Buenos Aires
(No. 2118a).

President
Arturo U. Illia
(1900-82)
A968

2000, Aug. 5 *Perf. 13½x13¼*
2119 A968 75c multi 1.75 1.00

José de San
Martín (1778-
1850)
A969

2000, Aug. 26 *Perf. 13½*
2120 A969 75c multi 1.75 1.00

Dalmacio Vélez Sarsfield (1800-75),
Writer of Civil Code — A970

Perf. 13½x13¼
2000, Sept. 23 **Litho.**
2121 A970 75c multi 1.75 1.00

2000 Summer Olympic,
Sydney — A971

No. 2122: a, Windsurfing. b, Field hockey. c,
Volleyball. d, Pole vault.

2000, Sept. 23 *Perf. 13½*
2122 A971 75c Block of 4, #a-d 7.50 7.50

Horses
A972

No. 2123: a, Argentine Petiso. b, Argentine Carriage Horse. c, Peruvian. d, Criolla. e, Argentine Saddle Horse. f, Argentine Polo.
No. 2124: a, Horse-drawn mail coach. b, Horse's head.

2000, Oct. 7   **Perf. 13¾x13½**
2123		Sheet of 6 + 2 labels	7.00	7.00
a.-b.	A972	25c Any single	.85	.50
c.-d.	A972	50c Any single	1.00	.85
e.-f.	A972	75c Any single	1.60	1.25

Souvenir Sheet
Perf. 14
2124		Sheet of 2	3.50	2.75
a.	A972	25c multi	1.25	1.00
b.	A972	75c mutli	1.75	1.50

España 2000 Intl. Philatelic Exhibition.

Archaeological
Artifacts — A973

Designs: 10c, Ceremonial hatchet, Santa Maria culture. 25c, Musical pipes. 50c, Loom, Mapuche culture. 60c, Poncho. 75c, Funerary mask, Tafi culture. 1p, Basket, Mbayá Indians. 2p, Drum, Mapuche culture. 3.25p, Ceremonial mask, Chané culture. 5p, Funerary urn, Belén culture. 9.40p, Rhea-feather costume.

Perf. 13½x13¾ Syncopated
2000   **Litho.**
2125	A973	10c multi	.25	.25
2126	A973	25c multi	.60	.50
2127	A973	50c multi	1.00	.80
2128	A973	60c multi	1.25	1.00
2129	A973	75c multi	1.60	1.25
2130	A973	1p multi	2.10	1.75
2131	A973	2p multi	4.25	3.00
2132	A973	3.25p multi	8.00	5.50
2133	A973	5p multi	10.50	7.00
2134	A973	9.40p multi	20.00	9.50
		Nos. 2125-2134 (10)	49.55	30.55

Issued: 10c, 60c, 11/16; 25c, 50c, 9.40p, 10/26; 1p, 2p, 9/13; 3.25p, 5p, 8/30. See Nos. 2495, 2670-2672.

Natl. Atomic
Energy
Commission,
50th Anniv.
A974

2000, Nov. 11   **Litho.**   **Perf. 13½**
| 2135 | A974 | 75c multi | 1.75 | 1.00 |

Fileteado Art Style and the
Tango — A975

No. 2136: a, Left side of Fileteado design. b, Right side of Fileteado design. c, Musicians. d, Tango dancers.

2000, Nov. 11   **Perf. 13¾x13½**
| 2136 | A975 | 75c Block of 4, #a-d | 7.50 | 7.50 |

Organ
Donation
Campaign
A976

2000, Nov. 25   **Perf. 13½**
| 2137 | A976 | 75c multi | 1.75 | 1.00 |

Christmas
A977

2000, Nov. 25
| 2138 | A977 | 75c multi | 1.75 | 1.00 |

Medicinal
Plants — A978

Designs: No. 2139, 75c, Mirabilis jalapa. No. 2140, 75c, Senna corymbosa. No. 2141, 75c, Eugenia uniflora. No. 2142, 75c, Commelina erecta.

2000, Nov. 25
| 2139-2142 | A978 | Set of 4 | 6.50 | 4.50 |

Pre-Columbian Art — A979

Various artifacts. Background colors: a, Bright orange. b, Red orange. c, Green. d, Red violet.

2000, Dec. 9
| 2143 | A979 | 75c Block of 4, #a-d | 7.50 | 7.50 |

A979a

Serpentine Die Cut 11¼x11
2001, Feb. 6   **Litho.**   **Self-Adhesive**
Background Color
2143E	A979a	10c blue grn	.25	.25
2143F	A979a	25c brt green	.65	.55
2143G	A979a	60c orange	1.40	1.40
2143H	A979a	75c red	2.00	1.60
2143I	A979a	1p blue	2.60	2.10
2143J	A979a	3p red brn	8.00	6.50
2143K	A979a	3.25p yel green	8.75	7.00
2143L	A979a	5.50p rose	15.00	12.00
		Nos. 2143E-2143L (8)	38.65	31.40

Nos. 2143E-2143L are broken at right by five die cut wavy lines. Sold at Unidad Postal outlets. See Nos. 2217-2224A.

Miniature Sheet

Cenozoic Mammals — A980

No. 2144: a, Megaterio (Megatherium americanum). b, Gliptodonte (Doedicurus clavicaudatus). c, Macrauquenia (Macrauchenia patachonica). d, Toxodonte (Toxodon platensis).

2001, Mar. 10   **Perf. 13¾x13½**
| 2144 | A980 | 75c Sheet of 4, #a-d | 10.00 | 6.50 |

Antarctic Bases, 50th Anniv. — A981

Map and: No. 2145, 75c, Cormorant, Base Brown. No. 2146, 75c, Skua, Base San Martín.

Perf. 13¾x13½
2001, Mar. 24   **Litho.**
| 2145-2146 | A981 | Set of 2 | 3.50 | 2.50 |

Apiculture — A982

No. 2147: a, Bee on flower. b, Bees on honeycomb. c, Bees, apiarist, and hives. d, Honey, pollen.

2001, Apr. 7   **Perf. 13½x13¼**
| 2147 | | Block of 4 | 9.00 | 6.50 |
| a.-d. | A982 | 75c Any single | 1.60 | 1.00 |

Souvenir Sheet

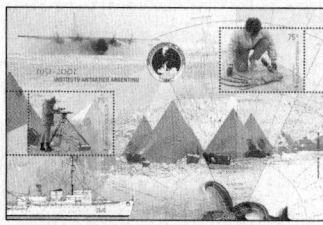

Argentine Antarctic Institute, 50th
Anniv. — A983

No. 2148: a, Scientist with fossils. b, Scientist with mapping equipment.

2001, Apr. 21   **Perf. 14**
| 2148 | A983 | 75c Sheet of 2, #a-b | 5.00 | 5.00 |

Spain to Argentina Flight of Plus Ultra
Seaplane, 75th Anniv. — A984

2001, Apr. 28   **Perf. 13¾x13½**
| 2149 | A984 | 75c multi | 1.75 | 1.25 |

Art in Silver — A985

No. 2150: a, Bridle (Freno). b, Stirrups (Estribos). c, Spurs (Espuelas). d, Gaucho's ornament (Rastra).

2001, May 19   **Litho.**   **Perf. 13¾x13½**
| 2150 | A985 | 75c Block of 4, #a-d | 7.50 | 6.50 |

World Youth Soccer
Championships — A986

Designs: No. 2151, 75c, Player kicking ball. No. 2152, 75c, Goalie catching ball.

2001, June 16
| 2151-2152 | A986 | Set of 2 | 3.25 | 2.50 |

Souvenir Sheet

Belgica 2001 Intl. Stamp Exhibition,
Brussels — A987

No. 2153: a, 25c, Washerwoman by the Banks of the Belgrano, by Prilidiano Pueyrredón. b, 75c, The Hay Harvest, by Pieter Breughel, the Elder.

2001, June 16   *Perf. 14*
2153 A987   Sheet of 2, #a-b   3.50 2.50

2001 Census — A988

Perf. 13½x13¾ Syncopated
2001, July 14
2154 A988 75c multi   1.75 1.00

SAC-C Satellite, Birds and Flowers A989

2001, July 14   *Perf. 13¾x13½*
2155 A989 75c multi   1.75 1.25
Environmental protection.

Bandoneón Recital — 1990, by Aldo Severi — A990

2001, July 28   *Perf. 13½x13¾*
2156 A990 75c multi   1.75 1.25
The tango in art.

Souvenir Sheet

Phila Nippon '01, Japan — A991

No. 2157: a, Tango dancers, musical score. b, Kabuki dancer.

2001, July 28   *Perf. 14*
2157 A991 75c Sheet of 2, #a-b   5.00 3.50
Exists imperf. Value, pair $200.

Miniature Sheet

Wild Cats — A992

No. 2158: a, 25c, Puma. b, 25c, Jaguar. c, 50c, Jaguarundi and young. d, 50c, Ocelot. e, 75c, Mountain cat. f, 75c, Huiña.

2001, July 28   *Perf. 13¾x13½*
2158 A992   Sheet of 6, #a-f,
      +2 labels   9.00 6.50

Enrique Santos Discépolo (1901-51), Tango Lyricist — A993

2001, Aug. 4   *Perf. 13½x13¾*
2159 A993 75c multi   2.25 1.25

America Issue — UNESCO World Heritage — A994

No. 2160 — Buildings and artifacts from Jesuit Block and Estancias of Cordoba: a, Denomination at UL. b, Denomination at UR.

2001, Aug. 11   *Perf. 13¾x13½*
2160 A994 75c Horiz. pair, #a-b   4.00 4.00

Prevention of Breast Cancer — A995

2001, Sept. 1   *Perf. 13½x13¾*
2161 A995 75c multi   1.75 1.25

World Championship Race Cars of Juan Manuel Fangio — A996

No. 2162 — Cars and track layouts: a, Alfa Romeo 159 Alfetta, Barcelona, 1951. b, Mercedes-Benz W196, Reims, France, 1954. c, Lancia-Ferrari D50, Monte Carlo, Monaco, 1956. d, Maserati 250F, Nürburgring, Germany, 1957.

2001, Oct. 6   *Perf. 13¾x13½*
2162 A996 75c Block of 4, #a-d   7.00 6.50

Politicians — A997

Designs: No. 2163, 75c, Roque Sáenz Peña (1851-1914). No. 2164, 75c, Justo José de Urquiza (1801-70).

2001, Oct. 20
2163-2164 A997   Set of 2   3.50 2.50

Bulnesia Sarmientoi A998

2001, Oct. 20 Litho.   *Perf. 13½x13¾*
2165 A998 75c multi   1.75 1.25

Souvenir Sheet

Hafnia 01 Philatelic Exhibition, Copenhagen — A999

No. 2166: a, 25c, Argentine post rider, 18th cent. b, 75c, European post rider, 17th cent.

2001, Oct. 27 Litho.   *Perf. 14*
2166 A999   Sheet of 2, #a-b   3.50 2.75

Items in Argentine Museums A1000

Designs: No. 2167, 75c, Ammonite, skeleton of Carnotaurus sastrei, from Argentine Naural Science Museum. No. 2168, 75c, Letter from Buenos Aires, stagecoach "La Pobladora," from Enrique Udaondo Graphic Museum Complex. No. 2169, 75c, Icons from

Averias culture, funerary urn from Las Mercedes culture, from Emilio and Duncan Wagner Museum of Anthropological and Natural Sciences, vert. No. 2170, 75c, Crucifix of Juan Martin de Pueyrredon, and detail, from Pueyrredon Museum, vert.

Perf. 13¾x13½, 13½x13¾
2001, Nov. 10   Litho.
2167-2170 A1000   Set of 4   7.50 6.00

Aviators and Their Airplanes A1001

Designs: No. 2171, 75c, Carola Lorenzini (1899-1941) and Focke Wulf 44-J. No. 2172, 75c, Jean Mermoz (1901-36) and "Arc-en-Ciel."

2001, Nov. 24   *Perf. 13¾x13½*
2171-2172 A1001   Set of 2   3.50 2.50
No. 2171 exists imperf. Value, pair $150.

Christmas A1002

2001, Nov. 24   *Perf. 13½x13¾*
2173 A1002 75c multi   1.75 1.25

Dances A1003

No. 2174: a, Flamenco. b, Waltz. c, Zamba. d, Tango.

Perf. 13¾x13½
2001, Nov. 29   Litho.
2174   Booklet pane of 4   8.00 —
  a.-d.   A1003 75c Any single   1.50 1.50
     Booklet, #2174   6.00

Dancers' Day A1004

2001, Dec. 1 Litho.   *Perf. 13¾x13½*
2175 A1004 75c multi   2.25 1.25

Argentine Television, 50th Anniv. — A1005

No. 2176: a, Television, camera, microphone, test pattern. b, Televisions and videotape reels. c, Television, astronaut and satellite dish. d, Televisions, cables and VCR remote control.

2001, Dec. 1   *Perf. 13¾x13½*
2176 A1005 75c Block of 4, #a-d 7.00 6.00

Argentina in the Antarctic A1006

Designs: No. 2177, 75c, Esperanza Base, 50th anniv. No. 2178, 75c, First air and sea courier service, 50th anniv.

2002, Mar. 9
2177-2178 A1006   Set of 2   3.00 2.50

America Issue — Education A1007

No. 2179: a, School and Argentine flag. b, Children playing hop scotch.

2002, Mar. 23
2179 A1007 75c Vert. pair, #a-b 3.00 2.50

Falkland Islands Birds A1008

Designs: No. 2180, 50c, Charadrius falklandicus. No. 2181, 50c, Larus scoresbii. No. 2182, 75c, Chloephaga rubidiceps, vert. No. 2183, 75c, Aptenodytes patagonicus, vert.

Perf. 13¾x13½, 13½x13¾
2002, Apr. 13   Litho.
2180-2183 A1008   Set of 4   6.00 4.00

2002 World Cup Soccer Championships, Japan and Korea — A1009

No. 2184: a, Flags, soccer ball and field (38mm diameter). b, Soccer players, years of Argentinian championships.

2002, Apr. 27   Litho.   *Perf. 12¾*
2184 A1009 75c Horiz. pair, #a-b 2.50 2.50
    See Brazil No. 2840, France No. 2891, Germany No. 2163, Italy No. 2526, Uruguay No. 1946.

Anniversaries — A1010

No. 2185, 25c: a, Rosario riverfront, Ship on Paraná River, arms. b, Rosario riverfront, National Flag Monument.
No. 2186, 50c: a, Mt. Fitzroy, Nahuel Huapi Natl. Park. b, Dr. Francisco P. Moreno.
No. 2187, 75c: a, Flower, aerial view of San Carlos de Bariloche. b, Church and town map.

2002, May 11 Litho. *Perf. 13½x13¾*
Horiz. Pairs, #a-b
2185-2187 A1010   Set of 3   6.00 4.00

Pan-American Health Organization, Cent. — A1011

2002, June 1
2188 A1011 75c multi   1.50 1.00

Doctors — A1012

No. 2189: a, Cosme Mariano Argerich (1758-1820), founder of Military Health Service. b, José María Ramos Mejía (1849-1914), psychiatric educator. c, Salvador Mazza (1886-1946), Chagas' disease specialist. d, Carlos Arturo Gianantonio (1926-95), pediatrician.

Perf. 13¾x13½   Litho.
2002, June 15
2189 A1012 50c Block of 4, #a-d 4.00 3.00

Landscapes — A1013

No. 2190: a, Seven-colored Mountain, Jujuy Province. b, Iguaçu Falls, Misiones Province. c, Talampaya Natl. Park, La Rioja Province. d, Mt. Aconcagua, Mendoza Province. e, Rose Garden, Buenos Aires. f, San Jorge Lighthouse, Chubut. g, Perito Moreno Glacier, Santa Cruz Province. h, Lapataia Bay, Tierra del Fuego Province.

2002, July 29   *Perf. 14x13½*
2190   Block of 8   12.00 6.00
  a.-h. A1013 75c Any single   1.50 .60

Eva Perón (1919-52) A1014

No. 2191: a, Official portrait. b, Embossed profile. c, At microphone. d, Painting by Nicolas Garcia Uriburu.

Litho., Litho & Embossed (#2191b)
2002, July 27   *Perf. 13½x13¾*
2191   Horiz. strip of 4   6.00 4.00
  a.-d. A1014 75c Any single   1.25 .60

Worldwide Fund for Nature (WWF) — A1015

No. 2192: a, Ozotoceros bezoarticus. b, Vicugna vicugna. c, Pudu puda. d, Catagonus wagneri.

2002, July 27 Litho. *Perf. 13¾x13½*
2192 A1015 $1 Block of 4, #a-d 6.00 4.50

Souvenir Sheet

Philakorea 2002 World Stamp Exhibition, Seoul — A1016

No. 2193: a, Argentine soccer player (blue and white shirt). b, Korean soccer player (red shirt).

2002, Aug. 10   *Perf. 14*
2193 A1016 1.50p Sheet of 2,
        #a-b   6.00 4.50

Sports — A1016a

10c, Cycling. 25c, Tennis. 50c, Auto racing. 75c, Parachuting. 1p, Horse racing. 2p, Golf. 5p, Sailing.

Perf. 13½x13¾ Syncopated
2002, Sept. 6   Litho.
2193C A1016a 10c multi 1.50 .25
2193D A1016a 25c multi 1.50 .25
2193E A1016a 50c multi 1.50 .30
2193F A1016a 75c multi 2.60 .50
2193G A1016a 1p multi 2.60 .70
2193H A1016a 2p multi 4.50 1.40
2193I A1016a 5p multi 6.50 3.50
  Nos. 2193C-2193I (7)   20.70 6.90

Nos. 2193C-2193I were sold only to customers who met certain mailing requirements but could be used on mail by anyone without restrictions.

Valdés Peninsula Tourism — A1017

Whale breaching: a, Head. b, Tail.

2002, Sept. 14   *Perf. 13½x13¾*
2194 A1017 75c Horiz. pair, #a-b 1.75 1.75

Insects A1018

Designs: 25c, Edessa meditabunda. 50c, Elaechlora viridis. 75c, Chrysodina aurata. 1p, Steirastoma breve.

2002, Sept. 21   *Perf. 13¾x13½*
2195-2198 A1018   Set of 4   4.00 3.00

Men's Volleyball World Championships A1019

Various players with background colors of: No. 2199, 75c, Blue green (shown). No. 2200, 75c, Light blue. No. 2201, 75c, Yellow green. No. 2202, 75c, Orange.

Perf. 13½x13¾
2002, Sept. 28 A1019 Set of 4   Litho.
2199-2202 A1019   Set of 4   3.50 2.50
On Nos. 2199-2202 portions of the design were applied by a thermographic process producing a shiny, raised effect.

Argentine Highway Association, 50th Anniv. — A1020

2002, Oct. 5   *Perf. 13¾x13½*
2203 A1020 75c multi   .90 .60

Argentine Personalities — A1021

Designs: No. 2204, 75c, Roberto Arlt (1900-42), novelist. No. 2205, 75c, Beatriz Guido (1924-88), writer. No. 2206, 75c, Niní Marshall (1903-96), actress. No. 2207, 75c, Luis Sandrini (1905-80), actor.

2002, Oct. 19
2204-2207 A1021   Set of 4   3.50 2.50

Immigrant Agricultural Colonies A1022

Flags of France, Switzerland, Spain and Italy and: a, Hotel for immigrants, mother and son, stamped passport. b, Two immigrants and ship. c, Two immigrants, Provisory Hotel for immigrants, French immigrant instruction book. d, Farmer plowing field, family of immigrants.

2002, Oct. 19   Litho.   Perf. 13½x13¾
2208   Horiz. strip of 4   3.00 3.00
a.-d.   A1022 75c Any single   .90   .50

Argentine Federation of Philatelic Entities, 50th Anniv. — A1023

Designs: No. 2209, 75c, Stamped cover, stagecoach, EXFICEC '56 exhibition cancel, Head of Ceres from Corrientes issue. No. 2210, 75c, ESPAMER '98 Cancel, postman, ship and map, coat of arms.

2002, Nov. 2   Perf. 13¾x13½
2209-2210 A1023   Set of 2   2.00 1.00

Christmas — A1024

2002, Nov. 16
2211 A1024 75c multi   .90   .50

Folk Musicians A1025

Designs: No. 2212, 75c, Gustavo "Cuchi" Leguizamón (1917-2000). No. 2213, 75c, Armando Tejada Gómez (1929-92). No. 2214, 75c, Carlos Vega (1898-1966). No. 2215, 75c, Andrés Chazarreta (1876-1960).

2002, Dec. 7   Perf. 13½x13¾
2212-2215 A1025   Set of 4   3.00 1.50

Puppets A1026

No. 2216: a, Marionette of woman. b, King and fish hand puppets. c, Rod puppet of man. d, Shadow theater.

2002, Dec. 7   Perf. 13¾x13½
2216   Booklet pane of 4   3.00 1.50
a.-d.   A1026 75c Any single   .90   .50
    Booklet, #2216   3.50

Unidad Postal Type of 2001
Perf. 13¾x13½ Syncopated
2002   Litho.
Size: 35x24mm (10p, 35x25mm)
Background Color
2217 A979a 10c blue green   .25   .25
2218 A979a 25c brt green   .50   .35
2219 A979a 50c tan   1.00   .50
2220 A979a 75c red   1.50   .75
2221 A979a 1p blue   2.25 1.00
2222 A979a 2p gray   4.50 1.50
2223 A979a 3p brown   5.50 1.75
2224 A979a 5p olive bister   8.50 2.25
2224A A979a 10p yellow   17.00 3.00
    Nos. 2217-2224A (9)   41.00 11.35

Issue dates: Nos. 2217-2224, 6/02; 10p, 8/16/02.
Nos. 2217-2224A were sold only at Unidad Postal outlets.

Communal Vegetable Gardens — A1027

Designs: No. 2225, 75c, Cabbage. No.2226, 75c, Corn, vert.

Perf. 13¾x13½, 13½x13¾
2003, Mar. 8
2225-2226 A1027   Set of 2   1.50   .75

Native Handicrafts — A1028

Designs: No. 2227, 75c, Sieve, by Mbyá people, fork and spoon by Wichi people. No. 2228, 75c, Woven waistband of Pilagal'ek people, Bag by Nam Qom people.

2003, Mar. 8   Perf. 13¾x13½
2227-2228 A1028   Set of 2   1.50   .75

National Parks — A1029

Animals and parks: No. 2229, 50c, Lama guanicoe, Los Cardones National Park. No. 2230, 50c, Piaya cayana, Colonia Benítez Natural Reserve. No. 2231, 50c, Mazama gouazoupira, Copo National Park. No. 2232, 75c, Tinamotis pentlandii, Campo de los Alisos National Park. No. 2233, 75c, Spheniscus magellanicus, Monte León, planned National Park.

2003, Mar. 22   Perf. 14x13½
2229-2233 A1029   Set of 5   3.50 2.00

Paintings A1030

Designs: No. 2234, 25c, Composición con Trapo Rejilla, by Kenneth Kemble. No. 2235, 25c, Pintura, by Roberto Aizenberg, vert. 50c, Pantalla, by Rómulo Macció, vert. No. 2237, 75c, La Giaconda, by Guillermo Roux. No. 2238, 75c, Hacerse Humo, by Antonio Seguí. 1p, San P., by Xul Solar (with attached label).

Perf. 13¾x13½, 13½x13¾
2003, Apr. 12
2234-2239 A1030   Set of 6   3.50 1.75

Nos. 2234-2238 were each printed in sheets of 4; No. 2239 was printed in sheets of 2 + 2 labels.

Argentina, Champions of 2002 Intl. Sporting Events — A1031

Designs: No. 2240, 75c, Women's field hockey. No. 2241, 75c, Soccer for blind players.

Litho., Litho. & Embossed (#2241)
2003, May 3   Perf. 13¾x13½
2240-2241 A1031   Set of 2   1.75 1.00

Comic Strips — A1032

No. 2242: a, 25c, Mago Fafa, by Alberto Bróccoli. b, 25c, Astronaut, by Crist (Cristóbal Reinoso). c, 50c, Hijitus, by Manuel García Ferré. d, 50c, Savarese, by Domingo Mandrafina and Robin Wood. e, 75c, Sónoman, by Oswal (Oswaldo Walter Viola). f, 75c, El Tipito, by Daniel Paz and Rudy (Marcelo E. Rudaeff). g, 75c, La Vaca Aurora, by Domingo Mirco Repetto. h, 75c, Diógenes y el Linyera, by Tabaré (Gómez Laborde), Jorge Guinzberg and Carlos Abrevaya.

2003, May 17   Litho.   Perf. 13½x13¾
2242 A1032   Sheet of 8, #a-h   5.00 5.00

Silver Tableware — A1033

No. 2243: a, Soup bowl with lid (sopera). b, Kettle and burner, maté kettle and drinking tube. c, Chocolate pot and jar with handle. d, Sugar bowl (azucarera).

2003, May 24   Perf. 13¾x13½
2243 A1033 75c Block of 4, #a-d 3.00 3.00

Food — A1034

Designs: Nos. 2244a, 2245a, Empanadas (red denomination). Nos. 2244b, 2245b, Locro (orange denomination) Nos. 2244c, 2246a, Parrillada (green denomination) Nos. 2244d, 2246b, Pastelitos (blue denomination).

2003, June 7   Perf. 13¾x13½
2244 A1034 75c Vert strip of 4,
    #a-d, + 4 labels   3.00 3.00

Booklet Panes
Perf. 14
2245 A1034 75c Pane of 2, #a-b,
    + 2 labels   2.50 2.00
2246 A1034 75c Pane of 2, #a-b,
    + 2 labels   2.50 2.00
    Complete booklet, #2245-2246   5.50

Size of stamps in booklet panes: 40x30mm.

Miniature Sheet

Children's Games — A1035

No. 2247: a, El Elástico. b, La escondida (hide and seek). c, La mancha (tag). d, Martín Pescador.

2003, July 12   Perf. 13¾x13½
2247 A1035 50c Sheet of 4, #a-d 2.50 2.50

Landscapes — A1036

No. 2248: a, Mbiguá Marsh, Formosa Province. b, Dead Man's Salt Flats, Catamarca Province. c, Quilmes Ruins, Tucumán Province. d, Iberá Marshes, Corrientes Province. e, Ischigualasto Provincial Park, San Juan Province. f, Mar del Plata, Buenos Aires Province. g, Caleu Caleu Department, La Pampa Province. h, Lanín National Park, Nequén Province.

2003, July 19   Perf. 14x13¾
2248 A1036 75c Block of 8, #a-h   6.00 6.00

Opening of Nuestra Señora del Rosario Bridge and Roadway, Rosario-Victoria — A1037

No. 2249: a, 25c, Bridge, map of roadway. b, 75c, Bridge and cross-section.

Perf. 13½x13¾

2003, Aug. 23				Litho.
2249	A1037	Horiz. pair, #a-b	1.25	1.25

Argentine History A1038

Designs: No. 2250, 75c, Dr. Vicente Fidel López (1815-1903), Education minister, headquarters of Province of Buenos Aires Bank. No. 2251, 75c, First page of constitution, medal and signature of Juan Bautista Alberdi. No. 2252, 75c, Emblem and squadron of General San Martín Mounted Grenadiers Regiment. No. 2253, 75c, Presidential sash and staff, Casa Rosada. No. 2254, 75c, Arms of Río Negro Province, vert.

Perf. 13¾x13½, 13½x13¾

2003, Sept. 6				
2250-2254	A1038	Set of 5	4.00	2.00

Constitution, 150th anniv. (No. 2251), Revival of General San Martín Mounted Grenadiers Regiment, cent. (No. 2252), Presidential inauguration (No. 2253).

Souvenir Sheet

Bangkok 2003 World Philatelic Exhibition — A1039

No. 2255: a, Quebrada de Humahuacha black demon mask, Argentine flag. b, Phi Ta Khon Festival mask, Thailand flag.

Litho. with Foil Application

2003, Oct. 4				Perf. 14
2255	A1039	75c Sheet of 2, #a-b	1.50	1.50

America Issue — Flora and Fauna A1040

Designs: No. 2256, 75c, Nothofagus pumilio. No. 2257, 75c, Vultur gryphus.

2003, Oct. 11	Litho.	Perf. 13¾x13½
2256-2257	A1040	Set of 2	2.00	1.00

Jubany Base, Antarctica, 50th Anniv. — A1041

2003, Oct. 18				
2258	A1041	75c multi	1.00	.50

Rescue of Swedish Scientific Expedition by A. R. A. Uruguay, Cent. — A1042

Designs: No. 2259, Welcome, (ship and penguins) by Eduardo De Martino. No. 2260: a, A. R. A. Uruguay. b, A. R. A. Uruguay and Lt. Julián Irízar.

2003, Oct. 18		Perf. 13¾x13½
2259	A1042	75c multi	1.00	.50

Souvenir Sheet
Perf. 14

2260	A1042	75c Sheet of 2, #a-b	1.50	1.50

No. 2260 contains two 40x30mm stamps.

Agricultural and Industrial Products — A1043

Designs: No. 2261, 75c, Cattle. No. 2262, 75c, Soybeans. No. 2263, 75c, Aluminum. No. 2264, 75c, Teradi 800 cobalt therapy machine.

2003, Oct. 18		Perf. 13¾x13½
2261-2264	A1043	Set of 4	3.00	1.50

Christmas A1044

Designs: No. 2265, 75c, Purmamarca clay creche figures. No. 2266, 75c, Gaucho Birth, carved wood creche figures by Eloy López.

2003, Nov. 8		Perf. 13½x13¾
2265-2266	A1044	Set of 2	1.50	.75

20th Century Architecture A1045

Designs: No. 2267, 75c, Barolo Palace, Buenos Aires, by Mario Palanti, 1923. No.

2268, 75c, Tucumán Province Bank Building, San Miguel de Tucumán, by Alejandro Virasoro, 1928. No. 2269, 75c, Córdoba Province Savings Bank Building, Córdoba, by Jaime Roca, 1929. No. 2270, 75c, Minetti Palace, Rosario, by Juan B. Durand, Leopoldo Schwarz and José Gerbino, 1930.

2003, Nov. 8				
2267-2270	A1045	Set of 4	3.00	1.50

Orcadas Base, Antarctica, Cent. — A1046

Designs: No. 2271, Helicopter, Orcadas Base. No. 2272: a, #127 with 1904 South Orcadas cancel, vert. b, Meteorological observatory and weather vane.

2004, Feb. 21		Perf. 13¾x13½
2271	A1046	75c multi	1.00	.50

Souvenir Sheet
Perf. 14

2272	A1046	75c Sheet of 2, #a-b	2.50	2.50

No. 2272 contains one 30x40mm and one 40x30mm stamp.

Quebrada de Humahuaca UNESCO World Heritage Site — A1047

No. 2273 — View of Rio Grande Valley and: a, Decorated llama, rock painting, person in front of door. b, Santa Rosa de Lima Church, costumed carnival participants.

2004, Mar. 27		Perf. 13½x13¾
2273	A1047	75c Horiz. pair, #a-b	1.50	.75

America Issue — Forest Conservation — A1048

No. 2274 — Forest and timeline charting hectares of forest with years: a, 1914, 1956. b, 1989, 2004.

2004, Mar. 27		
2274	A1048	75c Horiz. pair, #a-b	1.50	.75

No. 2274b has large hole in center of stamp.

La Voz del Interior Newspaper, Cent. — A1049

2004, Apr. 17		Perf. 13¾x13½
2275	A1049	75c multi	.75	.40

Landscapes — A1050

No. 2276: a, Molinos, Salta Province. b, Pampa del Indio Provincial Park, Chaco Province. c, Rio Hondo Dam, Santiago del Estera Province. d, Bridge, Santa Fe de la Vera Cruz, Santa Fe Province. e, San Roque Lake, Córdoba Province. f, El Palmar National Park, Entre Rios Province. g, Potrero de los Funes, San Luis Province. h, Mt. Tronador, Río Negro Province.

2004, Apr. 17		Perf. 14x13½
2276	A1050	75c Block of 8, #a-h	6.00	6.00

FIFA (Fédération Internationale de Football Association), Cent. — A1051

Paintings of soccer players by Rubén Ramonda: No. 2277, 75c, The Tunnel (blue background). No. 2278, 75c, El Picado (orange background).

2004, May 22	Litho.	Perf. 13¾x13½
2277-2278	A1051	Set of 2	1.50	.75

Souvenir Sheet

España 2004 World Philatelic Exhibition — A1052

No. 2279: a, Return of the Fishing Fleet, by Joaquín Sorolla y Bastida. b, A Stop in the Pampas, by Angel Della Valle, vert.

2004, May 22		Perf. 14
2279	A1052	75c Sheet of 2, #a-b	1.75	1.75

Naval Hydrographic Service, 125th Anniv. — A1053

No. 2280 — Nautical chart and: a, Binnacle. b, Sextant. c, Cabo Vírgenes Lighthouse. d, Oceanographic ship Puerto Deseado.

2004, June 5		Perf. 13¾x13½
2280	A1053	75c Block of 4, #a-d	3.00	3.00

Printed in sheets of four blocks separated by a central column of labels.

Souvenir Sheet

Circus — A1054

No. 2281: a, Trained dogs. b, Clown on stilts, trapeze artist. c, Clown juggling on unicycle. d, Bareback rider.

2004, June 12
2281 A1054 50c Sheet of 4, #a-d 2.50 2.50

Characters From Comic Strip "Patoruzito," by Dante Quinterno — A1055

No. 2282: a, 25c, Isidorito. b, 25c, Upita. c, 50c, Patoruzito. d, 50c, Malén. e, 75c, Pamperito. f, 75c, Chacha.
No. 2283: a, Patoruzito (20x60mm). b, Pamperito (20x60mm). c, Isidorito (30x30mm)
No. 2284: a, Malén (30x40mm). b, Upita (30x40mm). c, Chacha (30x40mm)

2004, July 10 Litho. Perf. 13½x13¾
2282 A1055   Sheet of 6 + 2 labels   3.50 3.50

Booklet Panes
Perf. 14
2283	Booklet pane of 3 + label	2.50	2.50
a.-c.	A1055 75c Any single	.75	.45
2284	Booklet pane of 3 + label	2.50	2.50
a.-c.	A1055 75c Any single	.75	.45
	Complete booklet, #2283-2284	5.50	

Fish of the Falkland Islands Area A1056

Designs: No. 2285, 75c, Salilota australis. No. 2286, 75c, Patagonotothen ramsayi. No. 2287, 75c, Dissostichus eleginoides. No. 2288, 75c, Bathyraja griseocauda.

2004, July 17 Litho. Perf. 13¾x13½
2285-2288 A1056   Set of 4   3.00 1.50

Assistance Dogs — A1057

Designs: No. 2289, 75c, Rescue dog. No. 2290, 75c, Seeing-eye dog, vert.

Perf. 13¾x13½, 13½x13¼
2004, July 17
2289-2290 A1057   Set of 2   1.50 .75

2004 Summer Olympics, Athens — A1058

No. 2291: a, Cycling. b, Judo. c, Swimming. d, Tennis.

2004, Aug. 7   Perf. 13¾x13½
2291 A1058 75c Block of 4, #a-d 3.00 3.00

Legends A1059

Designs: No. 2292, 75c, El Pehuén. No. 2293, 75c, La Yacumama. No. 2294, 75c, La Pachamama. No. 2295, 75c, La Difunta Correa.

2004, Aug. 21
2292-2295 A1059   Set of 4   4.00 2.00

Souvenir Sheet

World Stamp Championship 2004, Singapore — A1060

No. 2296: a, Mangifera indica. b, Syagrus romanzoffiana.

2004, Aug. 21   Perf. 14
2296 A1060 75c Sheet of 2, #a-b 2.00 2.00

Centenaries — A1061

Designs: No. 2297, 75c, Agronomy and Veterinary Science Institute for Higher Learning, Buenos Aires. No. 2298, 75c, City of Neuquén. No. 2299, 75c, Philatelic Association of Rosario.

2004, Sept. 11   Perf. 13¾x13½
2297-2299 A1061   Set of 3   2.00 1.00

Prevention of Uterine Cancer A1062

2004, Sept. 18   Perf. 13½x13¾
2300 A1062 75c multi   .70 .35

Preservation of Water Resources — A1063

No. 2301: a, Hourglass with clean water. b, Hourglass with polluted water.

2004, Sept. 18   Perf. 13¾x13½
2301 A1063 75c Vert. tete beche
                    pair, #a-b   1.50 .75

Landmarks in Argentina — A1063a

Designs: 25c, Ruins of San Ignacio Miní, Misiones Province. 50c, Iruya. 1p, Buenos Aires. 2p, Aconcagua Provincial Park. 3p, Valdes Peninsula. 5p, Mina Clavero. 10p, Ushuaia.

Perf. 13¾x13½ Syncopated
2004, Sept. 24   Litho.
2301C	A1063a	25c multi	.25	.25
2301D	A1063a	50c multi	.35	.35
2301E	A1063a	1p multi	.70	.70
2301F	A1063a	2p multi	1.40	1.40
2301G	A1063a	3p multi	2.10	2.10
2301H	A1063a	5p multi	3.50	3.50
j.		With label	2.60	2.60
2301I	A1063a	10p multi	6.75	6.75
	Nos. 2301D-2301I (6)		14.80	14.80

Issued: No. 2301Hj, 5/11/10.
See Nos. 2357, 2586-2587, 2678-2679.

The Nativity A1064

Virgin Mary — A1065

2004, Oct. 16 Litho. Perf. 13½x13¾
2302 A1064 75c multi   .65 .35
2303 A1065 75c multi   .65 .35
Christmas, Stained glass windows, St. Felicitas Church, Buenos Aires.

Numismatics — A1066

No. 2304 — Halves of 1813 silver 1 real coin and 1813 gold 8 escudos coin: a, Obverse (sun). b, Reverse (coat of arms).

2004, Oct. 23
2304 A1066 75c Horiz. pair, #a-b 1.25 1.25

Andrés Bello and Front Page of Spanish Grammar for Americans — A1067

2004, Nov. 6   Perf. 13¾x13½
2305 A1067 75c multi   .70 .35
Third Intl. Spanish Language Congress, Rosario.

Buenos Aires Commodities Exchange, 150th Anniv. — A1068

2004, Nov. 6
2306 A1068 75c multi   .70 .35

Medicinal Plants A1069

Designs: No. 2307, 75c, Aloysia citriodora. No. 2308, 75c, Minthostachys mollis. No. 2309, 75c, Lippia turbinata. No. 2310, 75c, Tagetes minuta.

2004, Nov. 20   Perf. 13½x13¾
2307-2310 A1069   Set of 4   2.50 1.25

12th Pan-American Scout Jamboree — A1070

2005, Jan. 15   Perf. 13¾x13½
2311 A1070 75c multi   .70 .35

Argentina — Thailand Diplomatic Relations, 50th Anniv. A1071

Designs: No. 2312, 75c, Tango dancers, Argentina. No. 2313, 75c, Tom-tom dancers, Thailand.

2005, Feb. 5   **Perf. 13½x13¾**
2312-2313 A1071   Set of 2   1.40   .40

Paintings by Antonio Berni (1905-81) A1072

Designs: No. 2314, Woman with a Red Sweater.
No. 2315 — Details from Manifestation: a, 75c, Bearded man, man looking up (40x50mm). b, 75c, Child, two men with hats in foreground, horiz. (50x40mm).

2005, Mar. 12   **Perf. 13½x13¾**
2314 A1072 75c shown   .70   .35
     Souvenir Sheet
     Perf. 14
2315 A1072   Sheet of 2, #a-b   1.75 1.75

Rotary International, Cent. — A1073

2005, Mar. 19   **Perf. 13¾x13½**
2316 A1073 75c multi   .80   .40

Writers A1074

Designs: No. 2317, 75c, Silvina Ocampo (1903-93). No. 2318, 75c, Ezequiel Martínez Estrada (1895-1964).

2005, Mar. 19   **Perf. 13½x13¾**
2317-2318 A1074   Set of 2   1.40   .70

Argentine Motor Vehicles — A1075

Designs: No. 2319, 75c, Graciela sedan. No. 2320, 75c, Justicialista Sport. No. 2321, 75c, Rastrojero Diesel truck. No. 2322, 75c,

Siam Di Tella 1500. No. 2323, 75c, Torino 380 W.

2005, Apr. 9 Litho.   **Perf. 13¾x13½**
2319-2323 A1075   Set of 5   3.50 1.75

A portion of the design of each stamp is coated with a glossy varnish.

Intl. Year of Physics A1076

Designs: No. 2324, 75c, José Antonio Balseiro, founder of Balseiro Institute, nuclear reactor. No. 2325, 75c, Albert Einstein, front page of Einstein's theory of relativity.

2005, Apr. 23 Litho.   **Perf. 13¾x13½**
2324-2325 A1076   Set of 2   1.40   .70

Balseiro Institute, 50th anniv.

Pope John Paul II (1920-2005) A1077

Designs: No. 2326, Pope waving.
No. 2327: a, Pope with crucifix, Papal arms. b, Pope and crowd.

2005, Apr. 23   **Perf. 13½x13¾**
2326 A1077 75c shown   1.25   .60
     Souvenir Sheet
     Perf. 14
2327 A1077 75c Sheet of 2, #a-b 2.75 2.75

No. 2327 contains two 40x50mm stamps.

General Workers Confederation, 75th Anniv. A1078

La Capital Newspaper, Mar del Plata, Cent. — A1079

Sunday Blue Law No. 4661, Cent. — A1080

2005, May 21 Litho.   **Perf. 13½x13¾**
2328 A1078 75c multi   .70   .35
2329 A1079 75c multi   .70   .35
2330 A1080 75c multi   .70   .35
   Nos. 2328-2330 (3)   2.10 1.05

César Milstein (1927-2002), 1984 Nobel Laureate in Physiology or Medicine — A1081

2005, June 4   **Perf. 13¾x13½**
2331 A1081 75c multi   .70   .35

Volunteer Firefighters A1082

Designs: No. 2332, 75c, Orestes Liberti (1860-1936), first commander of volunteer firefighter brigade, horse-drawn fire engine. No. 2333, 75c, Fire fighters in action, fire truck.

2005, June 4   **Perf. 13½x13¾**
2332-2333 A1082   Set of 2   1.40   .70

Argentine Red Cross, 125th Anniv. — A1083

2005, June 11   **Perf. 13¾x13½**
2334 A1083 75c multi   .70   .35

Juan Filloy (1894-2000), Writer — A1084

2005, July 16
2335 A1084 75c multi   .70   .35

Miniature Sheet

Cats — A1085

No. 2336: a, 25c, Birman. b, 25c, Siamese. c, 50c, Oriental. d, 50c, Persian. e, 75c, Abyssinian. f, 75c, European.

2005, July 16
2336 A1085   Sheet of 6, #a-f, +   2 labels   3.00 3.00

Wine Regions — A1086

Glass of wine, map, vineyard in: No. 2337, 75c, Salta Province, Torrontés grapes. No. 2338, 75c, Mendoza Province, Malbec grapes. No. 2339, 75c, San Juan Province, Syrah grapes. No. 2340, 75c, Río Negro Province, Merlot grapes.

2005, July 16   **Perf. 14x13½**
2337-2340 A1086   Set of 4   2.75 1.40

Historic Houses of Worship A1087

Designs: No. 2341, 75c, Our Lady of the Rosary of Candonga Chapel, Sierra Chicas. No. 2342, 75c, Al Ahmad Mosque, Buenos Aires. No. 2343, 75c, Temple of the Israelite Congregation, Buenos Aires. No. 2344, 75c, Vision of the Middle Buddhist Temple, Buenos Aires.

2005, Aug. 6   **Perf. 13¾x13½**
2341-2344 A1087   Set of 4   2.75 1.40

Local Grocery Stores A1088

Designs: No. 2345, 75c, Pulpería de Cacho di Catarina, Mercedes. No. 2346, 75c, Pulpería El Torito, Baradero. No. 2347, 75c, Pulpería Perucho, General Lavalle. No. 2348, 75c, Pulpería Impini, Larroque.

2005, Sept. 10
2345-2348 A1088   Set of 4   2.75 1.40

Antarctic Science A1089

Designs: No. 2349, Iceberg, Antarctic Treaty emblem

No. 2350: a, Major General Hernán Pujato and members of First Argentine Polar Expedition air crew. b, Divers, raft, iceberg.

2005, Sept. 24   *Perf. 13¾x13½*
2349 A1089 75c multi   .90 .45

Souvenir Sheet
Perf. 14
2350 A1089 75c Sheet of 2, #a-b 3.00 3.00
No. 2350 contains two 40x30mm stamps.

Colón Theater Companies, 80th Anniv. — A1090

No. 2351: a, Dancer Julio Bocca, ballet dancers, Colón Theater building. b, Orchestra, choir, opera singers.

2005, Sept. 24   *Perf. 13½x13¾*
2351 A1090 75c Horiz. pair, #a-b 1.40 .70

Alternative Energy Sources A1091

Designs: 75c, Solar power. 4p, Wind power.

2005, Oct. 15
2352-2353 A1091 Set of 2   4.00 2.00

Christmas A1092

Details from altarpiece by Elena Storni: No. 2354, Madonna and Child.

No. 2355: a, The Annunciation, Mary and Elizabeth. b, Nativity. c, Magi. d, Presentation of Jesus in the Temple.

2005, Oct. 15   *Perf. 13½x13¾*
2354 A1092 75c shown   .70 .35

Souvenir Sheet
Perf. 14
2355 A1092 75c Sheet of 4, #a-d 3.00 3.00
No. 2355 contains four 40x40mm stamps.

Fourth Summit of the Americas, Mar del Plata — A1093

2005, Oct. 29   Litho.   *Perf. 13¾x13½*
2356 A1093 75c multi   .70 .35

Landmarks Type of 2004

Design: Perito Moreno Glacier

Perf. 13¾x13½ Syncopated
2005, Nov. 18
2357 A1063a 4p multi   3.50 3.50

Immigrants to Argentina — A1095

Designs: No. 2358, 75c, German immigrants in Cañada de Gómez, bandoneon. No. 2359, 75c, Slovakian immigrants in Buenos Aires, weather indicator. No. 2360, 75c, Welsh immigrants, Chubut Central Railway train, railway lantern. No. 2361, 75c, Jewish settlers, Moisés Ville, wheat.

2005, Nov. 19   *Perf. 13¾x13½*
2358-2361 A1095 Set of 4   3.00 1.50

Boxers A1096

Designs: No. 2362, 75c, Lius Angel Firpo (1894-1960). No. 2363, 75c, Nicolino Locche (1939-2005).

2005, Dec. 17   *Perf. 13½x13¾*
2362-2363 A1096 Set of 2   1.40 .70

Argentine Design — A1097

Designs: No. 2364, 75c, Image and sound design. No. 2365, 75c, Clothes and textile design, vert. No. 2366, 75c, Industrial design, vert. No. 2367, 75c, Graphic design.

Perf. 13¾x13½, 13½x13¾
2005, Dec. 17
2364-2367 A1097 Set of 4   3.00 1.50

Pres. Bartolomé Mitre (1821-1906) — A1098

2006, Jan. 21   *Perf. 13¾x13½*
2368 A1098 75c multi   .70 .35

Esquel, Cent. A1099

2006, Feb. 18
2369 A1099 75c multi   .70 .35

Wine Producing Regions — A1100

No. 2370: a, Merlot grapes and wine, Alto Valle, Río Negro (70x30mm). b, Wine flowing from vat (50x30mm).

No. 2371: a, Wine barrels (50x30mm). b, Torrontés grapes and wine, Cafayate, Salta (70x30mm).

No. 2372: a, Grape harvesters (50x30mm). b, Syrah grapes and wine, Valle del Zonda, San Juan (70x30mm).

No. 2373: a, Malbec grapes and wine, Valle del Tupungato, Mendoza (70x30mm). b, Wine in glass and bottle (50x30mm).

2006, Mar. 3   Litho.   **Perf. 14**
2370	A1100	Booklet pane of 2	4.00	—
a.		50c multi	.40	.25
b.		3.50p multi	3.00	1.50
		Complete booklet, #2370	4.50	
2371	A1100	Booklet pane of 2	4.00	—
a.		75c multi	.65	.35
b.		3.25p multi	2.75	1.40
		Complete booklet, #2371	4.50	
2372	A1100	Booklet pane of 2	4.00	—
a.		1p multi	.90	.45
b.		3p multi	2.75	1.40
		Complete booklet, #2372	4.50	
2373	A1100	Booklet pane of 2	5.00	—
a.		1.25p multi	1.50	.85
b.		2.75p multi	3.25	1.75
		Complete booklet, #2373	5.50	
		Nos. 2370-2373 (4)	17.00	

Dr. Ramón Carrillo (1906-56), Neurologist — A1101

Perf. 13¾x13½
2006, Mar. 11   Litho.
2374 A1101 75c multi   .70 .35

Musical Instruments A1102

Designs: 75c, Charango. 3.50p, Drum.

2006, Mar. 11   *Perf. 13½x13¾*
2375-2376 A1102 Set of 2   4.00 2.00

Miniature Sheet

Lighthouses — A1103

No. 2377: a, Primero de Mayo. b, Año Nuevo. c, El Rincón. d, Recalada a Bahía Blanca.

2006, Mar. 18
2377 A1103 75c Sheet of 4, #a-d 3.00 3.00

Souvenir Sheet

Start of Military Dictatorship, 30th Anniv. — A1104

No. 2378: a, Man, left side of Navy Mechanics School. b, Flower, right side of Navy Mechanics School.

2006, Mar. 25   **Perf. 14**
2378 A1104 75c Sheet of 2, #a-b 1.50 1.50

Silver Religious Objects — A1105

No. 2379: a, Crown. b, Candelabra. c, Chalice. d, Viaticum.

2006, Apr. 8   *Perf. 13¾x13½*
2379 A1105 75c Block of 4, #a-d 3.00 3.00

Auto
Racing
A1106

Races and winning automobiles: No. 2380, 75c, Rally Nacional A8, Toyota Corolla WRC. No. 2381, 75c, Turismo Carretera, Ford Falcon. No. 2382, 75c, Turismo Competición 2000, Ford Focus. No. 2383, 75c, Class 3 Turismo Nacional, Ford Escort.

2006, May 6
2380-2383 A1106 Set of 4 3.00 1.50

Miniature Sheet

Dogs — A1107

No. 2384: a, 25c, Springer spaniel. b, 25c, Yorkshire terrier. c, 50c, Argentino dog. d, 50c, Miniature schnauzer. e, 75c, Poodle. f. 75c, Chow chow.

2006, May 20
2384 A1107 Sheet of 6 #a-f, +
2 labels 3.00 3.00

A1108

2006 World Cup Soccer
Championships — A1109

No. 2386: a, Serbia & Montenegro player. b, Argentina player, blue and white background. No. 2387: a, Ivory Coast player. b, Netherlands player.

2006, May 20 Litho. Perf. 13¾x13½
2385 A1108 4p shown 3.75 3.75

Booklet Panes
Perf. 14¼

2386 Pane of 2 2.25 —
a.-b. A1109 1p Either single 1.00 .70
2387 Pane of 2 2.25 —
a.-b. A1109 1p Either single 1.00 .70
Complete booklet, #2386-2387 5.00

Souvenir Sheet

2388 A1109 1.50p shown 3.00 3.00

World No Tobacco Day — A1110

2006, May 27 Litho. Perf. 14x13½
2389 A1110 75c multi .70 .35

Intl. Year of Deserts and
Desertification — A1111

Designs: No. 2390, 75c, Lizard and plant. No. 2391, 75c, Impression of lizard in sand, dead plant.

Perf. 13¾x13½
2006, June 10 **Litho.**
2390-2391 A1111 Set of 2 1.40 .70

Famous
Men — A1112

Designs: No. 2392, 75c, Tato Bores (1927-96), television actor. No. 2393, 75c, Rodolfo Walsh (1927-77), kidnapped journalist.

2006, June 10 Perf. 13½x13¾
2392-2393 A1112 Set of 2 1.40 .70

Winter Sports — A1113

No. 2394: a, Alpine skiing. b, Snowboarding. c, Cross-country skiing. d, Biathlon.

2006, June 17 Perf. 13¾x13½
2394 A1113 75c Block of 4, #a-d 3.00 3.00

Tango
Dancing
A1114

Designs: 75c, Musician. 4p, Dancers.

2006, June 24
2395-2396 A1114 Set of 2 4.75 2.50
See France Nos. 3224-3225.

Patoruzito Riding Pamperito — A1115

2006, July 8
2397 A1115 75c multi .70 .35

Endangered Animals — A1116

Designs: No. 2398, 75c, Eubalaena australis. No. 2399, 75c, Hippocamelus bisulcus. No. 2400, 75c, Hippocamelus antisensis. No. 2401, 75c, Panthera onca.

2006, July 8 Perf. 14x13¾
2398-2401 A1116 Set of 4 3.00 1.50

30th Mercosur
Common
Market Council
and Summit of
Presidents,
Córdoba
A1117

2006, July 22 Perf. 13¾x13½
2402 A1117 3.50p multi 2.75 1.50

Souvenir Sheet

First British Invasion of Buenos Aires
and Reconquest, Bicent. — A1118

2006, July 22 Perf. 14
2403 A1118 1.50p multi 2.00 2.00

Energy Conservation — A1119

Winning designs in children's art contest: No. 2404, 75c, Light bulb, house and electrical cord, by Florencia Tovi. No. 2405, 75c, Plant in sunlight, unplugged lamp, by Camila Suárez.

2006, July 22 Perf. 13¾x13½
2404-2405 A1119 Set of 2 1.40 .70

First Postage Stamps of Corrientes,
150th Anniv. — A1120

Designs: 75c, August 21, 1856 Corrientes cancel. 1.50p, Corrientes #1.

Litho. & Embossed
2006, Aug. 19 Perf. 13¾x13½
2406 A1120 75c multi .70 .35

Souvenir Sheet
Litho.
Perf. 14
2407 A1120 1.50p multi 2.00 2.00
No. 2407 contains one 40x40mm stamp.

Interjurisdictional Committee on the
Colorado River, 50th Anniv. — A1121

Perf. 13½x13¾
2006, Aug. 26 **Litho.**
2408 A1121 75c multi .70 .35

Patricios
Infantry Corps,
Bicent.
A1122

2006, Sept. 9
2409 A1122 75c multi .70 .35

Grapes, Wines and
Vineyards — A1123

Designs: No. 2410, 75c, Syrah grapes and wine, Catamarca vineyards. No. 2411, 75c, Torrontés Riojano grapes and wine, La Rioja vineyards. No. 2412, 75c, Pinot Noir grapes and wine, Neuquén vineyards.

2006, Sept. 16 Perf. 14x13½
2410-2412 A1123 Set of 3 2.10 1.00

Col.
Ramón
L.
Falcón
Federal
Police
Cadet
School,
Cent.
A1124

2006, Oct. 14 Litho. Perf. 13¾x13½
2413 A1124 75c multi .70 .35

Border Bridges — A1125

Designs: No. 2414, 75c, Pres. Tancredo Neves Intl. Bridge. No. 2415, 75c, San Roque González de Santa Cruz Intl. Bridge.

2006, Oct. 14   **Perf. 14x13¾**
2414-2415 A1125   Set of 2   1.40   .70

Christmas
A1126

Paintings by Alfredo Guttero: No. 2416, 75c, Madonna and Dove. No. 2417, 75c, The Annunciation, horiz.

Perf. 13½x13¾, 13¾x13½
2006, Oct. 21
2416-2417 A1126   Set of 2   1.40   .70

Natl. Institute of Agricultural and Cattle Ranching Technology, 50th Anniv. — A1127

Perf. 13¾x13½
2006, Nov. 11   **Litho.**
2418 A1127 75c multi   .70   .35

Rock Musicians
A1128

Designs: No. 2419, 75c, Tanguito (1945-72). No. 2420, 75c, Luca Prodan (1953-87). No. 2421, 75c, Miguel Abuelo (1946-88). No. 2422, 75c, Pappo (1950-2005).

2006, Nov. 18   **Perf. 13½x13¾**
2419-2422 A1128   Set of 4   3.00 1.50

Caciques
A1129

Designs: No. 2423, 75c, Valentín Sayhueque (1823-1903), Huilliche cacique. No. 2424, 75c, Casimiro Biguá, Tehuelche cacique.

2006, Dec. 2
2423-2424 A1129   Set of 2   1.40   .35

Frigate Hercules, Detail From *Battle of Martín García Island,* by Emilio Biggeri — A1130

2007, Mar. 10   **Perf. 13¾x13½**
2425 A1130 75c multi   .70   .35
   Adm. Guillermo Brown (1777-1857).

Wine-Growing Regions — A1131

No. 2426: a, Hand picking bunch of grapes. b, Vineyard, grapes, bottle of Pinot Noir, Neuquén Region (60x30mm).
No. 2427: a, Harvester cutting grapes from vine. b, Vineyard, grapes, bottle of Torrontés Riojano, La Rioja Region (60x30mm).
No. 2428: a, Harvester inspecting grapes on vine. b, Vineyard, grapes, bottle of Syrah, Catamarca Region (60x30mm).

2007, Mar. 10   **Litho.**   **Perf. 14**
2426   Booklet pane of 2   4.00   —
   a. A1131 75c multi   .75   .50
   b. A1131 3.25p multi   3.00 2.25
     Complete booklet, #2426   4.25
2427   Booklet pane of 2   4.00   —
   a. A1131 75c multi   .75   .50
   b. A1131 3.25p multi   3.00 2.25
     Complete booklet, #2427   4.25
2428   Booklet pane of 2   4.00   —
   a. A1131 75c multi   .75   .50
   b. A1131 3.25p multi   3.00 2.25
     Complete booklet, #2428   4.25

Complete booklets include a plastic wine bottle spout.

Falkland Islands War, 25th Anniv. A1132

Map of the Falkland Islands and: No. 2429, 75c, Argentina #C90 in changed colors with Islas Malvinas cancel. No. 2430, 75c, IAI Dagger fighters. No. 2431, 75c, Battle cruiser ARA General Belgrano. No. 2432, 75c, Decorated war veteran. No. 2433, 75c, War decoration, vert.

Perf. 13¾x13½, 13½x13¾
2007, Mar. 31   **Litho.**
2429-2433 A1132   Set of 5   4.00 2.00

Postal and Telecommunications Workers Federation, 50th Anniv. — A1133

2007, Apr. 14   **Perf. 13¾x13½**
2434 A1133 75c multi   .70   .35

Map of Antarctica, Icebreaker Almirante Irízar — A1134

No. 2436 — Antarctic fauna: a, Phalacrocorax atriceps. b, Leptonychotes weddellii. c, Sterna vittata, denomination at UR. d, Sterna vittata, denomination at UL. e, Pygoscelis adeliae. f, Chionis alba. g, Pygoscelis papua, denomination at UR. h, Pygoscelis papua, denomination at UL.

2007, Apr. 21
2435 A1134 4p shown   3.75 1.50
2436   Sheet of 8   6.00 6.00
   a.-h. A1134 75c Any single   .50   .50

Miniature Sheet

Toys — A1135

No. 2437: a, Rocking horse. b, Tea set. c, Toy train and stations. d, Toy soldiers.

2007, May 5   **Litho.**   **Perf. 13¾x13½**
2437 A1135   Sheet of 4   3.00 3.00
   a.-d.   75c Any single   .35   .35

Museums — A1136

Designs: 75c, Latin American Art Museum, Buenos Aires. 3.25p, High Mountain Archaeological Museum, Salta.

2007, May 5
2438-2439 A1136   Set of 2   3.00 1.50

Road Safety Year — A1137

2007, May 19   **Litho.**   **Perf. 13½x13¾**
2440 A1137 75c red & silver   .70   .35

Souvenir Sheet

Intl. Polar Year — A1138

2007, June 2   **Perf. 14**
2441 A1138 4p multi + label   3.50 2.00

Defense of Buenos Aires From British Attack, Bicent. A1139

Perf. 13¾x13½
2007, June 23   **Litho.**
2442 A1139 75c multi   .70   .35

Pierre Auger Observatory A1140

2007, July 14   **Litho.**   **Perf. 13½x13¾**
2443 A1140 75c multi   .70   .35

St. Joseph Calasanctius (1557-1648) A1141

2007, July 14
2444 A1141 1p multi   1.00   .65

Souvenir Sheet

Campo del Cielo Meteorite — A1142

2007, July 28   **Perf. 14**
2445 A1142 6p multi   6.00 6.00

No. 2445 was sold with, but unattached to, a booklet cover, and 3-D glasses.

Homero Manzi
(1907-51),
Political
Leader, Tango
Lyricist
A1143

Perf. 13½x13¾
2007, Aug. 11 Litho.
2446 A1143 1p multi .90 .65

Tourism Along
Route
40 — A1144

No. 2447: a, Road to San Carlos de
Bariloche (30x30mm). b, El Acay Pass
(40x30mm). c, Road to Perito Moreno
(70x30mm). d, La Trochita locomotive
(40x30mm). e, Lanin Volcano (40x30mm). f,
Rio Grande (50x30mm). g, Animals on road,
San José Jachal (40x30mm). h, Cuesta de
Miranda (50x30mm) i, Nuestra Senora del
Tránsito Chapel (30x30mm). j, Quilmes Ruins
(30x30mm). k, Road to Oratorio (40x30mm).

2007, Aug. 25 Litho. **Perf. 14**
2447 Sheet of 11 10.00 10.00
a.-b. A1144 50c Either single .45 .30
c.-k. A1144 1p Any single .90 .65

Souvenir Sheet

Diplomatic Relations Between
Argentina and Germany, 150th
Anniv. — A1145

2007, Sept. 8
2448 A1145 4p multi 3.75 2.75

Prevention of Carbon Monoxide
Accidents — A1146

Children's art by: No. 2449, 1p, Julieta Saa-
vedra Barragán. No. 2450, 1p, Leandro
Ventancour. No. 2451, 1p, Efraín Osvaldo
Rost, vert. No. 2452, 1p, Camila M. Alvarez
Petrone, vert.

Perf. 13¾x13½, 13½x13¾
2007, Sept. 8
2449-2452 A1146 Set of 4 3.60 2.60

San Lorenzo
de Almagro
Athletic Club,
Cent. — A1147

2007, Sept. 22 **Perf. 13½x13¾**
2453 A1147 1p multi .90 .65

Beatification of Ceferino Namuncurá
(1886-1905) — A1148

2007, Oct. 13 Litho. **Perf. 13¾x13½**
2454 A1148 1p multi .90 .65

Contemporary Art — A1149

Designs: No. 2455, 1p, Corrientes Esquina
Uruguay, photograph by Horacio Coppola. No.
2456, 1p, 0611, painting by Pablo Siquier. No.
2457, 1p, Diálogo, digital photograph by
Liliana Porter, vert. No. 2458, 1p, Imaginando
el Estupor, mosaic by Marta Minujin, vert.

Perf. 13¾x13½, 13½x13¾
2007, Oct. 27
2455-2458 A1149 Set of 4 3.60 2.60
Nos. 2455-2458 each were printed in sheets
of 4.

Christmas
A1150

Designs: 25c, Adoration of the Magi. 1p,
Holy Family.

2007, Nov. 10 **Perf. 13½x14**
2459-2460 A1150 Set of 2 1.80 1.30

First
Balloon
Crossing
of Río de
la Plata,
Cent.
A1151

Perf. 13¾x13½
2007, Nov. 24 Litho.
2461 A1151 1p multi .90 .65

Discovery of Oil and Gas in Argentina,
Cent. — A1152

2007, Nov. 24
2462 A1152 1p multi .90 .65

2007
Presidential
Inauguration
A1153

2007, Dec. 15 **Perf. 13½x13¾**
2463 A1153 1p multi .90 .65

Festivals
A1154

Designs: No. 2464, 1p, National Chamamé
Festival, Corrientes Province. No. 2465, 1p,
National Poncho Festival, Catamarca Prov-
ince. No. 2466, 1p, National Festival of
Dressage and Folklore, Jesús María, Cordoba
Province. No. 2467, 1p, National Snow Festi-
val, San Carlos de Bariloche, Río Negro
Province.

2007, Dec. 15
2464-2467 A1154 Set of 4 3.00 1.50

2008 Summer
Olympics,
Beijing
A1155

Designs: No. 2468, 50c, Mountain biking.
No. 2469, 50c, Taekwondo. 1p, Basketball. 4p,
Pole vault.

Perf. 13½x13¾
2008, Mar. 29 Litho.
2468-2471 A1155 Set of 4 4.00 2.00

Natl. Scientific and Technical Research
Council, 50th Anniv. — A1156

Designs: No. 2472, 1p, Bone tissue bridges
with 45S5 bioactive glass particles. No. 2473,
1p, Pollen grain of Polygonum sp. No. 2474,
1p, Remnants of Supernova W44. No. 2475,

1p, Cave paintings, Epuyén River Valley. No.
2476, 1p, Gas heater device.

2008, Apr. 12 **Perf. 13¾x13½**
2472-2476 A1156 Set of 5 3.00 1.50

Association of Argentine Private Radio
Stations, 50th Anniv. — A1157

2008, Apr. 26
2477 A1157 1p multi .70 .35

Pres. Arturo Frondizi (1908-95), Oil
Pumps — A1158

2008, Apr. 26
2478 A1158 1p multi .70 .35

Birds — A1159

Male and female: 1p, Sturnella loyca. 4p,
Xanthopsar flavus.

2008, Apr. 26 **Perf. 13½x13¾**
2479-2480 A1159 Set of 2 3.50 1.75

Argentine Aero Club, Cent. — A1160

2008, May 10 **Perf. 14x13½**
2481 A1160 1p multi .70 .35

Colón Theater, Buenos Aires,
Cent. — A1161

2008, May 24
2482 A1161 1p multi .70 .35

Aimé Bonpland (1773-1858), Founder of Corrientes Natural Sciences Museum — A1162

2008, May 24　　　**Perf. 13¾x13½**
2483　A1162　1p multi　　　　　.70　.35

Dr. Marcos Sastre (1808-87), Textbook Writer, and Text from Reading Book, Anagnosia — A1163

Perf. 13¾x13½
2008, June 21　　　　　**Litho.**
2484　A1163　1p multi　　　　　.70　.35

Luciano-Honorato Valette (1880-1957), Antarctic Naturalist — A1164

Disappearance of Rescue Ship ARA Guaraní, 50th Anniv. — A1165

2008, June 28
2485　A1164　1p multi　　　　　.70　.35
2486　A1165　1p multi　　　　　.70　.35

Characters From "The Mail Song," by María Elena Walsh A1166

Character From "Big Brother," by Silvia Schujer A1167

Characters From "Letters to Santa Claus," by Luis María Pescetti — A1168

Character From "Mammarachos por Carta," by Ricardo Mariño — A1169

Perf. 13½x13¾, 13¾x13½
2008, July 26
2487　A1166　1p multi　　　　　.65　.35
2488　A1167　1p multi　　　　　.65　.35
2489　A1168　1p multi　　　　　.65　.35
2490　A1169　1p multi　　　　　.65　.35
　　Nos. 2487-2490 (4)　　　2.60　1.40
Children's songs and literature.

Scenes From "The Mail Song," by María Elena Walsh — A1170

Scenes From "Mamarrachos por Carta," by Ricardo Mariño — A1171

Characters From "Letters to Santa Claus," by Luis María Pescetti — A1172

Characters From "Big Brother," by Silvia Schujer — A1173

No. 2491: a, Bird holding Argentina #2216b in beak. b, Mailbox. c, Paper airplane, letters. d, Post office, letters. e, Smokestacks behind open envelope with letter. f, Philatelic office, Argentina #2236, #2239 and its adjacent label.

No. 2492: a, Postman holding letter. b, Postman and woman reading letter. c, Bird reading letter. d, Man with pipe. e, Birds on mail box. f, Monkey with banana.

No. 2493: a, Child writing letter to Santa Claus. b, Santa Claus reading letter from child.

No. 2494: a, Girl at table playing card game (40x50mm). b, Boy and mother, horiz. (70x40mm).

2008, July 26　Litho.　Perf. 13½x13¾
Booklet Stamps
2491　A1170　Block of 6　　4.00　4.00
a.-f.　　1p Any single　　　　.65　.65
g.　　Booklet pane, 2 #2491　8.00　—

2492　A1171　Block of 6　　4.00　4.00
a.-f.　　1p Any single　　　　.65　.65
g.　　Booklet pane, 2 #2492　8.00

Perf. 14¼
2493　A1172　Booklet pane of 2　　　　　　　　　5.25　—
a.-b.　　4p Either single　　2.60　2.60

Perf. 14
2494　A1173　Booklet pane of 2　　　　　　　　　5.25　—
a.-b.　　4p Either single　　2.60　2.60
　　Complete booklet, #2491g, 2492g, 2493, 2494　　26.50

Complete booklet is a spiral-bound book containing the four booklet panes, postal cards, text pages and pieces for a children's card game.

Archaeological Artifacts Type of 2000

Design: Jar, Yocavil culture.

Perf. 13½x13¾ Syncopated
2008, Aug. 2
2495　A973　10p multi　　　6.75　6.75

Souvenir Sheet

Olympex 2008 World Stamp Exhibition, Beijing — A1174

Litho. With Foil Application
2008, Aug. 2　　　　　**Perf. 14**
2496　A1174　4p multi　　　3.00　3.00

Immigrants to Argentina — A1175

Designs: No. 2497, 1p, Cherry blossoms, koi, immigrants from Japan. No. 2498, 1p, Metal decorative plates and immigrants from Lebanon. No. 2499, 1p, Tiles, guitar and immigrants from Portugal. No. 2500, 1p, Wooden decorative box, embroidered silk, Ugaritic alphabet and immigrants from Syria.

Perf. 13¾x13½
2008, Sept. 20　　　　**Litho.**
2497-2500　A1175　Set of 4　2.60　1.30

Souvenir Sheets

National Flower Festival — A1176

Designs: No. 2501, 5p, Gerbera daisy, gardenia and rose (shown). No. 2502, 5p, Carnation, gold-banded lily and delphinium.

2008, Sept. 27   *Perf. 14*
2501-2502 A1176   Set of 2   6.50 6.50

Nos. 2501-2502 are impregnated with a floral scent.

Souvenir Sheets

Sports Personalities — A1177

Designs: No. 2503, 5p, Hand of Manu Ginobili, basketball and hoop. No. 2504, 5p, Rugby football kicked by Hugo Porta, goal posts, silhouettes of rugby player kicking ball. No. 2505, 5p, Silhouette of golfer putting, foot of Roberto De Vicenzo, vert. No. 2506, 5p, Juan Manuel Fangio in race car, vert.

2008, Oct. 11   *Perf. 14*
2503-2506 A1177   Set of 4   12.00 12.00

See Nos. 2541-2544, 2632-2635.

Science Teaching Year — A1178

2008, Oct. 25   *Perf. 13¾x13½*
2507 A1178 1p multi   .70 .35

Flowers
A1179

Designs: No. 2508, 1p, Ceiba chodatii. No. 2509, 1p, Nelumbo nucifera.

2008, Oct. 25
2508-2509 A1179   Set of 2   1.25 .60

See Viet Nam Nos. 3343-3344.

Souvenir Sheet

First Stamps of Argentina, Buenos Aires and Cordoba,150th Anniv. — A1180

No. 2510: a, Cordoba #2 (30x30mm). b, Buenos Aires #4 (40x30mm). c, Argentina #3 (30x40mm).

2008, Nov. 1   *Perf. 14*
2510 A1180 1p Sheet of 3, #a-c   1.90 1.90

Christmas
A1181

2008, Nov. 15   *Perf. 13½x13¾*
2511 A1181 1p multi   .60 .60

Dances
A1182

Designs: No. 2512, 1p, Malambo sureño dancer, Argentina. No. 2513, 1p, Hoy-nazan dancers, Armenia.

2008, Nov. 22   *Litho.*
2512-2513 A1182   Set of 2   1.25 .60

See Armenia Nos. 790-791.

El Cronista Comercial Newspaper, Cent. — A1183

2008, Dec. 13   *Perf. 13¾x13½*
2514 A1183 1p multi   .60 .30

School of Forestry, 50th Anniv.
A1184

2008, Dec. 13   *Perf. 13½x3¾*
2515 A1184 1p multi   .60 .30

Festivals
A1185

Designs: No. 2516, 1p, Chaya Festival, La Rioja Province. No. 2517, 1p, Natl. Grape Harvest Festival, Mendoza Province. No. 2518, 1p, Natl. Cherry Festival, Los Antiguos, Santa

---

Cruz Province. No. 2519, 1p, Natl. Sea Festival, Mar del Plata, Buenos Aires Province.

2009, Feb. 14   *Perf. 13½x13¾*
2516-2519 A1185   Set of 4   2.25 1.20

Souvenir Sheet

Preservation of Polar Regions and Glaciers — A1186

No. 2520: a, Retreat of Piedras Blancas Glacier. b, Retreat of Argentine Antarctic Territory ice.

2009, Mar. 7   *Perf. 14*
2520 A1186 5p Sheet of 2, #a-b   5.50 5.50

Bishop Colombres Memorial Experimental Agribusiness, Cent. — A1187

2009, Mar. 21   *Perf. 13¾x13½*
2521 A1187 1p multi   .55 .30

Souvenir Sheet

New Year 2009 (Year of the Ox) — A1188

Litho. & Embossed, Margin With Foil Application
2009, Apr. 4   *Perf. 14*
2522 A1188 5p multi   3.00 3.00

China 2009 World Stamp Exhibition, Luoyang.

Holy Cross Exaltation Parish, Puerto Santa Cruz, Cent. — A1189

2009, Apr. 18   *Litho.*   *Perf. 13½x13¾*
2523 A1189 1p multi   .55 .30

Argentine Exports — A1190

Designs: 1p, Wine. 5p, Agricultural machines.

2009, Apr. 18   *Perf. 13¾x13½*
2524-2525 A1190   Set of 2   3.25 1.50

Endangered Species
A1191

Designs: No. 2526, 1p, Harpyhaliaetus coronatus. No. 2527, 1p, Chelonoidis chilensis, horiz.

Perf. 13½x13¾, 13¾x13½
2009, Apr. 18
2526-2527 A1191   Set of 2   1.10 .60

Pres. Raúl Ricardo Alfonsín (1927-2009)
A1192

2009, May 9   *Perf. 13½x13¾*
2528 A1192 1p multi   .55 .30

Children of the Holy Virgin of the Garden Congregation in Argentina, 150th Anniv.
A1193

2009, May 23
2529 A1193 1p multi   .55 .30

Raúl Scalabrini Ortiz (1898-1959), Writer — A1194

2009, May 23
2530 A1194 1p multi   .55 .30

Political and Military Command of the Malvinas (Falkland Islands), 180th Anniv. A1195

Paintings: 1p, Luis Vernet, governor of the Malvinas, by Luisa Vernet Lavalle Lloveras. 5p, Ship and houses near cliff, by Vernet, map of Malvinas.

2009, June 13   *Perf. 13½x13¾*
2531 A1195 1p multi   .55 .30

Souvenir Sheet
Perf. 14
2532 A1195 5p multi   3.00 3.00
No. 2532 contains one 70x30mm stamp.

Water — A1196

No. 2533: a, Droplets. b, Drops, clouds and hand, vert.

2009, June 27   *Perf. 14*
2533   Sheet of 2, unscratched   5.50 5.50
    a. A1196 5p multi   2.75 2.75
    b. A1196 5p multi, unscratched   2.75 2.75
    c. As "b," scratched   2.75
No. 2533b and sheet margin have scratch-off panels.

Flora and Fauna A1197

Designs: No. 2534, 1p, Polybetes pythagoricus. No. 2535, 1p, Passiflora caerulea.

2009, July 25   *Perf. 13¾x13½*
2534-2535 A1197   Set of 2   1.10 .55

Amusement Park Rides — A1198

No. 2536: a, Bumper cars. b, Roller coaster. c, Ferris wheel. d, Ghost train.

2009, Aug. 1
2536   Horiz. strip of 4 + flanking label   2.25 2.25
    a.-d. A1198 1p Any single   .55 .55

Miniature Sheet

Sheep — A1199

No. 2537: a, Merino ram. b, Romney Marsh yearling. c, Corriedale ewe and lamb. d, Hampshire Down ewe and lamb. e, Lincoln ewe. f, Frisian ewe.

2009, Aug. 22
2537 A1199 1p Sheet of 6, #a-f, + 2 labels   3.25 3.25

Soil Erosion — A1200

No. 2538 — Erosion by: a, Water. b, Wind.

2009, Sept. 12   *Perf. 14x13½*
2538   Horiz. pair   1.10 1.10
    a.-b. A1200 1p Either single   .55 .55

A1201

America Issue, Education For All — A1202

Perf. 13¾x13½
2009, Sept. 12   Litho.
2539 A1201 1p multi   .55 .30
2540 A1202 1p multi   .55 .30

Sports Personalities Type of 2008
Designs: No. 2541, 5p, Delfo Cabrera running in 1948 Summer Olympics, vert. No. 2542, 5p, Tennis ball and shorts of Guillermo Vilas (38mm diameter). No. 2543, 10p, Field hockey players, stick of Luciana Aymar, vert. No. 2544, 10p, Cyclists chasing Juan Curuchet, vert.

Perf. 14, Perf. (No. 2542)
2009, Sept. 26   Litho.
2541-2544 A1177   Set of 4   16.00 16.00
The tennis ball on No 2542 is covered with flocking.

National Technological University, 50th Anniv. A1203

2009, Oct. 17   *Perf. 13½x13¾*
2545 A1203 1p multi   .55 .30

Souvenir Sheets

A1204

Italia 2009 Intl. Philatelic Exhibition, Rome — A1205

No. 2546: a, La Scala Theater, Milan. b, Colon Theater, Buenos Aires.
No. 2547: a, Froilán González racing in Ferrari 375 (85x30mm rhomboid) b, Ferrari F60 race car (60x20mm).

2009, Oct. 24   Litho.   *Perf. 14*
2546 A1204 6p Sheet of 2, #a-b   6.50 6.50
2547 A1205 6p Sheet of 2, #a-b   6.50 6.50

Intl. Year of Astronomy — A1206

Designs: 1p, Telescope, National University of Córdoba Astronomical Observatory. 10p, Galileo Galilei (1564-1642), diagram of solar system orbits.

2009, Oct. 24   Litho.   *Perf. 13¾x13½*
2548 A1206 1p multi   .55 .30

Souvenir Sheet
Perf. 14
2549 A1206 10p multi   5.25 5.25
No. 2549 contains one 80x20mm stamp.

Children's Art — A1207

Winning art in "I Can Slow TB Down" children's stamp design contest: No. 2550, 1p, Boxing gloves hitting "TB," by Alberto Penayo Pardo. No. 2551, 1p, Lungs with bandage, by Candela Alemany Fiandrino. No. 2552, 1p, Boy coughing, doctor holding sign, by Rocío Cabrera, vert. No. 2553, 1p, Hands holding lungs, by Juliana Benzo, vert.

Perf. 13¾x13½, 13½x13¾
2009, Nov. 14   Litho.
2550-2553 A1207   Set of 4   2.10 2.10

Christmas A1208

2009, Nov. 21   *Perf. 13½x14*
2554 A1208 1p multi   .55 .30

Historic Buildings — A1209

No. 2555, 1p — San Martín Mansion, 1910: a, Exterior. b, Interior.
No. 2556, 1p — Ortiz Basualdo Mansion, 1918: a, Exterior. b, Interior.
No. 2557, 1p — Fernandez-Anchorena Mansion, 1909: a, Exterior. b, Interior.
No. 2558, 1p — Duhau Mansion, 1934: a, Exterior. b, Interior.

Perf. 13¾x13½
2009, Dec. 12   Litho.
Horiz. Pairs, #a-b
2555-2558 A1209   Set of 4   4.25 2.40
Nos. 2555-2558 each were printed in sheets containing 8 pairs and 4 labels.

Festivals A1210

Designs: No. 2559, 1.50p, National Apple Festival, General Roca, Río Negro Province. No. 2560, 1.50p, National Sun Festival, San Juan, San Juan Province. No. 2561, 1.50p, National Students Festival, San Salvador de Jujuy, Jujuy Province. No. 2562, 1.50p, National Tradition Festival, San Antonio de Areco, Buenos Aires Province.

2010, Feb. 20   *Perf. 13½x13¾*
2559-2562 A1210   Set of 4   3.25 1.60

South American Sails 2010 Regatta A1211

Designs: 1.50p, Argentine Navy frigate Libertad.
No. 2564: a, Chilean Navy schooner Esmerelda. b, Libertad, diff.

Perf. 13¾x13½ Syncopated
2010, Feb. 20
2563 A1211 1.50p multi .80 .40

Souvenir Sheet
Perf. 14
2564 A1211 6p Sheet of 2,
#a-b, + 12 la-
bels 6.25 6.25

No. 2564 contains two 40x50mm stamps.

May Revolution,
Bicent. — A1212

Perf. 13½x13¾ Syncopated
2010, Mar. 6
2565 A1212 1.50p multi .80 .40

National
Symbols
A1213

Designs: No. 2566, 1.50p, Coat of arms.
No. 2567, 1.50p, Flag, horiz.

Perf. 13½x13¾, 13¾x13½
2010, Mar. 27
2566-2567 A1213 Set of 2 1.60 .80

A Culture of Peace — A1214

No. 2568: a, Dove. b, Map of South
America.

2010, Apr. 24 Litho. Perf. 13½x13¾
2568 A1214 1.50p Horiz. pair,
#a-b 1.60 1.60

Buenos Aires City Symphony,
Cent. — A1215

2010, Apr. 24 Perf. 14x13½
2569 A1215 1.50p multi .80 .40

Argentine
Army, Bicent.
A1216

2010, May 8 Perf. 13½x13¾
2570 A1216 1.50p multi .80 .40

Argentine Naval Command,
Bicent. — A1217

2010, May 29 Perf. 13¾x13½
2571 A1217 1.50p multi .80 .40

Bicentenary
Mural — A1218

No. 2572: a, Cabildo, Buenos Aires
(30x50mm). b, General Manuel Belgrano, flag
of Argentina on pole, Casa de Tucumán, San
Miguel de Tucumán (30x50mm). c, Gen. José
de San Martín on horseback, raising sword
(40x80mm). d, National Constitution
(30x50mm). e, Ships unloading immigrants
(30x50mm). f, Sword battle, people voting,
"1910," horiz. (70x30mm). g, National Congress, Blind Justice (30x50mm). h, Trolley, film
set, bridge, horiz. (40x30mm). i, Palm tree,
crowd, banners, men with feet in fountain,
baby with umbilical cord (30x60mm). j, Military
with guns, cardinal, man smoking cigar, eyes,
"the disappeared" in pit (30x40mm). k,
Mothers of the Plaza de Mayo holding pictures
of the disappeared, May Pyramid statue
(40x60mm). l, Motorcyclist, men with brief-
cases holding cellular phones, man on computer, airplanes (40x60mm).

2010, May 29 Litho. Perf. 14
2572 Sheet of 12 9.75 9.75
a.-l. A1218 1.50p Any single .80 .80

Gazeta de
Buenos-Ayres,
Bicent.
A1219

2010, June 5 Litho. Perf. 13½x13¾
2573 A1219 1.50p multi .80 .40

A1220

2010 World Cup Soccer
Championships, South Africa — A1221

2010 World Cup emblem and stylized player
from: No. 2574, 1.50p, Nigeria. No. 2575,

1.50p, Greece, vert. 5p, South Korea. 7p,
Argentina, vert.
No. 2578, 5p, Argentina player sliding to
kick ball. No. 2579, 5p, Argentina player heading ball into net. No. 2580, 5p, Argentina
player making scissor kick. No. 2581, 5p,
Goalie making save, vert.

Perf. 13¾x13½, 13½x13¾
2010, June 5
2574-2577 A1220 Set of 4 7.75 4.00

Souvenir Sheets
Perf. 14
2578-2581 A1221 Set of 4 10.50 10.50

Nos. 2578-2579 each contain one
70x40mm stamp, No. 2580 contains one
60x40mm stamp, and No. 2581 contains one
40x60mm stamp.

World Junior Rugby Championships,
Argentina — A1222

2010, June 19 Perf. 13¾x13½
2582 A1222 1.50p multi .80 .40

Souvenir Sheet

First Government Junta,
Bicent. — A1223

2010, July 24 Perf. 14
2583 A1223 5p multi 2.60 1.25

Miniature Sheet

Toys and Games — A1224

No. 2584: a, Sulky-cycle (sulky-ciclo). b,
Cup and ball (balero). c, Top (trompo). d, Hoop
(aro). e, Doll (muñeca).

Perf. 13½x13¾ Syncopated
2010, July 24 Litho.
2584 A1224 2p Sheet of 5, #a-e,
+ 15 labels 5.25 5.25

The stamps and labels of No. 2584 are puzzle pieces that when separated and rear-
ranged form a picture.

Jorge Luis
Borges (1899-
1986), Writer
A1225

Perf. 13¾x13½ Syncopated
2010, Aug. 14 Litho.
2585 A1225 7p multi 3.50 1.75

2010 Frankfurt Book Fair. See Germany No.
2585.

Landmarks Type of 2004

Designs: 1.50p, Parana River, Corrientes.
6p, Les Eclaireurs Lighthouse, Tierra del
Fuego.

Perf. 13¾x13½ Syncopated
2010 Litho.
2586 A1063a 1.50p multi + label .80 .40
2587 A1063a 6p multi 3.25 1.60

Issued: 1.50p, 5/11; 6p, 2/12.

Mountain Lakes — A1226

Flags of Romania and Argentina and: 1.50p,
Lake Ballea, Romania. 7p, Lake Nahuel
Huapi, Argentina.

2010, Aug. 14 Perf. 13¾x13½
2588-2589 A1226 Set of 2 4.50 2.25

See Romania Nos. 5201-5202.

Women's Field Hockey World Cup
Championships, Rosario — A1227

2010, Aug. 28
2590 A1227 1.50p multi .80 .40

Games
A1228

Designs: No. 2591, 1.50p, Truco (card
game). No. 2592, 1.50p, Bocce.

2010, Aug. 28 Perf. 13½x13¾
2591-2592 A1228 Set of 2 1.60 .80

2010 Census
A1229

Perf. 13¾x13½ Syncopated

2010, Sept. 18
2593 A1229 1.50p multi   .75   .40

Juan Bautista Alberdi (1810-84), Lawyer and Diplomat — A1230

2010, Sept. 18   **Perf. 13½x13¾**
2594 A1230 1.50p multi   .75   .40

National Library, Bicent. A1231

2010, Sept. 18   **Perf. 13¾x13½**   **Litho.**
2595 A1231 1.50p multi   .75   .40

Souvenir Sheet

Weather Stations in Austria and Argentina — A1232

No. 2596 — Weather station in: a, Stadtpark, Vienna. b, Buenos Aires Botanical Garden.

2010, Oct. 16   **Perf. 14**
2596 A1232 5p Sheet of 2, #a-b   5.25 5.25
   See Austria No. 2283.

The Child of Bethlehem, by Aldo Severi — A1233

2010, Nov. 13   **Perf. 13¾x13½**
2597 A1233 1.50p multi   .75   .40
   Christmas.

Federal Electric Power Council, 50th Anniv. A1234

2010, Nov. 27   **Perf. 13½x13¾**
2598 A1234 1.50p multi   .75   .40

Souvenir Sheets

Lighthouses — A1235

Portuguese Ceramic Tile — A1236

No. 2599: a, Querandí Lighthouse, Argentina. b, Santa Marta Lighthouse, Portugal.

2010, Sept. 25   **Perf. 14**
2599 A1235 5p Sheet of 2, #a-b   5.25 5.25
2600 A1236 10p multi   5.25 5.25

Portugal 2010 Intl. Philatelic Exhibition, Lisbon. Portions of the designs of Nos. 2599a-2599b were applied by a thermographic process producing a shiny, raised effect.

World Post Day — A1237

2010, Oct. 9   **Litho.**   **Perf. 13½x13¾**
2601 A1237 1.50p multi   .75   .40

A Song to Work, Sculpture by Rogelio Yrurtia — A1238

2010, Oct. 16   **Perf. 14x13½**
2602 A1238 1.50p multi   .75   .40

Dakar Rally in Argentina — A1239

No. 2603 — Photographs of 2009 and 2010 Rallies: a, Starting line of Rally, Buenos Aires (60x40mm). b, Motorcycle No. 107 (50x50mm). c, Car No. 300 on dirt road (60x40mm). d, Truck No. 502 on dirt road, (50x50mm). e, Vehicles on dirt road (50x50mm). f, Quad No. 251 (40x80mm). g, Quad No. 277 (40x80mm).
No. 2604: a, Car No. 375 on dirt road (60x50mm). b, Two quad riders in sand near hill (60x40mm). c, Car No. 377 in air (60x40mm). d, Motorcycle No. 1 (40x50mm).

---

e, Tree near Laguna del Pescado (40x50mm). f, White clouds over mountain near Tucumán (40x50mm). g, Road and bridge near Jujuy (40x50mm). h, Truck No. 500 in water (70x50mm).

2010, Dec. 11   **Perf. 14**
2603   Booklet pane of 7   9.75   —
 a.-e.   A1239 1.50p Any single   .75   .75
 f.   A1239 5p multi   2.50 2.50
 g.   A1239 7p multi   3.50 3.50
2604   Booklet pane of 8   10.50   —
 a.-g.   A1239 1.50p Any single   .75   .75
 h.   A1239 10p multi   5.00 5.00
   Complete booklet, #2603-2604
   + post card   20.50

Intl. Year of Forests A1240

2011, Mar. 19   **Perf. 13½x13¾**
2605 A1240 2p multi   1.00   .50

Postal Union of the Americas, Spain and Portugal (UPAEP), Cent. — A1241

2011, Mar. 19   **Perf. 13¾x13½**
2606 A1241 8p multi   4.00 2.00

Buenos Aires, 2010 World Book Capital — A1242

No. 2607 — Stylized buildings spelling: a, "Buenos Aires Capital." b, "Mundial del Libro 2011."

2011, Apr. 16   **Perf. 14x13½**
2607   Horiz. pair   2.00 2.00
 a.-b.   A1242 2p Either single   1.00   .40

A1243

Antarctic Treaty, 50th Anniv. — A1244

Designs: 2p, Iceberg and Antarctic Treaty emblem.
No. 2609: a, Pygoscelis papua. b, Scientist and equipment.

2011, Apr. 16   **Perf. 13¾x13½**
2608 A1243 2p multi   1.00   .50

Souvenir Sheet
Perf. 14

2609 A1244 8p Sheet of 2, #a-b   8.00 8.00

34th Antarctic Treaty Consultative Meeting, Buenos Aires.

Mariano Moreno (1778-1811), Politician — A1245

2011, May 21   **Perf. 13¾x13½**
2610 A1245 2p multi   1.00   .50

World Blood Donor Day — A1246

Perf. 13¾x13½ Syncopated
2011, May 21
2611 A1246 5p multi   2.50 1.25

Year of Decent Labor, Health and Safety for Workers A1247

2011, June 4   **Perf. 13¾x13½**
2612 A1247 2p multi   1.00   .50

Pres. Domingo Faustino Sarmiento (1811-88) A1248

2011, June 25   **Perf. 13½x13¾**
2613 A1248 2.50p multi   1.25   .60

May Pyramid, Buenos Aires, Bicent. — A1249

2011, June 25   **Perf. 13½x14**
2614 A1249 2.50p multi   1.25   .60

America Cup Soccer
Tournament — A1250

No. 2615 — Players from Group A teams: a, Argentina and Bolivia. b, Colombia and Costa Rica.
No. 2616 — Players from Group B teams: a, Venezuela and Brazil. b, Paraguay and Ecuador.
No. 2617 — Players from Group C teams: a, Peru and Uruguay. b, Mexico and Chile.

2011, June 25   **Perf. 14**
2615   Wheel with 2 sheets   5.00   —
a.-b.   A1250 5p Either sheet   2.50   2.50
2616   Wheel with 2 sheets   5.00   —
a.-b.   A1250 5p Either sheet   2.50   2.50
2617   Wheel with 2 sheets   5.00   —
a.-b.   A1250 5p Either sheet   2.50   2.50
          Nos. 2615-2617 (3)   15.00

Nos. 2615a-2615b, 2616a-2616b and 2617a-2617b are attached to wheels with a metal grommet at the center of the wheels.

Launch of SAC-D/Aquarius
Satellite — A1251

2011, July 23   Litho.   Perf. 13¾x13½
2618   A1251 2.50p multi   1.25   .60

Mailboxes — A1252

Designs: No. 2619, 2.50p, Corneta type mailbox, cancel. No. 2620, 2.50p, Pillar box, handwritten letter, vert.

Perf. 13¾x13½, 13½x13¾
2011, Aug. 20
2619-2620   A1252   Set of 2   2.40   1.20

Festivals
A1253

Designs: No. 2621, 2.50p, National Beer Festival, Villa General Belgrano. No. 2622, 2.50p, National Horse Festival, San Cristóbal. No. 2623, 2.50p, Foreign Communities Fair, Comodoro Rivadavia. No. 2624, 2.50p, National Tea Festival, Campo Viera.

2011, Sept. 10   **Perf. 13½x13¾**
2621-2624   A1253   Set of 4   4.75   2.40

Orchids
A1254

Designs: No. 2625, 2.50p, Zygopetalum maxillare. No. 2626, 2.50p, Sacoila lanceolata, vert.

Perf. 13¾x13½, 13½x13¾
2011, Sept. 24
2625-2626   A1254   Set of 2   2.40   1.20

Train on the Clouds — A1255

No. 2627: a, Train cars, bridge (yellow orange panel). b, Locomotive, bridge (blue panel). c, Train on curved bridge (orange panel). d, Train on curved bridge, diff. (red panel).

2011, Sept. 24   **Perf. 14**
2627   Sheet of 4   9.75   9.75
a.-d.   A1255 5p Any single   2.40   2.40

Argentine Pediatric Society,
Cent. — A1256

2011, Oct. 22   **Perf. 13¾x13½**
2628   A1256 2.50p multi   1.25   .60

Miniature Sheet

Pig Breeds — A1257

No. 2629: a, Landrace. b, Hampshire. c, Pietrain. d, Duroc Jersey. e, Spotted Poland. f, Yorkshire.

2011, Oct. 29   **Litho.**
2629   A1257 2.50p Sheet of 6,
       #a-f, + 2 la-
       bels   7.25   7.25

Christmas
A1258

Litho. With Glitter Affixed
2011, Oct. 29   Perf. 13¾ Syncopated
2630   A1258 2.50p multi   1.25   .60

Souvenir Sheet

Pres. Néstor Carlos Kirchner (1950-2010), and Casa Rosada — A1259

2011, Nov. 26   Litho.   Perf. 14
2631   A1259 5p multi   2.40   2.40

Sports Personalities Type of 2008
Souvenir Sheets

Designs: No. 2632, 10p, Horse and mallet of Adolfo Cambiaso, polo player, vert. No. 2633, 10p, Chessboard and Miguel Najdorf (1910-97), chess player, vert. (50x60mm). No. 2634, 10p, Sailboard of Carlos Espinola, sailboarder, vert. (50x60mm). No. 2635, 10p, Roller skates of Nora Vega, roller skater (60x40mm).

2011, Nov. 12
2632-2635   A1177   Set of 4   19.00   19.00

Rights of the
Child — A1260

Winning art in children's stamp design contest by: No. 2636, 2.50p, Nicolás Agustín Bernachea (blue panels). No. 2637, 2.50p, Sofía Panagópulo (pink panels). No. 2638, 2.50p, Ezequiel Catalano Segesso (yellow green panels). No. 2639, 2.50p, Laura Florencia Martinessi (orange panels).

2011, Nov. 26   **Perf. 13½x13¾**
2636-2639   A1260   Set of 4   4.75   2.40

Souvenir Sheet

Creation of Argentine Flag and Pledge
of Allegiance, Bicent. — A1261

2012, Mar. 3   Litho.   Perf. 14
2640   A1261 5p multi   2.25   2.25

First Argentine Flight Landing at South
Pole, 50th Anniv. — A1262

2012, Mar. 3   Litho.   Perf. 13¾x13½
2641   A1262 2.50p multi   1.25   .60

Monument to Gen. Manuel Belgrano,
Buenos Aires, and Argentine
Flag — A1263

2012, Mar. 31   **Perf. 14x13¾**
2642   A1263 2.50p multi   1.25   .60

Argentine Claims of Sovereignty Over
British South Atlantic Islands — A1264

Argentine flag and map of: No. 2643, 2.50p, Falkland Islands (Isla Gran Malvina and Isla Soledad). No. 2644, 2.50p, South Georgia (Isla San Pedro). No. 2645, 2.50p, South Sandwich Islands (Islas Traverse, Islas Candelaria, Islas Saunders, Isla Jorge, Isla Blanca and Grupo Tule del Sur), vert. (28x67mm).

Perf. 13¾x13½, 13¾x14 (#2645)
2012, Mar. 31
2643-2645   A1264   Set of 3   3.50   1.80

Presidential
Staff and
Argentine
Flag — A1265

2012, Apr. 14   **Perf. 13½x13¾**
2646   A1265 2.50p multi   1.25   .60

Presidential mandate of Cristina Fernández Kirchner for 2011-15.

Monument to Gen. José de Martín, First Deed of Río Gallegos Town Council — A1266

2012, Apr. 14   **Perf. 14x13¾**
2647 A1266 2.50p multi   1.25 .60

Río Gallegos Town Council, cent.

Alernative Energies — A1267

Designs: 2.50p, Biogas, biomass and biocombustibles. 9.50p, Solar, wind and hydroelectric energy.

2012, Apr. 28   **Litho.**   **Perf. 14x13½**
2648-2649 A1267   Set of 2   5.50 2.75

Argentine Natural History Museum, Bicent. A1268

Museum emblem and: No. 2650, 2.50p, Skeleton of Dahlia the Elephant. No. 2651, 2.50p, Skull of Bonatitan reigi (dinosaur). No. 2652, 2.50p, Agrias narcissus butterflies, horiz. No. 2653, 2.50p, Display in Hall of Birds, horiz.

Perf. 13½x13¾, 13¾x13½
2012, Apr. 28
2650-2653 A1268   Set of 4   4.50 2.40

Intl. Year of Cooperatives — A1269

2012, June 16   **Perf. 13¾x13½**
2654 A1269 2.50p multi   1.10 .60

Passage of Sáenz Peña Universal Male Suffrage Law, Cent. — A1270

2012, June 16   **Perf. 13½x13¾**
2655 A1270 2.50p multi   1.10 .60

Paintings of Historical Events of 1812 — A1271

Painting of: No. 2656, 2.50p, Jujuy Exodus, by unknown artist. No. 2657, 2.50p, Battle of Tucuman, by Tomas del Villar.

2012, June 16   **Perf. 13¾x13½**
2656-2657 A1271   Set of 2   2.25 1.20

Argentine School of Military Aviation, Cent. — A1272

2012, July 21   **Perf. 14x13½**
2658 A1272 2.75p multi   1.25 .60

Operation Southern Cross for Naval Assistance in Antarctica — A1273

2012, July 21   **Perf. 13¾x13½**
2659 A1273 5p multi   2.25 1.20

Souvenir Sheet

Eva Perón (1919-52) — A1274

2012, Sept. 1   **Perf. 14**
2660 A1274 10p multi   4.50 4.50

Alzheimer's Disease Awareness A1275

2012, Sept. 15   **Perf. 13½x13¾**
2661 A1275 3p multi   1.40 .70

Festivals A1276

Designs: No. 2662, 3p, National Artisans Festival, Colón. No. 2663, 3p, Maní National Festival, Hernando. No. 2664, 3p, National Orange Festival, Bella Vista. No. 2665, 3p, National Calf Festival and Branding Day, Ayacucho.

2012, Sept. 25
2662-2665 A1276   Set of 4   5.25 2.60

General San Martín Mounted Grenadiers Regiment, 200th Anniv. — A1277

2012, Oct. 13   **Perf. 13¾x13½**
2666 A1277 3p multi   1.25 .60

Christmas A1278

2012, Nov. 17   **Perf. 13½x13¾**
2667 A1278 3p multi   1.25 .60

Miniature Sheet

Bats — A1279

No. 2668: a, Sturnira lillium in flight. b, Sturnira lillium hanging and close-up of head. c, Histiotus laephotis. d, Histiotus montanus. e, Chrotopterus auritus in flight. f, Head of Chrotopterus auritus. g, Head of Noctilio leporinus. h, Noctilio leporinus in flight.

2012, Dec. 22   **Perf. 13¾x13½**
2668 A1279 3p Sheet of 8, #a-h   9.75 9.75

Battle of Salta, 200th Anniv. — A1280

2013, Feb. 23   **Perf. 14x13½**
2669 A1280 3.50p multi   1.40 .70

Archaeological Artifacts Type of 2000

Designs: 30p, Ceremonial hatchet, Tehuelche culture. 40p, Basket with handle, Selk'nam culture. 50p, Basket with handle and lid, Wichi culture.

Perf. 13½x13¾ Syncopated
2013, Mar. 1
2670 A973 30p multi   12.00 12.00
2671 A973 40p multi   16.00 16.00
2672 A973 50p multi   20.00 20.00
   Nos. 2670-2672 (3)   48.00 48.00

General Constituent Assembly of 1813, 200th Anniv. A1281

2013, Mar. 9   **Perf. 13½x13¾**
2673 A1281 3.50p multi   1.40 .70

Festivals A1282

Designs: No. 2674, 3.50p, National Folklore Festival, Cosquín. No. 2675, 3.50p, National Trout Festival, Junín de los Andes. No. 2676, 3.50p, National Lemon Festival, Tafí Viejo, vert. No. 2677, 3.50p, National Petroleum Festival, Comodoro Rivadavia, vert.

Perf. 13¾x13½, 13½x13¾
2013, Mar. 23
2674-2677 A1282   Set of 4   5.50 2.75

Landmarks Type of 2004

Designs: 3.50p, Cancha de Bochas, Ischigualasto National Park. 30p, Hill of Seven Colors, Jujuy.

Perf. 13¾x13½ Syncopated
2013, Mar.
2678 A1063a 3.50p multi   1.40 .70
2679 A1063a 30p multi   12.00 6.00

Souvenir Sheet

Partido de Esteban Echeverría Area of Buenos Aires, Cent. — A1283

No. 2680: a, Door on building built in 1789. b, Plaza and flags, horiz.

2013, Apr. 13   **Litho.**   **Perf. 14**
2680 A1283   Sheet of 2   4.00 4.00
  a.-b.   5p Either single   2.00 2.00

National University of Córdoba, 400th Anniv. — A1284

2013, Apr. 27   **Perf. 14x13½**
2681 A1284 3.50p multi   1.40 .70

Election of Pope Francis A1285

No. 2682 — Arms of Pope Francis and: a, Pope Francis, flags of Vatican City, Italy and Argentina. b, Pope Francis in profile, flags of Vatican City and Argentina. c, Pope Francis waving, flags of Vatican City and Argentina. d, Pope Francis holding cross, flags of Vatican City and Argentina.

2013, May 2		Perf. 13¾x13½	
2682	Vert. strip of 4	12.50	12.50
a.-b.	A1285 3.50p Either single	1.40	1.40
c.	A1285 10p multi	4.00	4.00
d.	A1285 14p multi	5.50	5.50

See Italy No. 3179, Vatican City Nos. 1523-1526.

African Union, 50th Anniv. A1286

2013, June 1 Litho.	Perf. 13½x13¾		
2683 A1286 4p multi		1.50	.75

Villa Carlos Paz, Cent. A1287

2013, July 27 Litho.	Perf. 13¾x13½		
2684 A1287 4p multi		1.50	.75

Souvenir Sheet

125th Session of the International Olympic Committee, Buenos Aires — A1288

No. 2685: a, Runners, Pierre de Coubertin (1863-1937), founder of Intl. Olympic Committee (60x30mm). b, Gymnast, flag of Argentina, *Floralis Generica*, sculpture by Eduardo Catalano (60x40mm).

2013, Sept. 14 Litho.	Perf. 14		
2685 A1288 5p Sheet of 2, #a-b		3.75	3.75

Birds A1289

Designs: No. 2686, 4p, Furnarius rufus. No. 2687, 4p, Podiceps gallardoi. No. 2688, 4p, Campephilus magellanicus, vert. No. 2689, 4p, Gubernatrix cristata, vert.

Perf. 13¾x13½, 13½x13¾			
2013, Oct. 19			Litho.
2686-2689 A1289	Set of 4	5.50	3.00

A1290

A1291

A1292

Winning Designs in "Right to Identity" Children's Art Contest A1293

2013, Oct. 22 Litho.	Perf. 13¾x13½		
2690 A1290 4p multi		1.40	.70
2691 A1291 4p multi		1.40	.70
Perf. 13½x13¾			
2692 A1292 4p multi		1.40	.70
2693 A1293 4p multi		1.40	.70
Nos. 2690-2693 (4)		5.60	2.80

Sergeant Juan Bautista Cabral (c. 1789-1813), Hero in Battle of San Lorenzo A1294

San Martín Regiment of Mounted Grenadiers in Battle of San Lorenzo — A1295

2013, Nov. 9 Litho.	Perf. 13½x13¾		
2694 A1294 4p multi		1.40	.70
Perf. 14x13½			
2695 A1295 4p multi		1.40	.70

Battle of San Lorenzo, 200th anniv.

Campaign Against Discrimination — A1296

No. 2696 — Stylized people with joined hands and background color of: a, 4p, White. b, 13p, Black.

2013, Nov. 9 Litho.	Perf. 13½x13¾		
2696 A1296	Horiz. pair, #a-b	5.75	3.00

America Issue.

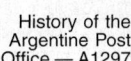

History of the Argentine Post Office — A1297

No. 2697: a, Queen Juana of Castile, coat of arms, postal runner, map of Peru (opening of first post office in Lima, Peru, 1514) (30x30mm). b, Manuel Belgrano, Mariano Moreno, Cabildo, Buenos Aires (Post Office of the May Revolution, 1810) (30x40mm). c, President Juan Perón, and his wife, Eva (creation of Post Office and Telecommunications Secretariat, 1949) (30x40mm). d, Mail box, postal workers, flag of Argentina (renationalization of Postal Service, 10th anniv., 2013) (30x40mm). e, Pres. Nelson Kirchner, people with flags, mail boxes (renationalization of Postal Service, 2003) (63mm diameter).

Litho., Litho. With Foil Application (10p)

2013, Nov. 19		Perf. 14	
2697	Miniature sheet of 5	9.75	9.75
a.-d.	A1297 5p Any single	1.60	1.60
e.	A1297 10p multi	3.25	3.25

Souvenir Sheet

Brasiliana 2013 Intl. Philatelic Exhibition, Rio de Janeiro — A1298

No. 2698: a, 4p, Dolichandra unguis-cati. b, 13p, Alouatta guariba, vert.

2013, Nov. 23 Litho.	Perf. 14		
2698 A1298 Sheet of 2, #a-b		5.50	5.50

Argentine National Anthem, 200th Anniv. A1299

Perf. 13½x13¾			
2013, Nov. 30			Litho.
2699 A1299 4p multi		1.25	.60

Christmas A1300

Perf. 13½x13¾			
2013, Nov. 30			Litho.
2700 A1300 4p multi		1.25	.60

New Laws, Policies, and Regulations Affecting Argentina Society — A1301

Designs; 25c, New national idenification cards (resolution 1800/09). 50c, Marriage

equality (law 26,618). 1p, Soccer balls (free television broadcasts of local soccer games). 2p, Airplane, oil well, envelope and mail box (nationalization of industries). 5p, Flasks and chemical symbols (law 26,421 establishing program to support Network of Argentinian Researchers and Scientists Abroad). 10p, Family, hands, roof (establishment of Pro.Cre.Ar. loan program). 30p, End of Impunity laws and reopening of criminal trials of Argentina's military dictatorship (law 25,779). 40p, Mandatory open primary elections with obligatory voting. 50p, Open digital television.

Perf. 13½x13¾ Syncopated			
2014, Jan. 20			Litho.
2701 A1301 25c multi		.25	.25
2702 A1301 50c multi		.25	.25
2703 A1301 1p multi		.25	.25
2704 A1301 2p multi		.50	.30
2705 A1301 5p multi		1.25	.60
2706 A1301 10p multi		2.50	1.25
2707 A1301 30p multi		7.50	3.75
2708 A1301 40p multi		10.00	5.00
2709 A1301 50p multi		12.50	6.00
Nos. 2701-2709 (9)		35.00	17.65

New Laws, Policies and Regulations Affecting Argentina Society — A1302

Designs: 25c, Nationalization of pension funds (law 26,425). 50c, Argentina Connected national telecommunications plan. 1p, Argentina-Bolivia pipeline integration. 2p, Latin American integration (Union of South American Nations). 3p, Creation of universities. 4p, Law regulating audiovisual communication services (law 26,522). 5p, Argentina Works Program. 6p, National Assisted Fertilization Act (law 26,862). 10p, National child allowance decrees (Decree 1602/09). 30p, Suffrage for 16-year-olds (law 26,774). 50p, Restructuring of national debt.

Perf. 13½x13¾ Syncopated			
2014			Litho.
2710 A1302 25c multi		.25	.25
2711 A1302 50c multi		.25	.25
2712 A1302 1p multi		.25	.25
2713 A1302 2p multi		.50	.30
2714 A1302 3p multi		.75	.40
2715 A1302 4p multi		1.00	.50
2716 A1302 5p multi		1.25	.60
2717 A1302 6p multi		1.50	.75
2718 A1302 10p multi		2.50	1.25
2719 A1302 30p multi		7.50	3.75
2719A A1302 50p multi		12.00	12.00
Nos. 2710-2719A (11)		27.75	20.30

Issued: No. 2710-2719, 1/20; 50p, 8/25.

Jorge A. Newbery (1875-1914), Pilot, Airplane and Hot Air Balloon — A1303

2014, Mar. 5 Litho.	Perf. 13¾x13½		
2720 A1303 4.50p multi		1.25	.60

Hugo Chávez (1954-2013), President of Venezuela — A1304

Chávez: No. 2721, 10p, Waving, wearing presidential sash. No. 2722, 10p, Holding map of South America.

2014, Mar. 5 Litho.	Perf. 13¾x13½		
2721-2722 A1304	Set of 2	5.00	2.50

America Issue.

Argentine Presence in the Antarctic, 110th Anniv. — A1305

No. 2724 — Latin American Antarctic Progam Administrators emblem and: a, Scientific researcher and penguin (30x60mm). b, Plesiosaurs (60x30mm).

Perf. 13¾x13½
2014, Mar. 25   **Litho.**
2723 A1305 4.50p shown   1.25   .60

Souvenir Sheet
Perf. 14
2724   Sheet of 2   3.00 3.00
a.-b.   A1305 6p Either single   1.50 1.50

25th reunion of Latin American Antarctic Program Administrators, Buenos Aires (No. 2724).

Flora and Fauna of Iguazu Falls Area A1306

No. 2725: a, Doxocopa linda mileta (40x40mm). b, Billbergia zebrina (30x40mm). c, Iguazu Falls and Toco toucan (70x40mm). d, Iguazu Falls (90x30mm)

Litho. & Silk-Screened
2014, Apr. 14   **Perf. 14**
2725   Miniature sheet of 4   9.00 9.00
a.-b.   A1306 8p Either single   2.00 2.00
c.-d.   A1306 10p Either single   2.50 2.50

Souvenir Sheet

Renationalization of YPF Energy Company — A1307

2014, May 5   **Litho.**   **Perf. 14**
2726 A1307 16p multi   4.00 4.00

Battle of Montevideo, 200th Anniv. — A1308

2014, May 19   **Litho.**   **Perf. 14x13½**
2727 A1308 4.50p multi   1.10   .60

National University of Tucuman, Cent. — A1309

2014, May 26   **Litho.**   **Perf. 14x13½**
2728 A1309 4.50p multi   1.10   .60

2014 World Cup Soccer Championships, Brazil — A1310

No. 2729 — Shirts and schedules of Group F teams: a, Argentina. b, Bosnia & Herzegovina. c, Iran. d, Nigeria.

2014, May 12   **Litho.**   **Perf. 13½x13¾**
2729   Horiz. strip of 4   —   —
a.-d.   A1310 10p Any single   —   —

No. 2729 was quickly withdrawn from sale.

Myths and Legends A1311

Designs: No. 2733, 10p, La Flor del Ceibo (the Ceibo flower). No. 2734, 10p, El Viento Zonda (the Zonda wind).

Perf. 13½x13¾
2014, June 30   **Litho.**
2733-2734 A1311   Set of 2   5.00 5.00

America Issue.

El Enterriano, by Eleodoro Ergasto Marenco (1914-96) A1312

2014, July 14   **Litho.**   **Perf. 13½x13¾**
2735 A1312 5p multi   1.25 1.25

Commercial Aircraft — A1313

Designs: No. 2736, 5p, Comet IV. No. 2737, 5p, Boeing 747-200. No. 2738, 5p, Boeing 737-800NG. No. 2739, 5p, Airbus 340-300.

2014, July 21   **Litho.**   **Perf. 14x13½**
2736-2739 A1313   Set of 4   5.00 5.00

Control of Aerolíneas Argentinas by Argentine Government, 6th Anniv. — A1314

Litho. & Silk-Screened
2014, July 21   **Perf. 14**
2740 A1314 20p multi   5.00 5.00

Souvenir Sheet

PhilaKorea 2014 Intl. Philatelic Exhibition, Seoul — A1315

No. 2741: a, Bird in flight (29mm diameter). b, Three birds (38mm diameter)

Litho. & Silk-Screened With Foil Application
2014, Aug. 11   **Perf.**
2741 A1315 15p Sheet of 2, #a-b 7.25 7.25

Luis Alberto Spinetta (1950-2012), Rock Musician A1316

Perf. 13½x13¾
2014, Sept. 22   **Litho.**
2742 A1316 10p multi   2.40 2.40

Monument to the Army of the Andes, Cent. — A1317

Perf. 13½x13¾
2014, Sept. 25   **Litho.**
2743 A1317 5p multi   1.25 1.25

Festivals A1318

Designs: No. 2744, 5p, Cuevas de las Manos Festival, Perito Moreno. No. 2745, 5p, National Mate Festival, Paraná. No. 2746, 5p, 70th National Agriculture Festival, Esperanza. No. 2747, 5p, National Steam Train Festival, El Maitén.

Perf. 13½x13¾
2014, Sept. 29   **Litho.**
2744-2747 A1318   Set of 4   4.75 4.75

Souvenir Sheet

1813 Coins of the United Provinces of the River Plate — A1319

No. 2748: a, Gold 8-escudo and silver 8-real coins. b, Silver coins, horiz.

2014, Oct. 14   **Litho.**   **Perf. 14**
2748 A1319 6p Sheet of 2, #a-b   3.00 3.00

Julio Cortázar (1914-84), Writer — A1320

Prize-winning art in Cortázar stamp design contest by: No. 2749, 5p, Gastón Martino. No. 2750, 5p, José Rivadulla. No. 2751, 5p, Lucía Valentina Piuzzi, vert. No. 2752, 5p, Ana Gauna, vert.

Perf. 13¾x13½, 13½x13¾
2014, Oct. 20   **Litho.**
2749-2752 A1320   Set of 4   4.75 4.75

Non-Direct Blood Transfusions by Dr. Luis Agote, Cent. — A1321

2014, Nov. 10   **Litho.**   **Perf. 14x13½**
2753 A1321 5p multi   1.25 1.25

Nativity, by Raúl Soldi (1905-94) A1322

Perf. 13½x13¾
2014, Nov. 21   **Litho.**
2754 A1322 10p multi   2.40 2.40

Christmas. See Vatican City No. 1581.

Movie
Stars — A1323

Designs: No. 2755, 5p, Tita Merello (1904-2002), actress. No. 2756, 5p, Alfredo Alcón (1930-2014), actor.

Perf. 13½x13¾
2014, Nov. 25   **Litho.**
2755-2756 A1323   Set of 2   2.40   2.40
Mar del Plata Intl. Film Festival, 60th anniv.

Nelson Mandela (1918-2013),
President of South Africa — A1324

Perf. 13¾x13½
2014, Dec. 15   **Litho.**
2757 A1324 10p multi   2.40   2.40

Antarctopelta Oliveroi — A1325

Perf. 13¾x13½
2015, Mar. 9   **Litho.**   **Perf. 13¾x13½**
2758 A1325 6p multi   1.40   1.40
Souvenir Sheet
Perf. 14
2759 A1326   Sheet of 2, #a-b   5.75   5.75
Argentine exploration and science projects in Antarctica.

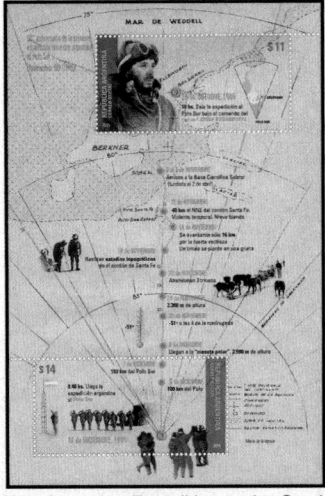

First Argentine Expedition to the South
Pole, 50th Anniv. — A1326

No. 2759: a, 11p, Map and Col. Jorge Edgard Leal, expedition leader. b, 14p, Expedition members saluting flag of Argentina.

Festivals
A1327

Designs: No. 2760, 6p, National Festival of the Longest Night, Ushuaia. No. 2761, 6p, National Drum Festival, Frías. No. 2762, 6p, National Chocolate Festival, Bariloche. No. 2763, 6p, National Cotton Festival, Presidencia Roque Sáenz Peña.

2015, Apr. 27   **Litho.**   **Perf. 13½x13¾**
2760-2763 A1327   Set of 4   5.50   5.50

Miniature Sheet

Trees — A1328

No. 2764: a, Handroanthus impetiginosus. b, Araucaria araucana. c, Salix humboldtiana. d, Cercidium praecox.

2015, Apr. 27   **Litho.**   **Perf. 13½x13¾**
2764 A1328 6p Sheet of 4, #a-d   5.50   5.50

Souvenir Sheet

Exterior of Néstor Kirchner Cultural
Center, Buenos Aires — A1329

2015, May 26   **Litho.**   **Perf. 14**
2765 A1329 20p multi + 6 labels   4.50   4.50

Free Peoples
Congress,
200th Anniv.
A1330

Perf. 13½x13¾
2015, June 29   **Litho.**
2766 A1330 10p multi   2.25   2.25

A1331

No. 2767: a, Dr. René G. Favaloro (1923-2000), cardiac surgeon. b, Heart with bypass pioneered by Dr. Favaloro.

2015, July 13   **Litho.**   **Perf. 13½x13¾**
2767 A1331 10p Horiz. pair, #a-b   4.50   4.50

International Telecommunication
Union, 150th Anniv. — A1332

2015, Aug. 21   **Litho.**   **Perf. 14x13½**
2768 A1332 10p multi   2.25   2.25

United
Nations,
70th
Anniv.
A1333

Perf. 13¾x13½
2015, Aug. 31   **Litho.**
2769 A1333 10p multi   2.25   2.25

Souvenir Sheet

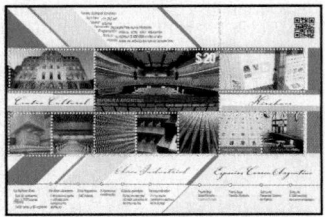

Interior of Nestor Kirchner Cultural
Center, Buenos Aires — A1334

2015, Sept. 14   **Litho.**   **Perf. 14**
2770 A1334 20p multi + 9 labels   4.25   4.25

Miniature Sheet

Birds — A1335

No. 2771: a, Ramphastos dicolorus. b, Ramphastos toco. c, Pteroglossus bailloni. d, Selenidera maculirostris.

Perf. 13¾x13½
2015, Sept. 22   **Litho.**
2771 A1335 7p Sheet of 4, #a-d   6.00   6.00

Miniature Sheet

Mammals — A1336

No. 2772: a, Lama pacos. b, Lama guanicoe. c, Vicugna vicugna. d, Lama glama.

Perf. 13¾x13½
2015, Sept. 22   **Litho.**
2772 A1336 7p Sheet of 4, #a-d   6.00   6.00

A1337

A1338

A1339

A1340

Gustavo Cerati (1959-2014), Rock
Musician — A1341

2015, Oct. 9   **Litho.**   **Perf. 13¾x13½**
2773 A1337 7p multi   1.50   1.50
2774   Horiz. strip of 4   8.50   8.50
   a. A1338 10p multi   2.10   2.10
   b. A1339 10p multi   2.10   2.10
   c. A1340 10p multi   2.10   2.10
   d. A1341 10p multi   2.10   2.10

Souvenir Sheet

Ciudad Evita — A1342

No. 2775: a, Man and house. b, Apartment complex.

Litho. (Sheet Margin Litho. & Embossed)
2015, Oct. 13   **Perf. 14**
2775 A1342 25p Sheet of 2,
          #a-b   10.50 10.50

Christmas
A1343

2015, Nov. 2   Litho.   Perf. 13½x13¾
2776 A1343 10p multi   2.10 2.10

Souvenir Sheet

Pres. Juan D. Perón (1895-
1974) — A1344

2015, Nov. 17   Litho.   Perf. 14
2777 A1344 29p multi   6.00 6.00

2015 Inauguration
of Pres. Mauricio
Macri — A1345

2016, May 9   Litho.   Perf. 13½x14
2778 A1345 8p multi   1.25 1.25

Campaign Against Human
Trafficking — A1346

No. 2779 — Inscription starting with: a, "Yo
le digo. . ." b, "Explotación. . ."

2016, May 23   Litho.   Perf. 13½x13¾
2779 A1346 8p Horiz. pair, #a-b   2.50 2.50
          America Issue.

Argentine Naval Aviation,
Cent. — A1347

2016, June 6   Litho.   Perf. 14x13½
2780 A1347 10p multi   1.40 1.40

Rubén Darío (1867-1916),
Poet — A1348

Perf. 13¾x13½
2016, June 10   Litho.
2781 A1348 20p multi   2.75 2.75

Independence, 200th
Anniv. — A1349

Perf. 13½x13¾ Syncopated
2016, June 27   Litho.
2782 A1349 10p multi   1.40 1.40

Open Cabildo of Buenos Aires of May
25, 1810 — A1350

Battle of
Tucumán
and
Members of
the Second
Triumvirate,
1812
A1351

Argentine Declaration of
Independence, 200th Anniv. — A1352

2016, July 7   Litho.   Perf. 14
2783   Sheet of 3   4.25 4.25
   a. A1350 10p multi   1.40 1.40
   b. A1351 10p multi   1.40 1.40
   c. A1352 10p multi   1.40 1.40
          Road to Argentine Independence.

A1353

Coats of
Arms — A1354

No. 2784 — Arms of: a, Argentina. b, Corri-
entes Province. c, Chaco Province. d, For-
mosa Province. e, Misiones Province. f, Cata-
marca Province. g, Jujuy Province. h, La Rioja
Province. i, Salta Province. j, Santiago del
Estero Province. k, Tucumán Province. l, Men-
doza Province. m, San Juan Province. n, San
Luis Province. o, Autonomous City of Buenos
Aires. p, Buenos Aires Province. q, Córdoba
Province. r, Entre Ríos Province. s, La Pampa
Province. t, Santa Fe Province. u, Chubut
Province. v, Neuquén Province. w, Río Negro
Province. x, Santa Cruz Province. y, Tierra del
Fuego, Antarctica and Southern Atlantic
Islands Province.

2016, July 7   Litho.   Perf. 14
2784   Sheet of 25   35.00 35.00
   a. A1353 10p multi   1.40 1.40
   b.-y. A1354 10p Any single 1.40 1.40

Souvenir Sheet

July 9, 1816, Bas-relief by Lola
Mora — A1355

No. 2785: a, Deputies at Congress of
Tucumán, facing right. b, Three deputies, facing left, behind table.

2016, July 7   Litho.   Perf. 14
2785 A1355 10p Sheet of 2, #a-
          b, + label   2.75 2.75

SEMI-POSTAL STAMPS

Samuel F. B.   Globe — SP2
Morse — SP1

Landing of
Columbus — SP5

Designs: 10c+5c, Alexander Graham Bell.
25c+15c, Rowland Hill.

Wmk. RA in Sun (90)
1944, Jan. 5   Litho.   Perf. 13
B1 SP1 3c +2c lt vio & sl bl   1.00 1.50
B2 SP2 5c +5c dl red & sl bl   .80 .50
B3 SP1 10c +5c org & slate   1.50 .50
B4 SP1 25c +15c red brn & sl
             bl   2.25 1.10
B5 SP5 1p +50c lt grn & sl
             bl   9.50 10.00
    Nos. B1-B5 (5)   15.05 13.60

The surtax was for the Postal Employees
Benefit Association.

Map of
Argentina — SP6

1944, Feb. 17   Wmk. 90   Perf. 13
B6 SP6 5c +10c ol yel & slate   1.10 .50
B7 SP6 5c +50c vio brn &
             slate   5.00 1.50
B8 SP6 5c +1p dl org & slate   13.50 7.00
B9 SP6 5c +20p dp bl & slate   30.00 30.00
    Nos. B6-B9 (4)   49.60 39.00

The surtax was for the victims of the San
Juan earthquake.

Souvenir Sheets

National Anthem and Flag — SP7

1944, July 17   *Imperf.*
B10 SP7 5c +1p vio brn & lt
bl   9.00   5.00
B11 SP7 5c +50p bl blk & lt
bl   425.00 275.00

Surtax for the needy in the provinces of La Rioja and Catamarca.

> **Catalogue values for unused stamps in this section, from this point to the end of the section, are for Never Hinged items.**

Stamp Designing SP8

1950, Aug. 26   **Photo.**   *Perf. 13½*
B12 SP8 10c +10c violet   .25   .25
Nos. B12,CB1-CB5 (6)   20.95 15.40

Argentine Intl. Philatelic Exhibition, 1950.

Poliomyelitis Victim — SP9

1956, Apr. 14   *Perf. 13½x13*
B13 SP9 20c +30c slate   .30   .25

The surtax was for the poliomyelitis fund. Head in design is from Correggio's "Antiope," Louvre.

Stamp of 1858 and Mail Coach on Raft — SP10

Designs: 2.40p+1.20p, Album, magnifying glass and stamp of 1858. 4.40p+2.20p, Government seat of Confederation, Parana.

1958, Mar. 29   **Litho.**   *Perf. 13½*
B14 SP10 40c +20c brt grn &
dl pur   .50   .50
B15 SP10 2.40p +1.20p ol gray &
bl   .50   .50
B16 SP10 4.40p +2.20p lt bl & dp
claret   .50   .50
Nos. B14-B16,CB8-CB12 (8)   6.20 5.50

Surtax for Intl. Centennial Philatelic Exhibition, Paraná, Entre Rios, Apr. 19-27. Nos. B14-B16 exist imperf. Value, set of pairs, $200.

View of Flooded Land — SP11

1958, Oct. 4   **Photo.**   *Perf. 13½*
B17 SP11 40c +20c brown   .25   .25
Nos. B17,CB13-CB14 (3)   1.55 1.30

The surtax was for flood victims in the Buenos Aires district. Exists imperf. Value, pair $37.50.

Child Receiving Blood — SP12

1958, Dec. 20   **Litho.**   **Wmk. 90**
B18 SP12 1p +50c blk & rose red   .75   .25

The surtax went to the Anti-Leukemia Foundation. Exists imperf. Value, pair $25.

Runner SP13

Designs: 50c+20c, Basketball players, vert. 1p+50c, Boxers, vert.

1959, Sept. 5   *Perf. 13½*
B19 SP13 20c +10c emer & blk   .25   .25
B20 SP13 50c +20c yel & blk   .25   .25
B21 SP13 1p +50c mar & blk   .25   .25
Nos. B19-B21,CB15-CB16 (5)   1.75 1.50

3rd Pan American Games, Chicago, Aug. 27-Sept. 7, 1959.

Condor — SP14

Birds: 50c+20c, Fork-tailed flycatchers. 1p+50c, Magellanic woodpecker.

1960, Feb. 6
B22 SP14 20c +10c dk bl   .40   .25
B23 SP14 50c +20c dp vio bl   .40   .25
B24 SP14 1p +50c brn & buff   .40   .25
Nos. B22-B24,CB17-CB18 (5)   2.15 1.35

The surtax was for child welfare work. See Nos. B30, CB29.

Souvenir Sheet

Uprooted Oak Emblem — SP15

1960, Apr. 7   **Wmk. 90**   *Imperf.*
B25 SP15 Sheet of 2   1.40 1.40
   a.   1p + 50c bister & carmine   .50   .50
   b.   4.20p + 2.10p app grn & dp clar   .50   .50

WRY, July 1, 1959-June 30, 1960. The surtax was for aid to refugees.

Jacaranda — SP16

Flowers: 1p+1p, Passionflower. 3p+3p, Orchid. 5p+5p, Tabebuia.

1960, Dec. 3   **Photo.**   *Perf. 13½*
B26 SP16 50c +50c deep blue   .25   .25
B27 SP16 1p +1p bluish grn   .25   .25
B28 SP16 3p +3p henna brn   .55   .35
B29 SP16 5p +5p dark brn   .95   .60
Nos. B26-B29 (4)   2.00 1.45

"TEMEX 61" (Intl. Thematic Exposition). For overprints see Nos. B31-B34.

Type of 1960

Bird: 4.20p+2.10p, Blue-eyed shag.

1961, Feb. 25   **Wmk. 90**   *Perf. 13½*
B30 SP14 4.20p +2.10p chest
brn   .65   .35

Surtax for child welfare work. See No. CB29.

Nos. B26-B29 Ovptd. in Black, Brown, Blue or Red

1961, Apr. 15
B31 SP16 50c +50c deep blue   .35   .25
B32 SP16 1p +1p bluish grn
(Brn)   .35   .25
B33 SP16 3p +3p hen brn (Bl)   .65   .25
B34 SP16 5p +5p dk brn (R)   .95   .40
Nos. B31-B34 (4)   2.30 1.15

Day of the Americas, Apr. 14.

Cathedral, Cordoba SP17

Design: 10p+10p, Cathedral, Buenos Aires.

Perf. 13½
1961, Oct. 21   **Wmk. 90**   **Photo.**
B35 SP17 2p +2p rose claret   .25   .25
B36 SP17 3p +3p green   .30   .25
B37 SP17 10p +10p brt blue   .70   .60
   a.   Souvenir sheet of 3   2.50 1.50
Nos. B35-B37 (3)   1.25 1.10

1962 International Stamp Exhibition. No. B37a contains three imperf. stamps similar to Nos. B35-B37 in dark blue.

Flight into Egypt, by Ana Maria Moncalvo — SP19

1961, Dec. 16   **Litho.**
B38 SP19 2p +1p lilac & blk brn   .25   .25
B39 SP19 10p +5p lt & dp clar   .40   .25

The surtax was for child welfare.

Mimus Saturninus Modulator SP20

Design: 12p+6p, Zonotrichia capensis hypoleuca.

1962, Dec. 29   *Perf. 13½*
B40 SP20 4p +2p bis, brn & bl
grn   1.10   .65
B41 SP20 12p +6p gray, yel, grn
& brn   1.75 1.25

The surtax was for child welfare. See Nos. B44, B47, B48-B50, CB32, CB35-CB36.

Soccer — SP21

No. B43, Horsemanship.

1963, May 18   *Perf. 13½*
B42 SP21 4p +2p multi   .25   .25
B43 SP21 12p +6p multi   .45   .35
   a.   Dark carmine (jacket) omitted   15.00
Nos. B42-B43,CB31 (3)   1.30 1.10

4th Pan American Games, Sao Paulo.

Bird Type of 1962

4p +2p, Pyrocephalus rubineus rubineus.

1963, Dec. 21   **Litho.**
B44 SP20 4p +2p multi   .60   .30

The surtax was for child welfare. See No. CB32.

Fencers — SP22

4p+2p, National Stadium, Tokyo, horiz.

1964, July 18   **Wmk. 90**   *Perf. 13½*
B45 SP22 4p +2p red, ocher &
brn   .25   .25
B46 SP22 12p +6p bl grn & blk   .35   .25
Nos. B45-B46,CB33 (3)   1.50 1.20

18th Olympic Games, Tokyo, Oct. 10-25, 1964. See No. CB33.

Bird Type of 1962

4p +2p, Cardinal paroaria coronata.

1964, Dec. 23   **Litho.**
B47 SP20 4p +2p multi   .90   .30

The surtax was for child welfare. See No. CB35.

SP22a

Stamp of 1862 — SP18

Designs: 8p+4p, Belonopterus cayennensis lampronotus. 10p+5p, Amblyramphus holosericeus, horiz. 20p+10p, Chloroceryle amazona.

1966-67   **Perf. 13½**
B48	SP22a	8p +4p blk, ol, brt grn & red	.80	.35
B49	SP22a	10p +5p blk, bl, org & grn	.80	.55
B50	SP22a	20p +10p blk, yel, bl & pink	.40	.35

Nos. B48-B50,CB36,CB38-CB39 (6)   5.00   3.50

The surtax was for child welfare. Issue dates: 8p+4p, Mar. 26, 1966. 10p+5p, Jan. 14, 1967. 20p+10p, Dec. 23, 1967.

Grandmother's Birthday, by Patricia Lynch; Lions Emblem — SP23

Perf. 12½x13½
B51	SP23	40p + 20p multi	.45	.40

1st Lions Intl. Benevolent Phil. Exhib. Surtax for the Children's Hospital Benevolent Fund.

1968, Dec. 14   Litho.   Wmk. 90

White-faced Tree Duck — SP24

1969, Sept. 20   Wmk. 365   Perf. 13½
B52	SP24	20p + 10p multi	.50	.35

Surtax for child welfare. See No. CB40.

Slender-tailed Woodstar (Hummingbird) SP25

1970, May 9   Wmk. 365   Perf. 13½
B53	SP25	20c + 10c multi	.45	.40

The surtax was for child welfare. See Nos. CB41, B56-B59, B62-B63.

Dolphinfish — SP26

1971, Feb. 20   Unwmk.   Perf. 12½
Size: 75x15mm
B54	SP26	20c + 10c multi	.50	.45

Surtax for child welfare. See No. CB42.

Children with Stamps, by Mariette Lydis — SP27

1971, Dec. 18   Litho.   Perf. 13½
B55	SP27	1p + 50p multi	.50	.30

2nd Lions Intl. Solidarity Stamp Exhib.

Bird Type of 1970

Birds: 25c+10c, Saffron finch. 65c+30c, Rufous-bellied thrush, horiz.

1972, May 6   Unwmk.   Perf. 13½
B56	SP25	25c + 10c multi	.30	.25
B57	SP25	65c + 30c multi	.45	.30

Surtax was for child welfare.

Bird Type of 1970

Birds: 50c+25c, Southern screamer (chaja). 90c+45c, Saffron-cowled blackbird, horiz.

1973, Apr. 28
B58	SP25	50c + 25c multi	.55	.30
B59	SP25	90c + 45c multi	.75	.55

Surtax was for child welfare.

Painting Type of Regular Issue

Designs: 15c+15c, Still Life, by Alfredo Guttero, horiz. 90c+90c, Nude, by Miguel C. Victorica, horiz.

1973, Aug. 28   Litho.   Perf. 13½
B60	A472	15c + 15c multi	.35	.25
B61	A472	90c + 90c multi	1.10	.75

Bird Type of 1970

Birds: 70c+30c, Blue seed-eater. 1.20p+60c, Hooded siskin.

1974, May 11   Perf. 13½
B62	SP25	70c + 30c multi	.60	.35
B63	SP25	1.20p + 60c multi	1.00	.50

Surtax was for child welfare.

Painting Type of 1974

Design: 70c+30c, The Lama, by Juan Batlle Planas.

1974, May 11   Litho.   Perf. 13½
B64	A477	70c + 30c multi	.35	.25

PRENFIL-74 UPU, Intl. Exhib. of Phil. Periodicals, Buenos Aires, Oct. 1-12.

Plushcrested Jay — SP28

Designs: 13p+6.50p, Golden-collared macaw. 20p+10p, Begonia. 40p+20p, Teasel.

1976, June 12   Litho.   Perf. 13½
B65	SP28	7p + 3.50p multi	.60	.30
B66	SP28	13p + 6.50p multi	.70	.35
B67	SP28	20p + 10p multi	.80	.40
B68	SP28	40p + 20p multi	1.10	.60

Nos. B65-B68 (4)   3.20   1.65

Argentine philately.

Telegraph, Communications Satellite — SP29

Designs: 20p+10p, Old and new mail trucks. 60p+30p, Old, new packet boats. 70p+35p, Biplane and jet.

1977, July 16   Litho.   Perf. 13½
B69	SP29	10p + 5p multi	.30	.25
B70	SP29	20p + 10p multi	.60	.60
B71	SP29	60p + 30p multi	1.25	.85
B72	SP29	70p + 35p multi	1.40	.90

Nos. B69-B72 (4)   3.55   2.60

Surtax was for Argentine philately. No. B70 exists with wmk. 365.

Church of St. Francis Type, 1977

Inscribed "EXPOSICION ARGENTINA '77"

1977, Aug. 27
B73	A515	160p + 80p multi	2.50	2.00

Surtax was for Argentina '77 Philatelic Exhibition. Issued in sheets of 4. Value $12

No. B73 Overprinted with Soccer Cup Emblem

1978, Feb. 4   Litho.   Perf. 13½
B74	A515	160p + 80p multi	4.50	4.25
a.		Souvenir sheet of 4	22.50	20.00

11th World Cup Soccer Championship, Argentina, June 1-25.

Spinus Magellanicus SP30

Birds: No. B76, Variable seedeater. No. B77, Yellow thrush. No. B78, Pyrocephalus rubineus. No. B79, Great kiskadee.

1978, Aug. 5   Litho.   Perf. 13½
B75	SP30	50p + 50p multi	1.60	1.00
B76	SP30	100p + 100p multi	1.60	1.00
B77	SP30	150p + 150p multi	2.50	1.50
B78	SP30	200p + 200p multi	2.50	1.75
B79	SP30	500p + 500p multi	4.50	3.50

Nos. B75-B79 (5)   12.70   8.75

ARGENTINA '78, Inter-American Philatelic Exhibition, Buenos Aires, Oct. 27-Nov. 5. Nos. B75-B79 issued in sheets of 4 with marginal inscriptions commemorating Exhibition and 1978 Soccer Championship. Value, set $62.50.

Caravel "Magdalena," 16th Century — SP31

Sailing Ships: 500+500p, 3 master "Rio de la Plata," 17th cent. 600+600p, Corvette "Descubierta," 18th cent. 1500+1500p, Naval Academy yacht "A.R.A. Fortuna," 1979.

1979, Sept. 8   Litho.   Perf. 13½
B80	SP31	400p +400p multi	3.50	2.25
B81	SP31	500p +500p multi	4.25	2.50
B82	SP31	600p +600p multi	6.00	3.25
B83	SP31	1500p +1500p multi	14.00	8.00

Nos. B80-B83 (4)   27.75   16.00

Buenos Aires '80, Intl. Philatelic Exhibition, 10/24-11/2/80. Issued in sheets of 4. Value, set $125.

Purmamarca Church SP32

Churches: 200p + 100p, Molinos. 300p + 150p, Animana. 400p + 200p, San Jose de Lules.

1979, Nov. 3   Litho.   Perf. 13½
B84	SP32	100p + 50p multi	.30	.25
B85	SP32	200p + 100p multi	.45	.25
B86	SP32	300p + 150p multi	.65	.30
B87	SP32	400p + 200p multi	.90	.50

Nos. B84-B87 (4)   2.30   1.30

Buenos Aires No. 3, Exhibition and Society Emblems — SP33

Argentine Stamps: 750p+750p, type A580. 1000p+1000p, No. 91. 2000p+2000p, type A588.

1979, Dec. 15   Litho.   Perf. 13½
B88	SP33	250p + 250p	1.50	1.25
B89	SP33	750p + 750p	2.75	2.25
B90	SP33	1000p + 1000p	8.00	6.00
B91	SP33	2000p + 2000p	6.75	6.00

Nos. B88-B91 (4)   19.00   15.50

PRENFIL '80, Intl. Philatelic Literature and Publications Exhib., Buenos Aires, Nov. 7-16, 1980.

Minuet, by Carlos E. Pellegrini SP34

Paintings: 700p+350p, Media Cana, by Carlos Morel. 800p+400p, Cielito, by Pellegrini. 1000p+500p, El Gato, by Juan Leon Palliere.

1981, July 11   Litho.   Perf. 13½
B92	SP34	500p + 250p multi	.80	.45
B93	SP34	700p + 350p multi	1.20	.80
B94	SP34	800p + 400p multi	1.25	1.00
B95	SP34	1000p + 500p multi	1.60	1.40

Nos. B92-B95 (4)   4.85   3.65

Espamer '81 Intl. Stamp Exhib. (Americas, Spain, Portugal), Buenos Aires, Nov. 13-22.

Canal, by Beatrix Bongliani (b. 1933) — SP35

Tapestries: 1000p+500p, Shadows, by Silvia Sieburger, vert. 2000p+1000p, Interpretation of a Rectangle, by Silke R. de Haupt, vert. 4000p+2000p, Tilcara, by Tana Sachs.

1982, July 31   Litho.   Perf. 13½

B96	SP35 1000p + 500p multi	.40	.40
B97	SP35 2000p + 1000p multi	.50	.50
B98	SP35 3000p + 1500p multi	.60	.60
B99	SP35 4000p + 2000p multi	.70	.70
	Nos. B96-B99 (4)	2.20	2.20

Boy Playing Marbles SP36

No. B101, Jumping rope. No. B102, Hopscotch. No. B103, Flying kites. No. B104, Spinning top.

1983, July 2   Litho.   Perf. 13½

B100	SP36 20c + 10c shown	.30	.30
B101	SP36 30c + 15c multi	.35	.30
B102	SP36 50c + 25c multi	.70	.60
B103	SP36 1p + 50c multi	.90	.70
B104	SP36 2p + 1p multi	1.25	1.00
	Nos. B100-B104 (5)	3.50	2.90

Surtax was for natl. philatelic associations. See Nos. B106-B110.

Compass, 15th Cent. — SP37

ARGENTINA '85 Intl. Stamp Show: b, Arms of Spain, Argentina. c, Columbus' arms. d-f, Columbus' arrival at San Salvador Island. Nos. B105d-B105f in continuous design; ships shown on singles range in size, left to right, from small to large. Surtax was for exhibition.

1984, Apr. 28   Litho.   Perf. 13½

B105	Block of 6	4.00	4.00
a.-f.	SP37 5p + 2.50p, any single	.60	.40

Children's Game Type of 1983

No. B106, Blind Man's Buff. No. B107, The Loop. No. B108, Leap Frog. No. B109, Rolling the loop. No. B110, Ball Mold.

1984, July 7   Litho.   Perf. 13½

B106	SP36 2p + 1p multi	.35	.25
B107	SP36 3p + 1.50p multi	.35	.30
B108	SP36 4p + 2p multi	.50	.40
B109	SP36 5p + 2.50p multi	.50	.40
B110	SP36 6p + 3p multi	.70	.60
	Nos. B106-B110 (5)	2.40	1.95

Butterflies — SP38

No. B111, Rothschildia jacobaeae. No. B112, Heliconius erato phyllis. No. B113, Precis evarete hilaris. No. B114, Cyanopepla pretiosa. No. B115, Papilio androgeus.

1985, Nov. 9   Litho.   Perf. 13½

B111	SP38 5c + 2c multi	.90	.90
B112	SP38 10c + 5c multi	.90	.60
B113	SP38 20c + 10c multi	1.25	.75
B114	SP38 25c + 13c multi	1.90	1.50
B115	SP38 40c + 20c multi	2.50	2.25
	Nos. B111-B115 (5)	7.45	5.40

Children's Drawings — SP39

No. B116, N. Pastor, vert. No. B117, T. Valleistein. No. B118, J.M. Flores, vert. No. B119, M.E. Pezzuto. No. B120, E. Diehl.

1986, Aug. 30   Litho.

B116	SP39 5c + 2c multi	.25	.25
B117	SP39 10c + 5c multi	.35	.35
B118	SP39 20c + 10c multi	.60	.60
B119	SP39 25c + 13c multi	.85	.85
B120	SP39 40c + 20c multi	1.25	1.25
	Nos. B116-B120 (5)	3.30	3.30

Surtax for natl. philatelic associations.

Miniature Sheets

Fresh-water Fish — SP40

No. B121: a, Metynnis maculatus. b, Cynolebias nigripinnis. c, Leporinus solarii. d, Aphyocharax rathbuni. e, Corydoras aeneus. f, Thoracocharax securis. g, Cynolebias melanotaenia. h, Cichlasoma facetum.
No. B122: a, Tetragonopterus argenteus. b, Hemigrammus caudovittatus. c, Astyanax bimaculatus. d, Gymnocorymbus ternetzi. e, Hoplias malabaricus. f, Aphyocharax rubripinnis. g, Apistogramma agassizi. h, Pyrrhulina rachoviana.

1987, June 27

B121	SP40 Sheet of 8	1.50	1.50
a.-h.	10c +5c, any single	.25	.25
B122	SP40 Sheet of 8	3.00	3.00
a.-h.	20c +10c, any single	.45	.35

PRENFIL '88, Intl. Philatelic Literature and Media Exhibition, Buenos Aires, Nov. 25-Dec. 2 — SP41

Locomotives and railroad car: No. B123, Yatay locomotive, 1888. No. B124, FCCA electric passenger car, 1914. No. B125, B-15 locomotive, 1942. No. B126, GT-22 No. 200 locomotive, 1988.

1988, June 4   Litho.   Perf. 13½

B123	SP41 1a +50c multi	.80	.60
B124	SP41 1a +50c multi	.80	.60
B125	SP41 1a +50c multi	.80	.60
B126	SP41 1a +50c multi	.80	.60
	Nos. B123-B126 (4)	3.20	2.40

Nos. B123-B125 each issued in sheets of 4. Value, set $16.

Horses SP42

Paintings: No. B127, *The Waiting*, by Gustavo Solari. No. B128, *Mare and Foal*, by E. Castro. No. B129, *Saint Isidor*, by Castro. No. B130, *At Lagoon's Edge*, by F. Romero Carranza. No. B131, *Under the Tail*, by Castro.

1988, Oct. 29   Litho.   Perf. 13½

B127	SP42 2a +1a multi	1.10	.60
B128	SP42 2a +1a multi	1.10	.60
B129	SP42 2a +1a multi	1.10	.60
B130	SP42 2a +1a multi	1.10	.60
B131	SP42 2a +1a multi	1.10	.60
	Nos. B127-B131 (5)	5.50	3.00

PRENFIL '88 — SP43

Covers of philatelic magazines: No. B132, *Cronaca Filatelica,* Italy. No. B133, *CO-Fi,* Brazil. No. B134, *References de la Poste,* France. No. B135, *Postas Argentinas.*

1988, Nov. 26   Litho.   Perf. 13½

B132	SP43 1a +1a multi	.50	.40
B133	SP43 1a +1a multi	.50	.40
B134	SP43 1a +1a multi	.50	.40
B135	SP43 2a +2a multi	.50	.40
	Nos. B132-B135 (4)	2.00	1.60

Nos. B132-B135 printed in sheets of 4. Value, set $14.

Souvenir Sheet

ARBRAPEX '88 — SP44

Designs: No. B136a, *Candel Delivery at San Ignacio*, by Leonie Matthis, Cornelio Saavedra Museum, Buenos Aires. No. B136b, *Immaculate Conception*, a statue in the Isaac Fernandez Blanco Museum, Buenos Aires.

1988, Nov. 26   Perf. 12

B136	SP44 Sheet of 2	3.00	3.00
a.	2a +2a multi	1.00	.75
b.	3a +3a multi	1.75	1.25

Fish SP45

Designs: No. B137, Diplomystes viedmensis. No. B138, Haplochiton taeniatus. No. B139, Percichthys trucha. No. B140, Galaxias platei. No. B141, Salmo fario.

1989, June 24   Litho.   Perf. 13½

B137	SP45 10a +5a multi	.60	.40
B138	SP45 10a +5a multi	.60	.40
B139	SP45 10a +5a multi	.60	.40
B140	SP45 10a +5a multi	.60	.40
B141	SP45 10a +5a multi	.60	.40
	Nos. B137-B141 (5)	3.00	2.00

Nos. B137-B141 printed in sheets of 4. Value, set $15.

Discovery of America 500th Anniv. (in 1992) and ESPAMER '90 — SP46

Documents and chronicles: No. B142, Columbus's coat of arms, *Book of Privileges* title page. No. B143, Illustration from *New Chronicle and Good Government*, by Guaman Poma de Ayala. No. B144, Illustration from *Discovery and Conquest of Peru*, by Pedro de Cieza de Leon. No. B145, Illustration from *Travel to the River Plate*, by Ulrico Schmidl.

**1989, Sept. 16   Litho.   Perf. 13½
Yellow, Rose Violet & Black**

B142	SP46 100a +50a	1.00	.85
B143	SP46 150a +75a	1.00	.85
B144	SP46 200a +100a	1.00	.85
B145	SP46 250a +100a	1.00	.85
	Nos. B142-B145 (4)	4.00	3.40

Nos. B142-B145 printed in sheets of 4. Value, set $17.

Insects SP47

Designs: No. B146, *Podisus nigrispinus.* No. B147, *Adalia bipunctata.* No. B148, *Nabis punctipennis.* No. B149, *Hippodamia convergens.* No. B150, *Calleida suturalis.*

1990, June 30   Litho.   Perf. 13½

B146	SP47 1000a +500a multi	1.00	.85
B147	SP47 1000a +500a multi	1.00	.85
B148	SP47 1000a +500a multi	1.00	.85
B149	SP47 1000a +500a multi	1.00	.85
B150	SP47 1000a +500a multi	1.00	.85
	Nos. B146-B150 (5)	5.00	4.25

Nos. B146-B150 printed in sheets of 4. Value, set $24.

Souvenir Sheet

First Natl. Exposition of Aerophilately — SP48

a, Lieut. Marcos A. Zar, Macchi seaplane. b, Capt. Antonio Parodi, Ansaldo SVA biplane.

1990, July 14   Litho.   Perf. 12

B151	SP48 Sheet of 2	7.00	5.00
a.	2000a +2000a multi	3.00	2.50
b.	3000a +3000a multi	3.00	2.50

Souvenir Sheet

1992 Summer Olympics,
Barcelona — SP49

Designs: a, Shot put. b, High jump. c, Hurdles. d, Pole vault.

1990, Dec. 15   **Litho.**   **Perf. 13½**
B152   SP49   Sheet of 4   11.00 11.00
   a.-d.   2000a +2000a multi   2.50   2.50

Espamer '91 Philatelic Exhibition.
See No. B155.

Souvenir Sheet

Discovery of America, 500th Anniv. (in
1992) — SP50

Voyage of Alesandro Malaspina, 1789-1794:
a, Sailing ship. b, Malaspina. c, Indian, hut. d,
Indian, horse, artist drawing.

1990, Oct. 13   **Litho.**   **Perf. 13½**
B153   SP50   Sheet of 4   7.00 6.00
   a.-d.   2000a +1000a, any single   1.60 1.60

Espamer '91, Buenos Aires.

Souvenir Sheet

Race Cars and Drivers — SP51

Designs: a, Juan Manuel Fangio. b, Juan
Manuel Bordeu. c, Carlos Alberto Reutemann.
d, Oscar and Juan Galvez.

1991   **Litho.**   **Perf. 13½**
B154   SP51   Sheet of 4   6.50 6.50
   a.-d.   2500a +2500a, any single   1.40 1.25

Espamer '91.

1992 Summer Olympics Type of 1990
Souvenir Sheet

Women's gymnastics routines: a, Floor
exercise. b, Uneven parallel bars. c, Balance
beam. d, Rhythmic gymnastics.

1991, June 29   **Perf. 13½**
B155   SP49   Sheet of 4   6.50 6.50
   a.-d.   2500a +2500a, any single   1.40 1.25

Espamer '91.

Iberoprenfil '92 — SP52

Designs: No. B156, Castor missile. No.
B157, Satellite LUSAT 1.

1991, Dec. 28   **Litho.**   **Perf. 13½**
B156   SP52   4000a +4000a multi   3.00 3.00
B157   SP52   4000a +4000a multi   3.00 3.00

Dinosaurs
SP53

No. B158, Carnotaurus. No. B159,
Amargasaurus.

1992, May 2   **Litho.**   **Perf. 13½**
B158   SP53   38c +38c multi   1.75 1.75
B159   SP53   38c +38c multi   1.75 1.75
   a.   Pair, #B158-B159   4.50 4.50

Iberoprenfil '92, Buenos Aires — SP54

Paintings by Raul Soldi (b. 1905): No. B160,
The Fiesta. No. B161, Church of St. Anne of
Glew.

1992, Sept. 5   **Litho.**   **Perf. 13½**
B160   SP54   76c +76c multi   3.75 3.00
B161   SP54   76c +76c multi   3.75 3.00

Parafil
'92 — SP55

1992, Nov. 21   **Litho.**   **Perf. 13½**
B162   SP55   76c +76c multi   3.75 3.00

2nd Argentine-Paraguayan Philatelic Exhibition, Buenos Aires.

Souvenir Sheet

Birds — SP56

a, Egretta thula. b, Amblyramphus holosericeus. c, Paroaria coronata. d, Chloroceryle
amazona.

1993, July 17   **Litho.**   **Perf. 13½**
B163   SP56   38c +38c Sheet of 4   8.00 8.00

Souvenir Sheet

Latin American Air Post Philatelic
Exhibition — SP57

Designs: a, 25c+25c, Antoine de Saint-Exupery (1940-44), pilot, author. b, 75c+75c,
"The Little Prince," vert.

1995, June 3   **Litho.**   **Perf. 12**
B164   SP57   Sheet of 2, #a.-b.   7.00 7.00

For overprint see No. B180.

Souvenir Sheet

Exploration of Antarctica — SP58

75c+25c, Transport ship ARA Bahia Aguirre.
1.25p+75c, Argentine Air Force Hercules C-130.

1995, July 8
B165   SP58   Sheet of 2, #a.-b.   8.00 8.00

Aerofila
'96
SP59

Historic airplanes, pilots: No. B166, "Plus
ultra," Ramón Franco Bahamonde (1896-1938). No. B167, 14 Bis, Alberto Santos-Dumont (1873-1932). No. B168, Spirit of St.
Louis, Charles A. Lindbergh (1902-1974). No.
B169, Buenos Aires, Eduardo A. Olivero
(1896-1966).

1996, July 13   **Litho.**   **Perf. 13½**
B166   SP59   25c +25c multi   1.20 1.20
B167   SP59   25c +25c multi   1.20 1.20
B168   SP59   50c +50c multi   2.40 2.40
B169   SP59   50c +50c multi   2.40 2.40
   Nos. B166-B169 (4)   7.20 7.20

Ceramic
Murals
from
Buenos
Aires
Subway
SP60

1996, Sept. 21   **Litho.**   **Perf. 13½**
B170   SP60   1p +50c Dragon   3.50 2.75
B171   SP60   1.50p +1p Bird   5.25 4.50

MEVIFIL '97,
1st Intl.
Exhibition of
Audio-Visual
and Philatelic
Information
Media — SP61

Designs: No. B172, France Type A1. No.
B173, Spain Type A3. No. B174, Argentina
Type A4. No. B175, Buenos Aires Type A1.

1997, May 10   **Litho.**   **Perf. 13½**
B172   SP61   50c +50c multi   2.00 2.00
B173   SP61   50c +50c multi   2.00 2.00
B174   SP61   50c +50c multi   2.00 2.00
B175   SP61   50c +50c multi   2.00 2.00
   a.   Block of 4, #B172-B175   9.00 9.00

Issued in sheets of 16 stamps + 4 labels.

Trains — SP62

Designs: No. B176, Las Nubes (Train to the
Clouds), Salta. No. B177, Historical train, Buenos Aires. No. B178, Old Patagonian Express,
Rio Negro-Chubut. No. B179, Southern
Fueguino Railway, Tierra Del Fuego.

1997, Sept. 6   **Litho.**   **Perf. 13**
B176   SP62   50c +50c multi   2.50 2.50
B177   SP62   50c +50c multi   2.50 2.50
B178   SP62   50c +50c multi   2.50 2.50
B179   SP62   50c +50c multi   2.50 2.50
   Nos. B176-B179 (4)   10.00 10.00

No. B164 Overprinted in Red Violet

1997, Sept. 27   **Litho.**   **Perf. 12**
B180   SP57   Sheet of 2   7.50 7.50

Cartography — SP63

Maps of the Buenos Aires area from:
25c+25c, 1546. No. B182, 17th century. No.
B183, 1910. 75c+75c, 1999.

Perf. 13¾x13½
1999, Nov. 20   **Litho.**
B181   SP63   25c + 25c multi   1.00 1.00
B182   SP63   50c + 50c multi   2.00 2.00
B183   SP63   50c + 50c multi   2.00 2.00
B184   SP63   75c + 75c multi   3.00 3.00
   a.   Block of 4, #B181-B184   13.00 13.00

Methods of Transportation — SP64

No. B185: a, Bicycle. b, Graf Zeppelin. c, Train. d, Trolley.

2000, Oct. 21   Litho.   Perf. 14x13½
B185	Block of 4	8.00	8.00
a.	SP64 25c +25c multi	1.00	1.00
b.-c.	SP64 50c +50c Any single	2.00	2.00
d.	SP64 75c +75c multi	3.00	3.00

Cetaceans — SP65

No. B186: a, Burmeister's porpoise (Mariposa espinosa). b, River Plate dolphin. c, Minke whale. d, Humpback whale (Yubarta).

2001, Sept. 15   Litho.   Perf. 14x13½
B186	Block of 4	8.00	8.00
a.	SP65 25c +25c multi	1.00	1.00
b.-c.	SP65 50c +50c Any single	2.00	2.00
d.	SP65 75c +75c multi	3.00	3.00

Reptiles — SP66

No. B187: a, Boa constrictor occidentalis. b, Caiman yacare. c, Tupinambis merianae. d, Chelonoidis carbonaria.

2002, Aug. 24   Litho.   Perf. 14x13½
B187	Block of 4	6.00	6.00
a.	SP66 25c +25c multi	.75	.75
b.-c.	SP66 50c +50c Either single	1.25	1.25
d.	SP66 75c +75c multi	2.00	2.00

Bicycles — SP67

No. B188: a, Velocipede, 1855, Cycling Club champions, 1902. b, Velocipede, 1867, postman with delivery tricycle. c, Coventry Eagle touring bicycle, 1949, cyclists in park. d, Racing bicycle, 1960s, Palermo Velodrome, 1902.

2003, Aug. 9   Litho.   Perf. 14x13¾
B188	Block of 4	3.00	3.00
a.	SP67 25c+25c multi	.40	.40
b.-c.	SP67 50c+50c Either single	.65	.65
d.	SP67 75c+75c multi	1.00	1.00

Ships — SP68

No. B189: a, A. R. A. Villarino. b, A. R. A. Pampa. c, A. R. A. Bahia Thetis. d, A. R. A. Cabo de Hornos.

2004, Aug. 21   Litho.   Perf. 14x13½
B189	Block of 4	3.75	3.75
a.	SP68 25c +25c multi	.40	.40
b.-c.	SP68 50c +50c either single	.60	.60
d.	SP68 75c +75c multi	1.00	1.00

Merchant Ships — SP69

No. B190: a, Río de la Plata. b, Libertad. c, Campo Durán. d, Isla Soledad.

2005, Sept. 24   Litho.   Perf. 14x13½
B190	Block of 4	3.50	3.50
a.	SP69 25c +25c multi	.35	.35
b.-c.	SP69 50c +50c either single	.65	.65
d.	SP69 75c +75c multi	1.00	1.00

River Boats — SP70

No. B191: a, Ciudad de Buenos Aires. b, Lambaré. c, Madrid. d, Rawson.

2006, Aug. 19   Litho.   Perf. 14x13½
B191	Block of 4	3.50	3.50
a.	SP70 25c +25c multi	.40	.40
b.-c.	SP70 50c +50c either single	.75	.75
d.	SP70 75c +75c multi	1.10	1.10

Scouting, Cent. — SP71

No. B192: a, Scouts at campfire. b, Scout saluting near tent. c, Scout saluting, Scout with patrol flag. d, Scouts pulling rope.

2007, July 28   Litho.   Perf. 13½x14
B192	Horiz. strip of 4	4.00	4.00
a.	SP71 25c +25c multi	.35	.35
b.	SP71 50c +50c multi	.70	.70
c.	SP71 75c +75c multi	1.00	1.00
d.	SP71 1p +1p multi	1.25	1.25

Shells — SP72

Designs: 25c+25c, Calliostoma militaris. 50c+50c, Epitonium fabrizioi. 75c+75c, Odontocymbiola magellanica. 1p+1p, Trophon geversianus.

Perf. 13½x13¾
2008, Aug. 23   Litho.
B193-B196	Set of 4	4.00	4.00

Astronomical Observatories — SP73

Designs: No. B197, 50c+50c, Radio telescope, Argentine Institute of Radioastronomy. No. B198, 50c+50c, Telescope, La Plata

Astronomical Observatory. No. B199, 1p+1p, El Lioncito Astronomical Complex. No. B200, 1p+1p, Telescope, Félix Aguilar Astronomical Observatory.

2009, Aug. 22   Litho.   Perf. 14x13½
B197-B200	SP73	Set of 4	3.25	3.25

Girl Guides and Girl Scouts, Cent. — SP74

Designs: No. B201, 75c+75c, Girl Scout salute. No. B202, 75c+75c, Hands of five Girl Scouts joined. No. B203, 1p+1p, Hands of Girl Scouts joined, campfire. No. B204, 1p+1p, Hand on shoulder of Girl Scout.

2010, Aug. 21   Litho.   Perf. 13½x14
B201-B204	SP74	Set of 4	3.75	3.75

Minerals SP75

Designs: No. B205, 1.25p+1.25p, Rhodochrosite (rodocrisita). No. B206, 1.25p+1.25p, Sulphur (azufre). No. B207, 1.25p+1.25p, Pyrite (pirita). No. B208, 1.25p+1.25p, Quartz (cuarzo).

2011, Aug. 20   Perf. 13¾x13½
B205-B208	SP75	Set of 4	4.75	4.75

Minerals Type of 2011

Designs: No. B209, 1.50p+1.50p, Agate (agata). No. B210, 1.50p+1.50p, Amethyst (amatista). No. B211, 1.50p+1.50p, Fluorite (fluorita). No. B212, 1.50p+1.50p, Malachite (malaquita).

2012, Aug. 25
B209-B212	SP75	Set of 4	5.25	5.25

Extreme Sports — SP76

Designs: No. B213, 2p+2p, Skiing. No. B214, 2p+2p, Skateboarding. No. B215, 2p+2p, BMX cycling. No. B216, 2p+2p, Surfing.

2013, Dec. 21   Litho.   Perf. 14x13½
B213-B216	SP76	Set of 4	5.00	5.00

Volcanoes — SP77

Designs: No. B217, 5p+5p, Payú Liso. No. B218, 5p+5p, Llullaillaco. No. B219, 5p+5p, Lanín. No. B220, 5p+5p, Maipo.

Perf. 13¾x13½
2014, Aug. 19   Litho.
B217-B220	SP77	Set of 4	9.50	9.50

Clocks and Sundials SP78

Designs: No. B221, 7p+7p, Los Colosos de Siemens Clock, Buenos Aires. No. B222, 7p+7p, Palacio Fuentes Clock Tower, Rosario. No. B223, 7p+7p, Jesuit Estate Sundial, Alta Gracia. No. B224, 7p+7p, Miroglio Brothers Clock, Buenos Aires.

2015, Dec. 4   Litho.   Perf. 13½x13¾
B221-B224	SP78	Set of 4	11.50	11.50

AIR POST STAMPS

Airplane Circles the Globe — AP1   Eagle — AP2

Wings Cross the Sea — AP3

Condor on Mountain Crag — AP4

Perforations of Nos. C1-C37 vary from clean-cut to rough and uneven, with many skipped perfs.

Perf. 13x13½, 13½x13
1928, Mar. 1   Litho.   Wmk. 90
C1	AP1	5c lt red	1.50	.60
C2	AP1	10c Prus blue	2.50	1.10
C3	AP2	15c lt brown	2.50	1.00
C4	AP1	18c lilac gray	4.00	3.00
a.		18c brown lilac	4.50	3.00
b.		Double impression	375.00	
C5	AP2	20c ultra	3.00	1.00
C6	AP2	24c deep blue	5.00	3.00
C7	AP3	25c brt violet	5.00	1.60
C8	AP3	30c rose red	6.00	1.25
C9	AP4	35c rose	5.00	1.10
C10	AP1	36c bister brn	3.00	1.60
C11	AP4	50c gray black	5.00	.75
C12	AP2	54c chocolate	5.00	2.25
C13	AP2	72c yellow grn	6.00	2.25
a.		Double impression	350.00	
C14	AP3	90c dk brown	11.00	2.00
C15	AP3	1p slate bl & red	13.00	.90
C16	AP3	1.08p rose & dk bl	18.00	5.00
C17	AP4	1.26p dull vio & grn	25.00	10.00
C18	AP4	1.80p blue & lil rose	25.00	10.00
C19	AP4	3.60p gray & blue	50.00	22.00
		Nos. C1-C19 (19)	195.50	70.40

The watermark on No. C4a is larger than on the other stamps of this set, measuring 10mm across Sun.

Zeppelin First Flight

Air Post Stamps of 1928 Overprinted in Blue

1930, May

C20	AP2	20c ultra	10.00	5.00
C21	AP4	50c gray black	20.00	10.00
a.		Inverted overprint	475.00	
C22	AP3	1p slate bl & red	25.00	12.50
a.		Inverted overprint	650.00	
C23	AP4	1.80p blue & lil rose	70.00	30.00
C24	AP4	3.60p gray & blue	200.00	90.00
		Nos. C20-C24 (5)	325.00	147.50

Overprinted in Green

C25	AP2	20c ultra	13.00	8.00
C26	AP4	50c gray black	15.00	10.00
C27	AP3	90c dark brown	13.00	8.00
C28	AP3	1p slate bl & red	25.00	15.00
C29	AP4	1.80p blue & lil rose	700.00	500.00
a.		Thick paper	850.00	
		Nos. C25-C29 (5)	766.00	541.00

Air Post Stamps of 1928 Overprinted in Red or Blue

On AP1-AP2

On AP3-AP4

1931

C30	AP1	18c lilac gray	2.00	1.50
C31	AP2	72c yellow green	14.00	10.50
C32	AP3	90c dark brown	14.00	10.50
C33	AP4	1.80p bl & lil rose (Bl)	30.00	22.50
C34	AP4	3.60p gray & blue	57.50	40.00
		Nos. C30-C34 (5)	117.50	85.00

1st anniv. of the Revolution of 1930.

Zeppelin Issue

Nos. C1, C4, C4a, C14 Overprinted in Blue or Red

On AP1

On AP3

1932, Aug. 4

C35	AP1	5c lt red (Bl)	3.00	2.00
C36	AP1	18c lilac gray (R)	12.50	9.00
a.		18c brown lilac (R)	100.00	60.00
C37	AP3	90c dark brown (R)	32.50	26.00
		Nos. C35-C37 (3)	48.00	37.00

Plane and Letter — AP5

Mercury — AP6

Plane in Flight — AP7

Perf. 13½x13, 13x13½

1940, Oct. 23 Photo. Wmk. 90

C38	AP5	30c deep orange	5.00	.25
C39	AP6	50c dark brown	7.50	.25
C40	AP5	1p carmine	1.75	.25
C41	AP7	1.25p deep green	.50	.25
C42	AP5	2.50p bright blue	1.25	.25
		Nos. C38-C42 (5)	16.00	1.25

Plane and Letter — AP8

Mercury and Plane — AP9

Perf. 13½x13, 13x13½

1942, Oct. 6 Litho. Wmk. 90

C43	AP8	30c orange	.25	.25
C44	AP9	50c dull brn & buff	.40	.25

No. C43 exists imperf. Value, pair $20.
See Nos. C49-C52, C57, C61.

Plane over Iguaçu Falls — AP10

Plane over the Andes — AP11

Perf. 13½x13

1946, June 10 Unwmk.

C45	AP10	15c dull red brn	.25	.25
C46	AP11	25c gray green	.25	.25

See Nos. C53-C54.

Allegory of Flight AP12

Astrolabe — AP13

Perf. 13½x13, 13x13½

1946, Sept. 25 Litho. Unwmk.
Surface-Tinted Paper

C47	AP12	15c sl grn, pale grn	.55	.25
C48	AP13	60c vio brn, ocher	.55	.35

Types of 1942

1946-48 Unwmk. Perf. 13½x13

C49	AP8	30c orange	1.40	.25
C50	AP9	50c dull brn & buff	2.50	.25
C51	AP8	1p carmine ('47)	1.25	.25
C52	AP8	2.50p brt blue ('48)	5.50	.75
		Nos. C49-C52 (4)	10.65	1.50

No. C51 exists imperf. Value, pair $30.

Types of 1946

1948 Wmk. 90

C53	AP10	15c dull red brn	.25	.25
C54	AP11	25c gray green	.25	.25

Atlas (National Museum, Naples) — AP14

Map of Argentine Republic, Globe and Caliper — AP15

Perf. 13½x13, 13x13½

1948-49 Photo. Wmk. 288

C55	AP14	45c dk brown ('49)	.40	.25
C56	AP15	70c dark green	.70	.40

4th Pan-American Reunion of Cartographers, Buenos Aires, Oct.-Nov., 1948.

Mercury Type of 1942

1949 Litho. Perf. 13x13½

C57	AP9	50c dull brn & buff	.40	.25

Marksmanship Trophy — AP16

1949, Nov. 4 Photo.

C58	AP16	75c brown	.75	.25

World Rifle Championship, 1949.

> **Catalogue values for unused stamps in this section, from this point to the end of the section, are for Never Hinged items.**

Douglas DC-3 and Condor AP17

Perf. 13x13½

1951, June 20 Wmk. 90

C59	AP17	20c dk olive grn	.50	.25

10th anniversary of the State air lines.

Douglas DC-6 and Condor — AP18

1951, Oct. 17 Perf. 13½

C60	AP18	20c blue	.50	.25

End of Argentine 5-year Plan.

Plane-Letter Type of 1942

1951 Litho. Perf. 13½x13

C61	AP8	1p carmine	.40	.25

No. C61 exists imperf. Value, pair $20.

Jesus by Leonardo da Vinci (detail, "Virgin of the Rocks") AP19

Perf. 13½x13

1956, Sept. 29 Photo. Wmk. 90

C62	AP19	1p dull purple	.80	.25

Issued to express the gratitude of the children of Argentina to the people of the world for their help against poliomyelitis.

Battle of Montevideo AP20

Leonardo Rosales and Tomas Espora AP21

Guillermo Brown — AP22

1957, Mar. 2 Perf. 13½

C63	AP20	60c blue gray	.25	.25
C64	AP21	1p brt pink	.30	.25
C65	AP22	2p brown	.30	.25
		Nos. C63-C65 (3)	.85	.75

Cent. of the death of Admiral Guillermo Brown, founder of the Argentine navy.

Map of Americas & Arms of Buenos Aires — AP23

1957, Aug. 16

C66	AP23	2p rose violet	.50	.25

Issued to publicize the Inter-American Economic Conference in Buenos Aires.

Modern locomotive
AP24

1957, Aug. 31   Wmk. 90   Perf. 13½
C67 AP24 60c gray   .45 .25
Centenary of Argentine railroads.

AP25

No. C68, Globe, Flag,Compass Rose. No. C69, Key.

1957, Sept. 14
C68 AP25 1p multi   .25 .25
C69 AP25 2p multi   .30 .25
1957 International Congress for Tourism.

Birds Carrying Letters
AP26

1957, Nov. 6
C70 AP26 1p bright blue   .35 .25
Issued for Letter Writing Week, Oct. 6-12.

Early Plane AP27

1958, May 31   Perf. 13½
C71 AP27 2p maroon   .25 .25
50th anniv. of the Argentine Aviation Club.

Stamp Anniv. Type

Designs: 80c, Stamp of Buenos Aires and view of the Plaza de la Aduana. 1p, Stamp of 1858 and "The Post of Santa Fe."

1958   Litho.   Perf. 13½
C72 A270 80c pale bis & sl bl   .25 .25
C73 A270 1p red org & dk bl   .25 .25
Cent. of the 1st postage stamps of Buenos Aires & the Argentine Confederation.
Issue dates: 80c, Oct. 18; 1p, Aug. 23.

Comet Jet over World Map
AP29

1959, May 16   Perf. 13½
C74 AP29 5p black & olive   .40 .25
Inauguration of jet flights by Argentine Airlines.

Type of Regular Issue, 1960

"Cabildo" and: 1.80p, Mariano Moreno. 5p, Manuel Belgrano and Juan Jose Castelli.

Perf. 13½
1960, May 28   Wmk. 90   Photo.
C75 A287 1.80p red brown   .25 .25
  a.   Souvenir sheet of 3   1.40 .95
C76 A287 5p buff & purple   .35 .25
  a.   Souvenir sheet of 3   2.00 1.50

Souvenir sheets are imperf. No. C75a contains one No. C75 and 1p and 2p resembling Nos. 713-714; stamps in reddish brown. No. C76a contains one No. C76 and 4.20p and 10.70p resembling Nos. 715-716; stamps are in green.

Symbolic of New Provinces — AP30

1960, July 8   Litho.
C77 AP30 1.80p dp car & blue   .30 .25
Elevation of the territories of Chubut, Formosa, Neuquen, Rio Negro and Santa Cruz to provinces.

Type of Regular Issue, 1960
1960, Oct. 1   Photo.   Perf. 13½
C78 A291 1.80p rose lilac   .50 .25
C79 A291 10.70p brt grnsh blue   .70 .35

UNESCO Emblem AP31

1962, July 14   Litho.
C80 AP31 13p ocher & brown   .40 .25
15th anniv. of UNESCO.

Mail Coach AP32

1962, Oct. 6   Wmk. 90   Perf. 13½
C81 AP32 5.60p gray brn & blk   .75 .25
Mailman's Day, Sept. 14, 1962.

No. 695 and Type of 1959 Surcharged in Green

1962, Oct. 31   Photo.
C82 A277 5.60p on 5p brown   .30 .25
C83 A277 18p on 5p brn, grnsh   1.00 .25

UPAE Emblem — AP33

1962, Nov. 24   Photo.   Perf. 13½
C84 AP33 5.60p dark blue   .40 .25
50th anniv. of the founding of the Postal Union of the Americas and Spain, UPAE.

Skylark — AP34

Design: 11p, Super Albatros.

1963, Feb. 9   Litho.
C85 AP34 5.60p blue & black   .25 .25
C86 AP34 11p blue, blk & red   .40 .25
9th World Gliding Championships.

Symbolic Plane AP35

1963-65   Wmk. 90   Perf. 13½
C87 AP35 5.60p dk pur, car & brt grn   .40 .25
C88 AP35 7p black & bis ('64)   .55 .25
C88A AP35 7p black & bis ('65)   5.00 1.00
C89 AP35 11p blk, dk pur & grn   .60 .25
C90 AP35 18p dk pur, red & vio bl   1.25 .35
C91 AP35 21p brown, red & gray   1.75 .40
  Nos. C87-C91 (6)   9.55 2.50

"Argentina" reads down on No. C88, up on No. C88A. See Nos. C101-C104, C108-C111, C123-C126, C135-C141. For overprint and surcharges see Nos. C96, C146-C150.

Type of Regular Issue, 1964

Map of Falkland Islands (Islas Malvinas).

1964, Feb. 22   Perf. 13½
Size: 33x22mm
C92 A327 18p lt & dk bl & ol grn   2.75 .75

UPU Monument, Bern, and UN Emblem AP36

1964, May 23   Engr.   Perf. 13½
C93 AP36 18p red & dk brown   .60 .25
15th UPU Cong., Vienna, Austria, 5-6/64.

Discovery of America, Florentine Woodcut AP37

1964, Oct. 10   Litho.
C94 AP37 13p tan & black   .90 .35
Day of the Race, Columbus Day.

Lt. Matienzo Base, Antarctica AP38

1965, Feb. 27   Photo.   Perf. 13½
C95 AP38 11p salmon pink   .50 .25

Issued to publicize the national territory of Tierra del Fuego, Antarctic and South Atlantic Isles.

No. C88A Overprinted in Silver

1965, Mar. 17   Litho.
C96 AP35 7p black & bister   .30 .25

1st Rio de la Plata Stamp Show, sponsored jointly by the Argentine and Uruguayan Philatelic Associations, Montevideo, Mar. 19-28.

ITU Emblem — AP39

1965, May 11   Wmk. 90   Perf. 13½
C97 AP39 18p slate, blk & red   .40 .25
Centenary of the ITU.

Ascending Rocket — AP40

Design: 50p, Earth with trajectories and magnetic field, horiz.

1965, May 29   Photo.   Perf. 13½
C98 AP40 18p vermilion   .70 .30
C99 AP40 50p dp violet blue   1.25 .55

6th Symposium on Space Research, held in Buenos Aires, and to honor the Natl. Commission of Space Research.

Type of 1963-65 Inscribed "Republica Argentina"

1965, Oct. 13   Litho.   Wmk. 90
C101 AP35 12p dk car rose & brn   1.40 .25
C102 AP35 15p vio blue & dk red   1.50 .50
C103 AP35 27.50p dk bl grn & gray   2.50 1.00
C104 AP35 30.50p dk brown & dk bl   3.00 1.50
  Nos. C101-C104 (4)   8.40 3.25

Argentine
Antarctica Map
and Centaur
Rocket
AP41

1966, Feb. 19   Perf. 13½
C105 AP41 27.50p bl, blk & dp
                    org   1.10   .85
Launchings of sounding balloons and of a
Gamma Centaur rocket in Antarctica during
February, 1965.

Sea Gull
and
Southern
Cross
AP42

1966, May 14   Perf. 13½
C106 AP42 12p Prus blue, blk &
              red   .40   .25
50th anniv. of the Naval Aviation School.

Blériot Plane
Flown by
Fels,
1917 — AP43

1967, Sept. 2   Litho.   Perf. 13½
C107 AP43 26p olive, bl & blk   .30   .25
Flight by Theodore Fels from Buenos Aires
to Montevideo, Sept. 2, 1917, allegedly the 1st
intl. airmail flight.

**Type of 1963-65 Inscribed
"Republica Argentina" Reading
Down**

1967, Dec. 20   Perf. 13½
C108 AP35 26p brown   .60   .25
C109 AP35 40p violet   5.25   .30
C110 AP35 68p blue green   3.50   .45
C111 AP35 78p ultra   1.50   .60
  Nos. C108-C111 (4)   10.85 1.60

Vito
Dumas
and
Ketch
"Legh II"
AP44

1968, July 27   Litho.   Wmk. 90
C112 AP44 68p bl, blk, red & vio
              bl   .65   .40
Issued to commemorate Vito Dumas's one-
man voyage around the world in 1943.

Type of Regular Issue and

Assembly Emblem — AP45

40p, Globe and map of South America.

1968, Oct. 19   Litho.   Perf. 13½
C113 A395 40p brt pink, lt bl &
              blk   .75   .30
C114 AP45 68p bl, lt bl, gold &
              blk   1.25   .50
4th Plenary Assembly of the Intl. Telegraph
and Telephone Consultative Committee, Mar
del Plata, Sept. 23-Oct. 25.

Radar
Antenna,
Balcarce
Station
AP46

Perf. 13½
1969, Aug. 23   Wmk. 90   Photo.
C115 AP46 40p blue gray   .70   .25
Communications by satellite through Intl.
Telecommunications Consortium (INTELSAT).

Atucha
Nuclear
Center
AP47

1969, Dec. 13   Litho.   Wmk. 365
C116 AP47 26p blue & multi   2.00   .80
Completion of Atucha Nuclear Center.

**Type of 1963-65 Inscribed
"Republica Argentina" Reading
Down**

1969-71   Perf. 13½
C123 AP35 40p violet   5.75   .40
C124 AP35 68p dk blue grn
              ('70)   2.10   .60

Unwmk.
C125 AP35 26p yellow brn ('71) .35   .25
C126 AP35 40p violet ('71)   3.00   .40
  Nos. C123-C126 (4)   11.20 1.65

Old Fire
Engine
and Fire
Brigade
Emblem
AP48

1970, Aug. 8   Litho.   Unwmk.
C128 AP48 40c green & multi 1.50   .30
Centenary of the Fire Brigade.

Education Year
Emblem
AP49

1970, Aug. 29   Perf. 13½
C129 AP49 68c blue & blk   .80   .30
Issued for International Education Year.

Fleet Leaving Valparaiso, by Antonio
Abel — AP50

1970, Oct. 17   Litho.   Perf. 13½
C130 AP50 26c multicolored   1.00   .35
150th anniv. of the departure for Peru of the
liberation fleet from Valparaiso, Chile.

Sumampa Chapel — AP51

1970, Nov. 7   Photo.
C131 AP51 40c multicolored   1.00   .40
Bishopric of Tucuman, 400th anniversary.

Buenos Aires Planetarium — AP52

1970, Nov. 28   Litho.   Perf. 13½
C132 AP52 40c multicolored   .75   .25

Jorge
Newbery
and
Morane
Saulnier
Plane
AP53

1970, Dec. 19
C133 AP53 26c bl, blk, yel & grn   .45   .25
24th Aeronautics and Space Week.

Industries Type of Regular Issue
Design: 31c, Refinery.

1971, Oct. 16   Litho.   Perf. 13½
C134 A445 31c red, blk & yel   .80   .30

**Type of 1963-65 Inscribed
"Republica Argentina" Reading
Down**

1971-74   Unwmk.
C135 AP35 45c brown   3.50   .25
C136 AP35 68c red   .50   .25
C137 AP35 70c vio blue ('73) 2.75   .50
C138 AP35 90c emerald ('73) 2.75   .50
C139 AP35 1.70p blue ('74)   .60   .25
C140 AP35 1.95p emerald ('74) .60   .25
C141 AP35 2.65p dp claret ('74) .60   .25
  Nos. C135-C141 (7)   11.30 2.25
Fluorescent paper was used for Nos. C135-
C136, C138-C141. The 70c was issued on
both papers. Value, 70c on fluorescent paper
$5.50

Don Quixote,
Drawing by
Ignacio
Zuloaga
AP54

1975, Apr. 26   Photo.   Perf. 13½
C145 AP54 2.75p yellow, blk &
              red   .60   .35
Day of the Race and for Espana 75 Intl.
Philatelic Exhibition, Madrid, Apr. 4-13.

No. C87
Surcharged

1975, Sept. 15   Litho.   Wmk. 90
C146 AP35 9.20p on 5.60p   .90   .25
C147 AP35 19.70p on 5.60p   1.25   .45
C148 AP35 100p on 5.60p   5.50 2.25
  Nos. C146-C148 (3)   7.65 2.95

No. C87
Surcharged

1975, Oct. 15
C149 AP35 9.20p on 5.60p   .90   .30
C150 AP35 19.70p on 5.60p   1.50   .60

Argentine State Airline, 50th
Anniv. — AP55

No. C151, Junkers JU52-3M. No. C152,
Grumman SA-16. No. C153, Fokker F-27. No.
C154, Fokker F-28.

1990, Sept. 15   Litho.   Perf. 13½
C151 AP55 2500a multi   1.50   .90
C152 AP55 2500a multi   1.50   .90
C153 AP55 2500a multi   1.50   .90
C154 AP55 2500a multi   1.50   .90
  Nos. C151-C154 (4)   6.00 3.60

AIR POST SEMI-POSTAL STAMPS

Catalogue values for unused
stamps in this section are for
Never Hinged items.

Philatelic Exhibition Type
Designs: No. CB1, Stamp engraving. No.
CB2, Proofing stamp die. No. CB3, Sheet of
stamps. No. CB4, The letter. No. CB5, Gen.
San Martin.

Perf. 13½
1950, Aug. 26   Wmk. 90   Photo.
CB1 SP8 45c + 45c vio bl   .35   .25
CB2 SP8 70c + 70c dk brn   .60   .40
  a.   Souv. sheet of 3, #B12, CB1,
        CB2, imperf.   5.00 3.00
CB3 SP8 1p + 1p cerise   1.25 1.25
CB4 SP8 2.50p + 2.50p ol gray 8.50 6.00
CB5 SP8 5p + 5p dull grn   10.00 7.25
  Nos. CB1-CB5 (5)   20.70 15.15
Argentine Intl. Philatelic Exhib., 1950.

Pieta by
Michelangelo
SPAP2

1951, Dec. 22   **Perf. 13½x13**
CB6 SPAP2 2.45p +7.55p
grnsh blk   22.50 14.00

Surtax as for the Eva Peron Foundation.

Flower and
Child's Head
SPAP3

1958, Mar. 15   **Perf. 13½**
CB7 SPAP3 1p +50c deep claret   .30   .30

Surtax for National Council for Children.

Stamp of
1858 — SPAP4

1958, Mar. 29   **Litho.**   **Wmk. 90**
CB8 SPAP4 1p + 50c gray ol &
bl   .45   .35
CB9 SPAP4 2p + 1p rose lilac
& vio   .55   .45
CB10 SPAP4 3p + 1.50p green
& brown   .60   .55
CB11 SPAP4 5p + 2.50p gray ol
& car rose   1.10   .90
CB12 SPAP4 10p + 5p gray ol &
brn   2.00 1.75
Nos. CB8-CB12 (5)   4.70 4.00

The surtax was for the Intl. Centennial Philatelic Exhibition, Buenos Aires, Apr. 19-27.

Type of Semi-Postal Issue, 1958

Designs: 1p+50c, Flooded area. 5p+2.50p, House and truck under water.

1958, Oct. 4   **Photo.**   **Perf. 13½**
CB13 SP11 1p + 50c dull purple   .30   .25
CB14 SP11 5p + 2.50p grnsh
blue   1.00   .80

The surtax was for victims of a flood in the Buenos Aires district.

Type of Semi-Postal Issue

1959, Sept. 5   **Litho.**   **Perf. 13½**
CB15 SP13 2p + 1p Rowing   .40   .25
CB16 SP13 3p + 1.50p Woman
diver   .60   .50

Bird Type of Semi-Postal Issue

2p+1p, Rufous tinamou. 3p+1.50p, Rhea.

1960, Feb. 6   **Perf. 13½**
CB17 SP14 2p + 1p rose car &
sal   .45   .25
CB18 SP14 3p + 1.50p slate
green   .50   .35

The surtax was for child welfare work. See No. CB29.

Buenos Aires
Market Place,
1810
SPAP5

6p+3p, Oxcart water carrier. 10.70p+5.30p, Settlers landing. 20p+10p, The Fort.

1960, Aug. 20   **Photo.**   **Wmk. 90**
CB19 SPAP5 2 + 1p rose
brown   .25   .25
CB20 SPAP5 6 + 3p gray   .35   .25
CB21 SPAP5 10.70 + 5.30p blue   .60   .50
CB22 SPAP5 20 + 10p bluish
grn   1.00   .85
Nos. CB19-CB22 (4)   2.20 1.85

Inter-American Philatelic Exhibition EFIMAYO 1960, Buenos Aires, Oct. 12-24, held to for the sesquicentennial of the May Revolution of 1810.
No. CB22 exists imperf. Value, pair $40.
For overprints see Nos. CB25-CB28.

Seibo, National
Flower — SPAP6

#CB24, Copihue, Chile's national flower.

1960, Sept. 10   **Perf. 13½**
CB23 SPAP6 6 + 3p lilac
rose   .50   .30
CB24 SPAP6 10.70 + 5.30p ver   .70   .40

The surtax was for earthquake victims in Chile. Nos. CB23-CB24 exist imperf. Value, each pair $40.

Nos. CB19-
CB22
Overprinted

1960, Oct. 8
CB25 SPAP5 2 + 1p rose
brown   .25   .25
CB26 SPAP5 6 + 3p gray   .30   .30
CB27 SPAP5 10.70 + 5.30p blue   .50   .40
CB28 SPAP5 20 + 10p bluish
green   1.00   .75
Nos. CB25-CB28 (4)   2.05 1.70

United Nations Day, Oct. 24, 1960.

Type of Semi-Postal Issue, 1960

Design: Emperor penguins.

1961, Feb. 25   **Photo.**   **Wmk. 90**
CB29 SP14 1.80p + 90c gray   .40   .25

The surtax was for child welfare work. Exists imperf. Value, pair $50.

Stamp of
1862 — SPAP7

1962, May 19   **Litho.**
CB30 SPAP7 6.50p + 6.50p Prus
bl & grnsh
bl   .70   .65

Opening of the "Argentina 62" Philatelic Exhibition, Buenos Aires, May 19-29. Exists imperf. Value, pair $40.

Type of Semi-Postal Issue, 1963

1963, May 18   **Wmk. 90**   **Perf. 13½**
CB31 SP21 11p + 5p Bicycling   .60   .50

Exists imperf. Value, pair $40.

Type of Semi-Postal Issue, 1962

Design: Pitangus sulphuratus bolivianus.

1963, Dec. 21   **Perf. 13½**
CB32 SP20 11p + 5p multi   1.10   .60

The surtax was for child welfare.

Type of Semi-Postal Issue, 1964

1964, July 18   **Litho.**
CB33 SP22 11p + 5p Sailboat   .90   .70

Exists imperf. Value, pair $50.

Crutch, Olympic
Torch and
Rings — SPAP8

1964, Sept. 19   **Litho.**   **Perf. 13½**
CB34 SPAP8 18p + 9p bluish
grn, blk, red &
yel   .60   .60

13th "Olympic" games for the handicapped, Tokyo, 1964. Exists imperf. Value, pair $50.

Bird Type of Semi-Postal Issue, 1962

Design: Iridoprocne leucopyga.

1964, Dec. 23   **Litho.**   **Wmk. 90**
CB35 SP20 18p + 9p multi   1.10   .85

The surtax was for child welfare.

Furnarius
Rufus Rufus —
SP22a

1966, Mar. 26   **Perf. 13½**
CB36 SP22a 27.50p + 12.50p bl,
ocher, yel
& grn   1.10   .85

The surtax was for child welfare.

Coat of Arms — SPAP9

1966, June 25   **Litho.**   **Perf. 13½**
CB37 SPAP9 10p + 10p multi   1.75 1.40

ARGENTINA '66 Philatelic Exhibition held in connection with the sesquicentennial celebration of the Declaration of Independence, Buenos Aires, July 16-23. The surtax was for the Exhibition. Issued in sheets of 4.

Designs: 15p+7p, Thraupis bonariensis. 26p+13p, Ramphastos toco.

1967   **Litho.**   **Wmk. 90**
CB38 SP22a 15p + 7p blk, bl,
grn & yel   1.40 1.00
CB39 SP22a 26p + 13p blk, org,
yel & bl   .50   .40

The surtax was for child welfare.
Issued: 15p+7p, Jan. 14; 26p+13p, Dec. 23.

Bird Type of Semi-Postal Issue, 1969

Design: Ceophloeus lineatus.

1969, Sept. 20   **Wmk. 365**   **Perf. 13½**
CB40 SP24 26p + 13p multi   .75   .40

The surtax was for child welfare.

Bird Type of Semi-Postal Issue, 1970

Design: Phoenicopterus ruber chilensis.

1970, May 9   **Litho.**   **Wmk. 365**
CB41 SP25 40c + 20c multi   .75   .40

The surtax was for child welfare.

Fish Type of Semi-Postal Issue, 1971

Design: Odostethes platensis.

1971, Feb. 20   **Unwmk.**   **Perf. 12½**
         Size: 75x15mm
CB42 SP26 40c + 20c multi   .50   .40

The surtax was for child welfare.

OFFICIAL STAMPS

Regular Issues
Overprinted in Black —
a

1884-87   **Unwmk.**   **Perf. 12, 14**
O1 A29 ½c brown   40.00 25.00
O2 A23 1c red   12.00 8.00
  b.   Perf. 12   100.00 80.00
O3 A29 1c red   1.00 .50
  b.   Double overprint   100.00 100.00
O4 A20 2c green   1.00 .50
  b.   Double overprint   120.00 120.00
O5 A11 4c brown   1.00 .50
O6 A7 8c lake   1.00 1.00
O7 A8 10c green   100.00 50.00
O8 A23 12c ultra (#45)   1.50 1.00
  a.   Perf. 14   1,000. 250.00
O9 A29 12c grnsh blue   1.50 1.00
O10 A19 24c blue   2.00 1.50
O11 A21 25c lake   30.00 25.00
O12 A12 30c orange   80.00 70.00
O13 A13 60c black   50.00 40.00
O14 A14 90c blue   30.00 25.00
  b.   Double overprint   120.00 120.00
Nos. O1-O14 (14)   351.00 249.00

Inverted Overprint
O1a A29 ½c   30.00 20.00
O2a A23 1c Perf. 14   100.00 80.00
  c.   Perf. 12   75.00 —
O3a A29 1c   2.50 1.25
O4a A20 2c   120.00 120.00
O5a A11 4c   60.00 50.00
O6a A7 8c (Inverted overprint on reverse)   500.00 —
O8b A23 12c Perf. 12   — —
O9a A29 12c   300.00 250.00
O10a A19 24c   6.00 5.00
O13a A13 60c   150.00 120.00
O14a A14 90c   120.00 120.00

1884   **Rouletted**
O15 A17 16c green   3.00 2.00
  a.   Double overprint   25.00 —
  b.   Inverted overprint   300.00
O16 A18 20c blue   15.00 12.00
  a.   Inverted overprint   120.00 80.00
O17 A19 24c blue   2.00 1.50
  a.   Inverted overprint   6.00 5.00
  b.   Double ovpt., one inverted   250.00 —
Nos. O15-O17 (3)   20.00 15.50

Overprinted Diagonally in Red
1885   **Perf. 12**
O18 A20 2c green   3.00 2.00
  a.   Inverted overprint   100.00 100.00
O19 A11 4c brown   3.00 2.00
  a.   Inverted overprint   100.00 —
  b.   Double overprint   100.00 100.00
O20 A13 60c black   50.00 40.00
O21 A14 90c blue   450.00 275.00

1885   **Rouletted**
O22 A19 24c blue   27.50 20.00

On all of these stamps, the overprint is found reading both upwards and downwards. Counterfeits exist of No. O21 overprint and others.

Regular Issues
Handstamped
Horizontally in Black —
b

1884   *Perf. 12, 14*

O23	A23	1c red	100.00	50.00
a.		Perf. 12	400.00	300.00
O24	A20	2c green, diagonal overprint	60.00	40.00
a.		Horizontal overprint	450.00	300.00
O25	A11	4c brown	25.00	20.00
O26	A7	8c lake	25.00	10.00
O27	A23	12c ultra	60.00	50.00

Overprinted Diagonally

O28	A19	24c bl, rouletted	50.00	35.00
O29	A13	60c black	30.00	15.00

Counterfeit overprints exist.

Liberty Head — O1

Perf. 11½, 12 and Compound

1901, Dec. 1   *Engr.*

O31	O1	1c gray	.40	.25
b.		Vert. pair, imperf. horiz.	50.00	
c.		Horiz. pair, imperf. vert.	50.00	
O32	O1	2c orange brown	.40	.25
O33	O1	5c red	.45	.25
b.		Vert. pair, imperf. horiz.	50.00	
O34	O1	10c dark green	.90	.25
O35	O1	30c dark blue	5.00	1.60
O36	O1	50c orange	3.00	1.40
		Nos. O31-O36 (6)	10.15	4.00

Imperf, Pairs

O31a	O1	1c	80.00	
O32a	O1	2c	80.00	
O33a	O1	5c	100.00	
O34a	O1	10c	80.00	
O35a	O1	30c	100.00	
O36a	O1	50c	150.00	

Regular Stamps of
1935-51 Overprinted
in Black — c

Perf. 13x13½, 13½x13, 13

1938-54   *Wmk. RA in Sun (90)*

O37	A129	1c buff ('40)	.40	.25
O38	A130	2c dk brn ('40)	.40	.25
O39	A132	3c grn ('39)	1.00	.25
O40	A132	3c lt gray ('39)	.40	.25
O41	A134	5c yel brn	.40	.25
O42	A195	5c car ('53)	.40	.25
O43	A137	10c carmine	.55	.25
O44	A137	10c brn ('39)	.45	.25
O45	A140	15c lt gray bl, type II ('47)	.40	.25
O46	A139	15c slate blue	.75	.25
O47	A139	15c pale ultra ('39)	.45	.25
O48	A139	20c blue ('53)	1.10	.40
O49	A141	25c carmine	.40	.25
a.		Overprint 11mm	.55	.25
O49B	A143	40c dk violet	1.50	.35
O50	A144	50c red & org	.40	.25
a.		Overprint 11mm		.25
O51	A146	1p brn blk & lt bl ('40)	.45	.25
a.		Overprint 11mm	.45	.40
O52	A224	1p choc & lt bl ('51)	1.50	.25
a.		Overprint 11mm		.25
O53	A147	2p brn lake & dk ultra (ovpt. 11mm) ('54)	1.50	.25
		Nos. O37-O53 (18)	12.45	4.75

Overprinted in Black on Stamps and Types of 1945-47

Perf. 13x13½, 13½x13

1945-46   *Unwmk.*

O54	A130	2c sepia	3.00	1.75
O55	A132	3c lt gray	2.50	1.10
O56	A134	5c yel brn	.65	.25
O57	A195	5c dp car	.25	.25
O58	A137	10c brown	.25	.25
a.		Double overprint		
O59	A140	15c lt gray bl, type II	.30	.25
O61	A141	25c dull rose	.25	.25
O62	A144	50c red & org	.55	.25
O63	A146	1p brn blk & lt bl	.25	.25
O64	A147	2p brn lake & bl	.40	.25

O65	A148	5p ind & ol grn	.25	.25
O66	A149	10p dp cl & int blk	.45	.25
O67	A150	20p bl grn & brn	1.00	.80
		Nos. O54-O67 (13)	10.10	6.15

Overprinted in Black on Stamps and Types of 1942-50

Perf. 13, 13x13½

1944-51   *Wmk. 288*

O73	A132	3c lt gray	3.25	1.25
O74	A134	5c yellow brown	.70	.40
O75	A137	10c red brown	.35	.25
O76	A140	15c lt gray bl, type II	.25	.25
O77	A144	50c red & org (overprint 11 mm)	3.25	1.25
O78	A146	1p brn blk & lt bl (overprint 11mm)	3.25	1.25
		Nos. O73-O78 (6)	11.05	4.65

> Catalogue values for unused stamps in this section, from this point to the end of the section, are for Never Hinged items.

Nos. 600-606
Overprinted in Black
— d

1953   *Wmk. 90*   *Perf. 13*

O79	A228	5c gray	.40	.25
O80	A228	10c rose lilac	.40	.25
O81	A228	20c rose pink	.40	.25
O82	A228	25c dull green	.40	.25
O83	A228	40c dull violet	.40	.25
O84	A228	45c deep blue	.55	.30
O85	A228	50c dull brown	.40	.25

Nos. 611-617
Overprinted in Blue
— e

Perf. 13x13½, 13½x13

O86	A229	1p dk brown	.50	.25
O87	A229	1.50p dp green	.50	.25
O88	A229	2p brt carmine	.50	.25
O89	A229	3p indigo	.60	.35

Size: 30x40mm

O90	A229	5p red brown	.95	.55
O91	A228	10p red	5.00	4.00
O92	A229	20p green	50.00	30.00
		Nos. O79-O92 (14)	61.00	37.45

No. 612 Overprinted
in Blue — f

O93	A229	1.50p dp grn	1.50	.45

Regular Issues of 1954-59 Variously Overprinted in Black or Blue

g

h

Perf. 13½, 13x13½, 13½x13

1955-61   *Litho.*   *Wmk. 90*

O94	A237(c)	20c red (#629)	.40	.25
O95	A237(d)	20c red (#629)	.40	.25
O96	A237(d)	40c red, ovpt. 15mm (#630)	.40	.25

Engr.

O97	A239(g)	50c bl (#632)	.40	.25

Photo.

O98	A239(h)	1p brn (#635)	.40	.25
O99	A239(e)	1p brn (Bl, #635)	.40	.25
O100	A239(e)	1p brn (Bk, #635)	.40	.25

Engr.

O101	A239(h)	3p vio brn (#638)	.40	.25
O102	A240(h)	5p gray grn (#639)	.40	.25
O103	A240(h)	10p yel grn (#640)	.85	.25
O104	A240(f)	20p dl vio (#641)	1.00	.50
O105	A240(h)	20p dl vio (#641)	1.00	.50
a.		Perf 13½ (#641a)	1.00	.50
O106	A241(e)	50p ultra & ind (#642)	2.50	1.00
		Nos. O94-O106 (13)	8.95	4.50

The overprints on Nos. O99-O100 & O103-O104 are horizontal; that on No. O106 is vertical. On No. O106 overprint measures 23mm.

Issued: No. O102, 1957; Nos. O97, O101, O103, O105, 1958; Nos. O98-O99, O104, 1959; No. O100, 1960; No. O106, 1961.

No. 659 Overprinted Type "d"

1957   *Wmk. 90*   *Litho.*   *Perf. 13*

O108	A133	20c dl pur (ovpt. 15mm)	.40	.25

Nos. 666, 658 and 663 Variously Overprinted

1957   *Photo.*   *Perf. 13x13½, 13½*

O109	A261(g)	2p claret	.30	.25
O110	A254(e)	2.40p brown	.40	.25
O111	A258(c)	4.40p grnsh gray	.40	.25
		Nos. O109-O111 (3)	1.10	.75

Nos. 668, 685-687, 690-691, 693-705, 742, 742C and Types of 1959-65 Overprinted in Black, Blue or Red Types "e," "g," or

i

j

k

m

n

Lithographed; Photogravure

1960-68   *Perf. 13x13½, 13½*

O112	A128(g)	5c buff (vert. ovpt.)	.35	.25
O113	A275(j)	10c sl grn	.35	.25
O114	A275(j)	20c dl red brn	.35	.25
O115	A275(i)	50c bister	.35	.25
O116	A278(k)	1p brn	.45	.25
O117	A278(j)	1p brn, photo. (vert. ovpt.)	.45	.25
O117A	A278(j)	1p brn., litho., (down)	.40	.25
O118	A276(j)	2p rose red	.35	.25
O119	A312(m)	2p dp green	.50	.25
O120	A312(j)	2p brt grn (up)	.45	.25
O121	A312(j)	2p grn litho. (down)	.50	.25
O122	A277(e)	3p dk bl	.35	.25
O123	A277(j)	3p dk blue	.35	.25
O124	A276(j)	4p red, litho.	.60	.25
O125	A312(j)	4p rose red, litho. (down)	.45	.25
O126	A277(e)	5p brn (Bl) (horiz.)	.60	.25
O127	A277(e)	5p brn (Bk) (horiz.)	.45	.25
O128	A277(j)	5p sepia	.45	.25
O129	A277(e)	5p sepia (horiz. ovpt.)	.55	.25
O130	A276(j)	8p red	.35	.25
O131	A278(i)	10p lt red brn	.45	.25
O132	A276(j)	10p vermilion	.45	.25
O133	A278(j)	10p brn car (up)	2.25	1.00
O133A	A278(j)	10p brn car (down)	90.00	30.00
O134	A278(m)	12p dk brn vio (horiz.)	.40	.25
O135	A278(k)	20p Prus grn	.50	.25
O136	A278(j)	20p Prus grn (up)	.50	.25
O137	A276(j)	20p red, litho. (horiz.)	.45	.25
O138	A276(m)	20p red, litho. (horiz.)	.60	.25
O139	A278(j)	23p grn (vert. ovpt.)	1.10	.40
O140	A278(j)	25p dp vio, photo. (R) (up)	1.00	.45
O141	A278(j)	25p pur, litho. (R) (down)	1.75	.75
O142	A241(n)	50p dk blue	3.50	1.00
O143	A279(m)	100p bl (horiz. ovpt.)	2.50	1.00
O144	A279(m)	100p blue (up)	2.50	1.00
O145	A280(m)	300p dp violet (horiz.)	7.50	3.50
		Nos. O112-O133,O134-O145 (35)	34.10	15.85

The "m" overprint measures 15½mm on 2p; 14½mm on 12p, 100p and 300p; 13mm on 20p.

Issued: Nos. O122, O127, O135, 1961; Nos. O112-O114, O116, O118, 1962; No. O124, 1963; Nos. O119, O134, O143, 1964; Nos. O117, O125, O130, O139, O144, 1965; Nos. O120, O128, O132-O133, O136, O140, O142, O145, 1966; Nos. O121, O129, O137-O138, O141, 1967; No. O117A, 1968.

Nos. 699, 823-825, 827-829, and Type of 1962 Overprinted in Black or Red Types "j," "m," or "o"

o

Inscribed: "Republica Argentina"

Litho., Photo., Engr.

1964-67		Wmk. 90	Perf. 13½	
O149	A312(j)	6p rose red (down)	.55	.30
O153	A238a(m)	22p ultra	1.00	.45
O154	A238a(j)	43p dk car rose (down)	2.00	1.00
O155	A238a(j)	45p brn, photo. (up)	2.00	1.00
O156	A238a(j)	45p brn, litho. (up)	3.00	1.00
O157	A241(j)	50p dk bl (up) (R)	5.00	1.10
O158	A366(j)	90p ol bis (up)	6.00	2.75
O162	A495(o)	500p yel grn	12.50	5.50
	Nos. O149-O162 (8)		32.05	13.10

Issued: No. O153, 1964; No. O155, 1966; Nos. O149, O156-O162, 1967.

Type of 1959-67 Ovptd. Type "j"

1969		Litho.	Wmk. 365	Perf. 13½	
O163	A276	20p vermilion		.50	.25

Beginning with No. 2001, many Argentine stamps are inscribed "Correo Official," but are not official stamps.

OFFICIAL DEPARTMENT STAMPS

Regular Issues of 1911-38 Overprinted in Black
Ministry of Agriculture

No. OD1

1913		Type I	Perf. 13½x12½	
OD1	A88	2c choc (#181)	.50	.25
OD2	A88	1c ocher (#190)	.50	.25
OD3	A88	2c choc (#191)	1.00	.50
OD4	A88	5c red (#194)	1.00	.50
a.	Perf. 13½ (#194a)		3.00	1.00
OD5	A88	12c dp bl (#196)	1.00	.50
a.	Perf. 13½ (#196a)		3.00	.50
	Nos. OD2-OD5 (4)		3.50	1.75

1915				
OD6	A88	1c ocher (#208)	1.50	.50
OD7	A88	2c chocolate (#209)	1.00	.50
OD8	A88	5c red (#212)	1.00	.50
	Nos. OD6-OD8 (3)		3.50	1.50

No. OD9

1916			Perf. 13½	
OD9	A91	5c red (#220)	.50	.25

No. OD11   No. OD15

1918				
OD10	A94	12c blue (#238)	1.50	.50
OD11	A93	1c buff (#249)	.50	.25
OD12	A93	2c brown (#250)	.50	.25
OD13	A93	5c red (#253)	.50	.25
OD14	A94	12c blue (#255)	.50	.25
OD15	A94	20c ultra (#256)	.50	.25
	Nos. OD10-OD15 (6)		4.00	1.75

1920		Perf. 13½, 13½x12½ (OD16)		
OD16	A93	1c buff (#265)	1.00	.50
OD17	A93	2c brown (#266A)	4.00	1.00
OD18	A93	5c red (#269A)	.70	.30
a.	Perf. 13½x12½ (#269)		.70	.30
	Nos. OD16-OD18 (3)		5.70	1.80

1922			Perf. 13½	
OD19	A94	12c blue (#311)	2.00	.75
OD20	A94	20c ultra (#312)	75.00	

No. OD23

1923			Perf. 13½x12½	
OD21	A104	1c buff (#324)	1.00	.50
a.	Perf. 13½ (#324A)		5.00	2.00
OD22	A104	2c dk brn (#325)	.50	.25
OD23	A104	5c red (#328)	.50	.25
a.	Perf. 13½ (#328A)		1.00	.50
OD24	A104	12c deep blue (#330)	.80	.25
OD25	A104	20c ultra (#331)	.80	.25
a.	Perf. 13½ (#331A)		6.00	2.00
	Nos. OD21-OD25 (5)		3.60	1.50

1924				
OD26	A104	1c buff (#341)	.50	.25
a.	Inverted ovpt.		20.00	15.00
OD27	A104	2c dk brn (#342)	.50	.25
OD29	A104	5c red (#345)	.50	.25
OD30	A104	10c dl grn (#346)	.50	.25
OD31	A104	12c dp bl (#347)	.50	.25
OD32	A104	20c dp bl (#348)	.50	.25
a.	Inverted ovpt.		80.00	60.00
	Nos. OD26-OD32 (6)		3.00	1.50

No. OD34

1926				
OD34	A110	12c deep blue (#360)	.50	.25

No. OD28B

Type II

1931-36		Perf. 13x13½, 13½x13		
OD27B	A104	2c dk brn (#342)	5.00	2.00
OD28B	A104	3c green (#343)	.50	.25
OD29B	A104	5c red (#345)	.50	.25
OD30B	A104	10c dl grn (#346)	.50	.25
c.	Typo (coil) (#346a)		.50	.25
OD32B	A104	20c ultra (#348)	1.00	.50
c.	Typo (coil) (#348a)		.50	.25
OD33B	A104	30c claret (#351)	.50	.25
c.	Typo (coil) (#351a)		.50	.25

No. OD36

1936-38			Litho.	
OD35	A129	1c buff (#419)	.50	.25
OD36	A130	2c dk brn (#420)	.50	.25
OD37	A132	3c green (#422)	.50	.25
OD38	A134	5c yel brn (#427)	.50	.25
OD40	A139	15c lt gray bl (#436)	2.50	.30
OD41	A140	20c lt ultra (#437)	3.00	.30
OD42	A140	20c lt ultra (#438)	.80	.25
OD43	A141	25c car & pink (#441), perf. 13x13½	.50	.25
OD44	A142	30c org brn & yel brown (#442)	.50	.25
OD45	A145	1p brn blk & Lt bl (#445)	3.50	1.50
OD46	A146	1p brn blk & lt bl (#446)	.60	.30
	Nos. OD35-OD46 (11)		13.40	4.15

		Typo.	**Perf. 13½**	
OD38A	A134	5c yel brn (#427)	.50	.25
OD39A	A137	10c carmine (#430)	.50	.25
b.	Perf. 13½x13 (#430a)		1.00	.50

Ministry of War

No. OD47

1913		Type I	Perf. 13½x12½	
OD47	A88	2c choc (#181)	.80	.30
OD48	A88	1c ocher (#190)	.30	.25
OD49	A88	2c choc (#191)	4.00	.50
a.	Perf. 13½ (#191a)		15.00	3.00
OD50	A88	5c red (#194)	1.00	.50
a.	Inverted ovpt.		50.00	—
OD51	A88	12c dp bl (#196)	.50	.25
a.	Perf. 13½ (#196a)		5.00	1.00
	Nos. OD48-OD51 (4)		5.80	1.50

1915				
OD52	A88	1c ocher (#208)	30.00	6.00
OD53	A88	2c chocolate (#209)	4.00	.80
OD54	A88	5c red (#212)	4.00	.80
	Nos. OD52-OD54 (3)		38.00	7.60

1916			Perf. 13½	
OD55	A91	5c red (#220)	3.00	.50
OD56	A92	12c blue (#222)	3.00	.50

1918				
OD57	A93	1c buff (#232)	1.00	.50
a.	Perf. 13½x12½ (#232B)		8.00	3.00
OD58	A93	2c brown (#233)	5.00	.80
a.	Perf. 13½x12½ (#233B)		1.50	.50
OD59	A93	5c red (#236B) (Perf. 13½x12½)	1.50	.50
OD60	A94	12c blue (#238)	2.00	.80
	Nos. OD57-OD60 (4)		9.50	2.60

1918				
OD61	A93	1c buff (#249)	1.50	.50
a.	Perf. 13½x12½ (#249B)		6.00	5.00
OD62	A93	2c brown (#250)	.50	.25
a.	Perf. 13½x12½ (#250B)		1.00	.50
OD63	A93	5c red (#253)	1.00	.50
a.	Perf. 13½x12½ (#253B)		.50	.25
OD64	A94	12c blue (#255)	1.50	.50
OD65	A94	20c ultra (#256)	4.00	.60
	Nos. OD61-OD65 (5)		8.50	2.35

1920				
OD66	A93	2c brown (#266A)	2.50	.50
a.	Perf. 13½x12½ (#266)		.50	.25
OD67	A93	5c red (#269A)	1.50	.50
a.	Perf. 13½x12½ (#269)		1.00	.50
OD68	A94	12c blue (#271)	1.00	.50
	Nos. OD66-OD68 (3)		5.00	1.50

1921				
OD69	A94	12c blue (#299)	5.00	1.00

No. OD72

1922				
OD70	A93	1c buff (#305)	3.00	.30
OD71	A93	2c brown (13½x12½) (#306B)	5.00	1.00
OD72	A103	5c red (#309)	2.00	.50
OD73	A94	20c ultra (#312)	1.00	.50
	Nos. OD70-OD73 (4)		11.00	2.30

		Perf. 13½x12½		
OD74	A93	2c brown (#318A)	5.00	1.00

1923			Perf. 13½x12½	
OD75	A104	1c buff (#324)	1.00	.50
a.	Inverted ovpt.		20.00	18.00
b.	Perf. 13½ (#324A)		5.00	1.50
OD76	A104	2c dk brn (#325)	.50	.25
a.	Perf. 13½ (#325A)		2.00	.50
OD77	A104	5c red (#328)	.50	.25
a.	Inverted ovpt.		20.00	18.00
b.	Perf. 13½ (#328A)		1.50	.50
OD78	A104	12c dp bl (#330)	1.00	.50
OD79	A104	20c ultra (#331)	2.00	.50
a.	Perf. 13½ (#331A)		3.00	.50
b.	As "a," inverted ovpt.		20.00	18.00
	Nos. OD75-OD79 (5)		5.00	2.00

1924				
OD80	A104	1c buff (#341)	5.00	1.00
OD81	A104	2c dk brn (#342)	.50	.25
OD82	A104	3c green (#343)	.80	.25
OD83	A104	5c red (#345)	.50	.25
OD84	A104	10c dl grn (#346)	2.00	.25
OD85	A104	20c ultra (#348)	.50	.25
OD86	A104	30c claret (#351)	5.00	.50
OD87	A105	1p blue & red (#353)	5.00	.30
	Nos. OD80-OD87 (8)		19.30	3.05

No. OD88

1926				
OD88	A109	5c red (#359)	1.50	.25

No. OD82B

Type II

1931-36		Perf. 13½x12½, 13 (OD87B)		
OD82B	A104	3c green (#343)	1.50	.50
OD83B	A104	5c red (#345)	.60	.25
c.	Inverted ovpt.		—	60.00
OD84B	A104	10c dl grn (#346)	.50	.25
c.	Typo (coil) (346a)		1.50	.50
OD85B	A104	20c ultra (#348)	1.00	.30
c.	Typo (coil) (#348a)		5.00	.50
OD86B	A104	30c claret (#351)	.80	.25
c.	Typo (coil) (#351a)		2.00	.50
OD87B	A105	1p blue & red (#353)	5.00	.30
	Nos. OD82B-OD87B (6)		9.40	1.85

No. OD90

1936-38			Litho.	
OD89	A129	1c buff (#419)	.50	.25
OD90	A130	2c dk brn (#420)	.50	.25
OD91	A132	3c green (#422)	.50	.25
OD92	A134	5c yel brn (#427)	.50	.25
OD93	A137	10c car (#430)	.50	.25
OD94	A139	15c slate bl (#434)	.80	.25
OD95	A140	20c lt ultra (#437)	7.00	.50
OD96	A140	20c lt ultra (#438)	.50	.25
OD97	A141	25c car & pink (#441)	.50	.25
OD98	A142	30c org brn & yel brown (#442)	.50	.25
OD99	A144	50c red & org (#444)	.70	.25
OD100	A145	1p brn blk & lt bl (#445)	2.00	.60
OD101	A146	1p brn blk & lt bl (#446)	1.00	.50
	Nos. OD89-OD101 (13)		15.50	4.10

		Typo.	**Perf. 13½**	
OD92B	A134	5c yel brn (#427)	.50	.25
c.	Inverted ovpt.		20.00	15.00
OD93B	A137	10c car (#430)	.50	.25
c.	Inverted ovpt.		50.00	35.00
d.	Perf. 13½x13 (#430a)		1.00	.50

Ministry of Finance

No. OD102

1913 Type I Perf. 13½x12½
OD102	A88	2c choc (#181)	.50	.25
OD103	A88	1c ocher (#190)	.50	.25
OD104	A88	2c choc (#191)	.50	.25
OD105	A88	5c red (#194)	.50	.25
OD106	A88	12c dp bl (#196)	.50	.25
a.		Perf. 13½ (#196a)	90.00	35.00
Nos. OD103-OD106 (4)			2.00	1.00

1915
OD107	A88	2c choc (#209)	.50	.25
OD108	A88	5c red (#212)	.50	.25

1916 Perf. 13½
OD109	A91	5c red (#220)	.70	.30

1917
OD110	A93	2c brown (#233)	.50	.25
OD111	A93	5c red (#236)	4.00	.50
OD112	A94	12c blue (#238)	.50	.25
Nos. OD110-OD112 (3)			5.00	1.00

1918
OD113	A93	2c brown (#250)		100.00
OD114	A93	5c red (#253)	.50	.25
a.		Perf. 13½x12½ (#253b)	.70	.25
OD115	A94	12c blue (#255)	.70	.25
OD116	A94	20c ultra (#256)	1.00	.50
Nos. OD113-OD116 (4)			2.20	101.00

1920
OD117	A93	1c buff (#265)	3.00	1.00
OD118	A93	2c brown (#266)	4.50	1.50
OD119	A93	5c #269	6.00	1.50
a.		Perf. 13½ (#269A)	1.50	.30
OD120	A94	12c blue (#271) (perf. 13½)	1.50	.30
Nos. OD117-OD120 (4)			15.00	4.30

1922
OD121	A94	20c ultra (#312)	40.00	7.00

1923 Perf. 13½x12½, 13½
OD122	A104	1c buff (#324)	20.00	10.00
a.		Perf. 13½ (#324A)	2.00	1.00
OD123	A104	2c dk brn (#325)	.50	.25
a.		Perf. 13½ (#325A)	10.00	1.00
OD124	A104	5c red (#328)	.50	.25
a.		Inverted ovpt.	—	35.00
b.		Perf. 13½ (#328A)	1.00	.90
OD125	A104	12c dp bl (#330)	.70	.25
a.		Perf. 13½ (#330A)	3.00	.30
OD126	A104	20c ultra (#331)	.50	.25
a.		Perf. 13½ (#331A)	2.50	.30
Nos. OD122-OD126 (5)			22.20	11.00

1924 Perf. 13½x12½
OD127	A104	2c dk brn (#342)	250.00	250.00
OD128	A104	5c red (#345)	1.00	.25
OD130	A104	12c dp bl (#347)	40.00	17.50
OD131	A104	20c ultra (#348)	.50	.25
Nos. OD127-OD131 (4)			291.50	268.00

1926
OD134	A110	12c dp bl (#360)	30.00	12.50

No. OD129B   No. OD133B

1931-36 Type II
OD127B	A104	3c green (#343)	25.00	10.00
OD129B	A104	10c dl grn (#346)	.50	.25
c.		Typo (coil) (#346a)	.60	.25
OD131B	A104	20c ultra (#348)	1.00	.50
c.		Typo (coil) (#348a)	.50	.25
OD132B	A104	30c claret (#351)	.50	.25
c.		Typo (coil) (#351a)	1.50	.25

Perf. 13
OD133B	A105	1p blue & red (#353)	1.00	.50
Nos. OD127B-OD133B (5)			28.00	11.50

No. OD135

1936-38 Litho. Perf. 13½x13
OD135	A129	1c buff (#419)	.50	.25
OD136	A130	2c dk brn (#420)	.50	.25
OD137	A132	3c green (#422)	.50	.25
OD138	A134	5c yel brn (Perf. 13½) (#427d)	.50	.25
OD139	A137	10c car (#430)	.50	.30
OD140	A139	15c slate blue (#434) ('36)	2.00	.80
a.		Inverted ovpt.	—	80.00
OD141	A140	20c lt ultra (#437)	2.50	.25
OD142	A140	20c lt ultra (#438)	.50	.25
OD143	A142	30c org brn & yel brown (#442)	.50	.25
OD144	A145	1p brn blk & lt bl (#445)	5.00	1.50
OD145	A146	1p brn blk & lt bl (#446)	.60	.30
Nos. OD135-OD145 (11)			13.60	4.65

Typo. Perf. 13½
OD138A	A134	5c yel brn (#427)	.50	.25
b.		Inverted ovpt.	50.00	50.00
OD139A	A137	10c car (#430)	.50	.25
b.		Perf. 13½x13 (#430a)	18.00	1.50

Ministry of the Interior

No. OD147

1913 Type I Perf. 13½x12½
OD146	A88	2c choc (#181)	.90	.30
OD147	A88	1c ocher (#190)	.50	.25
OD148	A88	2c choc (#191)	2.50	.50
OD149	A88	5c red (#194)	1.00	.40
OD150	A88	12c dp bl (#196)	1.20	.50
a.		Perf. 13½ (#196a)	6.00	1.50
Nos. OD146-OD150 (5)			6.10	1.95

1915
OD151	A88	2c chocolate (#209)	2.00	.60
OD152	A88	5c red (#212)	2.00	.60

1916 Perf. 13½
OD153	A91	5c red (#220)	2.00	.80

1918
OD154	A93	5c red (#236B)	5.00	.50
OD155	A93	2c brown (#250)	.50	.25
OD156	A93	5c red (#253)	.70	.30
a.		Perf. 13½x12½ (#253B)	.50	.25
Nos. OD154-OD156 (3)			6.20	1.05

1920
OD157	A93	1c buff (13½x12½) (#265)	10.00	3.00
OD158	A93	5c red (#269)	5.00	1.00

1922 Perf. 13½
OD160	A103	5c red (#309)	6.00	2.00
OD161	A94	12c blue (#311)	2.00	.50
OD162	A94	20c ultra (#312)	2.00	.50
Nos. OD160-OD162 (3)			10.00	3.00

1923 Perf. 13½x12½
OD163	A104	1c buff (#324)	1.50	.50
a.		Perf. 13½ (#324A)	1.00	.50
OD164	A104	2c dark brown (#325)	.50	.25
a.		Perf. 13½ (#325A)	50.00	30.00
OD165	A104	5c red (#328)	.60	.25
a.		Perf. 13½ (#328A)	4.00	.50
OD166	A104	12c deep blue (#330)	6.00	.80
a.		Perf. 13½ (#330A)	45.00	20.00
OD167	A104	20c ultra (#331)	9.00	1.00
a.		Perf. 13½ (#331A)	7.00	1.00
Nos. OD163-OD167 (5)			17.60	2.80

1924
OD168	A104	1c buff (#341)	.50	.25
OD169	A104	2c dk brn (#342)	.50	.25
OD170	A104	3c green (#343)	3.00	.60
OD171	A104	5c red (#345)	.50	.25
OD173	A104	12c dp bl (#347)	1.00	.25
OD174	A104	20c ultra (#348)	10.00	8.00
Nos. OD168-OD174 (6)			15.50	9.60

No. OD172B

Type II

1931-36 Perf. 13½x12½
OD170B	A104	3c green (#343)	.70	.25
OD171B	A104	5c red (#345)	.70	.25
OD172B	A104	10c dull green (#346)	.50	.25
c.		Typo (coil) (#346a)	.50	.25
OD174B	A104	20c ultra (#348)	.50	.25
c.		Typo (coil) (#348a)	1.00	.50
OD175B	A104	30c claret (#351)	3.00	.50
c.		Typo (coil) (#351a)	6.00	2.00
Nos. OD170B-OD175B (5)			5.40	1.50

No. OD182A

1936-38 Litho. Perf. 13½x13
OD176	A129	1c buff (#419)	.50	.25
OD177	A130	2c dk brn (#420)	.50	.25
OD178	A132	3c green (#422)	.50	.25
OD178A	A134	5c yel brn (#427d)	.50	.25
OD180	A139	15c slate bl (#434) ('36)	.70	.30
OD181	A140	20c lt ultra (#437)	3.00	.50
OD182	A140	20c lt ultra (#438)	.50	.25
OD182A	A142	30c org brn & yel brown (#442)	.50	.25
OD182B	A145	1p brn blk & lt blue (#445)	5.00	2.00
OD182C	A146	1p brn blk & lt bl (#446) ('37)	.60	.30
Nos. OD176-OD182C (10)			12.30	4.60

Typo. Perf. 13½
OD178D	A134	5c yel brn (#427)	.60	.25
e.		Inverted ovpt.		75.00
OD179D	A137	10c car (#430)	.80	.30
e.		Perf. 13½x13 (#430a)	.50	.25

Ministry of Justice and Instruction

No. OD184

1913 Type I Perf. 13½x12½
OD183	A88	2c choc (#181)	3.00	.50
OD184	A88	1c ocher (#190)	4.00	.50
OD185	A88	2c choc (#191)	2.50	.50
a.		Perf. 13½ (#191a)	30.00	10.00
OD186	A88	5c red (#194)	1.00	.50
OD187	A88	12c dp bl (#196)	1.50	.50
Nos. OD184-OD187 (4)			9.00	2.00

1915
OD188	A88	1c ocher (#208)	1.00	.50
OD189	A88	2c chocolate (#209)	1.00	.50
OD190	A88	5c red (#212)	2.00	.80
Nos. OD188-OD190 (3)			4.00	1.80

1916 Perf. 13½
OD191	A91	5c red (#220)	1.00	.50
OD192	A92	12c blue (#222)	2.00	.80

1918
OD193	A93	1c buff (#232)	1.00	.50
a.		Perf. 13½x12½ (#232B)	1.00	.50
OD194	A93	2c brown (#233)	4.00	.50
a.		Perf. 13½x12½ (#233B)	2.00	.50
OD195	A93	5c red (#236)	9.00	1.00
a.		Perf. 13½x12½ (#236B)	2.00	.50
OD196	A94	12c blue (#238)	45.00	10.00
Nos. OD193-OD196 (4)			59.00	12.00

1920
OD197	A93	1c buff (#249)	.60	.30
a.		Perf. 13½x12½ (#249B)	20.00	7.00
OD198	A93	2c brown (#250)	.30	.25
a.		Perf. 13½x12½ (#250B)	.50	.25
OD199	A93	5c red (#253)	.50	.25
a.		Perf. 13½x12½ (#253B)	.60	.30
OD200	A94	12c blue (#255)	.50	.25
OD201	A94	20c ultra (#256)	.70	.25
Nos. OD197-OD201 (5)			2.60	1.35

1920 Perf. 13½x12½
OD202	A93	1c buff (#265)	.70	.25
OD203	A93	2c brown (#266)	.50	.25
OD204	A93	5c red (#269)	.50	.25
a.		Perf. 13½ (#269A)	8.00	2.50
OD205	A94	12c blue (perf. 13½) (#271)	1.00	.50
Nos. OD202-OD205 (4)			2.70	1.25

1922 Perf. 13½
OD206	A93	1c buff (#305)	3.00	1.00
a.		Perf. 13½x12½ (#305B)	.70	.25
OD207	A93	2c brown, (perf. 13½x12½) (#306B)	4.00	1.00
OD208	A103	5c red (#309)	.70	.25
a.		Perf. 13½x12½ (#309B)	.50	.25
OD209	A94	12c blue (#311)	20.00	4.00
OD210	A94	20c ultra (#312)	4.00	.60
Nos. OD206-OD210 (5)			31.70	6.85

1922 Perf. 13½x12½
OD211	A93	2c brown (#318A)	3.50	.70

1923
OD212	A104	1c buff (#324)	.60	.25
a.		Perf. 13½ (#324A)	1.20	.50
OD213	A104	2c dk brn (#325)	.50	.25
a.		Perf. 13½ (#325A)	1.00	.50
b.		As "a," inverted ovpt.	25.00	20.00
OD214	A104	5c red (#328)	.50	.25
a.		Perf. 13½ (#328A)	.50	.25
OD215	A104	12c dp bl (#330)	.50	.25
OD216	A104	20c ultra (#331)	.50	.25
a.		Perf. 13½ (#331A)	1.20	.30
Nos. OD212-OD216 (5)			2.60	1.25

1924
OD218	A104	1c buff (#341)	.50	.25
OD219	A104	2c dk brn (#342)	.50	.25
OD220	A104	3c green (#343)	.60	.25
OD221	A104	5c red (#345)	.50	.25
OD222	A104	10c dl grn (#346)	1.00	.50
OD223	A104	12c dp bl (#347)	.50	.25
OD224	A104	20c ultra (#348)	.50	.25
Nos. OD218-OD224 (7)			4.10	2.00

1926
OD227	A109	5c red (#359)	.50	.25
a.		Inverted ovpt.	35.00	30.00
OD228	A110	12c dp bl (#360)	.50	.25

No. OD217B

Type II

1931-36 Perf. 13½x12½, 13
OD217B	A104	½c red vio (#340)	5.00	2.00
OD218B	A104	1c buff (#341)	.50	.25
OD220B	A104	3c green (#343)	.50	.25
c.		Typo (coil) (#343b)	.50	.25
OD221B	A104	5c red (#345)	.50	.25
OD222B	A104	10c dl grn (#346)	.50	.25
c.		Typo (coil) (#346a)	.50	.25
OD223B	A104	12c dp bl (#347)	1.20	.30
OD224B	A104	20c ultra (#348)	.50	.25
c.		Typo (coil) (#348a)	.50	.25
OD225B	A104	30c claret (#351)	.50	.25
c.		Typo (coil) (#351a)	1.30	.50
OD226B	A105	1p blue & red (Perf. 13½) (#353)	1.00	.50
Nos. OD217B-OD226B (9)			10.20	4.30

No. OD229

1936-38 Perf. 13½x13
OD229	A129	1c buff (#419)	.50	.25
OD230	A130	2c dk brn (#420)	.50	.25
OD231	A132	3c green (#422)	.50	.25
OD232	A134	5c yel brn (#427d)	.50	.25
OD234	A139	15c slate bl (#434)	1.00	.25
OD234A	A140	20c lt ultra (#437)	.50	.25
OD234B	A140	20c lt ultra (#438)	.60	.25

OD234C A141 25c car & pink
(#441) .50 .25
OD234D A142 30c org brn & yel
brn (#442) .50 .25
OD234E A145 1p brn blk &l lt
bl (#445) 2.00 .60
OD234F A146 1p brn blk &l lt
bl (#446) 3.00 .30
Nos. OD229-OD234F (11) 10.10 3.15

		Typo.		Perf. 13½
OD232A A134 5c yel brn
(#427) .50 .25
OD233 A137 10c car (#430) .50 .25
a. Perf. 13½x13 (#430a) .50 .25

Ministry of Marine

No. OD236

1913 Type I **Perf. 13½x12½**
OD235 A88 2c choc (#181) .60 .25
a. Perf. 13½ (#181a) 150.00 75.00
OD236 A88 1c ocher (#190) .50 .25
OD237 A88 2c choc (#191) 8.00 .50
OD238 A88 5c red (#194) .50 .25
a. Perf. 13½ (#194a) 40.00 8.00
OD239 A88 12c dp bl (#196) .60 .30
Nos. OD236-OD239 (4) 9.60 1.30

1915
OD240 A88 2c chocolate (#209) 3.00 .50
OD241 A88 5c red (#212) 2.00 .25

1918
OD242 A93 1c buff (#232) .70 .30
OD243 A93 2c brown (#233) .70 .25
OD244 A93 5c red (#236) .70 .25
a. Perf. 13½ (#236B) 1.00 .50
Nos. OD242-OD244 (3) 2.10 .80

1920 **Perf. 13½**
OD245 A93 1c buff (#249) .50 .25
OD246 A93 2c brown (#250) .70 .25
a. Perf. 13½x12½ (#250) 1.00 .50
OD247 A93 5c red (#253) 3.50 .25
a. Perf. 13½x12½ (#253B) .60 .25
OD248 A93 12c blue (#255) 2.50 .30
OD249 A94 20c ultra (#256) 8.00 1.50
Nos. OD245-OD249 (5) 15.20 2.55

1920 **Perf. 13½**
OD250 A93 1c buff (#265A)
(perf. 13½x12½) .50 .25
OD251 A93 2c brown (#266A) .70 .30
a. Perf. 13½x12½ (#266) .80 .30
OD252 A93 5c red (#269A) .80 .25
Nos. OD250-OD252 (3) 2.00 .80

1922
OD253 A103 5c red (#309) 3.00 .50
a. Perf. 13½x12½ (#309B) 1.50 .30
OD254 A94 12c blue (#311) 30.00 10.00
OD255 A94 20c ultra (#312) 45.00 8.00
Nos. OD253-OD255 (3) 78.00 18.50

1923 **Perf. 13½x12½**
OD256 A104 1c buff (#324) .50 .25
a. Perf. 13½ (#324A) 87.50 50.00
OD257 A104 2c dk brn
(#325) 1.00 .50
a. Inverted overprint — 75.00
b. Perf. 13½ (#325A) 1.00 .50
OD258 A104 5c red (#328) 2.50 .25
a. Inverted overprint — 75.00
b. Perf. 13½ (#328A) 15.00 6.00
c. As "b," inverted overprint — 75.00
OD259 A104 12c deep blue
(#330) 1.20 .40
a. Perf. 13½ (#330A) 10.00 1.50
OD260 A104 20c ultra (#331) 2.00 .40
a. Perf. 13½ (#331A) 3.50 1.00
Nos. OD256-OD260 (5) 7.20 1.80

1924
OD261 A104 1c buff (#341) 3.00 1.00
OD262 A104 2c dk brn
(#342) .50 .25
OD264 A104 5c red (#345) .50 .25
OD266 A104 20c ultra (#348) 3.50 .25
Nos. OD261-OD266 (4) 7.50 1.75

1926
OD269 A109 5c red (#359) .50 .25

No. OD264B

Type II

1931-36 **Perf. 13½x12½, 13**
OD263B A104 3c grn (#343) 1.50 .40
OD264B A104 5c red (#345) 1.50 .25
OD265B A104 10c dl grn
(#346) 2.00 .50
c. Typo (coil) (#346a) .60 .25
OD266B A104 20c ultra (#348) 7.00 1.00
c. Typo (coil) (#348a) 5.00 .50
OD267B A104 30c claret
(#351) 3.00 .50
OD268B A105 1p blue & red
(Perf. 13½)
(#353) 40.00 20.00

No. OD270

1936-38 **Perf. 13½x13**
OD270 A129 1c buff (#419) .50 .25
OD271 A130 2c dk brn (#420) .50 .25
OD272 A132 3c green (#422) .50 .25
OD273 A134 5c yel brn
(#427d) .50 .25
OD275 A139 15c slate bl (#434)
('36) 1.00 .30
OD276 A140 20c lt ultra (#437) 1.20 .30
OD277 A140 20c lt ultra (#438) 1.00 .30
OD278 A142 30c org brn & yel
brn (#442)
('36) .60 .25
OD279 A145 1p brn blk & lt bl
(#445) ('36) 8.00 2.00
OD280 A146 1p brn blk & lt bl
(#446) ('37) 2.00 .50
Nos. OD270-OD280 (10) 15.80 4.65

		Typo.		Perf. 13½
OD273A A134 5c yel brn
(#427) .50 .25
a. Inverted overprint 25.00 25.00
OD274A A137 10c car (#430) 2.00 .25
b. Perf. 13½x13 (#430a) .60 .25

Ministry of Public Works

No. OD281

1913 Type I **Perf. 13½x12½**
OD281 A88 2c choc (#181) 1.00 .25
a. Perf. 13½ (#181a) 4.00 1.00
OD282 A88 1c ocher (#190) 1.00 .25
OD283 A88 5c red (#194) .80 .25
OD284 A88 12c dp bl (#196) 5.00 1.00
a. Perf. 13½ (#196a) 15.00 6.00
Nos. OD282-OD284 (3) 6.80 1.50

1916 **Perf. 13½**
OD285 A91 5c red (#220) 35.00 10.00

1918 **Perf. 13½x12½**
OD286 A93 2c brown (#233) 30.00 20.00
OD287 A93 5c red (#236) 18.00 9.00

1920 **Perf. 13½**
OD288 A93 2c brown (#266) 35.00 8.00
OD289 A93 5c red (#269) 5.00 1.00
OD290 A94 12c blue (#271) 50.00 20.00
Nos. OD288-OD290 (3) 90.00 29.00

1923 **Perf. 13½x12½**
OD291 A104 1c buff (#324) .60 .25
a. Perf. 13½ (#324A) 40.00 15.00
OD292 A104 2c dk brn
(#325) .50 .25
a. Perf. 13½ (#325A) .80 .25
OD293 A104 5c red (#328) .60 .30
a. Perf. 13½ (#328A) .80 .25
OD294 A104 12c dp bl (#330) .80 .30
a. Perf. 13½ (#330A) 2.00 .50
OD295 A104 20c ultra #331 2.00 .50
a. Perf. 13½ (#331A) 2.50 .50
Nos. OD291-OD295 (5) 4.50 1.60

1924
OD296 A104 1c buff (#341) .50 .25
OD297 A104 2c dk brn (#342) .50 .25
OD299 A104 5c red (#345) .50 .25
OD301 A104 12c dp bl (#347) 30.00 8.00
OD302 A104 20c ultra (#348) .50 .25
Nos. OD296-OD302 (5) 32.00 9.00

1926
OD305 A109 5c red (#359) .60 .25

No. OD299B

Type II

1931-36 **Perf. 13½x12½, 13**
OD298B A104 3c grn (#343) .50 .25
c. Typo (coil) (#343b) 25.00 5.00
OD299B A109 5c red (#345) .60 .25
OD300B A104 10c dl grn
(#346) .60 .25
c. Typo (coil) (#346a) 2.00 .25
OD301B A104 20c ultra typo
(coil) (#348b) 50.00 10.00
OD303B A104 30c claret
(#351) 1.00 .25
OD304B A105 1p blue & red
(13½)
(#353) 70.00 20.00
Nos. OD298B-OD304B (6) 122.70 31.00

No. OD307

1936-38 **Perf. 13½x13**
OD306 A129 1c buff (#419) .50 .25
OD307 A130 2c dk brn (#420) .50 .25
OD308 A132 3c green (#422) .50 .25
OD309 A134 5c yel brn
(#427d) .50 .25
OD311 A139 15c slate bl (#434) 1.50 .25
OD312 A140 20c lt ultra (#437) 2.00 .30
OD313 A140 20c lt ultra (#438) .50 .25
OD314 A142 30c org brn & yel
brn (#442)
('36) .60 .25
OD315 A144 50c red & org
(#444) ('36) .60 .30
OD316 A145 1p brn blk & lt bl
(#445) ('36) 4.00 1.00
OD317 A146 1p brn blk & lt bl
(#446) ('37) 1.20 .40
Nos. OD306-OD317 (11) 12.40 3.75

		Typo.		Perf. 13½
OD309A A134 5c yel brn
(#427) .60 .25
b. Inverted overprint — 75.00
OD310 A137 10c car (#430) 1.00 .30
a. Perf. 13½x13 (#430a) 1.00 .30

Ministry of Foreign Affairs and Religion

No. OD318

1913 Type I **Perf. 13½x12½**
OD318 A88 2c choc (#181) 45.00 9.00
OD319 A88 1c ocher (#190) .50 .25
OD320 A88 2c choc (#191) .50 .25
OD321 A88 5c red (#194) 1.20 .30
OD322 A88 12c dp bl (#196) .60 .25
a. Perf. 13½ (#196a) 50.00 20.00
Nos. OD319-OD322 (4) 2.80 1.05

1915
OD323 A88 5c red (#212) 1.00 .50

1916 **Perf. 13½**
OD324 A91 5c red (#220) 1.20 .50

1918
OD325 A94 20c ultra (#256) 5.00 2.00

1922
OD326 A93 1c buff, perf.
13½x12½ (#265) 1.00 .40
OD327 A93 5c red (#269) .50 .30

1922-23 **Perf. 13½x12½**
OD328 A93 2c brn (#306) 40.00 15.00
OD329 A103 5c red
(#309B) 100.00

			Perf. 13½
OD330 A93 12c blue
(#311) 100.00
OD330A A94 20c ultra
(#312) 100.00

1923 **Perf. 13½x12½**
OD331 A104 1c buff (#324) .60 .30
a. Perf. 13½ (#324A) 25.00 10.00
OD332 A104 2c dk brn
(#325) .50 .25
a. Perf. 13½ (#325A) 5.00 2.00
OD333 A104 5c red (#328) .50 .25
a. Perf. 13½ (#328A) 2.00 .30
OD334 A104 12c dp bl (#330) .50 .25
a. Perf. 13½ (#330A) 1.50 .50
OD335 A104 20c ultra (#331) .50 .25
Nos. OD331-OD335 (5) 2.60 1.30

No. OD344

1924
OD337 A104 1c buff (#341) .60 .25
OD338 A104 2c dk brn (#342) .50 .25
OD339 A104 3c green (#343) .50 .25
OD340 A104 5c red (#345) .50 .25
OD341 A104 10c dl grn (#346) 4.00 .50
OD342 A104 12c dp bl (#347) .60 .30
OD343 A104 20c ultra (#348) .60 .30
OD344 A104 30c claret (#351) .70 .30
Nos. OD337-OD344 (8) 8.00 2.40

1926
OD346 A110 12c dp bl (#360) .50 .25

Type II

1931-36 **Perf. 13½x12½, 13½**
OD336B A104 ½c red vio (#340) 2.50 1.00
OD341B A104 10c dl grn (#346) .60 .30
OD343B A104 20c ultra (typo,
coil) (#348a) .60 .30
OD344B A104 30c claret (typo,
coil) (#351a) .60 .30
OD345B A105 1p blue & red,
perf. 13½
(#353) .60 .30
Nos. OD336B-OD345B (5) 4.90 2.20

No. OD347

1935-37 **Typo.** **Perf. 13x13½**
OD347 A129 1c buff (#419) .50 .25
OD348 A130 2c dk brn
(#420) .50 .25
OD349 A132 3c green (#422) .50 .25
OD350 A134 5c yel brn
(#427d) .50 .25
OD352 A139 15c slate bl
(#434) .70 .30
OD353 A140 20c lt ultra
(#437) 1.00 .50
OD354 A140 20c lt ultra
(#438) .50 .25
OD355 A142 30c org brn & yel
brn (#442) .50 .25
OD356 A145 1p brn blk & lt
bl (#445) 6.00 2.50
OD357 A146 1p brn blk & lt
bl (#446) .70 .30
Nos. OD347-OD357 (10) 11.40 5.30

		Typo.		Perf. 13½
OD350B A134 5c yel brn (#427) .60 .25
OD351B A137 10c car (#430) .50 .25
c. Perf. 13½x13 (#430a) 2.00 .25

PARCEL POST STAMPS

PP1

Postal Service Headquarters, Buenos Aires — PP2

2001 Litho. _Serpentine Die Cut 11_

Self-Adhesive

Q1	PP1	1p red & black	20.00	20.00

Die Cut

Q1A	PP1	1p red & black	40.00	20.00
Q2	PP2	7p blue & black	27.50	20.00
Q3	PP2	11p brown & black	40.00	30.00
		Nos. Q1-Q3 (3)	87.50	70.00

Nos. Q1-Q3 were sold only at Unidas Postal outlets. No. Q3 is inscribed "Caja Envio 2."

Stamps of Type PP2 lacking "U.P." in denominations of 7p, 11p, 16p, and 23p were issued in 1999, but were applied by postal workers to packages brought to post offices by customers with large mailings (Grandes Clientes). These stamps were not to be given to any customers purchasing them. Value, set unused $160.

The same sale and use restrictions applied to four other non-denominated stamps for use by "Grandes Clientes," which are inscribed "Caja Normalizada," have blue, brown-violet, gray-green, and ocher frames, and were issued in 1995. Value, set unused $550.

Nos. Q2 and Q3, though inscribed "Grandes Clientes," apparently were available for purchase by any customers, at Unidas Postal outlets.

BUENOS AIRES

The central point of the Argentine struggle for independence. At intervals Buenos Aires maintained an independent government but after 1862 became a province of the Argentine Republic.

8 Reales = 1 Peso

> Values of Buenos Aires Nos. 1-8 vary according to condition. Quotations are for fine examples. Very fine to superb specimens sell at much higher prices, and inferior or poor stamps sell at reduced values, depending on the condition of the individual specimen.
>
> Nos. 1-8 are normally found without gum, and the values below are for such items. Examples with original gum sell for higher prices.

Steamship — A1

1858   Unwmk.   Typo.   _Imperf._

1	A1	1 (in) pesos lt brn	500.00	_300._
a.		Double impression		_700._
2	A1	2 (dos) pesos blue	300.00	_150._
b.		Diag. half used as 1p on cover		_7,500._
3	A1	3 (tres) pesos grn	1,500.	_950._
a.		3p dark green	2,000.	_1,500._
4	A1	4 (cuatro) pesos ver	5,000.	_4,500._
a.		Half used as 2p on cover		_25,000._
b.		4p chestnut brown (error)	30,000.	_40,000._
5	A1	5 (cinco) pesos org	5,000.	_3,000._
a.		5p ocher	5,000.	_3,000._
b.		5p olive yellow	5,000.	_3,000._

Issued: Nos. 2-5, Apr. 29; No. 1, Oct. 26.

1858, Oct. 26

6	A1	4 (cuatro) reales brown	350.00	_300._
a.		4r gray brown	400.00	_300._
b.		4r chestnut	350.00	_300._

1859, Jan. 1

7	A1	1 (in) pesos blue	200.	_100._
a.		1p indigo	300.	_150._
b.		Impression on reverse of stamp in blue	28,500.	
c.		Double impression	2,800.	_700._
d.		Vert. tête-bêche pair		_675,000._
e.		Horiz. tête-bêche pair		_—_
f.		Half used as 4r on cover		_7,500._
8	A1	1 (to) pesos blue	600.	_325._

No. 7e is valued with faults.

Nos. 1, 2, 3 and 7 have been reprinted on very thick, hand-made paper. The same four stamps and No. 8 have been reprinted on thin, hard, white wove paper.

Counterfeits of Nos. 1-8 are plentiful.

Liberty Head — A2

1859, Sept. 3

9	A2	4r green, _bluish_	400.00	275.00
10	A2	1p blue, fine impression	40.00	30.00
d.		Double impression	600.00	400.00
e.		Partial double impression	325.00	175.00
11	A2	2p vermilion, fine impression	500.00	300.00
a.		2p red, blurred impression	375.00	125.00
b.		Vert. half used as 1p on cover		4,000.

Both fine and blurred impressions of these stamps may be found. They have generally been called Paris and Local prints, respectively, but the opinion now obtains that the differences are due to the impression and that they do not represent separate issues. Values are for fine impressions. Rough or blurred impressions sell for less.

Many shades exist of Nos. 1-11.

1862, Oct. 4

12	A2	1p rose	350.00	150.00
13	A2	2p blue	350.00	90.00

All three values have been reprinted in black, brownish black, blue and red brown on thin hard white paper. The 4r has also been reprinted in green on bluish paper.

Values are for fine impressions. Rough or blurred impressions sell for less.

No. 13 exists with papermaker's wmk.

CORDOBA

A province in the central part of the Argentine Republic.

100 Centavos = 1 Peso

Arms of Cordoba — A1

Unwmk.
1858, Oct. 28   Litho.   _Imperf._
Laid Paper

1	A1	5c blue		_150._
2	A1	10c black		_3,000._

Cordoba stamps were printed on laid paper, but stamps from edges of the sheets sometimes do not show any laid lines and appear to be on wove paper. Counterfeits are plentiful.

CORRIENTES

The northeast province of the Argentine Republic.

1 Real M(oneda) C(orriente) =
12 ½ Centavos M.C. = 50 Centavos
100 Centavos Fuertes = 1 Peso
Fuerte

Nos. 1-2 were issued without gum. Nos. 3-8 were issued both with and without gum (values the same).

Ceres — A1

Unwmk.
1856, Aug. 21   Typo.   _Imperf._

1	A1	1r black, _blue_	100.00	40.00

No. 1 used is valued with pen cancellation.

Pen Stroke Through "Un Real"
1860, Feb. 8

2	A1	(3c) black, _blue_	600.00	_120.00_

No. 2 used is valued with pen cancellation.

Ceres — A2

1860-80

3	A2	(3c) black, _blue_	9.50	_30.00_
4	A2	(2c) blk, _yel grn_ ('64)	50.00	_100.00_
a.		(2c) black, _blue green_	92.50	_150.00_
5	A2	(2c) blk, _yel_ ('67)	7.50	_19.00_
6	A2	(3c) blk, _dk bl_ ('71)	3.00	_19.00_
7	A2	(3c) blk, _rose red_ ('76)	150.00	_70.00_
a.		(3c) black, _lil rose_ ('75)	200.00	_100.00_
8	A2	(3c) blk, _dk rose_ ('79)	8.00	_35.00_
a.		(3c) black, _red vio_ ('77)	75.00	_50.00_
		Nos. 3-8 (6)	228.00	_273.00_

Pen canceled examples of Nos. 3-8 that do not indicate the town of origin sell for much less.

Printed from settings of 8 varieties, 3 or 4 impressions constituting a sheet. Some impressions were printed inverted and tete beche pairs may be cut from adjacent impressions.

From Jan. 1 to Feb. 24, 1864, No. 4 was used as a 5 centavos stamp but examples so used can only be distinguished when they bear dated cancellations.

The reprints show numerous spots and small defects which are not found on the originals. They are printed on gray blue, dull blue, gray green, dull orange and light magenta papers.

ARMENIA

är-'mē-nē-ə

LOCATION — South of Russia bounded by Georgia, Azerbaijan, Iran and Turkey
GOVT. — Republic
AREA — 11,490 sq. mi.
POP. — 3,409,234 (est. 1999)
CAPITAL — Yerevan

With Azerbaijan and Georgia, Armenia made up the Transcaucasian Federation of Soviet Republics.

Stamps of Armenia were replaced in 1923 by those of Transcaucasian Federated Republics.

With the breakup of the Soviet Union on Dec. 26, 1991, Armenia and ten former Soviet republics established the Commonwealth of Independent States.

100 Kopecks = 1 Ruble
100 Luma = 1 Dram (1993)

> Catalogue values for unused stamps in this country are for Never Hinged items, beginning with Scott 430 in the regular postage section.

Counterfeits abound of all overprinted and surcharged stamps.

Watermark

Wmk. 171 — Diamonds

Perforations

Perforations are the same as the basic Russian stamps.

National Republic

Russian Stamps of 1902-19 Handstamped

At least thirteen types exist of both framed and unframed overprints ("a" and "c"). The device is the Armenian "H," initial of Hayasdan (Armenia). Inverted and double overprints are found.

Surcharged

Type I — Without periods (two types).
Type II — Periods after 1st "K" and "60."

Black Surcharge

			Perf.	14x14½
1919		**Unwmk.**		
1	A14	60k on 1k orange (II)	2.75	2.75
a.		Imperf. (I)	5.00	5.00
b.		Imperf. (II)	1.25	1.25

Violet Surcharge

2	A14	60k on 1k orange (II)	1.00	1.00

Handstamped in Violet a

6	A15	4k carmine	3.50	3.50
7	A14	5k claret, imperf.	9.00	9.00
a.		Perf.	8.00	8.00
9	A14	10k on 7k lt blue	6.00	6.00
10	A11	15k red brn & bl	3.50	3.50
11	A8	20k blue & car	2.50	2.50
13	A11	35k red brn & grn	4.75	4.75
14	A8	50k violet & green	4.25	4.25

15	A14	60k on 1k orange (II)	3.50	3.50
a.		Imperf. (I)	6.00	6.00
b.		Imperf. (II)	10.00	10.00
18	A13	5r dk bl, grn & pale bl	18.00	18.00
a.		Imperf.	9.00	9.00
19	A12	7r dk green & pink	35.00	15.00
20	A13	10r scar, yel & gray	40.00	15.00

Handstamped in Black

31	A14	2k green, imperf.	3.00	3.00
a.		Perf.	6.00	6.00
32	A14	3k red, imperf.	3.00	3.00
a.		Imperf.	10.00	10.00
33	A15	4k carmine	5.00	5.00
a.		Imperf.	10.00	10.00
34	A14	5k claret	1.25	1.25
a.		Imperf.	10.00	10.00
36	A15	10k dark blue	2.50	2.50
37	A14	10k on 7k lt blue	2.00	5.00
38	A11	15k red brn & bl	1.00	5.00
a.		Imperf.	5.00	15.00
39	A8	20k blue & car	2.00	5.00
40	A11	25k green & gray vio	2.00	5.00
41	A11	35k red brn & grn	2.00	4.00
42	A8	50k violet & green	3.00	5.00
43	A14	60k on 1k orange (II)	5.00	5.00
43A	A11	70k brown & org	3.00	3.00
b.		Imperf.	2.00	4.00
44	A9	1r pale brn, dk brn & org	3.00	5.00
a.		Imperf.	8.00	8.00
45	A12	3½r mar & lt grn, imperf.	3.00	6.00
a.		Perf.	6.00	6.00
46	A13	5r dk bl, grn & pale bl	6.00	6.00
a.		Imperf.	10.00	10.00
47	A12	7r dk green & pink	7.25	7.25
48	A13	10r scar, yel & gray	35.00	50.00

Handstamped in Violet c

Wove Paper

			Unwmk.	Perf.
62	A14	2k green, imperf.	12.00	12.00
a.		Perf.	18.00	18.00
63	A14	3k red, imperf.	2.50	2.50
a.		Perf.	15.00	15.00
64	A15	4k carmine	10.00	10.00
65	A14	5k claret	3.50	3.50
a.		Imperf.	3.50	3.50
67	A15	10k dark blue	5.00	10.00
68	A14	10k on 7k lt bl	3.50	3.50
69	A11	15k red brn & bl	3.00	5.00
70	A8	20k blue & car	3.00	5.00
71	A11	25k grn & gray vio	7.50	15.00
72	A11	35k red brn & grn	15.00	14.00
73	A8	50k violet & grn	5.00	10.00
74	A14	60k on 1k org (II)	6.00	8.00
a.		Imperf. (I)	6.00	8.00
b.		Imperf. (II)	6.00	8.00
75	A9	1r pale brn, dk brn & org	12.50	12.50
a.		Imperf.	10.00	10.00
76	A12	3½r mar & lt grn, imperf.	5.00	5.00
a.		Perf.	6.00	6.00
77	A13	5r dk bl, grn & pale bl, imperf.	12.50	12.50
a.		Perf.	8.00	8.00
78	A12	7r dk green & pink	20.00	20.00
79	A13	10r scar, yel & gray	20.00	20.00

Imperf

85	A11	70k brown & org	6.00	6.00

Handstamped in Black

Perf.

90	A14	1k orange	8.00	8.00
a.		Imperf.	10.00	10.00
91	A14	2k green, imperf.	1.25	1.25
a.		Perf.	8.00	8.00
92	A14	3k red, imperf.	5.00	10.00
a.		Perf.	2.00	2.00
93	A15	4k carmine	3.00	3.00
94	A14	5k claret	1.25	1.25
a.		Imperf.		3.50	5.00
95	A14	7k light blue	10.00	15.00
96	A15	10k dark blue	10.00	15.00
97	A14	10k on 7k lt bl	1.00	2.00
98	A11	15k red brn & bl	2.00	4.00
99	A8	20k blue & car	1.75	3.00
100	A11	25k grn & gray vio	2.00	5.00
101	A11	35k red brn & grn	2.00	4.00
102	A8	50k violet & grn	2.00	5.00
102A	A14	60k on 1k org, imperf. (I)	5.00	5.00
b.		Imperf. (II)	5.00	10.00
c.		Perf. (II)	5.00	5.00
103	A9	1r pale brn, dk brn & org	2.00	5.00
104	A12	3½r maroon & lt grn	4.75	8.00
a.		Imperf.	15.00	15.00

105	A13	5r dk bl, grn & pale bl	15.00	15.00
a.		Imperf.	6.00	6.00
106	A12	7r dk green & pink	5.00	10.00
107	A13	10r scar, yel & gray	20.00	45.00

Imperf

113	A11	70k brown & org	2.50	4.00

Handstamped in Violet or Black

Violet Surcharge, Type f

1920				**Perf.**
120	A14	3r on 3k red, imperf.	10.00	15.00
a.		Perf.	10.00	15.00
121	A14	5r on 3k red	10.00	10.00
122	A15	5r on 4k car	10.00	12.00
123	A14	5r on 5k claret, imperf.	5.00	12.00
a.		Perf.	12.00	20.00
124	A15	5r on 10k dk blue	20.00	30.00
125	A14	5r on 10k on 7k lt bl	20.00	30.00
126	A8	5r on 20k bl & car	10.00	15.00

Imperf

127	A14	5r on 2k green	12.00	12.00
128	A11	5r on 35k red brn & grn	12.00	12.00

Black Surcharge, Type f or Type g (#130)

Perf.

130	A14	1r on 1k orange	10.00	12.00
a.		Imperf.	15.00	15.00
131	A14	3r on 3k red	10.00	10.00
a.		Imperf.	5.00	5.00
132	A15	3r on 4k carmine	25.00	25.00
133	A14	5r on 2k grn, imperf.	2.50	2.50
a.		Perf.	5.00	5.00
134	A14	5r on 3k red	10.00	10.00
a.		Imperf.	5.00	5.00
135	A15	5r on 4k carmine	4.00	4.00
a.		Imperf.	10.00	10.00
136	A14	5r on 5k claret	4.00	4.00
a.		Imperf.	2.00	2.00
137	A14	5r on 7k lt blue	3.00	3.00
138	A15	5r on 10k dk blue	2.00	2.00
139	A14	5r on 10k on 7k lt bl	2.00	2.00
140	A11	5r on 14k bl & rose	2.50	2.50
141	A11	5r on 15k red brn & blue	1.00	1.00
a.		Imperf.	2.50	2.50
142	A8	5r on 20k bl & car	1.00	5.00
143	A11	5r on 20k on 14k bl & rose	75.00	100.00
144	A11	5r on 25k grn & gray vio	10.00	15.00

Black Surcharge, Type g or Type f (#148A, 151)

145	A14	10r on 1k org, imperf.	1.10	1.10
a.		Perf.	125.00	125.00
146	A14	10r on 3k red	175.00	175.00
147	A14	10r on 5k claret	18.00	18.00
a.		Imperf.	15.00	
148	A8	10r on 20k bl & car	15.00	15.00
148A	A11	10r on 25k grn & gray vio	10.00	10.00
149	A11	10r on 25k grn & gray vio	5.00	6.00
a.		Imperf.	10.00	20.00
150	A11	10r on 35k red brn & grn	2.00	2.00
151	A8	10r on 50k brn vio & grn	50.00	50.00
152	A8	10r on 50k brn vio & grn	3.00	4.00
152A	A11	10r on 70k brn & org, imperf.	5.00	5.00
b.		Perf.	240.00	240.00
152C	A8	25r on 20k bl & car	4.75	4.75
153	A11	25r on 25k grn & gray vio	5.00	5.00
154	A11	25r on 35k red brn & grn	20.00	20.00
a.		Imperf.	4.00	4.00

155	A8	25r on 50k vio & grn	5.00	5.00
a.		Imperf.	6.00	6.00
156	A11	25r on 70k brn & org	8.00	8.00
a.		Imperf.	5.00	5.00
157	A9	50r on 1r pale brn, dk brn & org, imperf.	2.00	2.00
a.		Perf.	10.00	15.00
158	A13	50r on 5r dk bl, grn & lt bl	25.00	25.00
a.		Imperf.	45.00	45.00
159	A12	100r on 3½r mar & lt grn	10.00	15.00
a.		Imperf.	10.00	10.00
160	A13	100r on 5r dk bl, grn & pale bl	12.00	12.00
a.		Imperf.	25.00	25.00
161	A12	100r on 7r dk grn & pink	12.00	15.00
a.		Imperf.	42.00	42.00
162	A13	100r on 10r scar, yel & gray	15.00	20.00

Wmk. Wavy Lines (168)
Perf. 11½
Vertically Laid Paper

163	A12	100r on 3½r blk & gray	120.00	120.00
164	A12	100r on 7r blk & yel	120.00	120.00

No. 168

1920		**Unwmk.**		**Imperf.**
		Wove Paper		
166	A14	(g) 1r on 60k on 1k org (I)	12.00	14.50
168	A14	(f) 5r on 1k orange	12.00	12.00
173	A11	(f) 5r on 35k red brn & grn	12.00	12.00
177	A11	(g) 50r on 70k brn & org	6.00	10.00
179	A12	(g) 50r on 3½r mar & lt grn	20.00	20.00
181	A9	(g) 100r on 1r pale brn, dk brn & org	20.00	20.00

Romanov Issues

No. 187   No. 187C

Surcharged Types g or f (#185-187, 190) on Stamps of 1913

1920				**Perf. 13½**
184	A16	1r on 1k brn org	175.00	175.00
185	A18	3r on 3k rose red	24.00	24.00
186	A19	5r on 4k dull red	12.00	12.00
187	A22	5r on 14k blue grn	50.00	50.00
187A	A19	10r on 4k dull red	40.00	
187B	A26	10r on 35k gray vio & dk grn		
187C	A19	25r on 4k dull red	20.00	20.00
188	A26	25r on 35k gray vio & dk grn	3.25	3.25
189	A28	25r on 70k yel grn & brn	3.25	3.25
190	A31	50r on 3r dk vio	2.50	2.50
190A	A16	100r on 1k brn org	125.00	125.00
190B	A17	100r on 2k green	125.00	125.00
191	A30	100r on 2r brown	12.50	12.50
192	A31	100r on 3r dk vio	12.50	12.50

On Stamps of 1915, Type g

Thin Cardboard
Inscriptions on Back
Perf. 12

193	A21	100r on 10k blue	20.00	
194	A23	100r on 15k brn	20.00	
195	A24	100r on 20k ol grn	18.00	

On Stamps of 1916, Type f

Perf. 13½

196	A20	5r on 10k on 7k brown	8.00	8.00
197	A22	5r on 20k on 14k bl grn	15.00	25.00

Surcharged Types f or g (#204-205A, 207-207C, 210-211) over Type c

Type c in Violet
Perf.

200	A15	5r on 4k car	6.00	8.00
201	A15	5r on 10k dk bl	25.00	25.00
202	A11	5r on 15k red brn & bl	5.00	5.00
203	A8	5r on 20k blue & car	10.00	10.00
204	A11	10r on 25k grn & gray vio	12.00	12.00
205	A11	10r on 35k red brn & grn	3.50	3.50
205A	A8	10r on 50k brn vio & grn	12.00	12.00
206	A8	25r on 50k brn vio & grn	150.00	150.00
207	A9	50r on 1r pale brn, dk brn & org, imperf.	30.00	30.00
a.		Perf.	30.00	30.00
207B	A12	100r on 3½r mar & lt grn	50.00	50.00
207C	A12	100r on 7r dk grn & pink	60.00	60.00

Imperf

208	A14	2k green	30.00	30.00
209	A14	5r on 5k claret	30.00	30.00
210	A11	25r on 70k brn & org	40.00	50.00
211	A13	100r on 5r dk bl, grn & pale bl	100.00	110.00

Surcharged Types g or f (212-213, 215, 219-219A, 221-222) over Type c

Type c in Black
Perf.

212	A14	5r on 7k lt bl	150.00	150.00
213	A14	5r on 10k on 7k lt bl	6.00	6.00
214	A11	5r on 15k red brn & bl	5.00	7.00
215	A8	5r on 20k blue & car	3.50	3.50
215A	A11	10r on 5r on 25k grn & gray vio	50.00	50.00
216	A11	10r on 35k red brn & grn	50.00	60.00
217	A8	10r on 50k brn vio & grn	12.00	15.00
217A	A9	50r on 1r pale brn, dk brn & org	35.00	50.00
b.		Imperf.	40.00	50.00
217C	A12	100r on 3½r mar & lt grn	30.00	30.00
218	A13	100r on 5r dk bl, grn & pale bl	35.00	40.00
a.		Imperf.	45.00	55.00
219	A12	100r on 7r dk grn & pink	35.00	50.00
219A	A13	100r on 10r scar, yel & gray	45.00	55.00

Imperf

220	A14	1r on 60k on 1k org (l)	35.00	35.00
221	A14	5r on 2k green	6.00	6.00
222	A14	5r on 5k claret	10.00	12.00

223	A11	10r on 70k brn & org	30.00	40.00
224	A11	25r on 70k brn & org	25.00	30.00

Surcharged Types g or f (#233) over Type a

Type a in Violet
Imperf

231	A9	50r on 1r pale brn, dk brn & org	170.00	170.00
232	A13	100r on 5r dk bl, grn & pale bl	100.00	110.00

Type a in Black

Perf.

233	A8	5r on 20k blue & car	6.00	6.00
233A	A11	10r on 25k grn & gray vio	20.00	20.00
234	A11	10r on 35k red brn & grn	175.00	175.00
235	A12	100r on 3½r mar & lt grn	10.00	10.00
a.		Imperf.	10.00	10.00

Imperf

237	A14	5r on 2k green	150.00	150.00
237A	A11	10r on 70k brn & org		

Surcharged Type a and New Value

Type a in Violet
Perf.

238	A11	10r on 15k red brn & blue	30.00	30.00

Type a in Black

239	A8	5r on 20k blue & car	4.00	5.00
239A	A8	10r on 20k blue & car	20.00	20.00
239B	A8	10r on 50k brn red & grn	30.00	40.00

Imperf

240	A12	100r on 3½r mar & lt grn	50.00	60.00

Surcharged Type c and New Value

Type c in Black

1920   **Perf.**

241	A15	5r on 4k red	6.00	8.00
242	A11	5r on 15k red brn & bl	4.00	6.00
243	A8	10r on 20k blue & car	20.00	20.00
243A	A11	10r on 25k grn & gray vio	12.00	15.00
244	A11	10r on 35k red brn & grn	45.00	50.00
a.		With additional srch. "5r"	—	—
245	A12	100r on 3½r mar & lt grn	10.00	15.00

No. 248

Imperf

247	A14	3r on 3k red	10.00	15.00
248	A14	5r on 2k green	3.00	7.00
249	A9	50r on 1r pale brn, dk brn & org	20.00	20.00

Type c in Violet

249A	A14	5r on 2k green	8.00	12.00

Russia AR1-AR3 Surcharged

A1   A2   A3

Perf. 14½x15
Wmk. 171

250	A1	60k on 1k red & buff	60.00	60.00
251	A2	1r on 1k red & buff	60.00	60.00
252	A3	5r on 5k green & buff	60.00	60.00
253	A3	5r on 10k brn & buff	60.00	60.00

Russian Semi-Postal Stamps of 1914-18 Srchd. with Armenian Monogram & New Values

On Stamps of 1914
Unwmk.   **Perf.**

255	SP5	25r on 1k red brn & dk grn, straw	72.50	72.50
256	SP5	25r on 3k mar & gray grn, pink	72.50	72.50
257	SP5	50r on 7 dk brn & dk grn, buff	90.00	90.00
258	SP5	100r on 1k red brn & dk grn, straw	90.00	90.00
259	SP5	100r on 3k mar & gray grn, pink	90.00	90.00
260	SP5	100r on 7k dk brn & dk grn, buff	90.00	90.00

No. 261

On Stamps of 1915-19

261	SP5	25r on 1k org brn & gray	100.00	100.00
262	SP5	25r on 3k car & gray	90.00	90.00
263	SP5	50r on 10k dk bl & brn	50.00	50.00
264	SP5	100r on 1k org brn & gray	90.00	90.00
265	SP5	100r on 10k dk bl & brn	90.00	90.00

These surcharged semi-postal stamps were used for ordinary postage.

A set of 10 stamps in the above designs was prepared in 1920, but not issued for postal use, though some were used fiscally. Value of set, $10. Exist imperf with "SPECIMEN" overprint. Value of set, $40. Reprints exist.

Soviet Socialist Republic

Hammer and Sickle — A7

Mythological Monster — A8

Symbols of Soviet Republics on Designs from old Armenian Manuscripts A9

Ruined City of Ani — A10

Mythological Monster — A11

Armenian Soldier — A12

Mythological Monster A13

Soviet Symbols, Armenian Designs — A14

Mt. Alagöz and Plain of Shirak A15

Fisherman on River Aras — A16

Post Office in Erevan and Mt. Ararat A17

Ruin in City of Ani — A18   Street in Erevan — A19

Lake Sevan and Sevan Monastery — A20

Mythological Subject from old Armenian Monument — A21

Mt. Ararat — A22

1921   Unwmk.   Perf. 11½, Imperf.

278	A7	1r gray green	.50	
279	A8	2r slate gray	.50	
280	A9	3r carmine	.50	
281	A10	5r dark brown	.50	
282	A11	25r gray	.50	.50
283	A12	50r red	.30	
284	A13	100r orange	.30	
285	A14	250r dark blue	.30	
286	A15	500r brown vio	.30	
287	A16	1000r sea green	.40	
288	A17	2000r bister	1.75	
289	A18	5000r dark brown	1.00	
290	A19	10,000r dull red	1.00	
291	A20	15,000r slate blue	1.25	
292	A21	20,000r lake	1.50	
293	A22	25,000r gray blue	2.00	
294	A22	25,000r brown olive	8.00	
		Nos. 278-294 (17)	20.60	

Except the 25r, Nos. 278-294 were not regularly issued and used. Counterfeits exist.
For surcharges see Nos. 347-390.

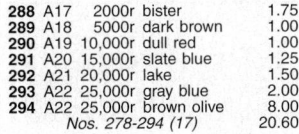

Russian Stamps of 1909-17 Surcharged

Lozenges of Varnish on Face

1921, Aug.   Wove Paper   Perf. 13½

295	A9	5000r on 1r	25.00
296	A12	5000r on 3½r	25.00
297	A13	5000r on 5r	25.00
298	A12	5000r on 7r	25.00
299	A13	5000r on 10r	25.00
		Nos. 295-299 (5)	125.00

Nos. 295-299 were not officially issued. Counterfeits abound.

A23

Mt. Ararat & Soviet Star — A24

Soviet Symbols — A25

Crane — A26

Peasant — A27

Harpy — A28

Peasant Sowing — A29

Soviet Symbols — A30

Forging — A31

Plowing A32

1922   Perf. 11½

300	A23	50r green & red	.85	
301	A24	300r slate bl & buff	1.00	
302	A25	400r blue & pink	1.00	
303	A26	500r vio & pale lil	1.00	
304	A27	1000r dull bl & pale bl	1.00	
305	A28	2000r black & gray	1.25	
306	A29	3000r black & grn	1.25	
307	A30	4000r black & lt brn	1.25	
308	A31	5000r blk & dull red	1.25	
309	A32	10,000r black & pale rose	1.25	
a.		Tête-bêche pair	42.50	
		Nos. 300-309 (10)	11.10	

Nos. 300-309 were not issued without surcharge.
Stamps of types A23 to A32, printed in other colors than Nos. 300 to 309, are essays.

Nos. 300-309 with Hstmpd. Srch. in Rose, Violet or Black

1922

310	10,000 on 50r (R)	90.00	90.00
311	10,000 on 50r (V)	60.00	60.00
312	10,000 on 50r	30.00	30.00
313	15,000 on 300r (R)	120.00	120.00
314	15,000 on 300r (V)	90.00	90.00
315	15,000 on 300r	30.00	30.00
316	25,000 on 400r (V)	60.00	60.00
317	25,000 on 400r	30.00	30.00
318	30,000 on 500r (R)	120.00	120.00
319	30,000 on 500r (V)	60.00	60.00
320	30,000 on 500r	30.00	30.00
321	50,000 on 1000r (R)	120.00	120.00
322	50,000 on 1000r (V)	60.00	60.00
323	50,000 on 1000r	25.00	25.00
324	75,000 on 3000r	30.00	30.00
325	100,000 on 2000r (R)	120.00	275.00
326	100,000 on 2000r (V)	60.00	60.00
327	100,000 on 2000r	25.00	25.00
328	200,000 on 4000r (V)	12.00	12.00
329	200,000 on 4000r	12.00	12.00
330	300,000 on 5000r (V)	60.00	60.00
331	300,000 on 5000r	25.00	25.00
332	500,000 on 10,000r (V)	60.00	60.00
333	500,000 on 10,000r	12.00	12.00
	Nos. 310-333 (24)	1,341.	1,496.

Forgeries exist.

Goose — A33   Armenian Woman at Well — A35

Armenian Village Scene A34

Mt. Ararat A36

Mt. Ararat A37

New Values in Gold Kopecks, Handstamped Surcharge in Black

1922   Imperf.

334	A33	1(k) on 250r rose	18.00	18.00
335	A33	1(k) on 250r gray	24.00	24.00
336	A34	2(k) on 500r rose	10.00	10.00
337	A34	3(k) on 500r gray	10.00	10.00
338	A35	4(k) on 1000r rose	10.00	10.00
339	A35	4(k) on 1000r gray	18.00	18.00
340	A36	5(k) on 2000r gray	10.00	10.00
341	A36	10(k) on 2000r rose	10.00	10.00
342	A37	15(k) on 5000r rose	62.50	62.50
343	A37	20(k) on 5000r gray	10.00	10.00
		Nos. 334-343 (10)	182.50	182.50

Nos. 334-343 were issued for postal tax purposes.
Nos. 334-343 exist without surcharge but are not known to have been issued in that condition. Counterfeits exist of both sets.

Regular Issue of 1921 Handstamped with New Values in Black or Red Short, Thick Numerals

1922   Imperf.

347	A8	2(k) on 2r (R)	60.00	60.00
350	A11	4(k) on 25r (R)	100.00	100.00
353	A13	10(k) on 100r (R)	24.00	24.00
354	A14	15(k) on 250r	3.50	3.50
355	A15	20(k) on 500r	18.00	18.00
a.		With "k" written in red	12.00	12.00
357	A22	50(k) on 25,000r bl (R)	300.00	300.00
358	A22	50(k) on 25,000r brn ol (R)	150.00	150.00
359	A22	50(k) on 25,000r brn ol		
		Nos. 347-358 (7)	655.50	655.50

Perf. 11½

360	A7	1(k) on 1r, imperf.	75.00	75.00
a.		Perf.	50.00	50.00
361	A7	1(k) on 1r (R)	45.00	45.00
a.		Imperf.	50.00	70.00
362	A8	2(k) on 2r, imperf.	47.50	47.50
a.		Perf.	50.00	50.00
363	A15	2(k) on 500r	100.00	125.00
a.		Perf.	100.00	100.00
364	A15	2(k) on 500r (R)	150.00	150.00
365	A11	4(k) on 25r, imperf.	30.00	30.00
a.		Perf.	50.00	50.00
366	A12	5(k) on 50r, imperf.	24.00	36.00
a.		Perf.	100.00	100.00
367	A13	10(k) on 100r	24.00	24.00
a.		Imperf.	50.00	50.00

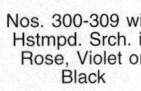

368	A21	35(k) on 20,000r,		
		imperf.	90.00	100.00
a.		With "k" written in violet	90.00	90.00
b.		Perf.	90.00	90.00
c.		As "a," perf.	90.00	90.00
d.		With "kop" written in violet, imperf.	90.00	90.00
		Nos. 360-368 (9)	585.50	632.50

Manuscript Surcharge in Red
Perf. 11½

371	A14	1k on 250r dk bl	50.00	50.00

Handstamped in Black or Red
Tall, Thin Numerals

No. 381

Imperf

377	A11	4(k) on 25r (R)	5.00	5.00
379	A13	10(k) on 100r	90.00	100.00
380	A15	20(k) on 500r	7.25	7.25
381	A22	50k on 25,000r bl	20.00	90.00
a.		Surcharged "50" only	60.00	60.00
382	A22	50k on 25,000r bl (R)	14.50	14.50
382A	A22	50k on 25,000r brn ol	29.00	29.00
		Nos. 377-382A (6)	165.75	245.75

On Nos. 381, 382 and 382A the letter "k" forms part of the surcharge.

Perf. 11½

383	A7	1(k) on 1r (R)	40.00	40.00
a.		Imperf.	100.00	
384	A14	1(k) on 250r	60.00	60.00
385	A15	2(k) on 500r	10.00	10.00
a.		Imperf.	24.00	24.00
386	A15	2(k) on 500r (R)	24.00	24.00
387	A9	3(k) on 3r	35.00	35.00
a.		Imperf.	40.00	40.00
388	A21	3(k) on 20,000r, imperf.	12.00	12.00
a.		Perf.	60.00	60.00
389	A11	4(k) on 25r	30.00	30.00
a.		Imperf.	120.00	120.00
390	A12	5(k) on 50r, imperf.	12.00	12.00
a.		Perf.	18.00	75.00
		Nos. 383-390 (8)	223.00	223.00

Catalogue values for unused stamps in this section, from this point to the end of the section, are for Never Hinged items.

Mt. Ararat — A45

a, 20k. b, 2r. c, 5r.

1992, May 28   Litho.   Perf. 14
430	A45	Strip of 3, #a.-c.	3.00	3.00

Souvenir Sheet
431	A45	7r Eagle & Mt. Ararat	55.00	55.00

AT & T Communications System in Armenia — A45a

1992, July 1   Litho.   Perf. 13x13½
431A	A45a	50k multicolored	4.50	4.50

A46

1992 Summer Olympics, Barcelona: a, 40k, Ancient Greek wrestlers. b, 3.60r, Boxing. c, 5r, Weight lifting. d, 12r, Gymnastics.

1992, July 25   Litho.   Perf. 14
432	A46	Strip of 4, #a.-d.	3.50	3.50

A47

20k, Natl. flag. 1r, Goddess Waroubini, Orgov radio telescope. 2r, Yerevan Airport. No. 436, Goddess Anahit. No. 437, Runic message, 7th cent B.C. 5r, UPU emblem. 20r, Silver cup.

1992-93   Litho.   Perf. 14½, 15x14½
433	A47	20k multicolored	.30	.30
434	A47	1r gray green	.30	.30
435	A47	2r blue	.40	.40
436	A47	3r brown	.60	.60
437	A47	3r bronze	.30	.30
438	A47	5r brown black	.90	.90
439	A47	20r gray	.70	.70
		Nos. 433-439 (7)	3.50	3.50

No. 435 is airmail. See Nos. 464-471, 521-524.

Issued: No. 436, 20k, 2r, 5r, 8/25/92; others, 5/12/93.

Religious Artifacts — A50

David of Sassoun, by Hakop Kojoian A50a

40k, Marker. 80k, Gospel page. 3.60r, Bas-relief, 13th cent. 5r, Icon of the Madonna.

1993, May 23   Litho.   Perf. 14
448	A50	40k multicolored	.25	.25
449	A50	80k multicolored	.30	.30
450	A50	3.60r multicolored	.90	.90
451	A50	5r multicolored	1.75	1.75
		Nos. 448-451 (4)	3.20	3.20

Souvenir Sheet
Perf. 14x13½
451A	A50a	12r multicolored	8.00	8.00

Scenic Views — A51

Designs: 40k, Garni Canyon, vert. 80k, Shaki Waterfall, Zangezur, vert. 3.60r, Arpa River Canyon, vert. 5r, Lake Sevan. 12r, Mount Aragats.

1993, May 24   Perf. 14
452	A51	40k multicolored	.25	.25
453	A51	80k multicolored	.25	.25
454	A51	3.60r multicolored	.50	.50
455	A51	5r multicolored	.70	.70
456	A51	12r multicolored	1.75	1.75
		Nos. 452-456 (5)	3.45	3.45

Yerevan '93 — A52

1993, May 25   Perf. 14½
457	A52	10r multicolored	.85	.85
a.		Min. sheet of 6 + 2 labels	5.50	5.50

For surcharges see Nos. 485-486.

Souvenir Sheet

Noah's Descent from Mt. Ararat, by Hovhannes Aivazovsky — A52a

1993, Aug. 4   Litho.   Perf. 14½
458	A52a	7r multicolored	4.50	4.50

Religious Relics, Echmiadzin — A53

Designs: 3r, Wooden panel, descent from cross, 9th cent. 5r, Gilded silver reliquary for Holy Cross of Khotakerats. 12r, Cross depicting right hand of St. Karapet, 14th cent. 30r, Reliquary for arm of St. Thaddeus the Apostle, 17th cent. 50r, Gilded silver vessel for consecrated ointment, 1815.

1994, Aug. 4   Litho.   Perf. 14x14½
459	A53	3d multicolored	.25	.25
460	A53	5d multicolored	.25	.25
461	A53	12d multicolored	.65	.65
462	A53	30d multicolored	1.25	1.25
463	A53	50d multicolored	2.00	2.00
		Nos. 459-463 (5)	4.40	4.40

Artifacts and Landmarks Type of 1993

Gods of Van (Urartu): 10 l, Shivini, god of the sun. 50 l, Tayshaba, god of elements. 10d, Khaldi, supreme god.
25d, Natl. arms.

1994, Aug. 4   Perf. 14½
464	A47	10 l black & brown	.25	.25
465	A47	50 l black & red brown	.25	.25
469	A47	10d black & gray	.85	.85
471	A47	25d red & bister	2.00	2.00
		Nos. 464-471 (4)	3.35	3.35

A54

1994, Dec. 31   Litho.   Perf. 14½x14
479	A54	16d No. 1a	.40	.40

First Armenian postage stamp, 75th anniv.

Early Printing Press — A54a

1994, Dec. 30   Litho.   Perf. 14x14½
480	A54a	30d multicolored	.60	.60

First Armenian periodical, 200th anniv.

Natl. Arms, Stadium — A54b

1994, Dec. 30   Litho.   Perf. 14x14½
481	A54b	30d multicolored	.65	.65

Natl. Olympic Committee.

Olympic Rings — A54c

1994, Dec. 30   Litho.   Perf. 14x14½
482	A54c	40d multicolored	1.00	1.00

Intl. Olympic Committee, Cent.

A54d

1994, Dec. 31   Litho.   Perf. 14x14½
483	A54d	50d multi + label	1.00	1.00

Ervand Otian (1869-1926)

A54e

1994, Dec. 31   Litho.   Perf. 14½x14
484	A54e	50d multi + label	1.00	1.00

Levon Shant (1869-1951).

No. 457 Surcharged in Blue or Red Brown

a — b

1994, Sept. 10   Litho.   Perf. 14
485 A52(a) 40d on 10r (Bl)   5.50 5.50
486 A52(b) 40d on 10r (RB)   5.50 5.50

Yerevan '94.

A55

Christianity in Armenia: 60d, Cross, 10th-11th cent. No. 488, Kings Abgar & Trdat, 1836. No. 489, St. Bartholomew, St. Thaddeus. 80d, St. Gregory, the Illuminator. 90d, Baptism of the Armenian people, 1892. 400d, Plan of Echmiadzin, c. 1660, engr. by Jakob Peeters.

1995, Apr. 3   Litho.   Perf. 14x15
487 A55 60d multicolored   .65   .65
488 A55 70d multicolored   .65   .65
489 A55 70d multicolored   .65   .65
490 A55 80d multicolored   1.00 1.00
491 A55 90d multicolored   1.10 1.10
    Nos. 487-491 (5)   4.05 4.05

Souvenir Sheet
492 A55 400d multicolored   5.50 5.50

Nos. 488-489 are 45x44mm.

A56

1995, Apr. 3
493 A56 150d gray & black   1.50 1.50

Vazgen I (1908-94), Catholikos of All Armenians.

Armenia Fund A57

1995, Apr. 27   Perf. 15x14
494 A57 90d multicolored   .90   .90

UN, 50th Anniv. A58

1995, Apr. 28
495 A58 90d multicolored   .90   .90

Cultural Artifacts — A59

Designs: 30d, Black polished pottery, 14th-13th cent. B.C. 60d, Silver cup, 5th cent. B.C. 130d, Gohar carpet, 1700 A.D.

1995, Apr. 27   Perf. 15x14
496 A59 30d multicolored   .35   .35
497 A59 60d multicolored   .65   .65
498 A59 130d multicolored   1.50 1.50
    Nos. 496-498 (3)   2.50 2.50

Birds — A60

1995, Apr. 27   Perf. 14
499 A60 40d Milvus milvus   .65   .65
500 A60 60d Aquila chrysaetos .95   .95

End of World War II, 50th Anniv. A61

Designs: No. 501, P. Kitsook, 408th Armenian Rifle Division. No. 502, A. Sargissin, N. Safarian, 89th Taman Armenian Triple Order-Bearer Division. No. 503, B. Chernikov, N. Tavartkeladze, V. Penkovsky, 76th Armenian Alpine Rifle Red Banner (51st Guards) Division. No. 504, S. Zakian, H. Babayan, I. Lyudnikov, 390th Armenian Rifle Division. No. 505, A. Vasillian, M. Dobrovolsky, Y. Grechany, G. Sorokin, 409th Armenian Rifle Division.
No. 506, vert.: a, Marshal Hovhannes Baghramian. b, Adm. Hovhannes Issakov. c, Marshal Hamazasp Babajanian. d, Marshal Sergey Khoudyakov.
No. 507: Return of the Hero, by Mariam Aslamazian.

1995, Sept. 30   Litho.   Perf. 15x14
501 A61 60d multicolored   .60   .60
502 A61 60d multicolored   .60   .60
503 A61 60d multicolored   .60   .60
504 A61 60d multicolored   .60   .60
505 A61 60d multicolored   .60   .60
    Nos. 501-505 (5)   3.00 3.00

Miniature Sheet
Perf. 15x14½
506 A61 60d Sheet of 4, #a.-d. 3.25 3.25

Souvenir Sheet
Perf. 15x14
507 A61 300d multicolored   4.00 4.00

Authors A62

Designs: No. 508, Ghevond Alishan (1820-1901). No. 509, Gregor Artsruni (1845-92), vert. No. 510, Franz Werfel (1890-1945), vert.

1995, Oct. 5   Litho.   Perf. 15x14
508 A62 90d blue & black   .85   .85
509 A62 90d cream, blk, gold .85   .85
510 A62 90d blue & maroon   .85   .85
    Nos. 508-510 (3)   2.55 2.55

Nos. 508-510 issued with se-tenant label.

A64

Prehistoric artifacts: 40d, Four-wheeled carriages, 15th cent. BC. 60d, Bronze model of geocentric solar system, 11-10th cent. BC, vert. 90d, Tombstone, Red Tufa, 7-6th cent. BC, vert.

1995, Dec. 5   Perf. 14½x15, 15x14½
512 A64 40d multicolored   .40   .40
513 A64 60d multicolored   .60   .60
514 A64 90d multicolored   .80   .80
    Nos. 512-514 (3)   1.80 1.80

A65

Christianity in Armenia — A66

Views of Yerevan: 60d, Brandy distillery, wine cellars. 80d, Abovian Street. 90d, Sports and concert complex. 100d, Baghramian Avenue. 120d, Republic Square.
400d, Panoramic photograph of Yerevan.

1995, Dec. 5   Perf. 15x14
515 A65 60d salmon & black   .50   .50
516 A65 80d pale org & blk   .60   .60
517 A65 90d buff & black   .70   .70

Size: 61x24mm
518 A65 100d pale yel bis & blk   .80   .80
519 A65 120d dull org & blk 1.00 1.00
    Nos. 515-519 (5)   3.60 3.60

Souvenir Sheet
520 A66 400d multicolored   4.25 4.25

No. 464 Surcharged in Green, Red, Blue Violet, or Red Brown

1996, Mar. 30   Litho.   Perf. 14½
521 A47 40d on 10l (G)   1.75 1.75
522 A47 100d on 10l (R)   3.50 3.50
523 A47 150d on 10l (BV)   5.00 5.00
524 A47 200d on 10l (RB)   7.00 7.00
    Nos. 521-524 (4)   17.25 17.25

Alexsandre Griboyedov (1795-1829), Writer — A67

1996, Apr. 24   Litho.   Perf. 14x14½
525 A67 90d multi + label   .90   .90

Khrimian Hayrik (1820-1907), Catholicos of All Armenians — A68

1996, Apr. 30   Perf. 14½x14
526 A68 90d brown & blue   .90   .90

No. 526 is printed se-tenant with label.

Admiral Lazar Serbryakov (1795-1862) — A69

1996, Apr. 30
527 A69 90d multi + label   .90   .90

Armenian Red Cross, 75th Anniv. — A70

1996, May 4   Perf. 14x14½
528 A70 60d multicolored   .60   .60

Motion Pictures, Cent. A71

1996, May 4   Perf. 14½x14
529 A71 60d multicolored   .60   .60

No. 529 exists imperf. Value $45.

Endangered Fauna — A72

1996, May 3   Perf. 14
530 A72 40d Carpa aegagrus   .70   .70
531 A72 60d Panthera pardus 1.10 1.10

1996 Summer Olympics, Atlanta — A73

Designs: a, 40d, Cyclist. b, 60d, Athletic event. c, 90d, Wrestling.

1996, July 25
532 A73 Strip of 3, #a.-c.   1.90 1.90

Modern Olympic Games, Cent. — A74

1996, July 25   Perf. 14x14½
533 A74 60d multicolored   .60   .60

Fridtjof Nansen (1861-1930), Arctic Explorer — A75

1996, May 20   Litho.   Perf. 14x14½
534 A75 90d multicolored   1.00 1.00

32nd Chess Olympiad, Yerevan — A76

Designs: No. 535, Petrosian-Botvinnik, World Championship match, Moscow, 1963. No. 536, Kasparov-Karpov, World Championship Match, Leningrad, 1986. No. 537, G. Kasparian, first prize winner, Contest of the Shakhmati v SSSR magazine, 1939. No. 538, 32nd Chess Olympiad, Yerevan.

1996, Sept. 15   Litho.   Perf. 14
535 A76 40d multicolored   .70   .70
536 A76 40d multicolored   .70   .55
537 A76 40d multicolored   .70   .70
538 A76 40d multicolored   .70   .70
a.   Booklet pane, #535-538   3.00
         Complete booklet, 2 #538a   7.50
         Nos. 535-538 (4)   2.80 2.65

No. 538a issued 9/24.
Nos. 535-538 also exist imperf. Value $30.

Tigran Petrosian, World Chess Champion, Chess House, Yerevan — A77

1996, Sept. 20   Perf. 14x15
539 A77 90d multicolored   .75   .75

No. 539 also exists imperf. Value $20.

Capra Aegagrus A78

World Wildlife Fund: 70d, Two running. 100d, One standing. 130d, One holding head down. 350d, Two facing forward.

1996, Oct. 20   Litho.   Perf. 14½x14
540 A78 70d multicolored   .60   .60
541 A78 100d multicolored   .70   .70
542 A78 130d multicolored   1.00 1.00
543 A78 350d multicolored   2.50 2.50
a.   Block of 4, #540-543   5.00 5.00
b.   Booklet pane, 2 #543a   10.00 10.00
         Complete booklet, #543b 12.00 12.00

Issued in sheets of 16 stamps.

Christianity in Armenia, 1700th Anniv. — A79

Armenian churches: No. 544, St. Catherine Church, St. Petersburg, 1780. No. 545, Church of the Holy Mother, Kishinev, 1803.

No. 546, Church of the Holy Mother, Samarkand, 1903. No. 547, Armenian Church, Lvov, 1370. No. 548, St. Hripsime Church, Yalta, 1913.
500d, Church of St. Gevorg of Etchmiadzin, Tbilisi, 1805.

1997, Mar. 19   Litho.   Perf. 14x15
544 A79 100d multicolored   1.00 1.00
545 A79 100d multicolored   1.00 1.00
546 A79 100d multicolored   1.00 1.00
547 A79 100d multicolored   1.00 1.00
548 A79 100d multicolored   1.00 1.00
         Nos. 544-548 (5)   5.00 5.00

Souvenir Sheet
549 A79 500d multicolored   4.00 4.00

First Armenian Printing Press, Etchmiadzin, 225th Anniv. — A80

1997, Mar. 26   Litho.   Perf. 15x14
550 A80 70d multicolored   1.00 1.00

Armenian Entertainers — A81

Designs: No. 551, Folk singer, Jivani (1846-1909). No. 552, Arno Babajanian (1921-83), composer, vert.

1997, Mar. 26   Perf. 15x14, 14x15
551 A81 90d multicolored   .60   .60
552 A81 90d multicolored   .60   .60

Paintings from Natl. Gallery of Armenia A82

Designs: No. 553, "One of my Dreams," by Eghishe Tadevossian. No. 554, "Countryside," by Gevorg Bashinjaghian. No. 555, "Portrait of Natalia Tehumian," by Hakob Hovnatanian. No. 556, "Salomé," by Vardges Sureniants.

1997, May 28   Litho.   Perf. 15x14
553 A82 150d multi   1.00 1.00
554 A82 150d multi   1.00 1.00
555 A82 150d multi, vert.   1.00 1.00
556 A82 150d multi, vert.   1.00 1.00
         Nos. 553-556 (4)   4.00 4.00

See Nos. 573-575.

Rouben Mamulian (1897-1987), Motion Picture Director — A83

1997, Oct. 8   Litho.   Perf. 15x14
557 A83 150d multicolored   1.00 1.00

Moscow '97, World Philatelic Exhibition — A84

170d, St. Basil's Cathedral.

1997, Oct. 17   Perf. 14x15
558 A84 170d multicolored   1.25 1.25

Eghishe Charents (1897-1937), Poet — A85

1997, Oct. 19   Perf. 15x14
559 A85 150d multicolored   1.00 1.00

A86

Europa (Stories and Legends): 170d, Hayk, the Progenitor of the Armenians. 250d, Vahagn, the Dragon Slayer.

1997, Oct. 18   Perf. 14x15
560 A86 170d multicolored   3.00 3.00
561 A86 250d multicolored   4.00 4.00

A87

40d, Iris lycotis. 170d, Iris elegantissima.

1997, Dec. 19   Litho.   Perf. 14
562 A87 40d multicolored   .30   .30
563 A87 170d multicolored   1.20 1.20

Religious Buildings — A88

Designs: No. 564, San Lazzaro, the Mekhitarian Congregation, Venice. No. 565, St. Gregory the Illuminator Cathedral, Anthelias. No. 566, St. Khach Armenian Church, Rostov upon Don. No. 567, St. James Monastery, Jerusalem. No. 568, Nercissian School, Tbilisi.
500d, Lazarian Seminary, Moscow.

1997, Dec. 22   Perf. 15x14, 14x15
564 A88 100d multi, horiz.   .70   .70
565 A88 100d multi   .70   .70
566 A88 100d multi   .70   .70
567 A88 100d multi, horiz.   .70   .70
         Size: 60x21mm
568 A88 100d multi, horiz.   .70   .70
         Nos. 564-568 (5)   3.50 3.50

Souvenir Sheet
569 A88 500d multicolored   3.00 3.00

Christianity in Armenia, 1700th anniv. (in 2001).

Christmas — A89

1997, Dec. 26   Perf. 14x15
570 A89 40d multicolored   .50   .50

Diana, Princess of Wales (1961-97) A90

1998, Apr. 8   Litho.   Perf. 15x14
571 A90 250d multicolored   2.00 2.00

No. 571 was issued in sheets of 5 + label.

Karabakh Movement, 10th Anniv. — A91

1998, Feb. 20   Litho.   Perf. 13½x14
572 A91 250d multicolored   2.75 2.75

Paintings from Natl. Gallery of Armenia Type of 1997

Designs: No. 573, "Tartar Women's Dance," by Alexander Bazhbeouk-Melikian. No. 574, "Family. Generations," by Yervand Kochar. No. 575, "Spring in Our Yard," by Haroutiun Kalents.

1998, Feb. 21   Perf. 15x14, 14x15
573 A82 150d multi   1.50 1.50
574 A82 150d multi, vert.   1.50 1.50
575 A82 150d multi, vert.   1.50 1.50
         Nos. 573-575 (3)   4.50 4.50

1998 World Cup Soccer Championships, France — A92

1998, June 10   Litho.   Perf. 14x15
576 A92 250d multicolored   2.25 2.25

No. 576 was issued in sheets of 10 and sheets of 8 + 2 labels. Value, sheet of 8 + 2 labels $20. Same, imperf $125.

National Holidays and Festivals A93

Europa: 170d, Couple jumping over fire, Trndez. 250d, Girls taking part in traditional ceremony, Ascension Day.

1998, June 24   Litho.   Perf. 15x14
577 A93 170d multicolored   1.50 1.50
578 A93 250d multicolored   2.50 2.50

Butterflies — A94

1998, June 26   Perf. 14
579 A94 170d Papilio alexanor 1.00 1.00
580 A94 250d Rethera komarovi 1.50 1.50

National Costumes — A95

1998, July 16   Litho.   Perf. 14x13½
581 A95 170d Ayrarat   1.25 1.25
582 A95 250d Vaspurakan   1.75 1.75
See Nos. 591-592.

Christianity in Armenia, 1700th Anniv. (in 2001) — A96

Churches: a, St. Forty Children's, 1958, Milan. b, St. Sargis, London, 1923. c, St. Vardan Cathedral, 1968, New York. d, St. Hovannes Cathedral, 1902, Paris. e, St. Gregory the Illuminator Cathedral, 1938, Buenos Aires.

1998, Sept. 25   Litho.   Perf. 11½
583 A96 100d Sheet of 5, #a.-e.   3.00 3.00

Memorial to Armenian Earthquake Victims A97

1998, Sept. 26   Perf. 15x14
584 A97 250d multicolored   2.25 2.25
No. 584 was issued in sheets of 10 and sheets of 8 + 2 labels. Value, sheet of 8 + 2 labels $35.

Minerals A98

1998, Oct. 23
585 A98 170d Pyrite   1.25 1.25
586 A98 250d Agate   1.75 1.75
See Nos. 616-617.

Valery Bryusov (1873-1924), Writer — A99

1998, Dec. 1   Perf. 14x15
587 A99 90d multicolored   .75 .75

Souvenir Sheet

Sergei Parajanov, Film Director, 75th Birth Anniv. — A100

1999, Apr. 19   Litho.   Perf. 14x14¾
588 A100 500d multicolored   4.00 4.00
  a.   IBRA 99 emblem in margin   4.50 4.50

State Reserves A101

1999, Apr. 22   Perf. 14¾x14¼
589 A101 170d Khosrov   1.50 1.50
590 A101 250d Kilijan   2.50 2.50
Europa.

National Costumes Type of 1998
1999, Apr. 20   Litho.   Perf. 14x13½
591 A95 170d Karin   1.25 1.25
592 A95 250d Zangezour   2.00 2.00

Council of Europe, 50th Anniv. — A102

1999, June 12
593 A102 170d multicolored   4.50 4.50

Cilician Ships A103

1999, Aug. 12   Litho.   Perf. 14¾x14
Sail Colors
594 A103 170d orange & blue   1.25 1.25
595 A103 250d red & white   2.00 2.00
With PhilexFrance 99 Emblem at LR
596 A103 250d red & white   2.25 2.25
  Nos. 594-596 (3)   5.50 5.50

Domesticated Animals — A104

1999, Aug. 19   Perf. 13¼x13¾
597 A104 170d Armenian gampr dog   1.25 1.25
598 A104 250d Van cat   2.00 2.00
With China 1999 World Philatelic Exhibition Emblem at LR
599 A104 250d Van cat   2.50 2.50
  Nos. 597-599 (3)   5.75 5.75

Souvenir Sheet

First Pan-Armenian Games — A105

1999, Aug. 28   Perf. 14¾x14
600 A105 250d multicolored   3.00 3.00

Souvenir Sheet

Christianity in Armenia, 1700th Anniv. (in 2001) — A106

Churches: a, St. Gregory the Illuminator, Cairo. b, St. Gregory the Illuminator, Singapore. c, St. Khach, Suceava, Romania. d, St. Savior, Worcester, Mass. e, Church of the Holy Mother, Madras, India.

1999, Aug.   Litho.   Perf. 13¼x13¾
601 A106 70d Sheet of 5, #a.-e.
                           + label   7.50 7.50

UPU, 125th Anniv. A107

1999, Oct.   Perf. 14¾x14¼
602 A107 270d multicolored   2.25 2.25

Politicians Assassinated Oct. 27, 1999 — A108

Designs: No. 603, Parliament Speaker Karen Demirchyan, Parliament building. No. 604, Prime Minister Vazgen Sargsyan, troops. 540d, Demirchyan, Sargsyan, Yuri Bakhshyan, Ruben Miroyan, Henrik Abrahamyan, Armenak Armenakyan, Leonard Petrossyan and Mikael Kotanyan.

Perf. 14¾x14¼
2000, Feb. 21   Litho.
603 A108 250d multi   2.50 2.00
604 A108 250d multi   2.50 2.00
  a.   Sheet, 5 each #603-604   65.00 65.00
Imperf
Size: 60x44mm
605 A108 540d multi   5.00 5.00

Fish — A109

Designs: 50d, Salmo ischchan. 270d, Barbus goktschaicus.

2000, May 23 Litho.   Perf. 13¼x13¾
606 A109 50d multi   1.00 1.00
607 A109 270d multi   2.00 2.00

Fairy Tales A110

70d, The Liar Hunter. 130d, The King and the Peddler.

2000, May 25   Perf. 14¾x14¼
608 A110 70d multicolored   .65 .65
609 A110 130d multicolored   1.25 1.25

Europa, 2000
Common Design Type
2000, June 19   Perf. 14¼x14¾
610 CD17 40d multi   .75 .75
611 CD17 500d multi   4.00 4.00

Christianity as State Religion, 1700th Anniv. — A111

No. 612: a, St. Gayane Church, Vagharshapat. b, Etchmiadzin Cathedral, Vagharshapat. c, Church of the Holy Mother, Khor Virap. d, St. Shoghakat Church, Vagharshapat. e, St. Hripsime Church, Vagharshapat.

2000, July 10 Litho.   Perf. 13¼x13¾
612 A111 70d Sheet of 5, #a-e, +
                            label   4.00 4.00

2000 Summer Olympics, Sydney — A112

Designs: 10d, Basketball. 30d, Tennis. 500d, Weight lifting.

2000, July 11   Perf. 13½x13¾
613-615 A112 Set of 3   5.00 5.00

Mineral Type of 1998
Designs: 170d, Quartz. 250d, Molybdenite.

2000, Sept. 4   Perf. 14¾x14
616-617 A98 Set of 2   3.25 3.25

A113

2000, Sept. 11   Perf. 14x14¾
618 A113 270d multi   2.00 2.00
Nerses Shnorhali (1100-73), poet and musician.

A114

2000, Sept. 15
619 A114 170d multi   1.40 1.40
Christmas.

Avetik Issahakian (1875-1957), Poet — A115

2000, Sept. 17   Perf. 14¾x14
620 A115 130d multi   .90 .90

Musical Instruments A116

Designs: 170d, Dhol. 250d, Duduk.

2000, Dec. 22 Litho.   Perf. 14x13¼
621-622 A116 Set of 2   3.50 3.50

Famous Armenians — A117

No. 623: a, Viktor Hambartsoumian (1908-96), cosmologist. b, Abraham Alikhanov (1904-70), physicist. c, Andranik Iossifian (1905-93), engineer. d, Sargis Saltikov (1905-83), metallurgist. e, Samuel Kochariants (1909-87), nuclear weapons scientist. f, Atrem Mikoyan (1905-70), aircraft designer. g, Norayr Sissakian (1907-66), biologist. h, Ivan Knuny-ants (1906-90), chemist. i, Nikoghayos Yenikolopian (1924-93), chemist.

No. 624: a, Nikoghayos Adonts (1871-1942), historian. b, Manouk Abeghian (1865-1944), grammarian. c, Hovhannes Toumanian (1869-1923), poet. d, Hrachya Ajarian (1876-1953), linguist. e, Gevorg Emin (1918-98), writer. f, Yervand Lalayan (1864-1931), anthro-pologist. g, Daniel Varoujan (1884-1915), poet. h, Paruyr Sevak (1924-71), writer. i, Wil-liam Saroyan (1908-81), writer.

No. 625: a, Hamo Beknazarian (1892-1965), actor. b, Alexandre Tamanian (1878-1936), architect. c, Vahram Papazian (1888-1968), actor. d, Vassil Tahirov (1859-1938), viticulturist. e, Leonid Yengibarov (1935-72), mime. f, Haykanoush Danielian (1893-1958), singer. g, Sergo Hambartsoumian (1910-83) "Strongest man on Earth". h, Hrant Shahinian (1923-96), gymnast. i, Toros Toramanian (1864-1934), architectural historian.

No. 626: a, Komitas (1869-1935), com-poser. b, Aram Khachatourian (1903-78), composer. c, Martiros Sarian (1880-1972), artist. d, Avet Terterian (1929-94), composer. e, Alexandre Spendiarian (1871-1928), com-poser. f, Arshile Gorky (1904-48), artist. g, Minas Avetissian (1928-75), artist. h, Levon Orbeli (1882-1958), physiologist. i, Hripsimeh Simonian (1916-98), artist.

2000, Dec. 23   *Perf. 14¾x14¼*
623	Booklet pane of 9	8.75	8.75
a.-i.	A117 110d Any single	.90	.90
624	Booklet pane of 9	8.75	8.75
a.-i.	A117 110d Any single	.90	.90
625	Booklet pane of 9	8.75	8.75
a.-i.	A117 110d Any single	.90	.90
626	Booklet pane of 9	8.75	8.75
a.-i.	A117 110d Any single	.90	.90
	Booklet, #623-626	45.00	

Souvenir Sheet

Battle of Avarayr, 1550th Anniv. — A118

No. 627: a, 170d, St. Vardan Mamikonian (388-451). b, 270d, Battle of Avarayr, 451.

2001, June 7   Litho.   *Perf. 14x14¾*
627 A118   Sheet of 2, #a-b   4.50 4.50

Record of Lamentations, by St. Grigor Narekatzi, 1000th Anniv. — A119

2001, June 8   Litho.   *Perf. 14¾x14*
628 A119 25d multi   2.00 2.00

Europa A120

Designs: 50d, Lake Sevan. 500d, Spandarian Reservoir.

2001, June 9
629-630 A120   Set of 2   5.75 5.75

Armenian Admission to Council of Europe A121

2001, June 11
631 A121 240d multi   2.25 2.25

Worldwide Fund for Nature (WWF) — A122

Sciurus persicus: a, 40d, On branch. b, 50d, Eating. c, 80d, Close-up. d, 120d, Digging.

     Perf. 13¼x13¾
2001, Aug. 25   Litho.
632 A122   Block of 4, #a-d   4.00 4.00

Souvenir Sheet

Second Pan-Armenian Games — A123

2001, Aug. 18   Litho.   *Perf. 14¾x14*
633 A123 300d multi   4.00 4.00

Souvenir Sheet

Christianity in Armenia, 1700th Anniv. — A124

Views of St. Gregory the Illuminator Cathe-dral, Yerevan: a, 50d, Front. b, 205d, Side (45x30mm). c, 240d, Side, diff. (45x30mm).

   Perf. 13¾x13¼, 13¼x13¾
2001, Aug. 27
634	A124	Sheet of 3, #a-c, + 6 labels	7.00	7.00
d.		As No. 634, with brown in-scriptions in margins	65.00	65.00

Marginal inscriptions on No. 634d read "INTERNATIONAL / PHILATELIC EXHIBI-TION / ARMENIA '01/ 10-16 September, 2001, Yerevan," in English, Armenian, Russian and French. Souvenir sheet can be formed into a box which shows cathedral from various angles.

Ivan Lazarev (1735-1801) and Institute of Eastern Languages, Moscow — A125

2001, Sept. 26   Litho.   *Perf. 14¾x14*
635 A125 300d multi   8.00 8.00

See Russia No. 6665.

Native Costumes — A126

Man and woman from: 50d, Javakhch. 250r, Artzakh.

2001, Sept. 27   *Perf. 14x13½*
636-637 A126   Set of 2   3.00 3.00

6th World Wushu Championships A127

2001, Oct. 3   *Perf. 13¼x13¾*
638 A127 180d black   2.75 2.75

Year of Dialogue Among Civilizations — A128

2001, Oct. 9   *Perf. 14x14¾*
639 A128 275d multi   6.00 6.00

Commonwealth of Independent States, 10th Anniv. — A129

2001, Nov. 29
640 A129 205d multi   2.25 2.25

European Year of Languages A130

2001, Dec. 21   *Perf. 14¾x14*
641 A130 350d multi   5.00 5.00

Independence, 10th Anniv. — A131

2001, Dec. 22
642 A131 300d multi   2.75 2.75

Transportation A132

Designs: 180d, Cart. 205d, Phaeton.

2001, Dec. 24   *Perf. 13½x14*
643-644 A132   Set of 2   3.75 3.75

Medicinal Plants — A133

Designs: 85d, Hypericum perforatum. 205d, Thymus serpyllum.

2001, Dec. 25   *Perf. 13¼x13¾*
645-646 A133   Set of 2   3.50 3.50

Eagle — A134

2002, Mar. 28   Litho.   *Perf. 14¾x14*
647	A134	10d brown	.60	.60
648	A134	25d green	.75	.75
649	A134	50d dk blue	1.00	1.00
	Nos. 647-649 (3)		2.35	2.35

See Nos. 674-676.

Industries A135

Designs: 120d, Calendar belt, 2nd cent. B.C., copper smelter. 350d, Containers, 7th cent. B.C., hops, barley, beer kettles.

2002, Apr. 26
650-651 A135   Set of 2   6.50 6.50

National Gallery Artworks — A136

Designs: No. 652, 200d, Lily, by Edgar Chahine. No. 653, 200d, Salomé, sculpture by Hakob Gurjian.

2002, Apr. 29   *Perf. 14x14¾*
652-653 A136   Set of 2   3.50 3.50

2002 World Cup Soccer Championships, Japan and Korea — A137

2002, May 2   *Perf. 14¾x14*
654 A137 350d multi   2.75 2.75

Souvenir Sheet

Hovsep Pushman (1877-1906), Artist — A138

2002, May 9
655 A138 650d multi   5.00 5.00

Hovhannes Tevossian (1902-58), Engineer — A139

2002, May 14
656 A139 350d multi   2.75 2.75

Europa — A140

Designs: 70d, Magician's hat. 500d, Clown.

2002, July 30   Litho.   Perf. 14x14¾
657-658 A140   Set of 2   4.00 4.00

Artemy Aivazian, Composer, Cent. of Birth A141

2002, July 31   Perf. 14¾x14
659 A141 600d multi   4.75 4.75

Souvenir Sheet

Cathedral of Ani, 1000th Anniv. (in 2001) — A142

**   Perf. 13¼x13¾**
2002, Sept. 24   Litho.
660 A142 550d multi   4.50 4.50

Intl. Year of Mountains A143

2002-03   Perf. 14¾x14
661 A143 350d multi   3.00 3.00
661a   Booklet pane of 3   9.00 9.00
   Issued: No. 661, 9/26/02. No. 661a, 2003.

Reptiles — A144

Designs: 170d, Lacerta armeniaca. 220d, Vipera raddei.

2002-03   Perf. 13¼x13¾
662-663 A144   Set of 2   3.50 3.50
663a   Booklet pane, 2 each #662-663   7.00 7.00
   Issued: Nos. 662-663, 9/27/02. No. 663a, 2003.

Women for Peace A145

2002, Dec. 20   Litho.   Perf. 14¾x14
664 A145 220d multi   2.00 2.00

Alexandrapol — Yeravan Railway, Cent. — A146

2002, Dec. 21
665 A146 350d multi   3.00 3.00

Flowers — A147

Designs: 150d, Galanthus artjuschenkoae. 200d, Merendera mirzoevae.

2002, Dec. 23   Perf. 13¼x13¾
666-667 A147   Set of 2   3.00 3.00
667a   Booklet pane, 2 each
     #666-667   6.00 —
   Complete booklet, #661a, 663a,
     667a   22.00
   Issued: No. 667a, 2003.

Space Research A148

Designs: 120d, Cosmic ray research. 220d, Orion 1 and Orion 2 space observatories.

2002, Dec. 24   Perf. 14¾x14
668-669 A148   Set of 2   3.00 3.00

Europa — A149

Poster art: 170d, Handle With Care!, by Artak Bagdassaryan. 250d, Armenia, Our Home, by Karen Koyojan.

**   Perf. 13½x13¼**
2003, June 24   Litho.
670-671 A149   Set of 2   3.50 3.50
671a   Booklet pane, 4 each #670-
     671   14.00 14.00
   No. 671a was sold with booklet cover, but was unattached to it.

Aram Khatchaturian (1903-78), Composer — A150

**   Perf. 13½x13¼**
2003, June 25   Litho.
672 A150 350d multi   3.00 3.00

Larus Armenicus A151

2003, June 26   Perf. 12½
673 A151 220d multi   1.60 1.60

Eagle Type of 2002
**   Perf. 13¼x13½**
2003, Sept. 23   Litho.
674 A134 70d red   .70 .70
675 A134 300d dk blue   2.50 2.50
676 A134 500d bister brn   5.00 5.00
   Nos. 674-676 (3)   8.20 8.20

Souvenir Sheet

Transport Corridor Europe — Caucausus — Asia (TRACECA), 10th Anniv. — A152

2003, Oct. 9   Perf. 13
677 A152 480d multi   6.50 6.50

First Armenian Postal Dispatch, 175th Anniv. A153

2003, Nov. 24   Perf. 13¼x13½
678 A153 70d multi   .75 .75

Introduction of Dram Currency, 10th Anniv. — A154

2003, Nov. 25
679 A154 170d multi   1.50 1.50

A155

2003, Nov. 25   Perf. 13½x13¼
680 A155 350d multi   3.25 3.25
   Siamanto (1878-1915), poet.

A156

2003, Nov. 27
681 A156 200d multi   2.00 2.00
   Vahan Tekeyan (1878-1945), poet.

Neurophysiology — A157

2003, Nov. 28   Perf. 13¼x13½
682 A157 120d multi   1.25 1.25

Souvenir Sheet

Third Pan-Armenian Games, Yerevan — A158

2003, Nov. 28
683 A158 350d multi   4.00 4.00

Souvenir Sheet

The Baptism, Miniature From Gospel of Ejmiatsin — A159

2003, Nov. 28   Perf. 13½x13¼
684 A159 550d multi   6.50 6.50

A160

Paintings in Museum of Russian Art: 200d, Still Life, by Alexander Shevchenko. 220d, In a Restaurant, by Konstantin Roudakov.

2004, Sept. 6   Litho.   Perf. 13½x13¼
685-686   A160   Set of 2   4.00 4.00

A161

2004, Sept. 9
687   A161   350d multi   3.50 3.50

FIFA (Fédération Internationale de Football Association), Cent.

Grapes — A162

Grape color: 170d, Yellow. 220d, Purple.

2004, Sept. 8   Perf. 12½
688-689   A162   Set of 2   4.00 4.00

Souvenir Sheet

Armenian Settlement of New Julfa, 400th Anniv. — A163

2004, Sept. 9   Perf. 13
690   A163   590d multi   6.00 6.00

Animated Films A164

Designs: 70d, Cat and Dog, 1937. 120d, Foxbook, 1975.

2004, Sept. 10   Perf. 13¼x13½
691-692   A164   Set of 2   2.00 2.00

Aramayis Yerzinkyan (1879-1931), Statesman — A165

2004, Sept. 11   Perf. 13½x13¼
693   A165   220d multi   2.50 2.50

Karabakh Horse — A166

2005, Feb. 14   Litho.   Perf. 12½
694   A166   350d multi   3.50 3.50

Dated 2004.

2004 Summer Olympics, Athens — A167

Hand: 70d, With Olympic Rings. 170d, As runner. 350d, As pistol.

2005, Feb. 14
695-697   A167   Set of 3   10.00 10.00

Dated 2004.

Intl. Day Against Desertification A168

2005, Feb. 21   Perf. 13½x13¼
698   A168   360d multi   3.25 3.25

Dated 2004.

Heart, Molecule and Chemistry Apparatus A169

2005, Feb. 22
699   A169   220d multi   2.25 2.25

Dated 2004.

Michael Nalbandian (1829-66), Writer — A170

2005, Feb. 23
700   A170   220d multi   2.25 2.25

Dated 2004.

Mouratsan (1854-1908), Writer — A171

2005, Feb. 24
701   A171   350d multi   3.50 3.50

Dated 2004.

Tigran Petrosian (1929-84), Chess Champion A172

2005, Feb. 25
702   A172   220d multi   3.00 3.00

Europa
A173   A174

2005, Mar. 16   Perf. 13½x13¼
703   A173   70d multi   1.50 1.50
704   A174   350d multi   2.50 2.50

Dated 2004.

Souvenir Sheet

Goshavank Monastery — A175

2005, Mar. 17   Perf. 12½
705   A175   480d multi   5.00 5.00

Dated 2004.

Armen Tigranian (1879-1950), Composer — A176

2005, Mar. 18   Perf. 13¼x13½
706   A176   220d multi   2.25 2.25

Dated 2004.

A177

2005, Apr. 21   Perf. 13½x13¼
707   A177   350d multi   3.25 3.25

Armenian genocide, 90th anniv.

A178

2005, Apr. 29
708   A178   350d multi   4.00 4.00

End of World War II, 60th anniv.
No. 708 was issued in sheets of 10 and sheets of 8 + 2 labels. Value, sheet of 8 + 2 labels $425.

Anushavan Arzumanian (1904-65), Educator — A179

2005, May 2   Perf. 13¼x13½
709   A179   220d multi   2.00 2.00

Dated 2004.

Paintings by Martiros Sarian (1880-1972)
A180   A181

2005, May 10   Perf. 13½x13¼
710   A180   170d Self-portrait   1.50 1.50
711   A181   200d Mount Aragats   1.75 1.75

Mother's Day A182

2005, Oct. 4   Litho.   Perf. 13¼x13½
712   A182   350d multi   3.25 3.25

A183

Europa: 70d, Bread. 350d, Porridge.

2005, Oct. 4   *Perf. 13½x13¼*
713-714 A183   Set of 2   4.00 4.00
714a   Booklet pane, 4 each #713-
      714   16.00 —

No. 714a was sold with booklet cover, but unattached to it.

A184

2005, Oct. 5
715 A184 70d multi   .75 .75

Armenian alphabet, 1600th anniv.

A185

2005, Oct. 5
716 A185 70d multi   .75 .75

Vardan Ajemian (1905-77), theater director.

A186

2005, Oct. 5
717 A186 170d multi   1.75 1.75

Anania Shirakatsi (605-85), scientist.

Mher Mkrtchian (1930-93),
Actor — A187

2005, Oct. 6   *Perf. 13¼x13½*
718 A187 120d multi   1.10 1.10

Artem Mikoyan (1905-70), Aircraft
Designer, and MiG Fighters — A188

2005, Oct. 6
719 A188 350d multi   3.25 3.25

Rugs — A189

Rugs from: 60d, 19th cent. 350d, 1904.
480d, 18th cent.

2005, Oct. 6   *Perf. 13½x13¼*
720-721 A189   Set of 2   3.50 3.50

Souvenir Sheet

722 A189 480d multi   4.50 4.50

No. 722 contains one 28x42mm stamp.

Armenia Year in Russia — A190

2006, Jan. 22   *Litho.*   *Perf. 11¼*
723 A190 350d multi   4.50 4.50

See Russia No. 6938.

Alexander Melik-Pashaev (1905-64),
Conductor — A191

2006, Mar. 27   *Perf. 13¼x13½*
724 A191 70d multi   .90 .90

Dated 2005.

St. Mary's Russian Orthodox
Cathedral, Yerevan — A192

2006, Mar. 27
725 A192 170d multi   2.00 2.00

Dated 2005.

Vakhtang Ananyan (1805-80),
Writer — A193

2006, Mar. 27
726 A193 170d multi   2.00 2.00

Dated 2005.

Raphael Patkanian
(1830-92),
Writer — A194

2006, Mar. 27   *Perf. 13½x13¼*
727 A194 220d multi   2.25 2.25

Dated 2005.

2006 Winter
Olympics,
Turin — A195

Mountains and: 120d, 2006 Winter Olympics emblem. 170d, Emblem, map of Italy on snowboard.

2006, Mar. 27   *Perf. 12½x12¾*
728-729 A195   Set of 2   3.25 3.25
729a   Miniature sheet, 5 each
     #728-729   30.00 30.00

Dated 2005.

Spiridon Melikian
(1880-1933),
Musician — A196

2006, Mar. 28   *Perf. 13½x13¼*
730 A196 350d multi   3.50 3.50

Dated 2005.

Souvenir Sheet

Miniature Art Depicting Nativity and
Adoration of the Magi — A197

2006, Mar. 28   *Perf. 13¼x13½*
731 A197 480d multi   5.50 5.50

Dated 2005.

Native
Costumes — A198

Costumes from: 170d, Sassoun. 200d,
Shatakhk.

2006, Mar. 28   *Perf. 13½x13¼*
732-733 A198   Set of 2   3.50 3.50

Dated 2005.

Insects — A199

Designs: 170d, Porphyrophora hamelii.
350d, Procerus scabrosus fallettianus.

2006, Mar. 28   *Perf. 12¾x12½*
734-735 A199   Set of 2   5.00 5.00

Dated 2005.

Europa Stamps,
50th
Anniv. — A200

Designs: Nos. 736, 740a, 70d, Orange panel and "C." Nos. 737, 740b, 70d, Blue panel and "E." Nos. 738, 740c, 70d, Red panel and "P." Nos. 739, 740d, 70d, Green panel and "T."

2006, Mar. 28   *Perf. 12¾x12½*
**Stamps With "Europa 1956-2006"
Inscription**
736-739 A200   Set of 4   3.50 3.50

Souvenir Sheet

**Stamps Without "Europa 1956-
2006" Inscription**
740 A200 70d Sheet of 4, #a-d   4.00 4.00

Dated 2005.

Souvenir Sheet

Independence, 15th Anniv. — A201

2006, Sept. 19   *Litho.*   *Perf. 12¾*
741 A201 480d multi   5.00 5.00

World
Peace — A202

2006, Oct. 16   *Perf. 13½x13¼*
742 A202 50d multi   .50 .50

Souvenir Sheet

Gospel of Haghpat to
Jerusalem — A203

2006, Oct. 16
743 A203 220d multi   2.50 2.50

2006 World Cup Soccer
Championships, Germany — A204

2006, Oct. 17   *Perf. 13¼x13½*
744 A204 350d multi   3.75 3.75

Europa
A205

Designs: 200d, Gears and clock hands.
350d, Keys.

2006, Oct. 17
745-746 A205 Set of 2   4.50 4.50

Sergei Merkyurov (1881-1952),
Sculptor — A206

2006, Oct. 18
747 A206 230d multi   2.25 2.25

Souvenir Sheet

Armenian General Benevolent Union,
Cent. — A207

No. 748: a, Boghos Nubar (1851-1930). b,
Signed document. c, Alex Manoogian (1901-
96).

2006, Oct. 18   *Perf. 13½x13¼*
748 A207 120d Sheet of 3, #a-c   3.75 3.75

On Nov. 30, 2006, the Armenian Postal Service was sold to a Dutch-owned
firm, HayPost CJSC, affiliated with the
Netherlands Postal Corporation. The
items illustrated below were released in
early 2007 by the stamp producer for
the Armenian Postal Service prior to
this sale, but as of December 2007,
were never put on sale at any HayPost
CJSC post office and were not valid for
postage. HayPost CJSC acquired the
remaining stock of these items from the
producer and is negotiating with the
Armenian government to place these
items on sale and make the items valid
for postage. All valid postage stamps
from 2007, starting with No. 749 below
are inscribed "Post." The items illustrated below do not have this inscription.

Swrnñ Taron

Çhruk Shirak

Smile of Reims, France — A208

Nativity, 15th Cent. Miniature, Armenia — A209

2007, May 22   Litho.   Perf. 13¼x13
749 A208   70d multi   1.50 1.50
750 A209   350d multi   7.50 7.50

See France Nos. 3335-3336.

Apricot — A210

2007, July 6   Perf. 13¼x13¾
751 A210   350d multi   4.00 4.00

King Tigran the Great (c. 140-55 B.C.) — A211

2007, July 19   Perf. 14¾x14
Background Color
752 A211   50d red   .60 .60
753 A211   60d olive green   .75 .75
754 A211   70d green   .90 .90
755 A211   120d blue   1.50 1.50
     Nos. 752-755 (4)   3.75 3.75

See Nos. 780-783. Compare with types A240, A256, A271-A272.

Europa A212

2007, Sept. 12
756 A212   350d multi   4.00 4.00

Scouting, cent.

Gusan Sheram (1857-1938), Composer — A213

2007, Sept. 13   Perf. 14x14¾
757 A213   280d multi   3.00 3.00

Margar Sedrakyan (1907-73), Cognac Producer A214

2007, Sept. 14   Perf. 14¾x14
758 A214   170d multi   2.00 2.00

Souvenir Sheet

Genocide Memorial, Tsitsernakaberd — A215

2007, Oct. 9   Perf. 14x14¾
759 A215   480d multi   3.50 3.50

Children's Art A216

2007, Oct. 24   Perf. 14¾x14
760 A216   35d multi   .55 .55

Rural Landscape, by Gevorg Bashinjaghyan (1857-1925) — A217

Kazbek, by Bashinjaghyan — A218

2007, Oct. 24   Litho.
761 A217   160d multi   1.50 1.50
762 A218   220d multi   2.25 2.25

Souvenir Sheet

Fourth Pan-Armenian Games, Yerevan — A219

2007, Oct. 25   Perf. 14x14¾
763 A219   360d multi   3.50 3.50

Jean Garzou (1907-2000), Painter — A220

Seda, by Garzou — A221

2007, Oct. 25   Perf. 14¾x14
764 A220   180d multi   1.75 1.75
765 A221   220d multi   2.25 2.25

Norayr Sisakyan (1907-66), Biochemist A222

2007, Oct. 26   Perf. 14¾x14
766 A222   120d multi   1.25 .90

Kamancha — A223

2007, Oct. 27   *Perf. 14x14¾*
767 A223 110d multi   1.10 .90

Birds — A224

Designs: 120d, Pelecanus crispus. 200d, Aegypius monachus.

2007, Oct. 27   *Perf. 13¼x13¾*
768-769 A224   Set of 2   4.00 3.00

Matenadaran Ancient Book Depository — A225

2007, Oct. 29   *Perf. 14¾x14*
770 A225 200d multi   2.00 2.00

Bagrat Nalbandyan (1902-90), Communications Administrator — A226

2007, Oct. 29   *Litho.*
771 A226 230d multi   2.25 1.75

N. Baghdasaryan (1907-88), Photojournalist A227

2007, Oct. 31   *Perf. 14x14¾*
772 A227 200d multi   2.00 1.75

Intl. Solar Year A228

2007, Nov. 7   *Perf. 14¾x14*
773 A228 170d multi   1.75 1.25

Busts of Goddesses — A229

Designs: 70d, Greek Goddess Aphrodite. 350d, Armenian Goddess Anahit.

2007, Dec. 14   *Litho.*   *Perf. 14x113½*
774-775 A229   Set of 2   5.00 5.00
    See Greece Nos. 2328-2329.

2008 Summer Olympics, Beijing — A230

    Perf. 13¼x13¾
2008, June 11   *Litho.*
776 A230 350d multi   3.50 3.50

Wood Carving — A231

2008, June 17   *Perf. 14x14¾*
777 A231 120d multi   1.25 1.25

Europa A232

2008, June 18   *Perf. 14¾x14*
778 A232 350d multi   3.50 3.50

Alexander Shirvanzade (1858-1935), Writer — A233

2008, June 19   *Perf. 14x14¾*
779 A233 280d multi   2.50 2.50

King Tigran the Great Type of 2007
2008, June 20   *Perf. 14¾x14*
    Background Color
780 A211   10d bright blue   .25   .25
781 A211   20d orange brn   .30   .25
782 A211   50d rose lilac   .60   .40
783 A211   1100d purple   9.00   9.00
    Nos. 780-783 (4)   10.15   9.90

Flowers — A234

Designs: 120d, Anemone fasciculata. 280d, Scabiosa caucasica.

2008, Oct. 9   *Litho.*   *Perf. 13¼x14*
784-785 A234   Set of 2   4.00 4.00

Yerevan State University of Architecture and Construction, 75th Anniv. — A235

2008, Oct. 28   *Perf. 14¾x14*
786 A235 220d multi   2.25 2.25

William Saroyan (1908-81), Writer — A236

2008, Oct. 29   *Perf. 14x14¾*
787 A236 350d multi   3.50 3.50

Victor Hambardzumyan (1908-96), Astrophysicist — A237

2008, Oct. 20   *Perf. 14¾x14*
788 A237 120d multi   1.25 1.25

Famous Men — A238

No. 789: a, Peyo Yavorov (1878-1914), Bulgarian poet. b, Andranik Ozanian (1865-1927), Armenian general who participated in Balkan Wars.

2008, Nov. 10   *Perf. 13*
789   Horiz. pair   4.00 4.00
  a.   A238 70d multi   .60   .60
  b.   A238 350d multi   3.40   3.40
    See Bulgaria No. 4492.

Dances — A239

Designs: 70d, Malambo sureño dancer, Argentina. 350d, Hoy-nazan dancers, Armenia.

2009, Apr. 4   *Perf. 12½x12¾*
790-791 A239   Set of 2   3.75 3.75
    See Argentina Nos. 2512-2513.

King Tigran the Great (c. 140-55 B.C.) — A240

2009, Apr. 8   *Perf. 13¼*
    Granite Paper
    Background Color
792 A240   10d olive green   .25   .25
793 A240   25d yel bister   .25   .25
794 A240   50d cerise   .45   .45
795 A240   70d brown   .65   .65
796 A240   120d purple   1.10   1.10
797 A240   220d dark blue   2.10   2.10
798 A240   280d dk bl violet   2.60   2.60
799 A240   350d plum   3.25   3.25
    Nos. 792-799 (8)   10.65   10.65

Numerals are in a different font than on Type A211. Compare with types A256, A271-A272.

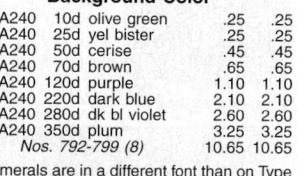

Van, Ancient Armenian Capital A241

2009, Apr. 29   *Perf. 14¾x14*
800 A241 220d multi   1.75 1.75

Europa — A242

2009, July 1   *Perf. 13¼x13¾*
801 A242 350d multi   2.75 2.75
    Intl. Year of Astronomy.

38th Chess Olympiad, Dresden, Germany A243

Designs: 70d, Chess board, Armenian players holding flag. 280d, Chess pieces, Armenian flag.

2009, July 29   *Perf. 13¾x13¼*
802-803 A243   Set of 2   3.50 3.50
803a   Miniature sheet of 10, 5
     each #802-803   25.00 25.00

European Court of Human Rights, 50th Anniv. A244

    Perf. 12¾x13¼
2009, Nov. 13   *Litho.*
804 A244 70d multi   7.00 7.00

Council of Europe, 60th Anniv. — A245

2009, Nov. 13   *Perf. 13¼x12¾*
805 A245 280d multi   7.00 7.00

Louis Braille (1809-52), Educator of the Blind A246

2009, Nov. 24　Litho.　Perf. 14¾x14
806　A246　110d multi　　1.10　1.10

No. 806 was issued in sheets of 10 and sheets of 8 + 2 labels. Value, sheet of 8 + 2 labels $12.

Daniel Varuzhan (1884-1915), Poet — A247

2009, Dec. 8　Perf. 13¼x12¾
807　A247　230d multi　　2.00　2.00

Souvenir Sheet

Davit of Sasun Monument, Yerevan, 50th Anniv. — A248

2009, Dec. 11　Perf. 14
808　A248　360d multi　　3.00　3.00

Souvenir Sheet

Olympic Champions — A249

No. 809: a, 70d, Hrant Shahinyan, gymnastics, 1952. b, 120d, Igor Novikov, pentathlon, 1956, 1964. c, 160d, Albert Azaryan, gymnastics, 1956, 1960.

2009, Dec. 11　Litho.
809　A249　Sheet of 3, #a-c　　3.25　3.25

Khachatur Abovyan (1809-1848), Writer A250

2009, Dec. 15　Perf. 12¾x13¼
810　A250　170d multi　　1.50　1.50

Animals — A251

Designs: 120d, Lutra lutra meridionalis. 160d, Ursus arctos syriacus.

2009, Dec. 16　Perf. 14
811-812　A251　Set of 2　　2.25　2.25
812a　　Miniature sheet of 10, 5
　　each #811-812　　12.00　12.00

Paintings in the National Gallery — A252

Designs: No. 813, 200d, Autumn. A Corner in Yerevan, by Sedrak Arakelyan. No. 814, 200d, Panna Paskevich, by Georgi Yakulov.

Perf. 13¼x12¾
2009, Dec. 16　Litho.
813-814　A252　Set of 2　　3.75　3.75

Vagharshapat Churches on UNESCO World Heritage List — A253

No. 815: a, Zvarnots Church. b, St. Hripsime Church. c, Mother See of Holy Etchmiadzin Church. d, St. Gayane Church.

2009, Dec. 18　Perf. 14
815　A253　70d Sheet of 4, #a-d　　6.00　6.00

Christmas A254

Madonna and Child with: 280d, Country name in white. 650d, Country name in black.

Perf. 13½x13¾
2009, Dec. 18　Litho.
816　A254　280d multi　　2.50　2.50

No. 816 was issued in sheets of 9 and sheets of 6 + 3 labels.

Souvenir Sheet
Perf. 14
817　A254　650d multi　　5.75　5.75

No. 817 contains one 30x60mm stamp.

New Year 2010 — A255

Litho. with Flocking
2009, Dec. 18　Perf. 14
818　A255　120d multi　　7.50　7.50

King Tigran the Great (c. 140-55 B.C.) — A256

2010, Jan. 29　Litho.　Perf. 13x13¼
Background Color
819　A256　10d cerise　　.25　.25
820　A256　25d dark blue　　.25　.25
821　A256　50d yel bister　　.50　.50
822　A256　70d vermilion　　.65　.65
823　A256　100d brown　　.85　.85
824　A256　120d maroon　　1.00　1.00
825　A256　200d gray　　1.75　1.75
826　A256　220d purple　　2.00　2.00
827　A256　280d red brown　　2.50　2.50
828　A256　650d yel green　　6.00　6.00
　　Nos. 819-828 (10)　　15.75　15.75

Self-Adhesive
Serpentine Die Cut 11¼
829　A256　10d cerise　　.25　.25
830　A256　25d dark blue　　.25　.25
831　A256　50d yel bister　　.40　.40
832　A256　70d vermilion　　.55　.55
833　A256　100d brown　　.75　.75
834　A256　120d maroon　　.90　.90
835　A256　200d gray　　1.50　1.50
836　A256　220d purple　　1.75　1.75
837　A256　280d red brown　　2.10　2.10
838　A256　650d yel green　　5.00　5.00
　　Nos. 829-838 (10)　　13.45　13.45

Type A256 has no lettering below king's neck. The country name is smaller than that found on types A211 and A240. Compare with types A271-A272.

Henrik Kasparyan (1910-95), Chess Player — A257

2010, Feb. 27　Perf. 14
839　A257　870d multi　　8.00　8.00

Victory in World War II, 65th Anniv. — A258

2010, May 6　Perf. 13¼x12¾
840　A258　350d multi　　2.75　2.75

Cemetery for Russian Officers, Gyumri — A259

2010, Aug. 20　Litho.　Perf. 13¼x13
Background Color
841　A259　350d light blue　　2.75　2.75
Souvenir Sheet
842　A259　650d maroon　　5.75　5.75

Mt. Ararat A260

Flag of Armenia — A261

2010, Sept. 21　Perf. 12½x13
843　A260　350d multi　　2.75　2.75
Perf. 13¼
844　A261　650d multi　　5.00　5.00

Independence Day.

Yerevan and Mt. Ararat — A262

Armenian Pavilion at Expo 2010, Shanghai — A263

2010, Sept. 22　Perf. 14
845　A262　280d multi　　2.25　2.25
Perf. 12½x13
846　A263　280d multi　　2.25　2.25
　　Expo 2010, Shanghai.

Europa — A264

2010, Oct. 8　Perf. 13¼
847　A264　350d multi　　2.50　2.50

2010 Youth Olympics, Singapore A265

2010, Nov. 26　Perf. 12½x13
848　A265　870d multi　　6.50　6.50

2010 World Cup Soccer Championships, South Africa — A266

2010, Nov. 26　Litho.
849　A266　1100d multi　　8.50　8.50

Souvenir Sheet

Olympic Champions — A267

No. 850: a, Vladimir Yengibaryan, boxing gold medalist, 1956. b, Faina Melnik, discus gold medalist, 1972. c, Yuri Vardanyan, weight lifting gold medalist, 1980.

2010, Nov. 26   **Perf. 13¼**
850 A267 160d Sheet of 3, #a-c   3.75 3.75

Souvenir Sheet

2010 Winter Olympics, Vancouver — A268

No. 851 — Skiers and 2010 Winter Olympics emblem at: a, 350d, Upper left. b, 500d, Center. c, 500d, Upper right.

2010, Nov. 26
851 A268   Sheet of 3, #a-c   11.00 11.00

Arakel Babakhanyan (1860-1932), Historian — A269

2010, Dec. 27   **Perf. 12½x13**
852 A269 220d multi   1.75 1.75

Raffi (Hakob Melik Hakobyan) (1835-88), Writer — A270

2010, Dec. 27   **Perf. 13x12½**
853 A270 220d multi   1.75 1.75

King Tigran the Great (c. 140-55 B.C.)
A271   A272

2011, Feb. 1   **Litho.**   **Perf. 13¼**
Granite Paper
Background Color

854	A271	10d dark blue	.25	.25
855	A272	35d gray brn	.30	.30
856	A272	50d green	.35	.35
857	A272	70d blue green	.55	.55
858	A272	120d org brown	.90	.90
859	A272	160d maroon	1.25	1.25
860	A272	220d dark red	1.75	1.75
861	A272	280d purple	2.10	2.10
862	A272	350d bister	2.75	2.75
863	A272	1100d dk brown	8.50	8.50
		Nos. 854-863 (10)	18.70	18.70

Nos. 854-863 lack the word "Post." Compare with Types A211, A240 and A256.

Ruben Sevak (1885-1915), Writer — A273

2011, Feb. 2   **Perf. 13¼**
864 A273 280d multi   2.00 2.00
Dated 2010.

A274

2011, Feb. 2   **Perf. 13¼**
865 A274 280d multi   2.00 2.00
Vahan Teryan (1885-1920), writer. Dated 2010.

A275

Paintings in National Gallery: No. 866, 450d, Portrait of Actress Khmara, by Haroutyun Kalents. No. 867, 450d, Catholicos Mkrtich Khrimyan, by Vardghes Sourenyants.

2011, Feb. 2   **Perf. 13x12½**
866-867 A275   Set of 2   6.50 6.50
Dated 2010.

Souvenir Sheet

Pepo, First Armenian Film With Sound, 75th Anniv. (in 2010) — A276

No. 868: a, 170d, Actors Avet Avetisyan and Davit Malyan. b, 200d, Actor Hrachya Nercissyan. c, 500d, Actress Tatiana Makhmuryan.

2011, Feb. 2   **Perf. 13¼**
868 A276   Sheet of 3, #a-c   6.50 6.50
Dated 2010.

Leonid Yenigbarov (1935-72), Circus Clown — A277

2011, Feb. 2   **Litho.**   **Perf. 13x12½**
869 A277 220d multi   1.60 1.60

Flora — A278

Designs: No. 870, 280d, Fritillaria armena. No. 871, 280d, Sambucus tigranii.

2011, Feb. 2   **Perf. 13¼**
870-871 A278   Set of 2   4.00 4.00

Souvenir Sheet

Easter — A279

2011, Apr. 15   **Litho.**   **Perf. 12½x13**
872 A279 1100d multi   7.50 7.50

Andranik Iossifian (1905-93), Designer of Meteorological Satellites — A280

First Man in Space, 50th Anniv. A281

2011, Apr. 18   **Perf. 13x12½**
873 A280 200d multi   1.50 1.50
               Perf. 12½x13
874 A281 350d multi   2.50 2.50

Capitals of Belarus and Armenia — A282

No. 875 — Buildings and arms of: a, Minsk, Belarus. b, Yerevan, Armenia.

2011, June 1   **Litho.**   **Perf. 13**
875 A282 200d Horiz. pair, #a-b   3.00 3.00
See Belarus No. 771.

Souvenir Sheet

Communications Regional Commonwealth, 20th Anniv. — A283

2011, June 1
876 A283 200d multi   1.50 1.50

Writers — A284

Designs: 120d, Hovhannes Tumanian (1869-1923). 230d, Valery Bryusov (1873-1924).

2011, June 1   **Perf. 12¾**
877-878 A284   Set of 2   3.00 3.00
878a   Vert. pair, #877-878   3.00 3.00

Nos. 877-878 each were printed in sheets of 9 + label. No. 878a was printed in sheets containing five pairs.
See Russia Nos. 7273-7274.

Souvenir Sheet

Fifth Pan-Armenian Games — A285

2011, Aug. 20
879 A285 380d multi   3.00 3.00

Birds — A286

Designs: 230d, Luscinia svecica. 330d, Parus major.

2011, Sept. 5   **Perf. 13¼**
880 A286 230d multi   1.75 1.75
881 A286 330d multi   2.75 2.75
a.   Horiz. pair, #880-881   4.50 4.50

Independence of Nagorno Karabakh From Azerbaijan, 20th Anniv. — A287

2011, Sept. 13 *Perf. 13x13¼*
882 A287 330d multi 2.50 2.50

Independence of Armenia, 20th Anniv. — A288

2011, Sept. 13
883 A288 380d multi 3.00 3.00

Fridtjof Nansen (1861-1930), Polar Explorer, Diplomat Assisting in Alleviating Armenian Refugee Crisis A289

2011, Nov. 9 *Perf. 13½*
884 A289 350d olive bister 2.75 2.75

Commonwealth of Independent States, 20th Anniv. — A290

2011, Dec. 1 *Perf. 13x12½*
885 A290 280d multi 2.10 2.10

Souvenir Sheet

Joint United Nations Program on AIDS — A291

No. 886 — AIDS ribbons: a, 200d. b, 280d.

2011, Dec. 1 *Perf. 13¼*
886 A291 Sheet of 2, #a-b 3.75 3.75

2011 Junior Eurovision Song Contest, Yerevan — A292

2011, Dec. 3 *Perf. 13¼x13*
887 A292 230d multi 1.75 1.75
a. Souvenir sheet of 4 7.00 7.00

No. 887 was printed in sheets of 8.

Europa A293

Photographs of forest in Dilijan Reserve with denominations at: No. 888, 350d, LL. No. 889, 350d, LR.

2011, Dec. 14 *Perf. 12½x13*
888-889 A293 Set of 2 5.00 5.00

Intl. Year of Forests.

Grigor Zohrap (1861-1915), Lawyer and Writer — A294

2011, Dec. 23 *Perf. 13¼x13*
890 A294 170d multi 1.25 1.25

Children — A295

No. 891: a, 100d, Girl holding grapes and bird, flag of Armenia. b, 120d, Boy holding wheat stalks, flag of Nagorno Karabakh.

2011, Dec. 27 *Litho.*
891 A295 Horiz. pair, #a-b 1.75 1.75
Youth philately. No. 891 was printed in sheets containing two pairs.

Souvenir Sheet

UNESCO World Heritage Sites — A296

No. 892: a, 230d, Sanahin Monastery. b, 330d, Haghpat Monastery.

2011, Dec. 27 *Perf. 13¼x13*
892 A296 Sheet of 2, #a-b 5.00 5.00

Christmas and New Year's Day — A297

2011, Dec. 27 *Perf. 13¼*
893 A297 220d multi 1.75 1.75

Armenian Army, 20th Anniv. — A298

Army coat of arms and: 200d, Soldiers, tank, military vehicle, airplanes. 280d, Armenian flag.

2012, Feb. 9 *Perf. 13¼x13*
894-895 A298 Set of 2 3.75 3.75

Admission to United Nations, 20th Anniv, A299

2012, Mar. 23 *Litho.* *Perf. 13x13¼*
896 A299 350d multi 2.60 2.60

Souvenir Sheet

Yerevan, World Book Capital — A300

2012, Apr. 22
897 A300 560d multi 5.00 5.00

Garegin Nzhdeh (1886-1955), Statesman A301

2012, May 3 *Perf. 13¼*
898 A301 200d multi 1.60 1.60

Misak Metsarents (1886-1908), Poet — A302

2012, May 3 *Perf. 13¼x13*
899 A302 280d black 2.10 2.10

Armenian Alphabet — A303

First seven letters of Armenian alphabet in capital and lower-case.

2012, May 14 *Perf. 13x13¼*
Color of Panel at Left
900 A303 10d dull rose .25 .25
901 A303 25d yel green .25 .25
902 A303 50d gray blue .45 .45
903 A303 70d dull blue .50 .50
904 A303 100d greenish gray .75 .75
905 A303 120d dull blue .95 .95
906 A303 280d lilac rose 2.10 2.10
Nos. 900-906 (7) 5.25 5.25

See Nos. 940-946, 983-989, 1066-1072.

Khachkars — A304

Khachkar: 200d, By Master Poghos, Goshavank, 1291. 280d, Arinj, 13th cent.

2012, June 14 *Perf. 13¼*
907-908 A304 Set of 2 3.50 3.50

Souvenir Sheet

Armenian Olympic Gold Medalists — A305

No. 909: a, Eduard Azaryan. b, Levon Julfalakyan. c, Hoksen Mirzoyan.

2012, June 15
909 A305 160d Sheet of 3, #a-c 3.50 3.50

Souvenir Sheet

Mesrop Mashtots (361-440), Monk — A306

2012, June 19 *Perf. 14½x14¼*
910 A306 560d multi 3.75 3.75

Hagigadar Monastery — A307

2012, Aug. 11　　*Perf. 13¼*
911 A307 380d multi　　2.75 2.75
　　a.　Souvenir sheet of 2 + 2 labels　5.50 5.50
　　See Romania No. 5383.

Armenian Membership in Organization for Security and Cooperation in Europe, 20th Anniv. — A308

2012, Sept. 7　　*Perf. 13x13¼*
912 A308 330d multi　　2.25 2.25

Ancient Artashat, Capital of Kingdom of Armenia, 185 B.C.-120 A.D. A309

2012, Oct. 30
913 A309 220d multi　　1.60 1.60

Mount Ararat and Alexander Misnikyan (1886-1925), Bolshevik Leader — A310

2012, Oct. 30
914 A310 230d multi　　1.50 1.50

Samvel Kocharyants (1909-93), Nuclear Physicist — A311

2012, Nov. 30　　*Perf. 14x13½*
915 A311 350d multi　　2.50 2.50

2012 Summer Olympics, London — A312

2012, Nov. 30　　*Perf. 13¼*
916　　Horiz. strip of 3　　4.50 4.50
　　a.　A312 170d Boxing　　1.25 1.25
　　b.　A312 200d Weight lifting　1.40 1.40
　　c.　A312 230d Wrestling　　1.75 1.75

Miniature Sheet

Armenian Olympic Gold Medalists — A313

No. 917: a, Hrachya Petikyan, shooting, 1992. b, Israyel Militosyan, weight lifting, 1992. c, Mnatsakan Iskandaryan, boxing, 1992. d, Armen Nazaryan, boxing, 1996.

2012, Nov. 30
917 A313 120d Sheet of 4, #a-d　3.50 3.50

Perch Proshyan (1837-1907), Writer — A314

2012, Dec. 4　　*Litho.*
918 A314 170d multi　　1.25 1.25

Lusine Zakaryan (1937-92), Opera Singer A315

2012, Dec. 4　　*Perf. 13x13¼*
919 A315 220d multi　　1.50 1.50

Religious Treasures of Etchmiadzin — A316

No. 920: a, 200d, Reliquary of Geghard, 1687. b, 220d, Cross with relic, 1746. c, 450d, Reliquary, Argadsz, St. Nshan, 13th cent.

2012, Dec. 4　　*Perf. 13¼x13*
920 A316　Horiz. strip of 3, #a-c　6.50 6.50

Ashot Hovhannisyan (1887-1977), First Secretary of Armenian Communist Party — A317

2012, Dec. 5　　*Perf. 13x13¼*
921 A317 170d black　　1.75 1.75

A318

2012, Dec. 5　　*Perf. 13¼x13*
922 A318 280d multi　　2.00 2.00
　Hovsep Orbeli (1887-1961), President of Armenian Academy of Arts and Sciences.

A319

2012, Dec. 5
923 A319 280d multi　　2.00 2.00
　Hayk Bzhishkyants (1887-1937), military leader.

Tigran Tchoukhadjian (1837-98), Composer — A320

2012, Dec. 6　　*Litho.*
924 A320 330d multi　　2.50 2.50

Hayastan All-Armenian Fund, 20th Anniv. — A321

2012, Dec. 12　　*Perf. 13x13¼*
925 A321 380d multi　　3.00 3.00

Collective Security Treaty Organization, 20th Anniv. — A322

2012, Dec. 17　　*Perf. 13¼x13*
926 A322 230d multi　　1.75 1.75

Tadevos Minasyants (1912-82), Minister of Communications — A323

2012, Dec. 27　　*Perf. 13x13¼*
927 A323 170d multi　　1.25 1.25

Tatev Monastery — A324

2012, Dec. 27　　*Litho.*
928 A324 350d multi　　2.50 2.50
　　a.　Sheet of 4 + 2 labels　　10.00 10.00
　　Europa.

Paintings in National Gallery of Armenia — A325

Designs: 220d, Dacha, by Marc Chagall. 280d, Self-portrait, by Rudolf Khachatryan.

2012, Dec. 27　　*Perf. 13¼x13*
929-930 A325　Set of 2　　3.50 3.50

Souvenir Sheet

Sayat-Nova (1712-95), Musician — A326

2012, Dec. 27
931 A326 560d multi　　4.25 4.25

Children's Art — A327

Designs: 100d, Trees. 120d, Soccer player.

2012, Dec. 28　　*Perf. 13¾*
932-933 A327　Set of 2　　1.60 1.60

Mammals A328

Designs: 230d, Allactaga elater. 330d, Ovis orientalis gmelinii.

2012, Dec. 28　　*Perf. 12½*
934 A328 230d multi　　1.50 1.50
935 A328 330d multi　　2.25 2.25
　　a.　Horiz. pair, #934-935　　4.00 4.00

Christmas and New Year's Day A329

2012, Dec. 28　　*Perf. 13x13¼*
936 A329 220d multi　　1.60 1.60

St. Sargis's Day — A330

2013, Jan. 29　　*Perf. 13¼x13*
937 A330 280d multi　　1.90 1.90

Souvenir Sheet

Churches — A331

No. 938: a, 160d, Holy Trinity Church, Yerevan. b, 200d, Church of Holy Archangels, St. Etchmiadzin. c, 200d, Church of St. Hakob of Msbin, Gyumri.

2013, Apr. 4　　　**Perf. 13¼**
938 A331　Sheet of 3, #a-c　4.00 4.00

Brandy Production in Armenia A332

2013, June 18　　**Perf. 13x13¼**
939 A332　300d multi　1.90 1.90

No. 939 was printed in sheets of 8 + 2 labels.

Armenian Alphabet Type of 2012

Second group of seven letters of Armenian alphabet in capital and lower-case.

2013, July 30　　**Perf. 13x13¼**
Color of Panel at Left
940 A303　10d olive bister　.25 .25
941 A303　35d salmon rose　.25 .25
942 A303　50d green　.40 .40
943 A303　60d blue　.45 .45
944 A303　70d rose　.55 .55
945 A303　100d greenish blue　.75 .75
946 A303　120d gray blue　.95 .95
　　Nos. 940-946 (7)　3.60 3.60

Europa A333

2013, Aug. 15　　Litho.
947 A333　350d multi　2.75 2.75
　a.　Souvenir sheet of 4　11.00 11.00

Johannes Lepsius (1858-1926), Documenter of Armenian Genocide — A334

James Bryce (1838-1922), Documenter of Armenian Genocide — A335

2013, Aug. 16　　**Perf. 13x13¼**
948 A334　280d multi　2.00 2.00
　　　　Perf. 13¼x13
949 A335　330d multi　2.50 2.50

Armenian Genocide, cent. (in 2015).

Souvenir Sheet

Church of St. Grigor, Kecharis Monastery, Tsakhkadsor — A336

2013, Aug. 24　Litho.　**Perf. 13¼x13**
950 A336　480d multi　4.00 4.00

Souvenir Sheet

Aurora Mardiganian (1901-94), Writer of Memoir "Ravished Armenia" — A337

　　　　Perf. 14¼x14½
951 A337　480d multi　4.00 4.00

Souvenir Sheet

Diplomatic Relations Between Armenia and Belarus, 20th Anniv. — A338

2013, Oct. 24　Litho.　**Perf. 13**
952 A338　650d multi　5.00 5.00

See Belarus No. 879.

Anton Kochinyan (1913-90), Politician A339

2013, Oct. 25　Litho.　**Perf. 13x13¼**
953 A339　230d multi　1.75 1.75

A340

Chess — A341

No. 954: a, 200d, Chess pieces and board, stylized globe. b, 280d, Chessboard with rook in background.
No. 955 — Half of trophy, globe, chess pieces and chess board with: a, 200d, Black squares. b, 280d, White squares.

2013, Nov. 6　Litho.　**Perf. 13¼**
954 A340　Horiz. pair, #a-b　4.00 4.00
　c.　Souvenir sheet of 4, 2 each
　　　#954a-954b　8.00 8.00
　d.　Souvenir sheet of 8, 4 each
　　　#954a-954b, + 8 labels　17.00 17.00
955 A341　Horiz. pair, #a-b　4.00 4.00
　c.　Souvenir sheet of 4, 2 each
　　　#955a-955b　8.00 8.00
　d.　Souvenir sheet of 8, 4 each
　　　#955a-955b, + 8 labels　17.00 17.00

Armenia as World Chess Team Champion (No. 954); Armenia as 3-time Chess Olympiad champion (No. 955).

Souvenir Sheet

Church of St. Hovhannes, Gandzasar Monastery — A342

2013, Nov. 8　Litho.　**Perf. 14¼x14½**
956 A342　560d multi　4.50 4.50

Gyumri, Cultural Capital of Commonwealth of Independent States — A343

2013, Nov. 11　Litho.　**Perf. 13x13¼**
957 A343　560d multi + 2 flanking
　　　　　labels　4.50 4.50

Award of the President of Armenia — A344

No. 958 — Medal depicting: a, 180d, Eagle. b, 220d, Coat of arms.

2013, Nov. 15　Litho.　**Perf. 13¼x13**
958 A344　Horiz. pair, #a-b　3.25 3.25

Ancient Capitals of Armenia A345

Designs: 160d, Armavir. 170d, Yervandashat.

2013, Nov. 19　Litho.　**Perf. 13x13¼**
959-960 A345　Set of 2　2.50 2.50

Beniamin Markarian (1913-85), Astrophysicist — A346

2013, Nov. 21　Litho.　**Perf. 13x13¼**
961 A346　170d multi　1.25 1.25

Armenian Chairmanship of Council of Europe in 2013 — A347

2013, Nov. 25　Litho.　**Perf. 13¼x13**
962 A347　380d multi　3.00 3.00

Paintings — A348

Designs: 230d, Family, by Ara Bekarian. 330d, Portrait of the Painter's Mother, by Stepan Aghajanian.

2013, Nov. 25　Litho.　**Perf. 13¼x13**
963-964 A348　Set of 2　4.50 4.50

Mushrooms A349

Designs: 230d, Macrolepiota rhacodes. 330d, Boletus edulis.

2013, Nov. 25　Litho.　**Perf. 12½**
965 A349　230d multi　1.75 1.75
966 A349　330d multi　2.75 2.75
　a.　Horiz. pair, #965-966　4.50 4.50

Nos. 965-966 each were printed in sheets of 8 + 2 labels. No. 966a was printed in a sheet containing 5 pairs.

Hakop Kojoian (1883-1959), Painter — A350

Armenian Herald, by Kojoian — A351

2013, Nov. 27　Litho.　**Perf. 13¼x13**
967 A350　240d multi　1.75 1.75
968 A351　240d multi　1.75 1.75
　a.　Horiz. pair, #967-968　3.50 3.50

Nos. 967-968 each were printed in sheets of 8. No. 968a was printed in sheets containing 4 pairs.

Dram Currency, 20th Anniv. A352

2013, Nov. 29　Litho.　**Perf. 13x13¼**
969 A352　380d multi　4.00 4.00

Souvenir Sheet

2014 Winter Olympics, Sochi, Russia — A353

No. 970: a, 350d, Cross-country skiing. b, 1100d, Alpine skiing.

2013, Dec. 2   Litho.   Perf. 13¼
970 A353   Sheet of 2, #a-b   10.00 10.00

Lord Byron (1788-1824), Poet and Compiler of Armenian-English Dictionary — A354

2013, Dec. 5   Litho.   Perf. 12½
971 A354   350d multi   2.75 2.75

Telephones in Armenia, Cent. A355

2013, Dec. 10   Litho.   Perf. 13x13¼
972 A355   170d multi   1.40 1.40

Vahran Papazian (1888-1968), Actor — A356

2013, Dec. 16   Litho.   Perf. 13x13¼
973 A356   230d multi   1.75 1.75

Chess A357

Designs: 100d, Chess pieces and boards. 120d, Chess pieces and board.

2013, Dec. 16   Litho.   Perf. 13x13¼
974-975 A357   Set of 2   1.75 1.75

Souvenir Sheet

Civil Aviation in Armenia, 80th Anniv. — A358

2013, Dec. 16   Litho.   Perf. 13¾
976 A358   500d multi   3.50 3.50

New Year 2014 A359

2013, Dec. 16   Litho.   Perf. 13x13¼
977 A359   220d multi   1.75 1.75

Wine Production in Armenia — A360

2013, Dec. 28   Litho.   Perf. 13x13¼
978 A360   330d multi + label   2.50 2.50

No. 978 was printed in sheets of 4 + 4 labels. Two different labels were made available on separate sheets.

Armenian Kingdom of Cilicia A361

Designs: 120d, King Levon III, ruler from 1270-89. 240d, Queen Keran, wife of King Levon III.

2013, Dec. 28   Litho.   Perf. 13x13¼
979-980 A361   Set of 2   2.75 2.75
980a   Horiz. pair, #979-980   2.75 2.75

Nos. 979-980 each were printed in sheets of 10. No. 980a was printed in sheets containing two pairs.

Souvenir Sheet

Artsakh Movement (Campaign to Transfer Jurisdiction of Nagorno-Karabakh to Armenia), 25th Anniv. — A362

2013, Dec. 28   Litho.   Perf. 13x13¼
981 A362   400d multi   3.00 3.00

Souvenir Sheet

Archaeological Items Found in Areni-1 Cave — A363

No. 982: a, 160d, Matting, c. 3500 B.C. b, 220d, Shoe, c. 3500 B.C.

2013, Dec. 28   Litho.   Perf. 13¼x13
982 A363   Sheet of 2, #a-b   3.00 3.00

Armenian Alphabet Type of 2012

Third group of seven letters of Armenian alphabet in capital and lower-case.

2014, May 8   Litho.   Perf. 13x13¼
Color of Panel at Left
983 A303   70d dull bl green   .60   .60
984 A303   120d rose lilac   1.00   1.00
985 A303   170d lilac   1.40   1.40
986 A303   220d gray green   1.75   1.75
987 A303   230d green blue   1.90   1.90

988 A303   280d blue   2.25   2.25
989 A303   380d rose   3.25   3.25
     Nos. 983-989 (7)   12.15 12.15

Intelligence Officers — A364

No. 990: a, Yakov Davtian (1888-1938). b, Ivan Agayants (1911-68). c, Haik Ovakimian (1898-1967). d, Ashot Akopian (1915-81). 350d, Gevork Vartanian (1924-2012).

2014, May 20   Litho.   Perf. 13x13¼
990 A364   230d Sheet of 4, #a-d   6.50 6.50

Souvenir Sheet
Perf. 13¼x13½
991 A364   350d multi   2.50 2.50

No. 991 contains one 45x28mm stamp.

Europa A365

Musical instruments: No. 992, 350d, Pku. No. 993, 350d, Zurna.

2014, May 23   Litho.   Perf. 13x13¼
992-993 A365   Set of 2   5.00 5.00

2014 World Cup Soccer Championships, Brazil — A366

2014, June 27   Litho.   Perf. 13x13¼
994 A366   380d multi   2.75 2.75

Armenian Kingdom of Cilicia A367

Map and: No. 995, 240d, Ruins, Ayas. No. 996, 240d, Anamur Fortress. No. 997, 240d, Korikos Fortress.

2014, July 4   Litho.   Perf. 13x13¼
995-997 A367   Set of 3   5.00 5.00
997a   Souvenir sheet of 6, 2
                 each #995-997   10.00 10.00

John Kirakossian (1929-85), Historian A368

2014, July 29   Litho.   Perf. 13x13¼
998 A368   330d multi   2.50 2.50

Armenian Genocide Monuments A369

Monument in: No. 999, 280d, Boston, Massachusetts. No. 1000, 280d, Montevideo, Uruguay, horiz. 380d, Paris, France.

Perf. 13¼x13, 13x13¼
2014, July 29   Litho.
999-1001 A369   Set of 3   7.00 7.00

Souvenir Sheet

Danish Mothers of Armenian Orphans — A370

No. 1002 — Medal and: a, Karen Jeppe (1875-1935). b, Maria Jacobsen (1882-1960).

2014, July 29   Litho.   Perf. 13¼x13
1002 A370   200d Sheet of 2, #a-b 3.00 3.00

Famous Men A371

Building and: No. 1003, 280d, Toros Toramanian (1864-1934), architect. No. 1004, 280d, Nikolay Marr (1864-1934), archaeologist, linguist and architect.

2014, Aug. 13   Litho.   Perf. 13x13¼
1003-1004 A371   Set of 2   4.00 4.00

Hounan Avetissian (1914-43), Military Hero — A372

2014, Aug. 15   Litho.   Perf. 13¼x13
1005 A372   170d multi   1.25 1.25

Ancient Capitals of Armenia A373

Designs: No. 1006, 240d, Dvin. No. 1007, 240d, Tigranakert.

2014, Aug. 21   Litho.   Perf. 13x13¼
1006-1007 A373   Set of 2   3.50 3.50

Hamo Sahian (1914-93), Poet A374

Stepan Zorian (1889-1967),
Writer — A375

2014, Sept. 5   Litho.   Perf. 13x13¼
1008 A374 220d multi   1.50 1.50
1009 A375 230d multi   1.75 1.75

Flora and
Fauna — A376

Designs: 230d, Dianthus gabrielianae.
330d, Upupa epops.

2014, Sept. 23   Litho.   Perf. 12¾
1010-1011 A376 Set of 2   4.00 4.00

Souvenir Sheet

Voskan Yerevantsi (1614-74), Book
Publisher — A377

Perf. 13¼x13½
2014, Sept. 26   Litho.
1012 A377 650d multi   5.00 5.00

Souvenir Sheet

World War I, Cent. — A378

2014, Sept. 29   Litho.   Perf. 13¼x13
1013 A378 480d multi   3.50 3.50

Cross Stones
(Khachkars)
A379

Designs: No. 1014, 240d, Holy Redeemer
khachkar, Urtz, 1279. No. 1015, 240d, Mas-
tara khachkar, 13th cent.

2014, Dec. 12   Litho.   Perf. 13¼
1014-1015 A379 Set of 2   3.50 3.50

Souvenir Sheet

Holy Transfiguration Cathedral,
Moscow — A380

2014, Dec. 12   Litho.   Perf. 13¼x13
1016 A380 870d multi   6.00 6.00

Skier — A381

2014, Dec. 15   Litho.   Perf. 13¼
1017 A381 350d multi   2.75 2.75

Dzitoghtyans House Museum,
Gyumri — A383

No. 1019: a, Building exterior. b, Dining
room.

2014, Dec. 30   Litho.   Perf. 13x13¼
1019 A383 280d Horiz. pair, #a-b 4.00 4.00

Shushi
A384

2014, Dec. 30   Litho.   Perf. 13x13¼
1020 A384 240d multi   1.75 1.75

Traditional
Costumes — A385

Designs: 120d, Man and woman from Yerevan. 230d, Man, woman and child from
Gyumri.

2014, Dec. 30   Litho.   Perf. 13¼x13
1021-1022 A385 Set of 2   2.75 2.75

A386

A387

Children's
Art — A388

2014, Dec. 30   Litho.   Perf. 13x13¼
1023 A386 100d multi   .75   .75

Perf. 13¼x13
1024 A387 100d multi   .75   .75
1025 A388 100d multi   .75   .75
     Nos. 1023-1025 (3)   2.25 2.25

Forget-me-not
A389

2015, Jan. 29   Litho.   Perf. 13¼x13
Background Color
1026 A389   70d white   .45   .45
1027 A389 120d pale yellow   .80   .80
1028 A389 240d pale peach   1.50 1.50
1029 A389 280d pale green   1.75 1.75
1030 A389 330d light blue   2.25 2.25
1031 A389 350d dull mauve   2.40 2.40
   a.   Souvenir sheet of 1   2.40 2.40
1032 A389 870d pale red vio   5.75 5.75
   a.   Souvenir sheet of 1   5.75 5.75
   b.   Sheet of 14, 2 each #1026-
        1032 + central label   30.00 30.00
     Nos. 1026-1032 (7)   14.90 14.90

Armenian Genocide, cent. Nos. 1026-1032
were each printed in sheets of 14 + central
label. See Nos. 1048-1050.

Paintings by Panos Terlemezian
(1865-1941) — A390

No. 1033: a, 230d, Self-portrait. b, 330d,
Mount Sipan from Ktuts Island.

2015, Mar. 3   Litho.   Perf. 13x13¼
1033 A390 Horiz. pair, #a-b   3.75 3.75

Melkonian Orphanage, Nicosia,
Cyprus — A391

2015, Apr. 2   Litho.   Perf. 14½x14¼
1034 A391 350d multi   2.40 2.40

See Cyprus No. 1232.

Anatole France (1844-1924),
Writer — A392

2015, Apr. 23   Litho.   Perf. 13x13¼
1035 A392 300d multi   2.25 2.25

Henry
Morgenthau,
Sr.
(1856-1946), U.S.
Ambassador to
the Ottoman
Empire — A393

2015, Apr. 23   Litho.   Perf. 13¼x13¼
1036 A393 300d multi   2.25 2.25

Souvenir Sheet

American Committee for Relief in the
Near East, Cent. — A394

2015, May 6   Litho.   Perf. 13
1037 A394 480d multi   3.75 3.75

Victory in
World War
II, 70th
Anniv.
A395

2015, May 8   Litho.   Perf. 13x13¼
1038 A395 230d multi   1.75 1.75

Eurasian
Economic
Union — A396

2015, May 12   Litho.   Perf. 13¼x13
1039 A396 560d multi   4.25 4.25

Missak Manouchian (1906-44), Poet — A397

2015, May 26   **Litho.**   *Perf. 13¼x13*
1040 A397 170d multi   1.40 1.40

Souvenir Sheet

Sixth Pan-Armenian Games — A398

2015, Aug. 5   **Litho.**   *Perf. 13½x13¼*
1041 A398 380d multi   3.25 3.25

Armenian Olympic Committee, 25th Anniv. — A399

2015, Sept. 29   **Litho.**   *Perf. 13¼*
1042 A399 230d multi   1.90 1.90

Souvenir Sheet

Blessing of the Holy Chrism — A400

2015, Sept. 29   **Litho.**   *Perf. 13¼x13*
1043 A400 480d multi   3.75 3.75

Constitutional Court, 20th Anniv. — A401

2015, Oct. 8   **Litho.**   *Perf. 13x13¼*
1044 A401 330d multi   2.40 2.40

Lazarev Institute, Moscow, 200th Anniv. A402

2015, Oct. 23   **Litho.**   *Perf. 13x13¼*
1045 A402 380d multi   3.00 3.00

Resistance to the Armenian Genocide — A403

No. 1046: a, 200d, Resistance in Van, Turkey. b, 280d, Resistance at Mount Musa.

2015, Oct. 29   **Litho.**   *Perf. 13x13¼*
1046 A403   Horiz. pair, #a-b   3.75 3.75

Armenian Genocide Museum and Institute, Yerevan — A404

No. 1047: a, 230d, Museum exterior and displays. b, 280d, Museum interior.

2015, Nov. 21   **Litho.**   *Perf. 13x13¼*
1047 A404   Horiz. pair, #a-b   4.25 4.25

Forget-me-not Type of 2015
2015, Dec. 24   **Litho.**   *Perf. 13¼x13*
Background Color
1048 A389 40d yellow orche   .35 .35
1049 A389 50d cobalt   .40 .40
1050 A389 60d rose   .50 .50
   Nos. 1048-1050 (3)   1.25 1.25

Nos. 1048-1050 were each printed in sheets of 14 + central label.

A405

Children's Art — A406

2015, Dec. 24   **Litho.**   *Perf. 13x13¼*
1051 A405 70d multi   .70 .70
1052 A406 70d multi   .70 .70

Top — A407

2015, Dec. 28   **Litho.**   *Perf. 13¼*
1053 A407 350d multi   2.75 2.75
   Europa.

Flora and Fauna — A408

Designs: 220d, Lynx lynx dinniki. 280d, Sorbus hajastana.

2015, Dec. 28   **Litho.**   *Perf. 12¾*
1054-1055 A408   Set of 2   3.75 3.75

Vladimir Vysotsky (1938-80), Singer A409

2015, Dec. 30   **Litho.**   *Perf. 13x13¼*
1056 A409 350d multi   2.75 2.75

Armenian State Philharmonia, Yerevan — A410

2015, Dec. 30   **Litho.**   *Perf. 13¼x13*
1057 A410 380d multi   3.00 3.00

Souvenir Sheet

Operation Nemesis — A411

2015, Dec. 30   **Litho.**   *Perf. 13¼x13*
1058 A411 360d multi   2.75 2.75
Operation Nemesis was a series of assassinations of people responsible for the Armenian Genocide.

Souvenir Sheets

A412

Medals and Orders for Fund-raising for Genocide Survivors — A413

No. 1059 — Order inscribed: a, Armenia. b, Servia, Syria, Armenia.
No. 1060 — Medal depicting: a, Two-headed bird. b, Cross.

2015, Dec. 30   **Litho.**   *Perf. 13¼*
1059 A412 280d Sheet of 2, #a-b 4.25 4.25
   Perf.
1060 A413 280d Sheet of 2, #a-b 4.25 4.25

Souvenir Sheet

2016 Posteurop Plenary Assembly, Yerevan — A414

2016, Apr. 20   **Litho.**   *Perf. 13¼*
1061 A414 870d multi   6.50 6.50

Souvenir Sheet

2016 World Stamp Show, New York — A415

2016, May 29   **Litho.**   *Perf.*
1062 A415 650d multi   5.00 5.00

Souvenir Sheet

2016 Summer Olympics, Rio de Janeiro — A416

2016, May 29   **Litho.**   *Perf. 13¼*
1063 A416 650d multi   5.00 5.00

Visit to Armenia of Pope Francis — A417

No. 1064: a, 170d, Pope Francis and Yerevan. b, 230d, Pope Francis, cupola of St. Peter's Basilica. c, 380d, Pope Francis, statue of St. Gregory the Illuminator. d, 480d, Pope Francis, Etchmiadzin Cathedral.
870d, Pope Francis, St. Peter's Basilica, Etchmiadzin Cathedral, horiz.

2016, June 24   **Litho.**   *Perf. 13¼*
1064 A417   Sheet of 4, #a-d, + label   9.50 9.50
Souvenir Sheet
Perf. 13¾x14
1065 A417 870d multi   6.50 6.50
   No. 1065 contains one 45x33mm stamp.

Armenian Alphabet Type of 2012

Fourth group of seven letters of Armenian alphabet in capital and lower-case.

2016, July 7   Litho.   Perf. 13x13¼
Color of Panel at Left
1066	A303	70d venetian red	.50	.50
1067	A303	120d apple green	.90	.90
1068	A303	170d mauve taupe	1.25	1.25
1069	A303	230d bister	1.75	1.75
1070	A303	280d brown olive	2.10	2.10
1071	A303	330d orange brown	2.50	2.50
1072	A303	380d greenish gray	3.00	3.00
		Nos. 1066-1072 (7)	12.00	12.00

2016 European Soccer Championships, France — A418

2016, July 15   Litho.   Perf. 13x13¼
1073	A418	500d multi	3.75	3.75

SEMI-POSTAL STAMPS

International Children's Day — SP1

2008, June 1   Litho.   Perf. 14¾x14
B1	SP1	70d +30d multi	1.00	1.00

Surtax (on sheet margin) was for UNICEF.

AIR POST STAMPS

AP1

Design: 90d, Artiom Katsian (1886-1943), world record holding pilot on range and altitude in 1909.

1995, Dec. 5   Litho.   Perf. 14x15
C1	AP1	90d multicolored	.75	.75

AP2

1996, Apr. 30   Litho.   Perf. 14x14½
C2	AP2	90d multicolored	.90	.90

Nelson Stepanian (1913-44), WWII fighter ace.

ARUBA

ə-'rü-bə

LOCATION — West Indies, north of Venezuela
AREA — 78 sq. mi.
POP. — 67,014
CAPITAL — Oranjestad

On Jan. 1, 1986 Aruba, formerly part of Netherlands Antilles, achieved a separate status within the Kingdom of the Netherlands.

100 Cents = 1 Gulden

> **Catalogue values for all unused stamps in this country are for Never Hinged items.**

> **Used values are for CTO or stamps removed from first day covers. Postally used examples sell for more.**

Traditional House — A1

Perf. 14x13
1986-87   Litho.   Unwmk.
1	A1	5c shown	.40	.25
2	A1	15c King William III Tower	.85	.40
3	A1	20c Loading crane	.60	.30
4	A1	25c Lighthouse	1.00	.35
5	A1	30c Snake	1.25	.70
6	A1	35c Owl	1.25	.70
7	A1	45c Shell	1.25	.70
8	A1	55c Frog	1.40	.80
9	A1	60c Water skier	1.50	1.00
10	A1	65c Net fishing	1.50	1.00
11	A1	75c Music box	1.50	1.10
12	A1	85c Pre-Columbian bisque pot	1.60	1.00
13	A1	90c Bulb cactus	2.00	1.25
14	A1	100c Grain	2.00	1.25
15	A1	150c Watapana tree	4.00	2.00
16	A1	250c Aloe plant	5.25	4.00
		Nos. 1-16 (16)	27.35	16.80

Issued: 5c, 30c, 60c, 150c, 1/1; 15c, 35c, 65c, 250c, 2/5; 20c, 45c, 75c, 100c, 4/7/87; 25c, 55c, 85c, 90c, 7/17/87.

Independence A2

25c, Map. 45c, Coat of arms, vert. 55c, Natl. anthem, vert. 100c, Flag.

1986, Jan. 1   Perf. 14x13, 13x14
18	A2	25c multicolored	1.25	.40
19	A2	45c multicolored	1.25	.75
20	A2	55c multicolored	1.25	1.25
21	A2	100c multicolored	1.75	1.75
		Nos. 18-21 (4)	5.50	4.15

Intl. Peace Year — A3

1986, Aug. 29   Litho.   Perf. 14x13
22	A3	60c shown	2.00	1.00
23	A3	100c Barbed wire	4.75	1.75

Princess Juliana and Prince Bernhard, 50th Wedding Anniv. — A4

1987, Jan. 7   Photo.   Perf. 13x14
24	A4	135c multicolored	4.00	2.25

State Visit of Queen Beatrix and Prince Claus of the Netherlands A5

60c, Prince William-Alexander.

1987, Feb. 16   Litho.   Perf. 14x13
25	A5	55c shown	2.00	1.00
26	A5	60c multicolored	2.00	1.00

Tourism — A6

1987, June 5   Litho.
27	A6	60c Beach and sea	2.00	1.25
28	A6	100c Rock and cacti	2.75	1.50

Aloe Vera Plant — A7

1988, Jan. 27   Litho.   Perf. 13x14
29	A7	45c Field	1.75	.90
30	A7	60c Plant	2.00	1.25
31	A7	100c Harvest	2.50	1.40
		Nos. 29-31 (3)	6.25	3.55

Coins — A8

1988, Mar. 16   Litho.   Perf. 13x14
32	A8	25c 25-cent	1.00	.40
33	A8	55c 50-cent	1.50	.90
34	A8	65c 5 and 10-cent	1.75	1.25
35	A8	150c 1-florin	3.25	2.25
		Nos. 32-35 (4)	7.50	4.80

Love Issue — A9

135c, Seashells, coastal scenery.

1988, May 4
36	A9	70c shown	1.75	1.00
37	A9	135c multicolored	2.50	1.75

A10

1988, Aug. 24
38	A10	35c shown	1.50	.75
39	A10	100c Emblems	2.50	1.40

Aruba, the 162nd member of the Intl. Olympic Committee (35c), 1988 Summer Olympics, Seoul (100c).

Carnival A11

1989, Jan. 5   Perf. 14x13
40	A11	45c Two children	2.00	.90
41	A11	60c Girl	2.00	.90
42	A11	100c Entertainer	2.50	1.25
		Nos. 40-42 (3)	6.50	3.05

Maripampun, Omphalophalmum Rubrum — A12

1989, Mar. 16   Litho.   Perf. 14x13
43	A12	35c Leaves	1.50	.70
44	A12	55c Pods	1.50	.90
45	A12	200c Blossom	4.00	2.75
		Nos. 43-45 (3)	7.00	4.35

New Year 1990 — A13

Dande band members playing instruments or singing: 25c, Violin, tambor, cuatro, marimba. 70c, Lead singer, guitar. 150c, Accordion, urri, guitar.

1989, Nov. 16   Litho.   Perf. 13x14
46	A13	25c multicolored	1.00	.50
47	A13	70c multicolored	1.40	.90
48	A13	150c multicolored	2.75	1.90
		Nos. 46-48 (3)	5.15	3.30

UPU — A14

1989, June 8   Litho.   Perf. 13x14
49	A14	250c multicolored	5.25	3.00

Crotalus durissus unicolor A15

1989, Aug. 24   Perf. 14x13
50	A15	45c shown	1.50	.75
51	A15	55c multi, diff.	1.75	.90
52	A15	60c multi, diff.	1.75	.90
		Nos. 50-52 (3)	5.00	2.55

Snake species in danger of extinction.

Man Living in Harmony with Nature — A16

1990, Feb. 7   Perf. 13x14, 14x13
53	A16	45c The land	1.25	.90
54	A16	55c shown	1.50	.90
55	A16	100c The sea	2.50	1.75
		Nos. 53-55 (3)	5.25	3.55

Environmental protection. Nos. 53, 55 horiz.

Marine
Life — A17

Designs: 60c, Giant caribbean anemone, Pederson's cleaning shrimp. 70c, Queen angelfish, red and orange coral. 100c, Banded coral shrimp, fire sponge, yellow boring sponge.

1990, Apr. 4   Litho.   Perf. 14x13
56	A17	60c multicolored	1.50	.90
57	A17	70c multicolored	2.00	1.25
58	A17	100c multicolored	2.75	2.25
		Nos. 56-58 (3)	6.25	4.40

A18

200c, Character trademark.

1990, May 30   Litho.   Perf. 13x14
59	A18	35c multicolored	1.25	.75
60	A18	200c multicolored	4.00	2.75

World Cup Soccer Championships, Italy.

A19

1990, Sept. 12
61	A19	45c Tools	1.25	.90
62	A19	60c Stone figure	1.50	.90
63	A19	100c Jar	2.75	1.40
		Nos. 61-63 (3)	5.50	3.20

Archeological discoveries.

Landscapes
A20

1991, Jan. 31   Litho.   Perf. 14x13
64	A20	55c Seashore	1.40	.90
65	A20	65c Desert	1.60	1.25
66	A20	100c Cactus, ocean view	2.25	1.40
		Nos. 64-66 (3)	5.25	4.05

Working
Women — A21

Designs: 35c, Taking care of others. 70c, Housewife. 100c, Women in society.

1991, Mar. 28   Litho.   Perf. 13x14
67	A21	35c multicolored	1.00	.45
68	A21	70c multicolored	1.50	1.25
69	A21	100c multicolored	2.00	1.75
		Nos. 67-69 (3)	4.50	3.45

Style of inscriptions varies.

Medicinal
Plants — A22

65c, Ocimum sanctum. 75c, Jatropha gossypifolia. 95c, Croton flavens.

1991, May 29
70	A22	65c multicolored	1.50	.90
71	A22	75c multicolored	1.75	1.25
72	A22	95c multicolored	2.00	1.40
		Nos. 70-72 (3)	5.25	3.55

A23

Aruban Handicrafts: 35c, Fish net, wood float, wooden needle. 250c, Straw hat, hat block.

1991, July 31   Litho.   Perf. 13x14
73	A23	35c lt bl, dk bl & blk	1.00	.75
74	A23	250c pink, lil rose & blk	4.50	3.50

A24

35c, Toucan. 70c, People shaking hands. 100c, Windmill.

1991, Nov. 29   Litho.   Perf. 13x14
75	A24	35c multicolored	1.00	.90
76	A24	70c multicolored	1.50	.90
77	A24	100c multicolored	2.50	1.75
		Nos. 75-77 (3)	5.00	3.55

Welcome to Aruba.

Aruba Postal
Service,
Cent. — A25

60c, Government decree, 1892, vert. 75c, First post office. 80c, Current post office.

Perf. 13x14, 14x13
1992, Jan. 31   Litho.
78	A25	60c multicolored	1.25	.90
79	A25	75c multicolored	1.50	.90
80	A25	80c multicolored	2.00	1.25
		Nos. 78-80 (3)	4.75	3.05

Equality
Day — A26

No. 81, People of five races. No. 82, Woman, man, scales.

1992, Mar. 25   Litho.   Perf. 14x13
81	A26	100c multicolored	2.00	1.40
82	A26	100c multicolored	2.00	1.40

Discovery of
America, 500th
Anniv. — A27

1992, July 30   Litho.   Perf. 13x14
83	A27	30c Columbus	1.25	.50
84	A27	40c Sailing ship	1.50	.75
85	A27	50c Natives, map	1.75	.95
		Nos. 83-85 (3)	4.50	2.20

Natural
Bridges in
Aruba — A28

Designs: 70c, Seroe Colorado Bridge, south coast. 80c, Natural Bridge, north coast.

1992, Nov. 30   Litho.   Perf. 14x13
86	A28	70c multicolored	1.50	.90
87	A28	80c multicolored	1.75	1.40

A29

1993, Jan. 29   Litho.   Perf. 13x14
88	A29	200c multicolored	4.00	2.75

Express mail service.

A30

Various rock formations found in Districts of Ayo and Casibari.

1993, Mar. 31   Litho.   Perf. 13x14
89	A30	50c multicolored	1.00	.90
90	A30	60c multicolored	1.25	.90
91	A30	100c multicolored	2.00	1.75
		Nos. 89-91 (3)	4.25	3.55

Folklore — A31

40c, String instruments, drum. 70c, Traditional music & games. 80c, Dera Gai song lyrics.

1993, May 28   Litho.   Perf. 13x14
92	A31	40c multicolored	1.00	.90
93	A31	70c multicolored	1.25	.90
94	A31	80c multicolored	1.50	1.40
		Nos. 92-94 (3)	3.75	3.20

Sailing Sports — A32

1993, July 30   Litho.   Perf. 13x14
95	A32	50c Sailboating	1.10	.90
96	A32	65c Land sailing	1.40	.90
97	A32	75c Wind surfing	1.60	1.10
		Nos. 95-97 (3)	4.10	2.90

Iguana
Iguana — A33

Perf. 14x13, 13x14
1993, Sept. 1   Litho.
98	A33	35c Young	1.25	.75
99	A33	60c Almost grown	1.50	1.25
100	A33	100c Mature, vert.	2.25	1.90
		Nos. 98-100 (3)	5.00	3.90

Burrowing
Owl — A34

5c, Two adults. 10c, Two adults, young. 35c, Adult with prey, vert. 40c, Adult, vert.

Perf. 14x13, 13x14
1994, Jan. 28   Litho.
101	A34	5c multicolored	1.50	.50
102	A34	10c multicolored	1.50	.75
103	A34	35c multicolored	2.00	1.00
104	A34	40c multicolored	2.00	1.50
		Nos. 101-104 (4)	7.00	3.75

World Wildlife Fund.

A35

Intl. Olympic Committee, Cent.: 90c, Baron Pierre de Coubertin (1863-1937), founder of modern Olympics.

1994, Mar. 29   Litho.   Perf. 13x14
105	A35	50c multicolored	1.25	1.00
106	A35	90c multicolored	1.75	1.40

A36

150c, Mascot, soccer ball.

1994, July 7   Litho.   Perf. 13x14
107	A36	65c shown	1.50	1.25
108	A36	150c multicolored	2.75	2.50

1994 World Cup Soccer Championships, US.

Wild Fruit — A37

Designs: 40c, Malpighia punicifolia. 70c, Cordia sebestena. 85c, Pithecellobium unguis-cati. 150c, Coccoloba uvifera.

1994, Sept. 28   Litho.   Perf. 13x14
109	A37	40c multicolored	1.00	.90
110	A37	70c multicolored	1.50	.90
111	A37	85c multicolored	1.75	1.40
112	A37	150c multicolored	3.25	2.50
		Nos. 109-112 (4)	7.50	5.70

Architectural
Landmarks
A38

Designs: 35c, Government building, 1888.
60c, Ecury residence, 1929, vert. 100c, Prot-
estant Church, 1846, vert.

1995, Jan. 27   Litho.   Perf. 14x13
113 A38 35c multicolored   .80 .70

Perf. 13x14
114 A38 60c multicolored   1.25 .85
115 A38 100c multicolored   2.10 1.75
     Nos. 113-115 (3)   4.15 3.30

UN, 50th
Anniv. — A39

Designs: 30c, Flags, sea, UN emblem,
dove, text from UN charter. 200c, World with
flags, doves, UN emblem.

1995, Mar. 29   Litho.   Perf. 13x14
116 A39 30c multicolored   1.25 .75
117 A39 200c multicolored   3.75 3.00

Interpaso
Horses — A40

Designs: 25c, 10-time champion Casanova
II, ribbons, horiz. 75c, Paso Fino, horiz. 80c,
Horse doing figure 8. 90c, Girl on horse.

1995, May 26   Perf. 14x13, 13x14
118 A40 25c multicolored   .75 .45
119 A40 75c multicolored   1.50 1.25
120 A40 80c multicolored   1.50 1.40
121 A40 90c multicolored   1.75 1.40
     Nos. 118-121 (4)   5.50 4.50

Vegetables — A41

25c, Vigna sinensis. 50c, Cucumis anguria.
70c, Hibiscus esculentus. 85c, Cucurbita
moschata.

1995, July 28   Litho.   Perf. 13x14
122 A41 25c multicolored   .75 .45
123 A41 50c multicolored   1.25 .90
124 A41 70c multicolored   1.40 1.25
125 A41 85c multicolored   1.60 1.50
     Nos. 122-125 (4)   5.00 4.10

Turtles — A42

1995, Sept. 27   Litho.   Perf. 14x13
126 A42 15c Hawksbill   1.40 .55
127 A42 50c Green   1.75 .90
128 A42 95c Loggerhead   2.25 1.50
129 A42 100c Leatherback   2.50 1.50
     Nos. 126-129 (4)   7.90 4.45

Separate Status,
10th Anniv. — A43

Statesmen and politicians: No. 130, Jan
Hendrik Albert Eman (1887-1957). No. 131,
Juan Enrique Irausquin (1904-62). No. 132,
Cornelis Albert Eman (1916-67). No. 133, Gil-
berto Francois Croes (1938-85).

1996, Jan. 1   Litho.   Perf. 13x14
130 A43 100c multicolored   1.75 1.40
131 A43 100c multicolored   1.75 1.40
132 A43 100c multicolored   1.75 1.40
133 A43 100c multicolored   1.75 1.40
     Nos. 130-133 (4)   7.00 5.60

The 1986 date on No. 133 is in error.

America
Issue — A44

National dresswear: 65c, Woman wearing
long, full dress, apron, vert. 70c, Man wearing
hat, bow tie, white shirt, black pants, vert.
100c, Couple dancing.

Perf. 13x14, 14x13
1996, Mar. 25   Litho.
134 A44 65c multicolored   2.00 .95
135 A44 70c multicolored   2.00 .95
136 A44 100c multicolored   2.75 1.60
     Nos. 134-136 (3)   6.75 3.50

1996 Summer
Olympic
Games,
Atlanta — A45

1996, May 28   Litho.   Perf. 14x13
137 A45 85c Runners   2.00 1.25
138 A45 130c Cyclist   2.75 2.10

A46

Famous Women: No. 139, Livia (Mimi)
Ecury (1920-91), nurse. No. 140, Lolita Euson
(1914-94), poet. No. 141, Laura Wernet-Pas-
kel (1911-62), teacher.

1996, Sept. 27   Litho.   Perf. 13x14
139 A46 60c multicolored   1.40 1.25
140 A46 60c multicolored   1.40 1.25
141 A46 60c multicolored   1.40 1.25
     Nos. 139-141 (3)   4.20 3.75

A47

Year of Papiamento 1997: 50c, Sign promoting use of Papiamento language, children
playing on beach, people in water, boat. 140c,
"Papiamento," sunrise.

1997, Jan. 23   Litho.   Perf. 13x14
142 A47 50c multicolored   1.00 1.00
143 A47 140c multicolored   2.50 2.50

Mailman on
Bicycle, 1936-
57
A48

America issue: 70c, Mailman handing mail
to woman, jeep, 1957-88. 80c, Mailman on
motor scooter placing mail in mailbox, 1995.

1997, Mar. 27   Litho.   Perf. 14x13
144 A48 60c multicolored   2.40 1.40
145 A48 70c multicolored   2.50 1.50
146 A48 80c multicolored   3.00 1.60
     Nos. 144-146 (3)   7.90 4.50

Aruban
Architectrue
A49

30c, Decorated cunucu house. 65c, Steps
with "popchi's." 100c, Arends's Building, vert.

1997, May 22   Litho.   Perf. 14x13
147 A49 30c multicolored   .90 .75
148 A49 65c multicolored   1.75 1.25

Perf. 13x14
149 A49 100c multicolored   2.00 1.75
     Nos. 147-149 (3)   4.65 3.75

Marine Life — A50

Designs: a, Marlin jumping out of water,
lighthouse. b, Dolphin jumping out of water,
trees, plants on beach. c, Iguana on rock,
beach. d, Dolphin, fish. e, Two dolphins, fish. f,
Fish, turtles, owl on beach. g, Various fish
among coral. h, Diver, shipwreck, fish, coral. i,
Various fish.

1997, May 29   Litho.   Perf. 12½x13
150 A50 90c Sheet of 9, #a.-i. 25.00 25.00
     PACIFIC 97.

Cruise
Tourism
A51

Designs: 35c, Ship at pier, tourists walking
toward ship. 50c, Ship with gangway lowered,
tourists. 150c, Ship out to sea, small boat.

1997, July 24   Litho.   Perf. 14x13
151 A51 35c multicolored   1.00 .85
152 A51 50c multicolored   1.25 1.10
153 A51 150c multicolored   3.00 2.50
     Nos. 151-153 (3)   5.25 4.45

Aruban Wild
Flowers
A52

50c, Erythrina velutina. 60c, Cordia dentata.
70c, Tabebuia billbergii. 130c, Guaiacum
officinale.

1997, Sept. 25
154 A52 50c multicolored   1.25 .95
155 A52 60c multicolored   1.50 1.25
156 A52 70c multicolored   1.75 1.25
157 A52 130c multicolored   2.75 2.00
     Nos. 154-157 (4)   7.25 5.45

Fort Zoutman,
Bicent. — A53

1998, Jan. 13   Litho.   Perf. 14x13
158 A53 30c sepia & multi   1.00 .75
159 A53 250c gray & multi   4.25 3.75

Total Solar Eclipse,
1998 — A54

100c, Map, track of eclipse.

1998, Feb. 26   Litho.   Perf. 13x14
160 A54 85c shown   2.75 1.50
161 A54 100c multicolored   3.50 2.00

Native
Birds — A55

50c, Mimus gilvus. 60c, Falco sparverius.
70c, Icterus icterus. 150c, Coereba flaveola.

Perf. 14x13, 13x14
1998, July 10   Litho.
162 A55 50c multi   1.60 1.00
163 A55 60c multi, vert.   2.00 1.25
164 A55 70c multi, vert.   2.25 1.25
165 A55 150c multi   3.50 2.75
     Nos. 162-165 (4)   9.35 6.25

World Stamp
1998 — A56

1998, Sept. 8   Litho.   Perf. 14x13
166 A56 225c multicolored   5.50 4.25

Endangered
Animals
A57

Equus asinus: 40c, Two standing on hill.
65c, Three standing, rocks, cacti, tree. 100c,
Adult, foal standing among rocks, cacti.

1999, June 21   Litho.   Perf. 14x13
167 A57 40c multicolored   1.40 .75
168 A57 65c multicolored   1.60 1.25
169 A57 100c multicolored   2.40 1.90
     Nos. 167-169 (3)   5.40 3.90

Cacti — A58

Designs: 50c, Opuntia wentiana. 60c,
Lemaireocereus griseus. 70c, Cephalocereus
lanuginosus. 75c, Cephalocereus lanuginosus
(in bloom).

1999, Mar. 31   Litho.   *Perf. 14x13*
170	A58	50c multicolored	1.25	.85
171	A58	60c multicolored	1.50	1.00
172	A58	70c multicolored	1.50	1.25
173	A58	75c multicolored	1.75	1.40
		Nos. 170-173 (4)	6.00	4.50

Dogs — A59

Various dogs, background: 40c, Trees. 60c, Cactus, aloe plant, rocks. 80c, Tree, sea. 165c, Sky, clouds.

1999, May 31   Litho.   *Perf. 13x14*
174	A59	40c multicolored	1.50	1.00
175	A59	60c multicolored	1.75	1.25
176	A59	80c multicolored	2.00	1.50
177	A59	165c multicolored	3.25	2.75
		Nos. 174-177 (4)	8.50	6.50

Discovery of Aruba, 500th Anniv. — A60

1999, Aug. 9   Litho.   *Perf. 14x13*
178	A60	150c shown	2.50	2.25
179	A60	175c Abstract paintings	3.00	2.50
a.		Souvenir sheet, #178-179	6.00	5.75

Natl. Library, 50th Anniv. — A61

1999, Aug. 20
180	A61	70c shown	1.50	1.40
181	A61	100c Original building	2.10	1.75

Christmas — A62

Coil Stamps

Die Cut Perf. 13x13½

1999, Dec. 1   Self-Adhesive   Litho.
182	A62	40c Magi on shore	1.60	1.00
183	A62	70c Magi in desert	2.25	1.25
184	A62	100c Holy Family	2.75	1.75
		Nos. 182-184 (3)	6.60	4.00

Tourist Attractions A62a

Reptiles A63

Tourist Attractions: 25c, Guadirikiri Cave. 55c, Cactus landscape. 85c, Hooiberg. 500c, Conchi. Reptiles: 40c, Norops lineatus. 60c, Iguana iguana, vert. 75c, Leptodeira annulata, vert. 150c, Cnemidophorus murinus.

2000   Litho.   *Perf. 14x13, 13x14*
185	A62a	25c multi	1.00	.50
186	A63	40c multi	1.25	.75
187	A62a	55c multi	1.40	1.00
188	A63	60c multi	1.40	1.25

189	A63	75c multi	1.60	1.25
190	A62a	85c multi	1.75	1.50
191	A63	150c multi	3.25	2.25
192	A62a	500c multi	8.50	7.25
		Nos. 185-192 (8)	20.15	15.75

Issued: 40c, 60c, 75c, 150c, 1/31; 25c, 55c, 85c, 500c, 6/5.
See Nos. 197-204.

America Issue, Campaign Against AIDS — A64

175c, Ribbon on globe, vert.

Perf. 14x13, 13x14
2000, Mar. 2   Litho.
193	A64	75c Flags	2.25	2.25
194	A64	175c multicolored	4.50	4.50

Organization Anniversaries A65

Designs: 150c, Aruba Bank N.V., 75th anniv. 165c, Alto Vista Church, 250th anniv.

2000, Apr. 20   Litho.   *Perf. 14x13*
195	A65	150c multi	2.75	2.25
196	A65	165c multi	3.00	2.50

Type of 2000

Animals: 5c, Cat. 15c, Shells. 30c, Tortoise. 35c, Mud house, vert. 50c, Rabbit. 100c, Balashi gold smelter, vert. 200c, Parakeet. 250c, Rock crystals.

Perf. 14x13, 13x14 (#200, 202)
2001   Litho.
197	A63	5c multi	1.00	.40
198	A62a	15c multi	.50	.40
199	A63	30c multi	1.00	.85
200	A63	35c multi	.90	.85
201	A63	50c multi	1.75	1.60
202	A62a	100c multi	2.75	2.10
203	A63	200c multi	4.25	4.00
204	A62a	250c multi	4.75	4.50
		Nos. 197-204 (8)	16.90	14.70

Issued: 5c, 30c, 500c, 200c, 1/31. 15c, 35c, 100c, 250c, 8/6.

Mascaruba, 40th Anniv. — A66

Actors on stage and audience in: 60c: Background. 150c, Foreground.

2001, Mar. 26   Litho.   *Perf. 14x13*
205-206	A66	Set of 2	4.00	3.50

Classic Motor Vehicles A67

Designs: 25c, 1930 Ford Crown Victoria Leatherback. 40c, 1933 Citroen Commerciale. 70c, 1948 Plymouth pickup truck. 75c, 1959 Ford Edsel.

2001, May 31
207-210	A67	Set of 4	7.00	5.00

Year of Dialogue Among Civilizations A68

2001, Oct. 9   Litho.   *Perf. 14x13*
211	A68	175c multi	3.50	3.00

Airport Views — A69

Designs: 30c, Dakota Airport, 1950. 75c, Queen Beatrix Airport, 1972. 175c, Queen Beatrix Airport, 2000.

2002, Jan. 31   Litho.   *Perf. 14x13*
212-214	A69	Set of 3	6.00	4.75

Royal Wedding A70

Prince Willem-Alexander, Maxima Zorreguieta and: 60c, Royal palace, golden coach. 300c, Bourse of Berlage, New Church.

2002, Feb. 2
215-216	A70	Set of 2	6.25	6.00

Water and Energy Company, 70th Anniv. — A71

Designs: 60c, Faucet and water drop, vert. 85c, Pipeline. 165c, Meter and meter-reading equipment, vert.

Perf. 13x14, 14x13
2002, June 3   Litho.
217-219	A71	Set of 3	5.50	5.25

America Issue — Youth, Education and Literacy — A72

Designs: 25c, Hand writing letters with quill pen. 100c, Child looking over wall of letters.

2002, July 15   Litho.   *Perf. 14x12¾*
220-221	A72	Set of 2	4.00	2.75

Aruba in World War II — A73

Designs: 60c, Attack on Lago Oil Refinery by German U-boat U-156. 75c, Torpedoing of ships by U-156. 150c, Statue of "Boy" Ecury, Aruban resistance fighter, Aruban militiaman, vert.

Perf. 14x13, 13x14
2002, Sept. 9   Litho.
222-224	A73	Set of 3	8.50	6.50

Mud Houses — A74

Various houses with frame color of: 40c, Yellow green. 60c, Blue green. 75c, Red.

2003, Jan. 31   Litho.   *Perf. 14x13*
225-227	A74	Set of 3	3.25	3.00

De Trupialen Performing Organization, 50th Anniv. — A75

Designs: 30c, Trupialen Boys' Choir. 50c, Play handbills. 100c, Emblems.

2003, Mar. 31   Litho.   *Perf. 14x13*
228-230	A75	Set of 3	3.25	3.00

Orchids — A76

Designs: 75c, Schomburgkia humboldtii. 500c, Brassavola nodosa.

2003, May 30   Litho.   *Perf. 14x13*
231-232	A76	Set of 2	10.00	10.00

Butterflies A77

Designs: 40c, Orange-barred sulphur. 75c, Monarch. 85c, Hairstreak. 175c, Gulf fritillary.

2003, July 31
233-236	A77	Set of 4	7.50	7.00

Endangered Animals A78

Turtles: 25c, Eretmochelys imbricata, vert. 60c, Dermochelys coriacea. 75c, Chelonia mydas, vert. 150c, Caretta caretta.

Perf. 13x14, 14x13
2003, Sept. 30   Litho.
237-240	A78	Set of 4	6.00	5.25

Carnival, 50th Anniv. — A79

Designs: 60c, Masks. 75c, Carnival Queen, vert. 150c, Aruba flag, Carnival participants.

Perf. 14x13, 13x14
2004, Jan. 30   Litho.
241-243	A79	Set of 3	3.75	3.75

Birds — A80

Designs: 70c, Sterna sandvicensis. 75c, Pelecanus occidentalis. 80c, Fregata magnificens. 90c, Larus atricilla.

2004, Mar. 31   *Perf. 13x14*
244-247	A80	Set of 4	5.50	4.50

Fish — A81

Designs: 40c, Parrotfish. 60c, Queen angelfish. 75c, Squirrelfish. 100c, Smallmouth grunt.

2004, May 31   Litho.   *Perf. 14x13*
248-251	A81	Set of 4	4.75	3.75

Christmas and New Year's Day — A82

Designs: 50c, Children, Christmas tree, gifts. 85c, Choir, stained glass window, candle, gifts. 125c, Fireworks display.

2004, Dec. 1   Litho.   Perf. 13x14
252-254 A82   Set of 3   3.25 3.25

Kingdom Statutes, 50th Anniv. — A83

Designs: 160c, Collage of Netherlands Antilles islands. 165c, Kingdom Statute Monument.

2004, Dec. 15   Perf. 14x13
255-256 A83   Set of 2   3.75 3.75

Greetings A84

Designs: 60c, Sun, flower (Thank you). 75c, Cacti and rabbits (Love). 135c, Fish (Get well soon). 215c, Balloons and flag (Congratulations).

2005, Jan. 31   Litho.   Perf. 14x13
257-260 A84   Set of 4   6.25 6.25

Drag Racing A85

Drag racers: 60c, One car going airborne. 85c, One car with chute deployed. 185c, Cars at start line.

2005, Mar. 16
261-263 A85   Set of 3   4.25 4.00

Souvenir Sheet

Reign of Queen Beatrix, 25th Anniv. — A86

No. 264: a, 30c, At coronation, 1980. b, 60c, Making speech, 1991. c, 75c, With Nelson Mandela, 1999. d, 105c, Visiting Aruba and the Netherlands Antilles, 1999. e, 215c, Speaking before European Parliament, 2004.

2005, Apr. 30 Litho. Perf. 13¼x13¾
264 A86   Sheet of 5, #a-e   6.50 6.50

Sunsets — A87

Designs: 60c, Birds and cacti. 100c, Palm tree. 205c, Pelicans and pilings.

2005, May 31   Perf. 13x14
265-267 A87   Set of 3   4.75 4.75

Birds of Prey — A88

Designs: 60c, Falco sparverius. 75c, Athene cunicularia. 135c, Pandion haliaetus. 200c, Polyborus plancus.

2005, July 29   Litho.   Perf. 14x13
268-271 A88   Set of 4   7.00 6.50
271a   Souvenir sheet, #268-271   7.00 7.00

A89

Corals: 60c, Staghorn coral. 75c, Blade fire coral. 100c, Deepwater sea fan. 215c, Smooth brain coral.

2005, Sept. 30   Litho.   Perf. 13x14
272-275 A89   Set of 4   6.00 6.00

A90

Children and philately: 75c, Girl, stamps. 85c, Boy with magnifying glass and stamp album. 125c, Boy with tongs and stock book.

2005, Oct. 31
276-278 A90   Set of 3   4.50 4.50

Paintings A91

Designs: 60c, House at Savaneta, by Jean Georges Pandellis. 75c, Haf di Rei, by Mateo Hayde. 185c, Landscape, by Julie Q. Oduber.

2006, Feb. 6   Litho.   Perf. 14x13
279-281 A91   Set of 3   5.00 5.00

Aruba YMCA, 50th Anniv. — A92

Designs: 75c, YMCA emblem. 205c, Children in playground, horiz.

Perf. 13x14, 14x13
2006, Apr. 3   Litho.
282-283 A92   Set of 2   4.25 4.25

Souvenir Sheet

Washington 2006 World Philatelic Exhibition — A93

No. 284 — Exhibition emblem and: a, Natural Bridge, head of iguana, tree and cactus. b, Cacti, tail of iguana, sailboat, vert.

2006, May 27   Litho.   Perf. 12¾
284 A93 500c Sheet of 2, #a-b   12.50 12.50

2006 World Cup Soccer Championships, Germany — A94

Designs: 75c, Children's drawing of goalie. 215c, Goalie's gloves and ball.

2006, June 5   Litho.   Perf. 14x13
285-286 A94   Set of 2   4.25 4.25

Hi-Winds Windsurfing Regatta, 20th Anniv. — A95

Designs: 60c, Hotel, windsurfers, kitesurfer, and fishing boats. 100c, Kitesurfers, windsurfer and flag in water. 125c, Windsurfers.

2006, July 3   Litho.   Perf. 14x13
287-289 A95   Set of 3   3.50 3.50

Fire Prevention A96

Designs: 60c, Fire prevention, safety and extinguishing strategies. 100c, Firemen at house fire. 205c, Fire trucks.

2006, Sept. 29   Litho.   Perf. 14x13
290-292 A96   Set of 3   4.50 4.50

Arikok National Park — A97

Designs: 75c, Cas di Torto, goat and garden, Cunucu Arikok. 100c, View of Miralamar, vert. 200c, Dunes of Boca Prins.

2006, Oct. 31   Litho.   Perf. 14x13
293-295 A97   Set of 3   4.50 4.50

Souvenir Sheet

New Year 2007 (Year of the Pig) — A98

No. 296: a, 205c, Pig. b, 215c, Dragon, vert.

2007, Feb. 15   Litho.   Perf. 12¾
296 A98   Sheet of 2, #a-b   5.25 5.25

Casa Cuna Children's Home Foundation, 50th Anniv. — A99

Designs: 50c, Original Casa Cuna building, Luciana Maria Koolman. 125c, Children in hands. 150c, New Casa Cuna building.

2007, Apr. 4   Perf. 14x13
297-299 A99   Set of 3   4.25 4.25

Museums in Oranjestad A100

Designs: 70c, Museum of Antiquities. 85c, Numismatic Museum. 100c, Archaeological Museum. 135c, Historical Museum.

2007, July 2   Litho.   Perf. 14x13
300-303 A100   Set of 4   5.00 5.00

Souvenir Sheet

Wrecks and Reefs — A101

No. 304: a, 200c, Pipeline system of wrecked oil tanker Pedernalis. b, 300c, Convair 400 airplane near Sonesta Island. c, 500c, Sea turtle, wreck of freighter Jane. d, 500c, Fish, wreck of freighter Antilla.

2007, Sept. 3   Litho.   Perf. 14x13
304 A101   Sheet of 4, #a-d   17.00 17.00

Christmas and New Year's Day — A102

Designs: 70c, Infant and mother. 100c, Girl with toys and gift box. 150c, Boy at New Year's celebration.

2007, Oct. 17
305-307 A102   Set of 3   4.00 4.00

Heineken Aruba Catamaran Regatta A103

Designs: 40c, Catamarans on beach. 80c, Catamarans racing near race buoy. 125c, Competitor leaning off side of catamaran. 130c, Row of catamarans in race.

2007, Nov. 8
308-311 A103 Set of 4   4.50 4.50

Alto Vista Church — A103a

2007-09 Litho. Perf. 14x13
Frame Color

311A	A103a	5c pink	.25	.25
311B	A103a	10c blue	.25	.25
311C	A103a	25c lt bl grn	.30	.30
311D	A103a	50c yel green	.55	.55
311E	A103a	85c green	.95	.95
311F	A103a	90c lt grnsh bl	1.00	1.00
311G	A103a	100c salmon	1.10	1.10
311H	A103a	125c violet	1.40	1.40
311I	A103a	130c lt blue	1.50	1.50
311J	A103a	135c beige	1.50	1.50
311K	A103a	140c violet	1.60	1.60
311L	A103a	200c dull org	2.25	2.25
311M	A103a	215c gray	2.40	2.40
311N	A103a	220c gray	2.50	2.50

Nos. 311A-311N (14)   17.45 17.45

Issued: 5c, 50c, 85c, 100c, 200c, 7/30/07; 135c, 9/3/08; 90c, 130c, 140c, 220c, 3/9/09. Others, 2007.

Queen Beatrix, 70th Birthday — A104

Queen Beatrix: 75c, As one-year old with Dutch dignitaries. 125c, With Prince Claus and newborn Crown Prince Willem Alexander. 250c, In royal robes on day of accession to throne. 300c, With family of Crown Prince Willem Alexander.

2008, Jan. 31 Perf. 13x14
312-315 A104 Set of 4   8.50 8.50

Aruban Cultural Year — A105

Designs: 80c, Carnival participants. 130c, Organ grinders. 205c, Dera Gai celebration. 275c, Dande musicians visiting home.

2008, Mar. 18 Litho. Perf. 14x13
316-319 A105 Set of 4   7.75 7.75

2008 Summer Olympics, Beijing A106

Designs: 50c, Running. 75c, Synchronized swimming. 100c, Men's rings, vert. 125c, Judo.

2008, Apr. 1 Perf. 14x13, 13x14
320-323 A106 Set of 4   5.00 5.00

Athene Cunicularia Arubensis — A107

Aruban burrowing owl: 100c, Entire bird. 150c, Two birds, horiz. 350c, Head of bird.

Perf. 13x14, 14x13
2008, June 2 Litho.
324-326 A107 Set of 3   7.50 7.50

Harley-Davidson Motorcycles — A108

Designs: 175c, FRX Super Glide Big Boy. 225c, Knucklehead. 305c, Roadking.

2008, July 4 Litho. Perf. 14x13
327-329 A108 Set of 3   8.00 8.00

Aruban Culture A109

Designs: No. 330, Poem by Federico Oduber. No. 331, 240c, Watapana Magazine covers, vert. No. 332, Henry Habibe and poem by Habibe, vert.

2008, July 8 Litho. Perf. 13¾

330	A109	240c multi	4.25	4.25
331	A109	240c multi	4.25	4.25
332	A109	240c multi	4.25	4.25

  a.   Souvenir sheet of 5, #330-332, Netherlands #1311, Netherlands Antilles #1187, + etiquette   17.50 17.50

Nos. 330-332 (3)   12.75 12.75

No. 332a sold for 10g. No. 330 also was available on Netherlands Nos. 1313a and 1313b and Netherlands Antilles No. 1189a.

Flowers — A110

No. 333: a, 100c, Calatropis procera. b, 215c, Passiflora foetida.
No. 334: a, 185c, Thespesia populnea. b, 200c, Cryptostegia grandiflora.

2008, Aug. 8 Litho. Perf. 13½
333 A110 Pair, #a-b   3.50 3.50
334 A110 Pair, #a-b   4.50 4.50

Drawings by Rembrandt (1606-69) — A111

Designs: 350c, Self-portrait, 1652. 425c, Self-portrait, 1630. 500c, Beggars at door, 1648.

2008, Sept. 30 Litho. Perf. 13x14
335-337 A111 Set of 3   14.50 14.50

Aruba in the Past — A112

Designs: 100c, Carting of potable water. 200c, Clay houses. 215c, Processing of aloe resin.

2008, Nov. 3 Litho. Perf. 14x13
338-340 A112 Set of 3   5.75 5.75

Louis Braille (1809-52), Educator of the Blind — A113

Designs: 200c, Braille. 215c, Walking stick for the blind.

2009, Jan. 5 Litho. Perf. 13x14
341-342 A113 Set of 2   5.50 5.50

Miniature Sheet

Carnival, 55th Anniv. — A114

No. 343: a, 75c, Miss Carnival on float. b, 100c, Clown on float. c, 175c, Float with "55" and champagne bottle. d, 225c, Carnival dancers.

2009, Feb. 6 Litho. Perf. 13¼x13¾
343 A114 Sheet of 4, #a-d   8.50 8.50

Caves A115

Designs: 175c, Tunnel of Love Cave. 200c, Fountain Cave. 225c, Guadirikiri Cave.

2009, Apr. 1 Perf. 14x13
344-346 A115 Set of 3   6.75 6.75

Souvenir Sheet

Global Warming — A116

No. 347: a, 200c, Hurricane over map of Caribbean. b, 250c, Map of polar regions, mountains, parched earth. c, 250c, Pollution

from industry and vehicles. d, 300c, Fluorescent light bulb, recycling symbols, windmill.

2009, June 2
347 A116 Sheet of 4, #a-d   11.50 11.50

Souvenir Sheet

Architecture — A117

No. 348: a, 175c, California Lighthouse. b, 250c, Plaza Daniel Leo, horiz. c, 275c, Henriquez Building, horiz. d, 325c, Ecury Complex main building.

2009, July 3 Perf. 12¾
348 A117 Sheet of 4, #a-d   11.50 11.50

National Library, 60th Anniv. — A118

Book reader: 185c, Girl. 300c, Woman.

2009, Aug. 20 Litho. Perf. 13x14
349-350 A118 Set of 2   5.50 5.50
350a   Vert. pair, #349-350   5.50 5.50

Dolphins A119

Designs: 125c, Stenella frontalis. 200c, Steno bredanensis. 300c, Two Stenella frontalis. 325c, Group of Steno bredanensis at surface.

2009, Sept. 30 Perf. 14x13
351-354 A119 Set of 4   14.00 14.00

Christmas A120

Designs: 75c Madonna and Child. 120c, Angel and stars. 125c, Hands, globe, stars, "2009." 210c, Shepherds and sheep.

2009, Oct. 19
355-358 A120 Set of 4   6.00 6.00

Miniature Sheet

Personalized Stamps — A120a

No. 358A: b, Church. c, House. d, Boat. e, Lizard and flower. f, Lighthouse. g, Tree.

2009, Dec. 18 Litho. Perf. 13¼x14
358A A120a (295c) Sheet of 6,
       #b-g   20.00 20.00

No. 358A sold for 1770c or $20 in U.S. currency. Stamps could be personalized. Butterfly images shown are generic.

Recycling
A121

Various works of art from recycled materials: 90c, Island landscape. 180c, Post office, tree, and animal. 325c, Fish.

2010, Jan. 22 Litho. Perf. 13¼
359-361 A121   Set of 3   6.75 6.75

Historic Airplanes — A122

No. 362: a, 250c, Seaplane. b, 500c, Seaplane and lighthouse.

2010, Mar. 26   Perf. 13¼x13
362 A122   Horiz. pair, #a-b   8.50 8.50

Scouting in Aruba, 10th
Anniv. — A123

No. 363: a, 85c, Scouts observing nature. b, 95c, Scouts building fire. c, 135c, Scout near tent. d, 180c, Scouts playing drums.

2010, Apr. 1   Litho.
363 A123   Block of 4, #a-d   5.50 5.50

End of World
War II, 65th
Anniv.
A124

No. 364: a, 140c, Large cannon. b, 200c, Beached torpedo. 275c, Equipment and ramp.

2010, May 4 Litho. Perf. 13¼x13
364 A124   Vert. strip of 3, #a-c   7.00 7.00

Parrots — A125

No. 365 — Various parrots: a, 85c. b, 90c. c, 180c.

2010, June 2   Perf. 13x13¼
365 A125   Horiz. strip of 3, #a-c   4.00 4.00

Paintings by Vincent Van
Gogh — A126

No. 366: a, 200c, Self-portrait with Gray Felt Hat. b, 250c, Still Life: Vase with Fifteen Sunflowers. c, 305c, Starry Night. d, 500c, Wheat Field with Crows.

2010, July 29   Perf. 13¼x13
366 A126   Block of 4, #a-d   14.00 14.00

Rum Shops
A127

No. 367: a, 100c, Essoville Rum Shop. b, 200c, Aruba Rum Shop. c, 255c, Caribbean Store.

2010, Sept. 13
367 A127   Vert. strip of 3, #a-c   7.50 7.50

Flowers — A128

No. 368: a, Caesalpinia pulcherrima. b, Dipladenia sanderi. c, Hibiscus. d, Adenium obesum. e, Bougainvillea. f, Ixora. g, Eichhornia crassipes. h, Passiflora caerulea. i, Allamanda cathartica. j, Nerium oleander.

2010, Sept. 29   Perf. 14
368   Block of 10   22.50 22.50
a.-j. A128 200c Any single   2.25 2.25

Houses of Worship — A129

No. 369: a, 85c, Synagogue. b, 90c, Church. c, 135c, Church, diff. d, 240c, Church interior.

2010, Oct. 28   Perf. 13x13¼
369 A129   Block of 4, #a-d   6.25 6.25

Birds — A130

No. 370: a, Falco sparverius. b, Icterus icterus. c, Mimus gilvus. d, Egretta alba. e, Aratinga pertinax. f, Pelecanus occidentalis. g, Athene cunicularia arubensis. h, Coerba flaveola. i, Polyborus plancus. j, Colibri thalassinus.

2010, Nov. 17 Litho. Perf. 14
370   Block of 10   22.50 22.50
a.-j. A130 200c Any single   2.25 2.25

Briareus Caribbean Reef
Octopus — A131

No. 371 — Various depictions of octopus: a, 100c. b, 175c. c, 255c. d, 300c.

2010, Nov. 30   Perf. 13¼x13
371 A131   Block of 4, #a-d   9.25 9.25

Butterflies — A132

No. 372: a, Zuleika. b, Blue morpho. c, Monarch. d, White peacock. e, Sulphur. f, Zebra. g, Malachite. h, Owl. i, Postman. j, Gulf fritillary.

2010, Dec. 22   Perf. 14
372   Block of 10   22.50 22.50
a.-j. A132 200c Any single   2.25 2.25

Separate Political Status, 25th
Anniv. — A133

No. 373 — Curved lines and: a, 200c, Star. b, 300c, "Status Aparte." c, 300c, F. B. Tromp, first governor of Aruba, and J. H. A. Eman, first prime minister of Aruba, country name in white at UL. d, 400c, A. J. Booi, first president of Parliament, and G. F. Croes, political party leader, country name in red at LR.

2011, Jan. 1
373 A133   Block of 4, #a-d   13.50 13.50

Flowers
A134

No. 374: a, Catharanthus roseus. b, Echinopsis lageniformis. c, Allamanda cathartica. d, Cordia sebestena. e, Ipomoea pes-caprae. f, Hibiscus rosa-sinensis. g, Cassia fistula. h, Bougainvillea glabra. i, Delonix regia. j, Nerium oleander.

2011, Feb. 16   Perf. 14
374   Block of 10   18.00 18.00
a.-j. A134 160c Any single   1.75 1.75

America
Issue
A135

No. 375 — Hands with flags of: a, 200c, Portugal, United States, Cuba and Brazil. b, 250c, Honduras, Canada, Colombia and Chile. c, 350c, United States, Brazil, Aruba and Panama. d, 400c, Suriname, Colombia, Chile and Spain.
No. 376: a, Like No. 375a. b, Like No. 375b. c, Like No. 375c. d, Like No. 375d.

2011, Mar. 23
375   Vert. strip of 4   13.50 13.50
a.   A135 200c multi   2.25 2.25
b.   A135 250c multi   2.75 2.75
c.   A135 350c multi   4.00 4.00
d.   A135 400c multi   4.50 4.50

Miniature Sheet
376 A135 300c Sheet of 4, #a-
       d   13.50 13.50
Postal Union of the Americas, Spain and Portugal (UPAEP), cent.

Bank Notes
A136

No. 377: a, 1964 Indonesia 25 sen note. b, 1986 Bhutan 2 ngultrum note. c, 1949 Philippines 50 centavo note. d, 1987 Sudan 25 piastre note. e, 1976 Mozambique 100 escudo note. f, 1993 Haiti 25 gourde note. g, 1917 Göttingen 25 pfennig note. h, 1997 Turkey 250,000 lira note. i, 1977 Solomon Islands 10 dollar note. j, 1915 Lille 25 centime note. k, 1985 Egypt 25 piastre note. l, 1976 Albania 100 lek note.

2011, Apr. 4
377   Block of 12   23.00 23.00
a.-l. A136 167c Any single   1.90   1.90

Maastricht Paper Money Fair.

Peonies — A137

No. 378 — Color of flowers: a, Dark red. b, Yellow. c, White. d, Pink.
350c, Pink peony.

2011, May 11   Litho.   Perf. 14
378 A137 110c Sheet of 4, #a-d   5.00   5.00
Souvenir Sheet
379 A137 350c multi   4.00   4.00

Fish — A138

No. 380: a, Holacanthus ciliaris. b, Chaetodon capistratus. c, Sparisoma viride. d, Pomacanthus paru. e, Balistes vetula. f, Lactophrys triqueter. g, Holocentrus rufus. h, Chaetodon striatus. i, Diodon holocanthus. j, Equetus punctatus.

2011, June 15
380   Block of 10   14.00 14.00
a.-j. A138 120c Any single   1.40   1.40

Chess — A139

No. 381 — Positions of chess pieces at end of 1956 match between Donald Byrne and winner Bobby Fischer: a, White queen on tan square. b, Black king on tan square. c, White knight on tan square, d, Black bishop on tan square. e, White pawn on tan square. f, Black bishop on green square. g, Black knight on tan square. h, Black rook on green square. i, White pawn on green square. j, White king on tan square. k, Black pawn on green square.

2011, July 22
381   Sheet of 15, #a-j, 5 #k +
             49 labels   30.00 30.00
a.-k. A139 180c Any single   2.00   2.00

Mail Boxes of the
World — A140

No. 382: a, Dark red rectangular pillar box. b, Orange red Estonian Post mail box. c, Yellow mail box. d, Blue USPS mail box. e, Yellow mail box inscribed "Postbriefkasten." f, Blue mail box with Cyrillic letters. g, Green pillar box

with Chinese inscriptions. h, Red mail box inscribed "Brieven Drukwerken." i, Green mail box with two legs. j, Red hexagonal British pillar box.

2011, Aug. 19
382   Block of 10   17.50 17.50
a.-j. A140 150c Any single   1.75   1.75

Paintings by Jan
Vermeer (1632-
75) — A141

No. 383: a, Girl with a Red Hat (red frame). b, The Milkmaid (blue frame). c, The Lacemaker (brown frame). d, Girl with a Pearl Earring (red frame).

2011, Sept. 21   Litho.   Perf. 14
383   Vert. strip of 4   11.50 11.50
a.   A141 200c multi   2.25   2.25
b.-c. A141 250c Either single   2.75   2.75
d.   A141 300c multi   3.50   3.50

Ships — A142

No. 384 — Various tall ships with panel color of: a, 200c, Blue violet. b, 225c, Maroon, horiz. c, 250c, Blue violet, horiz. d, 250c, Maroon, horiz. e, 275c, Maroon, horiz. f, 300c, Blue violet.

2011, Oct. 25
384 A142 Block of 6, #a-f   17.00 17.00

Butterflies
A143

Designs: No. 385, 160c, Diaethria neglecta. No. 386, 160c, Lycaena cupreus lapidicola. No. 387, 160c, Pyrrhogyra edocla. No. 388, 160c, Anartia amathea amathea. No. 389, 160c, Anglais urticae. No. 390, 160c, Morpho aega. No. 391, 160c, Junonia coenia coenia (red violet background). No. 392, 160c, Junonia coenia coenia (dark purple background). No. 393, 160c, Dione juno juno. No. 394, 160c, Lycaena heteronea austin.

2011, Dec. 1
385-394 A143 Set of 10   18.00 18.00

Nos. 385-394 were printed in sheets containing two of each stamp + a central label.

Birds — A144

No. 395: a, Pithecophaga jeffreyi. b, Harpia harpyja. c, Morphnus guaianensis. d, Caracara plancus. e, Lophaetus occipitalis. f, Stephanoaetus coronatus. g, Haliaeetus leucocephalus. h, Vultur gryphus. i, Aquila chrysaetos. j, Falco sparverius.

2012, Jan. 19
395   Block of 10   17.50 17.50
a.-j. A144 150c Any single   1.75   1.75

Aruban
Goats — A145

No. 396: a, Three goats on rocks. b, Two goats on rocks, horiz. c, Goat, horiz. d, Goat and cactus.

2012, Feb. 21
396   Strip of 4   11.00 11.00
a.   A145 175c multi   2.00   2.00
b.   A145 225c multi   2.50   2.50
c.   A145 275c multi   3.00   3.00
d.   A145 300c multi   3.50   3.50

2012 Summer Olympics,
London — A146

No. 397: a, Torch. b, Swimmer, horiz. c, Hurdler, horiz. d, "Olympia."

2012, Apr. 27
397 A146 500c Block of 4,
             #a-d   22.50 22.50
e.   Souvenir sheet of 4,
         #397a-397d   22.50 22.50

Whales
A147

No. 398: a, Delphinapterus leucas. b, Kogia breviceps. c, Balaena mysticetus. d, Orcinus orca. e, Physeter macrocephalus. f, Balaenoptera musculus. g, Globicephala macrorhynchus. h, Mesoplodon europaeus. i, Balaenoptera edeni. j, Megaptera novaeangliae.

2012, May 15
398   Block of 10   14.00 14.00
a.-j. A147 120c Any single   1.40   1.40

Women's Dresses — A148

No. 399: a, 175c, Woman. b, 200c, Woman with Aruban flag. c, 200c, Two women dancing. d, 250c, Two women, diff.

2012, June 21
399 A148 Block of 4, #a-d   9.25   9.25

2012 Rembrandt Regatta — A149

No. 400 — Various sailboats: a, 150c, Horiz. b, 150c, Vert. c, 175c, Horiz. d, 175c, Vert. e, 200c, Horiz. f, 200c, Vert.

2012, Aug. 7
400 A149 Block of 6, #a-f   12.00 12.00

A150

A151

A152

A153

A154

A155

A156

Cats — A157

2012, Sept. 20
401 A150 110c multi   1.25   1.25
402 A151 110c multi   1.25   1.25
403 A152 110c multi   1.25   1.25
404 A153 110c multi   1.25   1.25
405 A154 110c multi   1.25   1.25

406	A155	110c multi	1.25 1.25
407	A156	110c multi	1.25 1.25
408	A157	110c multi	1.25 1.25
	Nos. 401-408 (8)		10.00 10.00

Nos. 401-408 were printed in sheets containing two of each stamp and two labels.

Christmas and New Year's Day — A158

No. 409: a, 75c, Ornaments and tree. b, 120c, Gifts and Nativity manger. c, 125c, Candles. d, 210c, Fireworks and champagne flutes.

2012, Oct. 18
409 A158 Block of 4, #a-d   6.00 6.00

A159

A160

A161

A162

A163

A164

A165

A166

A167

Underwater Exploration A168

2012, Nov. 15

410		Block of 10	11.00 11.00
a.	A159	100c multi	1.10 1.10
b.	A160	100c multi	1.10 1.10
c.	A161	100c multi	1.10 1.10
d.	A162	100c multi	1.10 1.10
e.	A163	100c multi	1.10 1.10
f.	A164	100c multi	1.10 1.10
g.	A165	100c multi	1.10 1.10
h.	A166	100c multi	1.10 1.10
i.	A167	100c multi	1.10 1.10
j.	A168	100c multi	1.10 1.10

Orchids — A169

No. 411: a, Laelia xanthina. b, Dendrobium. c, Dendrobium convolutum. d, Brassavola nodosa. e, Rossioglossum grande. f, Cattleya aclandiae. g, Cattleya. h, Epidendrum cinnabarinum. i, Phragmipedium cardinale. j, Phragmipedium. k, Phalaenopsis. l, Cattleya gaskelliana.

2012, Dec. 20
411 A169 200c Block of 12, #a-l   27.00 27.00

Butterflies — A170

Designs: No. 412, 150c, Graphium sarpedon. No. 413, 150c, Danaus plexippus. No. 414, 150c, Danis danis. No. 415, 150c, Pseudacraea boisduvali. No. 416, 150c, Morpho peleides. No. 417, 150c, Scoptes alphaeus. No. 418, 150c, Jumonia oritya. No. 419, 150c, Palla ussheri. No. 420, 150c, Eryphanis polyxena. No. 421, 150c, Diaethria clymena. No. 422, 150c, Colias eurytheme. No. 423, 150c, Anthocharis cardamis.

2013, Jan. 16
412-423 A170 Set of 12   20.00 20.00

Nos. 412-423 were printed in sheets of 24 containing two of each stamp + a central label.

Wedding Dresses — A171

No. 424: a, Brown and green dress. b, Blue gray strapless dress. c, Brown dress with white veil. d, Lilac dress with sash. e, White dress with black ribbon. f, Red dress with gray collar.

2013, Feb. 28
424 A171 200c Block of 6, #a-f 13.50 13.50

Aruban Bank Notes — A172

No. 425: a, 10-florin banknote. b, 25-florin banknote. c, 50-florin banknote. d, 100-florin banknote. e, 500-florin banknote.

2013, Apr. 5

425		Horiz. strip of 5	11.50 11.50
a.-e.	A172	200c Any single	2.25 2.25

Printed in sheets containing two tete-beche strips.

A173

A174

A175

A176

Cruise Ships — A177

2013, May 16

426		Horiz. strip of 5	14.00 14.00
a.	A173	250c multi	2.75 2.75
b.	A174	250c multi	2.75 2.75
c.	A175	250c multi	2.75 2.75
d.	A176	250c multi	2.75 2.75
e.	A177	250c multi	2.75 2.75

No. 426 was printed in sheets containing two tete-beche strips.

A178

Paintings by Frans Hals (c. 1582-1666) — A179

Designs: Nos. 427a, 428a, Jester with a Lute. Nos. 427b, 428b, Singing Boy with a Flute.

2013, June 17
427 A178 500c Horiz. pair, #a-b   11.50 11.50

Souvenir Sheet
428 A179 500c Sheet of 2, #a-b   11.50 11.50

Birds — A180

No. 429: a, Coereba flaveola. b, Aratinga pertinax arubensis. c, Anas bahamensis. d, Zonotrichia capensis. e, Colinus cristatus. f, Columbigallina passerina. g, Egretta thula. h, Icterus icterus. i, Mimus gilvus. j, Pelecanus occidentalis. k, Sterna eurygnatha. l, Athene cunicularia.

2013, Aug. 1
429 A180 167c Block of 12, #a-l   22.50 22.50

Flowers — A181

No. 430: a, Passiflora. b, Canna. c, Bougainvillea. d, Aramyllis. e, Hibiscus. f, Ipomoea. g, Strelitzia. h, Lillium. i, Allamanda. j, Lantana.

2013, Sept. 5   Litho.   *Perf. 14*

430		Block of 10	22.50 22.50
a.-j.	A181	200c Any single	2.25 2.25

Printed in sheets containing two blocks that are tete-beche in relationship to each other.

Shells — A182

No. 431: a, 200c, Tonna maculosa. b, 200c, Nerita versicolor. c, 250c, Tellina radiata. d, 275c, Cymatium caribbaeum. e, 275c, Oliva caribaeensis. f, 300c, Voluta musica.

2013, Oct. 4   Litho.   Perf. 14
431   A182   Block of 6, #a-f   17.00 17.00

Nature Photography A183

No. 432: a, Blenchi, by Eddie Thodé. b, Dos Playa, by Lara Kuiperi. c, Iris, by r. Kock. d, Barancanan di Ayo, by Stan Kuiperi. e, Respeta nos Naturalesa, by Joost Howard. f, Un Tesoro, by Bruce Harms. g, Serenidad, by Melissa Sweerts. h, Cactus Landscape, by Lara Kuiperi. i, Palo di Bonchi, by J. Dania. j, Tres Burico, by Lara Kuiperi.

2013, Nov. 12   Litho.   Perf. 14
432   Block of 10   14.00 14.00
a.-j.   A183 120c Any single   1.40   1.40

Wildlife A184

No. 433: a, Agalychnis calidryas. b, Panthera onca with spotted fur. c, Ara macao. d, Ranitomega benedicta. e, Saimiri sciureus. f, Panthera onca with black fur. g, Ramphastos sulfuratus. h, Saguinus imperator.

2013, Dec. 16   Litho.   Perf. 14
433   Block of 8   16.00 16.00
a.-h.   A184 175c Any single   2.00   2.00

Paintings by Salvador Dalí (1904-89) — A185

No. 435: a, St. James of Compostela, 1957. b, Flores Surrealistas (Gala-Narciso), 1938. c, The Hallucinogenic Toreador, 1968-70. d, The Persistence of Memory, 1931, horiz. e, The Swallow's Tail, 1983, horiz. f, Elephants, 1948, horiz.

2014, Jan. 17   Litho.   Perf. 14
434   Block of 6   18.00 18.00
a.-f.   A185 258c Any single   3.00   3.00

Aruban Carnaval, 60th Anniv. — A186

No. 435: a, 300c, Woman with crown, vert. b, 300c, Woman with mask and feathered headdress, horiz. c, 325c, Woman with headdress, horiz. d, 325c, Woman with headdress and feathers, vert.

2014, Feb. 13   Litho.   Perf. 14
435   A186   Block of 4, #a-d   14.00 14.00

Automobiles A187

No. 436: a, Ford Thunderbird convertible. b, MG Midget convertible. c, Dodge Challenger. d, Ford Crown Victoria. e, Ford Mustang convertible. f, Chevrolet Corvette Sting Ray.

2014, Mar. 14   Litho.   Perf. 14
436   Block of 6   15.00 15.00
a.-f.   A187 225c Any single   2.50   2.50

Birds of Paradise — A188

No. 437: a, Paradisaea rudolphi. b, Lophorina superba, green background. c, Seleucidis melanoleuca. d, Paradisaea apoda. e, Paradisaea minor. f, Lophorina superba, yellow background. g, Ptiloris victoriae. h, Cicinnurus regius. i, Cicinnurus respublica. j, Parotia carolae.

2014, Apr. 24   Litho.   Perf. 14
437   Block of 10   27.50 27.50
a.-j.   A188 250c Any single   2.75   2.75

2014 World Cup Soccer Championships, Brazil — A189

No. 438 — World Cup trophy and: a, Player's foot approaching soccer ball. b, Two players attempting to head ball. c, Player making a diving kick. d, Player dribbling ball. e, Penalty kick. f, Soccer field.

2014, May 29   Litho.   Perf. 14
438   A189 400c Block of 6, #a-f 27.00 27.00

Astronomy — A190

No. 439: a, 350c, Twin planets in circle. b, 350c, Ringed planet. c, 375c, Venus. d, 375c, Star and planets.

2014, June 19   Litho.   Perf. 14
439   A190   Block of 4, #a-d   16.50 16.50

Miniature Sheets

Attacus Atlas — A191

Papilio Cresphontes — A192

No. 440: a, Latin name of moth, "2014," part of wing. b, Head of moth. c, Tip of upper wing. d, Large country name, tip of wing. e, Abdomen of moth, bottom of wing. f, Bottom of wing.

No. 441: a, "2014," "cresphontes," part of wing. b, Parts of wings. c, Edge of top wing. d, Large country name, "Papilio," head of butterfly. e, Abdomen of butterfly. f, Bottom of wing.

2014, Aug. 21   Litho.   Perf. 14
440   A191 200c Sheet of 6, #a-f   13.50 13.50
441   A192 200c Sheet of 6, #a-f   13.50 13.50

Fruit — A193

No. 442: a, Citrullus lanatus. b, Carica papaya. c, Mangifera indica. d, Annona muricata. e, Musa acuminata. f, Cucumis melo. g, Anacardium occidentale. h, Punica granatum.

2014, Sept. 26   Litho.   Perf. 14
442   A193 175c Block of 8, #a-h   16.00 16.00

Christmas A194

No. 443 — Ribbon with bow and: a, Bells. b, Gifts, candles, ornaments. c, Stars. d, Ornaments.

2014, Oct. 23   Litho.   Perf. 14
443   Vert. strip of 4   6.50 6.50
a.   A194 85c multi   .95   .95
b.   A194 130c multi   1.50 1.50
c.   A194 135c multi   1.50 1.50
d.   A194 220c multi   2.50 2.50

Fishing Boats — A195

No. 444: a, 250c, Six boats. b, 275c, Laly. c, 300c, Pikudito and other boats. d, 325c, Phasha and another boat.

2014, Nov. 19   Litho.   Perf. 14
444   A195   Block of 4, #a-d   13.00 13.00

Dutch Royalty — A196

Designs: No. 445, 300c, King Willem-Alexander. No. 446, 300c, Queen Máxima. No. 447, 300c, King Willem-Alexander and Queen Máxima. No. 448, 300c, King Willem-Alexander, Queen Máxima, Queen Beatrix, Princess Catharina-Amalia, Princess Alexia and Princess Ariane. No. 449, 300c, King Willem-Alexander, Queen Máxima, Princess Catharina-Amalia, Princess Alexia and Princess Ariane waving.

2015, Jan. 30   Litho.   Perf. 14
445-449 A196   Set of 5   17.00 17.00

Nos. 445-449 were printed in sheets of 10 containing two of each stamp + 2 labels.

Blue Flowers — A197

Designs: No. 450, 200c, Sisyrinchium angustifolium. No. 451, 200c, Lupinus lepidus. No. 452, 200c, Linum lewisii. No. 453, 200c, Amsonia tabernaemontana. No. 454, 200c, Ipomoea learii. No. 455, 200c, Guaiacum officinale. No. 456, 200c, Gentianopsis crinita. No. 457, 200c, Gentiana andrewsii. No. 458, 200c, Campanulastrum americanum. No. 459, 200c, Campanula rotundifolia.

2015, Feb. 26   Litho.   Perf. 14
450-459 A197   Set of 10   22.50 22.50

Nos. 450-459 were printed in sheets of 20 containing two of each stamp + a central label.

UNICEF — A198

No. 460: a, 225c, Child holding finger of adult. b, 250c, Child's hand on adult's hand. c, 325c, Adult hand holding child's hand. d, 350c, Adult's hands holding child's feet.

2015, Mar. 25   Litho.   Perf. 14
460   A198   Block of 4, #a-d   13.00 13.00

Paintings by Sandro Botticelli (c. 1445-1510) — A199

Paintings or Details: No. 461, The Birth of Venus (De geboorte van Venus). No. 462, The Madonna of the Book (Madonna del Libro). No. 463, Allegorical Portrait of a Woman, Possibly Simonetta Vespucci (Simonetta Vespucci als Maria Lactans). No. 464, The Annunciation (De Blijde Boodschap). No. 465, Madonna of the Magnificat (Madonna del Magnificat).

2015, Mar. 27   Litho.   Perf. 14
461   A199 275c multi   3.25 3.25
462   A199 275c multi   3.25 3.25
463   A199 275c multi   3.25 3.25
464   A199 275c multi   3.25 3.25

465 A199 275c multi   3.25   3.25
   a.   Block of 5, #461-465, + label   16.50   16.50
   Nos. 461-465 (5)   16.25   16.25

Nos. 461-465 were printed in sheets of 10 containing two of each stamp + 2 labels.

Butterflies — A200

No. 466: a, Colias hyale. b, Carcharodus lavatherae. c, Anthocharis cardamines. d, Carcharodus flocciferus. e, Colias palaeno. f, Euchloe ausonia. g, Gonepteryx cleopatra. h, Heteropterus morpheus. i, Ochlodes venatus. j, Pyrgus fritillarius.

2015, June 30   Litho.   *Perf. 14*
466 A200 220c Block of 10,
   #a-j   24.50   24.50

Cave Art — A201

No. 467: a, 350c, Black spirals in circle. b, 350c, Anthromorphic figure with curved arms and legs. c, 375c, Circles connected by lines. d, 375c, Oval with curved lines and dots.

2015, July 31   Litho.   *Perf. 14*
467 A201 Block of 4, #a-d   16.50   16.50

Struthio Camelus — A202

No. 468: a, Juvenile facing right, both feet on ground. b, Chick facing right, one foot raised. c, Adult facing left, bending with neck curved. d, Adult facing left with head up. e, Two chicks. f, Head of chick. g, Head of adult. h, Adult facing right. i, Head of adult near chick. j, Adult and juvenile.

2015, Aug. 28   Litho.   *Perf. 14*
468 A202 225c Block of 10,
   #a-j   25.00   25.00

Beaches — A203

No. 469 — Various beaches: a, 275c. b, 300c. c, 325c. d, 350c.

2015, Sept. 23   Litho.   *Perf. 14*
469 A203 Block of 4, #a-d   14.00   14.00

Historic Buildings — A204

No. 470: a, Old Hotel Colombia (red and white building with damaged wall). b, Quinta del Carmen. c, Eloy Arends Building (City Hall) (green and white building). d, Henriquez House (yellow building with red roof and stairway to second floor). e, Wild Family House (red and white building adjacent to parking lot). f, Former Aruba Bank Building (yellow building with red roof, cactus at right). g, Willem III Tower, Fort Zoutman (red and white tower), vert. h, San Nicolas Watertower (brown and yellow tower), vert.

2015, Oct. 16   Litho.   *Perf. 14*
470 A204 175c Block of 8, #a-
   h   16.00   16.00

Tourist Attractions — A205

No. 471: a, Alto Vista Chapel. b, Cruise liner. c, Bushiribana Gold Mill ruins. d, California Lighthouse. e, Double-decker streetcar. f, Rock formations

2015, Nov. 13   Litho.   *Perf. 14*
471 A205 250c Block of 6, #a-f   17.00   17.00

Fish — A206

Designs: 90c, Black beauty. 130c, Bluehead wrasse. 205c, Longfin damselfish. 220c, Blue Caribbean tang. 320c, Blackbar soldierfish.

Perf. 13¼x12¾
2016, Feb. 29   Litho.
472-476 A206 Set of 5   11.00   11.00

National Symbols — A207

Aruban: No. 477, 500c, Coat of arms. No. 478, 500c, Flag. No. 479, 500c, National anthem.

Perf. 12¾x13¼
2016, Mar. 16   Litho.
477-479 A207 Set of 3   17.00   17.00
   479a   Souvenir sheet of 3,
     #477-479   17.00   17.00

Burrowing Owls — A208

Designs: 140c, Two owls. 200c, One owl. 320c, Three owls. 65c, Owl in flight.

Perf. 13¼x12¾
2016, Mar. 31   Litho.
480-483 A208 Set of 4   15.00   15.00

Butterflies — A209

Designs: 85c, Graphium weiskei. 90c, Papilio glaucus. 100c, Jacoona amrita. 130c, Agrias claudina. 135c, Eunica eurota. 220c,

Papilio palinurus. 320c, Arginnis paphia. 420c, Aglais io.

2016, Apr. 29   Litho.   *Perf. 12¾x13¼*
484-491 A209 Set of 8   17.00   17.00

Medicinal Plants — A210

Designs: 100c, Aloe vera. 130c, Moringa olifera. 220c, Jatropha gossypiifolia. 250c, Lippia alba. 320c, Croton flavens.

2016, May 31   Litho.   *Perf. 12¾x13¼*
492-496 A210 Set of 5   11.50   11.50

2016 Summer Olympics, Rio de Janeiro A211

Designs: 100c, Synchronized swimming. 130c, Swimming. 220c, Sailing. 500c, Abstract design.

Perf. 13¼x12¾
2016, June 30   Litho.
497-500 A211 Set of 4   11.00   11.00

Vegetables — A212

Designs: 90c, Phaseolus vulgaris. 130c, Capsicum annuum. 205c, Cucumis savitus. 220c, Solanum melongena. 320c, Hibiscus esculentus.

2016, July 29   Litho.   *Perf. 12¾x13¼*
501-505 A212 Set of 5   11.00   11.00

Birds — A213

Designs: 50c, Tricolored herons. 85c, Snowy egrets. 90c, Roseate spoonbills. 100c, Blue-winged teals. 130c, Scarlet ibises. 220c, Black skimmers. 250c, Ruby-topaz hummingbird. 325c, Whistling heron.

Perf. 13¼x12¾
2016, Aug. 31   Litho.
506-513 A213 Set of 8   14.00   14.00

Insects A214

Designs: 50c, Odonata anisoptera. 90c, Blattaria periplaneta. 100c, Formicidae solenopsis. 130c, Tettigonia viridissima. 200c, Apis mellifera. 220c, Musca domestica. 275c, Vespula vulgaris. 320c, Psaltoda moerens.

Perf. 13¼x12¾
2016, Sept. 30   Litho.
514-521 A214 Set of 8   15.50   15.50

SEMI-POSTAL STAMPS

Surtax for child welfare organizations unless otherwise stated.

Solidarity
SP1

1986, May 7   Litho.   Perf. 14x13
B1 SP1 30c + 10c shown   1.75   .90
B2 SP1 35c + 15c Three ropes 1.75   .90
B3 SP1 60c + 25c One rope   2.50 1.40
        Nos. B1-B3 (3)   6.00 3.20

Surtax for social and cultural projects.

Child Welfare
SP2

No. B4, Boy, caterpillar. No. B5, Boy, cocoon. No. B6, Girl, butterfly.

1986, Oct. 29   Litho.   Perf. 14x13
B4 SP2 45c + 20c multi   2.50 1.00
B5 SP2 70c + 25c multi   2.75 1.75
B6 SP2 100c + 40c multi   3.50 2.25
        Nos. B4-B6 (3)   8.75 5.00

Christmas
(Child
Welfare)
SP3

No. B7, Boy on beach. No. B8, Drawing Christmas tree. No. B9, Child, creche figures.

1987, Oct. 27   Litho.   Perf. 14x13
B7 SP3 25c +10c multi   1.50   .75
B8 SP3 45c +20c multi   2.00   .90
B9 SP3 70c +30c multi   2.75 1.40
        Nos. B7-B9 (3)   6.25 3.05

Solidarity
SP4

YMCA emblem in various geometric designs.

1988, Aug. 3   Litho.   Perf. 14x13
B10 SP4 45c +20c shown   2.00   .90
B11 SP4 60c +25c multi, diff. 2.00 1.40
B12 SP4 100c +50c multi, diff.2.50 1.90
         Nos. B10-B12 (3)   6.50 4.20

11th YMCA world council.
Surtax for social and cultural projects.

Children's Toys (Child Welfare) — SP5

1988, Oct. 26   Perf. 13x14
B13 SP5 45c +20c Jacks   2.00 1.00
B14 SP5 70c +30c Top   2.00 1.40
B15 SP5 100c +50c Kite   3.00 1.90
         Nos. B13-B15 (3)   7.00 4.30

Child Welfare
SP6

No. B16, Baby spoon. No. B17, Chasing a ball. No. B18, Adult & child holding hands.

1989, Oct. 26   Perf. 14x13
B16 SP6 45c +20c multi   1.75 1.00
B17 SP6 60c +30c multi   2.00 1.00
B18 SP6 100c +50c multi   3.00 1.90
         Nos. B16-B18 (3)   6.75 3.90

Solidarity
SP7

No. B20, Family, house.

1990, July 25
B19 SP7 55c +25c shown   2.00 1.50
B20 SP7 100c +50c multi   3.50 2.50

Surtax for social and cultural projects.

Child Welfare — SP8

Christmas song: No. B21, Wind surfboards. No. B23, Kites, lizard.

1990, Oct. 24   Litho.   Perf. 13x14
B21 SP8 45c +20c multi   1.50   .90
B22 SP8 60c +30c shown   2.00 1.25
B23 SP8 100c +50c multi   3.00 2.25
         Nos. B21-B23 (3)   6.50 4.40

Child Welfare — SP9

Literacy: 45c+25c, Discovery of reading. 60c+35c, Pointing to letter. 100c+50c, Child reading.

1991, Oct. 25   Litho.   Perf. 13x14
B24 SP9 45c +25c multi   1.50 1.25
B25 SP9 60c +35c multi   2.00 1.40
B26 SP9 100c +50c multi   3.00 2.25
         Nos. B24-B26 (3)   6.50 4.90

Solidarity
SP10

55c+30c, Girl scouts, flag & emblem. 100c+50c, Hand holding cancer fund emblem, people.

1992, May 27   Litho.   Perf. 14x13
B27 SP10 55c +30c multi   2.00 1.50
B28 SP10 100c +50c multi 3.00 2.25

Surtax for social and cultural projects.

Postal Services of Aruba, Cent. (Child Welfare) SP11

Designs: 50c+30c, Heart. 70c+35c, Airplane, letters. 100c+55c, Pigeon with letter in beak, vert.

1992, Oct. 30   Litho.   Perf. 14x13
B29 SP11 50c +30c multi   1.75 1.25
B30 SP11 70c +35c multi   2.00 1.40

Perf. 13x14
B31 SP11 100c +50c multi 2.75 2.25
         Nos. B29-B31 (3)   6.50 4.90

Youth Foreign Study Programs (Child Welfare) SP12

Abstract designs of: 50c+30c, Landscapes. 75c+40c, Young man, scenes of other countries, vert. 100c+50c, Integrating cultures.

1993, Oct. 27   Perf. 14x13, 13x14
B32 SP12 50c +30c multi   1.50 1.25
B33 SP12 75c +40c multi   2.00 1.90
B34 SP12 100c +50c multi 2.50 2.25
         Nos. B32-B34 (3)   6.00 5.40

Solidarity
SP13

Intl. Year of the Family: 50c+35c, Family seated, reading, studying. 100c+50c, Family playing in front of house.

1994, May 30   Litho.   Perf. 14x13
B35 SP13 50c +35c multi   1.50 1.25
B36 SP13 100c +50c multi 2.75 2.50

Surtax for social and cultural projects.

Child Welfare
SP14

Designs: 50c+30c, Children on anchor with umbrella. 80c+35c, Children inside Sun. 100c+50c, Child riding owl.

1994, Oct. 27   Litho.   Perf. 14x13
B37 SP14 50c +30c multi   1.75 1.40
B38 SP14 80c +35c multi   2.25 1.90
B39 SP14 100c +50c multi 2.50 2.40
         Nos. B37-B39 (3)   6.50 5.70

Child Welfare — SP15

Children's drawings: 50c+25c, Children with balloons, house. 70c+35c, Three people with picnic basket on sunny day. 100c+50c, People gardening on sunny day.

1995, Oct. 26   Litho.   Perf. 13x14
B40 SP15 50c +25c multi   1.50 1.10
B41 SP15 70c +35c multi   2.00 1.60
B42 SP15 100c +50c multi 3.00 2.25
         Nos. B40-B42 (3)   6.50 4.95

Solidarity — SP16

El Sol Naciente Lodge, 75th Anniv.: 60c+30c, Masonic emblems. 100c+ 50c, Columns, terrestrial and celestial globes.

1996, July 26   Litho.   Perf. 13x14
B43 SP16 60c +30c multi   2.50 1.50
B44 SP16 100c +50c multi 3.50 2.50

Surtax for social and cultural projects (Solidarity)

Child Welfare
SP17

Cartoons: 50c+25c, Mother, baby rabbit waiting at school bus stop. 70c+35c, Mother, baby owl, outside school. 100c+50c, Children flying kite.

1996, Oct. 24   Litho.   Perf. 14x13
B45 SP17 50c +25c multi   1.75 1.25
B46 SP17 70c +35c multi   2.25 1.75
B47 SP17 100c +50c multi 2.50 2.40
         Nos. B45-B47 (3)   6.50 5.40

Child Welfare
SP18

Designs: 50c+25c, Girl sitting among aloe plants. 70c+35c, Boy, butterfly, cactus, vert. 100c+50c, Girl swimming under water, fish, coral.

Perf. 14x13, 13x14
1997, Oct. 23   Litho.
B48 SP18 50c +25c multi   1.50 1.10
B49 SP18 70c +35c multi   2.25 1.90
B50 SP18 100c +50c multi 2.50 2.40
         Nos. B48-B50 (3)   6.25 5.40

Solidarity
SP19

Service Organizations: 60c+30c, Globe, emblem of Lions Intl., wheelchair balanced on map of Aruba. 100c+50c, Child reading book, emblem of Rotary Intl., woman in rocking chair.

1998, May 29   Litho.   Perf. 14x13
B51 SP19 60c +30c multi   2.50 1.50
B52 SP19 100c +50c multi 3.50 2.75

Surtax for social and cultural projects.

Child Welfare — SP20

50c+25c, Girl performing traditional ribbon dance. 80c+40c, Boy playing a cuarta. 100c+50c, Two boys playing basketball.

1998, Oct. 22   Litho.   Perf. 13x14
B53 SP20 50c +25c multi   1.50 1.10
B54 SP20 80c +40c multi   2.25 2.10
B55 SP20 100c +50c multi 3.00 2.40
         Nos. B53-B55 (3)   6.75 5.60

Child Welfare
SP21

Designs: 60c+30c, Child on beach with man with fishing net. 80c+40c, Adult reading to children. 100c+50c, Mother, child, vert.

Left column (ARUBA continued)

Perf. 14x13, 13x14
1999, Oct. 21   Litho.

B56	SP21	60c +30c multi	1.50	1.25
B57	SP21	80c +40c multi	2.25	1.90
B58	SP21	100c +50c multi	2.75	2.40
		Nos. B56-B58 (3)	6.50	5.55

Solidarity
SP22

75c+35c, Children on playground equipment. 100c+50c, Children playing in sand.

2000, Aug. 28   Litho.   Perf. 14x13

B59-B60	SP22	Set of 2	5.00	4.00

Child Welfare
SP23

Children's art: 60c+30c, House with solar collectors. 80c+40c, House, girl, garbage can. 100c+50c, Flying automobiles.

2000, Oct. 26

B61-B63	SP23	Set of 3	7.00	5.75

Child
Welfare — SP24

Intl. Volunteers Year: 40c+20c, Children at crosswalk. 60c+30c, Boys walking dog. 100c+50c, Children depositing trash in can at beach.

2001, Oct. 31   Litho.   Perf. 13x14

B64-B66	SP24	Set of 3	6.25	4.75

Child
Welfare — SP25

Designs: 40c+20c, Boy, iguana and goat. 60c+30c, Girl, hawksbill turtle, red crab, horiz. 100c+50c, Boy, pelicans, parakeet, conch shell.

Perf. 13x14, 14x13
2002, Oct. 31   Litho.

B67-B69	SP25	Set of 3	6.50	5.00

Child Welfare
SP26

Children playing: 40c+20c, Baseball. 60c+30c, Volleyball. 100c+50c, Soccer.

2003, Oct. 31   Litho.   Perf. 14x13

B70-B72	SP26	Set of 3	6.00	6.00

Children's
Welfare — SP27

Children playing: 60c+30c, Maracas. 85c+40c, Steel drum. 100c+50c, Tambourine, wiri.

2004, Oct. 29   Litho.   Perf. 13x14

B73-B75	SP27	Set of 3	5.00	5.00

ASCENSION

ə-'sen_t_-shən

LOCATION — An island in the South Atlantic Ocean, 900 miles from Liberia
GOVT. — A part of the British Crown Colony of St. Helena
AREA — 34 sq. mi.
POP. — 1,117 (1993)

In 1922 Ascension was placed under the administration of the Colonial Office and annexed to the British Crown Colony of St. Helena. The only post office is at Georgetown.

12 Pence = 1 Shilling
20 Shillings = 1 Pound
100 Pence = 1 Pound (1971)

> **Catalogue values for unused stamps in this country are for Never Hinged items, beginning with Scott 50.**

Stamps and Types of St. Helena, 1912-22 Overprinted in Black or Red

Seal of
Colony — A3

1922   Wmk. 4   Perf. 14

1	A9	½p green & blk	8.00	27.50
2	A10	1p green	8.00	27.50
3	A10	1½p rose red	21.00	60.00
4	A9	2p gray & blk	21.00	16.00
5	A9	3p ultra	16.00	28.00
6	A10	8p dl vio & blk	34.00	62.50
7	A10	2sh ultra & blk, *blue*	120.00	150.00
8	A10	3sh vio & blk	175.00	200.00

Wmk. 3

9	A9	1sh blk, *gray grn* (R)	35.00	60.00
		Nos. 1-9 (9)	438.00	631.50
		Set, never hinged	675.00	

Seal of
Colony — A3

1924-33   Typo.   Wmk. 4   Perf. 14
Chalky Paper

10	A3	½p black & gray	6.75	19.00
11	A3	1p green & blk	7.00	17.00
12	A3	1½p rose red	10.00	50.00
13	A3	2p bluish gray & gray	25.00	13.00
14	A3	3p ultra	10.00	19.00
15	A3	4p blk & gray, *yel*	60.00	100.00
16	A3	5p ol & lil ('27)	24.00	29.00
17	A3	6p rose lil & gray	62.50	125.00
18	A3	8p violet & gray	21.00	52.50
19	A3	1sh brown & gray	25.00	62.50
20	A3	2sh ultra & gray, *blue*	72.50	115.00
21	A3	3sh blk & gray, *blue*	110.00	110.00
		Nos. 10-21 (12)	433.75	712.00
		Set, never hinged	675.00	

View of Georgetown — A4

Map of
Ascension — A5

Sooty Tern
Breeding
Colony
A9

Designs: 1½p, Pier at Georgetown. 3p, Long Beach. 5p, Three Sisters. 5sh, Green Mountain.

1934, July 2   Engr.

23	A4	½p violet & blk	1.10	1.00
24	A5	1p lt grn & blk	2.25	1.60
25	A4	1½p red & black	2.25	2.75
26	A5	2p org & black	2.25	3.00
27	A4	3p ultra & blk	2.75	1.90
28	A4	5p blue & black	2.75	4.00
29	A5	8p dk brn & blk	5.25	6.75
30	A9	1sh car & blk	22.50	12.00
31	A5	2sh6p violet & blk	57.50	50.00
32	A4	5sh brown & blk	62.50	70.00
		Nos. 23-32 (10)	161.10	153.00
		Set, never hinged	240.00	

Common Design Types pictured following the introduction.

Silver Jubilee Issue
Common Design Type

1935, May 6   Perf. 11x12

33	CD301	1½p car & dk blue	3.50	12.50
34	CD301	2p blk & ultra	10.00	37.50
35	CD301	5p ind & grn	22.50	30.00
36	CD301	1sh brn vio & indigo	22.50	40.00
		Nos. 33-36 (4)	58.50	120.00
		Set, never hinged	100.00	

25th anniv. of the reign of King George V.

Coronation Issue
Common Design Type

1937, May 19   Perf. 13½x14

37	CD302	1p deep green	.75	1.50
38	CD302	2p deep orange	1.00	.65
39	CD302	3p bright ultra	1.00	.60
		Nos. 37-39 (3)	2.75	2.75
		Set, never hinged	3.50	

Georgetown — A11

Designs: No. 41, 41A, 2p, 4p, Green Mountain. No. 41D, 6p, 10sh, Three Sisters. 1½p, 2sh6p, Pier at Georgetown. 3p, 5sh, Long Beach.

Perf. 13, 13½ (#41, 44, 45), 14 (#43C)
1938-53   Center in Black

40	A11	½p violet ('44)	.80	4.00
		Never hinged	1.50	
a.		Perf. 13½	4.00	4.00
		Never hinged	7.75	
41	A11	1p green	30.00	13.50
		Never hinged	45.00	
41A	A11	1p org yel ('42)	.25	.60
		Never hinged	.45	
b.		Perf. 14 ('49)	.40	16.00
		Never hinged	.70	
c.		Perf. 13½	8.00	9.00
		Never hinged	14.50	
41D	A11	1p green ('49)	.35	1.50
		Never hinged	.60	
42	A11	1½p red ('44)	.65	.80
		Never hinged	1.00	
a.		Perf. 14 ('49)	1.90	13.50
		Never hinged	3.50	
b.		Perf. 13½	5.75	1.40
		Never hinged	8.00	
42C	A11	1½p lilac rose ('53)	.30	6.50
		Never hinged	.55	
d.		Perf. 14 ('49)	1.35	1.10
		Never hinged	2.00	
e.		1½p carmine, perf 14	6.50	6.50
		Never hinged	12.00	
43	A11	2p orange ('44)	.50	.40
		Never hinged	.80	
a.		Perf. 14 ('49)	2.25	37.50
		Never hinged	3.50	

b.		Perf. 13½	5.75	1.00
		Never hinged	8.75	
43C	A11	2p red ('49)	.90	1.90
		Never hinged	1.35	
44	A11	3p ultra	65.00	30.00
		Never hinged	110.00	
44A	A11	3p black ('44)	.35	.80
		Never hinged	.70	
c.		Perf. 13½ ('40)	13.50	4.00
		Never hinged	21.00	
44B	A11	4p ultra ('44)	3.00	3.00
		Never hinged	5.25	
d.		Perf. 13½	10.00	3.75
		Never hinged	17.50	
45	A11	6p gray blue	7.25	2.50
		Never hinged	11.50	
a.		Perf. 13 ('44)	7.50	7.50
		Never hinged	12.50	
46	A11	1sh dk brn ('44)	3.50	2.00
		Never hinged	5.00	
a.		Perf. 13½	13.00	3.00
		Never hinged	22.50	
47	A11	2sh6p car ('44)	20.00	37.50
		Never hinged	30.00	
a.		Perf. 13½	30.00	11.50
		Never hinged	47.50	
b.		Frame printed doubly, one albino	3,750.	
		Never hinged	5,250.	
48	A11	5sh yel brn ('44)	25.00	42.50
		Never hinged	40.00	
a.		Perf. 13½	62.50	11.00
		Never hinged	100.00	
49	A11	10sh red vio ('44)	45.00	62.50
		Never hinged	62.50	
a.		Perf. 13½	65.00	50.00
		Never hinged	120.00	
b.		10sh brt aniline red pur, perf 13	65.00	50.00
		Never hinged	125.00	
		Nos. 40-49 (16)	202.85	210.00
		Set, never hinged	320.00	

> **Catalogue values for unused stamps in this section, from this point to the end of the section, are for Never Hinged items.**

Peace Issue
Common Design Type

Perf. 13½x14
1946, Oct. 21   Engr.   Wmk. 4

50	CD303	2p deep orange	.45	1.15
51	CD303	4p deep blue	.45	.65

Silver Wedding Issue
Common Design Types

1948, Oct. 20   Photo.   Perf. 14x14½

52	CD304	3p black	.55	.45

Engraved; Name Typographed
Perf. 11½x11

53	CD305	10sh red violet	60.00	57.50

> The stamps formerly listed as Nos. 54-56 have been merged into the rest of the George VI definitive series as Nos. 41//43C.

UPU Issue
Common Design Types

Engr.; Name Typo. on Nos. 58, 59
1949, Oct. 10   Perf. 13½, 11x11½

57	CD306	3p rose carmine	1.40	2.00
58	CD307	4p indigo	4.75	1.50
59	CD308	6p olive	1.75	3.50
60	CD309	1sh slate	4.50	3.00
		Nos. 57-60 (4)	12.40	10.00

Coronation Issue
Common Design Type

1953, June 2   Engr.   Perf. 13½x13

61	CD312	3p gray & black	1.25	2.50

Reservoir
A16

Designs: 1p, Map of Ascension. 1½p, Georgetown. 2p, Map showing Ascension between South America and Africa and cable lines. 2½p, Mountain road. 3p, Yellow-billed tropic bird. 4p, Longfinned tuna. 6p, Waves. 7p, Young green turtles. 1sh, Land crab. 2sh6p, Sooty tern (wideawake). 5sh, Perfect Crater. 10sh, View from Northwest.

1956, Nov. 19   Wmk. 4   Perf. 13
Center in Black

62	A16	½p brown	.25	.45
63	A16	1p lilac rose	2.75	1.75
64	A16	1½p orange	.85	.85

65	A16	2p carmine	3.00	1.75
66	A16	2½p org brown	1.50	2.00
67	A16	3p blue	3.75	1.10
68	A16	4p turq blue	1.25	1.75
69	A16	6p dark blue	1.25	2.00
70	A16	7p olive	2.50	1.10
71	A16	1sh scarlet	1.10	1.10
72	A16	2sh6p brown violet	30.00	8.00
73	A16	5sh bright green	40.00	19.00
74	A16	10sh purple	55.00	40.00
		Nos. 62-74 (13)	143.20	80.85

Brown Booby — A17

Birds: 1½p, Black tern. 2p, Fairy tern. 3p, Red-billed tropic bird in flight. 4½p, Brown noddy. 6p, Sooty tern. 7p, Frigate bird. 10p, Blue-faced booby. 1sh, Yellow-billed tropic bird. 1sh6p, Red-billed tropic bird. 2sh6p, Madeiran storm petrel. 5sh, Red-footed booby (brown phase). 10sh, Frigate birds. £1, Red-footed booby (white phase).

Perf. 14x14½

1963, May 23   Photo.   Wmk. 314

75	A17	1p multicolored	1.25	.30
76	A17	1½p multicolored	2.00	1.00
b.		Blue omitted	110.00	
77	A17	2p multicolored	1.60	.30
78	A17	3p multicolored	1.75	.30
79	A17	4½p multicolored	1.75	.30
80	A17	6p multicolored	1.60	.30
81	A17	7p multicolored	1.60	.30
82	A17	10p multicolored	1.60	.30
83	A17	1sh multicolored	1.60	.30
84	A17	1sh6p multicolored	5.00	2.25
		Complete booklet, 4 each #75, 76, 77, 78, 80 and 84, in blocks of 4	90.00	
85	A17	2sh6p multicolored	9.00	11.00
86	A17	5sh multicolored	9.00	11.00
87	A17	10sh multicolored	16.00	12.00
88	A17	£1 multicolored	24.50	13.00
		Nos. 75-88 (14)	78.25	52.65

Freedom from Hunger Issue
Common Design Type

1963, June 4   Wmk. 314

89	CD314	1sh6p car rose	1.00	1.00

Red Cross Centenary Issue
Common Design Type

1963, Sept. 2   Litho.   Perf. 13

90	CD315	3p black & red	3.00	.95
91	CD315	1sh6p ultra & red	5.25	1.75

ITU Issue
Common Design Type

Perf. 11x11½

1965, May 17   Litho.   Wmk. 314

92	CD317	3p mag & violet	.50	.40
93	CD317	6p grnsh bl & brn org	1.40	1.10

Intl. Cooperation Year Issue
Common Design Type

1965, Oct. 25   Wmk. 314   Perf. 14½

94	CD318	1p bl grn & claret	.40	.50
95	CD318	6p lt vio & green	.90	1.00

Churchill Memorial Issue
Common Design Type

1966, Jan. 24   Photo.   Perf. 14
Design in Black, Gold and Carmine Rose

96	CD319	1p bright blue	.50	.25
97	CD319	3p green	1.75	.90
98	CD319	6p brown	2.25	1.50
99	CD319	1sh6p violet	5.50	4.50
		Nos. 96-99 (4)	10.00	7.15

World Cup Soccer Issue
Common Design Type

1966, July 1   Litho.   Perf. 14

100	CD321	3p multicolored	1.00	.55
101	CD321	6p multicolored	1.50	1.25

WHO Headquarters Issue
Common Design Type

1966, Sept. 20   Litho.   Perf. 14

102	CD322	3p multicolored	2.10	1.10
103	CD322	1sh6p multicolored	4.50	2.40

Apollo Satellite Station, Ascension — A18

Wmk. 314

1966, Nov. 7   Photo.   Perf. 14

104	A18	4p purple & black	.25	.25
105	A18	8p blue grn & blk	.25	.25
106	A18	1sh3p brn ol & blk	.25	.25
107	A18	2sh6p brt grnsh blue & black	.40	.40
		Nos. 104-107 (4)	1.15	1.15

Opening of the Apollo communications satellite-earth station, part of the US Apollo program.

UNESCO Anniversary Issue
Common Design Type

1967, Jan. 3   Litho.   Perf. 14

108	CD323	3p "Education"	2.50	1.25
109	CD323	6p "Science"	3.50	1.90
110	CD323	1sh6p "Culture"	5.00	3.00
		Nos. 108-110 (3)	11.00	6.15

BBC Emblem A19

Photo.; Gold Impressed

1967, Dec. 1   Wmk. 314   Perf. 14½

111	A19	1p ultra & gold	.25	.25
112	A19	3p dk green & gold	.25	.25
113	A19	6p brt purple & gold	.25	.25
114	A19	1sh6p brt red & gold	.35	.35
		Nos. 111-114 (4)	1.10	1.10

Opening of the British Broadcasting Company's South Atlantic Relay Station on Ascension Island.

Human Rights Flame and Chain — A20

Perf. 14½x14

1968, July 8   Litho.   Wmk. 314

115	A20	6p org, car & blk	.25	.25
116	A20	1sh6p gray, mag & blk	.30	.30
117	A20	2sh6p brt grn, plum & blk	.40	.40
		Nos. 115-117 (3)	.95	.95

International Human Rights Year.

Blackfish A21

Fish: No. 119, Sailfish. 6p, Oldwife. 8p, Leather jackets. 1sh6p, Yellowtails. 1sh9p, Tuna. 2sh3p, Mako sharks. 2sh11p, Rock hind (jack).

Perf. 13x12½

1968-69   Wmk. 314   Litho.

118	A21	4p brt grnsh bl & blk	.30	.25
119	A21	4p red & multi	.35	.35
120	A21	6p yel olive & multi	.40	.40
121	A21	8p brt rose lil & multi	.60	.45
122	A21	1sh6p brown & multi	2.00	1.90
123	A21	1sh9p emer & multi	1.25	.95

Arms of R.N.S. Rattlesnake A22

124	A21	2sh3p ocher & multi	1.90	1.25
125	A21	2sh11p dp org & multi	3.75	3.25
		Nos. 118-125 (8)	10.55	8.80

Issue dates: No. 119, 6p, 1sh6p, 2sh11p, Mar. 3, 1969; others, Oct. 23, 1968.
See Nos. 130-133.

Coats of Arms of Royal Naval Ships: 9p, Weston. 1sh9p, Undaunted. 2sh3p, Eagle.

Perf. 14x14½

1969, Oct. 1   Photo.   Wmk. 314

126	A22	4p multicolored	.65	.50
127	A22	9p multicolored	.75	.60
128	A22	1sh9p multicolored	1.25	.75
129	A22	2sh3p multicolored	1.40	.85
a.		Min. sheet of 4, #126-129	8.50	8.50
		Nos. 126-129 (4)	4.05	2.70

See Nos. 134-137, 152-159, 166-169.

Fish Type of 1968

Deep-sea fish: 4p, Wahoo. 9p, Coalfish. 1sh9p, Dolphinfishes. 2sh3p, Soldierfish.

1970, Apr. 6   Litho.   Perf. 14

130	A21	4p bluish grn & multi	4.25	2.75
131	A21	9p org & multi	3.25	1.90
132	A21	1sh9p ultra & multi	5.50	3.00
133	A21	2sh3p gray & multi	5.50	3.00
		Nos. 130-133 (4)	18.50	10.65

Naval Arms Type of 1969

4p, Penelope. 9p, Carlisle. 1sh6p, Amphion. 2sh6p, Magpie.

Perf. 12½x12

1970, Sept. 7   Photo.   Wmk. 314

134	A22	4p ultra, gold & blk	1.25	.30
135	A22	9p lt bl, blk, gold & red	1.50	.55
136	A22	1sh6p grnsh bl, gold & blk	1.60	1.50
137	A22	2sh6p lt grnsh bl, gold & blk	2.25	2.10
a.		Miniature sheet of 4, #134-137	12.00	13.50
		Nos. 134-137 (4)	6.60	4.45

Decimal Currency Issue

Tycho Brahe's Observatory, Quadrant and Supernova, 1572 — A23

Man into Space: ½p, Chinese rocket, 1232, vert. 1p, Medieval Arab astronomers, vert. 2p, Galileo, his telescope and drawing of moon, 1609. 2½p, Isaac Newton, telescope and apple. 3½p, Harrison's chronometer and ship, 1735. 4½p, First American manned orbital flight (Project Mercury, 1962, vert.). 5p, Reflector of Palomar telescope and ring nebula in Lyra, Messier 57. 7½p, Jodrell Bank telescope. 10p, Mariner 7, 1969, and telescopic view of Mars. 12½p, Sputnik 2 and dog Laika, 1957. 25p, Astronaut walking in space, 1965 (Gemini 4; vert.). 50p, US astronauts and moon landing module, 1969. £1, Future space research station.

1971, Feb. 15   Litho.   Perf. 14½

138	A23	½p multicolored	.25	.25
139	A23	1p multicolored	.25	.25
140	A23	1½p multicolored	.30	.30
141	A23	2p multicolored	.35	.35
142	A23	2½p multicolored	1.10	.90
143	A23	3½p multicolored	2.25	.90
		Complete booklet, 4 each #138-143	30.00	
144	A23	4½p multicolored	1.50	.95
145	A23	5p multicolored	1.25	.90
146	A23	7½p multicolored	4.00	2.10
147	A23	10p multicolored	4.00	3.50
148	A23	12½p multicolored	5.00	3.75
149	A23	25p multicolored	6.00	3.50

Arms of H.M.S. Phoenix — A24

150	A23	50p multicolored	5.00	4.00
151	A23	£1 multicolored	5.00	5.00
		Nos. 138-151 (14)	36.25	26.65

For overprints see Nos. 189-191.
Booklet also exists with a date of 5/71 on the back cover. Value, $45.

Coats of Arms of Royal Naval Ships: 4p, Milford. 9p, Pelican. 15p, Oberon.

1971, Nov. 15   Photo.   Perf. 13½x13

152	A24	2p gold & multi	1.00	.25
153	A24	4p gold & multi	1.10	.45
154	A24	9p gold & multi	1.50	1.10
155	A24	15p gold & multi	1.60	1.75
a.		Souvenir sheet of 4, #152-155	8.50	8.50
		Nos. 152-155 (4)	5.20	3.55

Naval Arms Type of 1969

1½p, Lowestoft. 3p, Auckland. 6p, Nigeria. 17½p, Bermuda.

1972, May 22   Litho.   Perf. 14x14½

156	A22	1½p bl, gold & blk	.85	.65
157	A22	3p grnsh bl, gold & blk	.95	.70
158	A22	6p grn, gold, blk & bl	1.00	1.00
159	A22	17½p lil, gold, blk & red	1.50	1.75
a.		Miniature sheet of 4, #156-159	4.50	4.50
		Nos. 156-159 (4)	4.30	4.10

Course of Quest — A25

Designs: 4p, Shackleton and "Quest", horiz. 7½p, Shackleton's cabin and Quest in pack ice, horiz. 11p, Shackleton statue, London, and memorial cairn, South Georgia.

1972, Aug. 2   Perf. 14

160	A25	2½p multicolored	.55	.50
161	A25	4p multicolored	.60	.65
162	A25	7½p multicolored	.60	.70
163	A25	11p multicolored	.75	.90
a.		Souvenir sheet of 4, #160-163	3.00	3.00
		Nos. 160-163 (4)	2.50	2.75

Sir Ernest Henry Shackleton (1874-1922), explorer of Antarctica.

Silver Wedding Issue, 1972
Common Design Type

Design: Queen Elizabeth II, Prince Philip, land crab and shark.

1972, Nov. 20   Photo.   Perf. 14x14½

164	CD324	2p violet & multi	.25	.25
165	CD324	16p car rose & multi	.55	.55

Naval Arms Type of 1969

2p, Birmingham. 4p, Cardiff. 9p, Penzance. 13p, Rochester.

1973, May 28   Litho.   Wmk. 314

166	A22	2p blue & multi	2.40	1.50
167	A22	4p yel grn & multi	3.00	1.50
168	A22	9p lt blue & multi	3.75	1.75
169	A22	13p violet & multi	4.25	1.75
a.		Min. sheet of 4, #166-169	26.00	18.00
		Nos. 166-169 (4)	13.40	6.50

Turtles — A26

1973, Aug. 28   *Perf. 13½*
170 A26 4p Green   2.75 1.10
171 A26 9p Loggerhead   3.50 2.25
172 A26 12p Hawksbill   5.00 3.50
   Nos. 170-172 (3)   11.25 6.85

Light Infantry
Marine Sergeant,
1900 — A27

Uniforms (Royal Marines): 6p, Private, 1816. 12p, Officer, Light Infantry, 1880. 20p, Color Sergeant, Artillery, 1910.

1973, Oct. 31   *Perf. 14½*
173 A27 2p multicolored   2.00 1.50
174 A27 6p lt green & multi   3.00 1.90
175 A27 12p lt blue & multi   3.50 2.75
176 A27 20p lt lilac & multi   4.00 3.00
   Nos. 173-176 (4)   12.50 9.15

Departure of the Royal Marines from Ascension, 50th anniv.

Princess Anne's Wedding Issue
Common Design Type

1973, Nov. 14   *Perf. 14*
177 CD325 2p ocher & multi   .25 .25
178 CD325 18p multicolored   .40 .40

Letter
and UPU
Emblem
A29

UPU Cent.: 9p, Emblem and Mercury.

Wmk. 314
1974, Mar. 27   **Litho.**   *Perf. 14½*
179 A29 2p multicolored   .25 .25
180 A29 9p vio blue & multi   .50 .50

Young Churchill
and
Blenheim
Palace
A30

25p, Churchill and UN Headquarters, NYC.

1974, Nov. 30   **Litho.**   **Unwmk.**
181 A30 5p slate grn & multi   .25 .25
182 A30 25p purple & multi   .80 .80
  a. Souvenir sheet of 2, #181-182   2.00 2.25

Sir Winston Churchill (1874-1965).

Skylab over Photograph of Ascension
Taken by Skylab 3 — A31

Skylab Space Station: 18p, Command module and photo of Ascension from Skylab 4.

1975, Mar. 20   **Wmk. 314**   *Perf. 14½*
183 A31 2p multicolored   .25 .25
184 A31 18p multicolored   .80 .80

US Air Force C-141A Starlifter — A32

Aircraft: 5p, Royal Air Force C-130 Hercules. 9p, Vickers VC-10. 24p, U.S. Air Force C-5A Galaxy.

Perf. 13½x14
1975, June 19   **Litho.**   **Wmk. 314**
185 A32 2p multicolored   1.25 .60
186 A32 5p multicolored   1.75 .75
187 A32 9p multicolored   1.75 1.90
188 A32 24p multicolored   2.75 3.75
  a. Souvenir sheet of 4, #185-188   17.00 17.50
   Nos. 185-188 (4)   7.50 7.00

Wideawake Airfield, Ascension Island.

Nos. 144, 148-149
Overprinted

1975, Aug. 18   **Litho.**   *Perf. 14½*
189 A23 4½p multicolored   .30 .30
190 A23 12½p multicolored   .40 .40
191 A23 25p multicolored   .60 .60
   Nos. 189-191 (3)   1.30 1.30

Apollo Soyuz space test project (Russo-American cooperation), launching July 15; link-up, July 17.

HMS
Peruvian
and
Zenobia
Arriving
Oct. 22,
1815
A33

Designs: 5p, Water Supply, Dampiers Drip. 9p, First Landing, Oct. 1815. 15p, The Garden on Green Mountain. All designs after paintings by Isobel McManus.

1975, Oct. 22   **Wmk. 373**   *Perf. 14½*
192 A33 2p lt blue & multi   .25 .25
193 A33 5p lt blue & multi   .25 .25
194 A33 9p red & multi   .40 .40
195 A33 15p red & multi   .75 .75
   Nos. 192-195 (4)   1.65 1.65

British occupation, 160th anniv.

Canaries
A34

2p, Fairy tern, vert. 3p, Waxbills. 4p, Black noddy. 5p, Brown noddy. 6p, Common mynah. 7p, Madeira storm petrels. 8p, Sooty terns. 9p, White booby. 10p, Red-footed booby. 15p, Red-throated francolin. 18p, Brown booby. 25p, Red-billed bo'sun bird. 50p, Yellow-billed bo'sun bird. £1, Ascension frigatebird. £2, Boatswain Island Bird Sanctuary and birds.

Perf. 14x14½, 14½x14
1976, Apr. 26   **Litho.**   **Wmk. 373**
    Size: 35x27mm, 27x35mm
196 A34 1p multi   .50 2.10
197 A34 2p multi   .55 2.10
198 A34 3p multi   .55 2.10
199 A34 4p multi, vert.   .60 2.10
200 A34 5p multi   .75 2.10
201 A34 6p multi   .75 2.10
202 A34 7p multi   .75 2.10
203 A34 8p multi   .75 2.10
204 A34 9p multi, vert.   .75 2.10
205 A34 10p multi   .75 2.10
206 A34 15p multi, vert.   1.50 2.10

---

207 A34 18p multi, vert.   1.50 2.10
208 A34 25p multi   1.60 2.10
209 A34 50p multi   2.25 3.25
210 A34 £1 multi, vert.   2.75 4.00
    Perf. 13½
    Size: 46x33mm
211 A34 £2 multicolored   5.50 5.00
   Nos. 196-211 (16)   21.80 39.55

Great Britain Type A1 with Ascension
Cancel — A35

9p, Ascension #1, vert. 25p, Freighter Southampton Castle.

1976, May 4   *Perf. 13½x14, 14x13½*
212 A35 5p lt brn, car & blk   .25 .25
213 A35 9p gray grn, grn & blk   .25 .25
214 A35 25p blue & multi   .50 .50
   Nos. 212-214 (3)   1.00 1.00

Festival of Stamps 1976. See Tristan da Cunha No. 208a for souvenir sheet that contains one each of Ascension #214, St. Helena #297 and Tristan da Cunha #208.

US
Base
A36

Designs: 9p, NASA Station, Devil's Ashpit. 25p, Viking satellite landing on Mars.

Wmk. 373
1976, July 4   **Litho.**   *Perf. 13½*
215 A36 8p black & multi   .30 .30
216 A36 9p black & multi   .40 .40
217 A36 25p black & multi   .80 1.25
   Nos. 215-217 (3)   1.50 1.95

American Bicentennial. No. 215 also for the 20th anniv. of Bahamas Long Range Proving Ground (extension) Agreement.

Queen in Coronation Coach — A37

Designs: 8p, Prince Philip on Ascension Island, 1957, vert. 12p, Queen leaving Buckingham Palace in coronation coach.

Perf. 14x13½, 13½x14
1977, Feb. 7   **Litho.**   **Wmk. 373**
218 A37 8p multicolored   .25 .25
219 A37 12p multicolored   .25 .25
220 A37 25p multicolored   .35 .35
   Nos. 218-220 (3)   .85 .85

Reign of Queen Elizabeth II, 25th anniv.

Water Pipe in
Tunnel — A38

5p, Breakneck Valley wells. 12p, Break tank in pipe line, horiz. 25p, Dam & reservoir, horiz.

1977, June 27   **Litho.**   *Perf. 14½*
221 A38 3p multicolored   .25 .25
222 A38 5p multicolored   .25 .25
223 A38 12p multicolored   .40 .30
224 A38 25p multicolored   .75 .60
   Nos. 221-224 (4)   1.65 1.40

Water supplies constructed by Royal Marines, 1832 and 1881.

Mars
Bay
Site,
1877
A39

Designs: 8p, Mars Bay and instrument sites. 12p, Prof. and Mrs. Gill before their tent. 25p, Map of Ascension.

Perf. 13½x14
1977, Oct. 3   **Litho.**   **Wmk. 373**
225 A39 3p multicolored   .25 .25
226 A39 8p multicolored   .30 .25
227 A39 12p multicolored   .40 .40
228 A39 25p multicolored   .75 .75
   Nos. 225-228 (4)   1.70 1.65

Centenary of visit of Prof. David Gill (1843-1914), astronomer, to Ascension.

Elizabeth II Coronation Anniversary
Issue
Souvenir Sheet
Common Design Types
Unwmk.

1978, May 21   **Litho.**   *Perf. 15*
229   Sheet of 6   2.25 2.25
  a. CD326 25p Lion of England   .35 .35
  b. CD327 25p Elizabeth II   .35 .35
  c. CD328 25p Green turtle   .35 .35

No. 229 contains 2 se-tenant strips of Nos. 229a-229c, separated by horizontal gutter with commemorative and descriptive inscriptions and showing central part of coronation procession with coach.

East Crater
(Broken
Tooth) — A40

Volcanoes: 5p, Hollands Crater (Hollow Tooth). 12p, Bears Back. 15p, Green Mountain. 25p, Two Boats village.

1978, Sept. 4   **Litho.**   *Perf. 14½*
230 A40 3p multicolored   .25 .25
231 A40 5p multicolored   .25 .25
232 A40 12p multicolored   .40 .40
233 A40 15p multicolored   .50 .50
234 A40 25p multicolored   .80 .80
  a. Souvenir sheet, 2 each #230-234   3.00 4.25
  b. Strip of 5, #230-234   2.00 2.00

No. 234b shows panoramic view of volcanic terrain.

Resolution
A41

Capt. Cook's voyages: 8p, Cook's chronometer. 12p, Green turtle. 25p, Cook after Flaxman/Wedgwood medallion.

Litho.; Litho. & Embossed. (25p)
1979, Jan. 8   *Perf. 11*
235 A41 3p multicolored   .25 .25
236 A41 8p multicolored   .30 .30
237 A41 12p multicolored   .55 .55
238 A41 25p multicolored   .75 1.00
   Nos. 235-238 (4)   1.85 2.10

St. Mary's Church, Georgetown — A42

Designs: 12p, Old map of Ascension Island. 50p, Ascension, by Rembrandt.

Wmk. 373

1979, May 24   Litho.   Perf. 14½
239 A42 8p multicolored   .25   .25
240 A42 12p multicolored   .25   .25
241 A42 50p multicolored   .40   .40
      Nos. 239-241 (3)   .90   .90

Ascension Day.

Landing Cable at Comfortless Cove — A43

Eastern Telegraph Co., 80th anniv.: 8p, Cable Ship Anglia. 12p, Map showing cables across the Atlantic, vert. 15p, Cable-laying ship. 25p, Cable and earth station.

1979, Sept. 15
242 A43 3p rose car & black   .25   .25
243 A43 8p dk yel grn & black   .25   .25
244 A43 12p yel bister & black   .30   .30
245 A43 15p violet & black   .40   .40
246 A43 25p deep org & black   .50   .50
      Nos. 242-246 (5)   1.70   1.70

Ascension No. 45 — A44

1979, Dec. 17   Wmk. 373   Perf. 14
247 A44 3p shown   .25   .25
248 A44 8p No. 73   .25   .25
249 A44 12p No. 14, vert.   .25   .25
250 A44 50p Hill portrait, vert.   .55   .75
      Nos. 247-250 (4)   1.30   1.50

Sir Rowland Hill (1795-1879), originator of penny postage.

Anogramma Ascensionis A45

6p, Xiphopteris ascensionense. 8p, Sporobolus caespitosus. 12p, Sporobolus durus, vert. 18p, Dryopteris ascensionis, vert. 24p, Marattia purpurascens, vert.

1980, Feb. 18   Litho.   Perf. 14½
251 A45 3p shown   .25   .25
252 A45 6p multicolored   .25   .25
253 A45 8p multicolored   .25   .25
254 A45 12p multicolored   .25   .25
255 A45 18p multicolored   .30   .30
256 A45 24p multicolored   .40   .40
      Nos. 251-256 (6)   1.70   1.70

17th Century Bottle Post, London 1980 Emblem A46

12p, 36-gun frigate, 19th century. 15p, "Garth Castle," 1863. 50p, "St. Helena," Lockheed C141.

1980, May 1   Wmk. 373   Perf. 14
257 A46 8p shown   .25   .25
258 A46 12p multicolored   .30   .30
259 A46 15p multicolored   .35   .35
260 A46 50p multicolored   .75   .75
   a. Souvenir sheet of 4, #257-260 1.75   2.25
      Nos. 257-260 (4)   1.65   1.65

London 1980 Intl. Stamp Exhib., May 6-14.

Queen Mother Elizabeth Birthday
Common Design Type

1980, Aug. 11   Litho.   Perf. 14
261 CD330 15p multicolored   .50   .50

Lubbock's Yellowtail A47

10p, Resplendent angelfish. 25p, Hedgehog butterflyfish. 40p, Marmalade razorfish.

1980, Sept. 15   Litho.   Perf. 13½x14
262 A47 3p shown   .40   .40
263 A47 10p multicolored   .50   .50
264 A47 25p multicolored   1.00   .90
265 A47 40p multicolored   1.25   1.50
      Nos. 262-265 (4)   3.15   3.30

Tortoisen, by Thomas Maxon A48

Map of South Atlantic Ridge and Contintental Drift — A49

15p, Wideawake Fair, by Linton Palmer, 1866.

1980, Nov. 17   Perf. 13½, 14 (60p)
266 A48 10p multicolored   .25   .40
267 A48 15p multicolored   .35   .50
268 A49 60p multicolored   1.00   1.40
      Nos. 266-268 (3)   1.60   2.30

Royal Geographical Soc., 50th anniv.

Green Mountain Farm, 1881 — A50

Designs: 15p, Two Boats, 1881. 20p, Green Mountain and Two Boats farms, 1951. 30p, Green Mountain Farm, 1981.

1981, Feb. 15   Litho.   Perf. 14
269 A50 12p multicolored   .25   .25
270 A50 15p multicolored   .30   .30
271 A50 20p multicolored   .30   .30
272 A50 30p multicolored   .40   .40
      Nos. 269-272 (4)   1.25   1.25

Cable and Wireless Earth Station A51

1981, Apr. 27   Litho.   Perf. 14
273 Sheet of 10   4.00   4.00
   a. A51 15p multicolored   .40   .40

Flight of Columbia space shuttle. Gutter contains story of Ascension and space shuttle; margin shows craft and dish antenna.

Poinsettia — A52

2p, Clustererd wax flower. 3p, Kolanchoe, vert. 4p, Yellow pops. 5p, Camel's foot creeper. 8p, White oleander. 10p, Ascension lily, vert. 12p, Coral plant, vert. 15p, Yellow allamanda. 20p, Ascension euphorbia. 30p, Flame of the forest, vert. 40p, Bougainvillea. 50p, Solanum. £1, Ladies petticoat. £2, Red hibiscus.

1981, May 11   Wmk. 373   Perf. 13½
274 A52 1p shown   .90   .90
275 A52 2p multicolored   .70   .95
276 A52 3p multicolored   .70   .95
277 A52 4p multicolored   1.00   .95
278 A52 5p multicolored   1.00   .95
279 A52 8p multicolored   1.00   1.00
280 A52 10p multicolored   .65   .95
281 A52 12p multicolored   2.00   1.10
282 A52 15p multicolored   .75   .95
      Complete booklet, 4 ea. #275,
      276, 280 and 282, in blocks
      of 4   15.00
283 A52 20p multicolored   1.25   .95
284 A52 30p multicolored   1.50   1.60
285 A52 40p multicolored   1.50   3.25

Size: 42x53mm
286 A52 50p multicolored   1.60   3.50
287 A52 £1 multicolored   2.40   4.00
288 A52 £2 multicolored   4.00   7.00
      Nos. 274-288 (15)   20.95 29.00

1982, Aug. 27   Inscribed "1982"
275a A52 2p Clustererd wax flower .60   1.25
276a A52 3p Kolanchoe, vert.   .60   1.25
280a A52 10p Ascension lily, vert. .55   .75
282a A52 15p Yellow allamanda   .60   .75
283a A52 20p Ascension euphorbia 1.25   .75
287a A52 £1 Ladies petticoat   2.25   3.25
      Nos. 275a-287a (6)   5.85   8.00

For overprints see Nos. 321-322.

Linschoten's Map of Ascension, 1599. — A53

Maxwell's Map of Ascension, 1793 — A54

Old maps of Ascension: 12p, Maxwell, 1793, diff. 15p, Eckberg & Chapman, 1811. 40p, Campbell, 1819.

1981, May 22   Perf. 14½
289 A53 Sheet of 4   .60   .60
   a.-d. A54 10p any single   .25   .25
290 A54 10p shown   .25   .25
291 A54 12p multicolored   .35   .35
292 A54 15p multicolored   .40   .40
293 A54 40p multicolored   .75   .75
      Nos. 289-293 (5)   2.35   2.35

Royal Wedding Issue
Common Design Type

1981, July 22   Wmk. 373   Perf. 14
294 CD331 10p Bouquet   .25   .25
295 CD331 15p Charles   .25   .25
296 CD331 50p Couple   .60   .60
      Nos. 294-296 (3)   1.10   1.10

Nos. 294-296 each se-tenant with label.

Man Shining Cannon — A55

1981, Sept. 14   Litho.   Perf. 14
297 A55 5p shown   .25   .25
298 A55 10p Mountain climbing   .25   .25
299 A55 15p First aid treatment   .25   .25
300 A55 40p Duke of Edinburgh   .50   .50
      Nos. 297-300 (4)   1.25   1.25

Duke of Edinburgh's Awards, 25th anniv.

Scouting Year A56

10p, Parallel rope walking. 15p, 1st Ascension scout flag. 25p, Radio operators. 40p, Baden-Powell.

1982, Feb. 22   Litho.   Perf. 14
301 A56 10p multicolored   .25   .35
302 A56 15p multicolored   .40   .50
303 A56 25p multicolored   .60   .75
304 A56 40p multicolored   .75   1.10
   a. Souvenir sheet of 4   2.00   2.00
      Nos. 301-304 (4)   2.00   2.70

No. 304a contains stamps in designs of Nos. 301-304 (30x30mm, perf. 14½, diamond-shape).

Sesquicentennial of Charles Darwin's Visit — A57

1982, Apr. 19
305 A57 10p Portrait   .30   .30
306 A57 12p Pistols   .40   .40
307 A57 15p Rock crab   .55   .55
308 A57 40p Beagle   1.00   1.00
      Nos. 305-308 (4)   2.25   2.25

40th Anniv. of Wideawake Airfield — A58

5p, Fairey Swordfish. 10p, North American B25C Mitchell. 15p, Boeing EC-135N Aria. 50p, Lockheed Hercules.

1982, June 15   Litho.   Perf. 14
309 A58 5p multicolored   .95   .95
310 A58 10p multicolored   1.10   1.10
      Complete booklet, 4 ea. #309
      and 310, in blocks of 4   8.50
311 A58 15p multicolored   1.40   1.40
312 A58 50p multicolored   2.25   2.25
      Nos. 309-312 (4)   5.70   5.70

The cover of the booklet containing Nos. 309 and 310 exists with both brown and blue inscriptions. Same value.

Princess Diana Issue
Common Design Type
Perf. 14½x14

1982, July 1   Wmk. 373
313 CD333 12p Arms   .60   .60
314 CD333 15p Diana   .60   .60
315 CD333 25p Wedding   1.00   1.00
316 CD333 50p Portrait   1.75   1.75
      Nos. 313-316 (4)   3.95   3.95

Christmas and 50th Anniv. of BBC Overseas Broadcasting — A59

Anniv. Emblem and: 5p, Bush House (London headquarters). 10p, Atlantic relay station. 25p, Lord Reith, first director general. 40p, King George V delivering Christmas address, 1932.

1982, Dec. 20   Litho.   Perf. 14
317 A59 5p multicolored   .25 .25
318 A59 10p multicolored   .30 .30
319 A59 25p multicolored   .70 .70
320 A59 40p multicolored   1.10 1.10
        Nos. 317-320 (4)   2.35 2.35

Nos. 282a-283a Overprinted: "1st PARTICIPATION / COMMONWEALTH GAMES 1982"

1982   Litho.   Perf. 13½
321 A52 15p multicolored   .30 .30
322 A52 20p multicolored   .40 .40

12th Commonwealth Games, Brisbane, Australia, Sept. 30-Oct. 9.

A60

7p, Marasmius echinosphaerus. 12p, Chlorophyllum molybdites. 15p, Leucocoprinus cepaestipes. 20p, Lycoperdon marginatum. 50p, Marasmiellus distantifolius.

1983, Mar. 1   Perf. 14
323 A60 7p multicolored   .60 .30
324 A60 12p multicolored   .90 .50
325 A60 15p multicolored   1.00 .60
326 A60 20p multicolored   1.25 .70
327 A60 50p multicolored   1.60 1.75
        Nos. 323-327 (5)   5.35 3.85

View of Georgetown A61

15p, Farm, Green Mountain. 20p, Boatswain Bird Island. 60p, Telemetry Hill.

1983, May 12   Litho.   Perf. 14
328 A61 12p shown   .25 .25
329 A61 15p multicolored   .25 .25
330 A61 20p multicolored   .35 .35
331 A61 60p multicolored   1.00 1.00
        Nos. 328-331 (4)   1.85 1.85

See Nos. 359-362.

Manned Flight Bicentenary — A62

Military Aircraft: 12p, Wessex Five helicopter. 15p, Vulcan B2. 20p, Nimrod MR2P. 60p, Victor K2.

1983, Aug. 1   Wmk. 373   Perf. 14
332 A62 12p multicolored   .90 .75
333 A62 15p multicolored   1.10 .85
334 A62 20p multicolored   1.10 .80
335 A62 60p multicolored   1.75 1.40
        Nos. 332-335 (4)   4.85 3.80

Introduced Species A63

Tellina Antonii Philippi A64

1983, Sept.   Litho.   Wmk. 373
336 A63 12p Iguanid   .45 .40
337 A63 15p Rabbit   .55 .50
338 A63 20p Cat   .65 .60
339 A63 60p Donkey   1.50 1.50
        Nos. 336-339 (4)   3.15 3.00

12p, Nodipecten nodosus. 15p, Cypraea lurida oceanica. 20p, Nerita ascensionis gmelin. 50p, Micromelo undatus.

1983, Nov. 28   Litho.   Perf. 14½
340 A64 7p shown   .25 .25
341 A64 12p multicolored   .35 .35
342 A64 15p multicolored   .45 .45
343 A64 20p multicolored   .60 .60
344 A64 50p multicolored   1.25 1.25
        Nos. 340-344 (5)   2.90 2.90

St. Helena Colony, 150th Anniv. — A65

Designs: First issue inscribed Ascension instead of overprinted.

1984, Jan. 10   Litho.   Perf. 14
345 A65 12p No. 3   .30 .30
346 A65 15p No. 4   .40 .40
347 A65 20p No. 6   .55 .55
348 A65 60p No. 9   1.25 1.25
        Nos. 345-348 (4)   2.50 2.50

Souvenir Sheet

Visit of Prince Andrew — A66

1984, Apr. 10   Perf. 14½x14
349 A66   Sheet of 2   2.00 2.00
   a.   12p Andrew   .25 .25
   b.   70p In naval uniform   1.50 1.50

Lloyd's List Issue
Common Design Type

12p, Naval semaphore. 15p, "Southampton Castle". 20p, Pier Head. 70p, Dane.

1984, May 28
351 CD335 12p multicolored   .50 .25
352 CD335 15p multicolored   .60 .35
353 CD335 20p multicolored   .70 .45
354 CD335 70p multicolored   1.50 1.50
        Nos. 351-354 (4)   3.30 2.55

1984 Coins and Wildlife A67

12p, One penny, yellowfin tuna. 15p, Two pence, donkeys. 20p, Fifty pence, green turtle. 70p, One pound, sooty terns.

1984, June   Perf. 14
355 A67 12p multicolored   .80 .80
356 A67 15p multicolored   1.00 1.00
357 A67 20p multicolored   1.00 1.00
358 A67 70p multicolored   1.75 2.50
        Nos. 355-358 (4)   4.55 5.30

View Type of 1983

12p, Devil's Riding School. 15p, St. Mary's Church. 20p, Two Boats Village. 70p, Ascension Island.

1984, Oct.   Litho.   Wmk. 373
359 A61 12p multicolored   .25 .25
360 A61 15p multicolored   .35 .35
361 A61 20p multicolored   .50 .50
362 A61 70p multicolored   1.75 1.75
        Nos. 359-362 (4)   2.85 2.85

Trees — A68

7p, Bermuda cypress. 12p, Norfolk Island pine. 15p, Screwpine. 20p, Eucalyptus. 65p, Spore tree.

1985, Mar. 8   Litho.   Perf. 14½x14
363 A68 7p multicolored   .65 .55
364 A68 12p multicolored   .70 .60
365 A68 15p multicolored   .85 .70
366 A68 20p multicolored   .90 .90
367 A68 65p multicolored   2.25 2.25
        Nos. 363-367 (5)   5.35 5.00

Military Firearms A69

Large guns and insignia: 12p, Thirty-two pounder small bore muzzle loader, c. 1820; Royal Marines hat plate, c. 1816. 15p, Seven-inch rifled muzzle loader, c. 1866; royal cipher. 20p, Seven-pounder rifled muzzle loader, c. 1877; Royal Artillery badge. 70p, HMS Hood 5.5-inch gun; ship crest.

1985, July 21   Wmk. 373   Perf. 14½
368 A69 12p multicolored   .65 .65
369 A69 15p multicolored   1.00 1.00
370 A69 20p multicolored   1.00 1.00
371 A69 70p multicolored   2.50 2.50
        Nos. 368-371 (4)   5.15 5.15

Queen Mother 85th Birthday
Common Design Type

12p, With Duke of York, Balmoral, 1924. 15p, With Princes Andrew and Edward. 20p, At Ascot. 70p, Christening of Prince Henry, Windsor Castle. 75p, Leaving the QEII, 1968.

Perf. 14½x14
1985, June 7   Wmk. 384
372 CD336 12p multicolored   .55 .55
373 CD336 15p multicolored   .55 .55
374 CD336 20p multicolored   .75 .75
375 CD336 70p multicolored   1.75 1.75
        Nos. 372-375 (4)   3.60 3.60

Souvenir Sheet
376 CD336 75p multicolored   1.75 1.75

Intl. Youth Year, Girl Guides 75th Anniv. — A70

12p, Guides' banner. 15p, First aid. 20p, Camping. 70p, Lady Baden-Powell.

1985, Oct. 4   Wmk. 373
377 A70 12p multicolored   .60 .60
378 A70 15p multicolored   .65 .55
379 A70 20p multicolored   .75 .65
380 A70 70p multicolored   2.00 2.00
        Nos. 377-380 (4)   4.00 3.80

Wildflowers — A71

12p, Clerodendrum fragrans. 15p, Shell ginger. 20p, Cape daisy. 70p, Ginger lily.

Wmk. 384
1985, Dec. 6   Litho.   Perf. 14
381 A71 12p multicolored   .60 .60
382 A71 15p multicolored   .70 .70
383 A71 20p multicolored   .80 .80
384 A71 70p multicolored   1.60 2.00
        Nos. 381-384 (4)   3.70 4.10

Halley's Comet — A72

Designs: 12p, Newton's reflector telescope. 15p, Edmond Halley, Old Greenwich Observatory. 20p, Short's Gregorian telescope, comet, 1759. 70p, ICE space probe, Ascension satellite tracking station.

1986, Mar. 7
385 A72 12p multicolored   .60 .60
386 A72 15p multicolored   .70 .70
387 A72 20p multicolored   .75 .75
388 A72 70p multicolored   2.00 2.50
        Nos. 385-388 (4)   4.05 4.55

Queen Elizabeth II 60th Birthday
Common Design Type

Designs: 7p, Infant photograph, 1926. 15p, 1st worldwide Christmas broadcast, 1952. 20p, Garter Ceremony, Windsor Castle, 1983. 35p, Royal Tour, New Zealand, 1981. £1, Visiting Crown Agents' offices, 1983.

1986, Apr. 21   Perf. 14x14½
389 CD337 7p scarlet, blk & sil   .25 .25
390 CD337 15p ultra, blk & sil   .35 .35
391 CD337 20p green & multi   .45 .45
392 CD337 35p violet & multi   .50 .50
393 CD337 £1 rose vio & multi   1.25 1.25
        Nos. 389-393 (5)   2.80 2.80

For overprints see Nos. 431-435.

AMERIPEX '86 — A73

1986, May 22   Perf. 14½
394 A73 12p No. 183   .40 .40
395 A73 15p No. 260   .60 .60
396 A73 20p No. 215   .75 .75
397 A73 70p No. 310   1.50 1.50
        Nos. 394-397 (4)   3.25 3.25

Souvenir Sheet
398 A73 75p Statue of Liberty,
           New York Harbor   3.50 3.50

Statue of Liberty, cent.

Royal Wedding Issue, 1986
Common Design Type

Designs: 15p, Couple kissing. 35p, Andrew in navy uniform, helicopter.

Wmk. 384

1986, July 23		**Litho.**	**Perf. 14**	
399	CD338	15p multicolored	.50	.50
400	CD338	35p multicolored	1.10	1.10

Ships
A74

1p, Ganymede, c. 1811. 2p, Kangaroo, c. 1811. 4p, Trinculo, c. 1811. 5p, Daring, c. 1811. 9p, Thais, c. 1811. 10p, Pheasant, 1819. 15p, Myrmidon, 1819. 18p, Atholl, 1825. 20p, Medina, 1830. 25p, Saracen, 1840. 30p, Hydra, c. 1845. 50p, Sealark, 1840. 70p, Rattlesnake, 1868. £1, Penelope, 1889. £2, Monarch, 1897.

1986, Oct. 14		**Wmk. 384**	**Perf. 14½**	
401	A74	1p multicolored	.90	1.25
402	A74	2p multicolored	1.00	1.25
403	A74	4p multicolored	1.00	1.25
404	A74	5p multicolored	1.00	1.25
405	A74	9p multicolored	1.10	1.25
406	A74	10p multicolored	1.10	1.25
407	A74	15p multicolored	1.25	1.75
408	A74	18p multicolored	1.25	1.75
409	A74	20p multicolored	1.25	1.75
410	A74	25p multicolored	1.25	2.00
411	A74	30p multicolored	1.25	2.00
412	A74	50p multicolored	1.75	2.75
413	A74	70p multicolored	2.50	3.25
414	A74	£1 multicolored	3.50	4.25
415	A74	£2 multicolored	6.50	8.00
		Nos. 401-415 (15)	26.60	35.00

For surcharges see Nos. 502-504.

Edible Bush Fruits
A75

1987, Jan. 29			**Perf. 14**	
416	A75	12p Cape gooseberry	.90	.90
417	A75	15p Prickly pear	1.00	1.00
418	A75	20p Guava	1.10	1.10
419	A75	70p Loquat	2.00	2.00
		Nos. 416-419 (4)	5.00	5.00

1st American Manned Orbital Space Flight, 25th Anniv. — A76

15p, Ignition. 18p, Lift-off. 25p, Reentry. £1, Splashdown. 70p, Friendship 7 capsule.

1987, Mar. 30				
420	A76	15p multicolored	.85	.85
421	A76	18p multicolored	.95	.95
422	A76	25p multicolored	1.25	1.25
423	A76	£1 multicolored	4.00	4.00
		Nos. 420-423 (4)	7.05	7.05

Souvenir Sheet

424	A76	70p multicolored	2.50	2.50

Military Uniforms, 1815-20 — A77

Designs: a, Captains in full dress, 1st landing on Ascension. b, Surgeon and sailors at campsite. c, Seaman returning from Dampier's Drip with water supply. d, Midshipman at lookout post. e, Commander and surveyor.

1987, June 29				
425		Strip of 5	5.00	5.00
a.-e.	A77	25p multicolored	.85	.85

See Nos. 458, 482, 507.

Butterflies
A78

1987, Aug. 10			**Perf. 14½**	
426	A78	15p Painted lady	1.10	1.10
427	A78	18p Monarch	1.10	1.10
428	A78	25p Diadem	1.50	1.50
429	A78	£1 Long-tailed blue	4.00	4.00
		Nos. 426-429 (4)	7.70	7.70

See Nos. 436-439, 459-462.

Birds — A79

Designs: a, Ascension frigatebirds (males). b, Brown booby, frigatebird, white boobies. c, Frigatebird, white booby. d, Ascension frigatebirds (females). e, Adult frigatebird feeding young.

1987, Oct. 8		**Wmk. 373**	**Perf. 14**	
430		Strip of 5	12.00	12.00
a.-e.	A79	25p any single	2.00	2.00

No. 430 has continuous design.
See No. 453.

Nos. 389-393 Ovptd. "40TH WEDDING ANNIVERSARY" in Silver
Perf. 14x14½

1987, Dec. 7		**Wmk. 384**		
431	CD337	7p scar, blk & sil	.25	.25
432	CD337	15p ultra, blk & sil	.30	.30
433	CD337	20p green & multi	.50	.50
434	CD337	35p violet & multi	.75	.75
435	CD337	£1 rose vio & multi	2.00	2.00
		Nos. 431-435 (5)	3.80	3.80

40th wedding anniv. of Queen Elizabeth II and Prince Philip.

Insects Type of 1987

15p, Field cricket. 18p, Bush cricket. 25p, Ladybug. £1, Burnished brass moth.

1988, Jan. 18			**Perf. 14½**	
436	A78	15p multicolored	.80	.80
437	A78	18p multicolored	.90	.90
438	A78	25p multicolored	1.25	1.25
439	A78	£1 multicolored	4.25	4.25
		Nos. 436-439 (4)	7.20	7.20

Capt. William Bate (d. 1838), 1st Garrison Commander and Colonial Founder of Ascension
A80

Designs: 9p, Bate's Memorial, St. Mary's Church. 15p, Commodore's Cottage, Cross Hill. 18p, North East or Bate's Cottage, 1833. 25p, Landmarks on map. 70p, Bate and 3 soldiers.

1988, Apr. 14		**Litho.**	**Perf. 14**	
440	A80	9p multicolored	.30	.30
441	A80	15p multicolored	.50	.50
442	A80	18p multicolored	.60	.60
443	A80	25p multicolored	.85	.85
444	A80	70p multicolored	2.00	2.00
		Nos. 440-444 (5)	4.25	4.25

Australia Bicentennial Emblem and Ships Named HMS Resolution — A81

9p, 3-Masted squarerigger, 1667. 18p, 3-Masted squarerigger, 1772. 25p, Navy cruiser, 1892. 65p, Battleship, 1916.

1988, June 23		**Litho.**	**Perf. 14**	
445	A81	9p multicolored	1.25	.50
446	A81	18p multicolored	1.75	.80
447	A81	25p multicolored	2.00	1.10
448	A81	65p multicolored	3.50	2.50
		Nos. 445-448 (4)	8.50	4.90

Australia bicentennial.

Nos. 445-448 Overprinted

Wmk. 384

1988, July 30		**Litho.**	**Perf. 14**	
449	A81	9p multicolored	.75	.55
450	A81	18p multicolored	1.25	.90
451	A81	25p multicolored	1.25	.95
452	A81	65p multicolored	2.50	2.50
		Nos. 449-452 (4)	5.75	4.90

SYDPEX '88, July 30-Aug. 7.

Bird Type of 1987

Behaviors of the wideawake tern, Sterna fuscata: a, Two adults, flock overhead. b, Nesting (two birds). c, Nesting (three birds). d, Adult and young. e, Tern flapping its wings.

1988, Aug. 15			**Perf. 14**	
453		Strip of 5	10.00	10.00
a.-e.	A79	25p any single	1.90	1.90

No. 453 has continuous design.

Lloyds of London, 300th Anniv.
Common Design Type

8p, Lloyd's Coffee House, Tower Street, 1688. 18p, Cable ship Alert, horiz. 25p, Satellite recovery in space, horiz. 65p, Ship Good Hope Castle on fire off Ascension, 1973.

Wmk. 373

1988, Oct. 17		**Litho.**	**Perf. 14**	
454	CD341	8p multicolored	.40	.40
455	CD341	18p multicolored	.85	.85
456	CD341	25p multicolored	1.25	1.25
457	CD341	65p multicolored	2.50	2.50
		Nos. 454-457 (4)	5.00	5.00

Military Uniforms Type of 1987

Uniforms of the Royal Marines: a, Marines arrive in Ascension (marines), 1821. b, Semaphore station (officer, marine), 1829. c, Octagonal tank (sergeant), 1831. d, Water pipe tunnel (officers), 1833. e, Constructing barracks (officer), 1834.

1988, Nov. 21				
458		Strip of 5	8.50	8.50
a.-e.	A77	25p multicolored	1.50	1.50

Insect Type of 1987
Wmk. 384

1989, Jan. 16		**Litho.**	**Perf. 14½**	
459	A78	15p Plume moth	1.40	.85
460	A78	18p Green bottle	1.40	.85
461	A78	25p Weevil	1.10	1.10
462	A78	£1 Paper wasp	5.25	3.50
		Nos. 459-462 (4)	9.15	6.40

Land Crabs, Gecarcinus Lagostoma — A82

1989, Apr. 17				
463	A82	15p multicolored	.75	.75
464	A82	18p multi, diff.	.80	.80
465	A82	25p multi, diff.	1.25	1.25
466	A82	£1 multi, diff.	4.25	4.25
		Nos. 463-466 (4)	7.05	7.05

Background designs continuous

467	A82	15p multicolored	.55	.55
467A	A82	18p multi, diff.	.75	.75
467B	A82	25p multi, diff.	.95	.95
467C	A82	£1 multi, diff.	4.25	4.25
d.		Souvenir sheet of 4, #467-467C	8.00	8.00

Moon Landing, 20th Anniv.
Common Design Type

Apollo 7: 15p, Tracking Station, Ascension Is. 18p, Launch, Cape Kennedy. 25p, Mission emblem. 70p, Expended Saturn IVB stage. £1, Lunar landing profile for the Apollo 11 mission.

1989, July 20			**Perf. 14x13½**	
Size of Nos. 469-470: 29x29mm				
468	CD342	15p multicolored	.90	.65
469	CD342	18p multicolored	1.00	.75
470	CD342	25p multicolored	1.25	.95
471	CD342	70p multicolored	2.25	2.25
		Nos. 468-471 (4)	5.40	4.60

Souvenir Sheet

472	CD342	£1 multicolored	4.00	4.00

Souvenir Sheet

A83

1989, July 7			**Perf. 14x13½**	
473	A83	75p Emblems, No. 60	4.50	4.50

Miniature Sheet

World Stamp Expo '89, Washington, DC, and PHILEXFRANCE '89, Paris — A84

The Statue of Liberty and scenes from the centenary celebrations, 1986: a, Operation Sail. b, Face. c, Upper body. d, Three crown points. e, Ships in harbor, view of lower Manhattan. f, Ship in port, New York City.

1989, Aug. 21			**Wmk. 373**	
474	A84	Sheet of 6	5.25	5.25
a.-f.		15p any single	.75	.75

Devil's Ashpit Tracking Station A85

1989, Sept. 30   Wmk. 384   Perf. 14
475	Sheet, 5 each #a.-b.	10.50	10.50
a.	A85 18p shown	.70	.70
b.	A85 25p US space shuttle launch	1.10	1.10

Termination of NASA tracking operations, begun in 1965, at the station.

Shells and Mollusks A86

Designs: 8p, Strombus latus. 18p, Tonna galea. 25p, Harpa doris. £1, Charonia variegata.

Wmk. 384
1989, Nov. 6   Litho.   Perf. 14
476	A86	8p multicolored	.70	.45
477	A86	18p multicolored	1.25	.65
478	A86	25p multicolored	1.75	.90
479	A86	£1 multicolored	4.50	3.75
	Nos. 476-479 (4)		8.20	5.75

Donkeys — A87

Perf. 14 on 3 Sides
1989, Nov. 17   Litho.   Wmk. 384
Booklet Stamps
480	A87	18p shown	.80	1.00
a.		Booklet pane of 6	5.00	
481	A87	18p Green turtle	1.00	1.00
a.		Booklet pane of 4	4.25	

No. 480a sold for £1.

Military Type of 1987

Royal Navy equipment, c. 1815-1820: a, Seaman's pistol, hat, cutlass. b, Midshipman's belt buckle, button, sword, hat. c, Surgeon's hat, sword, instrument chest. d, Captain's hat, telescope, sword. e, Admiral's epaulet, megaphone, hat, pocket.

1990, Feb. 12   Litho.   Perf. 14
482	Strip of 5	6.50	6.50
a.-e.	A77 25p any single	1.10	1.10

World Wildlife Fund — A88

Frigate birds (Fregata aquila): 9p, Family group. 10p, Chick. 11p, Male in flight. 15p, Female and immature in flight.

Perf. 14½x14
1990, Mar. 5   Litho.   Wmk. 373
483	A88	9p multicolored	4.00	1.25
484	A88	10p multicolored	4.00	1.50
485	A88	11p multicolored	4.00	1.75
486	A88	15p multicolored	4.00	2.25
	Nos. 483-486 (4)		16.00	6.75

Great Britain Nos. 1-2 A89

Exhibition emblem and: 18p, Early Ascension cancellations. 25p, Unloading mail at

Wideawake Airfield. £1, Main P.O., Royal Mail van.

1990, May 3   Litho.   Perf. 14
487	A89	9p shown	.55	.55
488	A89	18p multicolored	.90	.90
489	A89	25p multicolored	1.25	1.25
490	A89	£1 multicolored	4.50	4.50
	Nos. 487-490 (4)		7.20	7.20

Penny Black 150th anniv., Stamp World London '90.

Queen Mother, 90th Birthday
Common Design Types

25p, Portrait, 1940. £1, King, Queen with soldiers.

1990, Aug. 4   Wmk. 384   Perf. 14x15
491	CD343 25p multi	1.25	1.40

Perf. 14½
492	CD344 £1 multi	3.50	4.25

Garth Castle, 1910 — A90

Designs: 18p, RMS St. Helena, 1982. 25p, Launching new RMS St. Helena, 1989. 70p, Duke of York launching new RMS St. Helena. £1, New RMS St. Helena.

Wmk. 373
1990, Sept. 13   Litho.   Perf. 14½
493	A90	9p multicolored	1.40	1.40
494	A90	18p multicolored	1.75	1.75
495	A90	25p multicolored	2.75	2.75
496	A90	70p multicolored	4.75	4.75
	Nos. 493-496 (4)		10.65	10.65

Souvenir Sheet
497	A90	£1 multicolored	7.50	7.50

See St. Helena Nos. 535-539, Tristan da Cunha Nos. 482-486.

Christmas — A91

Sculpture (8p) and paintings of Madonna and Child by: 8p, Felici. 18p, Unknown artist. 25p, Gebhard. 65p, Gritti.

1990, Oct. 24   Perf. 14
498	A91	8p multicolored	1.10	.80
499	A91	18p multicolored	1.90	1.40
500	A91	25p multicolored	2.75	1.90
501	A91	65p multicolored	4.25	4.25
	Nos. 498-501 (4)		10.00	8.35

Nos. 410, 412 & 414 Ovptd. in Silver "BRITISH FOR 175 YEARS"

1991, Feb. 5   Wmk. 384   Perf. 14½
502	A74	25p on #410	3.00	3.00
503	A74	50p on #412	3.50	3.50
504	A74	£1 on #414	4.75	4.75
	Nos. 502-504 (3)		11.25	11.25

Elizabeth & Philip, Birthdays
Common Design Types

1991, June 18
505	CD345	25p multicolored	1.40	1.60
506	CD346	25p multicolored	1.40	1.60
a.		Pair, #505-506 + label	3.50	3.75

Military Uniforms Type of 1987

Royal Marines Equipment 1821-1844: a, Officer's shako, epaulettes, belt plate, button. b, Officer's cap, sword, epaulettes, belt plate. c, Drum Major's shako with cords, staff. d, Sergeant's shako, chevrons, belt plate, canteen. e, Drummer's drum, sticks, shako.

1991, Aug. 1   Wmk. 373   Perf. 14
507	A77	25p Strip of 5, #a.-e.	10.00	10.00

Atlantic Relay Station, 25th anniv. A92

15p, BBC Atlantic relay station. 18p, English Bay transmitters. 25p, Satellite receiving station. 70p, Antenna support tower.

1991, Sept. 17   Wmk. 384   Perf. 14½
508	A92	15p multi	1.40	1.40
509	A92	18p multi	1.60	1.60
510	A92	25p multi, vert.	2.00	2.00
511	A92	70p multi, vert.	4.50	4.50
	Nos. 508-511 (4)		9.50	9.50

Christmas A93

Designs: 8p, St. Mary's Church, exterior. 18p, St. Mary's Church, interior. 25p, Grotto of Our Lady of Ascension, exterior. 65p, Grotto of Our Lady of Ascension, interior.

1991, Oct. 1   Perf. 14
512	A93	8p multicolored	.95	.80
513	A93	18p multicolored	1.75	1.40
514	A93	25p multicolored	2.25	1.95
515	A93	65p multicolored	4.25	5.00
	Nos. 512-515 (4)		9.20	8.95

Fish A94

1p, Blackfish. 2p, Five finger. 4p, Resplendent angelfish. 5p, Silver fish. 9p, Gurnard. 10p, Blue dad. 15p, Cunning fish. 18p, Grouper. 20p, Moray eel. 25p, Hardback soldierfish. 30p, Blue marlin. 50p, Wahoo. 70p, Yellowfin tuna. £1, Blue shark. £2.50, Bottlenose dolphin.

Wmk. 373
1991, Dec. 10   Litho.   Perf. 14
516	A94	1p multi	.70	.70
517	A94	2p multi	1.00	.75
518	A94	4p multi	1.10	.95
519	A94	5p multi	1.10	.95
520	A94	9p multi	1.50	1.10
521	A94	10p multi	1.50	1.10
522	A94	15p multi	2.00	1.10
523	A94	18p multi	2.00	1.25
524	A94	20p multi	2.00	1.50
525	A94	25p multi	2.00	1.60
526	A94	30p multi	2.00	1.75
527	A94	50p multi	2.50	2.50
528	A94	70p multi	3.25	4.00
529	A94	£1 multi	3.75	4.50
530	A94	£2.50 multi	7.50	9.50
	Nos. 516-530 (15)		33.90	33.25

Queen Elizabeth II's Accession to the Throne, 40th Anniv.
Common Design Type

Wmk. 373
1992, Feb. 6   Litho.   Perf. 14
531	CD349	9p multicolored	.45	.45
532	CD349	15p multicolored	.75	.75
533	CD349	18p multicolored	.90	.90
534	CD349	25p multicolored	1.25	1.25
535	CD349	70p multicolored	3.00	3.00
	Nos. 531-535 (5)		6.35	6.35

Discovery of America, 500th Anniv. — A95

9p, STV Eye of the Wind. 18p, STV Soren Larsen. 25p, Pinta, Santa Maria, & Nina. 70p, Columbus, Santa Maria.

Wmk. 373
1992, Feb. 18   Litho.   Perf. 14
536	A95	9p multicolored	1.50	.65
537	A95	18p multicolored	2.50	.95
538	A95	25p multicolored	3.00	1.25
539	A95	70p multicolored	5.75	2.75
	Nos. 536-539 (4)		12.75	5.60

World Columbian Stamp Expo '92, Chicago and Genoa '92 Intl. Philatelic Exhibitions.

Wideawake Airfield, 50th Anniv. — A96

15p, Control tower. 18p, Nose hangar. 25p, Construction work. 70p, Laying fuel pipeline.

Wmk. 373
1992, May 5   Litho.   Perf. 14
540	A96	15p multicolored	.95	.95
541	A96	18p multicolored	1.25	1.25
542	A96	25p multicolored	1.50	1.50
543	A96	70p multicolored	3.75	3.75
	Nos. 540-543 (4)		7.45	7.45

Ascension's Participation in Falkland Islands' Liberation, 10th Anniv. — A97

15p, Nimrod Mk.2. 18p, VC10. 25p, Wessex HU Mk.5 helicopter. 65p, Vulcan B2.
No. 548a, 15p + 3p like #544. b, 18p + 4p like #545. c, 25p + 5p like #546. d, 65p + 13p like #547.

Wmk. 373
1992, June 12   Litho.   Perf. 14
544	A97	15p multicolored	1.25	1.10
545	A97	18p multicolored	1.25	1.10
546	A97	25p multicolored	1.90	1.50
547	A97	65p multicolored	3.00	3.50
	Nos. 544-547 (4)		7.40	7.20

Souvenir Sheet
548	A97	Sheet of 4, #a.-d.	8.50	8.50

Surtax for Soldiers', Sailors' and Airmen's Families Association.

Christmas A98

Children's drawings: 8p, Snowman, rocks, candle. 18p, Underwater Santa, Christmas tree. 25p, Hello, bells. 65p, Nativity Scene, angel.

Wmk. 384
1992, Oct. 13   Litho.   Perf. 14
549	A98	8p multicolored	1.10	.90
550	A98	18p multicolored	1.60	1.25
551	A98	25p multicolored	1.90	1.50
552	A98	65p multicolored	3.75	3.75
	Nos. 549-552 (4)		8.35	7.40

Yellow Canary — A99

15p, Singing male. 18p, Adult male, female. 25p, Young calling for food. 70p, Mixed flock.

Wmk. 373

1993, Jan. 12   **Litho.**   *Perf. 14½*
553	A99	15p multicolored	1.25	1.25
554	A99	18p multicolored	1.40	1.40
555	A99	25p multicolored	1.75	1.75
556	A99	70p multicolored	4.50	4.50
		Nos. 553-556 (4)	8.90	8.90

Royal Air Force, 75th Anniv.
Common Design Type

Designs: 20p, Sopwith Snipe. No. 558, Supermarine Southampton. 30p, Avro Anson. 70p, Vickers Wellington 1C.

No. 561a, Westland Lysander. b, Gloster Meteor. c, DeHavilland Comet. d, British Aerospace Nimrod.

Wmk. 373

1993, Apr. 1   **Litho.**   *Perf. 14*
557	CD350	20p multicolored	2.10	1.50
558	CD350	25p multicolored	2.10	1.50
559	CD350	30p multicolored	2.25	1.60
560	CD350	70p multicolored	4.00	4.00
		Nos. 557-560 (4)	10.45	8.60

Souvenir Sheet

561	CD350	25p Sheet of 4, #a.-d.	6.25	6.25

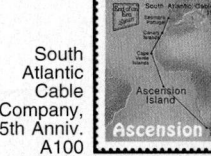

South Atlantic Cable Company, 25th Anniv. A100

Designs: 20p, Map showing cable route. 25p, Cable ship laying cable. 30p, Map of Ascension. 70p, Cable ship off Ascension.

Perf. 14x14½
1993, June 8   **Litho.**   **Wmk. 384**
562	A100	20p multicolored	1.25	1.25
563	A100	25p multicolored	1.50	1.50
564	A100	30p multicolored	1.75	1.75
565	A100	70p multicolored	4.00	4.00
		Nos. 562-565 (4)	8.50	8.50

Flowers A101

Perf. 14x14½
1993, Aug. 3   **Litho.**   **Wmk. 384**
566	A101	20p Lantana camara	1.50	.75
567	A101	25p Moonflower	1.75	.97
568	A101	30p Hibiscus	1.75	1.10
569	A101	70p Frangipani	4.00	3.50
		Nos. 566-569 (4)	9.00	6.32

Christmas A102

Designs: 12p, Child mailing Christmas card. 20p, Mail loaded onto Tristar. 25p, Plane in flight. 30p, Mail unloaded at Wideawake Airfield. 65p, Child reading card, Georgetown.

Perf. 14½x14
1993, Oct. 19   **Wmk. 373**
570	A102	12p multicolored	.75	.40
571	A102	20p multicolored	1.25	.45
572	A102	25p multicolored	1.40	.50
573	A102	30p multicolored	2.25	2.25
574	A102	65p multicolored	2.75	2.75
a.		Souvenir sheet of 5, #570-574	12.00	12.00
		Nos. 570-574 (5)	8.40	6.35

Stamps from No. 574a show a continuous design, while Nos. 570-574 have white borders on sides.

Prehistoric Aquatic Reptiles — A103

12p, Ichthyosaurus. 20p, Metriorhynchus. 25p, Mosasaurus. 30p, Elasmosaurus. 65p, Plesiosaurus.

1994, Jan. 25   **Wmk. 373**   *Perf. 14*
575	A103	12p multi	1.10	1.10
576	A103	20p multi	1.35	1.35
577	A103	25p multi	1.60	1.60
578	A103	30p multi	1.60	1.60
579	A103	65p multi	3.00	3.00
		Nos. 575-579 (5)	8.65	8.65

Ovptd. with Hong Kong '94 Emblem

1994, Feb. 18
580	A103	12p on #575	1.10	1.10
581	A103	20p on #576	1.75	1.75
582	A103	25p on #577	1.75	1.75
583	A103	30p on #578	1.90	1.90
584	A103	65p on #579	3.25	3.25
		Nos. 580-584 (5)	9.75	9.75

Green Turtle A104

20p, Four on beach. 25p, Crawling in sand. No. 587, Crawling from sea. 65p, Swimming. No. 589a, Side view, crawling from sea. b, Digging nest. c, Hatchlings heading to sea. d, Digging nest, diff.

1994, Mar. 22
585	A104	20p multicolored	2.25	2.25
586	A104	25p multicolored	2.75	2.75
587	A104	30p multicolored	2.75	2.75
588	A104	65p multicolored	4.25	4.00
		Nos. 585-588 (4)	12.00	11.75

Souvenir Sheet

589	A104	30p Sheet of 4, #a.-d.	14.00	14.00

Civilian Ships A105

Ships serving during Falkland Islands War, 1982: 20p, Tug Yorkshireman. 25p, Minesweeper support ship RMS St. Helena. 30p, Oil tanker British ESK. 65p, Cruise liner Uganda, hospital ship.

1994, June 14
590	A105	20p multicolored	2.75	2.75
591	A105	25p multicolored	3.00	3.00
592	A105	30p multicolored	3.00	3.00
593	A105	65p multicolored	5.25	5.25
		Nos. 590-593 (4)	14.00	14.00

Sooty Tern A106

1994, Aug. 16
594	A106	20p Chick	1.50	1.50
595	A106	25p Juvenile	1.60	1.60
596	A106	30p Brooding adult	1.90	1.90
597	A106	65p Displaying male	3.00	3.00
		Nos. 594-597 (4)	8.00	8.00

Souvenir Sheet

598	A106	£1 Dread	7.25	7.25

Christmas A107

Donkeys: 12p, Mare with foal. 20p, Young adult. 25p, Foal. 30p, Adult, egrets. 65p, Adult.

1994, Oct. 11   *Perf. 14x14½*
599	A107	12p multicolored	1.25	1.00
600	A107	20p multicolored	1.75	1.40
601	A107	25p multicolored	1.75	1.40
602	A107	30p multicolored	1.90	1.50
603	A107	65p multicolored	3.50	3.50
		Nos. 599-603 (5)	10.15	8.80

Flowers A108

20p, Leonurus japonicus. 25p, Periwinkle. 30p, Four o'clock. 65p, Blood flower.

1995, Jan. 10   *Perf. 14*
604	A108	20p multi, vert.	2.25	2.25
605	A108	25p multi	2.25	2.25
606	A108	30p multi, vert.	3.00	3.00
607	A108	65p multi	4.00	4.00
		Nos. 604-607 (4)	11.50	11.50

Island Scenes, c. 1895 A109

Designs: 12p, Horse-drawn wagon, Two Boats, Green Mountain. 20p, Island stewards' store. 25p, Royal Navy headquarters, barracks. 30p, Police office. 65p, Pier head.

1995, Mar. 7   **Wmk. 384**   *Perf. 14½*
608	A109	12p sepia	.80	.80
609	A109	20p sepia	1.10	1.10
610	A109	25p sepia	1.50	1.50
611	A109	30p sepia	2.75	2.75
612	A109	65p sepia	3.00	3.00
		Nos. 608-612 (5)	9.15	9.15

End of World War II, 50th Anniv.
Common Design Types

Designs: 20p, 5.5-inch guns taken from HMS Hood, 1941. 25p, Fairey Swordfish, first aircraft to land at Ascension. 30p, HMS Dorsetshire patrolling South Atlantic. 65p, HMS Devonshire patrolling South Atlantic. £1, Reverse of War Medal, 1939-45.

1995, May 8   **Wmk. 373**   *Perf. 14*
613	CD351	20p multicolored	2.25	2.25
614	CD351	25p multicolored	2.50	2.50
615	CD351	30p multicolored	3.00	3.00
616	CD351	65p multicolored	5.00	5.00
		Nos. 613-616 (4)	12.75	12.75

Souvenir Sheet

617	CD352	£1 multicolored	8.75	8.75
		Nos. 613-617 (5)	21.50	21.50

Butterflies — A110

20p, Long-tailed blue. 25p, Painted lady. 30p, Diadem. 65p, African monarch. £1, Red admiral.

1995, Sept. 1   **Wmk. 384**
618	A110	20p multi	2.10	2.10
619	A110	25p multi	2.40	2.40
620	A110	30p multi	2.50	2.50
621	A110	65p multi	4.00	4.00
		Nos. 618-621 (4)	11.00	11.00

Souvenir Sheet

622	A110	£1 multi	9.00	9.00

Singapore '95 (No. 622).

Christmas A111

Designs based on children's drawings: 12p, Santa on boat. 20p, Santa on wall. 25p, Santa in chimney. 30p, Santa on dolphin. 65p, South Atlantic run.

1995, Oct. 10   **Wmk. 373**
623	A111	12p multicolored	1.10	1.10
624	A111	20p multicolored	1.40	1.40
625	A111	25p multicolored	1.50	1.50
626	A111	30p multicolored	1.75	1.75
627	A111	65p multicolored	3.00	3.00
		Nos. 623-627 (5)	8.75	8.75

Mollusks A112

12p, Cypraea lurida. 25p, Cypraea spurca. 30p, Harpa doris. 65p, Umbraculum umbraculum.

Wmk. 384

1996, Jan. 10   **Litho.**   *Perf. 14*
628	A112	12p multicolored	2.25	2.25
629	A112	25p multicolored	2.75	2.75
630	A112	30p multicolored	3.00	3.00
631	A112	65p multicolored	3.75	3.75
a.		Strip of 4, #628-631	14.00	14.00

Queen Elizabeth II, 70th Birthday
Common Design Type

Various portraits of Queen, scenes of Ascension:
20p, St. Marys Church. 25p, The Residency. 30p, Roman Catholic Grotto. 65p, The Exiles Club.

Wmk. 384

1996, Apr. 22   **Litho.**   *Perf. 13½*
632	CD354	20p multicolored	.90	.90
633	CD354	25p multicolored	1.00	1.00
634	CD354	30p multicolored	1.25	1.25
635	CD354	65p multicolored	2.75	2.75
		Nos. 632-635 (4)	5.90	5.90

CAPEX '96 A113

Island transport: 20p, US Army Jeep. 25p, 1924 Citroen 7.5HP two seater. 30p, 1930 Austin Ten-four Tourer. 65p, Series 1 Land Rover.

Wmk. 384

1996, June 8   **Litho.**   *Perf. 14*
636	A113	20p multicolored	1.25	1.25
637	A113	25p multicolored	1.40	1.40
638	A113	30p multicolored	1.50	1.50
639	A113	65p multicolored	2.75	2.75
		Nos. 636-639 (4)	6.90	6.90

Birds and Their Young — A114

1p, Madeiran storm petrel. 2p, Red-billed tropicbird. 4p, Indian mynah. 5p, House sparrow. 7p, Common waxbill. 10p, White tern. 12p, Francolin. 15p, Brown noddy. 20p, Yellow canary. 25p, Black noddy. 30p, Red-footed booby. 40p, Yellow-billed tropicbird. 65p, Brown booby. £1, Masked booby. £2, Sooty tern. £3, Ascension frigate bird.

Wmk. 373

1996, Aug. 12		**Litho.**	**Perf. 13**	
640	A114	1p multicolored	.25	.25
641	A114	2p multicolored	.25	.25
642	A114	4p multicolored	.25	.25
643	A114	7p multicolored	.25	.25
644	A114	10p multicolored	.35	.45
645	A114	12p multicolored	.40	.50
646	A114	15p multicolored	.50	.65
647	A114	20p multicolored	.75	.90
648	A114	25p multicolored	.90	1.00
649	A114	30p multicolored	1.10	1.25
650	A114	40p multicolored	1.50	1.60
651	A114	65p multicolored	2.50	2.75
652	A114	£1 multicolored		
a.		Sheet of 1, perf. 14	4.50	4.50
653	A114	£1 multicolored	4.00	4.00
a.		Souvenir sheet of 1	4.50	4.50
654	A114	£2 multicolored	8.25	9.75
655	A114	£3 multicolored	11.00	12.50
		Nos. 640-655 (16)	32.50	37.10

No. 652a for Hong Kong '97. Issued 2/3/97. No. 653a for return of Hong Kong to China. Issued 7/1/97.

BBC Atlantic Relay Station, 30th Anniv. A115

Various views of relay station: 20p, 25p, Towers. 30p, Towers, buildings. 65p, Satellite dish, towers, beach.

1996, Sept. 9		**Wmk. 384**	**Perf. 14**	
656	A115	20p multicolored	.95	.95
657	A115	25p multicolored	1.10	1.10
658	A115	30p multicolored	1.25	1.25
659	A115	65p multicolored	2.75	2.75
		Nos. 656-659 (4)	6.05	6.05

Christmas A116

Santa Claus: 12p, On satellite dish. 20p, Playing golf. 25p, By beach. 30p, On RAF Tristar. 65p, Aboard RMS St. Helena.

1996, Sept. 23		**Perf. 14x14½**		
		Litho.	**Wmk. 373**	
660	A116	12p multicolored	.55	.55
661	A116	20p multicolored	1.00	1.00
662	A116	25p multicolored	1.00	1.00
663	A116	30p multicolored	1.25	1.10
664	A116	65p multicolored	2.75	2.50
		Nos. 660-664 (5)	6.55	6.15

UNICEF, 50th anniv.

A117

20p, Date palm. 25p, Mauritius hemp. 30p, Norfolk Island pine. 65p, Dwarf palm.

Wmk. 373

1997, Jan. 7		**Litho.**	**Perf. 14½**	
665	A117	20p multi	.85	.85
666	A117	25p multi	1.10	1.10
667	A117	30p multi	1.25	1.25
668	A117	65p multi	2.25	2.25
		Nos. 665-668 (4)	5.45	5.45

Hong Kong '97.

A118

Flag, ship or aircraft: 12p, Great Britain Red Ensign, tanker Maersk Ascension. 25p, RAF Ensign, Tristar. 30p, NASA emblem, Space Shuttle Atlantis. 65p, Royal Navy White Ensign, HMS Northumberland.

Wmk. 373

1997, Apr. 1		**Litho.**	**Perf. 14½**	
669	A118	12p multicolored	1.10	1.10
670	A118	25p multicolored	1.60	1.60
671	A118	30p multicolored	1.75	1.75
672	A118	65p multicolored	3.50	3.50
		Nos. 669-672 (4)	7.95	7.95

Herbs — A119

Designs: a, Solanum sodomaeum. b, Ageratum conyzoides. c, Leonurus sibricus. d, Cerastium vulgatum. e, Commelina diffusa.

Perf. 14x14½				
1997, June 7		**Litho.**	**Wmk. 373**	
673	A119	30p Strip of 5, #a.-e.	8.50	8.50

A120

Queen Elizabeth II and Prince Philip, 50th Wedding Anniv.: No. 674, Queen Elizabeth II. No. 675, Prince Philip playing polo. No. 676, Queen petting horse. No. 677, Prince Philip. No. 678, Prince Philip, Queen Elizabeth II. No. 679, Prince Harry, Prince William riding horses. £1.50, Queen Elizabeth, Prince Philip riding in open carriage.

Wmk. 384

1997, July 10		**Litho.**	**Perf. 13½**	
674	A120	20p multicolored	1.50	1.50
675	A120	20p multicolored	1.50	1.50
a.		Pair, #674-675	3.75	3.75
676	A120	25p multicolored	1.60	1.60
677	A120	25p multicolored	1.60	1.60
a.		Pair, #676-677	4.00	4.00
678	A120	30p multicolored	1.75	1.75
679	A120	30p multicolored	1.75	1.75
a.		Pair, #678-679	4.25	4.25
		Nos. 674-679 (6)	9.70	9.70

Souvenir Sheet

680	A120	£1.50 multicolored	9.00	9.00

Birds — A121

Booklet Stamps

Perf. 14 on 3 Sides

1997, Sept. 1		**Litho.**	**Wmk. 373**	
681	A121	15p like #644	2.75	2.75
682	A121	35p like #648	3.50	3.50
a.		Booklet pane, 2 ea #681-682	9.00	
		Complete booklet, #682a	9.00	

Game Fish — A122

12p, Black marlin. 20p, Atlantic sailfish. 25p, Swordfish. 30p, Wahoo. £1, Yellowfin tuna.

Perf. 14x14½				
1997, Sept. 3		**Litho.**	**Wmk. 373**	
683	A122	12p multi	.90	.90
684	A122	20p multi	1.40	1.40
685	A122	25p multi	1.50	1.50
686	A122	30p multi	1.60	1.60
687	A122	£1 multi	4.25	4.25
		Nos. 683-687 (5)	9.65	9.65

A123

St. Mary's Church (Christmas): 15p, Interior view. 35p, Stained glass window, Madonna and Child. 40p, Stained glass window, Falklands, 1982. 50p, Stained glass window.

Wmk. 384

1997, Oct. 1		**Litho.**	**Perf. 14**	
688	A123	15p multicolored	.90	.90
689	A123	35p multicolored	1.75	1.75
690	A123	40p multicolored	1.90	1.90
691	A123	50p multicolored	2.50	2.50
		Nos. 688-691 (4)	7.05	7.05

A124

Insects: 15p, Cactoblastis cactorum. 35p, Teleonemia scrupulosa. 40p, Neltumius arizonensis. 50p, Algarobius prosopis.

Wmk. 373

1998, Feb. 10		**Litho.**	**Perf. 14**	
692	A124	15p multicolored	1.90	1.90
693	A124	35p multicolored	2.50	2.50
694	A124	40p multicolored	3.25	3.25
695	A124	50p multicolored	3.25	3.25
		Nos. 692-695 (4)	10.90	10.90

Diana, Princess of Wales (1961-97)
Common Design Type

a, In polka-dotted dress. b, In yellow blouse. c, With longer hair style. d, Holding flowers.

Perf. 14½x14				
1998, Mar. 31		**Litho.**	**Wmk. 373**	
696	CD355	35p Sheet of 4, #a.-d.	5.50	5.50

No. 696 sold for £1.40 + 20p, with surtax from international sales being donated to the Princess Diana Memorial Fund and surtax from national sales being donated to designated local charity.

Royal Air Force, 80th Anniv.
Common Design Type of 1993
Re-inscribed

15p, Fairey Fawn. 35p, Vickers Vernon. 40p, Supermarine Spitfire F-22. 50p, Bristol Britannia C2.
No. 701: a, Blackburn Kangaroo. b, SE5a. c, Curtiss Kittyhawk III. d, Boeing Fortress II (B-17).

Wmk. 384

1998, Apr. 1		**Litho.**	**Perf. 14**	
697	CD350	15p multicolored	1.10	1.10
698	CD350	35p multicolored	2.25	2.25
699	CD350	40p multicolored	2.50	2.50
700	CD350	50p multicolored	3.00	3.00
		Nos. 697-700 (4)	8.85	8.85

Souvenir Sheet

701	CD350	50p Sheet of 4, #a.-d.	8.50	8.50

Birds — A125

Wmk. 373

1998, June 15		**Litho.**	**Perf. 14**	
702	A125	15p Swallow	1.25	1.25
703	A125	25p House martin	1.75	1.75
704	A125	35p Cattle egret	2.10	2.10
705	A125	40p Swift	2.10	2.10
706	A125	50p Allen's gallinule	2.50	2.50
		Nos. 702-706 (5)	9.70	9.70

Island Sports — A126

Wmk. 373

1998, Aug. 17		**Litho.**	**Perf. 14**	
707	A126	15p Cricket	2.50	.80
708	A126	35p Golf	3.25	1.50
709	A126	40p Soccer	2.50	1.50
710	A126	50p Trapshooting	2.50	1.50
		Nos. 707-710 (4)	10.75	5.30

Christmas A127

Designs: 15p, Children's nativity play. 35p, Santa arriving on Ascension. 40p, Santa arriving at a party. 50p, Carol singers.

Wmk. 373

1998, Oct. 1		**Litho.**	**Perf. 14**	
711	A127	15p multicolored	1.25	1.25
712	A127	35p multicolored	2.00	2.00
713	A127	40p multicolored	2.25	2.25
714	A127	50p multicolored	2.25	2.25
		Nos. 711-714 (4)	7.75	7.75

World War II Aircraft A128

15p, Curtiss C-46 Commando. 35p, Douglas C-47 Dakota. 40p, Douglas C-54 Skymaster. 50p, Consolidated Liberator Mk.V. £1.50, Consolidated Liberator LB-30.

Wmk. 373

1999, Jan. 20		**Litho.**	**Perf. 14**	
715	A128	15p multicolored	1.25	1.25
716	A128	35p multicolored	2.00	2.00
717	A128	40p multicolored	2.25	2.25
718	A128	50p multicolored	2.25	2.25
		Nos. 715-718 (4)	7.75	7.75

Souvenir Sheet

719	A128	£1.50 multicolored	12.50	12.50

Winston Churchill, 125th birth anniv.

Australia '99, World Stamp Expo A129

Union Castle Mail Ships: 15p, SS Glengorm Castle. 35p, SS Gloucester Castle. 40p, SS Durham Castle. 50p, SS Garth Castle. £1, HMS Endeavour.

Perf. 14½x14
1999, Mar. 5   Litho.   Wmk. 373
720 A129 15p multicolored 1.25 1.25
721 A129 35p multicolored 2.25 2.25
722 A129 40p multicolored 2.40 2.40
723 A129 50p multicolored 2.40 2.40
Nos. 720-723 (4) 8.30 8.30
Souvenir Sheet
724 A129 £1 multicolored 7.25 7.25

World Wildlife Fund — A130

Fairy tern: No. 725, Two on branch. No. 726, One on branch. No. 727, Adult feeding chick. No. 728, Two in flight.

Wmk. 384
1999, Apr. 27   Litho.   *Perf. 14½*
725 A130 10p multicolored .55 .45
726 A130 10p multicolored .55 .45
727 A130 10p multicolored .55 .45
728 A130 10p multicolored .55 .45
a. Sheet of 16, 4 each #725-728 9.00 9.00
Nos. 725-728 (4) 2.20 1.80

Wedding of Prince Edward and Sophie Rhys-Jones
Common Design Type
Perf. 13¾x14
1999, June 19   Litho.   Wmk. 384
729 CD356 50p Separate por- traits 1.90 1.90
730 CD356 £1 Couple 4.00 4.00

1st Manned Moon Landing, 30th Anniv.
Common Design Type

Designs: 15p, Command and service modules. 35p, Moon from Apollo 11. 40p, Devil's Ashpit Tracking Station. 50p, Lunar module lifts off moon. £1.50, Looking at earth from moon.

Perf. 14x13¾
1999, July 20   Litho.   Wmk. 384
731 CD357 15p multicolored 1.40 1.40
732 CD357 35p multicolored 1.75 1.75
733 CD357 40p multicolored 1.75 1.75
734 CD357 50p multicolored 1.75 1.75
Nos. 731-734 (4) 6.65 6.65
Souvenir Sheet
Perf. 14
735 CD357 £1.50 multicolored 7.25 7.25
No. 735 contains one 40mm circular stamp.

Queen Mother's Century
Common Design Type

Queen Mother: 15p, With King George VI, Winston Churchill. 35p, With Prince Charles. 40p, At Clarence House, 88th birthday. 50p, With drummers at Clarence House. £1.50, With Titanic.

Wmk. 384
1999, Aug. 20   Litho.   *Perf. 13½*
736 CD358 15p multicolored 1.25 1.25
737 CD358 35p multicolored 1.75 1.75
738 CD358 40p multicolored 2.00 2.00
739 CD358 50p multicolored 2.50 2.50
Nos. 736-739 (4) 7.50 7.50
Souvenir Sheet
740 CD358 £1.50 black 9.50 9.50

Christmas A131

Wmk. 384
1999, Oct. 6   Litho.   *Perf. 13¾*
741 A131 15p 3 children 1.25 1.25
742 A131 35p 2 children, hats 2.25 2.25
743 A131 40p 2 children, bed 2.25 2.25
744 A131 50p 4 children 2.25 2.25
Nos. 741-744 (4) 8.00 8.00

Cable and Wireless, Cent. A132

Perf. 13¼x13¾
1999, Dec. 13   Litho.   Wmk. 373
745 A132 15p CS Anglia 1.75 1.75
746 A132 35p CS Cambria 2.50 2.50
747 A132 40p Map 2.50 2.50
748 A132 50p CS Colonia 2.75 2.75
Nos. 745-748 (4) 9.50 9.50
Souvenir Sheet
749 A132 £1.50 CS Seine 9.00 9.00

Turtle Project — A133

15p, Young turtles. 35p, Turtle, trail at left. 40p, Turtle with tracking device on beach. 50p, Turtle with tracking device heading to sea.
No. 754: a, Turtle head, rock. b, Like 15p. c, Turtle on beach, sea. d, Turtle in surf.

2000, Mar. 8   Litho.   *Perf. 13¾*
750 A133 15p multi 1.10 1.10
751 A133 35p multi 1.90 1.90
752 A133 40p multi 1.90 1.90
753 A133 50p multi 2.10 2.10
Nos. 750-753 (4) 7.00 7.00
Souvenir Sheet
Perf. 14
754 A133 25p Sheet of 4, #a-d 8.50 8.50
e. With Stamp Show 2000 emblem in margin 8.50 8.50

No. 754 contains four 40x26mm stamps.
No. 754e issued 5/8.

Prince William, 18th Birthday
Common Design Type

William: 10p, As baby laying on stomach and stuffed animal. 15p, As toddler, vert. 35p, Wearing suit and wearing cap, vert. 40p, Holding flowers, and in parka. 50p, In suit and in checked shirt.

Perf. 13¾x14¼, 14¼x13¾
2000, June 21   Litho.   Wmk. 373
Stamps With White Border
755 CD359 15p multi 1.00 1.00
756 CD359 35p multi 1.75 1.75
757 CD359 40p multi 2.50 2.50
758 CD359 50p multi 3.00 3.00
Nos. 755-758 (4) 8.25 8.25
Souvenir Sheet
Stamps Without White Border
Perf. 14¼
759 Sheet of 5 9.50 9.50
a. CD359 10p multi .60 .60
b. CD359 15p multi .90 .90
c. CD359 35p multi 1.75 1.75
d. CD359 40p multi 2.00 2.00
e. CD359 50p multi 2.75 2.75

Forts A134

Designs: 15p, 1815 fortifications. 35p, Fort Thornton, 1817. 40p, Fort Hayes, 1860. 50p, Fort Bedford, 1940.

Wmk. 373
2000, Aug. 14   Litho.   *Perf. 14*
760-763 A134 Set of 4 10.00 10.00

Christmas — A135

Carols: 15p, I Saw Three Ships. 25p, Silent Night. 40p, Away in a Manger. 90p, Hark, the Herald Angels Sing.

2000, Oct. 16   Wmk. 384
764-767 A135 Set of 4 12.50 12.50

Souvenir Sheet

New Year 2001 (Year of the Snake) — A136

Turtles: a, 25p, Green. b, 40p, Loggerhead.

Wmk. 373
2001, Feb. 1   Litho.   *Perf. 14½*
768 A136 Sheet of 2, #a-b 5.25 5.25
Hong Kong 2001 Stamp Exhibition.

Sinking of the Roebuck, Tercentenary A137

Designs: 15p, Capt. William Dampier. 35p, Drawing of the Roebuck, horiz. 40p, Cave dwelling at Dampier's Drip, horiz. 50p, Map.

2001, Feb. 25   Litho.   *Perf. 14*
769-772 A137 Set of 4 11.00 11.00

Discovery of Ascension Island, 500th Anniv. — A138

Designs: 15p, Alfonso de Albuquerque. 35p, Portuguese caravel. 40p, Cantino map. 50p, Rear admiral Sir George Cockburn.

2001, Mar. 25   Litho.   *Perf. 14¾x14¼*
773-776 A138 Set of 4 11.50 11.50

The Age of Victoria A139

Designs: 15p, Great Britain Type A1 with Ascension cancel, vert. 25p, Parade, 1901. 35p, HMS Phoebe. 40p, The Red Lion, 1863. 50p, Queen Victoria, vert. 65p, Sir Joseph Dalton Hooker, botanist, vert. £1.50, Queen Victoria's Funeral.

Wmk. 373
2002, June 14   Litho.   *Perf. 14*
795-798 A142 Set of 4 6.50 6.50

Wmk. 373
2001, May 24   Litho.   *Perf. 14*
777-782 A139 Set of 6 12.00 12.00
Souvenir Sheet
783 A139 £1.50 multi 10.00 10.00

Souvenir Sheet

Belgica 2001 Intl. Stamp Exhibition, Brussels — A140

Ascension tourist sites: a, 35p, Islander Hostel. b, The Residency. c, 40p, The Red Lion. d, 40p, Turtle Ponds.

Wmk. 373
2001, June 9   Litho.   *Perf. 14¼*
784 A140 Sheet of 4, #a-d 11.00 11.00

Birdlife International World Bird Festival — A141

Ascension frigate bird: 15p, On rock with wings outstretched. 35p, Chick, with mouth open. 40p, Pair in flight, horiz. 50p, Close-up of bird, horiz.

Perf. 13¾x14¼, 14¼x13¾
2001, Oct. 1   Litho.   Wmk. 373
785-788 A141 Set of 4 8.50 8.50
Souvenir Sheet
789 Sheet, #785-788, 789a, perf. 14¼ 9.00 9.00
a. A141 10p Two birds on rock 1.25 1.25

Reign Of Queen Elizabeth II, 50th Anniv. Issue
Common Design Type

Designs: Nos. 790, 794a, 15p, Princess Elizabeth with dog. Nos. 791, 794b, 35p, In 1978. Nos. 792, 794c, 40p, In 1946. Nos. 793, 794d, 50p, In 1998. No. 794e, 60p, 1955 portrait by Annigoni (38x50mm).

Perf. 14¼x14½, 13¾ (#794e)
2002, Feb. 6   Litho.   Wmk. 373
With Gold Frames
790 CD360 15p multicolored 1.25 1.25
791 CD360 35p multicolored 1.75 1.75
792 CD360 40p multicolored 2.00 2.00
793 CD360 50p multicolored 2.25 2.25
Nos. 790-793 (4) 7.25 7.25
Souvenir Sheet
Without Gold Frames
794 CD360 Sheet of 5, #a-e 9.00 9.00

Falkland Islands War, 20th Anniv. — A142

Designs: 15p, Troops landing at English Bay. 35p, Weapons testing at Ascension. 40p, HMS Hermes and helicopter. 50p, Vulcan bomber at Wideawake Airfield.

Queen Mother Elizabeth (1900-2002)
Common Design Type

Designs: 35p, Wearing flowered bonnet (sepia photograph). 40p, Wearing pink hat. No. 801: a, 50p, Wearing hat (sepia photograph). b, £1, Wearing blue hat.

Wmk. 373
2002, Aug. 5   Litho.   Perf. 14¼
With Purple Frames
799 CD361 35p multicolored   1.25 1.25
800 CD361 40p multicolored   2.00 2.00
Souvenir Sheet
Without Purple Frames
Perf. 14½x14¼
801 CD361 Sheet of 2, #a-b   6.50 6.50

Flowers and Local Scenes — A143

Designs: 10p, Vinca, Travellers palm. 15p, Mexican poppy, Broken Tooth. 20p, Ascension lily, St. Mary's Church. 25p, Goatweed, Boatswain Bird Island. 30p, Mauritius hemp, Cannon. 35p, Frangipani, Guest House. 40p, Ascension spurge, Wideawake tern. 50p, Lovechaste, Pier head. 65p, Yellowboy, Sisters Peak. 90p, Persian lilac, Two Boats School. £2, Wild currant, Green turtle. £5, Coral tree, Wideawake Airfield.

Wmk. 373
2002, Aug. 28   Litho.   Perf. 14
802 A143 10p multi   .35   .45
803 A143 15p multi   .60   .70
804 A143 20p multi   .80   .95
805 A143 25p multi   1.00 1.10
806 A143 30p multi   1.25 1.25
807 A143 35p multi   1.50 1.80
808 A143 40p multi   1.60 1.90
809 A143 50p multi   2.00 2.40
810 A143 65p multi   2.75 3.25
811 A143 90p multi   3.50 4.00
812 A143 £2 multi   7.00 8.00
813 A143 £5 multi   17.50 20.00
   Nos. 802-813 (12) 39.85 45.80

Christmas — A144

Paintings: 15p, Ecce Ancilla Dominii, by Dante Gabriel Rossetti. 25p, The Holy Family and a Shepherd, by Titian, horiz. 35p, Christ Carrying the Cross, by Ambrogio Bergognone. 75p, Sketch for "The Ascension," by Benjamin West.

Perf. 14x14¼, 14¼x14
2002, Oct. 9   Litho.   Wmk. 373
814-817 A144 Set of 4   7.00 7.00

Ariane Downrange Tracking Station — A145

Designs: 35p, Ariane 4 on launchpad, vert. 40p, Map of downrange tracking stations. 65p, Automated Transfer vehicle in space. 90p, Ariane 5 launch, vert.

2003, Jan. 13   Litho.   Perf. 14½
818-821 A145 Set of 4   10.00 10.00
821a   Souvenir sheet, #818-821   10.00 10.00

Head of Queen Elizabeth II
Common Design Type

Wmk. 373
2003, June 2   Litho.   Perf. 13¾
822 CD362 £3 multi   13.50 13.50
   Nos. 822 (1)   13.50 13.50

Coronation of Queen Elizabeth II, 50th Anniv.
Common Design Type

Designs: Nos. 823, 825a, 40p, Queen in carriage. Nos. 824, 825b, £1, Queen with crown at coronation.

Perf. 14¼x14½
2003, June 2   Litho.   Wmk. 373
Vignettes Framed, Red Background
823 CD363 40p multicolored   1.75 1.75
824 CD363 £1 multicolored   5.00 5.00
Souvenir Sheet
Vignettes Without Frame, Purple Panel
825 CD363 Sheet of 2, #a-b   6.75 6.75

Prince William, 21st Birthday
Common Design Type

No. 826: a, Color photograph at right. b, Color photograph at left.

Wmk. 373
2003, June 21   Litho.   Perf. 14¼
826   Horiz. pair   7.50 7.50
a.-b. CD364 75p Either single   3.00 3.00

Powered Flight, Cent. — A146

Designs: 15p, Bleriot XI. 20p, Vickers VC-10. 35p, BAe Harrier FRS Mk 1. 40p, Westland Sea King HAS Mk 4. 50p, Rockwell Space Shuttle. 90p, General Dynamics F-16. £1.50, Fairey Swordfish Mk II.

Wmk. 373
2003, Aug. 12   Litho.   Perf. 14
Stamp + Label
827-832 A146 Set of 6   12.00 12.00
Souvenir Sheet
833   A146 £1.50 multi   8.50 8.50

Democracy, 1st Anniv., and Christmas — A147

Dove and: 15p, Casting ballot. 25p, Island council session. 40p, Higher education. £1, Government headquarters.

Wmk. 373
2003, Nov. 1   Litho.   Perf. 14
834-837 A147 Set of 4   8.25 8.25

Birdlife International — A148

Masked booby: 15p, Adult and chick. 35p, Two adults, vert. 40p, Adult in flight, vert. 50p, Adult with neck and wings extended. 90p, Adult.

Perf. 14¼x13¾, 13¾x14¼
2004, Feb. 6   Litho.   Wmk. 373
838-842 A148 Set of 5   11.00 11.00
842a   Souvenir sheet, #838-842, perf. 14¼   11.00 11.00

Royal Horticultural Society, Bicent. — A149

Flora: 15p, Bougainvillea glabra (red flowers). 35p, Bougainvillea glabra (red flowers). 40p, Bougainvillea glabra (white flowers). 90p, Bougainvillea spectabilis. £1.50, Pteris adscensionis.

Wmk. 373
2004, May 25   Litho.   Perf. 14
843-846 A149 Set of 4   8.50 8.50
Souvenir Sheet
847   A149 £1.50 multi   7.25 7.25

Fish — A150

Designs: 15p, Blue marlin underwater. 35p, Swordfish. 40p, Sailfish. 90p, White marlin. £1.50, Blue marlin breaching surface.

Wmk. 373
2004, July 26   Litho.   Perf. 13¾
848-851 A150 Set of 4   8.50 8.50
Souvenir Sheet
852   A150 £1.50 multi   7.25 7.25

The Moon — A151

Designs: 15p, Lunar eclipse from Hummock Point. 25p, Lunar eclipse from Sister's Peak. 35p, Lunar eclipse from Daly's Craggs. £1.25, Moon and birds from Mars Bay.

Wmk. 373
2004, Oct. 28   Litho.   Perf. 13½
853-856 A151 Set of 4   9.50 9.50
856a   Souvenir sheet of 1   6.25 6.25

Merchant Ships — A152

Designs: 15p, MV Ascension. 35p, RMS St. Helena. 40p, RMS Caronia. £1.25, MV Maersk Gannet.

2004, Nov. 26   Perf. 13¼
857-860 A152 Set of 4   10.50 10.50

Battle of Trafalgar, Bicent. — A153

Designs: 15p, British carronade on sliding carriage. 25p, Royal Marine drummer boy, 1805, vert. 35p, HMS Britannia, vert. 40p, Horatio Nelson, by Jean Frances Rigaud. 50p, HMS Neptune and Santissima Trinidad. 90p, HMS Victory.
No. 867, vert.: a, Horatio Nelson, by Lemuel Francis Abbott. b, HMS Ajax.

Wmk. 373, Unwmkd. (#866)
2005, Apr. 29   Litho.   Perf. 13½
861-866 A153 Set of 6   10.50 10.50
Souvenir Sheet
867   A153 £1 Sheet of 2, #a-b   9.00 9.00

No. 866 has particles of wood from the HMS Victory embedded in the areas covered by a thermographic process that produces a shiny, raised effect.

Birdlife International — A154

Birds: 15p, Fairy tern. 35p, White-tailed tropicbird. 40p, Brown booby. 50p, Brown noddy. £1.25, Red-billed tropicbird.

Wmk. 373
2005, May 27   Litho.   Perf. 13¾
868-872 A154 Set of 5   11.00 11.00
872a   Souvenir sheet, #868-872   11.50 11.50

Tuna Fish — A155

Designs: 35p, Three yellowfin tunas. 40p, Skipjack tunas. 50p, Albacore tunas. £1.25, Bigeye tunas. £1.50, Yellowfin tuna jumping.

Wmk. 373
2005, July 22   Litho.   Perf. 13¾
873-876 A155 Set of 4   10.00 10.00
Souvenir Sheet
877   A155 £1.50 multi   7.00 7.00

Pope John Paul II (1920-2005) — A156

Wmk. 373
2005, Aug. 18   Litho.   Perf. 14
878   A156 40p multi   2.25 2.25

Battle of Trafalgar, Bicent. — A157

Designs: 40p, HMS Victory. 65p, Ships in battle, horiz. 90p, Admiral Horatio Nelson.

Perf. 13¼
2005, Oct. 21   Litho.   Unwmk.
879-881 A157 Set of 3   10.00 10.00

Christmas — A158

Stories by Hans Christian Andersen (1805-75): 15p, The Little Fir Tree. 25p, The Mailcoach Passengers. 35p, The Little Match Girl. £1.25, The Snow Man.

2005, Oct. 3   Wmk. 373   Perf. 14
882-885 A158 Set of 4   9.00 9.00

Fish
A159

Designs: 20p, Black jack. 35p, Almaco jack. 50p, Horse-eye jack. £1, Rainbow runner. £1.50, Longfin crevalle jack.

Wmk. 373

2006, Jan. 24   Litho.   Perf. 13¾
886-889 A159   9.50 9.50
Souvenir Sheet
890 A159 £1.50 multi   6.50 6.50

Queen Elizabeth II, 80th Birthday
A160

"80" and Queen: 20p, As child. 40p, Wearing tiara. 50p, Wearing tiara, diff. £1.30, Wearing hat.
No. 895: a, Wearing tiara, diff. b, Without head covering.

Wmk. 373

2006, Apr. 21   Litho.   Perf. 14¼
891-894 A160 Set of 4   11.00 11.00
Souvenir Sheet
895 A160 £1 Sheet of 2, #a-b 9.50 9.50

Anniversaries — A161

No. 896, 20p: a, HMS Beagle. b, Charles Darwin.
No. 897, 35p: a, SS Great Britain. b, Isambard Kingdom Brunel.
No. 898, 40p: a, Niña. b, Christopher Columbus.
No. 899, 50p: a, Map with lines of magnetic variation of the compass. b, Edmond Halley.

Perf. 13x13¼

2006, July 24   Litho.   Wmk. 373
Horiz. Pairs, #a-b
896-899 A161 Set of 4   14.00 14.00
Darwin's voyage on the Beagle, 175th anniv., birth of Brunel, 200th anniv., death of Columbus, 500th anniv., birth of Halley, 350th anniv.

Greetings
A162

Designs: 15p, Long Beach (Greetings from Ascension). 25p, Sunset over lava flow (Merry Christmas). 35p, Dewpond (Seasons Greetings). £1.25, Boatswain Bird Island (Happy New Year).

Wmk. 373

2006, Oct. 30   Litho.   Perf. 14¼
900-903 A162 Set of 4   10.00 10.00

Worldwide Fund for Nature (WWF)
A163

Resplendent angelfish: 35p, Three fish. 40p, Seven fish. 50p, Three fish, diff. £1.25, Four fish.

Perf. 13¾

2007, Mar. 23   Litho.   Unwmk.
904-907 A163 Set of 4   9.00 9.00
907a   Sheet, 4 each #904-907 35.00 35.00

Falkland Islands War, 25th Anniv.
A164

Designs: Nos. 908, 913a, 35p, Handley Page Victor K Mk 2 tanker plane. Nos. 909, 912b, 40p, HMS Dumbarton Castle and Chinook helicopter. Nos. 910, 912c, 50p, HMS Fearless, landing craft and helicopters. Nos. 911, 913d, £1.25, Vulcan XM607 leaving Wideawake Airfield.
No. 912: a, 35p, RFA Tidespring refueling HMS Antrim. d, £1.25, Atlantic Conveyor and Harrier jet.
No. 913: b, 40p, Vickers VC 10 transport plane. c, 50p, Nimrod MR2 maritime reconnaisance plane.

2007, May 25   Perf. 13¼x13
Stamps With White Frames
908-911 A164 Set of 4   12.00 12.00
Stamps Without White Frames
912 A164 Sheet of 4, #a-d 12.00 12.00
913 A164 Sheet of 4, #a-d 12.00 12.00

Scouting, Cent.
A165

Lord Robert Baden-Powell blowing kudu horn and: 35p, Fleur-de-lis of scouts. 40p, Scouts rescuing turtle. 50p, Scouts on gun of HMS Hood. £1.25, Scouts on Land Rover.

2007, July 9   Perf. 14
914-917 A165 Set of 4   12.00 12.00

Mother Teresa (1910-97) and Princess Diana (1961-97) — A166

2007, Aug. 31
918 A166 50p multi   2.50 2.50

Wedding of Queen Elizabeth II and Prince Philip, 60th Anniv. — A167

No. 919: a, 35p, Couple in 1947. b, 90p, Wedding program. c, £1.25, Couple in 2006.

2007, Nov. 20   Litho.   Perf. 14¼
919 A167 Horiz. strip of 3,
           #a-c   12.00 12.00

British Ornithological Union Expedition, 50th Anniv. — A168

No. 920, 15p: a, British Ornithological Union base. b, Drawing of extinct rail.
No. 921, 25p: a, Scientist recording sounds of Wideawake tern. b, Wideawake terns.
No. 922, 40p: a, Boatswainbird Island outpost. b, Masked booby.
No. 923, 50p: a, Scientist pushing dinghy in surf. b, Red-footed booby.

2007, Dec. 10   Perf. 14¼
Horiz. Pairs, #a-b
920-923 A168 Set of 4   14.00 14.00

Oviparous Creatures — A169

Creature and eggs: 15p, Long-tailed blue butterfly. 20p, Ladybird beetle. 25p, Spiny lobster. 30p, Desert locust. 35p, Green turtle. 40p, Land crab. 50p, Red-footed booby. 65p, Coconut palm gecko. 90p, Common waxbill. £1, Yellowtail damselfish. £2.50, Madeiran storm petrel. £5, Red-necked francolin.

2008, Feb. 5   Litho.   Perf. 14¼
924 A169 15p multi   .60   .60
925 A169 20p multi   .80   .80
926 A169 25p multi   1.00 1.00
927 A169 30p multi   1.25 1.25
928 A169 35p multi   1.40 1.40
929 A169 40p multi   1.60 1.60
930 A169 50p multi   2.00 2.00
931 A169 65p multi   2.60 2.60
932 A169 90p multi   3.75 3.75
933 A169 £1 multi   4.00 4.00
934 A169 £2.50 multi   10.00 10.00
935 A169 £5 multi   20.00 20.00
  Nos. 924-935 (12)   49.00 49.00

Sharks
A170

Designs: 35p, Bluntnose sixgill shark. 40p, Scalloped hammerhead shark. 50p, Shortfin mako shark. £1.25, Whale shark. £1.50, Bigeye thresher shark.

2008, Mar. 14   Litho.   Perf. 14
936-939 A170 Set of 4   11.00 10.00
939a   Sheet of 16, 4 each
        #936-939   47.50 47.50
Souvenir Sheet
940 A170 £1.50 multi   7.00 7.00

National Aeronautical and Space Administration, 50th Anniv. — A171

Designs: No. 941, 35p, Bell X-1E airplane. No. 942, 35p, Apollo 11 Moon walk. 40p, Apollo 17 Lunar Rover. 50p, Space Shuttle Columbia. 65p, Hubble Space Telescope. 90p, International Space Station.

2008, May 23   Litho.   Perf. 14
941-946 A171 Set of 6   12.50 12.50

Royal Air Force, 90th Anniv.
A172

Airplanes: 15p, Sopwith 7F.1 Snipe. 35p, Vickers Wellington Mk 1C. 40p, Supermarine Spitfire Mk IX. 50p, Gloster Meteor F. IV. 65p, BAe Hawk. 90p, Typhoon F-2 Eurofighter.

Unwmk.

2008, June 20   Litho.   Perf. 14
947-952 A172 Set of 6   14.50 14.50

Botanists and Flowers — A173

Designs: 35p, Valerius Cordus (1515-44), and Cordia sebestena. 40p, Nehemiah Grew (1641-1712), and Grewia occidentalis. 50p, Charles Plumier (1646-1704), and Plumeria rubra. £2, Carl Peter Thunberg (1743-1828), and Thunbergia grandiflora.

2008, Aug. 28   Litho.   Perf. 14
953-956 A173 Set of 4   14.50 14.50

Christmas — A174

Santa Claus: 15p, Holding microphone. 25p, With reindeer in surf. 50p, On inflatable lounger in water. £2, Piloting flying sleigh.

2008, Nov. 22
957-960 A174 Set of 4   12.00 12.00

Longest-Reigning British Monarchs — A175

Designs: 35p, King Henry III and Tower of London. 40p, King James I and Stirling Castle. 50p, King George III and Windsor Castle. 65p, Queen Victoria and Osborne House. £1.25, Queen Elizabeth II and Buckingham Palace.

2008, Dec. 15
961-965 A175 Set of 5   12.00 12.00

Marine Mammals — A176

Designs: 35p, Bottlenose dolphins. 40p, Pantropical spotted dolphins. 50p, Sperm whale. £1.25, Gervais' beaked whales. £2, Humpback whale.

2009, Mar. 23   Perf. 14x14¾
966-969 A176 Set of 4   11.50 11.50
969a   Sheet, 4 each #966-969 40.00 40.00
Souvenir Sheet
970 A176 £2 multi   9.00 9.00

Naval Aviation, Cent. — A177

No. 971, 35p: a, Flight Sub-lieutenant Rex Warneford and Victoria Cross. b, Moraine-Saulnier L destroys Zeppelin LZ-37.
No. 972, 35p: a, Squadron Commander Richard Bell Davies and Victoria Cross. b, Nieuport 10 taking off.
No. 973, 40p: a, Lieutenant Commander Eugene Esmonde and Victoria Cross. b, Fairey Swordfish attacking German warships.
No. 974, 50p: a, Lieutenant Robert Hampton Gray and Victoria Cross. b, Corsair bombing Japanese warships.

2009, May 7   *Perf. 14*
Horiz. Pairs, #a-b
971-974 A177 Set of 4   12.00 12.00

Botany A178

Designs: No. 975, 35p, Raspberry. No. 976, 35p, Blue water lily. 40p, Prickly pear. 50p, Ascension lily. 65p, Yellowboy. 90p, Joseph Dalton Hooker (1817-1911), botanist.

2009, Sept. 7   *Perf. 14*
975-980 A178 Set of 6   11.00 11.00

Turtle Research and Conservation — A179

No. 981, 15p: a, Early turtle tracking and head of turtle. b, Dr. Archie Carr (1909-87) and map of Ascension.
No. 982, 35p: a, Turtle laying eggs and head of turtle. b, Turtle hatchlings and map of Ascension.
No. 983, 40p: a, Beach raking and head of turtle. b, Population monitoring and map of Ascension.
No. 984, 65p: a, Turtle rescue and head of turtle. b, Turtle rescue and map of Ascension.

2009, Oct. 1   *Perf. 13¾*
Horiz. Pairs, #a-b
981-984 A179 Set of 4   10.00 10.00

Charles Darwin (1809-82), Naturalist — A180

Darwin and: 35p, Woodpecker finch. 40p, Marine iguanas. 50p, Galapagos tortoise. £2, Galapagos penguins.

2009, Nov. 9   **Unwmk.**   *Perf. 14*
985-988 A180 Set of 4   13.00 13.00

White-tailed Tropicbird — A181

Designs: 35p, Bird in rock crevice. 40p, Bird on rock. 50p, Juvenile in flight. £1.25, Adult in flight.

2009, Dec. 4   **Litho.**   *Perf. 14*
989-992 A181 Set of 4   12.00 12.00
992a   Sheet, 4 each #989-992 48.00 48.00

Reef Fish — A182

Designs: 35p, Hardback soldier. 40p, Grouper. 50p, Five fingers. £1.25, Rock bullseye.
£2, Softback soldier.

2010, Mar. 19   *Perf. 13¾*
993-996 A182 Set of 4   12.00 12.00
996a   Sheet, 4 each #993-996 48.00 48.00
Souvenir Sheet
997 A182 £2 multi   8.50 8.50

A183

Girl Guides, Cent. — A184

Designs: 40p, Girl Guides wearing clown noses. 50p, Girl Guides and fish. 90p, Leaders holding cake. £1.25, Girl Guide climbing rock.
No. 1002: a, Olave Baden-Powell (1889-1977). b, Agnes Baden-Powell (1858-1945). c, Lord Robert Baden-Powell (1857-1941).

2010, Apr. 10   *Perf. 14*
998-1001 A183 Set of 4   12.00 12.00
Souvenir Sheet
1002 A184 £1 Sheet of 3, #a-
                c   12.00 12.00

Miniature Sheet

Battle of Britain, 70th Anniv. — A185

No. 1003: a, Supermarine Spitfire R6803. b, Hawker Hurricane V7383. c, Supermarine Spitfire X4036. d, Hawker Hurricane R4175. e, Supermarine Spitfire R6885. f, Hawker Hurricane V6684. g, Supermarine Spitfire K9998. h, Hawker Hurricane R4118.

2010, May 7   *Perf. 14*
1003 A185 50p Sheet of 8 #a-
                h   15.00 15.00
London 2010 Festival of Stamps.

Yellow Canary — A186

Designs: 15p, Juvenile. 35p, Adult male on branch. 60p, Adult female. 90p, Adult male on ground.

2010, Oct. 11   *Perf. 13¾*
1004-1007 A186 Set of 4   8.50 8.50
1007a   Miniature sheet of 16, 4
            each #1004-1007   35.00 35.00

Christmas — A187

Designs: 15p, Christmas lunch. 40p, Christmas parade. 50p, Christingle. £1.25, Nativity play.

2010, Nov. 17   *Perf. 14*
1008-1011 A187 Set of 4   9.00 9.00

Rediscovery of the Parsley Fern — A188

Ascension National Park emblem and: 15p, HMS Erebus and HMS Terror approaching Ascension, 1843. 15p, Parsley fern in situ. 35p, Parsley fern seedlings in pots. £1, Parsley fern cultivation at Kew Gardens.

2011, Feb. 16   *Perf. 13¾*
1012-1016 A188 Set of 5   8.00 8.00

Service of Queen Elizabeth II and Prince Philip — A189

Designs: 15p, Queen Elizabeth II. 25p, Queen and Prince Philip. 35p, Queen and Prince Philip, diff. 40p, Queen and Prince Philip, diff. 60p, Queen and Prince Philip, diff. £1.25, Prince Philip.
£2, Queen and Prince Philip, diff.

2011, Mar. 23   *Perf. 13¼*
1017-1022 A189 Set of 6   10.00 10.00
1022a   Sheet of 6, #1017-1022,
            + 3 labels   10.00 10.00
Souvenir Sheet
1023 A189 £2 multi   6.75 6.75

Royal Air Force Search and Rescue, 70th Anniv. — A190

Emblem and Sea King helicopter: 35p, On airplane's cargo ramp. 40p, Flying near Ascension. 90p, Approaching HMS Dumbarton Castle. £1, Approaching HMS Spartan submarine.
£2.50, Sea King helicopter in flight.

2011, May 19
1024-1027 A190 Set of 4   8.75 8.75
Souvenir Sheet
1028 A190 £2.50 multi   8.25 8.25

Miniature Sheet

Peonies — A191

No. 1029 — Peony color: a, Red. b, Gray lilac. c, Light orange. d, White.

2011, June 22   *Perf. 13¾*
1029 A191 50p Sheet of 4, #a-d 6.50 6.50

Wedding of Prince William and Catherine Middleton — A192

Couple, with Middleton: 35p, Wearing hat. 90p, Without hat. £1.25, Seated in coach in wedding dress.
£2, Couple standing on wedding day, vert.

2011, July 20   *Perf. 14*
1030-1032 A192 Set of 3   8.25 8.25
Souvenir Sheet
Perf. 14¾x14
1033 A192 £2 multi   6.50 6.50
No. 1033 contains one 29x45mm stamp.

Worldwide Fund for Nature (WWF) — A193

Phaethon aethereus: Nos. 1034, 1038a, 35p, Bird in rock crevice. Nos. 1035, 1038b, 40p, Two birds in flight. Nos. 1036, 1038c, 50p, Adult and juvenile in rock crevice. Nos. 1037, 1038d, £1.25, Bird in flight.

2011, Aug. 31
Stamps With White Frames
1034-1037 A193   Set of 4   8.00 8.00
Stamps Without White Frames
1038 A193   Strip of 4, #a-d   8.00 8.00

Nos. 1038a-1038d were printed in sheets of 16 stamps containing four strips.

Christmas — A194

Pantomimes: 15p, Mother Goose. 40p, Jack and the Beanstalk. 50p, Aladdin. £1.25, Cinderella.

2011, Nov. 16   **Perf. 14**
1039-1042 A194   Set of 4   7.25 7.25

Reign of Queen Elizabeth II, 60th
Anniv. — A195

Photographs of Queen Elizabeth II taken in: 15p, 2011. 25p, 1998. 35p, 1988. 40p, 1975. 60p, 1961. £1.25, 1953. £2, 1977.

2012, Feb. 6   **Perf. 13¼**
1043-1048 A195   Set of 6   9.50 9.50
1048a   Sheet of 6, #1043-1048, +
                 3 labels   9.50 9.50
Souvenir Sheet
1049 A195   £2 multi   6.50 6.50

Reef Fish
A196

Designs: 35p, Trumpetfish. 40p, Peacock flounder. 90p, Queen triggerfish. £1, Scrawled filefish. £2, Yellow goatfish.

2012, Apr. 15   Litho.   Perf. 13¾
1050-1053 A196   Set of 4   8.75 8.75
1053a   Sheet, 4 each #1050-
                 1053   35.00 35.00
Souvenir Sheet
1054 A196   £2 multi   6.50 6.50

Sinking
of the
Titanic,
Cent.
A197

Designs: 20p, The departure. 45p, The boat deck. 50p, The iceberg. £1, The sinking. £2, Abandoning ship.

2012, Aug. 1   **Perf. 14**
1055-1058 A197   Set of 4   6.75 6.75
Souvenir Sheet
1059 A197   £2 multi   6.25 6.25

Shackleton-Rowett Antarctic
Expedition, 90th Anniv. — A198

No. 1060, 45p: a, Sir Ernest Shackleton (36x36mm). b, John Quiller Rowett (18x36mm). c, Frank Wild (36x36mm).
No. 1061, 50p: a, Quest leaving London (36x36mm). b, Quest at Ascension (18x36mm). c, Quest in ice (36x36mm).

2012, Sept. 17   **Perf. 13¼**
Horiz. Strips of 3, #a-c
1060-1061 A198   Set of 2   9.25 9.25

Christmas
A199

Scenes from *A Christmas Carol*, by Charles Dickens: 25c, Ebenezer Scrooge passing Christmas carolers. 40p, Ghost visiting Scrooge. 50p, Scrooge carrying Tiny Tim, vert. £1.25, Scrooge watching boy deliver turkey, vert.

2012, Nov. 15   **Perf. 13¼x13½**
1062-1065 A199   Set of 4   7.75 7.75

Miniature Sheet

Wideawake Airfield, 70th
Anniv. — A200

No. 1066: a, 45p, Wideawake tern. b, 50p, Douglas DC-3 Dakota. c, £1, Eurofighter Typhoon. d, £1.45, Masked booby.

2012, Dec. 5   **Perf. 13¼**
1066 A200   Sheet of 4, #a-d   11.00 11.00

Aircraft
A201

Designs: 15p, Fairey Swordfish. 20p, North American B-25 Mitchell. 25p, Lockheed C-130K Hercules. 30p, Hawker Siddeley Nimrod MR2. 40p, BAE Sea Harrier FRS1. 45p, Lockheed C-5 Galaxy. 50p, Douglas DC-3 Dakota. 65p, Avro Vulcan. 90p, McDonnell Douglas Phantom F-4. £1, Eurofighter Typhoon. £2.50, Lockheed C-121. £5, Shorts Belfast.

2013, Jan. 15   **Perf. 13¾**
1067 A201   15p multi   .50   .50
1068 A201   20p multi   .65   .65
1069 A201   25p multi   .80   .80
1070 A201   30p multi   .95   .95
1071 A201   40p multi   1.25 1.25
1072 A201   45p multi   1.40 1.40
1073 A201   50p multi   1.60 1.60
1074 A201   65p multi   2.10 2.10
1075 A201   90p multi   3.00 3.00
1076 A201   £1 multi   3.25 3.25
1077 A201   £2.50 multi   8.00 8.00
1078 A201   £5 multi   16.00 16.00
            Nos. 1067-1078 (12) 39.50 39.50

Items Commemorating British
Coronations — A202

Coronation of Queen Elizabeth II, 60th
Anniv. — A203

Various items commemorating the coronation of: 45p, Queen Victoria. 50p, King Edward VII. 70p, King George V. £1.10, King George VI. £1.25, Queen Elizabeth II.

2013, Feb. 6   **Perf. 14**
1079-1083 A202   Set of 5   12.00 12.00
Souvenir Sheet
Perf. 14¾x14¼
1084 A203   £2 multi   6.00 6.00

British Settlement
of Ascension,
Bicent. (in
2015) — A204

Imprisonment of Napoleon Bonaparte on Ascension: 45p, Joséphine Bonaparte at Malmaison, by François Pascal Simon. 50p, Bonaparte at the Bridge of Arcole, by Antoine-Jean Gros. 60p, Napoleon and his General Staff, by Jean-Léon Gérôme. £1.45, Napoleon as First Consul, detail of painting by Jean-Baptiste Isabey.

2013, May 21   **Perf. 13¾**
1085-1088 A204   Set of 4   9.50 9.50

Lady Margaret
Thatcher (1925-
2013), British
Prime
Minister — A205

Photographs of Thatcher: 45p, Giving "Victory" sign, 1976. 50p, In cockpit of Sea Harrier jet, 1982. 60p, Holding teacup during visit to Ascension, 1992. £1.45, At Order of the Garter ceremony, 1995.

2013, June 14
1089-1092 A205   Set of 4   9.50 9.50

Ascension Frigatebirds — A206

Designs: 20p, Male and female. 45p, Male on egg. 50p, Chick. 60p, Female and chick. £1.10, Juvenile. £1.45, Male in flight.

2013, Aug. 16   **Perf. 13¼x13½**
1093-1098 A206   Set of 6   14.00 14.00

Shallow
Marine
Surveys
Group
A207

Marine life: Nos. 1099, 1103a, 45p, Fire worm. Nos. 1100, 1103b, 50p, Black bar soldier fish. Nos. 1101, 1103c, 60p, Endemic white hawk fish. Nos. 1102, 1103d, £1.45, Atlantic blue tang.
No. 1104a, £1, Anemone, vert.

2013, Aug. 29   **Perf. 13¼x13½**
Stamps With White Frames
1099-1102 A207   Set of 4   9.75 9.75
Stamps Without White Frames
1103 A230   Strip of 4, #a-d   9.75 9.75
Souvenir Sheet
Perf. 13½x13¼
1104 A207   Sheet of 3 (see
                footnote)   9.75 9.75
     a.   A207 £1 multi   3.25 3.25

No. 1104 contains No. 1104a, Falkland Islands No. 1107a and South Georgia and South Sandwich Islands No. 485a. This sheet was sold in Ascension, Falkland Islands and South Georgia and South Sandwich Islands.

Churches   Stained-
A208   Glass
                  Windows
                  A209

Designs: 45p, Grotto of Our Lady Catholic Church. 50p, Window depicting Madonna and Child. 60p, St. Mary's Anglican Church. £1, Window depicting St. Michael.

2013, Nov. 18   Litho.   Perf. 13¼
Stamps With White Frames
1105 A208   45p multi   1.50 1.50
1106 A209   50p multi   1.75 1.75
1107 A208   60p multi   2.00 2.00
1108 A209   £1 multi   3.25 3.25
            Nos. 1105-1108 (4)   8.50 8.50
Stamps Without White Frames
1109   Horiz. strip of 4   8.50 8.50
     a.   A208 45p multi   1.50 1.50
     b.   A209 50p multi   1.75 1.75
     c.   A208 60p multi   2.00 2.00
     d.   A209 £1 multi   3.25 3.25

Christmas.

British Settlement
of Ascension,
Bicent. (in
2015) — A210

The Napoleonic Years: 50p, Engraving of Napoleon Bonaparte after signing of Treaty of Amiens, 1802. 55p, Napoleon I in Coronation Robes, by François Gérard. 60p, Lord Horatio Nelson, by Lemuel Francis Abbott. £1.60, Napoleon at Wagram, by Emile Jean-Horace Vernet.

2014, Apr. 28   Litho.   Perf. 13¾
1110-1113 A210   Set of 4   11.00 11.00

Royal
Christenings
A211

Photograph from christening of: 50p, Queen Elizabeth II, 1926. 55p, Prince Charles, 1948. 60p, Prince William, 1982. £1.60, Prince George, 2013.

2014, May 21   Litho.   Perf. 13x13¼
1114-1117 A211   Set of 4   11.00 11.00

World War I,
Cent. — A212

Various poppies: 50p, 55p, 60p, £1.60.

2014, Aug. 4   Litho.   Perf. 14¾x14
1118-1121 A212   Set of 4   11.00 11.00

Royal Marines,
350th
Anniv. — A213

Designs: 20p, Duke of York and Albany's Maritime Regiment of Foot on man-of-war, 1664. 50p, Light Infantry and barracks on Ascension, 19th cent. 55p, Light Infantry at Gallipoli, 1915. 60p, Royal Marines Commandos at Eastney, 1970s. 65p, Royal Marines Band Service Bugler at Deal, 1996. £1, Royal Marines Commandos, 2014.

2014, Oct. 28   Litho.   Perf. 14
1122-1127 A213   Set of 6   11.50 11.50

Rosetta
Mission
A214

Designs: 35p, Ariane 5 launching Rosetta. 55p, Rosetta spacecraft. 65p, Deploying Philae lander. £1.60, Descent of Philae. £3, Comet 67P/Churyumov-Gerasimenko.

2014, Dec. 30   Litho.   Perf. 14
1128-1131 A214   Set of 4   9.75 9.75
Souvenir Sheet
1132 A214   £3 multi   9.25 9.25

British Settlement
of Ascension,
Bicent. — A215

The Napoleonic Wars: 55p, Napoleon Bonaparte on the Borodino Heights, by Vasily V. Vereshchagin. 60p, Napoleon at Fontainebleau, by Paul Delaroche. 65p, Arthur Wellesley, 1st Duke of Wellington, by Thomas Lawrence. £1.60, Napoleon dictating his memoirs in exile.

2015, Apr. 27   Litho.   Perf. 13¾
1133-1136 A215   Set of 4   10.50 10.50

Magna
Carta,
800th
Anniv.
A216

Designs: 50p, King John examining Magna Carta. 55p, Ascension Government building. 60p, Magistrate's Court, Ascension. £1.60, Arms of Ascension, King John.

2015, June 15   Litho.   Perf. 13
1137-1140 A216   Set of 4   10.50 10.50

Queen Elizabeth II, Longest-Reigning
British Monarch — A217

Queen Elizabeth II and events during her reign: 50p, Publications reporting on her coronation, 1953. 55p, First men on the Moon, 1969. 65p, Avro Vulcan (end of Cold War), 1991. £1.60, The Spirit of Chartwell in Diamond Jubilee celebration, 2012.

2015, Sept. 9   Litho.   Perf. 14
1141-1144 A217   Set of 4   10.00 10.00

British Settlement of Ascension,
Bicent. — A218

200th anniversary emblem and: 35p, King George III. 50p, Flag of Ascension. 55p, Coat of arms of Ascension. £1.60, Queen Elizabeth II.

2015, Oct. 22   Litho.   Perf. 14
1145-1148 A218   Set of 4   9.50 9.50

William Dampier
(1651-1715),
Explorer — A219

Designs: 25p, Dampier. 35p, Dampier's ship, HMS Roebuck. £1, Sinking of HMS Roebuck at Ascension Island, 1701. £1.60, Diver and bell of HMS Roebuck.

2015, Dec. 1   Litho.   Perf. 14
1149-1152 A219   Set of 4   9.75 9.75

Worldwide
Fund for
Nature
(WWF)
A220

Red-footed booby: 20p, Bird on rock. 50p, Adult and chick. 55p, Heads of brown and white morphs. £2, Juvenile.

Perf. 13¼x13½
2016, Feb. 22   Litho.
Stamps With White Frames
1153-1156 A220   Set of 4   9.50 9.50
Stamps Without White Frames
1157   Strip of 4   9.50 9.50
  a.   A220 20p multi   .60   .60
  b.   A220 50p multi   1.40 1.40
  c.   A220 55p multi   1.60 1.60
  d.   A220 £2 multi   5.75 5.75

Queen Elizabeth
II, 90th
Birthday — A221

Photograph of Queen Elizabeth II from: 50p, 1951. 55p, 1973. 65p, 1974. £1.60, 1995. £3, Queen Elizabeth II in 1961.

2016, Apr. 21   Litho.   Perf. 14
1158-1161 A221   Set of 4   9.75 9.75
Souvenir Sheet
1162 A221   £3 multi   9.00 9.00

British Broadcasting Corporation
Transmitting Station on Ascension,
50th Anniv. — A222

Designs: 20p, Original control desk. 25p, Klinka Klub and short wave antenna array towers, 1980s. 50p, Atlantic relay station, English Bay. 55p, Current transmitting station. 65p, BBC wind turbines, turtle. £1.60, Current transmitting station main office.

2016, July 3   Litho.   Perf. 13½
1163-1168 A222   Set of 6   10.00 10.00

Scenes from Plays by William
Shakespeare (1564-1616) — A223

Designs: 50p, Twelfth Night. 55p, Henry V. 65p, Hamlet. £1.60, Romeo and Juliet.

2016, Aug. 8   Litho.   Perf. 14
1169-1172 A223   Set of 4   8.75 8.75

Fish
A224

Designs: 50p, Resplendent angelfish. 55p, White hawkfish. 65p, Ascension wrasse. £1.60, Yellowtail damselfish.

2016, Oct. 17   Litho.   Perf. 13¼x13½
1173-1176 A224   Set of 4   8.25 8.25

AIR POST STAMPS

AP1

AP2

AP3

AP4

Green Turtles
AP5   AP6

2015, Feb. 14   Litho.   Perf. 13¼
Stamps With White Frames
C1 AP1 (50p) multi   1.60 1.60
C2 AP2 (50p) multi   1.60 1.60
C3 AP3 (50p) multi   1.60 1.60
C4 AP4 (50p) multi   1.60 1.60
C5 AP5 (50p) multi   1.60 1.60
C6 AP6 (50p) multi   1.60 1.60
  Nos. C1-C6 (6)   9.60 9.60
Miniature Sheet
Stamps Without White Frames
C7   Sheet of 6   9.75 9.75
  a.   AP1 (50p) multi   1.60 1.60
  b.   AP2 (50p) multi   1.60 1.60
  c.   AP3 (50p) multi   1.60 1.60
  d.   AP4 (50p) multi   1.60 1.60
  e.   AP5 (50p) multi   1.60 1.60
  f.   AP6 (50p) multi   1.60 1.60

POSTAGE DUE STAMPS

Outline Map of
Ascension — D1

1986   Litho.   Perf. 15x14
J1 D1   1p beige & brown   .25   .30
J2 D1   2p orange & brown   .25   .30
J3 D1   5p org ver & brn   .25   .30
J4 D1   7p violet & black   .25   .50
J5 D1   10p ultra & black   .35   .75
J6 D1   25p pale green & blk   .75 1.25
  Nos. J1-J6 (6)   2.10 3.40

AUSTRALIAN STATES

NEW SOUTH WALES

'nü sauth 'wā̧ə̧lz

LOCATION — Southeast coast of Australia in the South Pacific Ocean
GOVT. — British Crown Colony
AREA — 309,432 sq. mi.
POP. — 1,500,000 (estimated, 1900)
CAPITAL — Sydney

In 1901 New South Wales united with five other British colonies to form the Commonwealth of Australia. Stamps of Australia are now used.

12 Pence = 1 Shilling
20 Shillings = 1 Pound

Watermarks

Wmk. 12 — Crown and Single-lined A

Wmk. 13 — Large Crown and Double-lined A

Wmk. 49 — Double-lined Numerals Corresponding with the Value

Wmk. 51 — Single-lined Numeral

Wmk. 52 — Single-lined Numeral

Wmk. 53 — 5/-

Wmk. 54 — Small Crown and NSW

Wmk. 55 — Large Crown and NSW

Wmk. 56 — NSW

Wmk. 57 — 5/- NSW in Diamond

Wmk. 58 — 20/- NSW in Circle

Wmk. 70 — V and Crown

Wmk. 199 — Crown and A in Circle

Values for unused stamps are for examples with original gum as defined in the catalogue introduction except for Nos. 1-20 which are rarely found with gum and are valued without gum. Very fine examples of Nos. 35-100, F3-F5, J1-J10 and O1-O40 will have perforations touching the framelines or design on one or more sides due to the narrow spacing of the stamps on the plates and imperfect perforation methods. Stamps with perfs clear of the design on all four sides are scarce and will command higher prices.

Seal of the Colony — A1

A1 has no clouds. A2 has clouds added to the design, except in pos. 15.

1850   Unwmk.   Engr.   *Imperf.*

| 1 | A1 1p red, *yelsh wove* | 11,000. | 725.00 |
| b. | 1p red, *bluish wove* | 11,000. | 725.00 |

Seal of the Colony — A2

2	A2 1p red, *yelsh wove*	9,000.	600.00
b.	A2 1p carmine red, *yellowish laid*	14,500.	800.00
c.	A3 1p carmine red, *bluish wove*	9,000.	850.00
e.	1p carmine red, *bluish laid*		
f.	Hill unshaded	13,500.	925.00
g.	No clouds	13,500.	925.00
h.	No trees	13,500.	925.00

Printed in panes of 25 (5x5). Twenty-five varieties.
Stamps from early impressions of the plate sell at considerably higher prices.
No. 1 was reproduced by the collotype process in a souvenir sheet distributed at the London International Stamp Exhibition 1950. The paper is white.

Plate I — A3   Plate II — A4

Plate I: Vertically lined background.
Plate I re-touched: Lines above and below "POSTAGE" and "TWO PENCE" deepened. Outlines of circular band around picture also deepened.
Plate II (First re-engraving of Plate I): Horizontally lined background; the bale on the left side is dated and there is a dot in the star in each corner.
Plate II retouched: Dots and dashes added in lower spandrels.

Plate I
Late (worn plate) Impressions

| 3 | A3 2p blue, *yelsh wove* | 6,750. | 225.00 |
| a. | Early impression | 18,000. | 625.00 |

Printed in panes of 24 (12x2). Twenty-four varieties.

Plate I, Retouched

| 4 | A3 2p blue, *yelsh wove* | 9,500. | 400.00 |

Twelve varieties.

Plate II
Late (worn plate) Impressions

5	A4 2p blue, *yelsh wove*	7,250.	180.00
b.	2p 2p blue, *grayish wove*	7,250.	180.00
c.	"CREVIT" omitted	—	675.00
d.	Pick and shovel omitted	—	450.00
e.	No whip	10,000.	325.00
h.	Early impression	12,500.	375.00
5F	A4 2p blue, *bluish wove*	9,500.	300.00
g.	No whip	—	475.00
i.	"CREVIT" omitted	—	650.00

Eleven varieties.

Plate III A5   Plate IV A6

Plate III (Second re-engraving of Plate I): The bale is not dated and, with the exception of Nos. 7, 10 and 12, it is single-lined. There are no dots in the stars.
Plate IV (Third re-engraving of Plate I): The bale is double-lined and there is a circle in the center of each star.

1850-51   Wove Paper

6	A5 2p bl, *grayish wove*	8,500.	300.00
a.	Fan with 6 segments	—	650.00
b.	Double-lined bale	—	425.00
c.	No whip	—	475.00
7	A6 2p blue, *bluish wove ('51)*	8,000.	250.00
a.	2p blue, *bluish wove*	7,250.	180.00
b.	2p blue, *grayish wove*	8,000.	275.00
c.	Fan with 6 segments (Pos. 2/8)	—	425.00
d.	No clouds (Pos. 2/10)	—	425.00

Twenty-four varieties.

Plate V — A7

A8

Plate V (Fourth re-engraving of Plate I): There is a pearl in the fan-shaped ornament below the central design.

1850-51

8	A7 2p blue, *grayish wove ('51)*	8,000.	300.00
a.	2p ultra, *yellowish laid*	9,500.	425.00
b.	Fan with 6 segments (Pos. 2/8)	—	500.00
c.	Pick and shovel omitted (Pos. 2/5)	—	525.00
9	A8 3p green, *bluish wove*	9,500.	325.00
a.	3p green, *yellowish wove*	9,500.	375.00
b.	3p green, *yellowish laid*	12,500.	925.00
c.	3p green, *bluish laid*	12,500.	925.00
e.	No whip	—	600.00

Twenty-four varieties of No. 8, twenty-five of No. 9.

Queen Victoria — A9

TWO PENCE
Plate I — Background of wavy lines.
Plate II — Stars in corners.
Plate III (Plate I re-engraved) — Background of crossed lines.

1851   Yellowish Wove Paper

10	A9 1p carmine	4,500.	400.00
b.	No leaves to right of "SOUTH"	6,000.	1,000.
c.	Two leaves to right of "SOUTH"	6,000.	1,100.
d.	"WALE"	6,000.	1,100.
11	A9 2p ultra, Plate I	1,900.	135.00

1852   Bluish Laid Paper

12	A9 1p orange brown	6,750.	600.00
b.	As "a," no leaves to right of "SOUTH"		1,250.
c.	As "a," two leaves to right of "SOUTH"		1,300.
d.	As "a," "WALE"		1,300.

Queen Victoria — A10

SIX PENCE
Plate I — Background of fine lines.
Plate II (Plate I re-engraved) — Background of coarse lines.

1852-55
Bluish or Grayish Wove Paper

13	A9 1p red	1,900.	200.00
a.	1p carmine	2,000.	200.00
d.	As "c," no leaves to right of "SOUTH"	4,250.	400.00
e.	As "c," two leaves to right of "SOUTH"		475.00
f.	As "c," "WALE"		550.00
14	A9 2p blue, Plate I	1,350.	45.00
a.	2p ultramarine	1,700.	45.00
b.	2p slate	1,350.	45.00
15	A10 2p blue, Plate II ('53)	2,250.	125.00
a.	"WAEES"	3,000.	550.00
16	A9 2p blue, Plate III ('55)	1,000.	90.00
17	A9 3p green	3,500.	210.00
a.	3p emerald	4,000.	300.00
b.	As "a," "WACES"		800.00
18	A9 6p brown, Plate I	3,750.	450.00
a.	"WALLS"	4,500.	1,350.
b.	6p black brown	4,500.	1,250.
19	A9 6p brown, Plate II	4,500.	425.00
a.	6p bister brown	4,250.	425.00
20	A9 8p yellow ('53)	12,500.	1,100.
a.	8p orange	13,500.	1,100.
b.	No leaves to right of "SOUTH"		2,250.

The plates of the 1, 2, 3 and 8p each contained 50 varieties and those of the 6p 25 varieties.

The 2p, plate II, 6p, plate II, and 8p have been reprinted on grayish blue wove paper. The reprints of the 2p have the spandrels and background much worn. Most of the reprints of the 6p have no floreate ornaments to the right and left of "South." On all the values the wreath has been retouched.

Type of 1851 and

A11

A12

A13

A14

1854-55 Wmk. 49 Imperf.

23	A9	1p orange	450.00 57.50
a.		No leaves to right of "SOUTH"	975.00 200.00
b.		Two leaves to right of "SOUTH"	1,250. 225.00
c.		"WALE"	1,250. 225.00
24	A9	2p blue	400.00 27.50
a.		2p ultramarine	400.00 27.50
25	A9	3p green	575.00 57.50
a.		"WACES"	1,700. 225.00
b.		Watermarked "2"	7,250. 2,250.

Value for No. 25b is for copy with the design cut into.

26	A11	5p green	1,600. 800.00
27	A12	6p sage green	1,600. 110.00
28	A12	6p brown	1,600. 45.00
a.		Watermarked "8"	4,600. 175.00
29	A12	6p gray	1,600. 110.00
f.		As "e," watermarked "8"	4,500. 160.00
30	A13	8p orange ('55)	17,000. 1,900.
a.		8p yellow	18,000. 1,600.
31	A14	1sh pale red brown	4,250. 140.00
a.		1sh red	3,750. 110.00
c.		As "b," watermarked "8"	10,000. 250.00

See Nos. 38-42, 56, 58, 65, 67.
Nos. 38-42 exist with wide margins. Stamps with perforations trimmed are often offered as Nos. 26, 30, and 30a.

A15

1856 Imperf.

32	A15	1p red	350.00 27.50
a.		1p orange red	325.00 27.50
b.		As "a," printed on both sides	4,200. 2,750.
c.		Watermarked "2"	9,500.
33	A15	2p blue	300.00 16.00
a.		Watermarked "1"	9,500.
b.		Watermarked "5"	1,000. 110.00
c.		Watermarked "8"	8,250.
34	A15	3p green	1,600. 125.00
a.		3p yellow green	1,450. 125.00
b.		Watermarked "2"	5,000.
		Nos. 32-34 (3)	2,250. 168.50

The two known examples of No. 33c are in museums. Both are used.
The 1p has been reprinted in orange on paper watermarked Small Crown and NSW, and the 2p in deep blue on paper watermarked single lined "2." These reprints are usually overprinted "SPECIMEN."
See Nos. 34C-37, 54, 63, 90.

1859 Litho.

34C	A15	2p light blue	— 1,250.

1860-63 Engr. Wmk. 49 Perf. 13

35	A15	1p red	160.00 25.00
a.		1p orange	160.00 25.00
b.		Perf. 12x13	2,100.
c.		Perf. 12	250.00 25.00
36	A15	2p blue, perf. 12	225.00 15.00
a.		Watermarked "1"	4,000.
c.		Perf. 12x13	3,400. 250.00
37	A15	3p blue green	90.00 13.50
a.		3p yellow green	110.00 10.50
b.		3p deep green	110.00 10.00
c.		Watermarked "6"	225.00 16.00
d.		Perf. 12	900.00 55.00
38	A11	5p dark green	110.00 29.00
a.		5p yellow green	250.00 87.50
b.		Perf. 12	450.00 125.00
39	A12	6p brown, perf. 12	725.00 85.00
a.		6p gray, perf. 12	725.00 75.00
40	A12	6p violet	160.00 8.00
a.		6p aniline lilac	1,600. 170.00
b.		Watermarked "5"	850.00 32.50
c.		Watermarked "12"	800.00 27.50
e.		Perf. 12	625.00 22.50
41	A13	8p yellow	450.00 50.00
a.		8p orange	475.00 50.00
b.		As "a," perf. 12	6,250. 1,450.

c.		8p red orange	450.00 65.00
d.		As "c," perf 12	6,250. 1,450.
42	A14	1sh rose	300.00 9.00
a.		1sh carmine	250.00 10.00
b.		As "a," perf. 12	1,350. 75.00
		Nos. 35-42 (8)	2,220. 234.50

1864 Wmk. 50 Perf. 13

43	A15	1p red	80.00 27.50

A16

1861-80 Wmk. 53 Perf. 13

44	A16	5sh dull violet	350.00 77.50
a.		5sh purple	450.00 105.00
b.		5sh dull violet, perf. 12	2,250. 400.00
c.		5sh purple, perf. 12	— 110.00
d.		5sh purple, perf. 10	325.00 110.00
e.		5sh purple, perf. 12x10	475.00 110.00

See No. 101. For overprint see No. O11.
Reprints are perf. 10 and overprinted "REPRINT" in black.

A17

A18

1862-65 Typo. Unwmk. Perf. 13

45	A17	1p red ('65)	225.00 47.50
a.		Perf. 14	200.00 90.00
46	A18	2p blue	150.00 10.00
a.		Perf. 14	200.00 105.00

1863-64 Wmk. 50 Perf. 13

47	A17	1p red	77.50 9.00
a.		Watermarked "2"	225.00 35.00
b.		Horiz. pair, imperf between	2,800.
48	A18	2p blue	55.00 3.00
a.		Watermarked "1"	145.00 6.00

1862 Wmk. 49 Perf. 13

49	A18	2p blue	125.00 32.50
a.		Watermarked "5"	125.00 32.50
b.		Perf. 12x13	875.00 450.00
c.		Perf. 12	225.00 75.00

See Nos. 52-53, 61-62, 70-71.

A19

A20

1867, Sept. Wmk. 51, 52 Perf. 13

50	A19	4p red brown	125.00 9.50
a.		Imperf.	
51	A20	10p lilac	55.00 9.50
b.		Horiz. pair, imperf between	3,500.

See Nos. 55, 64, 91, 97, 117, 129.

A21

A22

A23

Typo.; Engr. (3p, 5p, 8p)
1871-84 Wmk. 54 Perf. 13

52	A17	1p red	35.00 3.50
a.		Perf. 10	325.00 45.00
b.		Perf. 13x10	35.00 2.50
c.		Horiz. pair, imperf between	3,250.
53	A18	2p blue	42.50 2.00
a.		Imperf.	
b.		Horiz. pair, imperf vert.	3,750.
c.		Perf. 10	400.00 27.50
d.		Perf. 13x10	35.00 1.50

e.		Perf. 12x13	
f.		2p Prussian blue, perf. 11x12	400.00 60.00
54	A15	3p green ('74)	85.00 8.00
a.		Perf. 11	225.00 130.00
b.		Perf. 12	— 225.00
c.		Perf. 10x12	225.00 50.00
d.		Perf. 11x12	175.00 45.00
e.		Perf. 10	160.00 17.50
f.		3p bright green, perf. 13x10	175.00 25.00
55	A19	4p red brown ('77)	125.00 20.00
a.		Perf. 10	275.00 95.00
b.		Perf. 13x10	85.00 5.00
c.		Perf. 10x13	175.00 27.50
56	A11	5p dk grn, perf. 10 ('84)	45.00 42.50
a.		Horiz. pair, imperf between	2,250.
b.		Perf. 12	325.00 125.00
c.		Perf. 10x12	140.00 72.50
d.		Perf. 10x13	
		12x10	67.50 42.50
57	A21	6p lilac ('72)	105.00 3.00
a.		Horiz. pair, imperf. between	— 3,500.
b.		Perf. 13x10	125.00 3.00
c.		Perf. 10	300.00 21.00
58	A13	8p yellow ('77)	225.00 30.00
a.		Imperf.	
b.		Perf. 10	550.00 45.00
c.		Perf. 13x10	250.00 42.50
59	A22	9p on 10p red brown, perf. 12 (Bk)	25.00 18.00
a.		Double surcharge, blk & bl	400.00
b.		Perf. 12x10	475.00 350.00
c.		Perf. 10	15.00 11.50
d.		Perf. 12x11	17.00 10.00
e.		Perf. 11x12	—
f.		Perf. 13	77.50 15.00
g.		Perf. 13x10	67.50 13.50
h.		Perf. 10x11	77.50 25.00
60	A23	1sh black ('76)	175.00 12.50
a.		Perf. 13x10	275.00 14.50
b.		Perf. 10	250.00 30.00
c.		Perf. 11	—
e.		Vert. pair, imperf between	3,500.
f.		Pair, imperf	2,800.
		Nos. 52-60 (9)	862.50 139.50

The surcharge on No. 59 measures 15mm.
See Nos. 66, 68. For overprints see Nos. O1-O10.

Typo.; Engr. (3p, 5p, 8p)
1882-91 Wmk. 55 Perf. 11x12

61	A17	1p red	10.00 1.40
a.		Perf. 10	22.50 2.50
b.		Perf. 10x13	140.00 11.00
c.		Perf. 10x12	310.00 75.00
d.		Perf. 12x11	135.00
e.		Perf. 10x11	135.00
f.		Perf. 11	550.00 175.00
g.		Perf. 13	1,100. 500.00
h.		Perf. 13x10	72.50 3.00
i.		Perf. 12x10	— 225.00
j.		Perf. 11x10	—
k.		Horiz. pair, imperf between	2,100.
62	A18	2p blue	14.50 1.10
a.		Perf. 10	67.50 1.25
b.		Perf. 13x10	170.00 8.50
c.		Perf. 13	550.00 125.00
d.		Perf. 12x10	500.00 125.00
e.		Perf. 11	125.00
f.		Perf. 12x11	500.00 125.00
g.		Perf. 11x10	550.00 190.00
h.		Perf. 12	2275.00
i.		Double impression	— 800.00
63	A15	3p green	11.00 11.00
a.		Imperf., pair	500.00
b.		Vert. pair, imperf. btwn.	—
c.		Horiz. pair, imperf. vert.	675.00 675.00
d.		Double impression	—
e.		Perf. 10	32.50 2.50
f.		Perf. 11	11.00 2.50
g.		Perf. 12	17.50 2.75
h.		Perf. 12x11	12.50 3.25
i.		Perf. 10x12	55.00 4.75
m.		Perf. 10x11	35.00 3.75
n.		Perf. 12x10	55.00 4.75
64	A19	4p red brown	85.00 3.00
a.		Perf. 10	— 17.00
b.		Perf. 10x12	250.00 75.00
c.		Perf. 12	300.00 225.00
65	A11	5p dk blue green	12.50 1.50
a.		Imperf., pair	550.00
b.		Perf. 10	12.50 1.50
c.		Perf. 10	17.50 2.00
d.		Perf. 12	28.00 2.00
e.		Perf. 10x12	175.00 47.50
f.		5p green, perf. 12x11	12.50 1.50
g.		5p green, perf. 11x10	90.00 90.00
h.		5p green, perf. 12x10	110.00 14.00
i.		5p green, perf. 10x11	90.00 90.00
j.		5p green, perf. 11	16.00 2.50
66	A21	6p lilac, perf. 10	105.00 2.75
a.		Horiz. pair, imperf. between	3,000.
b.		Perf. 10x12	110.00 2.00
c.		Perf. 11x12	145.00 16.50
d.		Perf. 12	145.00 11.50
e.		Perf. 11x10	125.00 125.00
f.		Perf. 10	145.00 9.00
g.		Perf. 10x13	— 400.00
67	A13	8p yellow, perf. 10	220.00 25.00
a.		Perf. 11	220.00 30.00
b.		Perf. 12	325.00 35.00
c.		Perf. 10x12	250.00 67.50
68	A23	1sh black	135.00 9.00
a.		Perf. 10x13	—
b.		Perf. 10	145.00 8.00
c.		Perf. 11	275.00 20.00
d.		Perf. 10x12	— 325.00
		Nos. 61-68 (8)	593.00 54.75

Nos. 63 and 65 exist with two types of watermark 55 — spacings of 1mm or 2mm between crown and NSW.

See No. 90. For surcharges and overprints see Nos. 92-94, O12-O19.
The 1, 2, 4, 6, 8p and 1sh have been reprinted on paper watermarked Large Crown and NSW. The 1, 2, 4p and 1sh are perforated 11x12, the 6p is perforated 10 and the 8p 11. All are overprinted "REPRINT," the 1sh in red and the others in black.

Perf. 11x12
1886-87 Typo. Wmk. 56
Bluish Revenue Stamp Paper

70	A17	1p scarlet	13.00 6.00
a.		Perf. 10	35.00 13.00
71	A18	2p dark blue	32.50 6.00
a.		Perf. 10	105.00 15.00

For overprint, see No. O20.

A24

Perf. 12 (#73-75), 12x10 (#72, 75A) and Compound
1885-86 "POSTAGE" in Black

72	A24	5sh green & vio	850.00 125.00
a.		Perf. 10	—
73	A24	10sh rose & vio	1,750. 275.00
74	A24	£1 rose & vio	9,000. —
a.		Perf. 13	— 5,250.

"POSTAGE" in Blue
Bluish Paper

75	A24	10sh rose & vio	325.00 80.00
b.		Perf. 10	1,350. 300.00
c.		Perf. 12x11	

White Paper

75A	A24	£1 rose & vio	6,750. 4,250.

For overprints, see Nos. O21-O23.
The 5sh with black overprint and the £1 with blue overprint have been reprinted on paper watermarked NSW. They are perforated 12x10 and are overprinted "REPRINT" in black.

"POSTAGE" in Blue
1894 White Paper

76	A24	10sh rose & violet, perf 12	450.00 105.00
b.		Double overprint	
		10sh mauve & claret, perf 10	850.00 275.00
c.		10sh mauve & violet, perf 11	750.00 190.00
d.		10sh mauve & violet, perf 12x11	425.00 125.00

See No. 108B.

View of Sydney
A25

Emu
A26

Captain Cook — A27

Victoria and Coat of Arms — A28

Lyrebird
A29

Kangaroo
A30

1888-89 Wmk. 55 Perf. 11x12

77	A25	1p violet	10.00 1.40
a.		Perf. 12	14.00 1.10
b.		Perf. 12x11½	42.50 2.40

78	A26	2p blue	16.00	1.40
a.		Imperf., pair	400.00	
b.		Perf. 12	25.00	.95
c.		Perf. 12x11½	29.00	.95
79	A27	4p brown	25.00	8.75
a.		Perf. 12x11½	87.50	20.00
b.		Perf. 12	72.50	10.00
c.		Perf. 11	700.00	200.00
d.		Imperf.		
80	A28	6p carmine rose	57.50	8.75
a.		Perf. 12	47.50	15.00
b.		Perf. 12x11½	57.50	8.75
81	A29	8p red violet	42.50	9.50
a.		Perf. 12	42.50	9.50
b.		Perf. 12x11½	75.00	20.00
82	A30	1sh maroon ('89)	57.50	8.75
a.		Imperf., pair	1,000.	
b.		Perf. 12x11½	57.50	4.25
c.		Perf. 12	72.50	4.25
		Nos. 77-82 (6)	208.50	38.55

First British settlement in Australia, cent.
For overprints see Nos. O24-O29.

1888 — Wmk. 56 — Perf. 11x12

83	A25	1p violet	35.00	4.00
84	A26	2p blue	115.00	6.00

See Nos. 104B-106C, 113-115, 118, 125-127, 130.

Map of Australia — A31

Governors Capt. Arthur Phillip (above) and Lord Carrington — A32

1888-89 — Wmk. 53 — Perf. 10

85	A31	5sh violet ('89)	475.00	105.00
86	A32	20sh ultra	600.00	225.00

See Nos. 88, 120. For overprints see Nos. O30-O31.

1890 — Wmk. 57 — Perf. 10

87	A31	5sh violet	400.00	77.50
a.		Perf. 11	450.00	100.00
b.		Perf. 10x11	550.00	77.50
c.		Perf. 12	700.00	115.00
f.		Horiz. pair, imperf btwn.		

Perf. 11x12, 12x11 — Wmk. 58

88	A32	20sh ultra	225.00	90.00
a.		Perf. 11	275.00	90.00
b.		Perf. 12	700.00	275.00
c.		20sh cobalt blue, perf 10	525.00	275.00

For overprints see Nos. O32-O33.

"Australia" — A33

1890, Dec. 22 — Wmk. 55 — Perf. 11x12

89	A33	2½p ultra	14.00	5.75
a.		Perf. 12	29.00	5.75
b.		Perf. 12x11½	87.50	—

For overprint see No. O35.

Type of 1856

1891 — Engr. — Wmk. 52 — Perf. 10

90	A15	3p green	15.00	100.00
a.		Double impression		

Type of 1867

1893 — Typo. — Perf. 11

91	A15	10p lilac	35.00	11.50
a.		Perf. 10	42.50	14.00
b.		Perf. 11x10 or 10x11	47.50	18.00
c.		Perf. 12x11	250.00	35.00

Types of 1862-84 Surcharged in Black

Halfpenny
a

SEVEN-PENCE HALFPENNY
b

1891, Jan. 5 — Wmk. 55 — Perf. 11x12

92	A17(a)	½p on 1p gray	21.00	14.00
a.		Imperf.		
b.		Surcharge omitted	—	
c.		Double surcharge	550.00	

93	A21(b)	7½p on 6p brown	21.00	14.00
a.		Perf. 10	21.00	14.00
b.		Perf. 11	20.00	11.50
c.		Perf. 12	24.00	14.00
d.		Perf. 10x12	24.00	14.00
94	A23(b)	12½p on 1sh red	14.00	12.00
a.		Perf. 11x12	22.50	22.50
b.		Perf. 10	29.00	25.00
c.		Perf. 11	30.00	25.00
d.		Perf. 12	35.00	25.00
		Nos. 92-94 (3)	56.00	40.00

For overprints see Nos. O34, O36-O37.

Victoria — A37

1892-97 — Perf. 11x12

95	A37	½p slate ('97)	5.75	.85
a.		Perf. 12x11½	5.75	.85
b.		Perf. 12	5.50	.85
c.		As #95, horiz. pair, imperf between	1,350.	
d.		½p gray, perf. 10	80.00	7.25
e.		As "d," perf. 10x12	140.00	18.00
f.		As "d," perf. 11	160.00	14.00
g.		As "d," perf. 11x12	2.25	.50

See Nos. 102, 109, 121. For overprint see No. O38.

Types of 1867-71

1897 — Perf. 11x12

96	A22	9p on 10p red brn (Bk)	20.00	17.50
a.		9p on 10p org brn (Bk)	20.00	17.50
b.		Surcharge omitted	—	
c.		Double surcharge	375.00	375.00
d.		Perf. 11	25.00	24.00
e.		Perf. 12	25.00	22.50
97	A20	10p violet	25.00	16.00
a.		Perf. 12x11½	25.00	16.00
b.		Perf. 11	47.50	22.50
c.		Perf. 12	35.00	17.50

The surcharge on No. 96 measures 13½mm.
For overprints see Nos. O39-O40.

Seal A38

Victoria A39

A40

ONE PENNY:
Die I — The first pearl in the crown at the left is merged into the arch, the shading under the fleur-de-lis is indistinct, and the "s" of "WALES" is open.
Die II — The first pearl is circular, the vertical shading under the fleur-de-lis is clear, and the "s" of "WALES" not so open.

2½ PENCE:
Die I — There are 12 radiating lines in the star on the Queen's breast.
Die II — There are 16 radiating lines in the star. The eye is nearly full of color.

1897 — Perf. 12

98	A38	1p rose red, II	4.75	.50
a.		Die I, perf. 11x12	5.75	.50
b.		Imperf., pair	—	
c.		Imperf. horiz. pair	700.00	
d.		Die I, perf. 12x11½	5.50	.50
e.		Die I, perf. 12	11.50	1.75
f.		Die I, perf. 12x11½	4.75	.50
g.		Die II, perf. 11x12	4.75	.50
99	A39	2p deep blue	13.50	.65
a.		Perf. 11x12	9.00	.65
b.		Perf. 12x11½	7.75	.65
100	A40	2½p dp purple, II	20.00	4.25
a.		Die I, perf. 12x11	22.50	4.75
b.		Die I, perf. 11	25.00	7.75
c.		Die II, perf. 11½x12	25.00	4.25
d.		Die II, perf. 11x12	21.00	4.25
e.		Die II, perf. 11½x12	25.00	4.25
		Nos. 98-100 (3)	38.25	5.40

Sixtieth year of Queen Victoria's reign.
See Nos. 103-104, 110-112, 122-124.

Type of 1861

1897 — Engr. — Wmk. 53 — Perf. 11

101	A16	5sh red violet	105.00	29.00
a.		Horiz. pair, imperf. btwn.	11,000.	
b.		Perf. 11x12 or 12x11	130.00	42.50
c.		Perf. 12	140.00	52.50

Perf. 12x11½, 11½x12

1899, Oct. — Typo. — Wmk. 55

HALF PENNY:
Die I — Narrow "H" in "HALF."

102	A37	½p blue green, I	3.50	.95
a.		Imperf., pair	190.00	325.00
103	A39	2p ultra	5.75	.95
a.		Imperf., pair	325.00	
104	A40	2½p dk blue, II	8.00	3.25
a.		Imperf., pair	325.00	
104B	A27	4p org brown	22.50	13.50
d.		As "c," imperf. pair	750.00	
105	A28	6p emerald	135.00	52.50
a.		Imperf., pair	600.00	
106	A28	6p orange	29.00	6.75
a.		6p yellow	26.00	10.75
b.		Imperf., pair	475.00	
106C	A29	8p magenta	42.50	8.00
		Nos. 102-106C (7)	246.25	85.90

Lyrebird — A41

1903 — Perf. 12x11½

107	A41	2sh6p blue green	87.50	42.50

See Nos. 119, 131.

"Australia" — A42

1903 — Wmk. 70 — Perf. 12½

108	A42	9p org brn & ultra	29.00	7.25
a.		Perf. 11	5,250.	1,850.

See No. 128.

Type of 1885-86

1904 — Wmk. 56 — Perf. 12x11 — "POSTAGE" in Blue

108B	A24	10sh brt rose & vio	325.00	125.00
c.		Perf. 11	525.00	200.00
d.		Perf. 14	400.00	135.00
e.		10sh aniline crimson & violet, perf 12	650.00	200.00
f.		As "e," perf 12x11	475.00	130.00
g.		10sh claret & violet, chalky paper, perf 12x11	475.00	175.00

The watermark (NSW) of No. 108B is 20x7mm, with rounded angles in "N" and "W." On No. 75, the watermark is 21x7mm, with sharp angles in the "N" and "W."

HALF PENNY:
Die II — Wide "H" in "HALF."

Perf. 11, 11x12½, 12x11½ and Compound

1905-06 — Wmk. 12

109	A37	½p blue grn, II	6.00	1.10
a.		½p blue green, I	6.25	1.10
b.		Booklet pane of 12	—	
110	A38	1p car rose, II	4.75	.50
a.		Booklet pane of 6	—	
b.		Booklet pane of 12	—	
111	A39	2p deep ultra	4.75	.50
112	A40	2½p dk blue, II	9.00	5.25
113	A27	4p org brown	21.00	8.75
114	A28	6p orange	29.00	6.00
a.		6p yellow	35.00	6.00
b.		Perf. 11	525.00	
115	A29	8p magenta	52.50	11.00
117	A20	10p violet	32.50	10.00
118	A30	1sh vio brown	57.50	5.75
119	A41	2sh6p blue green	77.50	40.00

Wmk. 199 — Perf. 12x11 or 11x12

120	A32	20sh ultra	225.00	87.50
		Nos. 109-115,117-120 (11)	519.50	176.35

1906-07 — Wmk. 13

121	A37	½p green, I	8.75	2.25
122	A38	1p rose, II	17.00	2.25
123	A39	2p ultra	17.00	2.25
124	A40	2½p blue, II	110.00	200.00
125	A27	4p org brown	29.00	25.00
126	A28	6p orange	67.50	37.50
127	A29	8p red violet	42.50	37.50

128	A42	9p org brn & ultra, perf. 12x11½ ('06)	22.50	4.50
a.		Perf. 11	175.00	140.00
129	A20	10p violet	62.50	87.50
130	A30	1sh vio brown	92.50	18.00
131	A41	2sh6p blue green	125.00	105.00
		Nos. 121-131 (11)	594.25	522.75

Portions of some of the sheets on which the above are printed show the watermark "COMMONWEALTH OF AUSTRALIA." Stamps may also be found from portions of the sheet without watermark.

SEMI-POSTAL STAMPS

SP1

Allegory of Charity SP2

1897, June — Wmk. 55 — Perf. 11

B1	SP1	1p (1sh) grn & brn	72.50	72.50
B2	SP2	2½p (2sh6p) rose, bl & gold	350.00	350.00

Diamond Jubilee of Queen Victoria. The difference between the postal and face values of these stamps was donated to a fund for a home for consumptives.

REGISTRATION STAMPS

Queen Victoria — R1

Unwmk.

1856, Jan. 1 — Engr. — Imperf.

F1	R1	(6p) orange & blue	1,700.	250.00
F2	R1	(6p) red & blue	1,800.	210.00
a.		Frame printed on back	13,500.	5,750.

1860 — Perf. 12, 13

F3	R1	(6p) orange & blue	950.00	75.00
F4	R1	(6p) red & blue	950.00	80.00

Nos. F1 to F4 exist also on paper with papermaker's watermark in sheet.

1863 — Wmk. 49

F5	R1	(6p) red & blue	225.00	25.00
c.		Double impression of frame	—	800.00

Fifty varieties.
Nos. F1-F2 were reprinted on thin white wove unwatermarked paper and on thick yellowish wove unwatermarked paper; the former are usually overprinted "SPECIMEN."
No. F4 was reprinted on thin white wove unwatermarked paper; perf. 10 and overprinted "REPRINT" in black.

POSTAGE DUE STAMPS

D1

Perf. 10, 11, 11½, 12 and Compound
1891-92 **Typo.** **Wmk. 55**

J1	D1	½p grn, perf 10	10.00	10.00
J2	D1	1p green	21.00	3.75
a.		Perf 12	45.00	9.00
J3	D1	2p green	29.00	5.75
a.		Perf 12x10	47.50	7.00
J4	D1	3p green	47.50	21.00
J5	D1	4p green	42.50	11.50
J6	D1	6p grn, perf 10	27.50	17.50
J7	D1	8p grn, perf 10	160.00	42.50
J8	D1	5sh grn, perf 10	325.00	105.00
a.		Perf 11	575.00	175.00
b.		Perf 11x12	—	300.00

Perf. 12x10

J9	D1	10sh green	600.00	—
a.		Perf. 10	750.00	80.00
J10	D1	20sh green	700.00	—
a.		Perf. 10	1,000.	125.00
b.		Perf. 12	1,350.	
		Nos. J1-J10 (10)	1,963.	217.00

Nos. J1-J5 exist on both ordinary and chalky paper.

Used values for Nos. J8-J10 are for c-t-o stamps.

OFFICIAL STAMPS

Regular Issues Overprinted in Black or Red

Perf. 10, 11, 12, 13 and Compound
1879-80 **Wmk. 54**

O1	A17	1p red	30.00	5.75
a.		Perf. 10	350.00	65.00
b.		Perf. 10x13	72.50	9.50
O2	A18	2p blue	47.50	5.25
a.		Perf. 11x12		525.00
b.		Perf. 10	525.00	77.50
O3	A15	3p green (R)	1,100.	550.00
O4	A15	3p green	350.00	60.00
a.		Watermarked "6"	—	925.00
b.		Double overprint	—	925.00
c.		3p yel grn, perf 10	350.00	60.00
d.		3p yel grn, perf 12	425.00	175.00
O5	A19	4p red brown	400.00	21.00
a.		Perf. 10x13	450.00	190.00
O6	A11	5p dark green	42.50	27.50
O7	A21	6p lilac	600.00	20.00
a.		Perf. 10	800.00	75.00
b.		Perf. 13x10	450.00	90.00
O8	A13	8p yellow (R)	1,750.	500.00
O9	A13	8p yellow	—	52.50
a.		Perf. 10	625.00	175.00
O10	A23	1sh black (R)	600.00	17.50
a.		Perf. 10	—	35.00
b.		Perf. 10x13	—	77.50
c.		Perf. 13x10	—	29.00

1880 **Wmk. 53**

O11	A16	5sh lilac, perf. 11	400.00	135.00
a.		Double overprint	4,500.	2,400.
b.		Perf. 10	1,000.	225.00
c.		Perf. 12x10	900.00	225.00
d.		Perf. 13	1,250.	200.00
e.		Perf. 10x12		—

1881 **Wmk. 55**

O12	A17	1p red	35.00	6.00
a.		Perf. 10x13		200.00
O13	A18	2p blue	21.00	2.40
a.		Perf. 10x13	400.00	200.00
O14	A15	3p green	17.50	8.50
a.		Double overprint		1,200.
b.		Perf. 12	325.00	200.00
c.		Perf. 11		
O15	A19	4p red brown	35.00	7.50
a.		Perf. 10x12	350.00	200.00
b.		Perf. 12	350.00	350.00
O16	A11	5p dark green	32.50	35.00
a.		Perf. 12	250.00	
b.		Perf. 12x10		
O17	A21	6p lilac	50.00	11.50
a.		Perf. 10		105.00
b.		Perf. 11x12		
c.		Perf. 12x11 ('85)	100.00	27.50
O18	A13	8p yellow	57.50	25.00
a.		Double overprint		
b.		Perf. 12	350.00	525.00

O19	A23	1sh black (R)	72.50	21.00
a.		Double overprint		525.00
b.		Perf. 10x13		140.00
c.		Perf. 11x12, comb.	57.50	21.00
		Nos. O12-O19 (8)	321.00	116.90

Beware of other red overprints on watermark 55 stamps.

No. O14 exists with two overprint types: "O" and "S" 7mm and 5.5mm apart. For detailed listings, see the Scott Classic Specialized catalogue.

1881 **Wmk. 56**

O20	A17	1p red	105.00	17.50

1887-90

O21	A24	10sh on #75	—	3,200.
O22	A24	£1 on #75A	19,500.	9,250.

No. 75 Overprinted

1889

O23	A24	10sh rose & vio	5,750.	1,450.
a.		Perf. 10	7,500.	3,500.

Overprinted

1888-89 **Wmk. 55**

O24	A25	1p violet	6.25	2.00
a.		Overprinted "O" only		
O25	A26	2p blue	9.50	1.40
O26	A27	4p red brown	25.00	9.50
O27	A28	6p carmine	18.00	12.00
O28	A29	8p red lilac	47.50	32.50
O29	A30	1sh vio brown	45.00	9.50
a.		Double overprint		
		Nos. O24-O29 (6)	151.25	66.90

Wmk. 53

O30	A31	5sh violet (R)	2,000.	800.00
O31	A32	20sh ultra	17,500.	1,150.

1890 **Wmk. 57**

O32	A31	5sh violet	400.00	150.00
a.		5sh, dull lilac, perf. 12	1,100.	250.00

Wmk. 58

O33	A32	20sh ultra	18,000.	1,750.

Centenary of the founding of the Colony (Nos. O24-O33).

1891 **Wmk. 55**

O34	A17(a)	½p on 1p gray & black	125.00	125.00
a.		Double overprint		
O35	A33	2½p ultra	24.00	14.00
O36	A21(b)	7½p on 6p brn & black	72.50	85.00
O37	A23(b)	12½p on 1sh red & black	125.00	140.00

1892

O38	A37	½p gray, perf 11x12	12.50	24.00
a.		Perf 10	16.00	27.50
b.		Perf 12	15.00	20.00
c.		Perf 12x11½	27.50	22.50

1894 **Wmk. 54**

O39	A22	9p on 10p red brn	1,100.	1,100.

Wmk. 52

O40	A20	10p lilac, perf. 13	325.00	175.00
a.		Perf. 11x10 or 10x11	475.00	450.00
b.		Perf. 10	400.00	

The official stamps became obsolete on Dec. 31, 1894. In Aug., 1895, sets of 32 varieties of "O.S." stamps, together with some envelopes and postal cards, were placed on sale at the Sydney post office at £2 per set.

These sets contained most of the varieties listed above and a few which are not known in the original issues. An obliteration consisting of the letters G.P.O. or N.S.W. in three concentric ovals was lightly applied to the center of each block of four stamps.

It is understood that the earlier stamps and many of the overprints were reprinted to make up these sets.

QUEENSLAND

ˈkwēnz-ˌland

LOCATION — Northeastern part of Australia
GOVT. — British Crown Colony
AREA — 670,500 sq. mi.
POP. — 498,129 (1901)
CAPITAL — Brisbane

Originally a part of New South Wales, Queensland was constituted a separate colony in 1859. It was one of the six British Colonies that united in 1901 to form the Commonwealth of Australia.

12 Pence = 1 Shilling
20 Shillings = 1 Pound

Values for unused stamps are for examples with original gum as defined in the catalogue introduction. Very fine examples of Nos. 4-73, 84-125, 128-140, and F1-F3b will have perforations touching the design on at least one or more sides due to the narrow spacing of the stamps on the plates. Stamps with perfs clear of the design on all four sides are scarce and will command higher prices.

Watermarks

Wmk. 5 — Small Star

Wmk. 6 — Large Star

Wmk. 12 — Crown and Single-lined A

Wmk. 13 — Crown and Double-lined A

Wmk. 65 — "Queensland Postage Stamps" in Sheet in Script Capitals

Wmk. 66

Wmks. 66 & 67 — "Queensland" in Large Single-lined Roman Capitals in the Sheet and Short-pointed Star to Each Stamp (Stars Vary Slightly in Size and Shape)

Wmk. 68 — Crown and Q

Wmk. 69 — Large Crown and Q

There are two varieties of the watermark 68, differing slightly in the position and shape of the crown and the tongue of the "Q."

Wmk. 70 — V and Crown

Queen Victoria — A1

Wmk. 6
1860, Nov. 1 **Engr.** **Imperf.**

1	A1	1p deep rose	6,600.	1,050.
2	A1	2p deep blue	16,250.	2,250.
3	A1	6p deep green	10,250.	1,050.

Clean-Cut Perf. 14 to 16

4	A1	1p deep rose	2,750.	375.
5	A1	2p deep blue	1,450.	140.
a.		Horiz. pair, imperf between	—	4,250.
6	A1	6p deep green	1,450.	110.

Clean-Cut Perf. 14 to 16

1860-61 **Wmk. 5**

6A	A1	2p blue	975.00	135.00
b.		Horiz. pair, imperf. between		11,500.
6D	A1	3p brown ('61)	775.00	110.00
6E	A1	6p deep green	1,350.	95.00
6F	A1	1sh gray violet	1,450.	120.00

Regular Perf. 14

6H	A1	1p rose	225.00	62.50
6I	A1	2p deep blue	625.00	105.00

Rough Perf. 14 to 16

7	A1	1p deep rose	115.00	57.50
8	A1	2p blue	300.00	52.50
a.		Horiz. pair, imperf between		10,250.
9	A1	3p brown ('61)	105.00	60.00
a.		Horiz. pair, imperf. vert.	10,250.	
10	A1	6p deep green	575.00	52.50
a.		6p dble deep green	675.00	42.50
11	A1	1sh dull violet	1,150.	140.00

Thick Yellowish Paper
Square Perf. 12½ to 13

1862-67 **Unwmk.**

12	A1	1p Indian red	575.00	115.00
13	A1	1p orange ('63)	140.00	22.50
a.		Perf. 13, round holes ('67)	160.00	42.50

No.	Type	Description	Unused	Used
b.		Horiz. pair, imperf. between	—	—
c.		Imperf., pair	—	3,000.
14	A1	2p deep blue	100.00	15.00
a.		2p pale blue	200.00	60.00
b.		Perf. 13, round holes ('67)	100.00	27.50
c.		Imperf., pair		2,750.
e.		Horiz. pair, imperf. between		16,000.
f.		Vert. pair, imperf. between	5,250.	
15	A1	3p brown ('63)	125.00	62.50
a.		Imperf.		
b.		Perf. 13, round holes ('67)	130.00	60.00
16	A1	6p yellow grn ('63)	195.00	32.50
a.		6p green	300.00	100.00
b.		Perf. 13, round holes ('67)	200.00	32.50
c.		Imperf., pair		2,850.
d.		Horiz. pair, imperf. between	—	17,500.
17	A1	1sh gray ('63)	500.00	47.50
b.		Imperf. horizontally		
c.		Horiz. pair, imperf. between	—	18,000.
d.		Perf. 13, round holes ('67)	500.00	47.50
e.		Vert. pair, imperf between	—	

White Wove Paper
1865   Wmk. 5   Rough Perf. 13

No.	Type	Description	Unused	Used
18	A1	1p orange	125.00	60.00
a.		Horiz. pair, imperf. between	5,750.	
19	A1	2p light blue	130.00	30.00
a.		Vert. pair, imperf. between	9,000.	
b.		Half used as 1p on cover		4,500.
20	A1	6p yellow green	240.00	45.00
		Nos. 18-20 (3)	495.00	135.00

1865   Perf. 12½x13

18B	A1	1p orange vermilion	175.00	85.00
19C	A1	2p blue	300.00	85.00

Perf. 13, Round Holes
1866   Wmk. 65

21	A1	1p orange vermilion	210.00	52.50
22	A1	2p blue	110.00	32.50
a.		Diagonal half used as 1p on cover		—

1865   Perf. 12½x13

21A	A1	1p orange vermilion	300.00	80.00
22C	A1	2p blue	300.00	80.00

1866   Unwmk.   Litho.   Perf. 13

23	A1	4p lilac	425.00	22.50
		4p slate	425.00	30.00
24	A1	5sh pink	1,150.	150.00
b.		Vert. pair, imperf between		9,000.

Wmk. 66, 67
1868-74   Engr.   Perf. 13

25	A1	1p orange ('71)	100.00	9.25
26	A1	2p blue	77.50	6.00
27	A1	3p grnsh brn ('71)	200.00	12.50
a.		3p brown	125.00	11.50
b.		3p olive brown	200.00	11.50
28	A1	6p yel grn ('71)	250.00	14.00
a.		6p deep green	325.00	35.00
30	A1	1sh grnsh gray ('72)	825.00	100.00
31	A1	1sh violet ('74)	425.00	37.50
a.		1sh brownish gray	850.00	110.00

Perf. 12

32	A1	1p orange	600.00	47.50
33	A1	2p blue	975.00	80.00
34	A1	3p brown	775.00	325.00
35	A1	6p deep green	1,900.	52.50
36	A1	1sh violet	900.00	87.50

Perf. 13x12

36A	A1	1p orange	250.00	
37	A1	2p blue	1,650.	50.00
37A	A1	2p blue	1,000.	

The reprints are perforated 13 and the colors differ slightly from those of the originals.

1868-75   Wmk. 68   Perf. 13

38	A1	1p orange	115.00	8.75
a.		Imperf pair	825.00	
39	A1	1p rose ('74)	105.00	17.00
40	A1	2p blue	90.00	5.00
a.		Vert. pair, imperf between	—	
b.		Imperf., pair	725.00	
41	A1	3p brown ('75)	140.00	21.00
42	A1	6p yel green ('69)	200.00	14.00
a.		6p apple green	240.00	17.50
b.		6p deep green	225.00	17.50
c.		As "a," imperf pair	725.00	
43	A1	1sh violet ('75)	400.00	87.50
		Nos. 38-43 (6)	1,050.	153.25

1876-78   Perf. 12

44	A1	1p orange	77.50	9.50
a.		Imperf.	775.00	
c.		Vert. pair, imperf between	—	
45	A1	1p rose	90.00	20.00
a.		1p salmon	125.00	20.00
46	A1	2p blue	75.00	2.40
a.		2p pale blue	160.00	29.00
47	A1	3p brown	125.00	17.50
48	A1	6p yellow green	275.00	9.50
a.		6p apple green	300.00	15.50
b.		6p deep green	265.00	16.00
49	A1	1sh violet	100.00	17.50
m.		Vert. pair, imperf between	—	
		Nos. 44-49 (6)	742.50	76.40

Nos. 44, 49 exist in vertical pairs, imperf. between.

Perf. 13x12

49B	A1	1p orange	250.00	
49C	A1	2p blue	1,500.	325.00
49D	A1	4p yellow	575.00	
49E	A1	6p deep green	575.00	

Perf. 12½x13

49G	A1	1p org ver	600.00	
49H	A1	2p deep blue	600.00	

The reprints are perforated 12 and are in paler colors than the originals.

1879   Unwmk.   Perf. 12

50	A1	6p pale emerald	450.00	40.00
a.		Horiz. pair, imperf. vert.		2,250.

A2

1875-81   Litho.   Wmk. 68   Perf. 13

50B	A1	4p yellow ('75)	2,000.	110.00

Perf. 12

51	A1	4p buff ('76)	1,675.	45.00
a.		4p yellow	1,675.	45.00
52	A1	2sh pale blue ('81)	170.00	62.50
		Fiscal cancellation		5.75
a.		2sh deep blue	200.00	62.50
b.		Imperf.		5.75
53	A2	2sh6p lt red ('81)	340.00	100.00
		Fiscal cancellation		5.75
54	A1	5sh org brn ('81)	475.00	150.00
		Fiscal cancellation		7.00
a.		5sh fawn	475.00	150.00
55	A1	10sh brown ('81)	875.00	250.00
		Fiscal cancellation		7.00
a.		Imperf., pair	1,750.	
56	A1	20sh rose ('81)	2,000.	400.00
		Fiscal cancellation		9.25
		Nos. 50B-56 (7)	7,535.	1,118.

Nos. 53-56, 62-64, 74-83 with pen (revenue) cancellations removed are often offered as unused.

A3

1879-81   Typo.   Wmk. 68   Perf. 12

57	A3	1p rose red	62.50	10.00
a.		1p red orange	87.50	11.00
b.		1p brown orange	115.00	10.00
c.		"QOEENSLAND"	675.00	125.00
d.		Imperf.	—	
e.		Vert. pair, imperf. horiz.		1,100.
f.		As "a" "OOGENSLAND"	275.00	47.50
g.		As "b" "OOGENSLAND"	550.00	65.00
58	A3	2p gray blue	90.00	5.00
a.		2p deep ultra	95.00	5.00
b.		Imperf.	—	
c.		"PENGE"	400.00	60.00
d.		"TW" joined	87.50	1.75
e.		Vert. pair, imperf. horiz.	1,750.	
59	A3	4p orange yellow	375.00	60.00
a.		Imperf.	—	
b.		Horiz. pair, imperf. vert.	12,750.	
60	A3	6p yellow green	200.00	8.00
a.		Imperf.	—	
b.		Horiz. pair, imperf. vert.	—	
61	A3	1sh pale violet ('81)	175.00	15.00
a.		1sh deep violet	190.00	14.00
		Nos. 57-61 (5)	902.50	98.00

The stamps of type A3 were electrotyped from plates made up of groups of four types, differing in minor details. Two dies were used for the 1p and 2p, giving eight varieties for each of those values.

Nos. 59-60 exist imperf. vertically.
For surcharge see No. 65.

Moiré on Back
1878-79   Unwmk.

62	A3	1p brown org ('79)	800.00	125.00
a.		"QOEENSLAND"		2,000.
63	A3	2p deep ultra ('79)	800.00	62.50
b.		"PENGE"	4,750.	800.00
64	A1	1sh red violet	250.00	115.00
		Nos. 62-64 (3)	1,850.	302.50

No. 57b Surcharged Vertically in Black

1880   Wmk. 68

65	A3	½p on 1p brn org	450.00	250.00
a.		"QUEENSLAND"	2,000.	1,400.

On No. 65, the surcharge reads from bottom to top. Stamps with surcharges reading downward are fakes.

A4

1882-83   Typo.   Perf. 12

66	A4	1p pale red	12.00	1.10
a.		1p rose	12.00	1.10
b.		Imperf. pair		
67	A4	2p gray blue	25.00	1.10
a.		2p deep ultra	25.00	1.10
b.		Horiz. pair, imperf between		
68	A4	4p yellow ('83)	42.50	4.75
a.		"PENGE"	325.00	70.00
b.		Imperf., single		
69	A4	6p yellow green	30.00	35.00
70	A4	1sh violet ('83)	60.00	11.00
		Nos. 66-70 (5)	169.50	52.95

There are eight minor varieties of the 1p, twelve of the 2p and four each of the other values. On the 1p there is a period after "PENNY." On all values the lines of shading on the neck extend from side to side.
Compare design A4 with A6, A10, A11, A15, A16.

1883   Perf. 9½x12

71	A4	1p rose	200.00	77.50
72	A4	2p gray blue	650.00	92.50
73	A4	1sh pale violet	350.00	95.00
		Nos. 71-73 (3)	1,200.	265.00

Beware of faked perfs.
See Nos. 94, 95, 100.

A5

Wmk. 68 Twice Sideways
1882-85   Engr.   Perf. 12
Thin Paper

74	A5	2sh ultra	275.00	70.00
75	A5	2sh6p vermilion	160.00	32.50
76	A5	5sh car rose ('85)	125.00	35.00
77	A5	10sh brown	275.00	60.00
78	A5	£1 dk grn ('83)	650.00	175.00
		Nos. 74-78 (5)	1,485.	372.50

The 2sh, 5sh and £1 exist imperf.
There are two varieties of the watermark on Nos. 74-78, as in the 1879-81 issue.
Stamps with revenue cancels sell for $3.25-6.50.

1886   Wmk. 69   Perf. 12
Thick Paper

79	A5	2sh ultra	300.00	67.50
80	A5	2sh6p vermilion	60.00	30.00
81	A5	5sh car rose	55.00	50.00
82	A5	10sh dark brown	140.00	55.00
83	A5	£1 dark green	350.00	90.00
		Nos. 79-83 (5)	905.00	292.50

High value stamps with cancellations removed are offered as unused.
Stamps with revenue cancels sell for $3.25-6.50.
See Nos. 126-127, 141-144.

A6

Redrawn
1887-89   Typo.   Wmk. 68   Perf. 12

84	A6	1p orange	17.50	1.00
85	A6	2p gray blue	17.50	1.00
a.		2p deep ultra	17.50	1.00
b.		Half used as 1c on cover		—
86	A6	2sh red brown ('89)	90.00	75.00

Perf. 9½x12

88	A6	2p deep ultra	450.00	90.00
		Nos. 84-88 (4)	575.00	167.00

The 1p has no period after the value.
In the redrawn stamps the shading lines on the neck are not completed at the left, leaving an irregular white line along that side.
Variety "LA" joined exists on Nos. 84-86, 88, 90, 91, 93, 97, 98, 102.
On No. 88 beware of faked perfs.

A7   A8

1890-92   Perf. 12½, 13

89	A7	½p green	14.00	2.00
90	A6	1p orange red	8.75	.50
a.		Imperf., pair	325.00	350.00
b.		Double impression		750.00
91	A6	2p gray blue	9.50	.50
92	A8	2½p rose carmine	17.00	2.75
93	A6	3p brown ('92)	9.50	4.25
94	A4	4p orange	27.50	4.75
a.		"PENGE" for "PENCE"	150.00	30.00
b.		4p orange yellow	30.00	5.50
c.		As "b," "PENGE" for "PENCE"	160.00	42.50
d.		4p yellow	17.50	4.75
e.		As "d," "PENGE" for "PENCE"	110.00	32.50
95	A4	6p green	11.50	2.50
96	A6	2sh red brown	45.00	57.50
		Nos. 89-96 (8)	142.75	74.75

The ½p and 3p exist imperf.

1895   Wmk. 69   Perf. 12½, 13
Thick Paper

98	A6	1p orange	5.00	.75
99	A6	2p gray blue	6.75	.75

Perf. 12

100	A4	1sh pale violet	42.50	25.00
		Nos. 98-100 (3)	54.25	26.50

A9   A10

Moiré on Back
1895   Unwmk.   Perf. 12½, 13

101	A9	½p green	11.00	7.00
a.		Without moire	80.00	
102	A6	1p orange	3.00	2.75
a.		"PE" missing	325.00	350.00
b.		1p reddish vermilion	2.75	2.75

Wmk. 68

103	A9	½p green	3.50	2.00
a.		½p deep green	3.50	2.00
b.		Printed on both sides	300.00	
c.		Double impression	—	
104	A10	1p orange	4.00	.50
105	A10	2p gray blue	37.50	.50

Wmk. 69
Thick Paper

106	A9	½p green, perf 12½	3.00	6.00
a.		Perf 13	3.00	6.00
b.		Perf 12	45.00	

1895-96   Unwmk.   Thin Paper
Crown and Q Faintly Impressed

107	A9	½p green	2.50	6.00
108	A10	1p orange	3.50	2.25
108A	A6	2p gray blue	13.00	175.00

A11   A12

A13

1895-96   Wmk. 68

109	A11	1p red	8.00	.75
110	A12	2½p rose	25.00	6.00
111	A13	5p violet brown	30.00	6.00
111A	A11	6p yellow green		22,500.

Only a few used examples of No. 111A are known, and readable cancels are from 1902. It is suggested that this otherwise unissued design was accidentally included in the plate of No. 120.

A14   A15

A16   A17

A18   A19

TWO PENCE:

Type I — Point of bust does not touch frame.
Type II — First redrawing. The top of the crown, the chignon and the point of the bust touch the frame. The forehead is completely shaded.
Type III — Second redrawing. The top of crown does not touch the frame, though the chignon and the point of the bust do. The forehead and the bridge of the nose are not shaded.

1897-1900   Perf. 12½, 13

112	A14	½p deep green	5.50	8.50
a.		Perf. 12		175.00
113	A15	1p red	3.00	.60
a.		Perf. 12	8.50	4.00
114	A16	2p gray blue (I)	8.00	7.50
a.		Perf. 12	1,100.	7.50
115	A17	2½p rose	18.00	30.00
116	A17	2½p violet, *blue*	10.00	3.50
117	A15	3p brown	8.50	3.25
118	A15	4p bright yellow	12.50	3.50
119	A18	5p violet brown	9.00	3.25
120	A15	6p yellow green	8.00	3.75
121	A19	1sh lilac	15.00	4.00
a.		1sh light violet	15.00	4.00
122	A19	2sh turq blue	55.00	50.00
		Nos. 112-122 (11)	132.50	117.85

See Nos. 130-140.

1898   *Serrated Roulette 13*

123	A15	1p scarlet	19.00	8.00
a.		Serrated and perf. 13	10.00	7.00
b.		Serrated in black	18.00	14.00
c.		Serrated without color and in black	20.00	27.50
d.		Same as "b," and perf. 13	80.00	100.00
e.		Same as "c," and perf. 13	100.00	110.00

Victoria — A20

1899   Typo.   Perf. 12, 12½, 13

124	A20	½p blue green	3.50	2.75

Unwatermarked stamps are proofs.

"Australia" — A21

NINE PENCE:
Type I — "QUEENSLAND" 18x1½mm.
Type II — "QUEENSLAND" 17½x1¼mm.

1903   Wmk. 70   Perf. 12½

125	A21	9p org brn & ultra, II	55.00	8.00
a.		Type I	42.50	8.00

— See No. 128. —

Type of 1882

1903-06   Wmk. 68   Perf. 12, 12½-13

Typographed, Perf. 12½-13 Irreg. ('03)

125B	A5	5sh rose	200.00	92.50
125C	A5	£1 dark green	2,250.	750.00

Lithographed, Perf. 12 ('05-'06)

126	A5	5sh rose	165.00	110.00
127	A5	£1 dark green	575.00	140.00
c.		Perf. 12½-13 Irreg.	1,100.	180.00

1907   Typo.   Wmk. 13   Perf. 12½

128	A21	9p yel brn & ultra, I	25.00	5.00
a.		Type II	80.00	6.50
b.		Perf. 11, type II	5,500.	825.00

1907   Wmk. 68   Perf. 12½, 13

129	A16	2p ultra, type II	11.00	6.00
129A	A18	5p dark brown	16.00	6.50
b.		5p olive brown	12.50	4.75

1907-09   Wmk. 12

130	A20	½p deep green	2.25	4.75
131	A15	1p red	3.25	.30
a.		Imperf., pair	425.00	
132	A16	2p ultra, II	32.50	3.75
133	A16	2p ultra, III	4.00	3.00
134	A15	3p pale brown	22.00	3.00
135	A15	4p bright yellow	11.50	4.75
136	A15	4p gray black ('09)	25.00	6.75
137	A15	5p brown	35.00	19.00
a.		5p olive brown	20.00	22.50
138	A15	6p yellow green	21.00	4.50
139	A19	1sh violet	21.00	3.75
140	A19	2sh turquoise bl	55.00	37.50

Wmk. 12 Sideways
Litho.

141	A5	2sh6p dp org	45.00	52.50
142	A5	5sh rose	85.00	70.00
143	A5	10sh dark brown	150.00	80.00
144	A5	£1 blue green	425.00	140.00
		Nos. 130-144 (15)	937.50	430.85

POSTAL FISCAL STAMPS

Authorized for postal use from Jan. 1, 1880. Authorization withdrawn July 1, 1892.

Used values are for examples with postal cancellations used from Jan. 1, 1880 through June 30, 1892.

Beware of stamps with a pen cancellation removed and a fake postmark added.

Queen Victoria — PF1

1866-74   Engr.   Unwmk.   Perf. 13

AR1	PF1	1p blue	105.00	47.50
AR2	PF1	6p violet	250.00	175.00
AR3	PF1	1sh green	240.00	140.00
AR4	PF1	2sh brown	260.00	140.00
AR5	PF1	2sh 6p red	475.00	275.00
AR6	PF1	5sh yellow	925.00	375.00
AR7	PF1	6sh yellow		1,250.
AR8	PF1	10sh yel grn	925.00	325.00
AR9	PF1	20sh rose	1,250.	500.00

Wmk. 68

AR10	PF1	1p blue	52.50	47.50
AR11	PF1	6p violet	115.00	115.00
AR12	PF1	6p blue	425.00	325.00
AR13	PF1	1sh green	125.00	92.50
AR14	PF1	2sh brown	200.00	110.00

AR15	PF1	5sh yellow	650.00	225.00
AR16	PF1	10sh yel grn	925.00	325.00
AR17	PF1	20sh rose	1,250.	500.00

Queen Victoria — PF2

1872-73   Wmk. 69   Perf. 13

AR18	PF2	1p lilac	35.00	29.00
AR19	PF2	6p brown	175.00	87.50
AR20	PF2	1sh green	200.00	105.00
AR21	PF2	2sh blue	325.00	140.00
AR22	PF2	2sh 6p ver	400.00	200.00
AR23	PF2	5sh org brn	275.00	120.00
AR24	PF2	10sh brown	600.00	225.00
AR25	PF2	20sh rose	1,100.	325.00

Perf. 12

AR26	PF2	1p lilac	35.00	29.00
AR27	PF2	6p brown	175.00	87.50
AR28	PF2	2sh blue	325.00	140.00
AR29	PF2	2sh 6p ver	200.00	100.00
AR30	PF2	5sh org brn	275.00	125.00
AR31	PF2	10sh brown	600.00	225.00
AR32	PF2	20sh rose	1,100.	325.00

Unwmk.
Perf. 13

AR33	PF2	1p lilac	40.00	20.00
AR34	PF2	6p lilac	200.00	100.00
AR35	PF2	6p brown	175.00	77.50
AR36	PF2	1sh green	115.00	47.50
AR37	PF2	2sh blue	140.00	115.00
AR38	PF2	2sh 6p ver	250.00	125.00
AR39	PF2	5sh org brn	400.00	140.00
AR40	PF2	10sh brown	650.00	225.00
AR41	PF2	20sh rose	1,100.	325.00

Perf. 12

AR42	PF2	1p lilac	40.00	20.00
AR43	PF2	6p lilac	200.00	100.00
AR44	PF2	6p brown	175.00	77.50
AR45	PF2	1sh green	115.00	47.50
AR46	PF2	2sh blue	140.00	115.00
AR47	PF2	2sh 6p ver	250.00	125.00
AR48	PF2	5sh org brn	400.00	140.00
AR49	PF2	10sh brown	650.00	225.00
AR50	PF2	20sh rose	1,100.	325.00

Queen Victoria — PF3

1878-79   Engr.   Unwmk.   Perf. 12

AR51	PF3	1p violet	275.00	140.00

Wmk. 68

AR52	PF3	1p violet	175.00	105.00

SEMI-POSTAL STAMPS

Queen Victoria, Colors and Bearers — SP1

SP2

1900, June 19   Wmk. 68

Perf. 12, 12½

B1	SP1	1p red lilac	150.00	135.00
B2	SP2	2p deep violet	400.00	300.00

These stamps were sold at 1sh and 2sh respectively. The difference was applied to a patriotic fund in connection with the Boer War.

REGISTRATION STAMPS

R1

Clean-Cut Perf. 14 to 16

1861   Wmk. 5   Engr.

F1	R1	(6p) olive yellow	675.00	125.00
a.		Horiz. pair, imperf. vert.		8,000.

Rough Perf. 14 to 16

F2	R1	(6p) dull yellow	110.00	72.50

1864   Perf. 12½ to 13

F3	R1	(6p) golden yellow	125.00	50.00
a.		Imperf.		
b.		Double impression	2,750.	2,750.

The reprints are watermarked with a small truncated star and perforated 12.

SOUTH AUSTRALIA

'sauth o-'strāl-yə

LOCATION — Central part of southern Australia
GOVT. — British Colony
AREA — 380,070 sq. mi.
POP. — 358,346 (1901)
CAPITAL — Adelaide

South Australia was one of the six British colonies that united in 1901 to form the Commonwealth of Australia.

12 Pence = 1 Shilling
20 Shillings = 1 Pound

Values for unused stamps are for examples with original gum as defined in the catalogue introduction.

Very fine examples of Nos. 10-60 and O1-O60 will have perforations slightly cutting into the framelines or design on one or more sides due to the narrow spacing of the stamps on the plates.

Stamps with perfs clear on all sides are scarce to rare and will command higher to substantially higher prices.

Watermarks

Wmk. 6 — Star with Long Narrow Points   Wmk. 7 — Star with Short Broad Points

Wmk. 70 — Crown and V   Wmk. 72 — Crown and SA

Wmk. 73 — Crown and SA, Letters Close

Wmk. 74 —
Crown and
Single-lined A

Queen Victoria — A1

1855-56 Engr. Wmk. 6 Imperf.
London Print

1	A1	1p dark green	9,750.	525.
2	A1	2p dull carmine	825.	100.
3	A1	6p deep blue	4,250.	200.
4	A1	1sh violet ('56)	26,500.	

1856-59 Local Print

5	A1	1p dp yel grn ('58)	9,750.	625.
a.		1p yellow green ('58)	8,750.	750.
6	A1	2p blood red	3,250.	90.00
a.		Printed on both sides		1,400.
b.		2p orange red ('56)	2,400.	92.50
7	A1	2p pale red ('57)	775.	55.00
a.		Printed on both sides		900.00
8	A1	6p slate blue ('57)	4,400.	200.00
9	A1	1sh orange ('57)	11,250.	500.00
a.		Printed on both sides	—	775.00
b.		1sh red orange		

1858-59 Rouletted

10	A1	1p yel grn ('59)	1,050.	70.00
a.		Horiz. pair, imperf. between	—	—
b.		1p pale yellow green ('59)	1,050.	75.00
11	A1	2p pale red ('59)	375.00	22.50
a.		Printed on both sides		875.00
12	A1	6p slate blue	850.00	70.00
13	A1	1sh orange ('59)	1,900.	55.00
c.		Printed on both sides		2,000.

See Nos. 14-16, 19-20, 25-26, 28-29, 32, 35-36, 41-43, 47, 51-52, 69-70, 73, 113, 118. For overprints see Nos. O1-O2, O5, O7, O9, O11-O13, O17, O20, O27, O30, O32, O39-O40, O42, O52, O76, O85.

A2

A3

Surcharge on #22-24, 34, 49-50

1860-69 Rouletted

14	A1	1p dl bl grn	150.00	55.00
a.		1p deep green	575.00	90.00
b.		1p bright green	145.00	55.00
15	A1	1p sage green	165.00	55.00
16	A1	2p ver ('62)	165.00	5.50
b.		Horiz. pair, imperf. btwn.	4,000.	775.00
d.		Rouletted and perf. all around	2,750.	700.00
		As "c," printed on both sides	—	575.00
18	A2	4p dull vio ('67)	175.00	45.00
19	A1	6p grnsh bl ('63)	275.00	4.75
20	A1	6p dull blue	350.00	7.50
a.		6p sky blue	275.00	7.75
b.		6p Prussian blue	1,050.	57.50
c.		Horiz. pair, imperf btwn.		3,250.
d.		6p ultramarine	275.00	4.95
e.		Horiz. pair, imperf. btwn. (#20f)	—	2,500.
f.		6p indigo blue		75.00
g.		Rouletted and perf. all around (#20f)		575.00
21	A3	9p gray lilac ('69)	165.00	10.50
a.		Double impression		
b.		Horiz. pair, imperf between		4,500.

c.		Rouletted and perf. all around	2,900.	275.00
22	A3	10p on 9p red org (Bl) ('66)	500.00	50.00
23	A3	10p on 9p yel (Bl) ('67)	750.00	35.00
24	A3	10p on 9p yel (Blk) ('69)	3,750.	90.00
a.		Inverted surcharge	—	7,500.
c.		Printed on both sides		1,250.
d.		Rouletted x perf. 10		
24E	A1	1sh yellow ('61)	1,375.	35.00
f.		Vert. pair, imperf. btwn.		6,000.
25	A1	1sh lake brn ('65)	350.00	14.00
a.		Horiz. pair, imperf. btwn.	—	2,500.
26	A1	1sh brown ('63)	425.00	35.00
a.		1sh chestnut ('64)	375.00	12.50
27	A2	2sh car ('67)	550.00	37.50
a.		Vert. pair, imperf. btwn.		2,750.

There are six varieties of the surcharge "TEN PENCE" in this and subsequent issues. Nos. 16b, 20g, 21c, 28a, 32c, 33a are rouletted remainders that were later perforated.

See Nos. 31, 33, 46, 48, 53, 63, 68, 72, 74, 112, 113B, 119-120. For surcharges & overprints see Nos. 34, 44-45, 49-50, 59, 67, 71, O4, O6, O8, O10, O16-O19, O18, O21, O26, O28-O29, O31, O33, O36-O38, O41, O41B, O43, O53. Compare with design A6a.

1867-72 Perf. 11½ to 12½xRoulette

28	A1	1p blue green	575.00	72.50
a.		Rouletted and perf. all around		775.00
29a	A1	1p bright green	375.00	27.50
31	A2	4p dull violet ('68)	3,250.	175.00
a.		4p purple ('69)		145.00
32	A1	6p Prus blue	900.00	22.00
b.		6p sky blue	950.00	22.00
c.		Rouletted and perf. all around	—	425.00
d.		6p indigo blue ('69)	1,000.	29.00
33	A3	9p gray lilac ('72)	—	300.00
34	A3	10p on 9p yel (Bl) ('68)	1,500.	40.00
a.		Printed on both sides		1,250.
35	A1	1sh chestnut ('68)	475.00	27.50
36	A1	1sh lake brown ('69)	475.00	25.00
a.		Rouletted and perf. all around	—	—

Nos. 44-45 Surcharged

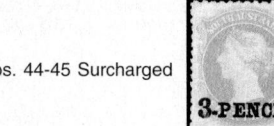

Perf. 10, 11½, 12½ and Compound
1867-74

41	A1	1p yel grn	185.00	25.00
42	A1	1p blue green	190.00	25.00
a.		Printed on both sides		
b.		Horiz. pair, imperf between		1,150.
43	A1	2p vermilion		1,500.
44	A2	3p on 4p sky blue (Blk) ('70)	625.00	20.00
a.		3p on 4p ultra, black surcharge	165.00	10.50
b.		Surcharge omitted	45,000.	22,500.
c.		Double surcharge		4,000.
d.		Surcharged on both sides		3,250.
45	A2	3p on 4p sl bl (Red) ('70)	1,400.	115.00
46	A2	4p dull violet	110.00	9.25
47	A1	6p Prussian blue	325.00	8.00
b.		6p sky blue	650.00	12.50
c.		Imperf. vert., pair		
48	A3	9p red lilac ('72)	120.00	9.00
a.		9p violet	220.00	9.00
b.		9p red violet	220.00	9.50
c.		Printed on both sides		925.00
49	A3	10p on 9p yel (Bl) ('68)	2,200.	55.00
50	A3	10p on 9p yel (Blk) ('69)	450.00	75.00
51	A1	1sh dp brn	185.00	12.50
52	A1	1sh red brown	200.00	12.50
a.		1sh chestnut	220.00	21.00
53	A2	2sh carmine	175.00	14.00
a.		Printed on both sides		800.00
b.		Horiz. pair, imperf. vert.	—	

See Nos. 67, O14, O28, O36.

A6

A6a

1868 Typo. Wmk. 72 Rouletted

54	A6a	2p orange red	160.00	3.50
a.		Imperf.		
b.		Printed on both sides		775.00
c.		Horiz. pair, imperf. btwn.		1,400.

1869 Perf. 11½ to 12½xRoulette

55	A6a	2p orange red		200.00

1870 Perf. 10xRoulette

56	A6a	2p orange red	550.00	42.50

Perf. 10, 11½, 12½ and Compound
1868-75

57	A6	1p bl grn ('75)	110.00	8.50
58	A6a	2p orange red	25.00	1.25
a.		Printed on both sides		450.00
b.		Horiz. pair, imperf. vert.		

Engr.

59	A3	10p on 9p yel (Bl)		1,800.

1869 Typo. Wmk. 6 Rouletted

60	A6a	2p orange red	190.00	25.00
a.		Imperf.		
b.		Printed on both sides		

Perf. 11½ to 12½xRoulette

61	A6a	2p orange red	2,250.	135.00

Perf. 11½ to 12½

61B	A6a	2p orange red	—	1,250.

See Nos. 62, 64-66, 97-98, 105-106, 115-116, 133-134, 145-146. For surcharges & overprints see Nos. 75, O3, O22-O25, O34-O35, O44-O47, O49, O55-O56, O62-O63, O68-O69, O74, O78-O79.

1871 Wmk. 70 Perf. 10

62	A6a	2p orange red	200.00	55.00

Engr.

63	A2	4p dull violet	5,750.	325.00
a.		Printed on both sides		4,750.

Examples of the 4p from edge of sheet sometimes lack watermark.

Perf. 10, 11½, 12½ and Compound
1876-80 Typo. Wmk. 73

64	A6	1p green	40.00	1.75
65	A6a	2p orange	50.00	.60
66	A6a	2p blood red ('80)	325.00	6.75
		Nos. 64-66 (3)	415.00	9.10

See Nos. 97-98, 105-106, 115-116, 133-134, 145-146.

No. 71

1876-84 Engr. Wmk. 7

67	A2	3p on 4p ultra (Blk)	175.00	32.50
a.		3p on 4p deep blue	140.00	22.50
b.		Double surcharge		1,900.
68	A2	4p reddish violet	100.00	6.50
a.		4p dull violet	100.00	8.00
69	A1	6p deep blue	150.00	5.00
a.		Horiz. pair, imperf. between	—	
b.		Imperf.		
70	A1	6p pale ultra ('84)	110.00	3.00
71	A3	8p on 9p bister brn	225.00	11.00
a.		8p on 9p yellow brown	200.00	10.50
b.		8p on 9p gray brown ('80)	190.00	10.00
d.		Double surcharge		2,750.
e.		Vert. pair, imperf between		3,250.
72	A3	9p rose lilac	16.00	5.00
a.		Printed on both sides		675.00
73	A1	1sh red brown	85.00	4.00
a.		1sh brown	90.00	4.00
c.		As "b," horiz. pair, imperf. btwn.		
d.			475.00	
74	A2	2sh carmine	50.00	8.00
a.		Horiz. pair, imperf. vert.		1,950.
b.		Imperf., pair		

For overprint see No. O41.

HALF-PENNY

Surcharged in Black

1882 Wmk. 73 Perf. 10

75	A6	½p on 1p green	15.00	12.50

A9

A10

A11

A12

Perf. 10, 11½, 12½ and Compound
1883-93 Typo.

76	A9	½p chocolate brown	17.50	2.50
a.		½p red brown ('89)	9.50	2.40
b.		½p bister brown	6.00	4.00
78	A10	3p deep green ('93)	24.00	5.50
a.		3p olive green ('90)	26.00	5.50
b.		3p sage green ('86)	26.00	3.25
79	A11	4p violet ('90)	60.00	3.25
80	A12	6p pale blue ('87)	65.00	4.00
		Nos. 76-80 (4)	166.50	15.25

See Nos. 96, 100-101, 104, 108-109, 111. For surcharges & overprints see Nos. 94-95, 99, O48, O50-O51, O54, O57-O61, O64, O66-O67, O71, O73, O75, O81-O82.

A13

1886-96 Perf. 10, 11½ to 12½

81	A13	2sh6p violet	90.00	10.00
82	A13	5sh rose	110.00	20.00
83	A13	10sh green	275.00	75.00
84	A13	15sh buff	875.00	275.00
85	A13	£1 blue	550.00	190.00
86	A13	£2 red brn	3,750.	550.00
87	A13	50sh rose red	4,500.	700.00
88	A13	£3 ol grn	5,500.	650.00
89	A13	£4 lemon	9,000.	1,450.
90	A13	£5 gray	8,750.	
90A	A13	£5 brn ('96)	5,500.	1,100.
91	A13	£10 bronze	8,500.	1,500.
92	A13	£15 silver	32,500.	2,400.
93	A13	£20 lilac	37,500.	2,750.

For overprints see Nos. O83-O84.

#94, 99

#95

Perf. 10, 11½x12½ and Compound
1891 Brown Surcharge

94	A11	2½p on 4p green	8.00	3.00
a.		"½" nearer the "2"	27.50	20.00
b.		Pair, imperf. between		3,750.
c.		Fraction bar omitted	125.00	90.00

Carmine Surcharge

95	A12	5p on 6p red brn	20.00	7.00
a.		No period after "D"	190.00	

See No. 99. For overprints see Nos. O48, O57, O59.

Many stamps of the issues of 1855-91 have been reprinted; they are all on paper watermarked Crown and SA, letters wide apart, and are overprinted "REPRINT."

1893 Typo. Perf. 15

96	A9	½p brown	12.50	1.60
a.		Horiz. pair, imperf. btwn	400.00	
b.		Pair, perf. 12 btwn; perf. 15 around	350.00	75.00
97	A6	1p brown	42.50	1.00
98	A6a	2p orange	25.00	1.00
a.		Vert. pair, imperf. between	1,000.	
99	A11	2½p on 4p green	55.00	3.00
a.		"½" nearer the "2"	135.00	35.00
b.		Fraction bar omitted		

No.	Type	Denom		Unused	Used
100	A11	4p	gray violet	42.50	4.25
101	A12	6p	blue	70.00	4.50
		Nos. 96-101 (6)		247.50	15.35

Kangaroo, Palm — A16   Coat of Arms — A17

1894, Mar. 1

102	A16	2½p	blue violet	45.00	6.50
103	A17	5p	dull violet	45.00	4.00

See Nos. 107, 110, 117, 135-136, 147, 151. For overprints see Nos. O65, O70, O72, O80.

1895-97   *Perf. 13*

104	A9	½p	pale brown	5.50	.50
105	A6	1p	green	12.50	.45
a.		Vert. pair, imperf. between			
106	A6a	2p	green	16.00	.25
107	A16	2½p	blue violet	10.00	2.25
108	A10	3p	olive green ('97)	6.00	3.50
109	A11	4p	bright violet	6.50	1.00
110	A17	5p	dull violet	11.00	1.75
111	A12	6p	blue	11.00	1.60
		Nos. 104-111 (8)		78.50	11.30

Some authorities regard the so-called redrawn 1p stamps with thicker lettering (said to have been issued in 1897) as impressions from a new or cleaned plate.

Perf. 11½, 12½, Clean-Cut, Compound
1896   **Engr.**   **Wmk. 7**

112	A3	9p	lilac rose	16.00	5.75
113	A1	1sh	dark brown	27.50	5.00
a.		Horiz. pair, imperf. vert.		475.00	
c.		Vert. pair, imperf. btwn.		650.00	
113B	A2	2sh	carmine	42.50	7.25
		Nos. 112-113B (3)		86.00	18.00

Adelaide Post Office — A18

1899   **Typo.**   **Wmk. 73**   *Perf. 13*

114	A18	½p	yellow green	8.00	1.50
115	A6	1p	carmine	10.00	1.50
a.		1p scarlet		9.00	1.50
116	A6a	2p	purple	6.50	.25
117	A17	2½p	dark blue	10.00	2.50
		Nos. 114-117 (4)		34.50	5.75

See Nos. 132, 144. For overprint see No. O77.

Perf. 11½, 12½
1901   **Engr.**   **Wmk. 72**

118	A1	1sh	dark brown	24.00	17.50
a.		1sh red brown		27.50	37.50
b.		Horiz. pair, imperf. vert.			
119	A2	2sh	carmine	27.50	12.50

1902

120	A3	9p	magenta	21.00	25.00

A19

Perf. 11½, 12½ and Compound
1902-03   **Typo.**   **Wmk. 73**

121	A19	3p	olive grn	17.50	3.00
a.		3p olive grn (20mm), perf 12		35.00	32.75
b.		Wmk sideways		1,850.	
122	A19	4p	red org	30.00	4.50
123	A19	6p	blue grn	12.50	3.00
124	A19	8p	ultra (value 19mm long)	9.00	17.50

124A	A19	8p	ultra (value 16½mm long) ('03)	12.50	17.50
b.		"EIGNT"		2,400.	3,250.
125	A19	9p	claret	15.00	11.00
a.		Vert. pair, imperf. between		2,750.	
b.		Horiz. pair, imperf. between			
126	A19	10p	org buff	18.50	19.00
127	A19	1sh	brn ('03)	27.50	9.00
a.		Horiz. pair, imperf. btwn.			
b.		Vert. pair, imperf. btwn.		2,750.	
c.		"Postage" and denomination in red brown		1,100.	1,000.
128	A19	2sh6p	purple	40.00	15.00
a.		2sh6p pale violet		90.00	50.00
129	A19	5sh	rose	135.00	80.00
130	A19	10sh	grn ('03)	225.00	100.00
131	A19	£1	blue	500.00	275.00
		Nos. 121-131 (12)		1,043.	554.50

1904   *Perf. 12x11½*

132	A18	½p	yellow green	8.50	2.75
133	A6	1p	rose	8.75	1.00
134	A6a	2p	purple	15.00	1.00
135	A16	2½p	dark blue	15.00	4.25
136	A17	5p	dull violet	21.00	2.25
		Nos. 132-136 (5)		68.25	11.25

A20

1904-08   *Perf. 12 and 12x11½*

137	A20	6p	blue grn	42.50	3.25
a.		Vert. pair, imperf. between		5,000.	
138	A20	8p	ultra ('06)	17.50	9.00
139	A20	9p	claret	24.00	7.00
139A	A20	10p	org buff ('07)	18.00	25.00
b.		Vert. pair, imperf. between		4,250.	
c.		Horiz. pair, imperf. between		3,000.	3,250.
140	A20	1sh	brown	32.50	4.25
a.		Vert. pair, imperf. between		2,750.	
b.		Horiz. pair, imperf between		3,000.	
141	A20	2sh6p	pur ('05)	85.00	42.50
142	A20	5sh	scarlet	85.00	52.50
142B	A20	10sh	grn ('08)	225.00	160.00
143	A20	£1	dp blue	240.00	175.00
		Nos. 137-143 (9)		769.50	478.50

See Nos. 148-150, 152-157.

1906-12   **Wmk. 74**

144	A18	½p	green	16.00	1.40
145	A6	1p	carmine	7.00	.25
146	A6a	2p	purple	8.00	.30
a.		Horiz. pair, imperf. between		2,500.	
147	A16	2½p	dk blue ('11)	11.00	13.50
148	A20	3p	ol grn (value 19mm long)	15.50	6.25
a.		Horiz. pair, imperf. between		6,000.	
149	A20	3p	ol grn (value 17mm long) ('09)	17.00	11.00
150	A20	4p	red org	25.00	9.00
151	A17	5p	dl vio ('08)	30.00	6.75
152	A20	6p	bl grn ('07)	8.50	9.50
a.		Vert. pair, imperf. between		2,000.	2,750.
153	A20	8p	ultra ('09)	13.50	22.50
154	A20	9p	claret	22.50	6.00
a.		Vert. pair, imperf. between		2,100.	
b.		Horiz. pair, imperf. between		5,000.	
155	A20	1sh	brown	13.00	5.50
a.		Horiz. pair, imperf. between		3,100.	
b.		Vert. pair, imperf. between		3,750.	
156	A20	2sh6p	pur ('09)	80.00	32.50
157	A20	5sh	lt red ('12)	145.00	145.00
		Nos. 144-157 (14)		412.00	269.45

OFFICIAL STAMPS

For Departments
Regular Issues Overprinted in Red, Black or Blue:

A. (Architect), A. G. (Attorney General), A. O. (Audit Office), B. D. (Barracks Department), B. G. (Botanical Gardens), B. M. (Bench of Magistrates), C. (Customs), C. D. (Convict Department), C. L. (Crown Lands), C. O. (Commissariat Officer), C. S. (Chief Secretary), C. Sgn. (Colonial Surgeon), C. P. (Commissioner of Police), C. T. (Commissioner of Titles), D. B. (Destitute Board), D. R. (Deed Registry), E. (Engineer), E. B. (Education Board),

G. P. (Government Printer), G. S. (Government Storekeeper), G. T. (Goolwa Tramway), G. F. (Gold Fields), H. (Hospital), H. A. (House of Assembly), I. A. (Immigration Agent), I. E. (Intestate Estates), I. S. (Inspector of Sheep), L. A. (Lunatic Asylum), L. C. (Legislative Council), L. L. (Legislative Library), L. T. (Land Titles), M. (Military), M. B. (Marine Board), M. R. (Manager of Railways), M. R. G. (Main Roads Department), N. T. (Northern Territory),

O. A. (Official Assignee), P. (Police), P. A. (Protector of Aborigines), P. O. (Post Office), P. S. (Private Secretary), P. W. (Public Works), R. B. (Road Board), R. G. (Registrar General of Births, &c.), S. (Sheriff), S. C. (Supreme Court), S.G. (Surveyor General), S. M. (Stipendiary Magistrate), S. T. (Superintendent of Telegraph), T. (Treasurer), T. R. (Titles Registry), V. (Volunteers), V. A. (Valuator), V. N. (Vaccination), W. (Waterworks).

1868-74   **Wmk. 6**   *Rouletted*

O1	A1	1p	green		350.00
O2	A1	2p	pale red		275.00
O3	A6a	2p	vermilion		120.00
O4	A2	4p	dull violet		275.00
O5	A1	6p	slate blue		275.00
O6	A3	9p	gray lilac		500.00
O7	A1	1sh	brown		275.00
O8	A2	2sh	carmine		275.00

Perf. 11½ to 12½ x Roulette

O9	A1	1p	green		275.00
O10	A2	4p	dull violet		850.00
O11	A1	6p	blue		210.00
O12	A1	1sh	brown		200.00

Perf. 10, 11½, 12½ and Compound

O13	A1	1p	green		160.00
O14	A2	3p	on 4p sl bl (Red)		750.00
O15	A2	3p	on 4p sl bl (Blk)		275.00
O16	A2	4p	dull violet		200.00
O17	A1	6p	deep blue		275.00
O18	A3	9p	violet		500.00
O19	A3	10p	on 9p yel (Blk)		500.00
O20	A1	1sh	brown	140.00	160.00
O21	A2	2sh	carmine		100.00

Rouletted
Wmk. 72

O22	A6a	2p	orange		120.00

Perf. 11 ½ x Roulette

O23	A6a	2p	orange		160.00
a.		Perf 10 x Roulette			275.00

Perf. 10, 11½, 12½ and Compound

O24	A6a	2p	orange		22.50

Wmk. 70
Perf. 10

O25	A6a	2p	orange		110.00
O26	A2	4p	dull violet		275.00

For General Use

Overprinted in Black

Perf. 10, 11½, 12½ and Compound
1874   **Wmk. 6**

O27	A1	1p	green	—	500.00
a.		1p dp yel green, perf 11½-12½x10		3,500.	400.00
b.		As "a," printed on both sides			1,275.
O28	A2	3p	on 4p ultra	8,750.	3,000.
a.		No period after "S"			3,000.
O29	A2	4p	dull violet	95.00	9.50
a.		Inverted overprint			
b.		No period after "S"			85.00
c.		Perf. 11½-12½x10		3,000.	600.00
O30	A1	6p	deep blue	240.00	10.00
a.		No period after "S"			110.00
b.		6p Prussian blue, perf 11½-12½x10		175.00	12.00
O31	A3	9p	violet	4,250.	1,700.
a.		No period after "S"		4,750.	2,400.
O32	A1	1sh	red brown	125.00	10.00
a.		Double overprint			225.00
b.		No period after "S"		400.00	90.00

O33	A2	2sh	carmine	275.00	30.00
a.		Double overprint			165.00
b.		No period after "S"			165.00
c.		2sh carmine, perf 11½-12½x10			160.00

1874-75   **Wmk. 72**

O34	A6	1p	blue green	240.00	37.50
a.		Inverted overprint			
O35	A6a	2p	orange	60.00	7.50

1876-86   **Wmk. 7**

O37	A2	4p	dull violet	75.00	6.00
O38	A2	4p	reddish vio	75.00	3.00
a.		Double overprint			
b.		Inverted overprint			300.00
c.		Dbl. ovpt., one inverted			
O39	A1	6p	dark blue	150.	5.50
a.		Double overprint			190.00
b.		Inverted overprint			
O40	A1	6p	ultramarine	150.00	5.50
a.		Double overprint			
b.		Inverted overprint			
O41B	A3	9p	violet	9,000.	
O42	A1	1sh	red brown	52.50	9.00
a.		Inverted overprint		750.00	275.00
b.		Double overprint			
O43	A2	2sh	carmine	300.00	9.00
a.		Double overprint			275.00
b.		Inverted overprint			325.00
c.		No period after "S"			90.00

1880-91   **Wmk. 73**

O44	A6	1p	blue green	12.00	1.00
a.		Inverted overprint			40.00
b.		Double overprint		52.50	35.00
c.		Dbl. ovpt., one inverted			750.00
O45	A6	1p	yellow green	14.50	1.00
O46	A6a	2p	orange	10.00	.80
a.		Inverted overprint			17.50
b.		Double overprint		70.00	32.50
c.		Overprinted sideways			
d.		Dbl. ovpt. inverted			
e.		Dbl. ovpt., both inverted			95.00
O47	A6a	2p	blood red	52.50	8.75
O48	A11	2½p	on 4p green	57.50	8.75
a.		"½" nearer the "2"			67.50
b.		Double overprint			
c.		Pair, one without ovpt.			
		Nos. O44-O48 (5)		146.50	20.30

1882-90   *Perf. 10*

O49	A6	½p	on 1p green	57.50	13.50
a.		Inverted overprint			
O50	A11	4p	violet	57.50	5.00
O51	A12	6p	blue	20.00	1.25
a.		Double overprint			
b.		No period after "S"			
		Nos. O49-O51 (3)		135.00	19.75

Overprinted in Black

Perf. 10, 11½, 12½ and Compound
1891   **Wmk. 7**

O52	A1	1sh	red brown	37.50	5.25
a.		No period after "S"			55.00
b.		1sh lake brown, perf 11½-12½		45.00	10.00
O53	A2	2sh	carmine	90.00	10.00
a.		Double overprint			
b.		No period after "S"		115.00	

1891-95   **Wmk. 73**

O54	A9	½p	brown	12.50	6.25
a.		No period after "S"		87.50	52.50
O55	A6	1p	blue green	17.50	2.00
a.		Double overprint		72.50	30.00
b.		No period after "S"		75.00	17.50
O56	A6a	2p	orange	12.00	.50
a.		No period after "S"			45.00
O57	A11	2½p	on 4p green	40.00	10.00
a.		"½" nearer the "2"		82.50	30.00
b.		Inverted overprint		145.00	
O58	A11	4p	violet	47.50	3.50
a.		Double overprint			
O59	A12	5p	on 6p red brn	50.00	14.50
O60	A12	6p	blue	18.50	2.50
a.		Double overprint			
b.		No period after "S"			
		Nos. O54-O60 (7)		198.00	39.25

1893   *Perf. 15*

O61	A9	½p	brown	24.00	7.75
O62	A6	1p	green	10.00	1.25
O63	A6a	2p	orange	10.00	.50
a.		Inverted overprint			16.50
b.		Double overprint			22.50
O64	A11	4p	gray violet	57.50	4.50
a.		Double overprint		160.00	32.50
O65	A17	5p	dull violet	72.50	10.00
O66	A12	6p	blue	24.00	3.00
		Nos. O61-O66 (6)		198.00	27.00

1896   *Perf. 13*

O67	A9	½p	brown	14.50	5.75
a.		Triple overprint		160.00	
O68	A6	1p	green	17.50	.60
a.		No period after "S"		52.50	10.00
O69	A6a	2p	orange	17.50	.50
a.		No period after "S"		50.00	10.00
O70	A16	2½p	blue violet	60.00	6.75
a.		No period after "S"			30.00

O71	A11	4p brt violet	60.00	3.00
a.		Double overprint	125.00	32.50
b.		No period after "S"	125.00	24.00
O72	A17	5p dull violet	62.50	12.00
a.		No period after "S"		
O73	A12	6p blue	27.50	2.00
a.		No period after "S"	90.00	60.00
		Nos. O67-O73 (7)	259.50	30.60

On No. O67a, one overprint is upright, two sideways.

Same Overprint in Dark Blue
1891-95   *Perf. 10*

O74	A6	1p green	200.00	7.50
O75	A12	6p blue		

Black Overprint
Perf. 11½, 12½, Clean-Cut
1897   **Wmk. 7**

O76	A1	1sh brown	35.00	5.50
a.		Double overprint		
b.		No period after "S"	375.00	

Overprinted in Black

1900   **Wmk. 73**   *Perf. 13*

O77	A18	½p yellow green	12.50	5.75
a.		Inverted overprint	110.00	
b.		No period after "S"	62.50	
c.		As "b," inverted overprint	—	
O78	A6	1p carmine rose	11.50	1.60
a.		Inverted overprint	45.00	32.50
b.		Double overprint	475.00	
c.		No period after "S"	82.50	22.50
O79	A6a	2p purple	12.50	.80
a.		Inverted ovpt.	40.00	22.00
b.		No period after "S"	77.50	21.00
O80	A16	2½p dark blue	75.00	18.50
a.		Inverted overprint		57.50
b.		No period after "S"	225.00	
O81	A11	4p violet	60.00	4.50
a.		Inverted overprint	165.00	
b.		No period after "S"	200.00	
O82	A12	6p blue	20.00	4.50
a.		No period after "S"	110.00	
		Nos. O77-O82 (6)	191.50	35.65

1901   *Perf. 10*

O83	A13	2sh6p violet	3,500.	2,500.
O84	A13	5sh rose	3,500.	2,500.

On Nos. O77-O82 the letters "O.S." are 11½mm apart; on Nos. O83-O84, 14½mm apart.

Overprinted in Black

1903   **Wmk. 72**   *Perf. 11½, 12½*

O85	A1	1sh red brown	47.50	11.00

TASMANIA
taz-'mā-nē-ə

LOCATION — An island off the southeastern coast of Australia
GOVT. — British Colony
AREA — 26,215 sq. mi.
POP. — 172,475 (1901)
CAPITAL — Hobart

Tasmania was one of the six British colonies that united in 1901 to form the Commonwealth of Australia. The island was originally named Van Diemen's Land by its discoverer, Abel Tasman, the present name having been adopted in 1853. Stamps of Australia are now used.

12 Pence = 1 Shilling
20 Shillings = 1 Pound

Watermarks

Wmk. 6 — Large Star

Wmk. 139 Double-lined Numeral

Wmk. 49 Double-lined Numeral

Wmk. 50 Single-lined "2"

Wmk. 75 Double-lined Numeral

Wmk. 51 Single-lined "4"

Wmk. 52 — Single-lined "10"

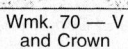
Wmk. 70 — V and Crown

Wmk. 13 — Crown & Double-lined A

Wmk. 76 — TAS

Wmk. 77 — TAS

Wmk. 78 — Multiple TAS

Values for unused stamps are for examples with original gum as defined in the catalogue introduction except for Nos. 1-2b and 10 which are valued without gum as few examples exist with any remaining original gum. Very fine examples of Nos. 17-75a will have perforations touching the design on one or more sides due to the narrow spacing of the stamps on the plates. Stamps with perfs clear of the design on all four sides are scarce and command higher prices.

Queen Victoria
A1   A2

Unwmk.
1853, Nov. 1   **Engr.**   *Imperf.*

1a	A1	1p blue, blurred impression, hard paper	11,000.	1,350.
2	A2	4p red orange	6,250.	550.00
a.		4p yellow orange	5,750.	425.00
		Cut to shape		25.00

Twenty-four varieties of each.
The 4p on vertically laid paper is believed to be a proof. Value, unused, $7,500.

The reprints are made from defaced plates and show marks across the face of each stamp. They are on thin and thick, unwatermarked paper and thin cardboard; only the first are perforated. Nearly all the reprints of Tasmania may be found with and without the overprint "REPRINT."

Nos. 1-47A with pen or revenue cancellations sell for a small fraction of the price of postally used examples. Stamps are found with pen cancellation removed.

Queen Victoria — A3

1855   **Wmk. 6**   **Wove Paper**

4	A3	1p dark carmine	10,500.	1,000.
5	A3	2p green	5,750.	500.00
a.		2p deep green	5,750.	600.00
6	A3	4p deep blue	5,000.	145.00

1856-57   **Unwmk.**

7	A3	1p pale red	13,500.	700.00
8	A3	2p emerald ('57)	16,500.	1,000.
9	A3	4p blue ('57)	2,650.	140.00

1856   **Pelure Paper**

10	A3	1p brown red	8,250.	800.00

1857-69   **Wmk. 49, 75**

11	A3	1p carmine ('67)	375.00	32.50
a.		1p orange red ('65)	375.00	37.50
b.		1p brown red	625.00	42.50
c.		Double impression	650.00	
e.		Wmk. 50 (error) ('69)		
12	A3	2p sage green ('60)	400.00	95.00
a.		2p yellow green	950.00	125.00
b.		2p green		67.50
d.		As "b," double impression		325.00
13	A3	4p pale blue	425.00	30.00
a.		4p blue	425.00	32.50
b.		Printed on both sides		
d.		As "a," double impression		275.00
		Nos. 11-13 (3)	1,200.	157.50

See Nos. 17-19, 23-25, 29-31, 35-37, 39-41, 45-47A.

A4   A4a

1858-67

14	A4	6p gray lilac ('63)	750.00	95.00
a.		6p red violet ('67)	1,150.	190.00
b.		Double impression ('63)		450.00
15	A4	6p blue gray ('65)	1,150.	150.00
16	A4a	1sh vermilion	825.00	90.00
		Nos. 14-16 (3)	2,725.	335.00

No. 15 watermarked large star was not regularly issued.
Issued: No. 14c, 16, 1/58; No. 14, 4/63; No. 15, 2/65; No. 14a, 4/67.

1864   *Rouletted*

17	A3	1p carmine	950.00	325.00
a.		1p brick red		500.00
18	A3	2p yellow grn	—	1,250.
19	A3	4p blue	—	475.00
21	A4	6p gray lilac	—	525.00
22	A4a	1sh vermilion	—	1,350.

Values for Nos. 17-22 are for stamps showing rouletting on two or three sides. Examples with full roulettes on all four sides are rare.

1864-69   *Perf. 10*

23	A3	1p brick red	175.00	65.00
a.		1p carmine	145.00	55.00
b.		1p orange red	175.00	55.00
c.		As "b," double impression		
24	A3	2p yellow green	825.00	160.00
a.		2p sage green	850.00	240.00
25	A3	4p blue	400.00	240.00
a.		Double impression		240.00
26	A4	6p gray lilac	575.00	42.50
a.		6p red lilac	850.00	105.00
27	A4	6p slate blue	775.00	105.00
28	A4a	1sh vermilion	575.00	52.50
a.		Horiz. pair, imperf. vert.		
		Nos. 23-28 (6)	3,325.	447.50

1864-91   *Perf. 12, 12½*

29	A3	1p carmine	120.00	25.00
a.		1p orange red	160.00	40.00
b.		1p brick red	140.00	62.50
c.		Double impression		
d.		Wmkd. "2"		3,000.
		As "d," pen cancel		325.00
30	A3	2p yellow green	625.00	100.00
a.		2p dark green	475.00	240.00
b.		2p sage green	475.00	240.00
31	A3	4p blue	325.00	26.00
a.		4p deep blue	325.00	25.00
b.		4p cobalt blue	—	67.50
32	A4	6p red lilac	170.00	47.50
a.		Horiz. pair, imperf between		
b.		Vert. pair, imperf between		
c.		6p violet	400.00	32.50
d.		As "c," Vert. pair, imperf between		—
e.		6p purple ('84)	175.00	22.50
g.		6p dull claret ('91)	52.50	15.00
33	A4	6p slate blue	775.00	110.00
34	A4a	1sh vermilion	450.00	75.00
a.		Double impression		200.00
b.		Horiz. pair, imperf. between		3,500.

The reprints are on unwatermarked paper, perforated 11½, and on thin cardboard, imperforate and perforated.

Perf. Pin-perf. 5½ to 9½, 13½ to 14½
1867

35	A3	1p carmine	1,250.	400.00
36	A3	2p yel grn		975.00
37	A3	4p blue		625.00
38	A4	6p gray		650.00
38A	A4	6p red lilac		1,350.
38B	A4a	1sh vermilion		

Oblique Roulette 14-15

39	A3	1p carmine		1,200.
40	A3	2p yel grn		1,600.
41	A3	4p blue		1,250.
42	A4	6p gray		2,000.
43	A4	6p red lilac		—
44	A4a	1sh vermilion		2,500.

1868   *Serrate Perf. 19*

45	A3	1p carmine	850.00	250.00
46	A3	2p yellow green		850.00
47	A3	4p blue	1,900.	250.00
47A	A3	6p purple	—	1,200.
47B	A3	1sh vermilion		

Queen Victoria — A5

1870-71 Typo. Wmk. 50 Perf. 11½
48	A5	2p blue green	200.00	10.00
a.		Double impression	5,500.	2,000.
b.		Perf. 12	210.00	11.00
c.		2p green	325.00	20.00
d.		As "c," perf. 12	200.00	11.00
e.		As "d," imperf, pair	—	

See Nos. 49-75, 98, 108-109.

Wmk. 51
49	A5	1p rose ('71)	150.00	60.00
a.		Imperf., pair	1,300.	1,200.
50	A5	4p blue	1,350.	525.00

Wmk. 52
51	A5	1p rose	130.00	21.00
a.		Imperf. pair	1,350.	1,350.
c.		Perf. 11½	1,350.	
52	A5	10p black	27.50	52.50
a.		Imperf. pair	750.00	
b.		Perf. 11½	52.50	52.50

The reprints are on unwatermarked paper. The 4p has also been reprinted on thin cardboard, imperf and perf.

1871-76 Wmk. 76 Perf. 11½
53	A5	1p rose	17.00	2.50
a.		Imperf.		
b.		Perf. 12	155.00	29.00
53B	A5	1p ver ('73)	325.00	80.00
54	A5	2p dp grn ('72)	80.00	2.75
a.		2p yellow green	375.00	5.00
b.		2p blue green	57.50	2.75
c.		Imperf. pair		1,750.
d.		2p green, perf. 12	700.00	150.00
e.		Double impression		
55	A5	3p brown	80.00	6.00
a.		3p purple brown	80.00	5.00
b.		As "a," imperf. pair		1,150.
56	A5	3p red brn ('71)	90.00	5.00
a.		3p indian red	75.00	5.00
b.		Imperf. pair	140.00	
c.		Vert. pair, imperf. horiz.		
d.		Perf. 12	145.00	24.00
57	A5	4p dull yel ('76)	150.00	45.00
a.		Perf. 12	375.00	25.00
58	A5	9p blue	32.50	9.00
a.		Imperf. pair	575.00	
b.		Perf. 12	60.00	52.50
59	A5	5sh bright violet	325.00	85.00
a.		Imperf.		
b.		Horiz. pair, imperf. vert.		
c.		Perf. 12	500.00	475.00
		Nos. 53-59 (8)	1,100.	235.25

The reprints are on unwatermarked paper, the 5sh has also been reprinted on thin cardboard; all are perforated.

1878 Wmk. 77 Perf. 14
60	A5	1p rose	11.00	1.25
61	A5	2p deep green	12.00	1.25
62	A5	8p violet brown	15.00	10.00
		Nos. 60-62 (3)	38.00	12.50

The 8p has been reprinted on thin unwatermarked paper, perforated 11½.

1880-83 Perf. 12, 11½
63	A5	3p indian red, perf. 12	10.00	9.00
a.		Imperf. pair	475.00	
b.		Horiz. pair, imperf. between	2,500.	
c.		Perf. 11½	25.00	5.50
64	A5	4p lem, perf. 11½ ('83)	80.00	20.00
a.		4p olive yellow, perf. 11½	160.00	30.00
b.		Printed on both sides	1,600.	
c.		Imperf.		
d.		4p deep yellow, perf. 12	140.00	32.50

Type of 1871
Surcharged in Black

1889 Perf. 14
65	A5	½p on 1p carmine	11.00	25.00
a.		"al" sideways in surcharge	2,000.	1,675.

No. 65 has been reprinted on thin cardboard, perforated 12, with the surcharge "Halfpenny" 19mm long.

1889-96 Perf. 11½
66	A5	½p red orange	3.25	3.50
a.		½p yellow orange	3.25	3.50
b.		Perf. 12	5.50	7.00
67	A5	1p dull red	15.00	3.50
a.		1p vermilion	11.00	3.00
68	A5	1p car, perf. 12	8.25	3.25
a.		1p pink, perf. 12	42.50	15.00
b.		1p salmon rose, perf. 12	35.00	12.50
c.		Imperf. pair	400.00	375.00

Perf. 12
69	A5	4p bister ('96)	16.00	7.50
70	A5	9p chalky bl ('96)	10.00	3.50
		Nos. 66-70 (5)	52.50	21.25

1891 Wmk. 76 Perf. 11½
71	A5	½p orange	80.00	10.00
a.		½p brown orange	52.50	45.00
b.		Imperf. pair	325.00	
c.		Perf. 12	70.00	45.00

72	A5	1p salmon rose	25.00	11.00
a.		1p carmine, perf. 12	45.00	42.50
73	A5	4p ol bis, perf. 12	25.00	32.50
		Nos. 71-73 (3)	130.00	93.50

See Nos. 98, 108-109.

Surcharged in Black

1891 Wmk. 77 Perf. 11½
Surcharge 14mm High
74	A5	2½p on 9p lt blue	17.50	9.25
a.		Dbl. surcharge, one invtd.	850.00	950.00
b.		Imperf. pair		

Perf. 12
Surcharge 15mm High
75	A5	2½p on 9p lt blue	8.50	7.75
a.		Surcharged in blue	10.00	6.50

No. 74 has been reprinted on thin unwatermarked paper, imperforate. There is also a reprint on thin cardboard, in deep ultramarine, with surcharge 16½mm high, and perforated 12.

A8   A9

1892-99 Typo. Perf. 14
76	A8	½p orange & vio	4.25	4.25
77	A9	2½p magenta	7.25	7.25
78	A8	5p pale bl & brn	11.50	7.25
79	A8	6p blue vio & blk	15.00	7.25
80	A8	10p red brn & grn ('99)	29.00	21.00
81	A8	1sh rose & green	15.00	7.25
82	A8	2sh6p brown & blue	47.50	35.00
83	A8	5sh brn vio & red	92.50	42.50
84	A8	10sh brt vio & brn	160.00	115.00
85	A8	£1 green & yel	700.00	450.00
		Nos. 76-85 (10)	1,082.	696.75

No. 80 shows the numeral on white tablet.
See Nos. 99, 110-111.

Lake Marion — A10

Mt. Wellington — A11

View of Hobart — A12

Tasman's Arch — A13

Spring River, Port Davey — A14

Russell Falls — A15

Mt. Gould and Lake St. Clair — A16

Dilston Falls — A17

1899-1900 Engr. Wmk. 78 Perf. 14
86	A10	½p dark green	16.00	12.00
87	A11	1p carmine	10.50	3.00
88	A12	2p violet	25.00	3.50
89	A13	2½p dark blue	35.00	17.50
90	A14	3p dark brown	18.00	9.00
91	A15	4p ocher	42.50	12.00
92	A16	5p ultramarine	47.50	29.00
93	A17	6p lake	45.00	37.50
		Nos. 86-93 (8)	239.50	123.50

See Nos. 94-97, 102-107, 114-117.

Perf. 11, 12½, 11x12½
1902-03 Litho., Typo. Wmk. 70
94	A10	½p green	8.00	2.75
95	A11	1p carmine	15.00	2.40
96	A11	1p dull red	22.50	3.00
97	A12	2p violet	14.00	1.40
98	A5	9p blue	15.00	7.25
a.		9p ultramarine	750.00	
b.		9p indigo	240.00	
c.		Perf. 11	15.00	15.00
99	A8	1sh rose & green	32.50	10.50
a.		Perf. 11	75.00	75.00
		Nos. 94-99 (6)	107.00	27.30

Nos. 94, 97 are litho., Nos. 96, 98-99 typo.
No. 95 was printed both ways.

No. 78 Surcharged in Black

1904 Wmk. 77 Perf. 14
100	A8	1½p on 5p blue & brn	2.75	2.75

Perf. 11, 12, 12½ and Compound
1905-08 Typo. Wmk. 13
102	A10	½p dull green	4.25	.95
a.		Booklet pane of 12		
103	A11	1p carmine	3.50	.60
a.		Booklet pane of 18		
104	A12	2p violet	18.00	.80
105	A14	3p dark brown	15.00	9.00
106	A15	4p ocher	25.00	7.25
107	A17	6p lake	70.00	12.50
108	A5	8p violet brown	35.00	16.00
109	A5	9p blue	130.00	8.00
110	A8	1sh rose & green	24.00	9.25
111	A8	10sh brt vio & brn	325.00	350.00
a.		Perf. 11	475.00	475.00
		Nos. 102-111 (10)	649.75	414.35

Nos. 104-107 also printed litho.

1911 Redrawn
114	A12	2p bright violet	15.00	7.50
115	A15	4p dull yellow	72.50	72.50
116	A17	6p lake	35.00	55.00
		Nos. 114-116 (3)	122.50	135.00

The redrawn 2p measures 33½x25mm instead of 32½x24½mm. There are many

slight changes in the clouds and other parts of the design.

The 4p is much lighter, especially the waterfall and trees above it. This appears to be a new or cleaned plate rather than a redrawn one.

In the redrawn 6p there are more colored lines in the waterfall and the river and more white dots in the trees.

No. 114 Surcharged in Red

1912
117	A12	1p on 2p brt vio	2.75	2.75

POSTAL FISCAL STAMPS

Authorized for postal use by Act of November 1, 1882. Authorization withdrawn Nov. 30, 1900.

Used values are for examples with postal cancellations used from Nov. 1, 1882 through Nov. 30, 1900.

Beware of stamps with a pen cancellation removed, often regummed or with a fake postmark added.

PF1   PF2

St. George and the Dragon
PF3   PF4

1863-80 Engr. Wmk. 139 Imperf.
AR1	PF1	3p green	450.00	200.00
AR2	PF2	2sh 6p car	450.00	180.00
AR3	PF3	5sh green	525.00	250.00
AR4	PF3	5sh brown	900.00	550.00
AR5	PF4	10sh sal ('80)	900.00	575.00
a.		10sh orange	1,200.	550.00

For overprint see No. AR32.

Perf. 10
AR6	PF1	3p green	475.00	300.00
AR7	PF2	2sh 6p car	450.00	
AR8	PF3	5sh brown	650.00	475.00
AR9	PF4	10sh orange	525.00	

Perf. 12
AR10	PF1	3p green	500.00	375.00
AR11	PF2	2sh 6p car	500.00	425.00
AR12	PF3	5sh green	500.00	350.00
AR13	PF3	5sh brown	950.00	
AR14	PF4	10sh orange	600.00	375.00

Perf. 12½
AR15	PF1	3p green	800.00	
AR16	PF2	2sh 6p car	375.00	
AR17	PF3	5sh green	650.00	
AR18	PF4	10sh orange	575.00	

Perf. 11½
AR19	PF1	3p green		
AR20	PF2	2sh 6p car	750.00	425.00
AR21	PF3	5sh green	300.00	200.00
AR22	PF4	10sh salmon	350.00	300.00
a.		10sh orange	300.00	140.00

Wmk. 77
Perf. 12
AR23	PF2	2sh 6p car	72.50	52.50

For overprint see No. AR33.

Duck-billed Platypus — PF5

1880 Engr. Wmk. 77 Perf. 14

AR24	PF5	1p slate	42.50	12.00
AR25	PF5	3p brown	29.00	7.75
AR26	PF5	6p lilac	140.00	21.00
AR27	PF5	1sh rose	200.00	35.00

For overprints see Nos. AR28-AR31.

Nos. AR24-AR27, AR2, AR23, 85 Overprinted "REVENUE"

1900, Nov. 15

AR28	PF5	1p slate	42.50	42.50
AR29	PF5	3p brown	42.50	45.00
AR30	PF5	6p lilac	300.00	140.00
AR31	PF5	1sh rose	500.00	240.00
AR32	PF2	2sh 6p car (#AR2)	675.00	525.00
AR33	PF2	2sh 6p car (#AR23)	450.00	
AR34	PF4	10sh orange	950.00	950.00
AR35	A8	£1 grn & yel (#85)	375.00	350.00

Nos. AR28-AR35 were not supposed to be postally used. Because of imprecise terminology, postal use was tolerated until all postal use of revenues ceased on Nov. 30, 1900.

Other denominations and watermarks were overprinted after postal use was no longer allowed.

VICTORIA

vik-'tōr-ē-ə

LOCATION — In the extreme south-eastern part of Australia
GOVT. — British Colony
AREA — 87,884 sq. mi.
POP. — 1,201,341 (1901)
CAPITAL — Melbourne

Victoria was one of the six former British colonies which united on Jan. 1, 1901, to form the Commonwealth of Australia.

12 Pence = 1 Shilling
20 Shillings = 1 Pound

Unused values for Nos. 1-16 are for stamps without gum as these stamps are seldom found with original gum. Otherwise, unused values are for stamps with original gum as defined in the catalogue introduction.

Very fine examples of all rouletted, perforated and serrate perforated stamps from Nos. 9-109 and F2 will have roulettes, perforations or serrate perforations touching the design. Examples clear on four sides range from scarce to rare and will command higher prices.

Watermarks

Wmk. 6 — Large Star

Wmk. 80

Wmk. 50   Wmk. 80a

Wmk. 81   Wmk. 139

Wmk. 49   Wmk. 75

Wmk. 70 — V and Crown   Wmk. 13 — Crown & Double-lined A

Queen Victoria — A1

A1 TYPES

1p:
Type I — "VICTORIA" very close to top of design, with very thin line of color between "VICTORIA" and frameline.
Type II — Thicker line of color between "VICTORIA" and frameline at top.

2p:
Type I — Border, two sets of nine wavy lines crisscrossing. Background, 22 groups of wavy triple lines below "VICTORIA."
Type II — Border, same. Background, 15 groups of wavy triple lines below "VICTORIA."
Type III — Border, two sets of five wavy lines crisscrossing. Background, same as type II.

3p:
Type I — Orb poorly defined, with white area at right and thicker at left. Central band of orb does not protrude at left.
Type II — Orb clearly defined, with white outlines at left and right. Central band of orb protrudes at left.

1850 Litho. Unwmk. Imperf.

1	A1	1p dull red, II	4,000.	225.00
a.		1p dull org ver, II	5,500.	750.00
b.		1p brownish red, II ('51)	1,500.	210.00
c.		1p dull brown, I	19,000.	2,500.
d.		1p orange vermilion, I	30,000.	5,500.
e.		1p orange brown, I		2,100.
2	A1	1p rose, II	3,500.	200.00
a.		1p pink, II	1,750.	190.00
b.		1p reddish brown, II ('51)	5,500.	190.00
3	A1	3p blue, I	6,500.	450.00
a.		3p light blue, II ('52)	2,250.	110.00
b.		3p bright blue, I	7,500.	625.00
4	A1	3p indigo, II	3,000.	600.00
a.		3p pale grnsh blue, II ('52)	3,500.	210.00
		Nos. 1-4 (4)	17,000.	975.00

Nos. 1-4 exist with and without frame line.

5	A1	2p lilac, I	7,500.	550.00
a.		2p brn lilac, I	7,000.	550.00
b.		2p orange brown, I		2,500.
6	A1	2p brn lilac, II	2,500.	250.00
a.		2p gray lilac, II	6,000.	200.00
7	A1	2p brn lilac, III	7,250.	200.00
a.		2p gray lilac, III	11,000.	500.00
b.		Value omitted, III		17,500.
8	A1	2p yel brn, III	3,000.	200.00

Rouletted 7

9	A1	1p vermilion		3,350.
10	A1	3p blue	2,500.	250.00
a.		3p deep blue	2,500.	300.00

Perf. 12

12	A1	3p blue	2,000.	175.00
a.		3p deep blue	2,000.	175.00

Victoria on Throne — A2

1852 Engr. Imperf.

14	A2	2p reddish brn	400.00	45.00
a.		2p chestnut		175.00
b.		2p purple brown	575.00	30.00

No. 14 was reprinted on paper with watermark 70, imperf. & perf. 12½, overprinted "REPRINT."

1854 Litho.

15	A2	2p gray brown	450.00	45.00
16	A2	2p brown lilac	300.00	40.00
a.		2p red lilac		37.50
b.		As "a," "TVO" for "TWO"	10,000.	1,500.

Fifty varieties.

A3   A4

1854-58 Typo.

17	A3	6p yellow orange	375.00	32.50
a.		6p dull orange	375.00	32.50
b.		6p reddish brown	725.00	72.50

See Nos. 19-20, 22-24A, 26-28.

Lithographed

18	A4	1sh blue	1,100.	35.00
a.		1sh greenish blue	1,250.	35.00
b.		1sh indigo blue		180.00

See Nos. 21, 25.

Typographed

19	A3	2sh green	3,000.	250.00

1857-58 Rouletted 7, 9½

20	A3	6p orange	—	87.50
a.		6p yellow orange		100.00
b.		6p reddish brown		115.00

Lithographed

21	A4	1sh blue	—	160.00
a.		1sh greenish blue	—	160.00

Typographed

22	A3	2sh green ('58)	7,000.	675.00

Small Serrate Perf. 19

23	A3	6p orange	—	125.00

Large Serpentine Perf. 10½

24	A3	6p orange	—	125.00

Serrate x Serpentine Perf.

24A	A3	6p orange	—	200.00

1859 Litho. Perf. 12

25	A4	1sh blue	250.00	25.00
a.		1sh greenish blue	275.00	27.50
b.		1sh indigo blue	—	52.50

Typographed

26	A3	2sh green	525.00	70.00

1861 Wmk. "SIX PENCE" (80)

27	A3	6p black	300.00	80.00

Wmk. Single-lined "2" (50)

1864 Perf. 12, 13

28	A3	2sh blue, green	350.00	13.00

A5

Wmk. Large Star (6)

1856, Oct. Engr. Imperf.

29	A5	1p green	250.00	42.50

1858 Rouletted 5½-6½

30	A5	6p blue	350.00	28.00
a.		6p light blue	450.00	45.00

Nos. 29 and 30 have been reprinted on paper watermarked V and Crown. They are imperforate and overprinted "REPRINT."

A6

1857-61 Typo. Imperf.
Wove Paper

31	A6	1p yellow green	175.00	25.00
a.		Printed on both sides		2,750.
32	A6	4p vermilion	450.00	15.00
a.		Printed on both sides		2,750.
33	A6	4p rose	375.00	15.00

Rouletted 7 to 9½

34	A6	1p yellow green	625.00	140.00
35	A6	4p rose	—	57.50
35A	A6	4p vermilion		575.00

Perf. 12

36	A6	1p yellow green	—	500.00

Unwmk. Imperf.

37	A6	1p blue green	425.00	22.50
38	A6	2p lilac	400.00	21.00
39	A6	4p rose	575.00	47.50

Examples of No. 39 printed in dull carmine on thin paper are regarded as printer's waste and of little value. They are also found printed on both sides.

Rouletted 7 to 9½

40	A6	1p emerald green	575.00	37.50
41	A6	2p lilac	1,150.	725.00
42	A6	4p rose pink	400.00	11.50
a.		Vert. pair, imperf. btwn.		750.00
b.		4p reddish pink		20.00

Perf. 12

43	A6	1p blue green	225.00	20.00
a.		1p yellow green	325.00	24.00
b.		Horiz. pair, imperf. btwn.		
44	A6	2p lilac		450.00
45	A6	4p rose	300.00	8.00
b.		Vert. pair, imperf. btwn.		

Rouletted 5½-6½

45C	A6	4p dull rose		1,250.

Serrate Rouletted 19

45A	A6	2p lilac	1,100.	600.00

Laid Paper
Imperf

46	A6	4p rose	825.00	35.00

Rouletted 5 to 7

47	A6	2p violet	275.00	10.50
a.		2p brown lilac	225.00	15.00
b.		2p dark lilac	300.00	25.00
48	A6	4p rose	250.00	7.25

Serrate Rouletted 19

48D	A6	4p rose red		825.00

Perf. 12

49	A6	1p green	300.00	25.00
50	A6	4p rose	200.00	15.00

Wove Paper
1860 Wmk. Value in Words (80)

51	A6	1p pale yellowish green	130.00	10.50
a.		Wmk. "FOUR PENCE" (error)		9,750.
52	A6	2p gray lilac	200.00	10.00
a.		2p brown lilac ('61)	—	52.50

Wmk. "THREE PENCE" (80)

53	A6	2p bluish gray ('63)	225.00	25.00

Single-lined "2" (50)

54	A6	2p lilac	300.00	18.00
a.		2p gray lilac	275.00	22.50
b.		2p brown lilac	225.00	21.00
c.		As "a," wmkd. single-lined "6"		7,750.

A7

1860 Unwmk. Laid Paper

56	A7	3p deep blue	625.00	77.50

Wmk. Value in Words (80)
Perf. 11½ to 12

1860-64 Wove Paper

57	A7	3p blue ('63)	240.00	12.50
a.		"TRREE" instead of "THREE" in watermark		800.00
58	A7	3p claret	180.00	37.50
a.		Perf. 13	240.00	47.50
59	A7	4p rose	200.00	7.75
60	A7	6p orange	5,750.	350.00

61	A7	6p black	250.00	10.50

Wmk. "FIVE SHILLINGS" (80)

62	A7	4p rose	*3,000.*	30.00

Wmk. Single-lined "4" (80a)

1863   *Imperf.*

63	A7	4p rose	—	*175.00*

Rouletted

64	A7	4p rose	*3,250.*	350.00

Perf. 11½ to 12

65	A7	4p rose	180.00	10.50

1863   **Unwmk.**   **Perf. 12**

66	A7	4p rose	625.00	30.00

A8   A9

1861-63   **Wmk. 80**   **Perf. 11½ to 12**

67	A8	1p green	140.00	17.00
68	A9	6p black	140.00	15.00

Wmk. Double-lined "1" (139)

69	A8	1p green	250.00	18.00
b.	Horiz. pair, imperf between		—	

Wmk. Single-lined Figures (50)

70	A8	1p green	115.00	11.50
71	A9	6p gray black	140.00	10.00

The 1p and 6p of 1861-63 are known on paper without watermark but were probably impressions on the margins of watermarked sheets.

A10   A11

A12   A13

Wmk. Single-lined Figures (50, 80a, 81)

1863-67   **Perf. 11½ to 13**

74	A10	1p green	120.00	8.50
a.	Double impression			1,500.
75	A10	2p gray lilac	120.00	15.00
a.	2p violet		115.00	11.50
76	A10	4p rose	140.00	5.00
a.	Double impression			1,500.
77	A11	6p blue	115.00	4.25
78	A10	8p orange	700.00	115.00
79	A12	10p brn, *rose*	200.00	10.50
80	A13	1sh blue, *blue*	200.00	6.50
	Nos. 74-80 (7)		1,595.	164.75

See Nos. 81-82, 84-96, 99-101, 108-112, 115-119, 124-126, 144, 188. Compare type A11 with type A54.

A14

Wmk. Double-lined "1" (139)

81	A10	1p green	125.00	7.00
82	A10	2p gray lilac	325.00	10.50
83	A14	3p lilac	325.00	100.00
84	A11	6p blue	115.00	9.50
	Nos. 81-84 (4)		890.00	127.00

See Nos. 97, 113, 114, 155, 186. Compare type A14 with type A51.

Wmk. Double-lined "2" (49)

85	A11	6p blue		*4,250.*

Wmk. Single-lined "4" (80a)

86	A10	1p green	200.00	30.00
87	A10	2p gray lilac	250.00	10.50
88	A11	6p blue		*2,750.*

Wmk. Double-lined "4" (75)

89	A10	1p green	2,500.	160.00
90	A10	2p gray lilac	250.00	8.00
91	A10	4p rose	300.00	9.50
92	A11	6p blue	325.00	35.00

Wmk. Single-lined "6" (50)

93	A10	1p green	325.00	42.50
94	A10	2p gray lilac	350.00	11.50

Wmk. Single-lined "8" (50)

95	A10	1p green	300.00	27.50
96	A10	2p gray lilac	325.00	10.50
97	A14	3p lilac	250.00	57.50
99	A12	10p slate	1,000.	200.00

Wmk. "SIX PENCE" (80)

100	A10	1p green	1,150.	57.50
100A	A10	2p slate gray		16,000.
101	A11	6p blue	800.00	42.50

All values of the 1864-67 series except the 3p and 8p are known on unwatermarked paper. They are probably varieties from watermarked sheets which have been so placed on the printing press that some of the stamps escaped the watermark.

One example of the 2p gray lilac, type A10, is reported to exist with only "PENCE" of watermark 80 showing. Some believe this is part of the "SIX PENCE" watermark.

1870   **Wmk. "THREE PENCE" (80)**

108	A11	6p blue	475.00	17.50

Wmk. "FOUR PENCE" (80)

109	A11	6p blue	800.00	52.50

A15

1867-78   **Wmk. (70)**   **Perf. 11½ to 13**

110	A10	1p green	115.00	5.75
111	A10	2p lilac	110.00	5.25
a.	2p gray lilac		125.00	9.50
112	A10	2p lilac, *lilac*	130.00	14.00
113	A14	3p red lilac	400.00	65.00
a.	3p lilac		475.00	72.50
114	A14	3p orange	47.50	6.50
a.	3p yellow		77.50	7.75
115	A10	4p rose	130.00	11.50
116	A11	6p blue	60.00	4.75
117	A11	6p ultra	72.50	5.00
a.	6p lilac blue		130.00	17.50
118	A10	8p brn, *rose*	140.00	10.50
119	A13	1sh bl, *blue*	325.00	17.50
120	A15	5sh bl, *yel*	3,250.	500.00
121	A15	5sh bl & rose	400.00	32.50
a.	Without blue line under crown		375.00	30.00
122	A15	5sh ultra & rose	325.00	42.50

See Nos. 126, 144, 188. For surcharge see No. 124.

For additional stamps of type A15, see No. 191. Compare type A15 with type A58.

A16

1870   **Perf. 13**

123	A16	2p lilac	115.00	2.60
a.	Perf. 12		125.00	3.50

No. 110 Surcharged in Red

1873, July 19   **Perf. 13, 12**

124	A10	½p on 1p green	100.00	24.00

No. 79 Surcharged in Blue

1871   **Wmk. Single-lined "10" (81)**

125	A12	9p on 10p brn, *rose*	650.00	25.00
a.	Double surcharge			*2,500.*

A19

1873-78   **Typo.**

126	A10	8p brown, *rose* ('78)	175.00	10.50
127	A19	9p brown, *rose*	175.00	27.50

For additional stamps of type A19, see Nos. 128-129, 174-175. Compare type A19 with type A55.

1875   **Wmk. V and Crown (70)**

128	A19	9p brown, *rose*	200.00	27.50

No. 128 Surcharged in Blue

1876

129	A19	8p on 9p brn, *rose*	350.00	32.50

A21   A22

A23   A24

A25

1873-81   **Perf. 13, 12**

130	A21	½p rose ('74)	24.00	2.00
131	A21	½p rose, *rose* ('78)	70.00	42.50
132	A22	1p grn ('75)	52.50	3.25
133	A22	1p grn, *gray* ('78)	240.00	110.00
134	A22	1p grn, *yel* ('78)	160.00	30.00
135	A23	2p violet	77.50	1.30
136	A23	2p vio, *grnsh* ('78)	325.00	40.00
137	A23	2p vio, *buff* ('78)	300.00	40.00
137A	A23	2p vio, *lil* ('78)	—	*1,200.*
138	A24	1sh bl, *bl* ('76)	130.00	6.75
139	A25	2sh bl, *grn* ('81)	240.00	35.00

See Nos. 140, 156A-158, 184, 189-190. Compare design A21 with design A46, A24 with A56, A25 with A57.

1878   **Double-lined Outer Oval**

140	A23	2p violet	77.50	3.75
b.	Vert. pair, lower stamp imperf horiz.			*3,000.*

A26   A27

A28

1880-84   **Perf. 12½**

141	A26	1p green ('84)	140.00	22.50
142	A27	2p brown	50.00	1.40
143	A27	2p lilac	37.50	2.25
144	A10	4p car rose	260.00	15.00
145	A28	4p car rose ('81)	115.00	10.00
	Nos. 141-145 (5)		602.50	51.15

See Nos. 156, 185, 187. Compare design A26 with design A47, A27 with A49, A28 with A52.

A29   A30

A31   A32

A33   A34

1884-86

146	A29	½p rose	22.50	2.25
147	A30	1p green	29.00	2.40
148	A31	2p violet	32.50	1.25
a.	2p lilac rose		32.50	1.25
149	A30	3p bister	20.00	2.40
a.	3p ocher		20.00	2.40
150	A32	4p magenta	110.00	6.25
a.	4p violet (error)		6,000.	1,250.
151	A30	6p bright blue ('85)	125.00	5.00
a.	6p ultramarine ('85)		85.00	4.75
b.	6p gray blue ('85)		82.50	4.75
152	A33	8p rose, *rose*	52.50	14.00
153	A34	1sh blue, *yel*	175.00	24.00
154	A33	2sh olive, *grn*	115.00	6.25
	Nos. 146-154 (9)		681.50	63.80

See Nos. 177-178, 192A. Compare designs A31-A32 with designs A37-A38.

Nos. 114, 145, 138-139 Ovptd. Vertically in Blue or Black

1885

155	A14	3p orange (Bl)	115.00	47.50
156	A28	4p car rose (Bl)	105.00	72.50
156A	A24	1sh bl, *bl* (Bl)		3,500.
	Revenue cancel			1,250.
157	A24	1sh bl, *bl* (Bk)	175.00	37.50
158	A25	2sh bl, *grn* (Bk)	175.00	35.00
	Nos. 155-156, 157-158 (4)		570.00	192.50

Reprints of 4p and 1sh have brighter colors than originals. They lack the overprint "REPRINT."

A35   A36

A37   A38

A39   A40

1886-87   **Perf. 12½**

159	A35	½p lilac	37.50	9.50
160	A35	½p rose	17.50	1.40
160A	A35	½p scarlet	7.75	1.40
161	A36	1p green	16.00	2.25
162	A37	2p violet	20.00	.55
a.		2p red lilac	11.50	.70
b.		Imperf.		1,100.
163	A38	4p red	22.50	2.40
164	A39	6p blue	37.50	3.25
165	A39	6p ultra	32.50	1.10
166	A40	1sh lilac brown	37.50	3.75
		Nos. 159-166 (9)	228.75	25.60

See No. 180.

A41

1889

167	A41	1sh6p blue	260.00	140.00
168	A41	1sh6p orange	35.00	15.00

A42   Southern Cross — A43

Queen Victoria — A44

1890-95   **Perf. 12½**

169	A42	1p org brn	10.00	.75
a.		1p chocolate brown	12.50	1.10
170	A42	1p yel brn	12.50	.55
171	A42	1p brn org, *pink* ('91)	10.50	4.50
172	A43	2½p brn red, *yel*	19.00	1.75
173	A44	5p choc ('91)	15.00	3.75
174	A19	9p green ('92)	45.00	16.00
175	A19	9p rose red	32.50	6.00
a.		9p rose ('95)	37.50	11.50
176	A40	1sh deep claret	37.50	2.40
a.		1sh red brown	32.50	1.40
b.		1sh maroon	87.50	5.25
177	A33	2sh yel grn	37.50	17.50
178	A33	2sh emerald	35.00	19.00
		Nos. 169-178 (10)	254.50	72.20

In 1891 many stamps of the early issues were reprinted. They are on paper watermarked V and Crown, perforated 12, 12½, and overprinted "REPRINT."
See Nos. 181, 183, 192. Compare type A43 with type A50, A44 with type A53.

A45

1897

179	A45	1½p yellow green	6.00	6.50

See No. 182. Compare type A45 with type A48.

1899

180	A35	½p emerald	25.00	5.75
181	A42	1p brt rose	11.50	.55
182	A45	1½p red, *yel*	5.75	3.50
183	A43	2½p dark blue	15.00	15.00
		Nos. 180-183 (4)	57.25	24.80

1901

184	A21	½p blue green	3.75	3.25
a.		"VICTCRIA"	110.00	62.50
185	A27	2p violet	14.00	3.00
186	A14	3p brown org	22.50	50.00
187	A28	4p bister	42.50	25.00
188	A11	6p emerald	17.50	13.00
189	A24	1sh orange yel	87.50	65.00
190	A25	2sh blue, *rose*	72.50	55.00
191	A15	5sh rose red & bl	90.00	72.50
		Nos. 184-191 (8)	350.25	286.75

1901

192	A42	1p olive green	11.50	7.50
192A	A30	3p sage green	40.00	19.00

Nos. 192-192A were available for postal use until June 30, 1901, and thereafter restricted to revenue use.

A46   A47

A48   A49

A50   A51

A52   A53

A54   A55

A56   A57

A58

1901   **Perf. 11, 12½ and Compound**

193	A46	½p blue green	5.75	1.40
194	A47	1p rose red	4.50	.65
a.		1p rose	14.00	1.00
195	A48	1½p red, *yellow*	3.75	1.25
a.		Perf. 11	110.00	110.00
196	A49	2p violet	21.00	1.10
197	A50	2½p blue	15.00	1.10
198	A51	3p brown org	15.00	2.50
199	A52	4p bister	10.50	1.25
200	A53	5p chocolate	17.50	1.10
201	A54	6p emerald	21.00	2.40
202	A55	9p rose	26.00	4.00

203	A56	1sh org yel	29.00	5.00
204	A57	2sh blue, *rose*	40.00	5.00
205	A58	5sh rose red & bl	110.00	35.00
a.		5sh carmine & blue	110.00	26.00
		Nos. 193-205 (13)	319.00	61.75

See Nos. 209-229, 232.

King Edward VII
A59   A60

1901-05

206	A59	£1 deep rose	350.00	150.00
a.		Perf. 11 ('05)	475.00	225.00
208	A60	£2 dk blue ('02)	700.00	450.00
a.		Perf. 11 ('05)	2,250.	1,400.

See Nos. 230-231.

1903   **Redrawn**

209	A56	1sh yellow	35.00	5.75
a.		1sh orange	32.50	4.75

No. 209 has the network lighter than No. 203. In the latter the "P" and "E" of "POST-AGE" are in a position more nearly horizontal than on No. 209.

Perf. 11, 12x12½, 12½, 12½x11

1905-10			**Wmk. 13**	
218	A46	½p blue green	4.75	.75
219	A47	1p rose red	2.40	.35
a.		1p carmine rose	15.00	3.00
220	A49	2p violet	9.25	.75
a.		2p purple	10.00	.90
221	A50	2½p blue	5.75	1.00
222	A51	3p brown org	15.00	3.00
a.		3p dull yellow	17.50	3.00
223	A52	4p bister	12.50	1.75
224	A53	5p chocolate	12.50	4.75
225	A54	6p emerald	24.00	2.00
226	A55	9p orange brown	24.00	5.00
a.		9p brown rose	26.00	5.25
227	A55	9p car rose	17.50	3.00
228	A56	1sh yellow ('08)	24.00	4.50
229	A58	5sh orange red & ultra	130.00	26.00
a.		5sh rose red & ultra	140.00	32.50
230	A59	£1 pale red ('07)	450.00	240.00
a.		£1 rose ('10)	350.00	240.00
231	A60	£2 dull blue	1,150.	725.00
		Nos. 218-229 (12)	281.65	52.85

No. 220 Surcharged in Red

1912, July 1

232	A49	1p on 2p violet	1.75	1.25

POSTAL-FISCAL STAMPS

On Jan. 1, 1884, all postage and fiscal stamps were made available for either purpose. Fiscal stamps became invalid after June 30, 1901.

Used values are for examples with postal cancellations used from Jan. 1, 1884 through June 30, 1901.

Beware of stamps with a pen cancellation removed, often regummed or with a fake postmark added.

Stamps inscribed "Stamp Duty" that were issued primarily in postal rates in the normal postage stamp size are listed in the postage section (Nos. 146-178, 180-183, 192-192A). The stamps meeting primarily fiscal rates and in the larger fiscal stamp size, are listed here in the Postal-Fiscal section.

Stamps Inscribed "Stamp Statute"

Victoria — PF1

PF1a (AR3)

PF1b (AR5)   PF1c (AR6)

Coat of Arms — PF2

PF3

Wmk. V and Crown (70)				
1870-83		**Typo.**		**Perf. 13**
AR1	PF1a	1p green	90.00	75.00
a.		Revenue cancel		7.25
		Perf. 12½	140.00	120.00
AR2	PF1	3p lilac	1,150.	600.00
		Revenue cancel		140.00
AR3	PF1a	4p red	1,000.	500.00
		Revenue cancel		125.00
AR4	PF1a	6p blue	125.00	45.00
		Revenue cancel		14.00
a.		Perf. 12	140.00	35.00
		Revenue cancel		10.50
AR5	PF1b	1sh blue, *blue*	140.00	45.00
		Revenue cancel		14.00
a.		Perf. 12	140.00	50.00
		Revenue cancel		17.50
b.		Perf. 12½	140.00	45.00
		Revenue cancel		14.00
c.		Wmk. 50, perf. 13	140.00	32.50
		Revenue cancel		11.50
d.		Wmk. 50, perf. 12	160.00	37.50
		Revenue cancel		13.00
AR6	PF1c	2sh blue, *grn*	225.00	130.00
		Revenue cancel		30.00
a.		Perf. 12	225.00	35.00
		Revenue cancel		35.00
b.		Wmk. 50, perf. 13	300.00	125.00
		Revenue cancel		17.50
c.		Wmk. 50, perf. 12	325.00	125.00
		Revenue cancel		21.00
AR7	PF2	2sh6p org, *yel*	650.00	260.00
		Revenue cancel		72.50
a.		Perf. 12	650.00	260.00
		Revenue cancel		72.50
b.		Perf. 12½	—	300.00
		Revenue cancel		87.50

AR8	PF1a	5sh blue, *yel*	600.00	140.00
		Revenue cancel		72.50
a.		Perf. 12	650.00	
b.		Perf. 12½	650.00	140.00
		Revenue cancel		72.50
AR9	PF1a	10sh brn, *rose*	1,600.	375.00
		Revenue cancel		90.00
a.		Perf. 12		
b.		Wmk. 50, perf. 13	1,600.	350.00
		Revenue cancel		75.00
c.		Wmk. 50, perf. 12		
AR10	PF1a	£1 lil, *yel*	1,250.	350.00
		Revenue cancel		90.00
a.		Perf. 12	1,150.	325.00
		Revenue cancel		90.00
b.		Perf. 12½	1,150.	325.00
		Revenue cancel		90.00
AR11	PF3	£5 blk, *grn*	10,000.	1,900.
		Revenue cancel		135.00
a.		Perf. 12		—
b.		Perf. 12½	10,000.	1,900.
		Revenue cancel		150.00

Nos. AR1-AR12 distributed for postal use from Jan. 1, 1884 through Apr. 23, 1884.

No. AR1 Surcharged "½d/HALF"
1879-96

AR12	PF1	½p on 1p grn	120.00	105.00
		Revenue cancel		42.50

Stamps Inscribed "Stamp Duty"

PF4 PF5 PF6 PF7 PF8 PF9 PF10 PF11 PF12 PF13 PF14 PF15

PF16 PF17 PF18 PF19 PF20 PF21 PF22 PF23 PF24 PF25

PF26 PF27 PF28

Wmk. V and Crown (70)

			Litho.	**Perf. 13**
1879-96				
AR13	PF4	1p green	140.00	45.00
		Revenue cancel		14.00
a.		Perf. 12	140.00	45.00
		Revenue cancel		14.00
b.		Perf. 12½	—	14.00
AR14	PF8	1sh 6p pink	375.00	50.00
		Revenue cancel		21.00
a.		Perf. 12	—	65.00
		Revenue cancel		26.00
b.		Perf. 12½	—	
AR15	PF11	3sh vio, *blue*	875.00	85.00
		Revenue cancel		21.00
a.		Perf. 12	1,000.	100.00
		Revenue cancel		21.00
b.		Perf. 12½	—	
AR16	PF12	4sh orange	175.00	35.00
		Revenue cancel		11.00
a.		Perf. 12	175.00	35.00
		Revenue cancel		11.00
b.		Perf. 12½	—	
AR17	PF14	6sh green	575.00	70.00
		Revenue cancel		12.50
a.		Perf. 12½	—	
AR18	PF15	10sh brn, *pink*	925.00	175.00
		Revenue cancel		62.50
a.		Perf. 12	—	
b.		Perf. 12½	—	
AR19	PF16	15sh lilac	1,750.	325.00
		Revenue cancel		125.00
AR20	PF17	£1 orange	800.00	110.00
		Revenue cancel		25.00
a.		Perf. 12½	800.00	110.00
AR21	PF18	£1 5sh *pink*	2,400.	450.00
		Revenue cancel		125.00
AR22	PF19	£1 10sh *olive*	2,750.	275.00
		Revenue cancel		75.00
AR23	PF20	35sh lilac	10,000.	
		Revenue cancel		350.00
AR24	PF21	£2 blue	—	240.00
		Revenue cancel		37.50
AR25	PF22	45sh violet	5,000.	425.00
		Revenue cancel		92.50
AR26	PF23	£5 rose	9,000.	1,000.
		Revenue cancel		125.00
AR27	PF24	£6 blue, *pink*	—	1,500.
		Revenue cancel		175.00
AR28	PF25	£7 vio, *blue*	—	1,500.
		Revenue cancel		175.00
AR29	PF26	£8 scarlet, *yel*	—	1,700.
		Revenue cancel		200.00
AR30	PF27	£9 green, *grn*	—	1,700.
		Revenue cancel		200.00

Typo.

AR31	PF4	1p green	105.00	45.00
		Revenue cancel		8.75
a.		Perf. 12	105.00	45.00
		Revenue cancel		8.75
b.		Perf. 12½	—	
AR32	PF5	1p brown	40.00	7.75
		Revenue cancel		1.40
a.		Perf. 12	40.00	9.25

b.		Perf. 12½	—	1.40
AR33	PF6	6p blue	140.00	22.50
				5.75
a.		Perf. 12	140.00	37.50
		Revenue cancel		5.75
b.		Perf. 12½		
AR34	PF7	1sh blue, *blue*	140.00	11.50
		Revenue cancel		5.75
a.		Perf. 12	140.00	14.00
		Revenue cancel		5.75
b.		Perf. 12½	140.00	13.00
		Revenue cancel		5.75
AR35	PF7	1sh blue, *yel*, perf 12½	200.00	45.00
		Revenue cancel		17.50
AR36	PF8	1sh 6p pink	260.00	50.00
		Revenue cancel		17.50
AR37	PF9	2sh blue, *grn*	325.00	45.00
		Revenue cancel		13.00
a.		Perf. 12	—	50.00
		Revenue cancel		13.00
b.		Perf. 12½	350.00	52.50
		Revenue cancel		13.00
AR38	PF10	2sh 6p org, perf 12½	175.00	37.50
a.		2sh6p yellow ('85)	115.00	17.50
b.		2sh6p lemon yellow ('92)	115.00	18.00
		Revenue cancel		5.75
AR39	PF11	3sh violet, *bl*, perf 12½	700.00	65.00
		Revenue cancel		14.00
AR40	PF11	3sh bister	125.00	29.00
		Revenue cancel		21.00
AR41	PF12	4sh org, perf 12½	140.00	26.00
		Revenue cancel		7.25
AR42	PF13	5sh claret, *yel*	110.00	11.50
		Revenue cancel		5.75
a.		Perf. 12	125.00	22.50
		Revenue cancel		5.75
b.		Perf. 12½	100.00	22.50
		Revenue cancel		5.75
AR43	PF13	5sh car *rose*	140.00	35.00
		Revenue cancel		7.25
AR44	PF14	6sh green	200.00	85.00
		Revenue cancel		16.00
AR45	PF15	10sh brn, *pink*	—	175.00
		Revenue cancel		57.50
a.		Perf. 12	—	
b.		Perf. 12½	—	
AR46	PF15	10sh green	325.00	65.00
		Revenue cancel		20.00
AR47	PF16	15sh brown	1,200.	145.00
		Revenue cancel		42.50
AR48	PF17	£1 org, *yel*, perf 12½	875.00	80.00
		Revenue cancel		25.00
a.		Perf. 12	1,100.	95.00
		Revenue cancel		30.00
AR49	PF18	£1 5sh *pink*	2,250.	160.00
		Revenue cancel		75.00
AR50	PF19	£1 10sh *olive*	1,750.	135.00
		Revenue cancel		50.00
AR51	PF21	£2 blue	1,350.	125.00
		Revenue cancel		27.50
a.		Perf. 12	—	200.00
		Revenue cancel		27.50
AR52	PF22	45sh gray lilac	5,000.	180.00
		Revenue cancel		62.50
AR53	PF23	£5 rose, perf. 12	—	900.00
		Revenue cancel		105.00
a.		perf. 12½	—	1,100.
		Revenue cancel		150.00
AR54	PF28	£10 lilac	5,500.	210.00
		Revenue cancel		62.50
a.		Perf. 12	5,500.	325.00
		Revenue cancel		62.50

Nos. AR49-AR52, AR54, used, are valued cto.

PF29

PF30

PF31

Wmk. V and Crown (70)

1879-1900		**Engr.**	**Perf. 12½**	
AR55	PF29	£25 green	—	900.00
		Revenue cancel		110.00
a.		Perf. 13		—
b.		Perf. 12		—
AR56	PF31	£50 violet	—	975.00
		Revenue cancel		125.00
a.		Perf. 13		—
AR57	PF31	£100 red	—	1,000.
		Revenue cancel		225.00
a.		Perf. 13		—
b.		Perf. 12		—
		Revenue cancel		225.00
		Typo.		
AR58	PF29	£25 green	—	325.00
a.		Lithographed		100.00
		Revenue cancel		140.00
AR59	PF30	£50 violet	—	500.00
a.		Lithographed		140.00
		Revenue cancel		225.00
AR60	PF31	£100 red	—	650.00
a.		Lithographed		225.00

Nos. AR55-AR60, used, are valued cto.

PF32

1887-90		**Typo.**		
AR61	PF32	£5 cl & ultra	4,000.	175.00
		Revenue cancel		82.50
AR62	PF32	£6 blue & yel	5,000.	200.00
		Revenue cancel		90.00
AR63	PF32	£7 blk & red	5,500.	225.00
		Revenue cancel		110.00
AR64	PF32	£8 org & lil	6,000.	250.00
		Revenue cancel		110.00
AR65	PF32	£9 red & green	6,500.	275.00
		Revenue cancel		135.00

Nos. AR61-AR65, used, are valued cto.

SEMI-POSTAL STAMPS

SP1

Queen Victoria and Figure of Charity SP2

Wmk. V and Crown (70)

1897, Oct.		**Typo.**	**Perf. 12½**	
B1	SP1	1p deep blue	27.50	27.50
B2	SP2	2½p red brown	140.00	110.00

These stamps were sold at 1sh and 2sh6p respectively. The premium was given to a charitable institution.

Victoria Cross — SP3

Scout Reporting SP4

1900				
B3	SP3	1p brown olive	125.00	75.00
B4	SP4	2p emerald	225.00	225.00

These stamps were sold at 1sh and 2sh respectively. The premium was given to a patriotic fund in connection with the South African War.

REGISTRATION STAMPS

R1

		Unwmk.		
1854, Dec. 1		**Typo.**	**Imperf.**	
F1	R1	1sh rose & blue	2,500.	225.00
1857			**Rouletted 7**	
F2	R1	1sh rose & blue	8,750.	425.00

LATE FEE STAMP

LF1

		Unwmk.		
1855, Jan. 1		**Typo.**	**Imperf.**	
I1	LF1	6p lilac & green	1,900.	275.00

POSTAGE DUE STAMPS

D1

Wmk. V and Crown (70)

1890		**Typo.**	**Perf. 12½**	
J1	D1	½p claret & blue	8.00	7.00
J2	D1	1p claret & blue	11.50	2.60
J3	D1	2p claret & blue	18.00	3.25
J4	D1	4p claret & blue	27.50	4.75
J5	D1	5p claret & blue	26.00	3.50
J6	D1	6p claret & blue	27.50	6.50
J7	D1	10p claret & blue	140.00	90.00
J8	D1	1sh claret & blue	90.00	14.00
J9	D1	2sh claret & blue	200.00	92.50
J10	D1	5sh claret & blue	300.00	140.00
		Nos. J1-J10 (10)	848.50	364.10

1891-94				
J11	D1	½p lake & blue	5.50	*7.75*
J12	D1	1p brn red & blue ('93)	15.00	2.75
J13	D1	2p brn red & blue ('93)	26.00	2.00
J14	D1	4p lake & blue ('94)	22.50	11.50
		Nos. J11-J14 (4)	69.00	24.00
1894-96				
J15	D1	½p bl grn & rose	9.50	3.00
J16	D1	1p bl grn & rose	9.00	3.00
J17	D1	2p bl grn & rose	18.00	3.50
J18	D1	4p bl grn & rose	18.00	3.00
J19	D1	5p bl grn & rose	22.50	22.50
J20	D1	6p bl grn & rose	20.00	14.00
J21	D1	10p bl grn & rose	45.00	20.00
J22	D1	1sh bl grn & rose	32.50	6.00
J23	D1	2sh yel grn & rose	115.00	37.50
J24	D1	5sh yel grn & rose	200.00	75.00
		Nos. J15-J24 (10)	489.50	187.50
1905-09			**Wmk. 13**	
J25	D1	½p yel grn & rose	10.00	*13.00*
J26	D1	1p yel grn & rose	12.00	4.50
J27	D1	2p yel grn & rose	29.00	5.25
J28	D1	4p yel grn & rose	35.00	21.00
		Nos. J25-J28 (4)	86.00	43.75

A 5p with wmk. 13 exists but was not issued.

WESTERN AUSTRALIA

'wes-tərn o-'strāl-yə

LOCATION — Western part of Australia, occupying about a third of that continent

GOVT. — British Colony

AREA — 975,920 sq. mi.

POP. — 184,124 (1901)

CAPITAL — Perth

Western Australia was one of the six British colonies that united on January 1, 1901, to form the Commonwealth of Australia.

12 Pence = 1 Shilling
20 Shillings = 1 Pound

Unused values for Nos. 1-10 are for stamps without gum as these stamps are seldom found with original gum. Otherwise, unused values are for stamps with original gum as defined in the catalogue introduction.

Very fine examples of all rouletted and perforated stamps from Nos. 6-34 have roulettes or perforations touching the design. Examples clear on all four sides range from scarce to rare and will command higher prices.

Watermarks

Wmk. 82 — Swan

Wmk. 83 — Crown and W A

Wmk. 70 — V and Crown

Wmk. 13 — Crown & Double-lined A

Wmk. 74 — Crown and Single-lined A

Swan A1   A2

1854-57		**Engr.** **Wmk. 82**	**Imperf.**	
1	A1	1p black	1,350.	275.
		Litho.		
2	A2	2p brown, *red*	4,000.	800.
		('57)		
a.		2p brown, *deep red* ('57)	4,250.	1,100.
b.		Printed on both sides	4,250.	950.

See Nos. 4, 6-7, 9, 14-39, 44-52, 54, 59-61. For surcharges see Nos. 41, 55-56.

A3

A4

3	A3	4p blue	450.	275.
a.		Frame inverted		95,000.
		As "a," cut to shape		27,500.
b.		4p slate blue	3,750.	1,350.
4	A2	6p bronze	6,000.	900.
		('57)		
5	A4	1sh pale brown	550.	400.
a.		1sh dark brown	700.	450.
b.		1sh dark red brown	2,250.	1,000.
c.		1sh pale red brown	26,500.	4,000.
		Engraved		
		Rouletted		
6	A1	1p black	3,200.	750.
		Lithographed		
7	A2	2p brn, *red*	9,500.	1,900.
		('57)		
a.		Printed on both sides		2,300.
8	A3	4p blue	—	675.
9	A2	6p bronze	12,500.	2,000.
		('57)		
10	A4	1sh brown	5,000.	1,000.

The 1p, 2p, 4p and 6p are known with pin-perforation but this is believed to be unofficial. No. 7a is only recorded used and with pin perforations.

1860		**Engr.**	**Imperf.**	
14	A1	2p vermilion	140.00	130.00
a.		2p pale orange	140.00	130.00
15	A1	4p blue	325.	*2,000.*
16	A1	6p dull green	2,100.	875.00
		Rouletted		
17	A1	2p vermilion	800.00	250.00
a.		2p pale orange	650.00	250.00
18	A1	4p deep blue	5,000.	—
19	A1	6p dull green	4,500.	750.00
1861		**Clean-Cut Perf. 14 to 16**		
20	A1	1p rose	700.00	200.00
21	A1	2p blue	140.00	45.00
a.		Imperf., pair		
b.		Horiz. pair, imperf. vert.		
22	A1	4p vermilion	1,550.	*2,400.*
a.		Imperf.		
23	A1	6p purple brn	525.00	92.50
a.		Imperf.		
24	A1	1sh green	875.00	140.00
a.		Imperf.		
		Rough Perf. 14 to 16		
24B	A1	1p rose	300.00	65.00
24C	A1	6p pur brn, *blu-ish*	3,500.	525.00
24D	A1	1sh deep green	2,500.	425.00
		Perf. 14		
25	A1	1p rose	400.00	110.00
25A	A1	2p blue	180.00	72.50
25B	A1	4p vermilion	450.00	300.00
		Unwmk.	**Perf. 13**	
26	A1	1p lake	115.00	7.75
28	A1	6p violet	240.00	77.50

1865-79 Wmk. 1 Perf. 12½

29	A1	1p bister	110.00	10.00
30	A1	1p yel ocher	130.00	15.00
31	A1	2p yellow	125.00	4.75
a.		2p lilac (error) ('79)	20,000.	17,500.
32	A1	4p carmine	120.00	8.75
a.		Double impression	42,500.	
33	A1	6p violet	160.00	11.50
a.		6p lilac	300.00	11.50
b.		6p red lilac	300.00	11.50
c.		Double impression	27,500.	
34	A1	1sh brt grn	200.00	21.00
a.		1sh sage green	525.00	45.00
		Nos. 29-34 (6)	845.00	71.00

1872-78 Perf. 14

35	A1	1p bister	180.00	7.25
36	A1	1p yellow ocher	115.00	5.00
37	A1	2p yellow	115.00	2.40
38	A1	4p carmine	750.00	140.00
39	A1	6p lilac	200.00	6.50
		Nos. 35-39 (5)	1,360.	161.15

 A5

1872 Typo.

40	A5	3p red brown	72.50	7.25
a.		3p brown	72.50	8.50

See Nos. 53, 92. For surcharges see Nos. 57, 69-72A.

No. 31 Surcharged in Green

ONE PENNY

1875 Engr. Perf. 12½

41	A1	1p on 2p yellow	625.00	80.00
a.		Pair, one without surcharge		
b.		"O" of "ONE" omitted		
c.		Triple surcharge	5,500.	

Forged surcharges exist.

1882 Wmk. 2 Perf. 12

44	A1	1p ocher yellow	125.00	8.00
46	A1	2p yellow	160.00	7.75
47	A1	4p carmine	300.00	60.00
48	A1	6p pale violet	575.00	60.00
		Nos. 44-48 (4)	1,160.	135.75

1882 Perf. 14

49	A1	1p ocher yellow	45.00	3.00
50	A1	2p yellow	50.00	3.00
51	A1	4p carmine	180.00	17.50
52	A1	6p pale violet	140.00	5.25
a.		6p violet	140.00	6.50

Typographed

53	A5	3p red brown	14.00	4.50
a.		3p brown	29.00	4.50
		Nos. 49-53 (5)	429.00	33.25

1883 Engr. Perf. 12x14

54	A1	1p ocher yellow	4,000.	300.00

Nos. 44 and 49 Surcharged in Red

½ / ONE PENNY

1884 Perf. 12

55	A1	½p on 1p ocher yel	18.00	32.50

Perf. 14

56	A1	½p on 1p ocher yel	30.00	40.00

No. 40 Surcharged in Green

1d.

1885 Typo. Wmk. 1

57	A5	1p on 3p red brown	87.50	26.00
a.		1p on 3p brown	115.00	27.50
b.		"1" with straight top	240.00	75.00

 A8

Wmk. Crown and C A (2)

1885 Typo. Perf. 14

58	A8	½p green	7.25	1.25

See No. 89.

1888 Engr.

59	A1	1p rose	35.00	5.75
60	A1	2p slate	90.00	2.75
61	A1	4p red brown	130.00	37.50
		Nos. 59-61 (3)	255.00	46.00

 A9   A10

A11 A12

1890-93 Typo.

62	A9	1p carmine rose	35.00	2.00
63	A10	2p slate	37.50	3.00
64	A11	2½p blue	20.00	3.25
65	A12	4p orange brown	14.00	2.75
66	A12	5p bister	15.00	5.00
67	A12	6p violet	21.00	6.50
68	A12	1sh olive green	26.00	7.50
		Nos. 62-68 (7)	168.50	30.00

See Nos. 73-74, 76, 80, 90, 94.

Nos. 40 and 53a Surcharged in Green

ONE PENNY

1893 Wmk. Crown and C C (1)

69	A5	1p on 3p red brown	16.00	7.75
a.		1p on 3p brown	16.00	7.50
b.		Double surcharge	1,600.	

Wmkd. Crown and C A (2)

70	A5	1p on 3p brown	77.50	10.50

Nos. 40a and 53a Surcharged in Green

Half-penny

1895 Wmk. Crown and C C (1)

71	A5	½p on 3p brown	13.00	35.00
a.		Double surcharge	1,250.	

No. 72 Surcharged in Green and Red

Half-penny

72	A5	½p on 3p brown	140.00	350.00

Wmk. Crown and C A (2)

72A	A5	½p on 3p brown	100.00	225.00

After the supply of paper watermarked Crown and C C was exhausted, No. 72A was printed. Ostensibly this was to provide samples for Postal Union distribution, but a supply for philatelic demands was also made.

Types of 1890-93 and

 A15

1899-1901 Typo. Wmk. 83

73	A9	1p carmine rose	7.75	1.75
74	A10	2p yellow	29.00	3.50
75	A15	2½p blue ('01)	14.00	4.75
		Nos. 73-75 (3)	50.75	10.00

 A16   A17

 A18 A19

 A20   A21

 A22 Southern Cross — A23

Queen Victoria

A24 A25

Perf. 12½, 12x12½

1902-05 Wmk. 70

76	A9	1p car rose	22.00	1.00
a.		1p salmon		
b.		Perf. 11	400.00	35.00
c.		Perf. 12½x11	1,200.	675.00
77	A16	2p yellow	22.50	4.75
a.		Perf. 11	400.00	57.50
b.		Perf. 12½x11	1,750.	1,100.
79	A17	4p org brn	29.00	4.00
a.		Perf. 11	1,400.	450.00
80	A12	5p ol bis, perf 12½ ('05)	175.00	115.00
a.		Perf. 11	90.00	100.00
81	A18	8p pale yel grn	30.00	4.75
82	A19	9p orange	50.00	17.50
b.		Perf. 11	175.00	185.00
83	A20	10p red	57.50	13.00
84	A21	2sh org red, yel ('06)	115.00	32.50
a.		Perf. 11	500.00	225.00
b.		2sh orange brown, yel ('11)	77.50	19.00
c.		2sh bright red, yel	130.00	19.00
d.		As "c," perf. 11	350.00	200.00
85	A22	2sh6p dk bl, rose	77.50	14.00
86	A23	5sh blue green	125.00	45.00
87	A24	10sh violet	300.00	130.00
a.		10sh bright purple	725.00	400.00
88	A25	£1 brown org	450.00	225.00
a.		£1 orange	750.00	425.00
		Nos. 76-88 (12)	1,454.	606.50

Perf. 12½, 12x12½

1905-12 Wmk. 13

89	A8	½p dp grn ('10)	8.00	9.25
a.		Perf 11	2,750.	
90	A9	1p rose	18.00	1.75
e.		Perf. 11	55.00	21.00
f.		Perf. 12½x11	1,100.	475.00
91	A16	2p yellow	11.50	3.25
a.		Perf. 11	65.00	32.50
b.		Perf. 12½x11	925.00	525.00
92	A5	3p brown	37.50	4.75
a.		Perf. 11	29.00	9.50
b.		Perf. 12½x11	—	1,200.
93	A17	4p orange brn	35.00	12.00
a.		4p bister brown	37.50	13.00
b.		Perf. 11	1,100.	290.00
94	A12	5p olive bis	29.00	15.00
a.		Perf. 11, pale olive bister	52.50	18.00
b.		Perf. 11, olive green	32.50	24.00
95	A18	8p pale yel grn ('12)	32.50	82.50
96	A19	9p orange	45.00	8.75
b.		Perf. 11	200.00	240.00
97	A20	10p red orange	37.50	35.00
98	A23	5s blue green	240.00	180.00
		Nos. 89-98 (10)	494.00	352.25

For surcharge see No. 103.

 A26   A27

1906-07 Wmk. 83 Perf. 14

99	A26	6p bright violet	40.00	3.25
100	A27	1sh olive green	50.00	6.50

1912 Wmk. 74 Perf. 11½x12

101	A26	6p bright violet	21.00	19.00
102	A27	1sh gray green	45.00	29.00
a.		Perf. 12½	2,750.	

No. 91 Surcharged

ONE PENNY

1912 Wmk. 13 Perf. 12½

103	A16	1p on 2p yellow	2.00	2.50
a.		Perf compound 12½x11	750.00	500.00

Stamps of Western Australia were replaced by those of Australia.

POSTAL-FISCAL STAMPS

Postal use of the 1p telegraph stamp was authorized beginning Oct. 25, 1886.

Used values are for examples with postal cancellations.

Beware of stamps with a pen cancellation removed and a fake postmark added.

PF1

1886 Wmk. 1 Perf. 14

AR1	PF1	1p bister	65.00	9.25

Perf. 12½

AR2	PF1	1p bister	65.00	7.75

Authorized for postal use by the Post and Telegraph Act of Sept. 5, 1893 were the current revenue stamps through the 1sh value.

Beware of stamps with a pen cancellation removed and a fake postmark added.

Because the Act specified current stamps, postally used examples from the provisional issue of of 1881 are not included here.

 PF2

1882 Wmk. 2 Perf. 14

AR3	PF2	1p purple	26.00	4.00
AR4	PF2	2p purple	260.00	100.00
AR5	PF2	3p purple	90.00	5.75
AR6	PF2	6p purple	105.00	7.75
AR7	PF2	1sh purple	180.00	15.00

The 6p is known postally used but was not authorized.

Wmk. 83

AR8	PF2	1p purple	22.50	4.50
AR9	PF2	3p purple	85.00	5.75
AR10	PF2	6p purple	85.00	6.00
AR11	PF2	1sh purple	180.00	22.50

Nos. AR7, AR11 have a rectangular outer frame and a circular frame around the swan.

Higher values are known with postal cancels, some postally used, but these were not authorized.

AUSTRALIA

o-'strāl-yə

LOCATION — Oceania, south of Indonesia, bounded on the west by the Indian Ocean
GOVT. — Self-governing dominion of the British Commonwealth
AREA — 2,967,909 sq. mi.
POP. — 17,892,423 (1996)
CAPITAL — Canberra

Australia includes the former British colonies of New South Wales, Victoria, Queensland, South Australia, Western Australia and Tasmania.

12 Pence = 1 Shilling
20 Shillings = 1 Pound
100 Cents = 1 Dollar (1966)

Catalogue values for unused stamps in this country are for Never Hinged items, beginning with Scott 197 in the regular postage section, Scott B1 in the semipostal section, Scott C6 in the air post section, Scott J71 in the postage due section, and all of the Australian Antarctic Territory.

Watermarks

Wmk. 8 — Wide Crown and Wide A

Wmk. 9 — Wide Crown and Narrow A

Wmk. 10 — Narrow Crown and Narrow A

Wmk. 11 — Multiple Crown and A

Wmk. 12 — Crown and Single-lined A

Wmk. 13 — Large Crown and Double-lined A

Wmk. 55 — Large Crown and NSW

Wmk. 203 — Small Crown and A Multiple

Wmk. 228 — Small Crown and C of A Multiple

Kangaroo and Map — A1

Die I — The inside frameline has a break at left, even with the top of the letters of the denomination.
Die II — The frameline does not show a break (repaired die).
Die III — The left inside frameline shows a break opposite the face of the kangaroo.
Die IV — As Die III, with a break in the top outside frameline above the "ST" of "AUSTRALIA." The upper right inside frameline has an incomplete corner.

Dies are only indicated when there are more than one for any denomination.

1913 Typo. Wmk. 8 Perf. 11½, 12

1	A1	½p green	11.50	7.50
		Never hinged	17.00	
2	A1	1p car (I)	17.50	1.75
		Never hinged	24.00	
h.		1p carmine (III)		2.25
		Never hinged	40.00	
3	A1	2p gray	70.00	10.00
		Never hinged	175.00	
4	A1	2½p dark blue	70.00	22.50
		Never hinged	190.00	
5	A1	3p ol bis, die I	140.00	17.50
		Never hinged	310.00	
a.		Die II	450.00	85.00
		Never hinged	850.00	
6	A1	4p orange	150.00	40.00
		Never hinged	700.00	
7	A1	5p org brn	150.00	50.00
		Never hinged	375.00	
8	A1	6p ultra (II)	140.00	30.00
		Never hinged	450.00	
b.		As #8, (III)	4,000.	1,300.
9	A1	9p purple	160.00	37.50
		Never hinged	575.00	
10	A1	1sh blue green	130.00	29.00
		Never hinged	700.00	
11	A1	2sh brown	300.00	140.00
		Never hinged	1,250.	
12	A1	5sh yel & gray	550.00	260.00
		Never hinged	2,000.	
13	A1	10sh pink & gray	1,600.	800.00
		Never hinged	4,250.	
14	A1	£1 ultra & brn	4,000.	2,500.
		Never hinged	9,250.	
15	A1	£2 dp rose & blk	8,500.	4,000.
		Never hinged	16,000.	
		Nos. 1-12 (12)	1,889.	645.75

On No. 4, "2½d" is colorless in solid blue background.
See Nos. 38-59, 96-102, 121-129, 206.

King George V
A2

Kookaburra (Kingfisher)
A3

1913-14 Unwmk. Engr. Perf. 11

17	A2	1p carmine	5.25	7.00
		Never hinged	8.00	
a.		Vert. pair, imperf. between	3,250.	
18	A3	6p lake brown ('14)	115.00	70.00
		Never hinged	260.00	

See No. 95.

A4

ONE PENNY
Die I — Normal die, having outside the oval band with "AUSTRALIA" a white line and a heavy colored line.
Die Ia — As die I with a small white spur below the right serif at foot of the "1" in left tablet.
Die II — A heavy colored line between two white lines back of the emu's neck. A white scratch crossing the vertical shading lines at the lowest point of the bust.
TWO PENCE
Die I — The numeral "2" is thin. The upper curve is 1mm. across and a very thin line connects it with the foot of the figure.
Die II — The "2" is thicker than in die I. The top curve is 1½mm across and a strong white line connects it with the foot of the figure. There are thin vertical lines across the ends of the groups of short horizontal lines at each side of "TWO PENCE."
THREE PENCE
Die I — The ends of the thin horizontal lines in the background run into the solid color of the various parts of the design. The numerals are thin and the letters of "THREE PENCE" are thin and irregular.
Die II — The oval about the portrait, the shields with the numerals, etc., are outlined by thin white lines which separate them from the horizontal background lines. The numerals are thick and the letters of "THREE PENCE" are heavy and regular.
FIVE PENCE
Die I — The top of the flag of the "5" is slightly curved.
Die II — The top of the flag of the "5" is flat. There are thin white vertical lines across the ends of the short horizontal lines at each side of "FIVE PENCE."

1914-24 Typo. Wmk. 9 Perf. 14

19	A4	½p emer ('15)	3.75	1.75
		Never hinged	8.50	
a.		Thin "½" at right	20,000.	5,750.
20	A4	½p org ('23)	4.00	4.00
		Never hinged	7.00	
21	A4	1p red (I)	11.00	1.75
		Never hinged	15.00	
a.		1p carmine rose (I)	22.50	4.00
		Never hinged	40.00	
b.		1p red (Ia)	550.00	9.75
		Never hinged	1,150.	
c.		1p carmine (II) ('18)	85.00	35.00
		Never hinged	175.00	
d.		1p scar (I), rough paper	22.50	9.75
e.		1p rose red (Ia), rough paper	800.00	29.00
f.		1p rose red (Ia), rough paper	750.00	115.00
22	A4	1p vio (I) ('22)	7.00	1.75
		Never hinged	11.50	
a.		1p red violet	10.50	5.25
		Never hinged	14.00	
23	A4	1p grn (I) ('24)	5.75	2.50
		Never hinged	10.50	
24	A4	1½p choc ('18)	7.50	2.25
		Never hinged	12.50	
a.		1½p red brown	8.00	2.50
		Never hinged	18.00	
b.		1½p black brown	7.00	2.50
		Never hinged	11.50	
25	A4	1½p emer ('23)	7.50	2.75
		Never hinged	12.50	
a.		Rough paper	260.00	160.00

26	A4	1½p scar ('24)	4.25	1.10
		Never hinged	7.00	
27	A4	2p brn org (I) ('20)	17.50	3.25
		Never hinged	32.50	
a.		2p orange (I) ('20)	17.50	2.50
		Never hinged	32.50	
b.		Booklet pane of 6		
28	A4	2p red (I) ('22)	17.50	3.25
		Never hinged	30.00	
29	A4	2p red brn (I) ('24)	22.50	12.50
		Never hinged	37.50	
30	A4	3p ultra (I) ('24)	32.50	7.75
		Never hinged	70.00	
31	A4	4p org ('15)	45.00	4.00
		Never hinged	92.50	
a.		4p yellow	140.00	32.50
		Never hinged	600.00	
32	A4	4p violet ('21)	22.50	21.00
		Never hinged	37.50	
33	A4	4p lt ultra ('22)	67.50	13.00
		Never hinged	140.00	
34	A4	4p ol bis ('24)	35.00	13.00
		Never hinged	70.00	
35	A4	4½p violet ('24)	27.50	6.75
		Never hinged	60.00	
36	A4	5p org brn (I) ('15)	37.50	7.25
		Never hinged	110.00	
37	A4	1sh4p lt blue ('20)	140.00	35.00
		Never hinged	475.00	
		Nos. 19-37 (19)	515.75	144.60

See Nos. 60-76, 113-120, 124.

1915 Perf. 11½, 12

38	A1	2p gray	160.00	17.00
		Never hinged	325.00	
39	A1	2½p dark blue	140.00	37.50
		Never hinged	300.00	
40	A1	6p ultra (II)	325.00	29.00
		Never hinged	875.00	
a.		Die III	4,250.	1,450.
41	A1	9p violet	325.00	60.00
		Never hinged	1,400.	
42	A1	1sh blue green	275.00	35.00
		Never hinged	1,250.	
43	A1	2sh brown	1,050.	125.00
		Never hinged	4,750.	
44	A1	5sh yellow & gray	1,500.	475.00
		Never hinged	3,250.	
		Nos. 38-44 (7)	3,775.	778.50

1915-24 Wmk. 10

45	A1	2p gray (I)	37.50	10.50
		Never hinged	62.50	
a.		Die II, shiny paper	45.00	17.50
		Never hinged	62.50	
46	A1	2½p dark blue	30.00	17.50
		Never hinged	47.50	
a.		"1" of fraction omitted	45,000.	50,000.
47	A1	3p ol bis (I)	37.50	9.50
		Never hinged	72.50	
a.		Die II	175.00	57.50
		Never hinged	325.00	
b.		3p lt olive (IV)	52.50	14.00
		Never hinged	92.50	
48	A1	6p ultra (II)	120.00	17.50
		Never hinged	275.00	
a.		6p chalky blue (III)	125.00	22.50
		Never hinged	250.00	
c.		6p ultra (IV)	120.00	20.00
		Never hinged	250.00	
49	A1	6p yel brn (IV, '23)	32.50	7.25
		Never hinged	62.50	
50	A1	9p violet (IV)	80.00	22.50
		Never hinged	190.00	
a.		9p lilac (II)	82.50	22.50
		Never hinged	200.00	
51	A1	1sh blue grn (II, '16)	72.50	14.00
		Never hinged	190.00	
b.		Die IV	75.00	14.00
52	A1	2sh brn ('16)	325.00	27.50
		Never hinged	975.00	
53	A1	2sh vio brn (II, '24)	140.00	37.50
		Never hinged	325.00	
54	A1	5sh yel & gray ('18)	325.00	125.00
		Never hinged	850.00	
55	A1	10sh brt pink & gray ('17)	1,050.	400.00
		Never hinged	1,750.	
56	A1	£1 ultra & brn org ('16)	3,450.	2,100.
		Never hinged	9,250.	
a.		£1 ultra & brn ('16)	3,250.	2,100.
		Never hinged	10,500.	
57	A1	£1 gray (IV, '24)	900.00	425.00
		Never hinged	2,250.	
58	A1	£2 dp rose & blk ('19)	7,000.	3,250.
		Never hinged	14,000.	
59	A1	£2 rose & vio brn ('24)	5,250.	3,250.
		Never hinged	12,500.	
		Nos. 45-54 (10)	1,200.	288.75

Perf. 14, 14½, 14½x14

1918-23 Wmk. 11

60	A4	½p emerald	3.50	3.25
		Never hinged	8.00	
a.		Thin "½" at right	140.00	160.00
61	A4	1p rose (I)	27.50	19.00
		Never hinged	45.00	
62	A4	1p dl grn (I) ('24)	9.25	9.25
		Never hinged	17.50	

63	A4	1½p choc ('19)	8.00 4.25
		Never hinged	17.50
a.		1½p red brown ('19)	12.50 4.50
		Never hinged	26.00
		Nos. 60-63 (4)	48.25 35.75

1924   Unwmk.   Perf. 14

64	A4	1p green (I)	5.75 6.25
		Never hinged	12.50
65	A4	1½p carmine	9.25 7.50
		Never hinged	17.50

Perf. 14, 13½x12½

1926-30   Wmk. 203

66	A4	½p orange	3.75 2.25
		Never hinged	7.00
a.		Perf. 14 ('27)	7.50 8.25
		Never hinged	11.50
67	A4	1p green (I)	3.75 1.10
		Never hinged	8.00
		1p green (Ia)	55.00 70.00
		Never hinged	75.00
b.		Perf. 14	4.50 1.75
		Never hinged	9.25
68	A4	1½p rose red ('27)	4.50 2.00
		Never hinged	9.25
c.		Perf. 14 ('26)	11.50 2.00
		Never hinged	22.50
69	A4	1½p red brn ('30)	6.25 4.50
		Never hinged	9.75
70	A4	2p red brn (II, '28)	9.25 5.75
		Never hinged	20.00
a.		Perf. 14 (I, '27)	45.00 29.00
		Never hinged	85.00
71	A4	2p red ('30)	11.50 3.25
		Never hinged	22.50
b.		Tête bêche pair	175,000.
c.		Unwmkd. (II '31)	2,000. 2,500.
72	A4	3p ultra (II) ('29)	35.00 5.50
		Never hinged	57.50
a.		3p ultra (I)	70.00 22.50
		Never hinged	150.00
b.		Perf. 14	45.00 11.50
		Never hinged	80.00
73	A4	4p ol bis ('29)	29.00 6.75
		Never hinged	52.50
a.		Perf. 14 ('28)	125.00 50.00
		Never hinged	300.00
74	A4	4½p dk vio ('27)	26.00 10.50
		Never hinged	45.00
a.		Perf. 13½x12½ ('28)	85.00 32.50
		Never hinged	150.00
75	A4	5p brn buff (II) ('30)	45.00 14.00
		Never hinged	85.00
76	A4	1sh4p pale turq bl ('28)	200.00 37.50
		Never hinged	500.00
a.		Perf. 14 ('27)	260.00 140.00
		Never hinged	775.00
		Nos. 66-76 (11)	374.00 93.10

For surcharges & overprints see Nos. 106-107, O3-O4.

Parliament House, Canberra A5

Unwmk.

1927, May 9   Engr.   Perf. 11

94	A5	1½p brown red	1.10 1.10
		Never hinged	2.00
a.		Vert. pair, imperf. btwn.	5,000. 4,250.
b.		Horiz. pair, imperf. btwn.	11,000. 11,000.

Opening of Parliament House at Canberra.

Melbourne Exhibition Issue
Kookaburra Type of 1914

1928, Oct. 29

95	A3	3p deep blue	5.50 8.00
		Never hinged	8.25
a.		Pane of 4	200.00 260.00
		Never hinged	300.00

No. 95a was issued at the Melbourne Intl. Phil. Exhib. No marginal inscription. Printed in sheets of 60 stamps (15 panes). No. 95a exists imperf. Value, $300,000.
No. 95 was printed in sheets of 120 and issued Nov. 2 throughout Australia.

Kangaroo-Map Type of 1913
Perf. 11½, 12

1929-30   Wmk. 203   Typo.

96	A1	6p brown	35.00 22.50
		Never hinged	57.50
97	A1	9p violet	75.00 26.00
		Never hinged	160.00
98	A1	1sh blue green	70.00 14.50
		Never hinged	165.00
99	A1	2sh red brown	150.00 29.00
		Never hinged	425.00
100	A1	5sh yel & gray	475.00 150.00
		Never hinged	1,000.
101	A1	10sh pink & gray	1,000. 725.00
		Never hinged	2,000.
102	A1	£2 dl red & blk ('30)	5,250. 925.00
		Never hinged	11,500.
		Nos. 96-102 (7)	7,055. 1,892.

For overprint see No. O5.

Black Swan — A6

Unwmk.

1929, Sept. 28   Engr.   Perf. 11

103	A6	1½p dull red	2.00 2.00
		Never hinged	3.25

Centenary of Western Australia.

Capt. Charles Sturt — A7

1930, June 2

104	A7	1½p dark red	1.25 1.25
		Never hinged	2.50
105	A7	3p dark blue	7.50 10.00
		Never hinged	11.00

Capt. Charles Sturt's exploration of the Murray River, cent.

Nos. 68 and 74a surcharged

1930   Wmk. 203   Perf. 13½x12½

106	A4	2p on 1½p rose red	2.50 1.25
		Never hinged	4.00
107	A4	5p on 4½p dark violet	14.00 15.00
		Never hinged	21.00

"Southern Cross" over Hemispheres A8

Perf. 11, 11½

1931, Mar. 19   Unwmk.

111	A8	2p dull red	1.25 1.25
		Never hinged	2.50
112	A8	3p blue	6.25 6.25
		Never hinged	10.00
		Nos. 111-112,C2 (3)	15.50 15.50

Trans-oceanic flights (1928-1930) of Sir Charles Edward Kingsford-Smith (1897-1935). See No. C3 for similar design. For overprints see Nos. CO1, O1-O2.

Types of 1913-23 Issues
Perf. 13½x12½

1931-36   Typo.   Wmk. 228

113	A4	½p org ('32)	7.50 7.50
		Never hinged	11.50
114	A4	1p green (I)	2.50 .40
		Never hinged	4.50
115	A4	1½p red brn ('36)	8.00 15.00
		Never hinged	12.50
116	A4	2p red (II)	2.50 .30
		Never hinged	4.50
117	A4	3p ultra (II) ('32)	32.50 2.25
		Never hinged	75.00
118	A4	4p ol bis ('33)	29.00 2.25
		Never hinged	55.00
120	A4	5p brn buff (II) ('32)	22.50 2.25
		Never hinged	35.00

Perf. 11½, 12; 13½x12½ (1sh4p)

121	A1	6p yel brn ('36)	30.00 37.50
		Never hinged	52.50
122	A1	9p violet ('32)	42.50 9.00
		Never hinged	115.00
124	A4	1sh4p lt blue ('32)	115.00 11.00
		Never hinged	160.00
125	A1	2sh red brn ('35)	7.50 5.25
		Never hinged	12.50
126	A1	5sh yel & gray ('32)	350.00 27.50
		Never hinged	925.00
127	A1	10sh pink & gray ('32)	600.00 225.00
		Never hinged	2,000.

128	A1	£1 gray ('35)	1,400. 375.00
		Never hinged	2,500.
129	A1	£2 dl rose & blk ('34)	4,500. 800.00
		Never hinged	9,250.
		Nos. 113-129 (15)	7,150. 1,520.

For redrawn 2sh see No. 206. For overprints see Nos. O6-O11.

Sydney Harbor Bridge — A9

Unwmk.

1932, Mar. 14   Engr.   Perf. 11

130	A9	2p red	4.50 5.25
		Never hinged	7.00
131	A9	3p blue	7.50 9.50
		Never hinged	11.50
132	A9	5sh gray green	575.00 350.00
		Never hinged	1,600.

**Wmk. 228
Perf. 10½
Typo.**

133	A9	2p red	4.00 2.25
		Never hinged	5.75

Opening of the Sydney Harbor Bridge on Mar. 19, 1932.
Value for 5sh, used, is for CTO examples.
For overprints see Nos. O12-O13.

Kookaburra — A14

1932, June 1   Perf. 13½x12½

139	A14	6p light brown	17.00 1.10
		Never hinged	27.50

Male Lyrebird — A16

**1932, Feb. 15   Unwmk.   Perf. 11
Size: 21½x25mm**

141	A16	1sh green	42.50 4.50
		Never hinged	110.00

See No. 175, 300. For overprint see No. O14.

Yarra Yarra Tribesman, Yarra River and View of Melbourne A17

Wmk. 228

1934, July 2   Engr.   Perf. 10½

142	A17	2p vermilion	3.00 1.75
		Never hinged	4.50
a.		Perf. 11½	10.50 4.50
		Never hinged	20.00
143	A17	3p blue	4.00 6.50
		Never hinged	10.00
a.		Perf. 11½	5.00 9.00
		Never hinged	9.00
144	A17	1sh black	55.00 27.50
		Never hinged	110.00
a.		Perf. 11½	65.00 32.50
		Never hinged	120.00
		Nos. 142-144 (3)	62.00 35.75

Centenary of Victoria.

Merino Sheep — A18

1934, Nov. 1   Perf. 11½

147	A18	2p copper red	8.00 2.00
		Never hinged	11.50
a.		Die II	15.00 5.75
		Never hinged	29.00
148	A18	3p dark blue	15.00 19.00
		Never hinged	20.00
149	A18	9p dark violet	35.00 50.00
		Never hinged	75.00
		Nos. 147-149 (3)	58.00 71.00

Capt. John Macarthur (1767-1834), "father of the New South Wales woolen industry."
Two dies of 2p: I, shading on hill in background uneven from light to dark. II, shading is uniformly dark.

Cenotaph in Whitehall, London — A19

1935, Mar. 18   Perf. 13½x12½

150	A19	2p red	2.50 .50
		Never hinged	5.25

Perf. 11

151	A19	1sh black	50.00 45.00

Anzacs' landing at Gallipoli, 20th anniv.
The 1sh perf 13½x12½ is a plate proof. Value, unused $2,250, mint never hinged $3,500.

George V on His Charger "Anzac" — A20

1935, May 2   **Perf. 11½**
152	A20	2p red	2.75	.35
		Never hinged	5.00	
153	A20	3p blue	8.00	12.50
		Never hinged	17.50	
154	A20	2sh violet	35.00	47.50
		Never hinged	85.00	
		Nos. 152-154 (3)	45.75	60.35

25th anniv. of the reign of King George V.

Amphitrite Joining Cables between Australia and Tasmania A21

1936, Apr. 1
157	A21	2p red	1.25	.60
		Never hinged	2.75	
158	A21	3p dark blue	3.75	3.50
		Never hinged	5.50	

Australia/Tasmania telephone link.

Edward VIII

A unique block of six unissued 2-penny King Edward VIII stamps realized the equivalent of U.S. $387,000 when it was sold at a London auction in 2014. A single stamp was separated from the block and sold at a Melbourne auction in 2015 for the equivalent of U.S. $123,600.

Proclamation Tree and View of Adelaide, 1936 — A22

1936, Aug. 3
159	A22	2p red	1.00	.60
		Never hinged	2.25	
160	A22	3p dark blue	3.75	3.75
		Never hinged	5.75	
161	A22	1sh green	14.00	10.00
		Never hinged	27.50	
		Nos. 159-161 (3)	18.75	14.35

Centenary of South Australia.

Gov. Arthur Phillip at Sydney Cove — A23

1937, Oct. 1   **Perf. 13x13½**
163	A23	2p red	1.00	.45
		Never hinged	3.25	
164	A23	3p ultra	3.75	3.25
		Never hinged	6.50	
165	A23	9p violet	15.00	13.00
		Never hinged	25.00	
		Nos. 163-165 (3)	19.75	16.70

150th anniversary of New South Wales.

Kangaroo A24

Queen Elizabeth A25

King George VI
A26   A27

Koala — A28

Merino Sheep — A29

Kookaburra (Kingfisher) A30

Platypus A31

Queen Elizabeth and King George VI in Coronation Robes
A32   A33

King George VI and Queen Elizabeth A34

Type I   Type II

Two Types of A25 and A26:
Type I — Highlighted background. Lines around letters of Australia Postage and numerals of value.
Type II — Background of heavy diagonal lines without the highlighted effect. No lines around letters and numerals.

Perf. 13½x14, 14x13½
1937-46   **Engr.**   **Wmk. 228**
166	A24	½p org, perf. 15x14 ('42)	.85	.70
		Never hinged	2.25	
a.		Perf. 13½x14 ('38)	1.40	.60
		Never hinged	3.50	
167	A25	1p emerald (I)	1.10	1.00
		Never hinged	2.25	
168	A26	1½p dull red brn (II)	6.25	5.75
		Never hinged	11.50	
a.		Perf. 15x14 ('41)	4.75	14.00
		Never hinged	8.00	
169	A26	2p scarlet (I)	1.10	.60
		Never hinged	2.25	

170	A27	3p ultramarine	40.00	24.00
		Never hinged	75.00	
a.		3p dp ultra, thin paper ('38)	40.00	4.50
		Never hinged	75.00	
171	A28	4p grn, perf. 15x14 ('42)	1.10	.30
		Never hinged	2.25	
a.		Perf. 13½x14 ('38)	3.25	3.00
		Never hinged	9.00	
172	A29	5p pale rose vio, perf. 14x15 ('46)	1.40	1.10
		Never hinged	2.25	
a.		Perf. 14x13½ ('38)	3.00	.90
		Never hinged	4.50	
173	A30	6p vio brn, perf. 15x14 ('42)	1.25	.30
		Never hinged	3.00	
a.		Perf. 13½x14	12.50	2.25
		Never hinged	26.00	
b.		6p chocolate, perf. 15x14	1.40	.55
		Never hinged	2.25	
174	A31	9p sep, perf. 14x15 ('43)	2.00	.45
		Never hinged	3.00	
a.		Perf. 14x13½ ('38)	4.50	2.25
		Never hinged	9.75	
175	A16	1sh gray grn, perf. 15x14 ('41)	1.40	.40
		Never hinged	2.00	
a.		Perf. 13½x14	27.50	3.50
		Never hinged	72.50	
176	A27	1sh4p mag ('38)	1.60	3.25
		Never hinged	3.50	

Perf. 13½
177	A32	5sh dl red brn ('38)	9.75	4.50
		Never hinged	26.00	
178	A33	10sh dl gray vio ('38)	35.00	20.00
		Never hinged	57.50	
179	A34	£1 bl gray ('38)	70.00	42.50
		Never hinged	115.00	
		Nos. 166-179 (14)	172.80	104.85

No. 175 measures 17½x21½mm.
See Nos.223A, 293, 295, 298, 300. For surch. & overprints see Nos. 190, M1, M4-M5, M7.

1938-42   **Perf. 15x14**
180	A25	1p emerald (II)	1.00	.70
181	A25	1p dl red brn (II) ('41)	.70	.60
181B	A26	1½p bl grn (II) ('41)	.70	2.25
182	A26	2p scarlet (II)	1.00	.30
182B	A26	2p red vio (II) ('41)	.40	.30
183	A27	3p dk ultra ('40)	29.00	4.50
		Never hinged	57.50	
183A	A27	3p dk vio brn ('42)	.40	.30
		Nos. 180-183A (7)	33.20	8.95
		Set, never hinged	72.50	

No. 183 differs from Nos. 170-170a in the shading lines on the king's left eyebrow which go downward, left to right, instead of the reverse. Also, more of the left epaulette shows.
For surcharges & ovpt. see Nos. 188-189, M3.

Coil Perforation
A special perforation was applied to stamps intended for use in coils to make separation easier. It consists of small and large holes (2 small, 10 large, 2 small) on the stamps' narrow side. Some of the stamps so perforated were sold in sheets.
This coil perforation may be found on Nos. 166, 181, 182, 182B, 193, 215, 223A, 231, 257, 315-316, 319, 319a and others.

Nurse, Sailor, Soldier and Aviator — A35

Perf. 13½x13
1940, July 15   **Engr.**   **Wmk. 228**
184	A35	1p green	1.10	3.25
		Never hinged	2.50	
185	A35	2p red	1.10	1.90
		Never hinged	2.50	
186	A35	3p ultra	8.00	12.50
		Never hinged	16.00	
187	A35	6p chocolate	17.00	27.50
		Never hinged	32.50	
		Nos. 184-187 (4)	27.20	45.15

Australia's participation in WWII.

No. 182 Surcharged in Blue

1941, Dec. 10   **Perf. 15x14**
188	A26	2½p on 2p red	.75	1.00
		Never hinged	1.50	

No. 183 Surcharged in Black and Yellow

189	A27	3½p on 3p dk ultra	.90	2.25
		Never hinged	1.75	

No. 172a Surcharged in Purple

Perf. 14x13½
190	A29	5½p on 5p pale rose vio	3.25	6.50
		Never hinged	5.00	
		Nos. 188-190 (3)	4.90	9.75

Queen Elizabeth
A36   A37

King George VI
A38   A39

George VI and Blue Wrens A40   Emu A41

1942-44   **Engr.**   **Perf. 15x14**
191	A36	1p brown vio ('43)	.45	.25
192	A37	1½p green	.70	.25
193	A38	2p lt rose vio ('44)	.70	.25
194	A39	2½p red	.70	.30
195	A40	3½p ultramarine	.95	.70
196	A41	5½p indigo	1.75	.35
		Nos. 191-196 (6)	5.25	2.10
		Set, never hinged	9.00	

See Nos. 224-225. For overprint see No. M2.

Catalogue values for unused stamps in this section, from this point to the end of the section, are for Never Hinged items.

Duke and Duchess of Gloucester A42

1945, Feb. 19   **Engr.**   **Perf. 14½**
197	A42	2½p brown red	.30	.25
198	A42	3½p bright ultra	.45	1.25
199	A42	5½p indigo	.55	1.25
		Nos. 197-199 (3)	1.30	2.75

Inauguration of the Duke of Gloucester as Governor General.

Official Crest and Inscriptions A43

Dove and Australian Flag A44

Angel of Peace; "Motherhood" and "Industry" A45

1946, Feb. 18   Wmk. 228   Perf. 14½
200 A43 2½p carmine   .25   .25
201 A44 3½p deep ultra   .65 1.75
202 A45 5½p deep yellow green .70 1.00
    Nos. 200-202 (3)   1.60 3.00

End of WWII. See Nos. 1456-1458.

Sir Thomas Mitchell and Map of Queensland A46

1946, Oct. 14
203 A46 2½p dark carmine   .25   .25
204 A46 3½p deep ultra   .75 1.60
205 A46 1sh olive green   .75   .60
    Nos. 203-205 (3)   1.75 2.45

Sir Thomas Mitchell's exploration of central Queensland, cent.

Kangaroo-Map Type of 1913 Redrawn

1945, Dec.   Typo.   Perf. 11½
206 A1 2sh dk red brown   5.50 5.50

The R and A of AUSTRALIA are separated at the base and there is a single line between the value tablet and "Two Shillings." On No. 125 the tail of the R touches the A, while two lines appear between value tablet and "Two Shillings." There are many other minor differences in the design.

For overprint see No. M6.

John Shortland A47

Pouring Steel A48

Loading Coal — A49

1947, Sept.   Engr.   Perf. 14½x14
207 A47 2½p brown red   .35   .25

Perf. 14½
208 A48 3½p deep blue   .65 1.50
209 A49 5½p deep green   .65   .75
    Nos. 207-209 (3)   1.65 2.50

150th anniv. of the discovery of the Hunter River estuary, site of Newcastle by Lieut. John Shortland. By error the 2½p shows his father, Capt. John Shortland.

Princess Elizabeth — A50

Perf. 14x14½
1947, Nov. 20   Wmk. 228
210 A50 1p brown violet   .40   .45

See No. 215.

Hereford Bull A51

Crocodile A52

1948, Feb. 16   Perf. 14½
211 A51 1sh3p violet brown   2.25 1.40
212 A52 2sh chocolate   2.25   .35

See No. 302.

William J. Farrer — A53

Design: No. 214, Ferdinand von Mueller.

1948   Perf. 14½x14
213 A53 2½p red   .50   .25
214 A53 2½p dark red   .45   .25

William J. Farrer (1845-1906), wheat researcher, and Ferdinand von Mueller (1825-1896), German-born botanist.
Issue dates: No. 213, July 12. No. 214, Sept. 13.

Elizabeth Type of 1947
1948, Aug.   Unwmk.   Perf. 14x14½
215 A50 1p brown violet   .40   .25

Scout in Uniform — A55

1948, Nov. 15   Engr.   Wmk. 228
216 A55 2½p brown red   .45   .25

Pan-Pacific Scout Jamboree, Victoria, Dec. 29, 1948 to Jan. 9, 1949. See No. 249.

Arms of Australia — A56

1949-50   Wmk. 228   Perf. 14x13½
218 A56 5sh dark red   4.50   .85
219 A56 10sh red violet   29.00 2.00
220 A56 £1 deep blue   45.00 8.50
221 A56 £2 green ('50)   200.00 26.00
    Nos. 218-221 (4)   278.50 37.35

Henry Hertzberg Lawson (1867-1922), Author and Poet — A57

Perf. 14½x14
1949, June 17   Unwmk.
222 A57 2½p rose brown   .50   .25

Outback Mail Carrier and Plane — A58

1949, Oct. 10
223 A58 3½p violet blue   .60   .55

UPU, 75th anniv.

Types of 1938, 1942-44 and

Aborigine — A59

1948-50   Unwmk.   Perf. 14½x14
223A A24 ½p orange ('49)   .45   .25
224 A37 1½p green ('49)   .35   .45
225 A38 2p lt rose violet   1.00   .55

Wmk. 228
226 A59 8½p dark brown ('50) .55   .45
    Nos. 223A-226 (4)   2.35 1.70

Issued: 2p, Dec.; ½p, Sept.; 1½p, 8/29; 8½p, 8/14.
See Nos. 248, 303.

John Forrest — A60

1949, Nov. 28   Wmk. 228
227 A60 2½p brown red   .50   .25

Forrest (1847-1918), explorer & statesman.

New South Wales A61

Victoria A62

First stamp designs.

Perf. 14½x14
1950, Sept. 27   Unwmk.
228 A61 2½p rose brown   .45   .25
229 A62 2½p rose brown   .45   .25
    a. Pair, #228-229   1.40 1.10

Cent. of Australian adhesive postage stamps. Issued in sheets of 160 stamps containing alternate copies of Nos. 228 and 229.

Elizabeth A63

George VI A64

1950-51   Engr.   Unwmk.
230 A63 1½p deep green   .85   .75
231 A63 2p yellow grn ('51) .30   .25
232 A64 2½p violet brn ('51) .30   .45
233 A64 3p dull green ('51) .35   .25
    Nos. 230-233 (4)   1.80 1.70

Issued: 1½p, 6/19; 2p, 3/28; 2½p, 5/23; 3p, 11/14.

A65

A66

1950-52   Wmk. 228
234 A64 2½p red   .25   .25
235 A64 3p red ('51)   .35   .45
236 A65 3½p red brown ('51) .35   .25
237 A65 4½p scarlet ('52)   .45   .90
238 A65 6½p choc ('52)   .35   .55
238A A65 6½p blue green ('52) .45   .25
239 A66 7½p deep blue ('51) .50   .55
    Nos. 234-239 (7)   2.70 3.20

Issued: 2½p, 4/12; 3p, 2/28; 7½p, 10/31; 3½p, 11/28; 4½p, No. 238, 2/20; No. 238A, 4/9.

A67

Founding of the Commonwealth of Australia, 50th Anniv. — A68

Designs: No. 240, Sir Edmund Barton. No. 241, Sir Henry Parkes. 5½p, Duke of York opening first Federal Parliament. 1sh6p, Parliament House, Canberra.

Perf. 14½x14
1951, May 1   Engr.   Unwmk.
240   3p carmine   1.60   .25
241   3p carmine   1.60   .25
    a. A67 Pair, #240, 241 3.50 3.50
242 A68 5½p deep blue   .90 3.00
243 A68 1sh6p red brown   1.40 1.40
    Nos. 240-243 (4)   5.50 4.90

Edward Hammond Hargraves — A69

Design: No. 245, Charles Joseph Latrobe (1801-1875), first governor of Victoria.

1951, July 2
244 A69 3p rose brown   1.00   .25
245 A69 3p rose brown   1.00   .25
    a. Pair, #244, 245   2.50 2.50

Discovery of gold in Australia, cent. (No. 244); Establishment of representative government in Victoria, cent. (No. 245). Sheets contain alternate rows of Nos. 244 and 245.

King George VI — A70

1952, Mar. 19 Wmk. 228 Perf. 14½
247 A70 1sh½p slate blue   2.50   .85

Aborigine Type of 1950 Redrawn
Size: 20½x25mm
248 A59 2sh6p dark brown   5.75 1.10

Portrait as on A59; lettering altered and value repeated at lower left. See No. 303.

Scout Type of 1948
Dated "1952-53"
Perf. 14x14½
1952, Nov. 19   Wmk. 228
249 A55 3½p red brown   .45   .25

Pan-Pacific Scout Jamboree, Greystanes, Dec. 30, 1952, to Jan. 9, 1953.

Modern Dairy, Butter Production — A71

Perf. 14½
1953, Feb. 11   Unwmk.   Typo.
250 A71 3p shown   .90   .40
251 A71 3p Wheat   .90   .40
252 A71 3p Beef   .90   .40
    a. Strip of 3, #250-252 8.00 9.25
253 A71 3½p shown   .90   .40
254 A71 3½p Wheat   .90   .40
255 A71 3½p Beef   .90   .40
    a. Strip of 3, #253-255 5.75 7.50
    Nos. 250-255 (6)   5.40 2.40

Both the 3p and 3½p were printed in panes of 50 stamps: 17 Butter, 17 Wheat and 16

Beef. The stamps were issued to encourage food production.

Queen Elizabeth II — A72

Perf. 14½x14

1953-54		Unwmk.	Engr.	
256	A72	1p purple	.30	.30
256A	A72	2½p deep blue ('54)	.45	.30
257	A72	3p dark green	.45	.25

Wmk. 228

258	A72	3½p dark red	.55	.45
258B	A72	6½p orange ('54)	3.25	.75
		Nos. 256-258B (5)	5.00	2.05

Issued: 3½p, 4/21; 3p, 6/17; 1p, 8/19; 2½p, 6½p, 6/23.
See Nos. 292, 296.

Coronation Issue

Queen Elizabeth II
A73

1953, May 25			Unwmk.	
259	A73	3½p rose red	.60	.25
260	A73	7½p violet	1.00	1.00
261	A73	2sh dull green	3.00	2.00
		Nos. 259-261 (3)	4.60	3.25

Boy and Girl with Calf — A74

1953, Sept. 3			Perf. 14½	
262	A74	3½p dp green & red brn	.50	.25

Official establishment of Young Farmers' Clubs, 25th anniv.

Lieut. Gov. David Collins — A75

Sullivan Cove, Hobart A76

Design: No. 264, Lieut. Gov. William Paterson (facing left).

1953, Sept. 23			Perf. 14½x14	
263	A75	3½p red brown	.45	.25
264	A75	3½p red brown	.60	.25
a.		Pair, #263-264	1.50	1.50
265	A76	2sh green	3.50	2.25
		Nos. 263-265 (3)	4.55	2.75

Settlement in Tasmania, 150th anniv. Sheets contain alternate rows of Nos. 263 and 264.

Tasmania Stamp of 1853 — A77

1953, Nov. 11			Perf. 14½	
266	A77	3p red	.35	.45

Tasmania's first postage stamps, cent.

Elizabeth II and Duke of Edinburgh — A78

Elizabeth II — A79

1954, Feb. 2		Perf. 14½x14, 14x14½		
267	A78	3½p rose red	.35	.25
268	A79	7½p purple	.40	.90
269	A78	2sh green	1.60	.75
		Nos. 267-269 (3)	2.35	1.90

Visit of Queen Elizabeth II and the Duke of Edinburgh, 1954.

Telegraph Pole and Key — A80

1954, Apr. 7		Engr.	Perf. 14	
270	A80	3½p dark red	.45	.25

Inauguration of the telegraph in Australia, cent.

Red Cross and Globe — A81

1954, June 9			Perf. 14½x14	
271	A81	3½p deep blue & red	.40	.25

Australian Red Cross Society.

Swan — A82

1954, Aug. 2		Unwmk.	Perf. 14½	
274	A82	3½p black	.40	.25

Western Australia's first postage stamp, cent.

Diesel and Early Steam Locomotives A83

1954, Sept. 13			Perf. 14x14½	
275	A83	3½p red brown	.45	.25

Centenary of Australian railroads.

Antarctic Flora and Fauna and Map — A84

1954, Nov. 17			Perf. 14	
276	A84	3½p black	.40	.25

Australia's interest in the Antarctic continent.

Olympic Circles and Arms of Melbourne — A85

1954, Dec. 1				
277	A85	2sh dark blue	3.00	2.00

16th Olympic Games to be held in Melbourne Nov.-Dec. 1956. See No. 286.

Globe, Flags and Rotary Emblem — A86

1955, Feb. 23			Perf. 14x14½	
278	A86	3½p carmine	.40	.25

Rotary International, 50th anniv.

Elizabeth II — A87

1955, Mar. 9		Wmk. 228	Perf. 14½	
279	A87	1sh ½p dk gray blue	2.75	1.00

See No. 301.

Top of US Monument, Canberra — A88

1955, May 4		Unwmk.	Perf. 14x14½	
280	A88	3½p deep ultra	.50	.25

Friendship between Australia and the US.

Cobb and Company Mail Coach A89

1955, July 6			Perf. 14½x14	
281	A89	3½p dark brown	.50	.25
282	A89	2sh brown	2.25	2.25

Pioneers of Australia's coaching era.

World Map, YMCA Emblem A90

Engr. and Typo.

1955, Aug. 10			Perf. 14	
283	A90	3½p Prus green & red	.40	.25
a.		Red omitted	25,000.	

Centenary of YMCA.

Florence Nightingale and Modern Nurse — A91

1955, Sept. 21		Engr.	Perf. 14x14½	
284	A91	3½p red violet	.40	.25

Centenary of Florence Nightingale's work in the Crimea and of the founding of modern nursing.

Queen Victoria — A92

1955, Oct. 17			Perf. 14½	
285	A92	3½p green	.40	.25

South Australia's first postage stamps, cent.

Olympic Type of 1954

1955, Nov. 30		Unwmk.	Perf. 14	
286	A85	2sh deep green	2.25	2.00

16th Olympic Games at Melbourne, Nov. 22-Dec. 8, 1956.

Queen Victoria, Queen Elizabeth II and Badges of Victoria, New South Wales and Tasmania A93

1956, Sept. 26			Perf. 14½x14	
287	A93	3½p brown carmine	.40	.25

Centenary of responsible government in Victoria, New South Wales and Tasmania.

Melbourne Coat of Arms — A94

Southern Cross, Olympic Torch — A95

Collins Street, Melbourne A96

Design: 2sh, Melbourne across Yarra River.

1956, Oct. 31		Engr.	Perf. 14½, 14	
288	A94	4p dark carmine	.50	.25

289 A95 7½p ultramarine .75 1.00

Photo.
Perf. 14x14½

290 A96 1sh multicolored .95 .50

Perf. 12x11½
Granite Paper

291 A96 2sh multicolored 1.60 1.25
Nos. 288-291 (4) 3.80 3.00

16th Olympic Games, Melbourne, 11/22-12/8.

A lithographed souvenir sheet incorporating reproductions of Nos. 288-291 in reduced size was of private origin and not postally valid.

Types of 1938-55 and

Queen Elizabeth II — A97

Perf. 14½x14, 14x15, 15x14, 14½

1956-57		Engr.	Unwmk.	
292	A72	3½p dark red	1.40	.55
293	A28	4p green	2.00	.45
294	A97	4p claret ('57)	.45	.25
a.		Booklet pane of 6 ('57)	12.50	
295	A30	6p brown violet	3.50	.55
296	A72	6½p orange	3.50	.25
297	A97	7½p violet ('57)	1.75	.55
298	A31	9p sepia	17.00	2.00
299	A97	10p gray blue ('57)	1.10	.55
300	A16	1sh gray green	7.25	1.10
301	A87	1sh7p redsh brn ('57)	5.50	.70
302	A52	2sh chocolate	14.00	1.10
303	A59	2sh6p brown ('57)	10.50	1.10
		Nos. 292-303 (12)	67.95	9.15

No. 300 measures 17½x21½mm. No. 303 measures 20½x25mm and is the redrawn type of 1952.

Issued: 3½p, 7/2; 2sh, 7/21; No. 293, 6p, 8/18; 6½p, Sept. 9p, 1sh, 12/13; 2sh6p, 1/30; 10p, 3/6; No. 294, 1sh7p, 3/13; 7½p, 11/13.

South Australia Coat of Arms — A99

1957, Apr. 17   Unwmk.   Perf. 14½
304 A99 4p brown red .40 .25

Centenary of responsible government in South Australia.
There are two types of No. 304.

Caduceus and Map of Australia A100

1957, Aug. 21   Perf. 14½x14
305 A100 7p violet blue .60 .30

Royal Flying Doctor Service of Australia.

Star of Bethlehem and Praying Child A101

1957, Nov. 6   Engr.
306 A101 3½p dull rose .35 .25
307 A101 4p pale purple .35 .25
Christmas.

Canberra War Memorial, Sailor and Airman A102

Design: No. 309, As No. 308 with soldier and service woman. Printed in alternate rows in sheet.

1958, Feb. 10   Unwmk.
308 A102 5½p brown carmine 1.00 .70
309 A102 5½p brown carmine 1.00 .70
a. Pair, #308-309 3.50 3.50

Sir Charles Kingsford-Smith and "Southern Cross" — A103

1958, Aug. 27   Perf. 14x14½
310 A103 8p brt violet blue 1.00 1.00

1st air crossing of the Tasman Sea, 30th anniv. See New Zealand No. 321.

Broken Hill Mine — A104

1958, Sept. 10   Perf. 14½x14
311 A104 4p brown .40 .25

Broken Hill mining field, 75th anniv.

Nativity — A105

1958, Nov. 5   Perf. 14½x15
312 A105 3½p dark red .30 .25
313 A105 4p dark purple .30 .25
Christmas.

A106

A107

A108

A109

A110

Platypus A111

Tasmanian Tiger A112

Flannel Flower — A113

Aboriginal Stockman Cutting Out a Steer A114

Designs: 3p, Queen Elizabeth II facing right. 6p, Banded anteater. 8p, Tiger cat. 9p, Kangaroos. 11p, Rabbit bandicoot. 1sh6p, Christmas bells (flower). 2sh3p, Wattle (flower). 2sh5p, Banksia (flower). 3sh, Waratah (flower).

FIVE PENCE

Die I — Four short lines inside "5" at right of ball; six short lines left of ball; full length line above ball is seventh from bottom. Odd numbered horizontal rows in each sheet are in Die I.

Die II — Five short lines inside "5" at right of ball; seven at left; full length line above ball is eighth from bottom. Even numbered horizontal rows in each sheet are in Die II.

Perf. 14½x14, 14x14½, 14½

1959-64		Engr.	Unwmk.	
314	A106	1p dull violet	.25	.25
315	A107	2p red brown	.70	.45
316	A108	3p bluish green	.35	.25
317	A108	3½p dark green	.25	.25
318	A109	4p carmine	2.25	.25
a.		Booklet pane of 6	29.00	
319	A110	5p dark blue (I)	1.10	.25
a.		5p dark blue (II)	1.10	.25
b.		Booklet pane of 6 ('60)	17.00	
320	A111	6p chocolate	2.25	.25
321	A111	8p red brown	2.25	.25
322	A111	9p brown black	2.25	.85
323	A111	11p dark blue	2.25	.25
324	A111	1sh slate green	4.50	.70
325	A112	1sh2p dk purple	2.25	.35
326	A113	1sh6p red, yellow	3.50	1.40
327	A113	2sh dark blue	2.25	.25
328	A113	2sh3p green, yel	2.25	.25
328A	A113	2sh3p yellow grn	7.00	2.25
329	A113	2sh5p brown, yellow	7.50	1.10
330	A113	3sh crimson	2.25	.45

Wmk. 228

331	A114	5sh red brown	24.00	2.25
		Nos. 314-331 (19)	69.40	12.30

Issued: 1p, 4p, 2/2; 3½p, 3/18; 2sh, 4/8; 3p, 5/20; 3sh, 7/15; 1sh, No. 328, 9/9; 5p, 10/1; 9p, 10/21; 1sh6p, 2/3/60; 2sh5p, 3/16/60; 8p, 5/11/60; 6p, 9/30/60; 11p, 5/3/61; 5sh, 7/26/61; 2p, 1sh2p, 3/21/62; No. 328A, 10/28/64.

Luminescent Printings

Paper with an orange red phosphorescence (surface coating), was used for some printings of the Colombo Plan 1sh, No. 340, the Churchill 5p, No. 389, and several regular postage stamps. These include 2p, 3p, 6p, 8p, 9p, 11p, 1sh2p, 1sh6p and 2sh3p (Nos. 315, 316, 365, 367, 321, 368, 323, 325, 369, 328A).

Stamps printed only on phosphorescent paper include the Monash 5p, Hargrave 5p, ICY 2sh3p and Christmas 5p (Nos. 388, 390-393) and succeeding commemoratives; the 2sh, 2sh6p and 3sh regular birds (Nos. 370, 372, 373); and most of the regular series in decimal currency.

Ink with a phosphorescent content was used in printing most of the 5p red, No. 366, almost all of the 5p red booklets, No. 366a, most of the decimal 4c regular, No. 397, and its booklet pane, No. 397a, and all of No. 398.

Postmaster Isaac Nichols Boarding Vessel to Receive Mail — A115

1959, Apr. 22   Perf. 14½x14
332 A115 4p dark gray blue .40 .25

First post office, Sydney, 150th anniv.

Parliament House, Brisbane, and Queensland Arms — A116

1959, June 5   Perf. 14x14½
333 A116 4p dk green & violet .40 .25

Cent. of Queensland self-government.

Approach of the Magi — A117

1959, Nov. 4   Perf. 15x14½
334 A117 5p purple .40 .25

Christmas.

Girl Guide and Lord Baden-Powell — A118

1960, Aug. 18   Perf. 14½x14
335 A118 5p dark blue .45 .25

50th anniversary of the Girl Guides.

The Overlanders by Sir Daryl Lindsay — A119

1960, Sept. 21   Perf. 14½
336 A119 5p lilac rose .40 .25

Exploration of Australia's Northern Territory, cent.

Melbourne Cup and Archer, 1861 Winner — A120

1960, Oct. 12   Unwmk.
337 A120 5p sepia .40 .25

Centenary of the Melbourne Cup.

Queen Victoria — A121

1960 Nov. 2   Engr.   Perf. 14½
338 A121 5p dark green .40 .25

Centenary of the first Queensland stamps.

Open Bible and Candle — A122

1960, Nov. 9   Unwmk.
339 A122 5p maroon .40 .25

Christmas; beginning of 350th anniv. year of the publication of the King James translation of the Bible.

Colombo Plan Emblem — A123

1961, June 30   *Perf. 14x14½*
340 A123 1sh red brown   .85 .30
Colombo Plan for the peaceful development of South East Asia countries, 10th anniv.

Dame Nellie Melba, by Sir Bertram Mackennal — A124

1961, Sept. 20   *Perf. 14½*
341 A124 5p deep blue   .45 .30
Dame Nellie Melba, singer, birth cent.

Page from Book of Hours, 15th Century A125

1961, Nov. 8   *Perf. 14½x14*
342 A125 5p reddish brown   .40 .25
Christmas; end of the 350th anniv. year of the publication of the King James translation of the Bible.

John McDouall Stuart — A126

1962, July 25   Unwmk.   *Perf. 14½*
345 A126 5p carmine   .40 .25
First south-north crossing of Australia by John McDouall Stuart, cent.

Nurse and Rev. Flynn's Grave — A127

1962, Sept. 5   Photo.   *Perf. 13½*
346 A127 5p multicolored   .50 .30
   a.   Red omitted   450.00
Australian Inland Mission founded by Rev. John Flynn, 50th anniv.

Woman and Globe — A128

1962, Sept. 26   Engr.   *Perf. 14x14½*
347 A128 5p dark green   .40 .25
World Conf. of the Associated Country Women of the World, Melbourne, Oct. 2-12.

Madonna and Child — A129

1962, Oct. 17   *Perf. 14½*
348 A129 5p deep violet   .40 .25
Christmas.

View of Perth and Kangaroo Paw — A130

Arms of Perth A131

1962, Nov. 1   Photo.   *Perf. 14*
349 A130   5p multicolored   .65 .25
   a.   Red omitted   5,500.

           Perf. 14½x14
350 A131 2sh3p emer, blk, red   3.50 3.50
              & ultra
British Empire and Commonwealth Games, Perth, Nov. 22-Dec. 1.
Perf 14x14¾ examples of Nos. 349-350 are from a booklet pane issued for the 2006 Commonwealth Games. These stamps were not valid for postage.

Elizabeth II — A132

Elizabeth II and Prince Philip — A133

1963, Feb. 18   Engr.   *Perf. 14½*
351 A132   5p dark green   .50 .25
352 A133 2sh3 red brown   3.00 3.00
Visit of Elizabeth II and Prince Philip.
Perf 14½x14 lithographed examples of Nos. 351-352 come from the booklet footnoted under No. 2507. These stamps were not valid for postage.

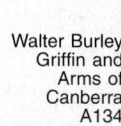

Walter Burley Griffin and Arms of Canberra A134

1963, Mar. 8   Unwmk.   *Perf. 14½x14*
353 A134 5p dark green   .40 .25
50th anniv. of Canberra; Walter Burley Griffin, American architect, who laid out plan for Canberra.

Red Cross Centenary Emblem — A135

1963, May 8   Photo.   *Perf. 13½x13*
354 A135 5p dk blue, red & gray   .50 .25
Centenary of the International Red Cross.

Explorers Blaxland, Lawson and Wentworth Looking West from Mt. York — A136

1963, May 28   Engr.   *Perf. 14½x14*
355 A136 5p dark blue   .40 .25
1st crossing of the Blue Mts., 150th anniv.

Globe, Ship, Plane and Map of Australia A137

1963, Aug. 28   **Unwmk.**
356 A137 5p red   .40 .25
Importance of exports to Australian economy.

Elizabeth II A138

Black-backed Magpie and Eucalyptus A139

Abel Tasman and Ship — A144

George Bass, Whaleboat — A145

Designs: 6p, Yellow-tailed thornbill, horiz. 1sh6p, Galah on tree stump. 2sh, Golden whistler. 2sh5p, Blue wren and bracken fern. 2sh6p, Scarlet robin, horiz. 3sh, Straw-necked ibis. 5sh, William Dampier and "Roebuck" sailing ship. 7sh6p, Capt. James Cook. 10sh, Matthew Flinders and three-master "Investigator." £2, Admiral Philip Parker King.

           Perf. 15x14
1963-65   **Unwmk.**   **Engr.**
365 A138   5p green   1.10 .25
   a.   Booklet pane of 6 ('64)   35.00
   b.   Pair, imperf. btwn.   2.00 2.00
366 A138   5p red   1.10 .25
   a.   Booklet pane of 6   45.00

           Photo.
           Perf. 13½
367 A139   6p multi   1.10 .50
   a.   Vert. pair, imperf. btwn.
368 A139   9p multi   2.00 2.75
369 A139 1sh6p multi   1.75 1.40
370 A139   2sh multi   2.25 .55
371 A139 2sh5p multi   5.25 3.50
372 A139 2sh6p multi   4.75 3.25
   a.   Red omitted   12,000. 12,000.
373 A139   3sh multi   4.75 1.75

           Engr.
   Perf. 14½x14, 14½x15
374 A144   4sh violet   3.75 .95
            blue

           Wmk. 228
375 A145   5sh red   4.50 2.50
            brown
376 A144 7sh6p olive   21.00 16.00
              green
377 A144 10sh deep   35.00 5.75
              claret
378 A145   £1 purple   57.50 30.00
379 A145   £2 brn blk   105.00 92.50
Nos. 365-379 (15)   250.80 161.90

No. 365a was printed in sheets of 288 which were sold intact by the Philatelic Bureau.

These sheets have been broken to obtain pairs and blocks which are imperf. between (see No. 365b).
    Issued: No. 365, 4sh, 10/9/63; 10sh, £1, 2/26/64; 9p, 1sh6p, 2sh5p, 3/11/64; 6p, 8/19/64; 7sh6p, £2, 8/26/64; 5sh, 11/25/64; 2sh, 2sh6p, 3sh, 4/21/65; No. 366, 6/30/65.
    See Nos. 400-401, 406-417, 1727-1728.

Star of Bethlehem — A146

1963, Oct. 25   Unwmk.   *Perf. 14½*
380 A146 5p blue   .40 .25
Christmas.

Cable Around World and Under Sea — A147

1963, Dec. 3   Photo.   *Perf. 13½*
381 A147 2sh3p gray, ver, blk   3.50 3.50
            & blue
Opening of the Commonwealth Pacific (telephone) cable service (COMPAC).
See New Zealand No. 364.

Bleriot 60 Plane, 1914 — A148

1964, July 1   Engr.   *Perf. 14½x14*
382 A148   5p olive green   .40 .25
383 A148 2sh3p red   3.25 3.25
50th anniv. of the first air mail flight in Australia; Maurice Guillaux, aviator.

Child Looking at Nativity Scene — A149

1964, Oct. 21   Photo.   *Perf. 13½*
384 A149 5p bl, blk, red &   .40 .25
          buff
   a.   Red omitted   6,250. 2,750.
   b.   Black omitted   2,750.
   c.   Buff omitted   3,500.
Christmas.
No. 384a used is valued on cover. The red ink can be removed from No. 384 by bleaching.

"Simpson and His Donkey" by Wallace Anderson — A150

1965, Apr. 14   Engr.   *Perf. 14x14½*
385 A150   5p olive bister   .50 .25
386 A150   8p dark blue   .90 .80
387 A150 2sh3p rose claret   3.00 3.00
Nos. 385-387 (3)   4.40 4.05
50th anniv. of the landing of the Australian and New Zealand Army Corps (ANZAC) at Gallipoli, Turkey, Apr. 25, 1915. Private John Simpson Kirkpatrick saved the lives of many wounded soldiers. The statue erected in his honor stands in front of Melbourne's Shrine of Remembrance.

Radio Mast and Satellite Orbiting Earth — A151

1965, May 10   Photo.   Perf. 13½
388 A151 5p multicolored   .65   .25
a.   Gray omitted   5,000.   5,000.

ITU, cent.

Winston Churchill — A152

1965, May 24
389 A152 5p lt bl, pale gray, dk gray & blk   .40   .25
a.   Pale gray omitted (white face)   5,500.
b.   Dark gray ("Australia") omitted   7,500.

Sir Winston Spencer Churchill (1874-1965), statesman and WWII leader.

Two examples of No. 389b recorded, one damaged. Value is for sound example.

See New Zealand No. 371.

John Monash and Transmission Tower — A153

1965, June 23   Photo.   Perf. 13½
390 A153 5p red, yel, blk & lt brn   .40   .25

Birth cent. of General Sir John Monash (1865-1931), soldier, Vice-Chancellor of University of Melbourne and chairman of the Victoria state electricity commission.

Lawrence Hargrave and Sketch for 1902 Seaplane A154

1965, Aug. 4   Unwmk.   Perf. 13½
391 A154 5p multicolored   .40   .25
a.   Purple (5d) omitted   600.00   600.00

50th anniv. of the death of Lawrence Hargrave (1850-1915), aviation pioneer.

ICY Emblem — A155

1965, Sept. 1   Photo.   Perf. 13½
392 A155 2sh3p lt blue & green   3.25   3.00

International Cooperation Year.

Nativity — A156

1965, Oct. 20   Unwmk.   Perf. 13½
393 A156 5p multicolored   .40   .25
a.   Gold omitted   5,500.
b.   Ultramarine omitted   1,000.
c.   Brown omitted (white faces)   5,000.

Christmas.

Types of 1963-65 and

Elizabeth II — A157   Humbug Fish — A158

Designs: No. 400, Yellow-tailed thornbill, horiz. 6c, blue-faced honeyeater, horiz. 8c, Coral fish. 9c, Hermit crab. 10c Anemone fish. 13c, Red-necked avocet. 15c, Galah on tree stump. 20c, Golden whistler. 24c Azure kingfisher, horiz. 25c, Scarlet robin, horiz. 30c Straw-necked ibis. 40c Abel Tasman and ship. 50c, William Dampier and "Roebuck" sailing ship. 75c, Capt. James Cook. $1, Matthew Flinders and three-master "Investigator." $2, George Bass and whaleboat. $4, Admiral Philip Parker King.

Perf. 14½x14 (A157); 13½ (A158, A139)

Engr. (A157), Photo. (A158, A139)
1966-71
394 A157 1c red brown   .45   .25
395 A157 2c olive green   .75   .25
396 A157 3c Prus green   .75   .25
397 A157 4c red   .30   .25
a.   Booklet pane of 5 + label   35.00
398 A157 5c on 4c red ('67)   .40   .25
a.   Booklet pane of 5 + label ('67)   7.00
399 A157 5c dk blue ('67)   .75   .25
a.   Booklet pane of 5 + label   12.50
400 A139 5c lt grn, blk, brn & yel   .55   .25
a.   Brown omitted   3,500.   —
401 A139 6c gray, blk, lem & bl   .80   .35
b.   Blue omitted   2,500.
401A A157 6c orange ('70)   .55   .25
402 A158 7c brn, ver, blk & gray   .85   .25
402A A157 7c dp rose lilac ('71)   .75   .25
403 A158 8c multicolored   .85   .55
404 A158 9c multicolored   .85   .35
405 A158 10c lt brn, blk, org & bl   .85   .25
a.   Orange omitted   4,250.
b.   Blue omitted   3,000.   2,000.
406 A139 13c lt bl grn, blk, gray & red   2.25   .45
a.   Red omitted   2,250.
b.   Gray omitted   2,100.
407 A139 15c lt grn, blk, gray & rose   2.25   1.10
a.   Rose omitted   4,500.
b.   Gray omitted   2,750.   750.00
408 A139 20c pink, blk, yel & gray   3.25   .30
a.   Yellow omitted   2,900.
b.   Gray omitted   750.00
409 A139 24c tan, blk, vio bl & org   1.10   1.10
410 A139 25c gray, grn, blk & red   3.75   .55
a.   Red omitted   5,750.
411 A139 30c lt grn, buff, blk & red   12.50   .85
a.   Red omitted   3,000.

Engr.
Perf. 14½x14, 14½x15
412 A144 40c violet blue   5.75   .25
413 A145 50c brown red   7.50   .25
414 A144 75c olive green   1.60   1.40
415 A144 $1 deep claret   2.60   .45
a.   Perf 15x14   125.00   32.50
416 A145 $2 purple   8.00   2.25
417 A145 $4 sepia   7.00   7.00
Nos. 394-417 (26)   67.00   19.95

No. 398 issued in booklets only.

Booklet panes of 10 of No. 399, and of 5 No. 400, are torn from sheets. They were issued for the use of "Australian Defence Forces," as the covers read, in Viet Nam.

Issued: Nos. 398, 399, 9/29/67; No. 401A, 9/28/70; No. 402A, 10/1/71; No. 415a, 1973; others, 2/14/66.

Coil Stamps
1966-67   Photo.   Perf. 15 Horiz.
418 A157 3c emerald, blk & buff   .85   .55
419 A157 4c org red, blk & buff   .70   .55
420 A157 5c blue, black & buff   .85   .25
Nos. 418-420 (3)   2.40   1.35

Issued: 5c, 9/29/67; others, 2/14/66.

Rescue A159

1966, July 6   Photo.   Perf. 13½
421 A159 4c blue, ultra & black   .30   .25

Royal Life Saving Society, 75th anniv.

Adoration of the Shepherds A160

1966, Oct. 19   Photo.   Perf. 13½
422 A160 4c olive & black   .30   .25
a.   Olive omitted   7,250.

Christmas.

Dutch Sailing Ship, 17th Century — A161

1966, Oct. 24   Photo.   Perf. 13½
423 A161 4c bl, blk, dp org & gold   .30   .25
a.   Deep orange omitted   6,000.
b.   Gold omitted   2,000.

350th anniv. of Dirk Hartog's discovery of the Australian west coast, and his landing on the island named after him.

Hands Reaching for Bible — A162

1967, Mar. 7   Photo.   Perf. 13½
424 A162 4c multicolored   .30   .25

British and Foreign Bible Soc., 150th anniv.

Combination Lock and Antique Keys — A163

1967, Apr. 5   Photo.   Perf. 13½
425 A163 4c emerald, blk & lt blue   .30   .25

150th anniv. of banking in Australia (Bank of New South Wales).

Lions Intl., 50th Anniv. — A164

1967, June 7   Photo.   Perf. 13½
426 A164 4c ultra, black & gold   .30   .25

YWCA Emblems and Flags A165

1967, Aug. 21   Photo.   Perf. 13½
427 A165 4c dk blue, lt bl & lilac   .30   .25

World Council Meeting of the YWCA, Monash University, Victoria, Aug. 14-Sept. 1.

Seated Women Symbolizing Obstetrics and Gynecology, Female Symbol A166

1967, Sept. 20   Photo.   Perf. 13½
428 A166 4c lilac, dk blue & blk   .30   .25

5th World Congress of Gynecology and Obstetrics, Sydney, Sept. 23-30.

Gothic Arches and Christmas Bell Flower A167

Cross, Stars of David and Yin Yang Forming Mandala — A168

1967   Photo.   Perf. 13½
429 A167 5c multicolored   .30   .25
430 A168 25c multicolored   2.00   2.00

Christmas.
Issue dates: 5c, Oct. 18; 25c, Nov. 27.

Satellite Orbiting Earth — A169

Satellite and Antenna, Moree, N.S.W. — A170

Design: 20c, World weather map connecting Washington, Moscow and Melbourne, and computer and teleprinter tape spools.

1968, Mar. 20   Photo.   Perf. 13½
431 A169 5c dull yel, red, bl & dk blue   .50   .25
432 A169 20c blue, blk & red   2.25   2.25
a.   Red omitted   3,000.
433 A170 25c Prus blue, blk & lt green   2.25   2.25
Nos. 431-433 (3)   5.00   4.75

Use of satellites for weather observations and communications.

Kangaroo Paw, Western Australia — A171

State Flowers: 13c, Pink heath, Victoria. 15c, Tasmanian blue gum, Tasmania. 20c,

Sturt's desert pea, South Australia. 25c, Cooktown orchid, Queensland. 30c, Waratah, New South Wales.

1968, July 10 Photo. Perf. 13½
Flowers in Natural Colors

434	A171	6c multicolored	.55	.65
435	A171	13c multicolored	.65	.55
436	A171	15c multicolored	1.00	.45
437	A171	20c multicolored	5.00	.75
438	A171	25c multicolored	2.25	.75
439	A171	30c multicolored	.75	.75
a.	Green omitted	3,750.	
	Nos. 434-439 (6)	10.20	3.40

A 1971 reprinting of No. 439 shows more areas of white in the pink petals. This is scarcer than the first printing. Value, $4.75.

Sturt's Desert Rose, Northern Territory — A171a

Designs: 5c, Golden wattle, national flower. 7c, 10c, Sturt's desert pea.

Coil Stamps

1970-75 Perf. 14½ Horiz.

439A	A171a	2c dk grn & multi	.25	.25
i.	Lettering and value bolder	.25	.25
439B	A171a	4c gray & multi	.70	.45
439C	A171a	5c gray & multi	.25	.25
439D	A171a	6c gray & multi	1.40	.55
h.	Green omitted	2,250.	
439E	A171a	7c blk, red & grn	.40	.25
f.	Green omitted	110.00	
439G	A171a	10c blk, red & grn	.35	.25
	Nos. 439A-439G (6)	3.35	2.00

Issued: 4c, 5c, 4/27; 6c, 10/28; 2c, 7c, 10/1/71; 10c, 1/15/75; No. 439Ai, 11/73.

Soil Testing Through Chemistry & by Computer A172

Hippocrates & Hands Holding Hypodermic A173

1968, Aug. 6 Photo. Perf. 13½

440	A172	5c multicolored	.30	.25
441	A173	5c multicolored	.30	.25

9th Intl. Congress of Soil Science, University of Adelaide, Aug. 6-16 (No. 440); General Assembly of World Medical Associations, Sydney, Aug. 6-9 (No. 441). Nos. 440-441 printed in sheets of 100 in two separate panes of 50 connected by a gutter. Each sheet contains 10 gutter pairs.

Runner and Aztec Calendar Stone — A174

Design: 25c, Aztec calendar stone and Mexican flag, horiz.

1968, Oct. 2

442	A174	5c multicolored	.55	.25
443	A174	25c multicolored	1.75	1.75
a.	Green omitted	3,500.	

19th Olympic Games, Mexico City, Oct. 12-27. Nos. 442-443 printed in sheets of 100 in two separate panes of 50 connected by a gutter. Each sheet contains 10 gutter pairs.

Symbolic House and Money — A175

1968, Oct. 16

444	A175	5c multicolored	.35	.35

11th Triennial Congress of the Intl. Union of Building Societies and Savings Associations, Sydney, Oct. 20-27.

View of Bethlehem and Church Window — A176

1968, Oct. 23 Photo. Perf. 13½

445	A176	5c lt bl, red, grn & gold	.30	.25
a.	Red omitted	3,500.	2,000.
b.	Gold omitted	850.00	500.00

Christmas.

Edgeworth David (1858-1934), Geologist — A177

Famous Australians: No. 447, Caroline Chisholm (1808-77), social worker, reformer. No. 448, Albert Namatjira (1902-59), aborigine, artist. No. 449, Andrew Barton (Banjo) Paterson 1864-1941), poet, writer.

1968, Nov. 6 Engr. Perf. 15x14

446	A177	5c green, greenish	.90	.35
a.	Booklet pane of 5 + label	4.75	
447	A177	5c purple, pink	.90	.35
a.	Booklet pane of 5 + label	4.75	
448	A177	5c dark brown, buff	.90	.35
a.	Booklet pane of 5 + label	4.75	
449	A177	5c indigo, lt blue	.90	.35
a.	Booklet pane of 5 + label	4.75	
	Nos. 446-449 (4)	3.60	1.40

Sir Edmund Barton (1849-1920) — A178

Prime Ministers: No. 451, Alfred Deakin (1856-1919). No. 452, John C. Watson (1867-1941). No. 453, Sir George H. Reid (1845-1918).

1969, Oct. 22 Engr. Perf. 15x14

450	A178	5c indigo, greenish	.90	.35
a.	Booklet pane of 5 + label	4.75	
451	A178	5c indigo, greenish	.90	.35
a.	Booklet pane of 5 + label	4.75	
452	A178	5c indigo, greenish	.90	.35
a.	Booklet pane of 5 + label	4.75	
453	A178	5c indigo, greenish	.90	.35
a.	Booklet pane of 5 + label	4.75	
	Nos. 450-453 (4)	3.60	1.40

Reginald C. and John R. Duigan, Aviators — A179

Famous Australians: No. 455, Lachlan Macquarie (1761-1824), Governor of New South Wales. No. 456, Adam Lindsay Gordon (1833-70), poet. No. 457, Edward John Eyre (1815-1901), explorer.

1970, Nov. 16 Engr. Perf. 15x14

454	A179	6c dark blue	.90	.35
a.	Booklet pane of 5 + label	4.75	

455	A179	6c dk brn, salmon	.90	.35
a.	Booklet pane of 5 + label	4.75	
456	A179	6c magenta, brt pink	.90	.35
a.	Booklet pane of 5 + label	4.75	
457	A179	6c brown red, salmon	.90	.35
a.	Booklet pane of 5 + label	4.75	
	Nos. 454-457 (4)	3.60	1.40

Nos. 446-457 were issued in booklet panes only; all stamps have 1 or 2 straight edges.

Macquarie Lighthouse — A180

1968, Nov. 27 Engr. Perf. 14½x13½

458	A180	5c indigo, buff	.45	.50

Macquarie Lighthouse, Outer South Head, Sydney, 150th anniv.

Surveyor George W. Goyder and Assistants, 1869; Building in Darwin, 1969 — A181

1969, Feb. 5 Photo. Perf. 13½

459	A181	5c black brn & dull yel	.30	.25

First permanent settlement of the Northern Territory of Australia, cent.

Melbourne Harbor Scene A182

1969, Feb. 26 Photo. Perf. 13½

460	A182	5c dull blue & multi	.30	.25

6th Biennial Conference of the Intl. Assoc. of Ports and Harbors, Melbourne, March 3-8.

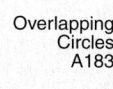

Overlapping Circles A183

1969, June 5 Photo. Perf. 13½

461	A183	5c gray, vio bl, bl & gold	.30	.25
a.	Gold omitted	3,000.	

ILO, 50th anniv.

Sugar Cane — A184

Primary industries: 15c, Eucalyptus (timber). 20c, Wheat. 25c, Ram, ewe, lamb (wool).

1969, Sept. 17 Perf. 13½x13

462	A184	7c blue & multi	.75	1.10
463	A184	15c emerald & multi	3.00	3.00
a.	Black omitted	1,750.	
464	A184	20c org brn & multi	1.00	.75
465	A184	25c gray, black & yel	1.25	1.10
	Nos. 462-465 (4)	6.00	5.95

Nativity — A185

Tree of Life — A186

Perf. 13½x13, 13x13½

1969, Oct. 15 Photo.

466	A185	5c multicolored	.30	.25
a.	Yellow omitted	1,800.	
b.	Magenta omitted	1,800.	
467	A186	25c multicolored	2.25	2.25

Christmas.

Vickers Vimy Flown by Ross Smith, England to Australia A187

Designs: No. 469, B.E. 2E plane, automobile, spectators. No. 470, Ford truck, surveyors Lieuts. Hudson Fysh & P.J. McGinness.

1969, Nov. 12 Perf. 13x13½

468	A187	5c bl, blk, cop red & ol	.55	.35
469	A187	5c bl, blk, cop red & ol	.55	.35
470	A187	5c cop red, black & ol	.55	.35
a.	Strip of 3, #468-470	3.25	3.25
	Nos. 468-470 (3)	1.65	1.05

1st England to Australia flight by Capt. Ross Smith & Lieut. Keith Smith, 50th anniv.
No. 470a had various combinations possible.

Diesel Locomotive and New Track Linking Melbourne, Sydney and Brisbane with Perth A188

1970, Feb. 11 Photo. Perf. 13x13½

471	A188	5c multicolored	.35	.25

Completion of the standard gauge railroad between Sydney and Perth.

EXPO '70 Australian Pavilion A189

Design: 20c, Southern Cross and Japanese inscription: "From the country of the south with warm feeling."

1970, Mar. 16 Photo. Perf. 13x13½

472	A189	5c bl, blk, red & brnz	.30	.25
473	A189	20c red & black	.75	.45

EXPO '70 Intl. Exhib., Osaka, Japan, Mar. 15-Sept. 13.

Queen Elizabeth II and Prince Philip A190

Australian Flag — A191

1970, Mar. 31
474 A190 5c yel bister & black .50 .30
475 A191 30c vio blue & multi 1.25 1.25

Visit of Queen Elizabeth II, Prince Philip and Princess Anne to Australia.

Steer, Alfalfa and Native Spear Grass A192

1970, Apr. 13 Photo. Perf. 13x13½
476 A192 5c emerald & multi .30 .35

11th Intl. Grasslands Congress, Surfers Paradise, Queensland, Apr. 13-23.

Capt. James Cook and "Endeavour" — A193

Designs: No. 478, Sextant, "Endeavour." No. 479, "Endeavour," landing party, kangaroo. No. 480, Daniel Charles Solander, Sir Joseph Banks, Cook, map, botanical drawing. No. 481, Cook taking possession with Union Jack; "Endeavour," coral. 30c, Cook, "Endeavour," sextant, kangaroo, aborigines.

1970, Apr. 20 Perf. 13½x13
Size: 24x35½mm
477 A193 5c org brn & multi .35 .25
478 A193 5c org brn & multi .35 .25
479 A193 5c org brn & multi .35 .25
480 A193 5c org brn & multi .35 .25
481 A193 5c org brn & multi .35 .25
a. Strip of 5, #477-481 1.75 1.75
Size: 62x29mm
482 A193 30c org brn & multi 1.75 1.75
a. Souv. sheet, #477-482, imperf 11.00 11.00
Nos. 477-482 (6) 3.50 3.00

Cook's discovery and exploration of the eastern coast of Australia, 200th anniv.
No. 481a has continuous design.
No. 482a with brown marginal overprint "Souvenir Sheet ANPEX 1970. . ." is of private origin. Value $25.

Snowy Mountains Hydroelectric Project A194

Designs: 8c, Ord River hydroelectric project (dam, cotton plant and boll). 9c, Bauxite and aluminum production (mine, conveyor belt and aluminum window frame). 10c, Oil and natural gas (off-shore drilling rig and pipelines).

1970, Aug. 31 Photo. Perf. 13½x13½
483 A194 7c multicolored .50 .40
484 A194 8c multicolored .25 .25
485 A194 9c multicolored .25 .25
486 A194 10c multicolored .35 .30
Nos. 483-486 (4) 1.35 1.20

Australian economic development.

Flame Symbolizing Democracy and Freedom of Speech — A195

1970, Oct. 2 Photo. Perf. 13½x13
487 A195 6c green & multi .30 .25

16th Commonwealth Parliamentary Assoc. Conference, Canberra, Oct. 2-9.

Herd of Illawarra Shorthorns and Laboratory A196

1970, Oct. 7 Perf. 13x13½
488 A196 6c multicolored .30 .25

18th Intl. Dairy Cong., Sydney, Oct. 12-16.

Madonna and Child, by William Beasley — A197

1970, Oct. 14 Perf. 13½x13
489 A197 6c multicolored .30 .25

Christmas.

UN Emblem, Dove and Symbols — A198

1970, Oct. 19
490 A198 6c blue & multi .30 .25

25th anniversary of the United Nations.

Qantas Boeing 707, and Avro 504 — A199

30c, Sunbeam Dyak powered Avro 504 on ground and Qantas Boeing 707 in the air.

1970, Nov. 2 Perf. 13x13½
491 A199 6c multicolored .40 .25
492 A199 30c multicolored 1.25 1.25

Qantas, Australian overseas airlines, 50th anniv.

Japanese Noh Actor, Australian Dancer and Chinese Opera Character — A200

15c, Chinese pipe, trumpet, Australian aboriginal didgeridoo, Thai fiddle, Indian double oboe, Tibetan drums. 20c, Red Sea dhow, Chinese junk, Australian lifeguard's surfboat, Malaysian & South Indian river boats.

1971, Jan. 6 Photo. Perf. 13½x13
493 A200 7c multicolored .45 .55
494 A200 15c multicolored .70 .70
495 A200 20c multicolored .70 .70
Nos. 493-495 (3) 1.85 1.95

Link between Australia and Asia; 28th Intl. Congress of Orientalists, Canberra, Jan. 6-12.

Southern Cross A201

1971, Apr. 21 Photo. Perf. 13x13½
496 A201 6c multicolored .30 .25

Australian Natives Assoc., cent.

Symbolic Market Graphs — A202

1971, May 5 Perf. 13½x13
497 A202 6c silver & multi .30 .25

Centenary of Sydney Stock Exchange.

Rotary Emblem A203

1971, May 17 Perf. 13x13½
498 A203 6c multicolored .30 .25

First Intl. Rotary Convention held in Australia, Sydney, May 16-20.

DH-9A, Australian Mirage Jet Fighters — A204

1971, June 9 Perf. 13½x13
499 A204 6c multicolored .55 .25

Royal Australian Air Force, 50th anniv.

Longnecked Tortoise, Painted on Bark — A206

Aboriginal Art: 25c, Mourners' body paintings, Warramunga tribe. 30c, Cave painting, Western Arnhem Land, vert. 35c, Graveposts, Bathurst and Melville Islands, vert.

Perf. 13x13½, 13½x13
1971, Sept. 29
504 A206 20c multicolored .45 .30
505 A206 25c multicolored .45 .45
506 A206 30c multicolored 1.00 .45
507 A206 35c multicolored .45 .45
Nos. 504-507 (4) 2.35 1.65

Three Kings and Star — A207

1971, Oct. 13 Photo. Perf. 13½x13
508 Block of 7 35.00 35.00
a. A207 7c brt grn, dk bl (Kings) & lil 2.00 .70
b. A207 7c lil, red brn, grn & dk bl 2.00 .70
c. A207 7c red brown & lilac 5.00 1.25
d. A207 7c lilac, red brn & brt grn 2.00 .70
e. A207 7c red brown & dark blue 2.00 .70
f. A207 7c lilac, green & dk blue 15.00 2.25
g. A207 7c brt grn, dk bl & lilac (Kings) 2.00 .70

Christmas. Nos. 508a-508g printed se-tenant in sheets of 50. Each sheet contains 2 green crosses formed by 4 No. 508g and three No. 508a.

Andrew Fisher (1862-1928) — A208

Prime Ministers: No. 515, Joseph Cook (1860-1947). No. 516, William Morris Hughes (1864-1952). No. 517, Stanley Melbourne Bruce (1883-1967).

1972, Mar. 8 Engr. Perf. 15x14
514 A208 7c dark blue .70 .40
a. Booklet pane of 5 + label 3.50
515 A208 7c dark red .70 .40
a. Booklet pane of 5 + label 3.50
516 A208 7c dark blue .70 .40
a. Booklet pane of 5 + label 3.50
517 A208 7c dark red .70 .40
a. Booklet pane of 5 + label 3.50
Nos. 514-517 (4) 2.80 1.60

Nos. 514-517 were issued in booklets only; all stamps have one or two straight edges.

Cameo Brooch — A209

1972, Apr. 18 Photo. Perf. 13½
518 A209 7c multicolored .35 .25

Country Women's Assoc., 50th anniv.

Apple and Banana A210

1972, June 14
519 A210 20c shown 1.50 1.50
520 A210 25c Rice 1.50 1.50
521 A210 30c Fish 1.50 1.50
522 A210 35c Cattle 3.00 3.00
Nos. 519-522 (4) 7.50 7.50

RSPCA Centenary — A205

Designs: 12c, Man and lamb (animal science). 18c, Kangaroo (fauna conservation). 24c, Seeing eye dog (animals' aid to man).

1971, July 5 Photo. Perf. 13½x13
500 A205 6c blk, brown & org .25 .25
501 A205 12c blk, dk grn & yel .45 .25
502 A205 18c brown & multi .65 .35
a. Litho., perf. 14¾x14, dated "2013" (#1003b) .45 .45
503 A205 24c blue & multi .70 .70
Nos. 500-503 (4) 2.05 1.55

Royal Society for Prevention of Cruelty to Animals in Australia, cent.
Issued: No. 502a, 5/10/2013.

Worker in Sheltered Workshop — A211

18c, Amputee assembling electrical circuit. 24c, Boy wearing Toronto splint, playing ball.

1972, Aug. 2   *Perf. 13½x13*
523	A211	12c grn & brn	.30 .25
524	A211	18c org & ol, horiz.	1.25 .60
525	A211	24c brn & ultra	.50 .25
	Nos. 523-525 (3)		2.05 1.10

Rehabilitation of the handicapped.

Overland Telegraph Line — A212

1972, Aug. 22   **Photo.**   *Perf. 13x13½*
526   A212   7c dk red, blk & lemon   .30   .30

Centenary of overland telegraph line.

Athlete, Olympic Rings — A213

1972, Aug. 28   *Perf. 13½x13*
527	A213	7c shown	.45 .45
528	A213	7c Swimming	.45 .45
529	A213	7c Rowing	.45 .45
530	A213	35c Equestrian	2.75 2.75
	Nos. 527-530 (4)		4.10 4.10

20th Olympic Games, Munich, 8/26-9/11.

Abacus, Numerals, Computer Circuits A214

1972, Oct. 16   **Photo.**   *Perf. 13x13½*
531   A214   7c multicolored   .30   .30

10th Intl. Congress of Accountants.

19th Cent. Combine Harvester A215

5c, Pioneer family, vert. 10c, Water pump, vert. 40c, Pioneer house. 50c, Cobb & Co. coach. 60c, Early Morse key, vert. 80c, Paddle-wheel steamer.

Perf. 13½x13, 13x13½
1972, Nov. 15   **Photo.**
532	A215	5c multicolored	.25 .25
533	A215	10c multicolored	.35 .25
534	A215	15c shown	.30 .25
535	A215	40c multicolored	.55 .25
536	A215	50c multicolored	.80 .25
537	A215	60c multicolored	.80 .55
538	A215	80c multicolored	1.00 .55
	Nos. 532-538 (7)		4.05 2.35

Australian pioneer life.

Jesus and Children A216

Dove, Cross and "Darkness into Light" — A217

Perf. 14½x14, 13½x13
1972, Nov. 29
539	A216	7c tan & multi	.35 .25
540	A217	35c blue & multi	6.50 6.50

Christmas.

Metric Conversion, Mass — A218

Metric conversion: No. 542, Temperature, horiz. No. 543, Length. No. 544, Volume.

1973, Mar. 7   **Photo.**   *Perf. 14x14½*
541	A218	7c pale vio & multi	.50 .30
542	A218	7c yellow & multi	.50 .30
543	A218	7c yel green & multi	.50 .30
544	A218	7c brt rose & multi	.50 .30
	Nos. 541-544 (4)		2.00 1.20

Conversion to metric system.

Stylized Caduceus and Laurel A219

1973, Apr. 4   **Photo.**   *Perf. 14½x14*
545   A219   7c dk bl, emer & lil rose   .40   .30

WHO, 25th anniv.

Dame Mary Gilmore, Writer — A220

Famous Australians: No. 547, William Charles Wentworth, explorer. No. 548, Sir Isaac Isaacs, lawyer, 1st Australian-born Governor-General. No. 549, Marcus Clarke, writer.

Engr. & Litho.
1973, May 16   *Perf. 15x14*
546	A220	7c bister & black	.65 .30
547	A220	7c bister & black	.65 .30
548	A220	7c black & violet	.65 .30
549	A220	7c black & violet	.65 .30
a.	Block of 4, #546-549		3.25 3.25

Shipping Industry — A221

Designs: 25c, Iron ore and steel. 30c, Truck convoy (beef road). 35c, Aerial mapping.

1973, June 6   **Photo.**   *Perf. 13½x13*
550	A221	20c ultra & multi	1.50 1.40
551	A221	25c red & multi	1.50 1.40
552	A221	30c ol brn & multi	1.50 1.40
553	A221	35c olive & multi	2.00 1.75
	Nos. 550-553 (4)		6.50 5.95

Australian economic development.

Banded Coral Shrimp — A222   Chrysoprase A223

Helichrysum Thomsonii A223a

Wombat A224

Radio Astronomy A225

Red Gums of the Far North, by Hans Heysen — A226

Coming South (Immigrants), by Tom Roberts — A226a

2c, Fiddler crab. 3c, Coral crab. 4c, Mauve stinger. 7c, Agate. 8c, Opal. 9c, Rhodonite. 10c, Star sapphire. 11c, Atomic absorption spectrophotometry. 25c, Spiny anteater. 30c, Brushtail possum. 33c, Immunology. 45c, Callistemon teretifolius, horiz. 48c, Oceanography. 75c, Feather-tailed glider.

Paintings: $1, Sergeant of Light Horse, by George Lambert. No. 575, On the Wallaby Track. $4, Shearing the Rams, by Tom Roberts. No. 577, McMahon's Point, by Arthur Streeton. No. 578, Mentone.

Perf. 14x15, 15x14 (A222, A223, A223a); Perf. 14x14½ (A224); Perf. 13x13½ (A225, A226, $1)
1973-84   **Photo.**
554	A222	1c shown	.25 .25
555	A222	2c multi	.25 .25
556	A222	3c multi	.25 .25
557	A222	4c multi	.25 .25
558	A223	6c shown	.25 .25
559	A223	7c multi	.30 .25
560	A223	8c multi	.30 .25
561	A223	9c multi	.30 .25
562	A223	10c multi ('74)	.35 .25
563	A223	11c multi ('75)	.65 .30
564	A223a	18c shown ('75)	.60 .25
565	A224	20c shown ('74)	.45 .25
566	A224	24c multi ('75)	1.10 .45
567	A224	25c multi ('74)	1.40 .40
568	A224	30c multi ('74)	.80 .25
569	A225	33c multi ('75)	1.10 1.10
570	A223a	45c multi ('75)	.95 .35
571	A225	48c multi ('75)	2.00 1.25
572	A224	75c multi ('74)	1.60 .85
573	A226a	$1 multi ('74)	2.00 .35

574	A226	$2 shown ('74)	3.75 .60
575	A226	$2 multi ('81)	3.75 .50
576	A226	$4 multi ('74)	7.50 3.25

Litho.
Perf. 14½
577	A226a	$5 multi ('79)	9.50 2.60
578	A226	$5 multi ('84)	9.50 1.40
579	A226a	$10 shown ('77)	15.00 3.75
	Nos. 554-579 (26)		64.15 20.15

Issued: 1c-9c, 7/11; 20c, 25c, 30c, 75c, 2/13; $1, No. 574, $4, 4/24; 10c, 10/16; 11c, 24c, 33c, 48c, 5/14; 18c, 45c, 8/27; $10, 10/19; No. 577, 3/14; No. 575, 6/17; No. 578, 4/4.

No. 560 Surcharged in Red

Perf. 15x14
580   A223   9c on 8c multi ('74)   .30   .35

Hand Protecting Playing Children A227

1973, Sept. 5   **Photo.**   *Perf. 13x13½*
581   A227   7c bis brn, grn & plum   .30   .25

50th anniv. of Legacy, an ex-servicemen's organization concerned with the welfare of widows and children of servicemen.

Baptism of Christ A228   The Good Shepherd A229

1973, Oct. 3   *Perf. 14x14½*
582	A228	7c gold & multi	.30 .25
a.		Perf. 14x15	3.00 .75

Perf. 13½
583   A229   30c gold & multi   2.25 2.25

Christmas.

Buchanan's Hotel, Townsville A230

St. James' Church, Sydney — A231

Designs: 7c, Opera House, Sydney. 40c, Como House, Melbourne.

1973, Oct. 17   **Photo.**   *Perf. 14½x14*
584	A230	7c lt blue & ultra	.35 .25
a.		Perf. 15x14	4.50 .90
585	A230	10c bister & black	.50 .35

Perf. 13x13½, 13½x13
586	A230	40c dl pink, gray & blk	.65 .75
587	A231	50c gray & multi	1.50 1.25
	Nos. 584-587 (4)		3.00 2.60

Australian architecture; opening of the Sydney Opera House, Oct. 14, 1973 (No. 584).

Radio and Gramophone Speaker A232

1973, Nov. 21 Photo. Perf. 13½x13
588 A232 7c dull blue, blk & brn .35 .25
Broadcasting in Australia, 50th anniv.

Supreme Court Judge on Bench — A233

1974, May 15 Photo. Perf. 14x14½
589 A233 7c multicolored .35 .25
150th anniv. of the proclamation of the Charter of Justice in New South Wales and Van Diemen's Land (Australia's Third Charter).

Australian Football — A234

1974, July 24 Photo. Perf. 14x14½
590 A234 7c shown .35 .25
591 A234 7c Cricket .35 .25
  a. Booklet pane of 1, litho., perf.
    14¾x14, dated "2007" .25 —
592 A234 7c Golf .35 .25
593 A234 7c Surfing .35 .25
594 A234 7c Tennis .35 .25
595 A234 7c Bowls, horiz. .35 .25
596 A234 7c Rugby, horiz. .35 .25
    Nos. 590-596 (7) 2.45 1.75

No. 591a issued 11/14/2007.

Carrier Pigeon A235

Designs: 30c, Carrier pigeons, vert.

1974, Oct. 9 Photo. Perf. 14½x14
597 A235 7c multicolored .35 .25
  a. Perf. 15x14 .60 .35

Perf. 13½x13
598 A235 30c multicolored 1.10 1.10
UPU, cent. A booklet containing a strip of 5 each of Nos. 597-598 was produced and sold for $4 Australian by the National Stamp Week Promotion Council with government approval.

William Charles Wentworth — A236

Typo. & Litho.
1974, Oct. 9 Perf. 14x15
599 A236 7c bister & black .40 .25
  a. Perf. 14x14½ 1.60 .40

Sesquicentennial of 1st Australian independent newspaper. W. C. Wentworth and Dr. Robert Wardell were the editors and the "A" is type from masthead of "The Australian."

Adoration of the Kings, by Dürer — A237

Christmas: 35c, Flight into Egypt, by Albrecht Dürer.

1974, Nov. 13 Engr. Perf. 14x14½
600 A237 10c buff & black .40 .25
601 A237 35c buff & black .90 .90

Pre-school Education A238

Correspondence Schools — A239

Science Education A240

Advanced Education — A241

Perf. 13x13½, 13½x13
1974, Nov. 20 Photo.
602 A238 5c multicolored .30 .25
603 A239 11c multicolored .30 .25
604 A240 15c multicolored .40 .30
605 A241 60c multicolored .75 .75
    Nos. 602-605 (4) 1.75 1.55

"Avoid Pollution" A242

"Road Safety" — A243

Design: No. 607, "Avoid bush fires."

1975, Jan. 29 Photo. Perf. 14½x14
606 A242 10c multicolored .55 .45
  a. Perf. 15x14 7.50 5.00
607 A242 10c multicolored .55 .45
  a. Perf. 15x14 1.75 1.10

Perf. 14x14½
608 A243 10c multicolored .55 .45
    Nos. 606-608 (3) 1.65 1.35
Environmental dangers.

Symbols of Womanhood, Sun, Moon — A244

1975, Mar. 12 Photo. Perf. 14x14½
609 A244 10c dk vio blue & grn .35 .25
International Women's Year.

Joseph B. Chifley (1885-1951) — A245

No. 611, John Curtin, 1885-1945. No. 612, Arthur W. Fadden, 1895-1973. No. 613, Joseph A. Lyons, 1879-1939. No. 614, Earle Page, 1880-1963. No. 615, John H. Scullin, 1876-1953.

1975, Mar. 26
610 A245 10c shown .30 .25
611 A245 10c multicolored .30 .25
612 A245 10c multicolored .30 .25
613 A245 10c multicolored .30 .25
614 A245 10c multicolored .30 .25
615 A245 10c multicolored .30 .25
    Nos. 610-615 (6) 1.80 1.50
Australian Prime Ministers.

Australian Postal Commission A246

Design: No. 617, Australian Telecommunications Commission.

1975, July 1 Photo. Perf. 14½x14
616 A246 10c red, black & gray .65 .45
  a. Perf. 15x14 .85 .45
617 A246 10c yel, black & gray .65 .45
  a. Pair, #616-617 1.60 1.25
  b. Perf. 15x14 .85 .45
  c. Pair, #616a, 617b 3.50 3.50

Formation of Australian Postal and Telecommunications Commissions. Printed checkerwise.

Edith Cowan, Judge and Legislator A247

Truganini, Last Tasmanian Aborigine A248

Portraits: No. 619, Louisa Lawson (1848-1920), journalist. No. 620, Ethel Florence (Henry Handel) Richardson (1870-1946), novelist. No. 621, Catherine Spence (1825-1910), teacher, journalist, voting reformer. No. 622, Emma Constance Stone (1856-1902), first Australian woman physician.

1975, Aug. 6 Photo. Perf. 14x14½
618 A247 10c olive grn & multi .45 .30
  a. Perf. 14x15 .45 .30
619 A247 10c yel bister & multi .45 .30
  a. Perf. 14x15 .45 .30
620 A248 10c olive & multi .45 .30
  a. Perf. 14x15 .45 .30
621 A248 10c gray & multi .45 .30
  a. Perf. 14x15 .45 .30
622 A248 10c violet & multi .45 .30
  a. Perf. 14x15 .45 .30
623 A248 10c brown & multi .45 .30
  a. Perf. 14x15 .45 .30
    Nos. 618-623 (6) 2.70 1.80
Famous Australian women.

Spirit House (PNG) and Sydney Opera House — A249

Bird in Flight and Southern Cross A250

1975, Sept. 16 Photo. Perf. 13½
624 A249 18c multicolored .45 .25
625 A250 25c multicolored .80 .65
Papua New Guinea independence, Sept. 16, 1975.

Adoration of the Kings — A251

"The Light Shineth in the Darkness" A252

1975, Oct. 29 Photo. Perf. 14½x14
626 A251 15c multicolored .40 .25
627 A252 45c silver & multi 1.50 1.50
Christmas.

Australian Coat of Arms A253

Type I

Type II

Type I — Kangaroo: eye is dot, right paw has 1 toe, left foot has 1 toe. Emu: feet have 1 toe.
Type II — Kangaroo: eye is line, right paw has 3 toes, left foot has 2 toes. Emu: feet have 2 toes.
Other differences exist.

1976, Jan. 5 Photo. Perf. 14½x14
628 A253 18c multicolored, type I .40 .25
  a. Type II .95 .40

"Williams' Coffin" Telephone, 1878 — A254

1976, Mar. 10 Photo. Perf. 13½
629 A254 18c buff & multi .40 .30
Centenary of first telephone call by Alexander Graham Bell, Mar. 10, 1876.

John Oxley
A255

Australian explorers: No. 631, Hamilton Hume and William Hovell. No. 632, John Forrest. No. 633, Ernest Giles. No. 634, Peter Warburton. No. 635, William Gosse.

1976, June 9   Photo.   Perf. 13½
630	A255	18c shown	.35	.25
631	A255	18c multicolored	.35	.25
632	A255	18c multicolored	.35	.25
633	A255	18c multicolored	.35	.25
634	A255	18c multicolored	.35	.25
635	A255	18c multicolored	.35	.25
		Nos. 630-635 (6)	2.10	1.50

Survey Rule, Graph, Punched Tape — A256

1976, June 15   Perf. 15x14
636	A256	18c multicolored	.40	.25

Commonwealth Scientific and Industrial Research Organization, 50th anniv.

Soccer Goalkeeper A257

Olympic Rings and: No. 638, Woman gymnast, vert. 25c, Woman diver, vert. 40c, Bicycling.

Perf. 13x13½, 13½x13
1976, July 14   Photo.
637	A257	18c multicolored	.30	.25
638	A257	18c multicolored	.30	.25
639	A257	25c multicolored	.40	.40
640	A257	40c multicolored	.60	.50
		Nos. 637-640 (4)	1.60	1.40

21st Olympic Games, Montreal, Canada, July 17-Aug. 1.

Richmond Bridge, Tasmania A258

Mt. Buffalo, Victoria — A259

Designs: 25c, Broken Bay, New South Wales. 35c, Wittenoom Gorge, Western Australia. 70c, Barrier Reef, Queensland. 85c, Ayers Rock, Northern Territory.

Perf. 14½x14, 14x14½
1976, Aug. 25   Photo.
641	A258	5c multicolored	.30	.25
642	A258	25c multicolored	.45	.25
643	A258	35c multicolored	.50	.30
644	A259	50c multicolored	.70	.30
645	A258	70c multicolored	.85	.40
646	A258	85c multicolored	1.00	.70
		Nos. 641-646 (6)	3.80	2.20

Blamire Young and Australia No. 59 — A260

1976, Sept. 27   Photo.   Perf. 13½
647	A260	18c apple grn & multi	.40	.25

Miniature Sheet
648		Sheet of 4	2.00	2.00
a.		A260 18c yellow & dark brown	.50	.50
b.		A260 18c rose, dk brown & yel	.50	.50
c.		A260 18c bl, dk brn, rose & yel	.50	.50

Natl. Stamp Week, Sept. 27-Oct. 3. Blamire Young (1862-1935), designer of Australia's 1st issue. No. 648 shows different stages of 4-color printing. The 4th stamp in sheet is identical with No. 647.

Virgin and Child, after Simone Cantarini A261

Holly, Toy Koala, Christmas Tree and Decoration, Partridge A262

1976, Nov. 1   Photo.   Perf. 14½x14
649	A261	15c brt car & lt blue	.40	.25

Perf. 13½
650	A262	45c multicolored	.80	.80

Christmas.

John Gould (1804-1881) Ornithologist A263

Famous Australians: No. 652, Thomas Laby (1880-1946), nuclear scientist. No. 653, Sir Baldwin Spencer (1860-1929), anthropologist (aborigines). No. 654, Griffith Taylor (1880-1963), geographer and antarctic explorer.

1976, Nov. 10   Perf. 15x14
651	A263	18c shown	.35	.25
652	A263	18c Laby	.35	.25
653	A263	18c Spencer	.35	.25
654	A263	18c Taylor	.35	.25
		Nos. 651-654 (4)	1.40	1.00

Violinists — A264

1977, Jan. 19   Photo.   Perf. 14x14½
655	A264	20c shown	.30	.25
656	A264	30c Dramatic scene	.35	.25
657	A264	40c Dancer	.45	.30
658	A264	60c Opera singer	.90	.40
		Nos. 655-658 (4)	2.00	1.20

Performing arts in Australia.

Elizabeth II — A265

Design: 45c, Elizabeth II and Prince Philip.

1977, Feb. 2   Perf. 14x14½
659	A265	18c multicolored	.40	.30
660	A265	45c multicolored	.75	.75

Reign of Queen Elizabeth II, 25th anniv. Perf 14½x14 examples of Nos. 659-660 are from a booklet pane containing 2 of each stamp, found in the booklet footnoted under No. 2507.

Wicket Keeper, Slip Fieldsman — A266

Cricket match, 19th century: No. 662, Umpire and batsman. No. 663, Two fieldsmen. No. 664, Batsman and umpire. No. 665, Bowler and fieldsman. 45c, Batsman facing bowler.

1977, Mar. 9   Photo.   Perf. 13½
661	A266	18c gray & multi	.45	.45
a.		Litho., perf. 14¾x14, dated "2007"	.55	.55
662	A266	18c gray & multi	.45	.45
a.		Litho., perf. 14¾x14, dated "2007"	.55	.55
663	A266	18c gray & multi	.45	.45
a.		Litho., perf. 14¾x14, dated "2007"	.55	.55
664	A266	18c gray & multi	.45	.45
a.		Litho., perf. 14¾x14, dated "2007"	.55	.55
665	A266	18c gray & multi	.45	.45
a.		Strip of 5, #661-665	3.00	3.00
b.		Litho., perf. 14¾x14, dated "2007"	.55	.55
666	A266	45c gray & multi	1.00	1.00
a.		Litho., imperf., dated "2007"	1.25	1.25
b.		Booklet pane of 6, #661a, 662a, 663a, 664a, 665b, 666a	4.00	—
		Nos. 661-666 (6)	3.25	3.25

Nos. 661a, 662a, 663a, 664a, 665b, 666a, 666b issued 11/14/2007.

Parliament House, Canberra A267

1977, Apr. 13   Perf. 14½x14
667	A267	18c multicolored	.40	.25

Parliament House, Canberra, 50th anniv.

Trade Union Workers A268

1977, May 9   Photo.   Perf. 13
668	A268	18c multicolored	.40	.25

Australian Council of Trade Unions (ACTU), 50th anniv.

Surfing Santa — A269   Virgin and Child — A270

1977, Oct. 31   Photo.   Perf. 14x14½
669	A269	15c multicolored	.40	.25

Perf. 13½x13
670	A270	45c multicolored	.75	.75

Christmas.

Australian Flag — A271

1978, Jan. 26   Photo.   Perf. 13x13½
671	A271	18c multicolored	.40	.30

Australia Day, 190th anniversary of first permanent settlement in New South Wales.

Harry Hawker and Sopwith "Camel" — A272

Australian Aviators and their Planes: No. 673, Bert Hinkler and Avro Avian. No. 674, Charles Kingsford-Smith and Fokker "Southern Cross." No. 675, Charles Ulm and "Southern Cross."

1978, Apr. 19   Litho.   Perf. 15½
672	A272	18c ultra & multi	.40	.30
673	A272	18c blue & multi	.40	.30
674	A272	18c orange & multi	.40	.30
675	A272	18c yellow & multi	.40	.30
a.		Souv. sheet, 2 each #674-675, imperf.	1.60	1.50
		Nos. 672-675 (4)	1.60	1.20

No. 675a for 50th anniv. of first Trans-Pacific flight from Oakland, Cal., to Brisbane.

Beechcraft Baron Landing A273

1978, May 15   Photo.   Perf. 13½
676	A273	18c multicolored	.40	.30

Royal Flying Doctor Service, 50th anniv.

Illawarra Flame Tree — A274

Australian trees: 25c, Ghost gum. 40c, Grass tree. 45c, Cootamundra wattle.

1978, June 1
677	A274	18c multicolored	.25	.25
678	A274	25c multicolored	.50	.50
679	A274	40c multicolored	.65	.65
680	A274	45c multicolored	.70	.70
		Nos. 677-680 (4)	2.10	2.10

Sturt's Desert Rose, Map of Australia — A275

1978, June 19   Litho.   Perf. 15½
681	A275	18c multicolored	.40	.25

Establishment of Government of the Northern Territory.

Hooded Dotterel — A276

Australian birds: 20c, Little grebe. 25c, Spur-wing Plover. 30c, Pied oystercatcher. 55c, Lotus bird.

1978		Photo.	Perf. 13½	
682	A276	5c multicolored	.25	.25
683	A276	20c multicolored	.40	.25
684	A276	25c multicolored	.45	.25
685	A276	30c multicolored	.70	.35
686	A276	55c multicolored	.90	.60
		Nos. 682-686 (5)	2.70	1.70

Issued: Nos. 683, 686, July 3; others, July 17. See Nos. 713-718, 732-739, 768.

Australia No. 95 on Album Page — A277

1978, Sept. 25		Litho.	Perf. 15½	
687	A277	20c multicolored	.40	.25
a.		Miniature sheet of 4	1.10	1.10

National Stamp Week; 50th anniv. of Melbourne Intl. Phil. Exhib., Oct. 1928.

Virgin and Child, by Simon Marmion — A278

Paintings from National Gallery, Victoria: 15c, Virgin and Child, after Van Eyck. 55c, Holy Family, by Perino del Vaga.

1978			Perf. 15	
688	A278	15c multicolored	.40	.25
689	A278	25c multicolored	.55	.55
690	A278	55c multicolored	1.00	.80
		Nos. 688-690 (3)	1.95	1.60

Christmas. Issued: 25c, 10/3; others, 11/1.

Tulloch A279

Race horses: 35c, Bernborough, vert. 50c, Phar Lap, vert. 55c, Peter Pan.

1978, Oct. 18			Perf. 15x14, 14x15	
			Photo.	
691	A279	20c multicolored	.40	.30
692	A279	35c multicolored	.70	.55
693	A279	50c multicolored	.90	.85
694	A279	55c multicolored	1.00	.95
		Nos. 691-694 (4)	3.00	2.65

Australian horse racing.

Flag Raising at Sydney Cove — A280

1979, Jan. 26		Litho.	Perf. 15½	
695	A280	20c multicolored	.40	.30

Australia Day, Jan. 26.

Passenger Steamer Canberra A281

Ferries and Murray River Steamers: 35c, M.V. Lady Denman. 50c, P.S. Murray River Queen. 55c, Hydrofoil Curl Curl.

1979, Feb. 14		Perf. 13½, 15x14 (20c)		
			Photo.	
696	A281	20c multicolored	.35	.30
697	A281	35c multicolored	.70	.55
698	A281	50c multicolored	.90	.90
699	A281	55c multicolored	1.00	.95
		Nos. 696-699 (4)	2.95	2.70

Port Campbell A282

Designs: Australian National Parks.

1979, Apr. 9		Litho.	Perf. 15½	
700	A282	20c shown	.35	.35
701	A282	20c Uluru	.35	.35
702	A282	20c Royal	.35	.35
703	A282	20c Flinders Ranges	.35	.35
704	A282	20c Nambung	.35	.35
a.		Strip of 5, #700-704	2.00	2.00
705	A282	20c Girraween, vert.	.35	.35
706	A282	20c Mount Field, vert.	.35	.35
a.		Pair, #705-706	.75	.75
		Nos. 700-706 (7)	2.45	2.45

Double Fairlie A283

Australian steam locomotives: 35c, Puffing Billy. 50c, Pichi Richi. 55c, Zig Zag.

1979, May 16		Perf. 13½, 15x14 (20c)		
			Photo.	
707	A283	20c multicolored	.40	.30
708	A283	35c multicolored	.75	.55
709	A283	50c multicolored	.90	.85
710	A283	55c multicolored	1.00	.95
		Nos. 707-710 (4)	3.05	2.65

"Black Swan" A284

1979, June 6		Photo.	Perf. 13½	
711	A284	20c multicolored	.40	.25

150th anniversary of Western Australia.

Children Playing, IYC Emblem A285

1979, Aug. 13		Litho.	Perf. 13½x13	
712	A285	20c multicolored	.40	.25

International Year of the Child.

Bird Type of 1978

Australian birds: 1c, Zebra finch. 2c, Crimson finch. 15c, Forest kingfisher, vert. 20c, Eastern yellow robin. 40c, Lovely wren, vert. 50c, Flame robin, vert.

1979, Sept. 17		Photo.	Perf. 13½	
713	A276	1c multicolored	.25	.25
714	A276	2c multicolored	.25	.25
715	A276	15c multicolored	.35	.25
716	A276	20c multicolored	.45	.25
717	A276	40c multicolored	.75	.35
718	A276	50c multicolored	1.00	.40
		Nos. 713-718 (6)	3.05	1.75

Christmas Letters, Flag-wrapped Parcels — A286

Christmas: 15c, Nativity, icon. 55c, Madonna and Child, by Buglioni.

1979		Litho.	Perf. 13	
719	A286	15c multicolored	.35	.25
720	A286	25c multicolored	.45	.30
721	A286	55c multicolored	1.00	.90
		Nos. 719-721 (3)	1.80	1.45

Issue dates: 25c, Sept. 24. Others, Nov. 1.

Trout Fishing — A287

Sport fishing: 35c, Angler. 50c, Black marlin fishing. 55c, Surf fishing.

1979, Oct. 24		Photo.	Perf. 14x14½	
722	A287	20c multicolored	.35	.30
723	A287	35c multicolored	.70	.55
724	A287	50c multicolored	.90	.75
725	A287	55c multicolored	1.00	.85
		Nos. 722-725 (4)	2.95	2.45

Matthew Flinders, Map of Australia A288

1980, Jan. 23		Litho.	Perf. 13½	
726	A288	20c multicolored	.40	.25

Australia Day, Jan. 28.

Dingo A289

1980, Feb. 20		Litho.	Perf. 13½x13	
727	A289	20c shown	.35	.25
728	A289	25c Border collie	.45	.45
729	A289	35c Australian terrier	.65	.65
730	A289	50c Australian cattle dog	.90	.85
731	A289	55c Australian kelpie	1.00	.90
		Nos. 727-731 (5)	3.35	3.10

Bird Type of 1978

10c, Golden-shoulder parrot, vert. 22c, White-tailed kingfisher, vert. 28c, Rainbow bird, vert. 35c, Regent bower bird, vert. 45c, Masked woodswallow. 60c, King parrot, vert. 80c, Rainbow pitta. $1, Western magpie, vert.

		Perf. 13x12½ (10c, 28c, 35c, 60c, $1), 14x15 (22c), 12½x13 (45c, 80c)		
1980		Litho., Photo. (22c)		
732	A276	10c multicolored	.30	.25
a.		Perf. 14½x14	1.40	.45
733	A276	22c multicolored	.45	.30
734	A276	28c multicolored	.55	.45
735	A276	35c multicolored	.70	.45
736	A276	45c multicolored	.95	.60
a.		Perf. 14x14½	2.50	1.80
737	A276	60c multicolored	1.25	.60
738	A276	80c multicolored	1.60	1.00
739	A276	$1 multicolored	2.00	.45
		Nos. 732-739 (8)	7.80	4.10

Issued: Nos. 733, 734, 737, 3/31; others, 7/1.

Queen Elizabeth II, 54th Birthday — A290

1980, Apr. 21		Litho.	Perf. 13x13½	
740	A290	22c multicolored	.35	.25

Wanderer — A291

1980, May 7		Lith.	Perf. 13x13½	
741		Strip of 5	2.00	2.00
a.	A291	22c shown	.35	.35
b.	A291	22c Stealing sheep	.35	.35
c.	A291	22c Squatter on horseback	.35	.35
d.	A291	22c Three troopers	.35	.35
e.	A291	22c Wanderer's ghost	.35	.35

"Waltzing Matilda", poem by Andrew Barton Patterson (1864-1941). No. 741 in continuous design.

High Court Building, Canberra — A292

1980, May 19				
742	A292	22c multicolored	.40	.25

Opening of High Court of Australia Building, Canberra, May 26.

Salvation Army Officers A294

No. 748, St. Vincent de Paul Society, vert. No. 749, Meals on Wheels, vert. No. 750, "Life. Be in it." (Joggers, bicyclists).

		Perf. 13x13½, 13½x13		
1980, Aug. 11				
747	A294	22c shown	.40	.30
748	A294	22c multicolored	.40	.30
749	A294	22c multicolored	.40	.30
750	A294	22c multicolored	.40	.30
		Nos. 747-750 (4)	1.60	1.20

Mailman c. 1900 — A295

1980, Sept. 29		Litho.	Perf. 13x13½	
751	A295	22c Mailbox	.40	.25
752	A295	22c shown	.40	.25
753	A295	22c Mail truck	.40	.25
754	A295	22c Mailman, mailbox	.40	.25
755	A295	22c Mailman, diff.	.40	.25
a.		Souvenir sheet of 3	1.50	1.50
b.		Strip of 5, #751-755	2.00	2.00
		Nos. 751-755 (5)	2.00	1.25

Natl. Stamp Week, Sept. 29-Oct. 5. Nos. 755a contains stamps similar to #751, 753, 755.

No. 755a overprinted "SYDPEX 80" was privately produced.

Holy Family, by Prospero Fontana — A296

Christmas: 15c, Virgin Enthroned, by Justin O'Brien. 60c, Virgin and Child, by Michael Zuern the Younger, 1680.

1980			**Perf. 13x13½**	
756	A296	15c multicolored	.30	.25
757	A296	28c multicolored	.55	.45
758	A296	60c multicolored	1.10	.65
		Nos. 756-758 (3)	1.95	1.35

Issued: 15c, 60c, Nov. 3; 28c, Oct. 1.

CA-6 Wackett Trainer, 1941 — A297

Designs: Australian military training planes.

1980, Nov. 19			**Perf. 13½x14**	
759	A297	22c shown	.40	.30
760	A297	40c Winjeel, 1955	.75	.55
761	A297	45c Boomerang, 1944	.80	.60
762	A297	60c Nomad, 1975	1.10	.80
		Nos. 759-762 (4)	3.05	2.25

Bird Type of 1978

1980, Nov. 17		**Litho.**	**Perf. 13½**	
768	A276	18c Spotted catbird, vert.	.50	.25

Flag on Map of Australia A298

1981, Jan. 21			**Perf. 13½x13**	
771	A298	22c multicolored	.40	.25

Australia Day, Jan. 21.

Jockey Darby Munro (1913-1966), by Tony Rafty — A299

Australian sportsmen (Caricatures by Tony Rafty): 35c, Victor Trumper (1877-1915), cricket batsman. 55c, Norman Brookes (1877-1968), tennis player. 60c, Walter Lindrum (1898-1960), billiards player.

1981, Feb. 18			**Perf. 14x13½**	
772	A299	22c multicolored	.40	.25
773	A299	35c multicolored	.65	.60
a.		Booklet pane of 1, perf. 14¾x14, dated "2007"	1.10	—
774	A299	55c multicolored	1.00	.90
775	A299	60c multicolored	1.10	1.00
		Nos. 772-775 (4)	3.15	2.75

No. 773a issued 11/14/2007.

Australia No. C2 and Cover A300

22c, Australia No. C2, vert.

Perf. 13x13½, 13½x13

1981, Mar. 25		**Litho.**		
776	A300	22c multicolored	.45	.45
777	A300	60c shown	1.10	.80

Australia-United Kingdom official airmail service, 50th anniv.

Map of Australia, APEX Emblem A301

1981, Apr. 6		**Photo.**	**Perf. 13x13½**	
778	A301	22c multicolored	.40	.25

50th anniv. of APEX (young men's service club).

Queen Elizabeth's Personal Flag of Australia A302

1981, Apr. 21		**Litho.**	**Perf. 13**	
779	A302	22c multicolored	.40	.25

Queen Elizabeth II, 55th birthday. Perf 14x14¾ examples in a booklet pane of 4 come from the booklet footnoted under No. 2507.

License Inspected, Forrest Creek, by S.T. Gill — A303

Gold Rush Era (Sketches by S.T. Gill): No. 781, Puddling. No. 782, Quality of Washing Stuff. No. 783, Diggers on Route to Deposit Gold.

1981, May 20			**Perf. 13x13½**	
780	A303	22c multicolored	.40	.30
781	A303	22c multicolored	.40	.30
782	A303	22c multicolored	.40	.30
783	A303	22c multicolored	.40	.30
		Nos. 780-783 (4)	1.60	1.20

Lace Monitor — A303a

Tasmanian Tiger — A304

Two Types of A304:
Type I — Indistinct line at right of ear, stripes even with base of tail.
Type II — Heavy line at right of ear, stripes longer.

3c, Corroboree frog. 5c, Queensland hairy-nosed wombat. 15c, Eastern snake-necked tortoise. 25c, Greater bilby, vert. 27c, Blue Mountains tree frog. 30c, Bridled nail-tailed wallaby, vert. 40c, Smooth knob-tailed gecko. 50c, Leadbeater's opossum. 55c, Stick-nest rat, vert. 65c, Yellow-faced whip snake. 70c, Crucifix toad. 75c, Eastern water dragon. 85c, Centralian blue-tongued lizard. 90c, Freshwater crocodile. 95c, Thorny devil.

1981-83			**Litho.**	
784	A303a	1c shown	.25	.25
785	A303a	3c multicolored	.25	.25
786	A304	5c multicolored	.35	.35
b.		Imperf., dated "2007"	.25	.25
787	A303a	15c multicolored	.35	.35
788	A304	24c Type I, photo. & litho.	.60	.40
a.		Shown, type II, litho.	.70	.40
b.		Imperf., dated "2007"	.50	.50
789	A304	25c multicolored	.70	.45
b.		Imperf., dated "2007"	.60	.60
790	A303a	27c multicolored	.60	.25
791	A304	30c multicolored	.90	.60
a.		Imperf., dated "2007"	.70	.70
792	A303a	40c multicolored	.85	.45
793	A304	50c multicolored	1.10	.70
b.		Imperf., dated "2007"	1.10	1.10
c.		Booklet pane, 2 each #788b, 793b	3.50	
794	A304	55c multicolored	1.10	.70
a.		Imperf., dated "2007"	1.25	1.25
b.		Booklet pane, #786b, 789b, 791a, 794a	2.75	
795	A303a	65c multicolored	1.40	.70
796	A303a	70c multicolored	1.40	.75
797	A303a	75c multicolored	1.60	.75
798	A303a	85c multicolored	1.90	1.10
799	A303a	90c multicolored	1.90	.90
800	A303a	95c multicolored	2.00	1.10
		Nos. 784-800 (17)	17.25	9.95

Perfs: 1c, 70c, 85c, 95c, 13½; 3c, 15c, 27c, 40c, 50c, 65c, 75c, 90c, 12½x13½; 5c, 25c, 30c, 55c, 13x12½; 24c, 13x13½.
Issued: 24c, 7/1/81; 5c, 25c, 30c, 50c, 55c, 7/15/81; 3c, 27c, 65c, 75c, 4/19/82; 15c, 40c, 90c, 6/16/82. 1c, 70c, 85c, 95c, 2/2/83.
Nos. 786b, 788b, 789b, 791a, 793b, 793c, 794a, 794b issued 6/26/07. No. 788b has wider spacing between text lines than on the original stamps.

1982-84			**Perf. 14x14½, 14½x14**	
785a	A303a	3c ('84)	.70	.45
786a	A304	5c ('84)	1.40	.50
787a	A303a	15c ('84)	1.25	.60
789a	A304	25c ('83)	1.40	.60
790a	A303a	27c	1.10	.30
792a	A303a	40c ('84)	3.00	1.10
793a	A304	50c ('83)	2.25	1.10
795a	A303a	65c ('84)	2.25	1.40
797a	A303a	75c ('84)	2.60	1.40
		Nos. 785a-797a (9)	15.95	7.45

Prince Charles and Lady Diana A305

1981, July 29		**Litho.**	**Perf. 13**	
804	A305	24c multicolored	.45	.25
805	A305	60c multicolored	1.25	1.50

Royal Wedding.

Fungi — A306

24c, Cortinarius cinnabarinus. 35c, Coprinus comatus. 55c, Armillaria lute-obubalina. 60c, Cortinarius austro-venetus.

1981, Aug. 19		**Litho.**	**Perf. 13**	
806	A306	24c multicolored	.55	.40
807	A306	35c multicolored	.70	.70
808	A306	55c multicolored	1.00	1.00
809	A306	60c multicolored	1.10	1.10
		Nos. 806-809 (4)	3.35	3.20

Intl. Year of the Disabled — A307

1981, Sept. 16			**Perf. 14x13½**	
810	A307	24c multicolored	.45	.30

Christmas Bush for His Adorning — A308

Christmas (Carols by William James and John Wheeler): 30c, The Silver Stars are in the Sky. 60c, Noeltime.

1981		**Litho.**	**Perf. 13x13½**	
811	A308	18c multicolored	.35	.25
812	A308	30c multicolored	.60	.55
813	A308	60c multicolored	1.10	1.00
		Nos. 811-813 (3)	2.05	1.80

Issue dates: 30c, Sept. 28; others, Nov. 2.

Globe — A309

1981, Sept. 30				
814	A309	24c multicolored	.55	.40
815	A309	60c multicolored	1.00	1.00

Commonwealth Heads of Government Meeting, Melbourne, Sept. 30-Oct. 7.

Yacht — A310

24c, Ocean racer. 35c, Lightweight sharpie. 55c, 12-Meter. 60c, Sabot.

1981, Oct. 14		**Litho.**	**Perf. 13x13½**	
816	A310	24c multicolored	.45	.30
817	A310	35c multicolored	.65	.50
818	A310	55c multicolored	1.00	.90
819	A310	60c multicolored	1.10	1.00
		Nos. 816-819 (4)	3.20	2.70

Australia Day, Jan. 26 A311

1982, Jan. 20		**Litho.**	**Perf. 13x13½**	
820	A311	24c multicolored	.45	.30

Sperm Whale A312

35c, Southern right whale, vert. 55c, Blue whale, vert. 60c, Humpback whale.

1982, Feb. 17			**Perf. 13x13½, 13½x13**	
821	A312	24c shown	.60	.55
822	A312	35c multicolored	.80	.70
823	A312	55c multicolored	1.00	1.00
824	A312	60c multicolored	1.10	1.10
		Nos. 821-824 (4)	3.50	3.35

A trial printing of No. 824 exists with a greenish blue background and no white streaks at the UL. A small number of these stamps were sold by mistake.

Elizabeth II, 56th Birthday — A313

1982, Apr. 21			**Perf. 13½**	
825	A313	27c multicolored	.50	.40

Roses — A314

27c, Marjorie Atherton. 40c, Imp. 65c, Minnie Watson. 75c, Satellite.

1982, May 19   Perf. 13x13½
826	A314	27c multicolored	.50	.30
827	A314	40c multicolored	.75	.60
828	A314	65c multicolored	1.10	1.00
829	A314	75c multicolored	1.25	1.10
		Nos. 826-829 (4)	3.60	3.00

50th Anniv. of Australian Broadcasting Commission A315

No. 830, Announcer, microphone. No. 831, Emblem.

1982, June 16   Perf. 13½x13
830	A315	27c multicolored	.45	.35
831	A315	27c multicolored	.45	.35
a.		Pair, #830-831	1.00	1.00

Nos. 830-831 se-tenant in continuous design.

Alice Springs Post Office, 1872 — A316

No. 833, Kingston, 1869. No. 834, York, 1893. No. 835, Flemington, 1890, vert. No. 836, Forbes, 1881, vert. No. 837, Launceston, 1889, vert. No. 838, Rockhampton, 1892, vert.

1982, Aug. 4   Perf. 13½x14, 14x13½
832	A316	27c shown	.50	.30
833	A316	27c multicolored	.50	.30
834	A316	27c multicolored	.50	.30
835	A316	27c multicolored	.50	.30
836	A316	27c multicolored	.50	.30
837	A316	27c multicolored	.50	.30
838	A316	27c multicolored	.50	.30
		Nos. 832-838 (7)	3.50	2.10

Christmas — A317

1st Australian Christmas cards, 1881. 21c, horiz.

1982   Litho.   Perf. 14½
839	A317	21c multicolored	.35	.25
840	A317	35c multicolored	.65	.40
841	A317	75c multicolored	1.25	1.00
		Nos. 839-841 (3)	2.25	1.65

Issue dates: 35c, Sept. 15; others, Nov. 1.

12th Commonwealth Games, Brisbane, Sept. 30-Oct. 9 — A318

1982, Sept. 22   Litho.   Perf. 14x14½
842	A318	27c Archery	.50	.40
843	A318	27c Boxing	.50	.40
844	A318	27c Weightlifting	.50	.40
a.		Souvenir sheet of 3, #842-844	1.75	1.75

845	A318	75c Pole vault	1.25	1.25
a.		Booklet pane of 4, #842-845, perf. 14x14¾ ('06)	3.00	—
		Nos. 842-845 (4)	2.75	2.45

Nos. 842-842 are perf 14½. No. 844a is perf 13½x13.
No. 845a issued 3/1/2006.

Natl. Stamp Week A319

1982, Sept. 27   Perf. 13x13½
846	A319	27c No. 132	.50	.30

A320

Design: Gurgurr (Moon Spirit), Bark Painting by Yirawala Gunwinggu Tribe.

1982, Oct. 12   Perf. 14½
847	A320	27c multicolored	.50	.30

Opening of Natl. Gallery, Canberra.

A321

Various eucalypts (gum trees): 1c, Pink-flowered marri. 2c, Gungurru. 3c, Red-flowering gum. 10c, Tasmanian blue gum. 27c, Forrest's marlock.

Perf. 12½x13½
1982, Nov. 17   Photo.
848	A321	1c multicolored	.25	.25
849	A321	2c multicolored	.25	.25
850	A321	3c multicolored	1.00	1.50
851	A321	10c multicolored	1.00	1.75
852	A321	27c multicolored	.55	.50
a.		Bklt. pane, #850-851, 2 #848-849, 3 #852 + label	4.00	
b.		Bklt. pane, 2 ea #848-849, 852	2.10	
		Nos. 848-852 (5)	3.05	4.25

Nos. 848-852 issued in booklets only.

Mimi Spirits Singing and Dancing, by David Milaybuma A322

Aboriginal Bark Paintings: Music and dance of the Mimi Spirits, Gunwinggu Tribe. 40c, Lofty Nabardayal. 65c, Jimmy Galareya. 75c, Dick Nguleingulei Murrumurru.

1982, Nov. 17   Litho.   Perf. 13½x14
853	A322	27c shown	.50	.30
854	A322	40c multicolored	.75	.70
855	A322	65c multicolored	1.10	.60
856	A322	75c multicolored	1.25	1.00
		Nos. 853-856 (4)	3.60	2.60

Historic Fire Engines A323

27c, Shand Mason Steam, 1891. 40c, Hotchkiss, 1914. 65c, Ahrens-Fox PS2, 1929. 75c, Merryweather Manual, 1851.

1983, Jan. 12   Perf. 13½x14
857	A323	27c multicolored	.50	.30
858	A323	40c multicolored	.75	.60
859	A323	65c multicolored	1.10	.90
860	A323	75c multicolored	1.25	1.00
		Nos. 857-860 (4)	3.60	2.80

Australia Day — A324

1983, Jan. 26   Litho.   Perf. 14½
861	A324	27c Sirius	.50	.45
862	A324	27c Supply	.50	.45
a.		Pair, #861-862	1.10	1.10

A325

1983, Feb. 2   Perf. 14x13½
863	A325	27c multicolored	.50	.30
863a		Perf. 14¾x14, dated "2013" (#1003b)	.70	.70

Australia-New Zealand Closer Economic Relationship agreement (ANZCER). Issued: No. 863a, 5/10/2013.

A326

No. 864, Equality, dignity. No. 865, Social justice, cooperation. No. 866, Liberty, freedom. No. 867, Peace, harmony.

1983, Mar. 9   Litho.   Perf. 14½
864	A326	27c multicolored	.50	.30
865	A326	27c multicolored	.50	.30
866	A326	27c multicolored	.50	.30
867	A326	75c multicolored	1.40	1.00
		Nos. 864-867 (4)	2.90	1.90

Commonwealth day.

Queen Elizabeth II, 57th Birthday A327

1983, Apr. 20   Perf. 14½
868	A327	27c Britannia	.50	.35

World Communications Year — A328

1983, May 18   Litho.   Perf. 13½x14
869	A328	27c multicolored	.50	.35

50th Anniv. of Australian Jaycees Youth Organization A329

1983, June 8
870	A329	27c multicolored	.50	.35

St. John Ambulance Cent. — A330

1983, June 8   Perf. 13½x14
871	A330	27c multicolored	.50	.35

Regent Skipper — A331

10c, Cairn's birdwing. 20c, Macleay's swallowtail. 27c, Ulysses. 30c, Chlorinda hairstreak. 35c, Blue tiger. 45c, Big greasy. 60c, Wood white. 80c, Amaryllis azure. $1, Sword grass brown.

1983   Perf. 13½, 14½x14 (30c)
872	A331	4c shown	.30	.25
873	A331	10c multicolored	.30	.25
874	A331	20c multicolored	.45	.25
875	A331	27c multicolored	.65	.25
875A	A331	30c multicolored	.85	.25
876	A331	35c multicolored	.70	.35
877	A331	45c multicolored	1.00	.45
878	A331	60c multicolored	1.40	.55
879	A331	80c multicolored	1.90	.80
880	A331	$1 multicolored	2.40	.90
		Nos. 872-880 (10)	9.95	4.30

Issue dates: 30c, Oct. 24; others, June 15.

The Sentimental Bloke, by C.J. Dennis, 1909 — A332

Folktale scenes: a, The bloke. b, Doreen-the intro. c, The stror at coot. d, Hitched. e, The mooch of life.

1983, Aug. 3   Perf. 14½
881		Strip of 5	2.50	2.50
a.-e.	A332	27c multi, any single	.45	.40

Kookaburra Bird Wearing Santa Hat — A333

24c, Nativity. 85c, Holiday beach scene.

1983   Litho.   Perf. 13½x14
882	A333	24c multicolored	.40	.30
883	A333	35c multicolored	.60	.35
884	A333	85c multicolored	1.50	.90
		Nos. 882-884 (3)	2.50	1.55

Christmas. Issued: No. 883, 9/14; Nos. 882, 884, 11/2.

Inland Explorers — A334

Clay sculptures by Dianne Quinn: No. 885, Ludwig Leichhardt (1813-48). No. 886, William John Wills (1834-61), Robert O'Hara Burke (1821-61). No. 887, Paul Edmund de Strzelecki (1797-1873). No. 888, Alexander Forrest (1849-1901).

1983, Sept. 26   *Perf. 14½*
885	A334	30c multicolored	.50	.35
886	A334	30c multicolored	.50	.35
887	A334	30c multicolored	.50	.35
888	A334	30c multicolored	.50	.35
		Nos. 885-888 (4)	2.00	1.40

Australia Day — A335

1984, Jan. 26   Litho.   *Perf. 13½x14*
889	A335	30c Cooks' Cottage	.50	.30

50th Anniv. of Official Air Mail Service — A336

Pilot Charles Ulm (1898-1934); his plane, "Faith in Australia," and different flight covers: No. 890, Australia-New Zealand. No. 891, Australia-Papua New Guinea.

1984, Feb. 22   Litho.   *Perf. 13½*
890	A336	45c multicolored	1.00	1.25
891	A336	45c multicolored	1.00	1.25
a.		Pair, #890-891	2.25	3.00

Thomson, 1898 — A337

Australian-made vintage cars: b, Tarrant, 1906. c, Australian Six, 1919. d, Summit, 1923. e, Chic, 1924.

1984, Mar. 14   *Perf. 14½*
892		Strip of 5	3.00	3.00
a.-e.	A337	30c any single	.45	.45

Queen Elizabeth II, 58th Birthday A338

1984, Apr. 18   *Perf. 14½*
893	A338	30c multicolored	.55	.30

Clipper Ships A339

30c, Cutty Sark, 1869, vert. 45c, Orient, 1853. 75c, Sobraon, 1866. 85c, Thermopylae, 1868, vert.

1984, May 23   *Perf. 14x13½, 13½x14*
894	A339	30c multicolored	.55	.45
895	A339	45c multicolored	.85	.80
896	A339	75c multicolored	1.25	1.10
897	A339	85c multicolored	1.50	1.25
		Nos. 894-897 (4)	4.15	3.60

Freestyle Skiing — A340

No. 899, Slalom, horiz. No. 900, Cross-country, horiz. No. 901, Downhill.

1984, June 6   Litho.   *Perf. 14½*
898	A340	30c shown	.50	.35
899	A340	30c multicolored	.50	.35
900	A340	30c multicolored	.50	.35
901	A340	30c multicolored	.50	.35
		Nos. 898-901 (4)	2.00	1.40

Coral Hopper — A341

3c, Jimble. 5c, Tasseled anglerfish. 10c, Stonefish. 20c, Red handfish. 25c, Orange-tipped cowrie. 30c, Choat's wrasse. 33c, Leafy sea dragon. 40c, Red velvet fish. 45c, Textile cone shell. 50c, Blue-lined surgeonfish. 55c, Bennett's nudibranch. 60c, Lionfish. 65c, Stingray. 70c, Blue-ringed octopus. 80c, Pineapple fish. 85c, Regal angelfish. 90c, Crab-eyed goby. $1, Crown of thorns starfish.

Perf. 13½, 14x14½ (30c, 33c)

1984-86   Litho.
902	A341	2c shown	.25	.25
903	A341	3c multicolored	.25	.25
904	A341	5c multicolored	.25	.25
905	A341	10c multicolored	.25	.25
906	A341	20c multicolored	.45	.35
907	A341	25c multicolored	.60	.35
908	A341	30c multicolored	.65	.25
909	A341	33c multicolored	.70	.25
910	A341	40c multicolored	.85	.60
911	A341	45c multicolored	.90	.70
912	A341	50c multicolored	1.00	.70
913	A341	55c multicolored	1.10	.90
914	A341	60c multicolored	1.25	.90
915	A341	65c multicolored	1.25	.90
916	A341	70c multicolored	1.40	1.00
917	A341	80c multicolored	1.60	1.00
918	A341	85c multicolored	1.75	1.10
919	A341	90c multicolored	1.75	1.10
920	A341	$1 multicolored	2.00	1.10
		Nos. 902-920 (19)	18.25	12.20

Issued: 2c, 25c, 30c, 50c, 55c, 85c, 6/18; 33c, 1/20/85; 5c, 20c, 40c, 80c, 90c, 6/12/85; 3c, 10c, 45c, 60c, 65c, 70c, $1, 6/11/86.

1984 Summer Olympics A342

Event stages: No. 922, Start (facing down). No. 923, Competing (facing right). No. 924, Finish, vert.

Perf. 13½x14, 14x13½

1984, July 25   Litho.
922	A342	30c multicolored	.60	.35
923	A342	30c multicolored	.60	.35
924	A342	30c multicolored	.60	.35
		Nos. 922-924 (3)	1.80	1.05

Ausipex '84 — A343

Designs: No. 926: a, Victoria #3. b, New South Wales #1. c, Tasmania #1. d, South Australia #1. e, Western Australia #1. f, Queensland #3.

1984   Litho.   *Perf. 14½*
925	A343	30c No. 2	.50	.35

Souvenir Sheet
926		Sheet of 7	4.00	4.00
a.-f.	A343	30c any single	.50	.40

No. 926 contains Nos. 925, 926a-926f. Issued: No. 925, Aug. 22; No. 926, Sept. 21.

Christmas — A344

24c, Angel and Child. 30c, Veiled Virgin and Child. 40c, Angel. 50c, Three Kings. 85c, Madonna and Child.

1984   Litho.   *Perf. 14x13½*
927	A344	24c multicolored	.45	.25
928	A344	30c multicolored	.55	.30
929	A344	40c multicolored	.75	.65
930	A344	50c multicolored	.90	.90
931	A344	85c multicolored	1.50	1.25
		Nos. 927-931 (5)	4.15	3.35

Stained-glass windows. Issue dates: 40c, Sept. 17; others, Oct. 30.

European Settlement Bicentenary A345

Design: No. 932, Bicentennial Emblem. Rock paintings: No. 933, Stick figures, Cobar Region, New South Wales. No. 934, Bunjil's Cave, Grampians, Western Victoria. No. 935, Quinkan Gallery, Cape York, Queensland. No. 936, Wandjina Spirit and Snake Babies, Gibb River, Western Australia. No. 937, Rock Python, Western Australia. No. 938, Silver Barramundi, Kakadu Natl. Park, Northern Territory. 85c, Rock Possum, Kakadu Natl. Park.

1984, Nov. 7   Litho.   *Perf. 14½*
932	A345	30c multicolored	.55	.30
933	A345	30c multicolored	.55	.30
934	A345	30c multicolored	.55	.30
935	A345	30c multicolored	.55	.30
936	A345	30c multicolored	.55	.30
937	A345	30c multicolored	.55	.30
938	A345	30c multicolored	.55	.30
939	A345	85c multicolored	1.75	2.00
		Nos. 932-939 (8)	5.60	4.10

Settlement of Victoria Sesquicentenary A346

No. 940, Helmeted honeyeater. No. 941, Leadbeater's possum.

1984, Nov. 19
940	A346	30c multicolored	.50	.50
941	A346	30c multicolored	.50	.50
a.		Pair, #940-941	1.25	1.25

Australia Day A347

No. 942, Musgrave Ranges, by Sidney Nolan. No. 943, The Walls of China, by Russell Drysdale.

1985, Jan. 25   Litho.
942		30c multicolored	.55	.55
a.		Pair, #942 tete-beche	2.50	2.50

943		30c multicolored	.55	.55
a.	A347	Pair, #942-943	1.50	1.50
b.		Pair, #943 tete-beche	2.50	2.50

Intl. Youth Year — A348

1985, Feb. 13   Litho.   *Perf. 14x13½*
944	A348	30c multicolored	.55	.40

Royal Victorian Volunteer Artillery — A349

Colonial military uniforms: b, Western Australian Pinjarrah Cavalry. c, New South Wales Lancers. d, New South Wales Contingent to the Sudan. e, Victorian Mounted Rifles.

1985, Feb. 25   *Perf. 14½*
945		Strip of 5	3.25	3.25
a.-e.	A349	33c any single	.55	.30

District Nursing Service Centenary — A350

1985, Mar. 13
946	A350	33c multicolored	.60	.40

Australian Cockatoo — A351

Perf. 14 Horiz. on 1 or 2 sides

1985, Mar. 13
947	A351	1c apple grn, yel & buff	3.00	4.00
948	A351	33c apple grn, yel, & lt grnsh blue	1.25	1.00
a.		Bklt. pane, 1 #947, 3 #948	6.50	

Issued in booklets only.

A352

No. 949, Abel Tasman, explorer. No. 950, The Eendracht. No. 951, William Dampier. No. 952, Globe and hand.

1985, Apr. 10   *Perf. 13*
949	A352	33c multicolored	.65	.45
950	A352	33c multicolored	.65	.45
951	A352	33c multicolored	.65	.45
952	A352	90c multicolored	1.90	2.25
a.		Souvenir sheet of 4, #949-952	5.50	5.50
		Nos. 949-952 (4)	3.85	3.60

Queen Elizabeth II,
59th
Birthday — A353

33c, Queen's Badge, Order of Australia.

1985, Apr. 22   **Perf. 14x13½**
953 A353 33c multicolored   .65 .45
a. Perf. 14¾x14, dated "2013"
      (#1003b)   .85 .85
    Issued: No. 953a, 5/10/2013.

A354

1985, May 15   Litho.   Perf. 14x13
954 A354 33c Soil   .60 .25
955 A354 50c Air   .90 .75
956 A354 80c Water   1.50 1.00
957 A354 90c Energy   1.60 1.25
    Nos. 954-957 (4)   4.60 3.25
    Environmental conservation.

A356

Illustrations from classic children's books: a,
Elves & Fairies, by Annie Rentoul. b, The
Magic Pudding, text and illustrations by Nor-
man Lindsay. c, Ginger Meggs, by James
Charles Bancks. d, Blinky Bill, by Dorothy
Wall. e, Snugglepot and Cuddlepie, by May
Gibbs.

1985, July 17   Litho.   Perf. 14½
960 A356 Strip of 5   3.00 3.00
a.-e.   33c any single   .50 .40

Electronic
Mail — A357

1985, Sept. 18   Litho.
961 A357 33c multicolored   .55 .30

Christmas
A358

Angel in a ship, detail from a drawing by
Albrecht Durer (1471-1528).

1985, Sept. 18   Litho.
962 A358 45c multicolored   .80 .35
    See Nos. 967-970.

Coastal
Shipwrecks
A359

Salvaged antiquities: 33c, Astrolabe from
Batavia, 1629. 50c, German beardman (Bel-
larmine) jug from Vergulde Draeck, 1656. 90c,
Wooden bobbins from Batavia, and scissors
from Zeewijk, 1727. $1, Silver buckle from
Zeewijk.

1985, Oct. 2   Litho.   Perf. 13
963 A359 33c multicolored   .65 .25
964 A359 50c multicolored   1.00 .95
965 A359 90c multicolored   1.90 1.75
966 A359 $1 multicolored   2.60 2.25
    Nos. 963-966 (4)   6.15 5.20

Christmas Type of 1985
Illustrations by Scott Hartshorne.

1985, Nov. 1   Litho.   Perf. 14
967 A358 27c Angel with trumpet   .50 .25
968 A358 33c Angel with bells   .60 .40
969 A358 55c Angel with star   1.00 .90
970 A358 90c Angel with orna-
              ment   1.50 1.50
    Nos. 967-970 (4)   3.60 3.05

Australia
Day — A360

1986, Jan. 24   Litho.   Perf. 14½
971 A360 33c Aboriginal painting   .55 .35

AUSSAT — A361

Various communications satellites.

1986, Jan. 24
972 A361 33c multicolored   .65 .30
973 A361 80c multicolored   1.60 1.60

South
Australia,
Sesquicent.
A362

No. 974, Sailing ship Buffalo. No. 975, City
Sign, sculpture by O.H. Hajek.

1986, Feb. 12   Perf. 13½x14
974 A362 33c multicolored   .50 .45
975 A362 33c multicolored   .50 .45
a.   Pair, #974-975   1.50 1.50

Cook's New
Holland
Expedition
A363

No. 976, Hibiscus merankensis. No. 977,
Banksia serrata. No. 978, Dillenia alata. No.
979, Corria reflexa. No. 980, Parkinson. No.
981, Banks.

1986, Mar. 12   Perf. 13
976 A363 33c multicolored   .65 .35
977 A363 33c multicolored   .65 .35
978 A363 50c multicolored   1.10 1.25
979 A363 80c multicolored   1.60 1.40
980 A363 90c multicolored   1.75 1.75
981 A363 90c multicolored   1.75 1.75
    Nos. 976-981 (6)   7.50 6.85
Australian bicentennial. Sydney Parkinson
(d. 1775), artist. Sir Joseph Banks (1743-
1820), naturalist.

Halley's
Comet — A364

33c, Radio telescope, trajectory diagram.

1986, Apr. 9   Perf. 14x13½
982 A364 33c multicolored   .65 .40

Elizabeth II, 60th
Birthday — A365

1986, Apr. 21   Perf. 14½
983 A365 33c multicolored   .65 .40

Horses
A366

33c, Brumbies. 80c, Stock horse mustering.
90c, Show-jumping. $1, Australian pony.

1986, May 21
984 A366 33c multicolored   .60 .30
985 A366 80c multicolored   1.50 1.50
986 A366 90c multicolored   1.60 1.60
987 A366 $1 multicolored   1.75 1.75
    Nos. 984-987 (4)   5.45 5.15

Click Go the
Shears, Folk Song
— A366a

Lines from the song: b, Old shearer stands.
c, Ringer looks around. d, Boss of the board.
e, Tar-boy is there. f, Shearing is all over.

1986, July 21   Litho.   Perf. 14½
987A   Strip of 5   3.00 3.00
b.-f. A366a 33c, any single   .50 .40
Amalgamated Shearers' Union, predeces-
sor of the Australian Workers' Union, cent.

Australia
Bicentennial
A367

Settling of Botany Bay penal colony: No.
988, King George III, c. 1767, by A. Ramsay.
No. 989, Lord Sydney, secretary of state,
1783-1789, by Gilbert Stuart. No. 990, Capt.
Arthur Phillip, 1st penal colony governor, by F.
Wheatley, 1786. $1, Capt. John Hunter, gover-
nor, 1795-1800, by W. B. Bennett, 1815.

1986, Aug. 6   Litho.   Perf. 13
988 A367 33c multicolored   .85 .70
989 A367 33c multicolored   .85 .70
990 A367 33c multicolored   .85 .70
991 A367 $1 multicolored   2.25 2.25
    Nos. 988-991 (4)   4.80 4.35

Wildlife — A368

Designs: a, Red kangaroo. b, Emu. c, Koala.
d, Kookaburra. e, Platypus.

1986, Aug. 13   Perf. 14½x14
992   Strip of 5   3.50 3.50
a.-e. A368 36c any single   .70 .60

Alpine
Wildflowers — A369

3c, Royal bluebell. 5c, Alpine marsh marigold. 25c, Mount Buffalo sunray. 36c, Silver
snow daisy.

Rouletted 9½ Vert. on 1 or 2 sides
1986, Aug. 25   Booklet Stamps
993 A369 3c multicolored   1.10 1.25
994 A369 5c multicolored   2.40 2.60
995 A369 25c multicolored   2.40 2.25
996 A369 36c multicolored   1.00 .70
a.   Bklt. pane, #993, #994, 2 #996   5.75
b.   Bklt. pane, #993, #995, 2 #996   6.00
    Nos. 993-996 (4)   6.90 6.80

Orchids — A370

36c, Elythranthera emarginata. 55c, Dendrobium nindii. 90c, Caleana major. $1,
Thelymitra variegata.

1986, Sept. 18   Perf. 14½
997 A370 36c multicolored   .75 .25
998 A370 55c multicolored   1.10 1.10
999 A370 90c multicolored   1.90 1.90
1000 A370 $1 multicolored   2.25 2.25
    Nos. 997-1000 (4)   6.00 5.50

America's Cup
Triumph '83 — A371

No. 1001, Australia II crossing finish line.
No. 1002, Trophy. No. 1003, Boxing kangaroo.

1986, Sept. 26   Perf. 14x13½
1001 A371 36c multicolored   .65 .50
1002 A371 36c multicolored   .65 .50
1003 A371 36c multicolored   .65 .50
a.   Perf. 14¾x14, dated "2013"
       (#1003b)   .95 .95
b.   Booklet pane of 4, #502a,
       863a, 953a, 1003a   3.50   —
    Nos. 1001-1003 (3)   1.95 1.50

Issued: Nos. 1003a, 1003b, 5/10/2013. No.
1003b was issued in a booklet also containing
Nos. 1284b, 3534d and 3918.

Intl. Peace Year — A372

1986, Oct. 22   Litho.   Perf. 14x13½
1004   A372   36c multicolored   .65   .35

Christmas A373

Kindergarten nativity play: No. 1005, Holy Family, vert. No. 1006, Three Kings, vert. No. 1007, Angels. No. 1008a, Angels, peasants. No. 1008b, Holy Family, angels, vert. No. 1008c, Shepherd, angels, vert. No. 1008d, Three Kings. No. 1008e, Shepherds.

1986, Nov. 3   Litho.
1005   A373   30c multicolored   .60   .35
  a.   Perf 14x13½   1.25 1.25
1006   A373   36c multicolored   .70   .55
1007   A373   60c multicolored   1.25 1.25
        Nos. 1005-1007 (3)   2.55 2.15

Souvenir Sheet
1008   Sheet of 5   3.25 3.25
  a.-e.   A373 30c any single   .60   .60

Perfs: Nos. 1005-1006, 1008c, 15x14½; Nos. 1007, 1008a 1008e, 14½x15. No. 1008b, 15x14½x15x15; No. 1008d, 14½x15x14½x14½.

Australia Day — A374

No. 1009, Flag, circuit board. No. 1010, Made in Australia campaign emblem.

1987, Jan. 23   Litho.   Perf. 13½x14
1009   A374   36c multicolored   .70   .40
1010   A374   36c multicolored   .70   .40

America's Cup — A375

Views of yachts racing.

1987, Jan. 28   Perf. 15x14½
1011   A375   36c multicolored   .70   .30
1012   A375   55c multicolored   1.10 1.25
1013   A375   90c multicolored   1.75 1.40
1014   A375 $1 multicolored   2.00 1.75
        Nos. 1011-1014 (4)   5.55 5.20

Fruits — A376

36c, Melons, grapes. 65c, Tropical fruit. 90c, Pears, apples, oranges. $1, Berries, peaches.

1987, Feb. 11   Perf. 14x13½
1015   A376   36c multicolored   .70   .30
1016   A376   65c multicolored   1.25 1.25
1017   A376   90c multicolored   1.75 1.40
1018   A376 $1 multicolored   2.00 1.75
        Nos. 1015-1018 (4)   5.70 4.70

Agricultural Shows — A377

1987, Apr. 10   Litho.   Perf. 14x13½
1019   A377   36c Livestock   .70   .30
1020   A377   65c Produce   1.25 1.25
1021   A377   90c Carnival   1.75 1.75
1022   A377 $1 Farmers   2.25 2.25
        Nos. 1019-1022 (4)   5.95 5.55

Queen Elizabeth II, 61st Birthday A378

1987, Apr. 21   Perf. 13½x14
1023   A378   36c multicolored   .70   .40

First Fleet Leaving England A379

Continuous design: No. 1024a, Convicts awaiting transportation. b, Capt. Arthur Phillip, Mrs. Phillip, longboat on shore. c, Sailors relaxing and working. d, Longboats heading from and to fleet. 4e, Fleet in harbor.
No. 1025a, Longboat approaching Tenerife, The Canary Isls. b, Fishing in Tenerife Harbor. $1, Fleet, dolphins.

1987   Perf. 13
1024   Strip of 5   3.50 3.50
  a.-e.   A379 36c any single   .70   .40
1025   Pair   1.50 1.50
  a.-b.   A379 36c any single   .70   .40
1026   A379 $1 multicolored   2.25 2.25
        Nos. 1024-1026 (3)   7.25 7.25

Australia bicent.; departure of the First Fleet, May 13, 1787; arrival at Tenerife, June 1787.
Issued: No. 1024, 5/13; Nos. 1025-1026, 6/3.

1987, Aug. 6
First Fleet arrives at Rio de Janeiro, Aug. 1787: a, Whale, storm in the Atlantic. b, Citrus grove. c, Market. d, Religious procession. e, Fireworks over harbor.
1027   Strip of 5   3.50 3.50
  a.-e.   A379 37c any single   .65   .40

No. 1027 has a continuous design.

1987, Oct. 13
First Fleet arrives at Cape of Good Hope, Oct. 1787: No. 1028a, British officer surveys livestock and supplies, Table Mountain. No. 1028b, Ships anchored in Table Bay. No. 1029, Fishermen pull in nets as the Fleet approaches the Cape.
1028   Pair   1.50 1.50
  a.-b.   A379 37c any single   .75   .75
1029   A379 $1 multicolored   2.25 1.40

No. 1028 has a continuous design.

1988, Jan. 26
Arrival of the First Fleet, Sydney Cove, Jan. 1788: a, Five aborigines on shore. b, Four aborigines on shore. c, Kangaroos. d, White cranes. e, Flag raising.
1030   Strip of 5   3.75 3.75
  a.-e.   A379 37c any single   .75   .45

Printed se-tenant in a continuous design.

The Early Years: Sydney Cove and Parramatta Colonies A380

Details from panorama "View of Sydney from the East Side of the Cove," 1808, painted by convict artist John Eyre to illustrate The Present Picture of New South Wales, published in London in 1811, and paintings in British and Australian museums: a, Government House, 1790, Sydney, by midshipman George Raper. b, Government Farm, Parramatta, 1791, attributed to the Port Jackson Painter. c, Parramatta Road, 1796, attributed to convict artist Thomas Watling. d, The Rocks and Sydney Cove, 1800, an aquatint engraving by Edward Dayes. e, Sydney Hospital, 1803, by George William Evans, an explorer and surveyor-general of New South Wales. Printed se-tenant in a continuous design.

1988, Apr. 13   Litho.   Perf. 13
1031   Strip of 5   3.50 3.50
  a.-e.   A380 37c any single   .65   .40

Australia Bicentennial.

The Man from Snowy River, 1890, Ballad by A.B. Paterson — A381

Excerpts: a, At the station. b, Mountain bred. c, Terrible descent. d, At their heels. e, Brought them back.

1987, June 24   Perf. 14x13½
1034   Strip of 5   3.50 3.50
  a.-e.   A381 36c any single   .70   .50

Printed se-tenant in a continuous design.

Fauna — A382

Designs: a, Possum. b, Cockatoo. c, Wombat. d, Rosella. e, Echidna.

1987, July 1   Perf. 14½x14
1035   Strip of 5   3.75 3.75
  a.-e.   A382 37c any single   .75   .45

Printed se-tenant in a continuous design.

Technology — A383

1987, Aug. 19   Perf. 14½
1036   A383   37c Bionic ear   .75   .30
1037   A383   53c Microchips   1.10   .75
1038   A383   63c Robotics   1.25 1.10
1039   A383   68c Zirconia ceramics   1.40 1.25
        Nos. 1036-1039 (4)   4.50 3.40

Children A384

37c, Crayfishing. 55c, Cat's cradle. 90c, Eating meat pies. $1, Playing with a joey.

1987, Sept. 16
1040   A384   37c multicolored   .75   .25
1041   A384   55c multicolored   1.10 1.25
1042   A384   90c multicolored   1.75 1.75
1043   A384 $1 multicolored   2.25 2.25
        Nos. 1040-1043 (4)   5.85 5.50

Christmas A385

Carolers: a, Woman, two girls. b, Man, two girls. c, Four children. d, Man, two women, boy. e, Six youths. 37c, three women, two men. Nos. 1044a-1044e are vert.

1987, Nov. 2   Litho.   Perf. 14½
1044   Strip of 5   3.25 3.25
  a.-e.   A385 30c any single   .60   .55

Perf. 13½x14
1045   A385   37c multicolored   .75   .45
1046   A385   63c shown   1.75 1.10
        Nos. 1044-1046 (3)   5.75 4.80

Carols by Candlelight, Christmas Eve, Sidney Myer Bowl, Melbourne.

Aboriginal Crafts — A386

Designs: 3c, Spearthrower, Western Australia. 15c, Shield, New South Wales. No. 1049, Basket, Queensland. No. 1050, Bowl, Central Australia. No. 1051, Belt, Northern Territory.

Perf. 15½ Horiz.

1987, Oct. 13   Photo.
1047   A386   3c multicolored   1.25 1.25
1048   A386   15c multicolored   4.50 4.50
1049   A386   37c multicolored   1.25 1.25
  a.   Bklt. pane, 2 ea #1047, 1049   5.75
1050   A386   37c multicolored   1.10 1.10
1051   A386   37c multicolored   1.25 1.25
  a.   Bklt. pane, #1048, 3 #1050, 2
            #1051   11.50
        Nos. 1047-1051 (5)   9.35 9.35

Issued only in booklets.

Caricature of Australian Koala and American Bald Eagle — A387

1988, Jan. 26   Perf. 13
1052   A387   37c multicolored   .75   .40

Australia bicentennial. See No. 1086 and US No. 2370.

Living Together — A388

Cartoons: 1c, Religion. 2c, Industry. 3c, Local government. 4c, Trade unions. 5c, Parliament. 10c, Transportation. 15c, Sports. 20c, Commerce. 25c, Housing. 30c, Welfare. 37c, Postal services. 39c, Tourism. 40c, Recreation. 45c, Health. 50c, Mining. 53c, Primary industry. 55c, Education. 60c, Armed Forces. 63c, Police. 65c, Telecommunications. 68c, The media. 70c, Science and technology. 75c, Visual arts. 80c, Performing arts. 90c, Banking. 95c, Law. $1, Rescue and emergency services.

1988   Perf. 14
1053   A388   1c multi   .25   .25
1054   A388   2c multi   .25   .25
1055   A388   3c multi   .25   .25
1056   A388   4c multi   .25   .25
1057   A388   5c multi   .25   .25

1058	A388	10c multi	.25	.25
1059	A388	15c multi	.35	.25
1060	A388	20c multi	.40	.25
1061	A388	25c multi	.50	.25
1062	A388	30c multi	.60	.25
1063	A388	37c multi	.75	.25
a.		Booklet pane of 10	7.50	
1063B	A388	39c multi	.80	.35
c.		Booklet pane of 10	8.00	
1064	A388	40c multi	.80	.45
1065	A388	45c multi	.90	.65
1066	A388	50c multi	1.00	.60
1067	A388	53c multi	1.75	1.00
1068	A388	55c multi	1.10	.75
1069	A388	60c multi	1.50	.90
1070	A388	63c multi	2.00	1.75
1071	A388	65c multi	1.50	1.10
1072	A388	68c multi	2.00	1.75
1073	A388	70c multi	1.50	.95
1074	A388	75c multi	1.60	.95
1075	A388	80c multi	1.75	1.10
1076	A388	90c multi	2.00	1.40
1077	A388	95c multi	2.00	1.10
1078	A388	$1 multi	2.25	1.40
		Nos. 1053-1078 (27)	28.55	18.95

Issued: 1c, 2c, 3c, 5c, 30c, 40c, 55c, 60c, 63c, 65c, 68c, 75c, 95c, 3/16; 39c, 9/28; others, 2/17.

Queen Elizabeth II, 62nd Birthday A389

1988, Apr. 21   **Perf. 14½**
1079   A389 37c multicolored   1.00 .50

EXPO '88, Brisbane, Apr. 30-Oct. 30 — A390

1988, Apr. 29   **Perf. 13**
1080   A390 37c multicolored   1.00 .50

Opening of Parliament House, Canberra A391

1988, May 9   **Perf. 14½**
1081   A391 37c multicolored   1.00 .50

Australia Bicentennial A392

Designs: No. 1082, Colonist, clipper ship. No. 1083, British and Australian parliaments, Queen Elizabeth II. No. 1084, Cricketer W.G. Grace. No. 1085, John Lennon (1940-1980), William Shakespeare (1564-1616) and Sydney Opera House. Nos. 1083a, 1085a have continuous design picturing flag of Australia.

1988, June 21   **Litho.**   **Perf. 13**
1082	A392	37c multicolored	.85	.50
1083	A392	37c multicolored	.85	.50
a.		Pair, #1082-1083	1.75	1.75
1084	A392	$1 multicolored	2.25	3.25
a.		Booklet pane of 1, imperf., dated "2007"	3.25	
1085	A392	$1 multicolored	2.25	3.25
a.		Pair, #1084-1085	4.50	6.25
		Nos. 1082-1085 (4)	6.20	7.50

No. 1084a issued 11/14/2007.
See Great Britain Nos. 1222-1225.

Caricature Type of 1988

Design: Caricature of an Australian koala and New Zealand kiwi.

1988, June 21   **Litho.**   **Perf. 13½**
1086   A387 37c multicolored   1.10 .60

Australia bicentennial. See New Zealand No. 907.

"Dream" Lore on Art of the Desert A393

Aboriginal paintings from Papunya Settlement in the Flinders University Art Museum: 37c, Bush Potato Country, by Turkey Tolsen Tjupurrula with by David Corby Tjapaltjarri. 55c, Courtship Rejected, by Limpi Puntungka Tjapangati. 90c, Medicine Story, anonymous. $1, Ancestor Dreaming, by Tim Leura Tjapaltjarri.

1988, Aug. 1   **Litho.**   **Perf. 13**
1087	A393	37c multicolored	1.00	.60
1088	A393	55c multicolored	1.40	1.40
1089	A393	90c multicolored	2.00	2.25
1090	A393	$1 multicolored	2.25	2.25
		Nos. 1087-1090 (4)	6.65	6.50

1988 Summer Olympics, Seoul — A394

37c, Basketball. 65c, Running. $1, Rhythmic gymnastics.

1988, Sept. 14   **Perf. 14½**
1091	A394	37c multicolored	1.00	.85
1092	A394	65c multicolored	1.60	1.60
1093	A394	$1 multicolored	2.60	2.60
		Nos. 1091-1093 (3)	5.20	5.05

34th Commonwealth Parliamentary Conference, Canberra — A395

37c, Scepter and mace.

1988, Sept. 19
1094   A395 37c multicolored   1.00 .50

Works in the Contemporary Decorative Arts Collection at the Natl. Gallery — A396

2c, "Australian Fetish," by Peter Tully. 5c, Vase by Colin Levy. 39c, Teapot by Frank Bauer.

Roulette 9 Horiz.

1988, Sept. 28   **Litho.**
1095	A396	2c multicolored	3.75	6.00
1096	A396	5c multicolored	4.25	6.00
1097	A396	39c multicolored	1.60	.40
a.		Bkt. pane of 3 (2c, 2 39c)	7.00	
b.		Bkt. pane of 6 (5c, 5 39c)	12.50	
		Nos. 1095-1097 (3)	9.60	12.40

Nos. 1095-1097 issued in booklets only.

Views — A397

1988, Oct. 17   **Photo.**   **Perf. 13**
1098	A397	39c The Desert	1.00	1.00
1099	A397	55c The Top End	1.60	1.60
1100	A397	65c The Coast	1.75	1.75
1101	A397	70c The Bush	1.90	1.90
		Nos. 1098-1101 (4)	6.25	6.25

Christmas A398

Children's design contest winning drawings: 32c, Nativity scene, by Danielle Hush, age 7. 39c, Koala wearing a Santa hat, by Kylie Courtney, age 6. 63c, Cockatoo wearing a Santa hat, by Benjamin Stevenson, age 10.

1988, Oct. 31   **Perf. 13½x13**
1102	A398	32c multicolored	.80	.30
1103	A398	39c multicolored	1.00	.60
1104	A398	63c multicolored	1.60	1.60
		Nos. 1102-1104 (3)	3.40	2.50

Sir Henry Parkes (1815-1896), Advocate of the Federation of the Six Colonies — A399

1989, Jan. 25   **Litho.**   **Perf. 14x13½**
1105   A399 39c multicolored   1.00 .50

Australia Day.

Sports — A400

1989, Feb. 13   **Perf. 14x14½**
1106	A400	1c Bowls	.30	.25
a.		Perf. 13¼x13¾ ('90)	.40	.35
1107	A400	2c Bowling	.25	.25
a.		Perf. 13¼x13¾ ('91)	.25	.25
1108	A400	3c Football	.35	.25
1109	A400	39c Fishing	1.10	.35
a.		Booklet pane of 10	11.00	
d.		Perf. 13¼x13¾ on sides ('90)	2.25	3.00
e.		Booklet pane of 10, #1109d	22.50	
1109B	A400	41c Cycling	1.10	.25
c.		Booklet pane of 10	11.00	
1110	A400	55c Kite-flying	1.10	.85
1111	A400	70c Cricket	2.25	1.10
a.		Imperf., dated "2007" (from booklet pane No. 1302b)	2.25	2.25
1112	A400	$1.10 Golf	2.25	1.40

No. 1109d also exists perfed on 4 sides from sheets. These are scarcer. Value, unused or used $17.50.
No. 1111a issued 11/14/2007.

1990-94
1114	A400	5c Kayaking, canoeing	1.40	1.10
a.		Perf. 13¼x13¾	.35	.25
1115	A400	10c Windsurfing	2.00	1.10
a.		Perf. 13¼x13¾	.70	.70
1116	A400	20c Tennis	2.00	.60
a.		Perf. 13¼x13¾	.60	.35
1117	A400	65c Rock climbing	2.60	2.25
a.		Perf. 13¼x13¾	1.40	1.40
1118	A400	$1 Running	2.25	2.25
a.		Perf. 13¼x13¾	4.75	3.50

Issued: Nos. 1114a, 1115a, 1116a, 1117a, 1118, 1/17/90; No. 1118a, 1/91; Nos. 1115, 1117, 2/92; No. 1116, 7/93; No. 1114, 3/94.

The 1990 year date on the original printing of No. 1117 is in serif type. The date on the 4 koala reprint of 2005 is in san-serif type.

1990, Aug. 27
1119	A400	43c Skateboarding	.85	.25
a.		Booklet pane of 10	8.50	

Perf. 13½
1120   A400 $1.20 Hang-gliding   2.60 1.10

1991, Aug. 22   **Perf. 14x14½**
1121	A400	75c Netball	1.50	.90
1122	A400	80c Squash	1.60	.85
1123	A400	85c Diving	1.75	.95
1124	A400	90c Soccer	1.75	1.10
		Nos. 1106-1124 (19)	29.00	17.15

For self-adhesive stamps see Nos. 1185-1186.

Botanical Gardens — A401

Designs: $2, Nooroo, New South Wales. $5, Mawarra, Victoria. $10, Palm House, Adelaide Botanical Garden. $20, A View of the Artist's House and Garden in Mills Plains, Van Diemen's Land by John Glover.

1989-90   **Litho. & Engr.**   **Perf. 14**
1132	A401	$2 multicolored	4.00	1.00
a.		Perf. 13¼x13¾ ('91)	10.00	4.00
1133	A401	$5 multicolored	10.00	2.25
a.		Perf. 13¼x13¾	20.00	9.25
1134	A401	$10 multicolored	20.00	4.50

Litho with Foil Application
Perf. 14½x14
1135	A401	$20 multicolored	40.00	11.00
		Nos. 1132-1135 (4)	74.00	18.75

Issued: $10, 4/12; $2, $5, 9/13; $20, 8/15/90.

Sheep A402

1989, Feb. 27   **Litho.**   **Perf. 13½x14**
1136	A402	39c Merino	.80	.80
1137	A402	39c Poll Dorset	.80	.80
1138	A402	85c Polwarth	1.75	1.75
1139	A402	$1 Corriedale	2.10	2.10
		Nos. 1136-1139 (4)	5.45	5.45

World Sheep and Wool Congress, Tasmania, Feb. 27-Mar. 6.

Queen Elizabeth II, 63rd Birthday — A403

1989, Apr. 21   **Litho.**   **Perf. 14½**
1140   A403 39c Statue by John Dowie   1.00 .40

Colonial Australia — A404

Pastoral Era: a, Immigrant ship in port, c. 1835. b, Pioneer's hut, wool bales in dray. c, Squatter's homestead. d, Shepherds. e, Explorers.

1989, May 10
1141	A404	Strip of 5	4.00	4.00
a.-e.		39c any single	.80	.65

Stars of Stage and Screen — A405

Performers and directors: 39c, Gladys Moncrieff and Roy Rene, the stage, 1920's. 85c, Charles Chauvel and Chips Rafferty, talking films. $1, Nellie Stewart and James Cassius Williamson, the stage, 1890's. $1.10, Lottie Lyell and Raymond Longford, silent films.

1989, July 12	Litho.	Perf. 14½	
1142 A405 39c multicolored		1.10	.25
a. Perf. 14x13½		11.50	11.50
1143 A405 85c multicolored		2.00	2.25
1144 A405 $1 multicolored		2.10	1.75
1145 A405 $1.10 multicolored		2.25	2.00
Nos. 1142-1145 (4)		7.45	6.25

Impressionist Paintings A406

Paintings by Australian artists: No. 1146, Impression for Golden Summer, by Sir Arthur Streeton. No. 1147, All on a Summer's Day, by Charles Conder, vert. No. 1148, Petit Dejeuner, by Frederick McCubbin. No. 1149, Impression, by Tom Roberts.

Perf. 13½x14, 14x13½			
1989, Aug. 23		Litho.	
1146 A406 41c shown		.80	.65
1147 A406 41c multicolored		.80	.65
1148 A406 41c multicolored		.80	.65
1149 A406 41c multicolored		.80	.65
Nos. 1146-1149 (4)		3.20	2.60

The Urban Environment — A407

1989, Sept. 1	Litho.	Perf. 15½	
Booklet Stamps			
1150 A407 41c Freeways		.80	.80
1151 A407 41c Architecture		.80	.80
1152 A407 41c Commuter train		.80	.80
a. Bklt. pane, 2 ea #1150, 1152, 3 #1151		5.50	
Nos. 1150-1152 (3)		2.40	2.40

No. 1152a sold for $3.

Australian Youth Hostels, 50th Anniv. A408

1989, Sept. 13		Perf. 14½	
1153 A408 41c multicolored		1.00	.50

Street Cars — A409

Designs: No. 1154, Horse-drawn tram, Adelaide, 1878. No. 1155, Steam tram, Sydney, 1884. No. 1156, Cable car, Melbourne, 1886. No. 1157, Double-deck electric tram, Hobart, 1893. No. 1158, Combination electric tram, Brisbane, 1901.

1989, Oct. 11	Litho.	Perf. 13½x14	
1154 A409 41c multicolored		.90	.80
1155 A409 41c multicolored		.90	.80
1156 A409 41c multicolored		.90	.80
a. Perf. 14½ on 3 sides		3.25	3.25
b. Booklet pane of 10, #1156a		32.50	

1157 A409 41c multicolored		.90	.80
1158 A409 41c multicolored		.90	.80
Nos. 1154-1158 (5)		4.50	4.00

Purchase of booklet containing No. 1156b included STAMPSHOW '89 admission ticket and a Melbourne one-day transit pass. Sold for $8.

Christmas — A410

Illuminations: 36c, Annunciation, from the Nicholai Joseph Foucault Book of Hours, c. 1510-20. 41c, Annunciation to the Shepherds, from the Wharncliffe Hours, c. 1475. 80c, Adoration of the Magi, from Parisian Book of Hours, c. 1490-1500.

1989, Nov. 1		Perf. 14x13½	
1159 A410 36c multicolored		.70	.40
a. Booklet pane of 10		7.00	
		Perf. 15x14½	
1160 A410 41c multicolored		.85	.65
1161 A410 80c multicolored		1.90	1.90
Nos. 1159-1161 (3)		3.45	2.95

Radio Australia, 50th Anniv. — A411

1989, Nov. 1		Perf. 14x13½	
1162 A411 41c multicolored		1.00	.60

Australia Day — A412

1990, Jan. 17	Litho.	Perf. 15x14½	
1163 A412 41c Golden wattle		1.00	.50

Special Occasions — A413

1990, Feb. 7		Perf. 14x13½	
1164 A413 41c Thinking of You		.90	.50
a. Booklet pane of 10		9.00	
b. Perf. 14½ on 3 sides		3.50	1.10
c. Booklet pane of 10, #1164b		35.00	

See No. 1193.

Women Practicing Medicine in Australia, Cent. A414

1990, Feb. 7		Perf. 14½x15	
1165 A414 41c Constance Stone		.80	.50

Dr. Constance Stone, Australia's first woman doctor.

A415

Fauna of the High Country: 41c, Greater glider. 65c, Spotted-tailed quoll. 70c, Mountain pygmy-possum. 80c, Brush-tailed rock-wallaby.

1990, Feb. 21		Perf. 14x13½	
1166 A415 41c multicolored		.85	.50
1167 A415 65c multicolored		1.40	1.40
1168 A415 70c multicolored		1.60	1.60
1169 A415 80c multicolored		1.90	1.90
Nos. 1166-1169 (4)		5.75	5.40

A416

No. 1170, Quit smoking. No. 1171, Don't drink and drive. No. 1172, Eat right. No. 1173, Medical check-ups.

1990, Mar. 14			
1170 A416 41c multicolored		.80	.55
1171 A416 41c multicolored		.80	.55
1172 A416 41c multicolored		.80	.55
1173 A416 41c multicolored		.80	.55
Nos. 1170-1173 (4)		3.20	2.20

Community health.

A417

Scenes from WW II, 1940-41: No. 1174, Anzacs at the front. No. 1175, Women working in factories, aircraft at the ready. 65c, Veterans and memorial parade. $1, Helicopters picking up wounded, cemetery. $1.10, Anzacs reading mail from home, 5 women watching departure of 2 ships.

1990-2005	Litho.	Perf. 14½	
1174 A417 41c shown		.85	.35
1175 A417 41c multicolored		.85	.35
1176 A417 65c multicolored		1.40	1.40
a. Booklet pane of 2, perf. 14½x14 ('05)		3.00	—
1177 A417 $1 multicolored		2.10	2.10
1178 A417 $1.10 multicolored		2.25	2.25
Nos. 1174-1178 (5)		7.45	6.45

Australia and New Zealand Army Corps (ANZAC).
Issued: Nos. 1174-1178, 4/12/90. No. 1176a, Apr. 2005.

A418

1990, Apr. 19		Perf. 14½	
1179 A418 41c multicolored		1.00	.50

Queen Elizabeth's 64th birthday.

Penny Black, 150th Anniv. A419

Stamps on stamps: a, New South Wales #44. b, South Australia #4. c, Tasmania #2. d, Victoria #120. e, Queensland #111A. f, Western Australia #3a.

1990, May 1		Perf. 13½x14	
1180 Block of 6		5.50	5.50
a.-f. A419 41c any single		.80	.50
g. Souvenir sheet of 6		5.75	5.75
h. As "g," with Stamp World London '90 emblem ovpt. in silver in sheet margin		14.50	14.50

No. 1180h issued 5/3.

The Gold Rush — A420

a, Off to the diggings. b, The diggings. c, Panning for gold. d, Commissioner's tent. e, Gold escort.

1990, May 16		Perf. 13	
1181 Strip of 5		4.00	4.00
a.-e. A420 41c any single		.80	.50

Cooperation in Antarctic Research A421

41c, Glaciology. $1.10, Krill (marine biology).

1990, June 13	Litho.	Perf. 14½x14	
1182 A421 41c multi		.80	.45
1183 A421 $1.10 multi		2.25	1.10
a. Min. sheet of 2, #1182-1183		3.25	3.25
b. #1183a overprinted		8.00	8.00

No. 1183 is overprinted in gold, in sheet margin only, for NZ 1990 International Stamp Exhibition, Auckland, Aug. 24-Sept. 2, 1990. See Russia Nos. 5902-5903.

Colonial Australia A422

Boom Time: a, Land boom. b, Building boom. c, Investment boom. d, Retail boom. e, Factory boom.

1990, July 12	Litho.	Perf. 13	
1184 Strip of 5		4.00	4.00
a.-e. A422 41c any single		.80	.55

Sports Type of 1989

1990-91	Typo.	Die Cut Perf. 11½	
		Self-Adhesive	
1185 A400 41c Cycling		1.00	.75
1186 A400 43c Skateboarding		1.00	.25
a. Litho.		1.00	.25

Blue background has large dots on No. 1186 and smaller dots on No. 1186a. No. 1186 is on waxed paper backing printed with 0 to 4 koalas. No. 1186a is on plain paper backing printed with one kangaroo.
Issued: 41c, 5/16; No. 1186, 8/27; No. 1186a, 1991.

Salmon Gums by Robert Juniper — A423

43c, The Blue Dress by Brian Dunlop.

Perf. 15½ Vert.

1990, Sept. 3   **Litho.**

Booklet Stamps

1191	A423	28c multicolored	3.75	3.50
a.		Perf. 14½ vert.	2.50	2.25
1192	A423	43c multicolored	1.00	.85
a.		Bklt. pane, #1191, 4 #1192	6.00	
b.		Perf. 14½ vert.	.90	.60
c.		Bkt. pane, #1191a, 4 #1192b	4.50	

Thinking Of You Type

1990, Sept. 3   **Perf. 14½**

1193	A413	43c multicolored	.85	.50
a.		Booklet pane of 10	8.50	

Christmas A424

1990, Oct. 31   **Litho.**   **Perf. 14½**

1194	A424	38c multicolored	.75	.35
a.		Booklet pane of 10	7.50	
1195	A424	43c Nativity, vert.	.85	.45
a.		Perf. 14¾x14, additionally dated "2013" (#3534b)	1.10	1.10
1196	A424	80c Opossum	1.60	1.60
		Nos. 1194-1196 (3)	3.20	2.40

Issued: No. 1195a, 5/10/2013.

Local Government in Australia, 150th Anniv. — A425

43c, Town Hall, Adelaide.

1990, Oct. 31

1197	A425	43c multi	1.00	.50

Flags A426

43c, National flag. 90c, White ensign. $1, Air Force ensign. $1.20, Red ensign.

1991, Jan. 10   **Litho.**   **Perf. 14½**

1199	A426	43c multi	.85	.45
1200	A426	90c multi	1.75	1.75
1201	A426	$1 multi	2.00	2.00
1202	A426	$1.20 multi	2.40	2.40
		Nos. 1199-1202 (4)	7.00	6.60

Australia Day.

Water Birds — A427

No. 1203, Black swan. No. 1204, Black-necked stork, vert. No. 1205, Cape Barren goose, vert. No. 1206, Chestnut teal.

1991, Feb. 14

1203	A427	43c multicolored	.95	.45
1204	A427	43c multicolored	.95	.45
1205	A427	85c multicolored	2.00	2.00
1206	A427	$1 multicolored	2.50	2.50
		Nos. 1203-1206 (4)	6.40	5.40

Women's Wartime Services, 50th Anniv. A428

50th Anniv: No. 1208, Siege of Tobruk. $1.20, Australian War Memorial, Canberra.

1991-2005   **Litho.**   **Perf. 14½**

1207	A428	43c shown	.90	.45
a.		Booklet pane of 4, perf. 14x14½ ('05)	3.75	—
1208	A428	43c multicolored	.90	.45
1209	A428	$1.20 multicolored	2.50	2.50
		Nos. 1207-1209 (3)	4.30	3.40

Issued: Nos. 1207-1209, 3/14/91. No. 1207a, Apr. 2005.

Queen Elizabeth II's 65th Birthday — A429

1991, Apr. 11   **Litho.**   **Perf. 14½**

1210	A429	43c multicolored	1.00	.80

Insects A430

No. 1211, Hawk moth. No. 1212, Cotton harlequin bug. No. 1213, Leichhardt's grasshopper. No. 1214, Jewel beetle.

1991, Apr. 11

1211	A430	43c multicolored	.95	.70
1212	A430	43c multicolored	.95	.70
1213	A430	80c multicolored	2.25	2.25
1214	A430	$1 multicolored	2.25	2.00
		Nos. 1211-1214 (4)	6.40	5.65

Australian Photography, 150th Anniv. — A431

Designs: No. 1215a, Bondi, by Max Dupain, 1939. No. 1215b, Gears for the Mining Industry, Vickers Ruwolt Melbourne, by Wolfgang Sievers, 1967. 70c, Wheel of Youth, by Harold Cazneaux, 1929. $1.20, Teacup Ballet, by Olive Cotton, 1935.

1991, May 13   **Litho.**   **Perf. 14½**

1215		Pair	1.75	1.75
a.-b.	A431	43c any single	.85	.75
1216	A431	70c blk, olive & cl	1.40	1.25
1217	A431	$1.20 blk, gray & Prus bl	2.40	2.25
		Nos. 1215-1217 (3)	5.55	5.25

Golden Days of Radio — A432

No. 1218, Music & variety shows. No. 1219, Soap operas. No. 1220, Quiz shows. No. 1221, Children's stories.

1991, June 13   **Litho.**   **Perf. 14½**

1218	A432	43c multicolored	.90	.55
1219	A432	43c multicolored	.90	.55
1220	A432	85c multicolored	1.75	1.75
1221	A432	$1 multicolored	2.10	1.90
		Nos. 1218-1221 (4)	5.65	4.75

Pets — A433

1991, July 25   **Litho.**   **Perf. 14½**

1222	A433	43c Puppy	1.00	.70
1223	A433	43c Kitten	1.00	.70
1224	A433	70c Pony	1.75	1.75
1225	A433	$1 Cockatoo	2.25	2.00
		Nos. 1222-1225 (4)	6.00	5.15

George Vancouver (1757-1798) and Edward John Eyre (1815-1901), Explorers — A434

1991, Sept. 26   **Litho.**   **Perf. 14½**

1226	A434	$1.05 multicolored	2.25	.65
a.		Souvenir sheet of 1	2.25	2.25
b.		As "a," overprinted in gold	3.50	3.50

Vancouver's visit to Western Australia, 200th anniv. and Eyre's journey to Albany, Western Australia, 150th anniv.

No. 1226b overprinted in sheet margin with show emblem and: "PHILANIPPON / WORLD STAMP / EXHIBITION / TOKYO / 16-24 NOV 1991" followed by Japanese inscription.

Issued: No. 1226b, Nov. 16.

Australian Literature of the 1890's A435

Designs: 43c, Seven Little Australians by Ethel Turner. 75c, On Our Selection by Steele Rudd. $1, Clancy of the Overflow by A.B. "Banjo" Paterson, vert. $1.20, The Drover's Wife by Henry Lawson, vert.

1991, Oct. 10

1227	A435	43c multicolored	.85	.40
1228	A435	75c multicolored	1.50	1.50
1229	A435	$1 multicolored	2.00	1.60
1230	A435	$1.20 multicolored	2.40	2.40
		Nos. 1227-1230 (4)	6.75	5.90

Christmas A436

38c, Shepherd. 43c, Baby Jesus. 90c, Wise man, camel.

1991, Nov. 1

1231	A436	38c multi	.75	.45
a.		Booklet pane of 20	15.00	
1232	A436	43c multi	.85	.50
1233	A436	90c multi	1.90	1.75
		Nos. 1231-1233 (3)	3.50	2.70

Thinking of You — A437

1992, Jan. 2   **Litho.**   **Perf. 14½**

1234	A437	45c Wildflowers	.90	.30
a.		Booklet pane of 10	9.00	

Threatened Species — A438

Designs: Nos. 1235a, 1241, Parma wallaby. Nos. 1235b, 1242, Ghost bat. Nos. 1235c, 1243, Long-tailed dunnart. Nos. 1235d, 1244, Little pygmy possum. Nos. 1235e, 1245, Dusky hopping mouse. Nos. 1235f, 1246, Squirrel glider.

1992, Jan. 2   **Litho.**   **Perf. 14x14½**

1235		Block of 6	5.50	5.50
a.-f.		A438 45c any single	.90	.70

Die Cut

Perf. 11½

Self-Adhesive

Size: 31x22mm

1241	A438	45c multicolored	1.40	.85
a.		Typo.	1.10	.85
1242	A438	45c multicolored	1.40	.85
a.		Typo.	1.10	.85
1243	A438	45c multicolored	1.40	.85
a.		Typo.	1.10	.85
1244	A438	45c multicolored	1.40	.85
a.		Typo.	1.10	.85
1245	A438	45c multicolored	1.40	.85
a.		Typo.	1.10	.85
1246	A438	45c multicolored	1.40	.85
a.		Typo.	1.10	.85
b.		Bklt. pane, 2 each #1241-1244, 1 each #1245-1246	14.00	
c.		Pane of 5, #1242-1246	11.50	
d.		Strip of 6, #1241-1246	8.50	
e.		Strip of 6, #1241a-1246a	7.00	
f.		#1246c overprinted	11.50	
g.		As "f," no die cutting	210.00	
		Nos. 1241-1246 (6)	8.40	5.10

Litho. stamps are sharper in appearance than typo. stamps, most notably on the black lettering. Nos. 1246b and 1246c have tagging bars which make the right portion of the stamps appear toned.

No. 1246f — overprinted in Gold on sheet margin of No. 1246c with emblem of "WORLD COLUMBIAN / STAMP EXPO '92 / MAY 22-31, 1992 - CHICAGO." Issued in May.

See Nos. 1271-1293.

Wetlands A439

20c, Noosa River, Queensland. 45c, Lake Eildon, Victoria.

Perf. 14½ Horiz.

1992, Jan. 2   **Litho.**

Booklet Stamps

1247	A439	20c multi	1.10	.85
a.		Perf. 14 horiz.	1.10	.85
1248	A439	45c multi	1.10	.85
a.		Bkt. pane, #1247, 4 #1248	5.75	
		Complete booklet, #1248a	5.75	
b.		Perf. 14 horiz.	.90	.65
c.		Bkt. pane, #1247a, 4 #1248b	4.75	
		Complete booklet, #1248c	4.75	

Sailing Ships A440

No. 1249, Young Endeavour. No. 1250, Britannia, vert. No. 1251, Akarana, vert. No. 1252, John Louis.

1992, Jan. 15   **Litho.**   **Perf. 14½**

1249	A440	45c multi	.90	.50
1250	A440	45c multi	.90	.50
1251	A440	$1.05 multi	2.10	2.10
1252	A440	$1.20 multi	2.25	2.25
a.		Sheet of 4, #1249-1252	6.75	6.75
b.		As "a," overprinted	9.25	9.25
c.		As "a," overprinted	10.50	10.50
		Nos. 1249-1252 (4)	6.15	5.35

Australia Day. Discovery of America, 500th anniv. (No. 1252a).

Overprint in gold on sheet margin of No. 1252b contains emblem and "WORLD COLUMBIAN / STAMP EXPO '92 / MAY 22-31, 1992-CHICAGO." No. 1252b issued in May.

Overprint in gold on sheet margin of No. 1252c contains emblem and "GENOVA '92 / 18-27 SEPTEMBER." No. 1252c issued in Sept.

Australian Battles, 1942 — A441

No. 1253, Bombing of Darwin. No. 1254, Milne Bay. No. 1255, Kokoda Trail. No. 1256, Coral Sea. No. 1257, El Alamein.

1992-2005		Litho.	Perf. 14½	
1253	A441	45c multi	.90	.45
1254	A441	75c multi	1.50	1.25
1255	A441	75c multi	1.50	1.25
1256	A441	$1.05 multi	2.10	2.10
a.	Booklet pane, #1253-1256, perf. 14x14½ ('05)		6.00	—
1257	A441	$1.20 multi	2.40	1.90
	Nos. 1253-1257 (5)		8.40	6.95

No. 1256a issued Apr. 2005.

Intl. Space Year — A442

45c, Helix Nebula. $1.05, The Pleiades. $1.20, Spiral Galaxy NGC 2997.

1992, Mar. 19

1258	A442	45c multi	.90	.45
1259	A442	$1.05 multi	2.10	1.40
1260	A442	$1.20 multi	2.40	1.60
a.	Sheet of 3, #1258-1260		6.25	6.25
b.	As "a," overprinted		14.00	14.00
	Nos. 1258-1260 (3)		5.40	3.45

Overprint on sheet margin of No. 1260b contains emblem of "WORLD COLUMBIAN / STAMP EXPO '92 / MAY 22-31, 1992-CHICAGO." No. 1260b issued in May.

Queen Elizabeth II, 66th Birthday A443

1992, Apr. 9 — Perf. 14x14½
1261 A443 45c Wmk. 228 & #258 .90 .25

Vineyard Regions A444

Designs: No. 1262, Hunter Valley New South Wales. No. 1263, North Eastern Victoria. No. 1264, Barossa Valley South Australia. No. 1265, Coonawarra South Australia. No. 1266, Margaret River Western Australia.

1992, Apr. 9

1262	A444	45c multicolored	.90	.80
1263	A444	45c multicolored	.90	.80
1264	A444	45c multicolored	.90	.80
1265	A444	45c multicolored	.90	.80
1266	A444	45c multicolored	.90	.80
	Nos. 1262-1266 (5)		4.50	4.00

Land Care — A445

a, Salt action. b, Farm planning. c, Erosion control. d, Tree planting. e, Dune care.

1992, June 11 — Litho. — Perf. 14½x14
1267 Strip of 5 4.50 4.50
a.-e. A445 45c Any single .90 .45

1992 Summer Olympics and Paralympics, Barcelona A446

1992, July 2 — Perf. 14½

1268	A446	45c Cycling	1.40	.60
1269	A446	$1.20 Weight lifting	2.50	2.50
1270	A446	$1.20 High jump	2.50	2.50
	Nos. 1268-1270 (3)		6.40	5.60

Threatened Species Type of 1992

Designs: 30c, Saltwater crocodile. 35c, Echidna. 40c, Platypus. No. 1274, Kangaroo. No. 1275, Adult kangaroo with joey. No. 1276, Two adult kangaroos. No. 1277, Four koalas. No. 1278, Koala walking. No. 1279, Koala in tree. 50c, Koala. 60c, Common brushtail possum. 70c, Kookaburra. Nos. 1283, 1283A, Pelican. 90c, Eastern gray kangaroo. 95c, Common wombat. $1.20, Pink cockatoo. $1.35, Emu.

1992-98		Litho.	Perf. 14x14½	
1271	A438	30c multi	.60	.25
1272	A438	35c multi	.70	.35
1273	A438	40c multi	.80	.30
1274	A438	45c orange & multi	.90	.80
a.	Brown panel		1.25	.90
b.	Bright orange panel		1.25	.90
c.	Additionally dated "2013" (#1284b)		1.25	1.25
1275	A438	45c orange & multi	.90	.80
a.	Brown panel		1.25	.90
b.	Bright orange panel		1.25	.90
c.	Additionally dated "2013" (#1284b)		1.25	1.25
1276	A438	45c orange & multi	.90	.80
a.	Sheet of 3, #1274-1276		2.75	2.75
b.	Brown panel		1.25	1.25
c.	Bright orange panel		1.25	1.25
d.	Additionally dated "2013" (#1284b)		1.25	1.25
1277	A438	45c orange & multi	.90	.80
a.	Brown panel		1.25	1.25
b.	Bright orange panel		1.25	1.25
1278	A438	45c orange & multi	.90	.80
a.	Brown panel		1.25	1.25
b.	Bright orange panel		1.25	1.25
1279	A438	45c orange & multi	.90	.80
a.	Block of 6, #1274-1279		5.50	5.50
b.	Souv. sheet, #1274-1279		15.00	15.00
c.	Brown panel		1.25	1.25
d.	Block, #1274a-1275a, 1276b, 1277a-1278a, 1279c		7.75	7.75
e.	Bright orange panel		1.25	1.25
f.	Block, #1274b-1275b, 1276c, 1277b-1278b, 1279e		7.75	7.75

On No. 1279a Australia and denomination are orange, "KANGAROO" is 9mm long, and date is 1½mm long. Date is 1mm long and "KANGAROO" 8mm long on Nos. 1279d and 1279f. No. 1279d comes from 2 Koala printing. No. 1279f comes from 3 Koala printing.

1280	A438	50c multi	1.00	.40
1281	A438	60c multi	1.25	.55
1282	A438	70c multi	1.40	.55
a.	"Australia 70c" in brn ('96)		1.60	1.40
1283	A438	85c peach panel at bottom	1.75	.80
1283A	A438	85c yellow panel at bottom	1.90	1.60
1284	A438	90c multi	1.75	.80
a.	Additionally dated "2013" (#1284b)		2.25	2.25
b.	Booklet pane of 4, #1274c, 1275c, 1276d, 1284a		6.00	—
1285	A438	95c multi	1.90	.80
1286	A438	$1.20 multi	2.40	2.25
a.	"Australia $1.20" in brown ('98)		4.25	3.25
1287	A438	$1.35 multi	2.75	2.00
	Nos. 1271-1287 (18)		23.60	15.45

PHILAKOREA '94 (No. 1279b). "Australia" and denominations on Nos. 1282, 1286 are in orange.

No. 1276a inscribed in sheet margin with "CHINA '96 — 9th Asian International Exhibition" in Chinese and English and exhibition emblems.

No. 1282a comes from 3 Koala or 1 Kangaroo and 1 Koala printing. No. 1286a comes from 1 Kangaroo printing.

No. 1283A is from the three koala printing.

Issued: 35c, 50c, 60c, 95c, 8/13; 40c, 70c, 90c, $1.20, 8/12/93; 30c, 85c, $1.35, 3/10/94; 45c, 5/12/94; No. 1279b, 8/94; No. 1282a, 3/96; No. 1276a, 5/18/96; No. 1283A, 1997; No. 1286a, 12/98; Nos. 1274c, 1275c, 1276d, 1284a, 1284b, 5/10/13. No. 1284b was issued

in a booklet also containing Nos. 1003b, 3534d and 3918.

Die Cut Perf. 11

1994, May 12 **Self-Adhesive** **Litho.**

1288	A438	45c like #1274	1.75	.75
1289	A438	45c like #1275	1.75	.75
1290	A438	45c like #1276	1.75	.75
1291	A438	45c like #1277	1.75	.75
1292	A438	45c like #1278	1.75	.75
1293	A438	45c like #1279	1.75	.75
a.	Bklt. pane, #1290, 1293, 2 each #1288-1289, 1291-1292		17.50	
b.	Strip of 6, #1288-1293		11.50	
	Nos. 1288-1293 (6)		10.50	4.50

Serpentine Die Cut 11½

1995 **Typo.** **Self-Adhesive**
Coil Stamps

1294	A438	45c Like #1274	1.00	.55
1294A	A438	45c Like #1275	1.00	.55
1294B	A438	45c Like #1276	1.00	.55
1294C	A438	45c Like #1277	1.00	.55
1294D	A438	45c Like #1278	1.00	.55
1295	A438	45c Like #1279	1.00	.55
a.	Strip of 6, #1294, 1294A-1294D, 1295		8.00	
	Nos. 1294-1295 (6)		6.00	3.30

Nos. 1294-1295 come from the third through seventh Koala printings by Pemara.

Opening of Sydney Harbor Tunnel, August 29 — A447

Sydney Harbor Bridge and Tunnel: a, Left side. b, Right side.

1992, Aug. 28 — Litho. — Perf. 14½
1296 A447 45c Pair, #a.-b. 8.50 8.50
c. Pair, #d.-e., perf 15½ 3.50 3.50

Buildings in Western Australia Goldfield Towns A448

Designs: No. 1297, Warden's Courthouse, Coolgardie. No. 1298, Post Office, Kalgoorlie. $1.05, York Hotel, Kalgoorlie. $1.20, Town Hall, Kalgoorlie.

1992, Sept. 17 — Litho. — Perf. 14x14½

1297	A448	45c multicolored	.90	.50
1298	A448	45c multicolored	.90	.50
1299	A448	$1.05 multicolored	2.10	2.10
1300	A448	$1.20 multicolored	2.40	2.40
	Nos. 1297-1300 (4)		6.30	5.50

Sheffield Shield Cricket Competition, Cent. — A449

Cricket match, 1890s: 45c, Bowler. $1.20, Batsman, wicket keeper.

1992, Oct. 15 — Litho. — Perf. 14½

1301	A449	45c multicolored	1.10	.55
a.	Perf. 14¾x14, dated "2007"		1.40	1.40
1302	A449	$1.20 multicolored	2.60	2.60
a.	Perf. 14¾x14, dated "2007"		3.75	3.75
b.	Booklet pane of 3, #1111a, 1301a, 1302a		7.50	—

Nos. 1301a, 1302a, 1302b issued 11/14/2007.

Christmas A450

Designs: 40c, Children dressed as Mary and Joseph with baby carriage. 45c, Boy jumping from bed Christmas morning. $1, Boy and girl singing Christmas carol.

1992, Oct. 30 — Litho. — Perf. 14x14½

1303	A450	40c multicolored	.80	.50
a.	Booklet pane of 20		16.00	
1304	A450	45c multicolored	.90	.35
1305	A450	$1 multicolored	2.00	1.75
	Nos. 1303-1305 (3)		3.70	2.60

Watercolor Paintings by Albert Namatjira — A451

Designs: No. 1306a, Ghost Gum, Central Australia. b, Across the Plain to Mount Giles.

1993, Jan. 14 — Litho. — Perf. 14x15
1306 A451 45c Pair, #a.-b. 2.25 2.25

Australia Day.

Dreamings — A452

Aboriginal paintings: 45c, Wild Onion Dreaming, by Pauline Nakamarra Woods. 75c, Yam Plants, by Jack Wunuwun, vert. 85c, Goose Egg Hunt, by George Milpurrurru, vert. $1, Kalumpiwarra-Ngulalintji, by Rover Thomas.

Perf. 14x14½, 14½x14

1993, Feb. 4 — Litho.

1307	A452	45c red & multi	.90	.75
1308	A452	75c org yel & multi	1.50	1.25
1309	A452	85c buff & multi	1.75	1.50
1310	A452	$1 salmon & multi	2.00	1.75
	Nos. 1307-1310 (4)		6.15	5.25

World Heritage Sites in Australia — A453

1993, Mar. 4 — Litho. — Perf. 14½x14

1311	A453	45c Uluru (Ayers Rock)	.90	.60
1312	A453	85c Fraser Island	1.75	1.60
1313	A453	95c Shark Bay	1.90	1.60
1314	A453	$2 Kakadu	4.00	2.75
	Nos. 1311-1314 (4)		8.55	6.55

See Nos. 1485-1488.

World War II Ships A454

45c, Cruiser HMAS Sydney II. 85c, Corvette HMAS Bathurst. $1.05, Destroyer HMAS Arunta. $1.20, Hospital Ship Centaur.

1993-2005 Litho. Perf. 14x14½
1315	A454	45c multicolored	.90	.60
1316	A454	85c multicolored	1.75	1.60
1317	A454	$1.05 multicolored	2.10	2.10
a.		Booklet pane, #1315, 1317		
		('05)	3.25	—
1318	A454	$1.20 multicolored	2.40	2.40
		Nos. 1315-1318 (4)	7.15	6.70

Issued: Nos. 1315-1318, 4/7/93. No. 1317a, April 2005.

Queen Elizabeth II, 67th Birthday — A455

1993, Apr. 7 Perf. 14½x14
| 1319 | A455 | 45c multicolored | .90 | .50 |

A456

Designs based on 19th cent. trade union banners: No. 1320, Baker, shoe maker. No. 1321, Stevedore, seamstresses. $1, Blacksmith, telephone operator, cook. $1.20, Carpenters.

1993, May 7 Litho. Perf. 14½x14
1320	A456	45c multicolored	.90	.70
1321	A456	45c multicolored	.90	.70
1322	A456	$1 multicolored	2.00	1.60
1323	A456	$1.20 multicolored	2.40	2.25
		Nos. 1320-1323 (4)	6.20	5.25

Working life in the 1890s.

Trains A457

Designs: No. 1324, Centenary Special, Tasmania. No. 1325, Spirit of Progress. No. 1326, Western Endeavour. No. 1327, Silver City Comet. No. 1328, Kuranda Tourist Train. No. 1329, The Ghan.

1993, June 1 Perf. 14x14½
1324	A457	45c multicolored	1.25	1.10
1325	A457	45c multicolored	1.25	1.10
1326	A457	45c multicolored	1.25	1.10
1327	A457	45c multicolored	1.25	1.10
1328	A457	45c multicolored	1.25	1.10
1329	A457	45c multicolored	1.25	1.10
a.		Block of 6, #1324-1329	7.75	7.75
		Nos. 1324-1329 (6)	7.50	6.60

Die Cut Perf. 11½x12
Self-Adhesive
1330	A457	45c like No. 1324	2.25	.70
1331	A457	45c like No. 1325	2.25	.70
1332	A457	45c like No. 1326	2.25	.70
1333	A457	45c like No. 1327	2.25	.70
1334	A457	45c like No. 1328	2.25	.70
1335	A457	45c like No. 1329	2.25	.70
a.		Strip of 6, #1330-1335	14.00	
b.		Bklt. pane, #1332, 1335, 2 ea #1330-1331, 1333-1334	14.00	
		Nos. 1330-1335 (6)	13.50	4.20

Aboriginal Art — A458

Aboriginal paintings: 45c, Black Cockatoo Feather, by Fiona Foley, vert. 75c, Ngarrgooroon Country, by Hector Jandany. $1, Ngak Ngak, by Ginger Riley. $1.05, Untitled work, by Robert Cole, vert.

Perf. 14½x14, 14x14½
1993, July 1 Litho.
1336	A458	45c henna brown & multi	.90	.35
1337	A458	75c brown & multi	1.50	1.10
1338	A458	$1 gray & multi	2.00	1.75
1339	A458	$1.05 olive & multi	2.10	1.75
		Nos. 1336-1339 (4)	6.50	4.95

Dame Enid Lyons, MP, and Sen. Dorothy Tangney A459

No. 1340, Stylized globe, natl. arms, Inter-Parliamentary Conf. emblem.

1993, Sept. 2 Litho. Perf. 14½
1340	A459	45c multicolored	1.10	.90
1341	A459	45c multicolored	1.10	.90
a.		Pair, #1340-1341	2.25	2.25

90th Inter-Parliamentary Union Conference (No. 1340). First women in Australian Federal Parliament, 50th anniv. (No. 1341). Nos. 1340-1341 printed in panes of 25 with 16 #1340 and 9 #1341. Panes with 16 #1341 and 9 #1340 were issued Nov. 19, but were available only through Philatelic Agency.

A460 A461

Dinosaurs: Nos. 1342, 1348, Ornithocheirus. Nos. 1343, 1349, Leaellynasaura. No. 1344, Allosaurus. No. 1345, Timimus. No. 1346, Muttaburrasaurus. No. 1347, Minmi.

1993, Oct. 1 Perf. 14x14½, 14½x14
1342	A460	45c multi, horiz.	.90	.70
1343	A460	45c multi	.90	.70
1344	A461	45c multi	.90	.70
1345	A461	45c multi	.90	.70

Size: 30x50mm
1346	A461	75c multi	1.50	1.00
1347	A461	$1.05 multi horiz.	2.10	2.10
a.		Souvenir sheet of 6, #1342-1347, perf. 14¼	8.25	8.25
b.		As "a," overprinted	10.00	10.00
c.		As "a," overprinted	10.00	10.00
		Nos. 1342-1347 (6)	7.20	5.90

Self-Adhesive
Die Cut Perf. 11½
1348	A460	45c multi horiz.	3.25	2.25
1349	A460	45c multi	3.25	2.25
a.		Bklt. pane, 5 each #1348-1349	32.50	

Overprint in gold on sheet margin of No. 1347b contains "BANGKOK 1993" show emblem and "WORLD PHILATELIC / EXHIBITION / BANGKOK 1-10 OCTOBER 1993."

Overprint in gold on sheet margin of No. 1347c contains dinosaur and "Sydney / STAMP & COIN / SHOW / 15-17 October 1993."

Christmas — A462

1993, Nov. 1 Litho. Perf. 14½x14
1354	A462	40c Goodwill	.80	.40
a.		Booklet pane of 20	16.00	
1355	A462	45c Joy	.90	.50
1356	A462	$1 Peace	2.00	1.60
		Nos. 1354-1356 (3)	3.70	2.50

Australia Day — A463

Landscape paintings: 45c, Shoalhaven River Bank-Dawn, by Arthur Boyd. 85c, Wimmera (from Mt. Arapiles), by Sir Sidney Nolan. $1.05, Lagoon, Wimmera, by Nolan. $2, White Cockatoos in Paddock with Flame Trees, by Boyd, vert.

Perf. 14½x14, 14x14½
1994, Jan. 13 Litho.
1357	A463	45c multicolored	.90	.45
1358	A463	85c multicolored	1.75	1.75
1359	A463	$1.05 multicolored	2.10	2.10
1360	A463	$2 multicolored	4.00	3.75
		Nos. 1357-1360 (4)	8.75	8.05

See Nos.1418-1421, 1476-1479, 1572-1574.

Royal Life Saving Society, Cent. A464

1994, Jan. 20 Litho. Perf. 14x14½
1361	A464	45c Vigilance	.90	.70
1362	A464	45c Education	.90	.70
1363	A464	95c Drill	1.90	1.90
1364	A464	$1.20 Fitness	2.40	2.10
		Nos. 1361-1364 (4)	6.10	5.40

Die Cut Perf. 11½
Self-Adhesive
1365	A464	45c like #1361	2.60	1.10
1366	A464	45c like #1362	2.60	1.10
a.		Pair, #1365-1366	5.75	
b.		Booklet pane, 5 #1366a	29.00	

Thinking of You — A465

1994, Feb. 3 Litho. Perf. 14x14½
1367	A465	45c Rose	.90	.50
1368	A465	45c Tulips	.90	.50
1369	A465	45c Poppies	.90	.50
a.		Pair, #1368-1369	1.75	1.75
b.		Booklet pane, 5 #1369a	8.75	
		Nos. 1367-1369 (3)	2.70	1.50

A466

1994, Apr. 8 Litho. Perf. 14½
| 1370 | A466 | 45c multicolored | 1.00 | .55 |

Queen Elizabeth II, 68th birthday.

1994, Apr. 8 Perf. 14½x14
| 1371 | A467 | 95c multicolored | 1.90 | 1.90 |

Opening of Friendship Bridge, Thailand-Laos.

A467

Intl. Year of the Family A468

Children's paintings of their families: 45c, Bobbie Lea Blackmore. 75c, Kathryn Teoh. $1, Maree McCarthy.

1994, Apr. 14 Litho. Perf. 14x14½
1372	A468	45c multicolored	.90	.55
1373	A468	75c multicolored	1.50	1.50
1374	A468	$1 multicolored	2.00	2.00
		Nos. 1372-1374 (3)	4.40	4.05

Australian Women's Right to Vote, Cent. A469

1994, June 9 Litho. Perf. 14x14½
| 1375 | A469 | 45c multicolored | 1.00 | .55 |

Bunyips Folklore Creatures A470

Types of Bunyips: No. 1376, Aboriginal legend. No. 1377, Nature Spirit. 90c, Berkeley's Creek. $1.35, Natural history.

1994, July 14 Litho. Perf. 14x14½
1376	A470	45c multicolored	1.10	1.10
1377	A470	45c multicolored	1.10	1.10
a.		Pair, #1376-1377	2.25	2.25
1378	A470	90c multicolored	2.25	2.25
1379	A470	$1.35 multicolored	3.00	3.00
		Nos. 1376-1379 (4)	7.45	7.45

World War II Prime Ministers A471

Designs: a, Robert Menzies. b, Arthur Fadden. c, John Curtin. d, Francis (Frank) Forde. e, Joseph Benedict (Ben) Chifley.

1994-2005
1380		Strip of 5	6.50	6.50
a.-e.		A471 45c any single	1.10	.90
f.		Booklet pane, #1380a, 1380c ('05)	2.60	—

Issued: No. 1380, 8/11/94. No. 1380f, April 2005.

Aviation Pioneers — A472

Designs: No. 1381, Lawrence Hargrave, box kites. No. 1382, Ross and Keith Smith, Vickers Vimy. $1.35, Ivor McIntyre, Stanley Goble, Fairey IIID A10-3 seaplane. $1.80, Freda Thompson, DeHavilland Moth Major.

1994, Aug. 29 Engr. Perf. 12
1381	A472	45c multicolored	1.00	1.00
1382	A472	45c multicolored	1.00	1.00
1383	A472	$1.35 multicolored	2.75	2.75
1384	A472	$1.80 multicolored	3.75	3.75
		Nos. 1381-1384 (4)	8.50	8.50

First England-Australia flight within 30-day time span (No. 1382). First aerial circumnavigation of Australia (No. 1383). First woman to fly solo from England-Australia (No. 1384).

A473   Australian Zoo
Animals — A474

Perf. 14x14½, 14½x14

1994, Sept. 28			**Litho.**	
1385	A473	45c Scarlet macaw	1.00	.90
1386	A473	45c Cheetah, vert.	1.00	.90
1387	A474	45c Fijian crested iguana	1.00	.90
1388	A474	45c Orangutan	1.00	.90

Size: 50x30mm
Perf. 14½x14

1389	A473	$1 Asian elephant	2.60	2.60
a.		Souv. sheet of 5, #1385-1389, perf. 14½	10.50	10.50
b.		As "a," ovptd.	10.50	10.50
c.		As "a," ovptd.	10.50	10.50
d.		As "a," ovptd.	10.50	10.50
e.		As "a," ovptd.	10.50	10.50
		Nos. 1385-1389 (5)	6.60	6.20

Self-Adhesive
Die Cut Perf. 11½

1390	A473	45c like #1385	3.00	2.25
1391	A473	45c like #1386	3.00	2.25
a.		Bklt. pane, 6 #1390, 4 #1391	30.00	

Denomination is in LL corner on No. 1391.
Overprint in gold on sheet margin:
No. 1389b, show emblem and "Brisbane Stamp Show Zoos / October 21-23, 1994."
No. 1389c, show emblem and "SYDNEY / STAMP / AND / COIN / SHOW / 30/9/94 TO 2/10/94."
No. 1389d, show emblem and "Stampshow '94 Melbourne October 27-30 / National/State Centennial Exhibition 1894-1994."
No. 1389e, show emblem and "STAMP SHOW 94 / Fremantle Convention Centre / 5-6 November 1994."

Christmas
A475

Details from Adoration of the Magi, by Giovanni Toscani: 40c, Madonna and Child, vert. 45c, One of Magi, horse and groom. $1, Joseph receiving frankincense from Magi. $1.80, Entire painting.

1994, Oct. 31		**Litho.**	**Perf. 14½x14**	
1392	A475	40c multicolored	.80	.50
a.		Booklet pane of 20	16.00	
		Complete booklet, #1392a	16.00	

Perf. 14x14½

1393	A475	45c multicolored	.90	.55
1394	A475	$1 multicolored	2.00	2.00

Size: 50x30mm

1395	A475	$1.80 multicolored	3.50	3.50
		Nos. 1392-1395 (4)	7.20	6.55

50th Sydney-Hobart Yacht
Race — A476

Designs: a, Yachts bow-on, Sydney Opera House, Harbor Bridge. b, Two yachts abeam.

1994, Oct. 31			**Perf. 14½**	
1396		Pair	3.50	3.50
a.-b.		A476 45c any single	1.10	1.10

Self-Adhesive
Die Cut Perf. 11½

1397	A476	45c like #1396a	3.50	3.50
1397A	A476	45c like #1396b	3.50	3.50

A477

Self-Adhesive
Booklet Stamps
Background Color
Die Cut Perf. 17

1994, Nov. 2			**Litho.**	
1398	A477	45c bluish green	1.40	1.40
1399	A477	45c blue	1.40	1.40
1400	A477	45c purple	1.40	1.40
1401	A477	45c yellow green	1.40	1.40
1402	A477	45c pale yel green	1.40	1.40
1403	A477	45c pale red brown	1.40	1.40
1404	A477	45c rose	1.40	1.40
1405	A477	45c orange yellow	1.40	1.40
a.		Booklet pane of 20	28.00	
		Nos. 1398-1405 (8)	11.20	11.20

No. 1405a contains 3 each of Nos. 1399, 1401, 1403, 1405 and 2 each of Nos. 1398, 1400, 1402, 1404. No. 1405a was sold in ATM machines, at the Natl. Philatelic Center, and Australian Philatelic Bureau.
Two printings differ slightly in shade and advertisement on back of pane.

Nos. 1406-1417 were deleted from the 2003 Standard catalogue. These self-adhesive stamps of design No. A438 have computer-generated denominations and exist with a large variety of different inscriptions for shows and other purposes.

Australia Day Type of 1994

Paintings: No. 1418, Back Verandah, by Russell Drysdale. No. 1419, Skull Springs Country, by Guy Grey-Smith. $1.05, Outcamp, by Robert Juniper. $1.20, Kite Flying, by Ian Fairweather.

1995, Jan. 12		**Litho.**	**Perf. 15x14½**	
1418	A463	45c multicolored	1.00	.60
1419	A463	45c multicolored	1.00	.60
1420	A463	$1.05 multicolored	2.10	1.90
1421	A463	$1.20 multicolored	2.40	2.10
		Nos. 1418-1421 (4)	6.50	5.20

St. Valentine's
Day — A478

Various designs: a, Red heart. b, Red & gold heart. c, Gold heart.

1995, Feb. 6		**Litho.**	**Perf. 14½x14**	
1422		Strip of 3	3.50	2.25
a.-c.		A478 45c any single	1.10	.55

See No. 1480.

Endeavour
A479

No. 1423: a, Captain Cook's Endeavour. b, Replica.

1995, Feb. 9		**Litho.**	**Perf. 14x14½**	
1423		Pair	3.75	3.75
a.-b.		A479 45c any single	1.10	.90

Booklet Stamps
Size: 44x26mm
Perf. 14 Horiz.

1424	A479	20c like #1423b	3.00	2.60
1425	A479	45c like #1423a	1.40	.70
a.		Bklt. pane, #1424, 4 #1425	8.50	
		Complete booklet, #1425a	8.50	

Natl. Trust,
50th Anniv.
A480

Designs: No. 1426a, Coalport plate, Regency style bracket clock. No. 1426b, 15th-16th cent. x-frame Italian style chair, 19th cent. Steiner doll. $1, Advance Australia teapot, neo-classical parian-ware statuette. $2, China urn, silver bowl.

1995, Mar. 16		**Engr.**	**Perf. 14x14½**	
1426		Pair	2.25	2.25
a.-b.		A480 45c any single	1.00	.55
1427	A480	$1 red brn & bl	2.10	1.90
1428	A480	$2 blue & green	4.00	4.00
		Nos. 1426-1428 (3)	8.35	8.15

Opals — A481

1995, Apr. 5		**Litho.**	**Perf. 14½x14**	
1429	A481	$1.20 Light opal	3.00	3.00
1430	A481	$2.50 Black opal	5.25	5.25

Nos. 1429-1430 each contain a holographic image. Soaking in water may affect the hologram.
See Nos. 1554-1555.

A482

1995, Apr. 20		**Litho.**	**Perf. 14½**	
1431	A482	45c multicolored	1.00	.55

Queen Elizabeth II, 69th birthday.

A483

Famous Australians from World War II — No. 1432, Sir Edward Dunlop. No. 1433, Mrs. Jessie Vasey. No. 1434, Tom Derrick. No. 1435, Rawdon Hume Middleton.

1995, Apr. 20			**Perf. 14½x14**	
1432	A483	45c multi	1.10	1.10
1433	A483	45c multi	1.10	1.10
1434	A483	45c multi	1.10	1.10
1435	A483	45c multi	1.10	1.10
a.		Block of 4, #1432-1435	4.75	4.75
		Nos. 1432-1435 (4)	4.40	4.40

Self-Adhesive
Die Cut Perf. 11½

1436	A483	45c like #1432	2.25	.85
1437	A483	45c like #1433	2.25	.85
1438	A483	45c like #1434	2.25	.85
1439	A483	45c like #1435	2.25	.85
a.		Booklet pane, 4 #1436, 2 each #1437-1439	22.50	
b.		Strip of 4, #1436-1439	9.75	
		Nos. 1436-1439 (4)	9.00	3.40

See Nos. 1452-1455.

UN, 50th
Anniv.
A484

1995, May 11		**Litho.**	**Perf. 14x14½**	
1440	A484	45c + label, multi	1.10	.55
a.		Block of 4 + 4 labels	5.75	4.50

No. 1440 was issued se-tenant with label in blocks of 4 + 4 labels in four designs. In alternating rows, labels appear on left or right side of stamp.

A485

Poster, scene from: No. 1441, The Story of the Kelly Gang, 1906. No. 1442, On Our Selection, 1932. No. 1443, Jedda, 1955. No. 1444, Picnic at Hanging Rock, 1970s. No. 1445, Strictly Ballroom, 1992.

1995, June 8		**Litho.**	**Perf. 14½x14**	
1441	A485	45c multicolored	1.25	1.00
1442	A485	45c multicolored	1.25	1.00
1443	A485	45c multicolored	1.25	1.00
1444	A485	45c multicolored	1.25	1.00
1445	A485	45c multicolored	1.25	1.00
a.		Strip of 5, #1441-1445	7.00	7.00
		Nos. 1441-1445 (5)	6.25	5.00

Self-Adhesive
Die Cut Perf. 11½

1446	A485	45c like #1441	3.25	.85
1447	A485	45c like #1442	3.25	.85
1448	A485	45c like #1443	3.25	.85
1449	A485	45c like #1444	3.25	.85
1450	A485	45c like #1445	3.25	.85
a.		Strip of 5, #1446-1450	20.00	
b.		Bklt. pane, 2 ea #1446-1450	32.50	
		Nos. 1446-1450 (5)	16.25	4.25

Motion Pictures, cent.
By its nature No. 1450b constitutes a complete booklet. The peelable backing serves as a booklet cover.

A486

People with Disabilities: No. 1451a, Person flying kite from wheelchair. b, Blind person playing violin, guide dog.

1995, July 13		**Litho.**	**Perf. 14½x14**	
1451		Pair	2.25	2.25
a.-b.		A486 45c any single	1.00	.55

Famous Australians from World War II Type of 1995

1995-2005		**Litho.**	**Perf. 14½x14**	
1452	A483	45c Leon Goldsworthy	1.25	.85
a.		Booklet pane, #1432, 1434, 1435, 1452 ('05)	5.75	—
1453	A483	45c Len Waters	1.25	.85
1454	A483	45c Ellen Savage	1.25	.85
a.		Booklet pane, #1433, 1454 ('05)	3.00	—
1455	A483	45c Percy Collins	1.25	.85
a.		Block of 4, #1452-1455	5.25	4.50
		Nos. 1452-1455 (4)	5.00	3.40

Issued: Nos. 1452-1455, 8/10/95. Nos. 1452a and 1454a, April 2005.

Peace Types of 1946
Perf. 14x14½, 14½x14

1995, Aug. 10			**Engr.**	
1456	A43	45c red brown	1.25	1.00
1457	A45	45c dark green	1.25	1.00
1458	A44	$1.50 dark blue	3.50	3.50
		Nos. 1456-1458 (3)	6.00	5.50

End of World War II, 50th anniv.

Wildlife
A487

Designs: a, Koalas. b, Pandas.

1995, Sept. 1   Litho.   Perf. 14
1459		Pair	2.25	2.25
a.-b.	A487 45c any single		1.10	1.10
c.	Souv. sheet #1459a, perf. 11x11½	2.25	2.25
d.	Souv. sheet #1459b, perf. 11x11½	2.25	2.25
e.	#1459c Ovptd. in sheet margin	4.50	4.50
f.	#1459d Ovptd. in sheet margin	4.50	4.50

Overprints read: No. 1459e: "AUSTRALIAN STAMP EXHIBITION." No. 1459f: "INTERNATIONAL STAMP & COIN EXPO. / BEIJING '95."

Issued: No. 1459f, 9/14/95.
See People's Republic of China Nos. 2597-2598.

Australian
Medical
Discoveries
A488

Designs: No. 1461a, Joseph Slattery, Thomas Lyle, Walter Filmer, x-ray pioneers. No. 1461b, Jean Macnamara, Macfarlane Burnet, viruses and immunology. No. 1461C, Fred Hollows, eye care, vert. $2.50. Howard Florey, co-discoverer of penicillin, vert.

1995, Sept. 7   Perf. 14x14½, 14½x14
1461		Pair	1.90	1.60
a.-b.	A488 45c any single		.85	.80
1461C	A488	45c multicolored	1.10	.55
1461D	A488	$2.50 multicolored	5.75	5.75
	Nos. 1461-1461D (3)		8.75	7.90

No. 1461D exists in sheetlets of 10.

The World
Down Under
A489

Designs: Nos. 1462a, 1465a, Flatback turtle. Nos. 1462b, 1465b, Flame angelfish, nudibranch. Nos. 1463a, 1465c, Potato cod, giant maori wrasse. Nos. 1463b, 1465d, Giant trevally. Nos. 1464a, 1465e, Black marlin. Nos. 1464b, 1465f, Mako & tiger sharks.

1995, Oct. 3   Litho.   Perf. 14x14½
1462		Pair	2.25	2.25
a.-b.	A489 45c any single		1.10	.90
1463		Pair	2.25	2.25
a.-b.	A489 45c any single		1.10	.90
1464		Pair	2.25	2.25
a.-b.	A489 45c any single		1.10	.90
	Nos. 1462-1464 (3)		6.75	6.75

Miniature Sheet of 6
1465	A489 45c #a.-f.		7.00	7.00
g.	Ovptd. in sheet margin	8.00	8.00
h.	Ovptd. in sheet margin	8.00	8.00
i.	Ovptd. in sheet margin	8.00	8.00
j.	Ovptd. in sheet margin	8.00	8.00
k.	Ovptd. in sheet margin	8.00	8.00

Nos. 1462-1464 have pale blue border on three sides. No. 1465 is a continuous design and does not have the pale border. Fish on No. 1465 are printed with additional phosphor ink producing a glow-in-the-dark effect under ultraviolet light.

Overprints in gold in sheet margin of No. 1465 include show emblems and text:

No. 1465g: "ADELAIDE / STAMP AND / COLLECTIBLES / FAIR / 14/10/95 - / 15/10/95."

No. 1465h: "SYDNEY / CENTREPOINT 95 / STAMPSHOW."

No. 1465i: "Brisbane Stamp Show / 20-22 October 1995."

No. 1465j: "Melbourne Stamp & Coin Fair / 27-29 October 1995."

No. 1465k: "Swanpex WA / 28-29 October 1995."

Booklet Stamps
Self-Adhesive
Die Cut Perf. 11½
1466	A489 45c like #1462a	1.10	.55
1467	A489 45c like #1462b	1.10	.55
1468	A489 45c like #1463a	1.10	.55
1469	A489 45c like #1463b	1.10	.55
1470	A489 45c like #1464a	1.10	.55
1471	A489 45c like #1464b	1.10	.55
a.	Booklet pane, #1470-1471, 2 each #1466-1469	14.00	
b.	Strip of 6, #1466-1471	14.00	
	Nos. 1466-1471 (6)	6.60	3.30

By its nature, No. 1471a constitutes a complete booklet. The peelable backing serves as a booklet cover.

Christmas — A490

Stained glass windows, Our Lady Help of Christians Church, Melbourne: 40c, Madonna and Child. 45c, Angel carrying banner. $1, Three rejoicing angels.

1995, Nov. 1   Litho.   Perf. 14½x14
1472	A490 40c multicolored	1.00	.70
1473	A490 45c multicolored	1.25	.75
1474	A490 $1 multicolored	2.25	2.00
	Nos. 1472-1474 (3)	4.50	3.45

Booklet Stamp
Self-Adhesive
Die Cut Perf. 11½
1475	A490 40c multicolored	1.40	.45
a.	Booklet pane of 20	28.00	

Madonna and Child on No. 1475 are printed with additional phosphor ink giving parts of the stamp a rough texture.

By its nature, No. 1475a constitutes a complete booklet. The peelable backing serves as a booklet cover, which also contains 20 labels. The complete booklet is available with backing showing two different advertisements.

Australia Day Type of 1994

Paintings by Australian women: 45c, West Australian Banksia, by Margaret Preston, vert. 85c, The Babe is Wise, by Lina Bryans, vert. $1, The Bridge in Curve, by Grace Cossington Smith. $1.20, Beach Umbrellas, by Vida Lahey.

Perf. 14x14½, 14½x14
1996, Jan. 16   Litho.
1476	A463 45c multicolored	1.00	.35
1477	A463 85c multicolored	1.90	1.60
1478	A463 $1 multicolored	2.10	1.90
1479	A463 $1.20 multicolored	2.40	2.10
	Nos. 1476-1479 (4)	7.40	5.95

Heart and
Roses
A491

1996, Jan. 30   Perf. 14x14½
1480	A491 45c gold & multi	1.00	.55

See No. 1422.

Military
Aviation
A492

Airplanes: No. 1481, Firefly, Sea Fury. No. 1482, Beaufighter, Kittyhawk. No. 1483, Hornet. No. 1484, Kiowa.

1996-2005   Litho.   Perf. 14x14½
1481	A492 45c multicolored	.90	.90
1482	A492 45c multicolored	.90	.90
a.	Booklet pane, #1481, 1482 ('05)	1.90	—
1483	A492 45c multicolored	.90	.90
1484	A492 45c multicolored	.90	.90
a.	Block of 4, #1481-1484	4.00	4.00

Issued: 1481-1484, 2/26/96. No. 1482a, April 2005.

Australian World Heritage Sites Type of 1993

Designs: 45c, Tasmanian Wilderness. 75c, Willandra Lakes. 95c, Fossil Cave, Naracoorte. $1, Lord Howe Island.

1996, Mar. 14   Litho.   Perf. 14½x14
1485	A453 45c multicolored	1.10	.95
1486	A453 75c multicolored	1.90	1.60
1487	A453 95c multicolored	2.00	2.00
1488	A453 $1 multicolored	2.25	1.90
a.	Booklet pane, #1311, 1314, 1485, 1488 ('06)	8.25	—
	Nos. 1485-1488 (4)	7.25	6.45

No. 1488a issued 3/15/2006.

Indonesian Bear
Cuscus — A493

No. 1489, Australian Spotted Cuscus.

1996, Mar. 22
1489	A493 45c multicolored	1.00	.80
1490	A493 45c multicolored	1.00	.80
a.	Pair, Nos. 1489-1490	2.50	2.50
b.	Souvenir sheet, No. 1490a	4.00	4.00
c.	As "b," with World Philatelic Youth Exhibition emblem in sheet margin	9.25	9.25

No. 1490a has continuous design.
See Indonesia Nos. 1640-1642.

Queen
Elizabeth II,
70th Birthday
A494

Litho. & Engr.
1996, Apr. 11   Perf. 14x14½
1491	A494 45c multicolored	1.00	.55

North Melbourne
Kangaroos
A495

Sydney
Swans — A497

Adelaide
Crows — A499

Richmond
Tigers — A501

Brisbane Bears
A496

Carlton
Blues — A498

Fitzroy
Lions — A500

St. Kilda
Saints — A502

Melbourne
Demons — A503

Collingwood
Magpies — A504

Fremantle
Dockers — A505

Footscray
Bulldogs — A506

West Coast
Eagles
A507

Essendon
Bombers
A508

Geelong
Cats — A509

Hawthorn
Hawks — A510

1996, Apr. 23   Litho.   Perf. 14½x14
1492	A495 45c multicolored	1.25	1.10
1493	A496 45c multicolored	1.25	1.10
1494	A497 45c multicolored	1.25	1.10
1495	A498 45c multicolored	1.25	1.10
1496	A499 45c multicolored	1.25	1.10
1497	A500 45c multicolored	1.25	1.10
1498	A501 45c multicolored	1.25	1.10
1499	A502 45c multicolored	1.25	1.10
1500	A503 45c multicolored	1.25	1.10
1501	A504 45c multicolored	1.25	1.10
1502	A505 45c multicolored	1.25	1.10
1503	A506 45c multicolored	1.25	1.10
1504	A507 45c multicolored	1.25	1.10
1505	A508 45c multicolored	1.25	1.10
1506	A509 45c multicolored	1.25	1.10
1507	A510 45c multicolored	1.25	1.10
a.	Min. sheet of 16, #1492-1507	20.00	
	Nos. 1492-1507 (16)	20.00	17.60

Booklet Stamps
Self-Adhesive
Serpentine Die Cut 11½
1508	A495 45c multicolored	1.40	.70
a.	Booklet pane of 10	14.00	
1509	A496 45c multicolored	1.40	.70
a.	Booklet pane of 10	14.00	
1510	A497 45c multicolored	1.40	.70
a.	Booklet pane of 10	14.00	
1511	A498 45c multicolored	1.40	.70
a.	Booklet pane of 10	14.00	
1512	A499 45c multicolored	1.40	.70
a.	Booklet pane of 10	14.00	
1513	A500 45c multicolored	1.40	.70
a.	Booklet pane of 10	14.00	
1514	A501 45c multicolored	1.40	.70
a.	Booklet pane of 10	14.00	
1515	A502 45c multicolored	1.40	.70
a.	Booklet pane of 10	14.00	
1516	A503 45c multicolored	1.40	.70
a.	Booklet pane of 10	14.00	
1517	A504 45c multicolored	1.40	.70
a.	Booklet pane of 10	14.00	
1518	A505 45c multicolored	1.40	.70
a.	Booklet pane of 10	14.00	
1519	A506 45c multicolored	1.40	.70
a.	Booklet pane of 10	14.00	
1520	A507 45c multicolored	1.40	.70
a.	Booklet pane of 10	14.00	
1521	A508 45c multicolored	1.40	.70
a.	Booklet pane of 10	14.00	
1522	A509 45c multicolored	1.40	.70
a.	Booklet pane of 10	14.00	

1523	A510	45c multicolored	1.40	.70
a.		Booklet pane of 10	14.00	

Nos. 1508-1523 (16) 　22.40　11.20

By their nature, Nos. 1508a-1523a are complete booklets. The peelable paper backing serves as a booklet cover.
Australian Football League, cent.

Flora and Fauna — A511

Designs: 5c, Leadbeater's possum. 10c, Powerful owl. 20c, Saltwater crocodile, Kangkong flower. 25c, Northern dwarf tree frog, red lily. No. 1528, Little kingfisher. No. 1529, Jacana. No. 1530, Jabiru. No. 1531, Brolga. $1, Big greasy butterfly, water lily. $2, Blackwood wattle. $5, Mountain ash, fern. $10, Kakadu Wetlands during lightning storm, great egret, red lily.

Perf. 14x14½, 14½x14 (#1535)
1996-99　　　　　　　　　**Litho.**

1524	A511	5c multi	.25	.25
1525	A511	10c multi	.30	.25
1526	A511	20c multi	.40	.40
1527	A511	25c multi	.55	.55
1528	A511	45c multi	.95	.95
1529	A511	45c multi	.95	.95
1530	A511	45c multi	.95	.95
1531	A511	45c multi	.95	.95
a.		Block of 4, #1528-1531	4.00	4.00
b.		Souvenir sheet of 2, #1530-1531	1.60	
1532	A511	$1 multi	2.10	1.40
1533	A511	$2 multi	4.00	2.50

Size: 30x50mm

1534	A511	$5 multi, vert.	10.00	6.50

Size: 50x30mm

1535	A511	$10 multi	20.00	12.00
a.		Souvenir sheet of 1	22.50	18.00
b.		As "a," ovptd in sheet margin	35.00	30.00
c.		As "a," ovptd in sheet margin	25.00	25.00
d.		As "a," ovptd in sheet margin	21.00	21.00

Nos. 1524-1535 (12) 　41.40　27.65

Self-Adhesive
Serpentine Die Cut 11½, 11¼ (#1539i)

1536	A511	45c like #1529	1.00	.55
1537	A511	45c like #1528	1.00	.55
1538	A511	45c like #1531	1.00	.55
1539	A511	45c like #1530	1.00	.55
a.		Booklet pane, 3 ea #1536, #1538, 2 ea #1537, #1539	10.50	
b.		Strip of 4, #1536-1539	4.50	
h.		Sheet of 5, #1537-1539, 2 #1536	5.75	
i.		Booklet pane, 5 each #1536-1539	20.00	

Serpentine Die Cut 12½x13

1539C	A511	45c like #1529	1.00	.55
1539D	A511	45c like #1528	1.00	.55
1539E	A511	45c like #1531	1.00	.55
1539F	A511	45c like #1530	1.00	.55
g.		Strip of 4, #1539C-1539F	4.50	

Nos. 1536-1539F (8) 　8.00　4.40

Nos. 1536-1539 are booklet stamps.
No. 1531b is inscribed in sheet margin with Shanghai '97 emblem and "International Stamp & Coin Exposition Shanghai '97" in Chinese and English.
No. 1535b is overprinted in silver in sheet margin with PACIFIC 97 emblem and "Australia Post Exhibition Sheet No. 4."
No. 1535c is overprinted in sheet margin for "Italia '98" in Milan.
No. 1535d is overprinted in copper in sheet margin with "PHILA NIPPON '01" and show emblem. Issued: No. 1535c, 8/1/01.
By its nature No. 1539a is a complete booklet. The peelable backing serves as a booklet cover.
Issued: 5c, 10c, $2, $5, 5/9/96; 20c, 25c, $1, $10, #1538a, 4/10/97; #1528-1531, 1536-1539, 6/2/97; #1531b, 11/17/97; #1539C-1539F, 11/13/99; No. 1539i, 9/1/98.
No. 1539i is a complete booklet.
See Nos. 1734-1746L, 1984-1995, 2060-2063, 2111-2114, 2159-2170, 2235-2238.

Modern Olympic Games, Cent. A512

Designs: No. 1540, Edwin Flack, 1st Australian gold medalist, runners. No. 1541, Fanny

Durack, 1st Australian woman gold medalist, swimmers. $1.05, Paralympics, Atlanta.

Litho. & Engr.
1996, June 6　　　　**Perf. 14x14½**

1540	A512	45c multicolored	1.00	.30
1541	A512	45c multicolored	1.00	.30
a.		Pair, #1540-1541	2.25	1.75
1542	A512	$1.05 multicolored	2.50	2.10

Nos. 1540-1542 (3) 　4.50　2.70

Transfer of Olympic Flag from Atlanta to Sydney
A513

1996, July 22　　　　　　**Litho.**

1543	A513	45c multicolored	1.10	.50

Issued in sheets of 10.

Children's Book Council, 50th Anniv.
A514

Covers from "Book of the Year" books: No. 1544, "Animalia." No. 1545, "Greetings from Sandy Beach." No. 1546, "Who Sank the Boat?" No. 1547, "John Brown, Rose and the Midnight Cat."

1996, July 4　Litho.　Perf. 14x14½

1544	A514	45c multicolored	1.00	1.00
1545	A514	45c multicolored	1.00	1.00
1546	A514	45c multicolored	1.00	1.00
1547	A514	45c multicolored	1.00	1.00
a.		Block of 4, #1544-1547	4.50	4.50

Nos. 1544-1547 (4) 　4.00　4.00

Serpentine Die Cut 11½
Self-Adhesive

1548	A514	45c like #1544	1.40	.70
1549	A514	45c like #1546	1.40	.70
1550	A514	45c like #1547	1.40	.70
1551	A514	45c like #1545	1.40	.70
a.		Booklet pane, 4 #1548, 2 each #1549-1551	15.50	
b.		Strip of 4, #1548-1551	7.00	

Nos. 1548-1551 (4) 　5.60　2.80

By its nature, No. 1551a is a complete booklet. The peelable paper backing serves as a booklet cover.

National Council of Women, Cent. — A515

Designs: 45c, Margaret Windeyer (1866-1939), honorary life president. $1, Rose Scott (1847-1925), founding executive member.

1996, Aug. 8　Litho.　Perf. 14½x14

1552	A515	45c claret & yellow	.95	.30
1553	A515	$1 blue & yellow	2.10	2.10

Gems Type of 1995
1996, Sept. 5　Litho.　Perf. 14½x14

1554	A481	45c Pearl	1.10	.30
1555	A481	$1.20 Diamond	3.00	3.00

No. 1555 contains a round foil design. Soaking in water may affect the design.

Arts Councils in Regional Australia
A516

Silhouettes of performing artists, outdoor scene: 20c, Ballet dancer, violinist, field, bales, trees. 45c, Violinist, hand holding flower, dancer, tree in field.

Perf. 14 Horiz.
1996, Sept. 12　　　　　**Litho.**
Booklet Stamps

1556	A516	20c multicolored	1.75	1.25
1557	A516	45c multicolored	.95	.85
a.		Bklt. pane, #1556, 4 #1557	5.75	
		Complete booklet, #1557a	5.75	

A517　　　　Pets — A518

1996-97　Perf. 14x14½, 14½x14

1558	A517	45c Cockatoo	1.10	1.10
1559	A517	45c Ducks, vert.	1.10	1.10
1560	A517	45c Dog, cat, vert.	1.10	1.10
a.		Pair, #1559-1560	2.60	2.60
1561	A518	45c Dog, puppy	1.10	1.10
1562	A518	45c Kittens	1.10	1.10
a.		Pair, #1561-1562	2.60	2.60

Size: 30x50mm

1563	A518	45c Pony mare, foal	1.10	.55
a.		Souvenir sheet, #1558-1563, perf. 14¼	7.75	7.75
b.		As "a," ovptd.	8.00	8.00
c.		As "a," ovptd.	8.00	8.00
d.		As "a," ovptd.	8.00	8.00
e.		As "a," ovptd.	8.00	8.00
f.		As "a," ovptd.	8.00	8.00
g.		As "a," ovptd.	8.00	8.00
h.		As "a," ovptd.	8.00	8.00

Nos. 1558-1563 (6) 　6.60　6.05

Self-Adhesive
Serpentine Die Cut 11½

1564	A518	45c like #1561	2.25	1.10
1565	A518	45c like #1562	2.25	1.10
a.		Bklt. pane, 6 #1564, 4 #1565	22.50	

No. 1563a is a continuous design.
Overprints in gold on sheet margin: No. 1563b, show emblem and "10TH ASIAN INTERNATIONAL PHILATELIC EXHIBITION 1996" in Chinese and English. No. 1563c, pets emblem and, "ASDA CENTREPOINT '96 STAMP AND COIN SHOW / 5-7 October 1996." No. 1563d, pets emblem and "ST PETERS STAMP & COLLECTIBLE FAIR / 12-13 OCTOBER 1996." No. 1563e, pets emblem and "MELBOURNE '96 NATIONAL PHILATELIC EXHIBITION / 17-20 OCTOBER 1996." No. 1563f, pets emblem and "QUEENSLAND SPRING STAMP AND COIN SHOW / 25-27 OCTOBER 1996." No. 1563g, pets emblem and "SWANPEX '96 / 26-27 OCTOBER 1996." No. 1563h: Hong Kong '97 emblem and "11TH ASIAN INTERNATIONAL STAMP EXHIBITION / 12-16 FEBRUARY 1997."
By its nature, No. 1565a is a complete booklet. The peelable paper backing serves as a booklet cover.
Issued: Nos. 1558-1563, 1563a, 1564-1565, 10/1/96; Nos. 1563b-1563g, 10/3/96; No. 1563h, 2/12/97.

Baron Ferdinand von Mueller (1825-96), Botanist — A519

1996, Oct. 9　　　　　　**Perf. 14**

1566	A519	$1.20 multicolored	2.50	2.50

See Germany No. 1949.

Christmas — A520

40c, Madonna and Child. 45c, Wise man. $1, Shepherd boy, lamb.

1996, Nov. 1　　　**Perf. 14½x14**

1567	A520	40c multicolored	.80	.80
1568	A520	45c multicolored	.90	.90
1569	A520	$1 multicolored	2.00	2.00

Nos. 1567-1569 (3) 　3.70　3.70

Self-Adhesive
Serpentine Die Cut 12

1570	A520	40c like #1567	2.25	.55
a.		Booklet pane of 20	45.00	

By its nature, No. 1570a is a complete booklet. The peelable paper backing serves as a booklet cover.

Exploration of Australian Coast & Christmas Island by Willem de Vlamingh, 300th Anniv. — A521

Portrait of a Dutch Navigator, by Jan Verkolje.

1996, Nov. 1　　　**Perf. 14x14½**

1571	A521	45c multicolored	.90	.30
a.		Pair, #1571 & Christmas Is. #404	2.25	2.25

Australia Day Type of 1994

Paintings: 85c, Landscape '74, by Fred Williams. 90c, The Balcony 2, by Brett Whiteley. $1.20, Fire Haze at Gerringong, by Lloyd Rees.

1997, Jan. 16　Litho.　Perf. 14½x14

1572	A463	85c multicolored	1.90	1.90
1573	A463	90c multicolored	2.00	2.00
1574	A463	$1.20 multicolored	3.00	3.00

Nos. 1572-1574 (3) 　6.90　6.90

Sir Donald Bradman, Cricketer
A522

1997, Jan. 23　Litho.　Perf. 14¼

1575	A522	45c Portrait	1.10	.55
a.		Without gold highlights, dated "2007"	1.40	1.40
1576	A522	45c At bat	1.10	.55
a.		Pair, Nos. 1575-1576	2.25	2.25
b.		Booklet pane of #1575-1576	1.90	
c.		Without gold highlights, dated "2007"	1.40	1.40

No. 1576b issued 1/24/07. Nos. 1575a, 1576c issued 11/14/2007.
See Nos. 1634-1646, 1719-1722, 1800-1807, 1933-1936, 1941-1942, 2021-2030, 2125-2132, 2207-2210.

Greetings — A523

1997, Jan. 29　　　**Perf. 14½x14**

1577	A523	45c Rose	.90	.90

Serpentine Die Cut 11½
Booklet Stamp
Self-Adhesive

1578	A523	45c like #1577	1.25	.30
a.		Booklet pane of 10	12.50	

By its nature, No. 1578a is a complete booklet. The peelable paper backing, which also contains 12 labels, serves as a booklet cover.

Classic
Cars — A524

Automobiles: No. 1579, 1934 Ford Coupe
Utility. No. 1580, 1948 GMH Holden 48-215
(FX). No. 1581, 1958 Austin Lancer. No. 1582,
1962 Chrysler Valiant R Series.

1997, Feb. 27   Litho.   Perf. 14x14½
1579	A524	45c multicolored	.90	.90
a.		Booklet pane of 4	3.75	
1580	A524	45c multicolored	.90	.90
a.		Booklet pane of 4	3.75	
1581	A524	45c multicolored	.90	.90
a.		Booklet pane of 4	3.75	
1582	A524	45c multicolored	.90	.90
a.		Booklet pane of 4	3.75	
b.		Block of 4, #1579-1582	4.50	4.50
		Complete booklet, #1579a, 1580a, 1581a, 1582a	19.00	
		Nos. 1579-1582 (4)	3.60	3.60

Complete booklet contains 2 postal cards
and 16 self-adhesive labels.

Serpentine Die Cut 12
Booklet Stamps
Self-Adhesive
1583	A524	45c like #1579	1.25	.55
1584	A524	45c like #1580	1.25	.55
1585	A524	45c like #1581	1.25	.55
1586	A524	45c like #1582	1.25	.55
a.		Bklt. pane, 2 ea #1583, 1585, 3 ea #1584, 1586	14.00	
b.		Strip of 4, #1583-1586	8.00	
		Nos. 1583-1586 (4)	5.00	2.20

By its nature, No. 1586a is a complete booklet. The peelable backing serves as a booklet
cover. The backing for No. 1586b is inscribed
with a 3x8mm black vertical box and "SNP
CAMBEC."

Circuses in
Australia, 150th
Anniv. — A525

Designs: No. 1591, Queen of the Arena,
May Wirth (1894-1978). No. 1592, Wizard of
the Wire, Con Colleano (1899-1973). No.
1593, Clowns. No. 1594, Tumblers.

1997, Mar. 13   Litho.   Perf. 14½x14
1591	A525	45c multicolored	1.00	.70
1592	A525	45c multicolored	1.00	.70
1593	A525	45c multicolored	1.00	.70
1594	A525	45c multicolored	1.00	.70
a.		Block of 4, #1591-1594	4.50	4.50
		Nos. 1591-1594 (4)	4.00	2.80

Queen Elizabeth II, 71st Birthday, 50th
Wedding Anniv.
A526

1997, Apr. 17   Engr.   Perf. 14x14½
1595	A526	45c Design A50	1.00	.55

A527

1997, Apr. 17   Perf. 14½x14
1596	A527	45c multicolored	1.00	.55

Lions Clubs of Australia, 50th anniv.

A528

Dolls and Teddy Bears: No. 1597, Doll wearing red hat. No. 1598, Bear standing. No.
1599, Doll wearing white dress holding teddy
bear. No. 1600, Doll in brown outfit. No. 1601,
Teddy bear seated.

1997, May 8   Litho.   Perf. 14½x14
1597	A528	45c multicolored	1.10	1.10
1598	A528	45c multicolored	1.10	1.10
1599	A528	45c multicolored	1.10	1.10
1600	A528	45c multicolored	1.10	1.10
1601	A528	45c multicolored	1.10	1.10
a.		Strip of 5, #1597-1601	5.50	5.50
		Nos. 1597-1601 (5)	5.50	5.50

Nos. 1597-1601 were printed in sheets containing two strips of five. Some sheets exist
overprinted in margin with picture of teddy
bear and inscription "Brisbane Stamp & Coin
Expo / 7-9 June 1997."

Emergency
Services
A529

Designs: No. 1602, Disaster victim evacu-
ated. No. 1603, Police rescue hiker. $1.05,
Rapid response saves home. $1.20, Ambu-
lance dash saves life.

1997, July 10   Litho.   Perf. 14x14½
1602	A529	45c multicolored	1.00	.80
1603	A529	45c multicolored	1.00	.80
a.		Pair, #1602-1603	2.25	2.25
1604	A529	$1.05 multicolored	2.10	2.00
1605	A529	$1.20 multicolored	2.40	2.10
		Nos. 1602-1605 (4)	6.50	5.70

Arrival of
Merino
Sheep in
Australia,
Bicent.
A530

Designs: No. 1606, George Peppin, Junior
(1827-76), breeder, Merino sheep. No. 1607,
"Pepe" chair, uses of wool.

1997, Aug. 7   Litho.   Perf. 14x14½
1606	A530	45c multicolored	1.00	.75
1607	A530	45c multicolored	1.00	.75
a.		Pair, #1606-1607	2.25	2.25

Scenes from
"The
Dreaming,"
Animated
Stories for
Children
A531

Designs: 45c, Dumbi the Owl. $1, The Two
Willy-Willies. $1.20, How Brolga Became a
Bird. $1.80, Tuggan-Tuggan.

1997, Aug. 21   Perf. 14½
1608	A531	45c multicolored	.90	.70
1609	A531	$1 multicolored	2.00	1.50
1610	A531	$1.20 multicolored	2.40	2.40
1611	A531	$1.80 multicolored	3.50	3.50
		Nos. 1608-1611 (4)	8.80	8.10

Prehistoric
Animals — A532

Designs: No. 1612, Rhoetosaurus brownei.
No. 1613, Mcnamaraspis kaprios. No. 1614,
Ninjemys oweni. No. 1615, Paracyclotosaurus
davidi. No. 1616, Woolungasaurus
glendowerensis.

1997, Sept. 4   Litho.   Perf. 14½x14
1612	A532	45c multicolored	.90	.65
1613	A532	45c multicolored	.90	.65
1614	A532	45c multicolored	.90	.65
1615	A532	45c multicolored	.90	.65
1616	A532	45c multicolored	.90	.65
a.		Strip of 5, #1612-1616	4.75	4.75
		Nos. 1612-1616 (5)	4.50	3.25

Printed in sheets of 10 stamps.

A533   Nocturnal
Animals — A534

No. 1617, Barking owl. No. 1618, Spotted-
tailed quoll. No. 1619, Platypus. No. 1620,
Brown antechinus. No. 1621, Dingo. No. 1622,
Yellow-bellied glider.

Perf. 14½x14, 14x14½
1997, Oct. 1   Litho.
1617	A533	45c multicolored	.90	.80
1618	A533	45c multicolored	.90	.80
a.		Pair, #1617-1618	2.25	2.25
1619	A534	45c multicolored	.90	.80
1620	A534	45c multicolored	.90	.80
1621	A534	45c multicolored	.90	.80
a.		Strip of 3, #1619-1621	3.25	3.25

Size: 50x30mm
1622	A534	45c multicolored	1.40	1.40
a.		Souvenir sheet, #1617-1622, perf. 14¼	8.00	8.00
		Nos. 1617-1622 (6)	5.90	5.40

No. 1622a is printed with additional
phosphor ink revealing a glow-in-the-dark spider and web under ultraviolet light.

Size: 21x32mm
Serpentine Die Cut Perf. 11½
Self-Adhesive
1623	A533	45c like #1617	2.25	.50
1624	A533	45c like #1618	2.25	.50
a.		Booklet pane, 5 each #1623-1624	22.50	
b.		Pair, #1623-1624	4.50	

By its nature No. 1624a is a complete booklet. The peelable paper backing serves as a
booklet cover.

Breast
Cancer
Awareness
A535

1997, Oct. 27   Litho.   Perf. 14x14½
1625	A535	45c multicolored	1.00	.55

Christmas
A536

Children in Christmas Nativity pageant: 40c,
Angels. 45c, Mary holding Baby Jesus. $1,
Three Wise Men.

1997, Nov. 3
1626	A536	40c multicolored	.85	.65
1627	A536	45c multicolored	1.10	.85
1628	A536	$1 multicolored	2.10	2.10
		Nos. 1626-1628 (3)	4.05	3.60

Booklet Stamps
Serpentine Die Cut Perf. 11½
Self-Adhesive
1629	A536	40c multicolored	1.10	.55
a.		Booklet pane of 20	22.00	

By its nature No. 1629a is a complete booklet. The peelable paper backing serves as a
booklet cover, which also contains 20 labels.

Maritime
Heritage — A537

1998, Jan. 15   Litho.   Perf. 14½x14
1630	A537	45c Flying Cloud	.90	.70
a.		Pane of 10	9.00	9.00
1631	A537	85c Marco Polo	1.75	1.40
a.		Sheet of 2, #1631 perf. 13½ & Canada #1779b	3.75	3.75
1632	A537	$1 Chusan	2.10	2.40
1633	A537	$1.20 Heather Belle	2.40	2.40
		Nos. 1630-1633 (4)	7.15	6.90

Australia '99 (No. 1630a). World Stamp
Expo. (No. 1631a).
See Canada No. 1779a.
Issued: No. 1630a, 6/17/98; No. 1631a,
3/19/99.

Legends Type of 1997

Olympians: No. 1634: a, Betty Cuthbert. b,
Cuthbert running. c, Herb Elliott. d, Elliott running. e, Dawn Fraser. f, Fraser swimming. g,
Marjorie Jackson. h, Jackson running. i, Murray Rose. j, Rose swimming. k, Shirley Strickland. l, Strickland clearing hurdle.

1998, Jan. 21   Perf. 14x14½
Size: 34x26mm
1634		Sheet of 12	14.00	14.00
a.-l.	A522	45c any single	1.10	1.10
m.		Booklet pane, #1634a-1634d	5.50	—
n.		Booklet pane, #1634e-1634h	5.50	—
o.		Booklet pane, #1634i-1634l	5.50	—

Booklet Stamps
Self-Adhesive
Serpentine Die Cut 11½
Size: 34x25mm
1635	A522	45c like #1634a	1.10	.65
1636	A522	45c like #1634b	1.10	.65
1637	A522	45c like #1634c	1.10	.65
1638	A522	45c like #1634d	1.10	.65
1639	A522	45c like #1634e	1.10	.65
1640	A522	45c like #1634f	1.10	.65
1641	A522	45c like #1634g	1.10	.65
1642	A522	45c like #1634h	1.10	.65
1643	A522	45c like #1634i	1.10	.65
1644	A522	45c like #1634j	1.10	.65
1645	A522	45c like #1634k	1.10	.65
1646	A522	45c like #1634l	1.10	.65
a.		Bklt. pane of 12, #1635-1646	13.50	
		Nos. 1635-1646 (12)	13.20	7.80

By its nature, No. 1646a is a complete booklet. The peelable backing serves as a booklet
cover. Nos. 1634m-1634o issued 1/24/07.

Greetings — A538

1998, Feb. 12   Litho.   Perf. 14½x14
1647	A538	45c Champagne roses	1.10	.65

Booklet Stamp
Self-Adhesive
Serpentine Die Cut 11½
1648	A538	45c like #1647	1.10	.65
a.		Booklet pane of 10	11.00	

By its nature No. 1648a is a complete booklet. The peelable paper backing, which contains 12 labels, serves as a booklet cover.

Queen
Elizabeth II,
72nd
Birthday
A539

1998, Apr. 9   Litho.   Perf. 14x14½
1649	A539	45c multicolored	1.10	.65

Royal Australian Navy Fleet Air Arm, 50th Anniv. A540

1998, Apr. 9
1650 A540 45c multicolored 1.10 .65

Farming in Australia A541

Designs: No. 1651, Sheep for producing wool. No. 1652, Sheaves of wheat. No. 1653, Herding cattle on horseback. No. 1654, Harvesting sugar cane. No. 1655, Dairy cattle, man on motorcycle.

1998, Apr. 21
1651 A541 45c multicolored .90 .75
1652 A541 45c multicolored .90 .75
1653 A541 45c multicolored .90 .75
1654 A541 45c multicolored .90 .75
1655 A541 45c multicolored .90 .75
  a. Strip of 5, #1651-1655 4.75 4.75
  Nos. 1651-1655 (5) 4.50 3.75

Booklet Stamps
Self-Adhesive
Serpentine Die Cut 11½
Size: 37x25mm

1656 A541 45c like #1651 1.75 .90
1657 A541 45c like #1652 1.75 .90
1658 A541 45c like #1653 1.75 .90
1659 A541 45c like #1654 1.75 .90
1660 A541 45c like #1655 1.75 .90
  a. Bklt. pane, 2 ea #1656-1660 17.50
  Nos. 1656-1660 (5) 8.75 4.50

The peelable backing of No. 1660a serves as a booklet cover.

Heart Health A542

1998, May 4 Litho. Perf. 14x14½
1661 A542 45c multicolored 1.10 .65

Rock and Roll in Australia A543

a, "The Wild One," by Johnny O'Keefe, 1958. b, "Oh Yeah Uh Huh," by Col Joye and the Joye Boys, 1959. c, "He's My Blonde-headed Stompie Wompie Real Gone Surfer Boy," by Little Pattie, 1963. d, "Shakin' All Over," by Normie Rowe, 1965. e, "She's So Fine," by The Easybeats, 1965. f, "The Real Thing," by Russell Morris, 1969. g, "Turn Up Your Radio," by The Masters Apprentices, 1970. h, "Eagle Rock," by Daddy Cool, 1971. i, "Most People I Know Think That I'm Crazy," by Billy Thorpe & the Aztecs, 1972. j, "Horror Movie," by Skyhooks, 1974. k, "It's a Long Way to the Top," by AC/DC, 1975. l, "Howzat," by Sherbet, 1976.

1998, May 26
1662 A543 Sheet of 12 11.50 11.50
  a.-l. 45c any single .90 .80

Coil Stamps
Self-Adhesive
Serpentine Die Cut 11½
Size: 37x25mm

1663 A543 45c like #1662a 1.25 .70
1664 A543 45c like #1662b 1.25 .70
1665 A543 45c like #1662c 1.25 .70
1666 A543 45c like #1662d 1.25 .70
1667 A543 45c like #1662e 1.25 .70
1668 A543 45c like #1662f 1.25 .70
1669 A543 45c like #1662g 1.25 .70
1670 A543 45c like #1662h 1.25 .70
1671 A543 45c like #1662i 1.25 .70
1672 A543 45c like #1662j 1.25 .70
1673 A543 45c like #1662k 1.25 .70

1674 A543 45c like #1662l 1.25 .70
  a. Strip of 12 + label 15.00
  Nos. 1663-1674 (12) 15.00 8.40

Endangered Birds — A544

World Wildlife Fund: No. 1675, Helmeted honeyeater. No. 1676, Orange-bellied parrot. No. 1677, Red-tailed black cockatoo. No. 1678, Gouldian finch.

1998, June 25 Perf. 14x14½
1675 A544 5c multicolored .80 .60
1676 A544 5c multicolored .80 .60
  a. Pair, #1675-1676 2.60 2.00
1677 A544 45c multicolored 1.40 1.10
1678 A544 45c multicolored 1.40 1.10
  a. Pair, #1677-1678 3.50 3.50

Performing and Visual Arts — A545

Young people: No. 1679, Playing French horn. No. 1680, Dancing.

1998, July 16 Litho. Perf. 14x14½
1679 A545 45c multicolored 1.00 .80
1680 A545 45c multicolored 1.00 .80
  a. Pair, #1679-1680 2.25 2.25

Orchids — A546

Designs: 45c, Phalaenopsis rosenstromii. 85c, Arundina graminifolia. $1, Grammatophyllum speciosum. $1.20, Dendrobium phalaenopsis.

1998, Aug. 6 Litho. Perf. 14x14
1681 A546 45c multicolored .90 .70
1682 A546 85c multicolored 1.75 1.60
1683 A546 $1 multicolored 2.00 1.90
1684 A546 $1.20 multicolored 2.40 2.10
  a. Souvenir sheet, #1681-1684 7.25 7.25
  Nos. 1681-1684 (4) 7.05 6.30

See Singapore Nos. 858-861b.

The Teapot of Truth, by Cartoonist Michael Leunig A547

Designs: No. 1685, Angel carrying teapot, bird with flower. No. 1686, Birds perched on heart-shaped vine. No. 1687, Characters using heads to pour tea into cup. $1, Stylized family. $1.20, Stylized teapot with face & legs.

1998, Aug. 13 Perf. 14x14½
1685 A547 45c multicolored 1.10 .55
  a. Booklet pane of 4 4.50
1686 A547 45c multicolored 1.10 .55
  a. Booklet pane of 4 4.50
1687 A547 45c multicolored 1.10 .55
  a. Booklet pane of 4 4.50

Size: 30x25mm

1688 A547 $1 multicolored 2.60 2.60
  a. Booklet pane of 2 5.25
1689 A547 $1.20 multicolored 3.25 3.25
  a. Booklet pane of 2 6.25
  Complete booklet, #1685a, 1686a, 1687a, 1688a, 1689a, 1 postal card & 16 self-adhesive labels 25.00
  Nos. 1685-1689 (5) 9.15 7.50

A548

Butterflies — No. 1690, Red lacewing. No. 1691, Dull oakblue. No. 1692, Meadow argus. No. 1693, Ulysses. No. 1694, Common red-eye.

1998, Sept. 3 Litho. Perf. 14½x14
1690 A548 45c multicolored 1.10 .85
1691 A548 45c multicolored 1.10 .85
1692 A548 45c multicolored 1.10 .85
1693 A548 45c multicolored 1.10 .85
1694 A548 45c multicolored 1.10 .85
  a. Strip of 5, #1690-1694 5.75 5.25
  b. Souv. sheet of 5, #1690-1694 5.50 4.25
  Nos. 1690-1694 (5) 5.50 4.25

No. 1694b for China 1999 World Philatelic Exhibition. Issued 8/21/99.

Self-Adhesive
Serpentine Die Cut 11½
1695 A548 45c like #1690 1.25 .70
1696 A548 45c like #1691 1.25 .70
1697 A548 45c like #1692 1.25 .70
1698 A548 45c like #1693 1.25 .70
1699 A548 45c like #1694 1.25 .70
  a. Strip of 5, #1695-1699 6.75
  Nos. 1695-1699 (5) 6.25 3.50

A549

Designs: No. 1700, Sextant, map of Bass Strait. No. 1701, Telescope, map of Van Diemen's Land (Tasmania).

1998, Sept. 10 Perf. 14½x14
1700 A549 45c multicolored 1.10 .70
1701 A549 45c multicolored 1.10 .70
  a. Pair, #1700-1701 2.25 2.25

Circumnavigation of Tasmania by George Bass (1771-c. 1803) and Matthew Flinders (1774-1814), bicent.

A550

Marine Life — A551

Designs: No. 1702, Fiery squid. No. 1703, Manta ray. No. 1704, Bottlenose dolphin. No. 1705, Weedy seadragon. No. 1706, Southern right whale. No. 1707, White pointer shark.

Perf. 14½x14, 14x14½
1998, Oct. 1 Litho.
1702 A550 45c multi 1.10 .85
1703 A550 45c multi, horiz. 1.10 .85
1704 A551 45c multi 1.10 .85
1705 A551 45c multi 1.10 .85
  a. Pair, #1704-1705 2.25 2.25

Size: 50x30mm

1706 A551 45c multi, horiz. 1.10 .85
1707 A551 45c multi 1.10 .85
  a. Souvenir sheet, #1702-1707 7.00 5.75
  Nos. 1702-1707 (6) 6.60 5.10

Booklet Stamps
Self-Adhesive
Serpentine Die Cut Perf. 11½
1708 A551 45c like #1704 1.10 .55
1709 A551 45c like #1705 1.10 .55
  a. Bklt. pane, 5 ea #1708-1709 11.00

No. 1709a is a complete booklet. The peelable paper backing serves as a booklet cover. Nos. 1708-1709 also exist in coils, issued in rolls of 100 with surrounding selvage removed. Value, set of singles $4.50.

Universal Declaration of Human Rights, 50th Anniv. — A552

1998, Oct. 22 Litho. Perf. 14½x14
1712 A552 45c multicolored 1.10 .70

Christmas A553

40c, Magi. 45c, Nativity. $1, Journey to Bethlehem.

1998, Nov. 2 Perf. 14x14½
1713 A553 40c multicolored .80 .55
1714 A553 45c multicolored .90 .80
1715 A553 $1 multicolored 2.00 2.00
  Nos. 1713-1715 (3) 3.70 3.35

Booklet Stamp
Self-Adhesive
Serpentine Die Cut Perf. 11½
1716 A553 40c multicolored 1.10 .55
  a. Booklet pane of 20 22.00

No. 1716a is a complete booklet.

Nationality and Citizenship Act, 50th Anniv. A554

1999, Jan. 14 Litho. Perf. 14x14½
1717 A554 45c multicolored 1.10 .80

Die Cut Perf. 11¾
Self-Adhesive
1718 A554 45c multicolored 1.10 .55

Legends Type of 1997

Designs: Nos. 1719, 1721, Arthur Boyd, artist. Nos. 1720, 1722, "Nebuchadnezzar on Fire Falling over a Waterfall," by Boyd.

1999, Jan. 22 Litho. Perf. 14x14½
1719 A522 45c multicolored 1.10 .85
1720 A522 45c multicolored 1.10 .85
  a. Pair, #1719-1720 2.25 2.25
  b. Booklet pane, #1719-1720 3.00

Booklet Stamps
Self-Adhesive
Serpentine Die Cut Perf. 11½
1721 A522 45c multicolored 1.10 .55
1722 A522 45c multicolored 1.10 .55
  a. Bklt. pane, 5 ea #1721-1722 11.00

No. 1722a is a complete booklet.
No. 1720b issued 1/24/07.

Love — A555

1999, Feb. 4 Perf. 14x14½
1723 A555 45c Red roses 1.00 .75

Booklet Stamp
Self-adhesive
Serpentine Die Cut Perf. 11½
1724 A555 45c like #1723 1.10 .55
  a. Booklet pane of 10 11.00

No. 1724a is a complete booklet.

Intl. Year of Older Persons A556

Designs: No. 1725, Woman walking with girl, man up close. No. 1726, Woman up close, man playing soccer with boy.

1999, Feb. 11   *Perf. 14x14½*
1725	A556	45c multicolored	.90	.65
1726	A556	45c multicolored	.90	.65
a.		Pair, #1725-1726	2.25	2.25

Early Navigators Type of 1963

No. 1727: a, like #374. b, like #376. c, like #377.
No. 1728: a, like #375. b, like #379. c, like #378.

Perf. 14x14½, 14½x14
1999, Mar. 19   Litho.
1727		Sheet of 3	3.25	3.25
a.-c.	A144 45c any single	1.00	1.00
d.	As #1727, imperf.	16.00	16.00
e.	As #1727, perfin "A99" in sheet margin	40.00	40.00
1728		Sheet of 3	3.25	3.25
a.-c.	A145 45c any single	1.00	1.00
d.	As #1728, imperf.	16.00	16.00
e.	As #1728, perfin "A99" in sheet margin	40.00	40.00

Australia '99, World Stamp Expo.
Nos. 1727e-1728e were made from Nos. 1727d-1728d at Australia '99. Examples different perforations or with the perforating and "A99" inverted were intentionally misperfed personally by patrons of the show.

Sailing Ships — A557

1999, Mar. 19   *Perf. 14½x14*
1729	A557	45c Polly Woodside	.90	.55
a.	Perf 14x14½	3.00	3.00
b.	Souvenir sheet of 2, #1729a, Ireland #1173a	7.00	7.00
1730	A557	85c Alma Doepel	1.75	1.75
1731	A557	$1 Enterprize	2.00	2.00
1732	A557	$1.05 Lady Nelson	2.10	2.10
	Nos. 1729-1732 (4)	6.75	6.40

Australia '99, World Stamp Expo (No. 1729a). See Ireland No. 1173.
No. 1729 was issued in sheets of 20 with a se-tenant label showing Australia '99 logo. Panes of 10 No. 1729 with labels were sold only at the show, where patrons could have their photos printed on the label.

Olympic Torch — A558

1999, Mar. 22
1733	A558	$1.20 #289	2.40	2.40

Flora & Fauna Type of 1996

Flowers: Nos. 1734, 1742A, 1743, 1746B, 1746I, Correa reflexa. Nos. 1735, 1744, 1746C, 1746J, Hibbertia scandens. Nos. 1736, 1745, 1746D, 1746K, Ipomoea pescaprae. Nos. 1737, 1746, 1746E, 1746L, Wahlenbergia stricta.
70c, Humpback whales, zebra volute. No. 1739, Brahminy kite, checkerboard helmet shell. No. 1740, Fraser Island, chambered nautilus. $1.05, Loggerhead turtle, baler. $1.20, White-bellied sea eagle, Campbell's stromb.

1999   Litho.   *Perf. 14x14½*
1734	A511	45c multicolored	.90	.75
1735	A511	45c multicolored	.90	.75
1736	A511	45c multicolored	.90	.75
1737	A511	45c multicolored	.90	.75
a.	Block of 4, #1734-1737	3.75	3.75
1738	A511	70c multicolored	1.40	1.40
1739	A511	90c multicolored	1.75	1.75
1740	A511	90c multicolored	1.75	1.75
a.	Pair, #1739-1740	3.50	3.50

1741	A511	$1.05 multicolored	2.10	1.90
1742	A511	$1.20 multicolored	2.40	2.40
	Nos. 1734-1742 (9)	13.00	12.20

Booklet Stamps
Serpentine Die Cut 11, 11¼
(#1742Df)
Self-Adhesive
1742A	A511	45c like #1734	1.10	.55
1742B	A511	45c like #1735	1.10	.55
1742C	A511	45c like #1736	1.10	.55
1742D	A511	45c like #1737	1.10	.55
e.	Booklet pane, 3 each #1742A, 1742C, 2 each #1742B, 1742D	11.00	
f.	Booklet pane, 5 each #1742A-1742D	22.50	

Die Cut perf. 12½x12¾
1743	A511	45c like #1734	1.10	.55
1744	A511	45c like #1735	1.10	.55
1745	A511	45c like #1736	1.10	.55
1746	A511	45c like #1737	1.10	.55
a.	Booklet pane, 3 each #1743, 1745, 2 each #1744, 1746	11.00	
g.	Strip of 4, #1743-1746		
	Nos. 1742A-1746 (8)	8.80	4.40

Nos. 1742De, 1746a are complete booklets.

Coil Stamps
Serpentine Die Cut 11½
1746B	A511	45c like #1734	1.10	.55
1746C	A511	45c like #1735	1.10	.55
1746D	A511	45c like #1736	1.10	.55
1746E	A511	45c like #1737	1.10	.50
f.	Strip of 4, #1746B-1746E	4.50	
h.	Pane, #1746B, 1746D-1746E, 2 #1746C	5.50	

Serpentine Die Cut 13
1746I	A511	45c like #1734	1.10	.55
1746J	A511	45c like #1735	1.10	.55
1746K	A511	45c like #1736	1.10	.55
1746L	A511	45c like #1737	1.10	.55
m.	Strip of 4, #1746I-1746K	4.50	
	Nos. 1746B-1746L (8)	8.80	4.35

Issued: Nos. 1738-1742, 7/8; 1746B-1746E, 1746I-1746L, 4/8.
No. 1742Df is a complete booklet.

Queen Mother and Queen Elizabeth II — A559

1999, Apr. 15   *Perf. 14x14½*
1747	A559	45c multicolored	1.00	.75

Queen Elizabeth II, 73rd birthday.

Children's Television Programs — A560

Designs: Nos. 1748, 1753, "Here's Humphrey." Nos. 1749, 1754, "Bananas in Pajamas." Nos. 1750, 1755, "Mr. Squiggle." Nos. 1751, 1756, Teddy bears from "Play School." Nos. 1752, 1757, Clock, dog, boy from "Play School."

1999, May 6   Litho.   *Perf. 14½x14*
1748	A560	45c multicolored	1.25	1.10
1749	A560	45c multicolored	1.25	1.10
1750	A560	45c multicolored	1.25	1.10
1751	A560	45c multicolored	1.25	1.10
1752	A560	45c multicolored	1.25	1.10
a.	Strip of 5, #1748-1752	6.75	6.75
	Nos. 1748-1752 (5)	6.25	5.50

Self-Adhesive
Serpentine Die Cut 11½x11¼
1753	A560	45c like #1748	1.50	.80
1754	A560	45c like #1749	1.50	.80
1755	A560	45c like #1750	1.50	.80
1756	A560	45c like #1751	1.50	.80
1757	A560	45c like #1752	1.50	.80
a.	Bklt. pane, 2 ea #1753-1757	15.00	
	Nos. 1753-1757 (5)	7.50	4.00

No. 1757a is a complete booklet.

Perth Mint, Cent. A561

1999, May 13   Litho.   *Perf. 14¼x14*
1758	A561	$2 gold & multi	4.00	4.00

Test Rugby in Australia, Cent. A562

Designs: Nos. 1759, 1763, Kicking ball, vert. Nos. 1760, 1764, Catching ball. $1, Diving with ball. $1.20, Being tackled.

1999, June 8   Litho.   *Perf. 14½x14*
1759	A562	45c multi	1.10	.85
1760	A562	45c multi, vert.	1.10	.85
a.	Pair, #1759-1760	2.25	2.25

Perf. 14x14½
1761	A562	$1 multi	2.25	2.25
1762	A562	$1.20 multi	2.50	2.50

Serpentine Die Cut 11½
Self-Adhesive
Coil Stamps
1763	A562	45c like #1759	1.75	.60
1764	A562	45c like #1760	1.75	.60
a.	Pair, #1763-1764	3.50	

Snowy Mountains Hydroelectric Projects, 50th Anniv. A563

Designs: No. 1765, Rock bolters at Tumut 2 Power Station Hall, driller at Tooma-Tumut Tunnel. No. 1766, English class for migrant workers at Cooma. No. 1767, Eucumbene Dam, Tumut 2 Tailwater Tunnel. No. 1768, Island Bend Dam, German carpenters.

1999, Aug. 12   Litho.   *Perf. 14x14½*
1765	A563	45c multicolored	1.10	.85
1766	A563	45c multicolored	1.10	.85
1767	A563	45c multicolored	1.10	.85
1768	A563	45c multicolored	1.10	.85
a.	Block of 4, #1765-1768	4.50	4.50
	Nos. 1765-1768 (4)	4.40	3.40

Self-Adhesive
Coil Stamps
Litho.
Serpentine Die Cut 11¾
1769	A563	45c Like #1765	1.25	.60
1770	A563	45c Like #1766	1.25	.60
1771	A563	45c Like #1767	1.25	.60
1772	A563	45c Like #1768	1.25	.60
a.	Strip of 4, #1769-1772	5.25	5.25
	Nos. 1769-1772 (4)	5.00	2.40

Teddy Bear — A564

Birthday cake — A564a

Roses, Rings — A564b

Pen, Letter — A564c

Christmas Ornament — A564d

Koala — A564e

1999-2003   Litho.   *Perf. 14½x14*
1773	A564	45c multicolored	.90	.65
1774	A564a	45c multicolored	.90	.65
1775	A564b	45c multicolored	.90	.65
a.	Booklet pane of 4 + 4 labels ('02)	3.75	—
	Booklet, 5 #1775a	19.00	
1776	A564c	45c multicolored	.90	.65
1777	A564d	45c multicolored	.90	.65
a.	Booklet pane of 4 + 4 labels	3.75	—
	Complete booklet, 5 #1777a	19.00	
1778	A564e	$1 multicolored	2.60	2.60
	Nos. 1773-1778 (6)	7.10	5.85

Greetings.
Nos. 1773-1778 each were printed with a se-tenant label at right in sheets of 20. Size of label is 24mm wide on No. 1777, 19mm wide on No. 1775a, 17mm on others. Labels were inscribed with phrases appropriate to the stamp design, or blank, upon which Australia Post printed photographs, sent to them through special orders. No. 1775a and 1777a each come with five different margins, each of which is found in the respective booklet, which sold for $9.95.
Issued: Nos. 1773-1778, 9/1/99; No. 1775a, 3/12/02. No. 1777a, 10/31/03.
See No. 1926.
Compare with types A631, A633, A634.

2000 Olympic Games, Sydney — A565

1999, Sept. 14   Litho.   *Perf. 14½x14*
1779	A565	45c multicolored	1.00	.75

Sydney Design 99, Intl. Design Congress A566

Designs: 45c, Australia Post emblem. 90c, Embryo chair. $1.35, Possum skin textile design. $1.50, Storey Hall, Royal Melbourne Institute of Technology.

1999, Sept. 16   Litho.   *Perf. 14x14½*
1780	A566	45c multicolored	.90	.50
1781	A566	90c multicolored	1.75	1.75
1782	A566	$1.35 multicolored	2.75	2.75
1783	A566	$1.50 multicolored	3.00	3.00
	Nos. 1780-1783 (4)	8.40	8.00

Pond Fauna — A567

Designs: Nos. 1784, 1790c, Roth's tree frog. Nos. 1785, 1790d, Dragonfly. Nos. 1786,

1790b, Sacred kingfisher. Nos. 1787, 1790f, Magnificent tree frog. Nos. 1788, 1790e, 1791, Northern dwarf tree frog. Nos. 1789, 1790a, 1792, Javelin frog.
No. 1793, Sacred kingfisher. No. 1794, Magnificent tree frog.

1999, Oct. 1   Litho.   *Perf. 14x14½*
1784	A567	45c multicolored	.95	.80
1785	A567	45c multicolored	.95	.80
a.		Pair, #1784-1785	2.25	2.25

Size: 26x38mm
Perf. 14½x14
1786	A567	45c multicolored	.95	.80
1787	A567	45c multicolored	.95	.80
a.		Pair, #1786-1787	2.25	2.25

Size: 25x30mm
1788	A567	50c multicolored	1.10	.90
1789	A567	50c multicolored	1.10	.90
a.		Pair, #1788-1789	2.40	2.40
		Nos. 1784-1789 (6)	6.00	5.00

Souvenir Sheet
Perf. 14½
1790	A567	Sheet of 6, #a-f	7.00	7.00
g.		Ovptd. in sheet margin for Bangkok 2000 Exhibition	8.00	8.00
h.		Ovptd. in gold in sheet margin for Adelaide Stamp '99 Exhibition	15.50	15.50

No. 1790d has foil impression on dragonfly's wings.
No. 1790 with overprints for Victorian and South Australian Philatelic Congresses in 1999 are unofficial.
No. 1790h was issued by Australia Post. Another, unofficial, overprint in black (with an orange and black sticker affixed) was applied to other souvenir sheets by the event organizers using the same logo.

Self-Adhesive
Serpentine Die Cut 11¼
Size: 25x30mm
1791	A567	50c multicolored	1.40	.60
1792	A567	50c multicolored	1.40	.60
a.		Bklt. pane, 5 ea #1791-1792	17.00	

Nos. 1791-1792 are booklet stamps. No. 1792a is a complete booklet.

Die Cut Perf. 11¾
Size: 26x38mm
1793	A567	45c multicolored	1.25	.60
1794	A567	45c multicolored	1.25	.60
a.		Pair, #1793-1794	3.00	3.00

Christmas
A568

1999, Nov. 1   *Perf. 14½x14*
1795	A568	40c Madonna and child, vert.	1.00	.75

Perf. 14x14½
1796	A568	$1 Tree	2.25	2.25

Booklet Stamp
Self-Adhesive
Serpentine Die Cut 11¾
1797	A568	40c Like #1795	1.10	.60
a.		Booklet pane of 20	22.50	

Celebrate 2000 — A569

1999, Nov. 1   Litho.   *Perf. 14½x14*
1798	A569	45c multicolored	1.10	.75

No. 1798 has a holographic image. Soaking in water may affect hologram.
Sheets of 10 exist with 10 labels inscribed "Celebrate 2000."
No. 1798 was also printed with a se-tenant label at right in sheets of 20. Labels were inscribed "Celebrate 2000" or blank, upon which Australia Post printed photographs, sent to them through special orders.
Sheets of 10 stamps plus 10 photo labels have been available at special events. These have the sheet selvage inscribed for each event. Most of these have been available only at the event and exist in very limited quantities.

Faces of Australia — A570

Ordinary people: a, Nicholle and Meghan Triandis, baby twins. b, David Willis, cattleman with hat. c, Natasha Bramley, with snorkel gear. d, Cyril Watson, Aboriginal boy. e, Mollie Dowdall, with red hat. f, Robin Dicks, in khaki uniform. g, Mary Simons, with gray hair. h, Peta and Samantha Nieuwerth, mother and daughter. i, Dr. John Matthews, with stethoscope. j, Edith Dizon-Fitzsimmons, with large earrings. k, Philippa Weir, with brown hat. l, John Thurgar, with suit, tie and hat. m, Miguel Alzona, with large, multicolored hat. n, Rachael Thomson, girl with wavy hair. o, Necip Akarsu, with mustache. p, Justin Allan, with HMAS Brisbane cap. q, Wadad Dennaoui, with checked blouse. r, Jack Laity, with hat and jacket. s, Kelsey Stubbin, with Australia cap. t, Gianna Rossi, with hand on chin. u, Paris Hansch, young girl. v, Donald George Whatham, in shirt and tie. w, Stacey Coull, Aboriginal girl in patterned blouse. x, Alex Payne, with bicycle helmet. y, John Lodge, with Salvation Army hat.

2000, Jan. 1   Litho.   *Perf. 14¾x13¾*
1799	A570	Sheet of 25	24.00	24.00
a.-y.		45c Any single	.95	.95

Legends Type of 1997
Aging veterans of World War I: Nos. 1800, 1804, Walter Parker. Nos. 1801, 1805, Roy Longmore. Nos. 1802, 1806, Alec Campbell. Nos. 1803, 1807, 1914-15 Star.

2000, Jan. 21   Litho.   *Perf. 14x14¾*
Size: 34x26mm
1800	A522	45c multi	.95	.95
1801	A522	45c multi	.95	.95
1802	A522	45c multi	.95	.95
1803	A522	45c multi	.95	.95
a.		Block of 4, #1800-1803	4.00	4.00
b.		Booklet pane, #1800-1803	6.00	—
		Nos. 1800-1803 (4)	3.80	3.80

Self-Adhesive
Die Cut Perf. 11¾
1804	A522	45c multi	1.40	.75
1805	A522	45c multi	1.40	.75
1806	A522	45c multi	1.40	.75
1807	A522	45c multi	1.40	.75
a.		Complete booklet, 2 each #1804-1806, 4 #1807	14.25	
		Nos. 1804-1807 (4)	5.60	3.00

No. 1803b issued 1/24/07.

A571

Arts festivals.

2000, Feb. 24   Litho.   *Perf. 14¾x14*
1808	A571	45c Perth	.95	.75
1809	A571	45c Adelaide	.95	.75
1810	A571	45c Sydney	.95	.75
1811	A571	45c Melbourne	.95	.75
1812	A571	45c Brisbane	.95	.75
a.		Strip of 5, #1808-1812	4.75	4.75
		Nos. 1808-1812 (5)	4.75	3.75

A572

Gardens: Nos. 1813, 1818, 1823, Coast banksia, false sarsaparilla, swamp bloodwood (denomination at UR). Nos. 1814, 1819, 1824, Swamp bottlebrush, Eastern spinebill (denomination at UL). Nos. 1815, 1820, 1825, Canna X generalis varieties (denomination at LL). Nos. 1816, 1821, 1826, Pond, roses, purple swamphen (denomination at UR). Nos. 1817, 1822, 1827, Pond, hibiscus, nerium oleander (denomination at UL).

2000, Mar. 23   Litho.   *Perf. 14¾x14*
1813	A572	45c multi	.95	.95
1814	A572	45c multi	.95	.95
1815	A572	45c multi	.95	.95
1816	A572	45c multi	.95	.95
1817	A572	45c multi	.95	.95
a.		Horiz. strip, #1813-1817	4.75	4.75
		Nos. 1813-1817 (5)	4.75	4.75

Booklet Stamps
Self-Adhesive
Serpentine Die Cut 11½x11¼
Pale Green Frames
1818	A572	45c multi	1.10	.75
1819	A572	45c multi	1.10	.75
1820	A572	45c multi	1.10	.75
1821	A572	45c multi	1.10	.75
1822	A572	45c multi	1.10	.75
a.		Booklet, 2 each #1818-1822	11.50	
		Nos. 1818-1822 (5)	5.50	3.75

Coil Stamps
Self-Adhesive
Serpentine Die Cut 11¾
Pale Green Frames
1823	A572	45c multi	1.25	.75
1824	A572	45c multi	1.25	.75
1825	A572	45c multi	1.25	.75
1826	A572	45c multi	1.25	.75
1827	A572	45c multi	1.25	.75
a.		Strip of 5, #1823-1827	7.00	
		Nos. 1823-1827 (5)	6.25	3.75

Queen Elizabeth II, 74th Birthday A573

2000, Apr. 13   Litho.   *Perf. 14x14¾*
1828	A573	45c multi	1.00	.75

Korean War, 50th Anniv. A574

2000, Apr. 18
1829	A574	45c multi	1.00	.75

Daisy — A575

Australia on Globe, Southern Cross — A576

Kangaroo and Flag — A577

Sand, Sea and Sky — A578

Rainforest A579

2000, May 11   *Perf. 14½x14*
1830	A575	45c multi + label	.95	.95
1831	A576	45c multi + label	.95	.95
1832	A577	45c multi + label	.95	.95
1833	A578	45c multi + label	.95	.95
1834	A579	45c multi + label	.95	.95
		Nos. 1830-1834 (5)	4.75	4.75

Nos. 1830-1834 each issued in sheets of 20 stamps and labels, with and without decorative selvage.
Sheets containing 10 No. 1831 with margins and ten labels that could be personalized were sold for $12, $2 of which was donated to volunteer organizations of the purchaser's choice. Volunteer organizations could purchase these sheets and offer them for resale in fundraising projects.
No. 1832 exists in a sheet of 10+10 labels that sold sold for $16. Sheet has decorative selvage and labels showing stock photo.

The Move Towards Federation — A580

Designs: No. 1835, Taking the vote. No. 1836, Waiting for the results. No. 1837, The fair new nation. No. 1838, Queen Victoria.

2000, May 22   *Perf. 14¾x14*
1835	A580	45c multi	1.10	.75
1836	A580	45c multi	1.10	.75
a.		Pair, #1835-1836	2.40	2.40

Size: 30x50mm
Perf. 14x14½
1837	A580	$1.50 multi	3.50	3.50
1838	A580	$1.50 multi	3.50	3.50
a.		Pair, #1837-1838	7.00	7.00
b.		Souvenir sheet, #1836a, 1838a	9.25	9.25
c.		As "b," with marginal inscription for The Stamp Show 2000, London	10.00	10.00
		Nos. 1835-1838 (4)	9.20	8.50

Tourist Attractions — A581

Designs: 50c, Sydney Opera House. $1, Nandroya Falls. $1.50, Sydney Harbour Bridge. $2, Cradle Mountain. $3, The Pinnacles. $4.50, Flinders Ranges. $5, Twelve Apostles. $10, Devils Marbles.

2000, June 20   Litho.   *Perf. 14½x14*
1839	A581	50c multi	1.00	.75
1840	A581	$1 multi	2.25	1.40
1841	A581	$1.50 multi	3.25	2.00
1842	A581	$2 multi	4.25	2.25
1843	A581	$3 multi	6.25	3.50

Size: 56x25mm
Perf. 14x14½

1844	A581	$4.50 multi	9.50	5.75
1845	A581	$5 multi	10.00	6.25
1846	A581	$10 multi	20.00	11.50
		Nos. 1839-1846 (8)	56.50	33.40

See Nos. 1925, 1979-1983, 2055-2059, 2077-2080, 2280-2283.

2000 Paralympics, Sydney — A582

Designs: Nos. 1847, 1855, Wheelchair tennis. Nos. 1848, 1856, Amputee running. Nos. 1849, 1853, Wheelchair basketball. Nos. 1850, 1852, Cycling for the visually impaired. Nos. 1851, 1854, Amputee shot put.

2000, July 3   Litho.   Perf. 14¾x14

1847	A582	45c multi	1.00	1.00
1848	A582	45c multi	1.00	1.00
a.		Pair, #1847-1848	2.40	2.40
1849	A582	49c multi	1.00	1.00
1850	A582	49c multi	1.00	1.00
1851	A582	49c multi	1.00	1.00
a.		Strip of 3, #1849-1851	3.50	3.50
		Nos. 1847-1851 (5)	5.00	5.00

Booklet Stamps
Self-Adhesive
Die Cut Perf. 11½x11¾

1852	A582	49c multi	1.40	.75
1853	A582	49c multi	1.40	.75
1854	A582	49c multi	1.40	.75
a.		Bklt., 4 ea #1852-1853, 2 #1854	14.50	

Coil Stamps
Self-Adhesive
Serpentine Die Cut 11¾

1855	A582	45c multi	1.10	.85
1856	A582	45c multi	1.10	.85
a.		Pair, #1855-1856	2.50	2.25
		Nos. 1852-1856 (5)	6.40	3.95

No. 1851 exists without Tasmania in the map of Australia at LL. Value $20.

Australian Victoria Cross, Cent. — A583

Designs: No. 1857, Sir Neville Howse. No. 1858, Sir Arthur Roden Cutler. No. 1859, Victoria Cross. No. 1860, Edward Kenna. No. 1861, Keith Payne.

2000, July 24   Litho.   Perf. 14¾x14

1857	A583	45c multi	.95	.95
1858	A583	45c multi	.95	.95
1859	A583	45c multi	.95	.95
1860	A583	45c multi	.95	.95
1861	A583	45c multi	.95	.95
a.		Horiz. strip of 5, #1857-1861	5.25	5.25
		Nos. 1857-1861 (5)	4.75	4.75

Olympic Sports — A584

Designs: Nos. 1862a, 1869, Water polo. Nos. 1862b, 1870, Women's field hockey. Nos. 1862c, 1863, Swimming. Nos. 1862d, 1865, Basketball. Nos. 1862e, 1866, Triathlon cycling. Nos. 1862f, 1871, Equestrian. Nos. 1862g, 1872, Tennis. Nos. 1862h, 1864, Rhythmic gymnastics. Nos. 1862i, 1867, Runner. Nos. 1862j, 1868, Rowing.

2000, Aug. 17   Litho.   Perf. 14¾x14

1862		Sheet of 10	11.50	11.50
a.-j.		A584 45c Any single	1.10	1.10
k.		As #1862, with inscription added in sheet margin	12.50	12.50

No. 1862k was issued 9/15/00 and has additional multicolored inscription in upper sheet margin reading "15-28 / September / 2000 / OLYMPHILEX 2000" and show emblem.

Booklet Stamps
Self-Adhesive
Serpentine Die Cut 11½x11¼

1863	A584	45c multi	1.25	.70
1864	A584	45c multi	1.25	.70
1865	A584	45c multi	1.25	.70
1866	A584	45c multi	1.25	.70
1867	A584	45c multi	1.25	.70
1868	A584	45c multi	1.25	.70
1869	A584	45c multi	1.25	.70
1870	A584	45c multi	1.25	.70
1871	A584	45c multi	1.25	.70
1872	A584	45c multi	1.25	.70
a.		Booklet, #1863-1872	13.75	
		Nos. 1863-1872 (10)	12.50	7.00

Sydney and Athens — A585

Olympic torch, flag and: 45c, Parthenon. $1.50, Sydney Opera House.

2000, Sept. 15   Litho.   Perf. 14½x14

1873	A585	45c multi + label	1.00	.60
1874	A585	$1.50 multi + label	3.50	3.50

Nos. 1873-1874 were issued in sheets of 20 stamps and 20 se-tenant labels. Labels were inscribed "Sydney Athens." These sheets could be ordered with personalized labels, as could sheets with a stock photo.
See Greece Nos. 1968-1969.

Australian Gold Medalists at 2000 Olympics A586

Cathy Freeman Lighting Olympic Flame — A587

Medal Winners: Nos. 1875, 1891, Ian Thorpe. Nos. 1876, 1892, Men's 4x100-meter freestyle relay swimming team. Nos. 1877, 1893, Michael Diamond. Nos. 1878, 1894, Three day event equestrian team. Nos. 1879, 1895, Susie O'Neill. Nos. 1880, 1896, Men's 4x200-meter freestyle relay swimming team. Nos. 1881, 1897, Simon Fairweather. Nos. 1882, 1898, Brett Aitken, Scott McGrory. Nos. 1883, 1899, Grant Hackett. Nos. 1884, 1900, Women's water polo team. Nos. 1885, 1901, Natalie Cook, Kerri Pottharst. Nos. 1886, 1902, Cathy Freeman. Nos. 1887, 1903, Lauren Burns. Nos. 1888, 1904, Women's field hockey team. Nos. 1889, 1905, Jenny Armstrong, Belinda Stowell. Nos. 1890, 1906, Tom King, Mark Turnbull.

2000   Digitally Printed   Perf. 14¼

1875	A586	45c multi	1.00	1.00
1876	A586	45c multi	1.00	1.00
1877	A586	45c multi	1.00	1.00
1878	A586	45c multi	1.00	1.00
1879	A586	45c multi	1.00	1.00
1880	A586	45c multi	1.00	1.00
1881	A586	45c multi	1.00	1.00
1882	A586	45c multi	1.00	1.00
1883	A586	45c multi	1.00	1.00
1884	A586	45c multi	1.00	1.00
1885	A586	45c multi	1.00	1.00
1886	A586	45c multi	1.00	1.00
1887	A586	45c multi	1.00	1.00
1888	A586	45c multi	1.00	1.00
1889	A586	45c multi	1.00	1.00
1890	A586	45c multi	1.00	1.00

Litho.

1891	A586	45c multi	1.10	1.10
1892	A586	45c multi	1.10	1.10
1893	A586	45c multi	1.10	1.10
1894	A586	45c multi	1.10	1.10
1895	A586	45c multi	1.10	1.10
1896	A586	45c multi	1.10	1.10
1897	A586	45c multi	1.10	1.10
1898	A586	45c multi	1.10	1.10
1899	A586	45c multi	1.10	1.10
1900	A586	45c multi	1.10	1.10
1901	A586	45c multi	1.10	1.10
1902	A586	45c multi	1.10	1.10
1903	A586	45c multi	1.10	1.10
1904	A586	45c multi	1.10	1.10
1905	A586	45c multi	1.10	1.10
1906	A586	45c multi	1.10	1.10
1907	A587	45c multi	1.10	1.10
		Nos. 1875-1907 (33)	34.70	34.70

Issued: Nos. 1875-1876, 9/17; No. 1877, 9/18; Nos. 1891-1892, 9/19; Nos. 1878-1880, 1893, 9/20; No. 1881, 9/21; Nos. 1882, 1894-1896, 9/22; No. 1897, 9/23; Nos. 1883-1884, 1898, 9/24; Nos. 1885-1886, 1899-1900, 9/26; Nos. 1887, 1901-1902, 9/28; Nos. 1888, 1903, 9/30; Nos. 1889-1890, 10/1; No. 1904, 10/2; Nos. 1905-1906, 10/3; No. 1907, 10/10.

Nos. 1875-1890 have shinier appearance than Nos. 1891-1906. Olympic rings, flag stars and flag edge on Nos. 1875-1890 has a more ragged appearance than Nos. 1891-1906, which have crisp details.

Nos. 1875-1907 printed in sheets of 10. Sheets of Nos. 1875-1890 exist rouletted at either the right or left and have one of six red animal imprints in lower right margin representing where the sheets were made (Platypus, Sydney; Kookaburra, Canberra; Koala, Brisbane; Swan, Perth; Kangaroo, Adelaide; Opossum, Melbourne). Sheets of Nos. 1875-1890 were placed on sale at 67 outlets within 24 hours of the awarding of the medals to the athletes. Sheets of Nos. 1891-1906, which have a straight-edged right margin and a red Australia map imprint in lower right margin, gradually became available nationwide as stocks were printed and shipped.

A sheet containing Nos. 1891-1907 and 8 labels was available only in the Australia Post annual collection. Value, $50.

Space — A588

Designs: Nos. 1908, 1914a, Flight crew. Nos. 1909, 1914b, Robots, vert. Nos. 1910, 1914c, 1915, 1917, Astronaut, vert. Nos. 1911, 1914d, 1916, 1918, Terrain, vert. Nos. 1912, 1914e, Spacecraft. Nos. 1913, 1914f, Launch site, vert.

Perf. 14x14½, 14½x14

2000, Oct. 3   Litho.

1908	A588	45c multi	.95	.95
1909	A588	45c multi	.95	.95

Size: 26x38mm

1910	A588	45c multi	.95	.95
1911	A588	45c multi	.95	.95
a.		Pair, #1910-1911	2.25	2.25

Size: 50x30mm

1912	A588	45c multi	.95	.95

Size: 30x50mm

1913	A588	45c multi	.95	.95
		Nos. 1908-1913 (6)	5.70	5.70

Souvenir Sheet
Litho. with Translucent Foil
Perf. 14½

1914		Sheet of 6	5.75	5.75
a.-f.		A588 45c any single	.95	.95
g.		As #1914, ovptd. in margin in gold	10.25	10.25

Booklet Stamps
Litho.
Self-Adhesive
Serpentine Die Cut 11½x11¼

1915	A588	45c multi	1.40	.60
1916	A588	45c multi	1.40	.60
a.		Booklet, 5 each #1915-1916	14.50	

Coil Stamps
Serpentine Die Cut 11½

1917	A588	45c multi	1.25	.60
1918	A588	45c multi	1.25	.60
a.		Pair, #1917-1918	2.75	2.00

Nos. 1915-1918 have pink and gray frames. No 1914g overprinted with emblem of Hong Kong 2001 Stamp Exhibition. Issued 2/1/01.

2000 Paralympics, Sydney — A589

Designs: No. 1919, Paralympics emblem. No. 1920, Runner with torch.

2000, Oct. 18   Litho.   Perf. 14½x14

1919	A589	45c multi + label	1.00	1.00
1920	A589	45c multi + label	1.00	1.00

Siobhan Paton, Paralympian of the Year — A590

2000, Oct. 31   Perf. 14¼

1921	A590	45c multi	1.00	.75

Christmas — A591

40c, Madonna and child. 45c, Manger.

2000, Nov. 1   Litho.   Perf. 14½x14

1922	A591	40c multi	.85	.80
1923	A591	45c multi	.95	.60
a.		Souvenir sheet, #1922-1923	2.25	2.25

Booklet Stamp
Serpentine Die Cut 11¾

1924	A591	40c multi	.85	.70
a.		Booklet of 20 + 20 stickers	17.25	

Tourist Attractions Type of 2000

2000, Nov. 1   Perf. 14½x14

1925	A581	80c Byron Bay	1.75	1.40

No. 1778 Digitally Overprinted in Dark Blue

2001, Jan.   Litho.   Perf. 14½x14

1926	A564	$1 multi + label	14.50	14.50

Federation of Australia, Cent. — A592

Designs: Nos. 1927, 1931, Federation Arch, Sydney. Nos. 1928, 1932, Sir Edmund Barton, first prime minister. No. 1929, National celebrations, horiz (50x30mm). No. 1930, State banquet (30x50mm).

Perf. 14¾x14, 14x14¾

2001, Jan. 1   Litho.

1927	A592	49c multi	1.10	1.00
1928	A592	49c multi	1.10	1.00
a.		Pair, #1927-1928	3.00	2.50
1929	A592	$2 multi	4.25	4.25
1930	A592	$2 multi	4.25	4.25
a.		Souvenir sheet, #1927-1930, perf. 14½	11.25	11.25
		Nos. 1927-1930 (4)	10.70	10.50

Self-Adhesive
Booklet Stamps
Serpentine Die Cut 11½x11

1931	A592 49c multi	1.10	.30
a.	Serpentine die cut 11½x11¾	—	—
1932	A592 49c multi	1.10	.30
a.	Booklet, 5 each # 1931-1932	11.50	

Australian Legends Type of 1997

Slim Dusty, musician: Nos. 1933, 1935, With guitar. Nos. 1934, 1936, Wearing blue shirt.

2001, Jan. 25   *Perf. 14x14¾*
Size: 34x26mm

1933	A522 45c multi	1.10	1.00
1934	A522 45c multi	1.10	1.00
a.	Pair, #1933-1934	2.75	2.75
b.	Booklet pane, #1933-1934	3.00	—

Self-Adhesive
Booklet Stamps
Serpentine Die Cut 11x11½

1935	A522 45c multi	1.10	.75
1936	A522 45c multi	1.10	.75
a.	Booklet, 5 each #1935-1936	11.50	
	Nos. 1933-1936 (4)	4.40	3.50

No. 1934b issued 1/24/07.

Australian Army, Cent. A593

Rising Sun badge and: No. 1937, Light Horse Brigade, 1940, soldiers in New Guinea, 1943. No. 1938, Soldier in UN peacekeeping mission carrying Rwandan child, 1995, soldiers on commando officer selection course, 1997.

2001-05   *Perf. 14x14¾*

1937	A593 45c multi	1.25	.85
a.	Additionally dated "2013" (#1938d)	1.10	1.10
1938	A593 45c multi	1.25	.85
a.	Pair, #1937-1938	2.75	2.75
b.	Booklet pane #1937-1938	3.00	—
c.	Additionally dated "2013" (#1938d)	1.10	1.10
d.	Booklet pane of 2, #1937a, 1938c	2.25	—
	Complete booklet, #1176a, 1207a, 1256a, 1317a, 1380f, 1452a, 1454a, 1482a, 1938b	40.00	

Issued: Nos. 1937-1938, 2/15/01. No. 1938b, 4/05. Complete booklet sold for $14.95.

Issued: Nos. 1937a, 1938c, 1938d, 3/5/13. No. 1938d was issued in booklet along with Nos. 2710c, 2869e, 3107c, 3349b and 3877a.

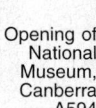

Opening of National Museum, Canberra A594

Designs: No. 1939, Museum floor plan. No. 1940, Pangk (wallaby sculpture), by George MacNaught and Joe Ngallametta.

2001, Mar. 8

1939	A594 49c multi	1.00	.85
1940	A594 49c multi	1.00	.85
a.	Pair, #1939-1940	2.25	2.25

Australian Legends Type of 1997

Similar to Nos. 1575-1576, but with cropped designs and "1908-2001" inscription added.

2001, Mar. 13   *Perf. 14¼*

1941	A522 45c Like #1575	1.00	.85
a.	Without gold highlights, dated "2007"	1.40	1.40
1942	A522 45c Like #1576	1.00	.85
a.	Pair, #1941-1942	2.25	2.25
b.	Without gold highlights, dated "2007"	1.40	1.40

Nos. 1941a, 1942b issued 11/14/07.

Rock Music A595

Designs: Nos. 1943a, 1953, Khe Sanh, by Cold Chisel, 1978. Nos. 1943b, 1952, Down Under, by Men at Work, 1981. Nos. 1943c, 1951, Power and the Passion, by Midnight Oil, 1983. Nos. 1943d, 1950, Original Sin, by INXS. Nos. 1943e, 1949, You're the Voice, by John Farnham, 1986. Nos. 1943f, 1948, Don't Dream It's Over, by Crowded House, 1986. Nos. 1943g, 1947, Treaty, by Yothu Yindi, 1991. Nos. 1943h, 1946, Tomorrow, by Silverchair, 1994. Nos. 1943i, 1945, Confide in Me, by Kylie Minogue, 1994. Nos. 1943j, 1944, Truly, Madly, Deeply, by Savage Garden, 1997.

2001, Mar. 20   **Litho.**   *Perf. 14x14¾*

1943	Sheet of 10	10.00	10.00
a.-j.	A595 45c Any single	1.00	1.00

Self-Adhesive
Serpentine Die Cut 11¼x11½

1944	A595 45c multi	1.25	.80
1945	A595 45c multi	1.25	.80
1946	A595 45c multi	1.25	.80
1947	A595 45c multi	1.25	.80
1948	A595 45c multi	1.25	.80
1949	A595 45c multi	1.25	.80
1950	A595 45c multi	1.25	.80
1951	A595 45c multi	1.25	.80
1952	A595 45c multi	1.25	.80
1953	A595 45c multi	1.25	.80
a.	Horiz. strip of 10, #1944-1953	13.75	
b.	Booklet, #1944-1953	13.75	
	Nos. 1944-1953 (10)	12.50	8.00

Queen Elizabeth II, 75th Birthday — A596

2001, Apr. 12   **Litho.**   *Perf. 14¾x14*

1954	A596 45c multi	1.00	.75

Flower — A597

Balloons — A598

Streamers — A599

Kangaroos — A600

Bayulu Banner — A601

Litho., Litho with Hologram (#1957)

2001-03   *Perf. 14½x14*

1955	A597 45c multi + label	.95	.95
1956	A598 45c multi + label	.95	.95
1957	A599 45c multi + label	.95	.95
1958	A600 $1 multi + label	2.25	2.25
a.	Booklet pane of 4 + 4 labels	9.25	
	Complete booklet, 2 #1958a	19.00	
1959	A601 $1.50 multi + label	3.50	3.50
a.	Booklet pane #1955-1959 (5)	8.60	8.60

Issued: Nos. 1955-1959, 4/24/01. No. 1958a, 10/31/03.

The complete booklet, which sold for $10.95, contains two panes of No. 1958a with different margins.

Federal Parliament, Cent. — A602

Designs: No. 1960, The Opening of the First Federal Parliament, 9 May 1901, by Charles Nuttall. No. 1961, Opening of the First Parliament of the Commonwealth of Australia by H.R.H. The Duke of Cornwall and York (Later King George V), May 9, 1901, by Tom Roberts.

2001, May 3   **Litho.**   *Perf. 14¼*

1960	A602 45c multi	1.10	.85
a.	Souvenir sheet of 1	1.25	1.25
1961	A602 $2.45 multi	5.25	5.25
a.	Souvenir sheet of 1	5.50	5.50

Outback Services A603

Designs: Nos. 1962, 1967, 1972, Telecommunications. Nos. 1963, 1968, 1973, Transport. Nos. 1964, 1969, 1974, School of the Air. Nos. 1965, 1970, 1975, Postal service. Nos. 1966, 1971, 1976, Royal flying Doctor Service.

2001, June 5   *Perf. 14x14½*

1962	A603 45c multi	1.00	1.00
1963	A603 45c multi	1.00	1.00
1964	A603 45c multi	1.00	1.00
1965	A603 45c multi	1.00	1.00
1966	A603 45c multi	1.00	1.00
a.	Horiz. strip, #1962-1966	5.75	5.75
	Nos. 1962-1966 (5)	5.00	5.00

Self-Adhesive
Coil Stamps
Serpentine Die Cut 11¼

1967	A603 45c multi	1.10	.95
1968	A603 45c multi	1.10	.95
1969	A603 45c multi	1.10	.95
1970	A603 45c multi	1.10	.95
1971	A603 45c multi	1.10	.95
a.	Horiz. strip, #1967-1971	5.75	

Booklet Stamps
Serpentine Die Cut 11¾

1972	A603 45c multi	1.10	.95
1973	A603 45c multi	1.10	.95
1974	A603 45c multi	1.10	.95
1975	A603 45c multi	1.10	.95
1976	A603 45c multi	1.10	.95
a.	Booklet, 2 each #1972-1976	11.50	
	Nos. 1967-1976 (10)	11.00	9.50

Dragon Boat Races A604

Dragon boats and: 45c, Hong Kong Convention and Exhibition Center. $1, Sydney Opera House.

2001, June 25   *Perf. 14x14½*

1977	A604 45c multi	1.10	.85
1978	A604 $1 multi	2.25	2.25
a.	Souvenir sheet, #1977-1978	3.50	3.50

See Hong Kong Nos. 938-939.

Tourist Attraction Type of 2000

Designs: 50c, Blue Mountains. $1, Murrumbidgee River. $1.50, Port Douglas. $20, Uluru.

Litho., Litho with Foil Application ($20)

2001, July 12   *Perf. 14½x14*

1979	A581 50c multi	.90	.90
1980	A581 $1 multi	1.90	1.90
1981	A581 $1.50 multi	2.75	2.75

Size: 56x25mm
Perf. 14x14½

1982	A581 $20 multi	23.00	25.75
	Nos. 1979-1982 (4)	28.55	31.30

Booklet Stamp
Self-Adhesive
Serpentine Die Cut 11¼x10½

1983	A581 50c multi	1.10	1.00
a.	Booklet, 10 #1983	11.50	

Flora & Fauna Type of 1996

Birds: Nos. 1984, 1988, 1992, Variegated fairy wren. Nos. 1985, 1989, 1993, Painted firetail. Nos. 1986, 1990, 1994, Crimson chat. Nos. 1987, 1991, 1995, Budgerigar.

2001-02   **Litho.**   *Perf. 14x14½*

1984	A511 45c multi	1.00	.90
1985	A511 45c multi	1.00	.90
1986	A511 45c multi	1.00	.90
1987	A511 45c multi	1.00	.90
a.	Block of 4, #1984-1987	4.25	4.25
	Nos. 1984-1987 (4)	4.00	3.60

Self-Adhesive
Coil Stamps
Die Cut Perf. 12½x12¾

1988	A511 45c multi	1.25	.75
1989	A511 45c multi	1.25	.75
1990	A511 45c multi	1.25	.75
1991	A511 45c multi	1.25	.75
a.	Horiz. strip of 4, #1988-1991	5.25	5.25

Booklet Stamps
Serpentine Die Cut 11¼

1992	A511 45c multi	1.25	.75
1993	A511 45c multi	1.25	.75
1994	A511 45c multi	1.25	.75
1995	A511 45c multi	1.25	.75
a.	Booklet pane, #1993, 1995	2.75	
b.	Booklet pane, #1992-1995, rouletted at bottom	5.75	
	Booklet, #1995a, 2 #1995b	11.50	
c.	Booklet pane, #1992-1995, rouletted at side	5.75	
	Booklet, 5 #1995c	28.75	
d.	Pane, #1992-1994, 2 #1995	6.25	
e.	Coil strip, #1992-1995	5.75	
f.	As "d," with Philakorea 2002 ovpt. in margin ('02)	9.00	
g.	As "d," with China 2002 Stamp & Coin Expo ovpt. in margin ('02)	9.00	
h.	As "d," with Hafnia '01 ovpt. in margin	19.00	
	Nos. 1988-1995 (8)	10.00	6.00

Issued: No. 1995f, 8/2/02; No. 1995g, 9/28/02. No. 1995h, 10/16/01. Rest of set, 8/9/01.

Daniel Solander (1733-82), Botanist on Endeavour A605

Designs: 45c, Barringtonia calyptrata and Solander. $1.50, Cachlospermum gillivraei and Endeavour.

Perf. 12½x12¾

2001, Aug. 16   **Litho. & Engr.**

1996	A605 45c multi	1.00	.75
1997	A605 $1.50 multi	3.50	3.50

See Sweden No. 2419.

Commonwealth Heads of Government Meeting, Brisbane — A606

2001, Sept. 4   Litho.   Perf. 14½x14
1998	A606	45c Southern Cross	1.00	.85
1999	A606	45c Australia on globe	1.00	.85
a.		Pair, #1998-1999	2.25	2.25

Christmas — A607

2001, Sept. 4   Perf. 14½x14
Stamp + Label
2000	A607	40c Christmas tree	.85	.85
2001	A607	80c Star	1.75	1.75

Nos. 2000-2001 were each printed in sheets of 20 + 20 labels. The labels could be personalized.

Birds of Prey — A608

Designs: No. 2002, Wedge-tailed eagle. No. 2003, Nankeen kestrel. No. 2004, Red goshawk, vert. No. 2005, Spotted harrier, vert.

Perf. 14x14½, 14½x14
2001, Sept. 11
2002	A608	49c multi	1.10	.85
2003	A608	49c multi	1.10	.85
a.		Pair, #2002-2003	2.50	2.50
2004	A608	98c multi	2.25	2.25
2005	A608	98c multi	2.25	2.25
a.		Pair, #2004-2005	5.00	5.00
		Nos. 2002-2005 (4)	6.70	6.20

Caricatures of Australian Wildlife by Roland Harvey — A609

Designs: Nos. 2006, 2012, Bilby and antechinus musicians, dancing cockatoo. Nos. 2007, 2013, Koala with birthday cake. Nos. 2008, 2014, Ring-tailed possums with drinks and food. Nos. 2009, 2015, Bilbies, crocodile, emu, koala and gifts. Nos. 2010, 2016, Wombat and ladder. Nos. 2011, 2017, Wallabies, echidnas, platypus and ladder.

2001, Oct. 2   Perf. 14½x14
2006	A609	45c multi	1.10	.80
2007	A609	45c multi	1.10	.80
2008	A609	45c multi	1.10	.80
a.		Horiz. strip of 3, #2006-2008	3.50	3.50
b.		Souvenir sheet, #2006-2008	3.50	3.50
2009	A609	45c multi	1.10	.80
2010	A609	45c multi	1.10	.80
2011	A609	45c multi	1.10	.80
a.		Horiz. strip, #2009-2011	3.50	3.50
b.		Souvenir sheet, #2009-2011	3.50	3.50
		Nos. 2006-2011 (6)	6.60	4.80

Self-Adhesive
Serpentine Die Cut 11½x11
2012	A609	45c multi	1.25	.80
2013	A609	45c multi	1.25	.80
2014	A609	45c multi	1.25	.80
2015	A609	45c multi	1.25	.80
2016	A609	45c multi	1.25	.80
2017	A609	45c multi	1.25	.80
a.		Coil strip, 2012-2017	9.25	
b.		Booklet #2014-2015, 2 each #2012-2013, 2016-2017	12.75	
		Nos. 2012-2017 (6)	7.50	4.80

Christmas — A610

Illuminations from the Wharncliffe Hours, by Maitre Francois: 40c, Adoration of the Magi. 45c, Flight into Egypt.

2001, Nov. 1   Perf. 14½x14
2018	A610	40c multi	1.10	.60
2019	A610	45c multi	1.10	.65

Self-Adhesive
Serpentine Die Cut 11½x11¼
2020	A610	40c multi	1.10	.25
a.		Booklet of 20 + 20 labels	24.00	

Australian Legends Type of 1997

Medical researchers: Nos. 2021, 2026, Sir Gustav Nossal. Nos. 2022, 2027, Nancy Mills. No. 2023, 2028, Peter Doherty. Nos. 2024, 2029, Fiona Stanley. Nos. 2025, 2030, Donald Metcalf.

2002, Jan. 23   Litho.   Perf. 14x14¾
Size: 34x26mm
2021	A522	45c multi	.95	.75
2022	A522	45c multi	.95	.75
2023	A522	45c multi	.95	.75
2024	A522	45c multi	.95	.75
2025	A522	45c multi	.95	.75
a.		Vert. strip, #2021-2025	5.25	5.25
b.		Booklet pane, #2021-2025	8.00	8.00
		Nos. 2021-2025 (5)	4.75	3.75

Booklet Stamps
Self-Adhesive
Serpentine Die Cut 11x11½
2026	A522	45c multi	1.10	1.00
2027	A522	45c multi	1.10	1.00
2028	A522	45c multi	1.10	1.00
2029	A522	45c multi	1.10	1.00
2030	A522	45c multi	1.10	1.00
a.		Booklet, 2 each #2026-2030	12.50	
		Nos. 2026-2030 (5)	5.50	5.00

No. 2025b issued 1/24/07.

Reign of Queen Elizabeth II, 50th Anniv. — A611

Queen: 45c, As young woman. $2.45, In 2000.

2002, Feb. 6   Perf. 14¾x14
2031	A611	45c multi	.95	.70
2032	A611	$2.45 multi	5.25	5.25
a.		Souvenir sheet, #2031-2032	6.25	6.25

A booklet pane containing 2 each of Nos. 2031-2032 is found in the booklet footnoted under No. 2507.

Gold Medalists at 2002 Winter Olympics, Salt Lake City — A612

Designs: No. 2033, Steven Bradbury. No. 2034, Alisa Camplin.

2002   Perf. 14¼
2033	A612	45c multi	1.10	1.00
2034	A612	45c multi	1.10	1.00

Issued: No. 2033, 2/20; No. 2034, 2/22.

Race Cars — A613

Designs: Nos. 2035, 2041, Victoria Austin 7 and Bugatti Type 40, Phillip Island, Victoria, 1928. Nos. 2036, 2042, Jaguar Mark II, Mallala, South Australia, 1963. Nos. 2037, 2043, Repco-Brabham, Sandown, Victoria, 1966. Nos. 2038, 2044, Holden Torana XU1 and Ford Falcon XY GTHO, Bathurst, New South Wales, 1972. Nos. 2039, 2045, Williams FW07 Ford, Calder, Victoria, 1980. Nos. 2040, 2046, Benetton-Renault, Albert Park, Victoria, 2001.

2002, Feb. 27   Perf. 14x14¾
2035	A613	45c multi	1.10	1.10
2036	A613	45c multi	1.10	1.10
2037	A613	45c multi	1.10	1.10
2038	A613	45c multi	1.10	1.10
2039	A613	45c multi	1.10	1.10
2040	A613	45c multi	1.10	1.10
a.		Block of 6, #2035-2040	7.00	7.00
		Nos. 2035-2040 (6)	6.60	6.60

Self-Adhesive
Serpentine Die Cut 11¼x11½
2041	A613	45c multi	1.10	.80
2042	A613	45c multi	1.10	.80
2043	A613	45c multi	1.10	.80
2044	A613	45c multi	1.10	.80
2045	A613	45c multi	1.10	.80
2046	A613	45c multi	1.10	.80
a.		Coil strip, #2041-2046	7.00	
b.		Booklet, #2045-2046, 2 each #2041-2044	11.50	
		Nos. 2041-2046 (6)	6.60	4.80

Lighthouses and Maps — A614

Designs: 45c, Macquarie, New South Wales. Nos. 2048, 2051, Troubridge Island, South Australia. Nos. 2049, 2052, Cape Naturaliste, Western Australia. $1.50, Cape Bruny, Tasmania.

2002, Mar. 12   Perf. 14½x14
2047	A614	45c multi	1.40	.60
a.		Booklet pane of 4	5.75	
2048	A614	49c multi	1.40	1.10
a.		Booklet pane of 2	2.75	
2049	A614	49c multi	1.40	1.10
a.		Horiz. pair, #2048-2049	2.75	2.75
b.		Booklet pane of 2	2.75	
2050	A614	$1.50 multi	3.50	3.50
a.		Booklet pane of 2	7.00	
b.		Booklet pane, #2047-2050	7.75	—
		Booklet, #2047a, 2048a, 2049b, 2050a, 2050b	25.75	

Booklet Stamps
Self-Adhesive
Serpentine Die Cut 11¾
2051	A614	49c multi	1.40	.85
2052	A614	49c multi	1.40	.85
a.		Booklet, 5 each #2051-2052	14.50	
		Nos. 2047-2052 (6)	10.50	8.00

Booklet containing Nos. 2047a-2050b sold for $9.95.

Encounter of Matthew Flinders and Nicolas Baudin, Bicent. A615

Map, ship and: 45c, Baudin and kangaroo. $1.50, Flinders and Port Lincoln parrot.

2002, Apr. 4   Perf. 14x14¾
2053	A615	45c multi	.95	.85
2054	A615	$1.50 multi	3.25	3.25

See France Nos. 2882-2883.

Tourist Attractions Type of 2000
Designs: 50c, Walker Flat. $1, Mt. Roland. $1.50, Cape Leveque.

2002, May 1   Perf. 14½x14
2055	A581	50c multi	1.10	1.00
2056	A581	$1 multi	2.25	2.25
2057	A581	$1.50 multi	3.25	3.25

Booklet Stamps
Self-Adhesive
Serpentine Die Cut 11¼x10½
2058	A581	50c multi	1.40	.85
2059	A581	$1 multi	2.25	2.00
a.		Booklet, 6 #2058, 4 #2059	18.00	
		Nos. 2055-2059 (5)	10.25	9.35

Flora & Fauna Type of 1996
Designs: 50c, Desert star flower. $1, Bilby. $1.50, Thorny devil. $2, Great Sandy Desert.

2002, June 4   Litho.   Perf. 14x14½
2060	A511	50c multi	1.00	1.00
2061	A511	$1 multi	2.25	2.25
2062	A511	$1.50 multi	3.25	3.25

Perf. 14½x14
Size: 50x30mm
2063	A511	$2 multi	4.25	4.25
		Nos. 2060-2063 (4)	10.75	10.75

See Nos. 2112-2114 for self-adhesive versions of 50c stamp.

Paintings by Albert Namatjira (1902-59) A616

Designs: Nos. 2064, 2068, Ghost Gum Mt. Sonder, MacDonnel Ranges. Nos. 2065, 2069, Mt. Hermannsburg. Nos. 2066, 2070, Glen Helen Country. Nos. 2067, 2071, Simpsons Gap.

2002, July 2   Litho.   Perf. 14x14¾
2064	A616	45c multi	.95	.95
a.		Booklet pane of 4	4.00	4.00
2065	A616	45c multi	.95	.95
a.		Booklet pane of 4	4.00	4.00
2066	A616	45c multi	.95	.95
a.		Booklet pane of 4	4.00	4.00
2067	A616	45c multi	.95	.95
a.		Block of 4, #2064-2067	4.25	4.25
b.		Souvenir sheet of 4, #2064-2067	4.25	4.25
c.		Booklet pane of 4	4.00	4.00
d.		Booklet pane, #2067b	4.25	4.25
		Booklet, #2064a, 2065a, 2066a, 2067c, 2067d	20.75	
		Nos. 2064-2067 (4)	3.80	3.80

Serpentine Die Cut 11x11½
Self-Adhesive
2068	A616	45c multi	1.10	1.10
2069	A616	45c multi	1.10	1.10
2070	A616	45c multi	1.10	1.10
2071	A616	45c multi	1.10	1.10
a.		Booklet pane of 10, 3 each #2068-2069, 2 each #2070-2071	12.50	
b.		Coil strip of 4, #2068-2071	5.25	
		Nos. 2068-2071 (4)	4.40	4.40

Australia — Thailand Diplomatic Relations, 50th Anniv. A617

Designs: 45c, Nelumbo nucifera. $1, Nymphaea immutabilis.

2002, Aug. 6   Litho.   Perf. 14x14½
2072	A617	45c multi	1.10	.85
2073	A617	$1 multi	2.25	2.00
a.		Souvenir sheet, #2072-2073	4.00	3.50
b.		As "a," overprinted in gold in margin	8.00	8.00

Overprint on margin of No. 2073b has IFSDA and APTA emblems and text reading "50th Anniversary International Federation / of Stamp Dealers Associations."
See Thailand Nos. 2028-2029.

Christmas — A618

Koala A619

Puja, by Ngarralja Tommy May — A620

2002 — Perf. 14¼x14

2074	A618	90c multi + label	1.90	1.90
2075	A619	$1.10 multi + label	2.25	2.25
2076	A620	$1.65 multi + label	3.50	3.50
a.		Booklet pane of 4 + 4 labels	13.75	—
		Complete booklet, 3 #2076a	42.00	
		Nos. 2074-2076 (3)	7.65	7.65

Issued: 2074-2076, 8/23. No. 2076a, 10/31.

Nos. 2074-2076 were each printed in sheets of 20 stamps + 20 labels. Labels on some sheets could be personalized for an additional fee.

The complete booklet, which sold for $20.75, contains three panes of No. 2076a with different margins.

Tourist Attractions Type of 2000

Designs: $1.10, Coonawarra. $1.65, Gariwerd-Grampians Natl. Park. $2.20, National Library. $3.30, Cape York.

2002, Aug. 23 — Litho. Perf. 14½x14

2077	A581	$1.10 multi	2.25	2.25
2078	A581	$1.65 multi	3.50	3.50
2079	A581	$2.20 multi	4.50	4.50
2080	A581	$3.30 multi	7.00	7.00
		Nos. 2077-2080 (4)	17.25	17.25

Aboriginal Food Plants — A621

Designs: Nos. 2081, 2088, Murnong. Nos. 2082, 2087, Acacia seeds. Nos. 2083, 2086, Quandong. Nos. 2084, 2090, Honey grevillea. Nos. 2085, 2089, Lilly-pilly.

2002, Sept. 3 — Litho. Perf. 14¾x14

2081	A621	49c multi	1.10	1.10
2082	A621	49c multi	1.10	1.10
2083	A621	49c multi	1.10	1.10
2084	A621	49c multi	1.10	1.10
2085	A621	49c multi	1.10	1.10
a.		Horiz. strip of 5, #2081-2085	5.75	5.75
b.		Tete beche block of 10, 2 each # 2081-2085	11.50	11.50
		Nos. 2081-2085 (5)	5.50	5.50

Booklet Stamps
Self-Adhesive
Serpentine Die Cut 11¾

2086	A621	49c multi	1.10	.90
2087	A621	49c multi	1.10	.90
2088	A621	49c multi	1.10	.90
2089	A621	49c multi	1.10	.90
2090	A621	49c multi	1.10	.90
a.		Booklet pane, 2 each #2086-2090	11.50	
		Nos. 2086-2090 (5)	5.50	4.50

Bunyip — A622   Fairy — A623

Gnome — A624   Goblin — A625

Wizard — A626   Sprite — A627

2002, Sept. 25 — Perf. 14¾x14

2091	A622	45c multi	1.10	1.10
2092	A623	45c multi	1.10	1.10
2093	A624	45c multi	1.10	1.10
a.		Horiz. strip of 3, #2091-2093	3.50	3.50
2094	A625	45c multi	1.10	1.10
2095	A626	45c multi	1.10	1.10
2096	A627	45c multi	1.10	1.10
a.		Horiz. strip of 3, #2094-2096	3.50	3.50
b.		Souvenir sheet, #2091-2096	5.75	5.75
		Nos. 2091-2096 (6)	6.60	6.60

Self-Adhesive
Serpentine Die Cut 11½x11

2097	A622	45c multi	1.10	.85
2098	A623	45c multi	1.10	.85
2099	A624	45c multi	1.10	.85
2100	A625	45c multi	1.10	.85
2101	A626	45c multi	1.10	.85
2102	A627	45c multi	1.10	.85
a.		Vert. coil strip of 6, #2097-2102	7.00	
b.		Booklet pane, #2097, 2102, 2 each #2098-2101	11.50	
		Nos. 2097-2102 (6)	6.60	5.10

Characters from The Magic Rainforest, by John Marsden.

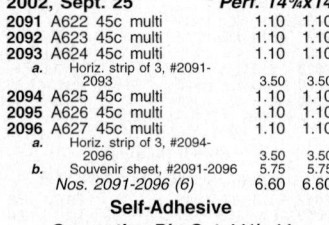

Race Horses A628

2002, Oct. 15 — Litho. Perf. 14x14½

2103	A628	45c Wakeful	1.10	.80
2104	A628	45c Rising Fast	1.10	.80
2105	A628	45c Manikato	1.10	.80
2106	A628	45c Might and Power	1.10	.80
2107	A628	45c Sunline	1.10	.80
a.		Horiz. strip of 5, #2103-2107	5.75	5.75
		Nos. 2103-2107 (5)	5.50	4.00

Christmas — A629

2002, Nov. 1 — Perf. 14½x14

2108	A629	40c Nativity	1.10	1.10
2109	A629	45c Magi	1.10	.70

Self-Adhesive
Booklet Stamp
Serpentine Die Cut 11¼

2110	A629	40c Nativity	1.10	.70
a.		Booklet pane of 20 + 20 labels	23.00	
		Nos. 2108-2110 (3)	3.30	2.50

Flora and Fauna Type of 1996

Designs: 50c, Desert star flower. $1.45, Blue orchid.

2003 — Litho. Perf. 14x14½

2111	A511	$1.45 multi	3.50	3.50

Self-Adhesive
Coil Stamps
Serpentine Die Cut 11¼

2112	A511	50c multi	1.10	.75

Serpentine Die Cut 12¾

2113	A511	50c multi	1.10	.75

Booklet Stamp
Serpentine Die Cut 11¼x11

2114	A511	50c multi	1.10	.75
a.		Booklet pane of 10	11.50	
b.		Booklet pane of 20	23.00	
		Nos. 2111-2114 (4)	6.80	5.75

Issued: 50c, 1/7; $1.45, 2/11.

Flowers — A630

Roses and Wedding Rings — A631

Roses and Hearts — A632

Birthday Cake, Balloons and Gifts — A633

Teddy Bear A634

Balloons and Streamers — A635

Kangaroo and Australian Flag — A636

Australia on Globe — A637

Automobile — A638

Rose and Wedding Rings — A639

2003 — Perf. 14½x14

2115	A630	50c multi + label	1.00	.85
a.		Booklet pane of 4 + 4 labels	4.25	
		Booklet, 5 #2115a	21.50	
2116	A631	50c multi + label	1.00	.85
a.		Booklet pane of 4 + 4 labels	4.25	
		Booklet, 5 #2116a	21.50	
2117	A632	50c multi + label	1.00	.85
a.		Booklet pane of 4 + 4 labels	4.25	
		Booklet, 5 #2117a	22.00	
b.		Strip of 3, #2115-2117, + 3 labels	3.25	
2118	A633	50c multi + label	1.00	.85
a.		Booklet pane of 4 + 4 labels	4.25	
		Booklet, 5 #2118a	22.00	
2119	A634	50c multi + label	1.00	.85
a.		Booklet pane of 4 + 4 labels	4.25	
		Complete booklet, 5 #2119a	22.00	
2120	A635	50c multi + label	1.00	.85
a.		Booklet pane of 4 + 4 labels	4.25	
		Booklet, 5 #2120a	22.00	
b.		Strip of 3, #2118-2120, + 3 labels	3.25	
2121	A636	50c multi + label	1.00	.85
2122	A637	50c multi + label	1.00	.85
a.		Booklet pane of 4 + 4 labels	4.25	
		Complete booklet, 5 #2122a	22.00	
2123	A638	50c multi + label	1.00	.85
a.		Strip of 3, #2121-2123, + 3 labels	3.25	
2124	A639	$1 multi + label	2.25	2.25
a.		Booklet pane of 4 + 4 labels	9.00	
		Booklet, 5 #2124a	45.00	
		Nos. 2115-2124 (10)	11.25	9.90

Issued: No. 2119a, 10/31/03; No. 2122a, 3/16/04. Rest of set, 1/7/03.

Panes of 20 stamps containing the same design could have labels personalized. The personalized panes sold for a higher price.

Nos. 2115a, 2116a, 2117a, 2118a, 2119a, 2120a, 2122a and 2124a come in complete booklets, each containing 5 panes, each pane having different margins. Some panes are found in a number of different booklets.

Australian Legends Type of 1997

Tennis players: Nos. 2125, 2129, Margaret Court with Wimbledon trophy. Nos. 2126, 2131, Court in action. Nos. 2127, 2130, Rod Laver with Wimbledon trophy. Nos. 2128, 2132, Laver in action.

2003, Jan. 24 — Perf. 14x14¾
Size: 34x26mm

2125	A522	50c multi	1.00	1.00
2126	A522	50c multi	1.00	1.00
2127	A522	50c multi	1.00	1.00
2128	A522	50c multi	1.00	1.00
a.		Block of 4, #2125-2128	5.25	5.25
b.		Booklet pane, #2125-2128	6.00	—
		Nos. 2125-2128 (4)	4.00	4.00

Self-Adhesive
Booklet Stamps
Serpentine Die Cut 11x11½

2129	A522	50c multi	1.25	.80
2130	A522	50c multi	1.25	.80
2131	A522	50c multi	1.25	.80
2132	A522	50c multi	1.25	.80
a.		Booklet pane, 3 each #2129-2130, 2 each #2131-2132	12.50	
		Nos. 2129-2132 (4)	5.00	3.20

No. 2128b issued 1/24/07.

Fish A640

2003, Feb. 11 — Perf. 14½x14

2133	A640	50c Snapper	1.10	.90
2134	A640	50c Murray cod	1.10	.90
2135	A640	50c Brown trout	1.10	.90
2136	A640	50c Yellowfin tuna	1.10	.90
2137	A640	50c Barramundi	1.10	.90
a.		Horiz. strip of 5, #2133-2137	5.75	5.75
		Nos. 2133-2137 (5)	5.50	4.50

Australian Cultivars — A641

Designs: Nos. 2138, 2143, Hari Withers camellia. Nos. 2139, 2144, Victoria Gold rose. Nos. 2140, 2145, Superb grevillea. Nos. 2141, 2146, Bush Tango kangaroo paw. Nos. 2142, 2147, Midnight rhododendron.

2003, Mar. 25 — Perf. 14¾x14

2138	A641	50c multi	1.00	.95
2139	A641	50c multi	1.00	.95
2140	A641	50c multi	1.00	.95
2141	A641	50c multi	1.00	.95
2142	A641	50c multi	1.00	.95
a.		Horiz. strip of 5, #2138-2142	5.25	5.25
		Nos. 2138-2142 (5)	5.00	4.75

Self-Adhesive
Serpentine Die Cut 11½x11¼

2143	A641	50c multi	1.10	.75
2144	A641	50c multi	1.10	.75
2145	A641	50c multi	1.10	.75
2146	A641	50c multi	1.10	.75
2147	A641	50c multi	1.10	.75
a.		Coil strip of 5, #2143-2147	5.75	
b.		Booklet pane, 2 each		
		#2143-2147	11.00	
		Nos. 2143-2147 (5)	5.50	3.75

Paintings — A642

Designs: No. 2148, Ned Kelly, by Sidney Nolan. No. 2149, Family Home, Suburban Exterior, by Howard Arkley. $1.45, Cord Drawn Long, Expectant, by Robert Jacks. $2.45, Girl, by Joy Hester.

2003, May 6 Litho. Perf. 14½x14

2148	A642	$1 multi	2.25	2.00
2149	A642	$1 multi	2.25	2.00
a.		Horiz. pair, #2148-2149	3.50	3.50
2150	A642	$1.45 multi	3.25	3.25
2151	A642	$2.45 multi	5.25	5.25
		Nos. 2148-2151 (4)	13.00	12.50

Coronation of Queen Elizabeth II, 50th Anniv. — A643

Designs: 50c, Queen Elizabeth II, 1953. $2.45, St. Edward's Crown.

2003, June 2 Litho. Perf. 14¾x14

2152	A643	50c multi	1.00	1.00
2153	A643	$2.45 multi	5.25	5.25
a.		Souvenir sheet, #2152-2153	6.50	6.50

Booklet Stamp
Self-Adhesive
Serpentine Die Cut 11½x11¼

2154	A643	50c multi	1.00	.85
a.		Booklet pane of 10	10.25	
		Nos. 2152-2154 (3)	7.25	7.10

Papunya Tula Aboriginal Art A644

Untitled works by: $1.10, Ningura Napurrula. $1.65, Naata Nungurrayi. $2.20, Graham Tjupurrula. $3.30, Dini Campbell Tjampitjinpa.

2003, June 17 Perf. 14½x14

2155	A644	$1.10 multi	2.25	2.25
2156	A644	$1.65 multi	3.50	3.50

Size: 56x25mm
Perf. 14x14½

2157	A644	$2.20 multi	4.50	4.50
2158	A644	$3.30 multi	7.00	7.00
		Nos. 2155-2158 (4)	17.25	17.25

Flora & Fauna Type of 1996

Designs: Nos. 2159, 2163, 2167, Orange-thighed tree frog. Nos. 2160, 2164, 2168, Green-spotted triangle butterfly. Nos. 2161, 2165, 2169, Striped possum. Nos. 2162, 2166, 2170, Yellow-bellied sunbird.

2003, July 8 Litho. Perf. 14x14¼

2159	A511	50c multi	1.00	.90
2160	A511	50c multi	1.00	.90
2161	A511	50c multi	1.00	.90
2162	A511	50c multi	1.00	.90
a.		Block of 4, #2159-2162	4.50	4.50
		Nos. 2159-2162 (4)	4.00	3.60

Self-Adhesive
Serpentine Die Cut 11¼

2163	A511	50c multi	1.00	.80
2164	A511	50c multi	1.00	.80
a.		Booklet pane of 2, #2163-2164	2.25	
2165	A511	50c multi	1.00	.80
2166	A511	50c multi	1.00	.80
b.		Booklet pane of 4, #2163-2166, rouletted at bottom	4.50	

	Complete booklet, #2164a, 2 #2166a		10.25
b.	Booklet pane of 4, #2163-2166, rouletted at side		4.50
	Complete booklet, 5 #2166b		23.00
c.	Coil strip of 4, #2163-2166		4.50

Coil Stamps
Serpentine Die Cut 12¾

2167	A511	50c multi	1.10	.80
2168	A511	50c multi	1.10	.80
2169	A511	50c multi	1.10	.80
2170	A511	50c multi	1.10	.80
a.		Strip of 4, #2167-2170	5.25	
		Nos. 2163-2170 (8)	8.40	6.40

Genetics A645

Map of Australia and: No. 2171, DNA molecule. No. 2172, Kangaroo chromosomes in cell division.

2003, July 8 Litho. Perf. 14x14¾

2171	A645	50c red & multi	1.00	.80
2172	A645	50c grn & multi	1.00	.80
a.		Horiz. pair, #2171-2172	2.25	1.75

Murray River Shipping, 150th Anniv. A646

Murray River vessels: Nos. 2173, 2178, Oscar W. Nos. 2174, 2179, Marion. Nos. 2175, 2180, Ruby. Nos. 2176, 2181, Pyap. Nos. 2177, 2182, Adelaide.

2003, Aug. 5 Litho. Perf. 14x14¾

2173	A646	50c multi	1.00	.90
a.		Booklet pane of 4	4.25	—
2174	A646	50c multi	1.00	.90
a.		Booklet pane of 4	4.25	—
2175	A646	50c multi	1.00	.90
a.		Booklet pane of 4	4.25	—
2176	A646	50c multi	1.00	.90
a.		Booklet pane of 4	4.25	—
2177	A646	50c multi	1.00	.90
a.		Booklet pane of 4	4.25	—
		Complete booklet, #2173a-2177a	29.00	
b.		Horiz. strip of 5, #2173-2177	7.50	7.50
		Nos. 2173-2177 (5)	5.00	4.50

Self-Adhesive
Serpentine Die Cut 11¼x11½

2178	A646	50c multi	1.10	.80
2179	A646	50c multi	1.10	.80
2180	A646	50c multi	1.10	.80
2181	A646	50c multi	1.10	.80
2182	A646	50c multi	1.10	.80
a.		Horiz. coil strip of 5, #2178-2182	5.75	
b.		Booklet pane, 2 each #2178-2182	11.00	
		Nos. 2178-2182 (5)	5.50	4.00

The booklet containing Nos. 2173a-2177a sold for $10.95.

Christmas — A647

2003, Aug. 5 Litho. Perf. 14½x14

2183	A647	50c Christmas tree	1.00	.90
a.		Sheet of 20 + 20 labels	35.00	
2184	A647	90c Star	1.90	1.75
a.		Sheet of 20 + 20 labels	40.00	

Labels on Nos. 2183a and 2184a could be personalized. No. 2183a sold for $23 on day of issue; No. 2184a for $32.

High Court of Australia, Cent. A648

Designs: 50c, Sir Samuel Griffith (1845-1920), first Chief Justice, text from Constitution about High Court. $1.45, "Justice," names of significant cases.

2003, Sept. 2 Litho. Perf. 14x14¾

2185	A648	50c multi	1.00	.85
2186	A648	$1.45 multi	3.25	3.25
a.		Souvenir sheet, #2185-2186	4.25	4.25

Insects A649

Designs: Nos. 2187, 2198, Ulysses butterfly. Nos. 2188, 2197, Leichhardt's grasshopper. Nos. 2189, 2196, Vedalia ladybird. Nos. 2190, 2195, Green mantid and damselfly. Nos. 2191, 2194, Emperor gum moth caterpillar. Nos. 2192, 2193, Fiddler beetle.

2003, Sept. 24 Perf. 14x14¾

2187	A649	50c multi	1.00	.90
2188	A649	50c multi	1.00	.90
2189	A649	50c multi	1.00	.90
a.		Horiz. strip, #2187-2189	3.50	3.50
2190	A649	50c multi	1.00	.90
2191	A649	50c multi	1.00	.90
2192	A649	50c multi	1.00	.90
a.		Horiz. strip, #2190-2192	3.50	3.50
b.		Souvenir sheet, #2187-2192	5.75	5.75
c.		As "b," with Bangkok 2003 emblem in margin in gold	8.00	8.00
		Nos. 2187-2192 (6)	6.00	5.40

Self-Adhesive
Serpentine Die Cut 11x11¼

2193	A649	50c multi	1.10	.90
2194	A649	50c multi	1.10	.90
2195	A649	50c multi	1.10	.90
2196	A649	50c multi	1.10	.90
2197	A649	50c multi	1.10	.90
2198	A649	50c multi	1.10	.90
a.		Horiz. coil strip, #2193-2198	7.50	
b.		Booklet pane, #2193-2194, 2 each #2195-2198	12.00	
		Nos. 2193-2198 (6)	6.60	5.40

No. 2193c issued 10/4.

2003 Rugby World Cup — A650

Designs: 50c, Players running with ball, hands and ball. $1.10, Webb Ellis Cup, Telstra Stadium. $1.65, Player kicking at goal, ball in hand.

2003, Oct. 8 Litho. Perf. 14½x14

2199	A650	50c multi	1.00	.85
a.		Booklet pane of 3	3.50	—
2200	A650	$1.10 multi	2.25	2.25
a.		Booklet pane of 3	7.00	—
2201	A650	$1.65 multi	3.50	3.50
a.		Booklet pane of 3	10.50	—
		Complete booklet, #2199a, 2200a, 2201a	21.00	
b.		Souvenir sheet, #2199-2201	7.00	7.00
		Nos. 2199-2201 (3)	6.75	6.60

Booklet sold for $10.95.

Active With Asthma A651

2003, Oct. 14 Perf. 14x14½

2202	A651	50c multi	1.00	.70

Christmas — A652

Designs: 45c, Madonna and Child with Angels. 50c, Three Wise Men. 90c, Angel Appearing to the Shepherds.

2003, Oct. 31 Perf. 14½x14

2203	A652	45c multi	.95	.95
2204	A652	50c multi	1.00	1.00
2205	A652	90c multi	1.90	1.90

Booklet Stamp
Self-Adhesive
Serpentine Die Cut 11½x11¼

2206	A652	45c multi	1.00	.60
a.		Booklet pane of 20 + 20 labels	21.00	
		Nos. 2203-2206 (4)	4.85	4.45

Australian Legends Type of 1997

Dame Joan Sutherland, opera singer: Nos. 2207, 2209, In costume. Nos. 2208, 2210, In black and red dress.

2004, Jan. 23 Litho. Perf. 14x14¾
Size: 37x26mm

2207	A522	50c multi	1.00	.90
2208	A522	50c multi	1.00	.90
a.		Horiz. pair, #2207-2208	2.25	2.25
b.		Booklet pane, #2207-2208	3.00	—

Booklet Stamps
Self-Adhesive
Serpentine Die Cut 11x11½

2209	A522	50c multi	1.00	.80
2210	A522	50c multi	1.00	.80
a.		Booklet pane, 5 each #2209-2210	10.50	
		Nos. 2207-2210 (4)	4.00	3.40

No. 2208b issued 1/24/07.

Settlement of Hobart Town, Tasmania, Bicent. A653

Segment of shell necklace, map of Tasmania and: No. 2211, Cheshunt House, Deloraine. No. 2212, Complete shell necklace. No. 2213, Mount Wellington. No. 2214, Hobart Town from Kangaroo Point, by John Glover.

2004, Feb. 3 Litho. Perf. 14x14½

2211	A653	50c multi	1.00	.80
2212	A653	50c multi	1.00	.80
a.		Pair, #2211-2212	2.25	2.25
2213	A653	$1 multi	2.25	2.00
2214	A653	$1 multi	2.25	2.00
a.		Pair, #2213-2214	4.50	4.50
b.		Souvenir sheet, #2211-2214	7.00	7.00
c.		As "b," ovptd. for Paris Exhib. 2004	35.00	35.00
d.		As "b," ovptd. for China 2005 exhibition	10.00	10.00
		Nos. 2211-2214 (4)	6.50	5.60

Historic Bridges A654

Designs: Nos. 2215, 2220, Ross Bridge, Tasmania, 1836. Nos. 2216, 2221, Lockyer Creek Bridge, Queensland, 1911. Nos. 2217, 2222, Sydney Harbour Bridge, 1932. Nos. 2218, 2223, Birkenhead Bridge, Adelaide, 1940. Nos. 2219, 2224, Bolte Bridge, Melbourne, 1999.

2004, Mar. 2 Litho. Perf. 14x14½

2215	A654	50c multi	1.00	.90
a.		Booklet pane of 4	4.25	
2216	A654	50c multi	1.00	.90
a.		Booklet pane of 4	4.25	
2217	A654	50c multi	1.00	.90
a.		Booklet pane of 4	4.25	
2218	A654	50c multi	1.00	.90
a.		Booklet pane of 4	4.25	
2219	A654	50c multi	1.00	.90
a.		Booklet pane of 4	4.25	
		Complete booklet, #2215a, 2216a, 2217a, 2218a, 2219a	21.00	
b.		Horiz. strip of 5, #2215-2219	5.25	5.25
c.		Booklet pane of 6 ('06)	6.25	
		Nos. 2215-2219 (5)	5.00	4.50

The complete booklet No. 2219a sold for $10.95.

No. 2219c issued 3/1/06.

Self-Adhesive
Serpentine Die Cut 11x11½

2220	A654	50c multi	1.40	.90
2221	A654	50c multi	1.40	.90
2222	A654	50c multi	1.40	.90
2223	A654	50c multi	1.40	.90
2224	A654	50c multi	1.40	.90
a.		Horiz. coil strip of 5, #2220-2224	7.25	
b.		Booklet pane, 2 each #2220-2224	14.50	
		Nos. 2220-2224 (5)	7.00	4.50

Southern Cross — A655

2004-05   **Perf. 14½x14**
2225 A655 50c multi   1.00   .80
   a.   Booklet pane of 4 + 4 labels   4.25
      Complete booklet, 5 #2225a   22.00

Issued: No. 2225, 3/16/04. No. 2225a, Jan. 2005. No. 2225a was issued in a variety of complete booklets, each containing 5 panes with different margins. Each complete booklet sold for $10.95.

Renewable Energy A656

Designs: Nos. 2226, 2230, Solar energy. Nos. 2227, 2231, Wind energy. Nos. 2228, 2232, Hydroelectric energy. Nos. 2229, 2233, Biomass energy.

2004, Mar. 30   **Perf. 14x14½**
2226 A656 50c multi   1.00 1.00
2227 A656 50c multi   1.00 1.00
2228 A656 50c multi   1.00 1.00
2229 A656 50c multi   1.00 1.00
   a.   Block of 4, #2226-2229   4.25 4.25
      Nos. 2226-2229 (4)   4.00 4.00

Coil Stamps
Self-Adhesive
Serpentine Die Cut 11x11½
2230 A656 50c multi   1.10   .85
2231 A656 50c multi   1.10   .85
2232 A656 50c multi   1.10   .85
2233 A656 50c multi   1.10   .85
   a.   Horiz. strip of 4, #2230-2233   4.50
      Nos. 2230-2233 (4)   4.40 3.40

Royal Visit, 50th Anniv. — A657

2004, Apr. 13   **Perf. 14½x14**
2234 A657 50c multi   1.00   .85
   a.   Booklet pane of 4   4.25 —
      Complete booklet, 5 #2234a   21.50

The booklet, which contains five panes with different margins, sold for $10.95. Another booklet pane, with a different margin, is found in the booklet footnoted under No. 2507.

Flora & Fauna Type of 1996
Designs: 5c, Red lacewing butterfly. 10c, Blue-banded eggfly butterfly. 75c, Cruiser butterfly. $2, Butterflies, Daintree National Park rainforest.

2004, May 4   **Litho.**   **Perf. 14x14½**
2235 A511 5c multi   .25   .25
2236 A511 10c multi   .25   .25
2237 A511 75c multi   1.60   .95

Size: 50x30mm
Perf. 14½x14
2238 A511 $2 multi   4.25 4.25
      Nos. 2235-2238 (4)   6.35 5.70

Australian Innovations A658

Designs: Nos. 2239, 2248, Black box flight recorder, 1961. Nos. 2240, 2247, Ultrasound imaging equipment, 1976. Nos. 2241, 2246, Racecam television sports coverage, 1979. Nos. 2242, 2245, Baby safety capsule, 1984. Nos. 2243, 2244, Polymer banknotes, 1988.

2004, May 18   **Perf. 14x14½**
2239 A658 50c multi   1.10   .90
2240 A658 50c multi   1.10   .90
2241 A658 50c multi   1.10   .90
2242 A658 50c multi   1.10   .90
2243 A658 50c multi   1.10   .90
   a.   Horiz. strip, #2239-2243   5.00 5.00
      Nos. 2239-2243 (5)   5.50 4.50

Booklet Stamps
Self-Adhesive
Serpentine Die Cut 11x11½
2244 A658 50c multi   1.10   .90
2245 A658 50c multi   1.10   .90
2246 A658 50c multi   1.10   .90
2247 A658 50c multi   1.10   .90
2248 A658 50c multi   1.10   .90
   a.   Booklet pane, 2 each #2244-2248   12.00
      Nos. 2244-2248 (5)   5.50 4.50

Passenger Ship Travel Posters — A659

Designs: 50c, Shaw Savill Lines. $1, Awatea, Union Steam Ship Co. $1.45, Orient Line. $2, Aberdeen & Commonwealth Line.

2004, June 1   **Litho.**   **Perf. 14½x14**
2249 A659 50c multi   1.00   .80
2250 A659 $1 multi   2.25 1.40
2251 A659 $1.45 multi   3.00 3.00
2252 A659 $2 multi   4.25 4.25
      Nos. 2249-2252 (4)   10.50 9.45

Serpentine Die Cut 11½x11¼
Syncopated
2252A A659 50c Like #2249, 2005   1.00   .80

Booklet Stamp
Self-Adhesive
Serpentine Die Cut 11½x11¼
2253 A659 50c multi   1.00   .90
   a.   Booklet pane of 10   10.25

Issued: Nos. 2249-2252, 2253, 6/1/04. No. 2252A, 2/22/05. No. 2252A issued in sheet of 10.

Eureka Stockade, 150th Anniv. A660

Designs: 50c, Eureka flag. $2.45, Peter Lalor (1827-89), leader of rebellious gold diggers.

2004, June 29   **Perf. 14x14½**
2254 A660 50c multi   1.00   .85
   a.   Booklet pane of 2   2.25
2255 A660 $2.45 multi   5.25 5.25
   a.   Booklet pane of 2   10.25
   b.   Booklet pane, #2254-2255   6.25
      Complete booklet, #2255a, 2255b, 2 #2254a   25.00
   c.   Souvenir sheet, #2254-2255   7.00 7.00

No. 2255b has perfs that extend to the right margin. No. 2255c does not have perfs that extend through the margin. The margin is larger on No. 2255b than on No. 2255c. The complete booklet sold for $10.95.

Tourist Attractions — A661

Designs: No. 2256, Koala, Eastern Australia, vert. No. 2257, Little penguin, Phillip Island, vert. $1.45, Clown anemonefish, Great Barrier Reef. $2.45, Beach, Gold Coast.

Perf. 14x14½, 14½x14
2004, July 13   **Litho.**
2256 A661 $1 multi   2.25 1.75
2257 A661 $1 multi   2.25 1.75
   a.   Horiz. pair, #2256-2257   4.50 4.50
2258 A661 $1.45 multi   3.00 2.00

Litho. With Foil Application
2259 A661 $2.45 multi   5.25 5.25
      Nos. 2256-2259 (4)   12.75 10.75

2004 Summer Olympics and Paralympics, Athens A662

2004, Aug. 3   **Litho.**   **Perf. 14x14½**
2260 A662 50c Swimmer   1.00   .90
2261 A662 $1.65 Swimmer   3.50 3.50
2262 A662 $1.65 Cyclist   3.50 2.75
      Nos. 2260-2262 (3)   8.00 7.15

Gold Medalists at 2004 Summer Olympics, Athens A663

Designs: No. 2263, Ian Thorpe, Men's swimming 400m freestyle. No. 2264, Women's 4x100m medley relay swimming team. No. 2265, Sara Carrigan, Women's cycling road race. No. 2266, Petria Thomas, Women's swimming 100m butterfly. No. 2267, Suzanne Balogh, Women's trap shooting. No. 2268, Ian Thorpe, Men's swimming 200m freestyle. No. 2269, Jodie Henry, Women's swimming 100m freestyle. No. 2270, Anna Meares, Women's cycling 500m time trial. No. 2271, James Tomkins and Drew Ginn, Men's rowing pairs. No. 2272, Grant Hackett, Men's swimming 1500m freestyle. No. 2273, Women's 4x100 freestyle relay swimming team. No. 2274, Chantelle Newbery, Women's diving 10m platform. No. 2275, Men's 4000m team pursuit cycling team. No. 2276, Ryan Bayley, Men's cycling individual sprint. No. 2277, Graeme Brown and Stuart O'Grady, Men's cycling Madison. No. 2278, Ryan Bayley, Men's cycling Keirin. No. 2279, Men's field hockey team.

2004   **Litho.**   **Perf. 14¼**
2263 A663 50c multi   1.00   .90
2264 A663 50c multi   1.00   .90
2265 A663 50c multi   1.00   .90
2266 A663 50c multi   1.00   .90
2267 A663 50c multi   1.00   .90
2268 A663 50c multi   1.00   .90
2269 A663 50c multi   1.00   .90
2270 A663 50c multi   1.00   .90
2271 A663 50c multi   1.00   .90
2272 A663 50c multi   1.00   .90
2273 A663 50c multi   1.00   .90
2274 A663 50c multi   1.00   .90
2275 A663 50c multi   1.00   .90
2276 A663 50c multi   1.00   .90
2277 A663 50c multi   1.00   .90
2278 A663 50c multi   1.00   .90
2279 A663 50c multi   1.00   .90
      Nos. 2263-2279 (17)   17.00 15.30

Issued: Nos. 2263-2264, 8/16; Nos. 2265-2266; Nos. 2267-2268, 8/18; Nos. 2269-2273, 8/23; No. 2274, 8/24; No. 2275, 8/25; No. 2276, 8/26; Nos. 2277-2278, 8/27; No. 2279, 8/30.

A sheet containing Nos. 2263-2279 was available only in the Australia Post annual collection. Value, $50.

Tourist Attractions Type of 2000
Designs: $1.20, Entrance Beach, Broome, Western Australia. $1.80, Mt. William National Park, Tasmania. $2.40, Potato Point, Bodalla, New South Wales. $3.60, Point Gibbon, South Australia.

2004, Sept. 6   **Perf. 14½x14**
2280 A581 $1.20 multi   2.50 1.75
2281 A581 $1.80 multi   3.75 2.75
2282 A581 $2.40 multi   5.25 4.00
2283 A581 $3.60 multi   7.50 6.25
      Nos. 2280-2283 (4)   19.00 14.75

Block of £2 Kangaroo & Map Stamps from Australia Post Archives — A664

2004, Sept. 7   **Perf. 14¼**
2284 A664 $5 multi   11.00 9.25

Souvenir Sheet
Self-Adhesive
Serpentine Die Cut 11¼
2285 A664 $5 multi   11.00 11.00

Australian Railways, 150th Anniv. A665

Designs: Nos. 2286, 2291, Melbourne to Sandridge line, 1854. Nos. 2287, 2292, Sydney to Parramatta line, 1855. Nos. 2288, 2293, Helidon to Toowoomba line, 1867. Nos. 2289, 2294, Kalgoorlie to Port Augusta line, 1917. Nos. 2290, 2295, Alice Springs to Darwin line, 2004.

2004, Sept. 7   **Perf. 14x14¾**
2286 A665 50c multi   1.00   .90
   a.   Booklet pane of 4   4.25 —
2287 A665 50c multi   1.00   .90
   a.   Booklet pane of 4   4.25 —
2288 A665 50c multi   1.00   .90
   a.   Booklet pane of 4   4.25 —
2289 A665 50c multi   1.00   .90
   a.   Booklet pane of 4   4.25 —
2290 A665 50c multi   1.00   .90
   a.   Booklet pane of 4   4.25 —
      Complete booklet, #2286a-2290a   22.00
   b.   Horiz. strip, #2286-2290   5.25 5.25
      Nos. 2286-2290 (5)   5.00 4.50

Complete booklet of Nos. 2286a-2290a sold for $10.95.

Self-Adhesive
With Designs Lightened at Stamp Edges
Serpentine Die Cut 11¼x11½
2291 A665 50c multi   1.10 1.00
2292 A665 50c multi   1.10 1.00
2293 A665 50c multi   1.10 1.00
2294 A665 50c multi   1.10 1.00
2295 A665 50c multi   1.10 1.00
   a.   Horiz. coil strip, #2291-2295   6.25
   b.   Booklet pane, 2 each #2291-2295   12.50
      Nos. 2291-2295 (5)   5.50 5.00

Cats and Dogs — A666

Designs: Nos. 2296, 2302, Cat (fish background). Nos. 2297, 2304, Cat (mouse background). Nos. 2298, 2301, Labrador retriever puppy (ball background). Nos. 2299, 2303, West Highland terriers (paw print background). $1, Jack Russell terrier (bone background).

2004, Sept. 21   **Perf. 14¾x14**
2296 A666 50c multi   1.00   .90
   a.   Booklet pane of 4   4.25 —
2297 A666 50c multi   1.00   .90
   a.   Horiz. pair, #2296-2297   2.25 2.25
   b.   Booklet pane of 4   4.25 —
   c.   Booklet pane, 2 each #2296-2297   4.50 —
      Complete booklet, #2296a, 2297b, 3 #2297c   21.00
2298 A666 50c multi   1.00   .90
   a.   Booklet pane of 4   4.25 —
2299 A666 50c multi   1.00   .90
   a.   Horiz. pair, #2298-2299   2.25 2.25
   b.   Booklet pane of 4   4.25 —
   c.   Booklet pane, 2 each #2298-2299   4.50 —

2300	A666	$1 multi	2.25	2.00
a.		Booklet pane of 2	4.25	—
		Complete booklet, #2298a, 2299b, 2300a, 2 #2299c	21.00	
b.		Souvenir sheet, #2296-2300	5.50	5.50
		Nos. 2296-2300 (5)	6.25	5.60

The complete booklets each sold for $10.95. The Cat booklet contains three examples of No. 2297c, each with different margins and stamp arrangements. The Dog booklet contains two examples of No. 2299c with different margins and stamp arrangements.

Self-Adhesive
Booklet Stamps
Serpentine Die Cut 11¼ Syncopated

2301	A666	50c multi	1.00	.90
2302	A666	50c multi	1.00	.90
2303	A666	50c multi	1.00	.90
a.		Booklet pane, 3 #2301, 2 #2303	5.25	
2304	A666	50c multi	1.00	.90
a.		Booklet pane, 3 each #2301-2302, 2 each #2303-2304	10.25	
b.		Booklet pane, 3 #2302, 2 #2304	5.25	
2305	A666	$1 multi	2.25	.90
a.		Booklet pane of 5	11.00	
		Nos. 2301-2305 (5)	6.25	4.50

Grand Prix Motorcycle Racing A667

Designs: Nos. 2306, 2311, Mick Doohan (motorcycle #1, red panel). Nos. 2307, 2312, Wayne Gardner (motorcycle #1, blue panel). Nos. 2308, 2313, Troy Bayliss (motorcycle #12, orange red panel). Nos. 2309, 2314, Daryl Beattie (motorcycle #4, green panel). Nos. 2310, 2315, Garry McCoy (motorcycle #8, yellow orange panel).

2004, Oct. 12 Litho. *Perf. 14x14¾*

2306	A667	50c multi	1.00	.90
2307	A667	50c multi	1.00	.90
2308	A667	50c multi	1.00	.90
2309	A667	50c multi	1.00	.90
2310	A667	50c multi	1.00	.90
a.		Horiz. strip of 5, #2306-2310	5.25	5.25
		Nos. 2306-2310 (5)	5.00	4.50

Self-Adhesive
Serpentine Die Cut 11¼ Syncopated

2311	A667	50c multi	1.10	1.00
2312	A667	50c multi	1.10	1.00
2313	A667	50c multi	1.10	1.00
2314	A667	50c multi	1.10	1.00
2315	A667	50c multi	1.10	1.00
a.		Horiz. coil strip, #2311-2315	6.25	
b.		Booklet pane, 2 each #2311-2315	12.50	
		Nos. 2311-2315 (5)	5.50	5.00

Christmas — A668

Designs: 45c, Madonna and Child. 50c, Shepherds. $1, Magi, horiz.

2004, Nov. 1 *Perf. 14¾x14, 14x14¾*

2316	A668	45c multi	.95	.85
2317	A668	50c multi	1.00	.90
2318	A668	$1 multi	2.25	1.90
		Nos. 2316-2318 (3)	4.20	3.65

Self-Adhesive
Booklet Stamps
Serpentine Die Cut 11¼ Syncopated

2319	A668	45c multi	.95	.85
a.		Booklet pane of 20 + 20 etiquettes	20.00	
2320	A668	$1 multi	2.25	1.75
a.		Booklet pane of 5	11.00	

Australian Tennis Open, Cent. A669

Designs: 50c, Male player, tennis court and stands, 1905. $1.80, Female player, tennis court and stands, 2005.

2005, Jan. 11 Litho. *Perf. 14x14¾*

2321	A669	50c multi	1.00	.85
a.		Booklet pane of 2	2.25	
2322	A669	$1.80 multi	3.75	3.00
a.		Booklet pane of 2	7.50	—
		Complete booklet, 2 each #2321a, 2322a	20.00	

The complete booklet contains two examples of Nos. 2321a and 2322a, each with different margins.

Australian Legends — Fashion Designers — A670

Designs: Nos. 2323, 2329, Prue Acton. Nos. 2324, 2330, Jenny Bannister. Nos. 2325, 2331, Collette Dinnigan. Nos. 2326, 2332, Akira Isogawa. Nos. 2327, 2333, Joe Saba. Nos. 2328, 2334, Carla Zampatti.

2005, Jan. 21 *Perf. 14¾x14*

2323	A670	50c multi	1.00	.95
2324	A670	50c multi	1.00	.95
a.		Horiz. pair, #2323-2324	2.25	2.00
b.		Booklet pane, #2323-2324	3.00	—
2325	A670	50c multi	1.00	.95
2326	A670	50c multi	1.00	.95
a.		Horiz. pair, #2325-2326	2.25	2.00
b.		Booklet pane, #2325-2326	3.00	—
2327	A670	50c multi	1.00	.95
2328	A670	50c multi	1.00	.95
a.		Horiz. pair, #2327-2328	2.25	2.00
b.		Booklet pane, #2327-2328	3.00	—
		Nos. 2323-2328 (6)	6.00	5.70

Self-Adhesive
Booklet Stamps
Serpentine Die Cut 11¼ Syncopated

2329	A670	50c multi	1.00	.95
2330	A670	50c multi	1.00	.95
a.		Booklet pane, 5 each #2329-2330	10.00	
2331	A670	50c multi	1.00	.95
2332	A670	50c multi	1.00	.95
a.		Booklet pane, 5 each #2331-2332	10.00	
2333	A670	50c multi	1.00	.95
2334	A670	50c multi	1.00	.95
a.		Booklet pane, 5 each #2333-2334	10.00	
		Nos. 2329-2334 (6)	6.00	5.70

Nos. 2324b, 2326b, 2328b, 1/24/07.

Sports Memorabilia A672

Parrots — A671

Designs: Nos. 2335, 2340, Princess parrot. Nos. 2336, 2344, Rainbow lorikeet. Nos. 2337, 2343, Green rosella. Nos. 2338, 2342, Red-capped parrot. Nos. 2339, 2341, Purple-crowned lorikeet.

2005, Feb. 8 *Perf. 14¾x14*

2335	A671	50c multi	1.25	.95
2336	A671	50c multi	1.25	.95
2337	A671	50c multi	1.25	.95
2338	A671	50c multi	1.25	.95
2339	A671	50c multi	1.25	.95
a.		Horiz. strip of 5, #2335-2339	6.25	6.25
		Nos. 2335-2339 (5)	6.25	4.75

A sheet containing Nos. 2335-2339 + 4 labels was available only with purchase of the "2005 Collection of Australian Stamps." Value $24.

Self-Adhesive
Coil Stamps
Serpentine Die Cut 11¼ Syncopated

2340	A671	50c multi	1.25	.85
2341	A671	50c multi	1.25	.85
2342	A671	50c multi	1.25	.85
2343	A671	50c multi	1.25	.85
2344	A671	50c multi	1.25	.85
a.		Vert. strip of 5, #2340-2344	6.25	
		Nos. 2340-2344 (5)	6.25	4.25

Designs: No. 2345, Sir Donald Bradman's cricket cap. No. 2346, Lionel Rose's boxing gloves. No. 2347, Marjorie Jackson's running spikes. No. 2348, Racing silks of Phar Lap's jockeys.

2005, Mar. 8 Litho. *Perf. 14¾x14*

2345	A672	50c multi	1.00	.95
a.		Booklet pane of 5, #1575a, 1576c, 1941a, 1942b, 2345 dated "2007"	7.50	—
2346	A672	50c multi	1.00	.95
a.		Horiz. pair, #2345-2346	2.25	2.00
2347	A672	$1 multi	2.25	2.00
2348	A672	$1 multi	2.25	2.00
a.		Horiz. pair, #2347-2348	4.50	4.50
		Nos. 2345-2348 (4)	6.50	5.90

No. 2345a issued 11/14/2007.

Child's Plush Toy — A673   Red Roses — A674

Gifts A675   Kangaroos A676

White Roses — A677   Yellow Roses and Woman's Hand — A678

Koala — A679   Shell on Beach — A680

Sydney Opera House — A681

2005, Mar. 22 *Perf. 14¾x14*

2349	A673	50c multi	1.00	1.00
2350	A674	50c multi	1.00	1.00
2351	A675	50c multi	1.00	1.00
2352	A676	50c multi	1.00	1.00
a.		Additionally dated "2013" (#3534d)	1.25	1.25
2353	A677	50c multi	1.00	1.00
a.		Horiz. strip, #2349-2353	5.25	5.25
2354	A678	$1 multi	2.25	2.00
2355	A679	$1.10 multi	2.25	2.25
2356	A680	$1.20 multi	2.40	2.40
2357	A681	$1.80 multi	3.75	3.75
		Nos. 2349-2357 (9)	15.65	15.40

Issued: No. 2352a, 5/10/2013.

Booklet Stamps
Self-Adhesive
Serpentine Die Cut 11x11¼ Syncopated

2358	A673	50c multi	2.25	2.25
a.		Booklet pane of 4	9.25	
		Complete booklet, 5 #2358a	45.00	
2359	A674	50c multi	2.25	2.25
a.		Booklet pane of 4	9.25	
		Complete booklet, 5 #2359a	45.00	
2360	A675	50c multi	2.25	2.25
a.		Booklet pane of 4	9.25	
		Complete booklet, 5 #2360a	45.00	
2361	A677	50c multi	2.75	2.75
a.		Booklet pane of 4	11.50	
		Complete booklet, 5 #2361a	57.50	
2362	A678	$1 multi	5.75	5.75
a.		Booklet pane of 4	23.00	
		Complete booklet, 5 #2362a	115.00	
2363	A679	$1.10 multi	8.00	8.00
a.		Booklet pane of 4	32.00	
		Complete booklet, 2 #2363a	65.00	
2364	A680	$1.20 multi	9.00	9.00
a.		Booklet pane of 2	18.00	
2365	A681	$1.80 multi	13.00	13.00
a.		Booklet pane of 2	26.00	
		Complete booklet, 2 each #2364a, 2365a	88.00	
		Nos. 2358-2365 (8)	45.25	45.25

Each pane in the various complete booklets has a different margin. The complete booklets containing Nos. 2358-2361 each sold for $10.95, the complete booklet containing No. 2362 sold for $20.95, and the complete booklets containing Nos. 2363-2365 sold for $12.95.

See Nos. 2439-2447.

First Australian Coin, 150th Anniv. A682

1855 One sovereign coin: Nos. 2366, 2368a, Obverse. Nos. 2367, 2368b, Reverse.

2005, Apr. 21 Litho. *Perf. 14x14¾*

2366	A682	50c multi	1.00	1.00
2367	A682	$2.45 multi	5.25	5.25
a.		Booklet pane, #2366-2367	7.75	—

Litho. & Embossed with Foil Application

2368		Sheet of 2	7.00	7.00
a.		A682 50c multi	1.00	1.00
b.		A682 $2.45 multi	5.25	5.25

UNESCO World Heritage Sites in Australia and Great Britain — A683

Designs: No. 2369, Wet Tropics of Queensland, Australia. No. 2370, Stonehenge, England. No. 2371, Greater Blue Mountains Area, New South Wales, Australia. No. 2372, Blenheim Castle, England. No. 2373, Purnululu National Park, Western Australia. No. 2374, Heart of Neolithic Orkney, Scotland. No. 2375, Ayers Rock, Uluru-Kata Tjuta National Park, Northern Territory, Australia. No. 2376, Hadrian's Wall, England.

2005, Apr. 21 Litho. *Perf. 14¼*

2369	A683	50c multi	1.00	.95
2370	A683	50c multi	1.00	.95
a.		Horiz. pair, #2369-2370	2.25	2.25
2371	A683	50c multi	1.00	.95
2372	A683	50c multi	1.00	.95
a.		Horiz. pair, #2371-2372	2.25	2.25
2373	A683	$1 multi	2.25	2.00
2374	A683	$1 multi	2.25	2.00
a.		Horiz. pair, #2373-2374	4.50	4.50
b.		Booklet pane, #2369-2370, 2373-2374, + 4 labels	7.75	—

2375	A683	$1.80 multi	3.75 3.50
2376	A683	$1.80 multi	3.75 3.50
a.		Horiz. pair, #2375-2376	7.50 7.50
b.		Booklet pane, #2371-2372, 2375-2376, + 4 labels	11.50 —
		Nos. 2369-2376 (8)	16.00 14.80

See Great Britain Nos. 2280-2287.

Creatures of the Slime
A684

2005, Apr. 21   Perf. 14x14¾

2377	A684	50c Tribrachidium	1.00 .95
2378	A684	50c Dickinsonia	1.00 .95
2379	A684	50c Spriggina	1.00 .95
2380	A684	50c Kimberella	1.00 .95
2381	A684	50c Inaria	1.00 .95
a.		Horiz. strip of 5, #2377-2381	5.25 5.25
2382	A684	$1 Charnodiscus	2.25 2.00
a.		Souvenir sheet, #2377-2382	7.50 7.50
b.		Booklet pane, #2377-2382	9.00 —
		Nos. 2377-2382 (6)	7.25 6.75

Rotary International, Cent. — A685

2005, Apr. 21   Perf. 14¾x14

2383	A685	50c multi	1.00 .90
a.		Imperf.	5.75 5.75

Self-Adhesive
Serpentine Die Cut 11½x11¼ Syncopated

2384	A685	50c multi	1.00 .90
a.		Booklet pane of 10	10.25
b.		Booklet pane of 1	1.40 —
		Complete booklet, #2367a, 2374b, 2376b, 2382c, 2384b	37.50

No. 2383a was sold at the Pacific Explorer Intl. Philatelic Exhibition 2005.

Queen Elizabeth II, 79th Birthday A686

2005, May 10   Perf. 14x14¾

2385	A686	50c multi	1.40 1.10
a.		Booklet pane of 4	5.75
		Complete booklet, 5 #2385a	29.00

2006 Commonwealth Games, Melbourne. No. 2385a was issued in a booklet that sold for $10.95, with the 5 panes having different margins.

Bush Wildlife A687

No. 2386, Superb lyrebird. Nos. 2387, 2390, Laughing kookaburra. Nos. 2388, 2391, Koala. Nos. 2389, 2392, Red kangaroo.

2005, June 7   Perf. 14x14¾

2386	A687	$1 multi	2.25 1.75
2387	A687	$1.10 multi	2.25 2.00
2388	A687	$1.20 multi	2.40 2.25
2389	A687	$1.80 multi	3.75 3.75
		Nos. 2386-2389 (4)	10.65 9.75

Serpentine Die Cut 11¼x11½ Syncopated
Self-Adhesive
Booklet Stamps

2390	A687	$1.10 multi	2.25 2.00
a.		Booklet pane of 5	11.50
2391	A687	$1.20 multi	2.40 2.25
a.		Booklet pane of 5	12.00
2392	A687	$1.80 Red kangaroo	3.75 3.75
a.		Booklet pane of 5	19.00
		Nos. 2390-2392 (3)	8.40 8.00

Wild Flowers — A688

Designs: Nos. 2393, 2397, 2401, Sturt's desert pea. Nos. 2394, 2398, 2402, Coarse-leaved mallee. Nos. 2395, 2399, 2403, Common fringe lily. Nos. 2396, 2400, 2404, Swamp daisy.

2005, July 5   Perf. 14x14½

2393	A688	50c multi	1.40 1.00
2394	A688	50c multi	1.40 1.00
2395	A688	50c multi	1.40 1.00
2396	A688	50c multi	1.40 1.00
a.		Horiz. strip of 4, #2393-2396	5.75 5.75
		Nos. 2393-2396 (4)	5.60 4.00

Self-Adhesive
Serpentine Die Cut 11¼x11

2397	A688	50c multi	1.40 .90
2398	A688	50c multi	1.40 .90
2399	A688	50c multi	1.40 .90
2400	A688	50c multi	1.40 .90
a.		Horiz. coil strip of 4, #2397-2400	5.75
b.		Booklet pane of 10, 3 each #2397-2398, 2 each #2399-2400	15.00
c.		Booklet pane of 20, 5 each #2397-2400	30.00
d.		Booklet pane of 5, #2398-2400, 2 #2397	7.25

Coil Stamps
Die Cut Perf. 12¾

2401	A688	50c multi	1.40 .90
2402	A688	50c multi	1.40 .90
2403	A688	50c multi	1.40 .90
2404	A688	50c multi	1.40 .90
a.		Horiz. coil strip of 4, #2401-2404	5.75
		Nos. 2397-2404 (8)	11.20 7.20

Australian Wine — A689

Designs: Nos. 2405, 2410, Grapevine, vineyard. Nos. 2406, 2411, Grapes, grape leaves. No. 2407, Grape pickers, basket of grapes, wine bottle. No. 2408, Wine bottle, corkscrew, wine barrels. $1.45, Wine glasses, cheese.

2005, July 19   Perf. 14x14¾

2405	A689	50c multi	1.00 1.00
2406	A689	50c multi	1.00 1.00
a.		Horiz. pair, #2405-2406	2.25 2.25
b.		Booklet pane, #2406a	2.25 —
c.		Booklet pane, 2 #2406a	4.50 —
2407	A689	$1 multi	2.25 2.25
2408	A689	$1 multi	2.25 2.25
a.		Horiz. pair, #2407-2408	4.50 4.50
b.		Booklet pane, 2 #2408a	9.25 —
2409	A689	$1.45 multi	3.25 3.25
a.		Booklet pane of 2	6.25 —
		Complete booklet, #2406b, 2406c, 2408b, 2409a	22.50
		Nos. 2405-2409 (5)	9.75 9.75

Booklet Stamps
Self-Adhesive
Serpentine Die Cut 11¼x11½ Syncopated

2410	A689	50c multi	1.25 1.25
2411	A689	50c multi	1.25 1.25
a.		Booklet pane, 5 each #2410-2411	12.50

Complete booklet sold for $10.95.

Trees A690

Designs: Nos. 2412, 2417, Snowgum. Nos. 2413, 2418, Wollemi pine. Nos. 2414, 2419, Boab. Nos. 2415, 2420, Karri. Nos. 2416, 2421, Moreton Bay fig.

2005, Aug. 8   Perf. 14x14¾

2412	A690	50c multi	1.10 1.10
2413	A690	50c multi	1.10 1.10
2414	A690	50c multi	1.10 1.10
2415	A690	50c multi	1.10 1.10
2416	A690	50c multi	1.10 1.10
a.		Horiz. strip of 5, #2412-2416	5.50 5.50
		Nos. 2412-2416 (5)	5.50 5.50

Coil Stamps
Serpentine Die Cut 11¼x11½ Syncopated

2417	A690	50c multi	1.10 1.00
2418	A690	50c multi	1.10 1.00
2419	A690	50c multi	1.10 1.00
2420	A690	50c multi	1.10 1.00
2421	A690	50c multi	1.10 1.00
a.		Horiz. strip of 5, #2417-2421	7.00
		Nos. 2417-2421 (5)	5.50 5.00

Nos. 2417-2421 have "frames" that are faded portions of the design.

Portion of Specimen Pane of New South Wales No. 86 from Australia Post Archives — A691

2005, Sept. 6   Litho.   Perf. 14¼

2422	A691	$5 multi	10.50 10.50

No. 2422 exists imperf.

Southern Cross — A692

Southern Cross and: 45c, Christmas tree. 50c, Map of Oceania and East Asia.

2005   Perf. 14½x14

2423	A692	45c multi	1.25 1.10
a.		Booklet pane of 4	5.25 —
		Complete booklet (see footnote)	23.00
2424	A692	50c multi	1.40 1.25

Issued: Nos. 2423, 2424, 9/6. No. 2423a, 11/1. No. 2423a exists with three different margins, each of which appear in a booklet also containing two examples of Christmas Island No. 452a. The complete booklet sold for $9.95.

Southern Cross With Personalized Picture — A692a

Serpentine Die Cut 11½x11¼ Syncopated

2005, Sept. 6   Litho.
Self-Adhesive

2425	A692a	45c Like #2423	2.50 2.50
2426	A692a	50c Like #2424	2.50 2.50

Nos. 2425-2426 were sold in sheets of 20 and have personalized pictures and a straight edge at right, and lack separations between the stamp and the picture. Sheets of 20 of No. 2425 sold for $22, and of No. 2426, $23.

Down on the Farm — A693

Designs: Nos. 2427, 2433, Hen and chicks. Nos. 2428, 2434, Lambs and insects. Nos. 2429, 2437, Goats and rabbit. Nos. 2430,

---

2435, Pigs and frog. Nos. 2431, 2436, Cow and bird. $1, Horse, dogs, birds, lizard.

2005, Oct. 4   Litho.   Perf. 14x14¾

2427	A693	50c multi	1.00 .95
a.		Booklet pane of 1	1.40
2428	A693	50c multi	1.00 .95
a.		Booklet pane of 1	1.40
2429	A693	50c multi	1.00 .95
a.		Booklet pane of 1	1.40
2430	A693	50c multi	1.00 .95
a.		Booklet pane of 1	1.40
2431	A693	50c multi	1.00 .95
a.		Booklet pane of 1	1.40
b.		Horiz. strip of 5, #2427-2431	5.25 5.25
2432	A693	$1 multi	2.25 2.00
a.		Booklet pane of 1	2.50
b.		Souvenir sheet, #2427-2432	8.00 8.00
c.		Booklet pane of 1 #2432b (120x190mm)	8.50
		Complete booklet, #2427a-2432a, 2432c	18.50
		Nos. 2427-2432 (6)	7.25 6.75

The complete booklet containing Nos. 2427a-2432a and 2432c sold for $9.95.

Booklet Stamps
Self-Adhesive
Serpentine Die Cut 11¼ Syncopated

2433	A693	50c multi	1.25 .90
2434	A693	50c multi	1.25 .90
2435	A693	50c multi	1.25 .90
2436	A693	50c multi	1.25 .90
2437	A693	50c multi	1.25 .90
a.		Booklet pane of 5, #2433-2437	6.25 —
b.		Booklet pane of 10, 2 each #2433-2437	12.50
c.		Booklet pane of 20, 4 each #2433-2437	25.00
2438	A693	$1 multi	1.90 1.50
a.		Booklet pane of 5	9.50 —
		Nos. 2433-2438 (6)	8.15 6.00

Greetings Types of 2005 With Personalized Photo at Right Like Type A692a
Serpentine Die Cut 11½x11¼ Syncopated

2005			**Self-Adhesive**
2439	A673	50c multi	2.75 2.75
2440	A674	50c multi	2.75 2.75
2441	A675	50c multi	2.75 2.75
2442	A676	50c multi	2.75 2.75
2443	A677	50c multi	2.75 2.75
2444	A678	50c multi	4.25 4.25
2445	A679	$1.10 multi	4.50 4.50
2446	A680	$1.20 multi	5.00 5.00
2447	A681	$1.80 multi	6.25 6.25
		Nos. 2439-2447 (9)	33.75 33.75

Nos. 2439-2447 were sold in sheets of 20 and have personalized pictures and a straight edge at right, and lack separations between the stamp and the picture. Sheets of 20 of Nos. 2439-2443 sold for $23 each, of No. 2444, $33.50, of No. 2445, $35, of No. 2446, $37, of No. 2447, $48.

Christmas — A694

Designs: Nos. 2448, 2450, Madonna and Child. Nos. 2449, 2451, Angel, horiz.

2005, Nov. 1   Litho.   Perf. 14½x14

2448	A694	45c multi	.95 .85

Perf. 14x14½

2449	A694	$1 multi	2.25 2.00

Booklet Stamps
Self-Adhesive
Serpentine Die Cut 11½x11¼ Syncopated

2450	A694	45c multi	.95 .85
a.		Booklet pane of 20	19.50

Serpentine Die Cut 11¼x11½ Syncopated

2451	A694	$1 multi	2.25 2.00
a.		Booklet pane of 5	11.00
		Nos. 2448-2451 (4)	6.40 5.70

Emblem of 2006
Commonwealth Games,
Melbourne — A695

Commonwealth Games
Athletes — A696

Highlights of Commonwealth
Games — A697

Medalists at Commonwealth
Games — A698

"Equality, Humanity, Destiny" — A699

"Destiny, Equality, Humanity" — A700

"Humanity, Destiny, Equality" — A701

Designs: Nos. 2455, 2458, Runner crouching before race. $1.25, Cyclist. $1.85, Athlete holding ball.

No. 2459 — Sheet #1: a, Trolley car with wings. b, Fish sculpture. c, Cat and mouse puppets. d, Queen Elizabeth II. e, Opening ceremony crowd and fireworks.

No. 2460 — Sheet #2: a, Anna Meares. b, Equality, Humanity, destiny. c, Stephanie Rice swimming. d, Destiny, Equality, Humanity. e, Ben Kersten.

No. 2461 — Sheet #3: a, Ryan Bayley holding flag. b, Adam Vella & Michael Diamond. c, Sean Finning. d, Deserie Baynes & Suzanne Balogh. e, Danni Miatke. f, Women's Artistic Gymnastics team. g, Kate Bates. h, Leisel Jones swim cap and waving. i, David Moore & Daniel Repacholi.

No. 2462 — Sheet #4: a, Brad Kahlfeldt. b, Libby Lenton, lane marker in background. c, Josh Jefferis on pommel horse. d, Emma Snowsill.

No. 2463 — Sheet #5: a, Leisel Jones wearing sweatsuit. b, Ryan Bayley wearing cycling helmet. c, Matthew Cowdrey in water. d, Chloe Sims. e, Sophie Edington in water. f, Women's 4x200m freestyle swim team. g, Ben Turner.

No. 2464 — Sheet #6: a, Katie Mactier. b, Russell Mark & Craig Trembath. c, Jessicah Schipper in water. d, Kerryn McCann. e, Lalita Yauhleuskaya & Dina Aspandiyarova.

No. 2465 — Sheet #7: a, Lauryn Mark & Natalia Rahman. b, Jane Saville. c, Libby Lenton, pushing on lane marker. d, Nathan Deakes in 20km walk. e, Lisa McIntosh.

No. 2466 — Sheet #8: a, Leisel Jones with fist raised. b, Men's triples lawn bowling team. c, Sophie Edington holding medal. d, Matthew Cowdrey wearing sweatsuit. e, Brooke Krueger-Billett. f, Josh Jefferis kissing medal. g, Natalie Grinham. h, Women's 4x100m freestyle swim team. i, Joanna Fargus.

No. 2467 — Sheet #9: a, Alex Karapetyan. b, Jessicah Schipper wearing sweatsuit. c, Nathan O'Neill. d, Lalita Yauhleuskaya holding medal.

No. 2468 — Sheet #10: a, Hollie Dykes. b, Men's 4x100m medley swim team. c, Oenone Wood. d, Women's 4x100m medley swim team. e, Stephanie Rice with arm raised. f, Damian Istria. g, Deborah Lovely.

No. 2469 — Sheet #11: a, Chantelle Newbery & Loudy Tourky. b, John Steffensen. c, Bree Cole & Sharleen Stratton. d, Lynsey Armitage & Karen Murphy.

No. 2470 — Sheet #12: a, Heath Francis. b, Jana Pittman. c, Lalita Yauhleuskaya wearing sight. d, Scott Martin. e, Loudy Tourky. f, Women's basketball team. g, Chris Rae. h, Bruce Scott.

No. 2471 — Sheet #13: a, Nathan Deakes in 50km walk. b, Bronwyn Thompson. c, Robert Newbery & Mathew Helm. d, Steven Hooker. e, Stuart Rendell. f, Kelvin Kerkow. g, Men's basketball team.

No. 2472 — Sheet #14: a, Women's 4x400m relay team. b, Kym Howe. c, Women's field hockey team. d, Mathew Helm. e, Men's 4x400m relay team. f, Bradley Pitt. g, Jarrod Fletcher.

No. 2473 — Sheet #15: a, Natalie Bates. b, Natalie Grinham & Joe Kneipp. c, Men's field hockey team. d, Rachael Grinham & Natalie Grinham. e, Mathew Hayman.

No. 2474 — Sheet #16: a, Dancer on hoops. b, Women wearing hats. c, Dancer. d, Lit-up stadium and fireworks. e, Darkened stadium and fireworks.

No. 2475 — Sheet #17 — Kerryn McCann: a, Running, with opponents in background. b, Drinking from water bottle. c, Running past opponent, profile. d, Running on track with opponent. e, With hands over mouth. f, Collapsed on track. g, With both arms raised. h, Holding flag. i, Raising flower bouquet. j, Holding medal.

2006	Litho.	Perf. 14¾x14		
2452	A695	50c shown	1.00	1.00
a.		Sheet of 9 + 9 labels	27.50	—
b.		Booklet pane of 4	4.25	

Self-Adhesive (#2453-2454)

Serpentine Die Cut 11¼ Syncopated

2453	A695	50c multi	1.00	1.00
a.		Booklet pane of 4	4.50	

With Personalized Photo at Right
Like Type A692a
Booklet Stamp

Serpentine Die Cut 11½x11¼ on 3 Sides, Syncopated

2454	A695	50c multi	4.50	5.75
a.		Booklet pane of 4	18.50	

Perf. 14x14¾

2455	A696	50c shown	1.00	1.00
2456	A696	$1.25 multi	2.50	2.50
2457	A696	$1.85 multi	3.75	3.75
a.		Souvenir sheet, #2455-2457, 142x75mm sheet	7.75	7.75
b.		Booklet pane, #2455-2457, in 168x118mm pane	7.75	
		Complete booklet, #1488a, 2457b, 2 each #2453a, 2454a, + 3 postal cards	42.50	
c.		Booklet pane, #2455-2457, in 156x103mm pane	7.75	
		Complete booklet #845a, 2219c, 2452b, 2457c	22.00	
		Nos. 2455-2457 (3)	7.25	7.25

Booklet Stamp
Self-Adhesive

Serpentine Die Cut 11¼ Syncopated

2458	A696	50c multi	1.00	1.00
a.		Booklet pane of 10	10.25	

Miniature Sheets

Perf. 14½x14

2459		Sheet of 5	7.25	15.00
a.-e.	A697	50c any single	1.40	3.00
2460		Sheet of 5	7.25	11.00
a.	A698	50c multi	1.40	3.00
b.	A699	50c multi	1.40	3.00
c.	A698	50c multi	1.40	3.00
d.	A700	50c multi	1.40	1.00
e.	A698	50c multi	1.40	3.00
2461		Sheet of 10, #2460b, 2461a-2461i	14.50	28.00
a.-i.	A698	50c any single	1.40	3.00

2462		Sheet of 5, #2460b, 2462a-2462d	7.25	13.00
a.-d.	A698	50c any single	1.40	3.00
2463		Sheet of 10, #2460b, 2460d, 2463a-2463h	14.50	24.00
a.-g.	A698	50c any single	1.40	3.00
h.	A701	50c multi	1.40	1.00
2464		Sheet of 5	7.25	15.00
a.-e.	A698	50c any single	1.40	3.00
2465		Sheet of 5	7.25	15.00
a.-e.	A698	50c any single	1.40	3.00
2466		Sheet of 10, #2460a-2466i	14.50	28.00
a.-i.	A698	50c any single	1.40	3.00
2467		Sheet of 5, #2460b, 2467a-2467d	7.25	13.00
a.-d.	A698	50c any single	1.40	3.00
2468		Sheet of 10, #2460b, 2460d, 2463h, 2468a-2468g	14.50	24.00
a.-g.	A698	50c any single	1.40	3.00
2469		Sheet of 5, #2460b, 2469a-2469d	7.25	13.00
a.-d.	A698	50c any single	1.40	3.00
2470		Sheet of 10, #2460b, 2460d, 2470a-2470h	14.50	26.00
a.-h.	A698	50c any single	1.40	3.00
2471		Sheet of 10, #2460b, 2460d, 2463h, 2471a-2471g	14.50	24.00
a.-g.	A698	50c any single	1.40	3.00
2472		Sheet of 10, #2460b, 2460d, 2463h, 2472a-2472g	14.50	24.00
a.-g.	A698	50c any single	1.40	3.00
2473		Sheet of 5	7.25	15.00
a.-e.	A698	50c any single	1.40	3.00
2474		Sheet of 5	7.25	15.00
a.-e.	A697	50c any single	1.40	3.00
2475		Sheet of 10	14.50	30.00
a.-j.	A697	50c any single	1.40	3.00
		Nos. 2459-2475 (17)	181.25	333.00

Issued: Nos. 2452-2453, 1/12; Nos. 2454, 2457b, 3/15; Nos. 2452b, 2455-2458, 2457c, 3/1; No. 2459, 3/16; No. 2460, 3/17; No. 2461, 3/18; Nos. 2462, 2463, 3/19; No. 2464, 3/20; Nos. 2465, 2466, 3/21; Nos. 2467, 2468, 3/22; No. 2469, 3/23; No. 2470, 3/24; No. 2471, 3/25; No. 2472, 3/26; Nos. 2473, 2474, 3/27; No. 2475, 3/28.

No. 2452a sold for $15.95. Labels could be personalized.

Complete booklet containing No. 2454 sold for $19.95. Labels could be personalized.

Complete booklet containing No. 2457c sold for $10.95 and included a booklet pane with perf. 14x14¾ lithographed examples of Nos. 349-350 which were not valid for postage.

A booklet issued 2/1, containing #2452b, an imperf booklet pane of 4 #2452, a booklet pane of 2 #2453, a booklet pane of 1 #2453 and four 50c coins, sold for $24.95.

Dame Edna
Everage in 2004
A702

Barry Humphries
A703

Inscriptions: Nos. 2476, 2481, Mrs. Norm Everage, 1969. Nos. 2477, 2482, Mrs. Edna Everage, 1973. Nos. 2478, 2483, Dame Edna Everage, 1982.

2006, Jan. 20	Litho.	Perf. 14½x14		
2476	A702	50c multi	1.00	1.00
2477	A702	50c multi	1.00	1.00
2478	A702	50c multi	1.00	1.00
2479	A702	50c shown	1.00	1.00
2480	A703	50c shown	1.00	1.00
a.		Horiz. strip of 5, #2476-2480	5.25	5.25
b.		Booklet pane, #2476-2480	5.25	—
		Complete booklet	45.00	
		Nos. 2476-2480 (5)	5.00	5.00

Booklet Stamps
Self-Adhesive

Serpentine Die Cut 11¼ Syncopated

2481	A702	50c multi	1.00	.90
2482	A702	50c multi	1.00	.90
2483	A702	50c multi	1.00	.90
a.		Booklet pane, 4 #2481, 3 each #2482-2483	10.25	

2484	A702	50c multi	1.00	.90
2485	A703	50c multi	1.00	.90
a.		Booklet pane, 5 each #2484-2485	10.25	
		Nos. 2481-2485 (5)	5.00	4.50

Edna Everage, stage character played by Barry Humphries.

No. 2480b issued 1/24/07. Complete booklet, which sold for $22.95, contains Nos. 1576b, 1634m, 1634n, 1634o, 1720b, 1803b, 1934b, 2025b, 2128b, 2208b, 2324b, 2326b, 2328b, and 2480b.

Rose
A704

2006, Jan. 27	Litho.	Perf. 14x14¾		
2486	A704	50c multi	1.00	1.00

With White Border
Self-Adhesive
Litho. & Typo.
Serpentine Die Cut 11¼ Syncopated

2487	A704	50c multi	1.00	.90

Booklet Stamp
Litho.

2488	A704	50c multi	1.00	.90
a.		Booklet pane of 10	8.50	

No. 2487 has a scratch-and-sniff area with a rose scent applied to the center of the rose, has a denomination composed of small black dots, and was printed in sheets of 10. No. 2488 lacks the scrach and sniff panel and has a solid gray denomination.

Flowers — A705

Designs: $1, Pincushion hakea. $2, Donkey orchid. $5, Mangles kangaroo paw. $10, Waratah.

2006, Feb. 7	Litho.	Perf. 14x14½		
2489	A705	$1 multi	2.25	1.40
2490	A705	$2 multi	4.25	2.75

Perf. 14½x14
Size:50x30mm

2491	A705	$5 multi	10.25	7.00
2492	A705	$10 multi	20.75	11.00
		Nos. 2489-2492 (4)	37.50	22.15

Souvenir Sheet
Litho. & Embossed

2493	A705	$10 multi	22.00	22.00

Dale Begg-Smith, Men's Moguls Gold Medalist at 2006 Winter Olympics, Turin — A706

2006, Feb. 15	Litho.	Perf. 14½		
2494	A706	50c multi	1.00	1.00

Animals
A707

Royal Exhibition
Building,
Melbourne — A708

Designs: 2495, 5c, Platypus. 2496, 25c, Short-beaked echidna. No. 2497, $1.25, Common wombat. Nos. 2498, $1.25, Koala, vert. No. 2499, $1.85, Tasmanian devil. 2501, $2.50, Greater bilby. 2502, $3.70, Dingo.

2006		Perf. 14x14¾, 14¾x14	
2495	A707	5c multi	.25	.25
2496	A707	25c multi	.50	.35
2497	A707	$1.25 multi	2.50	2.50
2498	A707	$1.25 multi	2.50	2.50
a.		Souvenir sheet of 1, with China 2006 emblem and Great Wall of China in sheet margin	2.25	2.25
b.		As "a," with Sydney landmarks in sheet margin	2.25	2.25
2499	A707	$1.85 multi	3.75	3.75
2500	A708	$1.85 multi	3.75	3.75
2501	A707	$2.50 multi	5.25	5.25
2502	A707	$3.70 multi	7.75	7.75
		Nos. 2495-2502 (8)	26.25	26.10

Self-Adhesive
Booklet Stamps
Serpentine Die Cut 11¼ Syncopated

2503	A707	$1.25 multi	2.50	2.50
a.		Booklet pane of 5	12.75	
b.		Booklet pane of 2	5.75	
		Complete booklet, 4 #2503b	23.00	
c.		As "a," with Washington 2000 Exhib. emblem added to lower right margin of bklt. pane	13.75	
2504	A708	$1.85 multi	3.75	3.75
a.		Booklet pane of 5	19.00	
b.		Booklet pane of 2	7.50	
		Complete booklet, 4 #2504b	30.00	

Issued: Nos. 2498, 2500, 2503, 2504, 5/2; No. 2503c, 5/27; others, 3/6.
Each of the four panes of Nos. 2503b and 2504b in the complete booklets have different margins. The complete booklet containing No. 2503b sold for $12.95; the booklet containing No. 2504b sold for $14.95.
Nos. 2498a-2498b issued 10/26.
See Nos. 2542-2543, 2674, 2676, 2678.

Queen Elizabeth II, 80th Birthday
A709　　　　A710

2006, Apr. 19		Perf. 14¾x14	
2505	A709	50c multi	1.00	1.00
a.		Booklet pane of 2	2.25	—
b.		Dated "2010"	2.00	1.00
2506	A710	$2.45 multi	5.25	5.25
a.		Booklet pane of 2	10.25	—
b.		Booklet pane, #2505-2506, 153x104mm pane size	6.25	—
		Complete booklet, #2506a, 2506b, 2 #2505a	21.00	
c.		Souvenir sheet, #2505-2506, 105x70mm sheet size	7.00	7.00

Self-Adhesive
Booklet Stamp
Serpentine Die Cut 11¼ Syncopated

2507	A709	50c multi	1.10	.90
a.		Booklet pane of 10	11.50	

Complete booklet containing Nos. 2505-2506 sold for $10.95.

A booklet commemorating royal visits to Australia containing a booklet pane of 2 each of lithographed, perf. 14x14¾ example of Nos. 474-475, a booklet pane of 4 lithographed, perf. 14x14¾ examples of No. 779, a booklet pane of 2 each of lithographed perf. 14½x14 examples of Nos. 659-660, a booklet pane of 2 each Nos. 2031-2032, a booklet pane of No. 2234a with a different margin, a booklet pane of 2 each of perf. 14½x14 examples of Nos. 351-352 (not valid for postage), and a 50c coin was released in 2006. It sold for $15.95.

Lighthouses
A711

Designs: Nos. 2508, 2513, Point Lonsdale Lighthouse, Victoria. Nos. 2509, 2514, Cape Don Lighthouse, Northern Territory. Nos. 2510, 2515, Wollongong Head Lighthouse, New South Wales. Nos. 2511, 2516, Casuarina Point Lighthouse, Western Australia. Nos. 2512, 2517, Point Cartwright Lighthouse, Queensland.

2006, May 2		Perf. 14¾x14	
2508	A711	50c multi	1.00	1.00
2509	A711	50c multi	1.00	1.00
2510	A711	50c multi	1.00	1.00
a.		Booklet pane, 2509, 2510, 2 #2508	4.25	—
b.		Booklet pane, 2508, 2509, 2 #2510	4.25	—
2511	A711	50c multi	1.00	1.00
2512	A711	50c multi	1.00	1.00
a.		Horiz. strip, #2508-2512	5.25	4.50
b.		Booklet pane, #2511, 2512, 2 #2509	4.25	—
c.		Booklet pane, 2510, 2512, 2 #2511	4.25	—
d.		Booklet pane, #2508, 2511, 2 #2512	4.25	—
		Complete booklet, #2510a, 2510b, 2512b, 2512c, 2512d	20.00	
		Nos. 2508-2512 (5)	5.00	5.00

Coil Stamps
Self-Adhesive
Serpentine Die Cut 11¼ Syncopated

2513	A711	50c multi	1.10	.90
2514	A711	50c multi	1.10	.90
2515	A711	50c multi	1.10	.90
2516	A711	50c multi	1.10	.90
2517	A711	50c multi	1.10	.90
a.		Vert. strip, #2513-2517	5.75	

Complete booklet sold for $10.95.

2006 World Cup Soccer
Championships, Germany — A712

Soccer player, 2006 World Cup emblem and word: Nos. 2518, 2522, "Play." Nos. 2519, 2523, "Goal." Nos. 2520, "Save." Nos. 2521, $1.85, "Shot."

2006, May 9		Perf. 14x14¾	
2518	A712	50c multi	1.00	1.00
2519	A712	50c multi	1.00	1.00
a.		Horiz. pair, #2518-2519	2.25	2.25
2520	A712	$1.25 multi	2.50	2.50
2521	A712	$1.85 multi	3.75	3.75
a.		Souvenir sheet, #2518-2521	8.50	8.50
b.		As "a," with 2006 Paris Exhib. ovpt.	9.25	9.25
		Nos. 2518-2521 (4)	8.25	8.25

Booklet Stamps
Self-Adhesive
Serpentine Die Cut 11¼ Syncopated

2522	A712	50c multi	1.10	1.10
2523	A712	50c multi	1.10	1.10
a.		Booklet pane, 5 each #2522-2523	11.50	

No. 2521b issued 6/17.

Postie
Kate — A713

Kate: Nos. 2524, 2529, Writing address on letter. Nos. 2525, 2530, On motorcycle, delivering letter. Nos. 2526, 2531, With van, delivering package. Nos. 2527, 2532, Riding motorcycle in rain. Nos. 2528, 2533, Waving.

2006, June 1		Litho.	Perf. 14x14¾	
2524	A713	50c multi	1.00	1.00
a.		Booklet pane of 1	1.75	
2525	A713	50c multi	1.00	1.00
a.		Booklet pane of 1	1.75	
2526	A713	50c multi	1.00	1.00
a.		Booklet pane of 1	1.75	
2527	A713	50c multi	1.00	1.00
a.		Booklet pane of 1	1.75	
2528	A713	50c multi	1.00	1.00
a.		Horiz. strip of 5, #2524-2528	5.25	5.25
b.		Booklet pane of 1	1.75	
		Nos. 2524-2528 (5)	5.00	5.00

Booklet Stamps
Self-Adhesive
Serpentine Die Cut 11¼ Syncopated

2529	A713	50c multi	1.10	.90
2530	A713	50c multi	1.10	.90
2531	A713	50c multi	1.10	.90
2532	A713	50c multi	1.10	.90
2533	A713	50c multi	1.10	.90
a.		Booklet pane, 2 each #2529-2533	11.50	
b.		Booklet pane, 4 each #2529-2533	22.50	
c.		Booklet pane, #2529-2533	5.75	
		Complete booklet, #2524a, 2525a, 2526a, 2527a, 2528b, 2533c	20.00	
		Nos. 2529-2533 (5)	5.50	4.50

Complete booklet sold for $9.95.

Worldwide
Fund for
Nature
(WWF)
A714

Designs: Nos. 2534, 2538, Humpback whale. Nos. 2535, 2539, Blue whale. $1.25, Fin whale. $1.85, Southern bottlenose whale.

2006, June 6		Perf. 14x14¾	
2534	A714	50c multi	1.10	1.00
2535	A714	50c multi	1.10	1.00
a.		Horiz. pair, #2534-2535	2.25	2.25
2536	A714	$1.25 multi	2.75	2.25
2537	A714	$1.85 multi	4.00	3.50
a.		Souvenir sheet, #2534-2537	9.50	9.50
		Nos. 2534-2537 (4)	8.95	7.75

Self-Adhesive
Serpentine Die Cut 11¼ Syncopated
Coil Stamps

2538	A714	50c multi	1.10	.95
2539	A714	50c multi	1.10	.95
a.		Horiz. pair, #2538-2539	2.25	

Booklet Stamps

2540	A714	$1.25 multi	2.75	2.25
a.		Booklet pane of 5	14.50	
2541	A714	$1.85 multi	4.00	3.50
a.		Booklet pane of 5	20.00	
		Nos. 2538-2541 (4)	8.95	7.65

Types of 2006 With Personalized Photo at Right Like Type A692a

Designs: $1.25, Koala. $1.85, Royal Exhibition Building.

Serpentine Die Cut 11½x11¼ Syncopated

2006			Litho.	

Self-Adhesive

2542	A707	$1.25 multi	3.75	3.75
2543	A708	$1.85 multi	4.50	4.50

Nos. 2542-2543 were sold in sheets of 20 and have personalized pictures and a straight edge at right, and lack separations between the stamp and the pictures. Sheets of 20 of No. 2542 sold for $38, and of No. 2543, $49.

Extreme
Sports
A715

Designs: 50c, Surfing. $1, Snowboarding. $1.45, Skateboarding. $2, Freestyle motocross.

2006, July 18		Litho.	Perf. 14x14¾	
2544	A715	50c multi	1.00	.90
2545	A715	$1 multi	2.25	1.75
2546	A715	$1.45 multi	3.25	2.75
2547	A715	$2 multi	4.25	4.25
		Nos. 2544-2547 (4)	10.75	9.65

Cars and
Trucks
A716

Designs: Nos. 2548, 2553, 1917 Ford TT Truck. Nos. 2549, 2554, 1956 Holden FE. Nos. 2550, 2555, 1961 Morris 850. Nos. 2551, 2556, 1976 Holden Sandman HX. Nos. 2552, 2557, 1985 Toyota Land Cruiser FJ60.

2006, Aug. 15		Perf. 14x14¾	
2548	A716	50c multi	1.00	1.00
a.		Booklet pane of 4	4.25	—
2549	A716	50c multi	1.00	1.00
a.		Booklet pane of 4	4.25	—
2550	A716	50c multi	1.00	1.00
a.		Booklet pane of 4	4.25	—
2551	A716	50c multi	1.00	1.00
a.		Booklet pane of 4	4.25	—
2552	A716	50c multi	1.00	1.00
a.		Complete booklet, #2548a-2552a	22.50	
b.		Horiz. strip of 5, #2548-2552	5.25	5.25
		Nos. 2548-2552 (5)	5.00	5.00

Booklet Stamps
Self-Adhesive
Serpentine Die Cut 11¼ Syncopated

2553	A716	50c multi	1.10	.90
a.		Booklet pane of 10	11.50	
b.		Missing 2006 date		
2554	A716	50c multi	1.10	.90
a.		Booklet pane of 10	11.50	
2555	A716	50c multi	1.10	.90
a.		Booklet pane of 10	11.50	
2556	A716	50c multi	1.10	.90
a.		Booklet pane of 10	11.50	
2557	A716	50c multi	1.10	.90
a.		Booklet pane of 10	11.50	
b.		Booklet pane, 2 each #2553-2557	11.50	
		Nos. 2553-2557 (5)	5.50	4.50

Complete booklet containing Nos. 2548a-2552a sold for $10.95.

Rock
Posters — A717

Designs: Nos. 2558a, 2559a, Sunbury Rock Festival, 1972. Nos. 2558b, 2559b, Magic Dirt Tour, 2002. Nos. 2558c, 2559c, The Masters Apprentices Parramatta concert, 1972. Nos. 2558d, 2559d, Goanna's Spirit of Place album, 1983. Nos. 2558e, 2559e, Angels, Sports and Paul Kelly and the Dots Latrobe concert, 1979. Nos. 2558f, 2559f, Midnight Oil, 1979. Nos. 2558g, 2559g, Big Day Out Festival, 2003. Nos. 2558h, 2559h, Apollo Bay Music Festival, 1999. Nos. 2558i, 2559i, Rolling Stones Australian Tour, 1973. Nos. 2558j, 2559j, Mental as Anything's Another Falcon Tour, 1990.

2006, Sept. 12		Litho.	Perf. 14½x14	
2558		Sheet of 10	10.00	10.00
a.-j.		A717 50c Any single	1.00	1.00
k.		Booklet pane of 2 #2558a	2.25	
l.		Booklet pane of 2 #2558b	2.25	—
m.		Booklet pane of 2 #2558c	2.25	—
n.		Booklet pane of 2 #2558d	2.25	—
o.		Booklet pane of 2 #2558e	2.25	—
p.		Booklet pane of 2 #2558f	2.25	—
q.		Booklet pane of 2 #2558g	2.25	—
r.		Booklet pane of 2 #2558h	2.25	—
s.		Booklet pane of 2 #2558i	2.25	—
t.		Booklet pane of 2 #2558j	2.25	—
		Complete booklet, #2558k-2558t	22.00	

Self-Adhesive
Serpentine Die Cut 11½x11¼ Syncopated

2559		Booklet pane of 10	10.50	
a.-j.		A717 50c Any single	1.00	1.00

Complete booklet containing Nos. 2558k-2558t sold for $10.95.

Dangerous
Australian
Wildlife
A718

Designs: Nos. 2560, 2566, White shark. Nos. 2561, 2567, Eastern brown snake. Nos. 2562, 2568, Box jellyfish. Nos. 2563, 2569, Saltwater crocodile. Nos. 2564, 2570, Blue-ringed octopus. Nos. 2565, 2571, Yellow-bellied sea snake.

2006, Oct. 3   Litho.   Perf. 14x14¾

2560	A718	50c multi	1.00	1.00
a.		Booklet pane of 2	2.25	
2561	A718	50c multi	1.00	1.00
2562	A718	50c multi	1.00	1.00
a.		Booklet pane of 2	2.25	
2563	A718	50c multi	1.00	1.00
a.		Booklet pane of 2	2.25	
2564	A718	50c multi	1.00	1.00
a.		Horiz. strip of 5, #2560-2564	5.25	5.25
b.		Booklet pane of 2	2.25	—
2565	A718	$1 multi	2.25	2.25
a.		Booklet pane, 2 each #2561, 2565	6.50	
b.		Booklet pane, #2560-2565 (page 26)	7.50	—
c.		Souvenir sheet, #2560-2565	7.75	7.75
		Complete booklet, #2560a, 2562a, 2563a, 2564b, 2565a, 2565b	25.00	
		Nos. 2560-2565 (6)	7.25	7.25

Self-Adhesive
Serpentine Die Cut 11 Syncopated

2566	A718	50c multi	1.00	.90
2567	A718	50c multi	1.00	.90
2568	A718	50c multi	1.00	.90
2569	A718	50c multi	1.00	.90
2570	A718	50c multi	1.00	.90
a.		Horiz. coil strip of 5, #2566-2570	5.25	
b.		Booklet pane, #2566-2570	5.25	
2571	A718	$1 multi	2.25	1.75
a.		Booklet pane of 5	11.00	
		Nos. 2566-2571 (6)	7.25	6.25

Complete booklet sold for $10.95. A souvenir sheet similar to No. 2565c containing partially perforated examples of Nos. 2560-2564 and a stamp that is assumed to be invalid depicting a red-back spider sold for $9.95. Value $20.

Television in
Australia,
50th Anniv.
A719

Television shows: Nos. 2572, 2577, IMT (In Melbourne Tonight). Nos. 2573, 2578, Homicide. Nos. 2574, 2579, Dateline. Nos. 2575, 2580, Neighbours. Nos. 2576, 2581, Kath & Kim.

2006, Oct. 24   Litho.   Perf. 14x14¾

2572	A719	50c multi	.90	.90
2573	A719	50c multi	.90	.90
2574	A719	50c multi	.90	.90
2575	A719	50c multi	.90	.90
2576	A719	50c multi	.90	.90
a.		Horiz. strip of 5, #2572-2576	4.50	4.50
		Nos. 2572-2576 (5)	4.50	4.50

Self-Adhesive
Serpentine Die Cut 11¼x11½ Syncopated

2577	A719	50c multi	.90	.30
a.		Booklet pane of 10 #2577	9.00	
2578	A719	50c multi	.90	.30
2579	A719	50c multi	.90	.30
2580	A719	50c multi	.90	.30
2581	A719	50c multi	.90	.30
a.		Booklet pane of 10 #2581	9.25	
b.		Booklet pane of 10, 2 each #2577-2581	9.25	
c.		Horiz. coil strip of 5, #2577-2581	4.50	
		Nos. 2577-2581 (5)	4.50	1.50

Melbourne
Summer
Olympics,
50th Anniv.
A720

1956 Melbourne Olympics emblem and: No. 2582, Australia #291, Olympic torch. No. 2583, View of Melbourne across Yarra River, 2006, Olympic torch. No. 2584, Australia #290, runners. No. 2585, Collins Street, Melbourne, 2006, runners.

2006, Nov. 1   Perf. 14¾x14

2582	A720	50c multi	.90	.70
2583	A720	50c multi	.90	.70
a.		Horiz. pair, #2582-2583	1.90	1.40
2584	A720	$1 multi	1.90	1.40
2585	A720	$1 multi	1.90	1.40
a.		Horiz. pair, #2584-2585	3.75	2.75
		Nos. 2582-2585 (4)	5.60	4.20

Christmas — A721

Designs: 45c, Madonna and Child. 50c, Magus with gift. $1.05, Shepherd and lamb.

2006, Nov. 1   Perf. 14¾x14

2586	A721	45c multi	.80	.80
2587	A721	50c multi	.90	.70
2588	A721	$1.05 multi	1.90	1.90
		Nos. 2586-2588 (3)	3.60	3.40

Self-Adhesive
Booklet Stamps
Serpentine Die Cut 11½x11¼ Syncopated

2589	A721	45c multi	.80	.30
a.		Booklet pane of 20	16.00	
2590	A721	$1.05 multi	1.90	.30
a.		Booklet pane of 5	9.25	

Australian Victory
in 2006 Ashes
Cricket
Match — A722

Designs: 50c, Players celebrating. $1.85, Players with Ashes Urn.

2007, Jan. 16   Litho.   Perf. 14½x14

2591	A722	50c multi	.85	.85
a.		Imperf.	1.60	1.60
2592	A722	$1.85 multi	3.50	3.50
a.		Souvenir sheet, #2591-2592	4.50	4.50
b.		Imperf.	15.00	12.00
c.		Booklet pane of 2, #2591a, 2592b	7.50	—
		Complete booklet, #591a, 666b, 773a, 1084a, 1302b, 2345a, 2592c	32.00	

Booklet Stamps
Self-Adhesive
Serpentine Die Cut 10¾x11¼ Syncopated

2593	A722	50c multi	.90	.30
a.		Booklet pane of 5	4.50	
2594	A722	$1.85 multi	3.50	1.75
a.		Booklet pane of 5	17.50	
		Nos. 2591-2594 (4)	8.75	6.40

Nos. 2591a, 2592b, 2592c issued 11/14/07. Complete booklet sold for $14.95 and was not made available to foreign addresses.

Horse Racing
Personalities
A723

Designs: Nos. 2595, 2607, Scobie Breasley, jockey, in silks. No. 2596, Breasley on horse. Nos. 2597, 2608, Bart Cummings, horse trainer, with binoculars. No. 2598, Cummings holding trophy. No. 2599, Roy Higgins, jockey, in silks. Nos. 2600, 2609, Higgins on horse. No. 2601, Bob Ingham, horse breeder. Nos. 2602, 2610, Ingham with horse. Nos. 2603, 2611, George Moore, jockey, in silks. No. 2604, Moore on horse. Nos. 2605, 2612, John Tapp, horse race announcer. No. 2606, Tapp with binoculars.

2007, Jan. 24   Perf. 14½x14

2595	A723	50c multi	.90	.90
2596	A723	50c multi	.90	.90
2597	A723	50c multi	.90	.90
2598	A723	50c multi	.90	.90
a.		Block of 4, #2595-2598	3.75	3.75

2599	A723	50c multi	.90	.90
2600	A723	50c multi	.90	.90
2601	A723	50c multi	.90	.90
2602	A723	50c multi	.90	.90
a.		Block of 4, #2599-2602	3.75	3.75
2603	A723	50c multi	.90	.90
2604	A723	50c multi	.90	.90
2605	A723	50c multi	.90	.90
2606	A723	50c multi	.90	.90
a.		Block of 4, #2603-2606	3.75	3.75
		Nos. 2595-2606 (12)	10.80	10.80

Booklet Stamps
Self-Adhesive
Serpentine Die Cut 11x11¼ Syncopated

2607	A723	50c multi	.90	.30
2608	A723	50c multi	.90	.30
a.		Booklet pane of 10, 5 each #2607-2608	9.25	
2609	A723	50c multi	.90	.30
2610	A723	50c multi	.90	.30
a.		Booklet pane of 10, 5 each #2609-2610	9.25	
2611	A723	50c multi	.90	.30
2612	A723	50c multi	.90	.30
a.		Booklet pane of 10, 5 each #2611-2612	9.25	
		Nos. 2607-2612 (6)	5.40	1.80

Flowers — A724

Designs: Nos. 2613, 2617, 2621, Tasmanian Christmas bell. Nos. 2614, 2618, 2622, Green spider flower. Nos. 2615, 2619, 2623, Sturt's desert rose. Nos. 2616, 2620, 2624, Phebalium whitei.

2007, Feb. 13   Litho.   Perf. 14½x14½

2613	A724	50c multi	.90	.90
2614	A724	50c multi	.90	.90
2615	A724	50c multi	.90	.90
2616	A724	50c multi	.90	.90
a.		Horiz. strip of 4, #2613-2616	3.75	3.75
		Nos. 2613-2616 (4)	3.60	3.60

Self-Adhesive
Serpentine Die Cut 11¼

2617	A724	50c multi	.90	.30
2618	A724	50c multi	.90	.30
2619	A724	50c multi	.90	.30
2620	A724	50c multi	.90	.30
a.		Horiz. coil strip of 4, #2617-2620	3.75	
b.		Booklet pane of 10, 3 each #2617-2618, 2 each #2619-2620	9.25	
c.		Booklet pane of 20, 5 each #2617-2620	18.50	

Coil Stamps
Die Cut Perf. 12¾

2621	A724	50c multi	.90	.30
2622	A724	50c multi	.90	.30
2623	A724	50c multi	.90	.30
2624	A724	50c multi	.90	.30
a.		Horiz. strip of 4, #2621-2624	3.75	
		Nos. 2617-2624 (8)	7.20	2.40

12th FINA World
Swimming
Championships,
Melbourne — A725

2007, Feb. 20   Perf. 14½x14

2625	A725	50c multi	.90	.90

Coil Stamp
Self-Adhesive
Serpentine Die Cut 11¼ Syncopated

2626	A725	50c multi	.90	.30

Islands
A726

Designs: 10c, Maria Island, Tasmania. 30c, Rottnest Island, Western Australia. $1.30, Green Island, Queensland. $1.95, Fraser Island, Queensland. $2.60, Kangaroo Island, South Australia. $3.85, Lord Howe Island, New South Wales.

2007, Mar. 5   Perf. 14x14½

2627	A726	10c multi	.25	.25
2628	A726	30c multi	.60	.30
2629	A726	$1.30 multi	2.25	2.25
2630	A726	$1.95 multi	3.50	3.50
2631	A726	$2.60 multi	4.50	2.25
2632	A726	$3.85 multi	7.00	3.50
		Nos. 2627-2632 (6)	18.10	12.05

Booklet Stamps
Self-Adhesive
Serpentine Die Cut 11¼ Syncopated

2633	A726	$1.30 multi	2.25	.30
a.		Booklet pane of 5	11.50	
2634	A726	$1.95 multi	3.50	.30
a.		Booklet pane of 5	17.50	

Surf Life
Saving
Australia,
Cent.
A727

Designs: Nos. 2635, 2639, Female lifeguard. Nos. 2636, 2640, Male lifeguards. $1, Surf boat crew. $2, Nippers (junior lifeguards). $2.45, Inflatable rescue boat and crew, vert. (30x50mm).

2007, Mar. 6   Litho.   Perf. 14x14½

2635	A727	50c multi	.90	.90
a.		Booklet pane of 1	1.25	
2636	A727	50c multi	.90	.90
a.		Horiz. pair, #2635-2636	1.90	1.90
		Booklet pane of 1	1.25	
2637	A727	$1 multi	1.90	1.40
a.		Booklet pane of 1	2.50	
2638	A727	$2 multi	3.75	2.75
a.		Booklet pane of 1	5.25	
		Nos. 2635-2638 (4)	7.45	5.95

Self-Adhesive
Coil Stamps (#2639-2640)
Serpentine Die Cut 11¼ Syncopated

2639	A727	50c multi	.90	.30
2640	A727	50c multi	.90	.30
a.		Horiz. pair, #2639-2640	1.90	

Litho. With Three-Dimensional Plastic Affixed

2641	A727	$2.45 multi	4.25	4.25
a.		Souvenir sheet of 2	8.50	
b.		Booklet pane, as "a," with rouletting at left of pane	12.50	
		Complete booklet, #2635a, 2636b, 2637a, 2638a, 2641b	23.00	

Complete booklet sold for $12.95. No. 2641a does not have rouletting at left side of sheet.

Signs of the
Zodiac — A728

Designs: Nos. 2642, 2654, 2665B, Aries. Nos. 2643, 2655, 2665C, Taurus. Nos. 2644, 2656, 2665D, Gemini. Nos. 2645, 2657, 2665E, Cancer. Nos. 2646, 2658, 2665F, Leo. Nos. 2647, 2659, 2665G, Virgo. Nos. 2648, 2660, 2665H, Libra. Nos. 2649, 2661, 2665I, Scorpio. Nos. 2650, 2662, 2665J, Sagittarius. Nos. 2651, 2663, 2665K, Capricorn. Nos. 2652, 2664, 2665L, Aquarius. Nos. 2653, 2665, 2665M, Pisces.

2007, Apr. 3   Litho.   Perf. 14½x14

2642	A728	50c multi	.95	.95
2643	A728	50c multi	.95	.95
2644	A728	50c multi	.95	.95
2645	A728	50c multi	.95	.95
a.		Block of 4, #2642-2645	4.00	
2646	A728	50c multi	.95	.95
2647	A728	50c multi	.95	.95
2648	A728	50c multi	.95	.95
2649	A728	50c multi	.95	.95
a.		Block of 4, #2646-2649	4.00	
2650	A728	50c multi	.95	.95
2651	A728	50c multi	.95	.95
2652	A728	50c multi	.95	.95
2653	A728	50c multi	.95	.95
a.		Block of 4, #2650-2653	4.00	
		Nos. 2642-2653 (12)	11.40	11.40

Booklet Stamps
Self-Adhesive
Serpentine Die Cut 11¼ Syncopated

2654	A728	50c multi	1.00	.30
a.		Booklet pane of 10	10.50	
2655	A728	50c multi	1.00	.30
a.		Booklet pane of 10	10.50	

2656	A728	50c multi	1.00	.30
a.		Booklet pane of 10	10.50	
2657	A728	50c multi	1.00	.30
a.		Booklet pane of 10	10.50	
2658	A728	50c multi	1.00	.30
a.		Booklet pane of 10	10.50	
2659	A728	50c multi	1.00	.30
a.		Booklet pane of 10	10.50	
2660	A728	50c multi	1.00	.30
a.		Booklet pane of 10	10.50	
2661	A728	50c multi	1.00	.30
a.		Booklet pane of 10	10.50	
2662	A728	50c multi	1.00	.30
a.		Booklet pane of 10	10.50	
2663	A728	50c multi	1.00	.30
a.		Booklet pane of 10	10.50	
2664	A728	50c multi	1.00	.30
a.		Booklet pane of 10	10.50	
2665	A728	50c multi	1.00	.30
a.		Booklet pane of 10	10.50	
		Nos. 2654-2665 (12)	12.00	3.60

With Personalized Photo at Right Like Type A692a
Serpentine Die Cut 11½x11¼ Syncopated
Self-Adhesive

2665B	A728	50c multi	2.50	*2.50*
2665C	A728	50c multi	2.50	*2.50*
2665D	A728	50c multi	2.50	*2.50*
2665E	A728	50c multi	2.50	*2.50*
2665F	A728	50c multi	2.50	*2.50*
2665G	A728	50c multi	2.50	*2.50*
2665H	A728	50c multi	2.50	*2.50*
2665I	A728	50c multi	2.50	*2.50*
2665J	A728	50c multi	2.50	*2.50*
2665K	A728	50c multi	2.50	*2.50*
2665L	A728	50c multi	2.50	*2.50*
2665M	A728	50c multi	2.50	*2.50*
		Nos. 2665B-2665M (12)	30.00	*30.00*

Nos. 2665B-2665M were sold in sheets of 20 and have personalized pictures and a straight edge at right, and lack separations between the stamp and the pictures. Sheets of 20 of Nos. 2665B-2665M each sold for $23.

Travel Posters of the 1930s — A729

Designs: 50c, At the Beach, by Percy Trompf. $1, Fishing, by John Vickery. $2, Riding in the Country, by James Northfield. $2.45, Winter Sport, by Northfield.

2007, Apr. 10   Perf. 14½x14

2666	A729	50c multi	.95	.75
2667	A729	$1 multi	2.00	1.60
a.		Booklet pane of 2, #2666-2667	3.25	—
2668	A729	$2 multi	4.00	3.00
2669	A729	$2.45 multi	5.00	3.75
a.		Booklet pane of 4, #2666-2669	12.00	—
b.		Booklet pane of 2, #2666, 2669	6.00	—
		Complete booklet (#2667a, 2669a, 2669b)	21.00	
		Nos. 2666-2669 (4)	11.95	9.10

Queen Elizabeth II, 81st Birthday A730

2007, Apr. 18   Perf. 14x14½

2670	A730	50c multi	.95	.75

Shipwrecks A731

Designs: 50c, Admella, 1859. $1, Loch Ard, 1878. $2, Dunbar, 1857.

2007, May 1   Litho.   Perf. 14x14½

2671	A731	50c multi	.95	.70
2672	A731	$1 multi	2.00	1.60
2673	A731	$2 multi	4.00	3.25
		Nos. 2671-2673 (3)	6.95	5.55

Animals Type of 2006 and

Sydney Harbour Bridge — A732

Design: $1.30, Yellow-footed rock wallaby, vert.

2007   Litho.   Perf. 14½x14

2674	A707	$1.30 multi	2.50	2.50
2675	A732	$1.95 multi	3.75	3.75
a.		Imperf. x perf. 14 x imperf. x imperf.	3.75	3.75
b.		Souvenir sheet, #2675, 2675a	7.50	7.50
c.		Souvenir sheet, 2 #2675	7.75	7.75
d.		As "b," with Sberatel Exhib., Prague ovpt.	9.75	9.75
e.		As "c," with Bangkok 2007 Exhib. ovpt.	9.75	9.75

Self-Adhesive
Booklet Stamps
Serpentine Die Cut 11¼ Syncopated

2676	A707	$1.30 multi	3.25	3.25
a.		Booklet pane of 2	6.25	
		Complete booklet, 4 #2676a	25.00	
2677	A732	$1.95 multi	4.00	4.00
a.		Booklet pane of 1	4.00	
b.		Booklet pane of 2	8.00	
		Complete booklet, #2677a, 3 #2677b	29.00	

With Personalized Photo at Right Like Type A692a
Serpentine Die Cut 11½x11¼

2678	A707	$1.30 multi	4.50	4.50
2679	A732	$1.95 multi	5.75	5.75

Issued: Nos. 2674-2679, 5/8; No. 2675b, 6/15. Complete booklet containing No. 2676 sold for $12.95. It contains four different examples of No. 2676a. The booklet containing No. 2677 sold for $14.95, and it contains three different examples of No. 2677b.

No. 2675c issued 6/15. Margin of No. 2675c is overprinted in gold with emblem for Sydney Philatelic Show.

Nos. 2678-2679 were sold in sheets of 20 and have personalized pictures and a straight edge at right, and lack separations between the stamp and the picture. A sheet of 20 of No. 2678 sold for $39; of No. 2679, $51.

Circus Performers — A733

Circus acts: Nos. 2680, 2685, 2690, Torch juggler. Nos. 2681, 2686, 2691, Contortionist. Nos. 2682, 2687, 2692, Trapeze artists. Nos. 2683, 2688, 2693, Acrobats. Nos. 2684, 2689, 2694, Human cannonball.

2007, May 15   Litho.   Perf. 14½x14

2680	A733	50c multi	.95	.95
2681	A733	50c multi	.95	.95
a.		Booklet pane of 2	2.50	—
2682	A733	50c multi	.95	.95
a.		Booklet pane of 2	2.50	—
2683	A733	50c multi	.95	.95
a.		Booklet pane of 2	2.50	—
2684	A733	50c multi	.95	.95
a.		Horiz. strip of 5, #2680-2684	5.00	5.00
b.		Booklet pane, #2680-2684	6.25	—
c.		Booklet pane, 2 each #2680, 2684	5.25	—
		Nos. 2680-2684 (5)	4.75	4.75

Booklet Stamps
Self-Adhesive
Serpentine Die Cut 11¼ Syncopated

2685	A733	50c multi	1.10	.40
2686	A733	50c multi	1.10	.40
2687	A733	50c multi	1.10	.40
2688	A733	50c multi	1.10	.40
2689	A733	50c multi	1.10	.40
a.		Booklet pane, 2 each #2685-2689	11.50	

Litho. With Foil Application

2690	A733	50c multi	1.40	1.40
2691	A733	50c multi	1.40	1.40
2692	A733	50c multi	1.40	1.40
2693	A733	50c multi	1.40	1.40
2694	A733	50c multi	1.40	1.40
a.		Booklet pane, #2690-2694	7.25	
		Complete booklet, #2681a, 2682a, 2683a, 2684b, 2684c, 2694a	25.00	
		Nos. 2685-2694 (10)	12.50	9.00

Complete booklet sold for $12.95. Nos. 2690-2694 each have gold stars and a portion of stamp covered by varnish.

Tourist Attractions — A734

Designs: Nos. 2695, 2700, Big Guitar, Tamworth, New South Wales. Nos. 2696, 2701, Big Lobster, Kingston Southeast, South Australia. Nos. 2697, 2702, Big Banana, Coffs Harbour, New South Wales. Nos. 2698, 2703, Big Merino Sheep, Goulburn, New South Wales. Nos. 2699, 2704, Big Pineapple, Nambour, Queensland.

2007, June 5   Perf. 14½x14

2695	A734	50c multi	.95	.95
2696	A734	50c multi	.95	.95
2697	A734	50c multi	.95	.95
2698	A734	50c multi	.95	.95
2699	A734	50c multi	.95	.95
a.		Horiz. strip of 5, #2695-2699	5.00	5.00
		Nos. 2695-2699 (5)	4.75	4.75

Booklet Stamps
Self-Adhesive
Serpentine Die Cut 11¼ Syncopated

2700	A734	50c multi	1.10	.40
2701	A734	50c multi	1.10	.40
2702	A734	50c multi	1.10	.40
2703	A734	50c multi	1.10	.40
2704	A734	50c multi	1.10	.40
a.		Booklet pane, 2 each #2700-2704	11.50	
		Nos. 2700-2704 (5)	5.50	2.00

Endangered Animals — A735

Designs: No. 2705, Gray-headed flying fox. No. 2706, Mountain pygmy possum. $1.25, Flatback turtle, horiz. $1.30, Wandering albatross, horiz.

2007, June 26   Perf. 14½x14

2705	A735	50c multi	.95	.70
a.		Booklet pane of 2 #2705	2.25	—
2706	A735	50c multi	.95	.70
a.		Horiz. pair, #2706	2.00	1.40
b.		Booklet pane of 2 #2706	2.25	—

Perf. 14x14½

2707	A735	$1.25 multi	2.40	1.90
a.		Booklet pane of 2	5.75	—
2708	A735	$1.30 multi	2.50	2.00
a.		Booklet pane of 2	6.00	—
		Complete booklet, #793c, 794b, 2705a, 2706b, 2707a, 2708a	23.00	

Complete booklet sold for $10.95.

Modern Architecture A736

Designs: No. 2709, Former ICI House, Melbourne. No. 2710, Academy of Science, Canberra. $1, Council House, Perth. $2.45, Sydney Opera House.

2007, July 10   Perf. 14x14¾

2709	A736	50c multi	.95	.70
2710	A736	50c multi	.95	.70
a.		Horiz. pair, #2709-2710	2.00	1.40
b.		Additionally dated "2013" (#2710c)	1.10	1.10
c.		Booklet pane of 2 #2710b	2.25	—
2711	A736	$1 multi	2.00	1.60
2712	A736	$2.45 multi	5.00	3.75
a.		Souvenir sheet, #2709-2712	9.00	9.00

Due to the arrangement of the stamps on No. 2712a, the left side of the top row of perfs on each of the stamps is perf. 14 and the right side of the top row is perf. 14¾.

No. 2712a exists imperf from a telephone drawing at a substantial premium over face value. Value for single souvenir sheet, $17.50.

Issued: Nos. 2710b, 2710c, 3/5/13. No. 2710c was issued in booklet along with Nos. 1939c, 2869e, 3107c, 3349b and 3877a.

Markets — A737

Designs: Nos. 2713, 2718, Queen Victoria Market, Melbourne. Nos. 2714, 2719, Rusty's Market, Cairns. Nos. 2715, 2720, Sydney Fish Market. Nos. 2716, 2721, Adelaide Central Market. Nos. 2717, 2722, Hume Murray Farmers Market, Albury Wodonga.

2007, July 24   Perf. 14½x14

2713	A737	50c multi	.95	.95
2714	A737	50c multi	.95	.95
2715	A737	50c multi	.95	.95
2716	A737	50c multi	.95	.95
2717	A737	50c multi	.95	.95
a.		Horiz. strip of 5, #2713-2717	5.00	5.00
		Nos. 2713-2717 (5)	4.75	4.75

Booklet Stamps
Self-Adhesive
Serpentine Die Cut 11¼ Syncopated

2718	A737	50c multi	1.10	.40
a.		Booklet pane of 10	11.50	
2719	A737	50c multi	1.10	.40
a.		Booklet pane of 10	11.50	
2720	A737	50c multi	1.10	.40
a.		Booklet pane of 10	11.50	
2721	A737	50c multi	1.10	.40
a.		Booklet pane of 10	11.50	
2722	A737	50c multi	1.10	.40
a.		Booklet pane of 10	11.50	
		Nos. 2718-2722 (5)	5.50	2.00

Asia-Pacific Economic Cooperation Forum, Sydney A738

2007, Aug. 28   Perf. 14x14½

2723	A738	50c multi	.95	.95

Coil Stamp
Self-Adhesive
Serpentine Die Cut 11¼x11½ Syncopated

2724	A738	50c multi	.95	.30

Special Air Service, 50th Anniv. A739

2007, Sept. 4   Perf. 14x14½

2725	A739	50c multi	.95	.75

This stamp exists with "SAS" insignia embossed with gold foil. This was a restricted issue sold at far more than face value by the Philatelic Bureau.

Botanical Gardens A740

Designs: Nos. 2726, 2731, Brisbane Botanic Gardens, Mt. Coot-tha. Nos. 2727, 2732, Kings Park and Botanic Gardens, Perth. Nos. 2728, 2733, Royal Botanic Gardens and Domain, Sydney. Nos. 2729, 2734, Royal

Botanic Gardens, Melbourne. Nos. 2730, 2735, Botanic Gardens of Adelaide.

2007, Sept. 12   Perf. 14x14½
2726	A740	50c multi	.95	.95
a.		Booklet pane of 4	4.25	—
2727	A740	50c multi	.95	.95
a.		Booklet pane of 4	4.25	—
2728	A740	50c multi	.95	.95
a.		Booklet pane of 4	4.25	—
2729	A740	50c multi	.95	.95
a.		Booklet pane of 4	4.25	—
2730	A740	50c multi	.95	.95
a.		Booklet pane of 4	4.25	—
		Complete booklet, #2726a-2730a	22.00	
b.		Horiz. strip of 5, #2726-2730	5.00	5.00
		Nos. 2726-2730 (5)	4.75	4.75

Self-Adhesive
Serpentine Die Cut 11¼x11½ Syncopated
2731	A740	50c multi	.95	.30
2732	A740	50c multi	.95	.30
2733	A740	50c multi	.95	.30
2734	A740	50c multi	.95	.30
2735	A740	50c multi	.95	.30
a.		Horiz. coil strip of 5, #2731-2735	5.00	
b.		Booklet pane of 20, 5 each #2731-2735, + 10 labels	19.50	
		Nos. 2731-2735 (5)	4.75	1.50

Complete booklet sold for $10.95.

Space Age, 50th Anniv. — A741

Designs: Nos. 2736, 2743, Sputnik, 1957. Nos. 2737, 2744, First space walk, 1965. Nos. 2738, 2745, First Moon walk, 1969. Nos. 2739, 2746, Voyager, 1977. Nos. 2740, 2747, International Space Station, 1998. Nos. 2741, 2742a, Hubble Space Telescope, 1990, horiz.

2007, Oct. 2   Litho.   Perf. 14½x14
2736	A741	50c multi	1.00	1.00
a.		Booklet pane of 2	2.40	—
2737	A741	50c multi	1.00	1.00
a.		Booklet pane of 2	2.40	—
2738	A741	50c multi	1.00	1.00
a.		Booklet pane of 2	2.40	—
2739	A741	50c multi	1.00	1.00
a.		Booklet pane of 2	2.40	—
2740	A741	50c multi	1.00	1.00
a.		Horiz. strip of 5, #2736-2740	5.25	5.25
b.		Booklet pane of 2	2.40	—
c.		Booklet pane of 5, #2736-2740	6.00	—
2741	A741	$1 multi, 50x30mm	2.25	2.25
a.		Booklet pane of 2	5.00	—
		Complete booklet, #2736a, 2737a, 2738a, 2739a, 2740b, 2740c, 2741a	23.00	
		Nos. 2736-2741 (6)	7.25	7.25

Souvenir Sheet
2742		Sheet of 6, #2736-2740, 2742a	7.50	7.50
a.		A741 $1 multi, 52x43mm	2.25	2.25

A souvenir sheet in the 50c denomination exists. It was sold in a restricted sale with a normal souvenir sheet and a coin at a price far in advance of face value.

Self-Adhesive
Booklet Stamps
Serpentine Die Cut 11¼ Syncopated
2743	A741	50c multi	1.00	.30
2744	A741	50c multi	1.00	.30
2745	A741	50c multi	1.00	.30
2746	A741	50c multi	1.00	.30
2747	A741	50c multi	1.00	.30
a.		Coil strip of 5, #2743-2747	5.25	
b.		Booklet pane, 2 each #2743-2747	10.00	
		Nos. 2743-2747 (5)	5.00	1.50

Complete booklet sold for $10.95.

Trailer Campers A742

People and trailer campers from: Nos. 2748, 2753, 1950s. Nos. 2749, 2754, 1960s. Nos. 2750, 2755, 1970s. Nos. 2751, 2756, 1980s. Nos. 2752, 2757, Today.

2007, Oct. 16   Perf. 14x14½
2748	A742	50c multi	1.10	1.10
a.		Booklet pane of 4	5.00	

2749	A742	50c multi	1.10	1.10
a.		Booklet pane, 2 each #2748-2749	5.00	—
2750	A742	50c multi	1.10	1.10
a.		Booklet pane of 4	5.00	
2751	A742	50c multi	1.10	1.10
a.		Booklet pane, 2 each #2750-2751	5.00	—
2752	A742	50c multi	1.10	1.10
a.		Horiz. strip of 5, #2748-2752	5.50	5.50
b.		Booklet pane of 4	5.00	—
		Complete booklet, #2748a, 2749a, 2750a, 2751a, 2752b	25.00	
		Nos. 2748-2752 (5)	5.50	5.50

Self-Adhesive
Booklet Stamps
Serpentine Die Cut 11¼ Syncopated
2753	A742	50c multi	1.10	.30
a.		Booklet pane of 10	11.00	—
2754	A742	50c multi	1.10	.30
a.		Booklet pane of 10	11.00	—
2755	A742	50c multi	1.10	.30
a.		Booklet pane of 10	11.00	—
2756	A742	50c multi	1.10	.30
a.		Booklet pane of 10	11.00	—
2757	A742	50c multi	1.10	.30
a.		Booklet pane of 10	11.00	—
b.		Booklet pane, 2 each #2753-2757	11.00	—
		Nos. 2753-2757 (5)	5.50	1.50

Complete booklet sold for $10.95.

Christmas — A743

Designs of past Australian Christmas stamps with original denominations removed: Nos. 2758, 2763, 1768. #669. Nos. 2759, 2764, 2769, #1195. Nos. 2760, 2765, #1567. Nos. 2761, 2766, #306, horiz. Nos. 2762, 2767, 2770, #931.

Perf. 14½x14, 14x14½
2007, Nov. 1   Litho.
2758	A743	45c multi	.95	.95
a.		Booklet pane of 4	4.25	—
2759	A743	45c multi	.95	.95
a.		Booklet pane of 4	4.25	
2760	A743	45c multi	.95	.95
a.		Horiz. pair, #2759-2760	2.00	2.00
b.		Booklet pane of 4	4.25	—
2761	A743	50c multi	1.10	1.10
a.		Booklet pane of 2	2.25	—
2762	A743	$1.10 multi	2.40	2.40
a.		Booklet pane of 1	2.50	—
		Nos. 2758-2762 (5)	6.35	6.35

Self-Adhesive
Serpentine Die Cut 11¼ Syncopated
2763	A743	45c multi	.95	.30
a.		With varnish block over stamp vignette	.95	.30
2764	A743	45c multi	.95	.30
a.		Booklet pane of 20	20.00	
2765	A743	45c multi	.95	.95
a.		Booklet pane of 20	20.00	
2766	A743	50c multi	1.10	1.10
a.		Booklet pane of 5	5.50	
2767	A743	$1.10 multi	2.40	2.40
a.		Booklet pane of 5	12.00	
b.		Souvenir sheet, #2763-2767	6.50	
c.		Booklet, #2763-2767	7.00	
		Complete booklet, #2758a, 2759a, 2760b, 2761a, 2762a, 2767c	25.00	
		Nos. 2763-2767 (5)	6.35	5.05

Complete booklet sold for $10.95. Size of No. 2767b is 156x100mm. Size of No. 2767c is 156x104mm.

With Personalized Photo at Right Like Type A692a
Serpentine Die Cut 11½x11¼ Syncopated
2768	A743	45c multi	2.40	2.40
2769	A743	45c multi	2.40	2.40
2770	A743	$1.10 multi	3.75	3.75
		Nos. 2768-2770 (3)	8.55	8.55

Nos. 2768-2770 were sold in sheets of 20 and have personalized pictures and a straight edge at right, and lack separations between the stamp and the pictures. Sheets of 20 of Nos. 2768 and 2769 sold for $22, and of No. 2770, $35.

A booklet entitled "Behind the Stamp," which contained four panes, sold for $19.95. The panes were in two designs, one containing Nos. 740, 1164, 1193, 1891 and a litho. reproduction of No. 277, the other containing Nos. 400, 616-617, 882, 1063 and a reproduction of No. 367. The stamps within both panes were dated "2007" and the panes were either perforated at a different gauge than the original stamps or imperforate.

Red Rose — A744

2008, Jan. 15   Litho.   Perf. 14
2771	A744	50c multi	1.00	1.00

Litho. With Foil Application
Serpentine Die Cut 11¼ Syncopated
Self-Adhesive
2772	A744	50c multi	1.00	.30

Booklet Stamp
Litho.
2773	A744	50c multi	1.10	.30
a.		Booklet pane of 4	4.50	
		Complete booklet, 5 #2773a	22.50	

With Personalized Photo at Right Like Type A692a
Serpentine Die Cut 11½x11¼ Syncopated
2774	A744	50c multi	2.40	2.40

No. 2772 was printed in a sheet of 10 + 10 labels, having rose-scented scratch and sniff areas on the rose and the labels. No. 2773 lacks the scratch and sniff areas. The complete booklet, which sold for $10.95, contains five examples of No. 2773a, each with a different margin.

No. 2774 was sold in sheets of 20 for $23 and have personalized pictures and a straight edge at right, and lack separations between the stamp and the personalized photo.

Philanthropists A745

Designs: Nos. 2775, 2782, Dame Elisabeth Murdoch. Nos. 2776, 2781, Victor and Loti Smogron. Nos. 2777, 2780, Lady Mary Fairfax. Nos. 2778, 2779, Frank Lowy.

2008, Jan. 23   Litho.   Perf. 14¾x14
2775	A745	50c multi	1.25	1.25
2776	A745	50c multi	1.25	1.25
2777	A745	50c multi	1.25	1.25
2778	A745	50c multi	1.25	1.25
a.		Horiz. strip of 4, #2775-2778	5.00	5.00
		Nos. 2775-2778 (4)	5.00	5.00

Coil Stamps
Self-Adhesive
Serpentine Die Cut 11¼ Syncopated
2779	A745	50c multi	1.00	.30
2780	A745	50c multi	1.00	.30
2781	A745	50c multi	1.00	.30
2782	A745	50c multi	1.00	.30
a.		Vert. strip of 4, #2779-2782	4.00	
		Nos. 2779-2782 (4)	4.00	1.20

Organ and Tissue Donation — A746

2008, Feb. 5   Perf. 14¾x14
2783	A746	50c multi	1.10	1.10

Booklet Stamp
Self-Adhesive
Serpentine Die Cut 11¼ Syncopated
2784	A746	50c multi	1.10	.30
a.		Booklet pane of 10	11.00	

Scouting in Australia, Cent. A747

Australian Scouting emblem and: 50c, Four scouts near tent. $1.35, Scouts from various nations. $2, Lord Robert Baden-Powell.

2008, Feb. 19   Perf. 14
2785	A747	50c multi	1.10	1.10
2786	A747	$1.35 multi	2.75	2.75
2787	A747	$2 multi	4.25	4.25
a.		Perf. 14x14½	4.25	4.25
b.		Souvenir sheet, 2 #2787a	8.50	8.50
		Nos. 2785-2787 (3)	8.10	8.10

Self-Adhesive
Serpentine Die Cut 11¼ Syncopated
Coil Stamp
2788	A747	50c multi	1.10	.30

Booklet Stamps
2789	A747	$1.35 multi	2.75	1.40
a.		Booklet pane of 5	14.50	
2790	A747	$2 multi	4.25	2.25
a.		Booklet pane of 5	22.00	
		Nos. 2788-2790 (3)	8.10	3.95

Canberra Stamp Show (No. 2787b).

Gorges — A748

Designs: $1.35, Grose River Gorge, New South Wales. $2, Walpa Gorge, Northern Territory. $2.70, Katherine Gorge, Northern Territory, horiz. $4, Geikie Gorge, Western Australia.

2008, Mar. 3   Litho.   Perf. 14
2791	A748	$1.35 multi	2.75	2.75
2792	A748	$2 multi	4.25	4.25
2793	A748	$2.70 multi	5.75	2.75
2794	A748	$4 multi	8.50	4.25
		Nos. 2791-2794 (4)	21.25	14.00

Booklet Stamps (#2795-2796)
Self-Adhesive
Serpentine Die Cut 11½x11¼ Syncopated
2795	A748	$1.35 multi	7.50	5.00
a.		Booklet pane of 5	37.50	
b.		Booklet pane of 2	15.00	
		Complete booklet, 4 #2795b	68.00	
2796	A748	$2 multi	9.00	7.50
a.		Booklet pane of 5	45.00	
b.		Booklet pane of 2	18.00	
		Complete booklet, 4 #2796b	72.00	

With Personalized Photo at Right Like Type A692a
2797	A748	$1.35 multi	8.00	8.00
2798	A748	$2 multi	12.00	12.00

Nos. 2797-2798 each were sold in sheets of 20 and have personalized pictures and a straight edge at right, and lack separations between the stamp and the personalized photo. Sheets of 20 of No. 2797 sold for $40, and of No. 2798, $52.

Complete booklet containing No. 2795b sold for $10.95, and containing No. 2796b, $16.95. Each booklet contains four panes with differing margins.

World Youth Day — A749

Various depictions of Pope Benedict XVI with "08" in: 50c, Light blue. $1.35, Pink. $2, Light green.

2008, Mar. 4			Perf. 14	
2799	A749	50c multi	1.10	.85
2800	A749	$1.35 multi	2.75	2.75
2801	A749	$2 multi	4.25	4.25
	Nos. 2799-2801 (3)		8.10	7.85

Booklet Stamps (#2802-2803)
Self-Adhesive
Serpentine Die Cut 11½x11¼ Syncopated

2802	A749	$1.35 multi	4.75	.40
a.	Booklet pane of 5		22.50	
2803	A749	$2 multi	7.50	2.50
a.	Booklet pane of 5		37.50	

With Personalized Photo at Right Like Type A692a

2804	A749	50c multi	5.00	3.00
2805	A749	$1.35 multi	8.00	8.00
2806	A749	$2 multi	10.00	10.00
	Nos. 2804-2806 (3)		23.00	21.00

Nos. 2804-2806 each were sold in sheets of 20 and have personalized pictures and a straight edge at right, and lack separations between the stamp and the personalized photo. Sheets of 20 of No. 2804 sold for $23, No. 2805, sold for $40, and No. 2806 sold for $52.

Rugby League, Cent. — A750

Players and teams: Nos. 2807, 2823, Andrew Ryan, Bulldogs. Nos. 2808, 2824, Scott Prince, Titans. Nos. 2809, 2825, Brett Kimmorley, Sharks. Nos. 2810, 2826, Danny Buderus, Knights. Nos. 2811, 2827, Johnathan Thurston, Cowboys. Nos. 2812, 2828, Darren Lockyer, Broncos. Nos. 2813, 2829, Matt Orford, Sea Eagles. Nos. 2814, 2830, Cameron Smith, Storm. Nos. 2815, 2831, Craig Fitzgibbon, Roosters. Nos. 2816, 2832, Alan Tongue, Raiders. Nos. 2817, 2833, Dean Widders, Rabbitohs. Nos. 2818, 2834, Tony Puletua, Panthers. Nos. 2819, 2835, Mark Gasnier, Dragons. Nos. 2820, 2836, Nathan Cayless, Eels. Nos. 2821, 2837, Robbie Farah, Wests Tigers. Nos. 2822, 2838, Steve Price, Warriors.

2008, Mar. 24			Perf. 14	
2807	A750	50c multi	1.10	1.10
2808	A750	50c multi	1.10	1.10
2809	A750	50c multi	1.10	1.10
2810	A750	50c multi	1.10	1.10
a.	Block of 4, #2807-2810		4.50	4.50
2811	A750	50c multi	1.10	1.10
2812	A750	50c multi	1.10	1.10
2813	A750	50c multi	1.10	1.10
2814	A750	50c multi	1.10	1.10
a.	Block of 4, #2811-2814		4.50	4.50
2815	A750	50c multi	1.10	1.10
2816	A750	50c multi	1.10	1.10
2817	A750	50c multi	1.10	1.10
2818	A750	50c multi	1.10	1.10
a.	Block of 4, #2815-2818		4.50	4.50
2819	A750	50c multi	1.10	1.10
2820	A750	50c multi	1.10	1.10
2821	A750	50c multi	1.10	1.10
2822	A750	50c multi	1.10	1.10
a.	Block of 4, #2819-2822		4.50	4.50
	Nos. 2807-2822 (16)		17.60	17.60

Booklet Stamps
Self-Adhesive
Serpentine Die Cut 11 Syncopated

2823	A750	50c multi	1.10	.30
a.	Booklet pane of 10		11.00	
2824	A750	50c multi	1.10	.30
a.	Booklet pane of 10		11.00	
2825	A750	50c multi	1.10	.30
a.	Booklet pane of 10		11.00	
2826	A750	50c multi	1.10	.30
a.	Booklet pane of 10		11.00	
2827	A750	50c multi	1.10	.30
a.	Booklet pane of 10		11.00	

2828	A750	50c multi	1.10	.30
a.	Booklet pane of 10		11.00	
2829	A750	50c multi	1.10	.30
a.	Booklet pane of 10		11.00	
2830	A750	50c multi	1.10	.30
a.	Booklet pane of 10		11.00	
2831	A750	50c multi	1.10	.30
a.	Booklet pane of 10		11.00	
2832	A750	50c multi	1.10	.30
a.	Booklet pane of 10		11.00	
2833	A750	50c multi	1.10	.30
a.	Booklet pane of 10		11.00	
2834	A750	50c multi	1.10	.30
a.	Booklet pane of 10		11.00	
2835	A750	50c multi	1.10	.30
a.	Booklet pane of 10		11.00	
2836	A750	50c multi	1.10	.30
a.	Booklet pane of 10		11.00	
2837	A750	50c multi	1.10	.30
a.	Booklet pane of 10		11.00	
2838	A750	50c multi	1.10	.30
a.	Booklet pane of 10		11.00	
b.	Booklet pane of 20, #2823-2829, 2831-2838, 5 #2830		22.00	
	Nos. 2823-2838 (16)		17.60	4.80

A booklet containing one Rugby League dollar coin, and panes containing Nos. 2810a, 2814a, 2818a, 2822a, and four No. 2814, each in perf. 14½x14, sold for $15.95.

Heavy Haulers — A751

Designs: Nos. 2839, 2844, 2849, Excavator. Nos. 2840, 2845, 2850, Dump truck. Nos. 2841, 2846, 2851, Road train. Nos. 2842, 2847, 2852, Locomotive and ore cars. Nos. 2843, 2848, 2853, Ore carrier MS Berge Stahl.

2008, Apr. 1			Perf. 14	
Without White Frames				
2839	A751	50c multi	1.10	1.10
2840	A751	50c multi	1.10	1.10
2841	A751	50c multi	1.10	1.10
2842	A751	50c multi	1.10	1.10
2843	A751	50c multi	1.10	1.10
a.	Horiz. strip of 5, #2839-2843		5.50	5.50
	Nos. 2839-2843 (5)		5.50	5.50

Booklet Stamps
Self-Adhesive
Serpentine Die Cut 11 Syncopated

2844	A751	50c multi	1.10	.60
2845	A751	50c multi	1.10	.60
2846	A751	50c multi	1.10	.60
2847	A751	50c multi	1.10	.60
2848	A751	50c multi	1.10	.60
a.	Booklet pane, 4 each #2844-2848		22.00	

Coil Stamps
With White Frames

2849	A751	50c multi	1.10	.60
2850	A751	50c multi	1.10	.60
2851	A751	50c multi	1.10	.60
2852	A751	50c multi	1.10	.60
2853	A751	50c multi	1.10	.60
a.	Vert. strip of 5, #2849-2853		5.50	
	Nos. 2844-2853 (10)		11.00	6.00

ANZAC Day — A752

Designs: Nos. 2854, 2863, Veterans marching. Nos. 2855, 2862, Laying of wreaths at memorial. Nos. 2856, 2861, Buglers. Nos. 2857, 2860, Veteran holding child. Nos. 2858, 2859, Young people at Gallipoli.

2008, Apr. 16			Perf. 14	
2854	A752	50c multi	1.10	1.10
a.	Perf. 14¾x14		1.10	1.10
b.	Booklet pane, 4 #2854a		5.00	—
2855	A752	50c multi	1.10	1.10
a.	Perf. 14¾x14		1.10	1.10
b.	Booklet pane, 4 #2855a		5.00	—
c.	Souvenir sheet of 4 #2856a		4.50	4.50
d.	Souvenir sheet, 2 each #2855-2856, perf. 14		4.50	4.50
2856	A752	50c multi	1.10	1.10
a.	Perf. 14¾x14		1.10	1.10
b.	Booklet pane, 4 #2856a		5.00	—
c.	Souvenir sheet of 4 #2856a		4.50	4.50
d.	Souvenir sheet, 2 each #2855-2856, perf. 14		4.50	4.50

2857	A752	50c multi	1.10	1.10
a.	Perf. 14¾x14		1.10	1.10
b.	Booklet pane, 4 #2857a		5.00	—
2858	A752	50c multi	1.10	1.10
a.	Perf. 14¾x14		1.10	1.10
b.	Booklet pane, 4 #2858a		5.00	—
	Complete booklet, #2854b-2858b		25.00	
c.	Souvenir sheet, #2854a-2858a		5.50	
d.	Horiz. strip of 5, #2854-2858		5.50	5.50
	Nos. 2854-2858 (5)		5.50	5.50

Coil Stamps
Self-Adhesive
Serpentine Die Cut 11 Syncopated

2859	A752	50c multi	1.10	.60
2860	A752	50c multi	1.10	.60
2861	A752	50c multi	1.10	.60
2862	A752	50c multi	1.10	.60
2863	A752	50c multi	1.10	.60
a.	Vert. strip of 5, #2859-2863		5.50	
	Nos. 2859-2863 (5)		5.50	3.00

Complete booklet sold for $10.95.
2008 World Stamp Championships, Israel (No. 2856c). Issued: Nos. 2855c, 11/3; No. 2856d, 11/5.

Queen's Birthday — A753

Designs: 50c, Queen Elizabeth II. $2, Order of Australia badge.

2008, Apr. 18			Perf. 14	
2864	A753	50c multi	1.10	.85
a.	Perf. 14¾x14		1.10	.85
b.	Dated "2010"		2.00	1.00
2865	A753	$2 multi	4.25	4.25
a.	Perf. 14¾x14		4.25	2.25
b.	Souvenir sheet, #2864a, 2865a		5.50	5.50

First Hot-air Balloon Flight in Australia, 150th Anniv. A754

Hot-air balloons over: Nos. 2866, 2870, Sydney Harbour Bridge and Sydney Opera House. Nos. 2867, 2871, Mount Feathertop, Victoria (red denomination). Nos. 2868, 2873, Western MacDonnell Ranges, Northern Territory (lilac denomination). Nos. 2869, 2872, Canberra.

2008, May 6	Litho.		Perf. 14x14¾	
2866	A754	50c multi	1.10	1.10
a.	Booklet pane of 4		5.00	
2867	A754	50c multi	1.10	1.10
a.	Booklet pane of 4		5.00	
2868	A754	50c multi	1.10	1.10
a.	Booklet pane of 4		5.00	
2869	A754	50c multi	1.10	1.10
a.	Booklet pane of 4		5.00	
b.	Booklet pane of 4, #2866-2869		5.00	—
	Complete booklet, #2866a-2869a, 2869b		25.00	
c.	Horiz. strip of 4, #2866-2869		4.50	4.50
d.	Additionally dated "2013" (#2869e)			
e.	Booklet pane of 2 #2869d		1.10	1.10
			2.25	
	Nos. 2866-2869 (4)		4.40	4.40

Issued: Nos. 2869d, 2869e, 3/5/13. No. 2869e was issued in booklet along with Nos. 1939c, 2710c, 3107c, 3349b and 3877a.

Booklet Stamps
Self-Adhesive
Serpentine Die Cut 11 Syncopated

2870	A754	50c multi	1.10	.30
2871	A754	50c multi	1.10	.30
2872	A754	50c multi	1.10	.30
2873	A754	50c multi	1.10	.30
a.	Booklet pane, 4 #2870, 2 each #2871-2873		11.00	
	Nos. 2870-2873 (4)		4.40	1.20

Complete booklet sold for $10.95.

Working Dogs — A755

Designs: Nos. 2874, 2879, German shepherd. Nos. 2875, 2880, Australian cattle dog. Nos. 2876, 2881, Beagle. Nos. 2877, 2882, Border collie. Nos. 2878, 2883, Labrador retriever.

2008, June 10	Litho.		Perf. 14¾x14	
2874	A755	50c multi	1.10	1.10
a.	Booklet pane of 4		5.00	
2875	A755	50c multi	1.10	1.10
a.	Booklet pane of 4		5.00	
2876	A755	50c multi	1.10	1.10
a.	Booklet pane of 4		5.00	
2877	A755	50c multi	1.10	1.10
a.	Booklet pane of 4		5.00	
2878	A755	50c multi	1.10	1.10
a.	Booklet pane of 4 #2874a-2878a		5.00	
	Complete booklet, #2874a-2878a		25.00	
b.	Horiz. strip of 5, #2874-2878		5.50	5.50
	Nos. 2874-2878 (5)		5.50	5.50

Booklet Stamps
Self-Adhesive
Serpentine Die Cut 11 Syncopated

2879	A755	50c multi	1.10	.30
a.	Booklet pane of 10 + 5 stickers		11.00	
2880	A755	50c multi	1.10	.30
a.	Booklet pane of 10 + 5 stickers		11.00	
2881	A755	50c multi	1.10	.30
a.	Booklet pane of 10 + 5 stickers		11.00	
2882	A755	50c multi	1.10	.30
a.	Booklet pane of 10 + 5 stickers		11.00	
2883	A755	50c multi	1.10	.30
a.	Booklet pane of 10 + 5 stickers		11.00	
b.	Booklet pane of 10, 2 each #2879-2883, + 5 stickers			
	Nos. 2879-2883 (5)		5.50	1.50

Complete booklet sold for $10.95.

2008 Summer Olympics, Beijing — A756

2008, June 24			Perf. 14¾x14	
2884	A756	50c multi	1.10	1.10

Coil Stamp
Self-Adhesive
Serpentine Die Cut 11 Syncopated

2885	A756	50c multi	1.10	.30

Ecology A757

Slogans: Nos. 2886, 2890, Save water. Nos. 2887, 2891, Reduce waste. Nos. 2888, 2892, Travel smart. Nos. 2889, 2893, Save energy.

2008, July 8	Litho.		Perf. 14x14¾	
2886	A757	50c multi	1.10	1.10
2887	A757	50c multi	1.10	1.10
2888	A757	50c multi	1.10	1.10
2889	A757	50c multi	1.10	1.10
a.	Block of 4, #2886-2889		4.50	4.50
	Nos. 2886-2889 (4)		4.40	4.40

Self-Adhesive
Serpentine Die Cut 11¼x11 Syncopated

2890	A757	50c multi	1.10	.30
a.	Booklet pane of 2		2.25	
2891	A757	50c multi	1.10	.30
a.	Booklet pane of 2		2.25	
2892	A757	50c multi	1.10	.30
a.	Booklet pane of 2		2.25	
2893	A757	50c multi	1.10	.30
a.	Booklet pane of 2		2.25	
b.	Booklet pane of 4, #2890-2893		4.50	

c.	Double-sided booklet pane of 8, 2 each #2890-2893	9.25	
	Complete booklet, #2890a, 2891a, 2892a, 2893a, 2893b, 2893c	24.00	
d.	Double-sided booklet of 20, 5 each #2890-2893	22.00	
e.	Horiz. coil strip of 4, #2890-2893	4.50	
	Nos. 2890-2893 (4)	4.40	1.20

Complete booklet sold for $10.95.

Quarantine Laws, Cent. — A758

2008, July 15   **Perf. 14¾x14**

2894	A758 50c multi	1.10	1.10

Coil Stamp
Self-Adhesive
Serpentine Die Cut 11x11¼ Syncopated

2895	A758 50c multi	1.10	.30

Australian Football, 150th Anniv. — A759

2008, July 29   **Perf. 14¾x14**

2896	A759 50c multi	1.10	.85

2008 Summer Olympics, Beijing — A760

No. 2897, Basketball. Nos. 2898, 2900, Cycling. Nos. 2899, 2901, Rhythmic gymnastics.

2008, Aug. 1

2897	A760 50c multi	1.10	.85
2898	A760 $1.30 multi	2.75	2.75
2899	A760 $1.35 multi	2.75	2.75
	Nos. 2897-2899 (3)	6.60	6.35

Litho.
Serpentine Die Cut 11¼ Syncopated
Booklet Stamps
Self-Adhesive

2900	A760 $1.30 multi	2.75	.30
a.	Booklet pane of 5	14.00	
2901	A760 $1.35 multi	2.75	.30
a.	Booklet pane of 5	14.50	

Scenes From World Youth Day — A761

Designs: No. 2902, Pilgrims at opening mass. No. 2903, Papal welcome. No. 2904, Stations of the Cross. No. 2905, Pilgrimage walk. No. 2906, Pope Benedict XVI at final mass.

2008, July 24   **Litho.**   **Perf. 14½x14**

2902	A761 50c multi	2.00	2.00
2903	A761 50c multi	2.00	2.00
2904	A761 50c multi	2.00	2.00
2905	A761 50c multi	2.00	2.00

2906	A761 50c multi	2.00	2.00
a.	Vert. strip of 5, #2902-2906	12.00	12.00
	Nos. 2902-2906 (5)	10.00	10.00

Aircraft A762

Designs: No. 2907, Bristol Tourer. No. 2908, Short S.30 Empire Flying Boat. No. 2909, Lockheed Super Constellation. $2, Airbus A380.

2008, Aug. 5   **Perf. 14**

2907	A762 50c multi	1.00	.80
a.	Perf. 14x14¾	1.25	1.25
b.	Booklet pane of 2, #2907a	2.50	—
2908	A762 50c multi	1.00	.80
a.	Perf. 14x14¾	1.25	1.25
b.	Booklet pane of 2, #2907a	2.50	—
2909	A762 50c multi	1.00	.80
a.	Perf. 14x14¾	1.25	1.25
b.	Booklet pane of 2, #2907a	2.50	—
c.	Horiz. strip of 3, #2907-2909	3.00	2.40
2910	A762 $2 multi	4.00	2.00
a.	Perf. 14x14¾	5.50	5.50
b.	Booklet pane of 1, #2907a	5.50	—
c.	Booklet pane of 4, #2907a-2910a	9.50	—
	Complete booklet, #2907b, 2908b, 2909b, 2910c, 2910a	23.00	
d.	Souvenir sheet, 2 each #2868, 2910a	9.50	9.50
	Nos. 2907-2910 (4)	7.00	4.40

Booklet Stamp
Self-Adhesive
Serpentine Die Cut 11¼ Syncopated

2911	A762 $2 multi	4.00	2.00
a.	Booklet pane of 5	20.00	

Complete booklet sold for $10.95. Issued: No./ 2910d, 8/22. SunStamp 2008 Philatelic Exhibition, Brisbane (No. 2910d).

Gold Medalists at 2008 Summer Olympics, Beijing A763

Designs: No. 2912, Stephanie Rice, Women's swimming 400m individual medley. No. 2913, Lisbeth Trickett, Women's swimming 100m butterfly. No. 2914, Leisel Jones, Women's swimming, 100m breaststroke. No. 2915, Stephanie Rice, Women's swimming 200m individual medley. No. 2916, Women's 4x200m freestyle relay swimming team. No. 2917, Drew Ginn and Duncan Free, Men's rowing pairs. No. 2918, David Crawshay and Scott Brennan, Men's rowing double sculls. No. 2919, Women's 4x100m medley relay swimming team. No. 2920, Emma Snowsill, Women's triathlon. No. 2921, Malcolm Page and Nathan Wilmot, Men's sailing 470 crew. No. 2922, Tessa Parkinson and Elise Rechichi, Women's sailing 470 crew. No. 2923, Ken Wallace, Men's single kayak 500m. No. 2924, Steven Hooker, Men's pole vault. No. 2925, Matthew Mitcham, Men's 10m platform diving.

2008, Aug.   **Litho.**   **Perf. 14¼**

2912	A763 50c multi	.95	.75
2913	A763 50c multi	.95	.75
2914	A763 50c multi	.95	.75
2915	A763 50c multi	.95	.75
2916	A763 50c multi	.95	.75
2917	A763 50c multi	.95	.75
2918	A763 50c multi	.95	.75
2919	A763 50c multi	.95	.75
2920	A763 50c multi	.95	.75
2921	A763 50c multi	.95	.75
2922	A763 50c multi	.95	.75
2923	A763 50c multi	.95	.75
2924	A763 50c multi	.95	.75
2925	A763 50c multi	.95	.75
	Nos. 2912-2925 (14)	13.30	10.50

Issued: Nos. 2912, 8/11; No. 2913, 8/12; No. 2914, 8/13; No. 2915, 8/14; No. 2916, 8/15; Nos. 2917-2919, 8/18; Nos. 2920-2922, 8/19; Nos. 2923-2925, 8/25. Nos. 2912-2925 were printed in sheets of 10. Digitally printed versions of Nos. 2912-2925 were printed in Beijing in sheets of 10. The digitally printed stamps were only available in complete sets of 14 sheets to collectors in Australia who pre-ordered the sets, and purchasers at the Olympex Stamp Exhibition in China. The digitally printed stamps have a larger dot pattern, most evident in the background and the

Olympic rings, and a browner cast to the orange background.

Waterfalls — A764

Designs: $1.40, Russell Falls, Tasmania. $2.05, Jim Jim Falls, Northern Territory. $2.80, Spa Pool, Hammersley Gorge, Western Australia. $4.10, Mackenzie Falls, Victoria.

2008, Sept. 8   **Litho.**   **Perf. 14¾x14**

2926	A764 $1.40 multi	2.50	2.50
2927	A764 $2.05 multi	3.75	3.75
2928	A764 $2.80 multi	5.25	2.50
2929	A764 $4.10 multi	7.50	3.75
	Nos. 2926-2929 (4)	19.00	12.50

Booklet Stamps
Self-Adhesive
Serpentine Die Cut 11¼ Syncopated

2930	A764 $1.40 multi	2.50	.30
a.	Booklet pane of 5	13.00	
b.	Booklet pane of 2	5.50	
	Complete booklet, 4 #2930b	22.00	
2931	A764 $2.05 multi	3.75	1.90
a.	Booklet pane of 5	19.00	
b.	Booklet pane of 2	7.75	
	Complete booklet, 4 #2931b	30.00	

With Personalized Photo at Right Like Type A692a
Serpentine Die Cut 11½x11¼ Syncopated
Self-Adhesive

2932	A764 $1.40 multi	3.75	3.75
2933	A764 $2.05 multi	5.00	5.00

Complete booklet containing No. 2930 sold for $11.95; booklet containing No. 2931, $16.95. Margins for each pane in the complete booklets differ.

Nos. 2932-2933 each were sold in sheets of 20 and have personalized pictures and a straight edge at right, and lack separations between the stamp and the personalized photo. Sheets of 20 of No. 2932 sold for $41, and No. 2933 sold for $53.

Tourist Areas of Cities — A765

Designs: Nos. 2934, 2941, 2945, Luna Park, Melbourne. Nos. 2935, 2942, 2946, South Bank, Brisbane. Nos. 2936, 2943, 2947, The Rocks, Sydney. Nos. 2937, 2944, 2948, Fishermans Wharf, Fremantle. $1.10, Foreshore, Cairns. $1.65, Salamanca Place, Hobart. $2.75, Glenelg, Adelaide (50x30mm).

2008, Sept. 8   **Litho.**   **Perf. 14x14½**

2934	A765 55c multi	.95	.95
2935	A765 55c multi	.95	.95
2936	A765 55c multi	.95	.95
2937	A765 55c multi	.95	.95
a.	Block of 4, #2934-2937	4.00	4.00
b.	Sheet of 4, #2934-2937	4.00	4.00
c.	Block of 4, #2934-2937, perf. 13½x14	18.00	18.00
2938	A765 $1.10 multi	2.00	1.60
2939	A765 $1.65 multi	3.00	2.25

Perf. 14½x14

2940	A765 $2.75 multi	5.00	2.40
	Nos. 2934-2940 (7)	13.80	10.05

Self-Adhesive
Coil Stamps
Die Cut Perf. 12¾

2941	A765 55c multi	.95	.30
2942	A765 55c multi	.95	.30
2943	A765 55c multi	.95	.30
2944	A765 55c multi	.95	.30
a.	Horiz. strip of 4, #2941-2944	4.00	

Booklet Stamps
Serpentine Die Cut 11¼

2945	A765 55c multi	.95	.30
a.	Booklet pane of 10	9.75	
2946	A765 55c multi	.95	.30
a.	Booklet pane of 10	9.75	
2947	A765 55c multi	.95	.30
a.	Booklet pane of 10	9.75	

2948	A765 55c multi	.95	.30
a.	Booklet pane of 10	9.75	
b.	Booklet pane of 20, 5 each #2945-2948	20.00	
	Nos. 2941-2948 (8)	7.60	2.40

Issued: No. 2937b, 5/14/09. Hong Kong 2009 Int'l. Stamp Exhibition (No. 2937b).

Australia and Southern Cross — A766

Balloons — A767   Bird and Beach — A768

Stylized Map A769   Sparklers A770

Flowers and Silver Wedding Rings — A771   Gold Wedding Rings — A772

Baby's Feet — A773   Heart and Roses — A774

Roses and Wedding Gown — A775

2008, Sept. 23   **Perf. 14½x14**

2949	A766 55c multi	.95	.95

Perf. 14¾x14

2950	A767 55c multi	.95	.95
2951	A768 55c multi	.95	.95
2952	A769 55c multi	.95	.95
a.	Souvenir sheet of 2 + 2 labels, Chips Rafferty in margin	4.25	4.25
b.	As "a," Errol Flynn in margin	4.25	4.25
2953	A770 55c multi	.95	.95
a.	Block of 4, #2950-2953	4.00	4.00
2954	A771 55c multi	.95	.95
2955	A772 55c multi	.95	.95
2956	A773 55c multi	.95	.95

2957	A774	55c multi	.95	.95
a.		Block of 4, #2954-2957	4.00	4.00
2958	A775	$1.10 multi	2.00	1.60
		Nos. 2949-2958 (10)	10.55	10.15

Nos. 2952a and 2952b were sold with Nos. 3009b and 3010d in a set for $12.95.

Booklet Stamps
Self-Adhesive
Serpentine Die Cut 11¼ Syncopated

2959	A767	55c multi	1.00	.30
a.		Booklet pane of 4	4.25	
		Complete booklet, 5 #2959a	22.00	
b.		Booklet pane of 10	10.50	
2960	A770	55c multi	1.00	.30
a.		Booklet pane of 4	4.25	
		Complete booklet, 5 #2960a	22.00	
b.		Booklet pane of 10	10.50	
2961	A771	55c multi	1.00	.30
a.		Booklet pane of 4	4.25	
		Complete booklet, 5 #2961a	22.00	
b.		Booklet pane of 10	10.50	
2962	A772	55c multi	1.00	.30
a.		Booklet pane of 4	4.25	
		Complete booklet, 5 #2962a	22.00	
b.		Booklet pane of 10	10.50	
2963	A773	55c multi	1.00	.30
a.		Booklet pane of 4	4.25	
		Complete booklet, 5 #2963a	22.00	
b.		Booklet pane of 10	10.50	
2964	A774	55c multi	1.00	.30
a.		Booklet pane of 4	4.25	
		Complete booklet, 5 #2964a	22.00	
2965	A775	$1.10 multi	2.00	2.00
a.		Booklet pane of 4	8.00	
		Complete booklet, 5 #2965a	41.00	
b.		Booklet pane of 10	20.00	
		Nos. 2959-2965 (7)	8.00	3.80

With Personalized Photo at Right Like Type A692a
Serpentine Die Cut 11½x11¼ Syncopated
Self-Adhesive

2966	A767	55c multi	2.25	2.25
2967	A768	55c multi	2.25	2.25
2968	A769	55c multi	2.25	2.25
2969	A770	55c multi	2.25	2.25
2970	A771	55c multi	2.25	2.25
2971	A772	55c multi	2.25	2.25
2972	A773	55c multi	2.25	2.25
2973	A774	55c multi	2.25	2.25
2974	A775	$1.10 multi	3.25	3.25
		Nos. 2966-2974 (9)	21.25	21.25

Issued: See Nos. 2959b, 2960b, 2962b, 2963b, 2965b, 3/2/09.

Complete booklet containing No. 2965 sold for $22.95; booklets containing Nos. 2959-2964 each sold for $11.95. Each booklet contained panes with five different margins.

Nos. 2966-2974 each were sold in sheets of 20 and have personalized pictures and a straight edge at right, and lack separations between the stamp and the personalized photo. Sheets of 20 of Nos. 2966-2973 each sold for $24, and No. 2974 sold for $35.

Large Extinct
Animals — A776

Designs: Nos. 2975, 2981, Genyornis. Nos. 2976, 2982, Diprotodon. Nos. 2977, 2983, Thylacoleo. Nos. 2978, 2984, Thylacine. No. 2979, Megalania, horiz. (52x37mm). No. 2980, Procoptodon, horiz. (52x37mm).

2008, Oct. 1   Litho.   Perf. 14½x14

2975	A776	55c multi	.95	.95
a.		Perf. 14	.95	.95
b.		Booklet pane of 2 #2975	2.25	
2976	A776	55c multi	.95	.95
a.		Perf. 14	.95	.95
b.		Booklet pane of 2 #2976	2.25	
2977	A776	55c multi	.95	.95
a.		Perf. 14	.95	.95
b.		Booklet pane of 2 #2977	2.25	
2978	A776	55c multi	.95	.95
a.		Perf. 14	.95	.95
b.		Horiz. strip of 4, #2975-2978	4.00	4.00
c.		Booklet pane of 2 #2978	2.25	
d.		Booklet pane of 4, #2975-2978	4.25	—
2979	A776	$1.10 multi	2.00	1.60
a.		Perf. 14	.95	.95
b.		Booklet pane of 2 #2979	4.25	
2980	A776	$1.10 multi	2.00	1.60
a.		Perf. 14	.95	.95
b.		Horiz. pair, #2979-2980	4.00	4.00
c.		Souvenir sheet of 2 #2975a-2980a	8.00	8.00
d.		Booklet pane of 2 #2980	4.25	
e.		Booklet pane of 2, #2979-2980	4.25	—
		Complete booklet, #2975b, 2976b, 2977b, 2978c, 2978d, 2979b, 2980b, 2980e	26.50	
f.		As "c," overprinted with Beijing 2008 Stamp Exposition emblem in margin	7.00	7.00
		Nos. 2975-2980 (6)	7.80	7.00

Self-Adhesive
Serpentine Die Cut 11¼ Syncopated

2981	A776	55c multi	.95	.30
2982	A776	55c multi	.95	.30
2983	A776	55c multi	.95	.30
2984	A776	55c multi	.95	.30
a.		Vert. coil strip of 4, #2981-2984	4.00	
b.		Booklet pane of 10, 3 each #2981-2982, 2 each #2983-2984	9.75	
		Nos. 2981-2984 (4)	3.80	1.20

Complete booklet sold for $13.95. Issued: No. 2980f, 10/24.

Matthew
Cowdrey,
Paralympian
of the
Year — A777

2008, Oct. 24   Litho.   Perf. 14¼

2985	A777	55c multi	.85	.70

Christmas
A778   A779

Star of Bethlehem and: Nos. 2987, 2992, 2995, Madonna and child. No. 2988, 2996, Angel. Nos. 2989, 2993, Magus.

2008, Oct. 31   Litho.   Perf. 14¾x14

2986	A778	50c multi	.80	.80
2987	A779	50c multi	.80	.80
2988	A779	55c multi	.85	.70
2989	A779	$1.20 multi	1.90	1.90
		Nos. 2986-2989 (4)	4.35	4.20

Booklet Stamps
Self-Adhesive
Litho. & Typo.
Serpentine Die Cut 11¼ Syncopated

2990	A778	50c multi	.80	.30
a.		Booklet pane of 10	8.00	

Litho.

2991	A778	50c multi	.80	.30
a.		Booklet pane of 20	16.00	
2992	A779	50c multi	.80	.30
a.		Booklet pane of 20	16.00	
2993	A779	$1.20 multi	1.90	.30
a.		Booklet pane of 5	9.25	
		Nos. 2990-2993 (4)	4.30	1.20

With Personalized Photo at Right Like Type A692a
Serpentine Die Cut 11½x11¼ Syncopated
Self-Adhesive

2994	A778	50c multi	1.75	1.75
2995	A779	50c multi	1.75	1.75
2996	A779	55c multi	1.75	1.75
		Nos. 2994-2996 (3)	5.25	5.25

Nos. 2994-2996 each were sold in sheets of 20 and have personalized pictures and a straight edge at right, and lack separations between the stamp and the personalized photo. Sheets of 20 of Nos. 2994-2995 each sold for $23, and No. 2996 sold for $24.

Posters for Popular
Australian
Films — A780

Poster for: Nos. 2997, 3002, The Adventures of Priscilla, Queen of the Desert. Nos. 2998, 3003, The Castle. Nos. 2999, 3004, Muriel's Wedding. Nos. 3000, 3005, Lantana. Nos. 3001, 3006, Gallipoli.

2008, Nov. 3   Litho.   Perf. 14¾x14

2997	A780	55c multi	.85	.85
2998	A780	55c multi	.85	.85
2999	A780	55c multi	.85	.85
3000	A780	55c multi	.85	.85
3001	A780	55c multi	.85	.85
a.		Horiz. strip of 5, #2997-3001	4.25	4.25
		Nos. 2997-3001 (5)	4.25	4.25

Self-Adhesive
Serpentine Die Cut 11¼ Syncopated

3002	A780	55c multi	.85	.30
a.		Booklet pane of 10	8.50	
3003	A780	55c multi	.85	.30
a.		Booklet pane of 10	8.50	
3004	A780	55c multi	.85	.30
a.		Booklet pane of 10	8.50	
3005	A780	55c multi	.85	.30
a.		Booklet pane of 10	8.50	
3006	A780	55c multi	.85	.30
a.		Booklet pane of 10	8.50	
b.		Booklet pane of 10, 2 each #3002-3006	8.50	
c.		Vert. coil strip of 5, #3002-3006	4.25	
d.		Souvenir sheet of 10, 1 ea #3002, 3004-3006, 6 #3003	11.00	
		Nos. 3002-3006 (5)	4.25	1.50

Academy Award-
winning Actors and
Actresses — A781

Designs: Nos. 3007, 3015, Nicole Kidman. Nos. 3008, 3016, Russell Crowe. Nos. 3009, 3018, Geoffrey Rush. Nos. 3010, 3017, Cate Blanchett. Nos. 3011, 3020, Crowe in *Gladiator.* Nos. 3012, 3019, Kidman in *Moulin Rouge!* Nos. 3013, 3021, Blanchett in *Elizabeth: The Golden Age.* Nos. 3014, 3022, Rush in *Shine.*

2009, Jan. 22   Litho.   Perf. 14¾x14

3007	A781	55c multi	.80	.80
a.		Booklet pane of 4	4.25	
3008	A781	55c multi	.80	.80
a.		Booklet pane of 4	4.25	
b.		Sheet of 10 + 10 labels	14.00	14.00
3009	A781	55c multi	.80	.80
a.		Booklet pane of 4	4.25	
b.		Souvenir sheet of 4	8.25	8.25
3010	A781	55c multi	.85	.85
a.		Booklet pane of 4	4.25	
b.		Block of 4, #3007-3010	3.50	3.50
c.		Booklet pane of 4, #3007-3010	4.25	—
d.		Souvenir sheet of 4, #3007-3010	8.25	8.25
3011	A781	55c multi	.85	.85
a.		Booklet pane of 4	4.25	
b.		Booklet pane of 4, 2 each #3008, 3011	4.25	
		Complete booklet, #3008a, 3010c, 3011a, 3011b	17.00	
3012	A781	55c multi	.85	.85
a.		Booklet pane of 4	4.25	
b.		Booklet pane of 4, 2 each #3007, 3012	4.25	
		Complete booklet, #3007a, 3010c, 3012a, 3012b	17.00	
3013	A781	55c multi	.85	.85
a.		Booklet pane of 4	4.25	
b.		Booklet pane of 4, 2 each #3010, 3013	4.25	
		Complete booklet, #3010a, 3010c, 3013a, 3013b	17.00	
3014	A781	55c multi	.85	.85
a.		Booklet pane of 4	4.25	
b.		Booklet pane of 4, 2 each #3009, 3014	4.25	
		Complete booklet, #3009a, 3010c, 3014a, 3014b	17.50	
c.		Block of 4, #3011-3014	3.50	3.50
		Nos. 3007-3014 (8)	6.65	6.65

Issued: No. 3008b, 5/6/10. Two sheets of 3008b, each sheet having different labels, were sold together as a set for $13.50. Nos. 3009b and 3010d were sold with Nos. 2952a and 2952b in a set for $12.95.

Self-Adhesive
Booklet Stamps
Serpentine Die Cut 11¼ Syncopated

3015	A781	55c multi	.85	.30
3016	A781	55c multi	.85	.30
3017	A781	55c multi	.85	.30
3018	A781	55c multi	.85	.30
3019	A781	55c multi	.85	.30
a.		Booklet pane of 10, 5 each #3015, 3019	8.50	
3020	A781	55c multi	.85	.30
a.		Booklet pane of 10, 5 each #3016, 3020	8.50	
3021	A781	55c multi	.85	.30
a.		Booklet pane of 10, 5 each #3017 3021	8.50	
3022	A781	55c multi	.85	.30
a.		Booklet pane of 20, 3 each #3015-3018, 2 each #3019-3022	17.00	

b.		Booklet pane of 10, 5 each #3019, 3022	8.50	
		Nos. 3015-3022 (8)	6.80	2.40

Each complete booklet sold for $10.95.

Roses — A782   Heart — A783

Flowers With Heart-
Shaped
Petals — A784

2009, Feb. 3   Litho.   Perf. 14¾x14

3023	A782	55c multi	.80	.80
3024	A783	55c gray blue	.80	.80
3025	A784	55c multi	.80	.80
a.		Pair, #3024-3025	1.60	1.60
		Nos. 3023-3025 (3)	2.40	2.40

Booklet Stamps
Self-Adhesive
Serpentine Die Cut 11¼ Syncopated

3026	A782	55c multi	.80	.80
a.		Booklet pane of 10	8.00	
3027	A783	55c gray blue	.80	.80
a.		Booklet pane of 10	8.00	
3028	A784	55c multi	.80	.80
a.		Booklet pane of 10	8.00	

Litho. With Foil Application

3029	A784	55c multi	.80	.80

Litho. With Flocking

3030	A783	55c gray blue	.80	.80
a.		Booklet pane of 10, 2 each #3029-3030	8.00	
		Nos. 3026-3030 (5)	4.00	4.00

With Personalized Photo at Right Like Type A692a
Syncopated Die Cut 11½x11¼ Syncopated
Self-Adhesive

3031	A782	55c multi	1.75	1.75
3032	A783	55c multi	1.75	1.75
3033	A784	55c multi	1.75	1.75
		Nos. 3031-3033 (3)	5.25	5.25

Nos. 3031-3033 each were sold in sheets of 20 and have personalized pictures and a straight edge at right and lack separations between the stamp and the personalized photo. Sheets of 20 of each stamp sold for $24.

Australian
Inventions — A785

Designs: Nos. 3034, 3039, Esky (insulated cooler), wine cask. Nos. 3035, 3040, Hills hoist (rotatable clothes line frame). Nos. 3036, 3041, Speedos (swim wear), zinc oxide cream. Nos. 3037, 3042, Ute (utility vehicle), B&D Roll-A-Door (garage door). Nos. 3038, 3043, Victa rotary lawnmower.

2009, Feb. 19   Litho.   Perf. 14¾x14

3034	A785	55c multi	.80	.80
a.		Booklet pane of 4	4.00	
b.		As #3034, perf. 14	.80	.80
3035	A785	55c multi	.80	.80
a.		Booklet pane of 4	4.00	
b.		As #3035, perf. 14	.80	.80
3036	A785	55c multi	.80	.80
a.		Booklet pane of 4	4.00	
b.		As #3036, perf. 14	.80	.80
3037	A785	55c multi	.80	.80
a.		Booklet pane of 4	4.00	
b.		As #3037, perf. 14	.80	.80
3038	A785	55c multi	.80	.80
a.		Booklet pane of 4	4.00	
		Complete booklet, #3034a, 3035a, 3036a, 3037a, 3038a	19.50	

b.	As #3038, perf. 14	.80	.80
c.	Souvenir sheet, #3034b-3038b	4.00	4.00
d.	Horiz. strip of 5, #3034-3038	4.00	4.00
	Nos. 3034-3038 (5)	4.00	4.00

Self-Adhesive
Serpentine Die Cut 11¼ Syncopated

3039	A785	55c multi	.80	.30
3040	A785	55c multi	.80	.30
3041	A785	55c multi	.80	.30
3042	A785	55c multi	.80	.30
3043	A785	55c multi	.80	.30
a.		Vert. coil strip of 5, #3039-3043	4.00	
b.		Booklet pane of 10, 2 each #3039-3043	8.00	
		Nos. 3039-3043 (5)	4.00	1.50

Complete booklet sold for $12.95.

Earth Hour — A786

Animals and slogan: Nos. 3044, 3047, Lights out. No. 3045, 3048, Switch off. $2.05, Save energy.

2009, Mar. 11   *Perf. 14¾x14*

3044	A786	55c multi	.90	.90
3045	A786	55c multi	.90	.90
a.		Horiz. pair, #3044-3045	1.90	1.90
3046	A786	$2.05 multi	3.50	3.50
		Nos. 3044-3046 (3)	5.30	5.30

Booklet Stamps
Self-Adhesive
Serpentine Die Cut 11¼ Syncopated

3047	A786	55c multi	.90	.30
3048	A786	55c multi	.90	.30
a.		Booklet pane of 20, 10 each #3047-3048	18.50	

Australia Post, Bicent. — A787

Inscriptions: Nos. 3049a, 3050, First postmaster. Nos. 3049b, 3051, Early post office. Nos. 3049c, 3052, Early posting box. Nos. 3049d, 3053, News from home. Nos. 3049e, 3054, Early air mail. Nos. 3049f, 3055, Home delivery. Nos. 3049g, 3056, Post-war immigration. Nos. 3049h, 3057, Retail post shop. Nos. 3049i, 3058, Express post. Nos. 3049j, 3059, Part of every day.

2009, Mar. 25   *Perf. 14¾x14*

3049		Sheet of 10	9.25	9.25
a.-j.	A787	55c Any single	.90	.90
k.		Booklet pane of 10, #3049a-3049j	11.00	—
l.		As "k," imperf.	11.00	
		Complete booklet, #3049l, 2 #3049k	32.50	

Self-Adhesive
Serpentine Die Cut 11¼ Syncopated

3050	A787	55c multi	.90	.30
3051	A787	55c multi	.90	.30
3052	A787	55c multi	.90	.30
3053	A787	55c multi	.90	.30
3054	A787	55c multi	.90	.30
3055	A787	55c multi	.90	.30
3056	A787	55c multi	.90	.30
3057	A787	55c multi	.90	.30
3058	A787	55c multi	.90	.30
3059	A787	55c multi	.90	.30
a.		Vert. coil strip of 10, #3050-3059	9.00	
b.		Booklet pane of 10, #3050-3059	9.00	
		Nos. 3050-3059 (10)	9.00	3.00

Complete booklet sold for $19.95. Compare with type A806.

Aboriginal Art — A788

Designs: No. 3060, Mamu, by Nura Rupert. No. 3061, All the Jila, by Jan Billycan. No. 3062, Mina Mina, by Judy Napangardi Watson. $1.40, Untitled work from the Mission Series, by Elaine Russell. $2.05, Natjula, by Tjuruparu Watson.

2009, Apr. 1   *Perf. 14x14¾*

3060	A788	55c multi	.90	.70
3061	A788	55c multi	.90	.70
3062	A788	55c multi	.90	.70
a.		Horiz. strip of 3, #3060-3062	2.75	2.00
3063	A788	$1.40 multi	2.25	1.10
3064	A788	$2.05 multi	3.50	1.75
		Nos. 3060-3064 (5)	8.45	4.95

Self-Adhesive
Booklet Stamps
Serpentine Die Cut 11¼ Syncopated

3065	A788	$1.40 multi	2.25	1.10
a.		Booklet pane of 5	11.50	
3066	A788	$2.05 multi	3.50	1.75
a.		Booklet pane of 5	17.50	

Queen's Birthday — A789

Queen Elizabeth II: 55c, In uniform. $2.05, Wearing green coat and hat.

2009, Apr. 15   *Perf. 14¾x14*

3067	A789	55c multi	.90	.70
a.		Booklet pane of 2	2.25	
b.		Dated "2010"	2.00	1.00
3068	A789	$2.05 multi	3.50	1.75
a.		Booklet pane of 2	8.50	
b.		Souvenir sheet of 2, #3067-3068	4.50	2.40
c.		Booklet pane, #3068b	5.25	—
		Complete booklet, #3068a, 3068c, 2 #3067a	18.50	

Complete booklet sold for $10.95.

Eponymous Desserts A790

Designs: Nos. 3069, 3073, Anna Pavlova and Pavlova. Nos. 3070, 3074, Dame Nellie Melba and Peach Melba. Nos. 3071, 3075, Baron and Lady Lamington and Lamingtons. Nos. 3072, 3076, ANZAC soldiers and ANZAC biscuits.

2009, May 15   *Litho.*   *Perf. 14x14¾*

3069	A790	55c multi	1.00	1.00
a.		Booklet pane of 4	5.25	—
3070	A790	55c multi	1.00	1.00
a.		Booklet pane of 4	5.25	—
3071	A790	55c multi	1.00	1.00
a.		Booklet pane of 4	5.25	—
3072	A790	55c multi	1.00	1.00
a.		Booklet pane of 4	5.25	—
		Complete booklet, #3069a-3072a	20.75	
b.		Horiz. strip of 4, #3069-3072	4.25	4.25
		Nos. 3069-3072 (4)	4.00	4.00

Booklet Stamps
Self-Adhesive
Serpentine Die Cut 11¼ Syncopated

3073	A790	55c multi	1.00	.30
3074	A790	55c multi	1.00	.30
3075	A790	55c multi	1.00	.30
3076	A790	55c multi	1.00	.30
a.		Booklet pane of 10, 3 each #3073-3074, 2 each #3075-3076	11.00	
		Nos. 3073-3076 (4)	4.00	1.20

Complete booklet sold for $10.95.

Worldwide Fund for Nature (WWF) A791

Designs: 55c, Spotted bottlenose dolphins. $1.35, Hourglass dolphins. $1.40, Southern right whale dolphins. $2.05, Dusky dolphins.

2009, May 26   *Perf. 14x14¾*

3077	A791	55c multi	1.00	.80
3078	A791	$1.35 multi	2.50	2.50
3079	A791	$1.40 multi	2.50	2.50
3080	A791	$2.05 multi	3.75	3.75
a.		Souvenir sheet, #3077-3080	10.00	10.00
		Nos. 3077-3080 (4)	9.75	9.55

Booklet Stamps
Self-Adhesive
Serpentine Die Cut 11¼ Syncopated

3081	A791	$1.35 multi	2.50	2.50
a.		Booklet pane of 5	13.00	
3082	A791	$1.40 multi	2.50	2.50
a.		Booklet pane of 5	13.00	
3083	A791	$2.05 multi	3.75	3.75
a.		Booklet pane of 5	19.00	
		Nos. 3081-3083 (3)	8.75	8.75

Queensland, 150th Anniv. — A792

Designs: 55c, Queensland Parliament, windmill. $2.75, Great Barrier Reef, red-eyed tree frog.

2009, June 9   *Litho.*   *Perf. 14¾x14*

3084	A792	55c multi	1.00	.80
3085	A792	$2.75 multi	5.25	4.00
a.		Souvenir sheet, #3084-3085	6.25	6.25

Australia's Favorite Stamps A793

Designs: Nos. 3086, 3091, 3095B, Australia #15. Nos. 3087, 3092, Australia #132. Nos. 3088, 3093, Australia #200. Nos. 3089, 3094, Australia #226. Nos. 3090, 3095, Australia #18.

2009, June 26   *Litho.*   *Perf. 14x14¾*

3086	A793	55c multi	1.00	1.00
a.		Booklet pane of 4	4.50	
3087	A793	55c multi	1.00	1.00
a.		Booklet pane of 4	4.50	
3088	A793	55c multi	1.00	1.00
a.		Booklet pane of 4	4.50	
3089	A793	55c multi	1.00	1.00
a.		Booklet pane of 4	4.50	
3090	A793	55c multi	1.00	1.00
a.		Booklet pane of 4	4.50	
		Complete booklet, #3086a-3090a	23.00	
b.		Horiz. strip of 5, #3086-3090	5.25	5.25
		Nos. 3086-3090 (5)	5.00	5.00

Self-Adhesive
Serpentine Die Cut 11¼ Syncopated

3091	A793	55c multi	1.00	.30
3092	A793	55c multi	1.00	.30
3093	A793	55c multi	1.00	.30
3094	A793	55c multi	1.00	.30
3095	A793	55c multi	1.00	.30
a.		Horiz. coil strip of 5, #3091-3095	5.25	
		Nos. 3091-3095 (5)	5.00	1.50

Litho. & Embossed
Serpentine Die Cut 11¼ Syncopated
Self-Adhesive

3095B	A793	55c multi	1.00	.30
c.		Sheet of 13, #3091-3095, 8 #3095B	14.00	

The complete booklet sold for $12.95. Nos. 3091-3095 each were printed by two different printers. There is no noticeable difference between single coil stamps, but Pemara-printed stamps are slightly closer to each other on the strip compared to the McKellar Renown-printed stamps.

Marsupials and Their Young — A794

Designs: $1.45, Koalas. $2.10, Eastern gray kangaroos. $2.90, Brushtail possums, horiz. $4.20, Common wombats, horiz.

2009, July 1   *Perf. 14¾x14*

3096	A794	$1.45 multi	2.75	2.75
3097	A794	$2.05 multi	4.00	4.00
a.		Additionally dated "2013" (#3534d)	5.50	5.50

Perf. 14x14¾

3098	A794	$2.90 multi	5.50	2.75
3099	A794	$4.20 multi	7.75	4.00
		Nos. 3096-3099 (4)	20.00	13.50

Issued: No. 3097a, 5/10/13.

Booklet Stamps
Self-Adhesive
Serpentine Die Cut 11¼ Syncopated

3100	A794	$1.45 multi	2.75	1.40
a.		Booklet pane of 5	14.00	
3101	A794	$2.10 multi	4.00	2.00
a.		Booklet pane of 5	20.00	

With Personalized Photo at Right Like Type A692a
Serpentine Die Cut 11¼ Syncopated
Self-Adhesive

3102	A794	$1.45 multi	4.00	4.00
3103	A794	$2.10 multi	5.25	5.25

Nos. 3102-3103 each were sold in sheets of 20 and have personalized pictures and a straight edge at right and lack separations between the stamp and the personalized photo. Sheets of 20 of No. 3102 sold for $42; No. 3103, for $54.

Parks and Gardens A795

Designs: Nos. 3104, 3109, Fitzroy Gardens, Melbourne. Nos. 3105, 3110, Roma Street Parkland, Brisbane. Nos. 3106, 3111, St. David's Park, Hobart. Nos. 3107, 3112, Commonwealth Park, Canberra. Nos. 3108, 3113, Hyde Park, Sydney.

2009, July 14   *Litho.*   *Perf. 14x14¾*

3104	A795	55c multi	1.10	1.10
a.		Booklet pane of 4	5.25	
b.		Sheet of 4, #3072, 3086, 3090, 3104	4.25	4.25
3105	A795	55c multi	1.10	1.10
a.		Booklet pane of 4	5.25	
3106	A795	55c multi	1.10	1.10
a.		Booklet pane of 4	5.25	
3107	A795	55c multi	1.10	1.10
a.		Booklet pane of 4	5.25	
b.		Additionally dated "2013" (#3107c)	1.25	1.25
c.		Booklet pane of 2 #3107b	2.50	
3108	A795	55c multi	1.10	1.10
a.		Booklet pane of 4	5.25	
		Complete booklet, #3104a-3108a	26.00	
b.		Horiz. strip of 5, #3104-3108	5.50	5.50
		Nos. 3104-3108 (5)	5.50	5.50

Issued: Nos. 3107b, 3107c, 3/5/13. No. 3107c was issued in booklet along with Nos. 1939c, 2710c, 2869e, 3349b and 3877a.

Coil Stamps
Self-Adhesive
Serpentine Die Cut 11¼ Syncopated

3109	A795	55c multi	1.10	.30
3110	A795	55c multi	1.10	.30
3111	A795	55c multi	1.10	.30
3112	A795	55c multi	1.10	.30
3113	A795	55c multi	1.10	.30
a.		Horiz. strip of 5, #3109-3113	5.25	
b.		Booklet pane of 10, 2 each # 3109-3113	11.00	
		Nos. 3109-3113 (5)	5.50	1.50

The complete booklet sold for $12.95.
Issued: No. 3104b, 7/23. Melbourne Stamp Show 09 (No. 3104b).

Insects and Spiders A796

Designs: Nos. 3114, 3120a, 3121, Hatchet wasp. Nos. 3115, 3120b, 3122, Praying mantis. Nos. 3116, 3120c, 3123, Ground beetle. Nos. 3117, 3120d, 3124, Jumping spider. Nos. 3118, 3120e, 3125, Ant. $1.10, Weevil.

2009, July 28 Litho. Perf. 14x14¾

3114	A796	55c multi	1.10	1.10
3115	A796	55c multi	1.10	1.10
3116	A796	55c multi	1.10	1.10
3117	A796	55c multi	1.10	1.10
3118	A796	55c multi	1.10	1.10
b.		Horiz. strip of 5, #3114-3118	5.25	5.25
3119	A796	$1.10 multi	2.25	1.60
		Nos. 3114-3119 (6)	7.75	7.10

Miniature Sheet
With Square of Thermochromic Ink
Covering Magnification Squares

3120		Sheet of 6	7.75	7.75
a.-e.		A796 55c Any single	1.10	1.10
f.		A796 $1.10 multi	2.25	2.25

Coil Stamps
Self-Adhesive
Serpentine Die Cut 11¼ Syncopated

3121	A796	55c multi	1.10	.30
3122	A796	55c multi	1.10	.30
3123	A796	55c multi	1.10	.30
3124	A796	55c multi	1.10	.30
3125	A796	55c multi	1.10	.30
a.		Horiz. strip of 5, #3121-3125	5.25	
		Nos. 3121-3125 (5)	5.50	1.50

Endangered
Wildlife — A797

Designs: Nos. 3126, 3132, Bridled nailtail wallaby. Nos. 3127, 3133, Norfolk Island green parrot. Nos. 3128, 3134, Subarctic fur seal. Nos. 3129, 3135, Christmas Island blue-tailed skink. Nos. 3130, 3136, Green turtle.

2009, Aug. 4 Litho. Perf. 14¾x14
"Australia" Above Denomination

3126	A797	55c multi	1.10	1.10
3127	A797	55c multi	1.10	1.10
3128	A797	55c multi	1.10	1.10
3129	A797	55c multi	1.10	1.10
3130	A797	55c multi	1.10	1.10
a.		Horiz. strip of 5, #3126-3130	5.25	5.25
		Nos. 3126-3130 (5)	5.50	5.50
3131	A797	55c Sheet of 5, #3126, 3128-3130, Norfolk Island #980	5.25	5.25

Booklet Stamps
Self-Adhesive
Serpentine Die Cut 11¼ Syncopated

3132	A797	55c multi	1.10	.30
3133	A797	55c multi	1.10	.30
3134	A797	55c multi	1.10	.30
3135	A797	55c multi	1.10	.30
3136	A797	55c multi	1.10	.30
a.		Booklet pane of 20, 4 each #3132-3136	22.00	
		Nos. 3132-3136 (5)	5.50	1.50

Inscribed on the left side of Nos. 3128 and 3134 is "Australian Antarctic Territory"; on Nos. 3129 and 3135, "Christmas Island," and on Nos. 3130 and 3136, "Cocos (Keeling) Islands." All recent stamps of the Australian possessions of Australian Antarctic Territory, Christmas Island and Cocos Islands are doubly-inscribed with "Australia" and the territory's name, and all stamps inscribed "Australia," "Australian Antarctic Territory," "Christmas Island," or "Cocos Islands," are valid for postage anywhere in those four areas. However, because Nos. 3128-3130 and 3134-3136 have the territorial inscriptions at the side rather than above the denomination like similar Norfolk Island stamps, Nos. 979-983, they will be listed here and not in the listings for each of these territories. No. 3131 is identical to Norfolk Island No. 984. Norfolk Island No. 980 has "Norfolk Island" above the denomination, which differentiates it from Australia No. 3127.

Corrugated Iron Water Tank, Fleurieu
Peninsula, South Australia
A798

Corrugated
Iron House,
Broken Hill,
New South
Wales
A799

Corrugated Iron Shearing Shed, Bushy
Park Cattle Station, Queensland
A800

Magney
House,
Bingie Bingie
Point, New
South Wales
A801

2009, Aug. 11 Perf. 14x14¾

3137	A798	55c multi	1.10	1.10
a.		Booklet pane of 4	5.25	
3138	A799	55c multi	1.10	1.10
a.		Booklet pane of 4	5.25	
3139	A800	55c multi	1.10	1.10
a.		Booklet pane of 4	5.25	
3140	A801	55c multi	1.10	1.10
a.		Booklet pane of 4	5.25	
		Complete booklet, #3137a-3140a	22.00	
b.		Horiz. strip of 4, #3137-3140	4.50	4.50
		Nos. 3137-3140 (4)	4.40	4.40

Self-Adhesive
Serpentine Die Cut 11¼ Syncopated

3141	A798	55c multi	1.10	.30
3142	A799	55c multi	1.10	.30
3143	A800	55c multi	1.10	.30
3144	A801	55c multi	1.10	.30
a.		Horiz. coil strip of 4, #3141-3144	4.50	
b.		Booklet pane of 20, 5 each #3141-3144	22.00	
		Nos. 3141-3144 (4)	4.40	1.20

Complete booklet sold for $10.95.

Intl. Year of
Astronomy
A802

Designs: 55c, Sombrero Galaxy (M104). $1.45, Reflection Nebula (M78). $2.10, Spiral Galaxy (M83).

2009, Aug. 25 Perf. 14x14¾

3145	A802	55c multi	1.10	.85
3146	A802	$1.45 multi	2.75	2.25
3147	A802	$2.10 multi	4.00	3.00
a.		Souvenir sheet, #3145-3147	8.00	6.00
		Nos. 3145-3147 (3)	7.85	6.10

No. 3147a exists imperf from a telephone drawing at a substantial premium over face value. Value for a single sheet, $22.

Birds — A803

Designs: 55c, Green catbird. $1.10, Noisy scrub-bird. $1.65, Mangrove golden whistler. $2.75, Scarlet honeyeater.

2009, Sept. 9 Litho. Perf. 14¾x14

3148	A803	55c multi	1.10	1.10
a.		Additionally dated "2013"	1.10	1.10
3149	A803	$1.10 multi	2.25	1.60
a.		Booklet pane of 2, #3148-3149	4.25	—
b.		Additionally dated "2013"	2.10	2.10
3150	A803	$1.65 multi	3.50	2.50
a.		Booklet pane of 2, #3149-3150	7.25	—
b.		Booklet pane of 2, #3148, 3150	6.75	—
c.		Additionally dated "2013"	3.25	3.25
3151	A803	$2.75 multi	5.50	4.25
a.		Booklet pane of 2, #3148, 3151	8.50	—
		Complete booklet, #3149a, 3150a, 3150b, 3151a	26.00	
b.		Additionally dated "2013"	5.50	5.50
c.		Booklet pane of 4, #3148a, 3149b, 3150c, 3151d	12.00	—
		Nos. 3148-3151 (4)	12.35	9.45

Issued: Nos. 3148a, 3149b, 3150c, 3151b, 3151c, 5/11/13. No. 3151c was issued in a booklet also containing Nos. 3376b, 3665b and 3925a.

Self-Adhesive
Serpentine Die Cut 11¼ Syncopated

3152	A803	55c multi	.95	.25
a.		Booklet pane of 20	19.00	

Complete booklet sold for $12.95.

Toys — A804

Children and: Nos. 3153, 3158, Cyclops pedal car. Nos. 3154, 3159, Test Match board game. Nos. 3155, 3160, Barbie doll. Nos. 3156, 3161, Malvern Star Dragstar bicycle. Nos. 3157, 3162, Cabbage Patch Kids doll.

2009, Sept. 25 Perf. 14¾x14

3153	A804	55c multi	1.10	1.10
a.		Booklet pane of 4	5.25	
3154	A804	55c multi	1.10	1.10
a.		Booklet pane of 4	5.25	
3155	A804	55c multi	1.10	1.10
a.		Booklet pane of 4	5.25	
b.		Sheet of 10 #3155 + 10 labels	22.00	22.00
3156	A804	55c multi	1.10	1.10
a.		Booklet pane of 4	5.25	
3157	A804	55c multi	1.10	1.10
a.		Booklet pane of 4	5.25	
		Complete booklet, #3153a, 3154a, 3155a, 3156a, 3157a	26.00	
b.		Horiz. strip of 5, #3153-3157	5.50	5.50
		Nos. 3153-3157 (5)	5.50	5.50

No. 3155b sold for $10.95.

Booklet Stamps
Self-Adhesive
Serpentine Die Cut 11¼ Syncopated

3158	A804	55c multi	1.10	.30
3159	A804	55c multi	1.10	.30
3160	A804	55c multi	1.10	.30
3161	A804	55c multi	1.10	.30
3162	A804	55c multi	1.10	.30
a.		Booklet pane of 10, 2 each #3158-3162	11.00	
		Nos. 3158-3162 (5)	5.50	1.50

Complete booklet sold for $12.95.

Children Playing
Sports — A805

"Let's get active" and children playing: Nos. 3163, 3169, Australian rules football. Nos. 3164, 3170, Basketball. Nos. 3165, 3171, Soccer. Nos. 3166, 3172, Netball. Nos. 3167, 3173, Cricket. Nos. 3168, 3174, Tennis.

2009, Oct. 6 Perf. 14¾x14

3163	A805	55c multi	1.10	1.10
3164	A805	55c multi	1.10	1.10
3165	A805	55c multi	1.10	1.10
3166	A805	55c multi	1.10	1.10
3167	A805	55c multi	1.10	1.10
3168	A805	55c multi	1.10	1.10
a.		Block of 6, #3163-3168	7.00	7.00
b.		Souvenir sheet, #3163-3168	7.00	7.00
		Nos. 3163-3168 (6)	6.60	6.60

Booklet Stamps
Self-Adhesive
Serpentine Die Cut 11¼ Syncopated

3169	A805	55c multi	1.10	.30
a.		Booklet pane of 10	11.50	
3170	A805	55c multi	1.10	.30
a.		Booklet pane of 10	11.50	
3171	A805	55c multi	1.10	.30
a.		Booklet pane of 10	11.50	

3172	A805	55c multi	1.10	.30
a.		Booklet pane of 10	11.50	
3173	A805	55c multi	1.10	.30
a.		Booklet pane of 10	11.50	
3174	A805	55c multi	1.10	.30
a.		Booklet pane of 10	11.50	
b.		Booklet pane of 10, #3172, 3174, 2 each #3169-3171, 3173	11.50	
		Nos. 3169-3174 (6)	6.60	1.80

Miniature Sheet

Australia Post Employees — A806

No. 3175: a, Patricia Crabb (with white blouse with red dots). b, Shirley Freeman (at counter, with brochures at left). c, Vinko Romank (lifting mail tubs). d, Valda Knott (sorting boxes in background). e, Gordon Morgan (motorcycle in background). f, Vongpradith Phongsavan (with conveyor belt in background). g, Norma Thomas (with contractor delivery automobile). h, John Marsh (with blue shirt and tie). i, Anne Brun (at desk, with computer keyboard at left). j, Russell Price (with beard).

2009, Oct. 13 Perf. 14¾x14

3175	A806	Sheet of 10	11.50	8.50
a.-j.		55c Any single	1.10	.85

Australia Post, bicent. Compare with Type A787.

Christmas
A807   A808

Designs: Nos. 3176, 3183, Madonna and Child. Nos. 3177, 3184, 3190, 3195, Candles in star frame. Nos. 3178, 3185, 3191, 3196, Tree ornaments in Christmas tree frame. Nos. 3179, 3186, 3192, 3197, Gifts in stocking cap frame. Nos. 3180, 3187, 3193, 3198, Ornaments in bell frame. Nos. 3181, 3188, 3194, 3199, Candy canes in stocking frame. $1.25, Magi.

2009, Nov. 2 Litho. Perf. 14¾x14

3176	A807	50c multi	1.10	1.10
3177	A808	50c multi	1.10	1.10
3178	A808	50c multi	1.10	1.10
3179	A808	50c multi	1.10	1.10
3180	A808	50c multi	1.10	1.10
3181	A808	50c multi	1.10	1.10
a.		Horiz. strip of 5, #3177-3181	5.50	5.50
3182	A808	$1.25 multi	2.75	2.75
a.		Souvenir sheet of 2, #3176, 3182	4.00	4.00
		Nos. 3176-3182 (7)	9.35	9.35

Booklet Stamps (#3183-3194)
Self-Adhesive
Serpentine Die Cut 11¼ Syncopated

3183	A807	50c multi	1.10	.30
a.		Booklet pane of 20	22.00	
3184	A808	50c multi	1.10	.30
3185	A808	50c multi	1.10	.30
3186	A808	50c multi	1.10	.30
3187	A808	50c multi	1.10	.30
3188	A808	50c multi	1.10	.30
a.		Booklet pane of 10, 2 each #3184-3188	11.00	
3189	A807	$1.25 multi	2.75	.30
a.		Booklet pane of 5	14.00	

Litho. With Foil Application
Frames in Gold

3190	A808	50c multi	1.10	.30
3191	A808	50c multi	1.10	.30
3192	A808	50c multi	1.10	.30
3193	A808	50c multi	1.10	.30
3194	A808	50c multi	1.10	.30
a.		Booklet pane of 10, 2 each #3190-3194	11.00	
		Nos. 3183-3194 (12)	14.85	3.60

With Personalized Photo at Right
Like Type A692a

3195	A808	50c multi	2.40	2.40
3196	A808	50c multi	2.40	2.40
3197	A808	50c multi	2.40	2.40

3198 A808 50c multi 2.40 2.40
3199 A808 50c multi 2.40 2.40
Nos. 3195-3199 (5) 12.00 12.00

Nos. 3195-3199 were sold in sheets of 20 containing 4 of each stamp, have personalized pictures and a straight edge at right and lack separations between the stamp and the personalized photo. Sheets of 20 of sold for $23.
No. 3197 exists without "Australia" and the denomination.

Authors — A809

Designs: Nos, 3200, 3212, Color photograph of Peter Carey. No. 3201, Black-and-white photograph of Carey. No. 3202, Black-and-white photograph of David Malouf. Nos. 3203, 3213, Color photograph of Malouf. Nos. 3204, 3214, Color photograph of Colleen McCullough. No. 3205, Black-and-white photograph of McCullough. No. 3206, Black-and-white photograph of Bryce Courtenay. Nos. 3207, 3215, Color photograph of Courtenay. Nos, 3208, 3216, Color photograph of Thomas Keneally. No. 3209, Black-and-white photograph of Keneally. No. 3210, Black-and-white photograph of Tim Winton. Nos. 3211, 3217, Color photograph of Winton.

2010, Jan. 21 Litho. Perf. 14¾x14
3200 A809 55c multi 1.10 1.10
3201 A809 55c black & gray 1.10 1.10
3202 A809 55c black & gray 1.10 1.10
3203 A809 55c multi 1.10 1.10
  a. Block of 4, #3200-3203 4.50 4.50
  b. Booklet pane of 4, #3203-3203 8.50 —
  c. As "b," with color separations of stamps 8.50 —
3204 A809 55c multi 1.10 1.10
3205 A809 55c black & gray 1.10 1.10
3206 A809 55c black & gray 1.10 1.10
3207 A809 55c multi 1.10 1.10
  a. Block of 4, #3204-3207 4.50 4.50
  b. Booklet pane of 4, #3204-3207 8.50 —
  c. As "b," with color separations of stamps 8.50 —
3208 A809 55c multi 1.10 1.10
3209 A809 55c black & gray 1.10 1.10
3210 A809 55c black & gray 1.10 1.10
3211 A809 55c multi 1.10 1.10
  a. Block of 4, #3208-3211 4.50 4.50
  b. Booklet pane of 4, #3208-3211 8.50 —
  c. As "b," with color separations of stamps 8.50 —
  Complete booklet, #3203b, 3203c, 3207b, 3207c, 3211b, 3211c 52.00
Nos. 3200-3211 (12) 13.20 13.20

Booklet Stamps
Self-Adhesive
Serpentine Die Cut 11¼ Syncopated
3212 A809 55c multi 1.10 .30
3213 A809 55c multi 1.10 .30
3214 A809 55c multi 1.10 .30
3215 A809 55c multi 1.10 .30
3216 A809 55c multi 1.10 .30
3217 A809 55c multi 1.10 .30
  a. Booklet pane of 20, 5 #3214, 3 each #3212-3213, 3215-3217 23.00
Nos. 3212-3217 (6) 6.60 1.80

Complete booklet sold for $24.95. Color separations were not valid for postage.

Rule of Governor Lachlan Macquarie, Bicent. — A810

Designs: No. 3218, Macquarie (1762-1824) and north view of Sydney. No. 3219, Port Jackson and Sydney Town. No. 3220, Parramatta Female Penitentiary. No. 3221, Governor's Sydney Stables.

2010, Feb. 16 Perf. 14x14¾
3218 A810 55c multi 1.10 .85
  a. Booklet pane of 4 5.75 —
3219 A810 55c multi 1.10 .85
  a. Booklet pane of 4 5.75 —
3220 A810 55c multi 1.10 .85
  a. Booklet pane of 4 5.75 —

3221 A810 55c multi 1.10 .85
  a. Booklet pane of 4 5.75 —
    Complete booklet, #3218a-3221a 23.00
  b. Block of 4, #3218-3221 4.50 3.50
Nos. 3218-3221 (4) 4.40 3.40
Complete booklet sold of $10.95.

Coinage of the Australian Commonwealth, Cent. — A811

1910 two shilling coin: Nos. 3222, 3224a, Reverse depicting Australian coat of arms. Nos. 3223, 3224b, Obverse depicting King Edward VII.

2010, Feb. 23 Litho. Perf. 14x14¾
3222 A811 55c multi 1.10 .85
3223 A811 $2.75 multi 5.75 2.75

Souvenir Sheet
Litho. & Embossed With Foil Application
3224 Sheet of 2 7.00 3.75
  a. A811 55c multi 1.10 .85
  b. A811 $2.75 multi 5.75 2.75

No. 3224 exists imperf from a telephone drawing at a substantial premium over face value. Value for single souvenir sheet, $14.

Gold Medalists at 2010 Winter Olympics, Vancouver A812

Designs: No. 3225, Torah Bright, Snowboard halfpipe. No. 3226, Lydia Lassila, Freestyle skiing aerials.

2010 Litho. Perf. 14¼
3225 A812 55c multi 1.10 .85
3226 A812 55c multi 1.10 .85

Issued: No. 3225, 2/25; No. 3226, 3/3.

Powered Flight in Australia, Cent. (in 2009) A813

Airplane of: 55c, Colin Defries. $1.45, John Duigan. $2.10, Harry Houdini.

2010, Mar. 9 Perf. 14x14¾
3227 A813 55c multi 1.10 .85
3228 A813 $1.45 multi 3.25 1.60
  a. Souvenir sheet, #3218, 3223, 3227, 3228 11.00 11.00
  b. Sheet of 4, 2 each #3227-3228 9.00 6.75
3229 A813 $2.10 multi 4.50 2.25
Nos. 3227-3229 (3) 8.85 4.70

Booklet Stamps
Self-Adhesive
Serpentine Die Cut 11¼ Syncopated
3230 A813 $1.45 multi 3.25 1.60
  a. Booklet pane of 5 16.00
3231 A813 $2.10 multi 4.50 2.25
  a. Booklet pane of 5 23.00

2010 Canberra Stamp Show (No. 3228a). London 2010 Festival of Stamps (No. 3228b). Issued: No. 3228a, 3/12. No. 3228b, 5/8.

Agricultural Shows — A814

Designs: Nos. 3232, 3237, Prize bull. Nos. 3233, 3238, Cake decorating competition. Nos. 3234, 3239, Horse competition. Nos. 3235, 3240, Wood chopping competition. Nos. 3236, 3241, Dog show.

2010, Mar. 23 Litho. Perf. 14¾x14
3232 A814 55c multi 1.10 1.10
  a. Booklet pane of 4 5.50 —
3233 A814 55c multi 1.10 1.10
  a. Booklet pane of 4 5.50 —
3234 A814 55c multi 1.10 1.10
  a. Booklet pane of 4 5.50 —
3235 A814 55c multi 1.10 1.10
  a. Booklet pane of 4 5.50 —
3236 A814 55c multi 1.10 1.10
  a. Booklet pane of 4 5.50 —
    Complete booklet, #3232a-3236a 27.50
  b. Horiz. strip of 5, #3232-3236 5.75 5.75
  c. Souvenir sheet, #3232-3236 5.75 5.75
Nos. 3232-3236 (5) 5.50 5.50

Booklet Stamps
Self-Adhesive
Serpentine Die Cut 11¼ Syncopated
3237 A814 55c multi 1.10 .30
3238 A814 55c multi 1.10 .30
3239 A814 55c multi 1.10 .30
3240 A814 55c multi 1.10 .30
3241 A814 55c multi 1.10 .30
  a. Booklet pane of 10, 2 each #3237-3241 11.50 —
Nos. 3237-3241 (5) 5.50 1.50

Complete booklet sold for $12.95.

Queen's Birthday — A815

2010, Apr. 6 Perf. 14¾x14
3242 A815 55c multi 1.25 1.25
  a. Sheet of 4, #2505b, 2864b, 3067b, 3242 8.00 4.00

Booklet Stamp
Self-Adhesive
Serpentine Die Cut 11¼ Syncopated
3243 A815 55c multi 1.25 .30
  a. Booklet pane of 10 12.75

Issued: No. 3242a, 5/8. London 2010 Festival of Stamps (No. 3242a).

Kokoda Campaign, 68th Anniv. — A816

Designs: Nos. 3244, 3249, Soldiers in battle. Nos. 3245, 3250, Injured Australian soldier, Papuan natives. Nos. 3246, 3251, Veterans of Kokoda Campaign, Papuan houses. Nos. 3247, 3252, Tourists at Kokoda. $1.45, Veterans at Kokoda Campaign Memorial, Isurava, Papua New Guinea.

2010, Apr. 20 Perf. 14¾x14
3244 A816 55c multi 1.10 1.10
3245 A816 55c multi 1.10 1.10
  a. Booklet pane of 4, 2 each #3244-3245 6.25 —
3246 A816 55c multi 1.10 1.10
3247 A816 55c multi 1.10 1.10
  a. Booklet pane of 4 6.25 —
  b. Horiz. strip of 4, #3244-3247 4.50 4.50
3248 A816 $1.45 multi 3.25 2.40
  a. Booklet pane of 4, 2 each #3246, 3248 11.50
    Complete booklet, #3245a, 3247a, 3248a 24.00
  b. Souvenir sheet, #3244-3248 7.75 7.75
Nos. 3244-3248 (5) 7.65 6.80

Self-Adhesive
Serpentine Die Cut 11¼ Syncopated
3249 A816 55c multi 1.10 .30
3250 A816 55c multi 1.10 .30
3251 A816 55c multi 1.10 .30
3252 A816 55c multi 1.10 .30
  a. Vert. coil strip of 4, #3249-3252 4.50
  b. Booklet pane of 10, 2 each #3250, 3252, 3 each #3249, 3251 11.50
Nos. 3249-3252 (4) 4.40 1.20

Complete booklet sold for $10.95. See Papua New Guinea Nos. 1455-1456.

Queen Victoria ("Chalon Head" Portrait of Tasmania and Queensland Stamps) — A817

2010, May 7 Litho. Perf. 14x13½
3253 A817 $5 multi 10.00 5.25
  a. Souvenir sheet of 1 10.00 5.25
  b. As "a," with London 2010 emblem in gold in sheet margin 8.25 8.25

No. 3253 has simulated toning. A souvenir sheet with a litho. and engraved stamp sold for $15.
Issued: No. 3253b, 5/8.

Railway Journeys A818

Designs: Nos. 3254, 3258, The Ghan. Nos. 3255, 3259, West Coast Wilderness Railway, Tasmania. Nos. 3256, 3260, The Indian Pacific. $2.10, Kuranda Scenic Railway, Queensland (50x30mm).

2010, May 7 Perf. 14¾x14¾
3254 A818 55c multi 1.10 1.10
3255 A818 55c multi 1.10 1.10
3256 A818 55c multi 1.10 1.10
  a. Booklet pane of 4, #3254, 3255, 2 #3256 6.50 —
  b. Booklet pane of 4, #3255, 3256, 2 #3254 6.50 —
  c. Booklet pane of 4, #3254, 3256, 2 #3255 6.50 —

Perf. 13½x14
3257 A818 $2.10 multi 4.25 2.25
  a. Booklet pane of 1 6.25
    Complete booklet, #3256a-3256c, 3257a 26.50
  b. Souvenir sheet of 1 4.25 2.25
  c. As "b," with London 2010 emblem in gold in sheet margin 3.50 3.50
Nos. 3254-3257 (4) 7.55 5.55

Self-Adhesive
Serpentine Die Cut 11¼ Syncopated
3258 A818 55c multi 1.10 .30
3259 A818 55c multi 1.10 .30
3260 A818 55c multi 1.10 .30
  a. Horiz. coil strip of 3, #3258-3260 3.50
  b. Booklet pane of 20, 8 each #3258-3259, 4 #3260 23.00

Serpentine Die Cut 11¼
3261 A818 $2.10 multi 4.25 2.25
  a. Booklet pane of 5 22.00
Nos. 3258-3261 (4) 7.55 3.15

No. 3257a has blue panels at the sides. Complete booklet sold for $12.95. Issued: No. 3257c, 5/8.

Expo 2010, Shanghai — A819

Designs: No. 3262, Australian Pavilion. No. 3263, Australian kookaburra mascot, Peng Peng.

2010, May 18 Perf. 14¾x14
3262 A819 55c multi 1.00 .80
3263 A819 55c multi 1.00 .80
  a. Pair, #3262-3263 2.00 1.60

UNESCO World Heritage Sites in Australia — A820

Designs: Nos. 3264, 3268, Purnululu National Park. Nos. 3265, 3269, Kakadu National Park. No. 3266, Gondwana Rainforests, horiz. No. 3267, Tasmanian Wilderness, horiz.

2010, May 25   **Perf. 14¾x14**
3264	A820	55c multi	1.00	1.00
3265	A820	55c multi	1.00	1.00
a.	Horiz. pair, #3264-3265		2.00	2.00

Perf. 14x14¾
3266	A820	$1.10 multi	2.25	1.60
3267	A820	$1.10 multi	2.25	1.60
a.	Horiz. pair, #3266-3267		4.50	3.25
	Nos. 3264-3267 (4)		6.50	5.20

Self-Adhesive
Serpentine Die Cut 11¼ Syncopated
3268	A820	55c multi	1.00	1.00
3269	A820	55c multi	1.00	1.00
a.	Vert. coil pair, #3268-3269		2.00	
b.	Booklet pane of 10, 5 each #3268-3269		10.00	

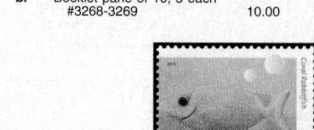

Fish — A821

Designs: 5c, Coral rabbitfish. Nos. 3271, 3278, 3283, Clown triggerfish. Nos. 3272, 3279, 3284, Spotted sweetlips. Nos. 3273, 3280, 3285, Golden damsel. Nos. 3274, 3281, 3286, Regal angelfish. $1.20, Saddle butterflyfish. $1.80, Chevron butterflyfish. $3, Orangefin anemonefish.

2010, June 21   **Litho.**   **Perf. 14x14½**
3270	A821	5c multi	.25	.25
3271	A821	60c multi	1.00	.25
3272	A821	60c multi	1.00	.25
a.	Souvenir sheet, #3271, 3272, 2 #3270		2.40	2.40
3273	A821	60c multi	1.00	.25
3274	A821	60c multi	1.00	.25
a.	Block or strip of 4, #3271-3274		4.00	1.00
3275	A821	$1.20 multi	2.00	1.00
3276	A821	$1.80 multi	3.00	1.50

Perf. 14½x14
Size: 50x30mm (#3277)
| 3277 | A821 | $3 multi | 5.00 | 2.50 |
| | Nos. 3270-3277 (8) | | 14.25 | 6.25 |

Coil Stamps
Self-Adhesive
Die Cut Perf. 12¾
3278	A821	60c multi	1.00	.25
3279	A821	60c multi	1.00	.25
3280	A821	60c multi	1.00	.25
3281	A821	60c multi	1.00	.25
a.	Horiz. strip of 4, #3278-3281		4.00	

Booklet Stamps
Serpentine Die Cut 11¼
3282	A821	5c multi	.25	.25
a.	Booklet pane of 20		4.00	
3283	A821	60c multi	1.00	.25
3284	A821	60c multi	1.00	.25
3285	A821	60c multi	1.00	.25
3286	A821	60c multi	1.00	.25
a.	Booklet pane of 10, 3 each #3283-3284, 2 each #3285-3286		10.00	
b.	Booklet pane of 20, 5 each #3283-3286		20.00	
	Nos. 3278-3286 (9)		8.25	2.25

Issued: No. 3272a, 8/4/10. Bangkok 2010 Intl. Stamp Exhibition (No. 3272a).

Beaches — A822

Designs: $1.50, Bay of Fires, Tasmania. $2.20, Cape Tribulation, Queensland. $4.30, Hellfire Bay, Western Australia, horiz.

2010, June 28   **Perf. 14¾x14**
| 3287 | A822 | $1.50 multi | 2.50 | 1.25 |
| 3288 | A822 | $2.20 multi | 3.75 | 1.90 |

Size: 50x30mm (#3289)
Perf. 14½x14
| 3289 | A822 | $4.30 multi | 7.25 | 3.75 |
| | Nos. 3287-3289 (3) | | 13.50 | 6.90 |

Booklet Stamps
Self-Adhesive
Serpentine Die Cut 11¼ Syncopated
3290	A822	$1.50 multi	2.50	1.25
a.	Booklet pane of 5		12.50	
3291	A822	$2.20 multi	3.75	1.90
a.	Booklet pane of 5		19.00	

With Personalized Photo at Right Like Type A692a
Serpentine Die Cut 11½x11¼ Syncopated
| 3292 | A822 | $1.50 multi | 3.75 | 3.75 |
| 3293 | A822 | $2.20 multi | 4.75 | 4.75 |

Nos. 3292-3293 each were printed in sheets of 20 and have personalized pictures and a straight edge at right, and lack separations between the stamp and the personalized photo. Sheets of 20 of No. 3292 sold for $43, and No. 3293 sold for $56.

Adopted Dogs — A823

Designs: Nos. 3294, 3299, Piper. Nos. 3295, 3300, Jessie. Nos. 3296, 3301, Buckley. Nos. 3297, 3302, Daisy. Nos. 3298, 3303, Tigger.

2010, June 29   **Perf. 14¾x14**
3294	A823	60c multi	1.00	1.00
3295	A823	60c multi	1.00	1.00
3296	A823	60c multi	1.00	1.00
3297	A823	60c multi	1.00	1.00
3298	A823	60c multi	1.00	1.00
a.	Horiz. strip of 5, #3294-3298		5.00	5.00
	Nos. 3294-3298 (5)		5.00	5.00

Self-Adhesive
Serpentine Die Cut 11¼ Syncopated
3299	A823	60c multi	1.00	.25
3300	A823	60c multi	1.00	.25
3301	A823	60c multi	1.00	.25
3302	A823	60c multi	1.00	.25
3303	A823	60c multi	1.00	.25
a.	Vert. coil strip of 5, #3299-3303		5.00	
b.	Booklet pane of 10, 2 each #3299-3303		10.00	
	Nos. 3299-3303 (5)		5.00	1.25

No. 3303a was produced by two different printers, Pemara and McKellar Renown. The stamps have the printer's name on the backing paper, but are essentially identical to each other.

Emergency Services — A824

000 Emergency Services emblem and: Nos. 3304, 3308, "Stay Focused, Stay Relevant, Stay on Line." Nos. 3305, 3309, Police Helicopter. Nos. 3306, 3310, Fire. Nos. 3307, 3311, Ambulance Cross.

2010, July 13   **Perf. 14¾x14**
3304	A824	60c multi	1.10	1.10
3305	A824	60c multi	1.10	1.10
3306	A824	60c multi	1.10	1.10
3307	A824	60c multi	1.10	1.10
a.	Horiz. strip of 4, #3304-3307		4.40	4.40
	Nos. 3304-3307 (4)		4.40	4.40

Self-Adhesive
Serpentine Die Cut 11¼ Syncopated
3308	A824	60c multi	1.10	.25
3309	A824	60c multi	1.10	.25
3310	A824	60c multi	1.10	.25
3311	A824	60c multi	1.10	.25
a.	Vert. coil strip of 4, #3308-3311		4.40	
b.	Booklet pane of 20, 5 each #3308-3311		22.00	
	Nos. 3308-3311 (4)		4.40	1.00

Southern Cross — A825

2010, July 19   **Perf. 14½x14**
3312	A825	60c Blue sky	1.10	.25
a.	Sheet of 20 + 20 labels		27.00	27.00
3313	A825	60c Purple & orange sky	1.10	1.10
a.	Horiz. pair, #3312-3313		2.25	2.25
b.	Sheet of 20 + 20 labels		27.00	27.00
c.	Perf. 14x14½, + label at bottom		1.40	1.40

Nos. 3312a and 3313b each sold for $12.95 and have labels depicting various National Rugby League and Australian Football League team emblems that could not be personalized. No. 3313c was issued in sheet of 10 + 10 labels depicting race horse Black Caviar that were sold in groups of 2 sheets that sold for $12.95.

Balloons — A826   Teddy Bear — A827

Wattle — A828   Flowers — A829

Tulips — A830   Roses — A831

Flowers and Champagne Flutes — A832   Wedding Rings — A833

2010, July 19   **Perf. 14¾x14**
3314	A826	60c multi	1.10	1.10
3315	A827	60c multi	1.10	1.10
3316	A828	60c multi	1.10	1.10
a.	Horiz. strip of 3, #3314-3316		3.30	3.30
3317	A829	60c multi	1.10	1.10
3318	A830	60c multi	1.10	1.10
3319	A831	60c multi	1.10	1.10
3320	A832	60c multi	1.10	1.10
a.	Block of 4, #3317-3320		4.40	4.40
3321	A833	$1.20 multi	2.25	2.25
	Nos. 3314-3321 (8)		9.95	9.95

Booklet Stamps
Self-Adhesive
Serpentine Die Cut 11¼ Syncopated
3322	A826	60c multi	1.10	.25
a.	Booklet pane of 10		11.00	
3323	A827	60c multi	1.10	.25
a.	Booklet pane of 10		11.00	
3324	A828	60c multi	1.10	.25
a.	Booklet pane of 10		11.00	
3325	A830	60c multi	1.10	.25
a.	Booklet pane of 10		11.00	
3326	A831	60c multi	1.10	.25
a.	Booklet pane of 10		11.00	
3327	A833	$1.20 multi	2.25	1.10
a.	Booklet pane of 10		22.50	
	Nos. 3322-3327 (6)		7.75	2.35

With Personalized Photo at Right Like Type A692a
Serpentine Die Cut 11½x11¼ Syncopated
3328	A826	60c multi	2.25	2.25
3329	A827	60c multi	2.25	2.25
3330	A828	60c multi	2.25	2.25
3331	A829	60c multi	2.25	2.25
3332	A830	60c multi	2.25	2.25
3333	A831	60c multi	2.25	2.25
3334	A832	60c multi	2.25	2.25
3335	A833	$1.20 multi	3.50	3.50
	Nos. 3328-3335 (8)		19.25	19.25

Nos. 3328-3335 each were printed in sheets of 20 and have personalized pictures and a straight edge at right, and lack separations between the stamp and the personalized photo. Sheets of 20 of Nos. 3328-3334 each sold for $25, and No. 3335 sold for $37. See No. 3401.

Australian Taxation Office, Cent. A834

2010, July 27   **Litho.**   **Perf. 14x14¾**
| 3336 | A834 | 60c multi | 1.10 | .85 |

Burke and Wills Expedition, 150th Anniv. A835

Designs: Nos. 3337, 3341, Explorers Robert Burke (1820-61) and William J. Wills (1834-61). Nos. 3338, 3342, Burke and Wills on horses leaving Melbourne. No. 3339, Expedition members returning from Gulf of Carpenteria. No. 3340, Expedition members heading towards Mt. Hopeless.

2010, Aug. 3   **Litho.**   **Perf. 14x14¾**
3337	A835	60c multi	1.10	1.10
a.	Booklet pane of 4		5.00	
3338	A835	60c multi	1.10	1.10
a.	Horiz. pair, #3337-3338		2.20	2.20
b.	Booklet pane of 4		5.00	
3339	A835	$1.20 multi	2.25	2.25
a.	Booklet pane of 2		5.00	
3340	A835	$1.20 multi	2.25	2.25
a.	Horiz. pair, #3339-3340		4.50	4.50
b.	Booklet pane of 2		5.00	—
	Complete booklet, #3337a, 3338b, 3339a, 3340b		20.00	
	Nos. 3337-3340 (4)		6.70	6.70

Coil Stamps
Self-Adhesive
Serpentine Die Cut 11¼ Syncopated
3341	A835	60c multi	1.10	.25
3342	A835	60c multi	1.10	.25
a.	Horiz. pair, #3341-3342		2.20	

Complete booklet sold for $10.95.
See Australian Antarctic Territory No. L149b.

Girl Guides, Cent. A836

Emblem, early Girl Guides and: 60c, Girl Guide with helmet and climbing rope. $1.50, Girl Guides wearing hats. $2.20, Olave Baden-Powell.

2010, Aug. 31   Litho.   Perf. 14x14¾

3343	A836	60c multi	1.10	1.10
3344	A836	$1.50 multi	2.75	2.75
3345	A836	$2.20 multi	4.00	4.00
	Nos. 3343-3345 (3)		7.85	7.85

Self-Adhesive
Serpentine Die Cut 11¼ Syncopated

3346	A836	60c multi	1.10	.25
a.	Booklet pane of 20		22.00	

Booklet Stamps

3347	A836	$1.50 multi	2.75	1.40
a.	Booklet pane of 5		14.00	
3348	A836	$2.20 multi	4.00	2.00
a.	Booklet pane of 5		20.00	
	Nos. 3346-3348 (3)		7.85	3.65

Dedication of National Service Memorial, Canberra A837

2010, Sept. 8   Litho.   Perf. 14x14¾

3349	A837	60c multi	1.10	1.10
a.	Additionally dated "2013" (#3349b)		1.25	1.25
b.	Booklet pane of 4 #3349a		5.00	

Issued: Nos. 3349a, 3349b, 3/5/13. No. 3349b was issued in booklet along with Nos. 1939c, 2710c, 2869e, 3107c and 3877a.

Booklet Stamp
Self-Adhesive
Serpentine Die Cut 11¼ Syncopated

3350	A837	60c multi	1.10	.25
a.	Booklet pane of 10		11.00	

Long Weekend Vacations A838

People on weekend vacations: Nos. 3351, 3356, Boating at beach, 1950s. Nos. 3352, 3357, Camping, 1960s. Nos. 3353, 3358, Surfing at beach, 1970s. Nos. 3354, 3359, Houseboating on river, 1980s. Nos. 3355, 3360, At winter resort, 1990s.

2010, Sept. 22   Perf. 14x14¾

3351	A838	60c multi	1.25	1.25
a.	Booklet pane of 4		5.50	
3352	A838	60c multi	1.25	1.25
a.	Booklet pane of 4		5.50	
3353	A838	60c multi	1.25	—
a.	Booklet pane of 4		5.50	
3354	A838	60c multi	1.25	1.25
a.	Booklet pane of 4		5.50	
3355	A838	60c multi	1.25	1.25
a.	Booklet pane of 4		5.50	
	Complete booklet, #3351a-3355a		27.50	
b.	Horiz. strip of 5, #3351-3355		6.25	6.25
	Nos. 3351-3355 (5)		6.25	6.25

Self-Adhesive
Serpentine Die Cut 11¼ Syncopated

3356	A838	60c multi	1.25	.25
3357	A838	60c multi	1.25	.25
3358	A838	60c multi	1.25	.25
3359	A838	60c multi	1.25	.25
3360	A838	60c multi	1.25	.25
a.	Horiz. coil strip of 5, #3356-3360		6.25	
b.	Booklet pane of 10, 2 each #3356-3360		12.50	
	Nos. 3356-3360 (5)		6.25	1.25

Complete booklet sold for $13.95.

Care for Wildlife — A839

Designs: Nos. 3361, 3367, Common wombat. Nos. 3362, 3368, Eastern gray kangaroo. Nos. 3363, 3369, Koala. Nos. 3364, 3370, Gray-headed flying fox. Nos. 3365, 3371, Southern boobook. $1.20, Ringtail possum.

2010, Oct. 5   Litho.   Perf. 14¾x14
Denomination Color

3361	A839	60c orange brown	1.25	1.25
3362	A839	60c blue	1.25	1.25
3363	A839	60c green	1.25	1.25
3364	A839	60c red brown	1.25	1.25
3365	A839	60c bister	1.25	1.25
a.	Horiz. strip of 5, #3361-3365		6.25	6.25
3366	A839	$1.20 red	2.40	1.75
a.	Souvenir sheet of 6, #3361-3366		8.75	8.75
	Nos. 3361-3366 (6)		8.65	8.00

Self-Adhesive
Serpentine Die Cut 11¼ Syncopated

3367	A839	60c orange brown	1.25	.25
3368	A839	60c blue	1.25	.25
3369	A839	60c green	1.25	.25
3370	A839	60c red brown	1.25	.25
3371	A839	60c bister	1.25	.25
a.	Vert. coil strip of 5, #3367-3371		6.25	
b.	Booklet pane of 10, 2 each #3367-3371		12.50	
	Nos. 3367-3371 (5)		6.25	1.25

Canonization of St. Mary MacKillop (1842-1909) A840

2010, Oct. 18   Perf. 14¾x14

3372	A840	60c multi	1.25	.95

Kingfishers A841

Designs: 60c, Red-backed kingfisher. $1.20, Sacred kingfisher. $1.80, Blue-winged kookaburra. $3, Yellow-billed kingfisher.

2010, Oct. 26   Perf. 14¾x14

3373	A841	60c multi	1.25	1.25
a.	Additionally dated "2013"		1.25	1.25
3374	A841	$1.20 multi	2.50	1.90
a.	Additionally dated "2013"		2.40	2.40
3375	A841	$1.80 multi	3.75	1.90
a.	Additionally dated "2013"		3.50	3.50
3376	A841	$3 multi	6.25	3.25
a.	Additionally dated "2013"		5.75	5.75
b.	Booklet pane of 4, #3373a, 3374a, 3375a, 3376a		13.00	—
	Nos. 3373-3376 (4)		13.75	8.30

Issued: Nos. 3373a, 3374a, 3375a, 3376a, 3376b, 5/11/13. No. 3376b was issued in a booklet also containing Nos. 3151c, 3665b and 3925a.

Self-Adhesive
Serpentine Die Cut 11¼ Syncopated

3377	A841	60c multi	1.25	.25
a.	Booklet pane of 10		12.50	

150th Running of the Melbourne Cup Horse Race — A842

Designs: No. 3378, Melbourne Cup. Nos. 3379, 3382, Carbine, 1890 winner. Nos. 3380, 3383, Phar Lap, 1930 winner, horiz. Nos. 3381, 3384, Saintly, 1996 winner, horiz.

2010, Nov. 1   Litho.   Perf. 14¾x14

3378	A842	60c multi	1.25	.95
a.	Booklet pane of 4		7.25	

Perf. 14x14¾

3379	A842	60c multi	1.25	1.25
a.	Booklet pane of 4		7.25	
3380	A842	60c multi	1.25	1.25
a.	Booklet pane of 4		7.25	

3381	A842	60c multi	1.25	1.25
a.	Booklet pane of 4		7.25	—
	Complete booklet, #3378a, 3379a, 3380a, 3381a		29.00	
b.	Souvenir sheet, #3378-3381		5.00	5.00
	Nos. 3378-3381 (4)		5.00	4.70

No. 3381b exists imperf from a telephone drawing at a substantial premium over face value. Value for single souvenir sheet, $15.

Booklet Stamps
Self-Adhesive
Serpentine Die Cut 11¼ Syncopated

3382	A842	60c multi	1.25	.25
3383	A842	60c multi	1.25	.25
3384	A842	60c multi	1.25	.25
a.	Booklet pane of 20, 7 each #3382-3383, 6 #3384		25.00	
	Nos. 3382-3384 (3)		3.75	75.00

Complete booklet sold for $13.95 and also included imperforate and gummed lithographed pages reproducing pairs of Nos. 337, 693, 694, 2104 and 2106 that were not valid for postage.

Christmas
A843   A844

Designs: Nos. 3385, 3390, 3393, 3396, Girl writing letter to Santa Claus. Nos. 3386, 3389, 3394, 3395, Santa Claus reading letter. Nos. 3387, 3391, Adoration of the Magi. $1.30, Adoration of the Shepherds.

2010, Nov. 1   Litho.   Perf. 14¾x14

3385	A843	55c multi	1.10	1.10
3386	A843	55c multi	1.10	1.10
a.	Horiz. pair, #3385-3386		2.25	2.25
3387	A844	55c multi	1.10	1.10
3388	A844	$1.30 multi	2.75	2.75
	Nos. 3385-3388 (4)		6.05	6.05

Booklet Stamps
Self-Adhesive
Serpentine Die Cut 11¼ Syncopated

3389	A843	55c multi	1.10	.25
3390	A843	55c multi	1.10	.25
a.	Booklet pane of 20, 10 each #3389-3390		22.00	
3391	A844	55c multi	1.10	.25
a.	Booklet pane of 20		22.00	
3392	A844	$1.30 multi	2.75	1.40
a.	Booklet pane of 5		14.00	

Litho. With Foil Application

3393	A843	55c multi	1.10	.25
a.	Booklet pane of 10		11.00	
3394	A843	55c multi	1.10	.25
a.	Booklet pane of 10		11.00	
	Nos. 3389-3394 (6)		8.25	2.65

With Personalized Photo at Right Like Type A692a
Litho.
Self-Adhesive
Serpentine Die Cut 11½x11¼ Syncopated

3395	A843	55c multi	2.50	2.50
3396	A843	55c multi	2.50	2.50

Nos. 3395-3396 were printed together in sheets of 20 (10 of each design), and have personalized pictures and a straight edge at right and lack separations between the stamp and the personalized photo. Sheets of 20 sold for $24.

Champagne Flutes Type of 2010 and

Roses — A845   Hearts and Flowers — A846

2011, Jan. 18   Perf. 14¾x14

3397	A845	60c multi	1.25	1.25
3398	A846	60c multi	1.25	1.25
a.	Horiz. pair, #3397-3398		2.50	2.50

Booklet Stamps
Self-Adhesive
Serpentine Die Cut 11¼ Syncopated

3399	A845	60c multi	1.25	.25
a.	Booklet pane of 12		12.50	
3400	A846	60c multi	1.25	.25
a.	Booklet pane of 12		12.50	
3401	A832	60c multi	1.25	.60
a.	Booklet pane of 12		12.50	
	Nos. 3399-3401 (3)		3.75	1.10

With Personalized Photo at Right Like Type A692a
Serpentine Die Cut 11½x11¼ Syncopated

3402	A845	60c multi	2.50	2.50
3403	A846	60c multi	2.50	2.50

Nos. 3395-3396 each were printed in sheets of 20 and have personalized pictures and a straight edge at right and lack separations between the stamp and the personalized photo. Sheets of 20 of Nos. 3402-3403 each sold for $25.
No. 3401 dated 2010.

Famous Women — A848

Designs: Nos. 3404, 3408, Eva Cox, feminist. Nos. 3405, 3409, Germaine Greer, writer on feminist topics. Nos. 3406, 3410, Elizabeth Evatt, jurist. Nos. 3407, 3411, Anne Summers, writer.

2011, Jan. 20   Perf. 14¾x14

3404	A848	60c multi	1.25	1.25
3405	A848	60c multi	1.25	1.25
3406	A848	60c multi	1.25	1.25
3407	A848	60c multi	1.25	1.25
a.	Horiz. strip of 4, #3404-3407		5.00	5.00
	Nos. 3404-3407 (4)		5.00	5.00

Booklet Stamps
Self-Adhesive
Serpentine Die Cut 11¼ Syncopated

3408	A848	60c multi	1.25	.25
3409	A848	60c multi	1.25	.25
3410	A848	60c multi	1.25	.25
3411	A848	60c multi	1.25	.25
a.	Booklet pane of 20, 5 each #3408-3411		25.00	
	Nos. 3408-3411 (4)		5.00	1.00

Intl. Women's Day, Cent. A849

2011, Feb. 15   Perf. 14x14¾

3412	A849	60c multi	1.25	.95
a.	Miniature sheet of 10		12.50	12.50

Military Aircraft A850

Designs: Nos. 3413, 3417, F-111. Nos. 3414, 3418, F/A-18F. $1.20, Wedge Tail. $3, C-17.

2011, Feb. 22   Perf. 14x14¾

3413	A850	60c multi	1.25	1.25
3414	A850	60c multi	1.25	1.25
3415	A850	$1.20 multi	2.40	1.90
a.	Souvenir sheet of 4, #3337, 3339, 3413, 3415		7.75	7.75
3416	A850	$3 multi	6.00	4.50
a.	Souvenir sheet of 4, #3413-3416		11.00	11.00
	Nos. 3413-3416 (4)		10.90	8.90

Booklet Stamps
Self-Adhesive
Serpentine Die Cut 11¼ Syncopated

3417	A850	60c multi	1.25	.25
3418	A850	60c multi	1.25	.25
a.		Booklet pane of 10, 5 each		
		#3417-3418	12.50	

Issued: No. 3415a, 3/31. Sydney Stamp Expo 2011 (No. 3415a).

Flowers — A851

Designs: Nos. 3419, 3424, Gerbera daisy. Nos. 3420, 3425, Jacarandas. Nos. 3421, 3426, Australian everlasting. Nos. 3422, 3427, Violet. Nos. 3423, 3428, Tulip.

2011, Mar. 8   Litho.   *Perf. 14¾x14*

3419	A851	60c multi	1.25	1.25
a.		Booklet pane of 4	5.25	
3420	A851	60c multi	1.25	1.25
a.		Booklet pane of 4	5.25	
3421	A851	60c multi	1.25	1.25
a.		Booklet pane of 4	5.25	
3422	A851	60c multi	1.25	1.25
a.		Booklet pane of 4	5.25	
3423	A851	60c multi	1.25	1.25
a.		Booklet pane of 4	5.25	—
		Complete booklet, #3419a, 3420a, 3421a, 3422a, 3423a	27.00	
b.		Horiz. strip of 5, #3419-3423	6.25	6.25
		Nos. 3419-3423 (5)	6.25	6.25

Self-Adhesive
Serpentine Die Cut 11¼ Syncopated

3424	A851	60c multi	1.25	.25
3425	A851	60c multi	1.25	.25
3426	A851	60c multi	1.25	.25
3427	A851	60c multi	1.25	.25
3428	A851	60c multi	1.25	.25
a.		Vert. coil strip of 5, #3424-3428	6.25	
b.		Booklet pane of 20, 4 each #3424-3428	25.00	
		Nos. 3424-3428 (5)	6.25	1.25

Complete booklet sold for $12.95.

Paintings of Flowers in National Gallery of Victoria A852

Paintings: Nos. 3429, 3434, A Bunch of Flowers, by Nora Heysen. Nos. 3430, 3435, Camellias, by Arnold Shore. Nos. 3431, 3436, Fruit and Flowers, by Vida Lahey. Nos. 3432, 3437, Still Life, Zinnias, by Roy de Maistre. Nos. 3433, 3438, A Cottage Bunch, by Hans Heysen.

2011, Mar. 22   *Perf. 14x14¾*

3429	A852	60c multi	1.25	1.25
3430	A852	60c multi	1.25	1.25
3431	A852	60c multi	1.25	1.25
3432	A852	60c multi	1.25	1.25
3433	A852	60c multi	1.25	1.25
a.		Horiz. strip of 5, #3429-3433	6.25	6.25
		Nos. 3429-3433 (5)	6.25	6.25

Self-Adhesive
Serpentine Die Cut 11¼ Syncopated

3434	A852	60c multi	1.25	.25
3435	A852	60c multi	1.25	.25
3436	A852	60c multi	1.25	.25
3437	A852	60c multi	1.25	.25
3438	A852	60c multi	1.25	.25
a.		Horiz. coil strip of 5, #3434-3438	6.25	
b.		Booklet pane of 10, 2 each #3434-3438	12.50	
		Nos. 3434-3438 (5)	6.25	1.25

Lake Eyre — A853

Lake Eyre: 60c, In dry season. $1.55, With new growth. $2.25, Bird life. $3.10, In flood.

2011, Apr. 4   *Perf. 14½x14*

3439	A853	60c multi	1.25	.65
3440	A853	$1.55 multi	3.25	3.25
3441	A853	$2.25 multi	4.75	4.75
3442	A853	$3.10 multi	6.50	3.25
		Nos. 3439-3442 (4)	15.75	11.90

Booklet Stamps
Self-Adhesive
Serpentine Die Cut 11¼

3443	A853	$1.55 multi	3.25	1.60
a.		Booklet pane of 5	16.50	
3444	A853	$2.25 multi	4.75	2.40
a.		Booklet pane of 5	24.00	

A854

Portraits of Queen Elizabeth II by: 60c, Brian Dunlop, 1984. $2.25, Rolf Harris, 2005.

2011, Apr. 5   *Perf. 14¾x14*

3445	A854	60c multi	1.25	.65
3446	A854	$2.25 multi	4.75	2.40
a.		Souvenir sheet of 2, #3445-3446	6.00	6.00

Queen Elizabeth II, 85th birthday.

A855

Background color: 60c, Pale olive green. $2.25, White.

2011, Apr. 12   *Perf. 14¾x14*

3447	A855	60c multi	1.25	1.25
3448	A855	$2.25 multi	4.75	2.40
a.		Souvenir sheet of 2, #3447-3448	6.00	6.00

Booklet Stamp
Self-Adhesive
Serpentine Die Cut 11¼ Syncopated

3449	A855	60c multi	1.25	.25
a.		Booklet pane of 10	12.50	

Wedding of Prince William and Catherine Middleton.

Wedding Photograph of Prince William and Wife Catherine A856

2011, May 4   *Perf. 14¼*

3450	A856	60c multi	1.25	1.25

Booklet Stamp
Self-Adhesive
Serpentine Die Cut 11¼ Syncopated

3451	A856	60c multi	1.25	.25
a.		Booklet pane of 10	12.50	

Dame Nellie Melba (1861-1931), Operatic Soprano — A857

2011, May 10   *Perf. 14¾x14*

3452	A857	60c multi	1.25	1.25

Booklet Stamp
Self-Adhesive
Serpentine Die Cut 11¼ Syncopated

3453	A857	60c multi	1.25	.25
a.		Booklet pane of 20	25.00	

Native Agricultural Products A858

Designs: Nos. 3454, 3458, Eucalyptus oil. Nos. 3455, 3459, Australian honey. Nos. 3456, 3460, Macadamia nuts. Nos. 3457, 3461, Tea tree oil.

2011, May 17   *Perf. 14x14¾*

3454	A858	60c multi	1.25	1.25
3455	A858	60c multi	1.25	1.25
3456	A858	60c multi	1.25	1.25
3457	A858	60c multi	1.25	1.25
a.		Horiz. strip of 4, #3454-3457	5.00	5.00
		Nos. 3454-3457 (4)	5.00	5.00

Self-Adhesive
Serpentine Die Cut 11¼ Syncopated

3458	A858	60c multi	1.25	.25
3459	A858	60c multi	1.25	.25
3460	A858	60c multi	1.25	.25
3461	A858	60c multi	1.25	.25
a.		Horiz. coil strip of 4, #3458-3461	5.00	
b.		Booklet pane of 10, 4 #3458, 2 each #3459-3461	12.50	
		Nos. 3458-3461 (4)	5.00	1.00

Southern Cross With Sports Team Emblem — A859

Booklet Stamps
Self-Adhesive
With Emblem of Australian Rules Football Team
Adelaide Crows
Serpentine Die Cut 10¾x11¼ Syncopated

2011, Apr. 12   Litho.

3462	A859	60c Emblem at R	1.50	.75
3463	A859	60c Emblem at L	1.50	.75
a.		Booklet pane of 10, 5 each #3462-3463	15.00	

Carlton Blues

3464	A859	60c Emblem at R	1.50	.75
3465	A859	60c Emblem at L	1.50	.75
a.		Booklet pane of 10, 5 each #3464-3465	15.00	

Essendon Bombers

3466	A859	60c Emblem at R	1.50	.75
3467	A859	60c Emblem at L	1.50	.75
a.		Booklet pane of 10, 5 each #3466-3467	15.00	

Geelong Cats

3468	A859	60c Emblem at R	1.50	.75
3469	A859	60c Emblem at L	1.50	.75
a.		Booklet pane of 10, 5 each #3468-3469	15.00	

Gold Coast Suns

3470	A859	60c Emblem at R	1.50	.75
3471	A859	60c Emblem at L	1.50	.75
a.		Booklet pane of 10, 5 each #3470-3471	15.00	

North Melbourne Kangaroos

3472	A859	60c Emblem at R	1.50	.75
3473	A859	60c Emblem at L	1.50	.75
a.		Booklet pane of 10, 5 each #3472-3473	15.00	

Port Adelaide Power

3474	A859	60c Emblem at R	1.50	.75
3475	A859	60c Emblem at L	1.50	.75
a.		Booklet pane of 10, 5 each #3474-3475	15.00	

West Coast Eagles

3476	A859	60c Emblem at R	1.50	.75
3477	A859	60c Emblem at L	1.50	.75
a.		Booklet pane of 10, 5 each #3476-3477	15.00	

Western Bulldogs

3478	A859	60c Emblem at R	1.50	.75
3479	A859	60c Emblem at L	1.50	.75
a.		Booklet pane of 10, 5 each #3478-3479	15.00	

Purple & Orange Sky
Brisbane Lions

3480	A859	60c Emblem at R	1.50	.75
3481	A859	60c Emblem at L	1.50	.75
a.		Booklet pane of 10, 5 each #3480-3481	15.00	

Collingwood Magpies

3482	A859	60c Emblem at R	1.50	.75
3483	A859	60c Emblem at L	1.50	.75
a.		Booklet pane of 10, 5 each #3482-3483	15.00	

Fremantle Dockers

3484	A859	60c Emblem at R	1.50	.75
3485	A859	60c Emblem at L	1.50	.75
a.		Booklet pane of 10, 5 each #3484-3485	15.00	

Hawthorn Hawks

3486	A859	60c Emblem at R	1.50	.75
3487	A859	60c Emblem at L	1.50	.75
a.		Booklet pane of 10, 5 each #3486-3487	15.00	

Melbourne Demons

3488	A859	60c Emblem at R	1.50	.75
3489	A859	60c Emblem at L	1.50	.75
a.		Booklet pane of 10, 5 each #3488-3489	15.00	

Richmond Tigers

3490	A859	60c Emblem at R	1.50	.75
3491	A859	60c Emblem at L	1.50	.75
a.		Booklet pane of 10, 5 each #3490-3491	15.00	

St. Kilda Saints

3492	A859	60c Emblem at R	1.50	.75
3493	A859	60c Emblem at L	1.50	.75
a.		Booklet pane of 10, 5 each #3492-3493	15.00	

Sydney Swans

3494	A859	60c Emblem at R	1.50	.75
3495	A859	60c Emblem at L	1.50	.75
a.		Booklet pane of 10, 5 each #3494-3495	15.00	

Blue Sky
With National Rugby League Emblems
North Queensland Cowboys

3496	A859	60c Emblem at R	1.50	.75
3497	A859	60c Emblem at L	1.50	.75
a.		Booklet pane of 10, 5 each #3496-3497	15.00	

St. George Illawarra Dragons

3498	A859	60c Emblem at R	1.50	.75
3499	A859	60c Emblem at L	1.50	.75
a.		Booklet pane of 10, 5 each #3498-3499	15.00	

Parramatta Eels

3500	A859	60c Emblem at R	1.50	.75
3501	A859	60c Emblem at L	1.50	.75
a.		Booklet pane of 10, 5 each #3500-3501	15.00	

Newcastle Knights

3502	A859	60c Emblem at R	1.50	.75
3503	A859	60c Emblem at L	1.50	.75
a.		Booklet pane of 10, 5 each #3502-3503	15.00	

Penrith Panthers

3504	A859	60c Emblem at R	1.50	.75
3505	A859	60c Emblem at L	1.50	.75
a.		Booklet pane of 10, 5 each #3504-3505	15.00	

Canberra Raiders

3506	A859	60c Emblem at R	1.50	.75
3507	A859	60c Emblem at L	1.50	.75
a.		Booklet pane of 10, 5 each #3506-3507	15.00	

Sydney Roosters

3508	A859	60c Emblem at R	1.50	.75
3509	A859	60c Emblem at L	1.50	.75
a.		Booklet pane of 10, 5 each #3508-3509	15.00	

Cronulla Sutherland Sharks

3510	A859	60c Emblem at R	1.50	.75
3511	A859	60c Emblem at L	1.50	.75
a.		Booklet pane of 10, 5 each #3510-3511	15.00	

Gold Coast Titans

3512	A859	60c Emblem at R	1.50	.75
3513	A859	60c Emblem at L	1.50	.75
a.		Booklet pane of 10, 5 each #3512-3513	15.00	

Purple & Orange Sky
Brisbane Broncos

3514	A859	60c Emblem at R	1.50	.75
3515	A859	60c Emblem at L	1.50	.75
a.		Booklet pane of 10, 5 each #3514-3515	15.00	

Canterbury-Bankstown Bulldogs

3516	A859	60c Emblem at R	1.50	.75
3517	A859	60c Emblem at L	1.50	.75
a.		Booklet pane of 10, 5 each #3516-3517	15.00	

South Sydney Rabbitohs

3518	A859	60c Emblem at R	1.50	.75
3519	A859	60c Emblem at L	1.50	.75
a.		Booklet pane of 10, 5 each #3518-3519	15.00	

Manly Warringah Sea Eagles

3520	A859	60c Emblem at R	1.50	.75
3521	A859	60c Emblem at L	1.50	.75
a.		Booklet pane of 10, 5 each #3520-3521	15.00	

Melbourne Storm

3522	A859	60c Emblem at R	1.50	.75
3523	A859	60c Emblem at L	1.50	.75
a.		Booklet pane of 10, 5 each #3522-3523	15.00	

New Zealand Warriors

3524	A859	60c Emblem at R	1.50	.75
3525	A859	60c Emblem at L	1.50	.75
a.		Booklet pane of 10, 5 each #3524-3525	15.00	

Wests Tigers

3526	A859	60c Emblem at R	1.50	.75
3527	A859	60c Emblem at L	1.50	.75
a.		Booklet pane of 10, 5 each #3526-3527	15.00	
		Nos. 3462-3527 (66)	99.00	49.50

Each booklet, Nos. 3463a-3527a, sold for $6.95. Stamps with team emblem at right have straight edge at right, and stamps with team emblem at left have straight edge at left.

Australian Navy, Cent. A860

Sailor and: Nos. 3528, 3530, HMAS Australia and biplane. Nos. 3529, 3531, HMAS Sydney and helicopter.

2011, June 14 — Perf. 14x14¾

3528	A860	60c multi	1.40	1.40
3529	A860	60c multi	1.40	1.40
a.		Horiz. pair, #3528-3529	2.80	2.80

Booklet Stamps
Self-Adhesive
Serpentine Die Cut 11¼ Syncopated

3530	A860	60c multi	1.40	.25
3531	A860	60c multi	1.40	.25
a.		Booklet pane of 20, 10 each #3530-3531	28.00	

A861

Baby animals: 60c, Bilby. $1.60, Dingo. $1.65, Kangaroo. $2.35, Koala. $4.70, Sugar glider.

2011, July 1 — Litho. — Perf. 14¾x14

3532	A861	60c multi	1.40	1.10
3533	A861	$1.60 multi	3.50	1.75
a.		Souvenir sheet of 1	3.50	3.50
3534	A861	$1.65 multi	3.50	3.50
a.		Souvenir sheet of 2, #3533-3534	7.00	7.00
b.		Souvenir sheet of 1	3.50	3.50
c.		Additionally dated "2013"	4.25	4.25
d.		Booklet pane of 4, #1195a, 2352a, 3097a, 3534c	12.50	—
3535	A861	$2.35 multi	5.00	5.00
a.		Souvenir sheet of 2	9.75	9.75
3536	A861	$4.70 multi	10.00	5.00
		Nos. 3532-3536 (5)	23.40	16.35

Issued: No. 3534a, 7/28; No. 3535a, 6/18/12. Nos. 3533a, 3534b, 11/11. PhilaNippon '11 World Stamp Exhibition, Yokohama (No. 3534a). 2012 World Stamp Championship, Indonesia (No. 3535a). China 2011 Intl. Stamp Exhibition, Wuxi (Nos. 3533a, 3534b). Nos. 3534c, 3534d, 5/10/13. No. 3534d was

---

issued in a booklet also containing Nos. 1003b, 1284b, and 3918.

Booklet Stamps
Self-Adhesive
Serpentine Die Cut 11¼ Syncopated

3537	A861	$1.65 multi	3.50	1.75
a.		Booklet pane of 5	17.50	
3538	A861	$2.35 multi	5.00	2.50
a.		Booklet pane of 5	25.00	

With Personalized Photo at Right
Like Type A692a
Serpentine Die Cut 11½x11¼ Syncopated

3539	A861	$1.60 multi	4.75	4.75
3540	A861	$1.65 multi	5.00	5.00
3541	A861	$2.35 multi	11.50	11.50
		Nos. 3539-3541 (3)	21.25	21.25

Nos. 3539-3541 each were printed in sheets of 20 and have personalized pictures and at straight edge at right, and lack separations between the stamp and the personalized photo. Sheets of 20 of No. 3539 sold for $45; No. 3540, $46; No. 3541, $106.

A862

2011, July 5 — Perf. 14¾x14

3542	A862	60c yellow & black	1.40	1.10

Amnesty International, 50th anniv.

Living Australian A863

Photographs of Australian scenes: Nos. 3543, 3548, Boy and dog on beach. Nos. 3544, 3549, Children with flags painted on faces hugging. Nos. 3545, 3550, Reflection in sunglasses of sports fans in stadium. Nos. 3546, 3551, Aboriginal boy performing wedge tail eagle dance. Nos. 3547, 3552, Kangaroo resting on beach.

2011, July 5 — Perf. 14x14¾
Denomination Color

3543	A863	60c orange	1.40	1.40
3544	A863	60c purple	1.40	1.40
3545	A863	60c green	1.40	1.40
3546	A863	60c red violet	1.40	1.40
3547	A863	60c blue	1.40	1.40
a.		Horiz. strip of 5, #3543-3547	7.00	7.00

Self-Adhesive
Serpentine Die Cut 11¼ Syncopated

3548	A863	60c orange	1.40	.25
3549	A863	60c purple	1.40	.25
3550	A863	60c green	1.40	.25
3551	A863	60c red violet	1.40	.25
3552	A863	60c blue	1.40	.25
a.		Horiz. coil strip of 5, #3548-3552	7.00	
b.		Booklet pane of 10, 2 each #3548-3552	14.00	
		Nos. 3548-3552 (5)	7.00	1.25

Skiing — A864

Designs: 60c, Child learning to ski. $1.60, Snowboarder, horiz. $1.65, Downhill skier, horiz.

2011, July 19 — Perf. 14¾x14

3553	A864	60c multi	1.25	1.25

Perf. 14x14¾

3554	A864	$1.60 multi	3.50	3.50
3555	A864	$1.65 multi	3.50	3.50
		Nos. 3553-3555 (3)	8.25	8.25

Self-Adhesive
Coil Stamp
Serpentine Die Cut 11¼ Syncopated

3556	A864	60c multi	1.25	.25

Booklet Stamps

3557	A864	$1.60 multi	3.50	1.75
a.		Booklet pane of 5	17.50	
3558	A864	$1.65 multi	3.50	1.75
a.		Booklet pane of 5	17.50	
		Nos. 3556-3558 (3)	8.25	3.75

Items Depicted on Australian States Stamps — A865

Designs: No. 3559, Kangaroo and lyrebird. No. 3560, Black swan and Southern Cross.

2011, July 28 — Perf. 14x13½

3559	A865	$2 pale grn & blue	4.25	2.10
3560	A865	$2 pink & blue	4.25	2.10
a.		Pair, #3559-3560	8.50	4.25
b.		Souvenir sheet of 2, #3559-3560	8.50	4.25

A limited edition of No. 3560b with a gold overprint in the sheet margin exists.

Worldwide Fund for Nature (WWF), 50th Anniv. A866

Designs: No. 3561, Quokka. No. 3562, Southern elephant seal. No. 3563, Dugong. No. 3564, Christmas Island shrew.

2011, Aug. 30 — Litho. — Perf. 14x14¾

3561	A866	60c multi	1.25	.95
3562	A866	60c multi	1.25	.95
3563	A866	60c multi	1.25	.95
3564	A866	60c multi	1.25	.95
a.		Block of 4, #3561-3564	5.00	4.00
b.		Souvenir sheet of 4, #3561-3564, #3561 at UL	5.00	5.00
c.		Souvenir sheet of 4, #3561-3564, #3562 at UL	5.00	5.00
d.		Souvenir sheet of 4, #3561-3564, #3563 at UL	5.00	5.00
e.		Souvenir sheet of 4, #3561-3564, #3564 at UL	5.00	5.00
		Nos. 3561-3564 (4)	5.00	3.80

Along with the "Australia" inscription at left, inscribed at the bottom above the animal's name is "Australian Antarctic Territory" on No. 3562, "Cocos (Keeling) Islands" on No. 3563, and "Christmas Island" on No. 3564. All recent stamps of the Australian possessions of Australian Antarctic Territory, Cocos Islands and Christmas Island are doubly-inscribed with "Australia" and the possession's name, and all stamps inscribed "Australia," "Australian Antarctic Territory," "Cocos Islands," or "Christmas Island" are valid for postage anywhere in those four areas. As there was no attempt to make the stamps bearing the names of these possessions in this set available separately in those locations they will be listed here only and not in the listings for each of the possessions.

2011 Presidents Cup Golf Tournament, Melbourne — A867

Designs: Nos. 3565, 3570, Hand on golf club. Nos. 3566, 3569B, 3571, Presidents Cup. Nos. 3567, 1572, Golf shoes, glove and ball. $1.65, Golf club and ball. $2.35, Clubs in golf bag.

2011, Sept. 27 — Perf. 14

3565	A867	60c multi	1.25	
3566	A867	60c multi	1.25	
3567	A867	60c multi	1.25	1..
a.		Horiz. strip of 3, #3565-3567	3.75	3.75
3568	A867	$1.65 multi	3.25	3.25
3569	A867	$2.35 multi	4.75	4.75
a.		Souvenir sheet of 5, #3565-3569	12.00	12.00
		Nos. 3565-3569 (5)	11.75	11.75

Litho. & Embossed With Foil Application

3569B	A867	60c multi	1.25	1.25

No. 3569B was printed in sheets of 15 that sold for $9.45.

Litho.
Self-Adhesive
Serpentine Die Cut 11¼ Syncopated

3570	A867	60c multi	1.25	.25
3571	A867	60c multi	1.25	.25
3572	A867	60c multi	1.25	.25
a.		Booklet pane of 10, 4 each # 3570-3571, 2 #3572	12.50	
b.		Vert. coil strip of 3, #3570-3572	3.75	
3573	A867	$1.65 multi	3.25	1.60
a.		Booklet pane of 5	16.50	
3574	A867	$2.35 multi	4.75	2.40
a.		Booklet pane of 5	24.00	
		Nos. 3570-3574 (5)	11.75	4.75

Mythical Creatures — A868

Designs: Nos. 3575, 3581, Fairy. Nos. 3576, 3582, Troll. Nos. 3577, 3583, Mermaid. Nos. 3578, 3584, Griffin. Nos. 3579, 3585, Unicorn. $1.20, Dragon.

2011, Oct. 4 — Litho. — Perf. 14¾x14

3575	A868	60c multi	1.25	1.25
3576	A868	60c multi	1.25	1.25
3577	A868	60c multi	1.25	1.25
3578	A868	60c multi	1.25	1.25
3579	A868	60c multi	1.25	1.25
a.		Horiz. strip of 5, #3575-3579	6.25	6.25
3580	A868	$1.20 multi	2.40	1.90
a.		Souvenir sheet of 6, #3575-3580	8.75	8.75
		Nos. 3575-3580 (6)	8.65	8.15

Booklet Stamps
Self-Adhesive
Serpentine Die Cut 11¼ Syncopated

3581	A868	60c multi	1.25	.25
3582	A868	60c multi	1.25	.25
3583	A868	60c multi	1.25	.25
3584	A868	60c multi	1.25	.25
3585	A868	60c multi	1.25	.25
a.		Booklet pane of 10, 2 each #3581-3585	12.50	
b.		Booklet pane of 20, 4 each #3581-3585	25.00	
		Nos. 3581-3585 (5)	6.25	1.25

Commonwealth Heads of Government Meeting, Perth — A869

2011, Oct. 18 — Perf. 14½x14

3586	A869	60c multi	1.25	.95

Diplomatic Relations Between Australia and South Korea, 50th Anniv. — A870

Designs: 60c, Korean woman playing haegeum. $1.65, Australian aborigine playing didgeridoo.

2011, Oct. 31 — Perf. 13¼x13

3587	A870	60c multi	1.25	.95

Stamp
...Adhesive
...ie Cut 11¼ Syncopated

	$1.65 multi	3.50	1.75
	Booklet pane of 5	17.50	

See South Korea No. 2373.

Christmas
A871   A872

Designs: Nos. 3590, 3595, Madonna and Child. Nos. 3591, 3596, 3599, 3601, Star on Christmas tree. Nos. 3592, 3597, 3600, 3602, Star and gift. 60c, Star and fruit tree branches. $1.50, Magi and camels, horiz.

2011, Oct. 31   Litho.   Perf. 14¾x14

3590	A871	55c multi	1.10	1.10
3591	A872	55c multi	1.10	1.10
3592	A872	55c multi	1.10	1.10
a.	Horiz. pair, #3591-3592		2.20	2.20
3593	A872	60c multi	1.25	1.25

Perf. 14x14¾

3594	A871	$1.50 multi	3.25	3.25
	Nos. 3590-3594 (5)		7.80	7.80

Booklet Stamps
Self-Adhesive
Serpentine Die Cut 11¼ Syncopated

3595	A871	55c multi	1.10	.25
a.	Booklet pane of 20 + 20 etiquettes		22.00	
3596	A872	55c multi	1.10	.25
3597	A872	55c multi	1.10	.25
a.	Booklet pane of 20, 10 each #3596-3597 + 20 etiquettes		22.00	
3598	A871	$1.50 multi	3.25	1.60
a.	Booklet pane of 5		16.50	

Litho. With Foil Application

3599	A871	55c multi	1.10	.25
a.	Booklet pane of 10		11.00	
3600	A872	55c multi	1.10	.25
a.	Booklet pane of 10		11.00	
	Nos. 3595-3600 (6)		8.75	2.85

Litho.
With Personalized Photo at Right
Like Type A692a
Serpentine Die Cut 11½x11¼
Syncopated

3601	A872	55c multi	2.50	2.50
3602	A872	55c multi	2.50	2.50
3603	A872	60c multi	2.60	2.60
	Nos. 3601-3603 (3)		7.60	7.60

Nos. 3601-3603 each were printed in sheets of 20 and have personalized pictures and a straight edge at right, and lack separations between the stamp and the personalized photo. Sheets of 20 of Nos. 3601 and 3602 each sold for $24, for No. 3603, $25.

Remembrance Day — A873

Lines from "In Flanders Fields," poem by John McCrae, and: 60c, Poppy, bugler. $1.20, Two poppies, two soldiers.

2011, Nov. 2   Litho.   Perf. 14x14¾

3604	A873	60c multi	1.25	1.25
3605	A873	$1.20 multi	2.50	1.90
a.	Souvenir sheet of 2, #3604-3605		3.75	3.25

Self-Adhesive
Serpentine Die Cut 11¼ Syncopated

3606	A873	60c multi	1.25	.25
a.	Booklet pane of 10		12.50	

No. 3606 was issued in coils and booklets.

Australian Lieutenant General Sydney F. Rowell, New Zealand Major General William Gentry, and U.S. Admiral Arthur Radford
A874

2011, Nov. 16   Perf. 14x14¾

3607	A874	60c multi	1.25	.95

ANZUS Treaty, 60th anniv.

Cupcake and Birthday Candle — A875

Teddy Bear — A876

Balloons and Streamers A877

"Love" and Hearts A878

Birds — A879   Rose — A880

2012, Jan. 17   Perf. 14¾x14

3608	A875	60c multi	1.25	1.25
3609	A876	60c multi	1.25	1.25
3610	A877	60c multi	1.25	1.25
3611	A878	60c multi	1.25	1.25
3612	A879	60c multi	1.25	1.25
a.	Horiz. strip of 5, $3608-3612		6.25	6.25
3613	A880	$1.20 multi	2.60	2.60
	Nos. 3608-3613 (6)		8.85	8.85

Booklet Stamps
Self-Adhesive
Serpentine Die Cut 11¼ Syncopated

3614	A875	60c multi	1.25	.25
a.	Booklet pane of 10 + 5 stickers		12.50	
3615	A876	60c multi	1.25	.25
a.	Booklet pane of 10 + 5 stickers		12.50	
3616	A877	60c multi	1.25	.25
a.	Booklet pane of 10 + 5 stickers		12.50	
3617	A878	60c multi	1.25	.25
a.	Booklet pane of 10 + 5 stickers		12.50	
3618	A879	60c multi	1.25	.25
a.	Booklet pane of 10 + 5 stickers		12.50	
3619	A880	$1.20 multi	2.75	1.40
a.	Booklet pane of 4		11.00	
	Complete booklet, 5 #3619a		55.00	
	Nos. 3614-3619 (6)		9.00	2.65

With Personalized Photo at Right
Like Type A692a
Serpentine Die Cut 11½x11¼
Syncopated

3620	A875	60c multi	2.75	2.75
3621	A876	60c multi	2.75	2.75
3622	A877	60c multi	2.75	2.75
3623	A878	60c multi	2.75	2.75
3624	A879	60c multi	2.75	2.75
3625	A880	$1.20 multi	4.00	4.00
	Nos. 3620-3625 (6)		17.75	17.75

Complete booklet sold for $24.95 and contains five booklet panes of No. 3619a, each with a different margin.

Nos. 3620-3625 each were printed in sheets of 20 and have personalized pictures and a straight edge at right, and lack separations between the stamp and the personalized photo. Sheets of 20 of Nos. 3620-3624 each sold for $25, for No. 3625, $37.

Athletes — A881

Designs: Nos. 3626, 3634, Ron Barassi, Australian Rules Football player. Nos. 3627, 3635, Gary Ablett, Jr., Australian Rules Football player. Nos. 3628, 3636, John Raper, Rugby League player. Nos. 3629, 3637, Billy Slater, Rugby League player. Nos. 3630, 3638, David Campese, Rugby Union player. Nos. 3631, 3639, David Pocock, Rugby Union player. Nos. 3632, 3640, Joe Marston, soccer player. Nos. 3633, 3641, Mark Schwarzer, soccer player.

2012, Jan. 20   Perf. 14¾x14

3626	A881	60c multi	1.25	1.25
a.	Booklet pane of 4		5.50	
3627	A881	60c multi	1.25	1.25
a.	Booklet pane of 4		5.50	
3628	A881	60c multi	1.25	1.25
a.	Booklet pane of 4		5.50	—
3629	A881	60c multi	1.25	1.25
a.	Booklet pane of 4		5.50	—
3630	A881	60c multi	1.25	1.25
a.	Booklet pane of 4		5.50	—
3631	A881	60c multi	1.25	1.25
a.	Booklet pane of 4		5.50	—
3632	A881	60c multi	1.25	1.25
a.	Booklet pane of 4		5.50	—
3633	A881	60c multi	1.25	1.25
a.	Booklet pane of 4		5.50	—
	Complete booklet, #3626a-3633a		44.00	
	Nos. 3626-3633 (8)		10.00	10.00

Booklet Stamps
Self-Adhesive
Serpentine Die Cut 11¼ Syncopated

3634	A881	60c multi	1.25	.25
a.	Booklet pane of 10		12.50	
3635	A881	60c multi	1.25	.25
a.	Booklet pane of 10		12.50	
3636	A881	60c multi	1.25	.25
a.	Booklet pane of 10		12.50	
3637	A881	60c multi	1.25	.25
a.	Booklet pane of 10		12.50	
3638	A881	60c multi	1.25	.25
a.	Booklet pane of 10		12.50	
3639	A881	60c multi	1.25	.25
a.	Booklet pane of 10		12.50	
3640	A881	60c multi	1.25	.25
a.	Booklet pane of 10		12.50	
3641	A881	60c multi	1.25	.25
	Nos. 3634-3641 (8)		10.00	2.00

Complete booklet sold for $19.95.

Technological Changes Through the Years — A882

Designs: Nos. 3642, 3647, Woman on pay telephone, 4G phone. Nos. 3643, 3648, Man carrying ice to icebox, modern refrigerator. Nos. 3644, 3649, Family watching black-and-white television, flat-screen television. Nos. 3645, 3650, Man with vinyl records and record player, digital media player. Nos. 3646, 3651, Man reading paper road map, global positioning system.

2012, Feb. 7   Perf. 14x14¾

3642	A882	60c multi	1.40	1.40
3643	A882	60c multi	1.40	1.40
3644	A882	60c multi	1.40	1.40
3645	A882	60c multi	1.40	1.40
3646	A882	60c multi	1.40	1.40
a.	Horiz. strip of 5, #3642-3646		7.00	7.00
b.	Souvenir sheet of 5, #3642-3646		7.00	7.00

Self-Adhesive
Serpentine Die Cut 11¼ Syncopated

3647	A882	60c multi	1.40	.25
3648	A882	60c multi	1.40	.25
3649	A882	60c multi	1.40	.25
3650	A882	60c multi	1.40	.25
3651	A882	60c multi	1.40	.25
a.	Horiz. coil strip of 5, #3647-3651		7.00	
b.	Booklet pane of 10, 2 each #3647-3651		14.00	
	Nos. 3647-3651 (5)		7.00	1.25

Transportation in State Capitals — A883

Designs: Nos. 3652, 3657, O-Bahn bus system, Adelaide. Nos. 3653, 3658, Ferry in Sydney Harbor. Nos. 3654, 3659, Train in Perth. Nos. 3655, 3660, St. Kilda-bound tram, Melbourne. Nos. 3656, 3661, North Sydney-bound double-decker train, Sydney.

2012, Feb. 21   Perf. 14x14¾

3652	A883	60c multi	1.40	1.40
a.	Booklet pane of 4		5.75	—
3653	A883	60c multi	1.40	1.40
a.	Booklet pane of 4		5.75	—
3654	A883	60c multi	1.40	1.40
a.	Booklet pane of 4		5.75	—
3655	A883	60c multi	1.40	1.40
a.	Booklet pane of 4		5.75	—
3656	A883	60c multi	1.40	1.40
a.	Booklet pane of 4		5.75	—
	Complete booklet, #3652a-3656a		29.00	
b.	Horiz. strip of 5, #3652-3656		7.00	7.00

Booklet Stamps
Self-Adhesive
Serpentine Die Cut 11¼ Syncopated

3657	A883	60c multi	1.40	.25
3658	A883	60c multi	1.40	.25
3659	A883	60c multi	1.40	.25
3660	A883	60c multi	1.40	.25
3661	A883	60c multi	1.40	.25
a.	Booklet pane of 20, 4 each #3657-3661		28.00	
	Nos. 3657-3661 (5)		7.00	1.25

Complete booklet sold for $12.95.

Ducks A884

Designs: Nos. 3662, 3666, Radjah shelduck. Nos. 3663, 3667, Pink-eared duck. $1.65, Australian shelduck. $2.35, Plumed whistling duck.

2012, Mar. 6   Perf. 14x14¾

3662	A884	60c multi	1.25	1.25
	Additionally dated "2013"		1.25	1.25
3663	A884	60c multi	1.25	1.25
	Additionally dated "2013"		1.25	1.25
3664	A884	$1.65 multi	3.50	3.50
	Additionally dated "2013"		3.25	3.25
3665	A884	$2.35 multi	5.00	5.00
	Additionally dated "2013"		4.50	4.50
b.	Booklet pane of 4, #3662a, 3663a, 3664a, 3665a		10.50	—
	Nos. 3662-3665 (4)		11.00	11.00

Issued: Nos. 3662a, 3663a, 3664a, 3665a, 3665b, 5/11/13. No. 3665b was issued in a booklet also containing Nos. 3151c, 3376a and 3925a.

Self-Adhesive
Serpentine Die Cut 11¼ Syncopated

3666	A884	60c multi	1.25	.25
3667	A884	60c multi	1.25	.25
a.	Horiz. coil pair, #3666-3667		2.50	
b.	Booklet pane of 10, 5 each #3666-3667		25.00	

Booklet Stamps

3668	A884	$1.65 multi	3.50	1.75
a.	Booklet pane of 5		17.50	
3669	A884	$2.35 multi	5.00	2.50
a.	Booklet pane of 5		25.00	
	Nos. 3666-3669 (4)		11.00	4.75

Farm Products — A885

Designs: 10c, Dairy cows. 20c, Pineapples. $1, Wine grapes. $3, Sunflowers. $5, Apples.

2012, Mar. 20   **Perf. 14x14½**

3670	A885	10c multi	.25	.25
3671	A885	20c multi	.40	.25
a.		As No. 3671, with part of design and 1mm wide white space separating designs at left side	1.10	1.10

Size: 50x30mm
Perf. 14½x14

3672	A885	$1 multi	2.10	1.10
3673	A885	$3 multi	6.25	3.25
3674	A885	$5 multi	10.50	5.25
		Nos. 3670-3674 (5)	19.50	10.10

No. 3671 has a white margin extending to the perforation tips at left. Four of the five stamps in the bottom row of the bottom pane in the sheet of 100 stamps (composed of two panes of 50) are No. 3671a.
See Nos. 3712-3723.

Compulsory Voting Enrollment, Cent. — A886

2012, Mar. 27   **Litho.**   **Perf. 14¾x14**

3675	A886	60c multi	1.25	.95

Reign of Queen Elizabeth II, 60th Anniv. — A887

Photograph of Queen Elizabeth II in: 60c, 1952. $2.35, 2012.

2012, Apr. 3   **Perf. 14¾x14**

3676	A887	60c multi	1.25	.95
3677	A887	$2.35 multi	5.00	5.00
a.		Souvenir sheet of 2, #3676-3677	6.25	6.00

Booklet Stamp
Self-Adhesive

Serpentine Die Cut 11¼ Syncopated

3678	A887	$2.35 multi	5.00	2.50
a.		Booklet pane of 5	25.00	

Medical Doctors — A888

Designs: Nos. 3679, 3684, Dr. Jane Stocks Greig (1872-1939), public health specialist. Nos. 3680, 3685, Dame Kate Campbell (1899-1986), pediatrician. Nos. 3681, 3686, Dr. Victor Chang (1936-91), cardiac surgeon. Nos. 3682, 3687, Dr. Fred Hollows (1929-93), ophthalmologist. Nos. 3683, 3688, Dr. Chris O'Brien (1952-2009), surgeon.

2012, Apr. 10   **Perf. 14¾x14**

3679	A888	60c multi	1.25	1.25
3680	A888	60c multi	1.25	1.25
3681	A888	60c multi	1.25	1.25
3682	A888	60c multi	1.25	1.25
3683	A888	60c multi	1.25	1.25
		Nos. 3679-3683 (5)	6.25	6.25

Coil Stamps
Self-Adhesive

Serpentine Die Cut 11¼ Syncopated

3684	A888	60c multi	1.25	.25
3685	A888	60c multi	1.25	.25
3686	A888	60c multi	1.25	.25
3687	A888	60c multi	1.25	.25
3688	A888	60c multi	1.25	.25
a.		Vert. coil strip of 5, #3684-3688	6.25	
		Nos. 3684-3688 (5)	6.25	1.25

Rising Sun Badge A889

Rising Sun Badge in use from: Nos. 3689, 3694, 1902-04. Nos. 3690, 3695, 1904-49. Nos. 3691, 3696, 1954-69. Nos. 3692, 3697, 1969-91. Nos. 3693, 3698, 1991-present.

2012, Apr. 17   **Perf. 14x14¾**

3689	A889	60c multi	1.25	1.25
3690	A889	60c multi	1.25	1.25
3691	A889	60c multi	1.25	1.25
3692	A889	60c multi	1.25	1.25
3693	A889	60c multi	1.25	1.25
a.		Horiz. strip of 5, #3689-3693	6.25	6.25
b.		Souvenir sheet of 5, #3689-3693	6.25	6.25

Booklet Stamps
Self-Adhesive

Serpentine Die Cut 11¼ Syncopated

3694	A889	60c multi	1.25	.25
3695	A889	60c multi	1.25	.25
3696	A889	60c multi	1.25	.25
3697	A889	60c multi	1.25	.25
3698	A889	60c multi	1.25	.25
a.		Booklet pane of 10, 2 each #3694-3698	12.50	
		Nos. 3694-3698 (5)	6.25	1.25

Limited editions of Nos. 3693b (part-perforate) and 3698a with a gold overprint in the margin exist.

Nudibranchs A890

Designs: Nos. 3699, 3705, Chromodoris westraliensis. Nos. 3700, 3706, Godiva sp. Nos. 3701, 3707, Flabellina rubrolineata. No. 3702, Phyllidia ocellata. No. 3703, Thorunna florens. $1.80, Nembrotha purpureolineata.

2012, May 8   **Perf. 14x14¾**

3699	A890	60c multi	1.25	1.25
a.		Booklet pane of 4	5.25	—
3700	A890	60c multi	1.25	1.25
a.		Booklet pane of 4	5.25	—
3701	A890	60c multi	1.25	1.25
a.		Booklet pane of 4	5.25	—
3702	A890	$1.20 multi	2.40	1.90
3703	A890	$1.20 multi	2.40	1.90
a.		Booklet pane of 4, #3699-3702	6.50	—
3704	A890	$1.80 multi	3.75	1.90
a.		Booklet pane of 4, #3699-3701, 3704	7.75	—
		Complete booklet, #3699a, 3700a, 3701a, 3703a, 3704a	30.00	
b.		Souvenir sheet of 6, #3699-3704	12.50	12.50
		Nos. 3699-3704 (6)	12.30	9.45

Booklet Stamps
Self-Adhesive

Serpentine Die Cut 11¼ Syncopated

3705	A890	60c multi	1.25	.25
3706	A890	60c multi	1.25	.25
3707	A890	60c multi	1.25	.25
a.		Booklet pane of 20, 7 each #3705-3706, 6 #3707	25.00	
		Nos. 3705-3707 (3)	3.75	.75

Complete booklet sold for $14.95.

Australian Flag, Olympic Rings, London Tourist Attractions — A891

2012, June 5   **Perf. 14¾x14**

3708	A891	60c multi	1.25	1.25

Self-Adhesive

Serpentine Die Cut 11¼ Syncopated

3709	A891	60c multi	1.25	.25
a.		Booklet pane of 10	12.50	

2012 Summer Olympics, London.

Colonial Heritage — A892

Designs: No. 3710, Redrawn vignette of New South Wales #1. No. 3710, Redrawn vignette of Tasmania #88.

2012, June 19   **Perf. 14x14½**

3710	A892	$2 yellow & blue	4.25	2.10
a.		Perf. 14x13½	4.25	2.10
3711	A892	$2 lt blue & blue	4.25	2.10
a.		Perf. 14x13½	4.25	2.10
b.		Horiz. pair, #3710-3711	8.50	4.25
c.		Souvenir sheet of 2, #3710a, 3711a	8.50	4.25

Farm Products Type of 2012

Designs: Nos. 3712, 3716, 3720, Beef cattle. Nos. 3713, 3717, 3721, Oranges. Nos. 3714, 3718, 3722, Sugar. Nos. 3715, 3719, 3723, Wool.

2012, June 26   **Litho.**   **Perf. 14x14½**

3712	A885	60c multi	1.25	.25
3713	A885	60c multi	1.25	.25
3714	A885	60c multi	1.25	.25
3715	A885	60c multi	1.25	.25
a.		Block of 4, #3712-3715	5.00	2.50
		Nos. 3712-3715 (4)	5.00	1.00

Coil Stamps
Self-Adhesive

Serpentine Die Cut 12¾

3716	A885	60c multi	1.25	.25
3717	A885	60c multi	1.25	.25
3718	A885	60c multi	1.25	.25
3719	A885	60c multi	1.25	.25
a.		Horiz. strip of 4, #3716-3719	5.00	

Booklet Stamps

Serpentine Die Cut 11¼

3720	A885	60c multi	1.25	.25
3721	A885	60c multi	1.25	.25
3722	A885	60c multi	1.25	.25
3723	A885	60c multi	1.25	.25
a.		Booklet pane of 10, 2 each #3720, 3722-3723, 4 #3721	12.50	
b.		Booklet pane of 20, 5 each #3720-3723	25.00	
		Nos. 3716-3723 (8)	10.00	2.00

Inland Exploration A893

Designs: No. 3724, Explorers crossing Blue Mountains, 1813. No. 3725, Explorers William Lawson, William Charles Wentworth and Gregory Blaxland. No. 3726, Explorer John McDouall Stuart. No. 3727, Stuart Overland Crossing Expedition planting flag on Indian Ocean coast.

2012, July 3   **Perf. 14x14¾**

3724	A893	60c multi	1.25	.95
3725	A893	60c multi	1.25	.95
a.		Horiz. pair, #3724-3725	2.50	1.90
3726	A893	$1.20 multi	2.50	2.00
3727	A893	$1.20 multi	2.50	2.00
a.		Horiz. pair, #3726-3727	5.00	4.00
b.		Souvenir sheet of 4, #3724-3727	7.50	6.00
		Nos. 3724-3727 (4)	7.50	5.90

Sports of the Summer Olympics A894

Designs: 60c, Swimming. $1.60, Pole V[...] $2.30, Rowing.

2012, July 17   **Perf. 14x14¾**

3728	A894	60c multi	1.25	1.25
3729	A894	$1.60 multi	3.50	3.50
3730	A894	$2.35 multi	5.00	5.00
		Nos. 3728-3730 (3)	9.75	9.75

Coil Stamp
Self-Adhesive

Serpentine Die Cut 11¼ Syncopated

3731	A894	60c multi	1.25	.25

Booklet Stamps

3732	A894	$1.60 multi	3.50	1.75
a.		Booklet pane of 5	17.50	
3733	A894	$2.35 multi	5.00	2.50
a.		Booklet pane of 5	25.00	
		Nos. 3731-3733 (3)	9.75	4.50

Photographs of Everyday Life in Australia — A895

Designs: Nos. 3734, 3740, Little Wonders, by Ann Clark (children on beach). Nos. 3735, 3742, The Godfathers, by Chevelle Williams (sheep in pen). Nos. 3736, 3741, Is There a Letter for Me?, by Wanda Lach (row of mailboxes in rural area). Nos. 3737, 3743, Lunch on the Harbor, by Damian Madden (seagull with French fry in beak). Nos. 3738, 3739, Fuel Ask at the Store Across the Road, by Ronald Rockman (rural gas station).

2012, July 24   **Perf. 14x14¾**

3734	A895	60c multi	1.25	1.25
3735	A895	60c multi	1.25	1.25
3736	A895	60c multi	1.25	1.25
3737	A895	60c multi	1.25	1.25
3738	A895	60c multi	1.25	1.25
a.		Horiz. strip of 5, #3734-3738	6.25	6.25
		Nos. 3734-3738 (5)	6.25	6.25

Booklet Stamps
Self-Adhesive

Serpentine Die Cut 11¼ Syncopated

3739	A895	60c multi	1.25	.25
3740	A895	60c multi	1.25	.25
3741	A895	60c multi	1.25	.25
3742	A895	60c multi	1.25	.25
3743	A895	60c multi	1.25	.25
a.		Booklet pane of 20, 4 each #3739-3742	25.00	
		Nos. 3739-3743 (5)	6.25	1.25

Souvenir Sheet

Emblem of Australia 2013 World Stamp Expo and Royal Exhibition Building, Melbourne — A896

2012, June 18   **Litho.**   **Perf. 14¾x14**

3744	A896	$1.85 multi	3.75	1.90

A limited edition of No. 3744 with a gold overprint in the sheet margin exists.

Australian Gold Medalists at 2012 Summer Olympics, London A897

Designs: No. 3745, Women's 4x100 meter freestyle swimming relay team. No. 3746, Tom Slingsby, men's Laser class sailing. No. 3747, Anna Meares, women's sprint cycling. No. 3748, Iain Jensen and Nathan Outteridge, men's 49er class sailing. No. 3749, Sally Pearson, women's 100 meter hurdles. No. 3750, Men's 1000 meter kayak fours team. No. 3751, Mathew Belcher and Malcolm Page, men's 470 class sailing.

Perf. 14¼

	...ti	1.25	.95
		1.25	.95
		1.25	.95
	..0c multi	1.25	.95
	60c multi	1.25	.95
A897	60c multi	1.25	.95
	Nos. 3745-3751 (7)	8.75	6.65

Nos. 3745-3751 each were printed in sheets of 10. Issued: No. 3745, 7/31; No. 3746, 8/9; No. 3747, 8/10; others, 8/13.

Portraits of Autralian Nobel Prize Winners — A898

Portrait of: Nos. 3752, 3757, Sir Frank Macfarlane Burnet, by Clifton Pugh. Nos. 3753, 3758, Sir John Carew Eccles, by Judy Cassab. Nos. 3754, 3759, Patrick White, by Brett Whiteley. Nos. 3755, 3760, Sir Howard Walter Florey, by Allan Gwynne-Jones. Nos. 3756, 3761, William Lawrence Bragg, by Sir William Dargie.

2012, Aug. 28   Litho.   Perf. 14¾x14

3752	A898 60c multi	1.25	1.25
3753	A898 60c multi	1.25	1.25
3754	A898 60c multi	1.25	1.25
3755	A898 60c multi	1.25	1.25
3756	A898 60c multi	1.25	1.25
a.	Horiz. strip of 5, #3752-3756	6.25	6.25
	Nos. 3752-3756 (5)	6.25	6.25

Self-Adhesive
Serpentine Die Cut 11¼ Syncopated

3757	A898 60c multi	1.25	.25
3758	A898 60c multi	1.25	.25
3759	A898 60c multi	1.25	.25
3760	A898 60c multi	1.25	.25
3761	A898 60c multi	1.25	.25
a.	Vert. coil strip of 5, #3757-3761	6.25	
b.	Booklet pane of 10, 2 each #3757-3761	12.50	
	Nos. 3757-3761 (5)	6.25	1.25

Road Trips — A899

Designs: Nos. 3762, 3769, Station wagon at Port Arthur, Tasmania. Nos. 3763, 3767, Volkswagen Bus at Great Barrier Reef, Queensland. Nos. 3764, 3768, Motorcyclists picnicking near Margaret River, Western Australia. $1.65, Station wagon at Phillip Island, Victoria. $2.35, Car at camel race, Alice Springs, Northern Territory.

2012, Sept. 18   Perf. 14¼

3762	A899 60c multi	1.25	1.25
3763	A899 60c multi	1.25	1.25
3764	A899 60c multi	1.25	1.25
a.	Horiz. strip of 3, #3762-3764	3.75	3.75
3765	A899 $1.65 multi	3.50	1.75
3766	A899 $2.35 multi	4.75	2.40
a.	Souvenir sheet of 5, #3762-3766	12.00	12.00
	Nos. 3762-3766 (5)	12.00	7.90

Booklet Stamps
Self-Adhesive
Serpentine Die Cut 11¼ Syncopated

3767	A899 60c multi	1.25	.25
3768	A899 60c multi	1.25	.25
3769	A899 60c multi	1.25	.25
a.	Booklet pane of 10, 3 each #3767, 3769, 4 #3768	12.50	
3770	A899 $1.65 multi	3.50	1.75
a.	Booklet pane of 5	17.50	
3771	A899 $2.35 multi	4.75	2.40
a.	Booklet pane of 5	24.00	
	Nos. 3767-3771 (5)	12.00	4.90

Compare with type A933.

Wilderness Areas — A900

Designs: $1.65, Nullarbor Plain, Western Australia. $2.35, Daintree National Park, Queensland. $4.50, Cradle Mountain, Tasmania.

2012, Sept. 25   Perf. 14¾x14

3772	A900 $1.65 multi	3.50	1.75
3773	A900 $2.35 multi	4.75	2.40
3774	A900 $4.50 multi	9.25	4.75
	Nos. 3772-3774 (3)	17.50	8.90

Booklet Stamps
Self-Adhesive
Serpentine Die Cut 11¼ Syncopated

3775	A900 $1.65 multi	3.50	1.75
a.	Booklet pane of 5	17.50	
3776	A900 $2.35 multi	4.75	2.40
a.	Booklet pane of 5	24.00	

Animals in Australian Zoos — A901

Designs: No. 3777, Sumatran tiger, Melbourne Zoo, Victoria. Nos. 3778, 3789, Wedge-tailed hawk, Healesville Sanctuary, Victoria. Nos. 3779, 3787, Sumatran orangutan, Perth Zoo, Western Australia. Nos. 3780, 3786, Giant panda, Adelaide Zoo, South Australia. Nos. 3781, 3785, Giraffe, Taronga Zoo, Sydney, New South Wales. Nos. 3782, 3788, Saltwater crocodile, Australia Zoo, Sunshine Coast, Queensland. Nos. 3783, 3784, Black rhinoceros, Taronga Western Plains Zoo, Dubbo, New South Wales.

2012, Sept. 28   Perf. 13¾x14

3777	A901 60c multi	1.25	.95

Size: 37x26mm
Perf. 14x14¾

3778	A901 60c multi	1.25	1.25
3779	A901 60c multi	1.25	1.25
3780	A901 60c multi	1.25	1.25
3781	A901 60c multi	1.25	1.25
3782	A901 60c multi	1.25	1.25
3783	A901 60c multi	1.25	1.25
a.	Souvenir sheet of 7, #3777-3783	8.75	8.75
	Nos. 3777-3783 (7)	8.75	8.45

Self-Adhesive
Serpentine Die Cut 11¼ Syncopated

3784	A901 60c multi	1.25	.25
3785	A901 60c multi	1.25	.25
3786	A901 60c multi	1.25	.25
3787	A901 60c multi	1.25	.25
3788	A901 60c multi	1.25	.25
3789	A901 60c multi	1.25	.25
a.	Horiz. coil strip of 6, #3784-3789	7.50	
b.	Booklet pane of 20, 4 each #3784-3785, 3 each #3786-3789	25.00	
	Nos. 3784-3789 (6)	7.50	1.50

Auto Racing at Bathurst, 50th Anniv. A902

Designs: Nos. 3790, 3794, Race car, country name in red. Nos. 3791, 3797, Mount Panorama Race Track, country name in yellow green. Nos. 3792, 3796, Race car, country name in blue. Nos. 3793, 3795, Race car, country name in yellow.

2012, Oct. 2   Perf. 14x14¾

3790	A902 60c multi	1.25	1.25
3791	A902 60c multi	1.25	1.25
3792	A902 60c multi	1.25	1.25
3793	A902 60c multi	1.25	1.25
a.	Block of 4, #3790-3793	5.00	5.00
b.	Souvenir sheet of 4, #3790-3793	5.00	5.00
	Nos. 3790-3793 (4)	5.00	5.00

Booklet Stamps
Self-Adhesive
Serpentine Die Cut 11¼ Syncopated

3794	A902 60c multi	1.25	.25
3795	A902 60c multi	1.25	.25
3796	A902 60c multi	1.25	.25
3797	A902 60c multi	1.25	.25
a.	Booklet pane of 10, 2 each #3794-3796, 4 #3797	12.50	
	Nos. 3794-3797 (4)	5.00	1.00

Susie O'Neill, Swimmer — A903

O'Neill: No. 3798, Wearing black jacket. No. 3799, Swimming in pool.

2012, Oct. 12   Perf. 14¾x14

3798	A903 60c multi	1.25	.95
3799	A903 60c multi	1.25	.95
a.	Pair, #3798-3799	2.50	1.90

Australian Ballet, 50th Anniv. — A904

Designs: Nos. 3800, 3802, One dancer. Nos. 3801, 3803, Two dancers.

2012, Oct. 16   Perf. 14¾x14

3800	A904 60c multi	1.25	1.25
3801	A904 60c multi	1.25	1.25
a.	Pair, #3800-3801	2.50	2.50

Coil Stamps
Self-Adhesive
Serpentine Die Cut 11¼ Syncopated

3802	A904 60c multi	1.25	.25
3803	A904 60c multi	1.25	.25
a.	Vert. pair, #3802-3803	2.50	

Lawn Bowling A905

Designs: 60c, Female bowlers. $1.20, Male bowlers.

2012, Nov. 1   Perf. 14x14¾

3804	A905 60c multi	1.25	.95
3805	A905 $1.20 multi	2.50	1.90
a.	Souvenir sheet of 2, #3804-3805	3.75	3.00

Christmas
A906   A907

Designs: Nos. 3806, 3811, Detail of Madonna and Child from Adoration of the Magi tapestry. Nos. 3807, 3812, 3815, 3817, Reindeer. Nos. 3808, 3813, 3816, 3818, Gifts. 60c, Bells. $1.60, Entire Adoration of the Magi tapestry (50x30mm), horiz.

2012, Nov. 1   Perf. 14¾x14

3806	A906 55c multi	1.25	1.25
3807	A907 55c multi	1.25	1.25
3808	A907 55c multi	1.25	1.25
3809	A906 60c multi	1.25	.60

Perf. 14½x14

3810	A906 $1.60 multi	3.50	1.75
	Nos. 3806-3810 (5)	8.50	6.10

Booklet Stamps
Self-Adhesive
Serpentine Die Cut 11¼ Syncopated

3811	A906 55c multi	1.25	.25
a.	Booklet pane of 20	25.00	
3812	A907 55c multi	1.25	.25
3813	A907 55c multi	1.25	.25
a.	Booklet pane of 20, 10 each #3812-3813	25.00	
3814	A906 $1.60 multi	3.50	1.75
a.	Booklet pane of 5	17.50	

Litho. With Foil Application

3815	A907 55c multi	1.25	.25
a.	Booklet pane of 10	12.50	

Litho. & Embossed With Foil Application

3816	A907 55c multi	1.25	.25
a.	Booklet pane of 10	12.50	
	Nos. 3811-3816 (6)	9.75	3.00

With Personalized Photo at Right Like Type A692a
Litho.
Serpentine Die Cut 11½x11¼ Syncopated

3817	A907 55c multi	2.50	2.50
3818	A907 55c multi	2.50	2.50

Nos. 3817-3818 each were printed in sheets of 20 and have personalized pictures and straight edge at right, and lack separations between the stamp an the personalized photo. Sheets of 20 of each stamp sold for $24.

Jacqueline Freney, Paralympian of the Year — A908

2012, Nov. 9   Perf. 14¼

3819	A908 60c multi	1.25	.95

Musical Legends — A909

Designs: Nos. 3820, 3830, AC/DC (rock band). Nos. 3821, 3831, Cold Chisel (rock band). Nos. 3822, 3832, INXS (rock band). Nos. 3823, 3833, John Farnham (singer). Nos. 3824, 3834, Kylie Minogue (singer). Nos. 3825, 3835, Men At Work (rock band). Nos. 3826, 3836, Ian "Molly" Meldrum (record producer). Nos. 3827, 3837, Olivia Newton-John (singer). No. 3828, 3838, Paul Kelly (singer). Nos. 3829, 3839, The Seekers (rock band).

2013, Jan. 18   Perf. 14¾x14

3820	A909 60c multi	1.25	1.25
a.	Booklet pane of 4	5.25	—
3821	A909 60c multi	1.25	1.25
a.	Booklet pane of 4	5.25	—
b.	Horiz. pair, #3820-3821	2.50	2.50
3822	A909 60c multi	1.25	1.25
a.	Booklet pane of 4	5.25	—
3823	A909 60c multi	1.25	1.25
a.	Booklet pane of 4	5.25	—
3824	A909 60c multi	1.25	1.25
a.	Booklet pane of 4	5.25	—
3825	A909 60c multi	1.25	1.25
a.	Booklet pane of 4	5.25	—
3826	A909 60c multi	1.25	1.25
a.	Booklet pane of 4	5.25	—
b.	Horiz. pair, #3824, 3826	2.50	2.50
3827	A909 60c multi	1.25	1.25
a.	Booklet pane of 4	5.25	—
b.	Horiz. pair, #3823, 3827	2.50	2.50
3828	A909 60c multi	1.25	1.25
a.	Booklet pane of 4	5.25	—
b.	Horiz. pair, #3822, 3828	2.50	2.50
3829	A909 60c multi	1.25	1.25
a.	Booklet pane of 4	5.25	—
b.	Horiz. pair, #3825, 3829	2.50	2.50
c.	Complete booklet, #3820a-3829a	52.50	
	Nos. 3820-3829 (10)	12.50	12.50

Booklet Stamps
Self-Adhesive
Serpentine Die Cut 11¼ Syncopated

3830	A909 60c multi	1.25	.25
a.	Booklet pane of 10	12.50	
3831	A909 60c multi	1.25	.25
a.	Booklet pane of 10	12.50	
3832	A909 60c multi	1.25	.25
a.	Booklet pane of 10	12.50	
3833	A909 60c multi	1.25	.25
a.	Booklet pane of 10	12.50	

3834	A909 60c multi	1.25	.25
a.	Booklet pane of 10	12.50	
3835	A909 60c multi	1.25	.25
a.	Booklet pane of 10	12.50	
3836	A909 60c multi	1.25	.25
a.	Booklet pane of 10	12.50	
3837	A909 60c multi	1.25	.25
a.	Booklet pane of 10	12.50	
3838	A909 60c multi	1.25	.25
a.	Booklet pane of 10	12.50	
3839	A909 60c multi	1.25	.25
a.	Booklet pane of 10	12.50	
	Nos. 3830-3839 (10)	12.50	2.50

Complete booklet sold for $24.95.

Eucalyptus
Leaves — A910

Map of
Australia — A911

Rose
Petal — A912

Orchid — A913

Gifts and
Champagne
Flutes — A914

2013, Feb. 5   Litho.   Perf. 14¾x14

3840	A910 60c multi	1.25	1.25
3841	A911 60c blue & multi	1.25	1.25
3842	A911 60c org & multi	1.25	1.25
3843	A912 60c multi	1.25	1.25
3844	A913 60c multi	1.25	1.25
a.	Horiz. strip of 5, #3840-3844	6.25	6.25
3845	A914 $1.20 multi	2.50	2.50
	Nos. 3840-3845 (6)	8.75	8.75

**Booklet Stamps
Self-Adhesive**

Serpentine Die Cut 11¼ Syncopated

3846	A910 60c multi	1.25	.25
a.	Booklet pane of 10 + 5 stickers	12.50	
3847	A911 60c blue & multi	1.25	.25
3848	A911 60c org & multi	1.25	.25
a.	Booklet pane of 10, 5 each #3847-3848, + 5 stickers	12.50	
3849	A912 60c multi	1.25	.25
a.	Booklet pane of 10 + 5 stickers	12.50	
3850	A913 60c multi	1.25	.25
a.	Booklet pane of 10 + 5 stickers	12.50	
3851	A914 $1.20 multi	2.50	1.25
a.	Booklet pane of 10 + 5 stickers	25.00	
b.	Booklet pane of 4	10.50	
	Complete booklet, 5 #3851b	52.50	
	Nos. 3846-3851 (6)	8.75	2.50

Complete booklet sold for $24.95 and contains five examples of No. 3851b, each with a different image in pane margin.

**With Personalized Photo at Right
Like Type A692a**
*Serpentine Die Cut 11½x11¼
Syncopated*

3852	A910 60c multi	2.60	2.60
3853	A911 60c blue & multi	2.60	2.60
3854	A911 60c org & multi	2.60	2.60
3855	A912 60c multi	2.60	2.60
3856	A913 60c multi	2.60	2.60
3857	A914 $1.20 multi	3.75	3.75
	Nos. 3852-3857 (6)	16.75	16.75

Nos. 3852-3857 each were printed in sheets of 20 and have personalized pictures and a straight edge at right and lack separations between the stamp and the personalized photo. Sheets of 20 of Nos. 3852-3856 sold for $25 each, No. 3857, $37.

Women and
Surfboards
A915

Surfer and
Stylized
Waves
A916

Surfboards
on
Automobile
Roof — A917

Surfer
A918

2013, Feb. 12   Litho.   Perf. 14¾x14

3858	A915 60c multi	1.25	1.25
a.	Booklet pane of 4	5.25	—
3859	A916 60c multi	1.25	1.25
a.	Booklet pane of 4	5.25	—
3860	A917 60c multi	1.25	1.25
a.	Booklet pane of 4	5.25	—
3861	A918 60c multi	1.25	1.25
a.	Booklet pane of 4	5.25	—
b.	Booklet pane of 4, #3858-3861, #3859 in UL	5.25	—
	Complete booklet, #3858a, 3859a, 3860a, 3861a, 3861b	26.50	
c.	Block of 4, #3851-3861	5.00	5.00
d.	Souvenir sheet of 4, #3858-3861, #3858 in UL	5.00	5.00
	Nos. 3858-3861 (4)	5.00	5.00

Self-Adhesive
Serpentine Die Cut 11¼ Syncopated

3862	A915 60c multi	1.25	.25
3863	A916 60c multi	1.25	.25
3864	A917 60c multi	1.25	.25
3865	A918 60c multi	1.25	.25
a.	Horiz. coil strip of 4, #3862-3865	5.00	
b.	Booklet pane of 10, 3 each #3862, 3865, 2 each #3863-3864	12.50	
	Nos. 3862-3865 (4)	5.00	1.00

Complete booklet sold for $12.95.

Dogs — A919

Designs: Nos. 3866, 3871, Miniature schnauzer. Nos. 3867, 3872, Miniature dachshund. Nos. 3868, 3873, Cavalier King Charles spaniel. Nos. 3869, 3874, Pug. Nos. 3870, 3875, Australian terrier.

2013, Feb. 19   Perf. 14¾x14

3866	A919 60c multi	1.25	1.25
3867	A919 60c multi	1.25	1.25
3868	A919 60c multi	1.25	1.25
3869	A919 60c multi	1.25	1.25
3870	A919 60c multi	1.25	1.25
a.	Horiz. strip of 5, #3866-3870	6.25	6.25
	Nos. 3866-3870 (5)	6.25	6.25

**Booklet Stamps
Self-Adhesive**

Serpentine Die Cut 11¼ Syncopated

3871	A919 60c multi	1.25	.25
a.	Booklet pane of 10 + 5 stickers	12.50	
3872	A919 60c multi	1.25	.25
a.	Booklet pane of 10 + 5 stickers	12.50	
3873	A919 60c multi	1.25	.25
a.	Booklet pane of 10 + 5 stickers	12.50	
3874	A919 60c multi	1.25	.25
a.	Booklet pane of 10 + 5 stickers	12.50	

3875	A919 60c multi	1.25	.25
a.	Booklet pane of 10 + 5 stickers	12.50	
	Nos. 3871-3875 (5)	6.25	1.25

Canberra,
Cent.
A920

Map and: 60c, National Portrait Gallery. $2.35, Parliament House.

2013, Mar. 5

3876	A920 60c multi	1.25	1.25
3877	A920 $2.35 multi	4.75	2.40
a.	Booklet pane of 4, 2 each #3876-3877	13.00	
	Complete booklet, #1938d, 2710c, 2869e, 3107c, 3349b, 3877a	27.50	

Self-Adhesive
Serpentine Die Cut 11¼ Syncopated

3878	A920 60c multi	1.25	.25
a.	Booklet pane of 20	25.00	

Complete booklet sold for $12.95. No. 3878 was issued in coils and booklet panes.

Paintings in National
Gallery of
Australia — A921

Designs: Nos. 3879, 3884, Dandenong Ranges from 'Beleura,' by Eugene von Guérard. Nos. 3880, 3885, In the Flinders - Far North, by Hans Heysen. Nos. 3881, 3886, Land of the Golden Fleece, by Arthur Streetson. Nos. 3882, 3887, Mr. Robinson's House on the Derwent, Van Diemen's Land, by John Glover. Nos. 3883, 3888, Studley Park at Sunrise, by Nicholas Chevalier.

2013, Mar. 19   Perf. 14¾x14

3879	A921 60c multi	1.25	1.25
3880	A921 60c multi	1.25	1.25
3881	A921 60c multi	1.25	1.25
3882	A921 60c multi	1.25	1.25
3883	A921 60c multi	1.25	1.25
a.	Horiz. strip of 5, #3879-3883	6.25	6.25
	Nos. 3879-3883 (5)	6.25	6.25

**Booklet Stamps
Self-Adhesive**

Serpentine Die Cut 11¼ Syncopated

3884	A921 60c multi	1.25	.25
3885	A921 60c multi	1.25	.25
3886	A921 60c multi	1.25	.25
3887	A921 60c multi	1.25	.25
3888	A921 60c multi	1.25	.25
a.	Booklet pane of 10, 2 each #3884-3888	12.50	
	Nos. 3884-3888 (5)	6.25	1.25

Baby
Animals — A922

Designs: $1.70, Kookaburra. $1.75, Wombat. $2.60, Echidna. $4.65, Platypus. $6.45, Possum.

2013, Apr. 2   Perf. 14¾x14

3889	A922 $1.70 multi	3.50	3.50
3890	A922 $1.75 multi	3.75	3.75
3891	A922 $2.60 multi	5.50	5.50
3892	A922 $4.65 multi	9.75	7.50
3893	A922 $6.45 multi	13.50	10.00
	Nos. 3889-3893 (5)	36.00	30.25

**Booklet Stamps
Self-Adhesive**

Serpentine Die Cut 11¼ Syncopated

3894	A922 $1.70 multi	3.50	1.75
a.	Booklet pane of 5	17.50	
3895	A922 $1.75 multi	3.75	1.90
a.	Booklet pane of 5	19.00	
3896	A922 $2.60 multi	5.50	2.75
a.	Booklet pane of 5	27.50	
	Nos. 3894-3896 (3)	12.75	6.40

**With Personalized Photo at Rig[ht]
Like Type A692a**
*Serpentine Die Cut 11½x11¼
Syncopated*

3898	A922 $1.75 multi	5.00	5.00
3899	A922 $2.60 multi	6.75	6.75

Nos. 3898-3899 each were printed in sheets of 20 and have personalized pictures and a straight edge at right and lack separations between the stamp and the personalized photo. Sheets of 20 of No. 3898 sold for $48, No. 3899, $65.

Coach — A923

Queen Elizabeth
II — A924

2013, Apr. 9   Litho.   Perf. 14¾x14

3900	A923 60c multi	1.25	.95
a.	Booklet pane of 1	1.25	—
3901	A924 $2.60 multi	5.50	5.50
a.	Souvenir sheet of 2, #3900-3901	6.75	6.75
b.	Booklet pane of 1	5.50	—
c.	Booklet pane of 3	16.50	—
	Complete booklet, #3901b, 2 each #3900a, 3901c, + 50c coin	41.00	

Complete booklet sold for $19.95.

**Booklet Stamp
Self-Adhesive**

Serpentine Die Cut 11¼ Syncopated

3902	A924 $2.60 multi	5.50	2.75
a.	Booklet pane of 5	27.50	

**Litho. & Embossed
Perf. 14¾x14**

3903	A923 60c multi	1.40	1.40

Coronation of Queen Elizabeth II, 60th anniv. Examples of No. 3901a with an overprint for the Australia 2013 World Stamp Expo were made given to the show organizers and sold only by them. No. 3903 was printed in sheets of 10 that sold for $6.45.

Botanical
Gardens
A925

Designs: Nos. 3904, 3909, Royal Tasmanian Botanical Gardens, Hobart. Nos. 3905, 3910, Australian National Botanic Gardens, Canberra. Nos. 3906, 3911, Blue Mountains Botanic Garden, Mount Tomah, New South Wales. Nos. 3907, 3912, Darwin Botanic Gardens, Darwin, Northern Territory. No. 3908, 3913, Royal Botanic Gardens, Cranbourne, Victoria.

2013, Apr. 23   Litho.   Perf. 14x14¾

3904	A925 60c multi	1.25	1.25
a.	Booklet pane of 4 + 2 labels	5.50	—
3905	A925 60c multi	1.25	1.25
a.	Booklet pane of 4 + 2 labels	5.50	—
3906	A925 60c multi	1.25	1.25
a.	Booklet pane of 4 + 2 labels	5.50	—
3907	A925 60c multi	1.25	1.25
a.	Booklet pane of 4 + 2 labels	5.50	—
3908	A925 60c multi	1.25	1.25
a.	Booklet pane of 4 + 2 labels	5.50	—
	Complete booklet, #3904a, 3905a, 3906a, 3907a, 3908a	27.50	
b.	Horiz. strip of 5, #3904-3908	6.25	6.25
	Nos. 3904-3908 (5)	6.25	6.25

**Coil Stamps
Self-Adhesive**

Serpentine Die Cut 11¼ Syncopated

3909	A925 60c multi	1.25	.25
3910	A925 60c multi	1.25	.25
3911	A925 60c multi	1.25	.25

1.25 .25
#3909-3913 1.25 .25
...913 (5) 6.25
6.25 1.25

...oklet sold for $12.95. Examples
...e booklets with overprints for the
...a 2013 World Stamp Expo were made
...to the show organizers and sold only by
...em.

Battle of
Beersheba,
96th Anniv. — A926

Designs: 60c, Statue of Australian Light
Horseman, by Peter Corlett, Beersheva, Israel.
$2.60, Australian Light Horsemen, photograph
of battle re-enactment.

2013, May 10   **Perf. 13x13½**
3914 A926 60c multi   1.25 .95
3915 A926 $2.60 multi   5.00 3.75

See Israel Nos. 1975-1976.

Black Caviar,
Undefeated
Racehorse — A927

2013, May 10   **Perf. 14¾x14**
3916 A927 60c multi   1.25 1.25

Booklet Stamp
Self-Adhesive

Serpentine Die Cut 11¼ Syncopated
3917 A927 60c multi   1.25 .25
   a.   Booklet pane of 10   12.50

Stamps like No. 3916 but with a white frame
were printed in limited-quantity sheets of 10
that were sold in special packages only at the
Australia 2013 World Stamp Expo.

Stamps Depicting Kangaroos — A928

2013, May 10   **Litho.**   **Imperf.**
3918 A928 $1.62 Booklet pane   3.50 —
   Complete booklet, #1003b,
   1284b, 3534d, 3918   25.00

No. 3918 contains imperforate examples of
Nos. 992a, 1030c, 1063B and 2121, but these
stamps were not valid for postage individually
as cutouts from the entire booklet pane. Complete booklet sold for $12.95, and also con-
tains a perforated booklet pane containing lithographed reproductions of Nos. 166 and 322
that is invalid for postage.

Kangaroo and Map
Stamps, Cent. — A929

2013, May 10   **Litho.**   **Perf. 14¼x14**
3919 A929 $10 red   19.00 9.50
   a.   Souvenir sheet of 1   19.00 9.50

A booklet containing an imperforate example of No. 3919 sold for $24.95.

First
Commonwealth of
Australia
Banknotes,
Cent. — A930

Designs: 60c, Scene from ceremony for
numbering first banknote. $2.60, Arms of
Australia.

2013, May 11   **Litho.**   **Perf. 14x13½**
3920 A930 60c multi   1.25 .95
3921 A930 $2.60 multi   5.00 3.75
   a.   Souvenir sheet of 2, #3920-
   3921   6.25 4.75

Examples of No. 3921a overprinted in the
margin with the emblem of the 2013 Melbourne World Stamp Expo were sold by the
exhibitions organizers for $15.

Pardalotes
A931

Designs: 60c, Forty-spotted pardalote.
$1.20, Spotted pardalote. $1.80, Red-browed
pardalote. $3, Striated pardalote.

2013, May 11   **Litho.**   **Perf. 14x14¾**
3922 A931 60c multi   1.25 1.25
3923 A931 $1.20 multi   2.25 2.25
3924 A931 $1.80 multi   3.50 2.60
3925 A931 $3 multi   5.75 4.50
   a.   Booklet pane of 4, #3922-
   3925   13.00
   Complete booklet, #3151c,
   3376b, 3665b, 3925a   48.50
   Nos. 3922-3925 (4)   12.75 10.60

Coil Stamp
Self-Adhesive

Serpentine Die Cut 11¼ Syncopated
3926 A931 60c multi   1.25 .25

Booklet Stamp
3927 A931 $1.20 multi   2.25 .50
   a.   Booklet pane of 5   11.50

Complete booklet sold for $24.95.

State
Government
Houses
A932

Government House of: Nos. 3928, 3932,
South Australia. Nos. 3929, 3933, Western
Australia. Nos. 3930, 3934, New South Wales.
Nos. 3931, 3935, Tasmania.

2013, June 11   **Litho.**   **Perf. 14x14¾**
3928 A932 60c multi   1.25 1.25
3929 A932 60c multi   1.25 1.25
3930 A932 60c multi   1.25 1.25
3931 A932 60c multi   1.25 1.25
   a.   Block of 4, #3928-3931   5.00 5.00
   Nos. 3928-3931 (4)   5.00 5.00

Self-Adhesive

Serpentine Die Cut 11¼ Syncopated
3932 A932 60c multi   1.25 .25
3933 A932 60c multi   1.25 .25
3934 A932 60c multi   1.25 .25
3935 A932 60c multi   1.25 .25
   a.   Horiz. coil strip of 4, #3932-
   3935   5.00
   b.   Booklet pane of 20, 5 each
   #3932-3935   25.00
   Nos. 3932-3935 (4)   5.00 1.00

Road
Trips — A933

Designs: Nos. 3936, 3942, Utility vehicle in
Sydney. Nos. 3937, 3941, Station wagon in
Melbourne. Nos. 3938, 3945, Car on roller
coaster tracks, Gold Coast. Nos. 3939, 3943,
Utility vehicle and camper in Adelaide. Nos.
3940, 3944, Car and camper in Canberra.

2013, July 2   **Litho.**   **Perf. 14¼**
3936 A933 60c multi   1.10 1.10
3937 A933 60c multi   1.10 1.10
3938 A933 60c multi   1.10 1.10
3939 A933 60c multi   1.10 1.10
3940 A933 60c multi   1.10 1.10
   a.   Souvenir sheet of 5, #3936-
   3940   5.50 5.50
   Nos. 3936-3940 (5)   5.50 5.50

Booklet Stamps
Self-Adhesive

Serpentine Die Cut 11¼ Syncopated
3941 A933 60c multi   1.10 .25
3942 A933 60c multi   1.10 .25
   a.   Booklet pane of 10, 5 each
   #3941-3942   11.00
3943 A933 60c multi   1.10 .25
3944 A933 60c multi   1.10 .25
3945 A933 60c multi   1.10 .25
   a.   Booklet pane of 20, 7 each
   #3943, 3945, 6 #3944   22.00
   Nos. 3941-3945 (5)   5.50 1.25

Aboriginal
Leaders — A934

Designs: Nos. 3946, 3951, Shirley Smith
(1921-98), justice and welfare advocate. Nos.
3947, 3952, Neville Bonner (1922-99), first
Aboriginal member of Australian Parliament.
Nos. 3948, 3953, Oodgeroo Noonuccal (1920-
93), poet. Nos. 3949, 3954, Eddie "Koiki"
Mabo (1936-92), plaintiff in historic Aboriginal
land rights lawsuit. Nos. 3950, 3955, Charles
Perkins (1936-2000), Secretary of the Department of Aboriginal Affairs.

2013, July 9   **Litho.**   **Perf. 14¾x14**
3946 A934 60c multi   1.10 1.10
   a.   Booklet pane of 4   4.75
3947 A934 60c multi   1.10 1.10
   a.   Booklet pane of 4   4.75
3948 A934 60c multi   1.10 1.10
   a.   Booklet pane of 4   4.75
3949 A934 60c multi   1.10 1.10
   a.   Booklet pane of 4   4.75
3950 A934 60c multi   1.10 1.10
   a.   Booklet pane of 4   4.75
   Complete booklet, #3946a,
   3947a, 3948a, 3949a,
   3950a   24.00
   b.   Horiz. strip of 5, #3946-3950   5.50 5.50
   Nos. 3946-3950 (5)   5.50 5.50

Coil Stamps
Self-Adhesive

Serpentine Die Cut 11¼ Syncopated
3951 A934 60c multi   1.10 .25
3952 A934 60c multi   1.10 .25
3953 A934 60c multi   1.10 .25
3954 A934 60c multi   1.10 .25
3955 A934 60c multi   1.10 .25
   a.   Vert. coil strip of 5, #3951-
   3955   5.50
   Nos. 3951-3955 (5)   5.50 1.25

Complete booklet sold for $12.95.

Birth of Prince
George of
Cambridge
A935

2013, July 22   **Litho.**   **Perf. 14¼**
3956 A935 60c multi   1.10 1.10

Booklet Stamp
Self-Adhesive

Serpentine Die Cut 11¼ Syncopated
3957 A935 60c multi   1.10 .25
   a.   Booklet pane of 10   11.00

Headline
News — A936

News stories of: Nos. 3958, 3962, August
15, 1945 (end of World War II). Nos. 3959,
3963, July 21, 1969 (first man on the Moon).
Nos. 3960, 3964, December 25, 1974
(destruction of Darwin by Cyclone Tracy). Nos.
3961, 3965, September 27, 1983 (victory of
Australia in America's Cup yacht races).

2013, July 23   **Litho.**   **Perf. 14¾x14**
3958 A936 60c multi   1.10 1.10
3959 A936 60c multi   1.10 1.10
3960 A936 60c multi   1.10 1.10
3961 A936 60c multi   1.10 1.10
   a.   Block of 4, #3958-3961   4.40 4.40
   b.   Souvenir sheet of 4, #3958-
   3961   4.40 4.40
   Nos. 3958-3961 (4)   4.40 4.40

Self-Adhesive

Serpentine Die Cut 11¼ Syncopated
3962 A936 60c multi   1.10 .25
3963 A936 60c multi   1.10 .25
3964 A936 60c multi   1.10 .25
3965 A936 60c multi   1.10 .25
   a.   Vert. coil strip of 4, #3962-
   3965   4.40
   b.   Booklet pane of 20, 5 each
   #3962-3965   22.00
   Nos. 3962-3965 (4)   4.40 1.00

Carnivorous
Plants — A937

Designs: Nos. 3966, 3970, Cephalotus fol-
licularis and ants. Nos. 3967, 3971, Drosera
rupicola and fly. Nos. 3968, 3972, Drosera
lowriei and butterfly. Nos. 3969, 3973, Nepen-
thes rowanae and frog.

2013, Aug. 13   **Litho.**   **Perf. 14¾x14**
3966 A937 60c multi   1.10 1.10
3967 A937 60c multi   1.10 1.10
3968 A937 60c multi   1.10 1.10
3969 A937 60c multi   1.10 1.10
   a.   Block of 4, #3966-3969   4.40 4.40
   Nos. 3966-3969 (4)   4.40 4.40

Booklet Stamps
Self-Adhesive

Serpentine Die Cut 11¼ Syncopated
3970 A937 60c multi   1.10 .25
3971 A937 60c multi   1.10 .25
3972 A937 60c multi   1.10 .25
3973 A937 60c multi   1.10 .25
   a.   Booklet pane of 10, 3 each
   #3970, 3972, 2 each
   #3971, 3973   11.00
   Nos. 3970-3973 (4)   4.40 1.00

Coral
Reefs
A938

Designs: Nos. 3974, 3979, Underwater view
of Ningaloo Reef, Western Australia. Nos.
3975, 3978, Underwater view of Great Barrier
Reef, Queensland. Nos. 3976, 3981, Aerial
veiw of Ningaloo Reef. Nos. 3977, 3980,
Aerial view of Great Barrier Reef.

2013, Aug. 20   **Litho.**   **Perf. 14½x14**
3974 A938 60c multi   1.10 1.10
   a.   Perf. 13½x14   1.10 1.10
3975 A938 60c multi   1.10 1.10
   a.   Horiz. pair, #3974-3975   2.20 2.20
   b.   Perf. 13½x14   1.10 1.10
3976 A938 $1.20 multi   2.25 2.25
3977 A938 $1.20 multi   2.25 2.25
   a.   Horiz. pair, #3976-3977   4.50 4.50
   b.   Perf. 13½x14   2.25 2.25
   c.   Souvenir sheet of 4, #3974a,
   3975b, 3976a, 3977b   6.75 6.75
   Nos. 3974-3977 (4)   6.70 6.70

Booklet Stamps
Self-Adhesive
Serpentine Die Cut 10½ Syncopated

3978	A938	60c multi	1.10	.25
3979	A938	60c multi	1.10	.25
a.	Booklet pane of 20, 10 each #3978-3979		22.00	
3980	A938	$1.20 multi	2.25	.50
3981	A938	$1.20 multi	2.25	.50
a.	Booklet pane of 5, 3 #3980, 2 #3981		11.50	
	Nos. 3978-3981 (4)		6.70	1.50

Poultry Breeds — A939

Designs: No. 3982, Australian Game hen and rooster. No. 3983, Australian Pit Game hen and chicks. Nos. 3984, 3985, Australorp hens (37x26mm).

2013, Sept. 3   Litho.   Perf. 14x13½

3982	A939	60c multi	1.10	.85
a.	Booklet pane of 4		4.75	—
3983	A939	60c multi	1.10	.85
a.	Booklet pane of 4		4.75	—
b.	Booklet pane of 4, 2 each #3982-3983		4.75	—

Perf. 14x14¾

3984	A939	60c multi	1.10	1.10
a.	Booklet pane of 4		4.75	—
b.	Souvenir sheet of 3, #3982-3984		3.30	3.30
	Complete booklet, #3982a, 3983a, 3983b, 2 #3984a		24.00	
	Nos. 3982-3984 (3)		3.30	2.80

Booklet Stamp
Self-Adhesive
Serpentine Die Cut 11¼ Syncopated

3985	A939	60c multi	1.10	.25
a.	Booklet pane of 10		11.00	

Complete booklet sold for $12.95 and contains two examples of No. 3984a having different margins.

Dinosaurs — A940

Designs: Nos. 3986, 3992, Koolasuchus. Nos. 3987, 3995, Serendipaceratops (26x37mm). No. 3988, Timimus (30x50mm). Nos. 3989, 3993, Diamantinasaurus, horiz. No. 3990, Qantassaurus, horiz. (50x30mm). Nos. 3991, 3994, Australovenator (26x37mm).

2013, Sept. 24   Litho.   Perf. 14½x14

3986	A940	60c multi	1.25	1.25
a.	Booklet pane of 4		5.00	—
b.	Perf. 14½		1.25	1.25

Perf. 14¾x14

3987	A940	60c multi	1.25	1.25
a.	Booklet pane of 4		5.00	—
b.	Perf. 14½		1.25	1.25

Perf. 14x14½

3988	A940	60c multi	1.25	1.25
a.	Perf. 14x13½		1.25	1.25
b.	Booklet pane of 2 #3988a		2.50	—
c.	Perf. 14½		1.25	1.25

Perf. 14x14½

3989	A940	60c multi	1.25	1.25
a.	Booklet pane of 4		5.00	—
b.	Perf. 14½		1.25	1.25

Perf. 14½x14

3990	A940	60c multi	1.25	1.25
a.	Perf. 13½x14		1.25	1.25
b.	Booklet pane of 2 #3990a		2.50	—
c.	Perf. 14½		1.25	1.25

Perf. 14¾x14

3991	A940	60c multi	1.25	1.25
a.	Booklet pane of 4		5.00	—
	Complete booklet, #3986a, 3987a, 3988b, 3989a, 3990b, 3991a		25.00	
b.	Perf. 14½		1.25	1.25
c.	Souvenir sheet of 6, #3986b, 3987b, 3988c, 3989b, 3990c, 3991b		7.50	7.50
	Nos. 3986-3991 (6)		7.50	7.50

Booklet Stamps
Self-Adhesive
Serpentine Die Cut 11¼

3992	A940	60c multi	1.25	.25
3993	A940	60c multi	1.25	.25
a.	Booklet pane of 10, 5 each #3992-3993		12.50	

Serpentine Die Cut 11¼ Syncopated

3994	A940	60c multi	1.25	.25
3995	A940	60c multi	1.25	.25
a.	Booklet pane of 20, 10 each #3994-3995		25.00	
	Nos. 3992-3995 (4)		5.00	1.00

Complete booklet sold for $12.95.

Historic Railroad Stations A941

Station at: Nos. 3996, 4000, Maryborough, Victoria. Nos. 3997, 4001, Quorn, South Australia. Nos. 3998, 4002, Hay, New South Wales. Nos. 3999, 4003, Normanton, Queensland.

2013, Oct. 8   Litho.   Perf. 14x14¾

3996	A941	60c multi	1.25	1.25
3997	A941	60c multi	1.25	1.25
3998	A941	60c multi	1.25	1.25
3999	A941	60c multi	1.25	1.25
a.	Block of 4, #3996-3999		5.00	5.00
	Nos. 3996-3999 (4)		5.00	5.00

Self-Adhesive
Serpentine Die Cut 11¼ Syncopated

4000	A941	60c multi	1.25	.25
4001	A941	60c multi	1.25	.25
4002	A941	60c multi	1.25	.25
4003	A941	60c multi	1.25	.25
a.	Horiz. coil strip of 4, #4000-4003		5.00	
b.	Booklet pane of 10, 3 each #4000-4001, 2 each #4002-4003		12.50	
	Nos. 4000-4003 (4)		5.00	1.00

Ludwig Leichhardt (1813-48), Explorer of Outback Region A942

2013, Oct. 15   Litho.   Perf. 14¼

4004	A942	60c multi	1.25	.95

See Germany No. 2752.

Early Australian Coinage A943

Designs: 60c, Holey dollar and dumps. $3, Holey dollars.

2013, Oct. 22   Litho.   Perf. 14x14¾

4005	A943	$3 multi	1.25	.95
4006	A943	$3 multi	5.75	4.50

Souvenir Sheet
Litho. & Embossed With Foil Application

4007		Sheet of 2	7.00	7.00
a.	A943 60c multi		1.25	.95
b.	A943 $3 multi		5.75	4.50

Christmas
A944   A945

Designs: Nos. 4008, 4014, Madonna and Child. Nos. 4009, 4015, 4019, Christmas tree.

Nos. 4010, 4016, 4020, Gift. 60c, Candle. Nos. 4012, 4017, Bell. Nos. 4013, 4018, Adoration of the Shepherds.

2013, Nov. 1   Litho.   Perf. 14¾x14

4008	A944	55c multi	1.10	1.10
4009	A945	55c multi	1.10	1.10
4010	A945	55c multi	1.10	1.10
a.	Horiz. pair, #4009-4010		2.20	2.20
4011	A944	60c multi	1.25	.95
4012	A944	$1.70 multi	3.25	1.60
4013	A944	$2.55 multi	4.75	2.40
a.	Souvenir sheet of 2, #4008, 4013		6.00	6.00
	Nos. 4008-4013 (6)		12.55	8.25

Booklet Stamps
Self-Adhesive
Serpentine Die Cut 11¼ Syncopated

4014	A944	55c multi	1.10	.25
a.	Booklet pane of 20 + 10 etiquettes		22.00	
4015	A945	55c multi	1.10	.25
4016	A945	55c multi	1.10	.25
a.	Booklet pane of 20, 10 each #4015-4016, + 10 etiquettes		22.00	
4017	A945	$1.70 multi	3.25	1.60
a.	Booklet pane of 5		16.50	
4018	A944	$2.55 multi	4.75	2.40
a.	Booklet pane of 5		24.00	

Litho. & Embossed With Foil Application

4019	A945	55c multi	1.10	.25
a.	Booklet pane of 10		11.00	
4020	A945	55c multi	1.10	.25
a.	Booklet pane of 10		11.00	
	Nos. 4014-4020 (7)		13.50	5.25

Christening of Prince George of Cambridge — A946

Duke and Duchess of Cambridge with Prince George: 60c, White background. $2.60, Yellow background.

2014, Jan. 7   Litho.   Perf. 14¾x14

4022	A946	60c multi	1.10	1.10
4023	A946	$2.60 multi	4.75	4.75
a.	Souvenir sheet of 2, #4022-4023		6.00	6.00

Booklet Stamps
Self-Adhesive
Serpentine Die Cut 11¼ Syncopated

4024	A946	60c multi	1.10	.25
a.	Booklet pane of 10		11.00	
4025	A946	$2.60 multi	4.75	2.40
a.	Booklet pane of 5		24.00	

Orchids — A947

Designs: Nos. 4026, 4030, Golden rock orchid. Nos. 4027, 4031, Bee orchid. Nos. 4028, 4032, Orange blossom orchid. Nos. 4029, 4033, Shirt orchid.

2014, Jan. 14   Litho.   Perf. 14¾x14

4026	A947	60c multi	1.10	1.10
4027	A947	60c multi	1.10	1.10
4028	A947	60c multi	1.10	1.10
4029	A947	60c multi	1.10	1.10
a.	Horiz. strip of 4, #4026-4029		4.40	4.40
	Nos. 4026-4029 (4)		4.40	4.40

Booklet Stamps
Self-Adhesive
Serpentine Die Cut 11¼ Syncopated

4030	A947	60c multi	1.10	.25
4031	A947	60c multi	1.10	.25
4032	A947	60c multi	1.10	.25
4033	A947	60c multi	1.10	.25
a.	Booklet pane of 10, 2 each #4030, 4032, 3 each #4031, 4033		11.00	
b.	Booklet pane of 20, 5 each #4030-4033		22.00	
	Nos. 4030-4033 (4)		4.40	1.00

Cooking Celebrities — A948

Designs: Nos. 4034, 4039, Margaret Fulton. Nos. 4035, 4040, Maggie Beer. Nos. 4036, 4041, Stephanie Alexander. Nos. 4037, 4042, Neil Perry. Nos. 4038, 4043, Kylie Kwong.

2014, Jan. 17   Litho.   Perf. 14¾x14

4034	A948	60c multi	1.10	1.10
a.	Booklet pane of 4		5.25	—
4035	A948	60c multi	1.10	1.10
a.	Booklet pane of 4		5.25	—
4036	A948	60c multi	1.10	1.10
a.	Booklet pane of 4		5.25	—
4037	A948	60c multi	1.10	1.10
a.	Booklet pane of 4		5.25	—
4038	A948	60c multi	1.10	1.10
a.	Booklet pane of 4		5.25	—
	Complete booklet, #4034a, 4035a, 4036a, 4037a, 4038a		22.00	
	Nos. 4034-4038 (5)		5.50	5.50

Booklet Stamps
Self-Adhesive
Serpentine Die Cut 11¼ Syncopated

4039	A948	60c multi	1.10	.25
a.	Booklet pane of 10		11.00	
4040	A948	60c multi	1.10	.25
a.	Booklet pane of 10		11.00	
4041	A948	60c multi	1.10	.25
a.	Booklet pane of 10		11.00	
4042	A948	60c multi	1.10	.25
a.	Booklet pane of 10		11.00	
4043	A948	60c multi	1.10	.25
a.	Booklet pane of 10		11.00	
	Nos. 4039-4043 (5)		5.50	1.25

Complete booklet sold for $14.95.

Victory of Australian Cricket Team in 2013-14 Ashes Test Matches — A949

Designs: 60c, Ashes urn. $2.60, Australian cricket team.

2014, Jan. 20   Litho.   Perf. 14¾x14

4044	A949	60c multi	1.10	.85
4045	A949	$2.60 multi	4.75	4.75
a.	Souvenir sheet of 2, #4044-4045		6.00	6.00

Booklet Stamp
Self-Adhesive
Serpentine Die Cut 11½x11¼

4046	A949	$2.60 multi	4.75	2.40
a.	Booklet pane of 5		24.00	

Hearts — A950   Rose — A951

2014, Feb. 4   Litho.   Perf. 14¾x14

4047	A950	60c multi	1.10	1.10
4048	A951	60c multi	1.10	1.10
a.	Pair, #4047-4048		2.20	2.20

Booklet Stamps
Self-Adhesive
Serpentine Die Cut 11¼ Syncopated

4049	A950	60c multi	1.10	.25
a.	Booklet pane of 10		11.00	
4050	A951	60c multi	1.10	.25
a.	Booklet pane of 20		22.00	

With Personalized Photo at Right Like Type A692a
Serpentine Die Cut 11½x11¼ Syncopated

4051	A950	60c multi	2.25	2.25
4052	A951	60c multi	2.25	2.25

Nos. 4051-4052 each were printed in sheets of 20 and have personalized pictures and a straight edge at right and lack separations between the stamp and the personalized photo. Sheets of 20 of each stamp sold for $25.

National and State Floral Emblems — A952

Designs: Nos. 4053, 4060, 4064, Tasmanian blue gum (Tasmania). Nos. 4054, 4061, 4065, Waratah (New South Wales). Nos. 4055, 4062, 4066, Golden wattle (Australia). Nos. 4056, 4063, 4067, Common heath (Victoria). $1.40, Cooktown orchid (Queensland). $2.10, Kangaroo paw (Western Australia). $3.50, Sturt's desert pea (South Australia).

2014, Mar. 24   Litho.   Perf. 14½x14

4053	A952	70c multi	1.40	1.40
4054	A952	70c multi	1.40	1.40
4055	A952	70c multi	1.40	1.40
4056	A952	70c multi	1.40	1.40
a.		Horiz. strip of 4, #4053-4056	5.60	5.60
4057	A952	$1.40 multi	2.60	1.40
4058	A952	$2.10 multi	4.00	2.00
4059	A952	$3.50 multi	6.50	3.25
		Nos. 4053-4059 (7)	18.70	12.25

Coil Stamp
Self-Adhesive
Serpentine Die Cut 12¾

4060	A952	70c multi	1.40	.25
4061	A952	70c multi	1.40	.25
4062	A952	70c multi	1.40	.25
4063	A952	70c multi	1.40	.25
a.		Vert. strip of 4, #4060-4063	5.60	

Booklet Stamps
Serpentine Die Cut 11¼

4064	A952	70c multi	1.40	.25
4065	A952	70c multi	1.40	.25
4066	A952	70c multi	1.40	.25
4067	A952	70c multi	1.40	.25
a.		Booklet pane of 10, 3 each #4064-4065, 2 each #4066-4067	14.00	
b.		Booklet pane of 20, 5 each #4064-4067	28.00	
		Nos. 4060-4067 (8)	11.20	2.00

Map of Australia on Beach
A953

Kangaroo
A954

Serpentine Die Cut 11¼ Syncopated
2014, Mar. 24   Litho.
Booklet Stamps
Self-Adhesive

4068	A953	(70c) multi	1.40	.25
4069	A954	(70c) multi	1.40	.25
a.		Booklet pane of 5, 2#4068, 3 #4069	7.25	

No. 4069a was made available to holders of Australia Post My Post Concession Account card and the general public. Pensioners, veterans, the disabled, and others typically on low or fixed incomes, could apply at their local post office to receive a Concession Account card. Those eligible to receive the card were sent a free example of No. 4069a, which was mailed with the card. Card holders, when showing the card at the post office and having the information recorded, could purchase up to ten No. 4069a every year for $3 (60c per stamp, lower than the 70c letter rate instituted on March 31). 10,000 examples of No. 4069a were made available to the public through the philatelic bureau, but these were sold for $3.95 (79c per stamp). There are no differences between the stamps offered to card holders and the general public, aside from the selling price. Nos. 4068 and 4069 were valid only on letters, and could not be used on parcels or international mail.

Queen Elizabeth II, 88th Birthday — A955

Queen Elizabeth II facing: 70c, Left. $2.60, Right.

2014, Apr. 8   Litho.   Perf. 14¾x14

4070	A955	70c multi	1.40	1.10
4071	A955	$2.60 multi	5.00	2.50
a.		Souvenir sheet of 2, #4070-4071	6.50	3.75

Booklet Stamp
Self-Adhesive
Serpentine Die Cut 11¼ Syncopated

4072	A955	$2.60 multi	5.00	2.50
a.		Booklet pane of 5	25.00	

Map of Australia
A956

Balloons and Streamers
A957

Baby's Mobile
A958

Fireworks
A959

Rose — A960

Stylized Flowers — A961

Champagne Flutes — A962

Wedding Rings and Roses — A963

Wedding Rings — A964

2014, Apr. 15   Litho.   Perf. 14¾x14

4073	A956	70c blue & multi	1.40	.70
4074	A956	70c red & multi	1.40	.70
a.		Horiz. pair, #4073-4074	2.80	1.40
4075	A957	70c multi	1.40	1.40
4076	A958	70c multi	1.40	1.40
4077	A959	70c multi	1.40	1.40
4078	A960	70c multi	1.40	1.40
4079	A961	70c multi	1.40	1.40
4080	A962	70c multi	1.40	1.40
4081	A963	70c multi	1.40	1.40
4082	A964	$1.40 multi	2.60	1.40
		Nos. 4073-4082 (10)	15.20	12.60

Booklet Stamps
Self-Adhesive
Serpentine Die Cut 11¼ Syncopated

4083	A957	70c multi	1.40	.25
a.		Booklet pane of 10	14.00	
4084	A958	70c multi	1.40	.25
a.		Booklet pane of 10	14.00	
4085	A959	70c multi	1.40	.25
a.		Booklet pane of 10	14.00	
4086	A960	70c multi	1.40	.25
a.		Booklet pane of 10	14.00	
4087	A961	70c multi	1.40	.25
a.		Booklet pane of 10	14.00	
4088	A962	70c multi	1.40	.25
a.		Booklet pane of 10	14.00	
4089	A963	70c multi	1.40	.25
a.		Booklet pane of 10	14.00	
4090	A964	$1.40 multi	2.60	1.40
a.		Booklet pane of 5	10.50	
		Complete booklet, 5 #4090a	52.50	
		Nos. 4083-4090 (8)	12.40	3.15

Complete booklet contains 5 examples of No. 4090a, each with different pane margins.

With Personalized Photo at Right Like Type A692a
Serpentine Die Cut 11½x11¼ Syncopated

4091	A956	70c blue & multi	2.50	2.50
4092	A957	70c multi	2.50	2.50
4093	A958	70c multi	2.50	2.50
4094	A959	70c multi	2.50	2.50
4095	A960	70c multi	2.50	2.50
4096	A961	70c multi	2.50	2.50
4097	A962	70c multi	2.50	2.50
4098	A963	70c multi	2.50	2.50
4099	A964	$1.40 multi	3.75	3.75
		Nos. 4091-4099 (9)	23.75	23.75

Nos. 4091-4099 each were printed in sheets of 20 and have personalized pictures and a straight edge at right and lack separations between the stamp and the personalized photo. Sheets of 20 of Nos. 4091-4098 sold for $27 each, No. 4099, $41.

World War I, Cent. — A965

Inscriptions: Nos. 4100, 4105, War Declared! Nos. 4101, 4106, Australians in Action. Nos. 4102, 4107, Troops Depart. Nos. 4103, 4108, Training, Mena Camp (Egypt). Nos. 4104, 4109, Our Boys.

2014, Apr. 22   Litho.   Perf. 14¼

4100	A965	70c multi	1.40	1.40
4101	A965	70c multi	1.40	1.40
4102	A965	70c multi	1.40	1.40
4103	A965	70c multi	1.40	1.40
4104	A965	70c multi	1.40	1.40
a.		Souvenir sheet of 5, #4100-4104	7.00	7.00
		Nos. 4100-4104 (5)	7.00	7.00

Booklet Stamps
Self-Adhesive
Serpentine Die Cut 11¼ Syncopated

4105	A965	70c multi	1.40	.25
4106	A965	70c multi	1.40	.25
4107	A965	70c multi	1.40	.25
4108	A965	70c multi	1.40	.25
4109	A965	70c multi	1.40	.25
a.		Booklet pane of 10, 2 each #4105-4109	14.00	
		Nos. 4105-4109 (5)	7.00	1.25

Australian Red Cross, Cent. A966

2014, May 6   Litho.   Perf. 14x14¾

4110	A966	70c multi	1.40	1.40

Coil Stamp
Self-Adhesive
Serpentine Die Cut 11¼ Syncopated

4111	A966	70c multi	1.40	.25

Poems by Andrew Barton "Banjo" Paterson (1864-1941) A967

Designs: Nos. 4112, 4116, Clancy of the Overflow. Nos. 4113, 4117, The Man from Snowy River. Nos. 4114, 4118, Waltzing Matilda. Nos. 4115, 4119, Mulga Bill's Bicycle.

2014, May 13   Litho.   Perf. 14x14¾

4112	A967	70c multi	1.40	1.40
a.		Booklet pane of 4	5.60	—
4113	A967	70c multi	1.40	1.40
a.		Booklet pane of 4	5.60	—
4114	A967	70c multi	1.40	1.40
a.		Booklet pane of 4	5.60	—
4115	A967	70c multi	1.40	1.40
a.		Block of 4, #4112-4115	5.60	5.60
b.		Souvenir sheet of 4, #4112-4115	5.60	5.60
c.		Booklet pane of 4 #4115	5.60	—
d.		Booklet pane of 4, #4112-4115	5.60	—
		Complete booklet, #4112a, 4113a, 4114a, 4115c, 2 #4115d	34.00	
		Nos. 4112-4115 (4)	5.60	5.60

Self-Adhesive
Serpentine Die Cut 11¼ Syncopated

4116	A967	70c multi	1.40	.25
4117	A967	70c multi	1.40	.25
4118	A967	70c multi	1.40	.25
4119	A967	70c multi	1.40	.25
a.		Horiz. coil strip of 4, #4116-4119	5.60	
b.		Booklet pane of 10, 3 each #4116-4117, 2 each #4118-4119	14.00	
		Nos. 4116-4119 (4)	5.60	1.00

The complete booklet sold for $16.95. In the complete booklet, one of the two examples of No. 4115d has a booklet pane margin similar to No. 4115b.

G20 Summit, Brisbane — A968

2014, June 3   Litho.   Perf. 14¾x14

4120	A968	70c multi	1.40	1.10

King George V Typographed Stamps, Cent. — A969

2014, June 17   Litho.   Perf. 14½x14

4121	A969	70c red	1.40	1.10
a.		Booklet pane of 4	5.60	—
4122	A969	70c red brown	1.40	1.10
a.		Booklet pane of 4	5.60	—
4123	A969	70c purple	1.40	1.10
a.		Booklet pane of 4	5.60	—
4124	A969	70c green	1.40	1.10
a.		Booklet pane of 4	5.60	—
b.		Booklet pane of 4, #4121-4124	5.60	—
c.		Booklet pane of 4, #4121-4124, imperf.	5.60	—
		Complete booklet, #4121a, 4122a, 4123a, 4124a, 4124b, 4124c	34.00	
d.		Block or strip of 4, #4121-4124	5.60	4.40
e.		Souvenir sheet of 4, #4121-4124	5.60	4.40
f.		Sheet of 10, 4 #4121, 2 each #4122-4124	14.00	11.00

Typo.

4125	A969	70c red	1.40	1.10
4126	A969	70c purple	1.40	1.10
4127	A969	70c green	1.40	1.10
4128	A969	70c red brown	1.40	1.10
a.		Horiz. strip of 4, #4125-4128	5.60	4.40
b.		Sheet of 10, 4 #4125, 2 each #4126-4128	14.00	11.00
		Nos. 4121-4128 (8)	11.20	8.80

Complete booklet sold for $16.95. Nos. 4124f and 4128b were sold together for $14.45.

First Air Mail in Australia, Cent. — A970

Designs: 70c, Spectators watching airplane in flight. $2.60, Maurice Guillaux piloting Bleriot XI airplane.

2014, July 1   Litho.   Perf. 14¼
4129 A970 70c multi 1.40 1.10
  a. Booklet pane of 4 .... 5.75 —
4130 A970 $2.60 multi 5.00 2.50
  a. Booklet pane of 4 .... 20.50 —
  b. Booklet pane of 2, #4129-4130 .... 6.50 —
    Complete booklet, #4130a, 4130b, 2 #4129a ... 38.50
  c. Souvenir sheet of 2, #4129-4130 .... 6.50 —

Complete booklet sold for $19.95. The two examples of No. 4129a in the booklet have different pane margins.

Visit of Duke and Duchess of Cambridge and Prince George A971

Designs: 70c, Duke and Duchess, Sydney Harbour Bridge. $2.60, Duke and Duchess, Prince George, and bilby.

2014, July 8   Litho.   Perf. 14¼
4131 A971 70c multi 1.40 1.40
4132 A971 $2.60 multi 5.00 5.00
  a. Souvenir sheet of 2, #4131-4132 .... 6.50 6.50

Booklet Stamps
Self-Adhesive
Serpentine Die Cut 11¼ Syncopated
4133 A971 70c multi .... 1.40 .25
  a. Booklet pane of 10 .... 14.00
4134 A971 $2.60 multi 5.00 2.50
  a. Booklet pane of 5 .... 25.00

Equestrian Events — A972

Designs: Nos. 4135, 4140, Pony Club. Nos. 4136, 4141, Polocrosse. Nos. 4137, 4142, Show jumping. Nos. 4138, 4143, Cross-country. Nos. 4139, 4144, Dressage.

2014, July 15   Litho.   Perf. 14¾x14
4135 A972 70c multi 1.40 1.40
4136 A972 70c multi 1.40 1.40
4137 A972 70c multi 1.40 1.40
4138 A972 70c multi 1.40 1.40
4139 A972 70c multi 1.40 1.40
  Nos. 4135-4139 (5) 7.00 7.00

Self-Adhesive
Serpentine Die Cut 11¼ Syncopated
4140 A972 70c multi .... 1.40 .25
  a. Booklet pane of 10 .... 14.00
4141 A972 70c multi .... 1.40 .25
  a. Booklet pane of 10 .... 14.00
4142 A972 70c multi .... 1.40 .25
  a. Booklet pane of 10 .... 14.00
4143 A972 70c multi .... 1.40 .25
  a. Booklet pane of 10 .... 14.00
4144 A972 70c multi .... 1.40 .25
  a. Booklet pane of 10 .... 14.00
  b. Vert. coil strip of 5, #4140-4144 .... 7.00
  Nos. 4140-4144 (5) 7.00 1.25

Norfolk Island Pine — A973

Norfolk Island Pine and: 70c, Cottesloe Beach, Western Australia. $1.40, Old Military Barracks, Kingston, Norfolk Island.

2014, July 22   Litho.   Perf. 14x14¾
4145 A973 70c multi 1.40 1.10
4146 A973 $1.40 multi 2.60 2.00

See Norfolk Island Nos. 1090-1091.

Australian Military Centenaries A974

Designs: Nos. 4147, 4149, Military aviation, cent. Nos. 4148, 4150, Submarines, cent.

2014, Aug. 5   Litho.   Perf. 14x14¾
4147 A974 70c multi 1.40 1.40
4148 A974 70c multi 1.40 1.40
  a. Vert. pair, #4147-4148 ... 2.80 2.80
  b. Souvenir sheet of 2, #4147-4148 .... 2.80 2.80

Booklet Stamps
Self-Adhesive
Serpentine Die Cut 11¼ Syncopated
4149 A974 70c multi .... 1.40 .25
4150 A974 70c multi .... 1.40 .25
  a. Booklet pane of 20, 10 each #4149-4150 .... 28.00

Mid-20th Century Advertisements A975

Advertisement for: Nos. 4151, 4156, Phillip Island Tourism. Nos. 4152, 4157, Harper's Empire Self-Raising Flour. Nos. 4153, 4158, Trans-Australian Airways. Nos. 4154, 4159, Jacko Shoe Polish. Nos. 4155, 4160, Swallow & Ariell's Teddy Bear Biscuits.

2014, Aug. 19   Litho.   Perf. 14¾x14
4151 A975 70c multi 1.40 1.40
4152 A975 70c multi 1.40 1.40
4153 A975 70c multi 1.40 1.40
4154 A975 70c multi 1.40 1.40
4155 A975 70c multi 1.40 1.40
  a. Horiz. strip of 5, #4151-4155 .... 7.00 7.00
  b. Souvenir sheet of 5, #4151-4155 .... 7.00 7.00
  Nos. 4151-4155 (5) 7.00 7.00

Coil Stamps
Self-Adhesive
Serpentine Die Cut 11¼ Syncopated
4156 A975 70c multi .... 1.40 .25
4157 A975 70c multi .... 1.40 .25
4158 A975 70c multi .... 1.40 .25
4159 A975 70c multi .... 1.40 .25
4160 A975 70c multi .... 1.40 .25
  a. Vert. strip of 5, #4156-4160 .... 7.00
  Nos. 4156-4160 (5) 7.00 1.25

Aurora Australis (Southern Lights) A976

Various photographs of auroras with denomination at: Nos. 4161, 4163, 4165, LL. Nos. 4162, 4164, 4166, LR.

2014, Aug. 26   Litho.   Perf. 14x14¾
4161 A976 70c multi 1.40 1.40
4162 A976 70c multi 1.40 1.40
  a. Horiz. pair, #4161-4162 .. 2.80 2.80
4163 A976 $1.40 multi 2.60 2.00
4164 A976 $1.40 multi 2.60 2.00
  a. Horiz. pair, #4163-4164 .. 5.20 4.00
  b. Souvenir sheet of 4, #4161-4164 .... 8.00 8.00
  Nos. 4161-4164 (4) 8.00 6.80

Booklet Stamps
Self-Adhesive
4165 A976 70c multi .... 1.40 .25
4166 A976 70c multi .... 1.40 .25
  a. Booklet pane of 10, 5 each #4165-4166 .... 14.00

On. No. 4164b, Nos. 4162a and 4164a are tete-beche in relationship to each other.

Gardens A977

Designs: Nos. 4167, 4172, Cruden Farm, Victoria. Nos. 4168, 4173, Mendel Gardens, Western Australia. Nos. 4169, 4176, Niwajiri, South Australia. Nos. 4170, 4174, Walcott Gardens, Australian Capital Territory. Nos. 4171, 4175, Wychwood, Tasmania.

2014, Sept. 2   Litho.   Perf. 14x14¾
4167 A977 70c multi 1.40 1.40
4168 A977 70c multi 1.40 1.40
4169 A977 70c multi 1.40 1.40
4170 A977 70c multi 1.40 1.40
4171 A977 70c multi 1.40 1.40
  a. Horiz. strip of 5, #4167-4171 .... 7.00 7.00
  Nos. 4167-4171 (5) 7.00 7.00

Booklet Stamps
Self-Adhesive
Serpentine Die Cut 11¼ Syncopated
4172 A977 70c multi .... 1.40 .25
4173 A977 70c multi .... 1.40 .25
4174 A977 70c multi .... 1.40 .25
4175 A977 70c multi .... 1.40 .25
4176 A977 70c multi .... 1.40 .25
  a. Booklet pane of 20, 4 each #4172-4176 .... 28.00
  Nos. 4172-4176 (5) 7.00 1.25

Venomous Creatures A978

Designs: Nos. 4177, 4186, European wasp. Nos. 4178, 4185, Lionfish. Nos. 4179, 4183, Bull ant. Nos. 4180, 4187, Tiger snake. Nos. 4181, 4188, Stonefish. Nos. 4182, 4184, Stingray.

2014, Sept. 23   Litho.   Perf. 14x14¾
4177 A978 70c multi 1.25 1.25
4178 A978 70c multi 1.25 1.25
4179 A978 70c multi 1.25 1.25
4180 A978 70c multi 1.25 1.25
  a. Souvenir sheet of 6, 2 each #4177, 4179, 4180, + 6 labels 7.75 7.75
4181 A978 70c multi 1.25 1.25
4182 A978 70c multi 1.25 1.25
  a. Souvenir sheet of 6, #4177-4182 .... 7.50 7.50
  b. Souvenir sheet of 6, 2 each #4176, 4181, 4182, + 6 labels 7.75 7.75
  Nos. 4177-4182 (6) 7.50 7.50

Booklet Stamps
Self-Adhesive
Serpentine Die Cut 11¼ Syncopated
4183 A978 70c multi .... 1.25 .25
4184 A978 70c multi .... 1.25 .25
4185 A978 70c multi .... 1.25 .25
4186 A978 70c multi .... 1.25 .25
4187 A978 70c multi .... 1.25 .25
4188 A978 70c multi .... 1.25 .25
  a. Booklet pane of 10, #4185, 4188, 2 each #4183-4184, 4186-4187 .... 12.50
  b. Booklet pane of 20, 3 each #4183, 4185, 4187, 4188, 4 each #4184, 4186 .... 25.00
  Nos. 4183-4188 (6) 7.50 1.50

A souvenir sheet of six containing one each of Nos. 4177-4182 + six labels was sold with a die and game pieces that sold for $9.95. Nos. 4180a and 4182b sold together as a set in a folder for $8.85.

National Parks — A979

Designs: $2.75, Alpine National Park, Victoria. $5.35, Blue Mountains National Park, New South Wales. $7.40, Judbarra/Gregroy National Park, Northern Territory.

Open Gardens Australia

2014, Oct. 1   Litho.   Perf. 14¾x14
4189 A979 $2.75 multi 5.00 2.50
4190 A979 $5.35 multi 9.50 4.75
4191 A979 $7.40 multi 13.00 6.50
  Nos. 4189-4191 (3) 27.50 13.75

Booklet Stamp
Self-Adhesive
Serpentine Die Cut 11¼ Syncopated
4192 A979 $2.75 multi 5.00 2.50
  a. Booklet pane of 5 .... 25.00

National Parks Type of 2014 With Personalized Photo at Right Like Type A692a
Serpentine Die Cut 11½x11¼ Syncopated
2014, Oct. 1   **Litho.**
Self-Adhesive
4193 A979 $2.75 multi 6.00 6.00

No. 4193 was printed in sheets of 20 and has personalized picture and a straight edge at right and lack separations between the stamp and personalized photo. Sheets of 20 of No. 4193 sold for $68.

Horse Racing Tracks A980

Designs: Nos. 4194, 4198, Eagle Farm, Queensland. Nos. 4195, 4199, Royal Randwick, New South Wales. Nos. 4196, 4200, Morphettville, South Australia. Nos. 4197, 4201, Flemington, Victoria.

2014, Oct. 7   Litho.   Perf. 14x14¾
4194 A980 70c multi 1.25 1.25
4195 A980 70c multi 1.25 1.25
4196 A980 70c multi 1.25 1.25
4197 A980 70c multi 1.25 1.25
  a. Horiz. strip of 4, #4194-4197 .... 5.00 5.00
  Nos. 4194-4197 (4) 5.00 5.00

Self-Adhesive
Serpentine Die Cut 11¼ Syncopated
4198 A980 70c multi .... 1.25 .25
4199 A980 70c multi .... 1.25 .25
4200 A980 70c multi .... 1.25 .25
4201 A980 70c multi .... 1.25 .25
  a. Horiz. coil strip of 4, #4198-4201 .... 5.00
  b. Booklet pane of 10, 3 each #4198-4199, 2 each #4200-4201 .... 12.50
  Nos. 4198-4201 (4) 5.00 1.00

Australian Defense Force, Cent. — A981

Poppies and: Nos. 4202, 4206, Cap of Royal Australian Navy. Nos. 4203, 4209, Hat of Australian Army. Nos. 4204, 4207, Cap of Royal Australian Air Force. Nos. 4205, 4208, Australian Defense Force badge.

2014, Oct. 21   Litho.   Perf. 14¼
4202 A981 70c multi 1.25 1.25
4203 A981 70c multi 1.25 1.25
4204 A981 70c multi 1.25 1.25
4205 A981 70c multi 1.25 1.25
  a. Souvenir sheet of 4, #4202-4205 .... 5.00 5.00
  Nos. 4202-4205 (4) 5.00 5.00

Booklet Stamps
Self-Adhesive
Serpentine Die Cut 11¼ Syncopated
4206 A981 70c multi .... 1.25 .25
4207 A981 70c multi .... 1.25 .25
4208 A981 70c multi .... 1.25 .25
4209 A981 70c multi .... 1.25 .25
  a. Booklet pane of 10, 2 each #4206, 4207, 4209, 4 #4208 .... 12.50

Christmas
A982   A983

Designs: Nos. 4210, 4216, Madonna and Child. Nos. 4211, 4217, 4221, Snowflake, ornament, Christmas tree, reindeer. Nos. 4212, 4218, 4222, Star, ornament, gift. 70c, Snowflake, ornament, holly leaves, dove, star. Nos. 4214, 4219, Snowflake and bells. Nos. 4215, 4220, Angels.

2014, Oct. 31   Litho.   Perf. 14¾x14
4210	A982	65c multi	1.10 1.10
4211	A983	65c green	1.10 1.10
4212	A983	65c red	1.10 1.10
4213	A983	70c blue green	1.25 .95
4214	A983	$1.70 pur & dk bl	3.00 1.50
4215	A982	$2.55 multi	4.50 2.25
a.		Souvenir sheet of 2, #4210, 4215	5.75 5.75
		Nos. 4210-4215 (6)	12.05 8.00

Self-Adhesive
Booklet Stamps
Serpentine Die Cut 11¼ Syncopated
4216	A982	65c multi	1.10 .25
a.		Booklet pane of 20 + 20 etiquettes	22.00
4217	A983	65c green	1.10 .25
4218	A983	65c red	1.10 .25
a.		Booklet pane of 20, 10 each #4217-4218, + 20 etiquettes	22.00
4219	A983	$1.70 pur & dk bl	3.00 1.50
a.		Booklet pane of 5	15.00
4220	A982	$2.55 multi	4.50 2.25
a.		Booklet pane of 5	22.50

Litho. With Foil Application
4221	A983	65c green	1.10 .25
a.		Booklet pane of 10	11.00
4222	A983	65c red	1.10 .25
a.		Booklet pane of 10	11.00
		Nos. 4216-4222 (7)	13.00 5.00

Marsupials
A984

Designs: Nos. 4225, 4234, Echidna. Nos. 4226, 4233, Common wombat. Nos. 4227, 4231, Eastern gray kangaroo. Nos. 4228, 4232, Koala. No. 4229, Numbat. No. 4230, Tasmanian devil.

2015, Jan. 13   Litho.   Perf. 14x14¾
4225	A984	70c multi	1.10 1.10
4226	A984	70c multi	1.10 1.10
4227	A984	70c multi	1.10 1.10
4228	A984	70c multi	1.10 1.10
a.		Block of 4, #4225-4228	4.40 4.40
4229	A984	$1.40 multi	2.25 1.75
4230	A984	$1.40 multi	2.25 1.75
a.		Vert. pair, #4229-4230	4.50 3.50
b.		Souvenir sheet of 6, #4225-4230	9.00 9.00
		Nos. 4225-4230 (6)	8.90 7.90

Booklet Stamps
Self-Adhesive
Serpentine Die Cut 11¼ Syncopated
4231	A984	70c multi	1.10 .25
4232	A984	70c multi	1.10 .25
4233	A984	70c multi	1.10 .25
4234	A984	70c multi	1.10 .25
a.		Booklet pane of 10, 3 each #4231-4232, 2 each #4233-4234	11.00
b.		Booklet pane of 20, 5 each #4231-4234	22.00
		Nos. 4231-4234 (4)	4.40 1.00

Victoria Cross
Recipients — A985

Designs: Nos. 4235, 4240, Ben Roberts-Smith. Nos. 4236, 4241, Cameron Baird

(1981-2013). Nos. 4237, 4242, Mark Donaldson. Nos. 4238, 4243, Dan Keighran. Nos. 4239, 4244, Keith Payne.

2015, Jan. 22   Litho.   Perf. 14¾x14
4235	A985	70c multi	1.10 1.10
4236	A985	70c multi	1.10 1.10
4237	A985	70c multi	1.10 1.10
4238	A985	70c multi	1.10 1.10
4239	A985	70c multi	1.10 1.10
a.		Souvenir sheet of 5, #4235-4239	5.50 5.50
		Nos. 4235-4239 (5)	5.50 5.50

Booklet Stamps
Self-Adhesive
Serpentine Die Cut 11¼ Syncopated
4240	A985	70c multi	1.10 .25
a.		Booklet pane of 10	11.00
4241	A985	70c multi	1.10 .25
a.		Booklet pane of 10	11.00
4242	A985	70c multi	1.10 .25
a.		Booklet pane of 10	11.00
4243	A985	70c multi	1.10 .25
a.		Booklet pane of 10	11.00
4244	A985	70c multi	1.10 .25
a.		Booklet pane of 10	11.00
		Nos. 4240-4244 (5)	5.50 1.25

Souvenir Sheet

Victoria Cross — A986

2015, Jan. 22   Litho.   Perf. 14x14¾
4245	A986	Sheet of 2	9.00 9.00
a.		70c olive green	1.10 .85
b.		$5 violet	7.75 5.75

Heart-Shaped
Items — A987

Designs: Nos. 4246, 4251, Kite. Nos. 4247, 4252, Airplane contrail. Nos. 4248, 4250, Hot-air balloon. Nos. 4249, 4253, Cloud.

2015, Feb. 3   Litho.   Perf. 14¾x14
4246	A987	70c multi	1.10 1.10
4247	A987	70c multi	1.10 1.10
4248	A987	70c multi	1.10 1.10
4249	A987	70c multi	1.10 1.10
a.		Horiz. strip of 4, #4246-4249	4.40 4.40
		Nos. 4246-4249 (4)	4.40 4.40

Booklet Stamps
Self-Adhesive
Serpentine Die Cut 11¼ Syncopated
4250	A987	70c multi	1.10 .25
4251	A987	70c multi	1.10 .25
4252	A987	70c multi	1.10 .25
4253	A987	70c multi	1.10 .25
a.		Booklet pane of 20, 7 each #4250-4251, 3 each #4252-4253	22.00
b.		Booklet pane of 10, 5 each #4252-4253	11.00
		Nos. 4250-4253 (4)	4.40 1.00

Clipper Ships
A988

Designs: No. 4254, Frances Henty. No. 4255, Phoenician. No. 4256, Arabian. No. 4257, Monkchester.

2015, Feb. 17   Litho.   Perf. 14x14¾
4254	A988	70c multi	1.10 .85
4255	A988	70c multi	1.10 .85
a.		Horiz. pair, #4254-4255	2.20 1.70
4256	A988	$1.40 multi	2.25 1.75
4257	A988	$1.40 multi	2.25 1.75
a.		Horiz. pair, #4256-4257	4.50 3.50
		Nos. 4254-4257 (4)	6.70 5.20

Tourist
Attractions — A989

Designs: Nos. 4258, 4262, Horse-drawn tram, Victor Harbour, South Australia. Nos. 4259, 4263, Seaplane, Whitsunday Islands, Queensland. Nos. 4260, 4264, Steam train, Dandenong Ranges, Victoria. Nos. 4261, 4265, Cruise boat, Katherine Gorge, Northern Territory.

2015, Mar. 3   Litho.   Perf. 14¾x14
4258	A989	70c multi	1.10 1.10
4259	A989	70c multi	1.10 1.10
4260	A989	70c multi	1.10 1.10
4261	A989	70c multi	1.10 1.10
a.		Horiz. strip of 4, #4258-4261	4.40 4.40
		Nos. 4258-4261 (4)	4.40 4.40

Self-Adhesive
Serpentine Die Cut 11¼ Syncopated
4262	A989	70c multi	1.10 .25
4263	A989	70c multi	1.10 .25
4264	A989	70c multi	1.10 .25
4265	A989	70c multi	1.10 .25
a.		Vert. coil strip of 4, #4262-4265	4.40
b.		Booklet pane of 10, 3 each #4262, 4264, 2 each #4263, 4265	11.00
		Nos. 4262-4265 (4)	4.40 1.00

Trees
A990

Designs: 70c, Lemon-scented gum tree. $1.40, Queensland bottle tree. No. 4268, Green fig tree. No. 4269, Moonah tree.

2015, Mar. 17   Litho.   Perf. 14x14¾
4266	A990	70c multi	1.10 .85
4267	A990	$1.40 multi	2.25 1.75
4268	A990	$2.10 multi	3.25 2.50
4269	A990	$2.10 multi	3.25 2.50
a.		Horiz. pair, #4268-4269	6.50 5.00
b.		Souvenir sheet of 4, #4266-4269	10.00 10.00
		Nos. 4266-4269 (4)	9.85 7.60

Self-Adhesive
Printed on Wood Veneer
Serpentine Die Cut 11¼ Syncopated
4270	A990	70c multi	1.25 1.25

No. 4270 was printed in sheets of 10. The sheet was sold only in a package, together with a sheet of 10 of No. 4266. The package sold for $14.95.

Australian and New
Zealand Army
Corps,
Cent. — A991

Soldier and bugler with bugler facing: 70c, Right. $1.85, Left.

2015, Apr. 7   Litho.   Perf. 14¾x14
4271	A991	70c multi	1.10 1.10
4272	A991	$1.85 multi	3.00 3.00
a.		Souvenir sheet of 2, #4271-4272	4.25 4.25

Booklet Stamps
Self-Adhesive
Serpentine Die Cut 11¼ Syncopated
4273	A991	70c multi	1.10 .25
a.		Booklet pane of 10	11.00
4274	A991	$1.85 multi	3.00 1.50
a.		Booklet pane of 5	15.00

See New Zealand Nos. 2584-2585.

Queen Elizabeth II,
89th
Birthday — A992

Hat color: 70c, Red. $2.75, Blue.

2015, Apr. 7   Litho.   Perf. 14¾x14
4275	A992	70c multi	1.10 .85
4276	A992	$2.75 multi	4.50 2.25
a.		Souvenir sheet of 2, #4275-4276	5.75 5.75
b.		Booklet pane of 2	9.00 —
c.		Booklet pane of 2, #4275-4276	5.75 —
		Complete booklet, #4276b, 4276c, 2 #4275a	24.50

Booklet Stamp
Self-Adhesive
Serpentine Die Cut 11¼ Syncopated
4277	A992	$2.75 multi	4.50 2.25
a.		Booklet pane of 5	22.50

Complete booklet sold for $14.95.

World War I,
Cent. — A993

Australian soldiers involved in Gallipoli campaign: Nos. 4278, 4283, Landing at Gallipoli. Nos. 4279, 4284, Lance Corporal Albert Jacka and Victoria Cross. Nos. 4280, 4285, At Lone Pine. Nos. 4281, 4286, With donkey used for recovering wounded soldiers. Nos. 4282, 4287, Near cannon before evacuation.

2015, Apr. 14   Litho.   Perf. 14¼
4278	A993	70c multi	1.10 1.10
a.		Booklet pane of 4	4.75
4279	A993	70c multi	1.10 1.10
a.		Booklet pane of 4	4.75
4280	A993	70c multi	1.10 1.10
a.		Booklet pane of 4	4.75
4281	A993	70c multi	1.10 1.10
a.		Booklet pane of 4	4.75
4282	A993	70c multi	1.10 1.10
a.		Booklet pane of 4	4.75
		Complete booklet, #4278a, 4279a, 4280a, 4281a, 4282a	24.00
b.		Horiz. strip of 5, #4278-4282	5.50 5.50
c.		Souvenir sheet of 5, #4278-4282	5.50 5.50
		Nos. 4278-4282 (5)	5.50 5.50

Booklet Stamps
Self-Adhesive
Serpentine Die Cut 11¼ Syncopated
4283	A993	70c multi	1.10 .25
4284	A993	70c multi	1.10 .25
4285	A993	70c multi	1.10 .25
4286	A993	70c multi	1.10 .25
4287	A993	70c multi	1.10 .25
a.		Booklet pane of 10, 2 each #4283-4287	11.00
		Nos. 4283-4287 (5)	5.50 1.25

Complete booklet sold for $14.95.

Cats — A994

Cats named: Nos. 4288, 4293, Charo. Nos. 4289, 4294, Bubu. Nos. 4290, 4295, Sweeie. Nos. 4291, 4296, Cato. Nos. 4292, 4297, Briony.

2015, May 5   Litho.   Perf. 14¾x14
4288	A994	70c multi	1.10 1.10
4289	A994	70c multi	1.10 1.10
4290	A994	70c multi	1.10 1.10
4291	A994	70c multi	1.10 1.10
4292	A994	70c multi	1.10 1.10
a.		Horiz. strip of 5, #4288-4292	5.50 5.50
		Nos. 4288-4292 (5)	5.50 5.50

Self-Adhesive
Serpentine Die Cut 11¼ Syncopated

4293	A994	70c multi	1.10	.25
a.		Booklet pane of 10	11.00	
4294	A994	70c multi	1.10	.25
a.		Booklet pane of 10	11.00	
4295	A994	70c multi	1.10	.25
a.		Booklet pane of 10	11.00	
4296	A994	70c multi	1.10	.25
a.		Booklet pane of 10	11.00	
4297	A994	70c multi	1.10	.25
a.		Booklet pane of 10	11.00	
b.		Vert. coil strip of 5, #4293-4297	5.50	
		Nos. 4293-4297 (5)	5.50	1.25

Items in Australian Museums — A995

Designs: Nos. 4298, 4303, 1907 Model automatic totalizer, from Museum of Applied Arts and Sciences, Sydney. Nos. 4299, 4302, Turtle sculpture by Ellarose Savage, Australian Museum, Sydney. Nos. 4300, 4305, Anchor of HMS Endeavour, National Museum of Australia, Canberra. Nos. 4301, 4304, Replica of "Welcome Stranger" gold nugget, Gold Museu, Sovereign Hill, Victoria.

2015, May 19   Litho.   Perf. 14¾x14

4298	A995	70c multi	1.10	1.10
4299	A995	70c multi	1.10	1.10
4300	A995	70c multi	1.10	1.10
4301	A995	70c multi	1.10	1.10
a.		Block of 4, #4298-4301	4.40	4.40
b.		Souvenir sheet of 4, #4298-4301	4.40	4.40
		Nos. 4298-4301 (4)	4.40	4.40

Coil Stamps
Self-Adhesive
Serpentine Die Cut 11¼ Syncopated

4302	A995	70c multi	1.10	.25
4303	A995	70c multi	1.10	.25
4304	A995	70c multi	1.10	.25
4305	A995	70c multi	1.10	.25
a.		Vert. strip of 4, #4302-4305	4.40	
		Nos. 4302-4305 (4)	4.40	1.00

Islands A996

Designs: Nos. 4306, 4310, Phillip Island, Victoria. Nos. 4307, 4311, Lady Musgrave Island, Queensland. $1.40, Bruny Island, Tasmania. $2.10, Buccaneer Archipelago, Western Australia.

2015, June 2   Litho.   Perf. 14x14¾

4306	A996	70c multi	1.10	1.10
4307	A996	70c multi	1.10	1.10
a.		Horiz. pair, #4306-4307	2.20	2.20
4308	A996	$1.40 multi	2.25	1.10
4309	A996	$2.10 multi	3.25	1.60
		Nos. 4306-4309 (4)	7.70	4.90

Booklet Stamps
Self-Adhesive
Serpentine Die Cut 11¼ Syncopated

4310	A996	70c multi	1.10	.25
4311	A996	70c multi	1.10	.25
a.		Booklet pane of 10, 5 each #4310-4311	11.00	

Walter and Eliza Hall Institute of Medical Research, Cent. — A997

2015, June 30   Litho.   Perf. 14¾x14

4312	A997	70c multi	1.10	.85
a.		Booklet pane of 4	4.50	
		Complete booklet, 5 #4312a	22.50	

Complete booklet sold for $14.95.

Lighthouses — A998

Designs: Nos. 4313, 4317, Cape Byron Lighthouse, New South Wales. Nos. 4314, 4318, Cape Leeuwin Lighthouse, Western Australia. Nos. 4315, 4319, North Reef Lighthouse, Queensland. Nos. 4316, 4320, Tasman Island Lighthouse, Tasmania.

2015, July 7   Litho.   Perf. 14¾x14

4313	A998	70c multi	1.10	1.10
a.		Booklet pane of 4	4.50	
4314	A998	70c multi	1.10	1.10
a.		Booklet pane of 4	4.50	
4315	A998	70c multi	1.10	1.10
a.		Booklet pane of 4	4.50	
4316	A998	70c multi	1.10	1.10
a.		Booklet pane of 4	4.50	—
b.		Booklet pane of 4, #4313-4316	4.50	—
		Complete booklet, #4313a, 4314a, 4315a, 4316a, 4316b	22.50	
c.		Block of 4, #4313-4316	4.40	4.40
		Nos. 4313-4316 (4)	4.40	4.40

Self-Adhesive
Serpentine Die Cut 11¼ Syncopated

4317	A998	70c multi	1.10	.25
4318	A998	70c multi	1.10	.25
4319	A998	70c multi	1.10	.25
4320	A998	70c multi	1.10	.25
a.		Booklet pane of 20, 5 each #4317-4320	22.00	
b.		Vert. coil strip of 4, #4317-4320	4.40	
		Nos. 4317-4320 (4)	4.40	1.00

Complete booklet sold for $14.95.

Hiking Trails A999

Designs: Nos. 4321, 4326, National Pass Track, New South Wales. Nos. 4322, 4328, Cape to Cape Track, Western Australia. Nos. 4323, 4325, Larapinta Trail, Northern Territory. Nos. 4324, 4327, Overland Track, Tasmania.

2015, July 14   Litho.   Perf. 14x14¾

4321	A999	70c multi	1.10	1.10
4322	A999	70c multi	1.10	1.10
4323	A999	70c multi	1.10	1.10
4324	A999	70c multi	1.10	1.10
a.		Horiz. strip of 4, #4321-4324	4.40	4.40
b.		Souvenir sheet of 4, #4321-4324	4.40	4.40
		Nos. 4321-4324 (4)	4.40	4.40

Self-Adhesive
Serpentine Die Cut 11¼ Syncopated

4325	A999	70c multi	1.10	.25
4326	A999	70c multi	1.10	.25
4327	A999	70c multi	1.10	.25
4328	A999	70c multi	1.10	.25
a.		Booklet pane of 10, 3 each #4325, 4327, 2 each #4326, 4328	11.00	
b.		Horiz. coil strip of 4, #4325-4328	4.40	
		Nos. 4325-4328 (4)	4.40	1.00

2015 Netball World Cup, Sydney — A1000

2015, Aug. 8   Litho.   Perf. 14¾x14

4329	A1000	70c multi	1.10	.85

Booklet Stamp
Self-Adhesive
Serpentine Die Cut 11¼ Syncopated

4330	A1000	70c multi	1.10	.25
a.		Booklet pane of 20	20.00	

Houses of Parliament A1001

Houses of Parliament in: 70c, Australia. $1.85, New Zealand. $1.95, Singapore.

2015, Aug. 14   Litho.   Perf. 14¼

4331	A1001	70c multi	1.10	.85
4332	A1001	$1.85 multi	2.75	1.40
4333	A1001	$1.95 multi	3.00	1.50
a.		Souvenir sheet of 3, #4331-4333	7.00	7.00
		Nos. 4331-4333 (3)	6.85	3.75

Diplomatic relations of Singapore with Australia and New Zealand, 50th anniv.
See New Zealand No. 2600, Singapore Nos. 1743-1745.

Birth of Princess Charlotte of Cambridge A1002

2015, Aug. 25   Litho.   Perf. 14¼

4334	A1002	70c multi	1.00	1.00

Booklet Stamp
Self-Adhesive
Serpentine Die Cut 11¼ Syncopated

4335	A1002	70c multi	1.00	.25
a.		Booklet pane of 10	10.00	

Neon Signs — A1003

Designs: Nos. 4336, 4339, Skipping Girl Vinegar sign, Abbotsford, Victoria, 1936. Nos. 4337, 4340, Pink Poodle Motel sign, Surfers Paradise, Queensland, 1967. $1.40, Dandy Pig sign for Gippsland Co-operative Bacon Curing Company, Dandenong, Victoria, 1950s.

2015, Sept. 1   Litho.   Perf. 14¾x14

4336	A1003	70c multi	1.00	1.00
4337	A1003	70c multi	1.00	1.00
4338	A1003	$1.40 multi	2.00	1.50
a.		Souvenir sheet of 3, #4336-4338	4.00	4.00
		Nos. 4336-4338 (3)	4.00	3.50

Self-Adhesive
Serpentine Die Cut 11¼ Syncopated

4339	A1003	70c multi	1.00	1.00
4340	A1003	70c multi	1.00	1.00
a.		Vert. coil pair, #4339-4340	2.00	
b.		Booklet pane of 10, 5 each #4339-4340	10.00	

A1004

A1006

A1007

Queen Elizabeth II, Longest-Reigning British Monarch — A1008

2015, Sept. 9   Litho.   Perf. 14¾x14

4341	A1004	70c black	1.00	.75
a.		Booklet pane of 4	4.25	—
4342	A1005	70c multi	1.00	.75
a.		Booklet pane of 4	4.25	—
4343	A1006	70c multi	1.00	.75
a.		Booklet pane of 4	4.25	—
b.		Horiz. strip of 3, #4341-4343	3.00	2.25
4344	A1007	$2.75 multi	4.00	4.00
a.		Booklet pane of 2	8.00	—
4345	A1008	$2.75 multi	4.00	4.00
a.		Booklet pane of 2	8.00	—
		Complete booklet, #4341a, 4342a, 4343a, 4344a, 4345a	29.00	
b.		Horiz. pair, #4344-4345	8.00	8.00
c.		Souvenir sheet of 5, #4341-4345	11.00	11.00
		Nos. 4341-4345 (5)	11.00	10.25

Booklet Stamps
Self-Adhesive
Serpentine Die Cut 11¼ Syncopated

4346	A1007	$2.75 multi	4.00	4.00
4347	A1008	$2.75 multi	4.00	4.00
a.		Booklet pane of 5, 2 #4346, 3 #4347	20.00	

Complete booklet sold for $19.95.

Planets — A1009

Designs: Nos. 4348, 4356a, Mercury. Nos. 4349, 4356b, Mars, horiz. Nos. 4350, 4356c, 4357, Earth. Nos. 4351, 4356d, 4358, Uranus. Nos. 4352, 4356e, 4359, Neptune, horiz. Nos. 4353, 4356f, 4360, Venus, horiz. Nos. 4354, 4356g, Jupiter. Nos. 4355, 4356h, Saturn, horiz.

Litho., Litho. & Silk-Screened (#4356)

2015, Sept. 22   Perf. 14½x14
Stamps With White Frames on Two Sides

4348	A1009	35c multi	.50	.40

Perf. 14x14½

4349	A1009	35c multi	.50	.40
a.		Pair, #4348-4349	1.00	.80

Size: 26x38mm
Perf. 14¾x14

4350	A1009	70c multi	1.00	1.00
4351	A1009	70c multi	1.00	1.00

Size:36x28mm
Perf. 14x14¾

4352	A1009	70c multi	1.00	1.00
4353	A1009	70c multi	1.00	1.00

Size: 30x50mm
Perf. 14x14½

4354	A1009	70c multi	1.00	1.00

Size: 50x30mm
Perf. 14½x14

4355	A1009	70c multi	1.00	1.00
		Nos. 4348-4355 (8)	7.00	6.80

Miniature Sheet
Stamps Without White Frames
Perf. 14½, 14x14½ (#4356e, 4356f)

4356		Sheet of 8	7.00	7.00
a.	A1009	35c multi	.50	.40
b.	A1009	35c multi	.50	.40
c.	A1009	70c multi, 26x38mm	1.00	.75
d.	A1009	70c multi, 26x38mm	1.00	.75
e.	A1009	70c multi, 38x28mm	1.00	.75
f.	A1009	70c multi, 38x28mm	1.00	.75
g.	A1009	70c multi, 30x50mm	1.00	.75
h.	A1009	70c multi, 50x30mm	1.00	.75

A1005

Litho.
Serpentine Die Cut 11¼ Syncopated
Booklet Stamps
Self-Adhesive
Size: 26x38mm
Stamps With White Frames on Two Sides

4357	A1009	70c multi	1.00	.25
4358	A1009	70c multi	1.00	.25
a.		Booklet pane of 20, 10 each #4357-4358	20.00	

Size: 38x26mm

4359	A1009	70c multi	1.00	.25
4360	A1009	70c multi	1.00	.25
a.		Booklet pane of 10, 5 each #4359-4360	10.00	
		Nos. 4357-4360 (4)	4.00	1.00

Humanitarians Honored by Australia — A1010

Designs: Nos. 4361, 4364, Mother Teresa (1910-97), Honorary Companion of the Order of Australia. Nos. 4362, 4365, Nelson Mandela (1918-2013), Honorary Companion of the Order of Australia. Nos. 4363, 4366, Raoul Wallenberg (1912-45), Honorary Citizen of Australia.

2015, Oct. 5   **Litho.**   **Perf. 14x14¾**

4361	A1010	70c multi	1.00	1.00
4362	A1010	70c multi	1.00	1.00
4363	A1010	70c multi	1.00	1.00
		Nos. 4361-4363 (3)	3.00	3.00

Booklet Stamps
Self-Adhesive
Serpentine Die Cut 11¼ Syncopated

4364	A1010	70c multi	1.00	.25
a.		Booklet pane of 10	10.00	
4365	A1010	70c multi	1.00	.25
a.		Booklet pane of 10	10.00	
4366	A1010	70c multi	1.00	.25
a.		Booklet pane of 10	10.00	
		Nos. 4364-4366 (3)	3.00	.75

Bicycles A1011

Designs: Nos. 4367, 4371, 1888 Basset & Co. penny-farthing. Nos. 4368, 4372, Sutherland ladies' safety bicycle, c. 1910. $1.85, Finlay Bros. men's sprung-frame saftey bicycle, 1930s. $2.75, Baum Cycles custom-made road bicycle, 2015.

2015, Oct. 13   **Litho.**   **Perf. 14¼**

4367	A1011	70c multi	1.00	1.00
a.		Booklet pane of 4	4.00	—
4368	A1011	70c multi	1.00	1.00
a.		Booklet pane of 4	4.00	—
b.		Horiz. pair, #4367-4368	2.00	2.00
4369	A1011	$1.85 multi	2.75	1.40
a.		Booklet pane of 2	5.50	—
4370	A1011	$2.75 multi	4.00	4.00
a.		Booklet pane of 2	8.00	—
		Complete booklet, #4367a, 4368a, 4369a, 4370a	21.50	
		Nos. 4367-4370 (4)	8.75	7.40

Booklet Stamps
Self-Adhesive
Serpentine Die Cut 11¼ Syncopated

4371	A1011	70c multi	1.00	.25
4372	A1011	70c multi	1.00	.25
a.		Booklet pane of 20, 10 each #4371-4372	20.00	
4373	A1011	$2.75 multi	4.00	2.00
a.		Booklet pane of 5	20.00	
		Nos. 4371-4373 (3)	6.00	2.50

Complete booklet sold for $14.95.

Animals in War — A1012

Poppies, soldiers and: Nos. 4374, 4379, Donkeys. Nos. 4375, 4380, Dogs. Nos. 4376, 4381, Horses. Nos. 4377, 4383, Pigeons. Nos. 4378, 4382, Camels.

2015, Oct. 27   **Litho.**   **Perf. 14¼**

4374	A1012	70c multi	1.00	1.00
4375	A1012	70c multi	1.00	1.00
4376	A1012	70c multi	1.00	1.00
4377	A1012	70c multi	1.00	1.00
4378	A1012	70c multi	1.00	1.00
a.		Souvenir sheet of 5, #4374-4378	5.00	5.00
		Nos. 4374-4378 (5)	5.00	5.00

Booklet Stamps
Self-Adhesive
Serpentine Die Cut 11¼ Syncopated

4379	A1012	70c multi	1.00	.25
4380	A1012	70c multi	1.00	.25
4381	A1012	70c multi	1.00	.25
4382	A1012	70c multi	1.00	.25
4383	A1012	70c multi	1.00	.25
a.		Booklet pane of 10, 2 each #4379-4383	10.00	
		Nos. 4379-4383 (5)	5.00	1.25

Christmas
A1013   A1014

Designs: Nos. 4384, 4389, 4394, Gift box with ribbon. Nos. 4385, 4390, 4395, Green doves. Nos. 4386, 4391, Nativity. Nos. 4387, 4392, Blue doves. Nos. 4388, 4393, Magi.

2015, Oct. 30   **Litho.**   **Perf. 14¾x14**

4384	A1013	65c multi	.95	.95
4385	A1013	65c multi	.95	.95
a.		Horiz. pair, #4384-4385	1.90	1.90
4386	A1014	65c multi	.95	.95
4387	A1013	$1.70 multi	2.50	2.50
4388	A1014	$2.55 multi	3.75	3.75
a.		Souvenir sheet of 2, #4386, 4388	4.75	4.75
		Nos. 4384-4388 (5)	9.10	9.10

Booklet Stamps
Self-Adhesive
Serpentine Die Cut 11¼ Syncopated

4389	A1013	65c multi	.95	.25
4390	A1013	65c multi	.95	.25
a.		Booklet pane of 20, 10 each #4389-4390	19.00	
4391	A1014	65c multi	.95	.25
a.		Booklet pane of 20	19.00	
4392	A1013	$1.70 multi	2.50	1.25
a.		Booklet pane of 5	12.50	
4393	A1014	$2.55 multi	3.75	1.90
a.		Booklet pane of 5	19.00	

Litho. & Silk-Screened

4394	A1013	65c multi	.95	.25
a.		Booklet pane of 10	9.50	

Litho. With Foil Application

4395	A1013	65c multi	.95	.25
a.		Booklet pane of 10	9.50	
		Nos. 4389-4395 (7)	11.00	4.40

Wildflowers A1015

Designs: Nos. 4398, 4402, 4405, Rose coneflower. Nos. 4399, 4403, 4406, Spiny mirbelia. Nos. 4400, 4404, 4407, Blue devil. $2, Golden rainbow.

2015, Dec. 15   **Litho.**   **Perf. 14¾x14**

4398	A1015	$1 multi	1.50	1.50
4399	A1015	$1 multi	1.50	1.50
4400	A1015	$1 multi	1.50	1.50
a.		Horiz. strip of 3, #4398-4400	4.50	4.50
4401	A1015	$2 multi	3.00	1.50
		Nos. 4398-4401 (4)	7.50	6.00

Self-Adhesive
Serpentine Die Cut 11¼ Syncopated

4402	A1015	$1 multi	1.50	.25
4403	A1015	$1 multi	1.50	.25
4404	A1015	$1 multi	1.50	.25
a.		Vert. coil strip of 3, #4402-4404	4.50	

---

b.		Booklet pane of 10, 4 #4402, 3 each #4403-4404	15.00	
c.		Booklet pane of 10, 8 #4402, 5 #4403, 7 #4404	30.00	
		Nos. 4402-4404 (3)	4.50	.75

With Personalized Photo at Right
Like Type A692a
Serpentine Die Cut 11½x11¼ Syncopated
Self-Adhesive

4405	A1015	$1 multi	2.40	2.40
4406	A1015	$1 multi	2.40	2.40
4407	A1015	$1 multi	2.40	2.40
4408	A1015	$2 multi	4.00	4.00
		Nos. 4405-4408 (4)	11.20	11.20

Nos. 4405-4408 were each printed in sheets of 20 and have personalized pictures and a straight edge at right and lack separations between the stamp and the personalized photo. Sheets of 20 of Nos. 4405-4407 sold for $33 each, No. 4408, $53.

Tennis Players — A1016

Designs: Nos. 4409, 4412, Tony Roche. Nos. 4410, 4413, Fred Stolle. Nos. 4411a, 4414, Pat Cash. Nos. 4411b, 4415, Ashley Cooper. Nos. 4411c, 4416, Roy Emerson. Nos. 4411d, 4417, Neale Fraser. Nos. 4411e, 4418, Evonne Goolagong Cawley. Nos. 4411f, 4419, John Newcombe. Nos. 4411g, 4420, Patrick Rafter. Nos. 4411h, 4421, Ken Rosewall. Nos. 4411i, 4422, Frank Sedgman. Nos. 4411j, 4423, Lleyton Hewitt.

2016, Jan. 21   **Litho.**   **Perf. 14¾x14**

4409	A1016	$1 multi	1.50	1.50
4410	A1016	$1 multi	1.50	1.50
a.		Vert. pair, #4409-4410	3.00	3.00
4411		Sheet of 10	15.00	15.00
a.-j.	A1016	$1 Any single	1.50	1.50

Booklet Stamps
Self-Adhesive
Serpentine Die Cut 11¼ Syncopated

4412	A1016	$1 multi	1.50	.25
a.		Booklet pane of 10	15.00	
4413	A1016	$1 multi	1.50	.25
a.		Booklet pane of 10	15.00	
4414	A1016	$1 multi	1.50	.25
a.		Booklet pane of 10	15.00	
4415	A1016	$1 multi	1.50	.25
a.		Booklet pane of 10	15.00	
4416	A1016	$1 multi	1.50	.25
a.		Booklet pane of 10	15.00	
4417	A1016	$1 multi	1.50	.25
a.		Booklet pane of 10	15.00	
4418	A1016	$1 multi	1.50	.25
a.		Booklet pane of 10	15.00	
4419	A1016	$1 multi	1.50	.25
a.		Booklet pane of 10	15.00	
4420	A1016	$1 multi	1.50	.25
a.		Booklet pane of 10	15.00	
4421	A1016	$1 multi	1.50	.25
a.		Booklet pane of 10	15.00	
4422	A1016	$1 multi	1.50	.25
a.		Booklet pane of 10	15.00	
4423	A1016	$1 multi	1.50	.25
a.		Booklet pane of 10	15.00	
		Nos. 4412-4423 (12)	18.00	3.00

White Roses — A1017   **Champagne Flutes — A1018**

Heart of Red Roses — A1019   **Cake — A1020**

Balloons A1021   **Handprints A1022**

Map of Australia A1023   **Flowering Gum A1024**

Wattle — A1025   **Engagement and Wedding Rings — A1026**

2016, Jan. 25   **Litho.**   **Perf. 14¾x14**

4424	A1017	$1 multi	1.50	1.50
4425	A1018	$1 multi	1.50	1.50
4426	A1019	$1 multi	1.50	1.50
4427	A1020	$1 multi	1.50	1.50
4428	A1021	$1 multi	1.50	1.50
4429	A1022	$1 multi	1.50	1.50
4430	A1023	$1 multi	1.50	1.10
4431	A1024	$1 multi	1.50	1.10
4432	A1025	$1 multi	1.50	1.10
4433	A1026	$2 multi	3.00	3.00
		Nos. 4424-4433 (10)	16.50	15.30

Booklet Stamps
Self-Adhesive
Serpentine Die Cut 11¼ Syncopated

4434	A1017	$1 multi	1.50	.25
a.		Booklet pane of 10 + 5 stickers	15.00	
4435	A1018	$1 multi	1.50	.25
a.		Booklet pane of 10 + 5 stickers	15.00	
4436	A1019	$1 multi	1.50	.25
a.		Booklet pane of 10 + 5 stickers	15.00	
4437	A1020	$1 multi	1.50	.25
a.		Booklet pane of 10 + 5 stickers	15.00	
4438	A1021	$1 multi	1.50	.25
a.		Booklet pane of 10 + 5 stickers	15.00	
4439	A1022	$1 multi	1.50	.25
a.		Booklet pane of 10 + 5 stickers	15.00	
4440	A1026	$2 multi	3.00	1.50
a.		Booklet pane of 4	12.00	
		Complete booklet, 4 #4440a	48.00	
		Nos. 4434-4440 (7)	12.00	3.00

Complete booklet sold for $32.95 and contains four examples of No. 4440a, each with a different pane margin.

With Personalized Photo at Right
Like Type A692a
Serpentine Die Cut 11½x11¼ Syncopated
Self-Adhesive

4441	A1017	$1 multi	2.40	2.40
4442	A1018	$1 multi	2.40	2.40
4443	A1019	$1 multi	2.40	2.40
4444	A1020	$1 multi	2.40	2.40
4445	A1021	$1 multi	2.40	2.40
4446	A1022	$1 multi	2.40	2.40
4447	A1023	$1 multi	2.40	2.40
4448	A1024	$1 multi	2.40	2.40
4449	A1025	$1 multi	2.40	2.40
4450	A1026	$2 multi	3.75	3.75
		Nos. 4441-4450 (10)	25.35	25.35

Nos. 4441-4450 were each printed in sheets of 20 and have personalized pictures and a straight edge at right and lack separations between the stamp and the personalized photo. Sheets of 20 of Nos. 4441-4449 sold for $33 each, No. 4450, $53.

Australian One Pound Banknote, One
Dollar Banknote and Coin — A1027

2016, Feb. 9   Litho.   Perf. 14½x14
4451	A1027	$1 multi	1.50	1.10
a.		Perf. 13½x14	1.50	1.10
b.		Booklet pane of 4 #4451a	6.00	
		Complete booklet, 5 #4451b	30.00	

Complete booklet sold for $20.95, and contained five examples of No. 4451b, each with different pane margins.

Items Starting With Same Letter — A1028

Designs: Nos. 4452, 4457, Numbat, nippers (junior lifeguards) on surfboard, New South Wales map. Nos. 4453, 4458, Quokka, quoll, queue sign, Quokkair plane, Queensland map. Nos. 4454, 4459, Surf, surfboard, sand castle, starfish, sausage, shark toy, shell, snail, South Australia map. Nos. 4455, 4460, Vegetables, Victa lawnmower, violins, Vegemite sandwich, Victoria map. Nos. 4456, 4461, Wombat, wattle, waratah, water hose, Western Australia Cricket Association bat and ball, Western Australia map.

2016, Mar. 1   Litho.   Perf. 14¾x14
4452	A1028	$1 multi	1.50	1.50
4453	A1028	$1 multi	1.50	1.50
4454	A1028	$1 multi	1.50	1.50
4455	A1028	$1 multi	1.50	1.50
4456	A1028	$1 multi	1.50	1.50
a.		Horiz. strip of 5, #4452-4456	7.50	7.50
		Nos. 4452-4456 (5)	7.50	7.50

**Booklet Stamps
Self-Adhesive**

Serpentine Die Cut 11¼ Syncopated
4457	A1028	$1 multi	1.50	.25
a.		Booklet pane of 10	15.00	
4458	A1028	$1 multi	1.50	.25
a.		Booklet pane of 10	15.00	
4459	A1028	$1 multi	1.50	.25
a.		Booklet pane of 10	15.00	
4460	A1028	$1 multi	1.50	.25
a.		Booklet pane of 10	15.00	
4461	A1028	$1 multi	1.50	.25
a.		Booklet pane of 10	15.00	
		Nos. 4457-4461 (5)	7.50	1.25

See Nos. 4520-4529.

Bridges
A1029

Designs: Nos. 4462, 4465, Gladesville Bridge, New South Wales. Nos. 4463, 4467, Story Bridge, Queensland. Nos. 4464, 4466, Tasman Bridge, Tasmania.

2016, Mar. 15   Litho.   Perf. 14x14¾
4462	A1029	$1 multi	1.60	1.60
4463	A1029	$1 multi	1.60	1.60
4464	A1029	$1 multi	1.60	1.60
a.		Horiz. strip of 3, #4462-4464	4.80	4.80
		Nos. 4462-4464 (3)	4.80	4.80

**Booklet Stamps
Self-Adhesive**

Serpentine Die Cut 11¼ Syncopated
4465	A1029	$1 multi	1.60	.25
4466	A1029	$1 multi	1.60	.25
4467	A1029	$1 multi	1.60	.25
a.		Booklet pane of 20, 7 each #4465-4466, 6 #4467	32.00	
		Nos. 4465-4467 (3)	4.80	.75

Queen Elizabeth II, 90th Birthday — A1030

Designs: $1, Queen Elizabeth II. $2.75, Golden wattle diamond brooch.

2016, Apr. 5   Litho.   Perf. 14¾x14
4468	A1030	$1 multi	1.60	1.25
4469	A1030	$2.75 multi	4.25	4.25
a.		Souvenir sheet of 2, #4468-4469	6.00	6.00

**Booklet Stamp
Self-Adhesive**

Serpentine Die Cut 11¼ Syncopated
4470	A1030	$2.75 multi	4.25	2.10
a.		Booklet pane of 5	21.50	

World War I, Cent. — A1031

Poppy and: Nos. 4471, 4476, Soldiers arriving on the Western Front. Nos. 4472, 4477, Somme Offensive. Nos. 4473, 4478, Referendum on conscription. Nos. 4474, 4479, Matron Grace Wilson of Australian Army Nursing Service, and Royal Red Cross, First Class. Nos. 4475, 4480, Soldier writing letter home.

2016, Apr. 12   Litho.   Perf. 14¼
4471	A1031	$1 multi	1.60	1.60
4472	A1031	$1 multi	1.60	1.60
4473	A1031	$1 multi	1.60	1.60
4474	A1031	$1 multi	1.60	1.60
a.		Booklet pane of 4, #4471-4474	6.50	—
4475	A1031	$1 multi	1.60	1.60
a.		Booklet pane of 4, #4472-4475	6.50	
b.		Booklet pane of 4, #4471, 4473-4475	6.50	
c.		Booklet pane of 4, #4471-4472, 4474-4475	6.50	
d.		Booklet pane of 4, #4471-4473, 4475	6.50	
		Complete booklet, #4474a, 4475a, 4475b, 4475c, 4475d	32.50	
e.		Souvenir sheet of 5, #4471-4475	8.00	8.00
		Nos. 4471-4475 (5)	8.00	8.00

**Booklet Stamps
Self-Adhesive**

Serpentine Die Cut 11¼ Syncopated
4476	A1031	$1 multi	1.60	.25
4477	A1031	$1 multi	1.60	.25
4478	A1031	$1 multi	1.60	.25
4479	A1031	$1 multi	1.60	.25
4480	A1031	$1 multi	1.60	.25
a.		Booklet pane of 10, 2 each #4476-4480	16.00	
		Nos. 4476-4480 (5)	8.00	1.25

Complete booklet sold for $20.95.

Butterflies
A1032

Designs: Nos. 4481, 4485, Pale triangle butterfly. Nos. 4482, 4487, Bordered rustic butterfly. Nos. 4483, 4486, Cairns birdwing butterfly. $2.75, Chequered swallowtail butterfly.

2016, May 3   Litho.   Perf. 14x14¾
4481	A1032	$1 multi	1.50	1.50
4482	A1032	$1 multi	1.50	1.50
4483	A1032	$1 multi	1.50	1.50
4484	A1032	$2.75 multi	4.00	4.00
a.		Souvenir sheet of 4, #4481-4484	8.50	8.50
		Nos. 4481-4484 (4)	8.50	8.50

Self-Adhesive

Serpentine Die Cut 11¼ Syncopated
4485	A1032	$1 multi	1.50	.25
4486	A1032	$1 multi	1.50	.25
4487	A1032	$1 multi	1.50	.25
a.		Horiz. coil strip of 3, #4485-4487	4.50	

b.		Booklet pane of 20, 7 each #4485, 4487, 6 #4486	30.00	

Booklet Stamp
4488	A1032	$2.75 multi	4.00	2.00
a.		Booklet pane of 5	20.00	
		Nos. 4485-4488 (4)	8.50	2.75

Returned and Services League of Australia, Cent. — A1033

2016, May 31   Litho.   Perf. 14¾x14
4489	A1033	$1 multi	1.50	1.50

**Booklet Stamp
Self-Adhesive**

Serpentine Die Cut 11¼ Syncopated
4490	A1033	$1 multi	1.50	.25
a.		Booklet pane of 20	30.00	

Early 20th Century Fruit Crate Labels
A1034

Labels for: Nos. 4491, 4495, Paterson & Co. "Red Gum Pack" Apples. Nos. 4492, 4496, The River's Pride Navel Oranges. Nos. 4493, 4497, L. H. Kile "Robin" Apples. Nos. 4494, 4498, W. H. Price Ltd. Special Ohanez Grapes.

2016, June 7   Litho.   Perf. 14x14¾
4491	A1034	$1 multi	1.50	1.50
a.		Booklet pane of 4	6.50	
4492	A1034	$1 multi	1.50	1.50
a.		Booklet pane of 4	6.50	
4493	A1034	$1 multi	1.50	1.50
a.		Booklet pane of 4	6.50	
4494	A1034	$1 multi	1.50	1.50
a.		Booklet pane of 4	6.50	
		Complete booklet, #4491a, 4492a, 4493a, 4494a	26.00	

Self-Adhesive

Serpentine Die Cut 11¼ Syncopated
4495	A1034	$1 multi	1.50	.25
4496	A1034	$1 multi	1.50	.25
4497	A1034	$1 multi	1.50	.25
4498	A1034	$1 multi	1.50	.25
a.		Horiz. coil strip of 4, #4495-4498	6.00	
b.		Booklet pane of 10, 3 each #4496-4497, 2 each #4497-4498	15.00	
		Nos. 4495-4498 (4)	6.00	1.00

Complete booklet sold for $16.95.

Owls — A1035

Designs: Nos. 4499, 4505, Rufous owl. Nos. 4500, 4503, Eastern grass owl. Nos. 4501, 4504, Sooty owl. Nos. 4502, 4506, Southern boobook owl.

2016, July 5   Litho.   Perf. 14x13½
4499	A1035	$1 multi	1.50	1.50
a.		Booklet pane of 2	3.25	
4500	A1035	$1 multi	1.50	1.50
a.		Booklet pane of 2	3.25	
b.		Booklet pane of 2, #4499-4500	3.25	
4501	A1035	$1 multi	1.50	1.50
a.		Booklet pane of 2	3.25	
b.		Booklet pane of 2, #4500-4501	3.25	
4502	A1035	$1 multi	1.50	1.50
a.		Booklet pane of 2	3.25	
b.		Booklet pane of 2, #4501-4502	3.25	
c.		Booklet pane of 2, #4499, 4502	3.25	
		Complete booklet, #4499a, 4500a, 4500b, 4501a, 4501b, 4502a, 4502b, 4502c	26.00	

d.		Souvenir sheet of 4, #4499-4502	6.00	6.00
		Nos. 4499-4502 (4)	6.00	6.00

**Booklet Stamps
Self-Adhesive**

Serpentine Die Cut 11¼x10¾ Syncopated
4503	A1035	$1 multi	1.50	.25
4504	A1035	$1 multi	1.50	.25
4505	A1035	$1 multi	1.50	.25
4506	A1035	$1 multi	1.50	.25
a.		Booklet pane of 10, 2 each #4503, 4506, 3 each #4504-4505	15.00	

Complete booklet sold for $16.95.

Play School Children's Television Program, 50th Anniv. — A1036

Designs: $1, Jemima and Humpty. $2, Big Ted and Little Ted.

2016, July 26   Litho.   Perf. 14¾x14
4507	A1036	$1 multi	1.50	1.50
4508	A1036	$2 multi	3.00	2.25
a.		Souvenir sheet of 2, #4507-4508	4.50	4.50

**Booklet Stamp
Self-Adhesive**

Serpentine Die Cut 11¼ Syncopated
4509	A1036	$1 multi	1.50	.25
a.		Booklet pane of 10	15.00	

With Personalized Photo at Right Like Type A692a

Serpentine Die Cut 11½x11¼ Syncopated

Self-Adhesive
4510	A1036	$1 multi	2.50	2.50

No. 4510 was printed in a sheet of 20 and has personalized pictures and a straight edge at right and lack separations between the stamp and the personalized photo. Sheets of 20 sold for $33 each.

2016 Summer Olympics, Rio de Janeiro
A1037

2016, Aug. 2   Litho.   Perf. 14x14¾
4511	A1037	$1 multi	1.50	1.10

Australian Gold Medalists at 2016 Summer Olympics, Rio de Janeiro
A1038

Designs: No. 4512, Mack Horton, men's 400-meter freestyle. No. 4513, Women's 4x100 meter freestyle relay team. No. 4514, Catherine Skinner, women's trap shooting. No. 4515, Women's rugby sevens team. No. 4516, Kyle Chalmers, men's 100-meter freestyle. No. 4517, Kimberley Brennan, women's single sculls. No. 4518, Tom Burton, men's Laser class sailing. No. 4519, Chloe Esposito, women's individual modern pentathlon.

2016   Litho.   Perf. 14¼
4512	A1038	$1 multi	1.50	1.10
4513	A1038	$1 multi	1.50	1.10
4514	A1038	$1 multi	1.50	1.10
4515	A1038	$1 multi	1.50	1.10
4516	A1038	$1 multi	1.50	1.10
4517	A1038	$1 multi	1.50	1.10
4518	A1038	$1 multi	1.50	1.10
4519	A1038	$1 multi	1.50	1.10
		Nos. 4512-4519 (8)	12.00	8.80

Nos. 4512-4519 were each printed in sheets of 10. Issued: Nos. 4512-4514, 8/8; No. 4515, 8/9; No. 4516, 8/11; No. 4517, 8/15; No. 4518, 8/17; No. 4519, 8/18.

Items Starting With Same Letter Type of 2016

Designs: Nos. 4520, 4525, Ant, Australian Rules Footballer players and ball, ANZAC memorial. Nos. 4521, 4526, Couple at campfire with Canberra map, crocodile, cockatoo. Nos. 4522, 4527, Lace monitor, lyrebird on lounge, Lamingtons on log. Nos. 4523, 4528, Rugby ball, refrigerator, rocket, reel, ruler, rope, Red Center poster. Nos. 4524, 4529, Tasmania map, Tasmanian devil, tradesman in tinnie (boat) with toolbelt.

2016, Aug. 16   Litho.   Perf. 14¾x14

4520	A1028	$1 multi	1.50	1.50
4521	A1028	$1 multi	1.50	1.50
4522	A1028	$1 multi	1.50	1.50
4523	A1028	$1 multi	1.50	1.50
4524	A1028	$1 multi	1.50	1.50
		Nos. 4520-4524 (5)	7.50	7.50

Self-Adhesive
Serpentine Die Cut 11¼ Syncopated

4525	A1028	$1 multi	1.50	.25
a.		Booklet pane of 10	15.00	
4526	A1028	$1 multi	1.50	.25
a.		Booklet pane of 10	15.00	
4527	A1028	$1 multi	1.50	.25
a.		Booklet pane of 10	15.00	
4528	A1028	$1 multi	1.50	.25
a.		Booklet pane of 10	15.00	
4529	A1028	$1 multi	1.50	.25
a.		Booklet pane of 10	15.00	
b.		Vert. coil strip of 5, #4525-4529	7.50	
		Nos. 4525-4529 (5)	7.50	1.25

Jewel Beetles — A1039

Designs: Nos. 4530, 4534, Stigmodera gratiosa. Nos. 4531, 4535, Castiarina klugii. No. 4532, Temognatha alternata. No. 4533, Julodimorpha bakewellii.

2016, Sept. 6   Litho.   Perf. 14¾x14

4530	A1039	$1 multi	1.60	1.60
4531	A1039	$1 multi	1.60	1.60
a.		Horiz. pair, #4530-4531	3.20	3.20
4532	A1039	$2 multi	3.25	2.40
4533	A1039	$2 multi	3.25	2.40
a.		Horiz. pair, #4532-4533	6.50	4.80
		Nos. 4530-4533 (4)	9.70	8.00

Self-Adhesive
Serpentine Die Cut 11¼ Syncopated

4534	A1039	$1 multi	1.60	.25
4535	A1039	$1 multi	1.60	.25
a.		Vert. coil pair, #4534-4535	3.20	
b.		Booklet pane of 20, 10 each #4534-4535	32.00	

Landing of Dirk Hartog in Western Australia, 400th Anniv. — A1040

2016, Sept. 13   Litho.   Perf. 14¾x14

4536	A1040	$2 multi	3.25	2.40

A1041

Endangered Animals — A1042

Designs: No. 4537, Orange-bellied parrots. No. 4538, Northern quolls. Nos. 4539, 4544,

Snow leopards. Nos. 4540, 4545, Western swamp tortoise. Nos. 4541, 4546, Western lowland gorillas. Nos. 4542, 4547, Asian elephants. Nos. 4543, 4548, Southern corroboree frog.

2016, Sept. 20   Litho.   Perf. 14x14¾

4537	A1041	50c multi	.80	.60
4538	A1041	50c multi	.80	.60
a.		Horiz. pair, #4537-4538	1.60	1.20
4539	A1041	$1 multi	1.60	1.60
4540	A1041	$1 multi	1.60	1.60
4541	A1041	$1 multi	1.60	1.60
4542	A1041	$1 multi	1.60	1.60

Perf. 13¾x14

4543	A1042	$1 multi	1.60	1.60
a.		Souvenir sheet of 7, #4537-4543	9.75	9.75
		Nos. 4537-4543 (7)	9.60	9.20

Self-Adhesive
Serpentine Die Cut 11¼ Syncopated

4544	A1041	$1 multi	1.60	.25
4545	A1041	$1 multi	1.60	.25
4546	A1041	$1 multi	1.60	.25
4547	A1041	$1 multi	1.60	.25
a.		Horiz. coil strip of 4, #4544-4547	6.40	
b.		Booklet pane of 20, 6 each #4544-4545, 4 each #4546, 4547	32.00	

Booklet Stamp
Serpentine Die Cut 10¾x11 Syncopated

4548	A1042	$1 multi	1.60	.25
a.		Booklet pane of 10	16.00	
		Nos. 4544-4548 (5)	8.00	1.25

Taronga Zoo, cent. (Nos. 4543, 4548).

Monotremes A1043

Designs: $2.10, Platypus. $2.95, Short-beaked echidna.

2016, Sept. 26   Litho.   Perf. 14¾x14

4549	A1043	$2.10 multi	3.25	3.25
4550	A1043	$2.95 multi	4.50	4.50
a.		Souvenir sheet of 2, #4549-4550	7.75	7.75

Booklet Stamps
Self-Adhesive
Serpentine Die Cut 11¼ Syncopated

4551	A1043	$2.10 multi	3.25	1.60
a.		Booklet pane of 5	16.50	
4552	A1043	$2.95 multi	4.50	2.25
a.		Booklet pane of 5	22.50	

With Personalized Photo at Right Like Type A692a
Serpentine Die Cut 11½x11¼ Syncopated

4553	A1043	$2.10 multi	4.25	4.25
4554	A1043	$2.95 multi	5.50	5.50

Nos. 4553-4554 were each printed in sheets of 20 and have personalized pictures and a straight edge at right and lack separations between the stamp and the personalized photo. Sheets of 20 of No. 4553 sold for $55 each, No. 4554, $72.

Australian Involvement in Viet Nam War — A1044

Poppies and inscription: Nos. 4555, 4560, In the field. Nos. 4556, 4561, Long Tan Cross. Nos. 4557, 4562, Aid and recreation. Nos. 4558, 4563, Opposition and withdrawal. Nos. 4559, 4564, Commemoration.

2016, Oct. 11   Litho.   Perf. 14¼

4555	A1044	$1 multi	1.60	1.60
a.		Booklet pane of 4	6.50	
4556	A1044	$1 multi	1.60	1.60
a.		Booklet pane of 4	6.50	
4557	A1044	$1 multi	1.60	1.60
a.		Booklet pane of 4	6.50	
4558	A1044	$1 multi	1.60	1.60
a.		Booklet pane of 4	6.50	

4559	A1044	$1 multi	1.60	1.60
a.		Booklet pane of 4	6.50	—
		Complete booklet, #4555a, 4556a, 4557a, 4558a, 4559a	32.50	
b.		Souvenir sheet of 5, #4555-4559	8.00	8.00
		Nos. 4555-4559 (5)	8.00	8.00

Booklet Stamps
Self-Adhesive
Serpentine Die Cut 11¼ Syncopated

4560	A1044	$1 multi	1.60	.25
4561	A1044	$1 multi	1.60	.25
4562	A1044	$1 multi	1.60	.25
4563	A1044	$1 multi	1.60	.25
4564	A1044	$1 multi	1.60	.25
a.		Booklet pane of 10, 2 each #4560-4564	16.00	
		Nos. 4560-4564 (5)	8.00	1.25

Complete booklet sold for $20.95.

Dylan Alcott, Paralympian of the Year — A1045

2016, Oct. 18   Litho.   Perf. 14¼

4565	A1045	$1 multi	1.60	1.25

No. 4565 exists in sheets of 10.

Christmas
A1046   A1047

Designs: Nos. 4566, 4571, 4576, 4578, Star and "Goodwill." Nos. 4567, 4572, 4577, 4579, Gift and "Joy." Nos. 4568, 4573, 4580, Madonna and Child. Nos. 4569, 4574, 4581, Angel, Nos. 4570, 4575, Magi.

2016, Oct. 31   Litho.   Perf. 14¾x14

4566	A1046	65c multi	1.00	1.00
4567	A1046	65c multi	1.00	1.00
a.		Horiz. pair, #4566-4567	2.00	2.00
4568	A1047	65c multi	1.00	1.00
4569	A1047	$1.70 multi	2.60	2.60
4570	A1047	$2.55 multi	4.00	4.00
a.		Souvenir sheet of 3, #4568-4570	7.75	7.75
		Nos. 4566-4570 (5)	9.60	9.60

Booklet Stamps
Self-Adhesive
Serpentine Die Cut 11¼ Syncopated

4571	A1046	65c multi	1.00	.25
4572	A1047	65c multi	1.00	.25
a.		Booklet pane of 20, 10 each #4971-4972, + 20 etiquettes	20.00	
4573	A1047	65c multi	1.00	.25
a.		Booklet pane of 20 + 20 etiquettes	20.00	
4574	A1047	$1.70 multi	2.60	1.40
a.		Booklet pane of 5	13.00	
4575	A1047	$2.55 multi	4.00	2.00
a.		Booklet pane of 5	20.00	

Litho. & Embossed With Foil Application

4576	A1046	65c multi	1.00	.25
a.		Booklet pane of 10	10.00	
4577	A1046	65c multi	1.00	.25
a.		Booklet pane of 10	10.00	
		Nos. 4571-4577 (7)	11.60	4.65

With Personalized Photo at Right Like Type A692a
Litho.
Serpentine Die Cut 11½x11¼ Syncopated

4578	A1046	65c multi	2.00	2.00
4579	A1046	65c multi	2.00	2.00
4580	A1047	65c multi	2.00	2.00
4581	A1047	$1.70 multi	3.50	3.50
		Nos. 4578-4581 (4)	9.50	9.50

Nos. 4578-4581 were each printed in sheets of 20 and have personalized pictures and a straight edge at right and lack separations between the stamp and the personalized photo. Sheets of 20 of No. 4578-4580 each sold for $26 each, No. 4581, $47.

SEMI-POSTAL STAMPS

Catalogue values in this section are for Never Hinged items.

Queensland Flood Relief — SP1

Designs: No. B1, Rescuer holding baby. No. B2, Flooded buildings, ground-level view. No. B3, Rescuers taking pet from house. No. B4, Kangaroo stranded on island in flood. No. B5, Flooded buildings, aerial view.

Serpentine Die Cut 11¼ Syncopated
2011, Jan. 27   Litho.
Self-Adhesive

B1	SP1	60c+(20c) multi	1.75	1.75
B2	SP1	60c+(20c) multi	1.75	1.75
B3	SP1	60c+(20c) multi	1.75	1.75
B4	SP1	60c+(20c) multi	1.75	1.75
B5	SP1	60c+(20c) multi	1.75	1.75
a.		Sheet of 10, 2 each #B1-B5	17.50	
		Nos. B1-B5 (5)	8.75	8.75

Surtax for Premier's Flood Relief Appeal.

Leaves in Ring and Hands — SP2

2012, June 26   Self-Adhesive

B6	SP2	60c+(20c) multi	1.75	1.75

Printed in sheets of 10. Surtax for Olivia Newton-John Cancer and Wellness Center.

AIR POST STAMPS

Airplane over Bush Lands — AP1

Unwmk.
1929, May 20   Engr.   Perf. 11

C1	AP1	3p deep green	9.25	8.50
		Never hinged	14.50	
a.		Booklet pane of 4 ('30)	450.00	

Kingsford-Smith Type of 1931
1931, Mar. 19

C2	A8	6p gray violet	8.00	8.00
		Never hinged	11.50	

AP3

1931, Nov. 4

C3	AP3	6p olive brown	17.00	14.00
		Never hinged	35.00	

For overprint see No. CO1.

Mercury and Hemispheres AP4

1934, Dec. 1   *Perf. 11*
C4 AP4 1sh6p violet brown   40.00 8.00
    Never hinged   97.50

Perf. 13½x14
1937, Oct. 22   **Wmk. 228**
C5 AP4 1sh6p violet brown   8.50 1.40
    Never hinged   14.50

> **Catalogue values for unused stamps in this section, from this point to the end of the section, are for Never Hinged items.**

Mercury and Globe — AP5

1949, Sept. 1   *Perf. 14½*
C6 AP5 1sh6p sepia   2.25 .60

1956, Dec. 6   **Unwmk.**
C7 AP5 1sh6p sepia   18.50 1.10

Super-Constellation over Globe — AP6

1958, Jan. 6   *Perf. 14½x14*
C8 AP6 2sh dark violet blue   2.75 2.25

Inauguration of Australian "Round the World" air service.

AIR POST OFFICIAL STAMP

No. C3 Overprinted

Perf. 11, 11½
1931, Nov. 17   **Unwmk.**
CO1 AP3 6p olive brown   35.00 35.00
    Never hinged   57.50

Issued primarily for official use, but to prevent speculation, a quantity was issued for public distribution.

POSTAGE DUE STAMPS

Very fine examples of Nos. J1-J38 will have perforations touching the design on one or more sides due to the narrow spacing of the stamps on the plates. Stamps with perfs clear of the design on all four sides are scarce and will command higher prices.

D1

1902 Typo. Wmk. 55 Perf. 11½, 12

J1	D1	½p emerald	11.50	11.50
J2	D1	1p emerald	17.50	11.50
a.		Perf. 11	2,800.	1,400.
b.		Perf. 11x11½	450.00	250.00
J3	D1	2p emerald	32.00	11.50
a.		Perf. 11x11½	600.00	200.00
J4	D1	3p emerald	32.00	21.00
J5	D1	4p emerald	45.00	25.00
J6	D1	6p emerald	70.00	17.00
J7	D1	8p emerald	180.00	140.00
J8	D1	5sh emerald	400.00	125.00
		Nos. J1-J8 (8)	788.00	362.50

D2

Perf. 11½, 12, Compound with 11

1902-04

J9	D2	½p emerald	17.50	11.50
a.		Perf. 11	775.00	400.00
J10	D2	1p emerald, Perf 12x11	17.00	5.75
a.		Perf. 11	200.00	42.50
b.		Perf 11½	400.00	200.00
c.		Perf 11x11½	37.50	11.50
J11	D2	2p emerald	23.00	5.75
a.		Perf. 11	260.00	57.50
b.		Perf 12	—	225.00
c.		Perf 11x11½	120.00	37.50
d.		Perf 11x12	140.00	45.00
J12	D2	3p emerald	160.00	26.00
a.		Perf. 11	225.00	63.00
b.		Perf 12	450.00	170.00
J13	D2	4p emerald	140.00	32.00
a.		Perf. 11	400.00	115.00
J14	D2	5p emerald	140.00	35.00
a.		Perf. 11	500.00	86.00
b.		Perf 12	100.00	23.00
J15	D2	6p emerald	160.00	29.00
a.		Perf. 11	260.00	32.00
J16	D2	8p emerald	325.00	120.00
J17	D2	10p emerald	175.00	29.00
a.		Perf 12x11½	150.00	29.00
J18	D2	1sh emerald	160.00	29.00
a.		Perf. 11	500.00	90.00
b.		Perf 12x11½	125.00	32.00
J19	D2	2sh emerald	200.00	32.00
a.		Perf 11½, 12	200.00	40.00
J20	D2	5sh emerald	500.00	57.50
a.		Perf. 11	1,700.	600.00

Perf. 11

J21	D2	10sh emerald	4,000.	3,200.
J22	D2	20sh emerald	8,500.	5,500.
		Nos. J9-J20 (12)	2,018.	412.50

Perf. 11½, 12 Compound with 11

1906   **Wmk. 12**

J23	D2	½p emerald	16.00	16.00
J24	D2	1p emerald	35.00	5.75
a.		Perf. 11	3,500.	1,450.
J25	D2	2p emerald	62.50	11.50
J26	D2	3p emerald	1,150.	450.00
J27	D2	4p emerald	140.00	27.50
a.		Perf. 11	4,600.	2,900.
J28	D2	6p emerald	490.00	35.00
		Nos. J23-J28 (6)	1,894.	545.75

1907   **Wmk. 13**   *Perf. 11½x11*

J29	D2	½p emerald	42.50	85.00
J30	D2	1p emerald	260.00	140.00
J31	D2	2p emerald	375.00	290.00
J32	D2	4p emerald	500.00	290.00
J33	D2	6p emerald	550.00	400.00
		Nos. J29-J33 (5)	1,728.	1,205.

D3

Perf. 11 (2sh, 10sh, 20sh), 11½x11 (1sh, 5sh)

1908-09   **Wmk. 12**

J34	D3	1sh emer ('09)	225.00	29.00
J35	D3	2sh emerald	1,800.	
J36	D3	5sh emerald	775.00	75.00
J37	D3	10sh emerald	5,200.	—
J38	D3	20sh emerald	29,000.	—

D4

1909-23   **Wmk. 13**   *Perf. 12x12½*

J39	D4	½p green & car	32.00	45.00
a.		Perf 11, green & rose ('14)	20.00	17.00

---

b.		Perf 12½, green & scarlet ('13)	37.50	29.00
c.		Perf 14 ('19)	20.00	17.00
J40	D4	1p green & car	23.00	9.75
a.		Perf 11, yel grn & rose, thicker paper, thick yellowish gum	4,600.	1,725.
b.		Perf 11, bright apple green & rose, thin paper, thin white gum ('14)	20.00	8.50
c.		Perf 14 ('14)	70.00	17.00
J41	D4	2p green & car	32.00	5.75
a.		Perf 11	—	
b.		Perf 14 ('18)	29.00	7.50
J42	D4	3p green & car	35.00	14.50
a.		Perf 14, green & rose ('16)	150.00	52.00
J43	D4	4p green & car	24.00	11.50
a.		Perf 14 ('21)	200.00	70.00
J44	D4	6p green & car	35.00	14.00
a.		Perf 11	—	
J45	D4	1sh green & car	33.00	9.25
a.		Perf 14, yel grn & scarlet ('23)	45.00	23.00
J46	D4	2sh green & car	115.00	16.00
J47	D4	5sh green & car	175.00	17.00
J48	D4	10sh green & car	450.00	325.00
a.		Perf 14, yel grn & scarlet ('21)	2,600.	
J49	D4	£1 green & car	1,100.	575.00
a.		Perf 14, yel grn & scarlet ('21)	1,600.	
		Nos. J39-J49 (11)	2,054.	1,043.

Nos. J39-J48 and J40a, J41a, J44a are from the 1909 printings and have thicker paper and thick yellowish gum. The other listings are from the 1912-23 printings on thinner paper with thin white gum.

1922-30   **Wmk. 10**   *Perf. 14, 11 (4p)*

J50	D4	½p grn & car ('23)	9.25	7.50
J51	D4	1p green & car	7.50	2.25
J52	D4	1½p green & rose ('25)	4.25	7.50
J53	D4	2p green & car	9.25	4.25
J54	D4	3p green & car	17.00	3.25
J55	D4	4p green & car ('30)	17.00	8.00
a.		Perf 14	52.00	23.00
J56	D4	6p green & car	37.50	18.50
		Nos. J50-J56 (7)	101.75	51.25
		Set, never hinged	200.00	

1931-36   **Wmk. 228**   *Perf. 11*

J57	D4	½p yel grn & rose ('34)	23.00	23.00
J58	D4	1p yel grn & rose ('32)	9.00	2.25
a.		Perf 14	14.00	11.50
J59	D4	2p yel grn & rose ('33)	10.50	2.25
a.		Perf 14	11.50	11.50
J60	D4	3p yel grn & rose ('36)	140.00	115.00
J61	D4	4p yel grn & rose ('34)	29.00	4.50
J62	D4	6p yel grn & rose ('36)	550.00	500.00
J63	D4	1sh yel grn & rose ('34)	70.00	30.00
		Nos. J57-J63 (7)	831.50	677.00
		Set, never hinged	1,400.	

D5

Engraved; Value Typo.
1938   *Perf. 14½x14*

J64	D5	½p green & car	3.50	3.50
J65	D5	1p green & car	12.50	1.10
J66	D5	2p green & car	12.50	2.25
J67	D5	3p green & car	55.00	23.00
J68	D5	4p green & car	16.00	1.10
J69	D5	6p green & car	100.00	45.00
J70	D5	1sh green & car	57.50	20.00
		Nos. J64-J70 (7)	257.00	95.95
		Set, never hinged	400.00	

> **Catalogue values for unused stamps in this section, from this point to the end of the section, are for Never Hinged items.**

Type of 1938
Value Tablet Redrawn

Original

Redrawn

Pence denominations: "D" has melon-shaped center in redrawn tablet. The redrawn 3p differs slightly, having semi-melon-shaped "D" center, with vertical white stroke half filling it.

1sh. 1938: Numeral "1" narrow, with six background lines above.

1sh. 1947: Numeral broader, showing more white space around dotted central ornament. Three lines above.

1946-57   **Wmk. 228**

J71	D5	½p grn & car ('56)	7.00	5.75
J72	D5	1p grn & car ('47)	4.50	1.10
J73	D5	2p green & car	8.00	1.10
J74	D5	3p green & car	10.00	1.10
J75	D5	4p grn & car ('52)	14.00	1.40
J76	D5	5p grn & car ('48)	18.50	2.25
J77	D5	6p grn & car ('47)	18.50	2.90
J78	D5	7p grn & car ('53)	8.00	7.00
J79	D5	8p grn & car ('57)	26.00	23.00
J80	D5	1sh grn & car ('47)	29.00	4.50
		Nos. J71-J80 (10)	143.50	50.10

1953-54

White Tablet, Carmine Numeral

J81	D5	1sh grn & car ('54)	10.00	6.25
J82	D5	2sh green & car	16.00	14.50
J83	D5	2sh green & car	15.00	8.50
		Nos. J81-J83 (3)	41.00	29.25

Issued: 2sh, 5sh, Aug. 26; 1sh, Feb. 17.

Redrawn Type of 1947-57

Two Types of Some Pence Values:
Type I — Background lines touch numeral, "D" and period.
Type II — Lines do not touch numeral, etc. Second engraving of 1sh has sharper and thicker lines.
The ½p type II has 7 dots under the "2."
The 8p type II has distinct lines in centers of "8" and between "8" and "D."

Engr.; Value Typo.
1958-60   **Unwmk.**   *Perf. 14½x14*

J86	D5	½p grn & car, II	7.00	4.25
a.		Six dots under the "2"	9.25	2.25
J87	D5	1p grn & car, II	5.75	1.10
a.		Type I	5.75	2.25
J88	D5	3p grn & car, II	5.75	4.50
J89	D5	4p grn & car, I	11.50	10.00
a.		Type II ('59)	9.25	9.25
J90	D5	5p grn & car, I	29.00	17.50
a.		Type II ('59)	100.00	40.00
J91	D5	6p grn & car, II	10.00	5.25
J92	D5	8p grn & car, II	29.00	29.00
a.		Indistinct lines	23.00	23.00
J93	D5	10p grn & car, II	17.00	6.25

White Tablet, Carmine Numeral

J94	D5	1sh green & car	29.00	7.00
a.		2nd redrawing ('60)	29.00	5.75
J95	D5	2sh grn & car	35.00	21.00
		Nos. J86-J95 (10)	179.00	105.85

Issued: 1sh, 9/8/58; 10p, 12/9/59; 2sh, 3/8/60; 3p, 6p, 5/25/60; others, 2/27/58.

MILITARY STAMPS

Nos. 166, 191, 183A, 173, 175, 206 and 177 Overprinted in Black

a   b

c

Perf. 14½x14, 15x14, 11½, 13½x13

1946-47   **Wmk. 228**
M1 A24(a) ½p orange   3.50 3.50
    Never hinged   5.75

M2	A36(b)	1p brown vio	3.50	3.50
		Never hinged	5.75	
a.		Blue overprint	115.00	77.50
		Never hinged	140.00	
M3	A27(b)	3p dk vio brn	3.50	3.50
		Never hinged	5.75	
a.		Double overprint	850.00	
M4	A30(a)	6p brn violet	12.00	11.50
		Never hinged	18.00	
M5	A16(a)	1sh gray green	12.00	11.50
		Never hinged	18.00	
M6	A1(c)	2sh dk red brn	35.00	45.00
		Never hinged	70.00	
M7	A32(c)	5sh dl red brn	140.00	200.00
		Never hinged	250.00	
		Nos. M1-M7 (7)	209.50	278.50

"B.C.O.F." stands for "British Commonwealth Occupation Force."

Issue dates: Nos. M1-M3, Oct. 11, 1946, Nos. M4-M7, May 8, 1947.

OFFICIAL STAMPS

Overprinted Official stamps are comparatively more difficult to find well centered than the basic issues on which they are printed. This is because poorly centered sheets that had been discarded were purposely chosen to be overprinted to save money.

Perforated Initials

In 1913-31, postage stamps were perforated "OS" for federal official use. The Scott Standard Catalogues do not list officials with perforated initials, but listings for these Australian stamps will be found in the *Scott Classic Specialized Catalogue*.

Overprinted

On Regular Issue of 1931

1931, May 4   Unwmk.   Perf. 11, 11½

O1	A8	2p dull red	160.00	45.00
O2	A8	3p blue	450.00	80.00

These stamps were issued primarily for official use but to prevent speculation a quantity was issued for public distribution.

Used values are for CTO examples. Counterfeit overprints exist.

On Regular Issues of 1928-32

1932   Wmk. 203   Perf. 13½x12½

O3	A4	2p red (II)	25.00	13.00
O4	A4	4p olive bister	40.00	26.00

Perf. 11½, 12

O5	A1	6p brown	97.50	90.00

1932-33   Wmk. 228   Perf. 13½x12½

O6	A4	½p orange	9.25	6.00
a.		Inverted overprint		
O7	A4	1p green (I)	6.00	2.00
O8	A4	2p red (II)	13.00	6.50
a.		Inverted overprint		
O9	A4	3p ultra (II) ('33)	18.00	9.25
O10	A4	5p brown buff	57.50	52.50

Perf. 11½, 12

O11	A1	6p yellow brown	45.00	35.00
a.		Inverted overprint		
		Nos. O6-O11 (6)	148.75	111.25
		Set, never hinged	275.00	

1932   Unwmk.   Perf. 11, 11½

O12	A9	2p red	7.25	6.00
O13	A9	3p blue	24.00	24.00
O14	A16	1sh gray green	72.50	52.50
		Nos. O12-O14 (3)	103.75	82.50
		Set, never hinged	160.00	

AUSTRALIAN ANTARCTIC TERRITORY

Catalogue values for all unused stamps in this section are for Never Hinged items.

All stamps, except Nos. L1-L7, are also valid for postage in Australia.

Edgeworth David, Douglas Mawson and A.F. McKay (1908-09 South Pole Expedition) — A1

Australian Explorers and Map of Antarctica — A2

Designs: 8p, Loading weasel (snow truck). 1sh, Dog team and iceberg, vert. 2sh3p, Emperor penguins and map, vert.

Perf. 14½, 14½x14, 14x14½

1957-59   Engr.   Unwmk.

L1	A1	5p brown	.65	.30
L2	A2	8p dark blue	2.75	2.25
L3	A2	1sh dark green	3.75	2.00
L4	A2	2sh ultra ('57)	1.75	1.00
L5	A2	2sh3p green	11.50	5.75
		Nos. L1-L5 (5)	20.40	11.30
		Set, hinged	9.75	

Nos. L1 and L2 were printed as 4p and 7p stamps and surcharged typographically in black and dark blue before issuance.

Sizes of stamps: No. L2, 34x21mm; Nos. L3, L5, 21x34mm; No. L4, 43½x25¼mm.

1961, July 5   Perf. 14½

L6	A1	5p dark blue	1.40	.45

The denomination on No. L6 is not within a typographed circle, but is part of the engraved design.

Sir Douglas Mawson — A3

1961, Oct. 18

L7	A3	5p dark green	.50	.40

50th anniv. of the 1911-14 Australian Antarctic Expedition.

Lookout and Iceberg — A4

Designs: 1c, Aurora australis and camera dome. 2c, Banding penguins. 5c, Branding of elephant seals. 7c, Measuring snow strata. 10c, Wind gauges. 15c, Weather balloon. 20c, Helicopter. 25c, Radio operator. 50c, Ice compression tests. $1, "Mock sun" (parahelion) and dogs. 20c, 25c, 50c and $1 horizontal.

Perf. 13½x13, 13x13½

1966-68   Photo.   Unwmk.

L8	A4	1c multicolored	.75	.40
L9	A4	2c multicolored	2.75	.90
L10	A4	4c multicolored	1.00	1.00
L11	A4	5c multicolored	2.25	1.10
L12	A4	7c multicolored	.75	.90
L13	A4	10c multicolored	1.00	1.00
L14	A4	15c multicolored	5.25	2.25
L15	A4	20c multicolored	8.00	2.75

L16	A4	25c multicolored	2.00	2.00
L17	A4	50c multicolored	7.50	7.50
L18	A4	$1 multicolored	25.00	15.00
		Nos. L8-L18 (11)	56.25	34.80
		Set, hinged	37.50	

Issued: 5c, 9/25/68; others, 9/28/66. Nos. L8-L18 are on phosphorescent helecon paper. Fluorescent orange is one of the colors used in printing the 10c, 15c, 20c and 50c.

Sastrugi Snow Formation A5

1971, June 23   Photo.   Perf. 13x13½

L19	A5	6c shown	.85	.85
L20	A5	30c Pancake ice	4.50	5.00

10th anniv. of the Antarctic Treaty pledging peaceful uses of and scientific cooperation in Antarctica.

Capt. Cook, Sextant, Azimuth Compass A6

Design: 35c, Chart of Cook's circumnavigation of Antarctica, and "Resolution."

1972, Sept. 13   Photo.   Perf. 13x13½

L21	A6	7c bister & multi	1.05	1.05
L22	A6	35c buff & multi	4.25	4.25

Bicentenary of Capt. James Cook's circumnavigation of Antarctica.

Plankton and Krill Shrimp — A7

Mawson's D.H. Gipsy Moth, 1931 — A8

Food Chain (Essential for Survival): 7c, Adelie penguin feeding on krill shrimp. 9c, Leopard seal pursuing fish, horiz. 10c, Killer whale hunting seals, horiz. 20c, Wandering albatross, horiz. $1, Sperm whale attacking giant squid.

Explorers' Aircraft: 8c, Rymill's DH Fox Moth returning to Barry Island. 25c, Hubert Wilkins Lockheed Vega, horiz. 30c, Lincoln Ellsworth's Northrop Gamma. 35c, Lars Christensen's Avro Avian and Framnes Mountains, horiz. 50c, Richard Byrd's Ford Tri-Motor dropping US flag over South Pole.

Perf. 13½x13, 13x13½

1973, Aug. 15

L23	A7	1c multicolored	.25	.25
L24	A8	5c multicolored	.25	.25
L25	A7	7c multicolored	1.40	.90
L26	A8	8c multicolored	.25	.50
L27	A7	9c multicolored	.25	.25
L28	A7	10c multicolored	2.50	1.75
L29	A7	20c multicolored	.70	.60
L30	A8	25c multicolored	.55	.60
L31	A8	30c multicolored	.55	.70
L32	A8	30c multicolored	.55	.70
L33	A8	50c multicolored	1.00	1.60
L34	A7	$1 multicolored	1.75	2.00
		Nos. L23-L34 (12)	10.00	10.10

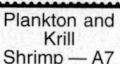

Adm. Byrd, Plane, Mountains A9

Design: 20c, Adm. Byrd, Floyd Bennett tri-motored plane, map of Antarctica.

1979, June 20   Litho.   Perf. 15½

L35	A9	20c multicolored	.40	.60
L36	A9	55c multicolored	.85	1.10

50th anniv. of first flight over South Pole by Richard Byrd (1888-1957).

"S.Y. Nimrod" A10

Designs: 1c, S.Y. Aurora. 2c, R.Y. Penola. 5c, M.V. Thala Dan. 10c, H.M.S. Challenger. No. L41, S.S. Morning. No. L42, S.Y. Nimrod, stern view. 20c, R.R.S. Discovery II. 22c, R.Y.S. Terra Nova. 25c, S.S. Endurance. 30c, S.S. Fram. 35c, M.S. Nella Dan. 40c, M.S. Kista Dan. 45c, L'Astrolabe. 50c, S.S. Norvegia. 55c, S.Y. Discovery. $1, H.M.S. Resolution.

2c, 5c, 22c, 25c, 40c, 55c, $1 are vertical.

Perf. 13½x13, 13x13½

1979-81   Litho.

L37	A10	1c multi	.25	.25
L38	A10	2c multi	.25	.25
L39	A10	5c multi	.25	.40
L40	A10	10c multi	.30	.70
L41	A10	15c multi	1.15	2.60
L42	A10	15c shown	.25	1.00
L43	A10	20c multi	.30	1.00
L44	A10	22c multi	.50	1.00
L45	A10	25c multi	.50	.70
L46	A10	30c multi	.50	1.30
L47	A10	35c multi	.60	1.30
L48	A10	40c multi	.80	1.30
L49	A10	45c multi	.80	1.30
L50	A10	50c multi	.80	1.00
L51	A10	55c multi	1.00	2.60
L52	A10	$1 multi	2.00	3.25
		Nos. L37-L52 (16)	10.25	19.95

Issued: 5c, 20c, 25c, 30c, 55c, 8/29; 1c, No. L41, 22c, 35c, $1, 5/21/80; 2c, 10c, No. L42, 40c, 45c, 50c, 9/9/81.

A11

1982, May 5   Litho.   Perf. 14x13½

L53	A11	27c Mawson, landscape	.35	.45
L54	A11	75c Mawson, map	1.00	1.40

Sir Douglas Mawson (1882-1958), explorer.

A12

Local Wildlife: a, Light-mantled sooty albatross. b, Macquarie Isld. shags. c, Elephant seals. d, Royal penguins. e, Antarctic prions.

1983, Apr. 6   Litho.   Perf. 14½

L55		Strip of 5, multi	3.50	3.50
a.-e.		A12 27c, any single	.70	.70

12th Antarctic Treaty Consultative Meeting, Canberra, Sept. 13-27 — A13

1983, Sept. 7   Litho.   Perf. 14½

L56	A13	27c multicolored	.45	.50

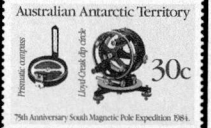

South Magnetic Pole Expedition, 75th Anniv. A14

1984, Jan. 16
L57 A14 30c Prismatic compass .50 .50
L58 A14 85c Aneroid barometer 1.50 *2.00*

Dog Team,
Mawson
Station
A15

2c, Summer afternoon. 10c, Evening. 15c, Prince Charles Mts. 20c, Morning. 25c, Sea ice, iceberg. 30c, Mt. Coates. 33c, Iceberg Alley. 36c, Winter evening. 45c, Brash ice, vert. 60c, Midwinter shadows. 75c, Coastline. 85c, Landing field. 90c, Pancake ice, vert. $1, Emperor penguins, Auster Rookery.

1984-87 **Litho.** **Perf. 14½x15**
L60 A15 2c multi .25 .25
L61 A15 5c shown .25 .25
L62 A15 10c multi .25 .25
L63 A15 15c multi .30 .25
L64 A15 20c multi .35 .30
L65 A15 25c multi .40 .35
L66 A15 30c multi .50 .45
L67 A15 33c multi .55 .45
L68 A15 36c multi .60 .50
L69 A15 45c multi .75 .65
L70 A15 60c multi 1.00 .80
L71 A15 75c multi 1.25 1.10
L72 A15 85c multi 1.50 1.25
L73 A15 90c multi 1.50 1.25
L74 A15 $1 multi 1.75 1.40
Nos. L60-L74 (15) 11.20 9.50

Issued: 5, 25, 30, 75, 85c, 7/18/84; 15, 33, 45, 90c, $1, 8/7/85; 2, 10, 20, 36, 60c, 3/11/87.

Antarctic Treaty,
25th Anniv. — A16

1986, Sept. 17 **Litho.** **Perf. 14x13½**
L75 A16 36c multicolored 1.00 .85

Environment,
Conservation
and
Technology
A17

No. L76: a, Hour-glass dolphins and the *Nella Dan.* b, Emperor penguins and Davis Station. c, Crabeater seal and helicopters. d, Adelie penguins and snow-ice transport vehicle. e, Gray-headed albatross and photographer.

1988, July 20 **Litho.** **Perf. 13**
L76 Strip of 5 6.00 6.00
  a.-e. A17 37c any single 1.05 1.05

Paintings by Sir
Sidney Nolan (b.
1917) — A18

No. L77, Antarctica. No. L78, Iceberg Alley. No. L79, Glacial Flow. No. L80, Frozen Sea.

1989, June 14 **Litho.** **Perf. 14x13½**
L77 A18 39c multicolored .90 .90
L78 A18 39c multicolored .90 .90
L79 A18 60c multicolored 2.00 2.00
L80 A18 80c multicolored 2.25 2.25
  Nos. L77-L80 (4) 6.05 6.05

Aurora
Australis
A19

Design: $1.20, Research ship Aurora Australis.

1991, June 20 **Litho.** **Perf. 14½**
L81 A19 43c multicolored .80 .80
L82 A19 $1.20 multicolored 2.25 2.25

Antarctic Treaty, 30th anniv. (No. L81).

Regional
Wildlife
A20

45c, Adelie penguin. 75c, Elephant seal. 85c, Northern giant petrel. 95c, Weddell seal. $1, Royal penguins. $1.20, Emperor penguin, vert. $1.40, Fur seals. $1.50, King penguins, vert.

Perf. 14x14½, 14½x14
1992-93 **Litho.**
L83 A20 45c multi .75 .65
L84 A20 75c multi 1.25 1.10
L85 A20 85c multi 1.50 1.40
L86 A20 95c multi 1.60 1.50
L86A A20 $1 multi 1.75 1.60
L87 A20 $1.20 multi 1.90 1.75
L88 A20 $1.40 multi 2.40 2.00
L89 A20 $1.50 multi 2.60 2.25
  Nos. L83-L89 (8) 13.75 12.25

Issued: $1, $1.40, $1.50, 1/14/93; others, 5/14/92.

The Last
Huskies
A21

45c, Dog up close, vert. 75c, Sled team. 85c, Dog seated, vert. $1.05, Three dogs.

1994, Jan. 13 **Litho.** **Perf. 14½**
L90 A21 45c multi 1.40 1.40
L91 A21 75c multi 2.00 2.00
L92 A21 85c multi 2.25 2.25
L93 A21 $1.05 multi 2.50 2.50
  Nos. L90-L93 (4) 8.15 8.15

Whales &
Dolphins
A22

1995, June 15 **Litho.** **Perf. 14½**
L94 A22 45c Humpback whale .95 .85
L95 A22 45c Hourglass
        dolphin, vert. .95 .85
L96 A22 45c Minke whale,
        vert. .95 .85
  a. Pair, #L95-L96 2.25 2.25
L97 A22 $1 Killer whale 2.50 2.50
  a. Souvenir sheet of 4, #L94-L97 7.75 7.75
  b. As "a," overprinted 65.00 65.00
  c. As "a," overprinted 40.00 40.00
  Nos. L94-L97 (4) 5.35 5.05

No. L97b is overprinted in gold in sheet margin with Singapore '95 emblem and: "Australia Post Exhibition Sheet No. 2," and, in both Chinese and English, with "Singapore 95 World Stamp Exhibition."
No. L97c is overprinted in gold in sheet margin with exhibition emblem, "Australian Post Exhibition Sheet No. 3" and CAPEX '96 WORLD PHILATELIC EXHIBITION / EXPOSITION PHILATELIQUE MONDIALE.
Issued: No. L97b, 9/1/95; No. L97c, 6/15/96.

Landscapes, by
Christian Clare
Robertson — A23

Designs: No. L98, Rafting sea ice. No. L99, Shadow on the Plateau. $1, Ice cave. $1.20, Twelve Lake.

1996, May 16 **Litho.** **Perf. 14½x14**
L98 A23 45c multicolored 1.25 .95
L99 A23 45c multicolored 1.25 .95
  a. Pair, Nos. L98-L99 2.50 2.25
L100 A23 $1 multicolored 3.00 2.50
L101 A23 $1.20 multicolored 4.25 3.75
  Nos. L98-L101 (4) 9.75 8.15

Australian
Natl.
Antarctic
Research
Expeditions,
50th Anniv.
A24

Designs: No. L102, Apple field huts. No. L103, Inside an apple hut. 95c, Summer surveying. $1.05, Sea ice research. $1.20, Remote field camp.

1997, May 15 **Litho.** **Perf. 14x14½**
L102 A24 45c multicolored 1.10 .90
L103 A24 45c multicolored 1.10 .90
  a. Pair, #L102-L103 2.25 2.25
L104 A24 95c multicolored 2.50 2.25
L105 A24 $1.05 multicolored 2.75 2.40
L106 A24 $1.20 multicolored 2.75 2.50
  Nos. L102-L106 (5) 10.20 8.95

Modes of
Transportion
A25

Designs: No. L107, Snowmobile. No. L108, Ship, "Aurora Australis." $1, Helicopter airlifting a four-wheel drive ATV, vert. $2, Antarctic Hagglunds (rubber-tracked vehicles with fiberglass cabins), vert.

Perf. 14x14½, 14½x14
1998, Mar. 5 **Litho.**
L107 A25 45c multicolored 1.90 1.75
L108 A25 45c multicolored 1.90 1.75
  a. Pair, #L107-L108 4.00 4.00
L109 A25 $1 multicolored 4.25 3.00
L110 A25 $2 multicolored 5.25 4.50
  Nos. L107-L110 (4) 13.30 11.00

Preservation
of Huts used
During
Mawson's
Antarctic
Expedition
A26

Designs: No. L111, Photograph of Mawson, sailing ship Aurora. No. L112, Photograph, "Home of the Blizzard," by Frank Hurley. 90c, Photograph, "Huskie Team," by Xavier Mertz. $1.35, Huts restoration.

1999, May 13 **Litho.** **Perf. 14x14½**
L111 A26 45c multicolored 1.50 1.50
L112 A26 45c multicolored 1.50 1.50
  a. Pair, #L111-L112 3.50 3.50
L113 A26 90c multicolored 3.50 3.00
L114 A26 $1.35 multicolored 4.00 3.50
  Nos. L111-L114 (4) 10.50 9.50

Penguins
A27

2000, July 24 **Litho.** **Perf. 13¾x14½**
L115 A27 45c Emperor penguins 3.50 3.25
L116 A27 45c Adélie penguins 3.50 3.25
  a. Pair, #L115-L116 7.00 7.00

Australians in the
Antarctic,
Cent. — A28

No. L117: a, Penguins and icicles. b, Louis Bernacchi, physicist. c, Nimrod. d, Scientists at South Magnetic Pole. e, Griffith Taylor and Frank Debenham, geologists. f, First radio used in Antarctica. g, First flight over Antarctica. h, Sir Douglas Mawson, explorer. i, BANZARE (British, Australian and New Zealand Antarctic Research Expedition). j, Australia's claim to territory. k, Establishment of ANARE (Australian National Antarctic Research Expeditions). l, Transport. m, Aurora Australis. n, Climate research. o, Cold-weather clothing. p, Nella Dan. q, First women on Antarctica. r, Communications. s, Tourism. t, Satellite view of Antarctica.

2001, May 17 **Litho.** **Perf. 14¾x14**
L117 Sheet of 20 28.50 28.50
  a.-e. A28 5c Any single 1.00 1.00
  f.-j. A28 10c Any single 1.10 1.10
  k.-o. A28 25c Any single 1.25 1.25
  p.-t. A28 45c Any single 1.40 1.40

Worldwide Fund for Nature
(WWF) — A29

No. L118: a, Leopard seal and pup on ice. b, Leopard seal and penguin on ice. c, Penguins, two leopard seals in water. d, Penguins, leopard seal in water.

2001, Sept. 11 **Litho.** **Perf. 14x14½**
L118 A29 Block of 4 9.00 8.00
  a.-d. 45c Any single 2.00 1.40

Antarctic Base Stations — A30

Maps showing station locations and : a, Light Detection and Ranging Instrument, aurora australis, Davis Station. b, Diatom, Casey Station. c, Wandering albatross, Macquarie Island Station. d, Adélie penguin, Mawson Station.

2002, July 2 **Litho.** **Perf. 14x14¾**
L119 A30 Block of 4, #a-d 10.50 10.50
  a.-d. 45c Any single 2.25 2.25

Ships — A31

Designs: No. L120, Kista Dan, No. L121, Magga Dan. $1, Thala Dan, vert. $1.45, Nella Dan, vert.

Perf. 14x14½, 14½x14
2003, Apr. 29 **Litho.**
L120 A31 50c multi 1.75 1.75
L121 A31 50c multi 1.75 1.75
  a. Horiz. pair, #L120-L121 3.75 3.75
L122 A31 $1 multi 3.75 3.75
L123 A31 $1.45 multi 5.50 5.50
  Nos. L120-L123 (4) 12.75 12.75

Mawson Station, 50th Anniv. — A32

Designs: No. L124, Naming ceremony, 1954. No. L125, Station buildings. $1, Barge and airplane. $1.45, Auster Emperor Penguin Rookery.

2004, Feb. 13   Litho.   Perf. 14x14½

L124	A32	50c multi	1.60	1.60
L125	A32	50c multi	1.60	1.60
a.		Horiz. pair, #L124-L125	4.00	4.00
L126	A32	$1 multi	3.00	3.00
L127	A32	$1.45 multi	5.25	5.25
		Nos. L124-L127 (4)	11.45	11.45

Aircraft A33

Designs: No. L128, Hughes 500 helicopter. No. L129, De Havilland DHC-2 Beaver. $1, Pilatus PC-6 Porter. $1.45, Douglas DC-3/Dakota C-47.

2005, Sept. 6   Litho.   Perf. 14x14½

L128	A33	50c multi	1.40	1.40
L129	A33	50c multi	1.40	1.40
a.		Horiz. pair, #L128-L129	3.50	3.50
L130	A33	$1 multi	2.75	2.75
L131	A33	$1.45 multi	4.50	4.50
		Nos. L128-L131 (4)	10.05	10.05

Fish — A34

Designs: No. L132, Mackerel icefish. No. L133, Lanternfish. No. L134, Eaton's skate. No. L135, Patagonian toothfish.

2006, Aug. 1   Litho.   Perf. 14x14¾

L132	A34	50c multi	1.50	1.50
L133	A34	50c multi	1.50	1.50
a.		Horiz. pair, #L132-L133	3.25	3.25
L134	A34	$1 multi	3.00	3.00
L135	A34	$1 multi	3.00	3.00
a.		Horiz. pair, #L134-L135	6.50	6.50
		Nos. L132-L135 (4)	9.00	9.00

Worldwide Fund For Nature (WWF) — A35

Royal penguins: No. L136, Four marching. No. L137, Nesting. No. L138, Two contesting territory (denomination at bottom), horiz. No. L139, Two courting (denomination at left), horiz.

2007, Aug. 7   Litho.   Perf. 14½x14

L136	A35	50c multi	1.40	1.00
L137	A35	50c multi	1.40	1.00
a.		Horiz. pair, #L136-L137	2.75	2.00

Perf. 14x14½

L138	A35	$1 multi	2.75	2.40
L139	A35	$1 multi	2.75	2.40
a.		Vert. pair, #L138-L139	5.75	4.75
		Nos. L136-L139 (4)	8.30	6.80

International Polar Year — A36

Designs: No. L140, Astronomy. No. L141, Glaciology. No. L142, Marine biology. No. L143, Oceanography.

Discovery of South Magnetic Pole, Cent. — A37

2008, Sept. 16   Litho.   Perf. 14x14½

L140	A36	55c multi	2.60	1.90
L141	A36	55c multi	2.60	1.90
a.		Vert. pair, #L140-L141	5.25	3.80
L142	A36	$1.10 multi	5.50	4.50
L143	A36	$1.10 multi	5.50	4.50
a.		Vert. pair, #L142-L143	11.00	9.00
b.		Souvenir sheet, #L140-L143	17.00	12.50
		Nos. L140-L143 (4)	16.20	12.80

Designs: No. L144, Crew unloading the Nimrod. No. L145, Crew depositing expedition provisions by automobile. No. L146, Men at Northern Party camp. No. L147, Alistair Mackay, Douglas Mawson, and Edgeworth David with flag at South Magnetic Pole.

2009, Jan. 8   Litho.   Perf. 14½x14

L144	A37	55c lt bl & blk	1.75	1.30
L145	A37	55c lt bl & multi	1.75	1.30
a.		Horiz. pair, #L144-L145	3.50	2.60
L146	A37	$1.10 lt bl & blk	3.75	2.50
L147	A37	$1.10 lt bl & blk	3.75	2.50
a.		Horiz. pair, #L146-L147	7.50	5.00
b.		Souvenir sheet, #L144-L147	11.50	8.00
		Nos. L144-L147 (4)	11.00	7.60

International Polar Year — A38

Designs: 55c, Snow petrel. $2.05, Jade iceberg.

2009, Mar. 4   Litho.   Perf. 14x14¾

L148	A38	55c multi	1.60	1.30
L149	A38	$2.05 multi	6.50	3.25
a.		Souvenir sheet, #L148-L149	8.00	4.50
b.		Sheet of 2, Australia #3337, Australian Antarctic Terr. #L149	10.00	10.00

Issued: No. L149b, 8/20/10. Stampex 2010, Adelaide (No. L149b).

Macquarie Island — A39

Designs: No. L150, Pleurophyllum hookeri (flower). No. L151, Southern elephant seal. No. L152, Mawson Point Stacks (green terrain). No. L153, Caroline Cove (brown terrain).

2010, Oct. 26   Litho.   Perf. 14¼

L150	A39	60c multi	2.00	1.50
L151	A39	60c multi	2.00	1.50
a.		Horiz. pair, #L150-L151	4.00	3.00
L152	A39	$1.20 multi	4.00	3.00
L153	A39	$1.20 multi	4.00	3.00
a.		Horiz. pair, #L152-L153	8.00	6.00
b.		Souvenir sheet, #L150-L153	12.00	12.00
		Nos. L150-L153 (4)	12.00	9.00

A40

A41

Icebergs A43

A42

2011, June 7   Litho.   Perf. 14x14¾

L154		Block of 4	7.00	7.00
a.		A40 60c multi	1.75	1.75
b.		A41 60c multi	1.75	1.75
c.		A42 60c multi	1.75	1.75
d.		A43 60c multi	1.75	1.75
e.		Souvenir sheet of 4, #L154a-L154d	8.00	8.00

Booklet Stamps
Self-Adhesive
Stamps With Grayed Frame
Serpentine Die Cut 11¼ Syncopated

L155	A40	60c multi	2.00	.30
L156	A41	60c multi	2.00	.30
L157	A42	60c multi	2.00	.30
L158	A43	60c multi	2.00	.30
a.		Booklet pane of 10, 3 each #L155-L156, 2 each #L157-L158	20.00	
		Nos. L155-L158 (4)	8.00	1.20

Australasian Antarctic Expedition, Cent. — A44

No. L159: a, Map and mast of SY Aurora. b, John King Davis (1884-1967), captain of the SY Aurora. c, SY Aurora and postmark. d, Expedition members landing at Macquarie Island. e, Birds on Macquarie Island.

2011, Aug. 2   Perf. 14¾x14

L159		Horiz. strip of 5	9.50	7.25
a.-e.		A44 60c Any single	1.90	1.40
f.		Souvenir sheet of 5, #L159a-L159e	9.50	7.25

Dr. Philip Law (1912-2010), Polar Explorer — A45

Designs: 60c, Law. $1.20, Map of Antarctica, Law and helicopter at Arthurson Bluff. $1.80, Map of Antarctica, opening of Mawson Station.

2012, Mar. 6   Litho.   Perf. 14¾x14

L160	A45	60c multi	1.75	1.40
L161	A45	$1.20 multi	3.50	2.75
L162	A45	$1.80 multi	5.50	2.75
a.		Souvenir sheet of 3, #L160-L162	11.00	8.50
		Nos. L160-L162 (3)	10.75	6.90

Australasian Antarctic Expedition, Cent. — A46

Designs: No. L163, Main hut. No. L164, Xavier Mertz and dogs. No. L165, Belgrave Ninnis and dogs. No. L166, Bow of SY Aurora, map of Cape Denison, penguins. No. L167, Stern of SY Aurora, expedition members carrying supplies from ship.

2012, Sept. 4

L163	A46	60c multi	1.75	1.30
L164	A46	60c multi	1.75	1.30
L165	A46	60c multi	1.75	1.30
a.		Horiz. strip of 3, #L163-L165	5.00	4.00
L166	A46	$1.20 multi	3.50	2.75
L167	A46	$1.20 multi	3.50	2.75
b.		Souvenir sheet of 5, #L163-L167	12.00	9.50
		Nos. L163-L167 (5)	12.25	9.40

Mountains A47

Designs: No. L168, Mt. Parsons. No. L169, Mawson Escarpment. $1.20, South Masson Range. $1.80, David Range.

2013, Mar. 12   Litho.   Perf. 14x14¾

L168	A47	60c multi	1.25	.95
L169	A47	60c multi	1.25	.95
a.		Horiz. pair, #L168-L169	2.50	1.90
L170	A47	$1.20 multi	2.50	1.90
L171	A47	$1.80 multi	3.75	3.00
a.		Souvenir sheet of 4, #L168-L171	8.75	8.75
		Nos. L168-L171 (4)	8.75	6.80

Australasian Antarctic Expedition, Cent. — A48

Designs: No. L172, Men walking in blizzard. No. L173, Man checking wind recorder. No. L174, Weddell seal, Cape petrels. No. L175, Wireless operator Walter Hannam. No. L176, Frank Wild, leader of Western Party of Expedition.

2013, Sept. 10   Perf. 14¾x14

L172	A48	60c multi	1.10	.85
L173	A48	60c multi	1.10	.85
L174	A48	60c multi	1.10	.85
a.		Horiz. strip of 3, #L172-L174	3.30	2.60
L175	A48	$1.20 multi	2.25	1.75
L176	A48	$1.20 multi	2.25	1.75
a.		Horiz. pair, #L175-L176	4.50	3.50
b.		Souvenir sheet of 5, #L172-L176	8.00	8.00
		Nos. L172-L176 (5)	7.80	6.05

Australasian Antarctic Expedition, Cent. — A49

Designs: No. L177, Scientific researchers with large net. No. L178, Expedition members on SY Aurora. No. L179, Sir Douglas Mawson (1882-1958), expedition leader. No. L180, Mawson on motor launch, Cape Denison. No. L181, Frank Hurley with movie camera.

2014, Feb. 18   Litho.   Perf. 14¾x14

L177	A49	60c multi	1.10	.85
L178	A49	60c multi	1.10	.85
L179	A49	60c multi	1.10	.85
a.		Horiz. strip of 3, #L177-L179	3.30	2.60
L180	A49	$1.20 multi	2.25	1.75
L181	A49	$1.20 multi	2.25	1.75
a.		Horiz. pair, #L180-L181	4.50	3.50
b.		Souvenir sheet of 5, #L177-L181	8.00	8.00
		Nos. L177-L181 (5)	7.80	6.05

Husky — A50

Designs: Nos. L182, L186, Gray husky (shown). Nos. L183, L186, Brown husky. No. L184, Dog team with drivers in orange parkas, horiz. No. L185, Dog team with drivers in black parkas, horiz.

Perf. 14³⁄₄x14, 14x14³⁄₄
2014, Sept. 9			Litho.	
L182	A50	70c multi	1.25	1.25
L183	A50	70c multi	1.25	1.25
a.		Horiz. pair, #L182-L183	2.50	2.50
L184	A50	$1.40 multi	2.50	2.00
L185	A50	$1.40 multi	2.50	2.00
a.		Horiz. pair, #L184-L185	5.00	4.00
b.		Souvenir sheet of 4, #L182-L185	7.50	7.50
		Nos. L182-L185 (4)	7.50	6.50

Booklet Stamps
Self-Adhesive
Serpentine Die Cut 11¼ Syncopated
L186	A50	70c multi	1.25	.25
L187	A50	70c multi	1.25	.25
a.		Booklet pane of 10, 5 each #L186-L187	12.50	

Antarctic Atmospheric Conditions
A51

Various Antarctic landscapes and atmospheric conditions with denomination at: No. L188, UR. No. L189, UL. No. L190, UR. No. L191, UL.

2015, May 26		Litho.	Perf. 14x14³⁄₄	
L188	A51	70c multi	1.10	.85
L189	A51	70c multi	1.10	.85
a.		Horiz. pair, #L188-L189	2.20	1.70
L190	A51	$1.40 multi	2.25	1.75
L191	A51	$1.40 multi	2.25	1.75
a.		Horiz. pair, #L190-L191	4.50	3.50
b.		Souvenir sheet of 4, #L188-L191	6.75	6.75
		Nos. L188-L191 (4)	6.70	5.20

Dogs Involved in Macquarie Island Pest Eradication
A52

Dogs and: No. L192, Penguins. No. L193, Man with backpack. No. L194, Woman. No. L195, Man in winter coat.

2015, Sept. 9		Litho.	Perf. 14x14³⁄₄	
L192	A52	70c multi	1.00	.75
L193	A52	70c multi	1.00	.75
a.		Horiz. pair, #L192-L193	2.00	1.50
L194	A52	$1.40 multi	2.00	1.50
L195	A52	$1.40 multi	2.00	1.50
a.		Horiz. pair, #L194-L195	4.00	3.00
b.		Souvenir sheet of 4, #L192-L195	6.00	6.00
		Nos. L192-L195 (4)	6.00	4.50

Photographs of Ernest Shackleton's Imperial Trans-Antarctic Expedition by Frank Hurley (1885-1962) — A53

Inscriptions: No. L196, Weddell Sea. No. L197, Ice-bound. No. L198, Ocean Camp. No. L199, Rescue Mission. $3, At Work.

2016, June 21		Litho.	Perf. 14³⁄₄x14	
L196	A53	$1 multi	1.50	1.10
L197	A53	$1 multi	1.50	1.10
a.		Horiz. pair, #L196-L197	3.00	2.25
L198	A53	$2 multi	3.00	2.25
L199	A53	$2 multi	3.00	2.25
a.		Horiz. pair, #L198-L199	6.00	4.50
L200	A53	$3 multi	4.50	3.50
a.		Souvenir sheet of 5, #L196-L200	13.50	13.50
		Nos. L196-L200 (5)	13.50	10.20

Ice Flowers (Frost Formations)
A54

Various ice flowers. Denomination at UR on Nos. L201, L203, L205a, L205c, L206, Denomination at UL on Nos. L202, L204, L205b, L205d, L207.

Litho., Litho & Embossed With Foil Application (#L205)
2016, Sept. 20			Perf. 14¼	
L201	A54	$1 multi	1.60	1.60
L202	A54	$1 multi	1.60	1.60
a.		Horiz. pair, #L201-L202	3.20	3.20
L203	A54	$2 multi	3.25	1.60
L204	A54	$3 multi	4.75	2.40
		Nos. L201-L204 (4)	11.20	7.20

Miniature Sheet
L205		Sheet of 4	11.50	6.50
a.-b.	A54	$1 Either single	1.60	1.25
c.	A54	$2 multi	3.25	1.60
d.	A54	$3 multi	4.75	2.40

Booklet Stamps
Self-Adhesive
Serpentine Die Cut 11¼ Syncopated
L206	A54	$1 multi	1.60	.25
L207	A54	$1 multi	1.60	.25
a.		Booklet pane of 10, 5 each #L206-L207	16.00	

album accessories

ADVANTAGE STOCK SHEETS
Advantage stock sheets fit directly in your 2-post or 3-ring National or Specialty album. Available with 1 to 8 pockets.

Sheets are sold in packages of 10.
- Stock sheets match album pages in every respect, including size, border, and color.
- Punched to fit perfectly in binder.
- Ideal for storing minor varieties and collateral material. A great place to keep new issues until the next supplement is available.
- Provides the protection of clear acetate pockets on heavyweight pages.

NATIONAL BORDER

Item			Retail	AA*
AD11	1 Pocket	242mm	$21.99	$19.99
AD12	2 Pockets	119mm	$21.99	$19.99
AD13	3 Pockets	79mm	$21.99	$19.99
AD14	4 Pockets	58mm	$21.99	$19.99
AD15	5 Pockets	45mm	$21.99	$19.99
AD16	6 Pockets	37mm	$21.99	$19.99
AD17	7 Pockets	34mm	$21.99	$19.99
AD18	8 Pockets	31mm	$21.99	$19.99

SPECIALTY BORDER

Item			Retail	AA*
AD21	1 Pocket	242mm	$21.99	$19.99
AD22	2 Pockets	119mm	$21.99	$19.99
AD23	3 Pockets	79mm	$21.99	$19.99
AD24	4 Pockets	58mm	$21.99	$19.99
AD25	5 Pockets	45mm	$21.99	$19.99
AD26	6 Pockets	37mm	$21.99	$19.99
AD27	7 Pockets	34mm	$21.99	$19.99
AD28	8 Pockets	31mm	$21.99	$19.99

SPECIALTY/NATIONAL SERIES BINDERS
National series pages are punched for 3-ring and 2-post binders. The 3-ring binder is available in two sizes. The 2-post binder comes in one size. All Scott binders are covered with a tough green leatherette material that is washable and reinforced at stress points for long wear.

3-RING BINDERS & SLIPCASES
With the three ring binder, pages lay flat and the rings make turning the pages easy. The locking mechanism insure that the rings won't pop open even when the binder is full.

Item			Retail	AA*
ACBR01D	Small 3-Ring Binder	Holds up to 100 pages	$41.99	$34.99
ACBR03D	Large 3-Ring Binder	Holds up to 250 pages	$41.99	$34.99
ACSR01	Small 3-Ring Slipcase.		$37.50	$26.99
ACSR03	Large 3-Ring Slipcase.		$37.50	$26.99

LARGE 2-POST BINDER & SLIPCASE
For the traditional Scott collector, we offer the standard hinge post binder. Scott album pages are punched with rectangular holes that fit on rectangular posts. The posts and pages are held by a rod that slides down from the top. With the post binder pages do not lie flat. However, filler strips are available for a minimal cost.

Item			Retail	AA*
ACBS03	Large 2-Post Binder	Holds up to 250 pages	$54.99	$46.99
ACSS03	Large 2-Post Slipcase		$37.50	$26.99

PAGE PROTECTORS
Protect your stamps and album pages with a clear archival quality plastic sleeve. Sleeves fits over the entire page and protects pages from creases, fingerprints and tears. Scott Page protectors are PVC-free and thin enough that they won't make your binder bulge. Page Protectors are available in two sizes. Sold in packages of 25.

2-Post Minuteman/International Pg Protectors

Item	Retail	AA*
ACC165	$13.99	$11.75

National/Specialty Series Pg Protectors*

Item	Retail	AA*
ACC166	$13.99	$11.75

*Punched to fit 2-post and 3-ring binder.

ALBUM PAGE DIVIDERS
Postage, air post, semi-postals; they're all right at your fingertips with Specialty Album Page Dividers. The dividers are a great way to keep your albums organized and save wear and tear on your pages.

Item		Retail	AA*
ACC145	Package of 10	$5.99	$4.99

BLANK PAGES
Ideal for developing your own album pages to be integrated with your album. Sold in packs of 20 pages.
Quadrille pages have graph pattern printed on page.

SPECIALTY SERIES PAGES (BORDER A)

Item		Retail	AA*
ACC110		$9.99	$7.99
ACC111	Quadrille*	$14.99	$12.99

NATIONAL SERIES PAGES (BORDER B)

Item		Retail	AA*
ACC120		$9.99	$7.99
ACC121	Quadrille*	$14.99	$12.99

Illustrated Identifier

This section pictures stamps or parts of stamp designs that will help identify postage stamps that do not have English words on them.

Many of the symbols that identify stamps of countries are shown here as well as typical examples of their stamps.

See the Index and Identifier for stamps with inscriptions such as "sen," "posta," "Baja Porto," "Helvetia," "K.S.A.", etc.

Linn's Stamp Identifier is now available. The 144 pages include more than 2,000 inscriptions and more than 500 large stamp illustrations. Available from Linn's Stamp News, P.O. Box 4129, Sidney, OH 45365-4129.

1. HEADS, PICTURES AND NUMERALS

GREAT BRITAIN

Great Britain stamps never show the country name, but, except for postage dues, show a picture of the reigning monarch.

Victoria

Edward VII   George V   Edward VIII

George VI

Elizabeth II

Some George VI and Elizabeth II stamps are surcharged in annas, new paisa or rupees. These are listed under Oman.

Silhouette (sometimes facing right, generally at the top of stamp)

The silhouette indicates this is a British stamp. It is not a U.S. stamp.

VICTORIA

Queen Victoria

INDIA

Other stamps of India show this portrait of Queen Victoria and the words "Service" (or "Postage") and "Annas."

AUSTRIA

YUGOSLAVIA

(Also BOSNIA & HERZEGOVINA if imperf.)

BOSNIA & HERZEGOVINA

Denominations also appear in top corners instead of bottom corners.

HUNGARY

Another stamp has posthorn facing left

BRAZIL

AUSTRALIA

Kangaroo and Emu

GERMANY

Mecklenburg-Vorpommern

SWITZERLAND

PALAU

37c   KAYANGEL

2. ORIENTAL INSCRIPTIONS

CHINA

中　中

Any stamp with this one character is from China (Imperial, Republic or People's Republic). This character appears in a four-character overprint on stamps of Manchukuo. These stamps are local provisionals, which are unlisted. Other overprinted Manchukuo stamps show this character, but have more than four characters in the overprints. These are listed in People's Republic of China.

         Some
              Chinese
         stamps show
              the Sun.

Most stamps of Republic of China show this series of characters.

Stamps with the China character and this character are from People's Republic of China.   人

Calligraphic form of
People's Republic of China

(一)	(二)	(三)	(四)	(五)	(六)
1	2	3	4	5	6
(七)	(八)	(九)	(十)	(一十)	(二十)
7	8	9	10	11	12

**Chinese stamps
without China character**

REPUBLIC OF CHINA

PEOPLE'S REPUBLIC OF CHINA

Mao Tse-tung

MANCHUKUO

Temple   Emperor Pu-Yi

The first 3 characters are common to
many Manchukuo stamps.

The last 3 characters are common to
other Manchukuo stamps.

Orchid Crest

Manchukuo
stamp
without
these
elements

JAPAN

Chrysanthemum Crest   Country Name

Japanese stamps without these elements

The number of characters in the
center and the design of dragons on
the sides will vary.

RYUKYU ISLANDS

Country Name

PHILIPPINES
(Japanese Occupation)

Country Name

NETHERLANDS INDIES
(Japanese Occupation)

Indicates Japanese Occupation

Java   Sumatra

Country Name   Country Name

Moluccas, Celebes and
South Borneo

Country Name

NORTH BORNEO
(Japanese Occupation)

Indicates Japanese   Country
Occupation   Name

MALAYA
(Japanese Occupation)

Indicates Japanese   Country
Occupation   Name

BURMA
Union of Myanmar

Union of Myanmar
(Japanese Occupation)

Indicates Japanese   Country
Occupation   Name

Other Burma Japanese Occupation stamps
without these elements

Burmese Script

KOREA

These two characters, in any order,
are common to stamps from the
Republic of Korea (South Korea) or of
the People's Democratic Republic of
Korea (North Korea).

This series of four characters can be found
on the stamps of both Koreas.
Most stamps of the Democratic People's
Republic of Korea (North Korea)
have just this inscription.

Indicates Republic of Korea (South Korea)

South Korean postage stamps issed after
1952 do not show currency expressed
in Latin letters. Stamps wiith "
HW," "HWAN," "WON,"
"WN," "W" or "W" with two lines through it,
if not illustrated in listings of stamps
before this date, are revenues.
North Korean postage stamps do not have
currency expressed in Latin letters.

Yin Yang appears on some stamps.

South Korean stamps show Yin Yang and
starting in 1966, 'KOREA" in Latin letters

Example of South Korean stamps lacking
Latin text, Yin Yang and standard Korean
text of country name. North Korean stamps
never show Yin Yang and starting in 1976
are inscribed "DPRK" or "DPR KOREA" in
Latin letters.

THAILAND

Country Name

King Chulalongkorn

King Prajadhipok and
Chao P'ya Chakri

---

3. CENTRAL AND EASTERN ASIAN INSCRIPTIONS

INDIA - FEUDATORY STATES

Alwar

Bhor

Bundi

Similar stamps come with different designs in corners and differently drawn daggers (at center of circle).

Dhar   Duttia

Faridkot

Hyderabad

Similar stamps exist with different central design which is inscribed "Postage" or "Post & Receipt."

Indore

Jammu & Kashmir

Text varies.

Jasdan

Jhalawar

Kotah

Size and text varies

Nandgaon

Nowanuggur

Poonch

Similar stamps exist
in various sizes with different text

Rajasthan

Rajpeepla

Soruth

Tonk

BANGLADESH

বাংলাদেশ

Country Name

NEPAL

Similar stamps are smaller, have squares in
upper corners and have five or nine
characters in central bottom panel.

TANNU TUVA   ISRAEL

GEORGIA

 This inscription
is found on other
pictorial stamps.

Country Name

ARMENIA

The four characters are found somewhere
on pictorial stamps. On some stamps only
the middle two are found.

4. AFRICAN INSCRIPTIONS

ETHIOPIA

5. ARABIC INSCRIPTIONS

١ ٢ ٣ ٤ ٥
1 2 3 4 5

٧ ٨ ٩ ٠
6 7 8 9 0

AFGHANISTAN

Many early Afghanistan stamps show Tiger's head, many of these have ornaments protruding from outer ring, others show inscriptions in black.

Arabic Script

Crest of King Amanullah

Mosque Gate & Crossed Cannons

The four characters are found somewhere on pictorial stamps. On some stamps only the middle two are found.

BAHRAIN

EGYPT

Postage

IRAN

Country Name

Royal Crown

Lion with Sword

Symbol

Emblem

IRAQ

JORDAN

LEBANON

Similar types have
denominations at top
and slightly different
design.

LIBYA

Country Name in various styles

Other Libya stamps show Eagle and
Shield (head facing either direction) or
Red, White and Black Shield (with or with-
out eagle in center).

Without Country Name

SAUDI ARABIA

Tughra (Central design)

← Palm Tree and Swords

20H

SYRIA

Arab Government Issues

THRACE　　**YEMEN**

PAKISTAN

PAKISTAN - BAHAWALPUR

→

→

Country Name in top panel, star and crescent

TURKEY

Star & Crescent is a device found on many Turkish stamps, but is also found on stamps from other Arabic areas (see Pakistan-Bahawalpur)

Tughra (similar tughras
can be found on stamps of
Turkey in Asia, Afghanistan
and Saudi Arabia)

Mohammed V

Mustafa Kemal

Plane, Star and Crescent

TURKEY IN ASIA

Other Turkey in Asia pictorials
show star & crescent.
Other stamps show tughra
shown under Turkey.

6. GREEK INSCRIPTIONS

GREECE

Country Name in various styles
(Some Crete stamps overprinted with the
Greece country name are listed in Crete.)

Lepta

ΔΡΑΧΜΗ   **ΔΡΑΧΜΑΙ**   ΛΕΠΤΟΝ
Drachma   Drachmas   Lepton
Abbreviated Country Name   ΕΛΛ

Other forms of Country Name

No country name

CRETE

Country Name

Crete stamps with a surcharge that have the year "1922" are listed under Greece.

EPIRUS

Similar stamps have text above the eagle.

IONIAN IS.

---

7. CYRILLIC INSCRIPTIONS

RUSSIA

Postage Stamp   Imperial Eagle

Postage in various styles

  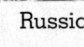

Abbreviation   Abbreviation   Russia
for Kopeck   for Ruble

Abbreviation for Russian Soviet Federated Socialist Republic RSFSR stamps were overprinted (see below)

Abbreviation for Union of Soviet Socialist Republics

This item is footnoted in Latvia

RUSSIA - Army of the North

"OKCA"

RUSSIA - Wenden

RUSSIAN OFFICES IN THE TURKISH EMPIRE

These letters appear on other stamps of the Russian offices.

The unoverprinted version of this stamp and a similar stamp were overprinted by various countries (see below).

ARMENIA

BELARUS

FAR EASTERN REPUBLIC

Country Name

FINLAND

Circles and Dots
on stamps similar
to Imperial
Russia issues

SOUTH RUSSIA

Country Name

BATUM

Forms of Country Name

TRANSCAUCASIAN FEDERATED REPUBLICS

Abbreviation for
Country Name

KAZAKHSTAN

Country Name

KYRGYZSTAN

Country
Name

ROMANIA

TAJIKISTAN

Country Name & Abbreviation

UKRAINE

Country Name in various forms

The trident appears
on many stamps,
usually as
an overprint.

Abbreviation for
Ukrainian
Soviet
Socialist
Republic

WESTERN UKRAINE

Abbreviation for
Country Name

AZERBAIJAN

AZƏRBAYCAN

Country Name

A.C.C.P.

Abbreviation for Azerbaijan
Soviet Socialist Republic

MONTENEGRO

ЦРНАГОРЕ

ЦРНА ГОРА

Country Name in various forms

Abbreviation
for country
name

No country name
(A similar Montenegro
stamp without coun-
try name has same
vignette.)

SERBIA

СРПСКА　**СРБИЈА**

Country Name in various forms

Abbreviation for country name

No country name

MACEDONIA

МАКЕДОНИЈА

Country Name

МАКЕДОНСКИ

Different form of Country Name

SERBIA & MONTENEGRO

YUGOSLAVIA

Showing country name

No Country Name

BOSNIA & HERZEGOVINA
(Serb Administration)

РЕПУБЛИКА СРПСКА

Country Name

РЕПУБЛИКЕ СРПСКЕ

Different form of Country Name

No Country Name

BULGARIA

No country name

Mung
in Mongolian

Country Name   Postage

Stotinka

Abbreviation
for Lev, leva

Tugrik
in Mongolian

MONGOLIA

Stotinki (plural)   Abbreviation for
Stotinki

Country Name in various forms and styles

Arms

No Country Name

Country name in   Tugrik in Cyrillic
one word

Country name in   Mung in Cyrillic
two words

New World of Technology

6-IN-1 LED POCKET MAGNIFIER/ MICROSCOPE (55X)

A powerful LED microscope (up to 55X magnification) teams up with two aspheric Perspex lenses (3X magnification large and 10X magnification small) to examine objects at various levels of detail. Built-in focus wheel ensures clarity. View objects even in low-light conditions with three lighting functions: three LED flashlight, simple UV light, one white LED. Black composite housing.

Item	Retail	AA*
MG61LED	$21.95	$19.95

5-IN-1 MULTI-FUNCTION POCKET MAGNIFIER 2.5X-10X LED

A sturdy stainless steel frame houses two aspheric lenses: 2.5X rectangular and 10X round, plus three lighting functions: 3-LED side flashlight, 1-LED research light, simple 395nm long-wave UV light. A mini ballpoint pen, available to take notes, tucks inside the acrylic housing. Leatherette case & 3 #LR927 batteries included.

Item	Retail	AA*
MG51	$15.95	$13.95

13W DUOFLEX MAGNIFIER DESK LAMP

The OttLite DuoFlex has a two-pronged approach to enhance your vision. First, the large 3X-5X magnifier enlarges your subject. Then the energy-efficient 13w "E" bulb spotlights the field. Flexible arms allow nearly infinite positioning. Long-term bulb is rated to last up to 10,000 hours.

Item	Retail	AA*
ACC213W	$109.99	$59.99

SCHAUBEK 10X LED & UV COMBO MAGNIFIER

This pocket-sized magnifier boasts 10X magnification with both LED and UV longwave light. Battery powered for maximum portability. Handy carrying case protects the 21mm magnifier while on the go.

Item	Retail	AA*
MG10XLUV	$39.99	$29.99

3.2X LED ILLUMINATED MAGNIFIER

This 7" aluminum 3.2X magnifier is both beautiful and functional. Six LEDs surround the 1.375" lens to provide glare-free illumination. Zippered protective case and 2 AA batteries included.

Item	Retail	AA*
MG32XL	$35.95	$31.95

LIGHTHOUSE DUAL WAVE ULTRAVIOLET LAMP

Examine your collectibles for both fluorescence (long wave) and phosphorescence (short wave) using one versatile ultraviolet lamp. Flip a switch to change quickly and easily between short and long UV rays (254 and 380nm). Short wave exposes tagging, while long wave reveals faults, tears, and repairs. Battery operated; requires 4x AA batteries (not included).

Item	Retail	AA*
LHL81	$71.95	$59.95

ZOOM 20X-40X MICROSCOPE WITH LED

This practical zoom microscope provides what collectors have been waiting for – outstanding clarity and resolution. Magnification is continuously adjustable between 20X and 40X. Powerful LED lighting illuminates the stage (3 #LR44 batteries included). Stand, examination slides, and slide covers also included.

Item	Retail	AA*
LHPM3	$29.95	$21.95

LIGHTHOUSE .1-500G DIGITAL SCALE

This portable-sized digital scale displays weight in six different units: g, oz, ozt, dwt, ct, gn. Illuminated LCD display with tare function is great for gold coins. Weight range 0.1-500 g with +/- 0.03 g tolerance. Requires 2 AA batteries, included.

Item	Retail	AA*
LHDW4	$29.95	$24.95

LIGHTHOUSE DIGITAL CALIPERS 6"

Sliding calipers measure from 1-150mm (0"-6") in .01mm increments with accuracy to 0.3mm. Six-digit LCD display easily switches from millimeters to inches. Batteries and padded case included.

Item	Retail	AA*
LHSL1	$49.95	$42.95

ZOOM 10X-300X USB DIGITAL MICROSCOPE, 5.0 MEGAPIXEL

The industry-leading 5.0 megapixel resolution makes the smallest details on coins and stamps visible on your computer screen via the included USB cable. Up to 10x - 300x magnification available with this high-end digital microscope

Item	Retail	AA*
LHDM4	$179.95	$169.95

PHONESCOPE DIGITAL MICROSCOPE

Clip this compact Lighthouse Phonescope lens on your smartphone or tablet to transform it into a powerful digital microscope. See the smallest details and instantly capture high-quality images and videos. The precision macro glass lens offers up to 60X magnification and requires no batteries. Field of view: 1/2" (13mm). Phonescope works with all popular smartphones without scratching display. Image resolution and zoom function dependent upon your device.

Item	Retail	AA*
LHSCOPE	$25.99	$21.99

ORDERING INFORMATION: *AA prices apply to paid subscribers of Amos Media titles, or orders placed online. Prices, terms and product availability subject to change. Taxes will apply in CA, OH, & IL. Shipping and handling rates will apply. See below.

Visit: AmosAdvantage.com
Call: 1-800-572-6885
Outside U.S. & Canada Call: 1-800-572-6885

SHIPPING & HANDLING: United States: Order total $0-$10.00 charged $3.99 shipping. United States - Order total $10.01-$79.99 charged $7.99 shipping. United States - Order total $80.00 or more charged 10% of order total for shipping. Maximum Freight Charge $45.00. Canada: 20% of order total. Minimum charge $19.99 Maximum charge $200.00. Foreign orders are shipped via FedExl Intl. or USPS and billed actual freight.

STOCKBOOKS

Stockbooks are a classic and convenient storage alternative for many collectors. These 9" x 12" Lighthouse stockbooks feature heavyweight archival quality paper with 9 pockets on each page and include double glassine interleaving between the pages for added protection.

Item	Binder Color	Pg Count	Pg Color	Retail	AA*	Item	Binder Color	Pg Count	Pg Color	Retail	AA*
LS4/8BK	Black	16 pgs	Black	$19.95	**$17.95**	LS4/32BK	Black	64 pgs	Black	$59.95	**$51.95**
LS4/8BL	Blue	16 pgs	Black	$19.95	**$17.95**	LS4/32BL	Blue	64 pgs	Black	$59.95	**$51.95**
LS4/8GR	Green	16 pgs	Black	$19.95	**$17.95**	LS4/32GR	Green	64 pgs	Black	$59.95	**$51.95**
LS4/8RD	Red	16 pgs	Black	$19.95	**$17.95**	LS4/32RD	Red	64 pgs	Black	$59.95	**$51.95**
LS4/16BK	Black	32 pgs	Black	$30.95	**$24.95**	LW4/8BK	Black	16 pgs	White	$17.95	**$15.95**
LS4/16BL	Blue	32 pgs	Black	$30.95	**$24.95**	LW4/8BL	Blue	16 pgs	White	$17.95	**$15.95**
LS4/16GR	Green	32 pgs	Black	$30.95	**$24.95**	LW4/8GR	Green	16 pgs	White	$17.95	**$15.95**
LS4/16RD	Red	32 pgs	Black	$30.95	**$24.95**	LW4/8RD	Red	16 pgs	White	$17.95	**$15.95**

COMFORT DELUXE STOCKBOOK

This new line of stockbooks features a padded green alligator-textured cover and gold-plated metal corners which are sure to impress. The double-sided black pages, made from extra-strong card stock, come with 9 clear strips and double glassine interleaves. They are double-linen hinged to lie completely flat.

Item	Binder Color	Pg Count	Pg Color	Retail	AA*
LBP4/32BL	Blue	64 pgs	Black	$67.95	**$59.95**
LBP4/32GR	Green	64 pgs	Black	$67.95	**$59.95**

Call 800-572-6885
Outside U.S. & Canada call: (937) 498-0800
Visit AmosAdvantage.com
P.O. Box 4129, Sidney, OH 45365

Vols. 1A-1B Number Additions, Deletions & Changes

Number in 2017 Catalogue	Number in 2018 Catalogue			

United States

new	370a
new	499i
new	689b
new	1476b
new	1929a
new	1930b
new	3632Ag
new	4125j
new	5036b

Computer Vended Postage

CVP75d	deleted
CVP75f-j	deleted
CVP75k-q	deleted
new	CVP75d
new	CVP75f-j
new	CVP85B
new	CVP87A
new	CVP87B
new	CVP88C
new	CVP89A
new	CVP89B
new	CVP89C
new	CVP91a
CVP93	CVP98
new	CVP93
new	CVP94-CVP97
new	CVP99-CVP100

Stamped Envelopes and Wrappers

new	U311b
new	UC3b
new	UC6b

Revenues

new	R1f
R163c	deleted
new	RW72d

Confederate States

new	21XU3B

Afghanistan

229a	deleted
232	231
234	232
239	233
241	234
243	235
245	236
236	236D
231	236E
233	236F
235	236G

AMOS ADVANTAGE
COVER SUPPLIES

COVER BINDERS AND PAGES

Padded, durable, 3-ring binders will hold up to 100 covers. Features the "D" ring mechanism on the right hand side of album so you don't have to worry about creasing or wrinkling covers when opening or closing binder. Cover pages sold separately. **Binders and pages are also sold in a money saving sets. Call or go online for more details.**

Item		Retail	AA*
COVER BINDERS		$16.99	**$12.99**

Choose from four classic colors: Black (CBBK); Blue (CBBL); Red/Burgundy (CBRD); Gray (CBGY)

COVER ALBUM PAGES WITH BLACK BACKGROUNDS

Item	Description	Retail	AA*
T2	Double-sided Page, 2 Pocket (25/pack)	$9.99	**$8.99**
SS2PG1B	Supersafe Page, 1 Pocket (10/pack)	$5.75	**$4.75**

COVER SLEEVES

Clear polyethylene sleeves protect your covers. **Sold in packages of 100.**

U.S. POSTAL CARD

3¹¹⁄₁₆"
5¾"

U.S. FIRST DAY COVER #6

3¹⁵⁄₁₆"
6⅞"

Item	Retail	AA*
CVB05	$2.75	**$2.25**

Item	Retail	AA*
CVB06	$3.25	**$2.75**

CONTINENTAL POSTCARD

4⅜"
6"

EUROPEAN FIRST DAY COVER

5⅛"
7¹³⁄₁₆"

Item	Retail	AA*
CVB07	$3.50	**$2.99**

Item	Retail	AA*
CVB09	$4.25	**$3.95**

#10 BUSINESS ENVELOPE

4¼"
9⅝"

Item	Retail	AA*
CVB10	$5.75	**$4.95**

MINT SHEET BINDERS & PAGES

Keep those mint sheets intact in a handsome, 3-ring binder. Just like the cover album, the Mint Sheet album features the "D" ring mechanism on the right hand side of binder so you don't have to worry about damaging your stamps when turning the pages. **Binders and pages are also sold in a money saving sets. Call or go online for more details.**

Item		Retail	AA*
MBRD	Red (Burgundy)	$21.99	**$17.99**
MBBL	Blue	$21.99	**$17.99**
MBGY	Gray	$21.99	**$17.99**
MBBK	Black	$21.99	**$17.99**
MS1	BLACK Mint Sheet Pages (25 per pack)	$16.99	**$14.99**
SSMP3C	CLEAR Mint Sheet Pages (12 per pack)	$9.95	**$8.95**

GLASSINE ENVELOPES

Perfect for organizing duplicates and sending approvals or mailing stamps. **Sold in packages of 100.**

Item	Size (Dimensions)	Retail	AA*
GE01	#1 (1¾" x 2⅞")	$4.99	**$4.49**
GE02	#2 (2⁵⁄₁₆" x 3⅝")	$5.49	**$4.99**
GE03	#3 (2½" x 4¼")	$5.99	**$5.49**
GE04	#4 (3¼" x 4⅞")	$6.99	**$5.99**
GE4H	#4½ (3⅛" x 5¹⁄₁₆")	$5.95	**$5.25**
GE05	#5 (3½" x 6")	$8.99	**$7.99**
GE06	#6 (3¾" x 6¾")	$9.50	**$8.50**
GE07	#7 (4⅛" x 6¼")	$10.00	**$9.00**
GE08	#8 (4½" x 6⅝")	$10.50	**$9.50**
GE10	#10 (4⅛" x 9½")	$16.99	**$14.99**
GE11	#11 (4½" x 10⅜")	$17.99	**$16.99**

GLASSINE BAGS

These larger glassine bags are ideal for storing panes, covers or prestige booklets. A handy accessory to keep around for all your collecting needs. Available in five different sizes. **Sold in packages of 100.**

Item	Size (Dimensions)	Retail	AA*
GB12	#12 (4⅝" x 6⅝")	$8.99	**$7.99**
GB13	#13 (5¾" x 7¾")	$9.99	**$8.99**
GB13A	#13A (6¾" x 9")	$10.99	**$9.99**
GB14	#14 (7¾" x 9¾")	$16.99	**$14.99**
GB15	#15 (8½" x 11")	$18.99	**$15.99**
GB16	#16 (11½" x 14")	$33.99	**$28.99**

Glassines are also available in boxes of 1,000 – call for pricing.

PRINZ CORNER MOUNTS

Clear, self-adhesive corner mounts are ideal for postal cards and covers. Mounts measure ⅞" each side and are made from transparent glass foil. There are 250 mounts in each pack.

Item	Retail	AA*
ACC176	$11.99	**$8.99**

AmosAdvantage.com • 1-800-572-6885
Outside U.S. and Canada, call (937) 498-0800
Mail to PO Box 4129, Sidney, OH 45365-4129

ORDERING INFORMATION: *AA prices apply to paid subscribers of Amos Media titles, or orders placed online. Prices, terms and product availability subject to change. Shipping and handling rates will apply. Taxes apply in CA, OH & IL.

SHIPPING & HANDLING: United States: Order total $0-$10.00 charged $3.99 shipping. Order total $10.01-$79.99 charged $7.99 shipping. Order total $80.00 or more charged 10% of order total for shipping. Maximum Freight Charge $45.00. **Canada:** 20% of order total. Minimum charge $19.99 Maximum charge $200.00. **Foreign:** Orders are shipped via FedEx Intl. or USPS and billed actual freight.

Currency Conversion

Country	Dollar	Pound	S Franc	Yen	HK $	Euro	Cdn $	Aus $
Australia	1.3427	1.7083	1.3287	0.0118	0.1731	1.4318	1.0106	—
Canada	1.3286	1.6904	1.3148	0.0117	0.1713	1.4167	—	0.9895
European Union	0.9378	1.1932	0.9281	0.0083	0.1209	—	0.7059	0.6984
Hong Kong	7.7555	9.8670	7.6749	0.0683	—	8.2699	5.8373	5.7760
Japan	113.56	144.48	112.38	—	14.643	121.09	85.473	84.576
Switzerland	1.0105	1.2857	—	0.0089	0.1303	1.0775	0.7606	0.7526
United Kingdom	0.7860	—	0.7778	0.0069	0.1013	0.8381	0.5916	0.5854
United States	—	1.2723	0.9896	0.0088	0.1289	1.0663	0.7527	0.7448

Country	Currency	U.S. $ Equiv.
Afghanistan	afghani	.0150
Aitutaki	New Zealand dollar	.7136
Albania	lek	.0078
Algeria	dinar	.0090
Andorra (French)	euro	1.0663
Andorra (Spanish)	euro	1.0663
Angola	kwanza	.0075
Anguilla	East Caribbean dollar	.3704
Antigua	East Caribbean dollar	.3704
Argentina	peso	.0628
Armenia	dram	.0021
Aruba	guilder	.5587
Ascension	British pound	1.2723
Australia	dollar	.7448
Australian Antarctic Territory	dollar	.7448
United Nations-New York	U.S. dollar	1.00
United Nations-Geneva	Swiss franc	.9728
United Nations-Vienna	euro	1.0615
United States	dollar	1.00

Source: **xe.com** Dec. 2, 2016. Figures reflect values as of Dec. 2, 2016.

INDEX TO ADVERTISERS
2018 VOLUME 1A

COMPLETE YOUR COLLECTION WITH THE
NATIONAL ALBUM SERIES

Here are the most complete and comprehensive U.S. album series you can buy.
There are spaces for every major U.S. stamp listed in the Scott Catalogue, including
Special Printings, Newspaper stamps and much more.

- Pages printed on one side.
- All spaces identified by Scott numbers.
- All major variety of stamps are either illustrated or described.
- Sold as page units only. Binders, slipcases and labels sold separately.

U.S. NATIONAL SERIES

Item	Description	Pages	Retail	AA*
100NTL1	1845-1934	108	$69.99	$59.49
100NTL2	1935-1976	108	$69.99	$59.49
100NTL3	1977-1993	117	$69.99	$59.49
100NTL4	1994-1999	96	$64.99	$55.24
100NTL5	2000-2005	99	$69.99	$59.49
100NTL6	2006-2009	68	$52.99	$45.04
100S010	2010 #78	14	$19.99	$16.99
100S011	2011 #79	18	$19.99	$16.99
100S012	2012 #80	18	$19.99	$16.99
100S013	2013 #81	21	$19.99	$16.99
100S014	2014 #82	19	$19.99	$16.99
100S015	2015 #83	13	$16.99	$14.44
100S016	**2016 #84**	**18**	**$22.99**	**$19.99**

Supplemented in February.

U.S. BOOKLET PANES

Item	Description	Pages	Retail	AA*
101BKP1	1900-1993	77	$52.99	$45.04
101BKP2	1994-1999	59	$44.99	$38.24
101BKP3	2000-2006	105	$69.99	$59.49
101S007	2007 #69	15	$19.99	$16.99
101S008	2008 #70	10	$13.99	$11.89
101S009	2009 #71	8	$13.99	$11.89
101S010	2010 #72	4	$9.99	$8.49
101S011	2011 #73	5	$9.99	$8.49
101S012	2012 #74	5	$9.99	$8.49
101S013	2013 #75	10	$13.99	$11.89
101S014	2014 #76	8	$13.99	$11.89
101S015	2015 #77	3	$6.99	$5.94
101S016	**2016 #78**	**8**	**$16.99**	**$13.99**

Supplemented in April.

U.S. COMMEMORATIVE PLATE BLOCKS

Item	Description	Pages	Retail	AA*
120CPB1	1901-1940	80	$57.99	$49.29
120CPB2	1940-1959	78	$52.99	$45.04
120CPB3	1959-1968	70	$49.99	$42.49
120CPB4	1969-1973	47	$34.99	$29.74
120CPB5	1973-1979	86	$57.99	$49.29
120CPB6	1980-1988	100	$69.99	$59.49
120CPB7	1989-1995	77	$52.99	$45.04
120CPB8	1996-2000	59	$44.99	$38.24
120CPB9	2001-2009	88	$57.99	$49.29
120S010	2010 #61	8	$13.99	$11.89
120S011	2011 #62	16	$19.99	$16.99
120S012	2012 #63	15	$19.99	$16.99
120S013	2013 #64	8	$13.99	$11.89
120S014	2014 #65	6	$9.99	$8.49
120S015	2015 #66	7	$9.99	$8.49
120S016	**2016 #67**	**5**	**$19.99**	**$16.99**

Supplemented in April.

U.S. REGULAR & REGULAR AIR PLATE BLOCKS

Item	Description	Pages	Retail	AA*
125RPB0	1918-1991	99	$69.99	$59.49
125RPB2	1992-2006	44	$34.99	$29.74
125S007	2007 #27	5	$9.99	$8.49
125S008	2008 #28	4	$9.99	$8.49
125S009	2009 #29	3	$6.99	$5.94
125S011	2011 #30	4	$9.99	$8.49
125S012	2012 #31	6	$9.99	$8.49
125S013	2013 #32	6	$9.99	$8.49
125S014	2014 #33	7	$9.99	$8.49
125S015	2015 #34	5	$9.99	$8.49
125S016	**2016 #35**	**5**	**$11.99**	**$9.99**

Supplemented in April.

U.S. COMPREHENSIVE PLATE NUMBER COILS

Item	Description	Pages	Retail	AA*
114PNC1	1981-1988	114	$69.99	$59.49
114PNC2	1989-1994	72	$49.99	$42.49
114PNC3	1995-1998	74	$49.99	$42.49
114PNC4	1999-2002	118	$69.99	$59.49
114PNC5	2003-2006	92	$64.99	$55.24
114S007	2007 #20	22	$19.99	$16.99
114S008	2008 #21	12	$16.99	$14.44
114S009	2009 #22	18	$19.99	$16.99
114S010	2010 #23	7	$9.99	$8.49
114S011	2011 #24	14	$19.99	$16.99
114S012	2012 #25	12	$16.99	$14.44
114S013	2013 #26	13	$16.99	$14.44
114S014	2014 #27	11	$16.99	$14.44
114S015	2015 #28	8	$13.99	$11.89
114S016	**2016 #29**	**9**	**$19.99**	**$16.99**

Supplemented in January.

U.S. PLATE NUMBER COIL SINGLES

Item	Description	Pages	Retail	AA*
117PNC1	1981-1993	89	$57.99	$49.29
117PNC2	1994-1998	65	$44.99	$38.24
117PNC3	1999-2003	112	$69.99	$59.49
117PNC4	2004-2008	107	$69.99	$59.49
117S009	2009 #21	21	$19.99	$16.99
117S010	2010 #22	5	$9.99	$8.49
117S011	2011 #23	12	$16.99	$14.44
117S012	2012 #24	12	$16.99	$14.44
117S013	2013 #25	13	$16.99	$14.44
117S014	2014 #26	11	$16.99	$14.44
117S015	2015 #27	8	$13.99	$11.89
117S016	**2016 #28**	**9**	**$17.99**	**$15.99**

Supplemented in January.

U.S. SIMPLIFIED PLATE NUMBER COILS

Item	Description	Pages	Retail	AA*
113PNC1	1981-1997	49	$39.99	$33.99
113PNC2	1997-2009	44	$34.99	$29.74
113S010	2010 #21	3	$6.99	$5.94
113S011	2011 #22	5	$9.99	$8.49
113S012	2012 #23	6	$9.99	$8.49
113S013	2013 #24	4	$9.99	$8.49
113S014	2014 #25	5	$9.99	$8.49
113S015	2015 #26	4	$9.99	$8.49
113S016	**2016 #27**	**3**	**$9.99**	**$8.99**

Supplemented in January.

ID GUIDE TO U.S. STAMPS

Through the use of charts and
illustrations get the vital information
you need to make confident
identification of classic and early
20th century regular issues.

Item	Retail	AA*
Z802	$39.95	$32.50

U.S. POSTAL CARDS

Item	Description	Pages	Retail	AA*
110PCD1	1873-1981	95	$64.99	$55.24
110PCD2	1982-1995	124	$72.99	$62.04
110PCD3	1996-1999	67	$44.99	$38.24
110PCD4	2000-2006	108	$69.99	$59.49
110S007	2007 #31	26	$21.99	$18.69
110S008	2008 #32	18	$19.99	$16.99
110S009	2009 #33	30	$29.99	$25.49
110S010	2010 #34	18	$19.99	$16.99
110S011	2011 #35	5	$9.99	$8.49
110S012	2012 #36	12	$16.99	$14.44
110S014	**2014 #37**	**4**	**$9.99**	**$8.49**

Supplemented in April.

U.S. POSTAL STATIONERY

Item	Description	Pages	Retail	AA*
105PST0	1853-1999	105	$69.99	$59.49
105S002	2000-2002 #55	4	$9.99	$8.49
105S004	2003-2004 #56	6	$9.99	$8.49
105S007	2005-2007 #57	5	$9.99	$8.49
105S008	2008 #58	3	$6.99	$5.94
105S009	2009 #59	7	$9.99	$8.49
105S013	2013 #60	3	$6.99	$5.94
105S014	2014 #61	2	$6.99	$5.94
105S015	**2015 #62**	**3**	**$6.99**	**$5.94**

Supplemented in March.

U.S. SMALL PANES

Item	Description	Pages	Retail	AA*
118SMP1	1987-1995	59	$44.99	$38.24
118SMP2	1996-1999	125	$72.99	$62.04
118SMP3	2000-2002	106	$69.99	$59.49
118SMP4	2003-2006	117	$69.99	$59.49
118S007	2007 #13	37	$32.99	$28.04
118S008	2008 #14	36	$29.99	$25.49
118S009	2009 #15	31	$29.99	$25.49
118S010	2010 #16	23	$21.99	$18.69
118S011	2011 #17	35	$29.99	$25.49
118S012	2012 #18	44	$34.99	$29.74
118S013	2013 #19	35	$29.99	$25.49
118S014	2014 #20	26	$21.99	$18.69
118S015	2015 #21	32	$29.99	$25.49
118S016	**2016 #22**	**26**	**$34.99**	**$29.99**

Supplemented in April.

ORDERING INFORMATION: *AA prices apply to paid
subscribers of Amos Media titles, or orders placed online.
Prices, terms and product availability subject to change.
Shipping and handling rates will apply. Taxes apply in CA,
OH & IL. **SHIPPING & HANDLING: United States:** Order
total $0-$10.00 charged $3.99 shipping. Order total $10.01-
$79.99 charged $7.99 shipping. Order total $80.00 or more
charged 10% of order total for shipping. Maximum Freight
Charge $45.00. **Canada:** 20% of order total. Minimum
charge $19.99 Maximum charge $200.00. **Foreign:** Orders
are shipped via FedEx Intl. or USPS and billed actual freight.

Get yours today by visiting **AmosAdvantage.com**

Or call **1-800-572-6885** Outside U.S. & Canada Call: **1-937-498-0800**
P.O. Box 4129, Sidney, OH 45365

2018
VOLUME 1A
DEALER DIRECTORY
YELLOW PAGE LISTINGS

This section of your Scott Catalogue contains advertisements to help you conveniently find what you need, when you need it....!

Accessories

BROOKLYN GALLERY COIN & STAMP, INC.
8725 4th Ave.
Brooklyn, NY 11209
PH: 718-745-5701
FAX: 718-745-2775
info@brooklyngallery.com
www.brooklyngallery.com

Appraisals

MILLER'S STAMP COMPANY
12 Douglas Lane, Suite 11
Waterford, CT 06385
Stamps@millerstamps.com
PH: 860-908-6200

Argentina

GUILLERMO JALIL
Maipu 466,local 4
1006 Buenos Aires
Argentina
guillermo@jalilstamps.com
philatino@philatino.com
www.philatino.com
www.jalilstamps.com

Auctions

DUTCH COUNTRY AUCTIONS
The Stamp Center
4115 Concord Pike
Wilmington, DE 19803
PH: 302-478-8740
FAX: 302-478-8779
auctions@dutchcountryauctions.com
www.dutchcountryauctions.com

R. MARESCH & SON LTD.
5th Floor - 6075 Yonge St.
Toronto, ON M2M 3W2
CANADA
PH: 416-363-7777
FAX: 416-363-6511
www.maresch.com

Australia

COLONIAL STAMP COMPANY
5757 Wilshire Blvd. PH #8
Los Angeles, CA 90036
PH: 323-933-9435
FAX: 323-939-9930
Toll Free in North America
PH: 877-272-6693
FAX: 877-272-6694
info@colonialstampcompany.com
www.colonialstampcompany.com

**WORLDSTAMPS/
FRANK GEIGER PHILATELISTS**
PO Box 4743
Pinehurst, NC 28374
PH: 910-295-2048
info@WorldStamps.com
www.WorldStampsScott.com/Australia

Austria

**HENRY GITNER
PHILATELISTS, INC.**
PO Box 3077-S
Middletown, NY 10940
PH: 845-343-5151
PH: 800-947-8267
FAX: 845-343-0068
hgitner@hgitner.com
www.hgitner.com

**WORLDSTAMPS/
FRANK GEIGER PHILATELISTS**
PO Box 4743
Pinehurst, NC 28374
PH: 910-295-2048
info@WorldStamps.com
www.WorldStampsScott.com/Austria

Bangkok

COLONIAL STAMP COMPANY
5757 Wilshire Blvd. PH #8
Los Angeles, CA 90036
PH: 323-933-9435
FAX: 323-939-9930
Toll Free in North America
PH: 877-272-6693
FAX: 877-272-6694
info@colonialstampcompany.com
www.colonialstampcompany.com

Belgium

**WORLDSTAMPS/
FRANK GEIGER PHILATELISTS**
PO Box 4743
Pinehurst, NC 28374
PH: 910-295-2048
info@WorldStamps.com
www.WorldStampsScott.com/Belgium

Bermuda

COLONIAL STAMP COMPANY
5757 Wilshire Blvd. PH #8
Los Angeles, CA 90036
PH: 323-933-9435
FAX: 323-939-9930
Toll Free in North America
PH: 877-272-6693
FAX: 877-272-6694
info@colonialstampcompany.com
www.colonialstampcompany.com

British Asia

THE STAMP ACT
PO Box 1136
Belmont, CA 94002
PH: 650-703-2342
PH: 650-592-3315
FAX: 650-508-8104
thestampact@sbcglobal.net

British Commonwealth

**ARON R. HALBERSTAM
PHILATELISTS, LTD.**
PO Box 150168
Van Brunt Station
Brooklyn, NY 11215-0168
PH: 718-788-3978
arh@arhstamps.com
www.arhstamps.com

**COLLECTORS EXCHANGE
ORLANDO STAMP SHOP**
1814A Edgewater Drive
Orlando, FL 32804
PH: 407-620-0908
PH: 407-947-8603
FAX: 407-730-2131
jlatter@cfl.rr.com
www.BritishStampsAmerica.com
www.OrlandoStampShop.com

ROY'S STAMPS
PO Box 28001
600 Ontario Street
St. Catharines, ON
CANADA L2N 7P8
Phone: 905-934-8377
Email: roystamp@cogeco.ca

THE STAMP ACT
PO Box 1136
Belmont, CA 94002
PH: 650-703-2342
PH: 650-592-3315
FAX: 650-508-8104
thestampact@sbcglobal.net

**WORLDSTAMPS/
FRANK GEIGER PHILATELISTS**
PO Box 4743
Pinehurst, NC 28374
PH: 910-295-2048
info@WorldStamps.com
www.WorldStampsScott.com/British

British E. Africa

COLONIAL STAMP COMPANY
5757 Wilshire Blvd. PH #8
Los Angeles, CA 90036
PH: 323-933-9435
FAX: 323-939-9930
Toll Free in North America
PH: 877-272-6693
FAX: 877-272-6694
info@colonialstampcompany.com
www.colonialstampcompany.com

British Guiana

COLONIAL STAMP COMPANY
5757 Wilshire Blvd. PH #8
Los Angeles, CA 90036
PH: 323-933-9435
FAX: 323-939-9930
Toll Free in North America
PH: 877-272-6693
FAX: 877-272-6694
info@colonialstampcompany.com
www.colonialstampcompany.com

Canada

CANADA STAMP FINDER
54 Soccavo Crescent
Brampton, ON L6Y 0W3
PH: 905-488-6109
Toll Free in North America
PH: 877-412-3106
FAX: 323-215-2635
info@canadastampfinder.com
www.canadastampfinder.com

Canada

ROY'S STAMPS
PO Box 28001
600 Ontario Street
St. Catharines, ON
CANADA L2N 7P8
Phone: 905-934-8377
Email: roystamp@cogeco.ca

**WORLDSTAMPS/
FRANK GEIGER PHILATELISTS**
PO Box 4743
Pinehurst, NC 28374
PH: 910-295-2048
info@WorldStamps.com
www.WorldStampsScott.com/Canada

China - PRC

THE STAMP ACT
PO Box 1136
Belmont, CA 94002
PH: 650-703-2342
PH: 650-592-3315
FAX: 650-508-8104
thestampact@sbcglobal.net

Classics

GARY POSNER, INC.
265 Sunrise Hwy. Ste. 1-308
Rockville Centre, NY 11570
Toll Free: 800-323-4279
Cell: 917-538-8133
FAX: 516-599-2145
garyposnerinc@aol.com
www. garyposnerinc.com

Collections

GARY POSNER, INC.
265 Sunrise Hwy. Ste. 1-308
Rockville Centre, NY 11570
Toll Free: 800-323-4279
Cell: 516-599-2145
FAX: 516-599-2145
garyposnerinc@aol.com
www. garyposnerinc.com

Ducks

MICHAEL JAFFE
PO Box 61484
Vancouver, WA 98666
PH: 360-695-6161
PH: 800-782-6770
FAX: 360-695-1616
mjaffe@brookmanstamps.com
www.brookmanstamps.com

Europe-Western

**HENRY GITNER
PHILATELISTS, INC.**
PO Box 3077-S
Middletown, NY 10940
PH: 845-343-5151
PH: 800-947-8267
FAX: 845-343-0068
hgitner@hgitner.com
www.hgitner.com

**WORLDSTAMPS/
FRANK GEIGER PHILATELISTS**
PO Box 4743
Pinehurst, NC 28374
PH: 910-295-2048
info@WorldStamps.com
www.WorldStampsScott.com/Europe

German Colonies

COLONIAL STAMP COMPANY
5757 Wilshire Blvd. PH #8
Los Angeles, CA 90036
PH: 323-933-9435
FAX: 323-939-9930
Toll Free in North America
PH: 877-272-6693
FAX: 877-272-6694
info@colonialstampcompany.com
www.colonialstampcompany.com

Great Britain

COLONIAL STAMP COMPANY
5757 Wilshire Blvd. PH #8
Los Angeles, CA 90036
PH: 323-933-9435
FAX: 323-939-9930
Toll Free in North America
PH: 877-272-6693
FAX: 877-272-6694
info@colonialstampcompany.com
www.colonialstampcompany.com

Latin America

GUY SHAW
PO Box 27138
San Diego, CA 92198
PH/FAX: 858-485-8269
guyshaw@guyshaw.com
www.guyshaw.com

New Issues

DAVIDSON'S STAMP SERVICE
Personalized Service since 1970
PO Box 36355
Indianapolis, IN 46236-0355
PH: 317-826-2620
ed-davidson@earthlink.net
www.newstampissues.com

**WORLDSTAMPS/
FRANK GEIGER PHILATELISTS**
PO Box 4743
Pinehurst, NC 28374
PH: 910-295-2048
info@WorldStamps.com
www.WorldStampsScott.com/NI

Stamp Stores

California

**BROSIUS STAMP, COIN &
SUPPLIES**
2105 Main St.
Santa Monica, CA 90405
PH: 310-396-7480
FAX: 310-396-7455
brosius.stamp.coin@hotmail.com

COLONIAL STAMP COMPANY
5757 Wilshire Blvd. PH #8
Los Angeles, CA 90036
PH: 323-933-9435
FAX: 323-939-9930
Toll Free in North America
PH: 877-272-6693
FAX: 877-272-6694
info@colonialstampcompany.com
www.colonialstampcompany.com